AF772783

Financial Economics

Financial Economics

Antonio Mele

The MIT Press
Cambridge, Massachusetts
London, England

© 2022 Massachusetts Institute of Technology

All rights reserved. No part of this book may be reproduced in any form by any electronic or mechanical means (including photocopying, recording, or information storage and retrieval) without permission in writing from the publisher.

The MIT Press would like to thank the anonymous peer reviewers who provided comments on drafts of this book. The generous work of academic experts is essential for establishing the authority and quality of our publications. We acknowledge with gratitude the contributions of these otherwise uncredited readers.

This book was set in Sabon by Westchester Publishing Services. Printed and bound in the United States of America.

Library of Congress Cataloging-in-Publication Data

Names: Mele, Antonio, author.
Title: Financial economics / Antonio Mele, Università della Svizzera Italiana, Swiss Finance Institute, and Centre for Economic Policy Research.
Description: Cambridge, Massachusetts : The MIT Press, 2022. | Includes bibliographical references and index.
Identifiers: LCCN 2021018189 | ISBN 9780262046848 (hardcover)
Subjects: LCSH: Finance. | Economics.
Classification: LCC HG173 .M3977 2022 | DDC 332—dc23
LC record available at https://lccn.loc.gov/2021018189

10 9 8 7 6 5

Contents

Introduction

A A Brief Description of the Book

This book originates from a set of notes I wrote in support of graduate and advanced undergraduate lectures in financial economics, macroeconomic dynamics, financial econometrics, and financial engineering. These notes have circulated for about 20 years under the title *Lectures on Financial Economics*. Unifying these notes into a coherent book was tantamount to engaging in a long and patient journey into historical intellectual developments as well as the interactions of ideas and theories with actual markets behaviors. I have attempted to synthesize the state of knowledge accumulated during 70 years of initially intermittent, and later incessant contributions to this very important field of economics.[1]

Finance has the potential to oil the wheels of the real economy. While economists still debate about the benefits of finance for our society, more than a dozen scholars researching this field may be counted as Nobel Prize laureates in economic sciences. Progress was sometimes faster than any attempts at organizing our thoughts. Initially, efforts at synthesis were focused on the mathematical structures of the pioneering work underlying the foundations of finance. Later, synthesis became more problematic as research work proliferated through such disparate domains including, among others, the evaluation of derivatives instruments, the behavior of markets over the business cycle, information problems in corporate finance and asset markets, and last but not least, the then-nascent econometrics of financial markets. The initial classics would often cover nonoverlapping spaces, as reviewed in section C of this introduction. We are still struggling with the creation of a comprehensive treatment of financial economics. This book is an attempt at such a treatment, an attempt at linking various theories and ideas to empirical puzzles and, sometimes, established market practice.

Financial economics relies on sophisticated methods that have already received a comprehensive textbook treatment since at least the early classics. While this book still aims

1. In fact, a century of contributions, once we account for those portions of this book dealing with markets plagued by Knightian uncertainty (Keynes, 1921; Knight, 1921) and those market failures identified by Keynes (1936). In section B of this introduction, I review the early contribution of Bachelier (1900).

to provide foundations and methodology, it is intended as a narrative of the historic milestones in the progress of thought. Empirical puzzles have motivated the emergence of new explanations of financial market behaviors and then new foundations; likewise, new theories have prompted additional testable predictions. This virtuous interaction has led to immense knowledge that I try to account for while trying to connect various areas in a single piece. I would have liked to write a history of financial economics, but as noted, I only attempt to synthesize as much as I can. Section B of this introduction provides motivation and historical perspective regarding the progress of knowledge that occurred during the last many decades and a broad outline of the book.

Writing an account on the state of knowledge in financial economics is a significant challenge. I may count more than 200 models underlying the explanations in this book. Does model uncertainty disqualify financial economics from being a science? I am writing this introduction with a humble but decisively optimistic view, even though underlying this view is the acknowledgment that we are dealing with such a large and sometimes fragmented field that is still far from being unified. While we cannot rely on controlled experiments as in other fields, our models lead to predictions that are typically testable through the availability of myriads of data. I hope that this book will make the reader comfortable with the idea that financial economics is progressing on a well-defined path; that the 200 models I discuss belong to a common paradigm; and finally, that each of these models is very important by shedding light into specific angles of the varied and complex structure of financial markets. This project has the potential to produce a durable impact once these learning objectives are met.

B Overview and Coverage

This book aims to track the milestones achieved in the history of thought in financial economics. Its objective is to provide a comprehensive reference while attempting to organize approximately a century of work; while relying on a rigorous analytical framework, and finally, while providing methodological tools that try to make it self-contained. At the same time the book endeavors to help explain real phenomena and how these phenomena and sometimes market practice have helped economists reformulate previous theories. Further, the book includes many examples and solved problems that illustrate the main lessons conveyed by the models analyzed in the book. I don't provide supplementary material such as solutions, answers, or other material to accompany the book. I have tried to make the book self-contained. Likewise, all problems and analytical examples that illustrate theories, methods, or empirical regularities are not at end of each chapter; rather, they are presented in places I (probably mistakenly) thought were appropriate.

While our field is very large, I try to cover as much material as I can while maintaining a balance between theoretical explanations and empirical evidence and identifying the practical relevance of our knowledge. The outcome might still appear to be patchy—again, a reflection of the nature of our field but also of my limited abilities. However, I hope that I am managing to provide the reader with a coherent treatment of many disparate aspects of financial markets—those arising in idealized explanations (be they based on abstract or empirical methodologies), those that are most relevant to the market practice, and finally those that may be of interest to scholars working in related fields.

The book is organized in three parts: (I) Foundations, (II) Empirical Lessons and Market Inefficiencies, and (III) Asset Pricing and Reality.

Part I (Foundations) develops primordial tools of analysis while striving to keep track of historical backgrounds. For example, chapter 1 deals with portfolio selection problems arising in the early 1950s and the initial theories of asset prices of the 1960s, works that are understood to be at the origins of financial economics. The next chapters in this part provide refinements of the initial theories based on subsequent breakthroughs that clarify the role of asset prices in the general equilibrium of economies subject to uncertainty, in both static (chapter 2) and dynamic settings (chapters 3 and 4) and in markets with information frictions (chapter 5). Historically, the apex of these developments was reached in the 1970s with the advent of "continuous time finance" and its methods. Continuous time models would elegantly address difficult problems, including no-arbitrage pricing of redundant securities (derivatives, in some cases) or portfolio choices through dynamic programming. The martingale methods of the 1980s–1990s would seal this toolbox with additional instruments, but they also paved the way to the analysis of incomplete markets and other market imperfections. It is the golden age of financial theory, a famous expression proposed by Darrell Duffie in his classic *Dynamic Asset Pricing Theory* (2001, p. xiii).

This part covers details of this progress but it also provides perspective into its economic significance. The goal of this book is to understand financial market fluctuations and sometimes the behavior of firms, subject to financial constraints, or the role that these fluctuations and behaviors play in conveying information and resources back to society. Information asymmetries and market imperfections are actually a recurrent theme in this book. Thus, chapters 1 through 3 deal with the idealized markets, leading to the initial explanations of asset prices; for example, chapter 3 deals with financial markets and attempts to take a broad perspective, one in which finance is part of a general ecosystem; however, our discussions in this chapter (often, not always) rely on models without frictions. In these markets, asset prices relate to consumption, production, money, and the links that arise through the behavior of fully rational individuals. Next, chapter 4 shows the beauties of continuous time finance that is applied to classical problems such as no-arbitrage pricing or portfolio selection (relying on dynamic programming) and also incomplete markets or the theory of irreversible investments and real options. In a real option problem, decisions are triggered when some underlying signals reach some values. For example, one may decide to exercise an American option only when the underlying asset price hits some level. Likewise, a firm subject to cash constraints may decide to distribute dividends only when its reserves are sufficiently large. Finally, some investors subject to short sell constraints may wish to sell the securities they hold only when the underlying fundamentals reach a certain threshold. These frictions are then dealt with in more detail in other chapters (see, e.g., the liquidity and capital structure problems analyzed in chapters 5 and 14 [part III] or how, in chapter 9 [Part II], real option theory may help explain bubble formation in markets subject to short sell constraints).

Chapter 5 explains some famous conceptual difficulties in defining a general equilibrium. These issues exist due to asymmetric information and potentially lead to question the very existence of markets or the process of securities creation. Indeed, information problems have always been valuable sources of inspiration for economists. Chapter 5 does rely on these information problems and provides the reader with an overview of theories of financial contracting and theories of capital structure. According to classical irrelevance results, capital structure does not affect the value of a firm. Why then do corporations issue debt or equity, that is, financial assets that may subsequently trade on secondary markets? Or suppose that a firm receives funds to undertake a project; shouldn't then the same firm lose some of its initial motivation in undertaking the necessary care while handling the project? How do we incentivize this firm's manager to exert the efforts that would make their interests aligned to those of the investors? What is a firm's dividend distribution policy in the presence of liquidity constraints? Can we understand a firm's capital structure while making reference to theories of dynamic contracts? This chapter often relies on powerful tools in real option theory to illustrate theories of recursive contracts in continuous time.

Some theories are important because of their main qualitative conclusions, and they may not need to be tested for their "functional form." But financial economics is also a field that lends itself so naturally to vast empirical investigations, especially in contexts in which models may predict different outcomes according to parameter values. We need to assess the statistical relevance of certain theories, and even more fundamentally, we need to estimate a model to be used by decision makers, be they policy makers or private corporations. Chapter 6 covers theories and methods of statistical inference needed to deal with models arising in financial economics, relying on classical econometric tools such as maximum likelihood, methods of moments, and the relatively more modern simulation-based inference methods.

The purpose of Part II (Empirical Lessons and Market Inefficiencies) is to explain the main empirical facts and the challenges that these facts pose to financial economists. The first puzzles regard excess price volatility; that is, the difficulty of the early dynamic models to explain aggregate market behavior. According to the early models, market volatility (and the premium required by investors to invest in a volatile environment) is one order of magnitude less than that we observe in the markets. Chapter 7 is an introduction to these critical problems and in particular to their measurement methods. These methods were developed mainly during the 1980s, the 1990s, and (in part) the 2000s, and are obviously statistical in nature. At the same time, they rely on the principle of no arbitrage: There are many ways we can price assets while only requiring absence of arbitrage; however, there is a benchmark among these ways, solely relying on securities market data, that we can use to assess whether a model under scrutiny suggests implausible parameter values (such as, say, the investors' risk appetite).

To address the volatility puzzles, financial economists added explanations of financial market behavior based on a variety of assumptions: investors' attitude to risk taking (e.g., nonexpected utility or habit formation), idiosyncratic risk, incomplete markets or restricted market participation, heterogeneous beliefs, learning in markets with incomplete information, a fully specified production sector, or Knightian and model uncertainty. This progress was based on the foundational work made during the golden age of financial theory described in part I. It occurred in the 2000s–2010s and is described in chapters 8 and 9. Interestingly, these new models address relatively older issues; for example, they predict that, under certain conditions, the aggregate equity premium and stock market volatility are both countercyclical, a fact known from earlier empirical research. But while these models were developed, financial economists also realized that they could explain additional cross-sectional anomalies such as the value premium (the tendency for firms with low multiples to perform better in the future than those with high) or the hoary issue of predictability (the tendency of the market to reverse its trends after a while, maybe in tandem with the business cycle).

A common trait of these models is their adoption of the "separation hypothesis;" that is, the assumption that the real economy is not affected by financial market developments. Perhaps due to the dramatic counterfactual evidence brought about by the Great Recession of the late 2000s, a new research agenda relaxed this assumption, aiming to revitalize previous work made by macroeconomists on financial accelerator mechanisms: the power of financial markets to exacerbate business cycles through feedback effects. Financial markets then do not reflect just the fundamentals of the economy. The real economy is also affected by conditions in financial markets; to illustrate, it is more difficult to finance businesses when collateral values (financial assets, for example) for potential loans deteriorate, and this occurs precisely in bad times. Thus, financial markets may act as accelerators of adverse economic conditions. Integrating financial markets into the real sphere of the economy is the explicit intellectual acknowledgment of the crucial role that financial markets (frictions) play in society. Chapter 9 contains many links to this literature, and some of these links form the basis for additional discussions and formal analysis in various junctures of part III.

Chapter 10 concludes this part while pointing to other famous puzzles and frictions. Do financial markets provide useful information? How deep is price discovery; that is, how well do asset prices reflect the fundamentals in a world with heterogenous information? This chapter begins with the classical analysis of markets plagued with information problems. Investors obviously have different pieces of information, and some of them are even known to possess superior information. A lemon problem arises: What are the incentives to trade with better informed investors? One answer is that trading may only arise when markets are somehow (informationally) inefficient: when information is not available symmetrically in the marketplace, we can only trade once we know that our would-be trading counterparty is not necessarily better informed than us. One implication of this reasoning is that agents with less information would never be able to reverse engineer the information of better informed traders from the price, but this inefficiency (a price that is only partially revealing) may actually be what makes markets function.

For a long time, this price inefficiency has been modeled as a result of the presence of exogenous liquidity shocks. In fact, liquidity and information problems have long been understood as the two sides of the same coin. But liquidity is not only information, and this chapter describes alternative explanations for it. Remarkably, these information and related problems were tackled while, at the same time, economists were in the process of developing market microstructure theory; that is, the theory of price formation in trading venues relatively more realistic than those hypothesized during the golden age. However, financial markets and trading venues can be even much more complex than the literature had initially hypothesized: Chapter 10 explains that the presence of irrational traders, information networks, limits of arbitrage, segmented markets, or decentralized trading systems (e.g., over-the-counter markets) were all exciting topics of research from the 1990s through the 2010s and still promises to improve our understanding of such a complex phenomenon as the price formation process. Chapter 10 also contains surveys of topics regarding coordination failures and higher order beliefs in financial markets. Why do bank crises arise? What are the determinants of a bank run? What makes agents coordinate to equilibrium outcomes where prices can deviate from fundamentals, as in the famous beauty contests introduced by John Maynard Keynes in his *General Theory of Employment, Interest and Money* (1936, chapter 12)? Remember, in these contests, the winners are those who pick the most popular faces from many photographs and thus are incentivized to forecast the forecasts of others, and everyone else is trying to do the same thing. How do higher order beliefs affect price dynamics?

Part III (Asset Pricing and Reality) aims to bring to fruition the lessons drawn from part II and copes (through the main analytical tools discussed in part I) with the main challenges posed by actual financial markets, such as those arising from option pricing and trading, interest rate modeling, or credit risk and the associated derivatives. In a sense, part II is about the big puzzles we face in fundamental research while part III is about how to live within our current and certainly unsatisfactory paradigms so as to cope with demand for intellectual expertise.

The importance of these topics can never be emphasized enough. Investments or business cycles are clouded with uncertainty. While investing, decision makers put their jobs and the security of their families at risk, thereby affecting human capital accumulation and hence the lives of future generations. Sometimes, the effects of poorly informed choices can be devastating. The 2007 subprime crisis and the subsequent Great Recession certainly illustrate these mechanisms. In general, financial market volatility is huge, for one reason or another, as illustrated by the theories and facts in part II. It is thus a natural human response to try to find a solution to cope with these risks.

Derivative securities are instruments to insure against risks related to certain investment decisions. They are called derivatives because their value is drawn from that of other securities. For example, if we are long a number of shares, we may wish to purchase put options on these shares (or on a dedicated index of them), which pay off when the shares' value is down; intuitively, then, the price of these options decreases with the price of the underlying securities. Louis Bachelier's "Théorie de la spéculation" in 1900 is the first attempt at tackling these evaluation problems—problems that were tackled again during the golden age, using no-arbitrage principles.

At the heart of these principles lie different assumptions, and one of them dictates that the underlying securities (or risks in general) should be well understood by all market participants. For example, the shares underlying the previous options should be traded in reasonably liquid markets—a condition for price discovery. It is most likely the case not only with many derivative securities such as equity index options or US Treasury derivatives that are traded in well functioning exchanges but also with a variety of derivatives traded in over-the-counter markets (e.g., interest rate swaps or credit-related products). However, if risks are poorly understood and price discovery is scarce, derivatives may be mispriced. A case of toxicity may then arise: investors may inadvertently add too many complex derivatives in their portfolios than justified by their risk-return trade-off profile. Unfortunately, financial history shows many cases of toxicity. The last chapter of part III examines some details of one of them as related to the process of securitization of very risky mortgages.

Engineering can be defined as a set of processes and methods that attempt to use established scientific knowledge to solve practical problems, as with the case of steam engines utilized during the first Industrial Revolution. In fact, if it wasn't for the previous mishaps, it would have been very tempting to title this part "Financial Engineering." Instead, "Asset Pricing and Reality" reminds us that while our engines do certainly rely on scientific and rigorous knowledge, this knowledge seems to be more limited than in the domains of the physical sciences. It does not mean that financial economists are not in the process of building up financial engineering. Nor does it mean that financial innovation is unnecessary or toxic. We shall learn throughout the whole book that financial innovation may allow for risk sharing (the transfer of some risks from those who are not willing to bear them to those who are) when the preexisting markets are not diverse enough (i.e., are incomplete). In fact, and interestingly, not only are financial economists inspired by the events they see (as with the previous revival of the financial accelerator hypothesis motivated by the Great Recession), but sometimes, their work leads to institutional changes: option markets would most probably not exist today without the golden age revolution of the 1970s.

Yet our most successful inventions regard risks that can at least be identified. Some of these inventions attract liquidity that in turn generates price discovery and then liquidity again over a virtuous circle. Liquidity begets liquidity: a product is more likely to trade if a trader knows they could easily trade it when, in the future, they will decide to get out from their current trade. Financial products are a little bit like the fax machine at the time of its introduction: they have worth because others are willing to use them. Potential market makers and financial economists alike (see chapter 10) are well aware of this chicken-and-egg problem: coordination may fail even when risks are well identified. The exposition in this part is affected by a sort of survivorship bias: it regards products, trading methods, and processes that have been successful. The exception is the description of *some* credit-related products at the epicenter of the 2007–2009 crisis.

Chapter 11 illustrates well the scope of part III, while part II describes theories and facts regarding asset market volatility, this chapter analyzes ways investors may trade asset market volatility in the equity space. The technicalities can be actually complex: we have realized volatility, stochastic volatility, implied volatility and volatility surfaces, implied binomial trees, and local volatility. Some models can be useful to buy-side institutions; others to sell-side firms that are only interested in pure intermediation activities. Further, and somehow unexpectedly, the theory of financial derivatives witnessed important developments during the 1990s and the 2000s. These developments regarded new definitions of volatility and new instruments and contracts to trade this volatility, known as variance swaps. A variance swap enables a counterparty exposed to equity markets to experience constant volatility within a given horizon. Remarkably, and under certain conditions, this contract can be evaluated in a model-free fashion—that is, without any strong assumptions except absence of arbitrage. The fair value of these contracts was suggestive of new indicators of uncertainty and volatility in equity markets, known as VIX. New instruments were then introduced and referenced to VIX. This is another episode of financial history when theory had preceded market practice. Note that trading volatility enables us to mitigate uncertainty but has the potential to contribute new avenues to systemic risk that policy makers and regulators alike should be very well aware of. This section reviews such avenues within the broader context of feedback effects: certain trading strategies are procyclical in that they specify to sell in a falling market and to buy in a rising market. The nature of these strategies resembles the accelerator mechanisms in chapter 9 (part II): agents react to signals in a way that makes these signals persist. The result is a notion of endogenous market volatility that in some cases may take the extreme form of a market crash. This chapter reviews some of these crashes and analyzes the mechanisms behind them.

Chapters 12 and 13 repeat some of these analyses in the more sophisticated field that is fixed income. Fixed income securities are complex due to theoretical reasons (they track the time value of money) and technical reasons (they have multiple dimensions, such as expiration or tenors of the various contracts) and also because price discovery in these markets may be somehow hindered by their trading mechanisms (over-the-counter markets). Yet fixed income securities allow pension funds and other asset managers to mitigate interest rate risk, which can be much, much higher than equity market risk. Interest rates do also display some important business cycle properties that policy makers rely on while trying to predict the business cycle; for this reason, chapter 13 contains some links to a number of fascinating topics that also arise in macroeconomics. Finally, chapter 14 deals with the evaluation of debt subject to default risk, derivatives based thereon and methods to monitor both credit and systemic risk. While this chapter is focused on practical aspects, it also contains a few junctures devoted to the analysis of strategic default (by both firms and governments), the origins of the 2007 subprime crisis, and discussions of feedback effects of the type analyzed in chapter 9 (part II) and chapter 11.

Engineering can be civil or electronic engineering, among many others. Likewise, a would-be financial engineering field should not be only about derivatives and interest rates. For example, it should also deal with such issues as portfolio optimization in the presence of short-sale constraints, time-varying volatility (autoregressive conditional heteroskedastic [ARCH] models, for example), Bayesian learning, variance shrinkage methods, and many additional topics that would make a very long list. In general, this field should be a chameleon, just as it is in the physical sciences: it should take the colors of the specific set of problems it is helping to address in order to facilitate financial transactions, information processes (including, e.g., the design of volatility indices with data stemming out from over-the-counter markets), and methods both in the buy-side and sell-side worlds. Some of these topics are covered throughout the book, although their systematic treatment goes well beyond the scope of this work.

C Discussion of Related Work

Financial economics has evolved while crossing a variety of boundaries. How did we track this progress? Ingersoll (1987), Huang and Litzenberger (1988), and Duffie (2001) are the first classics organizing more than 30 years of conceptual analysis while O'Hara (1995) is the first classic organizing the theories of the 1980s on liquidity and market microstructure.

These works led to a sophisticated and consistent framework at the basis of subsequent progress—progress that occurred mostly in response to empirical challenges faced by the initial analyses; for example, during the mid 1990s and the early 2000s, new models were proposed to explain how aggregate market behavior links to the business cycle. Cochrane (2005), Back (2010), and Campbell (2017) provided further momentum to standardization of knowledge, teaching how part of this progress relates to the initial analyses. The early work of Campbell, Lo, and MacKinlay (1997) offered a quite exhaustive overview of many statistical instruments that are still of paramount importance in the empirical modeling or statistical testing of financial markets phenomena.

Foucault, Pagano, and Röell (2013) summarized further progress related to studies of market liquidity and microstructure. During the 2000s, Amaro de Matos (2001) and Tirole (2006) provided us with the first attempts at organizing knowledge acquired in the theory of corporate finance while during the 1990s Freixas and Rochet (1997) had already written a classic in the theory of banking. In the references section of this introduction, I list additional references on works that attempt at organizing knowledge in financial economics.

I like to represent this book as being complementary to these very important works. The added value of mine is to provide general perspective into a large variety of topics as well as details of the historical progress leading to our current understanding of each of these topics.

To illustrate, the Constantinides, Harris, and Stultz's *Handbook of the Economics of Finance* (vol. 1, 2003; vol. 2, 2013) currently undertakes the ambitious task of dealing with many disparate topics arising in financial economics. However, these works are works to which several authors have contributed, and are only partially coordinated. This book provides explicit linkages across chapters to possibly help a reader interested in learning or reviewing several topics while accessing a common language. For example, this book may be used as a reference in several courses in advanced training programs; adopting this book for a single course (e.g., a course in macrofinance) should allow the reader to access material for related courses (one in financial markets with frictions, say) while relying on a style that they are already familiar with. But the most remarkable feature of what I have tried to accomplish in this book is the ambition to cover a wide range of topics—the milestones in the history of thought in this field—while maintaining a balance across theory, empirical evidence, historical contexts, and also market practice. As explained previously, in the references section of this introduction I am bringing a few additional textbook treatments of the field to the reader's attention, noting that these represent my own preferred readings and apologizing to all omitted authors.

D Audience and Prerequisites

The main audience for this book will be academics studying, teaching, and researching financial economics. The book also aims to appeal to applied researchers and other professionals servicing investment banks, institutional investors, central banks, and governments. The inclusion of policy makers as part of the audience for this book is motivated by the widespread acknowledgment of the many interconnections between financial markets and the macroeconomy. Macrofinancial linkages arising through the business cycle (or, say, market liquidity, microstructure, and volatility) are themes that have motivated important work by financial economists; this book is very useful reading for those engaged in designing supervisory standards and macroprudential policies. However, the main audience for this book will be financial economists. I shall return to additional factors for potential audiences in section E.

The style of the book is eminently academic. It is primarily quantitative, even while on many occasions the book provides descriptions of markets and historical contexts. But appreciating this book in its entirety relies on a predisposition to quantitative reasoning. At the same time, quantitative reasoning is the means, not the goal of this work. Thus, in general, those who are genuinely passionate about economics will appreciate this book. Finally, the book is suitable to both theorists and empiricists or fellows searching for concrete applications. Applied researchers will have access to the clear theoretical background needed prior to undertaking meaningful empirical research. Theorists will learn the nature of the empirical regularities and puzzles that have characterized our field since its very beginnings—knowledge that is indispensable prior to undertaking meaningful theoretical research.

Reading the book requires knowledge of economics and mathematics at a level required from a candidate to an MS in finance and economics at the London School of Economics or to a PhD in finance at the Swiss Finance Institute, two programs where I delivered many of the lectures inspiring this work. I also believe that the book may be accessed by a well-motivated student enrolled in a program such as, say, a BS in economics and statistics at University College London. Therefore, reading this book requires maturity in both microeconomics and macroeconomics at the level of the Varian (1992) and Blanchard (2017) textbooks, respectively. Moreover, some readers might already have gained motivation for finance while exposed to introductory finance textbooks such as Berk and DeMarzo (2016) and Bodie, Kane, and Marcus (2014). Additional prerequisites include knowledge of calculus, basic knowledge of time series and statistics, and an introductory exposure to stochastic calculus. Many technicalities are introduced and explained in appropriate junctures of the book along with references to more advanced material.

E Usage of the Book

The reader of this book is a scholar in financial economics, a market practitioner, a policy maker, or a scholar in related fields such as macroeconomics.

A scholar in financial economics may (i) recommend this book to a specialized readership for a survey of work linked to their research articles; (ii) recommend portions of the book to advanced graduate or PhD classes as complements to their lecture notes; and finally (iii) value a book that attempts at a synthesis: for example, reading this book may help a young scholar develop a critical view of our current understanding of financial markets, thereby stimulating further and hopefully important research.

A market practitioner or a policy maker with an appropriate background (see section D) may find this book to be a source of valuable information. For example, certain parts of the book (part III as well as some chapters in part II) may provide a quantitative strategist or a risk manager with guidance on elaborating, estimating, and implementing models for signal generation. Even more importantly, the book may help gain intellectual perspective into the many details that arise in market or policy practice.

Finally, a reader of this book may be a scholar in other fields. For example, a macroeconomist might be interested in financial economics from a broad and still rigorous perspective; this book may help shed light into their own research and perhaps motivate them to recommend portions of it for their PhD classes. For example, some financial economists learned from some of the classics described in section C of this introduction while at the same time reading the beautiful *Lectures on Macroeconomics* of Blanchard and Fischer (1989), which helped shape some research into macrofinance. Similarly, one objective of this book is to attract the attention of scholars in other fields. Oftentimes did scholars in other fields make excursions into financial economics and provide marvelous contributions, for example, on the role of information in securities markets, idiosyncratic risk, or financial accelerator mechanisms. I hope that the general perspective I endeavor to follow in this book may attract scholars from other fields and help to render more frequent excursions.

This book contains material that may be accessed while learning about a number of topics and/or be used as a reference for a number of courses, such as:

- foundations of portfolio selection (chapter 1)
- foundations of financial economics (selected portions of chapters 2, 3, 4, 5 and 10)
- introduction to quantitative methods in finance (selected portions of chapters 3 and 4)
- statistical methods of financial model validation (chapters 6 and 7)
- financial markets and the macroeconomy (chapters 8 and 9)
- information and financial markets (chapters 5 and 10)
- financial markets, debt, and frictions (chapters 5 and 10; selected portions of chapters 9 and 14)
- option pricing and volatility trading (chapter 11)
- fixed income markets and derivatives (chapters 12 and 13)
- credit markets and derivatives (chapter 14)
- derivatives and financial engineering (selected portions of chapters 11 through 14)

The chapters indicated in parenthesis contain the relevant material for the suggested courses, which I have indeed been experimenting for the last 20 years or so.

F Acknowledgments and Disclaimers

I thank MIT Press's three anonymous reviewers for their invaluable comments and Emily Taber for her enthusiasm and patience on this project. Special words of gratitude go to Christian Di Marco, Andrey Pankratov, Gianpaolo Parise, Alessio Ruzza, and Federico Severino for their excellent research assistance while in Lugano. Finally, I thank the Swiss National Science Foundation for their research support. It goes without saying that I retain full responsibility for omissions and mistakes. However, I am not able to accept liabilities for any losses related to the use of models, data, and methods described or developed in this book.

March 2022

References

Amaro de Matos, J. (2001). *Theoretical Foundations of Corporate Finance*. Princeton, NJ: Princeton University Press.

Bachelier, L. (1900). "Théorie de la spéculation." *Annales Scientifiques de l'École Normale Supérieure* 3 (17), 21–86.

Back, K. (2010). *Asset Pricing and Portfolio Choice*. Oxford: Oxford University Press.

Berk, J. and P. DeMarzo (2016). *Corporate Finance*. Boston: Pearson Education.

Blanchard, O. (2017). *Macroeconomics*. 7th ed. Boston: Pearson Education.

Blanchard, O., and S. Fisher (1989). *Lectures on Macroeconomics*. Cambridge, MA: MIT Press.

Bodie, Z., A. Kane, and A. J. Marcus (2014). *Investments*. Berkshire, UK: McGraw-Hill Education.

Campbell, J. (2017). *Financial Decisions and Markets: A Course in Asset Pricing*. Princeton, NJ: Princeton University Press.

Campbell, J. Y., A. W. Lo, and C. MacKinlay (1997). *The Econometrics of Financial Markets*. Princeton, NJ: Princeton University Press.

Cochrane, J. (2005). *Asset Pricing*. Princeton, NJ: Princeton University Press.

Constantinides, G. M., M. Harris, and R. Stultz, eds. (2003). *Handbook of the Economics of Finance*. Vol. 1. Amsterdam: Elsevier.

Constantinides, G. M., M. Harris, and R. Stultz, eds. (2013). *Handbook of the Economics of Finance*. Vol. 2. Amsterdam: Elsevier.

Duffie, D. (2001). *Dynamic Asset Pricing Theory*. Princeton, NJ: Princeton University Press.

Foucault T., M. Pagano, and A. Röell (2013). *Market Liquidity: Theory, Evidence and Policy*. Oxford, UK: Oxford University Press.

Freixas, X., and J-Ch. Rochet (1997). *Microeconomics of Banking*. Cambridge, MA: MIT Press.

Huang, C.-F., and R. H. Litzenberger (1988). *Foundations for Financial Economics*. New York: North-Holland.

Ingersoll, J. E. (1987). *Theory of Financial Decision Making*. New York: Rowman & Littlefield.

Keynes, J. M. (1921). *A Treatise on Probability*. London: MacMillan.

Keynes, J. M. (1936). *The General Theory of Employment, Interest and Money*. London: Palgrave Macmillan.

Knight, F. H. (1921). *Risk, Uncertainty, and Profit*. New York: Houghton Mifflin.

O'Hara, M. (1995). *Market Microstructure Theory*. Cambridge, MA: Blackwell.

Tirole, J. (2006). *The Theory of Corporate Finance*. Princeton, NJ: Princeton University Press.

Varian, H. (1992). *Microeconomic Analysis*. New York: W.W. Norton.

Further Reading

Generic References

LeRoy, S. F., and J. Werner (2014). *Principles of Financial Economics*. Cambridge, UK: Cambridge University Press.

Lengwiler, Y. (2014). *Microfoundations of Financial Economics*. Princeton, NJ: Princeton University Press.

Munk, C. (2013). *Financial Asset Pricing Theory*. Oxford: Oxford University Press.

Pennacchi, G. (2008). *Theory of Asset Pricing*. Boston: Pearson Addison Wesley.

Financial Markets and the Macroeconomy

Altug, S., and P. Labadie (2008). *Asset Pricing for Dynamic Economies.* Cambridge: Cambridge University Press.

Hansen, L. P., and T. J. Sargent (2008). *Robustness.* Princeton, NJ: Princeton University Press.

Information and Other Market Frictions

Allen, F., and D. Gale (2007). *Understanding Financial Crises.* Oxford: Oxford University Press.

Bianconi, M. (2003). *Financial Economics, Risk and Information.* Singapore: World Scientific Publishing.

Brunnermeier, M. K. (2001). *Asset Pricing under Asymmetric Information.* Oxford: Oxford University Press.

Duffie, D. (2012). *Dark Markets.* Princeton, NJ: Princeton University Press.

Schleifer, A. (2000). *Inefficient Markets.* Oxford: Oxford University Press.

Shin, H. S. (2010). *Risk and Liquidity.* Oxford: Oxford University Press.

Vives, X. (2008). *Information and Learning in Markets.* Princeton, NJ: Princeton University Press.

Derivatives

Brigo, D., and F. Mercurio (2006). *Interest Rate Models: Theory and Practice.* New York: Springer Verlag.

Derman, E., and M. B. Miller (2016). *The Volatility Smile.* Hoboken, NJ: John Wiley.

Duffie, D., and K.J. Singleton (2003). *Credit Risk.* Princeton, NJ: Princeton University Press.

Lando, D. (2004). *Credit Risk Modeling.* Princeton, NJ: Princeton University Press.

McDonald, R. L. (2006). *Derivatives Markets.* Boston: Pearson Addison Wesley.

Veronesi, P. (2010). *Fixed Income Securities.* Hoboken, NJ: John Wiley.

I

Foundations

1

The Classic Capital Asset Pricing Model

1.1 Introduction

An investor is considering creating a portfolio of securities. How should they choose the proportions of these securities based on their attitude toward risk? What are the asset pricing implications of all the investors' portfolio choices? Are these choices consistent with the absence of arbitrage opportunities?

This chapter deals with these issues in the context of the static markets idealized in the first contributions that would give birth to financial economics. Section 1.2 explains how portfolio selection works when our investor optimizes a mean-variance criterion as in the seminal approach of Markovitz (1952). According to this criterion, an investor seeks to maximize the portfolio expected return for any given variance constraint—the celebrated "mean-variance model." The ensuing asset allocation leads, in equilibrium (supply equals demand for all assets), to a notion of "market portfolio" as well as a first theory of asset prices—the celebrated "capital asset pricing model (CAPM)" of Sharpe (1964), Lintner (1965), and Mossin (1966) (see section 1.3).

The market portfolio is the first instance of a "preference-free" construct in financial economics: the asset composition of this portfolio is independent of the investors' risk aversion. Remarkably, any desired profile in the investors' risk-return trade-off is obtained as a combination of a purely safe asset and the market portfolio (hence the name). We shall explain that there are nuances to be made regarding these preference-free attributes, but the notion of a market portfolio is important, representing as it does a benchmark for each individual asset evaluation: the striking conclusion of the CAPM is that each asset's expected return is proportional to the expected return on the market portfolio. The volatility (i.e., riskiness) of each asset return then increases with the asset exposure to market movements. This asset exposure is known as beta.

These explanations are elegant albeit quite coarse descriptions of asset markets. Section 1.4 develops the "arbitrage pricing theory (APT)" model of Ross (1976). The APT provides refinements of the CAPM and predicts that each asset's expected return links to a number of factors and not just the market, as the original CAPM suggests. For example, there might be macroeconomic forces explaining stock returns because investors require compensation (i.e., a risk premium) for investing in risky assets that perform poorly when the economy performs equally poorly, which is usually the norm. The APT formalizes these concepts very elegantly.

How successful were these initial explanations of asset price fluctuations? It is well known that the single-factor CAPM cannot explain the cross-section of stock returns. It is one of the first asset pricing puzzles that financial economists had to face while developing the field. Section 1.5. explains that the empirical evidence suggests that at least three factors explain the cross-section of stock returns. In fact, the literature has produced a huge amount of evidence regarding many additional factors. We shall succinctly discuss this evidence and the extent to which some of them are merely "lucky factors."

The important point of this empirical evidence is that it provides motivation and guidance to the formulation of new models. These models can be seen as dynamic extensions of the APT. For example, a recurrent theme in financial economics is how "cyclical forces" affect asset evaluation and, in turn, how capital market developments feed back the business cycle. The original APT framework was the initial reference for thinking about these themes as studied in detail in more advanced parts of the book (see, e.g., chapters 8 and 9). More generally, it was a milestone for all subsequent work aimed to address various "asset pricing puzzles."

The empirical literature abounds with additional instances of asset pricing "anomalies"; that is, difficulties the CAPM (and related static models) encounters while explaining market behavior. Some of these anomalies are now understood to link to frictions that are behind the very price formation process. Information problems, agency issues, limited rationality, capital immobility, and decentralized markets are all examples of hindrances to market efficiency. In fact, the notion of "market efficiency" is elusive; financial economists actually agree that some (rigorously defined) inefficiency is needed to have markets function in the first place—an equilibrium degree of disequilibrium, in the words of Grossman and Stiglitz (1980) (see chapters 5 and 10). For example, bid-ask spreads are needed to incentivize financial institutions to trade securities in their roles of intermediaries. While these topics are dealt with in many junctures of this book (e.g., in chapters 5 and 10), it is important to emphasize them in the first chapter of this book.

However, the CAPM has many undisputed potentially useful features. A striking feature of the basic portfolio allocation rules derived in this chapter is that they are simple to understand. Thus, mean-variance asset allocation roughly suggests to invest more in assets that have higher expected returns and less volatility. In fact, we have already explained that the CAPM has been the basic starting point for further developments in the history of thought. But how successful the CAPM allocation rules have been in the market practice? This chapter provides some perspective on these rules. For example, section 1.3 explains that implementing the mean-variance model may be very difficult; one reason is that one of its main ingredients, the assets' expected returns, can only be estimated with poor precision. We review alternative rules, based on a Bayesian framework, where portfolio decisions incorporate the user's views on the asset expected returns (the famous Black-Litterman model). We also review the basic principles underlying risk parity in asset allocation: because expected returns are difficult to estimate, a possibility may be to proceed while ignoring the assets' expected returns in the first place. In its basic version, risk parity would suggest creating portfolios that weigh more assets that have less volatility. In fact, section 1.3 provides some foundations for this portfolio rule, based on "Knightian uncertainty," a situation arising when decision makers do not understand the statistical laws underlying their environment; chapter 9 (in part II) studies the asset price implications of Knightian uncertainty in more detail (see section 9.6). Section 1.3 shows that risk parity is a portfolio strategy that investors adopt, in equilibrium, once Knightian uncertainty is high. More advanced parts of this book (see, e.g., chapters 9 or 11) explain that a wide adoption of risk parity trading strategies may be destabilizing as assets would be sold when market volatility is high, a circumstance which typically occurs when markets fall. Finally, section 1.5 briefly reviews developments in the industry practice based on factor investing. Because additional factors appear to help explain the cross-section of expected returns, it seems natural that investors should seek exposure to factors that go beyond the market. Factor investing aims to seek such exposures ("smart beta").

1.2 Portfolio Selection

This section describes the process of wealth allocation for a representative investor who cares about "mean-variance efficiency." This notion of efficiency constraints our investor to choices of portfolios that produce the highest expected return for a given level of risk.

1.2.1 Wealth Constraints

Our investor can invest into m risky assets and one safe asset. Let $S=[S_1,\cdots,S_m]$ be the risky asset's price vector, and let S_0 be the price of the riskless asset. We wish to determine the value of a portfolio of all these assets. Let $\theta=[\theta_1,\cdots,\theta_m]$, where θ_i is the number of the ith risky asset, and let θ_0 be the number of the riskless asset in this portfolio. The initial wealth is $w=S_0\theta_0+S\cdot\theta$. Terminal wealth is $w'=x_0\theta_0+x\cdot\theta$, where x_0 is the payoff promised by the riskless asset and $x=[x_1,\cdots,x_m]$ is the vector of the payoffs pertaining to the risky assets—that is, x_i is the payoff promised by the ith risky asset.

Let $R\equiv\frac{x_0}{S_0}$ and $\tilde{R}_i\equiv\frac{x_i}{S_i}$ denote the gross returns from investing into the safe asset and the ith risky asset. Accordingly, define $r\equiv R-1$ as the safe interest rate, $\tilde{\mu}\equiv[\tilde{\mu}_1,\cdots,\tilde{\mu}_m]^\top$, where $\tilde{\mu}_i\equiv\tilde{R}_i-1$ is the return on the ith risky asset and $\mu\equiv E(\tilde{\mu})$, the vector of the expected returns on the risky assets. Finally, we let $\pi=[\pi_1,\cdots,\pi_m]^\top$, where $\pi_i\equiv\theta_iS_i$ is the wealth invested in the ith asset. We have

$$w'=x_0\theta_0+\sum_{i=1}^{m}x_i\theta_i\equiv R\pi_0+\sum_{i=1}^{m}\tilde{R}_i\pi_i \quad\text{and}\quad w=\pi_0+\sum_{i=1}^{m}\pi_i. \tag{1.1}$$

Combining the two expressions for w' and w leaves

$$w'=\pi^\top(\tilde{R}-\mathbf{1}_mR)+Rw=\pi^\top(\mu-\mathbf{1}_mr)+Rw+\pi^\top(\tilde{\mu}-\mu).$$

We use the decomposition, $\tilde{\mu}-\mu=B\cdot\tilde{u}$, where B is a $m\times d$ volatility matrix, with $m\leq d$, and $\tilde{u}$ is a random vector with expectation zero and variance-covariance matrix equal to the identity matrix. With this decomposition, we can rewrite the budget constraint in eq. (1.1) as follows:

$$w'=\pi^\top(\mu-\mathbf{1}_mr)+Rw+\pi^\top B\tilde{u}. \tag{1.2}$$

We can now use eq. (1.2) and determine the expected return and the variance of the portfolio value. We have

$$E\left[w'(\pi)\right]=\pi^{\top}(\mu-\mathbf{1}_m r)+Rw \quad \text{and} \quad var\left[w'(\pi)\right]=\pi^{\top}\Sigma\pi, \tag{1.3}$$

where $\Sigma \equiv BB^{\top}$. Let $\sigma_i^2 \equiv \Sigma_{ii}$. We assume that Σ has full rank and that for all i, j, $\sigma_i^2 > \sigma_j^2 \Longrightarrow \mu_i > \mu_j$. The last condition does actually hold in the equilibrium of markets in which investors are averse to risk, a topic dealt with several times in this chapter; further, note more trivially that this condition implies that $r < \min_j(\mu_j)$.

1.2.2 Portfolio Choice: The "Capital Market Line"

We assume that the investor maximizes the expected return on their portfolio conditionally on a given level of uncertainty. That is, let $w^2 \cdot v_p^2$ define the maximum level of dollar variance the investor is willing to accept. We consider the following program based on eq. (1.3) and the uncertainty constraint:

$$\hat{\pi}\left(v_p\right)=\arg\max_{\pi\in\mathbb{R}^m} E\left[w'(\pi)\right] \quad \text{s.t.} \quad var\left[w'(\pi)\right]=w^2\cdot v_p^2. \tag*{[1.P1]}$$

The first-order conditions for [1.P1] are

$$\hat{\pi}\left(v_p\right)=(2\nu)^{-1}\Sigma^{-1}(\mu-\mathbf{1}_m r) \quad \text{and} \quad \hat{\pi}^{\top}\Sigma\hat{\pi}=w^2\cdot v_p^2,$$

where ν is a Lagrange multiplier for the variance constraint. Plugging the first condition into the second, we obtain $(2\nu)^{-1}=\mp\frac{w\cdot v_p}{\sqrt{\text{Sh}}}$, where

$$\text{Sh}\equiv(\mu-\mathbf{1}_m r)^{\top}\Sigma^{-1}(\mu-\mathbf{1}_m r) \tag{1.4}$$

is the *Sharpe market performance*. To ensure efficiency, we take the positive solution. Substituting the positive solution for $(2\nu)^{-1}$ into the first-order condition, we obtain the portfolio that solves [1.P1]:

$$\frac{\hat{\pi}\left(v_p\right)}{w}\equiv\frac{\Sigma^{-1}(\mu-\mathbf{1}_m r)}{\sqrt{\text{Sh}}}\cdot v_p. \tag{1.5}$$

We are ready to determine the value of [1.P1], $E\left[w'(\hat{\pi}\left(v_p\right))\right]$, and hence the expected portfolio return, defined as

$$\mu_p(v_p)\equiv\frac{E\left[w'(\hat{\pi}(v_p))\right]-w}{w}=r+\sqrt{\text{Sh}}\cdot v_p, \tag{1.6}$$

where the last equality follows by a simple calculation. Eq. (1.6) describes what is known as the *Capital Market Line* (CML).

1.2.3 Without the Safe Asset: The "Efficient Portfolio Frontier"

Next, assume that the investor's choice space does not include the riskless asset. Their current wealth is now $w=\sum_{i=1}^m \pi_i$ while their terminal wealth is $w'=\sum_{i=1}^m \tilde{R}_i\pi_i$, such that, and relying on the definition of $\tilde{\mu}_i$,

$$w'=\sum_{i=1}^m \tilde{\mu}_i\pi_i+\sum_{i=1}^m \pi_i=\pi^{\top}\mu+w+\pi^{\top}B\tilde{u}, \tag{1.7}$$

where B and $\tilde{u}$ are as defined as in eq. (1.2). We can use eq. (1.7) to determine the expected return and the variance of the portfolio value, which are

$$E\left[w'(\pi)\right]=\pi^{\top}\mu+w, \text{ where } w=\pi^{\top}\mathbf{1}_m \quad \text{and} \quad var\left[w'(\pi)\right]=\pi^{\top}\Sigma\pi. \tag{1.8}$$

The program our investor now solves is

$$\hat{\pi}\left(v_p\right)=\arg\max_{\pi\in\mathbb{R}} E\left[w'(\pi)\right] \quad \text{s.t. } var\left[w'(\pi)\right]=w^2\cdot v_p^2 \text{ and } w=\pi^{\top}\mathbf{1}_m. \qquad [1.P2]$$

In appendix 1.A, we show that, provided $AC-D^2>0$ (a second-order condition, as explained in appendix A.1), the solution to [1.P2] is

$$\frac{\hat{\pi}\left(v_p\right)}{w}=\frac{C\mu_p(v_p)-D}{AC-D^2}\Sigma^{-1}\mu+\frac{A-D\mu_p(v_p)}{AC-D^2}\Sigma^{-1}\mathbf{1}_m, \tag{1.9}$$

where $A\equiv\mu^{\top}\Sigma^{-1}\mu$, $D\equiv\mathbf{1}_m^{\top}\Sigma^{-1}\mu$ and $C\equiv\mathbf{1}_m^{\top}\Sigma^{-1}\mathbf{1}_m$ and $\mu_p(v_p)$ is the expected portfolio return, defined as in eq. (1.6). In appendix 1.A, we also show that

$$v_p^2=\frac{1}{C}\left[1+\frac{1}{AC-D^2}\left(\mu_p(v_p)C-D\right)^2\right]. \tag{1.10}$$

Based on eq. (1.10), we define the *global minimum variance (GMV) portfolio* as the portfolio that achieves a variance equal to $v_{\text{gmv}}^2\equiv C^{-1}$ and an expected return equal to $\mu_{\text{gmv}}\equiv D/C$. We shall return to this portfolio below (see section 1.2.5).

Note that for each v_p, there are two values of $\mu_p(v_p)$ that solve eq. (1.10). The optimal choice for our investor is that with the highest μ_p. We define the *efficient portfolio frontier* as the set of values (v_p,μ_p) that solve eq. (1.10) with the highest μ_p. It has the following expression:

$$\mu_p(v_p)=\frac{D}{C}+\frac{1}{C}\sqrt{\left(Cv_p^2-1\right)\left(AC-D^2\right)}. \tag{1.11}$$

The efficient portfolio frontier is increasing and concave in risk, v_p. It can be interpreted as a "production function"—that is, a technology through which expected returns are obtained using varying "levels of risk" as inputs (see, e.g., the two-asset case depicted in figure 1.1). Which portfolio on this frontier is selected by an investor depends on the investor's attitudes toward risk. We shall return to this selection problem in section 1.3.

1.2.4 Risk-Return Trade-Offs in the Two-Asset Case

Consider a simple example in which there are only two risky assets, $m=2$. This simplified version of the model illustrates some crucial points regarding diversification very clearly and is also at the basis of famous contributions going beyond financial economics, notably in macroeconomics (see section 1.3.5.4). In this two-asset case, the efficient portfolio frontier is the risk-return trade-off resulting from any feasible combination of the two assets and does not require any optimization, as above: the budget constraint, $\frac{\pi_1}{w}+\frac{\pi_2}{w}=1$, pins down a unique relation between the portfolio expected return and variance. Precisely, we have: $\mu_p=\frac{E\left[w'(\pi)\right]-w}{w}=\frac{\pi_1}{w}\mu_1+\frac{\pi_2}{w}\mu_2$, or

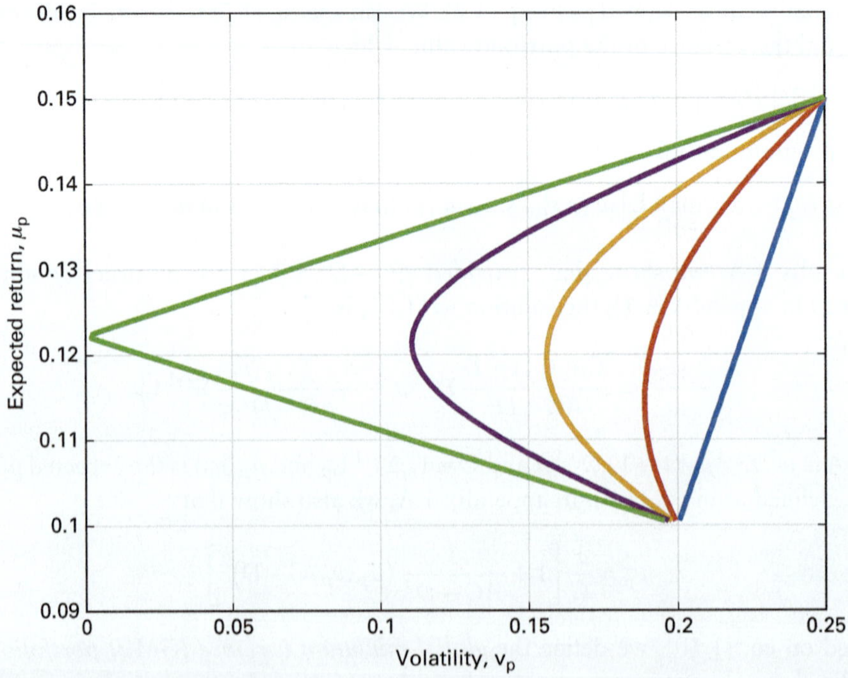

Figure 1.1
From top to bottom: portfolio frontiers corresponding to $\rho = -1, -0.5, 0, 0.5, 1$. Remaining parameter values are $\mu_1 = 0.10, \mu_2 = 0.15, \sigma_1 = 0.20, \sigma_2 = 0.25$. For each portfolio frontier, the efficient portfolio frontier includes those portfolios that yield the highest expected return for a given level of volatility.

$$\begin{cases} \mu_p = \mu_1 + (\mu_2 - \mu_1)\dfrac{\pi_2}{w} \\ v_p^2 = \left(1 - \dfrac{\pi_2}{w}\right)^2 \sigma_1^2 + 2\left(1 - \dfrac{\pi_2}{w}\right)\dfrac{\pi_2}{w}\sigma_{12} + \left(\dfrac{\pi_2}{w}\right)^2 \sigma_2^2 \end{cases}$$

whence

$$v_p = \frac{1}{\mu_2 - \mu_1}\sqrt{(\mu_2 - \mu_p)^2 \sigma_1^2 + 2(\mu_2 - \mu_p)(\mu_p - \mu_1)\rho\sigma_1\sigma_2 + (\mu_p - \mu_1)^2 \sigma_2^2}.$$

Note that when the returns on the two assets are perfectly correlated, $\rho = 1$, we have

$$\mu_p = \mu_1 + \frac{\mu_2 - \mu_1}{\sigma_2 - \sigma_1}(v_p - \sigma_1).$$

That is, the risk-return trade-off is linear. However, diversification pays as soon as the asset returns are not perfectly positively correlated: for any given expected return, the portfolio return volatility decreases as the asset correlation decreases. Figure 1.1 actually reveals that there are portfolios that are even less risky than the less risky asset and that risk can actually be zeroed in the extreme case where $\rho = -1$.

Naturally, in these examples, the portfolio frontier is given, in that the parameter values are given. However, these values should be determined in equilibrium. For example, the portfolio with zero volatility seems to offer investors too good opportunities: it yields positive expected returns with no risk. Can this be sustainable? Many investors would spot this opportunity and implement a trade that would make this opportunity disappear. Let us illustrate. If $\rho = -1$, the portfolio that achieves zero volatility has $\frac{\pi_2}{w} = \frac{\sigma_1}{\sigma_1+\sigma_2}$, and the expected return is $\mu_{o,p} \equiv \frac{\sigma_2}{\sigma_1+\sigma_2}\mu_1 + \frac{\sigma_1}{\sigma_1+\sigma_2}\mu_2$. But as more investors go long to exploit this portfolio's nice opportunity, the two asset prices go up, and their returns decrease. This process eventually stops once μ_1 and μ_2 adjust in a way such that $\mu_{o,p} = r$, the risk-free rate.

Naturally, it is a simple example, which relies on hypothetical price adjustments. However, this example illustrates the type of standard restrictions arising in financial economics, which make prices economically viable or free from arbitrage opportunities, as we shall explain in many junctures of this book. For example, in the context of this chapter, eq. (1.15) given below is the restriction that generalizes the previous reasoning to the case in which assets returns are not perfectly and negatively correlated.

1.2.5 Risk Parity and the Global Minimum Variance Portfolio

Note that the portfolio in eq. (1.9) can be decomposed into two components as follows:

$$\frac{\hat{\pi}(v_p)}{w} = \ell(v_p)\frac{\pi_d}{w} + [1-\ell(v_p)]\frac{\pi_{\text{gmv}}}{w}, \quad \ell(v_p) \equiv \frac{D(\mu_p(v_p)C - D)}{AC - D^2}, \tag{1.12}$$

where

$$\frac{\pi_d}{w} \equiv \frac{\Sigma^{-1}\mu}{D}, \quad \frac{\pi_{\text{gmv}}}{w} \equiv \frac{\Sigma^{-1}\mathbf{1}_m}{C}. \tag{1.13}$$

Therefore, any portfolio on the efficient portfolio frontier can be constructed by choosing a convex combination of two portfolios, π_d and π_{gmv}, with weights equal to $\ell(v_p)$ and $1 - \ell(v_p)$. It is a *mutual fund (or separation) theorem.*[1] We shall use this representation of efficient portfolios to derive the zero-beta CAPM of section 1.3.2.

The two portfolios in (1.13) may be described as follows. The first, π_d, achieves the expected return that makes $\ell(v_p) = 1$, that is, $(v_p, \mu_p) = \left(\frac{\sqrt{A}}{D}, \frac{A}{D}\right)$. The second portfolio, π_{gmv}, is the GBV portfolio introduced in section 1.2.3, for we know from eq. (1.10) that the minimum variance occurs at $(v_p, \mu_p) = (\sqrt{1/C}, D/C)$, that is, when $\ell(v_p) = 0$.[2] This portfolio displays a very peculiar and interesting property: it requires an asset composition that is independent of the market expectations on asset returns, μ. It is a remarkable property: in many instances of this book, portfolio weights are instead proportional to the assets' expected excess returns (see, e.g., eq. (1.18) or the extensions to its dynamic counterparts in chapter 4 [section 4.6]). It is then quite peculiar that such a portfolio does not carry any information on the expected returns.

To facilitate the interpretation of this portfolio, assume that all asset returns are uncorrelated, in which case π_{gmv} in (1.13) collapses to a vector, where each component is

1. But then any efficient portfolio can be constructed through a convex combination of any two arbitrary but distinct efficient portfolios (see appendix 1.A).

2. The covariance of the global minimum variance portfolio with any other portfolio is always C^{-1} (see appendix 1.A).

given by

$$\frac{\pi_{\text{gmv},i}}{w} \equiv \frac{1/\sigma_i^2}{\sum_{j=1}^m 1/\sigma_j^2}, \quad i=1,\cdots,m. \tag{1.14}$$

This portfolio expresses the rule to overweight assets that display lower volatility. It is the simplest example of a *risk parity* investment strategy, by which the risk contribution is the same for different assets: eq. (1.14) is an equally weighted portfolio in terms of risk and thus implicitly assumes that expected returns are the same for all assets. More advanced parts of this book (see, e.g., chapter 9 [section 9.11.5] or chapter 11 [section 11.10] explain that risk parity practice may feed endogenous risk: agents invested into such a strategy tend to sell when volatility increases, determining more volatility over a vicious circle. Roncalli (2014) provides an introduction to risk parity practice.

Note, finally, that if variances are all the same, $\sigma_i^2 = \bar{\sigma}^2$ for some $\bar{\sigma}^2$, then, the global minimum variance portfolio in (1.14) collapses to the famous one-over-N rule,

$$\frac{\pi_{\text{gmv},i}}{w} = \frac{1}{m},$$

where each asset is equally weighted and N stands for m in the notation of this chapter.

Implicit in these rules may be the acknowledgment of the idea that expected returns (and volatilities in the case of the one-over-N rule) are so difficult to calibrate that one may give up taking any assumptions on them in the first place. Indeed, it is well known that the actual performance of the mean-variance model is very sensitive to the estimates of the expected returns. Section 1.3.6 reviews a Bayesian approach to this problem, which enables a model user to incorporate their own views on market returns. Instead, section 1.3.7 proposes explanations for why investors would insist in using global minimum variance portfolios in a world of Knightian uncertainty where uncertainty reigns regarding the exact value taken by the assets' expected returns.

1.2.6 The Market Portfolio

The *market portfolio* is the portfolio at which the CML in eq. (1.6) and the efficient portfolio frontier in eq. (1.11) intersect. In fact, the market portfolio is the point at which the CML is *tangent* to the efficient portfolio frontier. For this reason, the market portfolio is also referred to as the "tangent portfolio." In figure 1.2, the market portfolio is at point M and has volatility equal to v_M and expected return equal to μ_M. At this point, the CML is tangent to the efficient portfolio frontier, AMC.[3] We now develop the reasons for referring to the tangent portfolio as the market portfolio.

1.2.6.1 Two-fund separation

Figure 1.2 illustrates that the CML dominates the efficient portfolio frontier AMC. Let us explain. On the one hand, the CML is the value of the investor's problem, [1.P1], obtained while investing in all the risky assets *and* the riskless asset. On the other hand, the efficient portfolio frontier is the value of the investor's problem, [1.P2], obtained while investing

3. The existence of the market portfolio requires a restriction on r, derived in eq. (1.15).

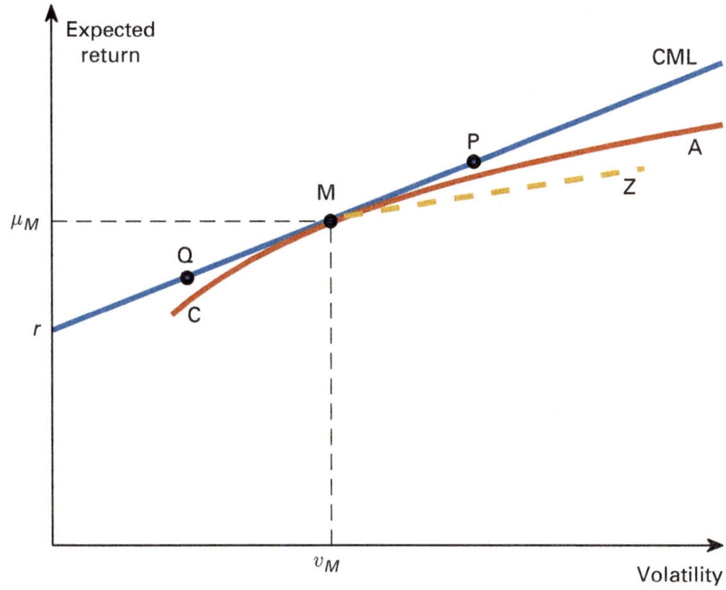

Figure 1.2
The capital market line and the market portfolio.

in the risky assets *only*.[4] Then, the CML and the efficient portfolio frontier can only be tangent to each other. If not, then there would exist a point on the efficient portfolio frontier that dominates some portfolio on the CML, and this is impossible. Likewise, the CML must have a portfolio in common with the efficient portfolio frontier—the portfolio that does not include the safe asset. We shall rely on these insights and provide an analytical characterization of the market portfolio.

So why do we term the market portfolio in this way? Figure 1.2 reveals that any portfolio on the CML can be obtained as a combination of the safe asset and the market portfolio M (a portfolio containing only the risky assets). Investors with high risk aversion would like to choose a portfolio such as Q, and investors with low risk aversion would perhaps pick a portfolio such as P. But no matter how risk averse an investor is, their optimal choice is a mix of the safe asset and the market portfolio M. Thus, the market portfolio allows an investor to calibrate their desired overall exposure to risk: they will invest those portions of their wealth in the market portfolio that makes their overall exposure to risk consistent with their risk appetite. It's a *two-fund separation theorem*. We shall make these statements more rigorous in the following sections.

This separation theorem has equilibrium implications that naturally lead us to refer the tangent portfolio to as "market portfolio." We know that any portfolio can be attained by investing in the portfolio M and by lending or borrowing funds in zero net supply. In

4. Figure 1.2 also depicts the dotted line MZ, which is the value of the investor's problem when they invest a proportion higher than 100% in the market portfolio, leveraged at an interest rate for borrowing higher than the interest rate for lending. In this case, the CML coincides with rM up to the point M. From M onward, the CML coincides with the highest between MZ and MA.

equilibrium, then, every investor must hold some proportions of M. But in aggregate, there is no net borrowing or lending, and all investors must then have portfolio holdings that sum up to the market portfolio, which is therefore the value-weighted portfolio of all the existing risky assets. This argument is formally developed in appendix 1.B.

Note, finally, that the market portfolio is a mere convex combination of all the existing risky assets. At first sight, it appears to be "preference-free" in that its construction is independent of the investors' risk attitudes. However, this proposition needs to be nuanced: below, we shall explain that the vector of expected returns μ still needs to be estimated and that models of risk and risk aversion might be needed to characterize μ.

1.2.6.2 *Asset allocation puzzles*

Do investors allocate wealth according to the previous predictions? Financial advisers are known to recommend that young investors hold more risky positions; they are also known to advise less conservative investors to increase their stock holdings compared with bonds. However, according to the theory in this section, the stocks-bonds mix in the market portfolio should be the same, regardless of the investors' attitude to risk (see the discussion around figure 1.2). It is an instance of asset allocation puzzles.

Campbell and Viceira (2002) provide an early synthesis of how these puzzles can be addressed through dedicated extensions of the framework in this section. These or additional analysts' recommendations could be understood while assuming that investors face more risks than those directly related to the price fluctuations of the assets in their portfolios. Some of these risks (not necessarily traded—e.g., labor income or random volatility) could indeed be hedged by investing more or less in risky positions than predicted by the simple theory in this section. Chapter 4 provides discussions of these cases while framing them into subsequently developed notions, according to which agents are assumed to have access to "stochastic opportunity sets."

1.2.6.3 *Analytical characterization*

We turn to characterize the market portfolio. We need to assume that the interest rate is sufficiently low to allow the CML to be tangent at the efficient portfolio frontier. The condition ensuring this outcome is that the return on the safe asset should be less than the expected return on the global minimum variance portfolio; namely,

$$r < \frac{D}{C} = \mu_{\text{gmv}}, \tag{1.15}$$

where μ_{gmv} is the global minimum variance portfolio identified through eq. (1.10). That is, we cannot find risky portfolios that yield less than the safe asset.

Next, let π_M be the market portfolio. To identify π_M, we note that it belongs to AMC if $\pi_M^\top \mathbf{1}_m = w$, where π_M also belongs to the CML and, therefore, by eq. (1.5), is such that

$$\frac{\pi_M}{w} = \frac{\Sigma^{-1}(\mu - \mathbf{1}_m r)}{\sqrt{\text{Sh}}} v_M. \tag{1.16}$$

Therefore, we search for the value v_M that solves

$$w = \mathbf{1}_m^\top \pi_M = \mathbf{1}_m^\top w \frac{\Sigma^{-1}(\mu - \mathbf{1}_m r)}{\sqrt{\text{Sh}}} v_M;$$

that is

$$v_M = \frac{\sqrt{\text{Sh}}}{D - Cr}. \tag{1.17}$$

Finally, we plug this value of v_M into the expression for π_M in eq. (1.16) and obtain

$$\frac{\pi_M}{w} = \frac{1}{D - Cr} \Sigma^{-1} \left(\mu - \mathbf{1}_m r\right). \tag{1.18}$$

Once again, the market portfolio belongs to the efficient portfolio frontier.[5] Indeed, on the one hand, the market portfolio cannot be above the efficient portfolio frontier as this would contradict the efficiency of the *AMC* curve (obtained by investing in risky assets only). On the other hand, by construction, the market portfolio belongs to the CML, and so it cannot be below the efficient portfolio frontier as the CML dominates the efficient portfolio frontier. Appendix 1.B makes this reasoning rigorous and shows that the market portfolio does indeed satisfy the tangency condition.

1.3 The Capital Asset Pricing Model

This section provides analysis that goes beyond the investors' efficient portfolio choices and derives the first asset evaluation formula appearing in the literature, based on the celebrated CAPM. First, we derive the CAPM, relying on arguments that have the same flavor as those in the original derivation of Sharpe (1964). Second, we derive the zero-beta CAPM of Black (1972), a model that does not require the existence of pure risk-free asset. Third, we explain how CAPM predictions relate to the behavior of risk averse investors. Finally, this section applies CAPM ideas and deals with such disparate topics as project evaluation or "speculative" demand of money.

1.3.1 Restrictions on Securities Expected Returns

Consider a portfolio comprising a proportion x of wealth invested in any asset i and the remaining proportion $1-x$ invested in the market portfolio. That is, we consider a portfolio that is parametrized by x. The expected return and volatility of this portfolio are

$$\begin{cases} \tilde{\mu}_p \equiv x\mu_i + (1-x)\mu_M \\ \tilde{v}_p \equiv \sqrt{(1-x)^2\sigma_M^2 + 2(1-x)x\sigma_{iM} + x^2\sigma_i^2} \end{cases} \tag{1.19}$$

where we have defined $\sigma_M \equiv v_M$. Clearly, the market portfolio M is a special case of this portfolio. Relying on the examples of section 1.2.4, we know that the curve in (1.19) has the same shape as the curve *BMi* in figure 1.3. The curve *BMi* lies below the efficient portfolio frontier *AMC* because the latter results from optimizing a mean-variance criterion over all the existing assets, which then dominates any portfolio that only comprises the two assets i and M.

5. While the market portfolio depends on r, this portfolio does not obviously include any shares in the safe asset.

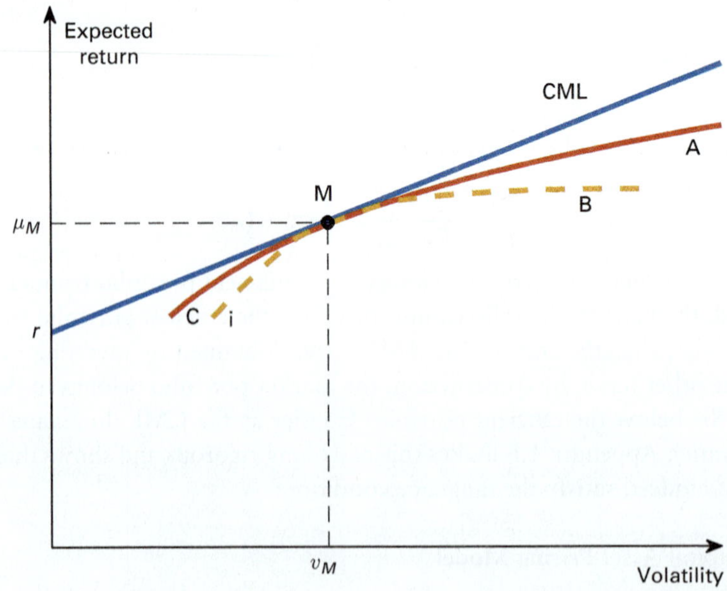

Figure 1.3
Construction of the capital asset pricing model.

For example, suppose that the *BMi* curve intersects the *AMC* curve. Then a feasible combination of assets in the *BMi* curve would dominate points on *AMC*, a contradiction, as *AMC* is the most efficient feasible combination of all existing assets. On the other hand, the *BMi* curve has a point in common with the *AMC* curve, which is *M* (the portfolio obtained with $x = 0$). Therefore, the curve *BMi* is tangent to the efficient portfolio frontier *AMC* at *M*, which is tangent to the CML at *M*, as we know.

That is, at *M*, the slopes of the *BMi* curve is the same as that of the efficient portfolio frontier *AMC*. This condition provides a restriction on the expected return μ_i on any asset *i* as we now show. Consider the *x*-parametrized curve (1.19). We determine its slope at *M* through the two slopes, $d\tilde{\mu}_p / dx$ and $d\tilde{v}_p / dx$, both evaluated at $x = 0$. We have

$$\frac{d\tilde{\mu}_p}{dx} = \mu_i - \mu_M, \quad \left.\frac{d\tilde{v}_p}{dx}\right|_{x=0} = -\frac{-(1-x)\sigma_M^2 + (1-2x)\sigma_{iM} + x\sigma_i^2|_{x=0}}{\tilde{v}_p|_{x=0}} = \frac{1}{\sigma_M}\left(\sigma_{iM} - \sigma_M^2\right).$$

Therefore,

$$\left.\frac{d\tilde{\mu}_p(x)}{d\tilde{v}_p(x)}\right|_{x=0} = \frac{\mu_i - \mu_M}{\frac{1}{\sigma_M}\left(\sigma_{iM} - \sigma_M^2\right)}. \tag{1.20}$$

On the other hand, the slope of the CML is $(\mu_M - r)/\sigma_M$, which, equated to the slope in eq. (1.20), yields

$$\mu_i - r = \beta_i\,(\mu_M - r), \quad \beta_i \equiv \frac{\sigma_{iM}}{v_M^2}, \quad i = 1, \cdots, m. \tag{1.21}$$

Eq. (1.21) is the celebrated *security market line* (SML) (see appendix 1.B for an alternative derivation). The assets for which $\beta_i > 1$ are usually referred to as "aggressive," and the assets for which $\beta_i < 1$ are called "conservative."[6] The rationale is the following. Assuming a positive beta, the higher this beta, the more volatile (and risky) the asset and the higher its expected return. Assets where beta is negative return on average less than the safe interest because they provide diversification. Thus, according to the model, assets that command an expected return less than the safe interest rate can still be quite volatile, notably when their (negative) beta is sizable.

The SML can be interpreted as a projection of the excess return on asset i (i.e., $\tilde{\mu}_i - r$) on the excess returns on the market portfolio (i.e. $\tilde{\mu}_M - r$). In other words,

$$\tilde{\mu}_i - r = \alpha_i + \beta_i(\tilde{\mu}_M - r) + \varepsilon_i, \quad i = 1, \cdots, m, \tag{1.22}$$

where $\alpha_i = 0$ provided the model is correctly specified. Section 1.5 provides discussion regarding the empirical evidence on the CAPM.

Eq. (1.22) leads to the following decomposition of the volatility regarding the return in the ith asset:

$$\sigma_i^2 = \beta_i^2 v_M^2 + var(\varepsilon_i), \quad i = 1, \cdots, m.$$

The quantity $\beta_i^2 v_M^2$ is known as *systematic* risk. The quantity $var(\varepsilon_i) \geq 0$ does, instead, capture the notion of *idiosyncratic* risk. In the next section, we shall show that idiosyncratic risk can be eliminated through a well-diversified portfolio—roughly, a portfolio that contains a large number of assets.

1.3.2 The Low-Beta Anomaly

Even though we discuss empirical properties of the CAPM in section 1.5, it is useful to discuss one of these properties now. Note that the SML line predicts that high-beta stocks should command higher returns than low beta (see eq. (1.21)). Yet historically, low-beta stocks have performed better on a risk-adjusted basis: stocks with lower beta tend to display a higher alpha (the intercept in eq. (1.22)) than stocks with higher beta. Why?

This anomaly has been known since at least Black, Jensen, and Scholes (1972). One explanation relies on market frictions. Consider an investor with a pronounced attitude toward risk-taking behavior. Theoretically, they might want to invest in a portfolio such as that indicated by point P in figure 1.2. This portfolio may be constructed through leverage: they should borrow money to invest more than 100% of their wealth into the market portfolio M. However, there may be constraints to leverage. To approximate the profit and loss (P&L) of a levered position, some investors may want to overweight their exposure to very risky assets; that is, those with high beta. High-beta stocks would display lower average returns as a result. Likewise, low-beta stocks may be underweighted and therefore might offer higher returns. There might also be investors able to borrow, and these investors

6. Interestingly, this notion of beta links to the following classical regression-based hedging context. Suppose we hold a perhaps highly illiquid asset that promises to deliver a return equal to $\tilde{z}$. To hedge against this stochastic return, go long a portfolio comprising a proportion π in the market portfolio and $1-\pi$ in a safe asset. We minimize the variance of the overall position by choosing $\hat{\pi} = \arg\min_x var[\tilde{z} - ((1-\pi)r + \pi\tilde{\mu}_M)] = \beta_{\tilde{z}} \equiv cov(\tilde{z}, \tilde{\mu}_M)/v_M^2$. That is, the beta of the asset is the proportion of the market portfolio that we use to hedge the asset against systematic market movements.

would be less exposed to the "weighting biases" the constrained are subject to. However, investors able to borrow are likely to be subject to margin requirements. The tighter the constraints, the higher the low-high beta spread.

It seems natural to assess how robust these insights are when judged against market conditions. Frazzini and Pedersen (2014) construct a betting-against-beta (BAB) factor: a portfolio that is long low-beta stocks and short high-beta stocks and engineered in a way to be market-neutral—that is, to have zero beta. Theoretically, this portfolio has a positive expected return. Empirically, this portfolio produces substantial risk-adjusted returns. However, in times of distress, when liquidity is tight, this portfolio's performance deteriorates, just as the theory suggests: a market distress comes with higher margin requirements; therefore, more cash should be held by the investors who are able to borrow, making their asset holdings more similar to the investors unable to borrow. The price of high-beta (or resp., low-beta) stocks increases (resp., decreases) as a result.

The previous examples cover quite advanced material, but it is useful to point them out in this introductory chapter. The objective is not only to inform the reader about the importance of market frictions (the CAPM is based on abstract frictionless markets) but also to explain how apparently spectacular risk-adjusted returns might then need to be assessed against realistic market conditions, such as those resulting from a liquidity dry-up. Moreover, the BAB factor is an example of a possible determinant of the cross-section of expected returns. Section 1.5 explains that hundreds of additional successful factors have been discovered in the empirical literature. While we may be inclined to be more lenient on factors suggested by economic reasoning (as the BAB of this section), we may want to create stringent statistical criteria for the purpose of avoiding a proliferation of factors arising from pure statistical analysis. Section 1.5.5 reviews work aimed at addressing such data-mining concerns.

1.3.3 Zero-Beta CAPM

The CAPM predicts that the market portfolio is a benchmark for all the assets' required returns. We can actually use any benchmark on the efficient portfolio frontier and not just the market portfolio to gauge each asset's expected return. In particular, we pick an arbitrary portfolio on the efficient frontier and consider another portfolio that has returns uncorrelated with the initial arbitrary portfolio. The spread generated by these two portfolios becomes the evaluation benchmark. Because we only deal with portfolios that have no riskless assets, the procedure may be useful when the risk-free asset is not available for trading.

So, consider any portfolio on the efficient frontier, which can be generated by eq. (1.12). Given a fixed weight equal to l, define $v_{p,l} : \ell\left(v_{p,l}\right) = l$, and let $\hat{\pi}_l \equiv \hat{\pi}\left(v_{p,l}\right)$. The return generated by the portfolio $\frac{\hat{\pi}_l}{w}$ is obviously $\mu_l \equiv \frac{\hat{\pi}_l^{\top}\tilde{\mu}}{w}$. The vector of the covariances of all the asset returns with μ_l is

$$cov(\tilde{\mu}, \tilde{\mu}_l) = \Sigma\frac{\hat{\pi}_l}{w} = \frac{l}{D}\mu + \frac{1-l}{C}\mathbf{1}_m. \tag{1.23}$$

In particular, we have that, for any asset i,

$$cov(\tilde{\mu}_i, \tilde{\mu}_l) = \frac{l}{D}\mu_i + \frac{1-l}{C}, \tag{1.24}$$

and then

$$var(\tilde{\mu}_l) = cov(\tilde{\mu}_l, \tilde{\mu}_l) = \frac{l}{D}\mu_l + \frac{1-l}{C}. \tag{1.25}$$

Eqs. (1.24) and (1.25) can be solved for $\frac{l}{D}$ and $\frac{1-l}{C}$, and the solutions can be replaced back into eq. (1.23), leaving

$$\mu = \frac{(var(\tilde{\mu}_l)\mu_i - cov(\tilde{\mu}_i, \tilde{\mu}_l)\mu_l)\,\mathbf{1}_m + cov(\tilde{\mu}, \tilde{\mu}_l)\,(\mu_l - \mu_i)}{var(\tilde{\mu}_l) - cov(\tilde{\mu}_i, \tilde{\mu}_l)}.$$

The previous expression simplifies for assets that have returns uncorrelated with $\tilde{\mu}_l$, say, some asset $z_l : cov(\tilde{\mu}_{z_l}, \tilde{\mu}_l) = 0$. We now have

$$\mu = \mu_{z_l}\mathbf{1}_m + \frac{cov(\tilde{\mu}, \tilde{\mu}_l)}{var(\tilde{\mu}_l)}\left(\mu_l - \mu_{z_l}\right). \tag{1.26}$$

Eq. (1.26) is Black's (1972) zero-beta CAPM. We may express expected returns in terms of "benchmark" returns, just as with the SML of eq. (1.21), without however having to rely on the market portfolio and a riskless asset. The spread referred to as at the beginning of this section is $\mu_l - \mu_{z_l}$, where μ_{z_l} is the expected return on an asset that has zero correlation with the benchmark portfolio on the efficient frontier (whence, zero-beta). It goes without saying that eq. (1.26) does not rely on whether riskless assets are actually available for trading or not.

1.3.4 An Excursion into Risk Premiums and Certainty Equivalents

1.3.4.1 Project evaluation

The CAPM is a model that determines the required return for any asset and, thus, is the very first tool that we can use to evaluate any risky project, not necessarily a very liquid one. The main prediction of the model is that the market is a pricing factor as it is the only source of risk against which we assess the expected return on any other asset. Let $\tilde{C}$ denote the future, random cash flow promised by a given project. Its return is $\tilde{\mu}_C = \frac{\tilde{C}}{V} - 1$, where V is the current value of the project; and by the CAPM, the risk-adjusted discount rate for this project is

$$\mu_C \equiv E(\tilde{\mu}_C) = r + \beta_C(\mu_M - r) = r + \frac{1}{V}\frac{cov(\tilde{C}, \tilde{\mu}_M)}{v_M}\lambda, \tag{1.27}$$

where $\lambda \equiv \frac{\mu_M - r}{v_M}$ is the unit market risk premium and $\beta_C = cov(\tilde{\mu}_C, \tilde{\mu}_M)/v_M^2$ is the project beta. The value of the project is

$$V = \frac{E(\tilde{C})}{1 + \mu_C}. \tag{1.28}$$

Replacing the expression for μ_C in eq. (1.27) into eq. (1.28) and rearranging terms gives us

$$V = \frac{E(\tilde{C}) - \frac{\lambda}{v_M}cov(\tilde{C}, \tilde{\mu}_M)}{1 + r}. \tag{1.29}$$

The project value is the discounted expectation of the random cash flow, $\tilde{C}$, "corrected for risk," in the following sense. According to the CAPM, the market is the only source of risk relevant for pricing, as explained. If the project cash flows are positively correlated with the market, investing in the project does not insulate the investments from this source of risk: the higher this correlation, the more aggressive the project is, just as we said in previous sections. But the more aggressive the project, the higher its expected return and, hence, the lower the project value. The risk-adjustment term, $\frac{\lambda}{v_M} cov(\tilde{C}, \tilde{x}_M)$, determines how low the project value has to be to induce an investor to undertake this project. This is the *risk premium* required to invest.

Were the project cash flows uncorrelated with the market (or were the market return the same as the riskless asset, $\lambda = 0$), eq. (1.29) would collapse to an actuarially fair evaluation formula, by which the project value is simply the discounted expectation of the future cash flows. Quite naturally, these statistical correlations occur under the probability laws generating returns and cash flows.

Is there any probability law such that the project value is the same as in eq. (1.29), but with the numerator replaced by the cash flow expectation under these hypothetical new laws and without any risk adjustments? The answer is in the affirmative. For obvious reasons, these laws are known as "risk neutral." They constitute indeed one fundamental pillar of asset evaluation, which this book heavily relies on.[7] Section 1.4 provides an introductory discussion to (and the next chapters provide a systematic treatment of) these foundational issues.

1.3.4.2 *With utility functions*

Consider an individual, who is considering entering into a gamble that yields a random payoff $\tilde{x}$ and costs V, with an initial wealth equal to w. We can think of this gamble as the investment decision in the previous section (*with* $\tilde{x} = \tilde{C}$) and set $r = 0$ to simplify the analysis. We assume the investor will enjoy a random utility $u(w - V + \tilde{x})$ from the project, where the function u is increasing and concave. The property by which the utility function is concave is tantamount to the assumption that our decision maker is risk averse. That is, the investor would prefer receiving the expected outcome of the project rather than exposing themselves to gambling for their utility. Formally, by Jensen's inequality, $E(u(w - V + \tilde{x})) \leq u(w - V + E(\tilde{x}))$.

We ask: What is the value V that induces the investor to enter into this project? Clearly, it cannot be higher than the solution V to

$$u(w) = E(u(w - V + \tilde{x})), \tag{1.30}$$

for otherwise the investor would be better off while staying away from the gamble (and experiencing utility equal to $u(w)$). We also assume that, should the project value be less than V, many additional investors with the same attitude for risk would step in and make this value increase to the extent that eq. (1.30) holds.

---

7. Informally, the project value can be expressed as $V = \frac{\mathbb{E}(\tilde{C})}{1+r}$, where $\mathbb{E}(\cdot)$ denotes the expectation under this risk neutral probability, say, Q. For the CAPM, the relation between Q and the original, natural probability, say P, is given by the so-called Radon-Nikodym derivative $\frac{dQ}{dP} = 1 - \frac{\lambda}{v_M}(\tilde{\mu}_M - \mu_M)$ (see section 1.4.2 for introductory details).

Next, define the demeaned payoff $\epsilon \equiv \tilde{x} - E(\tilde{x})$. We study the investor's attitude vis-à-vis risk in relation to the fair gamble, that is, the lottery that has payoff equal to ϵ. We have

$$u(w) = E\left(u\left(w + \Lambda + \epsilon\right)\right) \leq u\left(w + \Lambda\right), \tag{1.31}$$

where we have defined $\Lambda \equiv E(\tilde{x}) - V$. The first equality is simply eq. (1.30) (with the change in notation), and the inequality is Jensen's inequality again. Thus, Λ is positive. That is, due to risk aversion, the investor is willing to pay less than the expected cash flow to enter the project. For obvious reasons, we refer to Λ as the risk premium required to invest in the project.

Suppose, for example, that a representative investor has exponential utility, $u(w) = -e^{-\tau w}$, and that the cash flow is normally distributed, $\tilde{C} \sim N(E(\tilde{C}), \sigma_\epsilon^2)$, such that by eq. (1.30),

$$V = E(\tilde{C}) - \frac{1}{2}\tau\sigma_\epsilon^2. \tag{1.32}$$

The project value is at discount compared with the expected cash flow by a factor equal to $\Lambda = \frac{1}{2}\tau\sigma_\epsilon^2$, the risk premium. Note that this risk premium relates to the investor's risk aversion coefficient, τ: the higher τ, the higher the discount. We shall elaborate on this risk aversion coefficient below.

These conclusions are the utility counterparts to those of the CAPM in the previous section. According to the CAPM, the risk premium relates to the project exposure to market movements (see eq. (1.29)). In the model of this section, the risk premium arises to compensate a risk averse investor for the risk they would undertake in this specific project (see eq. (1.32)). Granted, in equilibrium, market movements may well be related to the investors' attitude vis-à-vis risk. However, the link to risk aversion is direct in this model. Section 1.3.5 clarifies how asset prices link to risk aversion in an equilibrium model—one in which agents choose amongst several alternatives, as in the CAPM.

Apart from exceptions (e.g., the previous Gaussian case), no closed-form solutions are available for V. We can, however, approximate Λ when the risks regarding the fair lottery are "small"; that is, when the variance of ϵ, σ_ϵ^2, say, is small. Appendix 1.C provides the following approximation to Λ in this small risks case:

$$\Lambda \approx \hat{\Lambda} \equiv -\frac{1}{2}\frac{u''(w)}{u'(w)}\sigma_\epsilon^2. \tag{1.33}$$

For example, if the representative investor has exponential utility, then $\hat{\Lambda} = \frac{1}{2}\tau\sigma_\epsilon^2$, which is the exact risk premium in the previous Gaussian case (see eq. (1.32)). Appendix 1.C. provides one additional example of evaluation models, in which no closed-form solutions are available for V, and discusses the quality of the approximations to V based on eq. (1.33).

1.3.4.3 With utility functions II: Certainty equivalents

An alternative albeit closely related notion of risk premium relies on the following reasoning. Assume that an individual *is entering* into a gamble—that is, they have no choice but to experience a random perturbation to their wealth, leaving them with $w + \tilde{x}$ dollars.[8]

8. As an example, think of these wealth fluctuations as those arising during the business cycles.

To illustrate, suppose that the individual expects a loss from this lottery, $E(\tilde{x}) < 0$. We ask, how much of their wealth would they be willing to give up if they were hypothetically asked to *avoid* the gamble?

If the individual were risk neutral, they would be glad to give up the expected loss. But if they are risk averse, they would be willing to give up more than the expected loss, say $-E(\tilde{x}) + \Pi$, for some positive Π interpreted as a risk premium. In other words, the individual would be glad to accept a *sure* reduction of their wealth to $w + E(\tilde{x}) - \Pi$, in exchange for avoiding to gamble,

$$u\left(w + E(\tilde{x}) - \Pi\right) = E\left(u\left(w + E(\tilde{x}) + \epsilon\right)\right) \leq u\left(w + E(\tilde{x})\right), \tag{1.34}$$

where the inequality is Jensen's inequality and shows that Π is positive. We refer to $\mathrm{CE}\,(w, \tilde{x}) \equiv E(\tilde{x}) - \Pi$ as the *certainty equivalent* for $\tilde{x}$ for an initial wealth equal to w. Naturally, the sign of $E(\tilde{x})$ can be anything.

The risk premium Π has an "insurance flavor." It relates to an economic premium that the individual is willing to pay to avoid a loss rather than to an economic incentive to undertake a risky project. However, it closely relates to the risk premium Λ defined in eq. (1.31). Consider, for example, the Gaussian project case in the previous subsection: if $\tilde{C}$ is Gaussian and the utility is exponential with risk aversion τ, the risk premium in this section is $\Pi = \frac{1}{2}\tau\sigma_\epsilon^2$, that is, the same as Λ in the previous section (see eq. (1.32)). Further, and just as with the approximation in eq. (1.33), the risk premium Π relates to the curvature of the utility function u, in that, in the small risks case, it can be approximated as follows (see appendix 1.C):

$$\Pi \approx \hat{\Pi} \equiv -\frac{1}{2}\frac{u''\left(w + E(\tilde{x})\right)}{u'(w + E(\tilde{x}))}\sigma_\epsilon^2. \tag{1.35}$$

Note that $\hat{\Pi}$ and $\hat{\Lambda}$ are the same as soon as the initial lottery is fair, $E(\tilde{x}) = 0$ (see eq. (1.33)). We now discuss alternative measures of risk premiums.

1.3.4.4 Constant and relative risk aversion

The notions of risk premiums investigated so far relate to *dollar* incentives to undertake (or avoid) risks. The expressions in eqs. (1.33) and (1.35) reveal that they are proportional to these risks (i.e., σ_ϵ^2) and that they increase with the "normalized curvature" of the utility function, $A\left(\cdot\right) \equiv -u''\left(\cdot\right)/u'\left(\cdot\right)$, a function we refer to as *absolute risk aversion*. The numerator of this function naturally measures how far the investor is from being risk neutral. The denominator of A makes this notion invariant to any positive and affine transformation of the original utility function: if two risk-averse investors have utilities u_1 and u_2, they have the same absolute risk aversion if and only if $u_1 = \varphi\left(u_2\right)$ and φ is an affine function. The exponential utility function hypothesized in the previous section is one for which absolute risk aversion is constant and equal to τ; it is known as constant absolute risk aversion (CARA) utility for this reason.

These notions can be extended to cover *relative* incentives to undertake (or avoid) risks. Consider, for example, the insurance risk premium of the previous section—one, however, regarding a multiplicative risk, that is, a lottery with an outcome equal to $\left(w + E(\tilde{x})\right)\left(1 + \tilde{g}\right)$ for some zero-mean random variable $\tilde{g}$, not $w + E(\tilde{x}) + \epsilon$ (an additive risk). The question we ask now is, what *proportion* of their wealth would the investor be willing to give up if hypothetically asked to avoid this lottery? The indifference condition in (1.34) is now replaced with

$$u\left(w+E(\tilde{x})\left(1-\Pi_r\right)\right)=E\left(u\left(\left(w+E(\tilde{x})\right)\left(1+\tilde{g}\right)\right)\right)\leq u\left(w+E(\tilde{x})\right), \tag{1.36}$$

where Π_r is a constant, relative (or percentage) risk premium. The previous inequality reveals that Π_r is positive. In appendix 1.C, we show that this relative risk premium can approximated as follows:

$$\Pi_r\approx\hat{\Pi}_r\equiv-\frac{1}{2}\frac{u''\left(w+E(\tilde{x})\right)\left(w+E(\tilde{x})\right)}{u'(w+E(\tilde{x}))}\sigma_g^2, \tag{1.37}$$

where σ_g^2 denotes the variance of $\tilde{g}$.

We refer the function $R_r(x)\equiv -u''(x)\,x/u'(x)$ to as *relative risk aversion*. Consider the utility function $u(x)=\frac{x^{1-\gamma}}{1-\gamma}$ for some constant $\gamma\neq 1$, or $u(x)=\ln x$ when $\gamma=1$. In this case, relative risk aversion is constant and equal to γ; it is known as constant relative risk aversion (CRRA) utility for this reason. Naturally, a CARA investor has increasing relative risk aversion. The implication of this property is that an investor keeps the same amount of dollars invested in risky assets as their wealth increases. However, the relative proportion of risky assets in their portfolio decreases with their wealth, as explained next. These notions of risk aversion are known since at least Pratt (1964) and Arrow (1965).

1.3.5 Back to CAPM: Equilibrium with Expected Utility

We explained that the investors' risk aversion determines the proportion of the market portfolio to hold and achieve any desired point of the risk-return trade-off. We formalize these explanations. We assume that our investors are risk averse: they prefer higher expected returns than lower, but for any expected portfolio return, they like portfolios that provide less volatility. We assume that investors are all the same and that the representative investor chooses portfolio holdings that maximize their utility derived from the expected returns and variance, namely,

$$\pi^*=\arg\max_{\pi} U\left(E\left[w'(\pi)\right], var\left[w'(\pi)\right]\right), \tag{1.P3}$$

where $U(\cdot,\cdot)$ is a concave utility function satisfying $U_1(\cdot,\cdot)>0$ and $U_2(\cdot,\cdot)<0$, subscripts denote partial derivatives, and the expressions for the portfolio expected return and variance are given in eq. (1.3).

Rearranging the first-order conditions to problem [1.P3] leads to the following portfolio choice:

$$\pi^*=\tau_*^{-1}\Sigma^{-1}\left(\mu-\mathbf{1}_m r\right), \quad \tau_*\equiv\frac{-2U_2^*}{U_1^*}, \tag{1.38}$$

where $U_j^*\equiv U_j\left(E\left[w'(\pi^*)\right], var\left[w'(\pi^*)\right]\right)$ and subscripts denote partial derivatives. That is, the investor's choice is a proportion of the market portfolio (see eq. (1.18)). Moreover, the more risk averse the investor is (i.e., the higher τ_*), the lower the proportion they desire to hold of the market portfolio.

The investor wishes to lend or to borrow according to whether $w-\mathbf{1}_m^\top\pi^*$ is positive or negative. If the riskless security is in zero net supply, then, in equilibrium,

$w-\mathbf{1}_m^\top\pi^*=0$—that is, the representative investor holds exactly the market portfolio, which is the value-weighted portfolio, $\pi_i^*=\bar{\theta}_i S_i$, where $\bar{\theta}_i$ is the number of the ith outstanding securities. Note, indeed, that if the riskless security is in zero net supply,

$$w=\mathbf{1}_m^\top\pi^*=\tau_*^{-1}\mathbf{1}_m^\top\Sigma^{-1}\left(\mu-\mathbf{1}_m r\right)=\tau_*^{-1}\left(D-Cr\right). \tag{1.39}$$

Replacing the previous relation into eq. (1.38) gives exactly the market portfolio, $\frac{\pi^*}{w}=\frac{\pi_M}{w}$, where π_M is as in eq. (1.18). Note that eq. (1.39) places a restriction on the safe interest rate, a restriction which we shall return below. Further, chapter 4 provides many additional instances of restrictions on the interest rate that link to investors' preferences (see, e.g., eq. (4.98)).

1.3.5.1 *Equilibrium expected returns*

What are the equilibrium expected returns? By eq. (1.38), we have that

$$\mu-\mathbf{1}_m r=\tau_* w\cdot\Sigma\frac{\pi^*}{w}=\tau_* w\cdot cov(\tilde{\mu},\tilde{\mu}_M), \tag{1.40}$$

where $\tilde{\mu}_M=\tilde{\mu}^\top\frac{\pi^*}{w}$ denotes the market return, and the second equality follows by results in appendix 1.B (see eq. (1.A12)). Moreover, note that, in equilibrium,

$$\mu_M=\frac{\pi^{*\top}}{w}\mu=r+\tau_* w\cdot\frac{\pi^{*\top}}{w}\Sigma\frac{\pi^*}{w}=r+\tau_* w\cdot v_M^2, \tag{1.41}$$

where the second equality follows by replacing μ from eq. (1.40). Eqs. (1.40) and (1.41) do obviously lead to the CAPM in eq. (1.21),

$$\mu-\mathbf{1}_m r=\frac{cov(\tilde{\mu},\tilde{\mu}_M)}{v_M^2}\left(\mu_M-r\right),$$

but they now also lead to a determination of the overall system of the expected excess returns: by eqs. (1.40) and (1.41), the expected excess returns on all assets (including the market portfolio) link to the representative agent's attitudes vis-à-vis risk.

1.3.5.2 *A parametric example: Exponential utility*

A simple example helps to illustrate the previous conclusions. Suppose the investor maximizes their expected utility of wealth, taken to be negative exponential, $u(w)=-e^{-\tau w}$, where τ is the absolute risk aversion. Assume that the asset returns are normally distributed, such that

$$\pi^*=\arg\max_\pi E\left[u\left(w'(\pi)\right)\right]=\arg\max_\pi\left(E\left[w'(\pi)\right]-\frac{\tau}{2}var\left[w'(\pi)\right]\right). \tag{1.42}$$

The solution to this problem is the same as that in eqs. (1.38), where τ^* collapses to the constant τ.[9] In equilibrium, the safe interest rate satisfies eq. (1.39), such that now the investor's equilibrium asset holdings coincide with the market portfolio.

9. Note that the investor desires to hold relative proportions of the risky assets (π^*/w) that are decreasing in w. This property follows by the assumption that this investor has constant absolute risk aversion.

We may elaborate on these results with a further simplification of this example, one with two risky assets that have uncorrelated payoffs. Assume also that the asset return volatilities are entirely driven by the asset payoffs, in that $\sigma_i^2 S_i^2 = \sigma_{x_i}^2$, where $\sigma_{x_i}^2$ is the variance of the ith asset payoff. It is easy to see that each asset demand is $\pi_i^* = (\tau\sigma_i^2)^{-1}(\mu_i - r) = \bar{\theta}_i S_i$, where the second equality is the equilibrium condition and, by the definition of μ_i, the equilibrium price is then

$$S_i = S_0\left(E(\tilde{x}_i) - \tau\bar{\theta}_i\sigma_{x_i}^2\right), \tag{1.43}$$

where we have set $x_0 \equiv 1$, such that $S_0 \equiv (1+r)^{-1}$. We assume that these prices are strictly positive.

To determine the equilibrium riskless rate r (or, equivalently, S_0), we use the zero net supply condition for the safe asset, that is, we aggregate the value of the asset holdings and set the result equal to the initial wealth, $\bar{\theta}_1 S_1 + \bar{\theta}_2 S_2 = w$, leaving us with

$$S_0 = \frac{w}{\bar{\theta}_1 E(\tilde{x}_1) + \bar{\theta}_2 E(\tilde{x}_2) - \tau(\bar{\theta}_1^2\sigma_{x_1}^2 + \bar{\theta}_2^2\sigma_{x_2}^2)}. \tag{1.44}$$

The single risky asset case is equally instructive. Assume that the second asset is not available for trading. In this case, the wealth of the representative investor equals $w = \bar{\theta}_1 S_1$, where S_1 is as in eq. (1.43) and the price of the safe asset is given by eq. (1.44), with $\bar{\theta}_2 \equiv 0$. That is, the equilibrium riskless rate simply forces the value of the risky asset holdings to equal initial wealth, $S_0 : \bar{\theta}_1 S_1 = w$.

1.3.5.3 *Mean-variance utility*

Next, suppose that, given a coefficient of variance aversion equal to τ, the agent maximizes a mean-variance criterion applying to portfolio *returns*, not to dollar positions, as in the case of the exponential utility in the previous section (see eq. (1.42)). That is, the investor chooses the following portfolio:

$$\pi_{\mathrm{mv}} = \arg\max_{\pi}\left(E\left[w'(\pi)/w\right] - \frac{\tau}{2}var\left[w'(\pi)/w\right]\right) = \frac{w}{\tau}\Sigma^{-1}(\mu - \mathbf{1}_m r), \tag{1.45}$$

where the last equality follows by a simple calculation. This solution differs from that in the previous section because the relative *proportions* of wealth invested in risky assets are now independent of w. Of course, exponential utility and mean-variance criterions would lead to the same outcome if exponential utility was referenced to portfolio returns, that is, if $u(w') = -e^{-\tau w'/w}$, in which case,

$$\pi^* = \arg\max_{\pi}\left(E\left[u\left(w'(\pi)/w\right)\right]\right) = \pi_{\mathrm{mv}}, \tag{1.46}$$

where π_{mv} is as in eq. (1.45).

Note that, in these cases, and in terms of the notation in (1.38), $\tau_* = \frac{\tau}{w}$, such that, by eq. (1.39), the equilibrium interest rate satisfies

$$r : \tau = D - Cr. \tag{1.47}$$

Section 1.3.7 relies on eq. (1.47) while discussing some foundational issues regarding risk parity portfolio allocations in equilibrium.

1.3.5.4 Tobin's reinterpretation of Keynesian money demand

One of the earliest applications of the ideas of portfolio selection occurred in monetary economics. In 1958, Tobin provided a new framework to think about money demand, aimed to provide microeconomic foundations to some traits of the monetary theory of Keynes (1936). In this novel framework, money demand arises as the agent invests their savings while optimizing over their risk-returns trade-offs based on their risk aversion. Tobin's work would actually inspire the very same Sharpe's ideas, leading to the CAPM. Let us review the main points underlying Tobin's contribution.

Tobin explains that taken at face value, Keynes's explanations of money demand would imply that agents end up making dichotomic choices: they would hold either money or bonds. That is, at the individual level, each agent holds money or bonds based on their own expectations about future interest rate levels. Yet at the aggregate level, money demand does inversely relate to nominal interest rates while being flat in correspondence of small rate values—a liquidity trap. Appendix 1.D provides a parametric example that clarifies the details of how these mechanisms operate.

Tobin formulates a theory of money demand in which agents do not make previous dichotomic choices. Consider the following specification of the examples in section 1.2.4. We interpret the safe asset as money, which is therefore such that its return and volatility are $\mu_1 \equiv 0$ and $\sigma_1 \equiv 0$; instead, bonds are risky, in that they provide a superior return but at the cost of some volatility. Therefore, the expected return and volatility of a portfolio comprising money and bonds are $\mu_p = \mu_2 \pi_2$ and $v_p = \pi_2 \sigma_2$, with straightforward notation, and initial wealth normalized to one.

An hypothetical representative agent optimizes a risk-return trade-off identical to that underlying eq. (1.42). Thus, their money demand is

$$1 - \pi_2 = 1 - \frac{\mu_2}{\tau \sigma_2^2}$$

and obviously decreases with the bond expected return. This simple model leads to some predictions regarding the effects of a decreased interest rate volatility. Suppose, for example, that a central bank has the power to lower both interest rates *and* interest rate volatility in such a way to keep the ratio μ_2 / σ_2 unchanged. Money demand decreases as a result. More generally, money demand is decreasing with interest rate volatility, σ_2. According to this very simple model, low interest rates may be targeted by merely lowering interest rate volatility.

1.3.6 The Black-Litterman Model

The mean-variance approach to asset allocation obviously requires knowledge of the assets expected returns. However, it has always been clear that the predictions of the mean-variance model were very sensitive to the assumptions underlying the assets expected returns. The main issue is that expected returns are very difficult to estimate. Moreover, even a small estimation error has the potential to lead to sizeable uncertainty around the accuracy of the model portfolio recommendations. This section provides a succinct description of a simple Bayesian approach to addressing these problems, originally developed by Black and Litterman (1991). Its key element is to acknowledge that the assets' expected returns, μ, are *unknown* and need to be estimated while having regard not only to data but also to the subjective views that investors might have about them. Fundamentally, this approach takes parameter uncertainty into account by allowing the model user to formulate their own *views*. We present succinct derivations of this approach. Meucci (2005) provides a comprehensive account of portfolio allocation in the presence of statistical risk.

1.3.6.1 *Views*

How do we estimate the assets' expected returns? A basic answer is to ask investors' opinions. Consider the following example. While the vector of expected returns, μ, is unknown, the model user may have views about some of its constituents. For example,

$$E(P\mu)=\mathcal{V}, \quad P=\begin{bmatrix} 1 & 0 & 0 & 0 & 0 & 0 \\ 0 & 0 & 0 & 0 & 1 & -1 \end{bmatrix}, \quad \mathcal{V}=\begin{bmatrix} 6\% \\ 1\% \end{bmatrix},$$

where the expectation is taken because μ is not known anymore and P is a matrix (also known as a pick matrix), which enables one to incorporate their own views across the whole spectrum of the expected returns. In this example with six assets, the first asset is expected to return 6% (an absolute view), and the fifth asset is expected to outperform the sixth by 1% (a relative view). We now discuss how the investor should update the estimation of the expected returns based on their views.

1.3.6.2 *Updating the estimates of the expected returns*

We assume that the assets expected returns satisfy

$$\begin{cases} \mu &= \bar{\mu}+\epsilon_\mu, \quad \epsilon_\mu \sim N(0,C), \quad C=c\Sigma \\ P\mu &= \mathcal{V}+\epsilon_v \quad \epsilon_v \sim N(0,\Omega), \end{cases} \tag{1.48}$$

where the second equation describes the investors' views; Σ is the usual variance-covariance matrix of the asset returns; $\bar{\mu}$, P, C, and Ω are vector or matrices of constants; and finally, c is a constant that measures the degree of intolerance to the investors' own prespecified belief, $\bar{\mu}$: the higher c, the higher the intolerance. We assume that Σ is known by the investors. A possible parametrization of Ω is $\Omega=P\Sigma P^\top/\psi$, where the constant ψ is a measure of the investors' confidence in their views.

We wish to determine the conditional distribution of μ given $\mathcal{V}$, say $\mu\,|\mathcal{V}$, that is, how the estimation of the expected returns changes with the views. This distribution can be obtained by an application of Bayesian methods that are reviewed in more advanced parts of the book (see, e.g., appendix 10.A in chapter 10). Appendix 1.E contains details of the proof that

$$\mu\,|\mathcal{V} \sim N\left(\mu_{bl}, \Sigma_*\right), \tag{1.49}$$

where

$$\mu_{bl}=\Sigma_*\left((c\Sigma)^{-1}\bar{\mu}+P^\top\Omega^{-1}\mathcal{V}\right), \quad \Sigma_*=c\left(\Sigma^{-1}+cP^\top\Omega^{-1}P\right)^{-1}. \tag{1.50}$$

A possible choice for the prior $\bar{\mu}$ is that implied by the mean-variance portfolio, obtained by inverting (1.45) for the expected excess returns,

$$\bar{\mu}=\mathbf{1}_m r+\tau\Sigma\frac{\pi_{\text{mv}}}{w}. \tag{1.51}$$

That is, we take the CAPM as the prior and update the assets expected returns by incorporating the views. Note that the asset returns, $\tilde{R} \sim N(\mu_{bl}, \Sigma_{bl})$, where $\Sigma_{bl} = \Sigma + \Sigma_*$. A mean-variance portfolio decision consistent with the investors' views is

$$\begin{aligned}\frac{\pi_{bl}}{w} &\equiv \frac{1}{\tau}\Sigma_{bl}^{-1}(\mu_{bl} - \mathbf{1}_m r) \\ &= \Sigma_{bl}^{-1} c^{-1} \Sigma_* \frac{\pi_{\text{mv}}}{w} + \frac{1}{\tau}\Sigma_{bl}^{-1}\left(\left(c^{-1}\Sigma_*\Sigma^{-1} - \mathbf{I}_m\right)\mathbf{1}_m r + \Sigma_* P^\top \Omega^{-1} \nu\right),\end{aligned} \tag{1.52}$$

where $\mathbf{I}_m$ denotes the m-dimensional identity matrix, the second line is obtained by replacing the expression for the CAPM prior $\bar{\mu}$ in (1.51) into (1.50) and, finally, by rearranging terms. Eq. (1.52) shows that the Black-Litterman portfolio with CAPM prior expected returns is a combination of the mean-variance portfolio (which obtains as a limit for $c \to 0$) and a term that tracks the investors' views.

1.3.7 Knightian Uncertainty and Global Minimum Variance Portfolio

This section describes a model by which investors react to parameter uncertainty by making conservative decisions. Compared with the Black-Litterman analysis, investors acknowledge that they might never learn about the true distribution affecting asset returns and are averse to this lack of knowledge. This situation is known as one of "Knightian uncertainty." Chapter 9 analyzes models with Knightian uncertainty, in which agents are unable to assess the probability distribution of asset returns and fundamentals (see section 9.6). In some cases, they take robust decisions; that is, decisions based on worst-case scenarios. In terms of the problems of this chapter, an investor lacks knowledge regarding the assets' expected returns but takes decisions *as if* a malevolent Nature had chosen the worst outcome for them. For example, the worst outcome could be the lowest expected return when the investor goes long and the highest expected return when they go short. Section 9.6 explains that these problems were introduced in finance since at least Dow and Werlang (1992) and provides a list of references and surveys, including the seminal contribution of Gilboa and Schmeidler (1989) on "maxmin" preferences (i.e., optimizing behavior under worst-case scenarios). This section is a slight variation on Garlappi, Uppal, and Wang (2007). It shows that, in equilibrium, investors tend to tilt their portfolios toward the global minimum variance portfolio defined in section 1.2.5, thereby providing some economic foundations to risk parity.

Consider the following very simple case first. An investor (with initial wealth $w = 1$) would like to build up a portfolio according to a mean-variance criterion, but they are concerned about parameter estimation error. Specifically, suppose the investor knows the asset returns' volatilities, and given a sample size T, they have obtained estimates of the asset expected returns μ_i, say $\hat{\mu}_i$, $i, \cdots, m$. They then solve the following program

$$\max_{\pi} \min_{\mu \in M} \left(\pi^\top(\mu - \mathbf{1}_m r) + R - \frac{\tau}{2}\pi^\top \Sigma \pi\right), \tag{1.P4}$$

where, for some prespecified values ϵ_i, $M = M_1 \times \cdots \times M_m$ and $M_i = \{\mu_i : (\mu_i - \hat{\mu}_i)^2 \leq \epsilon_i \sigma_i^2 / T\}$. In words, the investor selects their portfolio weights while assigning the worst-case outcome to each μ_i within some confidence band

$$\mu_i \in \left(\hat{\mu}_i - \frac{\sigma_i}{\sqrt{T}}\sqrt{\epsilon_i}, \hat{\mu}_i + \frac{\sigma_i}{\sqrt{T}}\sqrt{\epsilon_i}\right).$$

We shall soon return to explain the economic significance of this band while dealing with a similar decision problem (see (1.53) below). For now, note that the program [1.P4] can equivalently be cast as

$$\max_{\pi}\left(\pi^\top\left(\hat{\mu}_* - \mathbf{1}_m r\right) + R - \frac{\tau}{2}\pi^\top\Sigma\pi\right),$$

where each element of $\hat{\mu}_*$ is $\hat{\mu}_{*,i} = \hat{\mu}_i - \text{sign}\left(\pi_i\right)\frac{\sigma_i}{\sqrt{T}}\sqrt{\epsilon_i}$. That is, the investor acts so as to tilt the expected return toward the less favorable case (low when they buy, and high when they sell).

Next, consider a slightly different problem, where the set M in [1.P4] is, for a given constant η,

$$M = \left\{\mu : \left(\hat{\mu} - \mu\right)^\top \Sigma^{-1}\left(\hat{\mu} - \mu\right) \leq \eta\right\}, \tag{1.53}$$

a joint restriction on the admissible values for the unknown expected returns. The constant η may be interpreted in *cognitive terms*, in that the investor has information on the boundaries of their knowledge on the expected returns, μ, which is summarized by the set M. Another interpretation is that η is the agent's *aversion to parameter uncertainty*: the higher η, the more acute the worst-case scenarios they would implement while building up their portfolio choice.[10] Chapter 9 contains additional discussions on these topics (see section 9.6).

We assume that $\eta < \text{Sh}_* \equiv \left(\hat{\mu} - \mathbf{1}_m r\right)^\top \Sigma^{-1}\left(\hat{\mu} - \mathbf{1}_m r\right)$. In appendix 1.E, we show that the solution to this problem is

$$\hat{\pi} = \arg\max_{\pi}\left(\pi^\top\left(\hat{\mu} - \mathbf{1}_m r\right) + R - \frac{\tau}{2}\pi^\top\Sigma\pi - \sqrt{\eta\pi^\top\Sigma\pi}\right) = \frac{1}{\tau}\left(1 - \Omega\left(\eta\right)\right)\Sigma^{-1}\left(\hat{\mu} - \mathbf{1}_m r\right), \tag{1.54}$$

where $\Omega\left(\eta\right) \equiv \sqrt{\frac{\eta}{\text{Sh}_*}}$. We determine the equilibrium interest rate. Note that, by the expression in (1.54) and the definitions of C and D in section 1.2.3, the equilibrium condition, $1 = w = \mathbf{1}_m^\top\hat{\pi}$, leads to

$$r = \hat{r}_{\text{mv}} - \frac{\tau}{C}\frac{\Omega\left(\eta\right)}{1 - \Omega\left(\eta\right)}, \quad \hat{r}_{\text{mv}} \equiv \frac{\hat{D} - \tau}{C}, \tag{1.55}$$

where $\hat{D}$ is defined as D but with $\hat{\mu}$ replacing μ.

Based on this expression of the equilibrium interest rate, the solution (1.54) may be expressed as a weighted average of the mean-variance portfolio in (1.46) and the global

---

10. Assume, for example, that returns are normally distributed. Then $\frac{T(T-m)}{m(T-1)}\left(\hat{\mu} - \mu\right)^\top \Sigma^{-1}\left(\hat{\mu} - \mu\right) \sim \chi^2\left(m\right)$, i.e., a chi-square variate with m degrees of freedom. In this case, the constraint on the expected returns may be $\Pr(\left(\hat{\mu} - \mu\right)^\top \Sigma^{-1}\left(\hat{\mu} - \mu\right) \leq \eta) = 1 - p$, where $\eta = \epsilon\frac{m(T-1)}{T(T-m)}$, and ϵ is chosen so as to ensure a given probability $1 - p$ that the quadratic form lies within some chosen quintile.

minimum variance portfolio in (1.13),

$$\hat{\pi} = (1 - \Omega(\eta))\,\hat{\pi}_{\text{mv}} + \Omega(\eta)\,\pi_{\text{gmv}}, \quad \hat{\pi}_{\text{mv}} = \frac{1}{\tau}\Sigma^{-1}\left(\hat{\mu} - \mathbf{1}_m \hat{r}_{\text{mv}}\right). \tag{1.56}$$

Note that the mean-variance portfolio, $\hat{\pi}_{\text{mv}}$, is obtained while using estimated (not the true, unknown) expected returns.

Eq. (1.55) says that the equilibrium interest rate is equal to the interest rate in a mean-variance economy without parameter uncertainty, $\hat{r}_{\text{mv}}$ (i.e., r in (1.47) but with $\hat{D}$ replacing D), minus a wedge arising due to parameter uncertainty. In other words, agents react to parameter uncertainty by increasing their demand for safe assets, thereby decreasing the equilibrium interest rate. Thus, the model may be interpreted as one predicting flight-to-quality effects: the demand for safe assets increases with an hypothetical increase in η (interpreted as, say, an increase in uncertainty). Moreover, eq. (1.56) clearly shows that an increase in η results in a higher proportion of holdings in the global minimum variance portfolio: as uncertainty grows, agents tilt their portfolios toward asset compositions that are independent of the assets' expected returns; in the extreme case in which assets were uncorrelated, agents would tilt their portfolios toward risk parity after an increase in η.

1.4 The Arbitrage Pricing Theory

1.4.1 Exact APT

1.4.1.1 No-arb restrictions on expected returns

Suppose that asset returns are generated by the following *linear factor model*,

$$\underset{m\times 1}{\tilde{\mu}} = \underset{m\times 1}{\mu} + \underset{m\times k}{B} \cdot \underset{k\times 1}{f} \equiv \mu + cov(\tilde{\mu}, f)[var(f)]^{-1} \cdot f, \tag{1.57}$$

where μ and B are a vector and a matrix of constants and f is a k-dimensional vector of factors with zero mean, which are supposed to affect the asset returns, with $k \leq m$.

Let us normalize $[var(f)]^{-1} = I_{k\times k}$, so that $B = cov(\tilde{\mu}, f)$. With this normalization, we have

$$\tilde{\mu} = \mu + \begin{bmatrix} cov(\tilde{\mu}_1, f) \\ \vdots \\ cov(\tilde{\mu}_m, f) \end{bmatrix} \cdot f = \mu + \begin{bmatrix} \sum_{j=1}^{k} cov(\tilde{\mu}_1, f_j) f_j \\ \vdots \\ \sum_{j=1}^{k} cov(\tilde{\mu}_m, f_j) f_j \end{bmatrix}. \tag{1.58}$$

Next, consider a portfolio of m risky assets and a riskless asset. The wealth generated by this portfolio is given by eq. (1.2), and in this model is

$$w' = \pi^\top(\mu - \mathbf{1}_m r) + Rw + \pi^\top Bf. \tag{1.59}$$

An arbitrage opportunity arises, in this context, if there exists some portfolio π such that the wealth generated by this portfolio, w' in eq. (1.59), is certain and different from the safe gross interest rate R, that is, if $\exists \pi : \pi^\top B = 0$ and $\pi^\top(\mu - \mathbf{1}_m r) \neq 0$. Mathematically, this is ruled out whenever $\exists \lambda \in \mathbb{R}^k : \mu = \mathbf{1}_m r + B\lambda$. Substituting this relation into eq. (1.57) leaves

$$\tilde{\mu} = \mathbf{1}_m r + B\lambda + Bf = \mathbf{1}_m r + cov(\tilde{\mu}, f)\lambda + cov(\tilde{\mu}, f) f.$$

Taking expectations, we have for each asset return

$$\mu_i = r + (B\lambda)_i = r + \sum_{j=1}^{k} \underbrace{cov(\tilde{\mu}_i, f_j)}_{\equiv \beta_{i,j}} \lambda_j, \qquad i = 1, \cdots, m. \tag{1.60}$$

Let f_j be the jth component of the vector of risks in f. The economic interpretation of eq. (1.60) is that, to be induced to invest in a risky market, we need a risk premium that compensates us beyond the risk-free rate. This risk premium is $\sum_{j=1}^{k} \beta_{i,j}\lambda_j$. For each asset i, it is a linear combination of the betas $\beta_{i,j}$, which are the exposures of the asset return i to the sources of risks f_j times the unit risk premiums λ_j relating to each f_j. So naturally, the unit risk premiums are common to all asset returns, although of course the return exposures, $\beta_{i,j}$, can vary across i.

1.4.1.2 *Project evaluation*

Project evaluation under the exact APT is obtained under a straightforward generalization of eq. (1.28). For any project with random cash flow equal to $\tilde{C}_i$, we have that its random return is $\tilde{\mu}_i = \frac{\tilde{C}_i}{V_i} - 1$, such that the value, V_i, is given by

$$V_i = \frac{E(\tilde{C}_i)}{1 + \mu_i}, \tag{1.61}$$

where μ_i is as in eq. (1.60). In section 1.4.2, we shall explain how to represent the value of any project in terms of an alternative probability.

1.4.1.3 *APT and CAPM*

The APT collapses to the CAPM when the market portfolio is the only factor affecting asset returns. This property is easily seen. First, normalize the market portfolio return such that its variance equals one, consistent with eq. (1.60). Accordingly, let $\tilde{r}_M$ be the normalized market return, defined as $\tilde{r}_M \equiv v_M^{-1} \tilde{\mu}_M$, so that $var(\tilde{r}_M) = 1$. We have

$$\tilde{\mu}_i = \mu + \beta_i \tilde{r}_M, \qquad i = 1, \cdots, m,$$

where $\beta_i = cov(\tilde{\mu}_i, \tilde{r}_M) = v_M^{-1} cov(\tilde{\mu}_i, \tilde{\mu}_M)$. Then

$$\mu_i = r + \beta_i \lambda, \qquad i = 1, \cdots, m. \tag{1.62}$$

In particular, $\beta_M = cov(\tilde{\mu}_M, \tilde{r}_M) = v_M^{-1} var(\tilde{\mu}_M) = v_M$, and so, by eq. (1.62),

$$\lambda = \frac{\mu_M - r}{v_M}, \tag{1.63}$$

which is known as the *Sharpe ratio* on the market portfolio or the market price of risk.

By replacing $\beta_i = v_M^{-1} cov(\tilde{\mu}_i, \tilde{\mu}_M)$ and the expression for λ above into eq. (1.62), we obtain

$$\mu_i = r + \frac{cov(\tilde{\mu}_i, \tilde{\mu}_M)}{v_M^2} (\mu_M - r), \qquad i = 1, \cdots, m.$$

This is simply the SML in eq. (1.21).

1.4.2 Risk Neutral Tilts or the Fundamental Theorem of Asset Pricing

Only if the market were "risk neutral," would eq. (1.60) predict that the expected return on any risky asset collapse to the safe interest rate, $\mu_i = r$. But, is there a way to construct a risk neutral market—that is, one with a zero risk premium—from the original market where the risk premium $\sum_{j=1}^{k} \beta_{i,j}\lambda_j$ is different from zero? The answer is in the affirmative. It is a quite fundamental theme in financial economics. It links to the celebrated *fundamental theorem of asset pricing*, sometimes referred to as the "FTAP."

1.4.2.1 *Probability twists*

Let us develop intuition on such a beautiful result by elaborating a simple example. Assume that each of the risks f_j is standard normal, $P(df_j) = \frac{1}{\sqrt{2\pi}} \exp(-\frac{1}{2}f_j^2)df_j$, and next, that we tilt their densities by a factor equal to $\zeta(f_j) = \exp(-\frac{1}{2}\lambda_j^2 - \lambda_j f_j)$, where λ_j is the unit risk premium, as defined in section 1.4.1. This tilt defines a new probability under which each factor f_j is distributed. Let us determine this probability by tilting P through ζ,

$$Q(df_j) = \zeta(f_j)P(df_j) = \frac{1}{\sqrt{2\pi}} \exp\left(-\frac{1}{2}f_j^2 - \frac{1}{2}\lambda_j^2 - \lambda_j f_j\right) df_j = \frac{1}{\sqrt{2\pi}} \exp\left(-\frac{1}{2}\tilde{f}_j^2\right) d\tilde{f}_j, \tag{1.64}$$

where

$$\tilde{f}_j = f_j + \lambda_j. \tag{1.65}$$

Note that the new density, Q, is still that of standard normal variate. Yet under Q, it is $\tilde{f}_j$ that has zero expectation, not f_j. In other words, we have that under Q, (i) $\tilde{f}_j$ is standard normal and (ii) f_j is normal with unit variance but with an expectation equal to $-\lambda_j$. That is, assuming that $\lambda_j > 0$, f_j has a lower expectation under Q than under P—under P, this expectation is zero, and under Q, it is $-\lambda_j$.

We label the new probability Q risk neutral probability, for the following reasons. Consider eqs. (1.58) and (1.60), which say that under P,

$$\tilde{\mu}_i = r + \sum_{j=1}^{k} \beta_{i,j}\lambda_j + \sum_{j=1}^{k} \beta_{i,j} f_j. \tag{1.66}$$

We also know that under the new probability Q, each factor f_j is normally distributed with mean $-\lambda_j$. That is, replacing eq. (1.65) into eq. (1.66), we have that under Q,

$$\tilde{\mu}_i = r + \sum_{j=1}^{k} \beta_{i,j} \tilde{f}_j.$$

To summarize, the return on each assets $\tilde{\mu}_j$ has the following distributions under P and under Q:

$$\tilde{\mu}_j \sim N_P\left(r + \textstyle\sum_{j=1}^{k} \beta_{i,j}\lambda_j, \sigma_j^2\right), \quad \tilde{\mu}_j \sim N_Q\left(r, \sigma_j^2\right), \tag{1.67}$$

where $\sigma_j^2 = \Sigma_{jj}$, $\Sigma \equiv BB^\top$, as in eq. (1.3), and N_P and N_Q denote the Normal densities under P and under Q. That is, under Q, the expected return on each asset equals r, whence the risk neutral probability label. In later chapters, we shall use the celebrated Girsanov's theorem to elaborate on these topics and label the tilt ζ in eq. (1.64) as the Radon-Nikodym derivative of P against Q (see chapter 4, section 4.3.3).

1.4.2.2 *Evaluation of derivatives*

Why do we need to complicate everything with the previous probability changes? In fact, the entire building block underlying asset evaluation relies on similar risk neutral tilts. Consider the following example of derivative evaluation. We wish to price a quadratic derivative, that is, one that pays off the square of the cash flow promised by the first asset, $\tilde{C}_1^2$. It is challenging to evaluate this derivative through "APT software" in this Gaussian market because $\tilde{C}_1^2$ is obviously not normally distributed, which complicates the reasoning underlying its exposure to the factors f_j. In fact, in this Gaussian market, we cannot restrict the behavior of the expected return on this derivative without assuming something more. Let us explain.

Suppose we want to construct a portfolio of the existing assets to replicate the payoff of the quadratic derivative for each possible value this derivative could take. Can we do this? The answer is in the negative. We cannot use a finite number of assets to span an asset payoff, which could take a continuum of values, such as $\tilde{C}_1^2$. We say markets are *incomplete* in this context. In chapter 2, we shall see that the price of such and related derivatives can be found in a preference-free format as soon as the number of assets is at least as large as the number of states—markets are, then, *complete*. In this case, a portfolio that replicates the derivative's payoff can be found, and its value is the same as the derivative's, for two assets are worth the same whenever they promise the same payoff.

Chapter 2 explains that, in a world with complete markets, the price of the existing traded assets can be inverted for the shadow value of some elementary assets—those that pay off one unit of numéraire in a given state of the world and zero otherwise. The price of these elementary securities can then be used to price any derivative, which is redundant indeed. Chapter 4 explains how these results can be generalized to markets with a continuum of states, as soon as we assume that there exist a number of sufficiently diverse elementary securities, which guarantee a payoff could be delivered for each state of nature. To illustrate through the example of this section, consider the following elementary security, which promises the following payoff

$$\Pi(s) = \begin{cases} 1, & \text{if } \tilde{C}_1 \in (s, s+ds) \\ 0, & \text{otherwise} \end{cases}, \tag{1.68}$$

and let $\phi(s)ds$ be its current price. We shall refer these securities as Arrow-Debreu securities, for reasons explained in chapter 2.

We could utilize all of these Arrow-Debreu securities, that is, for all $s \in \mathbb{R}$, and replicate any generic function of the state, $\psi(s)$, including our original payoff, $\psi(s) = s^2$, $s \in \mathbb{R}$. Indeed, note that by purchasing $\psi(s)$ units of the security that pays off $\Pi(s)$ in eq. (1.68), we pay $\psi(s)\phi(s)\,ds$ today and are guaranteed to receive $1 \times \psi(s)$ tomorrow in state $\tilde{C}_1 \in (s, s+ds)$ and zero otherwise. Therefore, by purchasing all the securities that span $\mathbb{R}$, in proportion of $\psi(\cdot)$, we shall receive, for sure, $\psi(\tilde{C}_1)$ for any possible value of $\tilde{C}_1$ tomorrow and today pay

$$C_\psi \equiv \int_{-\infty}^{\infty} \psi(s)\,\phi(s)\,ds. \tag{1.69}$$

We call P_ψ such a portfolio. We claim that the value of the derivative, say V_ψ, is just C_ψ. For suppose not, and assume, for instance, that $V_\psi > C_\psi$. Then we could short sell the derivative for V_ψ, invest C_ψ into the portfolio P_ψ, and retain an arbitrage profit equal to $V_\psi - C_\psi$. It is an arbitrage profit because the portfolio P_ψ delivers the exact payoff we need to honor the short sale of the derivative.

The crucial point is to determine the value of ϕ. We claim that

$$\phi(s) = \frac{1}{1+r} q\left(s; V_1(1+r), \bar{\sigma}^2\right) \tag{1.70}$$

for some $\bar{\sigma}^2$, where $q(s; m, \bar{\sigma}^2)$ denotes the density of a normal distribution with mean and variance m and $\bar{\sigma}^2$. Indeed, let us take expectations of $\tilde{C}_1 = V_1(1+\tilde{\mu}_1)$ under Q, such that, by eq. (1.67),

$$V_1 = \frac{E_Q(\tilde{C}_1)}{1+r}. \tag{1.71}$$

On the other hand, let us apply eq. (1.69) to determine the value of the derivative that pays off, $\psi(\tilde{C}_1) = \tilde{C}_1$, which is

$$V_1 = \int_{-\infty}^{\infty} s\phi(s)\, ds. \tag{1.72}$$

Comparing eq. (1.71) and eq. (1.72) yields eq. (1.70).[11]

We are now ready to evaluate the quadratic derivative, by relying on eq. (1.69), and the expression of ϕ in eq. (1.70). We have for $\psi(s) = s^2$, that the value of the derivative, say V_C, can be expressed as a risk neutral expectation:

$$V_C = \int_{-\infty}^{\infty} s^2\phi(s)\, ds = \frac{E_Q(\tilde{C}_1^2)}{1+r}. \tag{1.73}$$

The expression in eq. (1.73) tells us that all we have to do is to recast the initial evaluation problem in terms of this new risk neutral setup. To fix ideas, suppose that the unit prices of risk λ_j are all positive. In this setup, the discounting factor is the safe interest rate, r. To compensate for such generous discounting, the expectation in the numerator of eq. (1.73) is lower than that under P because the distribution of $\tilde{C}_1$ is more skewed to the left under Q than under P, due to the factors driving the value of $\tilde{C}_1 = V_1(1+\tilde{\mu}_1)$ being skewed to take more pessimistic values under Q, on average, by a factor equal to $-\lambda_j$.

Let us proceed with the determination of V_C, by using eq. (1.73). We have that $E_Q(\tilde{C}_1^2) = V_1^2 E_Q((1+\tilde{\mu}_1)^2)$, where $1+\tilde{\mu}_1 \sim N_Q(1+r, \sigma_1^2)$ such that, by a direct calculation,

$$V_C = V_1^2\left(\frac{\sigma_1^2}{1+r} + 1 + r\right),$$

where V_1 is the value of the first asset, determined as usual through eq. (1.61). Note how simple this formula is. It links the value of the derivative to the square of the value of the

11. We can check that eq. (1.70) is consistent with the pricing of a pure discount bond. Such a bond has a payoff equal to $\psi(s) = 1$ for all s such that by eq. (1.69), $\frac{1}{1+r} = \int_{-\infty}^{\infty} \phi(s)\, ds$, which it does, by eq. (1.70).

underlying risk, V_1^2, and the discounted value of σ_1^2, reflecting that, after all, a quadratic derivative is about a play in volatility.

1.4.3 Uncertainty and Asset Evaluation

How asset prices relate to the volatility of fundamentals? It is a very old issue in financial economics.[12] Consider a two-period market for a cash ψ to be paid in the second period where we assume that $\psi = \psi(\tilde{C})$ for some random variable $\tilde{C}$. Accordingly, and generalizing eq. (1.73), $V_C \equiv (1+r)^{-1} E_Q[\psi(\tilde{C})]$ is the current value of a derivative that pays $\psi(\tilde{C})$.

We ask: How does the value V_C change when uncertainty regarding $\tilde{C}$ increases? For example, how does V_C change after a change in the variance of $\tilde{C}$? It is a complex question, and the answers to it depend on the assumptions we make about the uncertainty changes surrounding $\tilde{C}$. In this chapter, we begin with the simplest situation, one in which a change in the *uncertainty* of $\tilde{C}$ does not entail a change in the *expected value* of $\tilde{C}$. This case is actually very relevant. Suppose that that $\tilde{C}$ is the cash flow of a traded security with a given value V, such that its current value is, consistently with results in the previous sections, $E_Q(\tilde{C}) = V(1+r)$, which is clearly independent of the uncertainty surrounding $\tilde{C}$ once we take V to be given, just as we are doing.

Situations in which changes in the volatility of a random variable do not affect its mean are known as *mean-preserving spreads*. Appendix 1.C contains a succinct summary of these situations and develops results that predict that V_C does indeed increase after a mean-preserving spread in $\tilde{C}$, provided ψ is a convex function of $\tilde{C}$. Intuitively, a convex function exaggerates favorable realizations of $\tilde{C}$ and dampens the poor ones. The theory of mean-preserving spreads was introduced by Rothschild and Stiglitz (1970, 1971) and will be used at different junctures of this book.

1.4.4 The APT with Idiosyncratic Risk and a Large Number of Assets

Can idiosyncratic risk be eliminated? This section reviews conclusions on this question contained in the seminal work of Ross (1976) and its initial refinements made by Connor (1984) and Huberman (1983), among others. Consider eq. (1.22). Intuitively, we may form portfolios with a large number of assets so as to make idiosyncratic risk negligible by the law of large numbers. But would the APT relation in eq. (1.60) be still valid? The answer is in the affirmative, although it deserves some qualifications.

Consider the APT equation (1.57), and add a vector of idiosyncratic returns, ε, which are independent of f and have mean zero and variance σ_ε^2:

$$\tilde{\mu} = \mu + B \cdot f + \varepsilon.$$

We wish to show that, in the absence of some appropriate notion of arbitrage (to be defined below), it must be that the number of assets such that eq. (1.60) does *not* hold, $N(m)$ say, is bounded as m gets large, that is,

$$\left|\mu_i - \left((B\lambda)_i + r\right)\right| > 0, \quad i = 1, \cdots, N(m), \tag{1.74}$$

12. See, e.g., the classical work of Malkiel (1979), Pindyck (1984), Poterba and Summers (1985), Abel (1988), Barsky (1989), among others.

where

$$\lim_{m\to\infty} N(m) < \infty. \tag{1.75}$$

In other words, we wish to show that in a large market, eq. (1.60) does indeed hold for most of the assets, an approach close to that in Huang and Litzenberger (1988, 106–108).

By the same arguments leading to eq. (1.1), the wealth generated by a portfolio of the assets satisfying (1.74), $w'_{N(m)}$ say, is

$$w'_{N(m)} = \pi_{N(m)}^{\top}\left(\mu_{N(m)} - \mathbf{1}_{N(m)}r\right) + Rw_{N(m)} + \pi_{N(m)}^{\top}\left(B_{N(m)}f + \varepsilon_{N(m)}\right),$$

where μ_N, B_N and ε_N are (i) the vector of the expected returns, (ii) the factor exposures matrix, and (iii) the vector of idiosyncratic return components affecting these assets and, finally, where π_N and w_N are the portfolio and the initial wealth invested in these assets.

In this context, we may define an arbitrage as the portfolio $\pi_{N(m)}$ that in the limit, as the number of the existing assets m gets large, is riskless and yet delivers an expected return strictly larger than the safe interest rate, namely,

$$\lim_{m\to\infty} \frac{E[w'_{N(m)}]}{w_{N(m)}} > R, \quad \text{and} \quad \lim_{m\to\infty} var[w'_{N(m)}] \to 0. \tag{1.76}$$

We want to show that this situation does not arise under the condition in (1.75), thereby establishing that the linear APT relation in eq. (1.60) is valid for most of the assets in a large market.

So suppose the linear relation, $\mu_N - \mathbf{1}_N r = B_N \lambda$, doesn't hold. Then there exists a portfolio $\underline{\pi}$ such that

$$\underline{\pi}^{\top} B_N = 0 \quad \text{and} \quad \underline{\pi}^{\top}(\mu_N - \mathbf{1}_N r) \neq 0. \tag{1.77}$$

Consider the portfolio

$$\hat{\pi}_N = \frac{1}{N} \cdot sign\left(\underline{\pi}^{\top}(\mu_N - \mathbf{1}_N r)\right) \cdot \underline{\pi},$$

where $\underline{\pi}$ is as in (1.77). With this portfolio we clearly have $E[w'_N] = \hat{\pi}_N^{\top}(\mu_N - \mathbf{1}_N r) + Rw_N > Rw_N$, for each N and even for N large. That is, $\lim_{m\to\infty} E[w'_{N(m)}]/w_{N(m)} > R$, which is the first condition in (1.76). Regarding the second condition in (1.76), we have

$$var[w'_N] = \hat{\pi}_N^{\top}\left(B_N B_N^{\top} + \sigma_\varepsilon^2 I_{N\times N}\right)\hat{\pi}_N = \sigma_\varepsilon^2 \hat{\pi}_N^{\top}\hat{\pi}_N,$$

where the second equality follows by the first relation in (1.77). Clearly, $\lim_{m\to\infty} var[w'_{N(m)}] \to 0$ as $N(m) \to \infty$. Hence, in the absence of arbitrage, the condition in (1.75) must hold.

1.5 Empirical Evidence

This section contains a very succinct account regarding the empirical evidence on the CAPM, its factor extensions, and some of the market practice arising from it.

1.5.1 Fama-MacBeth Two-Step Regressions

How do we estimate eq. (1.22)? Consider a slightly more general version of eq. (1.22), one in which the riskless interest rate is time-varying:

$$\tilde{\mu}_{i,t} - r_t = \beta_i(\tilde{\mu}_{M,t} - r_t) + \varepsilon_{i,t}, \quad i = 1, \cdots, m,$$

where $\varepsilon_{i,t}$ denotes time-series residuals. Fama and MacBeth (1973) consider an estimation procedure based on two steps. In a first step, one obtains estimates of the market exposures for all stocks, $\hat{\beta}_i$ say, relying on monthly returns (or returns on other frequencies); we may approximate the market portfolio with some broad stock market index.[13] In the second step, we runs cross-sectional regressions, one for each month,

$$\tilde{\mu}_{i,t} - r_t = \alpha_t + \lambda_t \hat{\beta}_i + \eta_{i,t}, \quad t = 1, \cdots, T,$$

where T is the sample size and $\eta_{i,t}$ denotes "cross-sectional residuals." The time-series of cross-sectional estimates of the intercept α_t and the price of risk λ_t ($\hat{\alpha}_t$ and $\hat{\lambda}_t$, say) are then used to make statistical inference. For example, time-series averages and standard errors of $\hat{\alpha}_t$ and $\hat{\lambda}_t$ may lead to point estimates and standard errors for α (the unconditional expected return unexplained by the model) and λ (the price of risk predicted by the CAPM; see eqs. (1.62)–(1.63)). If the CAPM holds, estimates of α should not be significantly different from zero.

1.5.2 Macroeconomic Forces

Chen, Roll, and Ross (1986) use the Fama-MacBeth two-step estimation procedure and estimate a multifactor APT model, one built up along the lines of section 1.4. They identify macroeconomic forces driving asset returns with innovations in variables such as the term spread, expected and unexpected inflation, industrial production growth, or the corporate spread. They find that these sources of variation in the cross-section of asset returns are significantly priced.

The empirical literature subsequent to this work relies on testing procedures leading to mixed results. For example, Shanken and Weinstein (2006) find that industrial production growth seems to survive to their own testing methodology, although their evidence is less convincing regarding the previous factors. Part II of the book deals with related asset pricing puzzles and, more generally, with how financial markets relate to macroeconomic developments. The main objectives of part II are to strive against data mining (the process of searching for variables that explain asset returns) and, alternatively, to put economic reasoning at the core of the process that leads to suggestions for empirical relations. Section 1.5.5 provides further details on how data mining has been addressed in the empirical literature.

1.5.3 The Fama and French Model

Consider the SML introduced in section 1.3 (see eq. (1.21)). The CAPM predicts that each asset has an average excess return lying precisely on the SML. Assets delivering average

13. In tests of the CAPM, one uses proxies of the market portfolio, such as, say, the S&P 500. However, the market portfolio is unobservable. Roll (1977) points out that, as a result, the CAPM is inherently untestable as any test of the CAPM is a joint test of the model itself and of the closeness of the proxy to the market portfolio.

excess returns significantly away from the SML would point to evidence that this single factor version of the APT does not work; points A, B, C, and D in figure 1.4 illustrate this situation. Consider, for example, the asset corresponding to point A. A regression of the excess return of this asset onto the excess return on the market would produce a positive intercept, some $\alpha > 0$, such that its average excess return would equal $\alpha + \beta_i (\mu_M - r)$, thereby invalidating the SML in eq. (1.21).

Fama and French (1992, 1993) provide evidence that the standard CAPM is invalidated by the presence of two additional factors, size and value. Further, there is strong evidence of at least a third factor against the standard CAPM, momentum. These factors are discussed next.

(1) *Size* (Banz, 1981): Average returns for "small firms" are too high given their beta. Firm size is measured in terms of market capitalization: stock price times outstanding shares.
(2) *Value* (Stattman, 1980; Rosenberg, Reid, and Lanstein, 1985): Average returns on stocks with high book-to-market (BTM) ratios or "value stocks" are too high given their beta. In general, average returns on value stocks are higher than those on stocks with low BTM ratios or "growth stocks." The points A, B and C in figure 1.4 may identify examples of value stocks, with the average excess returns corresponding to point A relating to the firm with the highest BTM ratios; point D may be an example of a growth stock.[14]
(3) *Momentum* (Jegadeesh and Titman, 1993): Stocks with the highest returns in the previous 12 months tend to outperform in the next future.

What is the economic intuition for expecting these factors to explain the cross-section of asset returns? Fama and French (1992, 1993) provide empirical evidence that returns on both size and value are proxies for common risk factors. They argue that small and, especially, value stocks seem to display persistently low earnings. Size and value can then be proxies for profitability and sources of priced risk. However, there is still considerable debate regarding the economic interpretation of these factors. The interpretation of momentum as a factor is also very subtle. A natural explanation relies on the sensitivity of asset prices to news. For example, Pedersen (2015, 139) reviews the simple idea that prices underreact. If, for example, an asset price underreacts to good news, its subsequent increases lead to momentum. Chapter 10 provides additional explanations for underreaction based on "limits of arbitrage." Further, Chapter 8 reviews models by which volatility and expected returns actually increase on the upside (see section 8.6.3): when growth is very strong, asset price volatility and then premiums increase after good news, producing momentum; that is, returns are expected to increase precisely in good times.

The standard CAPM does not have the power to explain the cross-section of asset returns that are sorted by size, BTM, or momentum. Assets sorted in this way command

14. This example is highly hypothetical: it is well known that stocks with higher BTM ratios have higher betas (see Fama and French, 1993).

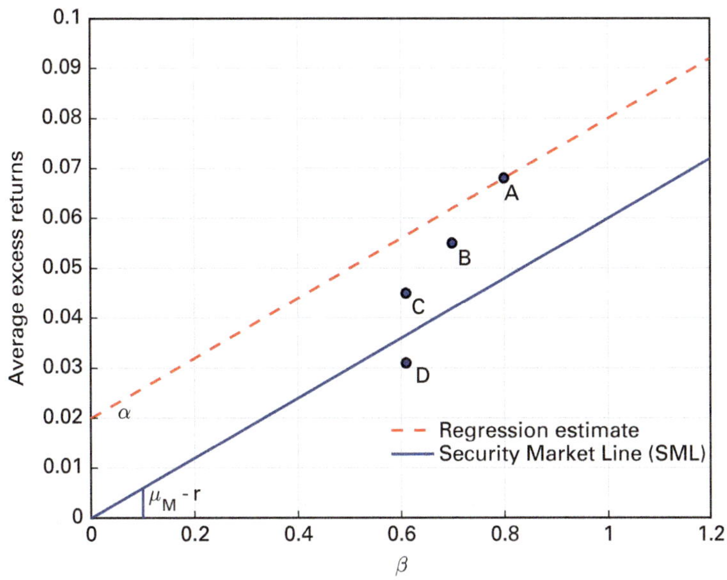

Figure 1.4
The solid line depicts the SML based on the assumption that the excess return on the market $\mu_M - r = 6\%$. The four points, A through D, identify hypothetical pairs of β estimates and average excess returns for four assets. The α on asset A is obtained while identifying the intercept of the line that passes through point A and is parallel to the SML.

a size premium, a value premium, and a momentum premium. Let us explain these facts relying on the original examples developed in the Fama and French (1993) paper. The original focus of this paper was the time series estimate of exposures to market, size and value. The returns to be explained relate to portfolios created as follows. First, portfolios are formed while sorting assets in a given universe through size and BTM. In each year, stocks are allocated into 5 size quintiles and 5 BTM quintiles, leading to a total of 25 portfolios obtained as intersections of the 5 size and the 5 BTM groups. Associated with each of these 25 portfolios are value-weighted monthly returns. The puzzle then, at least from the standard CAPM perspective, is that the CAPM cannot explain the expected returns on these 25 portfolios.

Fama and French (1993) show that the returns on these portfolios can be very much better understood by means of a multifactor model, in which both "size premiums" and "value premiums" are taken as "factor premiums." Fama and French consider three factors: (i) the *market premium*, defined as the monthly excess return on the market; (ii) the *small minus big (SMB) premium*, defined as the monthly difference between returns on assets with small and big size; (iii) the *high minus low (HML) premium*, defined as the monthly difference between returns on assets with high and low BTM ratios.

Precisely, stocks ranked by size are split into two groups (S: small; B: big) according to whether their market capitalization is below or above the median, and stocks ranked by BTM are broken into three groups based on the breakpoints for the bottom 30%

(L: low), middle 40% (M: medium) and top 30% (H: high) of the BTM ratios distribution. The result is a 2 × 3 matrix.

	Book-to-Market		
Size	L	M	H
S	(S,L)	(S,M)	(S,H)
B	(B,L)	(B,M)	(B,H)

The SMB premium is obtained as the difference between the average returns on small stocks minus that on big stocks; the HML premium is the difference between the average return on stocks with high BTM minus that on low; with obvious notation,

$$\begin{aligned} \text{SMB} &= \tfrac{1}{3}\left[(\text{S,L}) + (\text{S,M}) + (\text{S,H})\right] - \tfrac{1}{3}\left[(\text{B,L}) + (\text{B,M}) + (\text{B,H})\right] \\ \text{HML} &= \tfrac{1}{2}\left[(\text{S,H}) + (\text{B,H})\right] - \tfrac{1}{2}\left[(\text{S,L}) + (\text{B,L})\right]. \end{aligned}$$

That is, the two portfolios, SMB and HML, are *factor mimicking portfolios* and are recalculated at a regular frequency. Moreover, these portfolios are *dynamic*: some assets may exit from these portfolios and be replaced by new ones, whenever a criterion determines that they do not fall under the appropriate category at the date portfolios are recalibrated. The exposures to these portfolios are estimated while regressing each excess return on all factors:

$$\mu_i - r = \alpha_i + \beta_i\left(\mu_{Mt} - r\right) + \beta_{i,smb} SMB_t + \beta_{i,shml} HML_t + \varepsilon_{it}.$$

The model can be used to determine the expected return on each asset based on the predictive part of the previous regression. Carhart (1997) extends this model to one with a fourth factor: momentum. Returns on a momentum portfolio are the difference between monthly returns on assets with recent better performance minus returns on assets with recent worst performance. After the publication of Fama and MacBeth (1973), the literature has produced an enormous amount of work pointing to evidence of many additional factors, such as those identified in the Fama and French pieces; Bali, Engle, and Murray (2016) provide a review of this literature. Before we discuss some of this evidence in section 1.5.5, we provide a succinct review on how the "discovery" of factors has shaped investment practice.

1.5.4 "Smart Beta," or Factor Investing

The merit of the CAPM lies in its simple prediction that the risk of an asset and thus its premium relates to the asset returns' exposure to market fluctuations: its beta. But the empirical evidence reviewed in the previous section suggests the presence of additional factors, which the cross-section of expected returns may be exposed to. Thus, in the world of factor models, assets do not really have a meaning on their own in that their returns merely capture the factors they are exposed to. For example, in his extensive review of these topics, Ang (2014, 194) explains that "factors are to assets what nutrients are to food." In this world, investing is thus a means to capture variation in some of these factors and the premiums arising therefrom.

Market practice that emphasizes these ideas is known as *factor investing* or *smart beta*. This phenomenon is so important that smart beta is now part of "commoditization" efforts, notably occurring through smart beta exchange traded funds (ETFs).[15] These ETFs track smart beta indices—that is, indices that reflect the performance of an investment strategy that seeks exposure to some factors that are alternative to standard market capitalization indices. To simplify, while standard beta is exposure to market, smart beta is exposure to "something else." Which factors—or nutrients—and then premiums would any investor like to be exposed to? There is no theory or guidance to the variety of available products. The only assumptions underlying these products are that asset returns incorporate premiums related to their exposure to factors and then that there are dedicated portfolios of them that may isolate specific premiums. Some of these factors may be *macroeconomic factors*, such as economic growth, inflation, or volatility of financial markets; these factors are not traded and are difficult to mimic, with the exception of volatility in some cases as explained in chapter 11. But factors may be simply *investment styles*, such as value or momentum (see the previous section), or additional factors such as quality (embedded into stocks with stable earnings and balance sheets) or low volatility stocks (consistent with the risk parity examples of section 1.2.5). These factors are often dynamic: the investment strategy underlying them involves buying and selling over time, just as in the examples of the previous section.

1.5.5 "Lucky Factors"

How many factors have been reported in the literature, which are potentially able to explain the cross-section of expected returns? Harvey, Liu, and Zhu (2016) point to the existence of more than 300 such factors. This fact naturally raises a "data mining" concern: by force of trying with potentially new explanations of asset prices, we might end up finding some that work. How sure are we that the successful factors only worked by pure chance? This problem can be regarded as one of multiple testing: when we want to examine how plausible a new factor is, we are actually testing several null hypotheses (that the first factor is not significant, that the second is not significant, etc.). In this context, multiple testing is related to data mining simply because the significance of a new factor must be assessed while many variables (factors) are being tested on the same dataset.

Further, we may suspect that, in the underground, researchers have been trying with thousands of additional potential explanations and that none of them have seemed to work. Financial economists typically publish papers with positive results. Moreover, in the failed attempts, it is likely that some true explanations of asset markets were disregarded only because they were not successful given the particular samples on which they were tested. Intuitively, then, the higher the number of "hidden trials," the more likely it is that

15. An ETF is a portfolio of securities that may be traded on an exchange just like a common stock. Unlike a closed-end fund (that issues a fixed number of nonredeemable shares), which only trades once a day, an ETF trades all the time. While closed-end funds may trade at a discount or a premium, arbitrage forces tend to make an ETF more closely reflect its Net Asset Value. ETFs differ from open-end funds (which issue an open-ended number of redeemable shares) for a variety of reasons, such as the possibility to be traded on margin or to be sold short.

the discovered factors come out from pure data mining. This problem is one of sample selection bias of the type addressed by Heckman (1979).

More formally, let H_0 denote the null hypothesis that a given factor is not significant. According to standard terminology (see, e.g., Gouriéroux and Monfort, 2008), we may incur into two types of errors while in the process of statistical testing:

- *Type-I error*: rejecting H_0 when H_0 is true, leading to false positives outcomes;
- *Type-II error*: failing to reject H_0 when H_0 is false, leading to false negatives outcomes.

Associated with each of these errors is a probability of occurrence. Let $t_T(x)$ denote a statistic—that is, a function—of the sample of T observations, $(x_t)_{t=1}^T$. For example, $t_T(x)$ may be the t-statistic for the significance of a factor in a cross-sectional regression. The probabilities of making a Type-I and a Type-II error are, resp.,

$$\alpha_T(\theta) \equiv \Pr\left(t_T(x) \in \mathcal{C}_1 \middle| H_0\right), \quad \beta_T(\theta) \equiv \Pr\left(t_T(x) \in \bar{\mathcal{C}}_1 \middle| H_1\right),$$

where $\mathcal{C}_1$ denotes the critical region (and $\bar{\mathcal{C}}_1$, its complement), that is, the set of values such that H_0 is rejected if the statistic takes values belonging to it. The hypothesis H_1 is an alternative to H_0. The two probabilities are a function of the parameter θ underlying the data generating process. The probability α_T is known as the "size" of a test and $1-\alpha_T$ is its "significance." Instead, $1-\beta_T$ is the "power" of the test.

The critical region is chosen so as to represent the values of the statistics that we consider significantly different from those we would have observed under the null, H_0. Naturally, the higher $\alpha_T(\theta)$, the lower $\beta_T(\theta)$. How do we proceed in practice? In science, it seems reasonable to dislike Type-I errors more than Type-II. Typically, the null is the old theory, which we will retain until strong evidence mounts such that we may not maintain it anymore—"strong" meaning that the significance should be quite high. In a way, when abandoning a theory is costly, it might be better to guess that we are making errors without modifying our systems rather than that we are making errors while modifying it. This reasoning seems to be consistent with the Popperian account of science proceeding through falsifications of old hypotheses (Popper, 1959). In our context, Type-I errors lead to false discoveries, and Type-II errors lead to miss out true factors. Because we cannot simultaneously minimize the probabilities of both errors, one compromising approach is to fix a significance level, $1-\alpha_T$, and devise a testing procedure that maximizes power (the probability that true factors are not rejected) for the given significance level. However, note that power depends on the unknown parameters governing the alternative hypothesis.

To summarize, Harvey, Liu, and Zhu (2016) provide a thorough discussion of the statistical literature and the ensuing variety of tests that seem to work as appropriate benchmark for our testing concerns. Their conclusions are quite stringent: a t-statistic of at least three is required as evidence of a significant factor; many of the published successful factors are actually likely not true factors.

Appendix 1.A Portfolio Choice

We derive eq. (1.9), that is, the optimal portfolio allocation in the case without the safe asset. We solve two programs: (i) the primal program [1.P2] in the main text (maximize portfolio expected return for a given variance) and (ii) a dual program, to be introduced below, by which we minimize the portfolio return variance for a given expected return.

These derivations are in appendixes 1.A.1 and 1.A.2. Appendixes 1.A.3 and 1.A.4 provide derivations of selected results given in the main text.

1.A.1 The Primal Program

Given eq. (1.8), the Lagrangian function associated to [1.P2] is

$$\mathcal{L} = \pi^\top \mu + w - \nu_1(\pi^\top \Sigma \pi - w^2 v_p^2) - \nu_2(\pi^\top \mathbf{1}_m - w),$$

where ν_1 and ν_2 are two Lagrange multipliers. The first-order conditions are

$$\hat{\pi} = \frac{1}{2\nu_1}\Sigma^{-1}(\mu - \nu_2 \mathbf{1}_m), \quad \hat{\pi}^\top \Sigma \hat{\pi} = w^2 v_p^2, \quad \hat{\pi}^\top \mathbf{1}_m = w. \tag{1.A1}$$

Using the first and the third conditions leaves

$$w = \mathbf{1}_m^\top \hat{\pi} = \frac{1}{2\nu_1}(\underbrace{\mathbf{1}_m^\top \Sigma^{-1}\mu}_{\equiv D} - \nu_2 \underbrace{\mathbf{1}_m^\top \Sigma^{-1}\mathbf{1}_m}_{\equiv C}) \equiv \frac{1}{2\nu_1}(D - \nu_2 C).$$

We solve for ν_2, obtaining

$$\nu_2 = \frac{D - 2w\nu_1}{C}.$$

By replacing the solution for ν_2 into the first condition in (1.A1), we get

$$\hat{\pi} = \frac{w}{C}\Sigma^{-1}\mathbf{1}_m + \frac{1}{2\nu_1}\Sigma^{-1}\left(\mu - \frac{D}{C}\mathbf{1}_m\right). \tag{1.A2}$$

Next, we derive the value of the program [1.P2]:

$$E\left[w'(\hat{\pi})\right] - w = \hat{\pi}^\top \mu = \frac{w}{C}D + \frac{1}{2\nu_1}\left(A - \frac{D^2}{C}\right), \quad A \equiv \mu^\top \Sigma^{-1}\mu. \tag{1.A3}$$

It is easy to show that

$$\begin{aligned} var\left[w'(\hat{\pi})\right] &= w^2 v_p^2 \\ &= \hat{\pi}^\top \Sigma \hat{\pi} \\ &= \left[\frac{w}{C}\mathbf{1}_m^\top \Sigma^{-1} + \frac{1}{2\nu_1}\left(\mu^\top - \frac{D}{C}\mathbf{1}_m^\top\right)\Sigma^{-1}\right]\left[\frac{w}{C}\mathbf{1}_m + \frac{1}{2\nu_1}\left(\mu - \frac{D}{C}\mathbf{1}_m\right)\right] \\ &= \frac{w^2}{C} + \left(\frac{1}{2\nu_1}\right)^2\left(A - \frac{D^2}{C}\right). \end{aligned} \tag{1.A4}$$

Let us gather eqs. (1.A3) and (1.A4):

$$\begin{cases} \mu_p(v_p) \equiv \dfrac{E\left[w'(\hat{\pi})\right] - w}{w} = \dfrac{D}{C} + \dfrac{1}{2\nu_1 w}\left(A - \dfrac{D^2}{C}\right) \\ v_p^2 = \dfrac{1}{C} + \left(\dfrac{1}{2\nu_1 w}\right)^2\left(A - \dfrac{D^2}{C}\right) \end{cases} \tag{1.A5}$$

where we have emphasized the dependence of μ_p on v_p, which arises through the Lagrange multiplier v_1 as formally seen below (see eq. (1.A7)).

The first equation in (1.A5) can be solved for v_1 as follows:

$$\frac{1}{2v_1 w} = \left(AC - D^2\right)^{-1} \left(C\mu_p(v_p) - D\right). \tag{1.A6}$$

We use eq. (1.A6) and express $\hat{\pi}$ in eq. (1.A2) in terms of the portfolio expected return, $\mu_p(v_p)$. We have

$$\frac{\hat{\pi}}{w} = \frac{\Sigma^{-1}\mathbf{1}_m}{C} + \left(AC - D^2\right)^{-1} \left(C\mu_p(v_p) - D\right) \Sigma^{-1} \left(\mu - \frac{D}{C}\mathbf{1}_m\right).$$

By rearranging terms in the previous equation, we obtain eq. (1.9) in the main text.

Finally, we substitute eq. (1.A6) into the second equation of (1.A5), obtaining

$$v_p^2 = \frac{1}{C}\left[1 + \left(AC - D^2\right)^{-1} \left(C\mu_p(v_p) - D\right)^2\right],$$

which is eq. (1.10) in the main text. Note also that the second condition in (1.A5) reveals that

$$\left(\frac{1}{2v_1 w}\right)^2 = \frac{Cv_p^2 - 1}{AC - D^2}. \tag{1.A7}$$

Given that $AC - D^2 > 0$, the previous equation confirms the properties of the *global minimum variance portfolio* stated in the main text.

1.A.2 The Dual Program

Next, consider the following program:

$$\hat{\pi} = \arg\min_{\pi \in \mathbb{R}^m} var\left[\frac{w'(\pi)}{w}\right] \quad \text{s.t. } E\left[w'(\pi)\right] = E_p \text{ and } w = \pi^\top \mathbf{1}_m \tag{1.AP2-D}$$

for some constant E_p. The first-order conditions are

$$\frac{\hat{\pi}}{w} = \frac{\eta_1 w}{2}\Sigma^{-1}\mu + \frac{\eta_2 w}{2}\Sigma^{-1}\mathbf{1}_m, \quad \hat{\pi}^\top \mu = E_p - w, \quad w = \hat{\pi}^\top \mathbf{1}_m, \tag{1.A8}$$

where η_1 and η_2 are two Lagrange multipliers.

Combining the first and second conditions in (1.A8) leaves

$$E_p - w = \hat{\pi}^\top \mu = w^2 \left(\frac{\eta_1}{2}A + \frac{\eta_2}{2}D\right), \tag{1.A9}$$

and combining the first and third conditions in (1.A8) produces

$$w = \hat{\pi}^\top \mathbf{1}_m = w^2 \left(\frac{\eta_1}{2}D + \frac{\eta_2}{2}C\right). \tag{1.A10}$$

Next, let $\mu_p \equiv \frac{E_p - w}{w}$. By eqs. (1.A9) and (1.A10), the solutions for η_1 and η_2 are

$$\frac{\eta_1 w}{2} = \frac{C\mu_p - D}{AC - D^2}, \qquad \frac{\eta_2 w}{2} = \frac{A - D\mu_p}{AC - D^2}.$$

Therefore, the solution for the portfolio in eq. (1.A8) is

$$\frac{\hat{\pi}}{w} = \frac{C\mu_p - D}{AC - D^2}\Sigma^{-1}\mu + \frac{A - D\mu_p}{AC - D^2}\Sigma^{-1}\mathbf{1}_m.$$

Finally, the value of the program is

$$\begin{aligned} var\left[\frac{w'(\hat{\pi})}{w}\right] &= \frac{\hat{\pi}^\top}{w}\Sigma\frac{\hat{\pi}}{w} = \frac{\hat{\pi}^\top}{w}\left(\frac{C\mu_p - D}{AC - D^2}\mu + \frac{A - D\mu_p}{AC - D^2}\mathbf{1}_m\right) \\ &= \frac{C\mu_p^2 - 2D\mu_p + A}{AC - D^2}, \end{aligned}$$

where we have used the fact that (i) $\frac{\hat{\pi}^\top}{w}\mu = \mu_p$ and (ii) $\frac{\hat{\pi}^\top}{w}\mathbf{1}_m = 1$. Rearranging terms leaves eq. (1.10) in the main text.

To check that the second-order conditions apply, consider the bordered Hessian

$$H = \begin{bmatrix} \frac{\partial^2 \mathcal{L}}{\partial\pi\partial\pi} & \frac{\partial^2 \mathcal{L}}{\partial\pi\partial\eta_1} & \frac{\partial^2 \mathcal{L}}{\partial\pi\partial\eta_2} \\ \frac{\partial^2 \mathcal{L}}{\partial\eta_1\partial\pi} & \frac{\partial^2 \mathcal{L}}{\partial\eta_1\partial\eta_1} & \frac{\partial^2 \mathcal{L}}{\partial\eta_1\partial\eta_2} \\ \frac{\partial^2 \mathcal{L}}{\partial\eta_2\partial\pi} & \frac{\partial^2 \mathcal{L}}{\partial\eta_2\partial\eta_1} & \frac{\partial^2 \mathcal{L}}{\partial\eta_2\partial\eta_2} \end{bmatrix} = \begin{bmatrix} -2\eta_1\Sigma & -2\Sigma\pi & -\mathbf{1}_m \\ -2\pi\Sigma & 0 & 0 \\ \mathbf{1}_m^\top & 0 & 0 \end{bmatrix}.$$

It is negative (semi-) definite whenever the leading principal minors (formed through the last k columns and corresponding rows, for $k = 4, \cdots, m+2$) have determinants with signs that alternate, with the first one (formed with the last four rows and corresponding columns) having the sign of $(-1)^2 = +1$. This is possible whenever $\eta_1 > 0$, which is true by eq. (1.A6), whenever $AC > D^2$.

1.A.3 Efficient Portfolios Generate Efficient Portfolios

Let π_1 and π_2 be two portfolios on the efficient portfolio frontier. Then, $\pi_i = \ell_i \pi_d + (1 - \ell_i)\,\pi_{\text{gmv}}$ for some ℓ_i, and $i = 1, 2$. Solving for π_d and π_{gmv} leaves

$$\pi_d = \frac{1 - \ell_1}{\ell_2 - \ell_1}\pi_2 - \frac{1 - \ell_2}{\ell_2 - \ell_1}\pi_1, \quad \pi_{\text{gmv}} = \frac{\ell_2}{\ell_2 - \ell_1}\pi_1 - \frac{\ell_1}{\ell_2 - \ell_1}\pi_2.$$

Replacing these expressions for π_d and π_{gmv} into (1.12) leaves, for any given weight ℓ,

$$\hat{\pi} = \ell\pi_d + (1 - \ell)\,\pi_{\text{gmv}} = \omega(\ell_1, \ell_2)\,\pi_1 + (1 - \omega(\ell_1, \ell_2))\,\pi_2, \quad \omega(\ell_1, \ell_2) \equiv \frac{\ell_2 - \ell}{\ell_2 - \ell_1}.$$

That is, any arbitrary efficient portfolio can be generated by any other two arbitrary efficient portfolios, $\ell \neq \ell_1 \neq \ell_2$.

1.A.4 Covariance of Global Minimum Variance and Efficient Portfolio Returns

Let $\tilde{\mu}^p = \frac{\pi_p^\top}{w}\tilde{\mu}$ and $\tilde{\mu}^g = \frac{\pi_{\text{gmv}}^\top}{w}\tilde{\mu}$ be the returns that can be obtained by any portfolio π_p and π_{gmv}. The covariance of the global minimum variance portfolio with any other portfolio is

$$cov\left(\frac{\pi_p^\top}{w}\tilde{\mu}, \frac{\pi_{\text{gmv}}^\top}{w}\tilde{\mu}\right) = \frac{\pi_p^\top}{w}cov(\tilde{\mu}\tilde{\mu}^\top)\frac{\pi_{\text{gmv}}}{w} = \frac{\pi_p^\top}{w}\frac{\mathbf{1}_m}{C} = \frac{1}{C}.$$

Appendix 1.B The Market Portfolio and the Security Market Line

1.B.1 The Tangent Portfolio Is the Market Portfolio

Let us define the market capitalization for any asset i as the value of all the assets i that are outstanding in the market, namely,

$$\text{Cap}_i \equiv \bar{\theta}_i S_i, \quad i = 1, \cdots, m,$$

where $\bar{\theta}_i$ is the number of assets i outstanding in the market. The market capitalization of all the assets is simply

$$\text{Cap}_M \equiv \sum_{i=1}^{m} \text{Cap}_i.$$

The market portfolio, then, is the portfolio with relative weights given by

$$\bar{\pi}_{M,i} \equiv \frac{\text{Cap}_i}{\text{Cap}_M}, \quad i = 1, \cdots, m.$$

Next, suppose there are N investors and that each investor j has wealth w_j, which they invest in two funds: a safe asset and the tangent portfolio. Let w_j^f be the wealth investor j invests in the safe asset and $w_j - w_j^f$ the remaining wealth the investor invests in the tangent portfolio. The tangent portfolio is defined as $\bar{\pi}_T \equiv \frac{\pi_T}{w_j}$ for some π_T solution to [1.P2] and is obviously independent of w_j (see eq. (1.18) in the main text). The equilibrium in the stock market requires that

$$\text{Cap}_M \cdot \bar{\pi}_M = \sum_{j=1}^{N}\left(w_j - w_j^f\right)\bar{\pi}_T = \sum_{j=1}^{N} w_j \cdot \bar{\pi}_T = \text{Cap}_M \cdot \bar{\pi}_T,$$

where the second equality follows because the safe asset is in zero net supply and, hence, $\sum_{j=1}^{N} w_j^f = 0$ and the third equality holds because all the wealth in the economy is invested in stocks in equilibrium.

1.B.2 Tangency

We check that the CML and the efficient portfolio frontier have the same slope in correspondence of the market portfolio. Let us impose the following tangency condition of the CML to the efficient portfolio frontier in figure 1.2, AMC, at the point M:

$$\sqrt{\text{Sh}} = \frac{AC - D^2}{C\mu_M - D} v_M. \tag{1.A11}$$

The left-hand side (LHS) of this equation is the slope of the CML, obtained through eq. (1.6). The right-hand side (RHS) is the slope of the efficient portfolio frontier, obtained by differentiating $\mu_p(v)$ in the expression for the portfolio frontier in eq. (1.11) and setting $v = v_M$ in

$$\frac{d\mu_p(v)}{dv} = \sqrt{\left(Cv^2 - 1\right)^{-1}\left(AC - D^2\right)}v = \frac{AC - D^2}{C\mu_p(v) - D}v,$$

and where the second equality follows, again, by eq. (1.11). By eqs. (1.A11) and (1.17), we need to show that

$$\frac{C\mu_M - D}{AC - D^2} = \frac{1}{D - Cr}.$$

By plugging $\mu_M = r + \sqrt{\mathrm{Sh}} \cdot v_M$ into the previous equality and rearranging terms,

$$v_M = \frac{\sqrt{\mathrm{Sh}}}{D - Cr},$$

where we have made use of the equality $\mathrm{Sh} = A - 2Dr + Cr^2$, obtained by elaborating on the definition of the Sharpe market performance Sh given in eq. (1.4). This is indeed the variance of the market portfolio given in eq. (1.17).

1.B.3 Alternative Derivation of the SML

The vector of covariances of the m asset returns with the market portfolio are

$$cov(\tilde{\mu}, \tilde{\mu}_M) \equiv cov(\tilde{\mu}, \tfrac{\pi_M^\top}{w}\tilde{\mu}) = cov(\tilde{\mu}\tilde{\mu}^\top)\tfrac{\pi_M}{w} = \Sigma\frac{\pi_M}{w} = \frac{1}{D - Cr}\left(\mu - \mathbf{1}_m r\right), \qquad (1.\mathrm{A}12)$$

where we have used the expression for the market portfolio given in eq. (1.18). Next, premultiply the previous equation by $\frac{\pi_M^\top}{w}$ in eq. (1.16), and obtain

$$v_M^2 = \frac{\pi_M^\top}{w}\Sigma\frac{\pi_M}{w} = \underbrace{\frac{\left(\mu - \mathbf{1}_m r\right)^\top \Sigma^{-1}}{\sqrt{\mathrm{Sh}}}v_M}_{=\frac{\pi_M^\top}{w}} \cdot \underbrace{\frac{1}{D - Cr}\left(\mu - \mathbf{1}_m r\right)}_{=\Sigma\frac{\pi_M}{w}} \qquad (1.\mathrm{A}13)$$

or $v_M = \frac{\sqrt{\mathrm{Sh}}}{D - Cr}$, which confirms eq. (1.17).

Let us rewrite eq. (1.A12) component by component. That is, for $i = 1, \cdots, m$,

$$\sigma_{iM} \equiv cov(\tilde{\mu}_i, \tilde{\mu}_M) = \frac{1}{D - Cr}\left(\mu_i - r\right) = \frac{v_M}{\sqrt{\mathrm{Sh}}}\left(\mu_i - r\right) = \frac{v_M^2}{\mu_M - r}\left(\mu_i - r\right),$$

where the last two equalities follow by eq. (1.A13) and by the CML relation $\sqrt{\mathrm{Sh}} = \frac{\mu_M - r}{v_M}$. By rearranging terms, we obtain eq. (1.21).

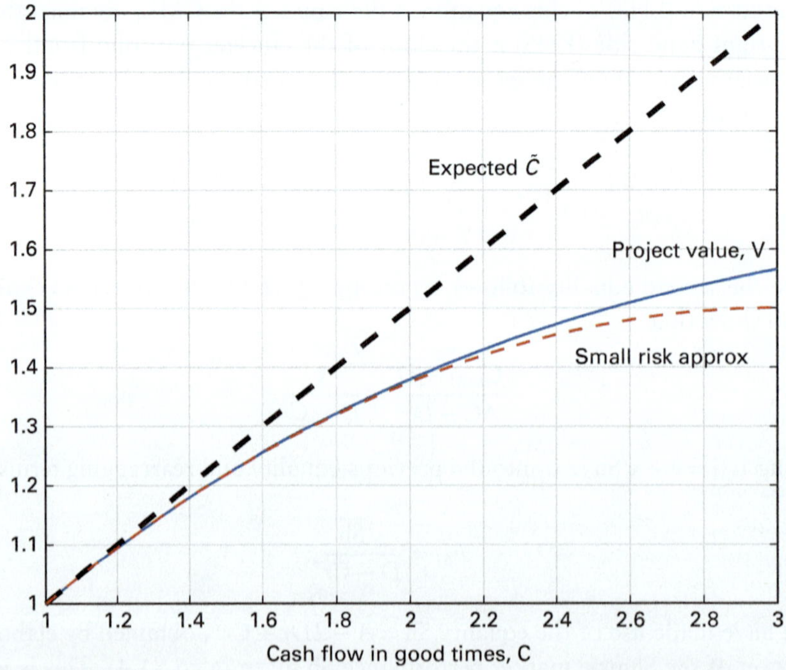

Figure 1.A1
The solid line depicts the value of the project, V, as a function of C, the project cash flow in good times. The thick dashed line depicts the expected value of the project, $E(\tilde{C}) = \frac{1}{2}(1 + C)$, and the thin dashed line is the "small risk approximation" to V in this example, obtained as $\hat{V} \equiv E(\tilde{C}) - \hat{\Lambda}$, where $\hat{\Lambda} \equiv \frac{1}{8}(C-1)^2$. The true risk premium is the difference $\Lambda = E(\tilde{C}) - V$.

Appendix 1.C Risk and Risk Aversion

1.C.1 Modeling and Approximating Risk Premiums

Project value in a representative investor model. We determine the value of the project discussed in section 1.3.4 in a simple model with a representative investor. This value is defined as the solution V to eq. (1.30), and we assume that the representative investor has initial wealth $w = 1$, exponential utility $u(w) = -e^{-\tau w}$ (with τ set equal to 1), and that the random cash flow $\tilde{C}$ is either 1 or $C > 1$ with equal probability. The value C is interpreted as the cash flow realization in "good times." In this example, a closed-form solution is not available for the value of V that satisfies eq. (1.30).

Figure 1.A1 depicts the numerical solution for V as a function of C. Note that due to risk aversion, V is lower than the expected cash flow, $E(\tilde{C}) = \frac{1}{2}(1 + C)$. An analytical approximation to the value of V based on eq. (1.33) is $\hat{V} \equiv E(\tilde{C}) - \hat{\Lambda}$, where the approximated premium, $\hat{\Lambda}$, is defined as

$$\Lambda \approx \hat{\Lambda} \equiv \frac{1}{2}\sigma_\epsilon^2 = \frac{1}{8}(C-1)^2$$

and the second equality follows by a simple calculation. Figure 1.A1 shows that the accuracy of the approximation, $\hat{V}$, deteriorates as the cash flow risk increases, that is, as the deviation of the cash flow in the good state of nature increases from that in the bad (i.e., one). We now turn to provide the rationale underlying the approximation in eq. (1.33).

The approximation in eq. (1.33). Consider a second-order Taylor's approximation of the RHS of the equality in eq. (1.31) around $\epsilon = \Lambda = 0$,

$$E\left(u\left(w+\Lambda+\epsilon\right)\right) \approx u\left(w\right)+u'\left(w\right)\Lambda+\frac{1}{2}u''\left(w\right)\sigma_\epsilon^2,$$

where σ_ϵ^2 denotes the variance of ϵ and where we have disregarded second-order terms in Λ. Using this approximation in eq. (1.31) leaves eq. (1.33).

The approximation in eq. (1.35). The rationale behind this approximation is similar to that underlying eq. (1.33). By a second-order Taylor's approximation of the RHS of the equality in eq. (1.34) around $\epsilon = 0$,

$$E\left(u\left(w+E(\tilde{x})+\epsilon\right)\right) \approx u\left(w+E(\tilde{x})\right)+\frac{1}{2}u''\left(w+E(\tilde{x})\right)\sigma_\epsilon^2,$$

and by a first-order approximation of the LHS,

$$u\left(w+E(\tilde{x})-\Pi\right) \approx u\left(w+E(\tilde{x})\right)-u'\left(w+E(\tilde{x})\right)\Pi.$$

Using these approximations in eq. (1.34) produces eq. (1.35).

The approximation in eq. (1.37). Approximate the RHS of the equality in eq. (1.36) with a second-order Taylor's expansion around $\tilde{g}=0$,

$$E\left(u\left(\left(w+E(\tilde{x})\right)\left(1+\tilde{g}\right)\right)\right) \approx u\left(w+E(\tilde{x})\right)+\frac{1}{2}u''\left(w+E(\tilde{x})\right)\left(w+E(\tilde{x})\right)^2\sigma_g^2,$$

and by a first-order approximation of the LHS,

$$u\left(w+E(\tilde{x})\left(1-\Pi_r\right)\right) \approx u\left(w+E(\tilde{x})\right)-u'\left(w+E(\tilde{x})\right)\left(w+E(\tilde{x})\right)\Pi_r.$$

Using these approximations in eq. (1.36) leaves eq. (1.37).

Certainty equivalents: examples. Consider a risk averse individual who is about to enter a gamble by which they will receive the outcome of rolling a dice. We assume that they have an initial wealth $w=1$ and utility function $u\left(w\right)=\ln w$. The expect payoff from the gamble is $E\left(\tilde{x}\right)=\frac{1}{6}\sum_{j=1}^{6} j=3.5$, and the variance is $\sigma_\epsilon^2=2.9167$. The certainty equivalent is defined as

$$\mathrm{CE}\left(w,\tilde{x}\right): u(w+\mathrm{CE}\left(w,\tilde{x}\right))=E\left(u\left(w+\tilde{x}\right)\right)=\frac{1}{6}\sum_{j=1}^{6}\ln\left(1+j\right)=1.4209,$$

where the last equality holds due to the assumption that $w=1$. That is, $\mathrm{CE}\left(1,\tilde{x}\right)=3.1408$. Accordingly, the (insurance) risk premium is $\Pi=E\left(\tilde{x}\right)-\mathrm{CE}\left(1,\tilde{x}\right)=0.3592$, whereas its approximation in eq. (1.35) is

$$\hat{\Pi}=-\frac{1}{2}\frac{u''\left(w+E(\tilde{x})\right)}{u'\left(w+E(\tilde{x})\right)}\sigma_\epsilon^2=\frac{1}{2}\frac{1}{1+3.5}2.9167=0.3241.$$

Alternatively, assume the individual has exponential utility $u(w) = -e^{-\tau w}$, with $\tau = 1$, and initial wealth still equal to one. The certainty equivalent is now solution to

$$\mathrm{CE}(w, \tilde{x}) : u(w + \mathrm{CE}(w, \tilde{x})) = E(u(w + \tilde{x})) = \frac{1}{6}\sum_{j=1}^{6}(-e^{-(1+j)}) = -3.5594 \times 10^{-2}.$$

That is, $\mathrm{CE}(1, \tilde{x}) = 2.3356$, such that the risk premium is now equal to $\Pi = E(\tilde{x}) - \mathrm{CE}(1, \tilde{x}) = 3.5 - 2.3356 = 1.1644$, whereas its approximation through eq. (1.35) is $\hat{\Pi} = 1.4584$.

1.C.2 Stochastic Dominance and Mean-Preserving Spreads

Variance is the notion of risk underlying the classical CAPM and other models in this chapter. But there are situations studied in this book where the choices of an expected utility maximizer are well understood while relying on a generalized notion of risk due to Rothschild and Stiglitz (1970, 1971). Moreover, this notion of risk can be utilized to characterize quite simply the relation between asset prices and the volatility of fundamentals described in section 1.4.3.

We begin with the following definition.

Definition 1.A1 (First-order stochastic dominance). *$\tilde{x}_2$ dominates $\tilde{x}_1$ if, for any utility function u increasing and concave, we have that $E[u(\tilde{x}_2)] \geq E[u(\tilde{x}_1)]$.*

We have:

Theorem 1.A1. *The following statements are equivalent: (a) $\tilde{x}_2$ dominates $\tilde{x}_1$, or $E[u(\tilde{x}_2)] \geq E[u(\tilde{x}_1)]$ for every increasing function u; (b) for each $x > 0$, $F_2(x)$ is more likely than $F_1(x)$ to pay more than x, that is, $F_1(x) \geq F_2(x)$, where $F_i(x)$ denotes the cumulative distribution of x_i.*

Proof. We prove this result in the case the support is compact, say $[a, b]$. First, we show that $(b) \Rightarrow (a)$. By integrating by parts,

$$E[u(x)] = \int_a^b u(x)dF(x) = u(b) - \int_a^b u'(x)F(x)dx,$$

where we have used the fact that $F(a) = 0$ and $F(b) = 1$. Therefore,

$$E[u(\tilde{x}_2)] - E[u(\tilde{x}_1)] = \int_a^b u'(x)\,[F_1(x) - F_2(x)]\,dx.$$

Next, we show that $(a) \Rightarrow (b)$. Indeed (a) implies that $\int_a^b u(x)\left(dF_2(x) - dF_1(x)\right) \geq 0$ for $u(x) = \mathbb{I}_{x \geq y}$ and $y \in (a, b)$, or $0 \leq \int_a^b \mathbb{I}_{x \geq y}\left(dF_2(x) - dF_1(x)\right) = \int_y^b \left(dF_2(x) - dF_1(x)\right) = F_1(y) - F_2(y)$. □

There is an alternative characterization of first-order stochastic dominance. Suppose there exists a strictly positive random variable η by which $\tilde{x}_2$ exceeds $\tilde{x}_1$, namely,

$$\eta > 0 : \tilde{x}_2 = \tilde{x}_1 + \eta. \tag{1.A14}$$

Then, we have that $\forall t \in [a,b]$, $F_1(t) \equiv \Pr(\tilde{x}_1 \leq t) = \Pr(\tilde{x}_2 \leq t + \eta) \geq \Pr(\tilde{x}_2 \leq t) \equiv F_2(t)$. That is, $\tilde{x}_2$ dominates $\tilde{x}_1$ if it can be expressed as in eq. (1.A14). It is quite an intuitive property, but at the same time, it does not insulate the pure component of risk. Instead, we would like to perform the thought experiment to ask every expected utility maximizer to choose between two distributions with the same mean. Consider the following definition of second-order stochastic dominance.

Definition 1.A2 (Second-order stochastic dominance). *Let $\tilde{x}_1$ and $\tilde{x}_2$ be two random variables with the same expectation. We say that $\tilde{x}_1$ is more risky than $\tilde{x}_2$ if, for every concave function u, we have that $E[u(\tilde{x}_1)] \leq E[u(\tilde{x}_2)]$.*

Next, consider a case in which the distribution of one variable $\tilde{x}_1$ is obtained from that of another variable $\tilde{x}_2$, as follows: we take weights from the middle part of the density and move them toward the tails by making sure that the new density has the same mean as the initial. This is equivalent to requiring that condition (b) in the following theorem holds true. We have:

Theorem 1.A2. *The following statements are equivalent: (a) $\tilde{x}_1$ is more risky than $\tilde{x}_2$; (b) $\tilde{x}_1$ has more weight in the tails than $\tilde{x}_2$, i.e. $\forall t$, $\int_{-\infty}^{t} [F_1(x) - F_2(x)]\, dx \geq 0$.*

Proof. As for $(a) \Rightarrow (b)$, consider the function $-b_y(x) = -\max\{y - x, 0\}$. It is increasing and concave and, hence, a candidate utility function. Therefore, it satisfies

$$\int_a^b (-b_y(x)) \left[dF_1(x) - dF_2(x)\right] \leq 0.$$

That is, using the definition of b_y,

$$\begin{aligned} 0 &\leq \int_a^y (y - x) \left[dF_1(x) - dF_2(x)\right] \\ &= y\left[F_1(y) - F_2(y)\right] - \int_a^y x \left[dF_1(x) - dF_2(x)\right] \\ &= \int_a^y \left[F_1(x) - F_2(x)\right] dx, \end{aligned}$$

where the last equality follows by an integration by parts. Next we prove that $(b) \Rightarrow (a)$. We have

$$\begin{aligned} E[u(\tilde{x}_1)] - E[u(\tilde{x}_2)] &= \int_a^b u(x) \left[f_1(x) - f_2(x)\right] dx \\ &= u(x)\left[F_1(x) - F_2(x)\right]\Big|_a^b - \int_a^b u'(x) \left[F_1(x) - F_2(x)\right] dx \\ &= -\int_a^b u'(x) \left[F_1(x) - F_2(x)\right] dx \\ &= -\left[u'(x) \left[\bar{F}_1(x) - \bar{F}_2(x)\right]\Big|_a^b - \int_a^b u''(x) \left[\bar{F}_1(x) - \bar{F}_2(x)\right] dx\right] \end{aligned}$$

$$= \int_a^b u''(x)\left[\bar{F}_1(x) - \bar{F}_2(x)\right]dx - u'(b)\left[\bar{F}_1(b) - \bar{F}_2(b)\right]$$

$$= \int_a^b u''(x)\left[\bar{F}_1(x) - \bar{F}_2(x)\right]dx,$$

where $\bar{F}_i(x) = \int_a^x F_i(u)du$. The last equality follows because, by integrating by parts,

$$-\int_a^b \left[F_1(x) - F_2(x)\right]dx = \int_a^b x\left[dF_1(x) - dF_2(x)\right] = 0,$$

where the last equality follows by the assumption that F_1 and F_2 have the same mean. Now, by $u'' < 0$ and $\bar{F}_1(x) > \bar{F}_2(x)$, the previous relation implies that $E[u(\tilde{x}_1)] < E[u(\tilde{x}_2)]$, that is, $\tilde{x}_1$ is more risky than $\tilde{x}_2$. □

Finally, we explain a link between the previous notions of risk and that of mean-preserving spreads utilized in section 1.4.4 of this chapter.

Mean-preserving spreads. We can now consider random variables that add up risk without affecting the mean: suppose that there exists a random variable $\epsilon : \tilde{x}_1$ has the same distribution as $\tilde{x}_2 + \epsilon$ and $E(\epsilon | \tilde{x}_2 = x_2) = 0$. We can think of an experiment in which after receiving a random payoff $\tilde{x}_2$, another random payoff could be offered to us, which has conditional expectation zero, thereby adding randomness without boosting the overall expected return. That is, $\tilde{x}_1$ is a *mean-preserving spread* of $\tilde{x}_2$. A variable that is a mean-preserving spread of another displays the properties stated in theorem 1.A2. Indeed,

$$\begin{aligned} E[u(\tilde{x}_1)] &= E[u(\tilde{x}_2 + \epsilon)] \\ &= E[E(u(\tilde{x}_2 + \epsilon) | \tilde{x}_2 = x_2)] \\ &\leq E[u(E(\tilde{x}_2 + \epsilon | \tilde{x}_2 = x_2))] \\ &= E[u(E(\tilde{x}_2 | \tilde{x}_2 = x_2))] \\ &= E[u(\tilde{x}_2)], \end{aligned}$$

where the inequality follows by concavity of u and by Jensen's inequality.

Appendix 1.D Money Demand and Liquidity Traps

We develop an example mentioned in the main text (see section 1.3.5.4) by which agents make dichotomic choices while either holding money or bonds based on their expectations on future interest rates. Assume the nominal yield curve is flat at i_0, and consider a perpetual bond with coupons equal to one, the price of which is $b_0 = \sum_{h=1}^{\infty} 1 \cdot (1 + i_0)^{-h} = i_0^{-1}$. There is a continuum of agents on $[0, 1]$, and each agent $j \in [0, 1]$ holds the belief that within a given period, i_0 will converge to a "normal" rate, say $i_e(j) \equiv 1/b_e(j)$. Therefore, the agent believes that the return on this bond over this period is

$$R_j(i_0) \equiv \frac{b_e(j) - b_0 + 1}{b_0} = \frac{i_0}{i_e(j)} - 1 + i_0,$$

such that there exists a value of i_0 for each j, such that $R_j(i_0) = 0$ and given by

$$\hat{\imath}_0(j) \equiv \frac{i_e(j)}{1 + i_e(j)}.$$

This rate is monotonically increasing in the normal rate for agent j and is critical in that agent j holds money if $i_0 < \hat{\imath}_0(j)$ and invests in bonds if $i_0 > \hat{\imath}_0(j)$. In other words, an investor invests in bonds when they believe that interest rates will fall by an amount sufficient to generate positive profits. Without loss of generality, assume that $\hat{\imath}_0(j)$ is monotonically decreasing.

How do open market operations affect interest rates in this example? For a given i_0, set $\bar{j} : \hat{\imath}_0(\bar{j}) = i_0$, such that investors $j < \bar{j}$ (resp. $j > \bar{j}$) only hold money (resp. bonds). Next, consider a central bank bond purchase operation. Given the current level of i_0, investors who are currently holding bonds are obviously *not* willing to tender any of their holdings: bondholders would be incentivized to sell at a price higher than b_0. Consider, for example, the price $b_0' \equiv (i_0 - \epsilon)^{-1}$, for some $\epsilon > 0$; then, the investors' break-even condition becomes $R_j(i_0 - \epsilon) = 0$. Now, would-be bondholders are those j such that $j > \bar{j}' > \bar{j}$, that is, a mass of investors equal to $\bar{j}' - \bar{j}$ are willing to sell at b_0': money demand decreases with the nominal interest rates.

Note that if the current interest rate i_0 was so low that $i_0 = \hat{\imath}_0(1) \equiv \underline{\xi}$, no agent would currently hold any bonds: everyone would now hold the belief that that interest rates may only rise. This situation is one of a *liquidity trap*: when $i_0 = \underline{\xi}$, an increase in money supply would not affect interest rates; there are no investors in the market to purchase bonds from, except the marginal investor $j = 1$. So if the central bank increases money supply, the marginal investor is willing to accept this new money and tender the bonds as they are obviously indifferent between investing in bonds or hoarding money. Actually, if the central bank decreases money supply, the marginal investor would also be willing to buy these bonds.

This description illustrates the very well-known Keynes's (1936) point that money demand should be negatively sloped at an aggregate level. Consider the following simple example, in which $i_e(j)$ is uniformly distributed, that is,

$$i_e(j) = \bar{\xi} - (\bar{\xi} - \underline{\xi})j, \quad j \in [0, 1]$$

for some two constants $\underline{\xi}$ and $\bar{\xi} > \underline{\xi}$. Then,

$$\hat{\imath}_0(j) = \frac{\bar{\xi} - (\bar{\xi} - \underline{\xi})j}{1 + \bar{\xi} - (\bar{\xi} - \underline{\xi})j}.$$

The jth agent money demand, $m^d(j)$ say, is dichotomic, in that

$$m^d(j) = \begin{cases} 1, & \text{if } \hat{\imath}_0(j) > i_0 \\ 0, & \text{otherwise} \end{cases}.$$

Yet aggregate money demand is

$$M^d \equiv \int_0^1 m^d(j)\,dj = \int_{j:\hat{\imath}_0(j)>i_0} dj = \frac{\bar{\xi} - (1+\bar{\xi})\, i_0}{(\bar{\xi} - \underline{\xi})(1 - i_0)},$$

Provided $i_0 < \frac{\bar{\xi}}{1+\bar{\xi}}$, aggregate money demand is positive. Moreover, it is always decreasing in i_0.

Appendix 1.E Parameter Uncertainty

Proofs of eq. (1.49). By the projection theorem (see appendix 10.A in chapter 10),

$$E(\mu\,|\mathcal{V}) = E(\mu) + cov(\mu, \mathcal{V})\, var(\mathcal{V})^{-1}(\mathcal{V} - E(\mathcal{V})),$$

and

$$var(\mu\,|\mathcal{V}) = var(\mu) - cov(\mu, \mathcal{V})\, var(\mathcal{V})^{-1}\, cov(\mu, \mathcal{V})^{\intercal},$$

where, by (1.48), $cov(\mu, \mathcal{V}) = cov(\mu, P\mu - \epsilon_v) = CP^{\intercal}$ and $var(\mathcal{V}) = PCP^{\intercal} + \Omega$. Therefore,

$$E(\mu\,|\mathcal{V}) = \bar{\mu} + CP^{\intercal}\left(PCP^{\intercal} + \Omega\right)^{-1}(\mathcal{V} - P\bar{\mu}), \quad var(\mu\,|\mathcal{V}) = C - CP^{\intercal}\left(PCP^{\intercal} + \Omega\right)^{-1} PC^{\intercal}.$$

The distribution in (1.49) follows by rearranging terms and using the definition $C = c\Sigma$. □

Proofs of eq. (1.54). Consider the Lagrangian function for the program [1.P4], where M is as in (1.53):

$$\mathcal{L} = \pi^{\top}(\mu - \mathbf{1}_m r) + R - \frac{\tau}{2}\pi^{\top}\Sigma\pi - \lambda\left(\eta - (\hat{\mu} - \mu)^{\top}\Sigma^{-1}(\hat{\mu} - \mu)\right), \qquad (1.A15)$$

where λ is the Lagrange multiplier. The first-order conditions for μ leads to $\hat{\mu} - \mu_* = \frac{1}{2\lambda}\Sigma\pi$, where μ_* is the optimal value for μ; replacing this expression and the first-order condition for λ into (1.A15) leaves

$$\mathcal{L} = \pi^{\top}(\hat{\mu} - \mathbf{1}_m r) + R - \frac{\tau}{2}\pi^{\top}\Sigma\pi - \frac{1}{2\lambda}\pi^{\top}\Sigma\pi. \qquad (1.A16)$$

The expression for the Lagrange multiplier, λ_* say, is obtained while using the constraint

$$\eta = (\hat{\mu} - \mu_*)^{\top}\Sigma^{-1}(\hat{\mu} - \mu_*) = \left(\frac{1}{2\lambda}\right)^2 \pi^{\top}\Sigma\pi,$$

leaving $2\lambda^* = \sqrt{\frac{\pi^{\top}\Sigma\pi}{\eta}}$. The objective function in eq. (1.54) in the main text follows by replacing λ_* into (1.A16). The second equality follows because the first-order conditions for this problem lead to

$$\hat{\pi} = \frac{\sigma_P}{\tau\sigma_P + \sqrt{\eta}}\Sigma^{-1}(\hat{\mu} - \mathbf{1}_m r), \quad \sigma_P \equiv \sqrt{\pi^{\top}\Sigma\pi}.$$

Replacing the expression for $\hat{\pi}$ into that for σ_P leads to the following equation satisfied by σ_P^2,

$$\sigma_P^2 = \left(\frac{\sigma_P}{\tau\sigma_P + \sqrt{\eta}}\right)^2 \mathrm{Sh}_*,$$

where Sh_* is defined in the main text. That is, $\tau\sigma_P + \sqrt{\eta} = \sqrt{\mathrm{Sh}_*}$. □

References

Abel, A. B. (1988). "Stock Prices under Time-Varying Dividend Risk: An Exact Solution in an Infinite-Horizon General Equilibrium Model." *Journal of Monetary Economics* 22, 375–393.

Ang, A. (2014). *Asset Management: A Systematic Approach to Factor Investing*. Oxford: Oxford University Press.

Arrow, K. J. (1965). "The Theory of Risk Aversion." In *Aspects of the Theory of Risk Bearing*. Helsinki: Yrjö Jahnssonin Säätiö.

Bali, T. G., R. F. Engle, and S. Murray (2016). *Empirical Asset Pricing: The Cross Section of Stock Returns*. Hoboken, NJ: John Wiley.

Banz, R. W. (1981). "The Relationship Between Return and Market Value of Common Stocks." *Journal of Financial Economics* 9, 3–18.

Barsky, R. B. (1989). "Why Don't the Prices of Stocks and Bonds Move Together?" *American Economic Review* 79, 1132–1145.

Black, F. (1972). "Capital Market Equilibrium with Restricted Borrowing." *Journal of Business* 45, 444–454.

Black, F., and R. Litterman (1991). "Asset Allocation: Combining Investor Views with Market Equilibrium." *Journal of Fixed Income* 1, no. 2, 7–18.

Black, F., M. C. Jensen, and M. Scholes (1972). "The Capital Asset Pricing Model: Some Empirical Tests." In *Studies in the Theory of Capital Markets*, edited by M. C. Jensen, 79–121. New York: Praeger.

Campbell, J. Y., and L. M. Viceira (2002). *Strategic Asset Allocation*. Oxford: Oxford University Press.

Carhart, M. (1997). "On Persistence of Mutual Fund Performance." *Journal of Finance* 52, 57–82.

Chen, N.-F., R. Roll, and S. A. Ross (1986). "Economic Forces and the Stock Market." *Journal of Business* 59, 383–403.

Connor, G. (1984). "A Unified Beta Pricing Theory." *Journal of Economic Theory* 34, 13–31.

Dow, J., and S. Werlang (1992). "Uncertainty Aversion, Risk Aversion, and the Optimal Choice of Portfolio." *Econometrica* 60, 197–204.

Fama, E. F., and K. R. French (1992). "The Cross-Section of Expected Stock Returns." *Journal of Finance* 47, 427–465.

Fama, E. F., and K. R. French (1993). "Common Risk Factors in the Returns on Stocks and Bonds." *Journal of Financial Economics* 33, 3–56.

Fama, E. F., and J. D. MacBeth (1973). "Risk, Return, and Equilibrium: Empirical Tests." *Journal of Political Economy* 38, 607–636.

Frazzini, A., and L. H. Pedersen (2014). "Betting Against Beta." *Journal of Financial Economics* 111, 1–25.

Garlappi, L., R. Uppal, and T. Wang (2007). "Portfolio Selection with Parameter and Model Uncertainty: A Multi-Prior Approach." *Review of Financial Studies* 20, 41–81.

Gilboa, I., and D. Schmeidler (1989). "Maxmin Expected Utility with a Non-Unique Prior." *Journal of Mathematical Economics* 18, 141–153.

Gouriéroux, C., and A. Monfort (2008). *Statistics and Econometric Models*. Vol. 2, *Themes in Modern Econometrics*. Cambridge, UK: Cambridge University Press.

Grossman, S. J., and J. E. Stiglitz (1980). "On the Impossibility of Informationally Efficient Markets." *American Economic Review* 70, 393–408.

Harvey, C. R., Y. Liu, and H. Zhu (2016). "... and the Cross-Section of Expected Returns." *Review of Financial Studies* 29, 5–68.

Heckman, J. (1979). "Sample Selection Bias as a Specification Error." *Econometrica* 47, 153–161.

Huang, C.-F., and R. H. Litzenberger (1988). *Foundations for Financial Economics*. New York: North-Holland.

Huberman, G. (1983). "A Simplified Approach to Arbitrage Pricing Theory." *Journal of Economic Theory* 28, 1983–1991.

Jegadeesh, N., and S. Titman (1993). "Returns to Buying Winners and Selling Losers: Implications for Stock Market Efficiency." *Journal of Finance* 48, 65–91.

Keynes, J. M. (1936). *The General Theory of Employment, Interest and Money*. London: Palgrave Macmillan.

Kyle, A. S. (1985). "Continuous Auctions and Insider Trading." *Econometrica* 53, 1335–1335.

Lintner, J. (1965). "The Valuation of Risk Assets and the Selection of Risky Investments in Stock Portfolios and Capital Budgets." *Review of Economics and Statistics* 47, 13–37.

Malkiel, B. (1979). "The Capital Formation Problem in the United States." *Journal of Finance* 34, 291–306.

Markovitz, H. (1952). "Portfolio Selection." *Journal of Finance* 7, 77–91.

Meucci, A. (2005). *Risk and Asset Allocation*. New York: Springer Verlag.

Mossin, J. (1966). "Equilibrium in a Capital Asset Market." *Econometrica* 34, 768–783.

Pedersen, L. H. (2015). *Efficiently Inefficient*. Princeton, NJ: Princeton University Press.

Pindyck, R. (1984). "Risk, Inflation and the Stock Market." *American Economic Review* 74, 335–351.

Popper, K. (1959). *The Logic of Scientific Discovery*. New York: Basic Books.

Poterba, J., and L. Summers (1985). "The Persistence of Volatility and Stock Market Fluctuations." *American Economic Review* 75, 1142–1151.

Pratt, J. W. (1964). "Risk Aversion in the Small and in the Large." *Econometrica* 32, 122–136.

Roll, R. (1977). "A Critique of the Asset Pricing Theory's Tests Part I: On Past and Potential Testability of the Theory." *Journal of Financial Economics* 4, 129–176.

Roncalli, T. (2014). *Introduction to Risk Parity and Budgeting*. London: Chapman & Hall.

Rosenberg, B., K. Reid, and R. Lanstein (1985). "Persuasive Evidence of Market Inefficiency." *Journal of Portfolio Management* 11, 9–17.

Ross, S. (1976). "Arbitrage Theory of Capital Asset Pricing." *Journal of Economic Theory* 13, 341–360.

Rothschild, M., and J. Stiglitz (1970). "Increasing Risk: I. A Definition." *Journal of Economic Theory* 2, 225–243.

Rothschild, M., and J. Stiglitz (1971). "Increasing Risk: II. Its Economic Consequences." *Journal of Economic Theory* 5, 66–84.

Shanken, J., and M. I. Weinstein (2006). "Economic Forces and the Stock Market Revisited." *Journal of Empirical Finance* 13, 129–144.

Sharpe, W. F. (1964). "Capital Asset Prices: A Theory of Market Equilibrium under Conditions of Risk." *Journal of Finance* 19, 425–442.

Stattman, D. (1980). "Book Values and Stock Returns." *The Chicago MBA: A Journal of Selected Papers* 4, 25–45.

Tobin, J. (1958). "Liquidity Preference as Behavior Towards Risk." *Review of Economic Studies* 25, 65–86.

2

Arbitrage, Equilibrium, and Pricing

2.1 Introduction

This chapter develops asset pricing restrictions that arise while also requiring that financial markets are free from arbitrage. Financial markets provide opportunities to trade assets that have exposure to different risks. Typically, these risks relate to the activity of entities such as private corporations, households, or governments. Ideally, these markets feature the property that, once an investor "enters" into them, they do not encounter difficulties while trying to "exit." These ideal markets are "liquid." In practice, markets may be illiquid and subject to a number of imperfections that are dealt with in other junctures of this book, as will be explained. Further, financial markets also obviously involve transactions among parties—say, "contracts" (such as a loan contract)—which may not necessarily be traded in secondary markets; some of these transactions are dealt with in chapter 5.

In some cases, the assets in the idealized markets of this chapter may be evaluated with no regard to "supply and demand" forces and therefore to determinants such as risk aversion or the bargaining power of the parties involved into a transaction. These assets may be priced while only relying on absence of arbitrage. How can this be possible? Suppose that the value of a given security can be "replicated" by means of a dedicated portfolio of other securities. In this case, the security value equals that of the replicating portfolio, regardless of supply and demand or of additional pricing guidance such as a law of large numbers. The reason is that two portfolios delivering the same payoff must be worth the same, for otherwise an arbitrage opportunity would arise: under conditions, one could trade the existing securities and make riskless profits. We say that, in this case, security evaluation is "preference free." It is, of course, an idealized situation but also a cornerstone in financial economics.

A foundational stone in this construction relies on the most elementary securities that we may imagine: those that only pay off a fixed amount of numéraire in a prespecified state of the world: say \$1 in the given state and zero otherwise. These assets are known as Arrow-Debreu securities in recognition of the founders of general equilibrium theory with uncertainty. Arrow-Debreu securities are conceptually very useful as the knowledge of their prices can be utilized to price any other asset. They link to what we commonly refer to as risk neutral probabilities, a concept introduced in chapter 1 and developed in detail in this and subsequent chapters. Not surprisingly, these idealized securities are also a useful tool in the market practice of asset pricing, as explained in part III. Thus, Arrow-Debreu securities constitute the bricks of the entire asset evaluation framework in financial economics, a bit like atoms in physics, so to speak.

Needless to say, many of the previous conclusions rely on a number of assumptions, such as the agents' symmetric information on the assets fundamentals, market completeness (i.e., the existence of an Arrow-Debreu security for each state of the world), absence of additional market frictions, or finally, perfect competition in the goods market. However, there are many examples of securities and other complex products that are difficult to replicate: their payoffs are exposed to risks that one may not be able to replicate while trading with existing securities (as in the case of markets with random equity volatility; see chapter 11). The present chapter has the humble task of introducing basic concepts and describes idealized markets without such imperfections, thereby setting foundations for more advanced analyses in other parts of the book. For example, we shall deal with more realistic market imperfections and information problems in chapters 4 and 5 and very often in part II (see, e.g., chapters 9 and 10); nevertheless, this chapter already contains an introduction to the theory of incomplete markets, a situation in which the payoff of certain financial securities cannot be replicated. In these cases, the value of these securities reflects supply and demand or agents' preferences.

We start from very far: we review the classical general equilibrium model in a context without uncertainty. In this model, equilibrium allocations are optimal according to Pareto's criterion. Financial securities play a critical role once these economies are subject to uncertainty. When these securities are diverse enough, resource allocations are still Pareto optimal in economies with uncertainty, just as in the classic general equilibrium model. Intuitively, a number of sufficiently diverse financial securities has the potential to deliver the payoffs we need in each future state of the world, thereby making markets function as if we were in a static world.

In fact, even when markets are incomplete, we can still define shadow prices of Arrow-Debreu securities, which may be used to evaluate any other asset. The challenge in this case is that absence of arbitrage does not allow us to determine a unique set of Arrow-Debreu prices (as in the complete markets case). Further assumptions are needed to determine these shadow prices. For example, in an economy in which agents optimize their consumption choices, Arrow-Debreu prices are pinned down in equilibrium. Indeed, an important task of this chapter is to link Arrow-Debreu prices to optimal consumption in equilibrium. It is natural. As financial economists, we would like to understand asset prices in economies where agents allocate their endowments across consumption and savings. This chapter provides introductions to these problems in the context of two-period economies, but many of its insights lead to asset pricing equations that are the logical antecedents to Euler's equations arising in multiperiod economies dealt with in more advanced parts of this book.

The chapter is organized as follows. The next section contains a succinct description of the static general equilibrium model and its properties and abstracts from decisions taken within the production sphere of the economy. Production-based economies are studied in more detail in chapter 3 as well as in part II (see, e.g., chapter 9). Section 2.3 illustrates the role financial securities can play in economies subject to uncertainty and some simple examples illustrating the meaning and use of Arrow-Debreu securities and their relations to the "risk neutral probability." Sections 2.4 and 2.5 provide theory based on the extension of the general equilibrium model of section 2.2 and include uncertainty. Section 2.4 provides the first important example of how we can evaluate assets solely based on requiring absence of arbitrage opportunities. Section 2.5 develops a more systematic treatment of markets in absence of arbitrage, in particular, the price implications in both complete and incomplete markets. Note that absence of arbitrage does not imply equilibrium, although the converse is true as explained in section 2.6. Section 2.6 then relates Arrow-Debreu security prices to risk neutral probabilities in both complete and incomplete markets and provides discussion on topics such as the role of financial markets as vehicles of risk sharing for a society. Section 2.7 provides a very first introduction to the theory of the consumption capital asset pricing model as well as its predictions on the equity premium. One appendix contains material omitted from the main text.

2.2 The Static General Equilibrium in a Nutshell

We consider an economy with n agents and m commodities. Let w_{ij} denote the amount of the ith commodity the jth agent is endowed with, and let $w^j = \left[w_{1j}, \cdots, w_{mj}\right]$. Let the price vector be $p = [p_1, \cdots, p_m]$, where p_i is the price of the ith commodity. Let $w_i = \sum_{j=1}^{n} w_{ij}$ be the total endowment of the ith commodity in the economy and $W = [w_1, \cdots, w_m]$ the corresponding endowments bundle in the economy.

The jth agent has utility function $u_j\left(c_{1j}, \cdots, c_{mj}\right)$, where $\left(c_{ij}\right)_{i=1}^{m}$ denotes their consumption bundle. We assume that the following standard conditions hold for the utility functions u_j.

Assumption 2.1 (Preferences). *The utility functions u_j satisfy the following properties: (i) monotonicity, (ii) continuity, and (iii) concavity. That is, $\frac{\partial u_j}{\partial c_{ij}}\left(c_{1j}, \cdots, c_{mj}\right) \geq 0$, and $\frac{\partial^2 u_j}{\partial c_{ij}^2}(c_{1j}, \cdots, c_{mj}) \leq 0$.*

Let $B_j(p_1, \cdots, p_m) = \left\{\left(c_{1j}, \cdots, c_{mj}\right) \in \mathbb{R}_+^m : \sum_{i=1}^{m} p_i c_{ij} \leq \sum_{i=1}^{m} p_i w_{ij} \equiv R_j\right\}$, a bounded, closed, and convex set. Each agent maximizes their utility function subject to the budget constraint

$$\max_{\{c_{ij}\}} u_j(c_{1j}, \cdots, c_{mj}) \quad \text{subject to } \left(c_{1j}, \cdots, c_{mj}\right) \in B_j(p_1, \cdots, p_m). \qquad \text{[2.P1]}$$

This problem certainly has a solution, for B_j is compact set, and by assumption 2.1, u_j is continuous, and a continuous function attains its maximum on a compact set. Moreover, appendix 2.A shows that this maximum is unique.

The first-order conditions to [2.P1] are, for each agent j,

$$\begin{cases} \dfrac{\frac{\partial u_j}{\partial c_{1j}}}{p_1} = \dfrac{\frac{\partial u_j}{\partial c_{2j}}}{p_2} = \cdots = \dfrac{\frac{\partial u_j}{\partial c_{mj}}}{p_m} \\ \displaystyle\sum_{i=1}^{m} p_i c_{ij} = \sum_{i=1}^{m} p_i w_{ij} \end{cases}. \qquad (2.1)$$

These conditions form a system of m equations with m unknowns. Let us denote the solution to this system with $[\hat{c}_{1j}(p, w^j), \cdots, \hat{c}_{mj}(p, w^j)]$. The total demand for the ith commodity is

$$\hat{c}_i(p, w) = \sum_{j=1}^{n} \hat{c}_{ij}(p, w^j), \quad i = 1, \cdots, m.$$

We emphasize that the economy we consider in this chapter abstracts from production. In this economy, prices determine resource allocation. This perspective is radically different from that of the classical school (Ricardo, Marx, and Sraffa), for which prices and resource allocation cannot be disentangled from the production side of the economy. In chapter 3 and in part II (see chapter 9), we discuss asset pricing implications of production economies while always relying on models and model refinements belonging to a neoclassical perspective.

2.2.1 Walras's Law

Let us plug the demand functions of the jth agent into the constraint of [2.P1] to obtain

$$\forall p, \quad 0 = \sum_{i=1}^{m} p_i \left(\hat{c}_{ij}(p, w^j) - w_{ij}\right). \tag{2.2}$$

Next, define the total excess demand for the ith commodity as $e_i(p, w) \equiv \hat{c}_i(p, w) - w_i$. By aggregating the budget constraint across all the agents, for each p,

$$0 = \sum_{j=1}^{n} \sum_{i=1}^{m} p_i \left(\hat{c}_{ij}(p, w^j) - w_{ij}\right) = \sum_{i=1}^{m} p_i e_i(p, w).$$

The previous equality is the celebrated *Walras's law.*

Next, multiply p by $\lambda \in \mathbb{R}_{++}$. Since the constraint to [2.P1] does not change, the excess demand functions are the same for each value of λ. In other words, *the excess demand functions are homogeneous of degree zero in the prices*, or $e_i(\lambda p, w) = e_i(p, w)$, $i = 1, \cdots, m$. This property of the excess demand functions is also sometimes referred to as *absence of monetary illusion.*

2.2.2 Competitive Equilibrium

A *competitive equilibrium* is a vector $\bar{p}$ in $\mathbb{R}^m_+$ such that $e_i(\bar{p}, w) \leq 0$ for all $i = 1, \cdots, m$, with at least one component of $\bar{p}$ being strictly positive. Further, if there exists a $j : e_j(\bar{p}, w) < 0$, then $\bar{p}_j = 0$.

2.2.2.1 *Back to Walras's law*

Walras's law holds by the mere aggregation of the agents' constraints. But the agents' constraints are accounting identities. In particular, Walras's law holds for any price vector and then for the equilibrium price vector,

$$0 = \sum_{i=1}^{m} \bar{p}_i e_i(\bar{p}, w) = \sum_{i=1}^{m-1} \bar{p}_i e_i(\bar{p}, w) + \bar{p}_m e_m(\bar{p}, w). \tag{2.3}$$

Now suppose that the first $m-1$ markets are in equilibrium, or $e_i(\bar{p},w)\leq 0$, for $i=1,\cdots,m-1$. By the definition of an equilibrium, we have that $\text{sign}\left(e_i(\bar{p},w)\right)\bar{p}_i=0$. Therefore, by eq. (2.3), we conclude that if $m-1$ *markets are in equilibrium, then the remaining market is also in equilibrium.*

2.2.2.2 *The notion of numéraire*

The excess demand functions are homogeneous of degree zero. Walras's law implies that if $m-1$ markets are in equilibrium, then the mth remaining market is also in equilibrium. We wish to link these two results. First, note that by Walras's law, the equations that define a competitive equilibrium are not independent. Once $m-1$ of these equations are satisfied, the mth remaining equation is also satisfied. In other words, there are $m-1$ independent relations and m unknowns in the equations that define a competitive equilibrium. So there exists an infinity of solutions. Suppose, then, that we choose the mth price to be a sort of exogenous datum. The result is that we obtain a system of $m-1$ equations with $m-1$ unknowns. Provided it exists, such a solution is a function f of the mth price, $\bar{p}_i=f_i(\bar{p}_m)$, $i=1,\cdots,m-1$. We may refer the mth commodity to as the *numéraire*.

In other words, the equations of general equilibrium may only determine a system of *relative* prices. The scale of the price system depends on the price of the numéraire. Precisely, it is easy to check that if the functions f_i are homogeneous of degree one, then multiplying p_m by a strictly positive number λ does not change the system of *relative* prices. Indeed, by the equilibrium condition, for all $i=1,\cdots,m$,

$$\begin{aligned}0 &\geq e_i\left(f_1(\lambda\bar{p}_m),\, f_2(\lambda\bar{p}_m),\cdots,\lambda\bar{p}_m,w\right)\\ &= e_i\left(\lambda\bar{p}_1,\lambda\bar{p}_2\cdots,\lambda\bar{p}_m,w\right)=e_i\left(\bar{p}_1,\bar{p}_2\cdots,\bar{p}_m,w\right),\end{aligned}$$

where the second equality is due to the homogeneity property of the functions f_i and the last equality holds because the excess demand functions e_i are homogeneous of degree zero. In particular, by defining relative prices as $\hat{p}_j=p_j/p_m$, one has that $p_j=\hat{p}_j\cdot p_m$ is a function that is homogeneous of degree one. That is, if $\lambda\equiv\bar{p}_m^{-1}$, then

$$0\geq e_i\left(\bar{p}_1,\cdots,\bar{p}_m,w\right)=e_i\left(\lambda\bar{p}_1,\cdots,\lambda\bar{p}_m,w\right)\equiv e_i\left(\frac{\bar{p}_1}{\bar{p}_m},\cdots,1,w\right).$$

2.2.3 Optimality

Let $c^j=\left(c_{1j},\cdots,c_{mj}\right)$ be the allocation to agent j, $j=1,\cdots,n$. The following definition contains the well-known concept of a Pareto optimum, that is, a criterion for a desirable resource allocation.

Definition 2.2 (Pareto optimum). *An allocation $\bar{c}=\left(\bar{c}^1,\cdots,\bar{c}^n\right)$ is a Pareto optimum if it is feasible, $\sum_{j=1}^n\left(\bar{c}^j-w^j\right)\leq 0$, and if there are no other feasible allocations $c=\left(c^1,\cdots,c^n\right)$ such that $u_j(c^j)\geq u_j(\bar{c}^j)$, $j=1,\cdots,n$, with one strict inequality for at least one agent.*

We have the following.

Theorem 2.3 (First welfare theorem). *Every competitive equilibrium is a Pareto optimum.*

Proof. Let us suppose on the contrary that $\bar{c}$ is an equilibrium but not a Pareto optimum. Then there exists a $c: u_{j^*}(c^{j^*})>u_{j^*}(\bar{c}^{j^*})$ for some j^*. Because $\bar{c}^{j^*}$ is optimal for agent j^*,

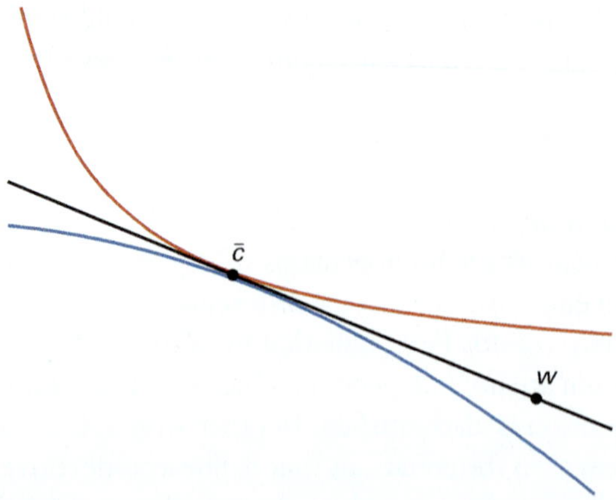

Figure 2.1
Decentralization of a Pareto optimum.

$c^{j*} \notin B_j(\bar{p})$, or $\bar{p}c^{j*} > \bar{p}w_j$ and by aggregating $\bar{p}\sum_{j=1}^{n} c^j > \bar{p}\sum_{j=1}^{n} w^j$, which is unfeasible. It follows that c cannot be an equilibrium. □

Next, we show that any Pareto optimal allocation can be "decentralized." That is, corresponding to a given Pareto optimum $\bar{c}$, there exist ways of redistributing endowments and a price vector $\bar{p}: \bar{p}\bar{c} = \bar{p}w$ that is an equilibrium for the initial set of resources.

Theorem 2.4 (Second welfare theorem). *Every Pareto optimum can be decentralized.*

The proof of theorem 2.4 is in appendix 2.A. This theorem can be interpreted as one that supports an *equilibrium with transfer payments*. For any given Pareto optimum $\bar{c}^j$, a social planner may endow each agent with $\bar{p}w^j$ (with $\bar{p}\bar{c}^j = \bar{p}w^j$; w^j is chosen by the planner), and agents choose $\bar{c}^j$ in equilibrium. Figure 2.1 depicts the famous Edgeworth's box, that is the decentralization in the two-agent, two-commodity case. Suppose that the objective is to achieve $\bar{c}$. Given an initial allocation w chosen by the planner, each agent is given $\bar{p}w^j$. *Laissez faire* leads to $\bar{c}$. In other words, agents are given a constraint of the form $\bar{p}c^j = \bar{p}w^j$. If w^j and $\bar{p}$ are chosen so as to induce each agent to choose $\bar{c}^j$, then $\bar{p}$ is a supporting equilibrium price. In this case, the marginal rates of substitution are identical as established by the following celebrated result.

Theorem 2.5 (Characterization of Pareto optima: I). *A feasible allocation $\bar{c} = (\bar{c}^1, \cdots, \bar{c}^n)$ is a Pareto optimum if and only if there exists a vector $\tilde{\phi} \in \mathbb{R}_{++}^{m-1}$ such that*

$$\tilde{\nabla}u_j = \tilde{\phi},\ j = 1, \cdots, n, \quad \textit{where } \tilde{\nabla}u_j \equiv \left(\frac{\frac{\partial u_j}{\partial c_{2j}}}{\frac{\partial u_j}{\partial c_{1j}}}, \cdots, \frac{\frac{\partial u_j}{\partial c_{mj}}}{\frac{\partial u_j}{\partial c_{1j}}} \right). \tag{2.4}$$

Proof. A Pareto optimum satisfies

$$\bar{c} \in \arg\max_{c \in \mathbb{R}_+^{m \cdot n}} u_1\left(c^1\right), \text{ subject to } \begin{cases} u_j(c^j) \geq \bar{u}_j,\ j = 2, \cdots, n \\ \sum_{j=1}^{n} (c^j - w^j) \leq 0 \end{cases}.$$

The Lagrangian function associated with this program is

$$L = u_1(c^1) + \sum_{j=2}^{n} \lambda_j \left(u_j(c^j) - \bar{u}_j\right) - \sum_{i=1}^{m} \phi_i \sum_{j=1}^{n} \left(c_{ij} - w_{ij}\right),$$

where λ_j, $j = 2, \cdots, n$, and ϕ_j, $i = 1, \cdots, m$ are multipliers. The first-order conditions are

$$\begin{cases} \dfrac{\partial u_1}{\partial c_{11}} & = & \phi_1 \\ & \cdots & \\ \dfrac{\partial u_1}{\partial c_{m1}} & = & \phi_m \end{cases} \qquad \begin{cases} \lambda_j \dfrac{\partial u_j}{\partial c_{1j}} & = & \phi_1 \\ & \cdots & \\ \lambda_j \dfrac{\partial u_j}{\partial c_{mj}} & = & \phi_m \end{cases}$$

where the second system holds for all $j = 2, \cdots, n$. In each of these two systems, we divide each equation by the first, obtaining eq. (2.4), with $\tilde{\phi} = \left(\frac{\phi_2}{\phi_1}, \cdots, \frac{\phi_m}{\phi_1}\right)$. The converse is left as an exercise. □

There is a simple and appealing interpretation of the Kuhn-Tucker multiplier ϕ of the constraints of theorem 2.5. Note that by eq. (2.1), in the competitive equilibrium,

$$\tilde{\nabla} u_j = \tilde{p} \equiv \left(\frac{p_2}{p_1}, \cdots, \frac{p_m}{p_1}\right).$$

But because a competitive equilibrium is also a Pareto optimum, then by theorem 2.5,

$$\tilde{\nabla} u_j = \tilde{\phi} \equiv \left(\frac{\phi_2}{\phi_1}, \cdots, \frac{\phi_m}{\phi_1}\right).$$

Hence, $\tilde{\phi}$ represents the vector of relative shadow prices arising within the centralized allocation process.

We provide a further characterization of Pareto optimal allocations.

Theorem 2.6 (Characterization of Pareto optima: II). *A feasible allocation $\bar{c} = (\bar{c}^1, \cdots, \bar{c}^n)$ is a Pareto optimum if and only if there exists a vector $\ell > 0$ such that $\bar{c}$ is solution to the following program:*

$$u(w, \ell) = \max_{c^1, \cdots, c^n} \sum_{j=1}^{n} \ell_j u_j(c^j), \text{ subject to } \sum_{j=1}^{n} c^j \leq w. \qquad [2.P2]$$

Proof. The *if* part is simple and at the same time instructive. Let us solve the program in [2.P2]. The Lagrangian is

$$L = \sum_{j=1}^{n} \ell_j u_j(c^j) - \sum_{i=1}^{m} \psi_i \sum_{j=1}^{n} \left(c_{ij} - w_{ij}\right)$$

for some multipliers ψ_j, $j = 1, \cdots, m$. The first-order conditions are, for $j = 1, \cdots, m$,

$$\ell_j \nabla u_j = \psi \equiv (\psi_1, \cdots, \psi_m)^\top, \quad \nabla u_j \equiv \left(\frac{\partial u_j}{\partial c_{1j}}, \cdots, \frac{\partial u_j}{\partial c_{mj}}\right)^\top. \tag{2.5}$$

That is, $\tilde{\nabla} u_j$ equals the same vector of constants for all the agents, just as in theorem 2.5. The converse to this theorem follows by an application of the usual separating theorem, as in Duffie (2001, chapter 1). □

Note that if $\ell_1 = 1$ and $\ell_j = \lambda_j$ for $j = 2, \cdots, n$, then $\psi_i = \phi_i$ $(i = 1, \cdots, m)$, and so the first-order conditions in theorems 2.5 and 2.6 would lead to the same allocation. More generally, we have the following theorem.

Theorem 2.7 (Centralization of competitive equilibrium through Pareto weighting). *The outcome of any competitive equilibrium can be obtained in an economy where a central planner solves the program in [2.P2], with system of social weights equal to $\ell_j = 1/\kappa_j$, where κ_j is the marginal utility of income for agent j.*

Thus, agents with high marginal utility of income (for a given price vector) receive little social weight in the centralized planner allocation procedure. This result and some of its extensions are particularly useful when one deals with economies with heterogeneous agents. Theorem 2.7 is also a point of reference when it comes to study asset prices in a world of incomplete markets. Chapter 9 contains several instances relying on these old but useful insights.

Proof of Theorem 2.7. In the competitive equilibrium,

$$\nabla u_j = \kappa_j p, \quad p \equiv (p_1, \cdots, p_m), \tag{2.6}$$

where κ_j are the Lagrange multipliers for the agents budget constraint so that κ_j is the agent j marginal utility of income:

$$\kappa_j = \frac{\partial}{\partial m_j} u_j \left(\hat{c}_{1j} \left(p, w_{1j}, \cdots, w_{mj} \right), \cdots, \hat{c}_{mj} \left(p, w_{1j}, \cdots, w_{mj} \right) \right), \quad m_j \equiv \sum_{i=1}^{m} p_i w_{ij}.$$

By comparing the competitive equilibrium solution in eq. (2.6) with the Pareto optimality property of the equilibrium in eq. (2.5), we deduce that a competitive equilibrium $(\bar{c}, p)$ can be implemented by a social planner acting as in theorem 2.6 and with $\ell_j = 1/\kappa_j$. Then, it also follows that, necessarily, $\psi = p$ by the aggregate resource constraint, $\sum_{j=1}^{n} c^j \leq w$, which intuitively has to hold both in the competitive and the centralized economy. Indeed, we have:

$$w_i = \sum_{j=1}^{n} \hat{f}_{ij} \left(\kappa_j p \right), \quad w_i = \sum_{j=1}^{n} f_{ij} \left(\kappa_j \psi \right), \quad i = 1, \cdots, m, \tag{2.7}$$

where $\hat{f}_{ij}$ and f_{ij} are the values taken by the inverse functions for consumption as implied by the private allocation in eq. (2.6) and the social in eq. (2.5). The first of eqs. (2.7) determines the general equilibrium price vector, p_*, say. The second of eqs. (2.7) is the aggregate constraint faced by the central planner with $\ell_j = 1/\kappa_j$, and clearly, this constraint is satisfied by a Lagrange multiplier ψ_*, say, which exactly matches p_*, namely, $\psi_* = p_*$, in which case $f_{ij} = \hat{f}_{ij}$. □

2.3 The Role of Financial Securities in Markets with Uncertainty

2.3.1 Commodity Markets

The theory of general equilibrium provides a convenient means to define subfields in economics in contexts with frictionless markets. Consider the following definition.

> A commodity is characterized by its physical properties, the date and the venue at which it will be available.
> — Gerard Debreu (1959, chapter 2)

In Debreu's own interpretation of this definition, by freezing time and physical properties, one obtains a theory of international commerce; by freezing venues and physical properties, one obtains a theory of finance. The previous definition does not incorporate the notion of uncertainty, a notion so important to describe the behavior of financial markets. To cope with uncertainty, Debreu (1959, chapter 7) extends the previous definition by highlighting that a commodity should still be described through a list of physical properties but with the structure of dates and venues replaced by an event structure.

The following example illustrates the difference between two contracts underlying the delivery of corn arising under conditions of certainty (case A) and uncertainty (case B).

A *An agent will deliver 5,000 tons of corn of a specified type to another agent, who will accept the delivery at date t and in venue ℓ.*

B *An agent will deliver 5,000 tons of corn of a specified type to another agent, who will accept the delivery in venue ℓ and in the event s_t at time t. If s_t does not occur at time t, no delivery shall take place.*

In both cases, the contract is paid at the time it is agreed. There are instances where we can actually use the model of the previous section to deal with contracts like that in case B. Consider, for example, a two-period economy, and suppose that in the second period, s_n mutually exhaustive and exclusive states of nature may occur. We can then recover the model of the previous section once we replace m (the number of commodities described by physical properties, dates and venues) with m^*, where $m^* = s_n \cdot m$. With m^* replacing m, the competitive equilibrium in this economy is defined as the competitive equilibrium in the economy of the previous section.

The assumption underlying this analogy is that markets exist in which commodities are traded for each state of nature. These "contingent" markets are *complete*: at the "dawn of history," all markets open for all goods in each future state of the world, and all transactions are executed then; in the future, there will only be "settlements" by which counterparties will deliver and accept the quantities in accordance with the signed contracts. Because this economy is formally the same as that without uncertainty, its resource allocation is Pareto optimal. However, the assumption that $s_n \cdot m$ contingent markets exist is strong. Next, we show how financial securities help mitigate this assumption.

2.3.2 Financial Securities and Rational Expectations

The assumption that markets only open at the "dawn of history" is clearly unrealistic. In reality, markets are open at all times. Indeed, Hicks (1939) had already developed a conceptual framework in which markets open in each period—a *temporary equilibrium theory*. In this framework, agents may well have incorrect expectations and could transfer value by trading securities in each period.

Arrow (1953) formalizes the Hicksian idea that markets open all the time in a context with uncertainty. What role do financial securities play in this context? Consider the following interpretation. Rather than signing contracts for delivery of *commodities* that are contingent on the realization of events, agents may agree on contracts generating *payoffs* that are contingent on the realization of events—that is, financial securities. The payoffs delivered by the assets in the various states of the world can then be collected to finance state-contingent consumption plans. In other words, it is now financial assets that are traded since the dawn of history; real markets will, instead, open in future states of the world where the asset payoffs will help finance a state-contingent consumption plan. This economy is formally the same as Debreu's, but the model emphasizes the presence of financial assets. Equally important, the model leads to a new and nuanced role of the equilibrium concept, the foundation to subsequent work on *rational expectations equilibrium*, later formalized by Radner (1968): at the dawn of history, the agents perfectly anticipate the equilibrium price of each good in each state of the world.

Let us illustrate. Consider a two-period economy. An asset $\mathcal{A}_i$ is a contract that promises to pay a payoff $v_i(s)$ in some state $s \in \mathcal{S}$ in the second period, where $\mathcal{S}$ denotes the set of all possible future events. We assume there exist M assets and that markets reopen for each commodity in each state of nature in the second period. Assets and commodities are linked as follows. At time zero, I purchase θ_i units of the asset $\mathcal{A}_i$. If state of nature s occurs in the second period, I utilize the payoff $v_i(s)$ and finance net transactions on the commodity markets reopening in the second period, namely,

$$p(s) \cdot e(s) = \sum_{i=1}^{M} \theta_i v_i(s), \quad \forall s \in \mathcal{S}, \tag{2.8}$$

where $p(s)$ and $e(s)$ denote the commodity price and excess demand vectors, which are both contingent on the realization of state s. In this context, "rational expectations" means that at time zero, I know what the price vector will be in state s, that is, I know the vector function $p(s)$.

Thus, financial assets transfer value across states of nature. Securities markets make this economy subject to uncertainty similar to that of the previous section, with one added feature: there are no such complicated markets that open at time zero for each state of nature in the future. There are, simply, commodity and asset markets in the first period and commodity markets that reopen in the second period. This economy, while more realistic than in the previous section, is perfectly isomorphic to the previous economy, provided eq. (2.8) holds true. However, in general eq. (2.8) does not hold. It would hold, provided that the number of assets is equal to the number of events in $\mathcal{S}$, that is, $M = s_n$. We say security markets are *complete* in this case.

What is the "fair value" of these securities? Section 2.5 provides basic foundations on security evaluation, which relies on absence of arbitrage and the way arbitrage links to economies with maximizing agents. Critical in this theoretical construction is the definition of a class of securities known as Arrow-Debreu securities. The remainder of this section develops some introductory examples regarding the evaluation of some basic gambles and some informal notions of arbitrage or fair value.

2.3.3 Laws of Large Numbers, Risk Aversion, and the Slicing of Risks

Securities promise random payoffs and trade at prices determined by a number of factors, such as supply and demand (e.g., bargaining power or risk aversion), market microstructure, and of course, absence of arbitrage. This section provides three examples of evaluation problems. The first discusses some limitations of the law of large numbers as a guidance for evaluating assets' payoff. The second focuses on agents' risk aversion. The third example explores how certain risks may be priced without any reference to risk aversion: in this example, we may slice a payoff into simpler constituents and rely on absence of arbitrage to determine restrictions on the value of some of these constituents.

2.3.3.1 Short-run bets and asymptotic arbitrage

A coin game delivers a payoff equal to the fraction of time a repeatedly tossed coin delivers heads (or tails). What is the fair value of this game? If we could only toss the coin many times, then, by the law of large numbers, the value of this gamble would approach 50% of a stake as the number of draws grows to avoid an "asymptotic arbitrage": that is, the probability to gain from betting for tails if the price for the tails is less than 50% of the stake over such a large number of trials—or selling tails, whenever this price is higher than 50%. Note that by allowing for the possibility to "sell tails," we are meaning that this gamble is, in fact, a tradable asset.

Yet assume (and realistically) that the number of trials is small, in which case the value of this gamble might well deviate from 50% of a stake, reflecting, for instance, preferences, bargaining power, or in general, supply and demand. The previous asymptotic arbitrage could not take place because tossing a coin only once, say, is far from guaranteeing an almost sure 50% frequency of tails outcomes. Thus, the fair value of this gamble does not necessarily reflect the probability of tails. The value of an unreplicable gamble may well reflect preferences and other factors—in short, supply and demand. In some cases, such a gamble may be evaluated by means of another probability of tails ("adjusted for risk"). In fact, in the next section, we show that factors such as bettors' preferences are not only necessary to value a gamble. These preferences would sometimes be needed for us to make conclusions about the logical consistency of the very same gamble.

2.3.3.2 The St. Petersburg paradox

Consider the following gamble, which leads to the famous *St. Petersburg paradox*. The gamble consists in tossing a coin a number of times and ends as soon as the outcome is a tail (say). The payoff doubles each time, that is, it is equal to $\$2^n$ if the gamble stops at n. Note that the probability of receiving $\$2^n$ at the nth trial is the probability that $n-1$ heads occur over the first $n-1$ trials and one tail in one trial, which (given the independence of the trials) is 2^{-n} in total. Therefore, the "fair value" of this gamble is

$$\sum_{n=1}^{\infty} (2^n) \times 2^{-n} = \infty.$$

However, this gamble is not riskless: the payoff, although positive, is not certain. Because the payoff is positive, we have to pay something to enter into this gamble, but no individuals should be willing to pay a large amount of money for it. Why? A moment's reflection suggests the payoff profile is quite unattractive. Note, for example, that there are almost 95% chances to obtain less than \$16. Bernoulli (1738) proposes to solve this puzzle by replacing outcomes with concave utilities of outcomes: concave utilities would dampen the occurrence of very positive returns. For example, a decision maker with log utility would have an expected utility equal to

$$\sum_{n=1}^{\infty} (\ln 2^n) \times 2^{-n} = \ln 4$$

and would not be willing to pay more than the certainty equivalent of the gamble, that is \$4. Thus, gambles may be quite subtle. Not only does their value depend on preferences. Risk-aversion may even be critical in ensuring their well-posedness.

2.3.3.3 *World Cup pricing, and arbitrage pricing*

The risks underlying the gambles of the previous examples cannot be evaluated in a preference-free fashion. As for the coin game, we would need a large number of draws to conclude its fair value is 50% of a stake. As for the coin game leading to the St. Petersburg paradox, we would actually need risk aversion to keep the value of the gamble finite. We now develop a third example where, again, the value of the gamble cannot be determined without making reference to supply and demand, although then we could price some of the elementary risks that make up this gamble in a preference-free fashion for the very simple reason that these risks are actually traded.

Consider, then, the odds posted by a bookmaker (displayed in table 2.1) against four hypothetical teams competing for the World Cup. In bookmaking language, odds set at a-b against a certain event mean that on a \$$b$ stake, the bettor receives \$$a$ if the given event occurs and loses their stake of \$$b$ otherwise. Therefore, odds of 5-1 against team B imply that the bookmaker stands ready to pay \$500 for a \$100 stake, should B win the World Cup. Let p be the probability of the event that a given team wins, under which the bettor's expected gain is zero, $p : a \times p + (-b) \times (1-p) = 0$, such that $\frac{a}{b}$ equals the odds ratio, $\frac{1-p}{p}$, with b being fixed to one in this example. Also shown in table 2.1 are these "implied break-even probabilities," calculated as $p_j = \frac{b_j}{b_j + a_j}$, where a_j-b_j are the odds against team j and p_j are the corresponding break-even probability, with $b_j \equiv 1$.

As in the coin game of section 2.3.3.1, the breakeven probabilities do not necessarily lead to the fair value of the gamble. Indeed, bookmakers typically make profits through

Table 2.1
Odds against teams in a World Cup.

Team	Odds against	Implied prob.
A	2-1	33.33%
B	5-1	16.67%
C	6-1	14.28%
D	9-1	10.00%

what is known as the "overround," the circumstance that quoted probabilities exceed 100%. But overrounds are obviously not arbitrage opportunities because a World Cup is an unique event, with its own weather conditions, teams, and many other factors: the chance of any team winning the competition has only a weak linkage to the objective (and, let's face it, hard-to-estimate) probability of winning over an hypothetically large number of matches. Once again, the price and then the quoted odds depend on both the bettors' risk appetite and the bookmakers' bargaining power.

Surprisingly though, while the single odds depend on supply and demand, we can price gambles for other events covered by bookmakers, independent of supply and demand. For example, what are the odds against either team A or team B winning the World Cup? It is a "derivative gamble," because its value depends on that of the constituent events. For convenience, let us convert the odds into "tickets," defined as follows. The cost of a ticket for a payoff equal to \$1 for a *a-b* odds is equal to $c: \$ (1-c) \times p + \$ (-c) \times (1-p) = 0$; that is, $c = \$\frac{b}{a+b}$: on paying c for the ticket, we are entitled to \$1 if the event occurs and \$0 otherwise. For example, the unit ticket for team A winning is worth \$0.33333 and for team B is \$0.16667. It easy to see then that the unit ticket value for the composite event needs to be \$0.33333 + \$0.16667 = \$0.5. If it was lower—say, \$0.4—we could sell the two bets for both A and B for \$0.5 and use the \$0.4 to ensure that we could honor the payoff that A or B will win. If the unit ticket value for the composite event was instead \$0.6, we could sell the composite bet and then bet for A and B separately to honor the payoff relating to the composite event.

Pricing derivatives in a preference-free format as in this example relies on the fact that markets are *complete*, in that we could replicate the composite risk by betting on each single team. The next sections extend this notion to various situation of interest that include financial security transactions. We begin with introducing the simplest securities, those that only pay off in specific states of nature, similar to the single bets of the World Cup of this section.

2.3.4 Arrow-Debreu Securities

We now discuss an introductory evaluation model that relies on the notion of quite simple securities: those that pay off one unit of numéraire in state s, if state s prevails, and zero otherwise. We refer these assets to as *Arrow-Debreu* securities in honor of Kenneth Arrow and Gérard Debreu. Naturally, Arrow-Debreu securities do not exist in reality for the very simple reason that it is impossible to determine states at such a pure level. States are simply part of a model's assumptions.

While Arrow-Debreu securities are model dependent, they can be used to price assets. This section develops a very intuitive link between asset prices and Arrow-Debreu security prices and explores how asset prices can then be recast as expectations of expected payoffs under a certain probability known as "risk neutral" probability. We conclude with a derivation of the price of these securities based on a simple equilibrium model.

2.3.4.1 *Pricing*

Consider a two-period economy where at time $t = 1$, three mutually exclusive states of the world may occur. We consider three Arrow-Debreu securities: the ith, AD_i, pays off \$1 in state i, and zero otherwise, as in figure 2.2.

		$t=1$	AD_1	AD_2	AD_3
	↗	state 1	$\$1$	0	0
$t=0$	→	state 2	0	$\$1$	0
	↘	state 3	0	0	$\$1$

Figure 2.2
Three Arrow-Debreu securities in a two-period economy.

		$t=1$	$\mathcal{A}_0$	$\mathcal{A}_1$	$\mathcal{A}_2$	$\mathcal{A}_3$
	↗	state 1	$\$D_1$	$\$D_1$	0	0
$t=0$	→	state 2	$\$D_2$	0	$\$D_2$	0
	↘	state 3	$\$D_3$	0	0	$\$D_3$

Figure 2.3
Payoffs of three assets that are rescaled versions of the three Arrow-Debreu securities in Figure 2.2.

Let ϕ_j be the price of the asset AD_j, and consider a portfolio that has one unit of each of the three assets. This portfolio yields one, for sure, at time $t=1$. Therefore, its price must be that of a pure discount bond or

$$\frac{1}{1+r}=\sum_{j=1}^{3}\phi_j, \tag{2.9}$$

where r denotes the riskless interest rate. More generally, consider an asset $\mathcal{A}_0$, which pays off D_i in state i, as in figure 2.3. Naturally, the values of D_i are known at zero—although of course we do not know which D_i will be drawn at time $t=1$. Also shown in this figure are the payoffs of three assets, $\mathcal{A}_i$, $i=1,2,3$, that are rescaled versions of Arrow-Debreu securities. Let us explain.

By definition, paying ϕ_1 yields \$1 if state 1 occurs and zero otherwise. Therefore, paying $\phi_1 \times D_1$ yields $1 \times D_1$ if state 1 occurs and zero otherwise. We can, then, slice the risks related to asset $\mathcal{A}_0$ into three by considering the three elementary assets, $\mathcal{A}_1$, $\mathcal{A}_2$, and $\mathcal{A}_3$. Each of these assets costs $\phi_j D_j$ at $t=0$. Moreover, a portfolio that has one unit of each of these three assets needs to have the same value of $\mathcal{A}_0$, say S,

$$S=\sum_{j=1}^{3}\phi_j D_j. \tag{2.10}$$

We can say more about S. Consider eq. (2.9), which we rewrite as $\sum_{j=1}^{3} Q_j=1$, where $Q_j=(1+r)\,\phi_j$. Thus, Q_j is a probability distribution. Replacing Q_j into eq. (2.10) reveals an important property of Q_j,

$$S = \frac{1}{1+r} \sum_{j=1}^{3} Q_j D_j = \frac{1}{1+r} E^Q(\tilde{D}).$$

The price of $\mathcal{A}_0$ can be expressed as the expectation of the future payoff, $\tilde{D}$, discounted with the riskless interest rate. It is as if we evaluated assets through actuarial methods but based on a probability different than the physical one. We shall refer to Q_j as risk neutral probability for this reason, and we shall discuss the properties of this benchmark probability in detail in the next sections.

To sum up, Arrow-Debreu securities would allow us to price any asset, relying on eq. (2.10). In section 2.5, we shall actually show that there are no arbitrage opportunities if and only if there exists a vector $\phi : S = \phi^\top V$, where S is a m-dimensional vector of security prices, V is a $m \times d$ matrix containing the securities payoffs, and d is the number of states. In this general context, ϕ carries the natural interpretation of the vector containing Arrow-Debreu security prices. Note also that the security we are evaluating in this specific example relies on the assumption that an appropriate set of Arrow-Debreu securities are available for trading. Alternatively, we may assume that only a selected number of Arrow-Debreu securities are available for trading, in which case markets become "incomplete," in a sense to be made precise in later sections. In this case, we shall explain, it is unlikely the given security could be given an unique price while only based on no-arbitrage restrictions.

Note, finally, an interesting property of Arrow-Debreu securities. Consider an economy with a finite number of states (not necessarily three), and define the random return of the ith security as $\tilde{R}_i = \frac{\tilde{x}_i}{\phi_i}$, where $\tilde{x}_i = 1$ in state i and zero otherwise. Given the objective probability distribution of the states, P_j, we have that each pair of asset returns is negatively correlated,

$$E(\tilde{R}_i) = \frac{P_i}{\phi_i}, \quad var(\tilde{R}_i) = \frac{P_i(1-P_i)}{\phi_i^2}, \quad corr(\tilde{R}_i, \tilde{R}_j) = -\sqrt{\frac{P_i P_j}{(1-P_i)(1-P_j)}}.$$

Arrow-Debreu securities pay off in mutually exclusive states of the world. It it, thus, natural that their returns are negatively correlated. Note that, as we decrease the number of states, we may expect that the correlation increases in absolute value, with an extreme case arising with only two states when $P_i = 1 - P_j$ and then $corr(\tilde{R}_i, \tilde{R}_j) = -1$. This property is natural: as we increase the number of states, there is a progressively higher number of states where any two Arrow-Debreu securities do not pay off, which may lead the returns correlations to increase. This correlation is still negative, however.

2.3.4.2 *Tying down Arrow-Debreu securities to consumption: an example*

Consider the previous two-period economy, where now there is a single agent, who maximizes

$$\max_{c_0, c_1} \left[u(c_0) + \beta E(u(c_1))\right], \quad \text{s.t. (i) } c_0 + \theta S = \omega_0 \text{ and } \text{(ii) } c_1 = \tilde{\omega}_1 + \theta\tilde{D},$$

where c_j is consumption at time $t = j$, ω_0 is endowment at time $t = 0$, $\tilde{\omega}_1$ is the random endowment at time 1, u is an increasing and concave utility function satisfying all regularity conditions that we need, E is the expectation taken under the physical probability, and remaining notation is as before. We then have two constraints. The first (i), says that endowment is split into time-0 consumption and investment, and the second (ii) says that time-1 consumption is financed by $\tilde{\omega}_1$ and the payoff provided by the asset.

Replacing the two constraints into the utility function, first-order conditions are obtained by differentiating the resulting objective function with respect to θ and lead to

$$S = \frac{\beta E(u'(\tilde{\omega}_1 + \theta \tilde{D})\tilde{D})}{u'(\omega_0 - \theta S)} = \frac{\beta E(u'(\tilde{\omega}_1)\tilde{D})}{u'(\omega_0)} = \sum_{j=1}^{3} \frac{\beta u'(\omega_{1,j})}{u'(\omega_0)} D_j P_j, \tag{2.11}$$

where $\omega_{1,j}$ is the endowment in state j and P_j is the probability of state j. The second equality follows by an equilibrium condition, namely, that the asset is in zero net supply, such that our single agent has to consume their endowment in each state.

Comparing eq. (2.10) and (2.11) allows us to identify Arrow-Debreu security prices as follows:

$$\phi_j = \frac{\beta u'(\omega_{1,j})}{u'(\omega_0)} P_j .$$

By concavity of the utility function, ϕ_j is high when $\omega_{1,j}$ is low. In other words, Arrow-Debreu prices for the "bad states" of nature are high: risk neutral probabilities assign high values to bad states. We shall come back to the interpretation of this result many times in this and subsequent chapters.

2.4 Arbitrage and Replication: Examples

We illustrate how absence of arbitrage leads asset prices to satisfy some restrictions. At this juncture, we cannot avoid explaining that the concept of arbitrage was first used in economics in a very famous contribution by Modigliani and Miller (1958). Modigliani and Miller showed that the value of a firm is independent of its capital structure. Chapter 5 discusses this important result in detail and develops explanations for the value of the firm for which this irrelevance result ceases to hold. This section aims to develop introductory examples to illustrate how absence of arbitrage works.

2.4.1 Rain and Sunshine

We consider a simple introductory example and discuss how absence of arbitrage leads to a unique price of "redundant securities." Consider an economy with complete markets, in which all uncertainty is regarding the event "tomorrow it will rain." Mr. Law is a decision maker who would like to implement the following state-contingent plan. If tomorrow will be sunny, he will need $c_s > 0$ units of numéraire to purchase sunglasses; if tomorrow will be rainy, he will need $c_r > 0$ to purchase an umbrella. Mr. Law has access to a financial market where m assets are traded. He builds up a portfolio θ aimed at delivering the payments he will need tomorrow:

$$\begin{cases} \sum_{i=1}^{m} \theta_i S_i (1 + x_i(r)) = c_r \\ \sum_{i=1}^{m} \theta_i S_i (1 + x_i(s)) = c_s \end{cases} \tag{2.12}$$

where S_i is the price of the ith asset, θ_i is the number of assets to put in the portfolio, and $x_i\,(r)$ and $x_i\,(s)$ are the net returns of asset i in the two states of nature, which are part of the information set available to Mr. Law. Finally, and remarkably, we are not making any assumptions regarding Mr. Law's preferences. We only know that he needs c_i in state i.

Eqs. (2.12) form a system of two equations with m unknowns $(\theta_1, \cdots, \theta_m)$. If $m < 2$, no perfect hedging strategies are available to Mr. Law—that is, eqs. (2.12) cannot be solved to obtain the desired pair $(c_i)_{i=r,s}$. We say markets are incomplete in this case. More generally, consider an economy with s_n states of nature, and define markets to be complete if and only if Mr. Law has access to s_n assets, which allow him to achieve any desired consumption plan, independent of his preferences. Preferences would only play a role when it comes to pick up a particular consumption plan among all possible.

Let us, then, define the following "payoff matrix":

$$V = \begin{bmatrix} S_1(1+x_1\,(s_1)) & & S_m(1+x_m\,(s_1)) \\ & \ddots & \\ S_1(1+x_1\,(s_n)) & & S_m(1+x_m\,(s_n)) \end{bmatrix},$$

where $x_i\,(s_j)$ is the return performed by the ith asset in state s_j. To implement any state contingent consumption plan $c \in \mathbb{R}^{s_n}$, Mr. Law needs to solve the following system,

$$c = V \cdot \theta,$$

where $\theta \in \mathbb{R}^m$, the portfolio. If $\operatorname{rank}(V) = s_n = m$, the previous system has a unique solution, given by $\hat{\theta} = V^{-1}c$. Consider, for example, the previous case where $s_n = 2$, and take $m = 2$ because any additional assets would be redundant in this case. Then,

$$\begin{cases} \hat{\theta}_1 = \dfrac{(1+x_2\,(r))c_s - (1+x_2\,(s))c_r}{S_1\,[(1+x_1\,(s))(1+x_2\,(r)) - (1+x_1\,(r))(1+x_2\,(s))]} \\ \hat{\theta}_2 = \dfrac{(1+x_1\,(s))c_r - (1+x_1\,(r))c_s}{S_2\,[(1+x_1\,(s))(1+x_2\,(r)) - (1+x_1\,(r))(1+x_2\,(s))]} \end{cases}.$$

Finally, assume that the second asset is safe or that it yields the same return in the two states of nature: $x_2\,(r) = x_2\,(s) \equiv r$. Let $x_s = x_1\,(s)$ and $x_r = x_1\,(r)$. Then, the pair $(\hat{\theta}_1, \hat{\theta}_2)$ can be rewritten as

$$\hat{\theta}_1 = \frac{c_s - c_r}{S_1\,(x_s - x_r)}, \quad \hat{\theta}_2 = \frac{(1+x_s)\,c_r - (1+x_r)\,c_s}{S_2\,(1+r)\,(x_s - x_r)}.$$

The issue we are dealing with relates to *replication* of random variables. Our random variable is a state contingent consumption plan $(c_i)_{i=r,s}$, where c_r and c_p are known, which we want to replicate for hedging purposes: tomorrow, Mr. Law will need either a pair of sunglasses or an umbrella. In this example, any two-state variable can be generated by investing into two assets with independent payoffs. The next step is to derive implications for the price of a security that would deliver exactly the same random variable $(c_i)_{i=r,s}$. Let H be the current price of such a security, say, $\mathcal{C}$. We claim that, in the absence of arbitrage,

$$H = w \equiv \hat{\theta}_1 S_1 + \hat{\theta}_2 S_2. \tag{2.13}$$

Indeed, if $w < H$, we can buy $\hat{\theta}$ and sell at the same time the third security C. The result is a sure profit equal to $H - w$, for $\hat{\theta}$ generates c_r if tomorrow it will rain and c_s if tomorrow it will not rain. In both cases, the portfolio $\hat{\theta}$ generates the payments we need to honor the sale of C. Likewise, we may show that the inequality $w > H$ would also lead to an arbitrage. Hence, eq. (2.13) must hold true.

We are left with the calculation of the RHS of eq. (2.13). We have

$$H = \frac{1}{1+r}\left[Qc_s + (1-Q)c_r\right], \quad Q = \frac{x_r - r}{x_s - x_r}. \tag{2.14}$$

Eq. (2.14) is an evaluation formula for C. It says that the price, H, can be expressed as the present value of the expected payoffs promised by C under a new probability, Q, termed *risk neutral probability*. Note that we are able to price C without any reference to agents' preferences. The reasons for this *preference-free* property is that we can replicate the payoffs of C through $\hat{\theta}$. Naturally, eq. (2.14) does not obviously require that any agent is using this portfolio. For example, some agents may be so poor that they could not even implement $\hat{\theta}$. Rather, the point is that $\hat{\theta}$ could be used to exploit an arbitrage opportunity arising as soon as eq. (2.13) does not hold. In this simple economy, any penniless agent could implement the arbitrage described above.

The next step is to extend eq. (2.14) to a dynamic setting. Suppose an additional day is available for trading, with the same description as before: the day after tomorrow, the payoffs of C are c_{ss} if it will be sunny, provided the previous day was sunny; c_{rs} if it will be sunny, provided the previous day was rainy, and so on. By the same arguments leading to eq. (2.14), we have that

$$H = \frac{1}{(1+r)^2}\left[Q^2 c_{ss} + Q(1-Q)\, c_{sr} + (1-Q)\, Qc_{rs} + Q^2 c_{rr}\right].$$

Finally, by extending the same reasoning to T trading days,

$$H = \frac{1}{(1+r)^T} E^Q\left(c_T\right), \tag{2.15}$$

where E^Q denotes the expectation taken under the risk neutral probability Q.

The key assumption underlying eq. (2.15) is that markets are complete at each trading day. It is true that, at the beginning of the trading period, Mr. Law faces 2^T mutually exclusive states of nature for T. If he did not have access to markets in each period, he would need 2^T securities to replicate the payoff of C. Yet in this example, only two assets *and* T trading periods are needed for replicating and pricing C. To emphasize this property, we say that assets and transaction dates make the markets *dynamically complete*. Dynamically complete markets allow the implementation of trading strategies that replicate the payoffs of C period by period. As a result, C is priced without any assumptions on the agents' preferences. The next section clarifies these issues further.

2.4.2 Replication and Pricing: The Role of Complete Markets

What are the origins of the preference-free formula in eq. (2.14)? Consider a general two-period model where the assets deliver a payoff matrix, V, and denote as usual with ϕ the vector of Arrow-Debreu prices, ϕ. We know that the initial price vector is, $S=\phi^\top V$. In a setting with complete markets, we can extract a unique vector of state prices from the previous relation,

$$\hat{\phi}^\top = SV^{-1}. \tag{2.16}$$

Next, we want to replicate any other security (e.g., a derivative) with final payoff c at the second period, through a portfolio comprising the initial assets. Denote the initial value of this portfolio with w and the value in the second period with w',

$$w \equiv S\theta, \quad w' \equiv V\theta. \tag{2.17}$$

We use this portfolio to replicate the derivative payoff, that is,

$$c = w' = V\theta \Longrightarrow \hat{\theta} = V^{-1}c.$$

We plug $\hat{\theta} = V^{-1}c$ into w of the first of eqs. (2.17) and obtain the initial value of the replicating portfolio,

$$\hat{w} \equiv S\hat{\theta} = SV^{-1}c = \hat{\phi}^\top c,$$

where the last equality follows by eq. (2.16). As usual, two portfolios that yield the same thing must be worth the same in the presence of frictionless markets. Therefore, the price of the derivative, H, is

$$H = \hat{w} = \hat{\phi}^\top c = \frac{1}{1+r} E^Q(c).$$

Done. We could price the given security in a preference-free fashion because markets are complete: the asset payoff can be replicated through securities that are actually traded. These traded securities "convey" information on Arrow-Debreu securities, ϕ, to the derivative, so to speak. Chapters 11–13 explain how this "extract-and-plug-in procedure" is used to evaluate complex derivative instruments in the market practice.

In the next sections, we study Arrow-Debreu securities within a more general perspective, relying on a general equilibrium economy without production and possibly with incomplete markets.

2.5 No-Arbitrage: Theory

This section formalizes the notion of absence of arbitrage and links this notion to the competitive equilibrium of section 2.2. We only consider markets with a single commodity.

2.5.1 Lands of Cockaigne

We consider a two-period economy. An agent may consume in both periods and also have the opportunity to invest in m assets. Let $v_i(\omega_s)$ be the payoff of asset i in state ω_s ($i = 1, \cdots, m$ and $s = 1, \cdots, d$). Consider the payoff matrix

$$V \equiv \begin{bmatrix} v_1(\omega_1) & & v_m(\omega_1) \\ & \ddots & \\ v_1(\omega_d) & & v_m(\omega_d) \end{bmatrix},$$

where we assume that $\text{rank}(V) = m \leq d$. Our agent has endowments for the second period in some states, which are collected in a vector $w^1 = [w_1, \cdots, w_d]^\top$. The vector of second period consumption is denoted, similarly, with c^1. The agent's budget constraints in the first and second period are, resp.,

$$c_0 - w_0 = -S\theta \quad \text{and} \quad c^1 - w^1 = V\theta. \tag{2.18}$$

An arbitrage opportunity is the possibility to create a portfolio that generates nonnegative payoffs, $V\theta > 0$, at no cost, $S\theta = 0$. By "nonnegative payoffs," we mean that, while all elements of the vector $V\theta$ are positive,[1] at least one of them is strictly positive. An arbitrage also arises if we can create a portfolio that is negatively valued, $S\theta < 0$, and that delivers no payoffs in each state, $V\theta = 0_d$. It is intuitive that an arbitrage cannot exist in a competitive equilibrium. Theorem 2.10 below shows indeed that the agents' programs would not be well defined in this case, implying arbitrarily large consumption.

To formalize the notion of arbitrage, we introduce the $(d+1) \times m$ matrix

$$W = \begin{bmatrix} -S \\ V \end{bmatrix},$$

and consider the following definition.

Definition 2.8. *An arbitrage opportunity is a strategy θ such that $W\theta > 0$.*

We elaborate on this notion and the matrix W. Define the vector subspace of $\mathbb{R}^{d+1}$,

$$\langle W \rangle = \left\{ z \in \mathbb{R}^{d+1} : z = W\theta, \ \theta \in \mathbb{R}^m \right\},$$

and the null space of $\langle W \rangle$,

$$\langle W \rangle^\perp = \left\{ x \in \mathbb{R}^{d+1} : xW = 0_m \right\}.$$

The vector subspace $\langle W \rangle$ is interpreted as the excess demand space in all the states of nature (including the present time), which is generated by the *income transfers across states* induced by θ. Naturally, $\langle W \rangle^\perp$ and $\langle W \rangle$ are orthogonal as $\langle W \rangle^\perp = \{x \in \mathbb{R}^{d+1} : xz = 0, z \in \langle W \rangle\}$. We shall return to the interpretation of $\langle W \rangle^\perp$ below (see eq. (2.21)). Thus, and in terms of W, requiring absence of arbitrage is equivalent to the following condition:

$$\langle W \rangle \bigcap \mathbb{R}_+^{d+1} = \{0\}. \tag{2.19}$$

That is, there are no portfolios generating income transfers that are (i) nonnegative and (ii) strictly positive in at least one state as in definition 2.8. Geometrically, $\langle W \rangle$ and the positive orthant, $\mathbb{R}_+^{d+1}$, cannot intersect. This condition enables one to derive powerful implications on asset prices as explained in the section below.

1. Given a vector $x \in \mathbb{R}^m$, $x > 0$ means that at least one component of x is strictly positive while the other components of x are nonnegative.

2.5.2 Enforced Asset Prices

The no-arbitrage condition in (2.19) implies that asset prices satisfy the following famous joint restriction.

Theorem 2.9. *There are no arbitrage opportunities if and only if there exists a strictly positive vector* $\phi : S = \phi^\top V$. *If* $m = d$, ϕ *is unique, and if* $m < d$, $\dim \left(\phi \in \mathbb{R}^d_{++} : S = \phi^\top V \right) = d - m$.

Theorem 2.9, proven in appendix 2.A, provides foundations to the main architecture that underlies asset evaluation in frictionless markets. Premultiply the second period budget constraint in (2.18) by $\phi^\top$, obtaining

$$\phi^\top (c^1 - w^1) = \phi^\top V\theta = S\theta = -(c_0 - w_0),$$

where the second equality follows by theorem 2.9 and the third equality is the first period budget constraint in (2.18). Critically, then, theorem 2.9 shows that, in the absence of arbitrage, each agent faces the following budget constraint,

$$0 = c_0 - w_0 + \phi^\top \left(c^1 - w^1 \right) = c_0 - w_0 + \sum_{s=1}^{d} \phi_s (c_s - w_s), \text{ with } \left(c^1 - w^1 \right) \in \langle V \rangle, \tag{2.20}$$

where $\langle V \rangle$ is the subspace generated by the payoffs induced by the portfolio choices,

$$\langle V \rangle = \left\{ e \in \mathbb{R}^d : e = V\theta, \ \theta \in \mathbb{R}^m \right\}.$$

Eq. (2.20) suggests interpreting ϕ as the vector of commodities prices in the various states of nature in the spirit of the Debreu (1959, chapter 7) quote and the proposals given in section 2.3.1. Note that first-period consumption is acting as the numéraire. Further, theorem 2.9 tells us that, because $S = \phi^\top V$, the vector ϕ is then the vector of *Arrow-Debreu state prices*. This conclusion generalizes the heuristic examples of section 2.4. Finally, we interpret the subspace $\langle W \rangle^\perp$ as follows. Let $\phi_1 \equiv [1 \ \phi]^\top$. Then, by eq. (2.20),

$$\phi_1^\top \in \langle W \rangle^\perp. \tag{2.21}$$

That is, the subspace $\langle W \rangle^\perp$ contains the vector of Arrow-Debreu state prices (in addition to the normalized price of the numéraire).

Note that our agent's budget constraint (2.20) is not precisely the constraint arising within the static general equilibrium model of section 2.2. It would only be that constraint if $m = d$, in which case $\langle V \rangle = \mathbb{R}^d$. Markets would, then, be complete. Theorem 2.9 then tells us that there exists a unique ϕ when markets are complete. When markets are incomplete, $m < d$, our agent has access to a "smaller" subspace of excess demands in the second period, $\langle V \rangle \subseteq \mathbb{R}^d$. Consider the following examples depicted in figure 2.4.

First, take $d = 2$ and $m = 1$, such that $\langle V \rangle = \left\{ e \in \mathbb{R}^2 : e = V\theta, \ \theta \in \mathbb{R} \right\}$, with $V = V_1$, where $V_1 = \binom{v_1}{v_2}$ say, and $\dim \langle V \rangle = 1$. The left panel of figure 2.4 depicts an example of $\langle V \rangle$: consumptions possibilities reduce to any pair on the straight line. The right panel depicts the case resulting when a new market opens for a second financial security that promises payoffs equal to $V_2 = \binom{v_3}{v_4}$. Then, $m = 2$, $V = (V_1 \ V_2)$, and $\langle V \rangle = \{ e \in \mathbb{R}^2 : e = \binom{\theta_1 v_1 + \theta_2 v_3}{\theta_1 v_2 + \theta_2 v_4}$,

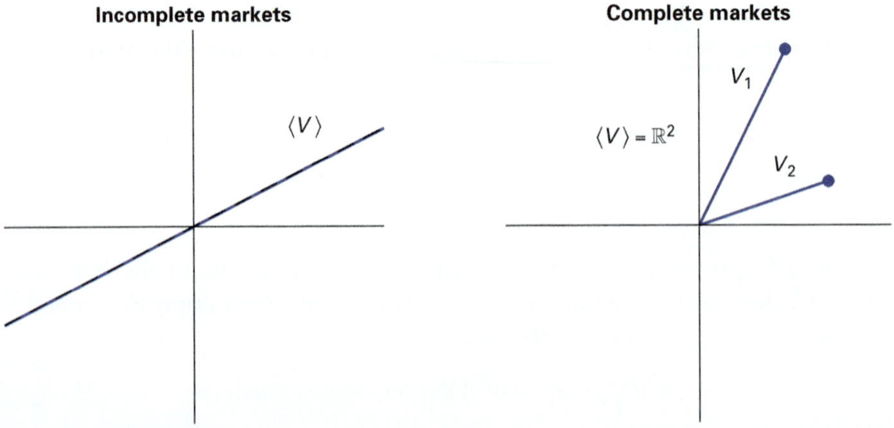

Figure 2.4
This picture depicts examples of the space of excess demands in a two-state economy in incomplete ($m=1$ security; left panel) and complete ($m=2$ securities; right) market cases.

$\theta \in \mathbb{R}^2\}$, i.e., $\langle V\rangle = \mathbb{R}^2$. Now, one may achieve to any desired excess demand in $\mathbb{R}^2$, just as in the economy of section 2.2.

2.6 Equivalent Martingales and Equilibrium

This section discusses how absence of arbitrage connects to the "risk neutral probability" and the concept of rational expectations in general equilibrium. It also explores a few basic properties of this equilibrium in the context of complete and incomplete markets.

2.6.1 Equilibrium with Financial Markets: Definition

We begin with a basic property regarding "viability" of the model that we are dealing with in this chapter. Let c_s^1 denote second period consumption in state s, and consider the following program

$$\left(\hat{c}_{0j}, \hat{c}_j^1\right) \in \arg\max_{(c_0, c^1)} \left(u_j(c_0) + \beta E(v_j(c^1))\right), \quad \text{subject to (2.20).} \qquad \text{[2.P3]}$$

We assume that the utility functions u_j and v_j satisfy assumption 2.1. This formulation of the agent's preferences ("additive") is made to simplify the presentation. Now we have the following theorem.

Theorem 2.10. *The program [2.P3] has a solution if and only if there are no arbitrage opportunities.*

Proof. Suppose, on the contrary, that the program [2.P3] has a solution but that there exists a $\theta : W\theta > 0$. With straightforward notation, the program constraint is $\hat{c} = w + W\hat{\theta}$. Then we can define a portfolio $\hat{\theta} + \theta$, such that $c = w + W(\hat{\theta} + \theta) = \hat{c} + W\theta > \hat{c}$, which contradicts optimality. For the converse, note that absence of arbitrage implies that there exists a strictly positive $\phi : S = \phi^\top V$, implying the budget constraint in (2.20) for a given ϕ. This constraint is clearly a closed subset of the compact budget constraint B_j in [2.P1] (in fact, it is B_j restricted to $\langle V \rangle$). Therefore, it is a compact set, and hence, the program [2.P3] has a solution as a continuous function attains its maximum on a compact set. □

From now on, we assume that financial assets are in zero net supply.

Definition 2.11. *An equilibrium is given by allocations and prices* $\{(\hat{c}_{0j})_{j=1}^n, ((\hat{c}_{sj})_{j=1}^n, \hat{\phi}_i)_{s=1}^d\}$, *where consumption allocations are solutions to program [2.P3] and satisfy*

$$0=\sum_{j=1}^{n}\left(\hat{c}_{0j}-w_{0j}\right), \quad 0=\sum_{j=1}^{n}\left(\hat{c}_{sj}-w_{sj}\right) \quad (s=1,\cdots,d), \quad 0=\sum_{j=1}^{n}\theta_{ij} \quad (i=1,\cdots,d).$$

In addition to the conditions in assumption 2.1, we also require that $\lim_{x\to 0} u_j'(x)=\infty$ and $\lim_{x\to\infty} u_j'(x)=0$ and that v_j satisfies the same properties. These assumptions help facilitate results on equilibrium existence. An equilibrium can then be solved as follows. First, we express demand functions in terms of the state prices; second, we search for the equilibrium state prices, that is, the state prices that clear the commodity markets. By Walras's Law, clearing in the commodity markets implies clearing in the financial market. Indeed, by aggregating any agent's constraints in the second period,

$$\sum_{j=1}^{n}\left(c_j^1-w_j^1\right)=V\sum_{j=1}^{n}\theta_{ij}.$$

We now discuss the notion of rational expectations that underlies equilibrium in this economy.

2.6.2 Rational Expectations

Asset prices are linear combinations of future payoffs, with weights equal to the state prices (see theorem 2.9). To equilibrium state prices, then, there must be corresponding equilibrium asset prices. Underlying these conclusions is the notion that agents *correctly* anticipate the state prices that arise, in equilibrium, for each state of nature. An equilibrium is, then, a probability distribution: the price is a function of the state, and the equilibrium distribution specifies the likelihood of any price realization in correspondence of each state. Note, then, the following properties. The agents' beliefs are *endogenous*: agents make decisions based on the equilibrium probability distribution of prices, a distribution that is also determined by agents' choices. In equilibrium, the agents' beliefs are entirely consistent with the probability distribution of the equilibrium prices.

Muth (1961, 315) explained that agents who take actions based on these endogenous beliefs have *rational expectations*: their expectations are the same as "the predictions of the relevant economic theory." Lucas (1972) relied on this concept to develop a monetary theory in an economy subject to uncertainty. As anticipated in section 2.3.2, Radner (1968) provided the first contribution on the theory of rational expectations in general equilibrium. In more advanced parts of this book (see, e.g., chapters 5 and 10), rational expectations are part of the assumption underlying models with asymmetric information. Consider the following examples.

Suppose that there are agents who trade an asset with less information than others. These uninformed agents take decisions based on the asset price they observe in equilibrium. The equilibrium price is a function of the state. The state is a noisy signal of the information possessed by the informed agents on the asset payoff. Call the asset payoff d and the noisy signal σ. We assume that the signal is the relevant piece of information that the uninformed investors rely on while making statistical inference on the asset payoff. In this market, "rational expectations" mean that uninformed agents correctly anticipate the functional form of the asset price: they (correctly) conjecture that the asset price is a function of the state of the world, say, σ. Accordingly, the uninformed agents' estimate of the asset payoff is $E\left(d \middle| P(\sigma)\right)$, where $P(\sigma)$ is the rational expectation price. This estimate is based on the equilibrium probability laws regarding the asset price. Based on this inference, the uninformed agents purchase $x_U(P(\sigma))$ (say) units of the asset and, in equilibrium, $Z = \lambda x_I(s) + (1-\lambda) x_U(P(\sigma))$, where Z is the random asset supply, λ is the proportion of informed agents, and $x_I(s)$ is their asset demand, a function of the realization of s (a signal on d). Chapter 10 reviews a famous model formulated by Grossman and Stiglitz (1980) where the rational expectation price is a function $P(\sigma)$ and where σ is a linear function of s and Z.

Crucial in this model is the assumption that Z is random as the uninformed agents cannot reverse engineer the information available to the informed, s. That is, prices are only partially revealing. Such an equilibrium is therefore known as *noisy* rational expectation equilibrium. We now proceed with the simpler models of this chapter, in which information is disseminated symmetrically across agents. Asymmetric information forms the basis of extensive analyses in other junctures of this book.

2.6.3 Pricing Kernels

Theorem 2.9 states that in the absence of arbitrage opportunities,

$$S_i = \phi^\top v_{\cdot,i} = \sum_{s=1}^{d} \phi_s v_{s,i}, \quad i = 1, \cdots, m. \tag{2.22}$$

We assume the first asset is safe, in that $v_{s,1} = 1 \; \forall s$, such that

$$S_1 \equiv \frac{1}{1+r} = \sum_{s=1}^{d} \phi_s. \tag{2.23}$$

Eq. (2.23) validates the economic interpretation of the state prices in eq. (2.20). Because the states of nature are exhaustive and mutually exclusive, ϕ_s is the price to be paid today in order to obtain one unit of numéraire tomorrow and in state s. Eq. (2.23) then confirms that the prices of all these rights sum up to the price of a pure discount bond; that is, the asset yielding one unit of numéraire tomorrow for sure.

We may elaborate on eq. (2.23) and develop another interpretation of the state prices in theorem 2.9. Define

$$Q_s \equiv (1+r)\phi_s. \tag{2.24}$$

By construction, $\sum_{s=1}^{d} Q_s = 1$. Therefore, we can interpret $Q \equiv (Q_s)_{s=1}^{d}$ as a probability distribution. Further, replacing Q in eq. (2.22) leaves

$$S_i = \frac{1}{1+r}\sum_{s=1}^{d} Q_s v_{s,i} = \frac{1}{1+r}E^{Q}\left(v_{\cdot,i}\right), \quad i = 1,\cdots,m. \tag{2.25}$$

Eq. (2.25) confirms eq. (2.14), obtained in the introductory example of section 2.3.4. It says that the price of any asset is the expectation of its future payoffs, taken under the probability Q, discounted at the risk-free interest rate r. For this reason, we usually refer to the probability Q as the *risk neutral* probability. In later chapters (see, e.g., chapter 4), eq. (2.25) is extended to a dynamic context. Intuitively, consider an asset that distributes dividends in every period; let S_t and D_t be the price and dividend paid off at time t, such that the "payoff" it promises for the next period is equal to $S_{t+1} + D_{t+1}$. Then, consistent with eq. (2.25), $S_t = (1+r)^{-1} E_t^{Q}\left(S_{t+1} + D_{t+1}\right)$, where E_t^{Q} denotes the risk neutral expectation given the information at time t, or by rearranging terms,

$$E_t^{Q}\left(\frac{S_{t+1} + D_{t+1} - S_t}{S_t}\right) = r. \tag{2.26}$$

That is, the expected return on the asset under Q equals the safe interest rate, r. In dynamic models, Q is also referred to as the *risk neutral martingale probability*, or *equivalent martingale measure*, for the following reason. Define a money market account as an asset with a value evolving over time as $M_t \equiv (1+r)^t$. Then, eq. (2.26) can be rewritten as $S_t/M_t = E_t^{Q}\left(\left(S_{t+1} + D_{t+1}\right)/M_{t+1}\right)$. That is, if $D_{t+1} = 0$ for some t, then the discounted process S_t/M_t is a martingale under Q.

Next, let us replace Q in (2.24) into the budget constraint in (2.20). The result is that, for $\left(c^1 - w^1\right) \in \langle V \rangle$,

$$\begin{aligned} 0 &= c_0 - w_0 + \sum_{s=1}^{d} \phi_s\left(c_s - w_s\right) \\ &= c_0 - w_0 + \frac{1}{1+r}\sum_{s=1}^{d} Q_s\left(c_s - w_s\right) \\ &= c_0 - w_0 + \frac{1}{1+r}E^{Q}\left(c^1 - w^1\right). \end{aligned} \tag{2.27}$$

For reasons developed below, it is also useful to derive an alternative representation of the budget constraint expressed in terms of the objective probability P, say. Accordingly, we introduce the state-dependent ratio ζ_s that indicates how far Q_s and P_s are:

$$\zeta_s = \frac{Q_s}{P_s}, \quad s = 1,\cdots,d.$$

We assume ζ_s is strictly positive and bounded; mathematically, it is tantamount to saying that Q and P are *equivalent* measures in that they assign the same weight to the null sets. We define the *pricing kernel* $m = (m_s)_{s=1}^{d}$ as

$$m_s \equiv \frac{1}{1+r}\zeta_s = \frac{1}{1+r}\frac{Q_s}{P_s} = \frac{\phi_s}{P_s}. \tag{2.28}$$

"Pricing kernel" is very standard terminology in financial economics. The reason behind this terminology is the following. Note that

$$\begin{aligned}\frac{1}{1+r}E^{Q}(c^{1}-w^{1}) &= \sum_{s=1}^{d}\frac{1}{1+r}Q_{s}(c_{s}-w_{s}) \\ &= \sum_{s=1}^{d}\frac{1}{1+r}\zeta_{s}(c_{s}-w_{s})P_{s} \\ &= E\left(m(c^{1}-w^{1})\right).\end{aligned}$$

Therefore, we can rewrite eq. (2.27) as

$$0=c_{0}-w_{0}+E\left(m(c^{1}-w^{1})\right),\quad (c^{1}-w^{1})\in\langle V\rangle.$$

Similarly, replacing m into eq. (2.25) leaves

$$S_{i}=\frac{1}{1+r}E^{Q}(v_{\cdot,i})=E(mv_{\cdot,i}),\quad i=1,\cdots,m. \tag{2.29}$$

We may refer to m as pricing kernel for two reasons. One, because m enables us to price ("pricing") any ("kernel") asset. The second reason is more technical. Further chapters will generalize this model to dynamic contexts. In these contexts, the asset price satisfies $s(d_{t})=\int K(t,u)\left(s(d_{u})+d_{u}\right)du$, where d_{σ} is the dividend paid in state σ and $K(\cdot,\cdot)$ is a function related to some appropriate pricing kernel (see, e.g., chapter 3). This pricing equation resembles the mathematical structure of a Fredholm equation (see, e.g., Ruston, 1986), where indeed the unknown is the pricing function and $K(\cdot,\cdot)$ is a known function referred to as kernel.

We now turn to discuss optimality conditions, their connections with the pricing kernel in equilibrium, and some issues arising in the context of incomplete markets.

2.6.4 Equilibrium, Risk Sharing, and Incomplete Markets

To summarize, in the absence of arbitrage, any agent j faces the following program:

$$\max_{(c_{0},c^{1})}\left(u_{j}(c_{0})+\beta E(v_{j}(c^{1}))\right)\quad \text{s.t. } 0=c_{0j}-w_{0j}+E\left(m(c_{j}^{1}-w_{j}^{1})\right),\ (c^{1}-w^{1})\in\langle V\rangle. \tag{2.P4}$$

The agent program [2.P4] conveniently summarizes the main issues the agent faces in an incomplete market setting: the excess demands in the second period are constrained to be in the subspace $\langle V\rangle$ as figure 2.4 illustrates in the two-state case, $d=2$. This section discusses a few properties of the equilibrium allocations based on this program and some indications of how to elaborate on it in the context of incomplete markets. The main conclusions in this section are generalized to dynamic contexts later in this book (see, e.g., chapters 4 or 9).

2.6.4.1 Complete markets, risk sharing, and mutuality

We already know that, when markets are complete, $\langle V\rangle = \mathbb{R}^d$, such that first-order conditions of [2.P4] are

$$u_j'\left(\hat{c}_{0j}\right) = \lambda_j, \quad \beta v_j'\left(\hat{c}_{sj}\right) = \lambda_j m_s, \quad s = 1, \cdots, d, \tag{2.30}$$

where λ_j is a Lagrange multiplier. It is very clear then that the properties of this model are the same as those of the static model in section 2.2 once we set $m-1=d$, where m is the dimension of the commodity space and $p_s = \phi_{s-1}$ is the price of the sth commodity, with $p_1 = 1$ (the numéraire). That is, an economy with uncertainty and complete markets can be understood by means of a static one.

These conclusions are practically relevant. In part II (see chapter 9), we analyze economies with heterogenous agents that have potentially interesting asset pricing implications. These implications can be conveniently analyzed while "centralizing" the original economy throughout a dedicated design of Pareto's weights, similar to theorem 2.7. Unfortunately, the assumption that markets are complete only leads to a simple benchmark: it seems unrealistic that agents may trade Arrow-Debreu securities for all states of the world; one reason financial innovation is so pervasive in practice is that markets are incomplete. Yet, chapter 9 explains that, in some cases, incomplete markets may be dealt with while relying on centralizing the original economy with "stochastic Pareto weights."

It is instructive to review some fundamental implications of the first-order conditions in equilibrium. For simplicity, let us just initially suppose that there is a single agent. In equilibrium, the pricing kernel is

$$m_s = \beta \frac{v'(w_s)}{u'(w_0)} \tag{2.31}$$

and can be interpreted as follows. The quantity,

$$-\left.\frac{dc_0}{dc_s}\right|_{c_0=w_0, c_s=w_s} = \beta \frac{v'(w_s)}{u'(w_0)} P_s = m_s P_s = \phi_s,$$

represents the present consumption the agent is willing to give up, at $t=0$, in order to achieve to additional consumption at $t=1$ and state s. In other words, ϕ_s is the price (expressed in terms of the present consumption numéraire) of one additional unit of consumption at $t=1$ and state s. It is the (state) price that makes this agent happy to consume their own endowment (i.e., the pricing leaving him without any further incentives to trade in the financial markets).

Note, also, that the risk neutral probability is

$$Q_s = \zeta_s P_s = (1+r)\, m_s P_s = (1+r)\, \beta \frac{v'(w_s)}{u'(w_0)} P_s.$$

By the property that $\frac{1}{1+r} = E(m)$, it is easy to verify that $\sum_{s=1}^{d} Q_s = 1$ and

$$\frac{Q_s}{P_s} = m_s (1+r) = m_s \beta^{-1} \frac{u'(w_0)}{E\left(v'(w_s)\right)} = \frac{v'(w_s)}{E\left(v'(w_s)\right)}.$$

We can achieve similar conclusions in economies with heterogenous agents, at least provided markets are complete. Note that, by the first-order conditions (see eq. (2.30))

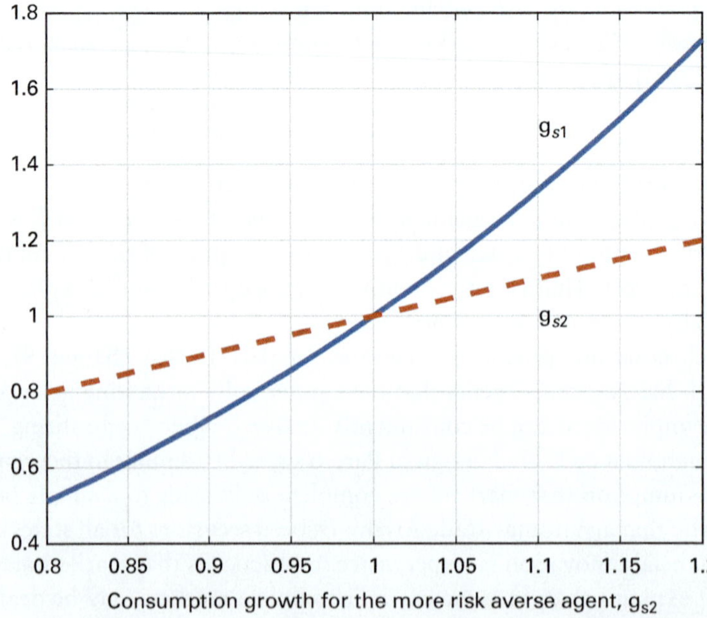

Figure 2.5
Equilibrium consumption growth rates of two agents with different risk aversion. The dashed line and solid line depict consumption growth of the more and, resp., less risk averse agents. The ratio of the two CRRA is equal to 3.

and eq. (2.28), the marginal rate of substitution for each agent is

$$\beta \frac{v_j'(\hat{c}_{sj})}{u_j'(\hat{c}_{0j})} P_s = \phi_s, \quad s = 1, \cdots, d, \quad j = 1, \cdots, n. \tag{2.32}$$

That is, in equilibrium, agents *do* have the same marginal rate of substitution. The reason is the following. The vector of state prices, ϕ, is unique if and only if markets are complete (see theorem 2.9), such that the LHS of (2.32) is independent of j. Note also that, as a result, the equilibrium allocation is a Pareto optimum by theorem 2.5 and the discussion made at the beginning of this section. The property that agents have the same marginal rates of substitution in each state of the world is known as *risk sharing*. Risk sharing means that, given an initial endowment distribution, the market mechanism makes it possible to redistribute risks in a way that higher risks are borne by the agents more willing to take them.

Consider the following simple example: an economy with two agents and the same discount rate but with different risk aversion. We assume that the first agent is less risk averse than the second, with a CRRA γ_1 less than that of the second agent, γ_2. These assumptions imply that $g_{s1} = g_{s2}^{\gamma_2/\gamma_1}$, where g_{si} denotes consumption growth in state s for agent i. In good times, when $g_{s2} > 1$, the more risk averse agent has a lower consumption growth rate, $g_{s2} < g_{s1}$. However, in bad times, when $g_{s2} < 1$, the more risk averse agent has a higher consumption growth rate, $g_{s2} > g_{s1}$. In other words, financial markets, when complete, operate in a way where the more risk averse agents face a less volatile consumption growth. Figure 2.5 illustrates these conclusions for the case $\gamma_2/\gamma_1 = 3$.

Risk sharing carries another meaning, that of "mutuality" (Wilson, 1968). Suppose that the distribution of endowments across agents is heterogeneous in that there are some states of the world in which some agents are better off than others. A system of complete markets would allow the agents to insure each other so that they would only bear the "macroeconomic risk," not the idiosyncratic risk. Let us illustrate. By eq. (2.32),

$$\frac{v_j'\left(\hat{c}_{sj}\right)}{u_j'\left(\hat{c}_{0j}\right)}=\frac{v_\ell'\left(\hat{c}_{s\ell}\right)}{u_\ell'\left(\hat{c}_{0\ell}\right)},\quad \text{for all agents } j,\ell, \text{ and state } s. \tag{2.33}$$

Suppose, then, that the aggregate endowment is higher in some state s than in some other state s'. We claim then that each agent has a strictly higher consumption in state s than in s'. In particular, note that this property implies that, in the absence of aggregate risk (when aggregate endowment is the same in each state), agents would bear no risk. To prove the claim, consider two distinct states s and s', and assume that the aggregate endowment satisfies $\omega_s > \omega_{s'}$. Then there must exist an individual j^* such that $\hat{c}_{sj^*} > \hat{c}_{s'j^*}$ and, hence, $v_{j^*}'\left(\hat{c}_{sj^*}\right) < v_{j^*}'\left(\hat{c}_{s'j^*}\right)$. By eq. (2.33), then, $v_\ell'(\hat{c}_{s\ell}) < v_\ell'(\hat{c}_{s'\ell})$ and, hence, $\hat{c}_{s\ell} > \hat{c}_{s'\ell}$ for any agent ℓ. Finally, note that because the utilities $v_j(\cdot)$ are state independent, the equilibrium distribution of the aggregate endowment does not depend on s.

Thus, the equilibrium allocations are state-independent functions of the aggregate endowment,

$$\hat{c}_{sj}=a_j\left(\omega_s\right),$$

for some strictly increasing function $a_j(\cdot)$. The conclusion is mutuality: if the aggregate endowment ω_s does not vary across states s, the equilibrium allocations would be independent of the state of the economy.[2] The functions $a_j(\cdot)$ are known as Pareto sharing rules.[3]

2.6.4.2 *Incomplete markets*

If markets are incomplete, the agents' marginal rates of substitution cannot be equal, except perhaps for a negligible set of endowment distribution. Magill and Quinzii (1996) review the main arguments and formal proofs of this statement and the literature on the existence of equilibrium in this case. We now review one approach to determine any agent's solution to their consumption problem. We know that the state price vector ϕ is not unique when markets are incomplete. That is, suppose that ϕ is an equilibrium state price; then,

---

2. To illustrate, consider an economy with two agents (A and B) and no aggregate risk. Pareto allocations can then be characterized within an Edgeworth's box where the axes indicate consumption in the two states s' and s. Note that the 45° line of the box is the set in which the two agents are perfecty insured across states. Moreover, the agents' indifference curves are tangent along the contract curve (i.e., the set of Pareto allocations), meaning that $dc_{s'A}/dc_{sA}=dc_{s'B}/dc_{sB}$. Because $-dc_{s'j}/dc_{sj}=v_j'(\hat{c}_{sj})P_s/v_j'(\hat{c}_{s'j})P_{s'}=\phi_{s'}/\phi_s$, this tangency condition is met only on the 45° line: Pareto allocations lead to mutuality.

3. Huang and Litzenberger (1988, chapter 5) review in detail further properties of these functions. In particular, $a_j(\cdot)$ are linear if and only if the utility functions take the following form, $v_i(c)=(\alpha_i+\gamma c)^{-1/\gamma}$, for some constants a_i and γ.

all the elements of

$$\Phi = \{\phi' \in \mathbb{R}^d_{++} : (\phi' - \phi)^\top V = 0\}$$

are also equilibrium state prices. In other words, there exist many equilibrium state prices that are consistent with the same observable asset price vector S, for $\phi'^\top V = \phi^\top V = S$.

How do we proceed in this case? Introduce the following budget constraint:

$$C = \left\{c \in \mathbb{R}^{d+1}_{++} : 0 = c_0 - w_0 + \phi^\top (c^1 - w^1),\ \ (c^1 - w^1) \in \langle V \rangle,\ \ \forall \phi \in \mathbb{R}^d_{++} : S = \phi^\top V\right\}.$$

Because Φ has many elements, the budget constraint C does, then, include many constraints to account for in a context with incomplete markets. Yet let $\text{Val}\,(P_I)$ be the value of the following program:

$$\max_{c \in C} \left(u_j\,(c_0) + \beta E(v_j(c^1))\right); \qquad [2.\text{P}_\text{I}]$$

consider the following constraint,

$$C_\phi = \left\{ \begin{array}{c} c \in \mathbb{R}^{d+1}_{++} : 0 = c_0 - w_0 + \phi^\top\,(c^1 - w^1),\ \ (c^1 - w^1) \in \mathbb{R}^d, \\ \text{for some given } \phi \in \mathbb{R}^d_{++} : S = \phi^\top V \end{array} \right\},$$

and let $\text{Val}\,(P_\phi)$ be the value of the program in some abstract complete markets case

$$\max_{c \in C_\phi} \left(u_j\,(c_0) + \beta E(v_j(c^1))\right). \qquad [2.\text{P}_\phi]$$

Clearly, $\text{Val}\,(P_I) \leq \text{Val}\,(P_\phi)$ for all ϕ, for the constraint in the incomplete markets case, C, is more stringent than that in any complete market setting, C_ϕ: the solution to the program in the incomplete markets case, [2.P$_\text{I}$], must satisfy the budget constraints in C, formed using *all* possible Arrow-Debreu state prices (including the Arrow-Debreu state price ϕ in C_ϕ) and constrained in a way that $(c^1 - w^1) \in \langle V \rangle$. These remarks suggest to define the following "min-max" Arrow-Debreu state price:

$$\phi^* = \arg\min_{\phi \in \Phi} \text{Val}\,(P_\phi)\,.$$

A natural issue is to ascertain whether

$$\text{Val}\,(P_I) = \text{Val}\,(P_{\phi^*})\,. \qquad (2.34)$$

Under regularity conditions, the previous equality does indeed hold. For the characterization of ϕ^*, let us assume that there exists $\hat{\phi} : \text{Val}\,(P_I) = \text{Val}(P_{\hat{\phi}})$. Then, $\hat{\phi} = \phi^*$. Indeed, suppose the contrary, that is, there exists $\phi' : \text{Val}(P_{\phi'}) < \text{Val}(P_{\hat{\phi}})$. Then we would have

$$\text{Val}\,(P_I) \leq \text{Val}(P_{\phi'}) < \text{Val}(P_{\hat{\phi}}) = \text{Val}\,(P_I)\,,$$

a contradiction. Note again that this is a characterization result of ϕ^*, not an existence proof. But eq. (2.34) holds true, as mentioned. He and Pearson (1991) do provide the first existence results in a dynamic setting. Chapter 4 provides additional discussion regarding these problems in a broader context of market imperfections.

A final comment is that the min-max state price does not give rise to any "pricing probability." It is a technical device that helps solve agents' programs when markets are incomplete. Consider, for example, the usual case dealt with in this chapter, in which agents have separable utilities. The counterparts to the first-order conditions in (2.30) is $u_j'(\hat{c}_{0j}) = \lambda_j$ and $\beta v_j'(\hat{c}_{sj}) = \lambda_j m_{s,j}^*$, where $m_{s,j}^*$ is the min-max pricing kernel for agent j. We obviously have as many min-max pricing kernels as agents. An equilibrium, provided it exists, may be found by market clearing. Naturally, in an economy with a single agent, the pricing probability is the min-max probability (i.e., the probability resulting from the min-max state price ϕ^*).

2.6.4.3 *Computation of the equilibrium*

We conclude this section by sketching some general steps to compute an equilibrium, provided it exists (at least in the complete markets case). The first-order conditions satisfied by any agent's program are

$$\hat{c}_{0j} = I_j(\lambda_j), \quad \hat{c}_{sj} = H_j\left(\beta^{-1}\lambda_j m_s\right), \tag{2.35}$$

where I_j and H_j denote the inverse functions of u_j' and v_j'. By assumption 2.1, I_j and H_j inherit the same properties of u_j' and v_j'. By replacing (2.35) into the budget constraints,

$$\begin{aligned} 0 &= \hat{c}_{0j} - w_{0j} + E\left(m(\hat{c}_j^1 - w_j^1)\right) \\ &= I_j(\lambda_j) + E\left(mH_j(\beta^{-1}\lambda_j m)\right) - \left(w_{0j} + E(mw_j^1)\right) \\ &\equiv z_j(\lambda_j) - \left(w_{0j} + E(mw_j^1)\right). \end{aligned}$$

Under standard conditions on $u_j'(x)$, we have that $\lim_{x\to 0} z_j(x) = \infty$, $\lim_{x\to\infty} z_j(x) = 0$, and $z_j'(x) < 0$. Therefore, there exists a unique solution for λ_j,

$$\lambda_j \equiv \Lambda_j\left(w_{0j} + E(mw_j^1)\right),$$

where $\Lambda(\cdot)$ denotes the inverse function of z. Plugging this solution back into (2.35) leaves

$$\hat{c}_{0j} = I_j\left(\Lambda_j\left(w_{0j} + E(mw_j^1)\right)\right), \quad \hat{c}_{sj} = H_j\left(\beta^{-1} m_s \Lambda_j\left(w_{0j} + E(mw_j^1)\right)\right).$$

To determine the general equilibrium, we need to pin down the pricing kernel, m. We need to solve a system of d unknowns (m_s, $s = 1, \cdots, d$) and $d+1$ equilibrium conditions (holding in the $d+1$ markets). By Walras's law, only d of these equations are independent. Consider the equilibrium conditions in the d markets in the second period,

$$\sum_{j=1}^{n} H_j\left(\beta^{-1} m_s \Lambda_j\left(w_{0j} + E(mw_j^1)\right)\right) = \sum_{j=1}^{n} w_{sj} \equiv w_s, \ s = 1, \cdots, d.$$

These conditions determine $(m_s)_{s=1}^d$, which enables one to compute prices and equilibrium allocations.

2.7 Consumption CAPM

An asset pricing theory is "consumption-based" when the assets' equilibrium expected returns, or the "risk premiums," link to the aggregate consumption behavior. Models with these features are referred to as consumption CAPM (CCAPM). The model in this chapter is the simplest version of a CCAPM. Many models in part II (see, e.g., chapters 8 and 9) are consumption based. How do these models relate to the classic CAPM of chapter 1, where the assets' expected returns link to the market portfolio?

We review conditions under which CCAPM models collapse to the CAPM—conditions that, to anticipate, appear to be stringent. A CCAPM links to equilibrium consumption. Its main prediction, we shall see, is that, under certain conditions, risk premiums are high for securities that pay high returns when consumption is high (i.e., when we don't need high returns) and that pay low returns when consumption is low (i.e., when we need high returns). The CAPM has a similar logic but replaces covariance between returns and consumption with covariance between asset returns and the market. Note that, in equilibrium, aggregate consumption and market should be related. This section aims at defining this type of relation such that CCAPM and CAPM are the same. One example where this linkage breaks down arises when securities are in zero net supply.

For the details, consider the asset pricing equation (2.29): for every asset that promises a gross return $\tilde{R}$,

$$1 = E(m\tilde{R}). \tag{2.36}$$

This equation holds for any asset, including a riskless asset that promises a gross return equal to R, such that $1 = E(mR)$. Combining this equation with (2.36) leaves $E(m(\tilde{R} - R)) = 0$ and, by rearranging terms,

$$E(\tilde{R}) = R - \frac{cov(v'(w^1), \tilde{R})}{E\left(v'(w^1)\right)}, \tag{2.37}$$

where the notation is as in section 2.6 (in particular, w^1 and v resp. denote the vector of endowments and the utility in the second period).

Eq. (2.37) can be rewritten as

$$E(\tilde{R}) - R = -\frac{cov(m, \tilde{R})}{E(m)} = -Rcov(m, \tilde{R}). \tag{2.38}$$

We also know from previous sections that in economies with a single agent (or in economies with complete markets, which may be centralized as in theorem 2.7), the pricing kernel m links to aggregate consumption (endowment) (see eq. (2.31)). However, note that the risk premium, $-Rcov(m, \tilde{R})$, links to how m covaries with the asset returns and that the asset returns may not necessarily be correlated with consumption endowment. In many models, they *are*. However, it is not a general property. For example, in an economy without aggregate risk (in which, that is, the second period aggregate endowments are constant) and assets in zero net supply, the risk premium would be zero. We now present some CCAPM models that provide more sensible predictions.

2.7.1 Risk Neutral Pricing and Macroeconomic Risks

We consider markets in which assets are in positive supply. For simplicity, we consider an economy with a representative agent endowed with θ_0 units of the asset (its supply). Their budget constraints are

$$c_1 + S\theta = S\theta_0 + w \quad \text{and} \quad \tilde{c}_2 = \tilde{d}\theta + \tilde{w}, \tag{2.39}$$

where S and θ are the asset price and demand, w is the initial endowment, c_1 is first period consumption, $\tilde{w}$ and $\tilde{d}$ are the second period random endowment and asset dividend, and $\tilde{c}_2$ is second-period consumption. We assume that $\tilde{d} > 0$.

We are assuming that the agent faces incomplete markets: they face two sources of risk (the asset dividend *and* endowment) but can only invest in one asset. Chapter 9 relies on this simple model to explain how incomplete markets may help explain some asset pricing puzzles (the fact, for example, that the excess expected returns predicted by CCAPM are too low compared with the average returns in the data) (see section 9.4). Now, in equilibrium, $\theta = \theta_0$, such that the asset price satisfies

$$S = \frac{E\left(\beta v'(\tilde{d}\theta_0 + \tilde{w})\tilde{d}\right)}{u'(w)}. \tag{2.40}$$

In the previous sections, $\theta_0 = 0$. Eq. (2.40) shows that, under standard conditions, the asset price S is decreasing with the asset supply, θ_0. This property is not merely a supply effect but a "risk premium," that is, one related to the state prices. Let us explain. By repeating the reasoning in section 2.6, the state price for state s is

$$\phi_s = \frac{\beta v'\left(d_s\theta_0 + w_s\right)}{u'(w)} P_s. \tag{2.41}$$

It is, as usual, the present consumption the agent is willing to give up, today, in order to obtain additional consumption tomorrow, in state s. Due to decreasing marginal utility, consumption demand in state s, $\hat{c}_s$, is decreasing in ϕ_s, $\hat{c} : \phi_s = \frac{\beta v'(\hat{c}_s)}{u'(\hat{c}_0)}$, for $s = 1, \cdots, d$. Therefore, in equilibrium, ϕ_s is decreasing the good supply in state s, $d_s\theta_0 + w_s$.

The previous "scarcity effect," by which a shrinkage in supply for state s determines an increase in the state price ϕ_s, is quite simple and yet powerful. It means that assets are evaluated by assigning high weights (i.e., by relying on high Arrow-Debreu state prices) to the bad states of nature. To illustrate, an increase in the asset supply θ_0, being uniform across all states of nature, mitigates the previous scarcity effect and then lowers the entire set of Arrow-Debreu prices, thereby reducing the asset price, S. The asset price decreases because consumption become cheaper in each state of the world.

We can study these issues from a slightly different angle. Note that eq. (2.40) can be rewritten as

$$S = \frac{E(\tilde{d})}{R(\theta_0)} + \frac{\beta}{u'(w)} cov\left(v'(\tilde{d}\theta_0 + \tilde{w}), \tilde{d}\right), \quad R(\theta_0) = \frac{u'(w)}{E\left(\beta v'(\tilde{d}\theta_0 + \tilde{w})\right)}. \tag{2.42}$$

The first term is an actuarial evaluation of the asset. The second term is a discount, assuming that $cov(\tilde{w}, \tilde{d}) > 0$ and due to decreasing marginal utility. Eq. (2.42) reveals that an increase in θ_0 leads to a heavier discounting effect: the interest rate, $R(\theta_0)$, increases with θ_0 as a result of a decreased demand for savings. The second term is negative, as explained: the asset pays off exactly when it is not needed.

Note that when $\theta_0 = \theta = 0$, Arrow-Debreu prices are low in bad states only due to a "pure endowment scarcity" channel: provided that $cov(\tilde{w}, \tilde{d}) > 0$, states in which endowments are lower command higher Arrow-Debreu prices.[4] To summarize, Arrow-Debreu state prices are independent of the asset returns when $\theta_0 = 0$. Instead, when $\theta_0 > 0$, one additional scarcity channel is activated, by which a drop in consumption is generated by a drop in the dividend. Suppose, for example, that the economy is in bad times. One may think of a fall in w_s as a result of a job loss (or reduction). So not only does w_s fall, but also the dividend likely falls. The dividend fall occurs precisely when agents would need a higher dividend to compensate for the job loss. Chapter 9 contains many models that elaborate on these simple ideas and tries to address some asset pricing puzzles that a basic CCAPM generates. We now provide simple conditions under which the CCAPM and the CAPM are the same.

2.7.2 CCAPM versus CAPM

Suppose that there is a portfolio delivering a return $\tilde{R}^m$ that is perfectly correlated with the pricing kernel, namely,

$$\tilde{R}_s^m = -c^{-1} v'(w_s), \text{ for all } s,$$

for some constant c. By eq. (2.38),

$$E(\tilde{R}) = R + c\frac{cov(\tilde{R}^m, \tilde{R})}{E(v'(w^+))}, \quad \text{and} \quad E(\tilde{R}^m) = R + c\frac{var(\tilde{R}^m)}{E(v'(w^+))}.$$

These two equations can be combined to yield

$$E(\tilde{R}) - R = \beta(E(\tilde{R}^m) - R), \quad \beta \equiv \frac{cov(\tilde{R}^m, \tilde{R})}{var(\tilde{R}^m)}.$$

That is, if a portfolio can be found that has returns that are perfectly correlated with the pricing kernel, the CCAPM collapses to the classic CAPM. In chapter 7, we explain that the CAPM can also be obtained by relying on a portfolio called the "maximum correlation portfolio," which is the portfolio that is the most highly correlated with the pricing kernel m.

Appendix 2.A Proofs of Selected Results

Uniqueness of a solution to [2.P1]. Suppose on the contrary that we have two maxima,

$$\bar{c} = (\bar{c}_{1j}, \cdots, \bar{c}_{mj}) \text{ and } \bar{\bar{c}} = (\bar{\bar{c}}_{1j}, \cdots, \bar{\bar{c}}_{mj}).$$

4. Note, finally, a special case of this model, resulting when $\theta_0 = 0$ and $\tilde{w}$ is constant. In this case, consumption is not random in the second period, and agents do not bear any risk. The asset price then is simply the discounted expected dividend, $S = E(\tilde{d})/R$.

These two maxima would satisfy $u_j(\bar{c}) = u_j(\bar{\bar{c}})$, with $\sum_{i=1}^{m} p_i \bar{c}_{ij} = \sum_{i=1}^{m} p_i \bar{\bar{c}}_{ij} = R_j$. Next, consider a point y lying between $\bar{c}$ and $\bar{\bar{c}}$, namely, $y = \alpha\bar{c} + (1-\alpha)\bar{\bar{c}}$, $\alpha \in (0,1)$. By assumption 2.1,

$$u_j(y) = u_j\left(\alpha\bar{c} + (1-\alpha)\bar{\bar{c}}\right) > u_j(\bar{c}) = u_j(\bar{\bar{c}}).$$

Moreover,

$$\sum_{i=1}^{m} p_i y_i = \sum_{i=1}^{m} p_i\left(\alpha\bar{c}_{ij} + (1-\alpha)\bar{\bar{c}}_{ij}\right) = R_j.$$

Hence, $y \in B_j(p)$ and is also strictly preferred to $\bar{c}$ and $\bar{\bar{c}}$, implying that $\bar{c}$ and $\bar{\bar{c}}$ are not optima—a contradiction. This establishes uniqueness of the solution to [2.P1].

Next, we provide a useful result, a well-known theorem on the separation of two convex sets. We use this theorem to deal with the proof of the second welfare theorem (theorem 2.4) and the existence of state prices tying up all asset prices (theorem 2.9).

Minkowski's separation theorem. *Let A and B be two non empty convex subsets of $\mathbb{R}^d$. If A is closed, B is compact, and $A \bigcap B = \emptyset$, then there exists a $\phi \in \mathbb{R}^d$ and two real numbers d_1, d_2 such that:*

$$a^\top \phi \le d_1 < d_2 \le b^\top \phi, \quad \forall a \in A, \forall b \in B.$$

We are now ready to prove theorems 2.4 and 2.9.

Proof of theorem 2.4. Let $\bar{c}$ be a Pareto optimum and $\tilde{B}_j = \{c^j : u_j(c^j) > u_j(\bar{c}^j)\}$. Let us consider the two sets $\tilde{B} = \bigcup_{j=1}^{n} \tilde{B}_j$ and $A = \{(c^j)_{j=1}^{n} : c^j \ge 0\, \forall j,\ \sum_{j=1}^{n} c^j = w\}$. A is the set of all possible combinations of feasible allocations. By the definition of a Pareto optimum, there are no elements in A that are also in $\tilde{B}$ or $A \bigcap \tilde{B} = \emptyset$. In particular, this statement is true for all compact subsets B of $\tilde{B}$ or $A \bigcap B = \emptyset$. Because A is closed, then, by the Minkowski's separating theorem, there exists a $p \in \mathbb{R}^m$ and two distinct numbers d_1, d_2 such that

$$p^\top a \le d_1 < d_2 \le p^\top b, \quad \forall a \in A, \forall b \in B.$$

Therefore, for all allocations $\left(c^j\right)_{j=1}^{n}$ preferred to $\bar{c}$, we have

$$p^\top \sum_{j=1}^{n} w^j < p^\top \sum_{j=1}^{n} c^j$$

or, by replacing $\sum_{j=1}^{n} w^j$ with $\sum_{j=1}^{n} \bar{c}^j$,

$$p^\top \sum_{j=1}^{n} \bar{c}^j < p^\top \sum_{j=1}^{n} c^j. \tag{2.A1}$$

Next we show that $p > 0$. Let $\bar{c}_i = \sum_{j=1}^{n} \bar{c}_{ij}$, $i = 1, \cdots, m$, and partition $\bar{c} = (\bar{c}_1, \cdots, \bar{c}_m)$. Let us apply the inequality in (2.A1) to $\bar{c} \in A$ and, for $\mu > 0$, to $c = (\bar{c}_1 + \mu, \cdots, \bar{c}_m) \in B$. We have $p_1\mu > 0$ or $p_1 > 0$. By repeating the argument for all i, $p_i > 0$. Finally, we choose $c^j = \bar{c}^j + \mathbf{1}_m \frac{\epsilon}{n}, j = 2, \cdots, n$, $\epsilon > 0$ in (2.A1), $p^\top \bar{c}^1 < p^\top c^1 + p^\top \mathbf{1}_m \epsilon$ or

$$p^\top \bar{c}^1 < p^\top c^1,$$

for ϵ sufficiently small. That is, $u_1(c^1) > u_1(\bar{c}^1) \Rightarrow p^\top c^1 > p^\top \bar{c}^1$, or $\bar{c}^1 = \arg\max_{c^1} u_1(c^1)$ s.t. $p^\top c^1 = p^\top \bar{c}^1$. By symmetry, $\bar{c}^j = \arg\max_{c^j} u_j(c^j)$ s.t. $p^\top c^j = p^\top \bar{c}^j$ for all j. □

Proof of theorem 2.9. Assume that there exists a strictly positive $\phi : S = \phi^\top V$. Then $S\theta = \phi^\top V\theta$, implying that no arbitrage (see definition 2.8) is possible. For the converse, note that the condition in (2.19) holds for any compact subset of $\mathbb{R}_+^{d+1}$. Therefore, it holds when it is restricted to the unit simplex in $\mathbb{R}_+^{d+1}$,

$$\langle W \rangle \bigcap S^d = \{0\}.$$

By Minkowski's separation theorem, $\exists \phi_1 \in \mathbb{R}^{d+1} : w^\top \phi_1 \le d_1 < d_2 \le \sigma^\top \phi_1$, $w \in \langle W \rangle$, $\sigma \in S^d$. By evaluating these inequalities at the simplex boundaries, we conclude that $d_1 < \phi_{1s}$, $s = 0, 1, \cdots, d$. Now, $0 \in \langle W \rangle$, such that $d_1 \ge 0$. Hence, $\phi_1 \in \mathbb{R}_{++}^{d+1}$. We claim that $\phi_1^\top \in \langle W \rangle^\perp$, that is, $w^\top \phi_1 = 0$. Assume the contrary—that is, there exists $w_* \in \langle W \rangle$ that also satisfies $w_*^\top \phi_1 \neq 0$. Then there would exist a real number ϵ with $\text{sign}(\epsilon) = \text{sign}(w_*^\top \phi_1)$, such that $\epsilon w_* \in \langle W \rangle$ and $\epsilon w_*^\top \phi_1 > d_2$, a contradiction. Therefore, it must be that $0 = \phi_1^\top W\theta = (-\phi_{10} S + \phi_{1(d)}^\top V)\theta$, $\forall \theta \in \mathbb{R}^m$, where $\phi_{1(d)}$ denotes the vector with the last d components of ϕ_1. It follows that $S = \phi^\top V$, where $\phi^\top = (\phi_{11}/\phi_{10}, \cdots, \phi_{1d}/\phi_{10})$.

Regarding the proof of the second part, note that $\dim \langle W \rangle + \dim \langle W \rangle^\perp = d + 1$. Since $\dim \langle W \rangle = \text{rank}(W)$ and, in the absence of arbitrage, $S = \phi^\top V$, $\dim \langle W \rangle = \dim \langle V \rangle = m$, whence $\dim \langle W \rangle^\perp = d - m + 1$. But, by the proof of the first part, $\phi_1^\top \in \langle W \rangle^\perp$, which implies the second statement of the theorem pertaining to $\phi = \phi_{1(d)}/\phi_{10}$. □

References

Arrow, K. J. (1953). "Le rôle des valeurs boursières pour la répartitition la meilleure des risques." *Econométrie* 41–48. CNRS, Paris. Translated as "The Role of Securities in the Optimal Allocation of Risk-Bearing." *Review of Economic Studies* 31 (1964), 91–96.

Bernoulli, D. (1738). "Specimen Theoriae Novae de Mensura Sortis." *Commentarii Academiae Scientiarum Imperialis Petropolitanae* V, 175-192. Translated as "Exposition of a New Theory on the Measurement of Risk." *Econometrica* 22 (1954), 23–36

Debreu, G. (1954). "Valuation Equilibrium and Pareto Optimum." *Proceedings of the National Academy of Sciences* 40, 588–592.

Debreu, G. (1959). *Theory of Value: An Axiomatic Analysis of Economic Equilibrium.* New Haven, CT: Yale University Press.

Duffie, D. (2001). *Dynamic Asset Pricing Theory.* Princeton, NJ: Princeton University Press.

Grossman, S. J., and J. E. Stiglitz (1980). "On the Impossibility of Informationally Efficient Markets." *American Economic Review* 70, 393–408.

He, H., and N. Pearson (1991). "Consumption and Portfolio Policies with Incomplete Markets and Short-Sales Constraints: The Infinite Dimensional Case." *Journal of Economic Theory* 54, 259–304.

Hicks, J. (1939). *Value and Capital.* Oxford: Oxford University Press.

Huang, C.-F., and R. H. Litzenberger (1988). *Foundations for Financial Economics.* New York: North-Holland.

Lucas, R. E. (1972). "Expectations and the Neutrality of Money." *Journal of Economic Theory* 4, 103–124.

Magill, M., and M. Quinzii (1996). *Theory of Incomplete Markets.* Cambridge, MA: MIT Press.

Modigliani, F., and M. Miller (1958). "The Cost of Capital, Corporation Finance and the Theory of Investment." *American Economic Review* 48, 261–297.

Muth, J. F. (1961). "Rational Expectations and the Theory of Price Movements." *Econometrica* 29, 315–335.

Radner, R. (1968). "Competitive Equilibrium under Uncertainty." *Econometrica* 36, 31–58.

Ruston, A. (1986). *Fredholm Theory in Banach Spaces.* Cambridge, UK: Cambridge University Press.

Wilson, R. (1968). "The Theory of Syndicates." *Econometrica* 36, 119–132.

3

Infinite Horizon Economies

3.1 Introduction

This chapter provides foundations for the study of dynamic economies and asset pricing. We consider a number of models by which aggregate consumption and production affect asset prices. Thus, these models generalize those in chapter 2 and, at least in principle, might already be taken to data. In fact, part II discusses many of their empirical limitations. Nonetheless, this chapter marks the starting point for the whole set of analytical results needed to implement dynamic models.

Lucas (1978) contains the first contribution to asset pricing in such a dynamic environment. In his model, asset prices are "discounted" expectations of future asset prices and dividends. The discounting factor reflects the agents' risk aversion. In this model, there is a representative agent with an infinite horizon. More generally, this chapter discusses infinite horizon models. We consider economies in which agents either live forever (as in Lucas's model) or belong to overlapping generations. These two types of models are workhorses in macroeconomics. We also rely on them without, of course, pursuing the ambitious objective of venturing in all details regarding the rich field of macroeconomics. Still, we aim at providing fundamental background that may well be useful to understand the behavior of asset prices. Ljungqvist and Sargent (2018) is an important reference in the field of dynamic macroeconomics; Blanchard and Fischer (1989) still represent an important and detailed introduction to some of the models in this chapter and these models' extensions for the purpose of macroeconomic analysis.

The chapter is organized as follows. Section 3.2 introduces simple consumption/saving problems for a representative agent. These plans may be formulated in a recursive setting: the agent's value function (i.e., their maximized intertemporal utility) equals their current utility plus the expected (discounted) future value function. These problems are formulated in an infinite horizon setting, which renders the resulting models stationary—a feature of many models dealt with in this book. This section contains Lucas's model as well as notions summarizing the trade-off of consuming at different points in time, such as the elasticity of intertemporal substitution. This notion is very important and will be used many times in this book (see, e.g., Chapter 9).

Lucas's model is an "endowment model," in that some trees (i.e., stocks) regularly deliver fruits (i.e., dividends) consumed by the agents. A richer model is one with production. Sections 3.3 and 3.4 provide an introduction to economies with production. We need to start from the roots and, thus, from some models that were initially developed in macroeconomics and that now also inform much research and knowledge in financial economics. According to these models, firms produce and distribute dividends regularly. Section 3.3 reviews the standard model of capital accumulation, and section 3.4 reviews "q-theory," that is, the asset pricing implications of this model.

The previous models rely on the presence of some representative agent. Section 3.5 provides some analysis of capital accumulation and asset pricing and also studies simple monetary economies based on another paradigm used to study dynamic economies: overlapping generations models. This model is used to study questions such as the existence of "bubbles." These questions appear to be more difficult to study in the context of models with a representative agent. Note that there are many more explanations for the existence of bubbles than those discussed in this chapter (see, e.g., chapter 9 [section 9.5] or chapter 14 [section 14.5]). However, the model in this chapter provides foundations for a very special bubble, resulting from (and somehow, correcting) resource allocations in economies that produce overaccumulation of capital. Finally, section 3.6 provides some foundational issues regarding questions of optimality in capital accumulation models. These issues may help understand the role of bubbles in the model of section 3.5.

The analysis of this chapter is in discrete time. However, appendixes 3.B and 3.C provide some analysis in continuous time. These two appendixes help further illustrate the analysis in the main text and contain results that also help bridge with the continuous time analysis of chapter 4.

3.2 Consumption-Based Asset Evaluation

3.2.1 Recursive Plans: Introduction

Consider the following simple benchmark economy. A decision maker is endowed with initial wealth equal to w_0, utility u over consumption c—satisfying $u'(c) \geq 0$ and $u''(c) \leq 0$—and discount factor $\beta < 1$. They need to solve the following problem

$$\begin{aligned} V(w_0) &\equiv \max_{(c_t)_{t=0}^{\infty}} \sum_{t=0}^{\infty} \beta^t u(c_t) \\ \text{s.t. } & w_{t+1} = (w_t - c_t) R_{t+1}, \quad (R_t)_{t=0}^{\infty} \text{ given.} \end{aligned} \tag{3.P1}$$

This problem can be reformulated in a recursive format

$$V(w_t) = \max_{c_t} \left(u(c_t) + \beta V(w_{t+1}) \right) \quad \text{s.t.} \quad w_{t+1} = (w_t - c_t) R_{t+1}. \tag{3.1}$$

It is easy to see that, by replacing the wealth constraint into the maximand of (3.1), the first-order conditions lead to $u'(c_t) = \beta V'(w_{t+1}) R_{t+1}$. Therefore, the consumption policy is a function of both wealth and the interest rate and is denoted with $c(w_t)$. The value function and the first-order condition can then be written as

$$V(w_t) = u(c(w_t)) + \beta V\left((w_t - c(w_t)) R_{t+1}\right), \quad u'(c(w_t)) = \beta V'\left((w_t - c(w_t)) R_{t+1}\right) R_{t+1}.$$

Differentiating the value function and using the first-order condition leaves the envelope condition

$$V'(w_t) = u'(c(w_t))\, c'(w_t) + \beta V'\left((w_t - c(w_t))\, R_{t+1}\right)\left(1 - c'(w_t)\right) R_{t+1} = u'(c(w_t)). \tag{3.2}$$

Therefore, $V'(w_{t+1}) = u'\left(c\left(w_{t+1}\right)\right)$, and by substituting back into the first-order condition,

$$\beta \frac{u'\left(c\left(w_{t+1}\right)\right)}{u'(c(w_t))} = \frac{1}{R_{t+1}}. \tag{3.3}$$

Eq. (3.3) is known as a *Euler condition*. This condition extends the results found in chapter 2. It says that, along an optimal consumption path, the present consumption that you give up at t to obtain additional consumption at $t+1$ has to equal the price at t of a pure discount bond. That is: the bond price is the relative price of consumption tomorrow relative to consumption today.

We can achieve the same conclusion relying on an alternative approach based on Lagrange multipliers. Consider the constraint in program [3.P1]. Savings at time t are $\text{sav}_t \equiv w_t - c_t$. Using this definition, the constraint in [3.P1] is $c_{t+1} + \text{sav}_{t+1} = R_{t+1}\text{sav}_t$, with $\text{sav}_{-1} = w_0$ given. Let λ_t be a sequence of Lagrange multipliers associated to these constraints. Consider the program

$$\mathcal{L}\left(\text{sav}_{-1}\right) \equiv \max_{(c_t, \text{sav}_t)_{t=0}^{\infty}} \sum_{t=0}^{\infty} \left(\beta^t u(c_t) - \lambda_t\left(c_t + \text{sav}_t - R_t \text{sav}_{t-1}\right)\right),$$

where λ_t is a sequence of Lagrange multipliers. The first-order conditions for consumption c_t are $\beta^t u'(c_t) = \lambda_t$, and the first-order conditions for savings sav_t lead to $\lambda_t = \lambda_{t+1} R_{t+1}$. Putting all together yields precisely eq. (3.3). Finally, note that these problems can be formulated in a recursive format,

$$\mathcal{L}\left(\text{sav}_{t-1}\right) = \max_{c_t, \text{sav}_t, \lambda_t} \left(u(c_t) - \lambda_t\left(c_t + \text{sav}_t - R_t \text{sav}_{t-1}\right) + \beta \mathcal{L}(\text{sav}_t)\right).$$

The first-order condition for consumption and savings are $u'(c_t) = \lambda_t$ and $\lambda_t = \beta \mathcal{L}'(\text{sav}_t)$, resp. Replacing the first-order conditions for λ_t (that is, the budget constraint) and differentiating $\mathcal{L}\left(\text{sav}_{t-1}\right)$ leaves $\mathcal{L}'\left(\text{sav}_{t-1}\right) = \beta \mathcal{L}'(\text{sav}_t) R_t$. These conditions lead to eq. (3.3).

As a simple example, consider a logarithmic utility function, $u(c) = \ln c$, and guess that the value function is $V(w_t) \equiv V(w_t; R_t) = a_t + b \ln w_t$. Substituting this guess into the envelope condition in (3.2) leaves $c(w) = b^{-1} w$. By eq. (3.3), then, $w_{t+1} = \beta w_t R_{t+1}$. Comparing the RHS of this equation with the RHS of the constraint in [3.P1] leaves $c(w_t) = (1-\beta)\, w_t$; in other terms, $b = (1-\beta)^{-1}$.[1]

Next, we introduce uncertainty and develop heuristic details regarding asset evaluation in this context.

1. To pin down the coefficient series a_t, use the definition of the value function, $V(w_t; R_t) \equiv u(c(w_t)) + \beta V\left(w_{t+1}; R_{t+1}\right)$. By plugging $V(w, R_t) = a_t + b \ln w$ and $c(w) = (1-\beta)^{-1} w$ into this definition leaves $a_t = \ln(1-\beta) + \beta a_{t+1} + \frac{\beta}{1-\beta} \ln\left(\beta R_{t+1}\right)$. If R is constant, a_t is also constant and is equal to $(\ln(1-\beta) + \frac{\beta}{1-\beta} \ln(\beta R)) / (1-\beta)$.

3.2.2 Asset Pricing: the Marginalist Argument

Consider the following thought experiment. At time t, you give up a small quantity of consumption equal to Δc_t. The reduction in your utility at t then equals $u'(c_t)\Delta c_t$. However, note that by investing Δc_t into a safe asset, you may consume $\Delta c_{t+1} = R_{t+1}\Delta c_t$ more at $t+1$. This additional consumption leads to an expected utility gain equal to $\beta E_t\left(u'\left(c_{t+1}\right)\Delta c_{t+1}\right)$, where E_t denotes the expectation conditional on time t information. If c_t and c_{t+1} are part of an optimal consumption plan, you should be left with no incentives to implement these intertemporal consumption transfers. Therefore, along an optimal consumption plan, any reduction and gain in welfare of this type must compensate

$$u'(c_t) = \beta E_t\left(u'(c_{t+1})R_{t+1}\right).$$

This relation generalizes eq. (3.3). Next, suppose that at time t, Δc_t can be invested in a risky asset whose price is S_t. You can buy $\Delta c_t / S_t$ units of this asset. Come time $t+1$, you could sell the asset for S_{t+1}, pocket its dividend D_{t+1}, and finance additional units of consumption equal to $\Delta c_{t+1} = \left(\Delta c_t / S_t\right) \cdot \left(S_{t+1} + D_{t+1}\right)$. The reduction in your current utility is $u'(c_t)\Delta c_t$. The boost in your expected utility at time $t+1$ is $\beta E_t\left(u'(c_{t+1})\Delta c_{t+1}\right)$. Again, if you are on an optimal consumption plan, there should be no incentives left to implement these intertemporal transfers. Therefore, the celebrated Lucas (1978) asset pricing equation holds:

$$u'(c_t) = \beta E_t\left(u'(c_{t+1})\frac{S_{t+1} + D_{t+1}}{S_t}\right). \tag{3.4}$$

Section 3.2.4 derives eq. (3.4) through dynamic programming methods. These methods are important not only because they enable us to formalize the current heuristic argument but also because they are very powerful and enable us to deal with more complex economies than the one considered in this section. Before turning to dynamic programming, we discuss a key concept which we often encounter in both financial economics and macroeconomics: the elasticity of intertemporal substitution.

3.2.3 Elasticity of Intertemporal Substitution

The elasticity of substitution between two consumption goods, c_A and c_B, is defined as the ratio

$$\mathrm{ES}\left(c_A, c_B\right) = -\frac{\partial\left(\frac{c_B}{c_A}\right)}{\partial\left(\frac{p_B}{p_A}\right)} \div \frac{\left(\frac{c_B}{c_A}\right)}{\left(\frac{p_B}{p_A}\right)},$$

where p_A and p_B are the prices of the two goods. It measures the percentage change in the relative consumption choice of two goods after a percentage change in their relative prices.

Similarly, define $\psi\left(c_t, c_s\right) \equiv \mathrm{ES}\left(c_t, c_s\right)$ as the elasticity of *intertemporal* substitution of consumption c_t and c_s at two points in time t and $s \geq t$. By the first-order conditions, $\beta\frac{u'(c_B)}{u'(c_A)} = \frac{p_B}{p_A}$,

$$\begin{aligned} \psi\left(c_t, c_s\right) &= -\frac{d\left(c_s / c_t\right)}{d\left(u'\left(c_s\right) / u'\left(c_t\right)\right)} \frac{u'\left(c_s\right) / u'\left(c_t\right)}{c_s / c_t} \\ &= -\frac{d\left(c_s / c_t\right)}{\left(c_s / c_t\right)} \div \frac{db}{b} = \frac{d\left(c_s / c_t\right) / \left(c_s / c_t\right)}{dR/R}, \end{aligned} \tag{3.5}$$

where b denotes the price of a zero-coupon bond and, accordingly, $b = \frac{\beta u'(c_s)}{u'(c_t)} \equiv R^{-1}$ and R denotes the gross interest rate from t to s. Note that we are assuming no uncertainty in these basic derivations.

The elasticity $\psi(c_t, c_s)$ is a measure of the percentage increase in the desired consumption tomorrow relative to today after a percentage decrease of the price of consumption tomorrow relative to today. Intuitively, high values of $\psi(c_t, c_s)$ describe a situation where the agent is quite sensitive about consuming at t and s: even a small increase in the interest rate R from t to s and hence a small percentage drop in b can induce them to a substantial relative increase of consumption in the future.

As $s \to t$, $\psi(c_t, c_s)$ collapses to the inverse of the elasticity of marginal utility with respect to consumption or simply the inverse of relative risk aversion

$$\begin{aligned}\frac{1}{\psi(c_t)} \equiv \lim_{s\to t} \frac{1}{\psi(c_t, c_s)} &= -\lim_{s\to t} \frac{c_s/c_t}{u'(c_s)/u'(c_t)} \frac{d\left(u'(c_s)/u'(c_t)\right)}{d\left(c_s/c_t\right)} \\ &= -\lim_{s\to t} \frac{d\left(1 + c_t \frac{u''(c_t)}{u'(c_t)}\left(\frac{c_s}{c_t} - 1\right)\right)}{d\left(\frac{c_s}{c_t}\right)} \\ &= -c_t \frac{u''(c_t)}{u'(c_t)},\end{aligned}$$

where the second equality follows by a first-order Taylor's expansion of the marginal utility of consumption at time s, $u'(c_s) = u'(c_t) + u''(c_t)(c_s - c_t) + O((c_s - c_t)^2)$. The expression for $\psi(c_t)$ is referred to as instantaneous "elasticity of intertemporal substitution."

For example, in the CRRA case and again in the deterministic case, we have that, along an optimal consumption path, $\frac{c_{t+1}}{c_t} = (\beta R)^{1/\gamma}$, where γ is the CRRA; as R increases, it becomes more attractive to save and postpone consumption. In a stylized equilibrium with a representative agent, $\ln R = -\ln \beta + \gamma g$, where g denotes the growth rate of the economy. When g is high, more consumption will be available in the future, which mitigates the incentives to save and drives the interest rate R up.

An agent with a low ψ has a quite inelastic demand for bonds. Intuitively, when the price of consumption in the future relative to today, b, drops, desired consumption tomorrow relative to today increases. But for an agent with a low ψ, the desired relative increase in future consumption is quite limited and so is their additional demand for bonds—the instruments that allow them to allocate intertemporal consumption.

3.2.4 Lucas's Model

3.2.4.1 The optimality condition

We consider markets for m "trees," that is, assets that distribute perishable fruits, the "dividends." We assume that the only source of risk stems from the fluctuation of the dividends' vector, $D = [D_1, \cdots, D_m]$. We assume D is a Markov process and denote its conditional distribution with $P\left(D_{t+1} \middle| D_t\right)$. A representative agent solves the program

$$\begin{aligned} V(\theta_t, D_t) = &\max_{(c_{t+i}, \theta_{t+i})_{i=0}^{\infty}} E_t\left(\sum_{i=0}^{\infty} \beta^i u(c_{t+i})\right) \\ \text{s.t. } &c_t + S_t\theta_{t+1} = (S_t + D_t)\,\theta_t \end{aligned} \qquad [3.P2]$$

where E_t denotes the expectation given the information set as of time t and $\theta_{t+1} \in \mathbb{R}^m$ is chosen at time t. The program [3.P2] may be solved while relying on a recursive approach very similar to that of section 3.2.1, at least once the due account is made of uncertainty. The Bellman's equation is

$$V(\theta_t, D_t) = \max_{c_t, \theta_{t+1}} E_t \left[u(c_t) + \beta V(\theta_{t+1}, D_{t+1})\right] \quad \text{s.t.} \quad c_t + S_t\theta_{t+1} = (S_t + D_t)\,\theta_t. \tag{3.6}$$

Similarly as in section 3.2.1, let us replace the budget constraint into the maximand in (3.6). The first-order conditions for θ_i are

$$0 = E_t\left[-u'\left((S_t + D_t)\,\theta_t - S_t\theta_{t+1}\right) S_{i,t} + \beta V_{1i}\left(\theta_{t+1}, D_{t+1}\right)\right], \tag{3.7}$$

where $V_{1i}(\theta, D) = \partial V(\theta, D)/\partial\theta_i$. The optimal policy, θ_{t+1}, is a function of the current state, (θ_t, D_t), say $\theta_{t+1} = \mathcal{T}(\theta_t, D_t)$. Differentiating the value function with respect to θ_i and using the previous first-order condition leaves us with

$$\begin{aligned} V_{1i}(\theta_t, D_t) &= E_t\left[u'(c_t)\left(S_{i,t} + D_{i,t} - \sum_{j=1}^{m} S_{j,t}\mathcal{T}_{1i}^{j}(\theta_t, D_t)\right)\right. \\ &\qquad \left. + \beta\sum_{j=1}^{m} V_{1j}\left(\theta_{t+1}, D_{t+1}\right)\mathcal{T}_{1i}^{j}(\theta_t, D_t)\right] \\ &= u'(c_t)\left(S_{i,t} + D_{i,t}\right), \end{aligned}$$

where $\mathcal{T}_{1j}^{i}(\theta_t, D_t) \equiv \partial\mathcal{T}_i(\theta, D)/\partial\theta_j$ and $\mathcal{T}_i$ is the ith component of the vector $\mathcal{T}$. Substituting this result into eq. (3.7) yields precisely the Lucas equation (3.4), holding for each asset i:

$$u'(c_t) = \beta E_t\left(u'\left(c_{t+1}\right)\frac{S_{i,t+1} + D_{i,t+1}}{S_{i,t}}\right). \tag{3.8}$$

It is easy to extend these conditions to the case in which the agent may also invest into a locally riskless asset, that is, an asset that expires in one period and delivers a certain payoff equal to one. In this case, the budget constraint in eq. (3.6) is $c_t + S_t\theta_{t+1} + S_{0,t}\theta_{0,t+1} = (S_t + D_t)\,\theta_t + \theta_{0,t}$, where $\theta_{0,t}$ denotes units of the locally riskless asset, $S_{0,t} \equiv e^{-r_t}$, and r_t is the riskless interest rate; and the Lucas equation for r_t would be $e^{-r_t} = \beta E_t\left(u'\left(c_{t+1}\right)/u'(c_t)\right)$.

3.2.4.2 *Rational expectations equilibrium*

The asset market clears when, for each t, $\theta_t = \mathbf{1}_m$ and $\theta_{0,t} = 0$. By the budget constraint, the market for goods also clears, $c_t = \sum_{i=1}^{m} D_{it} \equiv \bar{D}_t$. A *rational expectation equilibrium* is a sequence of asset prices $(S_t)_{t=0}^{\infty}$ such that the optimality condition in eq. (3.8) holds, the markets clear, $c_t = \bar{D}_t$, and each asset price is a function of the state, $S_{i,t} = S_i(D_t)$, say. That is,

$$u'(\bar{D}_t)S_i(D_t) = \beta\int u'(\bar{D}_{t+1})\left(S_i(D_{t+1}) + D_{i,t+1}\right) dP\left(D_{t+1}\middle| D_t\right). \tag{3.9}$$

Eq. (3.9) is a functional equation for $S_i(\cdot)$. We first focus on the independent and identically distributed (IID) case, $P\left(D_{t+1}\middle| D_t\right) = P\left(D_{t+1}\right)$. We shall comment on the notion of rational expectations in section 3.3.

IID shocks Eq. (3.9) simplifies to

$$u'(\bar{D}_t)S_i(D_t) = \beta \int u'(\bar{D}_{t+1})\left(S_i(\bar{D}_{t+1}) + D_{i,t+1}\right) dP\left(D_{t+1}\right). \tag{3.10}$$

Note that the RHS of this equation is independent of D. Therefore, $u'(\bar{D}_t)S_i(D_t)$ equals some constant κ_i (say); this constant may be found by substituting it back into the previous equation, leaving

$$\kappa_i = \frac{\beta}{1-\beta} \int u'(\bar{D}_{t+1}) D_{i,t+1} dP\left(D_{t+1}\right).$$

Therefore, the solution for $S_i(D)$ is

$$S_i(D_t) = \frac{\kappa_i}{u'(\bar{D}_t)}.$$

Note that the elasticity of the price to dividend equals $-\frac{u''(\bar{D})}{u'(\bar{D})} D_i$. It collapses to relative risk aversion in an economy with only one tree. For example, and assuming a CRRA equal to γ,

$$S(D_t) = \kappa \cdot D_t^{\gamma}, \quad \kappa \equiv \frac{\beta}{1-\beta} \int D^{1-\gamma} dP(D).$$

Thus, in this example, the asset price collapses to a constant, $\beta(1-\beta)^{-1}E(D)$, when the representative agent is risk neutral, $\gamma = 0$.

Dependent shocks Next, define the function $g_i(D) \equiv u'(\bar{D})S_i(D)$ and $h_i(D) \equiv \beta \int u'(\bar{D}_{t+1}) D_{i,t+1} dP(D_{t+1} | D)$. In terms of this new function, eq. (3.9) is

$$g_i(D) = h_i(D) + \beta \int g_i\left(D_{t+1}\right) dP\left(D_{t+1} \middle| D\right),$$

that is, a functional equation in g_i. We can show that, under regularity conditions, this equation has a unique solution. Consider the following result, known as the Blackwell's or "contraction" theorem.

Theorem 3.1. *Let $\mathcal{B}(X)$ the space of continuous bounded real functions on $X \subseteq \mathbb{R}^n$ endowed with the norm $\|f\| = \sup_X |f|$, $f \in \mathcal{B}(X)$. Consider the operator $T : \mathcal{B}(X) \mapsto \mathcal{B}(X)$ with the following properties:*

(i) *T is monotone: $\forall x \in X$ and $f_1, f_2 \in \mathcal{B}(X)$, $f_1(x) \leq f_2(x) \Longleftrightarrow T\left[f_1\right](x) \leq T\left[f_2\right](x)$;*
(ii) *$\forall x \in X$ and $c \geq 0$, $\exists \beta \in (0,1) : T\left[f + c\right](x) \leq T\left[f\right](x) + \beta c$.*

Then, $\forall f_0 \in \mathcal{B}(X)$, T has a unique fixed point $\lim_{\tau \to \infty} T^{\tau}\left[f_0\right] = f = T\left[f\right]$.

So let us introduce the following operator:

$$T\left[g_i\right](D) = h_i(D) + \beta \int g_i(D') \, dP\left(D' \middle| D\right).$$

The existence of g_i and hence S_i relies on the existence of a fixed point of $T : g_i = T[g_i]$. It is easily checked that conditions (i) and (ii) in theorem 3.1 hold. To establish that $T : \mathcal{B}(D) \mapsto \mathcal{B}(D)$ as well, it is sufficient to show that $h_i \in \mathcal{B}(D)$. A sufficient condition given by Lucas (1978) is that u is zero at the origin and bounded away by a constant $\bar{u}$.[2] Note that a log-utility agent would not satisfy this condition, yet this case can be easily solved in the case of a single tree, as shown next.

Suppose, then, that $u(c) = \ln c$ and that there is one single asset, such that eq. (3.9) collapses to

$$\frac{S(D_t)}{D_t} = \beta \int \left(\frac{S(D_{t+1})}{D_{t+1}} + 1 \right) dP(D_{t+1} | D_t).$$

The solution to this equation is a constant price-dividend ratio,

$$\frac{S(D_t)}{D_t} = \frac{\beta}{1-\beta}.$$

Note that this result does not depend on any distribution assumption on the dividend process. However, we cannot say more in the general CRRA case, and not even in the single asset case. Indeed, by eq. (3.9),

$$\frac{S(D_t)}{D_t} = \beta \int \left(\frac{D_{t+1}}{D_t} \right)^{1-\gamma} \left(\frac{S(D_{t+1})}{D_{t+1}} + 1 \right) dP(D_{t+1} | D_t).$$

It is easily seen that the solution to this functional equation is

$$\frac{S(D_t)}{D_t} = \frac{\beta \int \left(\frac{D_{t+1}}{D_t} \right)^{1-\gamma} dP(D_{t+1} | D_t)}{1 - \beta \int \left(\frac{D_{t+1}}{D_t} \right)^{1-\gamma} dP(D_{t+1} | D_t)},$$

such that the price-dividend ratio is constant whenever the distribution of the consumption endowment growth rate is independent of D_t. In chapter 7, we develop this case in more detail, assuming a log-normal distribution for D_{t+1}/D_t.

3.2.4.3 *Arrow-Debreu state prices*

The model makes sharp predictions regarding the price of the Arrow-Debreu securities. Relying on terminology introduced in chapter 2, we want to identify the *pricing kernel*. By the asset pricing equation (3.10), the pricing kernel is

$$m_{t+1} \equiv \beta \frac{u'(D_{t+1})}{u'(D_t)}.$$

Under regularity conditions, the Radon-Nikodym derivative of the risk neutral probability, Q, with respect to P, is

$$\left. \frac{dQ}{dP} \right|_{D_{t+1}|D_t} \equiv \frac{u'(D_{t+1})}{E\left[u'(D_{t+1} | D_t)\right]},$$

2. In this case, concavity of u implies that for each D, $0 = u(0) \leq u(D) + u'(D)(-D) \leq \bar{u} - Du'(D)$, which implies that for each D, $Du'(D) \leq \bar{u}$ and hence $h_i(D) \leq \beta\bar{u}$. Then it is possible to show that the solution is in $\mathcal{B}(D)$, which implies that $T : \mathcal{B}(D) \mapsto \mathcal{B}(D)$.

such that the Arrow-Debreu state price density is $dQ^*\left(D_{t+1}\middle|D_t\right)=R_t^{-1}dQ\left(D_{t+1}\middle|D_t\right)$. It is the price to pay in state D_t to obtain one unit of the good in the next period when the state is D_{t+1}. These conclusions generalize those of chapter 2 to the infinite horizon case. Parts II and III contain many examples of pricing kernels that are useful to address empirical puzzles or applied issues arising in both equity and fixed income markets.

3.2.4.4 *Multiple trees*

The Lucas model is actually quite complex: eq. (3.9) tells us that the price of any asset depends on the dividends paid by all the remaining assets. Therefore, the model may generate "contagion," in that a shock in the fundamentals that affects some asset returns may also affect all the remaining asset returns, even when dividends are not correlated. These interesting properties simply arise because there is a representative agent who is pricing all these assets. More generally, these properties would result even in economies with heterogenous agents: provided markets are not segmented, a shock to the pricing kernel, m_{t+1}, affects all the asset returns, $S_{i,t}$. Chapter 9 (see section 9.9) discusses additional channels and some tractable models, leading to correlation. Correlation may simply arise due to equilibrium forces that lead all asset prices to clear the markets.

3.3 Production: Foundational Issues

Many models in financial economics rely on the assumption that the asset payoffs are exogenously given. This book not only relies on such models but also provides some details regarding asset prices in production economies. Models of production economies are actually very important. To illustrate, corporations take production decisions while being subject to financial constraints, and financial constraints may depend on the state of the economy. Thus, the state of the economy may exacerbate business cycle conditions: after a negative shock, corporations may have more limited access to financing (due, for instance, to limited credit availability) and invest less, not only due to the initial shock but also to the financial frictions (the constraints). Chapter 9 provides more advanced discussions of these and related topics (see section 9.11). Chapter 5 also reviews some type of financial frictions that may be responsible for these phenomena.

This and the following section provide the basic analytical foundations that allow us to think about production economies in the *absence of frictions*. In these economies, firms maximize their value and set dividends endogenously. Accordingly, production and capital accumulation are endogenous. In this section, we review foundational issues for economies with productive capital. In section 3.4, we point to some asset pricing implications of these economies.

3.3.1 Decentralized Economy

We consider an economy with a continuum of identical firms, say, in $(0,1)$. These firms work while drawing resources from capital and labor markets. Technology is summarized by a production function $Y(K,N)$, which is continuous and twice differentiable in capital K and labor, N, with $Y_i(K,N)>0$, $y_{ii}(K,N)<0$, $\lim_{K\to 0+}Y_1(K,N)=\lim_{N\to 0+}Y_2(K,N)=\infty$, $\lim_{K\to\infty}Y_1(K,N)=\lim_{N\to\infty}Y_2(K,N)=0$, and subscripts denoting partial derivatives. We assume Y is homogeneous of degree one and then define per capita production as $y(k) \equiv Y(k,1)$, where $k \equiv K/N$ is per capita capital. Consumers' population grows at a rate equal to n: it satisfies $N_t/N_{t-1} = (1+n)$. Firms purchase capital and labor at prices $R = Y_1(K,N)$ and $w = Y_2(K,N)$. That is,

$$R = y'(k), \quad w = y(k) - ky'(k). \tag{3.11}$$

Consumers live forever. Each of them has an instantaneous utility over consumption c_t, denoted as $u(c_t)$ and a discount factor β and offers inelastically one unit of labor. The utility has standard properties such as $u' \geq 0$ and $u'' \leq 0$. To simplify the presentation in this section, assume that $N_0 = 1$ and $n = 0$. The resource constraint for our representative consumer is, then,

$$c_t + s_t = R_t s_{t-1} + w_t N_t, \quad N_t \equiv 1, \quad t = 1, 2, \cdots. \tag{3.12}$$

At each time $t-1$, the consumer saves s_{t-1} units of capital, which they lend to the firm: at time t, they receive the gross return on savings from the firm, $R_t s_{t-1}$, where $R_t = y'(k_t)$ plus the wage receipts $w_t N_t$. Their problem, then, is how to allocate these resources to consumption c_t and lending s_t. At time zero,

$$c_0 + s_0 = V_0 \equiv Y_1(K_0, N_0)K_0 + w_0 N_0, \quad N_0 \equiv 1.$$

Similarly, as in the two-period economies of chapter 2, we can write down a single budget constraint, obtained by iterating on eq. (3.12):

$$0 = c_0 + \sum_{t=1}^{T} \frac{c_t - w_t N_t}{\prod_{i=1}^{t} R_i} + \frac{s_T}{\prod_{i=1}^{T} R_i} - V_0.$$

We need to assume that the following transversality condition holds:

$$\lim_{T \to \infty} s_T \prod_{i=1}^{T} R_i^{-1} = 0, \tag{3.13}$$

such that the representative agent program is

$$\max_{(c_t)_{t=0}^{\infty}} \sum_{t=1}^{\infty} \beta^t u(c_t), \quad \text{s.t.} \quad V_0 = c_0 + \sum_{t=1}^{\infty} \frac{c_t - w_t N_t}{\prod_{i=1}^{t} R_i}. \tag*{[3.P3]}$$

The economic interpretation of the transversality condition (3.13) is the following. Note that the first-order conditions of the program [3.P3] are

$$\beta^t u'(c_t) = l \frac{1}{\prod_{i=1}^{t} R_i}, \tag{3.14}$$

where l is a Lagrange multiplier. In equilibrium, current savings equals next period capital or $k_{t+1} = s_t$. Therefore, eq. (3.13) is

$$\lim_{T \to \infty} \beta^T u'(c_T) k_{T+1} = 0. \tag{3.15}$$

The meaning of eq. (3.15) is that the value of capital (i.e., capital weighted by discounted marginal utility) becomes worthless eventually. We shall have to make sure that the model solution is consistent with eq. (3.15).

The first-order condition (3.14) leads to the usual Euler condition in eq. (3.3), where (now) $R_{t+1} = y'(k_{t+1})$. An equilibrium in this economy is a sequence $(c_t, k_t)_{t=0}^{\infty}$, satisfying

$$\begin{cases} k_{t+1} = y(k_t) - c_t \\ \beta \dfrac{u'(c_{t+1})}{u'(c_t)} = \dfrac{1}{y'(k_{t+1})} \end{cases} \tag{3.16}$$

and the transversality condition in eq. (3.15). The first equation of this system simply states that capital available for production at time $t+1$, k_{t+1}, is equal to savings, that is, $s_t \equiv y(k_t) - c_t$. It relies on the assumption that capital totally depreciates from one period to another, an assumption relaxed in the next section (and in appendix 3.B). The second is the Euler equation.

3.3.2 The Social Planner Solution

3.3.2.1 Recursive plan

The market solution (3.16) can be implemented by a social planner, who solves the following program,

$$\begin{aligned} V(k_0) &\equiv \max_{(c_t, k_t)_{t=0}^{\infty}} \sum_{i=0}^{\infty} \beta^i u(c_t) \\ \text{s.t. } k_{t+1} &= y(k_t) - c_t, \quad k_0 \text{ given} \end{aligned} \qquad [3.P4]$$

provided the transversality condition holds in eq. (3.15).

This program is easily solved. Replacing the constraint into the utility function and taking derivatives with respect to k_t leads directly to the second equation in (3.16). Alternatively, let us introduce the Lagrangian

$$\mathcal{L}(k_0) = \max_{(c_t, k_{t+1})_{t=0}^{\infty}} \sum_{t=0}^{\infty} \left(\beta^t u(c_t) - \lambda_t \left(k_{t+1} - y(k_t) + c_t\right)\right).$$

The first-order condition with respect to consumption is $\lambda_t = \beta^t u'(c_t)$, and the condition for capital is $\lambda_{t-1} = \lambda_t y'(k_t)$. Putting these conditions together leads to the second equation in (3.16). The same argument can be made following a recursive approach. We have:

$$\mathcal{L}(k_t) = \max_{c_t, k_{t+1}, \lambda_t} \left(u(c_t) - \lambda_t \left(k_{t+1} - y(k_t) + c_t\right) + \beta \mathcal{L}(k_{t+1})\right).$$

The first-order condition for consumption is $\lambda_t = u'(c_t)$ and for capital is $\lambda_t = \beta \mathcal{L}'(k_{t+1})$. Replacing the first-order condition for λ_t (i.e., the constraint in program [3.P4]) and differentiating with respect to k_t yields $\mathcal{L}'(k_t) = \beta \mathcal{L}'(k_{t+1}) y'(k_t)$. These three conditions lead, again, to the second equation in (3.16).

Finally, consider the Bellman's equation:

$$V(k_t) = \max_{c_t} \left(u(c_t) + \beta V(k_{t+1})\right), \quad \text{s.t. } k_{t+1} = y(k_t) - c_t.$$

The first-order condition leads to, $u'(c_t) = \beta V'(y(k_t) - c_t)$. Let us denote the policy function with $c_t = c(k_t)$. In terms of this function, the value function and the first-order conditions are

$$V(k_t) = u(c(k_t)) + \beta V(y(k_t) - c(k_t)), \quad u'(c(k_t)) = \beta V'(y(k_t) - c(k_t)).$$

By differentiating the value function,

$$V'(k_t) = u'(c(k_t))\, c'(k_t) + \beta V'(y(k_t) - c(k_t))\,(y'(k_t) - c'(k_t)) = u'(c(k_t))\, y'(k_t).$$

By replacing back into the first-order condition, we obtain the second equation in (3.16).

3.3.2.2 *Transversality condition again*

We may derive the transversality condition with the following arguments. Consider the following "truncated program"

$$\max_{(c_t, k_{t+1})_{t=0}^{T}} \sum_{t=0}^{T} \left(\beta^t u(c_t) - \lambda_t \left(k_{t+1} - y(k_t) + c_t\right)\right), \quad \text{s.t. } \lambda_T K_{T+1} = 0.$$

The first-order conditions are the usual ones. Moreover, replacing $\beta^T u'(c_T) = \lambda_T$ into the constraint of the program leaves $\beta^T u'(c_T) K_{T+1} = 0$. Taking the limit for T large yields eq. (3.15).

3.3.3 Dynamics

We study the dynamics of the system of eqs. (3.16) around a small neighborhood of the stationary state. The stationary state, or steady state, is defined as the pair (c, k), solution to

$$c = y(k) - k, \quad \beta = \frac{1}{y'(k)}.$$

A first-order expansion of each equation in (3.16) around (c, k) yields the following linear system:

$$\begin{pmatrix} \bar{k}_{t+1} \\ \bar{c}_{t+1} \end{pmatrix} = A \begin{pmatrix} \bar{k}_t \\ \bar{c}_t \end{pmatrix}, \quad A \equiv \begin{pmatrix} y'(k) & -1 \\ -\frac{u'(c)}{u''(c)} y''(k) & 1 + \beta \frac{u'(c)}{u''(c)} y''(k) \end{pmatrix}, \tag{3.17}$$

where $\bar{x}_t$ denotes the deviation of the value of any variable x_t from its stationary value, for example, $\bar{k}_{t+1} = k_{t+1} - k$. The solution to this system, obtained with the standard tools reviewed in appendix 3.A, is

$$\bar{k}_t = v_{11}\kappa_1\lambda_1^t + v_{12}\kappa_2\lambda_2^t, \quad \bar{c}_t = v_{21}\kappa_1\lambda_1^t + v_{22}\kappa_2\lambda_2^t, \tag{3.18}$$

where κ_i are constants that depend on the initial state, λ_i are the eigenvalues of A, and $\binom{v_{11}}{v_{21}}$, $\binom{v_{12}}{v_{22}}$ are the eigenvectors associated with λ_1 and λ_2. In appendix 3.A, we show that $\lambda_1 \in (0, 1)$ and $\lambda_2 > 1$. The proof in appendix 3.A provides some indications on how the model in this section may be modified in a way to lead to indeterminacies in the dynamics of consumption and capital. A critical step in that proof relies on the assumption of diminishing returns, that is, $y''(k) < 0$.

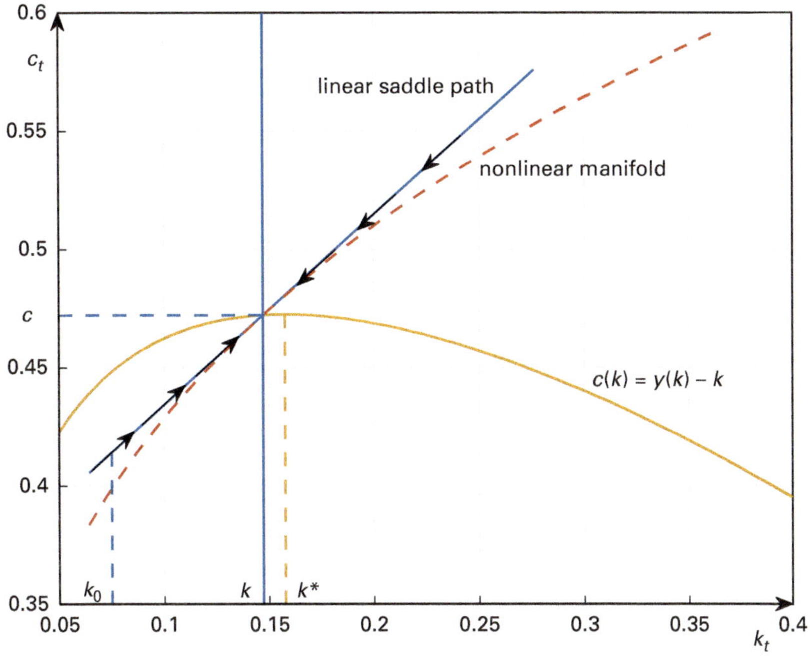

Figure 3.1
Dynamics of consumption and capital in the neoclassical model of capital accumulation. The linear saddle path equation is $c_0 = c + \frac{v_{21}}{v_{11}}(k_0 - k)$, which is a linear approximation to the equilibrium manifold. In this example, the nonlinear manifold is given by the first equation in (3.19), the vertical line is the equation $k = (y')^{-1}[\beta^{-1}] = 0.1471$, and the Golden Rule level of capital is $k^* = (y')^{-1}[1] = 0.1575$.

Let us return to eqs. (3.18). First, we need to rule out an explosive behavior of $\bar{k}_t$ and $\bar{c}_t$, for otherwise we would contradict that (c, k) is a stationary point and the optimality of the trajectories. Since $\lambda_2 > 1$, the only possibility is to "lock" the initial state $(\bar{k}_0, \bar{c}_0)$ in such a way that $\kappa_2 = 0$, which yields the following set of initial conditions: $\bar{k}_0 = v_{11}\kappa_1$ and $\bar{c}_0 = v_{21}\kappa_1$, or $\frac{\bar{c}_0}{\bar{k}_0} = \frac{v_{21}}{v_{11}}$. Therefore, the set of initial points that ensure a non explosive path must lie on the line $c_0 = c + \frac{v_{21}}{v_{11}}(k_0 - k)$. Since k is a predetermined variable, there exists one and only one value of c_0, which ensures a nonexplosive path of the system around its steady state (see figure 3.1). In figure 3.1, we define k^* as the solution of $1 = y'(k^*) \Leftrightarrow k^* = (y')^{-1}[1]$. It is the per capita capital that maximizes consumption in steady state (in the absence of the optimizing behavior). It is known as the *Golden Rule* of capital accumulation. Instead, $k = (y')^{-1}[\beta^{-1}]$ is the steady state in the economy of this section. Clearly, we have that $k < k^*$. We shall return to the notion of Golden Rule in section 3.6.

A linear approximation around the steady state needs to be interpreted with caution. The approximation may be poor while the system is far from the steady state. In fact, the phase diagram of figure 3.1 is related to the following example, in which $u(c) = \ln c$ and the production function is Cobb-Douglas $y(k) = k^\alpha$. It is easy to show that, in this case, the exact solution is

$$c_t = (1 - \beta\alpha)\, k_t^\alpha, \quad k_{t+1} = \beta\alpha k_t^\alpha. \tag{3.19}$$

The dashed line of figure 3.1 depicts the nonlinear manifold of this system (i.e., the first of the previous equations) and its linear approximation (the saddle path), assuming that $\beta = 0.95$ and $\alpha = 0.25$. These values imply that $\lambda_1 = 0.25$ and $\varphi \equiv \frac{v_{21}}{v_{11}} = 0.8026$, such that the linear saddle path is

$$c_t = c + \varphi\left(k_t - k\right), \quad k_t - k = \lambda_1\left(k_{t-1} - k\right), \text{ where } c = (1 - \beta\alpha)\, k^{\alpha}, \quad k = (\beta\alpha)^{1/(1-\alpha)}.$$

In this example, the quality of the approximation is seen to deteriorate as the system moves away from the steady state.

3.3.4 Stochastic Economies

> Real business cycle theory is the application of general equilibrium theory to the quantitative analysis of business cycle fluctuations.
> — Edward Prescott (1991, 3)

> The Kydland and Prescott model is a complete markets set-up, in which equilibrium and optimal allocations are equivalent. When it was introduced, it seemed to many—myself included—to be much too narrow a framework to be useful in thinking about cyclical issues.
> — Lucas (1994, 184)

In its simplest version, real business cycle theory is an extension of the neoclassical model of section 3.3.3, whereby technology is affected by random productivity shocks. The engine of fluctuations lies, then, within the real sphere of the economy. This explanation of economic fluctuations stands in sharp contrast with other approaches to the analysis of the business cycle, such as those developed by Lucas in the 1970s (see, e.g., Lucas, 1972). In Lucas's approaches that are based on information and money, the origins of fluctuations link to information delays with which agents discover the nature of a shock (real or monetary) (see, e.g., the short review in section 10.2 of chapter 10). Interestingly, Lucas's information-theoretic approach to the analysis of business cycles reveals to be very useful when understanding asset prices in models with asymmetric information. This link, often neglected in the literature, is instead emphasized in chapter 10.

The focus of this section is an introduction to the most basic version of real business cycle theory which (as in the information-based approach of Lucas) relies on *rational expectations*: macroeconomic fluctuations and then, as we shall explain, asset prices fluctuations stem from the optimal response of the agents vis-à-vis exogenous shocks: agents implement action plans that are state contingent, that is, they decide to consume, to work, and to invest according to the history of shocks as well as to the present shocks they observe. Chapter 2 contains introductory and succinct discussions of the notion of rational expectations and the historical intellectual developments leading to this concept (see, e.g., section 2.6). Note that the model of this section is very basic and relies on assumptions such as absence of frictions in goods and financial markets. The macroeconomic literature has produced well-known extensions (along the so-called new Keynesian tradition), which also accommodate for the presence of frictions and enable one to study the effects of monetary policy. Galí (2008) contains a useful review of some of the main extensions. Chapter 9 contains some details of models of business cycle fluctuations with financial frictions (see section 9.11).

3.3.4.1 *A basic model*

We consider an economy with complete markets and no frictions such that its equilibrium allocations are Pareto optimal. To characterize these allocations, note that they may be implemented through the following social planner program:

$$V(k_0, s_0) = \max_{(c_t)_{t=0}^{\infty}} E\left(\sum_{t=0}^{\infty} \beta^t u(c_t)\right), \tag{3.20}$$

subject to the capital accumulation constraint

$$I_t = K_{t+1} - (1-\delta) K_t, \tag{3.21}$$

where I_t denotes new investments and δ is a depreciation rate. That is, at time $t-1$, the available productive capital is K_t. At time t, a portion δK_t of this capital is lost due to depreciation. Therefore, at time t, the productive system is left with $(1-\delta) K_t$ units of capital. The capital available at time t, K_{t+1}, equals the capital already in place, $(1-\delta) K_t$, plus new investments, which is exactly what eq. (3.21) says.

Next, we keep on with the convention that the population is normalized to one such that $K_t = k_t$. The market clearing condition in the good market is

$$\tilde{y}(k_t, s_t) = c_t + I_t,$$

where $\tilde{y}(k_t, s_t)$ is the production function and s_t is the source of randomness, the engine for random fluctuations of the endogenous variables. By replacing eq. (3.21) into the equilibrium condition,

$$k_{t+1} = \tilde{y}(k_t, s_t) - c_t + (1-\delta) k_t. \tag{3.22}$$

So the planner maximizes the utility in eq. (3.20) under the capital accumulation constraint in eq. (3.22).

We assume that $\tilde{y}(k_t, s_t) \equiv s_t y(k_t)$, where y is as in section 3.2 and $(s_t)_{t=0}^{\infty}$ is the solution to

$$s_{t+1} = s_t^{\rho} \epsilon_{t+1}, \tag{3.23}$$

where $\rho \in (0,1)$ and $(\epsilon_t)_{t=0}^{\infty}$ is an IID sequence with support being such that $s_t > 0$. In this economy, every asset is priced as in the Lucas's model in section 3.2. Therefore, the gross return on savings $s_. y'(k_.)$ satisfies

$$u'(c_t) = \beta E_t\left(u'(c_{t+1})\left(s_{t+1} y'(k_{t+1}) + 1 - \delta\right)\right). \tag{3.24}$$

A rational expectation equilibrium is a stochastic process $(c_t, k_t)_{t=0}^{\infty}$, satisfying eq. (3.22) and the Euler equation in (3.24), for a given k_0 and s_0.

We show the existence of a saddle path for the linearized version of eqs. (3.22)–(3.24) and assuming no uncertainty takes place, which implies determinacy of a stochastic Markov equilibrium (at least in its linearized form).[3] We study the behavior of $(k, c, s)_t$ in

3. A stochastic Markov equilibrium is a situation that implies the existence of a stationary probability measure, defined as $p(\mathcal{X}') = \int \pi(\mathcal{X}'|\mathcal{X}) dp(\mathcal{X})$, where $\mathcal{X}$ is the state of the economy and π is a transition measure. In this section, the state at time t is given by c_t, k_t.

a neighborhood of $\epsilon \equiv E(\epsilon_t)$. Let (c, k, s) be consumption, capital, and productivity shock corresponding to ϵ and obtained replacing ϵ into eqs. (3.22)–(3.24)

$$c = sy(k) - \delta k, \quad s = \epsilon^{\frac{1}{1-\rho}}, \quad \beta = \frac{1}{sy'(k) + 1 - \delta}.$$

A first-order approximation to eqs. (3.22)–(3.24) around (k, c, s) leaves

$$\hat{z}_{t+1} = \Phi \hat{z}_t + Qu_{t+1}, \tag{3.25}$$

where we have defined $\hat{x}_t \equiv \frac{x_t - x}{x}$, and $\hat{z}_t = (\hat{k}_t, \hat{c}_t, \hat{s}_t)^\top$, $u_t = (u_{c,t}, u_{s,t})^\top$, $u_{c,t} = \hat{c}_t - E_{t-1}(\hat{c}_t)$, $u_{s,t} = \hat{s}_t - E_{t-1}(\hat{s}_t) = \hat{\epsilon}_t$, and finally

$$\Phi = \begin{pmatrix} \beta^{-1} & -\frac{c}{k} & s\frac{y(k)}{k} \\ -\frac{u'(c)}{cu''(c)} sky''(k) & 1 + \frac{\beta u'(c)}{u''(c)} sy''(k) & -\frac{\beta u'(c)}{cu''(c)} s(sy(k)y''(k) + \rho y'(k)) \\ 0 & 0 & \rho \end{pmatrix},$$

$$Q = \begin{pmatrix} 0 & 0 \\ 1 & 0 \\ 0 & 1 \end{pmatrix}.$$

Consider the characteristic equation

$$0 = \det(\Phi - \lambda I) = (\rho - \lambda) \det(A' - \lambda I) = (\rho - \lambda) \det(A - \lambda I),$$

where A' is the 2×2 matrix obtained by taking the last row and the last column out of Φ and where A is the same matrix in the deterministic system (3.17). Therefore, one solution is $\lambda_1 = \rho$, and relying on the deterministic case (see section 3.3.3 and appendix 3.A), we have $\lambda_2 \in (0, 1)$ and $\lambda_3 > 1$.[4] Similarly as in the deterministic case, we diagonalize the system by rewriting $\Phi = P\Lambda P^{-1}$, where Λ is a diagonal matrix that has the eigenvalues of Φ on the diagonal and P is a matrix of the eigenvectors associated to the roots of Φ. Eq. (3.25) is then

$$\hat{y}_{t+1} = \Lambda \hat{y}_t + w_{t+1}, \tag{3.26}$$

where $\hat{y}_t \equiv P^{-1}\hat{z}_t$ and $w_t \equiv P^{-1}Qu_t$. The third equation of this system is

$$\hat{y}_{3,t+1} = \lambda_3 \hat{y}_{3t} + w_{3,t+1}, \tag{3.27}$$

and $\hat{y}_3$ explodes unless $\hat{y}_{3t} = 0$ for all t, which is only possible when $w_{3t} = 0$ for all t.[5]

The condition that $w_{3t} = 0$ carries an interesting economic interpretation: it tells us that the only sources of uncertainty in this system can stem from shocks to the fundamentals or that there cannot be extraneous sources of noise, also called "sunspots." Let us explain. Define $\Pi \equiv P^{-1}$, such that $w_{3t} = 0$ implies that there is a linear relation between the two

4. In the linearized model of this section, the state variables are expressed in growth rates. To reformulate the model in terms of first differences, we pre- and postmultiply Φ by appropriate normalizing matrices. For example, if G is the 3×3 matrix that has $\frac{1}{k}$, $\frac{1}{c}$, and $\frac{1}{s}$ on its diagonal, (3.25) can be written as $E(z_{t+1} - z) = G^{-1}\Phi G(z_t - z)$, where $z_t = (k_t, c_t, s_t)$.

5. In other words, eq. (3.27) implies that $\hat{y}_{3t} = \lambda_3^{-(T-t)} E_t(\hat{y}_{3,t+T})$ for all T. Because $\lambda_3 > 1$, this relation holds only when $\hat{y}_{3t} = 0$ for all t.

expectational errors (in consumption and technology), namely,

$$\text{for all } t, \; u_{ct} = -\frac{\pi_{33}}{\pi_{32}} u_{st} \quad (\text{“no sunspots”}). \tag{3.28}$$

Eq. (3.28) is a “no sunspots” condition in that it says that expectational errors in consumption cannot be independent of those of the economic fundamentals—in this case, technological shocks. The term “sunspots” is used to describe a phenomenon that in principle, should not affect the fundamentals of the economy (such as, say, sunspot activity) but that in fact might affect them. In terms of the simple economy of this section, the source of uncertainty in this economy is the presence of technological shocks, and any remaining expectational errors can only be perfectly correlated to these shocks. There are no sunspots: no “extraneous” sources of risk may affect the economy. Cass and Shell (1983) studied sunspots in general equilibrium. Section 3.3.4.2 provides further discussion on sunspots and some references to literature reviews.

Let us elaborate further on the condition that $\hat{y}_{3t} = 0$. Let $\hat{y}_t = P^{-1}\hat{z}_t \equiv \Pi \hat{z}_t$, such that

$$0 = \hat{y}_{3t} = \pi_{31}\hat{k}_t + \pi_{32}\hat{c}_t + \pi_{33}\hat{s}_t. \tag{3.29}$$

Eq. (3.29) tells us that the three state variables, $\hat{k}_t$, $\hat{c}_t$, and $\hat{s}_t$, are mutually linked in a two-dimensional plane, a saddle path in which they exhibit a stable behavior. This stable manifold is defined as

$$\mathcal{S} = \left\{ x \in \mathbb{R}^3 \middle| \pi_{3.}x = 0 \right\}, \quad \pi_{3.} = (\pi_{31}, \pi_{32}, \pi_{33}),$$

and bears the same meaning as that borne by the stable saddle path in figure 3.1 in the deterministic case. Precisely, $\mathcal{S}$ is the convergent subspace, with $\dim(\mathcal{S}) = 2$, that is, the number of roots with modulus less than one. In other words, in this economy with two predetermined variables, $\hat{k}_0$ and $\hat{s}_0$, there exists one and only one value of $\hat{c}_0 \in \mathcal{S}$ that ensures a stable path, which is given by $\hat{c}_0 = -\frac{\pi_{31}\hat{k}_0 + \pi_{33}\hat{s}_0}{\pi_{32}}$. This reasoning generalizes that in the deterministic case (section 3.3.3) and is generalized further in appendix 3.A.

3.3.4.2 Indeterminacy and sunspots

In this economy, the equilibrium is determinate: the number of predetermined variables is the same as the dimension of the stable manifold. Appendix 3.A explains that the equilibrium would be indeterminate if the stable manifold had a higher dimension. Intuitively, there would be many initial conditions and then many equilibrium paths consistent with a stable manifold. A simple example developed below illustrates how such indeterminacy of equilibria relates to the notion of sunspots introduced in the previous section.

Sunspots in macroeconomics have made the object of extensive research during the 1990s (see, e.g., Farmer, 1998, for early introductory reviews). The motivation behind these topics is certainly related to the notion of “animal spirits” that Keynes (1936) utilized to describe agents’ behavior: at times, investment or consumption decisions may be related to instinctive behavior; that is, one that goes beyond an extent that could be rationally justified by the fundamentals. Further, sunspots may be empirically relevant: it is well known since at least Watson (1993) that the basic real business cycle model needs many extensions to stand up to the scrutiny of data. The main issue is that the model seems to provide limited space for a rich propagation mechanism. It largely relies on large productivity shocks (the impulses). Yet, as provocatively put by King and Rebelo (1999), "if these shocks are large and important, why can't we read about them in the *Wall Street Journal*?" Sunspots offer an interesting route to enrich the propagation mechanism. Finally, sunspots may be used to describe phenomena such as a "bank run" (see section 10.9.4 in chapter 10): even if a bank is perfectly solvent, depositors may rationally run if they believe others will.

So how is it that a deterministic economy might generate "stochastic outcomes," that is, outcomes driven by shocks entirely unrelated to the fundamentals of the economy? Assume this is indeed the case, and consider the deterministic model in section 3.3.3. In the presence of sunspots, optimal consumption and capital would then be random processes such that eqs. (3.17) may be rewritten as

$$\begin{pmatrix} \hat{k}_{t+1} \\ \hat{c}_{t+1} \end{pmatrix} = A \begin{pmatrix} \hat{k}_t \\ \hat{c}_t \end{pmatrix} + \begin{pmatrix} 0 \\ u_{c,t+1} \end{pmatrix},$$

where we define the expectational error $u_{c,t} \equiv \hat{c}_t - E_{t-1}(\hat{c}_t)$. We know that $\lambda_1 \in (0,1)$ and $\lambda_2 > 1$, and defining $A = P\Lambda P^{-1}$, we can write the previous system as follows:

$$\hat{y}_{t+1} = \Lambda \hat{y}_t + P^{-1}(0 \quad u_{c,t+1})^{\top}.$$

Note that, for $\hat{y}_{2t} = \lambda_2^{-T} E_t(\hat{y}_{2,t+T})$ to hold for all T, we need that $\hat{y}_{2t} = 0$ for all t. Therefore, the second element of $P^{-1}(0 \quad u_{c,t+1})^{\top}$ must be zero, or for all t,

$$0 = \pi_{22} u_{c,t} \Longleftrightarrow 0 = u_{c,t}.$$

That is, in this model, there is no room for expectational errors and hence sunspots. This property is clearly due to the fact that $\lambda_2 > 1$: the dimension of the saddle path is lower than the number of predetermined variables, just as discussed in the previous section. Instead, equilibria with sunspots may arise in economies in which the saddle path has a dimension larger than one, that is, when $\lambda_2 < 1$. The dynamics of consumption and capital would then be indeterminate. In these economies, indeterminacy and sunspots represent two sides of the same coin. Why do we get that $\lambda_2 > 1$? A close inspection of results in appendix 3.A reveals that this property is due to the assumptions made on the utility and production functions, u and y. It is not surprising as it is known that sunspots equilibria may not be consistent with a Pareto-optimal economy such as the one in this section. Market imperfections have the potential to be a source of sunspots. Sources of deviation from optimality may be incomplete markets. In macroeconomics, a body of the literature surveyed by Farmer (1998) has focused on economies with externalities and increasing returns. At the time of writing, the asset pricing implications of these economies do not seem to have been explored yet.

3.4 Production-Based Asset Pricing

This section considers the asset pricing implications of a simple production economy: one in which capital adjustment is costly. This economy displays a series of properties described as "q-theory." This theory enables one to connect the value of a firm to the replacement cost of its capital.

3.4.1 Firms

We consider an economy with a continuum of identical firms. Each of these firms faces a capital accumulation law that satisfies eq. (3.21), reproduced here for convenience:

$$K_{t+1} = (1-\delta) K_t + I_t. \tag{3.30}$$

We make the additional assumption that capital adjustment is costly: investing I_t per unit of capital already in place, K_t, entails a cost $\phi(\frac{I_t}{K_t})$, expressed in terms of the price of the final good. We allow investment goods to differ from the final good that the firm produces and take the final good to be the numéraire. An investment of I_t then leads to a cost $\phi(\frac{I_t}{K_t})K_t$, such that the profit the firm makes at time t is

$$D(K_t, I_t) \equiv \tilde{y}(K_t, N(K_t)) - w_t N(K_t) - p_t I_t - \phi\left(\frac{I_t}{K_t}\right) K_t, \tag{3.31}$$

where $\tilde{y}(K_t, N_t)$ is the firm's production at time t, obtained with capital K_t and labor N_t and subject to the productivity shocks described in section 3.3.4; w_t is the real wage; $N(K)$ is the labor demand schedule, solution to the optimality condition, $\tilde{y}_N(K_t, N(K_t)) = w_t$ for all t; and p_t is the real price of the investment goods or uninstalled capital. Finally, the adjustment cost function satisfies $\phi \geq 0$, $\phi' \geq 0$, $\phi'' \geq 0$. In other words, capital adjustment is costly when the adjustment is made quickly. Naturally, ϕ is zero in the absence of adjustment costs. In appendix 3.B, we show that $D(K, I)$ is homogenous of degree one.

Each firm maximizes the *value* of the profit. We rely on the Arrow-Debreu state prices introduced in chapter 2. From the perspective of time 0, the profit at time t and in state s is worth

$$\phi_{0,t}(s) D(K_t(s), I_t(s)) = m_{0,t}(s) D_t(K_t(s), I_t(s)) P_{0,t}(s),$$

where $\phi_{0,t}(s)$ is the value at time 0 of an Arrow-Debreu security that pays \$1 at time t and in state s and $m_{0,t}(s)$ and $P_{0,t}(s)$ are the corresponding *stochastic discount factor* and probabilities.[6] To simplify notation, we now set $m_{t+1}(\cdot) \equiv m_{t,t+1}(\cdot)$ (the familiar pricing kernel).

3.4.1.1 *The value of the firm*

We assume that the firm distributes all the profits in each period and that, for a given capital K_0, it maximizes its *cum dividend* value

$$V_c(K_0) = \max_{(K_t, I_{t-1})_{t=1}^{\infty}} \left(D(K_0, I_0) + E\left(\sum_{t=1}^{\infty} m_{0,t} D(K_t, I_t) \right) \right),$$

subject to the capital accumulation law (3.30).

6. Chapter 4 contains formal definitions of stochastic discount factors both in discrete and continuous time.

The value of the firm at time t, $V_c(K_t)$, can be found recursively through the Bellman's equation,

$$V_c(K_t) = \max_{I_t} \left(D(K_t, I_t) + E_t \left(m_{t+1} V_c(K_{t+1}) \right) \right),$$

where the expectation is taken with respect to the information set as of time t. The first-order conditions for I_t lead to

$$-D_I(K_t, I_t) = E_t \left(m_{t+1} V_c'(K_{t+1}) \right). \tag{3.32}$$

That is, along the optimal capital accumulation path, the marginal cost of new installed capital at time t, $-D_I$, equals the risk-adjusted expected marginal return on the investment, defined as the expected value of the marginal contribution of existing capital to the value of the firm at time $t+1$, $V_c'(K_{t+1})$. Note that I_t adds to already existing capital, which was costly to install in the first place. Intuitively, then, $-D_I$ should be higher than p_t, the cost of uninstalled capital. We now formalize this intuition.

By eq. (3.32), optimal investment is a function $I(K_t)$, and the value of the firm satisfies

$$V_c(K_t) = D(K_t, I(K_t)) + E_t \left(m_{t+1} V_c(K_{t+1}) \right).$$

Differentiating the value function in the previous equation with respect to K_t and using eq. (3.32) yields the following envelope condition:

$$\begin{aligned} V_c'(K_t) &= D_K(K_t, I(K_t)) + D_I(K_t, I(K_t)) I'(K_t) \\ &\quad + E_t \left(m_{t+1} V_c'(K_{t+1}) \left((1-\delta) + I'(K_t) \right) \right) \\ &= D_K(K_t, I(K_t)) - (1-\delta) D_I(K_t, I(K_t)). \end{aligned}$$

Replacing this expression for the value function back into eq. (3.32) leaves

$$-D_I(K_t, I(K_t)) = E_t \left[m_{t+1} \left(D_K(K_{t+1}, I(K_{t+1})) - (1-\delta) D_I(K_{t+1}, I(K_{t+1})) \right) \right]. \tag{3.33}$$

Along the optimal capital accumulation path, the marginal cost of new installed capital at time t is equal to the risk-adjusted expected value of (i) the very same marginal cost at time $t+1$, corrected for capital depreciation, $(1-\delta)$, plus (ii) capital productivity, net of adjustment costs. Note that, by differentiating D with respect to I, we find

$$-D_I(K_t, I(K_t)) = p_t + \phi' \left(\frac{I_t}{K_t} \right). \tag{3.34}$$

We now introduce a fundamental concept in investment theory.

3.4.1.2 *q-theory*

The Tobin's *marginal* q is defined as the ratio of the risk-adjusted expected marginal value of an additional unit of capital over its replacement cost:

$$\mathrm{TQ}_t \equiv \text{Tobin's marginal q} \equiv \frac{E\left[m_{t+1} V_c'(K_{t+1}) \right]}{p_t}.$$

We show that the numerator, $E\left[m_{t+1}V_c'\left(K_{t+1}\right)\right]$, is the shadow price of installed capital. Consider the Lagrangian at time t,

$$V_c\left(K_t\right)=\max_{I_t,K_{t+1},q_t}\left(D\left(K_t,I_t\right)-q_t\left(K_{t+1}-(1-\delta)K_t-I_t\right)+E_t\left(m_{t+1}V_c\left(K_{t+1}\right)\right)\right), \tag{3.35}$$

which, when integrated, gives rise to the value of the firm:

$$V_c\left(K_0\right)=\max_{\left(I_t,K_{t+1}q_t\right)_{t=0}^{\infty}}E\left(\sum_{t=0}^{\infty}m_{0,t}\left(D\left(K_t,I_t\right)-q_t\left(K_{t+1}-(1-\delta)K_t-I_t\right)\right)\right).$$

The first-order condition for investment I_t is $q_t=-D_I\left(K_t,I_t\right)=E\left(m_{t+1}V_c'\left(K_{t+1}\right)\right)$, where the second equality follows by eq. (3.32). Therefore, q_t is the risk-adjusted expected marginal return on the investment, that is, the shadow price of installed capital. Finally, we write Tobin's marginal q as the ratio of the shadow price of installed capital to its replacement cost

$$\mathrm{TQ}_t=\frac{q_t}{p_t}.$$

Replacing the condition $q_t=-D_I\left(K_t,I_t\right)$ into eqs. (3.33)–(3.34) leaves

$$q_t=E_t\left[m_{t+1}\left(D_K\left(K_{t+1},I_{t+1}\right)+(1-\delta)q_{t+1}\right)\right] \tag{3.36}$$

and

$$q_t=p_t+\phi'\left(\frac{I_t}{K_t}\right). \tag{3.37}$$

The shadow price of installed capital, q_t, is equal to the marginal cost of new installed capital and is larger than the price of uninstalled capital, p_t. It is an intuitive property; to install new capital requires some (marginal) adjustment costs, which add to the "row" price of uninstalled capital, p_t. Therefore, in the presence of adjustment costs, Tobin's marginal q is larger than one.

Eq. (3.36) can be solved forward, leaving

$$q_t=E\left(\sum_{s=1}^{\infty}(1-\delta)^{s-1}m_{0,t+s}D_K\left(K_{t+s},I_{t+s}\right)\right). \tag{3.38}$$

The shadow price of installed capital is worth the sum of all its risk-adjusted expected marginal net productivity, discounted at the capital depreciation rate: installed capital depreciates and its impact on future productivity does so as well. Moreover, eq. (3.37) can be inverted for I_t/K_t,

$$\frac{I_t}{K_t}=\phi'^{-1}\left(q_t-p_t\right), \tag{3.39}$$

where ϕ'^{-1} denotes the inverse of ϕ' and is increasing since ϕ' is increasing. Given K_t, and the fact that K_{t+1} is predetermined, the firm determines q_t through eq. (3.36) and then the level of new investments through eq. (3.39). These investments are increasing in the difference between the shadow price of installed capital, q_t, and that of uninstalled capital, p_t, as originally assumed by Tobin (1969).

In the absence of adjustment costs, when $q_t = p_t$, eq. (3.36) delivers the condition

$$1 = E_t\left[m_{t+1}\left(\tilde{y}_K\left(K_{t+1}, N\left(K_{t+1}\right)\right) + (1-\delta)\right)\right],$$

where we have set $p_t \equiv 1$ for all t, meaning that the firm's production is just the uninstalled capital. This can be interpreted as an evaluation equation for the firm equity returns (see section 9.10.1 in chapter 9). Empirically, however, the marginal productivity of capital, $\tilde{y}_K(K_t, N(K_t))$, is not volatile enough to rationalize asset returns, as explained in more detail in chapter 9. Further, we now explain that Tobin's marginal q may be well approximated by market-to-book ratios, which are typically time-varying. Therefore, adjustment costs are important for asset pricing.

Tobin's marginal q is difficult to estimate. Yet in the special case analyzed in this section, where firms act competitively and have access to an homogeneous production function and adjustment costs, Tobin's marginal q simplifies considerably. Let $V(K_t)$ denote the ex-dividend value of the firm, which is its stock market value since it nets out the dividend it pays to its holder in the current period. It is

$$V(K_t) \equiv V_c(K_t) - D(K_t, I(K_t)) = E_t\left(m_{t+1} V_c\left(K_{t+1}\right)\right).$$

Tobin's *average* q is defined as the ratio of the stock market value of the firm over the replacement cost of the capital

$$\text{Tobin's average q} \equiv \frac{\text{Firm market value}}{\text{Replacement cost of capital}} = \frac{V(K_t)}{p_t K_{t+1}}$$

and can be interpreted as the "market-to-book" value of a firm.

We now state a celebrated result, which Hayashi (1982) originally obtained in a continuous time setting.

Theorem 3.2. *Tobin's marginal q and average q coincide, that is,*

$$V(K_t) = q_t K_{t+1}.$$

Proof. By the homogeneity properties of the production function and the adjustment costs,

$$D(K_t, I_t) = D_K(K_t, I_t) K_t + D_I(K_t, I_t) I_t.$$

Therefore, the ex-dividend value of the firm is

$$\begin{aligned} V(K_0, I_0) &= E\left(\sum_{t=1}^{\infty} m_{0,t} D(K_t, I_t)\right) \\ &= E\left(\sum_{t=1}^{\infty} m_{0,t}\left(D_K(K_t, I_t) - (1-\delta) D_I(K_t, I_t)\right) K_t\right) \\ &\quad + E\left(\sum_{t=1}^{\infty} m_{0,t} D_I(K_t, I_t) K_{t+1}\right), \end{aligned}$$

where the second line follows by eq. (3.30). By eq. (3.33) and the law of iterated expectations

$$E\left(\sum_{t=1}^{\infty} m_{0,t}\left(D_K\left(K_t, I_t\right)-(1-\delta) D_I\left(K_t, I_t\right)\right) K_t\right)$$
$$=-D_I\left(K_0, I_0\right) K_1-E\left(\sum_{t=1}^{\infty} m_{0,t} D_I\left(K_t, I_t\right) K_{t+1}\right).$$

Hence, $V\left(K_0, I_0\right)=-D_I\left(K_0, I_0\right) K_1=q_0 K_1$. □

This theorem suggests that market-to-book values are larger than one in the presence of adjustment costs. Further, this result, in conjunction with that in eq. (3.37), provides a simple rule of thumb for investment decisions. Consider, for example, the case of quadratic adjustment costs, where $\phi(x)=\frac{1}{2}\kappa^{-1}x^2$ for some $\kappa>0$. Then eq. (3.39) is

$$I_t=\kappa\left(q_t-p_t\right) K_t=\kappa\left(\frac{\text{Firm market value}}{\text{Replacement cost of capital}}-1\right) p_t K_t,$$

where the second equality follows by theorem 3.2. Thus, according to q-theory, firms grow when they have a market value higher than capital replacement costs and shrink otherwise.

Intuitively, investments increase with profitability: a firm that expects an increase in profits adjusts its investments to take new opportunities into account. Now, the stock market value of the firm reflects precisely expected profitability (adjusted for risk). Then, q-theory simply compares the firm market value with the replacement costs of capital: a firm should invest if the market evaluation of already installed capital (firm market value) is higher than the market value of the same capital. Indeed, there is empirical evidence that investments and Tobin's q are correlated. However, it may just be that this relation is merely driven by the factors that affect future profitability and that are already embedded in Tobin's q.

3.4.2 Consumers

Finally, we need to determine the stochastic discount factor. We generalize the budget constraint in [3.P3] (see section 3.3.1) to the uncertainty case. We claim that, in this case, the relevant budget constraint is

$$V_0=c_0+E\left(\sum_{t=1}^{\infty} m_{0,t}\left(c_t-w_t N_t\right)\right). \tag{3.40}$$

Indeed, we have that $c_t+S_t\theta_{t+1}=\left(S_t+D_t\right)\theta_t+w_t N_t$ and then

$$E\left(\sum_{t=1}^{\infty} m_{0,t}\left(c_t-w_t N_t\right)\right)=E\left(\sum_{t=1}^{\infty} m_{0,t}\left(S_t+D_t\right)\theta_t\right)-E\left(\sum_{t=1}^{\infty} m_{0,t} S_t \theta_{t+1}\right)$$
$$=E\left(\sum_{t=1}^{\infty} \underset{t-1}{E}\left(\frac{m_{0,t}}{m_{t-1,t}} m_{t-1,t}\left(S_t+D_t\right)\theta_t\right)\right)$$

$$
\begin{aligned}
&-E\left(\sum_{t=2}^{\infty} m_{0,t-1} S_{t-1}\theta_t\right)\\
&=E\left(\sum_{t=1}^{\infty} m_{0,t-1} S_{t-1}\theta_t\right)-E\left(\sum_{t=2}^{\infty} m_{0,t-1} S_{t-1}\theta_t\right)\\
&=S_0\theta_1=V_0-c_0,
\end{aligned}
$$

where the third line follows by the properties of the pricing kernel, $\frac{m_{0,t}}{m_{t-1,t}}=m_{0,t-1}$ and $m_t \equiv m_{t-1,t}$.

Therefore, the program consumers solve is

$$
\max_{(c_t)_{t=0}^{\infty}} E\left(\sum_{t=1}^{\infty} \beta^t u\left(c_t, N_t\right)\right), \quad \text{s.t. eq. (3.40).}
$$

We now have two optimality conditions, one intertemporal and another, intratemporal:

$$
m_{t+1}=\beta\frac{u_1\left(c_{t+1}, N_{t+1}\right)}{u_1\left(c_t, N_t\right)} \text{ (\textit{inter}temporal); } \quad w_t=-\frac{u_2\left(c_t, N_t\right)}{u_1\left(c_t, N_t\right)} \text{ (\textit{intra}temporal).}
$$

3.4.3 Equilibrium

In equilibrium, output equals consumption plus investments and the adjustment costs resulting from these investments. That is, for all t,

$$
\tilde{y}\left(K_t, N_t\right)=c_t+p_t I_t+\phi\left(\frac{I_t}{K_t}\right) K_t. \tag{3.41}
$$

Naturally, this condition follows by Walras's law. Indeed, it is easily seen that the equilibrium in the financial market, $\theta_t=1$, implies that $c_t=D_t+w_t N_t$. Replacing this condition into eq. (3.31) delivers the equilibrium condition in eq. (3.41). Implicit in these derivations is the idea that adjustment costs are not paid to anyone. They may be interpreted as capital losses the firm incurs along its way of growth. Finally, in a one-sector model, the investment good is the numéraire, such that $p_t=1$.

3.5 Production, Money, and Asset Prices in Overlapping Generations Models

Overlapping generations models (OLGs) are alternative representations of the dynamics of consumption and capital. These models were introduced by Allais (1947) and Samuelson (1958) and have been used since then to study a variety of phenomena and institutional arrangements such as money, social security, or bubbles. Perhaps less used are these models in financial economics. This section provides foundational issues arising in OLG economies related to capital accumulation, the dynamics of asset prices and interest rates, and bubbles. We study endowment economies, monetary economies, and economies with capital accumulation.

3.5.1 Introduction: Endowment Economies

3.5.1.1 A deterministic model

We initially assume the population is constant and made up of one young and one old individual. The young agent maximizes their intertemporal utility subject to their budget constraint

$$\max_{(c_{1t},c_{2,t+1})} \left(u\left(c_{1t}\right)+\beta u\left(c_{2,t+1}\right)\right), \quad \text{subject to} \begin{cases} \text{sav}_t + c_{1t} = w_{1t} \\ c_{2,t+1} = \text{sav}_t R_{t+1} + w_{2,t+1} \end{cases} \qquad [3.\text{P5}]$$

where w_{1t} and $w_{2,t+1}$ are the endowments the agent receives at their young and old age, sav_t is the amount of savings planned for time t, and β and u are the discount factor and utility function and are taken to satisfy the usual properties. Note that the agent born at time $t-1$ faces the constraints $\text{sav}_{t-1}+c_{1,t-1}=w_{1,t-1}$ and $c_{2t}=\text{sav}_{t-1}R_t+w_{2t}$. By combining their second period constraint with the first period constraint of the agent born at time t,

$$\text{sav}_{t-1}R_t + w_t = \text{sav}_t + c_{1t} + c_{2t}, \quad w_t \equiv w_{1t} + w_{2t}. \qquad (3.42)$$

Note that young people may only lend to each other. In this example, there is only one individual in each generation. Therefore, the equilibrium in the lending market is defined by the condition

$$\text{sav}_t = 0. \qquad (3.43)$$

Eq. (3.43) implies that the goods market is also in equilibrium, that is, $w_t=\sum_{i=1}^{2} c_{i,t}$, for all t. Therefore, the equilibrium in this model is one of an autarky equilibrium, that is, one in which no trade takes place. The first-order conditions for the program [3.P5] require that the slope of the indifference curve be equal to the slope of the lifetime budget constraint, $c_{2,t+1}=-R_{t+1}c_{1,t}+R_{t+1}w_{1t}+w_{2,t+1}$, such that

$$\beta\frac{u'(c_{2,t+1})}{u'(c_{1,t})}=\frac{1}{R_{t+1}}. \qquad (3.44)$$

The equilibrium, then, is a sequence of gross returns R_t satisfying eqs. (3.42), (3.43), and (3.44), or

$$b_t \equiv \frac{1}{R_{t+1}} = \beta\frac{u'(w_{2,t+1})}{u'(w_{1t})}. \qquad (3.45)$$

We interpret b_t as the shadow price of a bond issued at t and paying one unit of numéraire at $t+1$. The equilibrium prices b_t satisfy eq. (3.45) and are such that the agents are happy with not being able to lend or borrow.

This model may be extended to the case in which agents are heterogeneous. The program each agent j solves now is

$$\max_{(c_{1j,t},c_{2j,t+1})} \left(u_j\left(c_{1j,t}\right)+\beta_j u_j\left(c_{2j,t+1}\right)\right), \quad \text{subject to} \begin{cases} \text{sav}_{j,t} + c_{1j,t} = w_{1j,t} \\ c_{2j,t+1} = \text{sav}_{j,t} R_{t+1} + w_{2j,t+1} \end{cases}$$

with obvious notation. The first-order conditions are, for all t and each agent j,

$$b_t \equiv \frac{1}{R_{t+1}} = \beta_j\frac{u_j'\left(c_{2j,t+1}\right)}{u_j'\left(c_{1j,t}\right)}.$$

An equilibrium is a sequence of bond prices b_t satisfying the previous relation and the equilibrium in the intrageneration lending market

$$\sum_{j=1}^{N} \text{sav}_{j,t} = 0, \tag{3.46}$$

where N denotes the number of agents in each generation, a constant.

Suppose, for example, that agents have all the same CRRA, γ, and the same discount factor, $\beta_j = \beta$. In this case,

$$\text{sav}_{j,t} = \frac{(\beta R_{t+1})^{\frac{1}{\gamma}} w_{1t} - w_{2,t+1}}{R_{t+1} + (\beta R_{t+1})^{\frac{1}{\gamma}}}.$$

The first term in the numerator reflects an income effect while the second is a substitution effect. The quantity $\frac{1}{\gamma}$ is the elasticity of intertemporal substitution (see section 3.2.3). Consider, for example, the log utility case, $\gamma = 1$. We have

$$\begin{aligned} c_{1j,t} &= \frac{1}{1+\beta}\left(w_{1j,t} + \frac{w_{2j,t+1}}{R_{t+1}}\right), \\ c_{2j,t+1} &= \frac{\beta}{1+\beta}\left(R_{t+1} w_{1j,t} + w_{2j,t+1}\right), \text{sav}_{j,t} = \frac{1}{1+\beta}\left(\beta w_{1j,t} - \frac{w_{2j,t+1}}{R_{t+1}}\right), \end{aligned} \tag{3.47}$$

and using the equilibrium condition in eq. (3.46),

$$b_t = \frac{1}{R_{t+1}} = \beta \frac{\sum_{j=1}^{N} w_{1j,t}}{\sum_{j=1}^{N} w_{2j,t+1}}. \tag{3.48}$$

3.5.1.2 *A tree in a stochastic economy*

Consider a tree that yields a stochastic dividend D_t in each period. Each agent solves

$$\max_{(c_{1t}, c_{2,t+1})} \left(u(c_{1t}) + \beta E_t\left(u\left(c_{2,t+1}\right)\right)\right), \quad \text{subject to} \begin{cases} S_t\theta_t + c_{1t} = w_{1t} \\ c_{2,t+1} = (S_{t+1} + D_{t+1})\theta_t + w_{2,t+1} \end{cases} \tag{3.P6}$$

where S_t denotes the asset price, θ denotes the units of the asset the agent chooses in their young age, and E_t is the expectation taken conditional on information available at time t. The agent born at time $t-1$ faces the constraints $S_{t-1}\theta_{t-1} + c_{1,t-1} = w_{1,t-1}$ and $w_{2t} + (S_t + D_t)\theta_{t-1} = c_{2,t}$. By combining the second period constraint of the agent born at time $t-1$ with the first period constraint of the agent born at time t,

$$(S_t + D_t)\,\theta_{t-1} - S_t\theta_t + w_t = c_{1,t} + c_{2,t}.$$

The clearing condition in the asset market, $\theta_t = 1$, implies that the goods market also clears: that is, for all t, we have that $D_t + w_{1t} + w_{2t} = c_{1,t} + c_{2,t}$. Further, in equilibrium, $\theta_t = 1$, implying that (i) $c_{1t} = w_{1t} - S_t$ and (ii) $c_{2,t+1} = S_{t+1} + D_{t+1} + w_{2,t+1}$. By plugging in the constraints of [3.P6], taking the first-order conditions and, finally, using (i) and (ii),

$$u'(w_{1t} - S_t)\,S_t = \beta E_t\left[u'\left(S_{t+1} + D_{t+1} + w_{2,t+1}\right)\left(S_{t+1} + D_{t+1}\right)\right].$$

Assume, for example, log utility, $u(c) = \ln c$, and set $\tilde{R}_{t+1} = \left(S_{t+1} + D_{t+1}\right)/S_t$. We have

$$\frac{1}{w_{1t} - \text{sav}_t^*} = \beta E_t\left(\frac{1}{\text{sav}_t^* \tilde{R}_{t+1} + w_{2,t+1}} \tilde{R}_{t+1}\right), \quad \text{where sav}_t^* \equiv S_t\theta_t,\ \theta_t = 1. \tag{3.49}$$

Note that in the previous deterministic model,

$$\frac{1}{w_{1t} - \text{sav}_t} = \beta \frac{1}{\text{sav}_t R_{t+1} + w_{2,t+1}} R_{t+1}, \quad \text{where sav}_t \equiv 0, \tag{3.50}$$

which leads to the equilibrium bond price in eq. (3.45). Eqs. (3.49) and (3.50) result from the optimality conditions of log utility investors. They differ because, in the tree economy, savings have to stay positive (the tree must be held by the young agent), such that in equilibrium, $\text{sav}_t^* \equiv S_t \geq 0$. Instead, in the previous economy *without* a tree, the interest rate, R_t, has to be such that savings are zero for all t, $\text{sav}_t = 0$.

Eq. (3.49) can be explicitly solved for the price of the tree, S_t, once we assume $w_{2t} = 0$ for all t. Note that in the absence of a tree, the endowments in the old age could not be zero as the autarky economy in this case would be such that the old generation would not consume anything. In the presence of a tree, this assumption is conceptually innocuous; in this case, the old generation could consume the fruits of the tree (in addition to the proceedings arising from selling the tree to the young generation). Solving eq. (3.49) for S_t when $w_{2t} = 0$, then, leads to the following price of the tree:

$$S_t = \frac{\beta}{1+\beta} w_{1t}. \tag{3.51}$$

The price of the tree wholly reflects preferences and endowments of the young generation. The higher the endowment at time t, the higher the savings is, and the better the asset valuation is. A low time discount (i.e., a high β) also leads to higher savings and then high asset valuations. Note that S_t does not even reflect the dividends the asset pays.

In the general case in which endowments are available at old age, we cannot solve the model in closed form. Let us make some simplifications. Suppose the asset distributes a constant dividend equal to $\bar{D}$, a perpetuity, and that the agents have deterministic endowments equal to w_1 and w_2. A stationary equilibrium is one in which the equilibrium price is constant. By eq. (3.49), this price, S, is a solution to

$$\frac{S}{w_1 - S} = \beta \frac{S + \bar{D}}{S + \bar{D} + w_2}. \tag{3.52}$$

It is easy to show that there exists a unique solution to eq. (3.52), $S_o\left(w_1, w_2, \beta, \bar{D}\right)$ say, satisfying

$$S_o\left(w_1, w_2, \beta, \bar{D}\right) \in \left(\beta \frac{\bar{D}}{\bar{D} + w_2}, \beta\right)$$

and that $S_o\left(w_1, w_2, \beta, \bar{D}\right)$ is increasing in β and w_1, decreasing in w_2, and finally increasing in $\bar{D}$.

The point of these models is that asset prices may fail to deliver predictions consistent with standard intuition in the infinite horizon case. We shall return to this point in chapter 10 while explaining that, in economies in which agents have limited investment horizons, irrational traders may have a durable impact on asset price dynamics even while they trade against more sophisticated traders (see section 10.9).

3.5.2 Monetary Economies

We consider a version of the previous model with endowments and assume that agents can now transfer value through a piece of paper interpreted as money. The young agent maximizes their intertemporal utility, subject to the budget constraint

$$\max_{(c_{1t},c_{2,t+1})} u\left(c_{1t}, c_{2,t+1}\right), \quad \text{subject to} \begin{cases} \frac{m_t}{p_t} + c_{1t} = w_{1t} \\ c_{2,t+1} = \frac{m_t}{p_{t+1}} + w_{2,t+1} \end{cases} \tag{3.P7}$$

where m_t is the amount of money they hold at time t and p_t is the price of the consumption good as of time t. We assume agents have a utility function more general than in the standard additive utility case as there are special cases of this utility that lead to closed-form solutions for quantities of interest.

Let

$$\text{sav}_t \equiv \frac{m_t}{p_t}, \quad R_{t+1} \equiv \frac{p_t}{p_{t+1}}. \tag{3.53}$$

Then the budget constraint in [3.P7] is formally identical to that in [3.P5]. The difference is that in the monetary economy of this section, the young agent may wish to transfer value over time by saving money, earning a gross "interest rate" equal to the rate of deflation: the lower the price level the next period, the higher the purchasing power of the money they transfer from a young to an old age.

Naturally, by aggregating the budget constraints of the young and the old generation, eq. (3.42) is obtained. However, sav_t and R_{t+1} are now defined as in (3.53). Further, sav_t is not necessarily zero in this monetary economy: money can be transferred from one generation to the next. Finally, in equilibrium, $\text{sav}_t = \frac{\bar{m}_t}{p_t}$, where $\bar{m}_t$ denotes money supply. Therefore, the real value of money (i.e., sav_t) is strictly positive once the equilibrium price p_t stays bounded over time, a property that may actually occur, as we shall see. In this sense, the role of money (a medium for transferring value) is similar to that of a tree in the stochastic OLG economy of the previous section.

Substituting the equilibrium savings $\text{sav}_t = \frac{\bar{m}_t}{p_t}$ and $R_{t+1} = \frac{p_t}{p_{t+1}}$ into eq. (3.42), we obtain $\bar{m}_{t-1} = \bar{m}_t + p_t (c_{1t} + c_{2t} - w_t)$, which used again in eq. (3.42), leaves

$$\text{sav}_{t-1} R_t = \text{sav}_t - \frac{\Delta \bar{m}_t}{p_t}. \tag{3.54}$$

We need a law of movement for money creation. We assume that $\frac{\Delta \bar{m}_t}{\bar{m}_{t-1}} = \mu_t$ for some bounded sequence μ_t.[7] Therefore, by eq. (3.54),

$$(1 + \mu_t)\, \text{sav}_{t-1} R_t = \text{sav}_t. \tag{3.55}$$

7. In this section, we assume that money transfers are made to the young generation: the money the young generation has to absorb is that from the old generation, $\bar{m}_{t-1}$, and that created by the "central bank," $\mu_t \bar{m}_{t-1}$. One might consider an alternative model in which transfers are made to the old generation.

Eq. (3.55) may be generalized to the case in which population grows: at time t, N_t individuals are born, and $\frac{N_t}{N_{t-1}} = (1+n)$ for some constant n, just as initially assumed in section 3.2. Total money supply is defined as $M_t \equiv N_t \bar{m}_t$, and we assume that for all t, $\frac{\Delta M_t}{M_{t-1}} = \mu_t$. We assume that μ_t is independent of R and that $\lim_{t\to\infty} \mu_t = \mu$ is a constant. Note that $(1+\mu_t) N_{t-1} \frac{\bar{m}_{t-1}}{p_{t-1}} \frac{p_{t-1}}{p_t} = N_t \frac{\bar{m}_t}{p_t}$ and, by rearranging terms,

$$\frac{1+\mu_t}{1+n} \operatorname{sav}(R_t) R_t = \operatorname{sav}(R_{t+1}), \tag{3.56}$$

where the notation $\operatorname{sav}(R_{t+1}) \equiv \operatorname{sav}_t$ emphasizes that real savings are a function of the interest rate, a property of the solution to [3.P7].

An equilibrium is a sequence of interest rate factors, $(R_t)_{t=0}^{\infty}$, a solution to (3.56). A stationary equilibrium is one for which $R_t = R$, a constant, for all t. There may be two stationary equilibria:

(1) The (almost) Golden Rule: $R_m = \frac{1+n}{1+\mu}$. Section 3.6.2 shows that a social planner might support this equilibrium, at least provided $\mu = 0$ (whence, "almost"). The price satisfies $p_t = \left(\frac{1+\mu}{1+n}\right)^t p_0$. It is left as an exercise to verify that the real money supply, $\frac{\bar{m}_t}{p_t}$, is bounded and strictly positive and that the agents' budget constraints are bounded as a result. This equilibrium, in which agents "trust" money, is referred to as a "monetary" equilibrium.

(2) Autarky state: $R_a : \operatorname{sav}(R_a) = 0$, or $\lim_{t\to\infty} \frac{\bar{m}_t}{p_t} \to 0$. This equilibrium is such that $R_a < R_m$: prices increase more rapidly than per capita monetary stocks.[8] In this stationary equilibrium, agents do not "trust" money.

To analyze the dynamics of interest rates, assume for simplicity that the saving function is differentiable and that its derivative is nowhere zero, that is, $\operatorname{sav}'(\cdot) \neq 0$. Consider differentiating (3.56) and obtain the following "slope":

$$\operatorname{sl}_{t+1} \equiv \frac{dR_{t+1}}{dR_t} = \frac{\operatorname{sav}'(R_t) R_t + \operatorname{sav}(R_t)}{\operatorname{sav}'(R_{t+1})} \frac{1+\mu_t}{1+n}. \tag{3.57}$$

A reasonable assumption is that the agents' preferences lead to gross substitutability, that is, $\operatorname{sav}'(R) > 0$. As the price of future consumption relative to present (that is, R^{-1}) decreases, agents wish to consume more in the second period and hence to save more. Note that a lower price tomorrow also generates an income effect. However, the intertemporal substitution effects dominate the income effect. Now, the slope at the stationary state is $\lim_{t\to\infty} \operatorname{sl}_t = \operatorname{sl}$, where

$$\operatorname{sl} = \frac{\operatorname{sav}'(R) R + \operatorname{sav}(R)}{\operatorname{sav}'(R)} \frac{1+\mu}{1+n}.$$

It is easy to verify that the slope corresponding to the autarky case, $R = R_a$, is always less than one and that, under the assumption of gross substitutability, the slope corresponding

8. Indeed, note that for large t, $\frac{\bar{m}_{t+1}}{p_{t+1}} < \frac{\bar{m}_t}{p_t}$. Rearranging terms leaves $R_m^{-1} < \frac{p_{t+1}}{p_t} \to R_a^{-1}$.

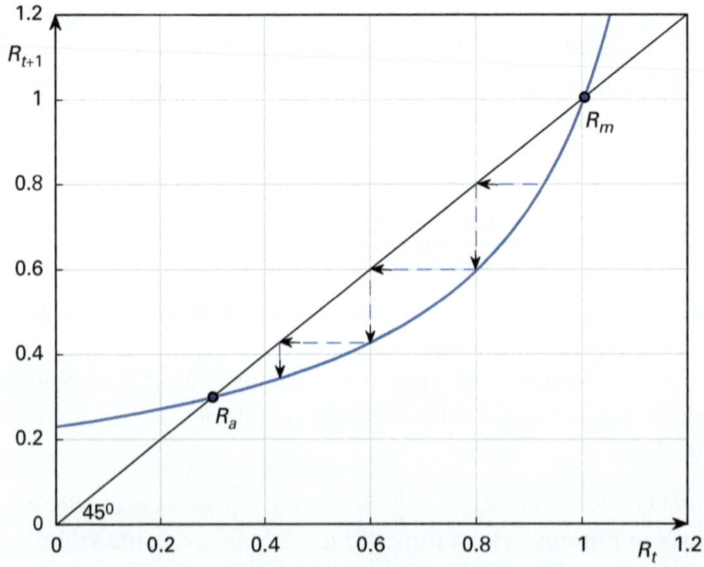

Figure 3.2
The dynamics of interest rate factors, R_t, predicted by model (3.59). The autarky (and stable) stationary equilibrium is $R_a = \phi = 0.30$, and the monetary (and unstable) stationary equilibrium is $R_m = \frac{1+n}{1+\mu}$, with $n = 1\%$ and $\mu = 0.5\%$.

to the monetary stationary state, sl_m say, is

$$\mathrm{sl}_m = \frac{\mathrm{sav}'(R_m)\, R_m + \mathrm{sav}(R_m)}{\mathrm{sav}'(R_m)\, R_m}, \tag{3.58}$$

and, thus, $\mathrm{sl}_m > 1$. That is, the autarky state is stable while, under gross substitutability, the monetary state is not.

Consider the following examples. Agents have a Cobb-Douglas utility function, $u(c_{1t}, c_{2,t+1}) = \sqrt{c_{1t}c_{2,t+1}}$, and constant endowments, $w_{it} = \bar{w}_i$ for each i and t, such that $\mathrm{sav}(R_{t+1}) = \frac{1}{2}\left(\bar{w}_1 - R_{t+1}^{-1}\bar{w}_2\right)$, at least provided $R_{t+1} \geq R_a = \phi \equiv \frac{\bar{w}_2}{\bar{w}_1}$, an assumption that holds in the numerical implementation provided below—that is, gross substitutability. Assuming that $\mu_t = \mu$, the dynamics of interest rates implied by (3.56) are

$$R_{t+1} = \frac{\phi R_m}{R_m - R_t + \phi}. \tag{3.59}$$

The two stationary equilibria are $R_a = \phi$ and R_m. Figure 3.2 depicts the mapping in (3.59) and displays its two stationary points.

All paths beginning from the right of R_m are explosive and then cannot be consistent with an economic equilibrium: a decreasing sequence of prices would eventually rule out the existence of a solution to the agents' programs. Therefore, an equilibrium path may only begin anywhere in $[R_a, R_m]$, although then we have no other information: there exists a continuum of points $R_0 \in [R_a, R_m]$ that are candidates for being the beginning of an equilibrium sequence.

The previous conclusions rely on the assumption of gross substitutability. Another possibility is that the agents' preferences imply complementarities, such that $\text{sav}'(R) < 0$: in this case, the income effect would dominate the substitution effect. If these complementarities are sufficiently strong, the mapping $R_t \mapsto R_{t+1}, f(\cdot)$, say, may bend backward. Further, if the slope (3.58) at the monetary stationary state is negative *and* less than one in absolute value, $|\text{sl}_m| < 1$, then the monetary equilibrium is stable: it can be reached from any initial value R_0 in a neighborhood of R_m. That is, and according to the (still undetermined) initial condition, there may be sequences of gross interest rates that converge either to the autarky state or to the monetary state. In fact, there are conditions under which this sequence may even never reach R_m but rather cycle around R_m. For example, in a cycle of order 2, we have that $R' = f(f(R'))$ for some R'.[9] In an important contribution, Grandmont (1985) shows that, in more general models, there may be cycles of any order, a property known as "chaos." In a chaotic system, the dynamics of the variables of interest appear to be random even when they are not. Chaotic systems in economics were investigated during the 1980s and the beginning of the 1990s, and this research is surveyed by Brock, Hsieh, and LeBaron (1991) and Medio (1992). While these pieces of work are theoretically important, the empirical evidence in support of chaos in macroeconomics and finance does not seem to be strong (see, e.g., LeBaron, 1994).

3.5.3 Capital Accumulation and Bubbles

This section analyzes the dynamics of capital accumulation in OLG models. One interesting property is that bubbles may exist in these economies. Bubbles are difficult to justify in economies with a finite number of agents (see Santos and Woodford, 1998). For example, chapter 4 provides a formal discussion of bubbles for Lucas's economy in section 3.2 (see section 4.2.6), explaining that their presence would not be consistent with the requirement of standard transversality conditions. Instead, OLG economies provide natural harbors of "chain-letter" phenomena where new agents enter to sustain a bubble already in place. This section describes these phenomena and is based on a re-elaboration of Diamond's (1965) OLG model made by Tirole (1985); in this formulation, bubbles exist in a deterministic setting. Weil (1987) first extended these results to stochastic bubbles. Interestingly, a condition for the existence of bubbles is a sort of inefficiency related to capital accumulation. An intrinsically useless and unbacked asset would be able to bring the economy to an efficient path.

In Diamond's model, firms produce a single good through the same production function as discussed in section 3.3. All agents still solve the program in [3.P5] although now w_{1t} is interpreted as the wage the young agent receives at time t. To simplify, we set $w_{2,t+1} = 0$ and denote $w_t = w_{1t}$. By the first-order conditions, $u'(w_t - \text{sav}_t) = \beta u'(\text{sav}_t R_{t+1}) R_{t+1}$. Thus, under regularity conditions, there exists a saving function, $\text{sav}_t \equiv \text{sav}(R_{t+1}, w_t)$. Note that, by the expressions of R_t and w_t given in section 3.3.1 (see eq. (3.11)), the agent's saving is, ultimately, a function of k_{t+1} and k_t; for simplicity, we denote savings with $\text{sav}(k_{t+1}, k_t)$.

9. More precisely, by eq. (3.56), a cycle of order 2 occurs provided there are two values R' and R'' such that $R''\text{sav}(R'') = R_m\text{sav}(R')$ and $R'\text{sav}(R') = R_m\text{sav}(R'')$. Thus, the two values satisfy $R'R'' = R_m^2$.

In turn, savings equal investments, $K_{t+1} = N_t \text{sav}(k_{t+1}, k_t)$, or

$$k_{t+1} = \frac{\text{sav}(k_{t+1}, k_t)}{1+n}. \tag{3.60}$$

The law of capital accumulation in (3.60) may give rise to complicated dynamics; some of them may resemble those mentioned in the previous section.

From now on, we assume that there exists a stationary and stable steady state, denoted as k_d. Rather than characterizing properties of this steady state, we generalize the model and discuss the properties of k_d as a special case of the more general model, one in which bubbles may possibly exist. In particular, we assume that, in addition to investing in capital, agents may purchase a piece of paper that has no intrinsic utility and is unbacked. In this deterministic setting, the price of this piece of paper at time $t+1$, B_{t+1}, should satisfy the no-arbitrage equation $B_{t+1} = y'(k_{t+1}) B_t$; that is, its gross return is the equilibrium interest rate factor R_{t+1}. In terms of per capita values, $b_t = B_t / N_t$,

$$b_{t+1} = b_t \frac{y'(k_{t+1})}{1+n}. \tag{3.61}$$

Thus, the bubble grows if the interest rate is larger than the growth rate of the economy, n. However, it is counterintuitive that bubbles grow more than the growth rate of the economy. A bubble should not explode. At the stationary state, $b_t = b$ and $k_t = k$ for all t and some $b > 0$, and $k > 0$, such that by eq. (3.61), $y'(k) = 1+n$. It is easy to see that the value of capital at this stationary state is k^*, the Golden Rule. Next, consider the law of capital accumulation. It generalizes that in eq. (3.60),

$$k_{t+1} = \frac{\text{sav}(k_{t+1}, k_t) - b_t}{1+n} \tag{3.62}$$

because agents now also invest into the piece of paper, thereby slowing capital accumulation. Evaluating (3.62) in steady state,

$$\begin{cases} b = \text{sav}(k,k) - (1+n)k \\ k = (y')^{-1}[1+n] \end{cases}. \tag{3.63}$$

Figure 3.3 depicts the two equations in (3.63), based on a parametric version of the model described below. The first equation is denoted as $(\Delta k_t = 0)$ as it is obtained while setting $b_t = b$ and $k_t = k$ in (3.62). The second equation is the vertical line for $k_t = k^*$. Displayed also is Diamond's stationary state, k_d, which occurs when $b = 0$. To summarize, bubble and capital evolve as in eq. (3.61) and eq. (3.62). A stationary state with a positive bubble exists if the two equations (3.63) intersect for levels of capital on the left of k_d, just as with point B. Section 3.6 explains that this condition implies that, in the absence of bubbles, the economy is dynamic inefficient in that it employs too much capital. A social planner would be able to improve resource allocation among generations with less capital. In this example, bubbles may make the economy dynamic efficient because they would slow down capital accumulation.

The system dynamics are as follows. First, consider the locus of points $(k, b) : \Delta b_{t+1} = 0$, that is,

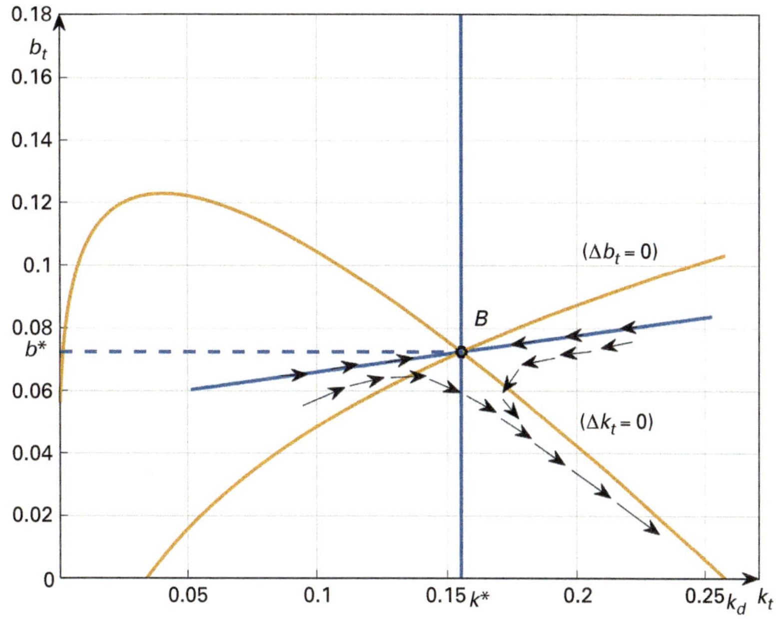

Figure 3.3
The dynamics of capital and bubbles. The curve denoted as $(\Delta k_t = 0)$ is the first equation in (3.63), and the curve denoted as $(\Delta b_t = 0)$ is eq. (3.64). The convergent space is the linear approximation $b - b^* = \varphi_b (k - k^*)$ to the system (3.61) and (3.62). The examples in this picture are based on the assumption that agents have log utility and that the production function is Cobb-Douglas. The Golden Rule and Diamond's steady state are $k^* = 0.1554$ and $k_d = 0.2578$, resp. Parameter values are in the main text.

$$(k, b) : b = \text{sav}(k^*, k) - (1 + n) k^*. \tag{3.64}$$

This locus is obtained as follows. By eq. (3.61), $\Delta b_{t+1} = b_t (y'(k_{t+1}) - (1+n)) / (1+n)$, where, by (3.62), $k_{t+1} = (\text{sav}(k_{t+1}, k_t) - b_t) / (1+n)$. Eq. (3.64) follows by imposing $\Delta b_{t+1} = 0$. Thus, the bubble grows for all points (k_t, b_t) on the left of this locus and decreases otherwise. On the other hand, capital grows for all points (k_t, b_t) below the $(\Delta k_t = 0)$ locus and decreases otherwise. Thus, the stationary state B lies on a stable saddle path. Given an initial level of capital k_0, there is a single bubble level that leads to the stationary point B. In other cases, such as those identified in figure 3.3, a bubble may last for a while and eventually fade.

Figure 3.3 illustrates the saddle path property of this state through the linear approximation to (3.61)–(3.62), based on an economy in which agents have log utility and the production function is the standard Cobb-Douglas, $u(c) = \ln c$ and $y(k) = k^\alpha$. Note that, in this case, the saving function is independent of the interest rate factor R_{t+1} and thus reduces to a function of k_t only, $\text{sav}(k_t)$ say,

$$\text{sav}(k_t) = \frac{\beta}{1+\beta} w_t = \frac{\beta}{1+\beta} (1 - \alpha) k_t^\alpha. \tag{3.65}$$

In this example, the laws of capital accumulation (3.60) (without bubbles) and (3.62) (with bubbles) hold, with the saving function $\text{sav}(k_t)$ in (3.65). The Diamond's level of capital is obtained by replacing $k_{t+1}=k_t=k_d$ into the resulting law of accumulation without bubbles; instead, the Golden Rule level of capital is $k^*=\left(y'\right)^{-1}[1+n]$. They are $k_d=(\beta(1-\alpha)/(1+\beta)(1+n))^{\frac{1}{1-\alpha}}$ and $k^*=(\alpha/(1+n))^{\frac{1}{1-\alpha}}$, resp. Thus, $k_d>k^*$ if and only if the subjective discounting factor is sufficiently large, $\beta>\alpha/(1-2\alpha)$. Intuitively, this condition implies that agents' propensity to save is so high that capital accumulates more than prescribed by the Golden Rule. This condition is satisfied in this example as $\beta=0.95$ and $\alpha=0.25$, just as in the examples of section 3.3.3. Likewise, the first of the equations for the steady state (3.63) is

$$b=\frac{\beta}{1+\beta}(1-\alpha)k^{\alpha}-(1+n)k,$$

where b^* is obtained by calculating the RHS of the previous equation at k^*. The locus $(\Delta b_t=0)$ depicted in figure 3.3 is obtained by replacing sav (k^*,k) with sav (k) in (3.64), with $n=0.01$. Finally, the linear stable subspace in the figure is obtained through a first-order expansion of (3.61) and (3.62) around the stationary state (b^*,k^*),

$$\begin{pmatrix}\bar{b}_{t+1}\\ \bar{k}_{t+1}\end{pmatrix}=H\begin{pmatrix}\bar{b}_t\\ \bar{k}_t\end{pmatrix},\quad H\equiv\begin{pmatrix}1-\frac{b^*y''(k^*)}{(1+n)^2} & \frac{b^*y''(k^*)\text{sav}'(k^*)}{(1+n)^2}\\ -\frac{1}{1+n} & \frac{\text{sav}'(k^*)}{1+n}\end{pmatrix},\tag{3.66}$$

where $\bar{b}_t=b_t-b^*$ and $\bar{k}_t=k_t-k^*$. Appendix 3.A shows that the eigenvalues of H are $\lambda_1<1$ and $\lambda_2>1$. Therefore, the linear subspace is $b-b^*=\varphi_b(k-k^*)$, where, given the parameter values, $\varphi_b\equiv\frac{v_{11}}{v_{21}}=0.1165$ and $\binom{v_{11}}{v_{21}}$ denotes the eigenvector associated with $\lambda_1=0.25$. We now turn to discuss in more detail the conditions underlying these bubbles.

3.6 Dynamic Efficiency

We consider the following question. What is the "efficient" level of capital in a dynamic economy, that is, one desirable by a social planner? The answer to this question is quite precise, at least in the context of the introductory capital accumulation models of this chapter. The efficient level of capital is the level of capital such that the marginal productivity of capital is larger than the population (gross) growth. Thus, and because marginal productivity is decreasing in capital, an economy is dynamically *inefficient* when it accumulates more capital than that predicted by the Golden Rule.

3.6.1 Production Economies

Consider the familiar law of capital accumulation: $K_{t+1}=Y(K_t,N_t)-C_t$, for K_0 given and where the production function satisfies the standard properties in section 3.3. Dividing both sides of this equation by N_t leaves

$$k_{t+1}=\frac{1}{1+n}\left(y(k_t)-c_t\right),\quad\text{for } k_0 \text{ given}\tag{3.67}$$

and where lowercase letters denote per capita variables. The stationary state of the economy is obtained when $k_{t+1}=k_t\equiv k$ and $c_{t+1}=c_t\equiv c$, such that

$$c=y(k)-(1+n)k.$$

In steady state, per capita consumption attains its maximum at

$$k^* : y'(k^*) = 1 + n. \tag{3.68}$$

The per capita capital steady state that satisfies eq. (3.68) describes the Golden Rule introduced in section 3.3 (see figure 3.1). Now, a social planner would be able to increase per capita consumption at the stationary state, provided $y'(k) < 1+n$. Indeed, suppose that we are in steady state. Then, because $y(k)$ is given, we can lower k, obtaining $dc = -(1+n)\,dk > 0$ immediately and $dc = \left(y'(k) - (1+n)\right) dk > 0$ in the next periods. This conclusion does actually hold for the whole capital accumulation path, not only in steady state. To prepare for a formal proof of this statement along the lines originally put forward by Cass (1972), consider the following definition. A path $(k, c)_{t=0}^{\infty}$ is consumption efficient (inefficient) if there does not exist (if there exists) another path $(\tilde{k}, \tilde{c})_{t=0}^{\infty}$ satisfying eq. (3.67) and such that $\tilde{c}_t \geq c_t$ for all t, with at least a strict inequality for one t. We have:

Theorem 3.3 (Dynamic efficiency). *A path $(k, c)_{t=0}^{\infty}$ is (i) consumption efficient if $\frac{y'(k_t)}{1+n} \geq 1$ for all t and (ii) consumption inefficient otherwise.*

Proof. As for part (i), suppose k_t is consumption efficient and consider an alternative consumption efficient path, $\tilde{k}_t = k_t + \epsilon_t$. Since k_0 is given, $\epsilon_0 = 0$. Moreover, by eq. (3.67),

$$(1+n)\,(\tilde{k}_{t+1} - k_{t+1}) = y(\tilde{k}_t) - y(k_t) - (\tilde{c}_t - c_t),$$

and because $\tilde{k}$ is consumption efficient, $\tilde{c}_t \geq c_t$, with at least one strictly equality for some t. Therefore, by concavity of y and the definition of $\tilde{k}_t$,

$$0 \leq y(\tilde{k}_t) - y(k_t) - (1+n)(\tilde{k}_{t+1} - k_{t+1}) < y'\left(k_t\right) \epsilon_t - (1+n)\,\epsilon_{t+1},$$

or $\epsilon_{t+1} < \frac{y'(k_t)}{1+n}\epsilon_t$. Evaluating this inequality at $t=0$ yields $\epsilon_1 < \frac{y'(k_0)}{1+n}\epsilon_0$, and since $\epsilon_0 = 0$, one has that $\epsilon_1 < 0$. Since $\frac{y'(k_t)}{1+n} \geq 1$ for all t, then $\epsilon_t \to -\infty$ as $t \to \infty$, which contradicts $\tilde{k}_t$ having bounded trajectories. The proof of part (ii) proceeds similarly, with $\liminf \epsilon_t >> -\infty$. □

We may rely on theorem 3.3 and examine the efficiency properties of some of the models studied in this chapter. Consider the representative agent model in section 3.3.3, in which the stationary state is $k = \left(y'\right)^{-1}[\beta^{-1}] < k^*$, where $k^* = \left(y'\right)^{-1}[1]$ is the Golden Rule level of capital (see figure 3.1). The economy is, then, dynamically efficient for any initial capital level $k_0 < k$. It is not surprising because the model of section 3.3.3 is one without any form of imperfections: resource allocation is Pareto optimal.

Consider, instead, the OLG models in section 3.5.3. In this case, eq. (3.67) still describes the capital accumulation path once we set $c_t \equiv \frac{C_t}{N_t} = c_{1t} + \frac{c_{2,t}}{1+n}$. This economy is dynamically inefficient if the interest rate is less than population growth. In this case, agents are saving more than socially desirable. The previous section identifies bubbles as a phenomenon that may theoretically bring an economy to dynamic efficiency. There exist additional channels that may slow down the capital formation process, such as the organization of the social security system. For example, it is well known that, while a defined contributions system would generally not alter capital accumulation, a defined benefits (or a *pay-as-you-go*) system would generally slow down the capital accumulation process. If an economy is dynamically inefficient under *laissez-faire*, a defined benefits system would, then, make this economy efficient. Naturally, in an economy that is already dynamically efficient, a defined benefits system would only slow down the capital accumulation process.

3.6.2 Money

Consider the monetary OLG model in section 3.5.2. We wish to find first-best allocations, that is, allocations that a social planner would choose while acting directly on agents' consumption, that is, without "forcing" the agents to make use of money.[10] Consider the monetary state $R_m = \frac{1+n}{1+\mu}$. We show that R_m is a stationary state that the social planner would implement, in which consumptions and endowments are constant across generations and $\mu = 0$.

Note that the social planner allocates resources while not considering agents' demands for money. Their only constraint is the resource constraint $w \equiv w_1 + \frac{w_2}{1+n} = c_{1t} + \frac{c_{2t}}{1+n}$, and the objective then is

$$\max \sum_{t=0}^{\infty} \vartheta^t u\left(w - \frac{c_{2t}}{1+n}, c_{2,t+1}\right),$$

where ϑ^t is the weight given to the generation as of time t. The first-order conditions, $\frac{u_2}{u_1} = \frac{\vartheta}{1+n}$, lead to the "modified" Golden Rule in steady state (modified by the weight ϑ). Therefore, the modified Golden Rule may be attained in the market equilibrium when $\mu = 0$.

Appendix 3.A Finite Difference Equations and Determinacy

Let $z_0 \in \mathbb{R}^d$, and consider the following linear system of finite difference equations

$$z_{t+1} = A \cdot z_t, \quad t = 0, 1, \cdots, \tag{3.A1}$$

for some matrix A. The solution to eq. (3.A1) is

$$z_t = v_1 \kappa_1 \lambda_1^t + \cdots + v_d \kappa_d \lambda_d^t, \tag{3.A2}$$

where λ_i and v_i are the eigenvalues and the eigenvectors of A, and κ_i are constants to be determined below.

A standard proof of this result relies on the so-called diagonalization of eq. (3.A1). Consider the system of the characteristic equations for A, $(A - \lambda_i I)\, v_i = 0_{d\times 1}$, where λ_i is scalar and v_i a $d \times 1$ column vector for $i = 1, \cdots, n$, or in matrix form, $AP = P\Lambda$, where $P = (v_1, \cdots, v_d)$ and Λ is a diagonal matrix with λ_i on its diagonal. We set $P^\top = P^{-1}$. Postmultiplying by P^{-1} leaves the *spectral decomposition* of A:

$$A = P\Lambda P^{-1}. \tag{3.A3}$$

By replacing eq. (3.A3) into eq. (3.A1) and rearranging terms,

$$y_{t+1} = \Lambda \cdot y_t, \text{ where } y_t \equiv P^{-1} z_t.$$

10. In a second-best equilibrium, a social planner would let the market "play" first (at least in a thought experiment) while allowing the agents to use money. The planner would then parametrize these equilibria with μ_t, the monetary growth rate, and maximize an aggregator of the agents' indirect utility functions with respect to μ_t.

The solution for y is $y_{it} = \kappa_i \lambda_i^t$, and the solution for z is $z_t = P y_t = (v_1, \cdots, v_d) y_t = \sum_{i=1}^d v_i y_{it} = \sum_{i=1}^d v_i \kappa_i \lambda_i^t$, which is eq. (3.A2).

To determine the vector of constants $\kappa = (\kappa_1, \cdots, \kappa_d)^\top$, evaluate the solution at $t = 0$,

$$z_0 = (v_1, \cdots, v_d)\kappa = P\kappa,$$

whence

$$\hat{\kappa} \equiv \kappa(P) = P^{-1} z_0, \tag{3.A4}$$

where the columns of P are vectors belonging to the space of the eigenvectors. Naturally, there are many such vectors. However, the previous formula shows how the constants $\kappa(P)$ need to "adjust" so as to guarantee the stability of the solution with respect to changes in P.

Example 3.A1. Let $d = 2$, and suppose that $\lambda_1 \in (0, 1)$, $\lambda_2 > 1$. The resulting system is unstable for any initial condition except perhaps for a set with measure zero. This set of measure zero gives rise to the saddle path. We determine the coordinates of this set. We wish to find the set of initial conditions such that $\kappa_2 = 0$, which in turn rules out an explosive behavior due to the unstable root, $\lambda_2 > 1$. The solution at $t = 0$ is

$$\begin{pmatrix} x_0 \\ y_0 \end{pmatrix} = z_0 = P\kappa = (v_1 \; v_2) \begin{pmatrix} \kappa_1 \\ \kappa_2 \end{pmatrix} = \begin{pmatrix} v_{11}\kappa_1 + v_{12}\kappa_2 \\ v_{21}\kappa_1 + v_{22}\kappa_2 \end{pmatrix},$$

where we have set $z = (x, y)^\top$. Replacing the second equation into the first and solving for κ_2 yields

$$\kappa_2 = \frac{v_{11} y_0 - v_{21} x_0}{v_{11} v_{22} - v_{12} v_{21}},$$

which is zero when

$$y_0 = \frac{v_{21}}{v_{11}} x_0.$$

For this system, the saddle path is a line with a slope equal to the ratio of the two components of eigenvector for λ_1—the stable root. Figure 3.A1 depicts the phase diagram for this system, with the "divergent" line satisfying the equation $y_0 = \frac{v_{22}}{v_{12}} x_0$.

The saddle path can be interpreted in the following terms. If x is a *predetermined* variable, y must "jump" to the saddle path $y_0 = \frac{v_{21}}{v_{11}} x_0$ so as to ensure the system does not explode. Note, then, the following difficulty: if the system includes two predetermined variables, there are no stable solutions. However, this possibility is unusual in economics. Consider the next example.

Example 3A.2. Note that example 3.A1 covers the linearized version of the neoclassic growth model. Indeed, section 3.3.3 shows that in a small neighborhood of the stationary state (k, c), the deviations $(\bar{k}_t, \bar{c}_t)_{t=0}^\infty$ of capital and consumption from (k, c) satisfy eq. (3.17). The two eigenvalues of A are $\lambda_{1/2} = \frac{1}{2}(\text{tr}(A) \mp \sqrt{\text{tr}(A)^2 - 4\det(A)})$, where (i) $\det(A) = y'(k) = \beta^{-1} > 1$ and (ii) $\text{tr}(A) = \beta^{-1} + 1 + \beta \frac{u'(c)}{u''(c)} y''(k) > 1 + \det(A)$. Note that

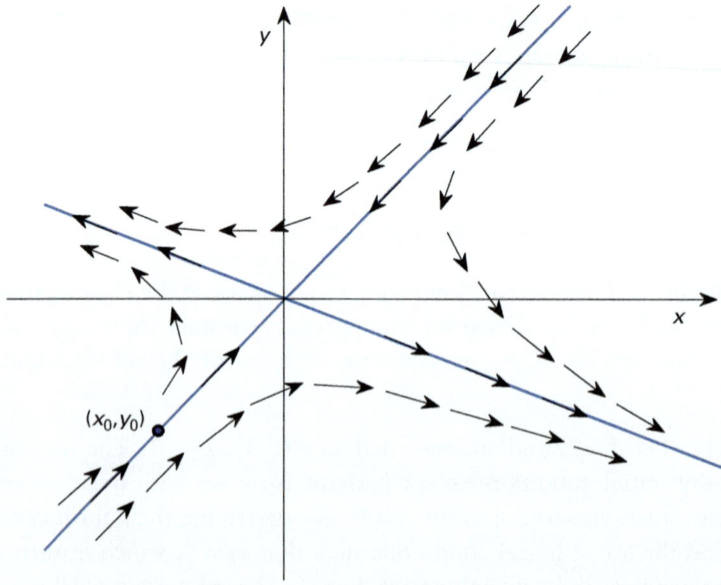

Figure 3A.1
Phase diagram for the system of eqs. (3A.1) in a two-dimensional space.

$$a \equiv \text{tr}(A)^2 - 4\det(A) = \left(\beta^{-1} + 1 + \beta\frac{u'(c)}{u''(c)}y''(k)\right)^2 - 4\beta^{-1} > \left(\beta^{-1}+1\right)^2 - 4\beta^{-1}$$
$$= \left(1-\beta^{-1}\right)^2 > 0,$$

where the first inequality follows by the standard assumption made on utility, u, and production, y. Therefore, $\lambda_2 = \frac{1}{2}\left(\text{tr}(A) + \sqrt{a}\right) > \frac{1}{2}\left(1 + \det(A) + \sqrt{a}\right) > 1 + \frac{1}{2}\sqrt{a} > 1$. Regarding λ_1, note that $\det(A) > 0$, such that $2\lambda_1 = \text{tr}(A) - \sqrt{\text{tr}(A)^2 - 4\det(A)} > 0$; moreover, $\lambda_1 < 1 \Longleftrightarrow \text{tr}(A) - \sqrt{\text{tr}(A)^2 - 4\det(A)} < 2$, or $(\text{tr}(A) - 2)^2 < \text{tr}(A)^2 - 4\det(A)$, which can be easily verified. Hence, $\lambda_1 \in (0,1)$.

Bubbles in the OLG model (3.66). The two eigenvalues of H in (3.66) are as in the previous example but with $\det(H) = \frac{sav'(k^*)}{1+n} > 0$ and $\text{tr}(H) = 1 - \frac{b^* y''(k^*)}{(1+n)^2} + \frac{sav'(k^*)}{1+n} > 1 + \det(H)$. Note also that $\phi = \text{tr}(H)^2 - 4\det(H) > \left(1 - \det(H)\right)^2 > 0$. Therefore, by the same arguments used in example 3.A2, $\lambda_2 > 1$ and $\lambda_1 < 1$.

We may extend the previous examples to higher dimensional spaces. A *convergent* or *stable subspace* is the counterpart to the saddle path in the $d=2$ case. It is the locus of points such that z_t in eq. (3.A2) does not explode. (In the case of nonlinear systems, this convergent subspace is termed *convergent* or *stable manifold.*) Let $\Pi \equiv P^{-1}$, and rewrite eq. (3.A4), that is, the system determining the solution for κ, as follows:

$$\hat{\kappa} = \Pi z_0.$$

We assume the elements of z and A are ordered in such a way that $\exists s : |\lambda_i| < 1$, for $i = 1, \cdots, s$ and $|\lambda_i| > 1$ for $i = s+1, \cdots, d$. Then we partition Π as follows:

$$\hat{\kappa} = \begin{pmatrix} \underset{s\times d}{\Pi_{\bar{s}}} \\ \underset{(d-s)\times d}{\Pi_u} \end{pmatrix} z_0.$$

Proceeding similarly as in example 3.A1, we search for conditions that ensure the system remains "trapped" in the convergent space: we require that $\hat{\kappa}_{s+1} = \cdots = \hat{\kappa}_d = 0$, or

$$\begin{pmatrix} \hat{\kappa}_{s+1} \\ \vdots \\ \hat{\kappa}_d \end{pmatrix} = \underset{(d-s)\times d}{\Pi_u} z_0 = 0_{(d-s)\times 1}.$$

Let $d \equiv k + k^*$, where k^* is the number of predetermined variables and k is the number of the remaining, or free, variables. Partition Π_u and z_0 in such a way to disentangle free from predetermined variables as follows:

$$0_{(d-s)\times 1} = \underset{(d-s)\times d}{\Pi_u} z_0 = \begin{pmatrix} \underset{(d-s)\times k}{\Pi_u^{(1)}} & \underset{(d-s)\times k^*}{\Pi_u^{(2)}} \end{pmatrix} \begin{pmatrix} \underset{k\times 1}{z_0^{\text{free}}} \\ \underset{k^*\times 1}{z_0^{\text{pre}}} \end{pmatrix} = \underset{(d-s)\times k}{\Pi_u^{(1)}} \underset{k\times 1}{z_0^{\text{free}}} + \underset{(d-s)\times k^*}{\Pi_u^{(2)}} \underset{k^*\times 1}{z_0^{\text{pre}}},$$

or

$$\underset{(d-s)\times k}{\Pi_u^{(1)}} \underset{k\times 1}{z_0^{\text{free}}} = - \underset{(d-s)\times k^*}{\Pi_u^{(2)}} \underset{k^*\times 1}{z_0^{\text{pre}}}. \tag{3.A5}$$

The k^* dimensional vector z_0^{pre} is obviously known as it is the vector of predetermined variables, and $\Pi_u^{(1)}, \Pi_u^{(2)}$ depend on the primitives of the economy embedded into the matrix A. Then eq. (3.A5) has $d-s$ equations with k unknowns, that is, the components of z_0^{free}. We assume that $\Pi_u^{(1)}$ has full rank.

We refer s to as the dimension of the convergent subspace, $\mathcal{S}$, say. To explain this terminology, consider the solution for z_t,

$$z_t = v_1 \hat{\kappa}_1 \lambda_1^t + \cdots + v_s \hat{\kappa}_s \lambda_s^t + v_{s+1} \hat{\kappa}_{s+1} \lambda_{s+1}^t + \cdots + v_d \hat{\kappa}_d \lambda_d^t.$$

For z_t to remain stuck in $\mathcal{S}$, it must be that

$$\hat{\kappa}_{s+1} = \cdots = \hat{\kappa}_d = 0,$$

in which case

$$\underset{d\times 1}{z_t} = \underset{d\times 1}{v_1} \hat{\kappa}_1 \lambda_1^t + \cdots + \underset{d\times 1}{v_s} \hat{\kappa}_s \lambda_s^t = (v_1 \hat{\kappa}_1, \cdots, v_s \hat{\kappa}_s) \cdot (\lambda_1^t, \cdots, \lambda_s^t)^\top,$$

that is,

$$\underset{d\times 1}{z_t} = \underset{d\times s}{\hat{V}} \cdot \underset{s\times 1}{\hat{\lambda}_t},$$

where $\hat{V} \equiv (v_1\hat{\kappa}_1, \cdots, v_s\hat{\kappa}_s)$ and $\hat{\lambda}_t \equiv (\lambda_1^t, \cdots, \lambda_s^t)^\top$. Finally, for each t, introduce the vector subspace:

$$\langle \hat{V} \rangle_t \equiv \{z_t \in \mathbb{R}^d : \underset{d\times 1}{z_t} = \underset{d\times s}{\hat{V}} \cdot \underset{s\times 1}{\hat{\lambda}_t}, \ \hat{\lambda}_t \in \mathbb{R}^s\}.$$

Clearly, for each t, $\dim\langle \hat{V} \rangle_t = \text{rank}(\hat{V}) = s$—whence the terminology.

There are three cases to consider.

(1) $d - s = k$, or $s = k^*$. The dimension of the divergent subspace is equal to the number of free variables; equivalently, the dimension of the convergent subspace is equal to the number of predetermined variables. The system dynamics are determined in this case because the predetermined variables identify one (and only one) point in the convergent space, at which the free variables can jump to ensure that the system remains in the convergent space, $z_0^{\text{free}} = -\Pi_u^{(1)-1}\Pi_u^{(2)} z_0^{\text{pre}}$—as is illustrated in example 3.A1 where $d = 2$ and $k = 1$ and x_0 is the predetermined variable: x_0 identifies one (and only one) point in the saddle path, (x_0, y_0), such that the system does not explode starting from that point.

(2) $d - s > k$, or $s < k^*$. There are no solutions in general lying in the convergent space—a case mentioned just before example 3.A2.

(3) $d - s < k$, or $s > k^*$. There are infinitely many solutions that lie on the convergent space, a phenomenon typically referred to as *indeterminacy*. It is in this case that *sunspots* equilibria have the potential to arise. To illustrate, consider again example 3.A1, in which $d = 2$ and $s = 1$. In this example, indeterminacy may only arise if no predetermined variables exist. Alternatively, in this two-dimensional example, indeterminacy would arise if $d = 2$, $s = 2$, and $k^* = 1$.

Appendix 3.B Neoclassic Growth in Continuous Time

3.B.1 Convergence from Discrete Time

3.B.1.1 Laws

Consider chopping time in the law of population growth as follows:

$$N_{hk} - N_{h(k-1)} = \bar{n} N_{h(k-1)} h, \quad k = 1, \cdots, \ell,$$

where $\bar{n}$ is an *instantaneous rate* and $\ell = \frac{t}{h}$ is the number of subperiods in the given time period t. The solution is $N_{h\ell} = (1 + \bar{n}h)^\ell N_0$, or $N_t = (1 + \bar{n}h)^{t/h} N_0$. Taking limits leaves

$$N_t = \lim_{h\downarrow 0} (1 + \bar{n}h)^{t/h} N_0 = e^{\bar{n}t} N_0.$$

We proceed similarly with the law of capital accumulation. We have

$$K_{h(k+1)} = (1 - \bar{\delta}h) K_{hk} + I_{h(k+1)} h, \quad k = 0, \cdots, \ell - 1,$$

where $\bar{\delta}$ is an instantaneous depreciation rate and $\ell = \frac{t}{h}$. By iterating,

$$K_t = (1 - \bar{\delta}h)^{t/h} K_0 + \sum_{j=1}^{t/h} (1 - \bar{\delta}h)^{t/h - j} I_{hj} h.$$

Taking the limits for $h \downarrow 0$ yields

$$K_t = e^{-\bar{\delta}t} K_0 + e^{-\bar{\delta}t} \int_0^t e^{\bar{\delta}u} I_u du, \tag{3.A6}$$

or in differential form,

$$\dot{K}_t = -\bar{\delta} K_t + I_t. \tag{3.A7}$$

By replacing the resource allocation constraint

$$Y_t = F(K_t, N_t) = C_t + I_t \tag{3.A8}$$

into eq. (3.A7), we obtain the law of capital accumulation

$$\dot{K}_t = F(K_t, N_t) - C_t - \bar{\delta} K_t. \tag{3.A9}$$

3.B.1.2 *Per capita dynamics*

Define c_t and k_t as per capita consumption and capital, and divide both sides of eq. (3.A9) by N_t,

$$\frac{\dot{K}_t}{N_t} = \frac{F(K_t, N_t)}{N_t} - c_t - \bar{\delta} k_t = y(k_t) - c_t - \bar{\delta} k_t,$$

where $k_t \equiv \frac{K_t}{N_t}$ and the second equality follows by standard homogeneity properties of the production function. That is,

$$\dot{k} = y(k_t) - c_t - (\bar{\delta} + \bar{n}) k_t. \tag{3.A10}$$

Eq. (3.A10) is the per capital accumulation constraint faced by a social planner, as we elaborate next.

3.B.2 The Model

We study the following social planner problem,

$$\begin{cases} \max_c \int_0^\infty e^{-\rho t} u(c_t) dt \\ \text{s.t. } \dot{k}_t = y(k_t) - c_t - (\bar{\delta} + \bar{n}) k_t \end{cases} \qquad [3.A\text{-}P1]$$

where all variables are per capita. We are about to derive optimality conditions while relying on standard optimization methods reviewed briefly in appendix 3.C. The first step is to consider the Hamiltonian, defined as

$$H_t = u(c_t) + \lambda_t \left(y(k_t) - c_t - (\bar{\delta} + \bar{n}) k_t \right),$$

where λ is a co-state variable. The first-order conditions are

$$\begin{cases} \dfrac{\partial H_t}{\partial c_t} = 0 \\ \dfrac{\partial H_t}{\partial \lambda_t} = \dot{k}_t \\ -\dfrac{\partial H_t}{\partial k_t} = \dot{\lambda}_t - \rho \lambda_t \end{cases}.$$

The first and the third conditions lead, resp., to

$$\begin{cases} \lambda_t &= u'(c_t) \\ \dot{\lambda}_t &= \left(\rho+\bar{\delta}+\bar{n}-y'(k_t)\right)\lambda_t \end{cases}. \tag{3.A11}$$

Differentiating the first equation in (3.A11) with respect to time yields

$$\dot{\lambda}_t = \left(\frac{u''(c_t)}{u'(c_t)}\dot{c}_t\right)\lambda_t,$$

and using the second equation in (3.A11),

$$\dot{c}_t = \frac{u'(c_t)}{u''(c_t)}\left(\rho+\bar{\delta}+\bar{n}-y'(k_t)\right). \tag{3.A12}$$

An equilibrium is the solution of a system comprising the constraint in [3.A-P1] and eq. (3.A12). We analyze the dynamics of this system around a small neighborhood of the stationary state. This stationary state is defined as the solution (c,k) of the constraint in [3.A-P1] and eq. (3.A12) when $\dot{c}(t)=\dot{k}(t)=0$, namely,

$$\begin{cases} c &= y(k)-\left(\bar{\delta}+\bar{n}\right)k \\ \rho+\bar{\delta}+\bar{n} &= y'(k) \end{cases}.$$

Consider a first-order approximation of both sides of the constraint in [3.A-P1] and eq. (3.A12) near (c,k),

$$\begin{cases} \dot{c}_t &= -\dfrac{u'(c)}{u''(c)}y''(k)\left(k_t-k\right) \\ \dot{k}_t &= \rho\cdot\left(k_t-k\right)-\left(c_t-c\right) \end{cases},$$

where we used the equality $\rho+\bar{\delta}+\bar{n}=y'(k)$. By setting $x_t\equiv c_t-c$ and $y_t\equiv k_t-k$, the previous system can be rewritten as follows

$$\dot{z}_t = A\cdot z_t, \quad A\equiv\begin{pmatrix} 0 & -\dfrac{u'(c)}{u''(c)}y''(k) \\ -1 & \rho \end{pmatrix},$$

where $z\equiv(x\ y)^{\top}$.

This system can be diagonalized through the spectral decomposition of A, namely, $A=P\Lambda P^{-1}$, where Λ is the diagonal matrix with the eigenvalues of A on the diagonal and P is the matrix of the eigenvectors with $P^{\top}=P^{-1}$, similarly as in the discrete time model of appendix 3.A. We have

$$\dot{v}_t = \Lambda\cdot v_t,$$

where $v\equiv P^{-1}z$. The eigenvalues are solutions of the following quadratic equation:

$$0=\lambda^2-\rho\lambda-\frac{u'(c)}{u''(c)}y''(k).$$

One may easily see that the roots to this equation (λ_1 and λ_2, say) are real and have the opposite sign, and we take $\lambda_1 < 0$. The solution for v_t is

$$v_{it} = \kappa_i e^{\lambda_i t}, \ i = 1, 2,$$

or

$$z_t = P \cdot v_t = v_1 \kappa_1 e^{\lambda_1 t} + v_2 \kappa_2 e^{\lambda_2 t},$$

where v_1 and v_2 are two-dimensional column vectors. We have

$$\begin{cases} x_t &= v_{11}\kappa_1 e^{\lambda_1 t} + v_{12}\kappa_2 e^{\lambda_2 t} \\ y_t &= v_{21}\kappa_1 e^{\lambda_1 t} + v_{22}\kappa_2 e^{\lambda_2 t} \end{cases}.$$

Let us evaluate this solution for $t = 0$,

$$\begin{pmatrix} x_0 \\ y_0 \end{pmatrix} = P\kappa = (v_1 \ v_2) \begin{pmatrix} \kappa_1 \\ \kappa_2 \end{pmatrix}.$$

By a reasoning nearly identical to that in appendix 3.A, we conclude that

$$\kappa_2 = 0 \Longleftrightarrow \frac{y_0}{x_0} = \frac{v_{21}}{v_{11}}.$$

Therefore, and similarly as with the discrete-time model, the saddle path is located along the line with slope equal to the ratio of the eigenvector elements corresponding to the negative root.

3.B.3 Tobin's q in a Deterministic Model

3.B.3.1 Homogeneity of profits

Consider the profit function (3.31) in the main text, and replace the optimality condition $\tilde{y}_N(K, N) = w$, such that

$$D(K, I) \equiv \tilde{y}(K, N(K)) - \tilde{y}_N(K, N(K)) N(K) - pI - \phi\left(\frac{I}{K}\right) K,$$

where $\tilde{y}(K, N)$ is homogeneous of degree one. We show that $D(K_t, I_t)$ is also homogeneous of degree one. This claim follows if

$$N(\lambda K) = \lambda N(K) \quad \text{and} \quad \tilde{y}_N(K_t, N(K_t)) = \tilde{y}_N(\lambda K_t, N(\lambda K_t)). \tag{3.A13}$$

We show that the two equalities in (3.A13) hold. Indeed, because $\tilde{y}(K, N)$ is homogeneous of degree one, $\tilde{y}_N(K, N)$ is homogeneous of degree zero, implying that $\tilde{y}_N(K, N) = \tilde{y}_N(\lambda K, \lambda N) = w$ and the two equalities in (3.A13) follow.

3.B.3.2 Marginal and average q

A firm maximizes future profits under a capital accumulation constraint

$$\begin{cases} V_t = \max_I \displaystyle\int_t^\infty R(t, u) D(K_u, I_u)\, du \\ \text{s.t. } \dot{K}_t = I_t - \bar{\delta} K_t \end{cases}$$

where $R(t,u) \equiv \exp\left(-\int_t^u r_s ds\right)$ and $r_s = r$ (a constant) is the riskless rate. The Hamiltonian (see appendix 3.C) is defined as

$$H_t = D(K_t, I_t) + q_t\left(I_t - \bar{\delta}K_t\right), \tag{3.A14}$$

where q_t is a co-state variable, interpreted as the shadow price of a unit of installed capital.

The first-order conditions are

$$\frac{\partial H_t}{\partial I_t} = 0 \quad \text{and} \quad -\frac{\partial H_t}{\partial K_t} = \dot{q}_t - rq_t \tag{3.A15}$$

and lead to

$$q_t = -D_I(K_t, I_t) = p_t + \phi'\left(\frac{I_t}{K_t}\right)$$

and

$$-\frac{\partial H_t}{\partial K_t} = -\left(D_K(K_t, I_t) - q_t\bar{\delta}\right) = \dot{q}_t - rq_t.$$

The last equation is

$$q_t = \int_t^\infty R(t,u)\, e^{-\bar{\delta}(u-t)} D_K(K_u, I_u)\, du.$$

It is the continuous time, deterministic counterpart to eq. (3.38) in the main text.

Next, note that

$$\begin{aligned}\frac{d}{dt}\left(q_t K_t R(0,t)\right) &= \left(\left(\dot{q}_t - r_t q_t\right)K_t + q_t\dot{K}_t\right)R(0,t)\\ &= \left(-\frac{\partial H_t}{\partial K_t}K_t + q_t\left(I_t - \bar{\delta}K_t\right)\right)R(0,t)\\ &= -D(K_t, I_t)\, R(0,t),\end{aligned}$$

where the last equality follows because H is homogenous of degree one and, hence, $H = H_K K + K_I I = H_K K$, where the last equality follows by the first optimality condition in (3.A15) and then by eq. (3.A14). Integrating the last equation leaves

$$q_T K_T R(0,T) - q_0 K_0 = -\int_t^T R(0,u)\, D(K_u, I_u)\, du \equiv V_{0,T}.$$

Therefore, assuming that the following transversality condition holds,

$$\lim_{T\to\infty} q_T K_T R(0,T) = 0,$$

we have that $V_0 = \lim_{T\to\infty} V_{0,T} = q_0 K_0$. That is, marginal and average q coincide, consistent with the discrete time, stochastic model in the main text.

Appendix 3.C Optimization of Continuous Time Systems

Consider the following optimization problem. For k_0 given,

$$\begin{cases} J(k_t,t,T) \equiv \max\limits_{(v_\tau)_{\tau\in[0,T]}} E_t\left(\int_t^T e^{-\rho(\tau-t)}u(k_\tau,v_\tau)\,d\tau + e^{-\rho(T-t)}B(k_T)\right) \\ \text{s.t. } dk_\tau = T(k_\tau,v_\tau)\,d\tau + \sigma(k_\tau,v_\tau)\,dW_\tau \end{cases} \tag{3.A16}$$

where u and B are an instantaneous and a terminal payoff, ρ is a subjective instantaneous rate, W_τ is a standard Brownian Motion, and finally, $T(k,v)$ and $\sigma(k,v)$ are given drift and diffusions functions.

We interpret k as a state variable and v as a control. In general, the control depends on the realization of k, although we assume that it cannot depend on future observations of k—it can only depend on past values of k. We confine attention to controls known as *feedbacks*, such that v only depends on the current value of k, $v_\tau(\omega) \equiv \hat{v}(\tau, k_\tau(\omega))$ for each sample path ω of the state variable $k_\tau(\omega)$. The function $\hat{v}$ makes the control and then the state variable k, Markovian.

We refer the value function $J(k_t,t,T)$ to as the *undiscounted* indirect utility, and based on famous derivations of Merton (1969, 24) in related contexts, we can define

$$I(k_t,t,T) \equiv e^{-\rho t}J(k_t,t,T) \tag{3.A17}$$

and call $I(\cdot)$ the *discounted* indirect utility. We shall come back to this discounted utility below (see eq. (3.A19)).

We apply what is known as the *stochastic programming principle*. Heuristically, we maximize up to an intermediate point in time, $t+\Delta t$, say, assuming the maximization for the remaining time period $[t+\Delta t, T]$ holds. We have:

$$\begin{aligned} J(k_t,t,T) &= \max_{(v_\tau)_{\tau\in[0,T]}} E_t\left(\int_t^T e^{-\rho(\tau-t)}u(k_\tau,v_\tau)\,d\tau + e^{-\rho(T-t)}B(k_T)\right) \\ &= \max_{(v_\tau)_{\tau\in[0,T]}} \left[E_t\left(\int_t^{t+\Delta t} e^{-\rho(\tau-t)}u(k_\tau,v_\tau)\,d\tau\right)\right. \\ &\quad \left. + e^{-\rho\Delta t}E_t\left(E_{t+\Delta t}\left(\int_{t+\Delta t}^T e^{-\rho(\tau-t-\Delta t)}u(k_\tau,v_\tau)\,d\tau + e^{-\rho(T-t-\Delta t)}B(k_T)\right)\right)\right] \\ &= \max_{(v_\tau)_{\tau\in[0,\Delta T]}} E_t\left(\int_t^{t+\Delta t} e^{-\rho(\tau-t)}u(k_\tau,v_\tau)\,d\tau\right) + e^{-\rho\Delta t}E_t\left(J(k_{t+\Delta t},t+\Delta t,T)\right), \end{aligned}$$

where the last two lines follow by the law of iterated expectations. By rearranging terms,

$$\begin{aligned} \left(\frac{1-e^{-\rho\Delta t}}{\Delta t}\right)J(k_t,t,T) &= \max_{(v_\tau)_{\tau\in[t,+\Delta t]}} E_t\left(\frac{1}{\Delta t}\int_t^{t+\Delta t} e^{-\rho(\tau-t)}u(k_\tau,v_\tau)\,d\tau\right) \\ &\quad + e^{-\rho\Delta t}E_t\left(\frac{1}{\Delta t}\left(J(k_{t+\Delta t},t+\Delta t,T) - J(k_t,t,T)\right)\right). \end{aligned}$$

For small Δt, and under regularity conditions, we have that by Itô's lemma,

$$0=\max_{v}\left(u(k,v)+\left(\frac{\partial}{\partial\tau}+L\right)J(k,\tau,T)-\rho J(k,\tau,T)\right), \tag{3.A18}$$

subject to the boundary condition $J(k,T,T)=B(k)$, where $LJ\equiv\frac{\partial J}{\partial k}T+\frac{1}{2}\frac{\partial^2 J}{\partial k^2}\sigma^2$.

Eq. (3.A18) is at the basis of the following derivations. However, these derivations could equivalently be based on the discounted utility $I(\cdot)$ in (3.A17). Note that

$$\left(\frac{\partial}{\partial\tau}+L\right)I(k,\tau,T)=e^{-\rho t}\left(\frac{\partial}{\partial\tau}+L-\rho\right)J(k,\tau,T),$$

and replacing into eq. (3.A18) leaves

$$0=\max_{v}\left(e^{-\rho t}u(k,v)+\left(\frac{\partial}{\partial\tau}+L\right)I(k,\tau,T)\right). \tag{3.A19}$$

However, we shall keep on relying on eq. (3.A18) rather than (3.A19).

The first-order condition for eq. (3.A18) is

$$0=u_v(k,\hat{v})+\frac{\partial J(k,\tau,T)}{\partial k}T_v(k,\hat{v})+\frac{1}{2}\frac{\partial^2 J(k,\tau,T)}{\partial k^2}\frac{\partial\sigma^2(k,\hat{v})}{\partial v},$$

which implicitly defines $\hat{v}\equiv\hat{v}(\tau,k)$, such that eq. (3.A18) can be written as:

$$\begin{aligned}\rho J(k,\tau,T)-\frac{\partial J(k,\tau,T)}{\partial\tau}&=u(k,\hat{v}(\tau,k))+\lambda(k,\tau,T)\,T(k,\hat{v}(\tau,k))\\&\quad+\frac{1}{2}\mu(k,\tau,T)\,\sigma^2(k,\hat{v}(\tau,k))\\&\equiv\hat{H}(\tau,k,\lambda(k,\tau,T),\mu(k,\tau,T)),\end{aligned} \tag{3.A20}$$

where

$$\lambda(k,\tau,T)\equiv\frac{\partial J(k,\tau,T)}{\partial k}$$

is interpreted as the marginal indirect utility in (3.A16) with respect to k and

$$\mu(k,\tau,T)\equiv\frac{\partial\lambda(k,\tau,T)}{\partial k}=\frac{\partial^2 J(k,\tau,T)}{\partial k^2}.$$

The function $\hat{H}$ is usually referred to as the optimized *Hamiltonian*, and eq. (3.A20) is the *Bellman equation* for diffusion processes.

By Itô's lemma,

$$d\lambda=\left(\frac{\partial\lambda}{\partial\tau}+\frac{\partial\lambda}{\partial k}T+\frac{1}{2}\frac{\partial^2\lambda}{\partial k^2}\sigma^2\right)d\tau+\frac{\partial\lambda}{\partial k}\sigma\,dW. \tag{3.A21}$$

Moreover, by differentiating both sides of the Bellman equation, that is, eq. (3.A20), with respect to k,

$$\begin{aligned}\rho\frac{\partial J}{\partial k}-\frac{\partial^2 J}{\partial k\partial\tau}&=\rho\lambda-\frac{\partial\lambda}{\partial\tau}\\&=\frac{\partial\hat{H}}{\partial k}+\frac{\partial\hat{H}}{\partial\lambda}\frac{\partial\lambda}{\partial k}+\frac{\partial\hat{H}}{\partial\mu}\frac{\partial\mu}{\partial k}\\&=\frac{\partial\hat{H}}{\partial k}+T\frac{\partial\lambda}{\partial k}+\frac{1}{2}\sigma^2\frac{\partial\mu}{\partial k},\end{aligned}\tag{3.A22}$$

where the first equality follows the definition of λ and the third equality holds by the definition of the optimized Hamiltonian function, $\hat{H}(\tau,k,\lambda,\mu)$. Plugging eq. (3.A22) into eq. (3.A21) leaves

$$d\lambda=\left(\rho\lambda-\frac{\partial\hat{H}}{\partial k}\right)d\tau+\frac{\partial\lambda}{\partial k}\sigma dW,$$

which shows that

$$\rho\lambda-\frac{\partial\hat{H}}{\partial k}=\frac{\mathrm{E}(d\lambda)}{d\tau}=\frac{\partial\lambda}{\partial\tau}+\frac{\partial\lambda}{\partial k}T+\frac{1}{2}\frac{\partial^2\lambda}{\partial k^2}\sigma^2.\tag{3.A23}$$

To summarize, we solve the problem in three steps.

(1) Maximize the Hamiltonian function,

$$H(\tau,k,\lambda,\mu)\equiv u(k,v)+\lambda\cdot T(k,v)+\frac{1}{2}\cdot\mu\cdot\sigma(k,v)^2,$$

with respect to the control v. The result is the optimized Hamiltonian function, $\hat{H}(\tau,k,\lambda,\mu)$.

(2) Impose the condition in eq. (3.A23).

(3) Solve the partial differential equation (3.A18) for J.

Succinctly,

$$\begin{cases}\dfrac{\partial\hat{H}}{\partial v}=0\\[2mm]\dfrac{\partial\hat{H}}{\partial\lambda}=T\\[2mm]\rho\lambda-\dfrac{\partial\hat{H}}{\partial k}=\dfrac{\partial\lambda}{\partial\tau}+\dfrac{\partial\lambda}{\partial k}T+\dfrac{1}{2}\dfrac{\partial^2\lambda}{\partial k^2}\sigma^2\end{cases}.\tag{3.A24}$$

Note that in the infinite horizon case (i.e., the problem in (3.A16) when $T=\infty$), eq. (3.A18) collapses to

$$0=\max_v\left(u(k,v)+LJ(k)-\rho J(k)\right),$$

subject to the transversality condition

$$\lim_{T\to\infty} e^{-\rho(T-t)} E_t\left(J\left(k_T\right)\right) = 0.$$

The deterministic model in appendix 3.B is a special case of the current setup.

References

Allais, M. (1947). *Economie et intérêt*. Paris: Imprimerie Nationale.

Blanchard, O, and S. Fischer (1989). *Lectures on Macroeconomics*. Cambridge, MA: MIT Press.

Brock, W., D. Hsieh, and B. LeBaron (1991). *Nonlinear Dynamics, Chaos, and Instability: Statistical Theory and Economic Evidence*. Cambridge, MA: MIT Press.

Cass, D. (1972). "On Capital Overaccumulation in the Aggregative, Neoclassical Model of Economic Growth: A Complete Characterization." *Journal of Economic Theory* 4, 200–223.

Cass, D., and K. Shell (1983). "Do Sunspots Matter?" *Journal of Political Economy* 91, 193–228.

Diamond, P. A. (1965). "National Debt in a Neoclassical Growth Model." *American Economic Review* 55, 1126–1150.

Farmer, R. (1998). *The Macroeconomics of Self-Fulfilling Prophecies*. Cambridge, MA: MIT Press.

Galí, J. (2008). *Monetary Policy, Inflation, and the Business Cycle*. Princeton, NJ: Princeton University Press.

Grandmont, J. M. (1985). "On Endogenous Competitive Business Cycles." *Econometrica* 53, 995–1045.

Hayashi, F. (1982). "Tobin's Marginal *q* and Average *q*: A Neoclassical Interpretation." *Econometrica* 50, 213–224.

Keynes, J. M. (1936). *The General Theory of Employment, Interest and Money*. London: Palgrave Macmillan.

King, R. G., and S. T. Rebelo (1999). "Resuscitating Real Business Cycles." In *Handbook of Macroeconomics*, edited by J. B. Taylor and M. Woodford. Amsterdam: Elsevier.

LeBaron, B. (1994). "Chaos and Nonlinear Forecastability in Economics and Finance." *Philosophical Transactions of the Royal Society of London* (A) 348, 397–404.

Ljungqvist, L., and T. J. Sargent (2018). *Recursive Macroeconomic Theory*. Cambridge, MA: MIT Press.

Lucas, R. E. (1972). "Expectations and the Neutrality of Money." *Journal of Economic Theory* 4, 103–124.

Lucas, R. E. (1978). "Asset Prices in an Exchange Economy." *Econometrica* 46, 1429–1445.

Lucas, R. E. (1994). "Money and Macroeconomics." In *General Equilibrium: 40th Anniversary Conference*, 184–187. Louvain-la-Neuve, Belg.: Center for Operations Research and Econometrics (CORE) Discussion Paper no. 9482.

Medio, A. (1992). *Chaotic Dynamics: Theory and Applications to Economics*. Cambridge: Cambridge University Press.

Merton, R. C. (1969). "Lifetime Portfolio Selection under Uncertainty: The Continuous-Time Case." *Review of Economics and Statistics* 51, 247–257.

Prescott, E. (1991). "Real Business Cycle Theory: What Have We Learned?" *Revista de Analisis Economico* 6, 3–19.

Samuelson, P. A. (1958). "An Exact Consumption-Loan Model of Interest With or Without the Social Contrivance of Money." *Journal of Political Economy* 66, 467–482.

Santos, M. S., and M. Woodford (1998). "Rational Asset Pricing Bubbles." *Econometrica* 65, 19–57.

Tirole, J. (1985). "Asset Bubbles and Overlapping Generations." *Econometrica* 53, 1499–1528.

Tobin, J. (1969). "A General Equilibrium Approach to Monetary Policy." *Journal of Money, Credit and Banking* 1, 15–29.

Watson, M. (1993). "Measures of Fit for Calibrated Models." *Journal of Political Economy* 101, 1011–1041.

Weil, P. (1987). "Confidence and the Real Value of Money in an Overlapping Generation Economy." *Quarterly Journal of Economics* 102, 1–22.

4

Continuous Time Models

4.1 Introduction

This chapter deals with models of asset prices and markets cast in continuous time. Continuous time does not obviously represent a novel economic concept *per se*. However, continuous time models may, at times, enable us to deal with issues arising in economies and markets more complex than those in the previous chapters. Moreover, on an applied perspective, continuous time models may be very conveniently used to evaluate derivative instruments that draw value from complex events, such as those relating to baskets of credit events, financial market volatility, or history-dependent developments in fixed income markets, to name a few (see part III). Continuous time models pose challenges to econometricians: we only observe a discrete realization of an idealized continuous time data-generating process. Chapter 6 surveys tools, based on simulations, which allow us to mitigate these challenges.

This chapter has three objectives. The first is to explain in detail how the principle of absence of arbitrage works in continuous time: how do asset prices need to "drift" to ensure that there is no arbitrage? How many possible "drifts" would we expect to see in arbitrage-free markets?

The second objective is to develop technical details about the properties of asset prices in continuous time. For example, we shall see that asset prices, once restricted by the absence of arbitrage, satisfy partial differential equations under regularity conditions. Yet asset prices are discounted expectations of their future payoffs, taken under the risk neutral probability. How are these properties tied together? We shall explain how these properties are tied to each other by introducing the celebrated Feynman–Kac theorem, which provides a probabilistic representation of the solution to a partial differential equation. Moreover, what is the relation between the risk neutral probability and the "physical" probability? How do we need to tilt the physical probability to determine the risk neutral? How many risk neutral probabilities exist in incomplete markets or in markets with frictions? Are there natural "pricing probabilities" arising in complex contexts, such as those in which interest rates are random? And how these pricing probabilities relate to the notion of *numéraires*? Girsanov theorem is the starting point that we need to deal with these fundamental questions.

The third objective is to begin describing some topics in real option theory. These topics are further developed in chapter 5 in order to address issues at the intersection of real option theory and corporate finance. The resulting framework of analysis allows us to deal with delicate problems regarding the interactions between financial markets and macroeconomic developments.

The models we consider in this chapter are diffusion models (with some extensions that accommodate for jumps), which are the workhorse in finance. Heuristically, diffusion models may be described as models by which changes in a variable of interest are driven by a deterministic component (the "drift") and a stochastic one (the "diffusion"). The diffusion component is normally distributed over an infinitesimal amount of time and is proportional to the changes of what is known as a "Brownian motion." Crucially, we typically assume that the fundamentals of the economy follow diffusion processes and that asset prices are "rational"; that is, they are a function of these fundamentals. Absence of arbitrage restricts the set of all possible rational pricing functions. The fundamental tool with which we link asset prices to fundamentals is Itô's lemma, a device we need to build new processes (in our case, the asset prices) from old ones (the fundamentals of the economy). The complication in finance is that these new processes, albeit a function of the fundamentals, are not given in advance; instead, they are the focus of research.

The chapter is organized as follows. The next section is an introduction to methods. It deals with details that originally led to the birth of continuous time finance: the Black–Scholes formula for evaluating European options; it also illustrates how continuous time models are obtained as limiting cases of discrete time models and also describes basic properties of long-lived asset prices, such as (i) the fundamental relations that link expected returns, volatilities (the "betas"), and risk premiums (the "lambdas"); and (ii) a representation of the price-dividend ratio in terms of certain possibly varying discount rates: the risk adjusted discount rates. These derivations help develop discussions regarding the properties of equity markets in chapters 8 and 9.

Sections 4.3, 4.4 and 4.5 deal with famous links between absence of arbitrage and martingales: section 4.3 explains how no-arbitrage restricts asset prices (rescaled by some numéraire) to be martingales under the risk neutral probability; section 4.4 deals with "martingale methods"; that is, methods for determining optimal consumption-portfolio pairs based on the previous "martingale probabilities" in contexts with complete markets; and section 4.5 deals with changes of probabilities under which asset prices (rescaled by the numéraires) are martingales. The content of these sections is fundamental to further developments in parts II and III: in particular, sections 4.3 and 4.4 contain material that help develop models of market fluctuations in part II; and section 4.5 provides helpful instruments in the context of asset evaluation in the equity, fixed income, and credit spaces (see part III).

Section 4.6 analyzes consumption-portfolio choices in both complete and incomplete markets and derives classical asset pricing results that generalize the static CAPM of chapter 1 and other models in chapter 2. Section 4.7 provides a succinct introduction to consumption-portfolio choices under market imperfections that generalize the incomplete market case in section 4.6. These sections help develop some of the models in chapter 9.

Section 4.8 is an introduction to real options theory, that is, the theory that analyzes choices based on some triggering events. It analyzes not only the pricing of American options but also irreversible investments and some theory of controlled Brownian motions. These models are used as benchmarks for dealing with some financial market frictions and macroeconomic developments in chapter 9.

Section 4.10 ends this chapter and introduces foundational issues on "discontinuities," that is, the fact that asset prices might undergo jumps—diffusion processes only have "continuous sample paths." It also develops the first extension in the literature of the Black–Scholes option pricing formula, based on a simple jump-diffusion model, known as Merton's pricing formula. Processes with jumps are also particularly useful to address evaluation problems regarding defaultable securities and will be used in chapter 14.

Finally, in addition to regular appendixes with technical details omitted from the main text, this chapter includes a self-contained appendix containing notions of stochastic calculus (appendix 4.A).

4.2 An Introduction to No-Arbitrage and Equilibrium

4.2.1 Time

By definition, long-lived assets do not have an expiration date, and their prices do not explicitly depend on calendar time,[1] at least insofar as the state variables driving them do not explicitly depend on time. Naturally, it does not mean that these prices cannot be time-varying or stochastic. On the contrary, they can well be driven by the random state variables, as we shall explain in a few sections.

Derivatives do, instead, have an expiration date, and their value reflects the time left to maturity, when they will be worth the terminal payoff. The presence of an expiration date implies that derivative prices solve partial differential equations, which also involve the price sensitivity to time. In the absence of any expiration date, asset prices are still solutions to partial differential equations, but their sensitivity to time is zero, at least provided that the state variables driving them are Markov variables. In the simple case of a single state variable, long-lived asset prices are then solutions to ordinary differential equations as in the Lucas model with a single state variable of section 4.2.6.

The next section develops the simplest possible setting where we can illustrate the main tools of continuous time finance, which is the Black and Scholes (1973) market leading to the evaluation formula for a European option. In the absence of arbitrage, the derivative price is solution to a certain partial differential equation, the solution of which we can represent as a conditional expectation taken under the risk neutral probability. In section 4.2.3, we provide the link between this risk neutral probability and the original probability.

4.2.2 The Origins: *Black–Scholes*

4.2.2.1 *Self-financed strategies*

With a self-financed portfolio, the change in a portfolio value between two instants t and $t + dt$ is determined as a mark-to-market P&L: the change in the asset prices multiplied by the quantities of the same assets held at time t. In other words, a self-financed portfolio can be implemented with no injection or withdrawal of funds over time. For example, let θ_t and S_t denote the number and the price of some risky security (say, some shares) at t

1. See, e.g., eq. (4.31).

and $\theta_{M,t}$ and M_t be the amount of riskless assets and their value at time t. Then, the value of a self-financed portfolio, $V = S\theta + \theta_M M$, satisfies

$$dV_t = \theta_t dS + \theta_{M,t} dM_t = \left(\frac{dS_t}{S_t} - \frac{dM_t}{M_t} \right) \pi_t + \frac{dM_t}{M_t} V_t,$$

where $\pi_t \equiv S_t \theta_t$ and the second equality follows by simple calculations. If the portfolio strategy involves trading into risky securities distributing an instantaneous dividend, D_t, and if c_t denotes instantaneous consumption, V_t then satisfies

$$dV_t = \left(\frac{dS_t}{S_t} + \frac{D_t}{S_t} dt - r dt \right) \pi_t + r V_t dt - c_t dt. \tag{4.1}$$

Appendix 4.B provides additional details regarding eq. (4.1).

4.2.2.2 *Black–Scholes partial differential equation*

Why are partial differential equations so important in finance? Suppose that the previous asset price is a geometric Brownian motion,

$$\frac{dS_t}{S_t} = \mu dt + \sigma dW_t, \; \mu, \sigma > 0, \tag{4.2}$$

and that there exists a riskless accounting technology or money market account (MMA) such that

$$\frac{dM_t}{M_t} = r dt,$$

where $r > 0$. Finally, suppose that there exists another asset, a "call option," which gives rise to a payoff equal to $(S_T - K)^+$ at some future date T, where K is the "strike," or exercise price of the option. Let $(C_t)_{t \in [0,T]}$ be the option price process. We wish to figure out what this price looks like while formulating as few assumptions as possible. We ignore dividend issues, assume there are no transaction costs, and rule out any other frictions. We assume *rational expectations*—that is, there exists a function $f : C_t = f(t, S_t)$, and assume that this function is as differentiable as needed for an application of Itô's lemma, such that:

$$dC = (Lf)\, dt + f_S \sigma S dW,$$

where Lf is the "infinitesimal generator," defined as $Lf = \frac{\partial f}{\partial t} + \frac{1}{2}\sigma^2 S^2 f_{SS} + \mu S f_S$, with subscripts denoting partial derivatives. Next, we create the following portfolio: θ_t units of the risky asset and, as a residual of wealth, $\theta_{M,t}$ units in the MMA, M_t. As explained, for any portfolio strategy to be "self-financed," the value V of the resulting portfolio satisfies eq. (4.1), that is, and assuming (4.2) and $D_t \equiv 0$,

$$dV_t = (\theta_t \mu S_t + r \theta_{Mt} M_t)\, dt + \theta_t \sigma S_t dW_t.$$

Now, set $V_0 = C_0$. Moreover, let us actually conjecture that we could choose θ_t and θ_{Mt} such that $V_t = C_t$ for all t, that is, that the self-financed strategy can replicate the option price. We obviously need to check this conjecture below. For now, note that if $V_t = C_t$ for all t, the drifts and diffusion coefficients of both V_t and C_t have to be the same, by a result stated in appendix 4.A, known as the *unique decomposition property*. Diffusion terms are the same when $\hat{\theta} = f_S$. Replacing this $\hat{\theta}$ into the dynamics of V produces

$$dV = \left(\mu S f_S + r\theta_M M\right) dt + f_S \sigma S dW. \tag{4.3}$$

Next, take $\hat{\theta}_M$: drift(V) = drift (C), that is,

$$\hat{\theta}_M = \frac{Lf - \mu f_S S}{rM}. \tag{4.4}$$

Because we are conjecturing that $V_t = C_t$ for all t:

$$f = C = \hat{V} \equiv \hat{\theta} S + \hat{\theta}_M \hat{M} = f_S S + \frac{Lf - \mu f_S S}{r}.$$

By the definition of L, and rearranging terms,

$$\frac{\partial f}{\partial t} + \frac{1}{2}\sigma^2 S^2 f_{SS} + rSf_S - rf = 0, \quad \forall (t, S) \in [0, T) \times \mathbb{R}_{++}, \tag{4.5}$$

subject to the "boundary condition" $f(T, S) = (S - K)^+$ for all S. Eq. (4.5) is a *partial differential equation*; that is, we are searching for an unknown function f, which has to be such that once it and its partial derivatives are plugged into the LHS of the first line, we obtain zero. Moreover, the same function must pick up the boundary condition. The solution to this is the celebrated Black and Scholes (1973) (hereafter, Black–Scholes) formula, $f(t, S) = C_{BS}(S, T - t; K, \sigma)$, where[2]

$$\begin{aligned} &C_{BS}(S_t, T - t; K, \sigma) \\ &= S_t \Phi(d_t) - K e^{-r(T-t)} \Phi(d_t - \sigma\sqrt{T-t}), \quad d_t \equiv \frac{\ln\left(\frac{S_t}{K}\right) + \left(r + \frac{1}{2}\sigma^2\right)(T - t)}{\sigma\sqrt{T-t}} \end{aligned} \tag{4.6}$$

and $\Phi(\cdot)$ denotes the cumulative normal distribution.

There are many ways to prove this very famous result. For example, we may rely on a direct calculation, similar to the one contained in appendix 4.C. In part III, we will review this formula again as this will be relied on while explaining many properties of market behavior under and beyond the assumptions underlying the Black–Scholes market. Remember, however, that the conjecture that $V_t = C_t$ holds for all t remains to be verified. We deal with this conjecture in section 4.2.2.4 while relying on a slightly more general perspective than that underlying the Black–Scholes market. Prior to verifying this important step, we study the nature of the strategy underlying the replication arguments in this section.

2. The case where $r = 0$ is dealt with similarly. If $r = 0$, we need to have $Lf = \mu f_S S$, by eq. (4.3) or, analogously, by eq. (4.4), which leads to eq. (4.5), with $r = 0$. In this case, the portfolio process is set equal to $\hat{M}_0 = V_0 - \hat{\theta}_0 S_0$ at inception of the strategy and then is constant, such that at each point in time, $V_t = \hat{\theta}_t S_t + \hat{M}_0$, with $dV_t = \hat{\theta}_t dS_t$.

4.2.2.3 *Replication by issuing debt*

We are interested in the sign of $\hat{\theta}_M$ in (4.4) in the context of the Black–Scholes option evaluation model. Note that

$$Lf - \mu f_S S = f_t + \frac{1}{2}\sigma^2 S^2 f_{SS} = rf\left(1 - S\frac{f_S}{f}\right) \leq 0,$$

where the first equality follows by the definition of the infinitesimal generator, the second by eq. (4.5) and, finally, the inequality follows by a property of the Black–Scholes formula (4.6) discussed in chapter 11 (see section 11.3). By (4.4), then, $\hat{\theta}_{Mt} \leq 0$. That is, in the Black–Scholes market, a European option can be replicated while investing θ_t in the underlying asset and issuing debt in proportions of $-\hat{\theta}_{Mt}$.

4.2.2.4 *Nonhedgeable claims*

Suppose that there exists a traded asset and that its price satisfies eq. (4.2). We want to replicate a generic "risk," a process $\varphi_t \equiv \varphi(S_t, t)$. By Itô's lemma,

$$d\varphi = \varphi_S dS + \left(\frac{\partial \varphi}{\partial t} + \frac{1}{2}\sigma^2 S^2 \varphi_{SS}\right) dt.$$

Consider as usual a self-financed strategy V_t; its value satisfies

$$dV_t = \theta_t dS_t + \theta_{M,t} dM_t.$$

We have

$$dV - d\varphi = (\theta - \varphi_S)\, dS + \left(r\theta_M M - \left(\frac{\partial \varphi}{\partial t} + \frac{1}{2}\sigma^2 S^2 \varphi_{SS}\right)\right) dt. \tag{4.7}$$

Therefore, and consistently with the Black–Scholes derivation in the previous subsection, a *necessary* condition for V_t to replicate φ_t is that

$$\hat{\theta}_t = \varphi_S(S_t, t), \quad \text{for all } t \in [0, T]. \tag{4.8}$$

Next, suppose φ is the price of a *traded* asset, one that delivers a payoff equal to $\varphi(S_T, T) = \psi(S_T)$ at time T, for some function ψ. Assume at the same time that the function $\varphi(S_t, t)$ satisfies the partial differential equation (4.9) below. We may ask: Wasn't the function $\varphi(S_t, t)$ given in advance? The answer is that, in the absence of arbitrage, we cannot be given a price of a traded risk in advance: this price must satisfy some restrictions, and we shall argue that this restriction is indeed summarized by eq. (4.9) below. It's a sort of Heisenberg principle: once we are able to replicate the value of a traded risk, the very same value must then satisfy some restrictions to prevent anyone from implementing an arbitrage strategy.

Indeed, suppose that we replicate the claim with $\hat{\theta}_t$ given by eq. (4.8), where $\varphi(S_t, t)$ satisfies (4.9). We need to have that $V_0 = \varphi(S_0, 0) = \varphi_0^{\$}$, where $\varphi_0^{\$}$ denotes the market price of the asset at time 0. Indeed, suppose this is not the case, for example, $V_0 < \varphi_0^{\$}$. We could make an immediate profit by going short the asset for $\varphi_0^{\$}$ and implementing a self-financing strategy with $\hat{\theta}_t$, such that $V_0 = \varphi(S_0, 0)$, where φ satisfies

$$L\varphi(S, t) = r\varphi(S, t) + (\mu - r)\varphi_S(S, t), \quad \text{with boundary condition } \varphi(S_T, T) = \psi(S_T). \tag{4.9}$$

We claim that $V_t = \varphi(S_t, t)$ for all $t \in [0, T]$. Indeed, by eq. (4.7),

$$dV - d\varphi = \left(r\theta_M M - \left(\frac{\partial \varphi}{\partial t} + \frac{1}{2}\sigma^2 S^2 \varphi_{SS} \right) \right) dt$$
$$= \left(r(V - \varphi_S S) - \left(\frac{\partial \varphi}{\partial t} + \frac{1}{2}\sigma^2 S^2 \varphi_{SS} \right) \right) dt$$
$$= r(V - \varphi)\, dt, \qquad (4.10)$$

where the first equality follows by eq. (4.8), the second by the self-financing condition $\theta_M M = V - \theta S$ and again by (4.8), and the third by (4.9). Because $V_0 = \varphi(S_0, 0)$, then (4.10) implies $V_t = \varphi(S_t, t)$ for all t, as claimed, and $V_T = \varphi(S_T, T) = \psi(S_T)$ too, which allows to honor the short sale of the asset.[3] The reasoning validates that the traded risk satisfies (4.9). Note that these arguments do not require that a market exists for this risk during the life of the contract.

The crucial assumption underlying the property that the strategy value replicates the risk $\varphi(S_t, t)$, $V_t = \varphi(S_t, t)$ for all t, is that $\varphi(S_t, t)$ *is the price of a traded asset*, that is, eq. (4.9) holds true. We can also show the converse. That is, suppose the strategy value replicates the risk through eq. (4.8). In this case, the LHS of (4.7) is zero, and by eq. (4.8),

$$\frac{\partial \varphi}{\partial t} + \frac{1}{2}\sigma^2 S^2 \varphi_{SS} = r\theta_M M = r(V - \theta S) = r(\varphi - \varphi_S S). \qquad (4.11)$$

Then the risk, φ, satisfies eq. (4.9).

Next, suppose that φ is *not* the price of a traded asset—for example, $\varphi(\cdot) = S^2$. Then the counterpart to (4.8) would be $\hat{\theta}_t = \varphi'(S_t)$, the counterpart to (4.10) would be

$$dV - d\varphi = \left(r\theta_M M - \frac{1}{2}\sigma^2 S^2 \varphi'' \right) dt, \qquad (4.12)$$

and the latter is identically zero when the following counterpart to (4.11) holds,

$$\frac{1}{2}\sigma^2 S^2 \varphi'' = r\theta_M M = r(V - \theta S) = r(\varphi - \varphi' S).$$

However, this ordinary differential equation cannot hold, unless $r + \sigma^2 = 0$. That is, assume that $V_t = \varphi(S_t)$ for all t; then, the LHS of eq. (4.12) cannot equal zero, contradicting that $V_t = \varphi(S_t)$ holds for all t.

All in all, we cannot replicate $\varphi(S_t) = S_t^2$ through a self-financed strategy. Naturally, we could replicate the payoff at maturity, S_T^2, provided a market exists for a claim to S_T^2 (see eq. (4.25) in the following section), not necessarily a market over the entire life of this derivative. The price of this asset is obviously not $\varphi(S_\tau) = S_\tau^2$ for each τ though. To

3. Suppose the opposite, that is, that $\varphi_0^\$ < V_0 = \varphi(0, S_0)$. We could then buy the asset for $\varphi_0^\$$ and, hence, claim for $\psi(S_T)$ at T. We could at the same time "short sell" the portfolio for $V_0 > \varphi_0^\$$ (guaranteeing a positive profit at time 0), which we could update through through the self-financed strategy $\hat{\theta}_t$ up to time T when it will deliver $-V_T = -\psi(S_T)$, which we could honor through the long static position in the asset initiated at time 0.

determine the *tracking error* of the portfolio, note that (assuming for brevity risk neutrality)

$$dV - d\varphi = \left(r\theta_M M - \frac{1}{2}\sigma^2 S^2 \varphi'' \right) dt$$
$$= \left(r(V - \varphi' S) - \frac{1}{2}\sigma^2 S^2 \varphi'' \right) dt$$
$$= \left(rV - \left(2r + \sigma^2\right) S^2 \right) dt. \tag{4.13}$$

Eq. (4.13) confirms that $dV = d\varphi$ only when $L\varphi = r\varphi$, which would imply that $r + \sigma^2 = 0$: an asset price equal to S_t^2 would be sustained only under this implausible parameter restriction.

An alternative to a self-financed strategy generating a tracking error is a strategy, which albeit not being self-financed, guarantees that the risk process is replicable. For example, one could set $\hat{\theta}_t = \varphi'(S_t)$ and

$$\hat{\theta}_{Mt} M_t = \varphi(S_t) - \hat{\theta}_t S_t. \tag{4.14}$$

While eq. (4.14) allows us by construction to replicate φ, it also obviously generates *a hedging cost* ε_t that satisfies $d\varepsilon_t = d\varphi - dV$. In the context of our example,

$$dV - d\varphi = \left(r\hat{\theta}_M M - \frac{1}{2}\sigma^2 S^2 \varphi'' \right) dt$$
$$= \left(r(\varphi - \varphi' S) - \frac{1}{2}\sigma^2 S^2 \varphi'' \right) dt$$
$$= -\left(r + \sigma^2 \right) S^2 dt, \tag{4.15}$$

where V is the value of the self-financed strategy implemented with $\hat{\theta}_t$.

In other words, the second line of (4.13) uses the *self-financing condition* $\hat{\theta}_{Mt} M_t = V_t - \hat{\theta}_t S_t$ while the second line of (4.15) relies on the *replicability condition* (4.14). Assuming $\varepsilon_t = 0$, the tracking error arising from (4.15) is a strictly positive process, and at time T it equals

$$\varepsilon_T = \left(r + \sigma^2 \right) \int_t^T e^{-(r+\sigma^2)(T-s)} V_s ds.$$

In section 4.3, we shall return to the issues regarding replicability of claims in the context of incomplete markets.

4.2.2.5 *Surprising cancellations*

The option price predicted by the Black–Scholes model is independent of the drift of the underlying asset. After reading this chapter, the reader will interpret this result as follows. Asset prices (rescaled by the MMA) are martingales under the so-called risk neutral probability (Q, say). Therefore, they are discounted expectations of payoffs under Q: Q is the probability under which asset prices drift proportionally to r. In other words, μ doesn't matter.

Let us analyze the details of this property in the context of the previous replicating arguments. Consider the following very simple example. Assume that

$$\begin{cases} \dfrac{dS_t}{S_t} &= \mu_t dt + \sigma dW_{1,t} \\ d\mu_t &= \mu_{D,t} dt + \sigma_{D,t} dW_{2,t} \end{cases} \tag{4.16}$$

where σ is a constant, μ_t, $\mu_{D,t}$ and $\sigma_{D,t}$ are some functions of time, and $W_{j,t}$, $j = 1, 2$, are two standard Brownian motions.

Consider the function $\varphi_t = \varphi(S_t, \mu_t, t)$, and assume it is solution to the following partial differential equation, generalizing (4.9),

$$\begin{aligned} &L^{S,\mu}\varphi = r\varphi + \varphi_S (\mu - r) S + \varphi_\mu (\mu_D - \hat{\mu}_D), \\ &\text{with boundary condition } \varphi(T, \mu_T, S_T) = \psi(S_T), \end{aligned} \tag{4.17}$$

where $L^{S,\mu}\varphi(S, \mu, t)$ is the infinitesimal generator of the diffusion process (4.16) and $\hat{\mu}_D$ is some function, interpreted as the drift of μ_t under the risk neutral probability. Note that once $\varphi_\mu = 0$ for each (t, S, μ), eq. (4.17) collapses to the Black–Scholes equation (4.9). We shall return to this point in a moment. Note that we are not saying $\varphi(S, \mu, t)$ is any option price.

Next, consider a self-financing strategy invested in the underlying asset and the MMA, just as in the previous section. We have, generalizing eq. (4.7), that

$$\begin{aligned} dV - d\varphi &= (\theta - \varphi_S) dS - \varphi_\mu d\mu \\ &\quad + \left(r\theta_M M - \left(\frac{\partial \varphi}{\partial t} + \frac{1}{2}\sigma^2 S^2 \varphi_{SS} + \frac{1}{2}\sigma_D^2 \varphi_{\mu\mu} \right) \right) dt. \end{aligned}$$

Let $\theta = \varphi_S$, use the definition of a self-financing strategy (i.e., $\theta_M M = V - \theta S = V - \varphi_S S$), and (4.17), such that the previous equation collapses to

$$dV - d\varphi = r(V - \varphi) dt - \varphi_\mu (d\mu - \varphi_\mu dt).$$

That is, taking $\varphi_\mu = 0$ implies that the strategy is self-financing and, by arguments similar to those in the previous section, replicates the option value. By no-arbitrage, the price of the option is then the Black–Scholes price even in this market with random drift. Chapter 11 explains that it is in general impossible to replicate the option when the asset return volatility is random: the Black–Scholes price is generally no longer the no-arbitrage price in a market with random volatility.

4.2.3 Asset Prices as Feynman–Kac Representations

4.2.3.1 A digression on more general partial differential equations

The Black–Scholes equation (4.5) is a typical (in fact, the first) example of partial differential equations in finance. It leads to an equation of the so-called parabolic type as we shall explain soon. More generally, let us be given

$$a_0 + a_1 F_t + a_2 F_S + a_3 F_{SS} + a_4 F_{tt} + a_5 F_{St} = 0, \tag{4.18}$$

subject to some boundary condition. This partial differential equation is called (i) elliptic, if $a_5^2 - 4a_3a_4 < 0$; (ii) parabolic, if $a_5^2 - 4a_3a_4 = 0$; or (iii) hyperbolic, if $a_5^2 - 4a_3a_4 > 0$.

The typical partial differential equations arising in finance are of the parabolic type. For example, the Black–Scholes function $F = e^{rt} f$ is parabolic. The following section explains how to provide a probabilistic representation to these parabolic partial differential equations.

4.2.3.2 *Feynman–Kac solutions to partial differential equations*

The typical situation that we encounter in finance is that the asset price is a function F that solves a parabolic partial differential equation, that is, a special case of eq. (4.18):

$$-r(x,t)F(x,t) + F_t(x,t) + \mu(x,t)F_x(x,t) + \frac{1}{2}\sigma^2(x,t)F_{xx}(x,t) = 0, \quad \forall (t,x) \in [0,T) \times \mathbb{R}, \tag{4.19}$$

with the boundary condition, $F(x,T) = g(x,T)$, for all x, with the function g being the final payoff. Somehow surprisingly, now define a stochastic differential equation with drift and diffusion μ and σ,

$$dZ_t = \mu(Z_t,t)\,dt + \sigma(Z_t,t)\,dW_t, \quad Z_0 = x, \tag{4.20}$$

where W_t is a Brownian motion. Under regularity conditions on μ, σ, r, the solution F to eq. (4.19) is

$$F(x,t) = E\left(e^{-\int_t^T r(Z_s,s)\,ds} g(Z_T,T) \middle| z_t = x \right), \tag{4.21}$$

where Z is solution to eq. (4.20) and the expectation is taken with respect to the distribution of Z in eq. (4.20). Note that the existence of the Feynman–Kac representation does not ensure per se the existence of a solution to a given partial differential equation.

Eq. (4.21) can be used to represent the solution to the Black–Scholes partial differential equation (4.5), with the "auxiliary" stochastic differential equation (4.20) collapsing to

$$\frac{dS_t}{S_t} = r\,dt + \sigma\,d\tilde{W}_t, \tag{4.22}$$

where $\tilde{W}_t$ is a Brownian motion defined under a certain probability, referred to as risk neutral probability, due to the property that the drift of $\frac{dS}{S}$ is the risk-free rate, r. That is, by eq. (4.21), the price of an option in a Black–Scholes market is the risk neutral expectation of the final payoff, discounted at the risk-free rate. We shall return to these notions in section 4.2.4 below.

The Feynman–Kac representation of the solution to partial differential equations is quite useful. First, computing expectations is generally both easier and more intuitive than finding a solution to partial differential equations through guessing and verification. Second, except for specific cases, the solution to asset prices is unknown, and a natural way to cope with this problem is to go for Monte Carlo methods—approximation of the expectation in eq. (4.21) through simulations and use of the law of large numbers. Finally, the Feynman–Kac representation theorem is useful for some theoretical reasons reviewed in appendix 4.D of this chapter.

4.2.3.3 *A few heuristic proofs*

We shall provide heuristic proofs of the Feynman–Kac representation theorem here; rigorous details of this proof are well beyond the scope of this book.[4] We shall consider a slightly more general case, in which

$$Lf + q - rf = 0, \tag{4.23}$$

subject to some boundary conditions. We interpret f as the asset price and q as its instantaneous dividend rate. We assume that q is some function $q(x,t) \equiv q_t$. We have, as usual, that $Lf = \frac{\partial f}{\partial t} + \mu f_x + \frac{1}{2}\sigma^2 f_{xx}$.

So, suppose that there exists a solution to eq. (4.23), and define

$$y_t \equiv e^{-\int_0^t r_u du} f(t, Z_t) + \int_0^t e^{-\int_0^u r_s ds} q_u du,$$

where Z_t is solution to eq. (4.20). By Itô's lemma,

$$dy = e^{-\int_0^t r_u du}\left((Lf + q - rf)dt + f_z \sigma dW\right) = e^{-\int_0^t r_u du} f_z \sigma dW,$$

where the second equality follows by eq. (4.23). Therefore, under regularity conditions, y is a martingale, with $y_0 = E(y_T)$, such that

$$f(0, Z_0) = y_0 = E(y_T) = E\left(e^{-\int_0^T r_t dt} f(T, Z_T)\right) + E\left(\int_0^T e^{-\int_0^u r_s ds} q_u du\right).$$

That is, the asset price at time 0, $f(0, z_0)$, equals the expected discounted value at T and the sum of the expected discounted dividends up to maturity. We now move to another pillar of continuous time evaluation: the Girsanov theorem.

4.2.4 The Girsanov Theorem

4.2.4.1 *Motivation again*

Consider the Black–Scholes partial differential equation (4.5). We now know that by the Feynman–Kac theorem, the price f can be represented as the discounted expectation of its terminal payoff, $f(T,S) = (S-K)^+$,

$$f(t, S_t) = e^{-r(T-t)}\mathbb{E}_t (S_T - K)^+, \tag{4.24}$$

where $\mathbb{E}_t$ denotes the expectation taken conditionally on the information set at t and, with respect to a new probability Q (say), under which S_t is solution to eq. (4.22), where $\tilde{W}$ is a Brownian motion under Q. We already explained that Q is referred to as the *risk neutral probability*, due to reasons similar to those explained in chapters 1–3: under Q, the expected rate of return of both the derivative and the underlying asset price is the riskless rate, r.

Note that the methodology leading to eq. (4.24) applies to derivatives other than Black–Scholes. Consider, for example, a "quadratic derivative,"that is, one that pays off the

4. For more technical details, excellent sources of reference are still Friedman (1975) and Karatzas and Shreve (1991).

square of the asset price at time T, S_T^2. The arguments made in the previous sections relating to the replication of this derivative are still the same—with a portfolio process that still includes $\hat{\theta} = f_S$ units of the risky assets, to be calculated below. The price of this derivative, then, still satisfies eq. (4.24), although the boundary condition is $f(T, S) = S^2$, such that the price can be expressed as

$$f(t, S_t) = e^{-r(T-t)}\mathbb{E}_t\left(S_T^2\right) = e^{-r(T-t)}S_t^2 e^{\left(2r+\sigma^2\right)(T-t)}. \tag{4.25}$$

This implies that the "hedging portfolio" is $\hat{\theta}_\tau = 2S_\tau e^{(r+\sigma^2)(T-\tau)}$. Indeed, it is easy to check that the value of the replicating strategy, $V_\tau = \hat{\theta}_\tau S_\tau + \hat{\theta}_{M_\tau} M_\tau$, coincides with eq. (4.25), using eq. (4.4). Chapter 11 provides a thorough discussion of the hedging portfolio in a Black–Scholes market.

4.2.4.2 *Relation between Q and P: Heuristic details*

How does the risk neutral probability Q relate to the physical one, P? Harrison and Kreps (1979) clarify this point while relying on Girsanov theorem. Consider the following heuristic details. Under P, S_t is solution to eq. (4.2), where W_t is a Brownian motion under P. Now, define $\eta_T \equiv \frac{dQ}{dP}$, and note that

$$\mathbb{E}_t(S_T - K)^+ = \int (S_T - K)^+ \, dQ = \int \eta_T (S_T - K)^+ \, dP = E_t\left(\eta_T (S_T - K)^+\right).$$

We claim that η_t is solution to

$$\frac{d\eta_t}{\eta_t} = -\lambda dW_t, \quad \eta_0 = 1,$$

where $\lambda = \frac{\mu - r}{\sigma}$. Indeed, define $y_t \equiv \eta_t f_t$. Because $f_T = (S_T - K)^+$, we have that $y_0 = f_0 = e^{-rT}E(y_T)$. That is, $e^{-rt}y_t$ is a martingale under the probability P. But by Itô's lemma,

$$d\left(e^{-rt}y\right) = e^{-rt}\eta\left(\frac{\partial f}{\partial t} + \frac{1}{2}\sigma^2 S^2 f_{SS} + (\mu - \lambda\sigma) S f_S - rf\right) dt + e^{-rt}\eta\left(\sigma S f_S - \lambda f\right) dW.$$

Under standard regularity conditions (including pathwise integrability), $e^{-rt}y_t$ is a martingale when

$$0 = \frac{\partial f}{\partial t} + \frac{1}{2}\sigma^2 S^2 f_{SS} + (\mu - \lambda\sigma) S f_S - rf. \tag{4.26}$$

On the other hand, we know that f is a solution to the Black–Scholes partial differential equation

$$0 = \frac{\partial f}{\partial t} + \frac{1}{2}\sigma^2 S^2 f_{SS} + rS f_S - rf. \tag{4.27}$$

Comparing eq. (4.26) and eq. (4.27) reveals $\lambda = \frac{\mu - r}{\sigma}$. The interpretation of λ is that of a *unit risk premium* for investing in the stock. We shall return to this important interpretation later.

The point of the previous derivations is that it is *as if* we start from the original probability space under which S_t is solution to eq. (4.2) and then define a new Brownian motion $d\tilde{W} = dW + \lambda dt$, such that replacing $\tilde{W}$ into eq. (4.2) delivers eq. (4.22) under some new probability space. Note that the Brownian motion we initially began with is obviously defined under P, although "pricing" is "operating" under a different space. This is among the most crucial concepts in financial economics and is formalized in the next section.

4.2.4.3 *The theorem*

Consider two probabilities Q and P, linked through $Q(A) = \int_A \eta dP$ for $A \in F$ (some event space), and the Radon-Nikodym derivative,

$$\left.\frac{dQ}{dP}\right|_{\mathbb{F}_T} = \eta_T = \exp\left(-\frac{1}{2}\int_0^T \|\lambda_t\|^2 dt - \int_0^T \lambda_t dW_t\right), \tag{4.28}$$

for some process λ_t, where $\mathbb{F}_T$ denotes the information set available at T;[5] W_t is a Brownian motion under P. Then,

$$\tilde{W}_t = W_t + \int_0^t \lambda_u du$$

is a Brownian motion under the probability Q.

The Girsanov theorem is the counterpart to the static and heuristic change of probability dealt with in chapter 1 (see section 1.4). Intuitively, in continuous time, a change in probability leads to a "mean-shift" of the random variable we are changing the distribution of. The fact that this change does not entail a change in volatility is well known in continuous time finance. The economic interpretation is that, all other things being equal, the shift toward the left reflects a more pessimistic assessment of the asset return distribution.

Finally, consider the following few additional details regarding asset evaluation. Suppose we wish to price a claim expiring at T. Heuristically, we have

$$\mathbb{E}_t(X_T) = \int X_T dQ = \int X_T \left(\frac{dQ}{dP}\right) dP = E_t\left[\left(\frac{dQ}{dP}\right) X_T\right] = E_t(\eta_T X_T).$$

Similarly, we can "update" the previous formula as time unfolds as follows:

$$\mathbb{E}_t(X_T) = \eta_t^{-1} E_t(\eta_T X_T),$$

where

$$\frac{d\eta_t}{\eta_t} = -\lambda_t dW_t, \quad \eta_0 = 1.$$

Section 4.4 explains additional properties regarding this change of probabilities. We now proceed to illustrate how these properties relate to the frameworks in the previous chapters. Precisely, we shall see that η_t relates to the pricing kernel through what we typically refer to as the "stochastic discount factor." Finally, we shall provide more economic structure on the risk premium λ_t, and we shall consider evaluation of long-lived assets.

---

5. This process is required to satisfy the so-called Novikov's condition, $E(\exp(\frac{1}{2}\int_0^T \|\lambda_t\|^2 dt)) < \infty$, which ensures that Q integrates to one, $E(\eta_T) = 1$, or $\int dQ = 1$.

4.2.5 The APT in Continuous Time

We explain how asset prices link to a number of state variables by deriving a continuous time version of the APT (see chapter 1) for a single asset, in which the asset's expected excess returns form a linear combination of the asset's exposures to factors, with weights equal to the unit risk premiums the market requires to bear the risk arising from each of these factors. We begin with a heuristic derivation of the pricing kernel in continuous time as the limit of a discrete time model; then we characterize the market expected returns in terms of the APT while relying on a diffusive model.

4.2.5.1 *Prices and pricing kernels from discrete to continuous time*

Let S_t be the price of a long-lived asset as of time t and $D_{t+h} \cdot h$ the dividend paid by this asset at t over a small trading period h. We know that in the absence of arbitrage, there exists a positive process $m_{t,\cdot}$, the *pricing kernel*, such that the price of any asset is the expectation of its future payoff, weighted with $m_{t,t+h}$,

$$S_t = E_t \left[m_{t,t+h} \left(S_{t+h} + D_{t+h} \cdot h \right) \right], \tag{4.29}$$

where E_t is the conditional expectation given the information set at time t. For example, in an economy with a representative risk neutral agent, we have that $m_{t,t+h} = e^{-r_t h}$, where r_t is the risk-free rate per unit of time.

Given the pricing kernel, we define the *stochastic discount factor* or state-price process, ξ_t, as the process that grows by the pricing kernel:

$$\xi_{t+h} = m_{t,t+h} \xi_t, \quad \xi_0 \equiv 1.$$

In terms of the stochastic discount factor, eq. (4.29) is $0 = E_t \left(\xi_{t+h} S_{t+h} - S_t \xi_t \right) + E_t \left(\xi_{t+h} D_{t+h} h \right)$, which, in the limiting case of h that tends to zero, is

$$0 = E_t \left[d \left(\xi_t S_t \right) \right] + \xi_t D_t dt. \tag{4.30}$$

Eq. (4.30) can be integrated to yield: $\xi_t S_t = E_t (\int_t^T \xi_u D_u du) + E_t \left(\xi_T S_T \right)$. Assuming that $\lim_{T \to \infty} E_t \left(\xi_T S_T \right) = 0$, the asset price satisfies

$$\xi_t S_t = E_t \left(\int_t^\infty \xi_u D_u du \right). \tag{4.31}$$

Note that $E_t \left(m_{t,t+h} \right) - 1 = e^{-r_t h} - 1 \approx -r_t h$,[6] from which it follows that

$$\frac{\xi_{t+h} - \xi_t}{\xi_t} \approx -r_t h + \left(m_{t,t+h} - E_t \left(m_{t,t+h} \right) \right). \tag{4.32}$$

In the presence of risk and risk averse agents, the innovations to the pricing kernel will drive fluctuations in the stochastic discount factor.

Many of the models in this chapter (and this book) are cast within a diffusion setting, such that the stochastic discount factor satisfies the continuous time limit to eq. (4.32),

$$\frac{d\xi_t}{\xi_t} = -r_t dt - \lambda_t \cdot dW_t, \tag{4.33}$$

6. Just set $S_{t+h} + D_{t+h} h \equiv 1$ in eq. (4.29), and interpret S_t as the price of a default-free zero coupon bond.

where W is a vector Brownian motion, which is assumed to drive fluctuations in asset prices, and λ is the vector of unit risk premiums.

The interpretation of ξ_t in eq. (4.33) is that it conveys information on the sources of variation in asset prices that agents need to be compensated for in order to invest. Without risk, $\xi_\tau = \xi_t e^{-r(\tau-t)}$; that is, ξ_τ reduces to the usual discount factor. Otherwise, ξ_τ varies stochastically, driven by potentially the same sources of variation that affect asset prices, dW_t. In particular, eq. (4.31) tells us that asset prices are expectations of future dividends discounted through ξ_τ. In more advanced sections of this chapter (see section 4.4), ξ_τ will be seen to relate to the continuous state counterpart of the Arrow-Debreu prices (see chapter 2). Heuristically, $\frac{\xi_\tau(\omega)}{\xi_t}dP$ is the value at time t of a unit of numéraire in some future state of the world ω at time τ, such that (4.31) is simply the sum of all dividend values.[7]

4.2.5.2 *Expected returns and the stochastic discount factors*

We determine the differential $d(\xi S)$ in eq. (4.30); by Itô's lemma,

$$d(\xi S) = Sd\xi + \xi dS + d\xi dS = \xi S\left(\frac{d\xi}{\xi} + \frac{dS}{S} + \frac{d\xi}{\xi}\frac{dS}{S}\right),$$

such that eq. (4.30) can be written as

$$E_t\left(\frac{dS}{S}\right) + \frac{D}{S}dt = -E_t\left(\frac{d\xi}{\xi}\right) - E_t\left(\frac{d\xi}{\xi}\frac{dS}{S}\right). \tag{4.34}$$

Eq. (4.34) holds for any asset price. Consider then, a locally riskless asset, that is, an asset with price dynamics given by $dS_{0t} = r_t S_{0t} dt$, where r_t is the short-term rate at t. This asset does not distribute dividends, such that $E_t(d\xi dS_0) = 0$. By (4.34), then $E_t(\frac{d\xi_t}{\xi_t}) = -r_t dt$. This result is the continuous time counterpart to eq. (4.32).

By eq. (4.34), the expected returns satisfy

$$E_t\left(\frac{dS}{S}\right) + \frac{D}{S}dt = rdt - E_t\left(\frac{d\xi}{\xi}\frac{dS}{S}\right). \tag{4.35}$$

We know (see section 4.2.3) that the expectations in eq. (4.35) can be reexpressed in terms of partial derivatives. Asset prices, then, solve partial differential equations as in some models in chapters 8 and 9. We now develop further details regarding the determinants of expected returns.

4.2.5.3 *Lambdas and betas*

Note that the asset price, S, is obviously driven by the same Brownian motions driving r and ξ, such that $E_t\left(\frac{d\xi}{\xi}\frac{dS}{S}\right) = -\text{Vol}\left(\frac{dS}{S}\right)\cdot\lambda dt$, where $\text{Vol}\left(\frac{dS}{S}\right)$ denotes the instantaneous volatility of asset returns (a vector, in case the asset price is driven by multiple state variables).

---

7. Finally, note that not all sources of variation in asset prices "receive compensation," and the elements of λ_t are zero precisely in correspondence of those sources of variation that do not require compensation.

Substituting this result into the RHS of eq. (4.35) leaves

$$E_t\left(\frac{dS}{S}\right)+\frac{D}{S}dt=rdt+\underbrace{\mathrm{Vol}\left(\frac{dS}{S}\right)}_{\text{"betas"}}\times\underbrace{\lambda}_{\text{"lambdas"}}\;dt. \tag{4.36}$$

Expected returns are equal to the short-term rate plus a risk premium due to the randomness of these very same returns. The premium is the product of the instantaneous risks related to the asset price fluctuations (the "betas," $\mathrm{Vol}\left(\frac{dS}{S}\right)$) times the unit risk premiums that compensate for each individual source of the instantaneous risks (the "lambdas," λ). Eq. (4.36) is, then, an APT relation, the continuous time counterpart to those developed in chapter 1. Indeed, the only assumption it relies on is absence of arbitrage; that is, a positive pricing kernel exists. We now proceed to a further decomposition of these expected returns.

4.2.5.4 *Risk adjusted discount rates*

How do we discount future cash flows in a model with multiple sources of risk? It seems that there is an obvious answer to this question: we should use the APT, that is, eq. (4.36). The answer to the question is actually subtle. Eq. (4.36) provides predictions on expected returns, but expected returns are not necessarily risk-adjusted discount rates. Naturally, expected returns and risk-adjusted discount rates would be the same if dividends and asset prices were driven by one and the same factor. However, the two notions deviate in a multifactor framework.

To illustrate these points in a simple case, we make the assumption that the price-dividend ratio, p say, is independent of the dividend level, D, and is driven by a vector of state variables, y, such that $S(D,y)=D\cdot p(y)$.[8] The asset price then satisfies $\frac{dS}{S}=\frac{dp}{p}+\frac{dD}{D}+\frac{dp}{p}\frac{dD}{D}$, such that by eq. (4.35),

$$E_t\left(\frac{dS}{S}\right)+\frac{D}{S}dt=\mathcal{R}dt-E_t\left(\frac{dp}{p}\frac{d\xi}{\xi}\right), \tag{4.37}$$

where

$$\mathcal{R}dt\equiv rdt-E_t\left(\frac{dD}{D}\frac{d\xi}{\xi}\right)=rdt+\underbrace{\sigma_0}_{\text{"cash-flow beta"}}\times\underbrace{\lambda_{CF}}_{\text{"cash-flow lambda"}}\;dt$$

and $\sigma_0\equiv\mathrm{Vol}\left(\frac{dD}{D}\right)$ (possibly a vector) and λ_{CF} denotes the unit-risk premium required to compensate for the randomness in the dividend process.

We refer to $\mathcal{R}$ as the *risk-adjusted discount rates*. They equal the safe interest rate r plus the premium, $-E_t(\frac{dD}{D}\frac{d\xi}{\xi})$, that arises to compensate for the stochastic fluctuations of dividends. Eq. (4.37) tells us that if the price-dividend ratio is constant, $E_t(\frac{dp}{p}\frac{d\xi}{\xi})=0$, the risk adjusted discount rates are the same as the expected returns, just as in the one-factor Lucas economy discussed in chapter 3.

If we assume that the price-dividend ratio is constant and that aggregate dividends D equal consumption, then σ_0 would be too small to make the expected returns predicted

8. This "scale-invariant" property occurs in many economies (see part II for more detailed discussion). For example, it occurs if (i) the dividends D are geometric Brownian motions and (ii) the distribution of y is independent of D.

by this model consistent with the data. This is the celebrated equity premium puzzle dealt with in much detail in part II. But eq. (4.37) reveals that expected returns could be inflated if the price-dividend ratio fluctuates, driven by additional state variables requiring compensation:

$$E_t\left(\frac{dp}{p}\frac{d\xi}{\xi}\right) = \underbrace{-\text{Vol}\left(\frac{dp}{p}\right)}_{\text{"price betas"}} \times \underbrace{\lambda_p}_{\text{"price lambdas"}} \quad dt. \tag{4.38}$$

This term does indeed represent a wedge between the expected returns and the risk-adjusted discount rates (see eq. (4.37)); therefore, it carries the potential to mitigate the equity premium puzzle. Note that eq. (4.38) describes the most natural channel through which expected returns are inflated: some state variable y fluctuates and leads the price-dividend ratio to fluctuate, thereby affecting the realized returns. If these fluctuations require compensation (meaning that their innovations affect the stochastic discount factor, $\lambda_p \neq 0$), they affect the expected returns. The "price betas" are the asset returns' exposure to factors arising through this channel, and the "price lambdas" are the corresponding unit premiums to bear these risks.

Chapter 8 explains that, in addition to the equity premium puzzle, time variation in *returns volatility* is a pervasive empirical property of asset prices. This property can be rationalized by time variation in risk-adjusted discount rates. Heuristically, note that returns volatility relates to the "price betas" in eq. (4.38). In a diffusion setting, the price beta relates to the semi-elasticity of the price-dividend ratio with respect to y, $\text{Vol}\left(\frac{dp}{p}\right) = \frac{p'(y)}{p(y)}\text{Vol}(dy)$; that is, the critical ingredient of the "price beta" is the very same price-dividend ratio in eq. (4.31).

Finally, note that under the assumptions made so far, eq. (4.31) can be rearranged, and further, by a change in probability, the price-dividend ratio can be reexpressed in terms of the risk-adjusted discount rates, as follows:

$$p(y_t) = \mathbb{E}\left(\int_t^\infty \frac{D_\tau^*}{D_t}\cdot e^{-\int_t^\tau \mathcal{R}(y_u)du}\,\middle|\, y_t\right), \quad \frac{D_\tau^*}{D_t} = e^{\left(g-\frac{1}{2}\sigma_0^2\right)(\tau-t)+\sigma_0\left(\hat{W}_\tau-\hat{W}_t\right)}, \tag{4.39}$$

where $\mathbb{E}$ and $\hat{W}_\tau$ denote expectation and Brownian motion under the risk neutral probability. Eq. (4.39) is a present value formula in which a fictitious risk-unadjusted dividend growth, D_τ^*/D_t, is discounted using the risk-adjusted discount rates, $\mathcal{R}(y_t)$.

Eq. (4.39) contains a representation of asset prices with its own interest. It also helps to illustrate some model mechanics of chapter 8, by which the sensitivity of the price-dividend ratio to changes in y_t is affected by how $\mathcal{R}(y_t)$ reacts to changes in y_t. Intuitively, if the risk-adjusted discount rates $\mathcal{R}(y_t)$ undergo large swings in bad times, the volatility predicted by eq. (4.39) would likely exhibit some of the interesting countercyclical statistics that we see in the data—statistics that are also reviewed in detail in chapter 8.

4.2.6 Example: No-Arbitrage in the Lucas Tree

4.2.6.1 Family of prices

Consider the Lucas (1978) model with one tree and one perishable good taken as the numéraire—the continuous time version of the model in chapter 3. We assume that the dividend is a geometric Brownian motion,

$$\frac{dD_t}{D_t} = gd\tau + \sigma_0 dW_t, \tag{4.40}$$

for two positive constants g and σ_0. We assume no sunspots and denote the rational pricing function with $S \equiv S(D)$. By Itô's lemma,

$$dS_t = \underbrace{gD_t S'(D_t) + \frac{1}{2}\sigma_0^2 D_t^2 S''(D_t)dt}_{\equiv \mu_{St} S_t} + \underbrace{\sigma_0 D_t S'(D_t) dW_t}_{\equiv \sigma_{St} S_t}. \tag{4.41}$$

Therefore, the law of accumulation for wealth satisfies eq. (4.1), with dividend and price dynamics given in eqs. (4.40) and (4.41).

In section 4.3, we explain that, in the absence of arbitrage, there must be some process λ, the "unit risk premium," such that

$$\mu_S + \frac{D}{S} - r = \lambda \sigma_S. \tag{4.42}$$

Let us assume that the short-term rate, r, and the risk premium, λ, are both constant. Below, we also show that this assumption is internally consistent in a general equilibrium economy. By the definition of μ_S and σ_S, eq. (4.42) can be written as

$$0 = \frac{1}{2}\sigma_0^2 D^2 S''(D) + (g - \lambda\sigma_0) DS'(D) - rS(D) + D. \tag{4.43}$$

Eq. (4.43) is a second-order differential equation. Its solution, provided it exists, is the rational price of the asset. To solve eq. (4.43), we initially assume that the solution, S_F say, takes the following simple form: $S_F(D_t) = K \cdot D_t$, where K is a constant to be determined. Next, we verify that this is indeed *one* solution to eq. (4.43). Indeed, if we guess that a solution has the same form as $S_F(D_t)$, then plugging this guess and its derivatives into eq. (4.43) leaves $K = (r - g + \lambda\sigma_0)^{-1}$; assuming, then, that K is bounded and positive, we obtain

$$S_F(D_t) = \frac{1}{r + \lambda\sigma_0 - g} D_t. \tag{4.44}$$

This is a Gordon-type formula. It merely states that prices are risk-adjusted expectations of future expected dividends, where the risk-adjusted discount rate is given by $r + \lambda\sigma_0$. Hence, in a comparative statics sense, stock prices are inversely related to the risk premium, a quite intuitive conclusion.

Eq. (4.44) can be thought as the Feynman–Kac representation to eq. (4.43), namely,

$$S_F(D_t) = \mathbb{E}_t\left(\int_t^\infty e^{-r(\tau - t)} D_\tau d\tau\right), \tag{4.45}$$

where $\mathbb{E}_t[\cdot]$ is the conditional expectation taken under the risk neutral probability Q (say), the dividend process follows

$$\frac{dD_t}{D_t} = (g - \lambda\sigma_0)\, d\tau + \sigma_0 d\tilde{W}_t,$$

and $\tilde{W}_\tau = W_\tau + \lambda(\tau - t)$ is a another standard Brownian motion defined under Q. Formally, the true probability, P, and the risk neutral probability, Q, are tied up by the Radon-Nikodym derivative, η_τ, defined as in (4.28), with a constant λ.

The reason we are referring to these prices as belonging to a "family of prices" is that we have not specified how preferences and beliefs affect the short-term rate, r, and the unit risk premium, λ. For example, we have assumed that r and λ are both constant. But when are r and λ constant? We now formulate an assumption regarding the agents' optimizing behavior that leads to the pricing results summarized so far. We will solve a model relying on solution methods known as *martingale methods*, which are reviewed again in section 4.4.

4.2.6.2 *Equilibrium with CRRA*

How precisely do agents' preferences affect asset prices? In eq. (4.44), the asset price depends on both the interest rate, r, and the unit risk premium, λ. We now formulate an assumption on the agents' behavior and pin down a particular expression for r and λ that arise in equilibrium. The impact of agents' preferences on the equilibrium interest rate and the risk premium may be subtle. For example, we shall see that when risk aversion is low, a small change in it implies that r and λ move in the same direction. However, if risk aversion is high, r and λ may move in different directions. The examples in this section show, then, how delicate it is to implement a thought experiment by which we try to change r while fixing λ, or vice versa.

Consider the dynamics of wealth in eq. (4.1). It is easy to show that, under the risk neutral probability Q, V is solution to

$$dV_t = (rV_t - c_t)\,d\tau + \pi_t \sigma_S d\tilde{W}_t. \tag{4.46}$$

This result is shown in more detail in section 4.3. The intuition now is that eq. (4.46) holds by plugging eq. (4.42) into eq. (4.1). We assume that the following transversality condition holds:

$$\lim_{T\to\infty} \mathbb{E}_t\left(e^{-r(T-t)}V_T\right) = 0. \tag{4.47}$$

Integrating eq. (4.46) and using the previous transversality condition leaves

$$V_t = \mathbb{E}_t\left(\int_t^\infty e^{-r(\tau-t)} c_\tau d\tau\right). \tag{4.48}$$

Now, in equilibrium, $D_t = c_t$, such that eqs. (4.45) and (4.48) imply that $S_t = V_t$: wealth equals the asset value.

Next, consider an economy with a single agent who has CRRA equal to γ. The agent has a subjective discount rate ρ and maximizes their intertemporal utility

$$\max_c E_t\left(\int_t^\infty e^{-\rho(\tau-t)} u(c_\tau)\,d\tau\right) \quad \text{s.t. } V_t = E_t\left(\int_t^\infty m_{t,\tau} c_\tau d\tau\right), \tag{4.P1}$$

where $u(c) = \frac{c^{1-\gamma}}{1-\gamma}$. The constraint in [4.P1] follows by a change of probability in eq. (4.48) after defining $m_{t,\tau} \equiv \frac{\xi_\tau}{\xi_t}$, where ξ_τ denotes, as usual, the stochastic discount factor.

Marginal utility and stochastic discount factor link similarly as explained in previous chapters (see, e.g., section 2.6 in chapter 2). Indeed, the first-order conditions for [4.P1] are $\kappa e^{\rho(\tau-t)} m_{t,\tau} = c_\tau^{-\gamma} = D_\tau^{-\gamma}$, where κ is a Lagrange multiplier and the last equality follows by the equilibrium condition, $c_\tau = D_\tau$. Now, apply Itô's lemma, and expand both sides of the first-order conditions,

$$dD_t^{-\gamma} = \left(-\gamma g + \frac{1}{2}\sigma_0^2 \gamma (\gamma+1)\right) D_t^{-\gamma} dt - \gamma D_t^{-\gamma} \sigma_0 dW_t = D_t^{-\gamma} \left((\rho - r)\, dt - \lambda dW_t\right).$$

But drifts and volatilities of the first and the second equality have to be the same, which leaves the following expressions for r and λ,

$$r = \rho + \gamma g - \frac{1}{2}\gamma(\gamma+1)\sigma_0^2, \quad \lambda = \gamma\sigma_0, \tag{4.49}$$

two constants.

Eq. (4.49) can be interpreted as follows. The first term, ρ, reflects subjective discounting. The second term is related to intertemporal substitution effects: the interest rate increases with g as higher growth incentivizes to save less. Further, note that γ is the inverse of the elasticity of intertemporal substitution (EIS) (see section 3.2.3 in chapter 3); so when the EIS is very high, the representative agent has a very elastic bond demand, such that the bond price and hence the interest rate is not very sensitive to changes in g. Finally, the third term is decreasing in γ, reflecting precautionary motives: these motives matter more for higher levels of uncertainty, σ_0^2. When γ is sufficiently low, intertemporal substitution effects prevail such that the interest is increasing in γ. When γ (or σ_0^2) is sufficiently high, precautionary motives prevail, and interest rates decrease with γ. These properties will be discussed again in many junctures of the book, notably in part II (see, e.g., section 7.2 in chapter 7 or section 9.2 in chapter 9).

Let us come back to determine the asset price. Replacing eqs. (4.49) into eq. (4.44) leaves

$$S(D_t) = \frac{1}{\rho - (1-\gamma)\left(g - \frac{1}{2}\gamma\sigma_0^2\right)} D_t. \tag{4.50}$$

We claim that the denominator in (4.50) is strictly positive if the transversality condition (4.47) holds in equilibrium, $S_t = V_t$. Indeed,

$$\begin{aligned}
\lim_{T\to\infty} \mathbb{E}_t\left(e^{-r(T-t)} V_T\right) &= \lim_{T\to\infty} \mathbb{E}_t\left(e^{-r(T-t)} S_T\right) \\
&= \lim_{T\to\infty} E_t\left(m_{t,T} S_T\right) \\
&= S_t \lim_{T\to\infty} e^{-(r-g+\sigma_0\lambda)(T-t)} \\
&= S_t \lim_{T\to\infty} e^{-\left(\rho-(1-\gamma)(g-\frac{1}{2}\gamma\sigma_0^2)\right)(T-t)} \\
&= 0.
\end{aligned} \tag{4.51}$$

We now further elaborate on the transversality condition (4.47).

4.2.6.3 Bubbles

We may refer (4.47) to as a *no-bubble condition*. Indeed, note that, in addition to $S_F(D)$, the function $\hat{S}(D) \equiv AD_\tau^\delta$ also satisfies eq. (4.43) for any arbitrary constant A. Now, plugging $\hat{S}(D)$ into eq. (4.43) shows that δ satisfies

$$0 = \delta(g - \lambda\sigma_0) + \frac{1}{2}\delta(\delta - 1)\sigma_0^2 - r. \tag{4.52}$$

This quadratic equation in δ has two solutions, say, $\delta_1 < 0$ and $\delta_2 > 0$. Therefore, the asset price does actually take the form

$$S(D_t) = S_F(D_t) + A_1 D_t^{\delta_1} + A_2 D_t^{\delta_2}, \tag{4.53}$$

where $\lim_{D \to 0} |S(D)| = \infty$ if $A_1 \neq 0$. We set $A_1 = 0$ to rule out that the price explodes as the dividend gets small, leaving

$$S(D_t) = S_F(D_t) + \mathcal{B}(D_t), \tag{4.54}$$

where $\mathcal{B}(D) \equiv A_2 D^{\delta_2}$.

The component $S_F(D)$ is the risk-adjusted present value of the expected dividends (see Eq. (4.45)) and, hence, is the asset's *fundamental value*. The second component may then be interpreted as a bubble, that is, the difference between the asset value $S(D)$ and the fundamental value $S_F(D)$. We seek conditions under which $S(D)$ in (4.54) satisfies the transversality condition in eq. (4.47). We have

$$\lim_{T\to\infty} \mathbb{E}_t\left(e^{-r(T-t)} S_T\right) = \lim_{T\to\infty} \mathbb{E}_t\left(e^{-r(T-t)} S_F(D_T)\right) + \lim_{T\to\infty} \mathbb{E}_t\left(e^{-r(T-t)} \mathcal{B}(D_T)\right).$$

By eq. (4.51), the fundamental value of the asset satisfies the transversality condition, provided the denominator in eq. (4.50) is strictly positive. Regarding the bubble, we have

$$\begin{aligned}\lim_{T\to\infty} \mathbb{E}_t\left(e^{-r(T-t)} \mathcal{B}(D_T)\right) &= A_2 \lim_{T\to\infty} \mathbb{E}_t\left(e^{-r(T-t)} D_T^{\delta_2}\right)\\ &= A_2 D_t^{\delta_2} \cdot \lim_{T\to\infty} e^{\left(\delta_2(g-\lambda\sigma_0)+\frac{1}{2}\delta_2(\delta_2-1)\sigma_0^2 - r\right)(T-t)}\\ &= A_2 D_t^{\delta_2},\end{aligned}$$

where the last line holds as δ_2 satisfies eq. (4.52). That is, the bubble cannot satisfy the transversality condition, and we set $A_2 = 0$. Thus, in this economy, the transversality condition in eq. (4.47) holds if and only if there are no bubbles.

4.2.6.4 Reflecting barriers and absence of arbitrage

Consider the following extension of the previous model. When the dividend D_t fluctuates above some level $\underline{D} > 0$, the dividend is "free" to fluctuate according to the geometric Brownian motion model of the previous section. However, when the dividend hits a "barrier" $\underline{D}$, it is "reflected" back with probability one. We describe these dynamics by saying that the dividend is a process with *reflecting barriers*. Alternatively, one may think that the firm has "infinitely deep pockets," in that it can always guarantee that the dividends it distributes are solutions to

$$\frac{dD_t}{D_t}=gdt+\sigma_0 dW_t+dU_t, \tag{4.55}$$

where U_t is a continuous, nonnegative process that increases only when D_t hits $\underline{D}$. We may think of the firm as operating on an "infinitesimal intervention" scale.

Eq. (4.55) generalizes eq. (4.40), in that D_t cannot decrease below a threshold. How does the asset price behave in this context? By Itô's lemma and eq. (4.55),

$$\begin{aligned} dS_t &= S'(D_t)\,dD_t+\frac{1}{2}\sigma_0^2D_t^2S''(D_t)\,dt \\ &=\left(S'(D_t)\,gD_t+\frac{1}{2}\sigma_0^2D_t^2S''(D_t)\right)dt+S'(D_t)\,\sigma_0D_tdW_t+S'(D_t)dU_t. \end{aligned} \tag{4.56}$$

We claim that to ensure absence of arbitrage, the following *smooth pasting* condition must hold:

$$S'(\underline{D})=0. \tag{4.57}$$

Indeed, the dividends D_t are reflected at the barrier $\underline{D}$; since reflection takes place with probability one, the asset is locally riskless at $\underline{D}$. To rule out arbitrage, we require that, at $\underline{D}$, the price only moves by its predictable component, the drift in (4.56). This condition is satisfied when $S'(D_t)=0$ for $D_t=\underline{D}$. In this case, the last component in (4.56) becomes $S'(\underline{D})dU_t=0$ for all t. Then, by standard arguments (i.e., eq. (4.42)),

$$\mu_{S,t}+\frac{D_t}{S_t}-r=\lambda\sigma_S(D_t)\equiv\lambda\frac{\sigma_0D_tS'(D_t)}{S(D_t)},$$

where $\mu_{S,t}\equiv\frac{d}{d\tau}E_t\left(\frac{S_\tau}{S_t}\right)\Big|_{\tau=t}$. By eq. (4.57), then, we have that, at $D_t=\underline{D}$,

$$\mu_S+\frac{\underline{D}}{S}=r.$$

In words, suppose that we hold the asset during the infinitesimal period in which "the reflection" takes place. During this time, the asset is locally riskless (due to reflection) and thus cannot earn more or less than the riskless rate. Indeed, by the previous relation and by imposing that $\sigma_S(\underline{D})=0$, we have that wealth satisfies (see eq. (4.1)),

$$dV=\left(\pi\left(\mu_S+\tfrac{\underline{D}}{S}-r\right)+rV-c\right)dt+\pi\sigma_S(\underline{D})dW=(rV-c)\,dt.$$

This example illustrates how arbitrage restrictions operate through eq. (4.42).

To solve the model, note that while dividends fluctuate above the barrier, $D_t>\underline{D}$, the price is still as in eq. (4.53),

$$S(D_t)=\frac{D_t}{r-g+\lambda\sigma_0}+A_1D_t^{\delta_1}+A_2D_t^{\delta_2}.$$

We set $A_2=0$, meaning that the effects of a lower barrier $\underline{D}$ on the price dynamics are not perceptible when dividends are large. To determine A_1, we pin down the price at the barrier $\underline{D}$. We have $K \equiv S_F(D)/D$ and

$$0 = S'(\underline{D}) = K + \delta_1 A_1 \underline{D}^{\delta_1 - 1}, \quad \underline{S} \equiv S(\underline{D}) = K\underline{D} + A_1 \underline{D}^{\delta_1},$$

where the second condition is the *value matching condition*, which we impose to ensure the continuity of the price with respect to D and hence absence of arbitrage. The solution to the previous system is

$$\underline{S} = \frac{1-\delta_1}{-\delta_1} K\underline{D} \quad \text{and} \quad A_1 = \frac{K}{-\delta_1} \underline{D}^{1-\delta_1}. \tag{4.58}$$

The price is an increasing and convex function of the fundamental, D.[9] Convexity reflects the "option-like" feature of the dividends barrier, $\underline{D}$.

Finally, note that $\underline{D}$ is exogenously given in this model. Chapter 5 (see section 5.7) considers models in which dividends' distribution is endogenous within a number of dynamic corporate finance theories. In these models, dividends are "controlled" as part of an optimization problem.

4.3 Martingales and Arbitrage I: Viability

4.3.1 Trees

We still consider a Lucas economy in which trees are exchanged without frictions and initially fix a finite horizon $T < \infty$. Let $(\Omega, \mathcal{F}, P)$ be a probability space and W be a standard d dimensional Brownian motion. Define $\mathbb{F} = (\mathbb{F}_t)_{t \in [0,T]}$ to be the P augmentation of the natural filtration $\mathbb{F}_\tau^W = \sigma(W_s,\ s \le \tau)$ generated by W, with $\mathbb{F} = \mathbb{F}_T$. We assume that prices, interest rates, and dividends are all adapted to $\mathbb{F}$. For further reference, we define $L^2_{0,T,d}$ to be the space of all $\mathbb{F}_t$-adapted processes x in $\mathbb{R}^d$ satisfying $\int_0^T \|x_u\|^2 du \in (0, \infty)$.

We consider m trees and an MMA. Section 4.6 considers extensions to markets with additional assets in zero net supply, such as derivatives. Let $S_{0\tau} = e^{\int_t^\tau r_u du}$ denote the value of a unit MMA, where r_t is the instantaneous or short-term interest rate taken to be adapted to $\mathbb{F}$; we assume that $E_t(S_{0\tau})$ is bounded. The trees entitle owners to receive dividends D_{it}, the numéraire, and the price of each tree at time t, S_{it}, satisfies

$$\frac{dS_{it}}{S_{it}} = \bar{\mu}_{it} dt + \sigma_{it} dW_t, \quad i = 1, \cdots, m, \tag{4.59}$$

where $\bar{\mu}_{it}$ is scalar and $\sigma_{it} \in \mathbb{R}^d$. We assume that $\bar{\mu}_{it}$ and σ_{it} satisfy regularity conditions that guarantee a solution to eq. (4.59). Let $\sigma_t \equiv [\sigma_{1t}, \cdots, \sigma_{mt}]^\top$, and assume that rank $(\sigma_t) = m \le d$ for all t. We assume that the dividend D_i is solution to

$$\frac{dD_{it}}{D_{it}} = g_{it} dt + \sigma_{0i,t} dW_t,$$

where g_{it} and $\sigma_{0i,t}$ are $\mathbb{F}_t$-adapted, with $\sigma_{0i} \in \mathbb{R}^d$.

---

9. This model takes the barrier $\underline{D}$ as given. However, one may be interested in "controlling" the dividend D_τ in a way that, as soon as the price S_τ hits an exogenous given level $\underline{S}$, the dividend is activated to induce the price to increase back. It is straightforward to see that the solution for the dividend level that triggers this "infinitesimal" intervention is obtained by inverting the first equation in (4.58) for the dividend threshold.

The value of an investment strategy net of dividends is $V_t \equiv \sum_{i=0}^{m} \theta_{it} S_{it}$, where θ_{it} denotes the number of assets i invested at time t. The vector of all such θ_i is taken to be a predictable process in $\mathbb{R}^{m+1}$, satisfying standard regularity conditions.[10] Similarly as in section 4.2, we say that a strategy is self-financing if its value V is the solution to

$$dV_t = \left(\pi_t^\top (\mu_t - \mathbf{1}_m r_t) + r_t V_t - c_t\right) dt + \pi_t^\top \sigma_t dW_t, \tag{4.60}$$

where $\mathbf{1}_m$ is an m-dimensional vector of ones, $\pi \equiv [\pi_1, \cdots, \pi_m]^\top$ with generic element $\pi_i \equiv \theta_i S$, and μ is an m-dimensional vector with generic element $\bar{\mu}_i + \frac{D_i}{S_i}$. We require V to be strictly positive.

4.3.2 Martingale Restrictions

Define the gain process for asset i as $\bar{g}_{it} = \frac{S_{it}}{S_{0t}} + \bar{z}_{it}$, where $d\bar{z}_{it} = \frac{1}{S_{0t}} D_{it} dt$. We generalize the notion of risk neutral probability introduced in section 4.2 by defining a set $\mathcal{Q}$ of probabilities under which $\bar{g}_{it}$ is a martingale. Then, and similarly as in previous formulations of no-arbitrage results,[11] the set $\mathcal{Q}$ is not empty if and only if the market is arbitrage free. We provide a heuristic proof of this result relying on Girsanov's theorem (see section 4.2.4). Given an $\mathbb{F}_t$-adapted process λ_t, define $\hat{W}_t = W_t + \int_0^t \lambda_u du$, a standard Brownian motion under a probability Q equivalent to P, with Radon-Nikodym derivative equal to

$$\eta_T^0 = \left.\frac{dQ}{dP}\right|_{\mathbb{F}_T} = \exp\left(-\frac{1}{2}\int_0^T \|\lambda_\tau\|^2 d\tau - \int_0^T \lambda_\tau^\top dW_\tau\right). \tag{4.61}$$

The dynamics of the gain process under Q are

$$d\bar{g}_{it} = \frac{S_{it}}{S_{0t}}\left((\mu_{it} - \sigma_{it}\lambda_t - r_t)\, dt + \sigma_{it} d\hat{W}_t\right).$$

Requiring $\bar{g}_i$ to be a martingale under any $Q \in \mathcal{Q}$ leads to the following restriction:

$$\mu_t - \mathbf{1}_m r_t = \sigma_t \lambda_t. \tag{4.62}$$

We now show that eq. (4.62) is a *martingale restriction* each asset price satisfies in the absence of arbitrage. First, note the implications of this restriction on the dynamics of wealth. By eqs. (4.60) and (4.62), we have that, for $\tau \in [t, T]$,

$$\frac{V_\tau}{S_{0\tau}} = V_t - \int_t^\tau \frac{c_u}{S_{0u}} du + \int_t^\tau \frac{\pi_u^\top \sigma_u}{S_{0u}} d\hat{W}_u. \tag{4.63}$$

Consider the following definition.

Definition 4.1 (Arbitrage opportunity). *A portfolio π is an arbitrage opportunity if, for any zero-consumption path $c_\tau \equiv 0$, one has that $V_t \le S_{0T}^{-1} V_T$ and* $\Pr\left(S_{0T}^{-1} V_T - V_t > 0\right) > 0$.

10. Namely, it is required that this vector θ (say) satisfies $E_t(\int_t^T \|\theta_\tau\|^2 d\tau) < \infty$ to rule out arbitrage through "doubling strategies"—doubling the bets until we win.
11. See, e.g., theorem 2.9 in chapter 2.

We have:

Theorem 4.2. *There are no arbitrage opportunities if and only if the set of risk neutral probabilities Q is not empty.*

A proof of this fundamental result is in appendix 4.C. Note that the "if" part follows easily by eq. (4.63). The "only if" part is more elaborate, and it can be outlined as follows. We want to claim that absence of arbitrage implies that Q is nonempty or, equivalently, by Girsanov's theorem, that there exists λ satisfying eq. (4.62). Now, if eq. (4.62) didn't hold, we could implement an arbitrage as follows. We could find a nonzero $\underline{\pi} : \underline{\pi}^\top \sigma = 0$ and $\underline{\pi}^\top (\mu - \mathbf{1}_m r) \neq 0$. Then, we could use $\underline{\pi}$ when $\mu - \mathbf{1}_m r > 0$ and $-\underline{\pi}$ when $\mu - \mathbf{1}_m r < 0$, thereby obtaining an appreciation rate of V larger than r in spite of having zeroed uncertainty through $\underline{\pi}^\top \sigma = 0$. Eq. (4.62) rules out this arbitrage because we have that, for each π, $\pi^\top (\mu - \mathbf{1}_m r) = \pi^\top \sigma \lambda$. More precisely, define

$$\langle \sigma^\top \rangle^\perp \equiv \left\{ x \in L^2_{t,T,m} : \sigma^\top x = 0_d \right\} \quad \text{and} \quad \langle \sigma \rangle \equiv \left\{ z \in L^2_{t,T,m} : z = \sigma u, \; u \in L^2_{t,T,d} \right\}.$$

Then we may formalize the previous reasoning as follows. The excess return vector, $\mu - \mathbf{1}_m r$, must be orthogonal to all vectors in $\langle \sigma^\top \rangle^\perp$, and since $\langle \sigma \rangle$ and $\langle \sigma^\top \rangle^\perp$ are orthogonal, $\mu - \mathbf{1}_m r \in \langle \sigma \rangle$, or $\exists \lambda \in L^2_{t,T,d} : \mu - \mathbf{1}_m r = \sigma \lambda$.[12]

4.3.3 Market Completeness

Consider the following definition.

Definition 4.3 (Dynamically complete markets). *Markets are* dynamically complete *if for each random variable $Y \in L^2(\Omega, \mathcal{F}, P)$, we can find a portfolio process such that the terminal wealth achieved with that process (when initial wealth is x) equals Y, that is, $\pi : V_T^{x,\pi} = Y$ a.s.*

The previous definition is the natural continuous time counterpart to that given in the discrete time case (see chapter 2). Consistent with the conclusions in chapter 2, we shall explain that, in continuous time, markets are dynamically complete if and only if (i) $m = d$ and (ii) the volatility matrix of the available asset (primitive assets and derivatives) returns is nonsingular. We shall provide a sketch of the proof for the sufficiency part of this statement, which regards the existence of spanning dynamic strategies.[13] So, given a $Y \in L^2$, let $m = d$, and suppose the volatility matrix σ is nonsingular. Let us consider the Q martingale,

$$M_\tau \equiv \mathbb{E}\left(S_{0T}^{-1} \cdot Y \middle| \mathbb{F}_\tau \right). \tag{4.64}$$

By a result known as representation of Brownian martingales[14] and often referred to as *martingale representation theorem*, a continuous local martingale can be expressed as a stochastic integral with respect to Brownian motions:[15] there exists a $\varphi \in L^2_{0,T,d}$ such that

$$M_\tau = M_t + \int_t^\tau \varphi_u^\top d\hat{W}_u.$$

12. Appendix 4.C provides the proof that $\langle \sigma \rangle$ and $\langle \sigma^\top \rangle^\perp$ are orthogonal.
13. Karatzas (1997, 8–9), for example, provides a proof of the converse.
14. See, e.g., theorem 4.15 (chapter 3) in Karatzas and Shreve (1991).
15. See, e.g., Karatzas and Shreve (1991, 170, theorem 4.2).

We wish to find a portfolio process π such that the discounted wealth process net of consumption, $S_{0\tau}^{-1}V_{\tau}$, equals M_{τ} under P or equivalently under Q. By eq. (4.63),

$$\frac{V_{\tau}^{x,\pi}}{S_{0\tau}} = x + \int_{t}^{\tau} \frac{\pi_u^{\top}\sigma_u}{S_{0u}} d\hat{W}_u,$$

such that, by identifying, the portfolio we are searching for is $\hat{\pi}^{\top} = S_0\varphi^{\top}\sigma^{-1}$. Set $x = M_t$. Then $M_{\tau} = S_{0\tau}^{-1}V_{\tau}^{M_t,\hat{\pi}}$, and in particular, $M_T = S_{0T}^{-1}V_T^{M_t,\hat{\pi}}$. Comparing with eq. (4.64) leaves $V_T^{M_t,\hat{\pi}} = Y$. Therefore—and because there exists a unique λ satisfying $\mu - \mathbf{1}_m r = \sigma\lambda \Longleftrightarrow m = d$—we have the following result.

Theorem 4.4. *$\mathcal{Q}$ is a singleton if and only if markets are complete.*

Similarly as in the discrete time models of chapter 2, when markets are incomplete, absence of arbitrage does not allow us to identify a unique risk neutral probability. The next results provide additional characterizations of the many risk neutral probabilities in $\mathcal{Q}$ in the incomplete markets case. Define $\langle\sigma\rangle^{\perp} \equiv \{x \in L_{0,T,d}^2 : \sigma_t x_t = 0_m\}$. Let

$$\hat{\lambda} = \sigma^{\top}\left(\sigma\sigma^{\top}\right)^{-1}(\mu - \mathbf{1}_m r).$$

Under the usual regularity conditions, $\hat{\lambda}$ can be interpreted as the process of unit risk premiums. In fact, *all* processes belonging to the set $\mathcal{Z} = \{\lambda : \lambda_t = \hat{\lambda}_t + \nu_t,\ \nu \in \langle\sigma\rangle^{\perp}\}$ are bounded and then are interpreted as unit risk premiums processes. More precisely, define the Radon-Nikodym derivative of Q with respect to P on $\mathbb{F}_T$,

$$\hat{\eta}_T \equiv \left.\frac{dQ}{dP}\right|_{\mathbb{F}_T} = \exp\left(-\frac{1}{2}\int_0^T \left\|\hat{\lambda}_t\right\|^2 dt - \int_0^T \hat{\lambda}_t^{\top} dW_t\right),$$

and the density process of all equivalent probabilities $Q \approx P$ on $(\Omega, \mathcal{F})$,

$$\eta_t = \hat{\eta}_t \cdot \exp\left(\frac{1}{2}\int_0^t \|\nu_u\|^2 du - \int_0^t \nu_u^{\top} dW_u\right), \quad t \in [0, T]),$$

a strictly positive P martingale. We then have the following result.

Theorem 4.5. *$Q \in \mathcal{Q}$ if and only if $Q(A) = E(1_A\eta_T)$, $\forall A \in \mathbb{F}_T$.*

To summarize, note that $\dim(\langle\sigma\rangle^{\perp}) = d - m$. This proposition shows very neatly that, when markets are incomplete, there are many risk neutral probabilities, a conclusion originally made in great generality by Harrison and Pliska (1983).[16] The representation of these probabilities in theorem 4.5 is known at least since He and Pearson (1991, 271, proposition 1) and Shreve (1991, 429, lemma 3.4).

16. The so-called Föllmer and Schweizer (1991) measure, or minimal equivalent martingale measure, is defined as $\hat{P}(A) \equiv E(1_A\hat{\eta}_T)$ for each $A \in \mathbb{F}_T$.

4.4 Martingales and Arbitrage II: Optimization

We refer to *martingale methods* as the approach to solve intertemporal consumption-portfolio problems relying on the previous martingale results. In a complete market setting, there is only one risk neutral probability under which asset prices, rescaled by the MMA, satisfy a martingale restriction. Due to this fact, the budget constraints reduce to a single, static constraint, just as in the introductory example of section 4.2.6. This property considerably simplifies the intertemporal problems faced by the consumer-investor. While the description of these methods initially require complete markets, the very same methods may work to deal with market imperfections that include restricted market participation (incomplete markets) or other forms of portfolio constraints. We defer the treatment of such imperfections to a later section (see section 4.7).

4.4.1 Complete Markets and Single Budget Constraints

Chapter 2 explains that, in a two-period economy, agents face a single budget constraint when markets are complete. We now derive a result that parallels these conclusions. Assume then that markets are complete, $m=d$. To illustrate the analogy with chapter 2, consider again the budget constraint in a two-period economy, which can be written in a compact way as follows:

$$0=c_0-w_0+E\left(m\cdot\left(c^1-w^1\right)\right), \tag{4.65}$$

where c and w resp. denote consumption and endowments and m is the pricing kernel.

It is instructive to review the steps to achieve eq. (4.65). Recall that the budget constraints at time 0 and time 1 are, resp., $c_0-w_0=-S\theta$ and $c^1-w^1=V\theta$, where we are using the same notation in chapter 2. Further, by absence of arbitrage, there exists a vector $\phi:S=\phi^\top V$. Each element of this vector is interpreted as the price of an Arrow-Debreu security or a state price. It is this vector that allows us to write a single budget constraint, eq. (4.65). Indeed, replacing the no-arbitrage security price vector S into the time 0 budget constraint and using the time 1 constraint leaves $c_0-w_0=-\phi^\top\left(c^1-w^1\right)$. Eq. (4.65) now follows, by properties of the Arrow-Debreu state prices,

$$\phi_s=m_s\cdot P_s,\quad m_s\equiv(1+r)^{-1}\eta_s,\quad \eta_s=\frac{Q_s}{P_s},$$

and by "taking the *sum* across all states of nature."

We follow a similar logic while dealing with the continuous time case. Define Arrow-Debreu state price *densities*,

$$\phi_T\equiv\xi_T dP,\quad \xi_T=S_{0T}^{-1}\eta_T,\quad \eta_T=\left.\frac{dQ}{dP}\right|_{\mathbb{F}_T}. \tag{4.66}$$

As in the finite state case, we want to determine the value of current consumption and the present value of future consumption. For a given $\omega\in\Omega$, define

$$C_{0,T}(\omega)\equiv\int_0^T\phi_u(\omega)\,c_u(\omega)\,du+\phi_T(\omega)\,V_T(\omega).$$

Now $C_{0,T}(\omega)$ is the counterpart to $c_0 + \phi_s(c_s - w_s)$. It is the value of current consumption (the numéraire) and consumption (net of endowments) in state ω. Following the steps in the two-period case, we now "take the *integral* over all states of nature," obtaining

$$V_0 = E_0\left(\int_0^T \xi_u c_u du + \xi_T V_T\right),$$

where V_0 is wealth at time 0, and where we have used the definitions in (4.66). Thus, in a dynamic setting, agents face an infinite number of trajectory (budget) constraints. However, when markets are complete, these constraints collapse to a single constraint, just as in the two-period market model. The reason is that when there is a single Q, there exists then a unique state price density ϕ that ensures asset prices satisfy the martingale restriction. Such a state price density is the basis for evaluating consumption in each state of nature.

These derivations may appear heuristic, but they are rigorously founded. Consider eq. (4.63), and take the time t conditional expectation under Q,

$$x \equiv V_t = \mathbb{E}_t\left(\int_t^T \frac{c_u}{S_{0u}}du + \frac{V_T}{S_{0T}}\right) = E_t\left(\int_t^T \frac{\xi_u}{\xi_t}c_u du + \frac{\xi_T}{\xi_t}V_T\right), \tag{4.67}$$

where the last equality follows by a change in probability, proven in appendix 4.C, and

$$\frac{\xi_\tau}{\xi_t} = \exp\left(-\int_t^\tau r_u du\right)\frac{\eta_\tau^0}{\eta_t^0}, \tag{4.68}$$

where η_τ^0 is as in eq. (4.61). We now proceed with problems faced by the consumer-investor in a complete market setting relying on the previous budget constraint.

4.4.2 Optimization

A representative agent maximizes their expected utility over consumption flows and terminal wealth under the budget constraint. We assume that markets are complete. We know then that the agent faces a single, static budget constraint, eq. (4.67). The agent problem is

$$J(t,x) = \max_{(c_\tau, V_T)} E\left(\int_t^T u(\tau, c_\tau)\,d\tau + U(T, V_T)\right), \quad \text{s.t. eq. (4.67) holds,} \tag{4.P2}$$

where u and U denote instantaneous and terminal utilities. For each $\tau \in [t, T)$, the first-order conditions are

$$u_c(\tau, c_\tau) = \kappa\frac{\xi_\tau}{\xi_t} \quad \text{and} \quad U_V\left(T, V_T^{x,\pi,c}\right) = \kappa\frac{\xi_T}{\xi_t}, \tag{4.69}$$

where κ is a Lagrange multiplier.

To determine the consumption-portfolio policy, note that for a generic $\mathbb{F}_T$-measurable random variable $\hat{v}$, the following martingale satisfies:

$$M_s \equiv E_s\left(\int_t^T \frac{\xi_u}{\xi_t}\hat{c}_u du + \frac{\xi_T}{\xi_t}\hat{v}\right).$$

By the martingale representation theorem (introduced in section 4.3), there exists a vector ϕ adapted to $\mathbb{F}_t$, such that

$$M_\tau = M_t + \int_t^\tau \phi_u^\top dW_u, \tag{4.70}$$

and by Itô's lemma,

$$\int_t^\tau \frac{\xi_u}{\xi_t} c_u du + \frac{\xi_\tau}{\xi_t} V_\tau = x + \int_t^\tau \frac{\xi_u}{\xi_t} \left(\pi^\top \sigma - V\lambda^\top\right)_u dW_u.$$

By an identification argument,

$$\pi_\tau^\top = \left(V_\tau \lambda_\tau^\top + \frac{\phi_\tau^\top}{\xi_\tau / \xi_t}\right) \sigma_\tau^{-1}. \tag{4.71}$$

4.4.3 Marginal Utility of Income

The Lagrange multiplier κ in eq. (4.69) carries the interpretation of marginal utility of income, similar to some derivations in chapter 2. We provide a proof of this quite intuitive "envelope property" by relying on an infinite horizon framework and instantaneous utility at t equal to $e^{-\rho t} u(c_t)$, a framework often utilized in part II. We then consider the following program, a special case of program [4.P2],

$$\mathcal{J}(V_0) \equiv \max_{(c_t)_{t\geq 0}} E_0 \left(\int_0^\infty e^{-\rho t} u(c_t)\, dt\right), \quad \text{s.t. } E_0 \left(\int_0^\infty \frac{\xi_t}{\xi_0} c_t dt\right) = V_0, \quad \xi_0 \equiv 1 \qquad [4.P3]$$

where V_0 denotes initial wealth and the notation $\xi_{t+\Delta} \equiv m_{t,t+\Delta}\xi_t$, generalizes that in section 4.2.

The optimality conditions are, as usual,

$$\hat{c}_t : e^{-\rho t} u'(\hat{c}_t) = \kappa \xi_t \Longrightarrow u'(\hat{c}_0) = \kappa. \tag{4.72}$$

Further, assuming enough regularity conditions, we can differentiate the intertemporal utility in [4.P3], obtaining

$$\mathcal{J}'(V_0) = E_0 \left(\int_0^\infty e^{-\rho t} u'(\hat{c}_t) \frac{\partial \hat{c}_t}{\partial V_0} dt\right) = \kappa E_0 \left(\int_0^\infty \xi_t \frac{\partial \hat{c}_t}{\partial V_0} dt\right) = \kappa, \tag{4.73}$$

where the second equality holds by the first of the optimality conditions (4.72) and the third by differentiating LHS and RHS of the budget constraint in [4.P3] with respect to V_0, as originally claimed.

Next, we determine κ, thereby pinning down $\hat{c}_0$ in the second of the optimality conditions in (4.72). Rather than performing this task within a general framework, we assume the agent has a CRRA equal to γ, such that the optimality conditions in (4.72) become $\hat{c}_t = \kappa^{-\frac{1}{\gamma}} \left(e^{\rho t} \xi_t\right)^{-\frac{1}{\gamma}}$. By replacing optimal consumption into the budget constraint of [4.P3] and rearranging terms,

$$\kappa = V_0^{-\gamma} \left(\int_0^\infty e^{-\frac{\rho}{\gamma} t} E_0 \left(\xi_t^{1-\frac{1}{\gamma}}\right) dt\right)^\gamma, \tag{4.74}$$

and by integrating out the objective in [4.P3],

$$\mathcal{J}(V_0) = E_0\left(\int_0^\infty e^{-\frac{\rho}{\gamma}t}\xi_t^{1-\frac{1}{\gamma}}dt\right)^\gamma \times \frac{V_0^{1-\gamma}}{1-\gamma}.$$

Finally, by the optimality conditions (4.72), initial consumption has to satisfy

$$\hat{c}_0 = \kappa^{-\frac{1}{\gamma}} = E_0\left(\int_0^\infty e^{-\frac{\rho}{\gamma}t}\xi_t^{1-\frac{1}{\gamma}}dt\right)^{-1} V_0 \equiv k_o^{-1}V_0, \tag{4.75}$$

where the second equality follows by the expression of κ in eq. (4.74). Assume, for instance, log utility, $\gamma = 1$, in which case $\hat{c}_0 = \rho V_0$ as in some of the models in chapter 3. In equilibrium, optimal consumption equals all dividends. For example, assuming one tree, the initial endowment has to satisfy the following constraint, $V_0 = k_o D_0$, where k_o is the constant in (4.75).

4.4.4 Example: Log Utility

Set $\rho \equiv 0$ and let $u(t,c) = \ln c$ and $U(T,v) = \ln v$. The optimality conditions (4.69) reduce to $\frac{1}{\hat{c}_\tau} = \kappa\frac{\xi_\tau}{\xi_t}$ and $\frac{1}{\hat{v}} = \kappa\frac{\xi_T}{\xi_t}$ and replacing these conditions into the budget constraint leaves the solution for the Lagrange multiplier, $\kappa = \frac{T-t+1}{x}$, such that $\hat{c}_\tau = \frac{x}{T-t+1}\frac{1}{\xi_\tau/\xi_t}$ and $\hat{v} = \frac{x}{T-t+1}\frac{1}{\xi_T/\xi_t}$. Regarding the portfolio process, we have that $M_\tau = x$, such that the representation in (4.70) implies that $\phi = 0$. Therefore, by (4.71), we have $\pi_\tau^\top = V_\tau^{x,\pi,\hat{c}}\lambda_\tau^\top\sigma_\tau^{-1}$. Next, note that $V_\tau^{x,\pi,\hat{c}}$ can be determined using $\hat{c}$ and $\hat{v}$ in Eq. (4.67) (for $t \equiv \tau$), leaving $V_\tau^{x,\pi,\hat{c}} = \frac{x}{\xi_\tau/\xi_t}\frac{T-\tau+1}{T-t+1}$. Therefore, the solution for the portfolio process is

$$\pi_\tau = \frac{x}{\xi_\tau/\xi_t}\frac{T-\tau+1}{T-t+1}\sigma_\tau^{-1}\lambda_\tau = \frac{x}{\xi_\tau/\xi_t}\frac{T-\tau+1}{T-t+1}\left(\sigma_\tau\sigma_\tau^\top\right)^{-1}(\mu_\tau - \mathbf{1}_m r_\tau),$$

where the last equality follows by the expression for the risk premium vector, $\mu - \mathbf{1}_m r = \sigma\lambda$.

4.4.5 Equilibrium

In a complete markets setting, an equilibrium is (i) a consumption-portfolio policy satisfying eqs. (4.69)–(4.71) and (ii) market clearing: for all $\tau \in [t,T)$,

$$c_\tau = D_\tau \equiv \sum_{i=1}^m D_{i\tau}, \quad \theta_{0\tau} = 0, \quad \pi_\tau = S_\tau. \tag{4.76}$$

We now derive equilibrium allocations and Arrow-Debreu state price densities. First, note that the dividend process, D, satisfies

$$\frac{dD_\tau}{D_\tau} = g_\tau d\tau + \sigma_{0\tau}dW_\tau,$$

where $gD \equiv \sum_{i=1}^m g_i D_i$ and $\sigma_0 D \equiv \sum_{i=1}^m \sigma_{0i}D_i$. In equilibrium, $c_\tau = D_\tau$, such that

$$d\ln u_c(\tau, D_\tau) = d\ln\xi_\tau = -\left(r_\tau + \frac{1}{2}\|\lambda_\tau\|^2\right)dt - \lambda_\tau^\top dW_\tau, \tag{4.77}$$

where the first equality follows by the first-order conditions in (4.69) and the second by the definition of ξ_τ in eq. (4.68).

Finally, by Itô's lemma, $\ln u_c(\tau, D_\tau)$ is solution to

$$d\ln u_c = \left(\frac{u_{\tau c}}{u_c} + gD\frac{u_{cc}}{u_c} + \frac{1}{2}\sigma_0^2 D^2\left(\frac{u_{ccc}}{u_c} - \left(\frac{u_{cc}}{u_c}\right)^2\right)\right)dt + \frac{u_{cc}}{u_c}D\sigma_0 dW. \tag{4.78}$$

By identifying drifts and diffusion terms in eqs. (4.77) and (4.78), we obtain, after a few simplifications, the expression for the equilibrium short-term rate and the prices of risk:

$$\begin{aligned} r_\tau &= -\left(\frac{u_{\tau c}(\tau, D_\tau)}{u_c(\tau, D_\tau)} + g_\tau D_\tau \frac{u_{cc}(\tau, D_\tau)}{u_c(\tau, D_\tau)} + \frac{1}{2}\sigma_{0\tau}^2 D_\tau^2 \frac{u_{ccc}(\tau, D_\tau)}{u_c(\tau, D_\tau)}\right) \\ \lambda_\tau^\top &= -\frac{u_{cc}(\tau, D_\tau)}{u_c(\tau, D_\tau)}\sigma_{0\tau} D_\tau. \end{aligned}$$

For example, consider the CRRA utility function if $u(\tau, c) = e^{-\rho(\tau - t)}\left(c^{1-\gamma} - 1\right)/(1-\gamma)$ and $m = 1$. Then r_τ and λ_τ are as in (4.49) but with g_τ replacing g and $\sigma_{0\tau}$ replacing σ_0.

Finally, we provide an equilibrium asset evaluation result. We assume that each asset i entitles the owner to some random terminal consumption δ_i at time T. Then the equilibrium asset prices satisfy

$$S_{it} = \mathbb{E}_t\left(\frac{S_{0t}}{S_{0T}}\delta_i + \int_t^T \frac{S_{0t}}{S_{0u}} D_{iu} du\right) = E_t\left(\frac{\xi_T}{\xi_t}\delta_i + \int_t^T \frac{\xi_u}{\xi_t} D_{iu} du\right),$$

where the second equality holds by the same arguments leading to eq. (4.67). Replacing the first-order condition in (4.69) and the equilibrium conditions in eq. (4.76),

$$S_{it} = E_t\left(\frac{U_V(T, \delta)}{u_c(t, D_t)}\delta_i + \int_t^T \frac{u_c(s, D_s)}{u_c(t, D_t)} D_{is} ds\right),$$

where $\delta \equiv \sum_{i=1}^m \delta_i$.

4.5 Martingales and Arbitrage III: Distorsions and Numéraires

Consider a framework where, given a strictly positive random variable x_T, we define a Radon-Nikodym derivative as

$$\left.\frac{dP_2}{dP_1}\right|_{\mathbb{F}_T} = \eta_T(T) = \frac{x_T}{E_t(x_T)},$$

where $\mathbb{F}_T$ denotes the information set at time T and $E_t(\cdot)$ is the expectation under P_1, conditional on the information set at time t. Define a corresponding *density process* for $\eta_T(\tau)$ as

$$\eta_T(\tau) = \frac{E_\tau(x_T)}{E_t(x_T)}, \quad \tau \in [t, T].$$

We obviously have that $E_\tau[\eta_T(T)] = \eta_T(\tau)$ for all τ and, in particular, $\eta_T(t) = 1$. Therefore, $\eta_T(\cdot)$ is a martingale starting from 1, with $\eta_T(t) = E_t[\eta_T(T)] = 1$, and P_2 is thus a probability.

We now develop a series of examples to illustrate how naturally changes of probability arise in finance. A leading example is one where P_1 is the physical probability and the random variable x_T is the marginal utility of consumption at T, $x_T = u'(c_T)$, as in (the continuous time version of) the consumption-based asset pricing models of chapters 2 and 3. Another fundamental example spans many fixed-income security pricing problems described in chapter 13. In these problems, x_T is the inverse of the MMA at T, $x_T = e^{-\int_t^T r_u du}$, and P_1 is the risk neutral probability, such that

$$\eta_T(\tau) = \frac{\mathbb{E}_\tau\left(e^{-\int_t^T r_u du}\right)}{P_t(T)} = \frac{e^{-\int_t^\tau r_u du} P_\tau(T)}{P_t(T)},$$

where $P_t(T)$ is the time t price of a zero coupon bond expiring at T.

The next section develops the leading example of a change of probabilities, the consumption-based probabilities, as a benchmark. Section 4.5.2 reviews general notions and examples of pricing, based on the numéraires being involved into the definition of a given asset pricing problem.

4.5.1 Leading Example: Consumption-Based Probabilities

4.5.1.1 Martingale restriction

Consider a basic consumption-based model where an investor can invest at two dates only, at t and at $T > t$, without any intermediate consumption, such that any asset price satisfies

$$S_t = E_t\left(\frac{e^{-\rho(T-t)}u'(c_T)}{u'(c_t)} S_T\right) = e^{-r(T-t)}\mathbb{E}_t(S_T),$$

with the usual notation. In this model, we define the risk neutral probability Q through the Radon-Nikodym derivative of Q against P,[17]

$$\left.\frac{dQ}{dP}\right|_{\mathbb{F}_T} = \underbrace{\frac{e^{-\rho(T-t)}E_t\left[u'(c_T)\right]}{u'(c_t)} e^{r(T-t)}}_{=1} \cdot \frac{u'(c_T)}{E_t\left[u'(c_T)\right]}, \tag{4.79}$$

where the equality in the RHS follows by the properties of a riskless bond. So, assuming decreasing marginal utility, the risk neutral probability distorts the physical as it assigns more weight to the bad states of nature, that is, those where consumption is low, consistent with the explanations regarding the static model in chapter 2.

We derive implications for a continuous time model where a representative agent has CRRA equal to γ. In equilibrium, $c_T = S_T$, such that if consumption is a geometric Brownian motion with parameters (μ, σ), we have the following density

17. This derivation relies on the assumption that the short-term rate is constant. Section 8.4.2 in chapter 8 contains a derivation of the more general case of stochastic interest rates in a Markov setting.

process:

$$\eta_T(\tau) = \frac{E_\tau\left(S_T^{-\gamma}\right)}{E_t\left(S_T^{-\gamma}\right)} = \left(\frac{S_\tau}{S_t}\right)^{-\gamma} e^{\left(\gamma\mu - \frac{1}{2}\sigma^2\gamma(\gamma+1)\right)(\tau - t)}, \tag{4.80}$$

such that

$$\frac{d\eta_T(\tau)}{\eta_T(\tau)} = -\gamma\sigma dW_\tau,$$

where W_τ is a Brownian motion under P. By Girsanov's theorem, then, we have that $\tilde{W}_t = W_t + (\gamma\sigma)t$ is a Brownian motion under Q, such that the stock price is the solution to

$$\frac{dS_t}{S_t} = \underbrace{\left(\mu - \gamma\sigma^2\right)}_{=r} dt + \sigma d\tilde{W}_t.$$

To reconcile prices in the risk neutral world with prices in the true, we need the average path of the stock price to be lower under the risk neutral probability than under the physical. Since the stock is traded, we also have that $\mu - \gamma\sigma^2 = r$, as indicated. In fact, in this model, the risk premium does not show up directly in the price of standard derivative instruments as we now discuss.

4.5.1.2 *Rubinstein's (1976) formula*

The bond price restriction in eq. (4.79) leads to the familiar expression for the interest rate, $r = \rho + \gamma\mu - \frac{1}{2}\sigma^2\gamma(\gamma+1)$. Replacing this expression for the interest rate into (4.80) leads to the following expression for the stochastic discount factor:

$$\frac{\xi_T}{\xi_t} \equiv e^{-r(T-t)} \frac{\eta_T(T)}{\eta_t(T)} = e^{-\rho(T-t)} \left(\frac{S_T}{S_t}\right)^{-\gamma},$$

such that the price of a European call option is then

$$\begin{aligned} C(S_t, T-t) = {} & S_t E\left[\mathbb{I}_{S_T>K}\left(\frac{S_T}{S_t}\right)^{1-\gamma}\right] e^{-\rho(T-t)} \\ & - K e^{-\rho(T-t)} E\left[\left(\frac{S_T}{S_t}\right)^{-\gamma} \mathbb{I}_{S_T>K}\right]. \end{aligned} \tag{4.81}$$

When $\gamma = 0$, the interest rate reduces to the impatience rate, $r = \rho$. It is easy to show that in this case, $C(S_t, T-t)$ collapses to the Black–Scholes formula in section 4.2 (see eq. (4.6)) and hence, does not depend on μ. In fact, eq. (4.81) collapses to the Black–Scholes formula for every γ (see appendix 4.C). The reason is that markets are complete, such that the option is redundant. The risk premium, $\mu - r$, is somehow "hidden" in the option price.

4.5.2 Numéraire Pricing

4.5.2.1 *Definition*

The derivations obtained so far relies on the risk neutral probability, that is, the probability under which the asset prices that are discounted by the value of the MMA are martingales: the MMA is the numéraire in this no-arbitrage context. We can formulate equivalent versions of this theorem, utilizing different numéraires and different equivalent probabilities. Consider the following definition, which we shall state assuming no dividends for simplicity.

Definition 4.6 (Numéraires and equivalent probabilities). A numéraire *is any asset with a price process $\mathcal{N}_t > 0$, say. Given a numéraire, a probability $Q^{\mathcal{N}}$ is an* equivalent probability *if any asset price process S_t normalized by $\mathcal{N}_\tau$ satisfies*

$$\frac{S_t}{\mathcal{N}_t} = E_t^{Q^{\mathcal{N}}}\left(\frac{S_T}{\mathcal{N}_T}\right).$$

A critical task in this and previous chapters is the formulation of the FTAP—markets are arbitrage free if and only if there exists an equivalent martingale probability. We now provide examples of existence of numéraires and associated probabilities $Q^{\mathcal{N}}$.

4.5.2.2 *Examples of numéraires and arbitrage pricing laws*

Risk neutral probability The risk neutral probability corresponds to the MMA numéraire, as mentioned, with the value process given by

$$\mathcal{N}_\tau^r \equiv e^{\int_0^\tau r_u du}.$$

Suppose, for example, that the short-term rate is constant. In terms of the consumption probabilities of section 4.5.1, we have that

$$\frac{S_t}{\mathcal{N}_t^r} = \mathbb{E}_t\left(\frac{S_T}{\mathcal{N}_T^r}\right), \quad \mathcal{N}_t^r = e^{rt}. \tag{4.82}$$

Alternatively, and still assuming that interest rates are constant, we may express eq. (4.82) as

$$\frac{S_t}{\mathcal{N}_t^P} = \mathbb{E}_t\left(\frac{S_T}{\mathcal{N}_T^P}\right), \quad \mathcal{N}_t^P = e^{-r(T-t)} \equiv P_t(T),$$

with the obvious condition that $\mathcal{N}_T^P = P_T(T) = 1$. If interest rates are constant, the MMA yields the same as an investment of $\frac{1}{P_t(T)}$ units of a zero coupon bond, such that we can reinterpret the zero coupon bond as the numéraire. Next, we generalize this context to one with stochastic interest rates.

Forward probability Suppose instead that interest rates are random, such that

$$S_t = \mathbb{E}_t\left(e^{-\int_t^T r_u du} S_T\right) = P_t(T) \cdot \mathbb{E}_t\left(\frac{e^{-\int_t^T r_u du}}{P_t(T)} S_T\right) = P_t(T) \cdot \mathbb{E}_t^{Q^{\mathcal{N}_P}}(S_T), \tag{4.83}$$

where $Q^{\mathcal{N}_P}$ is the so-called *forward probability*, defined through the Radon-Nikodym derivative against Q as follows:

$$\left.\frac{dQ^{\mathcal{N}_P}}{dQ}\right|_{\mathbb{F}_T} = \frac{e^{-\int_t^T r_u du}}{P_t(T)}. \tag{4.84}$$

Accordingly, in this context of random interest rates, we can define the zero coupon bond as a numéraire such that, by eq. (4.83),

$$\frac{S_t}{\mathcal{N}_t^P} = \mathbb{E}_t^{Q^{\mathcal{N}_P}}\left(\frac{S_T}{\mathcal{N}_T^P}\right), \quad \mathcal{N}_t^P = P_t(T), \tag{4.85}$$

where the equality follows by the boundary condition for the price of a zero coupon bond, $\mathcal{N}_T^P = 1$.

In chapter 13, we shall make reference to this probability to price interest rate derivatives without risk of default. The price of these derivatives is

$$C_t = \mathbb{E}_t\left(e^{-\int_t^T r_u du}\Psi\left((r_s)_{s\in[t,T]}\right)\right), \tag{4.86}$$

where $\Psi(\cdot)$ is the payoff, possibly a function(al) of the entire path of the short-term rate over the life of the derivative. Note the main difficulty in eq. (4.86). The discount factor $e^{-\int_t^T r_u du}$ obviously correlates with the payoff and complicates the evaluation of this derivative. However, we can use the forward probability to express C_t as follows:

$$C_t = P_t(T) \cdot \mathbb{E}_t^{Q^{\mathcal{N}_P}}\left(\Psi\left(\{r_s\}_{s\in[t,T]}\right)\right). \tag{4.87}$$

As the Radon-Nikodym derivative defined in eq. (4.84) makes clear, the new probability, $Q^{\mathcal{N}_P}$, distorts Q in that it assigns a higher weight to events where interest rates paths are lower. The drift of r under $Q^{\mathcal{N}_P}$ is indeed lower as formally shown in appendix 13.B of chapter 13.[18] In other words, by using eq. (4.87), we get rid of the random discount factor $e^{-\int_t^T r_u du}$ in eq. (4.86), but then we multiply the expected payoff by $P_t(T)$. At the same time, the expected payoff is calculated in a world ruled by a probability $Q^{\mathcal{N}_P}$ where interest rates are on average lower than under Q.

Note that the calculations underlying eq. (4.85) can be used to check the internal consistency of the definition of the new numéraire and equivalent probabilities with absence of arbitrage. There are no arbitrage opportunities if there exists a probability $Q^{\mathcal{N}_P}$ with Radon-Nikodym derivative against Q equal to

$$\left.\frac{dQ^{\mathcal{N}_P}}{dQ}\right|_{\mathbb{F}_T} = \frac{\mathcal{N}_t^r}{\mathcal{N}_T^r} \cdot \frac{\mathcal{N}_T^P}{\mathcal{N}_t^P}. \tag{4.88}$$

18. Note that this statement certainly holds when the short-term rate is a Markov process. In more complex models such as those with stochastic volatility, the bond price sensitivity to movements in the state variables may switch signs and render this statement model dependent.

Indeed, we have, simply, that

$$\frac{S_t}{\mathcal{N}_t^P} = \mathbb{E}_t^{Q^{\mathcal{N}_P}}\left(\frac{S_T}{\mathcal{N}_T^P}\right) = \mathbb{E}_t\left(\frac{S_T}{\mathcal{N}_T^P}\frac{\mathcal{N}_t^r}{\mathcal{N}_T^r}\cdot\frac{\mathcal{N}_T^P}{\mathcal{N}_t^P}\right),$$

which is the first equality in eq. (4.83).

Annuity probability Consider now a class of contracts where the payoff Π_T is given by the difference between a constant K and some risk of interest, which is not necessarily traded, rescaled by a variable measurable at time T,

$$\Pi_T \equiv \mathcal{N}_T^A \left(R_T - K\right). \tag{4.89}$$

The interpretation of Π_T in this section is that of the value of an interest rate "swap payer" at time T, whereby a party A shall pay a fixed interest rate K to counterparty B in exchange of the variable interest rate over a certain horizon, called the tenor. In eq. (4.89), R_T is the so-called swap rate, and $\mathcal{N}_T^A$ is the value at time T of an annuity of one dollar over the tenor of the swap. Swaps contracts are among the most important interest rate derivatives dealt with in practice and are motivated and explained in detail in chapter 13.

The annuity factor $\mathcal{N}_T^A$ is a valid numéraire in this market. Accordingly, let us define the *annuity probability* arising in this context through the counterpart to the Radon-Nikodym derivative in eq. (4.88),

$$\left.\frac{dQ^{\mathcal{N}_A}}{dQ}\right|_{\mathbb{F}_T} = \frac{\mathcal{N}_t^r}{\mathcal{N}_T^r}\cdot\frac{\mathcal{N}_T^A}{\mathcal{N}_t^A},$$

such that we can price all contracts in this market.[19] First, the value at t of a forward starting interest rate swap, that is, a swap agreed at time t, say Π_t, is given by

$$\frac{\Pi_t}{\mathcal{N}_t^A} = \mathbb{E}_t^{Q^{\mathcal{N}_A}}\left(\frac{\Pi_T}{\mathcal{N}_T^A}\right).$$

Likewise, the value of a swaption payer—that is, an option to enter into a future swap—is Π_t^+, where

$$\frac{\Pi_t^+}{\mathcal{N}_t^A} = \mathbb{E}_t^{Q^{\mathcal{N}_A}}\left(\frac{\max\{\Pi_T, 0\}}{\mathcal{N}_T^A}\right) = \mathbb{E}_t^{Q^{\mathcal{N}_A}}\left(R_T - K\right)^+.$$

Note that forward swap rate, defined as the value of K determined at time t such that Π_t is zero, satisfies

$$K = \mathbb{E}_t^{Q^{\mathcal{N}_A}}\left(R_T\right).$$

Accordingly, we can define the forward swap rate as the process $R_\tau = \mathbb{E}_\tau^{Q^{\mathcal{N}_A}}(R_T)$, for $\tau \leq T$, which is obviously a martingale under $Q^{\mathcal{N}_A}$. These properties are extremely useful when it comes to pricing these important derivatives.

19. Note that under this annuity probability, the events that matter most are those where interest rates paths are low, similar to the forward probability.

Defaultable probability Finally, we consider the so-called *survival-contingent probability*, studied in chapter 14, where the numéraire, $\mathcal{N}_T^{A^D}$, is a defaultable annuity of one dollar paid off over a certain tenor, which is interpreted as the period over which two counterparties exchange credit risk. The option to enter into this deal is called a credit default swaption, and the payoff is as in eq. (4.89), with $\Pi_T^+ \equiv \mathcal{N}_T^{A^D} (\text{cds}_T - K)^+$, where cds_T is the credit default risk premium as of time T and K is a constant.

4.5.2.3 *Martingales and numéraires*

The examples in the previous section can be gathered to provide a general insight. Consider a forward starting agreement, one that originated at time t, with a payoff equal to

$$\mathcal{N}_T (X_T - K),$$

where $\mathcal{N}_T$ is a numéraire, $Q^{\mathcal{N}}$ is an equivalent probability, and X_T is measurable at time T. Then the "forward risk," defined as

$$X_\tau = \mathbb{E}_\tau^{Q^{\mathcal{N}}} (X_T),$$

is a martingale under $Q^{\mathcal{N}}$ and $K = X_t$ is the value that sets the value of the forward starting agreement equal to zero.

4.5.2.4 *Marking-to-market updates of forward starting agreements*

Suppose we are long an amount θ_t of a forward starting agreement at time t that has a strike K_t such that the value of this agreement at t right after the trade is $\pi_{t+} \equiv \theta_t \mathcal{N}_t (X_t - K_t)$ and the value at $t+1$ before the trade is $\pi_{t+1} \equiv \theta_t \mathcal{N}_{t+1} (X_{t+1} - K_t)$. Choosing the strike K_t that clears π_{t+} delivers the forward risk, $K_t = X_t$, such that, by aggregating,

$$\begin{aligned}\sum_{t=1}^{n} \pi_{t+1} &= \sum_{t=1}^{n} \theta_t \mathcal{N}_{t+1} (X_{t+1} - X_t) \\ &= \sum_{t=1}^{n} \theta_t \left[\mathcal{N}_t (X_{t+1} - X_t) + (\mathcal{N}_{t+1} - \mathcal{N}_t)(X_{t+1} - X_t)\right].\end{aligned}$$

By chopping the trading interval into small pieces, we obtain that, under standard regularity conditions,

$$\pi_T - \pi_0 = \int_0^T \theta_t \mathcal{N}_t dX_t + \int_0^T \theta_t d\mathcal{N}_t dX_t.$$

4.6 Equilibrium with State Variables and a Representative Agent

This section considers equilibrium implications of portfolio choices in an environment where the state variables are diffusion processes. We assume that there is a representative agent. In a nutshell, we derive the optimal portfolio choices of an investor in a dynamic setting, thereby extending mean-variance results in chapter 1. In this section, we solve for these choices relying on dynamic programming, the approach introduced by Merton (1969). An equilibrium is defined as the situation in which, among others, the asset prices dynamics are such that the investor is happy with their portfolio holdings. These results are known due to Merton (1971, 1973) and Breeden (1979).

4.6.1 Constant Investment Opportunity Sets

An agent faces the following problem:

$$\mathcal{J}(V_t) = \max_c E_t\left(\int_t^\infty e^{-\rho(\tau-t)} u(c_\tau)\, d\tau\right), \quad \text{s.t. eq. (4.60) holds.}$$

Under regularity conditions, the value function $\mathcal{J}(\cdot)$ satisfies the following Hamilton-Jacobi-Bellman equation:

$$0 = \max_{c,\pi}\left(u(c) + \mathcal{J}'(V)\left(\pi^\top(\mu - \mathbf{1}_m r) + rV - c\right) + \frac{1}{2}\mathcal{J}''(V)\,\pi^\top\sigma\sigma^\top\pi - \rho\mathcal{J}(V)\right). \tag{4.90}$$

The first-order conditions lead to

$$u'(c) = \mathcal{J}'(V) \quad \text{and} \quad \pi = \left(\frac{-\mathcal{J}'(V)}{\mathcal{J}''(V)}\right)(\sigma\sigma^\top)^{-1}(\mu - \mathbf{1}_m r). \tag{4.91}$$

To solve for the value function, replace eqs. (4.91) into eq. (4.90); the result is an ordinary differential equation solved by $\mathcal{J}$. In the CRRA case, $u(c) = c^{1-\gamma}$, the solution is $\mathcal{J}(V) = a\frac{V^{1-\gamma}-b}{1-\gamma}$, for two constants a, b,[20] such that consumption and portfolio policies satisfy

$$c = a^{-\frac{1}{\gamma}} V, \qquad \frac{\pi}{V} = \frac{1}{\gamma}(\sigma\sigma^\top)^{-1}(\mu - \mathbf{1}_m r).$$

4.6.2 Stochastic Opportunity Sets

Next, we consider a case of potentially incomplete markets, in which an exogenous state process y_t drives asset prices. It is the solution to

$$dy_t = \varphi(y_t)\, dt + \Sigma(y_t)\, dW_t, \tag{4.92}$$

where W_t is a d-dimensional Brownian motion and φ and Σ are some vector and matrix valued functions that satisfy the usual regularity conditions. This setup is somehow abstract for now. These state variables can be inflation, exchange rates, industrial production growth, and so on. Naturally, an important task in financial economics is to explain how some of these variables in these examples (e.g., the rate of economic growth) are affected by asset prices, but the scope of this chapter is to examine market behavior in this simplified setting; part II contains more elaborate explanations of market behavior (see chapters 8 and 9). Similar to the discrete time model of Lucas (1978) (see chapter 3), we assume that there are assets that provide the right of receiving dividends (the numéraire) of m trees and that their prices are driven by y_t. That is, if S_{it} denotes the time t price of the ith

---

20. To determine these two constants, replace optimal consumption, $c = a^{-1/\gamma} V$, into eq. (4.90); use the conjecture for the value function $\mathcal{J}$; and solve for the undetermined coefficients, obtaining $a = \left(\frac{\rho - r(1-\gamma)}{\gamma} - \frac{(1-\gamma)Sh}{2\gamma^2}\right)^{-\gamma}$ and $b = (a\rho)^{-1}$, where $Sh \equiv (\mu - \mathbf{1}_m r)^\top(\sigma\sigma^\top)^{-1}(\mu - \mathbf{1}_m r)$. As $\gamma \to 1$, we have that $\mathcal{J}(V_t) = \frac{1}{\rho}\ln V_t$ and $c_t = \rho V_t$.

asset, S_{it} is some function $S_{it} \equiv S_i(t, y_t)$ (the price at t when the state process is y_t), which in some models shall be determined in equilibrium. We assume $S_i(t, y_t)$ is as differentiable as needed to apply Itô's lemma, such that

$$\frac{dS_{it}}{S_{it}} = \bar{\mu}_i(t, y_t)\, dt + \sigma_i(t, y_t)\, dW_t, \tag{4.93}$$

where

$$\bar{\mu}_i S_i = \frac{\partial S_i}{\partial t} + \frac{\partial S_i}{\partial y}\varphi + \frac{1}{2}\mathrm{Tr}\left(\Sigma\Sigma^\top \frac{\partial^2 S_i}{\partial y \partial y^\top}\right), \quad \sigma_i S_{it} = \frac{\partial S_i}{\partial y}\Sigma;$$

the remaining notation is straightforward. We also assume that there is a safe asset in zero net supply, that is, an asset with a price S_{0t} satisfying eq. (4.93) with $\bar{\mu}_0(t, y) \equiv r(t, y)$ (the short-term rate) and $\sigma_0(t, y) \equiv 0_m$.

Thus, eq. (4.93) is a specific version of the eq. (4.59) in section 4.3. In particular, σ is the $m \times d$ matrix with entry $\sigma_{ij}(t, y)$, that is, the ith asset price exposure to the jth source of risk in eq. (4.92). We assume that rank$(\sigma) = m \leq d$ for each τ, just as in section 4.3, such that the value V_t of a self-financed portfolio satisfies eq. (4.60). Finally, we assume that $D_{it} = D_i(t, y_t)$ for a given function D_i.

4.6.2.1 *Markets with nonproductive assets*

While the price system in (4.93) can lead to incomplete markets, we also consider a case in which markets could be (but are not necessarily) *completed* by "nonproductive" assets in zero net supply, interpreted as derivative instruments.[21] Let σ_F denote the volatility matrix of these contingent claims, defined similarly as σ. A condition under which these nonproductive contingent claims complete the market is that the augmented volatility matrix $\hat{\sigma} = \left[\sigma^\top \ \sigma_F^\top\right]^\top$ is square and has full rank. This condition is easy to interpret: rewrite the augmented price system as

$$\begin{pmatrix} \frac{dS_{1t}}{S_{1t}} \\ \cdots \\ \frac{dS_{mt}}{S_{mt}} \\ \frac{dF_{1t}}{F_{1t}} \\ \cdots \\ \frac{dF_{nt}}{F_{nt}} \end{pmatrix} = \begin{pmatrix} \bar{\mu}_{1t} \\ \cdots \\ \bar{\mu}_{mt} \\ \bar{\mu}^F_{1t} \\ \cdots \\ \bar{\mu}^F_{nt} \end{pmatrix} dt + \hat{\sigma}\, dW_t, \tag{4.94}$$

where F_{it} denotes the time t price of the ith contingent claim. Then, the condition rank$(\hat{\sigma}) = d$ means that observing the asset prices is equivalent to observing the sources of uncertainty in the market.

The notion that derivative assets can complete the market was first introduced by Ross (1976). Naturally, the presence of derivative securities does not guarantee that markets

21. We formulate a model that, according to parameter restrictions, can be interpreted in the spirit of the discrete time Lucas (1978) tree model and also in terms of the Cox, Ingersoll, and Ross model (1985a).

are complete; further conditions are required as discussed in the example of a stochastic volatility model (see eqs. (4.112) below).

Let us consider a frictionless economy with a representative agent[22] and derive the equilibrium restrictions on (4.94). The agent maximizes their intertemporal utility under a budget constraint that generalizes eq. (4.60); this new budget constraint reflects the agent's increased portfolio possibilities arising through nonproductive assets. Let us denote their value function with $\mathcal{J}(t, V_t, y_t) \equiv \max_c E_t(\int_t^T u(s, c_s)ds)$. Under regularity conditions, the decision problem is summarized by the Bellman equation, $0 = \max_{c,\pi} G(t, V, y; c, \pi, \pi_F)$, where

$$\begin{aligned} &G(t, V, y; c, \pi, \pi_F) \\ &\equiv u(t,c) + \mathcal{J}_t(t,V,y) + \mathcal{J}_V(t,V,y)\left(\pi^\top(\mu - \mathbf{1}_m r) + \pi_F^\top\left(\mu^F - \mathbf{1}_n r\right) + rV - c\right) \\ &\quad + \mathcal{J}_y(t,V,y)\,\varphi(y) + \frac{1}{2}\mathcal{J}_{VV}(t,V,y)\pi_a^\top\hat{\sigma}\hat{\sigma}^\top\pi_a + \pi_a^\top\hat{\sigma}\Sigma^\top\mathcal{J}_{Vy}(t,V,y) \\ &\quad + \frac{1}{2}\mathrm{Tr}\left(\Sigma\Sigma^\top\mathcal{J}_{yy}(t,V,y)\right) \end{aligned} \tag{4.95}$$

and where μ^F is a n-dimensional vector with generic element μ_j^F and μ_j^F is the cum-dividend expected return on the jth contingent claim (and a similar notation regarding μ, as usual); π_F is the n-dimensional vector process of wealth invested in the contingent claims; finally, $\pi_a = \left[\pi^\top \;\; \pi_F^\top\right]^\top$.

The first-order conditions are $0 = u_c - \mathcal{J}_V$, and

$$\begin{cases} 0_m = (\mu - \mathbf{1}_m r)\mathcal{J}_V + (\sigma\sigma^\top\pi + \sigma\sigma_F^\top\pi_F)\mathcal{J}_{VV} + \sigma\Sigma^\top\mathcal{J}_{Vy} \\ 0_m = (\mu^F - \mathbf{1}_n r)\mathcal{J}_V + (\sigma_F\sigma_F^\top\pi_F + \sigma_F\sigma^\top\pi)\mathcal{J}_{VV} + \sigma_F\Sigma^\top\mathcal{J}_{Vy} \end{cases}. \tag{4.96}$$

We now elaborate on these conditions and characterize portfolio choices and their asset pricing implications.

4.6.2.2 *Hedging demands and separation theorems*

We focus on portfolio selection while focusing on productive assets, thereby setting $\pi_F = 0_{d-m}$, and provide discussion regarding nonproductive assets below. By the first of eqs. (4.96), the assets demand is

$$\frac{\pi}{V} = \left(\sigma\sigma^\top\right)^{-1}(\mu - \mathbf{1}_m r)\frac{\mathcal{J}_V}{-V\mathcal{J}_{VV}} + \left(\sigma\sigma^\top\right)^{-1}\sigma\Sigma^\top\frac{\mathcal{J}_{Vy}}{-V\mathcal{J}_{VV}}. \tag{4.97}$$

Eq. (4.97) shows that our agent aims to a portfolio that has two components. The first is proportional to the "tangent portfolio" and the second is the "hedging portfolio," a term we use for reasons explained below. Tangent portfolios were mentioned in chapter 1: in

22. It is known since at least Huang (1987) that, in the diffusive case of this chapter and under conditions, there exists a representative agent economy supporting the prices in the initial economy when markets are complete. This result is based on the welfare theorems of chapter 2 and will be further reviewed in chapter 9.

the static mean-variance context, it is the portfolio on the efficient frontier that allows an investor to construct any desired asset allocation consistent with their risk-return trade-off profile. Precisely, any efficient risk-return complex (in the mean-variance sense) can be achieved by investing proportions of wealth in a risk-free asset *and* in the tangent portfolio. If the riskless asset is in zero-net supply, then all agents hold the tangent portfolio, which for this reason is also known as the market portfolio.

In the dynamic market of this section, the tangent portfolio also collapses to a market portfolio when the price system encompasses the whole information provided by the state variables. In this case, the value function ceases to directly depend on y, which makes $\mathcal{J}_y = \mathbf{0}$, where $\mathbf{0}$ denotes a vector of zeros. Premultiplying eq. (4.97) by $\mathbf{1}_m^\top$, assuming $\mathcal{J}_y = \mathbf{0}$, using the equilibrium condition that $\mathbf{1}_m^\top \pi = V$ (safe asset is in zero net supply) and finally rearranging terms, leaves the following restriction on the safe interest rate:[23]

$$(D - Cr)^{-1} = \frac{\mathcal{J}_V}{-V\mathcal{J}_{VV}}, \tag{4.98}$$

where $D = \mathbf{1}_m^\top \left(\sigma\sigma^\top\right)^{-1} \mu$ and $C = \mathbf{1}_m^\top \left(\sigma\sigma^\top\right)^{-1} \mathbf{1}_m$, consistently with similar notations introduced in chapter 1. Replacing eq. (4.98) into eq. (4.97) leaves, for $\mathcal{J}_{Vy} = \mathbf{0}$, the (continuous time diffusive equivalent to the) market portfolio in the mean-variance context of chapter 1, as claimed (see eq. (1.18)).

It is indeed a market portfolio: in equilibrium, $\pi_{it} = \bar{\theta}_i S_{it}$, where $\bar{\theta}_i$ is the number of outstanding securities; because we assume the safe asset is in zero net supply, our representative agent then holds the value-weighted portfolio of all existing securities in positive supply, $V_t = \sum_{i=1}^m \bar{\theta}_i S_{it}$. Finally, note that there is one more instance in which the tangent portfolio collapses to the market portfolio, arising when the indirect utility function is separable in V and y, such that $\mathcal{J}_{Vy} = \mathbf{0}$. This case occurs, for example, when the representative investor has instantaneous logarithmic utility, a case we shall return to below.

When the markets do not encompass all the information provided by the state variables, the value function depends directly on y and the asset demand also includes the second component in eq. (4.97), which we refer to as *hedging demand*. This second component captures investors' concerns to mitigate their risks beyond standard mean-variance diversification. It reflects a demand for d portfolios, where each portfolio maximizes the covariance of wealth with the state variable y_i for a given variance of wealth (i.e., each portfolio maximizes the correlation between wealth and y_i). Now we shall show these claims.

Let Σ_i denote the vector of exposures of factor y_i to the Brownian motions in eq. (4.92), that is, the ith row of Σ, and define

$$p_i^* = \arg\max_p cov_{p,y_i} \quad \text{s.t.} \quad p^\top \sigma\sigma^\top p = \sigma_p^2,$$

where $cov_{p,y_i} \equiv p^\top \sigma \Sigma_i^\top$ denotes the instantaneous covariance between wealth and the state variable y_i when wealth is invested in p and σ_p^2 is a given level of variance. We have

$$p_i^* = \frac{1}{2\ell_i}\left(\sigma\sigma^\top\right)^{-1} \sigma \Sigma_i^\top,$$

23. That is, we determine the restriction in (4.98) while simply requiring that the market for the safe asset clears, just as in the static model (see eq. (1.39) in chapter 1).

where ℓ_i is a Lagrange multiplier. The second component in eq. (4.97) is a weighted average of these d portfolios, with weights equal to $\frac{\mathcal{J}_{Vy_i}}{-V\mathcal{J}_{VV}}2\ell_i$.

Eq. (4.97) is, thus, a "$(d+2)$ separation theorem" that provides us with interesting generalizations of the static CAPM of chapter 1. It tells us that investors can achieve any asset allocation consistent with their risk-return trade-off profiles by means of $d+2$ "mutual funds" that invest into (i) the riskless security, (ii) the mean-variance portfolio, and finally, (iii) d portfolios that have the highest correlation with the d state variables. How much is invested in each of these funds depends on the investors' attitude to risk.

We now discuss some examples and then proceed with the asset pricing implications of the model.

4.6.2.3 *One example: Stochastic volatility and asset allocation puzzles*

The hedging demand can be understood from a different angle. Note that

$$p_i^* \propto \arg\min_p \left\| \Sigma_i - p^\top \sigma \right\|^2 = \left(\sigma\sigma^\top\right)^{-1} \sigma \Sigma_i^\top. \tag{4.99}$$

That is, p_i^* minimizes the "gap" (in the mean-square sense) between the dynamics of optimally invested wealth and those of the state variables. By attempting to mimic the factors' dynamics, the hedging demand provides the best (mean-square) hedge against fluctuations in the state variables. How much of this hedging demand is generated (and in which sign) depends on the investor's attitude to risk.

There is one case in which the hedging demand completely fills these gaps, which arises when markets are complete. Markets may be complete because there are exactly as many productive assets as state variables. In this case, $p_i^* \propto \left(\sigma^\top\right)^{-1} \Sigma_i^\top$, such that the correlation between the hedging portfolio returns and the state variable y_i is just one. Therefore, hedging demands arise even when markets are complete.

But markets may be complete even with relatively few productive assets, namely, when (i) the number of productive and nonproductive assets equals d and (ii) the augmented volatility matrix $\hat{\sigma}$ in eq. (4.94) has full rank, as previously explained. Consider the following example and a market for a single security with price equal to S_t at time t. Assume that W_t has two components and that asset returns exhibit *stochastic volatility*, in that

$$\frac{dS_t}{S_t} = \bar{\mu}\left(S_t, y_t\right) dt + s\left(y_t\right) dW_{1t}, \tag{4.100}$$

for some functions $\bar{\mu}(\cdot, \cdot)$ and $s(\cdot)$, and where y_t is solution to eq. (4.92).

Part III (see, e.g., chapter 11) contains surveys of these models with stochastic volatility, which seem to capture a few stylized features of market behavior and that, for this reason, are the workhorse in standard market practice. In this chapter, the volatility function $s(\cdot)$ is given by Mother Nature, an assumption further discussed below. Instead, the expected return $\bar{\mu}(\cdot, \cdot)$ is determined in the equilibrium of the model (see eq. (4.112) below).

In this example, the market is incomplete because there is only one asset against two standard Brownian motions. However, markets can be completed by a second asset, a nonproductive asset such as a European option written on the productive security. We shall return to this issue briefly below. Chapter 11 discusses more precise conditions under which derivatives can complete markets in this context (see section 11.5). We now proceed to explain some interesting features of this model that help rationalize standard advisory pratice regarding long-term portfolio choice.

Chapter 1 explains that mean-variance theory suggests efficient portfolios that clash with advisory pratice (see section 1.2). One "asset allocation puzzle" is that less risk averse investors are advised to increase their portfolio holdings of more risky assets. It is a puzzle from a mean-variance perspective because, in a mean-variance context, investors decide their exposure to risk while choosing appropriate proportions of the tangent portfolio and the risk-free asset. This puzzle (and a possible solution to it) can be illustrated within the context of the simple model in (4.100) (even if this is a single-asset model!). In terms of eq. (4.94), we have that $m=1$, $d=2$, and $\sigma=[s \;\; 0]$, and in terms of eq. (4.92), we have that y_t is a single state variable with $\Sigma=[\Sigma_1 \;\; \Sigma_2]$. Therefore, by eq. (4.97), the demand for the risky security is

$$\frac{\pi}{V}=\frac{\mu-r}{s^2}\frac{\mathcal{J}_V}{-V\mathcal{J}_{VV}}+\frac{\Sigma_1}{s}\frac{\mathcal{J}_{Vy}}{-V\mathcal{J}_{VV}}. \tag{4.101}$$

How does time-varying risk affect portfolio choice? The first term in (4.101) reflects standard mean-variance trade-offs, and the second is the hedging component, which is proportional to p_i^* in eq. (4.99). Campbell and Viceira (2002) and Chacko and Viceira (2005) rely on models along these lines to explain a number of asset allocation puzzles, that is, the circumstance that asset allocation practice does not precisely conform to the predictions of the static CAPM in chapter 1.

4.6.3 Arrow-Debreu Densities and Restrictions on Expected Returns

4.6.3.1 The martingale restriction

Finally, we study the equilibrium restrictions on the assets' expected returns. In equilibrium, $\pi_t=\text{Cap}_t$ and $\pi_{Ft}=0_n$, where Cap is the m-dimensional vector of market capitalizations, that is, $\text{Cap}_{it}=\bar{\theta}_i S_{it}$ for each i. Eqs. (4.96) then reduce to

$$\begin{pmatrix} \mu-1_m r \\ \mu^F-1_n r \end{pmatrix}=\hat{\sigma}\lambda, \quad \lambda\equiv-\left(\sigma^\top \text{Cap}\frac{\mathcal{J}_{VV}}{\mathcal{J}_V}+\Sigma^\top\frac{\mathcal{J}_{Vy}}{\mathcal{J}_V}\right). \tag{4.102}$$

The unit risk premiums, λ, relate to the curvature of the indirect utility function and the volatility of asset returns and the state variables as we should expect: the curvature reflects the investor's attitude toward risks, and the volatility determines the size of these risks. Importantly, eq. (4.102) shows that the agent's optimizing behaviors (and equilibrium) lead to a single risk neutral probability in the set $\mathcal{Q}$ (see section 4.3), regardless of whether asset markets are complete (see eqs. (4.62)).

Eqs. (4.102), then, amount to "martingale restrictions" on asset prices, thereby providing a theory of asset prices for both productive and nonproductive assets (such as options). For example, the price of the nonproductive assets is the solution to partial differential equations subject to appropriate boundary conditions, similar to the models of section 4.2.[24] Naturally, these prices are not preferencefree: even when markets are completed by their very same assets ($m+n=d$), no security is redundant in these markets.

Section 4.6.4 explains how to determine the last element of these markets: the safe interest rate, r. Prior to this, we provide additional discussion and illustrate how these martingale restrictions lead to famous generalizations of the CAPM.

4.6.3.2 Multibeta CAPM

We describe expected excess returns based on a representation that has the same flavor as the CAPM. Accordingly, we rely on derivations that are similar to those in chapter 1 (see appendix 1.B). Note that eq. (4.97) provides the weights of the market portfolio, which are split into the tangent (or mean-variance efficient) and the hedging portfolios. We now elaborate on the previous martingale restrictions by applying them to both the market and hedging portfolios. Appendix 4.C provides precise analytical details of the following derivations.

First, note that the first of eqs. (4.102) is

$$\mu - \mathbf{1}_m r = \mathrm{cov}_{S,M} \frac{-V\mathcal{J}_{VV}}{\mathcal{J}_V} + \sigma\Sigma^\top \frac{-\mathcal{J}_{Vy}}{\mathcal{J}_V}, \tag{4.103}$$

where $\mathrm{cov}_{S,M}$ is the instantaneous covariance between the productive assets returns and wealth invested in the market portfolio.

Next, premultiply eq. (4.103) by the market portfolio, obtaining

$$\mu_M - r = \mathrm{var}_M \frac{-V\mathcal{J}_{VV}}{\mathcal{J}_V} + \mathrm{cov}_{M,y} \frac{-\mathcal{J}_{Vy}}{\mathcal{J}_V}, \tag{4.104}$$

where $\mu_M \equiv \frac{\pi_M^\top}{V}\mu$, and $\pi_M^\top$ is as in eq. (4.97) and equal to Cap in equilibrium (such that $\pi_M^\top \mathbf{1}_m = V$), that is, μ_M is the market expected return; finally, var_M denotes the instantaneous variance of wealth invested in the market portfolio.

Further, premultiply eq. (4.103) by the d hedging portfolios, defined as

$$\frac{\pi_{H_i}}{V} \equiv \frac{\left(\sigma\sigma^\top\right)^{-1}\sigma\Sigma_i^\top}{\mathbf{1}_m^\top\left(\sigma\sigma^\top\right)^{-1}\sigma\Sigma_i^\top}, \quad i=1,\cdots,d. \tag{4.105}$$

We have, for each of the expected excess returns on the hedging portfolios, that

$$\mu_{H_i} - r = \mathrm{cov}_{H_i,M} \frac{-V\mathcal{J}_{VV}}{\mathcal{J}_V} + \mathrm{cov}_{H_i,y} \frac{-\mathcal{J}_{Vy}}{\mathcal{J}_V}, \quad i=1,\cdots,d \tag{4.106}$$

with notation similar to that in eq. (4.104).

Eqs. (4.104) and (4.106) can form a system of $d+1$ linear equations, which can be solved for the $d+1$ unknowns, $\frac{-V\mathcal{J}_{VV}}{\mathcal{J}_V}$ and $\frac{-\mathcal{J}_{Vy_i}}{\mathcal{J}_V}$. Replacing the solutions into eq. (4.103)

24. Such partial differential equations arise because, by Itô's lemma, asset price drifts and diffusions involve partial derivatives of asset prices with respect to state variables, just as μ and σ in eq. (4.93).

leaves the following restriction on each asset's expected excess returns:

$$\mu_i - r = \beta_{i,M}(\mu_M - r) + \sum_{j=1}^{d} \beta_{i,H_j}(\mu_{H_j} - r), \quad i = 1, \cdots, m, \tag{4.107}$$

where the coefficients $\beta_{i,M}$ and β_{i,H_j} are the coefficient estimates of the multiple regression of the excess returns of security i onto the excess returns on the market and the hedging portfolios.

Note that if the investor has log utility, $\mathcal{J}_{Vy} = 0$—or in the absence of stochastic opportunity sets—eqs. (4.103) and (4.104) immediately deliver

$$\mu - 1_m r = \frac{\text{cov}_{S,M}}{\text{var}_M}(\mu_M - r). \tag{4.108}$$

Eq. (4.108) is the continuous time equivalent to the static single beta CAPM of chapter 1.

4.6.3.3 *Consumption CAPM*

In equilibrium, instantaneous consumption equals the sum of the instantaneous dividend rates promised by all the securities. But we are assuming that these dividend rates depend on the exogenous state process y. Therefore, in equilibrium, consumption is driven by this state process. Note also that consumption may depend on y even when the dividend rates are independent of y but utility is state dependent. Part II contains many detailed discussions of these cases (see chapters 8 and 9). Our objective now is to derive a martingale restriction expressed in terms of equilibrium consumption, consistently with the introductory Lucas tree examples of section 4.2.6.

Consider the first-order conditions, $u_c = \mathcal{J}_V$, which can be expanded with respect to both V and y, leaving

$$\frac{\mathcal{J}_{VV}}{\mathcal{J}_V} = \frac{u_{cc}}{u_c} c_V, \quad \frac{\mathcal{J}_{Vy}}{\mathcal{J}_V} = \frac{u_{cc}}{u_c} c_y,$$

where c_V and c_y denote the partial derivatives of the equilibrium consumption with respect to V and y, resp. Based on the previous relations, the risk premium in the martingale restrictions in eqs. (4.102) can be restated as

$$\lambda = -\frac{c u_{cc}}{u_c}\left(\sigma^\top \text{Cap}\frac{c_V}{c} + \Sigma^\top \frac{c_y}{c}\right) \equiv -\frac{c u_{cc}}{u_c}\text{vol}_c^\top, \tag{4.109}$$

where, by Itô's lemma, vol_c can be recognized as the vector of consumption growth exposures to the primitive sources of risk,

$$\frac{dc}{c} = (\cdots)\, dt + \text{vol}_c dW.$$

These conclusions generalize those obtained in the introductory examples of section 4.2.6. Finally, there is an alternative way to express the martingale restriction. Consider the first of eqs. (4.102),

$$\mu - 1_m r = -\frac{c u_{cc}}{u_c}\sigma\,\text{vol}_c^\top \equiv -\frac{c u_{cc}}{u_c}\text{cov}_{S,c}, \tag{4.110}$$

where we have used eq. (4.109) and where $\text{cov}_{S,c}$ denotes the vector of the m instantaneous covariances of the securities returns with consumption. Premultiplying eq. (4.110) by an arbitrary portfolio weighting $\frac{\pi_p^\top}{V}$ yields $\mu_p - r = -\frac{cu_{cc}}{u_c}\text{cov}_{p,c}$, which we can replace back to eq. (4.110), leaving

$$\mu - \mathbf{1}_m r = \frac{\text{cov}_{S,c}}{\text{cov}_{p,c}}(\mu_p - r). \tag{4.111}$$

Eq. (4.111) is known as the consumption CAPM (CCAPM). Note that the portfolio p is not the market portfolio. But if there is a portfolio p that is perfectly correlated with changes in consumption, eq. (4.111) would imply that

$$\mu - \mathbf{1}_m r = \frac{\text{cov}_{S,c}}{\text{var}_c}(\mu_c - r),$$

where μ_c and var_c denote the average and the variance of consumption growth.

4.6.3.4 *Markets completed by options and equilibrium option prices*

Consider the previous example of a market with a single asset and random volatility (see eq. (4.100)), and to simplify, set $\theta_1 \equiv 1$. We now assume that there is a European option available for trading and that this option completes the market, an assumption that may be shown to hold through (see chapter 11 and the discussion below). The martingale restrictions in eq. (4.102) collapse to

$$\begin{pmatrix} \mu - r \\ \mu^F - r \end{pmatrix} = \hat{\sigma}\lambda, \quad \hat{\sigma} = \begin{pmatrix} s & 0 \\ \sigma_1^F & \sigma_2^F \end{pmatrix}, \quad \lambda = \begin{pmatrix} s\frac{-V\mathcal{J}_{VV}}{\mathcal{J}_V} + \Sigma_1 \frac{-V\mathcal{J}_{Vy}}{\mathcal{J}_V} \\ \Sigma_2 \frac{-V\mathcal{J}_{Vy}}{\mathcal{J}_V} \end{pmatrix}, \tag{4.112}$$

where we have used the equilibrium condition $V = S$.

The first equation in (4.112) provides a restriction on the expected excess returns on the primitive asset, $\mu - r$; the next section explains how the safe interest rate r is determined (see eq. (4.113)). To summarize, in equilibrium, $V_t = S_t$, where S_t is solution to eq. (4.100), with $\bar{\mu}(S_t, y_t) = \mu(S_t, y_t) - \frac{D_t}{S_t}$ and $\mu(S_t, y_t)$ restricted as just explained. The second condition is an option pricing theory. Chapter 11 explains that it is a partial differential equation that the price of an option solves, subject to the appropriate boundary condition (see section 11.5).

The risk premium reflects the representative investor attitudes to risk. If the discounted utility function exhibits CRRA, that is, $u(t, c) = e^{-\rho t}\frac{c^{1-\gamma}}{1-\gamma}$, with ρ and γ constants, then in equilibrium, $\mathcal{J}(V, y, t) = e^{-\rho t} g(y, t)\frac{V^{1-\gamma}}{1-\gamma}$ for some function g. Note that g is independent of y in the logarithmic utility case, $\gamma = 1$, such that $\mathcal{J}_{Vy} = 0$: the representative investor does not require compensation for bearing volatility risk,[25] an assumption that does not seem to receive empirical support.

When does the option complete markets? Note that the economic rationale for market completeness is critical. The equilibrium in this section relies on the assumption of

25. These results are known since at least Lewis (2000, 228, 232). Pham and Touzi (1996) first showed that the volatility risk premium (i.e., the second component in (4.112)) is zero when a representative investor has logarithmic utility.

a representative agent, an assumption that holds when markets are complete and under additional conditions identified by Huang (1987). In the market of this section, markets are complete once $\hat{\sigma}$ is invertible, as explained earlier. Assuming that s is strictly positive, $\hat{\sigma}$ is invertible if $\sigma_2^F \neq 0$ a.s. But then note that, by Itô's lemma, $\sigma_2^F = \frac{F_y}{F}\Sigma_2$, where F denotes the option price and F_y is the partial of F with respect to the volatility state variable, y. Assuming $\Sigma_2 \neq 0$ (for otherwise volatility would not make markets incomplete), markets are complete when the option price is monotonic in y. Naturally, the option price is endogenous, and a monotonicity property cannot be taken as an assumption, but Bajeux-Besnainou and Rochet (1996) and Romano and Touzi (1997) show that such a property holds under mild conditions, as discussed in chapter 11.

4.6.3.5 *Asset volatility and general equilibrium*

One aspect of the previous model with stochastic volatility is the assumption that the asset return volatility $s(y_t)$ is given by Mother Nature. While this assumption leads to tractable models with random volatility, an important task in financial economics is to elaborate on theoretical explanations for asset volatility that are consistent with market behavior. These explanations necessitate a further elaboration of the framework in this section and are provided in part II (see chapters 8 and 9). We now proceed to explain how interest rates are determined in the equilibrium of the model.

4.6.4 Interest Rates

4.6.4.1 *I: Consumption-based*

We know already that interest rates and risk premiums link to the marginal utility of consumption (see section 4.2). How do these facts relate to the predictions in this section? Recall that by the first-order conditions, an optimal consumption path satisfies $u_c = \mathcal{J}_V$; marginal utility of consumption equals marginal indirect utility of wealth. We wish to find the *equilibrium* dynamics of the marginal indirect utility of wealth, say, $\mathcal{J}_V^*$. First, note that by previous results on martingale approaches to arbitrage (see section 4.4), we have that, in equilibrium,

$$d \ln \mathcal{J}_V^* = \left(\frac{L\mathcal{J}_V^*}{\mathcal{J}_V^*} - \frac{1}{2} \|\lambda\|^2 \right) dt - \lambda dW,$$

where λ is just as it is in eq. (4.102).

Next, we determine the expected growth rate in the marginal utility of wealth. Let us differentiate the Bellman's equation with respect to V,

$$\begin{aligned}
0 &= G_V(t, V, y; c, \pi, \pi_F) \\
&= \mathcal{J}_{Vt}(t, V, y) + \mathcal{J}_{VV}(t, V, y) \left(\pi^\top (\mu - \mathbf{1}_m r) + \pi_F^\top \left(\mu^F - \mathbf{1}_n r \right) + rV - c \right) \\
&\quad + r\mathcal{J}_V(t, V, y) + \mathcal{J}_{Vy}(t, V, y)\varphi(y) + \frac{1}{2}\mathcal{J}_{VVV}(t, V, y)\pi_a^\top \hat{\sigma}\hat{\sigma}^\top \pi_a \\
&\quad + \pi_a^\top \hat{\sigma} \Sigma^\top \mathcal{J}_{VVy}(t, V, y) + \frac{1}{2}\mathrm{Tr}\left(\Sigma\Sigma^\top \mathcal{J}_{Vyy}(t, V, y) \right),
\end{aligned}$$

where G is defined in eq. (4.95). Evaluating the previous expression in equilibrium and re-arranging leaves[26]

$$r = -\frac{L\mathcal{J}_V^*(t, V, y)}{\mathcal{J}_V^*(t, V, y)} = -\frac{Lu_c(t, c)}{u(t, c)}. \tag{4.113}$$

That is, the interest rate equilibrium dynamics link to those of consumption. For example, if the dividends of the productive assets are exogenously specified (the assumption in this section), then the equilibrium dynamics of consumption relate to those of the sum of all the dividends and are determined by expanding the RHS of the second equality in (4.113).

4.6.4.2 *II: With exogenously given productive activities*

In a famous contribution, Cox, Ingersoll, and Ross (1985a) develop an asset pricing framework that is a variant of that in this section: productive assets are "linear activities," with average growth μ_t and volatilities σ_t given by Mother Nature. These production activities do not distribute payoffs during their life. They are called linear because investing S_{i0} in the ith of them at time 0 delivers S_{it} at time t.

We could derive the equilibrium interest rate in this framework by repeating the arguments leading to eq. (4.98), but it is instructive to consider an alternative formulation. Let us evaluate the first set of the first-order conditions (4.102) at the equilibrium, premultiply the result by $\pi^\top$, and use the additional equilibrium condition $\pi^\top 1_m = V$, leaving

$$r = \frac{\pi^\top}{V}\mu + var\left(\frac{dV}{V}\right)\frac{V\mathcal{J}_{VV}}{\mathcal{J}_V} + cov\left(\frac{dV}{V}, dy\right)\frac{\mathcal{J}_{Vy}}{\mathcal{J}_V}, \tag{4.114}$$

where the equilibrium dynamics of wealth are given by

$$dV_t = \left(\pi_t^\top \mu_t - c_t\right)dt + \pi_t^\top \sigma_t dW_t \tag{4.115}$$

and $\pi_t = \text{Cap}_t$ now denotes the vector of linear activities values.

Eq. (4.114) says that the safe interest rate equals the expected return on wealth plus additional factors reflecting risk aversion. Intuitively, the higher the investor's risk aversion, the lower the risky asset demand, which in equilibrium leads to lower interest rates needed to clear the market for the safe asset.

This model can be used to price the entire term structure of interest rates and may be analytically convenient under some simplifying assumptions. Cox, Ingersoll, and Ross (1985b) make such additional assumptions and derive a celebrated theory of the term structure of interest rates. Let us just consider an economy in which the investor can access a single production activity, such that $V = \pi_1 = \theta_1 S_1$, with $\theta_1 = 1$. We assume that (i) $\mu_t = \hat{\mu} y_t$ and $\sigma_t \sigma_t^\top = \Omega y_t$ for two constants $\hat{\mu}$ and Ω and that (ii) y_t in eq. (4.92) is a single state variable, that is the solution to

$$dy_t = \phi(\bar{y} - y_t)dt + v\sqrt{y_t}dW_t, \tag{4.116}$$

26. In particular, $L\mathcal{J}_V^* = \mathcal{J}_{Vt}^* + \mathcal{J}_{VV}^*\left(\pi^\top \mu - c\right) + \frac{1}{2}\mathcal{J}_{VVV}^* \text{Cap}^\top \sigma\sigma^\top \text{Cap} + \text{Cap}^\top \sigma \Sigma^\top \mathcal{J}_{VVy}^* + \frac{1}{2}\text{Tr}(\Sigma\Sigma^\top \mathcal{J}_{Vyy}^*)$.

for some d-dimensional vector of constants v and two constants ϕ and $\bar{y}$. Under these assumptions, $\pi = V$, and the equilibrium interest rate in eq. (4.114) reduces to

$$r_t = \left(\hat{\mu} + \Omega \frac{V \mathcal{J}_{VV}}{\mathcal{J}_V}\right) y_t + \sigma_t v^\top \frac{\mathcal{J}_{Vy}}{\mathcal{J}_V} \sqrt{y_t}. \tag{4.117}$$

This expression for the equilibrium interest rate further simplifies when the indirect utility of the representative investor is separable, that is, $\mathcal{J}_{Vy} = 0$. For example, this case occurs when the investor has logarithmic instantaneous utility and eq. (4.117) becomes

$$r_t = (\hat{\mu} - \Omega)\, y_t. \tag{4.118}$$

Assuming that $\hat{\mu} > \Omega$ and additional regularity conditions, the short-term rate is then strictly positive and inherits the "square-root dynamics" from y_t in eq. (4.116). Finally, in this economy, the risk premium in eq. (4.102) is $\lambda_t = \bar{\sigma}^\top \sqrt{y_t}$, where $\bar{\sigma}$ is some vector of constants such that $\|\bar{\sigma}\|^2 = \Omega$; by eq. (4.117), it can be expressed as a function of the short-term rate as follows:

$$\lambda_t = \bar{\sigma}^\top (\hat{\mu} - \Omega)^{-1/2} \sqrt{r_t}. \tag{4.119}$$

Chapter 13 examines this model in some more detail, but it also reviews another model along these lines that was developed by Longstaff and Schwartz (1992), which aims to richer dynamics for the short-term rate than those in eq. (4.118). The only more general assumption made by Longstaff and Schwartz is that the single linear activity is the solution to

$$\frac{dS_1}{S_1} = (\hat{\mu}_1 y_{1t} + \hat{\mu}_2 y_{2t})\, dt + \bar{\sigma} \sqrt{y_{2t}} dW_t,$$

where $\hat{\mu}_i$ are two constants; $\bar{\sigma}$ is a vector of constants with the same properties as that in the Cox, Ingersoll, and Ross (1985b) model; and

$$dy_{it} = \phi_i (\bar{y}_i - y_{it})\, dt + v_i \sqrt{y_{it}} dW_t, \quad i = 1, 2. \tag{4.120}$$

Under these assumptions, the short-term rate in eq. (4.114) and the risk premium in eq. (4.102) are

$$r_t = \hat{\mu}_1 y_{1t} + (\hat{\mu}_2 - \Omega)\, y_{2t}, \quad \lambda_t = \bar{\sigma}^\top \sqrt{y_{2t}}. \tag{4.121}$$

That is, the equilibrium interest rate follows a two-factor model. This model is a useful benchmark to think about in a world where bond return volatility is random as discussed in chapter 13.

4.7 Portfolio Constraints

This section analyzes portfolio choice in markets with limited participation (e.g., incomplete markets) and imperfections (e.g., short sale constraints). The point of departure is the Brownian model in sections 4.3–4.4 where we still assume that $m = d$: the number of securities equals the number of sources of uncertainty, such that in absence of any frictions, markets would be complete. To model portfolio frictions, we restrict the portfolio shares in the risky assets, $p_t \equiv \pi_t / V_t^{x,\pi,c}$, to lie in a closed convex set $K \in \mathbb{R}^d$.

We follow the approach put forward by Cvitanić and Karatzas (1992). This approach consists in "embedding" the *constrained* portfolio choice of the investor in a set of *unconstrained* portfolio optimization problems. Under regularity conditions, there exists one problem within this set of unconstrained problems, the solution of which is the solution of the original constrained problem. Therefore, we may solve the constrained problem by solving the unconstrained problem by means of the martingale methods of section 4.4. This approach is closely related to the minimax probability methods of He and Pearson (1991), briefly illustrated within the discrete-time framework with incomplete markets of chapter 2 (see section 2.6). The approach in this section leads to a more systematic methodology for implementing solutions to consumption and portfolio policies, one that generalizes the work of He and Pearson (1991), which only related to problems with incomplete markets. Karatzas and Shreve (1998, chapters 5 and 6) provide a systematic treatment of consumption and portfolio choices under constraints.

4.7.1 Admissible Portfolio Choices

We begin with some definitions. Let K denote the set of the admissible portfolio choices and consider the *support function* of $-K$,

$$\zeta(\nu) = \sup_{p \in K}(-p^\top \nu), \quad \nu \in \mathbb{R}^d, \tag{4.122}$$

and its *effective domain*,

$$\tilde{K} = \{\nu \in \mathbb{R}^d : \zeta(\nu) < \infty\}, \tag{4.123}$$

also known as the *barrier cone* of $-K$.

Corresponding to the sets K of admissible portfolios are different support functions ζ. Consider the following examples. *Unconstrained* portfolio choice occurs in the special circumstance in which $K = \mathbb{R}^d$, in which case $\tilde{K} = \{0\}$ and $\zeta = 0$ on $\tilde{K}$. *Prohibition of short-selling* is modeled by restricting the set of admissible portfolios to $K = [0, \infty)^d$, in which case $\tilde{K} = K$ and $\zeta = 0$ on $\tilde{K}$. The case with *incomplete markets*, originally covered by He and Pearson (1991), can be summarized by the set $K = \{p \in \mathbb{R}^d : p_{m+1} = \cdots = p_d = 0\}$ (i.e., only the first m assets can be traded), in which case $\tilde{K} = \{\nu \in \mathbb{R}^d : \nu_1 = \cdots = \nu_m = 0\}$.

Figures 4.1 and 4.2 illustrate these examples in the $\mathbb{R}^2$ case. To develop intuition on (4.123), consider for a given cone K, the set $\tilde{K}_- = \{\nu \in \mathbb{R}^2 : p^\top \nu \geq 0, \forall p \in K\}$ (see figure 4.1). Consider again the prohibition of *short selling*, in which case $K = [0, \infty)^2$. It is easy to see that, in this case, $\tilde{K}_- = K$, and that

$$\zeta(\nu) = \sup_{p \in [0,\infty)^2} (-p^\top \nu) = \begin{cases} 0, & \text{if } \nu \in \tilde{K}_- = [0, \infty)^2 \\ \infty, & \text{otherwise} \end{cases}.$$

That is, $\zeta(\nu)$ is finite only on $\tilde{K}_-$, such that the effective domain is $\tilde{K} = \tilde{K}_-$. As for the *incomplete markets* case, assume for sake of illustration that the second asset is not available for trading, such that $K = \{p \in \mathbb{R}^2 : p_2 = 0\}$ and

$$\begin{aligned} \tilde{K}_- &= \{\nu \in \mathbb{R}^2 : p_1\nu_1 + p_2\nu_2 \geq 0, \ \forall p_1 \in \mathbb{R} \text{ and } p_2 = 0\} \\ &= \{\nu \in \mathbb{R}^2 : p_1\nu_1 \geq 0, \ \forall p_1 \in \mathbb{R}\} \\ &= \{\nu \in \mathbb{R}^2 : \nu_1 = 0\}. \end{aligned}$$

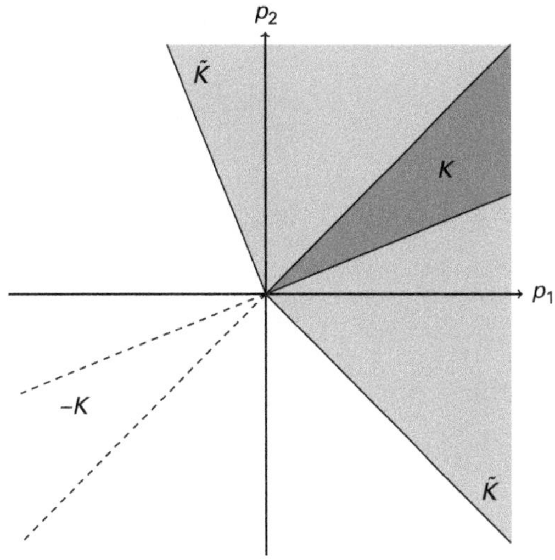

Figure 4.1
Portfolio choice under constraints. K denotes the set of admissible portfolios, and $\tilde{K}$ is the effective domain for the support function ζ in (4.122).

Note that the function $\zeta(\nu)$ is now

$$\zeta(\nu) = \sup_{p_1 \in \mathbb{R}} (-p_1 \nu_1) = \begin{cases} 0, & \text{if } \nu \in \tilde{K}_- \text{ (i.e. } \nu_1 = 0) \\ \infty, & \text{otherwise} \end{cases}.$$

Again, $\zeta(\nu)$ is finite only on $\tilde{K}_-$, such that the effective domain is $\tilde{K} = \tilde{K}_-$. The top panel in figure 4.2 illustrates this case. The remaining panels of this figure plot examples of less severe forms of constraints. In these examples, markets are still complete but access to them is constrained.

4.7.2 Artificial Markets

This section describes an unconstrained problem that can be solved through the martingale methods of section 4.4. This problem relies on some judiciously chosen "artificial" markets in which an investor makes unconstrained portfolio choices. The important property of this unconstrained problem is that one of the artificial markets leads the unconstrained investor to choose the same portfolio that they would have chosen in a market with portfolio constraints. Consider the Brownian model of sections 4.3–4.4. To build a family of artificial markets, we tilt the price dynamics in this model through the support function ζ in (4.122) as follows:

$$\frac{dS_{0t}}{S_{0t}} = r_t^{\nu} dt, \quad \frac{dS_{it}}{S_{it}} = \mu_{it}^{\nu} dt + \sigma_{it} dW_t, \quad i = 1, \cdots, d, \tag{4.124}$$

where

$$r^{\nu} \equiv r + \zeta(\nu), \quad \mu_i^{\nu} \equiv \mu_i + \nu + \zeta(\nu). \tag{4.125}$$

Let $\text{Val}(x; K)$ denote the value of the problem for an investor who faces a portfolio constraint $K \in \mathbb{R}^d$, when their initial wealth is x. Let $\text{Val}_{\nu}(x)$ be the value for the same investor

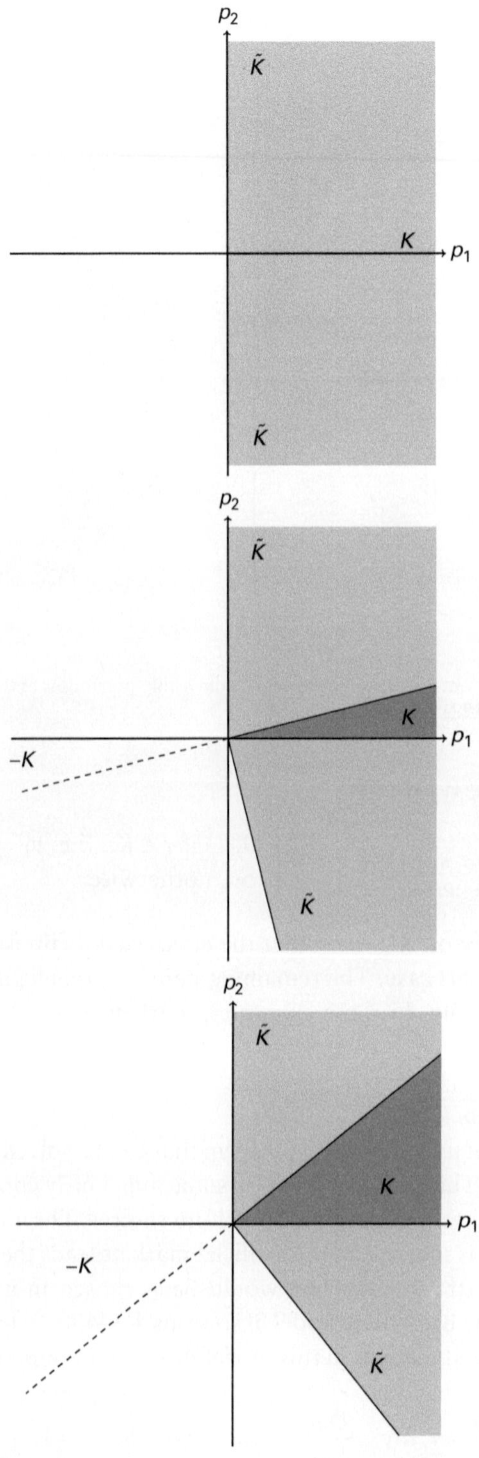

Figure 4.2
Portfolio constraints and incomplete markets. K denotes the set of admissible portfolios, and $\tilde{K}$ is the effective domain for the support function ζ in (4.122). From top to bottom, markets that impose impose progressively softer constraints on portfolio choice are displayed.

in the market (4.124). Clearly, the value for the investor in the market of sections 4.3–4.4 is just $\text{Val}_0(x)$. Now, for each $\nu \in \mathbb{R}^d$, the unconstrained program the investor faces in the market (4.124) can be dealt with through martingale methods. In this market, the risk neutral probability, Q^ν say, is defined by means of the following Radon-Nikodym derivative:

$$\eta_T^\nu \equiv \left. \frac{dQ^\nu}{dP} \right|_{\mathbb{F}_T} = \eta_T^0 \exp\left(-\int_0^T \left(\sigma_t^{-1}\nu_t\right)^\top dW_t - \frac{1}{2}\int_0^T \left\|\sigma_t^{-1}\nu_t\right\|^2 dt \right), \tag{4.126}$$

where η_T^0 is as in eq. (4.61). He and Pearson (1991) provide the analysis of a special instance of this setting, namely, when markets are incomplete, in which case the support function is $\zeta = 0$ as previously explained.

The main result is as follows. Under regularity conditions,

$$\text{Val}(x; K) = \inf_{\nu \in \tilde{K}} \left(\text{Val}_\nu(x)\right), \tag{4.127}$$

and optimal consumption and portfolio choices for this unconstrained problem are exactly those chosen by the investor constrained to have $p \in K$. Appendix 4.E provides a heuristic derivation of eq. (4.127). Consider the following example, in which our investor has log utility. It is left as an exercise to show that the $\hat{\nu}$ that equalizes the two value functions in (4.127) is

$$\hat{\nu} = \arg\min_{\nu \in \tilde{K}} \left(2\zeta(\nu) + \left\|\lambda + \sigma^{-1}\nu\right\|^2 \right),$$

where $\lambda = \sigma^{-1}(\mu - 1_d r)$ (see Cvitanić and Karatzas, 1992, 790).

4.8 Inaction: The Economics of American Options

This section provides an introduction to real options theory. In some situations, we take decisions in a discontinuous way. That is, we may decide not to take any action unless certain variables reach certain threshold values. For example, we may decide to exercise an American option when the underlying stock price touches a certain level. Sections 4.8.1 and 4.8.2 provide some simple introductory examples to these type of problems. Sections 4.8.3–4.8.5 derive evaluation results for American-style options in some simplified setting. Section 4.8.6 contains additional material on irreversible investments and exchange rate determination in economies with target zones. Chapter 5 builds on some of the models in this section and develops explanations regarding optimal capital structure in dynamic models of corporate finance and agency frictions.

4.8.1 Early Exercise Premiums: An Introductory Example

Consider two gambles referenced on the outcome from rolling a die. The first gamble is very simple: we roll a die and receive a payoff equal to $\pi \in \{1, \cdots, 6\}$, such that its fair value from the perspective of a risk neutral gambler is $v_0 \equiv \frac{1}{6}\sum_{j=1}^{6} j = 3.5$.[27] The second

27. This gamble is, thus, the risk neutral counterpart to one of the gambles described in appendix 1.C.1 of chapter 1.

Table 4.1
Payoffs of a gamble with early exercise decisions.

Panel A. Value after the 1st roll			Panel B. Value after the 2nd roll		
State j	Value at j, $p_1(j) = \max\{j, \bar{p}_2\}$	Decision	State j	Value at j, $p_2(j) = \max\{j, \bar{p}_3\}$	Decision
1	4.25	roll again	1	3.5	roll again
2	4.25	roll again	2	3.5	roll again
3	4.25	roll again	3	3.5	roll again
4	4.25	roll again	4	4	stop
5	5	stop	5	5	stop
6	6	stop	6	6	stop

gamble is more complex: we are now allowed to roll the die three times and decide to earn the payoff $\pi \in \{1, \cdots, 6\}$ and then stop the game at any of these draws. The design of the second gamble clearly aims to increase the chances of better outcomes and is expected to be valued more than the first: the right to "exercise the option" to restart the game two times more has a positive value. For example, in case the outcome in any of the draws is $j = 1$, we would for sure like to roll the die again, and in case the outcome is $j = 6$, we would for sure like to stop rolling the die. More generally now, we wish to find a state-contingent rule that maps states to a decision in order to stop the game.

We assume that we want to maximize the expected payoff, $\sup_{\tau \in \{1,2,3\}} \mathbb{E}(\pi_\tau)$, where π_τ denotes the payoff obtained on trial τ. We proceed recursively. Each time we roll the die, we stop, provided the outcome is favorable enough in that it is higher than the outcome we would expect from the next draw. Mathematically, the value of the game in each state is $\max\{j, \bar{p}'\}$, where $j \in \{1, \cdots, 6\}$ and $\bar{p}'$ denotes the expected payoff from rolling the die another time.

Table 4.1 provides the values of the second gamble on the first and second rolls for each state. Let us consider panel B. If the outcome after the second roll is 1 or 2 or 3, we roll the die again because the expected payoff from the third (and final) roll, $\bar{p}_3$ say, is obviously $\bar{p}_3 = v_0$ and is higher than that we would currently obtain, $\bar{p}_3 > 3$. However, we stop after the second roll, provided the outcome is larger than or equal to 4, as any of these outcomes is higher than $\bar{p}_3$. By a similar reasoning, the value of the gamble at the first roll in state j is $p_1(j) = \max\{j, \bar{p}_2\}$, where $\bar{p}_2 = \frac{1}{6}(3.5 \times 3 + 4 + 5 + 6) = 4.25$, leading to panel A of table 4.1. The value of the gamble is, then, the expected payoff from panel A, $\bar{p}_1 = \frac{1}{6}(4.25 \times 4 + 5 + 6) = 4.6667$.

The value of the first gamble is less than that of the second, $v_0 < \bar{p}_1$. We may interpret the second gamble as an "American option," which we can exercise at any time before its expiration, say, after having seen any of the first two rolls. The first gamble is, instead, interpreted as a "European option," with a payoff that only links to the third roll. The difference between the values of the two gambles compensates for the option to exercise early. In general, the value of the gamble after t rolls is

$$p_t(j) = \max\{j, \mathbb{E}_t(p_{t+1})\}, \quad p_T = \pi \in \{1, \cdots, 6\},$$

where the last equality is the terminal condition.

Table 4.2
Utilityof a risk averse gambler with early exercise decisions.

Panel A. Value after the 1st roll			Panel B. Value after the 2nd roll		
State j	value at j, $v_1(j) = \max\{\ln j, \bar{v}_2\}$	Decision	State j	Value at j, $v_2(j) = \max\{\ln j, \bar{v}_3\}$	Decision
1	1.3465	roll again	1	1.0965	roll again
2	1.3465	roll again	2	1.0965	roll again
3	1.3465	roll again	3	$\ln 3$	stop
4	$\ln 4$	stop	4	$\ln 4$	stop
5	$\ln 5$	stop	5	$\ln 5$	stop
6	$\ln 6$	stop	6	$\ln 6$	stop

Note that the "exercise boundaries" are $j \geq 5$ after the first roll and $j \geq 4$ after the second, meaning that the region where it is optimal to stop widens as the game goes through—the value to wait obviously decreases as the expiration approaches. Moreover, these boundaries are obviously endogenous in that we calculate them as a part of the decision process. Finally, the boundaries are time-varying in this *free-boundary* problem, although in the next section, we shall consider infinite horizon decision problems where the free boundary to be selected is constant.

4.8.2 Risk Aversion

How would a risk averse individual evaluate the previous gamble? We assume that our agent has logarithmic utility. They maximize the utility at the time they leave the gamble where this time is endogenous. Namely, the agent maximizes their expected utility as $\sup_{\tau\in\{1,2,3\}} \mathbb{E}\left(\ln \pi_\tau\right)$. The value function at time t and state j is equal to

$$v_t(j) = \max\left\{\ln j, E_t\left(v_{t+1}\right)\right\}.$$

The value function to be expected from a third roll is $\bar{v}_3 \equiv \frac{1}{6}\sum_{j=1}^{6} \ln j = 1.0965$, and because $\ln 2 < \bar{v}_3$ and $\ln 3 > \bar{v}_3$, the decision after the second roll is to draw again only when the roll delivers particularly poor outcomes, $j = 1$ or 2. Likewise, the value expected from rolling the die a second time is $\bar{v}_2 \equiv \frac{1}{6}\left(2 \times 1.0965 + \sum_{j=3}^{6} \ln j\right) = 1.3465$, such that and given that $\ln 3 < \bar{v}_2$ and $\ln 4 > \bar{v}_2$, the decision after the first roll is to stop as soon as the state is particularly favorable, that is, when j is at least as large as 4. Therefore, the value of this gamble from the perspective of the log utility gambler is $\bar{v}_1 = \frac{1}{6}\left(3 \times 1.3465 + \sum_{j=4}^{6} \ln j\right) = 1.4712$.

Note how cautious this risk averse individual is: they want to continue this game only when the outcome is lower than 3. By contrast, the risk neutral individual of the previous section continues the game even when the roll is equal to 4. We quantify how much (insurance) risk premium (see section 1.3.4 in chapter 1) is implied in the evaluation of this gamble. We consider the certainty equivalent of the gamble, $\hat{v} : \ln \hat{v} = 1.4712$, that is, $\hat{v} = 4.3545$. It is lower than the value given by a risk neutral gambler $\bar{p}_1 = 4.6667$. The difference is a risk premium. Still, the risk averse individual acknowledges this gamble carries a strictly positive early exercise premium in that $\bar{v}_1 - \bar{v}_3 > 0$.

As explained, evaluating the gamble in this section requires relying on factors such as risk aversion. The reason is that the asset underlying this gamble (rolling a die) is not traded and then does not satisfy martingale restrictions of the type considered in chapter 2. The next section develops an evaluation framework for traded assets with payoffs linking to other traded assets. In these cases, asset evaluation proceeds while relying on standard risk neutral arguments.

4.8.3 Real Options Theory

We build on the intuition developed through the example of the previous section and derive a continuous time approximation to the solution of the resulting problem by hinging on a series of heuristic arguments. We consider an "American option," that is, an option that we can exercise at any time before the expiry date, T. Once the option is exercised, it yields a payoff equal to a function of the underlying asset price, say, $\psi(S_t)$. Let C_t be the price of an American option as of time t. In discrete time, we have

$$C_t = \max\left\{\psi(S_t), e^{-r\Delta t}\mathbb{E}_t\left[C_{t+\Delta t}\right]\right\}. \tag{4.128}$$

We assume that the nature of the option, summarized by the payoff $\psi(S_t)$, is such that there are two regions, a stopping region and a continuation region, defined as follows.

(1) The stopping region, where time to maturity and the price of the asset underlying the option are such that it is optimal to exercise $C_t = \max\left\{\psi(S_t), e^{-r\Delta t}\mathbb{E}_t\left[C_{t+\Delta t}\right]\right\} = \psi(S_t)$, in which case, of course, $C_t \geq e^{-r\Delta t}\mathbb{E}_t\left[C_{t+\Delta t}\right]$. By rearranging terms,

$$0 \geq e^{-r\Delta t}\frac{\mathbb{E}_t\left[C_{t+\Delta t}\right] - C_t}{\Delta t} - \frac{1-e^{-r\Delta t}}{\Delta t}C_t. \tag{4.129}$$

The expected return on the option under the risk neutral probability is less than that on a bank deposit, which further clarifies why it is optimal to exercise early. Naturally, the fact the option is yielding less than the safe interest rate is not an arbitrage. We could simply not short the derivative as no one else is willing to buy it because it is not optimal to do so.

(2) The continuation region where time to maturity and the price of the asset underlying the option are such that it is optimal to wait $C_t = \max\left\{\psi(S_t), e^{-r\Delta t}\mathbb{E}_t\left[C_{t+\Delta t}\right]\right\} = e^{-r\Delta t}\mathbb{E}_t\left[C_{t+\Delta t}\right]$, or

$$0 = e^{-r\Delta t}\frac{\mathbb{E}_t\left[C_{t+\Delta t}\right] - C_t}{\Delta t} - \frac{1-e^{-r\Delta t}}{\Delta t}C_t. \tag{4.130}$$

The expected return on the option under the risk neutral probability is the same as that on a bank deposit.

Note that the existence of these two regions is not guaranteed. For example, as we shall see, it is never optimal to exercise early American calls written on assets that do not distribute dividends. When the two regions are instead well defined, they define an exercise "envelope," a function of the asset price underlying the option and time to maturity. It is a "free boundary" problem: we need to find a boundary that triggers some action, in this case, exercising the option. Moreover, this boundary is free in that it is not specified exogenously as with derivatives such as barrier options (see chapter 14).

The problem of finding the exercise envelope is analytically very challenging.[28] The problem, however, may considerably simplify when the expiry date, T, is infinite. Intuitively, in this case, the option price and hence the envelope depends only on the underlying asset price. Let us illustrate. Assume that $T=\infty$ and that the underlying price is a geometric Brownian motion with volatility parameter σ. Then, in the limit $\Delta t \to 0$, we have that the option price satisfies

$$\text{Stopping region:}\quad \mathcal{L}[C]-rC\leq 0 \text{ and } C=\psi(S) \tag{4.131}$$

$$\text{Continuation region:}\quad \mathcal{L}[C]-rC=0, \tag{4.132}$$

where $\mathcal{L}[C]=\frac{1}{2}\sigma^2S^2C''+rSC'$. Eqs. (4.131) and (4.132) are the continuous time counterparts to eqs. (4.129) and (4.130). To these two equations we need to add a number of conditions, discussed in the two examples in the subsections below.

We may cast this evaluation problem under an equivalent angle, one of an optimal stopping time problem,

$$C=\sup_{\tau\geq 0} E\left(e^{-r\tau}\psi(S_\tau)\right). \tag{4.133}$$

That is, we would like to find the time at which it is best to undertake an action, in this case, exercising the option. This *stopping time* links to the free-exercise boundary S^*, say, as follows:

$$\tau^*=\inf_{\tau\geq 0}\left\{\tau : S_\tau=S^*\right\},$$

where S^* is determined endogenously. It is a "real option" problem as it links nicely to the theory of evaluation of firms undertaking real economic activities (see section 4.8.6). We now describe this problem in detail in standard cases. Finally, note that the free boundary is constant because the model is stationary and maturity is $T=\infty$. The free boundary may well be time dependent in case any of these assumptions do not hold. For example, the free boundary in the die example of the previous section does depend on time.

4.8.4 Perpetual Puts

Consider a perpetual put, that is, an asset with a payoff equal to $\psi(S)=(K-S)^+$. Its price, p say, is a function of the underlying asset price S only and satisfies eqs. (4.131) and (4.132), with additional conditions. First, we assume and later verify that there exists a value for the underlying price—the free boundary, S_* say—such that it is optimal to exercise the option whenever $S<S_*$. That is, suppose that the current level of the asset price is $S_t>S_*$. To exercise the option, the price should fall to a *sufficiently low* level equal to S_*.

Let us determine S_*. First, eqs. (4.131) and (4.132) can be written as

$$\text{Stopping region } (S\leq S_*):\quad p(S_*)=K-S_* \tag{4.134}$$

$$\text{Continuation region } (S>S_*):\quad \mathcal{L}[p]-rp=0 \tag{4.135}$$

28. Barone-Adesi and Whaley (1987) provide classical approximations for the values of American options with finite maturity in models with constant volatility.

where K is the strike price of the option. Eq. (4.134) is a "value matching" condition. It ensures that the pricing function p is continuous as we move from the continuation region toward the stopping region. Second, we require the following boundary condition:

$$\lim_{S\to\infty} p(S) = 0. \tag{4.136}$$

That is, as the underlying price gets large, the put option value needs to approach zero, reflecting the fact that the probability of option exercise becomes negligible. Finally, the pricing function, $p(S)$, satisfies the following "smooth pasting" condition, obtained after taking the first-order derivative in eq. (4.134),

$$p'(S_*) = -1. \tag{4.137}$$

We conjecture that, in the continuation region, the pricing function p that solves eq. (4.135) has the form $p(S) = AS^{\gamma}$ for two constants A and γ. Plugging this guess into eq. (4.135) reveals, in fact, that the pricing function satisfying it has the following form:

$$p(S) = A_1 S^{\gamma_1} + A_2 S^{\gamma_2}, \tag{4.138}$$

where A_1 and A_1 are two constants to pin down, $\gamma_1 = -\frac{2r}{\sigma^2}$ and $\gamma_2 = 1$. To satisfy the boundary condition in eq. (4.136), we need that $A_2 = 0$, which leaves $p(S) = A_1 S^{\gamma_1}$. Evaluating this function at S_*, as in eq. (4.134), and using the smooth pasting condition in eq. (4.137) yields

$$\begin{cases} p(S_*) = A_1 S_*^{\gamma_1} = K - S_* \\ p'(S_*) = \gamma_1 A_1 S_*^{\gamma_1 - 1} = -1 \end{cases}. \tag{4.139}$$

The endogenous variables of this system are the two constants A_1 and S_*. We have

$$S_* = \frac{r}{r + \frac{1}{2}\sigma^2} K \tag{4.140}$$

and $A_1 = (K - S_*) S_*^{-\gamma_1}$, such that

$$p(S) = (K - S_*) \left(\frac{S}{S_*} \right)^{\gamma_1}.$$

A few comments are in order. First, eq. (4.140) shows that the value to wait increases with σ^2, as the exercise boundary decreases with σ^2. Heuristically, and in terms of eq. (4.128), the option price solves

$$p(S_t) \approx \max\left\{\psi(S_t), e^{-r\Delta t}\mathbb{E}_t\left[p(S_{t+\Delta t})\right]\right\}, \quad \psi(S_t) \equiv (K - S_t)^+,$$

and an increase in σ^2 leads to a higher value for the discounted expectation inside the max operator: it takes more time before the option may be exercised. Second, when the short-term rate is zero, $S_* = 0$, meaning it is never optimal to exercise and the option is worthless.

4.8.5 Perpetual Calls

Real option problems may not have a solution with well-defined stopping and continuation regions, such as those in eqs. (4.131) and (4.132). For example, for a perpetual call option—that is, for a payoff equal to $\psi(S) = (S-K)^+$—it is never optimal to exercise early if the underlying asset does not pay dividends. We illustrate this property while following the arguments in the previous subsection. The call price, $c(S)$, satisfies

$$\text{Stopping region } (S \geq S_*): \; c(S_*) = S_* - K \tag{4.141}$$

$$\text{Continuation region } (S < S_*): \; \mathcal{L}[c] - rc = 0. \tag{4.142}$$

The solution to eq. (4.142) has the same functional form as that in eq. (4.138), with the same values of γ_1 and γ_2. However, due to the conjectures on the location of the stopping and continuation regions in eqs. (4.141) and (4.142), this solution satisfies the boundary condition $\lim_{S\to 0} c(S) = 0$ rather than the boundary condition satisfied by the put price (see eq. (4.136)). Therefore, and because $\gamma_2 = 1$, we must have that $c(S) = A_2 S$, or

$$c(S_*) = A_2 S_* = S_* - K,$$

where the second equality follows by the value matching condition in eq. (4.141). Solving for S_* yields

$$S_* = \frac{K}{1 - A_2}.$$

As for the smooth pasting condition, we have that $c'(S_*) = A_2 = 1$, such that $S_* = \infty$. It is never optimal to exercise. In other words, there are no solutions to the counterparts to the two eqs. (4.139). The call option price fails to simultaneously satisfy the value matching and smooth pasting condition.

4.8.5.1 With dividends

If the underlying asset distributes any payouts over the life of the option—say, due to storage costs or even dividends—the problem has instead a well-defined solution. Assume that under the risk neutral probability, the underlying asset price satisfies

$$\frac{dS_t}{S_t} = (r - q)\, dt + \sigma \hat{W}_t,$$

where q is the constant payout ratio, $q \equiv \frac{D_t}{S_t}$, with D_t denoting the instantaneous payout (e.g., a dividend), and as usual, $\hat{W}_t$ denotes a Brownian motion under the risk neutral probability.

For this problem, eqs. (4.131) and (4.132) reduce to

$$\text{Stopping region } (S \geq S_*): \; c(S_*) = S_* - K \tag{4.143}$$

$$\text{Continuation region } (S < S_*): \; \mathcal{L}_q[c] - rc = 0 \tag{4.144}$$

where now the infinitesimal generator is $\mathcal{L}_q[c] = \frac{1}{2}\sigma^2 S^2 c'' + (r-q) S c'$. We can show that the solution to eq. (4.144) is

$$c(S) = A_1 S^{\gamma_1} + A_2 S^{\gamma_2},$$

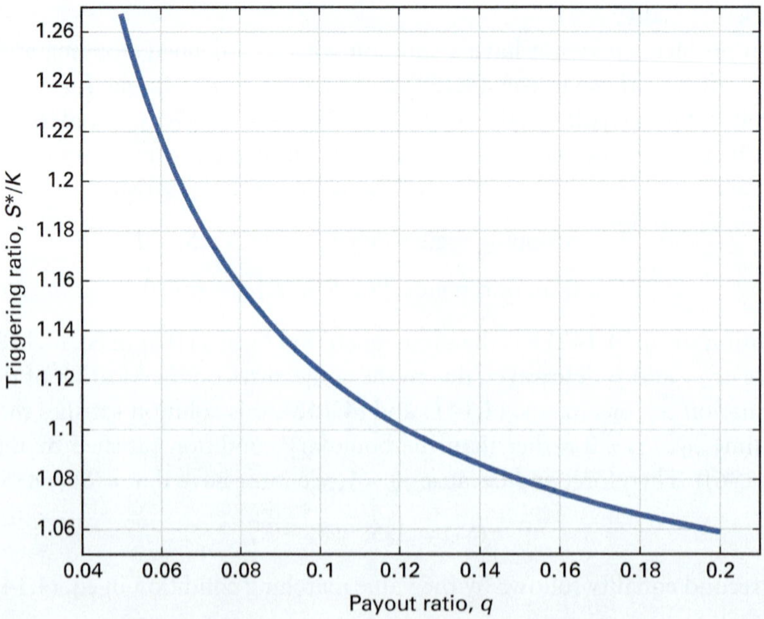

Figure 4.3
This picture depicts the price-to-strike ratio $\frac{S^*}{K}$ that triggers exercise of the American option as a function of the payout ratio q. Parameter values are $r = 1\%$ and $\sigma = 15\%$.

where $\gamma_{1/2} = \frac{1}{\sigma^2}\left(\alpha \mp \sqrt{\alpha^2 + 2\sigma^2 r}\right)$ and $\alpha \equiv q - r + \frac{1}{2}\sigma^2$. Clearly, $\gamma_1 < 0$, and it is possible to show that $\gamma_2 > 1$. The conjectures on the location of the stopping and continuation regions in eqs. (4.143) and (4.144) now deliver the boundary condition $\lim_{S \to 0} c(S) = 0$ and then

$$c(S) = A_2 S^{\gamma_2}. \tag{4.145}$$

The value matching condition and the smooth pasting conditions equivalent to the two eqs. (4.139) are now

$$\begin{cases} c(S_*) = A_2 S_*^{\gamma_2} = S_* - K \\ c'(S_*) = \gamma_2 A_2 S_*^{\gamma_2 - 1} = 1 \end{cases}.$$

The solution to this system is

$$A_2 = (S_* - K)\, S_*^{-\gamma_2}, \quad S_* = \frac{\gamma_2}{\gamma_2 - 1} K$$

such that the call option price in eq. (4.145) can be written as

$$c(S) = (S_* - K)\left(\frac{S}{S_*}\right)^{\gamma_2}.$$

Figure 4.3 depicts the ratio $\frac{S^*}{K}$ after which exercise is triggered, and expressed as a function of the payout ratio, q. Obviously, the triggering ratio blows up as q shrinks to zero. In general, the expected optimal stopping time is inversely related to q: the higher the payout ratio, the shorter the expected exercise time.

4.8.5.2 *American calls and incomplete markets*

American call options may have worth—even in the absence of dividends paid out by the underlying over their life—in the presence of incomplete markets. Consider the following example of a perpetual American call option written on the instantaneous variance (not the average expected volatility) of an asset return. Suppose that this variance, v_t say, is a solution to

$$dv_t = \kappa\,(\theta - v_t)\,dt + \sigma v_t dW_t,$$

where κ, θ and σ are parameters and W_t is a Brownian motion under the risk neutral probability. Let $\bar{v}$ denote the strike price of this option. Then the price of the American option price is a solution to

$$\text{Stopping region } (v \geq v_*): \quad c\,(v_*) = v_* - \bar{v}$$

$$\text{Continuation region } (v < v_*): \quad \mathcal{L}\,[c] - rc = 0$$

where

$$\mathcal{L}\,[c] = \kappa\,(\theta - v)\,\frac{\partial c}{\partial v} + \frac{1}{2}\sigma^2 v^2 \frac{\partial^2 c}{\partial v^2}. \tag{4.146}$$

Note that the smooth pasting condition is

$$c'\left(v^*\right) = 1,$$

and it may now hold. Intuitively, the risk neutral drift of v appears in the infinitesimal generator of eq. (4.146) because v is not traded; the risk neutral drift does not depend on r. This property parallels those arising in the previous models with dividends, and leads to a positive economic value for the American option.

4.8.6 Further Topics on Real Options and Controlled Brownian Motions

4.8.6.1 *Irreversible investments and the decision to invest*

We discuss a classical model of the optimal time at which a firm should start to sell its output, which was introduced by McDonald and Siegel (1986). Assume this firm has access to a technology such that at each instant of time t, an output x_t could be produced (and sold), which is a solution to

$$\frac{dx_t}{x_t} = \mu dt + \sigma dW_t,$$

where μ and σ are constants and W_t is a standard Brownian motion. The idea underlying the model is that the firm begins to produce only when x_t has reached a certain threshold and that the production cannot be interrupted once it starts—the investment is irreversible.

Note that if the firm decides to begin selling output for x_τ at τ, its net present value (NPV) is $\frac{x_\tau}{r-\mu} - c$, where r is the constant discounting rate, which needs to be larger than output growth to ensure finite NPV; $r > \mu$; and c is an initial constant cost incurred while starting the production. Therefore, the value of the firm that holds the potentiality to start producing at some future time τ when current potential output is x_0 is

$$G(x_0) = \sup_{\tau \geq 0} E\left(e^{-r\tau}\psi(x_\tau)\right), \quad \psi(x) \equiv \frac{x}{r-\mu} - c.$$

That is, the value of the firm is formally the same as that of a perpetual American option in (4.133). Accordingly, we conjecture that the optimal stopping time is determined as the first time x_t crosses a free boundary from below, x_o, say. In the continuation region,

$$0 = \mathcal{L}G(x) - rG(x) \quad \text{for } x < x_o, \tag{4.147}$$

where $\mathcal{L}G = \mu x G' + \frac{1}{2}\sigma^2 x^2 G''$. At the free boundary,

$$G(x_o) = \frac{x_o}{r-\mu} - c. \tag{4.148}$$

The solution to eq. (4.147) is $G(x) = A_1 x^{\gamma_1} + A_2 x^{\gamma_2}$, where $\gamma_1 < 0$, $\gamma_2 > 1$ and the parameter γ_2 is decreasing in σ^2.[29] Finally, A_1 and A_2 are constants to be determined. Note that it must be that $A_1 = 0$, for otherwise the value function would increase disproportionately as the output potential becomes arbitrarily small. Therefore, the economically viable solution to eq. (4.147) is the bounded value function

$$G(x) = A_2 x^{\gamma_2} \quad \text{for } x < x_o. \tag{4.149}$$

The free boundary x_o and the constant A_2 can now be determined by requiring that the two following conditions hold at the threshold x_o: (i) the value matching condition, that is, the value function in eq. (4.149), is the same as that in (4.148) and (ii) the smooth pasting condition, the derivatives agree. The result is

$$x_o = \frac{\gamma_2 (r-\mu)}{\gamma_2 - 1} c, \quad A_2 = \frac{x_o^{1-\gamma_2}}{\gamma_2 (r-\mu)}.$$

Therefore, the firm should start producing immediately unless it had to pay a cost c, in which case the threshold x^o from which it is optimal to begin producing increases proportionally with c. Note that, because γ_2 is decreasing in σ^2, x_o increases with σ^2. That is—and in analogy with the American put case of section 4.8.4—the value to postpone investments increases with uncertainty.

4.8.6.2 *A model of determination of exchange rates in target zones*

We provide one instance of policy intervention that can "force" asset prices to experience less long-term volatility than implied by economic fundamentals: an agreement between central banks to do "whatever it takes" to maintain the exchange rate within a given band. The main assumption underlying the model is that monetary interventions are fully credible and that interventions occur marginally in a way that the fundamentals behave as processes with reflecting barriers, just as in the dividend example given in section 4.2.6.4.

---

29. Replacing $G(x)$ into (4.147) shows that γ is the solution to $0 = f_\sigma(\gamma) \equiv \mu\gamma + \frac{1}{2}\sigma^2\gamma(\gamma-1) - r$. We have $-r = f_\sigma(0) < f_\sigma(1) = \mu - r < 0$. Therefore, it must be that the two roots satisfy $\gamma_1 < 0$ and $\gamma_2 > 1$. Moreover, it is easy to see that, for any $\sigma' > \sigma$, we have that $f_{\sigma'}(\gamma) > f_\sigma(\gamma)$ for all $\gamma > 1$. Thus, γ_2 decreases with σ^2.

Consider, first, the classical model of exchange rate determination, in which the exchange rate is tied down to the consumer price differentials between two countries through the purchasing power parity equation, $s_t = p_t - p_t^*$, where s_t denotes the log-spot exchange rate, p_t is the domestic log-price level at time t, and p_t^* is its foreign counterpart. Money demand increases with log-output y_t and decreases with the nominal interest rate i_t in a way that, in equilibrium, log-money supply is $m_t = p_t + ay_t - \alpha i_t + v_t$, where a and α are constants and v_t is some stochastic disturbance—α is thus the semi-elasticity of money demand to interest rates. An analogous, "starred" equation holds in the foreign country. Finally, the covered interest rate parity holds:

$$i_t = i_t^* + \frac{E(ds_t)}{dt}.$$

We can put this all together and conclude that the exchange rate is the solution to

$$s_t = x_t + \alpha \frac{E(ds_t)}{dt}, \tag{4.150}$$

where $x_t \equiv m_t - m_t^* - a(y_t - y_t^*) - (v_t - v_t^*)$. Assume that, were the exchange rate free to fluctuate, the fundamentals x_t would follow an arithmetic Brownian motion

$$dx_t = \mu dt + \sigma dW_t,$$

where μ and σ are constants and W_t is a Brownian motion. One can immediately see that this assumption regarding the fundamentals, eq. (4.150) and Itô's lemma, all imply that the equilibrium exchange rate, $s_t = s(x_t)$, is a solution to the following differential equation:

$$s(x) = x + \alpha \left(\mu s'(x) + \frac{1}{2}\sigma^2 s''(x) \right), \tag{4.151}$$

which is solved by

$$s_F(x_t) \equiv \alpha\mu + x_t.$$

Note that exchange rate volatility does not play any role in this context. In fact, there are many additional exchange rate functions on top of $s_F(x_t)$, which satisfy eq. (4.151),

$$s(x_t) = s_F(x_t) + B_1 e^{\beta_1 x_t} + B_2 e^{\beta_2 x_t}, \tag{4.152}$$

where $\beta_{1/2} = \frac{1}{\alpha\sigma^2}(-\alpha\mu \mp \sqrt{\alpha^2\mu^2 + 2\alpha\sigma^2})$ and B_1 and B_2 are two arbitrary constants. However, $s_F(x_t)$ is the only solution that we can interpret as one of expected fundamentals consistent with eq. (4.150), in that

$$E_t \left(\int_t^\infty e^{-\alpha^{-1}(\tau - t)} \alpha^{-1} x_\tau \, d\tau \right) = \alpha\mu + x_t \equiv s_F(x_t).$$

How would exchange rates behave once central banks are credible enough to modify the fundamentals and make the exchange rates lie within a given band? Krugman (1991) considers a model in which the exchange rate is maintained within a target zone, say, $s_t \in [\underline{s}, \bar{s}]$ for two given constants $\underline{s}$ and $\bar{s}$. The model's main assumption is that central banks control the fundamentals through "infinitesimal interventions," by injecting or withdrawing monetary base $m_t - m_t^*$ as soon as the fundamentals become too weak or too strong for the current exchange rate to be maintained within the band $[\underline{s}, \bar{s}]$. The fundamentals are then a solution to

$$dx_t = \mu dt + \sigma dW_t + dU_t - dL_t,$$

where U_t and L_t are continuous processes that only increase when the fundamentals reach hit some critical values $\underline{x}$ (U) and $\bar{x}$ (L) that ask for intervention, which will be determined below.

Through arguments entirely analogous to those utilized while pricing assets with dividends that have reflecting barriers (see eq. (4.56) in section 4.2.6.4), we now have that the exchange rate is solution to

$$ds(x_t) = \left(\mu s'(x_t) + \frac{1}{2}\sigma^2 s''(x_t)\right) dt + s'(x_t)\sigma dW_t + s'(x_t) dU_t - s'(x_t) dL_t.$$

Therefore, the exchange rate is still solution to the differential equation (4.151), and its general solution is therefore given by eq. (4.152). We can now determine the two constants, B_1 and B_2. First, note that analogous to the reflecting barrier case in section 4.2.6.4 (see eq. (4.57)), to rule out arbitrage, we need to ensure that the following smooth pasting conditions hold at the critical values $\underline{x}$ and $\bar{x}$:

$$s'(\underline{x}) = 0 \quad \text{and} \quad s'(\bar{x}) = 0. \tag{4.153}$$

Moreover, at the boundaries, we need to ensure that

$$s(\underline{x}) = \underline{s} \quad \text{and} \quad s(\bar{x}) = \bar{s}. \tag{4.154}$$

Eqs. (4.153) and (4.154) are four independent equations with four unknowns: the two constants of the exchange rate function, B_1 and B_2, and the two critical values of the fundamentals that trigger intervention, $\underline{x}$ and $\bar{x}$, which are all implicitly determined.

4.9 Jumps

Brownian motions are well suited to model the price behavior of liquid assets that are not subject to default risk. There is, however, a fair amount of interest in understanding asset prices as "discontinuous" processes. To illustrate, there may be events through which agents may mutate: for example, a liquidity shock (modeled as the realization of a "rare event") may make agents willing to sell the assets they hold, with important equilibrium dynamics (see, e.g., chapter 10). Fixed-income instruments may actually undergo liquidity dry-ups, default, or have infrequent movements and price discontinuities (see, e.g., section 13.4.6 in chapter 13 and chapter 14). This section is an introduction to a class of processes (Poisson processes), which is particularly useful in modeling all these issues.

4.9.1 Poisson Jumps

Let (t, T) be a given time interval, and consider events in this interval with the following properties.

(1) The number of event arrivals on all disjoint intervals of (t, T) are independent.

(2) For any two disjoint but equal intervals in (t, T), the probability of any event arrivals is the same in both intervals.

(3) The probability that more than one events arrive simultaneously in any interval is zero.

We rely on the previous properties and pin down the functional form of $P_k(\tau - t)$, that is, the probability that k events arrive during the interval of time $[t, \tau]$. First, note that $P_k(\tau - t)$ satisfies

$$P_0(\tau + d\tau - t) = P_0(\tau - t) P_0(d\tau) \tag{4.155}$$

with the boundary conditions $P_0(0) = 1$ and $P_k(0) = 0$ for $k \geq 1$. Eq. (4.155) and the first boundary condition are satisfied by the function $P_0(\tau) = e^{-v\tau}$ for some constant v; we take $v > 0$ to ensure that $P_0 \in [0, 1]$. Further, we have that

$$\begin{cases} P_1(\tau + d\tau - t) &= P_0(\tau - t) P_1(d\tau) + P_1(\tau - t) P_0(d\tau) \\ &\vdots \\ P_k(\tau + d\tau - t) &= P_{k-1}(\tau - t) P_1(d\tau) + P_k(\tau - t) P_0(d\tau) \\ &\vdots \end{cases}. \tag{4.156}$$

The first equation in (4.156) can be rearranged as follows:

$$\frac{P_1(\tau + d\tau - t) - P_1(\tau - t)}{d\tau} = -\frac{1 - P_0(d\tau)}{d\tau} P_1(\tau - t) + \frac{P_1(d\tau)}{d\tau} P_0(\tau - t).$$

For small $d\tau$, $P_1(d\tau) \approx 1 - P_0(d\tau)$ and $P_0(d\tau) \approx 1 - v d\tau$. Therefore, P_1 satisfies the following differential equation: $P_1'(\tau - t) = -v(P_1(\tau - t) - P_0(\tau - t))$. By a similar reasoning, P_k satisfies

$$P_k'(\tau - t) = -v(P_k(\tau - t) - P_{k-1}(\tau - t)).$$

The solution to this equation is

$$P_k(\tau - t) = \frac{v^k (\tau - t)^k}{k!} e^{-v(\tau - t)}. \tag{4.157}$$

We now provide heuristic details with regard to eq. (4.157) from a slightly different angle.

4.9.2 A Rare Event Interpretation

A Poisson model formalizes the notion of *rare events*. Note that, by the reasoning in the previous section, we have that $P_1(d\tau) \approx v d\tau$; that is, the probability that one event occurs in an infinitesimal amount of time is small and proportional to v. We usually refer v to as the *intensity* of event arrivals. Let us provide additional intuition. Consider the expression for the probability of k "arrivals" in n trials predicted by a binomial distribution

$$P_{n,k} = \binom{n}{k} p^k q^{n-k} = \frac{n!}{k!(n-k)!} p^k q^{n-k}, \qquad p, q > 0, \; p + q = 1,$$

where p is the probability of arrival in each trial. We want to model the probability p as a function of n, $p(n)$ say, while requiring that $\lim_{n\to\infty} p(n) = 0$. The last conditions would make each arrival "rare." One choice is $p(n) = \frac{a}{n}$ for some constant $a > 0$. Under this assumption, we have

$$\begin{aligned} P_{n,k} &= \frac{n!}{k!\,(n-k)!} p(n)^k \,(1-p(n))^{n-k} \\ &= \frac{n!}{n^k\,(n-k)!}\frac{a^k}{k!}\left(1-\frac{a}{n}\right)^n\left(1-\frac{a}{n}\right)^{-k} \\ &= \underbrace{\frac{n}{n}\cdot\frac{n-1}{n}\cdots\frac{n-k+1}{n}}_{k \text{ times}}\frac{a^k}{k!}\left(1-\frac{a}{n}\right)^n\left(1-\frac{a}{n}\right)^{-k}. \end{aligned}$$

By taking the limits,

$$\lim_{n\to\infty} P_{n,k} \equiv P_k = \frac{a^k}{k!}e^{-a}. \tag{4.158}$$

We may interpret these limiting results as follows. Consider an interval equal to $(\tau - t)$, which we split into n subintervals, each of them with length $\frac{\tau-t}{n}$. Then, the probability of one arrival in each subinterval is proportional to the subinterval length, that is,

$$p(n) = v\frac{\tau - t}{n}.$$

Thus, (4.157) and (4.158) are formally the same once we set $a \equiv v(\tau - t)$.

Finally, the heuristic argument by which $P_1(d\tau) \approx v d\tau$ and $P_0(d\tau) \approx 1 - v d\tau$ suggests a simple procedure to simulate a Poisson process. We simulate a uniform random variable $U(0,1)$ and approximate the continuous time process by Y, where

$$Y = \begin{cases} 0 & \text{if} \quad 0 \le U < 1 - vh \\ 1 & \text{if} \quad 1 - vh \le U < 1 \end{cases}$$

and h is a discretization interval.

4.9.3 Properties and Related Distributions

It is easy to check that P_k is a probability. We have

$$\sum_{k=0}^{\infty} P_k = e^{-a}\sum_{k=0}^{\infty}\frac{a^k}{k!} = 1,$$

where the last equality follows by a McLaurin expansion of e^a. The mean, μ_P say, of a random variable with a Poisson distribution is

$$\mu_P = \sum_{k=0}^{\infty} kP_k = e^{-a}\sum_{k=0}^{\infty} k\frac{a^k}{k!} = a. \tag{4.159}$$

A related distribution is the *exponential* (or Erlang) distribution, which may be derived as follows. Recall that probability of zero arrivals in $\tau - t$ predicted by the Poisson model is $P_0(\tau - t) = e^{-v(\tau-t)}$. It then follows that

$$G(\tau - t) \equiv 1 - P_0(\tau - t) = 1 - e^{-v(\tau-t)}$$

is the probability of at least one arrival in $\tau - t$. The function G can be also interpreted as the probability the first arrival occurred before τ, starting from t. The density function of G is

$$g(\tau - t) = \frac{\partial}{\partial \tau} G(\tau - t) = v e^{-v(\tau-t)}.$$

The first two moments of the exponential distribution, μ_e and σ_e^2 say, are

$$\mu_e = \int_0^\infty x v e^{-vx} dx = v^{-1}, \quad \sigma_e^2 = \int_0^\infty \left(x - v^{-1}\right)^2 v e^{-vx} dx = v^{-2}.$$

The expected time of the first arrival occurred before τ, starting from t equals v^{-1}. More generally, v^{-1} can be interpreted as the average time from one arrival to another.

A more general distribution than the exponential is the Gamma distribution with density

$$g_\gamma(\tau - t) = v e^{-v(\tau-t)} \frac{(v(\tau - t))^{\gamma-1}}{(\gamma - 1)!}.$$

The exponential distribution is obtained when $\gamma = 1$.

4.9.4 Cox Processes

In the previous sections, we have taken v to be constant. But we might take v to be a deterministic function of time, v_t say, and conclude that

$$\Pr(Z_\tau - Z_t = k) = \frac{\left(\int_t^\tau v_u du\right)^k}{k!} \exp\left(-\int_t^\tau v_u du\right), \quad k = 0, 1, \cdots.$$

More generally, the intensity function may be a function of some underlying state variable—for example, a state variable that follows a diffusion processes. Processes with random intensities are known as *Cox processes*. In chapter 14, we rely on such processes to model credit spreads, that is, the yield in excess of the safe interest rate that investors require to invest in certain securities subject to default risk (see section 14.3).

4.9.5 Asset Prices as Jump-Diffusion Processes

How do asset prices react to jumps in the underlying fundamentals? How do derivative prices change when the underlying asset is a jump-diffusion process? This section is a short introduction to models of asset prices driven by both Brownian motions and jump processes. We model jumps by interpreting the "arrivals" in the previous sections as those events on which a certain random variable experiences a jump of size $\mathcal{S}$, where $\mathcal{S}$ is another random variable with fixed probability p and support $\mathbb{S}$. A simple model is

$$dS_\tau = b(S_\tau)d\tau + \sigma(S_\tau)dW_\tau + \ell(S_\tau) \cdot \mathcal{S} \cdot dZ_\tau, \tag{4.160}$$

where b, σ, and ℓ are given functions (with $\sigma > 0$); W is a standard Brownian motion; and Z is a Poisson process with intensity equal to v, that is,

(1) $\Pr(Z_t) = 0$;

(2) $\forall t \le \tau_0 < \tau_1 < \cdots < \tau_N < \infty$, $Z(\tau_0)$ and $Z(\tau_k) - Z(\tau_{k-1})$ are independent for each $k = 1, \cdots, N$; and

(3) $\forall \tau > t$, $Z_\tau - Z_t$ is a random variable with Poisson distribution and expected value $v(\tau - t)$, that is,

$$\Pr(Z_\tau - Z_t = k) = \frac{v^k (\tau - t)^k}{k!} e^{-v(\tau - t)}.$$

Using the property in eq. (4.159), we have that $E(Z_T - Z_t) = v(T - t)$. In this framework, k is the number of jumps over the time interval $\tau - t$. Therefore, we have that $\Pr(Z_\tau - Z_t = 1) = v(\tau - t)\, e^{-v(\tau - t)}$ and, for $\tau - t$ small,

$$\Pr(dZ_\tau = 1) \equiv \Pr\left(Z_\tau - Z_t|_{\tau \to t} = 1\right) = v(\tau - t)\, e^{-v(\tau - t)}\Big|_{\tau \to t} \simeq v d\tau.$$

More generally, the process $(Z_\tau - v(\tau - t))_{\tau \ge t}$ is a martingale.

Armed with these preliminary facts, we can provide a heuristic derivation of Itô's lemma for jump-diffusion processes. Consider any function f with enough regularity conditions; that is, a function of time and S in eq. (4.160), that is, $f_\tau \equiv f(S_\tau, \tau)$. Consider the following expansion of f:

$$df_\tau = Lf(S_\tau, \tau)\, d\tau + f_S(S_\tau, \tau)\, \sigma(S_t) dW_\tau + \left[f(S_\tau + \ell(S_\tau)\mathcal{S}, \tau) - f(S_\tau, \tau)\right] \cdot dZ_\tau.$$

The first two terms result from a standard application of Itô's lemma, and L denotes the usual infinitesimal generator for diffusions. The third term is new and accounts for jumps. In case no jumps occur from the "pre-jump" time τ_- to τ, then $dZ_\tau = 0$. In case a jump occurs, then $dZ_\tau = 1$, such that the "rational" function f also instantaneously jumps to $f(S_\tau + \ell(S_\tau)\mathcal{S}, \tau)$. The jump equals $f(S_\tau + \ell(S_\tau)\mathcal{S}, \tau) - f(S_\tau, \tau)$. Clearly, this description collapses to the initial jump-diffusion model in eq. (4.160) in the trivial case $f(S, \tau) = S$.

We derive the infinitesimal generator for jump-diffusion processes, $L^J f$, say. Note heuristically that

$$\begin{aligned} E(df) &= (Lf)\, d\tau + E\left[(f(S + \ell\mathcal{S}, \tau) - f(S, \tau)) \cdot dZ_\tau\right] \\ &= (Lf)\, d\tau + E\left[(f(S + \ell\mathcal{S}, \tau) - f(S, \tau)) \cdot v d\tau\right]. \end{aligned}$$

That is,

$$L^J f \equiv Lf + v \int_{\mathbb{S}} \left[f(S + \ell\mathcal{S}, \tau) - f(S, \tau)\right] p(d\mathcal{S}),$$

where we recall that $\mathbb{S}$ and $p(\cdot)$ denote support and density of $\mathcal{S}$. Thus, $L^J f$ is the infinitesimal generator for jump-diffusion models in the simple example of this section.

If we interpret f as the price of some asset referenced to the more "primitive" asset price S (an option price, for example) and if the market was risk neutral, then under standard conditions this price would be the solution to $0 = L^J f - rf$. The general case where the market is not risk neutral is more articulated and is dealt with in appendix 4.F. The next section provides evaluation results for options that rely on a simple specification for the jump distribution.

4.9.6 An Option Pricing Formula

Merton (1976) developed the first option pricing formula that applied to markets in which the underlying asset is a jump-diffusion process. Suppose that some asset price S is the solution to eq. (4.160), with $\sigma(S) = \sigma S$, $\ell(S) = S$, and $\mathcal{S} = J - 1$ for some J to be interpreted below. For simplicity, assume that the distribution of J is the same under the physical probability P and the risk neutral Q. Note that the dynamics in eq. (4.160) are under the physical probability. Relying on results in appendix 4.F (see eq. (4.A32)), one may show that, under the risk neutral probability Q, S satisfies

$$\frac{dS_\tau}{S_\tau} = (r - \kappa)\,d\tau + \sigma d\hat{W}_\tau + (J - 1)\,dZ_\tau, \tag{4.161}$$

where $\kappa \equiv v_Q E(J - 1)$ and v_Q denotes the intensity under Q, which we take to be constant.

To solve the previous equation, denote the asset price right before a jump with S_{t-} such that, provided a jump occurs at time-τ_i with size J_{τ_i},

$$\frac{dS_{\tau_i}}{S_{\tau_i -}} = \frac{S_{\tau_i} - S_{\tau_i -}}{S_{\tau_i -}} = J_{\tau_i} - 1,$$

that is, $S_{\tau_i} = J_{\tau_i} S_{\tau_i -}$. The interpretation of J is then that of a percentage gross change in the asset price that is induced by a jump. We assume that $J_{\tau_i} \geq 0$ to ensure the asset price remains positive and denote its support with $\mathbb{J}$. Thus, conditional on $Z_t = k$ by T—that is, provided k jumps occur in the interval $[t, T]$—the asset price, denoted as $S_T^{(k)}$, is

$$S_T^{(k)} = S_t e^{\left(r - \kappa - \frac{1}{2}\sigma^2\right)(T-t) + \sigma\left(\hat{W}_T - \hat{W}_t\right)} \prod_{i=0}^{k} J_{\tau_i}, \tag{4.162}$$

where τ_i denote the "marks," that is, the jump times, and $J_{\tau_0} \equiv 1$.

We now proceed with evaluating an European call option that has a maturity equal to T and a strike equal to K. Its price, $C(S, \tau)$, appreciates as usual at the safe rate of return r under the risk neutral probability, that is, it is the solution to a partial-integral differential equation, $0 = \hat{L}^J C - rC$, where $\hat{L}^J$ denotes the infinitesimal generator for jump-diffusions in the risk neutral probability space,

$$\begin{aligned}\hat{L}^J C(S, \tau) = &\frac{\partial C(S, \tau)}{\partial \tau} + (r - \kappa) S \frac{\partial C(S, \tau)}{\partial S} \\ &+ \frac{1}{2}\sigma^2 S^2 \frac{\partial^2 C(S, \tau)}{\partial S^2} + v_Q \int_{\mathbb{J}} [C(SJ, \tau) - C(S, \tau)]\, p(dJ),\end{aligned}$$

and $C(S, T) = (S - K)^+$, the usual boundary condition.[30]

30. In other terms, the option price is the solution to eq. (4.A32) in appendix 4.F, where $S(x, \tau)$ is now interpreted as $C(S, \tau)$.

The Feynman–Kac representation for the option price is

$$C(S,t) = e^{-r(T-t)}\mathbb{E}_t (S_T - K)^+$$
$$= e^{-r(T-t)} \sum_{k=0}^{\infty} \frac{v_Q^k (T-t)^k}{k!} e^{-v_Q (T-t)} \mathbb{E}_t \left(S_T^{(k)} - K\right)^+, \qquad (4.163)$$

where the second equality follows by the expression of $S_T^{(k)}$ in eq. (4.162).

The option price may be given an explicit solution under the assumption that the jump size is log-normally distributed. Let $J_{\tau_i} = e^{j_i}$, where $j_i \sim N\left(\mu_J, \sigma_J^2\right)$ and $j_0 \equiv 0$. In terms of j, the asset price in (4.162) is therefore log-normally distributed,

$$S_T^{(k)} = S_t e^{\left(r-\kappa-\frac{1}{2}\sigma^2\right)(T-t)+\sigma\left(\hat{W}_T-\hat{W}_t\right)+\sum_{i=0}^k j_i} \equiv S_t e^{R_k}, \quad R_k \sim N\left(\mu_{R_k}, \sigma_{R_k}^2\right), \qquad (4.164)$$

where $\kappa = v_Q E\left(e^j - 1\right) = v_Q (e^{\mu_J + \frac{1}{2}\sigma_J^2} - 1)$, $\mu_{R_k} = \left(r - \kappa - \frac{1}{2}\sigma^2\right)(T-t) + k\mu_J$, and $\sigma_{R_k}^2 = \sigma^2 (T-t) + k\sigma_J^2$. In appendix 4.C.4, we calculate the expectations appearing in the summation (4.163) and determine the following closed-form solution for the option price:

$$C(S,t) = \sum_{k=0}^{\infty} \frac{v_Q^k (T-t)^k}{k!} e^{-v_Q (T-t)}$$
$$\times \left(S_t e^{-\kappa(T-t)+k\left(\mu_J+\frac{1}{2}\sigma_J^2\right)} \Phi(d_k) - e^{-r(T-t)} K \Phi\left(d_k - \sigma_{R_k}\right)\right), \qquad (4.165)$$

where

$$d_k \equiv \frac{\ln \frac{S_t}{K} + \left(r - \kappa + \frac{1}{2}\sigma^2\right)(T-t) + k\left(\mu_J + \sigma_J^2\right)}{\sqrt{\sigma^2 (T-t) + k\sigma_J^2}}.$$

The option price cannot be replicated by only trading the underlying asset. First, the underlying price is driven by two sources of risk: the Brownian motion and the jump process, as illustrated by the solution for S_τ under Q (see (4.161)). We might choose to rely on Black–Scholes delta and eliminate the Brownian risk but not jump risk. Second, we may not even choose to eliminate jump risk because a replicating strategy is based on pre-jump information. All in all, the option price jumps cannot be replicated by only trading the underlying asset. Therefore, the evaluation equation (4.165) is not preference free. Precisely, appendix 4.F shows that the risk neutral intensity v_Q appearing in (4.165) satisfies $v_Q = (1 + J_\xi)v$, where J_ξ denotes the change in the state-price density in the event of a jump in the asset price. Such a change does indeed depend on agents' preferences.

Appendix 4.A Introduction to Stochastic Calculus for Finance

This appendix provides some heuristic details on the foundations of Brownian motions and stochastic calculus, which are traditional workhorses in financial economics. Consider, again heuristically, a Brownian motion W on a probability space (Ω, F, P) and some

$T < \infty$: we write dW for the increment of W over an infinitesimal amount of time; that is, $dW_t = W_{t+\Delta t} - W_t$ as $\Delta t \to 0$. We may think of the "increment" dW_t as being normally distributed, $dW_t \sim N(0, dt)$, and use these increments as a means to build up a richer process X, say, a solution to

$$dX_t = \mu_t dt + \sigma_t dW_t, \tag{4.A1}$$

for some μ_t and σ_t to be defined later. Eq. (4.A1) describes a process known as Itô's process. The intuition on μ_t and σ_t is as follows. Heuristically, we have that $E(dX_t) = E(\mu_t)\,dt + \sigma E(dW_t) = E(\mu_t)\,dt$ such that μ_t relates to the instantaneous expected changes of dX. So this model is richer than a Brownian motion due to the presence of μ. Think of X as an asset price process. Eq. (4.A1) enables us to formalize the idea that, in an equilibrium with risk averse agents, investing in the asset requires that its expected capital gain be larger than zero, $\mu_t > 0$. Eq. (4.A1) also allows us to neatly define the asset return variance over the next infinitesimal amount of time, $var(dX_t) = E(dX_t - E(dX_t))^2 = E(\sigma_t dW_t)^2$, which, as it turns out, is $\sigma_t^2 dt$. Naturally, the important objective in financial economics is to single out the precise forces that determine μ_t and σ_t.

The "process" μ_t is called the *drift coefficient*, and the "process" σ_t is called the *diffusion coefficient* or the *volatility* of X_t. Clearly, the drift μ_t determines the trend, and the volatility σ_t determines the amount of noisiness of X_t around that trend. Both drift and diffusion coefficients need to be "adapted processes," as explained below. Examples of drift and diffusion coefficients are $\mu_t = W_t$ and $\sigma = 0$. In this case, $dX_t = W_t dt$, which shows that X_t still fluctuates randomly: μ_t is a stochastic process and so is X_t. Its infinitesimal variations can be "predicted," but its further developments cannot: we would say that X_t is *locally riskless* in this example.

Next, consider a more delicate example, which relates to *strategies and trading gains*. Suppose that a stock price is just a Brownian motion. The asset does not distribute dividends until some time T, and we hold θ_t units of it at time t. What are our trading gains from 0 to t? The answer to this question is given by the expression, $I_t \equiv \int_0^t \theta_s dW_s$. Intuitively, I_t is the sum of the instantaneous capital gains on the assets multiplied by the units of the asset that are held. This appendix provides more intuition on the "integrands" inside I_t. The expression I_t is known as a *stochastic integral*.

Why are we insisting on Brownian motions to model asset prices? We shall see that Brownian motions are "wild" in some precise sense, so wild that, as it turns out, they have unbounded variation on any interval of time. This property is very important. Harrison, Pitbladdo, and Schaefer (1984) show that in continuous time, asset prices must be "wild." Intuitively, if stock prices are continuous in time and have finite variation, they could be predicted in the immediate future. Processes with infinite variation facilitate the construction of reasonable models in financial economics, at least in continuous time.

We emphasize again that the material in this appendix is heuristic. This material does not provide all details. More technical treatments in order of descending difficulty can be found in Revuz and Yor (1999), Karatzas and Shreve (1991), Arnold (1974), Steele (2001), and Mikosch (1998).

4.A.1 Stochastic Integrals

4.A.1.1 *Motivation*

Consider a Brownian motion $W_t, t \geq 0$ on a probability space (Ω, F, P) and the associated natural filtration $\mathbb{F}_t$. We explore in which sense we need to understand the "integral"

$$I_t \equiv \int_0^t f(s) dW_s, \tag{4.A2}$$

where f is a progressively $\mathbb{F}_t$-measurable function. The motivation underlying (4.A2) relates to the Itô's process in (4.A1). As we will learn, a Brownian motion is actually nowhere differentiable. Therefore, eq. (4.A1) should be only understood as a shorthand for

$$X_t = X_0 + \int_0^t \mu_s ds + \int_0^t \sigma_s dW_s.$$

The term, $\int_0^t \sigma_s dW_s$ (or I_t) is known as a *stochastic integral.* What does this mean? In standard calculus, an integral can be defined from its differential. Unfortunately, we may not do the same in stochastic calculus: the stochastic integral is the real thing. We provide an introduction to this topic by first reviewing the ordinary Riemann integral and the Riemann-Stieltjes integral. These two notions to pathwise integration generically fail to provide a solid foundation to our stochastic integral. The main issue, as we will see, relates to the property that Brownian motions have unbounded variation in the sense that

$$\forall \omega \in \Omega, \; \sup_{\tau} \sum_{i=1}^{n} \left| W_{t_i}(\omega) - W_{t_{i-1}}(\omega) \right| = \infty,$$

where the supremum is taken over all partitions of $[0, T]$. We shall state conditions on how bounded the integrator and integrands in I_t should be in order to use a Riemann-Stieltjes approach to our stochastic integral. Unfortunately, these conditions are quite restrictive in finance applications. For example, Riemann-Stieltjes theory may still be used when $f(t) = 1$, or $f(t) = t$ in eq. (4.A2) but does not hold in more general contexts of interest.

4.A.1.2 *The Riemann integral*

Consider the mapping $x \mapsto f(x)$, $x \in (0, 1)$, and the following two definitions. First, a *partition* τ_n, defined as $\tau_n : 0 = t_0 < t_1 < \cdots < t_{n-1} < t_n = 1$ and $\Delta_i = t_i - t_{i-1}$, $i = 1, \cdots, n$. Second, an *intermediate partition* σ_n, defined as any collection of values y_i satisfying $t_{i-1} \leq y_i < t_i$, $i = 1, \cdots, n$. Then, for a given τ_n and σ_n, the Riemann sum is defined as

$$S_n(\tau_n, \sigma_n) \equiv \sum_{i=1}^{n} f(y_i) \Delta_i.$$

It is a "weighted average" of the values taken by $f(\cdot)$. Next, let mesh $(\tau_n) \equiv \max_{i=1,\cdots,n} \Delta_i$, and let mesh $(\tau_n) \to 0$ as $n \to \infty$. If the limit $\lim_{n\to\infty} S_n(\tau_n, \sigma_n)$, exists and is independent of τ_n and σ_n, it is called the *Riemann integral* of f on $(0, 1)$ and is written as

$$\int_0^1 f(t)\, dt.$$

Two properties are worth mentioning.

(1) *Linearity*: Given two constants c_1 and c_2, $\int_0^1 (c_1 f_1(t) + c_2 f_2(t))\, dt = c_1 \int_0^1 f_1(t)\, dt + c_2 \int_0^1 f_2(t)\, dt$.

(2) *Linearity on adjacent intervals*: $\int_0^1 f(t)\, dt = \int_0^a f(t)\, dt + \int_a^1 f(t)\, dt$ for every $a \in (0,1)$.

4.A.1.3 *The Riemann-Stieltjes integral*

The main idea underlying the Riemann-Stieltjes approach is to integrate one function, f, against another, g. A familiar example is the expectation of a random variable with distribution g. Heuristically, we have that

$$\int_0^1 t dg(t) \approx \sum_i t_i \left(g(t_i) - g(t_{i-1})\right).$$

More generally, consider again the definitions of τ_n, σ_n given earlier, and let $\Delta g_i = g(t_i) - g(t_{i-1})$, $i = 1, \cdots, n$. The Riemann-Stieltjes sum is defined as

$$S_n(\tau_n, \sigma_n) = \sum_{i=1}^{n} f(y_i)\, \Delta g_i.$$

Thus, the Riemann sum is a special case obtained with the identity function $g(t) = t$. Similarly as with Riemann integration, the *Riemann-Stieltjes integral* of f against g on $(0,1)$ is the limit, $\lim_{n\to\infty} S_n(\tau_n, \sigma_n)$, provided it exists and is independent of τ_n and σ_n. It is denoted as $\int_0^1 f_t dg_t$.

Our problem is: Can we use Riemann-Stieltjes integration theory and define integrals of functions against Brownian motions? That is, can we interpret $\int_0^1 f_t(\omega)\, dW_t(\omega)$ as a Riemann-Stieltjes integral, path by path, that is, for each $\omega \in \Omega$? Unfortunately not, except in very special cases. Indeed, a natural example of an integral of functions with respect to Brownian motion is $I_t(\omega) \equiv \int_0^t f(s) dW_s(\omega)$. But what does this representation mean? We know that a path of W_t is not differentiable. The issue relates to a quite peculiar property known as *unboundedness of Brownian motions*. To introduce this property, consider a continuous and continuously differentiable function f (see figure 4.A1) and its "first variation," defined as

$$\begin{aligned}
&\left[f(t_1) - f(t_0)\right] - \left[f(t_2) - f(t_1)\right] + \left[f(T) - f(t_2)\right] \\
&= \int_0^{t_1} f'(t)\, dt + \int_{t_1}^{t_2} \left(-f'(t)\right) dt + \int_{t_2}^{T} f'(t)\, dt \\
&= \int_{t_0}^{T} \left|f'(t)\right| dt,
\end{aligned}$$

where the points t_0, t_1, t_2 and T are selected as the stationary points (local minima or maxima) of f.

The first variation of f is, thus, a measure of the total amount of up and down motion of the path depicted by f. We can formalize this reasoning as follows. For a function of a real variable f, its variation in an interval $[a, b]$ is defined as

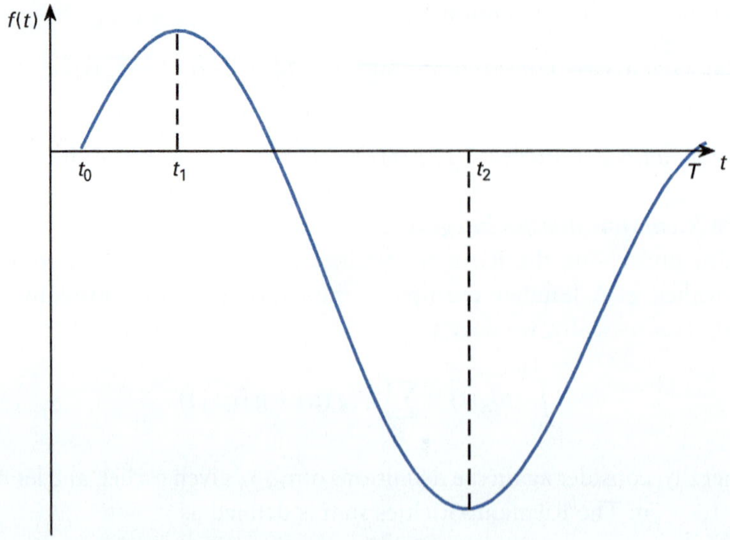

Figure 4.A1
Construction of the "first variation" for a continuous function f.

$$V_f([a,b]) = \sup \sum_{i=1}^{n} \left| f(t_i^{(n)}) - f(t_{i-1}^{(n)}) \right|,$$

where the supremum is taken over the partitions $a \equiv t_0^{(n)} < t_1^{(n)} < \cdots < t_n^{(n)} \equiv b$. Note that by the triangle inequality, $|f(x) - f(y)| = |f(x) - f(z) + f(z) - f(y)| \leq |f(x) - f(z)| + |f(z) - f(y)|$. That is, the sums in $V_f([a,b])$ can only increase as we include more into the partition. Therefore,

$$V_f([a,b]) = \lim_{\text{mesh}\to 0} \sum_{i=1}^{n} \left| f(t_i^{(n)}) - f(t_{i-1}^{(n)}) \right|.$$

Next, consider the following definition.

Definition 4.A1. *A real function h on $(0,1)$ has bounded p-variation, $p > 0$, if*

$$\sup_{\tau} \sum_{i=1}^{n} |h(t_i) - h(t_{i-1})|^p < \infty,$$

where the supremum is taken over all partitions of $(0,1)$.

We have:

Theorem 4.A2. *The Riemann-Stieltjes integral, $\int_0^1 f(t)dg(t)$, exists under the following conditions.*

(i) *The functions f and g do not have discontinuities at the same points.*
(ii) *f has bounded p-variation and g has bounded q-variation, with $\frac{1}{p} + \frac{1}{q} > 1$; that is, f, g satisfy $\sup_\tau \sum_{i=1}^n |f(t_i) - f(t_{i-1})|^p < \infty$ and $\sup_\tau \sum_{i=1}^n |g(t_i) - g(t_{i-1})|^q < \infty$ with $\frac{1}{p} + \frac{1}{q} > 1$.*

Now, it is well known that almost every path of W_t has bounded p-variation, for $p \geq 2$ and unbounded p-variation for $p < 2$, as argued below. Consider then the integral $I_t(\omega) = \int_0^t f(s) dW_s(\omega)$, where f is differentiable with bounded derivatives. By the mean value theorem, there exists a $K > 0$ such that: $|f(t) - f(s)| \leq K(t-s)$ for $s < t$. Therefore, $\sup_\tau \sum_{i=1}^n |f(t_i) - f(t_{i-1})| \leq K \sum_{i=1}^n (t_i - t_{i-1}) = K$. That is, f has bounded p-variation, with $p = 1$. By theorem 4.A2, we now have that, for almost every path of W_t, the Riemann-Stieltjes integral of f with respect to Brownian motions, $I_t(\omega)$, exists for every deterministic function f that is differentiable with bounded first-order derivative, as for $f(t) = 1$ or $f(t) = t$. But there are more complicated examples, such as $f_t(\omega) = W_t(\omega)$ and, in this case,

$$I_t(\omega) = \int_0^1 W_t(\omega) \, dW_t(\omega).$$

Let $p = 2 + \epsilon$, for some $\epsilon > 0$. Hence $p = q = 2 + \epsilon$, and so $\frac{1}{p} + \frac{1}{q} = \frac{2}{2+\epsilon} < 1$. We cannot employ the Riemann-Stieltjes integration theory and cope with this simple example. This is where the theory of Itô's stochastic integrals comes in.

4.A.1.4 A digression on unboundedness of Brownian motions

Why do Brownian motions have unbounded variation? Consider the "Brownian tree" in figure 4.A2. Time is Δt, and space is Δh. We claim that

$$\Delta h = \sqrt{\Delta t}. \tag{4.A3}$$

Indeed, and heuristically, we have that $var(\Delta W) = (\Delta h)^2$, which matched to $var(\Delta W) = \Delta t$, leaves precisely eq. (4.A3). Therefore, $E(|\Delta W|) = \Delta h = \sqrt{\Delta t}$. Next, we chop a time interval of length t in $n \equiv \frac{t}{\Delta t}$ parts. The total expected length traveled by a Brownian motion is

$$\frac{t}{\Delta t} \Delta h = \frac{t}{\Delta t} \sqrt{\Delta t} \to \infty \text{ as } \Delta t \to 0.$$

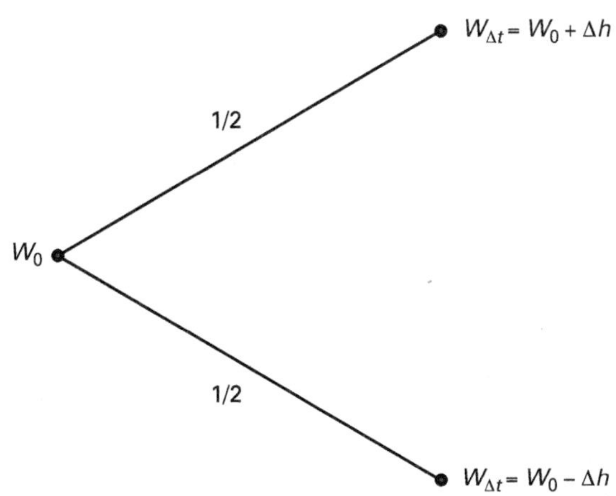

Figure 4.A2
The Brownian tree.

A formal proof of these results can be found in Revuz and Yor (1999, 25, corollary 2.5). A sketch of the more formal arguments proceeds as follows. We have

$$\sum_i \left(W_{t_i} - W_{t_{i-1}}\right)^2 \le \max_i \left|W_{t_i} - W_{t_{i-1}}\right| \cdot \sum_i \left|W_{t_i} - W_{t_{i-1}}\right|.$$

Moreover, $\max_i \left|W_{t_i} - W_{t_{i-1}}\right|$ converges to zero for each $\omega \in \Omega$ because $W_.$ is continuous and, by the Heine-Cantor theorem, continuous functions are uniformly continuous on finite intervals. Then, suppose that $W_{t.}$ has bounded variation, in which case we have that, for each $\omega \in \Omega$,

$$\lim_{\text{mesh}\to 0} \sum_i \left(W_{t_i} - W_{t_{i-1}}\right)^2 \to 0,$$

which is impossible as we shall now argue. Indeed, in the next section, we shall establish that $L_n \equiv \sum_i \left(W_{t_i} - W_{t_{i-1}}\right)^2 \overset{q.m}{\to} t$, implying that $\text{p}\lim_n L_n = t$. Therefore, there exists a sequence $n_k : L_{n_k} \to t$ for all $\omega \in \Omega$. (Convergence in probability does not imply almost sure convergence, yet it implies that there exists a suitable subsequence n_k that implies almost sure convergence, which is the only condition we require here.)

4.A.1.5 Itô

Let us begin with the following example, which helps explain the nature of the issues under study. Consider the definition

$$I_t(W, \omega) = \int_0^t W_s(\omega)\, dW_s(\omega)$$

and the following Riemann-Stieltjes sum

$$S_n = \sum_{i=1}^n W_{t_{i-1}} \Delta_i W, \quad \Delta_i W = W_{t_i} - W_{t_{i-1}}, \quad t_n = t,$$

where the intermediate partition relies on the left-end points $y_i = t_{i-1}$, $i = 1, \cdots, n$. Simple calculations leave

$$S_n = \frac{1}{2}\left(W_t^2 - Q_n(t)\right), \quad Q_n(t) \equiv \sum_{i=1}^n (\Delta_i W)^2.$$

The quantity $Q_n(t)$ is known as *quadratic variation*, a quite useful concept in financial econometrics. We have

$$E\left(Q_n(t)\right) = \sum_{i=1}^n E(\Delta_i W)^2 = \sum_{i=1}^n \Delta_i = t.$$

Moreover, $var\left((\Delta_i W)^2\right) = \Delta_i^2 var\left((\Delta_i W/\sqrt{\Delta_i})^2\right) = 2\Delta_i^2$, where the last equality follows because $\Delta_i W/\sqrt{\Delta_i} \sim N(0,1)$, such that $\left(\Delta_i W/\sqrt{\Delta_i}\right)^2 \sim \chi^2(1)$. Hence,

$$var\left(Q_n(t)\right) = \sum_{i=1}^n var\left(\Delta_i W^2\right) = 2\sum_{i=1}^n \Delta_i^2 \le 2\sum_{i=1}^n \text{mesh}(\tau_n)\cdot\Delta_i = 2t\cdot\text{mesh}(\tau_n) \to 0.$$

But $var\left(Q_n(t)\right) = E\left(Q_n(t) - E\left(Q_n(t)\right)\right)^2 = E\left(Q_n(t) - t\right)^2$. Therefore,

$$var\left(Q_n(t)\right) = E\left(Q_n(t) - t\right)^2 \to 0, \quad t \text{ pointwise.}$$

This type of convergence is called a *convergence in quadratic mean of $Q_n(t)$ to t* and is written as $Q_n(t) \overset{q.m.}{\to} t$, as explained in more detail in the appendixes of chapter 6. Now, by Chebyshev's inequality, convergence in quadratic mean implies convergence in probability:

$$\forall\delta > 0, \Pr\left\{\left|Q_n(t) - t\right| > \delta\right\} \leq \frac{E\left(Q_n(t) - t\right)^2}{\delta^2}.$$

That is, $I_t(W, \omega)$ does not exist as a Riemann-Stieltjes integral. Nevertheless, the previous facts suggest that a good definition of $I_t(W, \omega)$ may rely on the notion of a mean square limit, namely,

$$S_n = \sum_{i=1}^{n} W_{t_{i-1}} \Delta_i W = \frac{1}{2}\left(W_t^2 - Q_n(t)\right) \overset{q.m.}{\to} \frac{1}{2}\left(W_t^2 - t\right),$$

or, as we shall explain,

$$S_n = \sum_{i=1}^{n} W_{t_{i-1}} \Delta_i W \overset{q.m.}{\to} \int_0^t W_s dW_s,$$

where $\int_0^t W_s dW_s = \frac{1}{2}\left(W_t^2 - t\right)$ has the Itô's sense. Clearly, $\int_0^t W_s dW_s$ does not satisfy the usual Riemann-Stieltjes rule of integration: for any smooth function f such that $f(0) = 0$, the Riemann-Stieltjes integral $\int_0^t f(u) df(u) = \frac{1}{2} f^2(t)$. This property does not hold in this context because we still have to learn the chain rule of differentiation for paths of Brownian motions. This master rule is the celebrated Itô's lemma, which shall confirm that $\int_0^t W_s dW_s = \frac{1}{2}\left(W_t^2 - t\right)$.

The previous simple example illustrates that standard integration methods fail in our context. In fact, the timing of the integrands is also very important. For example, within standard Riemann integration theory, the integrand can be evaluated at any point in the interval. But in our context, we have that $\lim \sum_i f\left(W_{t_{i-1}}\right)\left(W_{t_i} - W_{t_{i-1}}\right)$ for the left boundary and $\lim \sum_i f\left(W_{t_i}\right)\left(W_{t_i} - W_{t_{i-1}}\right)$ for the right boundary. The two limits do not agree: by the law of iterated expectations, the expectation of the first is zero while the expectation of the second is not necessarily zero. Finally, integration theory in this context with Brownian motion relies on a different notion of convergence. Consider a short digression. The so-called Stratonovich stochastic integral selects as points of the intermediate partition the central ones,

$$\tilde{S}_n = \sum_{i=1}^{n} f\left(W_{y_i}\right) \Delta_i W, \quad y_i = \frac{1}{2}\left(t_{i-1} + t_i\right).$$

For the Stratonovich integral, the usual Riemann-Stieltjes rule applies, yet the Stratonovich stochastic integral cannot be dealt with using the standard Riemann-Stieltjes integration theory.

4.A.1.6 The Itô's stochastic integral for simple processes

Let $\mathbb{F}$ be the P augmentation of the filtration of W. Consider $[0,T]$ and partitions $\tau_n : 0 = t_0 < t_1 < \cdots < t_n = T$ and the following definition.

Definition 4.A3 (Simple processes). *The process* $C = (C_t,\ t \in [0,T])$ *is* simple *if:*

(1) *there exists a partition* τ_n *and a sequence of random variables* Z_i, $i = 1, \cdots, n$, *such that*

$$C_t = \begin{cases} Z_n, & \text{if } t = T \\ Z_i, & \text{if } t_{i-1} \le t < t_i,\ i = 1, \cdots, n \end{cases}$$

(2) *the sequence* (Z_i) *is* $\mathbb{F}_{t_{i-1}}$*-adapted,* $i = 1, \cdots, n$*; and*

(3) $E(Z_i^2) < \infty$ *for all* i *(*$L^2(P)$*, say).*

Consider, for example, $C_t = W_{t_{n-1}}$, if $t = T$, and $C_t = W_{t_{i-1}}$, if $t_{i-1} \le t < t_i$, $i = 1, \cdots, n$, and the following definition.

Definition 4.A4. *The Itô's stochastic integral of a simple process C is*

$$\int_0^T C_s dW_s = \sum_{i=1}^n C_{t_{i-1}} \left(W_{t_i} - W_{t_{i-1}}\right) = \sum_{i=1}^n Z_i \left(W_{t_i} - W_{t_{i-1}}\right), \text{ on } [0,T],$$

$$\int_0^t C_s dW_s = \sum_{i=1}^{k-1} C_{t_{i-1}} \left(W_{t_i} - W_{t_{i-1}}\right) + Z_k \left(W_t - W_{t_{k-1}}\right),\ t \in \left[t_{k-1}, t_k\right],$$

with the notation $\sum_{i=1}^0 m_i \equiv 0$.

The previous sums are Riemann-Stieltjes sums of C with respect to Brownian motions evaluated at *left-end* points.

We now list a set of useful properties.

Property 4.A5. $I_t(C) = \int_0^t C_s dW_s, t \in [0,T]$ *is an* $\mathbb{F}_t$*-martingale and has an expectation equal to zero.*

Proof. We check that $I_t(C)$ is an $\mathbb{F}_t$-martingale throughout three conditions: (i) $E\left|I_t(C)\right| < \infty$, for all $t \in [0,T]$; (ii) $I_t(C)$ is $\mathbb{F}_t$-adapted; and (iii) $E\left(I_t(C) \middle| \mathbb{F}_s\right) = I_s(C)$, $s < t$. Condition (i) follows by the isometry property to be introduced below. Condition (ii) is trivial. To show (iii), initially suppose that $s, t \in \left[t_{k-1}, t_k\right]$, $s < t$. We have:

$$\begin{aligned} I_t(C) &= \sum_{i=1}^{k-1} Z_i \left(W_{t_i} - W_{t_{i-1}}\right) + Z_k \left(W_t - W_{t_{k-1}}\right) \\ &= \sum_{i=1}^{k-1} Z_i \left(W_{t_i} - W_{t_{i-1}}\right) + Z_k \left(W_s - W_{t_{k-1}}\right) + Z_k \left(W_t - W_s\right) \\ &= I_s(C) + Z_k \left(W_t - W_s\right) \end{aligned}$$

$$\begin{aligned} E\left(I_t(C) \middle| \mathbb{F}_s\right) &= E\left(I_s(C) \middle| \mathbb{F}_s\right) + E\left(Z_k \left(W_t - W_s\right) \middle| \mathbb{F}_s\right) \\ &= I_s(C) + Z_k E\left(\left(W_t - W_s\right) \middle| \mathbb{F}_s\right) = I_s(C). \end{aligned}$$

The case $s \in [t_{l-1}, t_l]$ and $t \in [t_{k-1}, t_k]$, $l < k$ is proven similarly. Finally, $I_t(C)$ has zero expectation because it starts from the origin by the definition: $I_0(C) = 0 \Rightarrow E(I_t(C)) = 0$ for all t. That is, $\forall t$, $E(I_t(C)) = E(I_0(C)) = I_0(C) = 0$. □

Property 4.A6 (Isometry). $E\left(\int_0^t C_s dW_s\right)^2 = \int_0^t E\left(C_s^2\right) ds$, *for all* $t \in [0, T]$.

Proof. Without loss of generality, set $t = t_k$. We have

$$\begin{aligned} E\left(\int_0^t C_s dW_s\right)^2 &= E\left(\sum_{i=1}^k C_{t_{i-1}} \left(W_{t_i} - W_{t_{i-1}}\right)\right)^2 \\ &= E\left(\sum_{i=1}^k \sum_{j=1}^k C_{t_{i-1}} \left(W_{t_i} - W_{t_{i-1}}\right) C_{t_{j-1}} \left(W_{t_j} - W_{t_{j-1}}\right)\right) \\ &= E\left(\sum_{i=1}^k C_{t_{i-1}}^2 \left(W_{t_i} - W_{t_{i-1}}\right)^2\right), \end{aligned}$$

where the last equality follows because $W_{t_i} - W_{t_{i-1}}$ and $W_{t_j} - W_{t_{j-1}}$ are independent for all $i \neq j$. Then,

$$\begin{aligned} E\left(\int_0^t C_s dW_s\right)^2 &= E\left(\sum_{i=1}^k C_{t_{i-1}}^2 \left(W_{t_i} - W_{t_{i-1}}\right)^2\right) \\ &= E\left(\sum_{i=1}^k E\left(C_{t_{i-1}}^2 \left(W_{t_i} - W_{t_{i-1}}\right)^2 \middle| \mathbb{F}_{t_{i-1}}\right)\right) \\ &= E\left(\sum_{i=1}^k E\left(C_{t_{i-1}}^2 \middle| \mathbb{F}_{t_{i-1}}\right) \left(t_i - t_{i-1}\right)\right) \\ &= \sum_{i=1}^k E\left(C_{t_{i-1}}^2\right) \left(t_i - t_{i-1}\right) \\ &= \int_0^t E\left(C_s^2\right) ds. \end{aligned}$$

□

Property 4.A7 (Linearity and linearity on adjacent intervals).

Property 4.A8. $I_t(C)$ *has continuous sample paths.*

4.A.1.7 *The general Itô's stochastic integral*

Next, we consider a more general class of integrand processes C_t, satisfying $\int_0^T E\left(C_s^2\right) ds < \infty$ and belonging to $L^2(P \otimes dt)$, say. Let

$$\mathcal{H}^2 = \left\{\theta : \theta_t \text{ is measurable and } E\left(\int_0^T |\theta_t|^2 dt\right) < \infty \text{ a.s.}\right\}.$$

Clearly, $\mathcal{H}^2$ is a closed linear subspace of $L^2(P\otimes dt)$ ($\theta\in\mathcal{H}^2$ is also measurable). So let $\|\cdot\|_{L^2(P\otimes dt)}$ be the norm of $L^2(P\otimes dt)$ and $\mathcal{H}_0^2$ be the subset of $\mathcal{H}^2$ consisting of all simple processes. We now outline the construction of the stochastic integral, relying on four steps.

Step 1: ($\mathcal{H}_0^2$ is dense in $\mathcal{H}^2$). It is possible to show that, for any $C\in\mathcal{H}^2$, there exists a sequence of simple processes $C^{(n)}$ such that $\|C-C^{(n)}\|_{L^2(P\otimes dt)}\to 0$, that is, $\int_0^T E(C_s-C_s^{(n)})^2ds\to 0$.

Step 2: By step 1, $\{C^{(n)}\}$ is a Cauchy sequence in $L^2(P\otimes dt)$. By the isometry property of the Itô's integral for simple processes,

$$\left\|I_T(C^{(n)})-I_T(C^{(n')})\right\|_{L^2(P)}=\left\|C^{(n)}-C^{(n')}\right\|_{L^2(P\otimes dt)}.$$

Therefore, $I_T(C^{(n)})$ is a Cauchy sequence in $L^2(P)$. Now, it is well known that $L^2(P)$ is such that $I_T(C^{(n)})$ must converge to some element of $L^2(P)$, denoted as $I_T(C)$.

Step 3: This limit is called the *Itô's stochastic integral* of C and is written as

$$I_T(C)=\int_0^T C_s dW_s.$$

Finally, the limit is well defined: if there is another $C_*^{(n)}:\left\|C-C_*^{(n)}\right\|_{L^2(P\otimes dt)}\to 0$, then $\lim I_T(C_*^{(n)})=\lim I_T(C^{(n)})=I_T(C)$ in the $L^2(P)$ norm.

Step 4: (Itô's integral as a process) One may define a whole "continuum" of Itô's integrals at once. Step 3 is not enough because one needs uniform convergence on $[0,T]$. To deal with uniform convergence would require us to go well beyond the aim of this introductory appendix. The final result is that for any $C\in\mathcal{H}^2$, there exists a process $(I_t)_{t\in[0,T]}$, a continuous $\mathbb{F}_t$-martingale satisfying

$$I_t=\int_0^t C_s dW_s,\quad t\in[0,T],\quad P\otimes dt\text{-a.s.}$$

We provide some properties of the Itô's stochastic integral. Given a $\theta\in\mathcal{H}^2$, $I_t(\theta)=\int_0^t\theta_s dW_s$ satisfies the following properties: (i) continuous sample paths and $I_t(\theta)$ is an $\mathbb{F}_t$-martingale; (ii) an expectation equal to zero; (iii) Itô's isometry on $\mathcal{H}^2$, that is, $E(\int_0^t\theta_s dW_s)^2=\int_0^t E(\theta_s^2)\,ds<\infty$, $t\in[0,T]$, hence $E(|\int_0^t C_s dW_s|)^2\le E(\int_0^t C_s dW_s)^2=\int_0^t E(C_s^2)ds<\infty$; and (iv) linearity and linearity on adjacent intervals. A few remarks are in order. If $\theta\in\mathcal{H}^2$, then X_t, the solution to $dX_t=\theta_t dW_t$, is a martingale. If $\theta\notin\mathcal{H}^2$ but $\theta\in L^2(P)$, X_t is instead called a *local martingale*. The converse to these conclusions is known as the *martingale representation theorem*. This theorem states that if X is an $\mathbb{F}_t$-martingale, then there exists a $\theta\in\mathcal{H}^2: dX_t=\theta_t dW_t$. This result is utilized in the main text of this chapter when it helps us tell whether we live in a world with complete or incomplete markets.

4.A.1.8 Itô's lemma: Introduction

We provide an introduction to the technical details underlying the basic version of Itô's lemma. Let $f : \mathbb{R} \mapsto \mathbb{R}$ be twice continuously differentiable. We have

$$f(W_t) = f(W_0) + \int_0^t f'(W_s)\, dW_s + \frac{1}{2}\int_0^t f''(W_s)\, ds, \tag{4.A4}$$

where the first integral is an Itô's stochastic integral and the second one is a Riemann's integral. For example, let $f(B) = B^2$. Then,

$$W_t^2 = 2\int_0^t W_s dW_s + \int_0^t ds \Leftrightarrow \int_0^t W_s dW_s = \frac{1}{2}\left(W_t^2 - t\right). \tag{4.A5}$$

To provide a sketchy proof of eq. (4.A4), note that

$$f(W_t) - f(W_0) = \sum_{i=0}^{k-1} \left(f\left(W_{t_{i+1}}\right) - f\left(W_{t_i}\right)\right).$$

By a Taylor's expansion,

$$f\left(W_{t_{i+1}}\right) - f\left(W_{t_i}\right) = f'\left(W_{t_i}\right)\left(W_{t_{i+1}} - W_{t_i}\right) + \frac{1}{2} f''(\xi_i)\left(W_{t_{i+1}} - W_{t_i}\right)^2,$$

where $\min\left(W_{t_i}, W_{t_{i+1}}\right) < \xi_i < \max\left(W_{t_i}, W_{t_{i+1}}\right)$ (see figure 4.A3). Because W_t has continuous sample paths, then $\xi_i \equiv \xi_i(\omega) = W_{\tau_i(\omega)}$ for some τ_i depending on $\omega \in \Omega$, $\tau_i(\omega)$ such that $t_i \le \tau_i(\omega) \le t_{i+1}$.

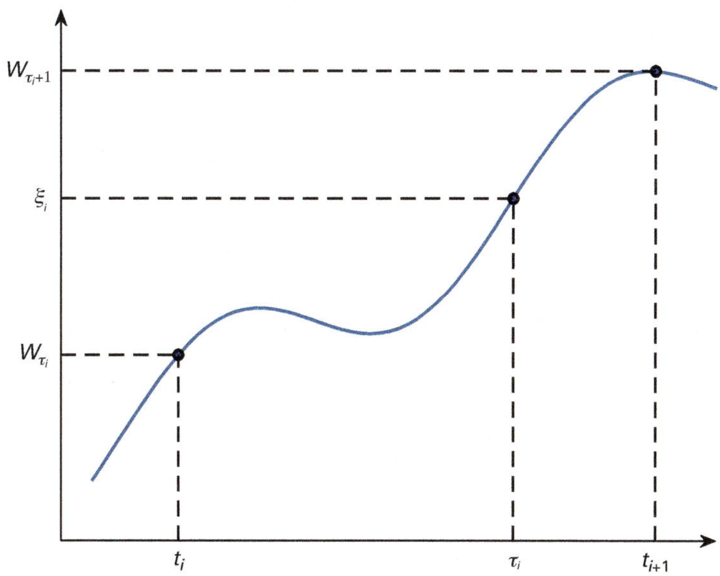

Figure 4.A3
Continuous sample paths of Brownian motions and Itô's lemma.

Therefore,

$$f(W_t) - f(W_0) = \sum_{i=0}^{k-1} f'(W_{t_i})(W_{t_{i+1}} - W_{t_i}) + \frac{1}{2}\sum_{i=0}^{k-1} f''(W_{\tau_i})(W_{t_{i+1}} - W_{t_i})^2.$$

We have

$$\sum_{i=0}^{k-1} f''(W_{\tau_i})(W_{t_{i+1}} - W_{t_i})^2 \approx \sum_{i=0}^{k-1} f''(W_{\tau_i})(t_{i+1} - t_i).$$

Finally,

$$\begin{aligned} \sum_i f'(W_{t_i})(W_{t_{i+1}} - W_{t_i}) &\rightarrow \int f'(W_s)\, dW_s \\ \sum_i f''(W_{\tau_i})(t_{i+1} - t_i) &\rightarrow \int f''(W_s)\, ds. \end{aligned}$$

4.A.2 Stochastic Differential Equations

4.A.2.1 Background

Consider the differential equation

$$dx_t = \mu(t, x_t)\, dt, \;\; x_0 = x,$$

for some function μ. With a stochastic differential equation, we can add randomness throughout the additional "Brownian part,"

$$dx_t = \mu(t, x_t)\, dt + \sigma(t, x_t)\, dW_t, \;\; x_0 = x.$$

We know that a sample path of a Brownian motion W_t is not differentiable. Therefore, the previous equation is only a shorthand notation for

$$x_t = x_0 + \int_0^t \mu(s, x_s)\, ds + \int_0^t \sigma(s, x_s)\, dW_s, \tag{4.A6}$$

where the first integral is Riemann and the second integral is an Itô's stochastic integral.

We have the following definitions. First, we say that an *Itô's process* is

$$dx_t = \mu_t dt + \sigma_t dW_t, \;\; x_0 = x,$$

for some progressively measurable processes μ_t and σ_t. Moreover, we say that an *Itô's diffusion process* is

$$dx_t = \mu(t, x_t)\, dt + \sigma(t, x_t)\, dW_t, \;\; x_0 = x.$$

It is well known that an Itô's diffusion process is a Markov process. The previous equation is also called a *stochastic differential equation* (SDE). In an SDE, randomness μ and σ occurs only through the current values of x_t. Finally, we say that a *time-homogeneous diffusion process* is

$$dx_t = \mu(x_t)\, dt + \sigma(x_t)\, dW_t, \;\; x_0 = x.$$

The *unique decomposition property* is a beautiful property used to price derivatives, which relies on replication arguments, as explained in the main text. This property says that, for any given two processes x_t and y_t with $x_0 = y_0$ and such that

$$dx_t = \mu_t^x dt + \sigma_t^x dW_t \quad \text{and} \quad dy_t = \mu_t^y dt + \sigma_t^y dW_t,$$

we have that $x_t = y_t$ almost surely if and only if $\mu_t^x = \mu_t^y$ and $\sigma_t^x = \sigma_t^y$, in the sense that $E(\int_0^T |a_t^x - a_t^y| \, dt = 0) = E(\int_0^T |b_t^x - b_t^y| \, dt) = 0$.

4.A.2.2 *Basic definitions, properties and regularity conditions*

We provide additional discussion regarding the Itô's integral representation $\int_0^t \sigma(s, x_s) \, dW_s$. We know this representation works, provided σ is $\mathbb{F}_t$-adapted and $\int_0^t E\left(\sigma(s, x_s)^2\right) ds < \infty$. But how do we know that these two basic conditions are satisfied if we do not know yet the *solution* of x_t? And, above all, what is a solution to an SDE? We have two concepts of such a solution: *strong* and *weak*.

Definition 4.A9 (Strong solution to an SDE). *A* strong *solution to eq. (4.A6) is a stochastic process* $x = (x_t, t \in [0, T])$ *such that*

(i) *x is $\mathbb{F}_t$-adapted;*
(ii) *the integrals in eq. (4.A6) are well defined in the Riemann's and Itô's sense and eq. (4.A6) holds almost surely,*
(iii) $E\left(\int_0^T |x_s|^2 \, ds\right) < \infty$.

In other words, the definition of a *strong* solution requires that a Brownian motion be "given in advance," and that the solution x_t constructed from it be then $\mathbb{F}_t$-adapted.

Next, suppose instead that we were only given x_0 and two functions $\sigma(t, x)$ and $\mu(t, x)$ and that we were asked to find a pair of processes $(\tilde{x}, \tilde{W})$ on some probability space $(\Omega, \tilde{\mathcal{F}}, P)$ such that eq. (4.A6) holds with $\tilde{x}$ being $\tilde{\mathbb{F}}_t$-adapted on some space, not necessarily the one in eq. (4.A6). (Clearly such a $\tilde{x}$ needs not be $\mathbb{F}_t$-adapted.) In this case, $(\tilde{x}, \tilde{W})$ is called a *weak solution* on $(\Omega, \tilde{\mathcal{F}}, P)$. In the case of a weak solution, we are given x, μ, σ, and then we have to find two things: a Brownian motion $\tilde{W}$ and an $\tilde{\mathbb{F}}_t$-adapted process $\tilde{x}$ such that $\tilde{x}_t = x_0 + \int_0^t \mu(s, \tilde{x}_s) \, ds + \int_0^t \sigma(s, \tilde{x}_s) \, d\tilde{W}_s$ holds almost surely. Clearly, a strong solution is also weak, but the converse is not true. Consider the following example.

Example 4.A10 (Tanaka's process). Let x_t satisfy

$$dx_t = \text{sign}(x_t) dW_t, \; x_0 = 0. \tag{4.A7}$$

This equation has no strong solutions. Indeed, define

$$y_t = \int_0^t \text{sign}(\hat{W}_s) d\hat{W}_s, \tag{4.A8}$$

where $\hat{W}$ is a Brownian motion. It can be shown that y_t is $\mathbb{G}_t$-measurable, where $\mathbb{G}_t$ is the σ-algebra generated by $|\hat{W}_t|$. Clearly $\mathbb{G}_t \subset \hat{\mathbb{F}}_t$, where $\hat{\mathbb{F}}_t$ is the σ-algebra generated by $\hat{W}_t$. Therefore, the σ-algebra generated by y_t is also strictly contained in $\hat{\mathbb{F}}_t$. Armed with this result, one can show that there are no strong solutions to eq. (4.A7). Indeed, assume the contrary; then, it would be possible to show that x_t is a Brownian motion. On the other hand, eq. (4.A7) can also be written as

$$dW_t = \text{sign}(x_t)dx_t,\ x_0 = 0,$$

or

$$W_t = \int_0^t \text{sign}(x_s)dx_s.$$

By the same reasoning used to to show that the σ-algebra generated by y_t is strictly contained in $\hat{\mathbb{F}}_t$ in eq. (4.A8), we conclude that the σ-algebra generated by W_t is strictly contained in the σ-algebra generated by x_t. But this contradicts that x_t is a strong solution to eq. (4.A7).

Incidentally, note that Tanaka's processes have been used to gain further insights into what is known as the theory of regulated Brownian motions (see, e.g., section 5.7 in chapter 5, and the additional comments provided here). Consider the following results.

Tanaka's equation. First, we provide well-known relations that link Dirac's delta to the indicator and the Heaviside function $H(x) \equiv \mathbb{I}_{x>0}$. We have

$$H(x) = \int_{-\infty}^{\infty} \mathbb{I}_{x>u}\delta(u)\,du = \int_{-\infty}^{x} \delta(u)\,du.$$

That is, $H' = \delta$. Now, note that the sign function satisfies $\text{sign}(x) = 2H(x) - 1$. Therefore, $\frac{d}{dx}\text{sign}(x) = 2H'(x)$. Next, consider the function $|W_\tau|$, where W_τ is a Brownian motion, and apply heuristically Itô's lemma and the previous properties of Dirac's delta,

$$|W_t| = \int_0^t \text{sign}(W_\tau)\,dW_\tau + \int_0^t \delta(W_\tau)\,d\tau. \tag{4.A9}$$

Eq. (4.A9) is known as *Tanaka's equation for Brownian local time*. It is possible to show that the first term is a Brownian motion starting from zero (see, e.g., Karatzas and Shreve, 1991, 209), say $\hat{W}_t$. The second integral is known as *local time*, a notion that chapter 5 relies on in its sections dedicated to dynamic contracting (see section 5.7). In this context, local time is a process that is positive and that only increases when W_t and hence $|W_t|$ hits zero.

We continue our discussion regarding the solution to stochastic differential equations. Clearly, we would need to impose conditions that enable one to distinguish between weak and strong solutions. However, from now on, we only discuss regularity conditions that guarantee existence and uniqueness of strong solutions—the case of interest in many continuous time problems in financial economics. We need two types of restrictions on μ and σ. Consider first the following definition. For a given function f, we say that it satisfies a Lipschitz condition in x if there exists a constant L such that for all $(x,y) \in \mathbb{R}^d \times \mathbb{R}^d$,

$$\|f(x,t) - f(y,t)\| \le L\,\|x-y\| \text{ uniformly in } t,$$

where $\|A\| \equiv \sqrt{\operatorname{Tr}\left(AA^\top\right)}$. In other words, f cannot change too much. We also say f satisfies a growth condition in x if there exists a constant G such that for all $(x,y) \in \mathbb{R}^d \times \mathbb{R}^d$,

$$\|f(x,t)\|^2 \leq G\left(1+\|x\|^2\right) \text{ uniformly in } t.$$

That is, f cannot grow too much.

Next, we turn to the concepts of existence and uniqueness of a solution to a stochastic differential equation. We say that, if $x_t^{(1)}$ and $x_t^{(2)}$ are both strong solutions to eq. (4.A6), then $x_t^{(1)} = x_t^{(2)}$ almost surely. We have:

Theorem 4.A11. *Suppose that μ, σ satisfy Lipschitz and growth conditions in x. Then, there exists a unique Itô's process x satisfying eq. (4.A6) which is continuous adapted Markov.*

Consider the following stochastic differential equation,

$$dx_t = \mu(a - x_t)\,dt + \sigma\sqrt{x_t}dW_t,$$

for some constants μ, a, σ. The solution to this equation is known as the *square-root process*. Part III reviews important instances where this process has been utilized in applied work in models of equity volatility (see chapter 11), the short-term rate (chapter 13), or the instantaneous probabilities of default by debt issuers (chapter 14). A technical point is that the diffusion component of this stochastic differential equation does not satisfy the conditions in theorem 4.A11. However, it is possible to show that, under parameter restrictions, there exists a strong solution; incidentally, the solution to this equation is still unknown in closed form.

When is a solution *unique*? It is well known that if μ, σ are locally Lipschitz continuous in x, then a strong solution is unique. However, a local Lipschitz condition is not necessarily sufficient to guarantee global existence (i.e., for all t) of a solution. This conclusion holds even for ordinary differential equations. For example, the following equation,

$$\frac{dx_t}{dt} = \mu(x_t) \equiv x_t^2,\ x_0 = 1,$$

has as unique solution:

$$x_t = \frac{1}{1-t},\ 0 \leq t < 1.$$

Yet is impossible to find a global solution, that is, one defined for all t. This is precisely the type of pathology ruled out by linear-growth conditions. More generally, linear-growth conditions ensure that $|x_t|$ is unique and does not explode in finite time. Naturally, Lipschitz and growth conditions are only *sufficient* conditions that guarantee the previous conclusions hold.

Note, finally, that the previous concepts are meant to relate to *strong* or *pathwise* uniqueness. There also exist definitions of *weak* uniqueness to mean that any two solutions (weak or strong) have the same finite-dimensional distributions. For example, Tanaka's equation (introduced earlier) has no strong solutions, yet it can be shown that it has a unique weak solution.

4.A.2.3 *Itô's lemma*

Itô's lemma is a fundamental tool of analysis in continuous time finance. It helps build up "new" processes from "old" processes. Two examples may clarify.

(1) A share price is certainly a function of its dividend process. If the dividend process is solution to some SDE, then the asset price is a solution to another SDE. Which SDE? Itô's lemma will give us the answer.

(2) As we know, derivatives are assets with a value depending on some underlying factors (whence the term "derivative"). In other words, derivative prices are functions of these factors. If factors are solutions to SDE, derivative prices are also solutions to SDE. Once again, Itô's lemma will provide us with the right SDE.

Naturally, the functional form linking the dividend process (or the factors) to the asset prices is unknown. But in situations of interest, no-arbitrage restrictions will help to pin down such a functional form.

Let us proceed with a few preliminary heuristic considerations. A useful heuristic definition is that the increments of a Brownian motion, dW_t, can be thought of as being equal to $\Delta W_t \equiv W_{t+\Delta t} - W_t \sim N(0, \Delta t)$ as $\Delta t \to 0$, just as we did at the beginning of this appendix. But then,

$$E(\Delta W_t) = 0 \text{ and } E\left(\Delta W_t^2\right) = \Delta t, \text{ hence } var(\Delta W_t) = \Delta t, \quad \text{and } var\left(\Delta W_t^2\right) = 2\Delta t^2,$$

where the second equality follows by the property of χ^2 distributions.

The point of the previous calculations is that for small Δt, the variance of ΔW_t^2, which is proportional to Δt^2, is negligible if compared with its expectation, which is Δt. Heuristically, $Q_n(t) \overset{q.m.}{\to} t$ and $dW_t^2 \equiv Q_n(dt) \overset{q.m.}{\to} dt$. These heuristic considerations lead to the celebrated Itô' multiplication table (see Table 4.A.1).

We may heuristically derive Itô's lemma based on table 4.A.1. Let x_t be the solution to

$$dx_t = \mu_t dt + \sigma_t dW_t,$$

and consider a function $f(x,t)$, which we assume to be as differentiable in (x,t) as many times as needed below. We expand f as follows:

$$df(x,t) = f_t(x,t)\,dt + f_x(x,t)\,dx + \frac{1}{2} f_{xx}(x,t)\,(dx)^2 + \text{remainder},$$

Table 4.A.1
Itô's multiplication table

$(dt)^n$	$=$	0	for $n > 1$
$dt \cdot dW$	$=$	0	
$(dW)^2$	$=$	dt	
$(dW)^n$	$=$	0	for $n > 2$
$dW_1 dW_2$	$=$	0	for two independent Brownian motions

where the remainder terms contains terms of order higher than $(dx)^2$ and $(dt)^2$, which we discard. We have

$$\begin{aligned} df &= f_t dt + f_x dx + \frac{1}{2} f_{xx} (dx)^2 \\ &= f_t dt + f_x (\mu dt + \sigma dW) + \frac{1}{2} f_{xx} (\mu dt + \sigma dW_t)^2 \\ &= f_t dt + f_x \mu dt + f_x \sigma dW + \frac{1}{2} f_{xx} \left(\mu^2 (dt)^2 + \sigma^2 (dW)^2 + 2\mu\sigma (dt \cdot dW) \right). \end{aligned}$$

By the Itô's multiplication table,

$$df = f_t dt + f_x \mu dt + f_x \sigma dW + \frac{1}{2} f_{xx} (\mu^2 \underbrace{dt^2}_{\equiv 0} + \sigma^2 \underbrace{dW^2}_{\equiv dt} + 2\mu\sigma \underbrace{dt \cdot dW}_{\equiv 0}).$$

By rearranging terms,

$$df(x,t) = \left(f_t(x,t) + f_x(x,t)\mu + \frac{1}{2} f_{xx}(x,t)\sigma^2 \right) dt + f_x(x,t)\sigma dW.$$

This is *Itô's lemma.*

To derive Itô's lemma in the case where x is multidimensional, apply Itô's multiplication table to the following expansion:

$$df(x,t) = f_t dt + f_x dx + \frac{1}{2} \sum_{i,j} f_{x_i x_j} dx_i dx_j.$$

We have:

Theorem 4.A12 (Itô's lemma, multidimensional). *Assume that the following process $x \in R^n$ is solution to*

$$dx_t = \mu(x_t, t) dt + \sigma(x_t, t) dW_t, \tag{4.A10}$$

where $\mu \in R^n$, σ is a $n \times d$ matrix and W is a d-dimensional standard Brownian motion. Consider the function $f(x,t)$, and assume it is twice continuously differentiable in x and differentiable in t. Then f is an Itô's process, solution to

$$df(x_t, t) = \mathcal{L}f(x_s, s) ds + f_x(x_s, s)\sigma(x_s, s) dW_s, \tag{4.A11}$$

where

$$\mathcal{L}f(x,t) = f_t(x,t) + f_x(x,t)\mu + \frac{1}{2} \mathrm{Tr}\left(\sigma\sigma^\top f_{xx}(x,t) \right)$$

and $f_x(x,t)$ and $f_{xx}(x,t)$ are the gradient and Hessian of f with respect to x.

Note that by eq. (4.A11) and provided $f_x\sigma \in \mathcal{H}^2$, f is a martingale whenever $\mathcal{L}f(x,t) = 0$, for all x, t. As a matter of terminology, the operator $\mathcal{A}f(x,t) = f_x(x,t)\mu + \frac{1}{2}\mathrm{Tr}\left[\sigma\sigma^\top f_{xx}(x,t)\right]$ is usually referred to as the *infinitesimal generator* of the diffusion process in eq. (4.A10).

Appendix 4.B Self-Financed Strategies

4.B.1 With Intermediate Consumption

Consider the standard budget equation of chapter 3 (see section 3.2),

$$c_t + S_t\theta_{1,t+1} + b_t\theta_{2,t+1} = (S_t + D_t)\,\theta_{1,t} + b_t\theta_{2,t} \equiv V_t + D_t\theta_{1,t},$$

where $\theta_{i,t}$ is the portfolio holding of asset i chosen at time $t-1$, $b_t\theta_{2,t}$ is the value of the MMA, and $V_t \equiv S_t\theta_{1,t} + b_t\theta_{2,t}$ denotes wealth net of dividends. We have

$$\begin{aligned}
V_t - V_{t-1} &= S_t\theta_{1,t} + b_t\theta_{2,t} - V_{t-1} \\
&= S_t\theta_{1,t} + b_t\theta_{2,t} - \left(c_{t-1} + S_{t-1}\theta_{1,t} + b_{t-1}\theta_{2,t} - D_{t-1}\theta_{1,t-1}\right) \\
&= \left(S_t - S_{t-1}\right)\theta_{1,t} + \left(b_t - b_{t-1}\right)\theta_{2,t} - c_{t-1} + D_{t-1}\theta_{1,t-1},
\end{aligned}$$

and, more generally,

$$V_t - V_{t-\Delta} = (S_t - S_{t-\Delta})\,\theta_{1,t} + \left(b_t - b_{t-\Delta}\right)\theta_{2,t} - (c_{t-\Delta}\cdot\Delta) + (D_{t-\Delta}\cdot\Delta)\,\theta_{1,t-\Delta}.$$

Next, let $\Delta \downarrow 0$ and assume that θ_1 and θ_2 are constant between t and $t-\Delta$. We have

$$dV_\tau = \left(dS_\tau + D_\tau d\tau\right)\theta_{1\tau} + db_\tau\theta_{2\tau} - c_\tau d\tau.$$

Assume that

$$\frac{db_\tau}{b_\tau} = r d\tau.$$

The budget constraint can then be written as:

$$\begin{aligned}
dV_\tau &= \left(dS_\tau + D_\tau d\tau\right)\theta_{1\tau} + rb_\tau\theta_{2\tau}d\tau - c_\tau d\tau \\
&= \left(dS_\tau + D_\tau d\tau\right)\theta_{1\tau} + r\left(V - S_\tau\theta_{1\tau}\right)d\tau - c_\tau d\tau \\
&= \left(dS_\tau + D_\tau d\tau - rS_\tau d\tau\right)\theta_{1\tau} + rVd\tau - c_\tau d\tau \\
&= \left(\frac{dS_\tau}{S_\tau} + \frac{D_\tau}{S_\tau}d\tau - rd\tau\right)\theta_{1\tau}S_\tau + rVd\tau - c_\tau d\tau \\
&= \left(\frac{dS_\tau}{S_\tau} + \frac{D_\tau}{S_\tau}d\tau - rd\tau\right)\pi_\tau + rVd\tau - c_\tau d\tau.
\end{aligned}$$

4.B.2 With Final Consumption Only

We may be interested in models in which consumption takes place only at the end of the period. Let $\bar{S} = \left(S^{(0)}, S\right)^\top$ and $\bar{\theta} = (\theta^{(0)}, \theta)$, where θ and S are both m-dimensional. Define, as usual, wealth at time t as $V_t \equiv \bar{S}_t\bar{\theta}_t$. We assume that assets do not distribute dividends over our investment horizon. A *self-financing* strategy $\bar{\theta}$ satisfies

$$\bar{S}_t\bar{\theta}_{t+1} = \bar{S}_t\bar{\theta}_t \equiv V_t, \quad t = 1, \cdots, T.$$

Therefore,

$$V_t = \bar{S}_t\bar{\theta}_t + \bar{S}_{t-1}\bar{\theta}_{t-1} - \bar{S}_{t-1}\bar{\theta}_{t-1}$$

$$= \bar{S}_t\bar{\theta}_t + \bar{S}_{t-1}\bar{\theta}_{t-1} - \bar{S}_{t-1}\bar{\theta}_t$$
$$= V_{t-1} + \Delta\bar{S}_t\bar{\theta}_t, \quad \Delta\bar{S}_t \equiv \bar{S}_t - \bar{S}_{t-1}, \quad t = 1, \cdots, T,$$

where the second line follows because $\bar{\theta}$ is self-financing. That is,

$$V_t = V_1 + \sum_{n=1}^{t} \Delta\bar{S}_n\bar{\theta}_n.$$

Next, suppose that

$$\Delta S_t^{(0)} = r_t S_{t-1}^{(0)}, \quad t = 1, \cdots, T,$$

with $\{r_t\}_{t=1}^T$ given and to be defined more precisely below. The term $\Delta\bar{S}_t\theta_t^+$ can then be rewritten as

$$\begin{aligned}
\Delta\bar{S}_t\bar{\theta}_t &= \Delta S_t^{(0)}\theta_t^{(0)} + \Delta S_t\theta_t \\
&= r_t S_{t-1}^{(0)}\theta_t^{(0)} + \Delta S_t\theta_t \\
&= r_t S_{t-1}^{(0)}\theta_t^{(0)} + r_t S_{t-1}\theta_t - r_t S_{t-1}\theta_t + \Delta S_t\theta_t \\
&= r_t\bar{S}_{t-1}\bar{\theta}_t - r_t S_{t-1}\theta_t + \Delta S_t\theta_t \\
&= r_t\bar{S}_{t-1}\bar{\theta}_{t-1} - r_t S_{t-1}\theta_t + \Delta S_t\theta_t \\
&= r_t V_{t-1} - r_t S_{t-1}\theta_t + \Delta S_t\theta_t,
\end{aligned}$$

where the fifth line follows because $\bar{\theta}$ is self-financing. Therefore, we have

$$V_t = (1 + r_t)\, V_{t-1} - r_t S_{t-1}\theta_t + \Delta S_t\theta_t,$$

or

$$V_t = V_1 + \sum_{n=1}^{t} \left(r_n V_{n-1} - r_n S_{n-1}\theta_n + \Delta S_n\theta_n\right).$$

Next, consider small time intervals. In the limit,

$$dV_t = r_t V_t dt - r_t S_t\theta_t dt + dS_t\theta_t.$$

For an alternative derivation of this equation, note that current wealth is simply initial wealth plus the cumulated gains from trade,

$$V_t = V_0 + \int_0^t d\bar{S}_u\bar{\theta}_u.$$

Therefore,

$$\begin{aligned}
dV_t &= d\bar{S}_t\bar{\theta}_t^+ \\
&= dS_{0t}\theta_{0t} + dS_t\theta_t \\
&= r_t S_{0t}\theta_{0t} dt + dS_t\theta_t \\
&= r_t\,(V_t - S_t\theta_t)\, dt + dS_t\theta_t \\
&= r_t V_t dt - r_t S_t\theta_t dt + dS_t\theta_t.
\end{aligned}$$

Finally, consider the problem of terminal wealth maximization, subject to the previous discrete time wealth accumulation constraints. The first-order conditions lead to

$$\hat{S}_t = \frac{E\left(u'(V_T)\cdot \hat{S}_{t+1}\middle|\, \mathbb{F}_t\right)}{E\left(u'(V_T)|\, \mathbb{F}_t\right)}, \quad t=0,\cdots,T-1,$$

where $\hat{S}_t = \frac{S_t}{M_t}$, that is, the prices expressed in terms of the money market numéraire.

The previous relations suggest that we can define a *martingale probability* Q for the price process (expressed in terms of the money market numéraire) by defining

$$\left.\frac{dQ}{dP}\right|_{\mathbb{F}_t} = \frac{u'(V_T)}{E\left(u'(V_T)|\, \mathbb{F}_t\right)}.$$

Appendix 4.C Proof of Selected Results

4.C.1 Proof of Theorem 4.2

First, we verify the claim in the main text that $\langle\sigma\rangle$ and $\langle\sigma^\top\rangle^\perp$ are orthogonal spaces. Indeed, note that

$$\begin{aligned}\left\{x\in L^2_{t,T,m} : x^\top z=0,\ z\in\langle\sigma\rangle\right\} &= \left\{x\in L^2_{t,T,m} : x^\top \sigma u=0,\ u\in L^2_{t,T,d}\right\}\\ &= \left\{x\in L^2_{t,T,m} : x^\top \sigma = 0_d\right\}\\ &= \left\{x\in L^2_{t,T,m} : \sigma^\top x = 0_d\right\}\\ &\equiv \langle\sigma^\top\rangle^\perp.\end{aligned}$$

Next, we provide the proof of theorem 4.2. Note that, by Girsanov's theorem, $\mathcal{Q}$ is nonempty if and only if eq. (4.62) holds true (see the discussion in the main text) Therefore, the proofs of this theorem rely on eq. (4.62).

If part. With $c\equiv 0$, eq. (4.63) is

$$\frac{V_\tau}{S_{0\tau}} = V_t + \int_t^\tau \frac{\pi_u^\top \sigma_u}{S_{0u}}\, d\hat{W}_u, \quad \tau\in[t,T],$$

or $V_t = E_t^Q\left(S_{0T}^{-1}V_T^{x,\pi,0}\right)$. An arbitrage opportunity is $V_t \le S_{0T}^{-1}V_T^{x,\pi,0}$ almost surely under Q, but the previous equality leaves $V_t = S_{0T}^{-1}V_T$ almost surely under Q (if a random variable $\tilde{y}\ge 0$ and $E_t(\tilde{y})=0$, then $\tilde{y}=0$ almost surely) and then almost surely under P. But this equality is in contradiction with $\Pr\left(S_{0T}^{-1}V_T - V_t > 0\right) > 0$ under zero-consumption paths as required by definition 4.1.

Only if part. We combine portions of proofs in Karatzas (1997, theorem 0.2.4) and Øksendal (1998, theorem 12.1.8b). We let

$$\begin{aligned}Z(\tau) &= \left\{\omega\in\Omega:\ \text{Eq. (4.62) has no solutions}\right\}\\ &= \left\{\omega\in\Omega : \mu_\tau(\omega) - 1_m r_\tau(\omega)\notin\langle\sigma\rangle\right\}\\ &= \left\{\omega\in\Omega : \exists \underline{\pi}_\tau(\omega) : \underline{\pi}_\tau(\omega)^\top\sigma_\tau(\omega)=0 \text{ and } \underline{\pi}_\tau(\omega)^\top\left(\mu_\tau(\omega)-1_m r_\tau(\omega)\right)\neq 0\right\},\end{aligned}$$

and, for some k, consider the following portfolio,

$$\hat{\pi}(\tau;w)=\begin{cases} k\cdot sign\left[\underline{\pi}_\tau(\omega)^\top(\mu_\tau(\omega)-\mathbf{1}_m r_\tau(\omega))\right]\cdot\underline{\pi}_\tau(\omega) & \text{for } \omega\in Z(\tau)\\ 0 & \text{for } \omega\notin Z(\tau)\end{cases}$$

Clearly $\hat{\pi}$ is $(\tau;\omega)$-measurable and, by eq. (4.60), generates wealth at time τ equal to

$$\begin{aligned}\frac{V_\tau}{S_{0\tau}}&=V_t+\int_t^\tau\frac{\hat{\pi}_u^\top(\mu_u-\mathbf{1}_m r_u)}{S_{0u}}\mathbb{I}_{Z_u}du+\int_t^\tau\frac{\hat{\pi}_u^\top\sigma_u}{S_{0u}}\mathbb{I}_{Z_u}dW_u\\&=V_t+\int_t^\tau\left(\frac{\hat{\pi}_u^\top(\mu_u-\mathbf{1}_m r_u)}{S_{0u}}\right)\mathbb{I}_{Z_u}du\\&\geq V_t.\end{aligned}$$

So the market has no arbitrage only if $\mathbb{I}_{Z_u}=0$, that is, only if eq. (4.62) has at least one solution. □

4.C.2 Details Regarding Multibeta CAPM

We provide precise definitions utilized in section 4.6.3.3. First, consider the covariance between asset and market returns,

$$cov\left(\sigma dW,\tfrac{dV_M}{V_M}\right)=\sigma\sigma^\top\frac{\text{Cap}}{V_M}dt\equiv\text{cov}_{S,M}dt,$$

where V_M is the solution to eq. (4.60) with π as in eq. (4.97) and is equal to Cap in equilibrium. Further, we have that

$$\begin{aligned}cov\left(\tfrac{dV_M}{V_M},dy\right)&=\frac{\text{Cap}^\top}{V_M}\sigma\Sigma^\top dt\equiv\text{cov}_{M,y}dt\\ var\left(\tfrac{dV_M}{V_M}\right)&=\frac{\text{Cap}^\top}{V_M}\text{cov}_{S,M}dt\equiv\text{var}_M dt\\ cov\left(\tfrac{dV_{H_i}}{V_{H_i}},\tfrac{dV_M}{V_M}\right)&=\frac{\pi_{H_i}^\top}{V_{H_i}}\sigma\sigma^\top\frac{\text{Cap}}{V_M}dt\equiv\text{cov}_{H_i,M}dt\end{aligned}$$

where V_H is now solution to eq. (4.60) with π as in eq. (4.105).

Based on these definitions, eq. (4.104) follows because

$$\mu_M-r=\frac{\pi_M^\top}{V_M}\text{cov}_{S,M}\frac{-V\mathcal{J}_{VV}}{\mathcal{J}_V}+\frac{\pi_M^\top}{V_M}\sigma\Sigma^\top\frac{-\mathcal{J}_{Vy}}{\mathcal{J}_V}=\text{var}_M\frac{-V\mathcal{J}_{VV}}{\mathcal{J}_V}+\text{cov}_{M,y}\frac{-\mathcal{J}_{Vy}}{\mathcal{J}_V},$$

and eq. (4.106) follows by similar arguments.

The solution to eqs. (4.104) and (4.106) is

$$\begin{pmatrix}\frac{-V\mathcal{J}_{VV}}{\mathcal{J}_V}\\ \frac{-\mathcal{J}_{Vy}}{\mathcal{J}_V}\end{pmatrix}=\begin{pmatrix}\text{var}_M & \text{cov}_{M,y}\\ \text{cov}_{H,M} & \text{cov}_{H,y}\end{pmatrix}^{-1}\begin{pmatrix}\mu_M-r\\ \mu_H-\mathbf{1}_d r\end{pmatrix},$$

where μ_H and $\text{cov}_{H,M}$ are two d-dimensional (column) vectors with generic components μ_{H_i} and $\text{cov}_{H_i,M}$, resp., and $\text{cov}_{H,y}$ is a $d \times d$ matrix with generic row $\text{cov}_{H_i,y}$. Replacing this result into eq. (4.103) leaves, for each $i = 1, \cdots, m$,

$$\mu_i - r = \begin{pmatrix} \text{cov}_{S_i,M} & \text{cov}_{S_i,y} \end{pmatrix} \begin{pmatrix} \text{var}_M & \text{cov}_{M,y} \\ \text{cov}_{H,M} & \text{cov}_{H,y} \end{pmatrix}^{-1} \begin{pmatrix} \mu_M - r \\ \mu_H - \mathbf{1}_d r \end{pmatrix},$$

where $\text{cov}_{S_i,y} \equiv \left(\sigma \Sigma^\top\right)_i$ relates to the vector of the instantaneous covariance between the ith asset returns and the state variables,

$$cov\left(\tfrac{dS_i}{S_i}, dy\right) = \left(\sigma \Sigma^\top\right)_i dt,$$

and eq. (4.107) follows by standard results on multiple regressions.

To illustrate, fix $d = 1$. Note that

$$\text{cov}_{S_i,y} = \kappa \text{cov}_{S_i,H}, \quad \text{cov}_{M,y} = \kappa \text{cov}_{H,M}, \quad \text{cov}_{H,y} = \kappa \text{var}_H,$$

where $\kappa \equiv \mathbf{1}_m^\top \left(\sigma \sigma^\top\right)^{-1} \sigma \Sigma_i^\top$, such that, for each $i = 1, \cdots, m$,

$$\mu_i - r = \begin{pmatrix} \text{cov}_{S_i,M} & \text{cov}_{S_i,H} \end{pmatrix} \begin{pmatrix} \text{var}_M & \text{cov}_{H,M} \\ \text{cov}_{H,M} & \text{var}_H \end{pmatrix}^{-1} \begin{pmatrix} \mu_M - r \\ \mu_H - r \end{pmatrix},$$

which can be regarded as the predictive part of a regression of the excess returns of security i onto the excess returns of the market and the (single) hedging portfolio.

4.C.3 Proof of Eq. (4.67).

We have

$$\begin{aligned}
V_t &= \mathbb{E}_t\left(\frac{V_T}{S_{0T}} + \int_t^T \frac{c_u}{S_{0u}} du\right) \\
&= \eta_t^{-1} E_t\left(\frac{\eta_T V_T}{S_{0T}} + \int_t^T \frac{\eta_T c_u}{S_{0u}} du\right) \\
&= \eta_t^{-1} E_t\left(\frac{\eta_T V_T}{S_{0T}} + \int_t^T E_u\left(\frac{\eta_T c_u}{S_{0u}}\right) du\right) \\
&= \eta_t^{-1} E_t\left(\frac{\eta_T V_T}{S_{0T}} + \int_t^T \frac{E_u(\eta_T) c_u}{S_{0u}} du\right) \\
&= \eta_t^{-1} E_t\left(\frac{\eta_T V_T}{S_{0T}} + \int_t^T \frac{\eta_u c_u}{S_{0u}} du\right) \\
&= E_t\left(\frac{\xi_T}{\xi_t} V_T + \int_t^T \frac{\xi_u}{\xi_t} c_u du\right),
\end{aligned}$$

where we used the law of iterated expectations, the martingale property of η_τ, and the definition of ξ_τ.

4.C.4 Rubinstein's Formula and Related Results

4.C.4.1 Rubinstein

We show that eq. (4.81) collapses to the Black–Scholes formula (see eq. (4.6)) for every γ. Define the ratio $x \equiv \frac{S_T}{S_t}$ such that, for a given m,

$$x^m = e^{\left(m\mu - \frac{1}{2}\sigma^2 m(1-m)\right)(T-t) - \frac{1}{2}v^2 + v\tilde{z}}, \quad v = m\sigma\sqrt{T-t},$$

where $\tilde{z} \sim N(0,1)$. We have

$$E\left(x^m \mathbb{I}_{x > \frac{K}{S_t}}\right) = e^{\left(m\mu - \frac{1}{2}\sigma^2 m(1-m)\right)(T-t)} E\left(e^{-\frac{1}{2}v^2 + v\tilde{z}} \mathbb{I}_{\tilde{z} > L}\right)$$
$$= e^{\left(m\mu - \frac{1}{2}\sigma^2 m(1-m)\right)(T-t)} \Phi(v - L),$$

where

$$L \equiv \frac{\ln\left(\frac{K}{S_t}\right) - \left(\mu - \frac{1}{2}\sigma^2\right)(T-t)}{\sigma\sqrt{T-t}}.$$

Let $m = 1 - \gamma$ such that

$$E\left(x^{1-\gamma} \mathbb{I}_{x > \frac{K}{S_t}}\right) = e^{\left((1-\gamma)\mu - \frac{1}{2}\sigma^2(1-\gamma)\gamma\right)(T-t)} \Phi\left((1-\gamma)\sigma\sqrt{T-t} - L\right)$$
$$= e^{\rho(T-t)} \Phi\left((1-\gamma)\sigma\sqrt{T-t} - L\right)$$
$$= e^{\rho(T-t)} \Phi\left(\frac{\ln\left(\frac{S_t}{k}\right) + \left(r + \frac{1}{2}\sigma^2\right)(T-t)}{\sigma\sqrt{T-t}}\right), \tag{4.A12}$$

where the second equality follows by using the expression for μ, $\mu = r + \gamma\sigma^2$, and the third by plugging the expression for L and, again, that for μ.

Next, let $m = -\gamma$ such that

$$E\left(x^{-\gamma} \mathbb{I}_{x > \frac{K}{S_t}}\right) = e^{\left(-\gamma\mu + \frac{1}{2}\sigma^2\gamma(1+\gamma)\right)(T-t)} \Phi\left(-\gamma\sigma\sqrt{T-t} - L\right)$$
$$= e^{-(r-\rho)(T-t)} \Phi\left(-\gamma\sigma\sqrt{T-t} - L\right)$$
$$= e^{-(r-\rho)(T-t)} \Phi\left(\frac{\ln\left(\frac{S_t}{K}\right) + \left(r - \frac{1}{2}\sigma^2\right)(T-t)}{\sigma\sqrt{T-t}}\right), \tag{4.A13}$$

where the second equality follows by the expression for r, $r = \rho + \gamma\mu - \frac{1}{2}\sigma^2\gamma(\gamma+1)$, and the third by the expression for the premium, $\mu = r + \gamma\sigma^2$. The result follows by replacing eqs. (4.A12) and (4.A13) into (4.81).

4.C.4.2 *Derivation of eq. (4.165)*

Define, as in the main text (see eq. (4.164)), $S_T^{(k)} = S_t e^{R_k}$, where $R_k \sim N\left(\mu_{R_k}, \sigma_{R_k}^2\right)$. Define $\tilde{z} \sim N(0,1)$. We have

$$\mathbb{E}\left(Se^{R_k} - K\right)^+ = Se^{\mu_{R_k}+\frac{1}{2}\sigma_{R_k}^2}\mathbb{E}\left(e^{-\frac{1}{2}\sigma_{R_k}^2+\sigma_{R_k}\tilde{z}}\mathbb{I}_{\tilde{z}>L_k}\right) - K\mathbb{E}\left(\mathbb{I}_{\tilde{z}>L_k}\right)$$

$$= Se^{\mu_{R_k}+\frac{1}{2}\sigma_{R_k}^2}\Phi\left(\sigma_{R_k}^2 - L_k\right) - K\Phi\left(-\sigma_{R_k}^2\right),$$

where

$$L_k \equiv \frac{\ln\frac{K}{S} - \mu_{R_k}}{\sigma_{R_k}},$$

and eq. (4.165) immediately follows with

$$d_k = \frac{\ln\frac{S}{K} + \mu_{R_k} + \sigma_{R_k}^2}{\sigma_{R_k}},$$

and by rearranging terms. □

Appendix 4.D The Green's Function

4.D.1 Setup

In section 4.4, it is shown that in frictionless markets, the value of a security as of time τ is

$$V(x_\tau, \tau) = E_\tau\left(\frac{\xi_T}{\xi_\tau}V(x_T, T) + \int_\tau^T \frac{\xi_s}{\xi_\tau}h(x_s, s)\,ds\right), \tag{4.A14}$$

where ξ_t is the stochastic discount factor and h is the instantaneous dividend.

The Arrow-Debreu state price density is usually defined as

$$\phi_{t,T} = \frac{\xi_T}{\xi_t}dP = \frac{S_{0t}}{S_{0T}}dQ.$$

We characterize this density as a solution to partial differential equations (PDEs). We provide some preliminary properties. By a reasoning similar to that in section 4.4, eq. (4.A14) can be rewritten as

$$V(x_\tau, \tau) = \mathbb{E}_\tau\left(a(\tau, T)\,V(x_T, T) + \int_\tau^T a(\tau, s)\,h(x_s, s)\,ds\right), \quad a(t', t'') \equiv \frac{S_{0t'}}{S_{0t''}}. \tag{4.A15}$$

Next, consider the state vector, $y_u \equiv (a(\tau, u),\ x_u)$, $\tau \leq u \leq T$, and let $q\left(y_{t'} \mid y_\tau\right)$ be the risk neutral density of y. We have

$$V(x_\tau, \tau) = \mathbb{E}_\tau\left(a(\tau, T)\,V(x_T, T) + \int_\tau^T a(\tau, s)\,h(x_s, s)\,ds\right)$$

$$= \int a(\tau,T)\, V(x_T,T)\, q\left(y_T \middle| y_\tau\right) dy_T + \int_\tau^T \int a(\tau,s)\, h(x_s,s)\, q\left(y_s \middle| y_\tau\right) dy_s ds.$$

Assuming that $V(x_T, T)$ and $a(\tau, T)$ are independent (and assuming the same for h),

$$V(x_\tau,\tau) = \int_X G(\tau,T) V(x_T,T)\, dx_T + \int_\tau^T \int_X G(\tau,s) h(x_s,s)\, dx_s ds.$$

The function G is known as *Green's function*,

$$G(t,\ell) \equiv G(x,t;x_\ell,\ell) = \int_{\mathbb{A}} a(t,\ell)\, q\left(y_\ell \middle| y_t\right) da,$$

where $\mathbb{A}$ denotes the support of a. This function is interpreted as the Arrow-Debreu state-price density, that is, the value at time t and in state $x \in R^d$ of a unit of numéraire at $\ell > t$ when future states are in a neighborhood of x_ℓ. The boundary condition for the Green's function is that it is Dirac's delta at $t = T$. To illustrate, consider a pure discount bond, $V(x,T) = h(x,s) + 1 \equiv 1$, such that

$$V(x_\tau,\tau) = \int_{\mathbb{X}} G(x_\tau,\tau;X,T)\, dX, \quad \text{with } \lim_{\tau \uparrow T} G(x_\tau,\tau;X,T) = \delta(x_\tau - X), \tag{4.A16}$$

where δ is the Dirac's delta and $\mathbb{X}$ denotes the support of x. The boundary condition ensures indeed that $\lim_{\tau\uparrow T} V(x_\tau,\tau) = 1$.

4.D.2 PDE Connection

We show that Green's function satisfies the same PDE satisfied by the asset price, with boundary condition as in (4.A16) and with the exception that it does not incorporate information on the instantaneous dividend.

We have

$$V(x_t,t) = \int_{\mathbb{X}} G(x_t,t;x_T,T)\, V(x_T,T)\, dx_T + \int_t^T \int_{\mathbb{X}} G(x_t,t;x_s,s) h(x_s,s)\, dx_s ds. \tag{4.A17}$$

Now, by eq. (4.A15) and the Feynman–Kac connection between PDEs and conditional expectations (see section 4.2), we have that, under regularity conditions, V is the solution to

$$0 = V_t + \mu V_x + \frac{1}{2}\sigma^2 V_{xx} - rV + h, \tag{4.A18}$$

where μ denotes the risk neutral drift of x. Next, take the partial derivatives of $V(x,t)$ in eq. (4.A17), obtaining

$$\begin{aligned} V_t &= \int_{\mathbb{X}} G_t V dX - \int_{\mathbb{X}} \delta(x - X)\, h dX + \int_t^T \int_{\mathbb{X}} G_t h dx_s ds \\ &= \int_{\mathbb{X}} G_t V dX - h + \int_\tau^T \int_{\mathbb{X}} G_t h dx_s ds \end{aligned}$$

$$V_x = \int_{\mathbb{X}} G_x V dX + \int_t^T \int_{\mathbb{X}} G_x h dx_s ds$$

$$V_{xx} = \int_{\mathbb{X}} G_{xx} V dX + \int_t^T \int_{\mathbb{X}} G_{xx} h dx_s ds$$

and replace them into eq. (4.A18) to obtain

$$0 = \int_{\mathbb{X}} \left(G_t + \mu G_x + \frac{1}{2}\sigma^2 G_{xx} - rG \right) V(x_T, T)\, dx_T$$
$$+ \int_t^T \int_{\mathbb{X}} \left(G_t + \mu G_x + \frac{1}{2}\sigma^2 G_{xx} - rG \right) h(x_s, s)\, dx_s ds.$$

That is, G is solution to

$$0 = G_t + \mu G_x + \frac{1}{2}\sigma^2 G_{xx} - rG, \quad \text{with} \ \lim_{t \uparrow T} G(x, t; X, T) = \delta(x - X),$$

where the boundary condition is precisely the boundary condition stated in (4.A16).

Appendix 4.E Portfolio Constraints

Let $V_{\nu t}^{x,p,c}$ denote the wealth process in the artificial market (4.124) when initial wealth is x, and portfolio and consumption processes are p and c. We are looking for a portfolio-consumption policy $(p_{\hat{\nu}}, c_{\hat{\nu}})$ such that

$$\text{Val}_{\hat{\nu}}(x) \equiv E\left(\int_0^T u(t, c_{\hat{\nu}t})\, dt + U\left(V_{\nu T}^{x, p_{\hat{\nu}}, c_{\hat{\nu}}} \right) \right) = \text{Val}(x; K). \qquad (4.\text{A}19)$$

That is, we are looking for a $\hat{\nu} : p_{\hat{\nu}t} \in K$ for all $t \in [0, T]$. Two small remarks on notation. We recall that we are defining, as in section 4.7, (i) $\text{Val}_\nu(x)$ as the value of the problem an investor faces in the *unconstrained* market in eqs. (4.124) and (ii) p_t as the *normalized* portfolio process, $p_t \equiv \frac{\pi_t}{V_t}$. The intuition underlying this problem is the following. As Cvitanić and Karatzas (1992) put it, we are searching for a member of a family of unconstrained problems (that is, those resulting from the market in eqs. (4.124)) with the property that the optimal portfolio satisfies the constraint (i.e., without imposing it) and thereby solves the original problem.

Note that because K contains the origin, the support function ζ in eq. (4.122) satisfies $\zeta(\nu) \geq 0$ for each $\nu \in \tilde{K}$. Moreover, by construction,

$$p \in K \Longleftrightarrow \zeta(\nu) + p^\top \nu \geq 0, \quad \forall \nu \in \tilde{K}. \qquad (4\text{A}.20)$$

Next, define the standard Brownian motion under the probability Q^ν, defined through the Radon-Nikodym in eq. (4.126):

$$W_{\nu t} = W_t + \int_0^t \left(\lambda_u + \sigma_u^{-1} \nu_u \right) du \equiv W_{0t} + \int_0^t \left(\sigma_u^{-1} \nu_u \right) du,$$

where $\lambda = \sigma^{-1}(\mu - \mathbf{1}_d r)$ and W_0 is the usual Brownian under the risk neutral probability in a market without frictions. If the price system is as in the artificial market of eqs. (4.124), then, for *any* unconstrained portfolio consumption (p, c), $V_{\nu t}^{x,p,c}$ is easily seen to satisfy

$$\begin{aligned} dV_\nu^{x,p,c} &= \left(\pi^\top(\mu^\nu - \mathbf{1}_d r^\nu) + r^\nu V_\nu^{x,p,c} - c\right) dt + \pi^\top \sigma dW, \\ &= \left(\left(p^\top \nu + \zeta(\nu)\right) V_\nu^{x,p,c} + r V_\nu^{x,p,c} - c\right) dt + V_\nu^{x,p,c} p^\top \sigma dW_0, \end{aligned}$$

where the second expression follows by a change in probability and the expressions for r^ν and μ^ν are given in eq. (4.125).

Therefore, for a given normalized portfolio-consumption policy (p, c), we have that the wealth difference, $\Delta_t \equiv \frac{V_{\nu t}^{x,\pi,c} - V_t^{x,\pi,c}}{S_{0t}}$, satisfies

$$d\Delta_t = \underbrace{\frac{V_{\nu t}^{x,\pi,c}}{S_{0t}}\left(p_t^\top \nu_t + \zeta(\nu_t)\right)}_{\equiv m(t)} dt + \Delta_t p_t^\top \sigma_t dW_{0t}, \quad \Delta_0 = 0.$$

Next, consider, the simpler equation,

$$d\bar{\Delta}_t = \bar{\Delta}_t p_t^\top \sigma_t dW_{0t}, \quad \bar{\Delta}_0 = 0. \tag{4.A21}$$

Because $m_t \geq 0$ by eq. (4A.20), then, by a comparison theorem (e.g., Karatzas and Shreve, 1991, 291–295), $\Delta_t \geq \bar{\Delta}_t = 0$, where the last equality follows because the solution to eq. (4.A21) is $\bar{\Delta}_t = \bar{\Delta}_0 L_t$ for some positive process L_t. Therefore, we have

$$V_{\nu t}^{x,p,c} \geq V_t^{x,p,c}, \quad \text{with an equality if} \quad \zeta(\nu_t) + p_t^\top \nu_t = 0 \text{ for all } t. \tag{4.A22}$$

Now, assume that there exists a portfolio the investor chooses in the artificial market (i.e., without imposing the constraint), which then *happens* to satisfy the constraint in the constrained market. Precisely, assume that there exists a $\hat{\nu}$ and a portfolio-consumption pair $(p_{\hat{\nu}}, c_{\hat{\nu}})$, such that

$$p_{\hat{\nu}t} \in K \quad \text{and} \quad \zeta(\hat{\nu}_t) + p_{\hat{\nu}t}^\top \hat{\nu}_t = 0. \tag{4.A23}$$

By the inequality in (4.A22), we have that, for all ν, $\mathrm{Val}_\nu(x) \geq \mathrm{Val}_0(x) \geq \mathrm{Val}(x; K)$, where the second inequality follows as the value of the constrained problem, $\mathrm{Val}(x; K)$, is less than the value of the problem in a frictionless market, $\mathrm{Val}_0(x)$. Therefore,

$$\mathrm{Val}(x; K) \leq \mathrm{Val}_{\hat{\nu}}(x) \quad \text{and} \quad \mathrm{Val}(x; K) \leq \inf_{\nu \in \tilde{K}} \left(\mathrm{Val}_\nu(x)\right). \tag{4.A24}$$

Moreover, we have

$$\begin{aligned} \mathrm{Val}(x; K) &= E\left(\int_0^T u(t, c_t)\, dt + U\left(V_T^{x,p,c}\right)\right), \quad p_t \in K \\ &\geq E\left(\int_0^T u(t, c_{\hat{\nu}t})\, dt + U\left(V_T^{x,p_{\hat{\nu}},c_{\hat{\nu}}}\right)\right) \end{aligned}$$

$$= E\left(\int_0^T u(t, c_{\hat{\nu}t})\,dt + U\left(V_{\hat{\nu}T}^{x,p_{\hat{\nu}},c_{\hat{\nu}}}\right)\right)$$

$$= \mathrm{Val}_{\hat{\nu}}(x),$$

where the second line holds because the value of the original problem is obviously larger than that of any constrained and not optimally chosen portfolio consumption $(p_{\hat{\nu}}, c_{\hat{\nu}})$; the third line follows by (4.A22) and (4.A23); and finally, the fourth line is the definition of $\mathrm{Val}_\nu(x)$. Therefore,

$$\mathrm{Val}(x;K) \geq \mathrm{Val}_{\hat{\nu}}(x) \geq \inf_{\nu\in\tilde{K}} (\mathrm{Val}_\nu(x)). \tag{4.A25}$$

Combining (4.A25) with the second inequality of (4.A24) leaves

$$\mathrm{Val}(x;K) = \inf_{\nu\in\tilde{K}} (\mathrm{Val}_\nu(x)).$$

Appendix 4.F Jumps

4.F.1 Radon-Nikodym Derivative

This section derives heuristic results on Radon-Nikodym derivatives for jump-diffusion processes. The reader is referred to Brémaud (1981) for precise mathematical details. Consider the jump times $0 < \tau_1 < \tau_2 < \cdots < \tau_n = T$. The probability of a jump in a neighborhood of τ_i is given by the "intensity," that is, $v_{\tau_i} d\tau_i$. To define the same probability under the risk neutral space, write $v_{Q,\tau_i} d\tau_i$ under Q, and set $v_Q = v\lambda^J$ for some λ_J. The probability that no jumps would occur between any two adjacent random points τ_{i-1} and τ_i *and* that a jump would occur at time τ_{i-1} is, for $i \geq 2$, proportional to

$$v_{\tau_{i-1}} e^{-\int_{\tau_{i-1}}^{\tau_i} v_u du} \quad \text{under } P$$

and to

$$v_{Q,\tau_{i-1}} e^{-\int_{\tau_{i-1}}^{\tau_i} v_{Q,u} du} = v_{\tau_{i-1}} \lambda^J_{\tau_{i-1}} e^{-\int_{\tau_{i-1}}^{\tau_i} v_u \lambda^J_u du} \quad \text{under } Q.$$

In fact, and as explained in section 4.9, these are densities of time intervals elapsing from one arrival to the next one.

Next, let A be the event of "marks," or jumps, at $\tau_1, \tau_2, \cdots, \tau_n$. The Radon-Nikodym derivative is the likelihood ratio of the two probabilities Q and P of the event A, namely,

$$\frac{Q(A)}{P(A)} = \frac{e^{-\int_t^{\tau_1} v_u \lambda^J_u du} \cdot v_{\tau_1} \lambda^J_{\tau_1} e^{-\int_{\tau_1}^{\tau_2} v_u \lambda^J_u du} \cdot v_{\tau_2} \lambda^J_{\tau_2} e^{-\int_{\tau_2}^{\tau_3} v_u \lambda^J_u du} \cdot \cdots}{e^{-\int_t^{\tau_1} v_u du} \cdot v_{\tau_1} e^{-\int_{\tau_1}^{\tau_2} v_u du} \cdot v_{\tau_2} e^{-\int_{\tau_2}^{\tau_3} v_u du} \cdot \cdots},$$

where we have used the property that, given that at $\tau_0 = t$ there are no jumps, the probability that no jumps would occur from t to τ_1 is $e^{-\int_t^{\tau_1} v_u du}$ under P and $e^{-\int_t^{\tau_1} v_u \lambda^J_u du}$ under Q. Simple algebra then yields

$$\frac{Q(A)}{P(A)} = \lambda^J_{\tau_1} \cdot \lambda^J_{\tau_2} \cdot e^{-\int_t^{\tau_1} v_u \left(\lambda^J_u - 1\right) du} \cdot e^{-\int_{\tau_1}^{\tau_2} v_u \left(\lambda^J_u - 1\right) du} e^{-\int_{\tau_2}^{\tau_3} v_u \left(\lambda^J_u - 1\right) du} \cdot \cdots$$

$$
\begin{aligned}
&= \prod_{i=1}^{n} \lambda_{\tau_i}^{J} \cdot e^{-\int_t^{\tau_n} v_u \left(\lambda_u^J - 1\right) du} \\
&= \exp\left[\ln\left(\prod_{i=1}^{n} \lambda_{\tau_i}^{J} \cdot e^{-\int_t^{\tau_n} v(u)\left(\lambda_u^J - 1\right) du}\right)\right] \\
&= \exp\left(\sum_{i=1}^{n} \ln \lambda_{\tau_i}^{J} - \int_t^{\tau_n} v_u \left(\lambda_u^J - 1\right) du\right) \\
&= \exp\left(\int_t^T \ln \lambda_u^J dZ_u - \int_t^T v_u \left(\lambda_u^J - 1\right) du\right),
\end{aligned}
\tag{4.A26}
$$

where the last equality follows by the definition of the Stieltjes integral.

The dynamics of this likelihood ratio are easily determined. Define $\eta_T \equiv e^{y_T}$, where

$$
y_\tau \equiv -\int_t^\tau v_u \left(\lambda_u^J - 1\right) du + \int_t^\tau \ln \lambda_u^J dZ_u.
$$

By applying Itô's lemma for jump processes,

$$
d\eta_\tau = -e^{y_\tau} v_\tau \left(\lambda_\tau^J - 1\right) d\tau + \left(e^{y_\tau + \ln \lambda_\tau^J} - e^{y_\tau}\right) dZ_\tau.
$$

That is,

$$
\frac{d\eta_\tau}{\eta_\tau} = \left(\lambda_\tau^J - 1\right) dM_\tau, \quad dM_\tau = dZ_\tau - v_\tau d\tau. \tag{4.A27}
$$

Note that the process M_t is a martingale as it is the difference between a Poisson process and its expected values. For this reason, it is sometimes referred to as a "compensated" Poisson process. We now turn to determine more precisely the relation between v and v_Q in the jump-diffusion case.

4.F.2 State Price Density

Assume that asset prices are driven by one source of uncertainty, which follows a jump-diffusion process

$$
dx_\tau = \mu(x_\tau) d\tau + \sigma(x_\tau) dW_\tau + S dZ_\tau,
$$

for some functions μ and σ and where remaining notation is as in the main text. Further, assume that the intensity under the physical probability is a function of the state x, $v(x)$ say. Finally, denote the jump component for the state price density ξ with $J_\xi(x)$. We have

$$
\frac{d\xi_\tau}{\xi_\tau} = -r(x_\tau) d\tau - \lambda(x_\tau) dW_\tau + J_\xi(x_\tau) dM_\tau, \quad \xi_t = 1, \tag{4.A28}
$$

where M_τ denotes the compensated Poisson process (see eq. (4.A27)) and, by (4.A27), the intensity under Q is

$$
v_Q(x) = v(x)\left(1 + J_\xi(x)\right). \tag{4.A29}
$$

We assume that the distribution of the jump, size $\mathcal{S}$, under the physical probability is the same as that under the risk neutral. We now rely on eq. (4.A28) and derive no-arbitrage pricing relations in a simple setting.

4.F.3 Arbitrage Restrictions

Assume that a price process S_τ of some asset is a function of the state, namely, $S \equiv S(x_\tau, \tau)$. For simplicity, we consider a finite horizon market, and we assume that the asset does not distribute dividends. By Itô's lemma for jump-diffusion processes,

$$\frac{dS(x_\tau, \tau)}{S(x_\tau, \tau)} = \mu_S(x_\tau, \tau)\, d\tau + \sigma_S(x_\tau, \tau)\, dW_\tau + J_S(x_\tau, \tau)\, dZ_\tau, \tag{4.A30}$$

where $\mu_S S = LS$, $\sigma_S S = \frac{\partial S}{\partial x}\sigma$, L is the generator for pure diffusion processes and, finally,

$$J_S(x, \tau) \equiv \frac{S(x_\tau + \mathcal{S}, \tau) - S(x_\tau, \tau)}{S(x_\tau, \tau)}.$$

Next, consider eq. (4.30), i.e., $0 = E_t\left[d(\xi_t S_t)\right]$. That is, by (4.34),

$$\begin{aligned} E_\tau\left(\frac{dS(x_\tau, \tau)}{S(x_\tau, \tau)}\right) &= -E_\tau\left(\frac{d\xi_\tau}{\xi_\tau}\right) - E_\tau\left(\frac{d\xi_\tau}{\xi_\tau}\frac{dS(x_\tau, \tau)}{S(x_\tau, \tau)}\right) \\ &= \left[r(x_\tau) + \lambda(x_\tau)\sigma_S(x_\tau, \tau) - v(x_\tau) J_\xi(x) E_\tau(J_S(x_\tau, \tau))\right] d\tau \\ &= \left[r(x_\tau) + \lambda(x_\tau)\sigma_S(x_\tau, \tau) - \left(v_Q(x_\tau) - v(x_\tau)\right) E_\tau(J_S(x_\tau, \tau))\right] d\tau, \end{aligned} \tag{4.A31}$$

where the second equality follows because

$$E_\tau\left(dM_\tau J_S(x, \tau)\, dZ_\tau\right) = E_\tau\left(J_S(x, \tau)\, dZ_\tau^2\right) = E_\tau\left(J_S(x, \tau)\, dZ_\tau\right) = E_\tau\left(J_S(x, \tau)\right) v d\tau$$

and the third by eq. (4.A29). Now, comparing (4.A30) and (4.A31) leaves

$$\mu_S(x_\tau, \tau) = r(x_\tau) + \lambda(x_\tau)\sigma_S(x_\tau, \tau) - v_Q(x) E_\tau\left(J_S(x, \tau)\right).$$

Next, we define the asset price dynamics under the risk neutral probability. Define as usual a Brownian motion under Q as $d\tilde{W}_\tau = dW_\tau + \lambda(x_\tau)\, d\tau$ such that, under Q,

$$\frac{dS(x_\tau, \tau)}{S(x_\tau, \tau)} = \left[r(x_\tau) - v_Q(x_\tau) E\left(J_S(x_\tau, \tau)\right)\right] d\tau + \sigma_S(x_\tau, \tau)\, d\tilde{W}_\tau + J_S(x_\tau, \tau)\, dZ_\tau. \tag{4.A32}$$

Note that we have not changed notation for the Poisson process: unlike in the Brownian motion case, we cannot define a Poisson process under Q through a spatial shift. The reason is that the paths of Z_τ are constant unless a jump that always has unit size occurs. Therefore, a change in probability for Poisson processes can be made through a shift in the intensity: if Z_τ is a Poisson process with intensity $v(\cdot)$ under probability P, then Z_τ is a Poisson process with intensity $v_Q(\cdot)$ under probability Q, where the Radon-Nikodym derivative of Q with respect to P is given by (4.A26).

More formally, note that

$$\eta_T Z_T = \eta_t Z_t + \int_t^T d(\eta_\tau Z_\tau) = \int_t^T d(\eta_\tau Z_\tau), \tag{4.A33}$$

where η_τ is as in (4.A27) and the second equality follows by $\eta_t = 1$ and $Z_t = 0$. By Itô's lemma,

$$d(\eta_\tau Z_\tau) = d\eta_\tau Z_\tau + \eta_\tau dZ_\tau + d\eta_\tau dZ_\tau$$
$$= \left(\left(\lambda_\tau^J - 1\right) dM_\tau\right) \eta_\tau Z_\tau + \eta_\tau dZ_\tau + \left(\lambda_\tau^J - 1\right) \eta_\tau dM_\tau dZ_\tau,$$

such that

$$E_\tau \left[d(\eta_\tau Z_\tau)\right] = \eta_\tau v_\tau d\tau + \left(\lambda_\tau^J - 1\right) \eta_\tau v_\tau d\tau = \eta_\tau v_{Q,\tau} d\tau.$$

Taking expectations in (4.A33) under Q and replacing the previous expression into the result yields

$$\begin{aligned}\mathbb{E}_t (Z_T) &= E_t \left(\frac{\eta_T}{\eta_t} Z_T\right) \\ &= \frac{1}{\eta_t} E_t \left(\int_t^T d(\eta_\tau Z_\tau)\right) \\ &= \frac{1}{\eta_t} E_t \left(\int_t^T E_\tau \left[d(\eta_\tau Z_\tau)\right]\right) \\ &= \frac{1}{\eta_t} E_t \left(\int_t^T \eta_\tau v_{Q,\tau} d\tau\right) \\ &= \mathbb{E}_t \left(\int_t^T v_{Q,\tau} d\tau\right). \end{aligned} \tag{4.A34}$$

That is, Z_τ is a Poisson process with intensity $v_Q(\cdot)$ under Q.

References

Arnold, L. (1974). *Stochastic Differential Equations: Theory and Applications.* New York: Wiley.

Bajeux-Besnainou, I., and J. C. Rochet (1996). "Dynamic Spanning: Are Options an Appropriate Instrument?" *Mathematical Finance* 6, 1–16.

Barone-Adesi, G., and R. E. Whaley (1987). "Efficient Analytic Approximation of American Option Values." *Journal of Finance* 42, 301–320.

Black, F., and M. Scholes (1973). "The Pricing of Options and Corporate Liabilities." *Journal of Political Economy* 81, 637–659.

Breeden, D. T. (1979). "An Intertemporal Asset Pricing Model with Stochastic Consumption and Investment Opportunities." *Journal of Financial Economics* 7, 265–296.

Brémaud, P. (1981). *Point Processes and Queues: Martingale Dynamics.* Berlin: Springer-Verlag.

Campbell, J. Y., and L. M. Viceira (2002). *Strategic Asset Allocation.* Oxford: Oxford University Press.

Chacko, G., and L. M. Viceira (2005). "Dynamic Consumption and Portfolio Choice with Stochastic Volatility in Incomplete Markets." *Review of Financial Studies* 18, 1369–1402.

Cox, J. C., J. E. Ingersoll, and S. A. Ross (1985a). "An Intertemporal General Equilibrium Model of Asset Prices." *Econometrica* 53, 363–384.

Cox, J. C., J. E. Ingersoll, and S. A. Ross (1985b). "A Theory of the Term Structure of Interest Rates." *Econometrica* 53, 385–407.

Cvitanić, J., and I. Karatzas (1992). "Convex Duality in Constrained Portfolio Optimization." *Annals of Applied Probability* 2, 767–818.

Föllmer, H., and M. Schweizer (1991). "Hedging of Contingent Claims under Incomplete Information." In *Applied Stochastic Analysis*, edited by M. Davis and R. Elliot, 389–414. New York: Gordon & Breach.

Friedman, A. (1975). *Stochastic Differential Equations and Applications*. Vol. 1. New York: Academic Press.

Harrison, J. M., and D. M. Kreps (1979). "Martingales and Arbitrage in Multiperiod Securities Markets." *Journal of Economic Theory* 20, 381–408.

Harrison, J. M., R. Pitbladdo, and S. M. Schaefer (1984). Continuous Price Processes in Frictionless Markets Have Infinite Variation." *Journal of Business* 57, 353–365.

Harrison, J. M., and S. Pliska (1983). "A Stochastic Calculus Model of Continuous Trading: Complete Markets." *Stochastic Processes and Their Applications* 15, 313–316.

He, H., and N. Pearson (1991). "Consumption and Portfolio Policies with Incomplete Markets and Short-Sales Constraints: The Infinite Dimensional Case." *Journal of Economic Theory* 54, 259–304.

Huang, C.-F. (1987). "An Intertemporal General Equilibrium Asset Pricing Model: The Case of Diffusion Information." *Econometrica* 55, 117–142.

Karatzas, I. (1997). *Lectures on the Mathematics of Finance*. Providence, RI: American Mathematical Society, CRM Monograph Series, Vol. 8.

Karatzas, I., and S. E. Shreve (1991). *Brownian Motion and Stochastic Calculus*. New York: Springer.

Karatzas, I., and S. E. Shreve (1998). *Methods of Mathematical Finance*. New York: Springer.

Krugman, P. (1991). "Target Zones and Exchange Rate Dynamics." *Quarterly Journal of Economics* 106, 669–682.

Lewis, A. L. (2000). *Option Valuation under Stochastic Volatility*. Newport Beach, CA: Finance Press.

Longstaff, F. A., and E. S. Schwartz (1992). "Interest Rate Volatility and the Term Structure: A Two-Factor General Equilibrium Model." *Journal of Finance* 47, 1259–1282.

Lucas, R. E. (1978). "Asset Prices in an Exchange Economy." *Econometrica* 46, 1429–1445.

McDonald, R. L., and D. R. Siegel (1986). "The Value of Waiting to Invest." *Quarterly Journal of Economics* 101, 707–727.

Merton, R. C. (1969). "Lifetime Portfolio Selection under Uncertainty: The Continuous-Time Case." *Review of Economics and Statistics* 51, 247–257.

Merton, R. C. (1971). "Optimum Consumption and Portfolio Rules in a Continuous-Time Model." *Journal of Economic Theory* 3, 373–413.

Merton, R. C. (1973). "An Intertemporal Capital Asset Pricing Model." *Econometrica* 41, 867–887.

Merton, R. C. (1976). "Option Pricing When Underlying Stock Returns Are Discontinuous." *Journal of Financial Economics* 3, 125–144.

Mikosch, T. (1998). *Elementary Stochastic Calculus with Finance in View*. Singapore: World Scientific.

Øksendal, B. (1998). *Stochastic Differential Equations*. Berlin: Springer.

Pham, H., and N. Touzi (1996). "Equilibrium State Prices in a Stochastic Volatility Model." *Mathematical Finance* 6, 215–236.

Revuz, D., and M. Yor (1999). *Continuous Martingales and Brownian Motion.* 3rd ed. New York: Springer.

Romano, M., and N. Touzi (1997). "Contingent Claims and Market Completeness in a Stochastic Volatility Model." *Mathematical Finance* 7, 399–412.

Ross, S. A. (1976). "Options and Efficiency." *Quarterly Journal of Economics* 90, 75–89.

Rubinstein, M. (1976). "The Valuation of Uncertain Income Streams and the Pricing of Options." *The Bell Journal of Economics* 7, 407–425.

Shreve, S. (1991). "A Control Theorist's View of Asset Pricing." In *Applied Stochastic Analysis*, edited by M. Davis and R. Elliot, 415–445. New York: Gordon & Breach.

Steele, J. M. (2001). *Stochastic Calculus and Financial Applications.* New York: Springer.

5

Information, Security Design, and Financial Contracting

5.1 Introduction

Many models that have been dealt with so far rely on the assumption that agents make investment decisions based on common sources of information. For example, chapter 3 contains generalizations of the static CAPM (see chapter 1), in which agents observe the assets' dividends and markets clear through standard mechanisms (i.e., in general equilibrium). However, in part II (see, e.g., chapters 9 and 10), we shall alternate between explanations based on frictionless dynamic stochastic general equilibrium models *and* models with frictions. Market imperfections are very important in theory and in practice. Financial efficiency is known to affect outcomes in the real economy. Rajan and Zingales (1998), for example, provided empirical evidence in support of the view that financial markets and institutions contribute to economic growth. A possible channel for this linkage is the fact that markets and institutions mitigate market imperfections, such as moral hazard or adverse selection, thereby reducing the cost of capital for firms. This chapter mostly focuses on such moral hazard and adverse selection problems, which amount to one of the most notable imperfections. Many areas of financial economics do incorporate these problems, and the process of addressing them results in a series of propositions that go well beyond the standard predictions of the frictionless dynamic stochastic general equilibrium models. This chapter provides an introduction to this literature. Part II deals with many additional instances and articulated models of financial markets with frictions, including noninformational frictions.

We begin with a review of information problems that helps the reader find the original sources and motivation for work in this important area of economics (see section 5.2). Section 5.3 discusses three models (and some of their variants) that illustrate information problems in financial economics. These problems challenge the main paradigm underlying theoretical constructs such as the CAPM. For example, why do certain derivative markets exist? Shouldn't asymmetric information be a deterrent to trading for those who have not enough information? This section contains a succinct introduction to problems of adverse selection, moral hazard, and signaling in financial markets; we illustrate the main ideas underlying some contracts that may mitigate these problems. The remainder of the chapter describes how the previous contracts may be made endogenous (i.e., optimal) among parties. Consider a firm that seeks financing. Is the firm going to issue debt or equity? In section 5.5, we review the classic Modigliani and Miller (1958) propositions on capital structure irrelevance and also point to potential frictions that may help restore a role for preferring debt to equity, for example. The remaining sections deal with theories of debt in the case of asymmetric information: section 5.5 show how debt may arise as an optimal contract in an environment with moral hazard. Section 5.6 analyzes debt in contexts with costly state verification. Finally, section 5.7 deals with dynamic theories of contracting.

5.2 Conceptual Challenges to Frictionless Markets: Information Problems

Why do certain assets exist? What makes corporations issue and, then, investors agree to trade equity or debt? Why would investors agree to trade even more complex securities? This chapter reviews theories of debt and the firm's capital structure that take into account informational asymmetries between investors and firms' managers. This section provides motivation underlying these theories and historical background around the economics of information. Section 5.3 develops three simple models that aim to illustrate these ideas.

5.2.1 The Economics of Information

Economic theory has been dealing with information problems for long time. The initial historical background includes very simple examples. Some agents may have more information than others. For example, insurance companies cannot verify the efforts made by insured individuals to avoid risks. In these cases, markets may fail to arise in the first place, a situation of "moral hazard" that Arrow (1963) explained very clearly in a famous contribution. As another example, and to remain in the theme of this book, consider an investor (the "principal") who contemplates investing in mortgage-backed securities; the investor cannot verify whether a bank (the "agent") is securitizing loans that are originated with good due diligence. This conflict of interest is an instance of what is referred to as an agency problem. Parallel to moral hazard is "adverse selection": to illustrate, a trader may only propose to sell some assets at $5 if they knew that these assets were worth less than $5. Further, how do firms "signal" their value, or how can they transmit credible information to the marketplace? How can borrowers or workers be incentivized to adopt behaviors in line with the interest of their "principal"?

Questions of this kind have been discussed since at least Adam Smith (1776) and then, for centuries, by many other economists, as explained in detail by Laffont and Martimort (2002). However, it was only during the 1970s that new models appeared to formalize these problems. Economists were stumbling into conceptual difficulties while attempting to incorporate such information asymmetries into elegant general equilibrium models. Their focus then became the analysis of simple market relationships among a few agents, covering adverse selection (Akerlof, 1970; Rothschild and Stiglitz, 1976), moral hazard (Ross, 1973, Mirrlees, 1974, 1975; Holmström, 1979; Shavell, 1979), and signaling (Spence, 1973, 1974; Riley, 1975). Salanié (1997) provides a very useful review of this literature.

5.2.2 Information Problems in Financial Markets

The earliest applications of information theory to finance were in the area of signaling (Leland and Pyle, 1977; Ross, 1977; Bhattacharya, 1979), followed by those in the area of adverse selection that aimed to deal with debt relationships (Townsend, 1979; Gale and Hellwig, 1985), credit markets (Stiglitz and Weiss, 1981), and asset markets (Glosten and Milgrom, 1985; Kyle, 1985) and then those that aimed to rationalize debt as a solution to moral hazard problems (Innes, 1990).

We review these information-based theories of financial markets in more advanced sections (from section 5.4) as well as in part II (e.g., in chapter 10), but this section illustrates some of their flavor. So far, securities have been given exogenously. However, in practice, securities may or may not exist or may or may not trade, according to market forces we have not analyzed so far. For example, how can we even consider purchasing any security at a price proposed to us? It may well be the case that our counterpart has information that the security will not likely perform and that the price we are offered is too high. It is an *adverse selection* problem: the only securities being proposed for sale are those with fundamental values below their proposed prices.

How can two parties trade in these conditions? They actually could, at least under additional conditions. For example, our reluctance to buy may weaken if we knew that a liquidity shock (not information) is the motivation underlying our counterparty's decision to sell. That is, we may buy some assets while assuming our counterparty is selling due to liquidity needs. However, the transaction price should reflect the buyer's concern of trading with an informed counterparty anyway. Thus, a potential buyer with limited information may treat a purely liquidity-motivated trade as one with a chance of having been initiated by an informed seller. It is interesting. Due to a buyer's concern of trading with an informed counterparty, a liquidity motivated trade can "move" prices. These "price impacts" are actually important. Now, we have that imperfectly liquid markets are also informationally inefficient. That is, prices may be affected by liquidity trades, that is, by reasons unrelated to the assets' fundamentals; yet, a transaction may take place anyway. The inefficiencies (unknown transaction motives) may actually make market function.

How informationally inefficient markets can be? Depending on the benefits of acquiring information relative to its costs, there may be investors deciding to remain uninformed. Indeed, by remaining uninformed, agents may still learn information held by informed traders while simply observing the equilibrium price: for example, a high price may reflect the fact that investors with superior information are buying, although this fact is still uncertain to the eyes of the uninformed agents. In equilibrium, agents remain uninformed when the costs related to this uncertainty are the same as the benefits of becoming informed—benefits regarding the ability to perform better trading decisions. It is the celebrated Grossman-Stiglitz "equilibrium degree of disequilibrium" (Grossman and Stiglitz, 1980). This chapter does not deal with these free-riding problems and, in general, with how information acquisition is determined in equilibrium; these issues are studied in part II (see chapter 10). Rather, it makes the preliminary point of illustrating how, and somehow paradoxically, the presence of liquidity motivated trades can help trading arise in a market plagued with asymmetric information.

A second information problem regards securities creation. Certain derivative assets draw value from events with a probability of occurrence that may be affected by security producers. For example, financial intermediaries can create and sell securities that are backed by mortgage loans. The resulting mortgages become "securitized" and possibly more liquid and easy to trade than the original loans. Chapter 14 provides some details of this securitization process. Securitization is a useful business model. On the one hand, outside investors may want to get some exposure to the original loans, but originating loans requires specialization. On the other hand, the originators of loans may only desire a partial exposure to these loans. Securitization would allow to share these risks.

The delicate point of securitization is that financial intermediaries need to be properly incentivized while originating the loans: anticipating that portions of these loans will be distributed to outside investors, financial intermediaries may well extend loans with poor credit standards (and pretend these standards are high), which are arguably less expensive to originate than loans with high credit standards. It is a *moral hazard* problem to be tackled while investors provide originators with adequate incentives. An incentive to originate good loans is to ensure that originators may become involved in losses should such losses materialize. This solution is consistent with standard remedies to moral hazard that have been proposed in the economics of information. To illustrate a standard insurance problem, a car driver may not be incentivized to drive properly when they are offered a full insurance contract. In our context, the originator needs to retain a sufficiently high proportion of securitized assets (have "skin in the game") to be incentivized in generating high quality mortgage loans.

A third instance of information problems regards the case in which a firm has a good project but is not able to credibly explain to the market that its project is good. Thus, the firm wants to issue bonds to finance the project, but investors walk away because the firm has not credibly explained that the project is of good quality. In the previous moral hazard example, a loan originator needs retain a sufficiently high proportion of the securitized assets. In this new example, the firm needs to signal the market that it is of a good type, and the signal has to be costly. For example, the firm may issue an option embedded into its debt, which gives the right but not the obligation to redeem its debt at some prespecified point; naturally, the option is expensive for the firm. The rationale behind this "callable bond" is that the firm wants investors to believe that the probability of default is really small and that this will be known at the time of the option exercise, when the cost of capital will be lower exactly for this reason. This is a *signaling problem*. Note that a market may arise (a bond market) due to the presence of a derivative (the callable option embedded into it). In this example, derivatives are "oiling the wheels of the economy." Interestingly, callable bonds are pervasive in the marketplace, and part III (see chapters 12 and 13) provides many pricing and modeling details for them.

The point of these models is to remind the reader that many attributes of securities should be endogenous. For example, the riskiness of a security in the moral hazard example may well depend on forces that the standard CAPM does not take into account. Alternatively, a market may even fail to arise in all the examples of this section. In fact, the CAPM was developed before the birth of the economics of information. Frictions and market failures would become the focus of economists only during the 1970s, as discussed. We now present models that illustrate these ideas in each of the previous three areas regarding information frictions: adverse selection, moral hazard, and signaling.

5.3 Three Information Problems

5.3.1 Adverse Selection and Trading

5.3.1.1 The lemons problem

Akerlof (1970) points out that asymmetric information raises a series of problems that may well lead to dysfunctional markets. Consider a market for a continuum of cars with quality q uniformly distributed in $(0, 1)$. First, assume that, for any specific car drawn from this distribution, the quality q is common knowledge. Potential buyers have a reservation value for cars equal to Kq, where $K > 1$ is a preference parameter; that is, buyers would be willing to buy at any price $s \leq Kq$. Instead, sellers would sell at any price $s > q$. Therefore, a transaction will take place for any price $\hat{s} \in (q, Kq)$.

Next, suppose that product quality uncertainty exists: the cars' quality q is *not* common knowledge; only the sellers know the true quality. In this case, an equilibrium may fail to emerge. Indeed, suppose s_o is an equilibrium price, which can only be acceptable by sellers when the true quality satisfies $q \leq s_o$. That is, the only sellers who sell are those proposing cars that have a quality worse than s_o: it is the adverse selection problem. The buyers anticipate this adverse selection and update their beliefs on the cars' quality to $E\left(q \mid q \leq s_o\right)$, where the (uniform) density of the cars' quality, conditional on $q \leq s_o$ is $\frac{1}{s_o}\mathbb{I}_{q\in(0,s_o)}$; thus, $E\left(q \mid q \leq s_o\right) = \frac{1}{2}s_o$. Buyers will then be willing to pay no more than $\frac{1}{2}Ks_o$, such that a transaction will occur (if any) only if $s_o < \frac{1}{2}Ks_o$: there are no equilibria unless the buyers have a sufficiently strong preference for cars, that is, $K > 2$. We now explain how the lemons problem can be mitigated when there is a probability that the motives for selling do not relate to quality problems.

5.3.1.2 Trading with noise

The lemons problem suggests that it is not trivial to explain how parties agree to trade financial securities: How do we know that those who want to sell a security do not already know they are selling us lemons? Investor protection laws certainly mitigate these concerns; however, regulation may only serve as a deterrent to episodes of misselling, and in many instances, it only applies after a trade is executed. Further, trading on the basis of asymmetric information may not necessarily be illegal: on the contrary, some institutional investors may have more information than others simply because they invest in (and pay for) research. Once again, how do we justify trading among parties that have access to information with different quality? It is an important and beautiful chapter in the history of thought that is discussed in detail in chapter 10. We now illustrate how trade may arise in spite of asymmetric information by relying on a famous mechanism: the presence of trades possibly motivated by liquidity needs.

Suppose, then, that there is a fraction of cars equal to $1 - p$ that is being sold because the owners need cash, and assume these cars' owners are ready to sell for any price. With complementary probability p, the car is still a lemon in that it may only be proposed for sale at a price exceeding its quality. Therefore, conditional on only observing a price equal to s_o the expected quality is

$$E\left(q \mid q \leq s_o\right) = pE_l\left(q \mid q \leq s_o\right) + (1-p)\,E_{nl}\left(q \mid q \leq s_o\right) = p\frac{1}{2}s_o + (1-p)\,\frac{1}{2}, \qquad (5.1)$$

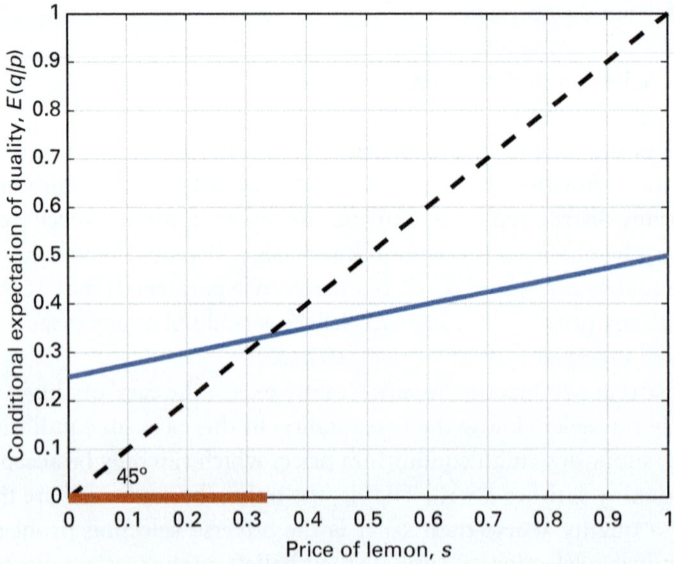

Figure 5.1
Equilibrium prices in a model of lemons with noise. The solid line depicts the conditional expectation $E(q|q<s)$ in eq. (5.1) for $p=\frac{1}{2}$. Trading takes place for all values of $s : s \le KE(q|q \le s)$, that is, assuming $K=1$ for all $s \in (0, \hat{s}_o]$, where $\hat{s}_o = \frac{1}{3}$.

where $E_l(\cdot)$ and $E_{nl}(\cdot)$ denote expectations conditional on s_0 and the car being sold as a lemon and not, resp. The second equality follows because $E_{nl}(q|\, q \le s_o) = E(q) = \frac{1}{2}$: by assumption, the car owners accept to sell at any price when hit by a liquidity shock, such that s_o carries no information content on q.

Trading occurs whenever the equilibrium price s_o satisfies

$$s_o \le KE(q|\, q \le s_o), \tag{5.2}$$

or for any equilibrium price $s_o \in (0, \hat{s}_o]$, where $\hat{s}_o = \frac{(1-p)K}{2-pK}$. The range of trading prices obviously increases with K. For example, when $K=2$, $\hat{s}_o=1$ and trading always takes place as in the lemons markets with $p=1$. But, and in contrast with the previous lemons market, trading can take place even when consumers have weaker preferences. The solid line of figure 5.1 depicts the conditional expectation in eq. (5.1) when $p=\frac{1}{2}$, which is obviously the same as the RHS of (5.2) once $K=1$. Note that, when $K=1$, there are equilibrium prices that were not in the previous lemons market with $p=1$, arising for all $s_o \in (0, \hat{s}_o]$, where $\hat{s}_o = \frac{1-p}{2-p}$. In figure 5.1, $\hat{s}_o = \frac{1}{3}$.

In these examples, noise is what makes markets plagued with asymmetric information work. A simple CAPM cannot explain these phenomena. However, markets microstructure and information problems are important aspects of market behavior and will be analyzed in greater detail in part II (see chapter 10).

5.3.2 Moral Hazard and Securitization

We study securities markets arising within a "originate-and-distribute" business model: a number of banks originate loans, which they can securitize to a number of sophisticated investors. Problems of this kind are extensively studied in frameworks of optimal contracting in the presence of asymmetric information.[1] This section discusses a streamlined model that is an introduction to the idea of skin in the game. However, this model does not address details on optimal financial contracting; optimal financial contracting is only studied in later sections of this chapter, although not precisely in the context of securitization.

We assume that investors are sophisticated in that they are able to obtain expected returns equal to ρ—the "alternative investments" return. Moreover, banks and investors act competitively and are specialists in their business: only investors have a reservation expected return equal to ρ, and only banks can manufacture securities out of the original loans. Chapter 14 provides a succinct description of the market for mortgage-backed securities—a very famous instance that illustrates the mechanisms in this section.

We consider a single, representative bank, which extends borrowers a loan of size equal to N that is subject to a loss. The loan rate is implied by the amount of resources made available to borrowers, kN, and their alternative usage: it is $1-k$, and is determined endogenously (see, e.g., (5.11) and figure 5.3). Loss is denoted with $\tilde{l}N$, where $\tilde{l} \in [0,1]$ is a random variable described below. Therefore, if the bank distributes the entire loan to investors, the expected return required by the investors on this loan satisfies $\frac{1-E(\tilde{l})}{s} \geq 1+\rho$, where $s \equiv \frac{S}{N}$ and S is the price of the loan paid by the investors. The inequality reflects the assumption that the investors would walk away from this deal should the price not be enough to guarantee an expected return at least as large as ρ. By the assumption of competition among investors,

$$s = \frac{1-E(\tilde{l})}{1+\rho}. \tag{5.3}$$

The bank is adverse to the risk of default on the loan that it has originated. To illustrate, the bank may be subject to value at risk (VaR) constraints,[2] which make it averse to uncertainties regarding loan performance. The bank can mitigate this risk while securitizing the loan: the bank can decide to sell a fraction χ of the loan it originated for a value equal to χs. First, we will study the bank's incentives to securitize these loans in a market with symmetric information; second, we will study if and how the bank's incentives could be aligned to those of investors in markets with moral hazard.

5.3.2.1 Full insurance, full securitization

Securitization resembles insurance: a bank that originates a loan may wish to resell this loan, thereby avoiding the risk of default. Similar to standard conclusions in the insurance literature and under conditions identified below, the bank finds it optimal to securitize the entire loan. This full insurance case can be understood through a very simple model with

1. For example, DeMarzo (2005) considers security designs arising through signaling: a bank retaining a portion of these loans would signal a good loan quality to investors. In Hartman-Glaser, Piskorski, and Tchistyi (2012), securitization is framed within a dynamic contracting model with moral hazard.

2. A VaR constraint imposes the bank to limit exposure to risk. Chapter 14 provides an overview regarding VaR in the credit space and existing regulation.

two states of nature, such that $\tilde{l} = l < 1$ with probability p and $\tilde{l} = 0$ with complementary probability. Therefore, in the bad state, the payoff to the bank is w_b, and in the good state, the payoff is w_g, where

$$\begin{cases} \dfrac{w_b}{N} = (1-\chi)(1-l) + \chi s - k \\ \dfrac{w_g}{N} = (1-\chi) + \chi s - k \end{cases} \tag{5.4}$$

and kN is the amount of money lent to the borrower. The bank payoffs are equal to the value of the securitized assets sold to the investors net of the resources originally lent to the borrowers, $\chi S - kN$, plus asset performance regarding the retained proportion of the original loan, $(1-\chi)(N - \tilde{l}N)$. Eqs. (5.4) clearly show that securitization allows the bank to smooth loan risks. Randomness is obviously eliminated with full securitization, $\chi = 100\%$. We will see that, if $\rho = 0$, it is indeed in the bank's interest to proceed with full securitization.

We model bank's aversion to risk while assuming the bank maximizes the following objective:

$$\max_{\chi \in [0,1]} pu(w_b) + (1-p)u(w_g),$$

where w_b and w_g are as in eqs. (5.4) and u is an increasing and concave function. The first-order conditions for this program lead to

$$\frac{u'(w_b)}{u'(w_g)} = \frac{1-p}{p} \frac{\rho + lp}{l(1-p) - \rho(1-l)},$$

where we have used eq. (5.3) to substitute for the equilibrium price and have used $E(\tilde{l}) = lp$.

We assume that ρ is small enough to make the ratio of the marginal utilities across states strictly positive and bounded. In the special case in which $\rho = 0$, we have that $u'(w_b) = u'(w_g)$, that is, $w_b = w_g$, which can only be achieved through $\chi = 1$: full securitization, as anticipated. This conclusion is reminiscent of well-known conclusions in the insurance literature: full insurance may result when insurers face perfect competition. The condition $\rho = 0$ parallels insurance markets outcomes, by which risks are priced through actuarial methods: securitized assets are valued as expected cash flows (see (5.3)). We now proceed with a tractable model that allows us to examine details of this securitization market in the presence of asymmetric information. We will first provide a framework in the symmetric information case.

5.3.2.2 *Symmetric information again*

Let us extend the two constraints in (5.4), assuming that losses are a continuous random variable, such that the final payoff to the bank is

$$\frac{\tilde{w}}{N} = (1-\chi)(1-\tilde{l}) + \chi s - k, \tag{5.5}$$

where $\tilde{l}$ is uniformly distributed on $(0, X)$ and $X < 1$; thus $E_X(\tilde{l}) = \frac{1}{2}X$ and $var_X(\tilde{l}) = \frac{1}{12}X^2$, where we emphasize the dependence on X for reasons discussed below. We assume that the bank has a mean-variance objective, thereby choosing a level of securitization equal to

$$\chi^* = \arg \max_{\chi \in [0,1]} E_X\left(\frac{\tilde{w}}{N}\right) - \frac{\tau}{2} var_X\left(\frac{\tilde{w}}{N}\right), \quad \tau > 0.$$

The trade-off of this optimization problem is the following. On the one hand, by increasing the extent of securitization, χ, the expected payoff increases due to the higher securitization proceeds, χs in eq. (5.5). On the other hand, a higher χ implies a lower recovery value, $(1-\chi)(1-\tilde{l})$. On average, the net benefit of an increase in securitization is obviously negative, because the price investors pay, s, is lower than the recovery value,

$$E_X(s - (1 - \tilde{l})) = -\frac{\rho}{1+\rho}(1 - E_X(\tilde{l})).$$

But to this expected negative marginal gain corresponds a positive marginal benefit due to a variance reduction, $\tau(1-\chi)\, var_X(\tilde{l})$. By equating the expected marginal gain to this marginal benefit and rearranging, we get the optimal retention rate:

$$1 - \chi^* = \frac{1 - E_X(\tilde{l})}{\tau var_X(\tilde{l})} \frac{\rho}{1+\rho}. \tag{5.6}$$

We assume parameter values are such that the solution is interior. Note the full insurance result: if $\rho = 0$, the optimal securitization rate is $\chi^* = 100\%$. In general, the retention rate $1 - \chi^*$ is increasing with ρ: the higher the expected return required by the sophisticated investors, the lower the securitization revenues (i.e., χs) and then the incentives to securitize. We now proceed to analyze how this conclusion is modified when the bank and the investors are asymmetrically informed on the loan quality.

5.3.2.3 *Asymmetric information: incentive-compatible constraint*

Credit standards have been assumed to be given so far. However, the borrowers' quality may be a decision variable: while anticipating that a significant proportion of the loans will be securitized (and, therefore, sold to outside investors) at a relatively high price, the bank may lose the incentives to adopt proper due diligence and, in general, to research for good borrowers. Moral hazard comes into play because the assets quality to end users (i.e., the likelihood of default of the original loans) now depends on the efforts the bank makes while originating the loans.

If the investors understood the bank's behavior, they would not be willing to pay the price they pay while assuming the bank sells products with good credit standards. To illustrate, and relying on previous notation, suppose that, if the bank does not make any efforts while selecting its borrowers, the upper limit to the loss distribution is $X = b$. Instead, if the bank invests in resources to improve the borrowers' credit standards, $X = b - \varepsilon$, where $\varepsilon \in (0, b)$. Now, these investments cost C, and the investors anticipate that the bank, unless properly incentivized, would not invest in these resources while selling the securitized assets for a high price (they would then misreport in having exerted all efforts). Absent these incentives, the investors are only willing to pay a price per notional equal to s_b, not the higher price $s_{b-\varepsilon}$, where, and consistent with eq. (5.3),

$$s_b = \frac{1 - E_b(\tilde{l})}{1+\rho}. \tag{5.7}$$

How can investors incentivize the bank to originate loans with high standards? It is a principal-agent problem, where investors act as the "principal" and the bank acts as the "agent." The investors want to ensure the bank invests in resources while originating the loans. In turn, a bank would do so, provided the post securitization increase in its payoff (due to a better loans quality) exceeds the costs of a better loan quality, namely,

$$\begin{aligned} &(1-\chi)(1-E_{b-\varepsilon}(\tilde{l})) + \chi s_{b-\varepsilon} - \frac{\tau}{2}(1-\chi)^2\, var_{b-\varepsilon}(\tilde{l}) - C \\ &\geq (1-\chi)(1-E_b(\tilde{l})) + \chi s_{b-\varepsilon} - \frac{\tau}{2}(1-\chi)^2\, var_b(\tilde{l}). \end{aligned} \tag{5.8}$$

The LHS of (5.8) is the payoff per notional accruing to the bank when it exerts an effort. The RHS is the payoff accruing to the bank when it does not.[3] Note that, in both cases, the investors are willing to pay the price that reflects the asset fundamentals when the bank puts efforts, $s_{b-\varepsilon}$. That is, the investors cannot observe whether the bank will exert (or have already exerted) any effort; however, they are willing to sign a contract in which they stand ready to pay the high price $s_{b-\varepsilon}$ but under the *incentive-compatibility* constraint (5.8).

In other words, the contract specifies a securitization rate $\bar{\chi}$ satisfying (5.8) and a securitization price $s_{b-\varepsilon}$, and the bank will then originate a loan retaining a proportion equal to $1-\bar{\chi}$ while securitizing this loan. In case the bank had already originated a loan with good credit standards (it may have, under parameter conditions specified below), the bank will then decide whether it is in its interest to securitize it at $\bar{\chi}$, as explained in detail in the next subsection. Note that if the bank had already originated the loan with no efforts and this fact becomes public information, there would not be obvious viable ways to proceed with contracting as explained in this section: the trivial solution would be that in the symmetric information case (see eq. (5.6)), with low securitization prices, $X=b$.

The contract is incentive compatible if the bank is able to retain a proportion $1-\chi>0$ of the securitized loans. By retaining risks, the bank signals to the investors that its interests are aligned regarding credit standards. Let us illustrate with a simple example. Assume the costs are $C=c\varepsilon$ for some constant c, and rewrite (5.8) as an equality

$$(1-\chi) + (1-\chi)^2 \frac{\tau}{12}(2b-\varepsilon) = 2c. \tag{5.9}$$

The LHS of this equation reflects the payoff increase the bank experiences while adopting good credit standards: (i) lower expected losses and (ii) lower volatility. The RHS

3. Both payoffs are calculated by including the amount k provided to the borrowers; this amount then cancels out from both sides of the inequality.

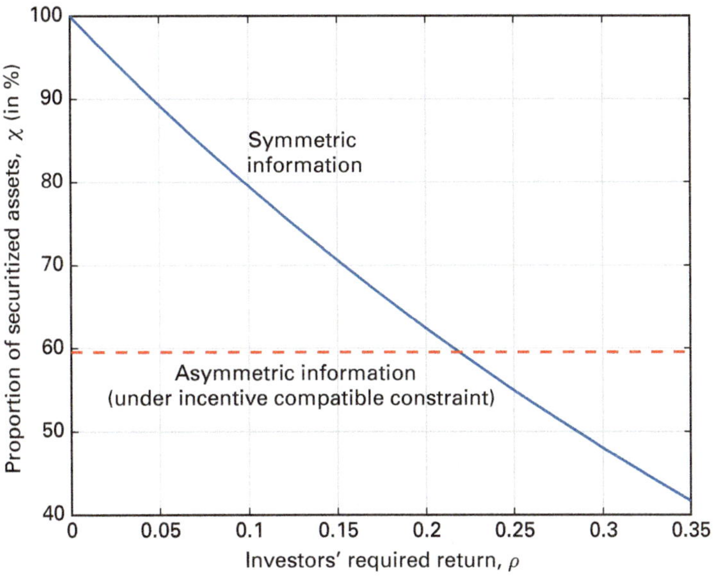

Figure 5.2
Proportion of securitized assets as a function of investors' sophistication. The solid line is this proportion in a market with symmetric information and poor credit standards (i.e., χ^* in eq. (5.6) with $X=b$). The dashed line is the proportion in a contract between banks and investors that is incentive compatible regarding the credit standards adopted by the bank (i.e., $\bar{\chi}$ solution to eq. (5.9)). Parameter values are $\tau=5, b=0.8$, $\varepsilon=0.2$ and $c=0.25$.

reflects costs for the adoption of a rigorous lending scheme. The contract is incentive compatible in correspondence of securitization levels $\bar{\chi}$ such that eq. (5.9) holds true. Given the parameter values in the legend of figure 5.2, we have $\bar{\chi}=0.59546$.[4] Figure 5.2 depicts the optimal securitization rate as a function of the investors' sophistication, that is, χ^* in eq. (5.6) as a function of ρ, assuming that $X=b$ (solid line). The horizontal dashed line is the retention rate $\bar{\chi}$.

Note that in a market with symmetric information, a bank would choose a retention rate $1-\chi^* \approx 40\%$ (approximately the same as in the market with moral hazard and contracting) only when the investors' expected return $\rho \approx 22\%$: the price of the securitized assets has to be sufficiently low to discourage the bank to securitize too much. But in a market plagued with moral hazard, and based on more realistic assumptions on investors' sophistication (i.e., $\rho < 22\%$), the retention rate suggested by the contract is higher (i.e., $\chi^* > \bar{\chi}$). The problem is that while securitizing more, the bank would not be properly incentivized to adopt the credit standards compatible with the promised amount of efforts.[5]

The point of this model is to emphasize that high retention rates may be needed to support securitization processes with underlying quality assets. Without such retention rates, a market may well fail to arise, especially when asset prices are high (in our examples, $s_{b-\varepsilon}$).

4. To illustrate, Chomsisengphet and Pennington-Cross (2006) report securitization rates in 2003 to amount for approximately 76% (conventional loans), 35% (jumbo), and 59% (subprime).

5. For example, consider the extreme case $\chi=100\%$. In this case, the equality in (5.9) is not satisfied in the presence of due diligence costs.

A default experience higher than that implied by asset prices may then be symptomatic of misselling or, at best, of the investors' poor understanding of the banks' incentive problems.[6] For example, during the 2007 subprime crisis, default frequencies for securitized loans were considerably higher for those loans that had higher ease of securitization (see Keys, Mukherjee, Seru, and Vig, 2010). We shall return to these observations in chapter 14, which describes additional critical aspects of the unfolding of the 2007–2008 credit crisis (see section 14.5).

5.3.2.4 *Participation constraints and loan rates*

In addition to being incentive compatible, the contract must be such that the bank cannot obtain better opportunities elsewhere. This condition gives rise to *participation constraints*: the bank must be incentivized to sign the contract in the first place.

First, the bank has the alternative of not securitizing the loans; therefore, the payoff accruing to the bank while securitizing at $\bar{\chi}$ must exceed the payoff it would obtain while not securitizing at all:

$$\begin{aligned}&(1-\bar{\chi})(1-E_{b-\varepsilon}(\tilde{l}))+\bar{\chi}s_{b-\varepsilon}-\frac{\tau}{2}(1-\bar{\chi})^2\, var_{b-\varepsilon}(\tilde{l})-C\\&\geq(1-E_b(\tilde{l}))-\frac{\tau}{2}var_b(\tilde{l}).\end{aligned}\tag{5.10}$$

Second, the bank has the alternative of not originating the loan and investing the original amount of cash kN in the risk-free asset and the market portfolio. Therefore, this alternative must yield a payoff that is less than that originating from securitization:

$$(1-\bar{\chi})(1-E_{b-\varepsilon}(\tilde{l}))+\bar{\chi}s_{b-\varepsilon}-\frac{\tau}{2}(1-\bar{\chi})^2\, var_{b-\varepsilon}(\tilde{l})-C-k\geq\frac{1}{2\tau}\lambda^2+Rk-k,\tag{5.11}$$

where $R\equiv 1+r$, r is the safe interest rate, and λ is the Sharpe ratio on the market portfolio (see eq. (1.63) in chapter 1).[7] This constraint determines the loan rate $1-k$.

The inequality (5.10) is satisfied for the parameter values of this exercise (and for the values of ρ in figure 5.2). Further, with these parameter values and without the option of securitizing, the bank would be better off exerting an effort rather than not (that is, (5.8) holds for $\chi=0$), and yet still, the bank prefers signing the contract for $\bar{\chi}$ rather than exerting an effort and retaining the loan (albeit for values of $\rho\leq 18\%$). Thus, securitization may allow the bank to mitigate risks consistent with its risk appetite.

Finally, figure 5.3 plots the loan rate the bank requires when (5.11) holds as an equality, the risk-free rate $r=0.01$, and the market Sharpe ratio is $\lambda=0.4$ (solid line); the dashed

6. In the model, the credit quality X (the upper limit of the distribution of $\tilde{l}$) can be inferred through eq. (5.7) as $X=2(1-s_X(1+\rho))$. The frequency of default decreases with the securitized price. Therefore, if the securitized asset is sold at $s_{b-\varepsilon}$ (when, in fact, the risk is $X=b$), one should observe a default frequency higher than predicted by the original sale price $s_{b-\varepsilon}$. Asset mispricing may lead to systemic risk (see section 14.5 in chapter 14).

7. Investing $w\equiv k$ in the risk-free asset and the market portfolio leaves next period wealth equal to $w'=\pi(\mu_M-r)+Rw+\pi B\tilde{u}$, consistent with the notation setup in chapter 1 (see sections 1.2 and 1.3). Given its mean-variance objective function, the bank would select a proportion of the market portfolio equal to π^* in eq. (1.42) (chapter 1), such that its value function, $E(w')-\frac{\tau}{2}var(w')$, would equal the first two terms of the RHS of (5.11).

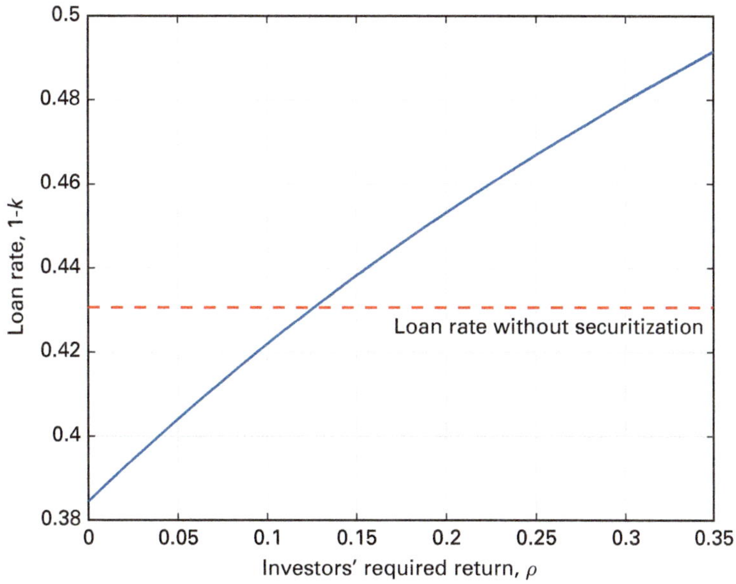

Figure 5.3
The solid line depicts the loan rate $1-k$ required by the participation constraint (5.11) (as an equality) as a function of investors' sophistication. The dashed line is the loan rate required when the bank makes an effort and does not securitize the loan. Parameter values are as in figure 5.2, and $r=0.01$ and $\lambda=0.4$.

line is the value of an hypothetical loan rate the bank would require when it generates and retains 100% of a high quality loan and pays a cost for it (and does not compare this investment with the market portfolio). For comparison, the expected loss is $E_{b-\varepsilon}(\tilde{l})=30\%$ and $E_b(\tilde{l})=40\%$. The required loan rate is increasing in ρ because a smaller securitized price, $s_{b-\varepsilon}$, requires a lower initial investment k to maintain the balance in (5.11).

5.3.3 Signaling: Callable Bonds, Equity, and Short-Term Debt

A continuum of entrepreneurs have the skills to undertake a project that delivers a random gross return $\tilde{R}$ in two periods. We assume that $\tilde{R}$ can take on three values, $\tilde{R}\in\{R_{uu},R_{ud},R_{dd}\}$, where $R_{uu}>R_{ud}\geq R_{dd}$, and that a partial resolution of uncertainty occurs at time $t=1$, as illustrated by figure 5.4. Precisely, the entrepreneurs have different types, and each type has a chance p to reach the upper node at $t=1$ from time 0. We assume that p is distributed on $(0,\bar{p})$ for some $\bar{p}$. Therefore, the higher p, the higher the project quality for the entrepreneur of type p.

From the upper node at time $t=1$, the chances of further upward movements are fixed. Notably, we assume that, at time $t=1$, the probabilities of events are known and independent of the firms' type. Thus, this model can be thought of as one in which economic performance results from both economy-wide productivity (the entrepreneurs' skills) and purely exogenous factors (such as business cycles). In the numerical example examined below, we assume that the probability of reaching node R_{uu} from node B_u is $\frac{2}{3}$. Note that the firm does not achieve any profits at $t=1$: in this model, passage of time only results in information revelation. Consistent with this description, we assume that any investments made at time 0 cannot be liquidated at time 1.

5.3.3.1 Project quality uncertainty

To start the project, the entrepreneurs need to invest some capital F, and we assume that their own capital (equity), W_0, may only cover a portion of these investment needs, that is, $W_0 < F$. Therefore, the entrepreneurs would like to access a financial market. For simplicity, we consider a standardized financial market, that is, one in which the only loans made available by investors, if any, have nominal size N, with $N \in (R_{ud}, R_{uu})$. Finally, we assume that both entrepreneurs and investors are risk neutral and that the interest rate paid on safe loans is zero. Crucially, potential investors are unaware of the entrepreneurs' quality—they are only aware of the upper bound $\bar{p}$.

We consider *debt contracts* as vehicles of resource transfer between firms and investors. Moreover, and because the project does not deliver any payoff until time 2, the firm ideally seeks for long-term financing, that is, a loan expiring at time 2, with no renegotiations at time 1, embedding, however, the optionalities described below.

In a market with symmetric information, investors know the entrepreneurs' types, and a firm of type p is able to raise $B = pB_u + (1-p)\,B_d$, where

$$B_u = \frac{2}{3}N + \frac{1}{3}R_{ud}, \quad B_d = \frac{2}{3}R_{ud} + \frac{1}{3}R_{dd}.$$

Figure 5.4 depicts the loan payoff at time 2 as well as the market value of the loan in the remaining nodes of the tree, B_u and B_d. It is straightforward to show that there is a threshold value of p depending on F, say $\underline{p}_F$, such that only entrepreneurs with $p \geq \underline{p}_F$ may be able to raise the capital needed to cover the initial costs, that is, $B \geq F - W_0$.

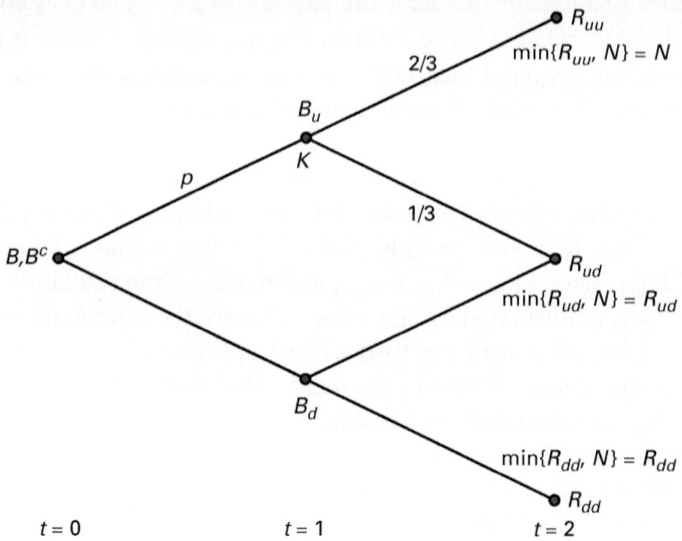

Figure 5.4
This figure depicts the payoffs of a straight bond and a callable bond on a binomial tree. Conditionally upon receiving funding, a firm may generate a random payoff $\tilde{R} \in \{R_{uu}, R_{ud}, R_{dd}\}$ at $t=2$. At time 0, each firm has probability to achieve upward movements equal to p. At time 1, the probability of upward movements is fixed and equal to $\frac{2}{3}$ in both the B_u and the B_d node. The value of the straight (resp., callable) bond at $t=1$ is either B_u or B_d (resp., K or B_d). At $t=0$, the value of the straight and callable bonds is denoted with B and B^c, resp.

In a market with asymmetric information, the entrepreneurs face the problem of credibly communicating their types to investors. Consider a high quality firm, that is, a firm with a high p. This firm has good chances of achieving node B_u at time 1 where it would benefit from improved financing conditions. Now, investors may obtain signals on the entrepreneur's skills only after the project is undertaken. As a way to implement an exchange mechanism, the entrepreneurs may try to transfer private pieces of information to investors while undertaking costly actions.

5.3.3.2 *Derivatives as signals*

To signal their value, entrepreneurs may issue a *callable bond*, that is, a contract giving the firm the right to redeem the loan at time 1 at a prespecifed strike $K \le B_u$. Upon exercise, the firm will issue another short-term bond at $t = 1$, valued at B_u. Thus, upon exercise, the firm receives a "money shower" equal to $B_u - K$ while still accessing the capital it needs to keep doing activities until time 2.

When the entrepreneurs credibly communicate their types, the decision whether to issue a callable or a straight bond does not affect the firm's profitability: the value of the option embedded in the callable bond is priced in at time 0, consistent with standard conclusions in frictionless financial markets. But we assume that there is a market imperfection: a bond callable at a strike K entails an intermediation cost equal to $\mathcal{C}(K) \equiv c(1 - K)$ for some constant c; the higher the "expropriation value" from the investors in case of exercise, the higher the intermediation fee. This assumption can be justified by arguing that, as K lowers, the resulting derivative embedded into the loan becomes more exotic, which necessitates more search or compliance costs.[8]

Therefore, the expected profits for an entrepreneur of type p are

$$\Pi(\pi, p, K) \equiv E_p(\tilde{R}) - E_p(\min\{\tilde{R}, N\}) + p(B_u - K) + B_\pi^c - \mathcal{C}(K) - F, \tag{5.12}$$

where $E_p(\cdot)$ denotes the expectation taken under the probability p. The first term in (5.12) is the return on the project and the second is (minus) the expected repayment. The second term is the same as the expected payoff from a straight bond: we are assuming that, upon exercise at time 1, the firm reissues a new bond, expiring at time 2 and with face value N. The third term is the money shower the entrepreneur expects in case of exercise. The fourth term is the value of the callable bond received at time 0, $B_\pi^c = \pi K + (1 - \pi) B_d$, where π denotes the probability conjectured by the investors. The last terms are the intermediation cost and the initial required investment.

In a market with symmetric information, $\pi = p$, such that the second, third, and fourth term in eq. (5.12) cancel out: the value of a callable bond (fourth term) equals the value of a straight bond (second) minus the option value to call (third). We want to study a mechanism such that, indeed, firms are able to signal their value, that is, $\pi = p$.

Rearrange eq. (5.12) as follows:

$$\Pi(\pi, p, K) = E_p(\tilde{R}) + B_\pi^c - B_p^c - \mathcal{C}(K) - F \tag{5.13}$$

8. We assume these costs are paid in advance. The predictions of the model would be similar if these costs were only paid contingent on the option exercise.

where $B^c_p \equiv pK + (1-p)\,B_d$ is the hypothetical price of the callable bond when $\pi = p$.[9] It is straightforward to calculate the price difference originating from the off-equilibrium difference in beliefs, $B^c_\pi - B^c_p$. To simplify the expression for this price difference, we assume that $R_{ud} = R_{dd} \equiv R_0$, such that the expected profits can be written as

$$\Pi(\pi, p, K) = R_0 + \frac{2}{3}p\,(R_{uu} - R_0) + (\pi - p)\,(K - R_0) - C(K) - F.$$

We now assume that the investors believe that the entrepreneurs signal their value by choosing a strike K. We conjecture that the investors rely on a *signaling schedule* $K \longmapsto \pi(K)$, that is, a schedule such that the strike price K proposed by a given firm reveals its true quality. For example, an entrepreneur with a probability $p = p_0$ truthfully signals their value by choosing a $K_0 : p_0 = \pi(K_0)$. In other words, the strike is a message the firm sends to the investors. How can the investors make sure this schedule incentivizes the entrepreneurs to send truthful messages? Consider the following "no-mimicking condition":

$$\Pi(\pi(K_0 + \Delta K), p_0, K_0 + \Delta K) \leq \Pi(\pi(K_0), p_0, K_0). \tag{5.14}$$

The LHS of (5.14) is the expected profit when a firm with $p = p_0$ announces, instead, to have a probability of success equal to $p_0' \equiv \pi(K_0 + \Delta K)$: by proposing $K_0 + \Delta K$, the firm leads investors to infer that the firm type is p_0' rather than p_0. The RHS is the expected profit for the same firm when it truthfully announces its type. The previous inequality states that the schedule $\pi(\cdot)$ must be such that no entrepreneur has incentives to pretend to be of a different type. Replacing $p_0 = \pi(K_0)$ into (5.14) and rearranging terms leaves

$$0 \geq \frac{\pi(K_0 + \Delta K) - \pi(K_0)}{\Delta K}(K_0 - R_0 + \Delta K) - \frac{C(K_0 + \Delta K) - C(K_0)}{\Delta K}.$$

Consider a signaling schedule that leaves the entrepreneur indifferent between mimicking or not and a small deviation from the truth, that is, $\Delta K \to 0$. Under regularity conditions, the previous condition becomes an ordinary differential equation

$$0 = \pi'(K)(K - R_0) - C'(K), \tag{5.15}$$

subject to appropriate boundary conditions discussed below. Given the previous assumption on C, the general solution to eq. (5.15) is

$$\pi(K) = A - c\ln(K - R_0), \tag{5.16}$$

for some constant A discussed below. We also provide a discussion regarding the domain of K below.

9. Eq. (5.13) follows by the assumption that time 1 probabilities are independent of the type. If these probabilities were still as they were at time 0, the third term in (5.12) should be replaced by $p\,(B_{u,\pi} - K)$, where $B_{u,\pi} = \pi N + (1-\pi)\,R_{ud}$ is the bond value conjectured by the investors. In this case, the RHS of eq. (5.13) should be corrected with an additional term equal to $p\,(B_{u,\pi} - B_{u,p})$. This additional term would complicate the analysis.

5.3.3.3 *Optimality and the Spence-Mirrlees condition*

The justification for having considered the no-mimicking condition at its marginal level (i.e., as an equality) is that eq. (5.15) is the first-order condition to the problem, $\max_K \Pi(\pi(K), p, K)$, evaluated at the equilibrium $p = \pi(K)$. Is this solution a maximum? Define the expected profits for firm p when the firm announces to be $\hat{p}$ through its message K, namely,

$$V(K(\hat{p}), p) \equiv R_0 + \frac{2}{3}p(R_{uu} - R_0) + (\hat{p} - p)(K(\hat{p}) - R_0) - C(K(\hat{p})) - F, \tag{5.17}$$

where $K(\cdot)$ denotes the inverse of the signaling schedule and $\hat{p} = \pi(K(\hat{p}))$. Appendix 5.A shows that, to be incentive compatible, the signaling schedule has to be such that

$$V_{12}(K(p), p) K'(p) \geq 0, \tag{5.18}$$

where subscripts denote partial derivatives. Indeed, it is straightforward to see that $V_{12}(K(\hat{p}), p)|_{\hat{p}=p} = -1$. Because $K'(p) < 0$, the schedule in eq. (5.16) is incentive compatible.

The condition (5.18) is known as *Spence-Mirrlees condition* and carries a very intuitive meaning. Note that $-V_1(K(\hat{p}), p)$ is the marginal benefit of decreasing K. Requiring that $-V_{12}(K(\hat{p}), p)|_{\hat{p}=p} > 0$ means that, in equilibrium, this marginal benefit increases as the project quality increases. Intuitively, the firm benefits from increasing the gap, $B_u - K$ (the "money shower"), and the expected benefit (the third term in (5.12)) increases with p and results in the previous expression for V_{12}.

5.3.3.4 *Signaling equilibria*

We now describe the equilibria in detail. First, we identify the lowest level of the strike $\underline{K}_A$ (say) that returns the exogenously given upper bound, $\bar{p}$. Using eq. (5.16), we find that

$$\pi(K) = \bar{p} + c \ln\left(\frac{\underline{K}_A - R_0}{K - R_0}\right), \quad \underline{K}_A \equiv R_0 + e^{\frac{1}{c}(A - \bar{p})}. \tag{5.19}$$

Second, we require that, for all $K \geq \underline{K}_A$, (i) $B^c(K) \equiv B^c_\pi > F - W_0$ (sufficient funding); (ii) $\Pi(\pi(K), \pi(K), K) \geq W_0$ (expected profits exceed initial investments); and (iii) $K \leq B_u$ (liquidity constraint at time 1). In the remainder, we fix $N = 1$.

There is a continuum of equilibria that satisfy the schedule in eq. (5.19) under the previous constraints and, thus, a set of continuum of signaling equilibria, each arising for some particular values of A. Precisely, both the domain and shape of the schedule depend on these values of A. And each of these equilibria is a *separating* equilibrium: the entrepreneurs send different messages to investors, and this communication is credible.[10] For each of these values of A, then, the signaling schedule acts as a *screening* device.

Figure 5.5 depicts two possible schedules resulting for $A = 0.10$ and $A = 0.20$. In these numerical examples, the strike domain is $[\underline{K}_A, \bar{K}_A]$, where $\bar{K}_A$ denotes the break-even strike for a given A, that is, $\bar{K}_A : \Pi(\pi(\bar{K}_A), \pi(\bar{K}_A), \bar{K}_A) = W_0$. The schedules thus coincide with

10. In a *pooling* equilibrium, the agents with superior information send the same messages to receivers, regardless of their type.

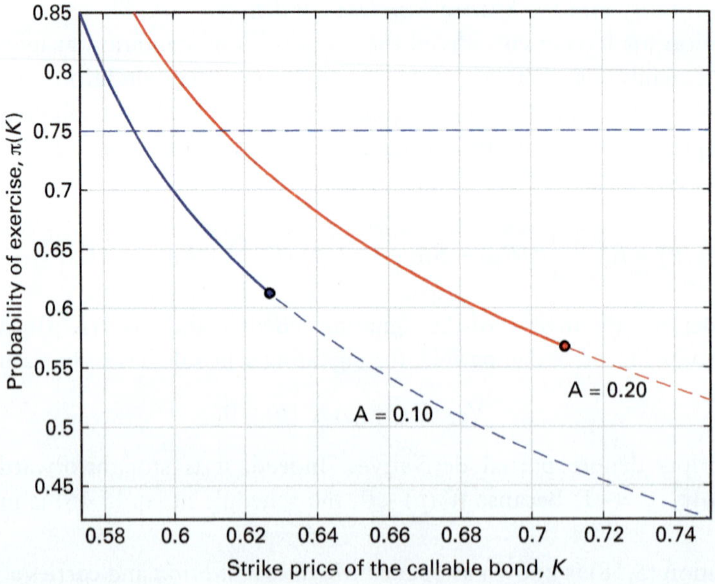

Figure 5.5
This picture depicts the signaling schedule $\pi(K)$ in eq. (5.19), a function of the strike price of the callable bond in the two equilibria with $A=0.10$ and $A=0.20$ and remaining parameters set equal to $R_0=0.55$, $F=0.60$, $\bar{p}=0.85$, $c=0.20$. In these examples, $W_0=0.10$ and $R_{uu}=1.10$, and the schedules coincide with the solid lines on the domain $[\underline{K}_A, \bar{K}_A]$. The dashed horizontal line identifies the strike values of the callable bond issued by an entrepreneur with $p=75\%$ in the two equilibria.

the solid lines between the points $(\underline{K}_A, \pi(\underline{K}_A))$ and $(\bar{K}_A, \pi(\bar{K}_A))$. In these examples, the previous conditions (i) and (iii) are satisfied; condition (ii) is not, in correspondence of the strikes beyond the breakeven $\bar{K}_A$, to which correspond the dashed curves.

Note that the message communicated by the entrepreneur changes from one equilibrium to another. Consider an entrepreneur with a probability of success $p=75\%$. In the equilibrium with $A=0.10$, they signal their quality by issuing a callable bond with strike price $K\approx 0.59$. In the equilibrium with $A=0.20$, the same entrepreneur issues a callable bond at a strike $K\approx 0.61$. Further, some entrepreneurs may start the project in some equilibrium and may not in others. For example, in the equilibrium with $A=0.10$, an entrepreneur with $p=60\%$ is only able to credibly sell at a strike beyond their breakeven: the entrepreneur has no incentives to issue debt and start any activity in the first place; however, the same entrepreneur issues debt and produces in the equilibrium with $A=0.20$.

5.3.3.5 Extensions

The model predictions in figure 5.5 rely on the assumption that, at time 1, the investor is either given K (and another short-term bond is issued at B_u) or R_0 (in which case the firm is in default). The investor can still claim the face value N but only from node B_u. The model can be extended for one additional period so as to allow the investor to have the potential to claim the face value even from node B_d at time 1, as in the bold path of figure 5.6. In other terms, in the model of figure 5.6, the callable bond may always be alive and lead to face value without any option exercise.

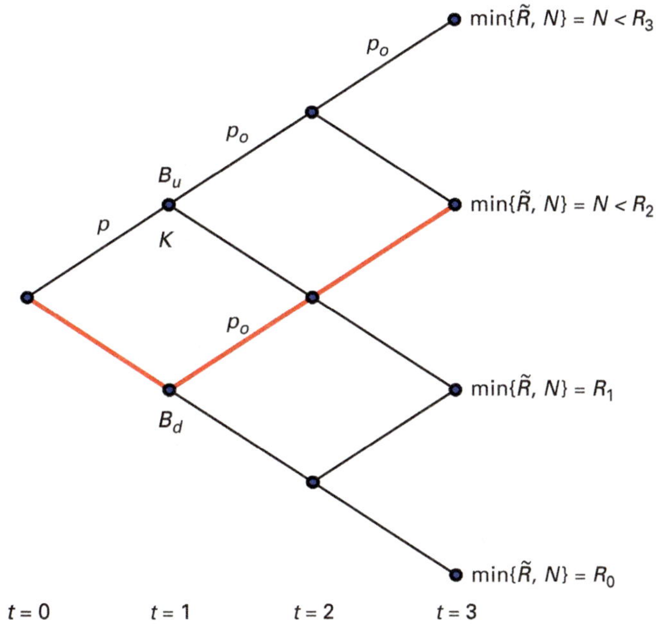

Figure 5.6
This figure depicts the payoffs of a callable bond on a binomial tree. Conditionally on receiving funding, a firm may generate a random payoff $\tilde{R} \in \left\{R_j\right\}_{j=\{0,1,2,3\}}$ at $t=3$. At time 0, each firm has probability to achieve upward movements equal to p. From time 1 on, upward movements probabilities are fixed and equal to p_o. The bold line identifies the path where the call option is not exercised and the investor receives the face value N.

In this model, there is a continuum of entrepreneurs, each of them having a probability to lead to upward movements at time 0 equal to p. From time 1 on, the probability of upward movements is fixed and publicly known to equal some p_o. Thus, the expression for the expected profits in eq. (5.12) is replaced by

$$\Pi(\pi, p, K) \equiv E_p(\tilde{R}) - E_p(\min\{\tilde{R}, N\}) + p(B_u - K) + B_\pi^c - C(K) - F,$$

where, now, $B_\pi^c = \pi K + (1-\pi) B_d$, and $B_d = p_o^2 N + 2p_o(1-p_o) R_1 + (1-p_o)^2 R_0$. It is straightforward to show that the signaling schedule still satisfies eq. (5.15), but with B_d replacing R_0.

5.3.4 Other Classical Problems: Short-Term Debt and Equity Sales

In the previous model, a transaction takes place due to signaling costs: issuing callable bonds costs may allow entrepreneurs to signal their activity is solid enough to justify the intermediation costs. In fact, a callable bond is a short-term contract—a contract, that is, by which an entrepreneur signals their quality while displaying no concerns for a costly renegotiation of terms at a future date.[11] In this section, we consider similar mechanisms. First, we briefly discuss the role of short-term debt as a signaling device: entrepreneurs

11. It has been known since at least Aghion and Bolton (1987) that short-term contracting enables rational agents to signal their type through their willingness to contract again in the future.

may signal their type by issuing short-term debt, which may be costly because refinancing may occur at adverse conditions. Thus, the more a firm issues short-term debt, the more it signals solid perspectives.

Second, we review a model in which entrepreneurs signal their types by issuing equity and retaining portions of it. In equilibrium, the more they retain, the more they signal their value. Finally, we end this section through a short digression on initial public offering (IPO). Issuing equity through an IPO seems to be a delicate issue because information may be asymmetrically dispersed among IPO investors. The result may be an underpricing of the IPO. Note that this digression is a variation on a theme: it regards a problem of asymmetric information among investors (adverse selection, as we shall see) rather than a problem of asymmetric information between the equity issuer and the investors' community (a signaling problem). We deal with IPO underpricing in this section because it complements the analysis of equity issuance in a signaling context.

5.3.4.1 Short-term debt

It is a well-established fact that firms with high credit ratings issue short-term debt such as commercial paper and that firms with lower ratings tend to finance through long-term liabilities. These facts may arise as a signaling outcome: firms may signal their value by securing less resources in the future than in the case with symmetric information, as in Diamond (1991). Tirole (2006, 254–256) considers another model along these lines based on moral hazard mechanisms and provides some additional discussion. Firms may be hurt by a liquidity shock, but firms of good type experience a lower chance of being hit by such a shock. Moral hazard is a friction that affects the refinancing market, which poses constraints on the extent to which borrowers may meet the liquidity shock. In a separating equilibrium, good firms are able to signal their value by willingly accepting a positive probability of discontinuing their project in case of a liquidity shock. This mechanism may be implemented throughout a "random credit line," by which firms of good type face a positive probability of not being able to access the funds they need to continue their activity. It is as if these firms were issuing higher debt (which, in some state of nature, they would not be able to repay) than in the case of symmetric information.

5.3.4.2 Equity

In a famous contribution, Leland and Pyle (1977) develop a model in which the entrepreneurs signal their value by selling proportions of ownership to outside investors. Thus, the proportion of retained ownership acts as a signal on the project quality: the higher the retained ownership, the higher the project quality. Intuitively, in the Leland and Pyle market, entrepreneurs are risk averse and would like to sell the whole project to outside investors. But, due to asymmetric information, they cannot. Since retaining ownership is costly, compared with the symmetric information market, they signal their value by retaining ownership. This mechanism works because, in the model, the better the project, the lower the costs of retaining ownership.

In the model, there is a continuum of entrepreneurs, each with a project that has normally distributed net returns, $\tilde{R} \sim N(\theta, \sigma^2)$, where σ^2 is constant and θ is uniformly distributed with support $[\underline{\theta}, \bar{\theta}]$.[12] The entrepreneur has some initial wealth W_0 but is risk averse and would like to sell this project to outside investors. In a market with symmetric information, this transaction would take place when risk sharing (see section 2.6.4 in chapter 2) is possible, for example, when the investors are risk neutral, an assumption we make in this section. Indeed, the investors would value the project at θ. However, the entrepreneur has utility function u, which satisfies

$$E[u(W_0 + \tilde{R})] < u(W_0 + E(\tilde{R})) = u(W_0 + \theta).$$

The LHS of this inequality is the utility of the entrepreneur when they do not sell the project, and the RHS is the utility when they do sell. That is, a transaction occurs due to risk sharing.

Next, assume that the entrepreneur's expected returns are only known to them, similar to the callable bond model of the previous section. We assume that the entrepreneur has CARA utility over their final wealth, $u(W) = -e^{-\tau W}$, $\tau > 0$. The investors' evaluation of the project would seem to be the average project quality, that is, a price $P \equiv \frac{1}{2}(\underline{\theta} + \bar{\theta})$. Therefore, an entrepreneur of type θ will accept to sell the project only if $E[u(W_0 + \tilde{R})] < u(W_0 + P)$. By the assumptions on the utility function, this inequality is satisfied if $\theta < \theta^* \equiv P + \frac{1}{2}\tau\sigma^2$. Therefore, the market becomes a market for lemons: only low quality projects are proposed to be sold.

We search for an equilibrium following the steps in section 5.3.1. We need to incorporate the investors' behavior while they anticipate adverse selection. The equilibrium price is a fixed point

$$P_o = E(\theta | \theta < \theta_o), \quad \theta_o = P_o + \frac{1}{2}\tau\sigma^2,$$

where $E(\theta | \theta < \theta_o) = \frac{1}{2}(\underline{\theta} + \theta_o)$. That is, $P_o = \underline{\theta} + \frac{1}{2}\tau\sigma^2$ and $\theta_o = \underline{\theta} + \tau\sigma^2$. Note that $P_o > P$, provided $\tau\sigma^2 > \bar{\theta} - \underline{\theta}$. In this case, all types would decide to go to the market. Otherwise, the high types, that is, those with $\theta \in [\theta_o, \bar{\theta}]$, prefer to pursue the project by self-financing it, and those who go to the market will sell "at discount," $P_o < P$, where the discount reflects a premium that even risk neutral investors would require due to asymmetric information: investors only know that low quality entrepreneurs ($\theta < \theta_o$) will go to the market and ignore who's who among them.

But, similarly as in the callable bond model of the previous section, the entrepreneurs may decide to transmit information to the investors. We assume that the entrepreneurs signal the quality of their projects by retaining a portion α of them. This portion, α, signals θ in that the investors believe in a signaling schedule $\alpha \longmapsto P(\alpha)$ that, in equilibrium, reveals the true expected return θ. Thus, and similarly as in the callable bond model, an entrepreneur of type θ chooses α to maximizes their expected utility, namely,

$$\begin{aligned} &\arg\max_{\alpha} E\left[u\left(W_0 + (1-\alpha)P(\alpha) + \alpha\tilde{R}\right)\right] \\ &= \arg\max_{\alpha}\left(W_0 + (1-\alpha)P(\alpha) + \alpha\theta - \frac{1}{2}\tau\alpha^2\sigma^2\right). \end{aligned}$$

12. The project requires an initial investment equal to \$1 (which the entrepreneurs can afford), and $\tilde{R}$ is the gain from this investment.

That is, if the entrepreneur retains α of the project, they will benefit from a random return equal to $\alpha\tilde{R}$ and an immediate cash-in equal to $(1-\alpha)P(\alpha)$, where $P(\alpha)$ is the project value conjectured by the investors.

The first-order conditions lead to

$$0=\theta-P(\alpha)+(1-\alpha)P'(\alpha)-\tau\sigma^2\alpha.$$

In equilibrium, $\theta=P(\alpha)$. The result is an ordinary differential equation solved by

$$P(\alpha)=A-\tau\sigma^2\left(\ln(1-\alpha)+\alpha\right)$$

for some constant A. Moreover, it is easy to check that the Spence-Mirrlees condition is satisfied with $Eu_{\alpha\theta}(\cdot)>0$: the marginal benefit of increasing α is increasing with the quality of the entrepreneur's project. Thus, there exists a set with a continuum of equilibria parametrized by the constant A, although some values of A may be ruled out, as discussed by Leland and Pyle.

5.3.4.3 *A variation on theme: IPO underpricing*

Why would a good firm go public and share its future profits with new investors? Very simply, the entrepreneurs may need capital necessary to expand their activities. While being public entails administrative and compliance costs, publicly listed companies have more visibility and may signal themselves as important market participants. An alternative to IPO is credit. However, credit may be expensive when financial intermediaries have high negotiation power. Finally, the entrepreneurs may be risk averse, and an IPO may be a way to implement risk sharing; however, due to asymmetric information, entrepreneurs may only be able to sell at discount, as in the previous section. The previous section also explains that signaling would enable entrepreneurs to transmit information to investors. We now focus on underpricing mechanisms arising from this asymmetric information, by which IPOs are made at discount.

That IPOs are made at discount is a well-known empirical regularity. Jenkinson and Ljungqvist (2001) contains an early review of the literature on IPOs. Note that IPOs are truly pervasive in practice to the extent that they give rise to dedicated investment strategies by professional investors. Thus, it seems unlikely that a price increase may systematically occur over the IPO's first day. We would need to focus on the very initial underpricing. This section describes a theoretical explanation inspired by work originally proposed by Rock (1982, 1986) and in an appendix of Beatty and Ritter (1986). The *winner's curse* is the mechanism at the heart of this explanation. It roughly works as follows. Suppose some investors are more informed than others regarding the value of the firm. The uninformed investors know that the informed investors will not participate in an overpriced IPO. Therefore, they know that the proportion of shares allocated to them will be higher when IPOs are overvalued. The winner's curse consists in being allocated more shares when these shares are overvalued—an instance of adverse selection. The model we describe is also useful because it allows us to anticipate an important theme, endogenous information acquisition: in the presence of informations costs, investors decide to become informed while comparing their utility with that of a would-be uninformed investor. This theme is dealt with in detail in chapter 10 (see section 10.6.1) when we describe the famous Grossman and Stiglitz (1980) model of the information content of asset prices.

So suppose that all investors are risk neutral and have initial resources to dedicate to IPOs that are equal to W. Informed investors pay a cost, C, in order to discover the asset value, v. Naturally, only once the cost is paid may investors come to know the asset value. By contrast, uninformed investors only know that v is random with some distribution, of which we provide some examples below. Let p be the underwriting IPO price. Naturally, informed investors do not participate in the IPO when $p > v$. Let N_I denote the number of informed investors, m the number of shares to allocate, and finally, α the proportion of shares allocated among the informed investors.

The expected profits accruing to all informed investors (before they pay the cost) are

$$\alpha m E(v-p)^+ - N_I C = 0, \tag{5.20}$$

where the equality follows by the risk neutrality assumption. Thus, information provides investors with an optionality: investors initially pay an initial cost, C, but they exercise the option to underwrite only when the IPO is underpriced, that is, when v is larger than the exercise price p. The problem truly resembles one in classic option pricing theory (see chapter 4). Instead, the expected profits of the uninformed investors satisfy

$$(1-\alpha) mE(v-p)^+ - mE(p-v)^+ = 0. \tag{5.21}$$

Now, eqs. (5.20) and (5.21) imply that

$$p = E(v) - \frac{N_I}{m} C. \tag{5.22}$$

That is, the IPO is underpriced.

We are not done yet because we need to determine N_I while imposing the condition that the expected profits for the uninformed and the informed are the same. To simplify this problem, we assume that the asset value is uniformed distributed, $v \sim U[0, \bar{v}]$, for some $\bar{v} > 0$. In appendix 5.A, we show that

$$E(v-p)^+ = \frac{1}{2\bar{v}} (\bar{v}-p)^2, \tag{5.23}$$

such that we can write (5.20) as

$$\alpha \frac{1}{2\bar{v}} (\bar{v}-p)^2 = \frac{N_I}{m} C. \tag{5.24}$$

To fix α, we assume that the uninformed investors' demand would always suffice to underwrite the IPO, that is, even if the IPO had to be deserted by the informed investors: the uninformed demand is at least equal to mp or, to simplify, equal to mp. Consider, therefore, the following rationing rule: $\alpha = \frac{N_I(W-C)}{N_I(W-C)+mp}$. Replacing this value of α into eq. (5.24) leaves

$$\frac{1}{2\bar{v}} (\bar{v}-p)^2 = \frac{N_I}{m} C + p \frac{C}{W-C}. \tag{5.25}$$

That is, using (5.22),

$$p = \frac{2C}{W-C} \bar{v}. \tag{5.26}$$

Finally, replacing (5.26) into (5.25) and rearranging leaves

$$N_I = \frac{1}{2}\frac{m}{C}\frac{W-5C}{W-C}\bar{v}.$$

That is, provided information costs are less than 20% of the resources devoted to the IPO, it pays to be informed. Note that N_I decreases with C but increases with m, W, and firm value uncertainty, $\bar{v}$.

5.4 The Classics: Capital Structure and Modigliani-Miller Propositions

Modigliani and Miller (1958) provide a fundamental analysis of the firms' capital structure. How does leverage affect the value of the firm? Their answer is that, in the presence of frictionless financial markets, the capital structure does not matter: the value of the firm is independent of how levered the firm is. This proposition is very important: it begs the questions of how to modify assumptions for the purpose of establishing non-neutrality propositions. In fact, Modigliani and Miller also offer new insights on a methodology perspective: their paper is the first to rely on the notion of absence of arbitrage and derive "asset price restrictions."

This section reviews these foundational stones in financial economics. It relies not only on their original arguments but also on relatively more modern arguments, based on Arrow-Debreu security pricing.

5.4.1 Irrelevance of Capital Structure

Modigliani and Miller (1958) consider an economy where firms can be sorted by the expected cash flows in the industry they operate. Let π be the constant, expected cash flows paid off by each firm within a representative industry and E_U be the price of an *unlevered* firm's share. Under standard conditions, we have that $E_U = \sum_{t=1}^{\infty}(1+\rho)^{-t}\pi$, where ρ is the risk-adjusted discount rate prevailing in a given industry such that the return on equity (ROE) for the unlevered firm can be expressed as

$$\rho = \frac{\pi}{E_U}.$$

Naturally the value of the firm is equal to the value of equity, $V_U = E_U$, say. Next, consider a *levered* firm operating within the same industry. This firm issues debt with nominal value equal to D and interest rate r and has equity value equal to E_L. Its value satisfies $V_L = E_L + D$. The following irrelevance result holds.

Theorem 5.1 (Modigliani and Miller). *In the absence of arbitrage and frictions, the market value of any firm is independent of its capital structure and is given by the discounted expected cash flows, that is,* $V_j = \frac{\pi}{\rho}$, *for any* $j \in \{U, L\}$.

In other words, the return on investment (ROI), defined as $\rho = \frac{\pi}{V_j}$, is the same for two firms that earn the same expected cash flows π, regardless of their capital structure. Naturally, ROE and ROI are the same for the unlevered firm.

Modigliani and Miller derive these results relying on the following arguments. Consider two firms: the first one is unlevered and the second, levered. Both firms earn the same expected cash flows, π, but have different values. An "arbitrageur" may then buy or sell shares of the firm and finance the net position with debt so as to achieve a zero-value portfolio that earns a strictly positive return, which would give rise to an arbitrage opportunity of the type discussed in chapter 2. Thus, value of the levered and the unlevered firm should be the same. Formally, let us be given an arbitrary constant $\alpha \in (0,1)$, and consider the following trade: (i) we buy $N_U = \alpha \frac{E_L + D}{E_U} = \alpha \frac{V_L}{V_U}$ of the unlevered firm or (ii) we sell $N_L = \alpha$ shares of the levered firm. These two trades make the balance of the position worth $-N_U E_U + N_L E_L = -\alpha D$, and so (iii) we borrow αD at the interest rate r to make this initial position worthless. This portfolio yields: (i) $+N_U \pi$, resulting from the purchase of the shares of the unlevered firm; (ii) $-N_L(\pi - rD)$, resulting from the sale of the shares of the levered firm; and (iii) $-r\alpha D$, arising to honor the debt needed to build up a zero-value portfolio at origination. Summing up, the profits are $N_U \pi - N_L(\pi - rD) - r\alpha D = \alpha\left(\frac{V_L}{V_U} - 1\right)\pi$, an arbitrage opportunity, provided $V_L > V_U$ (remember, the portfolio has zero value at origination). Therefore, arbitrage is ruled out by the condition that $V_L = V_U$. A similar argument shows that $V_L < V_U$ would also give rise to arbitrage. Therefore, it must be that $V_L = V_U = E_U = \frac{\pi}{\rho}$.

Naturally, equity returns are affected by leverage. Indeed, note that the ROI obviously satisfies $\pi = \text{ROI} \cdot V$, where V is the firm value, which, as shown, is *independent of its leverage*. Therefore,

$$\text{ROE} = \frac{\pi - rD}{E} = \frac{\text{ROI} \cdot (E + D) - rD}{E} = \text{ROI} + (\text{ROI} - r)\frac{D}{E}. \tag{5.27}$$

Provided $\text{ROI} > r$, the expected return on equity increases with leverage. An alternative formulation of the previous results is the following. We have that $V_U = E + D$ such that the return on V_U, that is, ROI, equals the weighted return on equity and debt, also known as the weighted average cost of capital (WACC), that is,

$$\text{ROI} = \frac{E}{E + D}\text{ROE} + \frac{D}{E + D} r \equiv \text{WACC}. \tag{5.28}$$

That is, the WACC is independent of leverage. Naturally, eqs. (5.27) and (5.28) are equivalent.

If the interest rate on debt is not affected by the firm's capital structure, ROE is increasing in the leverage ratio, $\frac{D}{E}$, once $\text{ROI} > r$. Underlying this result is the assumption that no-arbitrage trades may be implemented with a cost of borrowing money equal to that of the firm and that the firm is not subject to default risk. Consider a simple and heuristic example. Borrowers are concerned about the firm's leverage because, say, in bad times, the firm may not be solvent and so the probability of default increases with leverage. Assume that $r = f(\ell)$, where $\ell = \frac{D}{E}$ and in particular that $f(\ell) = 0.03\ell$. Then, we have that: $\text{ROE} = \text{ROI} + (\text{ROI} - 0.03\ell)\,\ell$. Figure 5.7 depicts ROE as a function of ℓ, assuming that $\text{ROI} = 5\%$ and that the risk-free rate in case of no such frictions is $r = 3\%$.

Consider the firm that has financing costs that vary with the leverage ratio, ℓ. When ℓ is low, the ROE increases with ℓ, magnifying the difference, $\text{ROI} - 0.03\ell$. When ℓ is sufficiently high, further increases of ℓ come at the expense of a much thinner wedge, $\text{ROI} - 0.03\ell$, which results into marginally lower ROE. In this example, there is an interior value for the leverage ratio that maximizes the ROE (approximately $\ell = 0.83$). While this

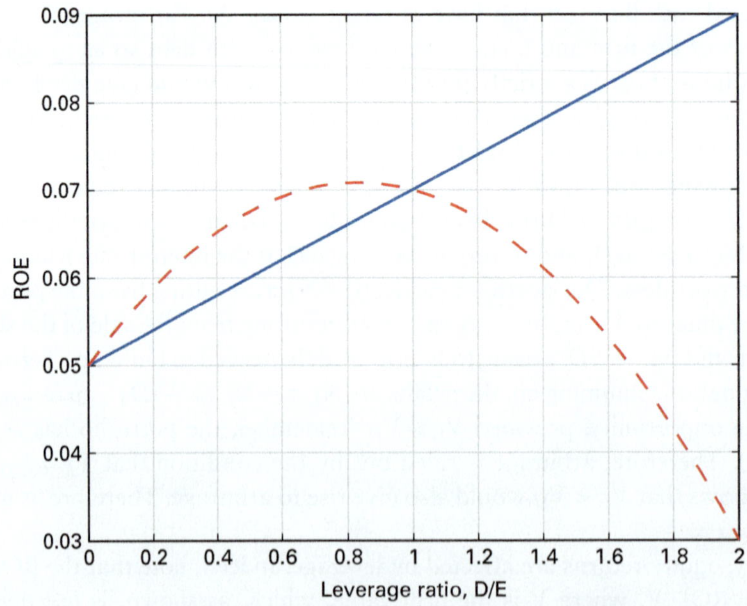

Figure 5.7
The solid line depicts the ROE for a firm that faces a cost of debt independent of the leverage ratio, with ROI $= 5\%$ and $r = 3\%$. The dashed line is the ROE for a firm that has a cost of debt increasing in the leverage ratio ℓ, $r(\ell) = 0.03\ell$.

example is very simple, it conveys the idea of the importance of frictions: in the example, financing costs depend on leverage, and ROE can be nonmonotonic in the leverage ratio. The remainder of this chapter reviews theories of debt by which capital structure affects the value of the firm. These theories rely on the assumption of asymmetric information between borrowers and lenders. Chapter 14 also presents dynamic models of the firm capital structure in which firm may strategically default and by which firm value is affected by leverage (see section 14.2).

5.4.2 Dynamic Versions of Irrelevance

The previous conclusions are easily seen to hold in dynamic economies that have no frictions. Consider the following continuous time framework. From chapter 4, we know that, in the absence of arbitrage opportunities, there exists a stochastic discount factor process, $\xi = (\xi_t)_{t \geq 0}$, that is, a system of Arrow-Debreu securities, under which all securities can be evaluated as expectations of future payoffs discounted with ξ. Suppose that a firm has a project, a "tree," which pays off a stream of fruits $(y_t)_{t \geq 0}$. Then, the value of the firm at time t, V_t say, satisfies

$$\xi_t V_t = E_t \left(\int_t^\infty \xi_u y_u du \right).$$

Next, suppose that this firm issues m_S shares and m_B bonds at prices S_0 and B_0, resp. Each bond yields an instantaneous coupon equal to C and is perpetual such that the dividend promised by each share is equal to $D_t = (y_t - m_B C) / m_S$. Consider then an investor who would like to become a shareholder in this firm. Suppose that the firm requires an initial investment I to start the project. Thus, our investor should invest an amount equal to $I - m_B B_0$ in this firm, where $m_B B_0$ is the initial debt value of the firm. The *net* shareholder value is equal to $m_S S_0 - (I - m_B B_0) = V_0 - I$. The question is: How do details on the firm capital structure affect V_0? We have $\xi_t S_t = E_t \left(\int_t^\infty \xi_u D_u du \right)$ and $\xi_t B_t = E_t \left(\int_t^\infty \xi_u C du \right)$, such that

$$\xi_t \left(m_S S_t + m_B B_t \right) = E_t \left(\int_t^\infty \xi_u y_u du \right) = \xi_t V_t .$$

That is, the value of the firm is independent of its capital structure and details such as, say, the coupon rate.

5.5 Debt and Moral Hazard

Why do firm issue debt? One possibility is risk sharing, that is, the possibility that market mechanisms allocate risks according to agents' attitude toward such risks (see section 2.6 in chapter 2). However, this explanation may be problematic as it leads to counterintuitive results. Section 5.5.1 reviews some of these results, and section 5.5.2 reviews a mechanism for debt issuance, which aims at mitigating moral hazard.

5.5.1 Symmetric Information Again: Full Insurance

Consider a risk averse entrepreneur who has access to a technology to produce a random output $\tilde{x} \in [0, \bar{x}]$ (for some $\bar{x} > 0$), drawn from a probability distribution with density g. The entrepreneur is penniless; they need an amount of capital equal to I to implement the production plan. Outside investors are willing to provide the entrepreneur with such capital and require an exogenous rate of return equal to ρ. The entrepreneur and outside investors both require limited liability. The contract between these two parties specifies a repayment schedule $D(\tilde{x})$ due to the investors, which maximizes the entrepreneur's utility, $\max_{D(\tilde{x}) \in [0, \tilde{x}]} E \left(u(\tilde{x} - D(\tilde{x})) \right)$, subject to the lender break-even condition $E \left(D(\tilde{x}) \right) = (1 + \rho) I$:

$$\max_{D(x) \in [0, x]} \int_0^{\bar{x}} u \left(x - D \left(x \right) \right) g \left(x \right) dx, \quad \text{s.t.} \quad (1 + \rho) I = \int_0^{\bar{x}} D \left(x \right) g \left(x \right) dx. \tag{5.29}$$

The first-order conditions for this problem are

$$\left(u' \left(x - D \left(x \right) \right) - \lambda \right) g \left(x \right) = \eta_0 \left(x \right) - \eta_1 \left(x \right),$$

where λ is the Lagrange multiplier for the lender break-even condition in (5.29) and $\eta_0 (x)$ and $\eta_1 (x)$ are the limited liability constraints ($D (x) \geq 0$ and $x \geq D (x)$, resp.).

When investors' limited liability is not binding, equity is constant—$\omega (x) \equiv x - D (x) = \bar{\omega}$—that is, investors simply redistribute income until the entrepreneur's marginal utility of equity is the same across states, similar to the "implicit contract theory" of real wages and employment of the 1970s.[13] When instead investors' limited liability is binding at zero, $\omega (x) = x$. All in all, debt and equity play roles that are somehow opposite to those we

13. See, e.g., chapter 9 in Blanchard and Fischer (1989).

would have expected. In part, these properties are due to the entrepreneur risk aversion. Thus, and somehow not surprisingly, risk-sharing motives do not justify the existence of standard debt contracts. We now proceed with theories of debt and capital structure relying on asymmetric information. In the following section, we also assume the entrepreneur is risk neutral, an assumption that helps lead to the typical "bang-bang" shape of debt and equity payoffs that we encounter in practice.

5.5.2 Moral Hazard

Innes (1990) provides an explanation of debt as a solution to a moral hazard problem: the role of a well-designed financial structure is to mitigate the underprovision of entrepreneurial efforts that may likely occur once a project is funded. Consider a risk neutral and penniless entrepreneur; they have access to a technology to produce a random payoff $\tilde{x} \in [0, \bar{x}]$ ($\bar{x} > 0$) through entrepreneurial effort and investment funds equal to I. Investors are willing to finance this project, but they can only observe the entrepreneur ex post output $\tilde{x}$, not the efforts they put in place; further, they require an expected return equal to ρ. We assume that $\tilde{x}$ is continuous with a probability density $g(x; e)$, where $e \geq 0$ denotes effort. Effort affects production favorably, in that the monotone likelihood ratio property (MLRP) holds:

$$\frac{\partial}{\partial x}\left(\frac{g_e(x; e)}{g(x; e)}\right) > 0, \tag{5.30}$$

where the subscript denotes a partial derivative; further, we assume that $\int x g(x; 0)\, dx = 0$. The interpretation of the MLRP property is that higher output realizations are more likely to have been generated by production processes with higher efforts. Finally, entrepreneurial efforts cost $c(e)$, for some increasing and convex function c. We assume that g and c satisfy all regularity conditions that lead to an interior solution to the contracting problem below.[14]

Entrepreneurs need to be incentivized to exert costly efforts once they receive funding. Investors propose a contract by which the entrepreneur repays $D(x)$ when the realization of output is $\tilde{x} = x$. Optimal contracting amounts to a repayment function $D(\cdot)$ that aligns the incentives of the principal (the investors) to those of the agent (the entrepreneur). Precisely, the contract aims to maximize the entrepreneur's utility or NPV (expected equity minus efforts),

$$\max_{\{D(x) \in [0,x], e\}} \int_0^{\bar{x}} (x - D(x))\, g(x; e)\, dx - c(e), \tag{5.31}$$

subject to the incentive compatibility constraint

$$c'(e) = \int_0^{\bar{x}} (x - D(x))\, g_e(x; e)\, dx \tag{5.32}$$

and the lender break-even condition

$$(1 + \rho) I = \int_0^{\bar{x}} D(x)\, g(x; e)\, dx. \tag{5.33}$$

14. In particular, the value of (5.31) is nonnegative as the entrepreneur can always choose to exert no effort and get a zero NPV (net of efforts).

Note that the repayment function $D(\cdot)$ in (5.31) is subject to limited liability on both sides. The incentive compatibility constraint in (5.32) reflects entrepreneurial trade-offs: marginal costs and benefits of effort compensate with each other. The Lagrangian for this problem is (assuming that limited liability is not binding):

$$\begin{aligned}\mathcal{L} = &\int_0^{\bar{x}} \omega(x)\left(1-\lambda+\mu\frac{g_e(x;e)}{g(x;e)}\right) g(x;e)\,dx \\ &+\lambda\left(\int_0^{\bar{x}} xg(x;e)\,dx-(1+\rho)I\right)-c(e)-\mu c'(e),\end{aligned} \tag{5.34}$$

where $\omega(x)\equiv x-D(x)$ denotes the entrepreneur's equity and μ and λ are Lagrange multipliers for (5.32) and (5.33). Therefore, provided the first multiplier is strictly positive, the optimal prepayment schedule $D(\cdot)$ is "bang-bang," and equity satisfies

$$\omega(x)=\begin{cases}0, & \text{if } \lambda>1+\mu\frac{g_e(x;e)}{g(x;e)}\\ x, & \text{if } \lambda<1+\mu\frac{g_e(x;e)}{g(x;e)}\end{cases}$$

such that, by the MLRP in (5.30), there exists a x^* such that

$$\omega(x)=\begin{cases}0, & \text{for } x<x^*\\ x, & \text{for } x>x^*\end{cases}. \tag{5.35}$$

The top panel of figure 5.8 depicts the equity schedule $\omega(x)$ (dashed line) and the bottom panel depicts the optimal repayment schedule $D(x)$ (dashed line). The repayment schedule is a debt contract in that it specifies a "variable payment" in the bad states of nature, that is, $D(x)=x$ for $x<x^*$. However, this contract is unusual: it is nonmonotonic and exhibits a downward jump—no payments are due to the lender in the good states of nature! To obviate this feature, we now impose a monotonic condition, stipulating that the optimal repayment schedule is nondecreasing.[15]

Consider the class of continuous but piecewise linear repayment schedules and then the equity schedules. It can be shown (see appendix 5.B) that for an optimal contract to exist, there must be a $D^*<x^*$ such that debt takes the standard form depicted in the bottom panel of figure 5.8, and accordingly, equity satisfies

$$\omega(x)=\max\{x-D^*,0\}. \tag{5.36}$$

It is instructive to consider the "first best" effort, which is the solution to (5.31) subject to (5.33) but not to the incentive compatibility constraint (5.32),

$$\hat{e}=\arg\max_e \int_0^{\bar{x}} xg(x;e)\,dx-(1+\rho)I-c(e).$$

15. Innes (1990) justifies this assumption by explaining that a nonmonotonicity would give the entrepreneur the incentive to secretly borrow from another party, report a high cash flow, reduce their repayment, and finally, repay the side loan.

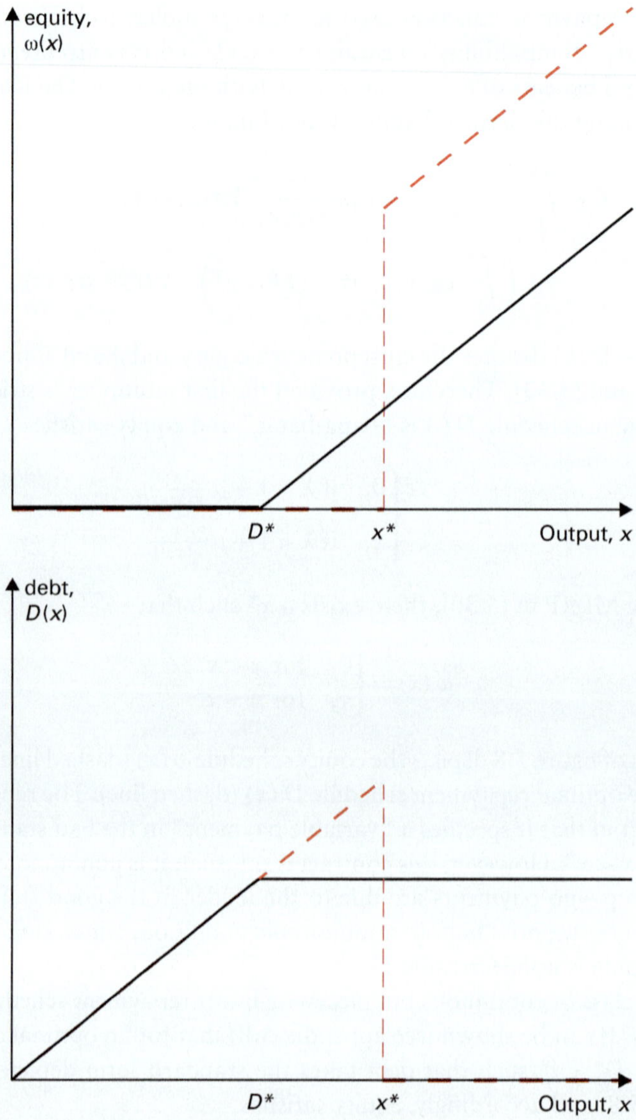

Figure 5.8
The top panel of this figure depicts the equity schedule $\omega(x)$ in (5.35) (dashed line) and in (5.36) (solid line) that arise while dispensing with and imposing the requirement of monotonicity for the repayment schedule of debt, $D(x)$. The bottom panel depicts the corresponding repayment schedules of debt.

It is possible to show that in the moral hazard model, effort is less than $\hat{e}$. The intuition is that because debt is monotonic in some regions (even without requiring it is always so), some of the efforts made by the entrepreneur are to the benefits of the investors.

5.6 Debt with Costly State Verification

In the previous models, the less informed agents are obviously never able to observe what the more informed agents know. This assumption may be relaxed while presuming that, on paying a cost, the less informed agents would be able to monitor some outcome. This section examines a model in which a borrower may declare bankruptcy. The lender then has the right to check the state of the borrower's assets and acquire these assets after bearing some auditing costs. Thus, verification costs could be interpreted as auditing or bankruptcy costs. Alternatively, they may be interpreted as the loss in value induced by the lender's seizure of the borrower's collateral assets. This interpretation should be particularly relevant. Investors might value collateral less than borrowers do; to illustrate, collateral assets might be problematic to resell, especially when potential users are financially constrained as during times of financial crises.

Models of this type are known as models with costly state verification. They were initially studied by Townsend (1979) in the context of implicit contracts and became more closely focused on credit markets after Gale and Hellwig (1985). This section provides a simplified presentation of the main mechanism underlying them as well as a parametric example based on Romer (2001).

5.6.1 Symmetric Information

A risk neutral entrepreneur (the "borrower") has an initial wealth equal to W and considers undertaking a project that requires an investment equal to \$1. We assume that the project output, y, has a cumulative distribution $F(\cdot)$ with support $[0, \bar{y}]$ for some $\bar{y}$. We assume the risk-free rate is exogenous and that outside investors ("lenders") are risk neutral and competitive; thus, they require an expected return equal to $(1+r)(1-W)$. Therefore, the borrower's expected return is $\Pi_b \equiv E(y) - (1+r)(1-W)$; they will invest in the project provided $\Pi_b > (1+r)W$, that is, $E(y) > 1+r$. This standard result is obtained due to the assumption that output, y, is observed by the lender. We now examine how this conclusion changes in the case with asymmetric information.

5.6.2 Asymmetric Information

We assume that the realization of output cannot be observed by the lender unless a fixed verification cost $c > 0$ is paid; that is, verifying the state is *costly*. It is possible to show that the optimal contract is a standard *debt contract* such that the entrepreneur borrows $1 - W$ and promises to pay the investors some fixed $D > 0$, where D is to be determined endogenously. Naturally, this payment is contingent on the entrepreneur not declaring bankruptcy. Instead, bankruptcy occurs when output is less than the promised D, in which case investors pay c, observe the output, and recover all the output they have observed. In each case, the entrepreneur obtains what is left. From now on, we shall refer to the two parties of the agreement as borrower and lender.

Because the lender is likely to incur into the verification costs, they would need to be compensated for these costs. Therefore, their required return is $\Pi_l = (1+r)(1-W) + \mathcal{C}$, where $\mathcal{C}$ denotes the expected verification costs. We denote the expected return's net of verification costs with $\Pi \equiv \Pi_l - \mathcal{C}$. The optimal debt contract is actually the one that minimizes the expected verification costs under the constraint that the lender obtains their required rate of return. Intuitively, the borrower keeps the output that is not paid to the lender, and therefore their income is maximized by minimizing the expected verification costs.

There are two cases to consider, according to whether the agreed-on nominal payment, D, is high or low compared with maximum production capacity, $\bar{y}$.

(1) Nominal payment is $D \leq \bar{y}$. In this case, the firm may either succeed and repay D or default. That is,
  - Success: output is $y \geq D$, which occurs with probability $1 - F(D)$, and the lender receives D without paying any verification cost.
  - Default: output is $y < D$, which occurs with probability $F(D)$, and the lender receives y after paying the verification cost c.

  Therefore, the lender's expected receipts net of verification costs are

$$\Pi_1(D) \equiv (1 - F(D))\, D + F(D)\left(E(y|\, y < D) - c\right).$$

  It is easy to see that $\lim_{D \to \bar{y}} \Pi_1(D) = E(y) - c$.

(2) Nominal payment is $D > \bar{y}$. In this case, the lender gets all output, although always after verification. The lender's expected payment is then $\Pi_2 \equiv E(y) - c$.

Thus, the lender's expected payments net of verification costs are $\Pi(D) = \Pi_1(D)\,\mathbb{I}_{D \leq \bar{y}} + \Pi_2 \mathbb{I}_{D > \bar{y}}$. In equilibrium, it must be that the lender obtains their required rate of return. That is, provided it exists, the nominal payment D^* (say) is any function $D^*(c, r, W)$ that satisfies

$$\Pi\left(D^*(c, r, W)\right) = (1+r)(1-W). \tag{5.37}$$

If such a function does not exist, the contract cannot be written and credit rationing is obtained as a result. We assume that this function exists and provide examples of it below. An obvious condition is that $\max_D \Pi(D) \geq (1+r)(1-W)$, an assumption we maintain from now on. We now describe some basic properties of the equilibrium nominal payment.

First, note that, by assuming that $1 - F'(0)\, c > 0$, the function $\Pi_1(D)$ is increasing for small values of D. This property reflects a "nominal payment effect": when D is small, the probability of success is high, and so a small increase in D benefits the lender without compromising too much the probability of default. However, larger values of D increase the probability of default, such that $\Pi_1(D)$ can be nonmonotonic in D. The function $D^*(c, r, W)$ is the smallest value of D such that $\Pi(D)$ solves eq. (5.37): in case multiple values of D existed, other lenders would undercut anyone who chooses any solution than the smallest value. Therefore, $D^*(c, r, W)$ is *increasing in c, increasing in r, and decreasing in W*.

Consider, for example, the following model parametrization, suggested by Romer (2001). Output is uniformly distributed, with $\bar{y}=2\gamma$. Then, $E(y)=\gamma$, $F(D)=\frac{D}{2\gamma}$, and $E(y|\, y<D)=\frac{1}{2}D$. The condition $1-F'(0)\,c>0$ is satisfied by requiring that verification costs are smaller than the maximum output capacity, that is, $c<2\gamma$. Plugging these values into eq. (5.37) leaves a quadratic equation in D; the smallest root of this equation is

$$D^*(c,r,W)=2\gamma-c-\sqrt{(2\gamma-c)^2-4\gamma(1+r)(1-W)}.$$

We shall return to the properties of $D^*(c,r,W)$ below and to this parametric example too.

5.6.3 Investments and Agency Costs

When do investments take place? The borrower undertakes their project if $E(y)-\Pi_l\geq(1+r)\,W$. The LHS of this inequality is the difference between the expected output and the gross return Π_l introduced earlier which is due to the lender (i.e., it is inclusive of the expected verification costs). Therefore, by the definition of Π_l, the borrower invests if

$$E(y)\geq(1+r)+\mathcal{C}. \tag{5.38}$$

We shall return to the inequality in (5.38) in more advanced parts of the book (see section 9.11.5 of chapter 9).

Agency problems complicate the decision to invest: due to $\mathcal{C}$, the borrower is now less likely to invest than in the case with asymmetric information in section 5.6.1. Agency costs are a wedge between the required return in the symmetric and asymmetric market. We may characterize these expected verification costs. They are given by the probability of an audit times the cost of the audit, namely,

$$\mathcal{C}=\mathcal{C}(c,r,W)\equiv F\left(D^*(c,r,W)\right)c.$$

Agency costs, then, inherit the properties of the equilibrium nominal payment $D^*(c,r,W)$. In terms of the previous parametric example based on uniform distributions, $\mathcal{C}(c,r,W)=\frac{D^*(c,r,W)}{2\gamma}c$: agency costs are proportional to the equilibrium nominal payments.

To summarize, agency costs raise the cost of external finance. But they decrease with the value of the assets owned by the borrowers, W. These assets can be interpreted as the borrower's liquid net worth. Chapter 9 discusses mechanisms of amplification of the business cycle based on these agency costs (see section 9.11). During a recession, the borrowers' net worth decreases, raising the cost of capital and discouraging investments, which reinforce the severity of the recession. Interestingly, investments decrease with the safe interest rate, r, due to one additional channel: agency costs. These costs increase with r because, as the lender's required return increases, the nominal payment must also increase for the lender to obtain their required rate of return (see eq. (5.37)). Finally, the model in this section may also serve as a benchmark taken to explain that, in bad times, it might be more difficult and hence more expensive to verify the state of collateral values (i.e., c is likely higher in bad times than in good). One may argue that issues in verifiability of collateral values might constitute one of the many reasons investments fell during periods such as the Great Depression of the 1930s and the Great Recession of the end of the 2000s.

5.7 Liquidity Management and Dynamic Security Design

We now discuss a few dynamic models designed to capture some important themes in corporate finance. How do firms distribute dividends when they face liquidity constraints? Intuitively, these firms may face bankruptcy when their reserves are exhausted. To avoid bankruptcy, it would be useful to begin distribute dividends only when such reserves reach some threshold value; section 5.7.1 deals with such a model.

Another theme we deal with regards security design. An entrepreneur is penniless but has skills to produce output. Financiers may provide entrepreneurs with the resources needed to run a firm. However, when would the entrepreneurs behave in the interest of the financiers? Section 5.7.2 discusses a dynamic model of contracting that can be implemented through standard securities. Naturally, this model predicts that Modigliani-Miller theorem cannot hold. The framework of analysis in this section relies on methods stemming from the real options theory rapidly discussed in chapter 4 (see section 4.8). However, this section provides more advanced tools of analysis that are needed to solve problems that are more complex than those in chapter 4. Note that Leland (1994) provides a famous model in which bankruptcy may be strategically chosen by shareholders such that the value of the firm is affected by capital structure. This model is dealt with in detail in chapter 14 (see section 14.2) as an important part of organized discussions on the evaluation of risky debt.

5.7.1 Liquidity Constraints and Optimal Dividend Policy

Jeanblanc-Picqué and Shirayev (1995) and Radner and Shepp (1996) consider a model in which a firm maximizes its value through a dividend policy that accounts for periods of inaction. Inaction occurs because of liquidity constraints. While it will be assumed that firm capital has positive growth, there may be bad times where it would not be optimal for the firm to distribute any dividends as this might trigger bankruptcy. This issue would not arise if shareholders were able to inject new funds or the firm could borrow from a bank or issue new securities.

Consider the simple frictionless case, in which the cash generated by the firm satisfies

$$dy_t = \mu dt + \sigma dW_t, \tag{5.39}$$

where μ and σ are parameters and W_t is a standard Brownian motion. The NPV of the firm that has initial cash equal to k_o is

$$\text{NPV}(k_0) \equiv \max\left\{0, k_0 + \frac{\mu}{r}\right\}, \tag{5.40}$$

where r is the constant discounting rate.

Next, consider the case in which the firm is liquidity constrained. The firm must always keep some positive cash, k_t, which can only be accumulated through retained earnings: injection of outside capital is not feasible due some frictions that are not being modeled in the first place. Now, it will be optimal to distribute dividends only after cash reaches a threshold, with the firm's capital being solution to

$$dk_t = \mu dt + \sigma dW_t - dD_t, \tag{5.41}$$

where D_t is a cumulative dividend process, which only increases once capital k_t has reached a sufficiently high level k^o, to be determined below. It is assumed that $k_0 > 0$, that bankruptcy occurs whenever k_t hits zero, and that the value of the firm is maximized by risk neutral managers as

$$V(k_0) = \sup E\left(\int_0^{\infty} e^{-rt} dD_t\right), \quad \text{s.t. eq. (5.41).} \tag{5.42}$$

The evaluation in (5.41) is quite different from that in eq. (5.40), as we now show, depending as it does on the dividend policy.

5.7.1.1 Bounded dividend policy

We initially assume that the dividend satisfies

$$dD_t = \omega(k_t)\, dt, \quad \text{with } 0 \leq \omega(k) \leq \bar{d} < \infty. \tag{5.43}$$

The limiting case, $\bar{d} = \infty$, is considered in the subsections below. By eqs. (5.41)–(5.43), the problem of the firm is then

$$V(k_0) = \sup E\left(\int_0^{\infty} e^{-rt} \omega(k_t)\, dt\right), \quad \text{s.t. } dk_t = (\mu - \omega(k_t))\, dt + \sigma dW_t, \tag{5.44}$$

such that the Bellman equation for the problem is

$$\begin{aligned} 0 &= \sup_{0 \leq \omega(k) \leq \bar{d}} \left[LV(k) - rV(k) + \omega(k)\right] \\ &= \mu V'(K) + \frac{1}{2}\sigma^2 V''(k) - rV(k) + \sup_{0 \leq \omega(k) \leq \bar{d}} \left[\omega(k)\left(1 - V'(k)\right)\right], \end{aligned} \tag{5.45}$$

where L denotes the usual infinitesimal generator of the constraint in (5.44).

The solution is

$$\omega(k) = \begin{cases} 0, & \forall k : V'(k) > 1 \text{ (inaction)} \\ \bar{d}, & \forall k : V'(k) \leq 1 \text{ (dividend distribution)} \end{cases}. \tag{5.46}$$

The details of this problem suggest the following interpretation of the solution: the firm should pay off as soon as the level of capital reaches a threshold level, at which the payout takes place at the maximal speed, $\bar{d}$. This interpretation needs to be corroborated by verifying that the marginal value of capital, $V'(k)$, is indeed decreasing in k. Intuitively, we expect capital value to increase as we move away from the firm bankruptcy boundary, $k = 0$, but at a decreasing pace: additional cash in the firm (retained earnings) would decrease the risk of default much more when k_t is low than when it is high. The interpretation of the optimal policy in (5.46) is neat: the firm pays out whenever the marginal value of capital kept in the firm is low (less than one).

Substituting eqs. (5.46) into eq. (5.45) and conjecturing that V is concave (decreasing returns to retaining earnings) over the inaction region yields that the firm does not distribute any dividends until k reaches a threshold, k^o (say),

$$\begin{cases} 0=\mu V'(k)+\frac{1}{2}\sigma^2 V''(k)-rV(k), & k<k^o \text{ (inaction region)} \\ 0=\frac{1}{\bar{d}}\left(\mu V'(k)+\frac{1}{2}\sigma^2 V''(k)-rV(k)\right)+(1-V'(k)), & k\geq k^o \text{ (payout region)} \end{cases} . \tag{5.47}$$

It is straightforward to verify that the solutions to the two equations in (5.47), $V_I(k)$ and $V_P(k)$ say, take the following form,

$$V_I(k)=A_{I1}e^{\alpha_1 k}+A_{I2}e^{\alpha_2 k} \quad \text{and} \quad V_P(k)=A_{P1}e^{\beta_1 k}+A_{P2}e^{\beta_2 k}+\frac{\bar{d}}{r},$$

for some coefficients A_{Ij} and A_{Pj} to be determined, and $\alpha_1<0$, $\alpha_2>0$, $\beta_1<0$ and $\beta_2>0$.

The bankruptcy condition stipulates that $V(0)=0$, such that $A_{I1}=-A_{I2}$, and then

$$V_I(k)=A_{I1}\left(e^{\alpha_1 k}-e^{\alpha_2 k}\right), \quad \text{for } k<k^o. \tag{5.48}$$

As for $V_P(k)$, note that because $\omega(k)$ is bounded by $\bar{d}$, then by eq. (5.44), V_P must be positive and bounded by $\frac{\bar{d}}{r}$, which requires $A_{P2}=0$. Therefore,

$$V_P(k)=A_{P1}e^{\beta_1 k}+\frac{\bar{d}}{r}, \quad \text{for } k\geq k^o. \tag{5.49}$$

To summarize, the value of the firm is given by eqs. (5.48) and (5.49), with three constants to be determined: the two coefficients, A_{I1}, P_{I1}, and the free boundary, k^o. The constants are determined by imposing (i) $V_I(k^o)=V_P(k^o)$ (value matching), (ii) $V_I'(k^o)=V_P'(k^o)$ (smooth pasting), and (iii) $V_I'(k^o)=1$ (free boundary). Note that these conditions in (5.47) imply that the following super-contact condition holds: $V_I''(k^o)=V_P''(k^o)$. The super-contact condition makes the second-order derivative continuous as required for an application of Itô's lemma to a function of a variable that takes values over the real line, $V(k)$. Finally, appendix 5.C shows that the coefficients determined in this way imply that V_I is positive, increasing, and concave for all $k<k^o$, thereby validating the conjectures underlying the two equations in (5.47). The difference between NPV (k_0) in eq. (5.40) and $V(k)$ in eqs. (5.48) and (5.49) is a cost accounting for the financial frictions faced by the firm.

5.7.1.2 *Reflected Brownian motions*

Next, we consider the limiting case in which $\bar{d}=\infty$. Below, we argue that the firm's capital would behave as a reflected Brownian motion in this case: when capital is below the threshold k^o, it is an arithmetic Brownian motion as in eq. (5.39), but as soon as capital reaches k^o, it is then reflected back to lower values with the capital in excess distributed as a dividend. Capital then is driven by a "regulated Brownian motion," that is, a Brownian motion that keeps the very same capital within k^o. It is also assumed that if the firm had to begin with cash larger than the threshold, the part exceeding k^o would be paid off as a dividend. Heuristically, eqs. (5.47) would hold in this case when

$$0=\mu V'(k)+\frac{1}{2}\sigma^2 V''(k)-rV(k) \quad \text{for } k<k^o \quad \text{and } V'(k^o)=1, \tag{5.50}$$

with the bankruptcy condition, $V(0)=0$ and

$$V(k)=k-k^o+V(k^o) \quad \text{for } k \geq k^o, \tag{5.51}$$

with the interpretation provided a moment earlier: were the firm to start with capital k_t higher than the threshold, the difference k_t-k^o would be immediately paid out as a dividend. Eq. (5.51) implies that the following super-contact condition must hold: $V''(k^o)=0$ for both left and right limits to k^o.

The solution to eq. (5.50) that satisfies the bankruptcy condition is

$$V(k)=\max\left\{0, \frac{e^{\alpha_2 k}-e^{\alpha_1 k}}{\alpha_2 e^{\alpha_2 k^o}-\alpha_1 e^{\alpha_1 k^o}}\right\}, \quad k \leq k^o, \tag{5.52}$$

where $\alpha_1<0$ and $\alpha_2>0$, just as in eq. (5.48). The threshold k^o is determined through the super-contact condition; it is $k^o=\frac{\ln(\alpha_1^2)-\ln(\alpha_2^2)}{\alpha_2-\alpha_1}$. Note that $V(k^o)=\frac{\mu}{r}$. Similarly as in the previous subsection, the difference between NPV (k_0) and $V(k)$ in eq. (5.52) is a cost accounting for the financial frictions faced by the firm. We now provide a few technical but heuristic details regarding the connection of this problem with reflected Brownian motions.

5.7.1.3 *Heuristic details on reflected Brownian motions*

We provide heuristic details that help develop intuition on reflected Brownian motions. A standard and rigorous source of references is Karatzas and Shreve (1991, 210–212). Define the *occupancy time* of a random process x_t in a set A up to time t as

$$m(A,t)=\int_0^t \mathbb{I}_{x_\tau \in A} d\tau,$$

where $\mathbb{I}_.$ denotes the indicator function. It measures how much time x_t spends in set A up to time t for a given realization on $[0,t]$. Below, it will be argued that there exists a function $\ell(x,t)$ called *local time* of x_t at a given point x, such that

$$m(A,t)=\int_A \ell(x,t)\,dx, \quad \ell(x,t)=\lim_{\epsilon \downarrow 0}\frac{1}{2\epsilon} m((x-\epsilon,x+\epsilon),t). \tag{5.53}$$

Note the following property. For any fixed x^o, and using the definitions of ℓ and m and that of the Dirac's function, we have, heuristically, that

$$\begin{aligned}
\ell(x^o,t) &= \int \delta(x-x^o)\,\ell(x,t)\,dx \\
&= \int \delta(x-x^o) \lim_{\epsilon \downarrow 0}\frac{1}{2\epsilon}\int_0^t \mathbb{I}_{x_\tau \in (x-\epsilon,x+\epsilon)} d\tau dx \\
&= \int_0^t \int \delta(x-x^o)\,\delta(x_\tau-x)\,dx d\tau \\
&= \int_0^t \delta(x_\tau-x^o)\,d\tau.
\end{aligned} \tag{5.54}$$

Note then that

$$\begin{aligned} m(A,t) &= \int_0^t \mathbb{I}_{x_\tau \in A} d\tau \\ &= \int_0^t \int \delta(x - x_\tau) \mathbb{I}_{x \in A} dx d\tau \\ &= \int \mathbb{I}_{x \in A} \int_0^t \delta(x - x_\tau) d\tau dx \\ &= \int_A \ell(x,t) dx, \end{aligned}$$

where the last equality follows by eq. (5.54). This is eq. (5.53).

Next, consider the solution for ω in eq. (5.46), which in the limiting case, $\bar{d} = \infty$, is $\omega(k_t) = \delta(k_t - k^o)$, where $\delta(\cdot)$ is Dirac's delta again. To simplify the presentation, set $\mu = 0$, $\sigma = 1$, and $k_0 = 0$, such that the firm's capital in eq. (5.41) now becomes

$$k_t = W_t - \int_0^t \delta(k_\tau - k^o) d\tau = W_t - \ell(k^o, t), \tag{5.55}$$

where the second equality follows by the property of local time in (5.54). Below, it is heuristically explained that local time in (5.55) satisfies

$$\ell(k^o, t) = \max_{0 \le \tau \le t} (W_\tau - k^o).$$

That is, local time constrains k_t to live below k^o: at each time that k_t increases above k^o, $\ell(k^o, t)$ increases and reflects k_t at k^o. In terms of the model, therefore, $\ell(k^o, \tau)$ represents the cumulative dividend as of time τ for all τ after capital has hit k^o for the first time. Eq. (5.55) describes a Brownian motion reflected at k^o: each time k_τ hits k^o from below, it is reflected back at k^o. The result is that cash reserves, k_τ, form a regulated Brownian motion. Harrison (1985) is a standard source of references and rigorous discussions around regulated Brownian motions.

Intuitively, it is optimal to pay out $\max\{k - k^o, 0\}$ such that the controlled cash reserve process $k_t \in [0, k^o]$. Indeed, for all $k \ge k^o$, $V'(k) = 1$, whence the instantaneous payment $k - k^o$ incorporated into (5.51). That is, the controlled process $K_t \equiv k^o - k_t$ is positive. Next, consider the following result (see, e.g., Karatzas and Shreve, 1991, 210).

Skorokhod problem. *Given a constant $k^o \ge 0$ and a Brownian motion W_t, there exists a unique process ℓ_t, such that*

$$X_t \equiv k^o - W_t + \ell_t \ge 0,$$

with the properties that (i) ℓ_t is nondecreasing, and (ii) ℓ_t increases only when $X_t = 0$. This process satisfies, $\ell_t = \left(\max_{0 \le s \le t} W_s - k^o\right)^+$.

Now, eq. (5.55) implies that

$$K_t \equiv k^o - k_t = k^o - W_t + \ell(k^o, t).$$

Because the controlled process K_t must be positive, we see that local time $\ell(k^o, t)$ fits the previous Skorokhod problem.

5.7.1.4 *Singular stochastic control*

We summarize the conclusions in the previous two subsections. A risk neutral manager maximizes the value of the firm,

$$V(k_0) = \sup E\left(\int_0^{\infty} e^{-rt} dD_t\right),$$

under the constraint that cash reserves are solution to

$$dk_t = \mu dt + \sigma dW_t - dD_t.$$

The solution is a cumulative dividend process, $D_t = \ell(k^o, t)$, the local time of k_t at k^o. To determine the barrier k^o, note that the Bellman equation is

$$0 = \max_{dD \geq 0}\left[\left(\mu V'(k) + \frac{1}{2}\sigma^2 V''(k) - rV(k)\right)dt + (1 - V'(k))\, dD\right]. \tag{5.56}$$

The optimal policy is to retain earnings (i.e., $dD = 0$) as long as $1 - V'(k) < 0$, and to distribute dividends (i.e., $dD > 0$) otherwise through an infinitesimal intervention. Therefore, in the inaction region, V is solution to eq. (5.50).

Eq. (5.50) can also be written in terms of the so-called Hamilton-Jacobi-Bellman variational inequality,

$$0 = \max\left\{\mu V'(k) + \frac{1}{2}\sigma^2 V''(k) - rV(k), 1 - V'(k)\right\},$$

with boundary condition $V(0) = 0$. The function V is given by (5.52) for $k \leq k^o$ and, by arguments nearly identical to those used to characterize V_I in (5.48) (see appendix 5.C), is increasing and concave. For $k \geq k^o$, V satisfies (5.51).

Finally, cumulative dividends satisfy

$$D_t = \left(\max_{0 \leq s \leq t}(k_s - k^o)\right)^+.$$

The next section deals with agency problems that may be cast in terms of a singular stochastic control problem similar to the one summarized in this section.

5.7.2 A Model of Continuous Time Contracting

Dynamic models with asymmetric information may be quite complex. Contracts are, in this case, "repeated," and the parties need to anticipate future behaviors and incentives. However, these models may be simplified by formulating them in a recursive setting. Earlier references to such a setting are Green (1987) or Spear and Srivastava (1987), where the agent's continuation utility is a state variable. DeMarzo and Sannikov (2006), DeMarzo and Fishman (2007), and Biais, Mariotti, Plantin, and Rochet (2007) consider dynamic models that allow one to derive theoretical propositions regarding the optimal capital structure of a firm in the presence of asymmetric information. Consider the following principal-agent relationship: an agent has skills to undertake a project but does not have resources; a principal has such financial resources, but not the skills. The agent and principal then establish a firm, and their problem is to design rules to share profits. We describe a contract that allows the agent and principal to run this firm and then some ways to implement this contract, which rely on the issuance of standard securities such as equity and debt.

5.7.2.1 Contract

We assume that the project generates instantaneous cash flows that satisfy eq. (5.39), that is,

$$dy_t = \mu dt + \sigma dW_t,$$

where μ and σ are constants and W_t is a standard Brownian motion. These cash flows are observed by the agent, not by the principal. The agent then may consider secretly divert funds from the firm for an instantaneous amount equal to $dy_t - d\hat{y}_t$ and only report cash flows equal to $d\hat{y}_t$. We assume that $dy_t - d\hat{y}_t > 0$, that is, the agent does not over-report; moreover, we assume that this fund diversion provides the agent with benefits equal to $\lambda\,(dy_t - d\hat{y}_t)$, where $\lambda \in [0,1]$ and the constant proportion $1-\lambda$ is interpreted as a deadweight cost of diverting funds.

The agent and the principal are both risk neutral, but the agent has a discount rate ρ and the principal has a discount rate r, where $r < \rho$: the principal is more patient than the agent; that is, in principle, the agent would be willing to borrow in order to finance consumption. The agent has limited liability but also limited wealth, as explained. The principal may cover the initial setup costs of the firm, I. Unlike in the model of section 5.7.1, we also assume that the principal has deep pockets and is able to cover the operating losses resulting from negative cash flow values. Finally, the principal has to pay the agent. They offer a contract, whereby the agent receives some instantaneous compensation equal to dD_t, up to some stopping time τ determined below. Let us analyze this contract.

The agent may consume

$$d\hat{c}_t = dD_t + \lambda\,(dy_t - d\hat{y}_t)\,, \tag{5.57}$$

and their utility, conditioned on reporting $\hat{y}_t$, is

$$\omega_t = E_t\left(\int_t^{\tau} e^{-\rho(u-t)}\,d\hat{c}_u + e^{-\rho(\tau-t)}R\right)$$

at $t=0$, where $R \geq 0$ is the terminal payoff the agent receives at the contract termination from an outside option. By contrast, the principal's total expected profit is

$$V_t = E_t\left(\int_t^{\tau} e^{-r(u-t)}(d\hat{y}_u - dD_u) + e^{-r(\tau-t)}L\right) \tag{5.58}$$

at $t=0$, where $L \geq 0$ is the expected value of the firm's assets at liquidation, that is, upon contract termination.

To study the contract that allows the principal and the agent to run this firm, we take the agent's continuation utility ω_t to be the state variable on which to base incentive compatible contracts. We characterize the agent continuation utility relying on the martingale representation theorem, which we already encountered in chapter 4.[16]

16. See discussions in sections 4.3 and 4.4 regarding complete markets and optimal consumption/portfolio choices.

First, define

$$\bar{\omega}_t \equiv E_t\left(\int_0^\tau e^{-\rho u} d\hat{c}_u + e^{-\rho\tau} R\right) = \int_0^t e^{-\rho u} d\hat{c}_u + e^{-\rho t}\omega_t, \tag{5.59}$$

where the second equality follows by simple calculations. Note that $\bar{\omega}_t$ is a martingale with respect to the information sets generated by $\hat{y}_t$. We focus on the truth-telling case, $y_t = \hat{y}_t$, and examine incentive compatibility later. By the martingale representation theorem, then, there exists a process adapted to y_t, say ϕ_t, such that

$$\bar{\omega}_t = \bar{\omega}_0 + \int_0^t \sigma e^{-\rho u}\phi_u dW_u. \tag{5.60}$$

By expanding (5.59) and (5.60) and rearranging terms,

$$d\omega_t = \rho\omega_t dt - d\hat{c}_t + \sigma\phi_t dW_t, \tag{5.61}$$

with $y_t = \hat{y}_t$. Eq. (5.61) can be interpreted as an arbitrage equation, implying as it does that $E(d\omega_t) + d\hat{c}_t = \rho\omega_t dt$: the expected relative change in the agent's continuation utility ω_t plus the agent instantaneous consumption (relative to ω_t) must equal the agent's discount rate, ρ.

The next step is to identify the set of values for ϕ_t such that the contract is incentive compatible. We claim that it must be that $\phi_t \geq \lambda$ for all t. Note, indeed, that ϕ_t is the sensitivity of the agent's continuation utility with respect to their reported earnings. Then, if the agent had to divert cash, they would (i) benefit for $\lambda(dy_t - d\hat{y}_t)$ but (ii) lose $\phi_t(dy_t - d\hat{y}_t)$ in their continuation payoff. In more detail, let $\hat{\omega}_t$ temporarily denote the agent's continuation utility under a report history equal to $(\hat{y}_u)_{u\leq t}$. We have:

$$\hat{\omega}_0 = \omega_0 + E\left(\int_0^\tau e^{-\rho t}(\lambda - \phi_t)\left(dy_t - d\hat{y}_t\right)\right).$$

Therefore, and because $dy_t - d\hat{y}_t \geq 0$, the contract incentivizes the agent not to divert funds when $\lambda \leq \phi_t$, in which case $\hat{\omega}_0 = \omega_0$.

We are now ready to formulate the contract in a singular stochastic control format. The principal problem is to maximize (5.58) such that (5.57) holds with $d\hat{y}_t = dy_t$, under the incentive compatibility constraint $\phi_t \geq \lambda$, that is,

$$\begin{aligned} V(\omega) = & \max_{\phi_t\geq\lambda,\ dD_t\geq 0} E\left(\int_0^\tau e^{-rt}(dy_t - dD_t) + e^{-r\tau}L\,\middle|\, \omega_0 = \omega\right), \\ & \text{s.t. } d\omega_t = \rho\omega_t dt - dD_t + \sigma\phi_t dW_t. \end{aligned} \tag{5.62}$$

Note the dependence of the principal discounted expected profits on the agent's continuation utility, $V(\omega)$. Similar to the previous section (see, e.g., eq. (5.56)), we may write the Bellman equation as follows:

$$0 = \max_{\phi\geq\lambda,\ dD\geq 0}\left[\left(\mu + \rho\omega V'(\omega) + \frac{1}{2}\sigma^2\phi^2 V''(\omega) - rV(\omega)\right)dt - \left(1 + V'(\omega)\right)dD\right].$$

In appendix 5.C, we show that the expected profits are concave, that is, $V''(\omega) \leq 0$, which implies that it must be that $\phi = \lambda$. Therefore, the Hamilton-Jacobi-Bellman variational inequality is

$$0 = \max\left\{\mu + \rho\omega V'(\omega) + \frac{1}{2}\sigma^2\lambda^2 V''(\omega) - rV(\omega), -\left(1 + V'(\omega)\right)\right\}, \quad V(R) = L, \quad (5.63)$$

where the second equality is the boundary condition: when the contract terminates and the agent accesses their outside option R, the principal obtains their liquidation payoff, L.

We now know how to solve this type of problems. Similar to the liquidity management problem of section 5.7.1, the contract is such that no payments are made available to the agent for all ω such that $-\left(1 + V'(\omega)\right) < 0$ and otherwise that payments are made ($dD > 0$) through an infinitesimal intervention. In particular, and because $V''(\omega) \leq 0$, we search for a threshold value of the agent's continuation utility, say ω^o, such that (i) for all $\omega \leq \omega^o$, $V(\omega)$ is solution to the second-order differential equation in (5.63) and (ii) for $\omega > \omega^o$, $V(\omega) = V(\omega^o) - (\omega - \omega^o)$ for $\omega > \omega^o$. The interpretation is simple. The principal may compensate the agent either by raising the agent's *promised* payoff, ω (which has a marginal cost equal to $-V'(\omega)$) or by providing the agent with an *immediate transfer*, which has a marginal cost equal to 1. Thus, when $-V'(\omega) < 1$, no payment is available to the agent. Payments are made only when $V'(\omega) = -1$.

The solution to (i) is subject to three boundary conditions: (a) $V(R) = L$, (b) $V'(\omega^o) = -1$ (free boundary), and (c) $V''(\omega^o) = 0$ (super contact). In appendix 5.C, we show that

$$V(\omega) = \frac{\mu}{r} + c_1 M\left(-\frac{r}{2\rho}, \frac{1}{2}, \frac{-\rho\omega^2}{\sigma^2\lambda^2}\right) + c_2 \frac{\sqrt{\rho}}{\sigma\lambda} M\left(-\frac{r}{2\rho} + \frac{1}{2}, \frac{3}{2}, \frac{-\rho\omega^2}{\sigma^2\lambda^2}\right)\omega, \quad \omega \leq \omega^o, \tag{5.64}$$

for two constants c_1 and c_2 determined in the appendix and where M denotes the confluent hypergeometric function of the first kind (see eq. (5.A9)).

Figure 5.9 depicts the solution in (5.64). Note that the first best is obtained with $V_0^{\text{fb}} = \frac{\mu}{r} - \omega_0$. Under asymmetric information, the principal continuation utility is, instead, lower than V_0^{fb}, provided $\rho > r$. The contract dynamics are as follows. First, the principal accepts to undertake this project if its NPV is positive, $V(\omega_0) \geq I$. Therefore, it must be the case that $\max_\omega V(\omega) \geq I$. If financial markets are competitive, the contract would be such that $\omega_0 = \max_{\omega \in (R, \omega^o)} \{\omega : V(\omega) = I\}$. Thus, the contract begins while the principal promises a continuation payoff ω_0 to the agent. The dynamics of ω_t are then determined by the constraint of (5.62) with $\phi_t = \lambda$, with no payments taking place until $\omega_t = \omega^o$. We now describe mechanisms to implement this contract by means of standard securities.

5.7.2.2 Implementation

DeMarzo and Sannikov (2006) show that this contract may be implemented through standard securities such as equity and debt as well as a credit line. Succinctly, the principal supplies funds to the firm through a credit line. The principal also holds a perpetual debt that has instantaneous coupons equal to $dC_t = \left(\mu - \frac{\rho}{\lambda}\omega^o\right) dt$ and $(1 - \lambda)$ fraction of equity. The agent holds the remaining λ of equity. Equity is a claim to a multiple of the agent compensation in the original contract that is equal to $\frac{1}{\lambda}$, that is, $\frac{dD_t}{\lambda}$.

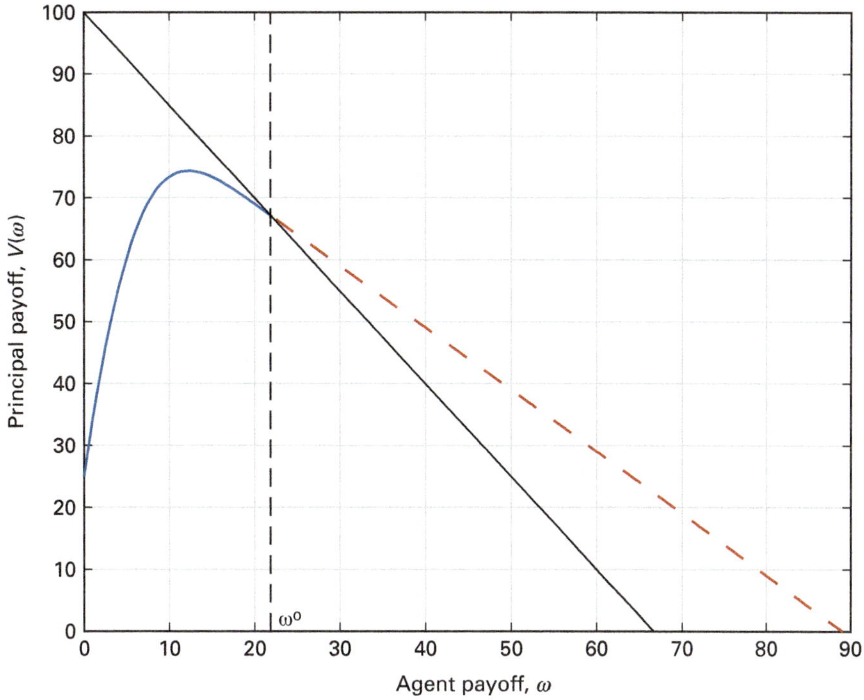

Figure 5.9
Principal and agent payoffs, $V(\omega)$ and ω. The blue solid line is the principal-agent payoff curve resulting when no payments are being made to the agent. Such payments are made when the agent's continuation payoff reaches ω^o. The black, thin line depicts the equation $V_c(\omega) = \frac{\mu}{r} - \frac{\rho}{r}\omega$: the solution to the second-order differential equation in (5.63) collapses to $V_c(\omega^o)$ under the free boundary and super-contact conditions. Parameters are $r = 0.10$, $\rho = 0.15$, $\lambda = 0.8$, $R = 0$, $L = 25$, $\sigma = 5$, and $\mu = 10$.

At each point in time, the firm can withdraw from and/or pay back the credit line for a credit limit equal to $\bar{\mathcal{B}} \equiv \frac{\omega^o - R}{\lambda}$. The outstanding balance, $\mathcal{B}_t$ (say), costs an interest rate equal to the agent's discount rate, ρ, and is set at $\mathcal{B}_t = \frac{\omega^o - \omega_t}{\lambda}$ for $\omega_t \in (R, \omega^o)$. It is the amount of funds that need to be repaid. It is easy to show that

$$d\mathcal{B}_t = \rho \mathcal{B}_t dt - dy_t + \frac{1}{\lambda} dD_t + dC_t.$$

The first term is the remuneration for the credit line services. The second term is the cash inflows that are used to repay the credit line; the third and the fourth terms represent dividends paid off to shareholders and coupons paid off to the bondholders. Dividends are only paid when the credit line is fully repaid, that is, when $\mathcal{B}_t = 0$. The firm is liquidated as soon as $\mathcal{B}_t = \bar{\mathcal{B}}$.

It is possible to show that this scheme provides the agent incentives to behave and that both principal and agent receive the same payments as in the original contract. While $\omega_t \in (R, \omega^o)$, the principal receives (a) dC_t (from the perpetual debt), (b) $dy_t - dC_t$ (from the credit line), and (c) remuneration from the outstanding balance, which does not generate any cash flows. Thus, and as in the original contract, the principal receives a total amount equal to dy_t. At $\omega = \omega^o$, the agent receives $\lambda \cdot \frac{1}{\lambda} dD_t$ (as in the original contract). Instead, the principal receives (a) dC_t (from the perpetual debt), (b) $dy_t - dC_t - \frac{1}{\lambda}dD_t$ (from the credit line), (c) remuneration from $\mathcal{B}_t$, and (d) $(1-\lambda)\frac{1}{\lambda}dD_t$ (from equity), for a total of $dy_t - dD_t$, just as in the original contract.

This implementation mechanism is not unique. Biais, Mariotti, Plantin, and Rochet (2007) consider the following proposal. The firm issues debt and equity. The "managers" (i.e., the agent) does not have to pay anything for starting this firm. Only "financiers" (i.e., the principal) does. How? Financiers contribute to the startup by providing resources that entitle them to a proportion $(1-\lambda)$ of equity and to a console bond (possibly up to some default time discussed below) with cumulative coupon at time t equal to C_t. Therefore, the financiers contribute to a total amount of resources equal to $(1-\lambda)S_0 + B_0$, where S_0 and B_0 denote equity and debt value at time 0. Equity is as in the previous implementation mechanism, a claim on future flows of dividends equal to $\frac{dD_t}{\lambda}$.

With these arrangements and resources, the firm pays the initial cost I and, for reasons explained below, also installs an initial level of cash equal to some M_0. It then starts produce output flows equal to dy_t. If cash earns the safe interest rate, r, its dynamics are given by

$$dM_t = rM_t dt + dy_t - \frac{dD_t}{\lambda} - dC_t. \tag{5.65}$$

The first term on the RHS of eq. (5.65) is the interest rate accruing to cash, the second is the output flow, the third is dividends' distribution, and the fourth is the bond coupon flow.

Now, suppose that cash reserves are set to be proportional to the agent's continuation utility (in excess of R), $M_t = \frac{\omega_t - R}{\lambda}$. By (5.61) and $\phi_t = \lambda$, M_t is solution to

$$dM_t = \rho\left(\frac{R}{\lambda} + M_t\right)dt + \sigma dW_t - \frac{dD_t}{\lambda}. \tag{5.66}$$

By comparing (5.65) and (5.66), it must be that $dC_t = E(dy_t) - \left(\rho\frac{R}{\lambda} + (\rho - r)M_t\right)dt$.

Dividends are distributed as soon as M_t reaches a sufficiently large value, that is, the threshold $M^o \equiv \frac{\omega^o - R}{\lambda}$, where ω^o is the free-boundary value for the agent's continuation utility determined in the previous section. The firm is liquidated once its cash reserves hit zero, that is, at time $\tau : M_\tau = 0$. On liquidation, the firm defaults on its bond obligations, and the bond holders receive the firm's scrap value, L. Therefore, the model predicts firm liquidation when cash is sufficiently small, similar to the model with optimal cash management of the previous section. The difference is that, in the present model, firm liquidation occurs due to the incentive scheme underlying the original contract, not because of liquidity reasons.

We need to determine the initial cash M_0 that the firm installs at origination. First, we determine equity and debt value. Equity value is[17]

$$S_t \equiv S(M_t) = E_t\left(\int_t^\tau e^{-r(u-t)}\frac{dD_u}{\lambda}\right). \tag{5.67}$$

17. That is, the price function is solution to the differential equation $0 = \rho(\frac{R}{\lambda} + m)S'(m) + \frac{1}{2}\sigma^2 S''(m) - rS(m)$, subject to the boundary conditions $S(0) = 0$ and $S'(m^o) = 1$. The two boundary conditions follow by arguments nearly identical to those leading to (5.63). Thus, there is an analytical solution to the stock price, which can be obtained by following the steps used to derive eq. (5.64) in appendix 5.C.

As explained, the firm distributes dividends as soon cash reserves reach the value $M^o \equiv \frac{\omega^o - R}{\lambda}$. It is possible to show that the equity price is increasing and concave in M; the interpretation of this property is the following. An increase in M lowers the default probability and then the probability of dividends' payment. Therefore, stock prices react positively to changes in M. However, stock prices react more in bad times (i.e., when M is low) than in good because the threat of default is more stringent in this case: stock prices are then concave in M. Chapter 8 (see, e.g., section 8.3) explains that price evaluations do indeed behave asymmetrically during the business cycle and offers additional explanations for this empirical regularity.

Likewise, the bond value is[18]

$$B_t \equiv B(M_t) = E_t\left(\int_t^\tau e^{-r(u-t)} dC_t + e^{-r(\tau-t)} L\right). \tag{5.68}$$

The initial cash M_0 is found, residually, from the firm's book value. Appendix 5.C shows that the book value is

$$M_t + I + G_t = S_t + B_t, \quad G_t \equiv \lambda S_t + (V(\omega_t) - I). \tag{5.69}$$

That is, the book value of securities (the "right hand" of the balance sheet) is equal to cash, plus initial investments, and a term, G_t, interpreted as the firm's goodwill (the present value to managers plus the NPV to financiers).[19] Note that, at time 0, the firm only receives financial resources equal to $(1-\lambda) S_0 + B_0$. By eq. (5.69), these resources are equal to $M_0 + V(\omega_0) \geq M_0 + I$ where the inequality follows by the assumption that the NPV to financiers is positive. If financial markets are competitive, this inequality turns into an equality, such that the initial resources gathered through the financiers' contribution are used to cover the initial costs, I, and the initial cash reserves M_0. Therefore, $M_0 : V(R + \lambda M_0) = I$.

Appendix 5.A Proofs for Section 5.3

5.A.1 Spence-Mirrlees Condition for the Callable Bond Model

Consider the problem $\max_{\hat{p}} V(K(\hat{p}), p)$, where $V(K(\hat{p}), p)$ is as in eq. (5.17) and $\hat{p} = \pi(K(\hat{p}))$. The first- and second-order conditions for this problem are

$$0 = V_1(K(\hat{p}), p) K'(\hat{p}) \quad \text{and} \quad V_{11}(K(\hat{p}), p) (K'(\hat{p}))^2 + V_1(K(\hat{p}), p) K''(\hat{p}) \leq 0. \tag{5.A1}$$

Evaluating the first-order condition at $\hat{p} = p$ yields

$$0 = V_1(K(p), p) K'(p), \tag{5.A2}$$

---

18. The debt value is solution to $0 = \rho(R/\lambda + m)B'(m) + \frac{1}{2}\sigma^2 B''(m) + \mu - (\rho\frac{R}{\lambda} + (\rho - r)m) - rB(m)$, subject to boundary conditions that follow by arguments similar to those in the previous footnote. They are $B(0) = L$ and $B'(m^o) = 0$.

19. In other words, eq. (5.69) says that, at time 0, for example, the present value to the financiers, $V(\omega_t) - I$, is equal to the value of equity assigned to them, $(1-\lambda) S_t$, minus the net investment into the firm, $I + M_t - B_0$.

which is eq. (5.15). Now, differentiate eq. (5.A2) with respect to p,

$$0 = V_{11}(K(p), p)(K'(p))^2 + V_{12}(K(p), p)K'(p) + V_1(K(p), p)K''(p). \tag{5.A3}$$

Evaluating the second-order condition in (5.A1) leaves

$$0 \geq V_{11}(K(p), p)(K'(p))^2 + V_1(K(p), p)K''(p) = -V_{12}(K(p), p)K'(p),$$

where the last equality follows by eq. (5.A3). The incentive-compatible condition (5.18) follows.

5.A.2 Proof of Eq. (5.23)

Note that the result follows very simply by calculating the conditional expectation and the probability in the third line of the following equalities:

$$\begin{aligned} E(v-p)^+ &= E\left[(v-p)\mathbb{I}_{v>p}\right] \\ &= E\left[(v-p)|\,\mathbb{I}_{v>p}=1\right]P\{\mathbb{I}_{v>p}=1\} \\ &= \left[E(v|\,v>p)-p\right]P\{v>p\}, \end{aligned}$$

where P denotes the probability under the uniform distribution. However, we provide a proof based on a change of probability. The proof is more cumbersome, but changes in probability of this type occur very often in financial economics (see, e.g., section 1.4.2 in chapter 1; section 4.5 in chapter 4; or the many instances occurring in part III, such as chapter 13).

So, note that, denoting $\mu = E(v)$,

$$E\left(v\mathbb{I}_{v>p}\right) = \mu E\left(\frac{v}{\mu}\mathbb{I}_{v>p}\right) = \mu E^{\mu}\left(\mathbb{I}_{v>p}\right),$$

where E^{μ} denotes a new probability P, defined as follows.

$$\frac{dP^{\mu}}{dP} = \frac{v}{\mu}.$$

Therefore,

$$dP^{\mu} = \frac{v}{\mu}dP = \frac{v}{\mu}\frac{1}{\bar{v}}dv.$$

We have

$$E(v-p)^+ = E\left((v-p)\mathbb{I}_{v>p}\right) = \mu E^{\mu}\left(\mathbb{I}_{v>p}\right) - pE\left(\mathbb{I}_{v>p}\right) = \mu P^{\mu}(v>p) - pP(v>p), \tag{5.A4}$$

where

$$P^{\mu}(v>p) = \int_p^{\bar{v}} dP^{\mu} = \frac{1}{\bar{v}^2}\left(\bar{v}^2 - p^2\right). \tag{5.A5}$$

Eq. (5.23) follows by replacing (5.A5), $\mu = \frac{1}{2}\bar{v}$, and $P(v>p) = \frac{1}{\bar{v}}(\bar{v}-p)$ into (5.A4).

Appendix 5.B Debt and Moral Hazard

Proof of eq. (5.36). Note, first, that monotonicity of $D(\cdot)$ requires that $\omega'(x) \leq 1$. We are considering continuous and piecewise linear equity schedules. We conjecture and later verify that there exists a $D^* < x^*$ that maximizes the entrepreneur's profits, such that

$$\omega(x) = \begin{cases} 0, & \text{for } x \in [0, D^*) \\ b_0 + b_1 x, & \text{for } x \geq D^* \end{cases}$$

for two constants b_0 and b_1. Because $\omega(x)$ is continuous, we need that $b_0 = -b_1 D^*$, such that $\omega(x) = b_1(x - D^*)$ for $x \geq D^*$. Therefore, the first term on the RHS of the Lagrangian $\mathcal{L}$ in the main text (see (5.34)) is

$$\mathcal{L}_1(D) \equiv \int_0^{\bar{x}} \omega(x) \underbrace{\left(1 - \lambda + \mu \frac{g_e(x;e)}{g(x;e)}\right) g(x;e) dx}_{\equiv \zeta(x)} = \underbrace{b_1 \int_D^{\bar{x}} (x - D)\, \zeta(x)\, dx.}_{\equiv \mathcal{L}_{11}(D)}$$

Maximizing $\mathcal{L}_1(D)$ with respect to D leads to the following first-order condition, D^*: $0 = \int_{D^*}^{\bar{x}} \zeta(x)\, dx$. By the MLRP, $\zeta(\cdot)$ changes its sign at x^*, with $\zeta(x) < 0$ for $x < x^*$ and $\zeta(x) > 0$ for $x > x^*$. Therefore, the first-order condition can only be satisfied if $D^* < x^*$. The second-order condition for a maximum is indeed $\mathcal{L}_1''(D^*) = \zeta(D^*) < 0$.

Further, because $\omega'(x) \leq 1$, we need that $b_1 \leq 1$. We claim that $\mathcal{L}_{11}(D^*) > 0$, in which case $b_1 = 1$ (i.e., the feasible value of b_1 that maximizes $\mathcal{L}_1(D)$), and eq. (5.36) follows. To show that $\mathcal{L}_{11}(D^*) > 0$, note that

$$\mathcal{L}_{11}(D^*) = \int_{D^*}^{\bar{x}} x\zeta(x)\, dx - D^* \int_{D^*}^{\bar{x}} \zeta(x)\, dx = \int_{D^*}^{\bar{x}} x\zeta(x)\, dx,$$

where the second equality follows by the first-order conditions. Therefore,

$$\begin{aligned} \mathcal{L}_{11}(D^*) &= \int_{D^*}^{x^*} x\zeta(x)\, dx + \int_{x^*}^{\bar{x}} x\zeta(x)\, dx \\ &> x^* \int_{D^*}^{x^*} \zeta(x)\, dx + \int_{x^*}^{\bar{x}} x\zeta(x)\, dx \\ &> x^* \int_{D^*}^{x^*} \zeta(x)\, dx + x^* \int_{x^*}^{\bar{x}} \zeta(x)\, dx \\ &= x^* \int_{D^*}^{\bar{x}} \zeta(x)\, dx \\ &= 0, \end{aligned}$$

where the first and the second inequalities follow as $\zeta(x) < 0$ for $x \in [D^*, x^*]$ and $\zeta(x) > 0$ for $x \in [x^*, \bar{x}]$ and the last equality follows by the first-order condition.

Appendix 5.C Dynamic Problems

We provide the proof of a statement made in section 5.7.1.

Proof that V_I and V_P in (5.48) and (5.49) are increasing and concave. Remember that $\alpha_1 < 0, \alpha_2 > 0$, and $\beta_1 < 0$. Note that conditions (ii) and (iii) in the main text imply that (a) $1 = V_I'(k^o) = A_{I1}\left(\alpha_1 e^{\alpha_1 k^o} - \alpha_2 e^{\alpha_2 k^o}\right)$ and (b) $1 = V_P'(k^o) = \beta_1 A_{P1} e^{\beta_1 k^o}$. Now, (a) implies that $A_{I1} < 0$; therefore, $V_I'(k) > 0$ for all $k \leq k^o$. Likewise, (b) implies that $A_{P1} < 0$ and therefore $V_P'(k) > 0$ for all $k \geq k^o$ and $V_P''(k) = \beta_1^2 A_{P1} e^{\beta_1 k^o} < 0$ for all $k \geq k^o$.

We are left to show that $V_I''(k) < 0$ for all $k \leq k^o$. First, we show that $V_I''(k^o - \varepsilon) < 0$ for any arbitrarily small $\varepsilon > 0$. Indeed, differentiating the first equation in (5.47) and evaluating the result at $k = k^o$,

$$\frac{1}{2}\sigma^2 V_I'''(k^o) = rV_I'(k^o) - \mu V_I''(k^o) > 0,$$

where the inequality follows by the fact that $V_I'(k^o) = 1$ and the super-contact property $V_I''(k^o) = V_P''(k^o) = 0$. Thus, for small $\varepsilon > 0$, we have $V_I''(k^o - \varepsilon) < V_I''(k^o) = 0$. Next, we show that $V_I''(k) < 0$ for all $k \leq k^o$. Suppose, instead, that there exists a k_* such that $V_I''(k) < 0$ for all $k \in (k_{**}, k^o)$ and $V_I''(k_*) = 0$; by continuity, then, it would follow that $V_I'''(k_*) < 0$. Next, differentiate the first equation in (5.47) and evaluate the result at $k = k_{**}$,

$$\frac{1}{2}\sigma^2 V_I'''(k_*) = rV_I'(k_*) - \mu V_I''(k_*) = rV_I'(k_*) > 0,$$

where the inequality follows by the fact that $V_I'(k_*) > 0$, a contradiction.

Next, we provide the proof of a statement in section 5.7.2.

Proof that V in (5.64) is concave. Since $V(\omega) = V(\omega^o) - (\omega - \omega^o)$ for $\omega > \omega^o$, then, by continuity, $V''(\omega^o) = 0$. Next, differentiate eq. (5.A6) below with respect to ω,

$$-(\rho - r)V'(\omega) = \rho\omega V''(\omega) + \frac{1}{2}\sigma^2\lambda^2 V'''(\omega),$$

and evaluate this result at $\omega = \omega^o$, obtaining

$$\frac{1}{2}\sigma^2\lambda^2 V'''(\omega^o) = \rho - r > 0,$$

where we have used the result that $V'(\omega^o) = -1$ and $V''(\omega^o) = 0$ and the inequality follows by the assumption that the principal is more patient than the agent. Whence, $V'''(\omega^o) > 0$, which then implies that $V''(\omega^o - \varepsilon) < V''(\omega^o) = 0$ for any arbitrarily small $\varepsilon > 0$. We show that $V''(\omega) < 0$ for all $\omega \leq \omega^o$ by arguments similar to the previous proof of statements made in section 5.7.1: the existence of a ω_* (the counterpart to k_*) such that $V''(\omega_*) = 0$ would now imply that $V'(\omega_*) > 0$, but evaluating eq. (5A.6) below at ω_* would also imply that $\rho\omega_* V'(\omega_*) = rV(\omega_*) - \mu < 0$, a contradiction.

Proof of eq. (5.64). For $\omega \leq \omega^o$, $V(\omega)$ is solution to the second-order differential equation in (5.63), that is,

$$0 = \mu + \rho\omega V'(\omega) + \frac{1}{2}\sigma^2\lambda^2 V''(\omega) - rV(\omega). \tag{5.A6}$$

The solution to (5.A6) takes the following form:

$$V(\omega) = \frac{\mu}{r} + v(\omega), \tag{5.A7}$$

where v satisfies the following equation:

$$0 = \frac{1}{2}\sigma^2\lambda^2 v''(\omega) + \rho\omega v'(\omega) - rv(\omega).$$

Note that the function $v(\omega) = u\left(\frac{-\rho}{\sigma^2\lambda^2}\omega^2\right)$ is solution to

$$0 = zu''(z) + (b - z)u'(z) - au(z), \quad a \equiv -\frac{r}{2\rho}, \quad b \equiv \frac{1}{2}. \tag{5.A8}$$

Eq. (5.A8) is known as Kummer's equation, and the general solution to it is given by (see chapter 13 in Abramowitz and Stegun, 1970) $u(z) = c_1 M(a, b, z) + c_2(-z)^{1-b} M(a + 1 - b, 2 - b, z)$, that is, eq. (5.64), with $z = \frac{-\rho}{\sigma^2\lambda^2}\omega^2$, and

$$M(a, b, z) = 1 + \sum_{n=1}^{\infty} \frac{(a)_n z^n}{(b)_n n!}, \quad (a)_n \equiv a(a+1)\cdots(a+n-1), \tag{5.A9}$$

and c_1 and c_2 are two constants to be determined through the boundary conditions stated in the main text, namely, (a) $v(R) = L - \frac{\mu}{r}$, (b) $v'(\omega^o) = -1$, and (c) $v''(\omega^o) = 0$. The function M is known as the confluent hypergeometric function of the first kind.

Condition (a) delivers

$$L - \frac{\mu}{r} = u\left(\frac{-\rho}{\sigma^2\lambda^2}R^2\right). \tag{5.A10}$$

Next, evaluate (5.A6) at $\omega = \omega^o$, and plug (5.A7) and conditions (b) and (c) into it, obtaining $v(\omega^o) = -\frac{\rho}{r}\omega^o$ or

$$-\frac{\rho}{r}\omega^o = u\left(\frac{-\rho}{\sigma^2\lambda^2}\omega^{o2}\right). \tag{5.A11}$$

Eqs. (5.A10) and (5.A11) form a system of two equations with two unknowns, c_1 and c_2. The solutions are functions of ω^o, which we denote with $c_1(\omega^o)$ and $c_2(\omega^o)$. Finally, we use condition (b) and determine the free boundary, ω^o.

As an example, suppose that $R = 0$, and denote $z(\omega) \equiv \frac{-\rho\omega^2}{\sigma^2\lambda^2}$. Eqs. (5.A10) and (5.A11) reduce to

$$c_1 = L - \frac{\mu}{r}, \quad c_2(\omega^o) = -\frac{\frac{\rho}{r}\omega^o + c_1 M(a, b, z(\omega^o))}{(-z(\omega^o))^{1-b} M(a + 1 - b, 2 - b, z(\omega^o))}. \tag{5.A12}$$

Condition (b) reads as

$$-1=v'(\omega^o)=u'(z(\omega^o))\,z'(\omega^o), \tag{5.A13}$$

where

$$\begin{aligned}u'(z(\omega))=&\,c_1M_z(a,b,z(\omega))\\&+c_2(\omega^o)(-z(\omega))^{1-b}M_z(a+1-b,2-b,z(\omega))\\&-(1-b)\,c_2(\omega^o)(-z(\omega))^{-b}M(a+1-b,2-b,z(\omega))\end{aligned}$$

and M_z denotes the derivative taken with respect to z; that is,

$$M_z(a,b,z)=\frac{a}{b}M(a+1,b+1,z).$$

Thus, ω^o is the solution to eq. (5.A13), and the value of c_2 is obtained by plugging this solution into $c_2(\omega^o)$ in (5.A12).

Proof of eq. (5.69). By eq. (5.65),

$$\begin{aligned}E\left(e^{-r(T\wedge\tau)}M_{T\wedge\tau}\right)=&\,M_0+E\left(\int_0^{T\wedge\tau}e^{-rt}dy_t\right)-E\left(\int_0^{T\wedge\tau}e^{-rt}\frac{dD_t}{\lambda}\right)\\&-E\left(\int_0^{T\wedge\tau}e^{-rt}dC_t\right),\end{aligned}$$

and, by taking the limits of both sides of this equation for $T\longrightarrow\infty$,

$$0=M_0+E\left(\int_0^{\tau}e^{-rt}dy_t\right)-E\left(\int_0^{\tau}e^{-rt}\frac{dD_t}{\lambda}\right)-E\left(\int_0^{\tau}e^{-rt}dC_t\right),$$

where we have used the property that $M_\tau=\frac{\omega_\tau-R}{\lambda}=0$. Replacing the definition of equity (see eq. (5.67)), debt (see eq. (5.68)), and finally, the principal's continuation value (see eq. (5.62)) leaves eq. (5.69) with $t=0$. It is straightforward to show that eq. (5.69) holds for any $\tau\in[0,\tau]$.

References

Abramowitz, M., and I. A. Stegun, eds. (1970). *Handbook of Mathematical Functions, with Formulas, Graphs, and Mathematical Tables*. 9th ed. New York: Dover.

Aghion, P., and P. Bolton (1987). "Contracts as a Barrier to Entry." *American Economic Review* 77, 388–401.

Akerlof, G. A. (1970). "The Market for 'Lemons': Quality Uncertainty and the Market Mechanism." *Quarterly Journal of Economics* 84, 488–500.

Arrow, K. J. (1963). "Uncertainty and the Welfare Economics of Medical Care." *American Economic Review* 53, 941–973.

Beatty, R. P., and J. R. Ritter (1986). "Investment Banking, Reputation, and the Underpricing of Initial Public Offerings." *Journal of Financial Economics* 15, 213–232.

Bhattacharya, S. (1979). "Imperfect Information, Dividend Policy, and the Bird in the Hand Fallacy." *Bell Journal of Economics* 10, 259–270.

Biais, B., T. Mariotti, G. Plantin, and J.-C. Rochet (2007). "Dynamic Security Design: Convergence to Continuous Time and Asset Pricing Implications." *Review of Economic Studies* 74, 345–390.

Blanchard, O., and S. Fischer (1989). *Lectures on Macroeconomics*. Cambridge, MA: MIT Press.

Chomsisengphet, S., and A. Pennington-Cross (2006). "The Evolution of the Subprime Mortgage Market." *Federal Reserve Bank of St. Louis Review* 88, 31–56.

DeMarzo, P. M. (2005). "The Pooling and Tranching of Securities: A Model of Informed Intermediation." *Review of Financial Studies* 18, 1–35.

DeMarzo, P. M., and M. J. Fishman (2007). "Optimal Long-Term Financial Contracting." *Review of Financial Studies* 20, 2079–2127.

DeMarzo, P. M., and Y. Sannikov (2006). "Optimal Security Design and Dynamic Capital Structure in a Continuous-Time Agency Model." *Journal of Finance* 61, 2681–2724.

Diamond, D. W. (1991). "Debt Maturity Structure and Liquidity Risk." *Quarterly Journal of Economics* 106, 709–737.

Gale, D., and M. Hellwig, (1985). "Incentive-Compatible Debt Contracts: The One-Period Problem." *Review of Economic Studies* 52, 647–663.

Glosten, L. R., and P. R. Milgrom (1985). "Bid, Ask and Transaction Prices in a Specialist Market with Heterogeneously Informed Traders." *Journal of Financial Economics* 14, 71–100.

Green, E. (1987). "Lending and the Smoothing of Uninsurable Income." In *Contractual Arrangements for Intertemporal Trade*, edited by E.C. Prescott and N. Wallace, 3–25. Minneapolis: University of Minnesota Press.

Grossman, S. J., and J. E. Stiglitz (1980). "On the Impossibility of Informationally Efficient Markets." *American Economic Review* 70, 393–408.

Harrison, J. M. (1985). *Brownian Motion and Stochastic Flow Systems*. New York: Wiley.

Hartman-Glaser, B., T. Piskorski, and A. Tchistyi (2012). "Optimal Securitization with Moral Hazard." *Journal of Financial Economics* 104, 186–202.

Holmström, B. (1979). "Moral Hazard and Observability." *Bell Journal of Economics* 10, 74–91.

Innes, R. D. (1990). "Limited Liability and Incentive Contracting with Ex-ante Action Choices." *Journal of Economic Theory* 52, 45–67.

Jeanblanc-Picqué, M., and A. N. Shirayev (1995). "Optimization of the Flow of Dividends." *Russian Mathematical Surveys* 50, 257–277.

Jenkinson, T., and A. Ljungqvist (2001). *Going Public*. Oxford: 2nd ed. Oxford University Press.

Karatzas, I., and S. E. Shreve (1991). *Brownian Motion and Stochastic Calculus*. 2nd ed. New York: Springer.

Keys, B., T. Mukherjee, A. Seru, and V. Vig (2010). "Did Securitization Lead to Lax Screening? Evidence from Subprime Loans." *Quarterly Journal of Economics* 125, 307–362.

Kyle, A. S. (1985). "Continuous Auctions and Insider Trading." *Econometrica* 53, 1335–1335.

Laffont, J.-J., and D. Martimort (2002). *The Theory of Incentives: The Principal-Agent Model*. Princeton, NJ: Princeton University Press.

Leland, H. E. (1994). "Corporate Debt Value, Bond Covenants and Optimal Capital Structure." *Journal of Finance* 49, 1213–1252.

Leland, H. E., and D. H. Pyle (1977). "Informational Asymmetries, Financial Structure, and Financial Intermediation." *Journal of Finance* 32, 371–387.

Mirrlees, J. (1974). "Notes on Welfare Economics, Information, and Uncertainty." In *Essays on Economic Behavior under Uncertainty*, edited by M. Balch, D. McFadden, and S. Wu. Amsterdam: North-Holland.

Mirrlees, J. A. (1975). "The Theory of Moral Hazard and Unobservable Behavior: Part I." Unpublished manuscript, Nuffield College, Oxford.

Modigliani, F., and M. Miller (1958). "The Cost of Capital, Corporation Finance and the Theory of Investment." *American Economic Review* 48, 261–297.

Radner, R., and L. Shepp (1996). "Risk vs. Profit-Potential: A Model for Corporate Strategy." *Journal of Economics Dynamics and Control* 20, 1373–1396.

Rajan, R. G., and L. Zingales (1998). "Financial Dependence and Growth." *American Economic Review* 88, 559–586.

Riley, J. (1975). "Competitive Signalling." *Journal of Economic Theory* 10, 174–186.

Rock, K. (1982). "Why New Issues are Underpriced." PhD diss., University of Chicago. Rock, K. (1986). "Why New Issues are Underpriced." *Journal of Financial Economics* 15, 187–212.

Romer, D. (2001). *Advanced Macroeconomics*. New York: McGraw-Hill.

Ross, S. A. (1973). "The Economic Theory of Agency: The Principal's Problem." *American Economic Review* 63, 134–139.

Ross, S. A. (1977). "The Determination of Financial Structure: The Incentive-Signalling Approach." *Bell Journal of Economics* 8, 23–40.

Rothschild, M., and J. Stiglitz (1976). "Equilibrium in Competitive Insurance Markets: An Essay on the Economics of Imperfect Information." *Quarterly Journal of Economics* 90, 29–649.

Salanié, B. (1997). *The Economics of Contracts: A Primer*. Cambridge, MA: MIT Press.

Shavell, S. (1979). "On Moral Hazard and Insurance." *Quarterly Journal of Economics* 93, 541–562.

Smith, A. (1776). *The Wealth of Nations*. New York: Modern Library.

Spear, S. E., and S. Srivastava (1987). "On Repeated Moral Hazard With Discounting." *Review of Economic Studies* 54, 599–617.

Spence, M. (1973). "Job Market Signaling." *Quarterly Journal of Economics* 87, 355–374.

Spence, M. (1974). *Market Signaling: Information Transfer in Hiring and Related Screening Processes*. Cambridge, MA: Harvard University Press.

Stiglitz, J. E., and A. Weiss (1981): "Credit Rationing in Markets with Imperfect Information." *American Economic Review* 71, 393–410.

Tirole, J. (2006). *The Theory of Corporate Finance*. Princeton, NJ: Princeton University Press.

Townsend, R. M. (1979). "Optimal Contracts and Competitive Markets with Costly State Verification." *Journal of Economic Theory* 21, 265–293.

6

Taking Models to Data

6.1 Introduction

This chapter surveys methods to estimate and test dynamic models of asset prices. Section 6.2 discusses foundational issues. Section 6.3 through 6.7 deal with classical estimation and testing methodologies.

Section 6.3 reviews maximum likelihood (ML) methods (Gauss, 1816; Fisher, 1912). ML relies on the principle that data are generated by some well-identified parametric model and that their realization is well summarized by a probability distribution, a distribution known up to the parameters; these parameters form the object of statistical inference. An ML estimator (MLE) is the value of the parameters that maximizes the probability of having observed our sample data.

Section 6.4 describes estimation and testing methods by which it is not necessary to specify the whole probability distribution of sample data. We only assume that these data are generated by some model and that they satisfy some restrictions; for example, our data are required to have finite moments (mean, variance, etc.), and these moments are functions of the model parameters, just as for the Lucas model in chapter 3 (see section 3.2). Then we estimate the model parameters while making sure that their value makes theoretical moments (that is, the moments implied by the theoretical model) and empirical moments (those we estimate from data) as close as possible. We call these restrictions moment conditions. This section sets up the stage for a general class of estimators, called M-estimators.

Section 6.5 explains that MLE may be understood as a M-estimator and that M-estimation may help test for model misspecification, the circumstance by which the model we are working with does not belong to the family of the true data generating process. Section 6.6 reviews methods of moments. The oldest is the "classical" method of moments where the number of moment conditions equals the dimension of the parameter vector (Pearson, 1894); this method has been generalized to the generalized method of moments (GMM) where the number of moment conditions exceeds the dimension of the parameter vector, leading to the so-called minimum chi-squared criterion (Neyman and Pearson, 1928; Hansen, 1982). Finally, section 6.7 reviews relatively more recent developments, relying on simulations. These methods aim to implement ML and GMM estimation for models that are analytically so complex that their probability or moments are unknown but can be simulated.

We emphasize that this chapter contains introductory material and that this material is, sometimes, dealt with heuristically. References to more rigorous treatments include classics such as Amemiya (1985), Gallant (1987), and White (1984) (for theory) and Hamilton (1994) (for the analysis of time series and the early applications in macroeconomics and finance). Further, at times, this chapter contains reviews that are not necessarily linked to details of this book; these reviews may be useful before reading more advanced material in other publications.

6.2 Data Generating Processes

6.2.1 Models: Specification and Identification

Given is a n-dimensional stochastic process y_t, generated by some *data generating process* (DGP), to be defined below. We use all available data to make inference into the probability distribution underlying y_t. Consider the following basic definitions. A DGP is a conditional law, say, the law of y_t, given the set of past values $\underline{y_{t-1}} = \{y_{t-1}, y_{t-2}, \cdots\}$ and some exogenous variable z_t, with $\underline{z_t} = \{z_t, z_{t-1}, z_{t-2}, \cdots\}$, denoted as $\ell_0(y_t | x_t)$, where $x_t = (\underline{y_{t-1}}, \underline{z_t})$. That is, ℓ_0 is the conditional density of the data, the true law. By "exogenous," we mean that the probability distribution of z_t is not affected by past or present values of y_t. Then we have three basic definitions. First, we define a *parametric model* as a set of conditional laws for y_t, indexed by a parameter vector $\theta \in \Theta \subseteq \mathbb{R}^p$,

$$(M) = \{\ell(y_t | x_t; \theta), \theta \in \Theta \subseteq \mathbb{R}^p\}. \tag{6.1}$$

We call Θ the parameter vector space. Second, we say that the model (M) is *well-specified* if

$$\exists \theta_0 \in \Theta : \ell(y_t | x_t; \theta_0) = \ell_0(y_t | x_t).$$

Third, we say that the model (M) is identifiable if θ_0 is unique. The main goal of this chapter is to review tools aimed at drawing inference about the true parameter θ_0 based on the observations of y_t. We need to rely on some assumptions that are described next.

6.2.2 Restrictions on the DGP

The previous definition of DGP is too rich to be practically relevant. This chapter deals with estimation methods applying to DGPs that satisfy a few restrictions. Two fundamental restrictions are usually imposed on the DGP:

- Restrictions on the *heterogeneity* of the stochastic process, leading to *stationary* random processes.
- Restrictions on the *memory* of the stochastic process, paving the way to *ergodic* processes.

6.2.2.1 *Stationarity*

Stationary processes describe phenomena that lead to long-run equilibria, in a statistical sense: as time unfolds, the probability generating the observations settles down to some long-run probability density, a time invariant probability. There are two basic notions of stationarity: (i) *strong* (or strict) *stationarity*, by which there is "homogeneity in law"; and (ii) *weak stationarity* or stationarity of order r by which there is "homogeneity in moments." Simply, strong stationarity requires that the joint probability distribution of data is the same for all the subsamples where we observed data and that this property will also hold in the future. Weak stationarity requires that these properties only hold for a limited number (i.e., r) of subsamples. One reason stationary processes are interesting is that their probability distribution is described by a limited number of parameters. A particularly convenient stationary process is a *covariance stationary* process, one for which means and autocovariances are all finite and independent of calendar time.

Stationary processes may have short or long memory. Consider the following examples: one for which $cov(y_t, y_{t+\tau}) = \tau^2$ and another for which $cov(y_t, y_{t+\tau}) = \exp(-|\tau|)$. The DGP is stationary in both cases. Yet, and regarding the first process, the dependence increases with τ; regarding the second, the dependence decreases with τ. Stationary processes may thus have long memory and "ergodicity" further restricts the DGP.

6.2.2.2 *Ergodicity*

We shall deal with DGPs where the dependence between y_{t_1} and y_{t_2} decreases with $|t_2 - t_1|$. To introduce some concepts and notation we shall say that two events A and B are independent when $P(A \cap B) = P(A)P(B)$. A stochastic process is *asymptotically independent* if, for some function β_τ,

$$\beta_\tau \geq \left| F(y_{t_1}, \cdots, y_{t_n}, y_{t_1+\tau}, \cdots, y_{t_n+\tau}) - F\left(y_{t_1}, \cdots, y_{t_n}\right) F\left(y_{t_1+\tau}, \cdots, y_{t_n+\tau}\right) \right|,$$

where we also have that $\lim_{\tau\to\infty} \beta_\tau \to 0$. A stochastic process is *N-dependent* if $\forall \tau \leq N$, $\beta_\tau \neq 0$. A stochastic process is *asymptotically uncorrelated* if there exists ρ_τ such that for all t, $\rho_\tau \geq cov(y_t, y_{t+\tau})/\sqrt{var(y_t)var(y_{t+\tau})}$, and that $0 \leq \rho_\tau \leq 1$ with $\sum_{\tau=0}^{\infty} \rho_\tau < \infty$. For example, $\rho_\tau = \tau^{-(1+\delta)}$, $\delta > 0$, in which case $\lim_{\tau\to\infty} \rho_\tau \to 0$.

Let $\mathbb{B}_1^t$ denote the σ-algebra generated by $\{y_1, \cdots, y_t\}$ and $A \in \mathbb{B}_{-\infty}^t$, $B \in \mathbb{B}_{t+\tau}^{\infty}$, and define

$$\alpha_\tau = \sup_\tau |P(A \cap B) - P(A)P(B)|, \quad \varphi_\tau = \sup_\tau |P(B \mid A) - P(B)|, \; P(A) > 0.$$

We say that (i) y is *strongly mixing* or *α-mixing* if $\lim_{\tau\to\infty} \alpha_\tau \to 0$ and (ii) y is *uniformly mixing* if $\lim_{\tau\to\infty} \varphi_\tau \to 0$. Clearly, a uniformly mixing process is also strongly mixing. A second-order stationary process is *ergodic* if $\lim_{T\to\infty} \sum_{\tau=1}^{T} cov(y_t, y_{t+\tau}) < \infty$. If a second-order stationary process is strongly mixing, it is also ergodic.

6.2.3 Parameter Estimation

Consider an estimator of the parameter vector θ of the model (6.1). Clearly, an estimator depends on the sample size and is thus denoted as $\hat{\theta}_T \equiv t_T(y)$. Of a given estimator $\hat{\theta}_T$, we say that it is:

- *unbiased* if $E(\hat{\theta}_T) = \theta_0$. The difference $E(\hat{\theta}_T) - \theta_0$ is called distortion, or bias.
- *weakly consistent* if $\text{plim}\, \hat{\theta}_T = \theta_0$. And *strongly consistent* if $\hat{\theta}_T \overset{a.s.}{\to} \theta_0$.

Finally, an estimator $\hat{\theta}_T^{(1)}$ is more *efficient* than another estimator $\hat{\theta}_T^{(2)}$ if, for any vector of constants c, we have that $c^\top \cdot var(\hat{\theta}_T^{(1)}) \cdot c < c^\top \cdot var(\hat{\theta}_T^{(2)}) \cdot c$.

6.2.4 Basic Properties of Density Functions

We assume we have T observations $y_T^1 = \{y_1, \cdots, y_T\}$, the realization of a T-dimensional random variable with joint density $f(\tilde{y}_1, \cdots, \tilde{y}_T; \theta) = f(\tilde{y}_1^T; \theta)$. We have momentarily put tildes on y_i to emphasize that we view each $\tilde{y}_i$ as a random variable. However, from now on and to simplify notation, we shall write y_i instead of $\tilde{y}_i$. Note that, by construction, $\int f(y|\theta)\, dy \equiv \int \cdots \int f(y_1^T|\theta)\, dy_1^T = 1$ for all $\theta \in \Theta$.

Next, suppose that the support of y is independent of θ. Under regularity conditions,

$$\nabla_\theta \int f(y;\theta)\, dy = \int \nabla_\theta f(y;\theta)\, dy = 0_p,$$

where 0_p is a column vector of zeros in $\mathbb{R}^p$ and ∇_θ denotes partial derivative with respect to θ. Moreover, for all $\theta \in \Theta$,

$$0_p = \int \nabla_\theta f(y;\theta)\, dy = E_\theta\left[\nabla_\theta \ln f(y;\theta)\right]. \tag{6.2}$$

Finally, we have

$$\begin{aligned} 0_{p\times p} &= \nabla_\theta \int \left[\nabla_\theta \ln f(y;\theta)\right] f(y;\theta)\, dy \\ &= \int \left[\nabla_{\theta\theta} \ln f(y;\theta)\right] f(y;\theta)\, dy + \int \left|\nabla_\theta \ln f(y;\theta)\right|_2 f(y;\theta)\, dy, \end{aligned}$$

where $|x|_2$ denotes the outer product, that is, $|x|_2 = x \cdot x^\top$. Hence, by eq. (6.2),

$$E_\theta\left[\nabla_{\theta\theta} \ln f(y;\theta)\right] = -E_\theta\left|\nabla_\theta \ln f(y;\theta)\right|_2 = -var_\theta\left[\nabla_\theta \ln f(y;\theta)\right] \equiv -\mathcal{J}(\theta),\ \forall\theta \in \Theta.$$

The matrix $\mathcal{J}$ is known as the Fisher's information matrix.

6.2.5 The Cramer-Rao Lower Bound

Let $t(y)$ some unbiased estimator of θ and assume, momentarily, that the dimension of the parameter space to $p = 1$. We have

$$E(t(y)) = \int t(y) f(y;\theta)\, dy.$$

Under regularity conditions,

$$\nabla_\theta E[t(y)] = \int t(y)\left[\nabla_\theta \ln f(y;\theta)\right] f(y;\theta)\, dy = cov\left(t(y), \nabla_\theta \ln f(y;\theta)\right).$$

By Cauchy-Schwartz inequality, $\left[cov\left(t(y), \nabla_\theta \ln f(y;\theta)\right)\right]^2 \le var[t(y)] \cdot var\left[\nabla_\theta \ln f(y;\theta)\right]$. Therefore,

$$\left[\nabla_\theta E(t(y))\right]^2 \le var[t(y)] \cdot var\left[\nabla_\theta \ln f(y;\theta)\right] = -var[t(y)] \cdot E\left[\nabla_{\theta\theta} \ln f(y;\theta)\right].$$

But if $t(y)$ is unbiased, or $E[t(y)] = \theta$,

$$var[t(y)] \ge \mathcal{J}(\theta)^{-1}.$$

The matrix $\mathcal{J}(\theta)^{-1}$ is the celebrated *Cramer-Rao lower bound*. The same results hold in the multidimensional case through a mere change in notation (see, e.g., Amemiya, 1985, 14–17).

6.3 Maximum Likelihood Estimation

6.3.1 Definition

The density of the data, $f(y_1^T | \theta)$, maps every possible sample and parameter values of θ on to positive numbers, the "likelihood" of occurrence of any given sample, given the parameter θ: $\mathbb{R}^{nT} \times \Theta \mapsto \mathbb{R}_+$. We trace the joint density of the entire sample through a thought experiment, in which we change the sample y_1^T. So the sample is viewed as the realization of a random variable.[1] We ask: Which value of θ makes the sample we observed the most likely to have occurred? We introduce the "likelihood function," $L(\theta | y_1^T) \equiv f(y_1^T; \theta)$. It is the function $\theta \mapsto f(y;\theta)$ for y_1^T given and equal to $\bar{y}$, say:

$$L(\theta | \bar{y}) \equiv f(\bar{y}; \theta).$$

Then, we maximize $L(\theta | y_1^T)$ with respect to θ. That is, we look for the value of θ that maximizes the probability to have observed our available sample data. The resulting estimator is called an MLE. As we shall see, the MLE attains the Cramer-Rao lower bound, provided the model is not misspecified.

6.3.2 Factorizations

Consider a series of events $\{A_i\}$. In appendix 6.B, we derive the following relation:

$$\Pr\left(\cap_{i=1}^{n} A_i\right) = \prod_{i=1}^{n} \Pr\left(A_i \middle| \cap_{j=1}^{i-1} A_j\right). \tag{6.3}$$

By eq. (6.3), then, the MLE satisfies

$$\hat{\theta}_T = \arg\max_{\theta \in \Theta} L_T(\theta) = \arg\max_{\theta \in \Theta} \left(\frac{1}{T} \ln L_T(\theta)\right).$$

In this section, we assume the data are IID data, such that

$$\ln L_T(\theta) \equiv \ln \prod_{t=1}^{T} f\left(y_t \middle| y_1^{t-1}; \theta\right) = \sum_{t=1}^{T} \ln f\left(y_t \middle| y_1^{t-1}; \theta\right) \equiv \sum_{t=1}^{T} \ln f(y_t; \theta) \equiv \sum_{t=1}^{T} \ell_t(\theta) \tag{6.4}$$

and $\ell_t(\theta)$ is the "log-likelihood" of a single observation. Appendix 6.C deals with MLE in the presence of dependent processes.

6.3.3 Asymptotic Properties

We show asymptotic normality in the IID case based on heuristic arguments and hint at more rigorous proofs and general results in appendix 6.B.

---

1. We make this description of maximum likelihood by relying on a standard, classical perspective. A Bayesian statistician would view the sample as *given*. We do not review Bayesian methods in this chapter.

6.3.3.1 The limiting problem

The MLE satisfies the following first-order conditions:

$$0_p = \nabla_\theta \ln L_T(\theta)\big|_{\theta=\hat{\theta}_T} \equiv \nabla_\theta \ln L_T(\hat{\theta}_T).$$

Consider a Taylor expansion of the first-order conditions around θ_0,

$$0_p = \nabla_\theta \ln L_T(\hat{\theta}_T) \overset{d}{=} \nabla_\theta \ln L_T(\theta_0) + \nabla_{\theta\theta} \ln L_T(\theta_0)(\hat{\theta}_T - \theta_0), \tag{6.5}$$

where the notation $x_T \overset{d}{=} y_T$ means that the difference $x_T - y_T = o_p(1)$ and θ_0 is defined as the solution to the limiting problem,

$$\theta_0 = \arg\max_{\theta\in\Theta}\left[\lim_{T\to\infty}\left(\frac{1}{T}\ln L_T(\theta)\right)\right] = \arg\max_{\theta\in\Theta}\left[E\left(\ell\left(\theta\right)\right)\right].$$

Finally, ℓ satisfies regularity conditions needed to ensure that

$$\theta_0 : E\left[\nabla_\theta \ell\left(\theta_0\right)\right] = 0_p. \tag{6.6}$$

To show that (6.6) is indeed the solution, suppose θ_0 is identified, that is, $\theta \neq \theta_0$ and $\theta, \theta_0 \in \Theta \Leftarrow f(y|\,\theta) \neq f(y|\,\theta_0)$. Assume further that, for each $\theta \in \Theta$, $E_\theta\left[\ln f(y|\,\theta)\right] < \infty$. Then we have that $\theta_0 = \arg\max_{\theta\in\Theta} E_\theta\left[\ln f(y|\,\theta)\right]$; this value of θ is unique. The proof is indeed very simple. We have

$$\begin{aligned}
E_{\theta_0}\left[-\ln\left(\frac{f(y|\,\theta)}{f(y|\,\theta_0)}\right)\right] &> -\ln E_{\theta_0}\left(\frac{f(y|\,\theta)}{f(y|\,\theta_0)}\right)\\
&= -\ln\int\frac{f(y|\,\theta)}{f(y|\,\theta_0)}f(y|\,\theta_0)dy\\
&= -\ln\int f(y|\,\theta)dy = 0.
\end{aligned}$$

6.3.3.2 Consistency and asymptotic normality

Provided the model is well-specified, we have that, under suitable regularity conditions, $\hat{\theta}_T \overset{p}{\to} \theta_0$ and even $\hat{\theta}_T \overset{a.s.}{\to} \theta_0$. One example of conditions required to obtain weak consistency is that the following uniform weak law of large numbers holds:

$$\lim_{T\to\infty} \Pr\left[\sup_{\theta\in\Theta}\left|\ell_T\left(\theta\right) - E\left(\ell\left(\theta\right)\right)\right|\right] \to 0.$$

Next, we may elaborate on the asymptotic expansion in eq. (6.5) and conclude that

$$\begin{aligned}
\sqrt{T}(\hat{\theta}_T - \theta_0) &\overset{d}{=} -\left[\frac{1}{T}\nabla_{\theta\theta}\ln L_T(\theta_0)\right]^{-1}\frac{1}{\sqrt{T}}\nabla_\theta \ln L_T(\theta_0)\\
&= -\left[\frac{1}{T}\sum_{t=1}^{T}\nabla_{\theta\theta}\ell_t(\theta_0)\right]^{-1}\frac{1}{\sqrt{T}}\sum_{t=1}^{T}\nabla_\theta \ell_t(\theta_0).
\end{aligned}$$

By the law of large numbers reviewed in appendix 6.A (weak law no. 1),

$$\frac{1}{T}\sum_{t=1}^{T}\nabla_{\theta\theta}\ell_t(\theta_0)\xrightarrow{p}E_{\theta_0}\left[\nabla_{\theta\theta}\ell_t(\theta_0)\right]=-\mathcal{J}(\theta_0).$$

Therefore, asymptotically,

$$\sqrt{T}(\hat{\theta}_T-\theta_0)\overset{d}{=}\mathcal{J}(\theta_0)^{-1}\frac{1}{\sqrt{T}}\sum_{t=1}^{T}\nabla_\theta\ell_t(\theta_0).$$

We also have

$$\frac{1}{\sqrt{T}}\sum_{t=1}^{T}\nabla_\theta\ell_t(\theta_0)\xrightarrow{d}N\left(0,\mathcal{J}(\theta_0)\right).$$

Indeed, let $\overline{\nabla_\theta\ell(\theta_0)_T}=\frac{1}{T}\sum_{t=1}^{T}\nabla_\theta\ell_t(\theta_0)$, and note that $E\left(\nabla_\theta\ell_t(\theta_0)\right)=0$. Then, by the central limit theorem (CLT) reviewed in appendix 6.A,

$$\frac{1}{\sqrt{T}}\frac{\sum_{t=1}^{T}\nabla_\theta\ell_t(\theta_0)}{\sqrt{var\left[\nabla_\theta\ell_t(\theta_0)\right]}}=\frac{\sqrt{T}\left(\overline{\nabla_\theta\ell(\theta_0)_T}-E\left(\nabla_\theta\ell_t(\theta_0)\right)\right)}{\sqrt{var\left[\nabla_\theta\ell_t(\theta_0)\right]}},$$

where, for each t, $var\left[\nabla_\theta\ell_t(\theta_0)\right]=\mathcal{J}(\theta_0)$.

Finally, by the Slutzky's theorem (see appendix 6.A),

$$\sqrt{T}(\hat{\theta}_T-\theta_0)\xrightarrow{d}N\left(0,\mathcal{J}(\theta_0)^{-1}\right).$$

Therefore, the MLE attains the Cramer-Rao lower bound.

6.4 M-Estimators

Consider a function g of the unknown parameters θ. Given a function Ψ, an M-estimator of the function $g(\theta)$ is the solution to

$$\max_{g\in G}\sum_{t=1}^{T}\Psi\left(x_t,y_t;g\right),$$

where y and x are stationary and ergodic. We assume that a solution to this problem exists, that it is interior, and that it is unique. Let us denote the M-estimator with $\hat{g}_T(x_1^T,y_1^T)$. Naturally, the M-estimator satisfies the following first-order conditions:

$$0=\frac{1}{T}\sum_{t=1}^{T}\nabla_g\Psi\left(y_t,x_t;\hat{g}_T(x_1^T,y_1^T)\right).$$

To simplify the presentation, we assume that (x,y) are independent in time and that they have the same law. By the law of large numbers,

$$\begin{aligned}\frac{1}{T}\sum_{t=1}^{T}\Psi\left(y_t,x_t;g\right)&\xrightarrow{p}\iint\Psi\left(y,x;g\right)dF(x,y)=\iint\Psi\left(y,x;g\right)dF\left(y\middle|x\right)dZ\left(x\right)\\&\equiv E_xE_0\left[\Psi\left(y,x;g\right)\right],\end{aligned}$$

where E_0 is the expectation operator taken with respect to the true conditional law of y given x and E_x is the expectation operator taken with respect to the true marginal law of x. The limit problem is

$$g_\infty = g_\infty(\theta_0) = \arg\max_{g \in G} E_x E_0 [\Psi(y, x; g)].$$

Under standard regularity conditions,[2] there exists a sequence of M-estimators $\hat{g}_T(x, y)$ converging almost surely to $g_\infty = g_\infty(\theta_0)$. Under additional regularity conditions, the M-estimator is also asymptotic normal as noted below.

Theorem 6.1. *Let* $\mathcal{I} \equiv E_x E_0 \left(\nabla_g \Psi(y, x; g_\infty(\theta_0)) \left[\nabla_g \Psi(y, x; g_\infty(\theta_0)) \right]^\top \right)$ *and assume that the matrix* $\mathcal{J} \equiv E_x E_0 \left[-\nabla_{gg} \Psi(y, x; g) \right]$ *exists and has an inverse. We have*

$$\sqrt{T} \left(\hat{g}_T - g_\infty(\theta_0) \right) \xrightarrow{d} N\left(0, \mathcal{J}^{-1} \mathcal{I} \mathcal{J}^{-1}\right).$$

Proof (Sketch). The M-estimator satisfies the following first-order conditions:

$$\begin{aligned} 0 &= \frac{1}{\sqrt{T}} \sum_{t=1}^{T} \nabla_g \Psi(y_t, x_t; \hat{g}_T) \\ &\stackrel{d}{=} \frac{1}{\sqrt{T}} \sum_{t=1}^{T} \nabla_g \Psi(y_t, x_t; g_\infty) + \sqrt{T} \left[\frac{1}{T} \sum_{t=1}^{T} \nabla_{gg} \Psi(y_t, x_t; g_\infty) \right] \cdot \left(\hat{g}_T - g_\infty \right). \end{aligned}$$

By rearranging terms,

$$\begin{aligned} \sqrt{T} \left(\hat{g}_T - g_\infty \right) &\stackrel{d}{=} \left[-\frac{1}{T} \sum_{t=1}^{T} \nabla_{gg} \Psi(y_t, x_t; g_\infty) \right]^{-1} \cdot \frac{1}{\sqrt{T}} \sum_{t=1}^{T} \nabla_g \Psi(y_t, x_t; g_\infty) \\ &\stackrel{d}{=} \left[E_x E_0 \left(-\nabla_{gg} \Psi(y, x; g) \right) \right]^{-1} \cdot \frac{1}{\sqrt{T}} \sum_{t=1}^{T} \nabla_g \Psi(y_t, x_t; g_\infty) \\ &\stackrel{d}{=} \mathcal{J}^{-1} \cdot \frac{1}{\sqrt{T}} \sum_{t=1}^{T} \nabla_g \Psi(y_t, x_t; g_\infty). \end{aligned}$$

By the limiting problem, $E_x E_0 \left[\nabla_g \Psi(y, x; g_\infty) \right] = 0$. Then, $var\left(\nabla_g \Psi \right) = E\left(\nabla_g \Psi \cdot \left[\nabla_g \Psi \right]^\top \right) = \mathcal{I}$, and then,

$$\frac{1}{\sqrt{T}} \sum_{t=1}^{T} \nabla_g \Psi(y_t, x_t; g_\infty) \xrightarrow{d} N(0, \mathcal{I}).$$

The result follows by the Slutzky's theorem and the symmetry of $\mathcal{J}$. □

2. Notably, G is compact; Ψ is continuous with respect to g and integrable with respect to the true law, for each g; $\frac{1}{T} \sum_{t=1}^{T} \Psi(y_t, x_t; g) \xrightarrow{a.s.} E_x E_0 [\Psi(y, x; g)]$ uniformly on G; and the limit problem has a unique solution $g_\infty = g_\infty(\theta_0)$.

One simple example of M-estimators is the nonlinear least squares estimator

$$\hat{\theta}_T = \arg\min_{\theta\in\Theta} \sum_{t=1}^{T} [y_t - m(x_t;\theta)]^2,$$

for some function m. In this case, $\Psi(x,y;\theta) = [y - m(x;\theta)]^2$.

6.5 Pseudo- or Quasi-Maximum Likelihood

The MLE is an M-estimator: set $\Psi = \ln L$, the log-likelihood function. Indeed, assume the model is well-specified, in which case $\mathcal{J} = \mathcal{I}$, which confirms we are back to the MLE.

Next, suppose that we implement the MLE to estimate a model, when in fact the model is *misspecified*. Misspecification means that the true DGP $\ell_0(y_t|x_t)$ does not belong to the family of laws spanned by our model, or

$$\ell_0(y_t|x_t) \notin (M) = \{f(y_t|x_t;\theta),\ \theta\in\Theta\}.$$

Yet suppose we insist in maximizing $\Psi = \ln L$, where $\ln L = \sum_t f(y_t|x_t;\theta)$. In this case,

$$\sqrt{T}(\hat{\theta}_T - \theta_0^*) \xrightarrow{d} N\left(0, \mathcal{J}^{-1}\mathcal{I}\mathcal{J}^{-1}\right),$$

where θ_0^* is the "pseudo-true" value[3] and

$$\mathcal{J} = -E_x E_0\left[\nabla_{\theta\theta}\ln f(y_t|\underline{y_{t-1}};\theta_0^*)\right],$$

$$\mathcal{I} = E_x E_0\left(\nabla_\theta \ln f(y_t|\underline{y_{t-1}};\theta_0^*)\cdot\left[\nabla_\theta \ln f(y_t|\underline{y_{t-1}};\theta_0^*)\right]^\top\right).$$

In the presence of specification errors, $\mathcal{J} \neq \mathcal{I}$. Comparing the two estimated matrices leads to detect specification errors. Finally, note that in this general case, the variance-covariance matrix $\mathcal{J}^{-1}\mathcal{I}\mathcal{J}^{-1}$ depends on the unknown law of (y_t, x_t). To assess the precision of the estimates of $\hat{g}_T$, one needs to estimate such a variance-covariance matrix. A common practice is to use the following almost sure consistent estimators:

$$\hat{J} = -\frac{1}{T}\sum_{t=1}^{T}\nabla_{gg}\Psi(y_t,x_t;\hat{g}_T), \quad \text{and} \quad \hat{\mathcal{I}} = -\frac{1}{T}\sum_{t=1}^{T}\left(\nabla_g\Psi(y_t,x_t;\hat{g}_T)\left[\nabla_g\Psi(y_t,x_t;\hat{g}_T)^\top\right]\right).$$

6.6 Generalized Method of Moments

Economic theory often places restrictions on models that have the following format:

$$E\left[h(y_t;\theta_0)\right] = 0_q, \tag{6.7}$$

where $h: \mathbb{R}^n \times \Theta \mapsto \mathbb{R}^q$, θ_0 is the true parameter vector, y_t is the n-dimensional vector of the observable variables, and $\Theta \subseteq \mathbb{R}^p$. Typically, then, the MLE cannot be used to estimate θ_0.

3. That is, θ_0^* is clearly the solution to some misspecified limiting problem. This θ_0^* has an appealing interpretation in terms of some entropy distance minimizer.

Moreover, MLE requires specifying a density function. Hansen (1982) proposed the GMM estimation procedure. Section 6.6.1 provides an account regarding the theoretical construction of this procedure. Section 6.6.2 reviews the early applications of GMM in financial economics.

6.6.1 Theory

Consider the sample counterpart to the population in eq. (6.7),

$$\bar{h}\left(y_1^T;\theta\right)=\frac{1}{T}\sum_{t=1}^{T}h\left(y_t;\theta\right), \tag{6.8}$$

where we have rewritten h as a function of the parameter vector $\theta\in\Theta$. The basic idea of GMM is to find a θ which makes $\bar{h}\left(y_1^{\top};\theta\right)$ as close as possible to zero. Precisely, consider the following definition.

Definition 6.2 (GMM estimator). The GMM estimator *is the sequence* $\hat{\theta}_T$ *satisfying*

$$\hat{\theta}_T=\arg\min_{\theta\in\Theta\subseteq\mathbb{R}^p}\underbrace{\bar{h}\left(y_1^T;\theta\right)^{\top}}_{1\times q}\cdot\underbrace{W_T}_{q\times q}\cdot\underbrace{\bar{h}\left(y_1^T;\theta\right)}_{q\times 1},$$

where $\{W_T\}$ *is a sequence of weighting matrices, with elements that may depend on the observations.*

When $p=q$, we say the GMM is *just identified* and is simply the MM, satisfying

$$\hat{\theta}_T:\bar{h}(y_1^T;\hat{\theta}_T)=0_q.$$

When $p<q$, we say the GMM estimator imposes *overidentifying* restrictions.

We analyze the IID case only. Under regularity conditions, there exists a matrix W_T that minimizes the asymptotic variance of the GMM estimator, which asymptotically satisfies

$$W=\left[\lim_{T\to\infty}T\cdot E\left(\bar{h}(y_1^T;\hat{\theta}_T)\cdot\bar{h}(y_1^T;\hat{\theta}_T)^{\top}\right)\right]^{-1}\equiv\Sigma_0^{-1}. \tag{6.9}$$

An estimator of Σ_0 can be

$$\Sigma_T=\frac{1}{T}\sum_{t=1}^{T}\left[h(y_t;\hat{\theta}_T)\cdot h(y_t;\hat{\theta}_T)^{\top}\right].$$

Note that $\hat{\theta}_T$ depends on the weighting matrix Σ_T, and the weighting matrix Σ_T depends on $\hat{\theta}_T$. Therefore, we need to implement an iterative procedure. The more one iterates, the less likely the final outcome depends on the initial weighting matrix $\Sigma_T^{(0)}$. For example, one can start with $\Sigma_T^{(0)}=\mathbf{I}_q$.

Now we have the following.

Theorem 6.3 (Asymptotic normality of GMM). *Consider a sequence of GMM estimators* $\hat{\theta}_T$ *with weighting matrix* Σ_T *converging to* Σ_0 *as in eq. (6.9) and such that* $\hat{\theta}_T\xrightarrow{p}\theta_0$. *We have*

$$\sqrt{T}(\hat{\theta}_T-\theta_0)\xrightarrow{d}N\left(0_p,\left[E\left(h_\theta\right)\Sigma_0^{-1}E\left(h_\theta\right)^{\top}\right]^{-1}\right),\quad \textit{where } h_\theta\equiv\nabla_\theta h(y;\theta_0).$$

Proof (Sketch). The assumption that $\hat{\theta}_T \xrightarrow{p} \theta_0$ holds under mild regularity conditions. Moreover, the GMM satisfies

$$0_p = \underset{p\times q}{\nabla_\theta \bar{h}(y_1^T;\hat{\theta}_T)} \underset{q\times q}{\Sigma_T^{-1}} \underset{q\times 1}{\bar{h}(y_1^T;\hat{\theta}_T)}. \tag{6.10}$$

Eq. (6.10) confirms that, if $p=q$, the GMM satisfies $\hat{\theta}_T : \bar{h}(y_1^T;\hat{\theta}_T)=0$. Indeed, $\nabla_\theta h \Sigma_T^{-1}$ is full rank with $p=q$, and eq. (6.10) can only be satisfied with $\bar{h}=0$. In the general case, $q>p$, we have

$$\underset{q\times 1}{\sqrt{T}\bar{h}(y_1^T;\hat{\theta}_T)} = \underset{q\times 1}{\sqrt{T}\bar{h}\left(y_1^T;\theta_0\right)} + \underset{q\times p}{\left[\nabla_\theta \bar{h}\left(y_1^T;\theta_0\right)\right]^\top} \sqrt{T}(\hat{\theta}_T-\theta_0) + o_p(1).$$

By premultiplying both sides of the previous equality by $\nabla_\theta \bar{h}(y_1^T;\hat{\theta}_T)\Sigma_T^{-1}$,

$$\begin{aligned}
&\sqrt{T}\nabla_\theta \bar{h}(y_1^T;\hat{\theta}_T)\Sigma_T^{-1}\cdot \bar{h}(y_1^T;\hat{\theta}_T) \\
&= \sqrt{T}\nabla_\theta \bar{h}(y_1^T;\hat{\theta}_T)\Sigma_T^{-1}\cdot \bar{h}\left(y_1^T;\theta_0\right) \\
&\quad + \nabla_\theta \bar{h}(y_1^T;\hat{\theta}_T)\Sigma_T^{-1}\cdot \left[\nabla_\theta \bar{h}\left(y_1^T;\theta_0\right)\right]^\top \sqrt{T}(\hat{\theta}_T-\theta_0) + o_p(1).
\end{aligned}$$

The LHS of this equality is zero by the first-order conditions in eq. (6.10). By rearranging terms,

$$\begin{aligned}
\sqrt{T}(\hat{\theta}_T-\theta_0) &\stackrel{d}{=} -\left(\nabla_\theta \bar{h}\left(y_1^T;\theta_0\right)\Sigma_T^{-1}\left[\nabla_\theta \bar{h}\left(y_1^T;\theta_0\right)\right]^\top\right)^{-1} \nabla_\theta \bar{h}(y_1^T;\hat{\theta}_T)\Sigma_T^{-1}\cdot\sqrt{T}\bar{h}\left(y_1^T;\theta_0\right) \\
&= -\left(\frac{1}{T}\sum_{t=1}^T \nabla_\theta h(y_t;\hat{\theta}_T)\Sigma_T^{-1}\frac{1}{T}\sum_{t=1}^T [\nabla_\theta h(y_t;\hat{\theta}_T)]^\top\right)^{-1} \\
&\quad \times \frac{1}{T}\sum_{t=1}^T \nabla_\theta h(y_t;\hat{\theta}_T)\Sigma_T^{-1}\sqrt{T}\bar{h}\left(y_1^T;\theta_0\right) \\
&\stackrel{d}{=} -\left(E\left(h_\theta\right)\Sigma_0^{-1}E\left(h_\theta\right)^\top\right)^{-1} E\left(h_\theta\right)\Sigma_0^{-1}\cdot\frac{1}{\sqrt{T}}\sum_{t=1}^T h\left(y_t;\theta_0\right).
\end{aligned}$$

Next, note that $\frac{1}{\sqrt{T}}\sum_{t=1}^T h\left(y_t;\theta_0\right) \xrightarrow{d} N\left(E(h), var(h)\right)$, where, by eq. (6.7), $E(h)=0$ and $var(h)=E\left(h\cdot h^\top\right)=\Sigma_0$. Hence,

$$\frac{1}{\sqrt{T}}\sum_{t=1}^T h\left(y_t;\theta_0\right) \xrightarrow{d} N\left(0,\Sigma_0\right).$$

Therefore, $\sqrt{T}(\hat{\theta}_T-\theta_0)$ is asymptotically normal with expectation 0_p and variance

$$\begin{aligned}
&\left(E\left(h_\theta\right)\Sigma_0^{-1}E\left(h_\theta\right)^\top\right)^{-1} E\left(h_\theta\right)\Sigma_0^{-1}\Sigma_0\Sigma_0^{-1}E\left(h_\theta\right)^\top\left(E\left(h_\theta\right)\Sigma_0^{-1}E\left(h_\theta\right)^\top\right)^{\top-1} \\
&= \left(E\left(h_\theta\right)\Sigma_0^{-1}E\left(h_\theta\right)^\top\right)^{-1}.
\end{aligned}$$

□

A widely used global specification test is that of the celebrated "overidentifying restrictions." Consider the following intuitive result:

$$\sqrt{T}\bar{h}\left(y_1^T;\theta_0\right)^{\top}\Sigma_0^{-1}\sqrt{T}\bar{h}\left(y_1^T;\theta_0\right)^{\top}\xrightarrow{d}\chi^2(q).$$

Now, would we expect that a similar result holds if we were to replace the true parameter θ_0 with the GMM estimator $\hat{\theta}_T$? It would seem that the answer is in the affirmative as $\hat{\theta}_T$ is a consistent estimator for θ_0. However, it turns out that it is not the case. Define

$$C_T=\sqrt{T}\bar{h}(y_1^T;\hat{\theta}_T)^{\top}\Sigma_T^{-1}\cdot\sqrt{T}\bar{h}(y_1^T;\hat{\theta}_T).$$

We have

$$\begin{aligned}
\sqrt{T}\bar{h}(y_1^T;\hat{\theta}_T) &\stackrel{d}{=}\sqrt{T}\bar{h}\left(y_1^T;\theta_0\right)+\nabla_\theta\bar{h}\left(y_1^T;\theta_0\right)\cdot\sqrt{T}(\hat{\theta}_T-\theta_0)\\
&\stackrel{d}{=}\sqrt{T}\bar{h}\left(y_1^T;\theta_0\right)-\left[\nabla_\theta\bar{h}\left(y_1^T;\theta_0\right)\right]^{\top}\left[E\left(h_\theta\right)\Sigma_0^{-1}E\left(h_\theta\right)^{\top}\right]^{-1}E\left(h_\theta\right)\Sigma_0^{-1}\cdot\sqrt{T}\bar{h}\left(y_1^T;\theta_0\right)\\
&\stackrel{d}{=}\sqrt{T}\bar{h}\left(y_1^T;\theta_0\right)-E\left(h_\theta\right)^{\top}\left[E\left(h_\theta\right)\Sigma_0^{-1}E\left(h_\theta\right)^{\top}\right]^{-1}E\left(h_\theta\right)\Sigma_0^{-1}\cdot\sqrt{T}\bar{h}\left(y_1^T;\theta_0\right)\\
&=\underset{q\times q}{(\mathbf{I}_q-\mathbf{P}_q)}\underset{q\times 1}{\sqrt{T}\bar{h}\left(y_1^T;\theta_0\right)},
\end{aligned}$$

where

$$\mathbf{P}_q\equiv E\left(h_\theta\right)^{\top}\left[E\left(h_\theta\right)\Sigma_0^{-1}E\left(h_\theta\right)^{\top}\right]^{-1}E\left(h_\theta\right)\Sigma_0^{-1}$$

is the orthogonal projector in the space generated by the columns of $E\left(h_\theta\right)$ by the inner product Σ_0^{-1}. Thus, we have shown that

$$C_T\stackrel{d}{=}\sqrt{T}\bar{h}\left(y_1^T;\theta_0\right)^{\top}\left(\mathbf{I}_q-\mathbf{P}_q\right)^{\top}\Sigma_T^{-1}\left(\mathbf{I}_q-\mathbf{P}_q\right)\sqrt{T}\bar{h}\left(y_1^T;\theta_0\right).$$

But,

$$\sqrt{T}\bar{h}\left(y_1^T;\theta_0\right)\xrightarrow{d}N\left(0,\Sigma_0\right),$$

and, by a classical result,

$$C_T\xrightarrow{d}\chi^2\left(q-p\right).$$

We now review early work aimed at estimating and testing asset pricing models.

6.6.2 Early Asset Pricing Tests

Hansen and Singleton (1982, 1983) started the literature on estimation and testing of dynamic asset pricing models based on a fully articulated rational expectations framework. Consider the Euler equations arising in the Lucas model (see section 3.2 in chapter 3),

$$E\left(\beta\frac{u'(c_{t+1})}{u'(c_t)}\left(1+r_{i,t+1}\right)-1\middle|\mathcal{F}_t\right)=0,\quad i=1,\cdots,m,$$

where u is the utility function of the representative agent, r_i is the return on asset i, β is the discount factor, $\mathcal{F}_t$ is the information set as of time t, and m is the number of assets. Consider the CRRA utility function, $u(x) = x^{1-\gamma}/(1-\gamma)$. If the model is well-specified, there exist some β_0 and γ_0 such that

$$\mathrm{E}\left(\beta_0 \left(\frac{c_{t+1}}{c_t}\right)^{-\gamma_0}(1+r_{i,t+1}) - 1 \middle| \mathcal{F}_t\right) = 0, \quad i = 1, \cdots, m.$$

To summarize, the parameter vector has dimension $p = 2$. To estimate the true parameter vector, $\theta_0 \equiv (\beta_0, \gamma_0)$, we can build up a system of orthogonality conditions by projecting observable variables predicted by the model onto some other variables included in the information set $\mathcal{F}_t$, called "instruments." Thus, a system of q orthogonality conditions is

$$E\left[h\left(y_t; \theta_0\right)\right] = 0_q,$$

where, for some vector of n instruments, say, $\mathcal{I}_t = [i_{1,t}, \cdots, i_{n,t}]^\top$,

$$\underset{q\times 1}{h\left(y_t; \theta\right)} = \begin{bmatrix} \left(\beta\left(\frac{c_{t+1}}{c_t}\right)^{-\eta}(1+r_{1,t+1}) - 1\right) \cdot \mathcal{I}_t \\ \vdots \\ \left(\beta\left(\frac{c_{t+1}}{c_t}\right)^{-\eta}(1+r_{m,t+1}) - 1\right) \cdot \mathcal{I}_t \end{bmatrix}, \quad q = mn.$$

Variables that we may include as candidates for instruments may be constants; past values of consumption growth, $\frac{c_{t+1}}{c_t}$; or past returns.

6.7 Simulation-Based Estimators

When the data probability distribution is fully specified, ML should be the ideal estimation method for the simple reason that its estimator achieves the Cramer-Rao lower bounds. However, economic theory places restrictions that make some models problematic to estimate through ML. Moreover, economic theory does not necessarily specify the distribution of the data that it tries to predict. In these cases, GMM is a natural estimation method. Unfortunately, GMM may also be unfeasible in some situations of interest. Let us illustrate.

Assume that the GDP can be summarized by the transition function,

$$y_{t+1} = H\left(y_t, \epsilon_{t+1}; \theta_0\right), \tag{6.11}$$

where $H: \mathbb{R}^n \times \mathbb{R}^d \times \Theta \mapsto \mathbb{R}^n$ and ϵ_t is a vector of IID disturbances in $\mathbb{R}^d$. We assume an econometrician knows the function H; for example, H may be suggested by economic theory. Next, let $z_t = (y_t, y_{t-1}, \cdots, y_{t-l+1})$, $l < \infty$. In many cases of interest, the function $\bar{h}$ in eq. (6.8) can be written as

$$\bar{h}\left(y_1^T; \theta\right) = \frac{1}{T}\sum_{t=1}^{T} \underbrace{\left[f_t^* - \mathrm{E}\left(f\left(z_t, \theta\right)\right)\right]}_{\equiv h(z_t, \theta)}, \tag{6.12}$$

where

$$f_t^* = f(z_t, \theta_0)$$

is a vector-valued moment function or "observation function," a function that summarizes the main predictions of the theory. For example, the Lucas model suggests that we may take $f_t^* = (1 + r_{i,t+1})^{-1}$ and $E(f(z_t, \theta)) = \beta E((\frac{c_{t+1}}{c_t})^{-\gamma})$. Then, we define consumption growth $y_{t+1} = \ln \frac{c_{t+1}}{c_t}$ and make assumptions on the transition law in (6.11). For example, we may assume y_{t+1} is log-normal as in some basic examples dealt with in part II (see, e.g., chapter 7). Armed with this assumption, we can determine $E(f(z_t, \theta))$ in closed form.

Our problems begin when we cannot determine the expectation $E(f(z_t, \theta))$ in closed form for each θ. In this case, the GMM estimator is unfeasible. Simulation-based methods have the potential to make methods of moments feasible.

6.7.1 Three Simulation-Based Estimators

The basic idea underlying simulation-based methods is quite simple. While the moment conditions are too complex to be determined analytically, the model in eq. (6.11) can be simulated. Accordingly, draw ϵ_t from its distribution, and save the simulated values $\hat{\epsilon}_t$. Compute recursively

$$y_{t+1}^{\theta} = H(y_t^{\theta}, \hat{\epsilon}_{t+1}, \theta),$$

and create simulated moment functions

$$f_t^{\theta} \equiv f(z_t^{\theta}, \theta).$$

Consider the following estimator:

$$\theta_T = \arg\min_{\theta \in \Theta} G_T(\theta)^{\top} W_T G_T(\theta), \tag{6.13}$$

where W_T is some weighting matrix, $G_T(\theta)$ is the simulated counterpart to $\bar{h}$ in eq. (6.12),

$$G_T(\theta) = \frac{1}{T} \sum_{t=1}^{T} \left(f_t^* - \frac{1}{S(T)} \sum_{s=1}^{S(T)} f_s^{\theta} \right),$$

and $S(T)$ is the simulated sample size, T; we express the simulated sample size as a function of T for reasons related to asymptotic theory.

The estimator θ_T in (6.13) is known as *simulated method of moments* (SMM) estimator. Intuitively, it aims to match the sample properties of the simulated processes f_t^{θ} to the actual ones. The estimator was introduced in a series of works by McFadden (1989), Pakes and Pollard (1989), Lee and Ingram (1991), and Duffie and Singleton (1993). The simulated pseudo-ML method of Laroque and Salanié (1989, 1993, 1994) can also be interpreted as an SMM estimator.

A second simulation-based estimator relies on the *indirect inference* principle (IIP) and was proposed by Gouriéroux, Monfort, and Renault (1993) and Smith (1993). Instead of minimizing the distance of some moment conditions, the IIP relies on minimizing the parameters of an "auxiliary," and not necessarily a well-specified model. Consider, for example, the following auxiliary parameter estimator:

$$\beta_T = \arg\max_{\beta} \ln L\left(y_1^T;\beta\right), \tag{6.14}$$

where L is the likelihood of some possibly misspecified model. Consider simulating S times the process y_t in eq. (6.11) and computing

$$\beta_T^s(\theta) = \arg\max_{\beta} \ln L(y_s(\theta)_1^T;\beta), \quad s=1,\cdots,S,$$

where $y_s(\theta)_1^T = (y_t^{\theta,s})_{t=1}^T$ are the simulated variables (for $s=1,\cdots,S$) when the parameter vector is θ. The IIP-based estimator is defined similarly as θ_T in eq. (6.13) but with the function G_T given by

$$G_T(\theta) = \beta_T - \frac{1}{S}\sum_{s=1}^{S}\beta_T^s(\theta). \tag{6.15}$$

Figure 6.1 illustrates the main ideas underlying the IIP.

Finally, Gallant and Tauchen (1996) propose a simulation-based estimation method, labeled *efficient method of moments* (EMM). Their estimator sets

$$G_T(\theta,\beta_T) = \frac{1}{N}\sum_{n=1}^{N}\frac{\partial}{\partial\beta}\ln f\left(y_n^{\theta}\middle|\, z_{n-1}^{\theta};\beta_T\right),$$

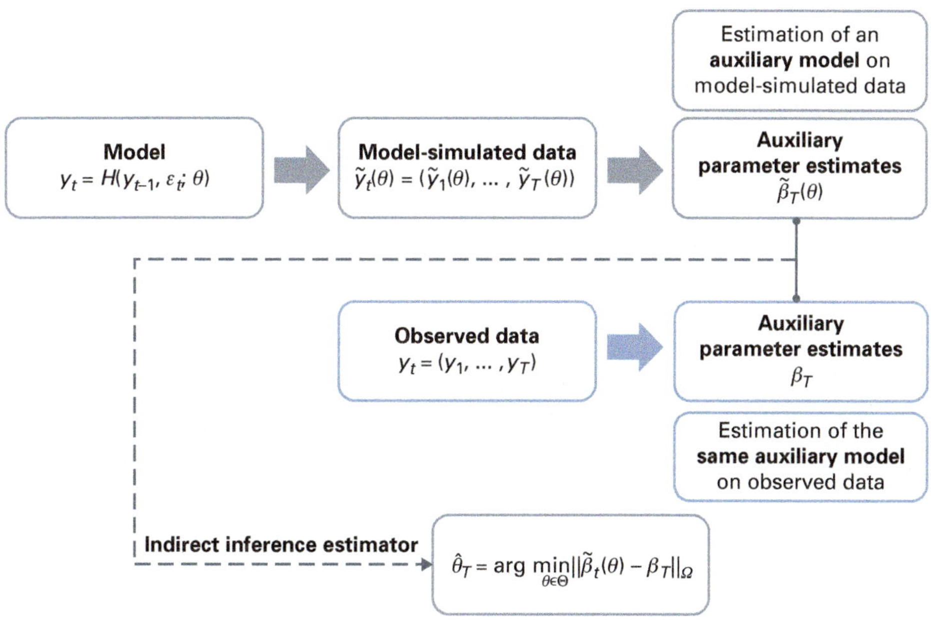

Figure 6.1
The Indirect Inference principle. Given the *true* model $y_t = H(y_{t-1},\epsilon_t;\theta)$, an estimator of θ based on the indirect inference principle ($\hat{\theta}_T$ say) makes the parameters of some *auxiliary* model $\tilde{\beta}_T(\hat{\theta}_T)$ as close as possible to the parameters β_T of *the same auxiliary* model estimated on the observations. That is, $\hat{\theta}_T = \arg\min_{\theta\in\Theta}\left\|\tilde{\beta}_T(\theta) - \beta_T\right\|_{\Omega}$, for some norm Ω.

where $\frac{\partial}{\partial\beta}\ln f\left(y|\,z;\beta\right)$ is the score of some auxiliary model f, also known as the score generator; β_T is the pseudo-ML estimator of the auxiliary model; and $(y_n^{\theta})_{n=1}^{N}$ is a long simulation (i.e., N is very large) of eq. (6.11), with the parameter vector set equal to θ. Finally, the weighting matrix W_T in eq. (6.13) is taken to be any matrix $\mathcal{I}_T^{-1}$ converging in probability to

$$\mathcal{I}=E\left[\left|\frac{\partial}{\partial\beta}\ln f\left(y_2|\,z_1;\beta\right)\right|_2\right]. \tag{6.16}$$

To motivate this choice of $G_T(\theta)$, note that the auxiliary score, $\frac{\partial}{\partial\beta}\ln f\left(y_t|\,z_{t-1};\beta_T\right)$, satisfies the following first-order conditions,

$$\frac{1}{T}\sum_{n=1}^{T}\frac{\partial}{\partial\beta}\ln f\left(y_t|\,z_{t-1};\beta_T\right)=0,$$

which represent the sample equivalent of

$$E\left[\frac{\partial}{\partial\beta}\ln f\left(y_2|\,z_1;\beta^*\right)\right]=0$$

for some β^*. Likewise, we must have that, with $\theta=\theta_0$, $G_T(\theta_0,\beta_T)=0$ *for large* N. All in all, the EMM searches for a parameter θ for the stochastic process $H\left(y_t,\epsilon_{t+1};\cdot\right)$ in (6.11), such that the expectation of the score of the auxiliary model is zero, a fundamental property of the score—one that holds even when the model is misspecified.

6.7.2 Asymptotic Normality

We provide heuristic derivations of asymptotic normality for the previous estimators and then define conditions under which the EMM may be asymptotically efficient.

6.7.2.1 *Simulated method of moments*

Let

$$\Sigma_0=\sum_{j=-\infty}^{\infty}E\left[\left(f_t^*-E\left(f_t^*\right)\right)\left(f_{t-j}^*-E\left(f_{t-j}^*\right)\right)^{\top}\right],$$

and suppose that

$$W_T\xrightarrow{p}W_0=\Sigma_0^{-1}.$$

We claim that under this condition, we have that, as $T\to\infty$ and $S(T)\to\infty$,

$$\sqrt{T}(\theta_T-\theta_0)\xrightarrow{d}N\left(0_p,(1+\tau)\left(D_0^{\top}\Sigma_0^{-1}D_0\right)^{-1}\right), \tag{6.17}$$

where $\tau=\lim_{T\to\infty}\frac{T}{S(T)}$, $D_0=E\left(\nabla_\theta G_\infty\left(\theta_0\right)\right)=E\left(\nabla_\theta f_\infty^{\theta_0}\right)$, and the notation G_∞ means that $G_.$ is drawn from its stationary distribution.

Indeed, the SMM in eq. (6.13) satisfies the first-order conditions

$$\begin{aligned}0_p &= [\nabla_\theta G_T(\theta_T)]^\top W_T G_T(\theta_T)\\ &= [\nabla_\theta G_T(\theta_T)]^\top W_T \cdot [G_T(\theta_0) + \nabla_\theta G_T(\theta_0)(\theta_T - \theta_0)] + o_p(1).\end{aligned}$$

That is,

$$\begin{aligned}\sqrt{T}(\theta_T - \theta_0) &\stackrel{d}{=} -\left([\nabla_\theta G_T(\theta_T)]^\top W_T \nabla_\theta G_T(\theta_0)\right)^{-1} [\nabla_\theta G_T(\theta_T)]^\top W_T \cdot \sqrt{T} G_T(\theta_0)\\ &\stackrel{d}{=} -\left(D_0^\top W_0 D_0\right)^{-1} D_0^\top W_0 \cdot \sqrt{T} G_T(\theta_T)\\ &= -\left(D_0^\top \Sigma_0^{-1} D_0\right)^{-1} D_0^\top \Sigma_0^{-1} \cdot \sqrt{T} G_T(\theta_0).\end{aligned} \tag{6.18}$$

We have

$$\begin{aligned}\sqrt{T} G_T(\theta_0) &= \sqrt{T} \cdot \frac{1}{T}\sum_{t=1}^{T}\left(f_t^* - \frac{1}{S(T)}\sum_{s=1}^{S(T)} f_s^{\theta_0}\right)\\ &= \frac{1}{\sqrt{T}}\sum_{t=1}^{T}\left(f_t^* - E\left(f_\infty^*\right)\right) - \frac{\sqrt{T}}{\sqrt{S(T)}} \cdot \frac{1}{\sqrt{S(T)}}\sum_{s=1}^{S(T)}\left(f_s^{\theta_0} - E\left(f_\infty^{\theta_0}\right)\right)\\ &\stackrel{d}{\to} N(0, (1+\tau)\Sigma_0),\end{aligned}$$

where we have used the fact that $E\left(f_\infty^*\right) = E\left(f_\infty^{\theta_0}\right)$. Using this result in eq. (6.18) produces the convergence in eq. (6.17). If $\tau = \lim_{T\to\infty} \frac{T}{S(T)} = 0$ (i.e., the number of simulations grows faster than the sample size), the SMM estimator is as efficient as the GMM estimator. Finally, and obviously, we need that $\tau = \lim_{T\to\infty} \frac{T}{S(T)} < \infty$: the number of simulations $S(T)$ cannot grow more slowly than the sample size.

6.7.2.2 *Indirect inference*

The IIP-based estimator works slightly differently. For this estimator, even if the number of simulations S is fixed, asymptotic normality is obtained without requiring that S goes to infinity faster than the sample size. Basically, the main requirement of the IIP is that ST goes to infinity.

By eq. (6.18) and the discussion in section 6.7.1, we know that the first-order conditions satisfied by the IIP-based estimator are, asymptotically:

$$\sqrt{T}(\theta_T - \theta_0) \stackrel{d}{=} -\left(D_0^\top W_0 D_0\right)^{-1} D_0^\top W_0 \cdot \sqrt{T} G_T(\theta_0),$$

where G_T is as in eq. (6.15), $D_0 = \nabla_\theta \beta(\theta)$, and $\beta(\theta)$ is solution to the limiting problem corresponding to the estimator in (6.14), namely,

$$\beta(\theta) = \arg\max_\beta \left(\lim_{T\to\infty} \frac{1}{T} \ln L\left(y_1^T; \beta\right)\right).$$

We determine the distribution of G_T in eq. (6.15). We have

$$\begin{aligned}\sqrt{T}G_T(\theta_0) &= \frac{1}{S}\sum_{s=1}^{S}\sqrt{T}\left(\beta_T - \beta_T^s(\theta_0)\right)\\ &= \frac{1}{S}\sum_{s=1}^{S}\sqrt{T}\left[(\beta_T - \beta_0) - \left(\beta_T^s(\theta_0) - \beta_0\right)\right]\\ &= \sqrt{T}(\beta_T - \beta_0) - \frac{1}{S}\sum_{s=1}^{S}\sqrt{T}\left(\beta_T^s(\theta_0) - \beta_0\right),\end{aligned}$$

where $\beta_0 = \beta(\theta_0)$. Hence, given the independence of the sample and the simulations,

$$\sqrt{T}G_T(\theta_0) \xrightarrow{d} N\left(0, \left(1 + \frac{1}{S}\right) \cdot \text{Asy.Var}\left(\sqrt{T}\beta_T\right)\right).$$

That is, asymptotically, S can be fixed with respect to T.

6.7.2.3 *Efficient method of moments*

We have

$$\theta_T = \arg\min_{\theta} G_T(\theta, \beta_T)^\top W_T G_T(\theta, \beta_T), \quad G_T(\theta, \beta_T) = \frac{1}{N}\sum_{n=1}^{N}\frac{\partial}{\partial\beta}\ln f\left(y_n^\theta \middle| z_{n-1}^\theta; \beta_T\right).$$

Therefore, the EMM estimator satisfies the following first-order conditions:

$$\begin{aligned}0 &= \nabla_\theta G_T(\theta_T, \beta_T)^\top W_T G_T(\theta_T, \beta_T)\\ &\stackrel{d}{=} \nabla_\theta G_T(\theta_0, \beta_T)^\top W_T\left(G_T(\theta_0, \beta_T) + \nabla_\theta G_T(\theta_0, \beta_T)(\theta_T - \theta_0)\right)\end{aligned}$$

or

$$\begin{aligned}&\sqrt{T}(\theta_T - \theta_0) \stackrel{d}{=}\\ &\quad -\left(\nabla_\theta G_T(\theta_0, \beta_T)^\top W_T \nabla_\theta G_T(\theta_0, \beta_T)\right)^{-1}\nabla_\theta G_T(\theta_0, \beta_T)^\top W_T\sqrt{T}G_T(\theta_0, \beta_T).\end{aligned}$$

We have, for some β^*,

$$\sqrt{T}G_T(\theta_0, \beta_T) \stackrel{d}{=} \mathcal{J}\sqrt{T}\left(\beta_T - \beta^*\right) \xrightarrow{d} N(0, \mathcal{I}),$$

where $\mathcal{J} = E\left(\frac{\partial}{\partial\beta\partial\beta^\top}\ln f\left(y_2 | y_1; \beta\right)\right)$ and $\mathcal{I}$ is as in eq. (6.16). Hence,

$$\sqrt{T}(\theta_T - \theta_0) \xrightarrow{d} N(0, V),$$

where

$$V = \left(\nabla_\theta G^\top W \nabla_\theta G\right)^{-1}\nabla_\theta G^\top W \mathcal{I} W^\top \nabla_\theta G\left(\nabla_\theta G^\top W \nabla_\theta G\right)^{-1}.$$

With $W = \mathcal{I}^{-1}$, this variance collapses to

$$V = \left(\nabla_\theta G^\top \mathcal{I}^{-1}\nabla_\theta G\right)^{-1}. \tag{6.19}$$

6.7.2.4 *Spanning scores*

This section provides a heuristic discussion of the conditions under which the EMM estimator achieves the Cramer-Rao lower bound. Consider the following definition. Of a given span of moment conditions s_f, say, that of the EMM, we say that it also spans the true score if

$$var\left(s|\, s_f\right) = 0, \tag{6.20}$$

where s denotes the true score. This definition is quite similar to one proposed by Tauchen (1997). From eq. (6.19), we know that the asymptotic variance of the EMM, say, var_{EMM}, satisfies

$$var_{\text{EMM}}^{-1} \equiv V^{-1} = \nabla_\theta G^\top var\left(s_f\right)^{-1} \nabla_\theta G.$$

By the linear projection,

$$s = Bs_f + \epsilon, \quad B = cov\left(s, s_f\right) var\left(s_f\right)^{-1},$$

we have

$$\begin{aligned} var_{\text{MLE}}^{-1} &= var\,(s) = Bvar\left(s_f\right) B^\top + var\left(s|\, s_f\right) \\ &= cov\left(s, s_f\right) var\left(s_f\right)^{-1} cov\left(s, s_f\right)^\top + var\left(s|\, s_f\right), \end{aligned} \tag{6.21}$$

where var_{MLE} denotes the asymptotic variance of the MLE. We claim that

$$cov\left(s, s_f\right)^\top = \nabla_\theta G. \tag{6.22}$$

Indeed, under regularity conditions,

$$\begin{aligned} \nabla_\theta G\left(\theta_0, \beta^*\right) &= \left[\frac{\partial}{\partial\theta}\left(\int \frac{\partial}{\partial\beta} \ln f\left(y; \beta^*\right) p\left(y, \theta\right) dy\right)\right]_{\theta=\theta_0} \\ &= \int \frac{\partial}{\partial\beta} \ln f\left(y; \beta^*\right) \frac{\partial}{\partial\theta} p\left(y, \theta_0\right) dy \\ &= \int \left(\frac{\partial}{\partial\beta} \ln f\left(y; \beta^*\right) \frac{\partial}{\partial\theta} \ln p\left(y, \theta_0\right)\right) p\left(y, \theta_0\right) dy \\ &= cov\left(s, s_f\right)^\top, \end{aligned}$$

where $p\,(y, \theta_0)$ is the true density. Next, replace eq. (6.22) into eq. (6.21),

$$var_{\text{MLE}}^{-1} = \nabla_\theta G^\top var\left(s_f\right)^{-1} \nabla_\theta G + var\left(s|\, s_f\right) = var_{\text{EMM}}^{-1} + var\left(s|\, s_f\right).$$

Therefore, the EMM estimator achieves the Cramer-Rao lower bound under the spanning condition in eq. (6.20).

6.7.3 A Fourth Estimator: Simulated Maximum Likelihood

Estimating the parameters of stochastic differential equations is a recurrent theme in empirical finance (see, e.g., chapters 11, 13, and 14). Consider a continuous time model,

$$dy\,(\tau) = b\,(y\,(\tau)\,; \theta)\, d\tau + \Sigma\,(y\,(\tau)\,; \theta)\, dW\,(\tau), \tag{6.23}$$

where $W(\tau)$ is a Brownian motion and b and Σ are two functions guaranteeing a strong solution to eq. (6.23). Except in special cases (e.g., the affine models reviewed in chapters 11 and 13), the likelihood function of the data generated by this process is unknown. We can then use one of the three estimators we have presented in section 6.7.1. An alternative method is simulated maximum likelihood, a method introduced in finance by Santa-Clara (1995) (also see Brandt and Santa-Clara, 2002). In this section, we only discuss the idea underlying this method, not the asymptotic theory. Danielsson (1994) is another early reference on simulated maximum likelihood methods applied to finance.

Suppose, then, that we observe discretely sample data generated by eq. (6.23): y_0, $y_1, \cdots, y_t, \cdots, y_T$, where T is the sample size. To implement MLE, we need to know the transition density, say, $p(y_{t+1}|\, y_t;\theta)$. We assume that we do not know p in closed form. Consider, then, the Euler approximation to eq. (6.23),

$$y_{(k+1)/n} = y_{k/n} + b\left(y_{k/n};\theta\right)\frac{1}{n} + \Sigma\left(y_{k/n};\theta\right)\sqrt{\frac{1}{n}}\epsilon_{k+1}, \tag{6.24}$$

where ϵ_k is a sequence of IID random variables with expectation zero and unit variance. This stochastic process is defined at the dates $\frac{k}{n}$, for k integer. Let $[Tn]$ denote the integer part of Tn, and for $k=1,\cdots,[Tn]$, set

$$\hat{y}_\tau^{(n)} = y_{k/n}, \text{ if } \frac{k}{n} \le \tau \le \frac{k+1}{n}.$$

In other words, we are chopping the time interval between two observations, $[t, t+1]$, in n pieces and then take n to be large. We know that as $n \to \infty$, $\hat{y}_t^{(n)} \Rightarrow y(t)$ as $n \to \infty$, where $\Rightarrow$ denotes "weak convergence," or "convergence in distribution," a concept used to explain that all finite dimensional distributions of $\hat{y}_t^{(n)}$ converge to those of $y(t)$ as $n \to \infty$.

The idea underlying simulated maximum likelihood is to estimate the transition density, $p(y_{t+1}|\, y_t;\theta)$, through simulations of eq. (6.24), performed using a large value of n. Note that there is no guarantee that the transition density is recovered by simulating eq. (6.24), not even for a large value of n. We can only perform an imperfect simulation of eq. (6.24).

So, consider the likelihood function

$$L = p(y_0;\theta)\prod_{t=0}^{T-1} p\left(y_{t+1}|\, y_t;\theta\right),$$

where $p(y_0;\theta)$ denotes the marginal density of the first observation, y_0. Let $p^n(y'|\, y;\theta)$ denote the transition density of the data generated by eq. (6.24). Then, assuming that ϵ is normally distributed,

$$p^n\left(y_{(k+1)/n}\middle|\, y_{k/n};\theta\right) = \varphi\left(y_{(k+1)/n}; y_{k/n} + b\left(y_{k/n};\theta\right)\frac{1}{n}; \Sigma^2\left(y_{k/n};\theta\right)\frac{1}{n}\right),$$

where $\varphi(u;\mu;\sigma^2)$ denotes the Gaussian density with mean μ and variance σ^2. Moreover, we have, approximately, that

$$\begin{aligned} p^n\left(y_{t+1}|\, y_t;\theta\right) &= \int p^n\left(y_{t+1}|\, x;\theta\right) p^n\left(x|\, y_t;\theta\right) dx \\ &= \int \varphi\left(y_{t+1}; x + b(x;\theta)\frac{1}{n}; \Sigma^2(x;\theta)\frac{1}{n}\right) p^n\left(x|\, y_t;\theta\right) dx, \end{aligned}$$

where we have set $x = y_{t+1-\frac{1}{n}}$. We may now draw values of x from $p^n(x|\, y_t;\theta)$, as we will explain in a moment, and estimate $p^n(y_{t+1}|\, y_t;\theta)$ with

$$p^{n,S}(y_{t+1}|\, y_t;\theta) \equiv \frac{1}{S}\sum_{j=1}^{S}\varphi\left(y_{(k+1)/n};\tilde{x}^j + b\left(\tilde{x}^j;\theta\right)\frac{1}{n};\Sigma^2\left(\tilde{x}^j;\theta\right)\frac{1}{n}\right),$$

where $\tilde{x}^j$ is obtained by iterating eq. (6.24) from time t to time $t+1-\frac{1}{n}$. Under regularity conditions, we have that, for all $\theta \in \Theta$, $\sup_{y',y}\left|p^{n,S}(y'|\, y;\theta) - p(y'|\, y;\theta)\right| \to 0$ as n and S get large, with $\frac{\sqrt{S}}{n} \to 0$.

6.7.4 Progress

The three estimators examined in sections 6.7.1 and 6.7.2 are general purpose. However, they do not lead to asymptotic efficiency unless the true score belongs to the span of the moment conditions as explained in section 6.7.2.4. There exist other simulation-based methods, which aim to approximate the likelihood function through simulations (e.g., Lee, 1995; Hajivassiliou and McFadden, 1998): for example, the simulated MLE in section 6.7.3 can be used to estimate the parameters of stochastic differential equations. While methods based on simulated likelihood lead to asymptotically efficient estimators, they address specific estimation problems, just as in the examples of section 6.7.3.

There exist estimators that are both general purpose and that can lead to asymptotic efficiency. Fermanian and Salanié (2004) consider an estimator that relies on approximating the likelihood function through kernel estimates obtained simulating the model of interest. Carrasco, Chernov, Florens, and Ghysels (2007) rely on a "continuum of moment conditions" by matching model-based (simulated) characteristic functions to data-based characteristic functions. Altissimo and Mele (2009) propose an estimator based on a continuum of moment conditions by minimizing a certain distance between conditional densities estimated with the true data and conditional densities estimated with data simulated from the model, where both conditional densities are estimated through kernel methods.

6.7.5 In Practice? Latent Factors and Identification

The estimation theory of this section does not rule out the situation in which some of the variables in eq. (6.11) are unobservable. The principle to follow is very simple: one applies any of the methods we have discussed to those variables simulated out of eq. (6.11), which correspond to the observed ones. Consider, for example, parameter estimation of the following model of the short-term rate $r(\tau)$,

$$\begin{aligned} dr(\tau) &= \kappa_r(\bar{r} - r(\tau))\,d\tau + \sqrt{v(\tau)}dW_1(\tau) \\ dv(\tau) &= \kappa_v(\bar{v} - v(\tau))\,d\tau + \xi\sqrt{v(\tau)}dW_2(\tau) \end{aligned} \tag{6.25}$$

where $v(\tau)$ is the short-term rate, instantaneous, stochastic variance, W_1 and W_2 are two standard Brownian motions, and the parameter vector of interest is $\theta = [\kappa_r\ \bar{r}\ \kappa_v\ \bar{v}\ \xi]$. This type of model is discussed at length in chapter 13 (see sections 13.4 and 13.5).

Consider, now, one of the methods discussed so far, say, indirect inference. The logical steps to follow are (i) to simulate eqs. (6.25) and (ii) to calibrate an auxiliary model to the short-term rate data simulated out of eqs. (6.25) in such a way that the calibrated parameters are as close as possible to the parameters of the same auxiliary model fitted on true data. Note that we may do so by neglecting the volatility data simulated out of eqs. (6.25): these data are obviously unobservable.

The question arises, therefore, as to whether the auxiliary model one chooses is rich enough to allow identification of the model parameter vector θ. There might be many combinations of unobserved random processes $v(\tau)$ that are consistent with the likelihood of any given auxiliary model. So, which auxiliary model do we use, in practice? This is a question that was asked by Gallant and Tauchen (1996), long time ago. The question is very challenging. Very simply, one requires the model to be identifiable, a property likely to hold once the auxiliary model is "rich enough." In an impressive series of applied work, Gallant and Tauchen and additional coauthors have proposed semi-nonparametric score generators as a way to get as close as possible to a "rich" model. Intuitively, by increasing the order of Hermite expansions, semi-nonparametric scores might converge to true ones. Alternatively, one might use a continuum of moment conditions as explained in section 6.7.4. For example, the nonparametric density estimators of Altissimo and Mele (2009) converge to the true parameter once the bandwidth parameters used to smooth out these kernel estimates get smaller and smaller.

Appendix 6.A Primers

This appendix contains useful reviews of concepts on which much of this chapter's analysis relies.

Convergence in probability. *A sequence of random vectors* $\{x_T\}$ converges in probability *to the random vector* $\tilde{x}$ *if for each* $\epsilon > 0$, $\delta > 0$, *and each* $i = 1, 2, \cdots, N$, *there exists a* $T_{\epsilon,\delta}$ *such that for every* $T \geq T_{\epsilon,\delta}$,

$$\Pr\left(|x_{Ti} - \tilde{x}_i| > \delta\right) < \epsilon.$$

This is succinctly written as $x_T \xrightarrow{p} \tilde{x}$ *or* $\text{plim}\ x_T = \bar{x}$, *if* $\tilde{x} \equiv \bar{x}$, *a constant.*

Convergence in probability generalizes the standard notion of a limit of a deterministic sequence. Of a deterministic sequence x_T, we say it converges to some limit $\bar{x}$ if, for $\kappa > 0$, there exists a T_κ such that, for each $T \geq T_\kappa$, we have that $|x_T - \bar{x}| < \kappa$. Convergence in probability can also be restated as saying that

$$\lim_{T\to\infty} \Pr\left(|x_{Ti} - \tilde{x}_i| > \delta\right) = 0.$$

The following definition contains a stronger notion of convergence.

Almost sure convergence. *A sequence of random vectors* $\{x_T\}$ converges almost surely *to the random vector* $\tilde{x}$ *if, for each* $i = 1, 2, \cdots, N$, *we have*

$$\Pr\left(\omega : x_{Ti}(\omega) \to \tilde{x}_i\right) = 1,$$

where ω *denotes the entire random sequence* x_{Ti}. *This type of convergence is succinctly written as* $x_T \xrightarrow{a.s.} \tilde{x}$.

Almost sure convergence implies convergence in probability. Convergence in probability means that, for each $\epsilon > 0$, $\lim_{T\to\infty} \Pr(\omega : |x_{Ti}(\omega) - \tilde{x}_i| < \epsilon) = 1$. Almost sure convergence requires that $\Pr(\lim_{T\to\infty} x_{Ti} \to \tilde{x}_i) = 1$ or that

$$\lim_{T'\to\infty} \Pr\left(\sup_{T\geq T'} |x_{Ti} - \tilde{x}_i| > \delta\right) = \lim_{T'\to\infty} \Pr\left(\bigcup_{T\geq T'} |x_{Ti} - \tilde{x}_i| > \delta\right) = 0.$$

Next, assume that the second-order moments of all x_i are finite. We have:

Convergence in quadratic mean. *A sequence of random vectors* $\{x_T\}$ converges in quadratic mean *to the random vector* $\tilde{x}$ *if for each* $i = 1, 2, \cdots, N$, *we have*

$$\lim_{T'\to\infty} E\left[(x_{Ti} - \tilde{x}_i)^2\right] \to 0.$$

This type of convergence is succinctly written as $x_T \overset{q.m.}{\to} \tilde{x}$.

Remark. Note that, by Chebyshev's inequality,

$$\Pr(|x_{Ti} - \tilde{x}_i| > \delta) \leq \frac{E[(x_{Ti} - \tilde{x}_i)^2]}{\delta^2}.$$

Therefore, convergence in quadratic mean implies convergence in probability.

We now turn to a weaker notion of convergence.

Convergence in distribution. *Let* $\{f_T(\cdot)\}_T$ *be the sequence of probability distributions (that is,* $f_T(x) = pr(x_T \leq x)$*) of the sequence of the random vectors* $\{x_T\}$. *Let* $\tilde{x}$ *be a random vector with probability distribution* $f(x)$. *A sequence* $\{x_T\}$ *converges in distribution to* $\tilde{x}$ *if, for each* $i = 1, 2, \cdots, N$, *we have*

$$\lim_{T\to\infty} f_T(x) = f(x).$$

This type of convergence is succinctly written as $x_T \overset{d}{\to} \tilde{x}$.

The following two results are particularly useful.

Slutzky's theorem. *If* $y_T \overset{p}{\to} \bar{y}$ *and* $x_T \overset{d}{\to} \tilde{x}$, *then*

$$y_T \cdot x_T \overset{d}{\to} \bar{y} \cdot \tilde{x}.$$

Cramer-Wold device. *Let* λ *be an N dimensional vector of constants. We then have*

$$x_T \overset{d}{\to} \tilde{x} \Leftrightarrow \lambda^\top \cdot x_T \overset{d}{\to} \lambda^\top \cdot \tilde{x}.$$

The following example illustrates the Cramer-Wold device. If $\lambda^\top \cdot x_T \overset{d}{\to} N(0; \lambda^\top \Sigma \lambda)$, then $x_T \overset{d}{\to} N(0; \Sigma)$.

We now state two results regarding convergence in probability.

Weak law (no. 1) (Khinchine). *Let* $\{x_T\}$ *be an IID sequence satisfying* $E(x_T) = \mu < \infty\ \forall T$. *We have* $\bar{x}_T \equiv \frac{1}{T}\sum_{t=1}^{T} x_t \xrightarrow{p} \mu$.

Weak law (no. 2) (Chebyshev). *Let* $\{x_T\}$ *be a sequence independent but not identically distributed, satisfying* $E(x_T) = \mu_T < \infty$ *and* $E\left[(x_T - \mu_T)^2\right] = \sigma_T^2 < \infty$. *If* $\lim_{T\to\infty} \frac{1}{T^2}\sum_{t=1}^{T}\sigma_t^2 \to 0$, *then*

$$\bar{x}_T \equiv \frac{1}{T}\sum_{t=1}^{T} x_t \xrightarrow{p} \bar{\mu}_T \equiv \frac{1}{T}\sum_{t=1}^{T}\mu_t.$$

We now state and provide a proof of the CLT in a simple setting.

Central Limit Theorem. *Let* $\{x_T\}$ *be an IID sequence satisfying* $E(x_T) = \mu < \infty$ *and* $E\left[(x_T - \mu)^2\right] = \sigma^2 < \infty\ \forall T$. *Let* $\bar{x}_T \equiv \frac{1}{T}\sum_{t=1}^{T} x_t$. *We have*

$$\frac{\sqrt{T}\,(\bar{x}_T - \mu)}{\sigma} \xrightarrow{d} N(0,1)\,.$$

The multidimensional version of this theorem requires a mere change in notation. For the proof, the classic method relies on the characteristic functions. Let

$$\varphi(t) \equiv E\left(e^{\mathrm{i}tx}\right) = \int e^{\mathrm{i}tx} f(x)dx,\ \mathrm{i} \equiv \sqrt{-1}\,.$$

We have $\left.\frac{\partial^r}{\partial t^r}\varphi(t)\right|_{t=0} = \mathrm{i}^r m^{(r)}$, where $m^{(r)}$ is the rth order moment. By a Taylor's expansion,

$$\varphi(t) = \varphi(0) + \left.\frac{\partial}{\partial t}\varphi(t)\right|_{t=0} t + \frac{1}{2}\left.\frac{\partial^2}{\partial t^2}\varphi(t)\right|_{t=0} t^2 + \cdots = 1 + \mathrm{i}m^{(1)}t - m^{(2)}\frac{1}{2}t^2 + \cdots\,.$$

Next, let $\bar{x}_T = \frac{1}{T}\sum_{t=1}^{T} x_t$, and consider the random variable

$$Y_T \equiv \frac{\sqrt{T}\,(\bar{x}_T - \mu)}{\sigma} = \frac{1}{\sqrt{T}}\sum_{t=1}^{T}\frac{x_t - \mu}{\sigma}\,.$$

The characteristic function of Y_T is the product of the characteristic functions of $a_t \equiv \frac{x_t - \mu}{\sqrt{T}\sigma}$, which are all the same: $\varphi_{Y_T}(t) = (\varphi_a(t))^T$, where $\varphi_a(t) = 1 - \frac{t^2}{2T} + \cdots$. Therefore,

$$\varphi_{Y_T}(t) = \varphi\left(\frac{t}{\sqrt{T}}\right)^T = \left(1 - \frac{1}{2}\frac{t^2}{T} + o\left(T^{-1}\right)\right)^T.$$

Clearly, $\lim_{T\to\infty}\varphi_{Y_T}(t) = e^{-\frac{1}{2}t^2}$, which is the characteristic function of a standard Gaussian variable.

Appendix 6.B Maximum Likelihood

First, we provide the proof of a result stated in the main text.

Proof of eq. (6.3) We have $P(A_1 \bigcap A_2) = P(A_1) \cdot P(A_2 | A_1)$. Consider the event $E \equiv A_1 \bigcap A_2$. We still have

$$\Pr(A_3 | A_1 \bigcap A_2) = \Pr(A_3 | E) = \frac{\Pr(A_3 \bigcap E)}{\Pr(E)} = \frac{\Pr(A_3 \bigcap A_1 \bigcap A_2)}{\Pr(A_1 \bigcap A_2)}.$$

That is,

$$\begin{aligned}\Pr\left(\bigcap_{i=1}^{3} A_i\right) &= \Pr(A_1 \bigcap A_2) \cdot \Pr(A_3 | A_1 \bigcap A_2) \\ &= \Pr(A_1) \cdot \Pr(A_2 | A_1) \cdot \Pr(A_3 | A_1 \bigcap A_2).\end{aligned}$$

Continuing, we obtain eq. (6.3). □

Next, we provide details regarding asymptotic normality for MLE. Assume then that $\hat{\theta}_T \overset{a.s.}{\to} \theta_0$ and that $H(\theta|y) \equiv \nabla_{\theta\theta} \ln L(\theta|y)$ exists and is continuous in θ uniformly in y, and finally that we can differentiate twice inside the integral $\int L(\theta|y)dy = 1$. We have

$$s_T(\theta) = \frac{1}{T} \sum_{t=1}^{T} \nabla_\theta \ln L(\theta | y).$$

Consider the c-parametrized curves $\theta(c) = c\Box(\theta_0 - \hat{\theta}_T) + \hat{\theta}_T$ where, for all $c \in (0,1)^p$ and $\theta \in \Theta$, $c\Box\theta$ denotes a vector in Θ that has $c^{(i)}\theta^{(i)}$ as its ith element. By the intermediate value theorem, there exists a c^* in $(0,1)^p$ such that we have, almost surely,

$$s_T(\hat{\theta}_T) = s_T(\theta_0) + H_T(\theta^*) \cdot (\hat{\theta}_T - \theta_0),$$

where $\theta^* \equiv \theta(c^*)$ and

$$H_T(\theta) = \frac{1}{T} \sum_{t=1}^{T} H(\theta | y_t).$$

The first-order conditions satisfied by the MLE tell us that $s_T(\hat{\theta}_T) = 0$. Hence,

$$0 = s_T(\theta_0) + H_T(\theta_T^*) \cdot (\hat{\theta}_T - \theta_0).$$

We also have that

$$\left|H_T(\theta_T^*) - H_T(\theta_0)\right| \leq \sup \left|H(\theta_T^* | y) - H(\theta_0 | y)\right|, \tag{6.A1}$$

where the supremum is taken over the set of all the observations. Since $\hat{\theta}_T \overset{a.s.}{\to} \theta_0$, we also have that $\theta_T^* \overset{a.s.}{\to} \theta_0$. Moreover, by the law of large numbers,

$$H_T(\theta_0) = \frac{1}{T} \sum_{t=1}^{T} H(\theta_0 | y_t) \overset{p}{\to} E[H(\theta_0 | y_t)] = -\mathcal{J}(\theta_0). \tag{6.A2}$$

Since H is continuous in θ uniformly in y, the inequality in (6.A1) and (6.A2) imply that

$$H_T\left(\theta_T^*\right) \overset{a.s.}{\to} -\mathcal{J}\left(\theta_0\right).$$

Therefore, as $T \to \infty$,

$$\sqrt{T}\left(\hat{\theta}_T - \theta_0\right) = -H_T^{-1}(\theta_0) \cdot s_T(\theta_0)\sqrt{T} = \mathcal{J}^{-1} \cdot \sqrt{T} s_T(\theta_0).$$

By the CLT, and $E\left(s_T\right) = 0$, the score, $s_T\left(\theta_0\right) = \frac{1}{T}\sum_{t=1}^T s\left(\theta_0, y_t\right)$, is such that

$$\sqrt{T} \cdot s_T\left(\theta_0\right) \overset{d}{\to} N\left(0, var\left(s\left(\theta_0, y_t\right)\right)\right),$$

where

$$var\left(s\left(\theta_0, y_t\right)\right) = \mathcal{J}.$$

The result follows by the Slutzky's theorem and the symmetry of $\mathcal{J}$.

Finally, one should show the existence of a sequence $\hat{\theta}_T$ converging almost surely to θ_0. Proofs on this type of convergence can be found in Amemiya (1985) or in Newey and McFadden (1994).

Appendix 6.C Maximum Likelihood Estimator for Dependent Processes

6.C.1 Weak Dependence

Let $\sigma_T^2 = var(\sum_{t=1}^T x_t)$, and assume that that $\sigma_T^2 = O(T)$, and that $\sigma_T^2 = O\left(T^{-1}\right)$. If

$$\sigma_T^{-1} \sum_{t=1}^T \left(x_t - E(x_t)\right) \overset{d}{\to} N(0, 1),$$

we say that $\{x_t\}$ is *weakly dependent*.

6.C.2 Central Limit Theorem for Martingale Differences

Let x_t be a sequence of martingale differences, with $E\left(x_t^2\right) = \sigma_t^2 < \infty$ for all t, and define $\bar{x}_T \equiv \frac{1}{T}\sum_{t=1}^T x_t$ and $\bar{\sigma}_T^2 \equiv \frac{1}{T}\sum_{t=1}^T \sigma_t^2$. Suppose that the following condition holds:

$$\forall \epsilon > 0, \ \lim_{T\to\infty} \frac{1}{T\bar{\sigma}_T^2} \sum_{t=1}^T x_t^2 \mathbb{I}_{|x_t| \geq \epsilon \cdot T \cdot \bar{\sigma}_T^2} = 0, \quad \text{and} \quad \frac{1}{T}\sum_{t=1}^T x_t^2 - \bar{\sigma}_T^2 \overset{p}{\to} 0.$$

Then,

$$\frac{\sqrt{T} \cdot \bar{x}_T}{\bar{\sigma}_T} \overset{d}{\to} N(0, 1).$$

This result is known as the CLT for martingale differences.

6.C.3 Asymptotic Normality

We use the CLT for martingale differences to prove asymptotic normality of the MLE in presence of weakly dependent processes. Therefore, the log-likelihood function in (6.4) is replaced with

$$\ln L_T(\theta)=\sum_{t=1}^{T}\ell_t(\theta),\quad \ell_t(\theta)\equiv\ell\left(\theta;y_t\middle|x_t\right).$$

The MLE satisfies the following first-order conditions:

$$0_p=\nabla_\theta \ln L_T(\theta)\big|_{\theta=\hat\theta_T}\stackrel{d}{=}\sum_{t=1}^{T}\nabla_\theta\ell_t(\theta)|_{\theta=\theta_0}+\sum_{t=1}^{T}\nabla_{\theta\theta}\ell_t(\theta)|_{\theta=\theta_0}(\hat\theta_T-\theta_0),$$

such that

$$\sqrt{T}(\hat\theta_T-\theta_0)\stackrel{d}{=}-\left[\frac{1}{T}\sum_{t=1}^{T}\nabla_{\theta\theta}\ell_t(\theta_0)\right]^{-1}\frac{1}{\sqrt{T}}\sum_{t=1}^{T}\nabla_\theta\ell_t(\theta_0). \tag{6.A3}$$

Now, note that (with obvious notation) $E_{\theta_0}\left[\nabla_\theta\ell_{t+1}(\theta_0)\middle|F_t\right]=0_p$, implying that $\nabla_\theta\ell_t(\theta_0)$ is a martingale difference. Further,

$$E_{\theta_0}\left(\left|\nabla_\theta\ell_{t+1}(\theta_0)\right|_2\middle|F_t\right)=-E_{\theta_0}\left(\nabla_{\theta\theta}\ell_{t+1}(\theta_0)\middle|F_t\right)\equiv\mathcal{J}_t(\theta_0).$$

Next, define $x_t\equiv c^\top\nabla_\theta\ell_t(\theta_0)$, for a given constant $c\in\mathbb{R}^p$. Clearly, x_t is also a martingale difference, with

$$E_{\theta_0}\left(x_{t+1}^2\middle|F_t\right)=c^\top\mathcal{J}_t(\theta_0)\,c,$$

and because x_t is a martingale difference, $E(x_tx_{t-i})=E\left[E\left(x_tx_{t-i}\mid F_{t-i}\right)\right]=E\left[E\left(x_t\middle|F_{t-i}\right)x_{t-i}\right]=0$, for all i. That is, x_t and x_{t-i} are uncorrelated. It follows that

$$\begin{aligned}
var\left(\sum_{t=1}^{T}x_t\right)&=\sum_{t=1}^{T}E\left(x_t^2\right)\\
&=\sum_{t=1}^{T}c^\top E_{\theta_0}\left(|\nabla_\theta\ell_t(\theta_0)|_2\right)c\\
&=\sum_{t=1}^{T}c^\top E_{\theta_0}\left[E_{\theta_0}\left(|\nabla_\theta\ell_t(\theta_0)|_2|F_{t-1}\right)\right]c\\
&=\sum_{t=1}^{T}c^\top E_{\theta_0}\left[\mathcal{J}_{t-1}(\theta_0)\right]c\\
&=c^\top\left[\sum_{t=1}^{T}E_{\theta_0}\left(\mathcal{J}_{t-1}(\theta_0)\right)\right]c.
\end{aligned}$$

Finally, define

$$\bar{x}_T\equiv\frac{1}{T}\sum_{t=1}^{T}x_t\quad\text{and}\quad\bar\sigma_T^2\equiv\frac{1}{T}\sum_{t=1}^{T}E\left(x_t^2\right)=c^\top\left[\frac{1}{T}\sum_{t=1}^{T}E_{\theta_0}\left(\mathcal{J}_{t-1}(\theta_0)\right)\right]c.$$

Under the conditions underlying the CLT for martingale differences, specified below, we have that

$$\frac{\sqrt{T}\bar{x}_T}{\bar{\sigma}_T} \xrightarrow{d} N(0,1).$$

By the Cramer-Wold device,

$$\left[\frac{1}{T}\sum_{t=1}^{T} E_{\theta_0}\left(\mathcal{J}_{t-1}(\theta_0)\right)\right]^{-1/2} \frac{1}{\sqrt{T}}\sum_{t=1}^{T} \nabla_\theta \ell_t(\theta_0) \xrightarrow{d} N\left(0, \mathbf{I}_p\right).$$

The conditions that need to be satisfied are

$$\frac{1}{T}\sum_{t=1}^{T} \nabla_{\theta\theta}\ell_t(\theta_0) - \frac{1}{T}\sum_{t=1}^{T} E_{\theta_0}\left[\mathcal{J}_{t-1}(\theta_0)\right] \xrightarrow{p} 0 \quad \text{and} \quad \text{plim}\frac{1}{T}\sum_{t=1}^{T} E_{\theta_0}\left[\mathcal{J}_{t-1}(\theta_0)\right] \equiv \mathcal{J}_\infty(\theta_0).$$

By eq. (6.A3), it follows, under these conditions, that

$$\sqrt{T}(\hat{\theta}_T - \theta_0) \xrightarrow{d} N\left(0_p, \mathcal{J}_\infty(\theta_0)^{-1}\right).$$

References

Altissimo, F., and A. Mele (2009). "Simulated Nonparametric Estimation of Dynamic Models." *Review of Economic Studies* 76, 413–450.

Amemiya, T. (1985). *Advanced Econometrics.* Cambridge, MA: Harvard University Press.

Brandt, M., and P. Santa-Clara (2002). "Simulated Likelihood Estimation of Diffusions with an Applications to Exchange Rate Dynamics in Incomplete Markets." *Journal of Financial Economics* 63, 161–210.

Carrasco, M., M. Chernov, J. P. Florens, and E. Ghysels (2007). "Efficient Estimation of General Dynamic Models with a Continuum of Moment Conditions." *Journal of Econometrics* 140, 529–573.

Danielsson, J. (1994). "Stochastic Volatility in Asset Price Estimation with Simulated Maximum Likelihood." *Journal of Econometrics* 64, 375–400.

Duffie, D., and K. J. Singleton (1993). "Simulated Moments Estimation of Markov Models of Asset Prices." *Econometrica* 61, 929–952.

Fermanian, J. D., and B. Salanié (2004). "A Nonparametric Simulated Maximum Likelihood Estimation Method." *Econometric Theory* 20, 701–734.

Fisher, R. A. (1912). "On an Absolute Criterion for Fitting Frequency Curves." *Messages of Mathematics* 41, 155–157.

Gallant, A. R. (1987). *Nonlinear Statistical Models.* New York: Wiley.

Gallant, A. R. and G. Tauchen (1996). "Which Moments to Match?" *Econometric Theory* 12, 657–681.

Gauss, C. F. (1816). "Bestimmung der Genanigkeit der Beobachtungen." *Zeitschrift für Astronomie und Verwandte Wissenschaften* 1, 185–196.

Gouriéroux, C., A. Monfort, and E. Renault (1993). "Indirect Inference." *Journal of Applied Econometrics* 8, S85–S118.

Hajivassiliou, V., and D. McFadden (1998). "The Method of Simulated Scores for the Estimation of Limited-Dependent Variable Models." *Econometrica* 66, 863–896.

Hamilton, J. D. (1994). *Time Series Analysis*. Princeton, NJ: Princeton University Press.

Hansen, L. P. (1982). "Large Sample Properties of Generalized Method of Moments Estimators." *Econometrica* 50, 1029–1054.

Hansen, L. P., and K. J. Singleton (1982). "Generalized Instrumental Variables Estimation of Nonlinear Rational Expectations Models." *Econometrica* 50, 1269–1286.

Hansen, L. P., and K. J. Singleton (1983). "Stochastic Consumption, Risk Aversion, and the Temporal Behavior of Asset Returns." *Journal of Political Economy* 91, 249–265.

Laroque, G., and B. Salanié (1989). "Estimation of Multimarket Fix-Price Models: An Application of Pseudo-Maximum Likelihood Methods." *Econometrica* 57, 831–860.

Laroque, G., and B. Salanié (1993). "Simulation-Based Estimation of Models with Lagged Latent Variables." *Journal of Applied Econometrics* 8, S119–S133.

Laroque, G., and B. Salanié (1994). "Estimating the Canonical Disequilibrium Model: Asymptotic Theory and Finite Sample Properties." *Journal of Econometrics* 62, 165–210.

Lee, B. S., and B. F. Ingram (1991). "Simulation Estimation of Time-Series Models." *Journal of Econometrics* 47, 197–207.

Lee, L. F. (1995). "Asymptotic Bias in Simulated Maximum Likelihood Estimation of Discrete Choice Models." *Econometric Theory* 11, 437–483.

McFadden, D. (1989). "A Method of Simulated Moments for Estimation of Discrete Response Models without Numerical Integration." *Econometrica* 57, 995–1026.

Newey, W. K., and D. L. McFadden (1994). "Large Sample Estimation and Hypothesis Testing." In *Handbook of Econometrics* (Vol. 4), edited by R. F. Engle and D. L. McFadden, 2111–2245. Amsterdam: Elsevier.

Neyman, J., and E. S. Pearson (1928). "On the Use and Interpretation of Certain Test Criteria for Purposes of Statistical Inference." *Biometrika* 20A, 175–240, 263–294.

Pakes, A., and D. Pollard (1989). "Simulation and the Asymptotics of Optimization Estimators." *Econometrica* 57, 1027–1057.

Pearson, K. (1894). "Contributions to the Mathematical Theory of Evolution." *Philosophical Transactions of the Royal Society of London*, Series A 185, 71–78.

Santa-Clara, P. (1995). "Simulated Likelihood Estimation of Diffusions with an Application to the Short Term Interest Rate." PhD diss. INSEAD.

Singleton, K. J. (2001). "Estimation of Affine Asset Pricing Models Using the Empirical Characteristic Function." *Journal of Econometrics* 102, 111–141.

Smith, A. (1993). "Estimating Nonlinear Time Series Models Using Simulated Vector Autoregressions." *Journal of Applied Econometrics* 8, S63–S84.

Tauchen, G. (1997). "New Minimum Chi-Square Methods in Empirical Finance." In *Advances in Econometrics: Theory and Applications, Seventh World Congress* (Vol. III), edited by D. Kreps and K. Wallis, 279–317. Cambridge: Cambridge University Press, Econometrics Society Monographs No. 28.

White, H. (1984). *Asymptotic Theory for Econometricians*. New York: Academic Press.

II

Empirical Lessons and Market Inefficiencies

7

Neoclassical Kernels and Puzzles

7.1 Introduction

This chapter provides an introduction to basic methodology of statistical inference for asset pricing models. The approach in this chapter still relies on "cross-equation restrictions" such as those of chapter 6 (see section 6.6) but is a bit more specific than that in chapter 6. It searches for very general quantitative implications of asset pricing models that can be taken to data, implications that are quite peculiar to our asset pricing models. Let us explain. Asset pricing models impose a number of restrictions on the dynamics of asset returns. These restrictions can be summarized by means a few convenient properties of the stochastic discount factor (or, similarly, the pricing kernel), a property consistent with the general data-reduction principle. This chapter discusses methods of statistical inference based on this principle. We discuss restrictions on the most basic statistical properties of the pricing kernel: its mean and standard deviation. These restrictions lead to the celebrated Hansen and Jagannathan (1991) bounds. In a nutshell, these bounds suggest that evidence against a given model mounts when the volatility of the pricing kernel falls below a certain threshold. We illustrate how these bounds work by revisiting a simplified version of the Lucas tree model introduced in chapter 3. This model predicts that assets' expected returns are too small than suggested by data, at least unless we assume that agents' risk aversion is implausibly high. This empirical failure of the model is well known as the *equity premium puzzle*.

The next section contains a simplified version of the Lucas model. This model is solved in closed form and then enables us to clearly understand the main issues underlying the puzzle through the lenses of the Hansen-Jagannathan bounds. Section 7.2 is, however, a simple introduction to the equity premium puzzle and another puzzle known as interest rate puzzle (the inability of the model to provide adequate predictions on the interest rate). Section 7.3 develops the central tool of analysis in this chapter—the "bounds." These bounds apply to the volatility of the pricing kernels of any model. They are nonparametric—that is, they do not depend on any model assumptions (except absence of arbitrage), only on securities data. We revisit the equity premium puzzle by applying these tools to the version of the Lucas model of section 7.2. Section 7.4 considers multifactor extensions of the basic Lucas model. These extensions consist of convenient assumptions on the stochastic discount factor. Note that, in spite of these added dimensionalities, the resulting models may well fail explain the dynamics of asset prices: a high volatility of the pricing kernel does not necessarily imply that the dynamics of asset prices are consistent with data. For example, chapter 8 explains that asset returns display time-varying and countercyclical statistics. Now, a model may not fail satisfy the Hansen-Jagannathan bounds and still predict that price-dividend ratios or expected returns are constant. Section 7.5 provides linkages between pricing kernels and the basic CAPM of chapter 1, and develops the "geometry" that unifies Hansen-Jagannathan bounds, the CAPM, and mean-variance efficiency. Section 7.6 concludes the chapter by reviewing the "conditional CAPM," a model which, contrary to that in section 7.4, has time-varying risk premiums. This model has been used to argue that a conditional version of the CAPM may pass standard asset pricing tests. We shall review the model and criticism around it.

7.2 The Equity Premium Puzzle

7.2.1 A Single-Factor Model

7.2.1.1 Assumptions

We consider an economy in which a representative agent has CRRA equal to γ and a constant discount factor β. We assume that cum-dividends gross returns, $(S_t + D_t)/S_{t-1}$, satisfy

$$\begin{cases} \ln(S_t + D_t) = \ln S_{t-1} + \mu_s - \frac{1}{2}\sigma_s^2 + \epsilon_{s,t} \\ \ln D_t = \ln D_{t-1} + \mu_d - \frac{1}{2}\sigma_d^2 + \epsilon_{d,t} \end{cases} \tag{7.1}$$

where

$$\begin{bmatrix} \epsilon_{s,t} \\ \epsilon_{d,t} \end{bmatrix} \sim NID\left(0_2; \begin{bmatrix} \sigma_s^2 & \sigma_{sd} \\ \sigma_{sd} & \sigma_d^2 \end{bmatrix}\right)$$

and where $\mu_s, \sigma_s, \mu_d, \sigma_{sd}$ are constants. We shall discuss these constants in a moment.

The second equation in (7.1) says that dividend growth is identically and independent distributed—dividends are log-normally distributed with exogenously given parameters μ_d and σ_d. The first equation is, instead, endogenous: we want to solve for the equilibrium in this Robinson Crusoe economy, in which asset returns are also log-normally distributed with parameters μ_s and σ_s. That is, and much in the line of derivations in part I, we search for an equilibrium price that satisfies the first equation in (7.1), and we also search for the constant covariance term, σ_{sd}.

All in all, we are searching for cross-equation restrictions such that eqs. (7.1) hold true. We begin with deriving Euler's restrictions and then proceed with pricing implications, assuming (and then verifying) that there are no sunspots—that is, there are no extraneous sources of randomness beyond those related to the dynamics of dividends.

7.2.1.2 *Euler's restrictions*

Optimality of the intertemporal plans leads to joint restrictions satisfied by the coefficients μ_s, μ_d, σ_s^2, σ_d^2, and σ_{sd}. By results in part I (see, e.g., section 3.2 in chapter 3), the Euler equations in this economy are

$$1 = E_t\left(m_{t+1} \cdot e^{Q_{t+1}}\right), \quad Q_{t+1} = \ln\left(\frac{S_{t+1} + D_{t+1}}{S_t}\right), \quad m_{t+1} \equiv e^{Z_{t+1}} \equiv \beta\left(\frac{D_{t+1}}{D_t}\right)^{-\gamma}, \tag{7.2}$$

where $E_t(\cdot)$ denotes the expectation taken given all the information available at time t and m_{t+1} is the pricing kernel. Eq. (7.2) holds for any asset. In particular, it holds for a one-period bond with price $S_t^b \equiv b_t$, $S_{t+1}^b \equiv 1$ and $D_{t+1}^b \equiv 0$. Define, then, $Q_{t+1}^b \equiv \ln b_t^{-1} \equiv \ln R_t$. By replacing R_t into (7.2) leaves $R_t^{-1} = E_t\left(e^{Z_{t+1}}\right)$, such that

$$\frac{1}{R_t} = E_t\left(m_{t+1}\right), \quad 1 = E_t\left(m_{t+1} e^{Q_{t+1}}\right). \tag{7.3}$$

Given our assumptions of normality (see eqs. (7.1)), we may rely on a very well-known result for log-normal distributions reviewed in appendix 7.A (see theorem 7.A1) and the definition of Z and determine the expectations in eqs. (7.3) in closed form,

$$\frac{1}{R_t} = E_t\left(e^{Z_{t+1}}\right) = e^{E_t(Z_{t+1}) + \frac{1}{2} var_t(Z_{t+1})} = e^{\ln\beta - \gamma\left(\mu_d - \frac{1}{2}\sigma_d^2\right) + \frac{1}{2}\gamma^2\sigma_d^2}. \tag{7.4}$$

Therefore, the equilibrium interest rate is constant, and its exact expression is given below (see the second of eqs. (7.5)). The second of eqs. (7.3) can be written as

$$1 = E_t\left(e^{Z_{t+1} + Q_{t+1}}\right) = e^{\ln\beta - \gamma\left(\mu_d - \frac{1}{2}\sigma_d^2\right) + \mu_s - \frac{1}{2}\sigma_s^2} \cdot E_t\left(e^{\tilde{n}_{t+1}}\right),$$

where $\tilde{n}_{t+1} \equiv \epsilon_{s,t+1} - \gamma\epsilon_{d,t+1} \sim N(0, \sigma_s^2 + \gamma^2\sigma_d^2 - 2\gamma\sigma_{sd})$. The expectation above can be determined again through standard properties of log-normal distributions, resulting in

$$\underbrace{\mu_s - r}_{\text{equity premium}} = \gamma\sigma_{sd}, \quad \text{and} \quad r_t \equiv \ln R_t = -\ln\beta + \gamma\mu_d - \frac{1}{2}\gamma\left(\gamma + 1\right)\sigma_d^2, \tag{7.5}$$

where we have used eq. (7.4) to calculate the continuously compounded interest rate, r.

Note that the expected gross return on the risky asset is

$$E_t\left(\frac{S_{t+1} + D_{t+1}}{S_t}\right) = e^{\mu_s - \frac{1}{2}\sigma_s^2} \cdot E_t\left(e^{\epsilon_{s,t+1}}\right) = e^{\mu_s} = e^{r + \gamma\sigma_{sd}}.$$

Therefore, if $\sigma_{sd} > 0$, then $E_t\left(\frac{S_{t+1}+D_{t+1}}{S_t}\right) > b_t^{-1}$, as expected.

The expressions for the equity premium and the short-term rate are the discrete-time counterpart to those derived in part I (see section 4.2.6 in chapter 4). Consider, for example, the interest rate. The second term, $\gamma\mu_d$, reflects "intertemporal substitution" effects: as μ_d increases, future consumption endowment increases, on average, which reduces the demand for bonds, thereby increasing the interest rate. The last term, instead, relates to "precautionary" motives: an increase in the uncertainty related to consumption endowment, σ_d, raises concerns, which our representative responds to while increasing their demand for bonds, thereby leading to a drop in the interest rate.

7.2.1.3 *Solution for the price-dividend ratio and absence of sunspots*

We will check the internal consistency of the model. The coefficients of the model satisfy some restrictions. In particular, the asset price volatility must be determined endogenously. Let us conjecture and later verify that the following "no sunspots" (see section 3.3 in chapter 3) condition holds, for each period t:

$$\epsilon_{s,t} = \epsilon_{d,t}. \tag{7.6}$$

By eqs. (7.5) and (7.6),

$$\mu_s - r = \lambda\sigma_d, \quad \lambda \equiv \gamma\sigma_d, \tag{7.7}$$

and by the definition of Z_{t+1} in eq. (7.2),

$$Z_{t+1} = -\left(r + \frac{1}{2}\lambda^2\right) - \lambda u_{D,t+1}, \quad u_{D,t+1} \equiv \frac{\epsilon_{d,t+1}}{\sigma_d},$$

such that, and consistent with derivations in part I (see section 4.2 in chapter 4), we can recursively define the stochastic discount factor ξ from the pricing kernel as follows:

$$\frac{\xi_{t+1}}{\xi_t} = m_{t+1} \equiv e^{Z_{t+1}}, \quad \xi_0 = 1.$$

It is the discrete-time counterpart to the continuous time representation of the Arrow-Debreu state price density in chapter 4.

Let us iterate the asset price equation (7.2),

$$E_t\left[\sum_{i=1}^{n}\left(\prod_{j=1}^{i} e^{Z_{t+j}}\right) D_{t+i} + \left(\prod_{j=1}^{n} e^{Z_{t+i}}\right) S_{t+n}\right] = \sum_{i=1}^{n} E_t\left(\frac{\xi_{t+i}}{\xi_t} D_{t+i}\right) + E_t\left(\frac{\xi_{t+n}}{\xi_t} S_{t+n}\right),$$

and let $n \to \infty$, such that, under a transversality condition discussed in a moment,

$$S_t = \sum_{i=1}^{\infty} E_t\left(\frac{\xi_{t+i}}{\xi_t} D_{t+i}\right). \tag{7.8}$$

The transversality condition underlying eq. (7.8) is that $\lim_{n\to\infty} E_t(\xi_{t+n} S_{t+n}) = 0$, which holds when the inequalities in (7.9) given below hold. These conditions parallel those analyzed for the continuous time models of chapter 4 (see section 4.2.6).

By properties of the log-normal distributions (see theorem 7.A1 in appendix 7.A), the expectations in eq. (7.8) are

$$E_t\left(\frac{\xi_{t+i}}{\xi_t} D_{t+i}\right) = E_t\left(e^{\sum_{j=1}^{i} Z_{t+j}} D_{t+i}\right) = D_t e^{(\mu_d - r - \sigma_d\lambda)i}.$$

Suppose the "risk-adjusted discount rate," $r + \sigma_d\lambda$, is higher than the dividend growth rate μ_d,

$$k \equiv \mu_d - r - \sigma_d\lambda < 0. \tag{7.9}$$

Under this condition, the summation in eq. (7.8) converges, leaving

$$\frac{S_t}{D_t} = \frac{e^k}{1 - e^k}. \tag{7.10}$$

Eq. (7.10) generalizes the celebrated Gordon's formula (Gordon, 1962). The price-dividend ratio increases with the expected dividend growth, μ_d, and decreases with the (risk-adjusted) discount rate, $r + \sigma_d \lambda$. The model predicts that price-dividend ratios are constant, a counterfactual prediction addressed in the next two chapters. Finally, the solution for the price-dividend ratio in eq. (7.10) is, of course, a special case of the Lucas model in part I (see section 3.2.4 in chapter 3), as explained in detail below.

We now check that the no-sunspots condition in eq. (7.6) holds and derive the asset price variance. By eq. (7.10), we have that (i) $\ln(S_t + D_t) = \ln D_t - \ln\left(1 - e^k\right)$ and (ii) $\ln S_{t-1} = \ln D_{t-1} + k - \ln\left(1 - e^k\right)$, or

$$\ln \frac{S_t + D_t}{S_{t-1}} = \ln \frac{D_t}{D_{t-1}} - k = \mu_d - \frac{1}{2}\sigma_d^2 - k + \epsilon_{d,t},$$

where the last equality follows by the second of eqs. (7.1). Identifying terms in the previous equation and the first of eqs. (7.1) leaves

$$\mu_s - \frac{1}{2}\sigma_s^2 = \mu_d - \frac{1}{2}\sigma_d^2 - k, \quad \epsilon_{s,t} = \epsilon_{d,t}, \text{ for each } t. \tag{7.11}$$

The second condition confirms that the no-sunspots condition in eq. (7.6) holds. It also informs us that $\sigma_s^2 = \sigma_{sd} = \sigma_d^2$. Replacing this into the first condition confirms indeed that $\mu_s = \mu_d - k = r + \sigma_d \lambda$.

Note also that by replacing the expression for the interest rate in the second of eqs. (7.5) and the equity premium in eq. (7.7) into eq. (7.9), the constant k simplifies to $e^k \equiv \beta e^{(1-\gamma)(\mu_d - \frac{1}{2}\gamma\sigma_d^2)}$, such that the price-dividend ratio in the log utility case, $\gamma = 1$, collapses to $\beta/(1-\beta)$, just as in chapter 3 (see section 3.2). This section provides a solution to the general CRRA case, under the additional assumption that dividend growth is normally distributed.

7.2.2 Equity Premium and Interest Rate Puzzles

> Average excess returns on the US stock market [the equity premium] is too high to be easily explained by standard asset pricing models.
>
> — Mehra and Prescott (1985)

Mehra and Prescott (1985) noted a difficulty with the Lucas model, which became widely known as the *equity premium puzzle*. To be consistent with US data, the equity premium in eq. (7.7), $\mu_s - r = \gamma\sigma_d^2$, must be an approximate 6% annualized. Now, if the asset we are trying to price is literally a *consumption claim*, then σ_d would be consumption volatility, which is, at most, a mere 3%. To rationalize an equity premium of about 6%, one would need a quite high value of relative risk aversion. We may reverse engineer this value by relying on the two equations in (7.7), obtaining $\gamma = \frac{0.06}{0.03^2} \approx 66$. Section 7.4

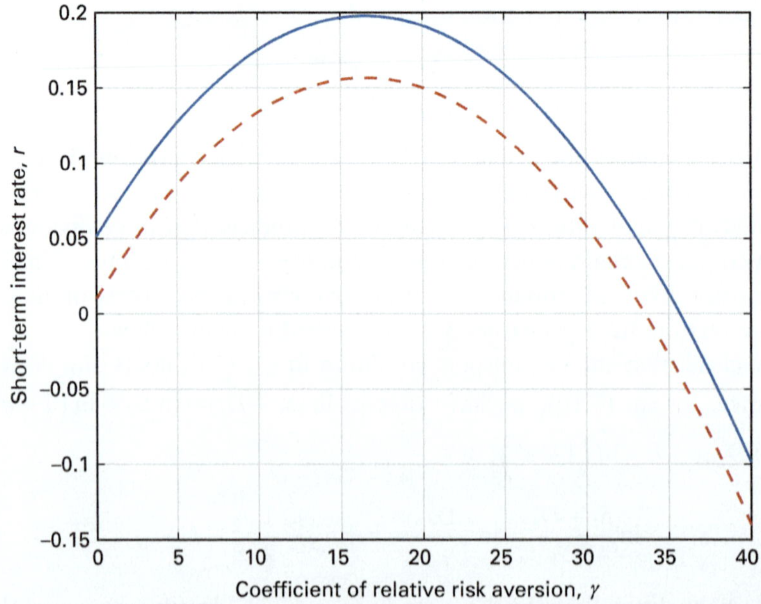

Figure 7.1
The interest rate puzzle. The two curves depict the interest rate in (7.5), based on the assumption that $\mu_d = 0.0183$ and $\sigma_d = 0.0328$. The solid line is obtained with $\beta = 0.95$ and the dashed line with $\beta = 0.99$.

explains this number may be improved to 35 once we also consider information provided by the volatility of short-term bonds.

One assumption underlying the previous calculations is that aggregate dividends and aggregate consumption are the same. This assumption is obviously not realistic. For example, assuming dividend growth volatility to be equal to 6%, the implied relative risk aversion becomes $\gamma = \frac{0.06}{0.06^2} \approx 17$, which mitigates the premium puzzle. Even in this case, the model fails deliver realistic predictions on return volatility: by eq. (7.11), return volatility would equal 6%, which is less than a half of aggregate equity volatility, as documented in detail in chapter 8 (see section 8.2). Further, the model would fail predict countercyclical statistics, such as countercyclical expected returns or dividend yields, topics dealt with in detail in the next chapters.

The size of the equity premium is not the only puzzle arising from this model. Even if we were comfortable with such large values of relative risk aversion, we would face another puzzle known as the *interest rate puzzle*. The expression for r in eqs. (7.5) shows—and figure 7.1 illustrates—that the interest rate would be very high with large value of γ. To lower the level of r, we need higher time discount factors, β. Interestingly, the interest rate decreases with γ as γ increases as precautionary motives become more stringent. However, it is not clear the extent to which precautionary motives may be considered as the main determinant of interest rate behavior.

Related to the interest rate puzzle is an *interest rate volatility* puzzle. In this model, the interest rate is constant. However, we may consider extensions of the model in which both the equity premium and interest rates change over time, driven by state variables related to preference shocks, time-varying expected dividend growth, or market imperfections (see

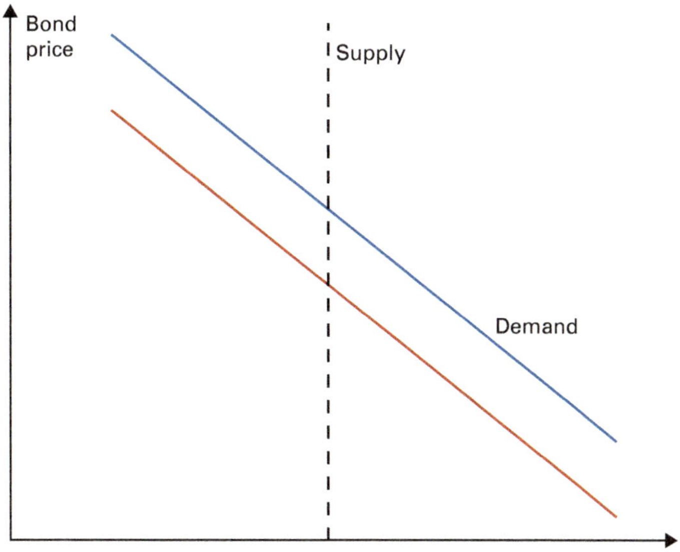

Figure 7.2
Interest rate volatility in a model with fixed bond supply.

chapter 9). In these models, the short-term interest rate would be too volatile. To illustrate, if expected dividend growth were time-varying, and equal to $\mu_{d,t}$, say, the expression for the short-term rate would be the same as in eq. (7.5) but with $\mu_{d,t}$ replacing the constant μ_d. It is easy to see that, in this case, the interest rate is quite volatile when γ is large. These themes are dealt with in detail in chapters 8 and 9.

To anticipate, one possibility is to assume that a representative agent has different intertemporal preferences than standard expected utility. From chapter 3 (see section 3.2.3), we know that, with standard expected utility, agents with low EIS have an inelastic demand for bonds (see section 3.2.3). With CRRA, a low EIS corresponds to a high CRRA as $\text{EIS} = \frac{1}{\gamma}$. So now suppose that the bonds demand shifts as a result of some exogenous shocks (say, a change in the expected dividend shock, $\mu_{d,t}$) as in figure 7.2.

In an economy with a representative agent, bonds supply is fixed. Thus, the combination of two assumptions (a representative agent with a low EIS) leads to the conterfactual conclusion that the volatility of the short-term interest rate is high.[1] To mitigate this issue, one may consider preferences that disentangle the EIS from risk aversion, such as those relying on nonexpected utility (Epstein and Zin, 1989, 1991; Weil, 1989) or models with multiple agents, in which bond supply has a positive slope as in the limited participation model of Guvenen (2009). Models with nonexpected utility are reviewed extensively in chapter 9. We now describe an ingenious procedure that enables us to tell whether a given model is consistent with securities data, a procedure based on the celebrated "Hansen-Jagannathan bounds."

1. See chapter 13 (e.g., section 13.4.5) for a description of the main stylized features on the short-term interest rate.

7.3 The Hansen-Jagannathan Cup

There seem to be many dimensions through which we may gauge models against data. In this section, we are mainly interested in the accuracy of a model's *quantitative* predictions. These predictions may be summarized by the statistical properties of the pricing kernel. Intuitively, the first two moments of the pricing kernel link to interest rates and risk premiums (see, e.g., chapter 4). To illustrate, the higher the volatility of the pricing kernel, the higher the risk premiums, at least for a given level of the interest rate. However, interest rates and risk premiums may simultaneously "change." For example, in the standard Lucas model, they both increase with risk aversion, γ, when γ is sufficiently low and they move in the opposite direction otherwise (see (7.5)). A model does not provide a good quantitative description of data if the variance of the pricing kernel is not large enough compared with its mean. The Hansen-Jagannathan bounds provide a measure of how large this variance should be. Remarkably, these bounds only depend on securities data. We now derive these bounds.

Consider an economy with n risky assets. The asset pricing equations for these assets are

$$1 = E_t\left[m_{t+1}\left(1+\tilde{r}_{j,t+1}\right)\right], \quad j=1,\cdots,n,$$

where $\tilde{r}_{j,t+1}$ denotes the net return on the jth asset at time $t+1$. Assuming $\tilde{r}_{j,t+1}$ is stationary and taking the unconditional expectation of both sides of the previous equation leaves

$$\mathbf{1}_n = E\left[m_t\left(\mathbf{1}_n+\tilde{r}_t\right)\right], \quad \tilde{r}_t = \left(\tilde{r}_{1,t},\cdots,\tilde{r}_{n,t}\right)^\top. \tag{7.12}$$

Next, let $\bar{m} \equiv E(m_t)$, and create a family of stochastic discount factors m_t^*, parametrized by $\bar{m}$, by projecting m on to the asset returns:

$$\text{Proj}\left(m \mid \mathbf{1}_n+\tilde{r}_t\right) \equiv m_t^*(\bar{m}) \equiv \bar{m} + \underset{1\times n}{\left[\tilde{r}_t - E(\tilde{r}_t)\right]^\top} \underset{n\times 1}{\beta_{\bar{m}}},$$

where[2]

$$\underset{n\times 1}{\beta_{\bar{m}}} = \underset{n\times n}{\Sigma^{-1}} \underset{n\times 1}{cov\left(m,\mathbf{1}_n+\tilde{r}_t\right)} = \Sigma^{-1}\left[\mathbf{1}_n - \bar{m}E\left(\mathbf{1}_n+\tilde{r}_t\right)\right]$$

and $\Sigma \equiv E[(\tilde{r}_t - E(\tilde{r}_t))(\tilde{r}_t - E(\tilde{r}_t))^\top]$. In appendix 7.A, it is shown that $m_t^*(m)$ is also a stochastic discount factor, that is,

$$\mathbf{1}_n = E\left[m_t^*(\bar{m})\cdot\left(\mathbf{1}_n+\tilde{r}_t\right)\right]. \tag{7.13}$$

We have

$$\sqrt{var\left(m_t^*(\bar{m})\right)} = \sqrt{\beta_{\bar{m}}^\top \Sigma \beta_{\bar{m}}} = \sqrt{\left[\mathbf{1}_n - \bar{m}E\left(\mathbf{1}_n+\tilde{r}_t\right)\right]^\top \Sigma^{-1}\left[\mathbf{1}_n - \bar{m}E\left(\mathbf{1}_n+\tilde{r}_t\right)\right]}. \tag{7.14}$$

Eq. (7.14) is the expression for the "base" of the celebrated *Hansen-Jagannathan "cup"*—after the work of Hansen and Jagannathan (1991). The following theorem reveals the importance of this expression as a means to assess the quality of a model through its pricing kernel.

2. We have $cov\left(m,\mathbf{1}_n+\tilde{r}\right) = E\left[m\left(\mathbf{1}_n+\tilde{r}\right)\right] - E(m)\,E\left(\mathbf{1}_n+\tilde{r}\right) = \mathbf{1}_n - \bar{m}E\left(\mathbf{1}_n+\tilde{r}\right)$.

Theorem 7.1. *Among all stochastic discount factors with fixed expectation $\bar{m}$, $m_t^*(\bar{m})$ is the one with the smallest variance.*

Proof. Consider another discount factor indexed by $\bar{m}$, that is, $m_t(\bar{m})$. Naturally, $m_t(\bar{m})$ satisfies $\mathbf{1}_n = E\left[m_t(\bar{m})\left(\mathbf{1}_n + \tilde{r}_t\right)\right]$. Moreover, by eq. (7.13),

$$\begin{aligned} 0_n &= E\left[\left(m_t(\bar{m}) - m_t^*(\bar{m})\right)\left(\mathbf{1}_n + \tilde{r}_t\right)\right] \\ &= E\left[\left(m_t(\bar{m}) - m_t^*(\bar{m})\right)\left(\left(\mathbf{1}_n + E(\tilde{r}_t)\right) + \left(\tilde{r}_t - E(\tilde{r}_t)\right)\right)\right] \\ &= E\left[\left(m_t(\bar{m}) - m_t^*(\bar{m})\right)\left(\tilde{r}_t - E(\tilde{r}_t)\right)\right] \\ &= cov\left[m_t(\bar{m}) - m_t^*(\bar{m}), \tilde{r}_t\right], \end{aligned} \tag{7.15}$$

where the third line follows because $E\left[m_t(\bar{m})\right] = E\left[m_t^*(\bar{m})\right] = \bar{m}$ and the fourth line holds by $E\left[\left(m_t(\bar{m}) - m_t^*(\bar{m})\right)\right] = 0$. But $m_t^*(\bar{m})$ is a linear combination of $\tilde{r}_t$, and hence by the previous equation, it must be that $0 = cov\left[m_t(\bar{m}) - m_t^*(\bar{m}), m_t^*(\bar{m})\right]$. Therefore,

$$\begin{aligned} var\left[m_t(\bar{m})\right] &= var\left[m_t^*(\bar{m}) + m_t(\bar{m}) - m_t^*(\bar{m})\right] \\ &= var\left[m_t^*(\bar{m})\right] + var\left[m_t(\bar{m}) - m_t^*(\bar{m})\right] + 2 \cdot cov\left[m_t(\bar{m}) - m_t^*(\bar{m}), m_t^*(\bar{m})\right] \\ &= var\left[m_t^*(\bar{m})\right] + var\left[m_t(\bar{m}) - m_t^*(\bar{m})\right] \\ &\geq var\left[m_t^*(\bar{m})\right]. \end{aligned}$$

□

Hansen and Jagannathan (1991) consider an extension of this result, in which the stochastic discount factor satisfies the nonnegativity constraint, $m > 0$. Moreover, note that the bounds in theorem 7.1 rely on the unconditional moments of asset returns. The analysis may be extended to include conditioning information as originally proposed by Gallant, Hansen, and Tauchen (1990) and Ferson and Siegel (2003). Ferson (2003) provides an early review of the literature on testing based on asset pricing bounds, with both conditional and unconditional information. We now proceed with illustrating the bounds of theorem 7.1, based on unconditional moments of securities data.

Consider, then, the curve, $\bar{m} \longmapsto var\left[m_t^*(\bar{m})\right]$, that is, the base of the cup. By theorem 7.1, for each possible $\bar{m}$, each pair $\left(\bar{m}, var\left[m_t(\bar{m})\right]\right)$ predicted by any model has to lie inside the cup delimited by $\left(\bar{m}, var\left[m_t^*(\bar{m})\right]\right)$. The idea is the following. Testing the validity of a model is tantamount to assessing how volatile its pricing kernel is. Consider, then, eq. (7.12), and assume that a candidate pricing kernel is parametrized by some vector $\theta \in \Theta$, such that $m_t(\bar{m}; \theta) \equiv m_t(\bar{m})$, say. We want to find values of θ, say $\hat{\theta}$, such that $m_t(\bar{m}; \hat{\theta})$ is a valid pricing kernel (i.e., $m_t(\cdot)$ must be such that it prices all the assets as in eq. (7.12)) and is "volatile enough." Requiring that it prices all the assets is actually an obvious condition.[3] The issue then is to ascertain whether $\left(\bar{m}, var\left[m_t(\bar{m})\right]\right)$ enters the cup for economically reasonable values of $\hat{\theta}$. Note that the cup relies on asset price data and does not require the existence of a risk-free asset.

To illustrate, consider the Lucas model of section 7.2. We calculate the Hansen-Jagannathan bounds in eq. (7.14) and ascertain whether there are parameter values of the model such that the pricing kernel curve hits the the bounds in the mean and standard

3. In particular, the proof shows that eq. (7.15) holds under this condition.

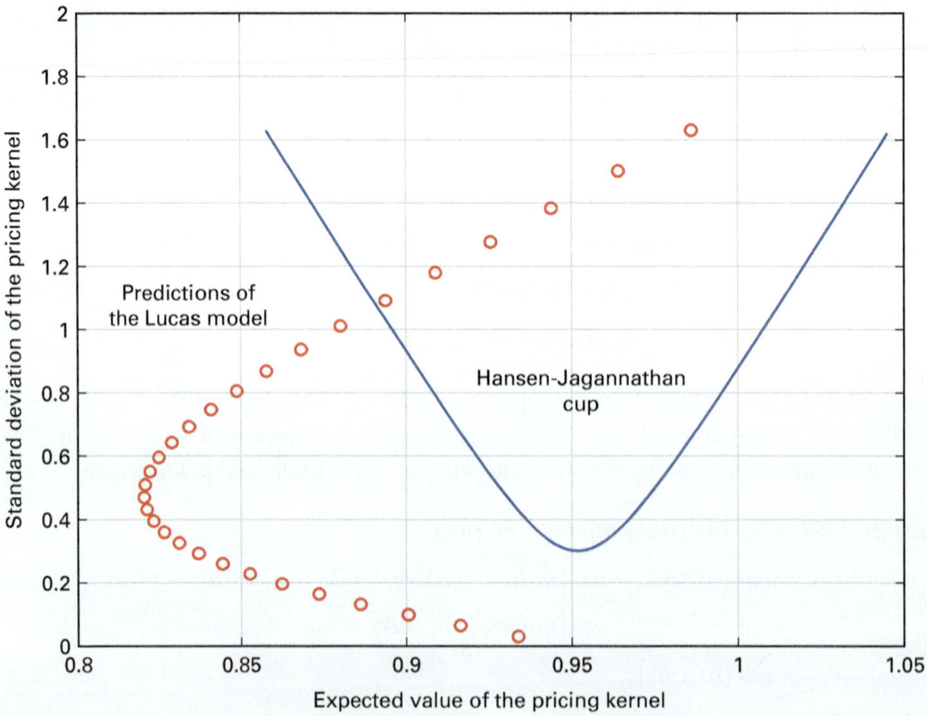

Figure 7.3
The solid line depicts the Hansen-Jagannathan bounds, obtained through eq. (7.14), and assuming that relevant information for securities data is summarized by three uncorrelated asset returns with annualized expected values and volatilities equal to [0.10 0.08 0.04] and [0.25 0.15 0.07], resp. The circles trace the "pricing kernel curve" predicted by the Lucas model (see eq. (7.16)), with parameters equal to $\beta = 0.95$, $\mu_d = 0.0183$, and $\sigma_d = 0.0328$ and γ ranging from 1 to 35. The circles inside the Hansen-Jagannathan cup are the pairs $(\bar{m}, \bar{\sigma}_m)$ in eq. (7.16) obtained with values of γ larger than 30. Progressively lower values of γ lead the pricing kernel curve to bend back.

deviation space. The pricing kernel of the model is

$$m_{t+1} = \frac{\xi_{t+1}}{\xi_t} = \exp\left(Z_{t+1}\right), \quad Z_{t+1} = -\left(r + \frac{1}{2}\lambda^2\right) - \lambda u_{D,t+1}, \quad u_{D,t+1} \equiv \frac{\epsilon_{d,t+1}}{\sigma_d}.$$

By the properties of log-normal distributions (see theorem 7.A1 in appendix 7.A), we have that the first two moments of m_t are

$$\bar{m} = E(m_t) = e^{-r} \quad \text{and} \quad \bar{\sigma}_m = \sqrt{var\left(m_t(\bar{m})\right)} = e^{-r + \frac{1}{2}\lambda^2}\sqrt{1 - e^{-\lambda^2}}, \qquad (7.16)$$

where r is as in eq. (7.5), and $\lambda = \gamma\sigma_d$, as usual. Note that, for given μ_d and σ_d^2, the two equations in (7.16) form a γ parametrized curve in the ($\bar{m}$-$\bar{\sigma}_m$) space. We refer this curve to as the "pricing kernel curve."

Does this curve enter the Hansen-Jagannathan cup? It is typically not the case, at least for plausible values of γ. Figure 7.3 depicts the bounds obtained with hypothetical (but plausible) figures regarding three asset returns. First, and for low values of γ, the pricing kernel curve bends back. The reason for this property is easily explained. In this example,

$\bar{\sigma}_m$ is always increasing in γ. When γ is low, the riskless interest rate r increases with γ, such that $\bar{m}$ decreases with γ. However, we expect that the pricing kernel curve bends back for any model where the intertemporal elasticity of substitution is confounded with relative risk aversion.

A bending pattern is indicative of conflicts between intertemporal elasticity of substitution and precautionary effects. Only when γ is sufficiently large, the interest rate decreases due to precautionary motives such that both $\bar{m}$ and $\bar{\sigma}_m$ increase. However, in the experiment depicted in figure 7.3, the pricing kernel curve hits the Hansen-Jagannathan cup only when γ is larger than 30.

The Lucas model predicts that the pricing kernel is not volatile. Subsequent chapters discuss departures from the Lucas benchmark that help increase the volatility of the pricing kernel. First, we will now explain how these tasks can be facilitated while increasing the number of state variables that affect asset evaluations. We simplify the presentation and only consider a market with a single risky asset.

7.4 Multifactor Extensions: The Aggregate Equity Market

If the pricing kernel has to be sufficiently volatile to stand to scrutiny of securities market data, a natural idea is to search for models with a sufficiently large number of factors. This section considers two possibilities: one in which returns are normally distributed and one in which returns are log-normally distributed. A multifactor model is naturally promising for its potential to boost the volatility of the pricing kernel and hence the equity premium. However, it may not necessarily deliver time-varying statistics (say, time-varying volatility), a robust empirical property that is discussed in detail in subsequent chapters.

7.4.1 Exponential Affine Pricing Kernels

This section considers a variant of the model in section 7.2. We determine expected returns while relying on the assumption that returns are normally distributed. We still maintain the assumption that the stochastic discount factor is exponential Gaussian, namely,

$$m_{t+1} = \exp\left(Z_{t+1}\right), \quad Z_{t+1} = -\left(r + \frac{1}{2}\lambda^2\right) - \lambda u_{D,t+1}, \quad u_{D,t+1} \sim \text{NID}\,(0,1),$$

where r and λ are some constants. In the absence of arbitrage,

$$1 = E(m_{t+1}\tilde{R}_{t+1}) = E\left(m_{t+1}\right)E(\tilde{R}_{t+1}) + cov(m_{t+1}, \tilde{R}_{t+1}), \quad \tilde{R}_{t+1} \equiv \frac{S_{t+1} + D_{t+1}}{S_t}.$$

By rearranging terms and using the fact that $E\left(m_{t+1}\right) = R^{-1}$,

$$E(\tilde{r}_{t+1}) - r = -R \cdot cov(m_{t+1}, \tilde{R}_{t+1}), \tag{7.17}$$

where $\tilde{r}_{t+1} \equiv \tilde{R}^e_{t+1} - 1$ and $r \equiv R - 1$.

The RHS of eq. (7.17) contains a covariance term, which cannot be determined without further assumptions on the data generating process. Suppose, for example, that $\tilde{r}$ is normally distributed. This assumption is only roughly consistent with those underlying the model in section 7.2, in which $\tilde{R}$ is *log*-normally distributed;[4] however, it is instructive to explore the implications of this new assumption on $\tilde{R}$. Now, we have that $\tilde{R}_{t+1}$ and Z_{t+1} are both normal and $m_{t+1} = m\left(Z_{t+1}\right) = \exp\left(Z_{t+1}\right)$. To determine the covariance between a normal variable, $\tilde{R}_{t+1}$, and the function of another normal variable, $m\left(Z_{t+1}\right)$, we may apply a result known as Stein's lemma (see theorem 7.A2 in appendix 7.A) and conclude that

$$cov(m_{t+1}, \tilde{R}_{t+1}) = E\left[m'\left(Z_{t+1}\right)\right] \cdot cov(Z_{t+1}, \tilde{R}_{t+1}) = -\lambda R^{-1} \cdot cov(u_{D,t+1}, \tilde{r}_{t+1}).$$

Replacing this expression into eq. (7.17) leaves

$$E(\tilde{r}_{t+1}) - r = \lambda \cdot cov(u_{D,t+1}, \tilde{r}_{t+1}).$$

We now extend the previous observations to a more general setup. Suppose that the stochastic discount factor is a function of K factors, $m\left(\epsilon_{1t}, \cdots, \epsilon_{Kt}\right)$, say. A particularly convenient analytical assumption is that m is exponential affine, with the "factors" $\left(\epsilon_{i,t}\right)_{i=1}^{K}$ being normally distributed, as in the following definition.

Definition 7.2 (Exponential affine pricing kernels). *An exponential affine pricing kernel (EAPK) is a pair (m_t, Z_t) and a function m, such that*

$$m_t = m(Z_t) = \exp(Z_t), \quad Z_t \equiv \phi_0 + \sum_{i=1}^{K} \phi_i \epsilon_{i,t}. \tag{7.18}$$

If $(\epsilon_{i,t})_{i=1}^{K}$ are jointly normal, and each $\epsilon_{i,t}$ has mean zero and variance σ_i^2, $i = 1, \cdots, K$, we say that the EAPK is a normal EAPK (NEAPK).

Next, assume that each $\epsilon_{i,t}$ has a zero mean; this assumption is without loss of generality because the constant ϕ_0 may encompass all constant terms stemming from the expectations of each factor. Further, suppose that $\tilde{R}$ is normally distributed. By Stein's lemma and assuming NEAPK,

$$\begin{aligned} cov(m_{t+1}, \tilde{R}_{t+1}) &= cov[\exp\left(Z_{t+1}\right), \tilde{R}_{t+1}] = R^{-1} cov(Z_{t+1}, \tilde{R}_{t+1}) \\ &= R^{-1} \sum_{i=1}^{K} \phi_i cov(\epsilon_{i,t+1}, \tilde{r}_{t+1}). \end{aligned}$$

Replacing the previous expression into eq. (7.17) leaves the linear factor representation

$$E(\tilde{R}_{t+1}) - R = -\sum_{i=1}^{K} \phi_i \underbrace{cov(\epsilon_{i,t+1}, \tilde{r}_{t+1})}_{\text{"betas"}}. \tag{7.19}$$

Thus, we have shown the implications summarized below.

---

4. According to the model in section 7.2, the equilibrium gross return is $\ln \tilde{R} = \mu_D - \frac{1}{2}\sigma_D^2 + \epsilon_S$, where ϵ_S is normally distributed. Chapter 4 (see section 4.2.5) shows that the normal model in this section may converge to a well-defined diffusive limit as the trading period tends to zero.

Proposition 7.3. *Suppose that $\tilde{R}$ is normally distributed. Then, assuming NEAPK implies a linear factor representation for asset returns.*

The APT theory underlying eq. (7.19) brings similarities with results known at least since the early work of Cochrane (1996).[5] Cochrane actually assumed that m is affine or that $m(Z_t) = Z_t$, where Z_t is affine, implying that $cov(m_{t+1}, \tilde{R}_{t+1}) = \sum_{i=1}^{K} \phi_i cov(\epsilon_{i,t+1}, \tilde{r}_{t+1})$. Replacing this expression into eq. (7.17) leaves

$$E(\tilde{r}_{t+1}) - r = -R \sum_{i=1}^{K} \phi_i cov(\epsilon_{i,t+1}, \tilde{r}_{t+1}), \quad \text{where } R = \frac{1}{E(m)} = \frac{1}{\phi_0}. \tag{7.20}$$

Instead, the assumption underlying definition 7.2 is that asset returns are normally distributed and that $m(Z_t)$ is exponential affine, where Z_t is affine, with the factors $\epsilon_{i,t}$ being normally distributed. Eq. (7.20) does not rely on the assumption that asset returns and factors are normally distributed. The only assumption is that the pricing kernel is affine. Eq. (7.20) is a convenient starting point for the discussion of more advanced models known as conditional CAPM (see section 7.6). We now discuss one additional class of models that can conveniently be solved in closed form.

7.4.2 With Log-Normal Returns

Next, assume that $\tilde{R}$ is *log*-normally distributed and that the NEAPK assumption in definition 7.2 holds. We have

$$\begin{aligned} 1 &= E_t\left(m_{t+1} \cdot \tilde{R}_{t+1}\right) \Longleftrightarrow \\ e^{-\phi_0} &= E_t\left(e^{\sum_{i=1}^{K} \phi_i \epsilon_{i,t+1}} \cdot \tilde{R}_{t+1}\right) \\ &= e^{E(y_{t+1}) + \frac{1}{2} var\left(\sum_{i=1}^{K} \phi_i \epsilon_{i,t+1} + y_{t+1}\right)}, \end{aligned} \tag{7.21}$$

where we have set $y_t = \ln \tilde{R}_t$. That is,

$$E_t(y_{t+1}) = -\phi_0 - \frac{1}{2}\left(\sigma_y^2 + \sum_{i=1}^{K} \phi_i^2 \sigma_i^2 + 2 \sum_{i=1}^{K} \phi_i \sigma_{y,\epsilon_i}\right),$$

where $\sigma_y^2 = var(\ln \tilde{R})$, and $\sigma_{y,\epsilon_i} = cov(\ln \tilde{R}, \epsilon_i)$. We repeat these arguments while applying eq. (7.21) to evaluate a zero coupon bond, obtaining

$$\ln R_{t+1} = -\phi_0 - \frac{1}{2} \sum_{i=1}^{K} \phi_i^2 \sigma_i^2.$$

5. To justify eq. (7.19) as an APT equation, consider the following reasoning. Suppose that the vector of returns satisfies $\tilde{R} = a + bf$ (for some vector a and matrix b), where f is a vector of K factors, each with zero mean and unit variance. Then, $b = cov(\tilde{R}, f)$. A portfolio π delivers $\pi^\top \tilde{R} = \pi^\top a + \pi^\top cov(\tilde{R}, f) f$. An arbitrage opportunity arises if there exists a π such that $\pi^\top cov(\tilde{R}, f) = 0$ and $\pi^\top a \neq r$. Relying on standard arguments (see, e.g., chapter 1), we may show that, in the absence of arbitrage, there exists a K-dimensional vector λ such that $a = cov(\tilde{R}, f)\lambda + r$. Therefore, $E(\tilde{R}) = r + cov(\tilde{R}, f)\lambda$.

Therefore, the expected excess returns are

$$E_t\left(y_{t+1}\right)-\ln R_{t+1}+\frac{1}{2}\sigma_y^2=-\sum_{i=1}^{K}\phi_i\sigma_{y,\epsilon_i}. \tag{7.22}$$

Eq. (7.22) illustrates properties of the model in section 7.2 through a different angle. Set $K=1$, and disregard momentarily the term $\frac{1}{2}\sigma_y^2$, a term arising due to Jensen's inequality effects. The model in this section collapses then to the Lucas model of section 7.2, once $\phi_1=-\gamma$ and $\sigma_{y,\epsilon_1}=\sigma_{d,\epsilon_1}$, as in the examples developed below. We know this model displays poor quantitative implications. The model in this section suggests that a reason for this empirical failure is that it explains asset returns with only one parameter in the stochastic discount factor, ϕ_1. Consider, then, the general case. Eq. (7.22) suggests that the equity premium may be arbitrarily large. Naturally, we would still need to achieve a clear understanding of the economic forces underlying the asset covariances, σ_{y,ϵ_i}, and the unit risk premiums, ϕ_i. Let us clarify while elaborating on the simple model of section 7.2, in which dividends are as in (7.1). Our objective is to determine the covariances, σ_{y,ϵ_i}. By eq. (7.8), the asset price is, formally,

$$S_t=\sum_{i=1}^{\infty}E_t\left(\frac{\xi_{t+i}}{\xi_t}D_{t+i}\right)=D_t\cdot\sum_{i=1}^{\infty}e^{\left(\mu_d+\phi_0+\frac{1}{2}\sum_{i=1}^{K}\phi_i\left(\phi_i\sigma_i^2+2\sigma_{d,\epsilon_i}\right)\right)\cdot i},\quad \sigma_{d,\epsilon_i}\equiv cov\left(\epsilon_d,\epsilon_i\right). \tag{7.23}$$

Assuming that

$$\hat{k}\equiv\mu_d+\phi_0+\frac{1}{2}\sum_{i=1}^{K}\phi_i\left(\phi_i\sigma_i^2+2\sigma_{d,\epsilon_i}\right)<0,$$

the series in (7.23) converges, and the price-dividend ratio equals

$$\frac{S_t}{D_t}=\frac{e^{\hat{k}}}{1-e^{\hat{k}}}.$$

Therefore, $\sigma_y^2=\sigma_d^2$ and $\sigma_{y,\epsilon_i}=\sigma_{d,\epsilon_i}$. That is, while the model is driven by multiple factors, the price-dividend ratio is constant. The next chapters explain that this property is counterfactual. Yet the model has the potential to address the equity premium puzzle (see eq. (7.22)), at least provided we are able to provide plausible explanations for the covariance terms, σ_{d,ϵ_i}. To illustrate these properties under a different angle, consider the stochastic discount factor predicted by this model. By the usual properties of log-normal distributions (see theorem 7.A1 in appendix 7.A), the first two moments of the stochastic discount factor are

$$E\left(m_t\right)=e^{E(Z_t)+\frac{1}{2}var(Z_t)},\quad \sqrt{var\left(m_t\right)}=e^{E(Z_t)+var(Z_t)}\sqrt{1-e^{-var(Z_t)}}.$$

Therefore, the model parameters may be calibrated to ensure that the first two moments of m_t enter the Hansen-Jagannathan cup. Still, remember that the model predicts that the price-dividend ratio is constant. That is, the model makes counterfactual predictions, a constant price-dividend ratio, despite the fact that the variance of its pricing kernel may be arbitrarily large. In other words, this example tells us that a model satisfying the Hansen-Jagannathan bounds of section 7.3 would need further scrutiny before it could be regarded as a potential explanation of asset price dynamics.

7.5 Relations to the Classic Capital Asset Pricing Model

7.5.1 Market Portfolios and Pricing Kernel Bounds

In part II (see section 2.7 in chapter 2), we explained that the CCAPM collapses to the classic CAPM, provided there is a portfolio that is perfectly correlated with the pricing kernel. Let us derive this result again from a slightly more general perspective than the CCAPM. Consider the model in the previous section, and let $\tilde{r}^e_{i,t+1} = \tilde{R}_{i,t+1} - R_{t+1}$ be the excess return on the risky asset i. We have

$$0 = E_t\left(m_{t+1}\tilde{r}^e_{i,t+1}\right) = E_t\left(m_{t+1}\right) E_t\left(\tilde{r}^e_{i,t+1}\right) + \rho_{im,t}\mathrm{Std}_t\left(m_{t+1}\right)\mathrm{Std}_t\left(\tilde{r}^e_{i,t+1}\right), \tag{7.24}$$

where $\mathrm{Std}_t(\cdot)$ denotes the standard deviation operator, conditional on time t information, and $\rho_{im,t} \equiv \mathrm{corr}_t(m_{t+1}, \tilde{r}^e_{i,t+1})$, a conditional correlation. Hence, the Sharpe ratio (on arithmetic returns) for asset i, $\mathcal{S}^i_t \equiv E_t(\tilde{r}^e_{i,t+1})/\mathrm{Std}_t(\tilde{r}^e_{i,t+1})$, satisfies

$$\left|\mathcal{S}^i_t\right| \leq \frac{\mathrm{Std}_t\left(m_{t+1}\right)}{E_t\left(m_{t+1}\right)}, \tag{7.25}$$

That is, the highest Sharpe ratio among all assets is bounded by the slope of the pricing kernel curve. This property may be used to ascertain whether a given pricing kernel is consistent with the universe of the observed Sharpe ratios. Unlike the Hansen-Jagannathan bounds (see section 7.3), these bounds require we observe the price of a risk-free asset. In section 7.5.4, we make the connection between these bounds and the Hansen-Jagannathan cup.

The equality in (7.25) holds for a hypothetical portfolio M with expected excess returns that are perfectly conditionally negatively correlated with the pricing kernel, $\rho_{Mm,t} = -1$. Moreover, if such a portfolio existed, the cross-section of the expected returns would satisfy the classic CAPM. Indeed, by eq. (7.24),

$$\begin{aligned} E_t(\tilde{r}^e_{i,t+1}) &= -\frac{\mathrm{Std}_t\left(m_{t+1}\right)}{E_t\left(m_{t+1}\right)}\rho_{im,t}\mathrm{Std}_t(\tilde{r}^e_{i,t+1}) \\ &= -\frac{E_t(\tilde{r}^e_{M,t+1})}{\mathrm{Std}_t(\tilde{r}^e_{M,t+1})}\rho_{im,t}\mathrm{Std}_t(\tilde{r}^e_{i,t+1}), \end{aligned}$$

where the second equality follows by the definition of $\mathcal{S}^M_t$ and the bound in eq. (7.25); rearranging terms and noticing that $\rho_{im,t} = -\rho_{iM,t}$ produces a CAPM equation

$$E_t(\tilde{r}^e_{i,t+1}) = \beta_{\tilde{r}^e_i,\tilde{r}^M} E_t(\tilde{r}^e_{M,t+1}), \tag{7.26}$$

with obvious notation.

7.5.2 A Semantic Digression on Market Portfolios

The classic CAPM would hold if portfolios could be created, with returns perfectly correlated with m. We are referring to these portfolios as market portfolios, consistent with standard CAPM terminology. However, it is problematic to rationalize market portfolios while relying on equally standard neoclassical models with fully optimizing agents. Consider, again, the single-factor, single-asset model in section 7.2. The appendix shows that the asset Sharpe ratio (on arithmetic returns) is

$$\mathcal{S} \equiv \frac{1 - e^{-\gamma \sigma_d^2}}{\sqrt{e^{\sigma_d^2} - 1}}. \tag{7.27}$$

Now, this asset is the only traded asset, and the appendix shows that the correlation between its returns and m is $\rho \equiv -\mathcal{S}(e^{\gamma^2 \sigma_d^2} - 1)^{-1/2}$. This correlation is, then, only approximately -1 (for low values of σ_d^2). While the asset returns and the pricing kernel are driven by the same source of randomness, $\epsilon_{d,t}$, they are not perfectly correlated because they are related in a nonlinear way. Therefore, in this model, the Sharpe ratio on the single asset is

$$\mathcal{S} < \frac{\mathrm{Std}_t(m_{t+1})}{\mathrm{E}_t(m_{t+1})} = \sqrt{e^{\gamma^2 \sigma_d^2} - 1},$$

where the inequality follows by the expression for ρ and the fact that $\rho > -1$. That is, in a single-tree economy, the very same tree may not be a market portfolio *à la* CAPM.

7.5.3 The Maximum Correlation Portfolio

Asset returns obey a joint CAPM restriction against one additional portfolio known as the *maximum correlation portfolio*. Let us elaborate. First, assume that there exists a portfolio that achieves a return equal to $\tilde{r}_{m^*,t} \equiv \frac{m_t^*}{\mathrm{E}((m_t^*)^2)} - 1$, where m_t^* is the minimum-variance pricing kernel leading to the Hansen-Jagannathan bounds (see section 7.3), $m_t^* \equiv m_t^*(\bar{m})$. Because m^* is linear in all asset returns, $\tilde{r}_{m^*}$ can actually be achieved through a portfolio of all tradable assets. Indeed, appendix 7.A shows that

$$1 = E_t\left(m_{t+1}\left(1 + \tilde{r}_{m^*,t+1}\right)\right). \tag{7.28}$$

Next, consider the conditional version of eq. (7.13) for any asset i

$$1 = E_t\left(m_{t+1}^*\left(1 + \tilde{r}_{i,t+1}\right)\right), \tag{7.29}$$

which can be viewed as the asset pricing equation (7.24) in the special case where the pricing kernel m_t happens to equal m_t^*. That is, eq. (7.29) can be interpreted as an asset pricing equation in a fictitious economy with pricing kernel m^*. Now, because $\tilde{r}_{m^*,t}$ is perfectly correlated with m^*, its Sharpe ratio achieves the bound in (7.25) in this fictitious economy and, by a reasoning similar to that leading to (7.26), eq. (7.29) implies that

$$E_t\left(\tilde{r}_{i,t+1}^e\right) = \beta_{\tilde{r}_i^e, \tilde{r}_{m^*}} E_t\left(\tilde{r}_{m^*,t+1}^e\right).$$

That is, the cross-section of expected returns aligns to $\tilde{r}_{m^*,t}$, similarly as with the classic CAPM. Note, however, that the portfolio with expected return $E\left(\tilde{r}_{m^*}^e\right)$ is not the market portfolio. Where is this portfolio located? Appendix 7.A shows that there are no portfolios yielding the same expected return with lower variance (that is, $\tilde{r}_{m^*}$ is mean-variance efficient) and that

$$E\left(\tilde{r}_{m^*}\right) = \mathrm{r} - \sqrt{\mathrm{Sh}}\sqrt{var\left(\tilde{r}_{m^*}\right)}, \tag{7.30}$$

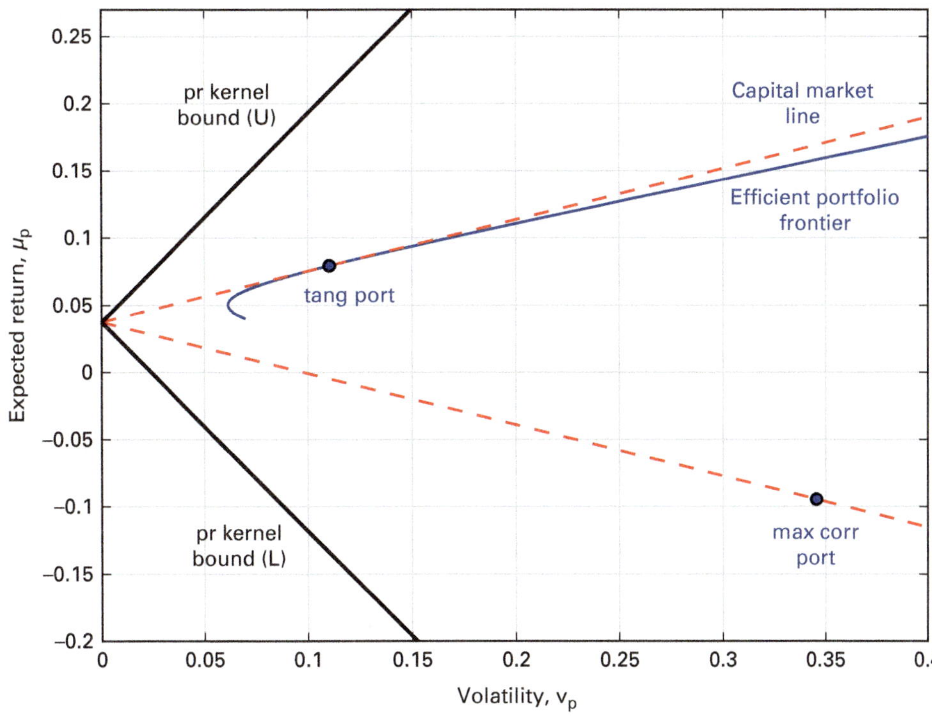

Figure 7.4
This figure plots pricing kernel bounds, the efficient portfolio frontier, and the CML in a hypothetical economy. Pricing kernel bounds (upper, U; lower, L) are obtained by restricting all assets' Sharpe ratios to satisfy the bound in (7.25) and assuming the truth is the Lucas model in section 7.2, with CRRA $\gamma = 33$ and the discretely compounded safe interest rate equal to $\bar{m}^{-1} - 1$. The origin of the CML is also equal to $\bar{m}^{-1} - 1$. The efficient portfolio frontier is constructed throughout the same hypothetical values for asset returns and volatilities used in figure 7.3. The tangent portfolio is the tradable portfolio with the highest Sharpe ratio, which is the negative of the Sharpe ratio on the equally tradable maximum correlation portfolio.

where $\mathrm{r} \equiv R - 1$ denotes the discretely compounded safe rate and Sh denotes the Sharpe market performance, a definition introduced in chapter 1.[6]

Figure 7.4 depicts the locus of all mean-variance efficient portfolios. The portfolio that achieves $E(\tilde{r}_{m^*})$ lies along the lower branch of the mean-variance efficient portfolios. Just above the upper branch is the CML, as explained in chapter 1,[7] and any portfolio with expected return $E(\tilde{r}_p)$ on it satisfies

$$E(\tilde{r}_p) = \mathrm{r} + \sqrt{\mathrm{Sh}}\sqrt{var(\tilde{r}_p)}. \tag{7.31}$$

The portfolio that achieves $E(\tilde{r}_{m^*})$ is called "maximum correlation portfolio," because, among all possible portfolios, $\tilde{r}_{m^*}$ is shown to be the one that has the highest correlation

6. See eq. (1.4) in chapter 1. Note that, in the present chapter, r denotes the continuously compounded safe rate, and r denotes its discretely compounded counterpart.
7. See eq. (1.6).

with any arbitrary m. Note that, due to eq. (7.28) and the definition of $\tilde{r}_{m^*}$, this correlation is positive and is precisely one when the true pricing kernel $m = m^*$.

7.5.4 Duality

By the definition of $\tilde{r}_{m^*,t}$ in the previous section, it is easy to show that the expected excess return on the maximum correlation portfolio is

$$E\left(1+\tilde{r}_{m^*,t}-\frac{1}{\bar{m}}\right)=-\frac{1}{\bar{m}}\frac{var\left(m_t^*\right)}{E\left(\left(m_t^*\right)^2\right)}, \tag{7.32}$$

where $\frac{1}{\bar{m}}$ is the gross return on an asset that does not correlate with the pricing kernel, for example, the risk-free rate.

Next, consider eq. (7.30) which is obtained assuming a risk-free rate. Comparing eq. (7.30) with eq. (7.32) and again using the definition of $\tilde{r}_{m^*,t}$ to conclude that $var\left(\tilde{r}_{m^*}\right) = \frac{var(m_t^*)}{E((m_t^*)^2)^2}$, we obtain

$$\sqrt{\text{Sh}}=\frac{\sqrt{var\left(m_t^*\right)}}{\bar{m}}\leq\frac{\sqrt{var\left(m_t\right)}}{\bar{m}}, \tag{7.33}$$

where the inequality follows by the Hansen-Jagannathan bounds in theorem 7.1.

Note that $\sqrt{\text{Sh}}$ is the slope of the CML in eq. (7.31) and is also the Sharpe ratio on the tangent portfolio. But, by construction, the tangent portfolio has the highest Sharpe ratio among all the assets. Therefore, eq. (7.33) shows that eq. (7.25) is the dual to the Hansen-Jagannathan bounds in theorem 7.1, in that $\min_m \frac{\text{Std}(m_t)}{\bar{m}} = \max_i S^i$.

To illustrate this duality, consider figure 7.4. This figure plots the pricing kernel bounds predicted by the Lucas model in section 7.2 for a CRRA coefficient $\gamma = 33$. It also depicts the efficient portfolio frontier (see chapter 1) in a hypothetical economy where the three risky assets have the same characteristics as those in figure 7.3 and the safe interest rate is equal to the prediction of the Lucas model, $\bar{m}^{-1} - 1$. The tangent portfolio is the portfolio that has the highest Sharpe ratio; if the Lucas model is correct, this Sharpe ratio cannot exceed the bound in (7.33) or, equivalently, (7.25). That is, while the Lucas pricing kernel curve has to hit the Hansen-Jagannathan cup in figure 7.3, the two dashed lines have to lie inside the pricing kernel bounds. This is the case in figure 7.4, although with the assumption of a very high γ.

In these examples, the tangent portfolio does not attain the upper pricing kernel bound and, thus, is far from acting as a market portfolio à la CAPM. However, all asset returns satisfy a CAPM restriction against the maximum correlation portfolio, also depicted in Figure 7.4. Finally, it is very instructive to note that the value of the safe interest predicted by the model is about 3.7%, which is obtained with a value of $\gamma = 33$. Figure 7.3 reveals that the Lucas model may hit the Hansen-Jagannathan cup even with lower values of γ. However, lower risk aversion would lead to an implausibly high value for the safe interest rate (see also figure 7.1)—the interest rate puzzle mentioned in section 7.2. That is, the bounds that this chapter considers regard the volatility of the pricing kernel, or the size of the equity premium, not the interest rate as already explained in section 7.2.

7.6 The Conditional Capital Asset Pricing Model

We now deal with an extension of the previous models, in which time variation in risk premiums has the potential to lead to time-varying returns statistics (e.g., a time-varying price-dividend ratio). Chapters 8 and 9 make several additional steps forward. First, they provide conditions under which these statistics have the same cyclical properties as in the data, such as, say, procyclical price-dividend ratios, countercyclical expected returns, and countercyclical realized volatility. Second, they provide economic rationale behind the forces that drive variations in asset returns. In many cases that we shall see, time variation in risk premiums is a key driver of these asset returns statistics. Note that time-varying risk premiums interact with risk. Intuitively, during recessions, risk premiums and firms' exposure to risk are both high; during expansions, risk premiums and exposures are both low. Therefore, "conditional betas" and "conditional lambdas" should be positively correlated. This correlation has the potential to improve the predictions of the standard CAPM.

This section provides a succinct analysis of the model implications of time-varying risk premiums without providing theoretical details regarding the forces underlying them. The starting point is eq. (7.20), derived under the assumption that the "lambdas" ϕ and the "betas," that is, the covariances between factors and returns, are all constant. Now, instead assume that they are time-varying, such that eq. (7.20) is generalized to

$$E_t(\tilde{r}_{t+1}) - r_t = -R_t \sum_{i=1}^{K} \phi_{it} cov_t(\epsilon_{i,t+1}, \tilde{r}_{t+1}), \tag{7.34}$$

with obvious notation. Eq. (7.34) describes an example of a conditional CAPM.

The obvious motivation underlying the conditional CAPM is that, despite the empirical evidence against the CAPM anticipated in chapter 1, a conditional version of it may be relatively more consistent with data. Let us illustrate. Consider the vector of factors at time $t+1$, $z_{t+1} = [1 \quad x_t \quad f_{t+1}^\top \quad f_{t+1}^\top x_t]^\top \equiv [1 \quad \bar{f}_{t+1}]^\top$, where $\bar{f}_{t+1}$ is K-dimensional, x_t is observed at time t, f_{t+1} is only observed at time $t+1$, and

$$m_{t+1} = \phi^\top z_{t+1},$$

for some vector of constants ϕ. We provide economic intuition on the "primitive factors" f_{t+1} and x_{t+1} below. Note that, *unconditionally*, eq. (7.20) holds true, that is,

$$E(\tilde{r}_{t+1}) - r = -R \sum_{i=1}^{K} \phi_i cov(\bar{f}_{i,t+1}, \tilde{r}_{t+1}).$$

However, conditionally on the information at time t, and setting $K=3$ for simplicity,

$$E_t(\tilde{r}_{t+1}) - r_t = -R_t \left[\phi_2 cov_t(f_{t+1}, \tilde{r}_{t+1}) + \phi_3 x_t cov_t(f_{t+1}, \tilde{r}_{t+1})\right],$$

where $R_t^{-1} = E_t\left(m_{t+1}\right)$. Thus, this formulation of the model is consistent not only with the idea of time-varying risk premiums, captured by the term $\phi_3 x_t$, but also with time-varying betas, that is, with returns covarying with the factors f_{t+1}. We may refer f_{t+1} to as fundamental factor. The role of x_t is to lead to time-varying risk premiums and may be referred to as a variable factor.

The next chapters explain indeed that the aggregate equity premium is countercyclical and that, during recessions, it increases more than it decreases during expansions. It is, then, natural to conjecture that variable factors may include conditioning information on macroeconomic developments. The literature has identified a variety of such factors, including, for example, the spread between low and high grade bonds (Jagannathan and Wang, 1996), aggregate consumption to wealth (Lettau and Ludvigson, 2001), the housing collateral ratio (Lustig and Van Nieuwerburgh, 2005), or labor income to consumption ratio (Santos and Veronesi, 2006).

Lewellen and Nagel (2006) provide some criticism regarding the ability of the conditional CAPM to explain the cross-section of expected returns. Consider the following simple example. Suppose that the pricing kernel is driven by one factor, the market, $m_{t+1} = a_t + b_t R_{m,t+1}$, where $R_{M,t}$ denotes the market portfolio at time t. We have

$$\begin{aligned} E_t(\tilde{r}_{i,t+1}) - r_t &= -R_t b_t cov_t(\tilde{R}_{M,t+1}, \tilde{R}_{i,t+1}) \\ &= \frac{cov_t(\tilde{R}_{M,t+1}, \tilde{R}_{i,t+1})}{var_t(\tilde{R}_{M,t+1})} (E_t(\tilde{r}_{M,t+1}) - r_t) \equiv \beta_{it}\gamma_t, \end{aligned} \tag{7.35}$$

with obvious notation and where the second equality follows by evaluating the first equality for $i = M$. Chapter 4 shows that this conditional CAPM representation holds in standard models with a log utility representative investor (see eq. (4.108) in section 4.6 in chapter 4).

Next, take the unconditional expectation of both sides of eq. (7.35),

$$E(\tilde{r}^e_{i,t+1}) = \bar{\beta}_i \bar{\gamma} + cov\,(\beta_{it}, \gamma_t)\,, \tag{7.36}$$

where $\tilde{r}^e_{i,t+1}$ denotes a return in excess of r_t and $\bar{\beta}_i$ and $\bar{\gamma}$ denote the unconditional expectations of β_{it} and γ_t. That is, a one-factor conditional CAPM implies a two-factor unconditional model. We explain the linkage between this unconditional version of the conditional CAPM and the unconditional CAPM. Note that, by definition,

$$E(\tilde{r}^e_{i,t+1}) = \alpha^u_i + \beta^u_i \bar{\gamma}, \tag{7.37}$$

where α^u_i and β^u_i are alpha and beta of the unconditional CAPM. Comparing (7.36) and (7.37) leaves

$$\alpha^u_i = \left(\bar{\beta}_i - \beta^u_i\right)\bar{\gamma} + cov\,(\beta_{it}, \gamma_t) \approx cov\,(\beta_{it}, \gamma_t) \leq \sqrt{var\,(\beta_{it})}\sqrt{var\,(\gamma_t)},$$

where the approximation is reasonable under conditions discussed by Lewellen and Nagel. The point is that asset exposures and market risk premium are typically too small to justify the magnitude of α^u_i that result from fitting a CAPM. Cross-sectional tests of the conditional CAPM based on eq. (7.36) should explicitly consider regressions with predictive parts equal to $E(\tilde{r}^e_{i,t+1}) = \bar{\beta}_i \bar{\gamma} + \chi \cdot cov\,(\beta_{it}, \gamma_t)$ and test the null that $\chi = 1$.

Appendix 7.A Proof of Selected Results

We state a celebrated result that we use in several parts of this chapter.

Theorem 7.A1 (First moments of log-normal distributions). *Let Z_{t+1} be normally distributed, conditionally upon the information set at time t. Then, for any $\alpha \in \mathbb{R}$,*

$$E_t\left(e^{-\alpha Z_{t+1}}\right) = e^{-\alpha E_t(Z_{t+1}) + \frac{1}{2}\alpha^2 var_t(Z_{t+1})}$$

$$\sqrt{var_t\left(e^{-\alpha Z_{t+1}}\right)} = e^{-\alpha E_t(Z_{t+1}) + \alpha^2 var_t(Z_{t+1})}\sqrt{1 - e^{-\alpha^2 var_t(Z_{t+1})}}$$

The following result is also very well known. For obvious reasons, it may be considered as the discrete time counterpart of Itô's lemma.

Theorem 7.A2 (Stein's lemma). *Suppose that two random variables x and y are jointly normal. Then,*

$$cov\left[g(x), y\right] = E\left[g'(x)\right] \cdot cov(x, y),$$

for any differentiable function g satisfying $E\left(\left|g'(x)\right|\right) < \infty$.

Next, we provide proofs of additional selected results stated in the main text.

Proof of eq. (7.13). We have

$$\begin{aligned}
E\left[m_t^*(\bar{m}) \cdot (\mathbf{1}_n + \tilde{r}_t)\right] &= E\left[\left(\bar{m} + (\tilde{r}_t - E(\tilde{r}_t))^\top \beta_{\bar{m}}\right)(\mathbf{1}_n + \tilde{r}_t)\right] \\
&= \bar{m}E(\mathbf{1}_n + \tilde{r}_t) + E\left[(\tilde{r}_t - E(\tilde{r}_t))^\top \beta_{\bar{m}}(\mathbf{1}_n + \tilde{r}_t)\right] \\
&= \bar{m}E(\mathbf{1}_n + \tilde{r}_t) + E\left[(\mathbf{1}_n + \tilde{r}_t)(\tilde{r}_t - E(\tilde{r}_t))^\top\right]\beta_{\bar{m}} \\
&= \bar{m}E(\mathbf{1}_n + \tilde{r}_t) + E\left[((\mathbf{1}_n + E(\tilde{r}_t)) + (\tilde{r}_t - E(\tilde{r}_t)))(\tilde{r}_t - E(\tilde{r}_t))^\top\right]\beta_{\bar{m}} \\
&= \bar{m}E(\mathbf{1}_n + \tilde{r}_t) + E\left[(\tilde{r}_t - E(\tilde{r}_t))(\tilde{r}_t - E(\tilde{r}_t))^\top\right]\beta_{\bar{m}} \\
&= \bar{m}E(\mathbf{1}_n + \tilde{r}_t) + \Sigma\beta_{\bar{m}} \\
&= \bar{m}E(\mathbf{1}_n + \tilde{r}_t) + \mathbf{1}_n - \bar{m}E(\mathbf{1}_n + \tilde{r}_t),
\end{aligned}$$

where the last line follows by the definition of $\beta_{\bar{m}}$.

Proof of eq. (7.28). Note that

$$E(m(1 + \tilde{r}_{m^*})) = \frac{E(m \cdot m^*)}{E\left[(m^*)^2\right]}$$

and that

$$\begin{aligned}
E\left(m \cdot m^*\right) &= \bar{m}^2 + E[m(\tilde{r}_t - E(\tilde{r}_t))^\top \beta_{\bar{m}}] \\
&= \bar{m}^2 + E[m(1 + \tilde{r}_t)^\top]\beta_{\bar{m}} - E[m(1 + E(\tilde{r}_t))^\top]\beta_{\bar{m}} \\
&= \bar{m}^2 + [\mathbf{1}_n - \bar{m}(1 + E(\tilde{r}_t))^\top]\beta_{\bar{m}}
\end{aligned}$$

$$
\begin{aligned}
&= \bar{m}^2 + [\mathbf{1}_n - \bar{m}\,(1 + E(\tilde{r}_t))^\top]\Sigma^{-1}[\mathbf{1}_n - \bar{m}\,(\mathbf{1}_n + E(\tilde{r}_t))] \\
&= \bar{m}^2 + var\,(m^*)\,,
\end{aligned}
$$

where the last line follows by the definition of m^*.

Proof that $\tilde{r}_{m^*}$ is mean-variance efficient. Let $p = (p_0, p_1, \cdots, p_n)^\top$ the vector of $n+1$ portfolio weights, where $p_i \equiv \pi^i / w$ denotes the asset i weight, such that $p^\top \mathbf{1}_{n+1} = 1$. Next, we build up an arbitrary portfolio that yields the expected return $E\,(r_{m^*})$, showing then that this arbitrary portfolio has a variance greater than $var\,(r_{m^*})$. Let $\underline{r} = (\bar{m}^{-1} - 1, \tilde{r}_1, \cdots, \tilde{r}_n)^\top$ and $r_p = p^\top \underline{r}$, such that $E(r_p) = E(r_{m^*})$. We have

$$
\begin{aligned}
cov\,(r_{m^*}, r_p - r_{r_{m^*}}) &= E[r_{m^*}\,(r_p - r_{m^*})] \\
&= E[r_{m^*}\,(R_p - R_{m^*})] \\
&= E\,(R_{m^*} R_p) - E\left(R_{m^*}^2\right) \\
&= \frac{E[m^*\,(1 + p^\top \underline{r})]}{E\,(m^{*2})} - \frac{E\,(m^{*2})}{[E\,(m^{*2})]^2} \\
&= \frac{1}{E\,(m^{*2})}[p^\top E\,(m^*\,(\mathbf{1}_{n+1} + \underline{r})) - 1] \\
&= 0.
\end{aligned}
\tag{7.A1}
$$

The first equality follows because, by construction, $E(r_p) = E(r_{m^*})$. The last equality follows because

$$
p^\top E\left[m^*\,(\mathbf{1}_{n+1} + \underline{r})\right] = p^\top \mathbf{1}_{n+1} = 1.
$$

Given eq. (7.A1), the claim follows directly:

$$
var\,(R_p) = var\left[R_{m^*} + (R_p - R_{m^*})\right] = var\,(R_{m^*}) + var\,(R_p - R_{m^*}) \geq var\,(R_{m^*})\,.
$$

Proof of eq. (7.30). Note that, by the definition of $\tilde{r}_{m^*,t}$,

$$
E\left(\tilde{r}_{m^*,t}\right) = \frac{\bar{m}}{E[(m^*)^2]} - 1. \tag{7.A2}
$$

Note that, in terms of the notation in chapter 1, m^* is, denoting $b = E(\tilde{r}_t)$,

$$
m^* = \bar{m} + (B\tilde{u})^\top \beta_{\bar{m}}, \; \beta_{\bar{m}} = \Sigma^{-1}\left[\mathbf{1}_n - \bar{m}\left(\mathbf{1}_n + b\right)\right],
$$

such that

$$
\begin{aligned}
E[(m^*)^2] &= \bar{m}^2 + \beta_{\bar{m}}^\top \Sigma \beta_{\bar{m}} \\
&= \bar{m}^2 + [\mathbf{1}_n^\top - \bar{m}(\mathbf{1}_n^\top + b^\top)]\Sigma^{-1}[\mathbf{1}_n - \bar{m}\left(\mathbf{1}_n + b\right)] \\
&= \frac{1}{(1+r)^2}\left(\mathrm{C}r^2 - 2\mathrm{D}r + A + 1\right),
\end{aligned}
\tag{7.A3}
$$

where the third equality follows by the equality $\bar{m}=(1+\mathrm{r})^{-1}$, with r denoting the simply compounded safe rate and where, consistent with notation in chapter 1,

$$A\equiv b^{\top}\Sigma^{-1}b,\quad C\equiv 1_n^{\top}\Sigma^{-1}1_n,\quad \text{and } D\equiv 1_n^{\top}\Sigma^{-1}b.$$

Further, note that, in terms of A, C, and D, the Sharpe market performance (see chapter 1) can be written as

$$\mathrm{Sh}\equiv\left(b-1_n r\right)^{\top}\Sigma^{-1}\left(b-1_n r\right)=\mathrm{Cr}^2-2D\mathrm{r}+A.$$

Replacing this expression for Sh into eq. (7.A3) and then (7.A2),

$$E\left(\tilde{r}_{m^*}\right)=\frac{\mathrm{r}-\mathrm{Sh}}{1+\mathrm{Sh}}. \tag{7.A4}$$

Next, note that, by straightforward calculations,

$$\sqrt{var\left(\tilde{r}_{m^*}\right)}=\frac{\sqrt{\beta_{\bar{m}}^{\top}\Sigma\beta_{\bar{m}}}}{E((m_t^*)^2)}=\frac{(1+\mathrm{r})\sqrt{\mathrm{Sh}}}{1+\mathrm{Sh}}.$$

Plugging this expression for $\sqrt{var\left(\tilde{r}_{m^*}\right)}$ into eq. (7.A4) leads to eq. (7.30) in the main text.

Maximum correlation portfolio. We wish to show that for any pricing kernel m, $|corr(m,R_{m^*})|\geq\left|corr(m,R_p)\right|$ for any portfolio that yields an expected return equal to $E\left(R_p\right)$. Define an ℓ-parametrized portfolio such that

$$E\left[(1-\ell)R_o+\ell R_p\right]=E\left(R_{m^*}\right),\ R_o\equiv\bar{m}^{-1}.$$

We have

$$\begin{aligned}
corr\left(m,R_p\right)&=corr\left[m,(1-\ell)R_o+\ell R_p\right]\\
&=corr\left[m,R_{m^*}+\left((1-\ell)R_o+\ell R_p-R_{m^*}\right)\right]\\
&=\frac{cov\left(m,R_{m^*}\right)+cov\left(m,(1-\ell)R_o+\ell R_{pt}-R_{m^*}\right)}{\sqrt{var(m)}\sqrt{var\left((1-\ell)R_o+\ell R_p\right)}}\\
&=\frac{cov\left(m,R_{m^*}\right)}{\sqrt{var(m)}\sqrt{var\left((1-\ell)R_o+\ell R_p\right)}},
\end{aligned}$$

where the last equality follows because

$$\begin{aligned}
cov\left(m,(1-\ell)R_o+\ell R_p-R_{m^*}\right)&=E\left[m\cdot\left((1-\ell)R_o+\ell R_p-R_{m^*}\right)\right]\\
&=(1-\ell)\cdot\underbrace{E\left(mR_o\right)}_{=1}+\ell\cdot\underbrace{E\left(mR_p\right)}_{=1}-\underbrace{E\left(m\cdot R_{m^*}\right)}_{=1}\\
&=0,
\end{aligned}$$

where the first line follows because $E((1-\ell)R_o+\ell R_p)=E(R_{m^*})$. Therefore,

$$corr\left(m,R_p\right)=\frac{cov\left(m,R_{m^*}\right)}{\sqrt{var(m)}\sqrt{var\left((1-\ell)R_o+\ell R_p\right)}}\leq\frac{cov\left(m,R_{m^*}\right)}{\sqrt{var(m)}\sqrt{var(R_{m^*})}}=corr\left(m,R_{m^*}\right),$$

where the inequality follows because R_{m^*} is mean-variance efficient, such that $var((1-\ell)R_o+\ell R_p)\geq var(R_{bt})$, for all R_p.

Proof of eq. (7.27) and related results. Note that the arithmetic returns, $\tilde{R}$, satisfy

$$\tilde{R}_{t+1}=e^{\mu_s-\frac{1}{2}\sigma_s^2+\epsilon_{s,t+1}},$$

such that, by theorem 7.A1,

$$E(\tilde{R}_{t+1})-R_{t+1}=e^{\mu_s}-e^r,\quad\sqrt{var(\tilde{R}_{t+1})}=e^{\mu_s-\frac{1}{2}\sigma_s^2}e^{\sigma_s^2}\sqrt{1-e^{-\sigma_s^2}},$$

leaving

$$\mathcal{S}=\frac{E(\tilde{R}_{t+1})-R_{t+1}}{\sqrt{var(\tilde{R}_{t+1})}}=\frac{e^{\mu_s}-e^r}{e^{\mu_s-\frac{1}{2}\sigma_s^2}e^{\sigma_s^2}\sqrt{1-e^{-\sigma_s^2}}}.$$

The result follows by the equilibrium condition $\mu_s=r+\gamma\sigma_s^2$, $\sigma_s^2=\sigma_d^2$ and by reorganizing terms.

Next, we prove the claim in the main text that

$$\rho\equiv corr(m,\tilde{R})=-\frac{\mathcal{S}}{\sqrt{e^{\gamma^2\sigma_d^2}-1}}. \tag{7.A5}$$

We have

$$\rho=\frac{cov(m,\tilde{R})}{\sqrt{var\,(m)}\sqrt{var(\tilde{R}_{t+1})}}=\frac{cov(m,\tilde{R})}{\left(E(\tilde{R}_{t+1})-R_{t+1}\right)\sqrt{var\,(m)}}\mathcal{S}, \tag{7.A6}$$

where

$$\begin{aligned}cov(m,\tilde{R})&=cov\left(e^{-\left(r+\frac{1}{2}\lambda^2\right)-\gamma\epsilon_{s,t+1}},e^{\mu_s-\frac{1}{2}\sigma_s^2+\epsilon_{s,t+1}}\right)\\&=e^{-\left(r+\frac{1}{2}\lambda^2\right)}e^{\mu_s-\frac{1}{2}\sigma_s^2}cov\left(e^{-\gamma\epsilon_{s,t+1}},e^{\epsilon_{s,t+1}}\right)\\&=e^{-\left(r+\frac{1}{2}\lambda^2\right)}e^{\mu_s-\frac{1}{2}\sigma_s^2}\left(e^{\frac{1}{2}(1-\gamma)^2\sigma_s^2}-e^{\frac{1}{2}\left(1+\gamma^2\right)\sigma_s^2}\right)\\\sqrt{var\,(m)}&=e^{-\left(r+\frac{1}{2}\lambda^2\right)}e^{\gamma^2\sigma_d^2}\sqrt{1-e^{-\gamma^2\sigma_d^2}},\end{aligned}$$

and $\lambda=\gamma\sigma_d$ and, again, $\sigma_s^2=\sigma_d^2$. Eq. (7.A5) follows by plugging the previous expressions and the premium, $E(\tilde{R}_{t+1})-R_{t+1}$, into (7.A6) and simplifying.

References

Cochrane, J. (1996). "A Cross-Sectional Test of an Investment-Based Asset Pricing Model." *Journal of Political Economy* 104, 572–621.

Epstein, L. G., and S. E. Zin (1989). "Substitution, Risk-Aversion and the Temporal Behavior of Consumption and Asset Returns: A Theoretical Framework." *Econometrica* 57, 937–969.

Epstein, L.G., and S. E. Zin (1991). "Substitution, Risk-Aversion and the Temporal Behavior of Consumption and Asset Returns: An Empirical Analysis." *Journal of Political Economy* 99, 263–286.

Ferson, W. E. (2003). "Tests of Multifactor Pricing Models, Volatility Bounds and Portfolio Perfomance." In *Handbook of the Economics of Finance* (Vol. 1B), edited by G. M. Constantinides, M. Harris, and R. M. Stulz, 743–802. Amsterdam: North-Holland.

Ferson, W. E., and A. F. Siegel (2003). "Stochastic Discount Factor Bounds with Conditioning Information." *Review of Financial Studies* 16, 567–595.

Gallant, R. A., L. P. Hansen, and G. Tauchen (1990). "Using the Conditional Moments of Asset Payoffs to Infer the Volatility of Intertemporal Marginal Rates of Substitution." *Journal of Econometrics* 45, 141–179.

Gordon, M. (1962). *The Investment, Financing, and Valuation of the Corporation.* Homewood, IL: Irwin.

Guvenen, F. (2009). "A Parsimonious Macroeconomic Model for Asset Pricing." *Econometrica* 77, 1711–1740.

Jagannathan, R., and W. Wang (1996). "The Conditional CAPM and the Cross-Section of Stock Returns." *Journal of Finance* 51, 3–53.

Hansen, L. P., and R. Jagannathan (1991). "Implications of Security Market Data for Models of Dynamic Economies." *Journal of Political Economy* 99, 225–262.

Lettau, M., and S. Ludvigson (2001). "Resurrecting the (C)CAPM: A Cross-Sectional Test When Risk Premia are Time-Varying." *Journal of Political Economy* 109, 1238–1287.

Lewellen, J., and S. Nagel (2006). "The Conditional CAPM Does Not Explain Asset-Pricing Anomalies." *Journal of Financial Economics* 82, 289–314.

Lustig, H., and S. Van Nieuwerburgh (2005). "Housing Collateral, Consumption insurance, and Risk Premia: An Empirical Perspective." *Journal of Finance* 60, 1167–1219.

Mehra, R., and E. C. Prescott (1985). "The Equity Premium: A Puzzle." *Journal of Monetary Economics* 15, 145–161.

Santos, T., and P. Veronesi (2006). "Labor Income and Predictable Stock Returns." *Review of Financial Studies* 19, 1–44.

Weil, P. (1989). "The Equity Premium Puzzle and the Risk-Free Rate Puzzle." *Journal of Monetary Economics* 24, 401–421.

8

Aggregate Fluctuations in Equity Markets

8.1 Introduction

This chapter discusses empirical regularities of the aggregate equity market, how these properties relate to the business cycle, and the extent to which a few benchmark models may account for them. This chapter is, thus, a natural development of the previous. Its motivation is still to explain how existing models can help rationalize the extant empirical evidence. However, its focus now regards how the aggregate stock market relates to macroeconomic fluctuations. When are stock returns procyclical? When is stock volatility countercyclical? This chapter aims to explain how to reverse engineer the *qualitative* behavior of economic forces that is consistent with such empirical properties of the aggregate stock market. Using a more technical language, we would like to identify pricing kernels that are consistent with the business cycle behavior of equity returns. We consider two broad and not mutually inconsistent explanations.

In the first explanation, agents evaluate assets relying on time-varying discount rates. In these economies, the cyclical properties of aggregate equity markets are explained by the agents' optimal response to shocks on the fundamentals–a response that consists in requiring high risk premiums in bad times and low risk premiums in good. The second relies on the idea that the expected growth of the economy is time-varying. For example, agents may have time-varying expectations of dividend growth because they have incomplete knowledge of the state of the economy and may try to infer this state from public signals. If the agents estimate that the probability of living in the good state is time-varying, they will view expected growth as being time-varying as well. This randomness becomes a source of fluctuations in market volatility. Naturally, expected growth may be time-varying for purely mechanical reasons, for example, because average dividend growth simply relates to underlying economic developments.

Time-varying risk premiums and agent inference about unknown fundamentals form the basis of more advanced discussions in chapter 9. This chapter is a basis for more advanced models that display the main qualitative empirical properties of aggregate stock market fluctuations. However, these models do not necessarily lead to a resolution of the *quantitative* puzzles surveyed in chapter 7. For example, even if a given model predicts interesting market dynamics (e.g., countercyclical volatility), further scrutiny is required regarding its predictions on the *size* of the equity premium. To illustrate, we may find a model that predicts countercyclical volatility, as in the data, and yet this volatility can be orders of magnitude lower than in the data.

How stable is the empirical linkage that the markets display vis-à-vis other macroeconomic variables? The empirical evidence reviewed in this chapter suggests that a few key market statistics are quite stationary in relation to their historical behavior over the business cycle. This property is interesting, especially in light of the fact that financial markets have undergone significant changes over time. Many of these changes have arguably affected various aspects of their *microstructure*, such as transactions technologies, price discovery, liquidity, volumes, to mention a few examples. How is it that the properties of the aggregate stock market reviewed in this chapter do not appear to be affected by these changes? One simple possibility is that market microstructure mainly affects the very high frequency behavior of markets. Instead, the analysis of this chapter (and chapter 9) regards slow, low frequency market movements, which should be relatively immune from changes in market microstructure details. Models of market microstructure are dealt with in chapter 10.

This chapter is organized as follows. The next section provides a succinct overview of empirical regularities of aggregate equity markets at the business cycle frequency; we explain that price-dividend ratios and aggregate equity returns are procyclical and that equity volatility and risk premiums are countercyclical. Section 8.3 analyzes in deeper detail the empirical behavior of aggregate equity volatility, providing some intuitive explanations for it. Section 8.4 develops tools of analysis needed to deal with more elaborated explanations of market dynamics. Sections 8.5 and 8.6 study market dynamics consistent with the two explanations referred to at the beginning of this introduction: time-varying risk premiums and time-varying expected growth. In both cases, we rely on an analytical framework to think about countercyclical statistics; this framework is developed in one of the technical appendixes to this chapter. Finally, note that the analysis of this chapter relies on price-dividend ratios. Many stocks do not distribute dividends for a while. Section 8.7 explains how to rely on alternative "multiples," such as market-to-book ratios, to achieve predictions comparable with those made in this chapter on price-dividend ratios.

8.2 Empirical Evidence: A Bird's Eye View

Financial economists seem to suggest different conclusions regarding aggregate stock market predictability. On the one hand, Fama provides seminal work and evidence that the aggregate equity market is unpredictable in the short run (see Fama, 2014); on the other hand, Shiller shows that the market moves much more than justified by the fundamentals (see Shiller, 2014). This *excess volatility* puzzle identified by Shiller is also associated with *predictability* in the medium term: in bad times (say, in recessions), the market requires high returns, and in good times, the market appetite for risk is high. These oscillations in investors' "moods" lead stock prices to wide and predictable fluctuations in the medium term, that is, excess volatility.

The conclusions of Fama and those of Shiller do not contradict each other. Fama's work centers on short-term fluctuations whereas Shiller's focus is on the medium term as explained. Chapter 10 focuses on short run problems and revisits Fama's work on market efficiency in light of information problems. This chapter and chapter 9 analyze aggregate stock market fluctuations at a lower frequency, that is, that of the business cycle. Note that, in most of the models in this chapter and the next, the investors' "mood" is rational, that is, linked to a rational assessment of risk or uncertainty in light of their preferences and beliefs.

8.2.1 Equity Markets and the Business Cycle

The evidence of a linkage between the aggregate stock market and the business cycle is indeed striking and has been well known for a while (see, e.g., the early survey in Campbell, 2003). This section aims to streamline how aggregate stock market fluctuations relate to general macroeconomic conditions. Note that we do not aim to establish any causality link among the various variables we analyze. Rather, the analysis in this section could be best described as one relying on "descriptive statistics." We use monthly data that cover the period from January 1948 through December 2011. Figures 8.1 through 8.3 plots series for the period from 1957 to 2011 whereas, unless otherwise stated, the analysis reported in table 8.1 and in all other tables and figures regard the sample period from 1948 to 2002. The analysis in this section is very robust to changes in the sampling periods.

We compute yearly returns at month t as $\sum_{i=1}^{12} \tilde{R}_{t+1-i}$, where $\tilde{R}_t = \ln(\frac{S_t + D_t}{S_{t-1}})$, S_t is the S&P Composite index at month t, and D_t is the aggregate dividend calculated by Robert Shiller. Table 8.1 provides basic statistics for both raw data such as the price-dividend ratio, realized returns, and stock volatility and expected returns. Stock volatility is calculated as follows:

$$\text{Vol}_t \equiv \sqrt{6\pi} \cdot \bar{\sigma}_t, \quad \bar{\sigma}_t \equiv \frac{1}{12} \sum_{i=1}^{12} \left| \tilde{R}_{t+1-i} - r_{t+1-i} \right|, \tag{8.1}$$

where r_t is the risk-free rate taken to be the one-month bill return.[1] Expected returns are calculated as explained below (see eq. (8.2)). With the exception of the price-dividend ratio, all figures are annualized percent.

We note the first main set of stylized facts.

Fact I. The price-dividend ratio and realized returns are procyclical.

For example, figure 8.1 reveals that the price-dividend ratio on the S&P 500 declines during *all* economic slowdowns as signaled by the recession indicator calculated by the National Bureau of Economic Research (NBER)—the NBER recessions. At the same time, during NBER expansions, price-dividend ratios seem to be driven by additional factors

1. The rationale behind this calculation is as follows. First, $\bar{\sigma}_t$ is an estimate of the average volatility occurring over the last 12 months. We annualize $\bar{\sigma}_t$ by multiplying it by $\sqrt{12}$. The term $\sqrt{6\pi}$ arises for the following reason. If we assume a given return $R = \sigma u$, where σ is a positive constant and u is a standard unit normal, then $E(|R|) = \sigma\sqrt{\frac{2}{\pi}}$. The definition Vol_t in eq. (8.1), then, follows by multiplying $\sqrt{12}\bar{\sigma}_t$ by $\sqrt{\frac{\pi}{2}}$. This correction term, $\sqrt{\frac{\pi}{2}}$, has been suggested by Schwert (1989a) in a related context.

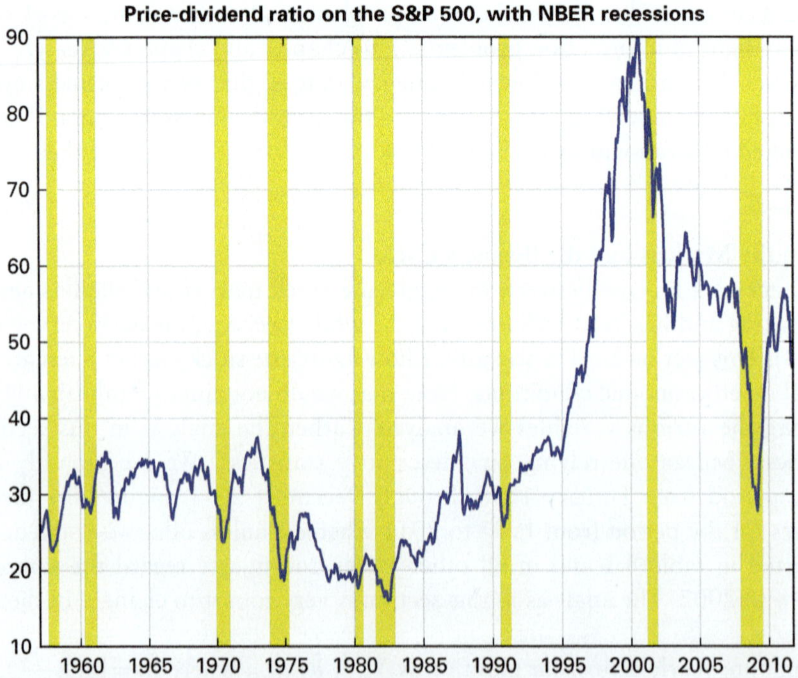

Figure 8.1
The price-dividend ratio, along with recession periods identified by the National Bureau of Economic Research (shaded areas).

Table 8.1
With the exception of the price-dividend-ratio levels, all figures are annualized percent.

	Total		NBER expansions		NBER recessions	
	Average	Std dev	Average	Std dev	Average	Std dev
P/D ratio	31.99	15.88	33.21	15.79	26.20	14.89
$\ln \frac{P/D_{t+1}}{P/D_t}$	2.01	12.13	3.95	10.81	−7.28	16.79
One-year returns	8.59	15.86	12.41	13.04	−9.45	15.49
Real risk-free rate	1.02	2.48	1.03	2.43	0.97	2.69
Excess return volatility	14.55	4.68	14.05	4.47	16.91	4.91
Expected returns	8.36	3.49	8.09	3.29	9.62	4.10

Note: P/D ratio = price-dividend ratio.

not necessarily related to the business cycle. For example, during the roaring 1960s, price-dividend ratios experienced two major drops that display the same order of magnitude as the decline at the very beginning of the chaotic 1970s. Realized returns follow similar patterns (see figure 8.2).

Table 8.1 also reports estimates of a key component of asset evaluation: the expected market return, that is, the return that investors expect while investing in the aggregate stock market. Appendix 8.A describes a procedure to estimate this unobserved variable.

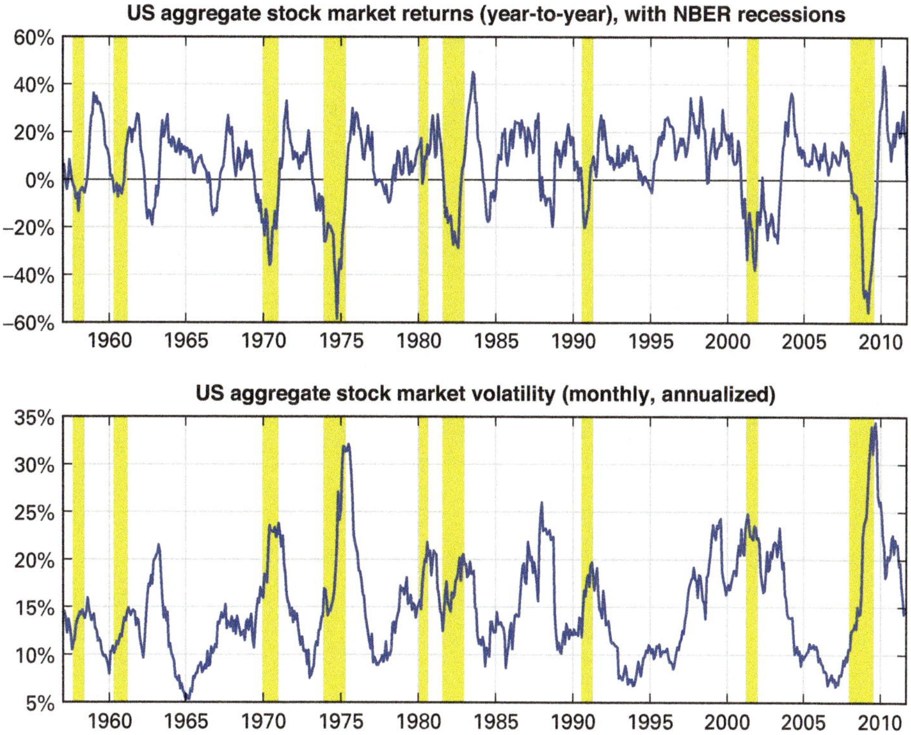

Figure 8.2
Monthly excess returns and volatility, in percentage, year-to-year.

This chapter relies on our reconstruction of yearly expected returns, defined as

$$\hat{\mathcal{E}}_t \equiv \sum_{j=1}^{12} P_t(\hat{R}_{t+j}), \tag{8.2}$$

where $\hat{R}_{t+j}$ is the expected return at time $t+j$ and $P_t(\hat{R}_{t+j})$ denotes the projection of $\hat{R}_{t+j}$ given the information at t, based on the model described in appendix 8.A.

The following fact summarizes the cyclical properties of realized volatility and expected returns.

Fact II. Stock volatility and expected returns are countercyclical.

That expected returns are countercyclical is a well-known fact since at least Fama and French (1989) and Ferson and Harvey (1991). Figures 8.2 through 8.4 are, indeed, suggestive of the business cycle pattern of the aggregate stock market. For example, Figure 8.3 depicts the statistical relation between stock volatility and the industrial production growth rate, which shows that stock volatility is largely countercyclical as it is higher during bad times than in good. There are, of course, exceptions. For example, stock volatility rocketed to almost 23% around the October 1987 crash—a crash occurring during one of the most enduring postwar expansion periods. Countercyclical volatility is a stylized fact extensively discussed in sections 8.3 and 8.4. An important lesson is that this empirical fact

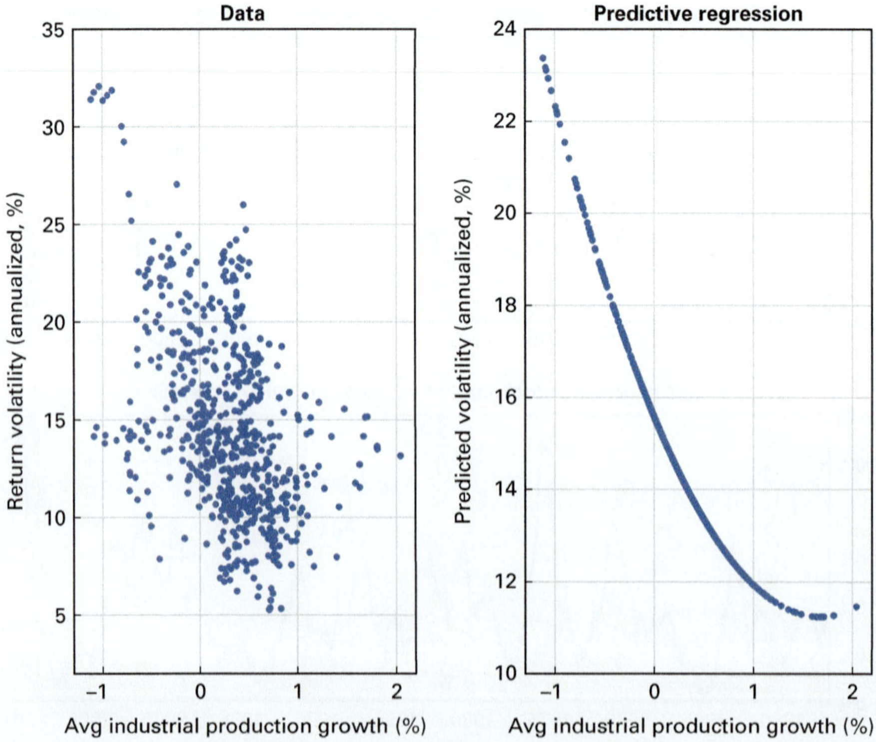

Figure 8.3
Stock volatility and business cycle conditions. The left panel plots stock volatility, Vol_t, against yearly (deseasoned) industrial production average growth rates, computed as $G_t \equiv \frac{1}{12}\sum_{i=1}^{12} g_{t+1-i}$, where g_t is the real, seasonally adjusted industrial production growth as of month t. The right panel depicts the prediction of the ordinary least squares regression: $Vol_t = \underset{(0.19)}{15.59} - \underset{(0.39)}{5.21} \cdot G_t + \underset{(0.41)}{1.56} \cdot G_t^2 + w_t$, where w_t is a residual term and robust standard errors are in parenthesis.

can be explained once the volatility of the price-dividend-ratio *changes* is countercyclical. Interestingly, table 8.1 reveals that price-dividend-ratio variations are more volatile during bad times than good. Finally, figure 8.3 suggests that stock volatility behaves asymmetrically over the business cycle in that it increases more in bad times than it decreases in good. This asymmetric behavior of stock volatility echoes its high frequency behavior documented at least since Glosten, Jagannathan, and Runkle (1993)—stock volatility increases more when returns are negative than it decreases when returns are positive.

A third set of stylized facts links to the asymmetric behavior of aggregate stock market fluctuations over the business cycle. We have already noted that volatility is countercyclical and behaves asymmetrically. We now turn to price multiples and expected returns.

Fact III. *Changes* in the price-dividend ratios and expected returns occur asymmetrically over the business cycle. The most volatile changes occur during the contractionary phases of the business cycle.

During recessions, price multiples and expected returns move more than they do in good times. For example, not only are expected returns countercyclical. On average, expected returns increase more during NBER recessions than they decrease during NBER

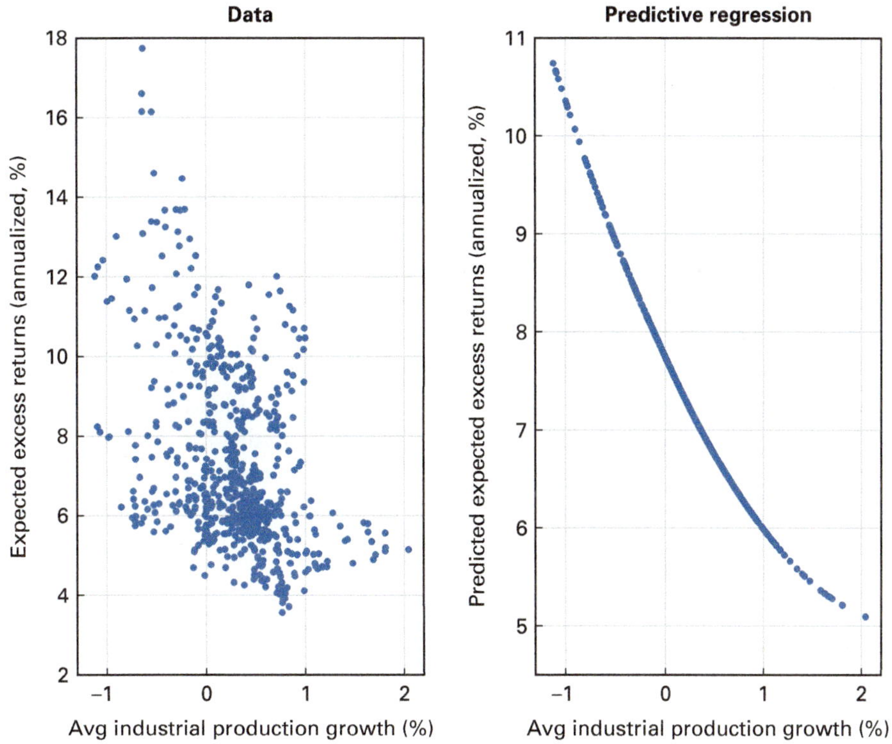

Figure 8.4
The left panel plots estimates of the expected returns (annualized, percent) ($\hat{\mathcal{E}}_t$ say) against yearly (de-seasoned) industrial production average growth rates, computed as $G_t \equiv \frac{1}{12}\sum_{i=1}^{12} g_{t+1-i}$, where g_t is the real, seasonally adjusted industrial production growth as of month t. Expected returns are estimated through eq. (8.2). The right panel depicts the prediction of the ordinary least squares regression: $\hat{\mathcal{E}}_t = \underset{(0.09)}{7.74} - \underset{(0.19)}{2.19} \cdot G_t + \underset{(0.19)}{0.43} \cdot G_t^2 + w_t$, where w_t is a residual term and robust standard errors are in parenthesis.

expansions—consistent with the summary statistics of table 8.1 and the informal pieces of evidence from figure 8.4. We shall return to this issue of countercyclical expected returns many times in this chapter.

Likewise, price-dividend ratios are not only procyclical. On average, price-dividend ratios increase less during NBER expansions than they decrease during NBER recessions. Further, this asymmetric behavior is quantitatively quite pronounced. Consider, for example, the changes in price-dividend ratios: on average, their percentage (negative) changes during recessions is nearly twice the percentage (positive) changes during expansions. Sections 8.3 and 8.4 aim to provide basic explanations of these facts.

8.2.2 Predictability

Fact I entails a quite intuitive consequence: price-dividend ratios convey information relating to future returns. After all, expansions are followed by recessions. Therefore, in good times, the stock market predicts that future returns will be negative. Define the excess return for the time period $[t, t+n]$ as $\tilde{R}^e_{t,t+n} \equiv \tilde{R}_{t,t+n} - r_{t,t+n}$, where $\tilde{R}_{t,t+n}$ is the asset return over $[t, t+n]$ and $r_{t,t+n}$ is the sum of the one-month US Treasury bill rate, taken over $[t, t+n]$. Consider the following regressions:

$$\tilde{R}^e_{t,t+n} = a_n + b_n \times \mathrm{P/D}_t + u_{n,t}, \quad n \geq 1, \tag{8.3}$$

where u_n is a residual term. Typically, the estimates of b_n are significantly negative, with a regression R^2 that increases with n.[2] However, while there is evidence on return predictability, it does not appear to be very strong; for example, figures 8.1 and 8.2 show that price-dividend ratios and market returns were both high during the 1990s. These topics will be dealt with again in chapter 9 (see, e.g., section 9.9).

Evidence on predictability exists, however. Where does it come from? Note that the previous regressions imply that $E(\tilde{R}^e_{t+n} | \mathrm{P/D}_t) = a_n + b_n \times \mathrm{P/D}_t$. Thus, they suggest that price-dividend ratios link to expected excess returns. In a somehow restrictive sense, countercyclical expected returns (fact II) and procyclical price-dividend ratios (fact I) might be two sides of the same coin. To investigate how this predictability links to business cycle developments, consider the following regression performed with monthly data from January 1948 to December 2002:

$$\tilde{R}^e_{t-12,t} = \underset{(1.04)}{14.64} - \underset{(1.37)}{9.09} \times \mathrm{G}_{t-12} - \underset{(2.67)}{14.27} \times \mathrm{Infl}_{t-12} + u_t, \quad \text{with } \mathrm{R}^2 = 11\%, \tag{8.4}$$

where robust standard errors are in parenthesis, u is a residual term, $\tilde{R}^e_{t-12,t}$ is the excess return from $t-12$ to t, G_t is the average industrial production growth over the previous 12 months as defined in figure 8.3, and Infl_t is defined similarly as G_t.

The negative signs of the coefficients in eq. (8.4) are to be expected. Economic activity does display mean-reverting behavior: bad times are followed by good. But good times are those where the stock market goes up. Therefore, a slowdown in economic activity is a predictor of high returns in the future. To illustrate with a simple example, assume that, over a prespecified sampling period, there is a *statistical* relation between the aggregate stock market and a single procyclical state variable tracking business cycle conditions–x_t, say–such that the log of the aggregate equity index is $\ln S_t = s_0 + s_x x_t$ for two constants s_0 and s_x, where $s_x > 0$ and where we are ignoring dividends. The additional critical assumption is that x_t is mean reverting, with unconditional expectation μ, speed of adjustment $\kappa > 0$, and some volatility coefficient $\sigma(x_t)$,

$$dx_t = \kappa(\mu - x_t)\, dt + \sigma(x_t)\, dW_t,$$

where W_t is a Brownian motion. It is easy to show that $E_{t-12}\left(\ln \frac{S_t}{S_{t-12}}\right) = a_0 - a_1 x_{t-12}$, where E_t denotes the expectation conditional on the information at t, $a_0 \equiv s_x\left(1 - e^{-12\kappa}\right)\mu$, and $a_1 \equiv s_x\left(1 - e^{-12\kappa}\right)$. That is, if x_t is mean reverting, $\kappa > 0$, and the aggregate stock market is procyclical ($s_x > 0$), expected returns are negatively related to past values of x_t, that is, $a_1 > 0$. This reasoning generalizes to a multivariate case, although the presence of feedbacks among macroeconomic variables might then dilute the contribution of each variable as a predictor of future expected returns.

The regression results in eq. (8.4) have the same nature as that underlying eq. (8.3): price-dividend ratios and market returns are procyclical. Note a final relation that reveals

2. See, e.g., the early empirical evidence summarized by Campbell (2003).

this procyclicality of market returns. At a contemporaneous level, the excess market returns are positively related to industrial production and negatively related to inflation,

$$\tilde{R}^e_{t-12,t} = \underset{(1.07)}{10.47} + \underset{(1.19)}{7.27} \times \mathrm{G}_t - \underset{(2.91)}{16.33} \times \mathrm{Infl}_t + w_t, \quad \text{with } \mathrm{R}^2 = 14\%, \tag{8.5}$$

where robust standard errors are in parenthesis and w is a residual term. Corradi, Distaso, and Mele (2013) estimate a continuous time model in which the aggregate stock market is driven by industrial production, inflation, and one unobserved factor; in this no-arbitrage model, the market return linkages to the two macroeconomic factors are similar to those summarized by the linear regression in eq. (8.5).

Finally, a seemingly puzzling feature is that price-dividend ratios do not appear to predict future dividend growth. Let $g_t \equiv \ln(D_t / D_{t-1})$. In regressions taking the following format,

$$g_{t+n} = a_n + b_n \times \mathrm{P/D}_t + u_{n,t}, \quad n \geq 1,$$

the predictive content of price-dividend ratios is poor, and estimates of b_n might often come with a wrong sign. To summarize, the previous regression estimates suggest that (i) price-dividend ratios are driven by time-varying expected returns, a proxy of the risk premium (as explained in detail in the next sections), and (ii) expected dividend growth does not seem to play a prominent role. Naturally, such evidence amounts to mere summary statistics. This and chapter 9 (see section 9.9) provide theoretical linkages with the purpose of explaining the origins of these statistical relations.

8.2.3 Risk-Return Trade-offs

Expected returns and stock volatility are both countercyclical, and hence they positively relate at a business cycle frequency. Figure 8.5 provides a scatterplot of expected returns against realized volatility. It is tempting to rely on this evidence and conclude that higher expected returns arise when the market requires compensation for higher volatility—a conclusion apparently consistent with the prediction of the CAPM (see chapter 1). This conclusion is, of course, misleading: the CAPM is wrong if volatility is random. If volatility is driven by business cycle factors, it is these very same factors that drive expected returns: volatility does, then, merely react to these factors. Let us elaborate with a simple model.

Consider an economy with a single asset and a representative agent. The asset price, S_t, is the solution to

$$\frac{dS_t}{S_t} = (\cdots)\, dt + \sigma_t dW_{1t},$$

and the asset return volatility σ_t is random:

$$d\sigma_t^2 = (\cdots)\, dt + \xi\,(\sigma_t) \left(\rho dW_{1t} + \sqrt{1-\rho^2} dW_{2t}\right),$$

where W_{it} are two standard Brownian motions, $\xi\,(\sigma_t)$ is a given function, and finally, ρ is the instantaneous (and constant) correlation between the asset returns and volatility. Now, by the results in part I (see eq. (4.97) in chapter 4), we have that, in equilibrium, the asset's

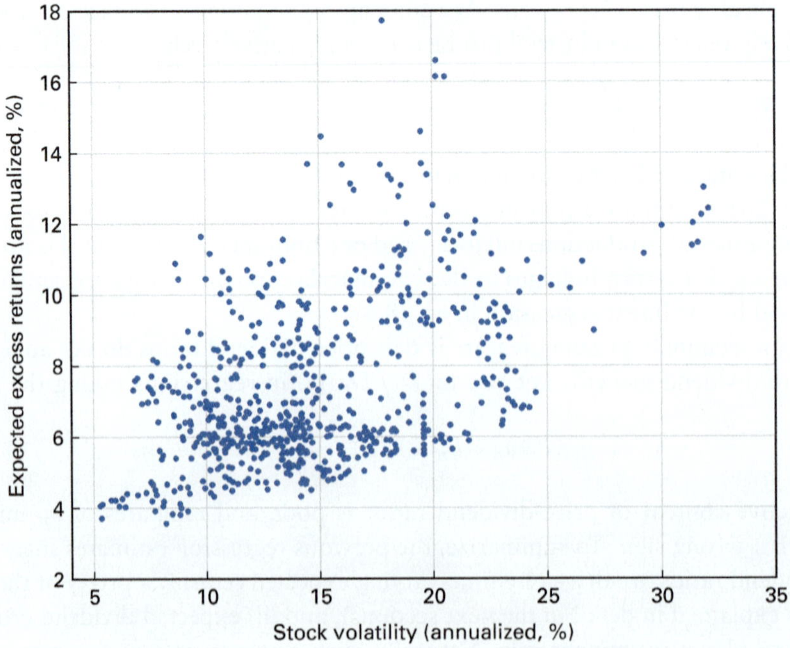

Figure 8.5
Expected returns and volatility.

expected excess returns are

$$\mu - r = \frac{-V\mathcal{J}_{VV}}{\mathcal{J}_V}\sigma_t^2 - \sigma_t \xi(\sigma_t)\rho\frac{\mathcal{J}_{V\sigma}}{\mathcal{J}_V}, \tag{8.6}$$

where $\mathcal{J}$ is the indirect utility of a representative agent (with subscripts denoting partial derivatives) and V is the agent's total wealth. That is, even in this simple model, a risk-return trade-off is not as clear-cut as the CAPM suggests: expected returns are driven not only by volatility but also by the volatility of volatility. Further, this relation can be strong or weak according to parameter values.

More fundamentally, this simple model takes volatility as exogenous. This chapter and chapter 9 remove this assumption. The objective is to analyze more realistic economies in which asset prices clear markets in general equilibrium, such that the dynamics of volatility are endogenous, resulting from the investors' optimal reaction to changes in the fundamentals. In these economies, eq. (8.6) is not the relevant pricing equation; rather, expected excess returns link to the primitive factors affecting the investors' choice space (see section 8.4). Investors require a premium to be compensated for these risk factors, not for realized volatility. In other words, market volatility results from the forces that affect expected returns. We now provide an overview of some plausible forces.

8.3 Volatility: A Business Cycle Perspective

A prominent feature of the US equity market is a close connection between aggregate volatility and business cycle developments as discussed in the previous section.

Understanding the origins and implications of these facts may be relevant to policy makers. Indeed, if stock market volatility is countercyclical, it must necessarily be encoding information about the development of the business cycle. Policy makers could then extract the signals that stock volatility brings on business cycle developments.

This section accomplishes three tasks. First, it mentions additional stylized facts relating aggregate stock volatility, expected returns, and price-dividend ratios over the business cycle (in section 8.3.1). Second, it attempts preliminary explanations of these facts (in section 8.3.2). Third, it investigates whether volatility contains any useful information regarding the business cycle (in section 8.3.3).

There are topics left over from this section. For example, we do not tackle statistical issues regarding volatility measurement.[3] Nor do we consider the role of volatility in applied asset evaluation. Instead, chapter 11 covers details regarding how time-varying volatility affects derivative pricing. The focus of this section is more fundamental: it explores the extent to which volatility movements may be given a wider business cycle perspective and also highlights some explanations underlying them.

8.3.1 Volatility Cycles

How does equity volatility relate to the business cycle? One of the first contributions to this literature is Schwert (1989a,b).[4] Schwert points out that low frequency fluctuations in equity volatility are difficult to explain through fluctuations in the volatility of other macroeconomic variables.

For example, industrial production volatility does not correlate with stock volatility. Let us calculate industrial production volatility as $\text{Vol}_{G,t} \equiv \frac{1}{\sqrt{12}} \sum_{i=1}^{12} |G_{t+1-i}|$, where G_t is the real, seasonally adjusted industrial production growth rate at month t (similarly as in eq. (8.1)). Figure 8.6 plots stock volatility against $\text{Vol}_{G,t}$; it does not reveal any obvious pattern between these two variables. These results are in striking contrast with those in figure 8.3, where instead stock volatility exhibits a quite clear countercyclical behavior. Table 8.1 reveals in more detail that stock market volatility is about 20% higher during NBER recessions than during NBER expansions.

In fact, Schwert also shows that stock volatility *is* countercyclical. The main focus of this section is to provide a few explanations of this evidence. This evidence would support the view that equity volatility relates to the business cycle, although not precisely to the *volatility* of other macroeconomic variables.

A seemingly unrelated but well-known stylized fact is that risk premiums are countercyclical, as summarized by fact II in the previous section. Particularly important is also fact III: the fall in expected returns during expansions is much smaller than their increase during recessions. Based on post war data, we find that, compared with an average of 8.36%, the expected returns increase by about 15% during recessions while they drop by a mere 3% during NBER expansions (see table 8.1). A final stylized fact is that price-dividend ratios behave asymmetrically over the business cycle. Table 8.1

3. See, e.g., Andersen, Bollerslev, and Diebold (2010) for an early survey regarding the many available statistical techniques to estimate volatility.

4. Additional important contributions include Hamilton and Lin (1996) and Brandt and Kang (2004). See Corradi, Distaso, and Mele (2013) for additional work and references.

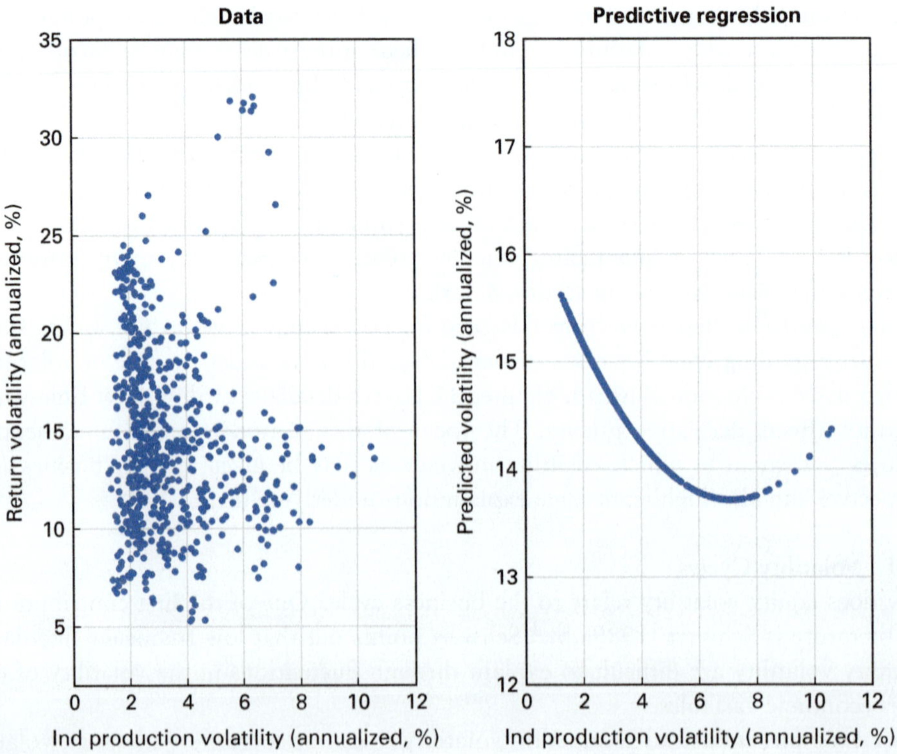

Figure 8.6
Return volatility and industrial production volatility. The left panel plots stock volatility, Vol_t, against industrial production volatility, $\text{Vol}_{G,t}$. The right panel depicts the prediction of the ordinary least squares regression: $\text{Vol}_t = \underset{(0.93)}{16.51} - \underset{(0.47)}{0.78} \cdot \text{Vol}_{G,t} + \underset{(0.05)}{0.05} \cdot \text{Vol}^2_{G,t} + w_t$, where w is a residual term and standard errors are in parenthesis.

reveals that price-dividend ratios are not only procyclical. Their downward changes during recessions are also more severe than their upward movements during expansions. Table 8.1 suggests that price-dividend ratios fluctuate much more in recessions than in expansions.

How can we rationalize these facts? A simple possibility is that the economy is frequently hit by shocks that display the same qualitative behavior of return volatility, expected returns, and price-dividend ratios. However, figure 8.6 suggests this channel is unlikely. Another possibility is that the economy reacts to shocks due to some mechanism endogenously related to the investors' maximizing behavior, which then activates the previous phenomena.

Section 8.3.2 puts forward explanations for countercyclical stock volatility relying on endogenous mechanisms. Section 8.3.3 provides additional empirical properties of equity volatility. The motivation is simple: because stock volatility is countercyclical, it might contain useful information about ongoing business cycle developments. The section, then, aims to provide answers to the following questions: (i) Do macroeconomic factors help explain the dynamics of stock market volatility? (ii) Conversely, what is the predictive content that stock market volatility brings about the business cycle?

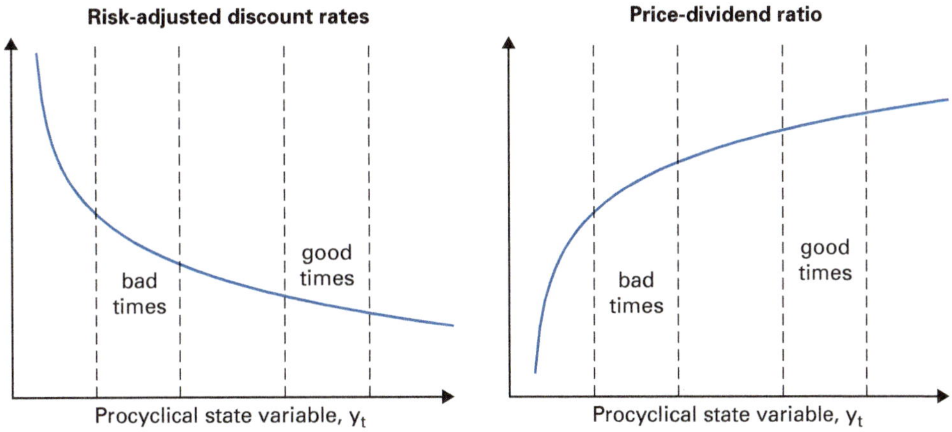

Figure 8.7
Countercyclical risk premiums and equity volatility. The left panel depicts a hypothetical relation between some variable y_t linked to the business cycle and risk-adjusted discount rates. If this relation is decreasing and sufficiently convex, the price-dividend ratio is concave in y_t, leading returns volatility to be higher during bad times than good.

8.3.2 Understanding the Empirical Evidence

This section is a broad introduction to the main determinants of aggregate stock market fluctuations. We develop a simple example of an economy where countercyclical volatility arises in conjunction with the property that investors' required returns are (i) countercyclical and (ii) *asymmetrically* related to business cycle developments. That is, in this economy, risk premiums increase more in bad times than they decrease in good, consistently with the evidence discussed earlier in this chapter.

8.3.2.1 Fluctuating compensation for risk

In frictionless markets, the price of a long-lived security is the risk-adjusted discounted expectation of its future payoffs. Intuitively, it is inversely related to the asset's expected return and, hence, the asset's risk premium. Thus, asset prices and price-dividend ratios should be procyclical because risk-adjusted discount rates are countercyclical.

Do countercyclical premiums also lead to countercyclical volatility? One additional property is required: *asymmetry*. Figure 8.7 depicts a heuristic example in which risk premiums are negatively related to a procyclical state variable, y_t say–that is, they are countercyclical; in this picture, they are also asymmetric in that they decrease less during good times than they increase during bad, consistent with the empirical evidence. Suppose that the economy enters a boom. Risk premiums decrease, and asset prices increase, on average. In this boom regime, when the fundamentals are hit by positive shocks, risk premiums decrease and asset prices increase. However, risk premiums (and hence asset prices) do not change as they would during a recession—we are assuming that risk premiums behave asymmetrically over the business cycle. Eventually, the boom ends, and a recession begins. As the economy leads to a recession, risk premiums increase, and asset prices decrease. Yet now, when the fundamentals are hit by negative shocks, risk premiums increase (and, hence, asset prices decrease) more than they moved during the boom. All in all, volatility increases on the downside. Once again, the asymmetric behavior occurs

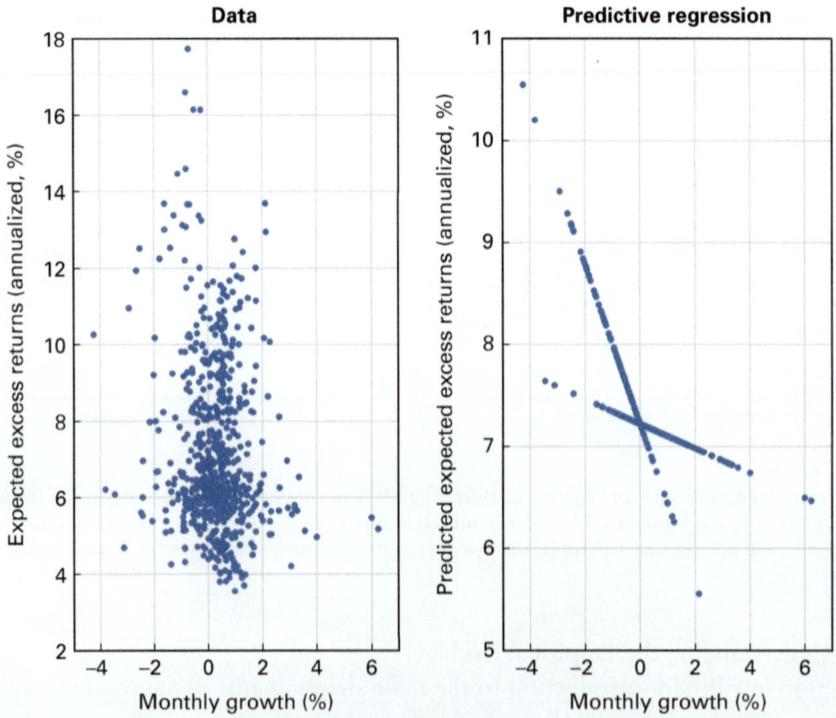

Figure 8.8
Expected returns and business cycle conditions. The left panel plots expected excess returns, $\hat{\mathcal{E}}_t$ in eq. (8.2) against real (de-seasoned) monthly industrial production growth, g_t. The right panel depicts the prediction of the ordinary least squares regression: $\hat{\mathcal{E}}_t = \underset{(0.099)}{7.225} - (\underset{(0.174)}{0.782} \cdot \mathbb{I}_{\text{Rec}_t} + \underset{(0.103)}{0.121} \cdot \mathbb{I}_{\text{Exp}_t}) \times g_t + w_t$, where $\mathbb{I}_{\text{Rec}_t}$ (resp., $\mathbb{I}_{\text{Exp}_t}$) is the indicator function that takes the value one during an NBER recession (resp. expansion) and zero otherwise, w_t is a residual term, and standard errors are in parenthesis.

due to the assumption that risk premiums change asymmetrically over the business cycle.[5] Naturally, there may be other risk premium channels that lead to an asymmetric behavior of price multiples. For example, chapter 5 (see section 5.7) explains that, in markets with asymmetric information, stock prices may be more sensitive to the business cycle during bad times than good because default is more likely in bad times, making dividend distribution less likely.

The empirical evidence in table 8.1 is supportive of a risk premium channel: expected returns seem to move more during recessions than expansions. Figure 8.8 connects this asymmetric behavior of the expected returns with short-run macroeconomic fluctuations. It depicts how expected returns relate to *monthly* industrial production growth, controlling for the business cycle.[6]

5. Mele (2007) develops a no-arbitrage framework to deal with these countercyclical issues, on which some parts of appendix 8.D are based.

6. Note that the relations in figures 8.3 and 8.4 are obtained by relying on (de-annualized) *year-to-year* growth, G_t, which likely captures low frequency business cycle components. These relations would not be as neat when only relying on monthly growth, g_t. The relations in figure 8.8 do relate to monthly growth, but they explicitly account for the business cycle.

To summarize, if risk premiums are more volatile during recessions than in booms, asset prices and price-dividend ratios are more responsive to changes in economic conditions during bad times than good, thereby leading to countercyclical volatility. Appendix 8.D formalizes these links, based on a continuous time framework, but the basic intuition is still the same as that in this section: asymmetry in discounting has to be sufficiently strong. Under this condition, the price-dividend ratio is, then, increasing and *concave* in the variables that summarize business cycle conditions, just as in figure 8.7. It is this concavity property that makes volatility increasing on the downside. We now provide a quantitative illustration of these results, based on a simple binomial tree model that is solved in closed form and shown to predict some of the stylized features surveyed in section 8.2. Sections 8.5 and 8.6 provide additional models that help understand the empirical evidence.

8.3.2.2 A simple model of countercyclical volatility

Consider an infinite horizon economy, a single asset, and a representative agent. In equilibrium, the agent consumes the dividends promised by asset. We also assume a safe asset is infinitely elastically supplied such that the interest rate is some constant $r > 0$. In the initial state, the dividend D is equal to one (see figure 8.9). In the second period, $D = e^{-\delta}$ ($\delta > 0$) with prob p (the bad state), or $D = e^{\delta}$ with prob $1 - p$ (the good state).

In the initial state, the agent's CRRA is $\gamma > 0$. In the good (resp., the bad) state, the agent's CRRA is γ_G (resp., γ_B) > 0. In the third period, the agent receives the final payoffs of figure 8.9, where M_S is the price of a claim to all future dividends, discounted consistent with a CRRA γ_S, where $S \in \{G, B, GB\}$ and $\gamma_{GB} = \gamma$.

Thus, this model is one with constant expected dividend growth but random risk aversion. Note that risk aversion is a source of "long-run risk"—once this risk is resolved, risk aversion remains fixed at its level forever.[7]

Table 8.2 provides calibration results for this model based on the statistics of table 8.1 (see appendix 8.A for details). Note that the model is calibrated using data for the aggregate dividend growth (not consumption), the volatility of which is about 6% annualized, almost twice that of consumption growth. In the Lucas model of chapter 7 (section 7.2), this figure would imply a CRRA equal to $17 \approx \frac{0.06}{0.06^2}$ to match an equity premium of 6%. However, the Lucas model would predict that return volatility is simply dividend growth volatility that is equal to 6%, which is less than a half of the average volatility in the data, 14.55%. Finally, the Lucas model predicts that the price-dividend ratio is constant and therefore cannot lead to the countercyclical statistics in table 8.1.

The model predicts that the average excess return volatility equals about 8%. Moreover, the average implied CRRA is now around 13, and the average expected excess returns are high. Finally, the model of this section predicts that stock volatility has swings that mimic those in the data, with levels reaching 13% in the bad state. In the bad state, however, the model overstates the expected returns by a few percentage points. Importantly, this

7. The literature on long-run risks is surveyed in chapter 9 (see section 9.2). In this literature, the expected dividend growth is affected by some unobservable and persistent factor, which generates countercyclical volatility due to the assumption that dividend growth and consumption volatility are countercyclical. The model in this section leads to countercyclical volatility without the assumption that the volatility of the fundamentals is countercyclical.

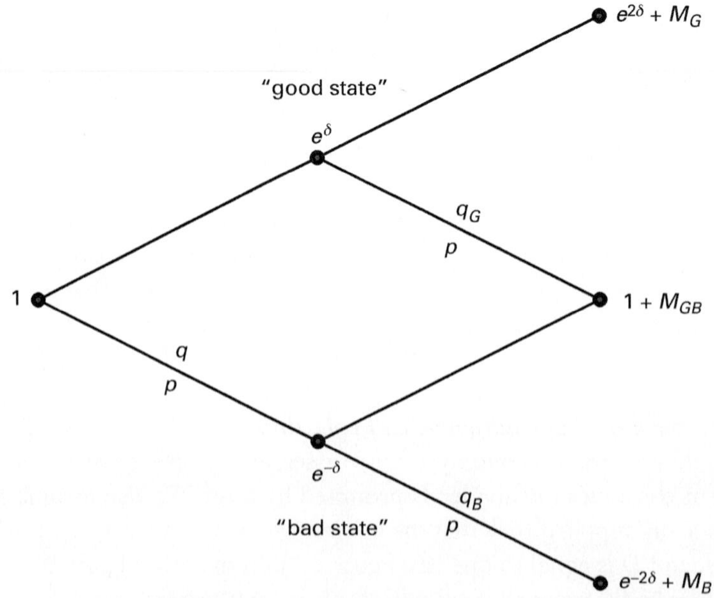

Figure 8.9
A model of random risk aversion and countercyclical volatility. The dividend D is normalized to one at the initial node of the tree. With probability p, D then decreases to $e^{-\delta}$ in the bad state. The risk neutral probability of this state is denoted as q. The risk neutral probability of further dividend movements depends on whether the economy is in a good or bad state (i.e., q_G or q_B). At time 3, the agent receives dividends plus the right to the stream of all future dividends. In the upper node, this right is worth M_G (obtained through the risk neutral probability q_G). In the central node, it is worth M_{GB} (through the risk neutral probability q). In the lower node, it is worth M_B (through the risk neutral probability q_B).

calibration exercise illustrates the asymmetric feature of expected returns and risk aversion. In this experiment, both expected returns and risk aversion increase more in bad times than they decrease in good.

8.3.2.3 *Alternative channels*

There are at least two broad mechanisms that explain aggregate stock market fluctuations: (i) time-varying risk premiums (as in this section) and (ii) time-varying expected dividend growth. Section 8.5 surveys more elaborated models than the tree of this section, aiming to rationalize countercyclical statistics based on the first channel. Section 8.6 examines models of "learning," in which volatility is time-varying due to the agents' attempt to learn about the state of the economy—these models predict that agents face time-varying expected dividend growth. In chapter 9, we survey many models relying on both channels, each of them focusing on particular economic mechanisms and specific predictions (e.g., idiosyncratic risk, restricted stock market participation, heterogeneous beliefs, bubbles, or Knightian uncertainty).

8.3.3 What to Do with Stock Market Volatility?

Equity volatility displays a pronounced business cycle pattern. Can we exploit this pattern for the purpose of forecasting? This section considers two exercises. In the first exercise, we forecast stock market volatility using past macroeconomic data. Stock volatility is an input

Table 8.2

This table reports calibration results for the infinite horizon tree model in figure 8.9 by perfectly matching the model-implied P/D ratios at time 3 to the data in the first row. The model-implied statistics in good, average, and bad states are those of time 2. The risk-adjusted rate is $r+\hat{\sigma}_0\lambda_S$, where r is the riskless rate; $\hat{\sigma}_0$ is dividend growth volatility; and λ_S is the Sharpe ratio on gross returns in state S, determined as $\lambda_S \equiv (q_S - p) \div \sqrt{p(1-p)}$ for $S=G$ (the good state) and $S=B$ (the bad state). Finally, p is the probability of the bad state, and q_S is the state-dependent risk-adjusted probability of the bad state (for $S\in\{G,B\}$). Implied risk aversion is the coefficient CRRA γ_S in the good state ($S=G$) and in the bad ($S=B$) implied by the calibrated model. The figures in the "average" column are the averages of the corresponding values in the good and bad states; averages are taken under $p=0.158$.

	Data		
	Expansions	Average	Recessions
P/D ratio	33.21	31.99	26.20
Excess return volatility	14.05	14.55	16.91
	Model calibration		
	Good state	Average	Bad state
P/D ratio	32.50	31.81	28.15
Excess return volatility	7.29	8.20	13.03
Risk-adjusted rate	8.95	9.07	9.71
Expected returns	10.16	11.46	18.42
Implied risk aversion	13.69	13.89	14.96

Note: P/D ratio = price-dividend ratio.

to many decision-making processes, ranging from portfolio selection to risk management; understanding how it links to ongoing business cycle conditions is therefore a natural exercise. The second exercise explores whether volatility helps predict economic activity. This exercise might help decision makers (e.g., policy makers) make informed decisions.

8.3.3.1 Macroeconomic constituents of stock market volatility

Table 8.3 reports results regarding the first exercise: How does volatility link to *past* macroeconomic data? We use year-to-year industrial production growth and inflation as the two macroeconomic factors that summarize the state of the economy at any given point in time. Volatility is positively related to past growth in the medium term (say between one and two years), a finding we can easily interpret. Bad times are followed by good. Because stock market volatility is countercyclical, high growth is followed by high volatility. These explanations are similar to those put forward in section 8.2 while elaborating on eq. (8.4). Equity volatility is also related to past inflation but in a more complex manner.

Figure 8.10 (top panel) depicts equity volatility and its in-sample forecasts when the regression model is fed with *past* macroeconomic data only. Naturally, the fit could be improved by providing the model with information about past volatility and past macroeconomic data. Nevertheless, it is remarkable that the fit relying on past macroeconomic information is more than 60% better than that relying on past volatility only as witnessed by the R^2s in table 8.3. Note that these results are not inconsistent with those reported

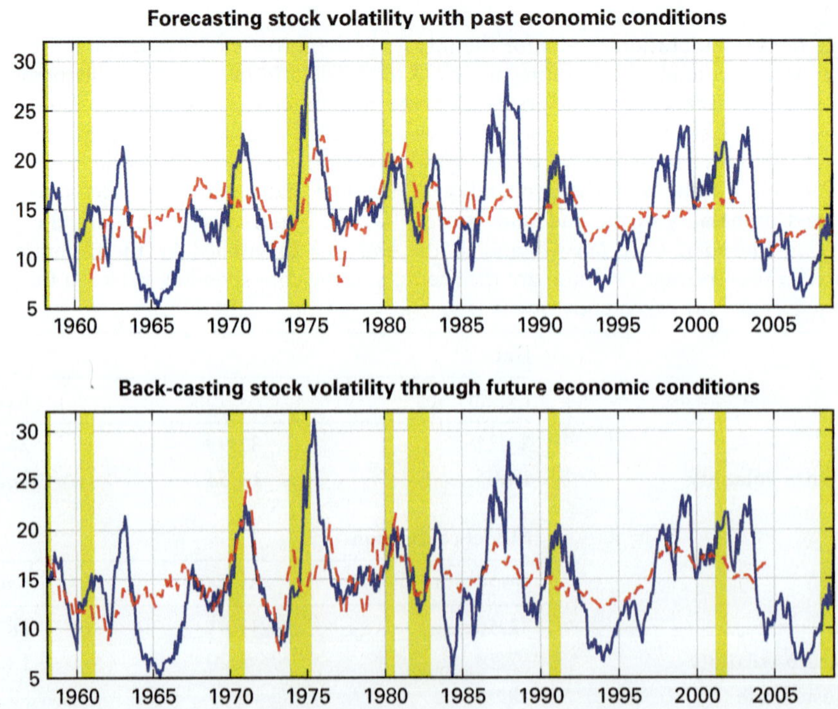

Figure 8.10
Predictions regarding equity market volatility. The top panel depicts stock market volatility (solid line) and its forecasts based on the sole use of *past* macroeconomic indicators (dashed), that is, the model estimates in the second column of table 8.3 ("past"). The bottom panel depicts stock market volatility and its prediction based on the realization of *future* values of macroeconomic indicators, that is, the model estimates in the third column of table 8.3 (future). Shaded areas are NBER recession and expansion episodes.

by Schwert (1989a,b). Indeed, this section relies on estimates regarding a frequency scale lower than those investigated by Schwert. More importantly, these estimates regard the linkages between stock market volatility and the *level* of macroeconomic variables, not their volatility.

The previous findings should not be interpreted as suggesting any causality link; they could be best regarded as descriptive statistics. They do suggest, however, that stock market volatility links to past macroeconomic developments. A natural question is how precisely it does that. Once again, the previous regressions capture mere statistical relations. Yet macroeconomic factors are likely part of the evaluation leading to the very same volatility. In terms of our daily jargon, macroeconomic factors could well be determinants of the pricing kernel. That is, stock volatility links to how the price responds to shocks in the fundamentals and hence macroeconomic conditions, but this linkage should be determined in absence of arbitrage.

Corradi, Distaso, and Mele (2013) pursue this topic in detail and build up a no-arbitrage model that reproduces the previous predictability results. In their model, there is a no-arbitrage nexus between equity volatility and macroeconomic factors. Christiansen, Schmeling, and Schrimpf (2012) and Paye (2012) provide evidence of Granger causality from past values of several macroeconomic variables to stock volatility, in out-of-sample experiments. However, Paye notes that we are still not able to exploit these linkages for

Table 8.3
The left part of this table ("Past") reports ordinary-least-squares estimates in linear regressions of one-year volatility (in %) onto, *past* one-year industrial production growth (in %), *past* one-year month inflation (in %), and *past* stock volatility. $\text{Growth}_{t-\Delta}$ is the one-year industrial production growth at time $t-\Delta$, etc. Time units are months. The second part of the table ("Future") is similar but contains coefficient estimates in linear regressions of volatility on to *future* industrial production growth and *future* inflation. Starred figures are not statistically distinguishable from zero at the 95% level. R^2 is the percentage, adjusted R^2.

Past				Future	
Const.	10.98	10.81	4.79	Const.	17.88
Growth_{t-12}	–	−0.15	−0.002*	Growth_{t+12}	0.02
Growth_{t-24}	–	0.16	0.24	Growth_{t+24}	−0.15
Growth_{t-36}	–	0.27	0.27	Growth_{t+36}	−0.43
Growth_{t-48}	–	0.23	0.20	Growth_{t+48}	−0.31
Infl_{t-12}	–	0.76	0.63	Infl_{t+12}	1.12
Infl_{t-24}	–	−0.97	−0.92	Infl_{t+24}	−1.09
Infl_{t-36}	–	−0.45	0.62	Infl_{t+36}	−1.03
Infl_{t-48}	–	0.31	0.15*	Infl_{t+48}	0.94
Vol_{t-12}	0.36	–	0.28		
Vol_{t-24}	−0.09	–	0.03*		
Vol_{t-36}	−0.10	–	−0.02*		
Vol_{t-48}	0.08	–	0.09		
R^2	12.50	21.91	27.24	R^2	24.30

forecasting purposes. It is an important result as it points to the possibility that, in the future, alternative data sets could do a better job than the datasets these authors are using. We make this point in section 8.3.3.3.

The distinction between Granger causality and forecasting accuracy is indeed subtle. A set of variables may well affect the probability distribution of stock volatility—it is the definition of Granger causality. At the same time, estimating, say, a linear regression linking past macroeconomic variables to stock volatility might not necessarily lead to a satisfactory performance. Intuitively, this relation can be subject to parameter estimation error, which increases the uncertainty surrounding the forecasts. This uncertainty might overwhelm bias reduction gains brought by a correctly specified model, that is, without omitted variables (macroeconomic variables). We illustrate this point in more detail below.[8]

8.3.3.2 Macroeconomic implications of stock market volatility

Does equity volatility also anticipate the business cycle? Table 8.3 suggests that stock volatility does indeed link to future business cycle developments. The bottom panel of Figure 8.10 depicts the predicting part of the regression in the last column of table 8.3, a "back-casting" exercise. Fornari and Mele (2013) have actually tackled this issue in some detail, both in sample and out of sample, concluding that stock volatility helps predict

8. The literature on statistical tests for Granger causality and forecasting accuracy is large. See, e.g., Clark and West (2007) for the former and Giacomini and White (2006) for the latter.

Table 8.4
This table reports ordinary least squares estimates of the parameters in eq. (8.7) for the postwar data and the two subsamples (i) prior and (ii) over the Great Moderation. Starred figures are not statistically distinguishable from zero at the 95% level.

	c	b_3	b_{12}	b_{24}	b_{36}	c_1	c_2
1957–2008	3.11	0.94	−0.15	−0.01*	−0.01*	0.48	1.51
1957–1982	3.60	0.98	−0.24	0.02*	−0.04	0.34*	1.87
1983–2008	2.88	0.94	−0.09	−0.05*	−0.01*	1.01	1.22

the business cycle in addition to traditional indicators such as the term spread and other financial variables.

To illustrate, note that stock volatility is not just countercyclical, that is, a coincident business cycle indicator. Figures 8.2 and 8.10 also seem to indicate that stock volatility tends to increase *before* recessions, a typical attribute of a *leading* indicator. Consider the following regression:

$$\sigma_t = c + \sum\nolimits_{i\in\{3,12,24,36\}} b_i\sigma_{t-i} + c_1\mathbb{I}_{t\in\mathcal{O}(\text{NBER}_t=1)} + c_2\mathbb{I}_{\text{NBER}_t=1} + \epsilon_t, \tag{8.7}$$

where σ_t is stock volatility at month t, $\mathbb{I}_{t\in\mathcal{O}(\text{NBER}_t=1)}$ is the indicator function that equals one in the 12 months preceding any NBER-dated recession and zero otherwise, $\mathbb{I}_{\text{NBER}_t=1}$ is the indicator function that equals one during any NBER-dated recession and zero otherwise; and ϵ_t is a residual term.

Table 8.4 reports estimates of this model parameters on a sample covering monthly data from January 1957 to September 2008. The table reports estimates for the whole sample and two subsamples, one before the "Great Moderation" (i.e., up to 1982) and the other, covering the Great Moderation and ending in 2008. A positive estimate of c_1 indicates that stock volatility increases ahead of recessions, and a positive estimate of c_2 indicates that stock volatility also increases during recessions.

It appears that stock volatility does anticipate economic downturns. This property is particularly important during the Great Moderation: presumably, the signaling power of volatility had strengthened due a more stable macroeconomic environment. These issues are actually quite delicate. The fact that stock volatility is countercyclical does not necessarily imply that it anticipates real economic activity. Even if it did, we would then need to identify the economic mechanisms behind this predicting power. *Post hoc ergo propter hoc?* Does stock market volatility affect investment decisions in the real sphere of the economy? Or rather, does volatility merely help predict the business cycle? The policy implications of these issues are obvious. If volatility only anticipates and does not affect the business cycle, there is little policy makers can do about it, even if its forecasting power is obviously significant per se. Interestingly, the literature has also identified longer term effects of volatility, resulting in a phenomenon sometimes referred to as volatility paradox (see, e.g., Brunnermeier and Sannikov, 2014; Daníelsson, Valenzuela, and Zer, 2018, 2020): periods of *low* volatility may encourage risk-taking behavior that would ultimately lead to crises. Chapter 9 provides details and additional references on the literature in which these properties may originate (see section 9.11.6).

8.3.3.3 *Forecasting with the wrong model*

The results in this section are in-sample. It may turn out that real-time forecasts could be disappointing. One reason could be data snooping: if we regress a variable of interest over thousands, there is a considerable chance that at least one out of those thousands nicely links to the endogenous variable, displaying a spectacular (in-sample) fit. However, precisely because this fit was obtained only by chance and not due to an economic linkage between this variable and the endogenous one, the out-of-sample performance of the model will likely disappoint.

An opposite situation can actually occur, in which a link between two variables really exists, which cannot be properly exploited for practical forecasting purposes. The intuitive reason for this difficulty is limited data. That is, we can only estimate a linkage between two variables by relying on a finite sample. Yet the finite-sample bias in the estimates of the linkage could be substantial and lead to large forecasting errors. Consider the following example, a data-generating process in which a variable x_t Granger causes a second one, y_t, as follows:

$$y_t = c + \beta x_t + \epsilon_t, \quad \epsilon_t \sim \text{NID}(0, \omega_\epsilon), \quad x_t \sim \text{NID}(\mu_x, \omega_x), \tag{8.8}$$

for five constants c, β, ω_ϵ, μ_x, and ω_x, the parameters of the model. We assume that μ_x and ω_x are known and consider making predictions of the variable y_t through two models.

The first model is misspecified in that we simply neglect that x_t Granger causes y_t, that is, $y_t = \psi + u_t$, for some constant ψ and some residual term u_t. We estimate the constant ψ of this misspecified model through ordinary least squares (OLS), obtaining

$$\hat{\psi} - c = \beta \bar{x}_T + \bar{\epsilon}_T,$$

where $\bar{x}_T$ and $\bar{\epsilon}_T$ denote the sample averages of x_t and ϵ_t and T is the sample size. The prediction error generated by this model for time $T+1$ is

$$\eta_{1,T+1} \equiv y_{T+1} - \hat{\psi} = \beta\left(x_{T+1} - \bar{x}_T\right) + \epsilon_{T+1} - \bar{\epsilon}_T.$$

Note that although $\hat{\psi}$ is biased for c, even asymptotically, the predictor of this misspecified model is unbiased because $E\left(\eta_{1,T+1}\right) = 0$.

Next, consider estimating the parameters of eq. (8.8) through OLS, and denote the estimators of c and β with $\hat{c}$ and $\hat{\beta}$. The prediction error pertaining to this model is

$$\begin{aligned}
\eta_{2,T+1} &\equiv y_{T+1} - \hat{c} - \hat{\beta} x_{T+1} \\
&= c - \hat{c} + (\beta - \hat{\beta}) x_{T+1} + \epsilon_{T+1} \\
&= (\beta - \hat{\beta})\left(x_{T+1} - \bar{x}_T\right) + \epsilon_{T+1} - \bar{\epsilon}_T,
\end{aligned} \tag{8.9}$$

where the second equality follows by (i) $\hat{c} = \bar{y}_T - \hat{\beta}\bar{x}_T$, with $\bar{y}_T$ denoting the sample average of y_t, and (ii) eq. (8.8), with

$$\beta - \hat{\beta} = -\frac{Cov_T\left(x_t, \epsilon_t\right)}{V_T\left(x_t\right)};$$

and where Cov_T and V_T stand for the sample covariance and variance of their arguments. The correctly specified model does, naturally, lead to an unbiased predictor in that $E(\eta_{2,T+1}) = 0$ by the second line in eq. (8.9).

Therefore, the two models we consider (the misspecified and the correctly specified) both lead to unbiased predictors. However, the second predictor is plagued by parameter estimation error and might actually lead to mean-squared prediction errors higher than those generated by the first predictor, especially when the sample variance of $\beta - \hat{\beta}$ is large. In other words, for large samples, $\beta - \hat{\beta}$ is of course quite small as $\hat{\beta}$ is consistent for β. In finite samples, however, this term can adversely affect the performance of the correctly specified model. The bottom line is this: the fact that volatility does not perform well as a predictor may not necessarily imply that it is not a predictor.

8.3.4 What Did We Learn?

Stock market volatility is higher in bad times than in good. Explaining this basic fact is challenging. We know very well how to model risk premiums and how these premiums should relate to the business cycle. We are more embarrassed when it comes to explaining volatility. This section explains that countercyclical volatility may result from risk premiums undergoing large swings as the economy moves away from good states, just as the data seem to suggest. This section focusses on the *fluctuations* of aggregate stock volatility and risk premiums, not their *average levels*. Not surprisingly, whether these fluctuations (and their average levels) can be consistent with the neoclassical model of rational evaluation is controversial just like with many topics at the intersection of financial economics and macroeconomics as vividly illustrated since the early debates (see, e.g., Campbell, 2003; Mehra and Prescott, 2003).

What are, then, the main empirical properties of stock volatility that we should always try to bear in mind? First, expected returns are strongly countercyclical and asymmetrically related to macroeconomic conditions. Second, equity volatility links to the business cycle (in-sample), although it cannot necessarily be forecast through macroeconomic variables (out-of-sample). Third, equity volatility contains information regarding business cycle developments. We now turn to theoretical explanations of aggregate stock market fluctuations.

8.4 Rational Market Fluctuations

This section provides a parsimonious framework that is used to address two general problems: (i) where prices are basically driven by time-varying risk premiums and (ii) where prices are driven by time-varying expected growth in the economic fundamentals. Section 8.4.1 provides a simple decomposition of the asset returns. Section 8.4.2 develops tools of analysis that are used in subsequent sections.

8.4.1 The Dynamics of Asset Returns

8.4.1.1 An identity

Dividend variability does not suffice to justify, quantitatively, fluctuations in the price-dividend ratio. Some additional state variables are needed to affect the dynamics of price-dividend ratios. However, chapter 7 explains that multifactor models are not necessarily exhaustive: these models may imply that the variance of the pricing kernel increases with the number of factors while at the same time keeping price-dividend ratios constant. What one really needs is a discipline on how to increase the dimension of a model. Let us elaborate.

Asset returns are the sum of payoffs *and* capital gains (prices). Consider the identity $\tilde{R}_{t+1} \equiv \frac{S_{t+1}+D_{t+1}}{S_t}$ or

$$\ln \tilde{R}_{t+1} \equiv g_{t+1} + \ln\left(\frac{p_{t+1}+1}{p_t}\right), \tag{8.10}$$

where $g_t \equiv \ln\left(\frac{D_t}{D_{t-1}}\right)$, the dividend growth, and $p_t \equiv \frac{S_t}{D_t}$, the price-dividend ratio. Thus, return volatility can be countercyclical because dividend growth and/or price-dividend ratio changes have countercyclical volatility.

The empirical evidence in section 8.2 suggests it is unlikely that, at the business cycle frequency, returns volatility links to the volatility of the fundamentals. Instead, the empirical evidence suggests a theoretical model should make at least two predictions. First, the price-dividend ratio should be volatile, and second, it should be more volatile in bad times than in good. For example, in an economy driven by a state variable linking to the business cycle, such as habit formation (see section 8.5), the price-dividend ratio should be increasing and *concave* in the business cycle variable (see section 8.3): this property ensures that volatility increases on the downside—the very definition of countercyclical volatility.

8.4.1.2 *Asymmetric behavior of the price-dividend ratio*

We rely on a simple model that bears the potential to predict an asymmetric behavior of the price-dividend ratio over the business cycle. Suppose that dividend growth is IID,

$$\frac{dD_t}{D_t} = g_0 dt + \sigma_0 dW_{1t},$$

where g_0 and σ_0 are two constants. We assume that *risk-adjusted discount rates* are driven by some state variable, y_t say, which summarizes business cycle conditions. That is, and relying on notation introduced in chapter 4 (see section 4.2.5), we assume that the risk-adjusted discount rates are

$$\mathcal{R}(y_t) = r(y_t) + \sigma_0 \lambda_{CF}(y_t),$$

where $r(\cdot)$ is the short-term rate and $\lambda_{CF}(\cdot)$ is the cash-flow lambda. We assume that y_t is a solution to

$$dy_t = \varphi(y_t)\,dt + v_1(y_t)\,dW_{1t} + v_2(y_t)\,dW_{2t}$$

for some functions φ and v_i. In the next sections and in chapter 9, we review models by which agents' preferences and beliefs lead to discount rates driven by such a state variable.

Given these assumptions and under regularity conditions, the price-dividend ratio is also driven by y_t as shown by the following expression:

$$p(y_t) = \mathbb{E}\left(\int_t^\infty \frac{D_\tau^*}{D_t} \cdot e^{-\int_t^\tau \mathcal{R}(y_u)du} d\tau \,\middle|\, y_t\right), \quad \frac{D_\tau^*}{D_t} = e^{\left(g_0 - \frac{1}{2}\sigma_0^2\right)(\tau - t) + \sigma_0\left(\hat{W}_{1\tau} - \hat{W}_{1t}\right)}, \tag{8.11}$$

where $\hat{W}_{1t}$ is a standard Brownian motion under the risk neutral probability Q and $\mathbb{E}$ denotes the expectation under Q.

Eq. (8.11) is derived in chapter 4 (see eq. (4.39) in section 4.2.5). It suggests that the sensitivity of p with respect to y links to the sensitivity of $\mathcal{R}$ with respect to y. Hence, whether volatility is countercyclical now depends on how the risk-adjusted discount rates change after shocks in y. Appendix 8.D formalizes this intuitive reasoning. It shows that if $\mathcal{R}$ increases in bad times sufficiently more than it decreases in good, the price-dividend ratio is concave in y and is therefore more volatile in bad times than in good, consistent with discussions in previous sections. More generally, appendix 8.D addresses the following issues.

(1) *Monotonicity*. Consider the price-dividend ratio in eq. (8.11). By Itô's lemma, stock volatility is $\sigma_0 + \frac{p'(y)}{p(y)}\text{Vol}(y)$, where $\text{Vol}(y) = \sqrt{v_1^2(y) + v_2^2(y)}$ is the volatility of y. Therefore, y helps inflate volatility if p increases with y.[9]

(2) *Negative convexity*. Suppose that y correlates with the business cycle. If Vol(y) is constant, stock volatility is countercyclical whenever p in eq. (8.11) is *concave* in y as in the simple reasoning underlying figure 8.7.

To address these issues, appendix 8.D revisits the option pricing literature on option price convexity and extends it to contexts with untraded risks. Chapter 11 contains additional explanations regarding these general properties of option prices that go beyond those needed for this chapter. Appendix 8.E introduces a class of models that are analytically convenient for reasons related to the analysis in appendix 8.D. The next section provides preliminary results on pricing kernels; some of these results are also used in the next chapter.

8.4.2 Markov Pricing Kernels, Asset Returns, and Volatility

8.4.2.1 *Pricing kernels*

We consider economies with a representative agent. In these economies, interest rates and risk premiums change randomly because the agent's utility depends on consumption *and* other variables. While complete markets naturally fit in the analysis of this section, incomplete markets can sometimes be analyzed relying on this framework (see chapter 9).

We elaborate on some foundational issues dealt with in chapter 4. Consider the pricing kernel in chapter 4, $m_t(\tau) \equiv \frac{\xi_\tau}{\xi_t}$, where the stochastic discount factor ξ_t satisfies

$$\xi_t \equiv \xi(D_t, x_t, t) = e^{-\int_0^t \rho(D_s, x_s)ds}\Upsilon(D_t, x_t), \quad \xi_0 = 1, \tag{8.12}$$

for some functions $\rho(D,x)$ and $\Upsilon(D,x)$ and some diffusion process x_t. $\Upsilon(D,x)$ is interpreted as the Radon-Nikodym derivative of the risk neutral probability with respect to the physical. We assume that ρ is bounded and positive and that Υ is twice continuously differentiable. We also assume that there is another process, y_t, such that $y_t = \mathcal{Y}(x_t)$ for some monotonic, continuous and twice continuously differentiable function $\mathcal{Y}$ and that

9. Further, note that this property ensures that volatility is strictly positive, making the agents' budget constraints well defined.

(D_t, y_t) are solutions to[10]

$$\begin{cases} dD_t = m(D_t, y_t)\,dt + \sigma_0(D_t)\,dW_{1t} \\ dy_t = \varphi(D_t, y_t)\,dt + v_1(D_t, y_t)\,dW_{1t} + v_2(D_t, y_t)\,dW_{2t} \end{cases}. \tag{8.13}$$

The assumption that $\mathcal{Y}(\cdot)$ is monotonic enables one to focus on economies in which asset prices, expected returns, and returns volatility are all functions of D and y only (see, e.g., eq. (8.17) below).

The stochastic discount factor is solution to

$$\frac{d\xi_t}{\xi_t} = -r_t dt - \lambda_{1t} dW_{1t} - \lambda_{2t} dW_{2t}, \tag{8.14}$$

where r is the short-term rate and $[\lambda_1, \lambda_2]$ is the vector of unit risk premiums. By applying Itô's lemma to ξ in eq. (8.12) and identifying the terms in eq. (8.14), one finds that the short-term rate r and risk premiums are both functions of the current state:

$$\begin{aligned} r(D,x) &= \rho(D,x) - \tfrac{L_x \Upsilon(D,x)}{\Upsilon(D,x)} \\ \lambda_1(D,x) &= -\left(\sigma_0(D)\tfrac{\partial \ln \Upsilon(D,x)}{\partial D} + v_{x1}(D,x)\tfrac{\partial \ln \Upsilon(D,x)}{\partial x}\right) \\ \lambda_2(D,x) &= -v_{x2}(D,x)\tfrac{\partial \ln \Upsilon(D,x)}{\partial x}, \end{aligned}$$

where L_x is the infinitesimal generator operator (see chapter 4) for (D,x) and $v_{xi}(D,x)$ denotes the diffusion coefficients of x_t.

For example, consider an infinite horizon economy in which aggregate dividends are a solution to eq. (8.13), with $v_2 \equiv 0$ and $v \equiv v_1$, and a representative agent solves the following program:

$$\max_{(c_t)_{t\geq 0}} E\left(\int_0^\infty e^{-\rho t} u(c_t, x_t)\,dt\right) \quad \text{s.t} \quad V_0 = E\left(\int_0^\infty \xi_t c_t dt\right), \quad V_0 > 0,$$

where $\rho > 0$, the instantaneous utility u is continuous and three times continuously differentiable, and x is the solution to

$$dx_t = \varphi_x(D_t, x_t)\,dt + v_x(D_t, x_t)\,dW_{1t}.$$

In equilibrium, optimal consumption equals aggregate dividends. In terms of ξ in eq. (8.12), we have that $\rho(D,x) = \rho$ and $\Upsilon(D_t, x_t) = \frac{u_1(D_t, x_t)}{u_1(D_0, x_0)}$ such that $\lambda_2 = 0$ and $\lambda \equiv \lambda_1$ and

$$\begin{aligned} r(D,x) = \rho &- \tfrac{u_{11}(D,x)}{u_1(D,x)} m(D,y) - \frac{1}{2}\sigma_0^2(D)\tfrac{u_{111}(D,x)}{u_1(D,x)} \\ &- \tfrac{u_{12}(D,x)}{u_1(D,x)}\varphi_x(D,x) - \frac{1}{2}v_x^2(D,x)\tfrac{u_{122}(D,x)}{u_1(D,x)} - v_x(D,x)\sigma_0(D)\tfrac{u_{112}(D,x)}{u_1(D,x)} \end{aligned} \tag{8.15}$$

$$\lambda(D,x) = -\tfrac{u_{11}(D,x)}{u_1(D,x)}\sigma_0(D) - \tfrac{u_{12}(D,x)}{u_1(D,x)} v_x(D,x). \tag{8.16}$$

10. Eqs. (8.13) are a slight generalization of eqs. (8.A26) in appendix 8.D.

8.4.2.2 *Expected returns and volatility under a scale-invariant assumption*

We study asset pricing implications of these stochastic discount factors. We rely on the continuous time formulation of the APT model in chapter 4 (see section 4.2.5), a *scale-invariant economy*, that is, an economy in which price-dividend ratios are independent of the dividend level. This assumption simplifies the analysis in this section and, presumably, provides useful guidance for empirical work. It is easy to see that a scale-invariant economy results from the assumption that dividend growth is independent of the dividend level D: in terms of eq. (8.13), we need to assume that (i) $m(D,y)=yD$, (ii) $\sigma_0(D)=\sigma_0 D$ for some constant σ_0, and (iii) the drift and diffusion coefficients of y are independent of D. Further, we still assume that y_t is some monotonic function $\mathcal{Y}(\cdot)$ of x_t in eq. (8.12); accordingly, we express the price-dividend ratio in terms of y_t.

Under these assumptions, the asset's expected returns are[11]

$$\begin{aligned}\mathcal{E}_t &\equiv \frac{d}{d\tau}E_t\left(\frac{S_\tau}{S_t}\right)\bigg|_{\tau=t}+\frac{D_t}{S_t}\\ &= \underbrace{r_t+\text{cash-flow beta}_t\times\text{cash-flow lambda}_t}_{\mathcal{R}_t\,\equiv\,\text{risk-adjusted discount rates}}+\underbrace{\text{price beta}_t\times\text{price lambda}_t}_{\mathcal{W}_t\,\equiv\,\text{price premium wedge}}\end{aligned}\tag{8.17}$$

where

$$\mathcal{R}_t=r_t+\sigma_0\lambda_1(y_t),\quad \mathcal{W}_t=\frac{p'(y_t)}{p(y_t)}\left(v_1(y_t)\lambda_1(y_t)+v_2(y_t)\lambda_2(y_t)\right),$$

and finally, returns volatility is

$$\text{Vol}(y_t)\equiv\begin{bmatrix}\text{Vol}_1(y_t)\\ \text{Vol}_2(y_t)\end{bmatrix}\equiv\begin{bmatrix}\sigma_0+v_1(y_t)\frac{p'(y_t)}{p(y_t)}\\ v_2(y_t)\frac{p'(y_t)}{p(y_t)}\end{bmatrix}.$$

Thus, expected returns do not compensate for volatility but for the risks that asset prices are linked to, y_t. However, note that, if $v_2(y_t)=0$, expected excess returns and return volatility align in a way that bears resemblance to the standard risk-return trade-off predicted by the CAPM (see chapter 1), that is,

$$\mathcal{E}_t-r_t=\text{Vol}(y_t)\lambda_1(y_t),\quad \text{Vol}(y_t)=\sigma_0+\frac{p'(y_t)}{p(y_t)}v_1(y_t).$$

That is, in this case, $\lambda_1(y_t)$, the cash-flow lambda, is also the Sharpe ratio. We rely on these predictions while analyzing a number of models in the following sections as well as in chapter 9.

8.5 Time-Varying Risk Premiums

Asset prices are what they are due to specific properties of the pricing kernel *and* the statistical properties of dividend growth. The focus of this section is to elaborate asset

11. See eq. (4.37) in chapter 4.

price explanations based on certain properties of the pricing kernel. We rely on simplifying assumptions, leading to a famous model proposed by Campbell and Cochrane (1999). In this model, dividend growth is IID. We explain how a pricing kernel may be consistent with dynamic properties of asset prices. Section 8.6 deals with economies in which growth is not IID but relying on simplifying assumptions on the pricing kernel.

In the economy of this section, agents display habit preferences: their utility of consumption derives from how consumption is far from some previously formed "habit consumption." In bad times, deviations from habit consumption decrease, leading risk averse agents to lower their portfolio holdings. That is, the equity premium increases in bad times. We rely on an analytical framework contained in appendix 8.D and show that this property may lead to countercyclical volatility, similar to the heuristic explanations of section 8.3. Moreover, the model is consistent with the findings on predictability in the empirical literature (see section 8.2). We conclude this section while referring to additional references in the literature stemming out of this model.

8.5.1 External Habit

External habit formation is a convenient mechanism that may rationalize the countercyclical statistics of this chapter. Campbell and Cochrane (1999) consider the following model. A representative agent with an infinite horizon has an undiscounted instantaneous utility,

$$u(c_t, x_t) = \frac{(c_t - x_t)^{1-\gamma} - 1}{1-\gamma}, \tag{8.18}$$

where c denotes consumption and x is a time-varying habit or exogenous "subsistence level." The habit process is defined residually through the "surplus consumption ratio," as we shall explain in a moment (see eq. (8.20)).

The total endowment process, D_t, satisfies[12]

$$\frac{dD_t}{D_t} = g_0 dt + \sigma_0 dW_t. \tag{8.19}$$

A measure of distance between consumption and the level of habit is the surplus consumption ratio, defined as

$$\mathcal{S}_t \equiv \frac{c_t - x_t}{c_t}. \tag{8.20}$$

The curvature of the instantaneous utility is inversely related to $\mathcal{S}$,

$$-\frac{u_{cc}(c,x)\,c}{u_c(c,x)} = \gamma \frac{c}{c-x} = \gamma \frac{D}{D-x} = \gamma \mathcal{S}^{-1}, \tag{8.21}$$

where subscripts denote partial derivatives; the second equality is the equilibrium condition, $c_t = D_t$; and the third follows by the definition of the surplus consumption ratio in

12. Campbell and Cochrane (1999) consider a discrete-time model in which log-consumption growth is Gaussian. Eq. (8.19) is the diffusion limit of their model.

equilibrium. By assumption, $\ln \mathcal{S}_t$ is an heteroskedastic autoregressive process,

$$dS_t = \underbrace{S_t \left((1-\phi)(\bar{s}_l - \ln S_t) + \frac{1}{2}\sigma_0^2 l^2 (S_t) \right)}_{\equiv \varphi(S_t)} dt + \underbrace{\sigma_0 S_t l(S_t) dW_t}_{\equiv v(S_t)}, \tag{8.22}$$

with some function $l(\cdot)$ discussed below. That is, the surplus ratio $\mathcal{S}_t$ is driven by output innovations (i.e., by dW_t): provided $v(\cdot) > 0$, the higher these innovations and hence consumption growth innovations, the higher the shocks to surplus ratio.[13]

This model of habit formation differs from previous formulations such as that of Ryder and Heal (1973) or Sundaresan (1989) and Constantinides (1990), due to three properties: (i) it is an "external" theory in that the habit x is "aggregate" and not consumption chosen by the individual, similarly as with Abel's (1990) "catching up with the Joneses" formulation or Duesenberry's (1949) relative income model; (ii) habit responds to consumption smoothly, not to each period's past consumption as in previous models of habit formation such as that of Ferson and Constantinides (1991); and (iii) it guarantees that marginal utility is always positive. The second of the previous properties produces slow mean reversions in the price-dividend ratio and long-horizon predictability and large predictable movements in stock volatility, which are empirical features reviewed in sections 8.2 and 8.3.

8.5.2 Countercyclical Statistics

In this economy, markets are complete: there is only one source of risk affecting the agent's choices—the dividend in eq. (8.19). Therefore, the Sharpe ratio is easily determined by relying on results in section 8.4 (see eq. (8.16)),

$$\lambda(D,x) = \frac{\gamma}{\mathcal{S}}\sigma_0 - \frac{\gamma}{\mathcal{S}D} v_x(D,x), \tag{8.23}$$

where v_x is the diffusion coefficient of the habit process in equilibrium, $x_t = D_t(1 - \mathcal{S}_t)$.

The first term on the RHS is proportional to the curvature of the instantaneous utility with respect to consumption (see eq. (8.21)); this term is thus countercyclical. The second term is proportional to the exposure of the marginal utility of consumption to changes in habit and has an opposite sign with respect to the curvature in (8.21): marginal utility of consumption increases with habit. This property may mitigate countercyclicality of the Sharpe ratio. By Itô's lemma, $v_x(D,x) = (1 - \mathcal{S} - \mathcal{S}l(\mathcal{S}))D\sigma_0$, which, replaced into eq. (8.23), leaves

$$\lambda(\mathcal{S}) = \gamma\sigma_0(1 + l(\mathcal{S})). \tag{8.24}$$

Let us explain. In this model, the stochastic discount factor $\xi_t \equiv e^{-\rho t}(\mathcal{S}_t D_t/\mathcal{S}_0 D_0)^{-\gamma}$. It is countercyclical because both $\mathcal{S}_t$ and D_t are procyclical. Moreover, it is more volatile than the Lucas stochastic discount factor, $e^{-\rho t}(D_t/D_0)^{-\gamma}$. Now, the Sharpe ratio, $\lambda(\mathcal{S})$, is the volatility of $\frac{d\xi_t}{\xi_t}$ and is made up of two components: the volatility of $\gamma\frac{dD_t}{D_t}$ (i.e., $\gamma\sigma_0$) and the volatility of $\gamma\frac{d\mathcal{S}_t}{\mathcal{S}_t}$ (i.e., $\gamma\sigma_0 l(\mathcal{S}_t)$), whence the expression in (8.24). Whether the

13. We may consider one additional Brownian motion in eq. (8.22) that is aimed at lowering the conditional correlation between output growth and the surplus consumption ratio. Moreover, in this model, asset returns are driven by a single state variable, $\mathcal{S}_t$, implying that the conditional correlation between consumption growth and stock returns is one. In the data, this correlation is much lower.

Sharpe ratio is countercyclical now depends on the volatility of a state variable driving the stochastic discount factor, $l(\cdot)$. We shall explain how this function is determined in a moment. For reasons clarified below, we first need to determine interest rates.

The real interest rate is, by eq. (8.15),

$$r(\mathcal{S}) = \rho + \gamma\left(g_0 - \frac{1}{2}\sigma_0^2\right) + \gamma(1-\phi)(\bar{s}_l - \ln\mathcal{S}) - \frac{1}{2}\gamma^2\sigma_0^2(1+l(\mathcal{S}))^2. \tag{8.25}$$

The third term reflects usual intertemporal substitution effects. Due to mean reversion, in bad times, when $\mathcal{S}$ is low, agents expect that the very same $\mathcal{S}$ will improve; in bad times, they would then expect their marginal utility to decrease. To compensate for this fall, they wish to decrease their future consumption, compared with today, while trying to save less (or to borrow more), thereby pushing interest rates up. The last term is a precautionary savings term.

Campbell and Cochrane (1999) choose the function l so as to satisfy three conditions: (i) the short-term rate r is constant and habit is predetermined both (ii) at the steady state and (iii) near the steady state. A constant r is consistent with the empirical evidence surveyed in section 8.2: that real interest rates are really not volatile compared with stock returns. Making habit predetermined at and near the steady state formalizes the idea that it takes time for consumption shocks to affect habit, at least at the steady state. Appendix 8.F shows that, under these conditions, the function l is

$$l(\mathcal{S}) = \bar{s}^{-1}\sqrt{1+2(\bar{s}_l - \ln\mathcal{S})} - 1, \tag{8.26}$$

where $\bar{s} = \sigma_0\sqrt{\frac{\gamma}{1-\phi}} = e^{\bar{s}_l}$. In turn, this function implies that the short-term rate in eq. (8.25) is constant.[14]

That is, the volatility of $\frac{d\mathcal{S}_t}{\mathcal{S}_t}$ is countercyclical. This feature is responsible of many interesting properties of the model. First, consider the Sharpe ratio. Figure 8.11 depicts $\lambda(\mathcal{S})$ in (8.24) relying on the expression for l in (8.26) and is obtained with the same parameter values as in Campbell and Cochrane (1999). It is decreasing in $\mathcal{S}$. Moreover, it is convex in $\mathcal{S}$ over the empirically relevant range of variation of $\mathcal{S}$. That is, the Sharpe ratio is countercyclical and moves asymmetrically over the business cycle, a property discussed below.

Next, consider the expected returns. By eq. (8.17), they are

$$\mathcal{E}(\mathcal{S}_t) = \mathcal{R}(\mathcal{S}_t) + \mathcal{W}(\mathcal{S}_t) = r(\mathcal{S}_t) + \underbrace{\left(\sigma_0 + \frac{p'(\mathcal{S}_t)}{p(\mathcal{S}_t)}v(\mathcal{S}_t)\right)}_{\equiv \text{Vol}(\mathcal{S}_t)}\lambda(\mathcal{S}_t), \tag{8.27}$$

where the risk-adjusted discount rates, $\mathcal{R}(\mathcal{S})$, and the wedge over them, $\mathcal{W}(\mathcal{S})$, are given by

$$\mathcal{R}(\mathcal{S}) = r(\mathcal{S}) + \sigma_0\lambda(\mathcal{S}) \quad \text{and} \quad \mathcal{W}(\mathcal{S}) = \frac{p'(\mathcal{S})}{p(\mathcal{S})}v(\mathcal{S})\lambda(\mathcal{S}), \tag{8.28}$$

14. Notably, it is $r = \delta + \gamma\left(g_0 - \frac{1}{2}\sigma_0^2\right) - \frac{1}{2}\gamma(1-\phi)$. Appendix 8.F considers a slightly more general model, in which the short-term rate is affine in $\ln s$.

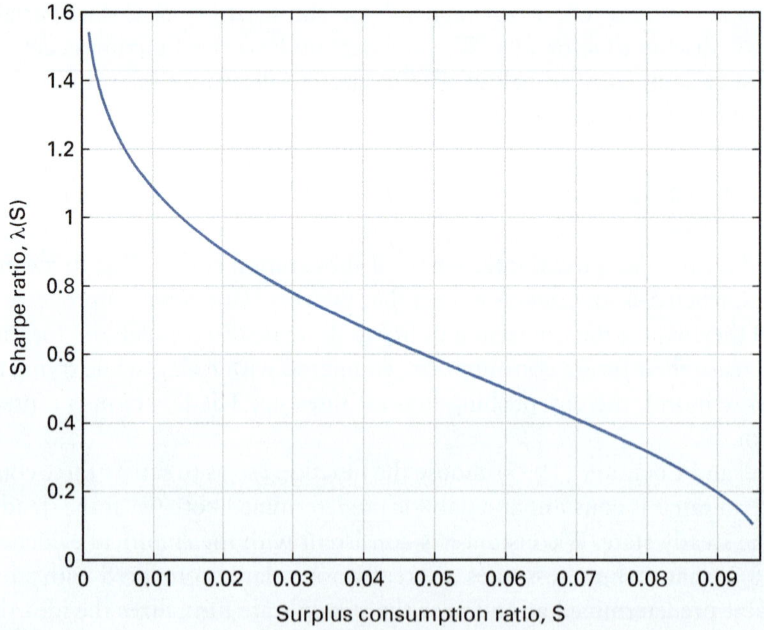

Figure 8.11
The Sharpe ratio in the Campbell and Cochrane (1999) habit formation model, $\lambda(\mathcal{S})$. Parameter values are $\gamma = 2$, $\sigma_0 = 0.0150$, and $\phi = 0.870$.

and $p(\cdot)$ is the price-dividend ratio, a function of $\mathcal{S}$, as explained below (see eq. (8.29)). The second equality in (8.27) follows easily: $\text{Vol}(\mathcal{S}_t)$ denotes the asset's return volatility such that, in this economy with a single source of risk, (8.27) represents the standard risk-return trade-off related to holding a security (see section 8.4.2).

How do movements in the surplus consumption ratio $\mathcal{S}$ affect expected returns? During economic downturns, the surplus consumption ratio $\mathcal{S}$ decreases, and agents require higher premiums, leading expected returns to increase and prices to decrease. If habit preferences are persistent (i.e., if ϕ is high), expected returns are then not only countercyclical but also slowly varying as with their empirical counterparts. Note that volatility is also countercyclical, provided the price-dividend ratio is sufficiently concave in $\mathcal{S}$, a condition ensuring a countercyclical wedge, $\mathcal{W}'(\mathcal{S}) < 0$. We now elaborate on this point.

Indeed, the calibrated model does suggest that the price-dividend ratio is concave in $\mathcal{S}$.[15] There is a link between convexity of the Sharpe ratio and concavity of the price-dividend ratio, a link illustrated heuristically in section 8.3.2. To explain this link in more detail, we would need to rely on technical details dealt with in appendix 8.D, which contains a canonical pricing problem that addresses asset price properties based on general

15. The solution of the model is not known in closed form, but this property results from a numerical solution of the model. Appendix 8.A describes a simple numerical method to solve the discrete-time version of this and related models.

assumptions on pricing kernels and expected growth (see appendix 8.D.3). Consider then the price-dividend ratio. In this economy, the short-term rate is constant, but for sake of generality, we may assume it is also state dependent, notably, a function of $\mathcal{S}$ (as, e.g., in appendix 8.F). By results in appendix 8.D (see eqs. (8.A27)–(8.A30)), the price-dividend ratio is

$$p(\mathcal{S}) = \int_0^\infty e^{g_0 t} \bar{\mathbb{E}} \left(e^{-\int_0^t \mathcal{R}(\mathcal{S}_u) du} \middle| \mathcal{S}_0 = \mathcal{S} \right) dt, \tag{8.29}$$

where $\mathcal{R}(\mathcal{S})$ are the risk-adjusted discount rates defined in (8.28) and $\mathcal{S}_t$ is now the solution to

$$d\mathcal{S}_t = \underbrace{(\varphi(\mathcal{S}_t) + (\sigma_0 - \lambda(\mathcal{S}_t))\, v(\mathcal{S}_t))}_{\equiv \bar{\varphi}(\mathcal{S}_t)} dt + v(\mathcal{S}_t)\, d\bar{W}_t,$$

where $\bar{W}_t = \hat{W}_t - \sigma_0 t$ is a Brownian motion under a certain probability, $\bar{Q}$, defined in appendix 8.D (see eq. (8.A29)); $\hat{W}_t$ is a Brownian motion under the risk neutral probability Q; and $\bar{\mathbb{E}}(\cdot)$ is the expectation taken under $\bar{Q}$. Intuitively, the expectation under $\bar{Q}$ is needed to deal with the correlation between consumption growth and habit.

The properties of the inner expectation in eq. (8.29) can be analyzed relying on theorem 8.A2 in appendix 8.D. We have:

(1) Suppose that the risk-adjusted discount rates are countercyclical, namely, $\mathcal{R}'(\mathcal{S}) \leq 0$. Then the price-dividend ratio is procyclical, viz $p'(\mathcal{S}) > 0$.
(2) Suppose that the price-dividend ratio is procyclical. Then the price-dividend ratio is also a concave function of $\mathcal{S}$ as soon as the risk-adjusted discount rates are convex in $\mathcal{S}$, namely, $\mathcal{R}''(\mathcal{S}) > 0$ and $\bar{\varphi}''(\mathcal{S}) \leq 2\mathcal{R}'(\mathcal{S})$.

The previous statements impose joint restrictions on the primitives such that the price-dividend ratio is consistent with asset price properties given in advance. The economic interpretation of convexity of $\mathcal{R}$ is similar to that anticipated in section 8.3 (see figure 8.7). The mechanism in this model is the following. In bad times, consumption c_t gets close to the subsistence level x_t such that $\mathcal{S}_t$ is very small. Risk premiums rise as a result, making agents more reluctant to invest in the stock market. That is, in bad times, risk-adjusted discount rates, $\mathcal{R}$, increase sharply, making the price-dividend ratio highly responsive to changes in economic conditions. Instead, in good times, and again due to convexity, $\mathcal{R}$ changes relatively less, and the price-dividend ratio is relatively less responsive to changes in economic conditions. Countercyclical volatility then results from the property that $\mathcal{R}$ is decreasing and convex in the surplus consumption ratio $\mathcal{S}$ such that the price-dividend ratio, p, is concave in $\mathcal{S}$: stock volatility increases on the downside, just as heuristically illustrated by figure 8.7.[16]

16. Alternatively, Mele (2007) shows that for any model in which the price-dividend ratio is driven by a diffusion variable y_t, there is a threshold y^* such that the price-dividend ratio is concave for all $y_t \leq y^*$ whenever $\lim_{y\to 0} \mathcal{R}(y) = \infty$. There are additional models with external habit formation that lead to countercyclical volatility (see, e.g., Menzly, Santos, and Veronesi, 2004; Mele, 2007).

8.5.3 Some Additional Literature

In addition to the previous qualitative properties, the model leads to quantitatively realistic risk premiums. However, the model does not lead to a resolution of the equity premium puzzle. This economy is indeed one with high risk aversion; to illustrate, the calibrated model produces an average value of $\gamma S^{-1} \approx 40$. Moreover, there has been some criticism on how realistic habit formation is as a channel to asset price volatility. For example, Brunnermeier and Nagel (2008) find that US investors do not change the composition of their risky asset holdings in response to changes in wealth. The authors interpret this evidence as being against external habit formation.

Naturally, time-varying risk premiums do not exclusively arise through external habit formation. For example, Barberis, Huang, and Santos (2001) develop a theory distinct from habit formation, which leads to time-varying risk premiums. Chapter 9 explains many alternative mechanisms by which risk premiums are time-varying. It also explains that habit formation does not necessarily lead to high risk aversion; for example, it shows (see section 9.3) that in an economy with heretogeneous agents, a mechanism similar to habit formation may lead to countercyclical statistics even with a limited average risk aversion. Finally, habit formation is a very convenient assumption that leads to asset prices with sensible properties, such as Shiller's excess volatility puzzles surveyed in section 8.2. Appendix 8.E explains that alternative assumptions on habit formation may lead to analytical solutions for quantities of interest that can conveniently be used in applied work. We now explore how habit formation may help model the dynamics of interest rates.

8.5.4 The Term Structure of Interest Rates

How does the yield curve relate to the business cycle? The yield curve is a very complex topic and deserves a separate treatment. Chapters 12 and 13 provide a comprehensive treatment of theories and market practice around the determination and management of risks affecting bond markets. It is useful, however, to briefly discuss the prediction of models with habit formation. Notably, by a simple extension of the basic model with constant interest rates (see appendix 8.F), the short-term rate is time-varying and equal to

$$r(S) = \rho + \gamma \left(g_0 - \frac{1}{2}\sigma_0^2 \right) - \frac{1}{2}\left(\gamma (1-\phi) - b\right) + b\left(\bar{s} - \ln S\right), \qquad (8.30)$$

where b is a constant. Wachter (2006) analyzes the term structure implications of this model in detail, both real and nominal, in an environment with time-varying expected inflation.

The role of the parameter b is to make interest rates time-varying. How do we ensure that eq. (8.30) is consistent with optimizing behavior? We know that the short-term rate depends on the sensitivity of habit to consumption shocks, a function of S, $l(S)$, through an effect due to precautionary savings: the higher this sensitivity, the higher the volatility of habit and hence the propensity to save, which drives interest rates down. This sensitivity $l(S)$ is free in that it is not restricted by theory. For example, the short-term rate also relates to habit due to intertemporal substitution effects and negatively due to mean reversion. Campbell and Cochrane chose $l(S)$ such that intertemporal substitution effects exactly offset precautionary savings, thereby making the short-term rate constant–or, at most, affine in the log surplus consumption ratio—as in eq. (8.30).

The question arises: Which sign should we empirically expect from the parameter b? Are real interest rates countercyclical? They *are*. It is somewhat puzzling from the perspective of the basic production economies analyzed in chapter 3 where real interest rates are procyclical because they are positively related to the marginal productivity of capital and hence to productivity shocks. However, economies with habit formation might be capable of generating countercyclical real rates due to intertemporal substitution effects. This is the case, for example, in models with frictions in the adjustment of capital supply to shocks (see Boldrin, Christiano, and Fisher, 2001), as further discussed in chapter 9 (see section 9.10). In endowment economies and habit formation, we may expect countercyclical real rates. Consider, for example, Menzly, Santos, and Veronesi's (2004) model of external habit formation (see appendix 8.E). This model predicts that the short-term rate is

$$r(\mathcal{S}_t) = \rho + g_0 - \sigma_0^2 + \beta\left(1 - \frac{\mathcal{S}_t}{\bar{s}}\right) - \sigma_0^2 \alpha\left(1 - \frac{\mathcal{S}_t}{\upsilon}\right). \tag{8.31}$$

Figure 8.12 depicts the short-term rate as a function of the surplus consumption ratio with parameter values similar to those used by Menzly, Santos, and Veronesi.

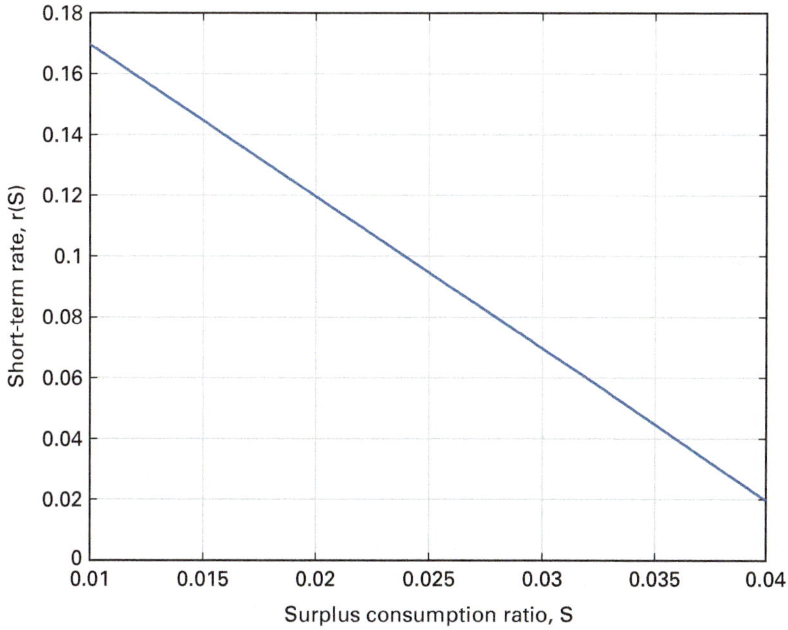

Figure 8.12
The short-term rate predicted by Menzly, Santos, and Veronesi's (2004) model of external habit formation. Parameter values are as in the following table.

g_0	σ_0	ρ	β	$\bar{s}$	α	υ	q
0.03	0.01	0.04	0.15	0.03	40	0.05	0.60

The fourth term of eq. (8.31) reflects intertemporal substitution effects and is the dominating term, leading to countercyclical interest rates due to the mean reversion in the surplus consumption ratio and similar to the Campbell and Cochrane model, as explained in section 8.5.2. Chapter 9 (see section 9.3) also reviews other models–such as the catching-up model of Chan and Kogan (2002)—that makes the same same prediction: real interest rates are countercyclical. We now continue our discussion on equity markets, leaving more space to fixed-income markets in part III of this book.

8.6 Large Price Swings As a Learning-Induced Phenomenon

This section considers economies in which expected dividend growth fluctuates randomly. This randomness may arise simply because the average growth of the economy is exposed to shocks as opposed to a simpler case where the growth rate is constant. That is, the drift of growth, while random, is fully observed by agents. This interpretation has always had an interest on its own (see, e.g., the early survey of Campbell, 2003). But a more interesting interpretation is that the state of the economy is not observed, and agents deal with their lack of knowledge by processing available data to estimate growth. These estimates lead them to face stochastic expected growth, a new state variable that has the potential to introduce interesting price dynamics.

The next section provides a succinct summary and motivation of the early literature on these models with unobserved growth. Section 8.6.2 contains heuristic derivations of learning dynamics as well as their asset pricing implications. Section 8.6.3 discusses two benchmark models. Chapter 9 contains more elaborated versions of learning mechanisms and asset price dynamics (see section 9.5).

8.6.1 Information

When the current state of the economy is unknown, agents may find that public signals help to reduce uncertainty on fundamentals. Thus, when public signals hit the market, agents make inferences by elaborating on them, thereby creating new state variables: the agents' own guesses on the state of the economy. These state variables become new sources of asset price fluctuations and time variation in market volatility.

Timmermann (1993, 1996) provides models along these lines relying on the assumption of exogenous discount rates. Learning increases equity volatility beyond the extent predicted by models with known fundamentals. Brennan and Xia (2001) generalize these models to a stochastic general equilibrium. Veronesi (1999) provides a rational expectations model with learning that displays nonlinear effects on the asset price. This section provides details on these mechanisms. One important point is "convexity," the property that asset prices are increasing and *convex* in the expected dividend growth, "g." This convexity property may give rise to price dynamics that resemble "an overreaction" in that, in good times, when g is high, asset prices become highly responsive to small changes in g.[17] It goes without saying that such "speculative enthusiasm" is fully rational: there is no overraction or other behavioral biases behind these properties.

17. The empirical relevance of this point was first acknowledged by Barsky and De Long (1990, 1993) in the context of a simple model. Naturally, prices may also be convex in g in economies with complete information.

In this section, information is incomplete, albeit symmetrically distributed among the agents. Symmetric information should not appear to be a strong assumption in this context. The models in this section aim to capture the idea that markets function in a context of "incompressible" uncertainty: there are no agents that have superior information on macroeconomic developments and asset markets. Chapter 10 considers models with both differential and asymmetric information, which appear to be more suited in describing markets for individual stocks. In these markets, it is plausible that agents with different information sets may wish to access information markets and that, as a result, some agents may infer signals while "reading the equilibrium asset prices." Indeed, while trading, agents with superior information impinge part of their information on the asset prices as explained in detail in chapter 10.

By contrast, it seems unrealistic that crucial information may be purchased regarding the direction of macroeconomic developments and that agents with less information attempt to learn from asset prices: while macroeconomic research helps to guide sophisticated asset managers, it seems implausible to imagine an articulated information market such as those described in chapter 10. Note that the assumption of symmetric information also simplifies the analysis. Agents only need to learn by elaborating public signals: prices merely convey the same information that any other agent already has.

8.6.2 An Introductory Model of Learning

Consider a two-period economy in which the dividend D has two components:

$$D = \theta + Z, \tag{8.32}$$

where θ and Z are independently distributed with $p \equiv \Pr(\theta = A) = 1 - \Pr(\theta = -A)$ and $\Pr(Z = A) = \Pr(Z = -A) = \frac{1}{2}$. Suppose that the "state" θ is unobserved. How should we update our prior probability p of the "good" state after observing D?

An application of the standard Bayes' theorem yields the posterior probabilities $\Pr(\theta = A|\, D_i)$ in table 8.5. Considered as a random variable defined over the observable states D_i, the posterior probability, $\Pr(\theta = A|\, D_i)$, has an expectation equal to $E\left[\Pr\left(\theta = A|\, D\right)\right] = p$ and a variance equal to $var\left[\Pr\left(\theta = A|\, D\right)\right] = \frac{1}{2}p\left(1 - p\right)$. Note that the variance is proportional to entropy. It is an inverse U-shaped function of p and takes a value of zero exactly when the prior on the state is degenerate (zero or one).

To derive the probabilities in table 8.5, indeed use Bayes' theorem: for any partition $(E_i)_i$ of a given state space,

$$\Pr\left(E_i|\, F\right) = \Pr\left(E_i\right) \frac{\Pr\left(F|\, E_i\right)}{\Pr\left(F\right)} = \Pr\left(E_i\right) \frac{\Pr\left(F|\, E_i\right)}{\sum_j \Pr\left(F|\, E_j\right) \Pr\left(E_j\right)}. \tag{8.33}$$

Table 8.5
Distribution of posterior probabilities, $\Pr\left(\theta = A|D\right)$.

D_i (observable state)	$D_1 = 2A$	$D_2 = 0$	$D_3 = -2A$
$\Pr(D_i)$	$\frac{1}{2}p$	$\frac{1}{2}$	$\frac{1}{2}(1-p)$
$\Pr\left(\theta = A|\, D = D_i\right)$	1	p	0

Applying eq. (8.33) to our example, we have

$$\Pr(\theta = A|\, D = D_1) = \Pr(\theta = A)\,\frac{\Pr(D = D_1|\,\theta = A)}{\Pr(D = D_1)} = p\frac{\Pr(D = D_1|\,\theta = A)}{\Pr(D = D_1)}.$$

But $\Pr(D = D_1|\,\theta = A) = \Pr(Z = D_1 - A) = \Pr(Z = A) = \frac{1}{2}$. Moreover, we have that $\Pr(D = D_1) = \frac{1}{2}p$. This leaves $\Pr(\theta = A|\, D = D_1) = 1$. These calculations are trivial, but one proceeds similarly while determining the other probabilities. We shall use (8.33) again soon.

This simple example illustrates the main ideas underlying *Bayesian learning*. As explained, the conditional variance of the posterior is proportional to entropy, $p(1-p)$. In many examples in the literature, however, this variance is proportional to squared entropy (see, e.g., chapters 8 and 9 in Liptser and Shiryaev, 2001a). These properties result from technical reasons, notably because Z is a discrete random variable. Indeed, assume that Z has some arbitrary but continuous density ϕ and zero mean and unit variance. Let $\pi(D) \equiv \Pr(\theta = A|\, D \in dD)$. By Bayes's rule in eq. (8.33),

$$\pi(D) = \Pr(\theta = A)\,\frac{\Pr(D \in dD|\,\theta = A)}{\Pr(D \in dD|\,\theta = A)\Pr(\theta = A) + \Pr(D \in dD|\,\theta = -A)\Pr(\theta = -A)}.$$

Now, we have that $\Pr(D \in dD|\,\theta = A) = \Pr(Z = D - A) = \phi(D - A)$ and similarly that $\Pr(D \in dD|\,\theta = -A) = \Pr(Z = D + A) = \phi(D + A)$. Simple calculations now yield

$$\pi(D) - p = p(1-p)\frac{\phi(D-A) - \phi(D+A)}{p\phi(D-A) + (1-p)\phi(D+A)}. \tag{8.34}$$

That is, the variance of the probability changes, $\pi(D) - p$, is proportional to $p^2(1-p)^2$.

8.6.2.1 Continuous time

We extend the previous heuristic results to a continuous time setting, assuming Z is a Brownian motion. Precisely, generalize eq. (8.32), and suppose that dividends satisfy

$$D_t = \theta t + \sigma_0 Z_t \tag{8.35}$$

for some constant σ_0 and where Z_t is a standard Brownian motion. We assume that the agent projects θ on to the information set generated by D_t. We can show that dividends can be represented as in the following decomposition:

$$D_t = E\left(\theta|\,(D_u)_{u\le t}\right)t + \sigma_0 W_t, \tag{8.36}$$

where W_t is a Brownian motion with respect to the agents' information set $\sigma(D_u, u \le t)$. In appendix 8.G, we show that $\pi_t \equiv \pi(D_t)$ satisfies

$$d\pi_t = 2A\frac{\pi_t(1-\pi_t)}{\sigma_0}dW_t, \quad \pi(D_0) \equiv p, \tag{8.37}$$

where $g_t \equiv E\left(\theta|\,(D_u)_{u\le t}\right)$ and $dW_t \equiv \sigma_0^{-1}(dD_t - g_t dt)$.

It is possible to show that if $\theta = A$ (resp. $\theta = -A$), then $\lim_{t\longrightarrow\infty}\pi_t = 1$ (resp. 0), almost surely. It is the strong law of large numbers for Brownian motions (e.g., Karatzas and Shreve, 1991, 104): $\lim_{t\longrightarrow\infty} D_t = \infty$ or $-\infty$ according to whether $\theta = A$ or $\theta = -A$.

Intuitively, if $\theta = A$, the Brownian noise in eq. (8.35) is dominated in the long run such that D_t becomes arbitrarily large, which leaves any agent confident that $\theta = A$. In other words, in this model, the agents are able to figure out the truth in the long run. Below, we shall specify an alternative model in which the agents can never completely learn.[18]

Note an interesting implication of this model. The "filter," g_t, is linear in π_t, that is, $g_t = A(2\pi_t - 1)$.[19] Therefore, the equilibrium in this economy with incomplete information is isomorphic in its pricing implications to that in a full information economy in which

$$\begin{cases} dD_t = g_t dt + \sigma_0 dW_t \\ dg_t = v(g_t)\, dW_t \end{cases}$$

where $v(g) \equiv (A - g)(g + A)/\sigma_0$.

8.6.2.2 *Asset valuation and convexity*

We now consider the asset pricing implications of an economy in which a representative agent solves the intertemporal consumption optimization problem

$$\max_{(c_t)_{t\geq 0}} E\left(\int_0^\infty e^{-rt} u(c_t)\, dt\right),$$

where r is the safe rate, assumed to be constant; the utility is exponential, $u(c) = -e^{-\alpha c}$; and α is the CARA coefficient. The risk premium coefficient in eq. (8.16) is then $\hat{\lambda} \equiv \alpha\sigma_0$, a constant. The dynamics of dividends under the risk neutral probability are

$$\begin{cases} dD_t = (g_t - \hat{\lambda}\sigma_0)dt + \sigma_0 d\hat{W}_t \\ dg_t = -\hat{\lambda} v(g_t)\, dt + v(g_t)\, d\hat{W}_t \end{cases} \tag{8.38}$$

where $\hat{W}$ is a Brownian motion under the risk neutral probability. Note that if the dividends are a geometric Brownian motion, and the agent has a CRRA equal to γ, then the dividend process is solution to

$$\frac{dD_t}{D_t} = (g_t - \sigma_0\hat{\lambda})dt + \sigma_0 d\hat{W}_t. \tag{8.39}$$

In this case, $\hat{\lambda}$ would equal $\gamma\sigma_0$, but g_t would be solution to the the same equation in (8.38).

In these economies, the instantaneous volatility of the expected dividend growth, g, is inverse U-shaped. Due to risk aversion, $\hat{\lambda} > 0$, the risk neutral drift of g (i.e., $\hat{\lambda} v(g_t)$) is then a convex function of g. Results in appendix 8.D (see theorem 8.A2) suggest that this property implies that the asset price is convex with respect to expected growth, g. The economic interpretation of the convex drift of g is simple. Our utility maximizing agent

18. Note that this derivation is heuristic. Liptser and Shiryaev (2001a) provide a rigorous derivation (see, e.g., their theorem. 8.1, p. 318, and example 1, p. 371). In particular, it can be shown that W_t is a Brownian motion with respect to the agents' information set $\sigma(D_u, u \leq t)$ (see their theorem 7.12, p. 273).

19. Conditional expectations of unobserved components of partially observed processes are sometimes referred to as a filters in the statistical literature.

requires compensation not only for dividend risk but also for the uncertainty around their estimated probability of living in the good state. In very good times and in very bad times, this probability is close to either one or zero, and there is no substantial uncertainty (i.e., $v(\cdot)$ is close to zero). Therefore, the drift of g_t under Q is small in very good and bad times; that is, it is convex in g_t. In the next subsection, we develop more intuition on these risk adjustments by relying on the portfolio choices of a representative agent.

The implications of these properties is that prices undergo large swings in good times. After a string of repeated positive news on growth, the agents find it very likely that the true dividend drift is $\theta = A$: the higher D_t is, the more likely it is that the asset is good. In these states of nature, the agents do not feel exposed to errors on π_t and therefore require little risk aversion corrections regarding g_t–corrections are made only regarding realized dividend growth, dD_t. Thus, asset prices go up both because dividends go up *and* due to repeated positive signals that the asset is good: these signals reduce the agents' exposure to the risk of not observing the asset quality.[20] Note that, in bad times, the agents are not exposed to these errors either, such that asset prices fall, albeit "moderately" so. That is, asset prices do go down because dividends are going down; however, their fall is somehow mitigated because the fall in dividends signals the asset is bad and thereby reduces the agent's exposure to the risk of not observing the asset quality. This convexity property may lead to fluctuations that an econometrician (say) could interpret as being generated by a bubble, even if no bubbles are present whatsoever.

Finally, it is instructive to provide the expression for expected returns and volatility predicted by this model, based on the analysis of section 8.4.2. For example, assuming that the representative agent has a CRRA equal to γ, we have that $\hat{\lambda} = \sigma_0 \gamma$, such that expected returns are

$$\mathcal{E}_t = \underbrace{r_t + \sigma_0^2 \gamma}_{\mathcal{R}_t} + \underbrace{\frac{p'(g_t)}{p(g_t)} \sigma_0 \gamma v(g_t)}_{\mathcal{W}_t} \tag{8.40}$$

and volatility is

$$\text{Vol}_t = \sigma_0 + \frac{p'(g_t)}{p(g_t)} v(g_t). \tag{8.41}$$

Below, we provide a more rigorous analysis of these convexity properties by relying on two famous (and more general) models of learning.

8.6.2.3 *With Bellman*

The previous explanations regarding risk aversion corrections can be illustrated while solving the agent's dynamic programming problem. In particular, the reader may verify, as an exercise, that the motives underlying the agent's investments in periods of uncertainty are captured by the hedging component of their portfolio.

20. In terms of eq. (8.39), the drift of dividend growth is tilted to the left due the risk-adjustment term, $\sigma_0 \hat{\lambda}$. Moreover, g_t is tilted to the left due to the negative drift, $-\hat{\lambda} v(g_t)$. The effects of $\hat{\lambda} v(g_t)$ are small in very good and very poor times because $v(\cdot)$ is small in these cases. The effects of $\sigma_0 \hat{\lambda}$ are independent of the state of the economy.

8.6.3 Convexity Again and Two Models of Learning

8.6.3.1 With a Markov chain

The model described by (8.38) is a special case of that considered by Veronesi (1999), in which an infinitely lived agent has a CARA $\alpha > 0$ and observes realizations of D, generated by

$$dD_t = \theta dt + \sigma_0 dZ_{1t}, \tag{8.42}$$

where Z_{1t} is a Brownian motion and θ is the expected dividend change that is supposed to follow a two-state $(\underline{\theta}, \bar{\theta})$ Markov chain. (See also David, 1997, for a related model.) In eqs. (8.38), the dividend is a "type," in that once nature draws θ, this θ is there forever. In eqs. (8.42), instead, θ is allowed to change according to a Markov chain, as explained.

Agents do not observe the expected dividend change, θ, and react to their lack of knowledge while attempting to infer the state in which they are living through Bayesian learning. It can be shown that the price in this economy is the same as that in a full information economy, in which the dividend is the solution to

$$\begin{cases} dD_t = g_t dt + \sigma_0 dW_t \\ dg_t = k(\bar{g} - g_t)\, dt + v(g_t)\, dW_t \end{cases} \tag{8.43}$$

where $v(g) = (\bar{\theta} - g)(g - \underline{\theta}) / \sigma_0$ and $k, \bar{g}$ are some positive constants.

Note that, while the diffusion terms in eq. (8.38) and in eq. (8.43) have the same functional form, the expected dividend change is a martingale in eq. (8.38) and is mean-reverting in eq. (8.43) under the *physical* probability, that is, when $\hat{\lambda} = 0$ in eq. (8.38). The reason for these differences is that in eq. (8.38), θ is drawn at time 0 and stays the same forever, whereas in eq. (8.43), θ is a Markov chain. In other words, in eq. (8.42), the agent will never figure out the truth, and g_t is mean-reverting toward its average rate.

Let us determine the asset price. Assume that the riskless asset is infinitely elastically supplied such that the interest rate r is constant. By the results in section 8.4, the cash-flow risk premium is constant and equal to $\lambda = \alpha\sigma_0$ (see eq. (8.16)), such that the dynamics of dividends and expected dividend growth under the risk neutral probability are

$$\begin{cases} dD_t = \left(g_t - \alpha\sigma_0^2\right) dt + \sigma_0 d\hat{W}_t \\ dg_t = \left(k(\bar{g} - g_t) - \alpha\sigma_0 v(g_t)\right) dt + v(g_t)\, d\hat{W}_t \end{cases} \tag{8.44}$$

and the asset price is

$$S(D, g) = \mathbb{E}\left(\int_0^\infty e^{-rt} D_t dt \,\middle|\, D, g \right) = \int_0^\infty C(D, g, t)\, dt,$$

where

$$C(D, g, t) = e^{-rt}\left(D - \alpha\sigma_0^2 t\right) + G(g, t), \quad \text{and} \quad G(g, t) \equiv e^{-rt} \int_0^t \mathbb{E}\left(g_u \middle| g\right) du. \tag{8.45}$$

The conditional expectation, $\mathbb{E}\left(g_u \middle| g\right)$, can be read as a special case of a certain problem introduced in appendix 8.D.3 (the "canonical pricing problem.") In particular, by theorem 8.A2 in this appendix, we have that $\mathbb{E}\left(g_u \middle| g\right)$ is convex in g whenever the drift of g in eq. (8.44) is convex. This condition holds true due to risk aversion, $\alpha > 0$. That is, the conditional expectation of g in eq. (8.45) inherits the same second-order properties (convexity) of this drift function.

The economic interpretation of these properties is the same as that behind eqs. (8.38) or (8.39). Prices are convex in the expected dividend growth because of a kind of "speculative enthusiasm": after a sequence of high realized growth, investors estimate that the likelihood is high that they are living in good times *and* that the likelihood is low that they are making mistakes in their assessments. Thus, asset prices increase, fueled by low risk premium discounts. Note that these low premiums regard the uncertainty the agents face while assessing the markets they are operating in. Their "speculative enthusiasm" is rational and not determined by "animal spirits." Finally, it is possible to show that returns volatility and expected returns are both increasing over most of the range of variation of g, although they both decrease as g approaches the "good state." The reason for this nonmonotonicity is that $\lim_{g \to \bar{\theta}} v(g) \to 0$, driving returns volatility $S_g(D,g)\,v(g)$ to zero. Explanations regarding the increasing part of expected returns and volatility are similar to those regarding a related model, which are given in section 8.6.3.3.

Some of the previous properties (notably, convexity) hold under the assumption that the riskless asset is infinitely elastically supplied. When investors' portfolio choices affect the safe asset, then the interest rate becomes a function of the expected growth, g, in equilibrium. Thus, when g increases, the increase in the asset price should be mitigated by the fact that the agents also wishes to save less: as g increases, more resources are likely to be available in the future; that is, the interest rate increases. Formally, by results in section 8.4, the short-term rate is $r(g) = \rho + \alpha g - \frac{1}{2}\alpha^2\sigma_0^2$ (see eq. (8.15)), such that the asset price is now

$$S_r(D,g) \equiv \mathbb{E}\left(\int_0^\infty e^{-\int_0^t r(g_s)ds} D_t dt \,\middle|\, D,g\right) = \int_0^\infty C_r(D,g,t)\,dt,$$

where

$$C_r(D,g,t) = \left(D - \alpha\sigma_0^2 t\right) B(g,t) + G_r(g,t)$$

$$B(g,t) \equiv \mathbb{E}\left(e^{-\int_0^t r(g_s)ds} \,\middle|\, g\right), \quad G_r(g,t) \equiv \mathbb{E}\left(e^{-\int_0^t r(g_s)ds} \bar{g}_t \,\middle|\, D,g,\bar{g}\right), \quad d\bar{g}_t = g_t dt.$$

Now, relying on results in appendix 8.D (see theorem 8.A2), we can show that the two functions, $B(g,t)$ and $G_r(g,t)$, are *affine* in g: once interest rates are determined endogenously, the asset price is no longer convex in the dividend expected growth. This is "unpleasant arithmetics." We know the short-term rate should not fluctuate too much, compared with stock returns. Assuming it is constant is empirically reasonable. However, when allowed to fluctuate in this setting, the previous interesting properties would be destroyed. Interestingly, the property that prices are linear in g with endogenous interest rates is not specific to economies in which dividends are as in eqs. (8.43) and agents have CARA. Veronesi (2000) shows that prices are still linear in scale invariant economies with a representative CRRA agent.

8.6.3.2 *With a continuum of states*

In the previous model, the asset price reacts asymmetrically to changes in the expected dividend growth, due to the assumption that agents learn on a *discrete* state space in a *continuous time* economy. We now describe another model, introduced by Brennan and Xia (2001), in which the agents learn about a *continuous* state in a *continuous time* economy.

In this model, an infinitely lived CRRA agent observes D which is a solution to

$$\frac{dD_t}{D_t} = \hat{g}_t dt + \sigma_0 dZ_{1t},$$

where Z_{1t} is a standard Brownian motion and the expected dividend growth, $\hat{g}_t$, is unobserved. Rather than assuming $\hat{g}_t$ to be on a countable number of states, Brennan and Xia postulate that it is an Ornstein-Uhlenbeck process:

$$d\hat{g}_t = k(\bar{g} - \hat{g}_t)dt + \sigma_1 dZ_{1t} + \sigma_2 dZ_{2t},$$

where $\bar{g}$, σ_1 and σ_2 are constants, and Z_{2t} is another standard Brownian motion.[21]

A representative agent updates their beliefs about $\hat{g}_t$ through Bayes's updating, similarly as in the previous section. This inference problem can be solved by relying on the general results stated in chapter 9 (see section 9.5.1). To simplify the presentation, we assume that $\sigma_1 = 0$: dividend growth is uncorrelated with the unobserved, expected dividend growth. Then it can be shown that, if the agent has a Gaussian prior on $\hat{g}_0$ with variance α_*^2 defined below, D_t satisfies

$$\begin{cases} \dfrac{dD_t}{D_t} = g_t dt + \sigma_0 dW_t \\ dg_t = k(\bar{g} - g_t)dt + v dW_t \end{cases}$$

where W_t is a standard Brownian motion, $v \equiv \frac{\alpha_*}{\sigma_0}$ and σ_0, k, $\bar{g}$, and α^* are constants. The constant α_* is chosen so as to make the learning environment stationary in that the volatility of dg_t is constant.[22]

Next, note that by eq. (8.16), the risk premium is constant and equal to $\lambda = \gamma\sigma_0$, where γ is the CRRA coefficient. Moreover, by eq. (8.15), the short-term rate is linear in g. Therefore, by the same reasoning leading to eq. (8.29), the price-dividend ratio is independent of D and is given by

$$p(g) = \int_0^\infty e^{-\sigma_0 \lambda t} \bar{\mathbb{E}} \left(e^{\int_0^t (g_u - r(g_u))du} \middle| g \right) dt, \tag{8.46}$$

where g_t is solution to

$$dg_t = \left(k(\bar{g} - g_t) + (\sigma_0 - \lambda) v\right) dt + v d\bar{W}_t, \tag{8.47}$$

$\bar{W}_t$ is a Brownian motion under $\bar{P}$, and $\bar{P}$ is defined similarly as in eq. (8.29).

Therefore, properties of the price-dividend ratio are inherited by those of the inner expectation in eq. (8.46). Precisely, an application of theorem 8.A2 in appendix 8.D leads to the following conclusions. The price-dividend ratio is increasing in the expected dividend

21. Brennan and Xia (2001) consider a more general model in which consumption and dividends differ.

22. Notably, α_* is the positive solution to the quadratic equation $0 = \alpha^2/\sigma_0^2 + 2k\alpha - \sigma_2^2$ (see eq. (9.45) in chapter 9). These results generalize those in Gennotte (1986) and are a special case of results shown in Detemple (1986). Gennotte and Detemple did not emphasize the impact of learning on the pricing function.

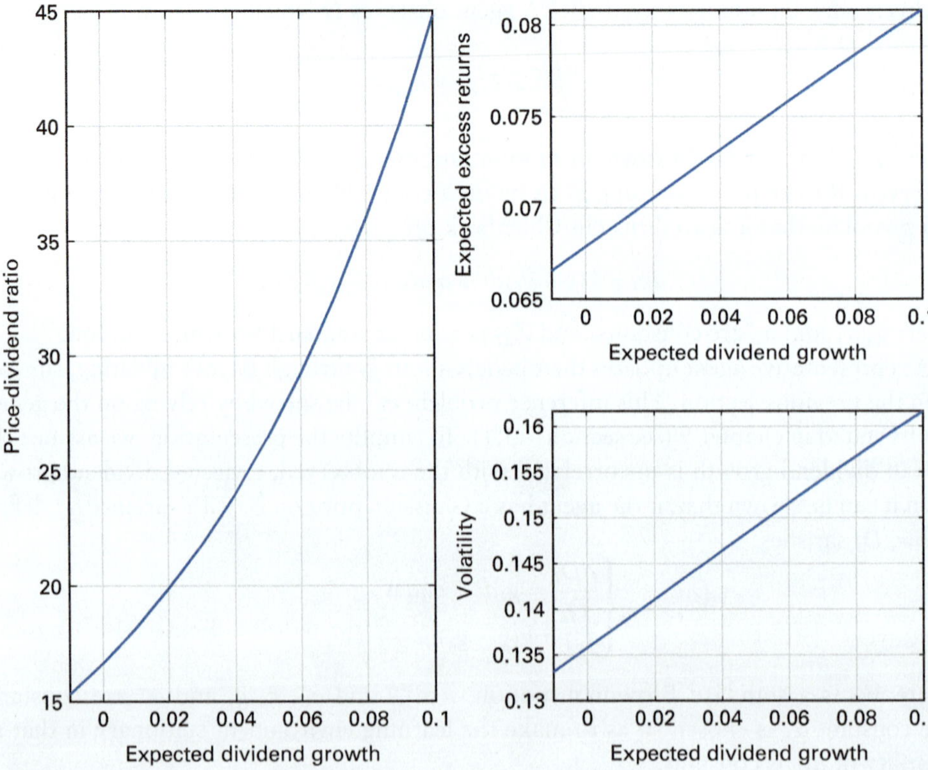

Figure 8.13
The price-dividend ratio, expected excess returns, and volatility predicted by a model with learning (see eqs. (8.46) and (8.49)). Parameter values are $\gamma = 10$, $\sigma_0 = 0.05$, $\bar{r} = 0.02$, $k = 0.05$, $\bar{g} = 0.05$, and $\sigma_2 = 0.015$. These values imply an approximate value of $v = 0.01$, used in the calculations.

growth, g, if and only if $r'(g) < 1$, and provided $r'(g) < 1$, it is always convex in g. Now, in equilibrium, $r'(g) = \gamma$, implying that these properties hold when $\gamma < 1$. Appendix 8.G provides all of the details of this reasoning and generalizes (8.47) to a more general process.

The condition that $\gamma < 1$ is too restrictive. We now assume that the bond price supply is infinitely elastic such that r is a constant and equal to some $\bar{r}$. Appendix 8.G shows that

$$p(g) = \int_0^\infty e^{A(t)+B(t)\left(g-\bar{r}-\gamma\sigma_0^2\right)} dt \tag{8.48}$$

for two functions A and B. By eqs. (8.40) and (8.41), expected returns and return volatility are

$$\mathcal{E}_t - \bar{r} = \gamma\sigma_0 \mathrm{Vol}_t, \quad \mathrm{Vol}_t = \sigma_0 + \frac{p'(g_t)}{p(g_t)} v. \tag{8.49}$$

Figure 8.13 plots the price-dividend ratio (8.48) and the expected excess returns and return volatility based on the parameter values indicated in the legend. Appendix 8.G provides additional details on the calculation of v in these examples. We comment on this figure in the next subsection.

8.6.3.3 Bubbles and volatility

The previous model predicts that the price-dividend ratio is convex in g. This property makes both expected returns and return volatility increasing in g_t. That is, risk increases on the upside, and risk premiums increase too: assets become more risky just when prices increase, which might be a route to momentum as reviewed in chapter 1 (see section 1.5.3).[23] These predictions should be compared with those in section 8.5 and with the empirical facts and other explanations in section 8.3 where risk and risk premiums do actually decrease on the upside. To put these conclusions in perspective, note that the focus of sections 8.3 and 8.5 is to capture the notion that price movements link to business cycles. In the models of this section, growth does, of course, likely link to the business cycle. It may, however, represent an *additional* channel of market fluctuations beyond business cycles: the point of the model is that growth may be so strong, and prices may then increase so fast, to make volatility and premiums increase on the upside.[24]

In fact, Pástor and Veronesi (2006) developed a model where price multiples (see section 8.7) exhibit a behavior similar to that predicted by the simple model in this section. They interpret the episodes around the "Nasdaq bubble" of the late 1990s—where volatility and premiums were both high (see also, figure 8.2 in section 8.2)—as ones that may be explained by the high uncertainty about firms' profitability. In their model, price multiples (such as market-to-book ratios) are increasing and convex in the expected profitability (similar to the model of this section) and therefore increase in the uncertainty around it. In the model of this section and under parameter restrictions, prices, returns volatility, and premiums do indeed increase with v. Thus, the large price swings these models generate may resemble bubbles. Nevertheless, it is very difficult to explain that large price increases always come through the patterns described in this section. For example, we know that the price increases around the first half of the 2000s were accompanied by *low* volatility and premiums. However, the models in this section point to important channels of asset price volatility that may well occur during periods of strong and sustained expected growth.

8.7 Retained Earnings and Market-to-Book Ratios

Firms do not necessarily distribute dividends on a regular basis. Typically, newly created firms do not actually distribute dividends at all for a while. Chapter 5 provides explanations by which an optimal policy is to start distributing dividends only when *sufficient* cash reserves are achieved (see section 5.7). Such a policy may arise not only due to liquidity reasons but also due to incentive problems. Much of the analytical framework in this and chapter 9 is based on the assumption that dividends are regularly paid. This section describes analytical frameworks that enable one to deal with alternative properties of the

23. Johnson (2002) provides an explanation of momentum based on mechanisms similar to the model in this section.

24. Note that, because g is mean-reverting, the price-dividend ratio, p, is mean-reverting too. Therefore, changes in p are negatively correlated with past values of g, similarly as with the explanations on predictability in section 8.2.2. This statistical relation is, of course, consistent with the property that the *total* expected return is increasing in g.

actual dividend distribution policy. The frameworks are very basic, and they may need to be extended in order to deal with actual behavior of price multiples.

Section 8.7.1 provides some simple intuition in a standard case, in which a firm not only distributes dividends regularly but also retains a portion of them to benefit from growth opportunities: reinvesting a retained proportion of earnings pays when the firm's future profitability is higher than the time-discount rate. Section 8.7.2 analyzes the situation in which the distribution of dividends occurs on an exogenously given, random date. The key "multiple" concept in this case is the market-to-book (MB) ratio, defined as the market value of the firm divided by its book values. MB ratios are often used both in academic research and in market practice. For example, chapter 1 discusses some very famous asset price anomalies while discussing measures related to MB ratios (see section 1.5.3).

8.7.1 Plowbacks and Growth Opportunities

Let A_t denote the total assets value that the firm has in place at time t. Assets grow because a portion b of the earnings, the "plowback ratio," is retained and then reinvested. Let ε_t and I_t denote earnings and investments at t, such that $I_t = b\varepsilon_t$, and dividends $D_t = (1-b)\,\varepsilon_t$. We assume firms have no debt such that ROE and ROI are the same. Thus, assuming that ROE is constant and equal to ρ, or $\varepsilon_t = \rho A_t$, we have that the assets' value evolves as $A_{t+\Delta t} - A_t = I_t \Delta t = b\varepsilon_t \Delta t = b\rho A_t \Delta t$. In continuous time,

$$\frac{dA_t}{At} = b\rho dt.$$

Dividend growth is equal to $b\rho$. Finally, we assume that the time-discount rate is constant and equal to $\mathcal{R}$ and that $\mathcal{R} > b\rho$ such that the price-dividend ratio is

$$\frac{P_0}{D_0} = \int_0^\infty e^{-\mathcal{R}t} E\left(\frac{D_t}{D_0}\right) dt = \int_0^\infty e^{-(\mathcal{R}-b\rho)} dt = \frac{1}{\mathcal{R} - b\rho}. \tag{8.50}$$

The reasoning underlying eq. (8.50) is very well known.[25] The asset price is $P_0(b) \equiv (1-b)\,\varepsilon_0 / (\mathcal{R} - b\rho)$, such that $P_0'(b) > 0$ if and only if $\rho > \mathcal{R}$. The difference, $P_0(b) - P_0(0)$, is known as the "present value of growth opportunities." When a firm's ROE exceeds the time-discount rate, asset prices always increase when part of the earnings are retained and reinvested. Even if dividends are temporarily lower than in the case without reinvestments, they will grow more as a result of the firm's relatively high profitability. Finally, note that the limiting price resulting as $b \to 1$ is not defined under the previous assumptions. This price actually diverges as $b \to R/\rho$. The next section provides a simple framework to deal with the case in which a firm does not distribute dividends for a while.

8.7.2 Random Dividends Distribution

We assume that firms have access to a technology that enables them to accumulate cash over time. Firms bear no debt. Thus, if B_0 denotes the initial cash a firm is endowed with, its book value at time t, B_t, is the solution to

$$dB_t = (\rho_t - \delta_t)\, B_t dt,$$

25. See, e.g., Bodie, Kane, and Marcus (2014, chap. 18).

where δ_t denotes the proportion of the firm's books that are distributed as an instantaneous dividend. The process, ρ_t—interpreted as the firm profitability, a ROI, or ROE—is a mean-reverting process

$$d\rho_t = k(\bar{\rho} - \rho_t)\, dt + \sigma dW_t \tag{8.51}$$

for three parameters k, $\bar{\rho}$, and σ, where W_t is a standard Brownian motion. While the model in this section is still tractable when $\delta_t > 0$ (under assumptions), we simplify the presentation and set $\delta_t \equiv 0$.

We assume that, at some future random T, say, the firm's value equals its book value. This assumption may be interpreted in a variety of ways. For example, we may assume that, while the firm does not distribute dividends, it is liquidated at some future date T, a date at which its cash will be entirely distributed to the shareholders. Thus, $M_T = B_T$, where M_T denotes the firm's market value. Alternatively, Pástor and Veronesi (2006), building on clean surplus relations in the accounting literature (Ohlson, 1995; Ang and Liu, 2001), interpret the date T as the date at which competition will eliminate a firm's abnormal earnings. We assume, as Pástor and Veronesi do, that under the risk neutral probability, T is exponentially distributed with constant intensity equal to λ and is independent of ρ_t Moreover, the short-term rate is constant and equal to $\bar{r}$. Under these conditions, the MB ratio, $\text{MB}(\rho) \equiv \frac{M_0}{B_0}$, is

$$\begin{aligned}\text{MB}(\rho) &= \mathbb{E}\left(e^{-\bar{r}T} \frac{B_T}{B_0} \middle| \rho \right) = \mathbb{E}\left(\int_0^\infty \lambda e^{-\lambda T} e^{-\bar{r}T} \frac{B_T}{B_0} dT \middle| \rho \right) \\ &= \lambda \int_0^\infty \mathbb{E}\left(e^{-(\lambda+\bar{r})T} \frac{B_T}{B_0} \middle| \rho \right) dT,\end{aligned} \tag{8.52}$$

where $\mathbb{E}(\cdot)$ denotes the expectation under the risk neutral probability. For example, assuming that ρ_t is constant and equal to $\bar{\rho}$ and that $\bar{\rho} < \bar{r} + \lambda$,

$$\text{MB}(\bar{\rho}) = \frac{\lambda}{\lambda + \bar{r} - \bar{\rho}}.$$

Intuitively, the MB ratio is increasing in $\bar{\rho}$. If $\bar{\rho} > \bar{r}$, this ratio is also decreasing in λ: if the rate of profitability is higher than the discount rate, the longer the expected period during which the book's value accumulates prior to T (i.e., the lower λ), the higher the expected discounted books' value at T is higher. For example, set $\lambda = 10^{-1}$ (the firm's expected time for T is equal to 10 years), $\bar{r} = 0.03$, and $\bar{\rho} = 0.10$; in this case, $\text{MB} = 3.33$.

Figure 8.14 plots eq. (8.52) in a risk neutral economy (see appendix 8.H for details on this graph). The MB ratio is increasing and convex in ρ_t. This model bears similarities with those in section 8.6. Whereas, in the previous models, expected dividend growth is the driver of the price-dividend ratio, it is now profitability that drives fluctuations in price multiples (the MB ratio).

Naturally, this model provides a very stylized description of MB ratios. As anticipated in chapter 3, production-based economies naturally lead to the definition of book-to-market values through Tobin's average q (see section 3.4). Works that contain predictions on MB ratios in production economies include the seminal paper of Berk, Green, and Naik (1999) or the earlier works of Gomes, Kogan, and Zhang (2003) and Zhang (2005), among others.

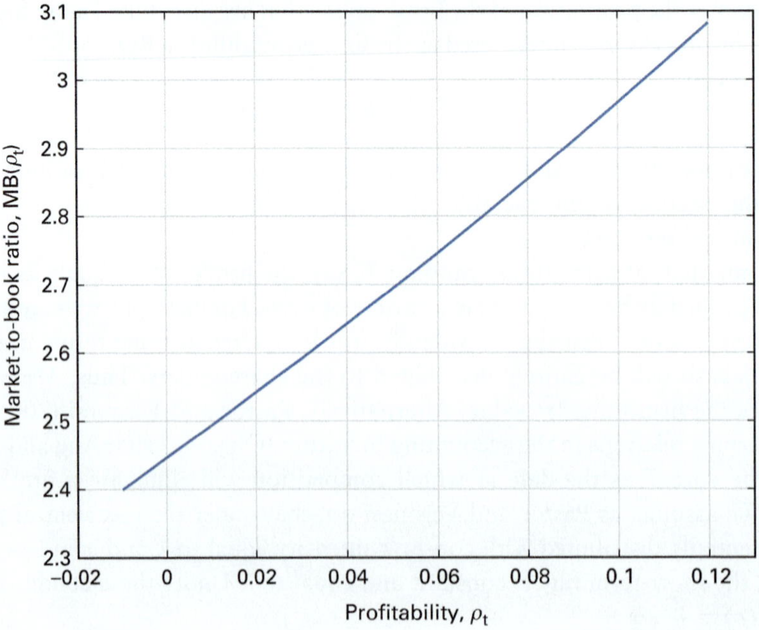

Figure 8.14
The MB ratio predicted by a model with random dividend distribution (see eq. (8.52)) as a function of profitability, ρ_t. Parameter values are $\lambda=20^{-1}$, $\phi=0.50$, $\bar{\rho}=0.07$, $\sigma=0.05$, and $\bar{r}=0.02$.

Appendix 8.A Estimation, Calibration, and Simulation Methods

8.A.1 Estimation of the Market Expected Return

We estimate yearly expected excess returns by relying on the following model:

$$\tilde{R}_t - r_t = a + \phi(\tilde{R}_{t-1} - r_{t-1}) + b^\top p_{t-1} + \epsilon_t, \tag{8.A1}$$

where a, ϕ, and b are coefficients (b is two-dimensional), p_t is a vector containing default and term spreads, and ϵ_t is a residual term that is assumed to be independent and identically normally distributed. Note that eq. (8.A1) may equivalently be cast as

$$\begin{cases} \tilde{R}_t - r_t = \hat{R}_t + (1-\phi L)^{-1}\epsilon_t \\ \hat{R}_t = a + \phi\hat{R}_{t-1} + b^\top p_{t-1} \end{cases} \tag{8.A2}$$

where L is the lag operator, $Lx_t \equiv x_{t-1}$.

The notion of yearly expected returns in the main text (see eq. (8.2)) relies on the projection $P_t(\hat{R}_{t+j})$ of $\hat{R}_{t+1}$ based on the model (8.A2). To calculate the projection terms in eq. (8.2), we could specify the dynamics of p_t in (8.A2). Alternatively, we proceed as follows. First, we estimate eq. (8.A1). Second, we reconstruct a time series of monthly expected returns, $\hat{R}_t$, in the second of eqs. (8.A2), given the estimates of a, ϕ, and b. Third, we fit an AR(1) model to the reconstructed series $\hat{R}_t$ and calculate projections on this series and estimate $\hat{\mathcal{E}}_t$ in eq. (8.2).

8.A.2 Calibration of the Tree in Section 8.3

SOLUTION AND CALIBRATION. We provide details regarding the calibration results in table 8.2 of the main text. In the first step, we estimate the two parameters p and δ of the dividend process. Let G be the yearly dividend gross growth rate. We calibrate p and δ by a perfect matching of the model's expected dividend growth, $\mu_D \equiv E(G) = pe^{-\delta} + (1-p)e^{\delta}$, and dividend variance, $\sigma_0^2 \equiv var(G) = \left(e^{\delta} - e^{-\delta}\right)^2 p(1-p)$, to their sample counterparts $\hat{\mu}_D = 1.0594$ and $\hat{\sigma}_0 = 0.0602$ that were obtained with US aggregate dividend data. The result is $(p,\delta) = (0.158, 0.082)$. Given these calibrated values of (p,δ), we fix $r = 1.0\%$, and proceed to calibrate the probabilities q, q_B, and q_G.

To calibrate (q, q_B, q_G), we need an explicit expression for all the payoffs at each node. We rely on the price of the claim, M_S, which we obtain in closed form as follows. For each state $S \in \{G, B, GB\}$, M_S is a solution to

$$\frac{M_S}{D_S} = e^{-r}\mathbb{E}_S\left(\frac{D_S'}{D_S} + \frac{M_S'}{D_S'}\frac{D_S'}{D_S}\right), \tag{8.A3}$$

where $\mathbb{E}_S(\cdot)$ is the expectation taken under the risk neutral probability q_S in state S; $S \in \{G, B, GB\}$; and $q_{GB} = q$, $D_G = e^{2\delta}$, $D_B = e^{-2\delta}$, $D_{GB} = 1$, and D_S' and M_S' are the dividend and the price of the claim as of the next period. Since risk aversion is constant from the third period on, the price-dividend ratio is constant as well from the third period on, which implies that $\frac{M_S}{D_S} = \frac{M_S'}{D_S'}$. Replacing this equality into eq. (8.A3) and solving for M_S yields

$$M_S = D_S \frac{q_S e^{-\delta} + (1-q_S)e^{\delta}}{e^r - \left[q_S e^{-\delta} + (1-q_S)e^{\delta}\right]}, \quad S \in \{G, B, GB\}. \tag{8.A4}$$

We calibrate $(q_G, q_B, q_{GB} = q)$ to make the "average" price-dividend ratio M_{GB}, the "good" price-dividend ratio $\frac{M_G}{e^{2\delta}}$, and the "bad" price-dividend ratio $\frac{M_B}{e^{-2\delta}}$ in eq. (8.A4) perfectly match the average price-dividend ratio, the average price-dividend ratio during NBER expansion periods, and the average price-dividend ratio during NBER recession periods (i.e., 31.99, 33.21, and 26.20, from table 8.1). Given $(p, \delta, r, q, q_B, q_G)$, we compute the price-dividend ratios in states G and B. For example, the price of the asset in state B is $P_B = e^{-r}[q_B(e^{-2\delta} + M_B) + (1-q_B)(1+M_{GB})]$. Given P_B, we compute the log-return in the bad state as $\ln(\frac{\tilde{\Pi}}{P_B})$, where

$$\tilde{\Pi} = \begin{cases} e^{-2\delta} + M_B & \text{with probability } p \\ 1 + M_{GB} & \text{with probability } 1-p \end{cases}.$$

Then, we compute the return volatility in state B. The price-dividend ratios, the expected log-return, and return volatility in state G are computed similarly. (Please notice that volatilities under p and under $\{q_S\}_{S \in \{G,B,GB\}}$ are not the same.)

Next, we recover the risk aversion parameter γ_S in the three states $S \in \{G, B, GB\}$ that are implied by the previously calibrated probabilities. As we shall show below, the relevant formula to use is

$$\frac{q_S}{p} = \frac{e^{\gamma_S \delta}}{pe^{\gamma_S \delta} + (1-p)e^{-\gamma_S \delta}}, \quad S \in \{G, B, GB\}. \tag{8.A5}$$

The values for the "implied" risk aversion parameter in table 8.2 are obtained by inverting eq. (8.A5) for γ_S, given the calibrated values of (p, δ, q_S).

Finally, we determine the risk-adjusted discount rate as $r + \hat{\sigma}_0 \lambda_S$, where λ_S is the Sharpe ratio. As shown below, this is equal to:

$$\lambda_S = \frac{q_S - p}{\sqrt{p(1-p)}}, \quad S \in \{G, B, GB\}. \tag{8.A6}$$

Proof of eq. (8.A5). We only provide the derivation of the risk neutral probability q_B since the proofs for the expressions of the risk neutral probabilities q_G and $q = q_{GB}$ are nearly identical. In equilibrium, the Euler equation for the stock price at the "bad" node is

$$P_B = \beta E\left[\frac{u'_B(\tilde{D}_S)}{u'_B(e^{-\delta})}\left(\tilde{D}_S + M_S\right)\right] = \beta E\left[\tilde{G}_S^{-\gamma_B}\left(\tilde{D}_S + M_S\right)\right], \quad S \in \{B, GB\}, \tag{8.A7}$$

where (i) β is the discount rate, (ii) the utility function for consumption C is state dependent and equal to $u_B(C) = C^{1-\gamma_B} / (1-\gamma_B)$, (iii) $E(\cdot)$ is the expectation taken under the physical probability p, and (iv) the dividend $\tilde{D}_S$ and the gross dividend growth rate $\tilde{G}_S$ are either $\tilde{D}_B = e^{-2\delta}$ and $\tilde{G}_B = \frac{e^{-2\delta}}{e^{-\delta}} = e^{-\delta}$ with probability p or $\tilde{D}_{GB} = 1$ and $\tilde{G}_{GB} = \frac{1}{e^{-\delta}} = e^{\delta}$ with probability $1-p$.

In the model, the asset is elastically supplied, or equivalently, there exists a storage technology with a fixed rate of return, $r = 1\%$. Let us derive the agent's private evaluation of this asset. The Euler equation for the safe asset is

$$e^{-r_B} = \beta E(\tilde{G}_S^{-\gamma_B}) = \beta \sum_{S \in \{B, GB\}} p_S \tilde{G}_S^{-\gamma_B}, \tag{8.A8}$$

where the safe interest rate, r_B, is state dependent, $p_B = p$ and $p_{GB} = 1-p$. Therefore,

$$q_B = \beta e^{r_B} p \tilde{G}_B^{-\gamma_B} \text{ and } 1 - q_B = \beta e^{r_B}(1-p)\tilde{G}_{GB}^{-\gamma_B} \tag{8.A9}$$

are a probability distribution. In fact, by plugging q_B and $1-q_B$ into eq. (8.A7), one sees that it is the risk neutral probability distribution. To obtain eq. (8.A5), note that by eq. (8.A8), $\beta e^{r_B} = 1 / E(\tilde{G}_S^{-\gamma_B})$, which when replaced into eq. (8.A9) yields

$$\frac{q_B}{p} = \frac{\tilde{G}_B^{-\gamma_B}}{E(\tilde{G}_S^{-\gamma_B})}.$$

Eq. (8.A5) follows by the definition of $\tilde{G}_S$ given above.

Proof of eq. (8.A6). Let e^{μ} be the gross expected return of the risky asset. The asset return can take two values: e^{R_l} with probability p and e^{R_h} with probability $1-p$, with $R_h > R_l$. Therefore, for each state, we have that

$$e^{\mu} = p e^{R_l} + (1-p) e^{R_h} \text{ and } e^{r} = q e^{R_l} + (1-q) e^{R_h} \tag{8.A10}$$

where we have omitted the dependence on the state S to alleviate the presentation. The standard deviation of the asset return is $\text{Std}_R = \left(e^{R_h} - e^{R_l}\right)\sqrt{p(1-p)}$. The Sharpe ratio is defined as

$$\lambda = \frac{e^{\mu} - e^{r}}{\text{Std}_R}.$$

By subtracting the two equations in (8.A10),

$$q = p + \frac{e^{\mu} - e^{r}}{\left(e^{R_h} - e^{R_l}\right)\sqrt{p(1-p)}}\sqrt{p(1-p)} = p + \lambda\sqrt{p(1-p)},$$

from which eq. (8.A6) follows immediately. Note also that, in terms of this definition of the Sharpe ratio, the risk neutral expectation of the dividend growth is $\mathbb{E}(G) = E(G) - \lambda\sigma_0$.

8.A.3 Simulation of Discrete-Time Pricing Models

Consider the pricing equation

$$S = E\left[m \cdot (S' + D')\right], \quad m = \beta\frac{u_c(D', x')}{u_c(D, x)} = \beta\left(\frac{s'}{s}\right)^{-\gamma}\left(\frac{D'}{D}\right)^{-\gamma}.$$

The price-dividend ratio, $p \equiv S/D$ say, satisfies

$$p = E\left[m\frac{D'}{D}\left(1 + p'\right)\right].$$

The previous equation is a functional equation in $p(s)$, say:

$$p(s) = E\left[g\left(s', s\right)\left(1 + p\left(s'\right)\right) \mid s\right], \quad g\left(s', s\right) = \beta\left(\frac{s'}{s}\right)^{-\gamma}\left(\frac{D'}{D}\right)^{1-\gamma}.$$

A numerical solution can be implemented as follows. Create a grid, and define $p_j = p\left(s_j\right)$, $j = 1, \cdots, N$, for some N. We have

$$\begin{bmatrix} p_1 \\ \vdots \\ p_N \end{bmatrix} = \begin{bmatrix} b_1 \\ \vdots \\ b_N \end{bmatrix} + \begin{bmatrix} a_{11} & \cdots & a_{N1} \\ \vdots & \ddots & \vdots \\ a_{1N} & \cdots & a_{NN} \end{bmatrix}\begin{bmatrix} p_1 \\ \vdots \\ p_N \end{bmatrix},$$

$$b_i = \sum_{j=1}^{N} a_{ji}, \quad a_{ji} = g_{ji} \cdot p_{ji}, \quad g_{ji} = g\left(s_j, s_i\right), \quad p_{ji} = \Pr\left(s_j \mid s_i\right) \cdot \Delta s,$$

where Δs is the integration step; $s_1 = s_{\min}$; $s_N = s_{\max}$; $s_{\min}$ and $s_{\max}$ are the boundaries in the approximation; and $\Pr\left(s_j \mid s_i\right)$ is the transition density from state i to state j, for example, a Gaussian transition density. Let $p = [p_1 \ \cdots \ p_N]^{\top}$, $b = [b_1 \ \cdots \ b_N]^{\top}$, and let A be a matrix with elements a_{ji}. The solution is

$$p = (I - A)^{-1} b. \tag{8.A11}$$

The model can be simulated in the following manner. Let $\underline{s}$ and $\bar{s}$ be the boundaries of the underlying state process. Fix $\Delta s = \frac{\bar{s} - \underline{s}}{N}$. Draw states. State s^* is drawn. Then

(1) if $\min\{s^*-\underline{s}, \bar{s}-s^*\}=s^*-\underline{s}$, let k be the smallest integer close to $\frac{s^*-\underline{s}}{\Delta s}$. Let $s_{\min}=s^*-k\Delta s$, and $s_{\max}=s_{\min}+N\cdot\Delta s$.

(2) if $\min\{s^*-\underline{s}, \bar{s}-s^*\}=\bar{s}-s^*$, let k be the biggest integer close to $\frac{s^*-\underline{s}}{\Delta s}$. Let $s_{\max}=s^*+k\Delta s$, and $s_{\min}=s_{\max}-N\cdot\Delta s$.

The previous algorithm avoids interpolations and ensures that during the simulations, p is computed in correspondence of exactly the state s^* that is drawn. Precisely, once s^* is drawn, we proceed to the following two steps: (i) create the corresponding grid $s_1=s_{\min}$, $s_2=s_{\min}+\Delta s, \cdots, s_N=s_{\max}$ according to the previous rules; and (ii) compute the solution from eq. (8.A11). In this way, one has $p(s^*)$ at hand—the simulated price-dividend ratio when state s^* is drawn.

Appendix 8.B A Multifactor Security Model

Consider a reduced-form model where an asset price, S_i say, is a twice-differentiable function of a number of factors, $S_i=S_i(y)$, $i=1,\cdots,m$, and $y=[y_1,\cdots,y_d]^\top$ is a vector of factors. We assume that the ith asset pays off an instantaneous dividend $D_i=D_i(y)$ and that y is a diffusion process

$$dy_t=\varphi(y_t)\,dt+v(y_t)\,dW_t,$$

where φ is d valued, v is $d\times d$ valued, and W is a d-dimensional Brownian motion. We assume the number of assets does not exceed the number of factors, $m\leq d$, consistent with the framework in chapter 4. By Itô's lemma,

$$\frac{dS_i}{S_i}=\frac{LS_i}{S_i}dt+\frac{\overbrace{\nabla S_i}^{1\times d}}{S_i}\overbrace{v}^{d\times d}dW,$$

where LS_i is the infinitesimal operator. Let r_t be the instantaneous short-term rate. By no arbitrage and under regularity conditions, there exists a measurable d vector process λ, the vector of unit prices of risk associated with the fluctuations of the factors, such that

$$\begin{bmatrix}\frac{LS_1}{S_1}-r+\frac{D_1}{S_1}\\ \vdots\\ \frac{LS_m}{S_m}-r+\frac{D_m}{S_m}\end{bmatrix}=\underbrace{\sigma}_{m\times d}\underbrace{\lambda}_{d\times 1},\qquad\text{where }\sigma=\begin{bmatrix}\frac{\nabla S_1}{S_1}\\ \vdots\\ \frac{\nabla S_m}{S_m}\end{bmatrix}\cdot v. \tag{8.A12}$$

To simplify, we take this economy to be Markov, assuming that $r_t\equiv r(y_t)$ and $\lambda_t\equiv\lambda(y_t)$.

Eqs. (8.A12) add up to a system of m uncoupled partial differential equations, and the solution is one no-arbitrage price system, assuming no bubbles.

Appendix 8.C Arrow-Debreu Partial Differential Equations

We develop an interesting connection relying on the assumptions of section 8.4.2.2. Note that by eq. (8.A12), S is the solution to

$$LS+D=rS+\left(S_D\sigma_0 D+S_y v_1\right)\lambda_1+S_y v_2\lambda_2,\quad\forall(D,y)\in\mathbb{R}\times\mathbb{R}. \tag{8.A13}$$

Under regularity conditions, the Feynman–Kac representation of the solution to eq. (8.A13) is

$$S(D,y)=\int_0^{\infty} C(D,y,t)\,dt,$$

where

$$C(D,y,t)=\mathbb{E}\left(e^{-\int_0^t r(y_u)du}\cdot D_t\Big|\, D,y\right)=E\left(m_t\cdot D_t|\, D,y\right)$$

and where m is the pricing kernel $m_t=\frac{\xi_t}{\xi_0}$, $\xi_0=1$, with ξ denoting the stochastic discount factor, as usual.

Alternatively, we represent the price S under the physical probability. Given the previous assumptions, we have that ξ necessarily satisfies

$$\frac{d\xi_t}{\xi_t}=-r(y_t)\,dt-\lambda_1(y_t)\,dW_{1t}+\lambda_2(y_t)\,dW_{2t}. \tag{8.A14}$$

Next, define the undiscounted "Arrow-Debreu adjusted" asset price process, defined as:

$$w(D,y)\equiv\Upsilon(D,y)\cdot S(D,y),$$

where $\Upsilon(D,y)$ is as in eq. (8.12),

$$\Upsilon(D_t,y_t)=\xi_t e^{\int_0^t \rho(D_s,y_s)\,ds}.$$

By the results in section 8.4.2, we know that the following price representation holds true:

$$S_t\xi_t=E\left(\int_t^{\infty}\xi_s D_s ds\right),\quad t\geq 0.$$

Under regularity conditions, the previous equation can then be understood as the unique Feynman–Kac stochastic representation of the solution to the following partial differential equation:

$$Lw(D,y)+f(D,y)=\rho(D,y)w(D,y),\quad \forall(D,y)\in\mathbb{R}\times\mathbb{R},$$

where $f\equiv\Upsilon D$. Eq. (8.A13) then follows by the definition of $Lw_t\equiv\frac{d}{ds}E\left[\Upsilon S\right]\Big|_{s=t}$.

Appendix 8.D Volatility, Options, and Convexity

8.D.1 The Maximum Principle

Consider the differential equation

$$\frac{dx_\tau}{d\tau}=\phi_\tau,\ \tau\in(t,T),\quad x_T=0,\quad \text{sign}(\phi_\tau)=\text{constant on }\tau\in(t,T), \tag{8.A15}$$

where ϕ is such that x is bounded on (t,T). We claim that

$$\text{sign}(x_t)=-\,\text{sign}(\phi_t). \tag{8.A16}$$

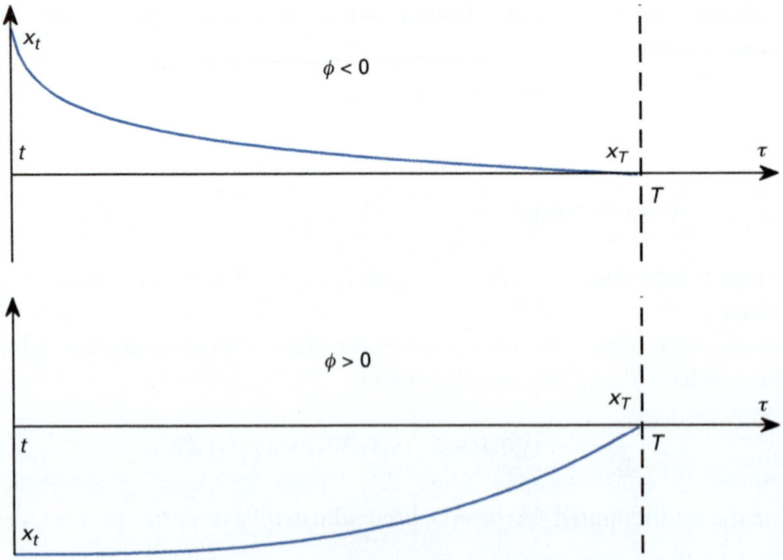

Figure 8.A1
Illustration of the maximum principle for ordinary differential equations.

Figure 8.A1 provides insights on (8.A16). If $\phi < 0$ for all $\tau \in (t, T)$, then x_τ is decreasing over time; but then, by the boundary condition $x_T = 0$, it follows that x_τ is positive on $\tau \in (t, T)$. Analytically, we have that

$$0 = x_T = x_t + \int_t^T \phi_\tau d\tau \Longrightarrow x_t = -\int_t^T \phi_\tau d\tau,$$

such that eq. (8.A16) holds.

Next, suppose that x_τ still satisfies eq. (8.A15), but that at the same time, x_τ is some function of a state variable y_τ and time

$$x_\tau = f(y_\tau, \tau),$$

where y_τ satisfies

$$\frac{dy_\tau}{d\tau} = b_\tau, \quad \tau \in (t, T).$$

Assuming enough regularity conditions, we have that

$$\frac{dx}{d\tau} = \left(\frac{\partial}{\partial\tau} + L\right) f, \quad \tau \in (t, T), \tag{8.A17}$$

where $Lf = \frac{\partial f}{\partial y} b$. Therefore, comparing eq. (8.A15) with eq. (8.A17) leaves

$$\left(\frac{\partial}{\partial\tau} + L\right) f = \phi, \quad \tau \in (t, T). \tag{8.A18}$$

Because $x_T = f(y_T, T) = 0$, the solution to eq. (8.A18) is

$$f(y_t, t) = -\int_t^T \phi_\tau d\tau. \tag{8.A19}$$

Therefore, and extending eq. (8.A16), we have the following result. Suppose that $x_T = f(y_T, T) = 0$ and that sign $(\phi_\tau) =$ constant on $\tau \in (t, T)$. Then, by eq. (8.A19),

$$\text{sign}\left(f\left(y_t, t\right)\right) = -\ \text{sign}\left(\phi_t\right).$$

These results can be extended to stochastic differential equations through the Feynman–Kac representation theorem (see chapter 4). Consider a more general version of eq. (8.A18), one that typical arises in models with Brownian motions:

$$0 = \left(\frac{\partial}{\partial \tau} + L - k\right) G + D, \quad \tau \in (t, T). \tag{8.A20}$$

Let

$$y_\tau \equiv e^{-\int_t^\tau k_u du} G_\tau + \int_t^\tau e^{-\int_t^u k_s ds} D_u du.$$

We claim that under regularity conditions, if eq. (8.A20) holds, then y is a martingale. Indeed,

$$\begin{aligned} dy_\tau &= -k_\tau e^{-\int_t^\tau k_u du} G_\tau d\tau + e^{-\int_t^\tau k_u du} dG_\tau + e^{-\int_t^\tau k_u du} D_\tau d\tau \\ &= -k_\tau e^{-\int_t^\tau k_u du} G_\tau d\tau + e^{-\int_t^\tau k_u du} \left[\left(\frac{\partial}{\partial \tau} + L\right) G_\tau\right] d\tau + e^{-\int_t^\tau k_u du} D_\tau d\tau + dM_\tau \\ &= e^{-\int_t^\tau k_u du} \left[-k_\tau G_\tau + \left(\frac{\partial}{\partial \tau} + L\right) G_\tau + D_\tau\right] d\tau + dM_\tau \\ &= dM_\tau, \end{aligned}$$

where M_τ is a local martingale and the last equality holds due to eq. (8.A20). But if y is a martingale,

$$y_t = G_t = E_t\left(y_T\right) = E_t\left(e^{-\int_t^T k_u du} G_T\right) + E_t\left(\int_t^T e^{-\int_t^\tau k_s ds} D_\tau d\tau\right),$$

where E_t is the expectation taken given the information at time t. Now, assume that $G_T = 0$ and that sign (D_τ) is constant for each $\tau \in (t, T)$. Then, sign $(y_\tau) =$ sign (D_t) for each τ.

We are now ready to use the maximum principle to study a few problems arising in this chapter.

8.D.2 Increasing Risk

We study the relation between contingent claims and the volatility of the fundamentals in the following setting:

$$c(x, T - s) \equiv \mathbb{E}\left(e^{-\int_s^T \rho(x_t) dt} \cdot \psi\left(x_T\right) \middle| x_s = x\right) \tag{8.A21}$$

where x is a diffusion process with drift b and diffusion a. We then have the following theorem.

Theorem 8.A1 (Increasing risk). *Consider two economies A and B with two fundamental volatilities a_A and a_B, and let $\pi_i(x) \equiv a_i(x) \cdot \lambda^i(x)$ and $\rho_i(x)$ $(i = A, B)$ be the corresponding risk premium and discount rate. If $a_A > a_B$, the price c^A in economy A is lower than the price price c^B in economy B whenever, for all $(x, \tau) \in \mathbb{R} \times [0, T]$,*

$$V(x,\tau) \equiv -\left(\rho_A(x) - \rho_B(x)\right) c^B(x,\tau) - \left(\pi_A(x) - \pi_B(x)\right) c^B_x(x,\tau) + \frac{1}{2}\left(a_A^2(x) - a_B^2(x)\right) c^B_{xx}(x,\tau) < 0. \tag{8.A22}$$

If X is the price of a traded asset, $\pi_A = \pi_B$. In addition, if ρ is constant, c is decreasing (increasing) in volatility whenever it is concave (convex) in x. This phenomenon is related to the "convexity effect" discussed in the main text. If X is not a traded risk, two additional effects are activated. The first effect relates to a discounting adjustment and is apparent through the first term in the definition of V. The second effect reflects risk premium adjustments and corresponds to the second term.

Proof of theorem 8.A1. The function $c(x, T-s)$ in eq. (8.A21) is the solution to

$$0 = -c_2(x, T-s) + L^* c(x, T-s) - \rho(x) c(x, T-s), \tag{8.A23}$$

subject to the boundary condition $c(x,0) = \psi(x)$, where $L^* c(x,u) = \frac{1}{2} a^2(x)\, c_{xx}(x,u) + b(x) c_x(x,u)$ and subscripts denote partial derivatives. Clearly, c^A and c^B are both solutions to eq. (8.A23) but with different coefficients. Let $b_A(x) \equiv b_0(x) - \pi_A(x)$, where b_0 is the drift under the physical probability. The price difference $\Delta c(x,\tau) \equiv c^A(x,\tau) - c^B(x,\tau)$ is the solution to

$$0 = -\Delta c_2(x, T-s) + \frac{1}{2}\sigma_A^2(x) \Delta c_{xx}(x, T-s) + b_A(x) \Delta c_x(x, T-s) - \rho_A(x) \Delta c(x, T-s) + V(x, T-s),$$

with $\Delta c(x, 0) = 0$ and V is as in eq. (8.A22) of the theorem. The result follows by the maximum principle. □

8.D.3 Stocks As Options

Chapter 1 (see section 1.4.3) introduces a standard pricing problem in a two-period market for a cash flow $\psi(\tilde{y})$, a function of some random variable $\tilde{y}$, to be paid in the second period. Assuming the yield curve is flat at zero, the fair value for this claim is $\bar{c} \equiv \mathbb{E}[\psi(\tilde{y})]$. We now consider a dynamic extension of this problem, in which $\tilde{y} = y_T$ for some future date T and $\tilde{y}$ is a random process, with $\tilde{y}_0 = y$, such that the price of the claim is now

$$c(y) = \mathbb{E}\left(\psi(y_T) \middle| y\right). \tag{8.A24}$$

The two pricing problems, $\mathbb{E}\left(\psi(y_T) \middle| y\right)$ and $\mathbb{E}(\psi(\tilde{y}))$, are clearly not the same. But they bear similarities. For example, suppose that (i) y is the price of a traded asset and (ii) y is a proportional process in that the risk neutral distribution of $\tilde{g} \equiv \frac{y_T}{y}$ is independent of y. Under these assumptions, the properties of $c(y)$ would be similar to $\bar{c}$: $c(y)$ increases following a mean-preserving spread in $\tilde{g}$ whenever ψ is convex. We now examine cases in which these assumptions may not hold.

Consider the following problem.

Canonical pricing problem. *Let y_t be the solution to*

$$dy_t = b(y_t)\,dt + a(y_t)\,d\bar{W}_t, \tag{8.A25}$$

where $\bar{W}$ is a multidimensional $\bar{P}$ Brownian motion (for some $\bar{P}$) and b and a are some given functions. Let ψ and ρ be two twice continuously differentiable positive functions, and define

$$c(y,T) \equiv \bar{\mathbb{E}}\left(e^{-\int_0^T \rho(y_t)dt} \cdot \psi(y_T)\Big| y\right). \tag{8.A25}$$

If $\bar{P} = Q$, the risk neutral probability, and ρ is the short-term rate, then $c(y,T)$ may be interpreted as the price of a derivative with payoff $\psi(\cdot)$. Further, note that if y_t is the price of a traded asset, the drift in eq. (8.A25) is $b(y) = y\rho(y)$. Instead, assuming y_t is not a traded risk, $b(y) = b_0(y) - a(y)\lambda(y)$, where b_0 denotes the drift of y_t under the physical probability and λ is a risk premium. This canonical pricing problem, then, covers a number of interesting cases. For example, we may assume $\psi(y) = 1$, $\rho(y) = y$, where y is a short-term rate, in which case c is the price of a zero coupon bond price.

However, $\bar{P}$ may not necessarily be the risk neutral probability. Consider the following "scale-invariant" economy, that is, an economy in which "price multiples" are independent of the dividend level. An asset distributing a dividend D, which is available for trading, is the solution to

$$\begin{cases} \dfrac{dD_t}{D_t} = m(y_t)\,dt + \sigma_0 dW_{1t} \\ dy_t = \varphi(y_t)\,dt + v_1(y_t)\,dW_{1t} + v_2(y_t)\,dW_{2t} \end{cases} \tag{8.A26}$$

where W_1 and W_2 are standard Brownian motions. This example generalizes that in section 8.5 because expected dividend growth, m, is now driven by the state variable y_t.

Note that, in this model, the distribution of $\frac{D_t}{D}$ is independent of D. We assume that the short-term rate r depends only on y_t. These assumptions imply that the price-dividend ratio is only a function of the current state, similar to section 8.4.1. However, due to stochastic expected dividend growth, the expression for p is slightly more general than that in eq. (8.11). It is

$$p(y) = \int_0^\infty c(y,t)\,dt, \tag{8.A27}$$

where, denoting as usual the risk-adjusted discount rate with $\mathcal{R}(y)$,

$$\begin{aligned} c(y,t) &\equiv \mathbb{E}\left(e^{-\int_0^t r(y_u)du}\frac{D_t}{D}\Big| y\right) \\ &= \mathbb{E}\left[e^{\int_0^t m(y_u)du}e^{-\int_0^t \mathcal{R}(y_u)du}\left(e^{-\frac{1}{2}\sigma_0^2 t + \sigma_0 \hat{W}_{1t}}\right)\Big| y\right] \\ &= \bar{\mathbb{E}}\left(e^{\int_0^t m(y_u)du}e^{-\int_0^t \mathcal{R}(y_u)du}\Big| y\right) \end{aligned} \tag{8.A28}$$

and $\mathbb{E}$ denotes, as usual, the expectation under Q, under which D and y satisfy

$$\begin{cases} \frac{dD_t}{D_t} = (m(y_t) - \sigma_0 \lambda_1(y_t))\, dt + \sigma_0 d\hat{W}_{1t} \\ dy_t = \left(\varphi(y_t) - \sum_{i=1}^{2} v_i(y_t) \lambda_i(y_t)\right) dt + v_1(y_t)\, d\hat{W}_{1t} + v_2(y_t)\, d\hat{W}_{2t} \end{cases}$$

where $\hat{W}_{it}$ are two Brownian motions under Q. The third line of eq. (8.A28) is obtained with a change of probability, and $\bar{\mathbb{E}}$ is the expectation taken under a conveniently changed probability $\bar{Q}$, defined by the Radon-Nikodym derivative,

$$\left.\frac{d\bar{Q}}{dQ}\right|_{F_t} = e^{-\frac{1}{2}\sigma_0^2 t + \sigma_0 \hat{W}_{1t}}, \tag{8.A29}$$

where F_t denotes the information set as of time t generated by $\hat{W}_{1t}$. By Girsanov's theorem, we have that under $\bar{Q}$,

$$dy_t = \underbrace{\left(\varphi(y_t) - \sum_{i=1}^{2} v_i(y_t) \lambda_i(y_t) + \sigma_0 v_1(y_t)\right)}_{\equiv \bar{\varphi}(y_t)} dt + v_1(y_t)\, d\bar{W}_{1t} + v_2(y_t)\, d\bar{W}_{2t}; \tag{8.A30}$$

$\bar{W}_i$ are Brownian motions under $\bar{Q}$.

Our canonical pricing problem allows us to analyze properties of prices relating to long-lived assets through those relating to c in eq. (8.A28), with y as in eq. (8.A30), once we set

$$\psi(y) \equiv 1; \quad \rho(y) \equiv \mathcal{R}(y) - m(y); \quad b(y) = \bar{\varphi}(y). \tag{8.A31}$$

The next theorem characterizes slope and convexity properties of the price c in the canonical pricing problem.

Theorem 8.A2. *We have*

(i) *Suppose that $\psi' > 0$; then, c is increasing whenever $\rho' \leq 0$. Further, if $\psi' = 0$, then c is decreasing (resp. increasing) whenever $\rho' > 0$ (resp. < 0).*
(ii) *Suppose that $\psi'' \leq 0$ (resp. $\psi'' \geq 0$) and that c is increasing; then, c is concave (resp. convex) whenever $b'' < 2\rho'$ (resp. $b'' > 2\rho'$) and $\rho'' \geq 0$ (resp. $\rho'' \leq 0$). Finally, if $b'' = 2\rho'$, c is concave (resp. convex) whenever $\psi'' < 0$ (resp. > 0) and $\rho'' \geq 0$ (resp. ≤ 0).*

This theorem generalizes previous results on monotonicity of option prices derived by Bergman, Grundy, and Wiener (1996). By the so-called *no-crossing property* of a diffusion, y is not decreasing in its initial condition y. Therefore, c inherits the same monotonicity features of ψ if discounting does not operate adversely as in the first part of the theorem. This simple observation allows us to address monotonicity properties of long-lived asset prices (see section 8.5).

Theorem 8.A2 generalizes a number of existing results on option price convexity. First, assume that ρ is constant and that y_t is the price of a traded asset such that $\rho' = b'' = 0$. Part (ii) then says that convexity of ψ propagates to convexity of c, a classical result surveyed earlier. Part (ii) also characterizes convexity in a more general context. Suppose, for example, that $\psi'' = \rho' = 0$ and that y_t is not a traded risk. Then, this theorem says that c

inherits convexity of the drift of y. As a final example, part (ii) extends a result in Mele (2003) on zero coupon bonds: let $\psi(y)=1$ and $\rho(y)=y$, such that c is the price of a zero coupon bond, where y is the short-term rate (see chapter 13 for details). By part (ii), c is convex whenever $b''<2$. Appendix 8.D.4 provides further details and intuition for this bound. Thus, option prices rely on both discounting and nonlinearities affecting the drift of the state variables when the underlying fundamentals are not traded. We shall now provide the proof of this result.

Proof of theorem 8.A2. By differentiating eq. (8.A23) two times with respect to x, we find that that $c^{(1)}(x,\tau)\equiv c_x(x,\tau)$ and $c^{(2)}(x,\tau)\equiv c_{xx}(x,\tau)$ are solutions to

$$\begin{aligned}0=&-c_2^{(1)}(x,T-s)+\frac{1}{2}a^2(x)c_{xx}^{(1)}(x,T-s)+\left(b(x)+\frac{1}{2}(a^2(x))'\right)c_x^{(1)}(x,T-s)\\&-\left(\rho(x)-b'(x)\right)c^{(1)}(x,T-s)-\rho'(x)c(x,T-s)\end{aligned}$$

and

$$\begin{aligned}0=&-c_2^{(2)}(x,T-s)+\frac{1}{2}a^2(x)c_{xx}^{(2)}(x,T-s)+\left(b(x)+(a^2(x))'\right)c_x^{(2)}(x,T-s)\\&-\left(\rho(x)-2b'(x)-\frac{1}{2}(a^2(x))''\right)c^{(2)}(x,T-s)\\&-\left(2\rho'(x)-b''(x)\right)c^{(1)}(x,T-s)-\rho''(x)c(x,T-s),\end{aligned}$$

subject to the boundary conditions $c^{(1)}(x,0)=\psi'(x)$ and $c^{(2)}(x,0)=\psi''(x)$. By results in appendix 8.D.1, $c^{(1)}(x,T-s)>0$ (resp. <0) whenever $\psi'(x)>0$ (resp. <0) and $\rho'(x)<0$ (resp. >0). This completes the proof of part (i); the proof of part (ii) is similar. □

Remark 8.A2 (Alternative proof). Related conclusions rely on the convexity property of the *payoff function* and a result due to Hajek (1985). This result says that if ψ is increasing and convex and x_1 and x_2 are two diffusion processes—both starting off from the same origin, with integrable drifts b_1 and b_2 and volatilities a_1 and a_2—then $E(\psi(x_{1\tau}))\le E(\psi(x_{2\tau}))$ whenever $b_1(t)\le b_2(t)$ and $a_1(t)\le a_2(t)$ for all $t\in(0,\tau)$. This result generalizes classic comparison theorems (e.g., Karatzas and Shreve, 1991, 291–295), where ψ is an increasing function and $a_1\equiv a_2$.

Remark 8.A3 (Bounds on convexity). An inspection of the previous proof reveals that prices are concave under less restrictive conditions than that given in part (ii) of the theorem. We would only need that

$$-\left(2\rho'(x)-b''(x)\right)c^{(1)}(x,T-s)-\rho''(x)c(x,T-s)<0$$

or that

$$\rho''(x)>-\left(2\rho'(x)-b''(x)\right)\frac{c^{(1)}(x,T-s)}{c(x,T-s)}. \tag{8.A32}$$

Assuming that $\rho'<0$ such that $\frac{c^{(1)}}{c}>0$, the inequality (8.A32) imposes a theoretical upper bound to the convexity of discount rates that ensure concavity of prices.

Additional notes

(1) The predictions on convexity around eq. (8.A24) are consistent with the celebrated Black and Scholes (1973) formula as further explained in chapter 11. This point was originally made by Jagannathan (1984, 429–430). As also explained in chapter 11, Bajeux-Besnainou and Rochet (1996, section 5); Bergman, Grundy, and Wiener (1996); El Karoui, Jeanblanc-Picqué, and Shreve (1998); and Romano and Touzi (1997) generalize these results to models with stochastic volatility.

(2) For regularity conditions underlying the Feynman–Kac theorem in infinite horizon settings and finance applications, see, for example, Huang and Pagès (1992, 53, theorem 3) and Wang (1993, 202, lemma 1). Huang and Pagès (1992, 41, proposition 1) also contains regularity conditions regarding the holds of Girsanov's theorem in infinite horizon settings.

(3) The derivation of eq. (8.A28) relies on a change in probability, which enables one to eliminate the $e^{-\frac{1}{2}\sigma_0^2\tau+\sigma_0\hat{W}_{1\tau}}$ term. This term is due to the positive correlation between dy and dD. The density of y under $\bar{Q}$ is right-shifted, compared with the density under Q, precisely due to this positive correlation.

(4) Kijima (2002) produces a counterexample where convexity of option prices might break down even if payoffs are convex in the underlying–and *traded*–assets. This property relies on an extension of the Black–Scholes model where the dividend process makes the drift of the underlying price concave. Theorem 8.A2 clarifies the origins of this property.

8.D.4 Bond Price Convexity Revisited

Consider a short-term rate process r_τ, and let $u(r_0, T)$ be the price of a bond expiring at time T when the current short-term rate is r_0:

$$u(r_0,T)=\mathbb{E}\left(e^{-\int_0^T r_\tau d\tau}\middle| r_0\right).$$

As pointed out in appendix 8.D.3, theorem 8.A2 (ii) implies that scalar models of the short-term rate (such as those dealt with in chapter 13) predict that $u_{11}(r_0,T)<0$ whenever $b''<2$, where b is the risk neutral drift of r. We now provide an alternative derivation under a set of simplifying assumptions. By eq. (6) in Mele (2003, 685),

$$u_{11}(r_0,T)=\mathbb{E}\left[\left(\left(\int_0^T \frac{\partial r_\tau}{\partial r_0}d\tau\right)^2-\int_0^T \frac{\partial^2 r_\tau}{\partial r_0^2}d\tau\right)e^{-\int_0^T r_\tau d\tau}\right].$$

Hence $u_{11}(r_0,T)>0$ whenever

$$\int_0^T \frac{\partial^2 r_\tau}{\partial r_0^2}d\tau<\left(\int_0^T \frac{\partial r_\tau}{\partial r_0}d\tau\right)^2. \tag{8.A33}$$

We assume that r_τ is solution to

$$dr_\tau=b(r_\tau)dt+a_0 r_\tau dW_\tau,$$

where a_0 is a constant. We have

$$\frac{\partial r_\tau}{\partial r_0} = \exp\left(\int_0^\tau b'(r_u)du - \frac{1}{2}a_0^2\tau + a_0 W_\tau\right) \quad \text{and} \quad \frac{\partial^2 r_\tau}{\partial r_0^2} = \frac{\partial r_\tau}{\partial r_0}\left[\int_0^\tau b''(r_u)\frac{\partial r_u}{\partial r_0}du\right]. \tag{8.A34}$$

Therefore, if $b'' < 0$, then $\partial^2 r_\tau/\partial r_0^2 < 0$, and by the inequality in (8.A33), $u_{11} > 0$.

This result can be improved. Suppose that $b'' < 2$ instead of $b'' < 0$. By the second of eqs. (8.A34),

$$\frac{\partial^2 r_\tau}{\partial r_0^2} < 2\frac{\partial r_\tau}{\partial r_0}\int_0^\tau \frac{\partial r_u}{\partial r_0}du,$$

and consequently,

$$\int_0^T \frac{\partial^2 r_\tau}{\partial r_0^2}d\tau < 2\int_0^T \frac{\partial r_\tau}{\partial r_0}\left(\int_0^\tau \frac{\partial r_u}{\partial r_0}du\right)d\tau = \left(\int_0^T \frac{\partial r_u}{\partial r_0}du\right)^2,$$

which is the inequality in (8.A33).

8.D.5 A "Macro-Asset" Derivative

We discuss an example regarding a highly conceptual asset, a "macro-asset" option, that is, one asset that delivers payoffs linked to aggregate outcomes. Let c_t be some exogenously given consumption process. The owner of the option has the right to receive a twice differentiable payoff $\psi(c_T)$ at some date T, where ψ is increasing and convex. We assume that c_t is solution to

$$\frac{dc_t}{c_t} = g_t dt$$

and that consumption growth satisfies

$$dg_t = \varphi(g_t)\,dt + v(g_t)\,dW_t,$$

where φ and v are some well-behaved functions and W_t is a standard Brownian motion. Let $p(c,g,t)$ be the option price when the state at t is $(c_t, g_t) = (c,g)$. We assume that p is as differentiable as needed below, that interest rates are constant, and that all agents are risk neutral.

By the usual connection between partial differential equations and conditional expectations (see chapter 4), the price $p(c,g,t)$ is the solution to

$$0 = \frac{\partial p}{\partial t} + gcp_c + \frac{1}{2}v^2 p_{gg} + \varphi p_g - rp, \quad \text{for all } c, g \text{ and } t \in [0,T), \tag{8.A35}$$

with the boundary condition $p(c,g,T) = \psi(c)$ for all c, g (subscripts denote partial differentiation).

First, we study the monotonicity of $p(c,g,t)$ with respect to both c and g, following two approaches. The first approach relies on the so-called *no-crossing property* of a diffusion process. Note that

$$p(c,g,t)=e^{-r(T-t)}\mathrm{E}\left[\psi\left(c_t\cdot e^{\int_t^T g_u du}\right)\Big| c_t=c,\ g_t=g\right]. \tag{8.A36}$$

Since ψ is increasing, p is increasing in c. Further, the no-crossing property of g implies that g_u is increasing in the initial condition g_t. Therefore, $p(c,g)$ is also increasing in g.

To analyze the convexity of p with respect to g, differentiate eq. (8.A35) and its boundary condition with respect to c, and find that $w\equiv p_c$ is the solution to

$$0=\frac{\partial w}{\partial t}+gcw_c+\frac{1}{2}v^2w_{gg}+\varphi w_g-(r-g)w,\quad \text{for all } c,g \text{ and } t\in[0,T),$$

with the boundary condition $w(c,g,T)=\psi'(c)$ for all c,g. The Feynman–Kac representation of the solution to the previous equation is

$$p_c(c,g,t)=e^{-r(T-t)}\mathrm{E}\left(e^{\int_t^T g_u du}\cdot\psi'(c_T)\Big| c_t=c,\ g_t=g\right), \tag{8.A37}$$

which is positive by the assumption that $\psi'>0$. This confirms the monotonicity properties established previously through no-crossing arguments. So, when is $p(c,g,t)$ *convex* in g? By differentiating eq. (8.A35) with respect to g, one obtains that $u\equiv p_g$ is the solution to

$$0=\frac{\partial u}{\partial t}+gcu_c+\frac{1}{2}v^2u_{gg}+(\varphi+\frac{1}{2}(v^2)')u_g-(r-\varphi')u+cp_c, \quad \text{for all } c,g \text{ and } t\in[0,T), \tag{8.A38}$$

with the boundary condition $u(c,g,T)=0$ for all c,g. By the Feynman–Kac representation theorem,

$$p_g(c,g,t)=\mathrm{E}\left(\int_t^T e^{-r(u-t)+\int_t^u\varphi'(g_s)ds}c_u p_c(c_u,g_u,u)du\Big| c_t=c,\ g_t=g\right).$$

By eq. (8.A37), $p_c>0$. Hence, p is increasing in g. By theorem 8.A2, p is strictly convex in g whenever the drift function of g is weakly convex. Indeed, by differentiating eq. (8.A38) with respect to g, we obtain that $\omega\equiv p_{gg}$ is the solution to

$$\frac{\partial\omega}{\partial t}+gc\omega_c+\frac{1}{2}v^2\omega_{gg}+(\varphi+(v^2)')\omega_g-(r-2\varphi'-\frac{1}{2}(v^2)'')\omega+k, \quad \text{for all } c,g \text{ and } t\in[0,T), \tag{8.A39}$$

where

$$k(c,g,t)\equiv 2cp_{cg}(c,g,t)+\varphi''(g)p_g(c,g,t), \tag{8.A40}$$

and the boundary condition $\omega(c,g,T)=0$ for all c,g.

By eq. (8.A37), we have that $p_c(c,g,t)=e^{-r(T-t)}\mathrm{E}_t\left(\frac{c_T}{c_t}\psi'(c_T)\right)$. Thus p_c is increasing in g by the assumption that ψ is increasing and convex and by the no-crossing property of a diffusion, by which g_u is increasing in the initial condition g_t. Therefore, $p_{cg} > 0$. Further, $p_g > 0$. Therefore, $k(c,g,t) > 0$ whenever $\varphi''(g) \geq 0$. By the Feynman–Kac theorem, then, p is *convex* in g whenever $\varphi''(g) \geq 0$.

The previous conclusions can hold even with a concave payoff function, say, $\psi(c) = \ln c$. In this case, eq. (8.A37) implies that $p_c(c,g,t) = e^{-r(T-t)}\frac{1}{c}$ such that the function k in eq. (8.A40) collapses to $k(c,g,t) = \varphi''(g)p_g(c,g,t)$. That is, the price $p(c,g,t)$ is convex (resp. concave) in g whenever φ is convex (resp., concave) in g. Note then that the price is linear in g whenever $\varphi'' = 0$ as can easily be verified by replacing $\psi(c) = \ln c$ into eq. (8.A36), leaving

$$p(c,g,t) = e^{-r(T-t)} \ln c + e^{-r(T-t)} E\left(\int_t^T g_u du \middle| g_t = g \right).$$

Appendix 8.E Linearity-Generating Processes

The focus of this chapter is a search for pricing kernels that make models qualitatively consistent with countercyclical statistics. In part, this search relies on theoretical test conditions such as those in appendix 8.D. We may actually use these conditions (e.g., theorem 8.A2) for another and somehow surprising purpose: searching for asset pricing models that have a closed-form solution. The idea is simple. Theorem 8.A2 provides conditions under which price-dividend ratios can be either concave or convex in the state variables driving them. Specifically, consider the expression for the price-dividend ratio in eqs. (8.A27)–(8.A30). In terms of the canonical pricing problem of appendix 8.D.3, we set the expressions in eqs. (8.A31) (reported here for convenience) as

$$\psi(y) \equiv 1, \quad \rho(y) \equiv \mathcal{R}(y) - m(y), \quad b(y) = \bar{\varphi}(y),$$

where, as usual, $\mathcal{R}(y) \equiv r(y) + \sigma_0 \lambda_{CF}(y)$ and, by eq. (8.A30),

$$\bar{\varphi}(y) \equiv \varphi(y) - \sum_{i=1}^{2} v_i(y)\lambda_i(y) + \sigma_0 v_1(y)$$

and $\varphi(y)$ denotes the drift of y under the physical probability.

Now, consider theorem 8.A2, and assume that (i) $\bar{\varphi}'' = 2(\mathcal{R}' - m')$. Then, c is concave (resp., convex) in y if (ii) $(\mathcal{R}'' - m'') \geq 0$ (resp., ≤ 0). But closed-form solutions are not available when these conditions are satisfied. How about ruling out the conditions leading to concavity *and* convexity? Obviously, then, price-dividend ratios must be affine. That is, the price-dividend ratios are affine in y if

$$\bar{\varphi}'' = 2(\mathcal{R}' - m') \quad \text{and} \quad \mathcal{R}'' - m'' = 0. \tag{8.A41}$$

Gabaix (2009) notes that price-dividend ratios are affine in the state variables driving them when the drift of these variables is quadratic. His remarks are consistent with theorem 8.A2 and the two conditions in (8.A41). In fact, Gabaix develops a theory of "linearity-generating processes," one that generalizes the single-state variable framework underlying theorem 8.A2 and related conditions in (8.A41). To illustrate, consider the model of external habit formation by Menzly, Santos, and Veronesi (2004). This model fits the class of linearity-generating processes. In detail, in this model, a representative agent maximizes

$$U = E\left(\int_0^\infty e^{-\rho t}\ln(c_t - x_t)\,dt\right), \tag{8.A42}$$

where x_t is the external habit. Relative risk aversion equals the inverse of the surplus consumption ratio, $\frac{1}{\mathcal{S}_t}$, with $\mathcal{S}_t = \frac{c_t - x_t}{c_t}$, which in equilibrium equals $\frac{D_t - x_t}{D_t}$, where D is consumption endowment. Menzly, Santos, and Veronesi assume that the surplus consumption ratio is a continuous time autoregressive process and the solution to

$$d\left(\frac{1}{\mathcal{S}_t}\right) = \beta\left(\frac{1}{\bar{s}} - \frac{1}{\mathcal{S}_t}\right)dt - \alpha\left(\frac{1}{\mathcal{S}_t} - \frac{1}{v}\right)\sigma_0 dW_t \tag{8.A43}$$

for some constants β, $\bar{s}$, α, and v. It can be shown that if α is small enough, $\mathcal{S}_t \in (0, v)$. Ljungqvist and Uhlig (2000) rely on similar assumptions to model productivity shocks in their model of catching up with the Joneses.

We shall verify that the two conditions in (8.A41) hold in this model. First, note that eq. (8.A43) implies that the surplus consumption ratio satisfies

$$d\mathcal{S}_t = \mathcal{S}_t\left(\beta\left(1 - \tfrac{\mathcal{S}_t}{\bar{s}}\right) + \alpha^2\sigma_0^2\left(1 - \tfrac{\mathcal{S}_t}{v}\right)^2\right)dt + \alpha\sigma_0\mathcal{S}_t\left(1 - \tfrac{\mathcal{S}_t}{v}\right)dW_t,$$

such that

$$\bar{\varphi}(\mathcal{S}) = \mathcal{S}\left(\beta\left(1 - \tfrac{\mathcal{S}}{\bar{s}}\right) + \alpha^2\sigma_0^2\left(1 - \tfrac{\mathcal{S}}{v}\right)^2\right) + (\sigma_0 - \lambda_{\text{CF}}(\mathcal{S}))\,\alpha\sigma_0\mathcal{S}\left(1 - \frac{\mathcal{S}}{v}\right).$$

By the results in section 8.4, the market Sharpe ratio is $\lambda(D, x) = \frac{1}{\mathcal{S}}(\sigma_0 - \frac{v(D,x)}{D})$, where $v(D, x)$ is the instantaneous volatility of the habit level, $x = D(1 - \mathcal{S})$ and by Itô's lemma equals $v(D, x) = D\sigma_0(1 - \mathcal{S}) - D\text{Vol}(d\mathcal{S})$, where $\text{Vol}(d\mathcal{S}) \equiv \alpha\sigma_0\mathcal{S}\left(1 - \frac{\mathcal{S}}{v}\right)$. Therefore, the market Sharpe ratio is

$$\lambda_{\text{CF}}(\mathcal{S}) \equiv \lambda(D, x) = \sigma_0\left(1 + \alpha\left(1 - \frac{\mathcal{S}}{v}\right)\right)$$

and is countercyclical. Finally, and again by the results in section 8.4,

$$r(\mathcal{S}) = \rho + g_0 - \sigma_0^2 + \beta\left(1 - \frac{\mathcal{S}}{\bar{s}}\right) - \sigma_0^2\alpha\left(1 - \frac{\mathcal{S}}{v}\right).$$

Therefore, we have that

$$\bar{\varphi}''(\mathcal{S}) = -2\frac{\beta}{\bar{s}}, \quad \mathcal{R}'(\mathcal{S}) = -\frac{\beta}{\bar{s}}, \quad m'(\mathcal{S}) = m''(\mathcal{S}) = 0,$$

implying that the two conditions in (8.A41) are satisfied and, thus, that the price-dividend ratio is affine in $\mathcal{S}$.

We may actually verify that the price-dividend ratio is affine in $\mathcal{S}$ through a direct calculation. Let $u(c, x) \equiv \ln(c - x)$ with $c = D$. By standard results, the price-dividend

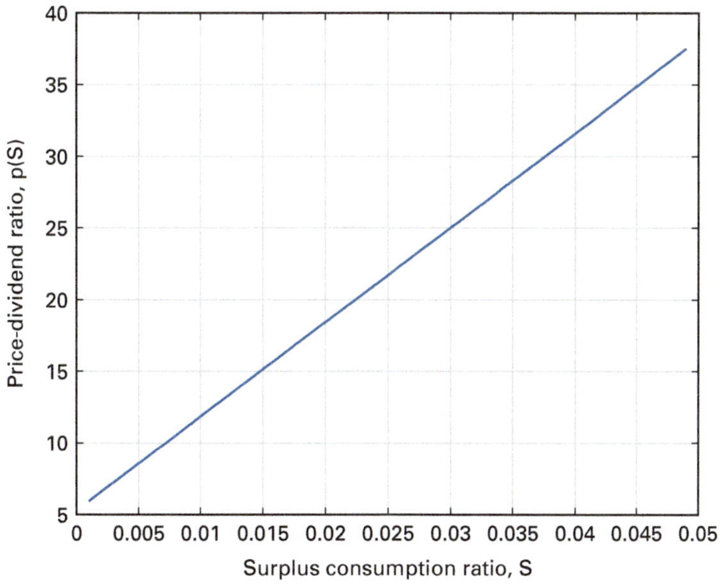

Figure 8.A2
The price-dividend ratio for an aggregate consumption claim predicted by Menzly, Santos, and Veronesi's (2004) model of external habit formation as a function of the surplus consumption ratio, $\mathcal{S}$ (see eq. (8.A44)), with parameter values, $\rho=0.04$, $\beta=0.15$, and $\bar{s}=0.03$.

ratio is

$$\begin{aligned} p\left(\mathcal{S}_0\right) &\equiv \mathrm{E}\left(\int_0^{\infty} e^{-\rho t} \frac{u_c\left(c_t, x_t\right)}{u_c\left(c_0, x_0\right)} \frac{c_t}{c_0} dt\right) \\ &= \mathcal{S}_0 \cdot \int_0^{\infty} e^{-\rho t} \mathrm{E}\left(\frac{1}{\mathcal{S}_t}\right) dt \\ &= \mathcal{S}_0 \cdot \int_0^{\infty} e^{-\rho t}\left(\frac{1}{\bar{s}}+e^{-\beta t}\left(\frac{1}{\mathcal{S}_0}-\frac{1}{\bar{s}}\right)\right) dt \\ &= \frac{1}{\rho+\beta}+\frac{\beta}{\rho \bar{s}(\rho+\beta)} \mathcal{S}_0 \end{aligned} \tag{8.A44}$$

and is plotted in figure 8.A2 as a function of the current surplus consumption ratio.

Appendix 8.F Habit

We derive eq. (8.26) by making a slightly more general assumption that the short-term rate we wish to come up with is affine in $\ln \mathcal{S}$, meaning that the last two terms in eq. (8.25) sum up to

$$\gamma(1-\phi)\left(\bar{s}_l-\ln \mathcal{S}\right)-\frac{1}{2} \gamma^2 \sigma_0^2(1+l(\mathcal{S}))^2=-\text{const.}+b\left(\bar{s}_l-\ln \mathcal{S}\right) \tag{8.A45}$$

for some b and where the constant (const.) is to be determined. The working paper version of Campbell and Cochrane (1999) considers exactly this case.

Define the log of the surplus ratio as

$$s_{l,\tau} \equiv \ln\left(1 - e^{x_{l,\tau} - c_{l,\tau}}\right), \tag{8.A46}$$

where $s_{l,\tau} \equiv \ln \mathcal{S}_\tau, x_l \equiv \ln x$, and $c_l \equiv \ln c$. Consider its first-order Taylor's expansion around the steady state $\overline{x_l - c_l} \equiv E\left(x_{l,\tau} - c_{l,\tau}\right)$,

$$s_{l,\tau} \approx \bar{s}_l + \left(1 - \frac{1}{\bar{s}}\right)\left(x_{l,\tau} - c_{l,\tau} - \overline{x_l - c_l}\right), \tag{8.A47}$$

where $\bar{s}_l \equiv \ln\left(1 - e^{\overline{x_l - c_l}}\right)$ and $\bar{s} \equiv e^{\bar{s}_l}$. Consider the discrete-time version of eq. (8.22),

$$s_{l,t+1} - \bar{s}_l \approx \phi\left(s_{l,t} - \bar{s}_l\right) + l\left(\mathcal{S}_t\right)\left(c_{l,t+1} - c_{l,t} - \left(g_0 - \frac{1}{2}\sigma_0^2\right)\right). \tag{8.A48}$$

Replacing eq. (8.A47), evaluated at $\tau = t$ and $\tau = t+1$, into both sides of the previous approximation and rearranging terms leaves

$$x_{l,t+1} - c_{l,t+1} - \overline{x_l - c_l} = \phi\left(x_{l,t} - c_{l,t} - \overline{x_l - c_l}\right) + \frac{l\left(\mathcal{S}_t\right)}{1 - \frac{1}{\bar{s}}}\left(c_{l,t+1} - c_{l,t} - \left(g_0 - \frac{1}{2}\sigma_0^2\right)\right). \tag{8.A49}$$

The function l in eq. (8.26) is found by imposing the following three conditions where the first is a slight generalization of that mentioned in the main text and the remaining two are the last two conditions in the main text.

- First, the short-term rate in eq. (8.25) is affine in $\ln \mathcal{S}$, that is, eq. (8.A45) holds, such that

$$l\left(\mathcal{S}\right) = \sqrt{2\frac{1}{\gamma^2\sigma_0^2}\left(\gamma\left(1-\phi\right) - b\right)\left(\bar{s}_l - \ln \mathcal{S}\right) + \frac{2}{\gamma^2\sigma_0^2}\text{const.} - 1}. \tag{8.A50}$$

- Second, habit is predetermined at the steady state, meaning that $x_{l,t+1}$ does not change with $c_{l,t+1}$, which, by eq. (8.A49), it does not change, when:

$$l\left(\bar{s}\right) = \frac{1}{\bar{s}} - 1. \tag{8.A51}$$

  Evaluating eq. (8.A50) at the steady state $\bar{s}$ and using the previous condition delivers $\frac{2}{\gamma^2\sigma_0^2}\text{const.} = \frac{1}{\bar{s}^2}$, such that eq. (8.A50) is

$$l\left(\mathcal{S}\right) = \sqrt{2\frac{1}{\gamma^2\sigma_0^2}\left(\gamma\left(1-\phi\right) - b\right)\left(\bar{s}_l - \ln \mathcal{S}\right) + \frac{1}{\bar{s}^2}} - 1. \tag{8.A52}$$

- Third, habit is predetermined near the steady state, meaning that

$$\frac{d}{ds_l}\left(\frac{dx_l}{dc_l}\right)\bigg|_{s=\bar{s}_l} = 0. \tag{8.A53}$$

We then need to find the dynamics of $x_{l,t+1}$, expressed as a function of $c_{l,t+1}$. By the definition of the log-surplus consumption ratio in eq. (8.A46), we have that $x_{l,t+1} = \ln\left(1 - e^{\sigma(c_{l,t+1})}\right) + c_{l,t+1}$, where $\sigma\left(c_{l,t+1}\right) \equiv s_{l,t+1}$ and $s_{l,t+1}$ is as in eq. (8.A48), such that, using eq. (8.A48),

$$\frac{dx_{l,t+1}}{dc_{l,t+1}} = 1 - \frac{1}{e^{-\sigma(c_{l,t+1})} - 1}\sigma'\left(c_{l,t+1}\right) = 1 - \frac{l_o\left(s_{l,t}\right)}{e^{-s_{l,t+1}} - 1},$$

where we have set $l_o\left(s_l\right) \equiv l(s)$. Therefore, eq. (8.A53) is, after simple computations and using eq. (8.A51),

$$l_o'\left(\bar{s}_l\right) = -\frac{1}{\bar{s}}.$$

Taking the derivative in eq. (8.A52), replacing it into the LHS of the previous equation, and solving for $\bar{s}_l$ yields

$$\bar{s} = \sigma_0\sqrt{\frac{\gamma^2}{\gamma(1-\phi) - b}},$$

which is the expression of the main text for $b = 0$. Replacing this expression of $\bar{s}$ into eq. (8.A52) leaves eq. (8.26) in the main text.

Finally, note that the expression of the short-term rate can now be found after simple calculations:

$$r(S) = \rho + \gamma\left(g_0 - \frac{1}{2}\sigma_0^2\right) - \frac{1}{2}\left(\gamma(1-\phi) - b\right) + b\left(\bar{s} - \ln S\right).$$

Appendix 8.G Learning

8.G.1 In Continuous Time

Here we provide heuristic details on eq. (8.37). The probability the dividend process in eq. (8.35) has the "good" drift $\theta = A$, conditional on the observation of $(D_t)_{t\leq\tau}$, is

$$\pi(\tau, D_\tau) = \frac{p\phi(D_\tau - A\tau)}{p\phi(D_\tau - A\tau) + (1-p)\phi(D_\tau + A\tau)} = \frac{p}{p + (1-p)e^{-\frac{2AD_\tau}{\sigma_0^2}}},$$

where the first equality follows by a straightforward generalization of the arguments leading to eq. (8.34) and the second holds by the assumption that $\sigma_0 Z_\tau$ is Gaussian with mean zero and variance $\sigma_0^2\tau$. Hence, we have that $\pi(\tau, D_\tau)$ is a function of the dividend only. To simplify notation, let $\pi(D_\tau) \equiv \pi(\tau, D_\tau)$. We have

$$\pi'(D) = 2\pi^2(D)\frac{1-p}{p}e^{-\frac{2AD}{\sigma_0^2}}\frac{A}{\sigma_0^2}, \quad \pi''(D) = \pi'(D)\frac{2A}{\sigma_0^2}\left(\frac{1-p}{p}2\pi(D)e^{-\frac{2AD}{\sigma_0^2}} - 1\right)$$

Note that

$$\frac{1-\pi(D)}{\pi(D)}=\frac{(1-p)\,e^{-\frac{2AD}{\sigma_0^2}}}{p}\quad\text{and}\quad g_\tau=E\left(\theta|\left(D_t\right)_{t\le\tau}\right)=A\left(2\pi\left(D_\tau\right)-1\right),$$

such that

$$\pi'(D)=\frac{2A}{\sigma_0^2}\pi(D)\left(1-\pi(D)\right),\quad \pi''(D)=-\pi'(D)\frac{2}{\sigma_0^2}g. \tag{8.A54}$$

Next, apply Itô's lemma to the function $\pi(D_\tau)$, where D_τ is solution to eq. (8.36). By the expressions in eq. (8.A54),

$$\begin{aligned}d\pi\left(D_\tau\right)&=\pi'\left(D_\tau\right)dD_\tau+\frac{1}{2}\pi''\left(D_\tau\right)dD_\tau^2\\&=\left(\pi'\left(D_\tau\right)g_\tau+\frac{1}{2}\pi''\left(D_\tau\right)\sigma_0^2\right)d\tau+\pi'\left(D_\tau\right)\sigma_0 dW_\tau\\&=\frac{2A}{\sigma_0}\pi\left(D_\tau\right)\left(1-\pi\left(D_\tau\right)\right)dW_\tau.\end{aligned}$$

8.G.2 Stochastic Growth and Convexity of Price-Dividend Ratios

We generalize the model (8.46) and assume that g_t is the solution to

$$dg_t=\left(\varphi\left(g_t\right)+\left(\sigma_0-\lambda\right)v\left(g_t\right)\right)dt+v\left(g_t\right)d\bar{W}_t$$

for some functions $\varphi(g)$ and $v(g)$. We then have the following.

(1) *If $r'(g)<1$, the price-dividend ratio is increasing in the expected dividend growth, g.*

(2) *Suppose that the price-dividend ratio is increasing in g. Then, it is also convex in g whenever $r''(g)<0$ and $\frac{d^2}{dg^2}\left(\varphi(g)+\left(\sigma_0-\lambda\right)v(g)\right)\ge-2+2r'(g)$.*

The proof of these statements follows by theorem 8.A2 in appendix 8.D. These statements generalize the claims in the main text that, in the model in (8.46)-(8.47), p is increasing and convex whenever $\gamma<1$.

8.G.3 The Solution and Calibration of the Uncountable States Model

First, we show eq. (8.48) and then provide some details on the plots in figure 8.13. Define $y_t\equiv\bar{r}+\sigma_0\lambda-g_t$, such that, by the definitions $\lambda=\gamma\sigma_0$ and $v=\frac{\alpha_*}{\sigma_0}$,

$$dy_t=k\left(\bar{y}-y_t\right)dt-v\,d\bar{W}_t,$$

where $\bar{y}\equiv\bar{r}+\gamma\sigma_0^2-\bar{g}+\frac{(\gamma-1)\sigma_0 v}{k}$. (We will determine α_* below.) Therefore, eq. (8.46) can be written as

$$p(g)=\int_0^\infty\bar{\mathbb{E}}\left(e^{-\int_0^t y_u du}\,\middle|\,y=\bar{r}+\gamma\sigma_0^2-g\right)dt=\int_0^\infty e^{A(t)-B(t)\left(\bar{r}+\gamma\sigma_0^2-g\right)}dt$$

where the second equality follows by results given in chapter 13: the integrand on the RHS of the first equality is the same as the price of a zero coupon bond predicted by a model of the yield curve known as an "affine model," which is solved in closed form. Accordingly, the two functions A and B are given by eqs. (13.39) in chapter 13; using the notation of this appendix, they are

$$A(t) = (B(t) - t)\, y_\infty - \frac{v^2}{4k} B^2(t), \quad B(t) = \frac{1}{k}\left(1 - e^{-kt}\right), \qquad (8.A55)$$
$$y_\infty = \bar{y} - \frac{1}{2}\left(\frac{v}{k}\right)^2.$$

The plots in figure 8.13 are obtained with a value of v calculated as follows. First, note that α_* is the solution to the following equation (see eq. (9.45) in chapter 9):

$$0 = \frac{1}{\sigma_0^2}\alpha^2 + 2k\alpha - \sigma_2^2.$$

Given the value $\sigma_2 = 0.015$, the solution to this quadratic equation is $\alpha_* = 6.3535 \times 10^{-4}$ such that $v = \frac{\alpha_*}{\sigma_0} = 1.2707 \times 10^{-2}$. Figure 8.13 is obtained with $v = 0.01$.

Appendix 8.H Market-to-Book Ratios

We provide detail regarding the MB ratio plotted in figure 8.14. The derivation of this ratio is similar to that in appendix 8.G.3. Define $y_t \equiv \lambda + \bar{r} - \rho_t$, where ρ_t is solution to (8.51) such that

$$dy_t = -d\rho_t = k(\bar{y} - y_t)\, dt - \sigma dW_t,$$

where $\bar{y} \equiv \lambda + \bar{r} - \bar{\rho}$. By eq. (8.52),

$$\begin{aligned} \mathrm{MB}(\rho) &= \lambda \int_0^\infty \mathbb{E}\left(e^{-(\lambda+\bar{r})t} \frac{B_t}{B_0} \middle| \rho \right) dt \\ &= \lambda \int_0^\infty \mathbb{E}\left(e^{-\int_0^t y_u dt} \middle| y = \lambda + \bar{r} - \rho \right) dt \\ &= \lambda \int_0^\infty e^{A(t) - B(t)(\lambda + \bar{r} - \rho)} dt, \end{aligned}$$

where the two functions are as in (8.A55) but with $\bar{y}$ defined as in this appendix and v replaced by σ.

References

Abel, A. B. (1990). "Asset Prices Under Habit Formation and Catching Up with the Joneses." *American Economic Review Papers and Proceedings* 80, 38–42.

Andersen, T. G., T. Bollerslev, and F. X. Diebold (2010). "Parametric and Nonparametric Volatility Measurement." In *Handbook of Financial Econometrics*, edited by Y. Aït-Sahalia and L. P. Hansen. Amsterdam: North-Holland/Elsevier.

Ang, A. and J. Liu (2001). "A General Affine Earnings Valuation Model." *Review of Accounting Studies* 6, 397–425.

Bajeux-Besnainou, I., and J.-C. Rochet (1996). "Dynamic Spanning: Are Options an Appropriate Instrument?" *Mathematical Finance* 6, 1–16.

Barberis, N., M. Huang, and T. Santos (2001). "Prospect Theory and Asset Prices." *Quarterly Journal of Economics* 116, 1–53.

Barsky, R. B., and J. B. De Long (1990). "Bull and Bear Markets in the Twentieth Century." *Journal of Economic History* 50, 265–281.

Barsky, R. B., and J. B. De Long (1993). "Why Does the Stock Market Fluctuate?" *Quarterly Journal of Economics* 108, 291–311.

Bergman, Y. Z., B. D. Grundy, and Z. Wiener (1996). "General Properties of Option Prices." *Journal of Finance* 51, 1573–1610.

Berk, J. B., R. C. Green, and V. Naik (1999). "Optimal Investment, Growth Options and Security Returns." *Journal of Finance* 54, 1153–1607.

Black, F., and M. Scholes (1973). "The Pricing of Options and Corporate Liabilities." *Journal of Political Economy* 81, 637–659.

Bodie, Z., A. Kane, and A. J. Marcus (2014). *Investments*. 10th ed. New York: McGraw-Hill Education.

Boldrin, M., L. Christiano, and J. Fisher (2001). "Habit Persistence, Asset Returns and the Business Cycle." *American Economic Review* 91, 149–166.

Brandt, M. W., and Q. Kang (2004). "On the Relationship between the Conditional Mean and Volatility of Stock Returns: A Latent VAR Approach." *Journal of Financial Economics* 72, 217–257.

Brennan, M. J., and Y. Xia (2001). "Stock Price Volatility and Equity Premium." *Journal of Monetary Economics* 47, 249–283.

Brunnermeier, M. K., and S. Nagel (2008). "Do Wealth Fluctuations Generate Time-Varying Risk Aversion? Micro-Evidence on Individuals' Asset Allocation." *American Economic Review* 98, 713–736.

Brunnermeier, M. K., and Y. Sannikov (2014). "A Macroeconomic Model with a Financial Sector." *American Economic Review* 104, 379–421.

Campbell, J. Y. (2003). "Consumption-Based Asset Pricing." In *Handbook of the Economics of Finance* (Vol. 1B), edited by G. M. Constantinides, M. Harris, and R. M. Stulz, 803–887. Amsterdam: North-Holland/Elsevier.

Campbell, J. Y., and J. H. Cochrane (1999). "By Force of Habit: A Consumption-Based Explanation of Aggregate Stock Market Behavior." *Journal of Political Economy* 107, 205–251.

Chan, Y. L., and L. Kogan (2002). "Catching Up with the Joneses: Heterogeneous Preferences and the Dynamics of Asset Prices." *Journal of Political Economy* 110, 1255–1285.

Christiansen, C., M. Schmeling and A. Schrimpf (2012). "A Comprehensive Look at Financial Volatility Prediction by Economic Variables." *Journal of Applied Econometrics* 27, 956–977.

Clark, T. E., and K. D. West (2007). "Approximately Normal Tests for Equal Predictive Accuracy in Nested Models." *Journal of Econometrics* 138, 291–311.

Constantinides, G. M. (1990). "Habit Formation: A Resolution of the Equity Premium Puzzle." *Journal of Political Economy* 98, 519–543.

Corradi, V., W. Distaso, and A. Mele (2013). "Macroeconomic Determinants of Stock Volatility and Volatility Premiums." *Journal of Monetary Economics* 60, 203–220.

Daníelsson, J., M. Valenzuela, and I. Zer (2018). "Learning from History: Volatility and Financial Crises." *Review of Financial Studies* 31, 2774–2805.

Daníelsson, J., M. Valenzuela, and I. Zer (2020). *Financial Volatility and Economic Growth, 1870–2016*. London: Systemic Risk Centre, The London School of Economics and Political Science.

David, A. (1997). "Fluctuating Confidence in Stock Markets: Implications for Returns and Volatility." *Journal of Financial and Quantitative Analysis* 32, 427–462.

Detemple, J. B. (1986): "Asset Pricing in a Production Economy with Incomplete Information." *Journal of Finance* 41, 383–391.

Duesenberry, J. S. (1949). *Income, Saving, and the Theory of Consumer Behavior*. Cambridge, MA: Harvard University Press.

El Karoui, N., M. Jeanblanc-Picqué, and S. E. Shreve (1998). "Robustness of the Black and Scholes Formula." *Mathematical Finance* 8, 93–126.

Fama, E. F. (2014). "Nobel Lecture: Two Pillars of Asset Pricing." *American Economic Review* 104, 1467–1485.

Fama, E. F., and K. R. French (1989). "Business Conditions and Expected Returns on Stocks and Bonds." *Journal of Financial Economics* 25, 23–49.

Ferson, W. E., and G. M. Constantinides (1991). "Habit Persistence and Durability in Aggregate Consumption: Empirical Test." *Journal of Financial Economics* 29, 199–240.

Ferson, W. E., and C. R. Harvey (1991). "The Variation of Economic Risk Premiums." *Journal of Political Economy* 99, 385–415.

Fornari, F., and A. Mele (2013). "Financial Volatility and Real Economic Activity." *Journal of Financial Management, Markets and Institutions* 1, 155–198.

Gabaix, X. (2009). "Linearity-Generating Processes: A Modelling Tool Yielding Closed Forms for Asset Prices." Working paper, New York University, Center for Business and Economic Research, and National Bureau of Economic Research.

Gennotte, G. (1986). "Optimal Portfolio Choice Under Incomplete Information." *Journal of Finance* 41, 733–746.

Giacomini, R., and H. White (2006). "Tests of Conditional Predictive Ability." *Econometrica* 74, 1545–1578.

Glosten, L., R. Jagannathan, and D. Runkle (1993). "On the Relation between the Expected Value and the Volatility of the Nominal Excess Return on Stocks." *Journal of Finance* 48, 1779–1801.

Gomes, J., L. Kogan, and L. Zhang (2003). "Equilibrium Cross-Section of Returns." *Journal of Political Economy* 111, 693–732.

Hajek, B. (1985). "Mean Stochastic Comparison of Diffusions." *Zeitschrift fur Wahrscheinlichkeitstheorie und Verwandte Gebiete* 68, 315–329.

Hamilton, J. D., and G. Lin (1996). "Stock Market Volatility and the Business Cycle." *Journal of Applied Econometrics* 11, 573–593.

Huang, C.-F., and Pagès, H. (1992). "Optimal Consumption and Portfolio Policies with an Infinite Horizon: Existence and Convergence." *Annals of Applied Probability* 2, 36–64.

Jagannathan, R. (1984). "Call Options and the Risk of Underlying Securities." *Journal of Financial Economics* 13, 425–434.

Johnson, T (2002). "Rational Momentum Effects." *Journal of Finance* 57, 585–608.

Karatzas, I., and S. E. Shreve (1991). *Brownian Motion and Stochastic Calculus*. Berlin: Springer-Verlag.

Kijima, M. (2002). "Monotonicity and Convexity of Option Prices Revisited." *Mathematical Finance* 12, 411–426.

Liptser, R. S., and A. N. Shiryaev (2001a). *Statistics of Random Processes*. Vol. I, *General Theory*. Berlin: Springer-Verlag.

Liptser, R. S., and A. N. Shiryaev (2001b). *Statistics of Random Processes*. Vol. II, *Applications*. Berlin: Springer-Verlag.

Ljungqvist, L., and H. Uhlig (2000). "Tax Policy and Aggregate Demand Management under Catching up with the Joneses." *American Economic Review* 90, 356–366.

Mehra, R., and E. C. Prescott (2003). "The Equity Premium in Retrospect." In *Handbook of the Economics of Finance* (Vol. 1B), edited by G. M. Constantinides, M. Harris, and R. M. Stulz, 889–938. Amsterdam: North-Holland/Elsevier.

Mele, A. (2003). "Fundamental Properties of Bond Prices in Models of the Short-Term Rate." *Review of Financial Studies* 16, 679–716.

Mele, A. (2007). "Asymmetric Stock Market Volatility and the Cyclical Befhavior of Expected Returns." *Journal of Financial Economics* 86, 446–478.

Menzly, L., T. Santos, and P. Veronesi (2004). "Understanding Predictability." *Journal of Political Economy* 111, 1, 1–47.

Ohlson, J. A. (1995). "Earnings, Book Values, and Dividends in Equity Valuation." *Contemporary Accounting Research* 11, 661–687.

Pástor, L. and P. Veronesi (2006). "Was There a NASDAQ Bubble in the Late 1990s?" *Journal of Financial Economics* 81, 61–100.

Paye, B. S. (2012). "Déjà Vol: Predictive Regressions for Aggregate Stock Market Volatility Using Macroeconomic Variables." *Journal of Financial Economics* 106, 527–546.

Romano, M., and N. Touzi (1997). "Contingent Claims and Market Completeness in a Stochastic Volatility Model." *Mathematical Finance* 7, 399–412.

Rothschild, M., and J. Stiglitz (1970). "Increasing Risk: I. A Definition." *Journal of Economic Theory* 2, 225–243.

Rothschild, M., and J. Stiglitz (1971). "Increasing Risk: II. Its Economic Consequences." *Journal of Economic Theory* 5, 66–84.

Ryder, H. E., and G. M. Heal (1973). "Optimal Growth with Intertemporally Dependent Preferences." *Review of Economic Studies* 40, 1–33.

Schwert, G. W. (1989a). "Why Does Stock Market Volatility Change Over Time?" *Journal of Finance* 44, 1115–1153.

Schwert, G. W. (1989b). "Business Cycles, Financial Crises and Stock Volatility." *Carnegie-Rochester Conference Series on Public Policy* 31, 83–125.

Shiller, R. J. (2014). "Nobel Lecture: Speculative Asset Prices." *American Economic Review* 104, 1486–1517.

Sundaresan, S. M. (1989). "Intertemporally Dependent Preferences and the Volatility of Consumption and Wealth." *Review of Financial Studies* 2, 73–89.

Timmermann, A. (1993). "How Learning in Financial Markets Generates Excess Volatility and Predictability in Stock Prices." *Quarterly Journal of Economics* 108, 1135–1145.

Timmermann, A. (1996). "Excess Volatility and Return Predictability of Stock Returns in Autoregressive Dividend Models with Learning." *Review of Economic Studies* 63, 523–577.

Veronesi, P. (1999). "Stock Market Overreaction to Bad News in Good Times: A Rational Expectations Equilibrium Model." *Review of Financial Studies* 12, 975–1007.

Veronesi, P. (2000). "How Does Information Quality Affect Stock Returns?" *Journal of Finance* 55, 807–837.

Wachter, J. A. (2006). "A Consumption-Based Model of the Term Structure of Interest Rates." *Journal of Financial Economics* 79, 365–399.

Wang, S. (1993). "The Integrability Problem of Asset Prices." *Journal of Economic Theory* 59, 199–213.

Zhang, L. (2005). "The Value Premium." *Journal of Finance* 60, 67–103.

9

Macrofinance

9.1 Introduction

This chapter discusses models that aim to address the empirical puzzles surveyed in chapters 7 and 8. The most prominent are the equity premium puzzle and its pattern over the business cycle as well as that of aggregate stock volatility. Because these puzzles mainly relate to the behavior of aggregate variables, it is natural to attempt to provide explanations hinging on macroeconomic variables such as consumption or output, whence the title of this chapter.

The equity premium puzzle is the difficulty that the neoclassical model has to predict expected returns that are quantitatively consistent with those in the data. In particular, chapter 7 explains that an implausibly high level of risk aversion is needed to reconcile models with data. Moreover, a high risk aversion implies a low elasticity of intertemporal substitution and hence an implausibly high volatility of the short-term interest rates, which gives rise to the "interest rate puzzle."

In the early attempts to address the equity premium puzzle, the assumption of a representative agent with CRRA preferences was replaced with that of a representative agent with nonexpected utility. In the nonexpected utility framework, risk aversion can be understood independently of the elasticity of intertemporal substitution. This approach, described in section 9.2, does not necessarily address the equity premium puzzle. We shall explain that the nonexpected utility model may only lead to a resolution of the puzzle when the price-dividend ratio is affected by a number of state variables. One instance of state variables identified in the literature is a long-run risk defined as a mechanism capable of turning even a small shock into an economic damage lasting for years. For example, it has been argued that expected consumption growth is highly persistent, such that shocks to expected growth have long-lasting implications. While the model has the potential to address the equity premium puzzle, we shall explain that there are nuances regarding the realism of this precise mechanism.

Section 9.3 explores channels that address the equity premium puzzle based on a variant of habit formation. The external habit formation model reviewed in chapter 8 relies on the existence of a representative agent with a high risk aversion. Alternatively, one can consider economies with heterogeneous agents, in which each agent has a consumption reference that they want to benchmark to—an assumption known as "catching up with the Joneses." The economy is heterogeneous in that each agent displays a different curvature of their utility function. In bad times, when markets are down, the less risk averse agents are those who suffer the most, reflecting their previous relatively more aggressive investment decisions. Thus, their relative wealth and hence, social weight decreases. That is, aggregate risk aversion increases in bad times, leading to the countercyclical mechanisms explained in chapter 8. This model has the potential to explain some empirical properties of the equity premium (its countercyclicality, for example) but is also subject to a number of caveats related to measurement issues.

Section 9.4 describes economies in which agents can be hit by idiosyncratic shocks, a risk that they cannot hedge against through security trading. How is it that idiosyncratic shocks may affect asset prices? The key assumption of the models we survey is that, while agents are the same ex ante, they will be affected by shocks that have different amplitude. A job loss is one important instance that illustrates how these models work. Recessions do not necessarily affect agents in the same way. Some agents can be hurt more than others. The possibility of a job loss can then induce agents to act prudently while investing in the stock market. That is, risk premiums are countercyclical. This explanation can lead to a potential resolution of the equity premium puzzle—theoretically, at least.

While idiosyncratic risk is a clear explanation, its empirical implications do not seem to be entirely exhaustive. Note that a natural hedge against idiosyncratic risk is self-insurance, that is, the ability to save in good times to cope with possible adversities occurring in bad times. Agents might actually eliminate a large portion of idiosyncratic risk by insuring themselves while having access to capital markets, thereby making idiosyncratic risk practically irrelevant to the explanation of the equity premium. For idiosyncratic risk to really matter, we would need to observe a large and persistent idiosyncratic risk or have capital markets transactions be so expensive so as to prevent agents from implementing self-insurance plans. But, empirically, idiosyncratic risks do not appear to be as large and persistent, and market transaction costs are not as large as required by our standard models with idiosyncratic risk. Naturally, there are historical instances in which idiosyncratic risk may have a better appeal: the Great Recession occurring after the 2007 crisis has the potential to teach us that idiosyncratic risks may be quite persistent.

Section 9.4 also considers an alternative channel: market incompleteness. Economies with incomplete markets are not necessarily consistent with a sizable equity premium. If agents have comparable access to equity markets, they share the same level of risk such that the premium required is similar to that in economies with complete markets. But market incompleteness has the potential to resolve the puzzle when a large fraction of the agents do not participate. The mechanism is simple. If markets are being shut down for a large proportion of agents, the agents who participate would be concerned about the aggregate macroeconomic risk they bear. This concern leads them to require a sizable premium.

Sections 9.5 and 9.6 deal with economies where agents have differences in beliefs and also face uncertainty (as opposed to risk) regarding the fundamentals. Section 9.5 contains natural developments from chapter 8: agents have differences in beliefs regarding some unobservable process (say, the expected dividend growth) and learn from past data. Their heterogeneity in the estimate of the state of the economy has the potential to explain not only bubbles (at least, provided the market is subject to short-sale constraints) but also additional volatility in the price of risk in general equilibrium economies without any frictions. Section 9.6 abandons the assumption that the agents know the very statistical laws of the fundamentals and develops models with *Knightian uncertainty*, which have the potential to explain the equity premium. Models with Knightian uncertainty are also considered in section 9.10.

Section 9.7 provides an introduction to models with government spending and the notion of *Ricardian equivalence*. One of the main predictions is that asset prices are decreasing in the government spending because interest rates are increasing in government spending.

Section 9.8 deals with a simple model and addresses an old issue in financial economics: how does a firm's leverage affect equity volatility? The role of this section is to illustrate how habit formation in asset pricing may help address a number of issues that go beyond those studied in chapter 8. However, the model is simple and consistent with the Modigliani-Miller propositions (see chapter 5).

Section 9.9 reviews some models with the potential to explain the cross-section of asset returns. These "multiple-tree" models are primarily the same as the basic Lucas (1978) model reviewed in chapter 3. The important difference is that the models in this section are solved analytically, helping to facilitate the interpretation of their predictions on the cross-section of expected returns.

Section 9.10 contains a succinct review on the relations underlying production, asset markets, and the hypothesis of "separation" between finance and macroeconomics. First it provides some famous arguments by which production-based economies would actually exacerbate the equity premium puzzle: in these economies, consumption is endogenous, and an increase in the agents' risk aversion may actually lead to decreased consumption volatility. One additional important difficulty in these economies is that capital supply is infinitely elastic and the price of capital is quite smooth. To increase capital price volatility, one needs hindrances in the capital formation process (e.g., adjustment costs) or an added volatility in the demand for capital (through, e.g., habit formation).

Which models do financial economists and macroeconomists have in common? Many of the models of this chapter aim to shed light into the behavior of asset prices over the business cycle; at the same time, these models rely on a substantial revamp of many of the old assumptions that underlie the classical real business cycle model reviewed in chapter 3. These new assumptions are not always incorporated in macroeconomics (at least not until the early 2000s). Section 9.10 provides an example of a modern version of a *dichotomy* between real and financial spheres of the economy, based on nonexpected utility. This example shows that one may model macroeconomic aggregates while safely ignoring all intricacies arising while trying to explain asset prices. However, section 9.11 emphasizes how financial markets and the macroeconomy may feed on each other. Adverse conditions in the real sphere of the economy may cause asset prices to drop. But when asset prices drop, financing conditions deteriorate (say, for example, because firms' collateral value decreases), which may lead to a reduced lending and then adverse macroeconomic developments, over a spiral. This section explains this type of "accelerator mechanisms" and additional asset price feedbacks.

9.2 Nonexpected Utility

The standard model of intertemporal additive utility confounds intertemporal substitution of consumption and attitudes toward risk. Epstein and Zin (1989, 1991) and Weil (1989) consider a class of recursive but not necessarily expected utility preferences, which has the potential of disentangling these two notions. This section provides details on this approach without insisting on the theoretic underpinnings: we provide basic definitions and derivations while focusing on the asset pricing implications of this class of preferences.

Consider how a decision maker allocates consumption across two periods of time, t and $t+1$. The notion of elasticity of intertemporal substitution, introduced in chapter 3 (see eq. (3.5)), captures how this intertemporal allocation is modified after a change in the safe interest rate,

$$\psi\left(c_{t+1}, c_t\right)=\frac{d\left(c_{t+1} / c_t\right) /\left(c_{t+1} / c_t\right)}{d R / R},$$

where R denotes the gross interest rate and c_t is consumption at time-t. Consider, for example, a two-period model where consumption at $t=1$ is known and equal to c_1 and consumption at $t=2$ is random and equal to $\tilde{c}_2$. We may wish to compare these two consumption levels while defining a certainty equivalent for consumption at time 2, $\hat{c}_2=u^{-1}E[u(\tilde{c}_2)]$, where $u(\cdot)$ is a decision-maker utility function. The certainty equivalent, $\hat{c}_2$, encodes information on the risk aversion attitude of our decision maker. This attitude should not help define how the decision maker would like to define their intertemporal substitution of consumption at two points in time.

To compare consumption at two different points in time, we may consider a dedicated function of c_1 and the certainty equivalent $\hat{c}_2$,

$$W \equiv W\left(c_1, \hat{c}_2\right). \tag{9.1}$$

This function, known as *aggregator*, enables one to disregard the risk aversion determinants that affect future consumption: it only aggregates known levels of consumption at two distinct points in time. For example, it turns out that, if $W=u^{-1}$, then the resulting aggregator will give rise to the standard additive utility model–intertemporal substitution and risk aversion would be confounded. Otherwise, the model is capable of disentangling these two notions. The next section provides details on these properties within a dynamic framework.

9.2.1 Recursive Formulations

Consider the standard case in which a decision maker has additive utility. The decision maker's continuation utility V_t satisfies

$$V_t=u\left(c_t\right)+\beta E_t\left(V_{t+1}\right) \equiv u\left(c_t\right)+\beta u\left(\hat{v}_{t+1}\right), \tag{9.2}$$

where u is a von Neumann-Morgenstern utility function and $\hat{v}_{t+1}$ is the certainty equivalent consumption, that is, $\hat{v}_{t+1}: u\left(\hat{v}_{t+1}\right)=E_t\left(V_{t+1}\right)$. Next, let us define the certainty equivalent continuation utility (expressed in consumption units) as $v_t: V_t=u\left(v_t\right)$, such that we can write eq. (9.2) as

$$v_t = W\left(c_t, \hat{v}_{t+1}\right) \equiv u^{-1}\left(u\left(c_t\right) + \beta u_R\left(\hat{v}_{t+1}\right)\right), \quad u_R\left(\cdot\right) \equiv u\left(\cdot\right),$$

where W is the *aggregator* and where, by construction, $\hat{v}_{t+1}$ is also the certainty equivalent utility at $t+1$, defined as $u_R\left(\hat{v}_{t+1}\right) = E_t\left[u_R\left(v_{t+1}\right)\right]$. The definition of u_R might appear to be a bit cumbersome, but setting such general notation will soon reveal to be useful.

Consider, for example, the standard CRRA utility function, in which case the aggregator is

$$W\left(c, \hat{v}\right) = \left(c^{1-\gamma} + \beta \hat{v}^{1-\gamma}\right)^{\frac{1}{1-\gamma}}.$$

In this formulation, the decision-maker's attitude vis-à-vis risk is encoded into the certainty equivalent $\hat{v}_{t+1}$ through the utility $u_R = u$. It is well known that the CRRA, γ, is the same as the reciprocal of the EIS (see chapter 3). However, there are no economic reasons for this coincidence. An alternative assumption on the aggregator W is that CRRA and EIS are not tied up. Consider the following aggregator:

$$\begin{aligned} &W\left(c, \hat{v}\right) = \left(c^{\rho} + \beta \hat{v}^{\rho}\right)^{1/\rho}, \quad \rho \neq 0, \quad \text{and} \\ &\hat{v}_{t+1} : u_R\left(\hat{v}_{t+1}\right) = E_t\left(u_R\left(v_{t+1}\right)\right), \quad u_R\left(\hat{v}\right) = \frac{\hat{v}^{1-\gamma}}{1-\gamma}, \end{aligned} \tag{9.3}$$

for three positive constants ρ, γ, and β.[1] The aggregator (9.3) generalizes W in eq. (9.1) to the dynamic case where the certainty equivalent utility $\hat{v}$ replaces the certainty equivalent consumption $\hat{c}_2$. In this formulation, the risk attitude for static wealth gambles is still the standard CRRA; however, this risk attitude, being encoded into a specific utility function u_R, does not affect how the agent thinks in terms of their intertemporal allocation of consumption. Precisely, we say that γ is the CRRA for static wealth gambles and that $\psi \equiv (1-\rho)^{-1}$ is the EIS.

Given these assumptions, we may now derive some model implications that we shall rely on while using the model for the purpose of asset evaluation. Then, by the definitions in (9.3), we have that

$$\hat{v}_{t+1} = \left(E_t(v_{t+1}^{1-\gamma})\right)^{\frac{1}{1-\gamma}},$$

such that the aggregator W then implies the following recursion,

$$v_t = \left(c_t^{\rho} + \beta\left(E_t(v_{t+1}^{1-\gamma})\right)^{\frac{\rho}{1-\gamma}}\right)^{\frac{1}{\rho}}. \tag{9.4}$$

Note that, in the absence of uncertainty, $v_t^{\rho} = c_t^{\rho} + \beta v_{t+1}^{\rho}$, which again clearly illustrates that ψ is the EIS. Moreover, it is immediately verified that when $\gamma = 1-\rho$ (CRRA equals the reciprocal of the EIS), the *certainty equivalent continuation utility*, v_t in eq. (9.4), collapses to the standard intertemporal additive utility, $v_t^{1-\gamma} = E\left(\sum_{n=0}^{\infty} \beta^n c_{t+n}^{1-\gamma}\right)$. The general

1. Section 9.10 deals with the case in which $\rho = 0$.

case is the focus of this and other sections in this chapter. In some cases (e.g., in section 9.10), it may be both convenient and intuitive to formulate the model in terms of the *continuation utility*, $V_t = u_R(v_t)$, such that eq. (9.4) collapses to

$$V_t = \frac{1}{1-\gamma}\left(c_t^{\rho} + \beta\left((1-\gamma)\,E_t(V_{t+1})\right)^{\frac{\rho}{1-\gamma}}\right)^{\frac{1-\gamma}{\rho}}. \tag{9.5}$$

Appendix 9.A relies on eq. (9.5) (see also eq. (9.8) below) and the Bellman equation associated with it while deriving the asset pricing implications of portfolio choices within a representative agent framework.

9.2.2 Preferences for Early Resolution of Uncertainty and Long-Run Risks

Nonexpected utility has the potential to address asset pricing puzzles through a mechanism known as the "preference for early resolution of uncertainty." It is instructive to provide intuition on this mechanism. The main idea is that a decision maker would value receiving information sooner than later. For example, it seems plausible that we would value receiving early signals on the likelihood of success of a given project on which we are investing resources. Based on this information, we would modify our allocation of resources and possibly plan for alternative projects (or invest even more resources in the given project). Likewise, it is possible that an agent concerned with an early resolution of uncertainty should require some premium for investing in stocks that have the potential of being affected by long-run risks. This theme is developed in detail in the following sections.

It turns out that, according to the standard expected utility model, an agent should be indifferent regarding the timing for uncertainty resolution. Nonexpected utility allows to deal with these problems. This section makes these statements clear while providing some simple examples. Consider the following finite horizon lotteries where consumption c_t takes place at $t = 1, 2, 3$ and first-period consumption is fixed at $c_1 = 1$.

- *Lottery A*. Consumption c_t is revealed at time t, for $t = 2, 3$. Moreover, $(c_t)_{t=2,3}$ is IID and equal to either c_h or c_l, with equal probability.
- *Lottery B*. Consumption c_t at $t = 2, 3$ is revealed at time 2, and $c_3 = c_2$.
- *Lottery C*. Consumption c_t at $t = 2, 3$ is revealed at time 2. Moreover, $(c_t)_{t=2,3}$ is IID and equal to either c_h or c_l, with equal probability.

Lottery B and lottery C clearly allow for early resolution of uncertainty. However, lottery B introduces a long-run risk: the realization of consumption at time 2 is the same as that at time 3. While this fact eliminates uncertainty at $t = 3$, it also creates the risk that a bad outcome at $t = 2$ would propagate to the next period. We will assume the agent is going to be averse to this risk: they underweight good outcomes at $t = 2, 3$ compared with bad outcomes. We want to identify parameter restrictions such that a decision maker with nonexpected utility, while still being concerned for long-run risks, does indeed prefer an early resolution of uncertainty. We evaluate these lotteries while relying on a finite horizon version of the Epstein-Zin model (9.4), namely while setting $v_3 = c_3$.

Figure 9.1 depicts the certainty equivalent utilities at $t = 1$ for the three lotteries while modeling consumption in the equally likely good and bad states of nature as $c_h = 1 + \sigma$ and $c_l = 1 - \sigma$, where σ is consumption volatility. In all the examples, we use the parameter

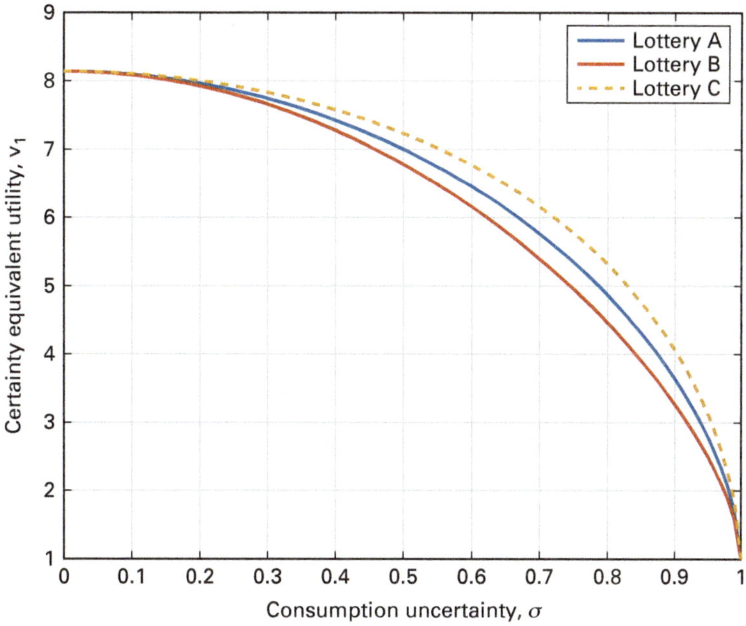

Figure 9.1
Certainty equivalent utilities at $t=1$ against consumption volatility for three lotteries in a three-period model with random consumption and Epstein-Zin preferences (9.4). In lottery A, consumption is IID for time 2 and time 3 and may take a value equal to $c_h = 1+\sigma$ and $c_l = 1-\sigma$ with equal probability, where σ is consumption volatility. In lotteries B and C, realization of consumption is revealed at time 2. In lottery B, consumption at time 3 is fixed at that of time 2; in lottery C, consumption at time 3, while drawn and revealed at time 2, is independent of consumption at time 2. Preference parameters are $\rho = \frac{1}{2}$, $\gamma = 2$, and $\beta = 0.95$.

restriction that $\rho > 1-\gamma$. Lottery B is less valuable precisely because of the long-run risk that it entails. Lottery C isolates the early resolution of uncertainty component, and it is the most preferred one. Indeed, it is well known that the condition $\rho > 1-\gamma$ formalizes the idea of a preference for an early resolution of uncertainty. In lottery B, however, such resolution comes together with a long-run risk. The next sections show how the parameter restriction $\rho > 1-\gamma$ may help address the equity premium puzzles.

The remainder of this section provides the analytical expressions for the certainty equivalent utilities at $t=1$ that lead to the outcomes depicted in figure 9.1.

9.2.2.1 Lottery A

We have

$$v_1^\rho = 1 + \beta \hat{v}_2^\rho, \quad \hat{v}_2 = \left(\frac{1}{2} \left(v_h^{1-\gamma} + v_l^{1-\gamma} \right) \right)^{\frac{1}{1-\gamma}}, \tag{9.6}$$

where the certainty equivalent continuation utility at $t=2$ is $v_s^\rho = c_s^\rho + \beta \hat{v}_3^\rho$ and either $s=h$ or $s=l$ with equal probability and, because $v_3 = c_3$, the certainty equivalent $\hat{v}_3$ is

$$\hat{v}_3 = \left(\frac{1}{2} \left(c_h^{1-\gamma} + c_l^{1-\gamma} \right) \right)^{\frac{1}{1-\gamma}}.$$

9.2.2.2 *Lottery B*

We obviously still have that eq. (9.6) holds, but the certainty equivalent continuation utility at $t=2$ is now

$$v_s^\rho = c_s^\rho + \beta \hat{v}_{3,s}^\rho, \quad s \in \{h, l\},$$

where, because time 3 consumption is known at time 2, the certainty equivalent $\hat{v}_{3,s}$ collapses to $\hat{v}_{3,s} = c_s$, $s \in \{h, l\}$.

9.2.2.3 *Lottery C*

Eq. (9.6) holds, but the certainty equivalent $\hat{v}_2$ is now affected by two sources of randomness at time 2: the realization of consumption at $t=2$ and at $t=3$. We have

$$\begin{aligned} \hat{v}_2 &= \left(E_1\left(v_2^{1-\gamma}\right)\right)^{\frac{1}{1-\gamma}} \\ &= \left(\frac{1}{2}E_1\left(E_1\left(v_2^{1-\gamma}\middle| c_3 = c_h\right)\right) + \frac{1}{2}E_1\left(E_1\left(v_2^{1-\gamma}\middle| c_3 = c_l\right)\right)\right)^{\frac{1}{1-\gamma}} \\ &\equiv \left(\frac{1}{4}\left(v_{h,h}^{1-\gamma} + v_{l,h}^{1-\gamma}\right) + \frac{1}{4}\left(v_{h,l}^{1-\gamma} + v_{l,l}^{1-\gamma}\right)\right)^{\frac{1}{1-\gamma}}, \end{aligned}$$

where v_2 is the certainty equivalent continuation utility at $t=2$, the second equality follows by the law of iterated expectations, and the third by simple calculations and the following definitions,

$$v_{s,\sigma}^\rho = c_s^\rho + \beta \hat{v}_{3,\sigma}^\rho, \quad \hat{v}_{3,\sigma} = c_\sigma, \quad (s, \sigma) \in \{h, l\},$$

and the expression for the certainty equivalent $\hat{v}_{3,\sigma}$ follows because time 3 consumption is revealed at time 2.

9.2.3 Testable Restrictions

Let us define cum-dividend wealth as $A_t \equiv \sum_{i=1}^m (P_{it} + D_{it})\, \theta_{it}$, where θ_{it} denotes the holdings of asset i chosen at time $t-1$. In appendix 9.A, we show that A_t is solution to

$$A_{t+1} = (A_t - c_t)\, \omega_t^\top \left(\mathbf{1}_m + \mathbf{r}_{t+1}\right) \equiv (A_t - c_t)\left(1 + r_{M,t+1}\right), \tag{9.7}$$

where ω is the vector of proportions of wealth invested in the m assets; $\mathbf{r}_{t+1}$ is the vector of asset returns, with any component i being equal to $r_{it+1} \equiv \frac{P_{it+1} + D_{it+1} - P_{it}}{P_{it}}$; and $r_{M,t}$ is the return on the market portfolio, defined as

$$r_{M,t+1} = \sum_{i=1}^m r_{it+1}\omega_{it}, \quad \omega_{it} \equiv \frac{P_{it}\theta_{it+1}}{\sum_i P_{it}\theta_{it+1}},$$

where P_{it} and D_{it} are the price and the dividend of asset i at time t: the usual convention is that the portfolio θ_{it+1} is chosen at time t. Note that the portfolio decision also includes a riskless asset, which can be interpreted by restricting the dividend on any of the previous assets to zero, as usual.

Consider an economy in which the underlying state is some Markov process y. We consider stationary consumption and investment plans. Accordingly, utility is a function $V(A,y)$ when current wealth is A and the state is y. By eq. (9.5),

$$V(A_t,y_t)=\frac{1}{1-\gamma}\max_{c,\omega}\left(c^\rho+\beta\left((1-\gamma)E_t(V(A_{t+1},y_{t+1}))\right)^{\frac{\rho}{1-\gamma}}\right)^{\frac{1-\gamma}{\rho}}. \tag{9.8}$$

Appendix 9.A relies on the Bellman equation associated with (9.8) and shows that the first-order conditions for the representative agent lead to the following Euler equation,

$$E_t\left[m\left(A_t,y_t;A_{t+1},y_{t+1}\right)\left(1+r_i\left(y_{t+1}\right)\right)\right]=1,\quad i=1,\cdots,m, \tag{9.9}$$

where the pricing kernel m is

$$m\left(A_t,y_t;A_{t+1},y_{t+1}\right)=\beta^\theta\left(\frac{c\left(A_{t+1},y_{t+1}\right)}{c\left(A_t,y_t\right)}\right)^{-\frac{\theta}{\psi}}\left(1+r_M\left(y_{t+1}\right)\right)^{\theta-1},\quad \theta\equiv\frac{1-\gamma}{1-\frac{1}{\psi}},\quad \psi\neq 1. \tag{9.10}$$

The pricing kernel in this model displays the interesting property to be affected by the market portfolio return, r_M, at least as soon as $\gamma\neq\frac{1}{\psi}$. In particular, the pricing kernel is countercyclical not only due to consumption growth but also (and provided $\theta<1$) due to the market return channel, giving more weight to states of nature when r_M is low rather than to states when r_M is high. Moreover, the pricing kernel may potentially inherit the excess volatility of market returns in a quite natural fashion. The condition that $\theta<1$ implies preference for early resolution for uncertainty, as explained.

Note, then, the interesting fixed-point problem in this model: market returns affect the pricing kernel, which affects market returns in turn. Due to this fixed point, asset prices predicted by these models are not known in closed form, apart from isolated exceptions. Further, the potential of this model to explain the empirical puzzles needs to be further qualified as discussed in the next section.

9.2.4 Risk Premiums and Interest Rates

So the Euler equation is

$$E_t\left(\beta^\theta\left(\frac{c_{t+1}}{c_t}\right)^{-\frac{\theta}{\psi}}\left(1+r_{M,t+1}\right)^{\theta-1}\left(1+r_{i,t+1}\right)\right)=1. \tag{9.11}$$

Eq. (9.11) obviously holds for the market portfolio and the risk-free asset. Therefore, taking logs in eq. (9.11) for $i=M$ and for the risk-free asset, $i=0$ say, yields the following conditions:

$$0=\ln E_t\left(e^{-\delta\theta-\frac{\theta}{\psi}\ln(c_{t+1}/c_t)+\theta R_{M,t+1}}\right),\quad R_{M,t}=\ln\left(1+r_{M,t}\right), \tag{9.12}$$

where $\delta\equiv-\ln\beta$ and

$$-R_{f,t}=-\ln\left(1+r_{0,t}\right)=\ln E_t\left(e^{-\delta\theta-\frac{\theta}{\psi}\ln(c_{t+1}/c_t)+(\theta-1)R_{M,t+1}}\right). \tag{9.13}$$

Next, suppose that consumption growth, $\ln \frac{c_{t+1}}{c_t}$, and the market portfolio return, $R_{M,t+1}$, are jointly normally distributed. In appendix 9.A, we show that the expected excess return on the market portfolio is given by

$$E_t(R_{M,t+1}) - R_{f,t} + \frac{1}{2}\sigma_{R_M}^2 = \frac{\theta}{\psi}\sigma_{R_M,c} + (1-\theta)\,\sigma_{R_M}^2, \tag{9.14}$$

where $\sigma_{R_M}^2 = var(R_M)$, $\sigma_{R_M,c} = cov(R_{M,t+1}, \ln(c_{t+1}/c_t))$, and the term $\frac{1}{2}\sigma_{R_M}^2$ in the LHS is a Jensen's inequality term. Note that eq. (9.14) is a mixture of the consumption CAPM (for the $\frac{\theta}{\psi}\sigma_{R_M,c}$ part) and the CAPM (for the $(1-\theta)\,\sigma_{R_M}^2$ part).

The risk-free rate is

$$R_{f,t} = \delta + \frac{1}{\psi}E_t\left(\ln\frac{c_{t+1}}{c_t}\right) - \frac{1}{2}(1-\theta)\,\sigma_{R_M}^2 - \frac{1}{2}\frac{\theta}{\psi^2}\sigma_c^2, \tag{9.15}$$

where $\sigma_c^2 = var(\ln(c_{t+1}/c_t))$.

Eqs. (9.14) and (9.15) can be elaborated further. In equilibrium, the asset price and hence the asset return is certainly related to consumption volatility. Precisely, assume that

$$\sigma_{R_M}^2 = \sigma_c^2 + \sigma_*^2, \quad \sigma_{R_M,c} = \sigma_c^2, \tag{9.16}$$

where σ_*^2 is a positive constant that may arise when the asset return is driven by some additional state variable.[2] Under the assumption that the asset return volatility is as in eq. (9.16), the equity premium in eq. (9.14) is

$$E_t(R_{M,t+1}) - R_{f,t} + \frac{1}{2}\sigma_{R_M}^2 = \gamma\sigma_c^2 + (1-\theta)\,\sigma_*^2 = \gamma\sigma_c^2 + \frac{\gamma - \frac{1}{\psi}}{1-\frac{1}{\psi}}\sigma_*^2. \tag{9.17}$$

Disentangling risk aversion from intertemporal substitution does not necessarily lead to a resolution of the equity premium puzzle. To raise the equity premium, we need to have $\sigma_*^2 > 0$, meaning that additional state variables are required to drive variation in asset returns. At the same time, the volatility of these state variables may affect asset returns only when risk aversion is distinct from the reciprocal of the EIS: if $\gamma = \psi^{-1}$, the price-dividend ratio would not even enter the Euler equation (see eq. (9.10)). To illustrate, suppose that σ_*^2 does not depend on γ and ψ and that $\psi > 1$. Then, the equity premium increases with σ_*^2 whenever $\gamma > \psi^{-1}$ (or $\theta < 1$). In other words, state variables have the potential to inflate the equity premium but only when they enter the pricing kernel through the market return. Section 9.2.6 illustrates this feature of the model through a mechanism relying on long-run risks.

Next, we derive the risk-free rate. Assume that $E(\ln(c_{t+1}/c_t)) = g_0 - \frac{1}{2}\sigma_c^2$, where g_0 is the expected consumption growth, a constant. Further, use the assumptions in eq. (9.16) to obtain the risk-free rate in eq. (9.15) is:

$$R_f = \delta + \frac{1}{\psi}g_0 - \frac{1}{2}\gamma\left(1+\frac{1}{\psi}\right)\sigma_c^2 - \frac{1}{2}\frac{\gamma - \frac{1}{\psi}}{1-\frac{1}{\psi}}\sigma_*^2. \tag{9.18}$$

2. This is, for example, the case of the Bansal and Yaron (2004) model described later in this chapter.

As we can see, we may increase relative risk aversion, γ, without substantially affecting the level of the risk-free rate, R_f. This is because the effects of γ on R_f have second-order importance (they multiply variances, which are orders of magnitude less than the expected consumption growth, g_0).

9.2.5 The Campbell-Shiller Approximation

Consider the definition of the market portfolio returns:

$$R_{M,t+1} = \ln\left(\frac{P_{t+1}+C_{t+1}}{P_t}\right) = \ln\left(\frac{e^{z_{t+1}}+1}{e^{z_t}}\right) + g_{t+1} \equiv f\left(z_{t+1}, z_t\right) + g_{t+1},$$

where P_t is the value of the market portfolio, $g_{t+1} = \ln \frac{C_{t+1}}{C_t}$ is the aggregate dividend growth, and $z_t = \ln \frac{P_t}{C_t}$ is the log of the aggregate price-dividend ratio. A first-order linear approximation of $f\left(z_{t+1}, z_t\right)$ around the average level of z leaves

$$R_{M,t+1} \approx \kappa_0 + \kappa_1 z_{t+1} - z_t + g_{t+1}, \tag{9.19}$$

where $\kappa_0 = \ln\left(\frac{e^{\bar{z}}+1}{e^{\bar{z}}}\right) + \frac{\bar{z}}{e^{\bar{z}}+1}$, $\kappa_1 = \frac{e^{\bar{z}}}{e^{\bar{z}}+1}$, and $\bar{z}$ is the average level of the log price-dividend ratio such that $\kappa_1 \approx 0.997$, using US data. The approximation in eq. (9.19) appears for the first time in Campbell and Shiller (1988).

This approximation allows us to isolate the forces that are potentially capable of addressing the equity premium puzzle. We know that agents require compensation for risk that goes well beyond that regarding consumption growth. Let us characterize, then, the innovations to the pricing kernel predicted by this model. By eq. (9.10),[3]

$$\ln m_{t,t+1} - E_t\left(\ln m_{t,t+1}\right) = -\gamma\left(g_{t+1} - E_t\left(g_{t+1}\right)\right) - (1-\theta)\kappa_1\left(z_{t+1} - E_t\left(z_{t+1}\right)\right), \tag{9.20}$$

where $g_{t+1} \equiv \ln \frac{C_{t+1}}{C_t}$ and $m_{t,t+1} \equiv m\left(A_t, y_t; A_{t+1}, y_{t+1}\right)$. That is, there can be additional sources of risk the agents require to be compensated for, provided that (i) the price-dividend ratio is random and (ii) agents have a *preference for early resolution of uncertainty* ($\theta < 1$). We now illustrate how this mechanism operates in the context of persistent risks.

9.2.6 Risks for the Long-Run

Bansal and Yaron (2004) consider a model in which *persistence* in the expected consumption growth has the potential to explain the equity premium puzzle. To illustrate the main points of this model, assume that consumption growth is the solution to

$$g_{t+1} = \ln \frac{C_{t+1}}{C_t} = g_0 - \frac{1}{2}\sigma_c^2 + x_t + \epsilon_{t+1}, \quad \epsilon_{t+1} \sim N\left(0, \sigma_c^2\right), \tag{9.21}$$

where x_t is a small persistent component in consumption growth and the solution to[4]

3. In other words, the LHS of eq. (9.20) describes innovations to the stochastic discount factor $\xi_{t+1} = m_{t,t+1}\xi_t$ (see chapter 7), as $\ln \frac{\xi_{t+1}}{\xi_t} - E_t\left(\frac{\xi_{t+1}}{\xi_t}\right) = \ln m_{t,t+1} - E_t\left(\ln m_{t,t+1}\right)$.

4. In this version of the model, the equity premium and volatility are constant. Bansal and Yaron assume that η_t is heteroskedastic to make the model consistent with time-varying statistics.

$$x_{t+1} = \rho x_t + \eta_{t+1}, \quad \eta_{t+1} \sim N\left(0, \sigma_x^2\right). \tag{9.22}$$

To find an approximate solution to the log of the price-dividend ratio, replace the Campbell-Shiller approximation in eq. (9.19) into the Euler equation (9.12) for the market portfolio:

$$0 = \ln E_t \left(e^{-\delta\theta - \frac{\theta}{\psi} \ln(C_{t+1}/C_t) + \theta\left(\kappa_0 + \kappa_1 z_{t+1} - z_t + g_{t+1}\right)} \right). \tag{9.23}$$

Conjecture that the log of the price-dividend ratio takes the simple form, $z_t = a_0 + a_1 x_t$, where a_0 and a_1 are two coefficients to be determined. Substituting this guess into eq. (9.23) and identifying terms leaves

$$z_t = a_0 + a_1 x_t, \quad a_1 \equiv \frac{1 - \frac{1}{\psi}}{1 - \kappa_1 \rho}, \tag{9.24}$$

where the constant a_0 is characterized in appendix 9.A.

Note that when growth is very persistent (i.e., $\kappa_1 \rho \approx 1$), even small changes in the expected dividend growth, x_t, lead to large swings in the price-dividend ratio. A model solved along these lines—where persistent processes would lead to highly volatile prices—was already available in the literature, at least since the discussion of Campbell, Lo, and MacKinlay (1997, 265) of a model with persistent expected returns:

> "If this standard deviation is small [i.e., the variability of expected stock returns], it is tempting to conclude that changing expected returns have little influence on stock prices .... This conclusion is too hasty: ... if expected returns vary in a persistent fashion, [prices] can be very variable even when the [expected returns are] not."

The model discussed by Campbell, Lo, and MacKinlay is one where expected returns are directly modeled as possibly persistent processes. Instead, the model of this section is one where expected growth is possibly persistent, and expected returns are persistent as a result. We shall soon see the implications of such a broader perspective. But note a crucial point. High volatility of the price-dividend ratio does not necessarily lead to a resolution of the equity premium puzzle. For example, in the context of nonexpected utility, eq. (9.17) suggests that in equilibrium, relative risk aversion and EIS should play together in the right direction as previously explained and that the variance σ_* should be equally important. Therefore, we need to check how this high volatility of the price-dividend ratio translates into a high equity premium.

We use the expression of $R_{M,t+1}$ in eq. (9.19) and determine σ_*^2 in (9.16), leading to the model prediction regarding the equity premium and the risk-free rate through eqs. (9.17) and (9.18). We have

$$\sigma_{R_M}^2 = \kappa_1^2 var_t\left(z_{t+1}\right) + \sigma_c^2 = \underbrace{\kappa_1^2 \left(\frac{1 - \frac{1}{\psi}}{1 - \kappa_1 \rho} \right)^2 \sigma_x^2 + \sigma_c^2}_{\equiv \sigma_*^2}.$$

That is, and as anticipated, nonexpected utility can lead to a resolution of the equity premium puzzle when asset returns are driven by sources of variation in addition to consumption growth. The previous expression for σ_*^2 shows precisely how long-run risks accomplish this: the added volatility stems from large fluctuations in the price-dividend ratio that arise due to the high persistence of the "small" component x_t in eq. (9.22). An alternative—albeit entirely consistent—way to explain these facts relies on the expression for the innovations to the pricing kernel (or the stochastic discount factor) in this model: by eq. (9.20),

$$\ln m_{t,t+1} - E_t\left(\ln m_{t,t+1}\right) = -\gamma\left(g_{t+1} - E_t\left(g_{t+1}\right)\right) - (1-\theta)\,\kappa_1 a_1\left(x_{t+1} - E_t\left(x_{t+1}\right)\right).$$

That is, long-run risks are priced, with this pricing materializing through the coefficient a_1, the sensitivity of the price-dividend ratio to changes in x_t (see eq. (9.24)): even if the innovations to x_t are small, a_1 is large, as explained, and leads to a large compensation for this risk, provided $\theta < 1$.

One difficulty with the model in this section is that it leads to constant expected returns and volatility. Bansal and Yaron (2004) consider a more general model in which the variance of consumption growth and that of expected growth are assumed to be the same and time-varying. This assumption leads to time-varying statistics. At the time of writing, it still remains unclear whether heteroskedasticity in consumption may be regarded as a plausible channel to time-varying asset returns statistics. For example, chapter 8 reviews empirical evidence that seems to be inconsistent with the idea that asset returns volatility links to fundamentals volatility. Nonetheless, the main features of this model seem sensible. Indeed, the literature on long-run risks has been prolific[5] and has been submitted to empirical scrutiny (see, e.g., Bansal, Kiku, and Yaron, 2012; Beeler and Campbell, 2012). In the model in this section, these risks coincide with a small albeit persistent growth component. It has been noted that, in practice, it is statistically difficult to detect a random process with such a small component (see Shephard and Harvey, 1990). But the economic mechanism underlying the model is plausible. Kaltenbrunner and Lochstoer (2010), for example, explain that optimal consumption smoothing in production economies may lead to the type of long-run risks studied in this section.

9.3 Heterogeneous Agents and "Catching up with the Joneses"

Chapter 8 explains that external habit formation has the potential to explain many of the stylized facts of aggregate stock market fluctuations. For example, the Campbell and Cochrane (1999) model produces predictions of asset prices and volatilities that are perfectly plausible due to a time-varying and countercyclical price of risk. However, this model still relies on an economy with a high risk aversion. This section presents a model, developed by Chan and Kogan (2002), where a countercyclical price of risk does not require the existence of a representative agent with a high risk aversion. In this model, there are heterogeneous agents with preferences displaying "catching up with the Joneses" features. These preferences were initially introduced by Abel (1990, 1999), and the model in this section extends Abel's analysis to economies with heterogeneous agents.

5. For example, it has addressed puzzles in international finance (see Colacito and Croce, 2011).

Consider a continuum of agents, each of them indexed by a risk aversion parameter $\gamma \in [1, \infty)$. The instantaneous utility of agent γ is

$$u_\gamma(c, x) = \frac{\left(\frac{c}{x}\right)^{1-\gamma}}{1-\gamma},$$

where c is consumption and x is the standard living of others, to be defined in a moment. The total endowment in the economy is D and follows a geometric Brownian motion,

$$\frac{dD_t}{D_t} = g_0 dt + \sigma_0 dW_t. \tag{9.25}$$

By assumption, the standard of living of others, x_t, is a weighted geometric average of the past realizations of the aggregate endowment D, namely,[6]

$$\ln x_t = \ln x_0 e^{-\theta t} + \theta \int_0^t e^{-\theta(t-s)} \ln D_s ds, \quad \text{with } \theta > 0.$$

Therefore, x_t satisfies

$$dx_t = \theta s_t x_t dt, \quad \text{where } s_t \equiv \ln\left(\frac{D_t}{x_t}\right). \tag{9.26}$$

By eqs. (9.25) and (9.26), s_t is the solution to

$$ds_t = \left(g_0 - \frac{1}{2}\sigma_0^2 - \theta s_t\right) dt + \sigma_0 dW_t.$$

This model can be interpreted as one displaying "catching up with the Joneses" features because the utility of each agent is affected by a benchmark, x_t, which is a weighted average of the past aggregate endowment D_t, the latter obviously being equal to aggregate consumption (see the constraint in [P1] below). This model is important. We already know (see chapter 8) that a realistically calibrated economy with habit formation and a representative agent relies on a high risk aversion. Moreover, an economy with "catching up with the Joneses" features and a representative agent would also rely on a high risk aversion, as argued below. Chan and Kogan (2002) show that their model, while capturing the spirit of habit formation through catching up with the Joneses, does not need to rely on a high risk aversion once we populate the economy with heterogeneous agents, thereby allowing habit formation and "catching up with the Joneses" features to perform a role in the explanation of the equity premium puzzle.

In this economy with complete markets, we can determine the asset price and solve the model by relying on the centralization of competitive equilibrium through Pareto weighting, along lines similar to those in theorem 2.7 of chapter 2. As explained in appendix 9.B, the equilibrium price process is the same as that in an economy with a representative agent

6. It is a distributed lags model in that the weights on $\ln x_0$ and $\ln D_s$ sum up to one. Alternatively, and assuming time starts infinitely far in the past, it is an infinite distributed lags model in that $\ln x_\tau = \int_{-\infty}^{\tau} \omega_{s,\tau} \ln D_s ds$, where the weights $\omega_{s,\tau} \equiv \theta e^{-\theta(\tau-s)}$ satisfy $\int_{-\infty}^{\tau} \omega_{s,\tau} ds = 1$.

with instantaneous utility,

$$u(D,x) \equiv \max_{c_\gamma} \int_1^\infty u_\gamma (c_\gamma, x) f_\gamma d\gamma \quad \text{s.t.} \quad \int_1^\infty c_\gamma d\gamma = D, \qquad \text{[P1]}$$

where ${f_\gamma}^{-1}$ is the marginal utility of income of the agent γ. Appendix 9.B provides further details on the derivation of the value function of the program [P1], which is

$$U(s) \equiv \int_1^\infty \frac{1}{1-\gamma} f_\gamma^{\frac{1}{\gamma}} \psi(s)^{\frac{\gamma-1}{\gamma}} d\gamma, \tag{9.27}$$

where ψ is a Lagrange multiplier, a function of the state s, satisfying

$$e^s = \int_1^\infty f_\gamma^{\frac{1}{\gamma}} \psi(s)^{-\frac{1}{\gamma}} d\gamma. \tag{9.28}$$

Finally, appendix 9.B shows that the unit risk premium predicted by this model is

$$\lambda(s) = \sigma_0 \frac{e^s}{\int_1^\infty \frac{1}{\gamma} f_\gamma^{\frac{1}{\gamma}} \psi(s)^{-\frac{1}{\gamma}} d\gamma}. \tag{9.29}$$

To summarize, eq. (9.28) determines the Lagrange multiplier, $\psi(s)$, which then feeds $\lambda(s)$ through eq. (9.29). Empirically, the Pareto weighting function, f_γ, can be parametrized by a function that can be calibrated to match selected characteristics of the asset returns and volatility. Note, finally, that this economy collapses to an otherwise identical homogeneous economy once the social weighting function $f_\gamma = \delta(\gamma - \bar{\gamma})$, the Dirac's mass at some $\bar{\gamma}$. In this case, $\lambda(s) = \sigma_0 \bar{\gamma}$, a constant. As anticipated, an economy with a single agent with "catching up with the Joneses" features is unlikely to resolve the equity premium puzzle or address other issues such as predictability because $\sigma_0 \bar{\gamma}$ is both small and constant.[7]

A technical but crucial assumption of this model is that the standard of living of others, x_t, is a process with *bounded* variation (see eq. (9.26)). This assumption implies that x_t is not a risk for which the agents require compensation. In this model, then, it is the agents' heterogeneity that drives variation in the risk premium $\lambda(s)$ (see eq. (9.29)). By calibrating the model to US data, Chan and Kogan find that $\lambda(s)$ is decreasing and convex in s.[8] The mechanism underlying the model predictions links to an endogenous redistribution of wealth. The less risk averse agents obviously invest a higher proportion of their wealth into risky assets, compared with the more risk averse. In the poor states of the world, when stock prices decrease, the wealth of the less risk averse agents lowers more than that of the more risk averse. The result is a reduction in the fraction of wealth held by the less risk averse individuals in the whole economy. Thus, in bad times, the contribution of these less risk averse individuals to aggregate risk aversion decreases, and hence, aggregate risk aversion increases and so does $\lambda(s)$ in eq. (9.29).

---

7. See Campbell (2003) for a similar critique.

8. Their numerical results also revealed that in their model, the *log* of the price-dividend ratio is increasing and *concave* in s. Finally, their lemma 5 (Chan and Kogan, 2002, 1281) establishes that in a homogeneous economy, the price-dividend ratio is increasing and *convex* in s.

Note that, in further work, Xiouros and Zapatero (2010) considered a model similar to that of Chan and Cogan, calibrate the distribution of f_γ to data (not financial market data), and argue that their model fails to produce a sufficiently volatile price of risk: heterogeneity of risk aversion does not seem to generate a significant redistribution of wealth, given the low level of consumption volatility. The economic mechanism underlying a countercyclical price of risk, while certainly plausible, seems to necessitate complementary channels in order to produce better quantitative predictions.

9.4 Idiosyncratic Risk and Incomplete Markets

Aggregate risk is too small to justify the size of the equity premium with a low level of risk aversion. Do individuals bear idiosyncratic risk—one that cannot be diversified away by trading in financial markets? And then, how can this risk affect asset evaluation? Shouldn't this risk be neutral to asset pricing? The answer to these questions is indeed subtle and relies on whether idiosyncratic risk affects agents' portfolio decisions and then equilibrium asset prices. This section presents and discusses models that activate these channels. It also reviews early models that explain the equity premium as a result of restricted stock market participation.

9.4.1 A Static Model of Idiosyncratic Risk

Mankiw (1986) is the first to point out the asset pricing implications of idiosyncratic risks. In his model, aggregate shocks to consumption do not affect individuals in the same way, ex post. Ex ante, individuals know that the business cycle may adversely change—an *aggregate* shock—although they also anticipate that the very same shock may be particularly severe to only a portion of them—an *idiosyncratic* shock. To illustrate, everyone faces a positive probability of experiencing a job loss during a recession, although only a part of the population will actually suffer from a job loss. Alternatively, it is one thing to say that a recession will lead to a salary reduction for everyone and another thing to say that a number of individuals will not be affected by the recession, although the remaining individuals may have to bear its entire burden.

Idiosyncratic risk may significantly affect agents' portfolio choice and hence asset evaluation. Naturally, in the presence of contingent claims that insure against these shocks, idiosyncratic risk would not matter. But the point is that, in reality, these contingent claims do not exist yet, due perhaps to moral hazard or adverse selection reasons. This source of market incompleteness might then potentially explain the aggregate stock market behavior in a way that the model with a standard representative agent cannot.

Mankiw considers the pricing of a risky asset in a two-period model, with the first period budget constraint given by $p\theta + m = w$ and the second period individual consumption equal to

$$c = \tilde{w} + \tilde{R}\theta + (w - p\theta)(1 + r) \equiv \tilde{w} + \tilde{X}\theta,$$

where $\tilde{w}$ is the second period endowment; m is the amount to invest in an MMA; r is the safe interest rate on the MMA, normalized to zero; w is the initial endowment, also normalized to zero; p is the price of the risky asset; $\tilde{R}$ is the payoff promised by the risky asset; and finally, $\tilde{X} \equiv \tilde{R} - p$ is the asset net payoff. That is, we may either endogenize the price p, given the payoff $\tilde{R}$, or just the net payoff, $\tilde{X}$, as described next. The asset is in zero

Table 9.1
Aggregate fluctuations and idiosyncratic risk

	Net asset payoff	Per capita consumption	Individual consumption ($\tilde{w}$)
Bad state	-1	$(1-\phi)\,\mu$	$\left(1-\frac{\phi}{\lambda}\right)\mu$ (consumed by λ) μ (consumed by $1-\lambda$)
Good state	$1+\pi$	μ	μ

net supply, and because agents are ex ante identical, we have that in equilibrium, $\theta=0$ such that $\tilde{w}$ equals per capita consumption, c.

There are two states of nature for the aggregate economy, both of which are equally likely. In the good state, the net asset payoff is $\tilde{X}=1+\pi$, and per capita consumption is $\tilde{w}=\mu$. In the bad state, the net asset payoff is instead $\tilde{X}=-1$, and per capita consumption is also adversely affected in that $\tilde{w}=(1-\phi)\,\mu$. The payoff in the good state, π, equals $2E(\tilde{X})$. Therefore, π measures a risk premium; of course it has to be determined in equilibrium.

How does this macroeconomic shock affect asset pricing in the presence of agents who could be heterogeneous ex post? The crucial feature of the model is the assumption that only a fraction λ of agents will absorb the macroeconomic risk in that, literally, a fraction $1-\lambda$ of individuals will not be hit by the aggregate shock and each of them will still consume μ for a total of $(1-\lambda)\,\mu$. The residual portion of the population will consume the residual, $(1-\phi)\,\mu-(1-\lambda)\,\mu=(\lambda-\phi)\,\mu$, such that each agent hit by the shock will consume $\left(1-\frac{\phi}{\lambda}\right)\mu$. The ratio, $\frac{\phi}{\lambda}$, is the per capita fall in consumption for any individual hit by the shock in the bad state of nature. If $\lambda=1$, the aggregate shock hits everyone. The highest concentration of the shock arises when $\lambda=\phi$, that is, when the fall in consumption is borne by the lowest possible fraction of the population. Table 9.1 summarizes payoffs, per capita consumption, and individual consumption in this economy.

To summarize, only a selected portion of individuals will bear and share a macroeconomic shock such that the burden of this shock will be particularly heavy should it materialize, especially when λ is small. Since the risky asset performs poorly in bad times, its evaluation should reflect not only business cycle risk but also the fact that the business cycle might be particularly severe to those who will be hurt by it.

To formalize this reasoning, consider the first-order conditions for any expected utility maximizer:

$$\begin{aligned} 0 &= E[\tilde{X}u'(\tilde{w}+\tilde{X}\theta)] \\ &= E[\tilde{X}u'(\tilde{w})] \\ &= \tfrac{1}{2}\cdot(-1)\left[u'\left(\left(1-\tfrac{\phi}{\lambda}\right)\mu\right)\lambda+u'(\mu)(1-\lambda)\right]+\tfrac{1}{2}\cdot(1+\pi)\,u'(\mu), \end{aligned}$$

where the second equality follows by the equilibrium condition, $\theta=0$, and u is an utility function satisfying standard regularity conditions. The premium, π, is

$$\pi=\lambda\frac{u'\left(\mu\left(1-\frac{\phi}{\lambda}\right)\right)-u'(\mu)}{u'(\mu)}.$$

Mankiw shows that, for utility functions leading to prudent behavior, $u''' > 0$, the premium π is decreasing in λ: an increase in the concentration of aggregate shocks leads to higher premiums. Moreover, it is easy to see that π can be made arbitrarily large, for λ arbitrarily close to ϕ once the utility function satisfies the Inada condition, $\lim_{c\to 0} u'(c) = \infty$, as we have that $\lim_{\lambda\to\phi} \pi = \infty$. For example, in the log utility case, we have that $\pi = \frac{\lambda\phi}{\lambda-\phi}$.

9.4.2 Idiosyncratic Shocks Unrelated to Aggregate Risk

Weil (1992) develops a simple model in which idiosyncratic shocks are unrelated to aggregate risk. In this model, there is a continuum of agents who are ex ante identical in that they have the same utility and the same endowments: some nonrandom ω endowment in the first period and a stochastic endowment $\tilde{\omega}$ in the second. The second period endowment is independent of dividends and IID across agents. The agents, then, face the following budget constraints:

$$\begin{cases} c_1 + S\theta = (S+d)\,\theta_0 + \omega \\ \tilde{c}_2 = \tilde{d}\theta + \tilde{\omega} \end{cases}$$

where θ_0 denotes the endowment of the risky asset, c_1 and $\tilde{c}_2$ are first- and second-period consumption, and d and $\tilde{d}$ are the dividends in the first and second period. We assume that $\theta_0 = 1$. Because agents are ex ante identical, although ex post heterogeneous, they have no incentives to trade. An autarkic equilibrium is therefore one where $\theta = 1$, $c_1 = d + \omega$, and $\tilde{c}_2 = \tilde{d} + \tilde{\omega}$. Markets are incomplete because $\tilde{\omega}$ cannot be spanned through the risky asset. The asset price satisfies

$$S = \frac{E(u'(\tilde{d}+\tilde{\omega})\tilde{d})}{u'(d+\omega)}.$$

Compare this price with that arising in a complete markets economy. In a complete markets economy, agents have the same marginal rate of substitution, state by state. If agents display identical preferences, risk-pooling is then the equilibrium outcome, and each agent consumes the same, $\tilde{c}_2 = \tilde{d} + E(\tilde{\omega})$, such that the asset price is

$$S_c = \frac{E(u'(\tilde{d}+E(\tilde{\omega}))\tilde{d})}{u'(d+\omega)}.$$

Because dividend and endowment risks are independent, then, assuming u' is convex, we have that $E(u'(\tilde{d}+E(\tilde{\omega}))\tilde{d}) \le E(u'(\tilde{d}+\tilde{\omega})\tilde{d})$. That is, (i) the risk-free rate in the incomplete market case lowers compared with that in the complete case, and (ii) $S_c \le S$.

The interpretation of the condition that u' is convex relates to prudence. This condition parallels that in the previous section, by which the equity premium in Mankiw's model is increasing in the concentration of aggregate shocks. In fact, Weil argues that both the risk-free rate and the equity premium puzzles might still be explained in economies with incomplete markets, in which agents make precautionary savings. One additional assumption is that agents display preferences with *decreasing absolute risk aversion (DARA)* and *decreasing absolute prudence (DAP)*.[9] The mechanism is the following.

9. A utility function u exhibits decreasing absolute prudence if the coefficient of absolute prudence, $-u'''(x)/u''(x)$, is decreasing.

Incomplete markets lead agents to act more prudently than they would if they had to face complete markets; their demand of both the riskless and the risky asset increases as a result, as explained previously. DARA and DAP ensure that the price of the risky asset increases less than the riskless asset: agents need to be less prone to bear dividend risk once they have nontraded labor income. Due to its reliance on DARA and DAP, the model seems somehow restrictive; however, many standard utility functions satisfy DARA and DAP. Duffie (1992) is one additional early reference to models with incomplete markets and a finite number of agents. In the early literature, models with idiosyncratic risk were static, and agents would not make self-insurance. The next section surveys some of the early dynamic models in which self-insurance plays a role.

9.4.3 Self-Insurance and Persistence of Idiosyncratic Shocks

The critical assumption underlying Mankiw's model is that once agents are hit by an idiosyncratic shock, the game is over. What happens once we allow agents to act in a multiperiod horizon? Intuitively, in a dynamic context, agents might implement self-insurance plans by accumulating financial assets after good shocks and selling or short selling after bad shocks have occurred. Telmer (1993) and Lucas (1994) show that if idiosyncratic shocks are not persistent, self-insurance is quite effective, and asset prices behave substantially the same as they would in a world without idiosyncratic risk. Therefore, to have asset prices significantly deviate from those arising within a complete market setting, one has to either (i) reduce the extent of risk sharing by assuming frictions such as transaction costs, short-selling constraints, or severe forms of market incompleteness or (ii) make idiosyncratic shocks persistent. With (i), we just merely eliminate the possibility that agents may implement self-insurance plans through capital market transactions. With (ii), we make idiosyncratic shocks so severe that no capital market transaction might allow agents to insure themselves and achieve portfolio solutions close to the complete market solution; intuitively, once any individual is hit by an idiosyncratic shock, they may short sell financial assets in the short run, although then they cannot persistently do so, given their wealth constraints.

Heaton and Lucas (1996) calibrate a model with idiosyncratic shocks using Panel Study of Income Dynamics and National Income and Product Accounts data. They find that idiosyncratic shocks are not quite persistent and that a large amount of transaction costs is needed to generate sizable levels of the equity premium. Naturally, idiosyncratic shocks are not always in the datasets as they were analyzed by Heaton and Lucas a long time ago. Models with idiosyncratic risk would actually help think about market behavior in periods such as the "Great Recession"—the recession occurred around 2009, when the persistence of idiosyncratic shocks would arguably be larger than over the "Great Moderation"—the period of low volatility of macroeconomic aggregates, starting after the monetary experiment in 1982 (e.g., Bernanke, 2004) and presumably ending in 2007.

9.4.4 Countercyclical Income Inequality

Constantinides and Duffie (1996) do actually take the issue of persistence in idiosyncratic risk to the extreme and consider a model without any transaction costs but with permanent idiosyncratic risk. They show that in fact, given an asset price process, it is always possible to find a cross-section of idiosyncratic risk processes compatible with a given asset price.

We now present this elegant model, which has a quite substantial theoretical importance per se. Indeed, the model makes transparent how some state variables that affect consumer choices can be reverse engineered from the observation of an asset price process.

Central to Constantinides and Duffie's analysis is the assumption that each individual i has a consumption equal to $c_{i,t}$ at time t, given by

$$c_{i,t} = \ell_{i,t} c_t, \quad \ell_{i,t} = \exp\left(\sum_{s=1}^{t} \left(\zeta_{i,s} y_s - \tfrac{1}{2} y_s^2 \right) \right),$$

where $\zeta_{i,t}$ are independent and standard normally distributed and y_t is a sequence of random variables interpreted as standard deviations of the cross-sectional distribution of the individual consumption growth shares, $\ln \frac{\ell_{i,t}}{\ell_{i,t-1}}$. Indeed,

$$\ln \left(\frac{c_{i,t+1}/c_{t+1}}{c_{i,t}/c_t} \right) \Bigg|_{\mathbb{F}_t \cup \{y_{t+1}\}} \sim N\left(-\frac{1}{2} y_{t+1}^2, y_{t+1}^2 \right), \tag{9.30}$$

where $\mathbb{F}_t$ is the information set as of time t. Denoting with $\mu(i)$ the measure of agent i, we have that, by eq. (9.30) and the law of large numbers, the cross-sectional variance of $\ln \frac{\ell_{i,t}}{\ell_{i,t-1}}$ is $\int (\ln \frac{\ell_{i,t}}{\ell_{i,t-1}} + \frac{1}{2} y_t^2)^2 d\mu(i) = y_t^2 \int \zeta_{i,t}^2 d\mu(i) = y_t^2$.

The meaning of the consumption share $\ell_{i,t}$ is that of an idiosyncratic shock every agent i receives on their consumption share at t. From the perspective of each agent, this shock is uninsurable in that it is unrelated to the asset returns. Moreover, by construction, the consumption share has a unit root as $\ln \ell_{i,t} - \ln \ell_{i,t-1} = \zeta_{i,t} y_t - \frac{1}{2} y_t^2$: a change in y_t and/or a shock in $\zeta_{i,t}$ have a permanent effect on the future path of $\ell_{i,t}$.

All agents have a CRRA utility function. We want to make sure this setup is consistent with any given equilibrium asset price process by requiring two conditions: (i) $\int c_{i,t} d\mu(i) = c_t$, that is, $\int \ell_{i,t} d\mu(i) = 1$, a condition satisfied by the law of large numbers, and (ii) the cross-sectional variances y_t^2 are reverse engineered so as to be consistent with any pricing kernel and hence any asset price process given in advance. To achieve (ii), note that by the law of iterated expectations, for any agent i, the value of an asset delivering a payoff equal to $\tilde{X}$ at time $t+1$ is

$$E\left[e^{-\rho} \left(\frac{c_{t+1}}{c_t} \right)^{-\gamma} E\left(e^{-\gamma\left(\zeta_{i,t+1} y_{t+1} - \frac{1}{2} y_{t+1}^2\right)} \Big| \mathbb{F}_t \cup \{y_{t+1}\} \right) \cdot \tilde{X} \Big| \mathbb{F}_t \right]$$

$$= E\left[e^{-\rho} \left(\frac{c_{t+1}}{c_t} \right)^{-\gamma} e^{\frac{1}{2}\gamma(\gamma+1) y_{t+1}^2} \cdot \tilde{X} \Big| \mathbb{F}_t \right],$$

where ρ is the discount rate and γ is the CRRA coefficient. It is independent of any agent i such that the stochastic discount factor is

$$\frac{\xi_{t+1}}{\xi_t} \equiv m_{t+1} \equiv e^{-\rho} \left(\frac{c_{t+1}}{c_t} \right)^{-\gamma} e^{\frac{1}{2}\gamma(\gamma+1) y_{t+1}^2}.$$

That is, given an aggregate consumption process and an arbitrage free asset price process, there exists a cross-section of idiosyncratic risk processes that supports the given price process. As a trivial example, consider the standard Lucas stochastic discount factor, which obtains when $y_t \equiv 0$.

Which properties of the pricing kernel are we looking for? Naturally, we wish to make sure m_t is countercyclical, and m_t may indeed be countercyclical when y_t^2—the dispersion of the cross-sectional distribution of the log-consumption growth—is. However, Lettau (2002) shows that empirically this dispersion is not enough, even when multiplied by $\frac{1}{2}\gamma(\gamma+1)$, unless we are willing to assume, again, a high level of risk aversion. Note that Lettau analyzes a situation that favorably biases his final outcome toward not rejecting the null that idiosyncratic risk matters, as he assumes agents cannot insure themselves at all: once they are hit by an idiosyncratic shock, they just have to consume their income. Constantinides, Donaldson, and Mehra (2002) consider overlapping generations models to mitigate the issue of persistence in the idiosyncratic risk process.

9.4.5 A Model with Restricted Market Participation

This section discusses a model that takes market incompleteness as *given* (e.g., it is not induced by idiosyncratic risks) and independent of the state of the economy. In this model, agents are heterogeneous ex ante in that they have unequal access to securities markets; by contrast, in the model of the previous section, agents are homogeneous ex ante but heterogeneous ex post, due to the realization of idiosyncratic shocks.

The model of this section considers an extreme form of market incompleteness, by which all the macroeconomic risk is borne by a handful portion of agents. There may be agents with access to the market for the risky asset ("equity") and agents without access. The equity premium is the expected excess return the first agents require to bear the risk in the equity market. This premium can be quite large, even in the presence of small risk aversion, because agents need to take on the entire aggregate macroeconomic risk. In particular, Basak and Cuoco (1998) consider the following model. An agent does not invest in the stock market and has logarithmic instantaneous utility, $u_n(c)=\ln c$. From the agent's perspective, markets are incomplete. A second agent can invest in the stock market and has instantaneous utility equal to $u_p(c)=(c^{1-\gamma}-1)/(1-\gamma)$. Both agents are infinitely lived. The competitive equilibrium of this economy cannot be Pareto efficient, and so aggregation results such as those underlying the economy in section 9.3 cannot be obtained. However, Basak and Cuoco show that aggregation is still obtained in this economy, once we define social weights in a judicious way.

Let $\hat{c}_{it}$ be the general equilibrium allocation of agent i, $i=p,n$. In equilibrium, $\hat{c}_p+\hat{c}_n=D$, where D is the instantaneous aggregate consumption, taken to be a geometric Brownian motion with parameters g_0 and σ_0,

$$\frac{dD_t}{D_t}=g_0dt+\sigma_0dW_t. \tag{9.31}$$

Define

$$s_t\equiv\frac{\hat{c}_{pt}}{D_t}, \tag{9.32}$$

which is the consumption share of the market participant.

Denoting the discounting rate with δ, the first-order conditions pertaining to the two agents intertemporal consumption plans are

$$u_p'(\hat{c}_{pt})=w_pe^{\delta t}\xi_t,\quad \hat{c}_{nt}^{-1}=w_ne^{\delta t-\int_0^t r_sds}, \tag{9.33}$$

where w_p, w_n are two constants, ξ is the pricing kernel process and the solution to

$$\frac{d\xi_t}{\xi_t} = -r_t dt - \lambda_t \cdot dW_t, \tag{9.34}$$

and finally, r is the short-term rate and λ is the unit risk premium, which equal

$$r(s) = \delta + \frac{\gamma g_0}{s + \gamma (1-s)} - \frac{1}{2} \frac{1}{s(s + \gamma(1-s))} \sigma_0^2 \gamma (1+\gamma), \tag{9.35}$$

and

$$\lambda(s) = \gamma \sigma_0 s^{-1}. \tag{9.36}$$

The expressions for r and λ in eqs. (9.35) and (9.36) are derived below. Appendix 9.B provides a further derivation that relies on the existence of a representative agent as originally put forward by Basak and Cuoco (1998) and as explained below.

In this economy, the marginal investor bears the entire macroeconomic risk. The risk premium this investor requires to invest in the aggregate stock market is large when their consumption share, s_t, is small. With just a risk aversion of $\gamma = 4$ and a consumption volatility of 3%, this model can reproduce realistic figures for the Sharpe ratio on the market aggregate, as illustrated by figure 9.2. For example, Mankiw and Zeldes (1991) estimate that the share of aggregate consumption held by stockholders is approximately 30%. In terms of this model, $s = 0.30$ translates into a Sharpe ratio equal to 0.4.

Guvenen (2009) makes an interesting extension of the Basak and Cuoco model. He considers two agents in which only the "rich agent" invests in the stock market, and in which this agent's EIS is higher than the EIS for a "poor" investor. Guvenen shows that, for the rich, a low EIS is needed to match the equity premium. However, US data show that the rich have a high EIS, which cannot match the equity premium.[10]

To derive eqs. (9.35) and (9.36), note that the consumption of the agent not participating in the stock market satisfies, by eq. (9.33),

$$\frac{d\hat{c}_{nt}}{\hat{c}_{nt}} = (r_t - \delta)\, dt. \tag{9.37}$$

Therefore, the consumption of the marginal investor, $\hat{c}_p = D - \hat{c}_n$, satisfies

$$\begin{aligned}\frac{d\hat{c}_{pt}}{\hat{c}_{pt}} &= \frac{dD_t}{D_t}\frac{D_t}{\hat{c}_{pt}} - \frac{d\hat{c}_{nt}}{\hat{c}_{nt}}\frac{\hat{c}_{nt}}{\hat{c}_{pt}} \\ &= \frac{1}{s_t}\left(g_0 - (r_t - \delta)(1 - s_t)\right) dt + \sigma_0 \frac{1}{s_t} dW_t, \end{aligned} \tag{9.38}$$

where the second equality follows by the definition of s in eq. (9.32) and by eqs. (9.31) and (9.37). Moreover, by the first-order conditions of the market participant in eq. (9.33)

10. Guvenen (2009) considers an extension of the model where we can disentangle EIS and CRRA for the rich investor.

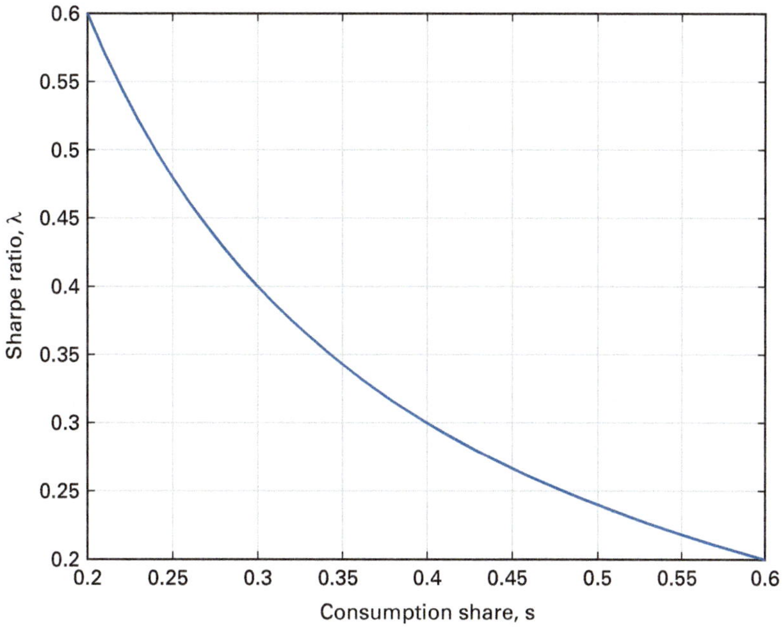

Figure 9.2
The Sharpe ratio, $\lambda(s)$ in eq. (9.36), in the Basak and Cuoco (1998) model as a function of the consumption share of the market participant, s. Parameter values are $\gamma = 3$ and $\sigma_0 = 3\%$.

and the CRRA assumption for u_p,

$$\gamma d \ln \hat{c}_{pt} = -\delta dt - d \ln \xi_t = -\left(\delta - r_t - \frac{1}{2}\lambda_t^2\right) dt + \lambda_t dW_t. \tag{9.39}$$

Using the relation $d \ln c = \frac{dc}{c} - \frac{1}{2}\left(\frac{dc}{c}\right)^2$ and then identifying terms in eq. (9.38) and eq. (9.39) delivers the two expressions for r and λ in eqs. (9.35) and (9.36).

How do these results technically relate to aggregation? Basak and Cuoco define the *instantaneous* utility of a representative agent, a social planner, as

$$U(D, x) \equiv \max_{c_p + c_n = D} \left[u_p(c_p) + x \cdot u_n(c_n)\right], \tag{9.40}$$

where

$$x \equiv \frac{u_p'(\hat{c}_p)}{u_n'(\hat{c}_n)} = u_p'(\hat{c}_p)\hat{c}_n$$

is a *stochastic social weight* and, once again, $\hat{c}_p$ and $\hat{c}_n$ are the private allocations, satisfying the first-order conditions in eqs. (9.33). By the definition of ξ and eqs. (9.33), x_t is the solution to

$$dx_t = -x_t \lambda_t dW_t. \tag{9.41}$$

Then, the equilibrium in this economy is supported by a fictitious representative agent with utility $U(D, x)$. Intuitively, the social planner allocations satisfy, by construction,

$$\frac{u_p'(c_{pt}^*)}{u_n'(c_{nt}^*)} = \frac{u_p'(\hat{c}_{pt})}{u_n'(\hat{c}_{nt})} = x_t,$$

where the starred variables denote the social planner's allocations. In other words, Basak and Cuoco's approach is to find a stochastic social weight process x_t such that the first-order conditions of the representative agent leads to the market allocations. The utility in eq. (9.40) can then be used to compute the short-term rate and risk premium and lead precisely to eqs. (9.35) and (9.36), as shown in appendix 9.B.

9.5 Disagreement and Learning

This is the first of two sections dealing with economies in which agents have a limited knowledge of the fundamentals, which they attempt to improve by processing publicly available signals. In this section, we assume agents have different opinions: while they all learn from signals, their learning pattern might differ for a variety of reasons—for example, agents might suffer from different cognitive biases regarding the real content of the signals they have access to.

We analyze the impact of disagreement on asset prices in two models. In both, the mechanism leading to disagreement is the agents' overconfidence about their ability to process information they consider as their own. In the first model, developed by Scheinkman and Xiong (2002), bubbles arise as a result of differences in opinion among risk neutral agents in the presence of short-sale constraints. In the second, agents' disagreement is cast within a more standard general equilibrium with complete markets, risk averse agents, and no short-sale constraints; a special case of this model is the two-person model of Dumas, Kurshev, and Uppal (2009), which we discuss in some detail.

To deal with the models in this section, we need a preliminary survey of tools, which allow us to think about how agents process information conveyed by multiple signals. These tools generalize the scope of those introduced in chapter 8 (section 8.6) and are in section 9.5.1. In section 9.5.2, we present details regarding the model of Scheinkman and Xiong, and in section 9.5.3, we analyze how differences in opinions are dealt with in general equilibrium in the absence of frictions. Section 9.5.3 also deals with issues of aggregation in markets with heterogeneous beliefs, providing a general framework to address a number of issues, from the analysis of survival of irrational traders to themes such as the equity premium puzzle or excess volatility in irrational markets.

Note that the vast majority of the explanations in this section have a behavioral slant. We are about to assume that agents have psychological biases in that they make systematic mistakes while assessing the probability distribution of the fundamentals: they emphasize aspects of the markets such as correlations or informativeness of signals, which are less pronounced than in the real markets they operate in. In section 9.6, we move to an alternative approach, relying on Knightian uncertainty: while agents still have a poor knowledge of the complex environment in which they take decisions, they behave rationally by explicitly acknowledging their ignorance and fearing the errors possibly arising from it.

9.5.1 Learning with Multiple Signals

We discuss filtering results on Bayesian learning that generalize those in chapter 8 while taking into account the possibility that agents might update beliefs relying on multiple signals.

Consider the following result—a special case of theorem 12.7 in Liptser and Shiryaev (2001, 36). Suppose that some unobservable process θ_t is a solution to

$$d\theta_t = (a_0 + a_1\theta_t)\, dt + bdZ_t, \tag{9.42}$$

where a_0 and a_1 are scalar constants, b is a k-dimensional vector of constants, and Z_t is a k-dimensional standard Brownian motion. Assume that an ℓ-dimensional vector of signals $\mathcal{S}_t$ on θ_t are observed and are the solution to

$$d\mathcal{S}_t = A\theta_t dt + BdZ_t, \tag{9.43}$$

where A and B are an ℓ-dimensional vector and an $\ell \times k$ matrix of constants. Define

$$\hat{\theta}_t \equiv E\left(\theta_t | \mathbb{F}_t\right),$$

where $\mathbb{F}_t$ is the information set available at time t. Then, $\hat{\theta}_t$ is a diffusion process with time-varying but deterministic volatility.

Assuming enough time has elapsed to make the variance of $\hat{\theta}_t$ stationary, we have

$$d\hat{\theta}_t = (a_0 + a_1\hat{\theta}_t)dt + \left(bB^\top + \alpha_* A^\top\right)(BB^\top)^{-1}(d\mathcal{S}_t - A\hat{\theta}_t dt), \tag{9.44}$$

where

$$\alpha_* : 0 = 2a_1\alpha_* + bb^\top - \left(bB^\top + \alpha_* A^\top\right)(BB^\top)^{-1}\left(bB^\top + \alpha_* A\right). \tag{9.45}$$

Note that the Brownian motions driving the unobservable θ_t and the signals $\mathcal{S}_t$ are (potentially) the same, such that the interpretation of $bB^\top$ into the variance term of eq. (9.44) is that of the instantaneous covariance between θ_t and $\mathcal{S}_t$,

$$cov\left(d\theta_t d\mathcal{S}_t\right) = bB^\top dt. \tag{9.46}$$

The next sections rely on these filtering results and evaluate how agents update their beliefs in light of new information in a number of models.

9.5.2 Overconfidence and Bubbles

Scheinkman and Xiong (2002) consider a market in which the *cumulative* dividend process D_t^c of an asset satisfies

$$dD_t^c = D_t dt + \sigma_d dZ_t^d, \tag{9.47}$$

where Z_t^d is a Brownian motion, σ_d is a constant, and D_t is the expected instantaneous dividend. Note that in all the models dealt with so far, the cumulative dividend is locally deterministic, that is, $\sigma_d = 0$ in eq. (9.47). So this model differs and relies on the additional assumption that D_t is not observed—only D_t^c is—and is known to be a mean-reverting process,

$$dD_t = \lambda\left(\bar{D} - D_t\right) dt + \sigma_f dZ_t^f, \tag{9.48}$$

where Z_t^f is a standard Brownian motion and λ and σ_f are two positive constants.

There are two sets of risk neutral agents, A and B, who observe signals on D_t, which satisfy

$$ds_t^i = D_t dt + \sigma_s dZ_t^i, \quad i \in \{A, B\}. \tag{9.49}$$

However, agent A thinks of s^A as being "their own signal" and believes its volatility is $\frac{\sigma_s}{\phi}$ for some $\phi \geq 1$, not σ_s, and agent B thinks the same regarding "their own signal" s^B. This overconfidence is the source of a behavioral bias similar to that considered in previous work by Kyle and Wang (1997) and Odean (1998): agents make systematic mistakes about the asset fundamentals while processing information by assigning higher weight to a signal they arbitrarily perceive as their own.

These assumptions are those appearing in the working paper version of Scheinkman and Xiong (2002). In the published version, the assumption is that agents perceive signals to be correlated with the fundamentals, even if they are not. These two alternative assumptions give rise to the same conclusions. We maintain the assumptions in this section because we deal with the latter assumption in section 9.5.3 while discussing another model, thereby providing the reader with an additional exercise about learning in an overconfidence context.[11] We now apply the filtering results in the previous section and analyze how overconfidence leads to disagreement formally. We then turn to the determination of an equilibrium and explain the mechanism leading to bubbles.

9.5.2.1 *The inference process*

We now provide a step-by-step derivation of the inference process. In terms of the framework of section 9.5.1, the expected instantaneous dividend D_t in eq. (9.48) is the unobservable θ_t, and the signals available to each agent, $\mathcal{S}_t$, are the cumulative dividend D_t^c in eq. (9.47) and the two signals s_t^i in eq. (9.49) where the latter are subject to behavioral biases as explained.

First, consider an agent who observes the cumulative dividend D_t^c in eq. (9.47) such that the Brownian motion in section 9.5.1 is $Z_t^\top = [Z_t^d \; Z_t^f]$ here, with the covariance term in eq. (9.46) being equal to zero, $cov\left(dD_t dD_t^c\right) = 0$. Then, by eq. (9.44), the expected instantaneous dividend at t given all available information, $\hat{D}_t \equiv E\left(D_t | \mathbb{F}_t\right)$, satisfies

$$d\hat{D}_t = \lambda(\bar{D} - \hat{D}_t)dt + \alpha_* \sigma_d^{-2}(dD_t^c - \hat{D}_t dt), \tag{9.50}$$

where α_* is the positive root of $0 = \sigma_d^{-2}\alpha_*^2 + 2\lambda\alpha_* - \sigma_f^2$. This is entirely consistent with the early models of learning reviewed in chapter 8.

Next, assume that agents also observe the signals s_t^i in eq. (9.49) but have no overconfidence. Then we shall argue that all agents update priors through new information as follows:

$$d\hat{D}_t = \lambda(\bar{D} - \hat{D}_t)dt + \alpha_* \left(\frac{1}{\sigma_d} dW_t^d + \frac{1}{\sigma_s} dW_t^A + \frac{1}{\sigma_s} dW_t^B\right), \tag{9.51}$$

11. Alternatively, we may think of agent A (resp. agent B) as having access to more precise information about signal A (signal B) than agent B (agent A). However, in this case, agents would not disagree once information is aggregated.

for some α_*, and where W_t^d is a Brownian motion under the information set $\mathbb{F}_t$ available to the agents and is defined as

$$dW_t^d \equiv \frac{1}{\sigma_d}(dD_t^c - \hat{D}_t dt).$$

The two Brownian motions W_t^i are defined similarly and will be dealt with later (see eqs. (9.55) below). Note that eq. (9.51) collapses to eq. (9.50) once we assume that agents have no access to the two signals s_t^i in eq. (9.49) or, equivalently, that these signals are uninformative, that is, $\sigma_s \to \infty$.

Finally, consider the case in which agents have overconfidence. Agent A, to start with, thinks of the signal s^B as being generated by eq. (9.49), but regarding s_t^A, they assume that

$$ds_t^A = D_t dt + \frac{\sigma_s}{\phi} dZ_t^A. \tag{9.52}$$

In terms of the filtering problem in section 9.5.1, the information set of this agent includes realizations of $\mathcal{S}_t^\top = [D_t^c \; s_t^A \; s_t^B]$ up to time t, where s_t^A is solution to eq. (9.52) and s_t^B is solution to eq. (9.49), such that b and B in eq. (9.42) and (9.43) are

$$b = [\sigma_f \;\; 0 \;\; 0 \;\; 0], \quad B = \begin{bmatrix} 0 & \sigma_d & 0 & 0 \\ 0 & 0 & \frac{\sigma_s}{\phi} & 0 \\ 0 & 0 & 0 & \sigma_s \end{bmatrix},$$

and then, by straightforward calculations and eq. (9.44), the dividend expected by agent A, $\hat{D}_t^A \equiv E\left(D_t | \mathbb{F}_t^A\right)$, satisfies

$$d\hat{D}_t^A = \lambda(\bar{D} - \hat{D}_t^A)dt + \alpha_* \left(\frac{1}{\sigma_d} dW_{At}^d + \frac{\phi}{\sigma_s} dW_{At}^A + \frac{1}{\sigma_s} dW_{At}^B\right), \tag{9.53}$$

where the Brownian motions will be defined in a moment and α_* is the positive root of $0 = (\frac{1}{\sigma_d^2} + \frac{\phi^2}{\sigma_s^2} + \frac{1}{\sigma_s^2})\alpha_*^2 + 2\lambda\alpha_* - \sigma_f^2$.

Likewise, the dividend expected by agent B, $\hat{D}_t^B \equiv E\left(D_t | \mathbb{F}_t^B\right)$, satisfies

$$d\hat{D}_t^B = \lambda(\bar{D} - \hat{D}_t^B)dt + \alpha_* \left(\frac{1}{\sigma_d} dW_{Bt}^d + \frac{1}{\sigma_s} dW_{Bt}^A + \frac{\phi}{\sigma_s} dW_{Bt}^B\right). \tag{9.54}$$

Finally, the Brownian motions in eqs. (9.53) and (9.54) satisfy

$$dW_{it}^d = \frac{1}{\sigma_d}(dD_t^c - \hat{D}_t^i dt), \quad dW_{it}^j = \frac{\phi_i}{\sigma_s}(ds_t^j - \hat{D}_t^i dt), \quad i, j \in \{A, B\}, \tag{9.55}$$

where

$$\phi_i = \begin{cases} 1, & \text{if } i \neq j \\ \phi \geq 1, & \text{if } i = j \end{cases}.$$

Naturally, the two standard Brownian motions W_t^A and W_t^B in eq. (9.51) are a special case of those in eq. (9.55), namely, for $\phi \equiv 1$.

Let us define the differences in beliefs as

$$g_t \equiv g_t^A \equiv \hat{D}_t^B - \hat{D}_t^A. \tag{9.56}$$

That is, a negative value of g_t is interpreted as a state in which agent A is more optimistic than B.

We wish to express the dynamics of g_t^A under the probability space of agent A and the dynamics of g_t^B under the probability space of agent B. Let us consider the terms of disagreement between the two types of agents. As regards the dynamics of cumulative dividends, we have by eq. (9.55) that

$$dW_{Bt}^d = dW_{At}^d - \frac{1}{\sigma_d} g_t dt,$$

and concerning the signals,

$$dW_{Bt}^A = \frac{1}{\phi} dW_{At}^A - \frac{g_t}{\sigma_s} dt, \quad \frac{1}{\phi} dW_{Bt}^B = dW_{At}^B - \frac{g_t}{\sigma_s} dt,$$

such that, using eqs. (9.53) and (9.54),

$$dg_t = -\rho g_t dt + \sigma_g dW_{At}^g, \tag{9.57}$$

for some positive constants ρ and σ_g, and a Brownian motion W_{At}^g.[12] Differences in beliefs are mean-reverting to zero. Intuitively, both agents believe that the long-term value of the instantaneous dividend is $\bar{D}$. Moreover, agents in group A think that future dividends will reflect their own beliefs, not the beliefs mistakenly held by agents in group B. Hence, they expect the difference in opinions to shrink over time. Naturally, agents in group B have a symmetrically opposite reasoning.

9.5.2.2 Bubbles as resale American options

The distinctive mark of the model is that trading occurs among agents due to difference in beliefs, and leads to bubbles arising as a result of short-selling constraints, consistent with previous insights of Harrison and Kreps (1979). Intuitively, at any point in time, the asset is held by the relatively more optimistic agent, whose asset evaluation is higher than their own assessment of the fundamentals as they are expecting to sell the asset to some future relatively more optimistic agent. Prices then deviate from any agent's fundamental evaluation because short-selling constraints bias the price toward the more optimistic agents' evaluation. We assume that all agents are risk neutral.

When is the optimal time to sell? It is a real option problem of the kind introduced in chapter 4. Let $S_{A,t}$ denote the asset price at t that agents in group A are willing to pay, such that

$$S_{A,t} = \sup_{\tau \geq 0} E_t^A \left(\int_t^{t+\tau} e^{-r(s-t)} dD_s^c + e^{-r\tau} \left(S_{B,t+\tau} - c \right) \right), \tag{9.58}$$

12. The constants are $\rho \equiv \lambda + (\frac{1+\phi^2}{\sigma_s^2} + \frac{1}{\sigma_d^2})\alpha_*$ and $\sigma_g \equiv (\phi^2 - 1)\sqrt{1+\phi^{-2}}\sigma_s^{-1}\alpha_*$, and the Brownian motion satisfies $\sqrt{1+\phi^{-2}} dW_{At}^g \equiv (dW_{At}^B - \frac{1}{\phi} dW_{At}^A)$.

where E_t^A denotes the time t conditional expectation of agents A, D_t^c is the cumulative dividend process in eq. (9.47), r is the constant interest rate, and c is a transaction cost, to be discussed later.

In other words, the price agents A are willing to pay at time t reflects the dividends paid out over the holding period and the price agents B are willing to pay at time $t+\tau$, net of the transaction cost. The conjecture is that the solution $S_{A,t}$ contains a bubble component,

$$S_{A,t} = \frac{\bar{D}}{r} + \frac{\hat{D}_t^A - \bar{D}}{r+\lambda} + \mathcal{B}(g_t). \tag{9.59}$$

The first two terms on the RHS of eq. (9.59) amount to the payoff of the asset over its life expected by agents in group A, $E_t^A(\int_t^\infty e^{-r(s-t)} dD_s^c)$—the fundamentals. According to the conjecture, agents A are willing to pay more than the fundamentals, with $\mathcal{B}(g_t)$ representing a bubble, a function of g_t, the difference in beliefs in eq. (9.56). The bubble arises exactly because agents in group A bid up the price to their own evaluations and agents in group B cannot sell short.

Replacing eq. (9.59) into eq. (9.58) and using the definition of g_t in eq. (9.56) leaves

$$\mathcal{B}(g_t) = \sup_{\tau \geq 0} E_t^A \left(e^{-r\tau} \left(\frac{g_{t+\tau}}{r+\lambda} + \mathcal{B}(-g_{t+\tau}) - c \right) \right). \tag{9.60}$$

The bubble is a resale option: it arises because the current asset holders have the option to resell it in the future at a price higher than their own evaluation. Eq. (9.60) shows that its value is determined through an optimal stopping time to sell, similarly as with a perpetual American option (see chapter 4), with the complication that the strike is endogenous, reflecting the value of the bubble as perceived by the future buyer at the optimal stopping time.

By results in chapter 4 (see section 4.8), one can conjecture that there exists a region of inaction where the asset owner holds the asset and a threshold g_* such that the optimal stopping time in eq. (9.60) is $\tau^* = \inf(\tau : g_{t+\tau} \geq g_*)$. In particular, in the continuation region, where the agent does not sell, the (discounted) bubble is a martingale such that by Itô's lemma and eq. (9.57),

$$\mathcal{L}[\mathcal{B}] - r\mathcal{B} = 0, \quad g \leq g_*, \tag{9.61}$$

where $\mathcal{L}[\mathcal{B}] = \frac{1}{2}\sigma_g^2 \mathcal{B}'' - \rho g \mathcal{B}'$ is the infinitesimal generator for g in (9.57). In the stopping region, where $\mathcal{L}[\mathcal{B}] - r\mathcal{B} \leq 0$,

$$\mathcal{B}(g) = \frac{g}{r+\lambda} + \mathcal{B}(-g) - c, \quad g \geq g_*. \tag{9.62}$$

Finally, a solution to this optimal stopping time satisfies the usual smooth-pasting conditions: (i) the function solution to eq. (9.61) for $g \leq g_*$ is the same as the function satisfying eq. (9.62) at $g = g_*$, and (ii) the derivatives of these two functions are the same at $g = g_*$. Scheinkman and Xiong (2002) show that there is a solution to this problem—and that $g_* \geq 0$, and that $g_* = 0$ only when the transaction cost $c = 0$. To illustrate, agent A needs to become sufficiently pessimistic ($g_t \geq g_* > 0$) to be able to justify the transaction cost while selling the asset. Intuitively, Brownian motions hit zero infinitely many times, such that agents will trade very often, driven by their ever-switching differences in opinions. The presence of a transaction cost mitigate, the occurrence of a such a trading frenzy.

9.5.3 General Equilibrium Without Frictions

We illustrate how to incorporate differences in beliefs in general equilibrium in a framework with complete markets. We begin with an introductory model, formulated by Kogan, Ross, Wang and Westerfield (2006) (KRWW, henceforth), which actually addresses an old and important question brought about at least since Friedman (1953): How long would irrational investors survive in financial markets?

The technical issue that arises while addressing this question links to how the agents' priors are aggregated in equilibrium: irrational agents are those who systematically believe in a model deviating from the truth and never wish to learn, thereby holding different beliefs than those of the rational agents. Section 9.5.3.1 studies such a model, and section 9.5.3.2 generalizes it to a context of learning, in which there are no agents who are more or less rational than others, along the lines of Scheinkman and Xiong (2002) but within a framework of frictionless markets without short-sale constraints. The "sentiment" model of Dumas, Kurshev, and Uppal (2009) is a special a case of this framework and vividly illustrates the main predictions arising from it; this will be discussed in section 9.5.3.3.

9.5.3.1 *Difference in beliefs and extinction of irrational traders*

KRWW analyze the implications of a drastic source of differences in beliefs, arising due to the irrationality of some agents. We briefly review this model because of both its outstanding economic importance and the aggregation techniques needed to solve it. The ensuing aggregation results are generalized in the following subsection devoted to the analysis of disagreement and learning in general equilibrium with multiple agents and frictionless markets.

Consider an economy in which there is a riskless asset in zero net supply, and one risky asset. The dividends paid by the risky asset follow a geometric Brownian motion under the physical probability P, with parameters μ and σ:

$$\frac{dD_t}{D_t} = \mu dt + \sigma dW_t, \tag{9.63}$$

with obvious notation. Rational agents correctly believe dividends are as in eq. (9.63). However, irrational agents think that the drift of the dividend process differs from that in eq. (9.63),

$$\frac{dD_t}{D_t} = \left(\mu + \upsilon\sigma^2\right) dt + \sigma dW_{2t}, \tag{9.64}$$

where υ is a constant and W_{2t} is a second Brownian motion, to be defined in a moment. Eq. (9.64) formalizes the idea that irrational agents understand the market under "their own" probability, P^2 (say), on which $dW_{2t} = dW_t - \upsilon\sigma dt$ is a Brownian motion increment by Girsanov's theorem. If $\upsilon > 0$, the irrational agent is "optimistic," in that they believe that dividends grow more than is justified by the true probability laws.

The change of probability from the benchmark rational agent to the irrational is given by the Radon-Nikodym derivative,

$$\eta_T \equiv \left.\frac{dP^2}{dP}\right|_{\mathbb{F}_T},$$

where $\mathbb{F}_T$ is the information set available to all agents and the density process η_t is the solution to

$$\frac{d\eta_t}{\eta_t} = \upsilon\sigma dW_t. \tag{9.65}$$

In this model, irrational agents do not attempt to learn from the history of dividends, and their cognitive bias is not eliminated as a result.

KRWW assume that all agents consume at some time T, that they have CRRA equal to γ, and that they have the same endowments.[13] Therefore, the rational and irrational investors maximize

$$E\left(\frac{c_{1T}^{1-\gamma}}{1-\gamma}\right) \quad \text{and} \quad E^2\left(\frac{c_{2T}^{1-\gamma}}{1-\gamma}\right) = E\left(\eta_T\frac{c_{2T}^{1-\gamma}}{1-\gamma}\right), \tag{9.66}$$

resp., where E^2 denotes the expectation under P^2 taken by the irrational agent and where the equality follows by a change of probability. Note that because η_T is strictly positive, the irrational agent becomes more and more aggressive as they disagree more with the rational agent, where disagreement is captured by η_T.

Because markets are complete, consumption allocations can be determined by solving a central planner program (just as explained in the static context of chapter 2), the value of which is

$$U_T = \max_{(c_i)_{i=1,2}: c_{1T}+c_{2T}=D_T}\left[f_1\frac{c_{1T}^{1-\gamma}}{1-\gamma} + f_2\eta_T\frac{c_{2T}^{1-\gamma}}{1-\gamma}\right], \tag{9.P1}$$

where f_i denotes the reciprocal of the marginal utility of income for agent i. The solution is

$$c_{1T} = \frac{1}{1+(b\eta_T)^{1/\gamma}}D_T, \quad c_{2T} = \frac{(b\eta_T)^{1/\gamma}}{1+(b\eta_T)^{1/\gamma}}D_T, \quad b \equiv \frac{f_2}{f_1}. \tag{9.67}$$

The irrational agent receives an allocation that increases with their disagreement: it is *as if* their utility function in (9.66) had a random weight, η_T, arising through how much they will disagree regarding the dividend path leading to D_T at the consumption date T.

We need to determine the ratio of marginal utilities of income, b. Replace the consumption allocations in (9.67) into the central planner program [9.P1], leaving

$$U(D_T, \eta_T) \equiv U_T = \left(f_1^{1/\gamma} + (\eta_T f_2)^{1/\gamma}\right)^\gamma \frac{D_T^{1-\gamma}}{1-\gamma},$$

such that, denoting partial derivatives with subscripts, the pricing kernel is given by

$$\xi_T = \frac{U_1(D_T, \eta_T)}{E_t[U_1(D_T, \eta_T)]} = \frac{(1+(b\eta_T)^{1/\gamma})^\gamma D_T^{-\gamma}}{E_t\left[(1+(b\eta_T)^{1/\gamma})^\gamma D_T^{-\gamma}\right]}. \tag{9.68}$$

13. Work on extinction by Cvitanić and Malamud (2011) relaxes the assumption that rational and irrational agents have the same mass.

Note that, because consumption only takes place at terminal date, T, the denominator of ξ_T contains the expectation of the representative agent's marginal utility, not its value at zero as is the standard case (chapter 8, section 8.4). As shown in chapter 4 (see appendix 4.B), ξ_T is the pricing kernel that determines the equilibrium prices using the MMA as the numéraire. KRWW show that (see appendix 9.B for a few steps underlying this derivation),

$$b = e^{-(1-\gamma)\upsilon\sigma^2 T}. \tag{9.69}$$

Eqs. (9.68) and (9.69) can now be used to determine the asset price and the relative consumption share. Regarding the asset price process (expressed in terms of the MMA numéraire), we have that, $S_t = E_t(\xi_T D_T)$. When agents have logarithmic preferences, $\gamma = 1$, the expression for S_t simplifies to

$$S_t = \frac{1+\eta_t}{1+\eta_t \cdot e^{-\upsilon\sigma^2(T-t)}} S_t^*, \quad S_t^* = e^{(\mu-\sigma^2)(T-t)} D_t, \tag{9.70}$$

where S_t^* denotes the price in an economy that is only populated by rational agents, that is, $\upsilon = 0$. That is, the presence of optimistic agents ($\upsilon > 0$) inflates asset prices beyond rational evaluations.

The density process can thus be interpreted as "sentiment," leading as it does to the following "euphoria." Suppose dividends are hit by a positive shock; then the asset price goes up because both S_t^* and η_t go up in eq. (9.70). That is, prices are driven by both rational evaluations and sentiment. The term "sentiment" has been used in a context with irrational agents and learning by Dumas, Kurshev, and Uppal (2009) (see section 9.5.3.3).

This property can be generalized to the case of any CRRA coefficient. Indeed, given the expression for ξ_τ in eq. (9.68), we can rely on results in chapter 8 (section 8.4.2), and determine the unit risk premium λ_τ in this economy. It is

$$\lambda_t = \sigma\gamma + \frac{(b\eta_t)^{1/\gamma}}{1+(b\eta_t)^{1/\gamma}} \frac{g}{\sigma}, \quad g \equiv -\upsilon\sigma^2, \tag{9.71}$$

and is less than that in the rational expectations economy, due to the permanent difference difference in beliefs, $E_t(\frac{dD_t}{D_t}) - E_t^2(\frac{dD_t}{D_t}) = g < 0$. All in all, the aggregate risk premium in this economy is lower, reflecting the optimistic view of the irrational agents: asset prices (expressed in terms of the money market numéraire) are higher in this economy than in the purely rational. Note also that the aggregate risk appetite is time-varying and driven by market sentiment, η_t. In good times (i.e., after a positive dividend shock), sentiment increases such that λ_t lowers in eq. (9.71), leading to "speculative enthusiasm" and higher asset evaluations.

Would irrational traders ever "disappear" in the long term? Define the relative consumption share of the rational agent against the irrational, which by eq. (9.67) and then (9.65) and (9.69) is

$$\frac{c_{2T}}{c_{1T}} = (b\eta_T)^{1/\gamma} = e^{-\frac{1}{\gamma}\left(1-\gamma+\frac{1}{2}\upsilon\right)\upsilon\sigma^2 T + \frac{1}{\gamma}\upsilon\sigma W_T}.$$

KRWW define *relative extinction* of irrational traders as occurring whenever $\lim_{T\to\infty}\frac{c_{2T}}{c_{1T}}=0$, almost surely. By the strong law of large numbers for Brownian motions (Karatzas and Shreve, 1991), we have that, given two constants a_0 and a_1,

$$\lim_{T\to\infty} e^{a_0 T+a_1 W_T}=\begin{cases}0, & a_0<0\\ \infty, & a_0>0\end{cases}$$

irrespective of the sign of a_1.

In the log utility case, $\gamma=1$, the irrational trader does not survive. For $\gamma>1$, relative extinction occurs whenever the irrational agent is either pessimistic, $\upsilon<0$, or too optimistic, $\upsilon>2(\gamma-1)$. However, the irrational trader would survive as soon as they are moderately optimistic, $0<\upsilon<2(\gamma-1)$, in which case the rational agent would not survive. The interpretation for the rational trader extinction is that the irrational trader has a price impact that makes low dividend states cheaper than the good, such that the rational trader accumulates more wealth in bad states than in the (relatively more likely) better states.

9.5.3.2 *Differences in beliefs in markets with multiple agents*

We consider an economy in which n agents hold different beliefs regarding the fundamentals of the economy, generalizing the two-person setting originally formulated by Detemple and Murthy (1994), Zapatero (1998), and others such as Basak (2000, 2005), Berrada (2006), or Buraschi and Jiltsov (2006). For example, an agent, the "benchmark," may think that output has expected growth $\hat{f}_t$ and constant volatility σ_0:

$$\frac{dD_t}{D_t}=\hat{f}_t dt+\sigma_0 dW_t. \tag{9.72}$$

We define agents with these beliefs as the benchmark in that any other agent's beliefs are about to be gauged against theirs, as explained below. Accordingly, and for a given T, consider the Radon-Nikodym derivative of the probability P^i of agent i against the benchmark $i=1$ and its density process, η_{it} say, which by Girsanov's theorem satisfies

$$\frac{d\eta_{it}}{\eta_{it}}=-g_{it}\frac{1}{\sigma_0}dW_t,\quad g_{it}\equiv\hat{f}_t-\hat{f}_{it}. \tag{9.73}$$

For each agent i, the dynamics of output is

$$\frac{dD_t}{D_t}=\hat{f}_{it}dt+\sigma_0 dW_{it}, \tag{9.74}$$

where $dW_{it}=dW_t+g_{it}\frac{1}{\sigma_0}dt$ is a Brownian motion under P^i. This example generalizes the model in the previous section, in which $\hat{f}_t$ and $\hat{f}_{it}$ are constant, as summarized by eq. (9.65).

We refrain from specifying additional examples and mechanisms leading to disagreement. For now, and until the next subsection, we focus on the determination of the equilibrium in this economy. Without loss of generality, define the first agent as the benchmark. We assume that markets are complete and that there is symmetric albeit incomplete information; denote with $\mathbb{F}_t$ the information set available to all agents. The

Radon-Nikodym derivatives,

$$\eta_{it} \equiv \left. \frac{dP^i}{dP^1} \right|_{\mathbb{F}_t}, \quad i \in \{2, \cdots, n\}, \tag{9.75}$$

formalize the notion of disagreement between agent i and the benchmark at t—a notion made more precise below. By convention, $\eta_{1t} = 1$.

Each agent maximizes their intertemporal utility, subject to the budget constraint

$$\max_{(c_{it})_{t\geq 0}} E^i \left(\int_0^\infty e^{-\rho t} u^i (c_{it})\, dt \right), \quad \text{s.t. } E^i \left(\int_0^\infty \xi_{it} c_{it} dt \right) = V_{0i}, \qquad [9.P2]$$

where E^i denotes expectation under P^i, V_{0i} is the initial wealth available to agent i, and ξ_{it} is the private state-price process or pricing kernel of agent i, a concept we elaborate on in a moment. The remaining notation is straightforward.

From part I, we know that a state-price process links to the evaluation of a consumption unit at some future prespecified state of nature. Heuristically, it is

$$\xi_{it} \equiv \left. \frac{dQ}{dP^i} \right|_{\mathbb{F}_t} e^{-\int_0^t r_u du}, \tag{9.76}$$

where Q denotes, as usual, the risk neutral probability, which links to the value of Arrow-Debreu securities, as we know. Note that ξ_{it} in eq. (9.76) can vary across agents due to difference in opinions, although then the agents need to agree on the price of the assets they observe—they do, simply, have different perspectives regarding the future developments of the assets' price.

To formalize the idea that agents disagree against the same benchmark, note that

$$\xi_{1t} = \eta_{it} \xi_{it},$$

and cast the program [9.P2] under the probability space of the benchmark agent, such that each agent i (note, i) maximizes their intertemporal utility subject to their budget constraint

$$\max_{(c_{it})_{t\geq 0}} E^1 \left(\int_0^\infty e^{-\rho t} \eta_{it} u^i (c_{it})\, dt \right), \quad \text{s.t. } E^1 \left(\int_0^\infty \xi_{1t} c_{it} dt \right) = V_{0i}. \qquad [9.P3]$$

The program [9.P3] is a standard, complete markets problem in which each agent has an instantaneous utility function equal to $\eta_{it} u^i (c_{it})$ and a commonly agreed state-price process ξ_{1t}—that of the benchmark agent. All agents do agree on the current price of all assets, although they now act more aggressively on their consumption as their divergence of opinion against the first agent widens, as summarized by a utility distortion factor η_{it}. The program [9.P3] is the intermediate-consumption, infinite-horizon extension to the program of maximizing terminal utility in (9.66).

Because markets are complete, we can study the asset pricing implications of this economy by centralizing it as usual. Consider a representative agent with instantaneous utility equal to

$$U_t = \max_{(c_i)_{i=1}^n} \sum_{i=1}^n \eta_{it} u^i (c_{it}) f_i, \quad \text{s.t.} \quad \sum_{i=1}^n c_{it} = D_t, \qquad [9.P4]$$

where D_t denotes output at t and f_i^{-1} is the marginal utility of *income* of agent i. We simplify the presentation, and to focus on the salient aspects of disagreement, we set $u^i \equiv u$ for all i. The first-order conditions of the program [9.P4] are

$$\eta_{it} u' (c_{it}) f_i = \psi_t,$$

where ψ_t is a Lagrange multiplier. Assuming agent have CRRA equal to γ, we can solve the previous equation for the consumption allocation to agent i, $c_{it} = \left(\frac{\psi_t}{\eta_{it}} \frac{1}{f_i}\right)^{-1/\gamma}$ and plug it into the constraint of the program [9.P4], thereby determining the Lagrange multiplier, $\psi_t = \left(D_t^{-1} \sum_{i=1}^n (\eta_{it} f_i)^{1/\gamma}\right)^\gamma$ and ultimately the sharing rule regarding consumption allocation,

$$c_{it} = \frac{(\eta_{it} f_i)^{1/\gamma}}{\sum_{i=1}^n (\eta_{it} f_i)^{1/\gamma}} D_t. \qquad (9.77)$$

Intuitively, and as anticipated, the more aggressive agents are, compared with the benchmark (i.e., the higher η_{it}), the higher their consumption allocation. Eq. (9.77) is, naturally, reminiscent of the consumption allocation in eq. (9.67) for the KRWW model. However, disagreement, η_{it}, is time-varying, possibly reflecting agents' learning in (9.73).

The value function for the central planner is obtained by replacing eq. (9.77) into the maximand of the program [9.P4],

$$U\left(D_t, (\eta_i)_{i=1}^n\right) \equiv U_t = \left(\sum_{i=1}^n (\eta_{it} f_i)^{1/\gamma}\right)^\gamma \frac{D_t^{1-\gamma}}{1-\gamma}. \qquad (9.78)$$

By standard arguments (see section 8.4.2 in chapter 8), the pricing kernel in this economy is given by $\xi_{1t} \equiv \xi_t$, where

$$\frac{\xi_t}{\xi_0} = e^{-\rho t} \frac{U_C\left(D_t, (\eta_{it})_{i=1}^n\right)}{U_C\left(D_0, (\eta_{i0})_{i=1}^n\right)}, \qquad (9.79)$$

where subscripts to U denote a partial derivative with respect to the first argument.

Note that to price any asset, we still need to determine the marginal utility of income for each agent i, f_i^{-1}. One approach could be to search for a cross-sectional distribution of Pareto weights that best fits selected moments of the price distribution as Chan and Kogan (2002) did in their model surveyed in section 9.3. Note that the cross-section of Pareto weights depends not only on wealth distribution but also on the beliefs' distribution. Indeed, by results in chapter 4 (see section 4.4.3), we have that the reciprocal of the marginal utility of income is

$$\frac{1}{f_i} = V_{0i}^{-\gamma} \left(\int_0^\infty e^{-\frac{\rho}{\gamma} t} E^1 \left(\eta_{it}^{\frac{1}{\gamma}} \xi_{1t}^{1-\frac{1}{\gamma}}\right) dt\right)^\gamma.$$

The asset market equilibrium can now be studied by determining the risk premiums, λ_t say, and interest rates as implied by the pricing kernel ξ_i for $i=1$ in eq. (9.76),

$$\xi_{1t} \equiv \left.\frac{dQ}{dP^1}\right|_{\mathbb{F}_t} e^{-\int_0^t r_u du} \equiv \eta_t^Q e^{-\int_0^t r_u du},$$

where

$$\frac{d\eta_t^Q}{\eta_t^Q} = -\lambda_t dW_t. \tag{9.80}$$

Finally, eq. (9.79) shows that agents' disagreement, as summarized by the cross-section $(\eta_{it})_{i=1}^n$, is a potential source of increased volatility of the pricing kernel and then resolution of the equity premium and other puzzles. The model in the next section discusses a special case of this framework that seems to illustrate this role.

9.5.3.3 *Two-person equilibrium*

Dumas, Kurshev, and Uppal (2009) (DKU, henceforth) consider a model in which agents disagree on the fundamentals due to overconfidence, similar to the model of Scheinkman and Xiong (2002) discussed in section 9.5.2. This model is a special case of that in the previous section: there are two agents ($n=2$) with the same CRRA coefficient γ, with one of them holding different beliefs due to overconfidence, as explained below.

The key assumptions of the model are that the expected growth of output D_t, f_t say, is unobserved and that the only available information is the observation of D_t and one additional signal that is totally uninformative about the state of the economy. However, an overconfident investor believes this signal is correlated with the economic fundamentals, whence a difference in beliefs between them and a second, rational investor, the benchmark.

In detail, output is solution to

$$\begin{cases} \dfrac{dD_t}{D_t} = f_t dt + \sigma_0 dZ_t^o \\ df_t = \zeta(\bar{f} - f_t)dt + \sigma_f dZ_t^f \end{cases} \tag{9.81}$$

where $\sigma_0, \zeta, \bar{f}$ and σ_f are constant and Z_t^0 and Z_t^f are standard Brownian motions. Investors also observe an uninformative signal that is a solution to

$$ds_t = \sigma_s dZ_t^s,$$

where Z_t^s is another standard Brownian motion. However, the overconfident investor believes that this signal is correlated with the fundamentals in that

$$s_t = s_t^* : ds_t^* = \sigma_s \left(\sqrt{1-\rho^2} dZ_t^s + \rho dZ_t^f \right).$$

These assumptions substantially match those in the published version of Scheinkman and Xiong (2002), as mentioned in section 9.5.2.

Let us solve the inference problem of the irrational investor, the problem of the rational being a special case, notably for $\rho=0$. In terms of the learning problem of section 9.5.1, we have that the vector Brownian motion is $Z_t^\top = [Z_t^o \; Z_t^s \; Z_t^f]$, such that b and B in eqs. (9.42) and (9.43) are

$$b = [0 \;\; 0 \;\; \sigma_f], \quad B = \begin{bmatrix} \sigma_0 & 0 & 0 \\ 0 & \sigma_s\sqrt{1-\rho^2} & \sigma_s\rho \end{bmatrix} \tag{9.82}$$

and the inferred output growth $f_t^* \equiv E\left(f_t \middle| \mathbb{F}_t^*\right)$ is

$$df_t^* = \zeta(\bar{f} - f_t^*)dt + \frac{\alpha_B}{\sigma_0}dW_t^* + \rho\sigma_f dW_{st}, \tag{9.83}$$

where $\mathbb{F}_t^*$ denotes the information set available to the irrational agent. Instead, the rationally expected output growth is $\hat{f}_t \equiv E\left(f_t \middle| \mathbb{F}_t\right)$ and satisfies

$$d\hat{f}_t = \zeta(\bar{f} - \hat{f}_t)dt + \frac{\alpha_A}{\sigma_0}dW_t, \tag{9.84}$$

where $\mathbb{F}_t$ is the information set available to the rational agent. Remaining notation is as follows: α_A and α_B are solutions to eq. (9.45), with $a_0 = \zeta\bar{f}$, $a_1 = -\zeta$, $A^\top = [1 \; 0]$, and the matrix B is as in eqs. (9.82), where α_A is determined by setting $\rho = 0$. Below, we shall define the two Brownian motions in eqs. (9.83) and (9.84).

We take the rational agent to be the benchmark. In terms of the model in the previous subsection, they think output is as in eq. (9.72), where $\hat{f}_t$ is their expected dividend growth and is the solution to eq. (9.84)—and by construction, the two Brownians in eqs. (9.72) and (9.84) coincide. The second investor disagrees and thinks that the expected dividend growth is f_t^* and is the solution to eq. (9.83).

As in the previous subsections, the density process summarizing the difference in opinions between the irrational and the benchmark is the process η_t solution to eq. (9.73) with $g_{it} \equiv g_t \equiv \hat{f}_t - f_t^*$. Thus, and consistent with similar conventions in previous sections, $g_t < 0$ is indicative of states in which the irrational agent is more optimistic than the rational agent. Note that from the perspective of the irrational agent, output is the solution to eq. (9.74), with $\hat{f}_{it} \equiv f_t^*$, and for the Brownian motion $W_{it} \equiv W_t^*$ in eq. (9.83), such that $dW_t^* = dW_t + g_t \frac{1}{\sigma_0} dt$. Finally, the Brownian motion W_{st} is simply defined as $\frac{ds_t^*}{\sigma_s}$ and is therefore uncorrelated with W_t. The dynamics of disagreement, g_t, are

$$dg_t = -\psi g_t dt + \sigma_g dW_t - \rho\sigma_f dW_{st},$$

where $\psi \equiv \zeta + \alpha_B/\sigma_0^2$ and $\sigma_g \equiv (\alpha_A - \alpha_B)/\sigma_0$.

DKU term the density process η_t "sentiment" to emphasize that it arises due to the agents' overconfidence in processing publicly available signals. In terms of the program [9.P3], sentiment is a "distortion factor" for the agents' utility. Because markets are complete, the asset pricing implications of this economy are obtained by relying on the instantaneous utility of a representative agent, which by eq. (9.78) is

$$U_t = \frac{D_t^{1-\gamma}}{1-\gamma}\left(f_1^{1/\gamma} + (\eta_t f_2)^{1/\gamma}\right)^\gamma,$$

where f_i denotes the reciprocal of the marginal utility of agent i, as usual.

By results in chapter 8 (section 8.4.2), we can determine interest rates, risk premium, and then the pricing measure, as indicated by eq. (9.80). By eq. (9.79), we have that the pricing kernel satisfies

$$\frac{\xi_t}{\xi_0} = e^{-\rho t} \frac{D_t^{-\gamma}}{D_0^{-\gamma}} \frac{\left(f_1^{1/\gamma} + (\eta_t f_2)^{1/\gamma}\right)^{\gamma}}{\left(f_1^{1/\gamma} + (\eta_0 f_2)^{1/\gamma}\right)^{\gamma}}, \tag{9.85}$$

such that the risk premium is

$$\lambda(\eta_t, g_t) = \sigma_0 \gamma + \frac{(f_2 \eta_t)^{1/\gamma}}{f_1^{1/\gamma} + (f_2 \eta_t)^{1/\gamma}} \frac{g_t}{\sigma_0}. \tag{9.86}$$

It is increasing in disagreement g_t, and increasing (resp. decreasing) in sentiment η_t if $g_t > 0$ (resp. $g_t < 0$). Similarly, one can show that the short-term rate at time t, r_t, is a function of $\hat{f}_t$, η_t, and g_t, that is, $r_t = r(\eta_t, g_t, \hat{f}_t)$ for some function $r(\cdot)$.

The risk premium in eq. (9.86), $\lambda(\eta_t, g_t)$, generalizes the risk premium in the Kogan, Ross, Wang and Westerfield (2006) market (see eq. (9.71) in section 9.5.3.1) in that the risk premium is now time-varying due to both sentiment and differences in opinion (differences in opinion never change in the model of section 9.5.3.1). When the irrational agent is optimistic, $g_t < 0$, an increase in sentiment lowers the risk premium to a level below that in the Lucas model. However, note that during times in which the irrational agent is pessimistic, $g_t > 0$, a higher sentiment η_t would exacerbate the equity premium.

Given the previous characterization of the risk premium and the interest rate, it follows that the price-dividend ratio is driven by the three state variables η_t, g_t, and $\hat{f}_t$ and is a solution to a partial differential equation that has one of the usual forms seen in chapter 8 for similar problems. DKU actually note that a closed-form solution exists under the parameter restriction that γ is an integer; they note that, by the binomial formula,

$$\left(f_1^{1/\gamma} + (\eta_t f_2)^{1/\gamma}\right)^{\gamma} = f_1 \sum_{k=0}^{\gamma} \binom{\gamma}{k} \left(\frac{f_2}{f_1}\eta_t\right)^{\frac{k}{\gamma}}.$$

Relying on this formula and the expression for the pricing kernel in eq. (9.85), one finds that the price-dividend ratio satisfies

$$\int_0^{\infty} E\left(\frac{\xi_t}{\xi_0}\frac{D_t}{D_0}\right) dt = \int_0^{\infty} e^{-\rho t} \sum_{k=0}^{\gamma} \binom{\gamma}{k} \frac{\left(\frac{f_2}{f_1}\eta_0\right)^{k/\gamma}}{\left(1 + \left(\frac{f_2}{f_1}\eta_0\right)^{1/\gamma}\right)^{\gamma}} E\left(\left(\frac{D_t}{D_0}\right)^{1-\gamma} \left(\frac{\eta_t}{\eta_0}\right)^{k/\gamma}\right) dt$$

$$\equiv p(\eta_0, g_0, \hat{f}_0),$$

where the dependence of p on g_0 and $\hat{f}_0$ arises through the expectation inside the integral, which DKU calculate in closed form.

Asset prices are then driven by three state variables: (i) sentiment, η_t; (ii) differences in opinion, g_t; and (iii) the correctly specified expected output growth, $\hat{f}_t$. The model generates plausible values of both volatility and the equity premium. The main determinant of the equity premium is the rational agent's risk aversion to the sources of risk introduced by the irrational, summarized by sentiment and difference in opinions η_t and g_t, as illustrated by the risk premium in eq. (9.86). Expected returns and volatility are then high compared with an economy with rational agents (i.e., with $\rho=0$), with rational investors increasing the proportion of their wealth in equity only when their evaluation of the expected fundamentals, $\hat{f}_t$, increases by a considerable amount. DKU also find that the time needed for the extinction of the irrational investors is quite high.

9.6 Coping with Knightian Uncertainty

9.6.1 Prelude

9.6.1.1 Knightian uncertainty

This section still studies asset prices in economies where agents have limited knowledge of the statistical laws for the fundamentals. The new element is that we assume that agents give up thinking of having a single model to decipher the signals they receive. Rather, they formulate *multiple priors* underlying the laws of the fundamentals and act while being averse to the uncertainty inherent their own priors.[14]

Note the difference between this approach and that in the previous section. In the previous section, limited knowledge of the fundamentals had led us to consider economies in which agents disagree on the "right" model. Naturally, disagreement is not a logical necessity, given limited knowledge; however, it is a natural assumption in this context as exemplified by the overconfidence bias models dealt with in section 9.5.2.[15] Still, the previous models of disagreement rely on the assumption that agents have a unique prior with which they interpret the complex world where they live. Instead, in this section, limited knowledge leads agents to be skeptical about their own ability to process complicated pieces of information. The agents acknowledge that many explanations are possible regarding how the economy works. We survey models that allow for this line of reasoning but, to simplify, consider only one representative agent.

The context in which agents operate in this section has come to be dubbed as *Knightian uncertainty* (Keynes, 1921; Knight, 1921) or *ambiguity*, that is, uncertainty that cannot be quantified probabilistically. In fact, one may argue that, since the dawn of financial economics, the entire building blocks of our models have been relying on the assumption that everything could be quantified probabilistically; the leading examples in these early developments are trivially easy to detect in the precursory mean-variance model of Markowitz (1952) and in the subsequent work leading to the CAPM (see chapter 1).

---

14. Consider the following examples. Remember the basic definitions in chapter 6 (see section 6.2): a model is a family of conditional laws for the data we observe at t, y_t, given past data and some exogenous variables, both collected in some vector x_t, $\ell\left(y_t \middle| x_t;\theta\right)$ say, where θ is a parameter vector (see eq. (6.1)). We say that the model is well-specified if there exists a parameter value θ_0 such that $\ell\left(y_t \middle| x_t;\theta_0\right)=\ell_0\left(y_t \middle| x_t\right)$, the true law. The parameter θ_0 is unknown and the object of statistical inference. In models with Knightian uncertainty, an agent is averse to this parameter uncertainty. In some models with Knightian uncertainty, the true law is unknown. Chapter 1 (see section 1.3.7) provides an example of models with Knightian uncertainty in the context of portfolio choice.

15. Differences in beliefs do not necessarily result from overconfidence. Cujean and Hasler (2017) develops a two-agent model in which expected dividend growth is unknown, with one agent thinking it is a continuous process and another thinking it is a discrete Markov chain instead.

But introducing Knightian uncertainty in economics is not a trivial task. We would need to know how to model rational decision makers who face uncertainty. Standard decision theory would not be helpful while thinking of uncertainty. We now proceed to a short survey of the literature on ambiguity while insisting on the key references in decision theory on which models can be built. In subsequent sections, we show how these decision-theoretic foundations can be relied upon to build up models that could be used to address the typical issues arising in financial economics.

9.6.1.2 *Notes regarding theoretic aspects of Knightian uncertainty*

An important issue from a theoretic standpoint is how to model aversion to uncertainty. One of the first approaches to emerge relies on the so-called "capacities," as explained in more detail below. This approach goes back to at least Schmeidler (1989). The idea underlying this approach is to make rigorous use of nonadditive measures to formalize the concept of "loss in probability" as an attitude toward uncertainty in the context of decision theory.

Dow and Werlang (1992) are the first to analyze the implications of this theory in the context of portfolio selection. First, they show that agents do not trade when prices are not favorable enough. Second, and within their simple introductory examples, they illustrate very clearly a fundamental albeit somehow technical result known since at least Schmeidler (1986) and further elaborated by Gilboa and Schmeidler (1989) in the context of decision theory: once capacities are convex, the agent's behavior is the same as that of an agent who has a max-min criterion. Max-min criteria are best described as decision rules the agents implement while believing nature will draw worst-case scenario events. Agents, then, make "robust" decisions in that their choices will lead to outcomes that are the ideal ones in bad times.

Max-min criterions lead to an analytically convenient framework utilized in both finance and macroeconomics. The approach to max-min in situations of uncertainty was originally advocated by Wald (1950), Ellsberg (1961), and Rawls (1971) and axiomatized by Gilboa and Schmeidler (1989). The max-min criterion of choice has been extended to "smooth" formulations that disentangle a cognitive notion of uncertainty from the attitude toward it. Gilboa and Marinacci (2011) provide a survey of Knightian uncertainty in economics and decision theory. Epstein and Schneider (2010) provide an early reference for a survey of models in financial economics.

9.6.1.3 *Plan of the section*

The next section provides an introduction to the main issues that agents face while having limited knowledge of the statistical law underlying their decision. Section 9.6.3 deals with the early models introduced in the literature (and extensions in the static case) to address Knightian uncertainty. Section 9.6.4 reviews a dynamic model that aims to address the equity premium puzzle.

9.6.2 Uncertainty Aversion and the Ellsberg Paradox

The Ellsberg paradox (Ellsberg, 1961) describes situations in which agents prefer to take considerable amounts of risk rather than to engage into situations plagued with ambiguity. To illustrate this paradox, consider the following example based on a two-period market,

Table 9.2
Arrow-Debreu securities in an uncertain market

Arrow-Debreu securities	States A	B	C
A	1	0	0
B	0	1	0
C	0	0	1
$A \cup C$	1	0	1
$B \cup C$	0	1	1

zero interest rates, Arrow-Debreu securities (see chapter 2), and a risk neutral Robinson Crusoe agent. Bossaerts, Ghirardato, Guarnaschelli and Zame (2010) also study Knightian uncertainty, relying on examples based on Arrow-Debreu security prices.

We assume that there are three Arrow-Debreu securities that pay off in three mutually exclusive states of the world—states A, B and C (see table 9.2). We initially assume that the probability of state A is $\frac{1}{3}$ and that of state B is $\frac{1}{4}$, such that the securities values, ϕ. say, are

$$\phi_{\mathrm{A}} = \frac{1}{3}, \quad \phi_{\mathrm{B}} = \frac{1}{4}, \quad \phi_{\mathrm{C}} = \frac{5}{12}, \tag{9.87}$$

with straightforward notation. Obviously, then, the value of a security paying off in states A or C is higher than that paying off in states B or C,

$$\phi_{\mathrm{A \cup C}} = \frac{9}{12}, \quad \phi_{\mathrm{B \cup C}} = \frac{8}{12}. \tag{9.88}$$

That is, the ranking of two portfolios is preserved once we include the *same* additional assets in each of these portfolios, provided the additional assets pay in states of the world in which the initial portfolios do not.

Next, suppose that the probability of state B, q say, is unknown. It is a situation of *uncertainty*, not *risk*. We have

$$\phi_{\mathrm{A}} = \frac{1}{3}, \quad \phi_{\mathrm{B}} = q, \quad \phi_{\mathrm{A \cup C}} = 1 - q, \quad \phi_{\mathrm{B \cup C}} = \frac{2}{3}.$$

How would we expect Mr. Crusoe to rank these assets? We are actually stuck without making additional assumptions regarding his attitude vis-à-vis uncertainty. We may proceed as follows. We assume that Mr. Crusoe is risk neutral but at the same time so averse to uncertainty that, if hypothetically asked to go long on these assets, he would evaluate them at the worst-case scenario. To formalize this uncertainty, we may assume that Mr. Crusoe may conceive a band within which the unknown probability q lies, $q \in (\underline{q}, \bar{q})$. The wider this band, the more averse he is to uncertainty regarding q. Note that $\underline{q}$ and $\bar{q}$ can be interpreted both in terms of *uncertainty aversion* and *cognitive* terms, that is, in terms of the "extent of ignorance" about q. We address this issue later; for now, we interpret this band as indicating Mr. Crusoe's aversion to uncertainty.

Table 9.3
Lotteries in an uncertain environment

	States		
Lotteries	A	B	C
f	1	0	0
g	0	1	0
f'	1	0	1
g'	0	1	1

How does asset evaluation reflect uncertainty aversion? Assuming that Mr. Crusoe evaluates the asset at worst-case scenarios,

$$\hat{\phi}_{\mathrm{B}} \equiv \min_{q \in (\underline{q}, \bar{q})} q = \underline{q} \quad \text{and} \quad \hat{\phi}_{\mathrm{A\cup C}} \equiv \min_{q \in (\underline{q}, \bar{q})} (1-q) = 1 - \bar{q}.$$

An interesting phenomenon results. The ranking summarized by eqs. (9.87) and (9.88) may break down. In particular, if Mr. Crusoe sets his band such that $\underline{q} = \frac{1}{3} - \epsilon_1$ and $\bar{q} = \frac{1}{3} + \epsilon_2$ for two positive numbers ϵ_1 and ϵ_2 small enough, then

$$\phi_{\mathrm{A}} > \hat{\phi}_{\mathrm{B}} \quad \text{and} \quad \hat{\phi}_{\mathrm{A\cup C}} < \phi_{\mathrm{B\cup C}}. \tag{9.89}$$

That is, uncertainty aversion might actually undermine a "sure thing" principle, a concept we shall return to in a moment.

The previous example is consistent with experimental evidence initially provided by Ellsberg (1961), who showed that individuals tend to avoid situations where it is difficult to describe events probabilistically. Klibanoff, Marinacci, and Mukerji (2005) explain this context by relying on the lottery of table 9.3, which is the counterpart to the Arrow-Debreu security example in table 9.2.

Savage's axiom P2, known as the *sure thing principle*, would tell us that, in this context and for any decision maker,

$$f \succ g \Longrightarrow f' \succ g'.$$

Yet assume that the probability of state B is unknown, similarly as in the example of table 9.2. Experimental evidence is consistent with the hypothesis that, in this case, decision makers would prefer the risky lottery g' (paying off \$1 with probability $\frac{2}{3}$) rather than the lottery f' (paying off \$1 with unknown probability), even if their preferences would lead them to choose f over g. In other words, aversion to uncertainty entails the following counterpart to the inequalities in (9.89),

$$f \succ g \quad \text{and} \quad f' \prec g'.$$

The previous examples reveal that there are new elements in asset evaluation in the presence of aversion to Knightian uncertainty. We now proceed with a few key models that provide new predictions in this context.

9.6.3 Portfolio Selection and Market Participation

9.6.3.1 A static model

Dow and Werlang (1992) model aversion to uncertainty relying on the notion of *capacities*. Heuristically, capacities are nonadditive measures in that they do not sum up to one from the perspective of an uncertainty averse decision maker. For example, an investor may be unaware of the distribution of the asset discounted payoff, yet they may consider that the asset discounted payoff is high (H) with a probability no lower than π or low (L) with a probability no lower than π', with these probabilities being such that $\pi + \pi' < 1$. In other words, the (unknown) probability that the asset payoff is H, π_o say, satisfies $\pi \leq \pi_o \leq 1 - \pi'$. We now illustrate how the fact that $\pi + \pi' < 1$ reflects the investor's aversion to uncertainty. We shall explain that, while the investor does not know the true distribution of the asset payoff, they evaluate the asset by assigning low chances of good outcomes.

Suppose a risk neutral agent is contemplating buying the asset. The worst-case scenario for them is that the asset payoff is L; however, there are chances this worst-case scenario could improve by an amount equal to $H - L$. That is, this improvement occurs with a probability at least equal to π. The minimum expected improvement is, thus, $\pi\,(H - L)$ such that the minimum expected return from being long is $\pi_b \equiv (L + \pi\,(H - L)) - p$, where p denotes the asset price, as usual. The expected improvement and expected returns are minimum because, by assumption, the true probability is taken to satisfy $\pi_o \geq \pi$. Now, consider a risk neutral agent who calculates expected returns at these minimum levels; they will buy the asset if $\pi_b > 0$, that is, whenever the price satisfies

$$p < \underline{p} \equiv L + \pi\,(H - L)\,. \tag{9.90}$$

Similarly, consider a risk neutral agent who contemplates selling the asset. Their worst-case scenario is that the asset is actually good, in which case their payoff is $-H$ and the minimum expected improvement is $\pi'\,(H - L)$, such that the expected return from being short the asset is $\pi_s \equiv -\left(H + \pi'\,(L - H)\right) + p$. Similarly, as in the buy case, the expected improvement is the minimum one because, by assumption, the true probability that the asset is L is $1 - \pi_o \geq \pi'$. Our agent would now sell the asset when $\pi_s > 0$, that is, when the price satisfies

$$p > \bar{p} \equiv H - \pi'\,(H - L)\,. \tag{9.91}$$

Note how aversion to uncertainty operates. Conditions (9.90) and (9.91) tell us that the lower π and π', the more averse to uncertainty an agent is. Aversion to uncertainty leads the agent to presume that $\pi + \pi' < 1$. Let us elaborate. By (9.90), the agent buys when $p < \underline{p}$, and by (9.91), the agent sells when $p > \bar{p}$, where $\underline{p} \leq \bar{p}$, with an equality holding only when $\pi + \pi' = 1$. That is, and unless the agent is uncertainty neutral (i.e., $\pi + \pi' = 1$), the agent will not participate in the market when the price $p \in (\underline{p}, \bar{p})$. When $p \in (\underline{p}, \bar{p})$, indeed, the price is too high to break even while deciding to buy, and too low to break even while deciding to sell. Dow and Werlang (1992, 200) define the quantity $1 - \pi - \pi'$ as "the amount of probability lost by the presence of uncertainty aversion."

9.6.3.2 *Worst-case scenario interpretation*

We can reinterpret the previous behavior in terms of decisions made under worst-case scenarios. That is, we may assume now that the agent relies on a set of additive priors, that is, on fully specified probability distributions. The previous model can then be interpreted as one in which the agent picks up the worst-case distribution according to the acts they make (buy or sell).

Let λ be the unknown probability that the asset payoff is good, such that the expected profits can be written as

$$\pi_\lambda \equiv (\lambda H + (1-\lambda) L - p) x,$$

where x denotes the position in the asset, with $|x|=1$ because we are assuming that the agent can only buy or sell one unit of the asset.

This model can be made consistent with the previous capacity framework. In the previous model, the asset is worth H with a probability *at least* π, meaning that the asset is worth L with probability *at most* $1-\pi$. Moreover, in the previous model, the asset is worth L with probability *at least* π', meaning that the asset is worth H with probability *at most* $1-\pi'$. Therefore, when the uncertainty averse agent buys, they do so while thinking that the probability $\lambda \in (\pi, 1-\pi')$ that the asset payoff is H is as small as possible. Similarly, when they sell, they do so while thinking that the probability $1-\lambda \in (\pi', 1-\pi)$ that the asset payoff is L is also as small as possible. That is, when the agent buys, the profits they expect are

$$\min_{\lambda \in (\pi, 1-\pi')} \pi_\lambda = L + \pi (H-L) - p = \underline{p} - p,$$

and when they sell,

$$\min_{1-\lambda \in (\pi', 1-\pi)} (-\pi_\lambda) = p - H + \pi' (H-L) = p - \bar{p}.$$

Thus, this model collapses to the previous capacity model. It also provides additional rationale regarding the probability bands underlying the Arrow-Debreu asset evaluation in section 9.6.2.

9.6.3.3 *Max-min preferences*

The previous model can be extended to one in which agents are risk averse. Suppose that an asset pays off a dividend $f \sim N\left(\mu, \sigma_f^2\right)$, where the mean μ is unknown albeit presumed to belong to a certain band, $\mu \in [\underline{\mu}, \bar{\mu}]$, for two constants $\underline{\mu}$ and $\bar{\mu}$. We shall come back to the interpretation of this band below. Suppose that a safe asset is elastically supplied at an interest rate equal to zero, and denote as usual the price of the risky asset with p. A risk averse agent (with CARA equal to τ) chooses to invest $x \cdot p$ dollars in the risky asset while solving the following optimization problem:

$$\hat{x} = \arg\max_x \min_{\mu \in [\underline{\mu}, \bar{\mu}]} E_\mu \left(-e^{-\tau W_x}\right), \tag{9.92}$$

where $W_x = (f-p)x$ and E_m denotes the expectation taken under the probability law that results when $\mu = m$.

Knightian uncertainty arises in this model due to lack of knowledge regarding the dividend distribution: while the agent knows f is normally distributed, they are unaware of its exact location, μ. The presumption that $\mu \in [\underline{\mu}, \bar{\mu}]$ might indicate their aversion to this uncertainty: the wider they presume this band is, the more uncertainty averse they are. One alternative interpretation of the band is that this very same band plays a merely cognitive role in that the agent *only knows* that there are two bounding constants to the truth, $\underline{\mu}$ and $\bar{\mu}$. In this model, it is actually impossible to disentangle the cognitive notion of uncertainty from the agent's attitude toward it. There are more general models of ambiguity in which these two notions can be separated, and they are surveyed in the next subsection.

The optimization problem in (9.92) is solved as follows. First, the agent solves for the inner problem; that is, they take a portfolio choice x as given and then figure out what a malevolent nature would pick up for them given their portfolio choice. For example, if the agent buys the asset, $x > 0$, it easy to see that the solution for the inner problem is $\hat{\mu} \equiv \underline{\mu}$. Analogously, if $x < 0$, then the inner solution is $\hat{\mu} \equiv \bar{\mu}$. In other words, the agent's aversion to uncertainty leads them to presume that nature will pick up a bad asset for them when they buy ($\hat{\mu} = \underline{\mu}$) and a good one when they sell ($\hat{\mu} = \bar{\mu}$).

Given the solution to the inner problem, $\hat{\mu}$, the agent proceeds with solving for their portfolio choice. The first-order conditions lead to

$$\hat{x} = \frac{E_{\hat{\mu}}(f) - p}{\tau \sigma_f^2}, \quad \hat{\mu} \in \left\{\underline{\mu}, \bar{\mu}\right\}.$$

We have that $\hat{x} > 0 \iff E_{\underline{\mu}}(f) > p$ and $\hat{x} < 0 \iff E_{\bar{\mu}}(f) < p$, such that the solution to the overall optimization problem in (9.92) is

$$\hat{x} = \begin{cases} \dfrac{E_{\underline{\mu}}(f) - p}{\tau \sigma_f^2}, & \text{for } p < E_{\underline{\mu}}(f) \quad \text{(buy region)} \\ 0, & \text{for } p \in [E_{\underline{\mu}}(f), E_{\bar{\mu}}(f)] \quad \text{(nonparticipation region)} \\ \dfrac{E_{\bar{\mu}}(f) - p}{\tau \sigma_f^2}, & \text{for } p > E_{\bar{\mu}}(f) \quad \text{(sell region)} \end{cases}. \tag{9.93}$$

The interpretation of the agent's behavior is similar to that regarding the Dow and Werlang model. The agent participates in the market if the price is sufficiently favorable to them, compared with the worst-case scenario: they buy (sell) when the price is lower (higher) than their own most pessimistic (optimistic) expectation of the asset payoff. In case the price is not favorable enough, the agent does not participate. Mele and Sangiorgi (2015) first provide the solution to a portfolio choice that generalizes $\hat{x}$ in (9.93) to markets with asymmetric information.

It is interesting to examine the equilibrium implications of the model. Suppose that the asset is in positive supply, $\bar{x}$, say. In equilibrium, $\hat{x} = \bar{x}$. Then, the equilibrium price is

$$p = E_{\underline{\mu}}(f) - \tau \sigma_f^2 \bar{x}.$$

That is, the equilibrium price reflects the most pessimistic evaluation of the dividend. This property propagates to dynamic models, as explained below.

9.6.3.4 *Smooth ambiguity aversion*

Klibanoff, Marinacci, and Mukerji (2005) (KMM, henceforth) introduce a model of ambiguity where the cognitive notion of uncertainty can be disentangled from the attitude toward it. We illustrate the main features of this model while extending the previous market as follows. Conditionally on μ, the asset payoff f is still normally distributed, but uncertainty aversion is modeled assuming that there exists an increasing and concave function $h:\mathbb{R}\to\mathbb{R}$, such that a decision maker prefers the portfolio holdings x' to x if and only if

$$E_{\mathcal{M}}\left[h\left(E_{\mu}\left(-e^{-\tau W_{x'}}\right)\right)\right]\geq E_{\mathcal{M}}\left[h\left(E_{\mu}\left(-e^{-\tau W_{x}}\right)\right)\right], \tag{9.94}$$

where $\mathcal{M}$ denotes the set of priors on μ. For example, Mele and Sangiorgi (2015) assume that $\mu\sim N\left(\mu_0,\sigma_\mu^2\right)$ in their model with asymmetric information, an assumption made in this section, too.

Concavity of h is crucial to the definition of ambiguity aversion. Let us explain. Lack of knowledge of μ is the source of uncertainty in the model, and concavity of h implies that a decision maker dislikes mean-preserving spreads in expected utility values that arise due to μ: they are thus ambiguity averse, unless h is linear, in which case they are ambiguity neutral. Therefore, in this model, Knightian uncertainty arises because μ is unknown, with σ_μ^2 measuring how acute uncertainty is. What makes the model new compared with one with only "second-order uncertainty" (i.e., the presence of a stochastic mean in the asset payoff) is the aversion to this second-order uncertainty arising through the concavity of h.

Regarding the functional function for h, one may consider $h\left(u\right)=-\frac{1}{\sigma}\left(e^{-\sigma u}-1\right)$, where the parameter σ measures "absolute ambiguity aversion," with the model collapsing to one with an ambiguity neutral agent only when $\sigma=0$. Based on KMM (2005, proposition 3), one can show that max-min expected utility obtains for σ large. This section follows Mele and Sangiorgi in that h is taken to lead to "constant relative ambiguity aversion," that is, $h\left(u\right)=-\left(-u\right)^{\alpha}$, for some constant $\alpha\geq1$. Thus, the model collapses to one with an ambiguity neutral agent only if $\alpha=1$; otherwise, the higher α, the more averse to ambiguity the agent is, independent of the extent of parameter uncertainty about μ, which is summarized by σ_μ^2, as explained.

The agent then solves the following optimization problem:

$$\hat{x}=\arg\max_{x}E_{\mathcal{M}}\left[h\left(E_{\mu}\left(-e^{-\tau W_{x}}\right)\right)\right], \tag{9.95}$$

where appendix 9.C shows that

$$\begin{aligned}&E_{\mathcal{M}}\left[h\left(E_{\mu}\left(-e^{-\tau W_{x}}\right)\right)\right]=\\&-\exp\left(-\alpha\tau\left(\mu_0-p\right)x+\frac{1}{2}\alpha\tau^2\left(\alpha\operatorname{var}\left(f\right)+\left(1-\alpha\right)\operatorname{var}\left(f\middle|\mu\right)\right)x^2\right).\end{aligned} \tag{9.96}$$

Thus, the program of this ambiguity averse agent resembles that of a mean-variance agent, although the "variance term" is replaced by a convex combination of the unconditional variance $\operatorname{var}\left(f\right)=\sigma_f^2+\sigma_\mu^2$ and the conditional variance $\operatorname{var}\left(f\middle|\mu\right)=\sigma_f^2$, such that $V\equiv\alpha\operatorname{var}\left(f\right)+\left(1-\alpha\right)\operatorname{var}\left(f\middle|\mu\right)=\sigma_f^2+\alpha\sigma_\mu^2$. If the agent were ambiguity neutral, $\alpha=1$, $V=\sigma_f^2+\sigma_\mu^2$, such that the problem would be indistinguishable from a standard mean-variance program with an increased variance: in other words, second-order uncertainty would not matter. Instead, second-order uncertainty matters when the agent is ambiguity averse, in which case the solution in (9.95) is

$$\hat{x} = \frac{\mu_0 - p}{\tau\left(\sigma_f^2 + \alpha\sigma_\mu^2\right)}.$$

The more averse to ambiguity the agent is, the higher α, and the less aggressive their portfolio holding will be for a given uncertainty level σ_μ^2. The equilibrium implications of the model are straightforward. With the asset in positive supply, $\bar{x}$, the equilibrium price is $p = \mu_0 - \tau\left(\sigma_f^2 + \alpha\sigma_\mu^2\right)\bar{x}$, with an "uncertainty premium" component being clearly related to both uncertainty, σ_μ^2, and uncertainty aversion, α.

9.6.4 A Model of Multiple Likelihoods

Leippold, Trojani, and Vanini (2008) (LTV, henceforth) develop a model in which the drift of dividend growth is unobservable, similar to the learning models of chapter 8 (see section 8.6) and the previous section 9.5. Their point of departure from these models is the assumption that agents do not know the statistical laws governing the unobserved dividend growth—in previous models, expected dividend growth is unobserved, but the underlying laws of movement are known. This lack of knowledge adds complexity and leads to interesting predictions regarding the equity premium.

In the model, agents are not sure about the unobservable drift of dividend growth, yet they formulate conjectures regarding the existence of a "cloud" of models containing the truth. In detail, this cloud is placed around a reference model for the dynamics of aggregate dividends,

$$\frac{dD_t}{D_t} = \theta dt + \sigma_0 dZ_t, \tag{9.97}$$

where σ_0 is a constant, θ is the unobservable expected dividend growth, and Z_t is a standard Brownian motion. Eq. (9.97), the reference model, is referred to as a "rough approximation to reality" by LTV, for reasons explained below.[16]

Eq. (9.97) is an approximation to reality, as mentioned. That is, the agents acknowledge that they are dealing with a possibly misspecified model, and this circumstance leads them to consider *multiple likelihoods* about the statistical laws of the fundamentals: they take eq. (9.97) as a benchmark but do not trust this benchmark. Precisely, they assume that the true, unknown model is contained in a "neighborhood" of this benchmark, that is, it belongs to the following family of models:

$$\frac{dD_t}{D_t} = \left(\theta + h(\theta)\,\sigma_0\right) dt + \sigma_0 dZ_{ht}, \tag{9.98}$$

for another Brownian motion Z_{ht}. In this family of models, the distortion function h generates deviations from the benchmark. It captures the idea that agents face Knightian

16. LTV assume that the agents also observe additional signals on θ; to simplify the presentation of the model, this section does not consider these signals.

uncertainty, in that they have limited knowledge regarding whether their reference model is correctly specified. Moreover, the agents assume that h satisfies

$$h^2(\theta) \leq \eta(\theta), \quad \text{for all } \theta, \tag{9.99}$$

and for some known function η. In words, eq. (9.98) contains model specifications that are statistically close to the reference model (9.97) and perhaps actually difficult to be statistically distinguishable. Naturally, in the absence of ambiguity, one has that $\eta \equiv 0$, such that this model would collapse to those seen in chapter 8.

Ambiguity, as described until now, is a source of second-order uncertainty, that is, one that adds uncertainty (the agents' acknowledgment of dealing with model misspecification) to an already unobserved process (the drift of dividend growth), which they may wish to learn about. The crucial point is how the agents behave vis-à-vis this added uncertainty. The behavioral assumption is that they *fear* model misspecification and choose consumption and portfolio policies (c_t, π_t) that maximize their worst-case scenario welfare, that is, their lifetime utility arising when a malevolent nature chooses the worst possible model in (9.98) for them:

$$\max_{(c_t,\pi_t)_{t\in(0,\infty)}} \inf_h E^h \left[\int_0^\infty e^{-\rho t} u(c_t)\, dt \right], \tag{9.100}$$

subject to the usual wealth constraints, and where E^h is the expectation taken under the statistical laws in eq. (9.98) arising with a distortion function equal to h, ρ is the instantaneous discounting rate, and $u(c)$ is the instantaneous utility with CRRA equal to γ. This formulation of the agent's problem has the same flavor as the max-min problem in the static market of section 9.6.3.

Regarding the unobserved drift in the reference model, θ, we may assume that θ is a continuous process or that it is a Markov chain on set of finite values, as explained in chapter 8 (section 8.6). One simplifying assumption is that θ takes a finite number of values, similarly as in the introductory example of learning of chapter 8 (see section 8.6.2).[17] Moreover, we assume that θ could only take two values, $\underline{\theta}$ and $\bar{\theta}$, and denote the family of drifts of the dividend growth with $\theta^h = \theta + h(\theta)\sigma_0$. As for the agents' inference process, let the conditional probability $\pi_t \equiv \Pr(\theta^h = \bar{\theta}^h \mid \mathbb{F}_t)$, where $\mathbb{F}_t$ denotes the information set available to agents at time t. Then, by results in chapter 8, we have that

$$d\pi_t = \frac{\bar{\theta}^h - \underline{\theta}^h}{\sigma_0} \pi_t (1 - \pi_t)\, dW_{ht}, \quad \pi_0 \equiv p,$$

where $dW_{ht} = \sigma_0^{-1} \left(\frac{dD_t}{D_t} - E^h \left(\theta^h | (D_s)_{s \leq t} \right) dt \right)$.

Note that, by results reviewed in chapter 8 (see section 8.6), π_t will converge to one or to zero according to whether $\theta^h = \bar{\theta}^h$ or $\theta^h = \underline{\theta}^h$. That is, in this market, the agent will eventually *learn about the model quality*, so to speak (i.e., high or low growth), although they will always be uncertain about the exact parameter values of the model.

---

17. Note, then, that with this assumption, the model does not generalize Veronesi's (2000) model of learning, in which the unobserved drift is a Markov chain (see section 8.6 in chapter 8). However, it captures the salient features brought up by Knightian uncertainty.

An equilibrium is one in which (i) a representative agent solves the optimization problem (9.100) and (ii) the optimal consumption equals dividends, $c_t = D_t$, for all t. To solve the optimization problem, and in analogy with the static max-min model of section 9.6.3, the agent first determines the infimum in (9.100) while taking as given the consumption and portfolio choices in the outer optimization problem. Given this, the agent solves for the outer portfolio policies while imposing the equilibrium condition that $c_t = D_t$. And, given this equilibrium condition, we have that the infimum is attained with

$$\hat{h}(\cdot) \equiv \arg\inf_h E^h\left[\int_0^\infty e^{-\rho t} u(D_t)\, dt\right].$$

Let $\Xi(\theta) \equiv \left\{\theta^h : (9.99) \text{ holds}\right\}$ and assume that $\Xi(\underline{\theta}) \cap \Xi(\bar{\theta}) = \emptyset$. Note that, because the drift of D_t in (9.98) is increasing in $h(\cdot)$, then by a comparison theorem (e.g., Karatzas and Shreve, 1991, 291–295), the previous expectation is increasing in $h(\cdot)$, such that[18]

$$\hat{h}(\theta) = -\sqrt{\eta(\theta)}. \tag{9.101}$$

In other words, asset prices are now evaluated *as if* the aggregate dividends dynamics were fully observed but with left-tilted bounds to growth,

$$\begin{cases} \dfrac{dD_t}{D_t} = \hat{g}_t dt + \sigma_0 dW_{\hat{h}t} \\ d\hat{g}_t = \frac{1}{\sigma_0}(\hat{g}_t - \underline{\theta}^{\hat{h}})(\bar{\theta}^{\hat{h}} - \hat{g}_t) dW_{\hat{h}t} \end{cases} \tag{9.102}$$

where $\hat{g}_t \equiv E^{\hat{h}}(\theta^{\hat{h}} | (D_s)_{s \leq t}) = \pi_t \bar{\theta}^{\hat{h}} + (1 - \pi_t)\underline{\theta}^{\hat{h}}$, such that, by results in chapter 8 (section 8.6), the equity premium $\mathcal{E}_t^h$, the short-term rate r_t, and volatility Vol_t are given by

$$\mathcal{E}_t^h = r_t + \gamma\sigma_0 \cdot \text{Vol}_t, \quad r_t = \rho + \gamma\hat{g}_t - \frac{1}{2}\gamma(\gamma+1)\sigma_0^2, \quad \text{Vol}_t = \sigma_0 + \frac{p'(\hat{g}_t)}{p(\hat{g}_t)} v(\hat{g}_t), \tag{9.103}$$

where $v(\cdot)$ denotes the diffusion coefficient of $\hat{g}_t$ in (9.102) and p is the price-dividend ratio.[19] By results given in chapter 8 (see section 8.4), the price-dividend ratio is an affine function of the dividend growth expected under the agent's worst-case scenario probability, $\hat{g}_t$. Appendix 9.C shows that

$$p(\hat{g}_t) = \underbrace{\frac{\hat{g}_t - \underline{\theta}^{\hat{h}}}{\bar{\theta}^{\hat{h}} - \underline{\theta}^{\hat{h}}}}_{=\pi_t} \frac{1}{\rho - (1-\gamma)(\bar{\theta}^{\hat{h}} - \frac{1}{2}\gamma\sigma_0^2)} + \underbrace{\frac{\bar{\theta}^{\hat{h}} - \hat{g}_t}{\bar{\theta}^{\hat{h}} - \underline{\theta}^{\hat{h}}}}_{=1-\pi_t} \frac{1}{\rho - (1-\gamma)(\underline{\theta}^{\hat{h}} - \frac{1}{2}\gamma\sigma_0^2)}. \tag{9.104}$$

18. Precisely, note that the value function in (9.100) that has to be extremized is $E^h\left[\int_0^\infty e^{-\rho t} u(D_t)\, dt\right] = \sum_{j=1}^2 \int_0^\infty \pi_j e^{-\rho t} E^h\left(u(D_t) | \theta_j\right) dt$, where $\theta_1 \equiv \underline{\theta}$, $\theta_2 \equiv \bar{\theta}$, $\pi_1 \equiv \pi$, $\pi_2 \equiv 1 - \pi_2$. The expectation in the integral is increasing in the drift of D_t by the said comparison theorem.

19. Note that the probability we are using while defining these statistics is that under the distorted beliefs: the agent prices the asset through $\hat{h}(\theta)$, as explained, and the statistics in (9.103) all originate from the pricing function $p(\cdot)$ given below (see eq. (9.104)). The expression for the equity premium under the reference model is given in eq. (9.105) below.

The price-dividend ratio is a weighted average (weighted with the posterior π_t) of the discounted lifetime expected dividends conditional on the up ($\bar{\theta}$) and down ($\underline{\theta}$) states of the world and under the worst-case drifts. Provided $\gamma < 1$, the price-dividend ratio is decreasing in the degree of ambiguity aversion, $\eta(\cdot)$.[20]

Note that the equity premium in (9.103) originates from the perspective of the worst-case probability in the family of models included in (9.98). To determine the equity premium under the reference model (9.97), note that $\hat{g}_t = g_t + \mathcal{A}_t\sigma_0$, where $g_t \equiv E(\theta | (D_s)_{s \le t}) = \pi_t\bar{\theta} + (1-\pi_t)\underline{\theta}$ is the growth estimate in the absence of any distortions and

$$\mathcal{A}_t \equiv \pi_t\hat{h}(\bar{\theta}) + (1-\pi_t)\hat{h}(\underline{\theta}),$$

is the average size of ambiguity aversion. Therefore, by Girsanov's theorem (see chapter 4), we can define a probability P_o with Radon-Nikodym derivative against the worst-case probability P^h (i.e., the probability under which $(D, \hat{g})$ are a solution to (9.102)),

$$\left.\frac{dP_o}{dP^h}\right|_{\mathbb{F}_t} = e^{-\frac{1}{2}\int_0^t \mathcal{A}_u^2 dt - \int_0^t \mathcal{A}_t dW_{\hat{h}u}},$$

such that $W_t = W_{\hat{h}t} + \int_0^t \mathcal{A}_u du$ is a Brownian motion under P^r. Then, under P^h, we have that

$$\begin{cases} \dfrac{dD_t}{D_t} = \underbrace{(\hat{g}_t - \mathcal{A}_t\sigma_0)}_{\equiv g_t} dt + \sigma_0 dW_t \\ d\hat{g}_t = -\mathcal{A}_t v(\hat{g}_t)dt + v(\hat{g}_t)dW_t \end{cases}.$$

Therefore, the equity premium under the reference model (9.97) is

$$\mathcal{E}_t = \mathcal{E}_t^h - \text{Vol}_t \cdot \mathcal{A}_t, \tag{9.105}$$

where $\mathcal{E}_t^h$ is the worst-case scenario equity premium in (9.102). Note that, by eq. (9.101), $\mathcal{A}_t < 0$, such that ambiguity aversion contributes positively to the equity premium.[21]

The rationale behind the definition of $\mathcal{E}_t$ in (9.105) relies on the following *interpretation* of the reference model. The ambiguity averse agent prices the asset at the worst-case scenario, yet nature draws aggregate dividends according to eqs. (9.97). Naturally, the agent is unsure of this statistical law and places a band around θ, a band that could be symmetric or asymmetric, reflecting the modeling assumption that the agent only knows that, for each regime (up or down), the expected dividend growth belongs to a certain band.[22]

---

20. The assumption that $\gamma < 1$ is standard in this context. The sensitivity of the short-term rate to growth is the agent's CRRA, γ (see (9.103)). Therefore, if $\gamma > 1$, growth changes would make discount rates change even more, such that the price-dividend ratio would be decreasing in growth and hence increasing in ambiguity aversion. Nonexpected utility would fix this seemingly counterintuitive issue while allowing the elasticity of intertemporal substitution to be disentangled from relative risk aversion (see section 9.2).

21. Eq. (9.105) follows by eq. (8.17) in chapter 8 and by the change in probability from P^h to P_o.

22. Precisely, the band is $[\underline{\theta} - \sqrt{\eta(\underline{\theta})}\sigma_0, \underline{\theta} + \sqrt{\eta(\underline{\theta})}\sigma_0]$ in the down regime, $\theta = \underline{\theta}$, and $[\bar{\theta} - \sqrt{\eta(\bar{\theta})}\sigma_0, \bar{\theta} + \sqrt{\eta(\bar{\theta})}\sigma_0]$ in the up regime, $\theta = \bar{\theta}$.

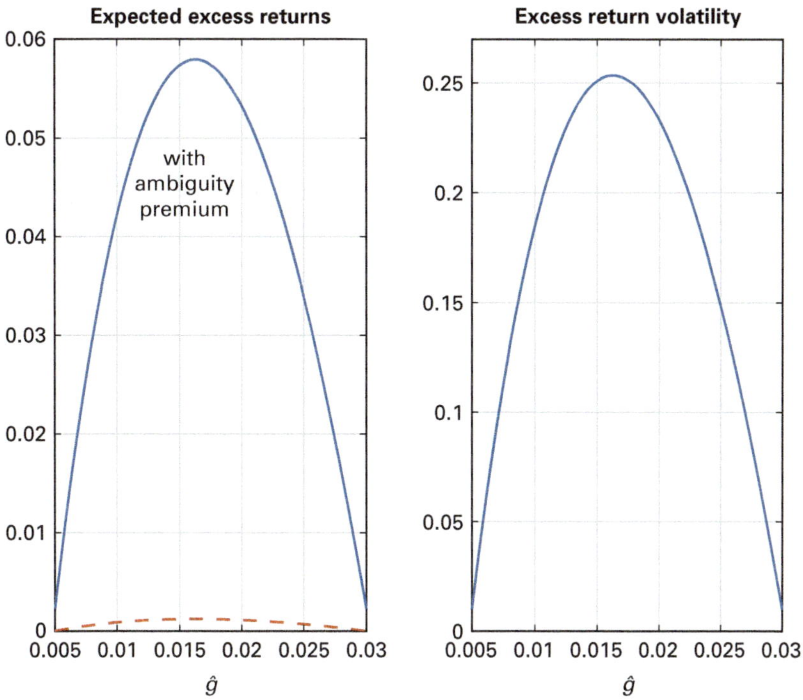

Figure 9.3
Left panel: The solid line depicts the equity premium under the reference probability, $\mathcal{E}_t - r_t$ in eq. (9.105), as a function of the expected growth, $\hat{g}_t$; the dashed line is the equity premium under the worst-case probability, $\mathcal{E}_t^h - r_t$ in eq. (9.103). Right panel: return volatility, Vol_t in eq. (9.103). In both panels, parameter values are $\underline{\theta} = 0.005$, $\bar{\theta} = 0.03$, $\sigma_0 = 0.01$, $\gamma = \frac{1}{2}$, $\rho = 0.04$, and finally, $\eta(\underline{\theta}) = \eta(\bar{\theta}) = \hat{\eta} = 0.05$.

It is easy to see that if the band is symmetric, with, say, $\eta(\underline{\theta}) = \eta(\bar{\theta}) \equiv \hat{\eta}$, the model predicts that the price-dividend ratio is the same as that in an economy without ambiguity but with a higher time preference rate (see eq. (9.A59) in appendix 9.C). However, this isomorphism breaks down once ambiguity aversion is state-dependent, $\eta(\underline{\theta}) \neq \eta(\bar{\theta})$. Further, even with homogeneous ambiguity aversion, the assumptions underlying the model leads to a sizable equity premium under the reference probability, $\mathcal{E}_t - r_t$ in (9.105), a premium that cannot arise in an economy without ambiguity.

The left panel of figure 9.3 plots the equity premium predicted by the model, with parameters fixed at the values given in the legend of figure 9.3. Note that the $\mathcal{E}_t^h$ component is small, whereas the ambiguity premium $\text{Vol}_t \cdot \mathcal{A}_t$ is able to boost the premium at the levels we need to rationalize the empirical evidence reviewed in chapter 8. Note, also, from the right panel of figure 9.3, that return volatility, Vol_t, has the right order of magnitude in the calibrated model. Finally, the price-dividend ratio, not shown, ranges from about 25 to 38.

Note that the equity premium is inverse U shaped against $\hat{g}_t$, a property arising mainly because return volatility is inverse U shaped. The origins of this property are clarified in chapter 8 (section 8.6). Models with multiple states (such as those considered by LTV) and mean-reverting behavior (ensured while assuming θ is a Markov chain) are natural candidates to make volatility and equity premiums visit their descending parts more often than their ascending parts, thereby leading to a countercyclical behavior.

9.7 Government Spending and Asset Prices

This section analyzes the impact of government spending on equity markets and interest rates. Government spending obviously requires financing. Governments finance their spending through taxes and/or debt accumulation. This section reviews the classical argument that, in the presence of complete markets and in the absence of any frictions, the particular mix of debt and taxes is irrelevant for the purpose of financing expenses. This proposition is the counterpart to the Modigliani-Miller theorem in chapter 5 (see section 5.4), by which the value of the firm is independent of the particular debt-equity mix. The economy in this section can also be described by a Ricardian proposition where consumption and portfolio choices and, hence, equilibrium asset prices do not depend on taxes or debt but only on output and expenses; the analytical details of these propositions date back to, at least, Barro (1974). The section, then, provides a simple example to illustrate how government expenses affect asset prices and interest rates.

9.7.1 Assumptions

We consider an infinite horizon economy in which output y_t is exogenously given as the solution to

$$\frac{dy_t}{y_t} = \mu dt + \sigma_0 dW_{1t},$$

for two parameters $\mu, \sigma_0 > 0$, and where W_{1t} is a standard Brownian motion. We denote government *spending* with G_t, and define g_t, government *size*, as the the ratio of government spending to output, that is, $G_t \equiv g_t y_t$. We assume that government spending is pure waste in that government spending does not enter the agents' utility function. Rather, a representative agent has an instantaneous utility over consumption c_t equal to $e^{-\rho t} u(c_t)$, where ρ is their subjective discount rate and $u(\cdot)$ denotes the agent's consumption utility. Finally, we assume that government spending is financed by debt and nondistortionary taxes and that agents have access to a system of complete state-contingent markets.

In equilibrium, private consumption equals $c_t = (1 - g_t) y_t$. To keep the model tractable, we assume that the inverse of the consumption-to-output ratio, that is, $i_t \equiv (c_t/y_t)^{-1} = (1 - g_t)^{-1}$, is a mean-reverting process,

$$di_t = k(\theta - i_t)\, dt + \sigma_I \left(i_t - \underline{i}\right)(\bar{\imath} - i_t)\, dW_{2t}, \tag{9.106}$$

where W_{2t} is a standard Brownian motion and k, θ, $\underline{i}$, and $\bar{\imath}$ are constants. Note that g_t is monotonically increasing in i_t and thus is mean-reverting. Moreover, under regularity conditions, the functional form of the instantaneous volatility in (9.106) ensures that $i_t \in (\underline{i}, \bar{\imath})$, which ensures that $g_t \in (\underline{g}, \bar{g})$ for all t, where $(\underline{g}, \bar{g})$ are such that $\underline{i} = (1 - \underline{g})^{-1}$ and $\bar{\imath} = (1 - \bar{g})^{-1}$.

9.7.2 Government Debt

We describe debt accumulation with a continuous time model that is the equivalent of those considered by Ljungqvist and Sargent (2018, section 13.10). We follow the same notation as—and derivations similar to—those in chapter 4 (see section 4.2.5). Let h be a small interval of time. Government expenses during this period are $G_t h$ and (nondistortionary) taxes are $\mathcal{T}_t h$, such that

$$G_t h = \mathcal{T}_t h + E_t \left(m_{t,t+h} d^{g}_{t+h} \right) - d^{g}_{t}, \tag{9.107}$$

where d^{g}_{t+h} is the amount of goods that, at time t, the government promises to pay at $t+h$ and $m_{t,t+h}$ is the standard pricing kernel (see section 4.2.5 of chapter 4), that is, $m_{t,t+h} = \xi_{t+h}/\xi_t$, where ξ_t is the stochastic discount factor. Government expenses can equivalently be financed through new debt issuance or taxes. Note that the payments d^{g}_{t+h} may be state-dependent, that is, stochastic.[23]

Eq. (9.107) simply says that government expenses are financed by taxes and net debt issuance (the second term on the RHS minus the third). Rearranging terms leaves $0 = E_t \left(\xi_{t+h} d^{g}_{t+h} - d^{g}_{t} \xi_t \right) + \xi_t \left(\mathcal{T}_t - G_t \right) h$. Taking the limits for $h \to 0$, integrating the result, and assuming the transversality condition, $\lim_{T \to \infty} E_t \left(\xi_T d^{g}_{T} \right) = 0$, leaves

$$\xi_t d^{g}_{t} = E_t \left(\int_t^{\infty} \xi_u \left(\mathcal{T}_u - G_u \right) du \right). \tag{9.108}$$

That is, debt value at t is the present value of future surpluses. The transversality condition is crucial in this derivation. From now on, we assume that tax proceedings are $\mathcal{T}_t = \mathcal{T}_{0,t} + \tau_t y_t$, where $\mathcal{T}_{0,t}$ are tax proceedings independent of output and τ_t is a tax rate on output.

9.7.3 Ricardian Equivalence

9.7.3.1 Agents' resource constraints

The representative agent invests their wealth in a safe asset issued by the government and a claim on the future flows of the after-tax aggregate consumption endowment y_t, the aggregate stock market. Government debt earns an interest rate equal to r_t. Under standard conditions (see chapter 4), the aggregate stock price, P_t, is the solution to

$$\frac{dP_t}{P_t} = \mu_t dt + \mathrm{Vol}_{1t} dW_{1t} + \mathrm{Vol}_{2t} dW_{2t}, \tag{9.109}$$

for some expected return μ_t and volatility processes Vol_{1t} and Vol_{2t}, which are endogenous. Thus, the agent's wealth, $V_t = \pi_t + d^{g}_{t}$, evolves as

$$\begin{aligned} dV_t = & \left[\left(\mu_t + \frac{(1-\tau_t)\, y_t}{P_t} - r_t \right) \pi_t + r V_t - \left(\mathcal{T}_{0,t} + c_t \right) \right] dt \\ & + \pi_t \left(\mathrm{Vol}_{1t} dW_{1t} + \mathrm{Vol}_{2t} dW_{2t} \right), \end{aligned} \tag{9.110}$$

where π_t is wealth invested in the stock. Thus, in the absence of arbitrage,

$$\mu_t + \frac{(1-\tau_t)\, y_t}{P_t} - r_t = \mathrm{Vol}_{1t} \lambda_{1t} + \mathrm{Vol}_{2t} \lambda_{2t},$$

23. For example, when d^{g}_{t+h} is deterministic, eq. (9.107) collpases to $(G_t - \mathcal{T}_t)\, h = R^{-1}_{t,h} d^{g}_{t+h} - d^{g}_{t}$, where $R_{t,h}$ is the safe interest rate factor for the period $[t, t+h]$.

where λ_{1t} and λ_{2t} are the unit prices of risk related to the fluctuation of W_{1t} and W_{2t}. Replacing the previous relation into (9.110), integrating and assuming the transversality condition, $\lim_{T\to\infty} E_t(\xi_T V_T)=0$, leaves

$$\xi_t V_t = E_t\left(\int_t^\infty \xi_u \left(\mathcal{T}_{0,u} + c_u\right) du\right), \tag{9.111}$$

where $\xi_t = e^{-\rho t}\frac{u'(c_t)}{u'(c_0)}$ is the solution to

$$\frac{d\xi_t}{\xi_t} = -r_t dt - \lambda_{1t} dW_{1t} - \lambda_{2t} dW_{2t}, \quad \xi_0 = 1. \tag{9.112}$$

9.7.3.2 *Equilibrium*

In equilibrium, $V_t = P_t + d_t^g$. Therefore, by the agents' resource constraint (9.111) and the government debt value in (9.108),

$$\begin{aligned}\xi_t P_t &= \xi_t\left(V_t - d_t^g\right)\\ &= E_t\left(\int_t^\infty \xi_u \left(\mathcal{T}_{0,u} + c_u - \mathcal{T}_u + G_u\right) du\right)\\ &= E_t\left(\int_t^\infty \xi_u (1-\tau_u) y_u du\right),\end{aligned} \tag{9.113}$$

where the last equality follows by the definition of the tax proceeding, $\mathcal{T}_t$, and the equilibrium condition $y_t = c_t + G_t$. Moreover, note that, in equilibrium, $\frac{\xi_t}{\xi_0} = e^{-\rho t}\frac{u'((1-g_t)y_t)}{u'((1-g_0)y_0)}$. Therefore, eq. (9.113) states that a claim for the *after-tax* consumption dividend is not affected by how the public deficit is financed (i.e., through taxes or debt).

Naturally, in this example, the stock price depends on the stochastic process for the dividend tax rate, τ_t: our tree is a claim to *net* dividends. The main point is that the system of Arrow-Debreu prices ξ_t is independent of taxes or debt. It is a Ricardian proposition: consumption and portfolio choices are independent of tax or debt strategies used to finance any given stream of expenses. Intuitively, eq. (9.108) says that debt at t must be repaid with future surpluses, and so the agents expect to use the proceedings of their bond holdings to pay future taxes.

So government spending, not the level of debt (or bonds' supply), affects asset prices. Chapter 10 describes a model with market imperfections in which bonds' supply may affect the whole yield curve (see section 10.9.3). Further, one of the crucial assumption underlying the previous conclusions is that governments do not default. Chapter 14 considers cases in which a government has the option to default (see section 14.2.4): in such economies, asset prices do depend on the level of accumulated debt. We now analyze how government spending affects asset prices and interest rates in the setting of this section.

9.7.4 Government Size and Asset Prices

In this economy, government spending may only affect the aggregate stock price through its effects on the system of Arrow-Debreu prices, ξ_t. In the model of this section, these effects operate through the equilibrium condition, $c_t = y_t - G_t$. For example, assuming that the representative agent has a log-utility of consumption, we have $\frac{\xi_t}{\xi_0} = e^{-\rho t} \frac{(1-g_0)y_0}{(1-g_t)y_t}$. Agents' preferences for government expenses may be an additional channel through which public spending may affect security evaluation. For simplicity, we only consider the equilibrium channel, and assume log-utility. It is left as an exercise to show that, under these conditions, the short-term rate and unit risk premiums in (9.112) are

$$r_t \equiv \rho + \mu - \sigma_0^2 - k\left(\theta\left(1 - g_t\right) - 1\right) \tag{9.114}$$

and

$$\lambda_{1t} = \sigma_0, \quad \lambda_{2t} = -\frac{\sigma_I}{\left(1-\underline{g}\right)\left(1-\bar{g}\right)} \frac{\left(g_t - \underline{g}\right)\left(\bar{g} - g_t\right)}{1 - g_t}.$$

The first unit premium, λ_{1t} is the standard Lucas tree unit premium in the case of log-utility; the second, λ_{2t}, is negative, but it makes the equity premium larger than in the standard Lucas model because the asset price reacts negatively to shocks to g_t (i.e., $\mathrm{Vol}_{2t} < 0$ in (9.109)), as shown next. The asset price is found by elaborating on eq. (9.113). For simplicity, set $\tau_t = \bar{\tau}$, a constant. We have

$$\begin{aligned} p\left(g_t\right) &\equiv \frac{P_t}{\left(1-\bar{\tau}\right) y_t} = E_t\left(\int_t^{\infty} e^{-\rho(u-t)} \frac{1-g_t}{1-g_u} du\right) \\ &= \frac{1}{\rho + k} + \frac{k\theta}{\rho\left(\rho + k\right)}\left(1 - g_t\right) \end{aligned} \tag{9.115}$$

where the last equality follows by the assumptions on the government expenses-to-output in (9.106) and simple calculations.

Figure 9.4 plots the price-dividend ratio, $p\left(g_t\right)$, and the short-term rate, $r_t \equiv r\left(g_t\right)$, against government size, g_t, based on the parameter values indicated in the legend. The short-term rate is increasing in g_t for the following reason. Agents expect that g_t will increase when it is currently low (due to mean reversion), thereby expecting that their marginal utility will increase. To compensate for this increase in marginal utility, agents then save more to finance more future consumption, pushing interest rates down. Given this property of the interest rate, the aggregate stock price is decreasing in g_t: in terms of definitions and results in chapter 8, price-dividend ratios are decreasing in any state variable y_t whenever the "risk-adjusted" discount rates (in this model, $r\left(y_t\right) + \sigma_0^2$, with $y_t = g_t$) are increasing in it.

9.8 Leverage and Volatility

Is firms' leverage responsible for a sustained stock volatility? Can leverage explain countercyclical stock volatility? We already know, from chapter 8, that ex post stock returns are high in good times, whence stock volatility is negatively related to ex post returns. According to the *leverage effect* hypothesis, this negative relation arises because, after a negative shock hits a stock price, the debt/equity ratio increases, and as a result, the firm becomes riskier, leading to an increase in stock volatility. It is often argued that the leverage effect is too weak empirically. Most of the contributions to these issues are empirical (e.g., Black, 1976; Christie, 1982; Schwert, 1989a,b; Nelson, 1991). Naturally, another possibility is

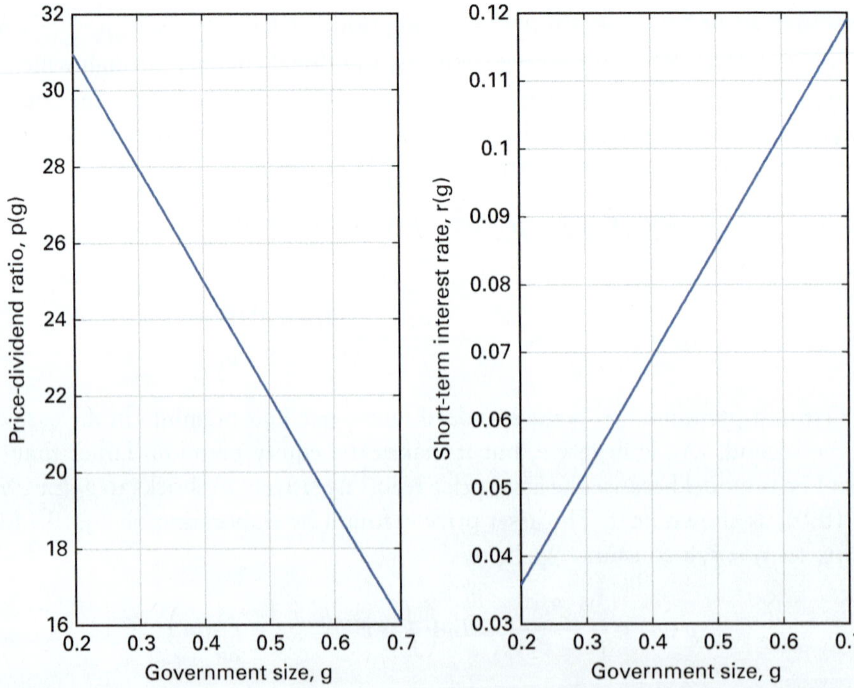

Figure 9.4
Government size, equity markets, and interest rates. The left panel depicts the price-dividend ratio in (9.115) against government size, defined as public spending over output ratio, $g_t = \frac{G_t}{y_t}$; the right panel depicts the short-term rate in (9.114). Parameter values in both panels are $\rho = 0.04$, $k = 0.10$, $\theta = (1 - 0.40)^{-1}$, $\mu = 0.03$, $\sigma_0 = 0.03$, and $\underline{g} = 0.20$ and $\bar{g} = 0.70$.

that stock volatility and returns are negatively related for reasons unrelated to the leverage effect. For example, stock volatility can be countercyclical because agents' preferences and beliefs, combined with macroeconomic conditions, lead precisely to this property as in the models discussed in chapter 7 and in the previous sections.

In this section, we explore an additional explanation, namely that countercyclical volatility arises as a result of a combined effect of the properties of the previous models and leverage. A difficulty is that, in many empirical studies, tests of the leverage effect hypothesis are performed without regard to a well-specified economic model. Gallmeyer, Aydemir, Hollifield (2007) show that the reasoning underlying this hypothesis can be made rigorous. They formulate a general equilibrium model with levered firms, which they realistically calibrate, to disentangle leverage effects from real effects, such as habit formation. They make use of a stochastic discount factor known to price assets fairly well and conclude that leverage effects do indeed have little effects in general equilibrium. This section develops a variant of their model, which has the mere merit to admit a closed-form solution.

9.8.1 Primitives

We consider an endowment economy, where total output, δ_t, is a geometric Brownian motion with parameters g_0 and σ_0. In this economy, a representative firm issues debt with maturity T and denoted with D_t. Denote equity with E_t. The firm distributes payoffs equal to $\delta_t = \delta_{Et} + \delta_{Dt}$, with obvious notation. Due to the Modigliani-Miller proposition, the value of the firm is $V_t \equiv E_t + D_t$ (see section 5.4 in chapter 5). A representative agent has habit formation preferences. To obtain closed-form solutions for the asset prices, we make reference to the Menzly, Santos, and Veronesi (2004) economy in chapter 8 (see section 8.5.4 and appendix 8.E). We denote the equilibrium surplus consumption ratio with $s_t = \frac{\delta_t - x_t}{\delta_t}$, where s is solution to

$$d\left(\frac{1}{s_t}\right) = \beta\left(\frac{1}{\bar{s}} - \frac{1}{s_t}\right)dt - \alpha\left(\frac{1}{s_t} - \frac{1}{\upsilon}\right)\sigma_0 dW_t$$

and $\beta, \bar{s}, \alpha$ and υ, are parameters. In this economy, Sharpe ratios are countercyclical and are equal to $\lambda(s) = \sigma_0\left(1 + \alpha\left(1 - \frac{s}{\upsilon}\right)\right)$. We assume debt services are $\delta_D = q\delta$ for some $q \in (0,1)$ and set the benchmark for debt maturity to $T = 10$ years.

It can be shown that a calibration of the model leads to the following results, (i) the price of debt is procyclical, (ii) return volatility is largely countercyclical, (iii) the leverage ratio is countercyclical, and finally, (iv) the contribution of leverage to equity returns volatility is quantitatively limited. We now provide the analytical framework that enables one to achieve these conclusions.

9.8.2 Equity Volatility and Leverage

From chapter 8, we know that the price-dividend ratio for the aggregate consumption claim is $p(s_t) \equiv a + bs_t$, for two constants a and b given below. It is easy to show that the debt value is

$$\frac{D_t}{\delta_t} = q\left(a_{T-t} + b_{T-t}s_t\right), \quad a_\tau = \frac{1 - e^{-(\rho+\beta)\tau}}{\rho + \beta}, \quad b_\tau = \frac{\beta\left(1 - e^{-\rho\tau}\right) + \rho\left(e^{-(\rho+\beta)\tau} - e^{-\rho\tau}\right)}{\rho(\rho+\beta)\bar{s}},$$

where ρ denotes the discounting rate and $a = \lim_{T\to\infty} a_\tau$ and $b = \lim_{T\to\infty} b_\tau$. Equity volatility is

$$\begin{aligned}\text{Vol}\left(\frac{dE}{E}\right) &= \sigma_V + (\sigma_V - \sigma_D)\frac{D}{E},\\ \sigma_V &= \sigma_0 + \frac{b}{a+bs}\text{Vol}(ds),\\ \sigma_D &= \sigma_0 + \frac{b_{T-t}}{a_{T-t} + b_{T-t}s}\text{Vol}(ds),\end{aligned} \tag{9.116}$$

where $\text{Vol}(ds) = \alpha\sigma_0 s\left(1 - \frac{1}{\upsilon}s\right)$. Note also that the leverage ratio, $\frac{D_t}{E_t}$, is endogenous and equal to

$$\frac{D_t}{E_t} = \frac{\left(a_{T-t} + b_{T-t}s_t\right)q}{a + bs_t - \left(a_{T-t} + b_{T-t}s_t\right)q}.$$

In other words, we only see what happens to $\frac{D_t}{E_t}$ and $\text{Vol}\left(\frac{dE_t}{E_t}\right)$ as the surplus s_t changes. We use the parameter values in figure 8.12 of chapter 8 (see section 8.5.4), with $q = 0.60$, and assess the predictions of the model. It is left as an exercise to verify that, given these parameter values, much of the action for the explanation of equity volatility in eq. (9.116)

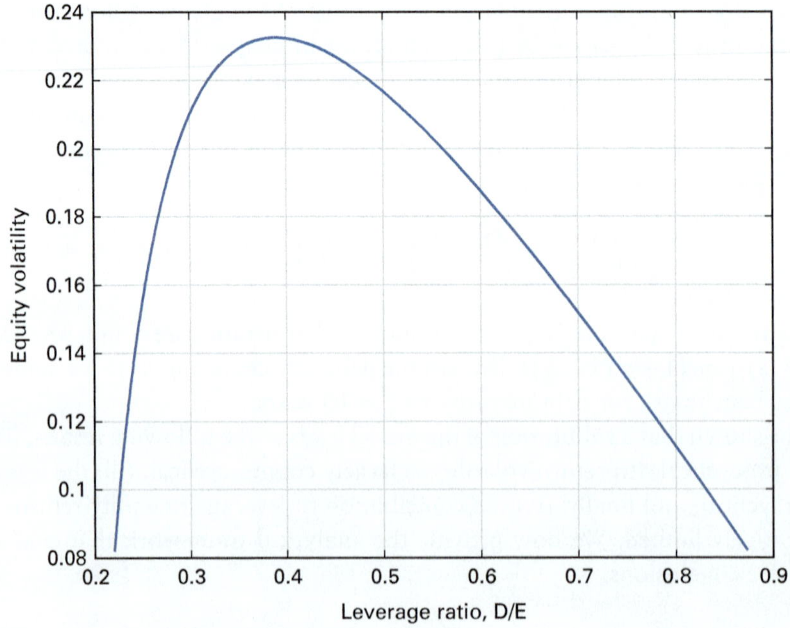

Figure 9.5
Leverage and equity volatility in a model with habit formation.

comes from the swings in the price-dividend ratio, $\frac{p'(s_t)}{p(s_t)} = \frac{b}{a+bs_t}$. What is the statistical relation between the leverage ratio $\frac{D}{E}$ and return volatility predicted by the model? Figure 9.5 depicts values of the leverage ratio and volatility consistent with the model. Naturally, figure 9.5 does not depict a causal relation as leverage and equity volatility are both driven by the same state variable, the surplus consumption ratio. It only tells us what we would expect to see in the data based on the predictions of this model.[24]

9.8.3 Bankruptcy

The previous model has no role for bankruptcy, which should play an obviously important role, as explained in great detail in chapter 14. To anticipate the importance of bankruptcy in a simple setting, consider a firm that issues debt for a nominal value equal to N and with a maturity of one year. In one year, the value of the firm, $\tilde{V}$, say, is equal to $\tilde{V} = V_b < N$, with probability p, or $\tilde{V} = V_g \geq N$, with complementary probability. We assume risk neutrality and no bankruptcy costs. Equity at time 0 is valued as $S_0 = (1-p)\left(V_g - N\right)$. At time 1, equity value is what is left after paying debt, that is, $S_1 = \mathbb{I}_{\tilde{V}=V_g}\left(V_g - N\right)$. Therefore, equity returns are $\tilde{R} = \frac{\tilde{S}_1 - S_0}{S_0}$, such that, by a simple calculation, return volatility is $\text{Vol}(\tilde{R}) = \sqrt{p/(1-p)}$. Even a small probability of default, say $p = 2\%$, may make return volatility quite high: in this example, $\text{Vol}(\tilde{R}) = 14.30\%$. Chapter 14 (see section 14.2) provides additional details regarding equity and debt volatility based on these simple ideas.

24. Does debt maturity lead to a greater contribution of leverage to volatility? No. Given the model parameter values, the effects of debt maturity on leverage can be shown to be quite limited.

9.9 Multiple Trees and the Cross-Section of Asset Returns

We consider markets for multiple securities and determine expected returns, volatilities, and comovements among the assets' realized returns. These markets feature contagion in the sense that a shock on a given asset returns affects the dynamics of other asset returns. Indeed, market expected returns are priced consistently (i.e., through the same pricing kernel). Further, asset evaluation operates across a portfolio of securities such that, in equilibrium, a shock on, say, the dividend paid off by some asset leads agents to rebalance their overall portfolio holdings. In these economies, the cross-section of the assets' expected returns and volatility are time-varying. This property enables one to explore issues regarding predictability (see section 8.2 in chapter 8) and how this predictability helps explain the cross-section of the expected returns.

Consider a model in which aggregate consumption and then output satisfies

$$\frac{dC_t}{C_t} = \mu_{ct}dt + \sigma_{ct} \cdot dW_t, \tag{9.117}$$

where W_t is a d-dimensional standard Brownian motion and μ_{ct} and σ_{ct} are drift and diffusion components, both possibly time-varying. In many models dealt with so far, σ_{ct} is a given constant and a small one. As we know, the equity premium puzzle is due precisely to this low volatility. This section provides extensions of the neoclassical models that still inherit this puzzle but that allow us to think about multi-asset economies. Interestingly, this puzzle may be addressed by models dealt with earlier to deal with the *aggregate* equity premium.

If consumption equals the sum of dividends, it may well fail being IID as both μ_{ct} and σ_{ct} may be time-varying due to the very same aggregation process. Cochrane, Longstaff, and Santa-Clara (2008) illustrated this property in a two-tree model, in which dividend processes are geometric Brownian motions. In a version of their model, they found a closed-form solution based on the assumption of a single log-utility investor. Martin (2013) contains extensions to multiple trees and CRRA investors. In early work, Menzly, Santos, and Veronesi (2004) derive closed-form solutions based on a framework in which consumption is actually IID and the dividends' shares (i.e., the proportions of each asset dividends to total consumption) are linear mean-reverting processes.

This section relies on a framework related to that in Menzly, Santos, and Veronesi (2004) (MSV, henceforth), and derives closed-form solutions in two cases: a first, in which aggregate consumption is not IID (due to aggregation process) and a second, in which consumption is IID, precisely as in MSV and in their habit formation model. Sections 9.9.1 and 9.9.2 deal with these two models and provide model predictions on predictability. Section 9.9.3 discusses further issues regarding predictability. Finally, section 9.9.4 presents a framework in which asset returns and volatilities are disentangled, based on a model known as a "string."

9.9.1 A Model of the Cross-Section of Expected Returns

We consider an economy in which aggregation leads to time-varying drifts and volatilities, just as in (9.117). We assume that there are N assets and that each asset i is a tree that pays off an instantaneous dividend equal to D_{it}, solution to

$$\frac{dD_{it}}{D_{it}} = g_{it}dt + \sigma_{di,t} \cdot dW_t, \quad i = 1, \cdots, N, \tag{9.118}$$

where the drift g_{it} is possibly time-varying and $\sigma_{di,t}$ is a d-dimensional vector that determines the volatility of asset i dividend. Define the aggregate dividend as the sum of the dividends paid off by all assets, that is, $D_t \equiv \sum_{i=1}^{N} D_{it}$. It is easy to show that D_t satisfies

$$\frac{dD_t}{D_t} = \sum_{i=1}^{N} \frac{dD_{it}}{D_{it}} s_{it} = \mu_{dt}dt + \sigma_{dt} \cdot dW_t, \tag{9.119}$$

where $\mu_{dt} \equiv \sum_{i=1}^{N} s_{it}g_{it}$, $\sigma_{dt} \equiv \sum_{i=1}^{N} s_{it}\sigma_{di,t}$, and $s_{it} \equiv \frac{D_{it}}{D_t}$ is the *dividend share* of asset i, that is, the proportion of the aggregate dividend that is attributable to asset i.

In equilibrium, the aggregate dividend equals aggregate consumption, $D_t = C_t$, such that, by identifying diffusion terms in (9.117) and (9.119), we have that $\sigma_{ct} = \sigma_{dt}$. Even if the assets dividends were all homoskedastic, aggregate consumption would be heteroskedastic. However, this point does not seem to be quantitatively important: we need to assume that σ_{ct} (or σ_{dt}) is small anyway, consistent with data.

9.9.1.1 *Cross-section restrictions*

We now derive cross-section restrictions for this model, assuming that a representative agent with infinite horizon has an instantaneous utility with CRRA equal to γ and discount rate ρ. Their first-order conditions are $e^{-\rho t}C_t^{-\gamma} = \xi_t$, where the stochastic discount factor ξ_t satisfies

$$\frac{d\xi_t}{\xi_t} = -r_t dt - \lambda_t \cdot dW_t,$$

with the usual notation. Therefore, the risk premium is[25]

$$\lambda_t = \gamma\sigma_{ct} = \gamma \sum_{i=1}^{N} s_{it}\sigma_{di,t}. \tag{9.120}$$

We determine the cross-section of expected returns. Let P_{it} be the price of asset i. The realized returns on this asset are

$$\frac{dP_{it} + D_{it}dt}{P_{it}} = \mathcal{E}_{it}dt + \sigma_{it} \cdot dW_t,$$

where $\mathcal{E}_{it}$ and σ_{it} are to be determined. The cross-section of expected returns is $\mathcal{E}_{it}$ for $i = 1, \cdots, N$. The d-dimensional vector σ_{it} determines the asset i volatility, $\|\sigma_{it}\|$. By standard arguments,

$$\mathcal{E}_{it} - r_t = \sigma_{it} \cdot \lambda_t = \gamma \sum_{j=1}^{N} s_{jt} cov_t (i, d_j), \quad cov_t (i, d_j) \equiv \sigma_{it} \cdot \sigma_{dj,t}. \tag{9.121}$$

where the last equality follows by the expression for λ in (9.120).

25. The expression for the equilibrium short-term rate, r_t, can be obtained in a standard way. It is omitted for brevity.

Eq. (9.121) tells us that the premium required to invest into a risky asset is proportional to the sum of the covariances of the asset returns with the dividends paid off by all the remaining assets, weighted by the assets dividend shares.[26] That is, correlations matter to explain the cross-section of the expected returns. However, the covariance that any asset i returns have with the dividend of a large stock (i.e., one with a large share) counts more than the same covariance for a small stock. We now provide more precise content around these general statements.

9.9.1.2 *Price multiples*

The representation in eq. (9.121) still needs to be narrowed down. One needs to determine the volatilities, σ_{it}, and then the covariance terms, $cov_t\left(i, d_j\right)$. It is not a trivial task, even assuming that dividend volatilities are all constant. Let us illustrate. Note that volatilities are determined through prices. Now, the price of asset i is

$$p_{it} \equiv \frac{P_{it}}{D_{it}} = E_t\left(\int_t^\infty \frac{\xi_u}{\xi_t}\frac{D_{iu}}{D_{it}}du\right) = E_t\left(\int_t^\infty \frac{\xi_u}{\xi_t}\frac{D_u}{D_t}\frac{s_{iu}}{s_{it}}du\right), \tag{9.122}$$

and a particularly convenient assumption is that $\gamma = 1$, in which case the price-dividend ratio for asset i simplifies to

$$p_{it} = E_t\left(\int_t^\infty e^{-\rho(u-t)}\frac{s_{iu}}{s_{it}}du\right). \tag{9.123}$$

The price-dividend ratio reflects information on the current size of the asset: other things being equal, the more the dividend share is expected to grow, the higher the price-dividend ratio is. It is a very intuitive property, but it also seems puzzling. We know that large stocks command small premiums; yet, according to a tractable version of the model, large stocks should have low prices (see, e.g., eq. (9.126)) and, in some cases, high expected returns as it will be argued below. Section 9.9.2 will explain a possible solution to this puzzle.

We formulate additional assumptions leading to an analytical solution for p_{it} in (9.123). To determine the dynamics of the shares, we apply Itô's lemma to $s_{it} = \frac{D_{it}}{D_t}$ and find that

$$\frac{ds_{it}}{s_{it}} = \underbrace{\left(g_{it} - \mu_{dt} + \left\|\sigma_{dt}\right\|^2 - \sigma_{di,t}\cdot\sigma_{dt}\right)}_{\equiv\mu_{it}^s}dt + \underbrace{\left(\sigma_{di,t} - \sigma_{dt}\right)}_{\equiv\Sigma_{it}}\cdot dW_t. \tag{9.124}$$

Note that the drift of s_{it} generally depends on all the asset shares, and the evaluation in eq. (9.123) is not analytically tractable. To render the problem tractable, we may instead assume that the drift of ds_{it}, that is, $\mu_{it}^s s_{it}$, is linear in s_{it}. In this case, the expectation in (9.123) may be evaluated even without making any assumption on Σ_{it}. However, an assumption made on the shares process would have implications on the dividend dynamics in (9.118) (notably, through the drift restrictions on g_{it} in (9.124)) and then the whole consumption process.

26. Note, obviously, that eq. (9.121) collapses to the standard prediction of the Lucas single tree model, provided the single asset dividend growth is IID.

For example, assume that g_{it} in (9.118) is restricted in a way such that the share process in (9.124) is

$$ds_{it} = \phi\left(\bar{s}_i - s_{it}\right) dt + s_{it}\Sigma_{it} \cdot dW_t, \tag{9.125}$$

where ϕ is a constant and $\bar{s}_i$ are constants satisfying $\sum_{i=1}^{N} \bar{s}_i = 1$. These restrictions ensure that the shares sum up to one.[27] Given these dynamics, the price-dividend ratio in (9.123) is

$$p_{it} = p\left(s_{it}\right) = \frac{1}{\rho+\phi} + \frac{\phi}{\rho\left(\rho+\phi\right)} \frac{\bar{s}_i}{s_{it}}. \tag{9.126}$$

The price-dividend ratio for each asset is decreasing in its dividend share. The intuition is that expected dividend growth for asset i is increasing in $\frac{\bar{s}_i}{s_{it}}$: the higher the current share, s_{it} (compared with $\bar{s}_i$), the lower the expected dividend growth.[28] We shall now explore the model implications on the cross-section of expected returns.

9.9.1.3 *The cross-section of expected returns*

The expected return on each asset depends on its asset return volatility. In this model, asset return volatility is

$$\sigma_{it} = \sigma_{di,t} + \sigma_{p_i,t}, \tag{9.127}$$

where $\sigma_{di,t}$ is the diffusion component of the asset i dividend (see eq. (9.118)) and σ_{p_it} is the diffusion component of the price-dividend ratio *log-changes* in asset i in (9.126). By Itô's lemma, $\sigma_{p_i,t} = \frac{p'(s_{it})}{p(s_{it})} s_{it}\Sigma_{it}$, and replacing this result into eq. (9.127) leaves

$$\sigma_{it} = \sigma_{dt} + \frac{1}{1+\frac{\phi}{\rho}\frac{\bar{s}_i}{s_{it}}} \Sigma_{it} = \frac{\sigma_{di,t} + \frac{\phi}{\rho}\frac{\bar{s}_i}{s_{it}}\sigma_{dt}}{1+\frac{\phi}{\rho}\frac{\bar{s}_i}{s_{it}}}. \tag{9.128}$$

Therefore, by eq. (9.121), $\gamma = 1$, and the second equality in (9.128), the cross-section of expected returns, is

$$\mathcal{E}_{it} - r_t = \sum_{j=1}^{N} s_{jt} cov_t\left(i, d_j\right), \quad cov_t\left(i, d_j\right) \equiv \frac{cov_{dt}\left(i, j\right) + \frac{\phi}{\rho}\frac{\bar{s}_i}{s_{it}} cov_t\left(d, j\right)}{1+\frac{\phi}{\rho}\frac{\bar{s}_i}{s_{it}}},$$

where $cov_{dt}(i, j) \equiv \sigma_{di,t} \cdot \sigma_{dj,t}$ and $cov_t(d, j) = \sigma_{dt} \cdot \sigma_{dj,t}$.

Note that we may rely on the first equality in (9.128) and achieve an alternative representation of the cross-section of expected returns, namely,

$$\mathcal{E}_{it} - r_t = \sigma_{dt}^2 + \frac{1}{1+\frac{\phi}{\rho}\frac{\bar{s}_i}{s_{it}}} cov_{cs_i,t}, \quad cov_{cs_i,t} = E\left(\frac{ds_{it}}{s_{it}}, \frac{dC_t}{C_t}\right) = \Sigma_{it} \cdot \sigma_{dt}. \tag{9.129}$$

---

27. Indeed, by the definition of σ_{dt} in eq. (9.119), we have that $\sum_i s_{it}\Sigma_{it} = \sum_i s_{it}\mu_{it}^s = 0$, such that $\sum_i ds_{it} = 0$, implying that, if $\sum_i s_{i0} = 1$, then $\sum_i s_{it} = 1$ for all t.

28. If the share process is as in eq. (9.125), then by Itô's lemma applied to $D_{it} = s_{it}D_t$, expected dividend growth, g_{it}, is increasing in $\frac{\bar{s}_i}{s_{it}}$. Obviously, the conditional expectation of s_{iT} is increasing in the initial condition s_{it} $(t < T)$. The point is that, by mean reversion, the lower the ratio $\frac{\bar{s}_i}{s_{it}}$, the lower the expected *increase* in the share in the future. Thus, a low s_{it} signals high dividend growth in the future to the extent of the relative distance of s_{it} from $\bar{s}_i$.

Eq. (9.129) shows that the premium for each asset is made of two components. The first component, σ_{dt}^2, is standard and is the same as the equity premium in the single Lucas tree, $N = 1$. The second component can take either sign. If the asset i dividend volatility is higher than the average, $\sigma_{di,t} > \sigma_{dt}$, then $\Sigma_{it} > 0$, such that the equity premium increases with s_{it}: as s_{it} increases, asset i pays a larger portion of consumption; it then becomes riskier than in the standard Lucas tree because the movements in its share and then its price-dividend ratio are positively correlated with consumption. But the premium decreases with s_{it} in the opposite case, $\sigma_{di,t} < \sigma_{dt}$. In this case, the asset serves as a partial hedge in bad times because the movements in its price-dividend ratio are negatively correlated with consumption shocks; an increase in its share would make the asset even more attractive.

Thus, the interplay between size and volatility determines the cross-section of expected returns: an asset's expected return decreases with its size (i.e., its dividend share) if and only if it has low dividend volatility. However, note that, in this case, its return falls to a level below the standard Lucas model, σ_{dt}^2. This property suggests that a multiple tree model may be consistent with sizable equity premiums through extensions such as those in this and chapter 8; for example, section 9.9.2 considers a multiple-tree model with habit formation.

9.9.1.4 *Stochastic singularity, volatility, and correlation*

A potential issue arising in these models is that, in the presence of a large number of assets, markets may exhibit stochastic singularity; that is, if $d < N$, the correlation matrix of the asset returns is degenerate. Alternatively, we may assume that markets are incomplete, $d > N$, or complete, $d = N$ (see chapter 4). However, in these cases, asset return volatility cannot be disentangled from correlation. Consider the covariance of the price-dividend ratios on any two assets

$$E\left(\frac{dp_{it}}{p_{it}}\frac{dp_{jt}}{p_{jt}}\right) = \frac{p'(s_{it})}{p(s_{it})}\frac{p'(s_{jt})}{p(s_{jt})}\Sigma_{it}\cdot\Sigma_{jt}s_{it}s_{jt}dt. \tag{9.130}$$

That is, the correlation of any two asset returns i and j links directly to the volatilities of these returns: we are not free to model volatilities independently of correlation. This property is due to the assumption that asset prices are driven by Brownian motions, and comparable properties have been well studied in the fixed income literature; chapter 13 explains these issues in detail in the context of forward interest rates modeling (see section 13.7.5). A way to cope with stochastic singularity is to model asset prices as strings, or random fields. These models are succinctly reviewed in section 9.9.4 below.

9.9.1.5 *Equity premiums and spillover effects*

Eq. (9.130) shows that asset returns can be correlated even while the fundamentals are not: the individual dividends in (9.118) may well be uncorrelated, and yet asset returns may be correlated. This property arises due to market clearing. In equilibrium, dividend shares have to sum up to one and are obviously correlated. This correlation translates to asset correlation because price-dividend ratios on each asset depend on the asset share. These phenomena have been known since at least Cochrane, Longstaff, and Santa-Clara (2008).

9.9.2 Exogenous Aggregate Output and Habit Formation

In the economy of the previous section, total output (and hence consumption) is the sum of all dividends: thus, dividends are exogenous, and consumption expected growth and volatility, μ_{ct} and σ_{ct}, are endogenous. This section presents a model, introduced by MSV, in which consumption volatility is constant and exogenously given. In this model, total output and dividend shares are given, and each dividend process obtains as a result of these assumptions. This assumption may, in some cases, lead to closed-form solutions in models with habit formation, as discussed below.

Precisely, assume that aggregate consumption in (9.117) is exogenously given, with constants μ_{ct} and σ_{ct}, denoted with μ_c and $\sigma_c \mathbf{e}_1$, where $\mathbf{e}_1$ denotes the vector that has all components equal to zero, except the first component, which is one. Also exogenously given is the share process, which is still as in eq. (9.125) but with exogenously given diffusion coefficients,

$$ds_{it} = \phi\left(\bar{s}_i - s_{it}\right) dt + s_{it}\sigma_{s,i}\left(\mathbf{s}_t\right) \cdot dW_t,$$

where $\sigma_{s,i}(\mathbf{s}_t) \equiv v_i - \sum_{j=1}^{N} s_{jt} v_j$, $v_i \equiv [v_i^1 \cdots v_i^d]$ is a vector of constants for each i, and $\mathbf{s}_t$ denotes the vector of all the shares.[29] This formulation renders the share process stationary: no asset share will shrink to zero or one.

By exogenously given diffusion coefficients, we mean that the vectors v_i in $\sigma_{s,i}(\mathbf{s}_t)$ are given. In contrast, the diffusion coefficients Σ_{it} in (9.124) or (9.125) result from the aggregation process. Given these assumptions, by Itô's lemma, the dividends paid off by each asset i, $D_{it} = s_{it} C_t$, satisfy eq. (9.118), with

$$g_{it} = \mu_c + \phi\left(\frac{\bar{s}_i}{s_{it}} - 1\right) + cov_{cs_i,t}, \quad \sigma_{di,t} = \sigma_c \mathbf{e}_1 + \sigma_{s,i}\left(\mathbf{s}_t\right),$$

where $cov_{cs_i,t} dt \equiv E\left(\frac{ds_{it}}{s_{it}} \frac{dC_t}{C_t}\right) = \sigma_c (v_i^1 - \sum_{j=1}^{N} s_{jt} v_j^1) dt$.

9.9.2.1 *Log-utility*

Assume initially that there is a representative agent with log utility and a discount rate ρ. Therefore, and similar to eq. (9.120), the risk premium in this model is $\lambda = \sigma_c \mathbf{e}_1$. Moreover, the price-dividend ratio is the same as in eq. (9.126), such that return volatility is (similar to eq. (9.128))

$$\sigma_{it} = \sigma_c \mathbf{e}_1 + \frac{1}{1 + \frac{\phi}{\rho} \frac{\bar{s}_i}{s_{it}}} \sigma_{s,i}\left(\mathbf{s}_t\right),$$

and the the cross-section of expected returns is

$$\mathcal{E}_{it} - r_t = \sigma_{it} \cdot \lambda = \sigma_c^2 + \frac{1}{1 + \frac{\phi}{\rho} \frac{\bar{s}_i}{s_{it}}} cov_{cs_i,t}. \tag{9.131}$$

29. MSV consider a model with N assets and one additional income flow, such that dividends plus income flow sum up to total consumption. With this assumption, the persistence parameter ϕ in the share process may vary in the cross-section.

Thus, the predictions of this model are nearly identical to those in section 9.9.1 (see eq. (9.129)). We now explain the analytical challenges faced while extending the model to incorporate more general assumptions on preferences such as habit formation.

9.9.2.2 *Habit*

Consider the last equality in eq. (9.122). The main analytical hurdle in this formula is that the aggregate dividends' *value*, $\xi_t D_t$, is correlated with the share process, s_{it}. In the log utility case, $\xi_t = e^{-\rho t} D_t^{-1}$, such that the aggregate dividends' value is independent of the share, which simplifies the expression in (9.122). Extending the model to include more general preferences requires additional assumptions for the purpose of tractability.

To illustrate, consider the following assumptions made by MSV. A representative agent has instantaneous utility $u(C_t, X_t, t) = e^{-\rho t} \ln(C_t - X_t)$, such that, in equilibrium,

$$\frac{\xi_u}{\xi_t}\frac{D_u}{D_t} = e^{-\rho(u-t)}\left(\frac{\mathcal{S}_u}{\mathcal{S}_t}\right)^{-1}, \quad \mathcal{S}_t \equiv \frac{C_t - X_t}{C_t},$$

where $\mathcal{S}_t$ is the surplus consumption ratio, a notion discussed in chapter 8 (see section 8.5; see also the discussion in section 9.3). Therefore, by eq. (9.122) and under regularity conditions,

$$p_{it} = \int_t^\infty e^{-\rho(u-t)} E_t\left(\frac{Y_u}{Y_t}\frac{s_{iu}}{s_{it}}\right) du, \tag{9.132}$$

where $Y_t \equiv \mathcal{S}_t^{-1}$, the inverse of the surplus consumption ratio. For tractability, assume that

$$dY_t = \beta\left(\bar{Y} - Y_t\right) dt - \alpha\left(Y_t - \underline{Y}\right)\sigma_c dW_{1t}, \tag{9.133}$$

for four constants β, $\bar{Y}$, α, and $\underline{Y}$ and where dW_{1t} denotes the first component of dW_t. In other words, $\sigma_c dW_{1t}$ is the diffusive component of aggregate consumption, consistent with the rationale underlying external habit formation. Under these assumptions, the stochastic discount factor is $\xi_t = e^{-\rho t}\frac{Y_t}{C_t}$ and is solution to

$$\frac{d\xi_t}{\xi_t} = -r_t dt - \left(1 + \alpha\left(1 - \underline{Y}\mathcal{S}_t\right)\right)\sigma_c dW_{1t}.$$

Chapter 8 contains a discussion of this model in the single-tree case and explains that the model belongs to the so-called "linearity-generating" family (see section 8.5.4 and appendix 8.E). A simple restriction that ensures a closed-form expression to p_{it} in (9.132) is that Y_t and s_{it} are not correlated, such that the inner expectation in (9.132) reduces to the product, $E_t(\frac{Y_u}{Y_t})E_t(\frac{s_{iu}}{s_{it}})$, which can be evaluated analytically. Therefore, assume that $v_i^1 = 0$ for all i (i.e., for all assets), such that $cov_{cs_i,t} = 0$.[30] Then, the price-dividend ratio is

$$p_{it} = a_{0i} + a_{1i}\mathcal{S}_t + a_{2i}\frac{\bar{s}_i}{s_{it}} + a_{3i}\frac{\bar{s}_i}{s_{it}}\mathcal{S}_t, \tag{9.134}$$

30. By contrast, note that it would be problematic to extend the model of section 9.9.1 to habit formation along these lines.

for some positive constants a_{xi}, and the cross-section of expected returns is given by

$$\begin{aligned}\mathcal{E}_{it} - r_t &= E\left(\frac{d\xi_t}{\xi_t}\left(\frac{dD_{it}}{D_{it}} + \frac{dp_{it}}{p_{it}}\right)\right)\\ &= \left(1+\alpha\left(1-\underline{Y}\mathcal{S}_t\right)\right)\left(1+\frac{k\bar{Y}\mathcal{S}_t\alpha\left(1-\underline{Y}\mathcal{S}_t\right)}{k\bar{Y}\mathcal{S}_t+\rho\left(1+f\left(\frac{\bar{s}_i}{s_{it}}\right)\right)}\right)\sigma_c^2,\end{aligned} \tag{9.135}$$

where f is some positive and decreasing function. Note that the assumption that $cov_{cs_i,t} = 0$ is strong as it implies that cash-flow risk plays no role in the cross-section of expected returns. To illustrate, this assumption would imply that the equity premium collapses to the standard Lucas prediction in the version of the model without habit (see eq. (9.131)). However, MSV show, numerically, that a model with cash-flow risks leads to conclusions very similar to those discussed below.

9.9.3 Discussion: Predictability

Chapter 8 explains that price multiples may explain expected returns but have less explanatory power on expected dividend growth (see section 8.2). In fact, the evidence on returns predictability does not seem to be very strong and, at times, is inconsistent across sample periods. The model of section 9.9.2 may provide a rationale for this puzzling behavior of price multiples, expected returns, and expected dividend growth. Let us illustrate.

Eqs. (9.134) and (9.135) show that price-dividend ratios and expected returns convey information on both business cycle conditions, $\mathcal{S}_t$, and expected dividend growth, $\frac{\bar{s}_i}{s_{it}}$. Now, variations in business cycle conditions lead to the standard *negative* relation between expected returns and price-dividend ratios: when, say, $\mathcal{S}_t$ decreases, p_{it} decreases, but $\mathcal{E}_{it} - r_t$ increases. However, time variation in expected dividend growth leads to a *positive* relation between these two variables: p_{it} and $\mathcal{E}_{it} - r_t$ are both increasing in the expected dividend growth. These two opposite forces weaken the predictive power of p_{it} on market returns and, in fact, destroy this power on expected dividend growth. The reason expected returns increase with expected dividend growth is that assets with a currently high $\frac{\bar{s}_i}{s_{it}}$ will obviously pay far in the future; their returns are then very exposed to shocks in the risk-adjusted discount rates (channeled by $\mathcal{S}_t$) and hence are volatile, commanding a high premium.[31] Interestingly, Santos and Veronesi (2010) show that a more general version of this model leads to a value premium, at least in the presence of sufficient heterogeneity in the cross-section of cash-flow risks.

9.9.4 Stochastic Strings

A stochastic string, or random field, can be thought of a probabilistic model by which each asset is driven by its own shock, and all shocks are correlated. Heuristically, while Brownian motions may be understood as particles that move randomly over time (see appendix 4.A of chapter 4), a two-parameter random field may be understood as the random motion

31. Note that in the model without habit, volatility and expected returns are increasing in dividend growth only when $\Sigma_{it} < 0$ as discussed after eq. (9.129).

of a string. An important point is that, in a string model, volatility is disentangled from correlation.

Let us explain the meaning of "two-parameters." Consider a market with a continuum of assets, in $(0,1)$, where the law of movement of each asset share in eq. (9.125) is replaced by

$$\frac{ds_{it}}{s_{it}} = \phi\left(\frac{\bar{s}_i}{s_{it}} - 1\right) dt + \sigma_{s,i}(\mathbf{s}_t)\, dZ_{it}, \quad i \in (0,1), \tag{9.136}$$

and, for each i and some constants $(\nu_{it})_{i\in(0,1)}$, the functional $\sigma_{s,i}(\mathbf{s}_t) \equiv \nu_i - \int_0^1 s_{jt}\nu_j dj$ guarantees that the shares sum up to one. Finally, dZ_{it} has zero mean and variance dt but is such that $dZ_{it}dZ_{jt} = \rho(i,j)\, dt$, for some function $\rho(i,j)$. This formulation allows one to separate volatility and correlation of the share process: there are two separate functions for volatility, $\sigma_{s,i}(\mathbf{s}_t)$, and correlation $\rho(i,j)$. Note that we are assuming that the volatility is a functional of the whole share process, $\mathbf{s}_t = (s_{it})_{i\in(0,1)}$.

Chapter 13 provides a more complete description of a string model in markets for fixed income securities. In this section, we illustrate how strings may be used to deal with equity returns.[32] In particular, note that, in (9.125), the share process is determined through aggregation. In contrast, in eq. (9.136), it is assumed that the share process is given, such that the dividend paid off by each asset follows by the identity $D_{it} \equiv s_{it}C_t$, where C_t is total consumption. In other words, in this model, total consumption is given exogenously, just as in the Brownian model of MSV in the previous section.

We assume that C_t subsumes all sources of uncertainty in the economy in that

$$\frac{dC_t}{C_t} = \mu_c dt + \int_0^1 \eta_{it} dZ_{it}, \tag{9.137}$$

where μ_c is a constant and $(\eta_{it})_{i\in(0,1)}$ is a series of processes adapted to Z_{it}. Further, we assume that there is a representative agent with log utility. It is easy to see that the price-dividend ratio for each asset i is still, then, $p(s_{it})$ in eq. (9.126). Moreover, by Itô's lemma, the dividend paid off by each asset satisfies

$$\frac{dD_{it}}{D_{it}} = (\cdots)\, dt + \sigma_{s,i}(\mathbf{s}_t)\, dZ_{it} + \int_0^1 \eta_{ut} dZ_{ut},$$

such that the returns of each asset are

$$\frac{dP_{it} + D_{it}dt}{P_{it}} = \mathcal{E}_{it}dt + \left(1 + \frac{p'(s_{it})}{p(s_{it})} s_{it}\right) \sigma_{s,i}(\mathbf{s}_t)\, dZ_{it} + \int_0^1 \eta_{ut} dZ_{ut}.$$

Now, given the assumption of log utility, the stochastic discount factor is $\xi_t = e^{-\rho t} C_t^{-1}$, such that, by eq. (9.137),

$$\frac{d\xi_t}{\xi_t} = -r_t dt - \int_0^1 \phi_{it} dZ_{it}, \quad \phi_{it} = \eta_{it},$$

32. Distaso, Mele, and Vilkov (2019) have developed a series of predictions on the cross-section of expected returns, based on random fields. This section explores the predictions of a string model based on a variant of their framework.

where the processes ϕ_{it} are interpreted as unit prices of risk for the realization of Z_{it}. The cross-section of expected excess returns is, thus,

$$\mathcal{E}_{it} - r_t = -cov\left(\frac{dP_{it}}{P_{it}}, \frac{d\xi_t}{\xi_t}\right) = \sigma_{ct}^2 + \underbrace{\frac{1}{1+\frac{\phi}{\rho}\frac{\bar{s}_i}{s_{it}}}\sigma_{s,i}(\mathbf{s}_t)\int_0^1 \eta_{ut}\rho(u,i)\,du}_{\equiv cov_{cs_i,t}}, \tag{9.138}$$

where $\sigma_{ct}^2 = \iint_{u,v\in[0,1]^2} \eta_{ut}\rho(u,v)\,\eta_{vt}dudv$, the second term on the RHS of eq. (9.138) follows by the expression for $p(s_{it})$, and the expression for the short-term rate is left to be found as an exercise.

Eq. (9.138) is formally the same as the prediction made by the MSV model (see eq. (9.131)), as indicated by the definition of $cov_{cs_i,t}$. However, this model is more flexible. Indeed, volatility and correlations are now clearly disentangled. To illustrate, the covariance between the price-dividend ratios on any two assets i and j is

$$\mathrm{E}\left(\frac{dp_{it}}{p_{it}}\frac{dp_{jt}}{p_{jt}}\right) = \frac{p'(s_{it})\,p'(s_{jt})}{p(s_{it})\,p(s_{jt})}\sigma_{s,i}(\mathbf{s}_t)\,\sigma_{s,j}(\mathbf{s}_t)\,\rho(i,j)\,dt.$$

Finally, note that this model can be extended to include habit formation just as for the MSV model. The counterpart for the inverse of the surplus consumption ratio in eq. (9.133) may be the solution to

$$dY_t = \beta(\bar{Y} - Y_t)\,dt - \alpha(Y_t - \underline{Y})\int_0^1 \eta_{it}dZ_{it}.$$

This model gives rise to predictions comparable to those discussed in sections 9.9.2 and 9.9.3.

9.10 Prices, Quantities, and the Separation Hypothesis

The models in this chapter are delivering a compelling lesson: to address asset pricing puzzles, we would need to substantially revamp some standard assumptions underlying neoclassic dynamic macroeconomic theory, namely, the basic version of the real business cycle theory reviewed in chapter 3. For example, section 9.10.1 argues that we would need to introduce adjustment costs in the capital formation process and some forms of agents' preferences such as habit formation. So how is it that, at least in the early years, macroeconomists had sometimes ignored the advances made by financial economists? Were macroeconomists too focused on explaining quantity dynamics? In a famous paper, Tallarini (2000) builds up a case for a "separation hypothesis." He considers a real business cycle model in which a representative agent has nonexpected utility as in section 9.2 and shows that price and quantity dynamics may be studied separately in an economy with a representative agent. These properties result from the circumstance that, in this model, risk aversion and EIS are two distinct concepts.

Is separation a realistic description of the economy? The Great Recession that followed the 2007–2009 subprime-related crisis (see chapter 14) has led economists to deeply rethink the role of financial markets in explaining macroeconomic developments. Thus, section 9.11 deals with explanations based on financial accelerator mechanisms, that is, mechanisms resulting from financial frictions, where financial market conditions feed macroeconomic developments, over over a spiral. Interestingly, these models have been known for a long time already as also reviewed in section 9.11. Nevertheless, Tallarini's hypothesis and analytical work are important. For example, they allow us to gain more intuition on the quantitative implications of nonexpected utility (see sections 9.10.2 and 9.10.3); moreover, and somehow surprising, Tallarini's examples on separation mechanisms allow us to link to other strands of the literature related to aversion to Knightian uncertainty (section 9.10.4).

9.10.1 Production Puzzles

Consider an economy where a representative firm produces a single good, $\tilde{y}(K_t, N_t)$ by means of capital K_t and labor N_t, just as in chapter 3 (see section 3.4). The firm pays off a dividend $D(K_t, I_t)$ in each period t, expressed as a function of capital K_t and investment I_t,

$$D(K_t, I_t) \equiv \tilde{y}(K_t, N(K_t)) - w_t N(K_t) - p_t I_t - \phi\left(\frac{I_t}{K_t}\right) K_t,$$

$$D_K(K_t, I_t) \equiv \tilde{y}_K(K_t, N(K_t)) - \frac{\partial}{\partial K}\left(\phi\left(\frac{I_t}{K_t}\right) K_t\right),$$

where subscripts denote partial derivatives. We know that Tobin's marginal q and average q are the same (see theorem 3.2 in chapter 3): the stock market value of the firm, $V(K_t)$, coincides with the value of installed capital, $V(K_t) = q_t K_{t+1}$, where q_t is Tobin's q under the assumption that the price of uninstalled capital is one. We determine equity returns in this economy. First, note that

$$\begin{aligned}
V(K_t) &= q_t K_{t+1} \\
&= E_t\left[m_{t+1}\left(D_K\left(K_{t+1}, I_{t+1}\right) K_{t+1} + (1-\delta) q_{t+1} K_{t+1}\right)\right] \\
&= E_t\left[m_{t+1}\left(D_K\left(K_{t+1}, I_{t+1}\right) K_{t+1} + q_{t+1}\left(K_{t+2} - I_{t+1}\right)\right)\right] \\
&= E_t\left[m_{t+1}\left(D_K\left(K_{t+1}, I_{t+1}\right) K_{t+1} - q_{t+1} I_{t+1} + V\left(K_{t+1}\right)\right)\right] \\
&= E_t\left[m_{t+1}\left(D\left(K_{t+1}, I_{t+1}\right) + V\left(K_{t+1}\right)\right)\right],
\end{aligned}$$

where the second line follows from q theory as reviewed in chapter 3; the third and fourth from the law of capital accumulation and the expression for $V\left(K_{t+1}\right)$; and the fifth from the condition $q_{t+1} = -D_I\left(K_{t+1}, I_{t+1}\right)$ and the homogeneity of the function D. Therefore, equity returns are given by

$$\begin{aligned}
\tilde{R}_{t+1} - 1 &\equiv \frac{D\left(K_{t+1}, I_{t+1}\right) + V\left(K_{t+1}\right) - V(K_t)}{V(K_t)} \\
&= \frac{D_K\left(K_{t+1}, I_{t+1}\right) K_{t+1} - q_{t+1} I_{t+1} + V\left(K_{t+1}\right) - V(K_t)}{V(K_t)}.
\end{aligned}$$

Without adjustment costs, $\phi \equiv 0$, Tobin's q collapses to one, $q_t = 1$, such that the capital gains, $V\left(K_{t+1}\right)/V(K_t) - 1 = -\delta + I_{t+1}/K_{t+1}$, and equity returns collapse to

$$\tilde{R}_t - 1 = \tilde{y}_K(K_t, N(K_t)) - \delta.$$

To match the volatility of equity returns, a model without adjustment costs requires a counterfactually high volatility of the marginal product of capital. Therefore, not only are adjustment costs needed to rationalize the existence of time-varying market-to-book ratios; adjustment costs would also have the potential to boost return volatility. In fact, the equity premium puzzle can only be exacerbated in a setting without adjustment costs. Note indeed that, by the usual representation of the equity premium (see section 7.5 of chapter 7),

$$E_t\left(r^e_{t+1}\right) = -\text{corr}_t(m_{t+1}, r^e_{t+1}) \cdot \frac{\text{Std}_t\left(m_{t+1}\right)}{E_t\left(m_{t+1}\right)} \cdot \text{Std}_t\left(r^e_{t+1}\right),$$

where r^e denotes the equity return in excess of the risk-free rate. Unless the excess returns predicted by the model are substantially and negatively correlated with the pricing kernel, the equity premium is small when $\text{Std}_t(r^e_{t+1})$ is small. Can higher risk aversion lead to a higher equity premium? Not necessarily. Indeed, in equilibrium, equity returns obviously relate to consumption; however, in a production economy, consumption smoothing may exacerbate the equity premium puzzle: Rouwenhorst (1995) originally pointed out that when consumption is endogenous, risk aversion makes it even smoother, thereby reducing $\text{Std}_t(r^e_{t+1})$ in equilibrium.

The main issue with the neoclassical model is that capital supply is perfectly elastic, such that the price of capital and hence capital gains are roughly constant. Jermann (1998) and Boldrin, Christiano, and Fisher (2001) note that one needs to consider some hindrance in the capital supply adjustment process to shocks. For example, Jermann assumes the existence of adjustment costs of the type considered in chapter 3. Instead, Boldrin, Christiano, and Fisher assume, among other things, that investment decisions can be thought of as being determined prior to the realization of the shocks. These contributions rely on the assumption that agents have habit preferences, an assumption that help generate high variability in the demand for capital and hence boost price volatility. Rigidities in capital formation and capital demand volatility seem to be needed to explain the equity premium. The next sections explore explanations of the equity premium based on alternative assumptions on agents' preferences and knowledge.

9.10.2 Risk-Sensitive Models

The model in section 9.2 relies on the assumption that the EIS is not one, that is, $\psi \neq 1$ or $\rho \neq 0$. We now relax this assumption. We only consider the case without production and briefly discuss the real sphere of the economy in the next subsection. In appendix 9.A (see eq. (9.A5)), we explain that, in a nonexpected utility setting, a representation of the pricing kernel alternative to m_{t+1} in eq. (9.10) is

$$m_{t+1} = \beta \left(\frac{c_{t+1}}{c_t}\right)^{\rho-1} \left(\frac{E_t\left(V_{t+1}\right)}{V_{t+1}}\right)^{\frac{\rho}{1-\gamma}-1}, \quad V_{t+1} = \frac{v_{t+1}^{1-\gamma}}{1-\gamma}, \tag{9.139}$$

where v_t denotes the certainty equivalent continuation utility expressed in consumption units, the solution to eq. (9.4). Next, define $z_t = (1-\beta)^{\frac{1}{\rho}} v_t$, which is obviously ordinally equivalent to v_t and satisfies

$$z_t = \left((1-\beta)\, c_t^{\rho} + \beta \left(E_t(z_{t+1}^{1-\gamma})\right)^{\frac{\rho}{1-\gamma}}\right)^{\frac{1}{\rho}}. \tag{9.140}$$

As $\rho \to 0$, the previous expression reduces to $z_t = c_t^{1-\beta}(E_t(z_{t+1}^{1-\gamma}))^{\frac{\beta}{1-\gamma}}$, such that, by defining $U_t : z_t \equiv e^{(1-\beta)U_t}$, we obtain

$$U_t = \ln c_t + \frac{\beta}{\sigma} \ln E_t(e^{\sigma U_{t+1}}), \quad \sigma \equiv (1-\gamma)(1-\beta). \tag{9.141}$$

Note that Hansen and Sargent (1995) provide an early formulation of eq. (9.141), which may be defined as a "risk-sensitive recursion." If $\sigma = 0$, then $U_t = \ln c_t + \beta E_t(U_{t+1})$, that is, the standard additive model. If instead, $\sigma \neq 0$, continuation utilities receive an additional reassessment for risk. The next section provides a further interpretation of (9.141).

Next, assume that consumption growth is a random walk with drift,

$$\ln \frac{c_{t+1}}{c_t} = \mu_g - \frac{1}{2}\sigma_c^2 + \epsilon_{t+1}, \quad \epsilon_{t+1} \sim N\left(0, \sigma_c^2\right). \tag{9.142}$$

for some constant μ_g. Note that eq. (9.142) describes a special case of the Bansal and Yaron (2004) model in section 9.2: it does not include the small persistent component x_t of eq. (9.21). We guess that $U_t = a + b \ln c_t$ and solve for the undetermined coefficients a and b using eq. (9.141), obtaining $a = \frac{2\beta\mu_g(1-\beta) - \beta(1-\beta-\sigma)\sigma_c^2}{2(1-\beta)^3}$ and $b = \frac{1}{1-\beta}$, such that eq. (9.139) collapses to

$$m_{t+1} = \beta \frac{c_t}{c_{t+1}} \frac{V_{t+1}}{E_t\left(V_{t+1}\right)} = \beta \frac{c_t}{c_{t+1}} \frac{e^{\sigma U_{t+1}}}{E_t\left(e^{\sigma U_{t+1}}\right)} = \beta e^{-\mu_g + \frac{1}{2}(2-\gamma)\gamma\sigma_c^2} e^{-\gamma\epsilon_{t+1}}.$$

We have

$$\bar{m} \equiv E_t\left(m_{t+1}\right) = \beta e^{-\mu_g + \gamma\sigma_c^2}, \quad \bar{\sigma} \equiv \sqrt{var_t\left(m_{t+1}\right)} = \bar{m}\sqrt{e^{\gamma^2\sigma_c^2} - 1}. \tag{9.143}$$

Figure 9.6 plots the Hansen-Jagannathan cup obtained with the same hypothetical parameter values used in chapter 7 (see figure 7.3) and the γ-parametrized curve in the $(\bar{m}, \bar{\sigma})$-space, referred to as the "pricing kernel curve" in chapter 7 (see section 7.3). The pricing kernel curve is constructed for two cases: the standard expected utility model (Lucas model) and the nonexpected utility case (referred to as the risk-sensitive model). Note that it takes a value of γ much lower than 30 to make the pricing kernel curve lie inside the cup. The reason is that, as γ increases, the volatility of the pricing kernel increases with γ (as in the Lucas model) but $E_t\left(m_{t+1}\right)$ remains substantially flat: quantitatively, interest rates mostly depend on the EIS, not γ. The reason is that, in the risk-sensitive model, there are no conflicts between intertemporal substitution and precautionary effects—the EIS is not necessarily the same as relative risk aversion.

Once again, this property reflects the fact that nonexpected utility solves the interest rate puzzle (see section 9.2). As also discussed in section 9.2, nonexpected utility does not necessarily imply a resolution of the equity premium puzzle: figure 9.6 suggests that we still need large values of γ to inflate the equity premium to empirically plausible levels. Alternatively, we need additional sources of variation in the primitives of the economy: it is precisely the contribution of Bansal and Yaron (2004) (reviewed in section 9.2), who relied on long-run risks in their attempt to explain the equity premium puzzle.

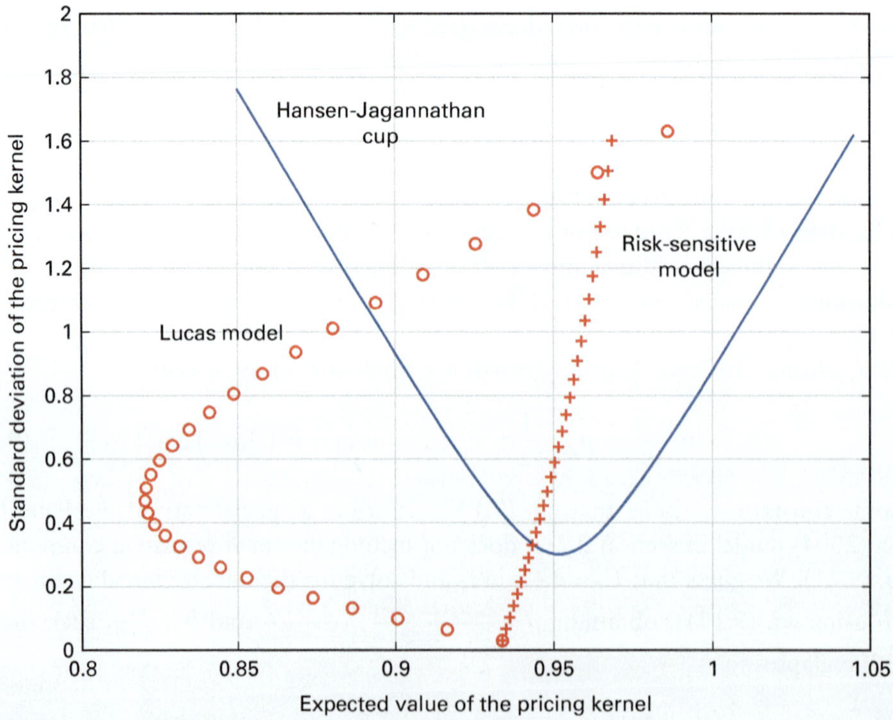

Figure 9.6
The solid line depicts the Hansen-Jagannathan bounds, obtained through eq. (7.14) and all the assumptions in chapter 7 (see section 7.3). The circles (resp. crosses) trace the "pricing kernel curve" predicted by the Lucas model (see eq. (7.16) in chapter 7) and the risk-sensitive model (see eq. (9.143)), with parameters equal to $\beta = 0.95$, $\mu_d = 0.0183$, and $\sigma_d = 0.0328$ and γ ranging from 1 to 35. The Lucas pricing kernel curve enters the cup with values of γ larger than 30. The pricing kernel curve predicted by the risk-sensitive model enters the cup with values of γ larger than 10.

9.10.3 Irrelevance

The main point of Tallarini regards an irrelevance result: we may understand asset markets and the real economy independently. This conclusion holds due to the assumption that the EIS is one, that is, $\rho = 0$, which leads to a simplification of the utility function. Naturally, the previous model does not take real aggregates into account, but Tallarini considers the following extension to eq. (9.141),

$$U_t = \ln c_t + \varphi \ln L_t + \frac{\beta}{\sigma'} \ln E_t \left(e^{\sigma' U_{t+1}} \right), \tag{9.144}$$

where the parameter $\varphi > 0$ now loads leisure, L_t, and is such that $\sigma' = \sigma / (1 + \varphi)$. Tallarini does not consider adjustment costs, and yet his model may explain the equity premium through a simple increase in the risk aversion parameter, σ', while maintaining intertemporal substitution constant, that is, by still assuming log consumption in the RHS of eq. (9.144). Interestingly, raising risk aversion does not affect the quantity dynamics macroeconomists are interested in, only intertemporal substitution might affect it.

Naturally, there are many other dimensions we should consider to make conclusions on any model's prediction about asset prices. For example, Tallarini's assumption of no adjustment costs implies that Tobin's q is one. More generally, section 9.11 explores a stream of the literature in which financial markets do matter, destroying the case for dichotomy in this section. Prior to this section, we review a few additional interesting observations made in the literature.

9.10.4 Preferences for Robustness and Detection Error Probabilities

Model uncertainty is the situation by which agents don't know the statistical laws underlying their benchmarks. Section 9.6 explains that this uncertainty may be formalized by assuming that agents formulate "multiple priors," that is, a "cloud of models" around some reference model: the agents take some model as a reference, but they don't trust it and the cloud is a measure of their mistrust. By positing such a cloud, the agents assume that their reference model is misspecified: the broader the cloud, the higher the size of model misspecification. The agents' aversion to misspecification can then be formalized by the size of misspecification: the higher this size, the higher the agents' aversion to model misspecification (and uncertainty). For example, in the model of section 9.6.4, $\eta(\cdot)$ in (9.99) represents such a size. Sometimes we refer to this type of preferences as preferences for robustness.

This section reviews a famous argument (see, e.g., chapter 14 of Hansen and Sargent, 2008) by which an economy with these features is essentially the same as that in the previous section. This argument is useful because, it has been argued, the model produces predictions consistent with Hansen-Jagannathan calculations, which rely on a realistic reinterpretation of the parameter γ in terms of aversion to uncertainty. Let us review these arguments.

The starting point is a reference model. We still assume that our agents take (9.142) as their point of reference. To formalize the idea that these agents cast doubts on this model, we assume that they "distort" the reference probability by means of a tilting factor, a martingale process G_t satisfying $G_{t+1}=g_{t+1}G_t$, such that their intertemporal utility is

$$W_0=\max_{c_t}\min_{g_{t+1}}\sum_{t=0}^{\infty}\beta^t E\left[G_t\left(\ln c_t+\beta\theta \mathrm{En}_t\left(g_{t+1}\right)\right)\right], \tag{9.145}$$

where $\mathrm{En}_t(\cdot)$ denotes the *conditional entropy* of g_t,

$$\mathrm{En}_t\left(g_{t+1}\right)\equiv E_t\left(g_{t+1}\ln g_{t+1}\right).$$

That is, while agents cast doubts on the reference probability, they add a penalty on the dispersion of their doubts, that is, the entropy $\mathrm{En}_t(\cdot)$. The higher θ, the higher this penalty. These types of preferences, reviewed in detail by Hansen and Sargent (2008), are known as "multiplier preferences" and clearly capture the same economic rationale underlying the max-min preferences discussed in section 9.6.3.

We explained that G_t is a martingale. Indeed, consider the following definitions:

$$G_{t+1}=\frac{\tilde{p}^{t+1}}{p^{t+1}}=\frac{\tilde{p}_{t+1}\tilde{P}^t}{p_{t+1}P^t}=g_{t+1}G_t,$$

where P_{t+1} denotes the (reference model) joint probability density of data up to time $t+1$ and $\tilde{P}_{t+1}$ is its distorted counterpart and p_{t+1} and $\tilde{p}_{t+1}$ are the corresponding conditional densities from t to $t+1$. Note then that $E_t\left(g_{t+1}\right)=1$, such that G_{t+1} is a martingale, and we set $G_0=1$. Moreover, this specification of G_t confirms that the expectation in (9.145) is taken under the distorted probabilities. Finally, the conditional entropy can be understood as the expected log-likelihood ratio (of $\tilde{p}_{t+1}$ over p_{t+1}) under the distorted probability, $\text{En}_t\left(g_{t+1}\right)=\tilde{E}_t\left(\ln g_{t+1}\right)$, where $\tilde{E}_t$ denotes the conditional expectation under the distorted probability.

Next, we cast (9.145) in a recursive format. To simplify notation, set $\pi_t \equiv \ln c_t + \beta\theta \text{En}_t\left(g_{t+1}\right)$. Consider the following heuristic recursive formulation of (9.145):

$$W_0 \equiv \sum_{t=0}^{\infty} \beta^t E\left(G_t \pi_t\right)=\pi_0+\beta \sum_{t=0}^{\infty} \beta^t E\left(g_{t+1} G_t \pi_{t+1}\right)=\pi_0+\beta \tilde{E}\left(W_1\right), \tag{9.146}$$

where the last equality follows by a change of probability and the law of iterated expectations. Thus, $W_0=\min_{g_1}\left(\pi_0+\beta E\left(g_1 W_1\right)\right)$ under the constraint that $E\left(g_1\right)=1$. By taking the first-order conditions and using the constraint, we find that the solution for g_1 is

$$g_1=\frac{e^{-\frac{1}{\theta} W_1}}{E\left(e^{-\frac{1}{\theta} W_1}\right)}.$$

Replacing this solution back into (9.146) leaves

$$W_t=\ln c_t-\beta\theta \ln E_t\left(e^{-\frac{1}{\theta} W_{t+1}}\right), \tag{9.147}$$

where $t=0$ and the reasoning generalizes to any t. Comparing (9.141) and (9.147) reveals that the model of this section is the same as the risk-sensitive model in the previous section: we would have to reinterpret the two parameters θ and σ as being linked by the relation $\theta=-\sigma^{-1}$.

Hansen and Sargent (2008, chapter 14) argue that this model has the potential to address the equity premium puzzle while relying on plausible values for the penalty parameter θ. They generate finite sample data both under the approximate (say, $\mathcal{A}$) and the "worst-case scenario" (say, $\mathcal{W}$) model. The density of the worst-case scenario model is obtained while tilting the approximate model density p_t by $g_{t+1}=\tilde{p}_{t+1}/p_{t+1}$ and obviously depends on the particular value of θ. A detection error probability is the probability that an econometrician falsely rejects $\mathcal{W}$ in favor of $\mathcal{A}$ (through, say, a log-likelihood test), say $p_{\mathcal{W}}$, and an overall detection error probability for a given θ can be defined as $p(\theta)=\frac{1}{2}\left(p_{\mathcal{A}}+p_{\mathcal{W}}\right)$. It is plausible that agents are likely to be concerned about not being able to distinguish between the two models, that is, about a high value of $p(\theta)$. Hansen and Sargent show that values of θ that generate small error detection probabilities also enable the model to come quite close to satisfy the Hansen-Jagannathan bounds.

9.11 Procyclicality and the Financial Accelerator Doctrine

9.11.1 Procyclicality

In the models of the previous sections, asset prices move in response to changes in the fundamentals: it is as if asset prices were "derivatives" written on a few key variables summarizing the state of the economy. But, can financial markets affect the real economy? The Great Recession of the late 2000s likely originated from the mortgage-driven credit crisis that erupted in 2007 (see chapter 14). Adverse developments in credit markets led financial intermediaries to losses, a diminished propensity to lend, and ultimately, a "credit crunch." In turn, the credit crunch exacerbated business cycle conditions, over a spiral.

These historical episodes are instances of "endogenous risk" or "procyclicality," by which a shock leads to adverse developments, which in turn reinforce the initial shock, creating a trend.[33] Specifically, a turmoil in capital markets may lead to adverse economic developments that reinforce the initial financial turmoil over a spiral. Even a relatively small shock, such as the initial subprime mortgage losses in 2007, has the potential to ultimately determine a severe development in the real aggregates. This thesis is known as the "financial accelerator" hypothesis. Understanding asset prices within such a general perspective would enable us to explain economic trends in contexts as critical as those underlying the Great Recession. Naturally, defining the details of these mechanisms leads to models based on alternative assumptions than those underlying the neoclassical model.

Fisher (1933) was one of the earliest proponents of a theory of procyclicality. His explanations were aimed at clarifying the origins of the Great Depression based on a debt-deflation spiral. In an economy with highly levered firms, such as that of the United States during the 1930s, a negative productivity shock leads to bankruptcy of a fraction of these firms, generating less investments and hence depressing aggregate demand and creating deflation. Debt (and its nominal rigidity) is the element that makes Fisher's explanations novel compared with neoclassical predictions. In particular, deflation boosts the real value of debt borne by firms, increasing the firms' burden and leading a higher fraction of these firms to default. This debt-deflation spiral results in a deterioration of the balance sheet of financial intermediaries because banks obviously bleed money as their borrowers default. The result is a contagion of defaults, one traveling from firms to financial intermediaries. Eventually, financial intermediation shrinks and the vicious feedback loop may continue for quite a while.[34]

---

33. The term "endogenous risk" is, by now, quite common in financial economics (see Danielsson and Shin, 2003). Chapter 11 discusses endogenous risk in the context of feedbacks resulting from a number of procyclical trading strategies (see section 11.10)

34. This explanation of the Great Depression was challenged by Friedman and Schwartz (1963), who proposed a "monetary view" instead. The monetary view holds that the prolonged recession and the banking crises in the 1930s are due to nonaccommodating monetary policies. Friedman and Schwartz find a statistical relation between monetary policy and real macroeconomic aggregates in the United States (from the Civil War through 1960): an expansionary monetary policy is associated with an expansion of real aggregates. They find that this linkage is particularly strong in the 1930s and suggest causality from monetary policy to real economic developments. According to Friedman and Schwartz, the role banks played during the Great Depression relates to the very same banking crises, which contributed to a low aggregate money supply via a reduced "money multiplier." (Chapter 14 provides further details on this and related channels; see section 14.5.) In particular, the

This section surveys models that have this financial accelerator flavor but focus on an amplification mechanism of a different nature. We explain how asset prices and credit market imperfections exert feedback effects into business cycles due to information asymmetries. Chapter 10 provides a systematic treatment of asset prices in markets with asymmetric information and other market imperfections but without insisting on feedbacks to the real economy. We rely on models with asymmetric information of the type succinctly reviewed in chapter 5. Firms have more information on their business perspectives (or production skills) than lenders. One main problem may be moral hazard: once resources are lent, borrowers may not necessarily exert the efforts required to act in the lenders' interest. In the seminal contribution of Kiyotaki and Moore (1997), for example, borrowers' human capital is inalienable; borrowers then might find it convenient to withdraw their labor and repudiate their debt. In the seminal contribution of Bernanke and Gertler (1989), asymmetric information is dealt with through costly state verification: financial intermediaries cannot observe idiosyncratic shocks but may monitor the borrowers' output on declaration of bankruptcy. In both contributions, the borrowers' net worth plays a primary role. In the amplification model of Kiyotaki and Moore, borrowers receive less funding in bad times as collateral values are also reduced in bad times. The ensuing lending shrinkage contributes to further depressing real economic activity and hence asset and collateral values, feeding a vicious feedback loop. The borrowers' net worth include asset values that have a forward-looking nature, and this loop may then intensify an initial shock. In the costly state verification model, a higher net worth decreases the cost of external finance. So, in bad times, the cost of external funds increases due to agency problems, discouraging investments even further.

These explanations constitute the pillars of the analytical framework in this section.[35] In particular, sections 9.11.3 and 9.11.4 deal with variants of the Kiyotaki and Moore (1997) model, in which small and temporary shocks generate large and persistent swings in asset prices and the business cycle. The mechanism parallels the multiplier channels in Bernanke and Gertler (1989), although its technical details do not rely on costly state verification. Bernanke, Gertler, and Gilchrist (1999) provide an early survey and a synthesis of models with costly state verification, which is described in section 9.11.5. In these models, asymmetric information relates to the observation of the borrowers' output, and an increase in the borrowers' net worth may lead to better financing conditions. Note that in

deflation of the early 1930s would not allow for any adjustment (a higher output following a higher *real* money supply) because real money supply did not substantially change due to a lowered multiplier. Friedman and Schwartz considered that the Fed should have targeted a much higher monetary base to mitigate these issues. The monetary view was subsequently complemented with the "credit view" as in the first contributions of Bernanke (1983), who emphasized the role of impaired credit intermediation and the cost of intermediation as an additional channel to the adverse developments. Bernanke and Blinder (1988) developed an early and simple model of the credit channel. This section describes further developments as part of financial accelerator mechanisms.

35. Additional interesting contributions have higlighted behavioral-type explanations of procyclicality. For example, in an early paper, Borio, Furfine, and Lowe (2001) explain that the agents' misperception of risk may contribute to amplification mechanisms. To illustrate, the credit/GDP ratio might be procyclical when financial intermediaries underestimate risk in good times, and over-estimate risk in bad, thereby lending too much in good times and too less in bad.

all these models, the source of persistence and amplification of business cycles is the asymmetric information on the borrowers' financial conditions. The literature has also studied mechanisms where endogenous risk is induced by lenders' conditions. This literature is also briefly reviewed in section 9.11.5. Section 9.11.6 concludes with a short summary of the state of current research and an indication of more complete surveys on topics relating to amplification mechanisms through financial markets.

Note that credit market imperfections and their impact on economic activity are very old topics of research in macroeconomics and are difficult to survey in more detail in this book devoted to financial economics. This concluding section of the chapter is mostly interested in the interactions between asset prices and the business cycle. However, we cannot skip describing a famous model developed by Stiglitz and Weiss (1981). In this model (described in section 9.11.2), asymmetric information relates to the riskiness of a project and may affect the size of loanable funds and lead to credit rationing. In the model, the loan rate may act as a screening device: an increase in the loan rate may deteriorate a bank's profitability. The bank may choose a loan rate that maximizes its expected profits but that does not necessarily clear the credit market. The result is credit rationing. Thus, because borrowers have limited liability, an increase in the loan rate attracts more risky projects. Blinder (1987) contains a simple exploration of the macroeconomic implications of credit rationing in a dynamic context. The remaining parts of this section deal with natural developments of mechanisms through which credit market imperfections may affect investments, business cycles, and interactions with asset prices.

9.11.2 Introduction: Credit Rationing

Credit rationing is perhaps one of the most clear instances that illustrates adverse selection in financial economics and macroeconomics.[36] Interest rates are typically taken as "exogenous" in neoclassical macrofinance models in that any loan rate required by a bank does not affect the riskiness of the project submitted to the bank. But in the presence of asymmetric information, an adverse selection problem may arise: after an increase in the required loan rate, a bank may well receive riskier loan applications to such an extent that the bank's expected profits could actually fall. We shall briefly explain that this property may imply credit rationing.

Stiglitz and Weiss (1981) formalize these ideas in a risk neutral environment. They consider a market with a number of potential borrowers indexed by a parameter θ, where each of them has a project with the same expected gross return $\bar{R}$—that is, $E_{\theta_i}(R) \equiv \int_0^\infty Rf(R;\theta_i)\,dR = \bar{R}$ for each borrower i and $f(R;\theta)$ denotes the density function of R for project θ. Critically, projects are ordered in a way that a greater θ implies a higher risk in the sense of mean-preserving spreads (see appendix 1.C in chapter 1). Equally critically, there is asymmetric information between any borrower and the bank in that the latter is unaware of the riskiness of the specific project that is being asked to be financed.

Loans are made at a nominal value B and rate r and are backed by the borrower's collateral C, such that the borrower is insolvent whenever the project return does not cover the firm's liabilities, that is, $C + R < B(1+r)$. We assume that $C < B(1+r)$, for otherwise the firm would be anticipated not to be in need of financing in the first place. In other

36. Chapter 5 contains introductory descriptions of adverse selection problems in financial markets.

words, the profits of the firm,

$$\Pi \equiv \max\{R - B(1+r), -C\}, \tag{9.148}$$

are increasing and convex in R. Thus, the expected profits $E_\theta(\Pi)$ are increasing in θ because, by construction, an increase in θ is a mean-preserving spread. Under regularity conditions, it then follows that there is a "break-even" level of risk, $\hat{\theta}$ say, such that the expected profits are zero for $\theta = \hat{\theta}$, that is, $E_{\hat{\theta}}(\Pi) = 0$. In other words, a firm is willing to borrow only when it carries a project that is sufficiently risky: firms for which $\theta < \hat{\theta}$ will not apply for a loan and firms for which $\theta \geq \hat{\theta}$ will apply for a loan. Note that these predictions result from convexity of Π: borrowers are willing to take more risks when allowed to default. Appendix 9.D provides a parametric example that illustrates this and additional properties of the model.

These properties lead to adverse selection: the riskiness of the borrowers applying for a loan increases after an increase in the required loan rate, r. Intuitively, any firm's profits lower after r increases, such that a higher risk is needed to raise expected profits so as to breakeven. In other words, $\hat{\theta}$ is an increasing function of r, $\hat{\theta}'(r) > 0$, say. The argument is very famous and is made in appendix 9.D.

Next, consider the bank profits

$$\Pi_b \equiv \min\{R + C, B(1+r)\}, \tag{9.149}$$

which are increasing and concave in R, such that the expected profits $E_\theta(\Pi_b)$ are decreasing in θ. What are the effects of an increase in r on the banks' expected profits? A first mechanical effect is that the banks' expected profits increase. But there is a second effect due to adverse selection: by increasing r, the pool of applicants becomes riskier because $\hat{\theta}'(r) > 0$, depressing the bank's expected profits. In other words, due to limited liability, higher risk borrowers have higher expected returns and thus are willing to pay higher interest rates. These two effects can take turns in dominating the overall bank's profitability such that $E_\theta(\Pi_b)$, considered as a function of r, can actually achieve a local maximum.

The equilibrium in the credit market is determined as follows. First, the bank determines the "screening schedule," $\hat{\theta}(r)$, and then, based on this schedule, calculates the posterior distribution of its profits. This posterior distribution is the distribution of Π_b conditional on the adverse selection outcome that only the riskiest potential borrowers would apply for a loan, $\theta \geq \hat{\theta}(r)$. Naturally, the bank is unable to understand who is the riskiest in the pool of applicants and utilizes the distribution of the types while determining the profits posterior distribution. Based on this posterior distribution, the bank determines the interest rate r^* to charge, and in this turn determines the overall demand for loans, $L^d(r^*) \equiv B\int_{\hat{\theta}(r^*)}^{\infty} \gamma(\theta)\, d\theta$, where $\gamma(\theta)$ is the distribution of the potential borrowers.

Note that $L^d(r)$ is decreasing in r, but there is no guarantee that the loanable funds supplied by the bank at the optimal r^* coincide with $L^d(r^*)$. Appendix 9.D develops a parametric example to illustrate this type of equilibrium credit rationing.

9.11.3 Credit Cycles I: Propagation

A standard critique to the basic versions of the neoclassical models of business cycles is that these models predict persistent aggregate fluctuations only based on the assumption of highly persistent technological shocks (see section 3.3.4 of chapter 3), an assumption often regarded with suspicion. This section examines a mechanism of propagation of productivity shocks with persistent effects, based on credit mechanisms. Kiyotaki and Moore (1997) provide a framework to think about business cycle fluctuations originating from and influencing asset prices movements. Persistence and amplification effects are the key predictions of this model. In fact, *persistence* can be understood without reference to asset prices: it may simply arise through the firms' financial constraints. Kiyotaki (1998) develops a model along these lines, which is analyzed in this section. The next section explains how introducing a financial asset allows a shock to be *amplified.*

9.11.3.1 *Farmers and gatherers*

Consider an economy with two types of agents: (i) "productive" or "farmers" and (ii) "unproductive" or "gatherers." Farmers invest k_t into a linear technology, obtaining output y_{t+1},

$$y_{t+1} = \alpha k_t. \tag{9.150}$$

Gatherers have access to a less productive technology: by investing $k_{g,t}$, their output, $y_{g,t+1}$, satisfies

$$y_{g,t+1} = \gamma k_{g,t}, \tag{9.151}$$

where

$$1 < \gamma < \alpha. \tag{9.152}$$

Productivity is random: in each period, farmers may become gatherers, and gatherers may become farmers. We provide more details on this assumption below. Intuitively, switching types is required to make sure both types survive.

All agents maximize the same intertemporal utility of consumption subject to their budget constraint. For example, the farmers' plan is

$$\max_{(c_{t+\tau})_{\tau=0}^{\infty}} E_t\left(\sum_{\tau=0}^{\infty} \beta^{\tau} \ln c_{t+\tau}\right), \quad \text{s.t.} \quad c_t + k_t = y_t + \frac{b_{t+1}}{R_t} - b_t, \tag{9.153}$$

where $\beta < 1$ denotes the subjective discounting factor, b_t is debt outstanding at time t, and R_t is the gross interest rate on debt for the period from t to $t+1$. The budget constraint says that at time t, consumption, c_t, and investments, k_t, are financed by output, y_t, and new issuance of debt, worth $\frac{b_{t+1}}{R_t}$, and net of repayments of current debt, b_t.

We are about to describe a mechanism by which gatherers lend to farmers as the latter "know how" to produce efficiently—they can make more money than just investing at the short-term rate. This mechanism works due to a friction in the lending market: while farmers are efficient, they might also default on their debt, and for this reason, gatherers are willing to only provide collateralized (that is, a limited amount of) loans. Thus, in the resulting economy, the gross interest rate $R_t = \gamma < \alpha$ can be sustained because farmers can only access to a limited amount of loans (due to the collateral constraint friction). Note that, if $R_t > \gamma$, gatherers would obviously not invest; if $R_t = \gamma$, they would be indifferent whether to invest or to lend money, although in equilibrium, they will do both.[37] To begin develop intuition on these results, we first analyze this economy in the frictionless case.

9.11.3.2 *A frictionless benchmark economy*

In the absence of frictions, the gross interest rate $R_t = \alpha$. Indeed, if $R_t > \alpha$, the farmers would never produce because the return on investment would be less than the real interest rate; and if $R_t < \alpha$, the farmers would be willing to borrow an infinite amount, which cannot be an equilibrium either. Note then that by eq. (9.152), the interest rate $R_t = \alpha$ and gatherers do not invest in this economy.

Define the farmers' net worth as $a_t \equiv y_t - b_t$. The flow-of-funds accounting relation in (9.153), the equilibrium condition $R_t = R \equiv \alpha$, and eq. (9.150) yield

$$a_{t+1} = (a_t - c_t)\, R. \tag{9.154}$$

The farmers' plan is then as in (9.153), subject to the flow-of-funds constraint in (9.154). The solution to this program is well known (see, e.g., section 3.2 in chapter 3).[38] Optimal consumption is $c_t = (1-\beta)\, a_t$. Then, by the constraint in (9.153) and the fact that aggregate borrowing is zero, aggregate investments are $K_t \equiv \beta W_t$, where W_t denotes aggregate net worth, which equals aggregate output, Y_{t+1} (again because aggregate borrowing is zero). To sum up,

$$W_{t+1} = Y_{t+1} = \alpha K_t = \alpha\beta W_t = \alpha\beta Y_t. \tag{9.155}$$

The growth of the economy is constant and equal to $\alpha\beta$. It is a very simple outcome, arising within a representative agent economy.[39] Note that, because of the high interest rate, farmers are the only agents to produce in this economy. Gatherers may produce in an economy in which the interest rate is lower than their marginal productivity, that is, $R \leq \gamma$. But this outcome cannot arise in absence of any frictions: farmers would find it optimal to borrow an infinite amount of funds and try to exploit this opportunity, which cannot be an equilibrium. An economy with farmers *and* gatherers necessitates some sort of hindrance in the borrowing opportunities opened to farmers—for example, a limit to the amount of borrowing.

9.11.3.3 *Financial constraints*

Kiyotaki (1998) proposes a variant on Kiyotaki and Moore (1997), the model described in the next section. In this variant, *only those who have initiated the investment* have the skills to produce the full output. Without those skills, one may only achieve to a fraction

---

37. A formal proof that $R_t = \gamma$ in this economy relies on the first-order conditions of the gatherers' problem (the equivalent to (9.153)) with respect to k_t and b_{t+1} and based on the production function in (9.151).

38. We shall assume that productivity shocks are a Markov chain in that farmers and gatherers may switch types. The value function of (9.153) is then $V(a_t) \equiv u(c_t) + \beta E_t\left(V\left(a_{t+1}\right)\right)$, where E_t denotes the expectation taken at time t, and so the results in section 3.2 of chapter 3 can still be utilized in the context of this model.

39. Moreover, eq. (9.155) confirms classical results (see chapter 3), namely, that in the steady state where $Y_{t+1} = Y_t$, the interest rate equals the subjective discount factor, $R = \alpha = \beta^{-1}$.

θ of the full output, even while having access to the producers' technology. Moreover, each producer can declare bankruptcy at any time after they start to produce. Anticipating this possibility of default, creditors will not lend more than can be obtained without the producers' skills,

$$b_{t+1} \leq \theta y_{t+1}. \tag{9.156}$$

That is, should any producer (and debtor) walk away, a creditor could then expropriate their technology and produce the output fraction θy_{t+1}. We can interpret this fraction as the "collateral" value of the producers' investments. In other words, creditors are "collaterizing" their loans.[40] We search for an equilibrium in which $R = \gamma$ around the stationary state and (9.156) holds as an equality. Below, we shall confirm that such an equilibrium exists by just verifying that the gatherers' investments are bounded and bounded away from zero.

The inequality (9.156) describes the friction that prevents farmers from borrowing in infinite amount even while the interest rate is less than their productivity. That is, farmers have access to "good" financing conditions, but they cannot borrow an infinite amount as they are credit constrained by (9.156). They will then borrow as much as they could, that is,

$$b_{t+1} = \theta y_{t+1} = \theta \alpha k_t. \tag{9.157}$$

The previous constraint imposes an upper limit to the farmers' investment, k_t. Using the budget constraint in (9.153), the equilibrium condition $R = \gamma$, and eq. (9.157), we find that this limit is

$$k_t = \frac{y_t - b_t - c_t}{1 - \frac{\theta \alpha}{\gamma}}. \tag{9.158}$$

Investments k_t are just mechanically derived from the budget constraint. The numerator in (9.158) equals the farmers' savings. It is the down payment that is used to invest, k_t, over and above the amount borrowed, $\frac{b_{t+1}}{R}$. Further, to ensure this investment plan is part of the equilibrium, it must be that $\theta \alpha < \gamma$. Under this condition, current borrowing is less than k_t, and the collateralized return (i.e., the percentage of loanable funds to the investment size, $\frac{b_{t+1}}{k_t}$) does not exceed the interest rate ($R = \gamma$). The flow-of-funds accounting relation is now

$$a_{t+1} \equiv y_{t+1} - b_{t+1} = (1 - \theta) \alpha k_t = \underbrace{\frac{(1 - \theta) \alpha}{1 - \frac{\theta \alpha}{\gamma}}}_{\equiv \tilde{\alpha}} (a_t - c_t). \tag{9.159}$$

9.11.3.4 *Investment plans*

The farmers seek to maximize their intertemporal utility in (9.153) subject to (9.159). We solve for consumption c_t, which then determines k_t in (9.158). The solution for consumption follows by the usual argument: for an agent with log utility, $c_t = (1 - \beta) a_t$. Replacing

40. Therefore, loans are collateralized due to "inalienability" of human capital, a mechanism put forward by Hart and Moore (1994).

into (9.158) and aggregating over all farmers leaves

$$\frac{K_t}{W_t} = \beta \frac{s_t}{\bar{s}}, \quad s_t \equiv \frac{A_t}{W_t}, \quad \bar{s} \equiv 1 - \frac{\theta \alpha}{\gamma}, \tag{9.160}$$

where capital letters denote aggregate variables and s_t is the farmers' aggregate share of net worth. Thus, investments depend on s_t. In fact, as we shall see, s_t is the state variable driving the dynamics of growth in the economy.

Under the conjecture that $R = \gamma$, gatherers are indifferent as to whether to invest or to lend. However, we can determine their investments from equilibrium conditions. Indeed, note that their aggregate savings are equal to $\beta A_{g,t}$, with obvious notation. Hence, in equilibrium, aggregate savings satisfy $S_t \equiv \beta \left(A_t + A_{g,t}\right) \equiv \beta W_t$, where $W_t = Y_t + Y_{g,t}$ because aggregate borrowing is zero. Therefore, the investment made by the gatherers can be determined in equilibrium by equating aggregate savings to aggregate investments, namely,

$$K_{g,t} = S_t - K_t = \beta W_t \left(1 - \frac{s_t}{\bar{s}}\right), \tag{9.161}$$

such that aggregate output satisfies $W_{t+1} = Y_{t+1} + Y_{g,t+1} = \alpha K_t + \gamma K_{g,t}$ or

$$\frac{W_{t+1}}{W_t} = \beta \left(\gamma + (\alpha - \gamma) \frac{s_t}{\bar{s}}\right). \tag{9.162}$$

Growth is increasing in s_t: the larger the relative size of productive agents, the higher the aggregate productivity. The mechanism is the following. The interest rate is such that gatherers may also invest, although with limited productivity, γ. Therefore, the higher s_t, the higher the investments made by the most productive agents, K_t, and then the higher total output growth. In other words, total output is now contributed to by both productive and nonproductive agents. Thus, provided $s_t < \bar{s}$ (a condition that is shown to hold in a neighborhood of the steady state), total growth is lower than in the unconstrained economy, $\alpha\beta$ (see eq. (9.155)). Naturally, the economy collapses to that with a representative agent once that $\gamma = \alpha$. Finally, note that by (9.161) and as soon as $s_t < \bar{s}$, the gatherers' investment $K_{g,t}$ is strictly positive and bounded, confirming that $R = \gamma$ is an equilibrium.

9.11.3.5 *Productivity shocks*

We determine aggregate output. Output dynamics depends on how farmers (P, for productive) and gatherers (U, for unproductive) switch their types. Assume that there is a mass $n:1$ of farmers to gatherers and that productivity is a Markov chain, as in this table of conditional probabilities:

$$\begin{array}{c|cc} & U_{t+1} & P_{t+1} \\ \hline U_t & 1 - n\delta & n\delta \\ P_t & \delta & 1 - \delta \end{array}.$$

It is easy to verify that, with the transition density in this table, the mass $n:1$ is constant over time.[41] Moreover, assume that the cross-type *distribution* of productivities is

41. Formally, a stationary density in this simple model is a 2×1 vector π solution to $\pi = \Pi \pi$, satisfying $\pi^{\top} \mathbf{1}_2 = 1$, where Π denotes the transition density of the Markov chain. For example, the

persistent in that $\Pr\left(U_{t+1} \middle| U_t\right) > \Pr\left(U_{t+1} \middle| P_t\right)$, that is,

$$1-\delta > n\delta. \tag{9.163}$$

In words, the probability of being a gatherer at time $t+1$ is higher for a gatherer than for a farmer at time t.

Requiring that agents can switch their types ($\delta > 0$) ensures that a stationary steady state exists, which is compatible with an equilibrium in which both types survive. Intuitively, if $\delta = 0$, the farmers' net worth would dominate, driven by the farmers' higher productivity. Moreover, persistence of the skills' distribution (see eq. (9.163)) ensures that a stationary steady state exists. We corroborate these claims next.

9.11.3.6 Net worth and aggregate output dynamics

The farmers' aggregate new worth at $t+1$ depends on the distribution of types in the economy. That is, A_{t+1} includes the net worth of time t farmers who are still farmers (and have a mass equal to $1-\delta$) and that of time t gatherers who become farmers (and have mass equal to $n\delta$),

$$A_{t+1} = (1-\delta)\left(Y_{t+1} - B_{t+1}\right) + n\delta\left(Y_{g,t+1} - B_{g,t+1}\right), \quad B_{g,t+1} = -B_{t+1}, \tag{9.164}$$

where again capital letters denote aggregate variables and the second equality is the equilibrium condition in the borrowing market.

We calculate the net worth of both farmers and gatherers and replace them into the farmers' law of net worth accumulation, eq. (9.164). Using optimal consumption $c_t = (1-\beta)\,a_t$ into (9.159) and aggregating yields the farmers' aggregate net worth *before* the productivity shock,

$$Y_{t+1} - B_{t+1} = \bar{\alpha}\beta A_t. \tag{9.165}$$

The gatherers' aggregate net worth is obtained by plugging eq. (9.160) into the farmers' aggregate debt obtained through eq. (9.157) and plugging $K_{g,t}$ from eq. (9.161) into $Y_{g,t+1} = \gamma K_{g,t}$, leaving

$$Y_{g,t+1} + B_{t+1} = \gamma\beta\left(W_t - A_t\right). \tag{9.166}$$

Finally, we plug eqs. (9.165) and (9.166) into eq. (9.164) and use the expression for $\frac{W_{t+1}}{W_t}$ in eq. (9.162), obtaining

$$s_{t+1} = \Phi\left(s_t\right) \equiv \frac{(1-\delta)\,\bar{\alpha}s_t + n\delta\gamma\left(1-s_t\right)}{\gamma + (\alpha-\gamma)\frac{s_t}{\bar{s}}}. \tag{9.167}$$

An equilibrium is a sequence $(s_t)_{t=0}^{\infty}$, for a given initial condition s_0. Note that $\Phi(0) = n\delta$ and $\Phi(1) = 1-\delta$. Therefore, (9.163) guarantees that a fixed point s^* exists and is such that $s^* = \Phi(s^*)$, with $s^* = 1$ when $\delta = 0$.[42] The condition $\delta > 0$ (positive probability of productivity switches across types) prevents this economy from reaching the trivial steady state with gatherers' extinction. Moreover, under conditions, there is a unique $s^* < \bar{s}$.

---

first condition is $\pi_1 = \Pr\left(U_{t+1} \middle| U_t\right)\pi_1 + \Pr\left(U_{t+1} \middle| P_t\right)\pi_2$, where π_1 denotes the stationary fraction of gatherers. The solution is $\pi_1 = \frac{1}{n+1}$, whence, $\frac{\pi_2}{\pi_1} = n$.

42. The unconstrained economy is obtained with $\alpha = \gamma$ and $\delta = 0$, in which case $\Phi(s) = s$.

Now, suppose we are at the steady state, $s^* < \bar{s}$, and that there is an *aggregate* but *temporary* productivity shock at t, in that both α and γ decrease by some Δ. After this shock, the farmers' aggregate net worth is, by eq. (9.164),

$$A_{t+1} = (1-\Delta)\left((1-\delta)\,\alpha K_t + n\delta\gamma K_{g,t}\right) - (1-\delta-n\delta)\,B_{t+1}.$$

That is, A_{t+1} obviously goes down, although proportionally more than aggregate output, $W_{t+1} = Y_{t+1} + Y_{g,t+1}$, due to leverage.[43] Therefore, after the aggregate shock, the farmers' aggregate share of net worth, s_{t+1} decreases, $s_{t+1} < s^*$, and due to the financial constraints, so do the farmers' investments and then aggregate output growth. It will now take some time for the farmers' aggregate share of net worth to catch up to its steady state, s^*, through eq. (9.167): because $\delta > 0$ and $\gamma < \alpha$, the economy experiences "productivity leakages," which prevent a full and instantaneous recovery to s^*. But the recovery process does take place: as s_t increases, more and more productive investments take place, leading to higher output growth and less stringent financial constraints, over a virtuous circle, and up to s^* again. Naturally, in the process, aggregate output growth, $\frac{W_{t+1}}{W_t}$, is lower than in the steady state (see eq. (9.162)), which in turn is lower than in the unconstrained economy, $\alpha\beta$.

The important lesson of the model is that propagation mechanisms may be solely due to financial constraints. Instead, in the unconstrained economy, a temporary shock only has a temporary impact (i.e., one period), after which growth stabilizes to $\alpha\beta$. Consistent with the real business cycle theory mentioned at the beginning of this section, the unconstrained economy in this section may witness persistent output fluctuations only through persistent shocks. Alternatively, the presence of financial constraints allows one to achieve conclusions regarding real economic developments. We now turn to review how financial constraints lead to amplification mechanisms of shocks occurring in the real sphere of the economy.

9.11.4 Credit Cycles II: Amplification

The previous model explains how propagation operates in an economy with borrowing constraints. However, one of the main mechanisms behind the financial accelerator doctrine relates to "amplification," that is, the fact that financial markets react to real economic shocks, thereby further affecting the real sphere of the economy, with real economic developments feeding back into financial markets in turn, over a vicious circle. This section relies on work by Kiyotaki and Moore (1997), which is analytically even simpler than that in the previous section; however, in the model of this section, there is a production factor, "land," which also acts as a collateral. In other words, in the model, durable assets play a dual role: they are factors of production and serve as collateral for loans. Amplification works as follows: in bad times, when the land value drops, the borrowing capacity decreases, which lowers future demand for land, thereby decreasing its current evaluations and depressing borrowing capacity even further.

43. That is, after the aggregate shock, $s_{t+1} = \frac{(1-\Delta)Y_{t+1}-(1-\Delta)B_{t+1}-\Delta B_{t+1}}{(1-\Delta)Y_{t+1}+(1-\Delta)Y_{g,t+1}} < \frac{Y_{t+1}-B_{t+1}}{Y_{t+1}+Y_{g,t+1}} = s^*$.

9.11.4.1 *Farmers and gatherers again*

Farmers and gatherers have both linear intertemporal utilities. Farmers' plans are

$$\max_{(c_{t+\tau})_{\tau=0}^{\infty}} \sum_{\tau=0}^{\infty} \beta^{\tau} c_{t+\tau}, \tag{9.168}$$

subject to a budget and further constraints (see (9.171) below) and where c_t denotes time t consumption. Gatherers have the same preferences, but the subjective discounting factor equals $\beta_g > \beta$. Farmers have access to constant returns to scale technology and may produce fruits through land. Their output is equal to

$$y_{t+1} = (a + \bar{c})\, k_t, \tag{9.169}$$

where k_t denotes land used at time t.[44] The portion ak_t of output in eq. (9.169) is assumed to be "tradable," and the portion $\bar{c}k_t$ is not and may only be immediately consumed. We take fruits to be the numéraire and denote the price at time t of land, the durable asset, with q_t.

The farmers' budget constraint is

$$c_t + q_t\left(k_t - k_{t-1}\right) = y_t + \frac{b_{t+1}}{R_t} - b_t. \tag{9.170}$$

It is similar to the budget constraint in (9.153). The difference is that new investments are now made into a *durable* asset, land, and the value of these investments amounts to $q_t\left(k_t - k_{t-1}\right)$. Farmers are credit constrained, just as in the previous section. However, they face a different constraint than (9.156). We now assume that land acts a collateral and that the amount of borrowing in each period cannot exceed the value of land in the next period, namely,

$$b_{t+1} \leq q_{t+1} k_t.$$

To sum up, the farmers' plan is to maximize lifetime utilities (eq. (9.168)), subject to the following constraints:

$$\begin{cases} c_t + q_t\left(k_t - k_{t-1}\right) = (a + \bar{c})\, k_{t-1} + \frac{b_{t+1}}{R_t} - b_t \\ c_t \geq \bar{c}k_{t-1}, \quad b_t \leq q_t k_{t-1} \end{cases}. \tag{9.171}$$

Kiyotaki and Moore show that the last two conditions are binding in a neighborhood of steady state.[45] That is, farmers only consume nontradable fruits and invest as much as they can. These policies leave them with the following law of capital accumulation:

$$\begin{cases} k_t = \dfrac{(a + q_t)\, k_{t-1} - b_t}{u_t}, \quad u_t \equiv q_t - R^{-1} q_{t+1} \\ b_t = q_t k_{t-1} \end{cases}. \tag{9.172}$$

---

44. Note that, in the model of the previous section, the good used for production (see eq. (9.150)) is the same as the consumption good, and the production factor is denoted with k_t. In this section, and with an abuse in notation, we denote land with k_t too.

45. This property is true when farmers are relatively impatient, $\beta < \beta_g$ (as assumed above), and when $a/(a + \bar{c}) < \beta$.

The reason the interest rate factor is assumed constant is clarified below. Note that the numerator of the RHS of the first equation is the farmers' net worth. Therefore, u_t (the denominator) is interpreted as the required down payment per unit of land k_t (the LHS) that is held by the farmers; in the model, the variable u_t plays one additional role, explained below (see eq. (9.173)).

Finally, there is a mass $m:1$ of gatherers to farmers. Gatherers may produce $y_{g,t+1}$ through the following technology:

$$y_{g,t+1} = G\left(k_{g,t}\right),$$

where $k_{g,t}$ denotes the land they use, the function G is increasing and concave and satisfies $G'(0) > aR > G'(\frac{\bar{k}}{m})$, and finally, $\bar{k}$ denotes the total supply of land,

$$\bar{k} = k_t + mk_{g,t}.$$

Underlying these assumptions is the further assumption that the interest rate factor, R, is constant. We now show this is indeed the case.

We assume that the previous production technology does not require any skills. Therefore, gatherers are not credit constrained. Their only constraint is (9.170), and their first-order conditions are

$$\begin{array}{ll} b_{t+\tau}: & R_{t+\tau-1} = \beta_g^{-1} \\ k_{t+\tau}: & 0 = -q_{t+\tau} + \beta_g\left(q_{t+\tau+1} + G'\left(k_{g,t+\tau}\right)\right) \end{array}.$$

The first condition shows that the interest rate that clears the loan market must be constant, that is, $R = \beta_g^{-1}$. By assumption, this rate is less than β; however, farmers cannot borrow an infinite amount because they are credit constrained. Combining the first and the second condition leaves

$$R^{-1}G'\left(k_{g,t}\right) = u_t \equiv q_t - R^{-1}q_{t+1}, \tag{9.173}$$

where we are using again the definition in (9.172). Note that u_t has a second and obvious interpretation in this model. It is the user opportunity cost of capital: to access land for one period, one buys land at time t and resells it at time $t+1$, and the present value of these transactions is equal to u_t. Now, by the gatherers' first-order conditions, the user cost of land is proportional to the gatherers' marginal productivity of land.

9.11.4.2 *Equilibrium*

By (9.173) and the land market-clearing condition,

$$k_t : u\left(k_t\right) \equiv R^{-1}G'\left(\frac{1}{m}\left(\bar{k} - k_t\right)\right) = u_t. \tag{9.174}$$

In equilibrium, the user cost of capital is increasing in k_t: if farmers' demand of land increases, the user cost has to increase in order to clear the land market. In equilibrium, then, the dynamics of farmers' capital in (9.172) satisfies

$$\begin{cases} u\left(k_t\right)k_t = \left(a + q_t\right)k_{t-1} - b_t \\ b_t = q_t k_{t-1} \end{cases}. \tag{9.175}$$

Next, we define the steady state and describe the system dynamics around the state following a productivity shock.

9.11.4.3 *Steady state*

By eqs. (9.172), the dynamics of the farmers' capital is

$$k_t = \frac{a}{u_t} k_{t-1},$$

such that, in the steady state,

$$a = u^* = \left(1 - \frac{1}{R}\right) q^*, \quad b^* = q^* k^*,$$

where starred variables denote values in their steady state. Therefore, assuming no bubbles, the asset price in the steady state is $q^* = \left(1 - \frac{1}{R}\right)^{-1} a$. Finally, we use eq. (9.174) and determine the user cost of capital in the steady state,

$$u\left(k^*\right) = u^* = a. \tag{9.176}$$

The last equation determines k^*, which in turn, given q_*, determines b^*.

9.11.4.4 *The effects of a productivity shock*

Suppose we are in steady state at time $t-1$ and that a temporary and unexpected productivity shock takes place at t, such that output produced at t is $a(1+\Delta)k^*$ for some $\Delta > 0$ (say). By (9.175), the system dynamics are given by

$$\begin{cases} u\left(k_t\right) k_t = \overbrace{\left(a(1+\Delta) + q_t - q^*\right)}^{\text{net worth}} k^* & . \\ u\left(k_{t+\tau}\right) k_{t+\tau} = a k_{t+\tau-1}, & \tau = 1, 2, \cdots \end{cases} \tag{9.177}$$

In the first equation in (9.177), $q_t - q^*$ is the capital gain on land holding: at time t, the value of land is $q_t k^*$ whereas debt repayment had been contracted at $q^* k^*$ at time $t-1$. In other terms, the farmers' net worth increases from $(a + q^*) k^* - b^* = ak^*$ (at time $t-1$) to $(a(1+\Delta) + q_t) k^* - b^* = (a(1+\Delta) + q_t - q^*) k^*$ (at time t). This increase results from two sources: the first direct source is the productivity shock, Δ; the second source is the asset price "jump." The second equation in (9.177) follows because the productivity shock is temporary.

We can linearize (9.177) around the steady state $\left(k_t = k^*, q_t = q^*, \Delta = 0\right)$, use (9.176) and the expression for q^*, and obtain

$$\begin{cases} \left(1 + \frac{1}{\eta}\right) \hat{k}_t = \Delta + \frac{R}{R-1} \hat{q}_t \\ \left(1 + \frac{1}{\eta}\right) \hat{k}_{t+\tau} = \hat{k}_{t+\tau-1}, & \tau = 1, 2, \cdots \end{cases} \tag{9.178}$$

where, for any variable x_t, we define the percentage deviation from the steady state as $\hat{x}_t \equiv \frac{x_t - x^*}{x^*}$ and η is the elasticity of the residual supply to farmers with respect to the user cost in the steady state, $\eta^{-1} \equiv u'\left(k^*\right) \div \frac{u(k^*)}{k^*}$.

Note that the impact of the asset price jump on capital accumulation is potentially substantial. However, the asset price after the shock is obviously endogenous, and we need to determine its expression. By eq. (9.173), we have that, in the absence of bubbles,

$$\begin{aligned} q_t &= \sum_{\tau=0}^{\infty} R^{-\tau} u\left(k_{t+\tau}\right) \\ &\approx \sum_{\tau=0}^{\infty} R^{-\tau}\left(u\left(k^*\right)+u'\left(k^*\right)k^*\hat{k}_{t+\tau}\right) \\ &= q^* + \frac{a}{\eta}\sum_{\tau=0}^{\infty} R^{-\tau}\left(1+\frac{1}{\eta}\right)^{-\tau}\hat{k}_t, \end{aligned} \tag{9.179}$$

where the approximation is a linear expansion made around the steady state and the last equality follows by (9.176) and the second of eqs. (9.178). We can now replace the expression for q^* into (9.179), rearrange terms, and obtain the following linear approximation of the asset price deviations from the steady state,

$$\hat{q}_t = \frac{1}{\eta}\frac{R-1}{R}\frac{1}{1-R^{-1}\left(1+\frac{1}{\eta}\right)^{-1}}\hat{k}_t. \tag{9.180}$$

Combining this expression with the first of eqs. (9.178) leaves the following solution for the asset price and capital deviations from the steady state:

$$\begin{cases} \hat{q}_t = \frac{1}{\eta}\Delta \\ \hat{k}_t = \frac{1}{1+\frac{1}{\eta}}\left(1+\frac{R}{R-1}\frac{1}{\eta}\right)\Delta \end{cases}. \tag{9.181}$$

At the time of the shock, the asset price and capital deviations from the steady state are given by eqs. (9.181). After the shock, capital evolves according to the second of eqs. (9.178), and accordingly, the asset price adjusts through eq. (9.180).

Eqs. (9.181) confirm that amplification effects may be substantial because the asset price reaction to a temporary productivity shock has the same order of magnitude as this very same shock. Further, the interaction between credit limits and asset prices may result into a persistent propagation mechanism, at least as soon as $\eta > 0$. Let us examine the main steps of the mechanism underlying amplification. We assume now that $\Delta < 0$ as we wish to highlight amplification effects that unfold in bad times. So, suppose that a negative shock takes place, such that the farmers' net worth falls down. This fall lowers the farmers' ability to borrow in the future and then the farmers' land demand at any date, present and future. This excess land supply is absorbed by the gatherers through a lower user cost at any date, present and future. The asset price falls, and the resulting capital loss is one additional channel of shrinkage in the farmers' net worth, which reinforces the previous credit-limit-driven propagation mechanism.

Particularly important in the amplification mechanism is the forward-looking nature of the asset price: the price reflects the future perspectives of the land, that is, the land user costs. To isolate these effects, suppose indeed that the future user costs didn't change (or were not supposed to change), such that $q_{t+1} = q^*$ and therefore

$$q_t = u(k_t) + \frac{q_{t+1}}{R} = u(k_t) + \frac{q^*}{R}.$$

By the usual linear expansion of $u(k_t)$ around the steady state, the asset price deviation from its steady state would be

$$\hat{q}_t = \frac{R-1}{R}\frac{1}{\eta}\hat{k}_t,$$

which can be replaced into the first of eqs. (9.177), leaving $\hat{k}_t = \Delta$. In this case, the effects of a productivity shock on capital, while still persistent, would only be limited to the size of the shock.

9.11.5 Financial Intermediation and Business Cycles: Additional Mechanisms

The remainder of this section describes alternative mechanisms through which market imperfections affect investments through amplification. We begin with a famous agency explanation, based on a model with costly state verification. We then examine models that focus on lenders' ("banks") capital rather than borrowers' net worth.

9.11.5.1 Costly state verification and business cycles

We examine a mechanism by which asymmetric information on the borrowers' output is dealt with the lenders' right to monitor this output in case of bankruptcy. Bernanke and Gertler (1989) are the early proponents of such explanations. Chapter 5 (see section 5.6) provides an introduction to models with costly state verification. In these models, borrowers invest when they expect better returns than in the standard case with symmetric information. The reason is that lenders lend while "transferring" verification costs to borrowers, so to speak. These verification costs are decreasing in the borrowers' wealth: borrowers with low wealth face higher cost of capital. Likewise, in the model of this section, a decrease in the borrowers' net worth in bad times may worsen financing conditions, which may then exacerbate real economic developments. This section relies on the framework proposed in the early review of Bernanke, Gertler, and Gilchrist (1999) (BGG, henceforth).

Consider an economy in which firms decide on capital investments by taking as given the price of capital goods and expected aggregate gross returns on capital, q_t and $E_t(R_{k,t+1})$, say. Naturally, q_t and $E_t(R_{k,t+1})$ are determined in general equilibrium. By convention, k^i_{t+1} denotes the capital purchased by firm i at time t and ready to be used in the next period. Given k^i_{t+1}, the firm needs to borrow $B^i_{t+1} \equiv q_t k^i_{t+1} - n^i_{t+1}$, where n^i_{t+1} denotes the entrepreneur's net worth. (Firm and entrepreneur are terms that we use interchangeably in this section.) Funds suppliers are financial intermediaries ("households"). Firms may fail to honor their debt obligations. However, financial intermediaries have the right to verify a firm's outcome upon declaration of bankruptcy. Debt nominal value and capital available for investing are then determined throughout a contract engineered along the lines of the costly state verification model dealt with in chapter 5 (see section 5.6).

First we consider the case with no aggregate risk. Let $\omega^i R_{k,t+1}$ denote the returns that a firm achieves, where ω^i is an IID random variable across firms (i.e., it represents idiosyncratic risk) and time, with $E(\omega^i)=1$; we denote density and cumulative distribution of ω^i with f and F. The contract works as follows. When the borrower can honor their debt obligation, the financial intermediary receives the nominal debt payment $\bar{\omega}^i R_{k,t+1} q_t k^i_{t+1}$ for some $\bar{\omega}^i$ to be determined endogenously, and the firm keeps $(\omega^i - \bar{\omega}^i) R_{k,t+1} q_t k^i_{t+1}$. If the firm declares bankruptcy, the financial intermediary has the right to check the borrower's returns and pays a verification cost equal to $\mu \omega^i R_{k,t+1} q_t k^i_{t+1}$ for some constant $\mu \in (0,1)$. The lender's expected profits then satisfy

$$\begin{aligned} R_{t+1} B^i_{t+1} &= E\left(\bar{\omega}^i \mathbb{I}_{\omega^i > \bar{\omega}^i} + (1-\mu)\,\omega^i \mathbb{I}_{\omega^i \le \bar{\omega}^i}\right) R_{k,t+1} q_t k^i_{t+1} \\ &= \left(\Gamma(\bar{\omega}^i) - \mu G(\bar{\omega}^i)\right) R_{k,t+1} q_t k^i_{t+1}, \end{aligned} \tag{9.182}$$

where R_{t+1} is the riskless interest rate factor and

$$\Gamma(\bar{\omega}^i) \equiv \bar{\omega}^i \left(1 - F(\bar{\omega}^i)\right) + G(\bar{\omega}^i), \quad G(\bar{\omega}^i) \equiv \int_0^{\bar{\omega}^i} \omega f(\omega)\, d\omega.$$

The first equality in (9.182) states that the lender cares about expected returns net of verification costs, consistent with the foundational model in chapter 5.[46] The expected profits to the borrower are then

$$E\left((\omega^i - \bar{\omega}^i)\mathbb{I}_{\omega^i > \bar{\omega}^i}\right) R_{k,t+1} q_t k^i_{t+1} = \left(1 - \Gamma(\bar{\omega}^i)\right) R_{k,t+1} q_t k^i_{t+1}.$$

The contract between lenders and borrowers specifies default boundaries so as to maximize the borrowers' expected profits under the constraint that lenders break even, namely,

$$\max_{k^i_{t+1}, \bar{\omega}^i} \left(1 - \Gamma(\bar{\omega}^i)\right) R_{k,t+1} q_t k^i_{t+1}, \quad \text{s.t. eq. (9.182) holds.} \tag{9.P5}$$

The first-order conditions (with respect to $\bar{\omega}^i$, k^i_{t+1}, and the Lagrange multiplier λ) for this problem lead to

$$\begin{aligned} 0 &= -\Gamma'(\bar{\omega}^i) + \lambda\left(\Gamma'(\bar{\omega}^i) - \mu G'(\bar{\omega}^i)\right) \\ 0 &= \left(1 - \Gamma(\bar{\omega}^i) + \lambda\left(\Gamma(\bar{\omega}^i) - \mu G(\bar{\omega}^i)\right)\right) s_{t+1} - \lambda \\ 0 &= \left(\Gamma(\bar{\omega}^i) - \mu G(\bar{\omega}^i)\right) s_{t+1} \mathcal{K}^i_{t+1} - (\mathcal{K}^i_{t+1} - 1) \end{aligned}$$

where $s_{t+1} \equiv R_{k,t+1}/R_{t+1}$ and $\mathcal{K}^i_{t+1} \equiv q_t k^i_{t+1}/n^i_{t+1}$. The interpretation of s_{t+1} is that of a "spread" between the return on capital and the safe rate, a premium on external finance. Instead, $\mathcal{K}^i_{t+1}$ is the capital/wealth ratio of firm i, that is, the inverse of the share of the firm's capital investment that is financed by net worth.

46. In the model, households are risk averse as explained below. However, the LHS of (9.182) is the relevant opportunity cost to financial intermediaries because loan risk can be perfectly diversifiable.

The first and the second of the first-order conditions for [9.P5] imply that there exists a function σ, such that

$$s_{t+1} = \sigma(\bar{\omega}^i), \tag{9.183}$$

and combining eq. (9.183) with the third of the first-order conditions leads to

$$\mathcal{K}^i_{t+1} = \Psi(\bar{\omega}^i) \tag{9.184}$$

for some function Ψ. Under regularity conditions,[47] the two functions σ and Ψ are both monotonically increasing. Therefore, eqs. (9.183) and (9.184) imply that there exists an increasing function $\mathcal{S}$, such that

$$s_{t+1} = \mathcal{S}(\mathcal{K}^i_{t+1}). \tag{9.185}$$

The function σ is increasing for the following reasons. The exogenous variable is the spread, s_{t+1}, such that default probabilities, $\bar{\omega}^i$, are increasing in this spread. This conclusion mirrors the predictions of the benchmark model in chapter 5 (see section 5.6): investments occur when the spread between the entrepreneur's project returns and the safe rate is sufficiently high to cover agency costs (see inequality (5.38)); the higher the default probability, the higher the wedge between the required return from investing in the project and the safe rate. The intuition underlying eq. (9.183) is the same: the higher the expected return, the higher the risk of default that can be borne in the loan contract. Thus, spreads and default probabilities are positively related. Further, in the stylized contract of chapter 5, default probabilities are decreasing in the borrower's wealth. Likewise, eq. (9.184) tells us that $\bar{\omega}^i$ is increasing in $\mathcal{K}^i_{t+1}$, that is, decreasing in the enterpreneur's net worth. We determine the equilibrium spread. Eq. (9.185) describes the capital supply, an increasing function of $\mathcal{K}^i_{t+1}$. The aggregate supply is obtained by a "horizontal sum" of the single capital supply functions (9.185)—that is, by aggregating the equation, $q_t k^i_{t+1} = \mathcal{S}^{-1}(s_{t+1}) n^i_{t+1}$, across firms, which leaves $s_{t+1} = \mathcal{S}(\frac{q_t k_{t+1}}{n_{t+1}})$, where k_{t+1} and n_{t+1} denote aggregate capital and aggregate net worth.

This description of the capital supply relies on the assumption that no aggregate risk is present. In the presence of aggregate risk, BGG explain that the contract can be simplified by assuming that risk neutral entrepreneurs guarantee that risk averse households are provided with a return that is free from any systematic risk: in other words, (9.182) should now hold for each realization of $R_{k,t+1}$. In this case, the aggregate supply is

$$E_t\left(R_{k,t+1}\right) = \mathcal{S}\left(\frac{q_t k_{t+1}}{n_{t+1}}\right) R_{t+1}. \tag{9.186}$$

Finally, entrepreneurs sell their capital to "retailers," an assumption BGG make to accommodate for price stickiness, a feature of the model that we will not comment on any further. Retailers then produce wholesale output through a technology with decreasing returns to capital and labor, $Y\left(k_{t+1}, \ell_{t+1}\right)$ say, where ℓ_{t+1} is labor input. The firms'

47. Namely, the function $\omega h(\omega)$ is increasing, where h denotes the hazard function for the idiosynchratic risk, $h \equiv f/(1-F)$.

expected return resulting from holding a unit of capital then is

$$E_t\left(R_{k,t+1}\right)=E_t\left(\frac{Y_k\left(k_{t+1},\ell_{t+1}\right)+(1-\delta)\,q_{t+1}}{q_t}\right), \tag{9.187}$$

where δ is the capital depreciation rate and Y_k denotes a partial derivative with respect to capital. The price, q_t, is determined by assuming that capital adjustment is costly and is increasing in k_t. Eq. (9.187) is the demand for capital and is decreasing in k_{t+1}.

Eqs. (9.186) and (9.187) determine the equilibrium capital. In the neoclassical model (see chapter 3), capital supply in (9.186) is a horizontal line as $E_t\left(R_{k,t+1}\right)=R_{t+1}$. In this model, it is increasing in k_{t+1} and shifts down with an increase in the aggregate net worth, n_{t+1}. The main mechanism underlying financial acceleration is the following. Aggregate net worth is made up of wealth that entrepreneurs accumulate not only by operating firms but also through wages. The capital supply schedule shifts to the left after a negative shock in net worth, n_{t+1}, and the equilibrium capital supply lowers. In turn, the price of capital lowers, thereby decreasing future net worth. Bernanke, Gertler, and Gilchrist provide a fully specified quantitative assessment of their model based on the assumption that lenders have log-utility and additional standard assumptions. Section 9.11.6 provides references on recent research on these accelerator mechanisms.

9.11.5.2 *Balance sheet capacity and risk premiums: Introduction*

One may identify two types of explanations of business cycles based on financial market conditions, among others. In one, considered in previous models, collateral constraints may lead to amplification of business cycle fluctuations. It is a *borrower*-induced channel. The literature has identified additional *lender*-induced channels where banks with reduced capital require higher compensation for their risky activity. In good times, though, when banks' capital is high, banks' leverage is very large. Shin (2010) and Adrian and Shin (2010a) provide surveys of these lender-induced channels. Geanakoplos (2010) reviews earlier work on the relation between leverage and business cycles.

The idea that financial intermediaries' capacity may affect security prices has been used in various junctures of the literature. For example, chapter 10 explains that arbitrageurs may fail to align asset prices to fundamentals due to a number of factors such as, say, limited risk-bearing capacity or frictions such as limited or temporary access to arbitrage capital. Chapter 14 attempts an explanation of the acceleration of the 2007–2009 subprime crisis based on risk-bearing capacity constraints (see section 14.5). Such constraints may indeed induce procyclicality, leading financial intermediaries to sell in bad times and buy in good, with balance sheets shrinking and expanding accordingly.

The emphasis of the balance sheet capacity channel is on the linkage between this procyclicality and the amount of credit provided to the economy. The role of bank equity is crucial in this explanation. A standard feature of credit models is that equity and debt depend on assets value (see, e.g., chapter 14). The idea underlying balance sheet capacities is that the direction of this relationship is reversed for banks, with assets values depending on equity. Let us explain with a simple example.

Banks lend money to the rest of the economy and thus give rise to assets values equal to A_t. Assume that the amount of these investments is limited by a value at risk (VaR) constraint,[48] such that equity value, E_t say, satisfies $E_t = \text{VaR}_t \times A_t$. A reasonable assumption is that VaR_t is countercyclical. For example, $\text{VaR}_t \approx \kappa\sigma_t$, where σ_t is the asset volatility and the fixed proportion, κ, is chosen by regulators or by the risk management directives of the banks. It is reasonable that σ_t is countercyclical. Thus, in bad times, when VaR_t increases, the leverage ratio, $\frac{A_t}{E_t} = \frac{1}{\text{VaR}_t}$, falls; in good times, the leverage ratio increases. Therefore, in these examples, the amount of loans depends on bank equity, E_t. Moreover, leverage is procyclical. There is indeed evidence that, at least prior to the 2007–2009 financial crisis, leverage is procyclical for the big investment banks (see, e.g., Adrian and Shin, 2010b), institutions that were at the epicenter of the financial crisis.[49] Moreover, there seems to be evidence that, while equity grows at a constant rate, assets values move more irregularly, suggesting that banks' equity may work as a state variable, consistent with these simple examples. The next section draws from Danielsson, Shin, and Zigrand (2011) and formalizes these ideas in a dynamic setting. Note that He and Krishnamurthy (2013) also consider a model in which financial intermediaries do contribute to countercyclical risk premiums. The model we review has the clear advantage that it can be described through closed-form solutions.

9.11.5.3 *A dynamic model of balance sheet capacity*

Consider an economy in which banks invest in "assets" while satisfying a VaR constraint. These assets may be understood as loans granted to the real sphere of the economy or as securities issued by the borrowers. However, the model does not take into account productivity or the effects of these loans on economic growth. Investors may provide banks with the money needed to invest, but they may also directly invest into the assets. The asset value satisfies

$$\frac{dS_t}{S_t} = \mu_t dt + \sigma_t dW_t, \tag{9.188}$$

where W_t is a standard Brownian motion, the origins of which will be clarified below, and the asset's expected returns and volatility, (μ_t, σ_t), will be determined in equilibrium.

"Traders" in the banks invest in the assets and also choose the amount of money M_t to borrow or to hoard, such that $E_t = A_t + M_t$, where A_t denotes the dollar demand for the assets, that is, $A_t = \theta_t S_t$, with θ_t denoting the assets units held by the banks. By standard conclusions on self-financing strategies in continuous time (see chapter 4), the banks' capital satisfies

$$dE_t = (A_t(\mu_t - r) + rE_t)\, dt + A_t \sigma_t dW_t, \tag{9.189}$$

where r denotes the exogenously given instantaneous rate on M_t.

---

48. Chapter 14 provides an overview of standard market practice in risk management, including VaR for loans subject to default risk (see section 14.4).

49. These conclusions are not trivial. Consider the simple counterexample of a household with a mortgage loan equal to D, and let H denote the house market value. The leverage ratio is $H/(H-D)$ and is decreasing with H, assuming D is constant. Adrian and Shin (2010b) document that the leverage of commercial banks is not related to asset values changes, suggesting a passive behavior of these banks.

The banks' problem is to maximize the expected instantaneous return on its equity, subject to a VaR constraint, that is,

$$\max_{A_t} E\left(dE_t\right) \quad \text{subject to} \quad \alpha\sqrt{var\left(dE_t\right)/dt} \leq E_t, \qquad [9.P6]$$

for some $\alpha > 0$. In other words, banks invest in the assets so that the expected volatility on their equity value, $\text{Vol}\left(dE_t/E_t\right)$, does not exceed a threshold number, the VaR, that is, $\text{Vol}\left(dE_t/E_t\right) \leq \alpha^{-1}$. Thus, the higher α, the more stringent the constraint faced by banks. This program can be interpreted as emanating from plans of managers living a short period of time within the banks in overlapping generations.

The first-order conditions for [9.P6] are

$$\mu_t - r = \gamma_t \alpha \sigma_t, \quad A_t = \frac{E_t}{\alpha \sigma_t}, \qquad (9.190)$$

where γ_t is the Langrange multiplier associated with the VaR constraint. Therefore, we may also express the solution to the banks' investment problem as

$$A_t = E_t \frac{\mu_t - r}{\gamma_t \alpha^2 \sigma_t^2}, \quad \gamma_t = \frac{\mu_t - r}{\alpha \sigma_t}.$$

Heuristically, the banks' investment solution resembles that of a CRRA investor with time-varying risk aversion, γ_t. When the Sharpe ratio is small, γ_t is low and banks *tend* to increase their assets' exposure. However, given the specific assumptions made on the banks constraints in [9.P6], this effect is entirely offset by a standard Merton's effect—the demand for an asset increases with its Sharpe ratio (the numerator of A_t). The result is that A_t is insensitive to the Sharpe ratio, as illustrated by the second of eqs. (9.190).

Interestingly, this form of the asset demand resembles *risk parity* practice as reviewed in chapter 1 (see section 1.2.5): banks invest in the assets in proportions inversely related to the assets' volatility and independent of the assets' expected excess returns. To the extent that volatility is decreasing in E_t, not only does asset demand increase due to the VaR constraint in [9.P6] (i.e., the numerator in $A_t = \frac{E_t}{\alpha \sigma_t}$) but it also increases due to this "risk parity" channel (i.e., the denominator).

In addition to banks, a number of "value investors" desire to be directly exposed to these securities. These investors are not subject to any constraint; they are value investors because their asset demand is price sensitive: they buy when the asset's value is sufficiently low.[50] Precisely, their dollar demand is assumed to equal

$$x_t \equiv \delta_0 \frac{Z_t - \ln S_t}{\sigma_t^2},$$

where δ_0 can be interpreted as a risk-tolerance parameter and Z_t is a demand shock, assumed to satisfy

$$dZ_t = r^* dt + \sigma_z dW_t$$

50. Value investors are more commonly defined as the investors who buy when asset prices are low relative to book assets.

for some constants r^* and σ_z. In equilibrium, $0 = A_t + \frac{1-\lambda}{\lambda} x_t$, such that

$$S_t = \exp\left(Z_t + \frac{1}{\alpha\delta}\sigma_t E_t\right), \tag{9.191}$$

where $\delta \equiv \frac{1-\lambda}{\lambda}\delta_0$, and λ denotes the mass of banks' asset demand.

Thus, the asset price is driven by the Brownian motion affecting Z_t. Asset returns volatility, σ_t, is endogenous in that its value depends on the realization of the state variable driving the asset price, S_t. Eq. (9.191) shows that E_t may be the only state variable to serve this purpose. Therefore, we conjecture that the assets' expected returns and volatility, (μ_t, σ_t), are a function of E_t. By Itô's lemma, then,

$$d\ln S_t = dZ_t + \frac{1}{\alpha\delta} d\left[\sigma\left(E_t\right) E_t\right], \tag{9.192}$$

where $\sigma\left(E_t\right) \equiv \sigma_t$ and

$$d\sigma\left(E_t\right) = \sigma'\left(E_t\right) dE_t + \frac{1}{2}\sigma''\left(E_t\right) dE_t^2, \tag{9.193}$$

and using eq. (9.189) and the solution for A_t in the second of eqs. (9.190),

$$\frac{dE_t}{E_t} = \left(\frac{\mu_t - r}{\alpha\sigma_t} + r\right) dt + \frac{1}{\alpha} dW_t. \tag{9.194}$$

Replacing eqs. (9.193) and (9.194) into eq. (9.192) and identifying diffusion and drift terms in (9.188) delivers the following restrictions:

$$0 = E^2\sigma'\left(E\right) + \left(E - \alpha^2\delta\right)\sigma\left(E\right) + \alpha^2\delta\sigma_z \tag{9.195}$$

and

$$\frac{\mu_t - r}{\sigma_t} = \frac{1}{2\alpha\sigma_z}\left[2\alpha\left(r^* - r\right) + \alpha\sigma_t^2 - \sigma_z + \left(\sigma_t - \sigma_z\right)\left(2\alpha^2 r + \frac{\alpha^2\delta}{E_t} - 2\right)\right]. \tag{9.196}$$

A general solution to (9.195) is[51]

$$\sigma\left(E_t\right) = \frac{1}{E_t} e^{\frac{-\alpha^2\delta}{E_t}}\left[c + \alpha^2\delta\sigma_z \operatorname{Re}\operatorname{Ei}\left(\frac{\alpha^2\delta}{E_t}\right)\right] \tag{9.197}$$

for some constant c. Note that there is a natural restriction satisfied by c, namely that $c = 0$. Indeed, we have that $\lim_{\delta\to 0}\sigma\left(E\right) = \frac{c}{E}$. However, when $\delta = 0$, the resulting economy is riskless, and volatility should be zero, whence $c = 0$. Finally, given the solution for $\sigma\left(E_t\right)$, we may determine the loan's expected return, $\mu_t = \mu\left(E_t\right)$, while using eq. (9.196) with $\sigma_t = \sigma\left(E_t\right)$.

51. The function $\operatorname{Ei}(x)$ denotes the so-called exponential integral, defined as $\operatorname{Ei}(x) = -\int_{-x}^{\infty}\frac{e^{-t}}{t}dt$, and it can be shown to be a complex function with imaginary part equal to $i\pi$. The real part, $\operatorname{Re}\operatorname{Ei}\left(\alpha^2\delta/E_t\right)$, is such that $\sigma\left(E\right)$ in eq. (9.197) is indeed solution to eq. (9.195).

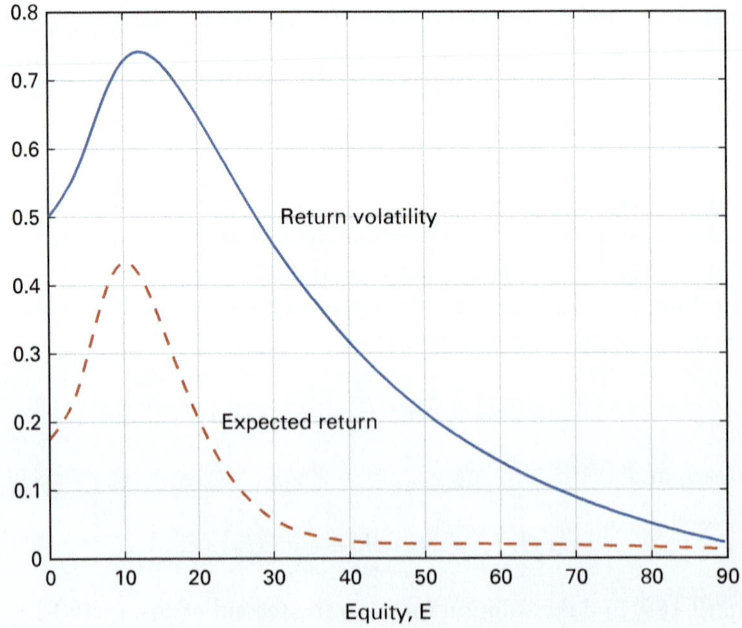

Figure 9.7
Expected returns and volatility on loans as a function of equity of financial intermediaries in an economy with lender-induced feedbacks. Parameters are $\alpha = 2.50$, $\delta = 6$, $\sigma_z = 0.50$, $r = 0.01$, and $r^* = 0.05$.

Figure 9.7 depicts the behavior of the expected returns and volatility on the loans as a function of equity, E, based on parameter values comparable to those used by Danielsson, Shin, and Zigrand (2011). When equity is low, the banks portfolio decisions have a little impact on asset prices, such that volatility and hence expected returns are small. When equity is large, financial intermediaries become basically unconstrained and risk neutral, such that the premium, $\mu_t - r_t$, and volatility, σ_t, both become small. Feedback effects are mostly important for intermediate levels of equity: a positive price shock (occurring through a shock on Z_t) leads to higher equity capital and then a higher assets demand, determining a further increase in asset valuations, thereby raising equilibrium volatility.

These conclusions are reminiscent of the literature in the mid-1990s on feedback effects of hedging strategies, reviewed in chapter 11 (see section 11.5). In this literature, "price spirals" occur as hedgers buy when asset prices increase and sell when asset prices decrease. In the model of this section, *procyclicality* occurs when banks increase their exposure to assets following a positive shock on the asset price.[52] Figure 9.8 depicts the amount of money invested or raised by banks as a function of the banks' equity and leverage. Leverage is largely procyclical, with banks borrowing at a level that disproportionately increases (accounted by a negative M) with equity values, resulting in balance sheet expansions.

52. Consider an alternative economy, in which banks maximize a mean-variance criterion, $\max_{A_t} E(dE_t) - \frac{a}{2} Var(dE_t)$, for some $a > 0$ and with the same value investors. The banks' asset demand is now independent of equity, i.e., $A_t = (\mu_t - r)/a\sigma_t^2$, and an equilibrium is satisfied by $\mu_t = r^* + \frac{1}{2}\sigma_z^2$ and $\sigma_t = \sigma_z$. There is no procyclicality arising in this economy.

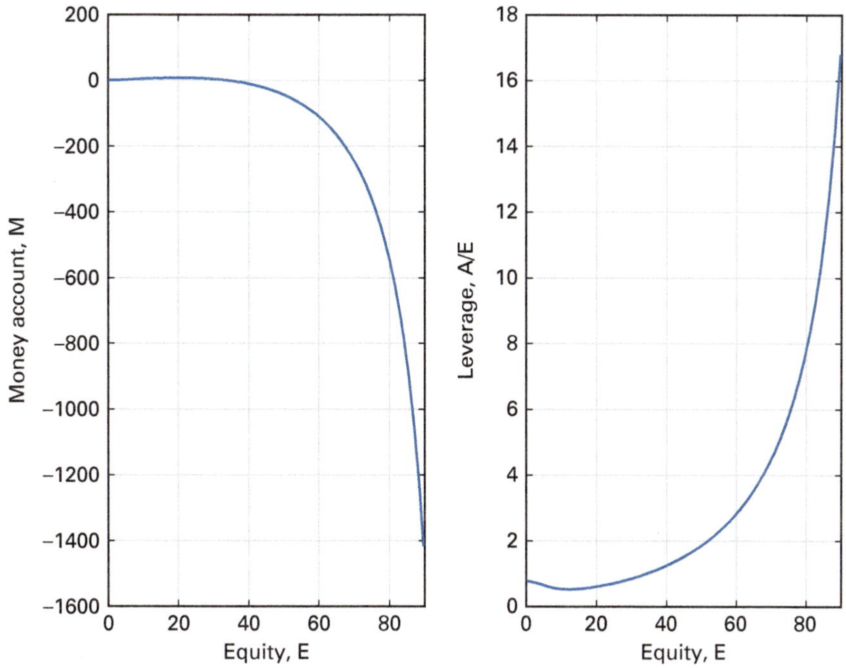

Figure 9.8
The left panel depicts the equilibrium level of the money accounts, $M_t = \left(1 - \frac{1}{\alpha\sigma(E_t)}\right) E_t$, as a function of E_t. The right panel depicts the equilibrium leverage, defined as $\frac{A_t}{E_t} = \frac{1}{\alpha\sigma(E_t)}$, as a function of E_t. Parameters values are as in figure 9.7.

Conversely, balance sheets undergo contractions as the banks' equity value decreases, also resulting in increasing expected returns. That is, in bad times, banks lend less, and the spread over the safe interest rates increases, consistent with the evidence of the financial crisis following the 2007–2009 subprime turmoil. However, this de-leveraging mechanism does not describe a credit crunch where banks hoard cash without lending it. Chapter 14 (see section 14.5) provides a discussion of how balance sheet contractions and credit crunches originated during the 2007–2009 crisis.

9.11.6 The State of Current Research

The literature on macroeconomics in the presence of financial frictions is, by now, truly vast. Interest in the study of amplification mechanisms certainly increased following the global financial crisis and the Great Recession of the late 2000s. This literature contains a series of generalizations and extensions of the models reviewed in this section. Brunnermeier, Eisenbach, and Sannikov (2014) and Moreno-Bromberg and Rochet (2018, chapter 8) contain detailed surveys of this recent literature.

Brunnermeier and Sannikov (2014) introduce a particularly rich and important paper. They consider a continuous time model in which the net worth of financial intermediaries is positive. The authors fully solve their model (i.e., without linearizations around a steady state) and show that system behavior differs according to whether the economy experiences normal times or times of crisis. During a crisis, when the economy is hit by a large shock, amplification mechanisms lead the economy toward a "regime" in which even small shocks are amplified. Interestingly, their model predicts that the economy may well be likely to experience a crisis in the future even if the volatility of fundamentals is low: intuitively, in their model, leverage increases when fundamental risk is low, which may lead to higher risks in the future that arise through amplification. Brunnermeier and Sannikov refer to this property of the model as a "volatility paradox." The reason it is a paradox is that we are used to thinking that periods of *high* volatility are typically followed by bad times. Chapter 8 explains that such is the empirical evidence (see section 8.3). However, this evidence refers to relatively short-term developments and does not examine the details of periods with particularly *low* volatility. It may be that the effects of leverage on the building up of risks may take a longer time, just as with the developments preceding the global financial crisis of the late 2000s.

Appendix 9.A Nonexpected Utility

9.A.1 Optimality

First, we derive the expression for the budget constraint provided in the main text.

Derivation of eq. (9.7). We have

$$\begin{aligned}
A_{t+1} &= \sum_i \left(P_{it+1} + D_{it+1}\right)\theta_{it+1} \\
&= \sum_i \left(P_{it+1} + D_{it+1} - P_{it}\right)\theta_{it+1} + \sum_i P_{it}\theta_{it+1} \\
&= \left(1 + \sum_i \frac{P_{it+1} + D_{it+1} - P_{it}}{P_{it}} \frac{P_{it}\theta_{it+1}}{\sum_i P_{it}\theta_{it+1}}\right) \sum_i P_{it}\theta_{it+1} \\
&= \left(1 + \sum_i r_{it+1}\omega_{it}\right)(A_t - c_t)
\end{aligned}$$

where the last line follows by the standard budget constraint $c_t + \sum P_{it}\theta_{it+1} = A_t$, the definition of r_{it+1}, and the definition of ω_{it} given in the main text. □

Optimality. Consider eq. (9.8) in the main text,

$$V(A_t, y_t) = \max_{c_t, \omega_t} \mathcal{W}\left(c_t, E_t\left(V\left(A_{t+1}, y_{t+1}\right)\right)\right),$$

$$\mathcal{W}(c, v) \equiv \frac{1}{1-\gamma}\left(c^\rho + \beta\left((1-\gamma)v\right)^{\frac{\rho}{1-\gamma}}\right)^{\frac{1-\gamma}{\rho}}.$$

The first-order condition for c_t yields

$$\begin{aligned}
&\mathcal{W}_1\left(c_t, E_t\left(V\left(A_{t+1}, y_{t+1}\right)\right)\right) = \\
&\quad \mathcal{W}_2\left(c_t, E_t\left(V\left(A_{t+1}, y_{t+1}\right)\right)\right) E_t\left[V_1\left(A_{t+1}, y_{t+1}\right)\left(1 + r_M\left(y_{t+1}\right)\right)\right],
\end{aligned} \tag{9.A1}$$

where subscripts denote partial derivatives. Thus, optimal consumption is some function of the state $c(A, y)$ such that

$$A_{t+1} = \left(A_t - c\left(A_t, y_t\right)\right)\left(1 + r_M\left(y_{t+1}\right)\right).$$

Next, differentiate the value function with respect to A_t,

$$V_1(A_t,y_t)=\mathcal{W}_1\left(c(A_t,y_t),E_t\left(V\left(A_{t+1},y_{t+1}\right)\right)\right)c_1(A_t,y_t)$$
$$+\mathcal{W}_2\left(c(A_t,y_t),E_t\left(V\left(A_{t+1},y_{t+1}\right)\right)\right)E_t\left[V_1\left(A_{t+1},y_{t+1}\right)\left(1+r_M\left(y_{t+1}\right)\right)\right]$$
$$\times(1-c_1(A_t,y_t)),$$

where again subscripts denote partial derivatives. Replacing eq. (9.A1) into the previous equation leaves the envelope condition for the dynamic programming problem,

$$V_1(A_t,y_t)=\mathcal{W}_1\left(c(A_t,y_t),E_t\left(V\left(A_{t+1},y_{t+1}\right)\right)\right). \tag{9.A2}$$

By replacing eq. (9.A2) back into eq. (9.A1) and rearranging terms,

$$E_t\left[\frac{\mathcal{W}_2(c(A_t,y_t),v(A_t,y_t))}{\mathcal{W}_1(c(A_t,y_t),v(A_t,y_t))}\mathcal{W}_1\left(c\left(A_{t+1},y_{t+1}\right),v\left(A_{t+1},y_{t+1}\right)\right)\left(1+r_M\left(y_{t+1}\right)\right)\right]=1,$$

where we have set $v(A_t,y_t)\equiv E_t\left(V\left(A_{t+1},y_{t+1}\right)\right)$.

By a similar argument, we now show that the same Euler equation applies to any asset $i=1,\cdots,m$,

$$E_t\left[\frac{\mathcal{W}_2(c(A_t,y_t),v(A_t,y_t))}{\mathcal{W}_1(c(A_t,y_t),v(A_t,y_t))}\mathcal{W}_1\left(c\left(A_{t+1},y_{t+1}\right),v\left(A_{t+1},y_{t+1}\right)\right)\left(1+r_i\left(y_{t+1}\right)\right)\right]=1. \tag{9.A3}$$

We have

$$V(A_t,y_t)=\max_{c_t,\omega_t}\mathcal{W}\left(c_t,E_t\left(V\left(A_{t+1},y_{t+1}\right)\right)\right)$$
$$=\max_{\theta_{t+1}}\mathcal{W}\left(A_t-\sum P_{i,t}\theta_{i,t+1},E_t\left(V\left(A_{t+1},y_{t+1}\right)\right)\right),$$

where $A_{t+1}=\sum\left(P_{i,t+1}+D_{i,t+1}\right)\theta_{i,t+1}$ and where the portfolio choice $\theta_{i,t+1}$ is made at time t. The first-order conditions are

$$\theta_{i,t+1}:0=-\mathcal{W}_1(\cdot)P_{i,t}+\mathcal{W}_2(\cdot)E_t\left[V_1\left(A_{t+1},y_{t+1}\right)\left(P_{i,t+1}+D_{i,t+1}\right)\right].$$

Replacing eq. (9.A2) into the previous equation leaves eq. (9.A3).

Derivation of eq. (9.9). We determine the pricing kernel in eq. (9.A3):

$$m\left(A_t,y_t;A_{t+1},y_{t+1}\right)=\frac{\mathcal{W}_2(c(A_t,y_t),v(A_t,y_t))}{\mathcal{W}_1(c(A_t,y_t),v(A_t,y_t))}\mathcal{W}_1\left(c\left(A_{t+1},y_{t+1}\right),v\left(A_{t+1},y_{t+1}\right)\right).$$

Note that

$$\mathcal{W}_1(c,v)=((1-\gamma)\mathcal{W}(c,v))^{1-\frac{\rho}{1-\gamma}}c^{\rho-1},$$
$$\mathcal{W}_2(c,v)=((1-\gamma)\mathcal{W}(c,v))^{1-\frac{\rho}{1-\gamma}}\beta((1-\gamma)v)^{\frac{\rho}{1-\gamma}-1}, \tag{9.A4}$$

such that, denoting $v_t \equiv v(A_t, y_t)$,

$$m(A_t, y_t; A_{t+1}, y_{t+1}) = \frac{\mathcal{W}_2(c_t, v_t)}{\mathcal{W}_1(c_t, v_t)} \mathcal{W}_1(c_{t+1}, v_{t+1})$$
$$= \beta \left(\frac{v_t}{\mathcal{W}(c_{t+1}, v_{t+1})} \right)^{\frac{\rho}{1-\gamma}-1} \left(\frac{c_{t+1}}{c_t} \right)^{\rho-1}$$
$$= \beta \left(\frac{E_t(V(A_{t+1}, y_{t+1}))}{V(A_{t+1}, y_{t+1})} \right)^{\frac{\rho}{1-\gamma}-1} \left(\frac{c_{t+1}}{c_t} \right)^{\rho-1}, \qquad (9.A5)$$

where we have used the property that, along an optimal consumption path, $V(A, y) = \mathcal{W}(c(A, y), v(A, y))$. Finally, we determine the term $\frac{E_t(V(A_{t+1}, y_{t+1}))}{V(A_{t+1}, y_{t+1})}$. By the envelope condition in (9.A2),

$$V_1(A_t, y_t) = \mathcal{W}_1(c(A_t, y_t), E_t(V(A_{t+1}, y_{t+1})))$$
$$= ((1-\gamma)\mathcal{W}(c(A_t, y_t), v(A_t, y_t)))^{1-\frac{\rho}{1-\gamma}} c(A_t, y_t)^{\rho-1}$$
$$= ((1-\gamma)V(A_t, y_t))^{1-\frac{\rho}{1-\gamma}} c(A_t, y_t)^{\rho-1},$$

where the first equality follows from eq. (9.A2), the second follows from the first of eqs. (9.A4), and the last is the optimality condition. We conjecture that $V(A, y) = b(y) \frac{A^{1-\gamma}}{1-\gamma}$ for some function b, such that the previous expression delivers the agent's optimal consumption,

$$c(A_t, y_t) = a(y_t) A_t, \quad a(y) \equiv b(y)^{\frac{\rho}{(1-\gamma)(\rho-1)}}. \qquad (9.A6)$$

Therefore,

$$A_{t+1} = (1 - a(y_t)) A_t (1 + r_M(y_{t+1})), \qquad (9.A7)$$

and

$$\frac{E_t(V(A_{t+1}, y_{t+1}))}{V(A_{t+1}, y_{t+1})} = \frac{E_t\left(b(y_{t+1})(1 + r_M(y_{t+1}))^{1-\gamma}\right)}{b(y_{t+1})(1 + r_M(y_{t+1}))^{1-\gamma}}. \qquad (9.A8)$$

Along any optimal path, $V(A, y) = \mathcal{W}(c(A, y), v(A, y))$. Using the expression of $\mathcal{W}$ in eq. (9.8) and again using the conjecture made on V,

$$V_t = b(y_t) \frac{A_t^{1-\gamma}}{1-\gamma}$$
$$= \frac{1}{1-\gamma} \left(a(y_t)^\rho A_t^\rho + \beta E_t \left(b(y_{t+1}) A_{t+1}^{1-\gamma} \right)^{\frac{\rho}{1-\gamma}} \right)^{\frac{1-\gamma}{\rho}}$$
$$= \frac{1}{1-\gamma} \left(a(y_t)^\rho A_t^\rho + \beta E_t \left(b(y_{t+1}) (1 - a(y_t))^{1-\gamma} A_t^{1-\gamma} (1 + r_M(y_{t+1}))^{1-\gamma} \right)^{\frac{\rho}{1-\gamma}} \right)^{\frac{1-\gamma}{\rho}},$$

and rearranging terms leaves

$$E_t\left(b\left(y_{t+1}\right)\left(1+r_M\left(y_{t+1}\right)\right)^{1-\gamma}\right)=\beta^{-\frac{1-\gamma}{\rho}}\left(\frac{a\left(y_t\right)}{1-a\left(y_t\right)}\right)^{\frac{(1-\gamma)(\rho-1)}{\rho}}. \tag{9.A9}$$

Moreover, using eq. (9.A6) and expressing $b(y)$ in terms of $a(y)$ yields

$$b\left(y_{t+1}\right)\left(1+r_M\left(y_{t+1}\right)\right)^{1-\gamma}=\left(a\left(y_{t+1}\right)\left(1+r_M\left(y_{t+1}\right)\right)^{\frac{\rho}{\rho-1}}\right)^{\frac{(1-\gamma)(\rho-1)}{\rho}}. \tag{9.A10}$$

Plugging eqs. (9.A9) and (9.A10) into eq. (9.A8),

$$\begin{aligned}\frac{E_t\left(V\left(A_{t+1},y_{t+1}\right)\right)}{V\left(A_{t+1},y_{t+1}\right)}&=\beta^{-\frac{1-\gamma}{\rho}}\left(\frac{a\left(y_t\right)}{\left(1-a\left(y_t\right)\right)a\left(y_{t+1}\right)\left(1+r_M\left(y_{t+1}\right)\right)^{\frac{\rho}{\rho-1}}}\right)^{\frac{(1-\gamma)(\rho-1)}{\rho}}\\&=\beta^{-\frac{1-\gamma}{\rho}}\left(\left(\frac{c_{t+1}}{c_t}\right)^{-1}\frac{A_{t+1}}{\left(1-a\left(y_t\right)\right)A_t\left(1+r_M\left(y_{t+1}\right)\right)^{\frac{\rho}{\rho-1}}}\right)^{\frac{(1-\gamma)(\rho-1)}{\rho}}\\&=\beta^{-\frac{1-\gamma}{\rho}}\left(\left(\frac{c_{t+1}}{c_t}\right)^{-1}\frac{1}{\left(1+r_M\left(y_{t+1}\right)\right)^{\frac{1}{\rho-1}}}\right)^{\frac{(1-\gamma)(\rho-1)}{\rho}},\end{aligned}$$

where the second equality follows by eq. (9.A6) and the third by eq. (9.A7). The result follows by replacing the previous expression into eq. (9.A5). □

Proof of eqs. (9.14) and (9.15). By the standard property that, if $\tilde{y}$ is normally distributed, $\ln E(e^{\tilde{y}})=E(\tilde{y})+\frac{1}{2}var(\tilde{y})$, we can elaborate on eq. (9.12), obtaining

$$\begin{aligned}0&=\ln E_t\left(e^{-\delta\theta-\frac{\theta}{\psi}\ln(c_{t+1}/c_t)+\theta R_{M,t+1}}\right)\\&=-\delta\theta-\frac{\theta}{\psi}E_t\left(\ln\frac{c_{t+1}}{c_t}\right)+\theta E_t(R_{M,t+1})+\frac{1}{2}\left(\left(\frac{\theta}{\psi}\right)^2\sigma_c^2+\theta^2\sigma_{R_M}^2-2\frac{\theta^2}{\psi}\sigma_{R_M,c}\right).\end{aligned} \tag{9.A11}$$

We do the same in eq. (9.13) and obtain

$$\begin{aligned}R_{f,t}=\delta\theta&+\frac{\theta}{\psi}E_t\left(\ln\frac{c_{t+1}}{c_t}\right)-(\theta-1)E_t(R_{M,t+1})\\&-\frac{1}{2}\left(\left(\frac{\theta}{\psi}\right)^2\sigma_c^2+(\theta-1)^2\sigma_{R_M}^2-2\frac{\theta(\theta-1)}{\psi}\sigma_{R_M,c}\right).\end{aligned} \tag{9.A12}$$

By replacing eq. (9.A12) into eq. (9.A11), we obtain eq. (9.14) in the main text.

To obtain the risk-free rate $R_{f,t}$ in eq. (9.15), we replace the expression for $E_t(R_{M,t+1})$ in eq. (9.14) into Eq. (9.A12). □

9.A.2 Long-Run Risks

Proof of eq. (9.24). By substituting the guess $z_t = a_0 + a_1 x_t$ into eq. (9.23),

$$
\begin{aligned}
0 &= (\kappa_0 - (1-\kappa_1)\,a_0 - \delta)\,\theta + \ln E_t\left(e^{-\frac{\theta}{\psi}\ln(C_{t+1}/C_t)+\theta\kappa_1 a_1 x_{t+1} - \theta a_1 x_t + \theta g_{t+1}}\right) \\
&= \theta\left(\left((\kappa_0 - (1-\kappa_1)\,a_0 - \delta) + \left(1-\frac{1}{\psi}\right)\left(g_0 - \frac{1}{2}\sigma_c^2\right)\right)\right) + \ln E_t\left(e^{\theta\left(1-\frac{1}{\psi}\right)\epsilon_{t+1} + \theta\kappa_1 a_1 \eta_{t+1}}\right) \\
&\quad + \theta\left((\kappa_1\rho - 1)\,a_1 + \left(1-\frac{1}{\psi}\right)\right)x_t \\
&\equiv \text{const}_1 + \text{const}_2 \cdot x_t,
\end{aligned}
$$

where the second equality follows by eqs. (9.21) and (9.22). Note then that this equality can only hold if the two constants, const_1 and const_2, are both zero. Imposing $\text{const}_2 = 0$ yields

$$
a_1 = \frac{1-\frac{1}{\psi}}{1-\kappa_1\rho}
$$

as in eq. (9.24) in the main text. Imposing $\text{const}_1 = 0$ and using the solution for a_1 yields the solution for the constant a_0. □

9.A.3 Continuous Time

Duffie and Epstein (1992a,b) extend the discrete time framework of nonexpected utility to continuous time. This appendix provides a heuristic introduction to this extension.

9.A.3.1 *Convergence to continuous time*

We begin with the definition of the certainty equivalent continuation utility in section 9.10 (see eq. (9.140)), $z_t = (1-\beta)^{\frac{1}{\rho}} v_t$, where $v_t : V_t = u_R(v_t)$ and satisfies eq. (9.4). We consider consumption taking place in discrete intervals of time and then take the continuous time limit. We define, consistently with (9.140),

$$
z_t = \left((1-e^{-\delta\Delta t})c_t^\rho + e^{-\delta\Delta t}\left(E_t(z_{t+\Delta t}^{1-\gamma})\right)^{\frac{\rho}{1-\gamma}}\right)^{\frac{1}{\rho}},
$$

and $\omega_t = \frac{z_t^{1-\gamma}}{1-\gamma}$, such that

$$
(1-\gamma)\,\omega_t = \left((1-e^{-\delta\Delta t})c_t^\rho + e^{-\delta\Delta t}\left((1-\gamma)\,E_t\left(\omega_{t+\Delta t}\right)\right)^{\frac{\rho}{1-\gamma}}\right)^{\frac{1-\gamma}{\rho}}. \tag{9.A13}
$$

It is easily checked that $\omega_t = (1-\beta)^{\frac{1-\gamma}{\rho}} V_t$, that is, ω_t is ordinally equivalent to V_t. Next, rearrange terms in eq. (9.A13), and take the limits for $\Delta t \to 0$, obtaining

$$
\begin{aligned}
\lim_{\Delta t\to 0}\frac{E_t\left(\omega_{t+\Delta t}\right)-\omega_t}{\Delta t} &= \lim_{\Delta t\to 0}\frac{\frac{1}{1-\gamma}\left((1-e^{\delta\Delta t})c_t^\rho + e^{\delta\Delta t}\left((1-\gamma)\,\omega_t\right)^{\frac{\rho}{1-\gamma}}\right)^{\frac{1-\gamma}{\rho}} - \omega_t}{\Delta t} \\
&= -\frac{\delta}{\rho}\frac{c_t^\rho - \left((1-\gamma)\,\omega_t\right)^{\frac{\rho}{1-\gamma}}}{\left((1-\gamma)\,\omega_t\right)^{\frac{\rho}{1-\gamma}-1}} \\
&\equiv -f\left(c_t,\omega_t\right),
\end{aligned} \tag{9.A14}
$$

where the second equality follows by l'Hôpital's rule. It is easy to check that the standard additive utility case is obtained once $\rho = 1-\gamma$. In the more general case, we integrate (9.A14) and, assuming that $\lim_{T\to\infty} E_t(\omega_T) = 0$, obtain

$$\omega_t = E_t\left(\int_t^\infty f(c_u, \omega_u)\, du\right).$$

We provide an alternative formulation. Define

$$z_{ot} = \left(c_t^\rho \Delta t + e^{-\delta\Delta t}\left(E_t\left(z_{o,t+\Delta t}^{1-\gamma}\right)\right)^{\frac{\rho}{1-\gamma}}\right)^{\frac{1}{\rho}}$$

and $\omega_{ot} = \frac{z_{ot}^{1-\gamma}}{1-\gamma}$. Repeating the same steps leading to (9.A14) yields

$$\begin{aligned}\lim_{\Delta t\to 0}\frac{E_t\left(\omega_{o,t+1}\right) - \omega_{o,t}}{\Delta t} &= -f_o\left(c_t, \omega_{ot}\right)\\ &\equiv -\frac{(1-\gamma)\,\omega_{ot}}{1-1/\psi}\left(\left(\frac{c_t}{\left((1-\gamma)\,\omega_{ot}\right)^{1/(1-\gamma)}}\right)^{1-1/\psi} - \delta\right).\end{aligned} \tag{9.A15}$$

While f in (9.A14) and f_o in (9.A15) are equivalent, all derivations in this appendix are based on f.

9.A.3.2 *Bellman equation and optimality conditions*

In the remainder, we assume that there is a set of state variables driven by Brownian motions, just as in section 4.6 of chapter 4. They are solution to eq. (4.92),

$$dy_t = \varphi(y_t)\, dt + \Sigma(y_t)\, dW_t,$$

for some vector and matrix valued functions φ and Σ and where W_t is a d-dimensional Brownian motion. These state variables may affect expected returns and volatility of m securities. We assume that there is a representative agent investing in such securities (and an MMA), such that the agent's wealth, V_t, satisfies the dynamics

$$dV_t = \left(\pi_t^\top(\mu_t - 1_m r_t) + r_t V_t - c_t\right) dt + \pi_t^\top \sigma_t dW_t,$$

with standard notation (see, e.g., eq. (4.60) in section 4.3 of chapter 4): μ_t and σ_t are vector- and matrix-valued securities' expected returns and volatilities, π_t are dollar holdings, and r_t is the short-term rate. We assume that μ_t, σ_t, and r_t may only depend on the current values of the state vector y_t.

Under these assumptions, the Bellman equation is

$$0 = \max_{c,\pi}\left[L\omega(V,y) + f(c, \omega(V,y))\right], \tag{9.A16}$$

where f is as in (9.A14) and

$$\begin{aligned}L\omega(V,y) &\equiv \omega_V(V,y)\left(\pi^\top(\mu - 1_m r) + rV - c\right) + \omega_y(V,y)\,\varphi(y)\\ &+\frac{1}{2}\omega_{VV}(V,y)\pi^\top\sigma\sigma^\top\pi + \pi^\top\sigma\Sigma^\top\omega_{Vy}(V,y) + \frac{1}{2}\mathrm{Tr}\left(\Sigma\Sigma^\top\omega_{yy}(V,y)\right),\end{aligned}$$

where subscripts denote partial derivatives.

The first-order conditions are

$$\begin{cases} 0 &= f_c(c,\omega(V,y)) - \omega_V(V,y) \\ 0_m &= (\mu - \mathbf{1}_m r)\,\omega_V(V,y) + \sigma\sigma^\top \pi\,\omega_{VV}(V,y) + \sigma\Sigma^\top \omega_{Vy}(V,y) \end{cases} \tag{9.A17}$$

where 0_m is a vector of zero and where we are omitting to note that μ, σ, Σ, and r may be a function of the state. We proceed along lines similar to those in the additive utility model (see section 4.6.3 in chapter 4) and derive a characterization of the cross-section of expected returns and the state prices.

9.A.3.3 *Cross-section of expected returns*

The second equation in (9.A17) implies that, in equilibrium, the cross-section of expected returns satisfies

$$\mu - \mathbf{1}_m r = -\sigma\sigma^\top \mathrm{Cap}\frac{\omega_{VV}(V,y)}{\omega_V(V,y)} - \sigma\Sigma^\top \frac{\omega_{Vy}(V,y)}{\omega_V(V,y)}, \tag{9.A18}$$

where we have used the market-clearing condition $\pi_t = \mathrm{Cap}_t$ and Cap is the vector of market capitalizations. Next, we determine the two ratios on the RHS of eq. (9.A18). Note then that the first equation in (9.A17) reveals that consumption is some function $c(V,y)$ and that by differentiating this equation with respect to V and y, we obtain

$$\frac{\omega_{VV}}{\omega_V} = \frac{f_{cc}}{f_c}c_V + f_{c\omega}, \quad \frac{\omega_{Vy}}{\omega_V} = \frac{f_{cc}}{f_c}c_y + \frac{f_{c\omega}}{f_c}\omega_y, \tag{9.A19}$$

where we have replaced the first-order condition, $\omega_V = f_c$, in the RHS of the previous relations. We replace these ratios into (9.A18) and obtain

$$\begin{aligned} \mu - \mathbf{1}_m r &= -\sigma\sigma^\top \mathrm{Cap}\left(\frac{f_{cc}}{f_c}c_V + f_{c\omega}\right) - \sigma\Sigma^\top\left(\frac{f_{cc}}{f_c}c_y + \frac{f_{c\omega}}{f_c}\omega_y\right) \\ &= \sigma\,\mathrm{vol}_c^\top \frac{-cf_{cc}}{f_c} - \sigma\sigma^\top \mathrm{Cap} f_{c\omega} - \sigma\Sigma^\top \frac{f_{c\omega}}{f_c}\omega_y \\ &\equiv \mathrm{cov}_{S,c}\frac{-cf_{cc}}{f_c} - V\mathrm{cov}_{S,M} f_{c\omega} - \sigma\Sigma^\top \frac{f_{c\omega}}{f_c}\omega_y, \end{aligned} \tag{9.A20}$$

where vol_c denotes the volatility vector of consumption growth and where we have used the relation

$$\mathrm{vol}_c \equiv \frac{c_V}{c}\mathrm{Cap}^\top \sigma + \frac{c_y^\top}{c}\Sigma, \tag{9.A21}$$

which holds by Itô's lemma and the definitions

$$\mathrm{cov}_{S,c} \equiv \sigma\,\mathrm{vol}_c^\top, \quad \mathrm{cov}_{S,M} \equiv \sigma\sigma^\top \frac{\mathrm{Cap}}{V}, \tag{9.A22}$$

which are interpreted as the covariance between asset returns and consumption ($\mathrm{cov}_{S,c}$) and the covariance between asset returns and market returns ($\mathrm{cov}_{S,M}$), consistent with the notation introduced in chapter 4 (see section 4.6.3).

Next, we determine the third term on the RHS of (9.A20). It is possible to show that $\omega(V,y) = \omega_0(y)\frac{V^{1-\gamma}}{1-\gamma}$ for some function $\omega_0(\cdot)$, such that $\omega_{Vy} = (1-\gamma)V^{-1}\omega_y$. Inserting this into the second relation of (9.A19) leaves

$$\omega_y = \frac{f_{cc}c_y}{(1-\gamma)V^{-1} - f_{c\omega}}.$$

Thus, the third term on the RHS of (9.A20) is

$$\begin{aligned} -\frac{f_{c\omega}}{f_c}\sigma\Sigma^\top\omega_y &= -\frac{cf_{cc}}{f_c}\frac{f_{c\omega}}{(1-\gamma)V^{-1} - f_{c\omega}}\sigma\Sigma^\top\frac{c_y}{c} \\ &= -\frac{cf_{cc}}{f_c}\frac{f_{c\omega}}{(1-\gamma)V^{-1} - f_{c\omega}}\mathrm{cov}_{S,c} + \frac{cf_{cc}}{f_c}\frac{f_{c\omega}\frac{c_V}{c}}{(1-\gamma)V^{-1} - f_{c\omega}}V\mathrm{cov}_{S,M}, \end{aligned}$$

where the second equality follows by the definitions of vol_c in (9.A21) (to replace $\Sigma^\top\frac{c_y}{c}$) and the definition of $\mathrm{cov}_{S,c}$ and $\mathrm{cov}_{S,M}$ in (9.A22). Thus, eq. (9.A20) can be written as

$$\begin{aligned} \mu - 1_m r = &\frac{-cf_{cc}}{f_c}\left(1 + \frac{f_{c\omega}}{(1-\gamma)V^{-1} - f_{c\omega}}\right)\mathrm{cov}_{S,c} \\ &+ \left(\frac{cf_{cc}}{f_c}\frac{f_{c\omega}\frac{c_V}{c}}{(1-\gamma)V^{-1} - f_{c\omega}} - f_{c\omega}\right)V\mathrm{cov}_{S,M}. \end{aligned} \tag{9.A23}$$

We now elaborate on the coefficient loadings for $\mathrm{cov}_{S,c}$ and $\mathrm{cov}_{S,M}$. First, note that, by the first of the optimality conditions in (9.A17) and the expression for f and ω, optimal consumption satisfies

$$\delta\left(\frac{c}{V}\right)^{\rho-1} = \omega_0^{\frac{\rho}{1-\gamma}}. \tag{9.A24}$$

Further, we take the appropriate derivatives of f in (9.A14) and obtain that $\frac{-cf_{cc}}{f_c} = 1-\rho$ and

$$f_{c\omega} = \delta(1-\gamma-\rho)\left(\frac{c}{V}\right)^{\rho-1}\omega_0^{-\frac{\rho}{1-\gamma}}V^{-1} = (1-\gamma-\rho)V^{-1}, \tag{9.A25}$$

where the second equality follows by (9.A24).

Therefore, regarding the loading on $\mathrm{cov}_{S,c}$ in (9.A23),

$$\frac{-cf_{cc}}{f_c}\left(1 + \frac{f_{c\omega}}{(1-\gamma)V^{-1} - f_{c\omega}}\right) = \frac{(1-\rho)(1-\gamma)}{\rho} = \frac{\theta}{\psi}, \tag{9.A26}$$

where we have used the definitions in the main text of the elasticity of intertemporal substitution (see section 9.2.1), $\psi \equiv (1-\rho)^{-1}$, and the parameter $\theta \equiv \frac{1-\gamma}{1-\psi^{-1}}$ (see eq. (9.10) in section 9.2.3).

Now, regarding the loading on $\mathrm{cov}_{S,M}$ in (9.A23), we have

$$\frac{cf_{cc}}{f_c}\frac{f_{c\omega}\frac{c_V}{c}}{(1-\gamma)V^{-1} - f_{c\omega}} - f_{c\omega} = -\frac{1-\gamma-\rho}{\rho}V^{-1} = (1-\theta)V^{-1}, \tag{9.A27}$$

where we have used the expression for $f_{c\omega}$ in (9.A25), the fact that, by (9.A24), $\frac{c_V}{c} = V^{-1}$; and again where we have used the definitions of ψ and θ. By replacing (9.A26) and (9.A27) into (9.A23) leaves

$$\mu - \mathbf{1}_m r = \frac{\theta}{\psi} \mathrm{cov}_{S,c} + (1-\theta)\, \mathrm{cov}_{S,M}. \tag{9.A28}$$

Note that eq. (9.A28) is the continuous time counterpart to the discrete time formulation in the main text (see, e.g., the pricing equation for the market portfolio, eq. (9.14) in the main text).

9.A.3.4 *State prices*

Finally, we derive the state prices predicted by the model. The proof is similar to others produced while deriving related results in the context of additive utility in chapter 4 (see section 4.6.4). Differentiating the Bellman equation (9.A16) with respect to V yields

$$f_\omega (c, \omega (V, y))\, \omega_V (V, y) = -\frac{\partial}{\partial V} L\omega (V, y) = -r\omega_V (V, y) - L\omega_V (V, y),$$

whence

$$-r = f_\omega (c, \omega (V, y)) + \frac{L\omega_V (V, y)}{\omega_V (V, y)} = f_\omega (c, \omega (V, y)) + \frac{Lf_c (c, \omega (V, y))}{f_c (c, \omega (V, y))},$$

where the second equality follows by the first of the optimality conditions in (9.A17). The previous equality suggests that the stochastic discount factor, ξ_t, is the solution to

$$\frac{d\xi}{\xi} = f_\omega (c, \omega (V, y))\, dt + \frac{df_c (c, \omega (V, y))}{f_c (c, \omega (V, y))},$$

which we integrate to obtain

$$\frac{\xi_T}{\xi_t} = \exp\left(\left(\int_t^T f_\omega (c_u, \omega (V_u, y_u))\, du \right) \frac{f_c (c_T, \omega (V_T, y_T))}{f_c (c_t, \omega (V_t, y_t))}. \right.$$

Any claim for time T, D_T say, can be priced as $E_t \left(\frac{\xi_T}{\xi_t} D_T \right)$.

Appendix 9.B Economies with Heterogeneous Agents

9.B.1 Economies with a Continuum of Agents

We study asset prices in economies with complete markets by relying on a centralized decision mechanisms that delivers the same outcome as that of the decentralized market-based approach. This approach was developed by Huang (1987) and extends the approach used to deal with the classical model in chapter 2.

We consider a set containing a continuum of agents, A, indexed by an instantaneous utility function $u_a (c)$, where for each $a \in A$, c is consumption. The case with a discrete number of agents is dealt with a change in notation and is analyzed in some of the examples below. Because markets are complete, the market allocation is Pareto efficient, and by the second welfare theorem, it can be "implemented" by means of the program

$$\max_{c_a} E\left[\int_0^\infty e^{-\delta t}\left(\int_{a\in A} u_a(c_{at}) f_a da\right) dt\right], \quad \text{s.t.} \quad \int_{a\in A} c_{at} da = D_t,$$

or, because there is no intertemporal transfer of resources,

$$U(D) \equiv \max_{(c_a)_{a\in A}} \int_{a\in A} u_a(c_a) f_a da, \quad \text{s.t.} \quad \int_{a\in A} c_a da = D, \qquad [9.A\text{-}P1]$$

where D is the aggregate endowment in the economy.

We explain how the equilibrium price system is determined as the Arrow-Debreu state price density in an economy with a single agent endowed with the aggregate endowment D and an instantaneous utility function $U(D)$ and where the social weighting function f_a is the reciprocal of the marginal utility of income for agent $a \in A$. Indeed, the first-order conditions for the program [9.A-P1] are

$$u_a'(c_{at}) f_a = \psi_t, \quad \text{for all } a \in A, \tag{9.A29}$$

where $u_a'(c_a)$ denotes the derivative of u_a with respect to c_a and ψ_t is a Lagrange multiplier. Moreover, by differentiating U with respect to D,

$$U_C(D_t) = \int_{a\in A} u_a'(c_{at}) \frac{\partial c_{at}}{\partial D_t} f_a da = \psi_t \int_{a\in A} \frac{\partial c_{at}}{\partial D_t} da = \psi_t, \tag{9.A30}$$

where $U_C(D)$ denotes the derivative of U with respect to D. The second equality in eq. (9.A30) follows by the optimality conditions (9.A29), and the third, by differentiating the constraint of the social plan [9.A-P1]. Combining eqs. (9.A29) and (9.A30) leaves

$$\frac{U_C(D_t)}{U_C(D_0)} = \frac{u_a'(c_{at})}{u_a'(c_{a0})}, \quad \text{for all } a \in A. \tag{9.A31}$$

On the other hand, the market general equilibrium allocation satisfies

$$e^{\delta t}\frac{\xi_t}{\xi_0} = \frac{u_a'(c_{at})}{u_a'(c_{a0})}, \quad \text{for all } a \in A. \tag{9.A32}$$

To show that the allocations in eq. (9.A31) and in eq. (9.A32) are the same, we need to show that

$$U_C(D_t) = e^{\delta t}\xi_t. \tag{9.A33}$$

We show that eq. (9.A33) holds true once the social weight $f_a = \kappa_a^{-1}$, where κ_a is the marginal utility of income of agent a. Indeed, in this case, eq. (9.A29) and the optimality conditions for the decentralized economy lead to, for all $a \in A$,

$$u_a'(c_{at}) = \kappa_a \psi_t \quad \text{and} \quad u_a'(c_{at}) = \kappa_a e^{\delta t}\xi_t. \tag{9.A34}$$

Aggregating the first and second of the previous conditions leaves

$$D_t = \int_{a\in A} \varphi_a(\kappa_a \psi_t)\, da, \quad D_t = \int_{a\in A} \hat{\varphi}_a\left(\kappa_a e^{\delta t}\xi_t\right) da,$$

where φ_a and $\hat{\varphi}_a$ denote the inverse functions for consumption, as implied by the social and private allocations in (9.A34). Eq. (9.A33) follows by an argument similar to that used to show theorem 2.7 in chapter 2 and by the envelope theorem in eq. (9.A30). Therefore, the pricing kernel in this economy with heterogeneous agents and complete markets has the same pricing implication as the economy with a single agent as explained, namely,

$$\frac{\xi_t}{\xi_0} = e^{-\delta t} \frac{U_C(D_t)}{U_C(D_0)}. \qquad (9.A35)$$

The practical merit of this approach is that, while the marginal utility of income is unobservable, the Arrow-Debreu state price density we constructed depends on the "infinite dimensional parameter" f, which could be calibrated to match selected quantitative features of consumption and asset price data.

We now apply this approach and derive the equilibrium conditions in two models and then move to study the allocation process in an incomplete market setting.

9.B.2 Catching Up with the Joneses

We provide additional details on the Chan and Kogan (2002) model. In this model, markets are complete, and we have that $A = [1, \infty]$ and the instantaneous utility of agent γ is $u_\gamma(c_\gamma, x) = (c_\gamma / x)^{1-\gamma} / (1-\gamma)$, where x is the "standard of living of others," as explained in the main text.

The static optimization problem for the social planner in [9.A-P1] can be written as

$$u(D,x) = \max_{c_\gamma} \int_1^\infty \frac{(c_\gamma / x)^{1-\gamma}}{1-\gamma} f_\gamma d\gamma, \quad \text{s.t.} \int_1^\infty \frac{c_\gamma}{x} d\gamma = \frac{D}{x}. \qquad (9.A36)$$

The first-order conditions for this problem lead to

$$\left(\frac{c_\gamma}{x}\right)^{-\gamma} f_\gamma = \psi\left(\frac{D}{x}\right), \qquad (9.A37)$$

where ψ is a Lagrange multiplier, a function of the aggregate endowment D, normalized by x. This is determined by eq. (9.28), which is obtained by replacing eq. (9.A37) into the budget constraint of the social planner, the second of eqs. (9.A36). The value function in eq. (9.27) of the main text follows by replacing eq. (9.A37) into the maximized value of the intertemporal utility, the first of eqs. (9.A36). General equilibrium allocations and prices are obtained by setting $f(\gamma)$ equal to the reciprocal of the marginal utility of income for agent γ.

The expression for the unit risk premium in eq. (9.29) follows by results given in section 8.4.2 of chapter 8,

$$\lambda(s(D,x)) = -\left(\frac{\partial^2 U(s(D,x))}{\partial D^2} \bigg/ \frac{\partial U(s(D,x))}{\partial D}\right) \sigma_0 D, \quad s(D,x) \equiv \ln \frac{D}{x}, \qquad (9.A38)$$

where $U(s)$ is the value function in eq. (9.27). To evaluate the previous expression for λ, first note that

$$\frac{\partial U(s(D,x))}{\partial D} = -\frac{\psi'(s(D,x))}{D} \int_1^\infty \frac{1}{\gamma} f_\gamma^{\frac{1}{\gamma}} \psi(s(D,x))^{-\frac{1}{\gamma}} d\gamma. \qquad (9.A39)$$

Moreover, differentiating eq. (9.28) with respect to D, using eq. (9.A39), and rearranging terms leads to $\partial U(s(D,x))/\partial D = \psi(s(D,x))/x$. Differentiating this expression for $\partial U/\partial D$ with respect to D again produces

$$\frac{\partial^2 U(s(D,x))}{\partial D^2} = \frac{\psi'(s(D,x))}{x}\frac{1}{D}. \tag{9.A40}$$

Replacing eqs. (9.A39) and (9.A40) into eq. (9.A38) yields eq. (9.29) in the main text. In this fictitious representative agent economy, the short-term rate is the expectation of the stochastic discount factor. Again, by results given in chapter 8 (see section 8.4.2), it equals

$$\begin{aligned} r(D,s,x) &= \rho - g_0 \frac{\partial^2 U(s(D,x))/\partial D^2}{\partial U(s(D,x))/\partial D} D - \theta \frac{\partial^2 U(s(D,x))/\partial D \partial x}{\partial U(s(D,x))/\partial D} sx \\ &\quad - \frac{1}{2}\sigma_0^2 \frac{\partial^3 U(s(D,x))/\partial D^3}{\partial U(s(D,x))/\partial D} D^2 \\ &= \rho + \frac{g_0}{\sigma_0}\lambda(s(D,x)) - \theta\left(1 + \frac{\psi'(s(D,x))}{\psi(s(D,x))}\right) s(D,x) \\ &\quad - \frac{1}{2}\sigma_0^2 \left(\frac{\psi''(s(D,x)) - \psi'(s(D,x))}{\psi(s(D,x))}\right). \end{aligned}$$

It is instructive to compare the first-order conditions of the social planner in eq. (9.A37) with those in the decentralized economy. Because markets are complete, the optimality conditions in the decentralized economy satisfy

$$e^{-\delta t}\left(\frac{c_{\gamma t}^{\mathrm{m}}}{x_t}\right)^{-\gamma} = \kappa_\gamma \xi_t x_t, \tag{9.A41}$$

where κ_γ is the marginal utility of income for agent γ, as usual. Aggregating the market allocations c_γ^{m} in eq. (9.A41),

$$D_t = \int_1^\infty c_{\gamma t}^{\mathrm{m}} d\gamma. \tag{9.A42}$$

By aggregating the social weighted allocations, $c_{\gamma t}^{\mathrm{s}}$ say, in eq. (9.A37), with $f = \kappa^{-1}$,

$$D_t = \int_1^\infty c_{\gamma t}^{\mathrm{s}} d\gamma. \tag{9.A43}$$

Comparing (9.A42) and (9.A43) leads to the conclusion that the social allocations, with $f = \kappa^{-1}$, are the same as the private allocations and that the counterpart to eq. (9.A35) is

$$\frac{\xi_t}{\xi_0} = e^{-\delta t}\frac{x_t^{-1}\psi\left(\frac{D_t}{x_t}\right)}{x_0^{-1}\psi\left(\frac{D_0}{x_0}\right)} = e^{-\delta t}\frac{U_C(D_t,x_t)}{U_C(D_0,x_t)}.$$

9.B.3 Restricted Stock Market Participation

We provide additional details on the Basak and Cuoco (1998) model. Given eq. (9.41) and results given in section 8.4 of chapter 8, the unit risk premium, $\lambda(D,x)$, solves a fixed-point problem,

$$\lambda(D,x) = -\frac{U_{11}(D,x)}{U_1(D,x)}\sigma_0 D + \frac{U_{12}(D,x)x}{U_1(D,x)}\lambda(D,x).$$

That is,

$$\lambda(D,x) = -\frac{U_1(D,x)U_{11}(D,x)}{U_1(D,x) - U_{12}(D,x)x} \cdot \frac{\sigma_0 D}{U_1(D,x)}. \tag{9.A44}$$

We claim that

$$U_1(D,x) = u_p'(c_p^*) \text{ and } \frac{U_1(D,x)U_{11}(D,x)}{U_1(D,x) - U_{12}(D,x)x} = u_p''(c_p^*), \tag{9.A45}$$

where c_p^* and c_n^* are the social planner consumption allocations. Replacing eqs. (9.A45) into eq. (9.A44) and using the definition of u_p and s leads to the expression for λ in eq. (9.36). The expression for the short-term rate r in eq. (9.35) can be found similarly and again through the results given in section 8.4 of chapter 8.

We now show that eq. (9.A45) holds true. Consider the Lagrangean for the maximization problem in eq. (9.40),

$$L = u_p(c_p) + x u_n(c_n) + \nu(c - c_p - c_n),$$

where ν is a Lagrange multiplier, $x = \frac{u_p'(\hat{c}_p)}{u_n'(\hat{c}_n)}$, and $\hat{c}_p$ and $\hat{c}_n$ are the market consumption allocations. The first-order conditions for the social planner lead to social allocation functions $c_p^* = c_p(D,x)$ and $c_p^* = c_n(D,x)$ and Lagrange multiplier $\nu(D,x)$, satisfying

$$u_p'(c_p(D,x)) = \nu(D,x) = x u_n'(c_n(D,x)). \tag{9.A46}$$

Accordingly, the value of the problem in eq. (9.40) is

$$U(D,x) = u_p(c_p(D,x)) + x u_n(c_n(D,x)),$$

such that

$$\begin{aligned} U_1(D,x) &= u_p'(c_p(D,x))\frac{\partial c_p(D,x)}{\partial D} + x u_n'(c_n(D,x))\frac{\partial c_n(D,x)}{\partial D} \\ &= u_p'(c_p(D,x))\left(\frac{\partial c_p(D,x)}{\partial D} + \frac{\partial c_n(D,x)}{\partial D}\right) \\ &= u_p'(c_p(D,x)), \end{aligned} \tag{9.A47}$$

where the second equality follows by the first-order conditions in eq. (9.A46) and the third equality holds by differentiating the equilibrium condition

$$D = c_p(D,x) + c_n(D,x), \tag{9.A48}$$

with respect to D.

Eq. (9.A47) establishes the first claim in eqs. (9.A45). To prove the second claim, invert the first-order condition with respect to v, obtaining, $c_p(D,x) = u_p'^{-1}[v(D,x)]$ and $c_n(D,x) = u_n'^{-1}[v(D,x)/x]$. Then replace these inverse functions into eq. (9.A48),

$$D = u_p'^{-1}[v(D,x)] + u_n'^{-1}[v(D,x)/x], \tag{9.A49}$$

where, by eq. (9.A46) and eq. (9.A47),

$$v(D,x) = u_p'\left(c_p(D,x)\right) = U_1(D,x). \tag{9.A50}$$

Differentiating eq. (9.A49) with respect to x and D and using eq. (9.A50) leaves:

$$0 = \frac{1}{u_p''\left(c_p(D,x)\right)} U_{12}(D,x) + \frac{1}{u_n''(c_n(D,x))} \frac{U_{12}(D,x)x - U_1(D,x)}{x^2} \tag{9.A51}$$

and

$$1 = \frac{1}{u_p''\left(c_p(D,x)\right)} U_{11}(D,x) + \frac{1}{u_n''(c_n(D,x))} \frac{U_{11}(D,x)}{x}. \tag{9.A52}$$

Replacing eq. (9.A52) into Eq. (9.A51) leaves

$$0 = \frac{U_{12}(D,x)}{u_p''\left(c_p(D,x)\right)} + \left(\frac{1}{U_{11}(D,x)} - \frac{1}{u_p''\left(c_p(D,x)\right)}\right) \frac{U_{12}(D,x)x - U_1(D,x)}{x}.$$

The second relation in eqs. (9.A45) follows by rearranging terms in the previous relation.

9.B.4 Extinction

Derivation of eq. (9.69). Denote with W_{0i} the initial wealth of agent i. Note that the budget constraints faced by the two agents are $W_{0i} = E(\xi_T c_{iT})$, $i = 1, 2$, such that by using the expressions for ξ_T and c_{it} in eqs. (9.67) and (9.68),

$$1 = \frac{W_{02}}{W_{01}} = \frac{E(\xi_T c_{2T})}{E(\xi_T c_{1T})} = \frac{E\left((b\eta_T)^{1/\gamma}(1 + (b\eta_T)^{1/\gamma})^{\gamma-1} D_T^{1-\gamma}\right)}{E\left((1 + (b\eta_T)^{1/\gamma})^{\gamma-1} D_T^{1-\gamma}\right)}, \tag{9.A53}$$

where the first equality follows by the assumptions that rational and irrational agents have the same initial endowments.

Let us introduce a new probability, $\check{P}$, defined through the Radon-Nikodym derivative,

$$\left.\frac{d\check{P}}{dP}\right|_{\mathbb{F}_T} = \frac{D_T^{1-\gamma}}{E(D_T^{1-\gamma})},$$

such that eq. (9.A53) can be rewritten as

$$\check{E}\left((b\eta_T)^{1/\gamma}(1 + (b\eta_T)^{1/\gamma})^{\gamma-1}\right) = \check{E}\left((1 + (b\eta_T)^{1/\gamma})^{\gamma-1}\right), \tag{9.A54}$$

where $\breve{E}$ denotes the expectation under $\breve{P}$. By Girsanov's theorem, we have that under $\breve{P}$,

$$\eta_T = e^{\left((1-\gamma)\upsilon\sigma^2 - \frac{1}{2}\sigma^2\upsilon^2\right)T + \sigma\upsilon\breve{W}_T},$$

where $\breve{W}_t$ is a Brownian motion under $\breve{P}$. That is, utilizing the expression for b in eq. (9.69), eq. (9.A54) can be written as

$$\breve{E}\left(\breve{\eta}_T^{1/\gamma}(1+\breve{\eta}_T^{1/\gamma})^{\gamma-1}\right) = \breve{E}\left((1+\breve{\eta}_T^{1/\gamma})^{\gamma-1}\right), \quad \breve{\eta}_T \equiv e^{-\frac{1}{2}\sigma^2\upsilon^2 T + \sigma\upsilon\breve{W}_T}. \tag{9.A55}$$

KRWW show indeed that eq. (9.A55) holds true.

Derivation of eq. (9.70). We determine the equilibrium asset price in the logarithmic preferences case. We have

$$S_t = E_t(\xi_T D_T) = \frac{E_t(1+\eta_T)}{E_t\left((1+\eta_T)D_T^{-1}\right)} = \frac{1+\eta_t}{E_t\left((1+\eta_T)D_T^{-1}\right)},$$

where the third equality follows by the martingale property of η_τ. To determine the denominator of the previous ratio, note that

$$\begin{aligned} E_t\left[(1+\eta_T)\left(\frac{D_T}{D_t}\right)^{-1}\right] &= e^{-(\mu-\sigma^2)(T-t)} + E_t\left[\eta_T\left(\frac{D_T}{D_t}\right)^{-1}\right] \\ &= e^{-(\mu-\sigma^2)(T-t)} + \eta_t E_t^2\left[\left(\frac{D_T}{D_t}\right)^{-1}\right] \\ &= e^{-(\mu-\sigma^2)(T-t)} + \eta_t e^{-(\mu-\sigma^2)(T-t)} \cdot e^{-\upsilon\sigma^2(T-t)}, \end{aligned}$$

where the second equality follows by a change in probability and the third, by Girsanov's theorem and eq. (9.64). Therefore,

$$S_t = D_t \frac{1+\eta_t}{E_t\left((1+\eta_T)\left(\frac{D_T}{D_t}\right)^{-1}\right)} = D_t \frac{1+\eta_t}{e^{-(\mu-\sigma^2)(T-t)}\left(1+\eta_t \cdot e^{-\upsilon\sigma^2(T-t)}\right)}. \tag{9.A56}$$

The price prevailing in a rational market, S_t^*, is determined once we set $\upsilon = 0$ and $\eta_\tau = 1$ for all τ, such that by eq. (9.A56),

$$S_t^* = D_t \frac{1}{e^{-(\mu-\sigma^2)(T-t)}}.$$

Replacing this value for S_t^* back to eq. (9.A56) produces eq. (9.70).

Appendix 9.C Knightian Uncertainty

9.C.1 Smooth Ambiguity Aversion

Given the assumptions on h in the main text, we have

$$E_{\mathcal{M}}\left[h\left(E_{\mu}\left(-e^{-\tau W_x}\right)\right)\right]=-E\left[\left(E\left(e^{-\tau W_x}\middle|\mu\right)\right)^{\alpha}\right]$$
$$=-E\left[\exp\left(-\alpha\tau\left(E\left(f|\mu\right)-p\right)x+\frac{1}{2}\alpha\tau^2\text{var}\left(f|\mu\right)x^2\right)\right].$$

Note that $E(f|\mu)$ is normally distributed with, say, a mean $\mu_E\equiv E\left[E(f|\mu)\right]$ and variance $\sigma_E^2\equiv\text{var}\left[E(f|\mu)\right]$, such that

$$E_{\mathcal{M}}\left[h\left(E_{\mu}\left(-e^{-\tau W_x}\right)\right)\right]$$
$$=-E\left[\exp\left(-\alpha\tau\left(\mu_E-p\right)x+\frac{1}{2}\alpha^2\tau^2\sigma_E^2x^2+\frac{1}{2}\alpha\tau^2\text{var}\left(f|\mu\right)x^2\right)\right]. \tag{9.A57}$$

By the law of iterated expectations,

$$\mu_E\equiv E\left[E\left(f|\mu\right)\right]=E\left(f\right)=\mu_0.$$

Regarding σ_E^2, note that by the law of total variance,

$$\text{var}\left(f\right)=\text{var}\left[E\left(f|\mu\right)\right]+E\left[\text{var}\left(f|\mu\right)\right]\equiv\sigma_E^2+\text{var}\left(f|\mu\right).$$

Replacing the values of μ_E and σ_E^2 implied by the previous two equalities into eq. (9.A57) leaves eq. (9.96).

9.C.2 Multiple Likelihoods

Consider the APT equation delivering $\mathcal{E}_t^h$, that is, the asset's expected returns under the distorted probability in (9.98),

$$\mathcal{E}^h=\frac{L^hP}{P}+\frac{D}{P}$$
$$=r_t+\gamma\sigma_0\cdot\text{Vol}_t$$
$$=\rho+\gamma x-\frac{1}{2}\gamma\left(\gamma+1\right)\sigma_0^2+\gamma\sigma_0\left(\sigma_0+\frac{p'(x)}{p(x)}v\left(x\right)\right) \tag{9.A58}$$

where L^h denotes the infinitesimal generator of $(D,\hat{g})$ in (9.102) and the last two lines follow by eqs. (9.103). That is, the price-dividend ratio is the solution to the following partial differential equation:

$$0=L^hp\left(x\right)+\sigma_0v\left(x\right)\left(1-\gamma\right)p'\left(x\right)-\left(\rho-\left(1-\gamma\right)x-\frac{1}{2}\gamma\left(\gamma+1\right)\sigma_0^2+\gamma\sigma_0^2\right)p\left(x\right)+1.$$

Conjecture that $p(x)=\alpha_0+\alpha_1x$ for two positive constants. Plugging this guess back to the previous equation confirms that the price-dividend ratio is indeed affine in the expected growth. To determine α_0 and α_1, one may proceed through the following intuitive arguments. Note that

$$\begin{aligned} p\left(\hat{g}_0\right) &= \int_0^{\infty} e^{-\rho t} E^{\hat{h}}\left(\frac{D_t}{D_0}\right)^{1-\gamma} dt \\ &= \pi_0 \frac{1}{\rho-(1-\gamma)\left(\bar{\theta}^{\hat{h}}-\frac{1}{2}\gamma\sigma_0^2\right)}+\left(1-\pi_0\right) \frac{1}{\rho-(1-\gamma)\left(\underline{\theta}^{\hat{h}}-\frac{1}{2}\gamma\sigma_0^2\right)}, \end{aligned}$$

where the first equality is a standard evaluation formula and the second relies on eq. (9.102). Replacing the definition of expected dividend growth into the previous equation, $\hat{g}_t=\pi_t\bar{\theta}^{\hat{h}}+(1-\pi_t)\underline{\theta}^{\hat{h}}$, delivers eq. (9.104).

Finally, note that the expression for the price-dividend ratio in eq. (9.104) simplifies when ambiguity aversion is the same in all states of nature. Precisely, assume that $\eta\left(\underline{\theta}\right)=\eta\left(\bar{\theta}\right)\equiv\hat{\eta}$, in which case $\mathcal{A}_t$ collapses to $-\sqrt{\hat{\eta}}$, and $g_t=\hat{g}_t+\sqrt{\hat{\eta}}\sigma_0$, such that the aggregate dividends under the distorted dynamics are

$$\begin{cases} \dfrac{dD_t}{D_t}=\left(g_t-\sqrt{\hat{\eta}}\sigma_0\right)dt+\sigma_0 dW_{ht} \\ dg_t=\frac{1}{\sigma_0}(g_t-\underline{\theta})(\bar{\theta}-g_t)dW_{ht} \end{cases}$$

and the price-dividend ratio is

$$p\left(g_t\right)=\frac{1}{\bar{\theta}-\underline{\theta}}\left(\frac{g_t-\underline{\theta}}{\rho_\eta-(1-\gamma)\left(\bar{\theta}-\frac{1}{2}\gamma\sigma_0^2\right)}+\frac{\bar{\theta}-g_t}{\rho_\eta-(1-\gamma)\left(\underline{\theta}-\frac{1}{2}\gamma\sigma_0^2\right)}\right) \tag{9.A59}$$

where $\rho_\eta\equiv\rho+(1-\gamma)\sqrt{\hat{\eta}}\sigma_0$. The analysis summarized by figure 9.3 is based on this expression for the price-dividend ratio.

Appendix 9.D Credit Rationing

We provide proofs of selected results regarding the Stiglitz and Weiss (1981) model as well as a parametric example to illustrate the model.

Risk increases with loan rates. Consider the definition of Π in eq. (9.148) and the break-even level of risk $\hat{\theta}$, defined as the function of the loan rate r that solves the following equation:

$$\begin{aligned} \hat{\theta}\left(r\right):0 &= \bar{\Pi}(r,\hat{\theta}\left(r\right)) \\ &\equiv E_{\hat{\theta}(r)}\left(\Pi\right) \\ &= \int_0^{B(1+r)-C}(-C)f(R;\hat{\theta}\left(r\right))dR+\int_{B(1+r)-C}^{\infty}(R-B\left(1+r\right))f(R;\hat{\theta}\left(r\right))dR, \end{aligned} \tag{9.A60}$$

such that

$$0=\frac{\partial\bar{\Pi}(r,\hat{\theta}\left(r\right))}{\partial r}+\frac{\partial\bar{\Pi}(r,\hat{\theta}\left(r\right))}{\partial\theta}\hat{\theta}'\left(r\right). \tag{9.A61}$$

The first term on the RHS of the previous equality is always negative, reflecting a mechanical effect by which the expected firm's profits lower with the cost of capital,

$$\frac{\partial \bar{\Pi}(r, \hat{\theta}(r))}{\partial r} = -B \int_{B(1+r)-C}^{\infty} f(R; \hat{\theta}(r)) dR.$$

The second term in eq. (9.A61) must, then, be strictly positive, but because $\frac{\partial \bar{\Pi}(r, \hat{\theta}(r))}{\partial \theta} > 0$, it must be that $\hat{\theta}'(r) > 0$.

A parametric model of credit rationing. Assume that there exists a continuum of projects in $(0, 1)$ and that the gross return on any project i can be either $R_i > 0$ with probability $1 - \theta_i$ or zero with complementary probability, an assumption borrowed from De Meza and Webb (1987). In the absence of borrowing, all projects have the same expected return, that is, $\bar{R} \equiv (1 - \theta_i) R_i$ for each i. We assume that $\bar{R} > B(1+r)$: the expected return on the project is at least as large as that on the loan rate, that is, entrepreneurs know how to produce, and they know better than bankers do. The variance of the project is $\theta_i (1 - \theta_i) R_i^2 = \bar{R}^2 \frac{\theta_i}{1-\theta_i}$, which is increasing in the probability of project failure θ_i; a change in θ_i is a mean-preserving spread.

The expected return to any firm that carries a project with risk θ_i is

$$\begin{aligned} \bar{\Pi}(r, \theta_i) &\equiv E_{\theta_i}(\Pi) = (-C)\theta_i + (R_i - B(1+r))(1 - \theta_i) \\ &= \bar{R} - B(1+r) + (B(1+r) - C)\theta_i \end{aligned}$$

and parallels the expected return in the continuous case (see eq. (9.A60)). We require that $C < B(1+r)$ (which parallels the "convexity" property in the main text), such that $\frac{\partial \bar{\Pi}(r,\theta)}{\partial \theta} > 0$, and we also have $\frac{\partial \bar{\Pi}(r,\theta)}{\partial r} = -B(1-\theta) < 0$, provided that $\theta < 1$. Therefore, by the same reasoning underlying eq. (9.A61), the credit market has adverse selection in that $\hat{\theta}'(r) > 0$, provided the cutoff function $\hat{\theta}(r) < 1$. We provide regularity conditions on $\hat{\theta}(r)$ below.

We slightly generalize the analysis in the main text, assuming that the cutoff function $\hat{\theta}(r)$ satisfies $(1 + r_f) W = \bar{\Pi}(r, \hat{\theta}(r))$, where r_f is the return on a safe asset and W is the borrower's wealth, which we take equal to the collateral that the borrower posts, $W = C$. We shall explain the rationale of this assumption in a moment. Under this assumption, the cutoff function satisfies

$$\hat{\theta}(r) = \frac{C(1+r_f) + B(1+r) - \bar{R}}{B(1+r) - C}, \quad \bar{R} \in \left(C(2+r_f), B(1+r) + C(1+r_f)\right), \tag{9.A62}$$

where the conditions on $\bar{R}$ ensure that $\hat{\theta}(\cdot) \in (0, 1)$. The assumption the entrepreneur has access to a safe technology is made to guarantee that $\bar{R} > B(1+r)$, still.

We assume that θ is drawn from a distribution with density $b(\theta)$, such that the posterior density, that is, the density the bank estimates based on the adverse selection outcome $(\theta \geq \hat{\theta}(r))$, is

$$b_r(\theta) \equiv \frac{b(\theta)}{\int_{\hat{\theta}(r)}^{1} b(\theta) d\theta}, \quad \theta \in (\hat{\theta}(r), 1).$$

Conditioning on a given risk θ, the bank's expected profits are $\bar{\Pi}_b(r;\theta) \equiv E_\theta(\Pi_b)$, where Π_b is as in eq. (9.149) of the main text. That is,

$$\bar{\Pi}_b(r;\theta) = C\theta + B(1+r)(1-\theta),$$

such that the posterior profits for the bank are

$$\bar{\Pi}_b(r) \equiv \int_{\hat{\theta}(r)}^{1} \bar{\Pi}_b(r;\theta)\, b_r(\theta)\, d\theta.$$

We set $B=100$, $C=50$, $\bar{R}=160$, and $r_f=0.03$. Regarding $b(\cdot)$, we consider a simple situation, which parallels one in Stiglitz and Weiss (1981), in which there are only two types, that is, $\theta=\theta_l=0.20$ with mass $\lambda=0.95$ and $\theta=\theta_u=0.30$ with mass $1-\lambda$. Taking into account (9.A62), the posterior profits for the bank are

$$\bar{\Pi}_b(r) = \begin{cases} C\bar{\theta} + B(1+r)\left(1-\bar{\theta}\right) & \text{for all } r : \hat{\theta}(r) \leq \theta_l \\ C\theta_u + B(1+r)(1-\theta_u) & \text{for all } r : \theta_l < \hat{\theta}(r) \leq \theta_u \\ 0 & \text{for all } r : \theta_u < \hat{\theta}(r) \end{cases}$$

where $\bar{\theta} = \lambda\theta_l + (1-\lambda)\theta_u$, and the loan demand schedule is

$$L^d(r) = \begin{cases} B & \text{for all } r : \hat{\theta}(r) \leq \theta_l \\ B(1-\lambda) & \text{for all } r : \theta_l < \hat{\theta}(r) \leq \theta_u \\ 0 & \text{for all } r : \theta_u < \hat{\theta}(r) \end{cases}.$$

The top panel of figure 9.A1 depicts the banks' posterior returns, defined as $\rho^b(r) \equiv \frac{\bar{\Pi}_b(r)}{B} - 1$, as a function of the loan rate r. Note that $\rho^b(r)$ achieves a local maximum at $r=23.10\%$, which is the threshold level of the loan rate after which the good applicants drop out of the market: for values of the loan rate higher than this threshold, the banks' posterior returns experience a discrete drop, reflecting the deterioration of the borrowers' creditworthiness. In other words, if the loan rate had to slightly increase from below 23.10%, the banks' posterior returns would plummet by more than 6 percentage points as a result of adverse selection. This extreme prediction is due to the highly asymmetric distribution of loan applicants.

The bottom panel of figure 9.A1 plots supply and demand of loans, where we assume that the loan supply satisfies $L^s(r) \equiv 0.9\bar{\Pi}_b(r)$. We justify this functional form by positing that the loan supply is an increasing function of $\rho^b(r)$, notably, $L^s(r) = 0.9\left(1+\rho^b(r)\right)B$. The properties of the loan supply are obviously inherited by those of the banks' posterior returns and imply the existence of a *local* maximum at about 23%. However, the *global* maximum is achieved at $r=33.57\%$, which is the loan rate at which type θ_u loses their interest as a potential borrower. In this case, $\rho^b(r^*) = 8.5\%$. The previous characterization of the global maximum does not depend on parameter values and shall be formally proved below.

The fact that the global maximum is a corner solution is not a merely technical detail. There would be credit rationing if the banks' space choice did not include loan rates in a neighborhood of $r^* = 33.57\%$. In this case, the banks' profits would be maximized at the

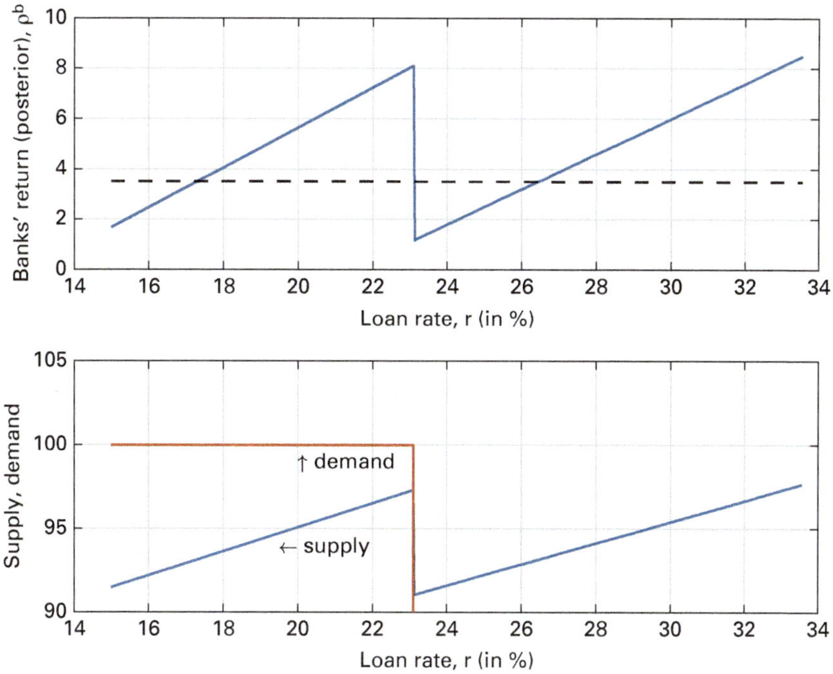

Figure 9.A1
Adverse selection and credit rationing.

local maximum, $r=23.10\%$, which would imply credit rationing. Naturally, it is problematic to justify these constraints. At least theoretically, a better route to credit rationing would perhaps result from the assumption that banks face Bertrand competition. Suppose a bank fixes a loan rate equal to r^* to maximize its profits. Then, competitors would lower loan rates to attract borrowers, and the process would continue up to the point where the banks' expected profits equal the operating costs. For example, if the operating costs absorb 3.5% of the posterior profits, there would be two equilibria (the loan rates at which the posterior banks returns intersect with the 3.5% line in the top panel of figure 9.A1). In this example, credit rationing would arise in the leftmost equilibrium. The assumption of Bertrand competition seems to be empirically questionable, however.

The difficulty in ensuring that an interior maximum of the banks' posterior profits is also a global maximum is not specific to this model but a specific case of results known since at least Riley (1987). Let us characterize r^* in the example of this appendix. First, note obviously that $\bar{\Pi}_b(r;\theta_i)=\bar{R}-\bar{\Pi}(r;\theta_i)$, $i\in\{l,u\}$, and that $\bar{\Pi}(r;\theta_i)\geq C(1+r_f)$ for all $\theta_i\geq\hat{\theta}(r)$, with a strict inequality for $\theta_i=\theta_u$ and $r<r_*$, where r_* is defined as the loan rate at which the riskiest firm (type θ_u) ceases to demand funds, $\hat{\theta}(r_*)=\theta_u$. Therefore, $E(\bar{\Pi}(r;\theta)|\,\theta_i\geq\hat{\theta}(r))>C(1+r_f)$ for $r<r_*$, such that the posterior profits for the bank are, for a given $r<r_*$,

$$E(\bar{\Pi}_b(r;\theta_i)|\,\theta_i\geq\hat{\theta}(r))=\bar{R}-E(\bar{\Pi}(r;\theta)|\,\theta_i\geq\hat{\theta}(r))\leq\bar{R}-C(1+r_f),$$

where the equality holds because the expected return $\bar{R}$ on a project is the same, independent of any risk. However, we have that $\bar{\Pi}(r_*;\theta_u) = \bar{\Pi}(r_*;\hat{\theta}(r_*)) = C(1+r_f)$, such that the previous weak inequality holds as an equality for $r = r^*$. Therefore, the unique global maximum is achieved by $r = r^*$.

References

Abel, A. B. (1990). "Asset Prices under Habit Formation and Catching up with the Joneses." *American Economic Review Papers and Proceedings* 80, 38–42.

Abel, A. B. (1999). "Risk Premia and Term Premia in General Equilibrium." *Journal of Monetary Economics* 43, 3–33.

Adrian, T., and H. S. Shin (2010a). "Financial Intermediaries and Monetary Economics." In *Handbook of Monetary Economics* (Vol. 3), edited by B. M. Friedman and M. Woodford, 601–650. Amsterdam: Elsevier.

Adrian, T., and H. S. Shin (2010b). "Liquidity and Leverage." *Journal of Financial Intermediation* 19, 418–437.

Bansal, R., D. Kiku, and A. Yaron (2012). "An Empirical Evaluation of the Long-Run Risks Model for Asset Prices." *Critical Finance Review* 1, 183–221.

Bansal, R., and A. Yaron (2004). "Risks for the Long Run: A Potential Resolution of Asset Pricing Puzzles." *Journal of Finance* 59, 1481–1509.

Barro, R. J. (1974). "Are Government Bonds Net Wealth?" *Journal of Political Economy* 82, 1095–1117.

Basak, S. (2000). "A Model of Dynamic Equilibrium Asset Pricing with Heterogeneous Beliefs and Extraneous Risk." *Journal of Economic Dynamics and Control* 24, 63–95.

Basak, S. (2005). "Asset Pricing with Heterogeneous Beliefs." *Journal of Banking and Finance* 29, 2849–2881.

Basak, S., and D. Cuoco (1998). "An Equilibrium Model with Restricted Stock Market Participation." *Review of Financial Studies* 11, 309–341.

Beeler, J., and J. Y. Campbell (2012). "The Long-Run Risks Model and Aggregate Asset Prices: An Empirical Assessment." *Critical Finance Review* 1, 141–182.

Bernanke, B. S. (1983). "Nonmonetary Effects of the Financial Crisis in the Propagation of the Great Depression." *American Economic Review* 73, 257–276.

Bernanke, B. S. (2004). "The Great Moderation." Presented at the Eastern Economic Association, Washington, DC, February 20.

Bernanke, B. S., and A. S. Blinder (1988). "Credit, Money, and Aggregate Demand." *American Economic Review Papers and Proceedings* 78, 435–439.

Bernanke, B. S., and M. Gertler (1989). "Agency Costs, Net Worth, and Business Fluctuations." *American Economic Review* 79, 14–31.

Bernanke, B. S., M. Gertler, and S. Gilchrist (1999). "The Financial Accelerator in a Quantitative Business Cycle Framework." In *Handbook of Macroeconomics* (Vol. 1C), edited by J. B. Taylor and M. Woodford, 1341–1393. Amsterdam: Elsevier/North-Holland.

Berrada, T. (2006). "Incomplete Information, Heterogeneity, and Asset Pricing." *Journal of Financial Econometrics* 4, 136–160.

Black, F. (1976). "Studies of Stock Price Volatility Changes."In *Proceedings of the 1976 Meeting of the American Statistical Association*, 177–181. Washington, DC: American Statistical Association.

Blinder, A. S. (1987). "Credit Rationing and Effective Supply Failures." *Economic Journal* 97, 327–352.

Boldrin, M., L. Christiano, and J. Fisher (2001). "Habit Persistence, Asset Returns and the Business Cycle." *American Economic Review* 91, 149–166.

Borio, C., C. Furfine, and P. Lowe (2001). "Procyclicality of the Financial System and Financial Stability: Issues and Policy Options." In *Marrying the Macro- and Micro-Prudential Dimensions of Financial Stability* No. 1, Bank for International Settlements, 1–57. Basel.

Bossaerts, P., P. Ghirardato, S. Guarnaschelli, and W. R. Zame (2010). "Ambiguity in Asset Markets: Theory and Experiment." *Review of Financial Studies* 23, 1325–1359.

Brunnermeier, M. K., T. M. Eisenbach, and Y. Sannikov (2014). "Macroeconomics with Financial Frictions: A Survey."In *Advances in Economics and Econometrics: Tenth World Congress* (Vol. 2), edited by D. Acemoglu, M. Arellano, and E. Dekel, 4–94. Cambridge: Cambridge University Press.

Brunnermeier, M. K., and Y. Sannikov (2014). "A Macroeconomic Model with a Financial Sector." *American Economic Review* 104, 379–421.

Buraschi, A., and A. Jiltsov (2006). "Model Uncertainty and Option Markets with Heterogeneous Beliefs." *Journal of Finance* 61, 2841–2897.

Campbell, J. Y. (2003). "Consumption-Based Asset Pricing."In *Handbook of the Economics of Finance* (Vol. 1B), edited by G. M. Constantinides, M. Harris, and R. M. Stulz, 803–887. Amsterdam: North-Holland/Elsevier.

Campbell, J. Y., and J. H. Cochrane (1999). "By Force of Habit: A Consumption-Based Explanation of Aggregate Stock Market Behavior." *Journal of Political Economy* 107, 205–251.

Campbell, J. Y., A. W. Lo, and C. MacKinlay (1997). *The Econometrics of Financial Markets.* Princeton, NJ: Princeton University Press.

Campbell, J. Y., and R. Shiller (1988). "The Dividend-Price Ratio and Expectations of Future Dividends and Discount Factors." *Review of Financial Studies* 1, 195–228.

Chan, Y. L., and L. Kogan (2002). "Catching up with the Joneses: Heterogeneous Preferences and the Dynamics of Asset Prices." *Journal of Political Economy* 110, 1255–1285.

Christie, A. A. (1982). "The Stochastic Behavior of Common Stock Variances: Value, Leverage, and Interest Rate Effects." *Journal of Financial Economics* 10, 407–432.

Cochrane, J. H., F. A. Longstaff, and P. Santa-Clara (2008). "Two Trees." *Review of Financial Studies* 21, 347–385.

Colacito, R. and M. M. Croce (2011). "Risks for the Long Run and the Real Exchange Rate." *Journal of Political Economy* 119, 153–181.

Constantinides, G. M., J. B. Donaldson, and R. Mehra (2002). "Juniors Can't Borrow: A New Perspective on the Equity Premium Puzzle." *Quarterly Journal of Economics* 117, 269–296.

Constantinides, G. M., and D. Duffie (1996). "Asset Pricing with Heterogeneous Consumers." *Journal of Political Economy* 104, 219–240.

Cujean, J., and M. Hasler (2017). "Why Does Return Predictability Concentrate in Bad Times?" *Journal of Finance* 72, 2717–2758.

Cvitanić, J., and S. Malamud (2011). "Price Impact and Portfolio Impact." *Journal of Financial Economics* 100: 201–225.

Danielsson, J., and H. S. Shin (2003). *Endogenous Risk.* In *Modern Risk Management: A History*, edited by P. Field. London: Risk Books.

Danielsson, J., H. S. Shin, and J.-P. Zigrand (2011). "Balance Sheet Capacity and Endogenous Risk." Financial Markets Group Discussion Papers DP 665, Financial Markets Group, London School of Economics and Political Science, London.

De Meza, D., and D. C. Webb (1987). "Too Much Investment: A Problem of Asymmetric Information." *Quarterly Journal of Economics* 102, 281–292.

Detemple, J., and Murthy, S. (1994). "Intertemporal Asset Pricing with Heterogeneous Beliefs." *Journal of Economic Theory* 62, 294–320.

Distaso, W., A. Mele, and G. Vilkov (2019). "Cross-Section without Factors: Correlation Risk, Strings and Asset Prices." London: Center for Economic and Policy Research, CEPR Discussion Paper No. DP13873.

Dow, J., and S. Werlang (1992). "Uncertainty Aversion, Risk Aversion, and the Optimal Choice of Portfolio." *Econometrica* 60, 197–204.

Duffie, D. (1992). "The Nature of Incomplete Security Markets." In *Advances in Economic Theory: Sixth World Congress* (Vol. II), edited by J.-J. Laffont, 214–262. Cambridge: Cambridge University Press.

Duffie, D., and L. G. Epstein (1992a). "Asset Pricing with Stochastic Differential Utility." *Review of Financial Studies* 5, 411–436.

Duffie, D., and L. G. Epstein (with C. Skiadas) (1992b). "Stochastic Differential Utility." *Econometrica* 60, 353–394.

Dumas, B., A. Kurshev, and R. Uppal (2009). "Equilibrium Portfolio Strategies in the Presence of Sentiment Risk and Excess Volatility." *The Journal of Finance* 64, 579–629.

Ellsberg, D. (1961). "Risk, Ambiguity and the Savage Axioms." *Quarterly Journal of Economics* 75, 643–669.

Epstein, L. G., and M. Schneider (2010). "Ambiguity and Asset Markets." *Annual Reviews of Financial Economics* 2, 315–334.

Epstein, L. G., and S. E. Zin (1989). "Substitution, Risk-Aversion and the Temporal Behavior of Consumption and Asset Returns: A Theoretical Framework." *Econometrica* 57, 937–969.

Epstein, L. G., and S. E. Zin (1991). "Substitution, Risk-Aversion and the Temporal Behavior of Consumption and Asset Returns: An Empirical Analysis." *Journal of Political Economy* 99, 263–286.

Fisher, I. (1933). "The Debt-Deflation Theory of Great Depressions." *Econometrica* 1, 337–57.

Friedman, M. (1953). "The Case for Flexible Exchange Rates." In *Essays in Positive Economics*. Chicago, IL: University of Chicago Press.

Friedman, M., and A. J. Schwartz (1963). *A Monetary History of the United States: 1867–1960*. Princeton, NJ: Princeton University Press.

Gallmeyer, M., A. C. Aydemir, and B. Hollifield (2007). "Financial Leverage and the Leverage Effect: A Market and a Firm Analysis." Working paper Carnegie Mellon.

Geanakoplos, J. (2010). "The Leverage Cycle." In *NBER Macroeconomic Annual 2009* (Vol. 24), edited by D. Acemoglu, K. Rogoff, and M. Woodford, 1–65. Chicago, IL: University of Chicago Press.

Gilboa, I., and M. Marinacci (2011). "Ambiguity and the Bayesian Paradigm." In *Advances in Economics and Econometrics: Tenth World Congress* (Vol. 1), edited by D. Acemoglu, M. Arellano, and E. Dekel, 179–242. Cambridge: Cambridge University Press.

Gilboa, I., and D. Schmeidler (1989). "Maxmin Expected Utility with a Non-Unique Prior." *Journal of Mathematical Economics* 18, 141–153.

Guvenen, F. (2009). "A Parsimonious Macroeconomic Model for Asset Pricing." *Econometrica* 77, 1711–1740.

Hansen, L. P., and T. J. Sargent (1995). "Discounted Linear Exponential Quadratic Gaussian Control." *IEEE Transactions on Automatic Control* 40, 968–971.

Hansen, L. P., and T. J. Sargent (2008). *Robustness*. Princeton, NJ: Princeton University Press.

Harrison, J. M., and D. M. Kreps (1978). "Speculative Investor Behavior in a Stock Market with Heterogeneous Expectations." *Quarterly Journal of Economics* 92, 323–336.

Hart, O. D., and J. Moore (1994). "A Theory of Debt Based on the Inalienability of Human Capital." *Quarterly Journal of Economics* 109, 841–879.

He, Z., and A. Krishnamurthy (2013). "Intermediary Asset Pricing." *American Economic Review* 103, 732–770.

Heaton, J., and D. J. Lucas (1996). "Evaluating the Effects of Incomplete Markets on Risk Sharing and Asset Pricing." *Journal of Political Economy* 104, 443–487.

Huang, C.-f. (1987). "An Intertemporal General Equilibrium Asset Pricing Model: The Case of Diffusion Information." *Econometrica* 55, 117–142.

Jermann, U. J. (1998). "Asset Pricing in Production Economies." *Journal of Monetary Economics* 41, 257–276.

Kaltenbrunner, G., and L. Lochstoer (2010). "Long-Run Risk Through Consumption Smoothing." *Review of Financial Studies* 23, 3141–3189.

Karatzas, I., and S. E. Shreve (1991). *Brownian Motion and Stochastic Calculus*. New York: Springer Verlag.

Keynes, J. M. (1921). *A Treatise on Probability*. London: Macmillan.

Kiyotaki, N. (1998). "Credit and Business Cycles." *Japanese Economic Review* 49, 18–35.

Kiyotaki, N., and J. Moore (1997). "Credit Cycles." *Journal of Political Economy* 105, 211–248.

Klibanoff, P., M. Marinacci, and S. Mukerji (2005). "A Smooth Model of Decision Making under Ambiguity." *Econometrica* 73, 1849–1492.

Knight, F. H. (1921). *Risk, Uncertainty, and Profit*. New York: Houghton Mifflin.

Kogan, L., S. Ross, J. Wang, and M. Westerfield (2006). "The Survival and Price Impact of Irrational Traders." *Journal of Finance* 61, 195–229.

Kyle, A. S., and F. A. Wang (1997). "Speculation Duopoly with Agreement to Disagree: Can Overconfidence Survive the Market Test?" *Journal of Finance* 52, 2073–2090.

Leippold, M., F. Trojani, and P. Vanini (2008). "Learning and Asset Prices under Ambiguous Information." *Review of Financial Studies* 21, 2565–2597.

Lettau, M. (2002). "Idiosyncratic Risk and Volatility Bounds, or, Can Models with Idiosyncratic Risk Solve the Equity Premium Puzzle?" *Review of Economics and Statistics* 84, 376–380.

Liptser, R. S., and A. N. Shiryaev (2001). *Statistics of Random Processes*, Vol. II: *Applications*. Berlin: Springer-Verlag.

Ljungqvist, L., and T. J. Sargent (2018). *Recursive Macroeconomic Theory*. Cambridge, MA: MIT Press.

Lucas, D. J. (1994). "Asset Pricing with Undiversifiable Income Risk and Short Sales Constraints: Deepening the Equity Premium Puzzle." *Journal of Monetary Economics* 34, 325–341.

Lucas, R. E. (1978). "Asset Prices in an Exchange Economy." *Econometrica* 46, 1429–1445.

Mankiw, N. G. (1986). "The Equity Premium and the Concentration of Aggregate Shocks." *Journal of Financial Economics* 17, 211–219.

Mankiw, N. G., and S. P. Zeldes (1991). "The Consumption of Stockholders and Non-Stockholders." *Journal of Financial Economics* 29, 97–112.

Markowitz, H. (1952). "Portfolio Selection." *Journal of Finance* 7, 77–91.

Martin, I. (2013). "The Lucas Orchard." *Econometrica* 81, 55–111.

Mele, A., and F. Sangiorgi (2015). "Uncertainty, Information Acquisition and Price Swings in Asset Markets." *Review of Economic Studies* 82, 1533–1567.

Menzly, L., T. Santos, and P. Veronesi (2004). "Understanding Predictability." *Journal of Political Economy* 112, 1–47.

Moreno-Bromberg, S., and J.-C. Rochet (2018). *Continuous-Time Models in Corporate Finance, Banking and Insurance*. Princeton, NJ: Princeton University Press.

Nelson, D. B. (1991). "Conditional Heteroskedasticity in Asset Returns: A New Approach." *Econometrica* 59, 347–370.

Odean, T. (1998). "Volume, Volatility, Price, and Profit When All Traders Are Above Average." *Journal of Finance* 53, 1887–1934.

Rawls, J. (1971). *A Theory of Justice*. Cambridge, MA: Harvard University Press.

Riley, J. G. (1987). "Credit Rationing: A Further Remark." *American Economic Review* 77, 224–227.

Rouwenhorst, G. K. (1995). "Asset Returns and Business Cycles." In *Frontiers of Business Cycle Research*, edited by T. F. Cooley, 294–330. Princeton, NJ: Princeton University Press.

Santos, T., and P. Veronesi (2010). "Habit Formation, the Cross Section of Stock Returns and the Cash-Flow Risk Puzzle." *Journal of Financial Economics* 98, 385–413.

Scheinkman, J. A., and W. Xiong (2002). "Overconfidence and Speculative Bubbles." *Journal of Political Economy* 111, 1183–1219.

Schmeidler, D. (1986). "Integral Representation Without Additivity." *Proceedings of the American Mathematical Society* 97, 255–261.

Schmeidler, D. (1989). "Subjective Probability and Expected Utility Without Additivity." *Econometrica* 57, 571–587.

Schwert, G. W. (1989a). "Why Does Stock Market Volatility Change Over Time?" *Journal of Finance* 44, 1115–1153.

Schwert, G. W. (1989b). "Business Cycles, Financial Crises and Stock Volatility." *Carnegie-Rochester Conference Series on Public Policy* 31, 83–125.

Shephard, N. G., and A. C. Harvey (1990). "On the Probability of Estimating a Deterministic Component in the Local Level Model." *Journal of Time Series Analysis* 11, 339–347.

Shin, H. S. (2010). *Risk and Liquidity*. Clarendon Lectures in Finance. Oxford: Oxford University Press.

Stiglitz, J. E., and A. Weiss (1981). "Credit Rationing in Markets with Imperfect Information." *American Economic Review* 71, 393–410.

Tallarini, T. (2000). "Risk-Sensitive Real Business Cycles." *Journal of Monetary Economics* 45, 507–532.

Telmer, C. I. (1993). "Asset-Pricing Puzzles and Incomplete Markets." *Journal of Finance* 48, 1803–1832.

Veronesi, P. (2000). "How Does Information Quality Affect Stock Returns?" *Journal of Finance* 55, 807–837.

Wald, A. (1950). *Statistical Decision Functions*. New York: Wiley.

Weil, P. (1989). "The Equity Premium Puzzle and the Risk-Free Rate Puzzle." *Journal of Monetary Economics* 24, 401–421.

Weil, P. (1992). "Equilibrium Asset Prices with Undiversifiable Labor Income Risk." *Journal of Economic Dynamics and Control* 16, 769–790.

Xiouros, C., and F. Zapatero (2010). "The Representative Agent of an Economy with External Habit Formation and Heterogeneous Risk Aversion." *Review of Financial Studies* 23, 3017–3047.

Zapatero, F. (1998). "Effects of Financial Innovations on Market Volatility when Beliefs Are Heterogeneous." *Journal of Economic Dynamics and Control* 22, 597–626.

10

Information and Other Market Frictions

10.1 Introduction

The previous chapters consider economies in which the equilibrium outcomes do not convey more information than that available to each agent. In those economies, information, while sometimes incomplete, is disseminated *symmetrically* across decision makers—for example, asset prices aggregate information that the agents already know, such that the agents' inference on the asset fundamentals would not improve were it also based on the equilibrium prices.

This chapter considers markets in which equilibrium outcomes aggregate information dispersed across agents, which the very same agents find useful while updating beliefs. This information is useful because agents have access to pieces of information that are not the same; now, therefore, asset prices contain information about the fundamentals that some agents might not directly observe and that are made publicly available (so to speak) through the trading activity. We study markets with *asymmetric* information where some agents have more precise information than others and markets with *differential* information where agents know different pieces of information that have the same quality. In the economies of the previous chapters, the price only determines the budget constraints. While the price still determines budget constraints in the markets that we analyze in this chapter, this price now plays an additional, fundamental role: it conveys information to investors.

Note how subtle the equilibrium concept needs to be in the markets of this chapter. If agents find it useful to condition their choices on the information conveyed by an equilibrium outcome, these very same choices may well affect the information contained in the equilibrium outcome, over a fixed point. Provided it exists, this fixed point leads to implications regarding the informational role of asset prices, that is, the equilibrium amount of information. In the asymmetric information case, we say that the price "transmits" information from the more informed investors to the less. In the differential information case, we say that the price "aggregates" information dispersed among investors. Both cases play outstanding roles in financial economics.

Consider the asymmetric information case: if uninformed investors can learn from the equilibrium price, what are the incentives left to purchase information? In other words, what is the value of information? The differential information case is equally important.

The welfare theorems reviewed in chapter 2 suggest that a Pareto optimal allocation can be "centralized." However, this solution cannot be implemented when portfolio decisions are made on the basis of "local" information. The market solution proves useful as the price would now aggregate dispersed information, making it available to investors initially not having direct access to it. These ideas go back to Hayek (1945) at least.

There are a number of conceptual issues in these markets. Namely, how much information does a price need to convey for an equilibrium to exist? Intuitively, if the asset price conveys information that is too precise and eventually becomes a sufficient statistics for the overall information available in the marketplace, the agents would not even need to condition their portfolio decisions on their own information. But then, if agents trade while only relying on the equilibrium price (and not on their own signals), how can the price aggregate information? This is the Grossman (1976) paradox. Further, it is intuitive that the price cannot reveal all private information when information is costly, for otherwise there would be no incentives left to purchase information in the first place: it is the Grossman and Stiglitz (1980) paradox.

A standard approach to deal with these conceptual difficulties is to assume that prices convey "noisy" signals on the information that investors have. As Black (1986) discussed, noise makes markets function when information problems would otherwise lead them not to arise in the first place. The mechanism is simple. In equilibrium, the price incorporates not only the information on which informed investors trade but also other factors that are possibly unrelated to the fundamentals, such as liquidity shocks—"noise." In this case, an uninformed investor cannot tell whether a large price swing is due to information or a liquidity shock because now the price only *partially reveals* the information informed investors have. So uninformed investors learn from the price, but the information conveyed by the price is imperfect such that informed investors still have superior information, even after the uninformed learn from the observation of the asset price. Thus, it can pay to purchase information. All in all, *partial* revelation of information is the key to make asset markets work in this context.

The equilibrium concept to deal with these markets is an extension of the rational expectations equilibrium (REE) the previous chapters have relied on and is called noisy REE (NREE). It is in macroeconomics that we seem to find the first example of an equilibrium in which agents confuse fundamentals with noise. In an attempt to explain the relation between the conduct of monetary policy and the business cycle, Phelps (1970) and Lucas (1972) consider an economy in which agents have imperfect information regarding the fundamentals of the economy. This information-based approach to the business cycle is summarized in Lucas (1981) and was somehow abandoned in favor of the real business cycle theory (see chapter 3), perhaps because it may be unrealistic to hypothesize that information is the main engine of macroeconomic fluctuations. However, the interplay between macroeconomics and information helped Lucas (1972) develop the notion of rational expectations within a "noisy" economy. In section 10.2, we present a simplified version of the Lucas framework, which helps pave the way to the study of asset markets in subsequent sections.

A central theme of this chapter is the role of information in asset markets. In many of the models of this chapter, noise is what makes these markets work, as explained. Liquidity shocks are the most natural example that illustrates this concept. In fact, the models in this chapter make sharp predictions on how liquidity shocks affect asset prices. For example, we shall explain that in non competitive markets (markets beyond the standard NREE), uninformed trades may have a price impact because market makers confuse information with noise: being unsure about the nature of the orders they see (information-driven or liquidity shocks), market makers price the assets in a way that even a liquidity shock (noise) gets impounded in equilibrium. It is a clear case of adverse selection: the prices set by market makers attract the "wrong trades," that is, market makers will be potentially buying from those who hold bad news about the asset and selling to those who hold good news. However, these markets work because market makers are not sure that each of the orders they receive is informed order or noise. But then, liquidity-motivated trades are hurt because market makers would set prices, taking into account the fact they might not be such. Therefore, in this type of explanation, liquidity in asset markets constitutes the other side of the same coin (against information).

The core of this chapter is then to analyze how information affects asset markets. Section 10.3 discusses the classical notions of informational efficiency in the early empirical literature and how the subsequent theory literature has helped shape these notions. The theory literature is reviewed next. First, sections 10.4 and 10.5 explain that the standard notions of a Walrasian equilibrium and REE are not sufficient to deal with markets in which agents have asymmetric or diverse information. Section 10.6 then deals with NREE. Sections 10.7 and 10.8 cover markets with non competitive players. Section 10.9 examines a number of additional mechanisms that may affect the asset price formation process, such as the presence of irrational (or noise) traders and additional market imperfections that lead to limits to arbitrage and other forms of capital immobility. Sections 10.6 and 10.9 also provide a succinct review of a few models of coordination failure among market participants that is able to explain phenomena such as bank runs or beauty contests.

While information plays a prominent role in explaining prices and liquidity in the asset market "microstructure," information cannot be the only driver of market liquidity. Liquidity in markets driven by macroeconomic news (government bonds, for example) cannot be only driven by investors with superior or diverse information. Further, markets are not necessarily centralized and necessitate "search" and "bargaining" for achieving trading. Section 10.10 studies liquidity in markets where information plays a more limited role, with the focus shifting to the search nature of decentralized, over-the-counter (OTC) markets.

10.2 Prelude: Imperfect Information in Macroeconomics

We consider a simplified version of the model developed by Lucas (1973), in which n goods are produced in n distinct "islands." Let y_i^s denote log-production supplied in the ith island. (All variables are in logs in this section.) Below, we explain which sources of randomness affect this economy (see eqs. (10.3) and (10.4)). It is assumed that production supplied is set so as to equal the expected wedge of the (log-) price in the island, p_i, over the average price in the economy, p,

$$y_i^s = E\left(p_i - p \middle| p_i\right), \quad \text{where} \quad p = \frac{1}{n}\sum_{j=1}^{n} p_j. \tag{10.1}$$

Eq. (10.1) follows, approximately, once we assume that the average price, p, is common knowledge, just as it is, for example, in the monopolistic competition model of Blanchard and Kiyotaki (1987). When p is not common knowledge as in the analysis of this section, eq. (10.1) can still be thought of as arising through a plausible decision mechanism. The specific functional form for the average price is the most important approximation made while deriving eq. (10.1) based on a rigorous micro-founded setup. Appendix 10.E contains a discussion of these issues.

Information is disseminated differentially (not asymmetrically), in that producers in the ith island are not aware of the price in the remaining islands and make statistical inferences on economic developments occurring in the other islands with the same precision. We assume exogenous variables are normally distributed. Further, we conjecture and later verify that all endogenous variables are also normally distributed. We shall show that this normality property implies the price index p gathers all information efficiently; that is, p is a sufficient statistics for all that information.

By the projection theorem reviewed in appendix 10.A, we have that

$$y_i^s = E\left(p_i - p \middle| p_i\right) \equiv \beta\left(p_i - E\left(p\right)\right),$$

where we have used the fact that information is symmetrically disseminated and therefore (i) the expectation $E\left(p_i\right) = E\left(p_j\right) = E\left(p\right)$ for every i and j and (ii) both the numerator and denominator of the ratio, $\beta \equiv \frac{cov(p_i - p, p_i)}{var(p_i)}$, are the same across all islands. This coefficient will be determined below as a part of the equilibrium.

Aggregating across all islands yields the celebrated *Lucas supply* equation

$$y^s \equiv \frac{1}{n}\sum_{j=1}^{n} y_j^s = \beta\left(p - E\left(p\right)\right). \tag{10.2}$$

Next, assume the demand for the good produced in the ith island is given by, for some $\theta > 0$,

$$y_i^d = m - p + u_i - \theta\left(p_i - p\right), \quad \text{where} \quad u_i \sim N\left(0, \sigma_u^2\right) \tag{10.3}$$

and m is money supply, which we assume to satisfy

$$m = E\left(m\right) + \epsilon, \quad \text{where} \quad \epsilon \sim N\left(0, \sigma_\epsilon^2\right). \tag{10.4}$$

Finally, we assume that $E\left(u_i \epsilon\right) = 0$ and that u_i are sectorial shocks in that $\sum_{j=1}^{n} u_j = 0$. The functional form for the demand function, y_i^d, follows after assuming the goods in the islands are imperfect substitutes (see appendix 10.E).

The equilibrium price in the islands plays two roles in this economy. A first and standard role is to clear the markets so that $y_i^s = y_i^d$ or

$$\beta\left(p_i - E\left(p\right)\right) = m - p + u_i - \theta\left(p_i - p\right), \quad \text{for all } i. \tag{10.5}$$

The second role the price performs is to convey information to agents regarding the two shocks: (i) the macroeconomic, monetary shock, ϵ, and (ii) the real shocks occurred in all the islands, u_j, $j = 1, \cdots, n$. We conjecture that the only real shock that determines the price in the ith island is u_i, that is, that the price is a function $p_i \equiv p(\epsilon, u_i)$. We also conjecture this price is affine in ϵ and u_i, namely,

$$p(\epsilon, u_i) = a + b\epsilon + cu_i, \tag{10.6}$$

where the coefficients a, b, and c have to be determined in equilibrium. Under these conditions, the average price is a function $p \equiv \bar{p}(\epsilon)$ satisfying

$$\bar{p}(\epsilon) = a + b\epsilon. \tag{10.7}$$

Let us replace eqs. (10.6), (10.7), and (10.4) into the equilibrium condition, eq. (10.5). By rearranging terms,

$$0 = (\beta b + b - 1)\,\epsilon + (\beta c + \theta c - 1)\,u_i + a - E(m).$$

The previous equation has to hold for all ϵ and u_i. Therefore,

$$a = E(m),$$

and the coefficients for ϵ and u_i must both equal zero, leading to the following expressions for b and c:

$$b = \frac{1}{1+\beta}, \quad c = \frac{1}{\theta+\beta}. \tag{10.8}$$

We are left with determining β. Given eqs. (10.6), (10.7), and (10.8), it is easy to show that

$$\beta = \frac{cov(p_i - p, p_i)}{var(p_i)} = \frac{\sigma_u^2}{\sigma_u^2 + \left(\frac{\theta+\beta}{1+\beta}\right)^2 \sigma_\epsilon^2}. \tag{10.9}$$

The previous equation has a unique and positive fixed point for β, which can then be replaced back into eqs. (10.8), yielding the solutions for b and c, which are both positive.

We can study some implications of this equilibrium. Replacing eqs. (10.6) and (10.7) into the Lucas supply equation (10.2) leaves

$$y^s = \beta b\epsilon. \tag{10.10}$$

Eq. (10.10) describes Lucas's neutrality result. Anticipated monetary policy, $E(m)$, does not affect the equilibrium outcome, y^s. The monetary shock affects y^s. Agents in any island do not observe the price in the remaining islands and hence the aggregate price level, p. Therefore, they are unable to tell whether an increase in the price of the good they produce, p_i, is due to a real shock, u_i, or to a monetary shock, ϵ. Precisely, they cannot disentangle a monetary shock from a real shock. If the agents were informed about real shocks, they would of course infer ϵ, and a monetary shock would not exert any effect on the equilibrium production.

Precisely, in equilibrium, the price difference is $p_i - p = cu_i$, which does not depend on ϵ. It is a "dichotomy" prediction reminiscent of the classical theory. However $p_i - p$ is not observed because p is not observed. Instead, producers in the ith island rely on the following estimate:

$$p_i - E(p|\,p_i) = \beta\,(b\epsilon + cu_i).$$

In other words, the price difference covaries positively with the observed price, p_i, that is, $cov(p_i - p, p_i) = c^2\sigma_u^2$. This covariance would be zero only when there is perfect knowledge regarding real shocks, $\sigma_u^2 = 0$, in which case $\beta = 0$. If knowledge is imperfect, producers extract signals from the average price and act on the basis of a positive statistical relation between prices and average prices, $cov(p_i - p, p_i) > 0$. Finally, note the following simple dynamic extension. Suppose that $E(m) = m_{-1}$, money supply in the previous period. Then, it follows by eq. (10.7) that the inflation rate $p - p_{-1} = b\epsilon + (1 - b)\,\epsilon_{-1}$. Therefore, output and inflation are positively correlated—a "Phillips curve." However, policy makers cannot exploit this curve because anticipated monetary policy, $E(m)$, is rationally "factored out" and does not affect output. Output and inflation are positively correlated only through the channel of unanticipated monetary shocks. This phenomenon is part of a set of results in macroeconomics known as Lucas's critique (Lucas, 1977).

In the next sections, we analyze asset markets that work through similar mechanisms in the following sense. Why should we ever buy some assets from people who insist on in selling them? Trading seems to be a difficult phenomenon to explain in a world with imperfect information. Yet trading does occur if imperfect information has the same nature as that of the Lucas model. Agents might well be imperfectly informed about the nature of, say, unusually high market orders. For example, sell orders might arrive to the market either because the asset is a lemon or because the agents selling the assets are hit by a liquidity shock. In the models of this chapter, an equilibrium with rational expectation exists precisely because of this "noise"—liquidity, in this example. There is a chance the sell order arrives to the market simply because the agents selling it are hit by a liquidity shock. Imperfectly informed agents, therefore, might be willing to buy if it is in their interest to do so.

10.3 Informational Efficiency: A Road Map

Informational efficiency is an attribute of asset markets that we gauge through equilibrium outcomes—typically, the price. It is an old and somehow controversial topic in financial economics. How do we define informational efficiency? We would like to rely on definitions that formalize the idea that, in efficient markets, prices reflect available information somehow accurately and rapidly. This definition is obviously loose, but now our objective is to illustrate how the process of narrowing this definition down leads to topics that have been controversial for some time. In particular, we need to qualify the (i) type and (ii) quality of information embedded into and revealed by the price: What type of information does the price reveal? How accurately can the price convey information?

The first question, relating to the type of information, has been addressed in a famous contribution by Fama (1970), who considers three forms of informational efficiency: (i) *strong* efficiency, arising when the price reflects all private and public information; (ii) *semi-strong* efficiency, the situation in which the price conveys all public information; and (iii) *weak* efficiency, arising when the price only conveys information regarding past (price) data.

At least initially, the motivation to define "efficient" markets (in the informational sense) was to illustrate that markets cannot be in a state of "disequilibrium." For example, if asset prices tend to be high on Friday and decline on Monday, a profitable trading opportunity might seem to arise. An equilibrium, the motivation goes, is informationally efficient (weakly so, in this example), should the average return from this opportunity be small enough to discourage trading on it. We know this reasoning has fallacies. Even if the average gain is statistically large, we might have no agent attempting it due to risk aversion or trading frictions. Therefore, we would never know whether even a potentially large gain (in statistical terms) is a market inefficiency or rather, say, compensation for risk, a classical "joint hypothesis" problem.

The theoretical literature has refined the notion of informational efficiency by shifting its focus on the second question formulated at the beginning of this section: How accurately *can* the price convey information? The approach followed to address this question relies on models in which rational agents obviously trade not only on their information but also on the information the price reveals in equilibrium, which depends on the agents' portfolio decisions, over a fixed point, as anticipated in the introduction. This fixed point can lead to asset prices that are *fully revealing* in that they reveal all private and public information. These models rely on rational agents and, not surprisingly, predict that no money could be ever "left on the table." We also have a refinement of this fully revealing concept: we say that markets with fully revealing prices are strongly informationally efficient if the prices reveal a sufficient statistic for all the private information. Note that strong efficiency in this theoretical sense differs from its meaning in the empirical literature, signifying as it does that a simple statistic (say, the average of the signals dispersed across the agents' population) is enough to forecast the asset fundamentals.

As discussed in the introduction, markets with fully revealing prices are problematic. They lead to paradoxes. First, the Grossman (1976) paradox. If markets are strongly efficient, the agents should abandon their own signals while formulating portfolio decisions, although in this case the price could not, obviously, contain any piece of *private* information, contradicting the initial presumption that markets are strongly efficient.

Second, the Grossman and Stiglitz (1980) paradox. If markets are strongly efficient, informed agents make losses once information is costly and would rather become "uninformed," free riding on an informative price, although in this case, the price could not obviously contain information anymore. To resolve this paradox, Grossman and Stiglitz (1980, 393) propose markets which they famously describe to be ones in which there is an "equilibrium degree of disequilibrium." That is, in their model, prices cannot be fully revealing but can be *partially revealing*, meaning that the informed agents do not give all of their information away to the uninformed. "Disequilibrium" means prices are not fully revealing, and "equilibrium degree of disequilibrium" means that the price informativeness depends on how many agents are informed—an endogenous variable in the model. Now note that "disequilibrium" allows markets to function, a perspective somehow distinct from the early attempts to define efficiency in the empirical literature.

The next three sections aim to formalize these ideas. Section 10.4 shows that money is indeed "left on the table" once agents take portfolio decisions while ignoring the information content of asset prices. Then we introduce progressively more appropriate notions of equilibrium where prices are fully (section 10.5) and partially (section 10.6) revealing.

10.4 Walrasian Equilibria as Informationally Inefficient Outcomes

We consider a two-period market. In the second period, a riskless asset (the numéraire) yields a gross return equal to R and a risky asset pays off $d \sim N\left(\bar{d}, \sigma_d^2\right)$ at time 2. The budget constraint faced by each agent is $W = (W_0 - (x - \omega_0)\, p)\, R + xd$, where W_0 is the agent's initial wealth and ω_0 denotes the initial endowment of the risky asset, p is the price of the risky asset, x is the asset holding chosen at time 1, and finally, W is the agent's terminal wealth. We assume that each investor maximizes a CARA expected utility function against terminal wealth, $E\left(-e^{-\tau W}\middle|\,\mathbb{F}_i\right)$, $\tau > 0$, where $\mathbb{F}_i$ denotes the information set available to agent i.

We derive the equilibrium in this market while assuming asymmetric information and treat differential information as a special case of this setting. We assume that there is a total of n agents. Of these n agents, n_I are informed in that they observe a signal on the asset value equal to

$$s^i = d + u^i, \quad i = 1, \cdots, n_I, \tag{10.11}$$

where the noise component of the signal s^i is $u^i \sim N\left(0, \sigma_u^2\right)$, for each investor i.

Let π_d and π_u denote the precisions of the dividend and noise distribution, that is, $\pi_d \equiv \sigma_d^{-2}$ and $\pi_u \equiv \sigma_u^{-2}$. The demand for the risky asset formulated by any informed investor is

$$\begin{aligned}\hat{x}_I^i &= \arg\max_x E\left(-e^{-\tau W}\middle|\, s^i\right) \\ &= \arg\max_x \left(-e^{-\tau E\left(W|s^i\right)+\frac{1}{2}\tau^2 var\left(W|s^i\right)}\right) \\ &= \gamma \pi_{d|s^i}\left(E(d|s^i) - Rp\right),\end{aligned} \tag{10.12}$$

where the second line follows because both d and s^i are normally distributed; $\gamma \equiv \tau^{-1}$, interpreted as *risk tolerance*; and by the projection theorem,

$$E(d|s^i) = \bar{d} + \frac{\pi_u}{\pi_d + \pi_u}\left(s^i - \bar{d}\right) \tag{10.13}$$

and $\pi_{d|s^i}$ denotes the precision of the asset payoff d conditional upon having observed s^i,

$$\pi_{d|s^i} = \pi_d + \pi_u, \quad \text{for all } i. \tag{10.14}$$

For simplicity, we are referring to $\hat{x}_I^i$ in eq. (10.12) (and in subsequent junctures of this chapter) as the asset demand. Note that $\hat{x}_I^i$ represents asset holdings and that the asset demand is $\hat{x}_I^i - \omega_0$.

There are also $n_U = n - n_I$ uninformed agents who do not observe the signal s^i in eq. (10.11). Their demand for the risky asset is $\hat{x}_U^i$, say, and is a special case of the informed asset demand in eq. (10.12), namely, for $\pi_u = 0$,

$$\hat{x}_U \equiv \hat{x}_U^i = \gamma\pi_d(\bar{d} - Rp). \tag{10.15}$$

The equilibrium price of the risky asset is found by aggregating demand; setting supply equal to aggregate demand,

$$z \equiv n\omega_0 = \sum_{i=1}^{n_I} \hat{x}_I^i + n_U \hat{x}_U; \tag{10.16}$$

and solving for p after replacing eq. (10.12) and eq. (10.15) into eq. (10.16) and using eqs. (10.14) and (10.13), yielding

$$p = \frac{\bar{d}}{R} + \frac{\pi_u n_I (\hat{s} - \bar{d})}{R\left(\left(\pi_d + \pi_u\right) n_I + \pi_d n_U\right)} - \frac{z}{R\gamma\left(\left(\pi_d + \pi_u\right) n_I + \pi_d n_U\right)}, \tag{10.17}$$

where $\hat{s}$ denotes the average signal, namely,

$$\hat{s} \equiv \frac{1}{n_I} \sum_{i=1}^{n_I} s^i. \tag{10.18}$$

The equilibrium price in eq. (10.17) has three components. The first is the discounted payoff. The second term reveals that the price aggregates information dispersed across the informed investors through the average signal, $\hat{s}$. That is, $\hat{s}$ is a sufficient statistics for all of the signals observed by each informed agent, $(s^i)_{i=1}^{n_I}$, with respect to the equilibrium price. This second term thus adds or subtracts value according to whether the average signal, $\hat{s}$, is higher than the unconditional guess, $\bar{d}$. The third term is a risk premium: the higher the average supply, the higher the risk the agents have to bear in equilibrium, which is evaluated proportionally to their risk aversion, $\gamma^{-1} = \tau$.

The main issue with a Walrasian equilibrium is that, while the price conveys information informed investors have, the uninformed investors do not condition on this informative price while formulating their asset demand in eq. (10.15). They only use the price to determine their budget constraint. The resulting equilibrium is conceptually problematic as a result. Consider, for example, a market with a large number of agents. By the law of large numbers, we have that, in this market,

$$\operatorname*{plim}_{n\to\infty} p = \bar{p} \equiv \frac{\bar{d}}{R} + \frac{\pi_u \bar{\lambda}(d - \bar{d})}{R\left(\bar{\lambda}\left(\pi_d + \pi_u\right) + \left(1 - \bar{\lambda}\right)\pi_d\right)} - \frac{\omega_0}{R\gamma\left(\bar{\lambda}\left(\pi_d + \pi_u\right) + \left(1 - \bar{\lambda}\right)\pi_d\right)},$$

where $\bar{\lambda} \equiv \lim_{n\to\infty} \frac{n_I}{n}$. That is, in this limit, the price perfectly reveals the asset payoff, d, provided of course the proportion of informed agents is asymptotically significant, $\bar{\lambda} > 0$.

It is an arbitrage opportunity. Any investor who understands this market (including any uninformed investor!) can make large profits whenever $R\bar{p} \neq d$. The investor will observe the price $\bar{p}$, and infer d. For example, if $R\bar{p} < d$, the investor will borrow $\bar{p}$ and use this to invest in the risky asset. In the second period, they will pay back $R\bar{p}$ and receive the asset payoff d with a sure profit equal to $d - R\bar{p} > 0$.

10.5 Rational Expectations Equilibrium

If the equilibrium price reveals information, any agent will find it convenient to update their knowledge about the asset payoff, d, while conditioning on their information set, comprising both the agent's own signal s^i and the equilibrium price. We term the equilibrium in this market *rational expectations equilibrium* (REE, henceforth). The term "rational expectations" is used to indicate that the agents correctly understand that the equilibrium asset price incorporates information disseminated across the market and make statistical inference and take investment decisions accordingly. We shall return to this point in a moment.

We solve for the equilibrium as follows. First, we conjecture that the equilibrium price does indeed incorporate information on the average signal, $\hat{s}$, just as the equilibrium price does in the Walrasian case in (10.17),

$$p = a + b(\hat{s} - \bar{d}), \tag{10.19}$$

for two constants a and b. In this market, then, a state of the world is the realization of a random variable that is the average signal and the asset price is a function of this variable: it takes values according to the realization of $\hat{s}$. Furthermore, we search for an equilibrium with *endogenous beliefs* or *rational expectations* (see chapter 2), where the statistical properties of the equilibrium price are fully consistent with the probability distribution that agents have regarding the very same equilibrium price conditionally on their information set.

Naturally, the two constants a and b cannot be the same as those in eq. (10.17): if the agents make an inference about the asset payoff while also conditioning on the equilibrium price, this equilibrium price should then differ from that arising in the Walrasian case. To determine the equilibrium, first note that the informed agents formulate a demand function equal to

$$\hat{x}_I^i = \gamma \pi_{d|s^i,\hat{s}} \left(E(d|s^i, \hat{s}) - Rp \right). \tag{10.20}$$

This demand schedule generalizes the one in eq. (10.12) in that the conditioning information now contains both the signal available to the informed investor, s^i, and the equilibrium price in (10.19) (or equivalently the average signal $\hat{s}$, at least provided that $b \neq 0$). However, it is easy to check that, by the projection theorem,

$$E(d|s^i, \hat{s}) = E\left(d \middle| \hat{s}\right) = \bar{d} + \frac{n_I \pi_u}{\pi_d + n_I \pi_u} (\hat{s} - \bar{d}) \tag{10.21}$$

and

$$\pi_{d|s^i,\hat{s}} = \pi_{d|\hat{s}} = \pi_d + n_I \pi_u. \tag{10.22}$$

That is, the average signal is a sufficient statistic for the distribution of the asset payoff. We shall discuss the economic implications of this conclusion below once we have solved for the equilibrium.

Regarding the uninformed investors, their demand schedule differs from the one in (10.15), in that they will update their beliefs about the asset payoff after having learned the price realization, p in (10.19) (or equivalently the average signal $\hat{s}$, at least provided that $b \neq 0$). But then note that each uninformed agent will have exactly the same demand schedule as the informed in (10.20) due to eqs. (10.21) and (10.22), namely,

$$\hat{x}_I^i = \hat{x}_U^j = \gamma \pi_{d|\hat{s}} \left(E\left(d \middle| \hat{s}\right) - Rp \right), \quad i = 1, \cdots, n_I, \quad j = 1, \cdots, n_U.$$

We determine the coefficients a and b of the equilibrium price in (10.19) by plugging the previous demand schedules into the market-clearing condition, eq. (10.16), leaving

$$p = \frac{\bar{d}}{R} + \frac{n_I \pi_u}{R\left(\pi_d + n_I \pi_u\right)} (\hat{s} - \bar{d}) - \frac{\omega_0}{R\gamma\left(\pi_d + n_I \pi_u\right)}. \tag{10.23}$$

In turn, the equilibrium asset allocation is, simply,

$$\hat{x}_I^i = \hat{x}_U^j = \omega_0, \quad i = 1, \cdots, n_I, \quad j = 1, \cdots, n_U.$$

The equilibrium price in (10.23) fully reveals the average information disseminated in the market, $\hat{s}$, just as in the Walrasian case (see eq. (10.17)). However, this equilibrium differs from the Walrasian: the REE collapses to Walrasian only (i) in the absence of uninformed agents attempting to extract information about the price, $n_U = 0$, and (ii) when the informed agents have access to the same signal, $s^i = s^j$ for all i, j (in which case we would set $n = 1$ in (10.23)). Finally, note that arbitrage is now ruled out in a market with a large number of agents. Assuming that n_I diverges with n (e.g., $n = \bar{\lambda} n_I$, for some $\bar{\lambda}$, just as in the previous sections), we have that

$$\operatorname*{plim}_{n \to \infty} p = p_* \equiv \frac{d}{R}.$$

The mechanism in this model is the following. While trading, the informed agents embed pieces of information into the equilibrium price—they "set" the information content of the price system so to speak. The uninformed agents free ride on these prices. The price now performs two roles: one (classical) is to determine the agents' budget constraint; the second (less mechanical) is to inform the uninformed agents about knowledge other investors have. Thus, when an uninformed agent observes a low price, they will increase their demand as their budget constraints soften. However, a low price reveals to the uninformed agents that the informed might have received bad information about the asset quality, which decreases their demand. In equilibrium, the two effects compensate exactly with each other, leading to a price-inelastic demand, $\hat{x}_U^j = \omega_0, j = 1, \cdots, n_U$. Given this, the informed agents can only be allocated their initial asset endowment as well, $\hat{x}_I^i = \omega_0, i = 1, \cdots, n_I$. The mathematics of this price inelasticity will be made more clear once we examine the NREE in the following section.

This model leads to a number of puzzling predictions. First, a feature of the model pointed out earlier, known as the *Grossman's paradox* (Grossman, 1976). By eqs. (10.21) and (10.22), any informed agent i gives up their knowledge about their own signal, s^i, relying as they do on the average signal, $\hat{s}$. But if no agent is using their own information while trading, we may now wonder how the price can end up aggregating information in the first place?

A second implication of the model regards the equilibrium allocation. Because each investor is allocated their own endowment in equilibrium, informed and uninformed investors make the same expected profits and hence have the same welfare. This raises the following issue, known as the *Grossman-Stiglitz paradox* (Grossman and Stiglitz, 1980): information (i.e., the signals, s^i) should cost, but then why would we be willing to purchase it if we could freely "read" from the equilibrium price? Now, precisely because there are no incentives to purchase information, the price should then not reflect any.

We now explain that these paradoxes could be solved by assuming the presence of "noise" in the equilibrium mechanisms, leading to a partially revealing price: when the uninformed agents make inference on the private information investors have, based on the price, they can only extract part of this information: while part of their information is given for free to the uninformed, uniformed investors can still have incentives to acquire information.

10.6 Noisy Rational Expectations Equilibrium

A natural way to cope with the issues arising in a REE is to assume that the risky asset supply is random. This assumption has an economic interpretation: random realizations of the asset supply might be viewed as liquidity shocks. The mechanism through which this assumption allows us to deal with the conceptual difficulties inherent the REE is the following. In equilibrium, the asset price embeds all of the private information *and* the realization of a liquidity shock. However, investors cannot extract both upon observing the price. The price system, therefore, conveys information, albeit in an imperfect way. This is "lucky" in a way—as Grossman and Stiglitz (1980, 393) put it—for were it to do it perfectly, an equilibrium would not exist. This is the role of "noisy" information famously pointed out by Black (1986) and discussed in the introduction of this chapter.

We consider two models: one with asymmetric information and another, with differential information.

In the model with asymmetric information, the uninformed investors trade at disadvantage compared with the informed. An equilibrium in the market for information is obtained once the welfare of the two types of agents (informed and uninformed) are equalized, controlling for the cost of information. An equilibrium in the asymmetric information market thus involves a fixed point. For a given number of informed agents, the price reveals some information to the uninformed agents, who determine the asset demand on the basis of the probabilistic distribution of the price. But, in equilibrium, prices depend on the uninformed demand. In the Grossman and Stiglitz (1980) market reviewed in section 10.6.1, there is a simple solution to this *information transmission* problem. In equilibrium, prices are informative to the extent that the incentives to purchase information decrease with the number of already informed agents—information choices are strategic substitutes.

In the differential information market of section 10.6.2, there are no agents with superior information. The models that formalize this market are introduced by Hellwig (1980) and Diamond and Verrecchia (1981). They aim to study issues regarding *information aggregation*: how does the market help aggregate information dispersed across investors? This question has very distant origins in economics (see section 2.2 in chapter 2). A competitive equilibrium leads to Pareto optimal allocations (the first welfare theorem); conversely, a given (desired) Pareto optimal allocation can be decentralized through a dedicated redistribution of wealth (the second welfare theorem). Pushed to the extreme, the second welfare theorem may seem to suggest that any desired market outcome could be implemented through a centralized, socialist-type planning system, as in the planning literature following the work of Lange (1936, 1942); that is, once the planner fixes a given outcome as an objective, this outcome could be achieved through a dedicated redistribution of resources that leads agents to the desired objective under *laissez faire*. Hayek (1945) rejects these ideas: we cannot implement this mechanism while missing data regarding information that is local. After all, the second welfare theorem regards Walrasian equilibria, not the equilibria we are examining in this chapter.

The Hellwig and Diamond-Verrecchia models formalize the process of information aggregation in the context of financial markets. It is a complex task because, compared with the previous REE markets, agents now cannot extract all the information that others know from the price and need to condition on their own signals and forecast both the signals and forecasts of others over a fixed point. An equilibrium in this market exists once all these forecasts are mutually and internally consistent and the price is only partially revealing of all the information disseminated in the market.

Finally, section 10.6.3 deals with a variation on theme: How much may price deviate from fundamentals in contexts where the law of iterated expectations may fail to hold? Keynes (1936) famously proposed that market evaluations may resemble those in a "beauty contest." In this contest, participants are asked to pick up the prettiest faces from a list and are remunerated according to average preferences of all the competitors. Clearly, the competitors need to forecast the forecasts of others. As it turns out, these forecasts may fail satisfy the law of iterated expectations and prices may consequently deviate from the fundamentals. In these cases, market evaluations are biased toward public signals, not the agents' own signals. Thus, asset prices still reflect average opinion as well as average opinion about average opinion, but in the way suggested by Keynes. We review a simplified version of a model developed by Allen, Morris, and Shin (2006) that illustrates these conclusions.

10.6.1 Asymmetric Information: Information Transmission

Grossman and Stiglitz (1980) consider a model with asymmetric information, in which investors can acquire information on the asset payoff after agreeing to pay a fee, C, say. Once the investors agree (say, at time t_0) to pay the fee (say, once payoffs are revealed), they observe a signal on the asset payoff and then trade at $t_1 > t_0$ based on their private information. The uninformed investors trade while making inferences on this private information based on the equilibrium price that they are seeing. In equilibrium, we shall see, uninformed investors can only infer part of the information possessed by the informed.

In the first step, we study the equilibrium in the asset market for a given number of informed investors. Due to asymmetric information, informed investors have a higher welfare than the uninformed (before paying C). In the second step, we determine the number of informed investors by requiring that the welfare of the uninformed and the informed are the same once we account for the cost C. It turns out that in this model, the higher the number of informed agents, the lower the incentives to acquire information.

10.6.1.1 Asset market equilibrium

Each informed investor agrees to pay the constant cost C and observes the same signal on the asset payoff, $s^i = s^j \equiv s$ for all i, j in eq. (10.11). That is, acquiring information only leads to a partial resolution of risk.[1] We assume and later justify that the equilibrium price

1. In their original formulation of the model, Grossman and Stiglitz assume that the asset payoff is $d = \delta + \epsilon$, where both δ and ϵ are normally distributed and where the informed investors observe δ for a fee. The formulation of the model in this section is equivalent. Moreover, to simplify the presentation, we are assuming that the information fee is only paid once payoffs are revealed (rather than at t_0).

in this market does not reveal more information than is already possessed by the informed agents. Therefore, the asset demand of the informed agents is the same as in the Walrasian market, eq. (10.12), namely,

$$\hat{x}_I \equiv \hat{x}_I^i = \gamma \pi_{d|s} \left(E\left(d|\, s \right) - Rp \right), \quad i = 1, \cdots, n_I, \tag{10.24}$$

with the agent's i conditional estimate and precision of the asset payoff being the same as in (10.13) and (10.14),

$$E\left(d|\, s \right) = \bar{d} + \frac{\pi_u}{\pi_d + \pi_u} (s - \bar{d}), \quad \pi_{d|s} = \pi_d + \pi_u. \tag{10.25}$$

We know from the previous section that the assumptions formulated so far lead to an equilibrium in which the uninformed investors free ride on the equilibrium price as the latter is fully revealing. Obviously, prices *do* reveal information that informed investors use. The issue is to ascertain whether *some* of this information could not be revealed for free to uninformed investors. Grossman and Stiglitz do indeed study an equilibrium with partial information revelation. One of their key assumptions is that the asset supply is random, such that markets now reveal both fundamental and non fundamental sources of information that an uninformed investor cannot tell apart. Specifically, assume that the total asset supply is random and equal to

$$nZ \equiv n\omega_0 + n\omega, \quad \omega \sim N\left(0, \sigma_z^2\right). \tag{10.26}$$

We interpret ω as a "liquidity shock." For example, a positive and large realization of ω could be interpreted as an asset sell-off due to non fundamental reasons (say, asset owners who monetize their investments due to unexpected consumption contingencies).

The partial revelation mechanism operates as follows. First, note that the uninformed investors now formulate their asset demand conditional upon having learned about the equilibrium price,

$$\hat{x}_U \equiv \hat{x}_U^j = \gamma \pi_{d|p} \left(E\left(d|\, p \right) - Rp \right), \quad j = 1, \cdots, n_U. \tag{10.27}$$

Replacing eqs. (10.24) and (10.27) into the market-clearing condition,

$$Z = \lambda \hat{x}_I + (1 - \lambda)\, \hat{x}_U, \quad \lambda \equiv \frac{n_I}{n}, \tag{10.28}$$

reveals that—provided the equilibrium price p is normally distributed, an assumption made below—p is also informationally equivalent to the "compound signal" θ, defined as

$$\theta \equiv (s - \bar{d}) - c\,(Z - \omega_0), \quad c \equiv (\lambda \gamma \pi_u)^{-1}. \tag{10.29}$$

The compound signal θ (or equivalently, the price) does reveal information about fundamental information, $s - \bar{d}$; however, it does so imperfectly, conveying as it does additional information regarding possible liquidity shocks, $Z - \omega_0$. An uninformed investor who observes the price now cannot tell how much of a price increase is due to good news (say, a high s) or a negative liquidity shock (say, a low Z). Therefore, we expect that, in the equilibrium of this market, informed agents have a higher welfare (before paying C) due to their superior information: they know s, and of course, they know the price p and then Z; that is, they know everything (but d).

We search for a linear equilibrium, that is, an equilibrium in which the asset price is a linear function of the compound signal, θ in eq. (10.29),

$$p = a + b\theta, \tag{10.30}$$

for two constants a and b to be determined. We determine a and b by replacing the asset demands of the informed and uninformed investors into the market-clearing condition, eq. (10.28). We proceed as follows.

First, we determine the conditional expectation, $E\left(d \mid p\right)$, and the conditional precision, $\pi_{d|p}$, in eq. (10.27). Note that the equilibrium price p in eq. (10.30) is affine in θ, and θ is normally distributed, such that $p \sim N\left(a, b^2\sigma_\theta^2\right)$. Therefore,

$$E\left(d \mid p\right) = \bar{d} + b_p\left(p - a\right), \quad \pi_{d|p} = \pi_d + \ell\pi_u, \quad b_p \equiv \frac{cov\left(d, p\right)}{\sigma_p^2}, \tag{10.31}$$

where

$$b_p = \frac{\pi_\theta}{b\pi_d}, \quad \ell = \frac{\pi_z}{\pi_z + c^2\pi_u}, \quad \frac{1}{\pi_\theta} = \sigma_d^2 + \sigma_u^2 + c^2\sigma_z^2, \tag{10.32}$$

such that the uninformed asset demand in (10.27) is

$$\hat{x}_U = \gamma\pi_{d|p}(\bar{d} + \underbrace{b_p\left(p - a\right)}_{\text{info revelation}} - \underbrace{Rp}_{\text{budget constraint}}). \tag{10.33}$$

Regarding the informed asset demand, we have by eqs. (10.24) and (10.25) that

$$\hat{x}_I = \gamma\pi_{d|s}\left(\bar{d} - Rp\right) + \gamma\pi_u\left(s - \bar{d}\right). \tag{10.34}$$

We shall develop the economic interpretation of both the uninformed and the informed asset demand schedules below.

Second, we plug (10.33) and (10.34) into eq. (10.28), obtaining the equilibrium price conjectured in (10.30),

$$p = \underbrace{\frac{\bar{d}}{R} - \frac{\omega_0}{\gamma R\left(\lambda\pi_{d|s} + (1-\lambda)\pi_{d|p}\right)}}_{=a} + \underbrace{\frac{\lambda\pi_u + (1-\lambda)\pi_{d|p}\frac{\pi_\theta}{\pi_d}}{R\left(\lambda\pi_{d|s} + (1-\lambda)\pi_{d|p}\right)}}_{=b} \cdot \theta.$$

The model leads to a number of important predictions. First, in equilibrium, the price does not reveal all private information to the uninformed agents but only a noisy version of it, θ: we say the price is *partially revealing*. Thus, the model provides a resolution to the Grossman-Stiglitz paradox: as the next subsection will show, there exist equilibria in which it is valuable to purchase information.

Second, consider the uninformed demand, $\hat{x}_U$ in eq. (10.33). One the one hand, it decreases with the price p as a mechanical implication of the agent's budget constraint. On the other hand, the uninformed demand increases with p due to information. In the REE, the two effects exactly compensate with each other as explained in the previous section. Straightforward calculations do instead reveal that, in the equilibrium of this model,

$$b_p - R \leq 0,$$

with an equality only holding once $\sigma_z^2 = 0$. That is, the uninformed asset demand in (10.33) "slopes down." The interpretation is simple: in the NREE, the effects of information revelation are weaker than in the REE case as the price is partially revealing, as explained.

Third, the constant c determines the price impact of a *liquidity shock*. The higher c, the higher the impact of a liquidity shock, $Z - \omega_0$, compared to information, $s - \bar{d}$. Its inverse, $c^{-1} = \lambda \gamma \pi_u$, is a measure of the risk-bearing capacity of the informed agents vis-à-vis information. Note, indeed, that the informed agent's demand $\hat{x}_I$ in (10.34) has two components. The first relates to how high the price is compared to the unconditional guess of the asset value; it increases (in absolute value) with the conditional precision of the value estimate given private information, $\pi_{d|s}$. The second component relates to how good news is compared to unconditional guesses; it increases (in absolute value) with the conditional precision of the noise (i.e., with the informational advantage), reflecting a better quality of private information. Thus, as anticipated, the term c^{-1} measures the total effect of the informed agent demand with respect to information. The higher the value of this term, the easier it becomes for the price system to absorb a liquidity shock, $Z - \omega_0$.

Finally, consider the conditional precision of the asset payoff on observation of the price, that is, $\pi_{d|p}$ in eq. (10.31): it is a measure of *price informativeness*. In particular, the constant ℓ in (10.32) reflects asymmetric information: it increases with π_u; that is, it decreases with the size of the noisy component of private information, σ_u^2. Moreover, it decreases with c; that is, it increases with the risk-bearing capacity of the informed agents. In other words, price informativeness decreases as private information becomes more noisy and increases with the risk-bearing capacity of the informed agents. Finally, note that, because $\ell < 1$,

$$\pi_{d|p} = \pi_d + \ell \pi_u < \pi_d + \pi_u = \pi_{d|s}. \tag{10.35}$$

That is, prices provide less information than private signals. This property is very intuitive and has important welfare implications, which are discussed below.

10.6.1.2 *The value of information*

The uninformed agents do not entirely learn about the private information other investors have acquired. Whilst observing the equilibrium price, they confuse fundamentals, $s - \bar{d}$, with liquidity shocks, $Z - \omega_0$ and sometimes, then, trade against the informed. Uninformed investors should therefore expect lower profits and welfare than the informed (before information costs). In appendix 10.B, we will show that

$$\frac{E\left(-e^{-\tau(W_I - C)}\right)}{E\left(-e^{-\tau W_U}\right)} = \sqrt{\frac{\pi_{d|p}}{\pi_{d|s}}} \cdot e^{\tau C}, \tag{10.36}$$

where $W_I - C$ and W_U denote the terminal wealth of the informed and the uninformed agent. Define the ex ante certainty equivalent profits of the informed and the uninformed agents as the two values C_I and C_U that solve

$$-e^{-\tau C_I} = E\left(-e^{-\tau(W_I - C)}\right) \quad \text{and} \quad -e^{-\tau C_U} = E\left(-e^{-\tau W_U}\right).$$

We define the *value of information* as the net gain of becoming informed in terms of the previous certainty equivalents (i.e., a monetary gain), which is, by eq. (10.36),

$$C_I - C_U = \frac{1}{2\tau} \ln\left(\frac{\pi_{d|s}}{\pi_{d|p}}\right) - C. \tag{10.37}$$

Because prices provide less information than private signals, $\pi_{d|s} > \pi_{d|p}$ (see eq. (10.35)), the informed agent is always better off compared to the uninformed, before accounting for the information cost C. Moreover, note that the conditional precision of the asset value estimate made by the informed agents, $\pi_{d|s}$, is independent of the number of informed agents, λ. Instead, that of the uninformed, $\pi_{d|p}$, is increasing in λ as discussed in the previous section. Therefore, the value of information is strictly decreasing in λ: the higher the number of informed agents, the less valuable it is to acquire private information. An interior equilibrium in the market for information is given by the proportion of informed agents λ^* such that $C_I - C_U = 0$.

Figure 10.1 depicts the value of information as a function of the proportion of informed agents for given constellations of parameter values. The examples in this figure come with interior equilibria. For example, when the cost of information is $C = 0.20$ and all remaining parameters are set equal to one (the benchmark), the equilibrium obtains with $\lambda^* = 71\%$. This equilibrium is stable in the following sense. When the proportion of informed agents is less than this equilibrium, $\lambda < \lambda^*$, there are incentives to become informed, $(C_I - C_U > 0)$, such that more agents will become informed until λ^* is reached. The opposite occurs when $\lambda > \lambda^*$. There might be non interior equilibria. For example, the cost of information could be so prohibitive that it would make $C_I - C_U < 0$ in (10.37) for all λ; in this case, the equilibrium would be $\lambda^* = 0$. In general, non interior equilibria are defined as $\lambda^* = 0$ if $C_I - C_U < 0$ for all λ and $\lambda^* = 1$ if $C_I - C_U > 0$.

The comparative statics in figure 10.1 are easy to explain. In the left panel, we compare a market in which liquidity shocks have a higher variability than in the benchmark. The value of information is higher than in the benchmark as prices reveal less information than in the benchmark and the equilibrium proportion of informed agents increase. In the right panel, the benchmark is compared with a market in which the quality of private information deteriorates as captured by a lower value of π_u. The value of information in this market now deteriorates, and the equilibrium proportion of informed agents decreases as a result.

10.6.1.3 *Information sales*

Where does private information come from? Financial intermediation services cover many spaces, and one of them is the production and sale of information. This section describes a simple model of information sale as developed by Admati and Pfleiderer (1986).

We consider the same market in the previous section where the risky asset promises a payoff $\tilde{d} \sim N(\bar{d}, \pi_d^{-1})$ and has a total supply equal to nZ, just as in eq. (10.26). In the

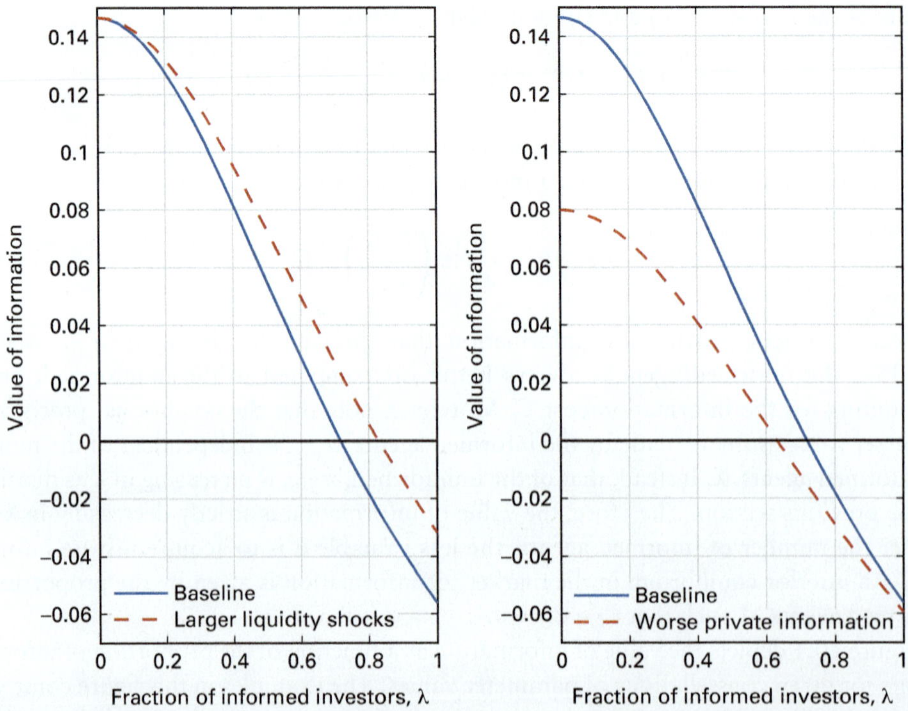

Figure 10.1
This figure depicts the value of information, $C_I - C_U$ in (10.37), when the cost of information is $C = 0.20$ and parameters are set equal to $\tau = \pi_d = \pi_u = \pi_z = 1$, which is the benchmark solid line in both panels. The left and right panels compare the benchmark with the value of information arising when the size of liquidity shocks increases so as to make $\pi_z = \frac{3}{4}$ (left panel, dashed line) and when the precision of information acquired by the informed agent decreases such that $\pi_u = \frac{3}{4}$ (right panel, dashed line).

model we are about to describe, traders become informed while purchasing information from a monopolistic seller of information. Precisely, we assume that a risk neutral agent has private information on the asset value: they observe a signal,

$$s = d + u, \tag{10.38}$$

where $u \sim N\left(0, \pi_u^{-1}\right)$.

This agent would like to sell this piece of information to the market through a "newsletter" that will tell readers about s. For simplicity, we assume that this monopolistic seller will not trade on their own account. The target market for information is a set of risk averse traders, each with a CARA coefficient equal to τ, just as in the previous section. In particular, we assume that, after paying a cost C, a fraction $\lambda = \frac{n_I}{n}$ of the traders have access to the newsletter, and the remaining fraction, $1 - \lambda$, will remain uninformed. We assume that the safe gross interest rate is R.

We know that, for a fixed λ, the asset price is as in the standard Grossman and Stiglitz (1980) model (see eq. (10.30)); we also know that the ratio of the indirect utility of informed agents to that of the uninformed is given by eq. (10.36), such that the value of the fee C that equalizes the informed and uninformed investors' welfare is

$$C(\lambda) \equiv \frac{1}{2\tau} \ln\left(\frac{\pi_{d|s}}{\pi_{d|p}}\right). \tag{10.39}$$

In other words, the indifference condition as to being informed or not translates to the fee level such that the value of information is equal to zero (see eq. (10.37)). The information seller should indeed sell information for a unit fee equal to $C(\lambda)$ once the size target is equal to λ. Indeed, suppose that, for a given target λ, the fee was some $C^* < C(\lambda)$; in this case, the value of information would be positive, and the given proportion λ would be willing to pay more than just C^* and purchase information. On the other hand, if the fee was some $C^* > C(\lambda)$, the value of information would be negative, and the given proportion λ of the population would not be willing to purchase information.

Because $\pi_{d|p}$ is increasing in λ (and $\pi_{d|s}$ is independent of λ), this fee, $C(\lambda)$, is decreasing in λ: the higher the number of agents to whom the seller decides to sell information, the lower the incentives for the uninformed traders to acquire information, and hence, the lower the fees required to zero the value of information.

The monopolist seller now wishes to determine the "optimal circulation size" for the newsletter, that is, the value of λ that maximizes the monopolist's total profits, namely,

$$\hat{\lambda} = \arg\max_{\lambda} \lambda C(\lambda).$$

Under regularity conditions on the model parameters, there exists an interior solution to this problem, leading to the equilibrium in the market for information and, consequently, the market for the risky asset, as usual.

This model can be made richer. For example, the monopolistic seller may decide to sell a newsletter with "photocopied" noise, that is, a newsletter containing the following signal: $s + \eta$, where s is still as in eq. (10.38) and η is some noise, $\eta \sim N(0, \pi_\eta^{-1})$. This model extension appears to be a mere change in notation; however, it actually adds flexibility that enables us to think about the seller's ability to control the information precision in the newsletter, as we now discuss.

First, clearly, the equilibrium fee is still as in eq. (10.39), and the conditional precisions are the same as in the previous section but with $\pi_{u+\eta}$ replacing π_u, where

$$\pi_{u+\eta} = \frac{\pi_u \pi_\eta}{\pi_u + \pi_\eta}.$$

Now suppose that the monopolistic seller has perfect information on $\tilde{d}$, that is, $\pi_u = \infty$. In this case, it is clearly in the interest of the seller to sell a newsletter with noise, for otherwise prices would be perfectly revealing to those who would decide not to purchase information: as a result, no trader would purchase information in the first place. In this case, what is the optimal amount of noise that the monopolist should plug into the newsletter? First, note that

$$\lim_{\pi_u \to \infty} \pi_{d|s} = \pi_d + \pi_\eta, \quad \lim_{\pi_u \to \infty} \pi_{d|p} = \pi_d + \frac{\pi_z \pi_\eta^2}{\pi_z \pi_\eta + (\lambda\gamma)^{-2}}.$$

The level of precision π_η that maximizes the monopolist's total profits for a given λ is

$$\hat{\pi}_\eta(\lambda) = \arg\max_{\pi_\eta} \lambda C(\lambda) = (\lambda\gamma)^{-1}\sqrt{\frac{\pi_d}{\pi_z}},$$

where the last equality follows by a direct calculation. By plugging $\hat{\pi}_\eta(\lambda)$ back into the expression for the fee in eq. (10.39), we have that the monopolist problem becomes

$$\hat{y} = \arg\max_y \left(\frac{1}{y}\ln\left(\frac{(1+y)^2}{1+2y}\right)\right) \approx 1.534,$$

where we have set $y = (\lambda\gamma)^{-1}\sqrt{\frac{1}{\pi_d\pi_z}}$ and where the last approximation is obtained numerically. That is, the optimal circulation size is $\hat{\lambda} \approx \sqrt{\frac{1}{\pi_d\pi_z}}0.652\tau$, provided it is less than one. The newsletter becomes more and more "exclusive" as the market becomes less and less noisy.

10.6.2 Differential Information: Information Aggregation

Hellwig (1980) and Diamond and Verrecchia (1981) consider models in which, unlike in the previous section, there are no investors with superior information. The key feature of these models is that, in equilibrium, investors learn about the asset fundamentals from both the price *and* the signals they observe. This property is due to reasons similar to those explained in the asymmetric information market of the previous section: due to the asset being in random supply, the equilibrium price is partially revealing, such that the signals available to each investor are useful while formulating the inference process leading to asset demands.[2]

In detail, we assume that each investor observes a signal on the asset fundamental (thus, $n_U \equiv 0$ and $n_I \equiv n$), which is the same as s^i in eq. (10.11), and that the total asset supply, nZ, is as in eq. (10.26). The asset demand of each agent is

$$\hat{x}^i = \gamma\pi_{d|s,p}\left(E\left(d|\,s^i,p\right) - Rp\right), \quad i = 1, \cdots, n, \tag{10.40}$$

where, as usual, p denotes the equilibrium price and where the conditional precision of the payoff estimate is assumed to be the same for each agent, $\pi_{d|s,p} \equiv \pi_{d|s^i,p}$. This conjecture on the conditional precision will be confirmed below.

We shall formulate conjectures regarding p in a moment. For now, we assume that the price p is a random variable that helps each investor forecast the asset payoff, d. The rationale behind this conjecture is that, in equilibrium,

$$nZ = \sum_{i=1}^{n}\hat{x}^i, \tag{10.41}$$

2. The two models are similar, except that Diamond and Verrecchia consider endowment shocks as the channel leading to partially revealing prices. The agents' inference process in Diamond and Verrecchia is also more elaborated than in Hellwig as each agent information set includes the price, the signal on the dividend, and the endowment shock. In Hellwig, there are no endowment shocks, as explained.

such that the clearing price aggregates the signals all investors observe, which are potentially useful for each investor's inference problem.

Further, we conjecture that the conditional expectation is

$$E\left(d|\, s^i, p\right) = \bar{d} + \chi_s(s^i - \bar{d}) + \chi_p\,(p - a)\,, \tag{10.42}$$

for two constants χ_s and χ_p, and a is the unconditional expectation of p. If p were exogenous, these two constants could be readily determined through the projection theorem. However, p is endogenous, and these coefficients could well depend on how the equilibrium price aggregates all available information. In other words, due to the endogeneity of the price, p, we need to check whether the projection theorem representation in (10.42) holds and whether it is unique.

There is a natural conjecture to make regarding the equilibrium price, which we shall justify in a moment—namely, that p is an affine function of the average signal and the per capita supply,

$$p - a = b_s(\hat{s} - \bar{d}) - b_z(Z - \omega_0), \tag{10.43}$$

where $\hat{s}$ denotes the average signal in eq. (10.18). The rationale underlying this conjecture is the following. Note that replacing eq. (10.42) into the asset demand $\hat{x}^i$ in (10.40) and then plugging the result into the equilibrium condition (10.41) yields, after rearranging terms, that

$$p - a = \underbrace{\frac{-Ra + \bar{d} - \frac{1}{\gamma\pi_{d|s,p}}\omega_0}{R - \chi_p}}_{\equiv 0} + \underbrace{\frac{\chi_s}{R - \chi_p}}_{\equiv b_s}(\hat{s} - \bar{d}) - \underbrace{\frac{1}{\gamma\pi_{d|s,p}\left(R - \chi_p\right)}}_{\equiv b_z}(Z - \omega_0)\,, \tag{10.44}$$

where the identities under the brackets follow by the conjecture made in (10.43).

The first restriction in (10.44) delivers the value of a in (10.43),

$$a = \frac{\bar{d}}{R} - \frac{1}{\gamma R\pi_{d|s,p}}\omega_0. \tag{10.45}$$

Instead, the coefficients b_s and b_z depend on the coefficient updates in the conditional expectation of eq. (10.42), χ_s and χ_p,

$$b_s = \frac{\chi_s}{R - \chi_p}, \quad b_z = \frac{1}{\gamma\pi_{d|s,p}\left(R - \chi_p\right)}, \tag{10.46}$$

where the very same χ_X, $X \in \{s, p\}$ depend on b_Y, $Y \in \{s, z\}$ over a a fixed point.

Intuitively, the statistical distribution of the equilibrium price depends on the agents' beliefs because the latter determines the asset demand; however, the agents' beliefs depend on the equilibrium distribution that generates the conditioning information the agents rely on while formulating their very same beliefs: the price. It is a fixed point that leads to endogenous beliefs, that is, to (noisy) rational expectations. More in detail, the price coefficients, $b_\cdot$, depend on the agents' coefficient updates, $\chi_\cdot$, as the agents' conditional expectation of the dividend (and hence $\chi_\cdot$) determine their asset demand, thereby contributing to the equilibrium price (through eq. (10.41)). In turn, the agents' coefficient updates $\chi.$ depend on the statistical distribution of the equilibrium price (and hence $b.$), as the latter is a conditioning variable for the agents' expectations of the dividends. Appendix 10.B shows that there is a unique solution to this fixed point and that the price in eq. (10.43) can be expressed as

$$p-a=\frac{\pi_u\left(\left(1-\frac{1}{n}\right)\pi_z+\psi_*^2\pi_u\right)}{R\left(\left(1-\frac{1}{n}\right)\left(\pi_u+\frac{1}{n}\pi_d\right)\pi_z+\psi_*^2\left(\pi_u+\pi_d\right)\pi_u\right)}\cdot\theta, \tag{10.47}$$

where θ is the compound signal, defined as

$$\theta=\left(\hat{s}-\bar{d}\right)-\psi_*\left(Z-\omega_0\right), \tag{10.48}$$

and ψ_* is a strictly positive and bounded constant defined in appendix 10.B (see eq. (10.A18)).

The fact that $\psi_*>0$ implies that the price only partially reveals the average signal, $\hat{s}$. Similar to the constant c in the Grossman and Stiglitz (1980) model (see eq. (10.29)), the constant ψ_* in this model determines the price impact of a liquidity shock. Below, we shall see a striking similarity between these two constants in the limiting case of a large number of agents.

The compound signal in eq. (10.48) is the differential information counterpart to θ in (10.29). That is, in the differential information market of this section, the price is partially revealing as θ conveys noisy information about the asset fundamentals. The equilibrium in this market then addresses a number of issues that the REE cannot. First, eqs. (10.47) and (10.48) reveal that b_s and b_z are both positive. Moreover, χ_s and χ_p are both positive, provided that the conditional precision $\pi_{d|s,p}>0$,[3] a condition that can be shown to hold. That is, every agent now conditions on both their own signal and the price while formulating their demand function—a resolution to the Grossman (1976) paradox. The coefficient χ_s is positive because the agents' signals are obviously positively correlated with the dividend, and the coefficient χ_p is also positive because the equilibrium price is positively correlated with the asset dividend.

The solution in eq. (10.47) is not known in closed form because the constant ψ_* is not either. Note that this constant determines the price sensitivity to the average signal and liquidity shocks, b_s and b_z, and also the conditional precision, $\pi_{d|s,p}$ in (10.45). However, a solution is available in the limiting case, in which the number of agents is large. This case provides intuition regarding the finite case.

So suppose that the number of agents is large such that, by the law of large numbers, the price in (10.47) satisfies

$$\operatorname*{plim}_{n\to\infty} p=\bar{p}\equiv\underbrace{\frac{\bar{d}}{R}-\frac{1}{R\gamma\bar{\pi}_{d|s,p}}\omega_0}_{\equiv\bar{a}_s}+\underbrace{\frac{\pi_u\left(1+\gamma^2\pi_u\pi_z\right)}{R\left(\pi_d+\left(1+\gamma^2\pi_u\pi_z\right)\pi_u\right)}}_{\equiv\bar{b}_s}\cdot\upsilon, \tag{10.49}$$

3. Assume momentarily that $\chi_p>0$. Because $b_z>0$, the second of eqs. (10.46) implies that $\chi_p<R$. Hence, by the first of eqs. (10.46) and $b_s>0$, it must be that $\chi_s>0$. The fact that $\chi_p>0$ follows by eq. (10.A12) in appendix 10.B.

where υ is the compound signal,

$$\upsilon \equiv \left(d-\bar{d}\right)-\bar{\psi}\left(Z-\omega_0\right), \quad \bar{\psi} \equiv \left(\gamma \pi_u\right)^{-1}, \tag{10.50}$$

and $\bar{\pi}_{d|s,p}$ denotes the limiting conditional precision,

$$\bar{\pi}_{d|s,p}=\lim_{n\to\infty} \pi_{d|s,p}=\left(\pi_d+\pi_u\right)+\gamma^2\pi_z\pi_u^2. \tag{10.51}$$

The price now reveals better information about the asset fundamentals than in the finite agents case as the signal υ embeds more precise information about the asset payoff than θ in (10.48). Naturally, each agent still finds it useful to condition their demand on both their own signal and the equilibrium price. Moreover, the price is partially revealing in this limiting case too. Now note that the limiting coefficient, $\bar{\psi}$, is the same as c in the Grossman and Stiglitz (1980) model when $\lambda=1$ (see eq. (10.29)). In other words, in this market, liquidity shocks are absorbed in a way comparable to that in the asymmetric information market, despite the obviously different mechanisms underlying these two markets.[4]

Finally, the conditional precision in (10.51) is the sum of the precision of the payoff given each agent's signal, $\pi_{d|s}=\pi_d+\pi_u$, plus a second component, $\gamma^2\pi_z\pi_u^2$. This second component is increasing in γ: the agent's demand becomes more aggressive as risk tolerance increases, leading to a more informative equilibrium price. The second component is also increasing in both π_z and π_u. The effects regarding an increase in π_z are explained by the price being more responsive to fundamentals than noise as σ_z^2 decreases. The effects regarding an increase in π_u link to each agent providing more information over the equilibrium aggregation while trading more aggressively on less noisy signals.

10.6.3 Higher Order Beliefs and Beauty Contests

Consider a market for an asset traded by overlapping generations of agents. The asset delivers a random payoff d, which is only known at time $T+1$, and as usual, we assume that $d\sim N(\bar{d},\sigma_d^2)$. Each generation has unit mass, and each trader in their generation has exponential utility as in the previous section, with a risk tolerance γ, and one period life. Each trader i at time t observes a signal s_t^i on the asset payoff, which has the same distribution as that of the signals in previous sections (see, e.g., eq. (10.11)),

$$s_t^i=d+u_t^i,$$

where u_t^i is normal and independent distributed with zero mean, variance equal to σ_u^2, and such that $\int_0^1 u_t^i di=0$. We assume that the total supply in each period t is IID and equal to Z_t, where $Z_t\sim N\left(0,\sigma_z^2\right)$. To simplify the presentation, we fix the safe interest rate to zero, that is, $R\equiv 1$.

4. Note that, in the Grossman-Stiglitz model, the compound signal contains the informed agents' *signal* on the fundamental value and information regarding per capita supply shocks. The term $(d-\bar{d})$ in (10.50) appears due to the law of large numbers.

Thus, at the final trading date, T, each trader's demand is

$$x_T^i = \gamma\pi_{d|\mathbb{F}_T^i}\left(E_T^i(d) - p_T\right),$$

where p_T is the equilibrium price at time T and where $E_T^i(d)$ and $\pi_{d|\mathbb{F}_T^i}$ denote the expectation and the precision of d of trader i, conditional upon all the information available to the trader at time T, $\mathbb{F}_T^i$: past prices and past realizations of the asset supply. In equilibrium, $\int_0^1 x_T^i di = Z_T$, and in a symmetric equilibrium, the conditional precisions are all the same, $\pi_{d|\mathbb{F}_T^i} \equiv \pi_{d|\mathbb{F}_T}$. Therefore, in a symmetric equilibrium, the price satisfies

$$p_T = \bar{E}_T(d) - \frac{1}{\gamma\pi_{d|\mathbb{F}_T}} Z_T,$$

where $\bar{E}_T(d)$ denotes the "average market opinion" of the asset value, that is, the cross-sectional average of the agents' conditional expectations,

$$\bar{E}_T(d) \equiv \int_0^1 E_T^i(d)\, di.$$

We may repeat the same arguments for the equilibrium at time $T-1$,

$$p_{T-1} = \bar{E}_{T-1}(p_T) - \frac{1}{\gamma\pi_{d|\mathbb{F}_{T-1}}} Z_{T-1} = \bar{E}_{T-1}\bar{E}_T(d) - \frac{1}{\gamma\pi_{d|\mathbb{F}_{T-1}}} Z_{T-1},$$

where the first equality follows because the traders at time $T-1$ may sell the asset at time T for p_T and the second equality holds as Z_t is zero mean and independently distributed. Therefore, the equilibrium price in any trading period is

$$p_t = \bar{E}_t\bar{E}_{t+1}\cdots\bar{E}_T(d) - \frac{1}{\gamma\pi_{d|\mathbb{F}_t}} Z_t. \tag{10.52}$$

That is, the equilibrium price reflects the average opinion of future average opinions on the asset value, d. In general, it depends on the whole history of prices and hence past signals and supply shocks. The price is, thus, partially revealing. Allen, Morris, and Shin (2006) solve for this equilibrium price. We may illustrate some of their main conclusions while ignoring that prices also depend on past prices. Neglecting this dependence does, of course, only lead to an approximation to the model solution, denoted as $\hat{p}_t$. This approximation only regards the first term on the RHS of eq. (10.52). So, consider the estimate of the asset value made by agent i at time t,

$$E_t^i(d) = \bar{d} + \chi(s_t^i - \bar{d}),$$

for some constant $\chi \in (0,1)$ (see, e.g., the first of eqs. (10.25)). Then, the average expectation is $\bar{E}_t(d) = \bar{d} + \chi(d - \bar{d})$, and the expectation of the average expectation of others is

$$E_{t-1}^i\bar{E}_t(d) = \bar{d} + \chi\left(E_{t-1}^i(d) - \bar{d}\right),$$

such that the second-order belief on the average expectation is $\bar{E}_{t-1}\bar{E}_t(d) = \bar{d} + \chi^2(d - \bar{d})$. Continuing,

$$\hat{p}_t = \bar{E}_t\bar{E}_{t+1}\cdots\bar{E}_T(d) = \bar{d} + \chi^{T-t}(d - \bar{d}).$$

So, in this approximation, prices are perfectly revealing. Naturally, they are not perfectly revealing in the full version of the model. However, the approximated prices display some interesting properties, which also hold in the general case. First, note that

$$\hat{p}_t - d = -(1 - \chi^{T-t})(d - \bar{d}) = \frac{1 - \chi^{T-t}}{1 - \chi}\left(\bar{E}_t(d) - d\right)$$

or

$$\left|\hat{p}_t - d\right| > \left|\left(\bar{E}_t(d) - d\right)\right|.$$

Similarly, prices are biased toward public knowledge, $\bar{d}$, in that

$$\hat{p}_t - \bar{E}_t(d) = (1 - \chi^{T-t-1})(\bar{d} - \bar{E}_t(d))$$

or sign $\left(\hat{p}_t - \bar{E}_t(d)\right) = \text{sign}(\bar{d} - \bar{E}_t(d))$.

Prices deviate from fundamentals more than average opinions on the same fundamentals. That is, they do not fully reflect the average consensus on the asset value. Similar to the Keynes beauty contest mentioned in the introduction of this section, agents evaluate assets by having in mind their market value and need, then, forecast the forecasts of others. These higher order beliefs (the forecasts of the forecasts of others) do not satisfy the law of iterated expectations, such that $\hat{p}_t \neq \bar{E}_t(d)$.

10.7 Dealers Markets: Introduction

Asset prices fluctuate even in the absence of important public news about the fundamentals and exhibit pronounced volatility at high frequency scales such as intraday. Information problems could be a market driver. Indeed, the previous sections emphasize that asset prices can incorporate private information conveyed by investors, albeit in a partially revealing fashion. Intuitively, changes in private information can be incorporated into asset prices more or less precisely, but once prices are partially revealing, they can fluctuate even while the asset demand is driven by reasons unrelated to fundamentals.

This and the following section formalize the previous reasoning and build on the insights of the previous section to develop information-based explanations of asset price fluctuations. While the models in the previous sections provide the necessary foundations to the role information plays in asset markets, the organization of financial markets and trading systems have institutional details that go beyond those underlying the previous models. These details include the timing of the market-clearing mechanism (when), the geography (where), and the trading operations (how).

The *timing* of the clearing mechanism can be best illustrated by two main organization protocols: (i) call auctions (batch markets) where trading occurs over prespecified windows of time and (ii) continuous auctions where trading occurs continuously. The *geography* of markets is varied. There are centralized markets such as those for products listed on an exchange. There are decentralized markets (e.g., OTC markets). There are dealership markets, in which end users trade through a number of dealers; dealership markets are therefore decentralized markets: a hypothetical end user who is not satisfied with the quotes a dealer provides them with can search for better opportunities offered by another dealer. Interdealer markets are markets in which only dealers can operate while adjusting their desired balances from those carried over while trading with end users. While dealers typically operate in OTC markets, they can also operate on exchanges like the London Stock Exchange. Section 10.10 provides an introductory account of how search theories help explain the microstructure of OTC markets. Finally, the *trading operations* in the market-clearing mechanism or order submissions can broadly take on two forms: (i) market orders or (ii) limit orders. These two forms may well affect market conditions. For example, market orders (i.e., those most likely to be initiated by informed/"active" investors) "consume" limit orders and decrease market liquidity while limit orders (most likely to be initiated by passive investors) improve market liquidity.

We analyze the role of information in the price formation mechanism while taking into account some of the previous "market microstructure" details. We study markets in which there are traders submitting market orders and dealers who operate as market makers and set prices. Market makers can be competitive or not. This section displays an important example of a market outcome in a setting where market makers are competitive with a famous model developed by Glosten and Milgrom (1985). The model is a cornerstone in the theory of market microstructure and helped develop empirical measures of liquidity. We hinge on this model to illustrate how information matters in dealers markets and also to explain how the model may be used as guidance for constructing such empirical liquidity estimates.

10.7.1 Markets with Symmetric Information

Suppose that market makers are perfectly competitive and risk neutral and that they receive market orders from potentially informed traders. The latter are potentially informed in that the market makers do not know whether the orders they receive emanate from an informed trader or a liquidity trader—an assumption that parallels those leading to partial revelation in the NREE models of the previous section. As usual, informed traders are those who observe a signal on the asset payoff, d. Denote with $\mathbb{F}_t$ the information set that is available to market makers at time t; this only includes buy or sell orders arriving sequentially to them in addition to some public information only released at time zero ($\mathbb{F}_0$). Clearly, $\mathbb{F}_t = \mathbb{F}_{t-1} \bigcup o_t$, where o_t can be either a buy or a sell order, that is, $o_t \in \{\text{buy}_t, \text{sell}_t\}$. For simplicity, we will assume that interest rates are zero.

Now suppose that no trader is "informed," such that the knowledge of o_t does not help predict d. Then, if dealer i receives a buy order and is risk neutral, they will set the ask price at t, a_{it} say, such that

$$0 = E\left(a_{it} - d \middle| \mathbb{F}_{t-1}, o_t = \text{buy}_t\right) = E\left(a_{it} - d \middle| \mathbb{F}_{t-1}\right), \tag{10.53}$$

where the second equality follows because the buy order is totally uninformative; that is, it has no predictive power on d in addition to $\mathbb{F}_{t-1}$.

Likewise, if dealer i receives a sell order, they will set the bid price at t, b_{it} say, such that

$$0 = E\left(d - b_{it} \middle| \mathbb{F}_{t-1}, o_t = \text{sell}_t\right) = E\left(d - b_{it} \middle| \mathbb{F}_{t-1}\right). \tag{10.54}$$

The expected profits in (10.53) and (10.54) are set equal to zero due to the assumption that dealers are perfectly competitive, and the second equalities in both (10.53) and (10.54) follow by the assumption that trades arrive to dealers while not carrying any information on d that was not already contained in $\mathbb{F}_{t-1}$. Therefore, the bid-ask spread is zero for each dealer, and the asset price p_t collapses to

$$p_t = a_{it} = b_{it} = E\left(d \middle| \mathbb{F}_{t-1}\right).$$

In the absence of public news about d, the price p_t will not change. It is counterfactual, as explained. Glosten and Milgrom (1985) show how the bid-ask spread can be positive in a model in which dealers face informed investors. We will present a simplified version of their model next.

10.7.2 With Asymmetric Information: Bid-Ask Spreads

Suppose the asset payoff d has a binary distribution: it is high, d_h, with a probability α, or low, d_l, with complementary probability. Denote with α_t the probability that $d = d_h$ conditionally upon the entire history of orders seen by the market makers up to t,

$$\alpha_t = \Pr\left(d = d_h \middle| \mathbb{F}_t\right).$$

Trades arrive sequentially to the market makers. The latter believe there is (i) a probability π the order at t is information driven and (ii) a probability $1 - \pi$ the order at t is liquidity driven and, in this case, a 50% chance the liquidity-motivated order, is a buy or a sell. Note that the order now might contain private information regarding the asset payoff. While market makers are not sure about whether the order is informative, they post order-contingent rules that reflect updated information: a bid price if the order they receive is a sell and an ask price if the order is a buy.

For example, regarding a sell order, competition leads a representative market maker to post the following bid price:

$$b_t = E\left(d \middle| \mathbb{F}_{t-1}, o_t = \text{sell}_t\right) = \alpha_{t-1}\left(\text{sell}_t\right) d_h + \left(1 - \alpha_{t-1}\left(\text{sell}_t\right)\right) d_l, \tag{10.55}$$

where, by Bayes's law,

$$\alpha_{t-1}\left(\text{sell}_t\right) \equiv \Pr\left(d = d_h \middle| \mathbb{F}_{t-1}, o_t = \text{sell}_t\right) = \frac{\Pr\left(o_t = \text{sell}_t \middle| d = d_h, \mathbb{F}_{t-1}\right)}{\Pr\left(o_t = \text{sell}_t \middle| \mathbb{F}_{t-1}\right)} \alpha_{t-1}. \tag{10.56}$$

Once again, note that the market maker posts bid and ask prices before knowing whether they will receive a sell or buy order. As explained, this is a posting rule and actually a *regret-free* rule: once the order is filled, market makers will not regret having executed at the prices they had previously posted given the information of the time. This rule is, of course, entirely consistent with market practice.

To determine the probabilities of the ratio in (10.56), note that, conditionally on $d = d_h$, informed traders would never sell such that the probability to receive a sell order in this case is simply the probability that the order is liquidity motivated, $1 - \pi$, times the probability that a liquidity trader sells, $\frac{1}{2}$,

$$\Pr\left(o_t = \text{sell}_t \middle| d = d_h, \mathbb{F}_{t-1}\right) = \frac{1}{2}(1-\pi). \tag{10.57}$$

Further,

$$\Pr\left(o_t = \text{sell}_t \middle| \mathbb{F}_{t-1}\right) = \alpha_{t-1} \cdot \frac{1}{2}(1-\pi) + (1-\alpha_{t-1}) \cdot \left(\pi + \frac{1}{2}(1-\pi)\right). \tag{10.58}$$

The first term on the RHS of the previous equality arises because, conditionally on $d = d_h$ (which has α_{t-1} likelihood, given $\mathbb{F}_{t-1}$), only sell trades can be liquidity motivated—trades that occur with probability $\frac{1}{2}(1-\pi)$, as explained while deriving eq. (10.57). The second term on the RHS of (10.58) is due to the fact that conditionally on $d = d_l$ (which has $1-\alpha_{t-1}$ likelihood, given $\mathbb{F}_{t-1}$), the probability of receiving a sell order is the sum of (i) the probability of an informed trade, π, plus (ii) the probability of a liquidity motivated order, $\frac{1}{2}(1-\pi)$.

Replacing eqs. (10.57) and (10.58) into eq. (10.56) leaves

$$\alpha_{t-1}(\text{sell}_t) = \frac{\frac{1}{2}(1-\pi)}{\frac{1}{2}(1-\pi) + (1-\alpha_{t-1})\pi} \alpha_{t-1}. \tag{10.59}$$

An analogous reasoning leads to the following expression for the ask price posted by a representative market maker:

$$a_t = E\left(d \middle| \mathbb{F}_{t-1}, o_t = \text{buy}_t\right) = \alpha_{t-1}(\text{buy}_t)\, d_h + (1-\alpha_{t-1}(\text{buy}_t))\, d_l, \tag{10.60}$$

where

$$\begin{aligned}
\alpha_{t-1}(\text{buy}_t) &\equiv \Pr\left(d = d_h \middle| \mathbb{F}_{t-1}, o_t = \text{buy}_t\right) \\
&= \frac{\Pr\left(o_t = \text{buy}_t \middle| d = d_h, \mathbb{F}_{t-1}\right)}{\Pr\left(o_t = \text{buy}_t \middle| \mathbb{F}_{t-1}\right)} \alpha_{t-1} \\
&= \frac{\frac{1}{2}(1+\pi)}{\frac{1}{2}(1-\pi) + \alpha_{t-1}\pi} \alpha_{t-1}.
\end{aligned} \tag{10.61}$$

It is easy to check that

$$\alpha_{t-1}(\text{buy}_t) \geq \alpha_{t-1}(\text{sell}_t);$$

that is, the order flow is informative.

To summarize, eqs. (10.55) and (10.60) form a stochastic difference system where the conditional probability the asset is good, α_t, is

$$\alpha_t = \begin{cases} \alpha_{t-1}(\text{sell}_t), & \text{as in eq. (10.59), with prob. } \bar{\pi}(d) \\ \alpha_{t-1}(\text{buy}_t), & \text{as in eq. (10.61), with prob. } 1-\bar{\pi}(d) \end{cases} \tag{10.62}$$

and $\bar{\pi}(d)$ denotes the probability of a sell order when the true asset value is $d \in \{d_l, d_h\}$, notably[5]

$$\bar{\pi}(d_h) = \frac{1}{2}(1-\pi) \quad \text{and} \quad \bar{\pi}(d_l) = \pi + \frac{1}{2}(1-\pi).$$

Note that $\bar{\pi}(d_l) > 1 - \bar{\pi}(d_l)$ and $1 - \bar{\pi}(d_h) > \bar{\pi}(d_h)$; that is, the probability that sell orders (resp., buy orders) arrive when there is bad (good) information is higher than 50%.

The model implies that *adverse selection costs* are borne by liquidity motivated orders. To motivate the emphasis on adverse selection, note that we are describing a market where the agents who hold private information would selectively trade to benefit from their knowledge: they buy when the asset is good (and the price is low) and sell when the asset is bad (and the price is high), such that the market would actually collapse without noise, similarly as in the standard lemon problem described in chapter 5.

In particular, consider the fair value of the asset, that is, the value resulting in the absence of any information frictions (i.e., prior to possibly informed trades arriving at t), defined as

$$p_{t-1} = E\left(d \mid \mathbb{F}_{t-1}\right) = \alpha_{t-1} d_h + \left(1 - \alpha_{t-1}\right) d_l. \tag{10.63}$$

It is the price we would observe absent any adverse selection. We have, accordingly, using eq. (10.55), eq. (10.59), and eq. (10.63),

$$b_t - p_{t-1} = s_t^b \cdot \left(d_h - d_l\right), \tag{10.64}$$

where

$$s_t^b \equiv \alpha_{t-1}\left(\text{sell}_t\right) - \alpha_{t-1} = -\frac{\left(1-\alpha_{t-1}\right)\pi}{\frac{1}{2}(1-\pi) + \left(1-\alpha_{t-1}\right)\pi}\alpha_{t-1} \leq 0.$$

The bid price is less than the fair value because once a market maker receives a sell order, they will be unsure about whether the sell order is liquidity motivated: it could be information motivated. This correlation between the order flow and the asset value leads the market maker to evaluate the asset less than based on their information set prior to the received order. The spread, s_t^b (posted at $t-1$ in anticipation of a sell order possibly occurring at t) measures the change in the market maker's belief occurring after receiving a sell order. Adverse selection costs are borne by liquidity traders: those affected by a liquidity shock will sell the asset at a price b_t that is lower than the fundamental value (i.e., the value based on the information set not including their own order, p_{t-1}).

Likewise, using eq. (10.60), eq. (10.61) and eq. (10.63),

$$a_t - p_{t-1} = s_t^a \cdot \left(d_h - d_l\right), \tag{10.65}$$

where

$$s_t^a \equiv \alpha_{t-1}\left(\text{buy}_t\right) - \alpha_{t-1} = \frac{\left(1-\alpha_{t-1}\right)\pi}{\frac{1}{2}(1-\pi) + \alpha_{t-1}\pi}\alpha_{t-1} \geq 0.$$

5. The model can be simulated as follows. We take as given the true value of the asset payoff, say $d \in \{d_l, d_h\}$, and simulate the conditional probabilities in eqs. (10.62), thereby generating bid and ask prices according to eqs. (10.55) and (10.60).

Now, those who want to buy an asset for liquidity reasons and, accordingly, place a buy order will buy at a price a_t higher than p_t, bearing an adverse selection cost.

Note also that the fact that $s_t^b \leq 0$ and $s_t^a \geq 0$ imply that transaction prices (bid, when a sell order is placed, and ask, when a buy order is placed) move in the direction of the order flow. Moreover, the two spreads, s_t^a and s_t^b, cannot be the same. In particular, we have that

$$-s_t^b > s_t^a \Longleftrightarrow \alpha_{t-1} > \frac{1}{2}.$$

That is, if the conditional probability that the asset payoff is high, α_t, is growing (say, for example, because we are observing more buy orders than sell orders), adverse selection on the ask side will be less and less severe as informed traders are "giving them away." Indeed, it is possible to show that the model predicts the price is asymptotically *strongly* efficient in that $\alpha_t \to 0$ if $d = d_l$ and $\alpha_t \to 1$ if $d = d_h$. Intuitively, chances become higher and higher that the asset payoff is truly low after a large number of sell orders arrives to the market maker's trading desk.

Finally, the model predicts that the bid-ask spread predicted by the model is

$$a_t - b_t = \left(s_t^a - s_t^b\right)(d_h - d_l).$$

It is increasing in the volatility of the asset payoff, consistent with empirical evidence. It is zero only when $\pi = 0$ (no asymmetric information) or, asymptotically, when either $\alpha_t \to 0$ or $\alpha_t \to 1$.

The insights of the model are very important, although the model has limitations. First, the only source of the bid-ask spread relies on information asymmetries and the inherent adverse selection: the market maker may receive buy orders from investors who know the asset payoff is good or sell orders from investors who know the asset is a lemon. That is, the order flow correlates with the asset payoff, which leads to "price impacts" of trades not related to fundamentals—the liquidity shocks: whenever a liquidity trader trades, they will move the price above or below the fundamentals because the market maker anticipates that the order they observe could be information driven.[6] Further, two assumptions of the model are that informed traders do not act strategically and that the order size is fixed. Section 10.8 analyzes markets in which traders understand that their trades can have a price impact and accordingly can optimize on their order size and also "distribute" their order sizes optimally over time. We first analyze how we may use this framework to model additional phenomena such as inventory risk or liquidity measurement.

10.7.3 Inventory Risk And Bid-Ask Spreads

Bid-ask spreads are an important determinant of liquidity but liquidity has many dimensions. Traders obviously would always like to "get in" when needed but, at the same time, "they would also like to get out" of a trade. Narrow bid-ask spreads "do not help" if trades are difficult to execute as books lack depth. One possible reason for low depth in a market could be that inventories are subject to market fluctuations. So, not only does

6. Section 10.10 provides additional explanations that capture the spirit of bid-ask spreads, based on search frictions.

market makers' risk aversion lead to positive bid-ask spreads that compensate for this "inventory risk"; this risk aversion may lead market makers to maintain finite inventories. This section develops a model that focuses on the bid-ask spread aspect of this complex problem. It is based on a variant of a formulation originally proposed by Stoll (1978).

Consider an asset market in which a liquidity supplier (a dealer, say) has concerns regarding their inventory risk. The dealer is ready to buy the asset at some bid price and sell the same asset at some ask price, and therefore they perform a purely intermediating role. It is possible that in performing this role, the dealer ends up with a non zero net position, say some positive asset holding. Inventory risk is the risk that the dealer's asset holding may change in value. Aversion to this risk leads to a bid-ask spread, even in the absence of asymmetric information.

Consider a two-period market in which such dealers are competitive. Let p_t the price of the asset at time t, and let W_t be the dealer's wealth, ω_t the dealer's asset inventory, x_t the asset holdings, and $n_t = \omega_t - x_t$ the asset units that are traded at time t. The dealer is selling the risky asset if n_t is positive and is buying if n_t is negative. Assume that investing in cash produces a zero net return, that is, set $R = 1$. We know, since the beginning of section 10.4, that the wealth constraint of any trader should satisfy $W = (W_0 - (x - \omega_0)\,p)\,R + xd$, where W_0 denotes the trader's initial wealth and ω_0 denotes their initial endowment of the asset. We can rely on this budget constraint to conclude that the dealer's wealth at time $t+1$ is

$$W_{t+1} = n_t p_t + (\omega_t - n_t)\,p_{t+1} + c_t,$$

where c_t denotes cash available at t.[7] Note that asset inventories at time $t+1$ is simply the inventories at t minus the asset units sold at t, namely,

$$\omega_{t+1} = \omega_t - n_t. \tag{10.66}$$

We assume that at time $t+1$, the asset pays off d, which is normally distributed with mean $\bar{d}$ and variance σ_d^2, as usual. Obviously, then, in this two-period market, $p_{t+1} = d$. In this model, we can interpret the difference $d - \bar{d}$ as information regarding the asset value that leads to market fluctuations. It is this risk that the dealer is averse to. Precisely, we assume that the dealer maximizes the expected utility of their final wealth with respect to n_t, and assume that this utility is CARA with coefficient $\tau > 0$. The first-order conditions for the dealer lead to the following dealer's supply function:

$$n_t = \omega_t + \gamma\pi_d(p_t - \bar{d}), \tag{10.67}$$

where we have denoted $\gamma \equiv \tau^{-1}$ (constant risk tolerance) and $\pi_d \equiv \sigma_d^{-2}$ (the dividend precision), as usual.

The dealer is willing to sell more than allowed by their current inventory should the asset price p_t be above its unconditional expectation $\bar{d}$. That is, if $p_t > \bar{d}$, then $n_t > \omega_t$, such that $\omega_{t+1} < 0$ (see eq. 10.66)): the dealer enters into a short position. Instead, should the price p_t be below $\bar{d}$, the dealer would then be willing to supply less than the inventory,

7. Just set $c_t \equiv W_0$, $x_t \equiv x$, $\omega_t \equiv \omega_0$, $p_{t+1} \equiv d$.

such that $\omega_{t+1} > 0$, resulting in a long position. The dealer's willingness to serve the market in this way increases with their risk-bearing capacity $\gamma\pi_d$.

Finally, consider the equilibrium in this market. At time t, the dealer receives an order—a random variable $o_t = +1$ (in case of a buy order) or $o_t = -1$ (in case of a sell order). In equilibrium, $n_t = o_t$, such that, by eq. (10.67)

$$p_t = \begin{cases} m_t + \frac{1}{\gamma\pi_d} & \text{if } o_t = +1 \text{ (ask price)} \\ m_t - \frac{1}{\gamma\pi_d} & \text{if } o_t = -1 \text{ (bid price)} \end{cases}$$

where $m_t \equiv \bar{d} - \frac{\omega_t}{\gamma\pi_d}$ is the mid-quote. The bid-ask spread is equal to $\frac{2}{\gamma\pi_d}$ and decreases with the dealer's risk-bearing capacity.

10.7.4 Empirical Measures of Liquidity

We often define *liquidity* as the easiness at which traders are able to trade. How do we measure liquidity? In practice, measuring liquidity requires modeling the details of market transactions. For example, according to the Glosten and Milgrom (1985) model reviewed in the previous section, bid-ask spreads force traders to trade at disadvantage compared with what they would be able to do based on the asset fundamentals. Thus, the higher the bid-ask spreads, the lower the asset liquidity. In the previous model, then, liquidity results from the presence of asymmetric information.

Roll (1984) developed an ingenious way to measure liquidity that does not rely on asymmetric information. Suppose that bid and ask prices are given by $b_t = p_t - \frac{1}{2}S$ and $a_t = b_t + S$, where S is the bid-ask spread, a constant, and the "fundamentals" p_t follow a random walk: $p_t = p_{t-1} + \epsilon_t$, where ϵ_t is IID. Therefore, the transaction price is

$$P_t = p_t + \frac{1}{2}Sq_t,$$

where $q_t = 1$ (resp., $q_t = -1$) if the trade is initiated by a buyer (resp. a seller). We assume that q_t is IID, with $\Pr(q_t = 1) = \frac{1}{2}$. This simple model captures the salient features of the Glosten and Milgrom model. It relies on the assumption that transactions take place at bid and ask prices, although this feature of the model is not derived from first principles (e.g., based on a model with asymmetric information); however, the model is flexible enough to be amenable to empirical work easily.

Note that the return from a single transaction is $\Delta P_t \equiv P_t - P_{t-1} = \frac{1}{2}S(q_t - q_{t-1}) + \epsilon_t$, such that

$$cov(\Delta P_t, \Delta P_{t-1}) = \left(\frac{1}{2}S\right)^2 cov(\Delta q_t, \Delta q_{t-1}) = -\left(\frac{1}{2}S\right)^2 var(q_{t-1}) = -\left(\frac{1}{2}S\right)^2. \tag{10.68}$$

Intuitively, returns are negatively correlated because transaction prices "bounce back." Suppose initially that the fundamentals are constant. When the price hits its "down" (the bid), it may only increase (in case of a subsequent buy order) or stay constant (in case of a subsequent sell order). Likewise, when the price hits its "up" (the ask), it may only decrease or stay constant. Transaction returns are then negatively correlated. This property also holds when fundamentals follow a random walk because ϵ_t is IID. Eq (10.68) may now be inverted for the spread,

$$S = 2\sqrt{-cov\left(\Delta P_t, \Delta P_{t-1}\right)}. \tag{10.69}$$

Eq. (10.69) is Roll's proposal for estimating the bid-ask spread, and its clear advantage is that it may be easily implemented.

The empirical literature contains a variety of additional empirical measures of market liquidity. For example, Amihud (2002) proposes to estimate illiquidity by the extent to which the order flow is able to move asset prices,

$$ILL \equiv \frac{1}{D}\sum_{t=1}^{D}\frac{|\Delta P_t|}{V_t}, \tag{10.70}$$

where ΔP_t and V_t are the observed price change and the gross order flow (i.e., buy plus sell orders) at time t and D is the number of days included in the average calculation. The intuition behind (10.70) is that the impact of transaction orders on prices should be high when the underlying market is not very liquid. The next section provides a rationale for this intuition, based on the celebrated Kyle (1985) model.[8] The reader who is interested in reviews of additional empirical measures of illiquidity is referred to Hasbrouck (2007) or de Jong and Rindi (2009).

10.8 Markets with Strategic Players

Investors with superior information do affect asset prices in all the markets analyzed so far. The question arises as to how such investors should trade if they had to make the best use of their information. In the markets of the previous sections, agents do not understand they have a price impact. This section removes this assumption and considers dealer markets in which investors with superior information make a strategic use of their information while realizing they have a price impact. The models we study make sharp predictions regarding how liquidity conditions are affected by the extent of information asymmetry between traders and dealers.

How does an informed trader trade while realizing that their trade has a price impact? On the one hand, an investor with superior information (an "insider trader," say) should trade aggressively on their information advantage against the market makers. On the other hand, prices likely move against the insider trader while they trade aggressively: they increase when the insider buys and decrease when the insider sells. So a large trade is not optimal because prices could move adversely, but then a small trade could just be "underutilized information."

In Kyle's (1985) model, a trading size optimizes the previous trade-off, given the market makers' pricing rule. Regarding this pricing rule, we assume that the market makers fully understand that the "order flow" they observe comprises both informed trading and

8. A better definition is one by which V_t is replaced with the net order flow (buy *minus* sell orders). However, net order flow seems to be more difficult to estimate than gross order flows.

noise. But similarly as in the Glosten and Milgrom (1985) model, they cannot disentangle the two components. Therefore, liquidity traders bear an adverse selection cost: the order flow has a price impact, such that liquidity traders will buy (sell) at higher (lower) price than the fundamental value, controlling for the informed trading. A price impact actually exists because the market makers understand that there might be informed traders.

Kyle (1985) solves for the equilibrium of this game and shows that the price impact and hence liquidity conditions relate to the information asymmetry between traders and dealers. Sections 10.8.1 analyzes the static, baseline version of his model. Section 10.8.2 reviews extensions of this model to deal with the presence of multiple traders, heterogeneous private information, information networks, or multiple dealers. Section 10.8.3 analyzes and discusses dynamic extensions of the baseline model and explains the model implications in terms of trading patterns and general market behavior. Finally, sections 10.8.4 and 10.8.5 deal with issues regarding market polarization and markets in which insiders are required to disclose their trades.

10.8.1 Kyle's Baseline Model

Kyle (1985) considers a market in which prices are determined in a *sequential equilibrium*, similar to the Glosten and Milgrom (1985) market. An insider trader knows the value of the asset payoff, d, and submits their order, x. The market maker (many of them, actually) observes the aggregate order flow, defined as the sum of the insider trade and a liquidity shock, Z, that is, $y \equiv x + Z$. We assume that $d \sim N(\bar{d}, \sigma_d^2)$ and $Z \sim N(0, \sigma_z^2)$ and that fundamentals (d) and noise (Z) are independent. The insider and the market maker are both risk neutral.

Given the order flow they observe and perfect competition, the representative market maker sets the asset price according to semi-strong informational efficiency,

$$p = E(d|y). \tag{10.71}$$

Thus, in Glosten and Milgrom (1985), market makers set prices in advance of the orders they receive (but they are conditional on a buy or sell), and these orders can be either informed or uninformed. In Kyle (1985), market makers set the price on observing an order flow that comprises both uninformed and informed trades. Only the market maker observes the order flow.

We conjecture that the price is linear in the aggregate order flow,

$$p = \bar{d} + \lambda y, \tag{10.72}$$

where the coefficient, λ, known as "Kyle's lambda," measures the price impact of the order flow. In other words, its inverse, $1/\lambda$, is a measure of *market depth*, that is, the order flow that is needed to induce prices to change by one dollar. So because the order flow obviously contains liquidity shocks, the higher λ, the less liquid the market is. We shall determine the value of λ below as part of the equilibrium of the game between the informed trader and the market maker. Needless to mention, this coefficient is a measure of adverse selection in this model: a positive λ prevents the asset price to be equal to the fundamentals, $\bar{d}$.

The insider trader chooses their order size to maximize their profits while anticipating their price impact,

$$\max_x E\left((\tilde{d}-p)x \middle| \tilde{d}=d \right), \tag{10.73}$$

with the price p being as in eq. (10.72). This problem has an interior solution, and the first-order conditions lead to the following demand schedule:

$$x=\beta(d-\bar{d}), \quad \beta\equiv\frac{1}{2\lambda}. \tag{10.74}$$

That is, the insider trade is proportional to the informational advantage, $d-\bar{d}$, which is the difference between the insider's information about the asset payoff and the unconditional guess of the asset payoff, $\bar{d}$—the "fair value" of the asset. Naturally, the coefficient of proportionality, β, still has to be determined.

Regarding the market maker's beliefs, we have, by the projection theorem, that

$$p=E\left(d\middle| y\right)=\bar{d}+\frac{cov\,(d,y)}{var\,(y)}y=\bar{d}+\underbrace{\frac{\beta\sigma_d^2}{\beta^2\sigma_d^2+\sigma_z^2}}_{\equiv\lambda}\cdot y, \tag{10.75}$$

where the identity under the brackets follows by the conjecture made in (10.72).

To summarize, the equilibrium in this market is one in which the market maker sets the price p as in eq. (10.72), and the optimal trading size of the insider is given by x in eq. (10.74). The price impact, λ, in (10.72) and the trading aggressiveness coefficient, β, in (10.74), satisfy

$$\begin{cases} \beta &= \dfrac{1}{2\lambda} \\ \dfrac{1}{\lambda} &= \beta+\dfrac{\sigma_z^2}{\sigma_d^2}\dfrac{1}{\beta} \end{cases}. \tag{10.76}$$

The first condition says that when markets are deep (i.e., when the price impact λ is low), the price is obviously less likely to move against the insider, who will therefore trade aggressively on their informational advantage, $d-\bar{d}$. The second condition says that the market maker makes the markets deep both when the insider does not trade so aggressively on their information advantage (i.e., when β is low) and when they trade so aggressively that they reveal much of their information (i.e., when β is high). An equilibrium of this game is the solution to (10.76),

$$\beta=\frac{\sigma_z}{\sigma_d}, \quad \lambda=\frac{1}{2}\frac{\sigma_d}{\sigma_z}. \tag{10.77}$$

The insider trades more and more aggressively as liquidity trades become large (i.e., as σ_z becomes large) because it is easier to hide their information in this case. That is, the probability the order flow contains information decreases with σ_z, mitigating adverse selection and then leading the market maker to lower λ; the informed traders trade more aggressively as a result. Likewise, the insider's informational advantage increases with σ_d, leading the market maker to raise the adverse selection costs λ and the insider to trade less aggressively.

Price discovery leads to halving the initial uncertainty about the asset payoff,

$$var\left(d\middle|\,p\right)=\sigma_d^2-\frac{cov^2\left(d,p\right)}{var\left(p\right)}=\frac{1}{2}\sigma_d^2, \tag{10.78}$$

where the first equality follows by the projection theorem and the second by a direct calculation.

Finally, the expected profits to the trader are, unconditionally,

$$E\left(\left(d-p\right)x\right)=\frac{1}{2}\sigma_z\sigma_d.$$

They increase with the insider's informational advantage, measured by σ_d, and with the insider's ability to hide their orders, measured by σ_z.

10.8.2 Markets with Multiple Traders and Dealers

We consider four extensions of the Kyle baseline model: one where there are multiple insiders with the same information; a second where insiders have differential information; a third where differential information may be studied within a context of information networks; and a fourth where there are multiple dealers.

10.8.2.1 Identical private information

When N traders observe the asset payoff, the market maker will see an order flow equal to $y\equiv Nx+Z$ and will set the price as in eq. (10.71). We still conjecture that this price is linear in y as in eq. (10.72) and search for a symmetric equilibrium, that is, an equilibrium in which each insider trades on their information advantage according to

$$x=\beta(d-\bar{d}). \tag{10.79}$$

Note that while formulating their trading rule, each insider now knows that they will have a price impact but that the other agents will have price impact too. A Cournot-Nash equilibrium is one in which (i) each trader formulates their optimal trading decision while taking the trading rules adopted by their peers as being as in (10.79) and (ii) still finds (10.79) as being optimal. The reason this market is referred to as being Cournotian is because it parallels the Cournot (1838) model in industrial organization where a finite number of firms compete for the same product[9] (and, hence, the same price) and act by maximizing their profits based on "residual demands," just as in the model of this section. Naturally, traders formulate their strategies while also conjecturing that the market maker bases their inference on the aggregate order flow, as explained.

Each trader maximizes their expected profits as follows:

$$\max_x E\left((\tilde{d}-p)x\middle|\,\tilde{d}=d\right),\quad p=\bar{d}+\lambda\cdot\left((N-1)\,\beta(d-\bar{d})+x+Z\right),$$

9. Chamberlin's (1933) model of monopolistic competition deals with markets in which firms compete for products that have imperfect substitutes.

leading to the following first-order conditions,

$$x = \underbrace{\frac{1-\lambda(N-1)\beta}{2\lambda}}_{\equiv\beta}(d-\bar{d}),$$

where the identity under the brackets follows by the conjecture made in eq. (10.79). That is,

$$\beta = \frac{1}{(N+1)\lambda}, \tag{10.80}$$

and one determines λ similar to (10.75),

$$\lambda = \frac{cov(d, Nx+Z)}{var(Nx+Z)} = \frac{N\beta\sigma_d^2}{N^2\beta^2\sigma_d^2+\sigma_z^2}. \tag{10.81}$$

The solution to eqs. (10.80) and (10.81) is

$$\beta = \frac{1}{\sqrt{N}}\frac{\sigma_z}{\sigma_d}, \quad \lambda = \frac{\sqrt{N}}{N+1}\frac{\sigma_d}{\sigma_z}. \tag{10.82}$$

The interpretation regarding the effects of σ_z and σ_d on strategies and pricing is the same as in the previous section. Regarding N, note that in the market of this section, traders trade less aggressively as their number increases. The reason is that the overall price impact of information is $\lambda N\beta = \frac{N}{N+1}$, which is increasing in N, making the probability of an informed trade increasing in N as well. Intuitively, then, as more traders trade on the same information, prices move more against them, which leads each trader to be less aggressive. Note, however, that markets become more liquid with N as the expression for λ in (10.82) suggests.

Further, note that while each trader trades less aggressively than in the baseline case where $N=1$ (see eqs. (10.77)), price discovery improves as N increases as a simple calculation reveals:

$$var(d|p) = \sigma_d^2 - \frac{cov^2(d,p)}{var(p)} = \frac{1}{N+1}\sigma_d^2.$$

Finally, competition among traders leads them to experience lower profits as their number increases,

$$E((d-p)x) = \frac{1}{\sqrt{N}(N+1)}\sigma_d\sigma_z.$$

We now explain that some of these properties do not hold in markets where traders have heterogeneous information.

10.8.2.2 *Heterogeneity in private information*

We now assume that each trader i observes a different signal s^i and that each s^i is as in eq. (10.11). The aggregate order flow is now $y \equiv \sum_{i=1}^N x_i + Z$, where each trader's demand x_i reflects their own informational advantage against the market maker. Below, we shall formulate conjectures about how this informational advantage is reflected in the trader's strategy (see eq. (10.84)). We will initially focus on explaining the gaming of this market with heterogeneous information.

First, as usual, market making makes the price semi-strong informationally efficient, just as in eq. (10.71). Second, we conjecture that this price is linear in y as in eq. (10.72). Third, we analyze this market as being a Cournot-Nash one as in the previous section: each trader trades so as to maximize their expected profits given the trading strategies of the other players and the market maker's inference. Finally, we search for a symmetric equilibrium. So, each trader maximizes their expected profits as follows:

$$\max_{x_i} E((\tilde{d}-p)x_i|s^i), \quad p=\bar{d}+\lambda\cdot\left(\sum_{j\neq i} x_j+x_i+Z\right).$$

It is instructive to analyze the first-order conditions of this problem,

$$0=E(\tilde{d}-\bar{d}|s^i)-\lambda\sum_{j\neq i} E\left(x_j\middle|\, s^i\right)-2\lambda x_i. \tag{10.83}$$

Note that while determining the optimal asset demand x_i, each agent needs to forecast the demand of their peers given the information they have access to (that is, they are determining $E\left(x_j\middle|\, s^i\right)$) while at the same time fully understanding that their peers are doing exactly the same in that x_j reflects agent j's expectation of agent i's (plus all other agents') expectations, given s^j. Forecasting the forecasts of others leads to an "infinite regress" problem where agents end up making conjectures about the conjectures others are making about them, ad infinitum.

There is no guarantee that a fixed point exists to this reasoning. However, in a linear equilibrium, a solution exists and is easy to describe. Conjecture that each agent trades on their informational advantage according to

$$x_i=\beta\left(s^i-\bar{d}\right). \tag{10.84}$$

Then, each agent's forecasts of the forecasts of others simplifies: traders now simply need to forecast the signals and then the informational advantage of their peers, $E\left(x_j\middle|\, s^i\right)=\beta E(s^j-\bar{d}|s^i)$. Therefore, in this linear equilibrium, each agent i can determine their optimal demand from the first-order conditions (10.83) as follows:

$$x_i=\frac{E\left(d-\bar{d}\middle|\, s^i\right)-\lambda\beta\,(N-1)\,E\left(s^1-\bar{d}\middle|\, s^i\right)}{2\lambda}=\underbrace{\frac{\rho\,(1-\lambda\beta\,(N-1))}{2\lambda}}_{\equiv\beta}\left(s^i-\bar{d}\right) \tag{10.85}$$

where we have used the conjecture that each agent trades according to (10.84) and the symmetry $E\left(x_j\middle|\, s^i\right)=\beta E(s^1-\bar{d}|s^i)$ for each j; the second equality follows because by the projection theorem,

$$E\left(d-\bar{d}\middle|\, s^i\right)=E\left(s^1-\bar{d}\middle|\, s^i\right)=\underbrace{\frac{\sigma_d^2}{\sigma_d^2+\sigma_u^2}}_{\equiv\rho}\left(s^i-\bar{d}\right); \tag{10.86}$$

and finally, the identity under the brackets in (10.85) follows by the conjecture made in eq. (10.84).

Note that eq. (10.86) says that the slope regression estimates of dividends and signals are the same and equal to ρ. Moreover, ρ is also the correlation coefficient between the signals traders have access to. The model collapses to the identical information market in the previous section once $\sigma_u^2 = 0$, that is, $\rho = 1$.

By eq. (10.85),

$$\beta = \frac{\rho}{\lambda\left(2 + \rho\left(N - 1\right)\right)}, \tag{10.87}$$

and regarding the price impact, appendix 10.B shows that

$$\lambda = \frac{cov\left(d, y\right)}{var\left(y\right)} = \frac{N\beta\rho\sigma_d^2}{N\beta^2\sigma_d^2\left(1 + \left(N - 1\right)\rho\right) + \rho\sigma_z^2}, \tag{10.88}$$

such that

$$\beta = \sqrt{\frac{\rho}{N}}\frac{\sigma_z}{\sigma_d}, \quad \lambda = \frac{\sqrt{\rho N}}{2 + \left(N - 1\right)\rho}\frac{\sigma_d}{\sigma_z}. \tag{10.89}$$

In equilibrium, trading aggressiveness, β, increases with the correlation of the traders' signals. Intuitively, in this model, the signals the traders observe become less and less correlated as their quality deteriorates,

$$\rho = \frac{n}{1 + n},$$

where $n = \frac{\sigma_d^2}{\sigma_u^2}$ is a measure of the signals quality. That is, as the noise component increases (i.e., σ_u^2 increases), each trader has access to more and more idiosyncratic, albeit noisy, pieces of information. Each trader then trades less aggressively as their signal becomes less precise.[10]

The price impact in (10.89), λ, is increasing in ρ, provided N is small enough. The mechanism is the following. The market maker anticipates that an increase in the quality of the traders' information (reflected by a higher ρ) results in a more informative trading, making adverse selection more severe—λ increases with ρ as a result. In other words, market makers have few traders (N is small), who in addition are equipped with high quality information, and λ increases with ρ as a result. Note that when N is large, λ can be decreasing in ρ provided the latter is large enough. The reason is that as N increases, the order flow becomes more informative (as $N\beta$ is increasing in N)—informed traders are then "revealing their presence," and an increase in ρ would make their presence revealed even more, so to speak: adverse selection costs lower as a result.

10. In section 10.8.3, we discuss alternative signals' structures such that a decrease in correlation does not necessarily imply less precise signals but an increase in monopolistic information power.

Price discovery deteriorates as the correlation decreases as it can be easily verified that

$$var(d|p) = \sigma_d^2 - \frac{cov^2(d,p)}{var(p)} = \frac{2-\rho}{2+(N-1)\rho}\sigma_d^2.$$

Finally, appendix 10.B shows that the expected profits for each trader i are

$$E((d-p)x_i) = \sqrt{\frac{\rho}{N}}\frac{1}{2+(N-1)\rho}\sigma_d\sigma_z. \tag{10.90}$$

When N is small, expected profits increase as ρ increases, reflecting the fact that agents observe signals with better quality. As N increases, the expected profits might actually fall with ρ when ρ is sufficiently high, reflecting a lower (ex post) informational advantage as explained earlier while commenting on λ in (10.89).

10.8.2.3 *Information networks*

The information structure in the previous section may conveniently be relied on to build models of information networks. An information network is an information structure where traders may share pieces of information. Some traders may share more information, and others may share less information. The network defines the granularity of the architecture underlying these types of information-sharing relationships among traders.

Colla and Mele (2010) consider a model with a "circular" information network. Two traders are geographically connected when they have access to the same information linkages. Assuming that traders and linkages are placed on a circle, traders then form an information network: the closer they are, the more linkages they share. Eventually, it may be that two "distant traders" have no common information linkages at all. However, in other cases, some traders may still share some information even if they are unable to access the signals available at the location of each other: the reason is that such traders may have access to information linkages even while these linkages are not available at their own location. This property is reminiscent of the "small worlds" phenomenon in the network literature (see, e.g., Watts and Strogatz, 1998): highly clustered networks may exhibit the property that its nodes (the traders, in this model) have a low average distance. Colla and Mele show that markets with such networks feature higher volume and better price discovery.

Ozsoylev (2006) is a paper contemporaneous with Colla and Mele's article and analyzes networks when traders have no market power. The information network literature has developed quite extensively, and Ozsoylev and Walden (2011) and Ozsoylev, Walden, Yavuz, and Bildik (2014) are also early references to theoretical work in this area. Goyal (2007) and Jackson (2008) provide early surveys of the literature on the broader area of the economics of networks.

10.8.2.4 *Multiple dealers*

Kyle (1989) considers a model in which uninformed and informed traders coexist and act strategically. Foucault, Pagano, and Röell (2013) consider a simplified version of this model where all traders are risk neutral and the "uninformed" traders are interpreted as "dealers." These dealers compete through a call auction mechanism, leading to an equilibrium price such that the dealers make profits on average. As in Kyle (1985), the order flow is $y = \sum_{i=1}^{N} x_i + Z$ but, in the presence of M dealers acting in an imperfectly competitive market,

$$y = \sum_{j=1}^{M} y_j(p), \tag{10.91}$$

where $y_j(p)$ is the supply schedule submitted by dealer j, a function of the price. The auctioneer sets a price such that the demand schedules of the dealers sum up to the order flow.

Each dealer j maximizes their expected profits taking the other dealers (and the informed traders) actions as given as in a Cournot-Nash market,

$$\max_{y_j} E\left(\left(p-d\right) y_j \middle| y\right), \tag{10.92}$$

and one constraint that takes into account the nature of imperfect competition among dealers as we now explain.

Assume that the other dealers supply schedules are, for each i,

$$y_i(p) = \gamma\left(p - \bar{d}\right), \quad i \neq j, \tag{10.93}$$

for some γ to be determined in the equilibrium of the game. The meaning of y_i is that dealer i sells if $y_i > 0$ and buys if $y_i < 0$. Replacing eq. (10.93) into eq. (10.91) leaves the residual demand function for any dealer j,

$$p = \bar{d} + \frac{y - y_j}{\gamma (M-1)}. \tag{10.94}$$

The maximization problem faced by each dealer j is therefore that in (10.92) under the constraint (10.94). The solution is

$$y_j = \frac{1}{2}\left(y - \gamma (M-1)\left(E\left(d \middle| y\right) - \bar{d}\right)\right) = \frac{1}{2}\left(1 - \gamma (M-1)\lambda\right) y \tag{10.95}$$

where the last equality follows by the projection theorem and, as usual, assuming for simplicity a single insider trader,

$$\lambda = \frac{cov\left(d, \beta(d-\bar{d}) + Z\right)}{var\left(\beta(d-\bar{d}) + Z\right)} = \frac{\beta\sigma_d^2}{\beta^2\sigma_d^2 + \sigma_z^2}. \tag{10.96}$$

The previous expression is the same as the usual Kyle lambda (see eq. (10.75)), although it is not the price impact in this model unless M is large.

We determine γ in eq. (10.93), and then we search for an equilibrium price by solving eq. (10.91). First, eliminate y from eq. (10.94) and eq. (10.95), such that

$$y_j(p) \equiv \underbrace{\frac{\left(1 - \gamma (M-1)\lambda\right)\gamma (M-1)}{1 + \gamma (M-1)\lambda}}_{\equiv \gamma} \left(p - \bar{d}\right)$$

where the identity under the brackets follows by the conjecture made in eq. (10.93). Therefore,

$$\gamma = \frac{M-2}{\lambda M(M-1)}. \tag{10.97}$$

Finally, eq. (10.91), eq. (10.93), and eq. (10.97) imply that the equilibrium price is

$$p = \bar{d} + \bar{\lambda} y, \quad \bar{\lambda} = \frac{M-1}{M-2}\lambda, \quad M > 2. \tag{10.98}$$

To determine the overall equilibrium, we need to determine β in (10.96) and then $\bar{\lambda}$ in eq. (10.98). The usual maximization problem of the insider trader leads to

$$\beta = \frac{1}{2\bar{\lambda}}. \tag{10.99}$$

Eq. (10.96) and eq. (10.99) imply that

$$\beta = \sqrt{\frac{M-2}{M}}\frac{\sigma_z}{\sigma_d}, \quad \bar{\lambda} = \frac{1}{2}\sqrt{\frac{M}{M-2}}\frac{\sigma_d}{\sigma_z}. \tag{10.100}$$

Dealers' market power makes asset markets less deep than in the perfect competition case of Kyle (1985) because the price impact, $\bar{\lambda}$, is decreasing in M as (10.100) reveals. Price discovery converges to that in Kyle (1985) (see eq. (10.78)) only for large M,

$$var(d|p) = \frac{1}{2}\frac{M}{M-1}\sigma_d^2.$$

Intuitively, the insider trades less in the perfectly competitive case (see (10.74)) than in the imperfectly competitive case (see (10.99)).

Finally, the expected profits to the insider trader are

$$E((d-p)x) = \frac{1}{2}\sqrt{\frac{M-2}{M}}\sigma_z\sigma_d$$

and are increasing in the number of dealers M, converging to the perfectly competitive case as M gets large.

10.8.3 Dynamic Markets

10.8.3.1 Positions in discrete time

Consider an asset that pays off a dividend d at some future point in time. The asset can be traded in N distinct periods before the dividend is paid off. A trader's cumulative *position* at the end of the trading period is $\theta_N = \sum_{i=1}^{N} \Delta x_i$, where Δx_i denotes the position in the asset at the trading period i (these positions are not part of a self-financed strategy). The trader's final profit is

$$\tilde{J} \equiv \theta_N d - S,$$

where $S \equiv \sum_{i=1}^{N} \Delta x_i p_i$ denotes the sum of the values of all the positions over the trading period. Therefore,

$$\tilde{J} = \sum_{i=1}^{N} (d - p_i)\,\Delta x_i. \tag{10.101}$$

Below, we shall utilize the continuous time counterpart to this expression while reviewing a dynamic extension of the Kyle model.

10.8.3.2 *Monopolistic trader*

How does the insider trader dilute information when allowed to trade over different batch auctions? We analyze the continuous time version of Kyle's model, in which trading occurs over a finite horizon fixed to $[0,1]$. As in the baseline market, the insider trades based on the available information, and the market maker (many of them, actually) updates their beliefs regarding the fundamental asset value d, based on their observation of the aggregate order flow.

The aggregate cumulative orders at any $t\in[0,1]$, y_t say, comprise two components: (i) the insider's cumulative demand, $x_t\equiv\int_0^t\theta_\tau d\tau$, and (ii) the cumulative orders by the liquidity traders, $\sigma_z Z_t$, where σ_z is a constant and Z_t is a standard Brownian motion. Therefore, $y_t=x_t+\sigma_z Z_t$, such that the aggregate order flow satisfies

$$dy_t=\theta_t dt+\sigma_z dZ_t. \tag{10.102}$$

The market maker does not make any profits while they set the price according to the semi-strong efficiency rule paralleling that in eq. (10.71),

$$p_t=E\left(d\middle|\,(y_\tau)_{\tau\in[0,t]}\right). \tag{10.103}$$

The insider trader maximizes their expected gains from trade, the continuous time version of $\tilde{J}$ in eq. (10.101):

$$J(t,p_t)|_{t=0}\equiv\max_{(\theta_t)_{t\in[0,1]}} E\left(\int_0^1(\tilde{d}-p_t)\theta_t dt\middle|\,\tilde{d}=d\right). \tag{10.104}$$

Motivated by the market behavior in the static setting of the previous sections, we conjecture that the optimal trading strategy in (10.104) is

$$\theta_t=\beta_t\left(d-p_t\right) \tag{10.105}$$

for some deterministic function β_t, such that the order flow in eq. (10.102) can be written as

$$dy_t=\beta_t\left(d-p_t\right)dt+\sigma_z dZ_t. \tag{10.106}$$

To determine the dynamics of the price in eq. (10.103), note heuristically that

$$\begin{aligned}
p_{t+dt}&=E\left(d\middle|\,(y_\tau)_{\tau\in[0,t]},y_{t+dt}-y_t\right)\\
&=E\left(d\middle|\,(y_\tau)_{\tau\in[0,t]}\right)+\frac{cov(d,y_{t+dt}-y_t|\,(y_\tau)_{\tau\in[0,t]})}{var(y_{t+dt}-y_t|\,(y_\tau)_{\tau\in[0,t]})}\left(y_{t+dt}-y_t\right)\\
&=p_t+\frac{\beta_t\Sigma_t dt}{\beta_t^2\Sigma_t dt^2+\sigma_z^2 dt}\left(y_{t+dt}-y_t\right),
\end{aligned} \tag{10.107}$$

where the second equality follows by the projection theorem, and the third by eq. (10.103) and eq. (10.106) and by the following definition of "residual variance,"

$$\Sigma_t \equiv E\left((d - p_t)^2 \Big| (y_\tau)_{\tau\in[0,t]} \right). \tag{10.108}$$

The residual variance, Σ_t, can be interpreted as a gauge of informational efficiency or price discovery process, that is, the market maker's inference about the asset payoff. We shall see that, in equilibrium, price discovery will be complete in that $\lim_{t\to 1} \Sigma_t = 0$.

In the limit, disregarding dt^2 terms, the price in (10.107) satisfies

$$dp_t = \lambda_t dy_t, \quad \lambda_t = \frac{\beta_t \Sigma_t}{\sigma_z^2}. \tag{10.109}$$

We now determine λ_t and Σ_t, and then use (10.109) to determine β_t, thereby having determined the trading strategy θ_t in eq. (10.105). Later, we shall verify that the determined strategy is indeed optimal. Regarding Σ_t, suppose that dy_t becomes available over the time interval dt. Then,

$$\begin{aligned}
\Sigma_{t+dt} &= E\left((d - p_t)^2 \Big| (y_\tau)_{\tau\in[0,t+dt]} \right) \\
&= E\left((d - p_t)^2 \Big| (y_\tau)_{\tau\in[0,t]} \right) - \frac{cov^2(d, y_{t+dt} - y_t | (y_\tau)_{\tau\in[0,t]})}{var(y_{t+dt} - y_t | (y_\tau)_{\tau\in[0,t]})} \\
&= \Sigma_t - \frac{\beta_t^2 \Sigma_t^2 dt^2}{\beta_t^2 \Sigma_t dt^2 + \sigma_z^2 dt} \\
&= \Sigma_t - \frac{\beta_t^2 \Sigma_t^2}{\sigma_z^2} dt,
\end{aligned}$$

such that in the limit, by the expression for λ_t in (10.109),

$$d\Sigma_t = -\lambda_t^2 \sigma_z^2 dt. \tag{10.110}$$

We conjecture that $\lambda_t = \lambda$, a constant, and that the equilibrium trading strategy in (10.105) leads to a complete price discovery process, $\lim_{t\to 1} \Sigma_t = 0$. Integrating eq. (10.110) and using the condition $\Sigma_0 = \sigma_d^2$ leaves $\Sigma_t = \sigma_d^2 - \lambda^2 \sigma_z^2 t$, and by the conjecture that $\Sigma_1 = 0$, we find that the price impact in (10.109) is

$$\lambda = \frac{\sigma_d}{\sigma_z} \tag{10.111}$$

and, accordingly,

$$\Sigma_t = \sigma_d^2 (1 - t). \tag{10.112}$$

That is, the pace of information revelation is constant in this market. Eqs. (10.111), (10.112), and (10.109) now imply that the trading aggressiveness in (10.105) is

$$\beta_t = \frac{1}{\lambda (1 - t)} = \frac{\sigma_z}{\sigma_d (1 - t)}. \tag{10.113}$$

Eqs. (10.111), (10.112), and (10.105) complete the description of the market equilibrium once we prove the trading strategy θ_t in eq. (10.105) is optimal with β_t as in (10.113). The proof proceeds in two steps. First, we show that the proposed θ_t leads the price process to converge to the fundamental d ("no money left on the table"), and second, we show that any strategy is optimal when it satisfies this property.

Regarding convergence to fundamental value, note that by replacing (10.102) into (10.109) and using the expressions for θ_t in (10.105) and the expressions for λ and β_t in (10.111) and (10.113),

$$dp_t = \frac{d - p_t}{1-t} dt + \sigma_d dZ_t. \tag{10.114}$$

Now, by Karatzas and Shreve (1991, 350–360), the process $W_t = \frac{p_t - \bar{d}}{\sigma_d}$ is a Brownian bridge from 0 to $\frac{d-\bar{d}}{\sigma_d}$, meaning that $W_0 = 0$ and $W_1 = \frac{d-\bar{d}}{\sigma_d}$. The latter equality implies that $p_1 = d$;[11] that is, the price is a Brownian bridge under the insider's information, although the end point of it is unknown to the market maker.

Regarding the previous convergence property as being one of the optimal trading strategies, consider the following Hamilton-Jacobi-Bellman equation satisfied by $J(t, p_t)$ in eq. (10.104),

$$0 = \max_{\theta_t} E_t\left(\left(d - p_t\right)\theta_t + J_t\left(t, p_t\right) + J_p\left(t, p_t\right)\lambda\theta_t + \frac{1}{2} J_{pp}\left(t, p_t\right)\lambda^2\sigma_z^2\right), \tag{10.115}$$

where the expectation is taken conditional on the price (and d) and where we have used $dp_t = \lambda dy_t$ and the expression of (10.102) for dy_t. As originally noted by Back (1992), the maximand in (10.115) is linear in θ_t such that the terms multiplying θ_t must sum up to zero, with the remaining terms summing up to zero as well, namely,

$$\begin{cases} d - p + J_p\lambda = 0 \\ J_t + \frac{1}{2} J_{pp}\lambda^2\sigma_z^2 = 0 \end{cases}. \tag{10.116}$$

Eqs. (10.116) and the boundary condition $J(1, p_1) = 0$ lead to the following expression for the value function in (10.104),

$$J(t, p_t) = \frac{1}{2\lambda}\left(d - p_t\right)^2 + \frac{1}{2}\lambda\sigma_z^2(1-t). \tag{10.117}$$

Indeed, we will argue that $J(1, p_1) = 0$ in a moment. Consider the value function in (10.104) for *any* θ_t, say $J^\theta(t, p_t)$. By Itô's lemma,

$$dJ^\theta = \left(LJ^\theta\right) dt + J_p^\theta \lambda_t \sigma_z dZ_t,$$

11. Note that the insider's cumulative orders x_t are bounded in probability as a result of this convergence. Indeed, by the definition of W_t, we have that $\sigma_d W_t = p_t - \bar{d} = \lambda\left(x_t + \sigma_z Z_t\right)$: boundedness in probability of W_t and Z_t implies that of x_t.

where LJ^{θ} denotes the usual infinitesimal generator, which by eq. (10.104) satisfies $0 = LJ^{\theta} + (d-p)\,\theta$. Therefore,

$$L_{\theta} \equiv E\left(\int_0^1 (\tilde{d}-p_t)\theta_t dt \middle| \tilde{d}=d\right) = J^{\theta}\,(0,p_0) - E\left(J^{\theta}\,(1,p_1)\right).$$

Note that by evaluating eq. (10.117) at $t=1$, we conclude that $J\,(1,p_1) = \frac{1}{2\lambda}\,(d-p_1)^2 \geq 0$. This means that for an optimal strategy $\hat{\theta}$ we have that $L_{\hat{\theta}} = J^{\hat{\theta}}\,(0,p_0) - E(J^{\hat{\theta}}\,(1,p_1)) \leq J^{\hat{\theta}}\,(0,p_0)$ and therefore that $E(J^{\hat{\theta}}\,(1,p_1)) = 0$; because $J\,(1,p_1) \geq 0$, it follows that $J\,(1,p_1) = 0$, that is, $p_1 = d$.

10.8.3.3 *Imperfectly competitive traders*

Foster and Viswanathan (1996) generalize the dynamic market of Kyle (1985) by relying on a discrete time setting with multiple traders (N, say), and a general correlation structure of the signals (still assumed to be Gaussian). They assume that each trader observes a signal correlated with the asset payoff, which has variance Λ_0, and that any two signals have the same correlation equal to $\rho \equiv \frac{\Omega_0}{\Lambda_0}$.[12]

One leading example of signals in this setting is the "exhaustive information structure," arising when the sum of all signals is the truth, that is, in a hypothetical market where all traders would form a "mega" Kyle trader upon information collusion, $d = \sum_{i=1}^{N} s^i$, where s^i is the signal available to trader i. It is immediate to verify that, for each i,

$$cov\,(s_i, d) = \Lambda_0 + (N-1)\,\Omega_0,$$

and that the variance of the asset payoff is

$$\sigma_d^2 = N\Lambda_0 + N\,(N-1)\,\rho\Lambda_0. \tag{10.118}$$

Eq. (10.118) can be inverted for ρ, leaving, for all i, j,

$$cov\,(s_i, s_j) \equiv \rho = \frac{1}{N\,(N-1)}\left(\frac{\sigma_d^2}{\Lambda_0} - N\right).$$

The correlation coefficient ρ is a measure of monopolistic information power among traders. The lower ρ, the more "unique" a signal is to each trader—and the higher the monopolistic power. Foster and Viswanathan (1996) show, numerically, that in a dynamic context, traders engage in a *rat race* once ρ is high: because traders have comparable information, they trade very aggressively since the beginning of the trading period to preempt being anticipated by others but then revealing virtually all their information over the first trading rounds. In fact, Back, Cao, and Willard (2000) consider a continuous time model along the same lines and conclude that an equilibrium fails to exist when $\rho = 1$ due to this behavior.

12. The variance-covariance matrix of the signals available to all traders is then invertible, provided $\Lambda_0 > -(N-1)\,\Omega_0$.

However, when ρ is small and the degree of monopolistic information power is high as a result, traders engage in a *waiting game*, trading little at the beginning of the trading period and aggressively toward the conclusion. These trading patterns lead to a price discovery process, which occurs at a slow pace at the beginning of the trading period and at a high pace at the end. These patterns of price discovery process cannot be generated by the constant information flow predicted by the single insider trader's model of Kyle (1985) as summarized by eq. (10.112).

10.8.4 Gravitational Pull Problems

A *chicken-and-egg problem* arises when the success of a market builds on the existence of a critical mass of users. Thus, the success of LinkedIn relies on the fact that many individuals and companies rely on it (among many other means) for the purpose of networking. Likewise, a market for a financial product is likely to be a success when it is liquid: a market with higher liquidity is likely to attract more traders, thereby making the market even more liquid over a virtuous circle. Alternatively, the circle may be vicious: a market with lower liquidity may remain as such because it is deserted by market participants in a self-reinforcing mechanism. Problems of this type were studied by, among others, Mendelson (1987), Pagano (1989), or Chowdhry and Nanda (1991) and are reviewed in great detail and simplified by Foucault, Pagano, and Röell (2013, chapter 7). This section relies on these simplified explanations to illustrate the previous self-reinforcing mechanisms.

Section 10.8.4.1 analyzes a simple model in which trading occurs in different venues. Trading venues are "fragmented" in that liquidity motivated trades are specific to each of these two venues. Despite the presence of an informed trader who is active in both markets, market fragmentation leads to price dispersion, that is, the circumstance by which the same asset can be traded at different prices. Naturally, price dispersion does not lead to any arbitrage opportunity: market fragmentation is, instead, a simple example of "limit of arbitrage." Section 10.9 provides a more systematic treatment of these topics. Section 10.8.4.2 considers a simple extension of this model, in which liquidity traders may choose which market to place their orders at. Section 10.8.4.3 interprets this model as one explaining motives for the adoption of a new financial product.

10.8.4.1 Market fragmentation

Consider a "fragmented" market for a risky security that pays off $\tilde{d} \sim N(\bar{d}, \sigma_d^2)$. The market is fragmented in that the security is traded in two venues, a and b, with liquidity traders being captive customers in one of these two venues. Let $z_a \sim N(0, \sigma_{za}^2)$ and $z_b \sim N(0, \sigma_{zb}^2)$ denote the demands of the liquidity traders in market a and in market b. Assume that all variables are independently distributed. A risk neutral trader (the "informed trader") knows the realization of $\tilde{d}$ and is able to simultaneously trade on both markets, placing an order x_a in market a and an order x_b in market b. This trader understands that their trade has a price impact, just as in the Kyle's model and his extensions. In each market, a market maker sets the price according to the semi-strong efficiency rule, and the informed trader understands that they have price impact.

A linear equilibrium in this fragmented market is given by two price functions (one for each market), $p_j = \bar{d} + \lambda_j (z_j + x_j)$, $j \in \{a, b\}$, for two constants λ_a and λ_b (the inverse of the two market depths), such that (x_a, x_b) maximize the informed trader's expected profits. Thus, in analogy with the objective function in the Kyle baseline model (see eq. (10.73) in section 10.8.1), the informed trader maximizes the following expected profits:

$$\max_{(x_a, x_b)} E\left((\tilde{d} - p_a)x_a + (\tilde{d} - p_b)x_b \middle| \tilde{d} = d \right).$$

The solution for the trade in each market is the same as the standard solution in Kyle's model (see eq. (10.74) and eq. (10.77)), that is, $x_j = (d - \bar{d})/2\lambda_j$, where

$$\lambda_j = \frac{1}{2}\frac{\sigma_d}{\sigma_{zj}}, \quad j \in \{a, b\}. \tag{10.119}$$

That is, the market is more liquid where σ_{zj}^2 is larger. The reasons underlying this conclusion are, of course, the same as those put forward to explain market liquidity in section 10.8.1. Naturally, the prices in the two markets differ not only due to the market depth but also due to the realization of the liquidity-motivated trades, z_a and z_b.

How would these conclusions change in a "consolidated market"? Consider a market in which the liquidity trades z_a and z_b are concentrated, such that liquidity trading is $z_a + z_b$. In this market, the price would be just as in Kyle's model (see eq. (10.72)), with

$$\lambda = \frac{1}{2}\frac{\sigma_d}{\sigma_z}, \quad \sigma_z \equiv \sqrt{\sigma_{za}^2 + \sigma_{zb}^2}.$$

Therefore, $\lambda < \min\{\lambda_a, \lambda_b\}$: the consolidated market is more liquid than each of the segmented markets. It is natural: liquidity demand is obviously concentrated in a consolidated market, making the order flow less informative. It is well beyond the scope of this chapter to explain market quality trade-offs arising while comparing trading structures of different type. It is useful, however, to review an argument by which market fragmentation actually results into some benefits: competition among trading venues may naturally lead to lower transaction fees.

10.8.4.2 Polarization

In the previous model, liquidity traders are captive customers in each of the two trading venues. We now assume that there are M additional liquidity traders who have discretion in choosing where to trade: m_a of them choose to trade in market a and m_b choose to trade in market b. Each of these "discretionary" traders has demand $z_{oi} \sim N(0, \sigma_o^2)$, $i = 1, \cdots, m \equiv m_a + m_b$, such that in market j, the total demand of liquidity traders is $\sum_{i=1}^{m_j} z_{o_i} + z_j$, for $j \in \{a, b\}$; Admati and Pfleiderer (1988) is the first paper to develop a notion of "discretionary liquidity trading," although in the context of intra day market fragmentation.

Suppose then, initially, that the number of discretionary traders in each market is fixed. It is easy to see that eq. (10.119) generalizes to

$$\lambda_j = \frac{1}{2}\frac{\sigma_d}{\bar{\sigma}_{zj}}, \quad \bar{\sigma}_{zj} \equiv \sqrt{m_j \sigma_o^2 + \sigma_{zj}^2}, \quad j \in \{a, b\}.$$

Now, suppose that, given m_j, market a is more liquid than b, that is, $\bar{\sigma}_{za} > \bar{\sigma}_{zb}$: discretionary traders in market b are incentivized to move to market a. As these traders migrate, market a becomes even deeper over a virtuous circle; but, to this virtuous circle in market a corresponds a vicious circle in market b. Eventually, all discretionary traders will move to market a, such that

$$\bar{\sigma}_{za} = \sqrt{m\sigma_o^2 + \sigma_{za}^2} > \sigma_{zb} = \bar{\sigma}_{zb}.$$

That is, the incentives for discretionary traders to move where liquidity is better result in market polarization: the depth of market b is only determined by the liquidity demand of the captive users in this market. Note that market polarization may arise even if the sizes of the captive liquidity users in each market are the same, $\sigma_{za} = \sigma_{zb}$. In this case, it would be sufficient that the initial number of discretionary traders m_a is only a bit larger than m_b to have all discretionary traders move to market a.

Note that it may well be the case that, without discretionary traders, market b is deeper than a, that is, $\sigma_{zb} > \sigma_{za}$. Yet, in the presence of discretionary traders, we would observe a "gravitational pull" toward market a if, initially, $\bar{\sigma}_{za} > \bar{\sigma}_{zb}$ as in the previous discussion. It is instructive to elaborate more on the case in which $\sigma_{zb} > \sigma_{za}$. In this case, the indifference condition under which discretionary traders in market b remain in this market is

$$\sigma_{zb}^2 - \sigma_{za}^2 = (m_a - m_b)\,\sigma_o^2.$$

No clusters occur if the captive demand in market b relative to a (the LHS of the previous equality) compensates for the higher discretionary demand in market a (the RHS). However, this equilibrium may be easily compromised: once again, clustering would be triggered should one single discretionary trader in market b move to a.

10.8.4.3 Market adoption of new products

"Liquidity-begets-liquidity" effects may help explain the reasons markets may fail or succeed in channeling financial innovation. Suppose that a new financial product is made available to trade. Call this new product—or its market—b. There may be many natural users of this product (a measure of its goodness) and maybe even more than the captive consumers of an old product that is already traded in the "old market," market a, say: thus, in principle, product b might receive higher demand than product a. In terms of the previous model, $\sigma_{zb} > \sigma_{za}$. Yet, this market may fail to arise if the discretionary traders in market b fail to coordinate toward the adoption of the new product, so as to lead to the inequality $\bar{\sigma}_{zb} > \bar{\sigma}_{za}$. Naturally, underlying this simple example is the assumptions that the new product is a perfect substitute of the old. However, the example helps highlight the role that liquidity clustering exerts in the process of financial innovation.

10.8.5 Mandatory Disclosure

In the aftermath of 1929, the Securities Exchange Act (SEA) of 1934 was created to ensure improved financial transparency and pricing accuracy in secondary markets and to mitigate investors' concerns on price or information manipulation in these markets. Insider trading should be an impediment to price efficiency due to the reasons reviewed in the previous sections. To illustrate, the market would evaluate assets at a discount or premium (according to the direction of the order flow) due to adverse selection. It is not surprising that securities laws try to mitigate some negative consequences of insider's trading. In practice, section 16(a) of the SEA requires that corporate insiders (directors, officers, and owners of at least 5 percent of equity securities) disclose their trades to the Securities and Exchange Commission within 10 days following the end of the month in which the trade occurs.[13]

How do such institutional details affect traders' behavior? Naturally, the Kyle baseline model cannot address this issue because its key feature is that traders don't disclose their trades. Huddart, Hughes, and Levine (2001) consider a model with disclosure where the informed traders' strategy is to add some noise (i.e., a randomly drawn buy or sell) to the asset demand related to the information these traders possess—a *mixed strategy*. A mixed strategy allows the insider trader to dissimulate their trade vis-à-vis the market maker, thereby still earning an information-related profit.

Consider a three-period market (the model may be extended to a multiperiod setting) where the insider trades at time 1 and time 2 and must disclose the trade at the close of the first trading round. We consider a second period of trading because, otherwise, the insider would disclose a trade that is perfectly revealing their information and the model would then collapse to the standard Kyle model; further, disclosure of time 2 trades is economically irrelevant because the asset pays off at time 3. Finally, we assume as usual that the payoff is some $\tilde{d} \sim N\left(\bar{d}, \sigma_d^2\right)$, and we denote noise trading at time $i = 1, 2$ as $Z_i \sim N\left(0, \sigma_z^2\right)$. Prices in all periods are set by the competitive market makers through the usual semi-strong efficiency rule: they are expectations of the asset payoff taken conditionally on the relevant available information.

The timing of trading is as follows. At time 1, the insider trades x_1, and the market maker sets a price equal to $p_1 = E(\tilde{d} \mid y_1)$, where $y_1 = x_1 + Z_1$ denotes the time 1 order flow. After trading x_1, the trader discloses x_1, and the market maker updates their estimate of the asset payoff from p_1 to $p_1^* = E(\tilde{d} \mid x_1, y_1) = E(\tilde{d} \mid x_1)$ where the second equality follows because y_1 obviously provides coarser information on $\tilde{d}$ than x_1. In a linear equilibrium, provided it exists,

$$p_1 = \bar{d} + \lambda_1 y_1, \quad p_1^* = \bar{d} + \gamma x_1, \tag{10.120}$$

where λ_1 and γ are determined endogenously. At time 2, the insider trader trades x_2, and the order flow is $y_2 = x_2 + Z_2$. Now, the time 2 price is $p_2 = E(\tilde{d} \mid x_1, y_2)$. In a linear equilibrium, provided it exists,

$$p_2 = p_1^* + \lambda_2 y_2,$$

where λ_2 is determined endogenously.

The informed trader solves their intertemporal problem by backward induction. First, they take their trade x_1 as given and then determine their time 2 trade to maximize the

13. At the time of writing, following the Sarbanes-Oxley Act of 2002, disclosure must actually occur within two business days following the transaction.

second-period profits, namely,

$$\hat{x}_2 = \arg\max_{x_2} E\left((\tilde{d} - p_2)x_2 \middle| \tilde{d} = d \right) = \beta_2 \left(d - p_1^*\right), \quad \beta_2 = \frac{1}{2\lambda_2}. \tag{10.121}$$

Accordingly, their expected profits at time 2 are

$$\pi\left(p_1^*\right) \equiv E\left((\tilde{d} - p_2)\hat{x}_2 \middle| \tilde{d} = d \right) = \frac{(d - p_1^*)^2}{4\lambda_2},$$

where p_1^* is as in eq. (10.120) and is thus a function of x_1.

At time 1, the insider chooses their trade at time 1, x_1, while maximizing the expected profits at time 1 and also taking into account the "information leakage" onto the second period generated by mandatory disclosure,

$$\hat{x}_1 = \arg\max_{x_1} E\left((\tilde{d} - p_1)x_1 + \pi\left(p_1^*\right) \middle| \tilde{d} = d \right).$$

We conjecture and later verify that there exists an equilibrium in which

$$\hat{x}_1 = \beta_1\left(d - \bar{d}\right) + \eta, \quad \eta \sim N\left(0, \sigma_\eta^2\right), \tag{10.122}$$

where β_1 and σ_η^2 are determined endogenously. The first-order conditions yield $0 = (1 - \frac{1}{2}\frac{\gamma}{\lambda_2})\left(d - \bar{d}\right) + (\frac{1}{2}\frac{\gamma^2}{\lambda_2} - 2\lambda_1)x_1$. Substituting eq. (10.122) into this equation reveals that it must be that

$$\lambda_1 = \lambda_2 \equiv \lambda, \quad \gamma = 2\lambda.$$

To determine λ_2, note that

$$\lambda_2 = \frac{cov(\tilde{d}, y_2\,|x_1, y_1)}{var\left(y_2 \middle| x_1, y_1\right)} = \frac{cov(\tilde{d}, y_2\,|x_1)}{var\left(y_2 \middle| x_1\right)} = \frac{\beta_2\sigma_{d|x_1}^2}{\beta_2^2\sigma_{d|x_1}^2 + \sigma_z^2}, \tag{10.123}$$

where $\sigma_{d|x_1}^2 = var(\tilde{d}\,|x_1) = \frac{1}{2}\sigma_d^2$ (see appendix 10.B). Therefore, $\beta_2 = \frac{1}{2\lambda_2}$ in (10.121) and (10.123) can be solved for explicitly, just as in the baseline Kyle model (see eqs. (10.76)), leaving

$$\beta_2 = \frac{\sigma_z}{\sigma_{d|x_1}}, \quad \lambda_2 = \frac{1}{2}\frac{\sigma_{d|x_1}}{\sigma_z}.$$

Finally, appendix 10.B proves that $\beta_1 = \frac{1}{2}\beta_2$ and that the variance of the noise in the mixed strategy is $\sigma_\eta^2 = \beta_1^2\sigma_d^2$. Note then that the insider trader sets the total variance of the trade equal to the noise variance,

$$var(\hat{x}_1) = \sigma_z^2.$$

Moreover, it is possible to show that price discovery and other market quality variables improve with mandatory disclosure if compared with the Kyle case.

10.9 Limits of Arbitrage and Further Frictions

A basic principle in financial economics is that assets are priced in the absence of arbitrage: two assets with the same payoffs are therefore valued the same. Consider, for example, a firm listed in two different stock exchanges. Once accounting for transaction costs, the share prices of this firm in the two exchanges should be the same because cash flows to the firm's owner are the same, regardless of where ownership is originated. Indeed, the standard argument goes, suppose that a price difference exists. One may then buy the cheap security and sell the expensive, thereby monetizing a profit and afterward holding the two hedged positions forever. This very basic reasoning implies that the would-be arbitrageur has an infinite horizon and incurs negligible transaction costs. Arbitrage forces would then keep prices close to fundamental values. This section describes situations in which these assumptions and conclusions may not hold.

There is empirical evidence of violations of arbitrage laws, at least those laws that are predicted by the neoclassical models in part I. Famous examples are provided by Rosenthal and Young (1990) and Froot and Dabora (1999), who showed that a persistent mispricing existed between dual-listed companies such as Royal Dutch/Shell (incorporated in both the Netherlands and in the United Kingdom but listed in a variety of exchanges around the world). Such deviations do not seem to be confined to "twin stocks." Most recent examples regard deviations from parity in fixed income securities markets during the 2007–2009 crisis as documented by Mercurio (2009).[14]

This section develops models in the spirit of the early explanations for this type of pricing anomaly.[15] We develop models in which arbitrage forces are not strong enough because arbitrage activity is risky. In these models, an asset price may diverge from the asset's fundamental value because arbitrageurs have finite horizons and price reversals leading to profits may arrive too late. In the model of section 10.9.1, prices deviate from fundamentals because of erratic demand of irrational traders. These traders may be those who, for instance, pick up stocks without accurate research or sometimes trade on the basis of signals that they mistakenly believe affect asset valuation. The point of the model is that the resulting mispricing can be persistent. Section 10.9.2 adds a complication: it considers a model in which the arbitrageurs manage external investors' capital and are subject to the risk of redemption from these investors. The higher this risk, the higher the equilibrium mispricing. The risk of early redemption is a complication similar to that encountered in section 10.9.4, which we will comment on in a moment.

In section 10.9.3, we consider a dynamic model that tries to explain the extent to which market segmentation is mitigated by arbitrageurs. That is, in this model, the source of mispricing is market segmentation, a market imperfection resulting from reasons not necessarily related to irrationality. Fixed income markets *are* segmented. Pension funds are consumers of long-term products whereas other intermediaries may be potential consumers of relatively shorter segments of the yield curve. In the model, arbitrageurs are

14. Chapter 13 explains market practice on "multiple curves" that aims at dealing with these imperfections (see section 13.9).

15. Shleifer (2000) provides a survey of this early work.

not subject to funding constraints but have limited risk-bearing capacity—say, a VaR constraint that limits their activity.[16] Prices then would be affected by these constraints and may well fail to be aligned with fundamentals.[17]

Finally, section 10.9.4 provides an introduction to a very important theme: the fragility of the banking system. Banks typically borrow through short-term liabilities (deposits, say) and invest in long-term assets. This "maturity mismatch" may create incentives for agents to withdraw their deposits early, exposing banks to the risk of not honoring their obligations. This risk may lead to a "liquidity crisis," even while, in principle, banks would be perfectly solvent. It is a "liquidity crisis": the market dysfunctionality arises due to the fact that it is costly to sell a long-term asset (i.e., illiquidity).

10.9.1 A Simple Model of Risky Arbitrage

DeLong, Shleifer, Summers, and Waldman (1990) focus on "convergence risks" faced by the arbitrageurs. They consider an asset market that features overlapping generations of traders. The asset promises a trivial stream of deterministic cash flows, but its evaluation is affected by some traders, called "irrational," who change their demand from a period to another in a random fashion. The presence of these traders raises a number of issues. In a famous contribution, Friedman (1953) argued that the profits of the irrational traders, if any, would be eliminated because rational investing would bring prices to their fundamental values. Chapter 9 presents an infinite horizon model where this conclusion does not necessarily hold (see section 9.5.3).

The model in this section examines these questions in the more radical setting where rational traders have a *finite* investment horizon. Suppose that the irrational traders bid up the asset price. In principle, the rational traders may sell the asset because the price should converge sooner or later. However, there is no guarantee this convergence takes place over the rational traders' life spans. Rational traders may have limited life spans due to a variety of reasons. They may simply have received an investment mandate from other clients for a limited amount of time. The next section considers the risk of redemption a bit more in detail.

The asset that is traded is a simple coupon bearing bond, as anticipated: it pays the interest rate r in each period, in perpetuity. The ex-coupon fundamental value of this asset to an investor with infinite horizon would then be one.[18] Investors also have access to an

16. Chapter 9 explains the importance of such constraints in the context of balance sheet capacity and the credit cycle (see section 9.11). Chapter 14 reviews market practice around this and related risk management tools.

17. The literature has identified quite a few additional channels through which prices do not reflect or adjust to fundamentals. Duffie (2010) reviews the literature on "capital immobility," with investors only infrequently adjusting their portfolios, and focuses on investment inattention. Section 10.10 deals with search models; these models also capture forms of capital immobility and predict that prices adjust slowly after an initial over reaction to some shocks.

18. Chapter 3 contains an example of an OLG economy in which the price of a tree is $S_t = \frac{\beta}{1+\beta} w_{1t}$, where w_{1t} is the young generation endowment at time t and β is the impatience rate (see eq. (3.51)); that is, the price reflects the preferences of a short-sighted investor and is independent of the dividend that it pays. By contrast, we know very well that, in an infinite horizon setting and under standard assumptions, the price of a tree should reflect its current dividend. For example, chapter 7 explains

MMA that yields a return equal to r. All traders live for two periods; they trade, say, at time t and consume at time $t+1$. Both rational and irrational traders have exponential utility over their final consumption. The rational trader program, therefore, is

$$\hat{x}_{Rt} = \arg\max_{x_{Rt}} E_t\left(-e^{-\tau W_{t+1}}\right), \quad W_{t+1} = (W_0 - x_{Rt}p_t)\,R + x_{Rt}\,(r + p_{t+1}),$$

where p_t is the asset price at time t. We have

$$\hat{x}_{Rt} = \gamma \frac{E_t\,(p_{t+1}) + r - Rp_t}{var_t\,(p_{t+1})} \tag{10.124}$$

and $\gamma \equiv \tau^{-1}$, as usual.

The irrational investors have a misperception of the statistical laws underlying the asset price. Their demand is assumed to be

$$\hat{x}_{It} = \hat{x}_{Rt} + \gamma \frac{\rho_t}{var_t\,(p_{t+1})}, \tag{10.125}$$

where $\rho_t \sim N(\bar{\rho}, \sigma_\rho^2)$ for two constants $\bar{\rho}$ and σ_ρ^2, that is, noise unrelated to the fundamentals. When $\sigma_\rho^2 = 0$, the irrational investors are consistently biased; this bias will then be incorporated by the equilibrium price.

The market-clearing condition is

$$\lambda \hat{x}_{Rt} + (1-\lambda)\,\hat{x}_{It} = Z, \tag{10.126}$$

where Z is a constant and λ denotes the mass of the rational traders. We conjecture that the equilibrium price equals the fundamental value to an infinite-horizon investor, \$1, plus some terms reflecting the asset demand of the irrational traders,

$$p_t = 1 + \alpha + \beta(\rho_t - \bar{\rho}). \tag{10.127}$$

Under this conjecture, $E_t\,(p_{t+1}) = 1 + \alpha$ and $var_t\,(p_{t+1}) = \beta^2\sigma_\rho^2$. Replacing these expressions into eqs. (10.124) and (10.125) and then into the market-clearing condition (10.126) leaves a linear equation: $A + B\rho_t = 0$ for two constants A and B. Setting $A = B = 0$ delivers the following restrictions for the coefficients of the equilibrium price in (10.127),

$$\alpha = \frac{(1-\lambda)\,\bar{\rho} - \tau\beta^2\sigma_\rho^2 Z}{r}, \quad \beta = \frac{1-\lambda}{1+r}.$$

That is, the price equals the asset fundamental value only in the absence of the irrational investors, $\lambda = 1$. Note that when irrational investors are biased, $\sigma_\rho^2 = 0$, $\rho_t = \bar{\rho}$, and the equilibrium price collapses to $p_t = 1 + (1-\lambda)\,\bar{\rho}/r$ such that the sign of the mispricing is the same as the sign of $\bar{\rho}$.

---

that if dividends are log-normally distributed, $S_t = \frac{e^k}{1-e^k} D_t$ for some $k < 0$, where D_t is the time t dividend (see eq. (7.10)). Assuming dividends are constant and equal to D, $S_t = \frac{1}{r} D$, where r is discretely compounded. The price of a perpetuity with $D = r$ is one.

It is interesting to determine the difference in the expected excess returns for the two type of traders, defined as

$$\Delta_t \equiv (\hat{x}_{It} - \hat{x}_{Rt}) \left(E_t \left(p_{t+1}\right) + r - Rp_t\right) = \frac{\gamma \rho_t}{\beta^2 \sigma_\rho^2} \left(-\alpha r - (1+r) \beta(\rho_t - \bar{\rho})\right),$$

such that

$$E(\Delta_t) = Z\bar{\rho} - \frac{\gamma (1+r)^2 \left(\bar{\rho}^2 + \sigma_\rho^2\right)}{\sigma_\rho^2 (1-\lambda)}. \tag{10.128}$$

Eq. (10.128) shows that there exist parameter values such that the expected returns of the irrational investors may well be higher than those of the rational. The range of these parameter values increases with the mass of irrational investors, $1-\lambda$. Not only do prices deviate from fundamentals; the profits of the irrational investors may also be larger than those of the rational traders. The model is consistent with Friedman's original claims only for values of λ that are sufficiently large.

10.9.2 Funding and Early Liquidation Constraints

10.9.2.1 Pairs trading and the collapse of LTCM

Convergence arbitrage is a trading strategy that aims at exploiting price differences arising for a set of securities that deliver comparable payoffs. For example, Long-Term Capital Management (LTCM) was a hedge fund launched in 1994 and specializing in trading bonds issued at different dates but having roughly the same maturity. To illustrate, consider a newly issued Treasury bond with maturity equal to five years ("on-the-run") and a 10-year Treasury issued five years ago, which will then expire in five years ("off-the-run"). In a frictionless market, the two securities would be valued the same. However, it is often the case that liquidity concentrates around the on-the-run bond. Because it is then much easier to purchase newly issued Treasuries than off-the-run Treasuries on OTC markets, the off-the-run bonds typically trade at a discount against the on-the-run. The convergence trade for LTCM was to buy the off-the-run and sale short the on-the-run. The rationale behind this simple strategy is that the on-the-run/off-the-run spread would narrow, leading the trade to unwind at a profit.[19]

LTCM made use of a large amount of leverage to run these strategies[20] because the spread is typically quite tiny. Overall, at the beginning of 1998, the company had about \$5 billion in equity and \$125 billion borrowed, with off-balance sheet derivative positions (mostly in the fixed income space) amounting to about \$1.25 trillion. The risk of convergence arbitrage for LTCM was a scenario of widening spreads accompanied by early redemption requests from the investors. Moreover, in such scenarios, LTCM

---

19. Realistically, the trade may be implemented by just buying, say, a 9-year and 9-month maturity Treasury and short selling a newly issued 10-year bond; three months make a small difference, requiring heavy investments in the strategy. The trade is then updated through new issuance cycles—the spreads typically fall with new issuances, leading to profits.

20. Naturally, LTCM would run additional strategies in the fixed income space, such as the swap spread arbitrage reviewed in chapter 12 (see section 12.3).

might have become a source of systemic risk: the price pressure resulting from its trading activity had the potential to trigger an analogous trading behavior from other market participants over a feedback loop similar to those dealt with in chapter 11 (see section 11.10) or chapter 14 (see section 14.5), with market participants buying assets with increasing prices and selling assets with decreasing prices. All in all, LTCM was likely to be a player with a significant price impact.

The 1997 Asian financial crisis spread an increased global risk aversion, and some institutional investors withdrew from the market, generating an increase in the type of spreads that LTCM was trading. The increase in these spreads most probably followed because the investors leaving the market were making similar trades as LTCM (and hence they had to reverse their trades) or more generally because liquidity conditions were worsening as a result of an increased risk aversion. All in all, the spreads LTCM was trading at began to be heavily affected by liquidity conditions. This situation escalated in August 1998 when Russia declared a "debt moratorium," determining a dramatic widening of credit spreads and liquidity-driven spreads all over the world, making the LTCM's "market-to-market" position precarious. The fund had to raise capital or liquidate assets to meet the losses from marking to market. This liquidity pressure contributed to panics, leading to additional liquidity spirals. Given the systemic importance of these events, the Federal Reserve Bank of New York had to orchestrate a $4 billion bailout that involved the largest investment banks of the time.

10.9.2.2 *A model with optimal mispricing and funding constraints*

Thus, arbitrage may be risky: mispricing may be persistent, and arbitrage activities around this mispricing are subject to the risk of redemption or, in general, early liquidation. We illustrate these ideas by developing a variant on a celebrated model that, remarkably, Shleifer and Vishny (1997) had proposed even before the collapse of LTCM. In our variant, arbitrageurs understand they have a price impact, and the investors may "run" the arbitrageurs with some exogenously given probability.[21] The fact that arbitrageurs internalize their price impact has implications on the extent to which inefficiencies may be removed through their trading activity.

We assume that there are two "riskless" securities, in that they promise to pay $1 in three periods, and we set $r=0$. The fair value of the two bonds should thus be $1 at all times. However, we assume that, at time 1, one of the two assets is mispriced. This mispricing may give rise to an arbitrage opportunity in the idealized markets of part I of this book. The point of this section is that arbitrage forces may not be strong enough to restore parity. Let us elaborate.

We assume that, without the arbitrageurs, the value of the "mispriced bond" at time 1 would be equal to $1-\varepsilon_1$ for some constant $\varepsilon_1 \in (0,1)$. Moreover, we assume that the arbitrageurs have a price impact equal to the dollar value of their purchases made while trying to exploit the arbitrage, $x \geq 0$, say, such that the bond price at time 1 equals $p_1(x) = 1-\varepsilon_1 + x$. The arbitrageurs trade based on the capital V_0 they receive from their investors as elaborated below. Moreover, we assume that $V_0 < \varepsilon_1$. We do not model the

21. In Shleifer and Vishny, arbitrageurs are price takers, but some of the funds made available to the arbitrageurs in bad times are determined endogenously.

contract governing the sharing rules among the investors and the arbitrageurs. At time 1, the arbitrageurs buy $x/p_1(x)$ units of the mispriced bond and sell the very same number of the correctly priced bond for \$1, thereby achieving an amount of resources equal to

$$V_1(x) \equiv \frac{x}{p_1(x)}(1 - p_1(x)) + V_0. \tag{10.129}$$

We assume that $x < V_0$, which may be interpreted as a collateral requirement due to the short sale of the correctly priced bonds.

At time 2, the mispricing may persist with probability q or disappear with complementary probability (in which case arbitrage activities may not be implemented anymore). In case the mispricing persists, then with probability ϑ, the investors "run," that is, they claim for an early redemption of their funds. In this case, the arbitrageurs shall need to reverse their time 1 trade: they will sell back the previously purchased units of the mispriced bond for $p_{2,a} = 1 - \varepsilon_2$ for some $\varepsilon_2 \in (0, 1)$ (i.e., without price impact, a simplifying assumption) and buy back the same units of the correctly priced bond for \$1, incurring into a loss equal to $-V_{2,a}(x)$, where

$$V_{2,a}(x) \equiv \frac{x}{p_1(x)}\left(p_{2,a} - 1\right).$$

The occurrence of this loss, although uncertain, acts as a deterrent for implementing arbitrage activity at time 1. In equilibrium, we shall see, the trade aggressiveness of arbitrageurs decreases with ϑ, the likelihood of a run.

In case of no runs, an event with a probability equal to $1 - \vartheta$, the arbitrageurs will invest all the resources gathered at time 1, that is, $V_1(x)$, into the arbitrage trade without being subject to any collateral constraint. Alternatively, we may assume that in case of no runs, the arbitrageurs invest some optimally chosen quantity $x_2 < V_1(x)$. Our assumption simplifies the model. Finally, we assume that this arbitrage trade has a price impact such that the time 2 price is $p_{2,b}(x) = 1 - \varepsilon_2 + V_1(x)$. The arbitrageurs' profits resulting from this trade are then equal to

$$V_{2,b}(x) \equiv \frac{V_1(x)}{p_{2,b}(x)}\left(1 - p_{2,b}(x)\right).$$

The problem of the arbitrageurs is to maximize the total expected profits with respect to their initial "intervention" x, namely,

$$\hat{x} \equiv \arg \max_{x \in (0, V_0)} \left[V_1(x) + q\vartheta V_{2,a}(x) + q(1 - \vartheta) V_{2,b}(x)\right]. \tag{10.130}$$

Figure 10.2 depicts results obtained after solving the model numerically. The left panel depicts the asset price at time 1, that is, $p_1(\hat{x})$, under different assumptions on the probability of an early redemption; the right panel depicts the price at time 2 in the event of no runs, $p_{2,b}(\hat{x})$. Prices are depicted as a function of $\frac{V_0}{\varepsilon_1}$, the ratio of the investors' capital to the initial mispricing. Figure 10.3 plots the solution to the arbitrageurs' problem, $\frac{\hat{x}}{\varepsilon_1}$, as a function of $\frac{V_0}{\varepsilon_1}$.

Consider the price at time 1. It increases with the investors' capital, V_0, when V_0 is small. Figure 10.3 does indeed show that, when V_0 is small, the arbitrageurs use all the

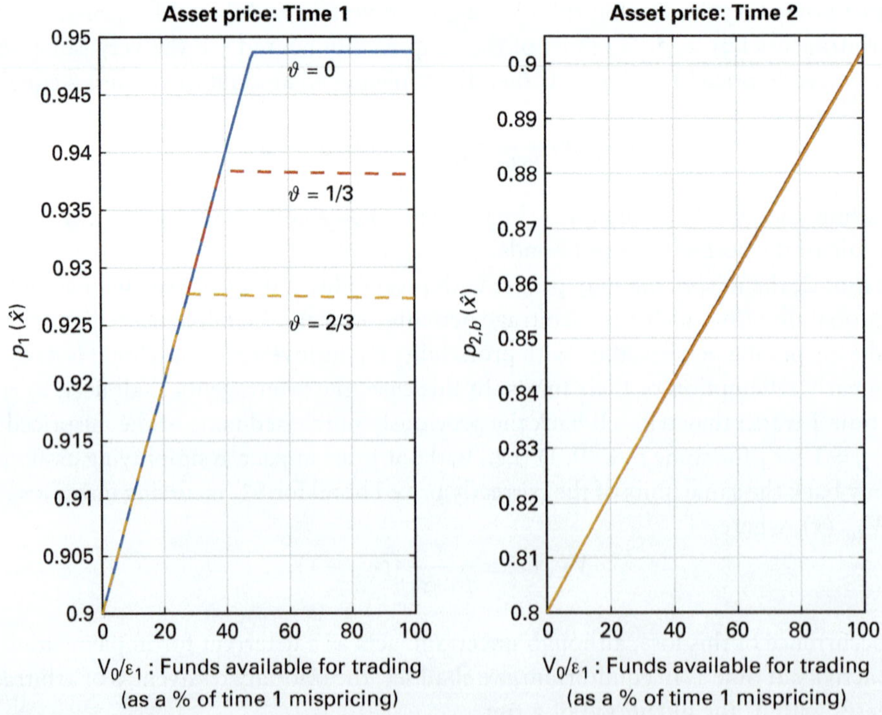

Figure 10.2
The left panel depicts the price $p_1(\hat{x}) = 1 - \varepsilon_1 + \hat{x}$, where $\hat{x}$ is the arbitrageurs' optimal investment at time 1 as a function of the funds made available to them by the investors, V_0/ε_1. The solid line is obtained by assuming there are no early redemptions; the dashed lines are obtained with probabilities of an early redemption of $\vartheta = 1/3$ and $2/3$. The remaining parameter values are $q = 1/3$ (the probability of a persistent mispricing), $\varepsilon_1 = 0.10$, and $\varepsilon_2 = 0.20$. The right panel depicts the price $p_{2,b}(\hat{x}) = 1 - \varepsilon_2 + V_1(\hat{x})$, where $V_1(\hat{x})$ is the total amount of resources the arbitrageurs have access to at time 1 as a function of V_0/ε_1.

investors' resources in the arbitrage trade, thereby pushing prices up. However, as V_0 gets larger, the arbitrageurs make limited use of the investors' capital. The reason is that the arbitrageurs take the price impact of their trades into account. Figure 10.3 shows that the higher V_0, the lower the proportion of funds used in the arbitrage trade at time 1. This proportion actually decreases with the investors' capital even when the probability of a run is zero, $\vartheta = 0$; however, in this case, $\hat{x}$ is flat against V_0 when V_0 is large enough, leading to a similar property for the time 1 price.

To summarize, even if the capital available to the arbitrageurs were as large as the initial mispricing, the arbitrageurs would not use all these funds and remove the mispricing—the solution $\hat{x}$ in (10.130) is interior. These conclusions are reminiscent of market practice. Hedge funds that aim at exploiting price anomalies may not accept "too many" investors: price impacts require not too much capital to be deployed in order to trade the anomalies, which could undermine alpha preservation.[22]

22. The price impacts mentioned at the beginning of this section regard the systemic impact of a loss of large institutional players such as LTCM. In the model, price impacts are not meant to capture the systemic effects of such losses.

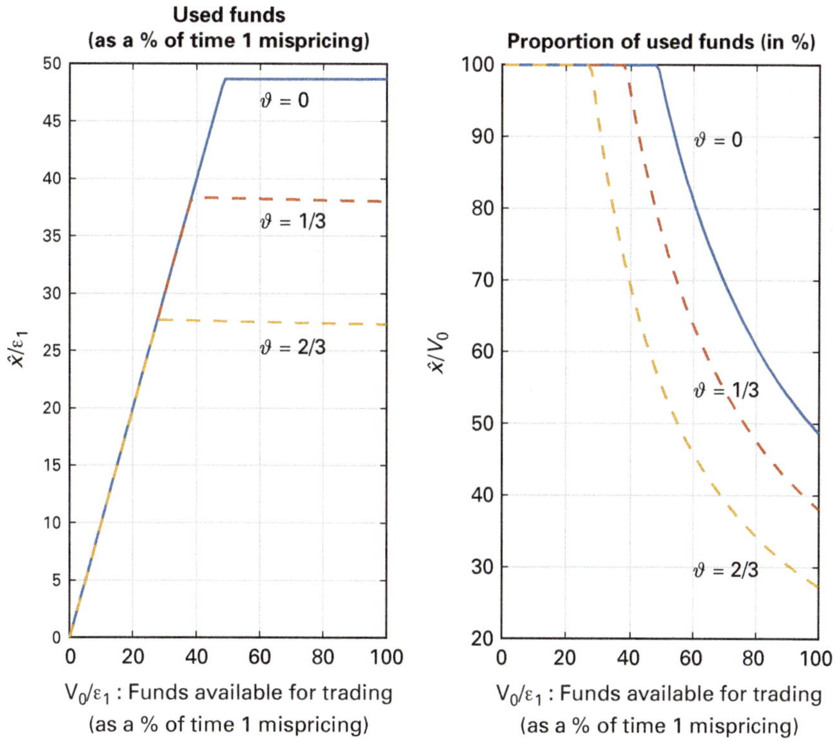

Figure 10.3
The left panel depicts the funds used by the arbitrageurs as a proportion of the time 1 pricing, $\hat{x}/\varepsilon_1$, where $\hat{x}$ is the arbitrageurs' optimal investment at time 1 as a function of the funds made available to them by the investors, V_0/ε_1. The solid line is obtained by assuming there are no early redemptions; the dashed lines are obtained by assuming that the probability of an early redemption is equal to $\vartheta = 1/3$ and $2/3$. The remaining parameter values are $q = 1/3$ (the probability of a persistent mispricing), $\varepsilon_1 = 0.10$, and $\varepsilon_2 = 0.20$. The right panel depicts the proportion of funds used by the arbitrageurs as a proportion of the initial capital, $\hat{x}/V_0$, as a function of V_0/ε_1.

As the probability of a run increases, the arbitrageurs slightly postpone part of their trades to time 2, with their time 1 trade $\hat{x}$ decreasing with V_0 and implying a similar property for the time 1 price. The price at time 1 would be less than parity even if the initial investors' capital, V_0, were able to offset the initial mispricing, ε_1, just as in the case with $\vartheta = 0$. Further, in equilibrium, the mispricing at time 1 becomes more and more severe with the likelihood of a run, as anticipated.

Finally, the price at time 2 is only marginally affected by the likelihood of a run. The reason is that this is the price resulting in the event that no runs have occurred; therefore, ϑ may affect the capital used in the time 2 arbitrage only through $V_1(\hat{x})$, that is, the total amount of resources collected as a result of time 1 decisions (see eq. (10.129)). This total amount is only marginally sensitive to the likelihood of a run. In all cases, the price at time 2 is then increasing in the initial capital. For sufficiently high V_0, this price would converge to parity even while the time 1 price would not.

10.9.3 Market Segmentation and Bond Supply Shocks

The 1990s were years of strong growth for the US economy, implying high tax receipts and decreasing federal budget deficits. In 1998, the federal budget was in a $70 billion surplus for the first time in about thirty years. At the time, the Congressional Budget Office was predicting steady increases in this surplus over subsequent years, with a more than $380 billion surplus forecast for 2009. The average maturity of government debt was increasing as a result: short-term bonds were naturally coming to expiration, with the remaining longer-term debt outstanding. Average government interest costs were then likely to increase provided that the yield curve kept on being increasing in maturity (long yields higher than short)—a typical situation that is explained in detail in chapter 13 (see section 13.3). In January 2000, US Treasury Secretary Lawrence Summers announced that the Treasury would implement a debt buyback program, that is, a purchase of Treasury debt with a subsequent reduction of that debt. Between March 2000 and April 2002, the Treasury conducted 45 reverse auctions to achieve a debt reduction of more than $65 billion. Thirty-year yields would drop by nearly 60 basis points within a few weeks after the announcement, with short-term yields staying substantially the same.

How can we rationalize these facts? Standard arbitrage theory links the price of a bond to a number of factors through a series of very well-known "cross-section restrictions." Chapters 11 and 12 contain thorough discussions of this theory along with many examples and applications in the space of dedicated fixed income derivatives and additional products. However, there is another view of bond markets known as the *preferred-habitat* view, by which bond markets are segmented: the yield on a certain maturity is determined by changes in supply and demand of investor clientèles around the given maturity. To illustrate, pension funds are mostly active in the long-term segment of the yield curve (longer than 15 years), whereas treasury managers of corporations or banks are mostly active in a shorter-term segment (say, less than 10 years). This theory is known at least since Culbertson (1957) and Modigliani and Sutch (1966), and its conclusions are well known by market participants.

Markets with preferred habit seem to be consistent with the yield curve reaction to the episodes around the 2000 buyback program. Indeed, standard theory might seem to predict a different story. Chapter 9, for example, explains that in the neoclassical model, asset prices (and hence the yield curve) do not relate to details regarding how government spending is financed and/or the level of debt—asset prices only depend on government spending (see section 9.7).[23] So how can we reconcile these two views? Greenwood and Vayanos (2014) consider a model where arbitrageurs invest in the whole yield curve and try to "fill the gaps" resulting from market segmentation. Without the arbitrageurs, a certain parametrization of the model would imply completely different dynamics for yields of nearby maturities. The model is related to previous work by Gromb and Vayanos (2002), who consider markets in which arbitrageurs face liquidity constraints similar to those described in the previous section. Instead, Greenwood and Vayanos (2014) consider markets in which arbitrageurs face no funding constraints but have limited risk-bearing capacity.

23. In chapter 14 (see section 14.2), we analyze models in which government bond prices depend on the level of accumulated debt in models where governments default strategically and face costs in case of default.

To illustrate the role of risk-bearing capacity, consider a frictionless market with risk neutral agents, in which the time t price of a bond expiring at T is

$$P_t(T) \equiv E_t\left(e^{-\int_t^T r_u du}\right), \tag{10.131}$$

where r_t is the instantaneous or short-term interest rate, defined as $r_t \equiv \lim_{\tau\to 0} R_t(\tau)$, and $R_t(\tau) \equiv -\frac{1}{\tau}P_t(\tau)$. Suppose that r_t is the solution to

$$dr_t = \kappa_r(\bar{r} - r_t)dt + \sigma_r dW_{1t} \tag{10.132}$$

for three constants, κ_r, $\bar{r}$, and σ_r and where W_{1t} is a standard Brownian motion. The two equations (10.131) and (10.132) form the basis for the celebrated Vasicek (1977) model so often used in the interest rate derivative literature (see chapter 13). Greenwood and Vayanos consider a model where each maturity is actually driven by supply-specific factors. However, arbitrageurs "cut and paste" over the whole curve, albeit with a limited risk-bearing capacity. In their model, bond prices collapse to (10.131) and (10.132) only when this risk-bearing capacity is large. However, when risk-bearing capacity and then "arbitrage forces" are limited, prices reflect the details of market segmentation with supply shocks affecting the yield curve. For example, a supply shock on the long-term segment of the yield curve may lead to an inversion in the yield curve. This section describes the main elements of this model.

10.9.3.1 Model

Available for trading are a continuum of bonds on $[0, T]$ for some fixed T. The dollar value of the supply of these bonds originates with the government and the investors; for each maturity τ, it is assumed to be given by

$$s_t(\tau) \equiv \zeta(\tau) + \theta(\tau)\beta_t, \tag{10.133}$$

for some deterministic functions $\zeta(\tau)$ and $\theta(\tau)$. The supply factor satisfies

$$d\beta_t = -\kappa_\beta \beta_t dt + \sigma_\beta dW_{2t},$$

for two parameters, κ_β and σ_β, where W_{2t} is a standard Brownian motion.

For example, we may assume that $\zeta(\tau)$ also depends on calendar time, such that $\zeta(\tau) = \zeta_0 R_t(\tau)$ for some constant ζ_0 and that $\theta(\tau) = -\zeta_0 b(\tau)$ for some deterministic function $b(\tau)$, such that $s_t(\tau) = \zeta_0\left(R_t(\tau) - b(\tau)\beta_t\right)$. Assuming that no arbitrageurs are in the market, an equilibrium is obtained once $s_t(\tau) = 0$ for each τ, yielding an extreme version of the preferred-habitat view where each yield is determined by the preference of the investor clientèle for maturity τ, $R_t(\tau) = b(\tau)\beta_t$. More generally, arbitrage forces would lead to a continuity of the yield curve; it is the task of this model to formalize how these arbitrage forces operate and guarantee continuity of the yield curve. Precisely, the model assumption is that arbitrageurs invest in all the bonds through a self-financed strategy where the value V_t satisfies

$$dV_t = \int_0^T \pi_t(\tau)\frac{dP_t(\tau)}{P_t(\tau)}d\tau + \left[V_t - \int_0^T \pi_t(\tau)\,d\tau\right]r_t dt,$$

where $\pi_t(\tau)$ denotes the dollar investment in the bond with maturity τ. Moreover, arbitrageurs are myopic. They come through overlapping generations, live for an infinitesimal time interval and solve the problem

$$\max_{(\pi_t(\tau))_{\tau\in[0,T]}} \left[E_t(dV_t) - \frac{a}{2}var_t(dV_t)\right], \qquad [10.P1]$$

for some risk aversion parameter $a > 0$.

We conjecture and later verify that the price of a zero coupon bond is

$$P_t(T) \equiv P_t(r_t, \beta_t, T) = e^{-A_r(T-t)r_t - A_\beta(T-t)\beta_t + C(T-t)},$$

for some functions $A_r(T-t)$, $A_\beta(T-t)$, and $C(T-t)$ that only depend on time to maturity $T-t$ and satisfying boundary conditions such that $P_T(r_t, \beta_t, T) = 1$. Under this conjecture, by Itô's lemma, the bond price satisfies

$$\frac{dP_t(T)}{P_t(T)} = \mu_t(T)\,dt - \sigma_r A_r(T-t)\,dW_{1t} - \sigma_\beta A_\beta(T-t)\,dW_{2t}$$

for some function $\mu_t(T)$, briefly discussed below.

10.9.3.2 *Cutting and pasting the yield curve*

The arbitrageurs' problem [10.P1] is

$$\max_{(\pi_t(\tau))_{\tau\in[0,T]}} \left[\int_0^T \pi_t(\tau)(\mu_t(\tau) - r_t)\,d\tau dt - \frac{a}{2}var_t(dV_t)\right]. \qquad [10.P2]$$

Appendix 10.C shows that the first-order conditions for [10.P2], along with the equilibrium condition, $s_t(\tau) = \pi_t(\tau)$, lead to

$$\mu_t(\tau) - r_t = a\left[\sigma_r^2 A_r(\tau)\int_0^T s_t(u)A_r(u)\,du + \sigma_\beta^2 A_\beta(\tau)\int_0^T s_t(u)A_\beta(u)\,du\right]. \qquad (10.134)$$

Note that, by Itô's lemma, $\mu_t(\cdot)$ is a function of $A_j(\cdot)$ for $j = r, \beta$, $C(\cdot)$ and their derivatives, such that eq. (10.134) gives rise to three differential equations solved by $A_j(\cdot)$ and $C(\cdot)$. The appendix shows that $A_r(\cdot) > 0$ and that, under conditions on $\theta(\cdot)$ (to be explained in a moment), $A_\beta(\cdot) \geq 0$. The conditions under which the second property holds are that (i) $\int_0^T \theta(\tau)\,d\tau \geq 0$ and (ii) there exists a maturity $\tau^* \geq 0$, such that $\theta(\tau) < 0$ for $\tau \leq \tau^*$ and $\theta(\tau) \geq 0$ for $\tau \geq \tau^*$. The first condition means that an increase in the "common supply factor" β_t in (10.133) leads to an increase in the total dollar value of bonds supply. The second condition covers cases in which the dollar value of short-term bonds supply decreases with β_t even while the total supply increases.

Eq. (10.134) provides "cross-equation restrictions" on the bonds' expected excess returns. The arbitrageurs require compensation for investing that relates to the overall portfolio exposures to the two factors, r_t and β_t. Only if[24] $a = 0$ would these premiums

24. However, a needs to be small enough to guarantee the existence of an equilibrium.

collapse to zero.[25] The fact that $A_r(\cdot)$ and $A_\beta(\cdot)$ are both positive guarantees that the expected excess return on any bond increases with a positive supply shock on any maturity $s_t(\cdot)$. This property arises because the first-order conditions for [10.P2] are simply eq. (10.134) for $s_t(\tau)=\pi_t(\tau)$: the more arbitrageurs are exposed to a given maturity, the higher the expected return is for the bonds' universe.

The property that $A_\beta(\cdot)\geq 0$, with $A_\beta(0)=0$, implies that a negative supply shock (i.e., a decrease in β_t) may well affect long-term yields more than short-term yields and even lead to a yield curve inversion. Interestingly, though, the yields on short-term bonds also decrease even when a negative supply shock is mostly local to long-term maturities (i.e., $\tau^*>0$). The reason for this property is that arbitrageurs are operating through global portfolio choices, thereby "cutting and pasting" the yield curve: a shock on a 30-year bond has implications on the exposure of the arbitrageurs' overall position to this shock, and the risk premium on each of these bonds reflects this exposure. Naturally, premiums are larger for longer-term bonds, given their higher *duration*[26] (i.e., sensitivity to r_t) and sensitivity to β_t, summarized by the two functions $A_r(\cdot)$ and $A_\beta(\cdot)$.

10.9.4 Liquidity and Runs

This section considers the implications of illiquidity on agents' behavior: runs. Banks invest in long-term assets by relying on short-term liabilities—typically, deposits that may be withdrawn at any time. In some circumstances, depositors may withdraw in anticipation that others might do the same. This coordination failure may be such that a bank is unable to satisfy all depositors' requests, a "self-fulfilling prophecy." In fact, bank runs have been often observed for many years until the regulatory reforms of the 1930s. Sometimes, such crises would spread to the whole banking system, generating "bank panics." Since the reforms, these crises seemed to have been more limited. Bryant (1980) and Diamond and Dybvig (1983) provide seminal analysis of these phenomena. Freixas and Rochet (1998) and Allen and Gale (2007) provide thorough reviews of these crises, discussions of theoretical explanations, and possible remedies. This section provides basic foundations of some theoretical mechanisms that may potentially lead to a bank run.

10.9.4.1 The issue

When agents are subject to the risk of a liquidity shock, they face incomplete markets:[27] there cannot be securities with payoffs correlated with the liquidity shocks that hit each single agent. The allocation in this economy can be improved by a social planner; as it turns out, the resulting allocation can be obtained throughout a system of competitive banks. Intuitively, banks act as "pools of liquidity." They accept deposits and invest only a portion of them into long-term assets. The retained portion of deposits is kept as a *reserve* that banks may employ to satisfy future withdrawal requests by agents hit by liquidity

---

25. When $a\neq 0$, the bond price is $P_t(T)\equiv\mathbb{E}_t(e^{-\int_t^T r_u du})$, where $\mathbb{E}_t(\cdot)$ denotes the conditional expectation taken under the risk neutral probability, Q. When $a\neq 0$, the dynamics of β_t then matter for asset pricing because the drift of r_t under Q includes β_t as a result of Girsanov theorem. Chapter 13 (see, for example, section 13.4.2) provides details regarding these changes of probability.

26. Chapters 12 and 13 contain extensive discussions of the notion of duration in fixed income markets (see, e.g., sections 12.3 and 13.4).

27. Chapters 2 and 4 provide definitions of incomplete markets.

shocks. Thus, in addition to the standard intermediation role, banks perform another role: they provide insurance against individual liquidity shocks.

But things can go wrong. Reserves typically cover only a fraction of the whole amount of deposits.[28] If depositors believe that other depositors believe that this fraction is insufficient to satisfy withdrawal requests, there will be a bank run: the bank may still be solvent but may not have enough liquidity to meet all withdrawal requests. By "solvent," we mean that the bank may have all the resources needed to repay depositors back, although only in the long term. The remainder of this section provides more formal details of this reasoning.

10.9.4.2 Liquidity shocks and investment technologies

Consider a three-period economy, $t=0,1,2$, with a continuum of consumers. Each of these consumers is endowed with one unit of good that they wish to consume in the future, ideally at $t=2$. However, there is a probability that each of them becomes an "early" consumer and, accordingly, in need of consuming at $t=1$. In other words, consumers learn their type at $t=1$, and some of them may want to consume earlier than initially planned. The event of early consumption generates a shock that will be referred to as a "liquidity shock." Let $u(c_t)$ denote the (increasing and concave) utility that a consumer draws from consuming c_t units at time t. The ex ante utility of each consumer is

$$U(c_1,c_2)=\pi u(c_1)+(1-\pi)\rho u(c_2), \tag{10.135}$$

where π is the probability of a liquidity shock and $\rho<1$ is a discount factor.

At time 0, consumers decide how much to invest into the available storing technologies. There is a long-term and illiquid productive technology that delivers $R>1$ at time 2 but, critically, $L<1$ at time 1. The low return, L, reflects a liquidation cost. Further, there is an unproductive technology that delivers one good at any time upon investing one good one period earlier. We characterize the main properties of this economy while analyzing different variants of it: (i) one in which agents live in autarky; (ii) one in which agents may trade a (liquid) security at the time of the liquidity shock, $t=1$; (iii) one in which allocations are chosen by a social planner; and finally, (iv) one in which there is a banking system.

10.9.4.3 Autarky equilibrium

The agents' saving decisions at time 0 can be described very simply, independent of whether these agents live in autarky or have access to a financial market. Each of the agents invests $I\in(0,1)$ into long-term technology and stores the remaining $1-I$ into unproductive technology. In an autarky equilibrium, the budget constraints are

$$c=\begin{cases} c_1=1-I+LI, & \text{in case a liquidity shock occurs at } t=1 \\ c_2=1-I+RI, & \text{otherwise.} \end{cases} \tag{10.136}$$

In case of a liquidity shock, consumption equals the portion of endowment stored through the unproductive technology, $1-I$, plus the proceedings from liquidating the long-term asset, LI. If no liquidity shocks occur, consumption takes place at $t=2$ and equals $1-I$ plus the long-term return guaranteed by the productive technology, RI. It is easy to

28. The situation in which this fraction is 100% is known as "narrow banking."

verify that, given the assumptions made on L and R, the budget constraints imply that

$$c_1 \leq 1, \quad c_2 \leq R. \tag{10.137}$$

10.9.4.4 *Equilibrium with a financial market*

Next, suppose that at $t=1$, a market is open for trading a one-period zero coupon bond, the price of which is denoted with p. When agents may trade this asset, the budget constraints (10.136) are replaced with

$$c = \begin{cases} c_1 = 1 - I + pRI, & \text{in case a liquidity shock occurs at } t=1 \\ c_2 = \dfrac{1-I}{p} + RI, & \text{otherwise.} \end{cases} \tag{10.138}$$

Let us explain. The first constraint says that, at time 1, an agent hit by a liquidity shock may raise funding with a nominal size equal to RI. Consumption at $t=1$ equals $1-I$ plus the bond issuance, pRI. Note that, when $t=2$, the agent may use the long-term payoff of the productive asset they are invested in (i.e., RI) to honor the bond issued at $t=1$. The agents not hit by a liquidity shock are on the demand side of this asset market. They had stored $1-I$ into unproductive technology, which they may use to purchase the bond. Then, at $t=2$, they consume the payoff of the long-term asset, RI, plus that related to the bond purchased at $t=1$, that is, $\frac{1-I}{p}$.

It is left as an exercise to show that $I=\infty$ if $p > \frac{1}{R}$ and $I=0$ otherwise. Thus, to avoid trivial outcomes, the equilibrium bond price must be equal to $p=\frac{1}{R}$. Replacing this value into (10.138) leaves the following equilibrium consumption, c_i^f, say:

$$c_1^f = 1, \quad c_2^f = R. \tag{10.139}$$

In equilibrium, the bonds' supply, πpRI (i.e., the bond issuance times the fraction of agents hit by the liquidity shock), equals demand, $(1-\pi)(1-I)$, such that the equilibrium amount of resources invested into the long-term asset equals the proportion of agents not hit by a liquidity shock, $I=1-\pi$.

Comparing (10.137) with (10.139) shows that welfare improves in an economy with a financial market. By issuing bonds, early consumers may raise more cash than in the autarky case, thereby mitigating a liquidity shock. By purchasing bonds, consumers not hit by a liquidity shock may turn their unproductive savings into productive. Is this outcome Pareto optimal? It shouldn't be: markets are incomplete anyway as no securities are available for trading, which pay off in the states of nature with a liquidity shock. Indeed, we now study how a social planner would allocate resources in this economy.

10.9.4.5 *The social planner's solution*

What would a social planner do? Consider the following program

$$\max_{c_1, c_2, I} U(c_1, c_2), \quad \text{s.t. } \pi c_1 = 1 - I \text{ and } (1-\pi) c_2 = RI, \qquad [10.P3]$$

where $U(c_1, c_2)$ is the same as in (10.135). That is, a social planner maximizes a social welfare criterion by which the utility of each agent receives the same weight: the agents' utilities are then weighted according to the size of each agent's type. The constraints in [10.P3] have the following meaning. First, the social planner stores $1-I$ of the total endowment into the unproductive technology, which they use to finance consumption of all early consumers (first constraint). Second, the planner invests I in the long-term productive technology, which they use to finance consumption of all consumers not hit by the liquidity shock (second constraint). The solution, $\hat{c}_i$, to [10.P3] satisfies

$$\begin{cases} u'(\hat{c}_1) = \rho R u'(\hat{c}_2) \\ \pi \hat{c}_1 + (1-\pi)\frac{1}{R}\hat{c}_2 = 1. \end{cases} \tag{10.140}$$

In general, the equilibrium allocation with a financial market (i.e., c_i^f in (10.139)) is not Pareto optimal. Suppose, for example, that agents have CRRA equal to γ, that is, $u(c) = c^{1-\gamma}/(1-\gamma)$. If $\gamma > 1$, we have that

$$\rho R u'(c_2^f) = \rho R u'(R) = \rho R^{1-\gamma} < 1 = u'(c_1^f),$$

where we have made use of the expressions of c_i^f in (10.139). That is, the equilibrium allocations in an economy with a financial market can be improved by increasing the first-period consumption and/or decreasing the second-period consumption:

$$\hat{c}_1 \geq c_1^f = 1, \quad \hat{c}_2 \leq c_2^f = R.$$

As it turns out, a banking system might lead to the same outcome $(\hat{c}_1, \hat{c}_2)$ solution to (10.140).

10.9.4.6 *Banking with a fractional reserve system*

Now suppose that many identical and competitive banks (in short, a bank) may accept deposits. The bank accepts all of the consumers' endowments (equal to one consumption unit) as deposits, stores $1-I$ of these endowments (a "fractional reserve") into unproductive but liquid technology, and finally, invests I into the illiquid asset. The deposit contract specifies that the consumer has the right to withdraw c_t at time t. Note that competition forces the bank to maximize the welfare of the representative investor. Therefore, the bank solves the program [10.P3], and hence the deposit contract specifies that withdrawals are $(\hat{c}_1, \hat{c}_2)$, where $\hat{c}_t$ is as in (10.140).

Can this fractional reserve system be implemented in practice? That is, are patient consumers left with any incentives to withdraw at $t=1$ and then store until $t=2$? First, note that by (10.140), $\hat{c}_1 > \hat{c}_2$ if and only if $\rho R < 1$. Thus, if $\rho R < 1$, the deposit contract $(\hat{c}_1, \hat{c}_2)$ will be destabilized: the patient consumers will withdraw at $t=1$, store $\hat{c}_1$, and consume $\hat{c}_1$ at $t=2$, which is larger than the amount the contract allows one to withdraw by waiting until $t=2$, $\hat{c}_2$. If instead, $\rho R > 1$, patient consumers are offered a deposit contract such that $\hat{c}_1 < \hat{c}_2$; they will then will find it beneficial to wait. Meanwhile, at $t=1$, early consumers withdraw for $\pi\hat{c}_1$, which exactly equals the bank's reserves, $1-I$ (see the first constraint in [10.P3]): at $t=0$, the bank sets aside $\pi\hat{c}_1$ as reserves and invests $1-\pi\hat{c}_1$ into the illiquid asset. Therefore, in this equilibrium, the deposit contract can be implemented, and no bank runs occur. We now describe another equilibrium, in which all patient consumers try to withdraw at $t = 1$, even in the favorable circumstance that $\rho R > 1$.

10.9.4.7 Bank runs

Why would patient consumers run? The problem is a coordination failure. Consider a given patient consumer. If everyone runs, the bank may only satisfy withdrawal requests equal to its reserves, $\pi \hat{c}_1$, plus the amount of goods that can be recovered by liquidating the long-term asset, $(1 - \pi \hat{c}_1)L$. However (and assuming that agents have CRRA equal to $\gamma > 1$),

$$\pi \hat{c}_1 + (1 - \pi \hat{c}_1)L \leq \hat{c}_1.$$

That is, the bank is only able to absorb withdrawal requests for less than its liabilities, $\hat{c}_1$ (i.e., the maximum withdrawals the bank had committed for through the deposit contract stipulated at $t = 0$). Now, consider the behavior of a given patient consumer. If everyone else runs, then the bank would have no resources left that our consumer may withdraw from at $t = 2$. Then it would be optimal for the consumer to run. Thus, there is an equilibrium in which everyone runs.

In this model, bank runs occur because beliefs are self-fulfilling: if late consumers believe there will be a run, they will run; and if they believe that a run will not occur, they will not run. In fact, this problem can be formally cast in terms of "sunspots," by which some sources of risk extraneous to the economy might actually affect agents' behavior and economic outcomes.[29] In an equilibrium with sunspots, agents take the randomness of an equilibrium outcome (in this example: runs, no runs) into account while formulating decisions. In fact, empirical evidence suggests that bank runs mostly occur during periods of poor economic performance. Thus, an alternative route to bank runs is one where agents run in anticipation of problems that a bank may experience during a particularly adverse development of the economic cycle. Diamond and Dybvig (1983) describe bank runs in an economy without extrinsic uncertainty, just as we have describe so far. Bryant (1980) describes bank runs by taking into account uncertainty regarding economic fundamentals. Allen and Gale (2007) provide additional discussions on these distinctions and review the empirical evidence on the nature of bank runs.

The multiplicity of equilibria in the model of this section is due to a strategic complementarity: agents find it optimal to run when others runs. A focus in the most recent literature is to identify conditions for the uniqueness of equilibria. Goldstein and Pauzner (2005) rely on a model of global games along the lines set forth by Morris and Shin (1998) and assume that the long-term asset has an uncertain payoff, linked to economic conditions. If economic conditions are common knowledge, bank runs occur provided the fundamentals are sufficiently poor and do not occur when fundamentals are sufficiently good; multiple equilibria still exist when the state of the economy is in some intermediate region. However, these conclusions change when agents only observe a noisy signal on the economic fundamentals. Goldstein and Razin (2015, chapter 2) review these results and related literature and provide intuitive explanations and suggestions for additional readings.

29. See section 3.3 in chapter 3 for a basic introduction to the notion of sunpots in dynamic models of the business cycle.

10.10 Over-the-Counter Markets

10.10.1 Background

OTC trading venues are pervasive in financial markets and cover products such as corporate, government, and municipal bonds; interest rate derivatives (e.g., interest rate swaps, swaptions, caps, floors); currencies, credit products such as collateralized debt obligations, credit default swaps; or large blocks of equities. Many of these products are actually reviewed and priced in great detail in part III (see, e.g., chapters 13 and 14). Duffie (2012) is a very important introduction to much of the economics underlying OTC markets.

OTC markets differ from centralized exchanges as they operate through peculiar pricing mechanisms. In these markets, for example, traders may only be aware of "local" information: some traders might be negotiating a deal for a product at a time and geographical venue while ignoring information regarding a similar product in other areas. Once a trader receives a price quote (bid or ask) from a dealer (i.e., an entity that maintains a two-way market), they may well continue to search for better conditions and other counterparties. The dealer may revise their quotes over time, based on public news (e.g., news on broad macroeconomic developments) and the evidence gathered while maintaining their own market segment. Quotes may occur by phone or electronic communication, including screen-query systems. At the time of writing, brokerage is also important in some of these markets (e.g., interest rate swap markets)—brokers intermediate while not trading on their own accounts. Interdealer brokers are institutions that specialize in connecting dealers.

Why do OTC markets exist? Some financial products are particularly complex and are sometimes tailored to the need of clients requesting them. Only a few specialists may be able to understand risks and trade products originated through such bespoke deals. Centralizing these products on an exchange would not necessarily attract a more widespread market: widespread markets necessitate standardization and simplicity. By construction, bespoke products are not standardized. Moreover, they may be too complex.

Products that are initially bespoke may, however, gain the interest of other market participants and trigger volumes and liquidity that may justify standardization and the introduction to an exchange. The typical example that is often discussed is a product that comes from the interest rate derivative markets. By the end of June 2015, the notional amount of outstanding interest rate derivatives amounted to $435 trillion, approximately 80% of the global OTC derivatives market. Interest rate swaps make up $320 trillion of these figures, the largest share in this space.

There are many reasons that justify these enormous figures. One is certainly related to widespread hedging motives, discussed in detail in chapter 13. For example, pension funds would like to hold assets paying a flow of fixed payments—payments that are needed to honor their liability sides. An interest rate swap contract would allow a pension fund to receive fixed payments from a counterparty (say, an investment bank) against floating rates (obtained, perhaps, by investing current fund contributions) and over long horizon spans. The pension fund is then a "swap receiver." Chapter 13 explains reasons that may attract institutions to be on the other side of the deal (thus being long a "swap payer"). Now, a bank that gathers a deal from a client (say, a swap "payer" denominated in US dollars) may not want to carry this deal on its books. Our bank may then search for counterparties willing to take on this product; one simple solution would be to offset this position while initiating a new swap "receiver" with another counterparty. In turn, the latter may dislike holding a payer position and may successfully search for counterparties and initiate new receivers. The process may continue, contributing to a large market.

An exchange would probably eliminate some of this business due to its "netting" ability. It would also eliminate counterparty risk, that is, the risk of default by players in these markets. In OTC markets, counterparty risk can become systemic risk when the affected players perform a core role in the trading network. To illustrate, the Lehman Brothers failure in 2008 spread concerns on such networks—effects that were so deep so as to literally stop the financial system for several months, contributing to business cycle developments of the time. At the time of writing, such interest rate derivatives are still traded OTC. It is not clear how resilient a centralized venue would be to large shocks, even accounting for its netting abilities—an exchange is subject to default risk anyway. Moreover, OTC markets are not necessarily illiquid. In fact, interest rate swap (IRS) markets are an example of a very liquid market and a standardized one. We have IRSs for any reasonable maturity and derivatives on these contracts (known as swaptions) that are equally liquid and standardized.[30] But again, this liquidity may suddenly disappear in case of systemic events.

10.10.2 Search

The next section analyzes price mechanics that differ from an exchange. We focus on what arguably is the most important characteristic of OTC markets: search. The previous discussion suggests that, in the absence of centralized information, searching for trading counterparts is vital in OTC markets. We describe a model of search based on work by Duffie, Gârleanu, and Pedersen (2007), in which traders need to search for counterparts. Search is a friction that leads to quite novel predictions regarding price formation in market microstructure: notably, search leads to price discounts (compared to an otherwise purely Walrasian market) and makes prices recover slowly after an aggregate liquidity shock. The price discount is a liquidity premium and increases with searching frictions.

In a related model with market makers, Duffie, Gârleanu, and Pedersen (2005) do in fact show that bid-ask spreads decrease with the ability of traders to find trading counterparties. In other words, a sophisticated trader has access to good trading conditions. This conclusion is somehow the opposite to conclusions that are based on information-based explanations of market microstructure. The next section presents the simplest version of Duffie, Gârleanu, and Pedersen (2007), a model without market making.

10.10.3 A Model with Symmetric Information

Many products that are traded in OTC markets are reviewed in part III (e.g., chapters 13 and 14), as explained, and will be priced while partially ignoring the market mechanisms inherent in OTC markets. One embarrassing reason for this treatment is that academic research and market practice have only relatively recently begun dialoguing regarding the

30. However, at the time of writing, interest derivatives such as IRS are still not entirely standardized. These contracts are organized as forward contracts, and the cost of entering them depends on *when* one enters (see chapter 13). Future contracts work differently as explained in chapter 11 (see section 11.2).

details of these markets. However, part III will illustrate the main efforts made in the market practice to incorporate some imperfections that plague these markets (e.g., counterparty risk or "multiple curves" in interest rate swap markets). This section only aims at providing a simple framework to understand the impact of search frictions on prices.

We consider an infinite-horizon continuous time market for a consol, an asset that yields an instantaneous payoff equal to one unit of consumption. Traders are risk neutral, and we take their discounting rate equal to the riskless interest rate, r. There are four types of traders: traders having a low valuation of the asset and who own (lo) or don't own (ln) the asset and traders having a high valuation of the asset and who own (ho) or don't own (hn) the asset. Agents with low valuations incur an instantaneous holding cost equal to δ. The model does not incorporate counterparty risk.

Traders may switch their types from low to high with intensity λ_u and from high to low with intensity λ_d. Finally, any agent is matched to any other with intensity λ. Whether these agents will trade depends on their preferences and asset ownership, as elaborated below. Traders' masses are denoted with $\mu_{\mathcal{T}}$, $\mathcal{T} \in \{lo, ln, ho, hn\}$ with obvious notation, and they sum up to one. Per capita supply is denoted with s, $s = \mu_{lo} + \mu_{ho}$. A transaction may only occur if a lo (resp., hn) trader meets an hn (resp., lo) trader, which occurs with intensity $\lambda\mu_{hn}$ (resp., $\lambda\mu_{lo}$). The objective of the model is to determine the transaction price, P, say.

The law of movement for $\mu_{\mathcal{T}}$ is

$$\begin{cases} \dot{\mu}_{lo} = -\lambda\mu_{hn}\mu_{lo} - \lambda_u\mu_{lo} + \lambda_d\mu_{ho} \\ \dot{\mu}_{ln} = \lambda\mu_{hn}\mu_{lo} - \lambda_u\mu_{ln} + \lambda_d\mu_{hn} \\ \dot{\mu}_{ho} = \lambda\mu_{hn}\mu_{lo} - \lambda_d\mu_{ho} + \lambda_u\mu_{lo} \\ \dot{\mu}_{hn} = -\lambda\mu_{hn}\mu_{lo} - \lambda_d\mu_{hn} + \lambda_u\mu_{ln} \end{cases} . \tag{10.141}$$

Consider, for example, the second equation of (10.141). The mass of ln traders (i) increases by $\lambda\mu_{hn}\mu_{lo}$, the aggregate meeting rate of lo and hn traders (the first term on the RHS); (ii) decreases by $\lambda_u\mu_{ln}$, the mass of ln traders switching to hn type; and (iii) increases by $\lambda_d\mu_{hn}$, the mass of hn traders switching to ln type. A steady state of this system in defined as $\mu_{\mathcal{T}} : \dot{\mu}_{\mathcal{T}} = 0$ for all $\mathcal{T}$.

Each trader's continuation utility equals current wealth plus a component $V_{\mathcal{T}}$ that depends on the type $\mathcal{T}$. To determine these components in steady state, note that, given risk neutrality and under regularity conditions, the indirect utility grows at r such that[31]

$$\begin{cases} rV_{lo} = \lambda_u\left(V_{ho} - V_{lo}\right) + \lambda\mu_{hn}\left(P - \Delta V_l\right) + 1 - \delta \\ rV_{ln} = \lambda_u\left(V_{hn} - V_{ln}\right) \\ rV_{ho} = \lambda_d\left(V_{lo} - V_{ho}\right) + 1 \\ rV_{hn} = \lambda_d\left(V_{ln} - V_{hn}\right) + \lambda\mu_{lo}\left(\Delta V_h - P\right) \end{cases} \tag{10.142}$$

where

$$\Delta V_l \equiv V_{lo} - V_{ln}, \quad \Delta V_h \equiv V_{ho} - V_{hn}.$$

31. Eqs. (10.142) are Bellman equations evaluated in steady state when any trader type has utility equal to current wealth plus $E_t(\int_t^\infty e^{-r(\tau - t)} c_\tau d\tau)$, subject to a budget constraint, where c_t denotes instantaneous consumption; randomness is due to types being subject to switching and matching processes.

Consider the first equation of (10.142). The LHS is the expected growth in the *lo* trader's continuation utility. The first term of the RHS accounts for the jump in the utility the *lo* trader would experience in case they switched from low to high type (which occurs with probability λ_u); the second term accounts for the jump in the trader's utility, should they meet a trading counterparty, that is, an *hn* trader (which occurs with probability λ): the jump in utility would equal the price received from the transaction, P, plus the (negative) change in utility derived from switching from *lo* to *ln*, that is, $-\Delta V_l$; finally, the term $1-\delta$ is the consol instantaneous payoff net of its holding costs, which is immediately consumed. The remaining equations are interpreted similarly.

Note that ΔV_h is the asset reservation value for an *hn* trader (the seller) and ΔV_l is the minimum price required by a *lo* trader (the buyer). Therefore, any transaction price $P \in [\Delta V_l, \Delta V_h]$. It is assumed that, once two traders with opposite needs meet, they agree on a price achieved through bilateral bargaining,

$$P = (1-q)\,\Delta V_l + q\Delta V_h, \tag{10.143}$$

where $q \in (0,1)$ is an exogenous parameter: the higher the value of q, the higher the bargaining power of the seller.

In appendix 10.D, we show that eqs. (10.142) and (10.143) imply that

$$P = \frac{1}{r} - \frac{\delta}{r} \frac{\lambda_d + (r + \lambda\mu_{lo})(1-q)}{r + \lambda_u + \lambda_d + \lambda\left((1-q)\,\mu_{lo} + q\mu_{hn}\right)}. \tag{10.144}$$

The model predicts that the asset price equals its console value (the price in a Walrasian market) minus an illiquidity premium. The illiquidity premium is increasing in δ, the holding costs. We expect the illiquidity premium to increase with searching costs. The price is decreasing in λ_d and increasing in λ_u, *ceteris paribus*: these conclusions hold while taking μ_{lo} and μ_{hn} as fixed. However, the masses of *lo* and *hn* traders are endogenous, and evolve through eqs. (10.141). Appendix 10.D shows that, in steady state, μ_{lo} is the solution to the quadratic equation,

$$0 = \lambda\mu_{lo}^2 + \left(\lambda\left(\frac{\lambda_u}{\lambda_u + \lambda_d} - s\right) + (\lambda_u + \lambda_d)\right)\mu_{lo} - \lambda_d s, \tag{10.145}$$

and that (see eq. (10.A36) in appendix 10.D) μ_{hn} is given by

$$\mu_{hn} = \mu_{lo} + \frac{\lambda_u}{\lambda_u + \lambda_d} - s. \tag{10.146}$$

Figure 10.4 depicts the equilibrium price in eq. (10.144) as a function of the average time needed to sell (in days), determined below, with μ_{lo} and μ_{hn} given by (10.145) and (10.146). We set $\delta = 0.3$ and use the intensity parameters values of Duffie, Gârleanu, and Pedersen (2007),[32] the reference period being equal to a year. Thus, for example, a value of $\lambda = 1250$ means that there is an expected number of meetings equal to 1,250 per year

32. This section follows the convention of Duffie (2010), where the values of λ are twice those in Duffie, Gârleanu, and Pedersen (2007).

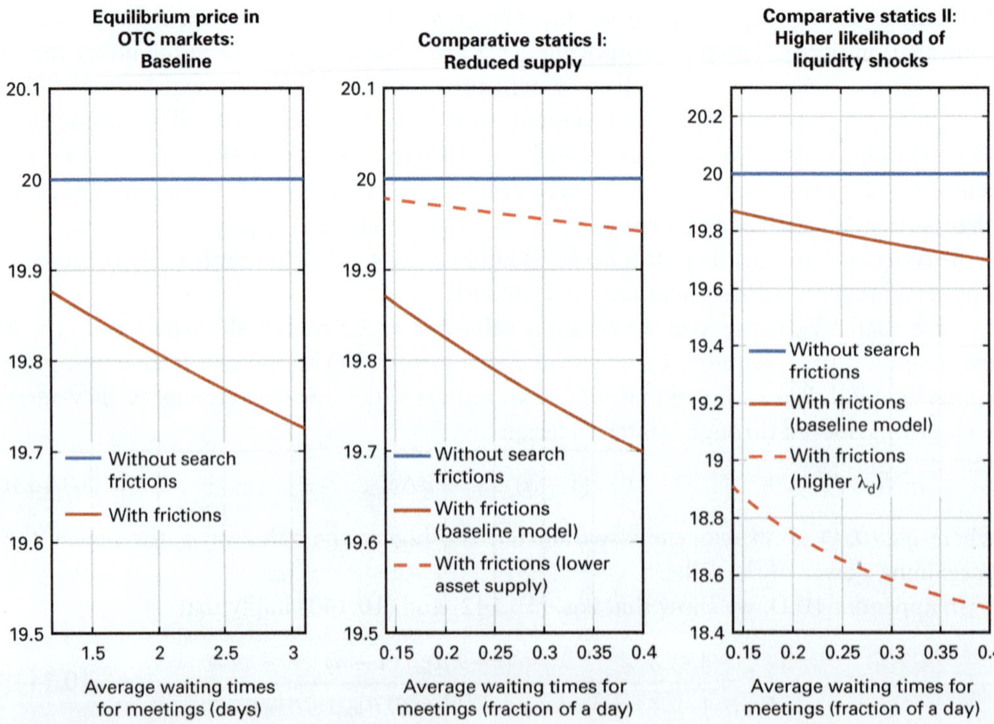

Figure 10.4
The left panel depicts the equilibrium price in eq. (10.144) as a function of the average waiting times for selling (days), defined as $(\mu_{hn}\lambda\Delta t)^{-1}$, where $\Delta t=\frac{1}{250}$. Parameter values are $r=5\%$, $\lambda_d=0.5$, $\lambda_u=5$, $s=0.8$, and $q=0.5$. The remaining panels depict comparative statics resulting from a lower asset supply ($s=0.6$, middle panel) and a higher likelihood of liquidity shock ($\lambda_d=1$, right) than in the baseline model; in both panels, the equilibrium prices are expressed as a function of the average waiting times for a meeting, expressed as a fraction of a day, $(\lambda\Delta t)^{-1}$.

or 5 per day;[33] on average, then, a *lo* trader expects to meet $\lambda\mu_{hn}=139.75$ *hn* traders every year, implying an average time to sell equal to almost two days. These values are obtained with $\mu_{hn}=0.1118$ (the steady state resulting in this example), and figure 10.4 extends price calculations to other average waiting times for selling.

The model predicts that the price is increasing in λ and confirms the intuition that the illiquidity premium increases with the intensity of liquidity shocks, λ_d. Further, the model predicts that the price increases as the asset supply s lowers. One of the most remarkable predictions is that illiquidity discounts deteriorate with search frictions: the higher the λ, the closer the OTC price is to its Walrasian counterpart. Finally, the price is increasing in q, the bargaining power of seller. Traders who want to sell will get prices closer to the buyers' reservation values, provided they have enough bargaining power. Duffie, Gârleanu, and Pedersen (2007) further examine the effects of an aggregate liquidity shock, obtained

33. For any Poisson model with intensity λ, the expected number of events on a time interval $T-t$ is equal to $\lambda\,(T-t)$ (see section 4.9 in chapter 4). Fixing $T-t=1$ is tantamount to "annualizing" λ.

while tilting the ergodic distribution of the traders toward one with many of the low type. The authors find that prices may recover quite slowly following a liquidity shock.

Appendix 10.A The Projection Theorem

Consider the following Gaussian environment, in which a random vector is normally distributed:

$$\begin{bmatrix} y \\ x \end{bmatrix} \sim N\left(\begin{bmatrix} \mu_y \\ \mu_x \end{bmatrix}, \begin{bmatrix} \Sigma_y & \Sigma_{yx} \\ \Sigma_{xy} & \Sigma_x \end{bmatrix} \right).$$

We have

$$E\left(y \middle| x\right) = \mu_y + \Sigma_{yx}\Sigma_x^{-1}\left(x - \mu_x\right) \tag{10.A1}$$

and

$$var\left(y \middle| x\right) = \Sigma_y - \Sigma_{yx}\Sigma_x^{-1}\Sigma_{xy}. \tag{10.A2}$$

A proof of this result can be obtained as follows. Consider the following "regression,"

$$\left(y - \mu_y\right) = B\left(x - \mu_x\right) + \epsilon, \tag{10.A3}$$

where ϵ is zero mean and orthogonal to x. By taking covariances in eq. (10.A3), $\Sigma_{yx} = B\Sigma_x$, yielding eq. (10.A1), and by taking variances in eq. (10.A3),

$$-B\Sigma_x B^\top + \Sigma_y = var\left(\epsilon\right) = var\left(y \middle| x\right).$$

Plugging $B = \Sigma_{yx}\Sigma_x^{-1}$ into the previous equation leaves eq. (10.A2).

We apply the projection theorem to study inference problems in which the conditioning variable x is a vector of signals, $x = s \equiv \left[s^1, \cdots, s^n\right]$, where

$$s^i = y + u^i, \quad u \sim N\left(0, \sigma_u^2\right), \quad i = 1, \cdots, n. \tag{10.A4}$$

Let $n = 1$ and let σ_y^2 denote the variance of y when $n = 1$. We have

$$E\left(y \middle| s\right) = \mu_y + \frac{\sigma_y^2}{\sigma_y^2 + \sigma_u^2}\left(s - \mu_y\right), \quad var\left(y \middle| s\right) = \sigma_y^2 \frac{\sigma_u^2}{\sigma_y^2 + \sigma_u^2}.$$

We can express the previous relations in terms of precision of the signals,

$$E\left(y \middle| s\right) = \mu_y + \frac{\pi_u}{\pi_y + \pi_u}\left(s - \mu_y\right), \quad var\left(y \middle| s\right) = \frac{1}{\pi_y + \pi_u}, \tag{10.A5}$$

where $\pi_\cdot$ denotes the precision of a random variable—for example, $\pi_u = \frac{1}{\sigma_u^2}$. Eq. (10.A5) is easily generalized to the case of multiple signals in (10.A4) with possibily different variances,

$$E\left(y \middle| s^1, \cdots, s^n\right) = \mu_y + \sum_{i=1}^{n} \frac{\pi_{u_i}}{\pi_y + \sum_{j=1}^{n} \pi_{u_j}}\left(s^i - \mu_y\right), \tag{10.A6a}$$

$$var\left(y|\,s^1,\cdots,s^n\right)=\frac{1}{\pi_y+\sum_{i=1}^n\pi_{u_i}}. \tag{10.A6b}$$

Eqs. (10.A6a) and (10.A6b) simplify once the precisions of the signals are all the same, $\pi_{u_i}=\pi_u$ for all i, leaving

$$E\left(y|\,s^1,\cdots,s^n\right)=\mu_y+\frac{n\pi_u}{\pi_y+n\pi_u}\left(\hat{s}-\mu_y\right),\quad var\left(y|\,s^1,\cdots,s^n\right)=\frac{1}{\pi_y+n\pi_u},$$

where $\hat{s}$ denotes the average signal,

$$\hat{s}\equiv\frac{1}{n}\sum_{i=1}^n s^i.$$

Appendix 10.B Proof of Selected Results

Proof of eq. (10.36) (Grossman and Stiglitz (1980) model). First, we determine the expected utility of the would-be uninformed investors. By the law of iterated expectations, it is

$$\mathcal{U}_U=E\left(E\left(-e^{-\tau W_U}\middle|\,p\right)\right)=E\left(-e^{-\tau E(W_U|p)+\frac{1}{2}\tau^2 Var(W_U|p)}\right),$$

where, by the expression of $\hat{x}_U$ in (10.27),

$$E(W_U|\,p)=(W_0+\omega_0 p)R+\gamma\pi_{d|p}\left(E\left(d|\,p\right)-Rp\right)^2,$$
$$Var(W_U|\,p)=\gamma^2\pi_{d|p}\left(E\left(d|\,p\right)-Rp\right)^2,$$

such that

$$\mathcal{U}_U=E\left(-e^{-\tau(W_0+\omega_0 p)R}\cdot e^{-\frac{1}{2}\pi_{d|p}(E(d|p)-Rp)^2}\right). \tag{10.A7}$$

Next, we calculate the expected utility of the would-be informed investors after accounting for information costs. By the law of iterated expectations, it is

$$\begin{aligned}\mathcal{U}_I&=E\left(E\left(-e^{-\tau(W_I-C)}\middle|\,p,s\right)\right)\\&=e^{\tau C}E\left(-e^{-\tau(W_0+\omega_0 p)R}\cdot e^{-\frac{1}{2}\pi_{d|s}(E(d|s)-Rp)^2}\right)\\&=e^{\tau C}E\left(-e^{-\tau(W_0+\omega_0 p)R}\cdot E\left(e^{-\frac{1}{2}\pi_{d|s}(E(d|s)-Rp)^2}\middle|\,p\right)\right).\end{aligned} \tag{10.A8}$$

To determine the inner expectation in the last line of (10.A8), we rely on the following distributional result, shown below:

$$\begin{aligned}&\sqrt{\pi_{d|s}}\left(E\left(d|\,s\right)-Rp\right)\Big|_p\sim N(E,V),\\&E\equiv\sqrt{\pi_{d|s}}\left(E\left(d|\,p\right)-Rp\right),\quad V\equiv\frac{\pi_{d|s}}{\pi_{d|p}}-1.\end{aligned} \tag{10.A9}$$

Now, it is well known that if $x \sim N(E, V)$, then

$$E\left(e^{-\frac{1}{2}x^2}\right) = \frac{1}{\sqrt{1+V}} e^{-\frac{1}{2}\frac{E^2}{1+V}}.$$

Applying this to determine the inner expectation in (10.A8) yields

$$\mathcal{U}_I = e^{\tau C}\sqrt{\frac{\pi_{d|p}}{\pi_{d|s}}} E\left(-e^{-\tau(W_0+\omega_0 p)R} \cdot e^{-\frac{1}{2}\pi_{d|p}((E(d|p)-Rp))^2}\right) = e^{\tau C}\sqrt{\frac{\pi_{d|p}}{\pi_{d|s}}} \cdot \mathcal{U}_U,$$

where the second equality follows by the expression of $\mathcal{U}_U$ in eq. (10.A7). Eq. (10.36) follows by the previous expression of $\mathcal{U}_I$.

We are left to show that (10.A9) holds true. Regarding the conditional expectation E, note that $E(d|s) = E(d|s,Z)$, such that, by the law of iterated expectations and the fact that the information content of p is coarser than that of (s, Z),

$$E(E(d|s)|p) = E(E(d|s,Z)|p) = E(d|p).$$

Regarding the expression for V in (10.A9), note that, due to the normality of d, s, and p, we have that

$$\begin{aligned}\sigma^2_{d|p} &\equiv var(d|p) \\ &= var(E(d|s)|p) + var(d - E(d|s)|p) \\ &= var(E(d|s)|p) + \sigma^2_{d|s},\end{aligned}$$

where the last line follows because $\sigma^2_{d|s}$ is independent of p. That is,

$$V = \pi_{d|s} \cdot var(E(d|s)|p) = \pi_{d|s} \cdot \left(\sigma^2_{d|p} - \sigma^2_{d|s}\right),$$

whence, the expression in (10.A9).

The equilibrium price in the differential information model (eq. (10.44)). By the projection theorem, the two coefficients appearing in the conditional expectation of (10.42) are

$$\begin{aligned}\begin{bmatrix}\chi_s \\ \chi_p\end{bmatrix}^\top &= \begin{bmatrix}cov(d,s^i) & cov(d,p)\end{bmatrix}\begin{bmatrix}var(s^i) & cov(s^i,p) \\ cov(s^i,p) & var(p)\end{bmatrix}^{-1} \\ &= \begin{bmatrix}cov(d,s^i) & cov(d,p)\end{bmatrix}\frac{1}{var(s^i)\,var(p) - cov^2(s^i,p)}\begin{bmatrix}var(p) & -cov(s^i,p) \\ -cov(s^i,p) & var(s^i)\end{bmatrix},\end{aligned} \tag{10.A10}$$

where, given the assumption on s^i in (10.11) and the conjectured equilibrium price in (10.43),

$$\begin{aligned}cov(d,s^i) &= \sigma^2_d, \\ cov(d,p) &= b_s\sigma^2_d,\end{aligned}$$

$$var(s^i) = \sigma_d^2 + \sigma_u^2,$$
$$cov(s^i, p) = b_s\left(\sigma_d^2 + \frac{1}{n}\sigma_u^2\right),$$
$$var\,(p) = b_s^2\left(\sigma_d^2 + \frac{1}{n}\sigma_u^2\right) + b_z^2\sigma_z^2, \tag{10.A11}$$

and the fourth equality follows because

$$cov\left(s^i, p\right) = b_s\left(\frac{1}{n}\sum_{i=1}^{n} cov\left(s^1, s^i\right)\right)$$
$$= b_s\frac{var\,(s^1) + (n-1)\,cov\,(s^1, s^2)}{n} = b_s\frac{\sigma_d^2 + \sigma_u^2 + (n-1)\,\sigma_d^2}{n}.$$

Plugging (10.A11) into eq. (10.A10) leaves, after tedious but straightforward calculations,

$$\begin{cases} \chi_s = \frac{1}{\Delta} b_z^2\sigma_z^2\sigma_d^2 \\ \chi_p = \frac{1}{\Delta} b_s\sigma_d^2\left(1 - \frac{1}{n}\right)\sigma_u^2 \end{cases}, \tag{10.A12}$$

where

$$\Delta \equiv var\left(s^i\right) var\,(p) - cov^2\left(s^i, p\right) = b_s^2\left(1 - \frac{1}{n}\right)\sigma_u^2\left(\sigma_d^2 + \frac{1}{n}\sigma_u^2\right) + b_z^2\sigma_z^2\left(\sigma_d^2 + \sigma_u^2\right). \tag{10.A13}$$

Next, replace (10.A12) into the expressions of the price coefficients, eqs. (10.46), which leaves the following expressions for b_s and b_z:

$$b_s = \frac{b_z^2\sigma_z^2\sigma_d^2}{R\Delta - b_s\sigma_d^2\left(1 - \frac{1}{n}\right)\sigma_u^2}, \quad b_z = \frac{\Delta}{\gamma\pi_{d|s,p}\left(R\Delta - b_s\sigma_d^2\left(1 - \frac{1}{n}\right)\sigma_u^2\right)}. \tag{10.A14}$$

We determine the conditional precision, $\pi_{d|s,p}$, prior to determining b_s and b_z in (10.A14). By the projection theorem,

$$\frac{1}{\pi_{d|s,p}} = \sigma_d^2 - \left[\begin{array}{cc} \chi_s & \chi_p \end{array}\right]\left[\begin{array}{c} cov\,(d, s^i) \\ cov\,(d, p) \end{array}\right] = \frac{1}{\Delta}\left(b_s^2\frac{1}{n}\left(1 - \frac{1}{n}\right)\sigma_u^2 + b_z^2\sigma_z^2\right)\sigma_u^2\sigma_d^2, \tag{10.A15}$$

where the second equality follows by (10.A11), the expressions for χ_s and χ_p in (10.A12), and that for Δ in (10.A13). Replacing eq. (10.A15) into the expression for b_z in (10.A14) and using (10.A13) leaves the following expressions for the asset price coefficients and the conditional precision:

$$\begin{cases} b_s = \dfrac{b_z^2 \sigma_z^2 \sigma_d^2}{R\Delta - b_s \sigma_d^2 \left(1 - \frac{1}{n}\right) \sigma_u^2} \\ \\ b_z = \dfrac{b_s^2 \frac{1}{n} \left(1 - \frac{1}{n}\right) \sigma_u^2 + b_z^2 \sigma_z^2}{\gamma \left(R\Delta - b_s \sigma_d^2 \left(1 - \frac{1}{n}\right) \sigma_u^2\right)} \sigma_u^2 \sigma_d^2 \end{cases} \tag{10.A16}$$

and

$$\pi_{d|s,p} = \frac{b_s^2 \left(1 - \frac{1}{n}\right) \sigma_u^2 \left(\sigma_d^2 + \frac{1}{n} \sigma_u^2\right) + b_z^2 \sigma_z^2 \left(\sigma_d^2 + \sigma_u^2\right)}{\left(b_s^2 \frac{1}{n} \left(1 - \frac{1}{n}\right) \sigma_u^2 + b_z^2 \sigma_z^2\right) \sigma_u^2 \sigma_d^2}. \tag{10.A17}$$

To show that there exists a unique solution for b_s and b_z, define the constant ψ through the following relation,

$$\psi \equiv \frac{b_z}{b_s} = \frac{b_s^2 \frac{1}{n} \left(1 - \frac{1}{n}\right) \sigma_u^2 + b_z^2 \sigma_z^2}{\gamma b_z^2 \sigma_z^2} \sigma_u^2 = \frac{\frac{1}{n} \left(1 - \frac{1}{n}\right) \sigma_u^2 + \sigma_z^2 \psi^2}{\gamma \sigma_z^2 \psi^2} \sigma_u^2 \tag{10.A18}$$

where the first equality follows by eqs. (10.A16) and the second by the very same definition of ψ. It is easy to see that there exists a unique solution for ψ to eq. (10.A18), ψ_*, say. Given ψ_*, we determine b_s in (10.A16) by expressing it as a function of ψ^* and relying on the definition of Δ in (10.A13) as follows:

$$b_s = \frac{b_z^2 \sigma_z^2 \sigma_d^2}{R\Delta - b_s \sigma_d^2 \left(1 - \frac{1}{n}\right) \sigma_u^2} = \frac{\psi_*^2 \sigma_z^2 \sigma_d^2}{R\kappa - \frac{1}{b_s} \sigma_d^2 \left(1 - \frac{1}{n}\right) \sigma_u^2}, \tag{10.A19}$$

where

$$\kappa \equiv \left(1 - \frac{1}{n}\right) \sigma_u^2 \left(\sigma_d^2 + \frac{1}{n} \sigma_u^2\right) + \psi_*^2 \sigma_z^2 \left(\sigma_d^2 + \sigma_u^2\right).$$

The solution for b_s and then b_z are obtained after rearranging terms in (10.A19) and using the definition of ψ:

$$b_s \equiv \frac{\sigma_d^2 \left(1 - \frac{1}{n}\right) \sigma_u^2 + \psi_*^2 \sigma_z^2 \sigma_d^2}{R\kappa}, \quad b_z = b_s \psi_*.$$

Eq. (10.47) follows after using the definitions of precisions in the previous expression and after rearranging terms.

The limiting case in eq. (10.49) is obtained after taking the limits in eq. (10.47) for n large and noting that

$$\lim_{n \to \infty} \psi_* = \bar{\psi} \equiv \frac{\sigma_u^2}{\gamma}.$$

Finally, the limiting conditional precision in (10.51) is obtained after taking the limit in eq. (10.A17) for n large and using the previous definition of $\bar{\psi}$.

Proof of eq. (10.88). By eq. (10.84), the order flow is

$$y=\sum_{i=1}^{N} x_i+Z=N\beta\left(\hat{s}-\bar{d}\right)+Z, \tag{10.A20}$$

where $\hat{s}$ denotes the average signal,

$$\hat{s}\equiv\frac{1}{N}\sum_{i=1}^{N} s^i=d+\frac{1}{N}\sum_{i=1}^{N} u^i. \tag{10.A21}$$

We have

$$cov\left(y,d\right)=N\beta\sigma_d^2 \tag{10.A22}$$

and, defining σ_s^2 as in (10.A24) below,

$$var\left(y\right)=N^2\beta^2 var(\hat{s})+\sigma_z^2=N^2\beta^2\frac{N\sigma_s^2+N\left(N-1\right)\rho\sigma_s^2}{N^2}+\sigma_z^2. \tag{10.A23}$$

Eq. (10.88) follows by eqs. (10.A22) and (10.A23) and by

$$\sigma_s^2\equiv\sigma_d^2+\sigma_u^2=\rho^{-1}\sigma_d^2. \tag{10.A24}$$

Proof of eq. (10.90). Note that by eq. (10.A20), the equilibrium price is

$$p=\bar{d}+\lambda\left(N\beta(\hat{s}-\bar{d})+Z\right).$$

Moreover, the trade of agent 1 is $x_1=\beta(s^1-\bar{d})$. Therefore, the expected profits for each trader are

$$\begin{aligned}E((d-p)x)&=\beta E((d-\bar{d})(s^1-\bar{d}))-\lambda N\beta^2E((\hat{s}-\bar{d})(s^1-\bar{d}))\\&=\beta\left((1-\lambda\beta N)\,\sigma_d^2-\lambda\beta\sigma_u^2\right)\\&=\beta\frac{(2-\rho)\,\sigma_d^2-\rho\sigma_u^2}{2+(N-1)\,\rho},\end{aligned}$$

where the second line follows by the expression for the average signal in eq. (10.A21) and by rearranging terms, and the third by using the expression for $\lambda\beta$ in eq. (10.87). Eq. (10.90) follows by the definition of ρ in (10.A24) and the expression for β in (10.89).

Proofs regarding the model with mandatory disclosure. By the projection theorem,

$$\lambda_1=\frac{cov(\tilde{d},y_1)}{var\left(y_1\right)}=\frac{\beta_1\sigma_d^2}{\beta_1^2\sigma_d^2+\sigma_\eta^2+\sigma_z^2},\quad \gamma=\frac{cov(\tilde{d},x_1)}{var\left(x_1\right)}=\frac{\beta_1\sigma_d^2}{\beta_1^2\sigma_d^2+\sigma_\eta^2}, \tag{10.A25}$$

and

$$\sigma^2_{d|x_1} = \sigma^2_d - \frac{cov^2(\tilde{d}, x_1)}{var(x_1)} = (1 - \gamma\beta_1)\,\sigma^2_d. \tag{10.A26}$$

We conjecture that

$$\sigma^2_\eta = \ell\beta_1^2\sigma^2_d \tag{10.A27}$$

for some constant ℓ. Then, by the second of eqs. (10.A25), $\gamma\beta_1 = (1+\ell)^{-1}$, and plugging this expression into eq. (10.A26), delivers

$$\sigma^2_{d|x_1} = \frac{\ell}{1+\ell}\sigma^2_d. \tag{10.A28}$$

Note also that $\gamma = 2\lambda_2$ and $2\lambda_2 = \frac{1}{\beta_2}$, such that $\gamma\beta_2 = 1$. Using this results and $\gamma\beta_1 = (1+\ell)^{-1}$ yields

$$\beta_2 = (1+\ell)\,\beta_1. \tag{10.A29}$$

Next, using the expressions for λ_1 in the first of eqs. (10.A25) and for λ_2 (see eq. (10.123)) into the equality, $\lambda_1 = \lambda_2$,

$$\frac{\beta_1\sigma^2_d}{\beta_1^2\sigma^2_d + \sigma^2_\eta + \sigma^2_z} = \frac{\beta_2\sigma^2_{d|x_1}}{\beta_2^2\sigma^2_{d|x_1} + \sigma^2_z}. \tag{10.A30}$$

Plugging (10.A27), (10.A28), and (10.A29) into (10.A30) leaves

$$\frac{\beta_1\sigma^2_d}{(1+\ell)\,\beta_1^2\sigma^2_d + \sigma^2_z} = \frac{\ell\beta_1\sigma^2_d}{\ell\,(1+\ell)\,\beta_1^2\sigma^2_d + \sigma^2_z}.$$

This equation is satisfied by $\ell = 1$. Replacing this solution into (10.A27), (10.A28), and (10.A29) leads to the results stated in the main text.

Appendix 10.C Market Segmentation

Proof of eq. (10.134). We have

$$\begin{aligned} var_t\,(dV_t) &= var_t\left(\int_0^T \pi_t(\tau)\,\frac{dP_t(\tau)}{P_t(\tau)}d\tau\right)dt \\ &= \left(\sigma_r^2\left(\int_0^T \pi_t(\tau)\,A_r(\tau)\,d\tau\right)^2 + \sigma_\beta^2\left(\int_0^T \pi_t(\tau)\,A_\beta(\tau)\,d\tau\right)^2\right)dt, \end{aligned}$$

such that the first-order conditions for [10.P2] lead to

$$\mu_t(\tau) - r_t = a\left[\sigma_r^2 A_r(\tau)\int_0^T \pi_t(u)\,A_r(u)\,du + \sigma_\beta^2 A_\beta(\tau)\int_0^T \pi_t(u)\,A_\beta(u)\,du\right].$$

Eq. (10.134) follows by the equilibrium condition $s_t(\tau) = \pi_t(\tau)$.

Proof that $A_r(\cdot) > 0$ *and* $A_\beta(\cdot) \geq 0$. Rewrite eq. (10.134) as follows:

$$\mu_t(\tau) - r_t = -\sigma_r A_r(\tau)\lambda_{r,t} - \sigma_\beta A_\beta(\tau)\lambda_{\beta,t},$$

where

$$\lambda_{j,t} = -a\sigma_j \int_0^T s_t(u) A_j(u)\, du, \quad j = r, \beta.$$

We have

$$P_t(r_t, \beta_t, T) = \mathbb{E}_t\left(e^{-\int_t^T r_u du}\right),$$

where $\mathbb{E}_t(\cdot)$ denotes the conditional expectation under the risk neutral probability and, by the Girsanov theorem (see chapter 4), the short-term rate is the solution to

$$dr_t = [\kappa_r(\bar{r} - r_t) - \sigma_r\lambda_{r,t}]\, dt + \sigma_r d\hat{W}_{1t}$$

and $\hat{W}_{1t}$ is a standard Brownian motion under the risk neutral probability. By results in chapter 8 (see appendix 8.D), it is easy to show that $\frac{\partial r_t}{\partial r_0} \geq 0$, which proves the claims that $A_r(\cdot) \geq 0$.

Regarding the sign of $A_\beta(\cdot)$, note that $y_t \equiv \frac{\partial r_t}{\partial \beta_0}$ is solution to

$$dy_t = -\left(\kappa_r y_t + \sigma_r \frac{\partial \lambda_{r,t}}{\partial \beta_0}\right) dt,$$

where

$$\frac{\partial \lambda_{r,t}}{\partial \beta_0} = -a\sigma_r \int_0^T \frac{\partial s_t(u)}{\partial \beta_0} A_r(u)\, du = -a\sigma_r \frac{\partial \beta_t}{\partial \beta_0} \int_0^T \theta(u) A_r(u)\, du$$

and where the second equality follows by the definition of $s_t(\cdot)$ in eq. (10.133). Note that $y_0 = 0$ and that $\frac{\partial \beta_t}{\partial \beta_0} > 0$. Moreover, it is possible to show that $A_r(u)$ is positive and increasing in u. Therefore, by the assumptions in the main text that $\int_0^T \theta(\tau)\, d\tau > 0$ and that $\theta(\tau) < 0$ for $\tau < \tau^*$ and $\theta(\tau) > 0$ for $\tau > \tau^*$, it is easy to show that $\frac{\partial \lambda_{r,t}}{\partial \beta_0} < 0$. Now, $z_t = e^{\kappa_r t} y_t$ is the solution to

$$dz_t = -e^{\kappa_r t}\sigma_r \frac{\partial \lambda_{r,t}}{\partial \beta_0} dt, \quad z_0 = 0,$$

such that $z_t \geq 0$ and then $y_t = \frac{\partial r_t}{\partial \beta_0} \geq 0$ for all t, then implying that $\frac{\partial P_t(r_t,\beta_t,T)}{\partial \beta_t} \leq 0$, thereby establishing that $A_\beta(\cdot) \geq 0$.

Appendix 10.D Search

Proof of eq. (10.144). Consider eqs. (10.142). Subtracting the second from the first equation and the fourth from the third leaves

$$\begin{cases} r\Delta V_l = \lambda_u(\Delta V_h - \Delta V_l) + \lambda\mu_{hn}(P - \Delta V_l) + 1 - \delta \\ r\Delta V_h = \lambda_d(\Delta V_l - \Delta V_h) + 1 - \lambda\mu_{lo}(\Delta V_h - P) \end{cases}.$$

Replacing the price P in (10.143) into the previous system and simplifying leads to

$$\begin{cases} r\Delta V_l = (\lambda_u + \lambda\mu_{hn}q)\left(\Delta V_h - \Delta V_l\right) + 1 - \delta \\ r\Delta V_h = -\left(\lambda_d + \lambda\mu_{lo}\left(1-q\right)\right)\left(\Delta V_h - \Delta V_l\right) + 1 \end{cases} \tag{10.A31}$$

which is solved by

$$\Delta V_h - \Delta V_l = \frac{\delta}{r + \lambda_u + \lambda_d + \lambda\mu_{lo}\left(1-q\right) + \lambda\mu_{hn}q}.$$

Replacing the previous expression for $\Delta V_h - \Delta V_l$ into the first of eqs. (10.A31) leads to an expression for ΔV_l. Replacing this expression for ΔV_l and the previous expression for $\Delta V_h - \Delta V_l$ into eq. (10.143) leaves the expression for the price in (10.144).

Determination of the steady state. Evaluating eqs. (10.141) at the steady state leaves

$$\begin{cases} 0 = -\lambda\mu_{hn}\mu_{lo} - \lambda_u\mu_{lo} + \lambda_d\mu_{ho} \\ 0 = \lambda\mu_{hn}\mu_{lo} - \lambda_u\mu_{ln} + \lambda_d\mu_{hn} \\ 0 = \lambda\mu_{hn}\mu_{lo} - \lambda_d\mu_{ho} + \lambda_u\mu_{lo} \\ 0 = -\lambda\mu_{hn}\mu_{lo} - \lambda_d\mu_{hn} + \lambda_u\mu_{ln} \end{cases} \tag{10.A32}$$

where all masses sum to one and asset supply is equal to s

$$1 = \mu_{lo} + \mu_{ln} + \mu_{ho} + \mu_{hn}, \quad s = \mu_{lo} + \mu_{ho}. \tag{10.A33}$$

Add the first and second (or, indifferently, the third and fourth) equations of (10.A32) and conclude that

$$\mu_{lo} + \mu_{ln} = \left(\mu_{ho} + \mu_{hn}\right)\frac{\lambda_d}{\lambda_u}. \tag{10.A34}$$

Combining the first of eqs. (10.A33) and eq. (10.A34) leaves

$$\mu_{lo} + \mu_{ln} = \frac{\lambda_d}{\lambda_u + \lambda_d}, \quad \mu_{ho} + \mu_{hn} = \frac{\lambda_u}{\lambda_u + \lambda_d}. \tag{10.A35}$$

Combining the second of eqs. (10.A33) and the second of eq. (10.A35) leaves

$$\mu_{hn} = \mu_{lo} + \frac{\lambda_u}{\lambda_u + \lambda_d} - s. \tag{10.A36}$$

Replacing the second of eqs. (10.A33) and eq. (10.A36) into the first equation of (10.A32) leaves the quadratic equation for μ_{lo} in the main text (see eq. (10.145)).

Appendix 10.E Introduction to Pricing Behavior in Macroeconomics

We provide a few arguments to justify the functional form for the supply and demand equations of section 10.2 (see eq. (10.1) and eq. (10.3)). We consider a variant of a model presented by Blanchard and Fischer (1989), which itself is a simplified version of Blanchard and Kiyotaki (1987). The model in this appendix differs from those above as it considers (i) a continuum of goods and (ii) taste shocks affecting each good. While the material in this appendix goes somehow beyond the scope of this book, it still helps keep the reasoning in this chapter self-contained.

Consumers-producers tastes and technology and markets. Consider a continuum of consumers-producers, each with a utility function equal to

$$U_i \equiv C_i^g \left(\frac{M_i}{P}\right)^{1-g} - d\frac{L_i^\beta}{\beta}, \quad i \in [0,1], \tag{10.A37}$$

where M_i is the nominal money holdings, P is a price index (to be determined below; see eq. (10.A44)), C_i is consumption of a basket of goods (to be defined in a moment), and L_i is labor supplied; the parameters satisfy $g \in (0,1)$, $d > 0$, $\beta \geq 1$. In other words, each producer enjoys consuming a basket of goods but experiences a disutility while working. Moreover, the agent's utility enjoys holding real money, M_i/P, an assumption that leads to a positive real money demand.

We assume that the basket of goods contains constant elasticity of substitution (CES) substitutes as in Dixit and Stiglitz (1977), that is,

$$C_i = \left(\int_0^1 Z_j^{1/\theta} C_{ij}^{(\theta-1)/\theta} dj\right)^{\frac{\theta}{\theta-1}}, \tag{10.A38}$$

where C_{ij} is consumer-producer i's consumption of the good j; Z_j is a taste shock for good j, assumed to be the same for all consumers-producers; and θ is the CES between any two consumption goods C_{ij} and $C_{i\ell}$. We assume that $\theta > 1$. We shall specify the properties of Z_j later.

Finally, we assume that (i) each producer specializes in the production of their own good according to the simple technology $Y_i = L_i$ and that (ii) the market is one with monopolistic competition; this market collapses to the perfectly competitive one when θ is large.

Each consumer-producer i maximizes the utility in (10.A37) subject to the budget constraint,

$$\int_0^1 P_j C_{ij} dj + M_i = P_i Y_i + \bar{M}_i \equiv I_i, \tag{10.A39}$$

where P_i is the price of the produced good and $\bar{M}_i$ is the money endowment. It is easy to see that the solution to this problem is symmetric in that each consumer-producer chooses the same basket *composition* (although then the *size* of this basket is determined by their income I_i). We can then define the price index in (10.A37) as the minimal expenditure needed to purchase a unit of the composite good C_i in eq. (10.A38),

$$P : PC_i = \int_0^1 P_j C_{ij} dj. \tag{10.A40}$$

We now determine the demand for both the single and the composite good.

Goods demand and price index. We determine C_i first. Replacing eq. (10.A40) into the budget constraint (10.A39) and maximizing (10.A37) subject to the resulting constraint,

$PC_i + M_i = I_i$, leads to a standard result:

$$C_i = g\frac{I_i}{P}, \quad M_i = (1-g)\, I_i. \tag{10.A41}$$

Next, we identify the optimal composition of each single good, C_{ij}. It is

$$\hat{C}_{ij} = \arg\max_{C_{ij}} C_i \quad \text{s.t.} \quad \int_0^1 P_j C_{ij} dj = I_i - M_i = gI_i, \tag{10.A42}$$

where the second equality of the constraint follows by eqs. (10.A41). Note that this program is simply the maximization of (10.A37) under the constraint (10.A39). The first-order conditions lead to

$$\left(\frac{Z_\ell}{Z_j}\right)^{-\frac{1}{\theta}} \left(\frac{C_{ij}}{C_{i\ell}}\right)^{1-\frac{1}{\theta}} = \frac{P_j C_{ij}}{P_\ell C_{i\ell}},$$

whence, the definition of θ as the CES between any two consumption goods. Note that, to simplify notation, we are now reverting to writing $C_{ij} \equiv \hat{C}_{ij}$. Replacing the previous optimality condition into the definition of the price index in (10.A40) and using the definition of the composite good in eq. (10.A38) leads to

$$C_{i\ell} = Z_\ell \left(\frac{P_\ell}{P}\right)^{-\theta} C_i = gZ_\ell \left(\frac{P_\ell}{P}\right)^{-\theta} \frac{I_i}{P}, \tag{10.A43}$$

where the second equality follows by (10.A41).

The price index is obtained by solving for P in eq. (10.A40) while relying on the first equality in eq. (10.A43), leaving

$$P = \left(\int_0^1 Z_j P_j^{1-\theta} dj\right)^{\frac{1}{1-\theta}}. \tag{10.A44}$$

Finally, we determine the indirect utility of consumer-producer i by replacing eqs. (10.A41) into eq. (10.A37),

$$U_i = \gamma \frac{I_i}{P} - d\frac{Y_i^\beta}{\beta} = \gamma \left(\frac{P_i}{P} Y_i + \frac{\bar{M}_i}{P}\right) - d\frac{Y_i^\beta}{\beta}, \tag{10.A45}$$

where γ is a constant and where we have used the agent budget constraint and the production technology $Y_i = L_i$. Note that this expression resembles the profit of a maximizing firm. One issue is whether the consumer-producer has pricing power, that is, whether P_i in $P_i Y_i$ is affected by their decisions regarding Y_i. We assume it is the case below, although this is not crucial for the interpretation of the pricing equations in section 10.2.

Production and equilibrium. The aggregate demand for the good produced by the consumer-producer ℓ is obtained by aggregating the individual demands for this good,

$$Y_\ell \equiv \int_0^1 C_{i\ell} di = gZ_\ell \left(\frac{P_\ell}{P}\right)^{-\theta} \int_0^1 \frac{I_i}{P} di = Z_\ell \left(\frac{P_\ell}{P}\right)^{-\theta} Y, \tag{10.A46}$$

where we have used the second equality in (10.A43) and where the last equality holds by the following definition of aggregate demand, Y,

$$PY \equiv \int_0^1 \left(\int_0^1 P_j C_{ij} dj \right) di = \int_0^1 PC_i di = g \int_0^1 I_i di. \tag{10.A47}$$

Let $\bar{M}$ denote the aggregate money endowment. We can solve for Y by noticing that

$$Y = g \int_0^1 \frac{I_i}{P} di = g \left(\int_0^1 \frac{P_i Y_i + \bar{M}_i}{P} di \right) = g \left(Y + \frac{\bar{M}}{P} \right), \tag{10.A48}$$

where the last equality follows by the fact that, in equilibrium, $\bar{M} = \int_0^1 M_i di$, such that

$$\int_0^1 P_i Y_i di = \int_0^1 PC_i di = PY,$$

where the first equality follows by aggregating the agents' budget constraint and the second by (10.A47). By eq. (10.A48), the solution for Y is then

$$Y = \frac{g}{1-g} \frac{\bar{M}}{P},$$

which, when replaced into eq. (10.A46), leaves the aggregate demand facing consumer-producer i:

$$Y_i = Z_i \left(\frac{P_i}{P} \right)^{-\theta} \frac{g}{1-g} \frac{\bar{M}}{P}. \tag{10.A49}$$

In the context of monopolistic competition of this appendix, one could solve for the optimal pricing rule. The latter is obtained by replacing eq. (10.A49) into eq. (10.A45) and maximizing with respect to P_i, leaving

$$\frac{P_i}{P} = \left[\frac{d\theta}{\gamma(\theta - 1)} \left(Z_i \frac{g}{1-g} \frac{\bar{M}}{P} \right)^{\beta - 1} \right]^{\frac{1}{1+\theta(\beta-1)}}. \tag{10.A50}$$

We now proceed with the interpretation of some basic assumptions in section 10.2 in light of the framework developed so far.

Relations with the model in section 10.2. Eq. (10.A49) provides foundations to the demand for each produced good in the model of section 10.2 (see eq. (10.3)). Regarding the supply equation (see eq. (10.1)), note that the assumption of market power and that P is common knowledge leads to eq. (10.A50), which could be replaced back into eq. (10.A49) to determine the equilibrium production in each market. Alternatively, one could simplify and remove the assumption of market power. Assume further that P is not common knowledge, in which case producers maximize their expected utility in eq. (10.A45):

$$\hat{Y}_i \equiv \arg\max_{Y_i} E \left(\gamma \frac{P_i Y_i}{P} - d \frac{Y_i^\beta}{\beta} \middle| P_i \right) = \left[\frac{\gamma}{d} E \left(\frac{P_i}{P} \middle| P_i \right) \right]^{\frac{1}{\beta - 1}}.$$

Assume that, conditionally on P_i, $\ln \frac{P_i}{P}$ is normally distributed. It is easy to verify that, in this case,

$$y_i^s \equiv \ln \hat{Y}_i = \kappa_0 + \kappa_1 E\left(p_i - p \middle| p_i\right) \tag{10.A51}$$

for two constant, κ_0 and κ_1. Naturally, the assumption that $p_i - p$ is conditionally normally distributed needs to be verified to hold in equilibrium. However, the price index in eq. (10.A44) reveals this to be problematic, unless a number of conditions hold true. For example, assume that the agents' distribution is such that there is a mass $\mu(i)$ of agents i, and suppose that taste shocks are centered around one, or $\int Z_i d\mu(i) = 1$, and that $\theta = 1$ such that

$$p = \int Z_i p_i d\mu(i).$$

Even in this case, the price index is not exactly the average log-price due to the presence of the taste shocks, such that eq. (10.A51) is only an approximation to eq. (10.1).

References

Admati, A. R., and P. Pfleiderer (1986). "A Monopolistic Market for Information." *Journal of Economic Theory* 39, 400–438.

Admati, A. R., and P. Pfleiderer (1988). "A Theory of Intraday Patterns: Volume and Price Variability." *Review of Financial Studies* 1, 3–40.

Allen, F., and D. Gale (2007). *Understanding Financial Crises*. Oxford: Oxford University Press.

Allen, F., S. Morris, and H. S. Shin (2006). "Beauty Contests and Iterated Expectations in Asset Markets." *Review of Financial Studies* 19, 719–752.

Amihud, Y. (2002). "Illiquidity and Stock Returns: Cross-Section and Time Series Effects." *Journal of Financial Markets* 5, 31–56.

Back, K. (1992). "Insider Trading in Continuous Time." *Review of Financial Studies* 5, 387–409.

Back, K., C. H. Cao, and G. A. Willard (2000). "Imperfect Competition Among Informed Traders." *Journal of Finance* 55, 2117–2155.

Black, F. (1986). "Noise." *Journal of Finance* 41, 529–543.

Blanchard, O. J., and S. Fischer (1989). *Lectures on Macroeconomics*. Cambridge, MA: MIT Press.

Blanchard, O. J., and N. Kiyotaki (1987). "Monopolistic Competition and the Effects of Aggregate Demand." *American Economic Review* 77, 647–666.

Bolton, P., and D. S. Scharfstein (1990). "A Theory of Predation Based on Agency Problems in Financial Contracting." *American Economic Review* 80, 93–106.

Bryant, J. (1980). "A Model of Reserves, Bank Runs, and Deposit Insurance." *Journal of Banking and Finance* 4, 335–344.

Chamberlin, E. H. (1933). *The Theory of Monopolistic Competition: A Re-orientation of the Theory of Value*. Cambridge, MA: Harvard University Press.

Chowdhry, B., and V. Nanda (1991). "Multimarket Trading and Market Liquidity." *Review of Financial Studies* 4, 483–511.

Colla, P., and A. Mele (2010). "Information Linkages and Correlated Trading." *Review of Financial Studies* 23, 203–246.

Cournot, A. A. (1838). *Recherches sur les Principes Mathématiques de la Théorie des Richesses*. Paris: Hachette.

Culbertson, J. (1957). "The Term Structure of Interest Rates." *Quarterly Journal of Economics* 71, 485–517.

de Jong, F., and B. Rindi (2009). *The Microstructure of Financial Markets*. Cambridge: Cambridge University Press.

DeLong, J. B., A. Shleifer, L. H. Summers, and R. J. Waldman (1990). "Noise Trader Risk in Financial Markets." *Journal of Political Economy* 98, 703–738.

Diamond, D. W. (1984). "Financial Intermediation and Delegated Monitoring." *Review of Economic Studies* 51, 393–414.

Diamond, D. W., and P. H. Dybvig (1983). "Bank Runs, Deposit Insurance and Liquidity." *Journal of Political Economy* 91, 401–419.

Diamond, D. W., and R. E. Verrecchia (1981). "Information Aggregation in a Noisy Rational Expectations Economy." *Journal of Financial Economics* 9, 221–235.

Dixit, A. K., and J. E. Stiglitz (1977). "Monopolistic Competition and Optimum Product Diversity." *American Economic Review* 67, 297–308.

Duffie, D. (2010). "Presidential Address: Asset Price Dynamics with Slow-Moving Capital." *Journal of Finance* 65, 1237–1267.

Duffie, D. (2012). *Dark Markets: Asset Pricing and Information Transmission in Over-the-Counter Markets* (Princeton Lectures in Finance). Princeton, NJ: Princeton University Press.

Duffie, D., N. Gârleanu, and L. H. Pedersen (2005). "Over-the-Counter Markets." *Econometrica* 73, 1815–1847.

Duffie, D., N. Gârleanu, and L. H. Pedersen (2007). "Valuation in Over-the-Counter Markets." *Review of Financial Studies* 20, 1865–1900.

Fama, E. (1970). "Efficient Capital Markets: A Review of Theory and Empirical Work." *Journal of Finance* 25, 383–417.

Foster, F. D., and S. Viswanathan (1996). "Strategic Trading When Agents Forecast the Forecasts of Others." *Journal of Finance* 51, 1437–1478.

Foucault T., M. Pagano, and A. Röell (2013). *Market Liquidity: Theory, Evidence and Policy*. Oxford: Oxford University Press.

Freixas, X., and J. C. Rochet (1998). *Microeconomics of Banking*. Cambridge, MA: MIT Press.

Friedman, M. (1953). *The Case for Flexible Exchange Rates—Essays in Positive Economics*. Chicago, IL: University of Chicago Press.

Froot, K. A., and E. M. Dabora (1999). "How Are Stock Prices Affected by the Location of Trade?" *Journal of Financial Economics* 53, 189–216.

Glosten, L. R., and P. R. Milgrom (1985). "Bid, Ask and Transaction Prices in a Specialist Market with Heterogeneously Informed Traders." *Journal of Financial Economics* 14, 71–100.

Goldstein, I., and A. Pauzner (2005). "Demand Deposit Contracts and the Probability of Bank Runs." *Journal of Finance* 60, 1293–1328.

Goldstein, I. and A. Razin (2015). *Three Branches of Theories of Financial Crises*. Foundations and Trends® in Finance. Hanover, MA: Now Publishers.

Goyal, S. (2007). *Connections*. Princeton, NJ: Princeton University Press.

Greenwood, R., and D. Vayanos (2014). "Bond Supply and Excess Bond Returns." *Review of Financial Studies* 27, 663–713.

Gromb, D., and D. Vayanos (2002). "Equilibrium and Welfare in Markets with Financially Constrained Arbitrageurs." *Journal of Financial Economics* 66, 361–407.

Grossman, S. J. (1976). "On the Efficiency of Competitive Stock Markets Where Traders Have Diverse Information." *Journal of Finance* 31, 573–585.

Grossman, S. J., and J. E. Stiglitz (1980). "On the Impossibility of Informationally Efficient Markets." *American Economic Review* 70, 393–408.

Hasbrouck, J. (2007). *Empirical Market Microstructure*. Oxford: Oxford University Press.

Hayek, F. A. (1945). "The Use of Knowledge in Society." *American Economic Review* 35, 519–530.

Hellwig, M. F. (1980). "On the Aggregation of Information in Competitive Markets." *Journal of Economic Theory* 22, 477–498.

Huddart. S., J. S. Hughes, and C. B. Levine (2001). "Public Disclosure and Dissimulation of Insider Trades." *Econometrica* 69, 665–681.

Jackson, M. O. (2008). *Social and Economic Networks*. Princeton, NJ: Princeton University Press.

Karatzas, I., and S. E. Shreve (1991). *Brownian Motion and Stochastic Calculus*. 2nd ed. New York: Springer-Verlag.

Keynes, J. M. (1936). *The General Theory of Employment, Interest and Money*. London: Palgrave Macmillan.

Kyle, A. S. (1985). "Continuous Auctions and Insider Trading." *Econometrica* 53, 1335–1355.

Kyle, A. S. (1989). "Informed Speculation with Imperfect Competition." *Review of Economic Studies* 56, 317–356.

Lange, O. (1936). "On the Economic Theory of Socialism: Part I." *Review of Economic Studies* 4: 53–71.

Lange, O. (1942). "The Foundations of Welfare Economics." *Econometrica* 10: 215–228.

Lucas, R. E. (1972). "Expectations and the Neutrality of Money." *Journal of Economic Theory* 4, 103–124.

Lucas, R. E. (1973). "Some International Evidence on Output-Inflation Tradeoffs." *American Economic Review* 63, 326–334.

Lucas, R. E. (1977). "Econometric Policy Evaluation: A Critique." *Carnegie-Rochester Conference Series on Public Policy* 1, 19–46.

Lucas, R. E. (1981). *Studies in Business-Cycle Theory*. Cambridge, MA: MIT Press.

Mendelson, H. (1987). "Consolidation, Fragmentation, and Market Performance." *Journal of Financial and Quantitative Analysis* 22, 189–207.

Mercurio, F. (2009). *Interest Rates and the Credit Crunch: New Formulas and Market Models*. New York: Bloomberg Education & Quantitative Research, Bloomberg Portfolio Research Paper No. 2010-01. https://papers.ssrn.com/sol3/papers.cfm?abstract_id=1332205.

Modigliani, F., and R. Sutch (1966). "Innovations in Interest-Rate Policy." *American Economic Review* 56, 178–197.

Morris, S., and H. S. Shin (1998). "Unique Equilibrium in a Model of Self-Fulfilling Currency Attacks." *American Economic Review* 88, 587–597.

Ozsoylev, H. (2006). "Asset Pricing Implications of Social Networks." Working Paper, Oxford, Said Business School.

Ozsoylev, H., and J. Walden (2011). "Asset Pricing in Large Information Networks." *Journal of Economic Theory* 146, 2252–2280.

Ozsoylev, H., J. Walden, D. Yavuz, and R. Bildik (2014). "Investor Networks in the Stock Market." *Review of Financial Studies* 27, 1323–1366.

Pagano, M. (1989). "Trading Volume and Asset Liquidity." *Quarterly Journal of Economics* 104, 255–274.

Phelps, E. S. (1970). "Introduction." In *Microeconomic Foundations of Employment and Inflation Theory*, edited by E. S. Phelps. New York: Norton.

Roll, R. (1984). "A Simple Implicit Measure of the Effective Bid-Ask Spread in an Efficient Market." *Journal of Finance* 39, 1127–1139.

Rosenthal, L., and C. Young (1990). "The Seemingly Anomalous Price Behavior of Royal Dutch Shell and Unilever N. V./PLC." *Journal of Financial Economics* 26, 123–141.

Shleifer, A. (2000). *Inefficient Markets: An Introduction to Behavioral Finance.* Clarendon Lectures in Finance. Oxford: Oxford University Press.

Shleifer, A., and R. Vishny (1997). "The Limits of Arbitrage." *Journal of Finance* 52, 35–55.

Stoll, H. R. (1978). "The Supply of Dealer Services in Securities Markets." *Journal of Finance* 33, 1133–1151.

Vasicek, O. (1977). "An Equilibrium Characterization of the Term Structure." *Journal of Financial Economics* 5, 177–188.

Watts, D. J., and S. H. Strogatz (1998). "Collective Dynamics of 'Small-World' Networks." *Nature* 393, 440–442.

III

Asset Pricing and Reality

11

Options and Volatility

11.1 Introduction

This is the first of four chapters that aim to illustrate how financial theory helps deal with the evaluation of derivatives and related instruments. We already know that the motivation underlying much of the theory in part I is the attempt to build on the breakthrough made by Black and Scholes (1973) and Merton (1973) on option pricing. How come we may price financial assets without any assumption on risk aversion? Part I (see, e.g., chapter 4) explains the rationale behind this and related results, which we will briefly review in a moment. This chapter aims to make many additional steps forward by dealing with derivative pricing in markets more realistic than those initially idealized by Black–Scholes and Merton.

We face a paradox known since at least Hakansson (1979). If the Black–Scholes formula is true, we should acknowledge that markets are complete, that is, that options are "redundant." Redundancy is at the heart of the whole Black–Scholes theoretical construct. However, note the following paradox. If options are redundant, why would anyone be willing to trade them in the first place? Alternatively, options are not redundant, and in practice, options are massively traded indeed; but then the Black–Scholes formula is wrong, relying as it does on the assumption that markets are complete. Indeed, in practice, many derivatives are traded over-the-counter, with financial intermediaries specializing in providing counterparties with payoffs. Financial intermediation is also about matching clients' needs of obtaining dedicated payoffs against a fee—in addition to the "fair value" of the derivative. The fee can be justified by the specialization required to cope with the sources of market incompleteness as well as the risks the intermediary incurs into losses while honoring the payoffs to be delivered to clients.

Derivatives exist because of market imperfections. Imperfections may be due to market incompleteness and dealers' specialization as in the previous examples. We would need to find some analytically tractable examples that illustrate the nature of these imperfections. In this chapter, we proceed through a very humble generalization of the Black–Scholes market. In this market, volatility is constant. From part II (see, e.g., chapter 8), we know that market volatility changes randomly over time and is driven by a number of forces such as changing risk aversion or agents' imperfect information of the economy's fundamentals.

Random volatility may indeed lead to market incompleteness in that it may not be hedged through the assets that underlie our derivatives. This chapter then explores how derivative pricing is affected in these contexts. Note that we are not querying about the origin of market volatility—queries dealt with in part II. We simply take the random character of volatility as given, with the purpose of performing option evaluation.

While the task of this chapter is quite focused, we will discuss volatility along a variety of dimensions from measurement to trading. Section 11.2 begins with a few basic definitions regarding the main derivatives that we deal with: forwards, futures, and options. A basic example of a forward contract is the promise to pay the difference between some future time T price and a fixed strike. The strike is chosen at $t < T$ in a way to make the value of the position equal to zero at t; the value of this strike is the forward price. This example is simple but can be extended to deal with other types of risks. For example, one may consider a contract by which one party pays a second party the difference between future realized market volatility and a certain fixed value of this volatility—a *variance swap*. Futures, we shall see, are contracts that achieve the same objectives as forwards while at the same time accommodating for standardization.

Options add important nonlinearities to these contracts. Their value stems from volatility. The higher the volatility, the higher the value of the right to exercise an option in the future. Options and volatility come hand in hand. In fact, one may trade volatility while constructing dedicated portfolios of derivatives. Sections 11.3 and 11.4 review some preliminary properties of option prices—properties that are at the basis of more advanced sections. For example, a dealer may wish to approximate the payoff of a derivative through *delta hedging*, that is, by building a portfolio including the underlying in proportions given by the Black–Scholes formula. Delta hedging may help trade volatility as argued shortly below.

Section 11.5 is a short review of stochastic volatility models both in discrete and continuous time. This review deals with both statistical models and *implied volatilities*. Implied volatilities are the hypothetical volatilities that make the Black–Scholes formula consistent with market data. They typically increase with the relative distance of spot prices from (low) strikes, giving rise to what is known as the *skew*. Stochastic volatility is a very natural explanation for the skew. In turn, the skew relates to the price of volatility—the value of a variance swap—as explained below.

By "trading volatility," we mean a trading activity aimed at generating P&Ls that are sensitive to changes in market volatility. However, option prices move because of the movement of both volatility and the underlying prices. Section 11.6 explains how delta hedging may help remove the price-movement component. It explains that, in practice, one may need a large number of options (and additional assumptions) to insulate volatility in a perfect way. This circumstance helps explain the success of products that help trade volatility, which are referenced to baskets of options, such as futures or options referenced to the VIX index of market volatility maintained by Chicago Board Options Exchange (Cboe).

We refer to the price of these volatility products as the price of market volatility. This price links theoretically to implied volatility, to baskets of skews, and interestingly to another concept of uncertainty, *local volatility*. What is the fair value of an exotic product? We need to look at the skew at a given instant of time, turn this skew into a certain function of the underlying price and calendar time, and then use this function to price an exotic product. That is, we transform an observed skew into a certain function that we use as the diffusion coefficient for the stock price. This function, called local volatility, is such that the resulting diffusion model reproduces the observed price of liquid products without error. The model then provides the fair value for products that have never been traded or more generally as a useful benchmark for an illiquid product. As mentioned, somehow surprisingly, local volatilities also link to the price of market volatility. Section 11.7 is an introduction to these concepts. Sections 11.8 and 11.9 contain a systematic treatment of the linkages among all these concepts of volatility. They present derivations of the fair value of variance swaps and the main derivatives referenced to this fair value, such as futures and options, and some basic evaluation models for these derivatives.

Finally, section 11.10 discusses the potential of certain trading strategies to lead to episodes of market dysfunctionalities, such as market crashes and other spikes of volatility that are not justified by the economic fundamentals. This topic relates to a theme known as "endogenous risk," the property that some initial shocks may turn into some self-reinforcing trends. Chapter 9 deals with this theme while insisting on linkages and amplification mechanisms between financial markets and the macroeconomy. This section focuses on feedback effects from derivative markets into the market for the underlying securities and the possible destabilizing outcomes that may result from them.

11.2 Forwards and Futures

A forward contract is an agreement to pay for the realization of a given risk at some maturity date, with the price being agreed at the contract's inception. The realized risk can be anything: an asset price, a commodity price, or an abstract index. The agreed price is called the *forward price* and is such that it makes the value of the contract equal to zero at inception. A standard situation is when the risk is a commodity price and when the two parties agree to trade at a price determined at inception, a situation we take as a benchmark in this chapter. In this case, we adopt the convention to say that the party with the obligation to buy the asset at the expiration has a long position and that the other party has a short position.

Forward contracts can lock in uncertainty relating to future events. Consider the following examples. A chocolate producer starts the production process at time T where they will need cocoa as an input. The output, chocolate, will be sold at time $S > T$:

cocoa chocolate

———— T ———— S ———→

Let $p_{\text{co},T}$ and $p_{\text{ch},S}$ denote the prices of cocoa and chocolate at time T and S, and let F_{co} and F_{ch} be the corresponding forward prices. To insure against the vagaries of cocoa prices, the producer can go *long* a forward contract. This contract guarantees a payoff equal to $p_{\text{co},T} - F_{\text{co}}$ at time T. This payoff, minus the unit input cost $p_{\text{co},T}$ to be incurred at time T, leaves exactly $-F_{\text{co}}$. That is, a forward contract allows the producer to freeze the sure amount F_{co} to be paid at T. Likewise, the producer may wish to be *short* a forward on the price of their own chocolate; indeed, this position would allow them to receive a payoff equal to $F_{\text{ch}} - p_{\text{ch},S}$ at S, and when this is added to the price of chocolate sold at S, it leaves the sure amount F_{ch}. This section deals with the pricing of such contracts.

11.2.1 Forwards: Definition and Pricing in Frictionless Markets

In a forward contract, a party (the long side of the trade) promises to pay another party (the short side) the difference between the value of some variable (a "risk") S_T and a fixed strike $F_t(T)$ at some future date T, that is,

$$\Pi_T = S_T - F_t(T),$$

where $F_t(T)$ is determined at the inception of the deal, time t. This agreement costs nothing at time t. Thus, assuming the short-term rate r is constant (and is the same for borrowing and lending), we have that $0 = \mathbb{E}_t(\Pi_T)$, where $\mathbb{E}_t$ denotes the risk neutral expectation. It must then be the case that $F_t(T) = \mathbb{E}_t(S_T)$. Let us elaborate more on this risk neutral expectation.

If markets are frictionless and the underlying asset is traded (a stock, say), forward contracts can be synthesized as follows. Let $P(t,T) = e^{-r(T-t)}$ be the price of a bond expiring at time T and S_t be the price of a stock. So at time t, borrow $P(t,T)F^*$, and buy the stock, choosing $F^* : P(t,T)F^* - S_t = 0$. The value of this portfolio at time T is $S_T - F^*$. But the portfolio is worthless at time t, so this trade is the same as a forward. Therefore, we have $F^* = F_t(T)$, where

$$F_t(T) = S_t e^{r(T-t)}. \tag{11.1}$$

Note that eq. (11.1) is saying that $F_t(T) = \mathbb{E}_t(S_T)$, consistent with previous derivations (see chapter 4). In this example, forwards are insensitive to volatility. They can actually be volatility sensitive under circumstances clarified below (see the discussion after eq. (11.2)) and in the following sections.

The pricing of a forward on a stock can be extended to cases where the underlying is not traded. Suppose that a risk materializes at time T—say, the level of average temperature over a certain period preceding T and over a prespecified geographical area or, say, the realized volatility experienced by the S&P 500 Index over the month preceding T. Denote this risk with $\tilde{X}_T$. The payoff of a forward contract from the perspective of its buyer is given by $\tilde{X}_T - F_t(T)$, such that, by risk neutral evaluation,

$$F_t(T) = \mathbb{E}_t(\tilde{X}_T). \tag{11.2}$$

Naturally, eq. (11.2) collapses to eq. (11.1), should $\tilde{X}_T$ be the price of a traded stock.

In general, and as expected from the very foundations in part I, eq. (11.2) reveals that it is unlikely that nontraded risk may be priced in a preference-free format. In these cases, the volatility of $\tilde{X}_T$ may well affect the forward price $F_t(T)$ due to risk premiums. However, there are exceptions in which the pricing in eq. (11.2) is model free even if $\tilde{X}_T$ is not traded. One important and relatively recent advance consists in having shown how to proceed with a model-free evaluation of nontraded risks while only relying on additional derivatives written on this risk. Section 11.8 explains that the VIX index of expected volatility maintained by the Cboe does rely on such advances.

11.2.2 Forwards as a Means to Borrow Money, and Pricing Again

Forward contracts can be used to borrow money. We can do the following: (i) go long a forward, which at time T delivers the payoff $-F+S_T$, or (ii) short sell the underlying asset, which at time T will give rise to a payoff of $-S_T$. So (i) and (ii) are such that, at t, we have access to S_t dollars due to (ii) and, at time T, we have a payoff equal to $-F$, that is, the sum of the two payoffs resulting from (i) and (ii). By eq. (11.1), this is tantamount to borrowing money at the interest rate r.

Section 11.2.5.2 elaborates on these ideas and explains that the inequality $F_t(T) < e^{r(T-t)}S_t$ would give rise to arbitrage in the absence of short-sale constraints. Likewise, the inequality $F_t(T) > e^{r(T-t)}S_t$ is an arbitrage opportunity: we may (i) short a forward contract and (ii) issue debt for S_t and invest the proceeds in the underlying asset. Come time T, the payoff from (i) is $F_t(T) - S_T$ and the payoff from (ii) is $S_T - S_t e^{r(T-t)}$, summing up to $F_t(T) - S_t e^{r(T-t)} > 0$. Therefore, eq. (11.1) holds in perfect capital markets.

11.2.3 Marking to Market

Consider a derivative that we go long at time $t=0$ when it is worthless. As time unfolds, its value changes and calls for marking to market it. Precisely, suppose the derivative pays off $\psi(S_T) - K_0$ at time T, where S_T is the price of some asset as of time T and K_0 is set so as to make the derivative worthless at time zero. Assuming that interest rates are constant, we have that $K_0 : e^{-rT}\mathbb{E}_0[\psi(S_T) - K_0] = 0$, where $\mathbb{E}_0$ is the expectation at time $t=0$ taken under the risk neutral probability. That is, $K_0 = \mathbb{E}_0[\psi(S_T)]$. The market value of the derivative at time t, say, MtM_t, is simply the present value of the expected payoff at T, under the risk neutral probability, $e^{-r(T-t)}\mathbb{E}_t[\psi(S_T) - K_0]$, or

$$\text{MtM}_t = e^{-r(T-t)}(K_t - K_0). \tag{11.3}$$

For more elaborate payoffs, such as those depending on the realizations of the underlying risks over the life of the contract, marking to market updates may be more intricate than that in eq. (11.3) (see, for example, the variance contracts discussed in section 11.8.3).

11.2.4 Futures

Forward contracts are typically traded in OTC markets, are not standardized, and may not trade after their inception. Futures are instead standardized. The cost of entering into a future contract is zero–the same as with a forward. However, a central feature of future contracts is *marking to market*, a feature that forces their value to be zero at any time we wish to enter them after inception. By contrast, note that we should generally have to pay (or be paid) to enter in a forward contract after its inception. Indeed, the payoff at T pertaining to a forward that we enter at time t is $S_T - F_t(T)$, such that, consistent with eq. (11.3), the value of the forward at τ (and originated at t) is as in the following mark to market update,

$$V_\tau^F(T) \equiv e^{-r(T-\tau)}\mathbb{E}_\tau(S_T - F_t(T)) = e^{-r(T-\tau)}(F_\tau(T) - F_t(T)).$$

By construction, forwards are not "standardized" in that their value (the cost of entering them) depends on when we enter them. Moreover, in OTC markets, it is often the case that the appropriate marking notion is that of a mark to model rather than mark to market.[1]

Futures work differently. First, trading of futures is organized through exchanges. Exchanges offer the advantage of eliminating counterparty risk: a party in a forward contract still faces the risk that its counterparty will fail to deliver a payoff. This failure may not result in a direct economic loss per se (as nothing is due until the contract expiration) but would deprive the given party from the hedging properties of an instrument that the party was counting on. By contrast, all future traders interface only with the exchange. The exchange then would net payoffs through dedicated clearing mechanisms. Needless to say, there still remains a risk regarding the ability of the exchange to maintain its operations.

Second, the cost of entering into futures is always zero as mentioned. Precisely, let $\mathcal{F}_\tau(T)$ be the price process of the future at time τ. Intuitively, while we hold a future position, we only pay or receive differences up to maturity T, $\mathcal{F}_{\tau_i}(T) - \mathcal{F}_{\tau_{i-1}}(T)$ over prespecified periods, $\tau_i - \tau_{i-1}$.[2] Finally, we could "close" any position at any time before T by just initiating an opposite position.

For reasons developed below, let us assume that the short-term rate r_τ is random. The two defining properties of $\mathcal{F}_\tau(T)$ are that (i) at maturity, the future "settles" at S_T, that is $\mathcal{F}_T(T) = S_T$ (a boundary condition that is part of the futures security design) and (ii) the gains generated by $d\mathcal{F}_\tau(T)$ are continuously credited from/debited to the future holder's account such that, in absence of arbitrage,

$$0 = \mathbb{E}_t\left(\int_t^T e^{-\int_t^\tau r_u du} d\mathcal{F}_\tau(T)\right).$$

The previous equality actually holds for any trading horizon $\ell \leq T$. Therefore, we have heuristically that $X_\ell \equiv \int_t^\ell e^{-\int_t^\tau r_u du} d\mathcal{F}_\tau(T)$ is a martingale under the risk neutral probability or $0 = \mathbb{E}_\ell(dX_\ell) = e^{-\int_t^\ell r_u du}\mathbb{E}_\ell(d\mathcal{F}_\ell(T))$, implying that $\mathcal{F}_\tau(T)$ is a martingale too. Therefore,

$$\mathcal{F}_t(T) = \mathbb{E}_t(S_T).$$

By contrast, it is easy to see that forward prices satisfy

$$F_t(T) = \frac{1}{P(t,T)}\mathbb{E}_t\left(e^{-\int_t^T r_u du} S_T\right).$$

In other words, the future price is a martingale under the risk neutral probability while the forward is not. In chapter 13, we show that forward prices are martingales under another probability (see section 13.8), referred to as the forward probability (see also chapter 4).

1. There are alternative OTC instruments that may not be affected by this issue. For example, in a "contract for difference," two counterparties agree that one of them shall pay the difference in value of any risk (an asset or commodity price—or an index) that comes into existence over a prespecified period. Note that such contracts would require searching for counterparties and would give rise to counterparty risk. This risk is eliminated while organizing trading on an exchange as we shall explain shortly.

2. In addition to these margins, one is typically due to provide an initial margin, which aims to mitigate concerns regarding the solvability of the trading parties.

Naturally, both futures and forward prices are martingales under the risk neutral probability once interest rates are constant or deterministic, although this case is obviously not relevant while dealing with the evaluation of fixed income securities.

11.2.5 Backwardation and Contango

Let us assume interest rates are constant, such that forwards and futures are valued the same. A natural question arises: do markets price forwards or futures at a "discount" or "premium"? We have two notions of discounts: one, regarding expectations of future prices, and a more operational notion, regarding current prices. We now elaborate on these notions and provide some explanations for such premiums and discounts.

11.2.5.1 Definitions

We say that markets are in *backwardation* if the forward price is lower than the expected spot price, $F_t(T) = S_t e^{r(T-t)} \leq E_t(S_T)$, and in *contango* otherwise, that is, $F_t(T) \geq E_t(S_T)$, where E_t denotes the expectation taken under the physical probability given the information at t. Clearly, markets are in backwardation if prices follow geometric Brownian motions as $E_t(S_T) = S_t e^{\mu(T-t)}$ and, crucially, $\mu > r$, where μ is the drift coefficient under the physical probability. Keynes (1930) and Hicks (1939) would refer to markets in backwardation as being the standard situation—one of *normal backwardation*. According to Keynes's and Hicks's normal backwardation hypothesis, commodity producers are more incentivized to hedge their risks than consumers, leading forward prices to be cheaper than their current expectations of future values. In terms of the introductory example in this section, risk averse chocolate producers would like to short forwards, and their risk aversion would make them likely to accept low forward prices for the chocolate they produce (i.e., a lower price than the chocolate price at which they expect to sell). Section 11.2.5.4 provides examples of transactions that occur due to such transfers of risks.

But expectations are difficult to estimate. Keynes and Hicks proposed to use *current* prices as estimates of expected prices. Forward prices should then be compared with current prices, not expected spot prices. Under this convention, markets are in backwardation if $F_t(T) \leq S_t$ and in contango otherwise, as illustrated by figure 11.1. It is easy to see that under this criterion, markets are now typically in contango as $F_t(T) = S_t e^{r(T-t)} > S_t$, as predicted by eq. (11.1).

11.2.5.2 Short-sale constraints

To restore backwardation, we need a mechanism by which spot prices are "rich." One possibility is to assume that the no-arbitrage arguments underlying eq. (11.1) break down. For example, suppose that $F_t(T) < S_t e^{r(T-t)}$. A standard argument suggests to go long a forward contract, short the asset, and invest the short-sale proceeds into an MMA. Come time T, the MMA would deliver $S_t e^{r(T-t)}$, and by honoring the forward at T, which costs $F_t(T)$, we would buy the asset and finally close the short-sale position. The net payoff at T would be equal to $S_t e^{r(T-t)} - F_t(T) > 0$. An informal argument at this juncture would be that, in the presence of a selling pressure aiming to exploit the arbitrage, the spot price would go down, thereby restoring eq. (11.1) and then contango. However, in the presence

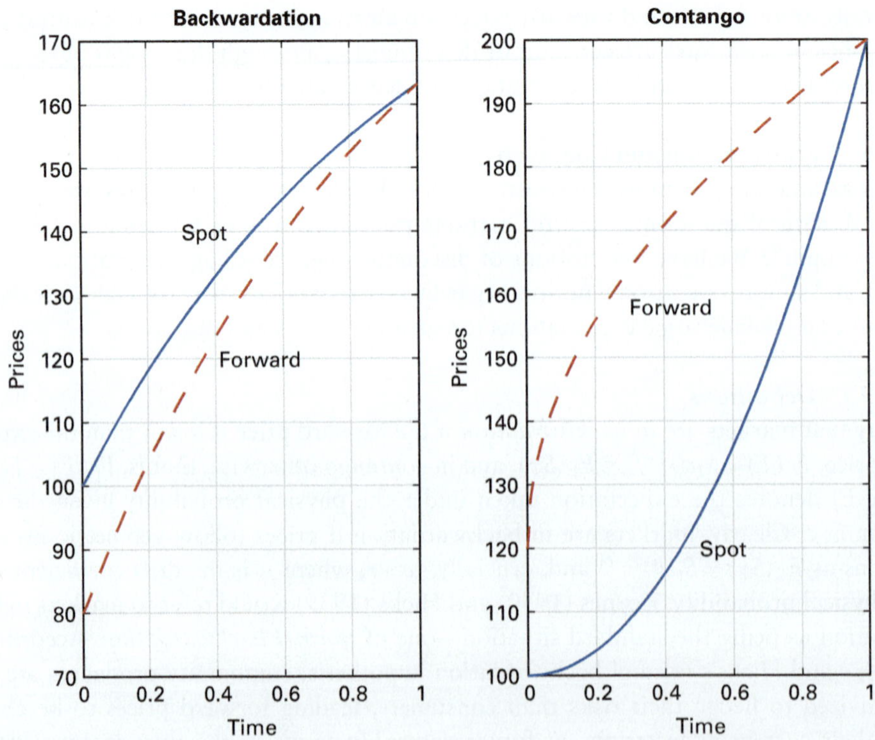

Figure 11.1
This picture depicts hypothetical price developments under deterministic market conditions. The left panel depicts a market in backwardation, and the right panel depicts contango. In both cases, forward and spots converge as time to maturity shrinks to zero.

of frictions such as short-sale constraints, the downward price pressure would not arise in the first place, leading to backwardation.

11.2.5.3 Convenience yields

The presence of a *convenience yield* is an alternative assumption to short-sale constraints, which we can make to restore backwardation. A convenience yield represents the flow of services accruing to the owner of the asset (not the owner of the forward). In the presence of a constant convenience yield, denoted with ψ, the forward price satisfies[3]

$$F_t(T) = S_t e^{(r-\psi)(T-t)}, \tag{11.4}$$

3. To prove eq. (11.4), we generalize the reasoning leading to eq. (11.1) as follows. Suppose to the contrary that $F_t(T) < S_t e^{(r-\psi)(T-t)}$. Then we go long a forward contract, short $\theta_t \equiv e^{-\psi(T-t)}$ shares at t, and invest the proceeds in an MMA. The short sale at t implies that we need to pay out the convenience yield ψS_τ at any time $\tau \in (t, T)$, which we finance by shorting additional ψ shares per shares already shorted, such that over any infinitesimal amount of time, we short $d\theta_\tau = \psi\theta_\tau d\tau$ additional shares. In total then, at time T, we would have shorted just one share as $\theta_T = \theta_t e^{\psi(T-t)} = 1$, which we buy back by honoring the forward, which costs $F_T(t)$, as usual. Finally, at time T, the MMA would yield $S_t e^{(r-\psi)(T-t)}$. Therefore, the net payoff at T would be equal to $S_t e^{(r-\psi)(T-t)} - F_t(T) > 0$, an arbitrage.

such that we have backwardation again for a large enough ψ.[4] Note, however, that contango would be a normal situation in storable commodity markets characterized by costs of "carry," such as warehousing fees or foregone interests—a cost of carry would imply a negative ψ in eq. (11.4). Thus, according to the sign and magnitude of ψ, we can have either backwardation or contango.

Some commodity markets can actually switch from being in backwardation to contango and in backwardation again through cycles. To account for these cycles, we may wish to consider a model with a stochastic convenience yield. For example, assume that, under the risk neutral probability, the spot price is a solution to

$$\begin{cases} \frac{dS_t}{S_t} = (r - \psi_t)\, dt + \sigma_S d\tilde{W}_{1t} \\ d\psi_t = \kappa \left(\alpha - \psi_t - \lambda \sigma_\psi\right) dt + \sigma_\psi d\tilde{W}_{2t} \end{cases} \tag{11.5}$$

where $\tilde{W}_{it}$ are standard Brownian motions under the risk neutral probability, κ, α and σ_ψ are constant parameters, and λ is a risk premium parameter, assumed to be constant. The parameter λ shows up because the stochastic convenience yield ψ_t is not tradable, and hence, $e^{-rt}\psi_t$ is not a martingale under the risk neutral probability.

The expression for the forward price would collapse to that in eq. (11.4) once we assume the convenience yield is constant. In the general case,

$$F_t(T) = \mathbb{E}_t(S_T) = S_t e^{r(T-t)} \mathbb{E}_t\left(e^{-\int_t^T \psi_u du}\right) \equiv S_t e^{r(T-t)} \varphi(\psi_t, T-t). \tag{11.6}$$

That is, a stochastic convenience yield may induce imperfect correlation between forwards and spots.

The expectation in eq. (11.6), $\varphi(\psi, T-t)$, is actually known in closed form. It is the same as the price of a zero coupon bond predicted by a model where the short-term rate is ψ_t and is the solution to the second equation in (11.5). This model, developed by Vasicek (1977), is discussed in chapter 13. The important implication of this model is that, according to the specific values taken by ψ_t, markets can either be in backwardation or in contango—both in terms of the criterion comparing the forward price with the current spot and the expected spot.

Finally, the relation between the fictitious "bond price" $\varphi(\psi, T-t)$ and the volatility parameter σ_ψ is indeterminate. As discussed in chapter 13, there are two effects that explain how the price of any zero coupon bond links to the volatility of the short-term rate: a "convexity" effect and a "risk premium" effect. The former acts so as to lead $\varphi(\psi, T-t)$ to be increasing in σ_ψ, and the latter acts in the same direction if $\lambda > 0$ and in the opposite direction if $\lambda < 0$. For short maturities, the risk premium effect dominates over convexity, such that $\varphi(\psi, T-t)$ and hence the forward price is decreasing in the volatility parameter σ_ψ, provided $\lambda < 0$. However, if $\lambda > 0$, the forward price is increasing in σ_ψ for any maturity.

---

4. In a continuous time setting, we have that, by no arbitrage, $\mathbb{E}_t\left(\frac{dS}{S}\right) + \delta dt = r dt$, where δ is the constant dividend yield. A convenience yield is simply $\psi \equiv \delta$. A storage cost is a negative convenience yield. Eq. (11.4) follows.

11.2.5.4 Risk aversion

If the markets for the underlying asset were liquid, the forward price would satisfy $F_t(T) = e^{r(T-t)}p_t$, where p_t denotes the underlying asset price and is independent of the expectations of the future price as explained in sections 11.2.1 and 11.2.2. Expectations and risk aversion play a crucial role when the assets underlying a forward deal are not traded in perfect capital markets or in the presence of convenience yields. This section provides examples of backwardation and contango benchmarked around the notion of expected prices (not spot prices) and are explained by risk aversion. In these examples, therefore, forward contracts are referenced to assets that are not traded in perfect capital markets. We will refer, then, to buy and sell sides of these contracts as buyers and sellers of insurance as appropriate.

Buyers of insurance may at times be long the risk they would like to hedge and at other times be short this risk. In the introductory examples of this section, a chocolate producer is *long* the risk of chocolate price movements: the producer gains when the chocolate price goes up and loses when this price goes down. To freeze this risk, the producer may pass the risk on to some insurance sellers. In this case, *insurance sellers go long* the forward contract. This risk transfer may work under conditions regarding the risk premiums that buyers and sellers of insurance are willing to pay and accept. We shall elaborate on this premium, based on the classical conceptual framework on risk premiums developed in chapter 1 (see section 1.3.4). From now on, we shall denote the utility functions of the buyers and sellers of insurance with $u_x(\cdot)$ and $x \in \{b, s\}$ and assume that these functions are continuous, increasing, and concave.

Potential buyers of insurance (who are long a risk) have the following alternative: either they buy insurance, in which case they will receive a sure amount $F_t(S)$ at time S (leading to the LHS of the first equality below), or they will face the vagaries of the chocolate price, receiving a random price $p_{\text{ch},S}$ at S (leading to the expected utility of the RHS in the first equality below). Therefore, at a very least, the forward price satisfies

$$u_b(w + F_t(S)) = E_t\left[u_b\left(w + p_{\text{ch},S}\right)\right] \leq u_b\left(w + E_t\left(p_{\text{ch},S}\right)\right),$$

where w denotes initial wealth. Precisely, by the previous inequality, there exists a constant $\Pi \geq 0$ depending on w and $u_b(\cdot)$, such that our chocolate producers are willing to sell at any forward price that satisfies $F_t(S) \geq F_t^b(S)$, where

$$F_t^b(S) \equiv E_t\left(p_{\text{ch},S}\right) - \Pi.$$

That is, buyers of insurance are willing to sell "at discount," that is, *at backwardation.* This example matches the certainty equivalent explanations given in chapter 1 (see section 1.3.4): a would-be buyer of insurance is exposed to randomness due to movements in the commodity price, and $F_t^b(S)$ is the certainty equivalent for this price; the buyer is then willing to avoid this "gamble," provided the forward price is higher than the certainty equivalent.

By contrast, sellers of insurance are not directly exposed to this risk and may well stay away from the gamble unless properly incentivized. Precisely, if they do not provide insurance, they will keep their initial wealth w, and if they provide insurance, they will receive a random payment equal to $p_{\text{ch},S} - F_t(S)$ at S. At a very least, their utility satisfies

$$u_s(w) = E_t\left[u_s\left(w + p_{\text{ch},S} - F_t(S)\right)\right] \leq u_s\left(w + E_t\left(p_{\text{ch},S}\right) - F_t(S)\right).$$

Precisely, there exists a constant $\Lambda \geq 0$ depending on w and $u_s(\cdot)$, such that these agents are willing to buy at any forward price $F_t(S) \leq F_t^s(S)$, where

$$F_t^s(S) \equiv E_t\left(p_{\text{ch},S}\right) - \Lambda.$$

That is, sellers of insurance may only buy at backwardation.

Putting this all together, we conclude that a risk transfer may take place for any forward price that satisfies $F_t(S) \in [F_t^b(S), F_t^s(S)]$. That is, the reservation forward price for the insurance seller must be higher than that for the insurance buyer or $\Pi \geq \Lambda$: the insurance premium the insurance buyer is willing to pay has to be at least as large as the premium required by the insurance seller. To illustrate, assume that $p_{\text{ch},S}$ is normally distributed with variance equal to σ^2, and suppose that the two types of agents have CARA utility such that the coefficients equal to τ_x, $x \in \{b, s\}$, with obvious notation. Then, $\Pi = \frac{1}{2}\tau_b\sigma^2$, and $\Lambda = \frac{1}{2}\tau_s\sigma^2$, such that a forward deal occurs whenever $\tau_b \geq \tau_s$; that is, insurance buyers should be more risk averse than insurance sellers.

Next, consider the case in which buyers of insurance are short their risk. In terms of the introductory examples of this section the chocolate producer is *short* the risk of cocoa price movements: they lose when this price goes up and gain when the price goes down. To hedge against this risk, they need to find a counterparty to transfer this risk to, that is, some insurance sellers. In this case, *insurance sellers go short* the risk. Consider another example, which is more related to themes dealt with in this chapter. An asset manager may be short the risk of market volatility—that is, the risk that volatility goes up. Then our asset manager may consider transferring this risk to some insurance provider, that is, one who would like to "sell volatility" to them, as in the *variance swap contracts* of section 11.8.

The two parties should agree on a transfer of these risks under conditions that match those mentioned above. Notably, the utility of an insurance buyer now must at least satisfy

$$u_b(w - F_t(T)) = E_t\left[u_b\left(w - p_{\text{co},T}\right)\right] \leq u_b\left(w - E_t\left(p_{\text{co},T}\right)\right),$$

such that their reservation forward price is now $F_t^b(T) \equiv E_t\left(p_{\text{co},T}\right) + \Pi$ for some $\Pi \geq 0$: the insurance buyer buys *at contango* whenever $F_t(T) \leq F_t^b(T)$. On the other hand, the utility of an insurance seller must at least satisfy

$$u_s(w) = E_t\left[u_s\left(w + F_t(T) - p_{\text{co},T}\right)\right] \leq u_s\left(w + F_t(T) - E_t\left(p_{\text{co},T}\right)\right),$$

and their reservation forward price is $F_t^s(T) \equiv E_t\left(p_{\text{co},T}\right) + \Lambda$ for some $\Lambda \geq 0$: the insurance sellers provides protection at contango whenever $F_t(T) \geq F_t^s(T)$. A forward deal now occurs whenever the forward price satisfies $F_t(T) \in [F_t^s(T), F_t^b(T)]$. That is, again, $\Pi \geq \Lambda$: insurance buyers should be willing to pay a premium larger than that required by insurance sellers.

11.3 Optionality and No-Arbitrage Bounds

This section reviews well-known properties of options. Options represent a right—but not the obligation—to buy or sell a given asset at a given price (the strike or exercise price) at some future date. Chapter 4 illustrates foundational issues regarding the evaluation of these contracts. This chapter describes additional properties that help explain their use in the market practice, such as those at the heart of important innovations in the space of volatility trading. This is the first section that illustrates a few properties of European options and provides some examples.

11.3.1 Model-Free Properties

Let C and p denote the prices of a call and put option and S the price of the asset underlying these contracts. Let K and T denote the exercise price and the expiration date, and let t be the current time. At expiration, $C_T = (S_T - K)^+$ and $p_T = (K - S_T)^+$. Figure 11.2 depicts the net profits generated by holding or short selling the option along with the underlying asset. To simplify the presentation, we set $r = 0$. Note that the exposure to losses with a long or short positioning in an asset can be mitigated while positioning into some appropriate option. For example, the left panel of figure 11.2 illustrates the idea that a long position in a call option exposes an investor less to negative market movements than a long position in the market, provided $C_t < S_t$, a no-arbitrage condition that will be discussed shortly. It is this "insurance" on the downside to make the option valuable.

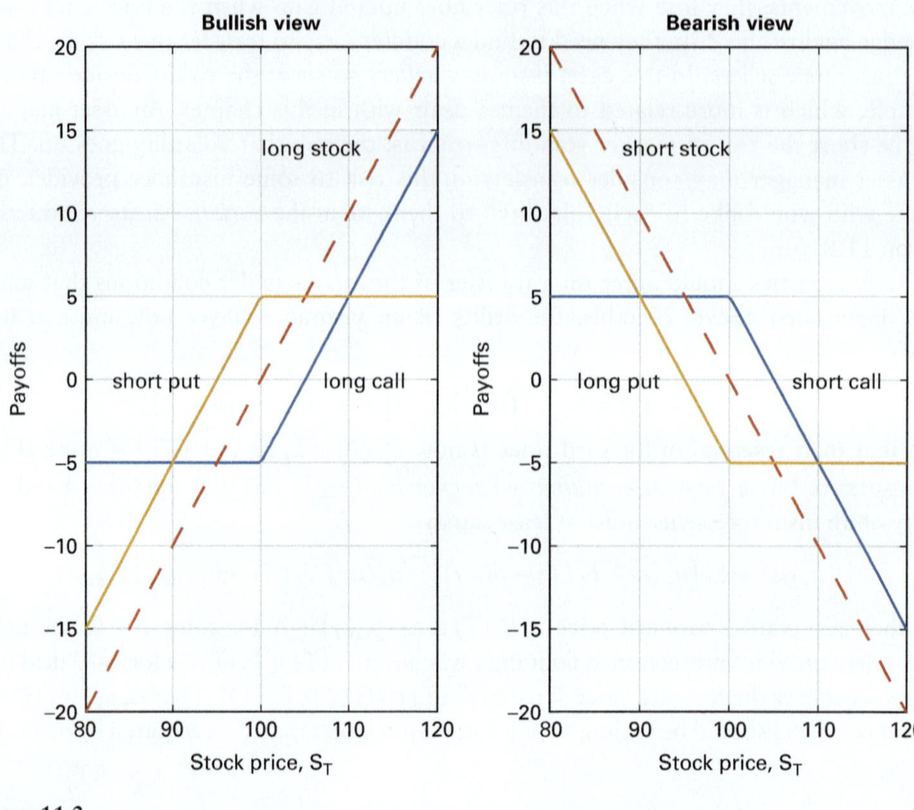

Figure 11.2
Left panel: One solid line depicts the P&L of an at-the-money European call option when the interest rate is zero, $(S_T - K)^+ - C_t$, where S_T is the stock price at expiration, $K = 100$ is the strike price, and $C_t = 5$ is the price of a call. The dashed line is the P&L from holding the stock, $S_T - S_t$, with $S_t = 100$. The remaining solid line is the payoff from the sale of a put option $p_t - (K - S_T)^+$, where, by the put-call parity, $p_t = C_t - S_t + KP(t, T) = 5$. The right panel depicts P&Ls from going long a put, $(K - S_T)^+ - p_t$ (one solid line); short the stock, $-(S_T - S_t)$ (the dashed line); and short a call $C_t - (S_T - K)^+$ (the remaining solid line).

Likewise, the right panel shows that a long position in a put option exposes an investor less to positive market movements than a short position in the market. The insurance is now on the upside. Finally, note that short positions in calls and puts are quite risky: while selling a put option, say, the investor may well cash in a premium; however, they would lose control of the optionality, so to speak, such that the counterpart may exercise against the investor in bad times, exposing them to large losses.

The prices of the call and put options satisfy a relation known as the *put-call parity*. That is, prices of a put and a call option that have the same exercise price K and the same expiration date T satisfy

$$p_t = C_t - S_t + KP(t, T). \tag{11.7}$$

To show that eq. (11.7) holds, consider two portfolios constructed as follows: (a) a long position in the call, a short position in the underlying asset, and an investment into an MMA for $KP(t, T)$; (b) a long position in one put. Table 11.1 indicates the value of the two portfolios at time t and time T.

Note that the two portfolios have the same value in each state of nature at time T. Therefore, their values at t must be the same. Alternatively, eq. (11.7) follows by taking conditional (risk neutral) expectations of the identity: $e^{-r(T-t)}(S_T - K)^+ \equiv e^{-r(T-t)}(K - S_T)^+ + e^{-r(T-t)}(S_T - K)$.

The put-call parity is a fundamental property with its own interest. It is also very useful, allowing as it does to derive properties of puts from properties of calls and vice versa (as, for example, in section 11.4). Consider a call option. Its price $C_t \equiv C(S_t; K, T - t)$ satisfies the following bounds:

$$(S_t - KP(t, T))^+ \leq C(S_t; K; T - t) \leq S_t. \tag{11.8}$$

Table 11.2 below provides us with the value of two portfolios at different times: (a) one with a long call and (b) one with a long asset and debt equal to $KP(t, T)$.

Table 11.1
Values of two portfolios: (a) One with a long position in one call, a short position in the underlying asset, and an investment into a MMA for KP(t, T); (b) a long position in one put.

		Value at T	
	Value at t	$S_T \leq K$	$S_T > K$
(a)	$C_t - S_t + KP(t, T)$	$-S_T + K$	$S_T - K - S_T + K$
(b)	p_t	$K - S_T$	0

Table 11.2

		Value at T	
	Value at t	$S_T \leq K$	$S_T > K$
(a)	C_t	0	$S_T - K$
(b)	$S_t - KP(t, T)$	$S_T - K$	$S_T - K$

Now note that the value of portfolio (a) dominates that of portfolio (b) at T. Therefore, at t, the value of (a) must be higher than the value of (b). Moreover, $C_t \geq 0$ because the option payoff is positive. Therefore, the first inequality in (11.8) is true. As for the second inequality, suppose the contrary, that is, $C_t > S_t$. Then, at time t, we could sell one call and buy the underlying asset, obtaining a profit equal to $C_t - S_t$. Come time T, the option will be exercised if $S_T > K$, in which case we shall sell the underlying asset and obtain K. If $S_T < K$, the option will not be exercised, and we will still hold the asset or sell it and realize an additional profit equal to S_T.

11.3.2 Limiting Behavior and Arbitrage Bounds

The bounds in (11.8) allow us to infer the asymptotic behavior of the call price. We have three properties: (i) $\lim_{S\to 0} C(S; K; T-t) \to 0$, (ii) $\lim_{K\to 0} C(S; K; T-t) \to S$, and (iii) $\lim_{T\to\infty} C(S; K; T-t) \to S$. Figure 11.3 illustrates the basic arbitrage bounds in (11.8) as well as the limiting behavior of the call price for S_t small and for S_t large. First, the price C_t must be in the region delimited by the AA and the BB lines—that is, it satisfies the bounds in (11.8). Moreover, C_t is small when S_t is small and large when S_t is large. However, C_t cannot lie outside the region within the AA line and BB lines: C may only get large by "sliding up" the BB line.

How does the option price behave in the region within the AA and BB lines? We cannot tell. Based on the boundary behavior of C_t, we may only say that, if C_t is convex in S_t, it is also increasing in S_t. In this case, the sensitivity of the option price with respect to changes in the stock price should be less than one. Intuitively, as the stock price increases, the option price will increase as the probability that the option will be exercised increases.

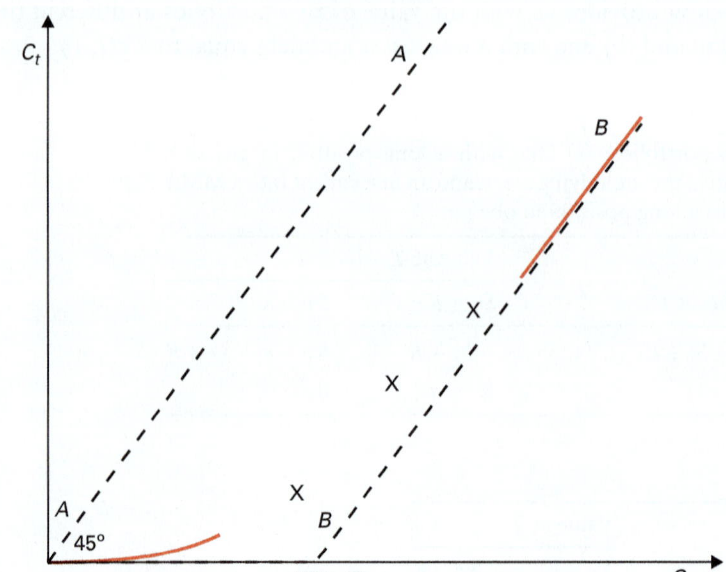

Figure 11.3
Option prices and no arbitrage bounds.

However, this probability is less than one, unless the stock price is really large, in which case option and stock prices increase by the same amount.

The convexity of C_t is a reasonable property, which holds for basic diffusive models (see section 11.4.5). A call option price that is increasing and convex seems to be empirically the relevant case. Theoretically, the Black–Scholes formula and many of its extensions predict such a behavior of the call pricing function. However, somehow surprisingly, note that these properties may not apply in some theoretical settings. Bergman, Grundy, and Wiener (1996) have provided several counterexamples in which C_t can be decreasing over some range of S_t due to the presence of jumps or stochastic volatility (see section 11.4.5 for further discussions).

11.3.3 Wasting Assets and Convexity

What is the economic meaning of convexity? An option with a convex payoff is unlikely to be exercised when S_t is small. So, when S_t is small, changes in S_t have little effect on C_t. However, as S_t gets large, the option becomes likely to be exercised, such that even a small change in S_t may result in a large change in C_t. In other words, the elasticity of the option price with respect to the asset price is larger than one, $\epsilon \equiv \frac{dC}{dS} \cdot \frac{S}{C} > 1$.[5] That is, option values are more volatile than the underlying asset prices.

Interestingly, convexity is responsible for explaining the behavior of option prices with respect to time to maturity. Call options are known as "wasting" assets: their value decreases over time. Figure 11.4 illustrates this property in a hypothetical Black–Scholes market: the option price decreases as time to maturity lowers. Let us explain. Convexity summarizes today the optionality an investor is given tomorrow. This optionality has a value that obviously decreases over time: with time, it becomes more and more certain which region of the state space the underlying price will be at the expiration. The final payoff is convex, and the option value inherits this property before the expiration. However, the higher the time to maturity, the less pronounced this convexity is for values of the underlying asset price around the at-the-money (ATM) price (e.g., around 100 in figure 11.4). We shall come back to these properties in more advanced sections of this chapter (see, e.g., sections 11.6.2 or 11.9.4).

11.3.4 Hedging

Financial intermediaries (investment banks, say) sell options that they want to hedge against: the main purpose in *intermediating* a derivative security is to receive fees from the transaction. The portfolio that "mimics" the option price must then display the properties discussed in section 11.3.1. For example, we need to ensure that the portfolio is increasing and convex in the underlying asset price, just as in figure 11.4. These properties are empirically the most relevant, as explained.

Thus, the hedging portfolio needs to exhibit a number of properties: (i) its value, V, should be increasing in S, a property ensured by including the underlying asset in the portfolio; (ii) the sensitivity of V with respect to S must be positive and bounded by one, $0 < \frac{dV}{dS} < 1$, a property ensured by including a proportion of underlying assets less than one;

5. For any function that is (i) increasing, (ii) convex and (iii) zero at the origin, the tangent is higher than the secant.

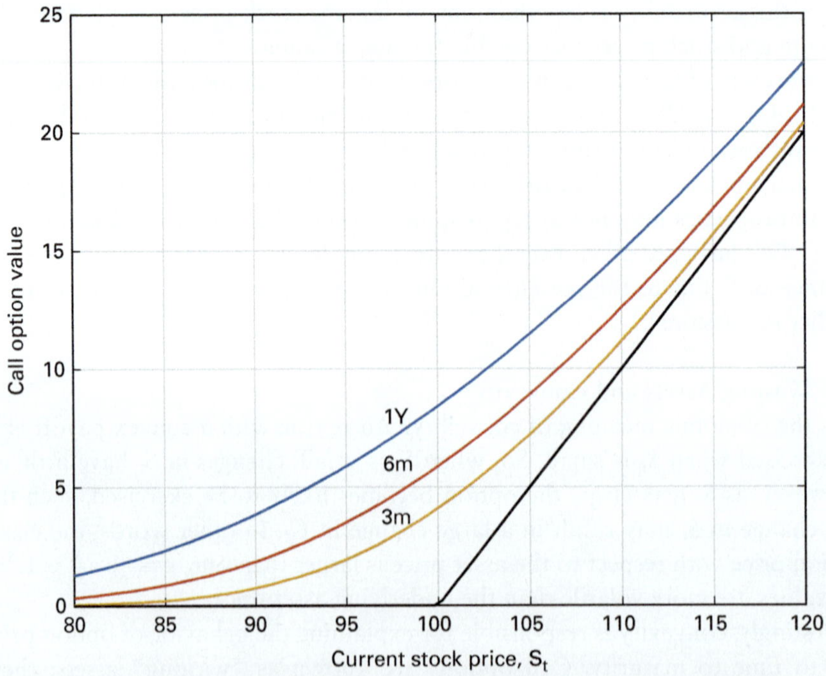

Figure 11.4
The value of a call option predicted by the Black–Scholes model for three maturity dates against the spot price, S_t. Strike price is $K = 100$, volatility parameter is $\sigma = 20\%$, and the short-term rate is $r = 1\%$. From top to bottom, the option values displayed are calculated for time to maturity $T = 1$ (one year), $T = 6/12$, and $T = 3/12$. The rightmost line is the intrinsic option value, $(S_t - K)^+$.

and (iii) the elasticity of V with respect to S must be larger then one, $\frac{dV}{dS}\frac{S}{V} > 1$, a property ensured while issuing debt. Denote the proportion of underlying assets with $\theta \in (0, 1)$ and the value of debt with D, such that the value of the replicating portfolio is $V = \theta S - D$. This portfolio has the potential to lead to these properties, just as in the Black–Scholes market, to be discussed in a moment.

In fact, hedging is dynamic in nature as option prices obviously change over time. Therefore, θ should be a function of both S and the option time to maturity. Chapter 4 clarifies these properties theoretically, and section 11.4 aims to revisit them. We would only need to explain that the portfolio we are discussing needs to satisfy some additional properties: (iv) the proportion of the underlying assets must increase with S and (v) the portfolio value should be virtually insensitive to changes in S when S is low; when S is large, the portfolio value should "slide up" as in the BB line in figure 11.3. These conditions are met if θ increases with S, with $\lim_{S \to 0} \theta(S) \to 0$ and $\lim_{S \to \infty} \theta(S) \to 1$. Finally, the portfolio needs to be self-financed because a long position in the option does not involve inflows or outflows until time to expiration. Therefore, any additional purchase (sale) of the underlying has to be financed by issuing new (shrinking some of the existing) debt. Section 11.4 shows that all these properties are satisfied for the hedging strategies in the Black–Scholes market.

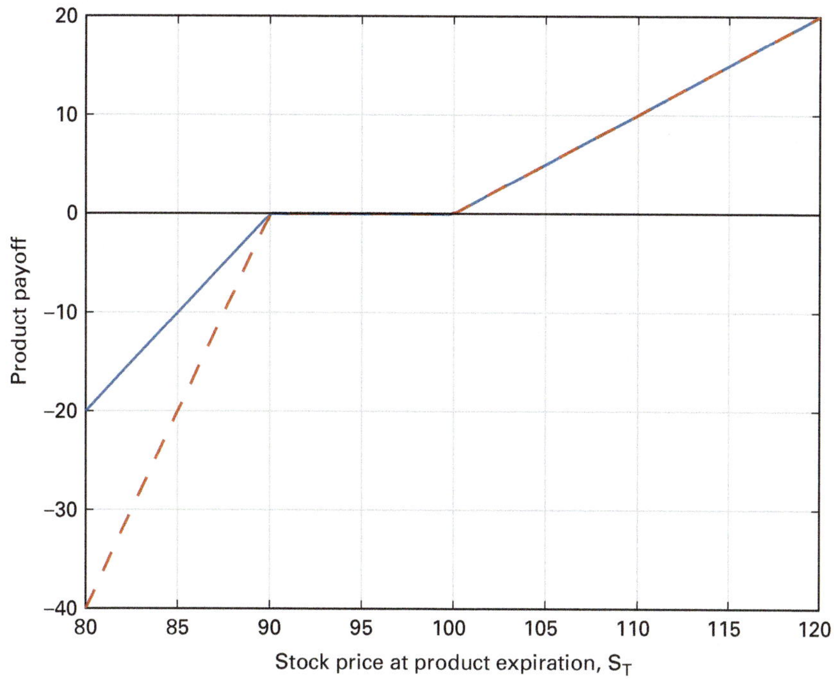

Figure 11.5
The solid line depicts the payoff promised by an "accumulator," a structured product that is long one call option and short n puts. In this example, the call strike price is $K_C = 100$, and the put strike price is $K_p = 90$. The solid and dashed lines depict the product payoffs resp. for $n = 2$ and $n = 4$.

11.3.5 A Case Study: Accumulators and Decumulators

Options can be used to build up dedicated structured products. Anecdotal evidence suggests that baskets of options may at times be popular among private bankers competing for clientèles. These products may be very risky. Consider, for example, an "accumulator." An accumulator is a portfolio which is long one call and short two or more puts. (A "decumulator" is short one accumulator.) The strike of the call is higher than the strike of the put. The rationale behind going long the call is to ensure profits are made once the market is up. Instead, puts are sold to finance the long position in the call so as to make the value of the accumulator equal to zero at its inception. In the example of figure 11.5, the strike of the call is $K_C = 100$. Note that, since the value of the accumulator is zero at inception, the picture depicts net profits.[6]

Suppose that the current market level is $S = 102$. In this example, an accumulator leads to profits, provided the market does not fall below the put strike, $K_p = 90$. However, accumulators are quite risky: the losses they lead to during market downturns are more severe than their gains in good times. The size of the losses obviously depends on how many puts we have sold, n, and their strike, K_p. As figure 11.5 illustrates, these losses widen with n.

6. Therefore, the assumptions underlying figure 11.5 are that the price of the put is $\frac{1}{2}$ (solid line) and $\frac{1}{4}$ (dashed line) the price of the call. These assumptions are made for illustrative purposes, and will be removed in section 11.5.3.

Note that we can decrease the probability of losses by fixing $K_p = 90$ and decreasing n; however, a lower n implies that less resources would be left to purchase the call. Another possibility is to go long a less expensive call by adding a knockout feature into the call contract (one, by which the option becomes worthless once the market reaches a certain level such as, say, 105 within the investment horizon) or by purchasing a call with a higher strike price. Alternatively, a product can be designed that carries more risk, but also more upside, by choosing some appropriate put strike. Obviously, puts become more valuable as their strike price increases. Therefore, we could increase K_p from 90 to 95, say, while keeping n constant. While selling put options with higher strikes increases the probability of losses, it also allows one to purchase more expensive calls—those with lower strikes, which leads to a higher probability of achieving positive returns.

Naturally, the previous reasoning relies on the assumption that the accumulator is self-financed at inception. This condition defines the type of options we may afford. Some call options can be too expensive and may require a large exposure to the short position in puts. For example, some calculations show that in a market with stochastic volatility, such as that of Heston (1993b), we may need to sale short approximately six puts when the current index level is $S = 102$ and $K_p = 95$. Section 11.5.3 develops a case study where these risks are quantified under a variety of alternative assumptions about strikes and market volatility.

11.4 Classical Evaluation and Properties

This section discusses evaluation, hedging, and additional properties of options in the markets idealized by Black and Scholes (1973) and Merton (1973). First, we review derivations of the Black–Scholes formula through the replication arguments introduced in chapter 4. We also rely on a general evaluation formula that applies to a variety of derivatives, such as futures, options or binary options.

This formula, provided in section 11.4.1, does actually rely on a framework that goes a bit beyond that underlying the Black–Scholes and Merton market; it is used in more advanced sections of this chapter, namely, when we attempt to price options in markets with stochastic volatility (see section 11.5.3). Section 11.4.2 then deals with evaluation and hedging in the Black–Scholes market, and section 11.4.3 provides the famous Black's formula—a formula that applies to price options on futures, the contract type that is encountered in standardized markets maintained by exchanges. Finally, in section 11.4.5, we discuss classical properties of options that will be used as benchmarks in later sections of the chapter.

11.4.1 A Pricing Formula

Forward and options obviously differ as they rely on the two distinct notions of obligation and optionality. However, we can encompass their payoffs into a single one, the value of which will be used a few times in this chapter. Consider again a contract similar to that in section 11.2.1 where, at time T, the payoff is given by $S_T - K$ for some constant value of K and where $S_T > 0$ denotes the value of some asset at T. We know that the current value of this payoff is

$$e^{-r(T-t)}\mathbb{E}_t\left(S_T - K\right) = S_t - e^{-r(T-t)}K, \tag{11.9}$$

which is zero, for $K = F^*$ (the forward value). We want to further analyze a situation by which this current value is not necessarily zero and show that the previous expression is a special case of a pricing formula. Consider a payoff at time T, equal to $S_T - K$, provided the stock price at T is at least as large as some positive constant $\ell \geq 0$,

$$(S_T - K)\,\mathbb{I}_{S_T \geq \ell}.$$

For $\ell = 0$, this payoff is just that of a forward, and for $\ell = K$, the payoff is that of a European call. We have

$$\begin{aligned} e^{-r(T-t)}\mathbb{E}_t\left[(S_T - K)\,\mathbb{I}_{S_T \geq \ell}\right] &= S_t\mathbb{E}_t\left(\eta_t(T)\,\mathbb{I}_{S_T \geq \ell}\right) - e^{-r(T-t)}K\mathbb{E}_t\left(\mathbb{I}_{S_T \geq \ell}\right) \\ &= S_t\hat{\mathbb{E}}_t\left(\mathbb{I}_{S_T \geq \ell}\right) - e^{-r(T-t)}K\mathbb{E}_t\left(\mathbb{I}_{S_T \geq \ell}\right) \\ &= S_t \cdot \hat{Q}_t\left(S_T \geq \ell\right) - e^{-r(T-t)}K \cdot Q_t\left(S_T \geq \ell\right), \end{aligned} \tag{11.10}$$

where $\eta_t(T) \equiv \frac{e^{-r(T-t)}S_T}{S_t}$, Q_t is the risk neutral probability given $\mathbb{F}_t$ (the information at time t), $\hat{Q}_t$ is a new probability with Radon-Nikodym derivative given by

$$\left.\frac{d\hat{Q}}{dQ}\right|_{\mathbb{F}_T} = \eta_t(T), \tag{11.11}$$

and finally, $\mathbb{E}_t$ denotes the expectation under Q_t and $\hat{\mathbb{E}}_t$ the expectation under $\hat{Q}_t$. Naturally, eq. (11.10) collapses to eq. (11.9) once $\ell = 0$, and it collapses to the celebrated Black and Scholes (1973) formula if S_t is a geometric Brownian motion and $\ell = K$, as explained in the following section. It is a general formula, and it turns out to be quite useful while dealing with difficult models such as those with random volatility (see section 11.5).

11.4.2 Black–Scholes

We assume that the stock price is a geometric Brownian motion with parameters (μ, σ),

$$\frac{dS_t}{S_t} = \mu dt + \sigma dW_t,$$

where W_t is a Brownian motion under the *physical* probability. Replicating the value of an asset, such as a European option, while trading in others is a theme framed in many junctures of part I. For the sake of completeness, we develop the arguments through some alternative lines of reasoning that ultimately lead to the Black–Scholes formula.

11.4.2.1 By replication: I

We invest θ units in the asset underlying a call option and θ_M in the MMA, and the value of this portfolio is $V = \theta S + \theta_M M$ with obvious notation. Once self-financed, the value of this portfolio satisfies

$$dV = \theta dS + \left(\theta_M \frac{dM}{dt}\right) dt, \tag{11.12}$$

whereas, by Itô's lemma, the call option price (C, say), satisfies

$$dC = \frac{\partial C}{\partial S} dS + \left(\frac{\partial C}{\partial t} + \frac{1}{2} \frac{\partial^2 C}{\partial S^2} \sigma^2 S^2 \right) dt. \tag{11.13}$$

We conjecture that the value of this portfolio does exactly replicate the option value, a conjecture verified in the subsection below. Comparing eq. (11.12) and eq. (11.13) leaves (i) the matching condition for dS, $\theta = \frac{\partial C}{\partial S}$ and (ii) the drift-matching condition,

$$\begin{aligned} \frac{\partial C}{\partial t} + \frac{1}{2} \frac{\partial^2 C}{\partial S^2} \sigma^2 S^2 &= \theta_M \frac{dM}{dt} \\ &= r\theta_M M \\ &= r(V - \theta S) \\ &= r\left(C - \frac{\partial C}{\partial S} S \right), \end{aligned} \tag{11.14}$$

where the second equality follows by $\frac{dM}{M} = r dt$, the third by the expression for the value of the replicating portfolio, and the fourth by the expression for θ in (i) and the equality $C = V$, due to the conjecture that the portfolio value is replicating the option value; see section 4.2 in chapter 4. Denote with $C(s, T-t; K, \sigma)$ the option price when the stock price is s, maturity is $T-t$, the strike is K, and finally, volatility is σ. Rearranging terms in (11.14) leaves

$$\frac{\partial C}{\partial t} + \frac{\partial C}{\partial S} rS + \frac{1}{2} \frac{\partial^2 C}{\partial S^2} \sigma^2 S^2 = rC, \tag{11.15}$$

subject to the boundary condition, $C(s, 0; K, \sigma) = (s - K)^+$.

The solution to eq. (11.15) is the celebrated Black and Scholes (1973) formula,

$$\begin{aligned} C_{BS}(S, T-t; K, \sigma) &= S\Phi(d) - Ke^{-r(T-t)}\Phi(d - \sigma\sqrt{T-t}), \\ d &= \frac{\ln(\frac{S}{K}) + (r + \frac{1}{2}\sigma^2)(T-t)}{\sigma\sqrt{T-t}}, \end{aligned} \tag{11.16}$$

where Φ denotes the cumulative standard normal distribution.

Finally, appendix 11.A derives eq. (11.15) by hinging on the original arguments developed by Black and Scholes (1973) and Merton (1973) where one considers a portfolio comprising the option, the underlying asset, and a portfolio strategy aiming to make the portfolio locally riskless.

11.4.2.2 By replication: II

Eq. (11.16) holds even without requiring that a market for the option exists during the option's life or that the pricing function $C(t, S)$ is differentiable. That the option price is differentiable is a result, not an assumption. Let us define the function $C(t, S)$ that solves eq. (11.15), with a boundary condition $C(T, S) = (S - K)^+$. Note that we are not assuming this function is the option price. Rather, we shall show that this is the option price. The argument is similar to those developed in chapter 4 (see section 4.2.2). Consider a self-financed portfolio of bonds and stocks, with $\pi = C_S S$. Its value satisfies

$$dV = (C_S S(\mu - r) + rV)\,dt + C_S \sigma S dW.$$

Moreover, by Itô's lemma, $C(t, S)$ is the solution to

$$dC = \left(C_t + \mu S C_S + \frac{1}{2}\sigma^2 S^2 C_{SS} \right) dt + C_S \sigma S dW.$$

Subtracting the previous two equations leaves

$$dV - dC = (\underbrace{-C_t - rSC_S - \frac{1}{2}\sigma^2 S^2 C_{SS}}_{=-rC} + rV)dt = r(V - C)\,dt.$$

Hence, we have that $V_\tau - C(\tau, S_\tau) = (V_0 - C(0, S_0))\, e^{r\tau}$ for all $\tau \in [0, T]$. Next, assume that $V_0 = C(0, S_0)$. Then, $V_\tau = C(\tau, S_\tau)$, and $V_T = C(T, S_T) = (S_T - K)^+$. That is, the portfolio $\pi = C_S S$ replicates the option payoff. Therefore, V_0 is the value of the option at time zero, even when a market for the option does not exist over its life.

11.4.2.3 By probabilistic arguments

Alternatively, we can use the general framework in section 11.4.1 and arrive at eq. (11.16). We simply set $\ell \equiv K$ in eq. (11.10) and determine the dynamics of the stock price under $\hat{Q}$ and under Q, and then determine $\hat{Q}_t(S_T \geq K)$ and $Q_t(S_T \geq K)$ in eq. (11.10). Under Q, the stock price is the usual geometric Brownian motion with drift equal to $rSdt$ and then $Q_t(S_T \geq K) = \Phi(d - \sigma\sqrt{T - t})$, which explains the second term in eq. (11.16). As for the first term, we can show that the Radon-Nikodym derivative, $\left.\frac{d\hat{Q}}{dQ}\right|_{\mathbb{F}_T} = \eta_t(T) \equiv \frac{e^{-r(T-t)}S_T}{S_t}$, is such that $\eta_\tau(T)$ is the solution to

$$\frac{d\eta_t(T)}{\eta_t(T)} = -(-\sigma)\, d\tilde{W}_t,$$

where $\tilde{W}_t$ is a Brownian motion under Q. By the Girsanov theorem (see chapter 4), then, the stock price is the solution to

$$d\ln S_t = \left(r + \frac{1}{2}\sigma^2\right) dt + \sigma d\hat{W}_t,$$

where $\hat{W}_t$ is a Brownian motion under $\hat{Q}$. It easily follows that $\hat{Q}_t(S_T \geq K) = \Phi(d)$, thereby completing the proof of the Black–Scholes formula.

11.4.2.4 Hedging

The "cloning" arguments in section 11.4.2.1 suggest how to replicate a call option in a Black–Scholes market. We set up a portfolio with an amount θ^* in the underlying asset and the remaining in the MMA, where

$$\theta_t^* \equiv \Delta_t^{\mathrm{BS}} \equiv \frac{\partial C_{\mathrm{BS}}(S_t, T - t; K, \sigma)}{\partial S} \tag{11.17}$$

and $C_{\mathrm{BS}}(\cdot)$ denotes the Black–Scholes formula.

Eq. (11.17) can actually be simplified. Note that the Black–Scholes formula is homogeneous of degree one in S and K; that is, $C_{\mathrm{BS}}(\lambda S, T-t; \lambda K, \sigma) = \lambda C_{\mathrm{BS}}(S, T-t; K, \sigma)$ for any constant λ. Therefore, by Euler's theorem,

$$C_{\mathrm{BS}}(S, T-t; K, \sigma) = \frac{\partial C_{\mathrm{BS}}(S, T-t; K, \sigma)}{\partial S} S + \frac{\partial C_{\mathrm{BS}}(S, T-t; K, \sigma)}{\partial K} K. \tag{11.18}$$

Comparing eq. (11.18) with the Black–Scholes formula in eq. (11.16) produces

$$\Delta_t^{\mathrm{BS}} = \Phi(d). \tag{11.19}$$

Why does anyone need to replicate derivatives in the first place? The reason is that financial intermediaries, such as investment banks, may simply be interested in mere intermediation activities and in the fees that accompany these activities. To illustrate, suppose that a bank receives an order to sell a put option. The bank would like to hedge against this derivative by creating a replicating portfolio, that is, a portfolio that delivers the same payoff needed to honor the initial sale. Standard market practice is to rely on the "Black–Scholes delta" in eq. (11.19) to achieve this objective.

Note that some market participants may be interested in trading securities while based on the Black–Scholes delta, even if for reasons not related to intermediation. Section 11.6 describes a number of strategies that aim at trading volatility. These strategies cannot merely rely on trading options: a view that market volatility will increase cannot be implemented with long positions in call options, say—call prices are increasing not only in volatility but also in the underlying price. A better solution is to go long options and delta hedge them through Black–Scholes, as we shall explain. Volatility trading may be one additional usage of the Black–Scholes hedge ratio in (11.19).

11.4.3 Future Options and Black's Formula

Consider a *future option*, one that gives the buyer the right, not the obligation, to enter into a future contract on a traded asset (expiring at $\mathcal{S}$) for a specified price K at time $T < \mathcal{S}$, such that the payoff at time T is $(F_T(\mathcal{S}) - K)^+$, where $F_\tau(\mathcal{S})$ denotes the future price in eq. (11.1), $F_\tau(\mathcal{S}) = S_\tau e^{r(\mathcal{S}-\tau)}$. It is easy to see that $F_\tau(\mathcal{S})$ is a martingale under the risk neutral probability Q. For example, assuming that S_t is a geometric Brownian motion with volatility σ, we have that

$$\frac{dF_\tau(\mathcal{S})}{F_\tau(\mathcal{S})} = \sigma d\tilde{W}_\tau, \quad \tau \in (t, \mathcal{S}), \tag{11.20}$$

where $\tilde{W}$ is a Brownian motion under Q. Therefore, the price of a future option as of time t is

$$\begin{aligned} C_{\mathrm{F}}(F_t(\mathcal{S}), T-t; K) &\equiv e^{-r(T-t)} \mathbb{E}_t (F_T(\mathcal{S}) - K)^+ \\ &= e^{-r(T-t)} \left(F_t(\mathcal{S}) \Phi(d) - K\Phi(d - \sigma\sqrt{T-t}) \right), \end{aligned} \tag{11.21}$$

where

$$d = \frac{\ln\left(\frac{F_t(\mathcal{S})}{K}\right) + \frac{1}{2}\sigma^2(T-t)}{\sigma\sqrt{T-t}},$$

and the second equality of eq. (11.21) follows by the Black–Scholes formula, eq. (11.16). Eq. (11.21) is the celebrated Black's (1976a) formula, which turns out to be very useful in the context of fixed income security pricing, as explained in chapter 13. Appendix 11.B provides an alternative derivation of eq. (11.21) based on the pricing approach of section 11.2 and the slightly more general assumption that the volatility of the future price in eq. (11.20) is time-varying—but deterministic.

Chapter 13 explains that the property that future prices are martingales under the risk neutral probability generalizes to one holding when interest rates are time-varying under a certain probability called *forward probability* (see section 13.8).

11.4.4 Surprising Cancellations and "Preference-Free" Formulae

Chapter 4 explains that, due to what Heston (1993a, 933), aptly terms "a surprising cancellation," the constant μ doesn't show up in the final option pricing formula. Heston (1993a) shows that this property is not robust to modifications of the assumptions on the asset price process. While the option price is independent of μ, even within a diffusion setting, the expected option *return* does of course depend on μ. Indeed, by eq. (11.15),

$$E\left(\frac{dC}{C}\right)=r+\underbrace{\frac{C_S}{C}\sigma S}_{\equiv\beta_S}\cdot\lambda, \tag{11.22}$$

where β_S is, by Itô's lemma, the instantaneous volatility of the option returns and λ is the unit risk premium related to the underlying asset price, $\lambda=(\mu-r)/\sigma$.

11.4.5 Properties of Options in Diffusive Models

We consider a simple model in which the stock price is the solution to

$$\frac{dS_t}{S_t}=\mu(S_t)\,dt+v(S_t)\,dW_t. \tag{11.23}$$

Let $C(S_t,t,T)$ be the price of a European-style option at time t, which pays off $\psi(S_T)>0$ at time T. We assume that $\psi(S)$ is differentiable, with $\psi'(S)>0$. In the absence of arbitrage, C satisfies the following partial differential equation,

$$0=C_t+C_S rS+\frac{1}{2}v^2(S)\,S^2C_{SS}-rC, \tag{11.24}$$

subject to the boundary condition, $C(S,T,T)=\psi(S)$. This section contains a succinct description of some useful properties of this model, properties discussed in more advanced parts of this chapter.

11.4.5.1 *Passage of time*

In section 11.3, we explain that call options are sometimes referred to as "wasting" assets. Their value "tends" to decrease over time because the value of optionality decreases over time. Define $\epsilon\equiv\frac{S}{C}C_S$, the elasticity of the option price with respect to the asset price. For a call option, we have that $\epsilon>1$ as noted in section 11.3, such that by eq. (11.24) and

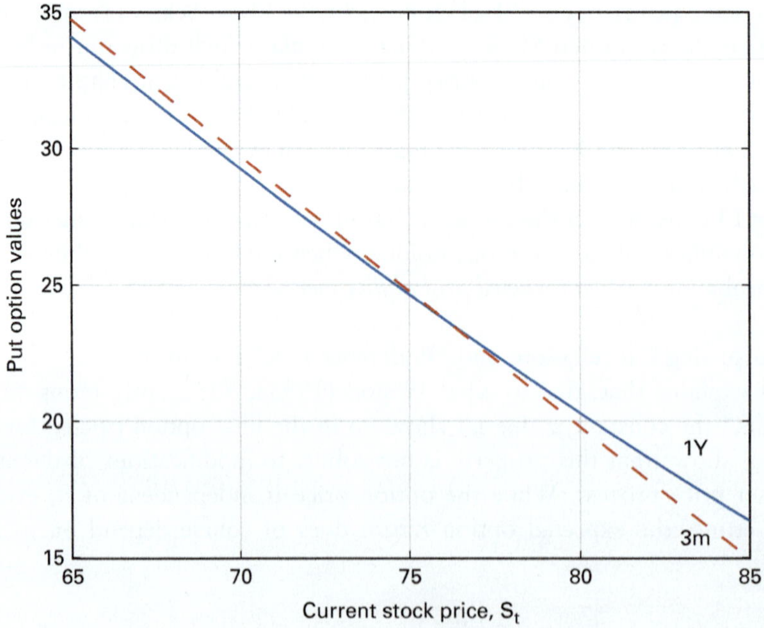

Figure 11.6
The value of a put option with strike $K = 100$ predicted by the Black–Scholes model, with a volatility $\sigma = 20\%$ and a short-term rate $r = 1\%$. The solid line is the price corresponding to time to maturity $T = 1$ (one year), and the dashed line is the price corresponding to time to maturity $T = 3/12$.

convexity of C, that is, $C_{SS} > 0$,

$$C_t = -r(\epsilon - 1)C - \frac{1}{2}v^2(S)C_{SS} < 0. \tag{11.25}$$

Now, convexity grows as time to maturity lowers. The limiting case is when time to maturity shrinks to zero, in which case C_{SS} shrinks to Dirac's delta. Therefore, the drop in value becomes the most severe for short maturities.

Naturally, these properties are not arbitrage opportunities. Consider the simple strategy of short selling a call option, which may be bought later. The difference should be a profit as the call values decreases over time. It is indeed a trading strategy but obviously not an arbitrage. To profit from a wasting asset, market volatility needs to be low in that the underlying asset price does not move too much as a result. Thus, this strategy may enable one to implement the view that market volatility would not increase. These observations are indeed the motivation for a basic trading strategy known as a "calendar spread," which is explained in some detail in section 11.6.1.

Finally, note that the elasticity of a European put with respect to the asset price is *negative*. Figure 11.6 reveals that this property can actually lead the RHS of eq. (11.25) to change sign.

11.4.5.2 Comparative statics of dynamic models

We derive properties of option prices in the context of diffusion processes, relying on methods suggested by Bergman, Grundy, and Wiener (1996) and in chapter 8 (see appendix

8.D). We establish that if the stock price is a solution to eq. (11.23), the price of a European-style option inherits the properties of the final payoff: it is increasing and convex in the underlying price if the payoff ψ is increasing and convex. These properties imply, we shall see, that the option price is increasing in the volatility of the underlying price.

Differentiate eq. (11.24) with respect to S. The result is that $H \equiv C_S$ satisfies

$$0 = H_t + \left(rS + \frac{1}{2}\frac{\partial}{\partial S}\left(v^2(S)\,S^2\right)\right) H_S + \frac{1}{2}v^2(S)\,S^2 H_{SS}, \tag{11.26}$$

subject to the boundary condition $H(S,\tau,T) = \psi'(S) > 0$. Therefore, we have that $H(S,\tau,T) = C_S(S,\tau,T) > 0$ for all S, due to results reviewed in chapter 8 (appendix 8.D). That is, in a scalar diffusion setting, a European-style option price is increasing in the underlying asset whenever the $\psi(S)$ is increasing.

Next, we find conditions under which $C_{SS} > 0$. We differentiate eq. (11.26) with respect to S, and $Z \equiv H_S = C_{SS}$ satisfies

$$\begin{aligned} 0 = Z_t &+ \left(rS + \frac{\partial}{\partial S}\left(v^2(S)\,S^2\right)\right) Z_S + \frac{1}{2}v^2(S)\,S^2 Z_{SS} \\ &- \left(-r - \frac{1}{2}\frac{\partial^2}{\partial S^2}\left(v^2(S)\,S^2\right)\right) Z, \end{aligned} \tag{11.27}$$

subject to the boundary condition $Z(S,\tau,T) = \psi''(S)$. We now have that $H(S,\tau,T) = C_{SS}(S,\tau,T) > 0$ whenever the payoff is convex, $\psi''(S) > 0$ for all S. That is, in a scalar diffusion setting, a European-style option price is convex in the underlying asset, provided the final payoff is convex.

We now show that the option price is increasing in volatility. Consider two markets A and B with prices $(C^i, S^i)_{i=A,B}$, in which the volatility of the asset price in market A is higher than that in market B, namely,

$$\frac{dS^i_\tau}{S^i_\tau} = r\,d\tau + v_i(S^i_\tau)\,d\tilde{W}_\tau, \quad i = A, B,$$

where $\tilde{W}$ is Brownian motion under the risk neutral probability and $v^A(s) > v^B(s)$ for all s. The price difference in the two markets, $\Delta C \equiv C^A - C^B$, satisfies

$$0 = \Delta C_t + rS\Delta C_S + \frac{1}{2}v_A^2 S^2 \Delta C_{SS} - r\Delta C + \frac{1}{2}\left(v_A^2 - v_B^2\right) S^2 C^B_{SS}. \tag{11.28}$$

By the same results used to analyze eq. (11.26) and (11.27), we now have that $\Delta C > 0$ whenever $C_{SS} > 0$. That is, if option prices are convex in the underlying price, they are increasing in the volatility of the asset price.

This result is reminiscent of the theory of mean-preserving spreads (see, e.g., appendix 8.D in chapter 8). By increasing the volatility of the underlying asset, the holder of an European call (say) would benefit from the upside while not suffering losses on the way down: risk neutral evaluation of traded assets benefits from an increasing volatility. Chapters 13 (see section 13.5.1) and 14 (see section 14.2) provide important examples in which this conclusion may not hold: the price of fixed income securities may not increase after an increase in the volatility of the fundamentals.

11.4.5.3 *Recovering risk neutral probabilities*

Consider the price of a European call,

$$C(S_t,t,T;K)=e^{-r(T-t)}\int_K^\infty (x-K)\,q(x|\,S_t)\,dx,$$

where q denotes the risk neutral density, not necessarily the log-normal density in the Black–Scholes market. Differentiating with respect to K leaves

$$\frac{\partial C(S_t,t,T;K)}{\partial K}=-e^{-r(T-t)}\int_K^\infty q(x|\,S_t)\,dx.$$

It is easy to see this relation is illustrated within the Black–Scholes model (see eq. (11.18)). Let us differentiate again:

$$\frac{\partial^2 C(S_t,t,T;K)}{\partial K^2}=e^{-r(T-t)}q(K|\,S_t). \tag{11.29}$$

Therefore, option prices can be used to retrieve the risk neutral density $q(S_T|\,S_t)|_{S_T=S}$ for any S by relying on eq. (11.29). These facts are used in applied work. They also help deal with the pricing of variance contracts reviewed in section 11.8.

11.5 Stochastic Volatility

11.5.1 Statistical Models of Changing Volatility

11.5.1.1 *ARCH and random variance models*

Asset returns have time-varying volatility (see chapter 8), and their empirical distributions seem to be both heavy peaked and thick tailed. These empirical regularities are very well known since at least the seminal work of Mandelbrot (1963) and Fama (1965). In his pioneering work, Mandelbrot proposed to model asset prices through stable Paretian distributions. In his equally pioneering work, Fama aimed to implement tests of the "random walk hypothesis." His work relates to his motivation to study market efficiency, a notion that he would elaborate in greater detail in a further contribution (Fama, 1970) discussed in chapter 10 (see section 10.3). At the same time, Fama also pointed to evidence of asset returns with thick-tailed distributions.

Approximately two decades later, Engle (1982) and Bollerslev (1986) introduced the first models that captured the random character of asset returns volatility. Engle's article would actually initially deal with the estimation of inflation volatility through his celebrated Auto Regressive Conditionally Heteroskedastic (ARCH) model. However, subsequent research made heavy use of ARCH models in the analysis of many aspects of financial econometrics, such as the term structure of interest rates, the pricing of options, or the presence of time-varying risk premiums in the foreign exchange market, as summarized by the classic survey of Bollerslev, Engle, and Nelson (1994). Early contributions that link changes in market volatility to variables with intuitive economic intuition include Clark (1973) and Tauchen and Pitts (1983), who assume that a stochastic process of information arrival generates a random number of intraday changes of the asset price.

An ARCH model works as follows. Let $\{\tilde{r}_t\}_{t=1}^N$ be a record of observations on some asset returns, $\tilde{r}_t = \ln S_t/S_{t-1}$, where S_t is the asset price. The variance of $\tilde{r}_t$ is then modeled as an autoregressive process,

$$\tilde{r}_t = a + \epsilon_t, \quad \epsilon_t | F_{t-1} \sim \mathrm{N}(0, \sigma_t^2), \quad \sigma_t^2 = w + \alpha\epsilon_{t-1}^2 + \beta\sigma_{t-1}^2, \tag{11.30}$$

where a, w, α, and β are parameters and F_t denotes the information set as of time t. This model is known as the GARCH(1,1) model (Generalized ARCH), and can be estimated through maximum likelihood methods. It was introduced by Bollerslev (1986) and collapses to the ARCH(1) model introduced by Engle (1982) once we set $\beta = 0$. In other words, the variance of the distribution of asset returns tomorrow is linear in the expectation error, $(E_{t-1}(\epsilon_t^2) - \epsilon_t^2)$, and rises linearly with the current "realized variance," ϵ_t^2, namely,

$$E_t(\epsilon_{t+1}^2) = w + (\alpha + \beta)\epsilon_t^2 + \beta\left(E_{t-1}(\epsilon_t^2) - \epsilon_t^2\right).$$

The quintessence of ARCH models is to make volatility dependent on the variability of past observations. An alternative formulation, initiated by Taylor (1986), makes volatility driven by some unobserved components. This formulation gives rise to the *stochastic volatility* model. Consider, for example, the following stochastic volatility model:

$$\tilde{r}_t = a + \epsilon_t, \quad \epsilon_t | F_{t-1} \sim \mathrm{N}\left(0, \sigma_t^2\right);$$
$$\ln \sigma_t^2 = w + \alpha \ln \epsilon_{t-1}^2 + \beta \ln \sigma_{t-1}^2 + \eta_t; \qquad \eta_t | F_{t-1} \sim \mathrm{N}\left(0, \sigma_\eta^2\right)$$

where a, w, α, β and σ_η^2 are parameters. The main difference between this model and the GARCH(1,1) model in eq. (11.30) is that the volatility as of time t, σ_t^2, is not predetermined by the past forecast error, ϵ_{t-1}. Rather, this volatility depends on the realization of the stochastic volatility shock η_t at time t. This makes the stochastic volatility model considerably richer than a simple ARCH model and also somehow more difficult to estimate: because volatility is not predetermined, maximum likelihood methods cannot be used to estimate this model. As for the ARCH model stochastic volatility models have also been intensively used, especially following the progress accomplished in the corresponding estimation techniques; some of these techniques involve simulation methods such as those reviewed in chapter 6 (see section 6.7).[7]

11.5.1.2 ARCH and diffusive models

Under regularity conditions, ARCH models and stochastic volatility models behave essentially the same as the sampling frequency gets sufficiently high. Precisely, Nelson (1990) shows that ARCH models converge in distribution to the solution of the stochastic differential equations, in the sense that the finite-dimensional distributions of the volatility process generated by ARCH models converge toward the finite-dimensional distributions of some diffusion process as the sampling frequency goes to infinity. To illustrate, consider

7. Mele and Fornari (2000) review the seminal contributions regarding estimation of stochastic volatility models.

the following model:

$$\begin{cases} d\ln S_\tau = (\cdots)\,d\tau + \sigma_\tau dW_\tau \\ d\sigma_\tau^2 = \left(\omega - \varphi\sigma_\tau^2\right)d\tau + \psi\sigma_\tau^2 dW_\tau^\sigma \end{cases} \tag{11.31}$$

where dW_τ and dW_τ^σ are correlated with correlation ρ and ω, φ, and ψ are some constants. Consider further the ARCH model

$$\begin{cases} y_{\Delta,n+1} = \epsilon_{\Delta,n+1}, \quad \epsilon_{\Delta,n} = \sigma_{\Delta,n}u_{\Delta,n}, \quad u_{\Delta,n} \sim \text{NID}(0,1) \\ \sigma_{\Delta,n+1}^2 = w_\Delta + \alpha_\Delta\left(|\epsilon_{\Delta,n}| - \gamma\epsilon_{\Delta,n}\right)^2 + \beta_\Delta\sigma_{\Delta,n}^2 \end{cases} \tag{11.32}$$

where $y_{\Delta,n+1} = \ln\left(S_{\Delta,n+1}/S_{\Delta,n}\right) - E\left(\ln\left(S_{\Delta,n+1}/S_{\Delta,n}\right)\right)$; n and Δ refer to the indexing of observed data and the sampling frequency (weekly, say); w_Δ, α_Δ, and β_Δ are positive parameters, possibly depending on the sampling frequency; and $\gamma \in (-1,1)$. The parameter γ allows to capture the Black-Christie-Nelson leverage effect discussed in chapter 9 (see section 9.8).[8] Note that the second of eqs. (11.32) can be written as

$$\begin{aligned} \sigma_{\Delta,n+1}^2 - \sigma_{\Delta,n}^2 &= \left[\Delta t^{-1}w_\Delta - \Delta t^{-1}\left(1 - \alpha_\Delta E\left(|u_{\Delta,n}| - \gamma u_{\Delta,n}\right)^2 - \beta_\Delta\right)\sigma_{\Delta,n}^2\right]\Delta t \\ &\quad + \Delta t^{-\frac{1}{2}}\alpha_\Delta\sigma_{\Delta,n}^2\sqrt{\Delta t}\,\Delta W_{\sigma,n}, \end{aligned} \tag{11.33}$$

and $\Delta W_{\sigma,n} \equiv \left(|u_{\Delta,n}| - \gamma u_{\Delta,n}\right)^2 - E\left(|u_{\Delta,n}| - \gamma u_{\Delta,n}\right)^2$. The first two terms define the drift term for the variance process, and the last term is the diffusive component. Then, under regularity conditions, the sample paths of S and σ^2 in eqs. (11.32) converge to those of S and σ^2 in eqs. (11.31) with a well-defined correlation coefficient ρ.[9]

11.5.2 Implied Volatility, Smiles, and Skews

In parallel to the previous time series research, research on option prices in the 1980s was challenging the Black–Scholes assumption of a constant volatility. As we know, the Black–Scholes model relies on the assumption that the underlying asset price is a geometric Brownian motion with constant volatility:

$$\frac{dS_t}{S_t} = \mu dt + \sigma dW_t,$$

where W is a Brownian motion and μ and σ are constants. As we also know, σ is the only parameter to enter the evaluation formula for a call option price.

---

8. See Black (1976b), Christie (1982), or Nelson (1991).

9. See Fornari and Mele (2006). We would need to assume that the sequence of parameters satisfies the following limits: $\lim_{\Delta t\downarrow 0}\Delta t^{-1}w_\Delta = \omega$, $\lim_{\Delta t\downarrow 0}\Delta t^{-1}(1 - \alpha_\Delta E\left(|u_{\Delta,n}| - \gamma u_{\Delta,n}\right)^2 - \beta_\Delta) = \varphi$, and $\lim_{\Delta t\downarrow 0}\Delta t^{-1/2}\sqrt{\text{var}\left(\Delta W_{2,n}\right)}\alpha_\Delta = \psi$. For example, suppose that $\gamma = 0$, in which case the random component of the diffusive term in eq. (11.33) collapses to $\Delta W_{\sigma,n} = u_{\Delta,n}^2 - E(u_{\Delta,n}^2)$, and the moment condition for the diffusive component is $\psi = \lim_{\Delta t\downarrow 0}\Delta t^{-1/2}\sqrt{2}\alpha_\Delta$. Intuitively, in this case ΔW_σ is an IID sequence of centered chi-square variates with one degree of freedom (and variance $\varpi = 2$) and stands for the discrete version of the Brownian motion increments dW_σ in the second of eqs. (11.31).

This dependence leads to a crucial point. Not only is the assumption of a constant σ inconsistent with the time series evidence reviewed in the previous section, but it is also inconsistent with empirical evidence on the *cross-section* of option prices. Let $C_t^{\$}(K,T)$ denote the time t market price of a call expiring at T with strike K. Consider the price predicted by the Black–Scholes model, $C_{\text{BS}}(S_t, T-t; K, \sigma)$ in eq. (11.16). Define the Black–Scholes *implied volatility*, IV say, as the value of σ that equates the Black–Scholes formula to the option market price:

$$\text{IV}: C_t^{\$}(K,T) = C_{\text{BS}}(S_t, T-t; K, \text{IV}). \tag{11.34}$$

We know from section 11.4.5 that the Black–Scholes option price is strictly increasing in σ. Further, it is left as an exercise to show that, provided the no-arbitrage bound (11.8) holds, the Black–Scholes price is less than the market price for small σ and higher for large σ. Therefore, there exists a unique value for IV such that eq. (11.34) holds true. In fact, it is market practice to quote options in terms of implied volatilities, not prices. Moreover, implied volatility is the same for both the call and the put. Indeed, by the put-call parity in eq. (11.7),

$$P_t^{\$}(K,T) = C_t^{\$}(K,T) - S_t + Ke^{-r(T-t)}. \tag{11.35}$$

This equation also holds for the Black–Scholes model for each σ, that is, $P_{\text{BS}}(S_t, T-t; K, \sigma) = C_{\text{BS}}(S_t, T-t; K, \sigma) - S_t + Ke^{-r(T-t)}$. Subtracting this equation from eq. (11.35) shows that the implied volatilities for a call and for a put options are the same.

If the Black–Scholes model holds, implied volatilities would be the same for each K. Yet, empirically, at least since 1987, the cross-section of implied volatilities exhibit striking characteristics. In particular, define the "moneyness" (by convention, call moneyness) as

$$mo \equiv \frac{S_t}{Ke^{-r(T-t)}}. \tag{11.36}$$

In the early formation years of equity option markets, the pattern of implied volatilities was a bit unclear. The most common pattern that seemed to emerge came in the form of a "smile," a U-shaped function of $\frac{1}{mo}$. After the 1987 crash, this pattern would change to one by which implied volatilities were decreasing in $\frac{1}{mo}$, a "smirk." This new pattern is often referred to as a "volatility skew." One possible explanation for these changes may relate to liquidity. Call and put options that are deep in the money and deep out of the money (OTM) are typically less liquid than ATM options and require a liquidity risk premium. Since the Black–Scholes option price is increasing in volatility, the implied volatility is U shaped in $\frac{1}{mo}$.

Figures 11.7 and 11.8 illustrate how smiles and skews result due to an alternative explanation, namely that asset returns display random volatility. We rely on the celebrated Heston (1993b) model in which volatility is random and refer the reader to section 11.5.3 (see eq. (11.56)) for additional details regarding this model.[10]

---

10. The densities in figure 11.8 are those of $1 - \Phi\left(d - \sigma\sqrt{T-t}\right)$ in eq. (11.16) (in the Black–Scholes market) and of $1 - P_2\left(\ln S, \sigma^2, t\right)$ in eq. (11.61) (in Heston's market). Both densities are with respect to K.

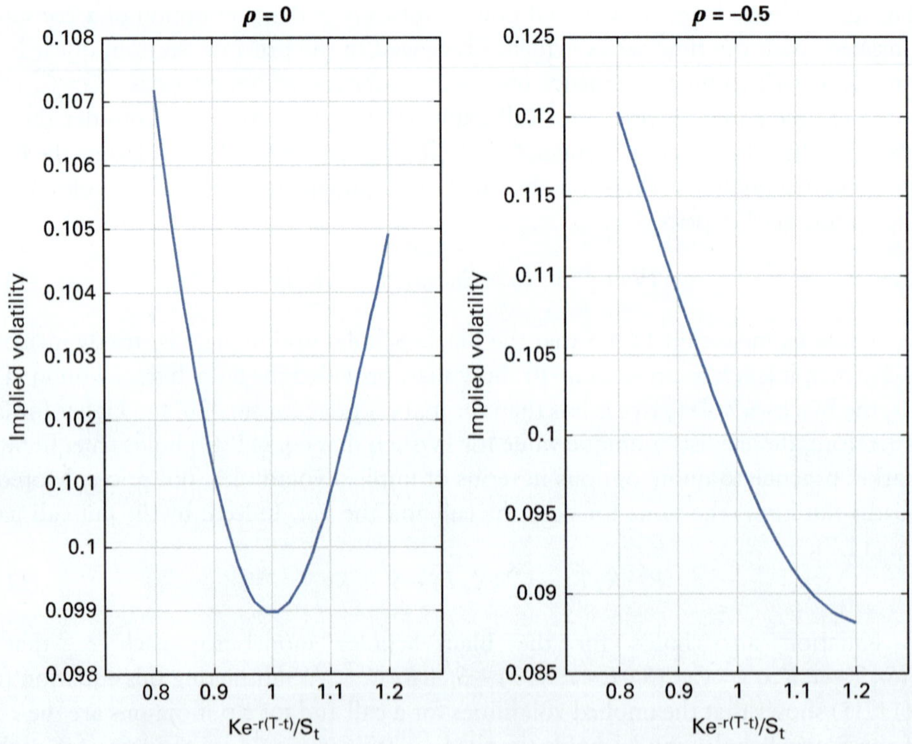

Figure 11.7
Smile and skew predicted by the Heston model (see eq. (11.56)). Model parameters are set to $\kappa = 2$, $\omega = 0.01$, $\xi = 0.1$. Moreover, in the left panel (the "smile"), $\rho = 0$, and in the right panel (the "skew"), $\rho = -0.5$. The current price is $S = 100$, the initial value of volatility is $\sqrt{v_t} = \sqrt{\omega}$, and the short-term rate is $r = 0$. The option maturity is six months.

The intuition underlying the patterns in figure 11.7 is the following. The Black–Scholes model relies on the assumption asset returns are log-normally distributed. However, this assumption is not correct: in a stochastic volatility model, market pricing operates through an alternative distribution, one for which tail events are given a larger weight due to market fears of extreme outcomes. To illustrate, the market may fear that the stock price will fall below a given level, say $\underline{K}$, more than the Black–Scholes model predicts. As a result, the market density should have a left tail thicker than the log-normal for values of $S < \underline{K}$.

Figure 11.8 illustrates this possibility. This picture depicts the risk neutral densities of the Black–Scholes model as well as the Heston model (with random volatility) where the latter is taken to be the truth. Heston's model does generate thick tails, as discussed later. To represent this property, figure 11.8 has magnified the left tail of the two densities. Then, a market density with a left tail thicker than that of Black–Scholes implies that the probability deep OTM *puts* (i.e., those with low strikes) will be exercised is higher under the market density than under the log-normal. For this reason, the implied volatility needed to price deep OTM *puts* is higher than that required to price ATM calls and puts.[11]

11. Note that if a call (put) option is OTM for a given strike, a put (call) is an in-the-money option for the same strike.

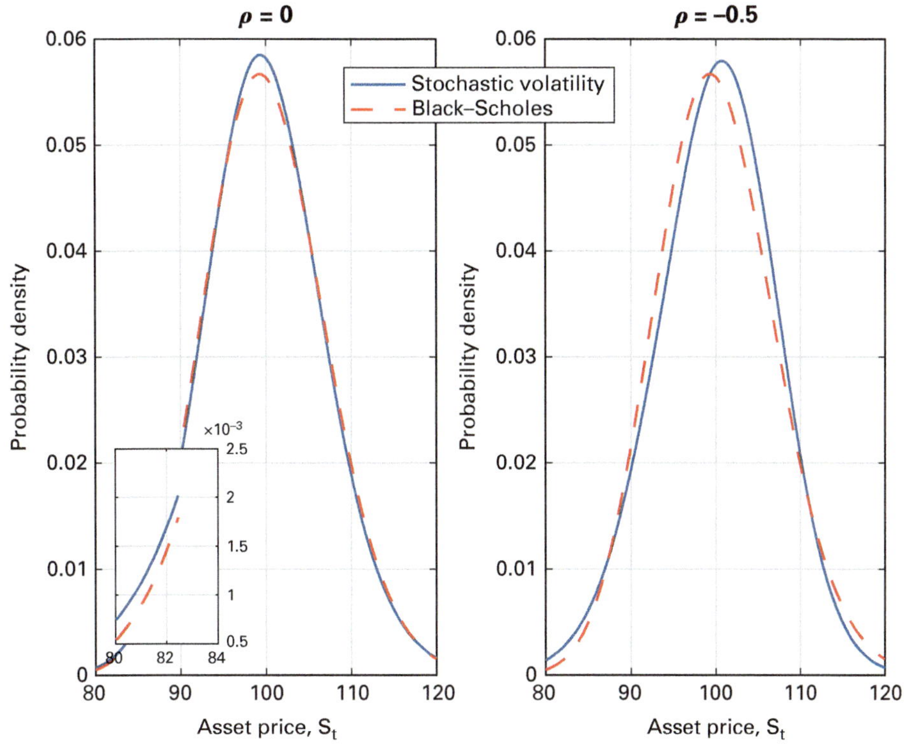

Figure 11.8
Six-month ahead risk neutral densities in the Black–Scholes market (dashed line) and the Heston market (see eq. (11.56)) (solid line) when the current asset price is $S = 100$. The parameters in the Heston's model are $\kappa = 2$, $\omega = 0.01$, $\xi = 0.1$, and $\rho = 0$ (left panel) and $\rho = -0.5$ (right panel), and the initial value of volatility is $\sqrt{v_t} = \sqrt{\omega}$. The Black–Scholes volatility parameter is set equal to $\sqrt{\omega}$. The small box on the left corner of the left panel magnifies the two densities at their left tails.

Suppose, for example, that given the current stock price, $S_t = 100$, Black–Scholes's implied volatility is 10% for a given maturity $T - t$ and a strike $K = 90$, that is,

$$P_{\text{BS}}(100, T-t; K, 10\%) = P_t^{\$}(K, T), \quad K = 90.$$

Next, consider an even lower strike, say, $K = 80$. In this case, the Black–Scholes put price would most likely not equal the market price: while the Black–Scholes and market prices both lower with a decreased strike, the Black–Scholes price decreases more because the probability of exercise is lower under this theoretical market than under the actual market:

$$P_{\text{BS}}(100, T-t; K, 10\%) < P_t^{\$}(K, T), \quad K = 80.$$

That is, Black–Scholes's implied volatility would now need to raise from 10% to 11%, say: when $K = 80$, $P_{\text{BS}}(100, T-t; K, 11\%) = P_t^{\$}(K, T)$.

At the other extreme, the market may attach a higher likelihood that the stock price will be above some $\bar{K}$ than predicted by Black–Scholes: the market density may have a right tail thicker than the log-normal for values of $S > \bar{K}$, implying a higher probability that deep

OTM *calls* (i.e., those with high strike prices) will be exercised compared with the lognormal. The left panel of figure 11.7 shows that, in this case, the implied volatility needed to price deep OTM *calls* exceeds the implied volatility needed to price ATM calls and puts. The second effect has disappeared since the 1987 crash, as mentioned, for reasons similar to those underlying the right panel of figure 11.8, leaving the "skew" of the right panel of figure 11.7.

This section suggests that OTM options contain important information regarding market expectations about future volatility. Indeed, the Cboe Volatility Index (Cboe-VIX) does aggregate the prices of OTM options to convey an estimate of the volatility expected to arise and corrected by risk. Section 11.8 develops details on this index and explains that it links to the fair value of a variance swap, that is, a contract in which a counterparty is insured against fluctuations in future volatility.

While these conclusions rely on numerical results, analytical explanations have existed since at least the early 1990s.[12] Consider the following model:

$$\begin{cases} \dfrac{dS_t}{S_t} &= \mu dt + \sigma_t dW_t \\ d\sigma_t^2 &= b(S_t, \sigma_t)dt + a(S_t, \sigma_t)dW_t^{\sigma} \end{cases} \tag{11.37}$$

where W_σ is a Brownian motion correlated with W with an instantaneous correlation equal to ρ and b and a are some functions satisfying regularity conditions. The drift function, b, is needed to generate mean-reverting behavior in stochastic volatility, σ_t^2. This property is required in the same spirit of the assumptions underlying the dynamics of interest rates (see chapter 13): volatility (or interest rates) cannot explode.

The option price is $C\left(S_t, \sigma_t^2, T-t\right) = e^{-r(T-t)}\mathbb{E}\left[(S_T - K)^+ \,|S_t, \sigma_t^2\right]$. Assume that the correlation $\rho = 0$. Then the implied volatility predicted by this model satisfies

$$\text{IV}: C\left(S_t, \sigma_t^2, T-t\right) = C_{\text{BS}}\left(S_t, T-t; K, \text{IV}\right)$$

and is U shaped with respect to $\frac{1}{mo}$. Indeed, let $X = \ln(mo)$, where mo is defined in eq. (11.36). In appendix 11.C, we show that, in a model with stochastic volatility and zero correlation, IV is approximately a quadratic function of X, IV $(X, T-t)$ say, with a minimum occurring at $X = 0$, just as in the left panel of figure 11.7, namely,

$$\text{IV}(X, T-t) \approx \mu_V(t) + \frac{1}{2}\left(\frac{X^2 - \left(\frac{1}{2}\mu_V^2(t)(T-t)\right)^2}{\mu_V^3(t)(T-t)}\right) var_t(\tilde{V}_{t,T}^{1/2}), \tag{11.38}$$

where $\mu_V(t) = \mathbb{E}_t(\tilde{V}_{t,T}^{1/2})$ and $\tilde{V}_{t,T}$ is the "average variance" or future realized variance, defined as

$$\tilde{V}_{t,T} \equiv \frac{1}{T-t}\int_t^T \sigma_\tau^2 d\tau. \tag{11.39}$$

12. See, e.g., Ball and Roma (1994) and Renault and Touzi (1996).

These properties link to a compelling lesson learned from the early literature on ARCH and random variance models: random changes in volatility lead to a return distribution with tails thicker than the normal—one with a kurtosis larger than three (Mandelbrot, 1963; Fama, 1965; Nelson, 1990)—a feature of the Heston model that is clear from figure 11.8. For example, we know that, even if unexpected returns are conditionally normally distributed, they are approximately and unconditionally Student's t once we assume their variance follows a GARCH(1,1) process (Nelson, 1990). Let us illustrate.

Denote the unexpected returns as of time t with ϵ_t, and suppose that $\epsilon_t = z_t \sigma_t$, where $z_t \sim \text{NID}(0,1)$ and σ_t, the conditional volatility of ϵ_t, is some random process. Then we have, by Jensen's inequality, that $E(\epsilon_t^4) = E(z_t^4)\, E(\sigma_t^4) \geq E(z_t^4)\,(E(\sigma_t^2))^2 = E(z_t^4)\,(E(\epsilon_t^2))^2$, which is an equality when σ_t is not random. It follows that the kurtosis is $\text{Kurt} \equiv \frac{E(\epsilon_t^4)}{(E(\epsilon_t^2))^2} \geq E(z_t^4) = 3$. That is, random volatility makes the unconditional return density leptokurtic even when the conditional is normal. Although these calculations relate to unconditional densities, similar conclusions would apply to conditional ones: random volatility makes a T day conditional density leptokurtic even when the one-day conditional is normal. As a result of this leptokurtosis, the probability that OTM options is exercised is larger than that implied by the log-normal distribution, whence, the smile effect. Instead, the smirk effect arises when $\rho < 0$ as shown by figure 11.7. Intuitively, when $\rho < 0$, the left tail of the return distribution is thicker than the right, thereby making OTM puts most valuable.

The model in eqs. (11.37) has been extended to accommodate for the presence of jumps. In these extensions, the asset return variance is still a mean-reverting process, but it may move discontinuously as in the following model:

$$d\sigma_t^2 = \kappa\left(\omega - \sigma_t^2\right)dt + \psi \sigma_t dW_t^{\sigma} + \mathcal{S} \cdot dJ_t,$$

where J_t is a Poisson process with intensity v, a process reviewed in chapter 4 (see section 4.9); $\mathcal{S} > 0$ is the size of the jump, assumed for simplicity to be constant; and finally, κ, ω, and ψ are constants. When $\rho < 0$, the model predicts that the left tail of the return distribution is thicker due to a positive likelihood of positive jumps, $v > 0$. Therefore, a high value of κ is needed to avoid a too thick-tailed distribution. Instead, if $v = 0$, a thicker distribution can be achieved with a lower value of κ.

The skew may result due to an even simpler mechanism than the random volatility model of this section. Assume that asset returns are driven by jumps, just as in the Merton's (1976) model reviewed in chapter 4 (see section 4.9):

$$\frac{dS_t}{S_t} = (\cdots)\,dt + \sigma dW_t - \mathcal{S} \cdot dJ_t, \tag{11.40}$$

where σ is now constant and $\mathcal{S} < 1$ is the jump size. Provided that $\mathcal{S} > 0$, this model predicts that the left tail of the return distribution is thicker than the right. Thus, downward jumps, especially if they are large, may be responsible for the skew. Naturally, this model may be extended to the case in which "Brownian volatility" σ is time-varying. The point of a simple model such as (11.40) is to emphasize that "crashophobia" may be an additional explanation for the skew: a model with jumps may explain the skew; further, option prices should incorporate some premium for the presence of jumps (see section 4.9.6 in chapter 4), and this premium may have the potential to provide additional explanation for the skew.

Finally, note that this section provides explanations of implied volatilities by highlighting the presence of *exogenous* processes of random volatility or jumps. During the 1990s, literature developed to account for markets with endogenous volatility. In these markets, there are feedback effects similar to those studied in chapter 9 (see section 9.11): when prices fall, some traders sell (say, for hedging reasons), making prices fall even more. These models, discussed in the last section of this chapter (see section 11.10), have the potential to explain the skew.

11.5.3 Option Pricing under Stochastic Volatility

Stochastic volatility has the potential to lead to *market incompleteness*,[13] the situation in which we cannot hedge against future contingencies based on trading available securities (see chapter 4). Precisely, the payoff of an option cannot be replicated while only trading the underlying asset: the number of assets available for trading (one stock) is less than the sources of risk—the two Brownian motions in eq. (11.37), W_τ^σ and W_τ. Intuitively, the option price is $C_\tau \equiv C(S_\tau, \sigma_\tau^2, T-\tau)$, thus being driven by both the asset price, S_τ, and the stochastic variance, σ_τ^2. The point is that σ_τ^2 and then C_τ, are driven by W_τ^σ while the value of a "would-be replicating" portfolio (only comprising the underlying asset) is driven by W_τ only. Because this portfolio cannot replicate the option, the option price cannot be preference free: as we know from part I, preference-free pricing relies on the ability to perfectly replicate a derivative, and the unique price of this derivative is then that of the replicating portfolio, independent of risk appetite.[14] Naturally, markets can be "completed" by the option, although in this case, option pricing is not preference free, as we shall show in the next sections.

Stochastic volatility entails two inextricable consequences: (i) there is an infinity of option prices consistent with absence of arbitrage, each of them corresponding to a particular risk neutral probability—there are many risk adjustments that we can make to the drift term of the variance process in eqs. (11.37); and (ii) there cannot be perfect hedging strategies only relying on the underlying asset. Regarding point (ii), we may either (a) use a strategy, which albeit not self-financed, would still allow for a perfect replication of the claim or (b) use a self-financed strategy that would apply to some misspecified model. In case (a), the strategy leads to a hedging cost process. In case (b), the strategy

13. Stochastic volatility might not necessarily lead to market incompleteness. Mele (1998, 88) considers a "circular" market with m asset prices where (i) asset price no. i exhibits stochastic volatility and (ii) this stochastic volatility is driven by the Brownian motion driving the $(i-1)$th asset price. Therefore, in this market, each asset price is a solution to eqs. (11.37), and yet markets are complete.

14. Note that the payoff of the option at the expiration T is $(S_T - K)^+$ and does not depend on σ_T^2. However, the value of the option at any $\tau < T$ does depend on σ_τ^2 because, intuitively, the risk neutral expectation of $(S_T - K)^+$, conditional on the information set at τ, is calculated through the risk neutral transition density π, say, which obviously depend on σ_τ^2.

leads to a tracking error process.[15] We begin with a short review on how asset prices may be replicated in a general context and then proceed to option evaluation in subsequent subsections.

11.5.3.1 Spanning and cloning

A set of securities spans a set of payoffs if any point in that set can be generated by a linear combination of the security prices. As explained in chapter 4, the set of payoffs may include those promised by a contingent claim, for example, that promised by a European call or final consumption. Chapter 4 relies on this "spanning" property and solves for consumption-portfolio choices through martingale methods. In this section, we show how spanning helps define replicating strategies with the purpose of pricing "redundant" assets. Consider the following model (introduced in chapter 4) where asset prices are assumed to be driven by a d-dimensional Brownian motion W_t,

$$dy_t = \varphi(y_t)\,dt + \Sigma(y_t)\,dW_t, \tag{11.41}$$

where φ and Σ are vector- and matrix-valued functions. The value of a portfolio is $V_t = \theta_t \cdot S_{+,t}$, where S_+ denotes the vector of the security prices and the MMA and θ_t is a portfolio process with the same notation as in chapter 4. As explained in that chapter (in section 4.3.1), the value of a self-financed portfolio satisfies $dV_t = \theta_t \cdot dS_{+,t}$ or

$$dV_t = \left(\pi_t^\top(\mu_t - 1_m r_t) + r_t V_t\right) dt + \pi_t^\top \sigma_t dW_t, \tag{11.42}$$

where $\pi \equiv (\pi_1, \cdots, \pi_m)^\top$, $\pi_i \equiv \theta_i S_i$, $\mu \equiv (\mu_1, \cdots, \mu_m)^\top$, S_i is the price of the ith asset, μ_i is its drift, and σ is the volatility matrix of the price process. Chapter 4 relies on the risk neutral probability and characterizes the securities span. But we may achieve a similar task under the physical probability, P. In our context, asset prices are semimartingales under P:

$$dA_t = dF_t + \tilde{\gamma}_t dW_t, \tag{11.43}$$

where F is a process with finite variation and $\tilde{\gamma}$ satisfies regularity conditions. Let us conjecture that $V_t = A_t$ for all t. By the *unique decomposition property* (see section 4.2 in chapter 4), drifts and diffusion components of V and A must be the same. Regarding the diffusion terms, the portfolio π_t in eq. (11.42) needs to satisfy

$$\tilde{\gamma}_t = \pi_t^\top \sigma_t. \tag{11.44}$$

Regarding the drifts, we equate those of V and F, obtaining

$$\frac{dF_t}{dt} = \pi_t^\top(\mu_t - 1_m r_t) + r_t V_t = \pi_t^\top(\mu_t - 1_m r_t) + r_t A_t, \tag{11.45}$$

where the second equality holds by the conjecture that $A_t = V_t$ for all t.

The conjecture that $A_t = V_t$ is indeed correct as A_t is the *price of a traded asset* and the *assumption of complete markets*. However, eq. (11.44) has no solutions for π when $m < d$,

15. There may be theoretical instances in which the claim may be "super-replicated," in which case strategies that deliver a payoff at least as large as that promised by the derivatives exist. Karatzas (1997) provides a quick guide to this type of results, which were developed during the 1990s.

such that there are no self-financing strategies that replicate A_t: the number of available assets is too small to span all possible events—markets are incomplete according to the definitions in chapter 4.

In the context of this chapter, a call price could be understood as being a differentiable function $C(t, y_t)$ and, by Itô's lemma, a special case of eq. (11.43),

$$dC = (LC)\, dt + (C_y \cdot \Sigma)\, dW,$$

where LC is the usual infinitesimal generator and C_y is the vector containing the partials of C with respect to each component of y. It can be replicated if at least $m = d$, in which case $C_y \Sigma = \pi^\top \sigma$. For example, in the context of Black–Scholes and Merton in section 11.4, we have that $m = d = 1$ and that the asset price S is the only state variable in eq. (11.41)—a geometric Brownian motion with parameters (μ, σ), that is, $\varphi(S) = \mu S$ and $\Sigma(S) = \sigma S$. Then, $C_y \cdot \Sigma = C_S \sigma S$ and $\pi = C_S S$, leading to the celebrated Black–Scholes hedge ratio in eq. (11.17).

How does replicability work in the context of stochastic volatility? It may actually work, although we may not have preference-free formulas, as we shall now explain.

11.5.3.2 *Replication*

Let us suppose that the price of the underlying asset is the solution to eqs. (11.37). The price of a European option is $C^i_\tau = C(S_\tau, \sigma^2_\tau, T_i - \tau)$. Suppose two such options are traded, with prices C^1_τ and C^2_τ, where we take $T_1 < T_2$. We cannot replicate C^1_τ by trading the underlying asset and the MMA. Indeed, let V be the value of a self-financed strategy, including the asset price and the MMA, which obviously satisfies

$$dV = (\pi(\mu - r) + rV)\, dt + \pi\sigma\, dW, \tag{11.46}$$

where π is the value of the underlying asset. Instead, the price of the first option satisfies

$$dC^1 = LC^1 dt + C^1_S \sigma S dW + C^1_{\sigma^2} a dW_\sigma, \tag{11.47}$$

where L is the infinitesimal generator, $LC^i \equiv \frac{\partial C^i}{\partial t} + \mu S C^i_S + b C^i_{\sigma^2} + \frac{1}{2}\sigma^2 S^2 C^i_{SS} + \frac{1}{2} a^2 C^i_{\sigma^2\sigma^2} + \rho a \sigma S C^i_{S\sigma^2}$. As we may see, we are unable to match the diffusion coefficients in eq. (11.46) to those in Eq. (11.47).

Instead, under conditions reviewed in section 11.5.3.3, we can replicate the price of the first option, C^1, through a self-financed portfolio strategy including (i) the underlying asset, (ii) the option expiring at T_2, and (iii) the MMA. The value V of this strategy satisfies

$$\begin{aligned} dV = &\left(\pi_1 (\mu - r) + \pi_2 \left(\frac{LC^2}{C_{T_2}} - r\right) + rV\right) dt \\ &+ \pi_1 \sigma dW + \pi_2 \left(\frac{C^2_S}{C^2} \sigma S dW + \frac{C^2_{\sigma^2}}{C^2} a dW_\sigma\right), \end{aligned} \tag{11.48}$$

where π_1 is the invested asset value and π_2 is the value of the investment in the second option. We match the diffusion coefficients of eq. (11.47) and eq. (11.48) and obtain

$$\pi_1 = \left(\frac{C^1_S}{C^2_S} - \frac{C^1_{\sigma^2}}{C^2_{\sigma^2}}\right) C^2_S S, \quad \pi_2 = \frac{C^1_{\sigma^2}}{C^2_{\sigma^2}} C^2. \tag{11.49}$$

Replacing these expressions into eq. (11.48) and equating the drift of eq. (11.48) to that of eq. (11.47) leaves

$$\frac{LC^1 - rC^1 - C_S^1(\mu - r)S}{C_{\sigma^2}^1} = \frac{LC^2 - rC^2 - C_S^2(\mu - r)S}{C_{\sigma^2}^2}.$$

These two ratios agree. They must then be equal to some process $a \cdot \Lambda^\sigma$, say, which is independent of the maturity of the option. Therefore, using the expression for the infinitesimal generator,

$$\frac{\partial C}{\partial t} + rSC_S + (b - a\Lambda^\sigma)\, C_{\sigma^2} + \frac{1}{2}\sigma^2 S^2 C_{SS} + \frac{1}{2}a^2 C_{\sigma^2\sigma^2} + \rho a\sigma SC_{S\sigma^2} = rC. \tag{11.50}$$

The interpretation of Λ^σ is that of the unit risk premium required to face the risk of stochastic fluctuations in volatility. Absence of arbitrage is not sufficient to recover a unique Λ^σ. By the Feynman–Kac stochastic representation of the solution to a partial differential equation, there are many solutions to eq. (11.50),

$$C(S_t, \sigma_t^2, T - t) = e^{-r(T-t)}\mathbb{E}_{Q^\Lambda}\left((S_T - K)^+ \,|\, S_t, \sigma_t^2\right), \tag{11.51}$$

where Q^Λ is *a* risk neutral probability, induced by the many Λ that are consistent with absence of arbitrage.

The previous derivation suggests two possible uses of the portfolio strategies of eqs. (11.49). The first, obvious, is hedging. We can always hedge the first option with π_1 and π_2 in eqs. (11.49). The second is more subtle. If we really think our evaluation model for the first option is better than the market, we can always synthesize the first option with the portfolio in eqs. (11.49) and replicate the payoff of the first option at expiration, $\psi(S_{T_1})$. This point will be developed below (see section 11.5.3.6).

Eq. (11.50) can be interpreted as APT relations. Indeed, let us define the unit risk premium as related to the fluctuations of the asset price, $\lambda = (\mu - r)/\sigma$. Then, (11.50) implies that

$$\frac{LC}{C} = E\left(\frac{dC}{C}\right) = r + \underbrace{\frac{C_S}{C}\sigma S}_{\equiv\beta_S} \cdot \lambda + \underbrace{\frac{C_{\sigma^2}}{C}a}_{\equiv\beta_{\sigma^2}} \cdot \Lambda^\sigma,$$

where β_S is the beta related to the volatility of the option price induced by fluctuations in the stock price, S, and β_{σ^2} is the beta related to the volatility of the option price induced by fluctuations in the return volatility. It is a generalization of the APT relation in eq. (11.22) that holds for the Black–Scholes model.

11.5.3.3 Market completeness

Implicit in the previous derivations is the assumption that derivatives enable any investor to face a complete market. Let us clarify. In this market, there are two sources of risk: the two Brownian motions W and W_σ. Now, by the results in chapter 4 (see Section 4.3), a market with the asset and a derivative on this asset may be complete, provided the volatility matrix of these two asset returns is nonsingular. It turns out that this condition is satisfied when

$|C_{\sigma^2}| > 0$ at all times: the option price must be responsive to changes in the asset returns volatility. Intuitively, eq. (11.48) shows that, under this condition, the value of a replicating strategy is able to incorporate information on W_σ. The point now is to ascertain whether this condition is satisfied. Intuitively, there must be conditions under which it should: we know that the option price is increasing in volatility in models without random volatility (see section 11.4.5). Bajeux-Besnainou and Rochet (1996) and Romano and Touzi (1997) do indeed show that, under certain conditions, this is the case: in models such as (11.37), option prices are strictly increasing in volatility, at least provided that the diffusion and drift of volatility equation are independent of the asset price.

11.5.3.4 *Pricing formulae*

Hull and White (1987), Scott (1987), and Wiggins (1987) developed the first option pricing models with stochastic volatility. Heston (1993b) provides an analytical solution, assuming an affine model for the variance process (to be defined below). In other cases in which a solution is not available, we would need to rely on numerical methods (say, through Monte Carlo simulations or the numerical solution to partial differential equations).

Hull and White Hull and White (1987) derive a first pricing formula based on a continuous time model where asset returns and volatility are uncorrelated:

$$\begin{cases} \frac{dS_t}{S_t} &= rdt + \sigma_t d\tilde{W}_t \\ \frac{d\sigma_t^2}{\sigma_t^2} &= \mu_v d\tau + \xi d\tilde{W}_t^\sigma \end{cases} \tag{11.52}$$

where $\tilde{W}$ and $\tilde{W}_\sigma$ are standard Brownian motions defined under the risk neutral probability. Appendix 11.C reviews the arguments leading to their famous pricing formula,

$$C(S_t, \sigma_t^2, T-t) = \mathbb{E}_t^{\tilde{V}}[C_{BS}(S_t, T-t; K, \tilde{V}_{t,T}^{1/2})], \tag{11.53}$$

where $C_{BS}(S_t, T-t; K, \tilde{V}_{t,T}^{1/2})$ is the Black–Scholes formula (see eq. (11.16)) evaluated at the average variance defined in eq. (11.39) and the conditional risk neutral expectation on the RHS is taken with respect to the laws generating $\tilde{V}_{t,T}$. According to eq. (11.53), the option price is simply the Black–Scholes formula averaged over all possible "values" taken by the future average variance, $\tilde{V}_{t,T}$. Accordingly, the authors provide a Taylor's expansion around the conditional expectation of $\tilde{V}_{t,T}$, $m_V(t) = \mathbb{E}_t(\tilde{V}_{t,T})$,

$$\begin{aligned} C(S_t, \sigma_t^2, T-t) &= C_{BS}(S_t, T-t; K, \sqrt{m_V}) \\ &+ \frac{1}{2} \left. \frac{\partial^2 C_{BS}(S_t, T-t; K, \sqrt{V})}{\partial V^2} \right|_{V=m_V(t)} var_t(\tilde{V}_{t,T}). \\ &+ \frac{1}{6} \left. \frac{\partial^3 C_{BS}(S_t, T-t; K, \sqrt{V})}{\partial V^3} \right|_{V=m_V(t)} skew_t(\tilde{V}_{t,T}) + \cdots \end{aligned} \tag{11.54}$$

In fact, eq. (11.54) is a general formula applying to models more general than that in eq. (11.52), say, one of the models encompassed by eqs. (11.37), provided of course W and W_σ are uncorrelated, as explained more formally in appendix 11.C.

In appendix 11.C, we also explain that the Hull and White equation (11.53) can be generalized to the case in which the two Brownian motions in (11.5.2) have instantaneous stochastic correlation equal to some ρ_τ. Romano and Touzi (1997) show that in this case, provided that ρ, b, and a in eqs. (11.37) are independent of S,

$$C\left(S_t, \sigma_t^2, \rho_\tau, T-t\right) = \mathbb{E}_t^{\tilde{V}}\left[C_{BS}\left(S_t L_{t,T}, T-t; K, \tilde{V}_{t,T}^{\rho\frac{1}{2}}\right)\right]$$
$$L_{t,T} \equiv e^{-\frac{1}{2}\int_t^T \rho_\tau^2 \sigma_\tau^2 d\tau + \int_t^T \sigma_\tau \rho_\tau dW_\tau^\sigma}, \quad \tilde{V}_{t,T}^{\rho} = \frac{1}{T-t}\int_t^T \sigma_\tau^2\left(1-\rho_\tau^2\right) d\tau. \tag{11.55}$$

Heston Heston (1993b) develops an analytical solution for European options in a model with stochastic volatility, in which the asset price is the solution to

$$\begin{cases} d\ln S_t &= \left(r - \frac{1}{2}\sigma_t^2\right) dt + \sigma_t d\tilde{W}_{1t} \\ d\sigma_t^2 &= \kappa\left(\omega - \sigma_t^2\right) dt + \xi\sigma_t\left(\rho d\tilde{W}_{1t} + \sqrt{1-\rho^2} d\tilde{W}_{2t}\right) \end{cases} \tag{11.56}$$

where κ, ω, ξ, and ρ are parameters. That is, the instantaneous variance is a square-root process under the risk neutral probability. We can evaluate the call relying on the general formula (11.10) in section 11.4.2. We have

$$\begin{aligned} C(S_t, \sigma_t^2; T-t, K) &= e^{-r(T-t)}\mathbb{E}_t\left(S_T - K\right)^+ \\ &= S_t \cdot \hat{Q}_t\left(S_T \geq K\right) - e^{-r(T-t)}K \cdot Q_t\left(S_T \geq K\right), \end{aligned} \tag{11.57}$$

where $\hat{Q}_t\left(S_T \geq K\right)$ and $Q_t\left(S_T \geq K\right)$ are two probabilities with (time t conditional) densities $\hat{q}_t^{\mathrm{m}}\left(S_T\right)$ and $q_t^{\mathrm{m}}\left(S_T\right)$; $q_t^{\mathrm{m}}\left(S_T\right)$ is the risk neutral marginal density of S_T; and $\hat{q}_t^{\mathrm{m}}\left(S_T\right)$ is another marginal density of S_T, with the Radon-Nikodym derivative with respect to $q_t^{\mathrm{m}}\left(S_T\right)$ given in eq. (11.11),

$$\eta_t(T) = \frac{\hat{q}_t^{\mathrm{m}}\left(S_T\right)}{q_t^{\mathrm{m}}\left(S_T\right)} = \frac{e^{-r(T-t)}S_T}{S_t}. \tag{11.58}$$

By the Girsanov theorem, the density process associated with $\eta_t(T)$ in eq. (11.58) satisfies

$$\frac{d\eta_t(\tau)}{\eta_t(\tau)} = -\left(-\sigma_\tau\right) d\tilde{W}_{1\tau},$$

such that the stock price is the solution to

$$\begin{cases} d\ln S_t &= \left(r + \frac{1}{2}\sigma_t^2\right) dt + \sigma_t d\hat{W}_{1t} \\ d\sigma_t^2 &= \left(\kappa\omega - \left(\kappa - \rho\xi\right)\sigma_t^2\right) dt + \xi\sigma_t\left(\rho d\hat{W}_{1t} + \sqrt{1-\rho^2} d\hat{W}_{2t}\right) \end{cases} \tag{11.59}$$

and $\hat{W}_{1t}$ is a Brownian motion under the new probability with density $\hat{q}_t^{\mathrm{m}}$ and with $d\hat{W}_{1t} = d\tilde{W}_{1t} - \sigma_t dt$.

Let $x \equiv \ln S$. In the Black–Scholes market, σ_t^2 is constant, and the two probabilities, $\hat{Q}_t\left(x_T \geq \ln K\right)$ and $Q_t\left(x_T \geq \ln K\right)$, can be expressed in closed form, using eq. (11.59) and eq. (11.56), resp., which leads to the celebrated formula in eq. (11.16) as explained in section 11.4.2.

Instead, in the Heston market, the two probabilities, $P_1\left(x_t, \sigma_t^2, t\right) \equiv \hat{Q}_t\left(x_T \geq \ln K\right)$ and $P_2\left(x_t, \sigma_t^2, t\right) \equiv Q_t\left(x_T \geq \ln K\right)$, are solutions to

$$\hat{L}P_1(x, \sigma^2, t) = 0, \quad LP_2(x, \sigma^2, t) = 0, \tag{11.60}$$

with the same boundary condition $P_j\left(x, \sigma^2, T\right) = \mathbb{I}_{x \geq \ln K}$, $j = 1, 2$, and where $\hat{L}$ and L are the infinitesimal generators associated with eq. (11.59) and eq. (11.56). Indeed, we have that: (i) probabilities are martingales due to $P_2\left(x_t, \sigma_t^2, T-t\right) = \mathbb{E}_t\left(\mathbb{I}_{x_T \geq \ln K}\right) = \Pr\left(x \geq \ln K\right)$, and similarly for $P_1(\cdot)$, and (ii) probabilities are diffusion processes because the stock price is. Eq. (11.60) then follows by the Feynman–Kac representation theorem.

The solution to the two partial differential equations in (11.60) is unknown in closed form, though. However, their characteristic functions can be shown to be exponential affine in x and σ^2. Precisely, define the two characteristic functions:

$$f_1(x_t, \sigma_t^2, t; \phi) = \hat{\mathbb{E}}_t\left(e^{-\mathrm{i}\phi x_T}\right), \quad f_2(x_t, \sigma_t^2, t; \phi) = \mathbb{E}_t\left(e^{-\mathrm{i}\phi x_T}\right), \quad \mathrm{i} \equiv \sqrt{-1},$$

where $\hat{\mathbb{E}}_t$ denotes the expectation taken with respect to $\hat{q}_t^{\mathrm{m}}$ and $\mathbb{E}_t$ denotes the conditional expectation taken against q_t^{m}. The two functions f_j satisfy the same partial differential equations (11.60), but they can be solved in closed form because their boundary conditions are simply $f_j\left(x, \sigma^2, T\right) = e^{-\mathrm{i}\phi x}$. Indeed, a fundamental definition is that a model is affine if its characteristic function is exponential affine in its state variables. Affine models were already used to analyze the term structure of interest rates at least since Vasicek (1977) and Cox, Ingersoll, and Ross (1985), as we shall discuss in chapter 13. Heston's model is the option pricing counterpart to these models of the yield curve.

The solution to the two characteristic functions is given by

$$f_j(x, \sigma^2, t; \phi) = e^{C_j(T-t;\phi) + D_j(T-t;\phi)\sigma^2 + \mathrm{i}\phi x},$$

where

$$C_j\left(T-t; \phi\right) = r\phi \mathrm{i}\left(T-t\right) + \frac{\kappa\omega}{\xi^2}\left[\left(b_j - \rho\xi\phi\mathrm{i} + d_j\right)\left(T-t\right) - 2\ln\left(\frac{1 - g_j e^{d_j(T-t)}}{1 - g_j}\right)\right]$$

$$D_j\left(T-t; \phi\right) = \frac{b_j - \rho\xi\phi\mathrm{i} + d_j}{\xi^2}\left(\frac{1 - e^{d_j(T-t)}}{1 - g_j e^{d_j(T-t)}}\right)$$

$$g_j = \frac{b_j - \rho\xi\phi\mathrm{i} + d_j}{b_j - \rho\xi\phi\mathrm{i} - d_j}, \quad d_j = \sqrt{\left(b_j - \rho\xi\phi\mathrm{i}\right)^2 - \xi^2\left(2u_j\phi\mathrm{i} - \phi^2\right)}$$

$$b_1 = \kappa - \xi\rho, \quad b_2 = \kappa, \quad u_1 = \frac{1}{2}, \quad u_2 = -\frac{1}{2}.$$

We may now invert the characteristic function, obtaining[16]

$$P_j(x_t, \sigma_t^2, t) = \frac{1}{2} + \frac{1}{\pi}\int_0^\infty \mathrm{Re}\left[\frac{e^{-\mathrm{i}\phi \ln K} f_j\left(x_t, \sigma_t^2, t; \phi\right)}{\mathrm{i}\phi}\right] d\phi. \tag{11.61}$$

Replacing these two probabilities into eq. (11.57) yields the celebrated Heston formula.

11.5.3.5 Case study: Assessing accumulators in markets with stochastic volatility

How may stochastic volatility affect trading strategies in practice? We consider a simple experiment based on the "accumulator" portfolios described in section 11.3.5. These portfolios are short n puts with the same strike K_p and long one call with strike K_C, such that the initial cost of the portfolio is equal to zero. Let $K_C = 100$, and assume all options expire in six months. We consider two markets: the Black–Scholes market and a second market where the underlying price follows the Heston model in (11.56). We assume that the parameter values are the same as those in figures 11.7 and 11.8. We also assume that random fluctuations in volatility are not priced, such that the parameters κ and ω under the physical probability are the same as those under the risk neutral probability. We take $r = 0$. We shall address a number of issues aimed at exploring how stochastic volatility affects risk and return of these accumulators.

First, assume the current level of the index is $S = 98$. How many puts with strike $K_p = 90$ should we sell to finance the long position in the call option? Assuming that the current variance in the Heston model equals the steady state variance, $\sigma_t = \sqrt{\omega} = \sqrt{0.01}$, we find that in the Heston market, $n = 3.9399$. Regarding the Black–Scholes market, we also assume a standard deviation equal to $\sqrt{0.01}$ and find $n = 5.1617$. If instead we assumed that the current index level is $S = 102$ and decide for a put strike equal to $K_p = 95$, we would find that $n = 5.9338$ in the Heston market and $n = 6.9016$ in Black–Scholes. The interpretation is that by increasing the strike from $K_p = 90$ to $K_p = 95$, we move toward more expensive puts. At the same time, assuming that $S = 102$ (instead of $S = 98$) leads to the opposite effect on the put prices. Moreover, a higher index level obviously makes call options more expensive. Overall, with these changes, we would need to sell a higher number of puts to finance a long position in the call.

We assess the portfolio performance assuming that the initial index value equals $S = 98$ and choose a put strike $K_p = 90$. We consider three initial values for volatility: the benchmark, $\sigma_t = \sqrt{0.01}$; a volatility higher the benchmark, $\sigma_t = \sqrt{0.02}$; and a volatility lower than the benchmark, $\sigma_t = \sqrt{0.008}$. In the high volatility case, we find that $n = 2.9252$; in the low volatility case, we find that $n = 4.3249$. An increase in volatility makes both puts and calls increase in value, although the put prices increase more than the call. Finally, we assume that the expected index growth rate is $\mu = 3\%$. We use Monte Carlo simulations and calculate the average, standard deviations, and annualized average return-to-risk ratios of the P&Ls (see table 11.3). Figure 11.9 depicts the relative frequency of these P&Ls in all cases we consider. The benchmark for the annualized average-to-risk ratio should be about 0.30 in the Black–Scholes market for a linear product. Consider indeed a simple

16. Stuart and Ord (2010, chap. 4) provide classical introductions to inversions of characteristic functions.

Table 11.3
P&Ls of a six-month accumulator

	Average	Std dev	$\sqrt{2}\frac{av}{std}$
B&S	1.3322	7.2839	0.2597
Heston	1.2284	7.2025	0.2412
Heston (high vol)	1.3120	9.0382	0.2053
Heston (low vol)	1.2018	6.7701	0.2511

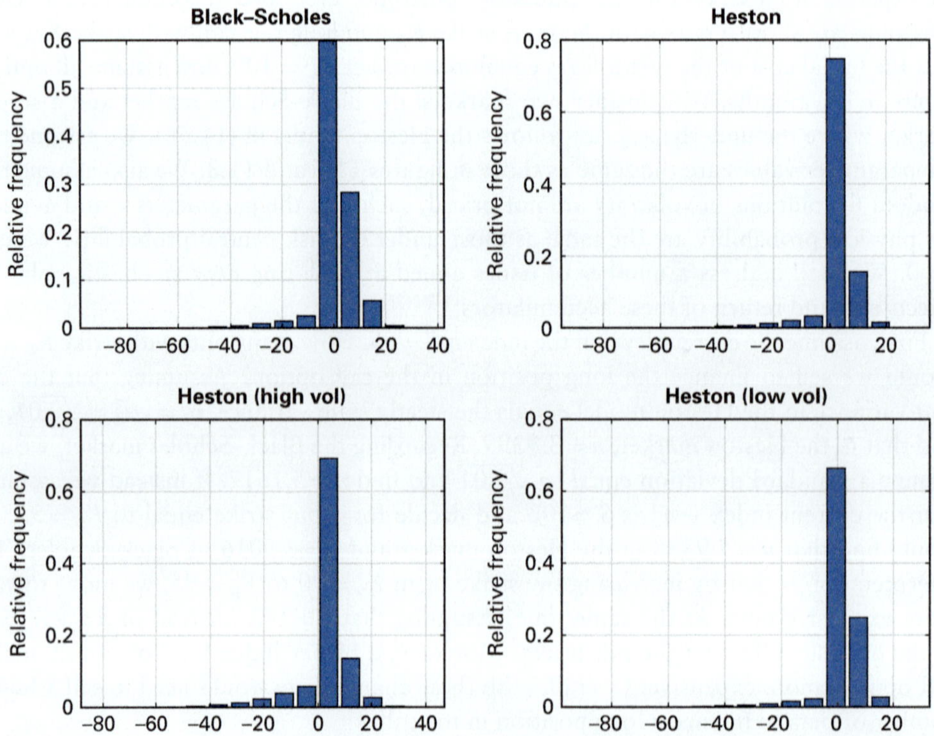

Figure 11.9
P&L frequencies of a six-month "accumulator" under different market assumptions: a Black–Scholes market (NW quadrant), the Heston market with current volatility fixed at its long-term value (NE), Heston's with current volatility lower than its long-term value (SE), and Heston's with current volatility higher than its long-term value (SW).

long strategy where we borrow \$98 at $r=0$, which we invest into an asset with growth rate of 3%. The dollar expected return in six months is $98{\cdot}e^{0.03\frac{1}{2}}-98=1.4811$, and by similar calculations, the standard deviation would be such that the annualized figure for the average returns-to-risk ratio would be 0.2974.

The accumulators display average-to-risk ratios that are comparable with the simple long strategy. However, they deliver payoffs with quite different distributions. These payoffs may be of interest to investors with a focus on tail events. In all cases, while the average P&Ls are positive, the frequency distributions have large standard deviations and long left tails: the downside risk is quite substantial, a feature obviously consistent with the description of the product payoff (see figure 11.5). In the Heston market, average profits are lower than in Black–Scholes because the density is more skewed to the left due to the negative correlation between asset returns and volatility. Within the Heston market, profits lower when we move to a low volatility scenario and increase in the opposite case, a property related to the sensitivity of the payoffs of the accumulators' derivatives with respect to the volatility environment.

11.5.3.6 *Taking stochastic volatility models to data*

How can we use option pricing models with stochastic volatility to generate trading signals? There are four main issues that make this question quite a delicate one. The first is that one would like to make sure that these models are *correctly (or well) specified* in the statistical sense made precise in Chapter 6. The second issue is that volatility is not observed, which complicates statistical inference. The third issue is that option prices and the underlying assets are obviously linked through no-arbitrage restrictions, which leads to additional difficulties regarding statistical inference. The fourth and final point regards model estimation; even if we manage to deal with the previous issues, parameter estimation error may complicate the interpretation of the model prediction.

There is obviously little we may do regarding the first and the last points, except perhaps unavoidable backtests and real-time experiments based on parameter values suggested by statistical inference. More subtle are the remaining points. The second point makes methods such as maximum likelihood unusable, as explained in chapter 6. However, there are alternative estimation methods that help dealing with estimation, and we will review one in a moment. The third point is equally challenging: one needs to be sure that the information provided by option and asset prices is not redundant.

A well-established estimation method relies on simulated methodologies introduced in chapter 6 (see section 6.7). Let $C_t\left(S_t, \sigma_t, K, T; \boldsymbol{\theta}\right)$ be the price of an option at time t when the state is (S_t, σ_t), the strike is K, maturity is T, and the parameter vector is $\boldsymbol{\theta}$.[17] We do not know $\boldsymbol{\theta}$ and σ_t and only observe the option market prices $C_t^{\$}\left(K_i, T_j\right)$ for a number of strikes i and/or time to maturities j and the underlying price S_t. But we may simulate the prices predicted by the model for each $\boldsymbol{\theta}$. Our parameter estimator, $\hat{\boldsymbol{\theta}}$ say, is such that the most salient statistical properties of data are captured by the data simulated out of $C_t(S_t, \sigma_t, K_i, T_j; \hat{\boldsymbol{\theta}})$ for the chosen strikes and time to maturities.

The previous step leads us to a collection of model-based prices, $C_t(S_t, \sigma_t, K_i, T_j; \hat{\boldsymbol{\theta}})$. We may assume that market prices are observed with error and find the value of σ_t, that is, the "filtered state" $(S_t, \hat{\sigma}_t)$[18] that minimizes some distance between $C_t(S_t, \sigma_t, K_i, T_j; \hat{\boldsymbol{\theta}})$ and $C_t^{\$}\left(K_i, T_j\right)$ for all i, j. By comparing $C_t(S_t, \hat{\sigma}_t, K_i, T_j; \hat{\boldsymbol{\theta}})$ with $C_t^{\$}\left(K_i, T_j\right)$, we may then focus on those segments of the option market that seem to be mispriced. When possible, we may synthesize the mispriced options based on a portfolio of relatively well-calibrated options, similar to the dynamically adjusted portfolio of section 11.5.3.2; for example,

17. Naturally, the parameter vector $\boldsymbol{\theta}$ has elements that keep track of the parameters under both P and Q. The parameters under Q enter the pricing function through risk premium adjustments.

18. We typically explain that we *estimate* an unknown parameter vector and that we *filter* the value of an unobserved random process.

we may synthesize a three-month ATM option with a portfolio invested in the underlying asset, another six-month ATM option and an MMA. In chapter 13, we explain how to rely on similar ideas in order to implement trading strategies in the fixed income space (see section 13.5.5).

11.6 Trading Volatility with Options

11.6.1 Option Portfolios and a Taxonomy

Volatility trading is the attempt at hedging against or implementing views regarding future movements in market volatility. It relies on a nondirectional view: the market direction does not matter; only the market's absolute changes are relevant.[19] It is market practice to distinguish between two types of volatility trading.

(1) *Vega trading* or *volatility surface* trading: A trade aiming to profit from the view that the term structure of implied volatilities will change—for example, from the expectation of a flattening or a steepening term structure of implied volatilities. It requires positioning into multiple options. For example, a "bull flattener" relies on the expectation that long-term implied volatilities will decrease faster than short-term ones, that is, the expectation the term structure of implied volatilities will flatten. This view may be implemented with a portfolio that is (a) long short-term options and (b) short long-term ones.
(2) *Gamma trading*: A trade aiming to profit from a realized volatility that deviates from current implied volatility. It relies on directional views regarding ongoing volatility developments. For this reason, gamma trading has a horizon that is typically shorter than that of vega trading. Gamma trading is implemented through portfolios comprising options and assets underlying these options. The most famous of these portfolios include "straddles," "strangles," "butterflies," "calendars," or delta-hedged options.

Figure 11.10 depicts hypothetical term structures of Black–Scholes ATM implied volatilities, that is, Black–Scholes ATM implied volatilities for maturities up to 12 months, assuming a Heston's market (see eq. (11.56)) under various scenarios. Not surprisingly, the term structure is increasing when current volatility, σ_t, is low and decreasing if σ_t is high: the term structure is "inverted" in bad times, that is, when volatility is high.[20] When σ_t^2 equals its long-term expected value, ω, the term structure is substantially flat.[21] Moreover, the higher the speed of mean reversion, κ, the higher the convergence of the curve to $\sqrt{\omega}$. Vega trading is a portfolio strategy that implements views based on expectations consistent with the patterns depicted in figure 11.10. In these examples, these

19. That is, the view may be directional regarding volatility developments.

20. Due to the presence of a "variance risk premium" (see section 11.8), we expect that the parameter ω under the risk neutral probability is higher than its counterpart under the physical probability. In this case, we would observe an increasing term structure of implied volatilities more often than a decreasing one.

21. Note that the black curve in figure 11.10 is slightly decreasing due to a Jensen's inequality effect: the ergodic mean of variance, $E_\infty(\sigma^2) \equiv \lim_{T\to\infty} E(\sigma_T^2|\sigma_t^2)$, satisfies $E_\infty(\sigma) < \sqrt{E_\infty(\sigma^2)}$.

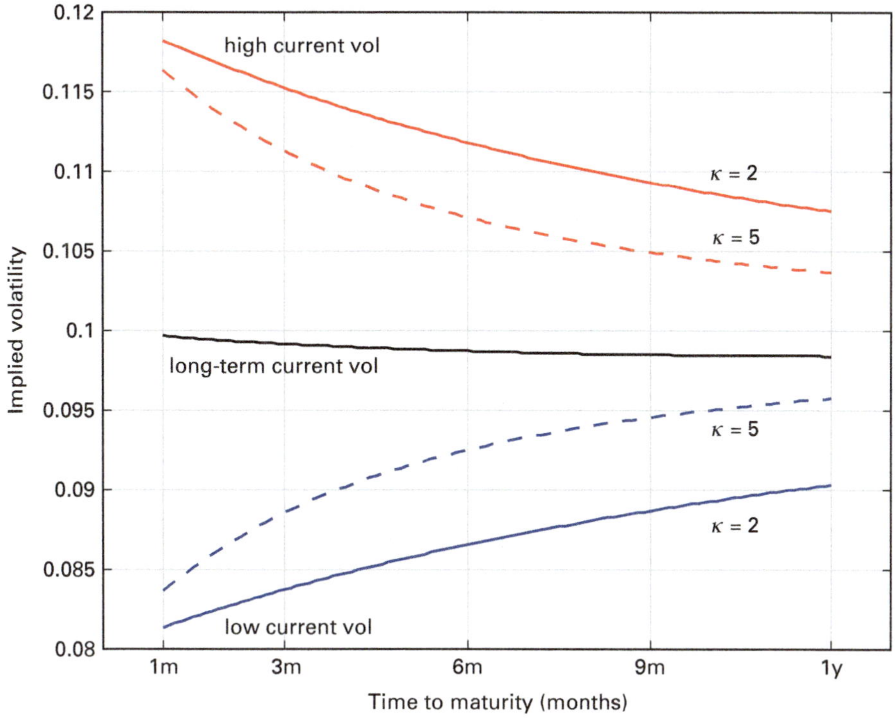

Figure 11.10
The term structure of Black–Scholes ATM-implied volatilities predicted by the Heston model (see eq. (11.56)) up to 12 months. Model parameters are set equal to $\omega = 0.01$, $\xi = 0.1$, and $\rho = -0.5$; the current price level is $S = 100$; and the short-term rate is $r = 0$. The middle curve is the term structure in correspondence of an initial value of volatility equal to $\sqrt{v_t} = \sqrt{\omega}$ and $\kappa = 2$. The increasing (resp. decreasing) curves are the term structures resulting from $\sqrt{v_t} = 0.80\sqrt{\omega}$ (resp. $1.20\sqrt{v_t} = \sqrt{\omega}$) and two assumptions on the speed of mean reversion ($\kappa = 2$ and $\kappa = 5$).

views are consistent with the assumptions underlying the Heston model. Another critical assumption underlying figure 11.10 is that the term structure regards ATM-implied volatilities. A more general "surface" strategy regards trading based on several strikes. Sections 11.8 and 11.9 describe more additional instruments that enable an investor to implement views that are "strikeless," that is, not depending on any specific option strike.

The focus of this section is on gamma trading. A natural question arises. In previous sections, we learned that option prices are generally increasing in volatility. So why does volatility trading necessitate portfolios of options *and* the underlying assets? In fact, option prices are increasing in both volatility and the asset price. Consider, for example, a market with stochastic volatility. In this market, the option price is $C\left(S_t, \sigma_t^2, t\right)$; if volatility, σ_t, increases, the option price in general increases as well. However, an increase in volatility may occur exactly when the asset price decreases. Note that this circumstance is likely to occur in light of the overwhelming empirical evidence on the negative correlation between σ_t and S_t (see section 11.5). Thus, in this case, the increase in C determined by an increase in σ_t may be offset by the fall in C following the drop in S_t.

Portfolios that only capture movements in volatility should, of course, be insensitive to changes in the underlying price. A natural way to achieve this property consists in taking positions in other options that offset movements in the initial option price due to changes in the underlying asset: it is the quintessence of gamma trading. Section 11.6.2 describes the rationale behind the simplest option portfolios obtained without hedging. Section 11.6.3 describes the hedging approach where one takes positions in the underlying asset that are proportional to Black–Scholes deltas, which offset movements in option prices resulting from changes in the underlying asset. In other words, a long position in a call option (say) may be partially offset by the short position in the "Black–Scholes replicating" portfolio—by construction, the Black–Scholes portfolio neutralizes movements in S_t, not σ_t. The result helps achieve a pure trade in volatility. Section 11.6.3 describes the P&L of this trade under some simplifying assumptions.

A difficulty with these strategies is that they are only imperfect substitutes for pure volatility trades: they deliver outcomes that still depend on the trajectory of the underlying price, a property known as "price dependence." Section 11.6.4, then, describes portfolios with many options. In these portfolios, options are weighted in a way that the portfolio's vega (the sensitivity to volatility) is insensitive to movements in the underlying price, at least in a Black–Scholes market. This insight was originally made by Demeterfi, Derman, Kamal, and Zou (1999). It is very important as it contributed to the creation of the main building blocks underlying modern volatility trading; these topics are reviewed in more detail in sections 11.8 and 11.9.

11.6.2 Delta-Neutral Portfolios

We consider portfolios of options with final payoffs driven by the same underlying price. The aim is to create portfolios for which the sum of the deltas of each option is equal to zero, that is, portfolios that have deltas equal to zero or "delta-neutral" portfolios. Intuitively, the payoffs of the options in these portfolios should be negatively correlated. For example, a *straddle* is a portfolio of one call option and one put option that have the same strike price and the same maturity. A *strangle* is the same as a straddle, with the difference being that the strike of the call differs from that of the put.

Figure 11.11 depicts an example of payoffs from going long a straddle. The left panel shows the intrinsic value of the straddle, $(K-S_T)^+ + (S_T-K)^+$, for $K=100$ as well as the value of the straddle at t in a Black–Scholes market, assuming a risk-free rate $r=1\%$, an instantaneous volatility $\sigma=10\%$, and two maturities—one month and three months. The right panel shows the P&L of the straddle, defined as $(K-S_T)^+ + (S_T-K)^+ - e^{r(T_i-t)}\text{Cost}_{i,t}$, where $\text{Cost}_{i,t} = p_{BS}(S_t, T_i-t; K, \sigma) + C_{BS}(S_t, T_i-t; K, \sigma)$, $C_{BS}(\cdot)$ is the Black–Scholes formula in eq. (11.16), $p_{BS}(\cdot)$ is the corresponding put price, and T_i-t is the straddle maturity, with $T_1-t=\frac{1}{12}$ and $T_2-t=\frac{3}{12}$. We assume that underlying price is $S_t=100$ such that the straddles are approximately at the money.[22]

The logic behind a straddle is that a call and a put have deltas that roughly compensate with each other—a property by which, in principle at least, straddle values change primarily due to volatility. Figure 11.11 illustrates that a straddle helps express views on volatility by paying off when the underlying price moves sufficiently away from its initial level, $S_t=100$.

22. The strike leading to at-the-money straddles is $K_i = S_t e^{r(T_i-t)}$, but to facilitate comparison, we set $K=100$ for both straddles.

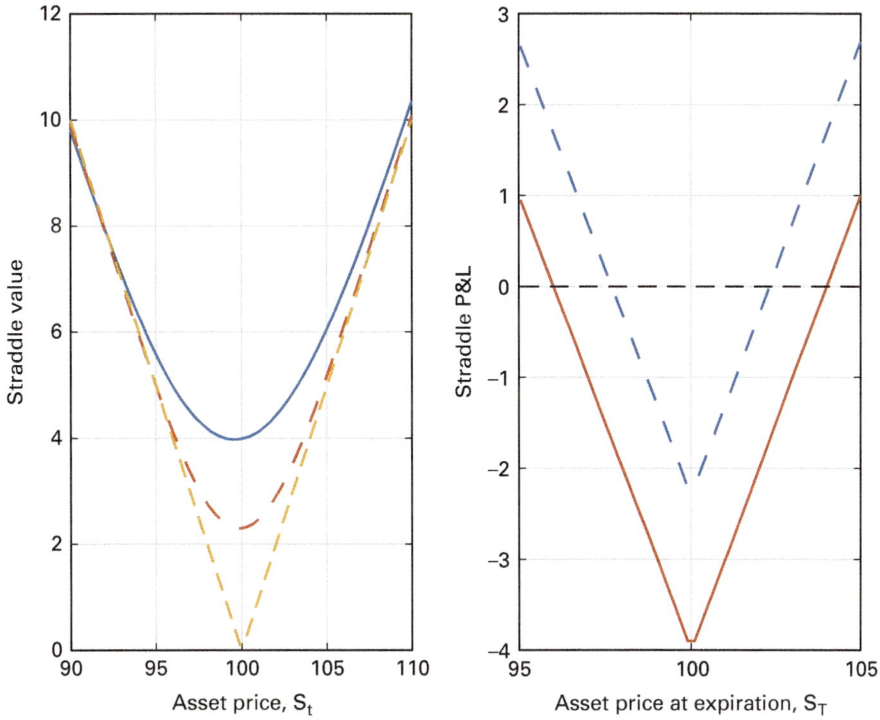

Figure 11.11
"Buying volatility." The left panel depicts the intrinsic value of a "straddle" with strike price $K=100$ (thin dashed line) as well as the value of a straddle with maturity $T_1-t=1/12$ (dashed line) and $T_2-t=3/12$ (solid line) in a Black–Scholes market when the current underlying price is S_t. The right panel depicts the P&Ls of roughly ATM straddles purchased at time t, defined as $(K-S_T)^+ + (S_T-K)^+ - e^{r(T-t)}\text{Cost}_{i,t}$, where $\text{Cost}_{i,t} = p_{BS}(S_t, T_i-t; K, \sigma) + C_{BS}(S_t, T_i-t; K, \sigma)$, with $T_1-t=1/12$ (dashed line) and $T_2-t=3/12$ (solid line), $r=1\%$, $\sigma=10\%$, and an underlying price $S_t=100$.

However, the delta of the straddle is not always zero, especially when the underlying price drifts away from moneyness. By eq. (11.19) and the put-call parity in eq. (11.7), in the Black–Scholes market the delta is $2\Phi(d)-1$, such that

$$\text{Straddle}(S,K) = C+p = S(2\Phi(d)-1) - Ke^{-r\tau}(2\Phi(d-\sigma\sqrt{\tau})-1),$$

where τ denotes time to maturity. Next, choose $K: S=Ke^{-r\tau}$ at inception, such that, *at inception*,

$$\begin{aligned}
\text{Straddle}_o^{atm}(S,K)\big|_{Ke^{-r\tau}=S} &\equiv 2S\left[\Phi\left(\frac{1}{2}\sigma\sqrt{\tau}\right) - \Phi\left(-\frac{1}{2}\sigma\sqrt{\tau}\right)\right] \\
&= 2S\left[2\Phi\left(\frac{1}{2}\sigma\sqrt{\tau}\right) - 1\right] \\
&\approx 2S\left[2\left(\Phi(0) + \phi(0)\frac{1}{2}\sigma\sqrt{\tau}\right) - 1\right] \\
&= 2S\frac{1}{\sqrt{2\pi}}\sigma\sqrt{\tau},
\end{aligned}$$

where the third line follows by Taylor's linear approximation around $\sigma\sqrt{\tau}$.

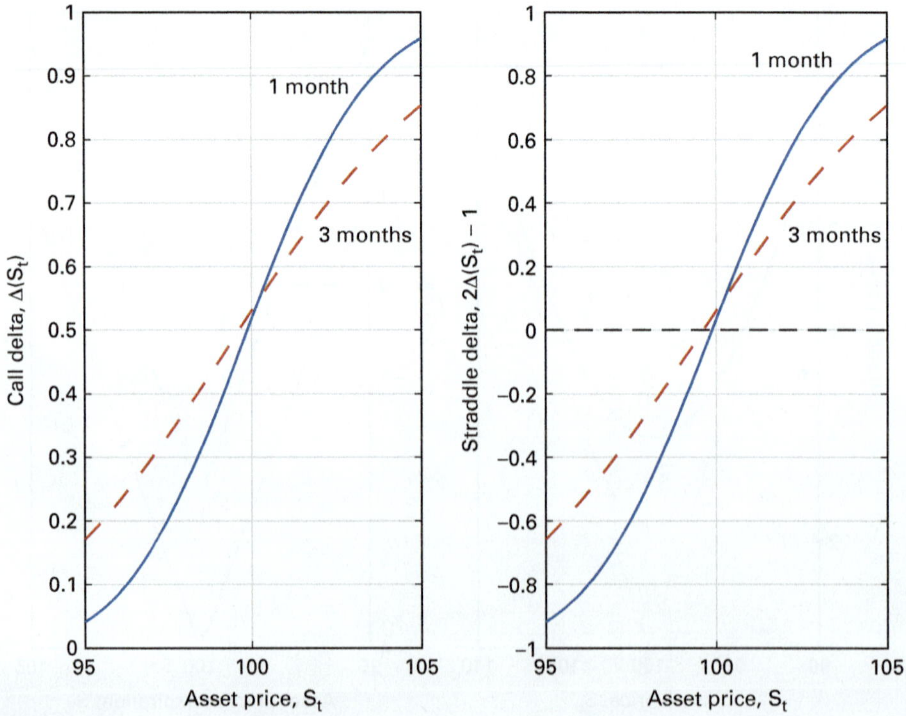

Figure 11.12
The delta of a call, $\Delta = \Phi$ (left panel), and that of a straddle, $2\Phi\,(d) - 1$ (right), where $\Phi\,(d)$ is the Black–Scholes delta in eq. (11.19), the strike is $K = 100$, and $r = 1\%$ and $\sigma = 10\%$ for maturity $T_2 - t = \frac{3}{12}$ (dashed line) and $T_1 - t = \frac{1}{12}$ (solid line).

Figure 11.12 depicts call deltas and straddle deltas as a function of the underlying price *after inception*.[23] For comparison, the picture plots delta for two maturities. The straddle delta deviates from zero as the underlying prices moves away from its initial level. The reason is that, as the asset price moves significantly, the straddle becomes a short or long position. When the price is up, the delta of the call is higher than the delta of the put in absolute value; the opposite happens when the asset price is down. The reason the straddle delta is roughly higher in absolute value for short-dated options will be clarified once we discuss some properties of calendars (see figure 11.14).

Naturally, going short a straddle leads to payoffs that have signs opposite to those in figure 11.11: being short a straddle relies on the expectation that markets are going to be stable; therefore, a short position in a straddle may be equivalent to selling volatility. Selling volatility is obviously very risky. In 1995, the 233-year old Barings Bank collapsed when one of its traders, Nick Leeson, was implementing a series of trades including short straddles on the Nikkei Index. A short straddle is a view that market volatility will not rise. However, in January 1995, a violent earthquake led the Nikkei index to crash by almost

23. Note that, by a standard homogeneity property, $\frac{\partial}{\partial S}\text{Straddle}\,(S, K) = 2\Phi\,(d) - 1$ and that, at inception, $\frac{\partial}{\partial S}\ \text{Straddle}\,(S, K)\big|_{Ke^{-r\tau}=S} \approx \frac{1}{\sqrt{2\pi}}\sigma\sqrt{\tau}$.

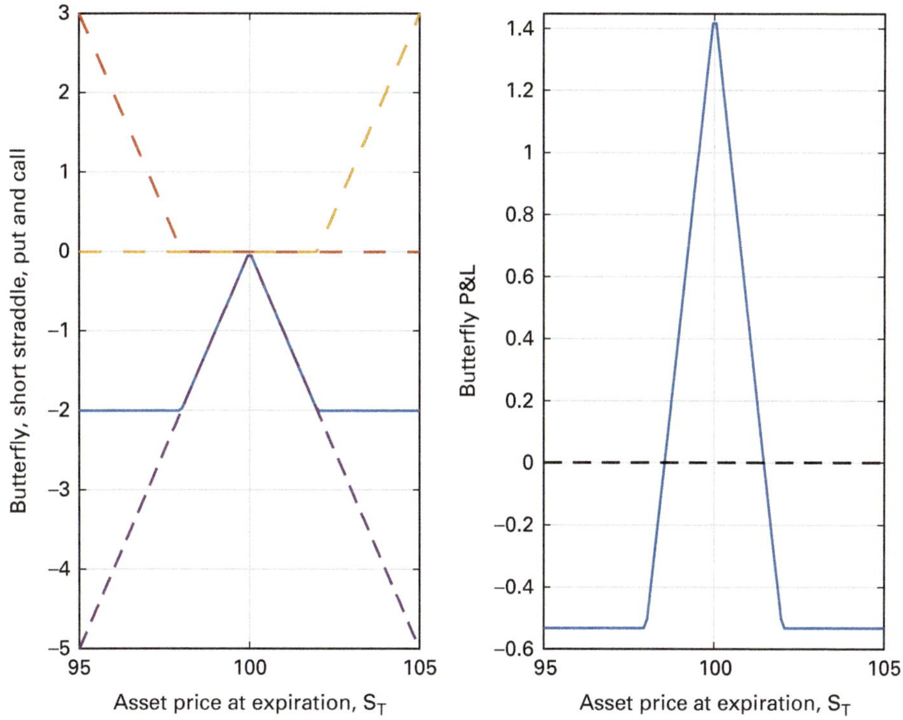

Figure 11.13
"Selling volatility." The left panel depicts the payoff of a "butterfly" with maturity equal to one month (solid line), which is (i) short one straddle (the thin dashed line) with strike $K = 100$ and (ii) long one OTM put, with strike $K_P = 98$ (the left dashed line), and one OTM call, with strike $K_C = 102$ (the right dashed line). The right panel depicts the P&L of the butterfly, $-[(K - S_T)^+ + (S_T - K)^+] + (K_p - S_T)^+ + (S_T - K_C)^+ - e^{r(T-t)}\text{Cost}_t$, where $T - t = \frac{1}{12}$ and Cost_t is the value of the butterfly at time t obtained in a Black–Scholes market with $r = 1\%$ and $\sigma = 10\%$ and the index level $S_t = 100$.

7% in a week. The straddle was "naked," that is, not delta hedged; it led to losses that were amplified by the trader's additional trades consistent with views that the index would stabilize. The index did not.

A trader may mitigate potential losses associated with a short position in a straddle by going long one additional portfolio comprising of (i) an OTM put, which pays exactly when the underlying asset price goes down, and (ii) an OTM call, which pays when the underlying asset price goes up. The result is known as a *butterfly spread*. Figure 11.13 depicts payoffs and the P&L of this portfolio, in which the (short) straddle has strike $K = 100$ with a maturity of one month (as one of the long straddles in figure 11.11) and the strikes of the OTM call and put are $K_C = 102$ and $K_p = 98$. The right panel shows the P&L of the butterfly, defined as $-\left[(K - S_T)^+ + (S_T - K)^+\right] + \left(K_p - S_T\right)^+ + (S_T - K_C)^+ - e^{r(T-t)}\text{Cost}_t$, where $T - t = \frac{1}{12}$ and Cost_t is the value of the butterfly at time t in the same Black–Scholes market considered in figures 11.11 and 11.12. Naturally, this cost is negative, due to the short position in the straddle.

Calendar spreads are alternative strategies to straddles with which to express views on volatility. They are portfolios long one call and short another call with the same strike

K where the first call has shorter maturity than the second. If the underlying asset price does not move too much, the calendar spread value drops because, due to the passage of time (see section 11.3), the price decay is more severe for the call with a shorter time to maturity. Intuitively, when maturity is large, a one-day passage of time may not affect uncertainty too much and, hence, the value of optionality embedded in the option price. When maturity is shorter, the option value may flatten to the intrinsic value much faster.

However, at any given point in time, the calendar spread increases in value as soon as the underlying price moves, regardless of the price direction. Let us explain. Suppose the underlying price increases from K. Then the lower the maturity, the higher the probability the option will be exercised and hence the higher the delta of the short-dated option. However, when the asset price decreases from K, the opposite happens: the lower the maturity, the lower the probability the option will be exercised and hence the lower the delta of the short-dated option. In other words, the delta is higher for short-term options when the price level is high and higher for long-term options when the price level is low as figure 11.12 illustrates in the *straddle* case.[24] Therefore, at any given point in time, when the underlying increases, the short-dated option value increases more than the long-dated option value; and when the underlying decreases, the short-dated option value decreases less than the long-dated one.

Thus, going long a calendar is consistent with the view that the underlying asset price will considerably fluctuate away from its current level, regardless of whether it is on its way up or down: (realized) market volatility is about to increase. Figure 11.14 depicts the payoff and the P&Ls of a calendar with strike $K=100$, an index level $S_t=100$, and maturities $T_1-t=\frac{1}{12}$ and $T_2-t=\frac{3}{12}$, assuming that the Black–Scholes market is the same as that underlying figures 11.12 and 11.13. The payoff one month after the initial positioning is $(S_T-K)^+ - C_{BS}(S_T,\frac{2}{12};K,\sigma)$, and the P&L is given by $(S_T-K)^+ - C_{BS}(S_T,\frac{2}{12};K,\sigma) - e^{r\frac{1}{12}}\left(C_{BS}\left(S_t,T_1-t;K,\sigma\right) - C_{BS}\left(S_t,T_2-t;K,\sigma\right)\right)$.

11.6.3 Delta-Hedged Strategies and Variance Risk Premiums

How do P&Ls look like for options portfolios? We illustrate the properties of such P&Ls under simplifying assumptions. We consider a simple situation, one in which we are long a call option, that we then hedge relying on the Black–Scholes model.[25] We consider both a Black–Scholes market and a market with stochastic volatility.

We will claim that this portfolio captures, albeit imperfectly so, a fundamental economic quantity known as *variance risk premium*. The variance risk premium compensates a trader who provides insurance to investors who are short realized volatility, that is, investors who will be hurt by high realized volatility. Precisely, if future realized volatility is random, we expect the economic value of this volatility, its expectation under Q, to be higher than the expected realized volatility (under P).

24. These properties can be further illustrated while comparing the intrinsic value of an option with the option value before maturity. The former is flat for relatively small values of the underlying price. Otherwise, it increases one-to-one with the underlying price.

25. This situation is a bit unrealistic. When intermediaries trade options, they do hedge them through through Black–Scholes or other models. However, they hedge books, not the single units adding up to the books.

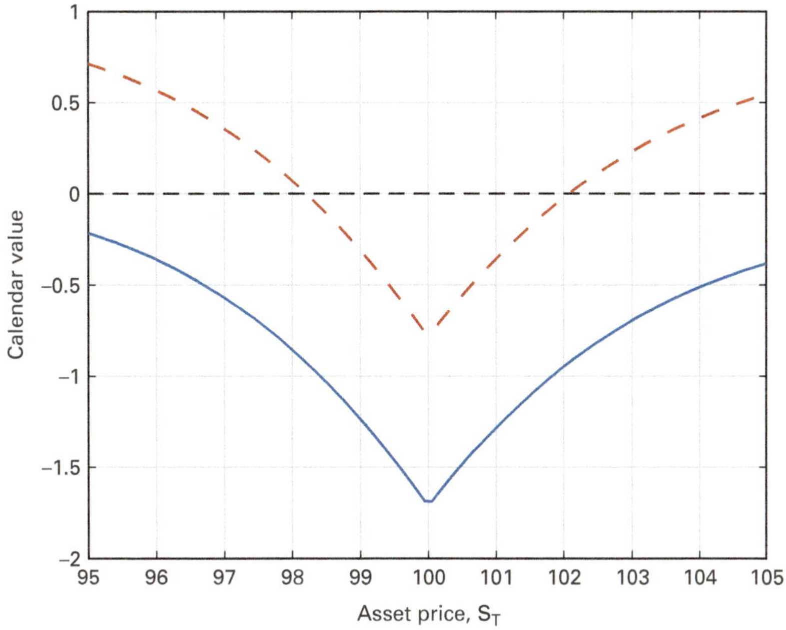

Figure 11.14
"Buying volatility." The payoff and P&L of a "calendar" with strike price $K=100$. This calendar is (i) long a call option with time to maturity $T_1-t=1/12$ and (ii) short a call option with time to maturity $T_2-t=3/12$. The solid line plots the payoff after one month from inception, defined as $\pi(S_T)\equiv(S_T-K)^+-C_{BS}(S_T,2/12;K,\sigma)$, and the dashed line is the payoff inclusive of the initial value of the position, $\pi(S_T)-e^{r/12}(C_{BS}(S_t,T_1-t;K,\sigma)-C_{BS}(S_t,T_2-t;K,\sigma))$, with an index level $S_t=100$.

Consider, for example, an asset manager committed to track a benchmark. This manager obviously relies on a selected subset of the assets that add up to the benchmark. The result is a tracking error, an error that may become particularly large in periods of high volatility. Missing a benchmark is problematic because it may be difficult to "catch up." This example merely tends to illustrate instances in which volatility may hurt: the asset manager is short volatility. To mitigate this problem, the asset manager may wish to "purchase volatility." One possibility is to purchase an option because its value increases with volatility. The immediate question is: At what price is anyone willing to sell such insurance to our asset manager? We know the option price is conveniently summarized by the Black–Scholes implied volatility. The previous question, then, becomes one involving implied volatility. The variance risk premium summarizes the difference between this implied variance and the future variance expected under P, that is, the difference between the Q- and P-expected variances.

We now develop these ideas in detail. We consider two idealized markets: a Black–Scholes and a stochastic volatility market. We calculate the P&L of going long a delta-hedged option in both cases. In the Black–Scholes market, the variance is constant such that the variance risk premium is zero. However, realized variance may be, on average, higher than the Black–Scholes implied variance if, for example, trading is made discretely, not continuously (as instead presumed by the Black–Scholes model). In this case, our delta-hedged option may well deliver a positive payoff: a trader bought an option at some value for the implied volatility but then realized volatility is higher than the implied volatility. In a market with stochastic volatility, a variance risk premium may well be positive even in the idealized setting with continuously rebalancing because future realized volatility may be higher than the implied volatility. Note that, in anticipation of these occurrences, markets with a relatively low risk appetite price options in a way that allows implied volatility to be higher than the realized volatility expected under P (see section 11.8); however, this section does not provide further discussions regarding the sign of the variance risk premium.

Note that the portfolios in this section are still surrogates for a pure play in volatility. A pure play in volatility may be implemented with dedicated "variance swaps" and will be dealt with in great detail in section 11.8. The key issue will be a search for the market price of volatility: How do markets evaluate the fair value of a variance swap, and how does this value reflect implied volatilities? The current section and the following section prepare the grounds to deal with these questions. Section 11.6.4 provides a quite substantial treatment of this issue.

11.6.3.1 *Black–Scholes market with discrete rebalancing*

Consider a Black–Scholes market where the short-term rate, r, is zero and μ is also zero. While volatility is constant in this market, there can be events in which the *realized* instantaneous variance, $(\Delta S_t/S_t)^2$, is higher than the *implied* variance, $\mathrm{IV}_0^2\Delta t$. In this context, the realized variance risk premium for a single trading date is the difference $\mathrm{IV}_0^2\Delta t - (\Delta S_t/S_t)^2$. On average, as the trading frequency increases, this premium is zero. But with discrete rebalancing, the premium may well be different from zero. What is the P&L of a portfolio that is long a call and is delta hedged through the Black–Scholes formula? Note that the value of this portfolio is equal to $\Pi_t = C_t - \Delta_{\mathrm{BS}}S_t$, such that, approximately, assuming discrete rebalancing,

$$\Delta\Pi_t = \underbrace{\Theta_t\Delta t + \frac{1}{2}\Gamma_t(\Delta S_t)^2 + \Delta_{\mathrm{BS}}\Delta S_t}_{=\Delta C_t} - \Delta_{\mathrm{BS}}\Delta S_t$$

$$= \left(-\frac{1}{2}\Gamma_t S_t^2 \mathrm{IV}_0^2\right)\Delta t + \frac{1}{2}\Gamma_t(\Delta S_t)^2 = \frac{1}{2}\Gamma_t S_t^2\left[\left(\frac{\Delta S_t}{S_t}\right)^2 - \mathrm{IV}_0^2\Delta t\right], \tag{11.62}$$

where $\Theta = \frac{\partial C}{\partial t}$ (theta), $\Delta_{\mathrm{BS}} = \frac{\partial C}{\partial S}$ (delta), and $\Gamma = \frac{\partial^2 C}{\partial S^2}$ (gamma) and the second equality follows by the Black–Scholes pricing equation (11.15). Intuitively, we are long the call option, and in the Black–Scholes market, this option value decays over time through $\Theta = -\frac{1}{2}\mathrm{IV}_0^2 S^2\Gamma$. At the same time, the option value increases with realized volatility due to convexity, $\frac{1}{2}\Gamma\Delta S^2$.

Aggregating up to the maturity of the option delivers the P&L of the portfolio at time T:

$$\mathrm{P\&L}_T \equiv \sum_{t=1}^{T}\Delta\Pi_t = \frac{1}{2}\sum_{t=1}^{T}\Gamma_t S_t^2\left[\left(\frac{\Delta S_t}{S_t}\right)^2 - \mathrm{IV}_0^2\Delta t\right]. \tag{11.63}$$

Note that the Black–Scholes delta is needed to compensate for those portions of the call price movements arising due to the movements in the underlying price—the term $\Delta_{\mathrm{BS}}\Delta S_t$

in the brackets of the first line of (11.62) contributes positively to the P&L when $\Delta S_t > 0$ and negatively otherwise. So the hedging is natural: the call price can go up because realized volatility (i.e., ΔS_t^2) increases or because the underlying price goes up. To isolate the views on volatility, we need to hedge against movements in the underlying price. Clearly, hedging through the Black–Scholes delta helps neutralize this effect.[26]

Eq. (11.63) says that the portfolio P&L delivers a positive payoff when the *realized* variance risk premium (the difference between implied and realized volatilities) is negative. The portfolio can then be a reasonable means to be long volatility, at least in the short term: the period-by-period profits $\Delta\Pi_t$ in eq. (11.62) only depend on how far realized volatility is from the initial Black–Scholes implied volatility.[27]

To illustrate, consider our introductory example. An asset manager is short volatility in that high price realizations may lead to high tracking errors. To simplify, assume that the asset manager utility over the next T trading days equals minus realized variance, that is, $-RV$, where $RV \equiv \sum_{t=1}^{T} (\Delta S_t/S_t)^2$. Ideally, the asset manager would like to access a *variance swap* market where, on the last trading day, some counterparty would pay them (minus) the realized variance risk premium, $-VRP \equiv \sum_{t=1}^{T} \left((\Delta S_t/S_t)^2 - \text{IV}_0^2 \Delta t \right)$. This variance swap would lock uncertainty in at $RV - VRP = -T \cdot \text{IV}_0^2 \Delta t$, that is, a constant. However, eq. (11.63) may imply that going long a hedged option may lead to a P&L different from $-VRP$: at any trading day, the difference between realized volatility and implied volatility, $(\Delta S_t/S_t)^2 - \text{IV}_0^2 \Delta t$, is weighted by dollar gamma, defined as $\Gamma_t S_t^2$. While dollar gamma is positive,[28] its value may be high or it may be low, according to the level of the underlying price, S_t. In fact, a negative P&L$_T$ may result despite the possibility that the terms $(\Delta S_t/S_t)^2 - \text{IV}_0^2 \Delta t$ are positive for most of the time. In other words, the P&L$_T$ depends on both the variance risk premium and the path of the underlying price: the portfolio may deliver profits in times of volatility depending on the price realization, a feature already mentioned and known as *price dependence*. Further, the notion of implied volatility in these examples is *strike dependent*: the option we are purchasing has an implied volatility that depends on the option strike. These features may be addressed with portfolios that comprise several options as explained in the following sections. Prior to accomplishing this task, we derive results that extend those in the previous Black–Scholes market while relying on a continuous time model with random volatility.

11.6.3.2 Stochastic volatility

Consider a market with stochastic volatility where the underlying price moves as in eqs. (11.37). At time t, we go long a call option with a market price equal to $C(S_t, \sigma_t^2, t)$. Let

---

26. Naturally, in the continuous time limit, assuming Black–Scholes is true, $\left(\frac{\Delta S_t}{S_t}\right)^2 \longrightarrow \text{IV}_0^2 dt$, such that eq. (11.63) shrinks to zero. Therefore, in the Black–Scholes market, views on realized volatility can be channeled only due to discrete rebalancing. Below, we shall explain that a nonzero P&L is obtained even in the continuous time limit, once the stock price displays stochastic volatility.

27. A similar P&L is obtained regarding straddles and calendars.

28. The Black–Scholes price is convex in S. Thus, gamma is positive, a very well-known property. We will return to properties of gamma in section 11.9 (see, e.g., figure 11.21).

us build up a self-financed portfolio with value V_t,

$$V_t = a_t S_t + b_t B_t, \tag{11.64}$$

where b_t are the units invested in a MMA, B_t is the MMA position, and

$$V_0 = C(S_0, \sigma_0^2, 0), \quad a_t = \Delta_{BS}(S_t, t; \text{IV}_0), \tag{11.65}$$

and IV_0 is the Black–Scholes implied volatility as of time $t = 0$, that is, the time at which we are taking a view on future volatility. Clearly, the model we are using to hedge is misspecified. However, the situation is, in some respects, similar to that examined earlier where we were relying on Black–Scholes hedge ratios while at the same time trading at discrete points in time.

Given these assumptions, El Karoui, Jeanblanc-Picqué, and Shreve (1998) make the following observations. Consider the value of the self-financed portfolio in eq. (11.64). Because this portfolio is self-financed,

$$\begin{aligned} dV_t &= a_t dS_t + r b_t B_t dt \\ &= rV_t dt + a_t (dS_t - rS_t dt) \\ &= [rV_t + a_t(\mu - r) S_t] dt + a_t \sigma_t S_t dW_t. \end{aligned}$$

Moreover, by Itô's lemma,

$$dC_{BS}(S_t, T-t; K, \text{IV}_0) = \left(\frac{\partial C_{BS}}{\partial t} + \mu S_t \frac{\partial C_{BS}}{\partial S} + \frac{1}{2}\sigma_t^2 S_t^2 \frac{\partial^2 C_{BS}}{\partial S^2} \right) dt + \sigma_t S_t \frac{\partial C_{BS}}{\partial S} dW_t,$$

where

$$\begin{aligned} &\frac{\partial C_{BS}}{\partial t} + \mu S_t \frac{\partial C_{BS}}{\partial S} + \frac{1}{2}\sigma_t^2 S_t^2 \frac{\partial^2 C_{BS}}{\partial S^2} \\ &= \underbrace{\frac{\partial C_{BS}}{\partial t} + rS_t \frac{\partial C_{BS}}{\partial S} + \text{IV}_0^2 S_t^2 \frac{\partial^2 C_{BS}}{\partial S^2}}_{\equiv rC_{BS}} + (\mu - r) S_t \frac{\partial C_{BS}}{\partial S} + \frac{1}{2}\left(\sigma_t^2 - \text{IV}_0^2\right) S_t^2 \frac{\partial^2 C_{BS}}{\partial S^2} \\ &= rC_{BS} + (\mu - r) S_t \frac{\partial C_{BS}}{\partial S} + \frac{1}{2}\left(\sigma_t^2 - \text{IV}_0^2\right) S_t^2 \frac{\partial^2 C_{BS}}{\partial S^2}. \end{aligned}$$

Therefore, the tracking error, or $\text{P\&L}_t$, defined as the difference between the Black–Scholes price and the portfolio value,

$$\text{P\&L}_t \equiv C_{BS}(S_t, T-t; K, \text{IV}_0) - V_t,$$

satisfies

$$d\text{P\&L}_t = \left(r\text{P\&L}_t + \frac{1}{2}\left(\sigma_t^2 - \text{IV}_0^2\right) S_t^2 \frac{\partial^2 C_{BS}}{\partial S^2} \right) dt.$$

At maturity T,

$$\begin{aligned}
\text{P\&L}_T &\equiv C_{\text{BS}}\left(S_T, T-T; K, \text{IV}_0\right) - V_T \\
&= \max\left\{S_T - K, 0\right\} - V_T \\
&= \frac{1}{2} e^{rT} \int_0^T e^{-rt} \frac{\partial^2 C_{\text{BS}}}{\partial S^2} S_t^2 \left(\sigma_t^2 - \text{IV}_0^2\right) dt.
\end{aligned} \tag{11.66}$$

This expression is the continuous time counterpart to eq. (11.63) in a market with stochastic volatility. Moreover, it can be shown that a delta-hedged straddle strategy leads to twice the expression in eq. (11.66), with the second partial of the straddle replacing the Black–Scholes gamma. Because the Black–Scholes price is convex, eq. (11.66) tells us that, even if we do not know exactly the law of movement of volatility but still hold the view that it will be persistently higher than the initial Black–Scholes implied volatility, we can obtain positive profits through (i) a long position in a call and (ii) a short position in the Black–Scholes replicating portfolio. Naturally, it isn't an arbitrage opportunity. The critical assumption is that volatility will increase.

Eq. (11.66) reveals that, even if the volatility σ_t is higher than IV_0 for most of the time, the final P&L may not necessarily lead to a profit. The reason is that the view on volatility developments for time t, $\sigma_t^2 - \text{IV}_0^2$, is weighted by dollar gamma, $S_t^2 \frac{\partial^2 C_{\text{BS}}}{\partial S^2}$. Similar to the discrete rebalancing case, "bad" realization of volatility, that is, $\sigma_t^2 < \text{IV}_0^2$, can occur precisely when the dollar gamma is large: it is the price-dependence issue mentioned while discussing eq. (11.63). Note also that this strategy is costly as it relies on delta hedging.

11.6.4 Perfect Hedging: Price Independence

How can we avoid price dependence? We may very naturally increase the number of options in the portfolio in a way to ensure that the portfolio vega is insensitive to changes in the underlying price. We assume a Black–Scholes market. Consider then a portfolio with a continuum of options, each bearing a weight equal to $\omega(K)$,

$$\pi\left(S_t, T-t; \sigma\right) = \int_0^\infty \omega(K)\, \mathcal{O}\left(S_t, T-t, K; \sigma\right) dK, \tag{11.67}$$

where $\mathcal{O}\left(S_t, T-t, K\right)$ denotes the price of an option with time to expiration equal to $T-t$ and strike K when the underlying price is S_t and the return volatility is σ. At this point, it is not crucial to specify whether the options in this portfolio are puts or calls. For simplicity, we initially assume that they are either puts or calls.

The objective is to find the density of portfolio weighting, $\omega(K)$, such that the portfolio has a vega that is insensitive to movements in S_t. Under regularity conditions, the portfolio vega is

$$\begin{aligned}
\frac{\partial \pi\left(S, T-t; \sigma\right)}{\partial \sigma} &= \int_0^\infty \omega(K) \frac{\partial \mathcal{O}\left(S, T-t, K; \sigma\right)}{\partial \sigma} dK \\
&= \int_0^\infty \omega(K)\, S\sqrt{T-t}\,\phi\left(d\left(\tfrac{K}{S}\right)\right) dK \\
&= \sqrt{T-t} \int_0^\infty \omega(xS)\, S^2 \phi\left(d(x)\right) dx,
\end{aligned} \tag{11.68}$$

where the second equality follows by the expression for the option vega (which is the same for a put and a call with the same strike), $d\left(\frac{K}{S}\right)$ is the same as d in eq. (11.16), and the third equality follows by a change of variables, $x \equiv \frac{K}{S}$. Inspection of eq. (11.68) reveals that the portfolio vega is independent of S for $\omega(K) \propto K^{-2}$. Demeterfi, Derman, Kamal, and Zou (1999) are the first to develop such results. Derman and Miller (2016) provide a comprehensive overview of the whole literature gravitating around these notions.

It is particularly important to investigate how the value of this portfolio changes with volatility. We consider a market with random volatility, the Heston model in section 11.5. The option prices we consider are now $\mathcal{O}(S_t, \sigma_t; T-t, K)$ with straightforward notation. Assume for simplicity that $r=0$, and pick all the options in the portfolio to be OTM, such that $\mathcal{O}(S_t, \sigma_t; T-t, K)$ is the Heston price of a put when volatility is σ_t and $K < S_t$ and the price of call when $K \geq S_t$. Section 11.8 shows that, when $\omega(K) = \frac{1}{T-t}K^{-2}$, the resulting portfolio has a value equal to

$$\mathbb{K} \equiv \frac{1}{T-t}\mathbb{E}_t\left(\int_t^T \sigma_u^2 du\right). \tag{11.69}$$

This value, we shall say, is the strike of a variance swap.

Naturally, this portfolio is unfeasible because it requires investing in a continuum of options. We may then examine the behavior of feasible portfolios. Figure 11.15 plots the square root of the portfolio value when the number of options is equal to $N=81$, 41, and 9 as a function of the current volatility, σ_t.[29] We call this value "VIX" for reasons explained in section 11.8. Also displayed is the theoretical value, determined through a direct calculation of $\mathbb{K}$ based on eq. (11.121) in section 11.9. The portfolio value matches the theoretical value quite well when the number of options is sufficiently high. It does, however, deviate from the theoretical value with a smaller number of options. A smaller number of options implies a lower sensitivity of the portfolio value to changes in market volatility.[30] We will return to these topics in sections 11.8 and 11.9. In the next section, we turn to another important issue, the issue of modeling the price of illiquid options based on the price of liquid options. Interestingly, this topic overlaps with the evaluation of variance swaps dealt with in section 11.8.

11.7 Local Volatility

This section generalizes the previous models with stochastic volatility in a way that enables one to price the entire cross-section of options (the "skew") without errors. The next section explains that there exists a beautiful connection between the model in this section

29. For $N=81$, the strike range is [80, 120] with increments of 0.5; for $N=41$, the strike range is [90, 110] with increments of 0.5; for $N=9$, the strike range is [98, 102] with increments of 0.5. In all cases, the spot price is $S_t=100$. Note that portfolios with a limited number of options may lead to underestimates or overestimates of $\mathbb{K}$, according to the combinations of strike range and intensity.
30. Note also that, with $N=81$ and 41, the sensitivity of the portfolio value to changes in volatility is independent of the asset price as these values are substantially the same as the theoretical ones, that is, $\mathbb{K}$ in (11.69) as $\mathbb{K}$ is, by construction, independent of the asset price.

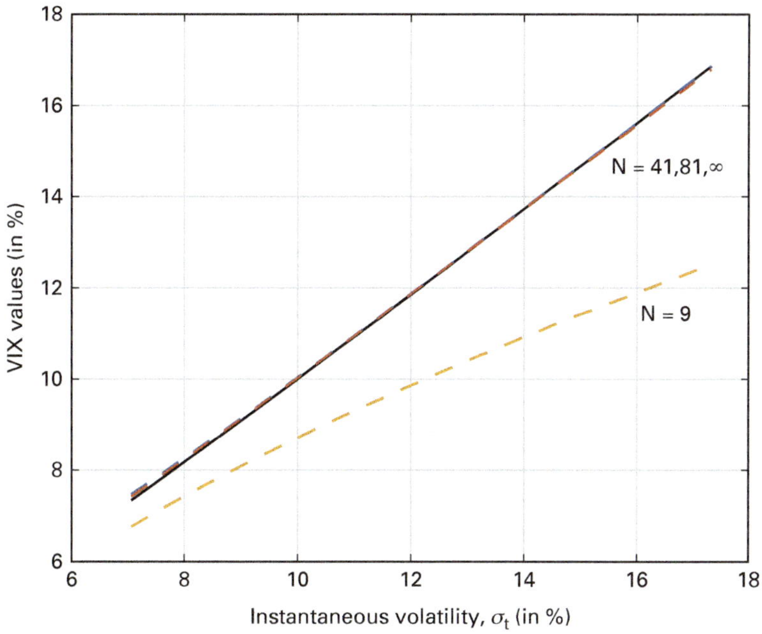

Figure 11.15
This picture depicts one-month VIX levels predicted by the Heston model as a function of current volatility, σ_t. Parameters are set equal to $\kappa = 2$, $\sqrt{\omega} = 0.1$, $\xi = 0.1$, and $\rho = -0.5$ as a function of current volatility, σ_t. The lines labeled with $N = 9$, 41, and 81 are VIX levels obtained with eq. (11.67) and $\omega(K) = \frac{1}{\Delta}K^{-2}$, $\Delta = \frac{1}{12}$, and 8, 40, and 80 out-of-the-money (and one ATM) Heston based option prices. The line labeled with ∞ is the truth calculated through $\text{VIX}^2_{t+\delta,\Delta}$ in eq. (11.121) (see section 11.9) and with $\delta = 0$.

and the *price* of volatility, that is, the price to be paid in dedicated "variance swaps" aimed to protect investors from changes in volatility over a fixed horizon.

11.7.1 Issues

Stochastic volatility models do provide interesting explanations for such properties as smiles and skews (see section 11.5.2). However, these models cannot allow for a *perfect* fit of the smile. Toward the end of the 1980s and the beginning of the 1990s, a modeling approach emerged to cope with issues relating to a perfect fit of the yield curve. As reviewed in chapters 12 and 13, this approach was a response to the need to price interest rate derivatives while relying on models in which the underlying assets in the banks' books (bonds, say) were priced without errors. In the early and mid-1990s, methods were developed to deal with equity options (Derman and Kani, 1994; Dupire, 1994; Derman, 1998), which we succinctly review in this section.

Why is it important to exactly fit all of the already existing options? Trading deals with both plain vanilla and less liquid or "exotic" derivatives. Suppose we wish to price exotic derivatives, say, a new product. We want to make sure the model we use to price the new product predicts that the plain vanilla option prices are identical to those we are trading. How can we trust a model that is not even able to pin down all outstanding contracts? Such a model could open arbitrage opportunities to unscrupulous users. To achieve these tasks, we need to feed the model with information regarding not only the current price but also the entire collection of available option prices. In the next sections, we deal with this task while relying on a discrete time (in section 11.7.2) as well as a continuous time (in section 11.7.3) model. In section 11.7.4, we provide some connections between this model and the Black–Scholes implied volatility.

11.7.2 Implied Binomial Trees

Trees have always been a standard tool of analysis since the seminal paper of Cox, Ross, and Rubinstein (1979). Binomial trees, for example, enable one to easily implement discrete time option pricing models. The idea underlying *implied* binomial trees is to enrich the basic Black–Scholes model with information regarding the very same asset that we are pricing (i.e., the options). While Black–Scholes and Cox-Ross-Rubinstein feed models with information only relating to the initial stock price, implied binomial trees also use information available through derivative data, and these data contribute to the modeling assumptions on the underlying stock price. The resulting model is one with time-varying volatility, in which each derivative price used to feed the model is fit without errors. By design, the model is able to price existing derivatives without pricing errors and thus can be used to price exotic derivatives. The model in this section relies on the work of Derman and Kani (1994) and Rubinstein (1994) and is the discrete time counterpart to the continuous time local volatility model of Dupire (1994) dealt with in section 11.7.3.

We assume that the short-term rate r is constant. We rely on the notion of Arrow-Debreu securities, that is, securities that pay off one unit of numéraire in a given state of the world and zero otherwise (see chapter 2). Let $p_s(\tau+1)$ be the price of an Arrow-Debreu security that pays off \$1 at time $\tau+1$ and in state s. The tree in figure 11.16 summarizes evaluation details at time τ.

In this tree, $q_s(\tau)$ is the risk neutral probability of an upward movement in the stock price at time τ in state s. Displayed are the values of the Arrow-Debreu security that pays at $(s,\tau+1)$, both at (s,τ) and $(s-1,\tau)$. By explanations given in chapter 2 (see section 2.3.4),

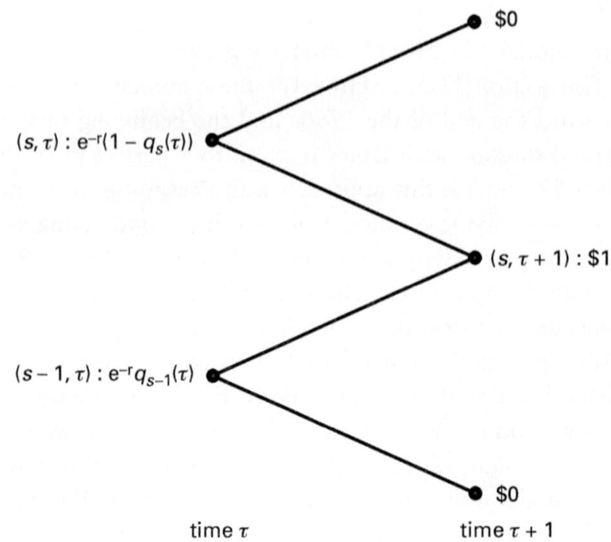

Figure 11.16
Binomial tree representation of Arrow-Debreu securities values.

we have that

$$p_s(\tau+1) = p_s(\tau)\, e^{-r}(1-q_s(\tau)) + p_{s-1}(\tau)\, e^{-r} q_{s-1}(\tau). \tag{11.70}$$

Eq. (11.70) is known as the forward equation for the set of all the Arrow-Debreu security prices. It can be solved recursively once we know $q_s(\tau)$ as r is given, as mentioned. To illustrate, suppose that the risk neutral probabilities are constant and equal to $\bar{q}$, such that the solution to eq. (11.70) is simply the discounted value of the risk neutral probability that s upward movements occur over $\tau+1$ trials:

$$p_s(\tau+1) = e^{-r(\tau+1)} \binom{\tau+1}{s} \bar{q}^s (1-\bar{q})^{\tau+1-s}.$$

This example can be used to price Arrow-Debreu securities in the context of the Cox-Ross-Rubinstein model of the previous section.

We now turn to a more general problem. Suppose we are given a set of European option prices. What are the values of $q_s(\tau)$ to be assigned in each node of the tree such that these options are priced without error? More generally, what are the values of $q_s(\tau)$ and those of the stock price in each node of the tree such that all the European options are priced without error?

In chapter 12, we rely on a general approach to price interest rate sensitive derivatives, by which one freezes the risk neutral probabilities while allowing the short-term rate r to be stochastic. That is, the approach enables one to address the "coupled need" of determining an implied binomial tree for the short-term rate *and* a perfect fit of the entire yield curve. In this chapter, we take r as given and determine an implied binomial tree for the risk neutral probabilities. Suppose then that we have filled all the nodes of the tree up to time τ, for example, $\tau = 2$, as in the example depicted in figure 11.17.

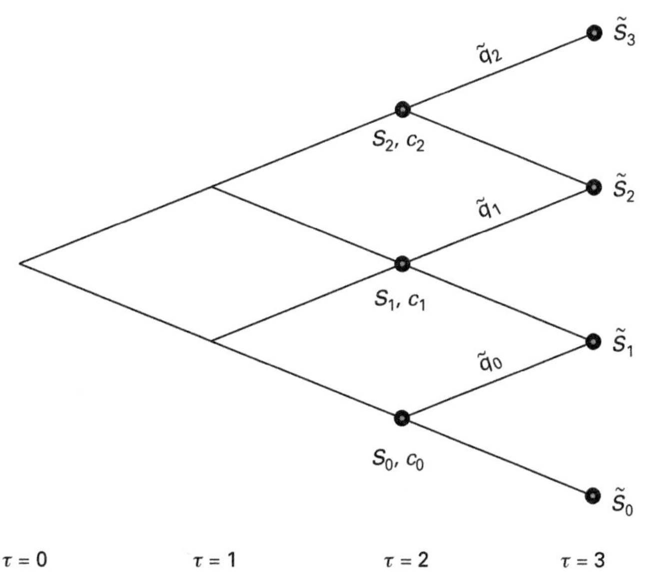

Figure 11.17
Binomial tree for option prices and underlying securities prices.

Let $S_i \equiv S_i\,(2)$ and c_i denote the stock and some derivative prices at time $\tau = 2$ and in node $i \in \{0, 1, 2\}$. Assume, as anticipated, that we have already determined them. We want to determine the values of the stock price at $\tau = 3$, that is, $\tilde{S}_i \equiv S_i\,(3)$ in node $i \in \{0, 1, 2, 3\}$, *and* the risk neutral probabilities at $\tau = 2$, that is, $\tilde{q}_i \equiv q_i\,(2)$ in node $i \in \{0, 1, 2\}$. In total, we want to determine 7 parameters, $\tilde{S}_i$ and $\tilde{q}_i$. Consider the case in which c_i are some European call option prices with strikes and maturity discussed in a moment.

In general, for any $\tau \equiv n - 1$, we want to determine $n + 1$ values of the stock price *and* n risk neutral probabilities for a total of $2n + 1$ parameters. Denote with $C_\$\,(K, \tau + 1)$ the market price of a European call option expiring at time $\tau + 1$ and struck at K. We consider n options struck at values taken by the stock in each node at time τ. The price of each of these options is the average of its values one period before expiration, weighted by the Arrow-Debreu securities prices for the states at time τ, namely,

$$C_\$\,(S_i, \tau + 1) = \sum_{j=0}^{\tau} p_j\,(\tau)\,c_j\,(S_i)\,, \quad i = 0, \cdots, \tau, \tag{11.71}$$

where $c_j\,(S_i)$ denotes the price at τ in node j of the same option struck at S_i and expiring at $\tau + 1$, and equals

$$c_j\,(S_i) = \begin{cases} e^{-r}\left(\tilde{q}_j(\tilde{S}_{j+1} - S_i) + (1 - \tilde{q}_j)(\tilde{S}_j - S_i)\right) & \text{if } j > i \\ e^{-r}\tilde{q}_j(\tilde{S}_{j+1} - S_i), & \text{if } j = i \\ 0 & \text{if } j < i \end{cases} . \tag{11.72}$$

Note that the strikes in eq. (11.71) are chosen such that the options are (roughly) ATM one period before their expiration. Accordingly, the expressions in eqs. (11.72) for the call option prices one period before the expiration follow because, by construction, $\tilde{S}_i \leq S_i \leq \tilde{S}_{i+1}$. While market prices for these options do not necessarily exist, we can interpolate the skew and predict the missing points needed to implement eq. (11.71).

To solve for the $2n + 1$ parameters, we use (i) the n pricing equations in (11.71); (ii) the n martingale conditions satisfied by the stock price at time τ,

$$S_i = e^{-r}\left(\tilde{q}_i\tilde{S}_{i+1} + (1 - \tilde{q}_i)\,\tilde{S}_i\right), \quad i = 0, \cdots, \tau; \tag{11.73}$$

and finally, (iii) some renormalization condition that is the $(2n + 1)$th condition needed to determine the solution to our system of prices.

Replacing eq. (11.73) into the first of eqs. (11.72) leaves

$$e^r c_j\,(S_i) = e^r S_j - S_i \quad \text{if } j > i. \tag{11.74}$$

Therefore, by eqs. (11.71), (11.72), and (11.74),

$$\begin{aligned} e^r C_\$\,(S_i, \tau + 1) &= p_i\,(\tau)\,e^r c_i\,(S_i) + \sum_{j=i+1}^{\tau} p_j\,(\tau)\,e^r c_j\,(S_i) \\ &= p_i\,(\tau)\,\tilde{q}_j(\tilde{S}_{i+1} - S_i) + \sum_{j=i+1}^{\tau} p_j\,(\tau)\left(e^r S_j - S_i\right). \end{aligned} \tag{11.75}$$

Let us solve eq. (11.73) for $\tilde{q}_i$,

$$\tilde{q}_i = \frac{e^r S_i - \tilde{S}_i}{\tilde{S}_{i+1} - \tilde{S}_i}. \tag{11.76}$$

Replacing eq. (11.76) into eq. (11.75) and rearranging terms leads to a recursive equation that the stock price satisfies over the nodes at time $\tau + 1$,

$$\tilde{S}_{i+1} = \frac{\tilde{S}_i \left(e^r C_\$ \left(S_i, \tau+1\right) - \sum_{j=i+1}^{\tau} p_j\left(\tau\right) \left(e^r S_j - S_i\right)\right) - p_i\left(\tau\right) S_i (e^r S_i - \tilde{S}_i)}{\left(e^r C_\$ \left(S_i, \tau+1\right) - \sum_{j=i+1}^{\tau} p_j\left(\tau\right) \left(e^r S_j - S_i\right)\right) - p_i\left(\tau\right) (e^r S_i - \tilde{S}_i)}. \tag{11.77}$$

One may proceed similarly while feeding the tree through European put options. Eq. (11.77) needs some renormalization, as mentioned. Once we solve for $\tilde{S}_{i+1}$, we can solve for $\tilde{q}_i$ by using eq. (11.76) and then update the price of the Arrow-Debreu securities in eq. (11.70) and solve for the tree recursively. Note that, in some cases, the algorithm may lead to negative risk neutral probabilities. We may not accept such a situation, which implies arbitrage. One remedy to this well-known problem is to change the definitions on the tree; for example, one may model the change of log-returns. We now turn to describe the continuous time approach to this type of problems.

11.7.3 The Perfect Fit in Continuous Time

We know that the only input to the option pricing problem is the instantaneous volatility of the underlying asset price. Which volatility should we use? At least we know that option prices are a function of this volatility. The idea is to find a volatility function such that this very same volatility delivers back the prices of all the already traded options. It's an "inverse" problem. Let us outline the steps we need to price new derivatives while avoiding any pricing errors regarding the existing ones.

(1) We take as given the prices of a set of actively traded European options. Let K and T be strikes and time to maturity of these liquid options. We aim to match model predictions to data, namely,

$$C_\$ \left(K, T\right) = C\left(K, T\right), \quad K, T \text{ varying}, \tag{11.78}$$

where $C_\$ \left(K, T\right)$ and $C\left(K, T\right)$ denote, resp., market option prices and model predictions for these prices. Note that we are assuming that a continuum of options exists and that the prices of these options are differentiable as much as we need to make our problem well defined; technically, we need that $\sigma_{\text{loc}}\left(K, T\right)$ in eq. (11.80) below be well defined. We ask: Does it mathematically make sense to consider a diffusive model for the asset price, such that the initial collection of option prices, $C_\$ \left(K, T\right)$, is predicted without errors, just as required by eq. (11.78)?

(2) The answer is in the affirmative. Consider a diffusion process for the stock price

$$\frac{dS_t}{S_t} = r dt + \sigma\left(S_t, t\right) d\tilde{W}_t, \tag{11.79}$$

where $\tilde{W}$ is a Brownian motion under the risk neutral probability. Then eq. (11.78) holds after "calibration" of the volatility function $\sigma\left(S_t, t\right)$, as explained next.

(3) In appendix 11.D, it is shown that eq. (11.78) holds if and only if $\sigma(S_t, t) = \sigma_{\text{loc}}(S_t, t)$, where

$$\sigma_{\text{loc}}(K, T) = \sqrt{2 \frac{\dfrac{\partial C_\$(K, T)}{\partial T} + rK \dfrac{\partial C_\$(K, T)}{\partial K}}{K^2 \dfrac{\partial^2 C_\$(K, T)}{\partial K^2}}}. \tag{11.80}$$

The function $\sigma_{\text{loc}}(S, t)$ is known as *local volatility*. Its square is the local variance, defined as the conditional expectation under Q of the instantaneous variance given the market level S at some future date τ,

$$\sigma_{\text{loc}}^2(S, \tau) = \mathbb{E}_t\left[\sigma^2(S_\tau, \tau) \middle| S_\tau = S\right], \tag{11.81}$$

where $\mathbb{E}_t[.|.]$ is a time t conditional expectation under the risk neutral probability. All in all, local volatility is the function $\sigma_{\text{loc}}(S, t)$ in eq. (11.80) such that the theoretical price generated by the model in eq. (11.79) equals the market prices of the initial collection of traded options.

(4) Finally, we can price illiquid options through numerical methods, for example, through simulations. In the simulations, we use

$$\frac{dS_t}{S_t} = rdt + \sigma_{\text{loc}}(S_t, t)\, d\tilde{W}_t.$$

Empirical evidence suggests that the local volatility surface $\sigma_{\text{loc}}(S, t)$ is typically decreasing in S for fixed t, a phenomenon known as the Black-Christie-Nelson leverage effect (see section 9.8 in chapter 9 and section 11.5.2). This empirical regularity may be relied on while assuming from the outset that $\sigma(x, t) = x^\alpha f(t)$ for some function f and some constant $\alpha < 0$. The resulting model is known as the constant elasticity of variance model.

One can also introduce models combining "local volatilities" with "stoch volatility" as follows

$$\begin{aligned} \frac{dS_t}{S_t} &= rdt + \sigma(S_t, t) \cdot v_t \cdot d\tilde{W}_t \\ dv_t &= \phi(v_t)dt + \psi(v_t)d\tilde{W}_t^v \end{aligned} \tag{11.82}$$

where $\tilde{W}^v$ is another Brownian motion (defined under the risk neutral probability) and ϕ and ψ are some functions. Appendix 11.D shows that, in this specific case, the initial set of all European options prices is pinned down by

$$\tilde{\sigma}_{\text{loc}}(K, T) = \frac{\sigma_{\text{loc}}(K, T)}{\sqrt{\mathbb{E}\left(v_T^2 \middle| S_T = K\right)}}, \tag{11.83}$$

where $\sigma_{\text{loc}}(K, T)$ is the same as in eq. (11.80). For this model, we simulate

$$\begin{cases} \dfrac{dS_t}{S_t} = rdt + \tilde{\sigma}_{\text{loc}}(S_t, t) v_t d\tilde{W}_t \\ dv_t = \phi(v_t)dt + \psi(v_t)d\tilde{W}_t^v \end{cases}.$$

Practitioners also heavily rely on the so-called SABR model, which is parametric in nature. This model is dealt with in chapter 13 (see section 13.10).[31]

11.7.4 Relations with Implied Volatility

11.7.4.1 Implied volatility as expected local volatility

Section 11.6.3.2 provides the expression of the P&L relating to a long position in a call option, delta hedged with the Black–Scholes model using an implied volatility fixed at an initial level IV_0,

$$\begin{aligned} \mathrm{P\&L}_T &\equiv C_{BS}(S_T, T; K, T, \mathrm{IV}_0) - V_T \\ &= \frac{1}{2} e^{rT} \int_0^T e^{-rt} \left(\sigma_t^2 - \mathrm{IV}_0^2\right) S_t^2 \frac{\partial^2 C_{BS}}{\partial S^2} dt. \end{aligned} \tag{11.84}$$

Naturally, we have that $e^{-rT}\mathbb{E}(\mathrm{P\&L}_T) = 0 \Leftrightarrow C_{BS}(S_0, 0; K, T, \mathrm{IV}_0) = V_0 = C(S_0, \sigma_0^2, 0)$, the true market price, consistently with eq. (11.65), such that by the last equality of eq. (11.84),

$$\mathrm{IV}_0^2 = \frac{\mathbb{E}\left[\int_0^T e^{-rt} S_t^2 \frac{\partial^2 C_{BS}}{\partial S^2} \cdot \sigma_t^2 dt\right]}{\mathbb{E}\left[\int_0^T e^{-rt} S_t^2 \frac{\partial^2 C_{BS}}{\partial S^2} dt\right]}.$$

Alternatively, we may consider another hedging positioning suggested by Gatheral (2006, chapter 3) where the delta hedging is made through some fictitious time-varying instantaneous but deterministic volatility equal to $\bar{\sigma}_t$, say, where

$$\bar{\sigma}_t^2 = \frac{1}{T-t} \int_t^T v_u du, \quad \bar{\sigma}_0^2 = \mathrm{IV}_0^2, \tag{11.85}$$

for some deterministic v_t. In this case, the P&L would be similar to that in eq. (11.84), with

$$\mathrm{P\&L}_T = \frac{1}{2} e^{rT} \int_0^T e^{-rt} \left(\sigma_t^2 - v_t\right) S_t^2 \frac{\partial^2 C_{BS}}{\partial S^2} dt.$$

Imposing the zero profit condition under Q leaves

$$v_t = \frac{\mathbb{E}\left(S_t^2 \frac{\partial^2 C_{BS}}{\partial S^2} \sigma_t^2\right)}{\mathbb{E}\left(S_t^2 \frac{\partial^2 C_{BS}}{\partial S^2}\right)} = \mathbb{E}_{Q^\Gamma}\left(\sigma_t^2\right), \tag{11.86}$$

where $\mathbb{E}_{Q^\Gamma}$ is the expectation taken under the probability Q^Γ, defined as

$$\frac{dQ^\Gamma}{dQ} = \frac{S_t^2 \frac{\partial^2 C_{BS}}{\partial S^2}}{\mathbb{E}\left(S_t^2 \frac{\partial^2 C_{BS}}{\partial S^2}\right)}. \tag{11.87}$$

31. Note that local volatility obviously depends on the initial state, that is, on when the calibration starts off. The calibration has to be re-performed all the time in order to incorporate new information.

We term Q^{Γ} *dollar gamma probability*. By eqs. (11.85) and (11.86),

$$\mathrm{IV}_0^2 = \frac{1}{T}\int_0^T \mathbb{E}_{Q^{\Gamma}}\left(\sigma_t^2\right) dt. \tag{11.88}$$

So implied volatilities *are* expectations of future realized volatilities but only under the dollar gamma probability. Clearly, then, they cannot be used as the fair value of a variance swaps unless we tilt the variance contract by a "random multiplier" coinciding with dollar gamma.

We can elaborate on eq. (11.88). We have

$$\begin{aligned}
\mathbb{E}_{Q^{\Gamma}}\left(\sigma_t^2\right) &= \mathbb{E}\left[\mathbb{E}\left(\sigma_t^2 \frac{dQ^{\Gamma}}{dQ}\middle| S_t\right)\right] \\
&= \mathbb{E}\left[\frac{dQ^{\Gamma}}{dQ}\mathbb{E}\left(\sigma_t^2\middle| S_t\right)\right] \\
&= \mathbb{E}\left[\frac{dQ^{\Gamma}}{dQ}\sigma_{\mathrm{loc}}^2\left(S_t, t\right)\right] \\
&= \mathbb{E}_{Q^{\Gamma}}\left[\sigma_{\mathrm{loc}}^2\left(S_t, t\right)\right] \\
&= \int \sigma_{\mathrm{loc}}^2\left(S_t, t\right) \frac{S_t^2 \frac{\partial^2 C_{\mathrm{BS}}}{\partial S^2} q\left(S_t | S_0\right)}{\mathbb{E}\left(S_t^2 \frac{\partial^2 C_{\mathrm{BS}}}{\partial S^2}\right)} dS_t \\
&\approx \sigma_{\mathrm{loc}}^2(\tilde{S}_t, t),
\end{aligned} \tag{11.89}$$

where $\tilde{S}_t$ will be defined in a moment, $q\left(S_t | S_0\right)$ denotes the conditional density of S_t given S_0, $\sigma_{\mathrm{loc}}^2\left(S_t, t\right)$ is the local variance (see section 11.7.3 and appendix 11.D), and the first equality follows by the law of iterated expectations.

The time path $(\tilde{S}_t)_{[t\in 0,T]}$ is a deterministic path, a sort of certainty equivalent for the local variance for fixed t. It is also known as the "most likely path" of S_t, after Gatheral (2006, chapter 3), meaning that the dollar gamma density dQ^{Γ} (see eq. (11.87)) peaks on a line that joins S_0 with the strike K. We also know that, at $t=T$, $\partial^2 C_{\mathrm{BS}}/\partial S^2$ is Dirac's delta centered at K such that we may safely condition $\tilde{S}_T = K$ and then view $\tilde{S}_t$ as a bridge starting from S_0 and ending at K. As a simple example, $\tilde{S}_t \approx S_0\left(K/S_0\right)^{t/T}$.

Using the approximation in eq. (11.89) delivers

$$\mathrm{IV}_0^2 = \frac{1}{T}\int_0^T \sigma_{\mathrm{loc}}^2(\tilde{S}_t, t) dt. \tag{11.90}$$

"Sticky smiles" can roughly be defined as those where the skew does not depend on the initial state. Suppose we have a very simple example where $\mathrm{IV}\left(t, T, K; S_t\right) = a - b\left(K + S_t\right) = a - b\left(\frac{K}{S_t} + 1\right) S_t$. As S_t falls, the skew goes up, consistent with the leverage effect. This skew does not depend on the initial price S_0. We can generate this skew by assuming the local variance does not depend on time, $\sigma_{\mathrm{loc}}^2\left(K, t\right) = a - b\left(K + S_0\right)$. Indeed, in light of eq. (11.90), we would then have that $\mathrm{IV}^2\left(0, T, K; S_0\right) = \mathrm{IV}_0^2 = a - b\left(K + S_0\right)$ and then, $\mathrm{IV}\left(t, T, K; S_t\right) = a - b\left(K + S_t\right)$ for each t.

11.8 The Price of (Equity) Volatility

How much volatility do we expect to prevail in the future after controlling for risk? The answer to this question has long been the volatility implied by ATM options. Eq. (11.90) seems to suggest this answer may somehow be correct. In fact, it is not. Expected volatility, adjusted for risk, is a weighted average of implied volatilities of a continuum of options as anticipated in section 11.6 (see eq. (11.69)). It is not only academic purism. Knowing expected volatility under the risk neutral probability enables an investor to trade assets with payoffs linked to future realized volatility, known as variance swaps. In fact, in September 2003, Cboe changed its volatility index VIX to approximate the variance swap rate of the S&P 500 index return (for 30 days), as explained later. In March 2004, Cboe launched Cboe Futures Exchange for the purpose of trading futures on the new VIX index; further, options referenced to VIX futures now trade with high volumes too.

There are compelling reasons why investors are interested in trading these contracts. One is the possibility of formulating views on market volatility without incurring the price-dependency issues pointed out in section 11.6. As also discussed in section 11.6, certain asset managers may also find these contracts useful because tracking errors widen in times of high volatility. Other institutional investors may find this type of contracts attractive as well, for example, those who invest in "relative value" strategies, attempting to profit from temporary price discrepancies. In times of high volatility, price discrepancies typically widen, and variance swaps help these institutions hedge against these events.

Figure 11.18 depicts the time series behavior of the new VIX index as well as volume on VIX options during the first years after their inception. The VIX index became known to a wide audience only during the 2007–2009 subprime crisis (see section 14.5 in chapter 14 for a review of the events leading to this crisis). The bottom panel of figure 11.18 reveals that trading in VIX derivatives would indeed become more relevant during this period. It is problematic to assess whether the increase in trading was determined by the "fear" events of the time. It may simply be that market making on VIX would take some time before its effects could be visible. In fact, too much volatility is not necessarily conducive to trading. The elevated levels of VIX during the 2007–2009 crisis reflect quite distressed markets, and this distress might have curbed traders' risk appetite and willingness to trade in the first place. Thus, the increase in trading at that time might have resulted despite, not because of, these historical circumstances. In fact, figure 11.18 suggests that trading would truly pick up *after* the 2007–2009 crisis.

This section provides some pricing details gravitating around VIX. The next section provides a simple example of a volatility product, one that may not always meet the needs of traders. Section 11.8.2 provides a derivation of the VIX as the fair value of a variance swap; sections 11.8.3 through 11.8.6 provide details on hedging and trading and marking to market such variance swaps; finally, section 11.8.7 contains some details related to skewness, which is another way to think about market volatility.

11.8.1 One Introductory Example: Range-Based Volatility

Straddles give rise to price dependency as explained in section 11.6: even in the presence of a highly volatile market within a reference period, the straddle may not deliver

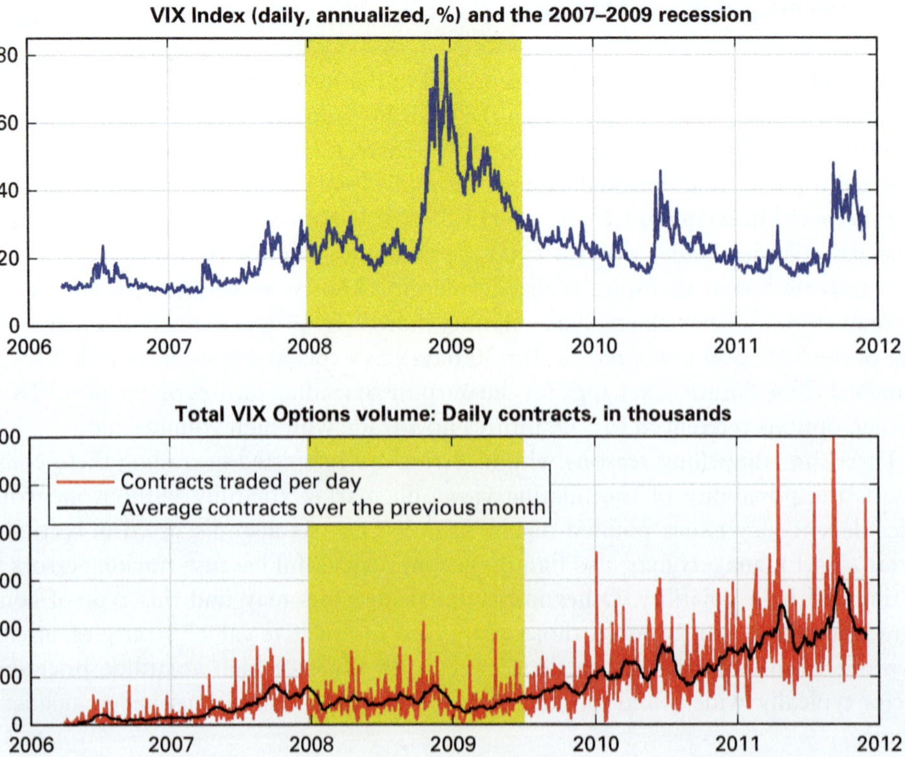

Figure 11.18
The top panel of this picture depicts daily values for VIX levels maintained by Cboe. The shaded area marks the recession as determined by NBER—the Great Recession episode. The bottom panel depicts the time series of total option contract volume.

a positive payoff unless the underlying price moves beyond the straddles' thresholds (see figure 11.11). This introductory section develops an example of a simple payoff that aims to track changes in volatility.

Consider a derivative with a payoff equal to the following estimate of stock volatility over a given time period $[t, T]$,

$$\pi (t, T) \equiv \max_{\tau \in [t,T]} (\ln S_\tau) - \min_{\tau \in [t,T]} (\ln S_\tau),$$

where S_τ denotes the asset price at τ. This volatility estimator relates to the Parkinson's (1980) "range estimator" of volatility, that is, one based on price ranges, defined as the difference between the highest and the lowest log price over a fixed sampling interval. This measure of realized volatility has drawbacks as a basis for volatility trading. Consider the following example, illustrated by figure 11.19, a market with some infrequent jumps. Specifically, suppose that for one month, the stock price never moves, except for three days (and only then) when it goes down by 7% (10th day) (discretely compounded), then overshoots by 1% (11th day), and finally gets back to its initial value (12th day) (a "flash crash"?). The payoff $\pi (t, T)$ is equal to $\ln \frac{B}{A} \approx 8.2\%$.

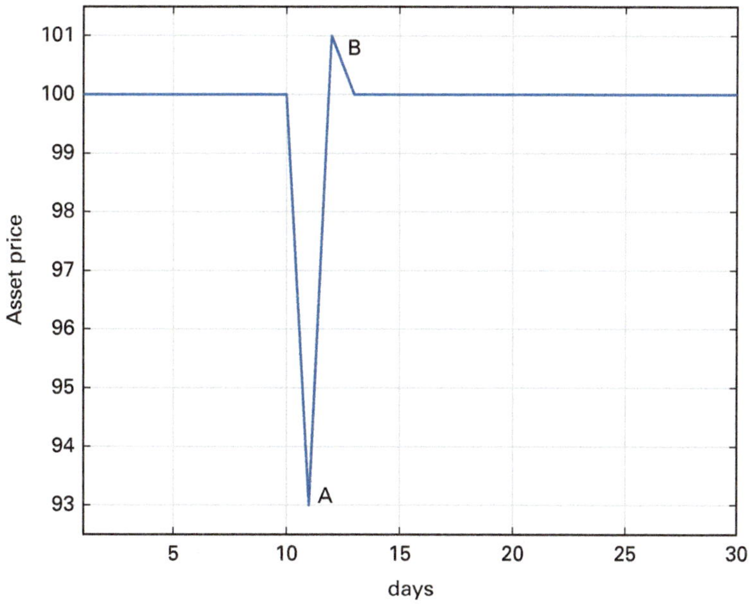

Figure 11.19
A market with infrequent jumps.

While this contract is clearly tracking volatility, it does so imperfectly. In this example, the stock price has not been volatile except for a few isolated days. We would like to make reference to contracts that pay off when volatility has been "sustained" over the whole month. The next section describes such contracts.

11.8.2 "Fear Gauge" Contracts

We are used to thinking that realized volatility determines option prices (see, e.g., section 11.5). This section deals with a different construct where option prices sum up to a sufficient statistics for market-adjusted (i.e., risk neutral) *expected* volatility. This notion of expected volatility is at the basis of major innovations on measurement and trading uncertainty in markets. These innovations began in the 1990s. This section analyzes some of its milestones.

11.8.2.1 Variance swaps and the VIX index

Let us consider the following price process S_t under the risk neutral probability

$$\frac{dS_t}{S_t} = rdt + \sigma_t d\tilde{W}_t, \tag{11.91}$$

where σ_t is $\mathbb{F}_t$-adapted; that is, $\mathbb{F}_t$ can be larger than that generated by the stock price, $\mathbb{F}_t^S \equiv \sigma\,(S_\tau : \tau \le t)$. Next, define the realized "integrated" variance within the time interval $[T_1, T_2]$, with $T_1 > t$:

$$\text{var}\,(T_1, T_2) \equiv \int_{T_1}^{T_2} \sigma_u^2 du.$$

We define a *variance swap* as a contract with zero value at the inception date, t, and a payoff at maturity T given by

$$\pi_T^{\text{var}} = \text{N} \times (\text{var}(t,T) - \mathbb{P}_{\text{var}}(t,T)), \tag{11.92}$$

where N is the notional value of the contract and $\mathbb{P}_{\text{var}}(t,T)$ is the variance swap rate agreed at t and paid off at time T.[32] Therefore, this contract is a forward, not a swap really. If r is deterministic, then the swap rate must satisfy

$$\mathbb{P}_{\text{var}}(t,T) = \mathbb{E}_t(\text{var}(t,T)).$$

It remains to determine $\mathbb{E}_t(\text{var}(t,T))$; below, we show that this is the same as a portfolio of OTM options. First, let us consider a simple case in which $r=0$. In this case, we can solve for $\mathbb{E}_t(\text{var}(t,T))$ while relying on previous results regarding local volatility. Indeed, note that, by eqs. (11.80) and (11.81) and the connection between risk neutral densities and convexity of the option price, eq. (11.29), we have

$$\mathbb{E}_t(\sigma_T^2) = 2e^{r(T-t)} \int_0^\infty \frac{\frac{\partial C_t(K,T)}{\partial T} + rK\frac{\partial C_t(K,T)}{\partial K}}{K^2} dK, \tag{11.93}$$

where $C_t(K,T)$ is the price as of time t of a call option expiring at T and struck at K. We can compute the risk neutral expectation of this realized variance under the assumption that $r=0$. By eq. (11.93),

$$\mathbb{E}_t(\text{var}(T_1,T_2)) = 2\int_0^\infty \frac{C_t(K,T_2) - C_t(K,T_1)}{K^2} dK. \tag{11.94}$$

Eq. (11.94) can be generalized to the case where $r>0$. In appendix 11.E, we show that, for $T_1 = t$, $T_2 \equiv T$,

$$\mathbb{E}_t(\text{var}(t,T)) = 2e^{r(T-t)} \left(\int_0^{F_t} \frac{P_t(K,T)}{K^2} dK + \int_{F_t}^\infty \frac{C_t(K,T)}{K^2} dK \right), \tag{11.95}$$

where F_t is the forward price $F_t = e^{r(T-t)} S_t$ and $P_t(K,T)$ is the price as of time t of a put option expiring at T and struck at K. A proof of eq. (11.95) is in appendix 11.E. The new VIX index maintained by Cboe is based on an approximation of the square root of $\mathbb{E}_t(\text{var}(t,T))$ in eq. (11.95) and annualized:

$$\text{VIX}(t,T) \equiv \sqrt{\frac{1}{T-t}\mathbb{E}_t(\text{var}(t,T))}, \tag{11.96}$$

32. Note that this contract relies on some notion of *realized* variance as a continuous record of returns is obviously unavailable. Moreover, it has long been market practice to define the variance notional in such a way that $\text{N} = \frac{\text{VN}}{2\sqrt{\mathbb{P}_{\text{var}}}}$, where VN is the "vega notional," that is, the notional expressed in volatility percentage points. Suppose, for example, that realized volatility is one "vega" (i.e., one volatility point) above the square root of the variance swap rate, $\text{var}(t,T) = (\sqrt{\mathbb{P}_{\text{var}}}+1)^2$, such that $\pi_T^{\text{var}} = (1 + \frac{1}{2\sqrt{\mathbb{P}_{\text{var}}}}) \times \text{VN} \approx \text{VN}$. That is, vega notional is approximately the notional for each vega realized volatility that exceeds the square root of the variance swap rate.

where $T-t$ is expressed as a fraction of a year. The approximation relies on a finite number of OTM options.

The VIX index is often referred to as a "fear gauge." The index composition justifies this terminology. By eqs. (11.95) and (11.96), VIX is indeed a weighted average of OTM option prices (and, hence, implied volatilities), which reflect the value of being insured against tail events. Thus, VIX may be interpreted as the market value of being insured against extreme movements in asset prices. This interpretation suggests a heuristic connection between VIX and aversion to Knightian uncertainty (see section 9.6 of chapter 9), a situation in which agents might come to evaluate economic outcomes while acting under worst-case scenarios. Note that, at the time of writing, these topics have yet to be explored in theoretical research. Finally, it is well known that VIX spikes when equity markets drop. However, eqs. (11.95) and (11.96) indicate that the index potentially reflects market fears regarding both tail events.[33]

Finally, section 11.7 explains that implied volatilities relate to local volatility. But how does expected variance in eq. (11.95) relate to the skew? Demeterfi, Derman, Kamal, and Zou (1999) show that, if implied volatility varies linearly with the strike,

$$\mathrm{IV} = \mathrm{IV}_{\mathrm{atm}} - b\frac{K-S}{S},$$

for some constant b, then

$$\mathrm{VIX}\,(t,T) \approx \mathrm{IV}_{\mathrm{atm}}\sqrt{1+3\,(T-t)\,b^2}.$$

That is, a "skew" ($b \neq 0$) increases the fair variance above ATM implied volatilities.

11.8.2.2 *A crash derivation of the general VIX formula*

The previous conclusions are quite remarkable. We know from section 11.2 that, for any generic risk $\tilde{X}_T$, its forward price is $\mathbb{E}_t(\tilde{X}_T)$, provided interest rates are constant such that $\mathbb{E}_t(\tilde{X}_T) = e^{r(T-t)}X_t$ as soon as X is traded. When X is not traded, we would expect to rely on a model in order to determine the expectation $\mathbb{E}_t(\tilde{X}_T)$. But the previous results regard a risk that is not traded, $\mathrm{var}\,(t,T)$—the value of which, $\mathbb{E}_t\,[\mathrm{var}\,(t,T)]$, we may still determine without relying on any model. In other words, we can price volatility in a model-free fashion: the annualized price of a variance swap is simply the square of the VIX index.

It is useful to review the steps that lead to eq. (11.95). The starting point is the so-called log contract, a concept first introduced by Neuberger (1994). This idealized contract is designed to guarantee a payoff equal to $\ln\frac{F_T}{F_t}$. Its fair value is obviously $\mathbb{E}_t\left(\ln\frac{F_T}{F_t}\right)$ and is negative as we will show in a moment. The intuitive reason the price of the log contract is negative is that the payoff $\ln\frac{F_T}{F_t}$ is skewed to the left due to the concavity of the logarithm function, such that the expected losses on the downside are larger than the expected gains

33. Mele and Obayashi (2015, chapter 2, proposition 2.3) show that, if the Black–Scholes implied volatilities are homogeneous of degree zero in (K, S_t), the expression in (11.95) is independent of S_t. The empirical evidence that the VIX spikes after large drops in the market suggests that implied volatilities and market drops might be moved by some common factor.

on the upside. Precisely, applying Itô's lemma to eq. (11.91) leaves

$$\mathbb{E}_t\left(\ln\frac{F_T}{F_t}\right)=-\frac{1}{2}\mathbb{E}_t\left[\mathrm{var}\left(t,T\right)\right]. \tag{11.97}$$

Therefore, the price of volatility is the same as the value of going short a log contract. Naturally, we are not done because we still don't know how to price the log contract in the first place. The pricing of this and related contracts relies on so-called "spanning arguments" as explained, for example, by Bakshi and Madan (2000) and Carr and Madan (2001). In appendix 11.E, it is shown that the payoff of the log contract can be written as

$$\ln\frac{F_T}{F_t}=\frac{1}{F_t}\left(F_T-F_t\right)-\left(\int_0^{F_t}\left(K-S_T\right)^+\frac{1}{K^2}dK+\int_{F_t}^{\infty}\left(S_T-K\right)^+\frac{1}{K^2}dK\right). \tag{11.98}$$

The expectation on the RHS of eq. (11.98) is (minus) half that on the RHS of eq. (11.95), assuming interest rates are constant. Eq. (11.95) then follows by eq. (11.97).

11.8.2.3 *Variance risk premiums*

Market-realized volatility obviously results from recent and ongoing market movements. How does realized volatility relate to expected volatility? The difference between expected and realized volatility links to the *variance risk premium* as anticipated in sections 11.2.5.4 and 11.6. Figure 11.20 depicts the VIX index (a measure of expected volatility) and realized volatility on the S&P 500, calculated as a rolling moving average with a window fixed at 30 days. The difference between the two is thus a measure of the variance risk premium. Note that this measure is positive for most of the time and is negative in correspondence of episodes of market turmoil, in which case realized volatility surpasses VIX even while both realized and expected volatilities are high.

What causes these patterns? Consider a variance swap. This contract is profitable to a protection seller due to the historical circumstance that the variance risk premium is generally positive, just as in the example depicted in figure 11.20. A protection seller then has the "statistical edge." However, the edge is simply the premium that compensates for entering into a variance swap: there may be episodes of market turmoil, such as the Lehman bankruptcy in September 2008 when protection sellers experienced large losses (i.e., the realized payoff in (11.92) is positive). The premium for taking such risks makes VIX higher on average than realized volatility.

The reason that the difference between VIX and realized volatility is being referred to as a "premium" is as follows. Assume for simplicity that interest rates are constant. Then note that, by results in chapter 4 (see, e.g., section 4.2.5), a premium for bearing a risk is equal to the covariance between that risk and the stochastic discount factor. But, for any variable measurable at T, X_T say, we have that

$$-cov\left(\frac{dQ}{dP},X_T\right)=E_t\left(X_T\right)-\mathbb{E}_t\left(X_T\right).$$

In many models, the Radon-Nikodym derivative, $\frac{dQ}{dP}$, is proportional to the marginal utility of a representative investor while being in state ω. The premium then is the difference between the expectations of the variable X_T under the risk-adjusted and the physical

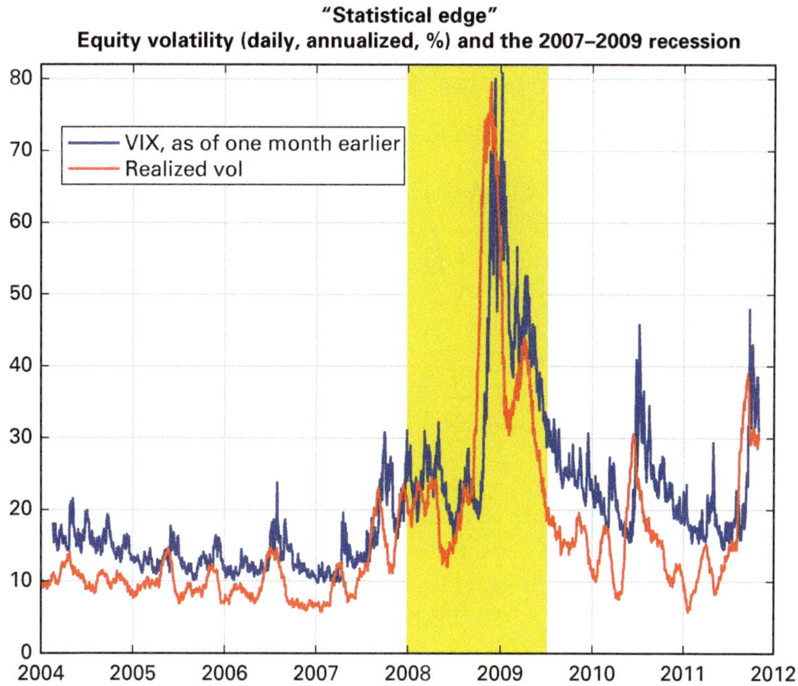

Figure 11.20
This picture depicts realized percentage volatility on the S&P 500 index and Cboe-VIX index as of one month earlier; the shaded area covers the 2007–2009 recession episode as defined by NBER. The sample period covers daily data from January 2, 2004, to October 28, 2011.

probabilities. To illustrate, $X_T(\omega)$ may be a variable positively related to stock market performance. Thus, under standard conditions (e.g., decreasing marginal utility), $\frac{dQ}{dP}$ and X_T are negatively correlated, resulting in a premium for investing in the market: the market delivers positive returns when we less need them (i.e., when marginal utility is low). Therefore, the premium is positive.

In our case, we interpret X_T as future realized volatility but expect $\frac{dQ}{dP}$ and X_T to be *positively* correlated: in bad times, marginal utility and realized volatility should both be high, leading to a *negative* premium: the expectation of volatility under P is lower than that under Q. Thus, according to these interpretations, the differences between VIX and realized volatility (proxies for expectations under Q and P) in figure 11.20 reflect a negative premium for investing in volatility markets.

11.8.3 Hedging Variance Swaps

A financial institution may merely be interested in intermediating a contract that then needs to be hedged against. For example, suppose that, at time t, you have sold protection by promising to pay the realized integrated variance $\text{var}(t,T)$ at time T. We want to replicate this integrated variance. By Itô's lemma,

$$\text{var}(t,T) = 2\int_t^T \frac{1}{S_u} dS_u - 2\ln\left(\frac{S_T}{S_t}\right) = 2\left(\int_t^T \frac{1}{S_u} dS_u - r(T-t)\right) - 2\ln\frac{F_T}{F_t}. \quad (11.99)$$

The first term can be replicated by continuously rebalancing a stock position that is always long $\theta_t = \frac{2}{S_t}$ shares of the stock and adjusted for the time value of money. Precisely, consider a self-financed portfolio (θ_τ, ψ_τ), such that its value satisfies

$$V_\tau = \theta_\tau S_\tau + \psi_\tau M_\tau,$$

where M_τ denotes the MMA. We choose

$$\hat{\theta}_\tau = \frac{1}{S_\tau}\frac{M_\tau}{M_T}, \quad \hat{\psi}_\tau = \left[\int_t^\tau \frac{1}{S_u} dS_u - 1 - r(\tau - t)\right]\frac{1}{M_T}. \tag{11.100}$$

It is easy to see that

$$\hat{V}_\tau = \left[\int_t^\tau \frac{1}{S_u} dS_u - r(\tau - t)\right]\frac{M_\tau}{M_T}, \tag{11.101}$$

such that (i) $\hat{V}_t = 0$ and (ii) $\hat{V}_T = \int_t^T \frac{1}{S_u} dS_u - r(T-t)$. Appendix 11.E shows that $(\hat{\theta}_\tau, \hat{\psi}_\tau)$ is self-financed. Therefore, the first term in eq. (11.99) can be hedged with a self-financed portfolio, $(2\hat{\theta}_\tau, 2\hat{\psi}_\tau)$, which costs nothing at time t.

To replicate the second term in eq. (11.99)—the payoff of the log contract—we simply replicate twice the payoff in (11.98). Therefore, we go short $2/F_t$ forwards, which are costless at time t, and long a continuum of OTM options with weights $2/K^2$. The cost of this position is

$$2\int_0^{F_t} \frac{P_t(K,T)}{K^2} dK + 2\int_{F_t}^\infty \frac{C_t(K,T)}{K^2} dK = e^{-r(T-t)} \mathbb{E}_t[\text{var}(t,T)]$$

where the equality follows by eq. (11.95). We borrow $e^{-r(T-t)}\mathbb{E}_t[\text{var}(t,T)]$ and purchase the options. Thus, $\text{var}(t,T)$ is replicated at time T because we have replicated both the first term and the second term in eq. (11.99). Finally, come time T, we pay back the amount due to our borrowing position, that is, $\mathbb{E}_t[\text{var}(t,T)]$. The ultimate outcome is a payoff equal to $\text{var}(t,T) - \mathbb{E}_t[\text{var}(t,T)]$.

11.8.4 Forward Volatility Trading

Let us consider the following example of volatility trading. Suppose we hold the view that expected market volatility will rise in one year's time to an extent that is inefficiently priced in by the term structure of the currently traded variance swaps. Precisely, our view is that the spot price of the variance swap in one year will exceed the "implied forward variance swap price,"that is,

$$\mathbb{P}_{\text{var}}(1,2) > \mathbb{P}_{\text{var}}(0,2) - \mathbb{P}_{\text{var}}(0,1). \tag{11.102}$$

To implement a trade consistent with this view, we may proceed as follows:

$$\begin{array}{lll} \text{(i)} & \text{long a two-year variance swap struck at } \mathbb{P}_{\text{var}}(0,2), & \text{with notional one} \\ \text{(ii)} & \text{short a one-year variance swap struck at } \mathbb{P}_{\text{var}}(0,1), & \text{with notional } e^{-r} \end{array} \tag{11.103}$$

Obviously, this strategy is costless at time 0.

The strategy in (11.103) generates profits whenever the inequality in (11.102) holds true. Suppose that eq. (11.102) holds true at time 1. Then, come time 1, we can go short another one-year variance swap struck at $\mathbb{P}_{\text{var}}(1,2)$. Intuitively, we do so because "we bought it cheap" according to (11.102). Going short this variance swap at time 1 generates the following payoff at time 2:

$$\pi_1(2) \equiv \mathbb{P}_{\text{var}}(1,2) - \text{var}(1,2). \tag{11.104}$$

Moreover, the two-year variance swap we went long at time 0 (component (i) of 11.103) gives rise to the following payoff at time 2:

$$\pi_2(2) \equiv \text{var}(0,2) - \mathbb{P}_{\text{var}}(0,2). \tag{11.105}$$

Adding eq. (11.104) and eq. (11.105) and using the relation, $\text{var}(0,2) = \text{var}(0,1) + \text{var}(1,2)$, leads to

$$\pi(2) \equiv \pi_1(2) + \pi_2(2) = \mathbb{P}_{\text{var}}(1,2) + \text{var}(0,1) - \mathbb{P}_{\text{var}}(0,2).$$

Finally, the one-year variance swap with notional e^{-r} that we went short at time 0 (component (ii) of 11.103) leads to the following payoff at time 1:

$$\pi(1) \equiv (\mathbb{P}_{\text{var}}(0,1) - \text{var}(0,1))\, e^{-r}. \tag{11.106}$$

Investing $\pi(1)$ for another year at the safe interest rate delivers $\pi(1)\, e^{r}$ at time 2, such that the total profits at time 2 are

$$\pi_{\text{tot}} \equiv \pi(2) + \pi(1)\, e^{r} = \mathbb{P}_{\text{var}}(1,2) - \mathbb{P}_{\text{var}}(0,2) + \mathbb{P}_{\text{var}}(0,1) > 0, \tag{11.107}$$

where the inequality follows by eq. (11.102).

11.8.5 Marking to Market

Suppose a variance contract expiring at time T is issued at time t, when it is costless. How much is this contract worth at time $\tau \in (t, T)$? Let us take the time τ risk neutral discounted expectation of π_T^{var} in eq. (11.92),

$$\begin{aligned} \mathbb{E}_\tau\left(\pi_T^{\text{var}}\right) &= Ne^{-r(T-\tau)}\mathbb{E}_\tau\left(\text{var}(t,\tau) + \text{var}(\tau,T) - \mathbb{P}_{\text{var}}(t,T)\right) \\ &= Ne^{-r(T-\tau)}\left(\text{var}(t,\tau) + \mathbb{P}_{\text{var}}(\tau,T) - \mathbb{P}_{\text{var}}(t,T)\right), \end{aligned} \tag{11.108}$$

where $\mathbb{E}_\tau$ denotes the risk neutral expectation conditional on the information available at time τ.

Marking to market suggests an alternative way to implement the forward volatility trading of the previous section. Suppose then again that we have a view that markets for volatility will be such that (11.102) holds true at time 1, and accordingly, consider the strategy in (11.103). If (11.102) holds true at time 1, we may close the position (i) in (11.103) at time 1. By eq. (11.108), the market value of the two-year variance swap we went long at time 0 is

$$\hat{\pi}(1) \equiv (\text{var}(0,1) + \mathbb{P}_{\text{var}}(1,2) - \mathbb{P}_{\text{var}}(0,2))\, e^{-r}. \tag{11.109}$$

At time 1, we obtain $\hat{\pi}(1) + \pi(1)$, which we can invest at the safe interest rate for one additional period, delivering the profit π_{tot} in eq. (11.107) for time 2.

11.8.6 Stochastic Interest Rates

When interest rates are stochastic but still independent of volatility, the expressions given for the contract and indices do not hold anymore. In these cases, there will be a number of adjustments to make. Mele and Obayashi (2015) provide a comprehensive treatment of variance contracts in case interest rates are stochastic in their attempt to model the price of volatility in the fixed income space. Appendix 11.E provides some elementary results that help deal with the equity case. In this section, we simply explain how one may modify the forward volatility trading strategy in (11.103) in the case of stochastic interest rates:

Consider, for example, the following strategy:

$$\begin{array}{lll} \text{(i)} & \text{long a two-year variance swap, struck at } \mathbb{P}_{\text{var}}(0,2), & \text{with notional one} \\ \text{(ii)} & \text{short a one-year variance swap, struck at } \mathbb{P}_{\text{var}}(0,1), & \text{with notional } \frac{P(0,2)}{P(0,1)} \end{array}$$

Come time 1, we may liquidate (i), access the payoff relating to (ii) for a total payoff equal to

$$(\text{var}(0,1)+\mathbb{P}_{\text{var}}(1,2)-\mathbb{P}_{\text{var}}(0,2))\,P(1,2)+(\mathbb{P}_{\text{var}}(0,1)-\text{var}(0,1))\,\frac{P(0,2)}{P(0,1)}$$
$$=(\mathbb{P}_{\text{var}}(1,2)-\mathbb{P}_{\text{var}}(0,2)+\mathbb{P}_{\text{var}}(0,1))\,P(1,2)$$
$$+(\text{var}(0,1)-\mathbb{P}_{\text{var}}(0,1))\left(P(1,2)-\frac{P(0,2)}{P(0,1)}\right),$$

where the first term on the LHS results from the liquidation of (i) and eq. (11.109) and the second term results from (ii). By eq. (11.102), the first term on the RHS is positive. If the short-term interest rate is deterministic, $P(1,2)=\frac{P(0,2)}{P(0,1)}$, and the second term on the RHS would be zero. If interest rates are stochastic, the second term can take on any sign although, then, its absolute value should be very low compared with the first term on the RHS.

11.8.7 A Digression on Skewness

What is the value to hedge against left tail risks? In fact, equity volatility accounts for left tail risk due to its negative correlation with the market. However, volatility does not uniquely track these risks. Skewness does. Model-free skewness contracts may be designed to deal with tail risk. Indices based on skewness are maintained by Cboe since January 2011. These indices are interesting because it seems that, at times, their value correlates with the variance risk premium: the higher the variance risk premium, the higher the expected skewness (under Q).

To evaluate a skewness contract, consider the following general perspective. Appendix 11.E shows that, for any twice differentiable function f,

$$e^{-r(T-t)}\mathbb{E}_t\left[f(F_T)-f(F_t)\right]=\int_0^{F_t} f''(K)\cdot\text{Put}_t(K,T)\,dK + \int_{F_t}^{\infty} f''(K)\cdot\text{Call}_t(K,T)\,dK, \tag{11.110}$$

where $F_t = e^{r(T-t)} S_t$, the forward rate, and the remaining is the usual notation. Eq. (11.110) shows that any Markov payoff can be spanned through a set of European options. For example, if $f(x) = \ln x$, we can price a log contract, which leads to price variance swaps (see section 11.8). We now rely on eq. (11.110) to evaluate skewness contracts.

Consider the following payoff, $f_{\text{v}}(F_T) \equiv \left(\ln \frac{F_T}{F_t}\right)^2$. By construction, $f_{\text{v}}(F_t) = 0$, such that by eq. (11.110),

$$\mathbb{E}_t\left[f_{\text{v}}(F_T)\right] = e^{r(T-t)}\left(\int_0^{F_t} \omega_{\text{v},t}(K) \cdot \text{Put}_t(K,T)\, dK + \int_{F_t}^{\infty} \omega_{\text{v},t}(K) \cdot \text{Call}_t(K,T)\, dK\right),$$

$$\omega_{\text{v},t}(K) \equiv f_{\text{v}}''(K) = \frac{2}{K^2}\left(1 - \ln \frac{K}{F_t}\right).$$

Which contract does the payoff $f_{\text{v}}(F_T)$ relate to? Clearly, $f_{\text{v}}(F_T)$ relates to the second moment of the cumulative return, $\ln \frac{F_T}{F_t}$. But this second moment is distinct from the realized variance that we always defined as the sum of instantaneous return variances, $\int_t^T \left(\frac{dF_u}{F_u}\right)^2$. Precisely, note that by Itô's lemma,

$$\mathbb{E}_t\left[f_{\text{v}}(F_T)\right] = \mathbb{E}_t\left[2\int_t^T \ln\left(\frac{F_\tau}{F_t}\right)\frac{dF_\tau}{F_\tau} + \int_t^T \left(1 - \ln \frac{F_\tau}{F_t}\right)\left(\frac{dF_\tau}{F_\tau}\right)^2\right]. \tag{11.111}$$

This variance contract is currently a bit unusual: the standard notion of variance we use to price is $\int_t^T \left(\frac{dF_u}{F_u}\right)^2$, not $\left(\ln \frac{F_T}{F_t}\right)^2$.

The current literature and practice on skewness contracts display a similar "cumulative return" flavor. Consider the following payoff, introduced by Bakshi, Kapadia, and Madan (2003):

$$f_{\text{sk}}(F_T) \equiv \left[\ln \frac{F_T}{F_t} - \mathbb{E}_t\left(\ln \frac{F_T}{F_t}\right)\right]^3, \quad f_{\text{sk}}(F_t) = 0.$$

The payoff $f_{\text{sk}}(F_T)$ relates to the third moment of the cumulative return over a certain investment horizon. The notion of a "realized skewness" relies on the third moments of the instantaneous returns and are averaged over a given horizon. Pricing realized skewness is presently unexplored territory. Let us instead consider the payoff $f_{\text{sk}}(F_T)$ and the definition of skewness, adjusted for risk:

$$\text{Skew} \equiv \frac{\mathbb{E}_t\left[f_{\text{sk}}(F_T)\right]}{\mathbb{E}_t\left[f_{\text{vv}}(F_T)\right]^{\frac{3}{2}}},$$

where

$$f_{\text{vv}}(F_T) \equiv \left[\ln \frac{F_T}{F_t} - \mathbb{E}_t\left(\ln \frac{F_T}{F_t}\right)\right]^2, \quad f_{\text{vv}}(F_t) = 0.$$

This concept of skewness is "adjusted for risk" because expectations are taken under the risk neutral probability. Note that $f_{vv}(F_T)$ is the demeaned version of $f_v(F_T)$, such that its expectation is

$$\mathbb{E}_t\left[f_{vv}(F_T)\right] = \mathbb{E}_t\left[f_v(F_T)\right] - \mathbb{E}_t\left[f_{\log}(F_T)\right]^2,$$

where $f_{\log}(F_T) = \ln\frac{F_T}{F_t}$ (the log contract), and

$$-\mathbb{E}_t\left[f_{\log}(F_T)\right] = e^{r(T-t)}\left(\int_0^{F_t}\frac{1}{K^2}\cdot \text{Put}_t(K,T)\,dK + \int_{F_t}^{\infty}\frac{1}{K^2}\cdot \text{Call}_t(K,T)\,dK\right).$$

Likewise,

$$\mathbb{E}_t\left[f_{sk}(F_T)\right] = e^{r(T-t)}\left(\int_0^{F_t}\omega_{sk,t}(K)\cdot \text{Put}_t(K,T)\,dK + \int_{F_t}^{\infty}\omega_{sk,t}(K)\cdot \text{Call}_t(K,T)\,dK\right),$$

$$\omega_{sk,t}(K) \equiv f''_{sk}(K) = \frac{3}{K^2}\left(\ln\frac{K}{F_t} - \mathbb{E}_t\left[f_{\log}(F_T)\right]\right)\left(2+\mathbb{E}_t\left[f_{\log}(F_T)\right] - \ln\frac{K}{F_t}\right).$$

11.9 VIX Derivatives

Volatility may be traded through VIX futures and options. In section 11.9.1, we provide a model-free approximation of VIX future values, based on a certain number of OTM and ATM options, and relying on insights originally made by Carr and Wu (2006) and Dupire (2006). In sections 11.9.2 and 11.9.3, we comment on a simple parametric model of VIX futures and options. Section 11.9.4 explains how the model-free approximation works, in practice, based on the hypothetical parametric benchmark; in particular, we provide experiments and gauge the goodness of the approximation when we decrease the number of options.

11.9.1 Model-Free Future Pricing

11.9.1.1 VIX-squared

For a Δ-forward looking volatility gauge (e.g., $\Delta = \frac{1}{12}$), we have that

$$\text{VIX}_{t,\Delta}^2 \equiv \mathbb{E}_t\left(\frac{1}{\Delta}\int_t^{t+\Delta}\sigma_\tau^2\,d\tau\right), \tag{11.112}$$

where the expectation is taken under the risk neutral probability. Consider the fair value of a future on VIX expiring at $t+\delta$,

$$\mathcal{F}_{t,t+\delta} \equiv \mathbb{E}_t\left(\text{VIX}_{t+\delta,\Delta}\right). \tag{11.113}$$

VIX squared is the expected value of a time-weighted average of realized instantaneous variances. Yet, we need to find the expected value of future VIX levels, not squared levels. We proceed with some approximations. We find the fair value of a hypothetical future on VIX squared, from which we find $\mathcal{F}$ in (11.113) while adding a convexity adjustment.

Then we will approximate $\mathcal{F}$ while ignoring the convexity adjustment. The interest in this approximation is that the approximated value for $\mathcal{F}$ is the square root of the difference of two VIX and is then model independent.

11.9.1.2 Approximated value of VIX futures

Consider the expected VIX squared at $t+\delta$:

$$\begin{aligned}
\hat{\mathcal{F}}^2_{t,t+\delta+\Delta} &\equiv \mathbb{E}_t\left(\mathrm{VIX}^2_{t+\delta,\Delta}\right) \\
&= \mathbb{E}_t\left(\frac{1}{\Delta}\int_{t+\delta}^{t+\delta+\Delta}\sigma_\tau^2 d\tau\right) \\
&= \frac{1}{\Delta}\mathbb{E}_t\left(\int_t^{t+\delta+\Delta}\sigma_\tau^2 d\tau - \int_t^{t+\delta}\sigma_\tau^2 d\tau\right) \\
&= \frac{1}{\Delta}\mathbb{E}_t\left(\frac{\delta+\Delta}{\delta+\Delta}\int_t^{t+\delta+\Delta}\sigma_\tau^2 d\tau - \frac{\delta}{\delta}\int_t^{t+\delta}\sigma_\tau^2 d\tau\right) \\
&= \frac{\delta+\Delta}{\Delta}\mathrm{VIX}^2_{t,\delta+\Delta} - \frac{\delta}{\Delta}\mathrm{VIX}^2_{t,\delta},
\end{aligned} \tag{11.114}$$

where the second line follows by the law of iterated expectations. For example, fix $\Delta = \frac{1}{12}$, and set the future month maturity equal to $\delta = n\Delta$ for integer n, such that

$$\hat{\mathcal{F}}^2_{t,t+(n+1)\Delta} = \mathbb{E}_t\left(\mathrm{VIX}^2_{t+n\Delta,\Delta}\right) = (n+1)\,\mathrm{VIX}^2_{t,(n+1)\Delta} - n\mathrm{VIX}^2_{t,n\Delta}. \tag{11.115}$$

Next, note that $\mathcal{F}_{t+n\Delta,t+n\Delta} = \mathrm{VIX}_{t+n\Delta,\Delta}$, such that

$$\begin{aligned}
\mathbb{E}_t\left(\mathcal{F}_{t+n\Delta,t+n\Delta}\right)^2 &= \mathbb{E}_t\left(\mathrm{VIX}^2_{t+n\Delta,\Delta}\right) - var_t\left(\mathcal{F}_{t+n\Delta,t+n\Delta}\right) \\
&= \hat{\mathcal{F}}^2_{t,t+(n+1)\Delta} - var_t\left(\mathcal{F}_{t+n\Delta,t+n\Delta}\right),
\end{aligned}$$

where the second equality follows by eq. (11.115). Therefore, by neglecting the term $var_t\left(\mathcal{F}_{t+n\Delta,t+n\Delta}\right)$, we obtain

$$\begin{aligned}
\mathcal{F}_{t,t+n\Delta} &= \mathbb{E}_t\left(\mathcal{F}_{t+n\Delta,t+n\Delta}\right) \approx \hat{\mathcal{F}}_{t,t+(n+1)\Delta} \\
&= \sqrt{(n+1)\,\mathrm{VIX}^2_{t,(n+1)\Delta} - n\mathrm{VIX}^2_{t,n\Delta}}.
\end{aligned} \tag{11.116}$$

That is, a variance future is approximated by the difference of two VIX: a long-dated skew minus a short-dated one. The value of this variance future is increasing in volatility, a property shown below.

11.9.1.3 Marking to market

Consider a generic $\tau \in [t, t+\delta]$ and a marking-to-market update of $\hat{\mathcal{F}}^2$:

$$\hat{\mathcal{F}}^2_{\tau,t+\delta+\Delta} \equiv \mathbb{E}_\tau\left(\frac{1}{\Delta}\int_{t+\delta}^{t+\delta+\Delta}\sigma_u^2 du\right). \tag{11.117}$$

By calculations similar to those leading to eq. (11.114), we have that, for $\tau \in [t, t+\delta]$,

$$\begin{aligned}
\hat{\mathcal{F}}^2_{\tau,t+\delta+\Delta} &\equiv \frac{1}{\Delta}\mathbb{E}_\tau\left(\int_\tau^{t+\delta+\Delta}\sigma_u^2 du - \int_\tau^{t+\delta}\sigma_u^2 du\right)\\
&= \frac{1}{\Delta}\mathbb{E}_\tau\left(\frac{\delta+\Delta-(\tau-t)}{\delta+\Delta-(\tau-t)}\int_\tau^{t+\delta+\Delta}\sigma_u^2 du - \frac{\delta-(\tau-t)}{\delta-(\tau-t)}\int_\tau^{t+\delta}\sigma_u^2 du\right)\\
&= \frac{\delta+\Delta-(\tau-t)}{\Delta}\mathrm{VIX}^2_{\tau,\delta+\Delta-(\tau-t)} - \frac{\delta-(\tau-t)}{\Delta}\mathrm{VIX}^2_{\tau,\delta-(\tau-t)}.
\end{aligned} \tag{11.118}$$

Note that the forward variance is still the same as a position in two skews (long the long-dated skew, short the short-dated one). Naturally, eq. (11.118) confirms that

$$\lim_{\tau\to t}\hat{\mathcal{F}}^2_{\tau,t+\delta+\Delta} = \hat{\mathcal{F}}^2_{t,t+\delta+\Delta} = \mathbb{E}_t\left(\mathrm{VIX}^2_{t+\delta,\Delta}\right)$$

(i.e., eq. (11.114)) and

$$\lim_{\tau\to t+\delta}\hat{\mathcal{F}}^2_{\tau,t+\delta+\Delta} = \mathrm{VIX}^2_{t+\delta,\Delta}$$

(i.e., eq. (11.112) evaluated at time $t+\delta$).

11.9.1.4 *The impact of a variance shock*

What is the impact of a shock on the instantaneous variance at τ on $\hat{\mathcal{F}}^2_{\tau,t+\delta+\Delta}$? By eq. (11.117), we have that

$$\hat{\mathcal{F}}^2_{\tau,t+\delta+\Delta} = \frac{1}{\Delta}\int_{t+\delta}^{t+\delta+\Delta}\mathbb{E}_\tau\left(\sigma_u^2\right)du.$$

If σ_t^2 is Markov, a positive shock at τ leads to an increase in $\mathbb{E}_\tau\left(\sigma_u^2\right)$ for all u. Therefore, the value of a future always increases after a positive variance shock occurred at time τ.

11.9.2 A Simple VIX Future Pricing Model

Assume that the variance is a mean-reverting process, similar to the Heston market of section 11.5,

$$d\sigma_t^2 = \kappa(\omega - \sigma_t^2)dt + v(\sigma_t^2)d\tilde{W}_t, \tag{11.119}$$

where κ and ω are constants, v is a function that guarantees a solution to eq. (11.119), and $\tilde{W}_t$ is a Brownian motion under the risk neutral probability. We shall mention additional literature and models related to and extending (11.119) in section 11.9.2.3.

11.9.2.1 *Evaluation*

We have

$$\mathbb{E}_\tau\left(\sigma_u^2\right) = \mathbb{E}\left(\sigma_u^2|\sigma_\tau^2\right) = \left(1-q_{\tau,u}\right)\omega + q_{\tau,u}\sigma_\tau^2, \quad q_{\tau,u} \equiv e^{-\kappa(u-\tau)} \in [0,1),$$

such that

$$\hat{\mathcal{F}}^2_{\tau,t+\delta+\Delta} = \left(1-q_\tau\right)\omega + q_\tau\sigma_\tau^2, \quad q_\tau \equiv e^{-\kappa(t+\delta-\tau)}\frac{1-e^{-\kappa\Delta}}{\kappa\Delta} \in (0,1). \tag{11.120}$$

That is, $\hat{\mathcal{F}}^2_{\tau,t+\delta+\Delta}$ increases with σ^2_τ, independent of whether the current variance value, σ^2_τ, is lower or higher than its long-term value, ω.

11.9.2.2 Contango and backwardation

We define, consistent with section 11.2, a market for volatility at a given maturity to be in contango if the value of the future is higher than the spot and in backwardation otherwise. How would the market behave, then, assuming volatility is mean reverting as in eq. (11.119)? Note that the VIX squared predicted by the model is

$$\lim_{\tau\to t+\delta} \hat{\mathcal{F}}^2_{\tau,t+\delta+\Delta} = \text{VIX}^2_{t+\delta,\Delta} = (1-q)\,\omega + q\sigma^2_{t+\delta}, \quad q \equiv \frac{1-e^{-\kappa\Delta}}{\kappa\Delta} \in (0,1). \tag{11.121}$$

Combining the previous equation with (11.120) leaves

$$\hat{\mathcal{F}}^2_{t,t+\delta+\Delta} = \text{VIX}^2_{t,\Delta} + q\left(1-e^{-\kappa\delta}\right)\left(\omega - \sigma^2_t\right). \tag{11.122}$$

According to this simple model, the market is in contango, provided the current variance is lower than its long-term value, that is, $\sigma^2_t < \omega$, and in backwardation otherwise. Historically, VIX future markets are typically in contango (see figure 11.24), a circumstance we shall return to later (see section 11.10.2). Because ω is a parameter defined under the risk neutral probability, this property implies a smaller value for the corresponding parameter under the physical probability.

11.9.2.3 Volatility, not variance

The future contracts in the previous sections are referenced to a notion of variance, that is, to VIX^2. However, market standards typically reference to a notion of volatility, that is, to VIX. To evaluate futures on VIX, we need to rely on the model predictions on VIX values based on eq. (11.121). Accordingly, the price at time t of a VIX future expiring at time T is

$$\mathcal{F}_t\left(T, \text{VIX}_{t,\Delta}\right) \equiv \mathbb{E}_t\left(\text{VIX}_{T,\Delta}\right) = \int \sqrt{(1-q)\,\omega + q\sigma^2_T}\,\phi(\sigma^2_T, T \,|\, \sigma^2_t, t)\,d\sigma^2_T, \tag{11.123}$$

where $\phi(\sigma^2_T, T|\,\sigma^2_t, t)$ denotes the transition density of σ^2_T given σ^2_t and the notation for the future value $\mathcal{F}_t\left(T, \text{VIX}_{t,\Delta}\right)$ on $\text{VIX}_{t,\Delta}$ is justified by the fact that, by eq. (11.121), $\sigma^2_t = \frac{\text{VIX}^2_{t,\Delta}-(1-q)\omega}{q}$. Then, VIX future values generally depend on the volatility of volatility, $v(\cdot)$ in eq. (11.119), as in the following example.

To make eq. (11.123) explicit, we need to specify $v(\cdot)$ in eq. (11.119), thereby obtaining the transition density $\phi(\sigma^2_T|\,\sigma^2_t)$. For example, it is well known that the transition density for the Heston model (see eq. (11.56)), that is, eq. (11.119) with $v\left(\sigma^2_t\right) = \xi\sigma_t$, is a noncentral chi-square density with $2(q+1)$ degrees of freedom and noncentrality parameter $2u_1$, namely,

$$\phi\left(\sigma^2_T, T \,\middle|\, \sigma^2_t, t\right) = ce^{-u_1-u_2}\left(\frac{u_2}{u_1}\right)^{q/2} I_q\left(2\sqrt{u_1u_2}\right), \tag{11.124}$$

where

$$c \equiv \frac{2\kappa}{\xi^2\left(1-e^{-\kappa(T-t)}\right)}, \quad u_1 \equiv ce^{-\kappa(T-t)}\sigma_t^2, \quad u_2 \equiv cv_T^2, \quad q \equiv \frac{2\kappa\omega}{\xi^2}-1,$$

and $I_q(\cdot)$ is the modified Bessel function of the first kind of order q. Cox, Ingersoll, and Ross (1985) used this result while modeling interest rate sensitive derivatives; their model is reviewed in chapter 13 (see section 13.4).

This model does, naturally, make some simplifications regarding the dynamics of volatility in equity markets. To illustrate, the literature contains models in which volatility may be mean reverting around a time-varying long-term value (as in, e.g., Egloff, Leippold, and Wu, 2010; Bates, 2012; Mencía and Sentana, 2013). In these models, futures may be evaluated by determining the expectation in (11.123); accordingly, the future value predicted by these models is a function of the state variables affecting VIX, some of which are unobserved. Statistical inference for these richer models needs to rely on simulation methods such as those introduced in chapter 6 (see section 6.7).

11.9.3 Options and the Volatility of Volatility

We rely on the model of the previous section and price European-style options written on VIX. Options may enable one to hedge against tail events. Consider, for example, a call option on VIX, struck at some $K=30$, and expiring in one month: the payoff to the option holder in one month equals the difference between the VIX value and 30, provided this difference is positive. Consider a call option contract expiring at time $t+\delta_1$ and referenced to a future written on VIX, where the VIX future has maturity equal to $t+\delta_1+\delta_2$. Its value is $C_t(\delta_1,\delta_2)=e^{-r(T-t)}\mathbb{E}_t\left(\mathcal{F}_{t+\delta_1}(t+\delta_1+\delta_2)-K\right)^+$, where $\mathcal{F}_{t+\delta_1}(t+\delta_1+\delta_2)$ denotes the value at $t+\delta_1$ of a future expiring at $t+\delta_1+\delta_2$.

Consider, for example, the model in (11.119). In this case, the future price is

$$\mathcal{F}_{t+\delta_1}\left(t+\delta_1+\delta_2, \text{VIX}_{t+\delta_1,\Delta}\right)=\int\sqrt{(1-q)\,\omega+q\sigma_{t_{\delta_1+\delta_2}}^2}\,\phi(\sigma_{t_{\delta_1+\delta_2}}^2, t_{\delta_1+\delta_2}|\sigma_{t_{\delta_1}}^2, t_{\delta_1})d\sigma_{t_{\delta_1+\delta_2}}^2,$$

where we denote $t_{\delta_1+\delta_2}\equiv t+\delta_1+\delta_2$, such that the call option is valued as

$$\begin{aligned}&C_t\left(\delta_1,\delta_2,\text{VIX}_{t,\Delta}\right)\\&\equiv e^{-r(T-t)}\int\left(\int\sqrt{(1-q)\,\omega+qx}\phi(x,t_{\delta_1+\delta_2}|\,\sigma_{t_{\delta_1}}^2,t_{\delta_1})dx-K\right)^+\phi(\sigma_{t_{\delta_1}}^2,t_{\delta_1}|\sigma_t^2,t)d\sigma_{t_{\delta_1}}^2,\end{aligned}$$

where the dependence of the call option value on the current levels of VIX is justified by the same reasons underlying notation in eq. (11.123). Note that, if the option was referenced to VIX levels rather than VIX futures, then $\delta_2=0$, such that

$$C_t\left(\delta_1,0,\text{VIX}_{t,\Delta}\right)=e^{-r(T-t)}\int\left(\sqrt{(1-q)\,\omega+q\sigma_{t+\delta_1}^2}-K\right)^+\phi(\sigma_{t+\delta_1}^2,t+\delta_1\middle|\sigma_t^2,t)d\sigma_{t+\delta_1}^2.$$

Thus, in this case, the evaluation of VIX options simplifies. By contrast, evaluating options on VIX futures is analytically more intricate because, at least for this model, it would require a double integration. At the time of writing, market practice is such that listed options are referenced to futures.

11.9.4 Replicating Variance Futures

We know variance futures are valued as the difference between two skews that are weighted by the inverse of K^2, a long-term skew minus a short-term skew, a portfolio that resembles a "short calendar." This section provides some insight into the reasons a short calendar may allow us to take a long volatility view and also discusses some errors made when approximating the value of a variance future while only relying on a finite number of options.

11.9.4.1 Calendars

At first glance, variance futures seem to rely on *short* positions on calendars. However, variance futures are clearly designed to provide long exposure to market volatility, which seems to contradict our intuition on calendars: going *long* a calendar is known to give us long exposure to volatility (see section 11.6.2). We clarify the subtle nature of these statements.

Consider the P&L of a calendar based on an ATM option with a given strike equal to K. We assume a Black–Scholes market with $r=0$ and the underlying expected return $\mu=0$, just as in the experiments of section 11.6.3. Being short a calendar spread is a long position in an option with maturity T_2 and a short position in the option with a shorter maturity, T_1. Suppose we take these positions, delta hedge both of them through Black–Scholes, and finally, aggregate the results. By eq. (11.63) and the fact that, in a Black–Scholes market, implied volatilities are obviously flat at some IV_0, the resulting P&L is

$$\text{P\&L}_T^h \equiv \frac{1}{2}\sum_{t=1}^{T} S_t^2 \Delta\Gamma_t \left[\left(\frac{\Delta S_t}{S_t}\right)^2 - \text{IV}_0^2 \Delta t\right], \tag{11.125}$$

where $\Delta\Gamma_t \equiv \Gamma_{2t} - \Gamma_{1t}$.

The sign of $\Delta\Gamma$ is, thus, crucial. If $\Delta\Gamma_t > 0$, going short a "hedged calendar" would actually enable one to benefit from an increase in volatility. When is $\Delta\Gamma$ positive, then? Clearly, the lower the maturity, the more the asset price density is peaked about K. By results that link this density to option price convexity (see eq. (11.29)), we now have that $\Delta\Gamma_t > 0$ when the asset price moves sufficiently away from the options' strike, for example, $K=100$ in figure 11.21. In other words, provided the asset price undergoes sufficiently wide fluctuations, going *short* a *hedged* calendar enables one to cash in the variance risk premium. A short hedged calendar is thus a position that aims to profit from realized volatility being higher than the implied volatility.

How do we reconcile these facts with our intuition that going long a calendar provides us with long exposure to volatility? In fact, as explained in section 11.6.2, a long exposure to volatility may be attempted through a long position into a *naked* calendar, that is, through unhedged option positions. The P&L of being long a short calendar, $\text{P\&L}_T^o$ say, should then pull the delta-hedging parts back from $\text{P\&L}_T^h$, that is,

$$\text{P\&L}_T^o \equiv \text{P\&L}_T^h + \sum_{t=1}^{T} \delta\Delta_{\text{BS},t} \cdot \Delta S_t, \quad \delta\Delta_{\text{BS},t} \equiv \Delta_{\text{BS},2t} - \Delta_{\text{BS},1t},$$

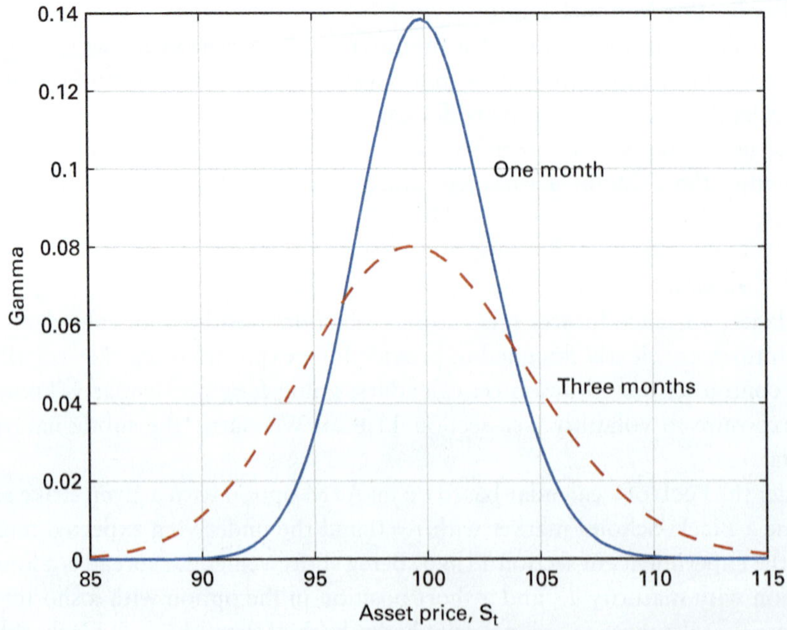

Figure 11.21
The Black–Scholes gamma as a function of the current asset price for a strike $K=100$ and $r=1\%$, $\sigma=10\%$, for maturity $T_2-t=\frac{3}{12}$ (dashed line) and $T_1-t=\frac{1}{12}$ (solid line).

where $\Delta_{BS,jt}$ is the Black–Scholes delta at time t for a maturity equal to T_j. We already know that $\delta\Delta_{BS,t}$ is negative (resp., positive) when the asset price increases (resp., decreases) sufficiently away from K (as discussed in section 11.6.2; see, e.g., figure 11.12). Therefore, the second term of $P\&L_T^o$ may well lead to losses in episodes of high volatility by overwhelming the first term, $P\&L_T^h$, consistent with the explanations of section 11.6.2 (see, e.g., figure 11.14): being long a unhedged calendar is a long exposure in volatility.

Yet, by delta hedging a short calendar, the result is a P&L that may be consistent with a long exposure in market volatility. However, we know that this P&L may be "dirty" so to speak: there is no guarantee that $\Delta\Gamma_t$ will be weighting large realizations of $(\Delta S_t/S_t)^2$ in such a way to enable one to monetize a variance risk premium. The problem is price dependence, just as we explained in section 11.6.3. We now proceed with analyzing how price dependence may be eliminated in a few numerical exercises in which more options are utilized to hedge against asset price movements.

11.9.4.2 Approximations

How well does a skew with a finite number of options approximate the truth? We address this issue while relying on the parametric model of section 11.9.2 and the same parameter values used in figure 11.15. Figure 11.22 shows that the truth is accurately approximated when trading two skews of $N=81$ options each. The approximation worsens with $N=41$ options for skew. As the number of options decreases (e.g., with $N=9$), the approximation deteriorates, and the sensitivity of the portfolio value to changes in the instantaneous volatility lowers.

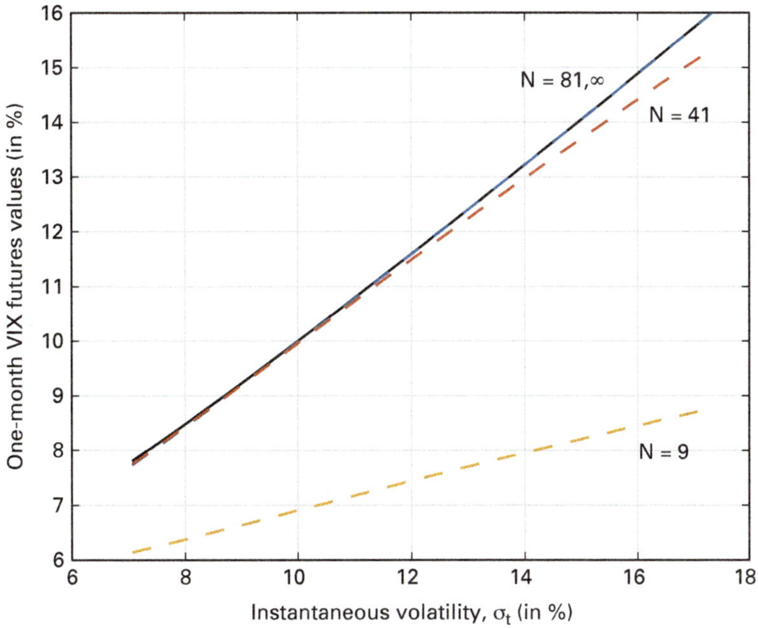

Figure 11.22
This picture depicts the square root of the variance future in the Heston model as a function of current volatility, σ_t. Parameters are set equal to $\kappa = 2$, $\sqrt{\bar{\omega}} = 0.1$, $\xi = 0.1$, and $\rho = -0.5$. The solid line depicts the square root of the truth, that is, $\hat{\mathcal{F}}_{t,t+\delta+\Delta}$ in (11.122) for $\delta = \Delta = \frac{1}{12}$. The dashed lines show the model-free approximation to the truth, obtained through the square root of a short calendar, that is, $\hat{\mathcal{F}}_{t,t+\delta+\Delta}$ in (11.116), using $N = 81$, 41, and 9 options. The truth is the solid line, which is nearly indistinguishable from the $N = 81$ approximation.

Finally, figure 11.23 depicts the value of both VIX levels and VIX futures, calculated with the truth as well as the portfolio approximation. The picture identifies the regions of contango and backwardation: given the parameter values, backwardation occurs when volatility is larger that 10% annualized.

11.10 Endogenous Risk and Market Dysfunctionalities

This section discusses how hedging activities and other trading strategies may increase the volatility of the underlying asset. We deal with strategies that are *procyclical*, that is, strategies that specify buying when markets are up and to sell otherwise. Many models in this chapter are based on the assumption that derivative prices depend on the underlying asset price. This section deals with "feedback effects" where the procyclical nature of some strategies has the power to feed back onto the underlying asset price.

Feedback effects are part of broader phenomena known as *endogenous risk*. Chapter 9 has already dealt with these phenomena while analyzing the delicate interplay between financial markets and real economic activity (see section 9.11).[34] Endogenous risk is the

34. The term "endogenous risk," already employed in chapter 9 (see section 9.11), actually appears to be more appropriate to describe episodes of extreme market volatility (see, for example, Danielsson, Shin, and Zigrand, 2012). Chapter 14 describes additional instances of endogenous

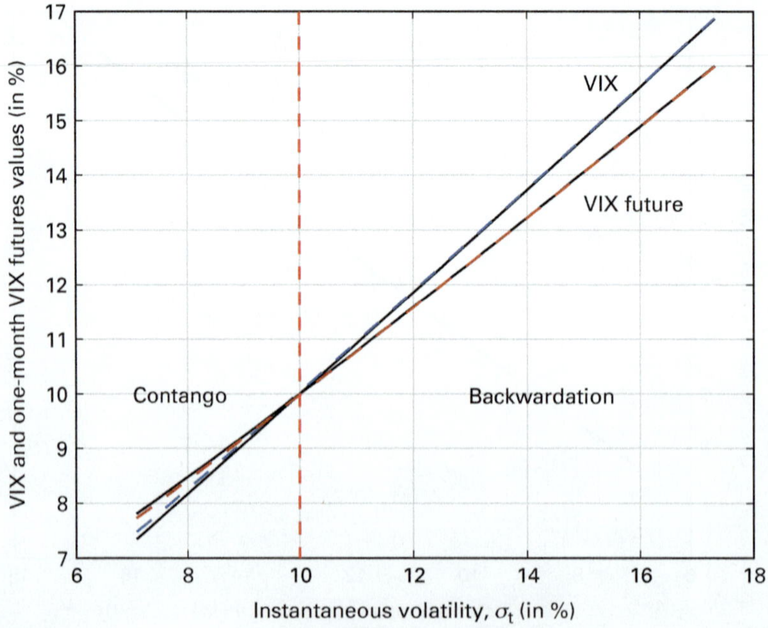

Figure 11.23
This picture depicts the square root of VIX levels and the variance future in the Heston model as a function of current volatility, σ_t. Parameters are set equal to $\kappa=2$, $\sqrt{\bar{\omega}}=0.1$, $\xi=0.1$, and $\rho=-0.5$. The solid line depicts the square root of the truth, that is, $\hat{\mathcal{F}}_{t,t+\delta+\Delta}$ in (11.122) for $\delta=\Delta=\frac{1}{12}$. The dashed lines show the model-free approximation to the truth (depicted as solid lines), obtained through the square root of a short calendar, that is, $\hat{\mathcal{F}}_{t,t+\delta+\Delta}$ in (11.116), and using $N=81$ options. The vertical dashed line separates the backwardation from the contango region.

property by which some initial shock may turn into a persistent trend. In this chapter, the benchmark example of endogenous risk is a market in which some institutions implement procyclical strategies with a price impact. Suppose the market is hit by a shock and then falls. Due to hedging activities, some institutions sell, amplifying the initial market drop. Some agents may not know that the overall drop is also caused by hedging activities. Such "uninformed" agents may infer that the market was initially hit by quite a bad piece of news; they will then sell into an already depressed market, causing a further drop. This drop may trigger additional hedging activities. Under certain conditions, the market may ultimately experience the most drastic form of volatility: a crash.

Gennotte and Leland (1990) develop a model that formalizes this reasoning and show that such "technical crashes" may occur even if the hedging activity is very small. While this model seems to explain the Black Monday crash of October 19, 1987,[35] the mechanism underlying the model is at the heart of many other historical instances of crashes, including the Black Tuesday crash of October 29, 1929. This section provides additional examples and descriptions of such crashes and also provides a simplified model that helps capture the salient features of a crash generated through such self-reinforcing mechanisms.

---

risk that have possibly occurred during the global financial crisis of the the late 2000s (see section 14.5).

35. The Dow Jones Industrial Average lost more than 22% on this day, the largest in its history.

Section 11.10.1 explains when a hedging strategy may be procyclical; section 11.10.2 provides a succinct description of a number of market crashes that presumably occurred due to self-reinforcing mechanism, and a simple model.

11.10.1 Cyclical Hedging

A financial intermediary would like to hedge a portfolio of derivatives it is exposed to. When will its hedging activity be procyclical? We need to consider two properties of this portfolio: delta and convexity.[36] Section 11.4 deals with delta in a Black–Scholes market. Convexity, or *gamma*, is the second-order derivative of a derivative price against its underlying asset price and is discussed in section 11.6. Note that gamma should be positive for long calls and puts (see figure 11.2). Naturally, going short calls and puts produces negative gamma. We now explain that hedging activities may or may not be procyclical, depending on the sign taken by delta and gamma. Even if the gamma is negative, delta hedging may still involve buying on the way up and selling on the way down. Precisely, consider the following four hedging portfolios.

(i) Positive gamma ("buying on the way up and selling on the way down")

(i.1) Hedging portfolios with positive delta—as required, for example, to hedge against the *sale* of (or, in general, to replicate) a call. Positive delta means that the hedging portfolio specifies *buying* the assets underlying the call. Delta increases with the price of these assets, and the hedging activity is such that one keeps on buying the assets as their price increases. Likewise, as the asset price decreases and delta lowers, the hedging activity now implies holding less assets, thereby leading to selling the assets precisely during market drops.

(i.2) Hedging portfolios with negative delta—as required, for example, to hedge against the *sale* of (or to replicate) a put. Due to negative delta, the hedging portfolio specifies *selling* the assets underlying the put. Since gamma is positive, delta is up when the underlying asset price is up, that is, the hedging activity consists in selling less as the asset price rises. For example, delta may have gone from -0.50 to -0.25, implying that a trader needs to buy back some of the underlying assets. When instead the underlying price lowers, delta lowers too, requiring a trader to sell the underlying asset precisely during a falling market.

(ii) Negative gamma (buying on the way down and selling on the way up)

(ii.1) Hedging portfolios with positive delta—as required, for example, to hedge against a portfolio that is *long* puts. The hedging portfolio consists in long positions on the assets underlying the put. Negative gamma now implies that a trader needs to buy the underlying asset less (resp., more) as its price goes up (resp., down). The hedging activity is countercyclical: a trader sells the underlying asset as its price increases and buys it otherwise.

---

36. The properties in this section hold for hedging portfolios calibrated to the Black–Scholes model. Section 11.5 explains that perfect replication cannot be achieved in incomplete markets such as those with stochastic volatility. In this case, replicating the payoff of an option may require trading on an MMA, the underlying asset, and another option.

(ii.2) Hedging portfolios with negative delta—as required, for example, to hedge against a portfolio that is *long* calls. Hedging requires a trader to *sell* the assets. Negative gamma implies that a trader needs to sell the underlying asset more (resp., less) as its price increases (resp., decreases). Hedging is countercyclical.

The next section provides a succinct description of a number of crash episodes that may be related to the existence of procyclical strategies that are similar to those in this section, and a model that rationalizes such episodes.

11.10.2 Market Crashes

11.10.2.1 Old and new

Endogenous risk is understood to be at the origin of many episodes of market dysfunctionalities. The Brady Commission, set up to inquire into the causes underlying the market crash of 1987, concluded that procyclical strategies might have been responsible for this crash (Brady 1988). The explanations for the 1987 crash actually help clarify asset price developments in many other circumstances. For example, stop-loss orders may well have contributed to the market crash in 1929: a stop-loss order specifies selling an asset exactly when the price of this asset falls below a given threshold. Similarly, margin calls may lead to liquidity spirals, as in bad times when prices fall and investors' demand decreases. Brunnermeier and Pedersen (2009) consider a model of such liquidity spirals.

The 1987 crash may be regarded as an early prototype of market dysfunctionalities. On May 6, 2010, the Dow Jones Industrial Average dropped by almost 9% in only a few minutes, an episode known as a "flash crash." What happened? This day appeared to be filled with bad news regarding the unfolding of the European debt crisis of the time. This news contributed to increasing volatility and deteriorating liquidity conditions. Then, according to explanations in a joint report by the Commodity Futures Trading Commission and the Security Exchange Commission (CFTC and SEC, 2010), a mutual fund (the "Seller") began an automated execution algorithm regarding an unusually large number of E-mini futures on the S&P 500. This trade was partially absorbed by high frequency trading (HFT) firms and also by cross-market arbitrageurs, who began to go long these futures and short the equity names underlying the SPY (that is, the ETF that tracks the S&P 500 index). To unwind these positions normally requires traders with fundamental views ("real money investors"). However, trading mainly emanated from HFT algorithms in the few minutes after the Seller's trade. Presumably, these algorithms were instructed to sell in order to keep limited inventories, a circumstance that would certainly occur in the absence of real money investors; as a result, these trades would have contributed to consuming limit order books. Now the Seller's sale algorithm was programmed to sell at execution rates that were increasing in past volumes (perhaps based on the assumption that higher volume may lead to high liquidity). So past volumes would trigger sales and additional volume generated by HFT algorithms that were simply trading with each other over a self-reinforcing mechanism. Cross-market arbitrageurs would then help to transfer this selling pressure onto equity. The market crashed in just a few minutes, as anticipated. The CFTC and SEC's explanation was based on the "hot potato" presumption that HFT algorithms would engage into a frenzy activity among themselves. Kirilenko, Kyle, Samadi, and Tuzun (2017) provide further empirical and granular evidence on the origins of these events.

11.10.2.2 Volatility begets volatility

This chapter describes expected volatility as a proxy to risk and uncertainty. However, since at least the mid-2010s, some market participants have been explaining that expected volatility may become a *source* of risk. For example, Christopher Cole of hedge fund Artemis Capital Management once explained that trading strategies based on machine learning or risk parity may lead to self-reinforcing mechanisms (see Cole, 2015). To illustrate, he mentioned that models based on machine learning might "recognize patterns in data that they themselves influence resulting in feedback loops" (Cole, 2015, 8). The mechanics behind the 2010 flash crash may not describe these dynamics, but they come close to capturing these descriptions: strategies reacted to signals not strictly related to the fundamentals (volume), and these reactions themselves became new signals.

Risk parity is particularly relevant to themes dealt with in this section. Chapter 1 explains that risk parity is a portfolio by which assets are weighted less when they are more volatile (see section 1.2.5). Now, suppose that some initial (and not fully observed) shock hits the markets and that equity markets subsequently drop. Then expected volatility would likely increase. Indeed, investors' risk appetite and more generally risky assets' demand diminishes as declining markets may signal that bad news is about to arrive: falling prices reveal information, albeit only partially, consistent with the asymmetric information explanations of chapter 10. Demand for protection then increases, and the smile goes up: the VIX rises. When VIX is used as an input to risk parity, the equity market falls further, and realized volatility also increases. The feedback loop consists of falling equity markets and rising volatility (both expected and realized). Although this section does not provide a more rigorous explanation of these dynamics, chapter 9 provides a formal model along these lines in a related area (feedback effects in the context of financial intermediaries' balance sheet capacities) (see section 9.11.5.3).[37]

Remarkably, Cole also noted that short volatility exchange traded products (ETPs) had surpassed long volatility ETPs and mentioned that short volatility ETPs might have introduced "self-reflexivity" (e.g., Cole, 2015, 8, 22): managing these products requires buying volatility exactly when volatility rises. On February 5, 2018, the VIX index touched levels never seen since the early 2010s. This episode became known as the volatility armageddon ("Volmageddon"), and procyclical strategies might indeed have well contributed to it, a circumstance equally acknowledged in policy reports (see, e.g., Pagano, Sánchez Serrano, and Zechner, 2019).[38] Let us explain.

The preliminary important question is: What were the forces behind the strong demand for short volatility ETPs? Section 11.9.2.2 mentions that VIX future markets are typically in contango, and figure 11.24 illustrates this circumstance for the "VIX basis," defined (in this picture) as the difference between one-month VIX futures and VIX. The VIX basis is often in contango and switches to backwardation during periods of acute uncertainty.

37. Chapter 14 also develops a model in which financial intermediaries with limited risk-bearing capacity may accelerate a crisis (see section 14.5).

38. Armageddon is the translation of the ancient Greek word $A\rho\mu\alpha\gamma\varepsilon\delta\hat{\omega}\nu$, which may denote the (possibly idealized) location of the end-of-the-world battle in the New Testament of the Christian Bible. In chapter 14, no-armageddon arbitrage is briefly mentioned as the market evaluation methodology of credit indices that accounts for the event that all names in an index may defaut in a finite time (see section 14.3.4.2).

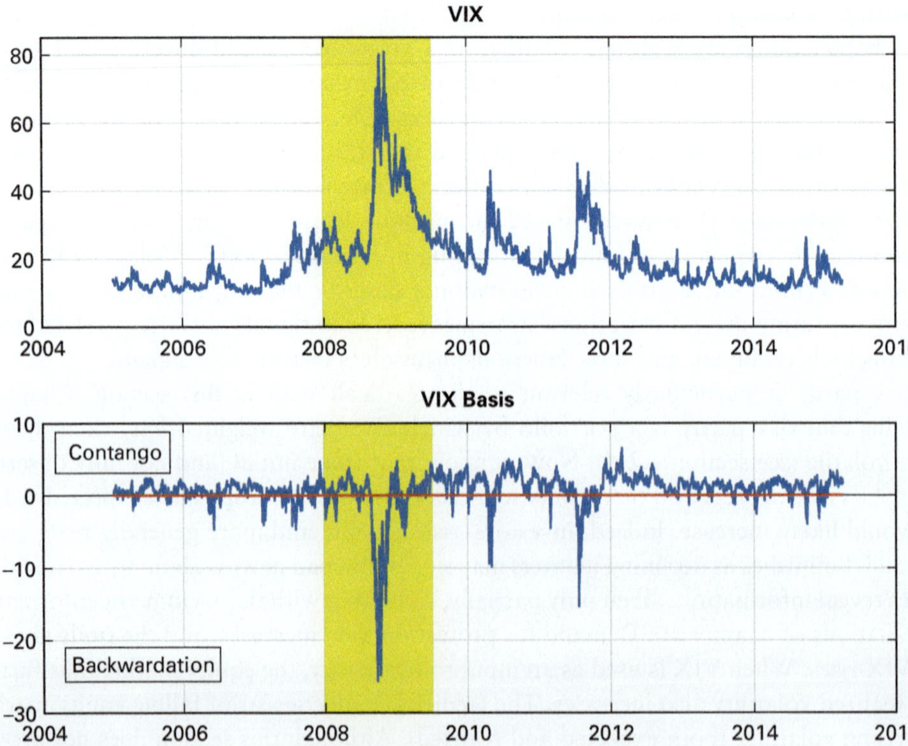

Figure 11.24
The top panel depicts the Cboe-VIX index. The bottom panel displays the VIX basis, defined as the difference between one-month VIX future values minus VIX; a positive (resp., negative) basis defines a contango (resp., backwardation) regime. The shaded area in both panels covers the 2007–2009 recession episode as defined by NBER. The sample period covers daily data from January 3, 2005, to April 17, 2015.

Contango reflects the premium required by investors who decide to insure other investors who are short volatility, similar to the explanations given for the premium on variance swap contracts (see section 11.2.5.4). Backwardation episodes occur in quite bad times: in these adverse circumstances, insurance costs become "negative," so to speak, driven by the expectation that, by mean reversion, future market volatility would drop. Figure 11.24 reveals that contango has always been the norm, even before the global financial crisis of the late 2010s. It appears to be equally important that VIX spikes (and backwardation) occur in bad times.

These properties suggest the very rudimentary investment strategy of systematically initiating short positions in VIX futures and then rolling these positions down. If market volatility doesn't spike, this strategy leads to "harvesting a contango premium." In a way, being short VIX futures is akin to the equally rudimentary strategy to systematically sell OTM put options on the S&P 500. In fact, as explained, investors of the early to mid-2010s were already heavily invested in selling volatility through VIX futures. This investment thesis was so popular to have become productized. In 2010, Credit Suisse had launched VelocityShares XIV (XIV), an inverse ETP that used to track short positions in VIX futures; the product had totalled returns of nearly 600% from inception to the end of January 2018 (and a market value approaching $2billion). Naturally, the risk of XIV was that, from time to time, the VIX would spike and jeopardize this performance.[39] On February 5, XIV did collapse by more than 80% and it was taken off the market only a few days later.

The collapse of XIV coincided with the likely presence of feedback effects. The important market movements began with the release of macroeconomic news. On February 2 (a Friday), the US government reported a strong rise in wages, fueling fears of inflation (and Fed tightening) and then, an increase in Treasury yields and subsequently a drop of equity markets amid higher bond yields and rising wages, with the S&P 500 losing about 2%. On February 5, the S&P 500 lost an additional 4%, and the VIX index increased about 20 percentage points to 37 points. However, the reaction of VIX was much stronger than suggested by the usual negative relation between VIX and S&P 500 returns mentioned in section 11.8.2 (see, e.g., Sushko and Turner, 2018). Therefore, the VIX dynamics might be explained by internal causes. These causes relate to the very mechanism underlying inverse volatility products, at least partially. As VIX increased, short volatility ETP managers needed to buy VIX futures in order to maintain the product sought exposure, and this activity contributed to the feedback. The Bank for International Settlements (2018) estimated that short volatility ETPs amounted to about $4 billion in market value at the time. Another product, ProShares SVXY, an inverse volatility ETF (at the time of writing, only leveraged at –0.5x), had both size and loss comparable with XIV. Finally, additional short volatility investors might well have contributed to the feedback while exerting buying pressure for VIX futures in a likely attempt at closing positions to mitigate losses in a rising VIX environment.

Naturally, these feedback effects also involved equity markets (risk-parity investing might have been a channel), and by February 8, the S&P 500 had lost nearly 9% since the initial publication of the US report on wages. These episodes are very important. They teach us how volatility markets may ultimately affect the aggregate stock market. Ironically, methods and systems that are conceived (at least in principle), to mitigate uncertainty and volatility in equity markets may, at times and through feedback effects, adversely affect some of the main channels of financing for the firms that are representative of the economy. In fact, feedback effects are, by now, acknowledged to be an important aspect of the price formation process in spaces beyond volatility markets. Ben-David, Franzoni, and Moussawi (2018) show that assets underlying ETFs are more volatile than others. We now present a model that captures the salient effects of some of these feedback effects, a simplifying variant of many models proposed in the literature so far.

11.10.2.3 A model of market feedbacks

Consider a market for a security that has a fixed supply equal to one and a price equal to S_t at time t. This security is traded by a number of investors endowed with some income equal to y_t in each period t. These investors can be interpreted as financial intermediaries,

39. An example of a *long volatility* ETP is Barclays VXX, a product that maintains long positions in VIX futures, launched for the period 2009–2019 and twined through VXXB for the period 2018–2048. Due to contango bleeding, these products are "rides to zero": an investor who is long in these products would likely lose all of their initial investment eventually. In exchange, a long volatility ETP delivers positive returns in periods of market distress.

and y_t can be interpreted as the amount of funds that are available to them. The role of this variable in the model is to lead to changes in the investors' asset demand such that, in equilibrium, the asset price, S_t, is driven by y_t. Consider the following example, a slight generalization of one suggested by Frey and Stremme (1997). The asset distributes a dividend equal to δ_t at time t and is traded through overlapping generations of investors. When young, each of these investors formulates the following asset demand:

$$D(S_t, y_t) = \arg\max_{d_t \geq 0} E_t \left(u \left(y_t + (S_{t+1} + \delta_{t+1} - S_t) \, d_t \right) \right),$$

where u is each investor's utility, one with a CRRA equal to γ. That is, the investor born at time t receives some income endowment y_t and trades a positive amount of assets; when old, the investor consumes all the wealth resulting from this investment and the endowment y_t, that is, assuming that the safe interest rate is zero, the argument of $u(\cdot)$. The first-order conditions for this problem are

$$0 = E_t \left[\left(y_t + (S_{t+1} + \delta_{t+1} - S_t) \, D(S_t, y_t) \right)^{-\gamma} (S_{t+1} + \delta_{t+1} - S_t) \right].$$

Now, suppose that the equilibrium asset price process satisfies $S_{t+1} + \delta_{t+1} = \tilde{s}_{t+1} S_t$ for some IID random variable $\tilde{s}_{t+1}$. Then it is easy to see that, under regularity conditions on $\tilde{s}_{t+1}$, the asset demand takes the following simple form,

$$D(S_t, y_t) = \kappa \frac{y_t}{S_t}, \tag{11.126}$$

for some positive constant κ. We refer to investors with this asset demand as "reference investors."

If reference investors were the only market participants, the asset price would be just $S_t = \kappa y_t$ due to the equilibrium condition $1 = D(S_t, y_t)$. Then, the variable $\tilde{s}_{t+1}$ would be proportional to the income growth (at least assuming a constant dividend-yield ratio). However, we assume that, in addition to reference investors, there is a number of traders motivated by hedging reasons of the type discussed in the previous section. Each period, each hedger trades $\Delta(S_t, \bar{t})$ asset units, where $\Delta(S_t, \bar{t})$ denotes the Black–Scholes hedging ratio for a put option for some fixed maturity $\bar{t}$, $\Delta(S_t, \bar{t}) = \Delta_t^{\text{BS}} - 1$, and Δ_t^{BS} is as in eq. (11.17); protection strategies based on puts were indeed predominant at the time of the 1987 crash. We assume that the proportion of hedgers is equal to χ, and that the reference investors' beliefs are such that their demand is still as in (11.126), such that in equilibrium,

$$1 = (1 - \chi) \, D(S_t, y_t) + \chi \Delta(S_t, \bar{t}). \tag{11.127}$$

Figure 11.25 (left panel) depicts four examples of total demand (the RHS of (11.127)). We assume that $\kappa \equiv 1$ in (11.126) and consider a put strike (or protection level) equal to $K = 100$, a fixed maturity $\bar{t}$ equal to one month, $r = 0.01$, volatility $\sigma = 0.10$, and finally, a mass of hedgers equal to $\chi = 30\%$. The four curves are obtained with income levels y_t equal to 200, 170, 152, and 120. Note that the total demand is nonmonotonic in all cases. The reason for this property is that the hedging demand, $\Delta(S_t, \bar{t})$, is procyclical, that is, increasing in S_t. The right panel of figure 11.25 suggests that the hedgers' demand is substantially flat only for asset price levels sufficiently away from $S_t = K = 100$; however,

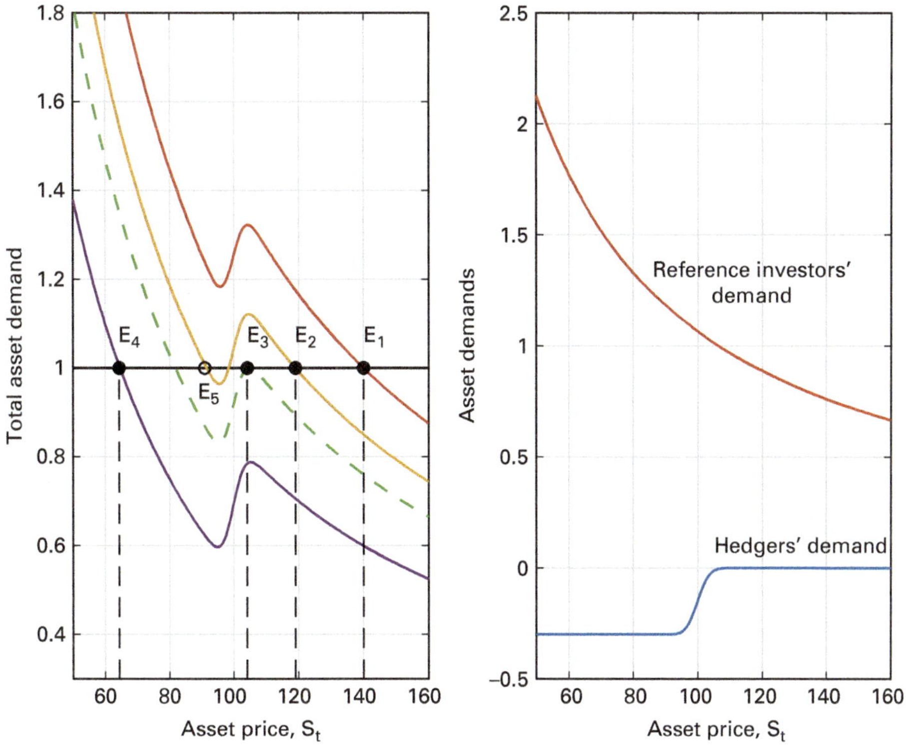

Figure 11.25
The left panel of this picture depicts the total asset demand as a function of the asset price when the reference investors' income decreases from $y_t = 200$ (top curve), to $y_t = 170$ and 152 (intermediate), and finally, to $y_t = 120$ (bottom) when $\chi = 30\%$ of investors follow a put replicating strategy with protection level $K = 100$ for one-month maturity with $r = 0.01$ and volatility $\sigma = 0.10$. Asset supply is fixed and equal to one such that the points E_1, E_2, E_3, and E_4 identify equilibrium prices under the four market conditions. The empty circle identifying point E_5 is discussed in the main text. The right panel depicts the components of the total asset demand (reference investors and hedgers) when $y_t = 152$.

it is quite steep around K, and this property translates into the nonmonotonicity of the total demand and sometimes a multiplicity of equilibria.

These properties of the total demand may be responsible for the occurrence of market crashes. Let us illustrate. Assume that, initially, the reference investors' income is $y_t = 200$, such that the equilibrium price is identified by the point E_1. As y_t decreases, the total demand curve shifts down, and the equilibrium price lowers. For example, when $y_t = 170$, there are three equilibria (occurring at the intersection with the horizontal line), but we assume that the new equilibrium is reached at E_2 (the closest to E_1). As y_t decreases further, total demand shifts down too, and the equilibrium price decreases smoothly with y_t. However, when $y_t = 152$, the total demand is tangent to the horizontal supply line (point E_3). From this point on, a further decrease in y_t (no matter how small this change might be) cannot lead to a smooth change in the equilibrium price: the price experiences a *discrete* change, that is, a jump. Consider, for example, the demand curve that is obtained with $y_t = 120$. The left panel shows that, in this case, the equilibrium price is quite low, correspond to point E_4; the market has experienced a crash before reaching this level. The market behavior after the crash and point E_5 are analyzed below.

Note that the market equilibrium details are very standard in the absence of hedgers: a lower y_t would lead to a lower demand, and the price would adjust accordingly. Instead, in a market with hedgers, the total asset demand decreases as the price lowers around $S_t = K$ and market clearing fails for prices in this neighborhood. It is as if the hedging demand were creating some additional supply exactly when the price is already falling. The standard clearing mechanisms would operate only when the price is sufficiently low (and the put option is, then, sufficiently OTM) to make $\Delta(S_t, \bar{t})$ substantially insensitive to S. All in all, a new equilibrium is possible only through a discrete change in the equilibrium price.

Gennotte and Leland (1990) provide the first model in which the equilibrium price can be "discontinuous with respect to fundamental information." Their model is more complex than the model in this section. In their model, some agents may not be aware of the hedging activities that may likely lead to the amplification mechanisms highlighted so far. Thus, consistent with the predictions of models of markets with asymmetric information (see chapter 10), such uninformed investors infer that, in the presence of large price movements, some bad news must have likely hit the fundamentals. In this market, even a fairly small amount of hedging activity (5%, in the calibration of the model) may lead to sizable market crashes. By contrast, in the stylized model of this section, hedging activity takes 30% of overall trading but is fully observed by the reference investors.

The predictions of these models are consistent with the market behavior around the 1987 crash. This crash did not seem to have been preceded by any particular devastating piece of news; rather, the markets were witnessing to a series of relatively negative trends, such as the interest rate increases subsequent to the Fed tightening of the time. In the model of this section, total demand slows down as y_t decreases, and at least initially, the price adjusts smoothly. A crash occurs after y_t lowers to some critical point and, ironically, is precisely due to hedging activity. Interestingly, Gennotte and Leland document that the dollar amount corresponding to portfolio replication strategies was relatively limited at the time of the 1987 crash, just as in their calibrated model.

What happens after the crash? The market may be stuck in a relatively low evaluation "regime." Let us explain. Note that, due to the nonmonotonicity of the total demand, there may exist multiple equilibria. For example, even if the state variable recovers to a level $y_t = 170$, the equilibrium price is not necessarily identified by point E_2 in figure 11.25. Rather, if we assume that equilibrium prices change by being as close as possible to their immediately previous values (an assumption we already made), the new equilibrium price should now correspond to point E_5 (the empty circle) and thus be lower than the price in point E_2. More generally, prices are lower after the crash, at least until y_t reaches some value that triggers an *upward* price jump. Figure 11.26 shows the equilibrium price dynamics: asset prices are initially in the "boom regime" and precipitate into the "bust regime" after a crash. Prices may then remain in the bust regime for a while and "rally" toward the boom regime only after y_t gets sufficiently high. The reason for this rally is the same as that for the crash: as prices recover, hedging demand increases over a feedback loop, and a new equilibrium is possible only through a discrete price change.

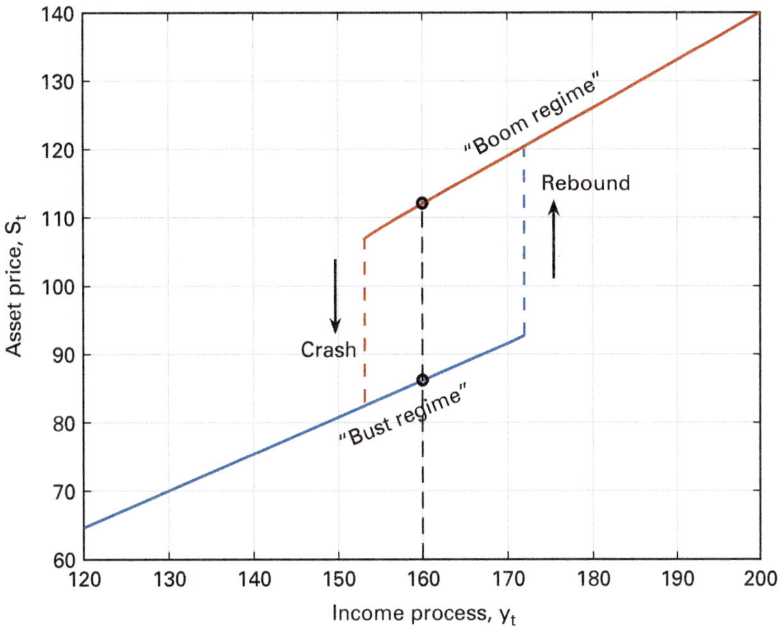

Figure 11.26
Non-Markovian asset price dynamics. This picture depicts the equilibrium asset price S_t as a function of the income process y_t in the boom and bust regimes. If two equilibrium prices are possible for a single value of y_t (as for $y_t = 160$), the current equilibrium price is in the boom or in the bust regime according to the most recent price history. Parameter values are as in the legend of figure 11.25.

Note, then, that there exist levels of y_t for which we may not be able to identify an equilibrium price independent of its most recent history. For example, a boom and a bust regime are both compatible with $y_t = 160$. Which equilibrium price will prevail? The price would be in the bust regime if it already was in the bust regime and in the boom regime otherwise. Such types of dynamics are known as *non-Markovian*: equilibrium prices are history dependent, a property that goes beyond many of the standard assumptions made in this book (see, e.g., chapter 4). Naturally, the Gennotte and Leland model features these non-Markovian properties too. Further, the literature has identified other information mechanisms by which equilibrium prices may crash and rally and be history dependent. Mele and Sangiorgi (2015) show that, in markets subject to Knightian uncertainty (see section 9.6 in chapter 9), there can be complementarities in information acquisition: the agents' incentives to purchase information increase with the number of agents who have already purchased it. These complementarities result in information frenzies and price rallies. When information frenzies stop, markets may crash.[40]

Finally, note the following interesting conceptual problem with the model in this section, a problem raised since at least Platen and Schweizer (1998) in their related model of

40. Veldkamp (2006) provides early work on information frenzies based on decreasing costs of information acquisition. García and Strobl (2011) study a mechanism of information complementarities based on relative wealth concerns. Mele and Sangiorgi (2015) mention additional references on information complementarities.

feedback effects. The price behavior underlying figure 11.26 is obviously inconsistent with the assumptions underlying the Black–Scholes hedging demand behind this very same behavior: prices are not geometric Brownian motions anymore. Therefore, a more appropriate modeling assumption is that the hedging demand should be based on the equilibrium price process depicted in figure 11.26. However, assuming such a hedging demand would change the equilibrium price process that would then necessitate a new assumption about the hedging demand, and so forth. Platen and Schweizer (1998, 74) explain that, ideally, sophisticated hedgers should base their strategies on a fixed point of this mechanism. It is an open question whether such a fixed point does exist. Alternatively, the hedgers' level of sophistication is costly enough to justify the model misspecifications that result from using Black–Scholes hedging.

Appendix 11.A The Original Formulation of Black–Scholes

The arguments in Black and Scholes (1973) and Merton (1973) rely on the assumption the option is traded. Accordingly, create a self-financed portfolio of $\bar{n}_S$ units of the underlying asset and n_C units of the European call option, where $\bar{n}_S$ is an arbitrary number. Such a portfolio is worth $V = \bar{n}_S S + n_C C$, and since it is self-financed, it satisfies

$$\begin{aligned} dV &= \bar{n}_S dS + n_C dC \\ &= \bar{n}_S dS + n_C \left[C_S dS + \left(C_\tau + \frac{1}{2}\sigma^2 S^2 C_{SS} \right) d\tau \right] \\ &= (\bar{n}_S + n_C C_S)\, dS + n_C \left(C_\tau + \frac{1}{2}\sigma^2 S^2 C_{SS} \right) d\tau, \end{aligned}$$

where the second line follows by Itô's lemma. Therefore, the portfolio is locally riskless whenever

$$n_C = -\bar{n}_S \frac{1}{C_S},$$

in which case V would appreciate at the safe rate,

$$\frac{dV}{V} = \frac{n_C \left(C_\tau + \frac{1}{2}\sigma^2 S^2 C_{SS} \right) d\tau}{\bar{n}_S S + n_C C} = \frac{-\frac{1}{C_S} \left(C_\tau + \frac{1}{2}\sigma^2 S^2 C_{SS} \right)}{S - \frac{1}{C_S} C} d\tau = r d\tau.$$

The last equality and the boundary condition lead to the Black–Scholes partial differential equation (11.15).

Appendix 11.B Black 1976

We wish to derive results that are known as the "Black 1976" formula (see Black, 1976a). We want to evaluate the following expectation:

$$\mathbb{E}_t (x_T - K)^+,$$

where

$$x_T = x_t e^{-\frac{1}{2}\int_t^T \gamma_\tau^2 d\tau + \int_t^T \gamma_\tau d\tilde{W}_\tau}.$$

Let $\mathbb{I}_{\text{exe}}$ be the indicator of all events such that $x_T \geq K$. We have

$$\begin{aligned}
\mathbb{E}_t (x_T - K)^+ &= \mathbb{E}_t (x_T \cdot \mathbb{I}_{\text{exe}}) - K \cdot \mathbb{E}_t (\mathbb{I}_{\text{exe}}) \\
&= x_t \cdot \mathbb{E}_t \left(\frac{x_T}{x_t} \cdot \mathbb{I}_{\text{exe}} \right) - K \cdot \mathbb{E}_t (\mathbb{I}_{\text{exe}}) \\
&= x_t \cdot \mathbb{E}_t^{Q^x} (\mathbb{I}_{\text{exe}}) - K \cdot \mathbb{E}_t (\mathbb{I}_{\text{exe}}) \\
&= x_t \cdot Q^x (x_T \geq K) - K \cdot Q (x_T \geq K)
\end{aligned}$$

where the probability Q^x is defined as

$$\frac{dQ^x}{dQ} = \frac{x_T}{x_t} = e^{-\frac{1}{2}\int_t^T \gamma_\tau^2 d\tau + \int_t^T \gamma_\tau d\tilde{W}_\tau},$$

a Q martingale starting at one. Under Q^x, $dW_\tau^x = d\tilde{W}_\tau - \gamma d\tau$ is a Brownian motion, such that

$$x_T = x_t e^{\frac{1}{2}\int_t^T \gamma_\tau^2 d\tau + \int_t^T \gamma_\tau dW_\tau^x}.$$

Note that $Q (x_T \geq K) = \Phi(d_2)$ and $Q^x (x_T \geq K) = \Phi(d_1)$, where

$$d_{2/1} = \frac{\ln\left(\frac{x_t}{K}\right) \mp \frac{1}{2}\int_t^T \gamma_\tau^2 d\tau}{\sqrt{\int_t^T \gamma_\tau^2 d\tau}}.$$

Appendix 11.C Stochastic volatility

11.C.1 The Hull and White Equation

We assume that the asset price and its volatility solve eqs. (11.37) but that the two Brownian motions W and W_σ are uncorrelated. Note first that, conditionally on the variance path $(\sigma_\tau^2)_{\tau\in[t,T]}$, $\ln\left(\frac{S_T}{S_t}\right)$ is normally distributed under the risk neutral probability,

$$\ln\left(\frac{S_T}{S_t}\right) = r(T-t) - \frac{1}{2}\int_t^T \sigma_\tau^2 d\tau + \int_t^T \sigma_\tau dW_\tau,$$

with

$$\mathbb{E}_t \left[\ln\left(\frac{S_T}{S_t}\right) \mid \left(\sigma_\tau^2\right)_{\tau\in[t,T]} \right] = r(T-t) - \frac{1}{2}(T-t)\,\tilde{V}_{t,T}$$

$$var_t \left[\ln\left(\frac{S_T}{S_t}\right) \mid \left(\sigma_\tau^2\right)_{\tau\in[t,T]} \right] = \int_t^T \sigma_\tau^2 d\tau = (T-t)\,\tilde{V}_{t,T}.$$

Then, we use the law of iterated expectations and elaborate on eq. (11.51) and arrive to eq. (11.53) as follows:

$$
\begin{aligned}
C\left(S_t,\sigma_t^2,T-t\right) &= e^{-r(T-t)}\mathbb{E}_t\left[(S_T-K)^+ \mid S_t,\sigma_t^2\right] \\
&= \mathbb{E}_t\left[\mathbb{E}\left(e^{-r(T-t)}\,(S_T-K)^+ \mid S_t,\left(\sigma_\tau^2\right)_{\tau\in[t,T]}\right)|S_t,\sigma_t^2\right] \\
&= \mathbb{E}_t[C_{\text{BS}}(S_t,T-t;K,\tilde{V}_{t,T}^{1/2})|S_t,\sigma_t^2] \\
&= \mathbb{E}_t[C_{\text{BS}}(S_t,T-t;K,\tilde{V}_{t,T}^{1/2})|\sigma_t^2] \\
&= \int C_{\text{BS}}(S_t,T-t;K,\tilde{V}_{t,T}^{1/2})\phi(\tilde{V}_{t,T}|\sigma_t^2)d\tilde{V}_{t,T} \\
&\equiv \mathbb{E}_t^{\tilde{V}}[C_{\text{BS}}(S_t,T-t;K,\tilde{V}_{t,T}^{1/2})],
\end{aligned}
\tag{11.A1}
$$

where $\phi(\tilde{V}_{t,T}|\sigma_t^2)$ denotes the density of $\tilde{V}_{t,T}$ conditional on the current level of the variance, σ_t^2. The third and fourth equalities follow by the assumption that W and W_σ are uncorrelated, such that

$$\phi(\tilde{V}_{t,T}|S_t,\sigma_t^2)=\phi(\tilde{V}_{t,T}|\sigma_t^2),$$

for otherwise the current level of the index, S_t, would help predict $\tilde{V}_{t,T}$. In other words, eq. (11.A1) reveals that the price of an option in this stochastic volatility market is the Black–Scholes formula weighted with the probability density of the realized variance.

11.C.2 Extensions

Romano and Touzi (1997) extend the Hull and White equation to the case where asset returns and volatility are correlated. Consider the following model:

$$
\begin{cases}
\dfrac{dS_t}{S_t}=rdt+\sigma_t\left(\rho_t dW_t^\sigma+\sqrt{1-\rho_t^2}dZ_t\right) \\
d\sigma_t^2=b\left(\sigma_t\right)dt+a\left(\sigma_t\right)dW_t^\sigma
\end{cases}
$$

where the correlation process, ρ_t, does not depend on S_t, and W_σ and Z are two independent Brownian motions, such that

$$S_T=S_tL_{t,T}\cdot e^{r(T-t)-\frac{1}{2}\int_t^T\sigma_\tau^2\left(1-\rho_\tau^2\right)d\tau+\int_t^T\sigma_\tau\sqrt{1-\rho_\tau^2}dZ_\tau},$$

where $L_{t,T}$ is as in eq. (11.55) of the main text. We have, using the law of iterated expectations,

$$
\begin{aligned}
&C\left(S_t,\sigma_t^2,\rho_t,T-t\right) \\
&= e^{-r(T-t)}\mathbb{E}_t\left[(S_T-K)^+ \mid S_t,\sigma_t^2,\rho_t\right] \\
&= \mathbb{E}_t\left[\mathbb{E}\left(e^{-r(T-t)}\,(S_T-K)^+ \mid S_t,\left(\sigma_\tau^2,\rho_\tau\right)_{\tau\in[t,T]}\right)|S_t,\sigma_t^2,\rho_t\right] \\
&= \mathbb{E}_t[C_{\text{BS}}(S_tL_{t,T},T-t;K,(\tilde{V}_{t,T}^\rho)^{1/2})|S_t,\sigma_t^2,\rho_t],
\end{aligned}
$$

where $\tilde{V}^{\rho}_{t,T}$ is as in eq. (11.55) of the main text. The third equality follows because, by assumption, both the variance and correlation processes are independent of $\{Z_\tau\}_{\tau\in[t,T]}$, such that conditionally on the variance and the correlation paths, $(\sigma_\tau^2)_{\tau\in[t,T]}$ and $(\rho_\tau)_{\tau\in[t,T]}$, $\ln\left(\frac{S_T}{S_t L_{t,T}}\right)$ is normally distributed under the risk neutral probability,

$$\ln\left(\frac{S_T}{S_t L_{t,T}}\right) = r(T-t) - \frac{1}{2}\int_t^T \sigma_\tau^2\left(1-\rho_\tau^2\right)d\tau + \int_t^T \sigma_\tau\sqrt{1-\rho_\tau^2}dZ_\tau,$$

with

$$\mathbb{E}_t\left[\ln\left(\frac{S_T}{S_t L_{t,T}}\right) \mid \left(\sigma_\tau^2,\rho_\tau\right)_{\tau\in[t,T]}\right] = r(T-t) - \frac{1}{2}(T-t)\tilde{V}^{\rho}_{t,T}$$

$$var_t\left[\ln\left(\frac{S_T}{S_t L_{t,T}}\right) \mid \left(\sigma_\tau^2,\rho_\tau\right)_{\tau\in[t,T]}\right] = \int_t^T \sigma_\tau^2 d\tau = (T-t)\tilde{V}^{\rho}_{t,T}.$$

The fourth line follows by the same arguments leading to eq. (11.A1).

11.C.3 Smile Analytics

We develop the approximation stated in eq. (11.38). The assumption is that the asset price and its volatility solve eqs. (11.37), with the Brownians W and W_σ being uncorrelated such that the market price of the option is that generated by the Hull and White equation (11.53). By definition, the Black–Scholes implied volatility, IV, satisfies

$$C_t^{\$} = \mathbb{E}_t[C_{\mathrm{BS}}(S,T-t,K;(\tilde{V}_{t,T}^{1/2})] = C_{\mathrm{BS}}(S,T-t;\mathrm{IV}(X,T-t)), \quad X \equiv \ln\frac{S_t e^{r(T-t)}}{K}. \tag{11.A2}$$

Let $\mu_V(t) = \mathbb{E}_t(\tilde{V}_{t,T}^{1/2})$ be the expected average volatility, and consider a Taylor's second-order expansion of the Black–Scholes function about $\mu_V(t)$,

$$\begin{aligned}&\mathbb{E}_t[C_{\mathrm{BS}}(S,T-t,K;\tilde{V}_{t,T}^{1/2})]\\ &\approx C_{\mathrm{BS}}(S,T-t,K;\mu_V^{1/2}(t)) + \frac{1}{2}\left.\frac{\partial^2 C_{\mathrm{BS}}(S,T-t;K,\sqrt{V})}{\partial\sqrt{V}^2}\right|_{\sqrt{V}=\mu_V(t)} var_t(\tilde{V}_{t,T}^{1/2})\end{aligned}$$

and

$$\begin{aligned}&C_{\mathrm{BS}}(S,T-t;\mathrm{IV}(X,T-t))\\ &\approx C_{\mathrm{BS}}(S,T-t,K;\sqrt{\mu_V(t)}) + \left.\frac{\partial C_{\mathrm{BS}}(S,T-t;K,\sqrt{V})}{\partial\sqrt{V}}\right|_{\sqrt{V}=\mu_V(t)}(\mathrm{IV}(X,T-t) - \mu_V(t)).\end{aligned}$$

Plugging these two approximations into eq. (11.A2) leaves

$$\mathrm{IV}(X,T-t) \approx \mu_V(t) + \frac{1}{2}\left.\frac{\partial^2 C_{\mathrm{BS}}(S,T-t;K,\sigma)/\partial\sigma^2}{\partial C_{\mathrm{BS}}(S,T-t;K,\sigma)/\partial\sigma}\right|_{\sigma=\mu_V(t)} var_t(\tilde{V}_{t,T}^{1/2}). \tag{11.A3}$$

The vega, $\partial C_{BS}/\partial\sigma$, and the volga, $\partial^2 C_{BS}/\partial\sigma^2$, for the Black–Scholes model are well known. They are

$$\frac{\partial C_{BS}(S,T-t;\sigma)}{\partial\sigma}=S\sqrt{T-t}\phi\left(\frac{X+\frac{1}{2}\sigma^2(T-t)}{\sigma\sqrt{T-t}}\right)$$

$$\frac{\partial^2 C_{BS}(S,T-t;K,\sigma)}{\partial\sigma^2}=\left(\frac{X^2-\left(\frac{1}{2}\sigma^2(T-t)\right)^2}{\sigma^3(T-t)}\right)\frac{\partial C_{BS}(S,T-t;K,\sigma)}{\partial\sigma}.$$

Replacing these expressions into eq. (11.A3) yields the approximation in eq. (11.38) of the main text.

Appendix 11.D Local volatility

The arguments underlying the derivation of the local volatility function in this appendix rely on Derman and Kani (1994), Dumas (1995), and Britten-Jones and Neuberger (2000). In all the following proofs, all expectations are taken to be conditional on $\mathbb{F}_t$, but to simplify notation, we write $\mathbb{E}(\cdot|\cdot)\equiv\mathbb{E}(\cdot|\cdot,\mathbb{F}_t)$.

Proof of eqs. (11.83) and (11.93). We first derive eq. (11.83), a result encompassing eq. (11.80). We assume that, under the risk neutral probability, the stock price is a solution to

$$\frac{dS_t}{S_t}=rdt+\sigma_t d\hat{W}_t, \tag{11.A4}$$

where σ_t is some $\mathbb{F}_t$-adapted process. For example, $\sigma_t\equiv\sigma(S_t,t)\cdot v_t$ for all t, where v_t is solution to the second of eqs. (11.82). Next, we assume that we are given a continuum of option prices $C_\$(K,T)$ along the two dimensions of strikes K and time to maturities T. We want to match the prediction of the model with the market prices,

$$C_\$(K,T)=e^{-r(T-t)}\mathbb{E}_t(S_T-K)^+, \tag{11.A5}$$

where S_τ is solution to eq. (11.A4).

Let us expand the term inside the expectation on the RHS of eq. (11.A5) with respect to time to maturity for fixed K,

$$d_T(S_T-K)^+=\left(\mathbb{I}_{S_T\geq K}rS_T+\frac{1}{2}\delta(S_T-K)\sigma_T^2S_T^2\right)dT+\mathbb{I}_{S_T\geq K}\sigma_TS_Td\hat{W}_T,$$

where δ is the Dirac's delta. By using the identity $(S_T-K)^++K\mathbb{I}_{S_T\geq K}=S_T\mathbb{I}_{S_T\geq K}$ and the properties of Dirac's delta (see, e.g., appendix 4.A in chapter 4),

$$\frac{d\mathbb{E}_t(S_T-K)^+}{dT}=r\left(\mathbb{E}_t(S_T-K)^++K\mathbb{E}_t\left(\mathbb{I}_{S_T\geq K}\right)\right)+\frac{1}{2}\mathbb{E}_t\left(\delta(S_T-K)\sigma_T^2S_T^2\right),$$

where

$$\mathbb{E}_t\left(\delta(S_T-K)\sigma_T^2S_T^2\right)=\iint\delta(S_T-K)\sigma_T^2S_T^2\underbrace{\phi_T(\sigma_T|S_T)\phi_T(S_T)}_{\equiv\text{ joint density of }(\sigma_T,S_T)}dS_Td\sigma_T$$

$$
\begin{aligned}
&= \int \sigma_T^2 \left(\int \delta (S_T - K) S_T^2 \phi_T (S_T) \phi_T (\sigma_T | S_T) dS_T \right) d\sigma_T \\
&= K^2 \phi_T (K) \int \sigma_T^2 \phi_T (\sigma_T | S_T = K) d\sigma_T \\
&\equiv K^2 \phi_T (K) \mathbb{E}_t \left(\sigma_T^2 \middle| S_T = K \right),
\end{aligned}
$$

such that

$$
\begin{aligned}
& e^{-r(T-t)} \frac{d\mathbb{E}_t (S_T - K)^+}{dT} \\
&= r \left(e^{-r(T-t)} \mathbb{E}_t (S_T - K)^+ + K e^{-r(T-t)} \mathbb{E}_t \left(\mathbb{I}_{S_T \geq K} \right) \right) \\
&\quad + \frac{1}{2} K^2 e^{-r(T-t)} \phi_T (K) \mathbb{E} \left(\sigma_T^2 \middle| S_T = K \right). \qquad (11.A6)
\end{aligned}
$$

Next, differentiate both sides of eq. (11.A5) with respect to T,

$$
\frac{\partial}{\partial T} C_\$ (K, T) = -r C_\$ (K, T) + e^{-r(T-t)} \frac{\partial \mathbb{E}_t (S_T - K)^+}{\partial T} \qquad (11.A7)
$$

and twice with respect to K,

$$
\frac{\partial}{\partial K} C_\$ (K, T) = -e^{-r(T-t)} \mathbb{E}_t \left(\mathbb{I}_{S_T \geq K} \right), \quad \frac{\partial^2 C_\$ (K, T)}{\partial K^2} = e^{-r(T-t)} \phi_T (K), \qquad (11.A8)
$$

where the second relation is simply the famous relation in eq. (11.29) of the main text. Replacing eqs. (11.A5), (11.A7), and (11.A8) into eq. (11.A6) leaves

$$
\frac{\partial}{\partial T} C_\$ (K, T) = -rK \frac{\partial C_\$ (K, T)}{\partial K} + \frac{1}{2} K^2 \frac{\partial^2 C_\$ (K, T)}{\partial K^2} \mathbb{E} \left(\sigma_T^2 \middle| S_T = K \right). \qquad (11.A9)
$$

This is

$$
\mathbb{E} \left[\sigma_T^2 \middle| S_T = K \right] = 2 \frac{\dfrac{\partial C_\$ (K, T)}{\partial T} + rK \dfrac{\partial C_\$ (K, T)}{\partial K}}{K^2 \dfrac{\partial^2 C_\$ (K, T)}{\partial K^2}} \equiv \sigma_{\text{loc}}^2 (K, T). \qquad (11.A10)
$$

That is, if eq. (11.A5) holds true, volatility must be restricted to satisfy eq. (11.A10). As an example, let $\sigma_t \equiv \sigma (S_t, t) \cdot v_t$, where v_t is solution to the second of eqs. (11.82). Then,

$$
\begin{aligned}
\sigma_{\text{loc}}^2 (K, T) &= \mathbb{E} \left(\sigma_T^2 \middle| S_T = K \right) \\
&= \mathbb{E} \left(\sigma^2 (S_T, T) \cdot v_T^2 \middle| S_T = K \right) \\
&= \sigma^2 (K, T) \mathbb{E} \left(v_T^2 \middle| S_T = K \right) \\
&\equiv \tilde{\sigma}_{\text{loc}}^2 (K, T) \mathbb{E} \left(v_T^2 \middle| S_T = K \right),
\end{aligned}
$$

which proves eq. (11.83).

The converse also holds true. Consider, for example, the case where $v_t \equiv 1$. That is, suppose that $u(x,t;K,T)$ is the solution to the *terminal value problem*,

$$\begin{cases} 0 = u_t + \frac{1}{2}\sigma^2(x,t)\,x^2 u_{xx} + rxu_x - ru, & t \in [0,T] \\ u(x,t;K,T) = (x-K)^+ \end{cases}$$

where x denotes the stock price at expiration. Then, define $C_\$(K,T) \equiv u(x,t;K,T)$ such that, by eq. (11.A10), $C_\$(K,T)$ solves the *initial value problem*,

$$\begin{cases} 0 = -\frac{\partial}{\partial T}C_\$(K,T) - rK\frac{\partial C_\$(K,T)}{\partial K} + \frac{1}{2}K^2\sigma_{\mathrm{loc}}^2(K,T)\frac{\partial^2 C_\$(K,T)}{\partial K^2}, & T>0 \\ C_\$(K,0) = (x-K)^+ \end{cases}$$

where x denotes the initial price. The previous partial differential equation is known as the *Dupire equation*.

Appendix 11.E Spanning and Variance Contracts

We provide proofs of results regarding spanning of derivative payoffs and variance contracts.

Proof of eq. (11.93). We have

$$\begin{aligned} \mathbb{E}_t\left(\sigma_T^2\right) &= \int_0^\infty \mathbb{E}\left(\sigma_T^2 \middle| S_T = K\right)\phi_T(K)\,dK \\ &= 2\int_0^\infty \frac{\frac{\partial C_t(K,T)}{\partial T} + rK\frac{\partial C_t(K,T)}{\partial K}}{K^2\frac{\partial^2 C_t(K,T)}{\partial K^2}}\phi_T(K)\,dK \\ &= 2e^{r(T-t)}\int_0^\infty \frac{\frac{\partial C_t(K,T)}{\partial T} + rK\frac{\partial C_t(K,T)}{\partial K}}{K^2}dK, \end{aligned}$$

where the second line follows by eq. (11.A10) and the third line follows by eq. (11.29). □

Proof of eq. (11.95). By a Taylor expansion with remainder, we have that, for any function f smooth enough,

$$\begin{aligned} f(x) &= f(x_0) + f'(x_0)(x-x_0) + \int_{x_0}^{x}(x-t)f''(t)\,dt \\ &= f(x_0) + f'(x_0)(x-x_0) + \int_0^{x_0} f''(t)(t-x)^+\,dt + \int_{x_0}^{\infty} f''(t)(x-t)^+\,dt. \end{aligned} \tag{11.A11}$$

Apply this result to $x = F_T$ and $x_0 = F_t$, where $F_\tau = e^{r(T-\tau)}S_\tau$, the forward rate. Multiplying both sides of the resulting equation by $e^{-r(T-t)}$ and taking expectations yields eq. (11.110) in the main text.

Next, apply eq. (11.A11) to $\ln F_T$,

$$\ln F_T = \ln F_t + \frac{1}{F_t}(F_T - F_t) - \int_0^{F_t} (K - F_T)^+ \frac{1}{K^2} dK - \int_{F_t}^{\infty} (F_T - K)^+ \frac{1}{K^2} dK$$

$$= \ln F_t + \frac{1}{F_t}(F_T - F_t) - \int_0^{F_t} (K - S_T)^+ \frac{1}{K^2} dK - \int_{F_t}^{\infty} (S_T - K)^+ \frac{1}{K^2} dK. \quad (11.A12)$$

Therefore, because $\mathbb{E}_t(F_T) = F_t$,

$$-\mathbb{E}_t\left(\ln \frac{F_T}{F_t}\right) = e^{r(T-t)} \left[\int_0^{F_t} \frac{P_t(K,T)}{K^2} dK + \int_{F_t}^{\infty} \frac{C_t(K,T)}{K^2} dK\right]. \quad (11.A13)$$

Note also that, by Itô's lemma,

$$\mathbb{E}_t\left(\int_t^T \sigma_u^2 du\right) = -2\mathbb{E}_t\left(\ln \frac{F_T}{F_t}\right). \quad (11.A14)$$

Replacing eq. (11.A14) into eq. (11.A13) yields eq. (11.95). □

Remark. The previous results hold when the short-term rate is constant. Dealing with stochastic interest rates requires making reference to the so-called *forward probability*, introduced in chapter 4 (see section 4.5) and more systematically dealt with in many junctures of chapter 13. We shall next highlight some properties of the forward probability, which will allow us to solve for the fair price of variance contracts. Mele and Obayashi (2015) (and some of their works mentioned within) is the earliest reference for this type of problem.

So, suppose that interest rates are stochastic, in that the short-term rate r_τ is another random process satisfying enough regularity conditions to justify the following derivations. Eq. (11.A13) generalizes to

$$-\mathbb{E}_t\left(e^{-\int_t^T r_\tau d\tau} \ln \frac{F_T}{F_t}\right) = -\mathbb{E}_t\left(e^{-\int_t^T r_\tau d\tau}\left(\frac{F_T - F_t}{F_t}\right)\right)$$

$$+ \int_0^{F_t} \frac{P_t(K,T)}{K^2} dK + \int_{F_t}^{\infty} \frac{C_t(K,T)}{K^2} dK. \quad (11.A15)$$

The LHS of eq. (11.A15) can be written as

$$\mathbb{E}_t\left(e^{-\int_t^T r_\tau d\tau} \ln \frac{F_T}{F_t}\right) = P(t,T)\,\mathbb{E}_t\left(\frac{e^{-\int_t^T r_\tau d\tau}}{P(t,T)} \ln \frac{F_T}{F_t}\right) = P(t,T)\,\mathbb{E}_t^{Q^F}\left(\ln \frac{F_T}{F_t}\right), \quad (11.A16)$$

where $\mathbb{E}_t^{Q^F}$ denotes the expectation taken at time t under the forward probability, defined as

$$\left.\frac{dQ_F^T}{dQ}\right|_{\mathbb{F}_T} = \frac{e^{-\int_t^T r_\tau d\tau}}{P(t,T)},$$

and where $\mathbb{F}_T$ is the information set up to time T. Now, the first term on the RHS of eq. (11.A15) is zero as a forward has no value at inception, such that

$$F_t = \mathbb{E}_t\left(\frac{e^{-\int_t^T r_\tau d\tau}}{P(t,T)} F_T\right) = \mathbb{E}_t^{Q^F}(F_T).$$

That is, the forward price is a martingale under the forward probability. Therefore, eq. (11.A14) is now replaced with

$$\mathbb{E}_t^{Q^F}\left(\int_t^T \omega_u^2 du\right) = -2\mathbb{E}_t^{Q^F}\left(\ln\frac{F_T}{F_t}\right), \qquad (11.A17)$$

where ω_t denotes the instantaneous volatility of the forward price. By combining eqs. (11.A15), (11.A16), and (11.A17), we obtain

$$\begin{aligned}\mathbb{E}_t^{Q^F}\left(\int_t^T \omega_u^2 du\right) &= \mathbb{E}_t\left(e^{-\int_t^T r_\tau d\tau}\int_t^T \omega_u^2 du\right)\\ &= \frac{2}{P(t,T)}\left[\int_0^{F_t}\frac{P_t(K,T)}{K^2}dK + \int_{F_t}^{\infty}\frac{C_t(K,T)}{K^2}dK\right].\end{aligned}$$

Finally, we claim that the fair value of a *forward* variance swap is model free. Indeed, note that the payoff of a forward variance contract is

$$\int_t^T \omega_u^2 du - \mathbb{P}_{\text{var}}(t,T),$$

such that the zero value condition at inception,

$$0 = \mathbb{E}_t\left[e^{-\int_t^T r_\tau d\tau}\left(\int_t^T \omega_u^2 du - \mathbb{P}_{\text{var}}(t,T)\right)\right],$$

leads to

$$\mathbb{P}_{\text{var}}(t,T) = \frac{1}{P(t,T)}\mathbb{E}_t\left(e^{-\int_t^T r_\tau d\tau}\int_t^T \omega_u^2 du\right) = \mathbb{E}_t^{Q^F}\left(\int_t^T \omega_u^2 du\right).$$

Proof that $(\hat{\theta}_\tau, \hat{\psi}_\tau)$ in eq. (11.100) is self-financed. For a portfolio strategy to be self-financed, we need to have $\psi_\tau M_\tau = V_\tau - \theta_\tau S_\tau$ and $dV_\tau = \theta_\tau dS_\tau + \psi_\tau dM_\tau$ or

$$dV_\tau = \theta_\tau S_\tau \frac{dS_\tau}{S_\tau} + \psi_\tau M_\tau \frac{dM_\tau}{M_\tau} = \theta_\tau S_\tau\left(\frac{dS_\tau}{S_\tau} - r d\tau\right) + rV_\tau d\tau, \qquad (11.A18)$$

where the second line follows by $\psi_\tau M_\tau = V_\tau - \theta_\tau S_\tau$. With $(\hat{\theta}_\tau, \hat{\psi}_\tau)$, we have that

$$\begin{aligned}d\hat{V}_\tau &= \hat{\theta}_\tau dS_\tau + \hat{\psi}_\tau dM_\tau\\ &= \frac{M_\tau}{M_T}\frac{dS_\tau}{S_\tau} + \hat{\psi}_\tau M_\tau r d\tau\end{aligned}$$

$$= \frac{M_\tau}{M_T}\frac{dS_\tau}{S_\tau} + \left(\hat{V}_\tau - \frac{M_\tau}{M_T}\right) r d\tau$$

$$= \frac{M_\tau}{M_T}\left(\frac{dS_\tau}{S_\tau} - r d\tau\right) + r\hat{V}_\tau d\tau, \tag{11.A19}$$

where we have used the portfolio weights in eq. (11.100) and the expression for the portfolio value $\hat{V}$ in eq. (11.101). Eq. (11.A19) is the same as eq. (11.A18) once we use the portfolio weight $\hat{\theta}_\tau$ in eq. (11.100). Therefore, $(\hat{\theta}_\tau, \hat{\psi}_\tau)$ is self-financed. □

References

Bajeux-Besnainou, I., and J. C. Rochet (1996). "Dynamic Spanning: Are Options an Appropriate Instrument?" *Mathematical Finance* 6, 1–16.

Bakshi, G., N. Kapadia, and D. Madan (2003). "Stock Return Characteristics, Skew Laws, and Differential Pricing of Individual Equity Options." *Review of Financial Studies* 16, 101–143.

Bakshi, G., and D. Madan (2000). "Spanning and Derivative Security Evaluation." *Journal of Financial Economics* 55, 205–238.

Ball, C. A., and A. Roma (1994). "Stochastic Volatility Option Pricing." *Journal of Financial and Quantitative Analysis* 29, 589–607.

Bank for International Settlements (2018). "International Banking and Financial Market Developments." *BIS Quarterly Review*, March.

Bates, D. S. (2012). "U.S. Stock Market Crash Risk, 1926–2010." *Journal of Financial Economics* 105, 229–259.

Ben-David, I., F. Franzoni, and R. Moussawi (2018). "Do ETFs Increase Volatility?" *Journal of Finance* 73, 2471–2535.

Bergman, Y. Z., B. D. Grundy, and Z. Wiener (1996). "General Properties of Option Prices." *Journal of Finance* 51, 1573–1610.

Black, F. (1976a). "The Pricing of Commodity Contracts." *Journal of Financial Economics* 3, 167–179.

Black, F. (1976b). "Studies of Stock Price Volatility Changes." *Proceedings of the 1976 Meeting of the American Statistical Association*, 177–181. Washington, DC: American Statistical Association.

Black, F., and M. Scholes (1973). "The Pricing of Options and Corporate Liabilities." *Journal of Political Economy* 81, 637–659.

Bollerslev, T. (1986). "Generalized Autoregressive Conditional Heteroskedasticity." *Journal of Econometrics* 31, 307–327.

Bollerslev, T., R. Engle, and D. Nelson (1994). "ARCH Models." In *Handbook of Econometrics* (Vol. 4), edited by D. McFadden and R. Engle, 2959–3038. Amsterdam: North Holland.

Brady, N. (1988). *Report of the Presidential Task Force on Market Mechanisms*. Washington, DC: US Government Printing Office.

Britten-Jones, M., and A. Neuberger (2000). "Option Prices, Implied Price Processes and Stochastic Volatility." *Journal of Finance* 55, 839–866.

Brunnermeier, M. K., and L. H. Pedersen (2009). "Market Liquidity and Funding Liquidity." *Review of Financial Studies* 22, 2201–2238.

Carr, P., and D. Madan (2001). "Optimal Positioning in Derivative Securities." *Quantitative Finance* 1, 19–37.

Carr, P., and L. Wu (2006): "A Tale of Two Indices." *Journal of Derivatives* 13, 13–29.

CFTC and SEC. See US Commodity Futures Trading Commission and US Securities and Exchange Commission.

Christie, A. A. (1982). "The Stochastic Behavior of Common Stock Variances: Value, Leverage, and Interest Rate Effects." *Journal of Financial Economics* 10, 407–432.

Clark, P. K. (1973). "A Subordinated Stochastic Process Model with Fixed Variance for Speculative Prices." *Econometrica* 41, 135–156.

Cole, C. (2015). "Volatility and the Allegory of the Prisoner's Dilemma." Austin, TX: Artemis Capital Management, white paper, October.

Cox, J. C., J. E. Ingersoll, and S. A. Ross (1985). "A Theory of the Term Structure of Interest Rates." *Econometrica* 53, 385–407.

Cox, J. C., S. A. Ross, and M. Rubinstein (1979). "Option Pricing: A Simplified Approach." *Journal of Financial Economics* 7, 229–263.

Danielsson, J., H. S. Shin, and J.-P. Zigrand (2012). "Endogenous Extreme Events and the Dual Role of Prices." *Annual Review of Economics* 4, 111–129.

Demeterfi, K., E. Derman, M. Kamal, and J. Zou (1999). "More Than You Ever Wanted To Know About Volatility Swaps." New York: Goldman Sachs, Quantitative Strategies Research Notes, March.

Derman, E. (1998). "Stochastic Implied Trees: Arbitrage Pricing with Stochastic Term and Strike Structure of Volatility." *International Journal of Theoretical and Applied Finance* 1, 61–110.

Derman, E., and J. Kani (1994). "Riding on a Smile." *Risk* 7, 32–39.

Derman, E., and M. B. Miller (2016). *The Volatility Smile*. Hoboken, NJ: Wiley.

Dumas, B. (1995). "The Meaning of the Implicit Volatility Function in Case of Stochastic Volatility." Unpublished working paper, INSEAD, Fontainebleu, France.

Dupire, B. (1994). "Pricing with a Smile." *Risk* 7, 18–20.

Dupire, B. (2006). "Model Free Results on Volatility Derivatives." Unpublished manuscript, Bloomberg, NY.

Egloff, D., M. Leippold, and L. Wu (2010). "Valuation and Optimal Investing in Variance Swaps." *Journal of Financial and Quantitative Analysis* 45, 1279–1310.

El Karoui, N., M. Jeanblanc-Picqué, and S. Shreve (1998). "Robustness of the Black and Scholes Formula." *Mathematical Finance* 8, 93–126.

Engle, R. F. (1982). "Autoregressive Conditional Heteroskedasticity with Estimates of the Variance of United Kingdom Inflation." *Econometrica* 50, 987–1008.

Fama, E. (1965). "The Behaviour of Stock Market Prices." *Journal of Business* 38, 34–105.

Fama, E. (1970). "Efficient Capital Markets: A Review of Theory and Empirical Work." *Journal of Finance* 25, 383–417.

Fornari, F., and A. Mele (2006). "Approximating Volatility Diffusions with CEV-ARCH Models." *Journal of Economic Dynamics and Control* 30, 931–966.

Frey, R., and A. Stremme (1997). "Market Volatility and Feedback Effects from Dynamic Hedging." *Mathematical Finance* 7, 351–374.

García, D., and Strobl, G. (2011). "Relative Wealth Concerns and Complementarities in Information Acquisition." *Review of Financial Studies* 24, 169–207.

Gatheral, J. (2006). *The Volatility Surface: A Practioner's Guide*. New York: John Wiley and Sons.

Gennotte, G., and H. Leland (1990). "Market Liquidity, Hedging and Crashes." *American Economic Review* 80, 999–1021.

Hakansson, N. (1979). "The Fantastic World of Finance: Progress and the Free Lunch." *Journal of Financial and Quantitative Analysis* 14, 717–734.

Heston, S. L. (1993a). "Invisible Parameters in Option Prices." *Journal of Finance* 48, 933–947.

Heston, S. L. (1993b). "A Closed-Form Solution for Options with Stochastic Volatility with Applications to Bond and Currency Options." *Review of Financial Studies* 6, 327–344.

Hicks, J. R. (1939). *Value and Capital*. Oxford: Oxford University Press.

Hull, J., and A. White (1987). "The Pricing of Options with Stochastic Volatilities." *Journal of Finance* 42, 281–300.

Karatzas, I. (1997). *Lectures on the Mathematics of Finance*. Providence, RI: American Mathematical Society, CRM Monograph Series, Vol. 8.

Keynes, J. M. (1930). *A Treatise on Money: The Applied Theory of Money*. London: Macmillan.

Kirilenko, A., A. S. Kyle, M. Samadi, and T. Tuzun (2017). "The Flash Crash: High Frequency Trading in an Electronic Market." *Journal of Finance* 72, 967–998.

Mandelbrot, B. (1963). "The Variation of Certain Speculative Prices." *Journal of Business* 36, 394–419.

Mele, A. (1998). *Dynamiques non linéaires, volatilité et équilibre*. Paris: Editions Economica.

Mele, A., and F. Fornari (2000). *Stochastic Volatility in Financial Markets. Crossing the Bridge to Continuous Time*. Boston, MA: Kluwer Academic.

Mele, A., and Y. Obayashi (2015). *The Price of Fixed Income Market Volatility*. Springer Finance Series. New York: Springer Verlag.

Mele, A., and F. Sangiorgi (2015). "Uncertainty, Information Acquisition and Price Swings in Asset Markets." *Review of Economic Studies* 82, 1533–1567.

Mencía, J., and E. Sentana (2013). "Valuation of VIX Derivatives." *Journal of Financial Economics* 108, 367–391.

Merton, R. C. (1973). "Theory of Rational Option Pricing." *Bell Journal of Economics and Management Science* 4, 637–654.

Merton, R. C. (1976). "Option Pricing When Underlying Stock Returns Are Discontinuous." *Journal of Financial Economics* 3, 125–144.

Nelson, D. B. (1990). "ARCH Models as Diffusion Approximations." *Journal of Econometrics* 45, 7–38.

Nelson, D. B. (1991). "Conditional Heteroskedasticity in Asset Returns: A New Approach." *Econometrica* 59, 347–370.

Neuberger, A. (1994). "Hedging Volatility: The Case for a New Contract." *Journal of Portfolio Management* 20, 74–80.

Pagano, M., A. Sánchez Serrano, and J. Zechner (2019). *Can ETFs Contribute to Systemic Risk?* Frankfurt am Main: European Systemic Risk Board, Reports of the Advisory Scientific Committee No. 9, June.

Parkinson, M. (1980). "The Extreme Value Method for Estimating the Variance of the Rate of Returns." *Journal of Business* 53, 61–68.

Platen, E., and M. Schweizer (1998). "On Feedback Effects from Hedging Derivatives." *Mathematical Finance* 8, 67–84.

Renault, E. (1997). "Econometric Models of Option Pricing Errors."In *Advances in Economics and Econometrics* (Vol. 3), edited by D. Kreps and K. Wallis, 223–278. Cambridge: Cambridge University Press.

Renault, E., and N. Touzi (1996). "Option Hedging and Implied Volatilities in a Stochastic Volatility Model." *Mathematical Finance* 6, no. 3, 279–302.

Romano, M., and N. Touzi (1997). "Contingent Claims and Market Completeness in a Stochastic Volatility Model." *Mathematical Finance* 7, 399–412.

Rubinstein, M. (1994). "Implied Binomial Trees." *Journal of Finance* 49, 771–818.

Scott, L. (1987). "Option Pricing when the Variance Changes Randomly: Theory, Estimation, and an Application." *Journal of Financial and Quantitative Analysis* 22, 419–438.

Stuart, A., and K. Ord (2010). *Kendall's Advanced Theory of Statistics*. Vol. 1, *Distribution Theory*. 6th ed. Oxford: Wiley.

Sushko, V., and Turner, G. (2018), "The Equity Market Turbulence of 5 February: The Role of Exchange-Traded Volatility Products." *BIS Quarterly Review*, March.

Tauchen, G., and M. Pitts (1983). "The Price Variability-Volume Relationship on Speculative Markets." *Econometrica* 51, 485–505.

Taylor, S. (1986). *Modeling Financial Time Series*. Chichester, UK: Wiley.

US Commodity Futures Trading Commission and US Securities and Exchange Commission (2010). *Findings Regarding the Market Events of May 6, 2010: Report of the Staffs of the CFTC and SEC to the Joint Advisory Committee on Emerging Regulatory Issues*. Washington, DC: CFTC and SEC. https://www.sec.gov/files/marketevents-report.pdf.

Vasicek, O. (1977). "An Equilibrium Characterization of the Term Structure." *Journal of Financial Economics* 5, 177–188.

Veldkamp, L. (2006). "Media Frenzies in Markets for Financial Information." *American Economic Review* 96, 577–601.

Wiggins, J. (1987). "Option Values and Stochastic Volatility: Theory and Empirical Estimates." *Journal of Financial Economics* 19, 351–372.

12

Engineering of Fixed Income Securities

12.1 Introduction

Fixed income markets represent one of the largest segments of the whole capital market universe. These markets help financial institutions reshape the risk profile acquired over their intermediation activities and involve corporate and government bonds, loans, mortgages, or instruments such as interest rate swaps and related derivatives. A pension fund may have liabilities that are difficult to hedge without the ability to access an interest rate swap market. Likewise, a derivative house may wish to create, evaluate, and hedge difficult products originated by specific needs of the clientèle.

According to statistics reported by the Bank for International Settlements, the notional amount outstanding in the global OTC derivatives market totaled nearly \$600 trillion in 2019. Of this notional amount, foreign exchange contracts contributed to about \$92 trillion, equity-linked contracts to \$6.8 trillion, and finally, interest rate derivatives to about \$449 trillion. These figures tell us that OTC markets are predominantly about interest rate derivatives. In the introduction to chapter 13, we provide additional statistics that specify which products are particularly important in the fixed income space. Interest rate products are also listed on exchanges such as Chicago Mercantile Exchange, Eurex, or NYSE LIFFE. The Bank for International Settlements reports that, in the dollar case for 2019, there were notional values for futures contracts of approximately \$35 trillion in the interest rate space and \$272 billion in the foreign exchange; in the same year, the corresponding option value was more than \$60 trillion for interest rate contracts and about \$116 billion for foreign exchange.

This chapter is an introduction to fixed income security pricing and paves the way to more advanced discussions in chapter 13. Fixed income securities, such as pure discount bonds, share similarities with equity derivatives. Consider, for example, a default-free bond. It draws value from movements in the underlying risks, that is, the interest rates the market requires to invest at different horizons safely. However, this bond is quite different from conceptually standard derivatives such as equity options. For example, its pricing is challenging as it is tied down to the time value of money. Bond values reflect intertemporal preferences and beliefs of market participants as illustrated many times in part I (see, e.g., chapter 2) and part II (e.g., chapters 8 and 9). Such pricing determinants are unobservable and, importantly, not traded. Thus, we cannot price bonds in a preference-free format, unlike in the instances conducive to the Black–Scholes (1973) formula reviewed in chapter 11 and throughout part I. We now explain how we deal with the pricing of fixed income securities.

12.1.1 No-Arbitrage Models

This chapter reviews models where we can *still* price derivatives written on bond prices and other securities in a preference-free setting. We rely on "no-arbitrage models," which are the fixed income counterparts to the local volatility models reviewed in chapter 11. In this framework, we give up modeling the current security prices in the first place. Rather, we take these prices as given and exploit all the information embedded in them to extract risk neutral probabilities of future price movements. Once risk neutral probabilities are reverse engineered, we can price any interest rate derivative in a preference-free format. "No-arbitrage model" means that the only assumption we are really making is the absence of arbitrage, in addition to standard statistical laws for price movements.

Ho and Lee (1986) developed the first model that illustrates this approach. This model is solved in closed form but relies on unrealistic assumptions and could lead to negative interest rates. We develop a calibration approach based on the extraction of Arrow-Debreu security prices that can accommodate for more realistic interest rate developments. Arrow-Debreu securities are abstract securities that pay off in mutually exclusive states of nature, as explained in part I (see, e.g., chapter 2), thus providing information regarding the risk neutral probability of the events in which they specifically pay off. While these assets are not tradable, we can extract their shadow value from the price of fixed income securities predicted by a model; we can then use these extracted values and price any interest rate derivative.

We center around these themes that we illustrate through simple numerical applications, including the pricing of interest rate derivatives such as options on bonds, swaps, caps, and callable or convertible bonds, emphasizing the joint behavior of derivative prices and the underlying asset price; for example, the derivative price predicted by a given model can tell us whether the underlying assets is mispriced. We rely on a discrete time analytical framework and, in particular, on the "implied binomial trees" utilized in chapter 11 to model equity derivatives. Chapter 13 deals with more advanced topics in interest rate modeling and derivative evaluation, including the empirical motivation underlying them as well as a systematic analysis through continuous time methods. Finally, this chapter does not cover credit risk, which is the focus of chapter 14.

12.1.2 Relative Pricing in Fixed Income Markets

While current bond prices cannot be given a preference-free representation, we may still aim to price interest rate derivatives in a preference-free fashion. The keyword is "relative pricing," that is, the situation in which we price a number of assets given the price of others while ensuring absence of arbitrage, as explained in many previous junctures of this book. Pricing options on traded assets is in general quite a different matter than pricing the underlying assets in the first place. Even in the equity case, we try to evaluate an option, say, in a preference-free fashion, even if the underlying asset price is not preference free.

By "preference free," we refer to the possibility to extract risk neutral probabilities, or Arrow-Debreu prices, from the price of already traded assets and price derivatives written on the states spanned by the extracted Arrow-Debreu prices.

We wish to achieve similar objectives in the fixed income space, although the task is more challenging. Consider, for example, the Black–Scholes formula. The logic leading to it cannot be exactly applied to evaluate fixed income securities. Indeed, the Black–Scholes model relies on the assumption of a constant volatility of the underlying price. In the context of interest rate derivatives, the volatility of the underlying asset price depends, instead, on the maturity of the underlying asset price, as it tends to zero as the time to maturity goes to zero.

More generally, we shall explain that pricing and hedging interest rate derivatives requires a model describing developments of the whole yield curve while at the same time ensuring the absence of arbitrage. An important objective of this chapter and chapter 13 is to ensure that the dynamics of the "pricers" under the risk neutral probability (e.g., the dynamics of the short-term rate) do not depend on risk aversion corrections. The reader who is impatient about being referred to a concrete illustration of these somewhat surprising statements is referred to eq. (12.43) in this chapter and the discussion around it or, in general, to chapter 13 (see section 13.7) where we describe the details of more advanced models such as the celebrated Heath, Jarrow, and Morton (1992) model.

12.1.3 Many Evaluation Paradigms

After reading this introductory chapter, we may find that there are many methods and models available for pricing interest rate derivatives. But derivatives houses do really have dozens of models with different houses possibly asking for different prices relating to the same product. This circumstance needs not be an arbitrage opportunity. Rate markets are typically OTC of the type studied in part II of this book (see chapter 10). Indeed, this chapter provides stylized examples of markets with different derivative prices predicted by models that match the same set of initially given market prices. Market incompleteness and segmentation may be responsible for these interesting features.

With dozens of methods available to price fixed income products, we do not see the emergence of a "single" model to price all of the extant fixed income products. Typically, each derivative house has its own proprietary models, with each of these models possibly targeting to different goals. For example, a bank might display a preference for a certain type of model as a result of (i) its culture and history or (ii) the particular business it is pursuing. To illustrate, chapter 13 explains that interest rate options such as "caps" may be conveniently evaluated based on the so called "market model" (see section 13.9). However, we will also explain that the adoption of a market model for caps does not lead to closed-form solutions for the price of a "swaption." That is, we may either price caps or swaptions in closed form but not both, and numerical methods are needed to price either caps or swaptions in order to be consistent with the market model. A preference for closed-form solutions for caps or swaptions depends on how exposed we are to these products. This is a simple example to illustrate how modeling choices may rely on very practical commercial trade-offs.

12.1.4 Plan of the Chapter

The chapter is organized as follows. Sections 12.2 and 12.3 develop basic definitions underlying fixed income securities, such as interest rate and market conventions, duration, convexity, and also provide introductory details regarding basic hedging and trading strategies.

Section 12.4 is the first section that deal with models fitting the initial yield curve without errors, which rely on binomial trees. We have two fundamental ways to achieve this goal. As for the first one, developed in section 12.4, we freeze "scenarios"—that is, the values taken by the short-term rate on the branches of a tree—and search for the risk neutral probabilities such that the prices predicted by the model agree with the market. As for the second, we fix risk neutral probabilities and search for scenarios where the model and the market are the same.

Sections 12.5 deals with the second approach, which constitutes the essence of the Ho and Lee (1986) model. But we also consider situations that go beyond this model, situations where we search for both probabilities and short-term rate scenarios that make models consistent with the markets. These situations are quite complex and necessitate a general framework of analysis, developed in section 12.6. We rely on the notion of Arrow-Debreu securities to implement calibration along these lines.

Sections 12.7 and 12.8 conclude this chapter through discussions of a number of additional applications of this chapter's methodology. Sections 12.7 deals with numerical examples and illustrates how to evaluate bonds that embed options to call and to convert (these contracts will receive a more systematic theoretical treatment in the following chapters). Section 12.8 contains a succinct description of the pricing of fed funds futures and how this pricing problem is used in practice to extract risk-adjusted probabilities of future movements in Federal Reserve interest rate targets.

12.2 Markets and Interest Rate Conventions

12.2.1 Markets for Interest Rates

We describe four main types of markets for interest rates: (i) the London Interbank Offer Rate (LIBOR), (ii) federal funds (known as fed funds), (iii) the Treasury, and (iv) repurchase agreements (repos). We briefly survey these markets and then review how to extract potentially useful information from them while constructing spreads.

12.2.1.1 LIBOR and the fed funds rate

Financial institutions lend to one another at maturities that range from just overnight to one year at a given currency. The LIBOR rate reflects an estimate of the rate at which financial institutions expect to borrow in these markets. It is an average indicative quote of the interbank lending market. It was once determined as follows. Each day, the British Bankers' Association surveyed a panel of major banks about the rate each of these banks expected to be charged by other banks for borrowing needs for a given maturity and a given currency. The four highest and the four lowest rates of these banks reports were ignored, and the remaining reports were aggregated for a number of currencies. At the time of writing, LIBOR is calculated by the Intercontinental Exchange in five currencies and published by Thompson Reuters. LIBOR is expected to be phased out shortly and replaced in the United States by the Secured Overnight Financing Rate, also known as SOFR. The left panel of figure 12.1 plots the LIBOR referenced to US dollars for a period in which aggregation was essentially the same as that just described.

The LIBOR is a fundamental point of reference to financial institutions, which look at it as an opportunity cost of capital. Moreover, many fixed income instruments are indexed to the LIBOR: forward rate agreements, interest rate swaps, or variable mortgage rates (see chapters 13 and 14). Because the banks submissions over the process of the LIBOR formation do not rely on trades (only on subjective estimates of the cost of capital), there might be incentives for report manipulation biased toward the rates that would make a given bank reap profits over LIBOR-sensitive derivatives, as hypothesized over the LIBOR scandals emerging in June 2012.

12.2.1.2 The federal funds rate

While the LIBOR reflects market conditions inherent the banking system for a given currency, the US fed funds rate more directly links to the liquidity to be deposited within the Federal Reserve. Banks have to maintain reserves with the Federal Reserve to partially back deposits and to clear financial transactions. These transactions involve banks with excess reserves with the Fed (which earn no interest) to banks with reserve deficiencies.

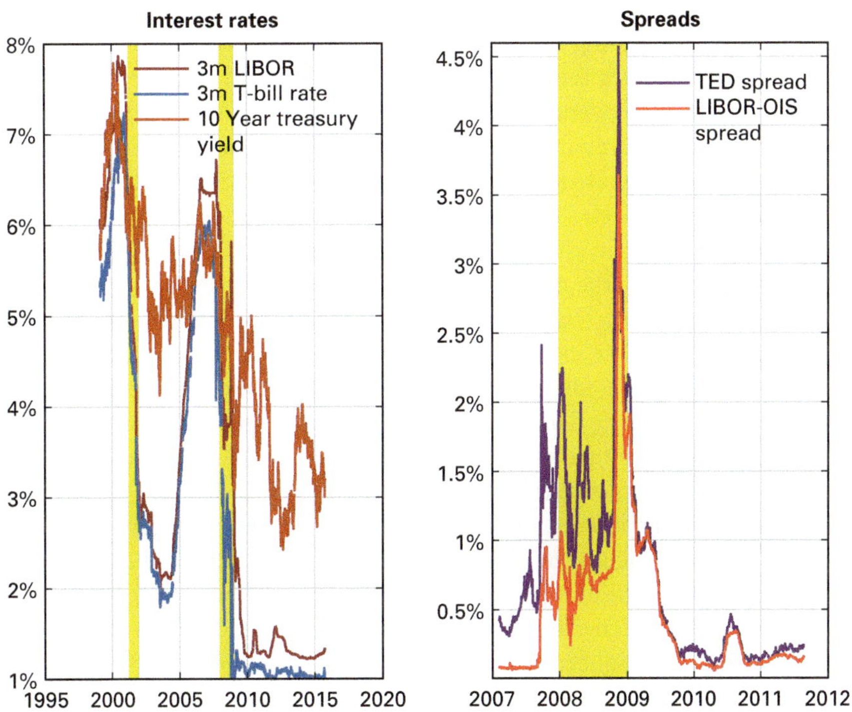

Figure 12.1
Left panel: The 3-month (3m) LIBOR referenced to the US dollar, the 3m T-bill rate, and the 10-year Treasury yield. Right panel: The TED spread (the difference between the 3m LIBOR and the 3m T-bill rate) and the LIBOR-OIS spread (the difference between the 3m LIBOR and the 3m OIS). The shaded areas mark recession periods identified by the National Bureau of Economic Research.

The fed funds rate is the overnight rate at which banks lend these reserves to each other. It is affected by the Federal Reserve Bank of New York and is kept at a rate that fluctuates within a range of the target rate decided by the governors at Federal Open Market Committee meetings. This range is "maintained" through open market operations.

12.2.1.3 *Treasury rate*

The Treasury rate is the rate at which a given government can borrow at a given currency. The left panel of figure 12.1 depicts the time behavior of the interest rate on short-term and long-term US government debt: the 3-month Treasury bill (T-bill) rate and the 10-year Treasury yield.

12.2.1.4 *Repurchase agreement rate*

A repo agreement is a contract by which one counterparty sells some assets to another with the obligation to buy these assets back at some future date. The assets act as collateral. The rate at which such a transaction is made is the repo rate. One-day repo agreements give rise to *overnight repos*. Longer-term agreements give rise to *term repos*.

12.2.1.5 *Interest rate spreads*

Interest rate spreads are the difference between interest rates applied to two different markets. Thus, they have the potential to remove pricing components that are incorporated in both markets, thereby isolating interesting pieces of information.

One important example is the LIBOR-OIS spread–the difference between the 3-month LIBOR minus the 3-month overnight indexed swap (OIS). The OIS rate is the swap rate in a swap agreement of fixed interest rate payments against variable interest rate payments where the variable interest rate is an overnight reference, typically an average, unsecured interbank overnight rate, such as the fed funds rate in the United States, SONIA (Sterling Overnight Index Average) in the United Kingdom, or EONIA in the Euro area.[1] The LIBOR interest rate reflects the monetary policy stance but should also incorporate a premium related to counterparty risk. Instead, the OIS is a mere interest rate swap; as such, it should primarily reflect the monetary policy stance. Therefore, the LIBOR-OIS spread has the potential to isolate credit views on financial institutions. Historically, the LIBOR-OIS spread has behaved quite flat, although it reached high record levels during the 2007 subprime crisis (see the right panel of figure 12.1). Chapter 13 discusses how these issues are dealt with in market practice (see section 13.9.4).

Another example of an interest rate spread commonly used in empirical research is the so-called TED spread, which is the difference between the LIBOR and the T-bill rate. The TED spread captures "flight to quality" effects that typically occur during times of crisis, when treasuries are considered particularly valuable by investors (see the right panel of figure 12.1). Due to this "flight to quality" reason, the TED spread might fail isolate views about developments in the interbank market.

On a historical note, the fed funds rate has been the object of much empirical research. In an attempt to explain how the "credit view" contributes to growth more than Friedman's monetary view, Bernanke and Blinder (1992) show that the fed funds rate

1. See the next chapter (section 13.8) for extensive discussions regarding interest rate swaps.

makes the predicting power of M1 money supply growth insignificant, as we shall review further in chapter 13 (see section 13.3). This finding initially spread enthusiasm about the ability of this rate to explain short-run aggregate fluctuations. However, as surveyed, for example, by Stock and Watson (2003), the explanatory power of the fed funds rate evaporates once we condition on the term spread. Chapter 13 contains discussions regarding the predicting power of the term spread (see section 13.3).

12.2.2 Mathematical Definitions of Interest Rates

12.2.2.1 Simply compounded interest rates

A simply compounded interest rate at time τ for the time interval $[\tau, T]$ is defined as the solution L to the following equation:

$$P(\tau, T) = \frac{1}{1 + (T - \tau) L(\tau, T)}. \tag{12.1}$$

This definition is intuitive and is the most widely used definition in the market practice. For example, LIBOR rates can be defined consistently with eq. (12.1), with $P(\tau, T)$ being the initial investment at τ that delivers \$1 at T. At times, we will write $P_t(T) = P(t, T)$.

12.2.2.2 Yield curves

The *yield to maturity* (YTM) or *spot rate* for some maturity date T is the yield on the zero maturing at T, denoted as $r(t, T)$. It is the solution to the following equation:

$$P(t, T) = \frac{1}{(1 + r(t, T))^T}. \tag{12.2}$$

With semiannual compounding, we have that $P(t, T) = (1 + \frac{r(t,T)}{2})^{-2T}$. In general, if the interest is compounded m times in a year at the annual rate r, then investing for T years yields $\left(1 + \frac{r}{m}\right)^{mT}$. Continuous compounding is obtained by letting $m \to \infty$ in the previous expression, leaving e^{rT}. Therefore, the *continuously compounded* spot rate is obtained as follows:

$$R(t, T) = -\frac{1}{T} \ln P(t, T).$$

It is a sort of "average rate" for investing from time t to time $T > t$. The function, $T \mapsto R(t, T)$, is known as the *yield curve* or as the *term structure of interest rates*.

A related and widely used concept is the *par yield curve*. Let $B(t, T)$ be the time t price of a bond that pays off the principal of \$1 at expiry T, and let $C(t, T)$ at $t+1, t+2, \cdots, T$, be a known sequence of constant coupons such that, in the absence of arbitrage and any other frictions,

$$B(t, T) = C(t, T) \sum_{i=1}^{T-t} P(t, t+i) + P(t, T).$$

Note that $C(t, T)$ is fixed at time t. A par bond is one that quotes at parity, $B(t, T) = 100\%$. The par yield curve is the sequence of coupon rates $C(t, T)$ for T varying, which corresponds to the par:

$$C(t,T)=\frac{B(t,T)-P(t,T)}{\sum_{i=1}^{T-t}P(t,t+i)},\quad B(t,T)=1. \tag{12.3}$$

In other words, the coupon rates $C(t,T)$ have to "adjust" to make the market happy to have the coupon-bearing bond quote at par, $B(t,T)=1$. An interesting interpretation of par yield is the following. Rewrite eq. (12.3) as follows: $1-P(t,T)=C(t,T)\cdot\sum_{i=1}^{T-t}P(t,t+i)$. The RHS of this equation is the present value of the flow of known coupons, $C(t,T)$, receivable at dates $t+1$, $t+2,\cdots,T$. The LHS is the present value of the flow of future and unknown LIBOR rates, $L(t+1-i,t+i)$ for $i=1,2,\cdots,T-1$, receivable at dates $t+1,t+2,\cdots,T$:

$$\sum_{i=1}^{T-t}\mathrm{Val}\left(\frac{1}{P(t+i-1,t+i)}-1\right)=\sum_{i=1}^{T-t}(P(t,t+i-1)-P(t,t+i))=1-P(t,T),$$

where $\mathrm{Val}(x)$ denotes the current price of receiving a random amount of x dollars at the maturity date when these are due and where we have used (i) the definition of the LIBOR rate in eq. (12.1) and (ii) a no-arbitrage relation, proven in chapter 13 (see section 13.2), namely, that the present value of $1/P(t+i-1,t+i)$ paid at $t+i$ is simply $P(t,t+i-1)$.

Therefore, we can interpret the par yield as the fixed rate in a swap contract that costs nothing at origination and where one party will pay another counterparty the fixed rate against the variable LIBOR—a *spot* swap rate. These swap contracts, of which section 12.4.4.2 gives a numerical example, are analyzed in detail in chapter 13 (see section 13.8).

12.2.2.3 *Forward rates*

In a *forward rate agreement* (FRA), two counterparties agree that the interest rate on a given principal (say, \$1) in a future time interval $[T,S]$ will be fixed at some level K. The FRA works as follows: at time T, the first counterparty receives \$1 from the second counterparty; at time $S>T$, the first counterparty pays back $\$[1+1\cdot(S-T)K]$ to the second counterparty. The amount K is agreed upon at time t. Therefore, the FRA makes it possible to lock in future interest rates. We consider simply compounded interest rates because this is the standard market practice.

The amount K for which the current value of the FRA is zero is known as the *simply compounded forward rate* as of time t for the time interval $[T,S]$ and is usually denoted as $F(t,T,S)$. We can rely on absence of arbitrage to express $F(t,T,S)$ in terms of bond prices as follows:[2]

$$\frac{P(t,T)}{P(t,S)}=1+(S-T)F(t,T,S). \tag{12.4}$$

Indeed, an investor in a zero from time t to time S is one who simultaneously makes (i) a *spot* loan from t to T, and (ii) a *forward* loan from T to S. In the absence of arbitrage,

2. Clearly, in the absence of any frictions, we have that $P(t,T)>P(t,S)$ for $S>T$. Indeed, suppose the contrary, that is, $P(t,T)<P(t,S)$. We may then buy the T-bond and sell the S bond, realizing a profit equal to $P(t,S)-P(t,T)$. Come time T, we will receive \$1, which we may reinvest in a riskless MMA until time S and honor the sale of the S bond.

it must be the case that,

$$\underbrace{[1+r(t,S)]^{S-t}}_{\text{zero loan}} = \underbrace{[1+r(t,T)]^{T-t}}_{\text{spot loan}} \times \underbrace{[1+(S-T)F(t,T,S)]}_{\text{forward loan}},$$

where $r(t,S)$ is the (discretely compounded) spot rate at time t for maturity S. Eq. (12.4) follows by the definition of $r(t,S)$ in Eq. (12.2).

Alternatively, consider the following portfolio implemented at time t. Go long one bond maturing at T and short $P(t,T)/P(t,S)$ bonds maturing at S, for the time period $[t,S]$. The initial cost of this portfolio is zero because,

$$-P(t,T)+\frac{P(t,T)}{P(t,S)}P(t,S)=0.$$

At time T, the portfolio yields \$1, which originates from the bond purchased at time t. At time S, we buy the $P(t,T)/P(t,S)$ bonds shorted at t and maturing at the very same S, which obviously costs \$ $P(t,T)/P(t,S)$. The portfolio, therefore, is acting as an FRA: it pays \$1 at time T and $-$\$ $P(t,T)/P(t,S)$ at time S. In addition, the portfolio costs nothing at time t. Therefore, the interest rate implicitly paid in the time interval $[T,S]$ must be equal to the forward rate $F(t,T,S)$ as stated in eq. (12.4).

12.2.3 Yields to Maturity on Coupon-Bearing Bonds

Finally, the YTM $\hat{y}$ on a bond is simply its rate of return. It is the single discount rate equating the present value of the payoff stream to its market price:

$$\hat{y}: B(0,T)=\sum_{i=1}^{n}\frac{C_{t_i}}{(1+\hat{y})^{t_i}}+\frac{1}{(1+\hat{y})^{T}}, \tag{12.5}$$

where $t \equiv 0 \leq t_1 < \cdots < t_n \equiv T$. Eq. (12.5) differs from the price formula $B(0,T) = \sum_{i=1}^{n}\frac{C_{t_i}}{(1+r(0,t_i))^{t_i}}+\frac{1}{(1+r(0,T))^{T}}$ because the same discount rate $\hat{y}$ is used to discount all future payments. Clearly, spot rates coincide with the YTM on a zero, that is, $\hat{y}=R(0,T)$.

Next, suppose that coupon payments are the same for each i—$C_{t_i}=\bar{C}$, say—and that the payment dates are set regularly. Eq. (12.5) then collapses to

$$B(0,T)=\left(1-Z^{T}\right)\frac{\bar{C}}{\hat{y}}+Z^{T}, \quad Z^{T}\equiv(1+\hat{y})^{-T}. \tag{12.6}$$

That is, the price of the coupon-bearing bond, $B(0,T)$, is a combination of the value of a perpetuity, $\frac{\bar{C}}{\hat{y}}$, and that of a zero expiring at T, Z^{T}. For large maturities, the bond value gets closer to that of a perpetuity; for low maturities, the bond value is closer to that of a zero coupon bond. If $\bar{C}>\hat{y}$, $B(0,T)\in\left(1,\frac{\bar{C}}{\hat{y}}\right)$; if $\bar{C}<\hat{y}$, $B(0,T)\in\left(\frac{\bar{C}}{\hat{y}},1\right)$. In the special case where $\bar{C}=\hat{y}$, the bond would quote at par.

The property to quote at par in this context arises as a special case of a more general characteristic of *floating rate bonds*. Floating rate bonds pay coupons equal to LIBOR and would quote at par at their first reset date (see section 13.2 in chapter 13). In the context of this preliminary example, $B(0,T)$ in (12.6) can be understood as the price of a "floating" rate bond in a market without uncertainty: if the coupon it pays is the same as the interest rate we use to discount future cash flows, our coupon-bearing bond is in fact a "floating" rate bond and would therefore need to quote at par.

Finally, note that we didn't specify how the relations introduced so far are obtained as a result of absence of arbitrage, and we didn't cover material regarding how to extract information on the yield curve while solely relying on the quotes of coupon-bearing bonds. Appendix 12.A provides standard material on topics such as "bootstrapping" (a way to determine the yield curve based on coupon-bearing bonds) as well as examples of how to implement trades to profit from temporary arbitrage opportunities arising in connection with misaligned coupon-bearing bond prices.

12.2.4 Accruals, Invoice, and Clean Prices on Coupon-Bearing Bonds

How do we price coupon-bearing bonds that trade at any date after issuance? Naturally, the price to pay at any date is still the present value of future coupons, although we still need to cope with issues relating to the discreteness of coupon payments. In the absence of arbitrage, the price of a coupon-bearing bond is

$$B_t(T_N) = \sum_{i=1}^{N} \frac{C_i}{n} P_t(T_i) + P_t(T_N),$$

where $\frac{C_i}{n}$ is a sequence of coupons paid off over some dates T_i, $i=1,\cdots,N$, and n is the frequency of coupon payments–for example, $n=2$ for semiannual coupon payments, in which case $T_i - T_{i-1} = \frac{1}{2}$, and in general, $T_i - T_{i-1} = \frac{1}{n}$. Finally, we define T_{i_t} as the first available coupon payment date a bondholder would have access to after time t, that is, $t: T_{i_t-1} \leq t < T_{i_t}$.

Due to the discreteness of coupon payments, discontinuities arise: at time T_{i_t}, the coupon is paid off, which leads to a discrete drop in the bond price. Precisely, we have

$$B_t(T_N) = \begin{cases} \frac{C_{i_t}}{n} P_t(T_{i_t}) + \sum_{i=i_t+1}^{N} \frac{C_i}{n} P_t(T_i) + P_t(T_N), & \text{for } t \in [T_{i_t-1}, T_{i_t}) \\ \sum_{i=i_t+1}^{N} \frac{C_i}{n} P_t(T_i) + P_t(T_N), & \text{for } t = T_{i_t} \end{cases} \tag{12.7}$$

such that the discrete price drop at time T_{i_t} is equal to

$$\frac{C_{i_t}}{n} P_t(T_{i_t}) = \frac{C_{i_t}}{n}, \quad \text{for } t = T_{i_t}.$$

It is market practice to avoid considering the effects relating to this drop in value while quoting bond prices. Define the "accruals" as that idealized portion of the coupon payments that occur between T_{i_t-1} and t:

$$\text{Accr}_t \equiv \begin{cases} \frac{C_{i_t}}{n} \frac{t - T_{i_t-1}}{T_{i_t} - T_{i_t-1}} & \text{for } t \in [T_{i_t-1}, T_{i_t}) \\ 0, & \text{for } t = T_{i_t} \end{cases}.$$

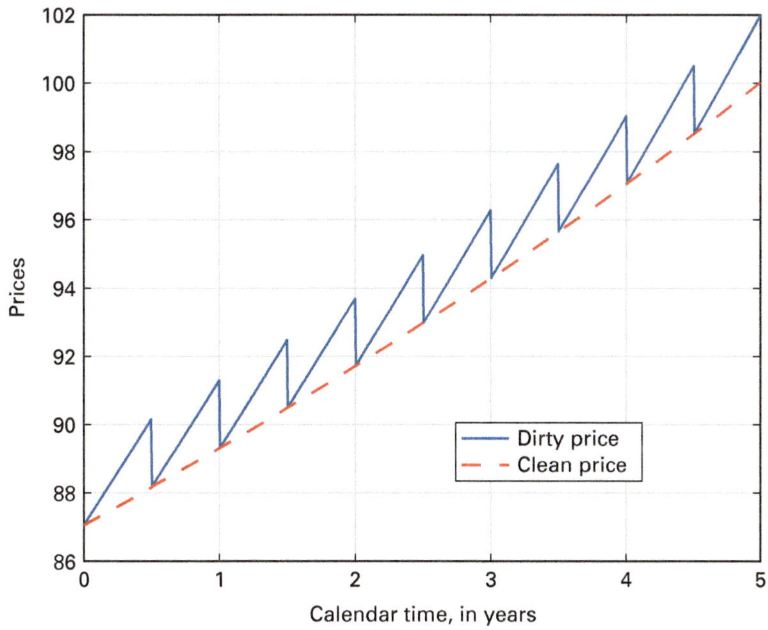

Figure 12.2
Hypothetical evolution of a bond price: Accounting for accruals (dirty) and not (clean).

Define a "clean price" as the difference between the "dirty price" $B_t(T_N)$ and the accruals:

$$B_t^c(T_N) \equiv B_t(T_N) - \text{Accr}_t$$
$$= \frac{C_{i_t}}{n}\left(P_t(T_{i_t}) - \frac{t - T_{i_t-1}}{T_{i_t} - T_{i_t-1}}\right) + \sum_{i=i_t+1}^{N} \frac{C_i}{n} P_t(T_i) + P_t(T_N). \tag{12.8}$$

It is easy to see that the clean price, $B_t^c(T_N)$, does not experience any jumps over the reset dates—the accruals drop by $\frac{C_{i_t}}{n}$, which is precisely the amount the dirty price drops by, such that the first term in the equality in eq. (12.8) is zero. Therefore, dirty and clean prices are the same at each coupon payment.

The dirty price, $B_t(T_N)$, is sometimes referred to as the "full price" or "invoice," reflecting the fact that it is the price at which buyers and sellers have to settle a transaction. US traders typically quote clean prices because dirty prices mainly reflect mechanical adjustments relating to coupon payments, whereas clean prices are more sensitive to changes in the general macroeconomic or the fixed income markets outlook as illustrated by a basic example below. However, on a transaction perspective, the real object of interest is the dirty price: $B_t(T_N)$ is the price to be paid and originating from the bond transaction.

Figure 12.2 depicts the typical shark-tooth pattern of the dirty price in an overly simplified world, where $C_i = 4$, annualized; $n = 2$; the yield curve is flat at the continuously compounded rate $r = 7\%$; and the maturity of the bond is $T = 5$ years. The sharp increase in the dirty price is mainly due to the term $2 \times P_t(T_{i_t})$ in eq. (12.7). This term increases roughly linearly over the payment dates and is much higher than the increase in value of the second term of eq. (12.7). The drop is precisely 2 at each payment date where the dirty price equals the clean price.

The pattern in the picture is of course not unique. For example, the clean price decreases over time when the yield curve is flat at a continuously compounded $r=2\%$. When the level of the yield curve is high, future coupons are heavily discounted such that the value of them is low when time to maturity is high. When the level of the yield curve is low, the current value of future coupons is high, and the clean price converges to 100 from above. We can determine a threshold value for r, say $\bar{r}$, such that the clean price is approximately constant at 100, using eq. (12.6). Because we assume the yield curve is flat at r continuously compounded and $n=2$, we need to find $r: e^{\bar{r}}=(1+\frac{\hat{y}}{2})^2$, with $\hat{y}=2\%$, whence $\bar{r}=3.96\%$.

12.3 Duration, Convexity Hedging, and Trading

The risk of a default-free bond is that the future spot rate could change. In other words, the bond's required return (i.e., the YTM) can obviously change in the future. Consider the definition of YTM $\hat{y}$ in eq. (12.5), and introduce the following function:

$$B(y;T) \equiv \sum_{i=1}^{n} \frac{C_{t_i}}{(1+y)^{t_i}} + \frac{1}{(1+y)^T}. \tag{12.9}$$

This function "mimics" how the market price $B(T)$ would behave after the initial YTM $\hat{y}$ changes to some value y and naturally is such that $B(\hat{y};T)=B(T)$. The function $y \mapsto B(y;T)$ is thus the simplest bond pricing model we could even formulate. It is perhaps too simple as it does not rely on absence of arbitrage. Nevertheless, we can use this very preliminary model and say something about interest rate risk.

We define a measure of risk of the bond based on the *sensitivity* of the hypothetical bond price $B(y;T)$ with respect to changes in y. We answer the following question: What happens to the hypothetical bond price $B(y;T)$ once we perturb the one rate $\hat{y}$ that discounts all the payoffs? The sensitivity we are dealing with is simply the first partial of the "bond pricing formula" in eq. (12.9) with respect to y,

$$B_y(y;T) = -\frac{1}{1+y}\left[\sum_{i=1}^{n} \frac{t_i \cdot C_{t_i}}{(1+y)^{t_i}} + \frac{T \cdot 1}{(1+y)^T}\right],$$

where the subscript denotes a partial derivative, that is, $B_y(y;T)=\frac{\partial}{\partial y}B(y;T)$. The sensitivity, $B_y(y;T)$, is the tangent to the price-yield relation, which figure 12.3 illustrates in the case of a zero coupon bond with a time to maturity equal to 10 years.

12.3.1 Duration

We define the "Macaulay duration" as

$$\mathrm{D_{Mac}} \equiv \frac{-B_y(y;T)}{B(y;T)}(1+y) = \sum_{i=1}^{n} \omega_{t_i} \cdot t_i + \hat{\omega}_T \cdot T,$$

where

$$\omega_{t_i} = \frac{C_{t_i}/(1+y)^{t_i}}{B(y;T)}, \quad \hat{\omega}_T = \frac{1/(1+y)^T}{B(y;T)}.$$

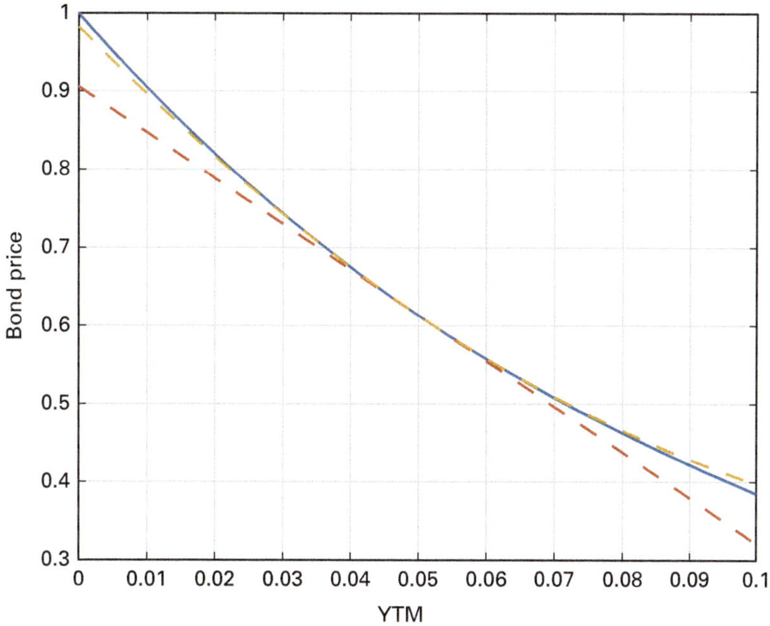

Figure 12.3
The relation between the YTM and the bond price and its first-order (duration) and second-order (convexity) approximations. The solid line depicts the price of a zero coupon bond expiring in 10 years as a function of the YTM, $(1 + \text{YTM})^{-10}$, and the two dashed lines are first-order and second-order Taylor's expansions around YTM = 5%.

In other words, the Macaulay duration is a weighted average of the payment dates. The weights ω_{t_i} are the discounted coupons at the various payment dates, $C_{t_i} / (1+y)^{t_i}$, related to the current market value of these coupons (the bond price $B(y; T)$) when the YTM is y. That is, the weights are the proportions of the bond's present value that is attributable to the payoff at date t. The weights satisfy $\sum_{i=1}^{n} \omega_{t_i} + \hat{\omega}_T = 1$. Therefore, $\mathrm{D_{Mac}} \leq T$. The Macaulay duration is a measure of how far in the future the bond pays off. For zero coupon bonds, $\mathrm{D_{Mac}} = T$.

For small y, $\mathrm{D_{Mac}}(y)$ is simply the semi-elasticity of the bond price with respect to the YTM. This semi-elasticity is also referred to as "modified duration":

$$\mathrm{D} \equiv \frac{-B_y}{B} = \frac{\mathrm{D_{Mac}}}{1+y}.$$

A simple computation reveals that the modified duration, D, satisfies $\frac{\partial \mathrm{D}}{\partial y} = \frac{-B_{yy}}{B} + \left(\frac{B_y}{B}\right)^2$. Therefore, the modified duration is *decreasing* in the YTM when the bond price is sufficiently convex in the YTM, which is certainly the case for long-term maturity dates. Interestingly, the modified duration is *increasing* in the YTM when the bond price is concave in the YTM, a property featured by callable bonds and mortgage-backed securities (MBSs) as explained in chapters 13 and 14 (also, see section 12.7 for some basic numerical examples). Intuitively, the incentives to proceed to early repayments "kick in" as the YTM decreases, which makes the duration of the MBS decrease. Finally, the derivative, $-B_y$, is also referred to as the dollar value of a basis point (DV01). It is a measure of the change in the price of a bond for one basis point change in the yield.

The Macaulay duration for *continuously compounded rates* is analytically a bit simpler. First, define the continuously compounded YTM as the single number $\hat{x}$ such that

$$B(\hat{x};T) = \sum_{i=1}^{n} c_{t_i} e^{-\hat{x}\cdot t_i} + e^{-\hat{x}\cdot T},$$

where $B(\hat{x};T)$ is the market price of a bond paying off the principal of one at maturity and the stream of payoffs c_{t_i}. Next, consider the function $x \mapsto B(x;T)$. Define the semi-elasticity of the bond price $B(x;T)$ with respect to the continuously compounded YTM x,

$$\frac{-B_x(x;T)}{B(x;T)} = \frac{\sum_{i=1}^{n} c_{t_i} t_i e^{-x\cdot t_i} + T\cdot e^{-x\cdot T}}{B(x;T)} = \sum_{i=1}^{n} w_{t_i}\cdot t_i + \hat{w}_T\cdot T,$$

where $B_x(x;T) = \frac{\partial B(x;T)}{\partial x}$, $w_{t_i} = \frac{c_{t_i} e^{-x\cdot t_i}}{B(x;T)}$, and $\hat{w}_T = \frac{e^{-x\cdot T}}{B(x;T)}$. Note that the weights are such that $\sum_{i=1}^{n} w_{t_i} + \hat{w}_T = 1$. Therefore, the "Macaulay duration" for continuously compounded rates is equal to the semi-elasticity of the bond price with respect to the continuously compounded YTM x.[3] This result may simplify some calculations.

12.3.2 Convexity

Convexity measures how the sensitivity, B_y, changes with y. It is the second partial of the bond price with respect to y, B_{yy}. Positive convexity means that the interest rate sensitivity declines as y increases as in figure 12.3. This property arises because $\frac{\partial}{\partial y}(-B_y) = -B_{yy} < 0$. Formally, convexity is defined as

$$\mathrm{C} \equiv \frac{B_{yy}}{B},$$

such that we can expand the bond price as follows:

$$\frac{\Delta B}{B} \approx -\mathrm{D}\cdot\Delta y + \frac{1}{2}\mathrm{C}\cdot(\Delta y)^2. \tag{12.10}$$

That is, duration may not be a safe measure of return for very "convex securities" as figure 12.3 illustrates.

12.3.3 Asset-Liability Management

12.3.3.1 Introductory issues

We can use duration to assess how exposed a bond portfolio is to interest rate movements and then "immunize" this portfolio value to interest rate changes. Duration is relevant to

3. Mathematically, we could have obtained this result in a straightforward manner as follows. Define the bond price function as $B(y(x))$, where, by definition, $y(x) = e^x - 1$. Hence, $B_x(y(x)) = B_y(y(x))\,y'(x) = B_y(y(x))\,e^x = B_y(y(x))\,(1+y)$. It follows that $\mathrm{D_{Mac}} = \frac{-B_y(1+y)}{B} = \frac{-B_x}{B}$.

asset-liability management. For example, pension funds have known streams of liabilities that must be matched by the assets they hold. In other words, the duration of the assets must equal the duration of the liabilities. For example, in the United Kingdom, pension funds must mark to market their liabilities. More generally, many institutions have guidelines recommending a small amount of net total duration of their balance sheets. One objective of these institutions is to immunize their liabilities against movements in interest rates.

Alternatively, consider the following basic example. A bank borrows \$100 at 2% for a year and lends this money at 4% for 5 years where the higher rate compensates for a variety of factors, such as business risk or the bank's market power. Assuming that the bank's borrower does not default, the bank generates profits of $\$(4\% - 2\%) \cdot 100 = \$2$ in the first year and in accordance with its books. However, the appropriate assessment of the current situation should not make reference to past market conditions. Suppose, for example, that after one year, the interest rate for borrowing increases from 2% to 5%, and remains such for 4 additional years. This assumption is unrealistic, but it gives an idea of where the action is. After one year, the market value of the assets will be $\$\frac{100 \cdot 1.04^5}{1.05^4} = \$100.09$; note that we discount at the 5% rate as this is the cost of capital for the bank.[4] The market value of the liabilities is, instead, $\$100 \cdot 1.02 = \$102$. The bank's problem is a duration mismatch.

Let us return to the pension fund example and consider the following extreme case. Thirty years from now, a pension fund is due to deliver \$100,000 to some future retiree. Suppose the current market situation is such that the yield curve is flat at 4%, such that the market value of this liability is $\$100,000 \cdot (1.04)^{-30} = \$30,832$. Accordingly, the would-be retiree invests \$30.832 in the pension fund. So, we have the following situation:

Cash	Pensions
\$30,832	\$30,832

Now suppose that the pension fund does not invest this cash. This strategy is of course inefficient, but it is precisely the point of this exercise to see why it is so.

Consider the following two extreme scenarios occurring within one week:

(i) "Up" scenario: The yield curve shifts up parallelly to 5%. Accordingly, the value of the liability for the pension fund becomes $\$100,000 \cdot (1.05)^{-30} = 23,138$.

Cash	Profit
\$30,832	\$7,694
	Pensions
	\$23,138

4. Alternatively, the 5% interest rate is just an opportunity cost of capital, defined as max {borrowing cost, lending rate}, where the borrowing cost also corresponds to the interest rate that a bank might obtain from other banks, for example.

(ii) "Down" scenario: The yield curve has a parallel shift down to 3%. Accordingly, the value of the liability for the pension fund is $\$100,000 \cdot (1.03)^{-30} = 41{,}199$.

Cash	Loss
\$30,832	−\$10,367
	Pensions
	\$41,199

A drop in the yield curve results in a loss for the pension fund: when interest rates go down, the pension fund faces a challenging situation as it has to honor its obligations in 30 years, but the financial market "yields less" than it promised one week earlier. Naturally, the pension fund would face the opposite situation were interest rates to go up as in the first scenario above.

There are many good ethical reasons we might dislike pension funds have to experience interest rate volatility. The volatility in this very basic example stems from the simple fact the pension fund receives \$30,832, which it then puts "under the pillow." The most efficient way to erase volatility would have been to invest \$30,832 in a 30-year bond at the market conditions of 4%. This strategy leads to a perfect hedging but relies on the assumption that we may invest into such a long-term bond. How do we deal with situations in which we cannot access to such a bond? The next sections illustrate these cases.

12.3.3.2 *Hedging*

Let us consider a portfolio of two bonds with different durations. Its value is given by

$$V = \theta_1 B_1(\hat{y}_1) + \theta_2 B_2(\hat{y}_2),$$

where $B_1(\hat{y}_1)$ and $B_2(\hat{y}_2)$ are the market value of the bonds, $\hat{y}_1$ and $\hat{y}_2$ are the YTM on the bonds, and finally, θ_1 and θ_2 are the quantities of bonds in the portfolio. Let us consider a small change in the two YTM $\hat{y}_1$ and $\hat{y}_2$. We have

$$dV = -\left[\theta_1 \mathrm{D}(\hat{y}_1) B_1(\hat{y}_1) d\hat{y}_1 + \theta_2 \mathrm{D}(\hat{y}_2) B_2(\hat{y}_2) d\hat{y}_2\right].$$

The question is: How should we choose θ_1 and θ_2 such that the value of the portfolio remains the same, even after a change in $\hat{y}_1$ and $\hat{y}_2$?

Let us assume a *parallel shift* in the term structure of interest rates. In this case, $d\hat{y}_1 = d\hat{y}_2$. The portfolio is said to be *immunized* if its value V does not change when $\hat{y}_1$ and $\hat{y}_2$ change, that is, when $dV = 0$

$$\theta_1 = -\frac{\mathrm{D}(\hat{y}_2) B_2(\hat{y}_2)}{\mathrm{D}(\hat{y}_1) B_1(\hat{y}_1)} \theta_2. \tag{12.11}$$

A useful interpretation of this portfolio is the following. We may be holding a bond with some duration—say, we hold θ_2 units of the second bond. Given these holdings, we may wish to sell another bond, possibly with a lower duration, to hedge against movements in the price of the bond we hold.

Alternatively, we can think of the second asset as a *liability* with a value that fluctuates after interest rates change. Then we may wish to purchase some *asset* to hedge against the liability. Mathematically, $\theta_2 < 0$, and $\theta_1 > 0$. Moreover, eq. (12.11) reveals that the number of assets to hold in order to hedge against the liability is high if the ratio of the two durations of the assets, $\mathrm{D}(\hat{y}_2)/\mathrm{D}(\hat{y}_1)$, is large. In this case, the hedging position is obviously inefficient. Asset-liability management and "immunizations" are costly when we hedge high duration liabilities with low duration assets. We now illustrate these claims through a few basic examples.

12.3.3.3 A first example: Hedging zeros with zeros

Suppose that we hold one bond, a zero coupon bond (or zero), with a maturity equal to 5 years. We want to hedge this risk through another bond, a zero with maturity equal to 1 year. Let us assume that the term structure is flat at 5%, discretely compounded. Then

$$B_1(\hat{y}_1) = \frac{1}{1+\hat{y}_1} = \frac{1}{1+0.05} = 0.95238, \quad \mathrm{D}(\hat{y}_1) = \frac{\mathrm{D_{Mac}}(\hat{y}_1)}{1+\hat{y}_1} = \frac{1}{1+0.05} = 0.95238$$

$$B_2(\hat{y}_2) = \frac{1}{(1+\hat{y}_2)^5} = \frac{1}{(1+0.05)^5} = 0.78353, \quad \mathrm{D}(\hat{y}_2) = \frac{\mathrm{D_{Mac}}(\hat{y}_2)}{1+\hat{y}_2} = \frac{5}{1+0.05} = 4.7619$$

and

$$\theta_1 = -\frac{\mathrm{D}(\hat{y}_2)\, B_2(\hat{y}_2)}{\mathrm{D}(\hat{y}_1)\, B_1(\hat{y}_1)}\theta_2 = -\frac{4.7619 \cdot 0.78353}{0.95238 \cdot 0.95238} \cdot 1 = -4.1135.$$

That is, to hedge the 5-year zero, we need to short sell approximately four 1-year zeros. The balance of this hedging position is

$$B_1(\hat{y}_1)\,\theta_1 + B_2(\hat{y}_2)\,\theta_2 = (-4.1135) \cdot 0.95238 + 0.78353 = -3.1341. \qquad (12.12)$$

This is quite an inefficient hedging position. One reason it is inefficient is that hedging long-term bonds with short-term bonds implies we should rebalance too often. Moreover, as time goes on, the sensitivity of the short-term bonds to changes in the YTM is very small (eventually, the price equals face value plus the coupon at maturity), compared with that of long-term bonds. Therefore, rebalancing becomes increasingly severe as time unfolds.

Next, we study how the value of this portfolio changes after large changes in the YTM. By the assumption that the initial term structure is flat at 5%, $\hat{y}_1 = \hat{y}_2 = 5\%$. Moreover, by rearranging eq. (12.12),

$$B_2(y = 5\%) = 4.1135 \cdot B_1(y = 5\%) - 3.1341. \qquad (12.13)$$

The LHS of eq. (12.13) is the price of the 5-year bond. The RHS is the value of a "replicating" portfolio, which consists of (i) approximately 4 units of the 1-year bond and (ii) the balance of the hedging position. Precisely, the RHS is a net obligation: it is the value of the assets we need to purchase back (approximately 4 units of the 1-year bond), net of some cash we already have ($3.1341), which we can use to partially purchase these assets.

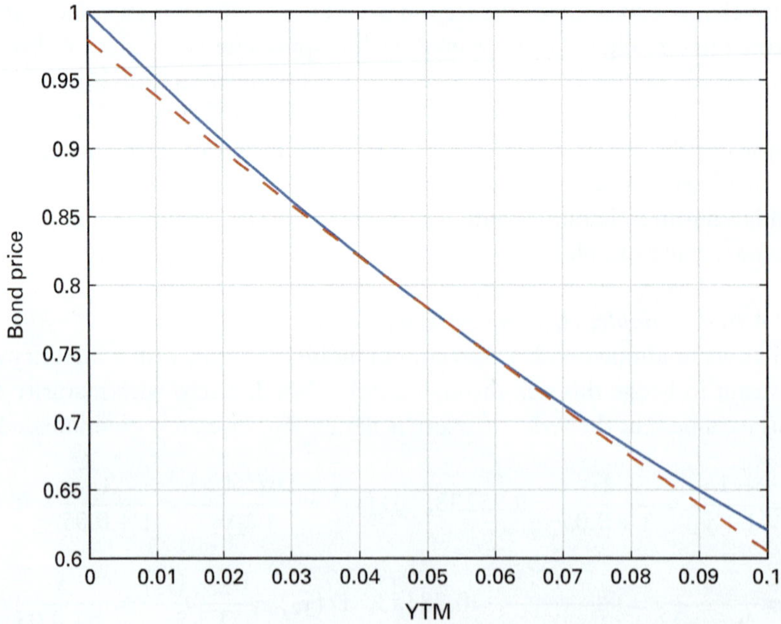

Figure 12.4
Solid line (top): The price of the 5-year zero, $B_2(y) = 1/(1+y)^5$, where y is the YTM. Dashed line (bottom): The value of the "replicating" portfolio consisting of (i) 4.1135 units of the 1-year zero and (ii) the balance of the hedging position, which is equal to $-\$3.1341$, that is, $4.1135 \cdot B_1(y) - 3.1341$, where $B_1(y) = 1/(1+y)$ is the 1-year zero price.

In other words, we can interpret this position as a trade where we buy the 5-year bond and sell approximately four 1-year bonds at some initial time t_0. Come some time $t_1 > t_0$, we liquidate by reversing the position.

If interest rates do not change, then, abstracting from passage of time, there will be no profits or losses once we liquidate or mark to market this position. If interest rates change, $y \neq 5\%$, eq. (12.13) can only approximately hold

$$B_2(y) \approx 4.1135 \cdot B_1(y) - 3.1341.$$

Figure 12.4 plots the LHS and the RHS of this relation.

What is going on? We are hedging the 5-year zero by selling approximately four 1-year zeros. In a neighborhood of $y = 5\%$, the value of the "synthetic" 5-year zero we sold, $4.1135 \cdot B_1(y) - 3.1341$, behaves as $B_2(y)$. However, the 5-year zero displays more convexity than the "synthetic" bond. This larger convexity implies that

- if interest rates go down, the price of the 5-year zero bond we hold increases more than the value of the "synthetic" bond we sold.
- if interest rates go up, the price of the 5-year zero bond we hold decreases less than the value of the "synthetic" bond we sold.

In both cases, we make profits. Profits are indeed equal to $(B_2^+ - \theta_1 B_1^+) - (B_2 - \theta_1 B_1) \equiv \Delta B_2 - \theta_1 \Delta B_1$, where B_1^+ and B_2^+ are the prices of the 1-year and 5-year bonds. But by convexity, B_2 increases more than $\theta_1 B_1$ when interest rates go down, and B_2 decreases less than $\theta_1 B_1$ when interest rates go up, or $\Delta B_2 - \theta_1 \Delta B_1 \geq 0$.

Naturally, we are not describing an arbitrage opportunity. The previous reasoning relies on the assumption of a parallel shift in the term structure of interest rates, that is, $d\hat{y}_1 = d\hat{y}_2$, where $\hat{y}_1$ is the spot rate for 1 year and $\hat{y}_2$ is the spot rate for 5 years. While parallel shifts in the term structure seem empirically relevant, they are not the only shifts that are likely to occur as explained in chapter 13 (see section 13.3).

To sum up, duration hedging is a useful tool but with quite important limitations. As eq. (12.10) makes clear, duration is only a first-order approximation to the price of a bond. Moreover, duration hedging obviously requires rebalancing, which might be substantial. As we know, a conventional bond is strictly convex in the YTM. Therefore, for large changes in the YTM, the duration-based hedging ratios should be updated. Readjustments are in order anyway, regardless of whether YTM changes or not, as the duration of conventional fixed income securities obviously decreases over time.

12.3.3.4 Duration trading: Barbell and bullet hedges

As a second example of duration hedging, consider a "barbell" trade. This trade aims to hedge some liability (a "bullet") with duration D_2 through two assets with durations D_1 and D_3, where $D_1 < D_2 < D_3$, that is, a trade by which we sell the middle duration, D_2, and purchase the tail ones, D_1 and D_3. A barbell trade provides positive returns once the yield curve flattens, with its short-end segment not increasing too much: being long the short-term segment of the curve is a simple device that may allow traders to invest elsewhere relatively rapidly once the first asset expires and if the bond market should go down.[5] We now illustrate some properties of a barbell trade assuming, first, that the curve moves through parallel shifts and, second, that the curves steepens or "twists."

Consider the example in the previous section, and suppose that another bond is available for trading, a zero with maturity equal to 10 years. We aim to hedge against movements in the price of the 5-year zero with a portfolio consisting of (i) one 1-year zero and (ii) the 10-year zero. We keep on assuming that the yield curve is flat at 5%, and only consider parallel shifts in the term structure of interest rates. We consider extensions below.

Such trade resembles the "butterfly" trade in chapter 11 (see section 11.6) as it relies on trading tail durations against middle duration as opposed to trading tail against middle strikes in the option strategies described in chapter 11. A barbell trade can be implemented as follows. We look for a portfolio of the 1-year and 10-year zero with the following properties: (i) the market value of the portfolio equals the market price of the 5-year zero,

$$B_2(\hat{y}_2) = B_1(\hat{y}_1)\theta_1 + B_3(\hat{y}_3)\theta_3; \tag{12.14}$$

and (ii) the local risk of the portfolio equals the local risk of the 5-year zero, $\partial B_2(\hat{y}_2)/\partial \hat{y}_2 = -\mathrm{D}(\hat{y}_2) B_2(\hat{y}_2)$, that is,

$$\mathrm{D}(\hat{y}_2) B_2(\hat{y}_2) = \mathrm{D}(\hat{y}_1) B_1(\hat{y}_1)\theta_1 + \mathrm{D}(\hat{y}_3) B_3(\hat{y}_3)\theta_3. \tag{12.15}$$

5. This barbell trade is thus one example of a "curve flattener." Instead, a "curve steepener" is a trade that aims to profit from an increased steepness of the yield curve. The next chapter (see section 13.3) provides some explanations regarding the determinants of the shape of the term structure of interest rates.

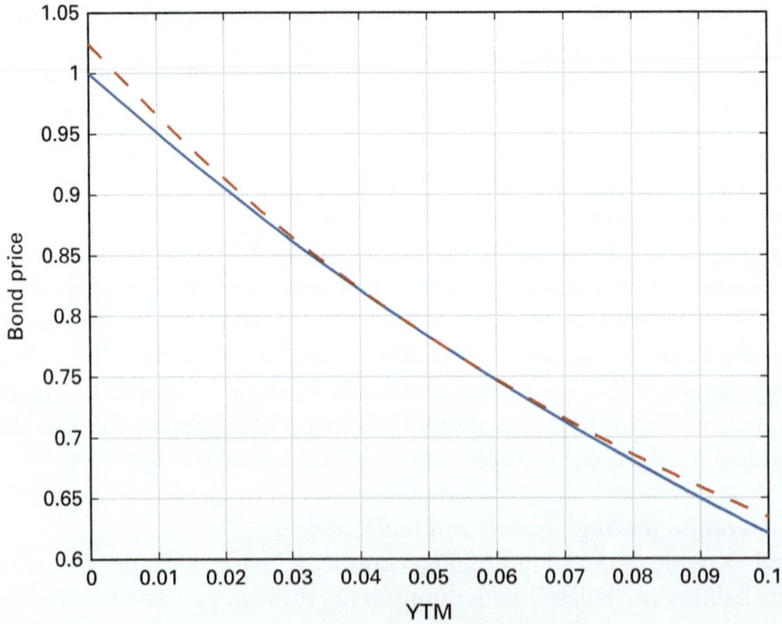

Figure 12.5
"Barbell trading." Solid line (bottom): The price of the 5-year zero, $B_2(y) = 1/(1+y)^5$, where y is the YTM. Dashed line (top): The value of the "barbell" portfolio consisting of (i) 0.45706 units of the 1-year zero and (ii) 0.56724 of the 10-year zero, that is, $B_1(y_1) \cdot 0.45706 + B_3(y_3) \cdot 0.56724$, where $B_1(y) = 1/(1+y)$ is the 1-year zero price and $B_3(y) = 1/(1+y)^{10}$ is the 10-year zero price.

The solution to eqs. (12.14) and (12.15) is given by

$$\theta_1 = \frac{\mathrm{D}(\hat{y}_3) - \mathrm{D}(\hat{y}_2)}{\mathrm{D}(\hat{y}_3) - \mathrm{D}(\hat{y}_1)} \frac{B_2(\hat{y}_2)}{B_1(\hat{y}_1)}, \quad \theta_3 = \frac{\mathrm{D}(\hat{y}_2) - \mathrm{D}(\hat{y}_1)}{\mathrm{D}(\hat{y}_3) - \mathrm{D}(\hat{y}_1)} \frac{B_2(\hat{y}_2)}{B_3(\hat{y}_3)}. \tag{12.16}$$

By the same calculation in the example of the previous section, we have that $B_3(\hat{y}_3) = 0.61391$ and $\mathrm{D}(\hat{y}_3) = 9.5238$. Using the figures in the previous example, we calculate θ_1 and θ_3 in eqs. (12.16),

$$\theta_1 = \frac{9.5238 - 4.7619}{9.5238 - 0.95238} \frac{0.78353}{0.95238} = 0.45706, \quad \theta_3 = \frac{4.7619 - 0.95238}{9.5238 - 0.95238} \frac{0.78353}{0.61391} = 0.56724.$$

Figure 12.5 depicts the behavior of the bullet price and the market value of the barbell as we change the YTM. Note that the barbell portfolio is more convex than the bullet. Moreover, the barbell trade is "self-financed." We may then sell the middle and buy the tails: by construction, the value of the bullet we sell equals the value of the barbell portfolio. Therefore, large movements in the YTM lead to profits under the assumption of parallel shifts in the yield curve.

Note that in this example, as in that of the previous section, the direction of interest rate movements does not matter for value creation. A "convexity trading" such as this might be the basis of a standard nondirectional strategy, resembling one where, say, we go long a number of "undervalued" stocks and short a number of "overvalued" stocks such that the initial value of the portfolio is zero. Then we likely make profits: in good

Table 12.1
Nonparallel shifts in the term-structure.

	YTM	Bullet price	Mod. dur.	Barbell value = $\theta_1 B_1(\hat{y}_1) + \theta_3 B_3(\hat{y}_3)$
Initial term structure				
1 year	$\hat{y}_1 = 4\%$	$B_1(\hat{y}_1) = 0.961$	$D(\hat{y}_1) = 0.961$	
5 years	$\hat{y}_2 = 5\%$	$B_2(\hat{y}_2) = 0.783$	$D(\hat{y}_2) = 4.762$	
10 years	$\hat{y}_3 = 6\%$	$B_3(\hat{y}_3) = 0.558$	$D(\hat{y}_3) = 9.434$	0.783
"Twist"				
1 year	$\hat{y}_1 = 6\%$	$B_1(\hat{y}_1) = 0.943$	$D(\hat{y}_1) = 0.943$	
5 years	$\hat{y}_2 = 5\%$	$B_2(\hat{y}_2) = 0.783$	$D(\hat{y}_2) = 4.762$	
10 years	$\hat{y}_3 = 4\%$	$B_3(\hat{y}_3) = 0.675$	$D(\hat{y}_3) = 9.615$	0.847
"Steepening"				
1 year	$\hat{y}_1 = 4\%$	$B_1(\hat{y}_1) = 0.961$	$D(\hat{y}_1) = 0.961$	
5 years	$\hat{y}_2 = 5\%$	$B_2(\hat{y}_2) = 0.783$	$D(\hat{y}_2) = 4.762$	
10 years	$\hat{y}_3 = 7\%$	$B_3(\hat{y}_3) = 0.508$	$D(\hat{y}_3) = 9.346$	0.751

times, the undervalued stock should increase in value more than the overvalued stock; in bad times, the drop in value of the undervalued stock should be less severe than that of the overvalued stock. For the barbell, the driver of value is convexity: as eq. (12.10) illustrates, the convexity term, C, is always positive and independent of the sign of Δy. Therefore, as soon as we hedge a bond with a portfolio that has the same duration as the given bond but higher convexity, the position leads to profits, given the assumptions made so far.

Naturally, a barbell trade does not lead to an arbitrage. The behavior of the bullet and the barbell in figure 12.5 and the positive P&L that they may have access to relies on the assumption of parallel shifts in the yield curve. However, as explained in chapter 13 (see section 13.3), it is not realistic to assume large *and* parallel movements in the yield curve. Historically, large shifts occurring over long horizons are accompanied by changes in the yield curve shape. In other words, factors affecting parallel movements in the yield curve are frequent, yet other factors also affect the yield curve. At least three factors are needed to explain the entire variation of the yield curve.

Table 12.1 considers the case of *nonparallel* shifts in the term structure. We assume that the initial term-structure is not flat. Then we consider two scenarios: (i) A "twist" in the term structure, that is, long-term rates lower than short-term, and (ii) a "steepening" of the term structure. We use the portfolio in eq. (12.16). Indeed, note that eq. (12.16) does not rely on the assumption that the yield curve is flat. It only relies on the assumption that subsequent movements in the yield curve are parallel. The exercise we are about to perform aims to explore the implications of a barbell trade once the assumption of parallel movements is incorrect.

By eq. (12.16), we find that, in correspondence of the initial term structure ($\hat{y}_1 = 4\%, \hat{y}_2 = 5\%, \hat{y}_3 = 6\%$), $\theta_1 = 0.449$ and $\theta_3 = 0.629$. We keep this portfolio fixed and determine the barbell value, $\theta_1 B_1(\hat{y}_1) + \theta_3 B_3(\hat{y}_3)$, occurring at the two scenarios "twist" and "steepening," with $B_2(\hat{y}_2) = 0.783$ in all cases. The trade is as follows: at time zero, we sale short the 5-year bond, which we hedge through the barbell portfolio (θ_1, θ_3) using the proceeds of the short sale. Then, at some future date, we purchase back the 5-year bond and sell back the portfolio (θ_1, θ_3). The convexity of the barbell trade is, in fact, a view about movements of long-term bond prices and leads to profits in the "twist" scenario. That is, by convexity, the price B_3 varies more than the price of shorter maturity zeros, thus leading to profits. Note, however, that this strategy leads to losses in the "steepening" scenario.

We need to state an important caveat. The previous conclusions rely on a comparative static analysis and abstract from the principle that term structure movements occur under no arbitrage. For example, the value of the zeros changes over the horizons we are designing scenarios for, even without any changes in the yield curve. Whether this effect is minor depends on the horizon. In section 12.5.7, we shall revisit the example of this section; in particular, we shall illustrate how passage of time and absence of arbitrage can be factored into the analysis and change some of the results described in table 12.1.

12.3.3.5 *Fixed income arbitrage strategies*

The previous "convexity trades" are examples of *yield curve arbitrage* strategies. They merely rely on convexity or, as discussed in the previous section, on directional views about interest rate movements. For example, we have explained that we may short 5-year bonds and go long 2-year and 10-year bonds if we believe that short-term interest rates will rise and medium-term interest rates will lower. This "butterfly" strategy is simple and may not be profitable as further discussed in section 12.5.7.

Swap spread arbitrage is another strategy. It seems to have been responsible for leading the hedge fund firm Long-Term Capital Management (LTCM) to a loss of about \$1.6 billion in 1998 (see Lowenstein, 2000).[6] The strategy works as follows: (i) enter a swap paying the floating LIBOR, L_t, and receiving a fixed rate $\bar{C}$; and (ii) short a par Treasury with the same maturity as the swap, thus paying the fixed coupon rate $\overline{CT}$ and invest the proceeds at the repo rate r_t. Thus, the payoff of the strategy is the fixed spread to be received, $F = \bar{C} - \overline{CT}$, minus the floating spread to be paid, $S_t = L_t - r_t$. So we go long or short this strategy according to whether we view F to be larger or smaller than the average floating spread S_t over the strategy horizon. Historically, the spread S_t has certainly been volatile but quite stable, so this strategy appears to be reasonable. However, the problem is that S_t can occasionally attain quite large values.

Trading strategies more sophisticated than the previous ones rely on *models* that aim to identify points of the yield curve that are misaligned from those predicted by the models. All in all, these strategies consist in buying the cheap and short the model-based rich, where the model-based rich is replicated through a portfolio with cash and the bonds that are well priced by the model, weighted with model-based delta. Chapter 13 provides more analytical details on this strategy in the context of no-arbitrage pricing (see section 13.4.2.2).

6. Chapter 10 succinctly reviews other strategies LTCM was invested in (see section 10.9).

12.3.3.6 *Negative convexity and market volatility*

What happens when bond prices have "negative convexity"? In chapter 13, we shall see that the value of a callable bond can be *concave* in the short-term rate (see section 13.8). MBSs display a similar property: they may be concave in the YTM. The reason for this negative convexity is that early repayments are likely to occur as the YTM decreases. This property implies two inextricable consequences: (i) the price of the MBS "increases less" than a conventional bond price after a decline in the YTM, especially when the YTM is low; and (ii) the duration of the MBS decreases as the YTM decreases.

Hedging against MBSs might lead to an increased volatility in rate markets. The mechanism is the following. Institutions that are long MBSs would typically short conventional bonds for hedging purposes, consistent with the prediction of eq. (12.11). However, the duration of MBSs increases as interest rates increase, due to negative convexity: $\frac{\partial \text{Duration}}{\partial r} = -\text{Convexity}$. Therefore, an interest rate increase can lead these institutions to short additional conventional bonds, which worsens liquidity and leads to a further increase in the interest rates, thereby feeding a vicious circle. Perli and Sack (2003) have estimated that in 2002 and 2003, this mechanism may have amplified the volatility of long-term US rates by a factor between 15% and 30%. It is an instance of "endogenous risk," the circumstance that the trend of a certain economic variable triggers actions from market participants that in turn reinforce the initial trend as in the case of the 1987 crash, discussed in chapter 11 (see section 11.10), or in the case of asset sell-offs in times of crisis, discussed in chapter 14 (see section 14.5).

12.4 Foundational Issues in Interest Rate Modeling

This section is an introduction to the design of binomial trees to price and fit already available market prices of fixed income securities. This design requires revising a few details pertaining the equity case examined in chapter 11. It is instructive to briefly review how binomial trees are used to represent price movements. Consider the example depicted in figure 12.6. Today, at the time of evaluation, we observe the state. In the next period, there can be two mutually exclusive states of nature: the state "up" occurring with probability p and the state "down" occurring with probability $1 - p$. After two periods, there are three mutually exclusive states of nature. This tree is also known as being a "recombining" tree because the "up-down" and the "down-up" nodes are the same.

We may use the previous tree as a guidance to price options written on stocks. The stock price unfolds through the branches of the tree. Then we figure out no-arbitrage movements of the option price along the tree. Our question is: Can we apply the same methodology and price an option written on a zero coupon bond? The answer is no: we cannot "exogenously" track the bond price movements in the same way we do with a stock price. A stock has no expiration. Instead, after one year, a 3-year zero (say) becomes a 2-year zero–a quite different security.

These issues can be mitigated by modeling the movements of the whole yield curve. Figure 12.7 summarizes the ideas underlying two modeling approaches. In the first, we model the dynamics of the short-term rate, defined as the interest rate on a loan with maturity equal to the time intervals in the tree. The resulting model, referred to as *model of the short-term rate*, has implications regarding the movements of the entire term structure.

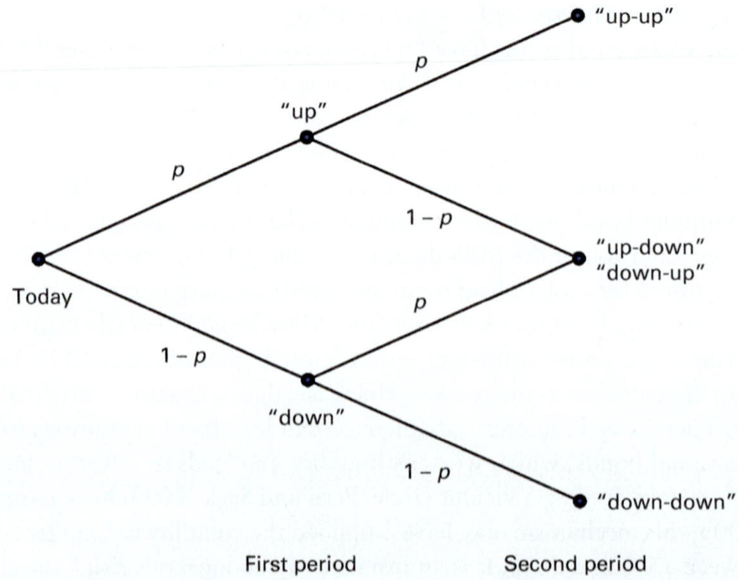

Figure 12.6
A recombining binomial tree.

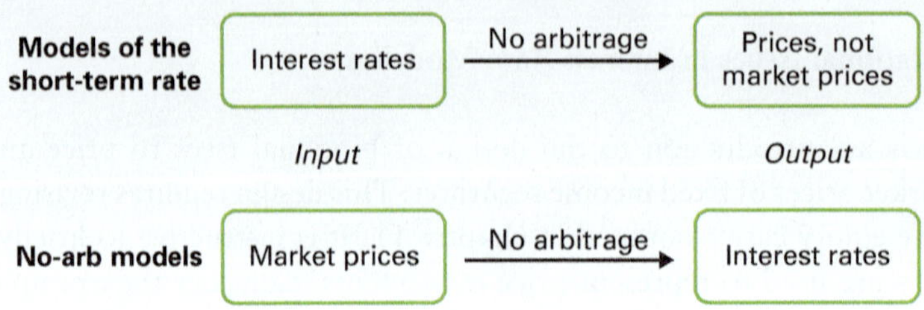

Figure 12.7
Two approaches to modeling the term structure of interest rates.

This approach, developed in the next section, leads to pricing outcomes where the current prices predicted by the *model* are not necessarily the same as the *market* prices. The second approach, based on *calibration*, leads to the so-called *no-arbitrage* models; these models describe the dynamics of the whole yield curve while predicting that its prices are the same as the market prices. We describe this approach in later sections of this chapter, relying on binomial trees; chapter 13 develops continuous time counterparts to this approach.

12.4.1 Tree Representation of the Short-Term Rate

12.4.1.1 Recursive evaluation

Consider a two-period two-state tree where the current short-term rate is r. The short-term rate prevailing in the next period, $\tilde{r}$, is random and can take two values: either r^+ with physical probability p or r^- with complementary probability. We assume that $r^+ > r^-$. Figure 12.8 summarizes the assumptions underlying this model.

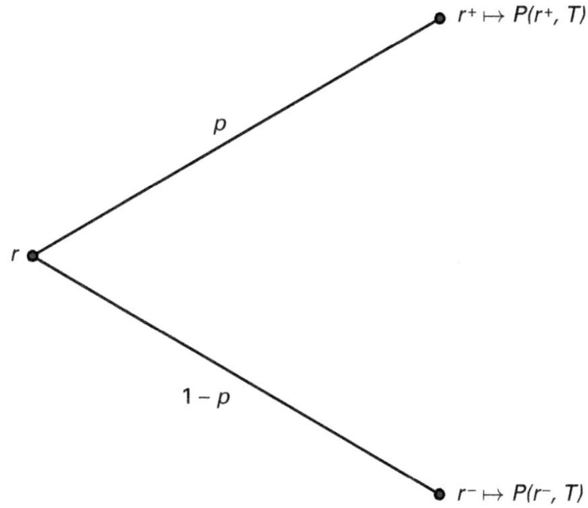

Figure 12.8
A two-period tree of prices and interest rate developments.

Let us explain. We are looking for a pricing function of r, say $P(x, T)$, such that it is $P\left(x = r^+, T\right)$ in the bad state of nature and $P\left(x = r^-, T\right)$ in the good state. Today the very same function is $P(x = r, T)$. When it comes to price options in a *complete* market setting (such as the Black–Scholes market), we take the stock price to be exogenous and then search for an endogenous option pricing function. The result is a preference-free pricing outcome. Let us review the arguments underlying this result, which we have discussed many times in this book (see, e.g., chapter 4). In the Black–Scholes market, the stock price is driven by one source of randomness, such that markets are completed by the very same asset and the option price can be expressed in a preference-free format through a replication argument. In this section, we shall still determine the price of a bond while relying on replication arguments. However, our pricing outcome will not be preference free because the risks affecting the bond prices are not traded—the short-term rate is not traded.

Let us elaborate. Suppose that two zeros with distinct maturities are available for trading. An MMA technology is also available. Investing \$1 in the MMA generates $\$1 \cdot (1 + r)$ in the second period. We build up a portfolio that contains one zero and the MMA. We then make sure the value of this portfolio in the second period replicates the value of the zero we wish to price. By no arbitrage, the value of the portfolio in the first period equals the value of the zero we wish to price. Appendix 12.B develops the arguments and shows that, in the absence of arbitrage, there is a function of r at most, say λ, such that the expected excess return on the bond satisfies

$$E\left[P(\tilde{r}, T)\right] - (1 + r) P(r, T) = \underbrace{\frac{\Delta P(\tilde{r}, T)}{\Delta \tilde{r}} \cdot \text{Vol}\,(\tilde{r} - r)}_{\text{price volatility}} \cdot \underbrace{\lambda}_{\text{unit risk premium}} \tag{12.17}$$

where $E\left[P(\tilde{r}, T)\right]$ denotes the expectation of the bond price under p and $\text{Vol}(\tilde{r} - r) \equiv \Delta\tilde{r} = r^+ - r^-$, which is interpreted as the volatility of the short-term rate.

The meaning of eq. (12.17) is quite simple. Suppose you invest $\$P(r,T)$ into an MMA. Its gross return is then $(1+r)P(r,T)$. Alternatively, suppose you invest $\$P(r,T)$ into a bond, yielding an expected gross return $E[P(\tilde{r},T)]$. The LHS of eq. (12.17) is then the expected excess (dollar) return on the bond, and the RHS is the prediction of the model. Eq. (12.17) is, in fact, an APT (see chapter 1) relation where λ is interpreted as a unit premium related to the risk of holding the bond over one period of time. It says that the expected excess return on the zero equals the volatility of its price multiplied by the unit price of risk. We call the term,

$$\frac{\Delta P(\tilde{r},T)}{\Delta \tilde{r}} \cdot \mathrm{Vol}\,(\tilde{r}-r),$$

"price volatility" because it measures the amplitude of the price variation due to changes in the short-term rate in the future, $\frac{\Delta P(\tilde{r},T)}{\Delta \tilde{r}}$, that is, the "price-sensitivity" where this price sensitivity is normalized by the volatility of the short-term rate, $\mathrm{Vol}(\tilde{r}-r)$.

We can elaborate on eq. (12.17) and bridge to continuous time APT relations (see chapter 4). The key observation is that eq. (12.17) relies on a tree with a trading period normalized to unity. When the trading period is equal to some Δt, the interest earned over that period is $r \cdot \Delta t$, and accordingly, $\lambda \cdot \Delta t$ is the premium that compensates for the risk of holding the bond over an amount of time equal to Δt. With these changes, eq. (12.17) can be cast as

$$E[P(\tilde{r},T)] - (1+r\cdot\Delta t)\,P(r,T) = \frac{\Delta P(\tilde{r},T)}{\Delta \tilde{r}} \mathrm{Vol}\,(\tilde{r}-r)\,\lambda\cdot\Delta t,$$

such that, by considering small Δt and rearranging terms,

$$\frac{E\,(dP(r,T))}{dt} - rP(r,T) = \frac{\partial P(r,T)}{\partial r} \mathrm{Vol}\,(dr)\,\lambda.$$

If we assume that r is solution to a stochastic differential equation, we may use Itô's lemma and turn the previous equation into a partial differential equation, subject to the boundary condition that the bond price is 1 at expiration. Chapter 13 contains a systematic treatment of these topics.

Eq. (12.17) can be cast in an alternative format that is equally easy to interpret. Rearranging terms leaves

$$P(r,T) = \frac{(p-\lambda)\,P(r^+,T) + [1-(p-\lambda)]\,P(r^-,T)}{1+r} = \frac{\mathbb{E}\,[P(\tilde{r},T)]}{1+r}, \tag{12.18}$$

where $\mathbb{E}(\cdot)$ denotes expectation under the risk neutral probability, q say, defined as $q \equiv p - \lambda$.

Assuming that $\lambda < 0$, $q \equiv p - \lambda > p$.[7] That is, the risk neutral probability of an upward movement is higher than the true probability, p. The sense around this reasoning is that, in this model, bond prices decrease with the short-term rate. Therefore, an investor who goes

7. To ensure that q is a probability, we need to have that (i) $q \equiv p - \lambda > 0 \Leftrightarrow -\lambda > -p$ and (ii) $q \equiv p - \lambda < 1 \Leftrightarrow -\lambda < 1 - p$. That is, $-\lambda \in (-p, 1-p)$.

long a bond is concerned by an increase in the short-term rate and hence "corrects" the true probability p by assigning a higher risk-adjusted probability to the "upward" state.

Eq. (12.18) says, simply, that there is no arbitrage if and only if there is a risk neutral probability such that prices earn an expected return equal to the short-term rate. As explained in part I (see, e.g., chapter 2), it does not mean that the market is risk neutral. Instead the market prices assets by discounting the assets future payoffs in a "generous" way through r. To compensate for this, the expectation in the numerator is taken under a probability which overweights the bad states of nature so as to lower back asset prices. It is as if we wished to price assets on planet Earth, a planet full of frictions, risk aversion, and the like, which are reflected in relatively poor asset evaluations. Then we search for another planet that has no frictions or risk aversion where the asset is evaluated through actuarial methods. To reconcile prices on these two planets, we need the idealized and peaceful planet to display a distorted probability, which assigns relatively higher chances to bad events than planet Earth does.

12.4.1.2 *One example*

Assume the current short-term rate equals 10%. We know that in one year, with (*physical*) probability p, r will increase by 2 percentage points, and with probability $1-p$, it will decrease by 2 percentage points. Finally, with the same probability p, the short-term rate prevailing from the next year to two years time will increase by 2 further percentage points from its previous value in one year time. We take the probability of an upward movement to be 20% and the absolute value of the Sharpe ratio to be 30%. Given these data, we use the formula and obtain an estimate of the *risk neutral probability* of an upward movement of the short-term rate equal to $q=p-\lambda=20\%-(-30\%)=50\%$.

Pricing zeros Let us price a zero maturing in two years while relying on the assumptions underlying the tree in figure 12.9. We can use eq. (12.18) to "fill-in" each node of the tree. We start from the end of the tree where the price of the 2-year zero is \$1, and then use eq. (12.18) to fill every node as illustrated in figure 12.9. In one year's time, the price of the zero is simply \$1 divided by the discount factor prevailing at the beginning of the next year. The price we are looking for is obtained by applying eq. (12.18), yielding

$$\frac{\mathbb{E}\left[P\left(\tilde{r},2\right)\right]}{1+r}=\frac{qP(r^{+},2)+(1-q)\,P(r^{-},2)}{1+r}=\frac{\frac{1}{2}0.8928+\frac{1}{2}0.9259}{1.10}=0.8267,$$

where $\mathbb{E}\left(\cdot\right)$ denotes, as usual, the expectation taken under the risk neutral probability q.

Convexity effects Does the 2-year spot rate equal to 10%? It is a natural question because, in this particular example, the short-term rate is a martingale under q. The answer is in the negative. Let us elaborate. The 2-year spot rate, $r\left(0,2\right)$, satisfies $0.8266=\left(1+r\left(0,2\right)\right)^{-2}$ or $r\left(0,2\right)=9.98\%$. That is,

$$0.8267=\frac{1}{1+r}\mathbb{E}\left(\frac{1}{1+\tilde{r}}\right)>\frac{1}{1+r}\frac{1}{1+\mathbb{E}(\tilde{r})}=0.8264.$$

In other words, suppose the interest rate is known with certainty to be 10% in the second period. Then the price should be 0.8264. That is, prices increase upon activation of

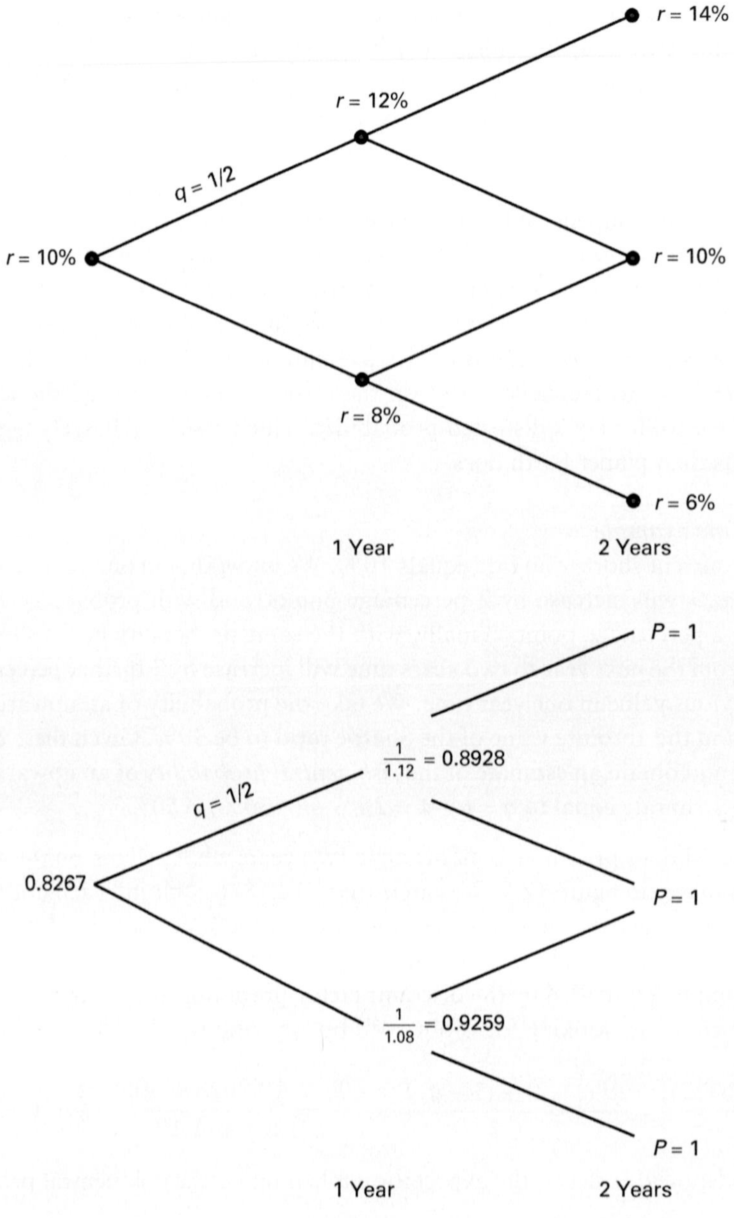

Figure 12.9
Top panel: assumptions regarding the dynamics of the short-term rate. Bottom panel: no arbitrage pricing of a 2-year bond.

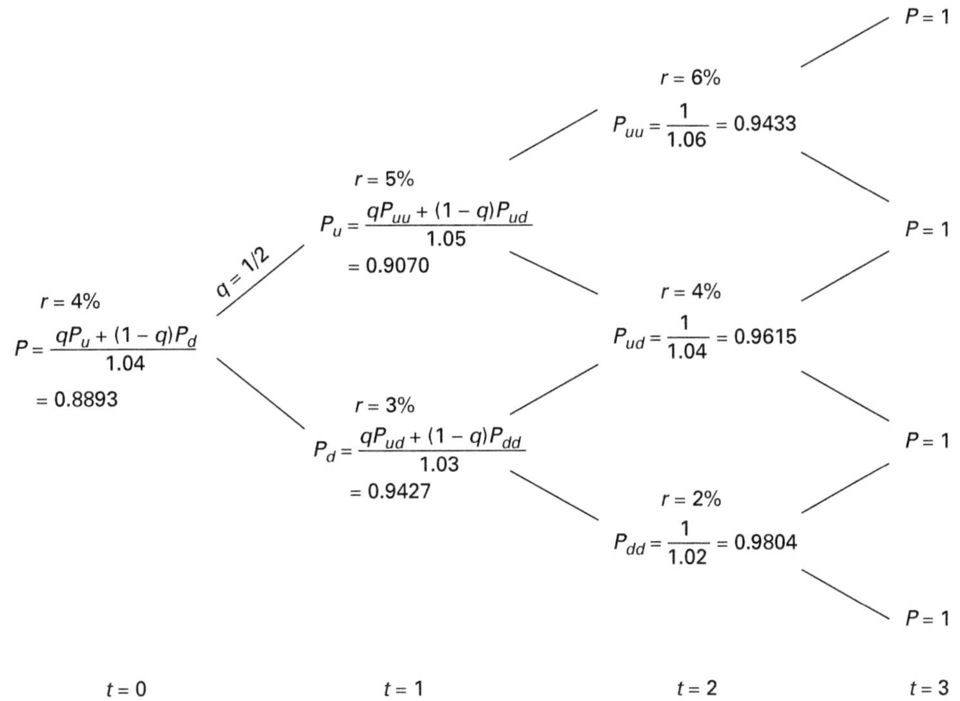

Figure 12.10
A multiperiod binomial tree.

uncertainty. It is a "convexity effect" dealt with in much greater detail in chapter 13 (see section 13.5.1).

12.4.2 Tree Pricing

The tree in figure 12.9 can be generalized to additional periods based on eq. (12.18) and by evaluating zeros at all nodes. Given q, we recursively use eq. (12.18) and calculate prices of zeros. We can then price any derivative written on these zeros. Naturally, this approach leads to a model by which the initial term structure is predicted with error. To illustrate, consider the tree in figure 12.10 where the current short-term rate for one year is $r = 4\%$. Also shown in this figure is the price of a 3-year zero at $t = 3$, the expiration date, and the price of the 3-year zero at $t = 2$. At $t = 3$, $P = 1$ in all states. At $t = 2$, the price satisfies $P(r, T) = \mathbb{E}[P(\tilde{r}, T)]/(1 + r) = 1/(1 + r)$ for $r = 6\%$, 4% and 2%. Next, we determine the price of the zero in the remaining nodes. We populate the tree through eq. (12.18). To determine $q = p - \lambda$, we need to estimate p and λ. Suppose once again we have that $q = \frac{1}{2}$. The tree in figure 12.10 provides the price of the zero in all the nodes at $t = 1$ and at the evaluation time $t = 0$. The final outcome is the current price of the 3-year zero, $P = 0.8893$.

Next, consider a European call option written on the 3-year zero with an expiration date equal to 2 years and a strike price $K = 0.95$. The tree in figure 12.11 indicates the option value predicted by the model on each node of the tree and a current option value equal to $C = 0.0124$.

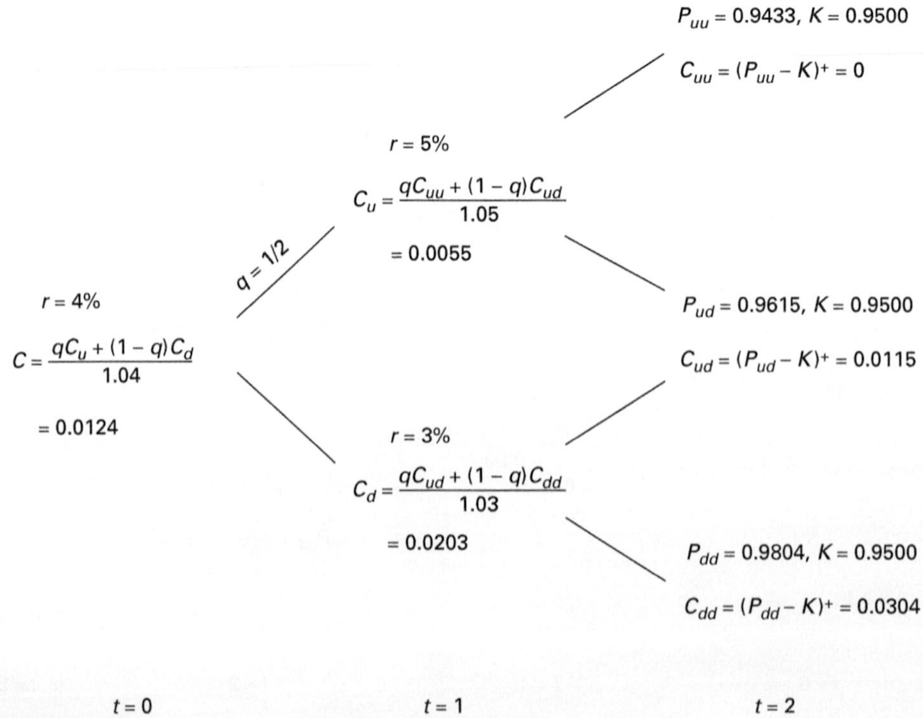

Figure 12.11
Pricing of an option on a zero coupon bond on a binomial tree.

12.4.3 Introduction to Calibration

Calibration is a procedure by which we search for model parameter values such that the model predictions coincide with (or reasonably approximate) selected empirical counterparts. For example, in the real business cycle literature reviewed in chapter 3, we calibrate a model's parameters and ensure that the correlation of asset returns with output is the same as that in the data. In this chapter, calibration is a procedure by which we search for a model's parameters that make the price predicted by the model equal to the market price.

12.4.3.1 Motivation

The *model* in the previous section *predicts* that the 3-year zero price is 0.8893. However, there is no guarantee that this price equals the market price of the zero. Suppose instead that the market price, $P_\$$ say, is 0.8700. What should we do to make the model-implied price of the 3-year zero equal to the market price? The question is important: How can we trust an option pricing model that is not even able to pin down the initial market value of the asset underlying the option contract? Alternatively, suppose the option is a bespoke product of a bank. The bank's client might question why the bank's evaluation model predicts a price of the bond to be so high (0.8893) compared with the observable and cheap market price (0.8700). We now discuss alternative option pricing procedures by which bond prices are predicted without errors.

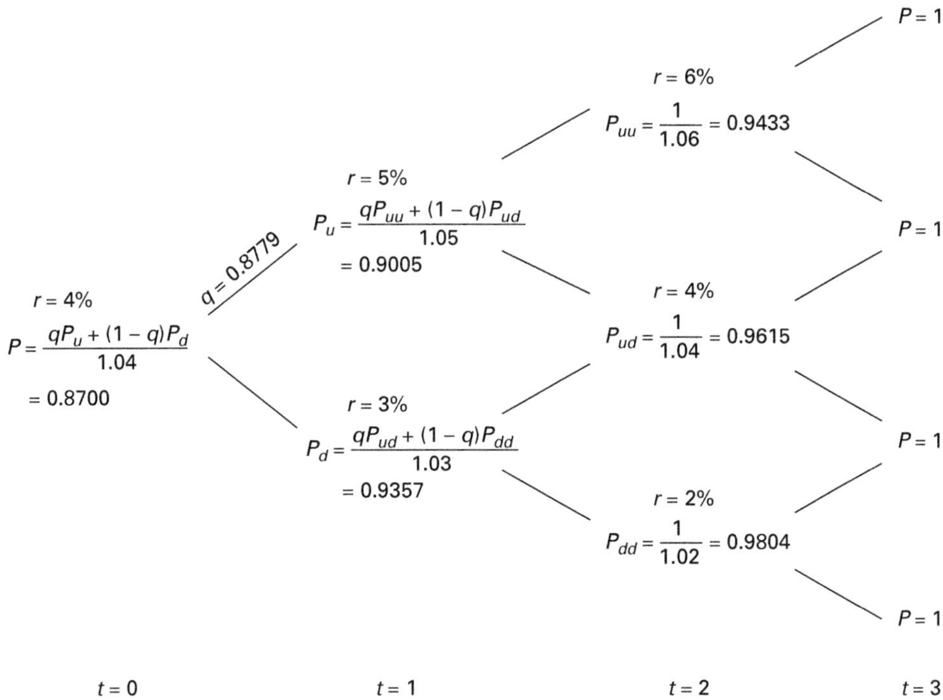

Figure 12.12
A multiperiod implied binomial tree: Pricing of a 3-year zero coupon bond.

12.4.3.2 Perfectly fitting trees

We search for perfectly fitting trees—that is, trees where risk neutral probabilities and/or short-term interest rates on each node are not given in advance but are such that the initial yield curve is fitted without error. These trees are called implied binomial trees ("implied" by the market prices), and they are the fixed income counterparts to the implied binomial trees in the equity space (see section 11.7 in chapter 11). Let us consider the example in the previous section. To ensure that the model-implied price is the same as the market price, $P_\$ = 0.8700$, we cannot take the risk neutral probability q as given. Rather, we *calibrate* q to the market price:

$$P_\$ = 0.8700 = \frac{1}{1.04}\left[q \cdot P_u + (1-q) \cdot P_d\right], \tag{12.19}$$

where P_u and P_d are the prices of the zero at time $t = 1$ in the event that the short-term rate is up to 5% or down to 3% (see figure 12.12).

Eq. (12.19) follows again by eq. (12.18). Now note that the price is not the unknown. Rather, the market price is given, and our goal is to calibrate the probability q. Naturally, to implement the calibration, we need to calculate the prices of the zero at $t = 1$, P_u, and P_d. These prices can be found by another application of eq. (12.18),

$$P_u = \frac{q \cdot 0.9433 + (1-q) \cdot 0.9615}{1.05}, \quad P_d = \frac{q \cdot 0.9615 + (1-q) \cdot 0.9804}{1.03}.$$

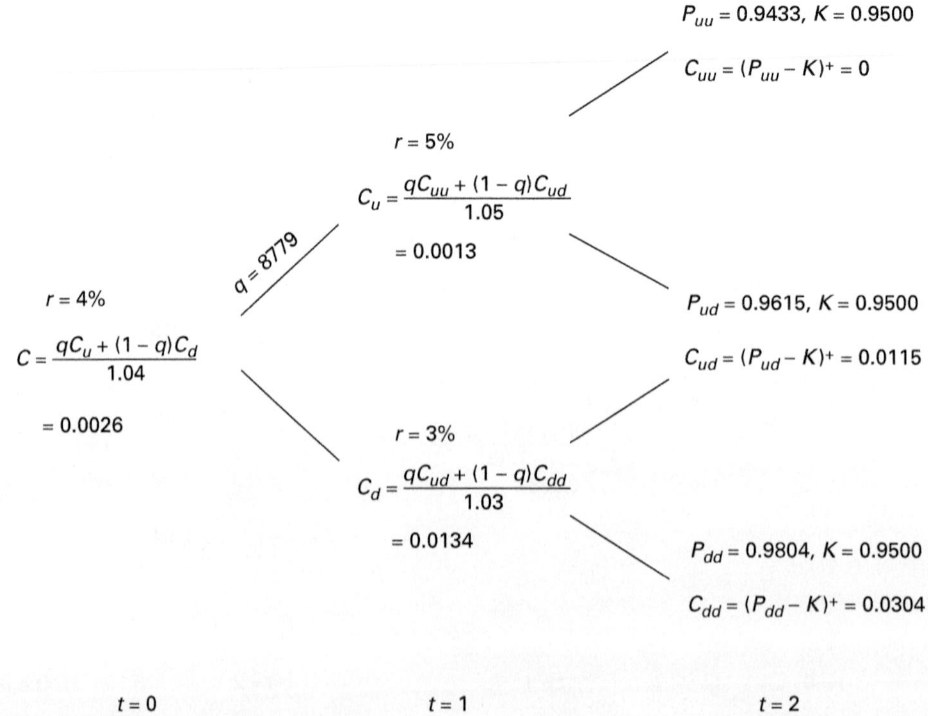

Figure 12.13
A multiperiod implied binomial tree: Pricing of a 2-year call written on the zero coupon bond.

By replacing the previous expressions for $P_1(5\%)$ and $P_1(3\%)$ into eq. (12.19), we obtain

$$\begin{aligned} P_{\$} &= 0.8700 \\ &= \frac{1}{1.04}\left(q \cdot \frac{q \cdot 0.9433 + (1-q) \cdot 0.9615}{1.05} + (1-q) \cdot \frac{q \cdot 0.9615 + (1-q) \cdot 0.9804}{1.03}\right). \end{aligned}$$

The positive solution to the previous quadratic equation is $q = 0.8779$, such that $P_u = 0.9005$, and $P_d = 0.9357$. Figure 12.12 depicts the *implied binomial tree*, that is, the tree that is obtained when the model-implied price matches the market price, $P_{\$} = 0.8700$.

Note that P_u and P_d are quite away from the values we found earlier while imposing that $q = \frac{1}{2}$ (see figure 12.10). In the "implied" tree, they are smaller than those obtained with $q = \frac{1}{2}$ (state by state). The reason for this divergence is that, in the implied binomial tree, $q = 0.8779$, such that the model can match a lower initial price, 0.8700. The implied tree puts more weight on those states of nature where the short-term rate is high or, equivalently, where bond prices are low.

We expect the price of the option in the implied binomial tree to be lower than that we found through the tree in figure 12.11 because call option prices decrease with the underlying asset price. Figure 12.13 depicts calculations of the option price based on the implied binomial tree. The option price predicted by the implied binomial tree is 0.0026, one order of magnitude less than the option price we found earlier in figure 12.11 (i.e.,

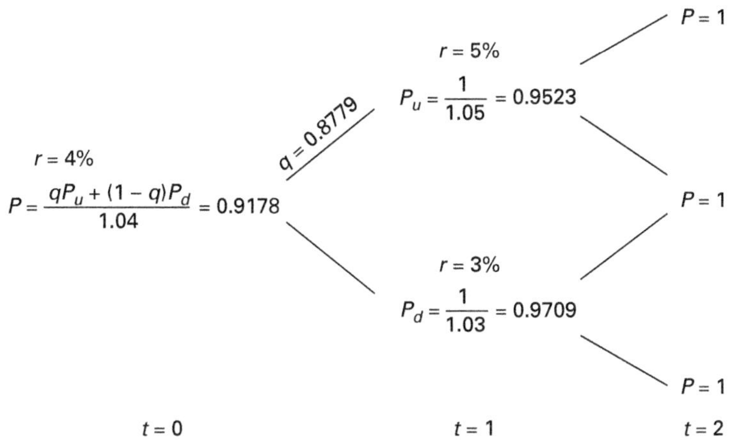

Figure 12.14
A multiperiod implied binomial tree: pricing of a 2-year zero coupon bond through a 3-year zero coupon bond.

0.0124). As anticipated, the implied risk neutral probability is much larger than $q = \frac{1}{2}$, such that the implied tree puts a relatively large weight on events where the short-term rate is high or bond prices are low; this weighting reduces the likelihood of option exercise and leads to a small option price.

12.4.3.3 *Another zero*

We might not be done yet. Suppose that we observe the price of a 2-year zero and that this price equals 0.9200. There is obviously no guarantee that the inputs to the pricing problem for the 3-year zero (in figure 12.12) are consistent with the price of the 2-year zero. Indeed, the calculations in figure 12.14, based on eq. (12.18), reveal that, if we used the pricing inputs for the 3-year zero, the price of the 2-year zero would equal 0.9178. That is, we cannot simultaneously fit the price of the 3-year and the 2-year zeros with the same risk neutral probability, $q = 0.8779$.

To simultaneously fit the price of the 3-year and the 2-year zeros, we should implement at least one of two approaches: (i) make the probabilities q time-varying or (ii) calibrate the entire movements of the short-term rates (i.e., on each node). We implement the first of these two approaches in the next subsection. Section 12.5 develops the second approach.

12.4.3.4 *Implementing implied binomial trees: Introduction*

We build up implied binomial trees in more general cases arising in the presence of several bond prices to be matched. Suppose the time interval is six months, such that the short-term rate is for six months. The current short-term rate is 3.99%, annualized. It may change to either 4.50% or 4.00%, with equal physical probability. This tree is depicted in figure 12.15, the title of which will become clear below. Now, suppose that two zeros are available for trading: a 6-month zero and a 1-year zero where the current price of the 1-year zero is 0.95974. The risk neutral probability implied by this tree must be such that the price of all the zeros are matched exactly.

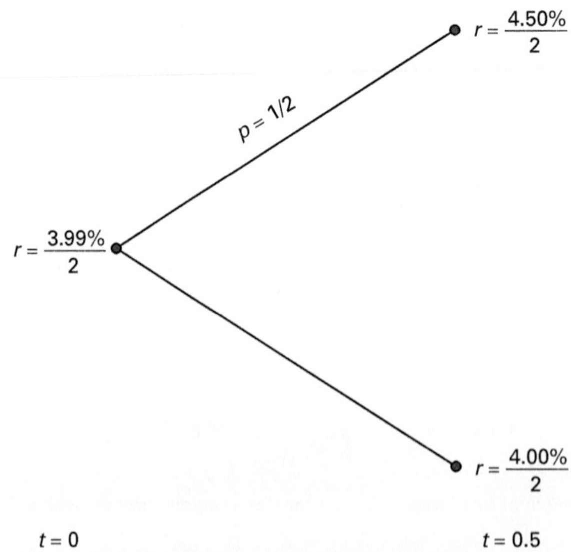

Figure 12.15
The dynamics of the short-term rate: A high interest rate scenario.

Naturally, the market price of a 6-month zero at $t=0$ equals $P_{\$}(0,0.5) = 1/\left(1+\frac{0.0399}{2}\right) = 0.9804$—the current short-term rate, 3.99%, is a mere definition. Next, we determine the no-arbitrage movements of the 1-year zero; figure 12.16 summarizes the calculations.

Note that the current market price, $P_{\$}(0,1) = 0.95974$, is less than the *expected* price to prevail tomorrow and discounted through the current interest rate,

$$\frac{1}{1+r}E[P(0.5,1)] = \frac{1}{1+\frac{0.0399}{2}}\left(\frac{1}{2}0.9779 + \frac{1}{2}0.9804\right) = 0.9599.$$

Hence, $p = \frac{1}{2}$ cannot be the risk neutral probability. Instead, the risk neutral probability satisfies

$$P_{\$}(0,1) = 0.95974 = \frac{1}{1+\frac{0.0399}{2}}\left[q \cdot 0.9779 + (1-q) \cdot 0.9804\right],$$

yielding $q = 0.605$.

We may now proceed with pricing derivatives. Consider a European call option written on the 1-year zero with an expiration date in six months and an exercise price equal to 0.9785 as in figure 12.17. The option value is

$$\begin{aligned} C &= \frac{1}{1+\frac{0.0399}{2}}\left[q \cdot 0 + (1-q) \cdot 0.0019\right] \\ &= 0.9804\left[0.395 \cdot 0.0019\right] = 7.3579 \times 10^{-4}. \end{aligned} \tag{12.20}$$

Next, we examine how the option value may change under an alternative assumption regarding the interest rate. Notably, we assume that the interest rate is as that in the tree of figure 12.18, not as that of figure 12.15.

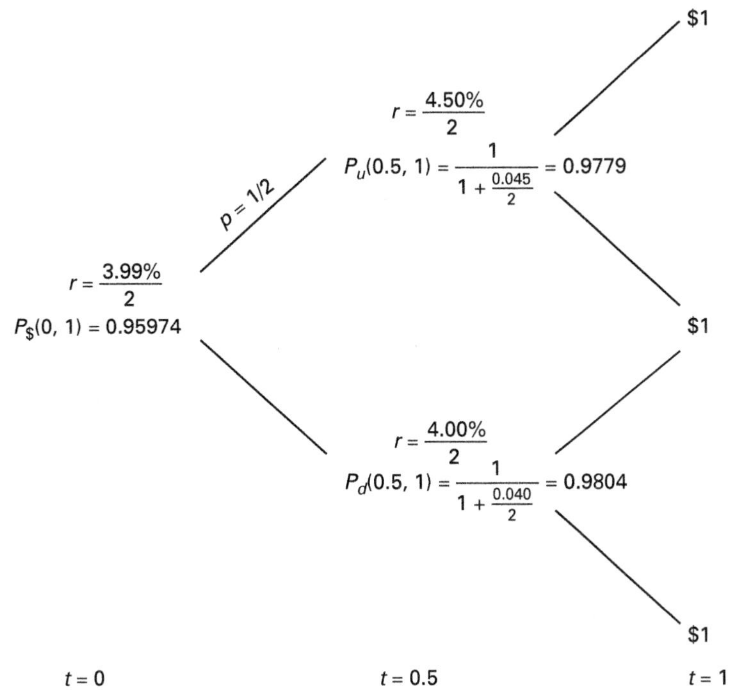

Figure 12.16
A binomial tree under the physical probability.

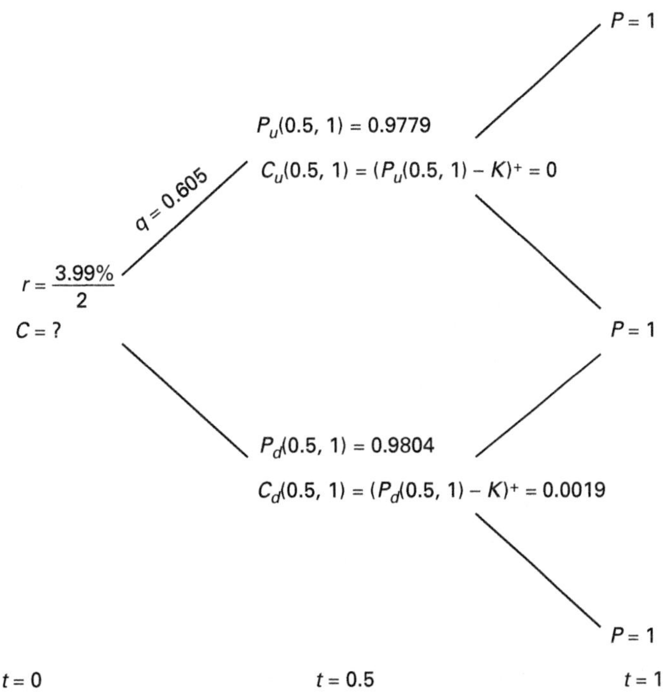

Figure 12.17
Option pricing in an implied binomial tree.

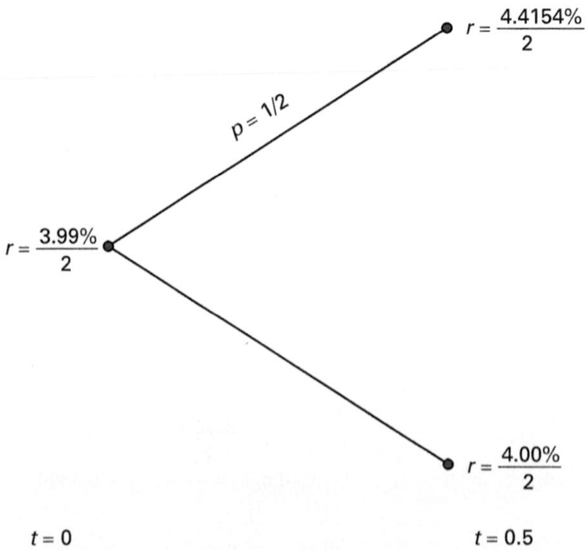

Figure 12.18
The dynamics of the short-term rate: A low interest rate scenario.

In the tree of figure 12.18, the short-term rate in the upper state of nature is $r = 4.4154\%$, not 4.50% as in figure 12.15. Thus, the 1-year bond price in 6 months in this state is now

$$P_{\text{up}}(0.5, 1) \equiv \frac{1}{1+\frac{r}{2}} = \frac{1}{1+\frac{4.4154\%}{2}} = 0.9784.$$

The risk neutral probability, q, solves

$$\begin{aligned} P_{\$}(0,1) &= 0.95974 \\ &= \frac{1}{1+r}\left[qP_{\text{up}}(0.5,1) + (1-q)\,P_{\text{down}}(0.5,1)\right] \\ &= \frac{1}{1+\frac{0.0399}{2}}\left[q \cdot 0.9784 + (1-q) \cdot 0.9804\right]. \end{aligned}$$

The solution, $q = 0.756$, is higher than the implied risk neutral probability underlying the tree of figure 12.15 (i.e., $q = 0.605$). Accordingly, the option price is now

$$\begin{aligned} C &= \frac{1}{1+\frac{0.0399}{2}}\left[q \cdot 0 + (1-q) \cdot 0.0019\right] \\ &= 0.9804\,[0.244 \cdot 0.0019] = 4.5451 \times 10^{-4}. \end{aligned} \tag{12.21}$$

Why is this price in eq. (12.21) smaller than in (12.20)? To match the initial bond price $P_{\$}(0,1) = 0.95974$, the model underlying figure 12.18 puts more weight on the up state of nature, that is, a higher implied risk neutral probability of future low bond prices, whence, a lower option price.[8] Note that the price is now almost half of that in (12.20): the optionalities give rise to nonlinear payoffs, and small deviations in the assumptions may lead to dramatic option pricing implications.

These simple calculations illustrate how financial intermediaries may behave in segmented markets. In such segmented markets, two investment banks (say) might have different views regarding current developments in the short-term rate (such as those summarized by figures 12.15 and 12.18). The first bank favors a "high" interest rate scenario but is not too concerned about this scenario ($r_{\text{up}} = 4.5\%$, $q = 0.605$). The second bank favors a "mild" interest rate scenario, although it assigns a higher risk-adjusted probability that this scenario may arise ($r_{\text{up}} = 4.4154\%$, $q = 0.756$). To illustrate, the first bank may display a quite conservative risk management system,[9] although then the option prices it proposes are higher than those of the second bank. While both institutions obviously agree on the initial bond price, $P_{\$}(0,1) = 0.95974$, they are able to sell the same product at different prices as they operate in segmented markets. For example, the clientèle of the first and the second banks might be unlikely to meet, and then the option prices proposed by the banks are not publicly known. Naturally, the two banks would need to agree on the option prices too in the absence of market imperfections (and arbitrage).

12.4.3.5 Adding periods

Next, we add one period to the previous trees and assume that the short-term rate is as that in the tree of figure 12.19. In this tree, q_0 is the risk neutral probability applying to the first period, and q_1 is the risk neutral probability applying to the second. We already know that $q_0 = 0.605$, and we assume that q_1 may differ from q_0. Finally, we assume that an additional zero is available for trading, a 1.5-year zero, with a current price equal to $P_{\$}(0,1.5) = 0.9382$. To determine q_1, we calibrate the implied tree for the 1.5-year zero (see figure 12.19).

We need the prices $P_u(0.5,1.5)$ and $P_d(0.5,1.5)$ to recover q_1 while relying on the previously calculated $q_0 = 0.605$. By no arbitrage, we have as usual that

$$P_u(0.5,1.5) = \frac{1}{1 + \frac{0.045}{2}} \left[q_1 0.9761 + (1 - q_1) 0.9789 \right], \tag{12.22}$$

$$P_d(0.5,1.5) = \frac{1}{1 + \frac{0.040}{2}} \left[q_1 0.9789 + (1 - q_1) 0.9808 \right]. \tag{12.23}$$

Naturally, q_1 is not known, and eqs. (12.22) and (12.23) are not enough to pin down the prices $P_u(0.5,1.5)$ and $P_d(0.5,1.5)$. But here is where calibration comes in. We rely

---

8. Mathematically, we have that $P_{\$}(0,1) = \frac{1}{1+r}(P_{\text{down}} - q\Delta P)$, where $\Delta P \equiv P_{\text{down}} - P_{\text{up}} > 0$. While P_{down} in figure 12.18 is the same as that in figure 12.15, the "bond price volatility" (i.e., ΔP) is lower. Therefore, q must increase in the tree of figure 12.18.

9. For example, in risk management systems that employ standard VaR methodologies (see, e.g., section 14.4 in chapter 14), calculations are performed under the physical probability (not the risk neutral). However, assumptions on interest rates levels do affect these calculations.

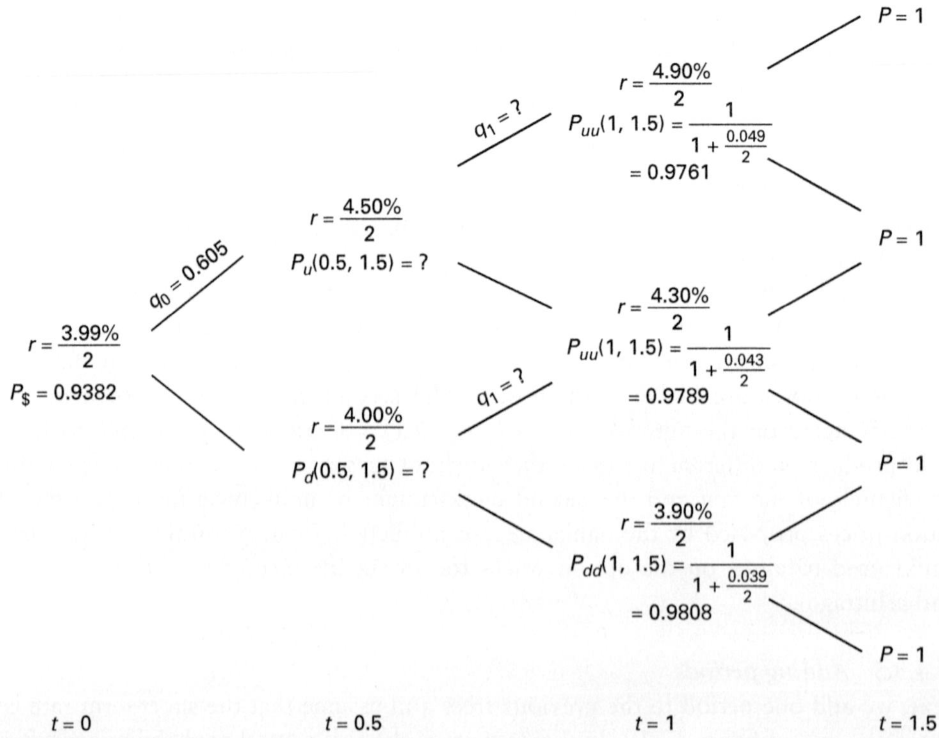

Figure 12.19
Implied binomial tree for a 1.5-year zero: Calibration of q_1.

on the price of the 1.5-year zero. In the absence of arbitrage,

$$P_\$ (0, 1.5) = 0.9382$$
$$= \frac{1}{1+\frac{0.0399}{2}} \left[q_0 P_u (0.5, 1.5) + (1 - q_0) P_d (0.5, 1.5)\right], \quad q_0 = 0.605 \tag{12.24}$$

Replacing eqs. (12.22) and (12.23) into eq. (12.24) leaves one equation with one unknown, solved by $q_1 = 0.8412$ such that $P_u (0.5, 1.5) = 0.9549$ and $P_d (0.5, 1.5) = 0.9600$. The final calculations are in the tree of figure 12.20.

We may now evaluate derivatives written on these zeros. Consider, for example, a call option on the 1.5-year zero, which expires in one year and has an exercise price equal to 0.9800. The option price at time $t = 0.5$ is either zero or $C = 0.00012$ as in the tree of figure 12.20, such that, with $q_0 = 0.605$, the current option price is

$$C = \frac{1}{1+\frac{0.0399}{2}} \left[0 \cdot q_0 + 0.00012 \cdot (1 - q_0)\right] = 4.647 \times 10^{-5}.$$

Finally, we may rely on the tree of figure 12.20 and price additional derivatives, such as, say, a call option on the 1.5-year zero, which has expiration date in six months, and an exercise price equal to 0.9580. Figure 12.21 summarizes the calculations.

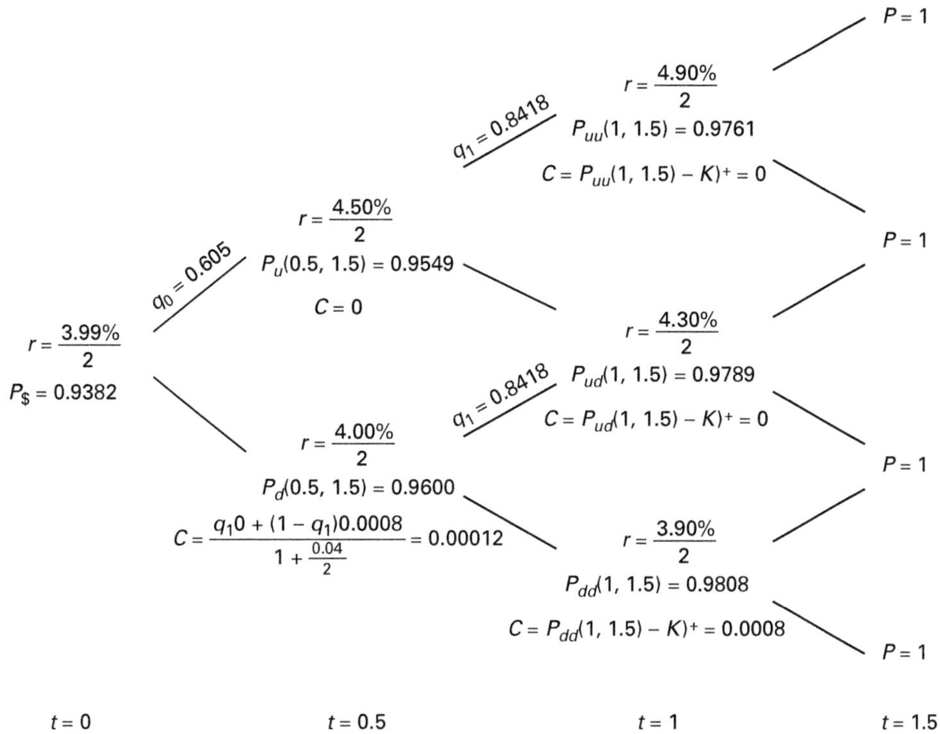

Figure 12.20
Implied binomial tree for a 1.5-year zero: Complete calibration.

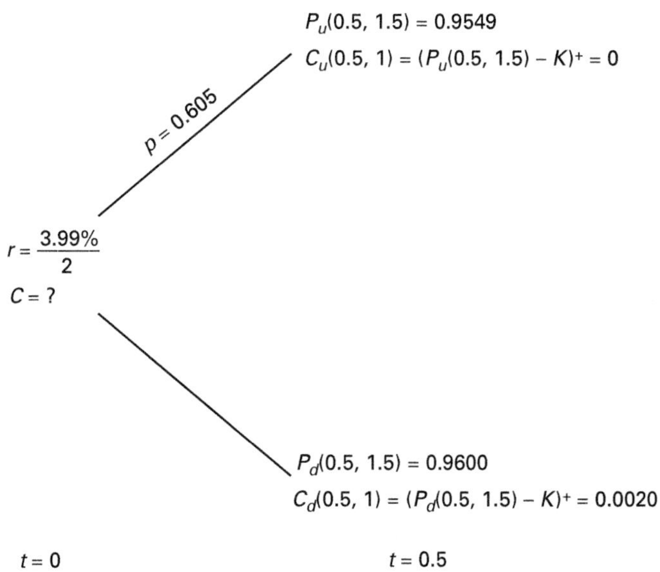

Figure 12.21
The price of call option on a 1.5-year zero.

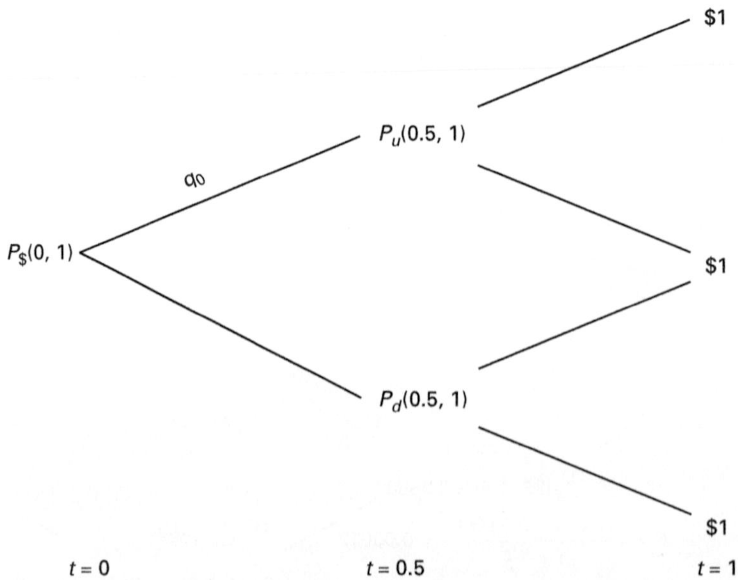

Figure 12.22
Calibration of q_0.

The no-arbitrage price of the option is

$$C = \frac{1}{1+\frac{0.039}{2}}\left[q_0 \cdot 0 + (1-q_0)\cdot 0.0020\right] = 0.9804\left[0.395 \cdot 0.0020\right] = 7.745 \times 10^{-4}.$$

12.4.3.6 *Summing up*

What have we done? In the trees of figure 12.19 and 12.20, we recovered the two risk neutral probabilities q_0 and q_1 for the time spans $(0, 0.5)$ and $(0.5, 1)$, based on the market price of two zeros (1-year and 1.5-year zeros). Precisely, given the 1-year zero bond price, $P_\$(0,1)$, q_0 could be recovered because $P_u(0.5,1)$ and $P_d(0.5,1)$ are next to the expiration and therefore are independent of q_0 (see figure 12.22).

Next, given q_0 ($\hat{q}_0$, say), we determined q_1 based on $P_\$(0,1.5)$ as illustrated in figure 12.23. Now, again, $P_{uu}(1,1.5)$, $P_{ud}(1,1.5)$ and $P_{dd}(1,1.5)$ are obviously independent of q_1; given these prices, we may then express $P_u(0.5,1.5)$ and $P_d(0.5,1.5)$ as two linear functions of q_1. Finally, by no arbitrage, the market price $P_\$(0,1.5)$ is linear in $P_u(0.5,1.5)$ and $P_d(0.5,1.5)$ (with known weights $\hat{q}_0$ and $1-\hat{q}_0$) and hence in q_1, which enabled us to recover q_1 ($\hat{q}_1$, say).

We can continue and consider one more period as in figure 12.24. We could recover q_2 based on the market price of a 2-year zero, $P_\$(0,2)$. We would proceed as follows. First, we determine the price of the 2-year zero at time $t=1.5$ on the filled nodes in figure 12.24 (say, $P_X(1.5,2)$ for $X=\{uu,ud,dd\}$), based on assumptions regarding the values of the short-term rate in those nodes. Second, given the prices $P_X(1.5,2)$ as well as the previously calibrated probabilities $\hat{q}_0$ and $\hat{q}_1$, no arbitrage enables us to express the current price $P_\$(0,2)$ as a linear function of q_2. Finally, we solve for q_2.

The calibration may continue through such a "forward propagation mechanism." We extend the tree by introducing additional periods. Then, we use the price of one additional

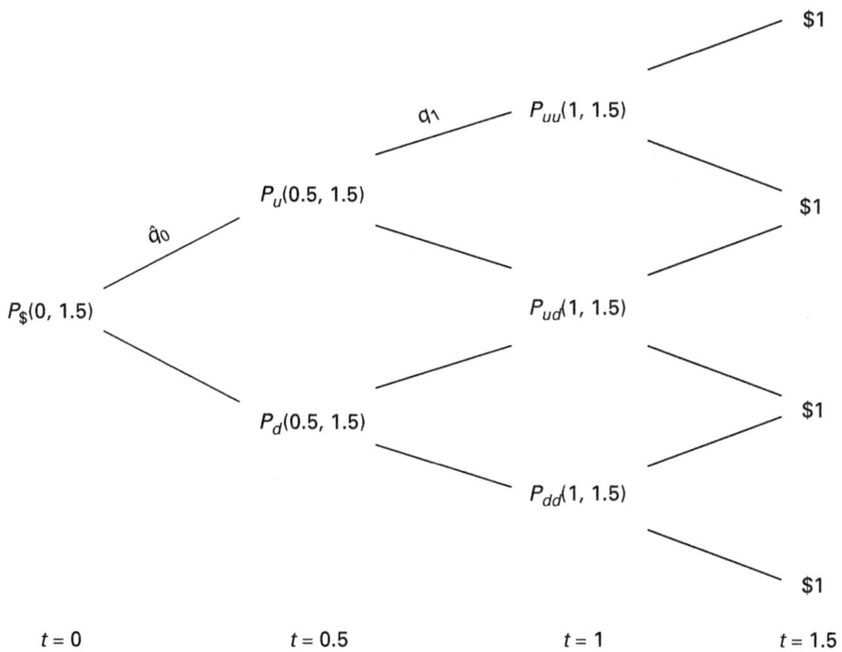

Figure 12.23
Calibration of q_1 by forward propagation.

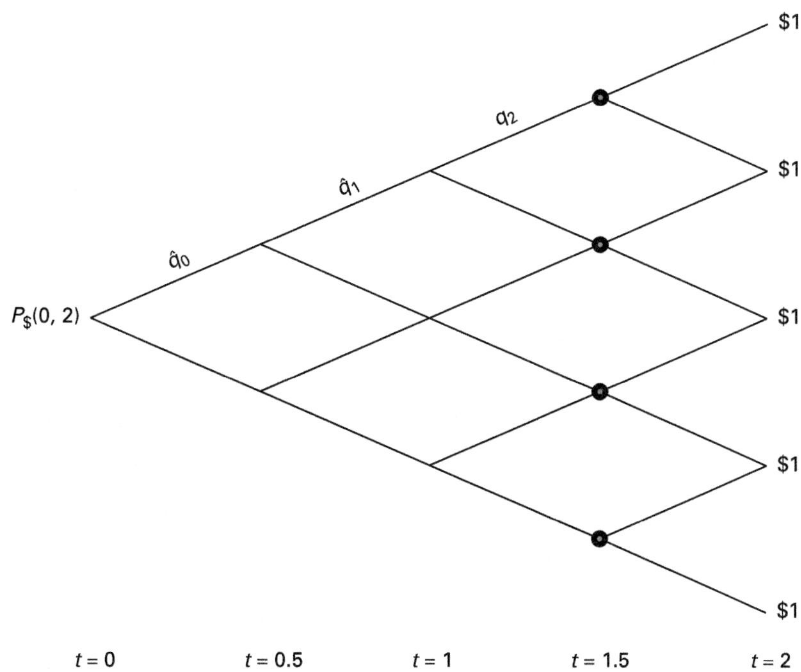

Figure 12.24
Calibration of q_2 by forward propagation.

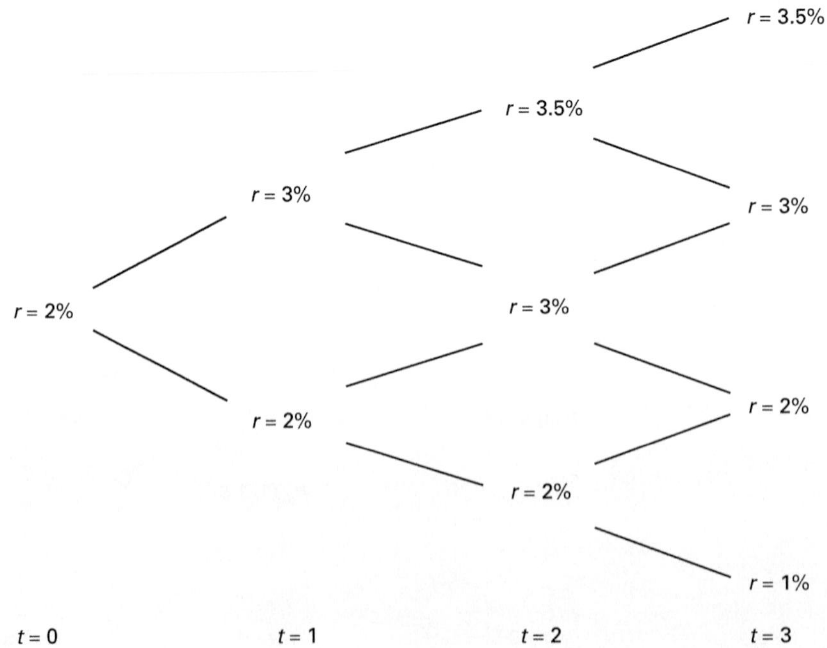

Figure 12.25
A binomial interest rate tree.

zero to recover time-varying risk neutral probabilities. Note that an alternative procedure may consist in (i) *fixing* the risk neutral probabilities q to some value at all times (e.g., $q = \frac{1}{2}$) and (ii) determining the "implied" values for the short-term rate in each node of the tree. Section 12.5 develops a systematic approach that allows us to implement this procedure.

12.4.4 Calibrating Probabilities Through Derivative Data

This section contains two numerical examples that illustrate how information on derivative data may be exploited to predict the price of the underlying assets. In particular, we use derivative data on zero coupon bonds and calibrate risk neutral probabilities that we use for the purpose of bond evaluation.

12.4.4.1 *Options*

Suppose that a 2-year zero coupon bond is traded for a price equal to $P_\$ (0,2) = 0.95500$. We assume that the short-term rate evolves over time according to the tree in figure 12.25.

Consider a European call option written on a 3-year zero coupon bond. This option has a strike price equal to 0.97000, expires in two years, and quotes for $C_\$ (0,2) = 1.0141 \cdot 10^{-3}$. We use the option price to find the no-arbitrage price of a 3-year coupon bearing bond that pays off 3% of the principal of \$1 every year. Precisely, we use the price of the 2-year zero and recover the risk neutral probability that applies to the first year; then, we recover the risk neutral probability applying to the second year from the option price. With these probabilities, we determine the no-arbitrage price of the 3-year bond.[10]

10. Note that we are assuming risk neutral probabilities are state independent. Otherwise, the price of additional assets would be required in order to reverse engineer state-dependent probabilities.

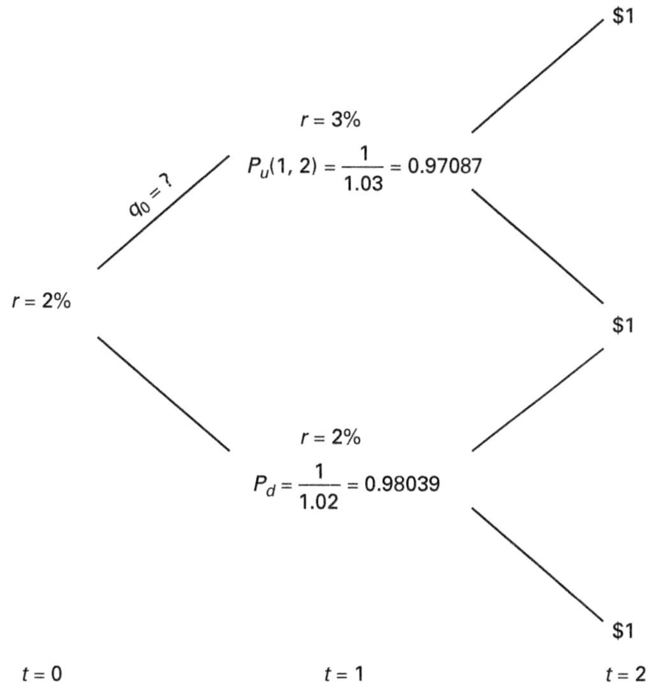

Figure 12.26
First-year probability implied by the price of two-year zero.

So we know that $P_\$ (0,2) = 0.95500$. Moreover, as illustrated in figure 12.26, we extract the price of the 2-year zero in the up and down states at time $t = 1$.

We can then solve for the risk neutral probability. We have

$$\begin{aligned} P_\$ (0,2) &= 0.95500 \\ &= \frac{1}{1.02} \left(q_0 \cdot P_u (1,2) + (1 - q_0) P_d (1,2)\right) \\ &= \frac{1}{1.02} (q_0 \cdot 0.97087 + (1 - q_0) 0.98039). \end{aligned}$$

That is, $q_0 = 0.6607$. Next, we use this probability and the price of the option, $C_\$ (0,2)$, to solve for the risk neutral probability that applies to the second period. Figure 12.27 illustrates the calculations. We assume that the option strike is $K = 0.97000$. Then, the option price at $t = 1$ can be either C_u or C_d, where

$$\begin{aligned} C_u &= \frac{1}{1.03} \left[q_1 \max\{P_{uu} (2,3) - K, 0\} + (1 - q_1) \max\left\{P_{ud} (2,3) - K, 0\right\}\right] \\ &= \frac{1}{1.03} (1 - q_1) 0.00087. \\ C_d &= \frac{1}{1.02} \left[q_1 \max\left\{P_{ud} (2,3) - K, 0\right\} + (1 - q_1) \max\left\{P_{dd} (2,3) - K, 0\right\}\right] \\ &= \frac{1}{1.02} \left[q_1 0.00087 + (1 - q_1) 0.01039\right]. \end{aligned}$$

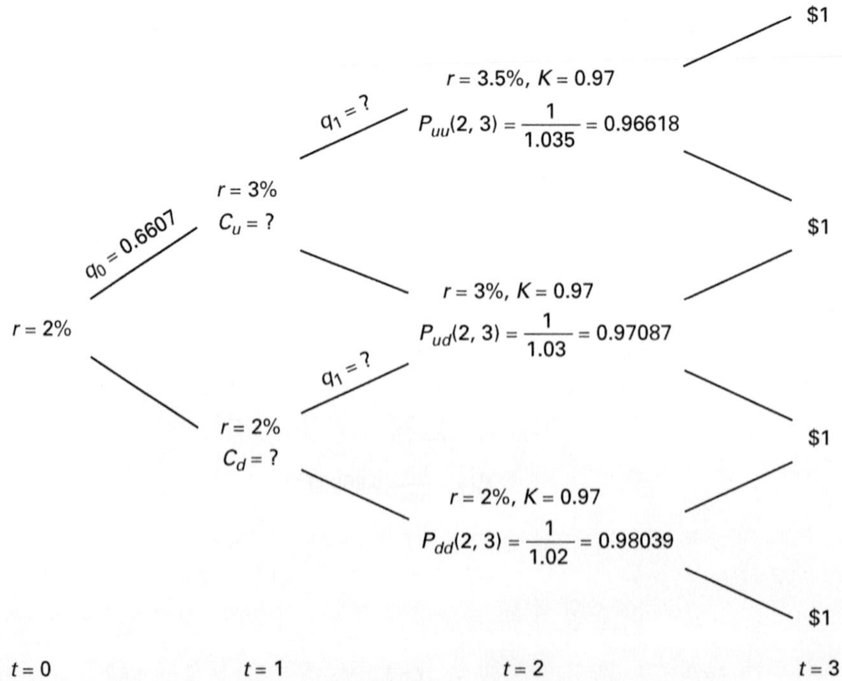

Figure 12.27
Second-year probability implied by the option price.

The option price satisfies

$$\begin{aligned} C_{\$}(0,2) &= 1.0141 \cdot 10^{-3} \\ &= \frac{1}{1.02}\left(q_0 C_u + (1-q_0) C_d\right) \\ &= \frac{1}{1.02}\left(0.6607 C_u + 0.3393 C_d\right). \end{aligned}$$

Replacing the previous expressions for C_u and C_d in this equation leaves an equation for q_1, which is solved by $q_1 = 0.8000$.

Finally, we determine the price of a zero maturing at $t = 3$, $P(0,3)$, that is embedded in the market prices, $P_{\$}(0,2)$ and $C_{\$}(0,2)$, based on the tree of figure 12.27.

We have

$$\begin{aligned} P_u(1,3) &= \frac{1}{1.03}\left[q_1 P_{uu}(2,3) + (1-q_1) P_{ud}(2,3)\right] \\ &= \frac{1}{1.03}(0.80 \cdot 0.96618 + 0.20 \cdot 0.97087) = 0.93895. \\ P_d(1,3) &= \frac{1}{1.02}\left[q_1 P_{ud}(2,3) + (1-q_1) P_{dd}(2,3)\right] \\ &= \frac{1}{1.02}(0.80 \cdot 0.97087 + 0.20 \cdot 0.98039) = 0.95370. \end{aligned}$$

Therefore,

$$P(0,3) = \frac{1}{1.02}\left[q_0 P_u(1,3) + (1-q_0) P_d(1,3)\right]$$
$$= \frac{1}{1.02}(0.6607 \cdot 0.93895 + 0.3393 \cdot 0.95370) = 0.92545.$$

The price of the 3-year bond bearing a 3% coupon is

$$B(0,3) = 0.03 \cdot \left[P_\$(0,1) + P_\$(0,2) + P(0,3)\right] + P(0,3)$$
$$= 0.03 \cdot (0.98039 + 0.95500 + 0.92545) + 0.92545 = 1.0113.$$

The previous calculations allow us to determine the discretely compounded yield curve: $r_{0,1} = 2.00\%$ (1 year); $r_{0,2} : 0.95500 = (1 + r_{0,2})^{-2}$ or $r_{0,2} = 2.328\%$ (2 years); and $r_{0,3}$: $0.92545 = (1 + r_{0,3})^{-3}$ or $r_{0,3} = 2.616\%$ (3 years). Remarkably, one may infer this curve without knowledge of all bond data and by simply inverting some of these data from the price of an option. We may then implement an arbitrage should the price of the "missing" bond become available and be misaligned from $P(0,3)$. Suppose, for example, that the market price is $P_\$(0,3) > P(0,3) = 0.92545$, say. Then we can sell short the 3-year zero and set up a dynamic, self-financing strategy aiming to replicate this zero, that is, capable of delivering \$1 at maturity.

We would proceed as follows. Consider again the tree in figure 12.27. Let us build a portfolio that is long the option and an MMA. We assume that the 3-year bond "converges" to the values P_{uu}, P_{ud}, and P_{dd}, for otherwise we might implement a trivial arbitrage from time $t = 2$ to $t = 3$. At time $t = 0$, we go long Δ_0 options and M_0 units of the MMA so as to make sure that the portfolio delivers $P_u(1,3)$ in the up state and $P_d(1,3)$ in the down state—thereby ensuring that the price of the bond is replicated at time $t = 1$. The value of this replicating strategy is, of course, $P(0,3)$, so by short selling the 3-year bond at $t = 0$, we obtain an initial profit equal to $P_\$(0,3) - P(0,3)$. Suppose then that at time $t = 1$, we are in the up node, such that the bond price is $P_u(1,3)$. In this node, we can build up another portfolio long Δ_1 options and M_1 units of the MMA. This portfolio aims at replicating the price of the bond at time $t = 2$—either $P_{uu}(2,3)$ or $P_{ud}(2,3)$. The value of this replicating portfolio would be just $P_u(1,3)$, which is the value of the replicating strategy implemented at $t = 0$. This strategy is self-financed as the following calculations reveal. By construction, $\Delta_0 C_u(1) + M_0(1+r) = P_u(1,3) = \Delta_1 C_u(1) + M_1$ (with $r = 2\%$), and $\Delta_1 \tilde{C}_{u\cdot}(2) + M_1(1+r) = \tilde{P}_{u\cdot}(2,3)$, where $r = 3\%$, and $\tilde{C}_{u\cdot}(2), \tilde{P}_{u\cdot}(2,3)$ are either $C_{uu}(2), P_{uu}(2,3)$, or $C_{ud}(2), P_{ud}(2,3)$, at $t = 2$, with straightforward notation. Therefore, we have that

$$\tilde{P}_{u\cdot}(2,3) - P_u(1,3) = \Delta_1\left(\tilde{C}_{u\cdot}(2) - C_u(1)\right) + rM_1$$
$$= \Delta_1\left(\tilde{C}_{u\cdot}(2) - C_u(1) - rC_u(1)\right) + rP_u(1,3),$$

that is, the definition of a self-financed strategy. Likewise, if instead at $t = 1$, we end up in the down node where the bond price (and the value of the strategy implemented at time $t = 0$) is $P_d(1,3)$, we can invest $P_d(1,3)$ in options and MMAs so as to replicate the price of the bond at time $t = 2$—either $P_{ud}(2,3)$ or $P_{dd}(2,3)$.

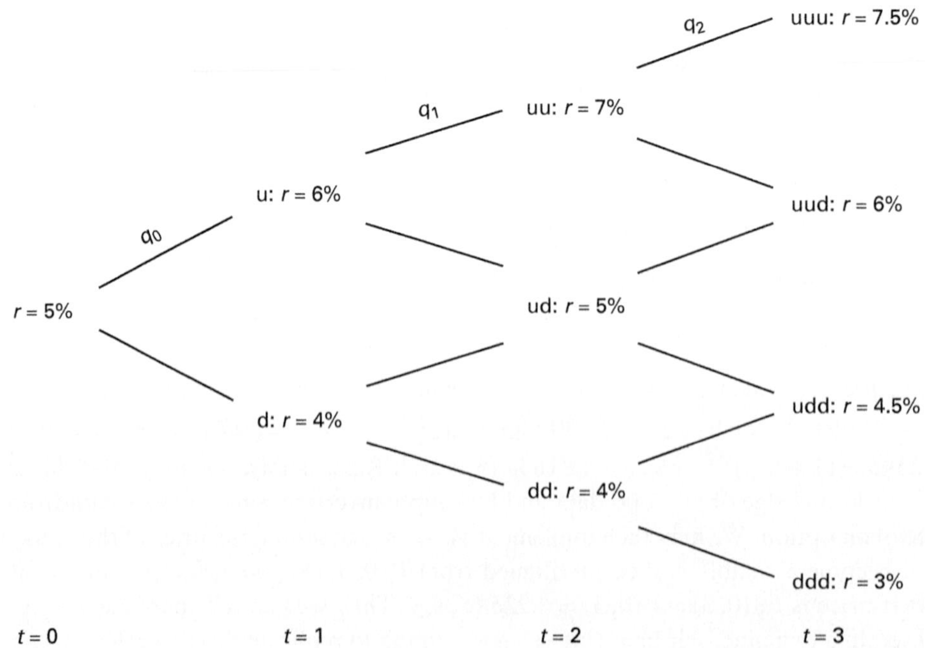

Figure 12.28
A binomial interest rate tree.

12.4.4.2 *Arrow-Debreu securities and the pricing of interest rate derivatives*

Arrow-Debreu securities are idealized assets that only pay over a specific state of nature (see chapter 2). In section 12.6, we rely on these securities to implement a methodology for achieving perfectly fitting models. This section is an introduction to such securities in the context of product evaluation in fixed income markets: we shall simply assume that some Arrow-Debreu securities are traded and extract risk neutral probabilities and evaluate interest rate derivatives such as "caplets" or "forward rate agreements." Likewise, note that this section is only a short introduction to interest rate derivative pricing. Chapter 13 provides a systematic treatment of these topics within a continuous time framework.

Extracting risk neutral probabilities from Arrow-Debreu securities Assume that the discretely compounded 1-year rate, the "short-term rate," evolves over time as in the tree of figure 12.28. We assume that three securities are traded: (i) a zero coupon bond expiring in two years, quoting for 0.91000; (ii) a zero coupon bond expiring in three years, quoting for 0.86500; and (iii) an Arrow-Debreu security, paying off \$1 only at time 3 in state "uuu," where the short-term rate equals 7.5%; we assume that this security is quoting for 0.10000.

We assume that the risk neutral probabilities of upward movements in the short-term rate change over time and take three values, q_0, q_1, and q_2, but are independent of the state of nature. We calibrate these probabilities to match all available market data. First, we derive q_0 based on the price of the 2-year zero, $P_\$ (0,2)$ say, as follows:

$$P_\$ (0,2) = 0.91000 = \frac{1}{1.05} \left(q_0 P_u (1,2) + (1 - q_0) P_d (1,2) \right),$$

where, with straightforward notation,

$$P_u(1,2)=\frac{1}{1.06}=0.94340, \quad P_d(1,2)=\frac{1}{1.04}=0.96154.$$

Solving for q_0 yields $q_0=0.33284$. Next, we calibrate q_1 such that the model price matches the price of the 3-year zero, $P_\$(0,3)$, say. We have

$$\begin{aligned}P_\$(0,3)=0.86500&=\frac{1}{1.05}\left(q_0 P_u(1,3)+(1-q_0)P_d(1,3)\right)\\&=\frac{1}{1.05}\left(0.33284\cdot P_u(1,3)+0.66716\cdot P_d(1,3)\right),\end{aligned}$$

where

$$P_u(1,3)=\frac{1}{1.06}\left(q_1 P_{uu}(2,3)+(1-q_1)P_{ud}(2,3)\right),$$

$$P_d(1,3)=\frac{1}{1.04}\left(q_1 P_{ud}(2,3)+(1-q_1)P_{dd}(2,3)\right),$$

and

$$P_{uu}(2,3)=\frac{1}{1.07}=0.93458, \quad P_{ud}(2,3)=\frac{1}{1.05}=0.95238, P_{dd}(2,3)=\frac{1}{1.04}=0.96154.$$

Solving for q_1 yields $q_1=0.66507$. Finally, we calibrate q_3 through the price of the Arrow-Debreu security paying in state "uuu." This price, denoted as $p_{uuu}^{\$}(3)$, is given by

$$\begin{aligned}p_{uuu}^{\$}(3)&=0.10000\\&=\frac{1}{1.05}\frac{1}{1.06}\frac{1}{1.07}q_0q_1q_2\\&=\frac{1}{1.05}\frac{1}{1.06}\frac{1}{1.07}0.33284\times 0.66507\times q_2,\end{aligned}$$

such that $q_2=0.53798$.

Pricing interest rate derivatives Next, we use the previously calibrated probabilities to price some interest rate derivatives. First, consider a "caplet" contingent on the rates prevailing at time $t=3$, paying off at time $t=4$, with a strike rate equal to 5%, and a notional value equal to \$100. The payoff of this product at $t=4$ is $\max\{L-5\%,0\}$, where L is the rate at $t=3$. That is, while uncertainty is resolved at $t=3$, payoffs are paid at $t=4$; this timing is entirely consistent with market conventions as explained in more detail in chapter 13 (see section 13.8).

Therefore, the discounted payoffs in each state of nature at $t=3$ are

uuu: $\frac{1}{1.075}\max\{7.5-5,0\}=2.32560$

uud: $\frac{1}{1.06}\max\{6-5,0\}=0.94340$

udd: $\frac{1}{1.045}\max\{4.5-5,0\}=0$

ddd: $\frac{1}{1.03}\max\{3-5,0\}=0.$

As for time $t=2$ and $t=1$, we have

$$t=2 \quad \text{uu:} \quad A_1 \equiv \tfrac{1}{1.07}\left(q_2 2.32560 + (1-q_2)\, 0.94340\right) = 1.5766$$

$$\text{ud:} \quad A_2 \equiv \tfrac{1}{1.05}\left(q_2 0.94340 + (1-q_2)\, 0\right) = 0.48336$$

$$\text{dd:} \quad A_3 \equiv 0$$

$$t=1 \quad \text{u:} \quad B_1 \equiv \tfrac{1}{1.06}\left(q_1 A_1 + (1-q_1)\, A_2\right) = 1.1419$$

$$\text{d:} \quad B_2 \equiv \tfrac{1}{1.04}\left(q_1 A_2 + (1-q_1)\, A_3\right) = 0.30910.$$

Therefore, the price of the caplet, Cap, say, is

$$\text{Cap} = \frac{1}{1.05}\left(q_0 B_1 + (1-q_0)\, B_2\right) = 0.55837.$$

Next, consider a forward rate agreement, where at $t=0$, two counterparties agree that at $t=4$, they will exchange with each other the variable short-term rate prevailing at $t=3$ against a fixed interest rate equal to K. We can use the previously calibrated probabilities to determine the *forward rate*, that is, the level of K that makes the value of this agreement equal to zero at $t=0$. We consider a "payer" forward agreement, one for which the discounted payoffs at $t=3$ are

$$\text{uuu:} \quad \pi_{uuu} \equiv \tfrac{1}{1.075}\,(7.5-K)$$

$$\text{uud:} \quad \pi_{uud} \equiv \tfrac{1}{1.06}\,(6-K)$$

$$\text{udd:} \quad \pi_{udd} \equiv \tfrac{1}{1.045}\,(4.5-K)$$

$$\text{ddd:} \quad \pi_{ddd} \equiv \tfrac{1}{1.03}\,(3-K).$$

At time $t=2$ and $t=1$, the payoffs are:

$$t=2 \quad \text{uu:} \quad \tilde{A}_{uu} \equiv \tfrac{1}{1.07}\left(q_2 \pi_{uuu} + (1-q_2)\, \pi_{uud}\right) = 5.9519 - 0.87506 \times K$$

$$\text{ud:} \quad \tilde{A}_{ud} \equiv \tfrac{1}{1.05}\left(q_2 \pi_{uud} + (1-q_2)\, \pi_{udd}\right) = 4.7950 - 0.90443 \times K$$

$$\text{dd:} \quad \tilde{A}_{dd} \equiv \tfrac{1}{1.04}\left(q_2 \pi_{udd} + (1-q_2)\, \pi_{ddd}\right) = 3.5215 - 0.92632 \times K$$

$$t=1 \quad \text{u:} \quad \tilde{B}_{u} \equiv \tfrac{1}{1.06}\left(q_1 \tilde{A}_{uu} + (1-q_1)\, \tilde{A}_{ud}\right) = 5.2495 - 0.83481 \times K$$

$$\text{d:} \quad \tilde{B}_{d} \equiv \tfrac{1}{1.04}\left(q_1 \tilde{A}_{ud} + (1-q_1)\, \tilde{A}_{dd}\right) = 4.2004 - 0.87669 \times K$$

We can now express the value of the contract as a function of the fixed rate K as follows:

$$\text{Fwd}\,(K) \equiv \frac{1}{1.05}\left(q_0 \tilde{B}_u + (1-q_0)\, \tilde{B}_d\right) = 4.3329 - 0.82167 \times K. \tag{12.25}$$

The forward rate is the value of K such that $\text{Fwd}\,(K)=0$, that is, $K=5.27330\%$. More generally, we can determine the value of the forward rate agreement in eq. (12.25) for any value of K. For example, we have that $\text{Fwd}\,(K=6) = 4.3329 - 0.82167 \times 6 = -0.59712$ in percentage terms.

Finally, we determine the no-arbitrage price of a bond expiring at $t=4$, $P(0,4)$, based on the forward rate relation (see eq. (12.4)), $\frac{P_{\$}(0,3)-P(0,4)}{P(0,4)}=5.27330\%$, leading to $P(0,4)=0.82170$. This value is indeed identical to that we may infer while pricing the bond on a tree as we will now show. At time $t=3$, we have that

uuu: $P_{uuu}(3,4)=\frac{1}{1.075}=0.93023$

uud: $P_{uud}(3,4)=\frac{1}{1.06}=0.94340$

udd: $P_{udd}(3,4)=\frac{1}{1.045}=0.95694$

ddd: $P_{ddd}(3,4)=\frac{1}{1.03}=0.97087.$

Then, we solve recursively, as usual:

$t=2$ uu: $P_{uu}(2,4)=\frac{1}{1.07}\left(q_2 P_{uuu}(3,4)+(1-q_2)P_{uud}(3,4)\right)=0.87506$

ud: $P_{ud}(2,4)=\frac{1}{1.05}\left(q_2 P_{uud}(3,4)+(1-q_2)P_{udd}(3,4)\right)=0.90443$

dd: $P_{dd}(2,4)=\frac{1}{1.04}\left(q_2 P_{udd}(3,4)+(1-q_2)P_{ddd}(3,4)\right)=0.92632$

$t=1$ u: $P_u(1,4)=\frac{1}{1.06}\left(q_1 P_{uu}(2,4)+(1-q_1)P_{ud}(2,4)\right)=0.83481$

d: $P_d(1,4)=\frac{1}{1.04}\left(q_1 P_{ud}(2,4)+(1-q_1)P_{dd}(2,4)\right)=0.87669.$

Finally, we calculate the price $P(0,4)=\frac{1}{1.05}\left(q_0 P_u(1,4)+(1-q_0)P_d(1,4)\right)=0.82167$ ≈ 0.82170 by rounding.

12.4.5 Extensions to Trinomial Trees

Trinomial trees model uncertainty as evolving through "trinary" events: each node in these trees would now give rise to three mutually exclusive events, not two, as in the standard binomial trees. Trinomial trees are useful to model mean reversion. In some cases, trinomial trees may be used to approximate the solution to partial differential equations.

12.5 The Ho-Lee Model

Ho and Lee (1986) introduce a revolutionary approach to modeling yield curve movements. This approach does not aim to a theory that *explains* the yield curve. Rather, it takes the observed yield curve as given and shifts its focus on modeling no-arbitrage *movements* of the entire curve. The model accomplishes the task of "matching" model prices to market prices. This matching is needed to ensure that the (model-implied) prices of the assets underlying derivative products coincide with market prices. Consider, for example, the Black–Scholes model, by which the underlying asset price is taken to be the market price. The Ho-Lee model aims to have the same objective in the more complex fixed income space. In chapter 13, we derive this model in continuous time and connect it to a more general approach to interest rate modeling developed later by Heath, Jarrow, and Morton (1992). Note that Ho and Lee originally derived their model in discrete time. This section also provides a derivation of the model in discrete time; the outcome may then be compared with alternative calibration methods in this chapter.

The main idea underlying the model is that the movements of the yield curve can be modeled through a binomial tree, much in the spirit of the Cox, Ross, and Rubinstein (1979) tree representation of Black and Scholes (1973). However, in Black and Scholes (1973) and Cox, Ross, and Rubinstein (1979), the underlying asset is a traded risk, and its price then satisfies the martingale condition. Instead, interest rate derivatives generally depend on risks that are not traded and therefore are not martingales. Further, because bond prices satisfy obvious boundary conditions, return volatility is time-varying. Ho and Lee address these issues by modeling the movements of the entire collection of bond prices. Note that there are three ways to achieve this task: (i) by making risk neutral probabilities time-varying for a given tree with predetermined values of the short-term rate (as in the previous sections), (ii) by assuming a constant risk neutral probability and searching for the values of the short-term rate on the tree, and (iii) by a combination of (i) and (ii) as in the implied binomial trees of chapter 11 (see section 11.7). The Ho-Lee model relies on the second modeling strategy. The key feature of this model is to determine no-arbitrage movements of the whole yield curve obtained while modeling the price of zero coupon bonds of any maturity.

12.5.1 The Tree

The Ho-Lee model determines no-arbitrage movements of bond prices that are consistent with the initial term structure of interest rates. Because forward rates link to bond prices (see, e.g., eq. 12.4)), the model is then a model of forward rate movements. In other words, the Ho-Lee is a *representation* of current bond prices (in terms of observed forward rates), rather than a *model* of current bond prices.

Assume that the price of any zero is generated by a binomial tree. Let $P_j(t,T)$ be the price of a pure discount bond at time t with a time to maturity $T-t$ after j *upstate price movements*. Let $j \sim B(t, 1-q)$, a binomial random variable, meaning that $\Pr(j) = \binom{t}{j}(1-q)^j q^{t-j}$, such that

$$E(j) = (1-q)\,t, \quad var(j) = q(1-q)\,t,$$

where $1-q$ is the risk neutral probability of a single upstate *price* movement. That is, if at time t, the number of upstate movements is equal to j, then at time $t+1$, the number of upstate movements can either increase to $j+1$ with probability $1-q$ or stay at j with probability q.[11] Figure 12.29 illustrates the price movements on this binomial tree.

Further, after one period, any zero is obviously one period closer to maturity. At maturity, $t=T$, the price of any zero is worth \$1, namely,

$$P_j(T,T) = 1, \quad \text{for all } j \text{ and } T.$$

Note that, in this model, it doesn't necessarily hold that $P_j(t+1,T) < P_j(t,T)$. Rather, we would have to expect that, as time to maturity approaches zero and the zero converges to par, $P_j(t+1,T) > P_j(t,T)$.

11. Therefore, we are now following the convention of having high values of bond prices in the upper parts of the tree.

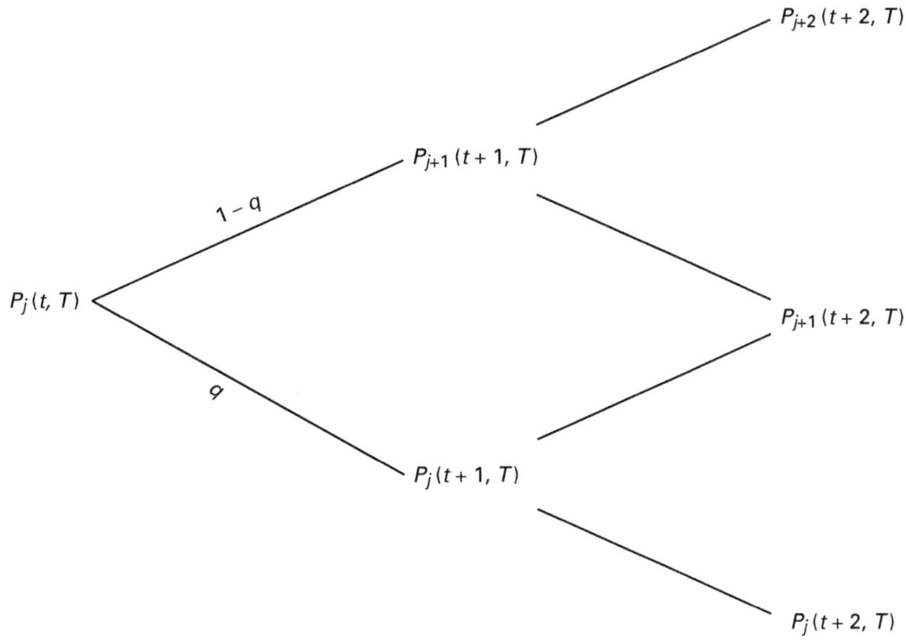

Figure 12.29
A binomial tree for a zero-coupon bond price.

12.5.2 Price Movements and the Martingale Restriction

In the absence of arbitrage, the expected return on the zero (under the risk neutral probability) at time t must equal the short-term rate, namely, $P_j(t,T) = e^{-r_j(t)}\mathbb{E}(P_{\cdot}(t+1,T))$, or

$$P_j(t,T) = P_j(t,t+1)\left[(1-q)P_{j+1}(t+1,T) + qP_j(t+1,T)\right], \tag{12.26}$$

where $P_j(t,t+1) = e^{-r_j(t)}$ and $r_j(t)$ is the continuously compounded short-term rate at time t after j upward movements. We call this condition the *martingale restriction.*

Let us introduce notation and assumptions regarding the price movements along the tree. We assume that

$$\underbrace{\frac{P_{j+1}(t+1,T)}{P_j(t,T)} = u(T-t)\frac{1}{P_j(t,t+1)}}_{\text{up at } t} \quad \text{and} \quad \underbrace{\frac{P_j(t+1,T)}{P_j(t,T)} = d(T-t)\frac{1}{P_j(t,t+1)}}_{\text{down at } t}. \tag{12.27}$$

The two functions, $u(\cdot)$ and $d(\cdot)$, also called "perturbation functions," are taken to be state independent and have to be determined endogenously. They capture the price movements in excess of the risk-free rate. Indeed, eqs. (12.27) tell us that the discounted gross return from going long a bond is

$$\underbrace{\frac{P(t+1,T)}{P(t,T)}}_{\text{Gross return}} \cdot \underbrace{P(t,t+1)}_{\text{Discount}} = \begin{cases} u(T-t) \text{ with probability } 1-q \\ d(T-t) \text{ with probability } q \end{cases}.$$

If there was no uncertainty, we would have $u(T-t)=d(T-t)=1$ for all $t \leq T$. It will be shown below that, in the general case, $d(T-t) \leq 1 \leq u(T-t)$.

Let us begin from the end. One period before expiration, that is, at $t=T-1$, our price is certain to jump to one, with a jump size equal to the short-term rate $r_j(t)$. Hence, the following boundary condition for the two functions $u(\cdot)$ and $d(\cdot)$ holds:

$$u(1)=d(1)=1. \tag{12.28}$$

In terms of the two functions $u(\cdot)$ and $d(\cdot)$, the martingale restriction in eq. (12.26) is

$$1=(1-q)\,u(T-t)+q d(T-t), \quad t \leq T. \tag{12.29}$$

Eq. (12.29) matches the "martingale restriction" introduced in chapter 11 (see section 11.7) in the equity case: stock prices are tied down to their future up-and-down movements through the risk neutral probability. In the Ho-Lee model, these movements depend on the bond maturity through the two functions $u(T-t)$ and $d(T-t)$, which are endogenous, making the evaluation problem more intricate.

12.5.3 The Recombining Condition and Interest Rate Volatility

Ho and Lee consider a recombining tree: the price $P_j(t,T)$ depends only on j, not on the exact sequence of movements leading to j. To summarize, then, we are looking for two functions $u(T-t)$ and $d(T-t)$ such that (i) the no-arbitrage condition in eq. (12.29) holds true and (ii) the tree is recombining (just as illustrated by figure 12.29). We now elaborate on the second condition (recombination). This condition implies that the price at time $t+2$ in the event of $j+1$ jumps, $P_{j+1}(t+2,T)$, can be generated by one of two paths that we track through the two equalities in (12.27):

(i) The "up-down" path, $P_j(t,T) \rightarrow P_{j+1}(t+1,T) \rightarrow P_{j+1}(t+2,T)$, where

$$P_{j+1}(t+2,T)=\underbrace{\overbrace{u(T-t)\frac{P_j(t,T)}{P_j(t,t+1)}}^{\equiv P_{j+1}(t+1,T),\text{ up at } t} \times d(T-t-1)\frac{1}{P_{j+1}(t+1,t+2)}}_{\text{down at } t+1}. \tag{12.30}$$

(ii) The "down-up" path, $P_j(t,T) \rightarrow P_j(t+1,T) \rightarrow P_{j+1}(t+2,T)$, where

$$P_{j+1}(t+2,T)=\underbrace{\overbrace{d(T-t)\frac{P_j(t,T)}{P_j(t,t+1)}}^{\equiv P_j(t+1,T),\text{ down at } t} \times u(T-t-1)\frac{1}{P_j(t+1,t+2)}}_{\text{up at } t+1}. \tag{12.31}$$

By equating eq. (12.30) and (12.31), we obtain

$$\frac{u(T-t)}{d(T-t)}=\frac{u(T-t-1)}{d(T-t-1)}\delta^{-1}, \quad \delta^{-1} \equiv \frac{P_{j+1}(t+1,t+2)}{P_j(t+1,t+2)} \in (1,\infty), \tag{12.32}$$

where δ is, by assumption, a constant, which we interpret in a moment. Eq. (12.32) is a finite-difference equation for the ratio $u(T-t)/d(T-t)$. Given the boundary conditions

(12.28), the solution is

$$\frac{u(T-t)}{d(T-t)}=\delta^{-(T-t-1)}. \tag{12.33}$$

The constant δ relates to the *volatility of the short-term rate*. Indeed, by taking logs in (12.32), we obtain

$$\ln\delta^{-1}=-\left[r_{j+1}(t+1)-r_j(t+1)\right]. \tag{12.34}$$

Moreover, conditionally on time t and price jumps equal to $j\leq t$, the short-term rate is binomially distributed and can take on two values: (i) $r_{j+1}(t+1)$ with probability $1-q$ and $r_j(t+1)$ with probability q. Then, the conditional variance of the short-term rate, $var_t[\tilde{r}(t+1)]$ say, satisfies

$$\sqrt{var_t[\tilde{r}(t+1)]}=\sqrt{q(1-q)}\cdot\left|r_{j+1}(t+1)-r_j(t+1)\right|=\sqrt{q(1-q)}\cdot\ln\delta^{-1}, \tag{12.35}$$

where the second equality follows by eq. (12.34).

There are no economic reasons to assume that δ is constant. Rather, the assumption that δ is time-varying and possibly state dependent may help match more than the initial yield curve (say European options), similarly as for the implied binomial trees for equity reviewed in chapter 11. At the same time, assuming δ is time-varying may lead to models without closed form solutions. Section 12.6 deals with models without a closed-form solution. The next section shows that the bond price can be expressed in closed form under the assumption that δ is constant.

12.5.4 Model Solution

12.5.4.1 Solution

Eq. (12.33) is the recombining condition, a "statistical" condition, so to speak (i.e., based on the probabilistic assumptions regarding the data-generating process). Instead, eq. (12.29) is the martingale condition that prevents arbitrage. Therefore, we are left with a system of two equations, eq. (12.33) and eq. (12.29), with two unknowns, $u(\cdot)$ and $d(\cdot)$:

$$\begin{cases} u(T-t)=\delta^{-(T-t-1)}d(T-t) \\ (1-q)\,u(T-t)+qd(T-t)=1 \end{cases}.$$

The solution to this system is

$$u(T-t)=\frac{1}{(1-q)+q\delta^{T-t-1}},\quad d(T-t)=\frac{\delta^{T-t-1}}{(1-q)+q\delta^{T-t-1}}. \tag{12.36}$$

So the problem is solved. Once we assign values to q and δ and an initial bond price $P(t,T)$, we plug eqs. (12.36) into eqs. (12.27) and populate the tree: we plug bond prices on each node of the tree. Then we may price interest rate derivatives, that is, assets with payoffs indexed to bond prices or interest rates over a given set of nodes. Note that eqs. (12.27) dictate the law of motion of the entire structure of bond prices along the trees, and they are silent regarding the initial condition (i.e., at time $t=0$). The condition is, naturally, that the market price is matched by the model price for any maturity, say, $P_0(0,T)=P_\$(0,T)$ for all T.

To sum up, the Ho-Lee model doesn't take any a priori stance regarding the dynamics of the short-term rate. Rather, it imposes (i) the martingale restriction on bond prices, an economic restriction, eq. (12.29), and (ii) the simplifying assumption the tree is recombining, a technical condition, eq. (12.27). These two conditions are sufficient to tell us about the dynamics of the short-term rate. While deliberately simple, this model has inspired a modern approach to interest rate modeling that is dealt with in much detail in chapter 13.

12.5.4.2 *Closed-form solution*

We may actually do more and develop a closed-form solution for the bond price. Let $F_S^j(t)$ be the forward rate as of time t after the occurrence of j upward price movements, and let the continuously compounded forward rate $\hat{F}_S^j(t)$ be defined as

$$\hat{F}_S^j(t) \equiv \ln\left(1 + F_S^j(t)\right), \quad j \leq t.$$

In appendix 12.C, we show that

$$P_j(t,T) = \frac{P_\$(0,T)}{P_\$(0,t)} e^{-\sum_{S=t}^{T-1}\left(\hat{F}_S^j(t) - \hat{F}_S(0)\right)}. \tag{12.37}$$

In appendix 12.C, we also show that the changes in the forward rate, $\hat{F}_S^j(t) - \hat{F}_S(0)$, satisfy

$$\hat{F}_S^j(t) = \hat{F}_S(0) + \ln\frac{u(S+1-t)}{u(S+1)} - (t-j)\ln\delta, \quad j \leq t. \tag{12.38}$$

Replacing eq. (12.38) into eq. (12.37) and using the solution for the perturbation function $u(\cdot)$ in (12.36) leaves

$$P_j(t,T) = \frac{P_\$(0,T)}{P_\$(0,t)} \delta^{(T-t)(t-j)} \prod_{S=t}^{T-1} \frac{(1-q)+q\delta^{S-t}}{(1-q)+q\delta^S}. \tag{12.39}$$

From the perspective of time 0, the price of the zero at t is, for each state j, a function of the initial yield curve, the volatility parameter δ, and the risk neutral probability q. Note in particular how important this volatility is. It is the only parameter to be estimated in addition to q. There is then an interesting parallel between this model and that of Black and Scholes (1973). In both models, the inputs are the volatilities of the fundamentals (the short-term interest rate in the Ho-Lee model and stock returns in the Black–Scholes model). However, in the Ho-Lee model, the "market" input does not link to the short-term rate but to the entire yield curve, and the output relates to future bond price movements. In the Black–Scholes model, the market input is the fundamental, the stock price, and the output is the initial option price.

Finally, the model displays the properties we would require from a perfectly fitting model (see figure 12.30). First, it matches each price at $t=0$ as can be easily verified. Second, it bridges to one when $t=T$. Third, the price is random at any time $t: 0<t<T$, that is, $P_j(t,T)$ occurs with probability $\binom{t}{j}(1-q)^j q^{t-j}$. Naturally, the values taken by $P_j(t,T)$ are determined by the equilibrium of the model, that is, by eq. (12.39). All in all, the model predicts random outcomes at time t while ensuring at the same time that the initial yield curve is fitted without errors. We are interested in random outcomes at t because we

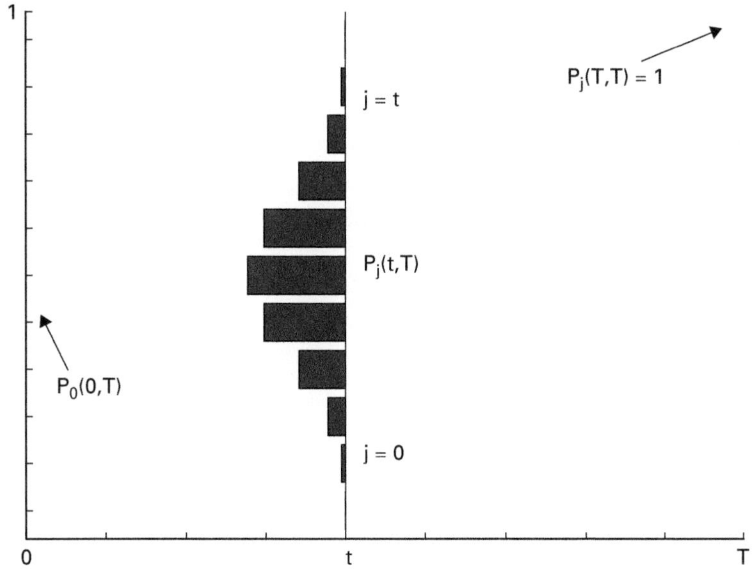

Figure 12.30
Probability distribution and boundary conditions for a zero-coupon bond price.

want to be able to evaluate options expiring at that date, based on model that predicts the underlying to be pinned down without errors.

12.5.5 Model Calibration

We need to "estimate" the value of δ. We can proceed as follows. Consider eq. (12.39), and let $T=t+1$. We have

$$P_j(t,t+1)=\frac{P_\$(0,t+1)}{P_\$(0,t)}\delta^{t-j}\frac{1}{(1-q)+q\delta^t},\quad j\leq t. \tag{12.40}$$

The continuously compounded short-term rate predicted by the model is

$$r_j(t)\equiv-\ln P_j(t,t+1)=\hat{F}_t(0)+\ln\left((1-q)+q\delta^t\right)-(t-j)\ln\delta,\quad j\leq t, \tag{12.41}$$

where $\hat{F}_t(0)\equiv\ln P(0,t)-\ln P(0,t+1)$. We also have that

$$r_j(1)-r(0)=\hat{F}_1(0)-\hat{F}_0(0)+\ln((1-q)+q\delta)+\ln\delta^{-1}\cdot(1-j).$$

Hence, the parameter δ can be chosen such that the volatility of the short-term rate predicted by the model matches exactly the volatility of the short-term rate that we see in the data. Concretely, we can take $\hat{\delta}=\exp(-\text{ Std}(\Delta r)/\sqrt{q(1-q)})$, where Std$(\Delta r)$ is the standard deviation of the short-term rate in the data.

12.5.6 An Example

Assume that three zero coupon bonds are available for trading, with current market prices of (i) $P_\$(0,1)=0.9851$ (the price of a 6-month zero), (ii) $P_\$(0,2)=0.9685$ (the price of a 1-year zero), and (iii) $P_\$(0,3)=0.9445$ (the price of a 18-month zero). We know that the price of one-period zero at time t, in the event of j upward *price* jumps from the current date to t, is given by eq. (12.40), where, in this example, each period is equal to 6 months. We assume that $q=\frac{1}{2}$ and $\delta=0.9802$.

12.5.6.1 *The dynamics of the short-term rate*

We determine the dynamics of the short-term rate for as many periods as possible, based on the market prices. We use eq. (12.40) to find the one-period zeros in each node.

- $t=0$. We have, trivially, $P(0,1)=P_\$(0,1)=0.9851$.
- $t=1$. We have two cases:
  - $j=0$: $P_0(1,2)=2\frac{P_\$(0,2)}{P_\$(0,1)}\delta\frac{1}{1+\delta}=0.9733$
  - $j=1$: $P_1(1,2)=2\frac{P_\$(0,2)}{P_\$(0,1)}\frac{1}{1+\delta}=0.9930$.
- $t=2$. We have three cases:
  - $j=0$: $P_0(2,3)=2\frac{P_\$(0,3)}{P_\$(0,2)}\delta^2\frac{1}{1+\delta^2}=0.9557$
  - $j=1$: $P_1(2,3)=2\frac{P_\$(0,3)}{P_\$(0,2)}\delta\frac{1}{1+\delta^2}=0.9750$
  - $j=2$: $P_2(2,3)=2\frac{P_\$(0,3)}{P_\$(0,2)}\frac{1}{1+\delta^2}=0.9947$.

Figure 12.31 summarizes these results.

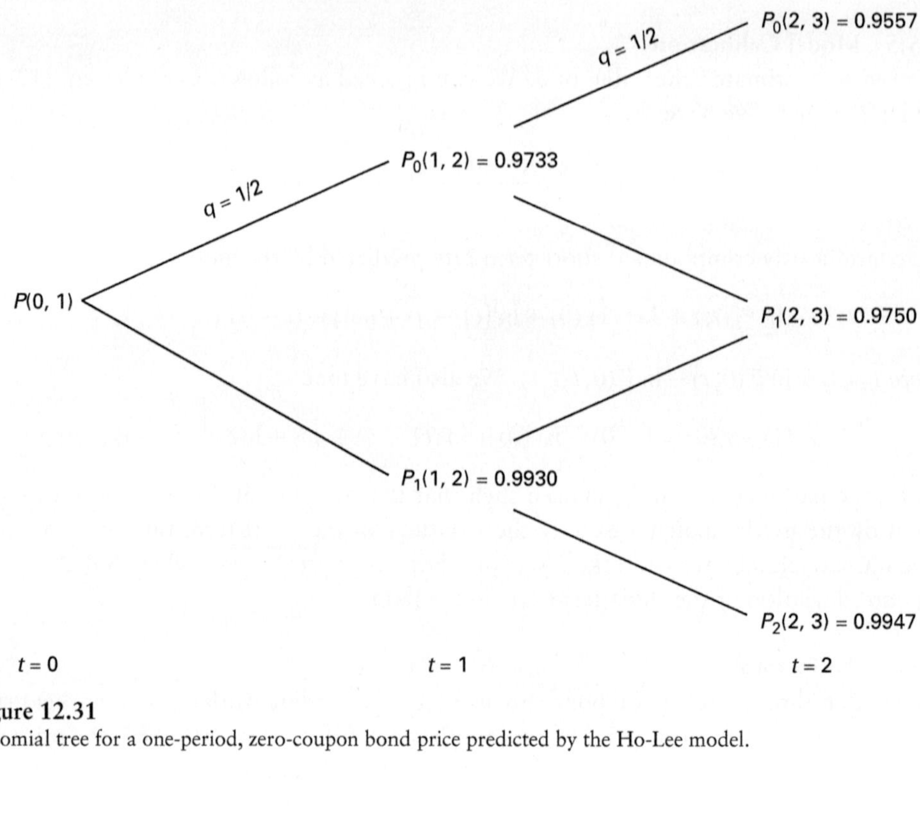

Figure 12.31
Binomial tree for a one-period, zero-coupon bond price predicted by the Ho-Lee model.

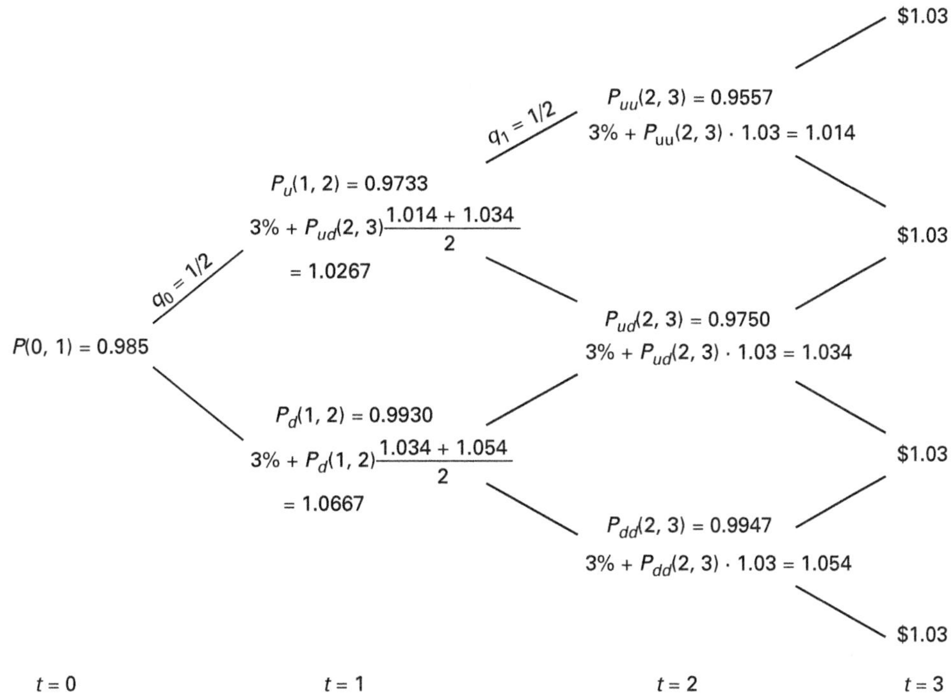

Figure 12.32
Values of a three-period, coupon-bearing bond price implied by the tree in figure 12.31.

12.5.6.2 *Pricing a coupon bearing bond*

Next, we consider pricing some additional bonds, e.g., a 1.5-year bond that pays (semiannually) coupons at 3% of the principal of $1. First, we need to find the value of this bond in each node of the tree. Note that, in each node, the price equals (i) the discounted expectation of its future value (including coupons) and (ii) the current coupons (see figure 12.32). That is, we follow the convention that the bond purchased at time t doesn't give the owner the right to receive any coupon at time t, but only from time $t+1$ onward.

Because the bond does not pay coupons at time zero, its current price is

$$P = P(0,1)\left(\frac{1}{2}1.0267 + \frac{1}{2}1.0667\right) = 0.9851\left(\frac{1}{2}1.0267 + \frac{1}{2}1.0667\right) = 1.0311.$$

Naturally, this price could be derived through the simple formula: $\left[P_{\$}(0,1) + P_{\$}(0,2) + P_{\$}(0,3)\right] \cdot 0.03 + P_{\$}(0,3)$. However, the derivation in this section is useful as it enables one to price dedicated derivatives written on the coupon bearing bond, as explained below.

12.5.6.3 *Pricing European options*

We consider pricing options on the previous 1.5-year bond: two call options that have the same strike price, $1, and maturities equal to 6 months and 1 year. First, we determine no-arbitrage movements of the *ex-coupon* bond price: if we purchase the bond today, we are entitled to receive coupons only starting from the next period. Figure 12.33 depicts

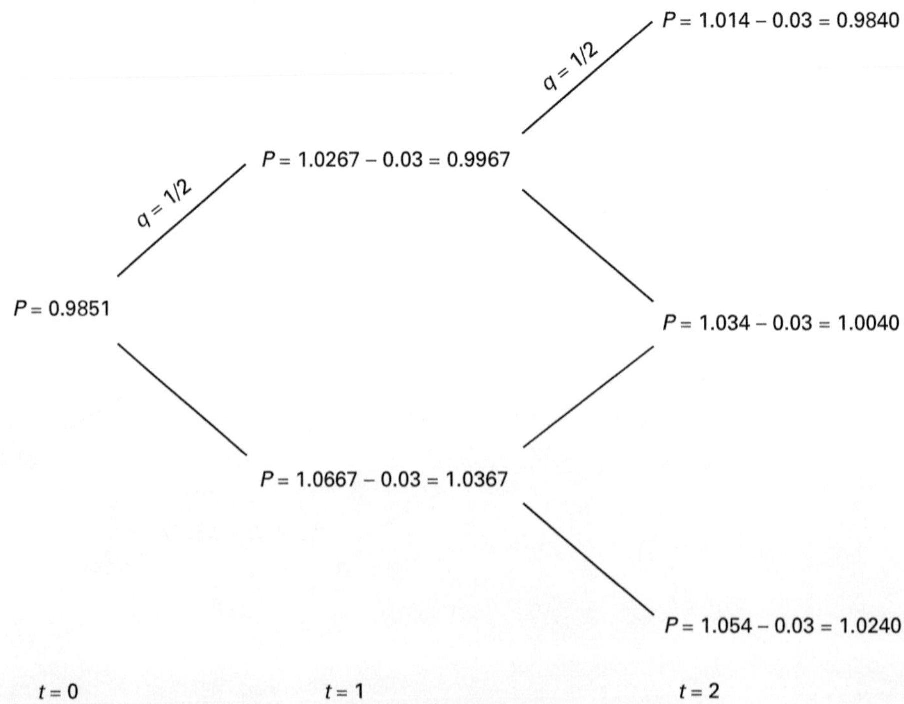

Figure 12.33
Ex-coupon values corresponding to the three-period bond prices in figure 12.32.

the relevant tree. We just subtract the coupon, 0.03, from each cum-coupon price in each node of the tree.

We may now price the two options. Figure 12.34 illustrates the evaluation of the 6-month maturity option. We have

$$C = 0.9851\left(\frac{1}{2}\cdot 0 + \frac{1}{2}\cdot 0.0367\right) = 1.808\times 10^{-2}.$$

The call option with a one-year maturity is dealt with similarly. Relying on the calculations displayed in figure 12.35, we have that

$$C = P(0,1)\left(\frac{1}{2}0.0019 + \frac{1}{2}0.014\right) = 0.9851\left(\frac{1}{2}0.0019 + \frac{1}{2}0.014\right) = 7.831\times 10^{-3}.$$

12.5.7 Continuous Time Approximations with an Application to Barbell Trading

Chapter 13 revisits the Ho-Lee model, explaining that it is part of a general class of models known as "HJM models" after the work of Heath, Jarrow, and Morton (1992) (see section 13.7); these models are typically formulated in continuous time. This section provides a heuristic derivation of the continuous time limit of the Ho-Lee model described in this chapter. It also relies on this continuous time extension to revisit the barbell strategies described in section 12.3. These strategies were assessed without making reference to a fully fledged no-arbitrage model, a task accomplished in this section.

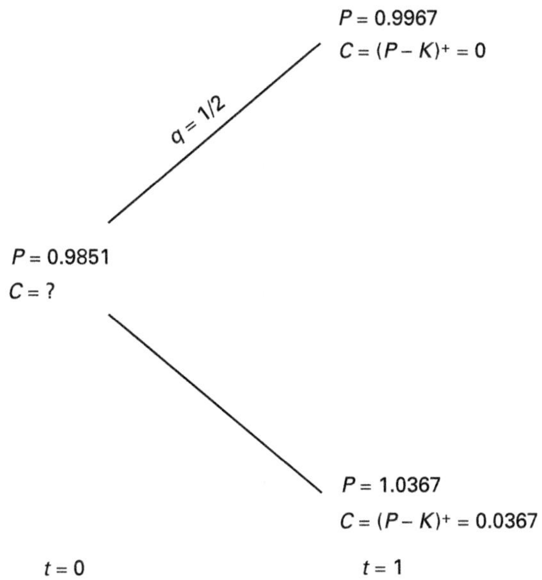

Figure 12.34
Binomial tree evaluation of a short-dated option on the three-period bond (with ex-coupon values in figure 12.33).

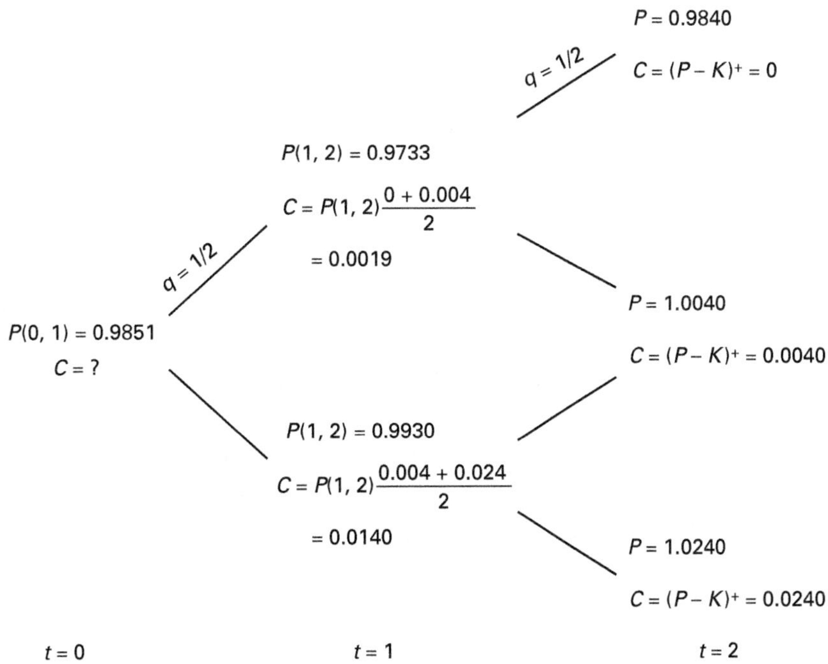

Figure 12.35
Binomial tree evaluation of a long dated option on the three-period bond (with ex coupon values in figure 12.33).

12.5.7.1 The approximation

Consider eq. (12.41), and define $r = -\Delta t^{-1} \ln P$ and $r_j^{\Delta}(t) \equiv r_j(t)\,\Delta t$, such that

$$r_j^{\Delta}(t) = \zeta_t - (t(1-q) - j)\ln\delta, \quad \zeta_t \equiv \hat{F}_t(0) + \ln\left(\delta^{-qt}(1-q) + \delta^{(1-q)t}q\right).$$

We have

$$\mathbb{E}_0\left[r_j^{\Delta}(t)\right] = \zeta_t, \quad \text{and} \quad \sigma^2 t \equiv \mathbb{V}_0\left[r_j^{\Delta}(t)\right] = \left(\ln\delta^{-1}\right)^2 q(1-q)\,t,$$

and we define $\ell \equiv \sigma/\sqrt{q(1-q)}$ such that, consistent with eq. (12.35), $\delta = e^{-\ell}$. Replacing δ into the definition of ζ_t and expanding terms up to the second order yields

$$\begin{aligned}
\zeta_t &= \hat{F}_t(0) + \ln\left(e^{\ell qt}(1-q) + e^{-\ell(1-q)t}q\right) \\
&\approx \hat{F}_t(0) + \ln\left(1 + \frac{1}{2}\ell^2 q(1-q)\,t^2\right) \\
&\approx \hat{F}_t(0) + \frac{1}{2}\ell^2 q(1-q)\,t^2 \\
&= \hat{F}_t(0) + \frac{1}{2}\sigma^2 t^2.
\end{aligned}$$

This expansion is accurate when ℓt is small. Now, note that

$$\mathbb{E}_0\left[r_j^{\Delta}(t)\right] = \hat{F}_t(0) + \frac{1}{2}\sigma^2 t^2, \quad \text{and} \quad \mathbb{V}_0\left[r_j^{\Delta}(t)\right] = \sigma^2 t. \tag{12.42}$$

Consistent with the previous calculations, chapter 13 shows that, in continuous time, the Ho-Lee model predicts that the short-term rate is the solution to

$$dr_t = \left(\frac{\partial}{\partial t} f_{\$}(0,t) + \sigma^2 t\right) dt + \sigma\, d\tilde{W}_t, \tag{12.43}$$

where $f_{\$}(0,t)$ is the instantaneous continuously compounded market forward rate, defined as $f_{\$}(0,T) = -\partial \ln P_{\$}(0,T)/\partial T$ (see section 13.2 of chapter 13), and $\tilde{W}_t$ is a Brownian motion defined under the risk neutral probability (see Section 13.6.2). In fact, chapter 13 shows that the Ho-Lee model counterpart to $f_{\$}(0,t)$, $f(0,t)$ say, is

$$f(s',t) - f(s,t) = \sigma^2 \int_s^{s'} (t-\tau)\,d\tau + \sigma(\tilde{W}_{s'} - \tilde{W}_s), \tag{12.44}$$

such that, for $r_{s'} = f(s',s')$,

$$r_{s'} - f(s,s') = \sigma^2 \int_s^{s'} (s'-\tau)\,d\tau + \sigma(\tilde{W}_{s'} - \tilde{W}_s). \tag{12.45}$$

Eq. (12.45) is the continuous time counterpart to the two conditions in eqs. (12.42). Combining eqs. (12.44) and (12.45) leaves

$$f(s',t) - f(s,t) = \sigma^2 (s'-s)(t-s') + r_{s'} - f(s,s'). \tag{12.46}$$

Chapter 13 (see section 13.7.1) explains that, for any model, it must hold that[12]

$$P(t,T)=\frac{P_\$(0,T)}{P_\$(0,t)}e^{-\int_t^T[f(t,u)-f(0,u)]du}. \tag{12.47}$$

Using the expression for $f(s',t)-f(s,t)$ in eq. (12.46) and integrating it leaves

$$\int_t^T [f(t,u)-f(0,u)]\,du=\frac{1}{2}\sigma^2(T-t)^2t+(T-t)\left(r_t-f(0,t)\right).$$

Replacing this expression into eq. (12.47) leaves

$$P(t,T)=\frac{P_\$(0,T)}{P_\$(0,t)}\exp\left(-\frac{1}{2}\sigma^2(T-t)^2t-\left(r_t-f(0,t)\right)(T-t)\right). \tag{12.48}$$

Eq. (12.48) provides a neat expression for the price of a zero coupon bond at time t. Our perspective is time 0. From this perspective, we view the price of the zero at time t, $P(t,T)$, as random, driven by the future value taken by the short-term rate, r_t. We may elaborate on this formula and use it for a variety of purposes. For example, we may price options consistent with the explanations given around figure 12.30. The next section develops an example by which this formula is used to evaluate the P&L of the barbell trade introduced in section 12.3.

12.5.7.2 *Application to barbell trading*

Section 12.3.3 argues that a barbell strategy may lead to positive profits due to "convexity" (see figure 12.5). However, this analysis does not take into account passage of time and no-arbitrage conditions; it may then lead us to misinterpret what represents a merely static analysis. We may use the Ho-Lee model and analyze the P&L of a barbell trade. We consider two situations: one in which the initial yield curve is flat and the other in which the initial yield curve is upward sloping.

We assume first that the yield curve is flat. We use the continuously compounded interest rate corresponding to the flat 5% of section 12.3.3, that is, $r=\ln 1.05=0.04879$. The portfolio includes units of bonds θ_1 and θ_2 determined through eq. (12.16). They are $\theta_1=0.45706$ and $\theta_3=0.56724$. Naturally, the instantaneous forward rate curve is flat and equal to $f_\$(0,t)=-\partial\ln P_\$(0,t)/\partial t=r$ for all t. We rely on eq. (12.48) and, assuming that $\sigma=0.03$, calculate the strategy value a few months later as follows:

$$\text{Bb}_t=100\times\left(\theta_1P(t,1)+\theta_3P(t,10)-P(t,5)\right). \tag{12.49}$$

Figure 12.36 depicts this strategy value for investment horizons equal to 1 month, 3 months, 6 months, and 1 year.

This trade is quite risky. Intuitively, the convexity effects depicted in figure 12.5 only kick in when the short-term rate leads toward its most extreme regions. Otherwise, time decay matters: by eq. (12.48), time decay would be irrelevant only when σ is small or when the investment horizon, t, is small. Thus, for long horizons, the barbell trade pays off when the short-term rate fluctuates significantly away from the initial value, $r=4.8790\%$.

12. For example, eq. (12.37) provides the discrete time counterpart to eq. (12.47).

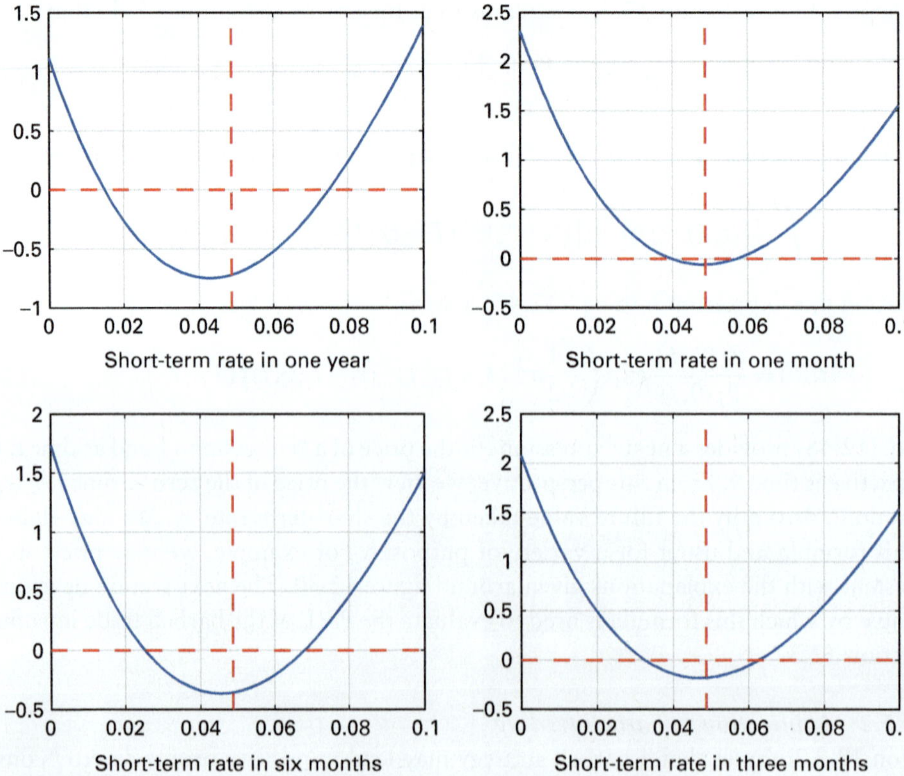

Figure 12.36
Barbell P&L, Bb_t in eq. (12.49), determined under the assumption that the yield curve is driven by the Ho-Lee model, eq. (12.48). The initial curve is flat at $r = 4.8790\%$. P&Ls for investment horizons of $t = 1/12$, $t = 3/12$, $t = 6/12$, and $t = 1$ are displayed in clockwise order. The vertical dashed lines pass through $r = 4.8790\%$, and the horizontal dashed lines pass through zero.

The required change in r_t diminishes with the investment horizon as explained. However, it still appears to be considerable: for example, at a one-month horizon, profits can be made when r_t moves to values either higher than about $r = 6\%$ or lower than $r = 4\%$. In fact, these calculations reveal that, in periods with low interest rate volatility, positive profits could be made with a *short* barbell trade (i.e., sell the barbell portfolio and long the 5-year bond). To roughly illustrate, for an investment horizon of 6 months, a short barbell trade leads to positive profits provided r_t will not fluctuate beyond the [2.5%, 6.8%] range.

Next, we assume that the initial yield curve is upward sloping and generate hypothetical prices as $P(0,t) = e^{-tY(t)}$, where $Y(t) \equiv 0.01(1 + \ln(1+t))$. We still determine the value of the portfolio according to eq. (12.16), that is, we rely on the self-financing condition in eq. (12.14) and both (i) the locally riskless condition in eq. (12.15), $dB_2(\hat{y}_2) = \theta_1 dB_1(\hat{y}_1) + \theta_3 dB_3(\hat{y}_3)$, and (ii) the (generically incorrect) assumption of parallel shifts in the yield curve, $\frac{\partial B_2(\hat{y}_2)}{\partial \hat{y}_2} = \frac{\partial B_1(\hat{y}_1)}{\partial \hat{y}_1}\theta_1 + \frac{\partial B_3(\hat{y}_3)}{\partial \hat{y}_3}\theta_3$. Figure 12.37 depicts P&Ls resulting from this trade. Similar to the P&Ls summarized by figure 12.36, the trade leads to profits only when r_t moves away, quite significantly, from its initial value, $r = 1\%$. In particular, only assuming

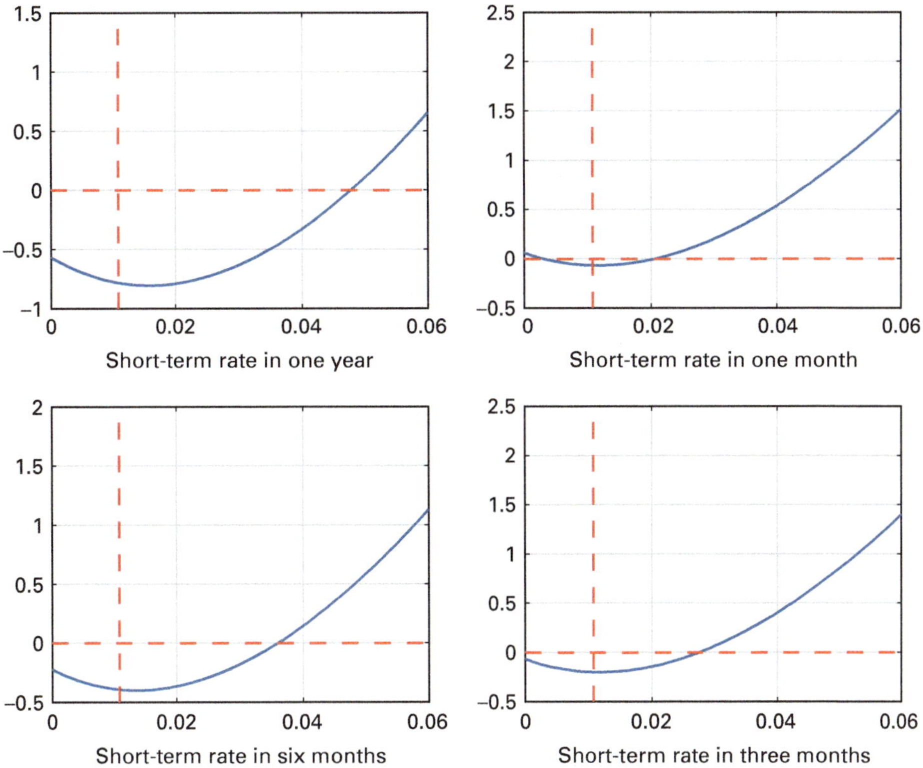

Figure 12.37
Barbell P&L, Bb (t) in eq. (12.49), determined under the assumption that the yield curve is driven by the Ho-Lee model, eq. (12.48). The initial yield curve is upward sloping as explained in the main text. P&Ls for investment horizons of $t = 1/12$, $t = 3/12$, $t = 6/12$, and $t = 1$ are displayed in clockwise order. The vertical dashed lines pass through the current short-term rate, $r = 1.0\%$, and the horizontal dashed lines pass through zero.

positive interest rates, profits can be made only when r_t increases to sufficiently high levels: the convexity effect materializes only with large changes in the short-term rate.

12.6 Beyond Ho-Lee: Calibration Through Arrow-Debreu Securities

The approach in the previous sections develops no-arbitrage restrictions on bond prices. These restrictions bear implications on forward rates and ultimately determine an *implied* stochastic process of the short-term rate. In this section, we determine no-arbitrage dynamics of the short-term rate in the first place. Under certain assumptions, the approach in this section enables one to implement recursive numerical solutions for models we don't know how to solve in closed form. Such numerical solutions are often required when our objective is that the model incorporates assumptions that lead to realistic dynamics of the short-term rate. To illustrate, the Ho-Lee model predicts that the short-term rate can take on negative values. Note that it is quite unusual that a model with realistic empirical predictions can also be solved in closed form.

The analysis of this section hinges on the Arrow-Debreu securities introduced in chapter 2 and parallels the work on equity options of Derman and Kani (1994), Rubinstein

(1994), and Dupire (1994), reviewed in chapter 11 (see section 11.7). Arrow-Debreu securities do not exist in practice for reasons mentioned in chapter 2: very simply, we may disagree on models and hence economically relevant events and states of nature. However, we can extract the shadow price of these securities from traded securities and use them to price interest rate derivatives. Naturally, these shadow prices are model dependent: Arrow-Debreu prices are, so to speak, the tip of the iceberg for any pricing model. We *do* need models to evaluate interest rate derivatives. However, the emphasis in this section differs from that in parts I and II. Previously, Arrow-Debreu prices were implied by model predictions, predictions based on the model primitives such as production possibilities or agents' preferences, and markets. By contrast, this section describes an approach by which we extract the Arrow-Debreu security prices from the price of already traded assets.

We describe this approach in two steps. First, we show how Arrow-Debreu prices can be employed to evaluate fixed income securities; in particular, we rely on these prices and replace the martingale restrictions of the previous sections into a set of equivalent conditions that are directly usable for practical purposes. Second, we develop algorithms to populate the short-term rate tree while ensuring that the initial yield curve is fitted without errors. We illustrate this procedure while relying on two models: (i) the Ho-Lee model and (ii) a model developed by Black, Derman, and Toy (1990). We obviously know the solution to the first model, but it is useful to review how it could alternatively be solved due to the insights on the mechanisms underlying the calibration algorithms of this section. In any case, retrieving Arrow-Debreu security prices is crucial even in the context of the Ho-Lee model as they help evaluate complex derivatives without a closed-form expression. Instead, not even the bond price is known in closed form in the second model.

12.6.1 Extracting Arrow-Debreu Securities from the Yield Curve

We know from chapter 2 that an Arrow-Debreu security is an asset that pays off \$1 in some prespecified state of the nature and pays zero otherwise. Consider, for example, the tree in figure 12.38. In this tree, q is the risk neutral probability of an upward movement of the short-term rate. A generic pair (s, τ) at each node tracks the number of upward movements of the short-term rate, s, and calendar time, τ; note that $s \leq \tau$ as there can only be one rate movement in each period. Consider the Arrow-Debreu security for state s at time $\tau + 1$. Let $p_s(\tau)$ denote the *current* price of an Arrow-Debreu security, one that pays off \$1 at time τ and in state s and pays zero otherwise. As we have learned from many junctures of this book, Arrow-Debreu securities can be used to price anything in a context with frictionless markets. For example, the current market price of a zero coupon bond maturing at time T is

$$P_{\$}(0, T) = \sum_{s=0}^{T} p_s(T). \tag{12.50}$$

More generally, consider a derivative that pays off $D_s(\tau)$ in node (s, τ), meaning that the derivative pays a dividend equal to $D_1(\tau)$ in state $s = 1$, $D_2(\tau)$ in state $s = 2, \cdots,$ and $D_\tau(\tau)$ in state $s = \tau$. Consistent with explanations given in chapter 2 (see section 2.3), the

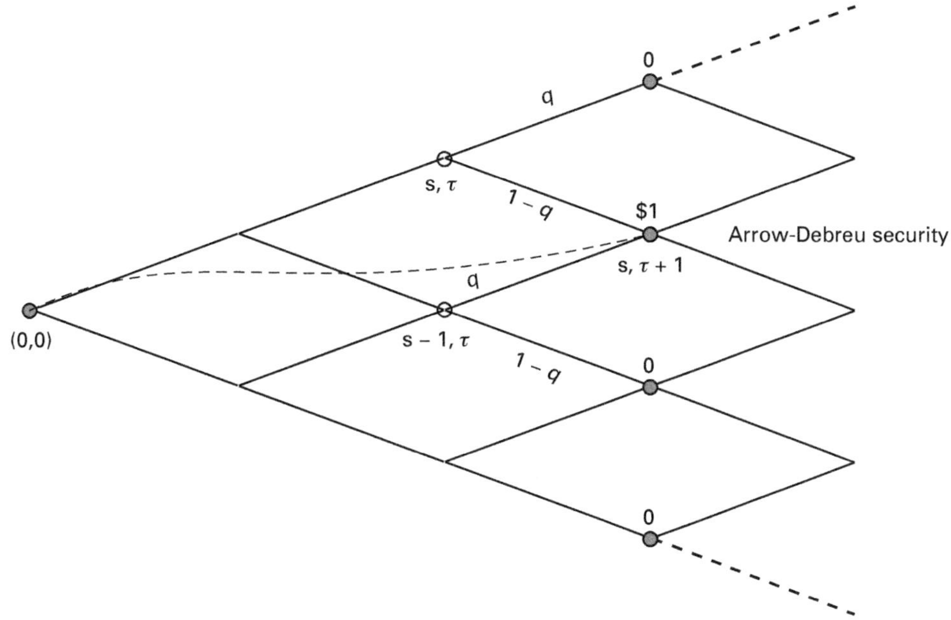

Figure 12.38
In the binomial tree of this section, an Arrow-Debreu security for state s at time $\tau+1$ is a security that pays \$1 at time $\tau+1$ in state s and zero otherwise. This section aims to show how to recover Arrow-Debreu prices from the price of fixed income securities.

price of this asset, denoted as $C_{\$}(0,T)$, is given by

$$C_{\$}(0,T)=\sum_{\tau=1}^{T}\sum_{s=0}^{\tau}p_s(\tau)\,D_s(\tau)\,. \tag{12.51}$$

We shall rely on eq. (12.51) and derive a recursive equation for the Arrow-Debreu security prices.

12.6.1.1 The forward equation for Arrow-Debreu security prices

We wish to retrieve the price of all Arrow-Debreu securities, that is, $p_s(\tau)$ for all s and τ, where $\tau\in\{1,\cdots,T\}$, based on the observation of the initial term structure of interest rates. Consider the Arrow-Debreu security that pays \$1 in node $(s,\tau+1)$ (see figure 12.38). Denote with $\pi_{j,\tau}[s,\tau+1]$ its value at time τ and in state j, $j\leq\tau$. What is this value at time τ in all states? A key observation is that, in this tree, the node $(s,\tau+1)$ (the filled circle) can only be "accessed" through the nodes (s,τ) and $(s-1,\tau)$ occurring at time τ (the two empty circles in figure 12.38). At time τ, then, the value $\pi_{j,\tau}[s,\tau+1]$ is zero in all the nodes (j,τ) except the empty circles (s,τ) and $(s-1,\tau)$: the node at which the Arrow-Debreu security pays off—the node $(s,\tau+1)$ (the filled circle)—cannot be reached if not through one of those nodes denoted with empty circles.

So we are left with finding the values $\pi_{j,\tau}[s,\tau+1]$ in the nodes corresponding to the empty circles (s,τ) and $(s-1,\tau)$, that is, $\pi_{s,\tau}[s,\tau+1]$ and $\pi_{s-1,\tau}[s,\tau+1]$. Let $r_s(\tau)$ be the continuously compounded short-term rate in node (s,τ). Consider the upper node, (s,τ).

We have

$$\pi_{s,\tau}[s,\tau+1]=e^{-r_s(\tau)}[0\cdot q+1\cdot(1-q)]=e^{-r_s(\tau)}(1-q).$$

Similarly, in the lower node, $(s-1,\tau)$,

$$\pi_{s-1,\tau}[s,\tau+1]=e^{-r_{s-1}(\tau)}[1\cdot q+0\cdot(1-q)]=e^{-r_{s-1}(\tau)}q.$$

We can think of our Arrow-Debreu security for $(s,\tau+1)$ as a derivative that, at time τ, delivers the following payoffs:

$$\begin{cases}\pi_{s,\tau}[s,\tau+1]=e^{-r_s(\tau)}(1-q)\\ \pi_{s-1,\tau}[s,\tau+1]=e^{-r_{s-1}(\tau)}q\\ \pi_{j,\tau}[s,\tau+1]=0, \quad \text{for all } j<s-1\end{cases}. \tag{12.52}$$

These "payoffs" are simply the market value of the Arrow-Debreu security for $(s,\tau+1)$ in the various states occurring at time τ, that is, the money the holder can make by selling the asset in the various states of nature occurring at τ. Therefore, we can apply eq. (12.51) and obtain

$$\begin{aligned}p_s(\tau+1)&=\sum_{j=0}^{\tau}p_j(\tau)\pi_{j,\tau}[s,\tau+1]\\ &=p_s(\tau)\pi_{s,\tau}[s,\tau+1]+p_{s-1}(\tau)\pi_{s-1,\tau}[s,\tau+1].\end{aligned}$$

By replacing the Arrow-Debreu prices in (12.52) into the previous equation, we obtain the *forward equation* for the Arrow-Debreu prices:

$$p_s(\tau+1)=p_s(\tau)e^{-r_s(\tau)}(1-q)+p_{s-1}(\tau)e^{-r_{s-1}(\tau)}q. \tag{12.53}$$

Eq. (12.53) is the counterpart to the forward equation used to fit European equity option prices (see eq. (11.70) in section 11.7.2). However, the approach in this section is distinct from that in chapter 11. Now, we take the risk neutral probability as constant and interest rates as time-varying and state dependent; by contrast, chapter 11 takes interest rates as exogenously given but allows the risk neutral probability to be time-varying and state dependent. Naturally, the approach in this section could be generalized to include stochastic risk neutral probabilities: generalizing this approach may be motivated by the need to fit derivative prices in addition to bond prices. We now explain how to fit bond prices.

12.6.1.2 *The bond price equation*

To implement an algorithm, we make a repeated and combined use of the forward equation (12.53) and the following zero pricing equation

$$P_{\$}(0,\tau+1)=\sum_{s=0}^{\tau}p_s(\tau)e^{-r_s(\tau)}. \tag{12.54}$$

The inputs to the algorithm are a number of zeros equal to the largest maturity date of the tree. Note an important feature of the calibration procedure. In order to extract Arrow-Debreu security prices, we need to rely on a given model for the underlying rate movements, $r_s(\tau)$. Accordingly, the following sections illustrate the algorithm based on two model examples. Instead, in the equity space, the cross section of option prices suffices to uniquely pin down the underlying price movements.

12.6.2 Implementation with Two Model Examples

12.6.2.1 The Ho-Lee model

We begin with the Ho-Lee model, assuming continuous compounding. By eq. (12.41), the short-term rate predicted by the Ho-Lee model is

$$r_j(\tau) = \hat{F}_\tau(0) + \ln\left((1-q) + q\delta^\tau\right) - (\tau - j)\ln\delta, \tag{12.55}$$

where $\hat{F}_\tau(0)$ is the continuously compounded forward rate at time zero for maturity $[\tau, \tau+1]$ and j is the number of *upward* movements of the entire set of *bond prices*. Define $s \equiv (\tau - j)$, which is the number of downward movements of the bond prices or, equivalently, the number of *upward* movements of the *short-term rate*. Hence, we can equivalently index the short-term rate by s and rewrite eq. (12.55) with a slight abuse in notation (replacing j with s) as follows:

$$r_s(\tau) = \underbrace{\hat{F}_\tau(0) + \ln\left((1-q) + q\delta^\tau\right)}_{\equiv r_0(\tau)} + \ln\delta^{-1}\cdot s, \tag{12.56}$$

such that $r_0(\tau)$ is the short-term rate at time τ in the event of zero upward movements in this rate and δ is the usual volatility parameter, which can be calibrated through $\ln\delta^{-1} = \frac{\text{Std}(\Delta r)}{\sqrt{q(1-q)}}$, with straightforward notation. Note, incidentally, that the short-term rate movements do depend on the specific value we assign to the risk neutral probability q.

Naturally, eq. (12.56) would be sufficient to populate the interest rate tree quite easily. However, even in the context of the Ho-Lee model, it is still quite important to retrieve Arrow-Debreu security prices as these would allow us to price all kinds of interest rate derivatives, including those for which a closed-form expression is unavailable.

Let us proceed. At time zero, the price of a zero maturing at time $\tau+1$ is

$$P_\$(0, \tau+1) = \sum_{s=0}^{\tau} p_s(\tau)\, e^{-r_s(\tau)} = e^{-r_0(\tau)} \sum_{s=0}^{\tau} \delta^s p_s(\tau),$$

where the second equality follows by the assumption that the short-term rate is solution to eq. (12.56).

By rearranging terms in the previous equation, we obtain a closed-form expression for the future short-term rate at time τ in the event of zero upward movements:

$$r_0(\tau) = \ln\left(\frac{\sum_{s=0}^{\tau} \delta^s p_s(\tau)}{P_\$(0, \tau+1)}\right). \tag{12.57}$$

This is the counterpart to zero pricing equation (12.54).

We use eq. (12.57) and the forward equation (12.53) to populate the interest rate tree under the assumption that $q = \frac{1}{2}$. Precisely, the algorithm proceeds as follows.

(i) Given the boundary condition for the Arrow-Debreu price, $p_0(0) = 1$, determine the initial value of the short-term rate, $r_0(0)$, using eq. (12.57), as $r_0(0) = \ln(1/P_\$(0,1))$.

(ii) Suppose we know the *future* value of the short-term rate at time $\tau-1$ in the event of no upward movements, that is, $r_0(\tau-1)$. Then, given the value of $r_0(\tau-1)$ and the price of the Arrow-Debreu securities $p_s(\tau-1)$ for $s\leq\tau-1$, determine $p_s(\tau)$ for $s\leq\tau$ through the forward equation (12.53),

$$p_s(\tau)=p_s(\tau-1)\,\delta^s e^{-r_0(\tau-1)}(1-q)+p_{s-1}(\tau-1)\,\delta^{s-1}e^{-r_0(\tau-1)}q,\quad q=\frac{1}{2},$$

where the last equation follows by plugging eq. (12.56) into eq. (12.53).

(iii) Given the Arrow-Debreu prices $p_s(\tau)$ for $s\leq\tau$, use eq. (12.57) to determine the *future* value of the short-term rate at time τ in the event of no upward movements, that is, $r_0(\tau)$.

(iv) If $\tau=T$, stop. Otherwise, go to (ii).

12.6.2.2 A model without closed-form solution

Next, we consider another old and well-known model proposed by Black, Derman, and Toy (1990). In this model, the short-term rate the is solution to

$$r_s(\tau)=\delta^s r_0(\tau),\tag{12.58}$$

where δ is, once again, a volatility parameter.[13] For computational convenience, this model assumes that the short-term rate in eq. (12.58) is discretely compounded. Accordingly, we rewrite the forward equation (12.53) in terms of discretely compounded rates:

$$p_s(\tau+1)=p_s(\tau)\frac{1}{1+r_s(\tau)}(1-q)+p_{s-1}(\tau)\frac{1}{1+r_{s-1}(\tau)}q.\tag{12.59}$$

The algorithm proceeds as follows.

(i) Determine the initial value of the short-term rate, $r_0(0)$, as the solution to $P_\$(0,1)=\frac{1}{1+r_0(0)}$.

(ii) Suppose we know the *future* value of the short-term rate at time $\tau-1$ in the event of no upward movements, that is, $r_0(\tau-1)$. Then, given the value of $r_0(\tau-1)$ and the price of the Arrow-Debreu securities $p_s(\tau-1)$ for $s\leq\tau-1$, determine $p_s(\tau)$ for $s\leq\tau$ through the forward equation (12.59),

$$p_s(\tau)=p_s(\tau-1)\frac{1}{1+\delta^s r_0(\tau-1)}(1-q)+p_{s-1}(\tau-1)\frac{1}{1+\delta^{s-1}r_0(\tau-1)}q,\quad q=\frac{1}{2},$$

where the last equation follows by plugging eq. (12.58) into eq. (12.59).

---

13. In its most general form, this model assumes that $r_s(\tau)=\delta_\tau^s r_0(\tau)$, where δ_τ is a volatility parameter that varies deterministically over time. This more general formulation leads to more flexibility, which is useful to fit the term structure of volatility.

(iii) Given the boundary condition $p_0(0) = 1$ and the Arrow-Debreu prices, $p_s(\tau)$ for $s \leq \tau$, use the pricing equation for the zero,

$$P_\$(0, \tau+1) = \sum_{s=0}^{\tau} p_s(\tau) \frac{1}{1+\delta^s r_0(\tau)},$$

to numerically solve for the *future* value of the short-term rate at time τ in the event of no upward movements, that is, $r_0(\tau)$. Note that we did not need this additional step for the solution of the Ho-Lee model as the short-term rate $r_0(\tau)$ is known in closed form in the Ho-Lee model (see eq. (12.57)). Note, since $r_0(\tau) > 0$, then we also have that $r_s(\tau) > 0$ by eq. (12.58).

(iv) If $\tau = T$, stop. Otherwise, go to (ii).

12.6.3 Numerical Examples

12.6.3.1 Ho and Lee again

We reexamine the numerical example in section 12.5.6, in which three zeros were traded (with maturities of 6 months, 1 year, and 1.5 years). By eq. (12.56), the short-term rate implied by the model is

$$r_s(\tau) = r_0(\tau) + (\ln \delta^{-1}) \cdot s. \tag{12.60}$$

We use eq. (12.60) and find the values of the short-term rate $r_s(\tau)$ in each node under the assumption that $q = \frac{1}{2}$ and that the standard deviation of the short-term rate is 0.014, annualized. We use a value of δ that matches this standard deviation, relying on eq. (12.35), $\frac{1}{\sqrt{2}}0.014 = \sqrt{q(1-q)} \ln \delta^{-1}$, and find that $\delta = 0.9804$. Further, the solution for $r_0(\tau)$ is known in closed form and is given by eq. (12.57). Given the term structure of prices $P_\$(0, \tau+1)$, $\tau = 0, 1, 2$, we "populate" the tree using eq. (12.57) and the forward Arrow-Debreu prices equation (12.53) that, by eq. (12.60), reduces to

$$p_s(\tau) = \frac{1}{2} e^{-r_0(\tau-1)} \left[\delta^s p_s(\tau-1) + \delta^{s-1} p_{s-1}(\tau-1) \right] \tag{12.61}$$

with the appropriate boundary conditions.

So we have to calculate interest rates and Arrow-Debreu prices for $\tau = 0, 1, 2$.

- $\tau = 0$. Eq. (12.57) is trivial. It leads to, $r_0(0) = \ln\left(\frac{1}{P_\$(0,1)}\right) = 0.015$. The forward equation for the Arrow-Debreu prices, eq. (12.61), is also trivial, $p_0(0) = 1$.
- $\tau = 1$. Let us use eq. (12.61), the forward equation for the Arrow-Debreu prices, to find $p_0(1)$ and $p_1(1)$. We have two cases:
  - $s = 0$. We have

$$p_0(1) = \frac{1}{2} e^{-r_0(0)} [p_0(0) + 0] = \frac{1}{2} e^{-r_0(0)} = 0.4925.$$

  The previous relation holds because $p_0(1)$ is the current price of the Arrow-Debreu security, which pays off \$1 in state 0 at time 1 as illustrated by figure 12.39.
  - $s = 1$. By a similar reasoning,

$$p_1(1) = \frac{1}{2} e^{-r_0(0)} [0 + p_0(0)] = \frac{1}{2} e^{-r_0(0)} = 0.4925.$$

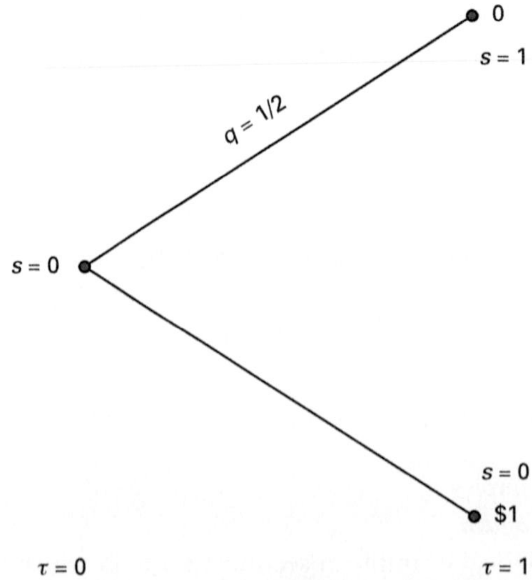

Figure 12.39
Determining the price of a short-term Arrow-Debreu security.

This Arrow-Debreu security is valued the same as that for state $s = 0$ because the risk neutral probability is 50%.

Eq. (12.57) is now

$$r_0(1) = \ln\left(\frac{p_0(1) + \delta p_1(1)}{P_\$(0,2)}\right) = \ln\left(\frac{0.4925 \cdot (1 + 0.9802)}{0.9685}\right) = 0.0069.$$

Hence, by eq. (12.60),

$$r_1(1) = r_0(1) + \left(\ln \delta^{-1}\right) = 0.0069 + 0.02 = 0.0270.$$

The tree depicted in figure 12.40 summarizes the results achieved so far.
We can now calculate the values of the short-term rate for one further period.

- $\tau = 2$. By eq. (12.61), the forward equation for the Arrow-Debreu prices, we have the following three cases:

$$(s=0) \qquad p_0(2) = \tfrac{1}{2} e^{-r_0(1)} \left[p_0(1) + 0\right] = 0.2446$$

$$(s=1) \qquad p_1(2) = \tfrac{1}{2} e^{-r_0(1)} \left[\delta p_1(1) + p_0(1)\right] = 0.4843$$

$$(s=2) \qquad p_2(2) = \tfrac{1}{2} e^{-r_0(1)} \left[0 + \delta p_1(1)\right] = 0.2397.$$

Figure 12.41 helps illustrate how to obtain these prices.

Consider, for example, $p_0(2)$, the price of the Arrow-Debreu security for time $\tau = 2$ under two consecutive downward movements of the short-term rate. This state can only be accessed to through the state $s = 0$ at time $\tau = 1$. But, in this state, the value of the Arrow-Debreu asset is $\frac{1}{2}e^{-r_0(1)}$. Hence, $p_0(2) = p_0(1) \cdot \frac{1}{2}e^{-r_0(1)}$. By a similar

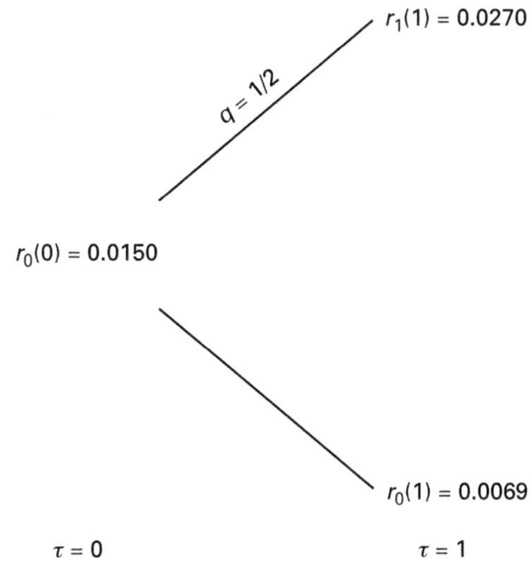

Figure 12.40
Short-term rate movements consistent with implied Arrow-Debreu security prices (first period).

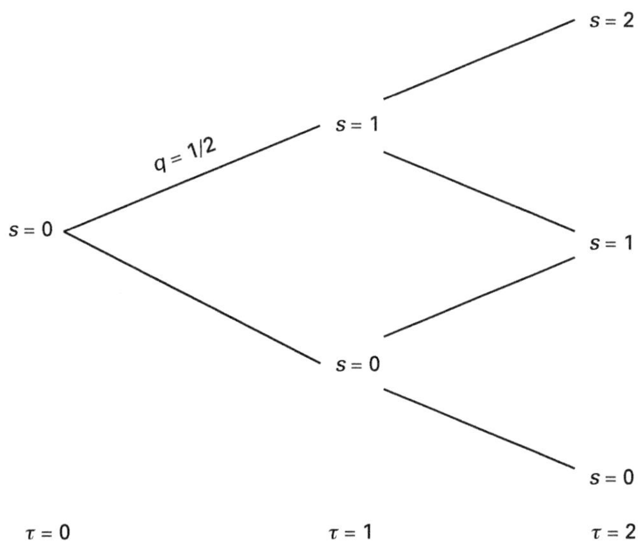

Figure 12.41
States of nature in the implied binomial tree.

reasoning, we have that $p_2(2) = p_1(1) \cdot \frac{1}{2} e^{-r_1(1)} = p_1(1) \cdot \frac{1}{2} e^{-r_0(1)} \delta$. Note that there is some symmetry in the distribution of Arrow-Debreu prices: the highest is $p_1(2)$, the price of the security that pays off with the highest likelihood. However, $p_0(2) > p_2(2)$, even if q is constant and equal to 50%; the reason is that discounting is more severe along the path leading to $s = 2$ than along that leading to $s = 0$.

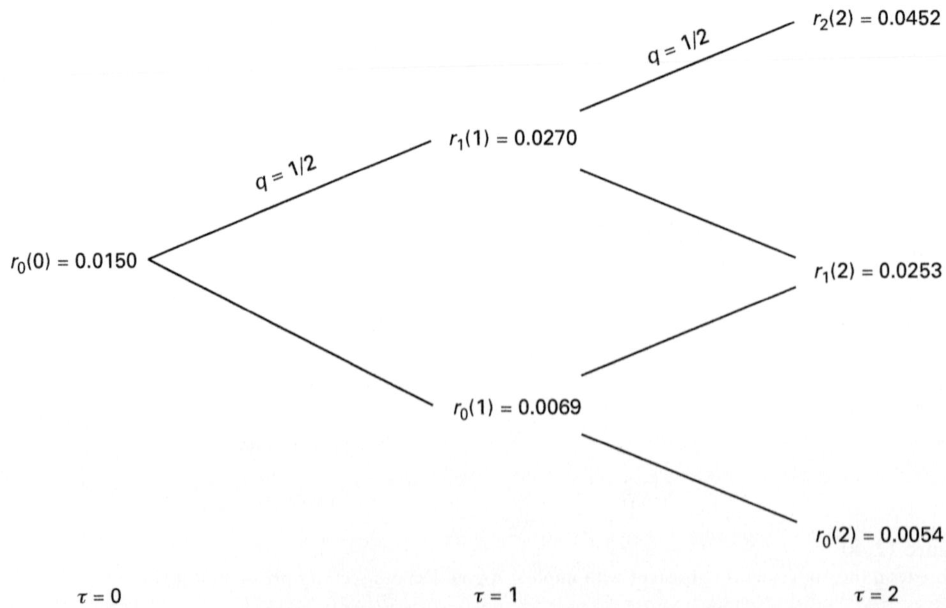

Figure 12.42
Short-term rate movements consistent with implied Arrow-Debreu security prices (first and second periods).

We can now calculate the values of the short-term rate for each node. Eq. (12.57) is now

$$r_0(2) = \ln\left(\frac{p_0(2) + \delta p_1(2) + \delta^2 p_2(2)}{P_\$(0,3)}\right)$$

$$= \ln\left(\frac{0.2446 + 0.9802 \cdot 0.4843 + (0.9802)^2 \cdot 0.2397}{0.9445}\right) = 0.0054.$$

Hence, by eq. (12.60),

$$r_s(2) = r_0(2) + \left(\ln \delta^{-1}\right) \cdot s = 0.0054 + 0.02 \cdot s, \qquad s = 0, 1, 2.$$

This yields the following values for the short-term rate: $r_0(2) = 0.0054$, $r_1(2) = 0.0253$, and $r_2(2) = 0.0452$.

The tree in figure 12.42 summarizes the implied tree for the short-term rate in this model. Naturally, the prices $P = e^{-r}$ in the nodes of the previous tree match those calculated in section 12.5.6, with the exception of discrepancies resulting from rounding errors.

12.6.3.2 A second example: Time-varying probabilities and interest rate volatility swaps

Assume that the spot yield curve is 2.5% for $t = 1$ year, 4.5% for $t = 2$ years, and 6% for $t = 3$ years, continuously compounded and annualized. Consider the following model:

$$r_s(t) = r_0(t) + a \cdot s, \tag{12.62}$$

where a is a constant and equal to 0.01, $r_s(t)$ is the continuously compounded short-term rate as of time t after s upward movements and finally the unit period of time is taken to be one year. As we know, the Ho-Lee model predicts that the price as of time 0 of an Arrow-Debreu security paying off in state s at time t, denoted as $p_s(t)$, satisfies the following forward equation for $t > 1$, $s \geq 0$, and $s \leq t$:

$$p_s(t) = e^{-r_0(t-1)} \left[(1-q)\left(e^{-a}\right)^s p_s(t-1) + q\left(e^{-a}\right)^{s-1} p_{s-1}(t-1) \right], \tag{12.63}$$

where q is the risk neutral probability of an upward movement in the short-term rate. Further, according to this model, the price of a zero coupon bond paying \$1 at time t, $P_\$(0,t)$, equals

$$P_\$(0,t) = e^{-r_0(t-1)} \sum_{s=0}^{t-1} \left(e^{-a}\right)^s p_s(t-1). \tag{12.64}$$

Suppose next that the risk neutral probability of an upward movement at any time t is not a constant q but a function of calendar time, say, q_t: q_t is, then, the probability of an upward movement in the short-term rate from time t to time $t+1$. Naturally, the assumption that q_t is time-varying makes this model markedly distinct from the Ho-Lee model. To calibrate this model, we consider the recursive equation for the Arrow-Debreu security prices:

$$p_s(t) = e^{-r_0(t-1)} \left[(1-q_{t-1})\left(e^{-a}\right)^s p_s(t-1) + q_{t-1}\left(e^{-a}\right)^{s-1} p_{s-1}(t-1) \right], \tag{12.65}$$

where q_{t-1} denotes the risk neutral probability of an upward movement in the short-term rate from time $t-1$ to time t. Eq. (12.65) can be derived through the same arguments in section 12.6.1. The boundary conditions are the usual ones: $p_0(0) = 1$, $p_s(t) = 0$, for $s \geq t$ and $s < 0$.

Next, suppose the risk neutral probability of an upward movement in the short-term rate in the first period equals $\frac{1}{2}$. Suppose, further, that available for trading is a derivative, which at time $t = 2$ pays off an amount of \$1 in state $s = 2$ and in state $s = 0$. The current price of this derivative equals 0.45514. The interpretation of the derivative is that of a contract that pays off when the interest rate experiences extreme movements (up-up or down-down)—a very basic *interest rate volatility contract*.[14] We refer to it as an "IR volatility security." Its price can be expressed as the sum of the two Arrow-Debreu securities for these extreme interest rate movements. The nominal value of the zero coupon bonds is \$1.

To populate the interest rate tree, we need to determine the three zero prices. They are

$$P_\$(0,1) = e^{-0.025} = 0.97531, \quad P_\$(0,2) = e^{-0.045 \times 2} = 0.91393,$$
$$P_\$(0,3) = e^{-0.06 \times 3} = 0.83527.$$

14. Chapter 11 deals with variance swaps in the equity case (see section 11.8). Mele and Obayashi (2015) deal with volatility in the fixed income space. Chapter 13 contains results pertaining to the Treasury case (see section 13.4.6).

We can start populate the tree. Eq. (12.64) can be rewritten as

$$r_0(t) = \ln\left(\frac{\sum_{s=0}^{t}\left(e^{-a}\right)^s p_s(t)}{P_{\$}(0,t+1)}\right). \tag{12.66}$$

We evaluate eq. (12.66) in each period.

- $t=0$. In this case, eq. (12.66) is

$$r_0(0) = \ln\left(\frac{1}{0.97531}\right) = 0.025.$$

- $t=1$. We have two nodes to fill: $s=0$ and $s=1$. We use eq. (12.65) as follows:
  - $s=0$: We have

$$p_0(1) = e^{-r_0(0)}(1-q_0)\,p_0(0) = 0.97531 \times 0.5 \times 1 = 0.48766.$$

  - $s=1$: We have

$$p_1(1) = e^{-r_0(0)} q_0 p_0(0) = 0.97531 \times 0.5 \times 1 = 0.48766.$$

  Then, eq. (12.66) is

$$r_0(1) = \ln\left(\frac{p_0(1) + \left(e^{-a}\right)p_1(1)}{P_{\$}(0,2)}\right) = \ln\left(\frac{0.48766 \times \left(1+e^{-0.01}\right)}{0.91393}\right) = 0.06$$

$$r_1(1) = r_0(1) + 0.01 = 0.07.$$

- $t=2$. There are now three nodes to be filled, which correspond to the states $s=0$, $s=1$, and $s=2$. We use eq. (12.65) as follows:
  - $s=0$: We have

$$p_0(2) = e^{-r_0(1)}(1-q_1)\,p_0(1) = e^{-0.06}(1-q_1)\,0.48766.$$

  - $s=1$: We have

$$\begin{aligned} p_1(2) &= e^{-r_0(1)}\left[(1-q_1)\,e^{-a}p_1(1) + q_1 p_0(1)\right] \\ &= e^{-0.06}\left[(1-q_1)\,e^{-0.01} + q_1\right]0.48766. \end{aligned}$$

  - $s=2$: We have

$$p_2(2) = e^{-r_0(1)} q_1 e^{-a} p_1(1) = e^{-0.06} q_1 e^{-0.01} 0.48766.$$

  We do not know q_1. Yet we can extract q_1 while relying on the price of the IR volatility security. This security quotes for 0.45514. At time $t=1$, its price is either $Z_u = e^{-0.07}q_1$ (in the up state of nature) or $Z_d = e^{-0.06}(1-q_1)$ (in the down state of nature). Therefore, its current price satisfies

$$0.45514 = \frac{1}{2}e^{-0.025}\left(Z_u + Z_d\right) = \frac{1}{2}e^{-0.025}\left[e^{-0.07}q_1 + e^{-0.06}(1-q_1)\right].$$

Solving for q_1 yields, $q_1 = 0.90$. Naturally, the same result is obtained by calibrating q_1 so as to make the price of the derivative, 0.45514, match the sum of the prices of the Arrow-Debreu securities paying off in states 0 and 2 at $t=2$, namely, $q_1 : 0.45514 = p_0(2) + p_2(2) = e^{-0.06}(1-q_1)\,0.48766 + e^{-0.06} q_1 e^{-0.01} 0.48766$. Now we can use $q_1 = 90\%$ and calculate the Arrow-Debreu prices, obtaining

$$p_0(2) = e^{-0.06}(1-.9)\,0.48766 = 0.04592$$

$$p_1(2) = e^{-0.06}\left[(1-.9)\,e^{-0.01} + .9\right] 0.48766 = 0.4588$$

$$p_2(2) = e^{-0.06}.9e^{-0.01} 0.48766 = 0.40922.$$

Note that the distribution of these Arrow-Debreu security prices has no symmetry at all. In particular, the price $p_0(2)$ is very low because q_1 is very high, such that the probability of reaching the lowest node of the tree at time $t=2$ is quite low.

Next, by eq. (12.66),

$$r_0(2) = \ln\left(\frac{p_0(2) + e^{-a}p_1(2) + e^{-2a}p_2(2)}{P_\$(0,3)}\right)$$

$$= \ln\left(\frac{0.04592 + e^{-0.01}0.4588 + e^{-2\times 0.01}0.40922}{0.83527}\right) = 0.07605,$$

and

$$r_1(2) = r_0(2) + 0.01 = 0.07605 + 0.01 = 0.08605$$

$$r_2(2) = r_0(2) + 2\times 0.01 = 0.07605 + 2\times 0.01 = 0.09605.$$

Finally, we wish to evaluate a European call option at time zero, written on the 3-year zero coupon bond with nominal value equal to \$1. This option expires at $t=2$ and has a strike price equal to \$0.91000. At expiry, the option pays off:

$$C_2(2) \equiv \left(e^{-r_2(2)} - 0.91\right)^+ = \left(e^{-0.09605} - 0.91\right)^+ = 0$$

$$C_1(2) \equiv \left(e^{-r_1(2)} - 0.91\right)^+ = \left(e^{-0.08605} - 0.91\right)^+ = 0.00755$$

$$C_0(2) \equiv \left(e^{-r_0(2)} - 0.91\right)^+ = \left(e^{-0.07605} - 0.91\right)^+ = 0.01677.$$

Then,

$$C_u = e^{-r_1(1)}\left(q_1 C_2(2) + (1-q_1)\,C_1(2)\right)$$

$$= e^{-0.07}(0.9\times 0 + 0.1\times 0.00755) = 7.0396\times 10^{-4}$$

$$C_d = e^{-r_0(1)}\left(q_1 C_1(2) + (1-q_1)\,C_0(2)\right)$$

$$= e^{-0.06}(0.9\times 0.00755 + 0.1\times 0.01677) = 7.9786\times 10^{-3}$$

which leads to $C = e^{-0.025}\frac{1}{2}(C_u + C_d) = 4.2341\times 10^{-3}$.

Finally, using all the data obtained so far, we evaluate a second European call option written on the 3-year bond, expiring in one year and struck at \$0.85. Its no-arbitrage price, denoted with C_T, is

$$C_T = e^{-0.025}\frac{1}{2}\left((P_u(1,3) - 0.85)^+ + (P_d(1,3) - 0.85)^+\right),$$

where

$$\begin{aligned} P_u(1,3) &= e^{-r_1(1)}\left(q_1 e^{-r_2(2)} + (1-q_1)e^{-r_1(2)}\right) \\ &= e^{-0.07}\left(0.90 \times e^{-0.09605} + 0.10 \times e^{-0.08605}\right) = 0.84786 \\ P_d(1,3) &= e^{-r_0(1)}\left(q_1 e^{-r_1(2)} + (1-q_1)e^{-r_0(2)}\right) \\ &= e^{-0.06}\left(0.90 \times e^{-0.08605} + 0.10 \times e^{-0.07605}\right) = 0.86498. \end{aligned}$$

That is, $C_T = e^{-0.025}\frac{1}{2}(0.01498) = 0.00730$. Suppose now that the option market value, $C_\$$, say, diverges from C_T, that is, $C_T \neq C_\$$. For example, $C_T < C_\$$. To implement this arbitrage opportunity, we can sell the option and use the proceeds to build up a portfolio comprising the bond expiring in three years and an MMA with an initial value

$$V_0 = \Delta P_\$(0,3) + M,$$

where Δ and M are chosen to match the payoffs promised by the option at time 1,

$$(\Delta, M) : \begin{cases} \Delta P_u(1,3) + Me^{r_0} = \pi_u \\ \Delta P_d(1,3) + Me^{r_0} = \pi_d \end{cases}$$

where π_u and π_d are the payoffs of the one-year option. The solution is

$$\hat{\Delta} = \frac{\pi_u - \pi_d}{P_u(1,3) - P_d(1,3)}, \quad \hat{M} = e^{-r_0}\frac{\pi_d P_u(1,3) - \pi_u P_d(1,3)}{P_u(1,3) - P_d(1,3)}.$$

Using the numerical values obtained so far, $\pi_u = 0$, $\pi_d = 0.01498$, $P_u(1,3) = 0.84786$, $P_d(1,3) = 0.86498$,

$$\hat{\Delta} = \frac{-0.01498}{0.84786 - 0.86498} = 0.875, \quad \hat{M} = e^{-0.025}\frac{0.01498 \times 0.84786}{0.84786 - 0.86498} = -0.72356.$$

The current value of this portfolio is

$$\hat{V}_0 = \hat{\Delta} P_\$(0,3) + \hat{M} = 0.875 \times 0.83527 - 0.72356 = 0.00730 = C_T.$$

Finally, if $C_T > C_\$$, we can buy the option, claim $[\pi_u, \pi_d]$ from the option seller, and sale short the previous $(\hat{\Delta}, \hat{M})$ portfolio. Net profits from the trade are $C_T - C_\$ > 0$ at time $t = 0$; at time $t = 1$, we use the claims from the option we purchased and honor the obligations resulting from the $(\hat{\Delta}, \hat{M})$ portfolio.

12.7 Callables, Puttables, and Convertibles with Trees

This section relies on binomial trees and provides introductory discussions and examples around callable, puttable, and convertible bonds, with and without credit risk. Chapter 13 considers a continuous time framework for the evaluation of callable and puttable bonds (see section 13.8.5), and chapter 14 contains a continuous time model to evaluate convertible bonds (see section 14.2.3).

12.7.1 Foundational Issues

Callable bonds are assets that can be called back by the issuer at a prespecified strike price, either at a fixed maturity date or at any fixed date before the expiration. One economic rationale behind this optionality may link to an agency problem: at the date of issuance, the issuers may not be able to credibly inform the investors about their future creditworthiness. By adding an option to call, the bond issuer might then signal its ability to refinance at some future date at hopefully better market conditions. Chapter 5 formalizes this reasoning based on a signaling model (see section 5.3.3). However, callable bonds may also exist for reasons not strictly related to agency problems or difference in beliefs (between the bond issuer and investors); they may be issued for purely hedging motives, for example, as a result of concerns that future interest rates may lower.

The right to call the bonds raises the cost of capital by the value of the (call) option to redeem the bonds. Let $V_t(T)$ denote the value of a callable zero coupon bond expiring at T. In this section, we assume that this value incorporates that of an American-style option to redeem the bonds, that is, a right that can be exercised at any point in time before the expiration. To alleviate notation, set $V_t \equiv V_t(T)$. For each t, the issuer decides to redeem the bonds whenever the exercise price K is less than the (discounted value of the) callable bond expected to prevail in the next period. The issuer, then, exercises at t when it expects its cost of capital will decrease (or equivalently, the market evaluation of its debt will increase) at $t+1$. Clearly, the price of a callable bond is just K in this case. Otherwise, the value of the callable bond is its discounted expected value over the next period. To summarize,

$$V_t = \min\{K, e^{-r_t}\mathbb{E}_t(V_{t+1})\} = e^{-r_t}\mathbb{E}_t(V_{t+1}) - \max\{e^{-r_t}\mathbb{E}_t(V_{t+1}) - K, 0\}. \qquad (12.67)$$

We can view this problem under the following slightly different angle. After having redeemed its (callable) bonds, an issuer may decide to issue *noncallable* zero coupon bonds. Note that we consider reissuance of noncallable debt as this assumption enables one to achieve a neat decomposition of the value of callable debt into that of a straight (i.e., non-callable) bond minus the option to call. Indeed, let $P_\tau(T)$ denote the price of a noncallable zero coupon bond, and suppose that, at some point in time τ^*, interest rates will decrease to the point that $P_{\tau^*}(T)$ is sufficiently large, as will be explained in a moment. The problem we want to study is actually one for which the issuer is seeking for an optimal stopping time τ^*, at which it can redeem the bonds for K and issue new noncallable debt at $\tau = \tau^*$ for a maturity equal to $T - \tau^*$ and priced at $P_{\tau^*}(T)$, thereby cashing in a difference equal to $P_{\tau^*}(T) - K$. The issuer then can still access capital until time T; further, the issuer can enjoy the additional "money shower," $P_{\tau^*}(T) - K$ at τ^*. Therefore, it is in the interest of the bond issuer to exercise at τ^* whenever the difference $P_{\tau^*}(T) - K$ is positive and sufficiently large.

How large does the difference $P_{\tau^*}(T) - K$ have to be? It is a real option problem of the kind studied in chapter 4 (see section 4.8), chapter 5 (see section 5.7), or chapter 9 (see section 9.5.2). The objective of the issuer is to maximize the present value of the "money shower" at some optimal stopping time τ^*, namely,

$$C_t \equiv \sup_{\tau} \mathbb{E}_t \left(e^{-\sum_{u=t}^{\tau} r_u} \left(P_\tau(T) - K\right)^+ \right), \tag{12.68}$$

which gives rise to a free-exercise boundary, $\tau^* = \inf_{\tau \in [t,T]} \{\tau : P_\tau(T) \geq P_\tau^*\}$. Note that, due to finite maturity, the free boundary P_τ^* may well be time dependent as in the dice examples of chapter 4 (see section 4.8).

We conjecture that the value of callable debt can be decomposed at any time as the value of a noncallable debt minus the American option price C_t in eq. (12.68):

$$V_t = P_t(T) - C_t. \tag{12.69}$$

Replacing eq. (12.69) into eq. (12.67) leaves

$$\begin{aligned} P_t(T) - C_t &= e^{-r_t}\mathbb{E}_t\left(P_{t+1}(T) - C_{t+1}\right) - \max\{e^{-r_t}\mathbb{E}_t\left(P_{t+1}(T) - C_{t+1}\right) - K, 0\} \\ &= P_t(T) - \max\{(P_t(T) - K)^+, e^{-r_t}\mathbb{E}_t\left(C_{t+1}\right)\}, \end{aligned}$$

where the second equality follows by the martingale property of the bond price rescaled by the MMA and by rearranging terms. That is,

$$C_t = \max\{(P_t(T) - K)^+, e^{-r_t}\mathbb{E}_t\left(C_{t+1}\right)\}. \tag{12.70}$$

In other words, the optimal stopping time problems (12.67) and (12.68) are equivalent.

Puttable bonds instead are assets that give the holder the right to sell the bonds back to the issuer at some exercise price, either at a fixed maturity date or any fixed date before the expiration. The bondholders would exercise their option to tender the bonds to the issuer when market conditions improve from the bondholders' perspective, that is, when interest rates are high enough so as to make bond prices lower than the exercise price. Therefore, issuing puttable bonds leads to a lower cost of capital to the extent of the value of the *put* option given to the bondholders to tender the bonds.

Suppose, for example, that the price of a *non*-puttable bond, $P_\tau(T)$, as usual, lowers to a level sufficiently lower than the strike price K, as will be clarified in a moment. The bondholders then will find it convenient to tender the bonds at K, buying conventional bonds at $P_\tau(T)$, thereby cashing in $K - P_\tau(T)$, and then wait until maturity. This trade would provide bondholders with a "money shower" equal to $K - P_\tau(T)$ at the exercise date. Alternatively, the bondholders would not exercise, and wait until maturity, in which case they would not receive the profit $K - P$ at the exercise date. Therefore, it is optimal to exercise when $K > P_\tau(T)$, that is, when the price is sufficiently low for some $\tau = \tau^*$, and it is obviously not so otherwise. Thus, the value of a puttable zero coupon bond,

$V_t^{\rm p} \equiv V_t^{\rm p}(T)$, say, satisfies

$$V_t^{\rm p} = \max\{K, e^{-r_t}\mathbb{E}_t(V_{t+1}^{\rm p})\} = e^{-r_t}\mathbb{E}_t\left(V_{t+1}\right) + \max\{K - e^{-r_t}\mathbb{E}_t(V_{t+1}^{\rm p}), 0\}. \qquad (12.71)$$

Conjecture that

$$V_t^{\rm p} = P_t(T) + \mathcal{P}_t, \qquad (12.72)$$

where $\mathcal{P}_t$ is the value of an American put on the zero coupon bond and is the solution to

$$\mathcal{P}_t = \max\{(K - P_t(T))^+, e^{-r_t}\mathbb{E}_t\left(\mathcal{P}_{t+1}\right)\}. \qquad (12.73)$$

Eq. (12.73) follows by substituting eq. (12.72) into eq. (12.71), and by arguments similar to those leading to eq. (12.70).

Convertible bonds provide the holder with the right to convert them into a prespecified number of shares of the issuing firm. First, consider the simple case in which conversion may only take place at some fixed date; in this case, these bonds are worth $\max\{\mathrm{CV}, P\} = P + \max\{\mathrm{CV} - P, 0\}$, where CV denotes the bonds conversion value, expressed in terms of the value of the issuer's shares, and P is the price of a conventional bond. That is, issuing convertible bonds lowers the cost of capital by the value of the optionalities provided to the bondholders. Convertible bonds can be made callable by the bond issuers at some strike K. Assume that the option to call can be exercised at the same date of the conversion decision. Further, if the bonds are called, the convertible bondholders have the option either to tender the bonds to the issuer or to convert them. Note that the only reason the bond issuers might call is that $P > K$. Therefore, the option to call places a ceiling on the convertible bonds' value equal to the strike K. Precisely, at the potential conversion date, the value of a *convertible callable* bond is $\max\{\mathrm{CV}, \min\{P, K\}\}$: the option to call back takes away some of the optionality from the bondholders, who in fact are forced to convert should the price P and the conversion value CV have increased beyond K.

In section 12.7.3, we will provide simple examples of convertible bonds with American-style exercise rights. Note, for now, some properties of these bonds (with conversion at any time), which arise in a discrete time framework. Denote with B_t the price of a convertible and callable bond at time t. We assume that, in the event bonds are called back, the issuer may issue callable bonds again. Consider the following triggering events. First, the issuer calls as soon as $K < B_t$, such that $\max\{\mathrm{CV}_t, \min\{B_t, K\}\} = \max\{\mathrm{CV}_t, K\}$. Then, the convertible bondholders convert when $\mathrm{CV}_t > K$, regardless of whether CV_t is higher than B_t. For example, it may be that $\mathrm{CV}_t < B_t$, in which case conversion would not have taken place without the issuer option to call at K. In other terms, with this option to call, we could have that

$$K < \mathrm{CV}_t < B_t. \qquad (12.74)$$

That is, the option to call provides investors with incentives to exercise the option to convert earlier: now, bondholders convert even if CV_t is less than the bond price.[15]

15. If $\mathrm{CV}_s < B_s$ for some $s < t$, and both CV_τ and B_τ are continuous, the inequalities in (12.74) could not hold. Indeed, if at time t, the bondholder has still not converted *and* $B_t > K$, the issuer would call the bond while providing the bondholder with the option to convert. But the bondholder would not convert because, due to continuity, CV_t would still be below K.

12.7.2 Callable Bonds

12.7.2.1 *Coping with credit risk: Option-adjusted spreads*

We can rely on no-arbitrage tree methods developed in this chapter and price callable bonds through trees while ensuring that the initial yield curve is fitted without errors. One issue to take into account is credit risk. We may proceed as follows.

(i) We "populate" a short-term rate tree through one of the no-arbitrage methods described in this chapter.

(ii) We rely on the implied short-term rate process of step (i) and price a callable coupon bearing bond without default risk. In each node of the tree, we compare the strike price K with the rolled-back (ex-coupon) bond value, take the minimum of the two, add the coupon to this minimum, and then find the market value of the callable bond at the relevant node,

$$V_t(s) = \min\{K, e^{-r_t(s)}\mathbb{E}_t(V_{t+1}|\, s)\} + \text{coupon},$$

where $V_t(s)$ denotes the value of the callable coupon bearing bond at time t and state s, $r_t(s)$ is the short-term process at t and state s, and $e^{-r_t(s)}\mathbb{E}_t(V_{t+1}|\, s)$ is the rolled-back bond value at time t and state s. As usual, this rolled-back value is found recursively, that is, by discounting the risk neutral expectation of the future values of the coupon-bearing callable bond value.

(iii) We correct for credit risk. The price of the callable bond in step (ii) is likely to exceed the market price of a defaultable bond. One then proceeds with adding a constant *spread* to the short-term rate process of step (i). The resulting credit risk-adjusted tree is used to implement step (ii). If the model-based callable bond is valued less than the market, one recalibrates the interest rate tree with a lower credit spread until convergence is achieved, by which market and model prices of the callable bonds are the same. The resulting spread is usually referred to as the *option-adjusted spread* to emphasize that it is determined while taking into account the optionalities regarding the callable bonds.

At this point, we may price derivatives written on callable defaultable coupon-bearing bonds (e.g., options).[16] Next, we illustrate a simple case: the pricing of a callable bond without credit risk.

12.7.2.2 *A numerical example: Without credit*

Assume that the discretely compounded six-month rate (taken to be the "short-term rate") evolves over time according to the tree in figure 12.43. Consider a bond expiring in two years, paying off coupon rates of 3% of the principal of \$1 every six months, and callable at any time by the issuer at par value; we label this bond "BCX." Three zero coupon bonds expiring in one year, eighteen months, and two years are also available for trading, with prices equal to, resp., 0.94632, 0.91876, and 0.89166. We use these data to calibrate the risk neutral probabilities of upward movements in the short-term rate in figure 12.43; we

16. Ho and Lee (2004, 274–278, chapter 8, section 8.3) contain exercises on the pricing of options on callable bonds relying on trees such as those described in this section.

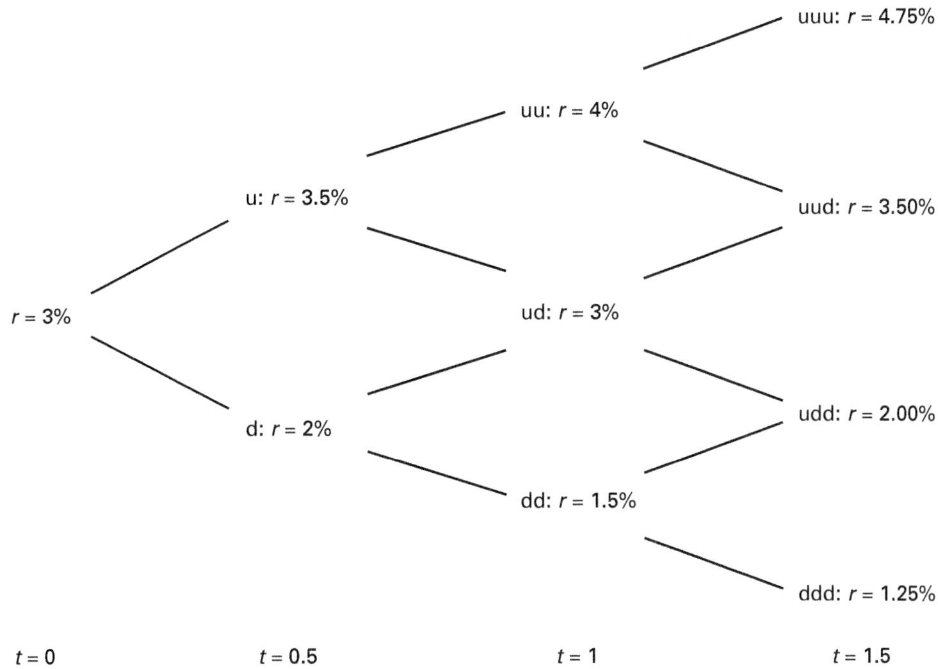

Figure 12.43
A binomial interest rate tree.

assume these risk neutral probabilities are time-varying but state independent. Finally, a conventional bond maturing in two years and paying coupons semiannually is also traded at 3% of the principal of \$1.

First we determine the price movements of the noncallable coupon-bearing 2-year bond. We have that $P_{\$}(0,0.5)=\frac{1}{1.03}=0.97087$. Further, regarding the zero expiring in one year,

$$P_{\$}(0,1)=0.94632=P_{\$}(0,0.5)\left(q_0\frac{1}{1.035}+(1-q_0)\frac{1}{1.02}\right),$$

which, solved for q_0, leaves $q_0=0.40$. As for the zero expiring in 1.5 years,

$$\begin{aligned}P_{\$}(0,1.5)&=0.91876=P_{\$}(0,0.5)\left(q_0 P_u(0.5,1.5)+(1-q_0)P_d(0.5,1.5)\right)\\&=0.97087\cdot\left(0.40\cdot P_u(0.5,1.5)+0.60\cdot P_d(0.5,1.5)\right),\end{aligned}$$

where

$$P_u(0.5,1.5)=\frac{1}{1.035}\left(q_1\frac{1}{1.04}+(1-q_1)\frac{1}{1.03}\right),$$

$$P_d(0.5,1.5)=\frac{1}{1.02}\left(q_1\frac{1}{1.03}+(1-q_1)\frac{1}{1.015}\right).$$

Solving for q_1 leaves $q_1 = 0.70$. As for the zero expiring in 2 years,

$$\begin{aligned} P_{\$}(0,2) &= 0.89166 = P_{\$}(0,0.5) \cdot (q_0 P_u(0.5,2) + (1-q_0) P_d(0.5,2)) \\ &= 0.97087 \cdot (0.40 \cdot P_u(0.5,2) + 0.60 \cdot P_d(0.5,2)), \end{aligned}$$

where

$$\begin{aligned} P_u(0.5,2) &= \frac{1}{1.035}(q_1 P_{uu}(1,2) + (1-q_1) P_{ud}(1,2)) \\ &= \frac{1}{1.035}(0.70 \cdot P_{uu}(1,2) + 0.30 \cdot P_{ud}(1,2)) \\ P_d(0.5,2) &= \frac{1}{1.02}(q_1 P_{ud}(1,2) + (1-q_1) P_{dd}(1,2)) \\ &= \frac{1}{1.02}(0.70 \cdot P_{ud}(1,2) + 0.30 \cdot P_{dd}(1,2)) \end{aligned}$$

and

$$\begin{aligned} P_{uu}(1,2) &= \frac{1}{1.04}\left(q_2 \frac{1}{1.0475} + (1-q_2)\frac{1}{1.035}\right) \\ P_{ud}(1,2) &= \frac{1}{1.03}\left(q_2 \frac{1}{1.035} + (1-q_2)\frac{1}{1.02}\right) \\ P_{dd}(1,2) &= \frac{1}{1.015}\left(q_2 \frac{1}{1.02} + (1-q_2)\frac{1}{1.0125}\right). \end{aligned}$$

Solving for q_2 leaves $q_2 = 0.60$. The price of a coupon bearing bond yielding 3% of the principal every six months is

$$B(0,2) = 0.03 \times (0.97087 + 0.94632 + 0.91876 + 0.89166) + 0.89166 = 1.0035. \tag{12.75}$$

Based on these calibrated risk neutral probabilities, we may evaluate the callable coupon-bearing bond. We discount the expected cash flows based on the following pay-off at each node of the tree: $\min\{B,1\} + 0.03$, where B is the present value of the future expected discounted cash flows promised at each node by a callable bond that has the same strike price K. In the following calculations, "wait" and "exercise" refer to the issuer's decision of, resp., not redeeming and redeeming the bonds. We have:

(i) At $t = 1.5$ years,

- uuu: $\frac{1.03}{1.0475} = 0.98329 < 1$. Decision: *wait*. $B = 0.98329$.
- uud: $\frac{1.03}{1.0350} = 0.99517 < 1$. Decision: *wait*. $B = 0.99517$.
- udd: $\frac{1.0300}{1.0200} > 1$. Decision: *exercise*. $B = 1$.
- ddd: $\frac{1.03}{1.0125} > 1$. Decision: *exercise*. $B = 1$.

(ii) At $t = 1$ year, $q = 60\%$, such that

- uu: $\frac{1}{1.04}(0.6 \times 0.98329 + 0.4 \times 0.99517 + 0.03) = 0.97889 < 1$. Decision: *wait*. $B = 0.97889$.

- ud: $\frac{1}{1.03}(0.6\times 0.99517+0.4\times 1+0.03)=0.99719<1$. Decision: *wait.* $B=0.99719$.
- dd: $\frac{1}{1.015}(0.6\times 1+0.4\times 1+0.03)=1.0148>1$. Decision: *exercise.* $B=1$.

(iii) At $t=0.5$ years, $q=70\%$, such that

- u: $\frac{1}{1.035}[(0.7\times 0.97889+0.3\times 0.99719)+0.03]=0.98008<1$. Decision: *wait.* $B=0.98008$.
- d: $\frac{1}{1.02}[(0.7\times 0.99719+0.3\times 1)+0.03]=1.0079>1$. Decision: *exercise.* $B=1$.

Finally, at the time of evaluation, we have that $q=40\%$, and, then, the price of the callable bond is

$$P^{c}=\frac{1}{1.03}(0.40\times 0.98008+0.60\times 1+0.03)=0.99226. \tag{12.76}$$

Naturally, the value of the callable bond is less than that of the conventional bond $B(0,2)$ in eq. (12.75): the difference is the value of the option given to the issuer to redeem these bonds. This option is exercised when interest rates become sufficiently low. That is, as rates decrease, prices increase less than in the conventional case, a property known as "negative convexity" (see section 13.8.5 in chapter 13).

How would we price the BCX bond when the previous market data were unavailable? In particular, suppose that (i) the risk neutral probabilities of upward movements in the short-term rate are (i.a) unknown from time zero to 0.5 years, (i.b) 70%, from 0.5 to one year, and (i.c) 60%, from one to 1.5 years; (ii) available for trading is a European call option written on the BCX bond; and (iii) this option, which quotes for $\$1.7226\times 10^{-3}$, expires in 1.5 years, is struck at \$0.99000, and becomes worthless as soon as the underlying callable bond is called back by the issuer, an assumption we shall refer to as "sudden death."

Now, note that at expiration, $t=1.5$ years, the payoffs of the option are

$$C_{uuu}=0,\quad C_{uud}=0.00517,$$

and, due to the sudden death assumption,

$$C_{udd}=C_{ddd}=0.00000.$$

At $t=1$ year, we have that $q=60\%$, and then

$$C_{uu}=\frac{1}{1.04}(0.6\times 0+0.4\times 0.00517)=1.9885\times 10^{-3}$$

$$C_{ud}=\frac{1}{1.03}(0.6\times 0.00517+0.4\times 0)=3.0117\times 10^{-3}$$

$$C_{dd}=0.$$

At $t = 0.5$ years, we have that $q = 70\%$, and then

$$C_u = \frac{1}{1.035}\left(0.70 \cdot C_{uu} + 0.30 \cdot C_{ud}\right)$$

$$= \frac{1}{1.035}\left(0.70 \cdot 1.9885 \times 10^{-3} + 0.30 \cdot 3.0117 \times 10^{-3}\right) = 2.2178 \times 10^{-3}.$$

$C_d = 0$, by the sudden death assumption.

At the time of evaluation, the call price is

$$C = 1.7226 \times 10^{-3} = \frac{1}{1.03}\left(qC_u + (1-q)\,C_d\right) = \frac{1}{1.03} \cdot q \cdot 2.2178 \times 10^{-3},$$

where q is the risk neutral probability of an upward movement in the short-term rate during the first six months. We can solve for q, obtaining $q = 80\%$ and then calculate the price of the callable bond. We have

$$P^{c\prime} = \frac{1}{1.03}\left(0.80 \times 0.98008 + 0.20 \times 1 + 0.03\right) = 0.98453.$$

It is lower than the price calculated in (12.76) because $P^{c\prime}$ assigns more weight (80%) than P^c (40%) to the occurrence of the state in which the interest rate goes up.

12.7.3 Convertible Bonds

12.7.3.1 *Evaluation issues*

Consider the following convertible and callable bond. Let K be the strike at which the bond can be called by the bond issuer, and let the parity, or *conversion value*, be $\text{CV} = \text{CR} \times S$, where S is the price of the common share and CR is the conversion ratio. We set the tree length equal to the time to expiration of the callable and convertible bond. Then we evaluate this bond through a binomial tree, relying on two steps.

(i) We model the stock price along the tree under the risk neutral probability.

(ii) We determine the bond value as $\max\{\text{CV}, \min\{B, K\}\}$, where B is the "rolled-back" value from the next nodes, obtained through the usual recursive, backward method: in each node in which conversion does not occur, its value is the present value of the risk neutral expectation of future payoffs. That is, define, on each node $B^* = \min\{B, K\}$, where B is the "rolled-back" bond value. Then, the payoff in each node is $\max\{\text{CV}, B^*\}$.

Note that this procedure relies on the assumption that we know the interest rates in each node. If the issuer was not subject to default risk, we would simply rely on a riskless interest rate tree. If the issuer is subject to default risk, we proceed as follows. In each node, the bond's value is decomposed into two parts: one part relating to the "pure debt component," discounted at the defaultable interest rate, and one part relating to the "pure equity component," discounted at the default-free interest rate.[17]

17. See, for instance, exercise 25.7 in Hull (2003, 653–654) for a very early example of this decomposition.

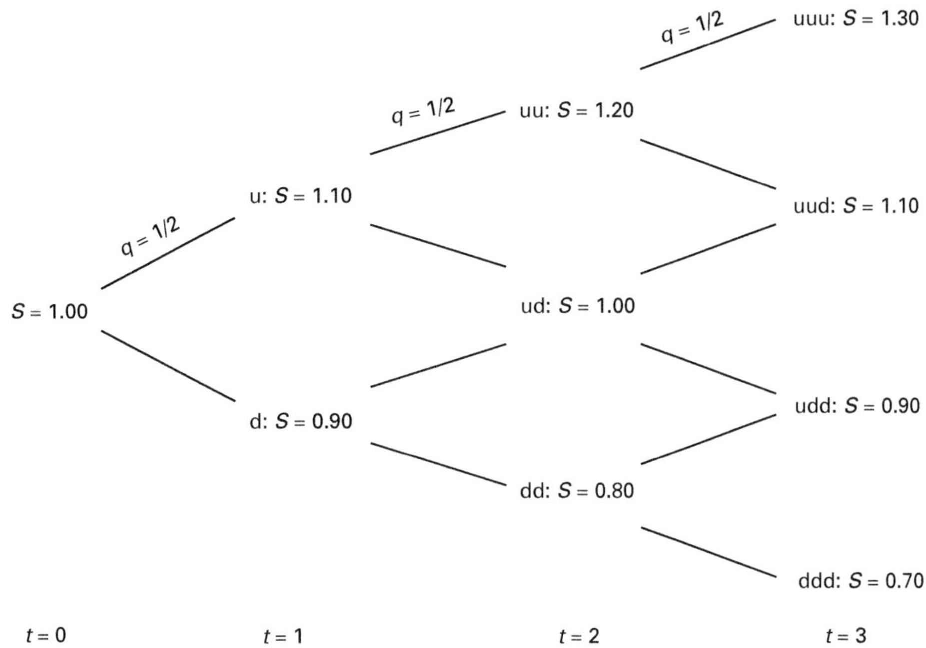

Figure 12.44
A binomial tree for the price of a share.

12.7.3.2 A numerical example: Without credit

Consider a 3-year convertible bond that can be converted at any time into one share of the underlying issuing firm's stock. The bond has a face value equal to 1, it is default free, and it pays off a coupon of 3% of the face value every year except the time at which it is issued. Moreover, in each period, it pays off the coupon, regardless of whether it will be converted. We assume that the share price is unaffected by any decision relating to bond conversion and that it evolves over time as in the tree of figure 12.44. In this tree, S denotes the share price, and $q=\frac{1}{2}$ is the constant risk neutral probability of price movements. Finally, we assume that the yield curve is flat at 3%, discretely compounded and that it will remain such over the next three periods and in each state.

We calculate the conversion value of the convertible bond in each node of the tree; then we identify the nodes where it is optimal for the bondholder to convert; finally, we determine the value of the convertible bond at $t=0$ as well as the value of the option to convert. As for the conversion value, we know it is simply the product of the conversion ratio times the current value of the outstanding stock, $\text{CV}_t=\text{CR}\cdot S_t=S_t$ (the conversion ratio is one). To find the current value of the convertible bond, we proceed recursively as explained and calculate, for each date t and in each node, $\max\{\text{CV}_t, B_t\}$, where B_t is the present value of the expected cash flows of the convertible bond, conditional on no conversion at time t. In the following calculations, "convert" refers to the bondholder's decision of converting the bonds.

The payoffs at time $t=3$ are

uuu: $\text{CV}=S=1.30$, $B_{uuu}\equiv\max\{\text{CV},1\}+0.03=1.33$. Decision: *convert.*

uud: $\text{CV}=S=1.10$, $B_{uud}\equiv\max\{\text{CV},1\}+0.03=1.13$. Decision: *convert.*

udd: $CV = S = 0.90$, $B_{udd} \equiv \max\{CV, 1\} + 0.03 = 1.03$.

ddd: $CV = S = 0.70$, $B_{ddd} \equiv \max\{CV, 1\} + 0.03 = 1.03$.

Payoffs in the next periods are

$t=2$ uu: $CV = S = 1.20$, $B_{uu} \equiv \max\{CV, A_1\} + 0.03$, $A_1 \equiv \frac{1}{1.03}\frac{1}{2}(B_{uuu} + B_{uud}) = \frac{1}{1.03}\frac{1}{2}(1.33 + 1.13) = 1.19420$. Hence $B_{uu} = 1.23000$. Decision: *convert*.

ud: $CV = S = 1.00$, $B_{ud} \equiv \max\{CV, A_2\} + 0.03$, $A_2 \equiv \frac{1}{1.03}\frac{1}{2}(B_{uud} + B_{udd}) = \frac{1}{1.03}\frac{1}{2}(1.13 + 1.03) = 1.04850$. Hence $B_{ud} = 1.07850$.

dd: $CV = S = 0.80$, $B_{dd} \equiv \max\{CV, A_3\} + 0.03$, $A_3 \equiv \frac{1}{1.03}\frac{1}{2}(B_{udd} + B_{ddd}) = 1$. Hence $B_{dd} = 1.03000$.

$t=1$ u: $CV = S = 1.10$, $B_u \equiv \max\{CV, L_1\} + 0.03$, $L_1 \equiv \frac{1}{1.03}\frac{1}{2}(B_{uu} + B_{ud}) = \frac{1}{1.03}\frac{1}{2}(1.23 + 1.07850) = 1.1206$. Hence $B_u = 1.15060$.

d: $CV = S = 0.90$, $B_d \equiv \max\{CV, L_2\} + 0.03$, $L_2 \equiv \frac{1}{1.03}\frac{1}{2}(B_{ud} + B_{dd}) = \frac{1}{1.03}\frac{1}{2}(1.07850 + 1.03000) = 1.0235$. Hence $B_d = 1.0535$.

Finally, the price of the convertible and callable bond is

$$B^{co} = \frac{1}{0.03}\frac{1}{2}(B_u + B_d) = \frac{1}{1.03}\frac{1}{2}(1.15060 + 1.0535) = 1.0700.$$

Instead, because the YTM is the same as the coupon rate, note that the value of a nonconvertible 3-year coupon bearing bond is 1 (see eq. (12.6)). Therefore, the option to convert is worth 0.07000.

Next, assume that the convertible bond is also callable by the issuer, at any time and at a strike value of 1.02000, and if it is called, the bondholder has the option to tender the bond or to convert it into one share. This convertible and callable bond can be evaluated as in the previous calculations, although the formula to use in each node is now $\max\{CV_t, \min\{B_t, K\}\}$ with $K = 1.02000$. The payoffs at time $t = 3$ are

uuu: $CV = S = 1.30$, $B_{uuu} \equiv \max\{CV, \min\{B = 1, 1.02\}\} + 0.03 = 1.33$. Decision: *convert*.

uud: $CV = S = 1.10$, $B_{uud} \equiv \max\{CV, \min\{B = 1, 1.02\}\} + 0.03 = 1.13$. Decision: *convert*.

udd: $CV = S = 0.90$, $B_{udd} \equiv \max\{CV, \min\{B = 1, 1.02\}\} + 0.03 = 1.03$.

ddd: $CV = S = 0.70$, $B_{ddd} \equiv \max\{CV, \min\{B = 1, 1.02\}\} + 0.03 = 1.03$.

We have

$t=2$ uu: $CV = S = 1.20$, $B_{uu} \equiv \max\{CV, \min\{A_1, 1.02\}\} + 0.03$, $A_1 \equiv \frac{1}{1.03}\frac{1}{2}(B_{uuu} + B_{uud}) = \frac{1}{1.03}\frac{1}{2}(1.33 + 1.13) = 1.19420$. Hence $B_{uu} = \max\{CV, 1.02\} + 0.03 = 1.23$. The bond is called and then converted.

ud: $CV = S = 1.00$, $B_{ud} \equiv \max\{CV, \min\{A_2, 1.02\}\} + 0.03$, $A_2 \equiv \frac{1}{1.03}\frac{1}{2}(B_{uud} + B_{udd}) = \frac{1}{1.03}\frac{1}{2}(1.13 + 1.03) = 1.04850$. Hence, $B_{ud} = \max\{CV, 1.02\} + 0.03 = 1.05$. The bond is called but not converted.

dd: $CV = S = 0.80$, $B_{dd} \equiv \max\{CV, \min\{A_3, 1.02\}\} + 0.03$, $A_3 \equiv \frac{1}{1.03}\frac{1}{2}(B_{udd} + B_{ddd}) = 1$. Hence $B_{dd} = \max\{CV, 1\} + 0.03 = 1.03000$.

$t = 1$ u: $CV = S = 1.10$, $B_u \equiv \max\{CV, \min\{L_1, 1.02\}\} + 0.03$, $L_1 \equiv \frac{1}{1.03}\frac{1}{2}(B_{uu} + B_{ud}) = \frac{1}{1.03}\frac{1}{2}(1.23 + 1.05) = 1.1068$. Hence $B_u = \max\{CV, 1.02\} + 0.03 = 1.13000$. The bond is called and then converted. The event at this node illustrates how the presence of the option to call the bond incentivizes investors to convert "early." Indeed, without this optionality opened to the issuer at $t = 1$, the bond value would be L_1, which is larger than the conversion value, $CV < L_1$, in which case the bondholder would not convert.

d: $CV = S = 0.90$, $B_d \equiv \max\{CV, \min\{L_2, 1.02\}\} + 0.03$, $L_2 \equiv \frac{1}{1.03}\frac{1}{2}(B_{ud} + B_{dd}) = \frac{1}{1.03}\frac{1}{2}(1.050 + 1.03000) = 1.0097$. Hence, $B_d = \max\{CV, 1.0097\} + 0.03 = 1.0397$. The bond is not called and is not converted.

Therefore, we have that

$$B^{\text{co-ca}} = \frac{1}{1.03}\frac{1}{2}(B_u + B_d) = \frac{1}{1.03}\frac{1}{2}(1.1300 + 1.0397) = 1.0533.$$

As expected, the value of a convertible callable is less than that of the convertible due to the option the bond issuers have acquired to call the bond.

12.8 Probabilities of Fed Funds Target Changes

Section 12.2 explains that the Fed affects the cost of capital related to reserve requirements of the banking system in the fed funds market. The Fed maintains a target fed funds rate and a range around this target as primordial tools for the conduct of its monetary policy. Market expectations about these targets are very important because they contribute to the pricing of other products (e.g., commercial loans, prime rates, consumer loans) and may affect general macroeconomic developments. This section explains how such market expectations may be reverse engineered from the price of dedicated derivatives aimed at limiting exposure to risk of fed funds target changes.

Consider a future contract with terminal value equal to the Federal target at some time T. Assume that, today (time t), the Federal Reserve target is equal to some FRT_t (say, 2%) and that at time T the Fed either may keep this target unchanged or may change it to $\text{FRT}_t + \Delta$, for some Δ. To illustrate, we assume that $\Delta > 0$, such that the Fed decision we are considering concerns a rate hike. Chapter 11 (see section 11.2.4) explains that the value of a future, $\mathcal{F}_t$ say, equals the risk neutral expectation of the future payoff, such that in our case,

$$\mathcal{F}_t = (1 - q_1)\,\text{FRT}_t + q_1\,(\text{FRT}_t + \Delta), \tag{12.77}$$

where q_1 denotes the risk neutral probability of a rate hike in the next period (see figure 12.45). Now, we may invert the previous relation for the probability of a hike, obtaining

$$q_1 = \frac{\mathcal{F}_t - \text{FRT}_t}{\Delta}. \tag{12.78}$$

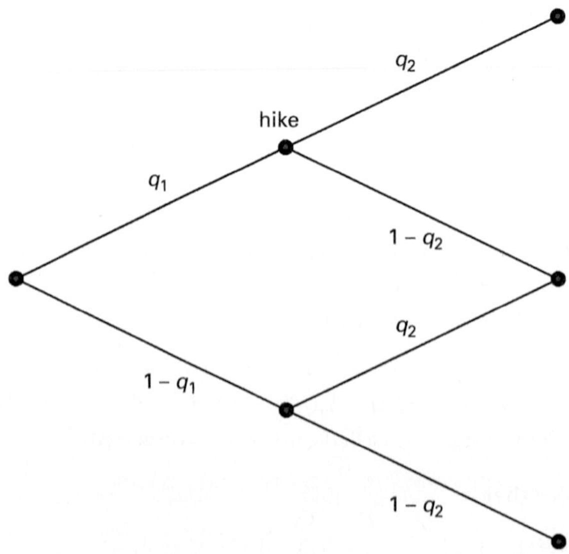

Figure 12.45
Recovery of probabilities of rate hikes through forward propagation.

Future markets on fed funds rely on the same rationale behind this simple example, although they are a bit more complicated. Mainly, the risk that these markets aim at protecting for is the *Federal Funds Effective Rate*, or FFER, defined as the weighted average rate at which banks lend to each other in the overnight fed funds market. The future contract is referenced to an average FFER.

Therefore, if a future contract on FFER begins at time t, then at any point in time τ, the future value incorporates two components: (i) a weighted average of the realized FFER up to τ and (ii) an expected FFER for the end of the month. Precisely, the simple fed funds future evaluation equation (12.77) is extended to time τ to

$$\mathcal{F}_\tau = \frac{\tau - t}{T-t}\overline{\text{FFER}}_{1,n} + \frac{T-\tau}{T-t}\mathbb{E}_\tau\left(\overline{\text{FFER}}_{n,m}\right), \qquad \overline{\text{FFER}}_{n,m} \equiv \frac{1}{m-n+1}\sum_{i=n}^{m}\text{FFER}_i, \tag{12.79}$$

where $\mathbb{E}_\tau(\cdot)$ is the risk neutral expectation taken conditional on the information at time τ, m is the number of days in the contract life, n is the number of days elapsed (at τ) from the beginning of the future contract, and FFER_i is the FFER on the ith day elapsed from the beginning of the future contract. CME Group currently lists 30-day fed funds futures, which corresponds to the assumption that $m = 30$.

Eq. (12.79) may be used as a basis for reverse engineering the probability of a change in the fed funds target. CME Group uses a FedWatch Tool and fed funds futures probability tree calculator that works as follows. Assume that we are on a Federal Open Market Committee (FOMC) “meeting month” and that we are on the nth day of a meeting month. One may consider a version of eq. (12.78) as a benchmark to extract probabilities of a rate hike,

$$q_1 = \frac{\mathrm{FRT}_{end} - \mathrm{FRT}_{start}}{\Delta}, \tag{12.80}$$

where FRT_{start} is the Federal Reserve target at the current time and FRT_{end} is the Federal Reserve target currently being anticipated by the market for the end of the month.

It remains to determine FRT_{start} and FRT_{end}. We rely on a variant of eq. (12.79) and consider the two cases: one with and one without an FOMC meeting having taken place in the current meeting month.

If, then, there was a FOMC meeting immediately before the meeting month, the FedWatch calculator relies on the following formula:

$$\mathrm{FRT}_{start} : \mathcal{F}_{current} = \frac{n}{m}\mathrm{FRT}_{start} + \frac{m-n}{m}\mathcal{F}_{next}, \quad \text{and} \quad \mathrm{FRT}_{end} = \mathcal{F}_{next}, \tag{12.81}$$

where $\mathcal{F}_{current}$ and $\mathcal{F}_{next}$ are the interest rate equivalents of the current and next month future contract.[18]

Alternatively, if there was no FOMC meeting immediately before the meeting month, the calculator assumes that

$$\mathrm{FRT}_{start} = \mathcal{F}_{previous} \quad \text{and} \quad \mathrm{FRT}_{end} : \mathcal{F}_{current} = \frac{n}{m}\mathcal{F}_{previous} + \frac{m-n}{m}\mathrm{FRT}_{end}, \tag{12.82}$$

where $\mathcal{F}_{previous}$ is the interest rate equivalent of the previous month's future contract.

In both cases, we use eqs. (12.81) and (12.82) into eq. (12.80) and estimate the risk neutral probability q_1 of a rate hike. This procedure may be extended to deal with the recovery of probabilities of rate hikes for more distant dates based on longer terms contracts. One assumes that probabilities are time-varying as in figure 12.45 and calibrates probabilities through "forward propagation," similar to other procedures illustrated in this chapter (see, e.g., figure 12.24). The outcome is a distribution of implied risk neutral probabilities of a number of rate hikes within a given time horizon.

Appendix 12.A Bootstrapping and No-Arbitrage Restrictions

12.A.1 Extracting Zeros from Bonds

Standard techniques are available to "extract" the price of zeros from that of coupon-bearing bonds, provided that at least a sufficient spread of bonds exists across maturities. Consider the following example, in which three coupon-bearing bonds are available for trading: the first pays off at T_1, the second pays off at T_1, T_2, and the third pays off at T_1, T_2, T_3. By no arbitrage,

$$B \equiv \begin{bmatrix} B(T_1) \\ B(T_2) \\ B(T_3) \end{bmatrix} = \begin{bmatrix} C_{11}+1 & 0 & 0 \\ C_{21} & C_{22}+1 & 0 \\ C_{31} & C_{32} & C_{33}+1 \end{bmatrix} \begin{bmatrix} P(T_1) \\ P(T_2) \\ P(T_3) \end{bmatrix} \equiv C \cdot P, \tag{12.A1}$$

18. We are referring to interest rate equivalents, because fed funds futures quote in prices, such that an interest rate equivalent of a future quote Q, say, is obtained as $100 - Q$.

for some coupons C_{ij}. We can use eq. (12.A1) to invert for the prices of the zeros, $P = C^{-1}B$. There is a mathematically equivalent inversion algorithm, a procedure known as "bootstrapping," based on the observation that the prices of the zeros can be solved recursively. Let B_i be the price of a bond that pays off coupons at on dates $t_1, t_2, \cdots, t_i$ and the principal of \$1 at t_i. Let P_i be the price of the zero maturing at t_i. Then, P_n can be estimated as follows:

$$P_n = \frac{B_n - \sum_{i=1}^{n-1} C_{ni} P_i}{C_{nn} + 1}, \quad n = 1, \cdots, N, \tag{12.A2}$$

where N is the largest available maturity. It is straightforward to verify this formula while relying on the example $N = 3$ in (12.A1). Naturally, eq. (12.A2) also follows by just rearranging eq. (12.3) in the special case C_{ni} is the same for all i.

To illustrate, suppose the bonds maturing at n have fixed coupons, $C_n \equiv C_{ni}$, for all i. We define the par yield in eq. (12.3) as the fixed sequence C_n such that the price B_n is forced to equal 100%. The example in the following table shows how to use eq. (12.A2), extract zeros and then reconstruct a discretely compounded yield curve.

Coupon	Maturity, n	Zero price	$\sum_{i=1}^{n} P_i$	Yield curve
6.00%	1	0.9434	0.9434	6.00%
7.00%	2	0.8728	1.8162	7.04%
8.00%	3	0.7914	2.6076	8.11%
9.50%	4	0.6870	3.2946	9.84%
9.00%	5	0.6454	3.9400	9.15%
10.50%	6	0.5306	4.4706	11.14%
11.00%	7	0.4579	4.9285	11.81%
11.25%	8	0.4005	5.3290	12.12%
11.50%	9	0.3472	5.6762	12.47%
11.75%	10	0.2980	—	12.87%

Note that eq. (12.A2) relies on the assumption that no maturities are missing. When some of the maturity dates are not available, the required coupon rate C_{ni} can be replaced with a linear interpolation $\hat{C}_{ni}$ between $C_{n,i-1}$ and $C_{n,i+1}$ as follows:

$$\hat{C}_{ni} = \frac{t_{i+1} - t_i}{t_{i+1} - t_{i-1}} C_{n,i-1} + \frac{t_i - t_{i-1}}{t_{i+1} - t_{i-1}} C_{n,i+1}.$$

The effects of the interpolation should be "visible" near the missing maturities.

12.A.2 Splines

There are techniques that are alternatives to bootstrapping that aim to cope with situations where the number of bonds is less than the maturity dates we want to fit. Suppose we observe N bonds, where the ith bond entitles one to receive coupons C_{ij}, for $j = 1, \cdots, M_i$, and that these prices are observed with errors or

$$B(M_i) = \sum_{j=1}^{M_i} C_{ij} P(t_j) + P(t_{M_i}) + \epsilon_i, \quad i = 1, \cdots, N,$$

where ϵ_i is the measurement error for the ith bond.

We aim to find the curve $T \mapsto P(T)$ that minimizes the errors in some statistical sense. The natural device is to "parametrize" the function $P(T)$ with a number of k parameters, where $k < N$. To parametrize the function $P(t_j)$ for a generic t_j, we can use *polynomials* as originally suggested by McCulloch (1971, 1975),

$$P(t_j) = 1 + a_1 t_j + a_2 t_j^2 + \cdots + a_k t_j^k,$$

where a_i are the parameters. *Cubic splines* are polynomials up to the third order and are very popular. The parameters a_i can be estimated by minimizing the sum of the squared errors, $\sum_{i=1}^{N} \epsilon_i^2$. A well-known pitfall of polynomials is that a high k might imply that, while the polynomial approximation works reasonably well near the observed maturities, it may exhibit an erratic behavior in between. To avoid this problem, we can use *local polynomials*, which are low-order polynomials (typically splines) fitted to nonoverlapping subintervals.

Naturally, we may also want to parametrize the spot rates, $R(T)$, as polynomials. Chapter 13 (section 13.3) explains that an alternative to polynomials are parametrizations introduced by Nelson and Siegel (1987), where

$$R(T) = \beta_1 + \beta_2 \left(\frac{1 - e^{-\lambda T}}{\lambda T} \right) + \beta_3 \left(\frac{1 - e^{-\lambda T}}{\lambda T} - e^{-\lambda T} \right) \tag{12.A3}$$

and β_i and λ are parameters. We provide interpretations of this parametrization in chapter 13 where we also explain how this has been used in practice to forecast the yield curve.

12.A.3 No-Arbitrage Restrictions

Bond prices need to satisfy restrictions that prevent arbitrage. We use figures taken from Tuckman (2002, 8–12) and illustrate how an arbitrage opportunity can arise and be exploited in this context. Our reasoning relies on Tuckman's. It also provides the explicit calculation and algorithmic details that could be used in cases that go beyond these specific sets of data.

12.A.3.1 Data

Suppose that, on some hypothetical date, say, February 15 (and year one, "y1"), we observe set I of bond prices in the left panel of the following table. Also shown in the right panel of the table are the implicit zeros obtained through bootstrapping. Assume that we observe additional bond prices—those in set II in the lower part of the table. Are these additional prices, those in Set II, compatible with those in set I in terms of arbitrage opportunities?

Set I: Treasury bond prices			Bootstrapped zeros	
Coupon	Maturity	Market price	Time to maturity	Implicit zero
7.875%	15-Aug-y1	101.400	0.5	$p(0, 0.5) = 0.97557$
14.250%	15-Feb-y2	108.980	1.0	$p(0, 1.0) = 0.95247$
6.375%	15-Aug-y2	102.160	1.5	$p(0, 1.5) = 0.93045$
6.250%	15-Feb-y3	102.570	2.0	$p(0, 2.0) = 0.90796$
5.250%	15-Aug-y3	100.840	2.5	$p(0, 2.5) = 0.88630$

Set II: Treasury bond prices

Coupon	Maturity	Market price
13.375%	15-Aug-y1	104.080
10.750%	15-Feb-y3	110.938
5.750%	15-Aug-y3	102.020
11.125%	15-Aug-y3	114.375

12.A.3.2 A basic no-arbitrage condition

We cast the problem in a more general format. Suppose we observe a vector of N bond prices with an $N \times N$ matrix C of coupons where each row of C gives the stream of the coupons promised by a given asset. We know that the $N \times 1$ vector of zeros P satisfies $B = CP$. That is, assuming that the matrix C is invertible,

$$P = C^{-1}B. \tag{12.A4}$$

Next, suppose there exists some asset that (i) promises to pay

$$c^* = [\ c_1^* \quad c_2^* \quad \cdots \quad c_N^* + 100\ ]$$

and (ii) has a price, b^*, such that

$$b^* < c^*P. \tag{12.A5}$$

The RHS of this inequality, c^*P, is the "no-arbitrage price" of the asset, which in this example is larger than the market price. The inequality gives rise to an arbitrage opportunity, which can be exploited by going long the asset and shorting a portfolio "synthesizing" it. To synthesize the asset one should go long for, we solve the following system of N equations with N unknowns:

$$\pi C = c^*, \tag{12.A6}$$

where the vector of unknowns, π, contains the number of assets in the synthesizing portfolio: by purchasing the portfolio π, one is entitled to receive πC in the future, which we want to equal c^*. The solution to eq. (12.A6) is

$$\hat{\pi} = c^* C^{-1}. \tag{12.A7}$$

Accordingly, the value of this portfolio, V say, is given by $V = \hat{\pi} B = c^* C^{-1} B = c^* P > b^*$ where the last equality follows by the "zero pricing equation" (12.A4) and the inequality holds by the inequality (12.A5).

To summarize, we now have the following situation: (i) the asset we hold produces the cash flows that are needed to pay out the coupons of the synthesizing portfolio we sold and (ii) the price of the asset we go long is less than the value of the portfolio that we went short. This situation is an arbitrage opportunity as initially claimed. We now use these insights to check whether arbitrage opportunities exist and can be exploited, using the previously given data.

First step: Detecting arbitrage opportunities First, we determine *no-arbitrage* prices of the bonds in set II using the implicit zeros extracted from set I. Denote these prices with B_1

(for the 6-month 13.375%), B_2 (for the 2-year 10.750%), B_3 (for the 2.5-year 5.750%), and B_4 (for the 2.5-year 11.125%). They are given by

$$B_1 = \left(\frac{13.375}{2} + 100\right) p(0, 0.5)$$

$$B_2 = \frac{10.750}{2}\left[p(0, 0.5) + p(0, 1) + p(0, 1.5)\right] + \left(\frac{10.750}{2} + 100\right) p(0, 2.0)$$

$$B_3 = \frac{5.75}{2}\left[p(0, 0.5) + p(0, 1.0) + p(0, 1.5) + p(0, 2.0)\right] + \left(\frac{5.75}{2} + 100\right) p(0, 2.5)$$

$$B_4 = \frac{11.125}{2}\left[p(0, 0.5) + p(0, 1.0) + p(0, 1.5) + p(0, 2.0)\right] + \left(\frac{11.25}{2} + 100\right) p(0, 2.5).$$

The next table provides the numerical values of these theoretical prices as compared to their market counterparts:

Set II: Treasury Bond prices

Coupon	Maturity	Market price	No-arb price
13.375%	15-Aug-y1	104.080	104.080
10.750%	15-Feb-y3	110.938	111.041
5.750%	15-Aug-y3	102.020	102.007
11.125%	15-Aug-y3	114.375	114.511

While there are no arbitrage opportunities for the 13.375% bond expiring in six months, the price of the 10.750% bond expiring in 2 years is less than its no-arbitrage price: this bond "trades cheap." In contrast, the 2.5 year 5.750% bond "trades rich," although the resulting arbitrage does not seem to be quite sensible.

Second step: Implementing the arbitrage We proceed to exploit the mispricing related to the 10.750% bond expiring in 2 years using the previous insights. We have $N = 4$ and $c^* = \left[\ \tfrac{1}{2}10.750 \quad \tfrac{1}{2}10.750 \quad \tfrac{1}{2}10.750 \quad \tfrac{1}{2}10.750 + 100\ \right]$. We use the first four bonds in set I to construct an arbitrage portfolio. In terms of the coupon matrix C, we have

$$C = \begin{bmatrix} \frac{1}{2}7.875 + 100 & 0 & 0 & 0 \\ \frac{1}{2}14.250 & \frac{1}{2}14.250 + 100 & 0 & 0 \\ \frac{1}{2}6.375 & \frac{1}{2}6.375 & \frac{1}{2}6.375 + 100 & 0 \\ \frac{1}{2}6.250 & \frac{1}{2}6.250 & \frac{1}{2}6.250 & \frac{1}{2}6.250 + 100 \end{bmatrix}.$$

We implement the following trade: (i) buy x 10.750% bonds expiring in 2 years, costing $110.938 \cdot x$, and (ii) create x portfolios satisfying eq. (12.A7),

$$\hat{\pi} = c^* C^{-1} = \left[0.0189 \quad 0.0197 \quad 0.0212 \quad 1.0218\right].$$

If we short x of these portfolios, then by construction, the coupons we need to pay are exactly matched by the coupons we receive from the x 10.750% bonds expiring in 2 years. However, the market value of the x portfolios we short is

$$x \cdot V = x \cdot \hat{\pi} B = x \cdot \left[0.0189 \quad 0.0197 \quad 0.0212 \quad 1.0218\right] \begin{bmatrix} 101.40 \\ 108.98 \\ 102.16 \\ 102.57 \end{bmatrix} = x \cdot 111.041,$$

where the vector of the market prices, B, is taken from set I. Therefore, the gains from this trade are $x \cdot (111.041 - 110.938) = 0.103 \cdot x$. For example, by trading \$1,000,000 at face value, that is, $x = 10{,}000$, then, arbitrage profits equal \$1,030.

Appendix 12.B Bond Sharpe Ratios

We provide a proof of eq. (12.17). Let $P(r, T_i)$ denote the price of a zero with a maturity T_i, $i = 1, 2$, when the interest rate is equal to r. We wish to replicate a zero with maturity T_1 by means of a portfolio that comprises of (i) Δ zeros with maturity T_2 and (ii) \$$M$ in the MMA. Let V_0 be the current value of this portfolio; it is clearly a function of the current short-term rate r and equals

$$V_0(r) = P(r, T_2)\,\Delta + M.$$

In the second period, the value of the portfolio is random as it depends on the development of the short-term rate $\tilde{r}$. Precisely, the value of the portfolio in the second period is

$$V(\tilde{r}) = \begin{cases} V(r^+) = P(r^+, T_2)\Delta + M(1+r), \text{ with probability } p \\ V(r^-) = P(r^-, T_2)\Delta + M(1+r), \text{ with probability } 1-p \end{cases}.$$

We also know that in the second period, the value of the second zero is

$$P(\tilde{r}, T_1) = \begin{cases} P(r^+, T_1), & \text{with probability } p \\ P(r^-, T_1), & \text{with probability } 1-p \end{cases}.$$

Next, we select Δ and M to make the portfolio value match that of the zero maturing at T_1 in each state of nature, namely,

$$V(\tilde{r}) = P(\tilde{r}, T_1) \quad \text{in each state.}$$

Mathematically, this is tantamount to solving the following system of two equations with two unknowns (Δ and M):

$$\begin{cases} V(r^+) = P(r^+, T_2)\,\Delta + M(1+r) = P(r^+, T_1) \\ V(r^-) = P(r^-, T_2)\,\Delta + M(1+r) = P(r^-, T_1) \end{cases}. \tag{12.A8}$$

The solution is

$$\hat{\Delta} = \frac{P(r^+, T_1) - P(r^-, T_1)}{P(r^+, T_2) - P(r^-, T_2)}, \quad \hat{M} = \frac{P(r^-, T_1)P(r^+, T_2) - P(r^+, T_1)P(r^-, T_2)}{[P(r^+, T_2) - P(r^-, T_2)](1+r)}.$$

By construction, the previous portfolio, $(\hat{\Delta}, \hat{M})$, replicates the value of the first zero in the second period. But if two assets (the portfolio and the first zero) yield the same payoffs in each state of nature, they must be worth the same in the absence of arbitrage. Therefore, we must have

$$V_0(r)|_{\Delta=\hat{\Delta}, M=\hat{M}} = P(r, T_2)\,\hat{\Delta} + \hat{M} = P(r, T_1)$$

or

$$(1+r)\,\hat{M} = (1+r)\,P(r, T_1) - (1+r)\,P(r, T_2)\,\hat{\Delta}. \tag{12.A9}$$

Next, let us figure out the prediction of the model in terms of the expected return it generates for the price of the bond maturing at T_2 when $(\Delta, M) = (\hat{\Delta}, \hat{M})$. To do this, multiply the first equation in (12.A8) by p, and multiply the second equation in (12.A8) by $1-p$. Add the result for $\Delta = \hat{\Delta}, M = \hat{M}$ to obtain

$$\left[pP(r^+, T_2) + (1-p)\,P(r^-, T_2)\right]\hat{\Delta} + \hat{M}(1+r) = pP(r^+, T_1) + (1-p)P(r^-, T_1).$$

Replacing eq. (12.A9) into the previous equation yields

$$\begin{aligned}&\left[\left(pP(r^+, T_2) + (1-p)\,P(r^-, T_2)\right) - (1+r)P\,(r, T_2)\right]\hat{\Delta}\\ &\quad = \left[pP(r^+, T_1) + (1-p)P(r^-, T_1)\right] - (1+r)P\,(r, T_1)\,.\end{aligned}$$

Finally, replacing the solution for $\hat{\Delta}$ into the previous equation leaves

$$\begin{aligned}&\frac{\left[pP(r^+, T_2) + (1-p)P(r^-, T_2)\right] - (1+r)P\,(r, T_2)}{P\left(r^+, T_2\right) - P\left(r^-, T_2\right)}\\ &\quad = \frac{\left[pP(r^+, T_1) + (1-p)\,P(r^-, T_1)\right] - (1+r)\,P\,(r, T_1)}{P\left(r^+, T_1\right) - P\left(r^-, T_1\right)}.\end{aligned}$$

The previous equation is easy to interpret. The numerators are the expected *excess* returns from holding the assets. They equal $E\left[P(\tilde{r}, T_i)\right] - (1+r)\,P\,(r, T_i)$, where $E\left[P(\tilde{r}, T_i)\right]$ is what the investors expect to receive the next period by investing $\$P\,(r, T_i)$ today in the bond and $(1+r)\,P\,(r, T_i)$ is what the investors expect to receive the next period by investing $\$P\,(r, T_i)$ today in the MMA. The denominators constitute a measure of volatility related to holding the assets. The previous equation then tells us that the Sharpe ratios (or the unit risk premiums) on the two zeros agree.

Let the Sharpe ratio on any zero be equal to some function λ of the short-term rate r only (and possibly of calendar time). This function, λ, does not clearly depend on the maturity of the zeros. Then, we have

$$\begin{aligned}&\left[pP(r^+, T_2) + (1-p)P(r^-, T_2)\right] - (1+r)\,P\,(r, T_2)\\ &\quad = \left[P(r^+, T_2) - P(r^-, T_2)\right]\lambda \qquad (12.\text{A}10)\\ &\quad = \frac{P(r^+, T_2) - P(r^-, T_2)}{r^+ - r^-}\cdot\left[(r^+ - r^-)\lambda\right].\end{aligned}$$

We can interpret $(r^+ - r^-)$ as a measure of interest rate volatility and define $\text{Vol}(\tilde{r} - r) \equiv (r^+ - r^-)$. Eq. (12.17) follows by rewriting eq. (12.A10) for a generic maturity date.

Appendix 12.C Ho-Lee Representations

Define the discretely compounded forward rate as the number $F_T\,(\tau) \equiv F\,(\tau, T, T+1)$, satisfying $\frac{P(\tau,T+1)}{P(\tau,T)} = \frac{1}{1+F_T(\tau)}$ as in eq. (12.4) of the main text. Iterating this equation leaves

$$P\,(\tau, T) = \prod_{S=\tau}^{T-1} \frac{1}{1+F_S\,(\tau)} = \frac{P\,(t, T)}{P\,(t, \tau)}\frac{P\,(t, \tau)}{P\,(t, T)}\prod_{S=\tau}^{T-1}\frac{1}{1+F_S\,(\tau)}.$$

Therefore, for any $t : t < \tau < T$, we have that

$$P(\tau, T) = \frac{P(t,T)}{P(t,\tau)} \prod_{S=\tau}^{T-1} \frac{1+F_S(t)}{1+F_S(\tau)}. \tag{12.A11}$$

Eq. (12.A11) is a convenient representation of the bond price at a future date τ: it is the ratio of the two *current* prices $P(t,T)$ and $P(t,\tau)$ and factors relating to the development of *forward rates* from the current time t to time τ, that is, $\frac{1+F_S(t)}{1+F_S(\tau)}$, for $S = \tau, \cdots, T-1$. Hence, once we model forward rates, we have implications for bond price movements.

We normalize the time line and set $t = 0$. Redefining $\tau = t$, eq. (12.A11) reduces to

$$P(t,T) = \frac{P(0,T)}{P(0,t)} \prod_{S=t}^{T-1} \frac{1+F_S(0)}{1+F_S(t)}. \tag{12.A12}$$

Eq. (12.37) in the main text follows by eq. (12.A12).

Next, we search for the model predictions on forward rates, that is, we prove eq. (12.38). The proof is by induction. Eq. (12.38) holds true for $t = 0$. Next, suppose that it holds at time t. We wish to show that in this case, eq. (12.38) would also hold at time $t+1$. At time $t+1$, we have two cases.

- *Case 1*: A *positive* price jump occurs between time t and time $t+1$. In this case,

$$\begin{aligned}
\hat{F}_S^{j+1}(t+1) &= \ln \frac{P_{j+1}(t+1,S)}{P_{j+1}(t+1,S+1)} \\
&= \ln\left[u(S-t)\frac{P_j(t,S)}{P_j(t,t+1)}\right] - \ln\left[u(S+1-t)\frac{P_j(t,S+1)}{P_j(t,t+1)}\right] \\
&= \ln \frac{u(S-t)}{u(S+1-t)} + \hat{F}_S^j(t) \\
&= \ln \frac{u(S+1-(t+1))}{u(S+1)} + \hat{F}_S(0) - [(t+1)-(j+1)]\ln\delta,
\end{aligned}$$

  where the first equality and the third follow by the definition of $\hat{F}_S^{j+1}(t)$, the second equality holds by the definition of the jump in eq. (12.27), and the fourth equality follows by eq. (12.38). Hence, eq. (12.38) holds at time $t+1$ in the occurrence of a *positive* price jump between time t and time $t+1$.
- *Case 2*: A *negative* price jump occurs between time t and time $t+1$. In this case,

$$\begin{aligned}
\hat{F}_S^{j}(t+1) &= \ln \frac{P_j(t+1,S)}{P_j(t+1,S+1)} \\
&= \ln\left[d(S-t)\frac{P_j(t,S)}{P_j(t,t+1)}\right] - \ln\left[d(S+1-t)\frac{P_j(t,S+1)}{P_j(t,t+1)}\right] \\
&= \ln \frac{d(S-t)}{d(S+1-t)} + \hat{F}_S^j(t) \\
&= \ln \frac{d(S-t)\,\delta^{-(S-t)+1}}{d(S+1-t)\,\delta^{-(S+1-t)+1}}\delta^{-1} + \hat{F}_S(0) + \ln\frac{u(S+1-t)}{u(S+1)} - (t-j)\ln\delta
\end{aligned}$$

$$= \ln \frac{u(S-t)}{u(S+1)} + \hat{F}_S(0) - [(t+1) - j] \ln \delta,$$

where the first four equalities follow by the same arguments produced in case 1, the fifth equality holds by the relation $u(T) = d(T)\,\delta^{-(T-1)}$ in eq. (12.33), and the last equality follows by rearranging terms. Hence, eq. (12.38) holds at time $t+1$ in the occurrence of a *negative* price jump between time t and time $t+1$.

References

Bernanke, B. S., and A. Blinder (1992). "The Federal Funds Rate and the Channels of Monetary Transmission." *American Economic Review* 82, 901–921.

Black, F., and M. Scholes (1973). "The Pricing of Options and Corporate Liabilities." *Journal of Political Economy* 81, 637–659.

Black, F., E. Derman, and W. Toy (1990). "A One-Factor Model of Interest Rates and its Application to Treasury Bond Options." *Financial Analysts Journal* 46, no. 1, 33–39.

Cox, J. C., S. A. Ross, and M. Rubinstein (1979). "Option Pricing: A Simplified Approach." *Journal of Financial Economics* 7, 229–263.

Derman, E., and J. Kani (1994). "Riding on a Smile." *Risk* 7, 32–39.

Dupire, B. (1994). "Pricing with a Smile." *Risk* 7, 18–20.

Heath, D., R. Jarrow, and A. Morton (1992). "Bond Pricing and the Term Structure of Interest Rates: A New Methodology for Contingent Claim Valuation." *Econometrica* 60, 77–105.

Ho, T. S. Y., and S.-B. Lee (1986). "Term Structure Movements and the Pricing of Interest Rate Contingent Claims." *Journal of Finance* 41, 1011–1029.

Ho, T. S. Y., and S.-B. Lee (2004). *The Oxford Guide to Financial Modeling.* Oxford: Oxford University Press.

Hull, J. C. (2003). *Options, Futures, and Other Derivatives.* 5th ed. Upper Saddle River, NJ: Prentice Hall.

Hull, J. C., and A. White (1990). "Pricing Interest Rate Derivative Securities." *Review of Financial Studies* 3, 573–592.

Lowenstein, R. (2000). *When Genius Failed: The Rise and Fall of Long-Term Capital Management.* New York: Random House.

McCulloch, J. (1971). "Measuring the Term Structure of Interest Rates." *Journal of Business* 44, 19–31.

McCulloch, J. (1975). "The Tax-Adjusted Yield Curve." *Journal of Finance* 30, 811–830.

Mele, A., and Y. Obayashi (2015). *The Price of Fixed Income Market Volatility.* New York: Springer.

Nelson, C. R., and A. F. Siegel (1987). "Parsimonious Modeling of Yield Curves." *Journal of Business* 60, 473–489.

Perli, R. and B. Sack (2003). "Does Mortgage Hedging Amplify Movements in Long-Term Interest Rates?" *Journal of Fixed Income* 13, no. 3, 7–17.

Rubinstein, M. (1994). "Implied Binomial Trees." *Journal of Finance* 49, 771–818.

Stock, J. H., and M. W. Watson (2003). "Forecasting Output and Inflation: The Role of Asset Prices." *Journal of Economic Literature* 41, 788–829.

Tuckman, B. (2002). *Fixed Income Securities.* 2nd ed. Hoboken, NJ: Wiley.

Vasicek, O. (1977). "An Equilibrium Characterization of the Term Structure." *Journal of Financial Economics* 5, 177–188.

13

Interest Rates

13.1 Introduction

The introduction to the previous chapter explains that fixed income securities are traded in one of the economically most significant segments of the whole capital market. Where do these markets come from? Figure 13.1 reveals that interest rate swaps contribute to more than 70% of the global interest rate derivative market.[1] Interest rate swaps are, at least in their vanilla version, contracts by which one party pays a counterparty a fixed interest rate against a variable. There are many institutional entities that benefit from these derivatives: banks concerned with inversions in the yield curve, pension funds committed to long-term liabilities, or intermediaries aiming to reshape the net duration of their balance sheets. Other institutions may be interested in "convexity," that is, in optionalities stemming from macroeconomic and, whence, interest rate developments; for example, an intermediary may have originated mortgages and would like to trade a swaption to hedge against prepayment related timing risk.

Chapter 10 (see section 10.10) explains one reason these over-the-counter markets are huge. An intermediary that originates a risk may wish to hedge with counterparties; in fact, it may immediately hedge the position by taking a position of the opposite side, and the process may continue, building on an already large notional asset base. To date, interest rate swaps are among the first financial innovations in the fixed income universe, with markets around them beginning to develop during the mid 1980s.

A thorough understanding of the pricing details in these markets necessitates a series of dedicated explanations. This is not only to provide the reader with a toolkit. Fixed income markets intimately link to macroeconomic developments. For example, monetary policy reacts to macroeconomic conditions, creating expectations on future developments of the yield curve. The yield curve does, indeed, display a number of interesting empirical

---

1. These figures refer to *notional* values. Gross *market values* are much less than those reported in figure 13.1. Gross market values are calculated using the replacement costs of all outstanding contracts; for example, they totalled \$8.35 trillion for interest rate contracts in 2019. Still, according to calculations made by Veronesi (2016), gross market values of interest rate derivatives were between 25% and 30% of global GDP from 2007 to 2013, approximately half of the total market capitalization of G-20 countries in 2012.

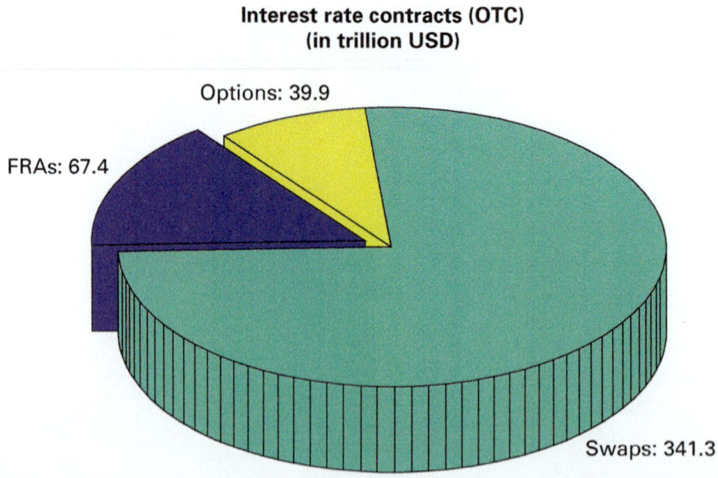

Figure 13.1
Notional value of interest rate derivative contracts in 2019.
Source: Bank for International Settlements.

properties that we need to survey. Therefore, this chapter surveys both empirical facts and models regarding the term structure of interest rates and derivatives based thereon. It expands from the previous chapter, relying as it does on continuous time methods and providing a systematic approach to a variety of important topics. These topics range from stylized facts such as the factors driving the yield curve, their business-cycle components, bond returns predictability, and volatility, to more conceptual aspects regarding how we would need to think about duration in a random environment or the pricing details of interest rate derivatives such as bond options, puttable and callable bonds, swaps, caps, floors, or swaptions, to mention a few.

From previous chapters, we know that an important objective that arises while pricing derivatives is to making sure that the underlying asset prices are pinned down without errors. This task is particularly challenging in the interest rate derivative space, because the yield curve is exposed to shocks that are typically not traded. Consider, for example, a model where the price of a zero coupon bond is only driven by random movements of the short-term rate—a one-factor model. This price depends on the assumed dynamics of the short-term rate (and, hence, productivity or monetary shocks) as well as market risk appetite. Models of this kind, and generalizations to multistate variables, are known as "models of the short-term rate," and are discussed in sections 13.4 and 13.5.

Models of the short-term rate are very important; once these models are made complex enough to address the main facts we see in the data, they might perform a series of tasks. For example, they can be used to forecast developments in fixed income markets. They could also be used for trading purposes if they reasonably point to market inefficiencies. Note that these models lead to pricing errors, and it is actually the presence of these errors to justify their potential use for trading purposes.

A second class of models that does not lead to pricing errors is that developed by Heath, Jarrow and Morton (1992), which generalizes the Ho and Lee (1986) model described in the previous chapter. In the previous chapter, we have seen tree-based instances of additional "no-arbitrage models." This chapter provides a systematic continuous time treatment of many of these models. The basic principle underlying these models is that current bond prices need not be modeled in the first place. Rather, current bond prices are taken as primitives, with the modeling focus being shifted to the ongoing development of forward rates, i.e., interest rates prevailing today for borrowing in the future. There is a relation linking bond prices to forward rates. No arbitrage then restricts the joint behavior of future bond prices and forward rates. We shall emphasize the use of these models to price derivatives.

In more detail, the plan of this chapter is as follows. The next section provides definitions of interest rates and markets, and foundational issues regarding two basic representations of bond prices—one in terms of the short-term rate and another in terms of forward rates. Section 13.3 contains an introduction to a number of very important empirical topics, such as bond return predictability, or the relation between the yield curve and the business cycle. Sections 13.4 and 13.5 deal with models of the short-term rate, and section 13.6 with some of their perfectly fitting extensions, i.e., the extensions that make these models fit the initial yield curve without errors. Section 13.7 contains a treatment of models that fit the yield curve, based on the Heath, Jarrow, and Morton (1992) framework. Section 13.8 is an introduction to the main interest rate derivatives, and describes how these assets can be priced relying on the models of the short-term rate (and their perfectly fitting extensions). Section 13.9 provides an alternative pricing framework, known as "market model," whereby derivatives are evaluated through Black's (1976) "pricers." Section 13.10 provides an introduction to the modeling of the skew (see chapter 11) in the fixed income space. A number of appendixes provides technical details omitted from the main text. This chapter does not assume default risk except in parts of section 13.4. Default risk is, instead, systematically dealt with in the next chapter.

13.2 Bond Prices and Interest Rates

13.2.1 A First Representation of Bond Prices

13.2.1.1 Zeros

Let $P(\tau, T)$ the price at τ of a zero coupon bond expiring at T, and consider the discretely compounded interest rate L for the time interval $[\tau, T]$ introduced in the previous chapter (see section 12.2), and defined as

$$P(\tau, T) = \frac{1}{1 + (T - \tau) L(\tau, T)}. \tag{13.1}$$

Given $L(\tau, T)$, the *short-term rate* process r is obtained as:

$$r_\tau \equiv \lim_{T \downarrow \tau} L(\tau, T).$$

Next, let Q be a risk neutral probability, and $\mathbb{E}_\tau(\cdot)$ denote the time τ conditional expectation under Q. By the FTAP, there is no arbitrage if and only if $P(\tau, T)$ satisfies, for all $\tau \in [t, T]$,

$$P(\tau, T) = \mathbb{E}_\tau\left(e^{-\int_\tau^T r_s ds}\right). \tag{13.2}$$

The proof of eq. (13.2) relies on arguments that are now quite standard in this book. Appendix 13.A reviews them again while relying on a multidimensional setting to highlight how they do specifically work in the context of bond evaluation.

13.2.1.2 *Fixed coupon and floating rate bonds*

Given a set of dates $\{T_i\}_{i=0}^n$, a fixed coupon bond pays off a known *coupon* stream, i.e., C_i at T_i, $i=1,\cdots,n$, and \$1 at T_n; typically, the coupon paid at at T_i compensates for the time interval $T_i - T_{i-1}$. By the FTAP, the value of a fixed coupon bond is

$$P_{\text{fcb}}(t, T_n) = P(t, T_n) + \sum_{i=1}^{n} C_i P(t, T_i).$$

A floating rate bond pays off coupons indexed to short-term rates,

$$C_i = \delta_{i-1} L(T_{i-1}, T_i) = \frac{1}{P(T_{i-1}, T_i)} - 1, \tag{13.3}$$

where $\delta_i \equiv T_{i+1} - T_i$, and where the second equality follows by eq. (13.1). By the FTAP, the price p_{frb} as of time t of a floating rate bond is:

$$\begin{aligned}
p_{\text{frb}}(t) &= P(t, T_n) + \sum_{i=1}^{n} \mathbb{E}_t\left(e^{-\int_t^{T_i} r_\tau d\tau} \delta_{i-1} L(T_{i-1}, T_i)\right) \\
&= P(t, T_n) + \sum_{i=1}^{n} \mathbb{E}_t\left(\frac{e^{-\int_t^{T_i} r_\tau d\tau}}{P(T_{i-1}, T_i)}\right) - \sum_{i=1}^{n} P(t, T_i) \\
&= P(t, T_n) + \sum_{i=1}^{n} P(t, T_{i-1}) - \sum_{i=1}^{n} P(t, T_i) \\
&= P(t, T_0).
\end{aligned} \tag{13.4}$$

where the second line follows by eq. (13.3) and the third line will be justified in a moment (see eq. (13.5) below). That is, a floating rate bond would quote at par at its first reset date, $p_{\text{frb}}(T_0) = P(T_0, T_0) = 100\%$.[2]

Regarding the third line of eq. (13.4),

$$P(t, T) = \mathbb{E}_t\left(\frac{e^{-\int_t^S r_\tau d\tau}}{P(T, S)}\right), \tag{13.5}$$

consider the following economic interpretation. Suppose that at time t, $\$P(t,T)$ are invested in a bond maturing at time T. At time T, this investment will obviously pay

2. This property also holds in a market where the floating rates continuously pay off the instantaneous short-term rate r. Indeed, let $T_0 = t$, and let p_{frb} be the solution to the partial differential equation (13.105) in section 13.8.2, with $\pi(r) = r$, and boundary condition $p_{\text{frb}}(T) = 1$. Then, it can be verified that $p_{\text{frb}} = 1$ is the solution to eq. (13.105).

off \$1. And at time T, \$1 can be further rolled over another bond maturing at time S, thus yielding \$ $1/P(T,S)$ at time S. In other words, an investment at t equal to \$$P(t,T)$, leads to a "payoff" at S equal to \$ $1/P(T,S)$, whence eq. (13.5).[3]

13.2.2 Forward Rates

The previous chapter provides the definition of a *forward rate agreement* (FRA) (see section 12.2), an agreement by which one party will borrow from a counterparty in the future. Forward rates are interest rates that make the value of a FRA equal to zero at origination. Forward rates at t, regarding a future time interval $[T,S]$, are denoted with $F(t,T,S)$. They link to bond prices through the following relation (see eq. (12.4) in chapter 12):

$$\frac{P(t,T)}{P(t,S)} = 1 + (S-T)\,F(t,T,S)\,. \tag{13.6}$$

Clearly, the forward rate agreed at T for the time interval $[T,S]$ is the short-term rate applying to the same period:

$$F(T,T,S) = L(T,S)\,. \tag{13.7}$$

FRAs can be seen as a means to exchange interest payments: fixed against variable. Consider the following agreement, by which one party shall (i) pay a counterparty an interest rate on a given principal at time T, fixed at some $K \neq F(t,T,S)$, and (ii) receive, in exchange, the future interest rate prevailing at time T for the time interval $[T,S]$, $L(T,S)$. The time S payoff originated by this forward starting "interest rate swap" is

$$\pi_{\text{fra}}(T,S) \equiv (S-T)\,[L(T,S) - K]\,. \tag{13.8}$$

Alternatively, we may think of (13.8) as the P&L to a party who, at time t, enters into a FRA as a future borrower for the time interval $[T,S]$. Come time T, the party will honor the FRA by borrowing \$1 for the time interval $[T,S]$ at a cost of K. At the same time, the party can lend this very same \$1 at the random interest rate $L(T,S)$. The time S payoff deriving from this trade is, of course, the same as $\pi_{\text{fra}}(T,S)$ in Eq. (13.8). In section 13.8, we shall deal with the evaluation of this and related payoffs. To anticipate, the forward rate, $F(t,T,S)$, is the value of K such that the payoff, $\pi_{\text{fra}}(T,S)$, is worth zero at *time t*. Note, then, that the rationale underlying this contract is precisely the same as that underlying the forward contracts in the equity space dealt with in chapter 11. For an equity contract, a forward price, is the price agreed at t for a transaction to take place at T, and such that nothing is due to any counterparty at inception. In the contract of this section, $F(t,T,S)$ is the value of the interest rate agreed at t for a borrowing position at T, and such that the value of this position is equal to zero at inception. In section 13.8, we continue to refer to the payoff in (13.8) as the payoff of a FRA.

3. Alternatively, note that the RHS of (13.5) follows by the law of iterated expectations: $\mathbb{E}_t\left(e^{-\int_t^S r_\tau d\tau}/P(T,S)\right) = \mathbb{E}_t\left(\mathbb{E}_T e^{-\int_t^T r_\tau d\tau} e^{-\int_T^S r_\tau d\tau}/P(T,S)\right) = P(t,T)$.

13.2.3 A Second Representation of Bond prices

13.2.3.1 Prices as forward-looking indicators

Bond prices can be expressed in terms of these forward interest rates, namely in terms of the "instantaneous" forward rates. First, rearrange terms in Eq. (13.6) so as to obtain

$$F(t,T,S)=-\frac{P(t,S)-P(t,T)}{(S-T)P(t,S)}. \tag{13.9}$$

The *instantaneous forward rate* $f(t,T)$ is defined as

$$f(t,T)\equiv\lim_{S\downarrow T}F(t,T,S)=-\frac{\partial\ln P(t,T)}{\partial T}. \tag{13.10}$$

It can be interpreted as the marginal rate of return from committing a bond investment for an additional instant. To express bond prices in terms of f, integrate Eq. (13.10), $f(t,\ell)=-\frac{\partial\ln P(t,\ell)}{\partial\ell}$, with respect to the maturity date ℓ, use the condition that $P(t,t)=1$, and obtain:

$$P(t,T)=e^{-\int_t^T f(t,\ell)d\ell}. \tag{13.11}$$

Eq. (13.11) suggests a natural modeling approach of the yield curve that emphasizes the dynamics of the forward rates, which is dealt with in detail in sections 13.6 and 13.7.

13.2.3.2 The marginal nature of forward rates

Consider the *yield-to-maturity* introduced in chapter 12 (see section 12.2), defined as the function $R(t,T)$ such that

$$P(t,T)\equiv e^{-(T-t)\cdot R(t,T)}. \tag{13.12}$$

Comparing Eq. (13.12) with Eq. (13.11) yields:

$$R(t,T)=\frac{1}{T-t}\int_t^T f(t,\tau)d\tau. \tag{13.13}$$

Differentiating Eq. (13.13) with respect to T yields:

$$\frac{\partial R(t,T)}{\partial T}=\frac{1}{T-t}\left[f(t,T)-R(t,T)\right]. \tag{13.14}$$

Eq. (13.14) underscores the "marginal nature" of forward rates: the yield curve, $R(t,T)$, is increasing in, decreasing in, or stationary at T, according to whether $f(t,T)$ exceeds, is lower, or equal the spot rate for maturity T. It is intuitive: forward rates summarize information on market expectations regarding future interest rates. For example, an increasing yield curve would signal high rates to be expected in the future, under conditions explained in section 13.3.

13.3 Stylized Facts

13.3.1 The Expectation Hypothesis

The *expectation hypothesis* holds that the *forward rates equal expected future short-term rates*, namely

$$f(t,T)=E_t(r_T), \tag{13.15}$$

where $E_t(\cdot)$ denotes expectation under the physical probability. Eq. (13.15) has two implications. First, through Eq. (13.13),

$$R(t,T) = \frac{1}{T-t}\int_t^T E_t(r_\tau)\,d\tau, \tag{13.16}$$

and second, by Eq. (13.14),

$$\frac{\partial R(t,T)}{\partial T} = \frac{1}{T-t}\left[E_t(r_T) - R(t,T)\right]. \tag{13.17}$$

Eq. (13.17) leads to a neat conclusion: the short-term rate that is expect to prevail at some future date T is high (compared to the corresponding yield) if and only if the yield curve is increasing in T. An increasing yield curve (i.e., a curve such that r_t is less than $R(t,T)$) signals that the market expects future short-term interest rates will increase. Likewise, an inverted yield curve signals the market expects future short-term rates will fall.[4] For example, in December 2012, the yield curve in the United Kingdom was substantially flat at less than 0.5% for maturities of less than three years, and then steadily increased to 2% for maturities of up to ten years. Taken at face value, the expectation hypothesis would simply imply that in December 2012, the market did not expect UK short-term to move over the following three years. Naturally, market expectations could have changed over new information.

A question naturally arises as to whether in the data the forward rate for maturity T is higher than the short-term rate expected to prevail at time T, namely

$$f(t,T) \geq E_t(r_T). \tag{13.18}$$

It is an old issue. One possibility is that (13.18) holds due to risk aversion. Consider the Hicks-Keynesian *normal backwardation* hypothesis reviewed in chapter 11 (see section 11.2).[5] In the context of this chapter, forward rates can be higher than expected spot rates as firms demand long-term funds with fund suppliers preferring to lend at shorter maturity dates. In this case, the market is cleared by intermediaries requiring a *liquidity premium* to be compensated for their risky activity of borrowing at short and lending at long maturities—intermediaries worry about their profits at time T, thereby lending at higher rates than the expected spots.[6]

Finally, consider the following definition of the *term-premium*, the difference between the spot rate and the future expected average short-term rate, for the same horizon, as follows:

$$\mathrm{TP}(t,T) \equiv R(t,T) - \frac{1}{T-t}\int_t^T E_t(r_\tau)\,d\tau = \frac{1}{T-t}\int_t^T \left[f(t,\tau) - E_t(r_\tau)\right]d\tau,$$

---

4. Section 13.4.4 explains that risk-aversion might also explain this property (see Eq. (13.42)).

5. Note that the *normal backwardation* hypothesis states that forward prices are lower than future expected spot prices, which implies the inequality in (13.18), stated in terms of rates.

6. The inequality in (13.18) cannot hold in a purely risk neutral market. Indeed, we have that, $e^{-\int_t^T f(t,\ell)d\ell} \equiv P(t,T) \geq e^{-\int_t^T \mathbb{E}_t(r_\tau)d\tau}$, which implies that $\int_t^T \left(f(t,\tau) - \mathbb{E}_t(r_\tau)\right)d\tau \leq 0$ for each T and therefore $f(t,\tau) \leq \mathbb{E}_t(r_\tau)$ for each τ, contradicting (13.18).

where the second equality follows by Eq. (13.13). We see that the expectation hypothesis, and possible violations of it, bring content to the term-premium. The next section aims to provide evidence of the expectation hypothesis, as linked to the predictability of bond returns.

13.3.2 Bond Returns Predictability

What does the empirical evidence suggest about the expectation hypothesis? How does the expectation hypothesis link to bond returns? First, we explain under which probability should the expectation hypothesis hold. Second, we succinctly review the main points regarding the empirical evidence.

13.3.2.1 Forward-adjusted expectation hypothesis

In more advanced sections of this chapter, we explain that forward rates cannot be unbiased expectations of the future spot rates, not even under the risk neutral probability. They are such only under a certain probability, known as forward probability, already introduced in chapter 4. Section 13.9.3, for example, shows that

$$f(t,T) = \mathbb{E}_{Q_F^T}(r_T), \tag{13.19}$$

where $\mathbb{E}_{Q_F^T}$ denotes the expectation under the forward probability, Q_T^F. This result points to a basic difficulty with the expectation hypothesis: Eq. (13.19) just tells us that the expectation hypothesis may only hold under the forward probability. There are two sources of risk, which might actually prevent the expectation theory from holding, in practice. To illustrate, let us elaborate on Eq. (13.19),

$$\begin{aligned} f(t,T) &= \mathbb{E}_{Q_F^T}(r_T) \\ &= \mathbb{E}_t(\eta_T(T)\, r_T) \\ &= \mathbb{E}_t(r_T) + cov_{Q,t}(\eta_T(T), r_T) \\ &= E_t(r_T) + cov_{P,t}\left(\eta_{P,T}(T), r_T\right) + cov_{Q,t}(\eta_T(T), r_T), \end{aligned} \tag{13.20}$$

where $\eta_{P,T}(T)$ (and $\eta_T(T)$) denotes the Radon-Nikodym derivatives of the risk neutral (and the forward) probability against the physical (and the risk neutral) probability; $\mathbb{E}_t$ and $cov_{Q,t}$ denote time t conditional expectation and covariance under the risk neutral probability, with E_t and $cov_{P,t}$ denoting the counterparts under the physical probability. That is, forward rates might deviate from future expected short-term rates, because of risk-aversion corrections (the second term in the last equality) and randomness in interest rates (the third term in the last equality).

13.3.2.2 The empirical evidence

Denote the continuously compounded returns on a zero expiring at some date T as $r_{t+1}^T = \ln \frac{P(t+1,T)}{P(t,T)}$. Using the definition of spot rates, $R(t,T)$, the excess returns, $\hat{r}_{t+1}^T$ say, can be expressed as

$$\hat{r}_{t+1}^T \equiv \ln \frac{P(t+1,T)}{P(t,T)} - \ln \frac{1}{P(t,t+1)}$$

$$
\begin{aligned}
&= \ln \frac{P(t+1,T)}{P(t,T)} - R(t,t+1) \\
&= -(T-t-1)\,R(t+1,T) + (T-t)\,R(t,T) - R(t,t+1)\,,
\end{aligned}
\tag{13.21}
$$

such that the expected change in the yield curve is negatively related to the expected excess returns and positively related to the slope of the yield curve:

$$
E_t\left[R(t+1,T) - R(t,T)\right] = -\frac{1}{T-t-1} E_t\left(\hat{r}_{t+1}^T\right) + \frac{1}{T-t-1}\left[R(t,T) - R(t,t+1)\right].
$$

Under the expectation hypothesis, the risk premium, $E_t\left(\hat{r}_{t+1}^T\right)$, is zero.[7] Then, we can test for the expectation theory by running the following regression:

$$
R(t+1,T) - R(t,T) = \alpha_T + \beta_T \frac{1}{T-t-1}\left[R(t,T) - R(t,t+1)\right] + \text{Residual}_t,
$$

and test for the null: $\alpha_T = 0$ and $\beta_T = 1$. A widely known empirical feature of US data is that the estimates of β_T are typically negative for all maturities T, and their absolute values are generally increasing with T. In fact, Fama and Bliss (1987) show that bond returns are predictable, in that the risk premium $E_t(\hat{r}_{t+1}^T)$ relates to the forward spreads, defined as $f_t^T - R(t,t+1)$, and that regressing,

$$
\hat{r}_{t+1}^T = \alpha_T + \beta_T \left(f_t^T - R(t,t+1)\right) + \text{Residual}_t,
$$

delivers statistically significant and positive values of β_T for many maturities T. The literature on bond return predictability has expanded starting from the 2000s, and focussed on rationalizing these empirical properties by means of dynamic models of the yield curve. We refer the reader to Singleton (2006, chaps. 9, 12, and 13) for an early and detailed review of this literature.

13.3.3 The Yield Curve and the Business Cycle

Yield curves do on average slope up. Underlying this pervasive property are two fundamental, not necessarily mutually exclusive, reasons: (i) on average, interest rates are expected to increase, (ii) investors are risk averse.[8] On average, the US yield curve is upward sloping at maturities from one up to ten years (see, e.g., figure 13.3). However, yield curves may invert. Moreover, there is strong empirical evidence, available since at least Kessel (1965) or, later, Laurent (1988, 1989), Stock and Watson (1989), Estrella and Hardouvelis (1991) and Harvey (1991, 1993), that inverted yield curves predict recessions with a lead time of about one to two years. Figure 13.2 illustrates these empirical facts through

7. Replace eq. (13.16) into (13.21), and use the law of iterated expectations to conclude.

8. Consider the following arguments. By Jensen's inequality, $e^{-(T-t)R(t,T)} \equiv P(t,T) = \mathbb{E}_t[e^{-\int_t^T r_\tau d\tau}] \geq e^{-\int_t^T \mathbb{E}_t(r_\tau) d\tau}$. Therefore, the yield curve satisfies: $R(t,T) \leq \frac{1}{T-t}\int_t^T \mathbb{E}_t(r_\tau)\,d\tau$. For example, suppose that r_t is a martingale under the risk neutral probability, viz $\mathbb{E}_t(r_\tau) = r_t$, such that $R(t,T) \leq r_t$. That is, the yield curve is not increasing in time to maturity, T, at least for small maturities. A yield curve may, then, slope up, because the r_t is *not* a martingale under the risk neutral probability.

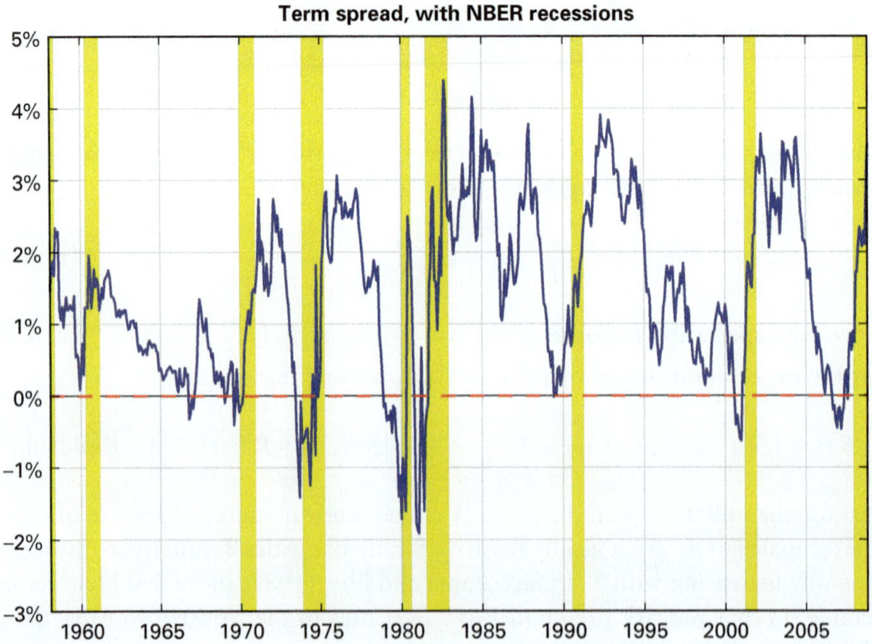

Figure 13.2
This picture depicts the time series of the term spread, defined as the difference between the 10-year yield minus the 3-month yield on US Treasuries. Sample data are monthly and cover the period from January 1957 to December 2008. The shaded areas mark recession periods, as defined by the National Bureau of Economic Research. The end of the last recession was announced to have occurred in June 2009.

a plot of the difference between long-term and short-term yields on Treasuries—in short, the "term spread."

There are, of course, recession episodes preceded by only mild yield curve inversions. But the really striking empirical regularity is the sharp movements of the term spread toward negative territory, occurring prior to any recession episode. Note, it is not really important whether it is the short-term rate that goes up or the long-term rate that goes down. The empirical regularity is that the *term spread* goes down and becomes negative prior to a recession. The explanations of these statistical facts are challenging, and might hinge upon both (i) the conduct of monetary policy and the expectations about it and (ii) the risk premium agents require to invest in long-term bonds. We discuss these two points below.

(i) *The monetary channel*:

- During expansions, monetary policy tends to be restrictive in an attempt at preventing the economy from heating up. At the height of an expansion, then, short-term yields go up. However, during recessions, interest rates are kept low in an attempt to fight against recessions.
- At the height of an expansion, the market may, then, anticipate an incoming recession, and expect central banks to lower future interest rates. The expectation hypothesis now predicts that the slope of the yield curve should decrease. Granted, we previously learned that the expectation hypothesis may not hold

empirically; bond markets command risk premiums. However, a risk premium channel would reinforce the conclusion that the slope of the yield curve decreases during expansions, as argued in the next point.

(ii) *The risk premium channel*: From chapter 8 we know that risk premiums are countercyclical, being high during recessions and low during expansions. The conditional equity premium is countercyclical, and so is the long-bond premium.[9] In fact, long-term yields and equity expected returns are likely to be driven by the same state variables affecting the pricing kernel of the economy.[10]

Let's summarize. On the one hand, countercyclical monetary policy may be responsible for the negative price changes affecting short-term bonds. On the other hand, expectations about countercyclical monetary policy as well as procyclical risk appetite may be responsible for positive price changes affecting long-term bonds. These price movements, we have argued, should occur at the height of an expansion. But, and somehow trivially, our sample data include expansions that are followed by recessions. Whence, the statistical facts regarding the predictive content of the yield curve. In section 13.4, we rely on a simple model to formalize this reasoning.

The empirical evidence that links yield curve inversions to recessions is quite important, but there are a few caveats. First, there may be other explanations for this evidence, relying on the presence of financial intermediaries. For example, Adrian and Shin (2011) discuss how interest rate margins (the difference between interest rates on each side of the banks' balance sheet) help banks' lending capacity. Now, inverted yield curves lead to negative margins. Arguably, this context may contribute to a reduced credit supply and, thus, to depress aggregate demand, feeding expectations of an imminent recession.[11] In turn, these expectations may lead to negative term spreads through the previous mechanisms, over a vicious circle. Finally, *expectations* may lead to yield curve inversions, in the following way. When financial intermediaries observe signals of economic contractions, they lend less, contributing to an upcoming contraction, similar as in the credit cycle mechanisms described in chapter 9 (see section 9.11). Furthermore, they expect future low interest rates, resulting from upcoming accommodating monetary policy; then, their demand for long-term bonds increases, leading long-term yield to decrease in the immediate term.

Interestingly, there is empirical evidence that yield curve inversions seem to link to business cycles even *prior* to the creation of the Federal Reserve system (see, e.g., Gerlach and Stuart, 2018). The creation of the US Central Bank, the Fed, is, thus, a "natural experiment" in this context. The conclusions from these empirical studies suggest that

9. An objection to this line of reasoning is that countercyclical risk premiums might lead to expect future bond prices to decrease over a future recession, thereby destroying the effects of a procyclical short-term rate. In section 13.4.4.2, we develop a model where these effects do not arise as soon as the effects of countercyclical risk premiums are assumed to be bounded.

10. That long term bonds and stock market are informally acknowledged to be tightly related is witnessed by a quite raw rule of thumb, whereby a stock market correction, such as a crash say, is deemed to be imminent when the spread 30 year bond yield minus the earning-price ratio is larger than 3%. This spread, which is usually around 1% or 2%—and on average, zero, once corrected for inflation—was indeed larger than 3% in 1987 and in 1997.

11. By standard q-theory (see section 3.4 in chapter 3), lower profits lead to lower investments. In our context, lower interest margins (and, hence, profits) lead bank to lend less.

additional forces may exist to explain the predictability power of the yield curve, beyond the gaming between central banks and market expectations regarding the future conduct of monetary policy.

Finally, an inverted yield curve may occur for reasons unrelated to the business cycle—in this case, some of the empirical evidence gathered so far might just have arisen by chance. For example, the inversion of the yield curve in 2006 is widely considered to have occurred due to a strong demand for long-term bonds, as warned by some policy makers at the time.[12] This demand pressure was exerted by institutional investors, for example, pension funds performing asset-liability management duties.[13] It is difficult to quantify this demand pressure and its contribution to the yield inversion of the time: since 2006, the Federal Reserve had started to target higher interest rates to deal with inflationary pressures, pressures at least partially originating from a quite expansionary policy that followed the 2001 recession, the Twin Towers attacks, and the 2003 corporate scandals. It is an open question as to whether the markets thought that this increased tightening was marking the end of an expansion, thereby feeding an expectation future interest rates would drop again in the near future. Historically, the Fed tightening would occur right when the financial system was about to enter into the 2007 subprime crisis and the crisis arising therefrom, developments dealt with in detail in the next chapter.

13.3.4 Additional Stylized Facts about the US Yield Curve

There are three additional features of data to be noted.

(i) Yields are highly correlated (say three-year yields with four-year yields, with five-year yields, etc.), and suggest the existence of common factors driving all of them, discussed in section 13.3.5 below.

(ii) Yields are also highly persistent, and this persistence bears important consequences for derivative pricing, as explained in section 13.8.1.

(iii) The term structure of unconditional yield volatility is often downward sloping, a feature also discussed in section 13.8.1.

13.3.5 Common Factors Affecting the Yield Curve

Which systematic factors affect the yield curve? How many factors are needed to explain variation in the yield curve? Risk management practice based on "duration hedging" relies on the assumption that most of this variation is captured by a single factor, one that produces parallel shifts in the yield curve (see chapter 12). How reliable is this idea in practice? This section reviews famous evidence that most of the variation in the US yield curve can be explained by just three factors: (i) a *level* factor, (ii) a *steepness* (slope) factor, and (iii) a *curvature* factor. Below, we explain the reasons underlying this terminology.

---

12. See, e.g., the *European Central Bank Monthly Bulletin*, February 2006, 27.

13. Likewise, note that the inversion of the yield curve in 2000 coincided with the Treasury buyback program discussed in chapter 10 (see section 10.9.3). In principle, this episode might have accounted for the inversion due to a diminished supply of long-term bonds.

It is intuitive that just a few factors may explain the yield curve. We should not expect too much difference between a 10Y zero and a 10Y+1day zero and, then, a 10Y+1day zero and a 10Y+2days zero. Repeating this reasoning ad infinitum suggests that most of the yield curve variations may well be driven by common sources. In a very famous study, Litterman and Scheinkman (1991) demonstrate that more than 95% of this variation is due to changes in the previous three factors. Their analysis relies on a *fixed-factor* model. Succinctly, suppose that p yields-to-maturity are generated by a linear factor model, with a fixed number k of factors,

$$\underset{p\times 1}{R_t} = \underset{p\times 1}{\bar{R}} + \underset{p\times k}{B}\ \underset{k\times 1}{F_t} + \underset{p\times 1}{\epsilon_t}, \tag{13.22}$$

where R_t is the vector of yields, $\bar{R}$ is the vector of unconditional expected yields, F_t is a zero-mean vector of common factors affecting the bond yields, and ϵ_t is a vector of idiosyncratic yields components. Finally, the matrix B contains factor loadings. Each row contains the factor loadings for all the common factors affecting a given yield, that is, the sensitivities of a yield with a given maturity to a change in the factors. Each column contains the *term structure of factor loadings*, that is, the changes in the whole yield curve determined by a change in a given factor.

13.3.5.1 Methodological details

Estimating the model in eq. (13.22) is challenging because the vector of factors F_t is unobservable. A simple method exists, known as *principal component analysis* (PCA, henceforth), which leads to empirical results qualitatively similar to those holding for the general model in eq. (13.22).[14] We discuss these empirical results in the next subsection. We now describe the main methodological points underlying PCA.

The main idea underlying PCA is to transform the original p correlated variables R into a set of new uncorrelated variables, the *principal components*. These principal components are linear combinations of the original variables, and are arranged in order of decreased importance: the first principal component accounts for as much as possible of the variation in the original data, the second component accounts for as much as possible of the remaining variation, and so on. We are looking for p linear combinations of the demeaned yields,

$$Y_{it} = C_i^\top \left(R_t - \bar{R}\right), \qquad i = 1, \cdots, p, \tag{13.23}$$

such that, for p vectors $C_i^\top$ of dimension $1 \times p$, (i) the new variables Y_i are uncorrelated, and (ii) their variances are arranged in decreasing order. The logic behind PCA is to ascertain whether a few components of $Y_t = [Y_{1t} \cdots Y_{pt}]^\top$ account for the bulk of variability of the original data. Let $C^\top = [C_1^\top \cdots C_p^\top]$ be a $p \times p$ matrix such that we can write eq. (13.23) in matrix format, $Y_t = C^\top \left(R_t - \bar{R}\right)$ or, by inverting,

$$R_t - \bar{R} = C^{\top -1} Y_t. \tag{13.24}$$

14. Appendix 13.C to this chapter provides some technical details on both PCA and estimation of factor models.

Next, suppose that the vector $Y_t^{(k)} = [Y_{1t} \cdots Y_{kt}]^\top$ accounts for most of the variability in the original data,[15] and let $C_{(k)}$ denote a $p \times k$ matrix extracted from the matrix $C^{\top -1}$ through the first k rows of $C^{\top -1}$. Since the components of $Y_t^{(k)}$ are uncorrelated and they are deemed largely responsible for the variability in the original data, it is natural to "disregard" the last $p-k$ components of Y in eq. (13.24),

$$\underset{p\times 1}{R_t - \bar{R}} \approx \underset{p\times k}{C_{(k)}} \underset{k\times 1}{Y_t^{(k)}}.$$

Should $Y_t^{(k)}$ really account for most of the movements of R_t, the previous approximation to eq. (13.24) should be fairly good.

Let us make more precise what the concept of variability is in the context of PCA. Suppose that the variance-covariance matrix of the yields, Σ, has p distinct eigenvalues, ordered from the highest to the lowest, as follows: $\lambda_1 > \cdots > \lambda_p$. Then, the vector C_i in eq. (13.23) is the eigenvector corresponding to the ith eigenvalue. Moreover,

$$var(Y_i) = \lambda_i, \qquad i = 1, \cdots, p.$$

Finally, we have that

$$R_{PCA} = \frac{\sum_{i=1}^k var(Y_i)}{\sum_{i=1}^p var(R_i)} = \frac{\sum_{i=1}^k \lambda_i}{\sum_{i=1}^p \lambda_i}. \tag{13.25}$$

It is in the sense of eq. (13.25) that we say that the first k principal components account for R_{PCA}% of the total variation of the data.

13.3.5.2 The empirical evidence

The striking feature of the empirical results uncovered by Litterman and Scheinkman (1991) is that they seem to be confirmed across different countries and sample periods. Moreover, these results bear the same interpretation, whether obtained through a rigorous factor analysis (see eq. (13.22)) or PCA. Figure 13.3 visualizes the effects that changes in these factors have on the yield curve.

- The first factor is called a "level" factor as its changes lead to parallel shifts in the term-structure of interest rates. Thus, this "level" factor produces essentially the same effects on the term structure as those underlying the "duration hedging" portfolio practice (see chapter 12). This factor explains approximately 80% of the total variation of the yield curve.
- The second factor is called a "steepness"(or "slope") factor as its variations induce changes in the slope of the term structure of interest rates. After a shock in this steepness factor, the short-end and the long-end of the yield curve move in opposite directions. The movements of this factor explain approximately 15% of the total variation of the yield curve.

15. There are no rigorous criteria to say what "most of the variability" means in this context. Instead, a likelihood-ratio test is most informative in the context of the estimation of eq. (13.22) by means of the methods explained in the previous footnote.

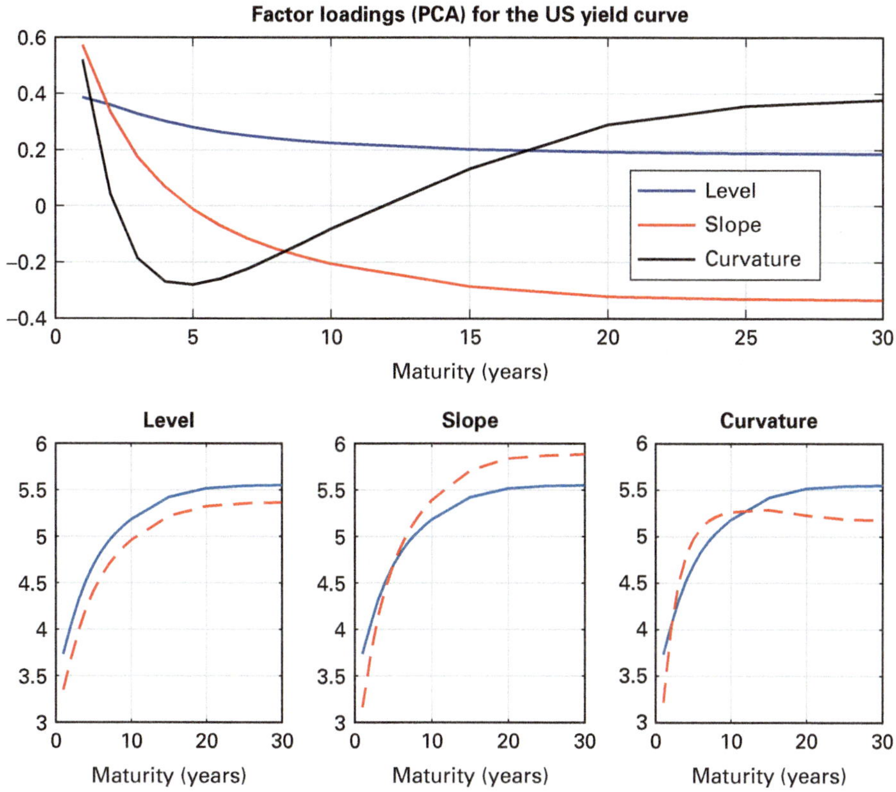

Figure 13.3
Top: Factor loadings. Bottom: Changes in the term structure of interest rates generated by changes in the "level," "slope," and "curvature" factors. Sample data are daily and cover the sample period from May 1998 to December 2009. The solid line is the average yield curve over the sample period. The dashed line is the yield curve obtained under a (one unit) negative shock in each factor.

- The third factor is called a "curvature" factor as its changes lead to changes in the curvature of the yield curve. That is, following a shock in the curvature factor, the middle of the yield curve and the short-end and the long-end of the yield curve move in opposite directions. This curvature factor accounts for approximately 5% of the total variation of the yield curve.

Understanding the origins of these three factors is still challenging to financial economists and macroeconomists. For example, macroeconomists explain that central banks affect the short-end of the yield curve, for example, by inducing variations in Federal Funds rate in the US. However, decisions taken by the Federal Reserve rely on current macroeconomic conditions. Therefore, the short-end of the yield curve likely links to macroeconomic developments. Instead, movements in the long-end of the yield curve should primarily depend on market expectations and risk aversion surrounding future interest rates and economic conditions. Financial economists, then, should expect to see the long-end of the yield curve as being driven by expectations of future economic activity, and by risk aversion.

Indeed, Ang and Piazzesi (2003) provide some empirical evidence that (i) macroeconomic factors such as inflation and real economic activity can explain movements at the short-end and the middle of the yield curve and, interestingly, (ii) the long-end of the yield curve is driven by unobservable factors. However, it is not clear whether such unobservable factors are driven by time-varying risk aversion or changing expectations. A compelling lesson is that models of the yield curve driven by only one factor are likely to be misspecified, due to the complexity of roles and objectives of the so many diverse participants in the fixed income markets and the macroeconomic linkages of decisions made by these institutions.

13.3.5.3 *Forecasting the yield curve*

Chapter 12 explains that simple techniques are available to fit the yield curve for the purpose of mere statistical descriptions of the data (see appendix 12.A). One, proposed by Nelson and Siegel (1987), and reproduced here for convenience, postulates that the yield curve can be modeled as:

$$R(T) = \beta_1 + \beta_2 \left(\frac{1 - e^{-\lambda T}}{\lambda T} \right) + \beta_3 \left(\frac{1 - e^{-\lambda T}}{\lambda T} - e^{-\lambda T} \right).$$

The three coefficients, β_1, β_2, and β_3, can be interpreted in terms of the three factors reviewed in this section. The coefficient β_1 governs the level of the yield curve. The coefficient β_2 relates to the slope, as an increase in this coefficient increases short yields more than long yields. The coefficient β_3 shapes the curvature, as an increase in this coefficient has little effect on very short and very long yields, but increases the middle of the yield curve. Moreover, the coefficient λ controls the exponential decay of the yield curve: small values of λ translate to slow decay and can better fit the curve at long maturities; large values of λ, instead, lead to a fast decay, which helps fit the short-end of the yield curve. Finally, λ determines where the loading on β_3 achieves its maximum. Diebold and Li (2006) rely on this model, and estimate β_i for each date, and then use these estimated time series of β_i to forecast future values of β_i through vector autoregressions and, then, the future yield curve.

13.4 Models of the Short-Term Rate: Introduction

The short-term rate is simply the growth rate, or velocity, at which "locally" riskless investments appreciate over the next infinitesimal amount of time. Naturally, this velocity is not a traded asset. Models where bond prices are tied up to interest rates are likely to be incomplete, in that to hedge against a bond, we cannot rely on anything underlying the bond price movements—what is traded is a money market account as well as the bond itself, not the interest rate. The evaluation framework in this context is one where bond prices can be replicated through other bond prices, as explained in a discrete time setting in chapter 12. These issues are similar to those encountered in chapter 11, where to price options in environments with random volatility, we needed to replicate options through other options.

13.4.1 Models versus Representations

The pricing formula in eq. (13.2) suggests a natural approach to model the arbitrage-free price P, based on the assumption that $(r_\tau)_{\tau\geq 0}$ is exogenously given. For example, we may assume that r_τ is the solution to

$$dr_\tau = b(r_\tau, \tau)\, d\tau + a(r_\tau, \tau)\, dW_\tau, \quad \tau \in (t, T], \tag{13.26}$$

where W_τ is a standard Brownian motion under the *physical* probability, and b, a are two functions that satisfy standard regularity conditions. Under this assumption, and additional regularity conditions,[16] eq. (13.2) is

$$P(r_t, t, T) = \mathbb{E}_t\left(e^{-\int_t^T r_u du}\right), \tag{13.27}$$

where we have emphasized that the price function is a function of the short-term rate only: because the short-term rate is a Markov process, then, by results reviewed in chapter 4 the conditional expectation on the RHS of (13.27) is only a function of the current short-term rate r_t.

What can we say about the two functions a and b? One possibility is to select functions that lead to a solution fast to compute in practice. Another possibility is that the chosen functions lead to empirically accurate model predictions. Well-known models solved in closed form are the celebrated "affine" models (see section 13.5.3). The point that any model should be accurate is more subtle. We may never achieve "perfect" accuracy in a model such as that in eqs. (13.26)–(13.27). This model is one that *determines* the yield curve and it cannot then *exactly fit* it. Instead, a perfect fit of the yield curve is crucial when the aim is to price interest rate derivatives, as discussed in chapter 12. However, we shall explain that the models in this section may well fit the yield curve, once equipped with an "infinite-dimensional" parameter calibrated to the observed yield curve.

Models with such a perfect accuracy are known as "no-arbitrage" models. They are the continuous time counterparts to the implied trees dealt with in chapter 12. In a sense, no-arbitrage models are *representations*, not *models* really. They force the short-term rate *process* to exactly pin down the yield curve at any instant and, for this reason, they likely lead to intertemporal inconsistencies—the parameters that pin down the yield curve today, likely differ from those as of tomorrow. The rationale underlying their use goes to the opposite extreme of what we are describing in this section. In this section, the short-term rate is the *input* to all subsequent movements of the term structure of interest rates. Instead, no-arbitrage models are a means through which we model future movements of the yield curve, by feeding information relating to the observed yield curve, not only the *current* short-term rate.

Models of the short-term rate are, then, and obviously, very useful, when the objective is to *explain* market behavior through a few inputs—a data reduction scientific principle. In these models, prices are economically admissible, i.e., no-arbitrage, and move while being driven by random changes in the state variables. The pricing errors they lead to may be seen as a virtue, not a defect. A permanent deviation of market data from the model

16. These conditions regard the change of probability that is necessary to express the dynamics of r_t under the risk neutral probability. This change in probability is discussed in section 13.4.2.

predictions might be a market anomaly rather than a model's imperfection, which the model could help exploit. Instead, and by construction, no-arbitrage models are needed to deal with pricing problems where bond prices have to match market data, and to change over time as a result of a probability distribution determined by the current market data, even when these market data are mispriced.

13.4.2 The Bond Pricing Equation

13.4.2.1 A first derivation

We assume and, later, verify that bond prices are solutions to the following stochastic differential equation

$$\frac{dP_i}{P_i} = \mu_{bi} d\tau + \sigma_{bi} dW, \tag{13.28}$$

where W is a standard d-dimensional Brownian, μ_{bi} and σ_{bi} are some progressively measurable functions (σ_{bi} is vector-valued), and $P_i \equiv P(\tau, T_i)$, for a collection of maturity dates T_i. The exact functional form of μ_{b_i} and σ_{b_i} is *not* given, as in the Black–Scholes market described in chapters 4 and 12. Rather, it is endogenous and must be found as a part of the equilibrium.

Based on general results given in chapter 4, we can show that the price system in (13.28) is arbitrage-free if and only if

$$\mu_{bi} = r + \sigma_{bi}\lambda, \tag{13.29}$$

for some d-dimensional process λ satisfying some basic regularity conditions. Even if eq. (13.29) follows by standard no-arbitrage arguments, appendix 13.A derives it again to emphasize how absence of arbitrage does specifically work in the context of bond markets.

The meaning of eq. (13.29) is better understood by replacing this equation into eq. (13.28), obtaining

$$\frac{dP_i}{P_i} = (r + \sigma_{bi}\lambda)\, d\tau + \sigma_{bi} dW.$$

The previous equation tells us that the growth rate of P_i is the short-term rate plus a *risk premium* equal to $\sigma_{bi}\lambda$. Note that there are no obvious economic arguments enabling us to sign this premium. However, it would be zero in a risk neutral world, where bond prices would, then, satisfy:

$$\frac{dP_i}{P_i} = r d\tau + \sigma_{bi} d\tilde{W},$$

where $\tilde{W} = W + \int \lambda d\tau$ is a Brownian motion under the risk neutral probability, Q. More formally, these changes in probability are justified by Girsanov's theorem (see chapter 4), and are needed to express r_t in (13.26) under the risk neutral probability.

To illustrate the derivation of eq. (13.29) when $d = 1$, consider the dynamics of the value V of a self-financed portfolio in two bonds and a money market account

$$dV = (\pi_1(\mu_{b1} - r) + \pi_2(\mu_{b2} - r) + rV)\, d\tau + (\pi_1\sigma_{b1} + \pi_2\sigma_{b2})\, dW,$$

where π_i is the wealth invested in a bond maturing at T_i: if θ_i denotes the units of bonds in the portfolio, $\pi_i = \theta_i P_i$. We can zero uncertainty by setting

$$\pi_1 = -\frac{\sigma_{b2}}{\sigma_{b1}} \pi_2.$$

By replacing the previous relation into the dynamics of V,

$$dV = \underbrace{\left(-\frac{\mu_{b1} - r}{\sigma_{b1}} \sigma_{b2} + (\mu_{b2} - r) \right)}_{\equiv \ell} \pi_2 d\tau + rV d\tau.$$

Note, now, that π_2 can always be chosen such that the value of this portfolio appreciates at strictly more than r: just set sign $(\pi_2) =$ sign (ℓ). Therefore, to rule out arbitrage, it must be that $\ell = 0$, or

$$\frac{\mu_{b1} - r}{\sigma_{b1}} = \frac{\mu_{b2} - r}{\sigma_{b2}}.$$

That is, the Sharpe ratio for any two bonds has to equal a process λ, say, and eq. (13.29) follows. Clearly, λ is independent of the two maturity dates, T_1 or T_2, which were arbitrary indeed. It is natural that λ is independent of any bond maturity, as this is the unit price of risk required to compensate for randomness in the short-term rate.

The two functions μ_{bi} and σ_{bi} in eq. (13.28) can be determined through Itô's lemma. Let $P(r, \tau, T)$ be the price at τ of a bond maturing at T when the state at τ is r—the "rational" bond pricing function. Because r is the solution to eq. (13.26), Itô's lemma implies that

$$dP = \left(\frac{\partial P}{\partial \tau} + bP_r + \frac{1}{2} a^2 P_{rr} \right) d\tau + aP_r dW,$$

where subscripts denote partial derivatives and, to simplify the presentation, we are still assuming that $d = 1$.

Comparing this equation with eq. (13.28), and identifying drifts and diffusion terms, we conclude that

$$\mu_b P = \frac{\partial P}{\partial \tau} + bP_r + \frac{1}{2} a^2 P_{rr} \quad \text{and} \quad \sigma_b P = aP_r.$$

Finally, replace these functions into eq. (13.29), and obtain that P satisfies the following partial differential equation (PDE, henceforth), for all r and $\tau \in [t, T)$:

$$\frac{\partial P}{\partial \tau} + bP_r + \frac{1}{2} a^2 P_{rr} = rP + \lambda a P_r, \tag{13.30}$$

with the boundary condition $P(r, T, T) = 1$, holding for all r. We will return to the the interpretation of this bond pricing equation in section 13.4.2.3.

13.4.2.2 *Derivation based on duration*

An alternative idea is to replicate the price of a bond expiring at some time T_1, say $P^1 \equiv P(r, \tau, T_1)$, with a self-financed portfolio comprising a money market account and a second bond expiring at time $T_2 > T_1$. This approach is the continuous time equivalent to the pricing approach in chapter 12 (see appendix 12.B). It is, also, the interest rate counterpart to option evaluation with stochastic volatility in chapter 11.

Let, then, V be the value of our self-financed portfolio, $V=\Delta\cdot P^2+M$, where Δ is the number of bonds maturing at T_2 to include in the portfolio, $P^2=P(r,\tau,T_2)$, and M is the dollar amount in the money market account. Since the portfolio is self-financed, standard arguments lead to

$$dV=\Delta\cdot dP^2+dM=\left(\Delta\cdot LP^2+rM\right)d\tau+\Delta\cdot aP_r^2 dW, \tag{13.31}$$

where $LP^2=\frac{\partial P^2}{\partial\tau}+bP_r^2+\frac{1}{2}a^2P_{rr}^2$; and obviously,

$$dP^1=\left(LP^1\right)d\tau+aP_r^1 dW. \tag{13.32}$$

Let the initial value of the portfolio match the bond price. Then, comparing the diffusive terms in eq. (13.31) and eq. (13.32), we find the delta to be:

$$\hat{\Delta}=\frac{\partial P(r,\tau,T_1)/\partial r}{\partial P(r,\tau,T_2)/\partial r}.$$

Comparing the drift terms in eq. (13.31) and eq. (13.32),

$$LP^1=\Delta\cdot LP^2+rM=\Delta\cdot LP^2+r\left(V-\Delta P^2\right)=\Delta\cdot LP^2+r\left(P^1-\Delta P^2\right),$$

where the last line follows because we are using the values (Δ,M), such that the portfolio value matches that of the first bond. Rearranging terms and evaluating the result at $\Delta=\hat{\Delta}$,

$$\frac{LP^1-rP^1}{P_r^1}=\frac{LP^2-rP^2}{P_r^2}\equiv\Lambda\equiv\lambda a,$$

for some Λ and λ independent of calendar time.

The delta, $\hat{\Delta}$, can be interpreted as the ratio of the durations of the two bonds, similarly as in the rudimentary duration hedging models of chapter 12 (see section 12.3). Such a duration-based derivation suggests a trading strategy. Suppose the first bond is mispriced against a given model, in that we believe that our model does better than the market is currently doing while pricing this bond. For example, we might observe that the model predicts that the price of this first bond is often lower than the market, $P^1<P_{\$}^1$, and that, at the same time, the very same model prices well bonds on other points of the curve. We can implement the following relative value trade. We sale short the first bond for $P_{\$}^1$, realize an initial gain equal to $P_{\$}^1-P^1$, with P^1 invested into the previously described portfolio, that is, a portfolio aiming at replicating the T_1-bond through a money market account and a T_2-bond. The assumption is, of course, that the model is better than the market, implying that such a replication is indeed possible. Veronesi (2010, chap. 16) develops examples that illustrate the performance of this strategy based on the models of the short-term rate dealt with in this section.

13.4.2.3 *Interpreting the bond pricing equation: Market incompleteness and preference-free evaluation*

Eq. (13.30) shows that the bond price, P, depends on both the drift of the short-term rate, b, and the risk-aversion correction, λ. Let us elucidate the circumstances leading to this fact. They link to market incompleteness.

Consider a benchmark complete market model, Black–Scholes, in which the option is redundant: in markets such as Black–Scholes, the stock price *is* the source of randomness, and markets are trivially completed by the very same asset; see part I (e.g., chapters 2 and 5). In the market of this section, the bond price is *not* the risk. Rather, the bond draws value from the interest rate risk, *as if* it was a "derivative" on r_t, where r_t is the risk, a risk that cannot be replicated: markets are, then, incomplete. Let us explain.

In chapter 2, we learned that a system of incomplete markets can be made complete by introducing a certain number of additional securities. For example, a market with two securities and three states is incomplete. Yet it may be completed once a third security is introduced, which together with the first two, can generate any consumption bundle in all states of the world—we only need that the payoff matrix of the three securities be nonsingular. Does this mean that the third security can be priced in a preference-free format? Of course not. By construction, the payoffs promised by the third security cannot be replicated by trading the first two. Its price, then, reflects the services it provides market participants with; thus, it cannot be preference-free. Note, however, that an hypothetical fourth security can be replicated by trading the three securities, and its price would then be preference-free.

Similarly, in the market of this section, r_t describes risk. Introducing one bond would then make markets complete. However, the price of this bond would not be preference-free. In chapter 11, we encountered an analogous situation, arising in equity markets with stochastic volatility: we had two sources of randomness, the stock price and its stochastic volatility, such that a portfolio with a stock *and* one additional option was needed to hedge against one given option—and no preference-free formulae are possible. Let us mention another example. In many models of part II, we were given a certain dividend risk, and the stock price could not, then, be expressed in a preference-free fashion: the dividend was the risk, and the stock price was like a derivative written on that risk, and able to complete the market but, still, not preference-free.

There is more. In this section, the bond completes the market, as explained. However, its price cannot be replicated "through the short-term rate," as r_t is not traded. Naturally, we can replicate a second bond price by trading the first (and a money market account). Yet the second bond price is not preference-free for the very reason the first is not. Hedging in these markets seems to be a bit intricate. Hedging may be possible, but requires leaving the preference-free territory. For example, we may try to replicate the price of an option written on a bond while trading on a market money account and the very same bond. It is possible, but we would need to match the volatility of the bond price to that of the option price. Because the volatility of the bond price is not exogenous (depending as it does on the price sensitivity with respect to r_t), the hedge is obviously not preference-free.

13.4.2.4 Modeling assumptions

These facts explain the reason the bond price depends on b and a. In this market, uncertainty is generated by an untraded risk, r_t, such that the initial market structure has one untraded risk, r_t, and zero assets, as explained. But because the short-term rate r_t is not a discounted martingale under Q, its drift does not equal to $r_t \cdot r_t = r_t^2$ under Q but, rather $b - \lambda a$, thereby leading to eq. (13.30). All in all, the bond price depends on the specific functional forms of b, a and λ.

This dependence on risk appetite may appear as a kind of hindrance. It may actually be a source of value, due to its potential to inform on agents' risk appetite λ: once two functions (b,a) are estimated, the yield curve could be "inverted" to infer the implied λ, which could help policy makers to take more informed decisions about how to affect the yield curve—admittedly, though, the task of estimating (b,a) is far from trivial.

By specifying (b,a) and identifying the risk premium λ, the PDE in eq. (13.30) can then be solved, either analytically or numerically. Choices concerning the exact functional form of b,a and λ are often made for analytical or empirical reasons. In section 13.4.4, we introduce the first, famous models in which b,a, and λ have a particularly simple form. Section 13.4.5 discusses analytical merits but major empirical drawbacks of these models. In section 13.4.6 we provide a very succinct description of models exhibiting jump (and default) phenomena. We, first, highlight how models of the short-term rate could be used to set up a metric of duration when this concept is more difficult to quantify than in the contexts outlined in chapter 12.

13.4.3 Stochastic Duration

Duration is a measure of risk tailored to capture the notion of fixed income volatility. Cox, Ingersoll, and Ross (1979) hinge upon models of the short-term rate and introduce the notion of *stochastic duration*, generalizing the notion of modified duration discussed in chapter 12. Suppose the price of a zero coupon bond is a function of the short-term rate only, $P(r, T-t)$. Define the *basis risk* as the semi-elasticity of the bond price with respect to the short-term rate

$$\Psi(r, T-t) \equiv -\frac{P_r(r, T-t)}{P(r, T-t)}.$$

Naturally, we want to make sure that any measure of duration equals time to maturity in the special case of a zero coupon bond. Therefore, Ψ cannot be a measure of duration: except in the trivial case in which r is constant, Ψ does not equal $T-t$ for a zero. The idea underlying "stochastic duration" of a given bond-related instrument is to search for the time to maturity T^*-t of a hypothetical zero coupon bond such that its basis risk is the same as that of the given bond (e.g., a coupon bearing bond or a callable bond), namely,

$$\Psi(r, T^*-t) = -\frac{B_r(r, S-t)}{B(r, S-t)},$$

where $B(r, S-t)$ is the price of the given bond-related instrument expiring at time S, and provided no events occur for expiry to occur prior to S (e.g., default or the exercise of the optionalities embedded into a callable bond). Stochastic duration is defined as the time to maturity T^*-t of an hypothetical zero coupon bond with the same basis risk as the bond-related instrument expiring at S:

$$T^*-t \equiv D(r, S-t) = \Psi^{-1}\left(-\frac{B_r(r, S-t)}{B(r, S-t)}\right), \tag{13.33}$$

where Ψ^{-1} denotes the inverse function of $\Psi(r, x)$ with respect to time to maturity x. It is immediate to verify that for a zero, $D(r, S-t) = S-t$. Moreover, the stochastic duration,

$D(r, T-t)$, collapses to the modified duration introduced in the previous chapter (see section 12.3) once the short-term rate is a constant.[17]

13.4.4 Some Famous Models

13.4.4.1 Vasicek

Vasicek (1977) derives a model of the yield curve assuming the short-term rate r_τ is a continuous time and mean-reverting process with constant basis point volatility, solution to:[18]

$$dr_\tau = \kappa(\bar{r} - r_\tau)\, d\tau + \sigma dW_\tau, \quad \tau \in (t, T], \tag{13.34}$$

where $\bar{r}$, κ and σ are positive constants. This model is more sensible than that of Merton (1973), where the short-term rate is an arithmetic Brownian motion. The intuition underlying the importance of mean-reversion is as follows. Suppose, first, that $\sigma = 0$, in which case,

$$r_\tau = \bar{r} + e^{-\kappa(\tau - t)}(r_t - \bar{r}). \tag{13.35}$$

If the current level of the short-term rate $r_t = \bar{r}$, it will be "locked-in" at $\bar{r}$ forever. If, $r_t < \bar{r}$, the short-term rate shall steadily increase, and converge to $\bar{r}$ as $\tau \to \infty$. Likewise, the short-term rate shall converge to $\bar{r}$ when $r_t > \bar{r}$. The speed of convergence of r to the long-term value $\bar{r}$ depends on the magnitude of κ: the higher κ, the higher the speed of convergence to $\bar{r}$.

In the general case, $\sigma \neq 0$, the solution to eq. (13.34) is,

$$r_\tau = \bar{r} + e^{-\kappa(\tau - t)}(r_t - \bar{r}) + \sigma e^{-\kappa\tau} \int_t^\tau e^{\kappa s} dW_s,$$

where the integral has to be understood in the Itô's sense. The interpretation of this solution is similar to that in the determinist case, in that the short-term rate now fluctuates around its "central tendency" $\bar{r}$. In other words, shocks are absorbed at a speed depending on the magnitude of κ, leading the short-term rate to display a mean-reverting behavior. Indeed, the conditional expectation of r is the same as that in eq. (13.35),

$$E(r_\tau | r_t) = \bar{r} + e^{-\kappa(\tau - t)}(r_t - \bar{r}). \tag{13.36}$$

Moreover, the conditional variance of r is:

$$var(r_\tau | r_t) = \frac{\sigma^2}{2\kappa}\left(1 - e^{-2\kappa(\tau - t)}\right).$$

Finally, it can be shown that r is normally distributed, with expectation and variance given by the two functions given above.

To solve for the entire term structure of interest rates, we need to make assumptions about the risk premium, λ. A closed-form expression for the bond price obtains, once we assume λ is a constant. Indeed, by replacing a constant risk premium λ and the functions

17. Indeed, note that if r is constant, then, $P(r, T-t) = e^{-r(T-t)}$, such that $\Psi^{-1}(x) = x$.

18. Note that Merton's (1973) seminal paper is also framed in a context with random interest rates solved in closed form. In Merton's model, the short-term rate is an arithmetic Brownian motion.

$b(r) = \kappa(\bar{r} - r)$ and $a(r) = \sigma$ into eq. (13.30), and denoting $r^* \equiv \bar{r} - \frac{\lambda\sigma}{\kappa}$, we obtain that the bond price P is the solution to:

$$0 = \frac{\partial P}{\partial \tau} + \kappa\left(r^* - r\right) P_r + \frac{1}{2}\sigma^2 P_{rr} - rP, \text{ for all } (r, \tau) \in \mathbb{R} \times [t, T), \tag{13.37}$$

with the usual boundary condition. Intuitively, $\kappa(r^* - r)$ is the drift of the short-term rate under Q, which is higher than under P for $\lambda < 0$, reflecting higher Arrow-Debreu state prices for the bad states of the world arising when interest rates are high.

It is instructive to see how this partial differential equation can be solved. We guess a solution of the form:

$$P(r, \tau, T) = e^{A(\tau,T) - B(\tau,T)\cdot r}, \tag{13.38}$$

for two functions A and B to be determined. Now suppose the guess in eq. (13.38) is true. By replacing the partial derivatives of P into eq. (13.37) leaves the equation $\phi_1(\tau) + \phi_2(\tau) r = 0$, where for all τ,

$$\phi_1(\tau) \equiv A_1(\tau, T) - \kappa r^* B(\tau, T) + \frac{1}{2}\sigma^2 B^2(\tau, T) \quad \text{and} \quad \phi_2(\tau) \equiv \kappa B(\tau, T) - B_1(\tau, T) - 1.$$

That is, $0 = \phi_1(\tau) = \phi_2(\tau)$, two ordinary differential equations subject to the boundary conditions $A(T, T) = 0$ and $B(T, T) = 0$. The solutions are:

$$A(\tau, T) = (B(\tau, T) - (T - \tau))\, r_\infty - \frac{\sigma^2}{4\kappa} B^2(\tau, T), \quad B(\tau, T) = \frac{1}{\kappa}\left(1 - e^{-\kappa(T-\tau)}\right), \tag{13.39}$$

where

$$r_\infty = r^* - \frac{1}{2}\left(\frac{\sigma}{\kappa}\right)^2.$$

The term structure of spot rates predicted by this model is, by the definition in eq. (13.12),

$$R(r, t, T) = -\frac{A(t, T)}{T - t} + \frac{B(t, T)}{T - t} r. \tag{13.40}$$

The quantity, r_∞, is interpreted as the "asymptotic" spot rate, as it is the limit of $R(r, t, T)$ for large T.

The model displays a number of features that match some empirical facts. Figure 13.4 depicts hypothetical examples of the yield curve predicted by the model. Due to mean-reversion, the yield curve may be increasing or decreasing according to whether the short-term rate is low or high; the curve may even exhibit a hump shape. The shapes in this figure depend, of course, on parameter values, which should be calibrated to reflect statistical properties of the yield curve; section 13.5.5 provides some details regarding such calibration procedures.

13.4.4.2 *A case study: Expectations and business cycles*

Vasicek's model can be taken to illustrate some aspects of the expectation hypothesis. We can also rely on a variant of this model and attempt at rationalizing the predicting power

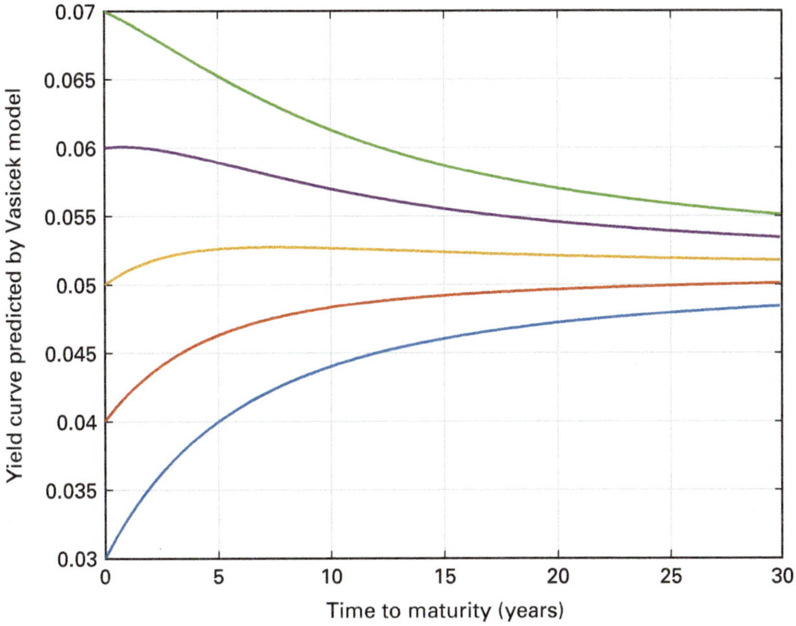

Figure 13.4
The yield curve predicted by the Vasicek model for levels of the short-term rate r_t equal to 3%, 4%, 5%, 6%, and 7%. Parameter values are $\kappa = 0.2$, $\bar{r} = 6\%$, $\sigma = 0.03$, and $\lambda = -0.015$. The asymptotic rate predicted by the model is $r_\infty = 5.10\%$.

of the term spread (see section 13.3). First, we express the yield curve in eq. (13.40) in a way that is more convenient to interpret. We mentioned earlier that the short-term rate is conditionally normally distributed. Now, the term $\int_t^T r_\tau d\tau$ is also conditionally normally distributed,[19] and, then, by eq. (13.2) and eq. (13.12),

$$R(r,t,T) = \mathbb{E}_t\left(\frac{1}{T-t}\int_t^T r_\tau d\tau\right) - \frac{1}{2}\frac{1}{T-t}\text{var}\left(\int_t^T r_\tau d\tau\right). \tag{13.41}$$

The second term in eq. (13.41) reflects Jensen's inequality effects. It equals

$$\frac{1}{2}\frac{1}{T-t}\text{var}\left(\int_t^T r_\tau d\tau\right) = \frac{1}{2}\left(1 - \frac{1-e^{-\kappa(T-t)}}{(T-t)\kappa}\right)\left(\frac{\sigma}{\kappa}\right)^2 - \frac{\sigma^2}{4(T-t)\kappa^3}\left(1-e^{-\kappa(T-t)}\right)^2,$$

and is much smaller than the first term when evaluated using realistic parameter values.

We approximate the yield curve with the first term of eq. (13.41), which is an expectation of the average short-term rate under the risk neutral probability. By eq. (13.36) and eq. (13.30), this expectation can be decomposed as the sum of the expectation under the physical probability plus risk premium terms, as follows

$$R(r,t,T) \approx \mathbb{E}_t\left(\frac{1}{T-t}\int_t^T r_\tau d\tau\right) = \frac{1}{T-t}\int_t^T E_t(r_\tau)\,d\tau + \frac{1}{T-t}\int_t^T \mathcal{E}_\tau d\tau, \tag{13.42}$$

19. See, for example, Lamberton and Lapeyre (1997, chap. 6).

where

$$\frac{1}{T-t}\int_t^T E_t(r_\tau)\,d\tau = \bar{r} + (r_t - \bar{r})\,\frac{1-e^{-\kappa(T-t)}}{\kappa(T-t)}, \quad \mathcal{E}_\tau \equiv -\frac{1-e^{-\kappa(\tau-t)}}{\kappa}\sigma\lambda.$$

Eq. (13.42) says that long-term rates reflect expectations of the future short-term rate and risk premium terms, defined as the average expected bond returns.

We can rely on this simple framework and describe a few, but key, business cycle properties of the yield curve. We assume that business cycle conditions can be summarized by the realization of a single state variable, y, which is the solution to

$$dy_t = \kappa(\bar{y} - y_t)\,dt + \sigma_y dW_t, \tag{13.43}$$

for three positive constants, κ, $\bar{y}$ and σ_y. Next, suppose that: (i) the *nominal* short-term rate is procyclical, in that $r_t \equiv A + By_t$, for two positive constants A and B, and that (ii) risk premiums are countercyclical in that, $\lambda_y(y) \equiv \lambda_0 - \lambda_1 y$, for two additional constants, where $\lambda_1 > 0$, to ensure countercyclicality, and λ_0 might in principle take any sign, although it is reasonable to assume that $\lambda_0 > 0$, which would imply that the constant portion of the risk premium is positive anyway. We shall return to the sign of λ_0 in a moment.[20]

Given the assumptions made so far, the short-term rate is the solution to eq. (13.34), with parameters $\bar{r} \equiv A + B\bar{y}$ and $\sigma \equiv B\sigma_y$. While the risk premium is time-varying, being equal to $\lambda(r) \equiv \lambda_0 - \frac{\lambda_1}{B}(r - A)$, the short-term rate is still conditionally normally distributed under the risk neutral probability, and the yield curve can be solved in closed form, with a solution like that in eq. (13.38), and an approximation like that in eq. (13.42). It is instructive to calculate the decomposition in eq. (13.42) predicted by this model. We have,

$$R(r,t,T) \approx \mathbb{E}_t\left(\frac{1}{T-t}\int_t^T r_\tau d\tau\right) = r^* + (r_t - r^*)\,\frac{1-e^{-\kappa^*(T-t)}}{\kappa^*(T-t)},$$

where $\kappa^* = \kappa - \sigma_y\lambda_1$, a strictly positive constant, and $r^* = \frac{\kappa\bar{r} - B\sigma_y\lambda_0 - A\sigma_y\lambda_1}{\kappa - \sigma_y\lambda_1}$: the model clearly collapses to Vasicek's for $\lambda_1 = 0$. A countercyclical risk premium, $\lambda_1 > 0$, leads to a tilt in the unconditional short-term rate, r^*, and, importantly, an increased persistence of the short-term rate, due to the fact that $\kappa^* < \kappa$. If risk premium effects are so large to make $\kappa^* < 0$, the model has no solutions for large T. Finally, note that while it is reasonable to assume $\lambda_0 > 0$, we may also wish to make sure λ_0 is small enough to ensure that for most of the time, $\lambda(r)$ is negative and, hence, expected excess returns are positive.

The term-spread (over the short-term rate) predicted by the model is

$$R(A + By_t, t, T) - r_t \approx B\left(\frac{1-e^{-\kappa^*(T-t)}}{\kappa^*(T-t)} - 1\right)(y_t - y^*), \tag{13.44}$$

where $y^* = \frac{\kappa\bar{y} - \sigma_y\lambda_0}{\kappa - \sigma_y\lambda_1}$ is the unconditional expectation of the procyclical variable y (under the risk neutral probability). The term spread is the product of three terms. The first reflects the

20. More generally, we may assume that the dynamics of y_t depend on r_t, by replacing Eq. (13.43) with, say, $dy_t = (\kappa(\bar{y} - y_t) - Cr_t)\,dt + \sigma_y dW_t$, for some constant C. Hördahl, Tristani, and Vestin (2006) propose models with similar feedback effects.

property that interest rates are procyclical, $B > 0$. The second term is negative when $\kappa^* > 0$, in which case the model formalizes explanations given in section 13.3.3. That is, before a "peak," i.e., when $y_t < y^*$, the yield curve is upward sloping. After this peak is achieved and, then, $y_t > y^*$, the probability the economy will enter into a recession is higher, given the mean-reverting nature of y_t, and the yield curve becomes inverted. In other words, at the peak of an expansion, when a recession is most likely, we expect that interest rates will lower due to their procyclicality, $B > 0$, whence the yield curve inversion. Long term interest rates are driven by expectations of future short-term rates.

Note that these effects take place once countercyclical risk aversion is mild enough to guarantee that $\kappa^* > 0$. If λ_1 was so large to make $\kappa^* < 0$, the model would generate the wrong predictions, with an inverted yield curve during the rising part of a boom, not the descending part. The mechanism would be that, during a peak, the future short-term rate would be expected to lower, but risk aversion would be expected to increase to a level so high to dwarf expectations effects and push future prices down: future countercyclical risk aversion would dominate procyclical effects generated by the short-term rate.

Naturally, this model is very simple, driven as it is by only one factor, the business cycle variable y_t. Its merit is that it makes a sharp prediction regarding the slope of the yield curve: a positive slope occurs before a peak, $y_t < y^*$, and a negative slope after the peak, $y_t < y^*$, the same as in the data. This model thus isolates the business cycle component of the yield curve that relates to its inversions. The crucial point is that the model is silent as regards the business cycle variable y_t. If we knew y_t, we could use it to forecast the business cycle in the first place.

13.4.4.3 Cox, Ingersoll, and Ross

Vasicek's model suffers from two main drawbacks. First, the short-term rate is normally distributed. This circumstance might be mitigated when σ is low, compared to $\bar{r}$, in which case the probability the short-term rate takes negative values can be small. At the same time, even a small probability of a negative interest rate might lead to severe mispricing in the case of interest rate derivatives, due to the nonlinearities induced by optionality. The previous chapter provides numerical examples for which small changes in assumptions lead to substantially different derivative prices (see, e.g., section 12.4.3).

The second drawback, related to the first, is that the short-term rate volatility is independent of the level of the short-term rate. It might be argued that short-term rate changes become more and more volatile as the level of the short-term rate increases, a phenomenon usually referred to as the *level-effect*.

Cox, Ingersoll, and Ross (1985) (CIR, henceforth) propose a model that addresses these two drawbacks at once. They rely on an equilibrium model in which the short-term rate can be expressed as the solution to (see eq. (4.118) in chapter 4)

$$dr_\tau = \kappa(\bar{r} - r_\tau)d\tau + \sigma\sqrt{r_\tau}dW_\tau, \quad \tau \in (t, T]. \tag{13.45}$$

The CIR model is also referred to as "square-root" process to emphasize that the diffusion function is proportional to the square-root of r. This feature makes the model address the level-effect phenomenon. The evidence about the level-effect is further discussed below (see section 13.4.5). Moreover, this property prevents r from taking negative values. Intuitively, when r wanders just above zero, it is pulled back to the strictly positive region at a strength of the order $dr = \kappa\bar{r}d\tau$.[21] The transition density of r is noncentral chi-square,[22] and its stationary density is a gamma distribution. The expected value is as in Vasicek.[23] It is left as an exercise to show that

$$var(r_\tau | r_t) = \frac{\bar{r}\sigma^2}{2\kappa} + (r_t - \bar{r})\frac{\sigma^2}{\kappa}e^{-\kappa(\tau-t)} + \frac{\sigma^2}{\kappa}\left(\frac{1}{2}\bar{r} - r_t\right)e^{-2\kappa(\tau-t)}.$$

Intuitively, the variance of the short-term rate depends on the unconditional expectation, $\bar{r}$, because the instantaneous variance of the short-term rate depends on r_τ.

CIR formulate assumptions on preferences and technology, which lead to a risk premium equal to $\lambda = \ell\sqrt{r}$, for some constant ℓ (see eq. (4.119) in chapter 4). By replacing this premium, and $b(r) = \kappa(\bar{r} - r)$ and $a(r) = \sigma\sqrt{r}$ into (13.30), one obtains that the bond price has the same functional form as that predicted by the Vasicek model (see eq. (13.38)), but with functions A and B satisfying the following differential equations

$$0 = A_1(\tau, T) - \kappa\bar{r}B(\tau, T) \quad \text{and} \quad 0 = -B_1(\tau, T) + (\kappa + \ell\sigma)B(\tau, T) + \frac{1}{2}\sigma^2 B^2(\tau, T) - 1,$$

subject to the boundary conditions, $A(T, T) = 0$ and $B(T, T) = 0$. The solution to the bond price is

$$P(r_t, T-t) = \Phi(T-t)\, e^{-B(T-t)r_t},$$

$$\Phi(T-t) = \left(\frac{2\gamma e^{\frac{1}{2}(\kappa_o+\gamma)(T-t)}}{(\kappa_o+\gamma)\left(e^{\gamma(T-t)}-1\right)+2\gamma}\right)^{\frac{2\kappa_o\bar{r}_o}{\sigma^2}}, \quad B(T-t) = \frac{2\left(e^{\gamma(T-t)}-1\right)}{(\kappa_o+\gamma)\left(e^{\gamma(T-t)}-1\right)+2\gamma},$$

$$\gamma = \sqrt{\kappa_o^2 + 2\sigma^2}, \quad \kappa_o = \kappa + \sigma\ell, \quad \bar{r}_o = \tfrac{\kappa}{\kappa+\sigma\ell}\bar{r}. \tag{13.46}$$

This model has been the reference in the industry for many years, and is still a reference. First, there are multidimensional extensions of this basic model, as reviewed in section 13.5.3. Second, square-root processes have revealed to be useful while modeling other important variables in finance that are strictly positive, such as equity or interest rate volatility (see section 11.5 in chapter 4 or section 13.5.1), the probability of default of a certain name (see section 14.3.3 in chapter 14). In the next subsection (section 13.4.6), we shall rely on a square-root process and model the probability of interest rate hikes.

---

21. This is only intuition. The exact condition under which the zero boundary is unattainable by r is $\kappa\bar{r} > \frac{1}{2}\sigma^2$. See Karlin and Taylor (1981, vol. 2, chap. 15) for a general analysis of attainability of boundaries for scalar diffusion processes.

22. Chapter 11 relies on a square-root process to model volatility in the equity space. Eq. (11.124) provides the functional form of this transition density.

23. The expected value of a mean-reverting processes with a linear drift is always as in Vasicek, independent of the assumption on the diffusion coefficient. This intuitive property (heteroskedasticity does not affect expected values) can be shown by applying methods introduced in chapter 8 (appendix 8.D).

13.4.4.4 *Negative interest rates*

Section 13.5.3 explains that the Vasicek and CIR models are part of a broader family of models, known as "affine models." Consider the following extension of the CIR model in (13.45),

$$dr_\tau = \kappa(\bar{r} - r_\tau)d\tau + \sigma\sqrt{\alpha + \beta r_\tau}\,dW_\tau, \quad \tau \in (t, T]. \tag{13.47}$$

The model collapses to Vasicek when $\beta = 0$, and to CIR when $\alpha = 0$. Under regularity conditions, the short-term rate predicted by this model is well defined, in that $r_\tau > -\frac{\alpha}{\beta}$. Thus, the model enables one to model negative interest rates and may be used to price derivatives in times where interest rates touch on negative values, as for example during the Quantitative Easing (QE, henceforth) programs implemented after the financial crisis of the late 2000s. Naturally, (13.47) is a very simple model, but section 13.5.3 shows how it may be generalized to account for several factors that may potentially affect the entire term structure of interest rates.

13.4.4.5 *Nonlinear drifts*

Models that are analytically tractable are truly valuable. Both Vasicek and CIR models lead to closed-form solutions as they both have a *linear* drift, among other things. What does the empirical evidence say about mean-reversion in the short-term rate? This issue is controversial. In the mid-1990s, three papers by Aït-Sahalia (1996), Conley et al. (1997), and Stanton (1997) produced evidence of nonlinear mean-reverting behavior. For example, Aït-Sahalia (1996) estimates a drift function that has the following form

$$b(r) = \beta_0 + \beta_1 r + \beta_2 r^2 + \beta_3 r^{-1}. \tag{13.48}$$

Figure 13.5 reproduces this function using the parameter values in his table 4, and relating to the sample period from 1983 to 1995. Similar results are reported in the other papers. To illustrate the action the short-term rate dynamics are under, figure 13.5 also depicts a linear drift, obtained with the parameter estimates of Aït-Sahalia (1996, table 4), and relating to a model with a CEV diffusion.

The nonlinear drifts in figure 13.5 might lead bond prices to exhibit unusual properties, though. As explained in chapter 8 (see appendix 8.D), bond prices are *concave* in the short-term rate if the risk neutralized drift function is sufficiently convex. While the empirical results summarized in figure 13.5 relate to drifts under the *physical* probability, the point is relevant: the shape of risk premiums (against r_t) should be quite unusual in order to destroy these nonlinearities (and induce bond prices to be convex in r_t).

The compelling lesson from figure 13.5 is that under the *nonlinear* dynamics, the short-term rate behavior resembles a martingale in its low/middle region, and is otherwise comparable to that under the linear dynamics. However, as the short-term rate moves to extreme regions, it is pulled back to the "center" in a very abrupt way. At the moment, it is still not clear the extent to which these preliminary empirical findings are robust. For example, Pritsker (1998) finds that certain tests for the goodness of fit based on nonparametric methods require a disproportionately huge amount of data in the presence of persistent

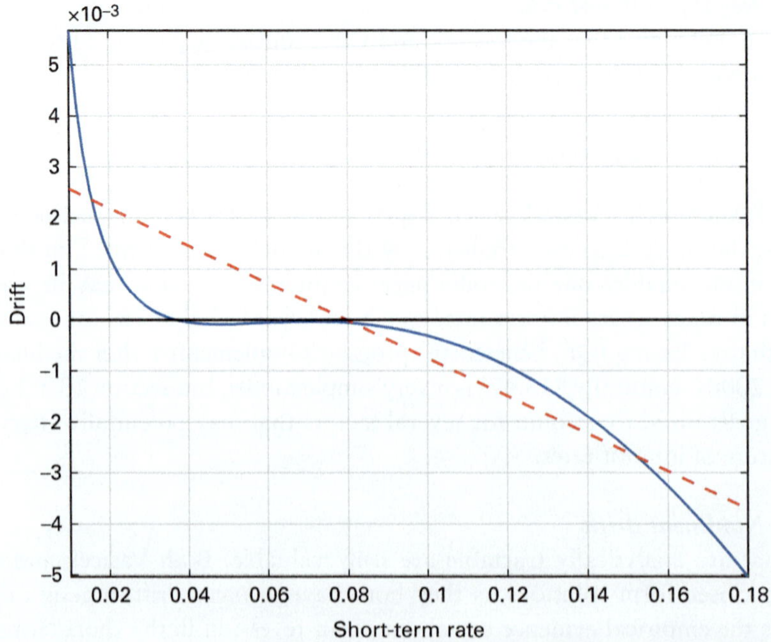

Figure 13.5
Nonlinear mean reversion? The solid line is the drift function in eq. (13.48), estimated by Aït-Sahalia (1996), and relating to a parametric model with a nonlinear diffusion function. The dashed line is the estimated linear drift relating to a model with a CEV diffusion.

data—the short-term rate is very persistent (see, e.g., discussions in section 13.4.5 and section 13.8.1).

More fundamentally, movements of the short-term rate over the tails of its distribution are obviously uncommon, making statistical inference a delicate exercise. Extreme behavior of economic variables do indeed occur during uncommon circumstances. To illustrate, the Great Recession period and the subsequent QE programs came as periods with very low interest rates and compressed volatility: a stubbornly high uncertainty would lead the Fed to stubbornly keep interest rates (and the expectation they would rise) low for a long period of time.[24] While the lessons from figure 13.5 would not apply in this case, this evidence should be kept well in mind while interpreting periods with much less elevated uncertainty than the Great Recession.

Finally, one possibility is that such *single-factor* models of the short-term rate are simply misspecified. For example, there is strong empirical evidence that the volatility of the short-term rate is time-varying, as we shall discuss in the next section. Moreover, the term structure implications of a single factor model are counterfactual, since we know that a single factor cannot explain the entire variation of the yield curve, as explained in section 13.3.5. We now describe more realistic models driven by more than one factor.

24. The next chapter contains discussions regarding the QE programs implemented after the Great Recession.

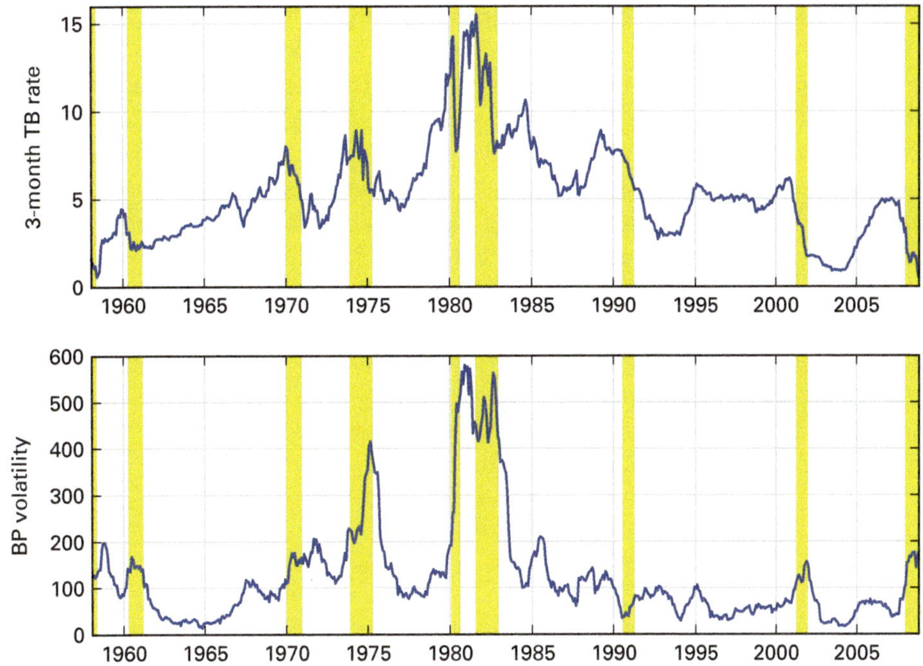

Figure 13.6
This picture depicts the time-series behavior of the 3-month TB rate (top panel, in percent) and the rolling, basis point volatility of the 3-month TB rate *changes*, $\mathrm{Vol}_{r,t}$ (bottom panel), over the sampling period from 1957:01 through 2008:12. The shaded areas mark recession episodes as defined by the National Bureau of Economic Research.

13.4.5 Interest Rate Volatility and the Business Cycle

One of the motivations underlying the early adoption of the CIR model in the industry was the property of the model to predict interest rate volatility to increase with the level of interest rates. Is this a robust empirical feature? It is a difficult question, as its answer varies according to historical episodes. To illustrate, consider the extraordinary monetary policy measures the Fed implemented around QE; interest rates were extremely low as a result, and accompanied by a suppressed volatility, especially after 2010, a theme we shall return to soon in this section. Interest rates and rate volatility were positively correlated during the Monetary Experiment too (between October 1979 and October 1982), when the Fed tightening of the time led interest rates and interest rate volatility to record highs.

Figure 13.6 depicts the time series behavior of the nominal short-term rate, as measured by the three-month TB rate, as well as the volatility of its changes expressed in basis points: $\mathrm{Vol}_{r,t} \equiv 100^2\sqrt{6\pi}\cdot\bar{\sigma}_{r,t}$, where $\bar{\sigma}_{r,t} \equiv \frac{1}{12}\sum_{i=1}^{12}\left|r_{t+1-i} - r_{t-i}\right|$, and r_t is the short-term rate as of month t.[25] Basis point volatility is, thus, a measure of uncertainty regarding interest rate movements. Suppose, for example, that interest rates were currently fluctuating at about 1% and the current basis volatility was equal to 80 and stable for one year. In a stationary Gaussian environment, then, we would roughly expect that interest rates will

25. This calculation follows that implemented to measure aggregate equity volatility in chapter 8 (see section 8.2).

be within a $1.96 \times \text{Vol}_{r,t}$ band from 1% with 95% probability in the next year (see Mele and Obayashi (2015, sec. 2.5)). Figure 13.7 plots a scatterplot of this basis point volatility against r_t (in percentage) for two sampling periods. For later use, define log volatility, or percentage volatility, as $\text{Vol}_{r,t}^{\%} \equiv \sqrt{6\pi} \cdot \bar{\sigma}_{r,t}^{\%}$, where $\bar{\sigma}_{r,t}^{\%} \equiv \frac{1}{12} \sum_{i=1}^{12} \left| \ln \left(r_{t+1-i}/r_{t-i} \right) \right|$.

One clear property is that interest rate volatility appears to be countercyclical, spiking in most of the NBER recession episodes. A natural explanation is that the Fed is more aggressive while decreasing interest rates in bad times than while increasing them in good. Moreover, we previously discussed the "level effect," i.e., the statistical relation by which the short-term rate volatility increases with the level of the short-term rate. One possible explanation of these episodes is that when liquidity is erratic, interest rates are high, reflecting a liquidity risk premium. But precisely because of erratic liquidity, interest rates are also very volatile in such periods.

A simple statistical model may help capture these stylized facts. Suppose that the short-term rate r_t has stochastic volatility, in that

$$\begin{cases} dr_t = \kappa \left(\mu - r_t \right) dt + \sqrt{v_t} r_t^{\eta} dW_{1t} \\ dv_t = \beta \left(\alpha - v_t \right) dt + \xi v_t^{\vartheta} \left(\rho dW_{1t} + \sqrt{1-\rho^2} dW_{2t} \right) \end{cases} \tag{13.49}$$

where W_{it} are standard Brownian motions under the physical probability, v_t is a factor affecting interest rate volatility, and remaining notation refers to the model parameters; in particular, ρ is the instantaneous correlation between dr_t and dv_t. This model generalizes the previous one-factor models. The yield curve may now be well driven by two factors, r_t and v_t. Section 13.5 studies models such as (13.49) in more detail. Note, now, that if $\eta > 0$, interest rate volatility increases with the level of r_t. Moreover, innovations to volatility are also and partly related to sources of volatility not directly affected by the *level* of the interest rate.

The empirical evidence underlying figure 13.7 does not lend much support to the level effect. Rather, it seems that interest rate volatility is quite flat against the level of rates. Section 13.5.4 explains that this property might relate to the possibility that fixed income markets are incomplete. But there are at least two notable exceptions that were already mentioned at the beginning of this section. The first occurred during the Monetary Experiment, when the Fed target was money supply, rather than interest rates. During this period, high volatility of money demand mechanically translated to high interest rate volatility through market clearing. Additionally, the monetary base in this period was kept deliberately low in an attempt to fight against inflation. Whence, both interest rate volatility and interest rates were very high. One additional reason for the high nominal rates at the time might link to a compensation for high *inflation volatility*—not only high inflation.

The second exception occurs at levels of the interest rate close to the "zero lower bound" (ZLB). When interest rates are small and their volatility is compressed, it seems that interest rate volatility becomes, then, increasing in the interest rate levels (see the top panels of figure 13.7). This property is emphasized by Filipović, Larsson, and Trolle (2017), who are able to telescope the joint behavior of interest rates and volatility in periods where interest rates were very close to the ZLB. This property seems natural: as the Fed succeeds in being credible in maintaining low interest rate levels during periods such as QE (not depicted in these pictures), interest rate volatility remains low. In this context, interest rate volatility may be read as a measure of monetary policy credibility.

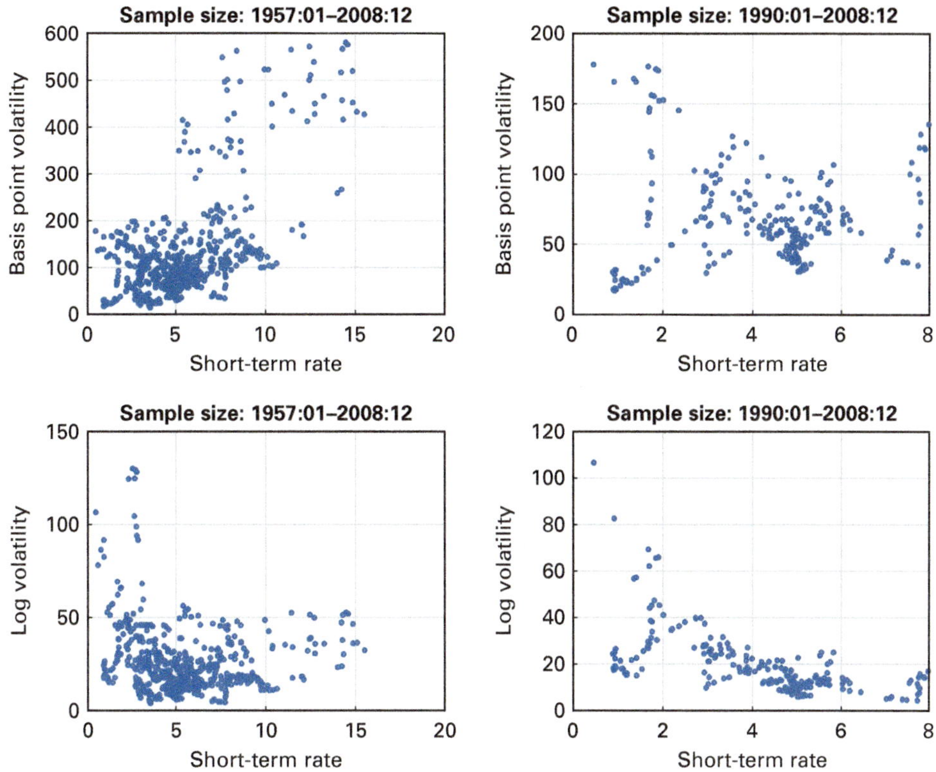

Figure 13.7
The top panels plot the basis point volatility of the short-term rate *changes*, $\mathrm{Vol}_{r,t}$, against the level of the short-term rate, for the sampling period 1957:01–2008:12 (left) and 1990:01–2008:12 (right). The bottom panels plot the log volatility counterparts. For the whole sample, average basis point and log volatility are equal to 123 and 24, resp. For the most recent sample, these figures lower to 68 and 19, resp.

Figure 13.7 is also suggestive of a change in regime that possibly occurred over a more recent past (at least until the QE period). From 1990 to 2008, interest rate volatility does not necessarily appear to positively link to rate levels, and there is evidence of the opposite. Figure 13.7 suggests that "percentage" volatility could actually be inversely related to the short-term rate, and over the more recent sample periods too.

All in all, it seems that we are left with mixed evidence regarding the relation between interest rate volatility and interest rates levels. The model described by eq. (13.49) has the interesting property by which interest rate volatility fluctuates while driven by its own source of risk, W_{2t}. Section 13.5 considers more general models of the yield curve with stochastic volatility. Section 13.4.6 below considers models by which the yield curve exhibits stochastic volatility because there are time-varying probabilities that interest rates may experience discontinuities.

We end this section by succinctly discussing an interesting property: the potential ability of the term spread to anticipate increases in interest rate volatility. This property seems to be natural; on the one hand, the term spread has anticipatory power on NBER dated recessions; on the other hand, interest rate volatility tends to increase during recessions, in

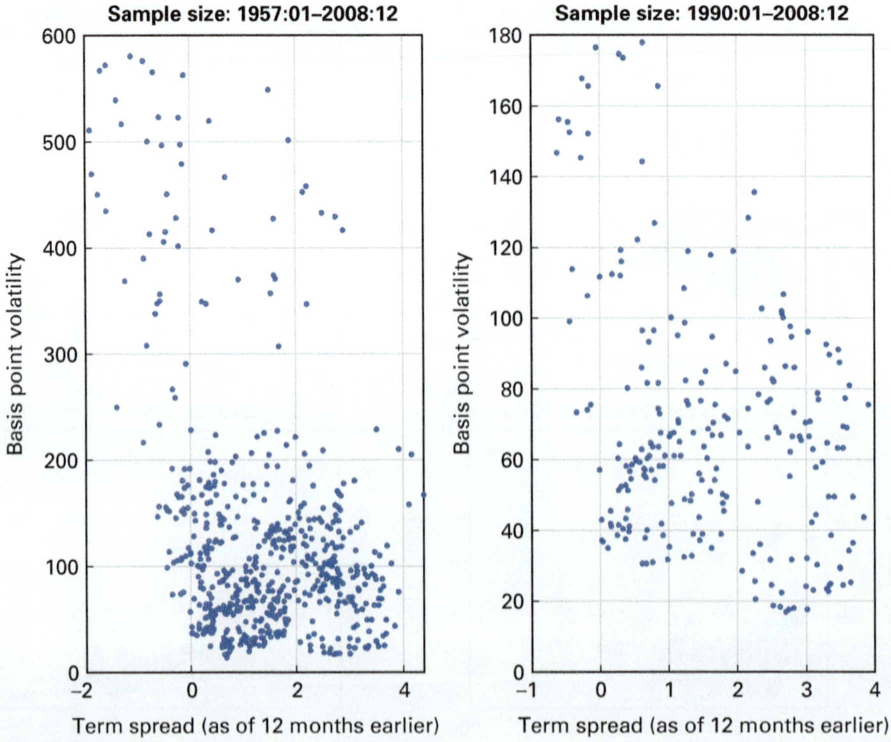

Figure 13.8
This picture depicts the basis point volatility of the short-term rate *changes*, $\text{Vol}_{r,t}$, against one-year lagged values of the term spread, defined as in figure 13.2, for the sampling period 1957:01–2008:12 (left) and 1990:01–2008:12 (right).

part because the Fed on average decreases interest rates more rapidly than it increases them. These properties would imply that the term spread has anticipatory power on interest rate volatility. Figure 13.8 suggests that this property is indeed in the data, and independent of the sampling period: an inverted yield curve, measured by a negative term spread, predicts an increase in basis point volatility one year later.

13.4.6 Jumps, Volatility, and Default

This chapter considers markets without "discontinuities." That is, asset prices move, driven by Brownian motions and under the assumption on no default for the underlying securities. How do prices behave in the presence of jumps in the short-term rate or default risk? This section provides some preliminary discussions on both themes, based on the jump-diffusion models introduced in chapter 4 (see section 4.9). We consider two models. In the first, we aim to model realized and expected volatility in Treasury markets while assuming that interest rates may experience jumps, interpreted as possibly induced by Fed decisions. The second model aims to capture one stylized feature of default, the fact that it often arrives unexpectedly; note that this model is very introductory and that default risk and associated derivatives are systematically dealt with in chapter 14.

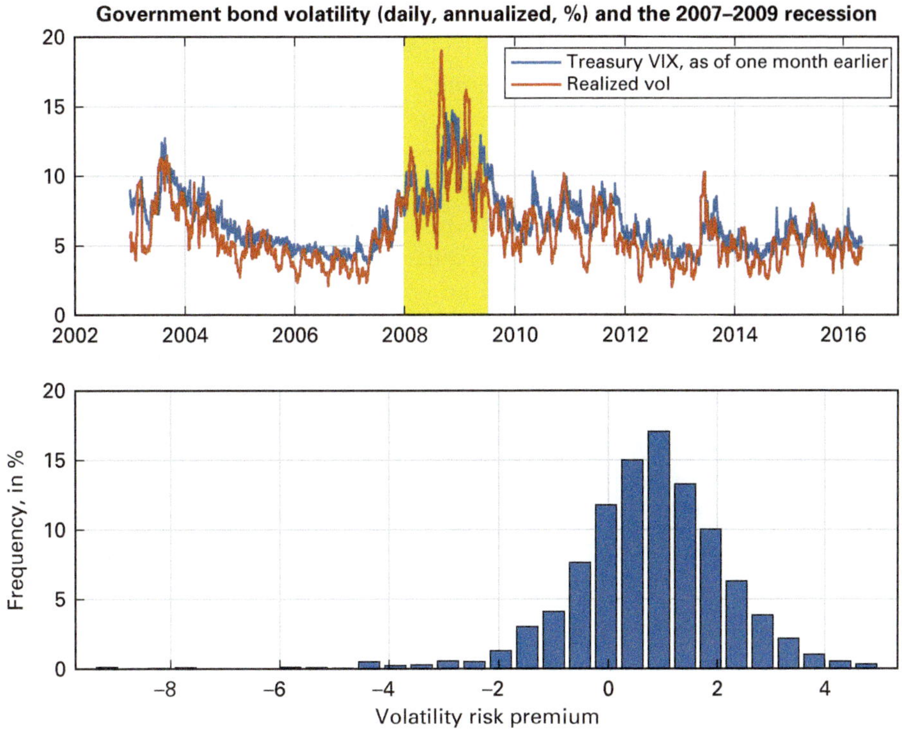

Figure 13.9

Top panel: Government bond volatility, realized and expected: realized percentage volatility on the 10-year Treasury future prices and Cboe Treasury VIX Index as of one month earlier; the shaded area covers the 2007–2009 NBER recession episode. Bottom panel: frequency distribution of the variance risk premium, defined as the difference between Treasury VIX minus realized volatility. The sample period covers daily data from January 2, 2003, to May 11, 2016.

13.4.6.1 Government bond volatility and expectations of interest rate hikes

It is well-known that expected volatility in fixed income markets is higher than realized volatility, similarly as in equity markets. For example, figure 13.9 (top panel) plots realized volatility for the 10-year Treasury future prices against the Cboe Treasury VIX.[26] The Treasury VIX is an index of expected volatility on the 10-year Treasury future prices and, thus, represents the government bond counterpart to the equity VIX reviewed in chapter 11 (sections 11.8 and 11.9); see Mele and Obayashi (2015, chap. 4). The bottom panel of figure 13.9 reveals that the volatility risk premium, defined as the difference between Treasury VIX and realized volatility, is positive for most of the time.

We consider a model that, at least qualitatively, may explain this premium. The model is particularly useful to think about market volatility around the QE period inaugurated by the Fed to cope with the Great Recession of the late 2000s. During QE, interest rates became so compressed to lead market participants to the expectation that interest rates might only have risen. We may model these episodes by assuming that interest rates can experience upward jumps. To illustrate, while these jumps were obviously not in the data

26. At the time of writing, this index is known as TYVIX.

during QE, it is plausible that market participants were actually expecting them. These expectations, we shall see, may lead both realized volatility and expected volatility to be time-varying, and to a volatility risk premium.

We focus on bond price volatility. We need to model the whole yield curve and, accordingly, determine price volatility while taking no-arbitrage restrictions into account. The model relies on the assumption that the yield curve is driven by two factors: the short-term rate r_t and the instantaneous intensity of an upward jump in the interest rate, v_t. Both r_t and v_t are diffusion processes. Volatility (both realized and expected) will be driven by v_t. The model predicts that, as the probability of an upward jump increases, expected volatility increases as well. Moreover, the model rationalizes a relatively lower realized price volatility despite the larger swings in expected volatility: according to the model, the volatility premium increases as a result of changes in the market probability of interest rate jumps, v_t.

Short-term rates as jump-diffusion processes We, first, consider a model where the short-term rate is a jump-diffusion process of the type considered in chapter 4 (see section 4.9). Ahn and Thompson (1988), while extending CIR, are the first to consider a model along these lines. Assume that, under the risk neutral probability, the short-term rate is a jump-diffusion process,

$$dr_t = b(r_t)\,dt + a(r_t)\,d\tilde{W}_t + \ell(r_t)\,S dN_t, \tag{13.50}$$

where $\tilde{W}_t$ is a standard Brownian motion, N_t is a Poisson process with intensity v_Q,[27] b and a are drifts and diffusion components, and $\ell(\cdot)\,S$ measures the size of the jumps when these occur, and S is a random variable with support $\mathbb{S}$. In the absence of arbitrage, the bond price $P(r,\tau,T)$ is the solution to

$$0 = (L-r)\,P(r,\tau,T) + v_Q \int_{\mathbb{S}} \left[P(r+\ell(r)\,S,\tau,T) - P(r,\tau,T)\right] p\,(dS), \tag{13.51}$$

where L is the usual infinitesimal generator, and, $P(r,T,T)=1$. Eq. (13.51) follows by the standard martingale property of P (see section 4.9 in chapter 4). The model can be extended to one with different qualities, or types, of jumps:

$$0 = (L-r)\,P(r,\tau,T) + \sum_{j=1}^{J} v_{Q,j} \int_{\mathbb{S}} \left[P(r+\ell S,\tau,T) - P(r,\tau,T)\right] p^j\,(dS),$$

where J is the number of jump types.

We now provide one simple example and address the pricing of government bond volatility. On the one hand, the example simplifies this framework as it only regards the case with $J=1$ and a deterministic jumps size; on the other hand, the example extends (13.50) to the case the intensity is time-varying.

Model We consider a simple model belonging to the affine jump-diffusion family studied by Duffie, Pan, and Singleton (2000).[28] We assume that, under the risk neutral probability,

27. This intensity is $v_Q = v\lambda^J$, where v is the jump intensity under the *physical* probability and λ^J is the risk premium related to the presence of jumps (see appendix 4.F in chapter 4).
28. Section 13.5.3 is a short introduction to multivariate affine models *without* jumps.

the short-term rate is the solution to

$$dr_t = k_r \left(r^* - r_t\right) dt + \sigma d\tilde{W}_{1t} + q dN_t,$$

where k_r, r^*, σ, and q are parameters, $\tilde{W}_{1t}$ is a standard Brownian motion, and N_t is a Poisson process with instantaneous intensity equal to v_t^Q. We assume that the market does not require compensation for jumps, and we denote $v_t^Q \equiv v_t$, where v_t is the intensity under the physical probability. We assume that

$$dv_t = k_v \left(v^* - v_t\right) dt + \xi \sqrt{v_t} d\tilde{W}_{2t},$$

where v_λ, v^* and ξ are parameters, and $\tilde{W}_{2t}$ is a standard Brownian motion under the risk neutral probability.

All in all, the model says that the short-term rate is mean-reverting, and that it may experience upward jumps that have a fixed size equal to $q > 0$. Moreover, the jump intensity is, itself, mean-reverting. We now provide model predictions.

Term structure implications We conjecture that the price of a zero coupon bond is a function of both the short-term rate and the jump intensity. Accordingly, let $P(r_t, v_t; t, T)$ denote the price of a zero at time t that has a time to maturity equal to $T - t$. By a slight extension of (13.51), $P(r_t, v_t; t, T)$ is the solution to

$$\begin{aligned} rP = & \frac{\partial P}{\partial t} + k_r \left(r^* - r\right) P_r + \frac{1}{2}\sigma^2 P_{rr} + k_v \left(v^* - v\right) P_v + \frac{1}{2}\xi^2 v P_{vv} \\ & + v \left(P\left(r + q, v; t, T\right) - P\left(r, v; t, T\right)\right), \end{aligned} \tag{13.52}$$

subject to the standard boundary condition $P(r, v; T, T) = 1$. This partial integro-differential equation can be solved, as in the pure diffusion case (see section 13.4.4), by conjecturing a specific functional form for the price and replacing this price and its partial derivatives into (13.52). In particular, the solution is exponential-affine,

$$P(r_t, v_t; t, T) = e^{A(T-t) - B(T-t) r_t - C(T-t) v_t}, \quad B(\tau) = \frac{1 - e^{-k_r \tau}}{k_r}, \tag{13.53}$$

where C, A are solutions to the following ordinary differential equations

$$\begin{cases} \dot{C}(\tau) = -\left(k_v C(\tau) + \frac{1}{2}\xi^2 C^2(\tau) + e^{-B(\tau)q} - 1\right), \\ A(\tau) = -k_r r^* \int_0^\tau B(u)\, du + \frac{1}{2}\sigma^2 \int_0^\tau B^2(u)\, du - k_v v^* \int_0^\tau C(u)\, du \end{cases}$$

and boundary conditions $A(0) = 0$ and $C(0) = 0$.

Appendix 13.D shows that $C(\tau) \geq 0$ for all τ. Therefore, the model predicts that the yield curve,

$$R(r_t, v_t; T - t) = -\frac{A(T-t)}{T-t} + \frac{B(T-t)}{T-t} r_t + \frac{C(T-t)}{T-t} v_t,$$

is uniformly increasing in both the short-term rate, r_t, and the instantaneous probability of a rate increase, v_t. Thus, the model is consistent with phenomena such as the "paper tantrum," i.e., the increase in US Treasury yields that was subsequent to the Fed announcement of QE tapering made in May 2013. The appendix actually also proves that the whole yield curve increases with q. The intuition underlying these conclusions is simple: the yield curve shifts up with an increase in the probability of an increase in the interest rate and with the size of this increase. To illustrate, assume, for example, that the short-term rate is a pure jump process, $dr_t = q dN_t$, and that the jump intensity is constant. In terms of the previous parametrization, we have that $k_r = \sigma = k_v = \xi = 0$, and we set $v_t \equiv v^*$ for all t. Then, $A(\tau) = 0$, $B(\tau) = \tau$, such that

$$R(r_t; T-t) = r_t + \frac{C(T-t)}{T-t} v^*, \quad C(\tau) = \tau - \frac{1-e^{-q\tau}}{q}.$$

The yield curve increases with both v^* and q.

We now rely on this simple model and turn attention to its implications on realized and expected government bond volatility.

Peso problems in the term structure of expected volatility A peso problem results from the circumstance that some events have not occurred in the past, but are likely to occur in the future. To illustrate, a Fed hike is obviously not in the data during the implementation of the QE program since the 2007–2009 recession; yet, markets might have, then, expected such a hike to happen at some point in time; on December 16, 2015, the Fed announced that such a hike would occur. We focus on the pricing of volatility related to a zero coupon bond price. The Cboe Treasury VIX is an index on a more complicated asset, the volatility of the 10-year Treasury future prices, which ultimately link to a coupon-bearing bond. We consider a zero coupon bond to simplify the analysis.[29]

Let us determine the dynamics of volatility predicted by the model and, then, the fair value of dedicated contracts referenced to this volatility. By Itô's lemma, the equilibrium bond price $P_t \equiv P(r_t, v_t, t, T)$ is the solution to

$$dP_t = (rP_t - v_t J_t)\, dt + \frac{\partial P_t}{\partial r} \sigma d\tilde{W}_{1t} + \frac{\partial P_t}{\partial v} \xi \sqrt{v_t} d\tilde{W}_{2t} + J_t dN_t, \tag{13.54}$$

where

$$J_t \equiv P(r_t + q, v_t; t, T) - P(r_t, v_t; t, T) = P(r_t, v_t; t, T)\left(e^{-B(T-t)q} - 1\right) \leq 0,$$

and the last equality follows because $B(\tau) \geq 0$. Therefore, and again by Itô's lemma, the bond price instantaneous variance is

$$\begin{aligned} V(v_t; t, T) \equiv var\left(d \ln P(r_t, v_t; t, T)\right) = \left(B^2(T-t)\sigma^2 + C^2(T-t)\xi^2 v_t\right) dt \\ + B^2(T-t) q^2 dN_t. \end{aligned} \tag{13.55}$$

Next, consider a government bond variance swap, defined as a contract by which, at time t, one party promises to pay the following payoff at time $\mathcal{T} < T$,

$$\Pi_{\mathcal{T}} \equiv \int_t^{\mathcal{T}} V(v_u; u, T)\, du - K,$$

29. Mele, Obayashi, and Yang (2020) analyze this more general case relying on a diffusion model without jumps.

for some strike K. The contract is costless at origination. This contract has been introduced by Mele and Obayashi (2015, chap. 4): it is the government bond counterpart to the equity variance swaps considered in chapter 11 (see section 11.8). The fair value of K, say $\hat{K}$, is found by imposing that, at origination, the contract value is zero, $\mathbb{E}_t(e^{-\int_t^{\mathcal{T}} r_u du}\Pi_{\mathcal{T}})=0$, and by rearranging terms,

$$\hat{K}=\frac{1}{P(r_t,v_t,T,\mathcal{T})}\mathbb{E}_t\left(e^{-\int_t^{\mathcal{T}} r_u du}\int_t^{\mathcal{T}} V(v_u;u,T)\,du\right)=\mathbb{E}_{Q_F^{\mathcal{T}}}\left(\int_t^{\mathcal{T}} V(v_u;u,T)\,du\right),$$

where $\mathbb{E}_{Q_F^{\mathcal{T}}}$ denotes the forward probability for maturity $\mathcal{T}$ introduced in Section 13.8.3.

An index of expected volatility is the square root of the annualized strike $\hat{K}$, $\text{T-VIX}_t^2(\mathcal{T})\equiv\frac{1}{\mathcal{T}-t}\hat{K}$, say. Appendix 13.D shows that

$$\text{T-VIX}_t(\mathcal{T})=\sqrt{\mathcal{A}(\mathcal{T}-t)+\mathcal{B}(\mathcal{T}-t)\,v_t}, \tag{13.56}$$

for two functions $\mathcal{A}(\cdot)$ and $\mathcal{B}(\cdot)$ given in the appendix (see eqs. (13.A11)).

That is, expected government bond volatility is driven by the instantaneous probability of an upward jump in the short-term rate. This model is stylized, but it makes the point that Treasury volatility may be driven by unobserved components related to market expectations of future Fed movements, v_t. Even if the Fed leaves interest rate targets unchanged, Treasury volatility may increase when market participants expect an imminent rate increase. Moreover, eq. (13.55) shows that realized volatility also increases with v_t. However, we have that for all $u>t$,

$$\mathbb{E}_{Q_F^{\mathcal{T}}}(V(v_u;u,T))>\mathbb{E}_{Q_F^{\mathcal{T}}}(V(v_u;u,T)|\,N_u=N_t)\,.$$

The previous inequality says that in the absence of jumps from time t to time u, expected volatility is higher than average volatility: because jumps occur infrequently, the model rationalizes the volatility risk premium that we see in the data.[30]

13.4.6.2 *Defaultable bonds*

But prices may "jump" due to credit risk, not only market risk. Consider a defaultable zero coupon bond, and assume that the event of default is a Poisson process N with intensity v. Assume, further, that in the event of default at τ, the bondholder receives a recovery payment $\bar{P}_\tau$, which may be deterministic or a function of the short-term rate.[31] Let $\hat{\tau}$ be the random time of default, and define

$$g=\begin{cases}0 & \text{if } t\leq\tau<\hat{\tau}\\ 1 & \text{otherwise}\end{cases}$$

30. Naturally, the volatility premium may be exacerbated when the intensity under the risk neutral probability is higher than the intensity under the physical probability.

31. The approach we are illustrating has a "reduced-form" flavor, and its derivations are based on the partial differential equations derived in Mele (2003). Chapter 14 contains a systematic treatment of the pricing of defaultable bonds.

such that, under the risk neutral probability,

$$\begin{cases} dr_t = b(r_t)\,d\tau + a(r_t)\,d\tilde{W}_t \\ dg_t = dN_t \end{cases} \tag{13.57}$$

Let $P^{(g)}(r,\tau,T)$ be the price at τ of a zero coupon bond maturing at T, and assume that, for all $\tau \leq T$, $P^{(1)} = \bar{P}_\tau < P^{(0)}$ and that the recovery value is independent of v. In the absence of arbitrage, the *pre-default* bond price $P^{\text{pre}} \equiv P^{(0)}$ satisfies

$$\begin{aligned} 0 &= (L - r)\,P^{(0)}(r,\tau,T) + v(r)\cdot\left[P^{(1)}(r,\tau,T) - P^{(0)}(r,\tau,T)\right] \\ &= (L - (r + v(r)))\,P^{(0)}(r,\tau,T) + v(r)\bar{P}_\tau, \end{aligned} \tag{13.58}$$

for all $\tau \in [t,T)$, with the boundary condition $P^{(0)}(r,T,T) = 1$. The solution is

$$P^{\text{pre}}(r_t,t,T) = \mathbb{E}_t^*\left(e^{-\int_t^T (r_\tau + v(r_\tau))d\tau}\right) + \mathbb{E}_t^*\left(\int_t^T e^{-\int_t^\tau (r_u + v(r_u))du} v(r_\tau)\bar{P}_\tau d\tau\right), \tag{13.59}$$

where $\mathbb{E}_t^*[\cdot]$ is the expectation taken with respect to only the first equation of system (13.57).

Eq. (13.59) can be simplified[32] after defining a percentage loss process $l_\tau \in [0,1] : \bar{P} = (1 - l)P^{(0)}$, which inserted into eq. (13.58) leaves a partial differential equation the solution of which is, by Feynman–Kac,

$$P^{\text{pre}}(r_t,t,T) = \mathbb{E}_t^*\left(e^{-\int_t^T (r_\tau + l_\tau \cdot v(r_\tau))d\tau}\right).$$

It is intuitive that the pre-default bond price P^{pre} is decreasing in the default intensity v. Appendix 13.D provides high-level assumptions that lead to this property.

13.5 Multifactor Models of the Short-Term Rate

The empirical evidence reviewed in section 13.3.4 suggests that one-factor models cannot explain the entire variation of the term structure of interest rates. We need at least three factors. This section contains a succinct review regarding the standard approaches that deal with this multidimensionality.

13.5.1 Stochastic Volatility

13.5.1.1 Convexity

How does volatility affect the yield curve? Consider the following two-period example. In the first period, the short-term rate is r and, in the second, it is either $\tilde{r} = r + d$ or $\tilde{r} = r - d$ with equal probability, where $d > 0$. The price of a two-period bond is $P(r,d) = m(r,d)/(1+r)$, where $m(r,d) = E\left(1/(1+\tilde{r})\right)$ is the discount factor expected to prevail at next period. By Jensen's inequality, $m(r,d) > 1/(1+E(\tilde{r})) = 1/(1+r) = m(r,0)$. That is, two-period bond prices increase upon activation of randomness. More generally, in this example, two-period bond prices are always increasing in the "volatility" parameter d, a

32. See Duffie and Singleton (1999, eq. (10), 696).

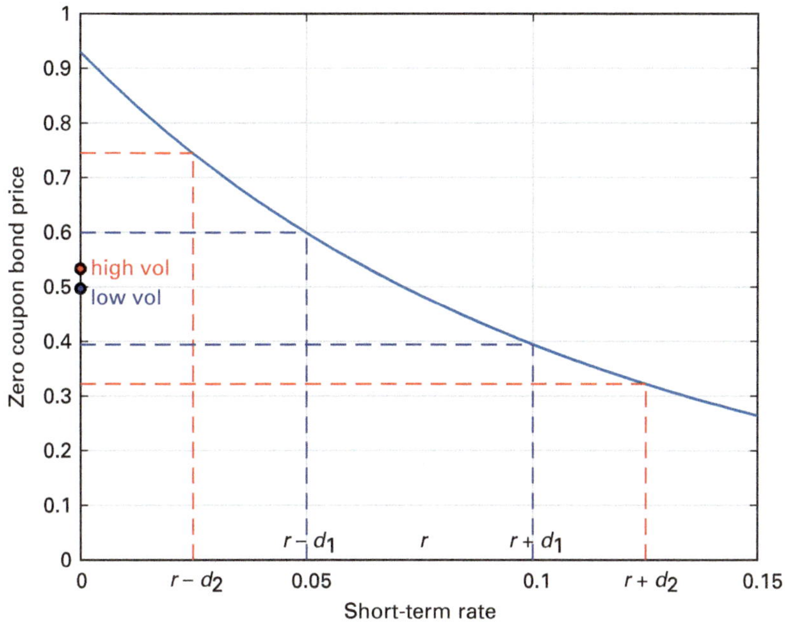

Figure 13.10

This picture depicts the price of a N-year zero coupon bond, $P(r,d) = \frac{1}{1+r}\mathbb{E}(\prod_{t=1}^{N-1}\frac{1}{1+r_t}) = \frac{1}{1+r}\mathbb{E}\left(\frac{1}{1+r+x}\right)^{N-1}$, where r is the current short term rate, and r_t is the short-term rate at time t, assumed to equal $r_t = r + x$ with equal probability, and for all t. Maturity is $N = 10$, $r = 0.075$, and $x = +d_i$ or $-d_i$. If $d_i = d_1 = 0.025$, the bond price is marked as "low vol" and, if $d_i = d_2 = 0.050$, the bond price is marked as "high vol."

property illustrated by figure 13.10 in a slightly more general case. The intuition underlying figure 13.10 is standard: the bond price is decreasing and convex in the short-term rate, such that the price is increasing in the interest rate volatility—the price drop in "bad times" (i.e., when the interest rate increases)—is less than the price increase in "good times."

These properties link to the theory of mean-preserving spreads (see, e.g., chapters 1, 8, and 11). In the example of figure 13.10, the "spread" in r is mean-preserving. In other words, we are assuming that the expected short-term rate is independent of d. These properties may well be destroyed in alternative settings. For example, consider a market in which an upward rate movement is more likely than a downward. As a second example, consider a multiplicative setting, in which either $\tilde{r} = r(1+d)$ or $\tilde{r} = r/(1+d)$ with equal probability. It can be shown that in these two examples, bond prices are decreasing in volatility for short maturities, and increasing for longer, a property originally illustrated by Litterman, Scheinkman, and Weiss (1991). Finally, consider a scenario different from that underlying Figure 13.10, by which the range of variation of r shifts to the right as d increases. This range shift may be so large to dwarf convexity effects, and bond prices may well fall after an increase in short-term volatility.

The next sections will illustrate that, due to risk aversion, changes in the expected short-term rate may actually well depend on "volatility" parameters such as d in these examples. Then, at short maturities, risk aversion dominates convexity effects, whereas convexities dominate over longer maturities. We now build on this intuition and explain the relation between interest rate volatility and the yield curve.

13.5.1.2 Two-factor models

In the CIR model, the instantaneous volatility of the short-term rate is stochastic, depending as it does on the level of r_τ, which is obviously stochastic. However, empirical evidence suggests that the short-term rate volatility depends on some additional factors, as discussed in section 13.4. Section 13.4.6 develops a model where stochastic volatility arises through time-varying intensities of Fed rate hikes. This section reviews a somehow more standard stochastic volatility model.

A natural extension of the CIR model is one in which the instantaneous volatility of the short-term rate depends on (i) the level of the short-term rate (as in the CIR model), and (ii) some additional random component. This additional component may be what we refer to as "stochastic volatility" of the short-term rate. It is the term structure counterpart to the stochastic volatility extension of the Black–Scholes (1973) model (see chapter 11).

Fong and Vasicek (1991) develop the first model in which the volatility of the short-term rate is stochastic. They assume that the short-term rate r_τ is the solution to

$$\begin{aligned} dr_\tau &= \kappa_r (\bar{r} - r_\tau)\, d\tau + \sqrt{v_\tau} r_\tau^\gamma dW_{1\tau} \\ dv_\tau &= \kappa_v (\bar{v} - v_\tau)\, d\tau + \xi_v \sqrt{v_\tau} dW_{2\tau} \end{aligned} \tag{13.60}$$

where κ_r, $\bar{r}$, κ_v, $\bar{v}$ and ξ_v are constants, and $[W_1 \; W_2]$ is a vector Brownian motion under the physical probability.[33]

The authors assume that $\gamma = 0$ and that the unit risk premiums that compensate for fluctuations in the short-term rate and its volatility are both proportional to $\sqrt{v_\tau}$, being $\lambda_r(v_\tau) \equiv \lambda_1 \sqrt{v_\tau}$ and $\lambda_v(v_\tau) \equiv \lambda_2 \sqrt{v_\tau}$, for two constants λ_1 and λ_2.[34] These assumptions lead to a solution for the price of a zero coupon bond given by

$$P(r_t, v_t, T-t) \equiv e^{A(T-t) - B(T-t) r_t + C(T-t) v_t}, \tag{13.61}$$

for three functions $A(T-t)$, $B(T-t)$, $C(T-t)$ characterized in appendix 13.E (see eqs. (13.A14)).

Due to randomness in the short-term rate volatility, bond return volatility now also fluctuates randomly, driven by sources of variation additional to r_t, i.e., v_t. It is possible to show that the short-term rate loading, $B(\cdot)$, is the same as that in the Vasicek model (see eq. (13.39)) and, thus, is always positive. Instead, the volatility loading $C(\cdot)$ can take on any sign. It is possible to show that in the absence of risk aversion corrections regarding r_τ (i.e., $\lambda_1 = 0$), C is positive, such that the whole yield curve lowers as volatility increases. However, when $-\lambda_1$ is large enough, the whole yield curve increases after an increase in volatility. Finally, for moderate values of $-\lambda_1$, $C(\cdot)$ can take both signs and is typically negative for shorter maturities and positive for longer: the short-end part of the yield curve increases in volatility while the longer-end part decreases. The next subsection provides intuition on these properties.

Longstaff and Schwartz (1992) propose another model in which the short-term rate exhibits stochastic volatility, making bond returns exhibit stochastic volatility driven by sources of variation additional to r_t. They rely on an equilibrium model reviewed in

33. In appendix 13.E, we consider an extension of this model, in which r_τ and v_τ are instantaneously correlated.

34. Thus, by Girsanov's theorem, $d\tilde{W}_{i\tau} = dW_{i\tau} + \lambda_i \sqrt{v_\tau} d\tau$ is a Brownian motion under Q.

chapter 4, in which the short-term rate is a linear combination of two factors,

$$r_\tau = \beta_1 y_{1\tau} + \beta_2 y_{2\tau}, \tag{13.62}$$

for two constants β_i and two uncorrelated processes $y_{i\tau}$ that satisfy the following square-root dynamics:

$$dy_{i\tau} = \hat{\kappa}_i(\bar{y}_i - y_{i\tau})d\tau + \sqrt{y_{i\tau}}\,d\tilde{W}_{it}, \tag{13.63}$$

where $\tilde{W}_{it}$ are standard Brownian motions under the risk neutral probability and $\hat{\kappa}_i$ and $\bar{y}_i$ are two constants (see eqs. (4.120)–(4.121) in chapter 4). It is easy to see that the bond price predicted by this model is

$$P(y_{1t}, y_{2t}, T-t) = \mathbb{E}_t\left(e^{-\int_t^T r_\tau d\tau}\right) = P^{\text{cir}}(\tilde{y}_{1t}, T-t; \theta_1)P^{\text{cir}}(\tilde{y}_{2t}, T-t; \theta_2), \tag{13.64}$$

where $\tilde{y}_{i\tau} \equiv \beta_i y_{i\tau}$ are solutions to

$$d\tilde{y}_{i\tau} = \hat{\kappa}_i(\hat{y}_i - \tilde{y}_{i\tau})d\tau + \hat{\sigma}_i\sqrt{\tilde{y}_{i\tau}}\,d\tilde{W}_{it},$$

with $\hat{y}_i \equiv \beta_i \bar{y}_i$, $\hat{\sigma}_i \equiv \sqrt{\beta_i}$ and $P^{\text{cir}}(\cdot, T-t, \theta_i)$ are the prices predicted by the CIR model (see eqs. (13.46)) when the parameter vector under the risk neutral probability is $\theta_i \equiv [\hat{\kappa}_i\ \hat{y}_i\ \hat{\sigma}_i]$.

Note that by eqs. (13.62) and (13.63), the instantaneous variance of the short-term rate is

$$v_\tau d\tau \equiv var(dr_\tau) = \left(\beta_1^2 y_{1\tau} + \beta_2^2 y_{2\tau}\right) d\tau,$$

such that we can now use the previous equation and eq. (13.62) and express $\tilde{y}_{1\tau}$ and $\tilde{y}_{2\tau}$ in terms of r_τ and v_τ,

$$\tilde{y}_{1\tau} = \frac{\beta_2 r_\tau - v_\tau}{\beta_2 - \beta_1}, \quad \tilde{y}_{2\tau} = \frac{v_\tau - \beta_1 r_\tau}{\beta_2 - \beta_1}.$$

Therefore, eq. (13.64) tells us that in this model, the price of a zero coupon bond is the same as that in eq. (13.61), for some functions $A(\cdot)$, $B(\cdot)$, and $C(\cdot)$. Section 13.5.3 explains the reasons both the Fong and Vasicek model and this model predict the bond price to have the same exponential-affine functional form in eq. (13.61).

Note, finally, the important feature of the models with random volatility in this section. They predict that the yield curve is now a function $R(r_t, v_t, T-t)$, depending on the level of the short-term rate, r_t, and one additional factor, the instantaneous variance of the short-term rate, v_t. Therefore, these models predict that we now have two factors that help explain the whole term structure of interest rates. Clearly, the short-end of the yield curve is not affected by volatility, as $\lim_{T\to t} R(r_t, v_t, T-t) = r_t$, for all v_t. Moreover, in these models, we have that $\lim_{T\to\infty} R(r_t, v_t, T-t) = \bar{R}$, where $\bar{R}$ is a constant and, hence, independent of v_t. Therefore, volatility may only affect the middle portion of the yield curve. For example, if the risk premium required to bear the interest rate risk is negative and sufficiently large, an upward movement in v_t may affect the yield curve in a way qualitatively similar to that depicted in figure 13.3 ("Curvature" panel), and would thus roughly mimic the "curvature" factor that we reviewed in section 13.3. We now provide additional details on how volatility affects the yield curve.

13.5.1.3 Volatility and the yield curve

How does volatility affect the yield curve? Consider the basic Vasicek (1977) model. Naturally, this model assumes that volatility is constant; however, it may be used to develop intuition on eqs. (13.60) and possibly other stochastic volatility models. It is possible to show that eq. (13.38) implies that

$$\frac{\partial R\left(r_t, T-t\right)}{\partial \sigma}=\frac{1}{T-t}\left(\text{Convex}_{t,T}+\text{Slope}_{t,T}\right), \tag{13.65}$$

where

$$\text{Convex}_{t,T} \equiv -\sigma \int_t^T p_r^2\,(T-s)\,ds, \quad \text{Slope}_{t,T} \equiv -\lambda \int_t^T p_r\,(T-s)\,ds,$$

and $p_r(T-t)=\partial \ln P(r,T-t)/\partial r=B(T-t)$ is as in section 13.4.4, and is independent of r. Eq. (13.65) shows that if $\lambda \geq 0$, the yield curve is decreasing in σ, a conclusion that parallels that for options, where option prices are increasing in the volatility of the asset price. As explained in chapter 11, options prices are increasing in volatility due to contract optionalities, i.e., convexity. This channel does still arise in the bond case of this chapter (see figure 13.10) and is represented by the term $\text{Convex}_{t,T}$ in eq. (13.65).

However, the empirical relevant case arises when $\lambda < 0$.[35] In this case, the sign of $\frac{\partial R(t,T)}{\partial \sigma}$ depends on both "convexity" and "slope" effects, effects that arise through the two terms $\text{Convex}_{t,T}$ and $\text{Slope}_{t,T}$. Now, if λ is negative, and sufficiently large in absolute value, these slope effects may dominate over convexity ones, and the yield curve may actually increase with σ. For intermediate values of λ, the term structure can be both increasing and decreasing in σ. At short maturities, convexity is typically dominated by slope effects, such that the short-end of the yield curve may increase with σ. For longer maturities, convexity may be quantitatively more important and, sometimes, dominates slope effects.

More generally, changes in interest rate volatility are not mean-preserving spreads for the risk neutral distribution, as eq. (13.65) illustrates in the case of the Vasicek model. In a world with complete markets, say Black–Scholes, the asset underlying the derivative contracts is traded. In the case under study, the short-term rate is not a traded risk. Therefore, its risk neutral drift depends on volatility through risk adjustments: to illustrate, in the Vasicek example, this dependence arises through the risk premium parameter, λ.

While eq. (13.65) relies on a model with constant volatility, the same reasoning may be made to interpret yield curve movements even when volatility is random.[36] In particular, suppose that the risk premium required to bear interest rate risk is negative and sufficiently large in absolute value. In this case, slope effects may dominate convexity ones at any maturity date, such that the whole yield curve, now, could be always increasing in volatility. Let us provide some intuition. It is reasonable to expect that in bad times (i.e., when interest rate volatility is high) risk premium effects dominate over convexity, such that the yield curve shifts up following an increase in volatility. However, in good times, we would expect

35. In this simple model, the assumption that $\lambda < 0$ is reasonable, as we observe positive risk premiums more often than negative risk premiums. In this model, $p_r < 0$. This property implies term premia are always positive with $\lambda < 0$.
36. See Mele (2003).

that convexity dominates, with the yield curve being decreasing in volatility. Thus, in these examples, if risk premiums are sufficiently sensitive to volatility, we would expect that, in good times, when volatility is small, convexity effects dominate and the yield curve lowers as volatility increases. In bad times, when volatility is high, we would expect that risk premium effects dominate, such that the yield curve increases following an increase in volatility.

To illustrate, assume that $\lambda = \bar{\lambda}\sigma^3$, for some constant $\bar{\lambda}$. This functional form of the risk premium ensures that the risk premium is quite small when σ is small, although then it substantially increases in bad times, i.e., when σ gets large. Replacing these expressions into eq. (13.65) clearly illustrates that risk premium effects become predominantly important as σ increases. In this respect, we may define a threshold value for σ, such that convexity effects are exactly offset by risk premium effects: for each time to maturity $T-t$, there exists a value of σ depending on $T-t$, say $\hat{\sigma}(T-t)$ such that $\frac{\partial R(r_t, T-t)}{\partial \sigma} = 0$. We might go on and define an average value of $\hat{\sigma}(T-t)$, say $\hat{\sigma}_* \equiv (T_2 - T_1)^{-1} \int_{T_1}^{T_2} \hat{\sigma}(u)\, du$, where T_1 and T_2 denotes the lowest and the highest time to maturity we want to consider. This threshold value, $\hat{\sigma}_*$, might lead to define what good or bad times can be, based on the term structure implications of a volatility shock.[37]

13.5.2 Three-Factor Models

We need at least three factors to explain the entire variation of the yield curve. A natural extension of the model in eqs. (13.60) is one in which the drift of the short-term rate contains some predictable component, $\bar{r}_\tau$, such that the yield curve is driven by the following three factor model:

$$\begin{cases} dr_\tau = \kappa_r (\bar{r}_\tau - r_\tau)\, d\tau + \sqrt{v_\tau} r_\tau^\gamma dW_{1\tau} \\ dv_\tau = \kappa_v (\bar{v} - v_\tau)\, d\tau + \xi_v \sqrt{v_\tau} dW_{2\tau} \\ d\bar{r}_\tau = \kappa_{\bar{r}} (\bar{\imath} - \bar{r}_\tau)\, d\tau + \xi_{\bar{r}} \sqrt{\bar{r}_\tau} dW_{3\tau} \end{cases} \tag{13.66}$$

where $\kappa_r, \gamma, \kappa_v, \bar{v}, \xi_v, \kappa_{\bar{r}}, \bar{\imath}$ and $\xi_{\bar{r}}$ are constants, and $[W_1\ W_2\ W_3]$ is a vector Brownian motion. Balduzzi et al. (1996) develop the first model in which the drift of the short-term rate is as in eqs. (13.66). Dai and Singleton (2000) estimate a number of models that generalize this model; section 13.5.5 contains some details regarding the estimation strategy of this type of models.

We are interested in the term structure implications of the model. First, and under regularity conditions, the yield curve is now a function $R(r_t, \bar{r}_t, v_t, T-t)$. Second, and intuitively, changes in the new factor $\bar{r}_t$ should primarily affect the long-end of the yield curve. Indeed, an empirical property is that the short-term rate reverts relatively quickly to the long-term factor $\bar{r}_\tau$ (i.e., κ_r is relatively large), where, instead, $\bar{r}_\tau$ mean-reverts slowly (i.e., $\kappa_{\bar{r}}$ is relatively low): the short-term rate is quite persistent anyway. Ultimately, the slow mean-reversion of $\bar{r}_\tau$ implies that changes in $\bar{r}_\tau$ last for the relevant part of the term

---

37. Naturally, we are referring to "bad times" as the periods where interest rates are volatile. Premiums were arguably very small during the QE period following the Great Recession, for the simple reason that the Fed was credibly fixing interest rates near zero, thereby compressing volatility (and premiums). That is, a period of low interest rate volatility does not necessarily imply a period with good economic developments.

structure we are usually interested in (i.e., up to 30 years), even if, theoretically, the limit, $\lim_{T\to\infty} R(r_t, \bar{r}_t, v_t, T-t)$, is independent of r_t, $\bar{r}_t$ and v_t.

However, it seems difficult to reconcile these properties with those of the factors discussed in section 13.3. First, the short-term rate cannot be taken as a "level factor," since its effects should die off along the yield curve. Instead, a *joint* change in both the short-term rate, r_t, and the "long-term" rate, $\bar{r}_t$, should be needed to mimic the "Level" panel of figure 13.3. But this interpretation is at odds with the assumption that the factors underlying the exercises in figure 13.3 are uncorrelated. Work by Ang, Bekaert, and Wei (2008) suggests that the term-structure of *real* interest rates is quite flat, on average, and that the increasing slope in the nominal curve primarily reflects inflation risk premiums. These findings suggest that inflation may play a very important role in explaining shape and dynamics of the yield curve.

13.5.3 Affine and Quadratic Term Structure Models

13.5.3.1 Affine

The Vasicek (1977) and CIR (1985) models predict that the price of a zero coupon bond is exponential-affine in the short-term rate r. Likewise, the models with stochastic volatility of Fong and Vasicek (1991) and Longstaff and Schwartz (1992) predict that the price of a zero is exponential-affine in the short-term rate r and its instantaneous variance v. These properties are the expression of a general phenomenon. For the simple one-factor case, it is indeed possible to show that bond prices are exponential-affine in r if and only if the functions b and a^2 are affine in r. Models that satisfy these conditions are known as *exponential-affine models*. These basic results extend to *multifactor* models (such as those of Fong and Vasicek or Longstaff and Schwartz), in which case bond prices are exponential-affine in the state variables.[38] In these models, the short-term rate can be written as a function $r(y)$ such that

$$r(y) = r^0 + r^1 \cdot y, \tag{13.67}$$

where r^0 is a constant, r^1 is a vector of constants, and y is a n-dimensional diffusion, solution to

$$dy_\tau = \kappa(\mu - y_\tau)\, d\tau + \Sigma V(y_\tau)\, dW_\tau, \tag{13.68}$$

where W is a d-dimensional Brownian motion, Σ is a full rank $n \times d$ matrix, and V is a full rank $d \times d$ diagonal matrix with elements,

$$V(y)_{(ii)} = \sqrt{\alpha_i + \beta_i^\top y}, \quad i = 1, \cdots, d, \tag{13.69}$$

for some scalars α_i and vectors β_i. Langetieg (1980) appears to be the first reference in the literature containing the first multifactor model constructed along these lines (in which, notably, $\beta_i = 0$).

38. More generally, we say that affine models are those that make the characteristic function exponential-affine in the state variables. In the case of multifactor interest rate models, this condition is equivalent to the condition that bond prices are exponential affine in the state variables.

Next, Let $V^{-}(y)$ be a $d \times d$ diagonal matrix with elements

$$V^{-}(y)_{(ii)} = \begin{cases} \frac{1}{V(y)_{(ii)}} & \text{if } \Pr\{V(y_t)_{(ii)} > 0 \text{ all } t\} = 1 \\ 0 & \text{otherwise} \end{cases}$$

and set

$$\Lambda(y) = V(y)\lambda_1 + V^{-}(y)\lambda_2 y, \tag{13.70}$$

for some d-dimensional vector λ_1 and some $d \times n$ matrix λ_2. Duffie and Kan (1996) explain the benefits of this model. In their formulation $\lambda_2 = 0_{d\times n}$, and the bond price is exponential-affine in the state variables y. That is, the price of the zero has the following functional form:

$$P(y, T-t) = e^{\mathcal{A}(T-t)+\mathcal{B}(T-t)\cdot y}, \tag{13.71}$$

for some functions $\mathcal{A}(\cdot)$ and $\mathcal{B}(\cdot)$ ($\mathcal{B}(\cdot)$ is vector-valued) satisfying $\mathcal{A}(0) = 0$ and $\mathcal{B}(0)_{(i)} = 0$ and characterized in appendix 13.E.

Duffee (2002) suggested the general functional form for Λ in eq. (13.70). The motivation underlying this function is that, in Treasury markets, risk premiums seem to relate to both *volatility* and *level* of the fundamentals. In this model, risk premiums reduce to $V(y)\Lambda(y) = V^2(y)\lambda_1 + \lambda_2 y$. Thus, the inclusion of the term $\lambda_2 y$ allows one to model the statistical relations linking risk premiums to fundamentals. Interestingly, in this model, bond prices still have an exponential-affine form, just as in eq. (13.71). When $\lambda_2 = 0_{d\times n}$, we say that the model is "completely affine," and "essentially affine," otherwise. The clear advantage of these affine models, then, is that they considerably simplify statistical inference, as explained in section 13.5.5 below.

Exponential-affine models have been extensively utilized, and surveying them further will fall well beyond the scope of this book. Piazzesi (2010) provides an extensive survey of these models.

13.5.3.2 Quadratic

Affine models are known to impose tight conditions on the volatilities of the state variables. These restrictions are needed in order to ensure that the square root in eq. (13.69) is real-valued. However, these constraints may hinder the model statistical performance. Another class of models, known as "quadratic," and introduced in great generality by Ahn, Dittmar, and Gallant (2002), overcome some of these difficulties while at the same time preserving analytical tractability.

13.5.3.3 No-arbitrage regressions and the macroeconomy

Ang and Piazzesi (2003) and Hördahl, Tristani, and Vestin (2006) (HTS, henceforth) introduce "no-arbitrage" regressions, to model the relations linking macroeconomic variables to the yield curve. In their models, the factors are taken to be a discrete-time version of eq. (13.68), where some components of y are observable, and others are unobservable. The observable variables may be macroeconomic factors such as inflation or industrial production. The authors, then, study how all these factors affect the yield curve, predicted by a pricing equation such as that in eq. (13.71). While HTS formulate a structural model of the macroeconomy, Ang and Piazzesi (2003) rely on a reduced-form model. "No-arbitrage regressions" is an expression used to emphasize that the linkages between the yield curve and the macroeconomic factors satisfy no-arbitrage restrictions. One simple example of a no-arbitrage regression model is in section 13.4.4 (see eq. (13.44)), where the term spread relates to some macroeconomic variable through no-arbitrage restrictions.

Reduced-form models may be exposed to the critique that some of their parameters may not be "variation-free." Let us explain. Sometimes, and especially in applied work, one may not be interested in making inference on all the parameters of a structural model. The theory of statistical reduction identifies conditions under which inference made on reduced-form models does not entail loss of information on the parameters of interest. Heuristically, consider the joint density function $f(y,z;\theta)$ of two sets of variables, y and z, where $\theta \in \Theta$ is some parameter vector. While researching for appropriate notions of exogeneity in econometrics, Engle, Hendry, and Richard (1983) defined a statistical *cut* as the property by which the joint density may be factored as $f(y,z;\theta) = f\left(y|\, z;\theta_1\right) f(z;\theta_2)$, where, for a partition of the parameter space $\Theta = \Theta_1 \times \Theta_2$, θ_1 and θ_2 are variation-free, in that $(\theta_1, \theta_1) \in \Theta_1 \times \Theta_2$.[39] In other words, parameters are variation-free if they have no linkages among them. In the context of this section, the occurrence of a statistical cut would allow one to focus on a certain model of interest, i.e., the conditional density $f\left(y|\, z;\theta_1\right)$, while at the same time safely disregarding the marginal density $f(z;\theta_2)$.

Naturally, this type of critiques applies to any reduced-form model and in any subfield of economics or social science. To see how this critique would apply to the models of this chapter, consider, for example, the simple Lucas model in part I, according to which the short-term rate is $r = \rho + \gamma\mu - \frac{1}{2}\sigma^2\gamma(1+\gamma)$, where ρ is the impatience rate, μ is the expected dividend growth, and γ is the representative agent's coefficient of relative risk aversion. In this model, a change in γ determines a change in the interest rate. This simple example reveals that there may be economies in which the risk aversion corrections in eq. (13.70) are not "free": tilting them may affect the parameters of the factor dynamics in eq. (13.68).

Reduced-form models have the advantage of bringing flexibility: they aren't "forced" to track any theoretical economy. No-arbitrage regressions give the data the power to say which parameter constellation make the model likely to perform, without imposing theoretical restrictions which the data might, then, be likely to reject. For example, the Lucas model clearly illustrates that some parameters may not be variation-free and, yet, this model may be simply wrong and, then, impose unreasonable data restrictions. Instead, in no-arbitrage models, cross-equations restrictions arise through the weaker requirement of absence of arbitrage.

13.5.4 Unspanned Stochastic Volatility

Are fixed income markets incomplete? Mele and Obayashi (2015) argue that the market for fixed income volatility is quite distinct from that for equity. Consequently, many of the investable products on the popular gauge of equity volatility, VIX (see chapter 11), may turn out to serve as nonexhaustive surrogates for exposure to fixed income volatility.

39. Barndorff-Nielsen (1978) and Florens and Mouchart (1980) provide earlier definitions of statistical cuts.

The "uniqueness" of fixed income volatility has actually been widely acknowledged in the literature. It has been well known since at least Collin-Dusfresne and Goldstein (2002) that fixed income market volatility does not appear to be priced only based on existing fixed income assets.

Simply, the authors showed that straddle returns on caps and floors (see section 13.8) cannot be explained by changes in the term structure of swap rates, but by other factors. That is, existing fixed income assets (such as bonds) do not help hedge rate volatility. The models proposed by Collin-Dusfresne and Goldstein to address these issues are known as leading to "unspanned stochastic volatility" (USV, henceforth). The reason for this terminology is the following. Consider any of the stochastic volatility models reviewed in chapter 11, in which a stock price S_t is the solution to

$$\frac{dS_t}{S_t} = \mu dt + \sigma_t dW_t, \tag{13.72}$$

under the physical probability, for some constant μ, a Brownian motion W_t, and a volatility process $(\sigma_t)_{t\geq 0}$ possibly driven by W_t *and* other Brownian motions. One example of these models is the celebrated Heston (1993) model, in which σ_t^2 is a square root process driven by a Brownian motion only partially correlated with W_t.

As we know from chapter 11, these models are typically understood to describe a situation of incomplete markets. Collin-Dusfresne and Goldstein (2002) propose to extend this notion to fixed income markets, by modeling bond prices in an incomplete markets setup. The idea is simple. If bond markets have stochastic volatility and are still incomplete, bond prices should satisfy dynamics in which their instantaneous returns have stochastic volatility, similarly as in eq. (13.72) for the equity case. At the same time, the bond price exposure to volatility should be zero, just as a stock price exposure to its own volatility is zero in the markets of chapter 11. In the context of the short-term rate models of this section (see, e.g., eqs. (13.66)), the latter condition is met when

$$\frac{\partial}{\partial v} P\left(r_t, \bar{r}_t, v_t, T-t\right) = 0. \tag{13.73}$$

Collin-Dufresne and Goldstein (2002) provide a characterization of the previous condition in multidimensional models. It is an open question whether existing models with USV compare to models without. In a nutshell, restrictions such as that in eq. (13.73) can hinder the ability of standard multifactor models to perform as accurately as they could do without restrictions. The authors argue that the Heath, Jarrow, and Morton (1992) (HJM, henceforth) models of section 13.7 are able to incorporate stochastic volatility and market incompleteness in a more flexible way. In any case, USV and incompleteness of fixed income markets both seem to be a quite robust and well-accepted empirical feature.

13.5.5 Topics Regarding Estimation and Trading Strategies

13.5.5.1 Univariate models

How to estimate the parameter vector $\theta = [\kappa, \mu, \eta, \beta, \alpha, \xi, \vartheta, \rho]^\top$ in eqs. (13.49)? Maximum Likelihood (ML) would be a feasible estimation method under two sets of conditions. *First*, the model in eqs. (13.49) should not have stochastic volatility at all, namely,

$\beta = \xi = 0$; in this case, the short-term rate would be solution to,

$$dr_t = \kappa(\mu - r_t)\,dt + \bar{\sigma} r_t^{\eta} dW_t,$$

where $\bar{\sigma}$ is now a constant. *Second*, the value of the elasticity parameter η is important. If $\eta = 0$, the short-term rate process is the Gaussian one proposed by Vasicek (1977). If $\eta = \frac{1}{2}$, we obtain the square-root process of Cox, Ingersoll, and Ross (1985). As we know, the transition density of r_t is Gaussian in the Vasicek market, and a noncentral chi-square in the CIR case. Therefore, in both Vasicek and CIR markets, we may write down the likelihood function of the diffusion process. Therefore, ML estimation is feasible in these two cases. In more general cases, such those in the next section, one needs to go for simulation methods, such as those described in chapter 6. However, we could still estimate multifactor affine models through ML.

13.5.5.2 More general models

Next, we outline estimation methodologies for models of the whole yield curve, i.e., models that go beyond the mere description of data in (13.49). These methods are based on a pricing model and, thus, share analogies with those described in chapter 11 to deal with models of option pricing with random volatility (see section 11.5). In particular, the unobservable variables may be filtered as a by product of the estimation strategy. We rely on three steps.

Step 1 We collect time series of three maturities of the yield curve, say 6-month, 5-year, and 10-year yields.

Step 2 We consider a pricing model. To illustrate, consider the three-factor model in eqs. (13.66), and assume that all Brownians are correlated, with ρ denoting the vector of all the correlations. The model predicts that the price of a zero coupon bond is

$$P^j(r_t, v_t, \bar{r}_t; \boldsymbol{\theta}, \boldsymbol{\lambda}) \equiv P(r_t, v_t, \bar{r}_t, T_j - t; \boldsymbol{\theta}, \boldsymbol{\lambda}) = \mathbb{E}\left(e^{-\int_t^{T_j} r_s ds} \,\middle|\, r_t, v_t, \bar{r}_t \right), \tag{13.74}$$

for some expiration dates T_j. The bond price depends on $\boldsymbol{\theta} = [\kappa_r, \kappa_v, \kappa_{\bar{r}}, \gamma, \bar{v}, \xi_v, \bar{\iota}, \xi_{\bar{r}}, \rho]^\top$ (the parameter vector under the physical probability) and, also, on $\boldsymbol{\lambda}$, the vector of risk premium coefficients.[40] The objective is to estimate both $\boldsymbol{\theta}$ and $\boldsymbol{\lambda}$. Consider the yield curve that the model predicts in correspondence of three maturities

$$R^j(r_t, v_t, \bar{r}_t; \boldsymbol{\theta}, \boldsymbol{\lambda}) \equiv -\frac{1}{T_j - t} \ln P^j(r_t, v_t, \bar{r}_t; \boldsymbol{\theta}, \boldsymbol{\lambda}), \quad j = 1, 2, 3. \tag{13.75}$$

Now, we can use observations, $R_{\$}^j$ say, model predictions, R^j, create moment conditions, and proceed to estimate $(\boldsymbol{\theta}, \boldsymbol{\lambda})$ by means of some method of moments (see chapter 6), provided of course the moments are enough to identify $(\boldsymbol{\theta}, \boldsymbol{\lambda})$.

---

40. Precisely, the Radon-Nikodym derivative of the risk neutral probability with respect to the physical is $\exp\left(-\frac{1}{2}\int \|\boldsymbol{\Lambda}_t\|^2 dt - \int \boldsymbol{\Lambda}_t dW_t\right)$, and $\boldsymbol{\Lambda}_t \equiv \boldsymbol{\Lambda}^{\mathrm{m}}(r_t, v_t, \bar{r}_t; \boldsymbol{\lambda})$, for some vector-valued function $\boldsymbol{\Lambda}^{\mathrm{m}}$ and parameter vector $\boldsymbol{\lambda}$. In this example, $\boldsymbol{\Lambda}^{\mathrm{m}}$ depends on the current value of the state vector $[r_t, v_t, \bar{r}_t]$. The model is, thus, Markov, consistent with the assumption that the bond price is a function of the current state only.

We encounter two difficulties. The first is that the volatility v_t and the long-term mean of the short-term rate, $\bar{r}_t$, are not observable. We can use simulation-based inference methods to cope with this issue: we simulate eqs. (13.66), and apply moment conditions or auxiliary models to observable variables, according to the procedure set forth in chapter 6 (see section 6.7). For example, we simulate eqs. (13.66) for a given value of $(\boldsymbol{\theta}, \boldsymbol{\lambda})$. For each simulation, we reconstruct a time series of interest rates R^j relying on eq. (13.75). Then, we obtain estimates of moment conditions or some auxiliary models on these artificial data that are as close as possible to those obtained from real data. In practice, our parameter estimator is the value of $(\boldsymbol{\theta}, \boldsymbol{\lambda})$ that minimizes a measure of distance between artificial and real data.

A second difficulty is that eq. (13.74) may not be known in closed-form. We may rely on affine models, as explained next.

Step 3 Affine models imply that

$$R^j\left(r_t, v_t, \bar{r}_t; \boldsymbol{\theta}, \boldsymbol{\lambda}\right) = A\left(j; \boldsymbol{\theta}, \boldsymbol{\lambda}\right) + \boldsymbol{B}\left(j; \boldsymbol{\theta}, \boldsymbol{\lambda}\right) \cdot \left[r_t, v_t, \bar{r}_t\right]^\top, \quad j = 1, 2, 3, \tag{13.76}$$

where $A(j; \theta, \lambda)$ and $\boldsymbol{B}(j; \theta, \lambda)$ are some functions of time to maturity $T_j - t$ ($\boldsymbol{B}$ is vector valued), and generally depend on the parameter vector $(\boldsymbol{\theta}, \boldsymbol{\lambda})$. Once eqs. (13.66) are simulated, we determine time series of yields R^j based on eq. (13.76).[41]

13.5.5.3 Filtering (and trading)

Given our parameter estimates, we make inference on the state $[r_t, v_t, \bar{r}_t]^\top$. We may invert eq. (13.76) given the observed values of the three yields. A conceptual difficulty with this approach is that the "estimates" of the state $[r_t, v_t, \bar{r}_t]^\top$ rely on the maturities we choose. Changing maturities may lead to different filtered states. A pragmatic assumption is that eq. (13.76) only holds with some observation error, such that we may, then, proceed while searching for the state that minimizes the error variance based on all available maturities. This procedure delivers the state for each observation; it is attractive, as it exploits market-based information that is summarized by the cross-section of yields.

This "no-arb" procedure to filter the state enables one to implement forecasting exercises. For example, we may fit a VAR to the time series of the filtered values of $[r_t, v_t, \bar{r}_t]^\top$ and, then, use this VAR to produce forecasts of the state and, finally, forecasts of yields using eq. (13.76).[42] We may try to replicate the segments of the yield curve that are mispriced through other segments of the yield curve that the model fits well, in analogy with exercises explained in the case of equity options in markets with stochastic volatility (see section 11.5.3 in chapter 11). Replication, in the current case, may be based on dynamically adjusted portfolios such as those described in section 13.4.2.2.

---

41. Dai and Singleton (2000) implement this estimation strategy, although they make use of data on swap rates.

42. An alternative is to simulate eqs. (13.66) beginning from a starting point equal to the state filtered at the most recent date. We simulate the system for a given time period, and obtain nonparametric estimates of the densities out of the simulated data (see, e.g., Pagan and Ullah (1999), for an introduction to nonparametric methods). Finally, we use these density estimates and determine conditional moment forecasts of any order.

13.6 No-Arbitrage Models: Early Formulations

Pricing interest rate derivatives necessitates taking the initial yield as *given* rather than *explaining* it. To illustrate, consider a European option written on a bond: only "explaining" the bond price is problematic as a model error on the bond price can generate a large option price error due to the nonlinearities induced by the optionality. Moreover, it would be problematic to rely on an option pricing model that cannot pin down the value of the underlying.

This section surveys the first attempts to deal with these issues within a continuous time framework, with of one them actually being the continuous time version of the Ho and Lee (1986) model in chapter 12. In section 13.6.1, we explain the main issues while relying on a benchmark option pricing formula; in sections 13.6.2 and 13.6.3, we provide details regarding two benchmark models.

13.6.1 Fitting the Yield Curve, Perfectly

Let again $P(r_\tau, \tau, S)$ be the time τ price of a zero coupon bond maturing at some time S. By no arbitrage, the price of a European call option on this bond, struck at K and expiring at $T < S$, is:

$$C^b(r_t, t, T, S) \equiv \mathbb{E}_t\left[e^{-\int_t^T r_\tau d\tau}\left(P(r_T, T, S) - K\right)^+\right].$$

In section 13.8, we show that

$$C^b(r_t, K; t, T, S) = P(r_t, t, S) \cdot Q_F^S[P(r_T, T, S) \geq K] - KP(r_t, t, T) \cdot Q_F^T[P(r_T, T, S) \geq K], \tag{13.77}$$

where Q_F^X is the so-called forward probability for maturity X (see eq. (13.111)).

The bond option price in eq. (13.77) bears some resemblance to the Black–Scholes formula, as further noted in section 13.8.4. However, this price depends on *theoretical* prices, $P(r_t, t, T)$ and $P(r_t, t, S)$, not *market* prices. This issue is problematic to sell-side institutions while engaged in intermediating derivatives: as explained many times, the need arises in this case to simultaneously match the yield curve at the time of evaluation. This section describes models that fit the yield curve without errors, which we call "perfectly fitting models." These models are simply a more elaborated, continuous time version of the no-arbitrage models introduced in chapter 12. They predict that the price of any bond, say a bond expiring at some S, is, of course, random, at time $T < S$, but also exactly equal to the *current* market price, that of time t. Finally, and naturally, this price must be arbitrage-free. The aim of this and subsequent sections is to show how to achieve this task by augmenting the models seen in the previous sections with a set of "infinite dimensional parameters."

A final remark. Section 13.8 explains that at least for the Vasicek model, the option price in eq. (13.77) does not explicitly depend on r because it only "depends" on $P(r_t, t, T)$ and $P(r_t, t, S)$, which could be set equal to their market value counterparts. So why do we look for perfectly fitting models in the first place? Wouldn't it be enough, then, to just replace the theoretical prices $P(r_t, t, T)$ and $P(r_t, t, S)$ with the market values, say $P^\$(t, T)$ and $P^\$(t, S)$? This way, the model *is* perfectly fitting. Apart from being logically inconsistent (you would have a model predicting something generically different from prices), this way of proceeding also has practical drawbacks.

Section 13.8 reveals indeed that option pricing formulae for European options might well agree "in notation" with those relating to perfectly fitting models. However, in section 13.8.6, we explain that as we move toward more complex interest rate derivatives, say options on *coupon* bearing bonds and *swaption* contracts, the situation becomes dramatically different. Finally, some maturity dates might not be actually traded. For example, $P^{\$}(t,T)$ might not be observed and, still, we might well be interested in the pricing of exotic products requiring knowledge of $P^{\$}(t,T)$. An intuitive procedure to deal with this difficulty is to interpolate across the traded maturities. In fact, the objective of perfectly fitting models is to allow for such an "interpolation" while preserving absence of arbitrage.

The remainder of this section discusses two specific, old, and yet very famous examples of perfectly fitting models: (i) the Ho and Lee (1986) model, and (ii) one generalization of it, introduced by Hull and White (1990). In section 13.7, we move on toward a general model-building principle that includes these two models as special cases.

13.6.2 Ho and Lee

Ho and Lee (1986) originally set their model in discrete-time, which is analyzed in chapter 12 along with alternative models. The model in this section represents the "diffusion limit" of the original Ho and Lee model, as put forward in chapter 12 (see section 12.5.7). In this continuous time version, the short-term rate is the solution to

$$dr_\tau = \theta_\tau d\tau + \sigma d\tilde{W}_\tau, \quad \tau \geq t, \tag{13.78}$$

where $\tilde{W}$ is a Brownian motion under Q, σ is a constant, and θ_τ is an "infinite dimensional" parameter, needed to pin down the initial, observed yield curve, as we now explain. The reason we refer to θ_τ as infinite dimensional is that θ_τ is taken to be a continuous function of calendar time $\tau \geq t$. We assume this function is known at t—whence, "parameter."

Clearly, eq. (13.78) is an affine model. Therefore, the bond price takes the following form

$$P(r_\tau, \tau, T) = e^{A(\tau,T) - B(\tau,T) r_\tau}, \tag{13.79}$$

for two functions A and B that can be determined in the usual way: replace the solution in (13.79) and its partial derivatives into (13.30), and conclude that A and B are solutions to differential equations, solutions given by

$$A(\tau,T) = \int_\tau^T \theta_s (s-T)\, ds + \frac{1}{6}\sigma^2 (T-\tau)^3, \quad B(\tau,T) = T - \tau.$$

Let $f_{\$}(t,\tau)$ denote the instantaneous, observed forward rate. By matching the instantaneous forward rate $f(\tau,T)$ predicted by the model to $f_{\$}(\tau,T)$ yields

$$f_{\$}(t,T) = f(t,T) = -\frac{\partial \ln P(r_t,t,T)}{\partial T} = \int_t^T \theta_s ds - \frac{1}{2}\sigma^2 (T-t)^2 + r_t. \tag{13.80}$$

Because $P_{\$}(t,T)=\exp(-\int_t^T f_{\$}(t,\tau)\,d\tau)$, the drift term θ_s satisfying eq. (13.80) guarantees an exact fit of the yield curve. Let us determine more precisely θ_τ. By differentiating eq. (13.80) with respect to T, leaves $\theta_T=\frac{\partial}{\partial T}f_{\$}(t,T)+\sigma^2(T-t)$, or:[43]

$$\theta_\tau=\frac{\partial}{\partial \tau}f_{\$}(t,\tau)+\sigma^2(\tau-t). \tag{13.81}$$

By eqs. (13.78) and (13.81), the short-term rate is then

$$r_t=f_{\$}(0,t)+\frac{1}{2}\sigma^2t^2+\sigma\tilde{W}_t, \tag{13.82}$$

such that both the conditional expectation and conditional variance of the short-term rate explode over time. Moreover, by eq. (13.80), and eq. (13.78), the instantaneous forward rate satisfies

$$d_\tau f(\tau,T)=-\theta_\tau d\tau+\sigma^2(T-\tau)\,d\tau+dr_\tau=\sigma^2(T-\tau)\,d\tau+\sigma d\tilde{W}_t. \tag{13.83}$$

Eq. (13.82) fully describes how this model works. The probability distribution of the short-term rate at any point in time is uniquely determined by absence of arbitrage: in particular, we did not make any assumptions regarding the drift of r_τ in eq. (13.78). This conclusion is in sharp contrast with the prediction of the standard models of the short-term rate, in which the risk-adjusted dynamics of the short-term rate inherits the assumptions made regarding the dynamics under the physical probability.

Note that the approach in this section is to infer the dynamics of the short-term rate from market prices. It is the same approach followed in chapter 12, but in continuous time. It is, then, useful to emphasize, again, an interesting parallel mentioned in chapter 12. In this particular model, we are searching for the function θ_τ that returns the initial yield curve. This search is similar to that in chapter 11, where a *local volatility* of the asset price is calibrated to return the observed option prices. Section 13.7 generalizes this approach and accounts for much richer market dynamics, resulting into the celebrated HJM framework. We now present an extension of Ho and Lee model that makes the market stationary, that is, a market in which interest rates are mean-reverting and conditional variances are bounded over time.

13.6.3 Hull and White

We now consider a model relatively more complex than the previous one. Why would we actually need a more complex model in the first place? After all, the Ho-Lee model can pin down the entire yield curve. The reason is that the yield curve may not be the only object that we want to fit. In general, we may want to price a large variety of derivatives, and fitting the yield curve may only be a necessary (not sufficient) working condition. For example, our goal could be to price complex interest rate derivatives while ensuring model predictions in line with some empirical evidence.

43. To verify that θ is indeed the fitting parameter we are searching for, we replace eq. (13.81) into eq. (13.80) and verify indeed that Eq. (13.80) holds as an identity.

Hull and White (1990) consider a variety of models that can fit the initial yield curve without errors, and amongst them, their simplest is

$$dr_\tau = \kappa\left(\frac{\theta_\tau}{\kappa} - r_\tau\right)d\tau + \sigma d\tilde{W}_\tau, \tag{13.84}$$

where $\tilde{W}$ is a Q-Brownian motion, and κ, σ are constants. The model generalizes the Ho and Lee model (1986) in eq. (13.78) and the Vasicek (1977) model in eq. (13.34). In the original formulation of Hull and White, κ and σ are both time-varying, but the main points of this model can be learned by working out this particularly simple case.

Eq. (13.84) also gives rise to an affine model. Therefore, the solution for the bond price is given by eq. (13.79). It is easy to show that the functions A and B are given by

$$A(\tau,T) = \frac{1}{2}\sigma^2\int_\tau^T B^2(s,T)\,ds - \int_\tau^T \theta_s B(s,T)\,ds, \tag{13.85}$$

and

$$B(\tau,T) = \frac{1}{\kappa}\left(1 - e^{-\kappa(T-\tau)}\right). \tag{13.86}$$

By reiterating the same reasoning produced to show (13.81), one shows (see appendix 13.E for details) that the solution for θ is

$$\theta_\tau = \frac{\partial}{\partial\tau}f_\$(t,\tau) + \kappa f_\$(t,\tau) + \frac{\sigma^2}{2\kappa}\left(1 - e^{-2\kappa(\tau-t)}\right). \tag{13.87}$$

That is, and contrary to the Ho-Lee model, mean-reversion ($\kappa > 0$) allows this model to keep the short-term rate stationary.

We now turn to a class of models that encompasses those in this section, in which the focus is to model forward rates in a way that prevents arbitrage, similarly to what we have done in this section, but without being restrictive regarding the particular relations linking bond prices to short-term rates (e.g., affine).

13.7 The Heath-Jarrow-Morton Framework

13.7.1 The Framework

The bond price representation in eq. (13.11),

$$P(\tau,T) = e^{-\int_\tau^T f(\tau,\ell)d\ell}, \quad \text{all } \tau \in [t,T], \tag{13.88}$$

underlies the modeling approach started by Heath, Jarrow, and Morton (1992). Given eq. (13.88), this approach takes as a primitive the stochastic evolution of the entire structure of forward rates, not only the special case of the short-term rate, $r_t = \lim_{\ell\downarrow t} f(t,\ell) \equiv f(t,t)$. The goal is to start with eq. (13.88), take the initial observed forward rates $\left(f(t,\ell)\right)_{\ell\in[t,T]}$ as given, and, then, find the no-abritrage, "cross-equation" restrictions on the stochastic behavior of $\left(f(\tau,\ell)\right)_{\tau\in(t,\ell]}$, for any $\ell \in [t,T]$.

By construction, the HJM approach allows for a perfect fit of the initial term structure. This point can be illustrated quite simply, as the bond price $P(\tau, T)$ is

$$\begin{aligned}
P(\tau, T) &= e^{-\int_\tau^T f(\tau,\ell)d\ell} \\
&= \frac{P(t,T)}{P(t,\tau)} \cdot \frac{P(t,\tau)}{P(t,T)} e^{-\int_\tau^T f(\tau,\ell)d\ell} \\
&= \frac{P(t,T)}{P(t,\tau)} \cdot e^{-\int_t^\tau f(t,\ell)d\ell + \int_t^T f(t,\ell)d\ell - \int_\tau^T f(\tau,\ell)d\ell} \\
&= \frac{P(t,T)}{P(t,\tau)} \cdot e^{\int_\tau^T f(t,\ell)d\ell - \int_\tau^T f(\tau,\ell)d\ell} \\
&= \frac{P(t,T)}{P(t,\tau)} \cdot e^{-\int_\tau^T (f(\tau,\ell) - f(t,\ell))d\ell}.
\end{aligned} \tag{13.89}$$

The previous relation holds independent of any model, but the first restriction we want to make is that the price at τ is consistent with the yield curve at t, such that eq. (13.89) can be written as

$$P(\tau, T) = \frac{P^{\$}(t,T)}{P^{\$}(t,\tau)} \cdot e^{-\int_\tau^T (f(\tau,\ell) - f(t,\ell))d\ell}, \tag{13.90}$$

where $P^{\$}(t, \cdot)$ denotes a market price at time t. Indeed, evaluating eq. (13.90) for $\tau = t$ leaves $P(t, T) = P^{\$}(t, T)$. Eq. (13.90) highlights a modeling perspective in a continuous time setting, which is the continuous time counterpart to the discrete time Ho-Lee model (see chapter 12). Indeed, it is shown, below, that the continuous time version of the Ho-Lee model (see eq. (13.83)) is a special case of the HJM framework.

Models of the short-term rate are obviously consistent with eq. (13.89) but cannot be consistent with eq. (13.90), because we know these models cannot fit the initial yield curve. Models of the short-term rate have implications regarding forward rates. Instead, models in the HJM framework begin while making assumptions on forward rates. In particular, the key points of the HJM methodology are (i) to take the current forward rates $f(t, \ell)$ as given (i.e., equal to those in the market) and, then, (ii) to model the future forward rate movements,

$$f(\tau, \ell) - f(t, \ell).$$

Therefore, in the HJM methodology, the current yield curve is perfectly fitted (see eq. (13.90)). In contrast, the approach in sections 13.4 and 13.5 consists in *modeling* the *current* bond price $P(t, T)$ through assumptions regarding the dynamics of the short-term rate. We know from previous sections and chapter 12 that fitting the initial term structure is critical for market making purposes. All in all, our objective is to describe a model that pins down the whole yield curve at time t while leaving uncertainty to a subsequent time T, a time, perhaps, at which an interest rate sensitive product will pay off, just as figure 12.30 in chapter 12 illustrates for the (discrete time) Ho and Lee model. Naturally, we model uncertainty while imposing discipline, namely, requiring absence of arbitrage.

13.7.2 The Model

13.7.2.1 *Primitives*

We assume that, for any given T, the instantaneous forward rate, $(f(\tau, T))_{\tau\in[t,T]}$, satisfies

$$d_\tau f(\tau, T) = \alpha(\tau, T)\, d\tau + \sigma(\tau, T)\, dW_\tau, \quad \tau \in (t, T], \tag{13.91}$$

for some processes α and σ, and where $f(t, T)$ is given. Note that in this model, the Brownian motion W_τ doesn't obviously "depend" on T. Strings models, analyzed in section 13.7.5, allow us to "index" W_τ with T, in a sense discussed below.

13.7.2.2 *No-arbitrage restrictions*

We derive restrictions on α that rule out arbitrage. Let $X_\tau \equiv -\int_\tau^T f(\tau, \ell) d\ell$. We have

$$dX_\tau = f(\tau,\tau)d\tau - \int_\tau^T (d_\tau f(\tau,\ell))\, d\ell = \left(r_\tau - \alpha^I(\tau,T)\right) d\tau - \sigma^I(\tau,T) dW_\tau,$$

where the second equality follows by $f(\tau,\tau) = r_\tau$, eq. (13.91) and the following definitions

$$\alpha^I(\tau,T) \equiv \int_\tau^T \alpha(\tau,\ell)d\ell, \quad \sigma^I(\tau,T) \equiv \int_\tau^T \sigma(\tau,\ell)d\ell.$$

By eq. (13.88), $P = e^X$. By Itô's lemma,

$$\frac{d_\tau P(\tau,T)}{P(\tau,T)} = \left(r_\tau - \alpha^I(\tau,T) + \frac{1}{2}\left\|\sigma^I(\tau,T)\right\|^2\right) d\tau - \sigma^I(\tau,T)dW_\tau.$$

By the FTAP, we have that

$$\frac{d_\tau P(\tau,T)}{P(\tau,T)} = \left(r_\tau - \alpha^I(\tau,T) + \frac{1}{2}\left\|\sigma^I(\tau,T)\right\|^2 + \sigma^I(\tau,T)\lambda_\tau\right) d\tau - \sigma^I(\tau,T)d\tilde{W}_\tau,$$

where $\tilde{W}_\tau = W_\tau + \int_t^\tau \lambda_s ds$ is a Q-Brownian motion, and λ satisfies

$$\alpha^I(\tau,T) = \frac{1}{2}\left\|\sigma^I(\tau,T)\right\|^2 + \sigma^I(\tau,T)\lambda_\tau. \tag{13.92}$$

By differentiating the previous relation with respect to T gives us the arbitrage restriction that we were looking for:

$$\alpha(\tau,T) = \sigma(\tau,T)\int_\tau^T \sigma(\tau,\ell)^\top d\ell + \sigma(\tau,T)\lambda_\tau. \tag{13.93}$$

13.7.3 The Dynamics of the Short-Term Rate

By eq. (13.91), the short-term rate satisfies

$$r_\tau \equiv f(\tau,\tau) = f(t,\tau) + \int_t^\tau \alpha(s,\tau)\, ds + \int_t^\tau \sigma(s,\tau)\, dW_s, \quad \tau \in (t, T]. \tag{13.94}$$

Differentiating with respect to τ yields

$$dr_\tau = \left(f_2(t,\tau) + \sigma(\tau,\tau)\lambda_\tau + \int_t^\tau \alpha_2(s,\tau)ds + \int_t^\tau \sigma_2(s,\tau)dW_s \right) d\tau + \sigma(\tau,\tau)dW_\tau, \quad (13.95)$$

where

$$\alpha_2(s,\tau) = \underbrace{\sigma_2(s,\tau) \int_s^\tau \sigma(s,\ell)^\top d\ell + \sigma(s,\tau)\sigma(s,\tau)^\top}_{\equiv \tilde{\alpha}_2(s,\tau)} + \sigma_2(s,\tau)\lambda_s. \quad (13.96)$$

Eq. (13.94) reveals that the short-term rate is in general non-Markov. A special case of eq. (13.94) is the Ho and Lee (1986) model, where $\sigma(s,\tau) = \sigma$, a constant, such that, by eq. (13.93), $\alpha(s,\tau) = \sigma^2(\tau - s) + \sigma\lambda_s$, consistently with eq. (13.82). The Hull and White (1990) model is dealt with in the next section.

Note that regarding the main objective of these models—pricing—we do not need to be concerned with "estimating" any risk premium, i.e., $\lambda(\cdot)$. We only need to consider the risk neutral dynamics of the "left corner" in the forward rate surface, that is, those of the short-term rate r_τ. By eq. (13.95) and Girsanov's theorem, these are given by

$$dr_\tau = \left(f_2(t,\tau) + \int_t^\tau \tilde{\alpha}_2(s,\tau)ds + \int_t^\tau \sigma_2(s,\tau)d\tilde{W}_s \right) d\tau + \sigma(\tau,\tau)d\tilde{W}_\tau, \quad (13.97)$$

where $\tilde{\alpha}_2(s,\tau)$ is defined in Eq. (13.96), and $\tilde{W}_\tau$ denotes, as usual, a Brownian motion under the risk neutral probability.

Eq. (13.97) can be easily simulated for the purpose of evaluating exotic products.

13.7.4 Embedding

Naturally, HJM models are not distinct from the short-term rate models of sections 13.4 and 13.5. Under "embeddability" conditions, HJM can be turned into short-term rate models—a property known as "universality" of HJM models.

13.7.4.1 Markovianity

Under which conditions do HJM models predict the short-term rate to be Markov? This question naturally links to the literature reviewed in sections 13.4 and 13.5, where the whole yield curve is driven by a scalar Markov process: the short-term rate. Carverhill (1994) and Ritchken and Sankarasubramanian (1995) study conditions under which the original state vector can be enlarged such that the resulting "augmented" state vector is Markov and at the same time, includes the short-term rate as a component. The resulting model quite resembles some of the short-term rate models surveyed in sections 13.4 and 13.5. In this model, the short-term rate is not Markov, yet it is part of a system that is Markov. We now illustrate these points within the simple Markov scalar case.

Assume the forward-rate volatility is deterministic and takes the following form:

$$\sigma(t,T) = g_1(t)g_2(T) \quad \text{all } t, T. \quad (13.98)$$

By eq. (13.97), then, r_τ satisfies

$$dr_\tau = \left(f_2(t,\tau) + \int_t^\tau \tilde{\alpha}_2(s,\tau)ds + g_2'(\tau) \int_t^\tau g_1(s)d\tilde{W}_s \right) d\tau + \sigma(\tau,\tau)d\tilde{W}_\tau$$

$$= \left(f_2(t,\tau) + \int_t^\tau \tilde{\alpha}_2(s,\tau)ds + \frac{g_2'(\tau)}{g_2(\tau)} g_2(\tau) \int_t^\tau g_1(s)d\tilde{W}_s \right) d\tau + \sigma(\tau,\tau)d\tilde{W}_\tau$$

$$= \left[f_2(t,\tau) + \int_t^\tau \tilde{\alpha}_2(s,\tau)ds + \frac{g_2'(\tau)}{g_2(\tau)} \left(r_\tau - f(t,\tau) - \int_t^\tau \tilde{\alpha}(s,\tau)ds \right) \right] d\tau + \sigma(\tau,\tau)d\tilde{W}_\tau .$$

Done. This is Markov. Precisely, the condition in eq. (13.98) ensures the HJM model predicts the short-term rate is Markov. Mean reversion, then, obtains assuming that $g_2'(T) < 0$ for all T. For example, take λ to be a constant, and

$$g_1(t) = \sigma \cdot e^{\kappa t}, \quad \sigma > 0, \quad g_2(t) = e^{-\kappa t}, \quad \kappa \geq 0,$$

such that $\sigma(t,T) = \sigma e^{-\kappa(T-t)}$, and the price volatility is $\int_\tau^T \sigma(\ell,T)\, d\ell = \sigma \frac{1-e^{-\kappa(T-\tau)}}{\kappa}$. This is the Hull-White model discussed in section 13.6.3, of which the Ho and Lee model is a particular case, namely for $\kappa = 0$.

13.7.4.2 *Short-term rate reductions*

When can models of the short-term rate be part of the HJM universe? Let the short-term rate be solution to:

$$dr_\tau = \bar{b}(\tau, r_\tau)d\tau + a(\tau, r_\tau)d\tilde{W}_\tau,$$

where $\tilde{W}$ is a Q-Brownian motion, and $\bar{b}$ is some risk neutralized drift function. The rational bond price function is $P(r_t,t,T)$, and the forward rate implied by the model is:

$$f(r_t,t,T) = -\frac{\partial}{\partial T} \ln P(r_t,t,T).$$

By Itô's lemma,

$$df = \left(\frac{\partial}{\partial t} f + \bar{b} f_r + \frac{1}{2} a^2 f_{rr} \right) d\tau + a f_r d\tilde{W}.$$

But for $f(r,t,T)$ to be consistent with the solution to eq. (13.91), it must be that

$$\begin{aligned} \alpha(t,T) - \sigma(t,T)\lambda_t &= \frac{\partial}{\partial t} f(r,t,T) + \bar{b}(t,r) f_r(r,t,T) + \frac{1}{2} a(t,r)^2 f_{rr}(r,t,T) \\ \sigma(t,T) &= a(t,r) f_r(t,r) \end{aligned} \quad (13.99)$$

and

$$f(t,T) = f(r,t,T). \quad (13.100)$$

In particular, the last condition can only be satisfied if the short-term rate model under consideration is of the perfectly fitting type.

13.7.5 Stochastic String Shocks Models

Chapter 9 (see section 9.9) provides a succinct introduction to a class of probabilistic models known as random fields, or stochastic string models. These models seem particular useful to deal with multi-asset markets, where the need arises to predict the outcome of several endogenous and possibly correlated variables. The focus of chapter 9 is a market for multiple trees. The concern of the present section is the forward interest rate market.

Kennedy (1994, 1997), Goldstein (2000), and Santa-Clara and Sornette (2001) provide seminal contributions in this area. Heaney and Cheng (1984) provide an early contribution more particularly focussed on portfolio selection in the presence of a continuum of bonds. This section provides a succinct derivation of the main asset price implications of strings in the fixed income space.

13.7.5.1 *Stochastic singularity*

Let $\sigma(\tau, T) = [\sigma_1(\tau, T), \cdots, \sigma_N(\tau, T)]$ in Eq. (13.91). For any $T_1 < T_2$,

$$E\left[df(\tau, T_1)\, df(\tau, T_2)\right] = \sum_{i=1}^{N} \sigma_i(\tau, T_1)\, \sigma_i(\tau, T_2)\, d\tau,$$

and,

$$c(\tau, T_1, T_2) \equiv corr\left[df(\tau, T_1)\, df(\tau, T_2)\right] = \frac{\sum_{i=1}^{N} \sigma_i(\tau, T_1)\, \sigma_i(\tau, T_2)}{\|\sigma(\tau, T_1)\| \cdot \|\sigma(\tau, T_2)\|}. \tag{13.101}$$

By replacing this result into eq. (13.93),

$$\begin{aligned} \alpha(\tau, T) &= \int_\tau^T \sigma(\tau, T) \cdot \sigma(\tau, \ell)^\top d\ell + \sigma(\tau, T)\lambda_\tau \\ &= \int_\tau^T \|\sigma(\tau, \ell)\|\, \|\sigma(\tau, T)\|\, c(\tau, \ell, T)\, d\ell + \sigma(\tau, T)\lambda_\tau. \end{aligned}$$

One drawback of this model is that the correlation matrix of any $(N+M)$-dimensional vector of forward rates is degenerate for $M \geq 1$. Stochastic string models overcome this difficulty by *modeling* the correlation structure $c(\tau, \tau_1, \tau_2)$ for all τ_1 and τ_2 in an independent way, rather than *implying* it from a given N-factor model (as in eq. (13.101)). In other terms, within the HJM methodology, one uses the functions σ_i to model both volatility and correlation structure of forward rates. The outcome might not be a good model, in practice. Instead, stochastic string models have two separate functions with which to model volatility and correlation. To illustrate, it may be that volatility and correlation are driven by different sets of state variables.

We consider a model, by which the forward rate is the solution to

$$d_\tau f(\tau, T) = \alpha(\tau, T)\, d\tau + \sigma(\tau, T)\, d_\tau Z(\tau, T),$$

where the *string* Z satisfies the following five properties:

(i) *For all* τ, $Z(\tau, T)$ *is continuous in* T;
(ii) *For all* T, $Z(\tau, T)$ *is continuous in* τ;
(iii) $Z(\tau, T)$ *is a* τ*-martingale and, hence, a local martingale, i.e.,* $E\left(d_\tau Z(\tau, T)\right) = 0$;
(iv) $var\left(d_\tau Z(\tau, T)\right) = d\tau$;
(v) $cov\left(d_\tau Z(\tau, T_1)\, d_\tau Z(\tau, T_2)\right) = \psi(T_1, T_2)\, d\tau$ *(say)*.

Properties (iii), (iv), and (v) make Z Markovian. The functional form for ψ is crucially important to guarantee this property. Given the previous properties, one can easily derive a key property of forward rates. We have

$$\sqrt{var\left(df\left(\tau,T\right)\right)}=\sigma\left(\tau,T\right)$$

$$c\left(\tau,T_1,T_2\right)\equiv corr\left(df\left(\tau,T_1\right)df\left(\tau,T_2\right)\right)=\frac{\sigma\left(\tau,T_1\right)\sigma\left(\tau,T_2\right)\psi\left(T_1,T_2\right)}{\sigma\left(\tau,T_1\right)\sigma\left(\tau,T_2\right)}=\psi\left(T_1,T_2\right).$$

As anticipated, we now have two separate functions that we may use to model volatility and correlation.

13.7.5.2 No-arbitrage restrictions

Similarly as in the HJM-Brownian case, let $X_\tau\equiv-\int_\tau^T f\left(\tau,\ell\right)d\ell$. We have

$$dX_\tau=f\left(\tau,\tau\right)d\tau-\int_\tau^T d_\tau f\left(\tau,\ell\right)d\ell=\left(r_\tau-\alpha^I\left(\tau,T\right)\right)d\tau-\int_\tau^T\left[\sigma\left(\tau,\ell\right)d_\tau Z\left(\tau,\ell\right)\right]d\ell,$$

where as usual, $\alpha^I\left(\tau,T\right)\equiv\int_\tau^T\alpha\left(\tau,\ell\right)d\ell$. But $P\left(\tau,T\right)=\exp\left(X_\tau\right)$. Therefore,

$$\begin{aligned}\frac{dP\left(\tau,T\right)}{P\left(\tau,T\right)}&=dX_\tau+\frac{1}{2}var\left(dX_\tau\right)\\&=\left(r_\tau-\alpha^I\left(\tau,T\right)+\frac{1}{2}\int_\tau^T\int_\tau^T\sigma\left(\tau,\ell_1\right)\sigma\left(\tau,\ell_2\right)\psi\left(\ell_1,\ell_2\right)d\ell_1 d\ell_2\right)d\tau\\&\quad-\int_\tau^T\left(\sigma\left(\tau,\ell\right)d_\tau Z\left(\tau,\ell\right)\right)d\ell.\end{aligned}$$

Next, suppose that the stochastic discount factor ξ satisfies

$$\frac{d\xi_\tau}{\xi_\tau}=-r_\tau d\tau-\int_{\mathbb{T}}\phi\left(\tau,T\right)d_\tau Z\left(\tau,T\right)dT,$$

where $\mathbb{T}$ denotes the set of all "risks" spanned by the string Z, and ϕ is the corresponding family of "unit risk premiums."

In absence of arbitrage,

$$0=E\left[d\left(P\xi\right)\right]=E\left[P\xi\cdot\left(\text{drift}\left(\frac{dP}{P}\right)+\text{drift}\left(\frac{d\xi}{\xi}\right)+cov\left(\frac{dP}{P},\frac{d\xi}{\xi}\right)\right)\right].$$

By exploiting the dynamics of P and ξ,

$$\alpha^I\left(\tau,T\right)=\frac{1}{2}\int_\tau^T\int_\tau^T\sigma\left(\tau,\ell_1\right)\sigma\left(\tau,\ell_2\right)\psi\left(\ell_1,\ell_2\right)d\ell_1 d\ell_2+cov\left(\frac{dP}{P},\frac{d\xi}{\xi}\right)/d\tau,$$

where

$$\begin{aligned}cov\left(\frac{dP}{P},\frac{d\xi}{\xi}\right)&=E\left(\int_{\mathbb{T}}\phi\left(\tau,S\right)d_\tau Z\left(\tau,S\right)dS\cdot\int_\tau^T\sigma\left(\tau,\ell\right)d_\tau Z\left(\tau,\ell\right)d\ell\right)\\&=\left(\int_\tau^T\int_{\mathbb{T}}\phi\left(\tau,S\right)\sigma\left(\tau,\ell\right)\psi\left(S,\ell\right)dSd\ell\right)d\tau.\end{aligned}$$

By differentiating α^I with respect to T we obtain,

$$\alpha(\tau,T)=\int_\tau^T \sigma(\tau,\ell)\,\sigma(\tau,T)\,\psi(\ell,T)\,d\ell+\sigma(\tau,T)\int_{\mathbb{T}}\phi(\tau,S)\,\psi(S,T)\,dS. \tag{13.102}$$

A proof of eq. (13.102) is in appendix 13.G.

13.8 Interest Rate Derivatives

This section provides the main definitions and an evaluation framework for the main interest rate derivatives, such as bond options, callable and puttable bonds, interest rate swaps, caps, floors, and swaptions.

We begin by addressing a simple fundamental question (in section 13.8.1). How come interest rate derivatives are so pervasive when, in fact, we know very well that the short-term rate displays little volatility? We explain this apparent puzzle by proposing that the bulk of interest rate volatility occurs for deals relating to long maturities. Granted, the short-term rate is not very volatile in the short term. However, it is very persistent. This persistence can be at the origins of wild volatility of interest rate deals that have larger maturities.

The remaining sections develop evaluation models of interest rate derivatives, which mainly rely on models of the short-term rate, and their perfectly fitting extensions. Section 13.9 contains details of the so-called market model, which is a HJM-style model intensively used by practitioners to evaluate these derivatives.

13.8.1 Persistence and Volatility in Fixed Income Markets

We know that the implied volatility on Treasury bonds with large maturities is quite high, and somehow comparable to the implied volatility in the equity space. Why is this implied volatility so large when, in fact, the volatility of the short-term rate is one order of magnitude less than that in equity markets? This section tackles these issues by elaborating on the notion of *realized* volatility, not implied volatility. To anticipate, the reasons for this high volatility lie in the fact that the short-term rate is very persistent, a sort of a "risk for the long run," similar to some explanations that attempt to rationalize the equity premium puzzle (see chapter 9).

Define, first, the *term structure of volatility*, as the function $\tau\mapsto \mathrm{Vol}(R(\tau))$, where $R(\tau)=-\frac{1}{\tau}\ln P(\tau)$, the yield for maturity τ, $P(\tau)$ is the price of the τ-maturity zero, and $\mathrm{Vol}(R(\tau))$ is the standard deviation of this spot-rate. It is instructive to calculate this volatility in a simple case. Consider the Vasicek model in eq. (13.34); by eq. (13.40), we have that

$$R(\tau)=-\frac{A(\tau)}{\tau}+\frac{1}{\tau}B(\tau)\,r,\quad B(\tau)=\frac{1-e^{-\kappa\tau}}{\kappa},$$

for some function $A(\tau)$. Therefore, we may define the *yield volatility* curve as

$$\mathrm{Vol}(R(\tau))=\frac{1}{\tau}\mathrm{Vol}_\infty(r)\,B(\tau), \tag{13.103}$$

where $\mathrm{Vol}_\infty(r)=\sqrt{\frac{\sigma^2}{2\kappa}}$ is the long-run volatility of the short-term rate. For example, if $\kappa=0.2$ and $\sigma=0.01$, then $\mathrm{Vol}_\infty(r)\approx 0.0158$.

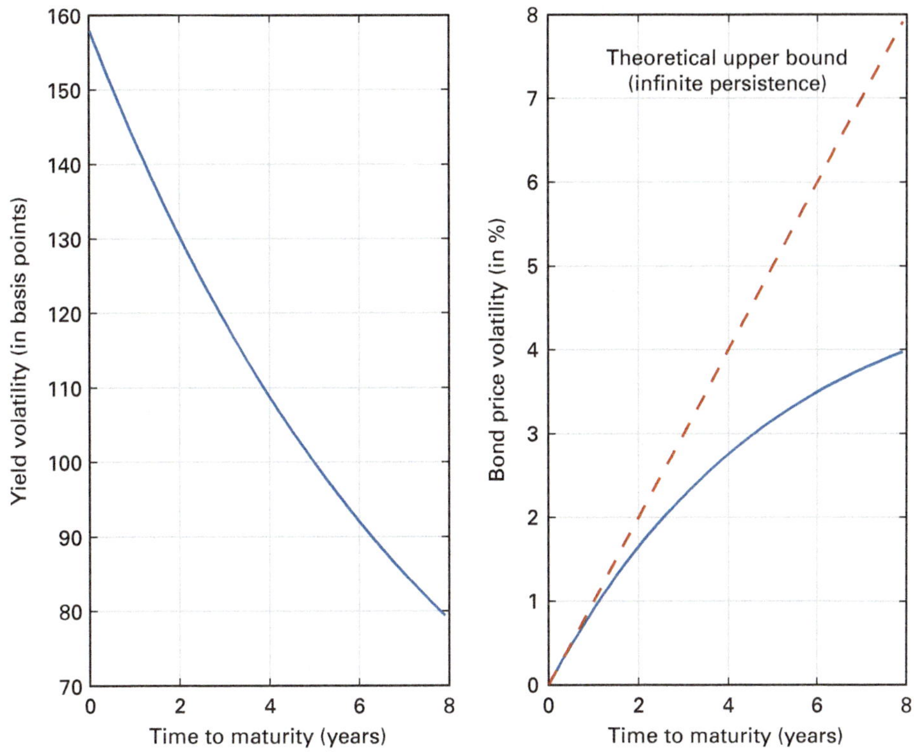

Figure 13.11
Left panel. The yield volatility curve predicted by the Vasicek model, i.e., $\text{Vol}\,(R\,(\tau))$ in eq. (13.103) expressed in basis points, with $\sigma = 0.01$ and $\kappa = 0.02$. Right panel. The term-structure of bond price volatility (solid line), i.e., $\text{Vol}\left(\frac{dP}{P}\right)$ in eq. (13.104) expressed in percentage, with $\kappa = 0.2$; the dashed line depicts the bond price volatility when persistence is infinite, i.e., $\kappa = 0$.

The left panel of figure 13.11 depicts the yield volatility curve, that is, eq. (13.103) expressed in basis points, $100^2 \times \text{Vol}\,(R\,(\tau))$. It is decreasing in time to maturity, attaining its maximum at $100^2 \times \text{Vol}_\infty\,(r) \approx 158$. These properties are natural: in this model, the yield curve flattens out to the asymptotic interest rate and, thus, yield curve volatility collapses to zero, asymptotically.

However, the *volatility of bond returns* can be quite high. Let us illustrate. In the Vasicek model, the dynamics of the bond price are, by Itô's lemma,

$$\frac{dP_t\,(\tau)}{P_t\,(\tau)} = (\cdots)\,dt + (-\sigma \cdot B\,(\tau))\,dW_t.$$

Therefore, the volatility of bond returns is,

$$\text{Vol}\left(\frac{dP}{P}\right) = \sigma B\,(\tau)\,. \tag{13.104}$$

Compare eq. (13.104) with eq. (13.103). The main difference between these two equations is that the RHS of eq. (13.103) is divided by τ, which makes $\text{Vol}\,(R\,(\tau))$ decreasing in τ; otherwise, $\text{Vol}_\infty\,(r)$ and σ have the same order of magnitude. The main point is that the

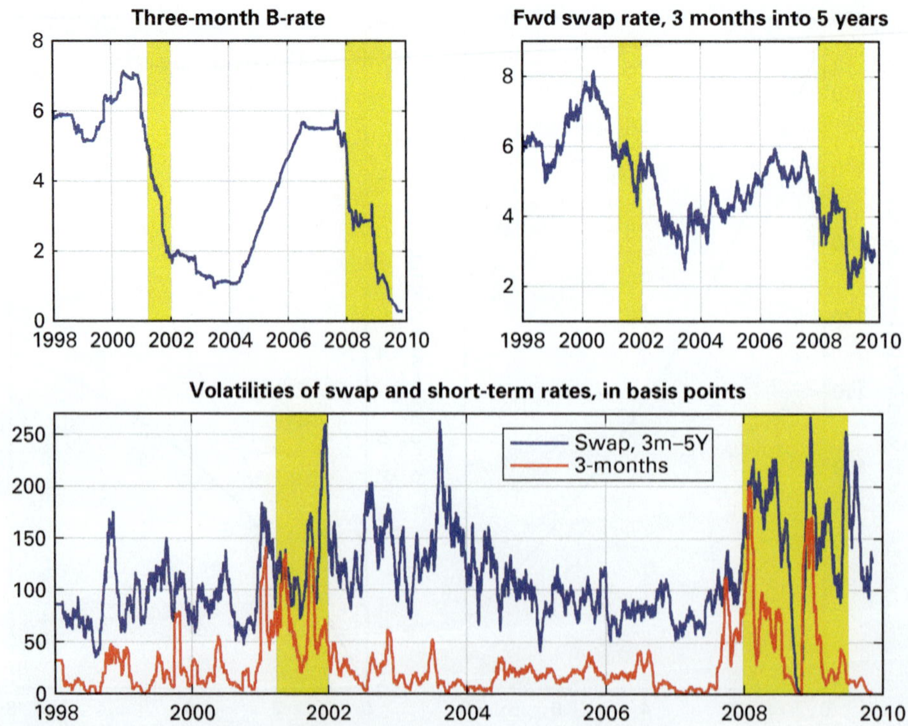

Figure 13.12
Interest rate volatility and deals' maturity. The top panels depict the 3m Bill rate (left) and the 3m–5Y swap rate (right); the 3m–5Y swap rate is constructed through the times series of cross-sections of zeros, based on eq. (13.128) below. The bottom panel depicts basis point volatilities calculated for both the 3m Bill rate and the 3m–5Y swap rate. Data are daily, annualized, and sampled from January 1998 to December 2009. The shaded areas mark recession periods as defined by the National Bureau of Economic Research.

yield $R(\tau)$ is an *average return* guaranteed when the purchased bond is held until expiry. This average return becomes less volatile as time to maturity increases, and tends to a constant. Instead, the bond return, $\frac{dP}{P}$, measures capital gains that can be realized by selling the bond at any time. Its volatility increases with the bond time to maturity. Even if σ is very small, the volatility in eq. (13.104) may be quite high. Assume, as in our examples, that $\sigma = 0.01$ and that κ is close to zero, an hypothetical case of "infinite persistence." In this case, $\text{Vol}\left(\frac{dP}{P}\right) \approx \sigma\tau$, which is 5% for a five year zero. The right panel of figure 13.11 depicts the term structure of bond price volatility, i.e., eq. (13.104) expressed in percentage points, and illustrates these properties in the case $\kappa = 0.2$.

The high persistence of the short-term rate, as measured by a low value of κ, makes long maturity bond returns quite volatile. Intuitively, this high persistence implies that a shock in the short-term rate has long-lasting effects on the future path of the short-term rate. This makes the short-term rate very volatile in the long run, which makes the value of long maturity zeros very volatile as a result. Put differently, interest rates exhibit inertia: (i) it takes a number of shocks to move interest rates away from their equilibrium paths and so, short-term bonds are not volatile; and (ii) it takes time for interest rates to absorb shocks and so, medium-/long-term bonds are volatile. For example, figure 13.12 depicts time series of the three-month rate and the three months into five years (3m–5Y) swap rate, a rate applying to deals that have 5-year maturity (see eq. (13.128) in section 13.8.7), along with their basis point volatilities.[44] The 3m–5Y swap rate is much more volatile than the short-term rate. The bottom panel of figure 13.12 tracks the two realized volatilities and reveals that, in this sample period, the basis point volatility of the 3m–5Y swap rate does consistently and significantly dominate that of the Bill rate. It goes without saying that the theoretical calculations in the right panel of figure 13.11 relate to bond price returns, not to interest rate levels. However, the point of figure 13.11 is very simple: volatility of bond returns and interest rates (not yields) should increase with time to maturity.

These observations are consistent with high levels of "implicit" (not implied) option-based volatility. In section 13.8.4 (see eq. (13.116)), we show that this volatility is

$$v=\sqrt{T-t}\cdot \mathrm{Vol}^{\mathrm{O}}, \quad \mathrm{Vol}^{\mathrm{O}}\equiv\sigma\sqrt{\frac{1-e^{-2\kappa(T-t)}}{2\kappa\,(T-t)}}\frac{1-e^{-\kappa(S-T)}}{\kappa}.$$

As κ gets small, $\mathrm{Vol}^{\mathrm{O}}$ tends to $\sigma\times(S-T)$, which increases with the bond's time to maturity left at its expiration, $S-T$, at the time of the option exercise.

The previous reasoning does, of course, still hold in the more realistic case of a three-factor model, such as that in eqs. (13.66). In that case, as explained, κ_r is large and $\kappa_{\bar{r}}$ is small: the short-term rate is quite persistent because it mean-reverts, quickly, to a persistent process, which we denoted as $\bar{r}_\tau$. Naturally, in such as a three-factor model, eq. (13.104) does not hold anymore, as we should add two more volatility components, related to stochastic volatility, v_τ, and the persistent process $\bar{r}_\tau$. However, bond return volatility would be boosted by the high persistence of $\bar{r}_\tau$.

13.8.2 Hypothetical Continuous Payoffs

Interest rate derivatives could be priced in an elegant way if their payoffs were paid out continuously, hypothetically. Let w denote the price of any such derivative, and $\pi\,(t,r)$ be its instantaneous payoff (a function of calendar time and r). Consider any model of the short-term rate in Section 13.4; to simplify, take $d=1$, such that r_t in eq. (13.26) carries all information. The price w is the solution to the following partial differential equation

$$\frac{\partial w}{\partial\tau}+\bar{b}w_r+\frac{1}{2}a^2w_{rr}+\pi=rw, \quad \text{for all } (r,\tau)\in\mathbb{R}\times[t,T), \tag{13.105}$$

subject to the appropriate boundary conditions. In eq. (13.105), $\bar{b}$ denotes, as usual, the drift of r_t under Q; and π needs to be added to the expected basis point appreciation of w under Q, such that, overall, $\mathbb{E}_t\left(dw\right)+\pi=rw$. While π may be taken to approximate many of the interest rate derivatives payoffs dealt with below, standard evaluation practice relies on payoffs defined in terms of LIBOR-type and, so, discretely compounded,

44. The volatilities in figure 13.12 are measured the same way as in section 13.4.5. Relying on daily data and assuming 25 days per month, we estimate basis point volatility as $\mathrm{Vol}_{x,t}\equiv 100^2\sqrt{\frac{\pi}{2}}\sqrt{300}\cdot\bar{\sigma}_{x,t}$, where $\bar{\sigma}_{x,t}\equiv\frac{1}{25}\sum_{i=1}^{25}\left|x_{t+1-i}-x_{t-i}\right|$, and x_t is the variable of interest on day-t, notably the 3m–5Y swap rate or the three month B-rate.

rates. Moreover, intermediate payments obviously only take place at discrete dates, not continuously.

In this and the following section, we elaborate within a framework that allows us to price interest rate derivatives based on more realistic assumptions than those underlying continuous payoffs. We begin by introducing a basic, but fundamental conceptual pillar in interest rate derivative evaluation: the so-called *forward probability*.

13.8.3 Forward Martingale Probabilities

We know from chapter 4 that asset prices normalized by the money market account are martingales, yet the money market account is not the only numéraire in markets where interest rates are random. Chapter 4 also explains we may use the price of zero coupon bonds as an alternative numéraire, which leads to the notion of *forward probabilities* (see section 4.4). This section develops this notion more closely, and hinges upon it to demonstrate useful results applying to the dynamic of interest rates, not only prices, which will be quite useful when pricing interest rate derivatives.

Consider a forward contract agreed at time t, and let $\varphi_T(t)$ be the T-forward price for a claim S_T at $T > t$. That is, $\varphi_T(t)$ is the price agreed at t, which will be paid at T for delivery of the claim at T, such that the agreement is worthless at t. Clearly,

$$0 = \mathbb{E}_t\left(e^{-\int_t^T r_u du}\left(S_T - \varphi_T(t)\right)\right).$$

But since $\varphi_T(t)$ is known at time t,

$$\mathbb{E}_t\left(e^{-\int_t^T r_u du} S_T\right) = \varphi_T(t)\, \mathbb{E}_t\left(e^{-\int_t^T r_u du}\right). \tag{13.106}$$

For example, assume S is the price of a *traded* asset, such that $\mathbb{E}_t(e^{-\int_t^T r_u du} S_T) = S_t$: Eq. (13.106) then collapses to the well-known formula: $\varphi_T(t)\, P(t,T) = S_t$ (as explained in chapter 11). Yet and as also explained in chapter 11, entering the forward contract originated at t, at a later date $\tau > t$, costs. To calculate the marking to market of the forward at time τ, note that the final payoff at time T is $S_T - \varphi_T(t)$. Discounting this payoff at $\tau \in [t,T]$ delivers $P(\tau,T)[\varphi_T(\tau) - \varphi_T(t)]$.

Next, let us elaborate on eq. (13.106). We can use the basic bond pricing equation (13.2) in section 13.2, and rearrange terms in eq. (13.106), to obtain:

$$\varphi_T(t) = \mathbb{E}_t\left(\frac{e^{-\int_t^T r_u du}}{P(t,T)} S_T\right) = \mathbb{E}_t\left(\eta_T(T) S_T\right), \tag{13.107}$$

where

$$\eta_T(T) \equiv \frac{e^{-\int_t^T r_u du}}{P(t,T)}.$$

Eq. (13.107) suggests that we can define a new probability Q_F^T, as follows

$$\eta_T(T) = \left.\frac{dQ_F^T}{dQ}\right|_{\mathbb{F}_T} \equiv \frac{e^{-\int_t^T r_u du}}{\mathbb{E}_t\left(e^{-\int_t^T r_u du}\right)}, \tag{13.108}$$

where $\mathbb{F}_T$ denotes the information set up to time T. Naturally, $\mathbb{E}_t[\eta_T(T)]=1$. Moreover, if the short-term rate process is deterministic, $\eta_T(T)$ equals one and Q and Q_F^T are the same.

In terms of this new probability Q_F^T, the forward price $\varphi_T(t)$ is:

$$\varphi_T(t)=\mathbb{E}_t(\eta_T(T)\cdot S_T)=\int(\eta_T(T)\cdot S_T)\,dQ=\int S_T dQ_F^T=\mathbb{E}_{Q_F^T}(S_T), \tag{13.109}$$

where $\mathbb{E}_{Q_F^T}(\cdot)$ is conditional expectation at t under Q_F^T. For reasons clarified in a moment, Q_F^T is referred to as the T-forward probability. Clearly, $\varphi_T(T)=S_T$. Therefore, eq. (13.109) is, also,

$$\varphi_T(t)=\mathbb{E}_{Q_F^T}(\varphi_T(T)).$$

That is, forward prices are martingales under the forward probability—whence, the expression, forward *martingale* probability, which we shall shorten to forward probability to simplify the presentation. Naturally, and as usual, future prices are martingales under the risk neutral probability, not the forward probability, as explained in chapter 11.

The forward probability is a useful tool, which helps pricing interest-rate derivatives, as we shall explain in detail below. It was introduced by Geman (1989) and Jamshidian (1989), and further analyzed by Geman, El Karoui, and Rochet (1995). Appendix 13.B provides additional details, and also relates forward prices to some certainty equivalents. We now rely on this probability to facilitate the calculation of options on bonds.

13.8.4 European Options on Bonds

13.8.4.1 A bond option pricing formula

Let T be the expiration date of a European call option on a zero coupon bond, and $S>T$ the expiration date of the bond. We consider a simple model of the short-term rate with $d=1$, such that the price of a zero is $P(r,\tau,S)$, with the usual notation. Consider the price of an option on this bond, maturing at T and with strike equal to K. It equals

$$C^b(r,t,T,S)=\mathbb{E}_t\left[e^{-\int_t^T r_\tau d\tau}\left(P(r_T,T,S)-K\right)^+\right]. \tag{13.110}$$

Finding a closed-form solution for this price looks formidable. Note indeed that C^b is the solution to a partial differential equation, subject to the boundary condition $C^b(r,T,T,S)=(P(r,T,S)-K)^+$, where $P(r,\tau,S)$ is also solution to another partial differential equation. Relying on the forward probability allows us to simplify this problem.

Let us, then, elaborate on eq. (13.110). The main issue we encounter is that the payoff $(P(r_T,T,S)-K)^+$ depends on r_T, and yet the discounting factor, $e^{-\int_t^T r_\tau d\tau}$, would also obviously depend on the realization of the short-term rate. As discussed in chapter 4, it is a general issue arising when evaluating fixed-income instruments, as interest rates are obviously random in this context. We overcome these details while turning the risk neutral expectation in (13.110) into the forward. That is, and denoting $P_T=P(r_T,T,S)$,

$$\begin{aligned}&C^b(r_t,t,T,S)\\&=\mathbb{E}_t\left(e^{-\int_t^T r_\tau d\tau}P(r_T,T,S)\cdot\mathbb{I}_{P_T\geq K}\right)-K\cdot\mathbb{E}_t\left(e^{-\int_t^T r_\tau d\tau}\cdot\mathbb{I}_{P_T\geq K}\right)\end{aligned}$$

$$= P(r_t, t, S) \cdot \mathbb{E}_t\left(\frac{e^{-\int_t^S r_\tau d\tau}}{P(r_t, t, S)} \cdot \mathbb{I}_{P_T \geq K}\right) - KP(r_t, t, T) \cdot \mathbb{E}_t\left(\frac{e^{-\int_t^T r_\tau d\tau}}{P(r_t, t, T)} \cdot \mathbb{I}_{P_T \geq K}\right)$$

$$= P(r_t, t, S) \cdot \mathbb{E}_{Q_F^S}\left(\mathbb{I}_{P_T \geq K}\right) - KP(r_t, t, T) \cdot \mathbb{E}_{Q_F^T}\left(\mathbb{I}_{P_T \geq K}\right)$$

$$= P(r_t, t, S) \cdot Q_F^S\left[P(r_T, T, S) \geq K\right] - KP(r_t, t, T) \cdot Q_F^T\left[P(r_T, T, S) \geq K\right], \quad (13.111)$$

where the second equality follows by a standard calculation,[45] Q_F^i is the i-forward probability, $i = T, S$; and, finally, $\mathbb{E}_{Q_F^i}(\cdot)$ is the expectation under the i-forward martingale probability.

The option pricing formula in (13.111) may be considered as the bond counterpart to Black–Scholes's formula. More generally, this formula and the steps toward its derivation extend those provided in chapter 11 in the equity case (see Eq. (11.10)). Eq. (13.111) is indeed the difference between two terms. The first is the product of the underlying asset price, $P(r_t, t, S)$, and a certain probability that the underlying asset is exercised, $Q_F^S[P(r_T, T, S) \geq K]$; the second is the discounted strike, $KP(r_t, t, T)$, times the probability that the underlying asset is exercised, $Q_F^T[P(r_T, T, S) \geq K]$, where Q_F^T is the probability under which the discounted underlying price is a martingale.

Below, we provide an important instance in which the probabilities in eq. (13.111) can be calculated in closed-form, based on the assumption that the short-term rate is Gaussian (see eqs. (13.115)). We actually present two models with a closed-form solution, one developed in a seminal paper by Jamshidian (1989), and the second one, simply, its perfectly fitting extension. We shall primarily deal with call options although the pricing of put options will be easily derived through a put-call parity, given next.

13.8.4.2 *A put-call parity arising in government bond markets*

Consider the identity

$$(K - P(T, S))^+ \equiv (P(T, S) - K)^+ + K - P(T, S), \quad T \leq S.$$

Taking the risk neutral, discounted expectations of both sides of this equation leaves,

$$\mathbb{E}_t\left(e^{-\int_t^T r_\tau d\tau}(K - P(T, S))^+\right)$$

$$= \mathbb{E}_t\left(e^{-\int_t^T r_\tau d\tau}(P(T, S) - K)\right)^+ + P(t, T)K - \mathbb{E}_t\left(e^{-\int_t^T r_\tau d\tau}P(T, S)\right)$$

$$= \mathbb{E}_t\left(e^{-\int_t^T r_\tau d\tau}(P(T, S) - K)\right)^+ + P(t, T)K - P(t, S),$$

45. By the law of iterated expectations,

$$\mathbb{E}_t\left[e^{-\int_t^T r_\tau d\tau}P(r_T, T, S)\mathbb{I}_{P_T \geq K}\right] = \mathbb{E}_t\left[e^{-\int_t^T r_\tau d\tau}\mathbb{I}_{P_T \geq K}\mathbb{E}_T\left(e^{-\int_T^S r_\tau d\tau}\right)\right] = \mathbb{E}_t\left[e^{-\int_t^S r_\tau d\tau}\mathbb{I}_{P_T \geq K}\right].$$

where the last equality follows by the same argument leading to eq. (13.111). Therefore, we have the put-call parity relation:

$$\text{Put}\,(t,T;P\,(t,S)\,,K)=\text{Call}\,(t,T;P\,(t,S)\,,K)+P\,(t,T)\,K-P\,(t,S)\,, \tag{13.112}$$

where $\text{Put}\,(t,T;P\,(t,S)\,,K)$ is the price of a European put written on a zero-coupon bond expiring at time S, expiring at time $T<S$, and struck at K, and $\text{Call}\,(\cdot)$ denotes the corresponding call price.

13.8.4.3 *Jamshidian-Vasicek model*

Next, suppose that the short-term rate is the solution to the Vasicek model considered in section 13.4 (see eq. (13.34)), such that under the risk neutral probability,

$$dr_t=\kappa\left(r^*-r_t\right)d\tau+\sigma d\tilde{W}_t,$$

where $\tilde{W}_t$ is a Q-Brownian motion and $r^*\equiv\bar{r}-\frac{\lambda\sigma}{\kappa}$, and remaining notation is as in section 13.4.4. As we know from Section 13.4, Eq. (13.38), the price of a zero predicted by the model is $P\,(r_\tau,\tau,S)=e^{A(\tau,S)-B(\tau,S)r_\tau}$, for some function A, and $B\,(t,T)=\frac{1}{\kappa}\left(1-e^{-\kappa(T-t)}\right)$. In section 13.6 (see eq. (13.77)), it was also argued (and eq. (13.111) proves) that the price of a European option on a zero is

$$\begin{aligned}C^b\,(r_t,K;t,T,S)&=\mathbb{E}_t\left(e^{-\int_t^T r_\tau d\tau}\,(P(r_T,T,S)-K)^+\right)\\&=P(r_t,t,S)\cdot Q_F^S\,[P(r_T,T,S)\geq K]-KP(r_t,t,T)\cdot Q_F^T\,[P(r_T,T,S)\geq K]\,,\end{aligned} \tag{13.113}$$

where Q_F^T denotes the T-forward probability.

In appendix 13.H, we show that the two probabilities in eq. (13.113) can be evaluated by the *changes of numéraire* described in section 13.8.3, such that the solution for $P\,(r,T,S)$ is

$$P\,(r,T,S)=\begin{cases}\dfrac{P\,(r,t,S)}{P\,(r,t,T)}e^{-\frac{1}{2}\sigma^2\int_t^T[B(\tau,S)-B(\tau,T)]^2d\tau-\sigma\int_t^T[B(\tau,S)-B(\tau,T)]dW_\tau^{Q_F^T}}, & \text{under } Q_F^T\\[2ex]\dfrac{P\,(r,t,S)}{P\,(r,t,T)}e^{\frac{1}{2}\sigma^2\int_t^T[B(\tau,S)-B(\tau,T)]^2d\tau-\sigma\int_t^T[B(\tau,S)-B(\tau,T)]dW_\tau^{Q_F^S}}, & \text{under } Q_F^S\end{cases} \tag{13.114}$$

where $W^{Q_F^T}$ is a Brownian motion under the forward probability Q_F^T. Therefore, by simple algebra,

$$\begin{aligned}&Q_F^S\,[P\,(r,T,S)\geq K]=\Phi\left(d_1\right),\quad Q_F^T\,[P\,(r,T,S)\geq K]=\Phi\left(d_1-v\right),\\&d_1=\frac{\ln\frac{P(r_t,t,S)}{KP(r_t,t,T)}+\frac{1}{2}v^2}{v},\end{aligned} \tag{13.115}$$

where

$$v^2=\sigma^2\int_t^T\left[B\,(\tau,S)-B\,(\tau,T)\right]^2d\tau=\sigma^2\frac{1-e^{-2\kappa(T-t)}}{2\kappa}B^2\,(T,S)\,. \tag{13.116}$$

This elegant solution for the bond option price resembles Black–Scholes formula in the equity space. The difference is that, in Black–Scholes, the volatility of the underlying is given. In the present context, bond price volatility is also given, but it links to both the short-term rate volatility, σ, and the price sensitivity to changes in the short-term rate, $B(t, T)$. The latter depends on the speed of mean-reversion, κ, which is particularly important: the higher the persistence (i.e., the lower κ), the higher bond price volatility and, hence, the option price.

In practice, options on zero coupon bonds are not currently traded. Instead, options on coupon bearing bonds are traded, over-the-counter. These options are dealt with in section 13.8.6. Chicago Mercantile Exchange lists options on the US Treasury Ten-Year note futures, which are priced and analyzed in detail by Mele, Obayashi, and Yang (2020). However, the bond option pricing model dealt with in this section is a very useful starting point for pricing more complex products. It also allows us to understand some basic properties, discussed in a moment, which extend to more complex models in less hypothetical situations.

Figure 13.13 depicts the call option price against both the short-term rate and the underlying bond price, based on the parameter values used in figure 13.4. It is decreasing in the short-term rate, due to the inverse relation between bond prices and interest rates in this model. Note that option prices increase as persistence increases: the solid lines are prices calculated while assuming a speed of mean reversion $\kappa = 0.20$; the dashed lines are prices calculated with an increased persistence, that is, with $\kappa = 0.10$.[46] In this comparative statics exercise, option prices do uniformly increase as κ lowers, consistent with earlier explanations on bond price volatility: higher persistence leads to higher uncertainty and, hence, makes options more valuable.

13.8.4.4 *Perfectly fitting extension*

Brigo and Mercurio (2006) survey a number of perfectly fitting models that go well beyond that in the previous section. The simplest relies on the Hull and White (1990) model in eq. (13.84) of section 13.6.3. Note that while eq. (13.110) is formally the same as in the previous section, the value of more complex derivatives depends on whether we use or not a perfectly fitting extension, as section 13.8.6 explains in further detail.

13.8.5 Callable Bonds and Convexity Risks

This section relies on a continuous time model to illustrate a few, key properties of callable and puttable bonds. As explained in chapter 12 (see section 12.7) *callable* bonds are assets that give the issuer the right to buy them back at certain times and predetermined prices; *puttable bonds*, instead, give the investor the right to sell them back to the issuer at certain times and strikes. Chapter 12 explains the pricing mechanism regarding these assets within a discrete time framework in which the option exercise is of the American type, relying on binomial trees. This section only considers European-style options (and zero coupon bonds), but leads to clear predictions and analytical evaluation formulae. For simplicity,

---

46. Note that, in figure 13.13, a decrease in κ implies a wider range of values taken by the underlying bond price, $P(r_t, t, S)$.

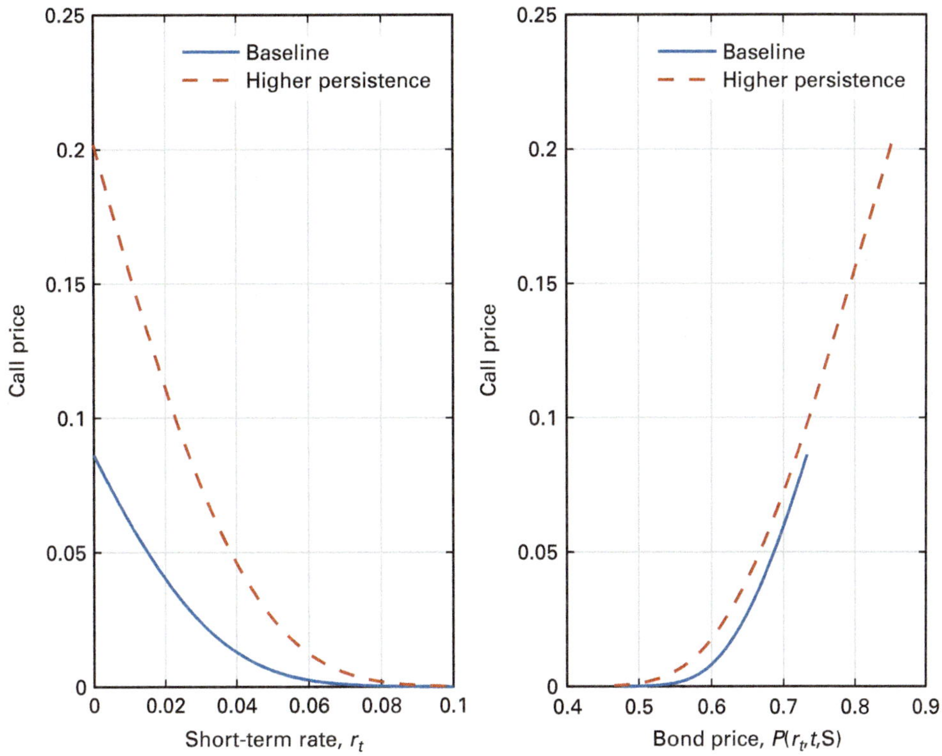

Figure 13.13
The price of a European call option written on a pure discount bond, $C^b(r_t, K; t, T, S)$ in eq. (13.113). Left and right panels depict the option price as a function of the short-term rate, r_t, and the bond price, $P(r_t, t, S)$, resp. The bond has a maturity $S-t=10$ years, and the option expires in six months and has a strike price $K=0.65$. Solid lines depict prices based on the Jamshidian-Vasicek model, with parameter values fixed to those in figure 13.4. Dashed lines depict prices calculated assuming a lower speed of mean reversion, $\kappa=0.10$.

we consider *nondefaultable* bonds. We review some pricing details of callable bonds and also some implications regarding hedging activity around these products and feedback effects.

13.8.5.1 Evaluation

Consider, first, a callable bond maturing at S, and let K be the strike at which the bond may be called. Suppose that the date of exercise, if any, is some future time $T<S$. Repeating some of the reasoning in chapter 12, assume exercise, in which case the issuer can buy its bonds back at K and reissue a zero coupon bond at better market conditions, P, where P denotes, as usual, the price of a *noncallable* bond. The difference, $P-K$, is just a net gain for the issuer. Therefore, the callable bond is worth K when $K<P$. Instead, if $K>P$, the issuer does not have any incentives to exercise and, then, the value of the callable bond is just that of a noncallable bond. Therefore, the callable bond is worth P when $K>P$. To sum up, the value at T of a callable bond is $\min\{P(T,S), K\}$. It easy to see that,

$$\min\{P, K\} = P - \max\{P-K, 0\}.$$

Therefore, we see that the price of a *callable* bond with maturity date S, equals the price of a *noncallable* bond with the same maturity date S, minus the value to call the bond, which equals the price of an hypothetical call option on the *noncallable* bond, struck at K.

We can apply these insights to price a callable bond in a concrete example. Consider, for example, the Vasicek model of the short-term rate. Then, if the short-term rate is r_t at time t, the value at time t of the nondefaultable zero coupon bond maturing at time S, callable at time $T < S$, at a strike price equal to K, is

$$P^{\text{callable}}(r_t, K; t, T, S) = P(r_t, t, S) - \text{Call}^b(r_t, K; t, T, S), \tag{13.117}$$

where $P(r_t, t, S)$ is the value of the *noncallable* zero maturing at time S, and $\text{Call}^b(r_t, K; t, T, S)$ is the value of a call option on the *noncallable* S-zero, maturing at time T and having a strike price equal to K. Eq. (13.117) shows that the presence of the option to call the bond raises the cost of capital for the issuer. Note that, assuming the short-term rate is as in the Vasicek market, the call option in eq. (13.117) is $\text{Call}^b(r_t, K; t, T, S) = C^b(r_t, K; t, T, S)$, that is, the Jamshidian's (1989) formula in eq. (13.113). In the next subsection, we shall use this framework and evaluate the callable bond, $P^{\text{callable}}(r_t, K; t, T, S)$, as well as additional attributes of this bond: duration and volatility.

The evaluation of puttable bonds proceeds along similar lines as those for callable bonds. As anticipated in chapter 12 (see section 12.7), the payoff at the expiration of the bondholders right to tender the bonds is

$$\max\{P, K\} = P + \max\{K - P, 0\},$$

where P is the price of a non-puttable bond. We can use, again, the Vasicek model to price the previous payoff. The price at t of a nondefaultable zero coupon bond maturing at time S, puttable at time $T < S$, at a strike price equal to K, when the short-term rate is r_t, is

$$\begin{aligned} P^{\text{puttable}}(r_t, K; t, T, S) &= P(r_t, t, S) + \text{Put}^b(r_t, K; t, T, S) \\ &= \text{Call}^b(r_t, K; t, T, S) + P(r_t, t, T)\, K, \end{aligned}$$

where $P(r_t, t, S)$ is the value of the *nonputtable* zero maturing at time S; $\text{Put}^b(r_t, K; t, T, S)$ is the value of a put option on the *nonputtable* zero maturing at S, maturing at T, and with strike equal to K; and the second equality follows by the put-call parity of eq. (13.112), with $\text{Call}^b(r_t, K; t, T, S)$ defined as in eq. (13.117).

13.8.5.2 *Stochastic duration*

Figure 13.14 depicts the behavior of the callable bond price in eq. (13.117), $P^{\text{callable}}(r_t, K; t, T, S)$, as a function of the short-term rate, r_t, for an exercise price $K = 0.65$, option maturity $T = 0.5$, and the bond maturity $S = 10$. To evaluate eq. (13.117), we make use of the closed-form solution in eqs. (13.38) and (13.113).

Figure 13.14 clearly illustrates that the convexity of the noncallable bond price is destroyed by the convexity of the price of the option embedded in the callable bond (see figure 13.13). Intuitively, as the short-term rate lowers, callable and noncallable bond prices increase. However, the price of callable bonds increases less, because, as bond prices

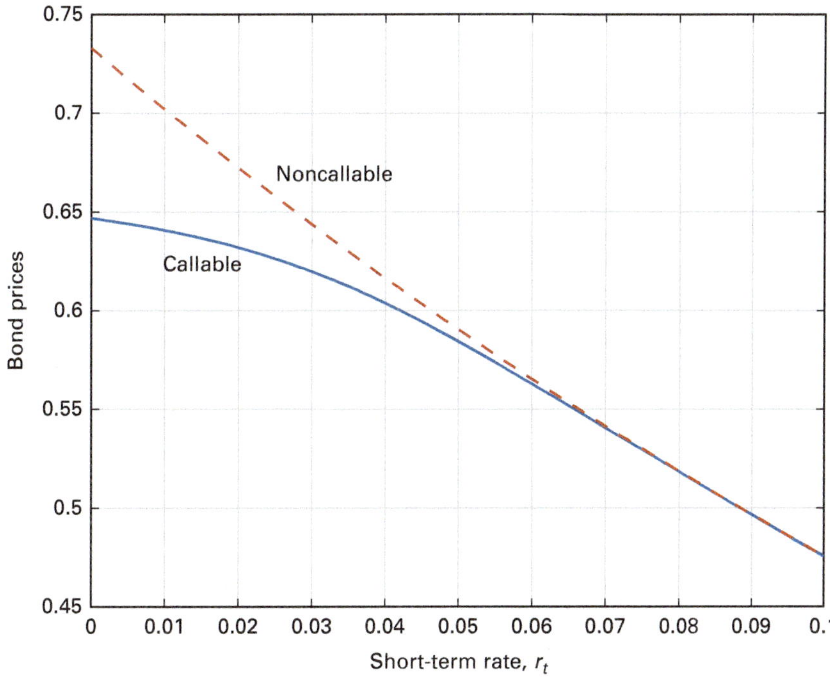

Figure 13.14
"Negative convexity." Solid line: the price of a callable bond. Dashed line: the price of a noncallable bond. The bond has a maturity $S-t=10$ years and can be called in six months at a strike $K=0.65$. Prices are based on the Jamshidian-Vasicek model and parameter values are the same as in figure 13.4. Negative convexity is the property the callable bond price exhibits vis-à-vis the short-term rate r_t.

increase, the probability the issuer will exercise the option increases. As a result, the risk neutral probability of the callable bond price shifts toward the strike price, $K=0.65$, implying a progressively lower decay rate for the price when r_t is low.

What is the duration of a callable bond? Roughly, when interest rates are sufficiently high, a 10-year callable bond resembles its conventional counterpart, because even a likely decrease in the yield curve would not lead the bond-issuer to redeem its debt at the strike price. The two bond prices (and their duration) diverge when interest rates become relatively smaller. To formalize this intuition, we determine the stochastic duration of the callable bond predicted by this model, based on eq. (13.33) (see section 13.4.3). For the Vasicek model, the semi-elasticity of the noncallable bond price with respect to r is $\Psi(r,T-t)=-\frac{1}{\kappa}\left(1-e^{-\kappa(T-t)}\right)$; its inverse with respect to time to maturity is

$$\Psi^{-1}(x)=-\frac{1}{\kappa}\ln(1+\kappa x).$$

Therefore, by eq. (13.33), the stochastic duration of the callable bond predicted by the Vasicek model is

$$D(r,t,T,S)=-\frac{1}{\kappa}\ln\left(1+\kappa\frac{P_r(r,t,S)-C_r^b(r,t,T,S)}{P(r,t,S)-C^b(r,t,T,S)}\right), \tag{13.118}$$

where subscripts denote partial derivatives. In appendix 13.I, we show that

$$C_r^b(r,K;t,T,S) = P_r(r,t,S)\,\Phi(d_1) - KP_r(r,t,T)\,\Phi(d_1 - v), \qquad (13.119)$$

where d_1 and v are as in eqs. (13.115) and (13.116). Appendix 13.I makes use of the previous expression and provides a closed-form solution for eq. (13.118) (see eq. (13.A21)).

Figure 13.15 (left panel) depicts the stochastic duration of the callable bond as a function of the initial level of the short-term rate, r_t, that is, $D(r_t,t,T,S)$ in eq. (13.118). As expected, stochastic duration increases with the level of r_t and, eventually, flattens out to 10 years when the short-term rate reaches a sufficiently high level to make exercise unlikely in six months.

13.8.5.3 Convexity risks

The right panel of figure 13.15 depicts the instantaneous volatility of the callable bond price. By Itô's lemma, it is

$$\text{Vol}(r_t,t,T,S) \equiv -\sigma \frac{P_r(r,t,S) - C_r^b(r,t,T,S)}{P(r,t,S) - C^b(r,t,T,S)}. \qquad (13.120)$$

Note that this volatility is increasing in the short-term rate, reflecting negative convexity:[47] prices move more when the short-term rate is high than when it is low because prices flatten out when interest rates are low, reflecting prepayment risk. Eventually, when prepayment risk is negligible, volatility flattens out to its upper bound, which is the price of a conventional bond.

These properties may help understand market behavior. Consider an economy in the process of recovering from a recession, with interest rates that are, then, increasing. During this process, the expected losses in a callable bond become more severe: by construction, the term $\text{Vol}(r_t,t,T,S)$ in (13.120) measures the sensitivity of the callable bond price with respect to changes in the short-term rate, and is proportional to the semi-elasticity of the price with respect to r_t.

How can investors find protection from these losses? One possibility is to take opposite positions that are proportional to the duration of the callable bond; for example, in the previous chapter (see section 12.3.3), we explained that, in an environment with raising interest rates, going short on conventional bonds may help mitigate losses in the market for mortgage-backed securities. We also explained that this hedging activity may lead to endogenous risk, or "feedback effects": as interest rates go up, more conventional bonds are sold, which makes interest rates rise more. Another possibility is that holders of convexity risks transfer these risks in the first place, by purchasing an interest rate option (say a call) to compensate for the short position embedded in the callable bond. It is indeed practice in the mortgage market, as we now explain, and also likely to lead to feedback effects.

47. We have defined volatility in absolute terms, due to the usual inverse relation between bond prices and interest rates.

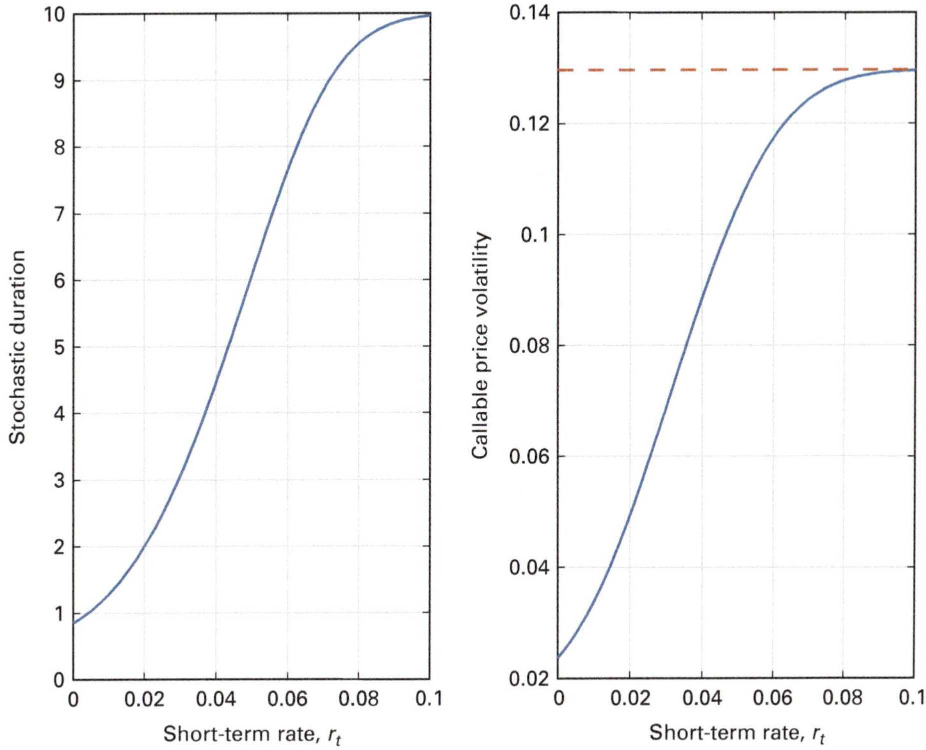

Figure 13.15
The left panel depicts the stochastic duration for a callable bond with time to maturity $S-t=10$ years, which can be called in six months at a strike $K=0.65$, i.e., $D(r,t,T,S)$ in eq. (13.118). The right panel depicts the instantaneous volatility of the same callable bond (solid line), i.e., $\text{Vol}(r_t,t,T,S)$ in eq. (13.120); the dashed line is the instantaneous volatility of a straight, non-callable bond price, i.e., $B(t,S)$ in eq. (13.38), and equals 13%. Prices are based on the Jamshidian-Vasicek model and parameter values are the same as in figure 13.4.

13.8.5.4 The mortgage market and the price of fixed income volatility

Mortgage-backed securities are securities with payoffs linked to the performance of an underlying mortgage pool, as reviewed in more detail in the next chapter. Their reference to mortgages makes them similar to callable bonds: holding a mortgage-backed security is, somehow, equivalent to buying a noncallable bond and selling an interest linked prepayment option. Let us explain.

In the early days, mortgages were extended for the relatively short-term and had consequently had to be frequently refinanced. During the Great Depression, when the housing market was falling precipitously, many borrowers lost access to the credit market (they could not roll over their debts) as a result of lowered collateral values as well as defaults in the very banking system. The borrowers' defaults would result into foreclosures and, then, a further negative price pressure in the housing market, over a vicious circle. The Federal National Mortgage Association (Fannie Mae) was created in 1938 in an attempt to liberate borrowers from house price volatility and increase house evaluations, by promoting long-term mortgages (up to 30 years) and fixed rates within local banks throughout financial support of the US Federal Government, and providing borrowers with prepayment options. These optionalities were very important, as they would accommodate borrowers' needs for geographic mobility, needs that have been typically high in the US.[48]

Prepayment is the feature that makes mortgages like callable bonds. The bank originating a loan, or the holder of a mortgage-backed security, has sold this option to the borrower. This option to prepay creates negative convexity. Concerns regarding negative convexity may act as an amplification mechanism. How? Some investors long in the mortgage market (e.g., servicers or large hedge funds)[49] may not wish to be short negative convexity risk, either due to risk aversion or, as explained in a moment, due to speculative reasons. These investors, then, offset expected changes due to prepayments by trading interest rate swaps. Alternatively, and importantly, these investors transfer convexity risks to dealers, a channel we now describe in more detail.

The hot potato is with the dealers, now. But dealers hedge. They have sold a "call option" such as that in figures 13.13 and 13.14 (for example, a swaption or some other interest rate sensitive derivative of the type studied in this chapter); they now manage the risk through dynamic hedging. Dynamic hedging may create feedback effects of the type identified in chapter 11 (see section 11.10): selling a call to the initial investors is positive gamma, leading dealers "to buy on the way up and to sell on the way down" over the performance of their hedging activity.

Thus, for example, when US interest rates are increasing, dealers may well hedge while selling US Treasuries or Eurodollar futures. This activity pushes interest rates into the direction they are moving, and may create additional volatility. Note that the origins of these episodes may not necessarily link to risk aversion. A hedge fund may speculate on mispriced mortgage-based securities. To illustrate, the fund may have originated long negative convexity, with the call it had implicitly sold being very expensive, compared to the call it may, then, buy from dealers. The process described earlier remains absolutely the same: once the dealers sell an option to the fund, they may, then, wish to hedge against it, creating volatility.

The story may not end here. This additional volatility may lead sophisticated market participants to anticipate a period of increased volatility, and to speculate on it, while purchasing insurance for interest rate volatility (straddles, for example). But demand for insurance against future fixed income market volatility may lead *implied* volatilities to increase, and these increased costs may, then, render fixed income portfolios quite expensive to hedge, creating the premises for additional difficulties. Endogenous risk and stability in fixed income markets may well be issues that macro-prudential authorities should take into account in a scenario with increasing rates.

13.8.6 Options on Fixed Coupon Bonds

For simplicity, we shall ignore issues regarding coupon accruals, and assume the expiration date of these options occurs at any of the coupon payment (or reset) dates. Therefore,

48. In the next chapter (see section 14.3.5), we shall discuss additional roles that Fannie Mae played in the process of securitization of these mortgages since the 1970s.

49. Or, in terms of the callable bond example, the investors who have bought the callable bond.

the payoff of an option maturing at T_0 on a fixed coupon bond paying off at dates $T_1, \cdots, T_n$ is

$$(P_{\text{fcb}}(T_0,T_n)-K)^+ = \left(P(T_0,T_n)+\sum_{i=1}^{n} c_i P(T_0,T_i)-K\right)^+. \tag{13.121}$$

Evaluating the expectation of the payoff in eq. (13.121) is somehow problematic: the maximum between zero and a sum is obviously not in general the same as the sum of the maxima between zero and each element of the sum. Even with a model in which bond prices are log-normal, the sum of log-normals is not log-normal. However, this issue can be dealt with through a well-known trick, described next.

Consider any of the models of the short-term rate reviewed in section 13.4, by which the price of a zero is some function $P(t,T)=P(r,t,T)$. Assume that $P(r,T,T)$ is decreasing in r,[50] such that (under additional conditions) there exists a unique value of r, say $r^*(K)$, which solves the following equation

$$P\left(r^*(K),T_0,T_n\right)+\sum_{i=1}^{n} c_i P\left(r^*(K),T_0,T_i\right)=K. \tag{13.122}$$

The payoff in eq. (13.121) can then be written as:

$$\left(\sum_{i=1}^{n}\bar{c}_i P\left(r_{T_0},T_0,T_i\right)-K\right)^+ = \left(\sum_{i=1}^{n}\bar{c}_i\left(P\left(r_{T_0},T_0,T_i\right)-P\left(r^*(K),T_0,T_i\right)\right)\right)^+,$$

where $\bar{c}_i = c_i$, $i=1,\cdots,n-1$, and $\bar{c}_n = 1+c_n$.

Next, note that the terms $P\left(r_{T_0},T_0,T_i\right)-P\left(r^*(K),T_0,T_i\right)$ have all the same sign for all i.[51] Therefore, the payoff in eq. (13.121) is

$$\left(\sum_{i=1}^{n}\bar{c}_i P(r_{T_0},T_0,T_i)-K\right)^+ = \sum_{i=1}^{n}\bar{c}_i\cdot\left(P(r_{T_0},T_0,T_i)-\mathcal{K}_i^*(K)\right)^+,$$
$$\mathcal{K}_i^*(K)\equiv P\left(r^*(K),T_0,T_i\right). \tag{13.123}$$

Each term of the sum in eq. (13.123) can be evaluated as an option on a pure discount bond with strike price equal to $P(r^*(K),T_0,T_i)$, where the threshold $r^*(K)$ is found numerically. The device for reducing the problem of an option on a fixed coupon bond to a problem involving the sum of options on zero coupon bonds was invented by Jamshidian (1989).

The price of the call on the fixed coupon bond is, therefore

$$\overline{\text{Call}}\left(t,T_0;P_{\text{fcb}}(t,T_n),K,v\right)=\sum_{i=1}^{n}\bar{c}_i\cdot\text{Call}\left(t,T_0;P(t,T_i),\mathcal{K}_i^*(K),v_i\right), \tag{13.124}$$

50. Bond prices are indeed always decreasing in the short-term rate in all one-factor stationary, Markov models of the short-term rate. However, this is not a general property in multifactor models (see Mele, 2003).

51. Suppose that $P(r_{T_0},T_0,T_1)>P(r^*,T_0,T_1)$. Because $P(\cdot,T_0,T_1)$ is decreasing, $r_{T_0}<r^*$. Hence, $P(r_{T_0},T_0,T_i)>P(r^*,T_0,T_i)$ for each i.

where r^* solves eq. (13.122), and

$$\text{Call}\left(t,T_0;P_i,\mathcal{K}_i^*(K),v_i\right)=P_i\Phi\left(d_{1,i}\right)-\mathcal{K}_i^*(K)\,P(t,T_0)\,\Phi\left(d_{1,i}-v_i\right),$$

$$d_{1,i}=\frac{\ln\frac{P_i}{\mathcal{K}_i^*(K)P(t,T_0)}+\frac{1}{2}v_i^2}{v_i},\quad v_i=\sigma\sqrt{\frac{1-e^{-2\kappa(T_0-t)}}{2\kappa}}B(T_0,T_i),\quad B(t,T)=\frac{1}{\kappa}\left(1-e^{-\kappa(T-t)}\right).$$

The price of a put can then be determined through the put-call parity in eq. (13.112).

Why are perfectly fitting models so important in practice? Suppose that in eq. (13.122), the critical value r^* is determined through Vasicek's model. This assumption is attractive because it leads to evaluate the payoff in eq. (13.124) through Jamshidian's formula of section 13.8.4, precisely as we have just done. However, this way of proceeding does not ensure that the yield curve is perfectly fitted. The natural alternative is to use the corresponding perfectly fitting extension, the Hull and White model in section 13.6.3, i.e., eq. (13.84), and use its price to calibrate r^* in eq. (13.122). Note, now, the importance of a perfectly fitting model. Both Jamshidian and its perfectly fitting extension agree regarding the price of an option on a zero. However, Jamshidian and its perfectly fitting extension would assign different values to options on coupon bearing bonds, because they would lead to different values for r^* in eq. (13.122) and, hence, different values for the fictitious strikes $P(r^*,T_0,T_i)$ in eq. (13.124).

13.8.7 Interest Rate Swaps

Savings and Loan associations (also known as "thrifts"; S&L, henceforth) are types of cooperative ventures that extend mortgage, car and personal loans to individual members, and are typically financed through retail savings; their governance is marked by the presence of voting and management rights extended to their depositors and borrowers members.

During the 1980s and through the beginning of the 1990s, S&Ls entered into a deep and persistent crisis, leading to a government bailout of about $125billion under George H. W. Bush's administration. There are many causes underlying this crisis, and one of them links to the rise in short-term rates arising as an attempt of the Fed to fight against inflation: the so-called Monetary Experiment discussed in section 13.4.5. Banking is risky precisely because it involves lending at horizons longer than those for borrowing. S&L "banking" is not immune to the risks inherent in such modus operandi. S&Ls had originated loans at interest rates that were surpassed by interest rates on deposits resulting after the rate hike of the early 1980s. Interest rate swaps are derivative instruments that could have helped coping with the yield curve compressions of the time. This section contains foundational pricing details regarding these instruments. First, we provide a simple introduction and motivation for them.

13.8.7.1 Motivation

An interest rate swap is an exchange of interest rate payments. Two counterparties exchange a fixed against a floating interest rate payment. Typically, the floating payment is referenced to a short-term interest rate. For example, the party receiving a floating interest rate payment has "good" (or only) access to markets for "variable" interest rates, but wishes to pay fixed interest rates. Alternatively, the party receiving a floating interest rate is exposed to interest rate risks in the short-term segment, risks that it wants to hedge, as it could have been the case with the S&Ls during the 1980s.

The party receiving a floating interest rate payment and paying a fixed interest rate K_{irs} has access to a payoff equal to

$$\delta_{i-1}\left(L\left(T_{i-1},T_i\right)-K_{\text{irs}}\right)$$

at time T_i, $i=1,\cdots,n$, where $\delta_{i-1}\equiv T_i-T_{i-1}$ as usual. Each of these payments is a FRA really, and can be evaluated with standard methodology (see section 13.2). By convention, we say that the *swap payer* is the counterparty who pays the fixed interest rate K_{irs}, and that the *swap receiver* is the counterparty paying the variable interest rates.

With dedicated interest rate swaps of this kind, a S&L could have "locked in the yield curve." Specifically, in this stylized example, the payoff of a swap payer for the S&L could have been

$$\begin{aligned}&\delta_{i-1}\left(L^{\text{long}}\left(T_{i-1},T_i\right)-L\left(T_{i-1},T_i\right)\right)+\delta_{i-1}\left(L\left(T_{i-1},T_i\right)-K_{\text{irs}}\right)\\&\quad=\delta_{i-1}\left(L^{\text{long}}\left(T_{i-1},T_i\right)-K_{\text{irs}}\right),\end{aligned}$$

where $L^{\text{long}}\left(T_{i-1},T_i\right)$ is the interest rate gained over long-term assets. Naturally, if short-term interest rates had to go down, relative to K_{irs}, the S&L would not have benefited from the increased long-term/short-term spread, $\delta_{i-1}\left(L^{\text{long}}\left(T_{i-1},T_i\right)-L\left(T_{i-1},T_i\right)\right)$.[52] Yet, insuring against yield curve inversions would be the appropriate course of action, if yield curve inversions had to lead to bankruptcy, and bankruptcy was costly. Below, we explain that additional products exist (caps, swaptions), which ensure against the upside while at the same time freeing up the downside.

More generally, financial institutions exposed to the risk of interest rate increases would find it optimal to enter into such agreements, provided that the losses feared on the upside (i.e., when interest rates increase) are higher than the benefits reaped on the downside (i.e., when interest rates decrease), i.e., when risk appetite is limited. To illustrate, risk appetite may be limited by bankruptcy costs, as in the previous example, or by the presence of financial constraints such as Value-at-Risk constraints of the type reviewed in the next chapter (see section 14.4).

Governments are another relevant example of institutions that might benefit from a swap payer, although with some important qualifications. Consider a government that, for reasons not modeled in this chapter, might have accumulated a considerable amount of debt and, then, be led to pay high interest rates, thereby being exposed to a considerable risk of default.[53] Governments obviously benefit from an interest rate swap payer in those events when interest rates increase. Naturally, the downside is that governments would have to give up to improved financing conditions, were interest rates to decrease. At first glance, it may seem that this downside may weigh less than the risk of default.

52. Under the normal backwardation hypothesis (see section 13.3.1) the value of K_{irs} that clears the FRA is higher than the expected future short-term rate, $L\left(T_{i-1},T_i\right)$.
53. The next chapter deals with problems regarding risk of default for sovereign entities (see section 14.2.4).

But the downside of an interest rate payer might actually be particularly severe. Indeed, an environment with persistently low interest rates may occur precisely when the economy experiences persistently bad times, as for example during the period of ultra-low interest rate policies implemented after the global financial crisis of the late 2000s. In such circumstances, government deficits are typically higher than on average and public debt becomes more vulnerable to default risk, weakening the case for a swap payer.

In turn, some other institutions would like to be on the opposite side of these deals. For example, pension funds may be interested in swap receivers, as anticipated in chapter 10 (see section 10.10). First, pension funds want to have access to long-term assets that distribute fixed payments, ideally, "coupons" (needed to honor payments to past funds' contributors). For all intents and purposes, a long-maturity receiver swap (that is, a high-tenor swap, according to terminology introduced below) may play such a role: a fund may simply pay a variable interest rate (obtained by investing current contributions into a variable interest rate market) against the payment of fixed interest rates. Second, and as explained in the previous chapter (see section 12.3), pension funds are quite adverse to decreasing interest rates, a scenario consistent with losses; a pension fund is particularly averse to such losses.

We now examine the pricing details regarding interest rate swaps.

13.8.7.2 FRA again

Interest rate swaps are baskets of the FRAs introduced in section 13.2.2. Consider the payoff $\pi_{\text{fra}}(T,S)$ in eq. (13.8), and denote its value at t with $\text{FRA}(t,T,S;K)$, where $S-T$ is the debt-servicing period, and K is the fixed rate, namely

$$\begin{aligned}
\text{FRA}(t,T,S;K) &= \mathbb{E}_t\left(e^{-\int_t^S r_\tau d\tau}(S-T)(L(T,S)-K)\right) \\
&= \mathbb{E}_t\left(e^{-\int_t^S r_\tau d\tau}(S-T)L(T,S)\right)-(S-T)P(t,S)K \\
&= \mathbb{E}_t\left(\frac{e^{-\int_t^S r_\tau d\tau}}{P(T,S)}\right)-(1+(S-T)K)P(t,S) \\
&= P(t,T)-(1+(S-T)K)P(t,S), \qquad (13.125)
\end{aligned}$$

where the third line holds by the definition of L and the fourth follows by arguments set forth in section 13.2 (see eq. (13.5)). Note that we may achieve the conclusions underlying eq. (13.125) through a different route. Indeed, the LIBOR, $L(T,S)$, while known at T, is only paid off at S, such that the value of $1+(S-T)L(T,S)$ (to be delivered at S) is simply one at T and, obviously, $P(t,T)$ at t. That is, the value of $(S-T)L(T,S)$ (to be delivered at time S) is $P(t,T)-P(t,S)$ at t, whence, the fourth equality.[54]

54. We are assuming, as it is standard, that settlements occur at S. When settlements occur at $T<S$, the value of $1+(S-T)L(T,S)$ at T is obviously higher than one, and the calculations leading to the last line of eq. (13.125) and the "model-free" expression for F would not go through. The technical issue is a "convexity effect" by which a payoff of $1+(S-T)L(T,S)$ at time T is equivalent to a payoff of $(1+(S-T)L(T,S))^2$ at time S. Brigo and Mercurio (2006, chap. 13) and Veronesi (2010, Chapter 21) explain the standard market practice to deal with this issue.

Thus, and as anticipated in section 13.2, the forward *forward interest rate* in Eq. (13.9), $F(t,T,S)$, is the value K that clears the agreement at origination, that is, the value that makes $\text{FRA}(t,T,S;K)=0$. We can provide a more intuitive expression for $\text{FRA}(t,T,S;K)$. Replacing the expression for the forward rate in (13.9) into eq. (13.125) leaves

$$\text{FRA}(t,T,S;K)=(S-T)(F(t,T,S)-K)\,P(t,S)\,. \tag{13.126}$$

That is, the value of the FRA can take on any sign, and is exactly zero when $K=F(t,T,S)$, where $F(t,T,S)$ solves eq. (13.6).

Interest rate swaps are baskets of FRAs, as mentioned: they consist in exchanges of payments occurring repeatedly and over a given time horizon, known as the *swap tenor*. We now proceed with evaluating them.

13.8.7.3 Forward starting interest rate swaps: Evaluation

Consider the value at t of a forward starting swap (i.e., a swap starting at $T_0>t$) *payer*, denoted as $\text{IRS}(t,T_0,\cdots,T_n;K_{\text{irs}})$,

$$\begin{aligned}\text{IRS}(t,T_0,\cdots,T_n;K_{\text{irs}}) &= \sum_{i=1}^{n}\mathbb{E}_t\left(e^{-\int_t^{T_i} r_\tau d\tau}\delta_{i-1}\left(L\left(T_{i-1},T_i\right)-K_{\text{irs}}\right)\right)\\ &= \sum_{i=1}^{n}\text{FRA}(t,T_{i-1},T_i;K_{\text{irs}}),\end{aligned} \tag{13.127}$$

where, by eq. (13.126),

$$\text{FRA}\left(t,T_{i-1},T_i;K_{\text{irs}}\right)=\delta_{i-1}\left(F\left(t,T_{i-1},T_i\right)-K_{\text{irs}}\right)P\left(t,T_i\right).$$

The *forward swap rate* F_{sw} is the value of K_{irs} such that $\text{IRS}(t,T_0,\cdots,T_n;K_{\text{irs}})=0$. Simple calculations yield

$$F_{\text{sw}}(t,T_0,\cdots,T_n)=\frac{\sum_{i=1}^{n}\delta_{i-1}P(t,T_i)\,F\left(t,T_{i-1},T_i\right)}{\sum_{i=1}^{n}\delta_{i-1}P(t,T_i)}=\frac{P(t,T_0)-P(t,T_n)}{\sum_{i=1}^{n}\delta_{i-1}P(t,T_i)}, \tag{13.128}$$

where the last equality holds by eq. (13.6) in section 13.2: $\delta_{i-1}F\left(t,T_{i-1},T_i\right)P\left(t,T_i\right)=P\left(t,T_{i-1}\right)-P\left(t,T_i\right)$. This expression collapses to the par coupon rate derived in chapter 12 (see section 12.2), once we set $t=T_0$. That is, the *spot* swap rate is a par yield. Furthermore, note that the first equality of eq. (13.128) suggests that the forward swap rate is a linear combination of forward rates and, thus, reflects expectations of future short-term rates,

$$F_{\text{sw}}(t,T_0,\cdots,T_n)=\sum_{i=1}^{n}\omega(t,T_i)\,F\left(t,T_{i-1},T_i\right),\quad \omega(t,T_i)\equiv\frac{\delta_{i-1}P(t,T_i)}{\sum_{i=1}^{n}\delta_{i-1}P(t,T_i)}. \tag{13.129}$$

In section 13.9.3.5, we use this property and discuss how to deal with the approximation of the value of derivatives referenced to interest rate swaps.

Finally, we provide an expression for the value of the forward starting swap, which we will rely upon while evaluating interest rate swaps derivatives. By plugging the expression for the forward swap rate in eq. (13.128) into eq. (13.127), we obtain the following intuitive expression for the forward swap payer:

$$\begin{aligned}
\text{IRS}\left(t, T_0, \cdots, T_n; K_{\text{irs}}\right) &= \sum_{i=1}^{n} \delta_{i-1} F\left(t, T_{i-1}, T_i\right) P\left(t, T_i\right) - K_{\text{irs}} \sum_{i=1}^{n} \delta_{i-1} P\left(t, T_i\right) \\
&= \sum_{i=1}^{n} \delta_{i-1} P\left(t, T_i\right) \left(F_{\text{sw}}\left(t, T_0, \cdots, T_n\right) - K_{\text{irs}}\right) \\
&\equiv \text{PVBP}_t\left(T_1, \cdots, T_n\right) \left(F_{\text{sw}}\left(t, T_0, \cdots, T_n\right) - K_{\text{irs}}\right), \qquad (13.130)
\end{aligned}$$

where $\text{PVBP}_t\left(T_1, \cdots, T_n\right)$ is the so-called swap "Price Value of the Basis Point," i.e., the present value impact of one basis point move in the forward swap rate at t.

13.8.7.4 *Marking to market*

While a forward starting swap is costless at origination, its marking to market updates are calculated as follows. Suppose to enter at τ into a forward starting swap originated at time t. Denoting with T_{i_τ} the first reset date to occur after time τ, the value of this position is

$$\begin{aligned}
&\text{IRS}^{\text{mtm}}\left(\tau, T_{i_\tau}, \cdots, T_n; K_{\text{irs}}\right) \\
&\equiv \sum_{i_\tau=1}^{n} \mathbb{E}_\tau\left(e^{-\int_\tau^{T_i} r_s ds} \delta_{i-1}\left(L\left(T_{i-1}, T_i\right) - F_{\text{sw}}\left(t; \cdot\right)\right)\right) \\
&= \sum_{i_\tau=1}^{n} \mathbb{E}_\tau\left(e^{-\int_\tau^{T_i} r_s ds} \delta_{i-1}\left(L\left(T_{i-1}, T_i\right) - F_{\text{sw}}\left(\tau; \cdot\right) + F_{\text{sw}}\left(\tau; \cdot\right)\right)\right) \\
&\quad - \text{PVBP}_\tau\left(T_1, \cdots, T_n\right) F_{\text{sw}}\left(t; \cdot\right) \\
&= \text{PVBP}_\tau\left(T_1, \cdots, T_n\right)\left(F_{\text{sw}}\left(\tau; \cdot\right) - F_{\text{sw}}\left(t; \cdot\right)\right),
\end{aligned}$$

where we have simplified notation for $F_{\text{sw}}\left(t, T_0, \cdots, T_n\right)$, and the last equality follows by the definition of a forward swap at τ.

13.8.8 Caps and Floors

A cap works as an interest rate swap, with the exception that the exchange of interest rates payments takes place only if actual interest rates are higher than some strike K. A cap protects against upward movements in interest rates, while freeing up the downside. By going long a cap, the S&L institution in the example of the previous section, then, would literally benefit from the downside in the short-term interest rates through a cap on them. Precisely, a cap is made up of *caplets*. The payoff as of time T_i of a caplet is:

$$\delta_{i-1}\left(L\left(T_{i-1}, T_i\right) - K\right)^+, \quad i = 1, \cdots, n.$$

Floors are defined in a similar way. They are baskets of single *floorlets* that pay off $\delta_{i-1}\left(K - L\left(T_{i-1}, T_i\right)\right)^+$ at time T_i, $i = 1, \cdots, n$.

We only discuss caps. By the FTAP, the a cap at time t is valued

$$p_{\text{cap}}(t) \equiv \sum_{i=1}^{n} \mathbb{E}_t \left(e^{-\int_t^{T_i} r_\tau d\tau} \delta_{i-1} \left(L\left(T_{i-1}, T_i\right) - K \right)^+ \right). \tag{13.131}$$

We can rely on models of the short-term rate to address this problem analytically. Consider the definition of simply compounded rates (see eq. (13.1) in section 13.2), viz $\delta_{i-1} L\left(T_{i-1}, T_i\right) = \frac{1}{P(T_{i-1}, T_i)} - 1$, and rewrite the caplet payoff as follows

$$\left(\delta_{i-1} L\left(T_{i-1}, T_i\right) - \delta_{i-1} K\right)^+ = \frac{1}{P\left(T_{i-1}, T_i\right)} \left(1 - (1 + \delta_{i-1} K) P(T_{i-1}, T_i)\right)^+.$$

We have

$$\begin{aligned} p_{\text{cap}}(t) &= \sum_{i=1}^{n} \mathbb{E}_t \left(\frac{e^{-\int_t^{T_i} r_\tau d\tau}}{P(T_{i-1}, T_i)} \left(1 - (1 + \delta_{i-1} K) P(T_{i-1}, T_i)\right)^+ \right) \\ &= \sum_{i=1}^{n} \mathbb{E}_t \left(e^{-\int_t^{T_{i-1}} r_\tau d\tau} \frac{1}{\mathcal{K}_i} \left(\mathcal{K}_i - P(T_{i-1}, T_i)\right)^+ \right), \quad \mathcal{K}_i = \left(1 + \delta_{i-1} K\right)^{-1}, \end{aligned} \tag{13.132}$$

where the last equality follows by a simple calculation (see eq. (13.A18) in appendix 13.H).

Jamshidian, and Hull and White models predict closed-form expressions for bond prices and, then, for the cap price in eq. (13.132). Precisely, eq. (13.132) suggests that a cap is a basket of puts on zero coupon bonds, with strikes $\mathcal{K}_i$. As such, it can be priced in closed form, using the models in sections 13.8.4. We have

$$p_{\text{cap}}(t) = \sum_{i=1}^{n} \frac{1}{\mathcal{K}_i} \text{Put}\left(t, T_{i-1}; P\left(t, T_i\right), \mathcal{K}_i, v\right), \tag{13.133}$$

where Put $(\cdot)$ satisfies the put-call parity in eq. (13.112), and, by the pricing formulae in section 13.8.4,

$$\text{Call}\left(t, T_{i-1}; P\left(t, T_i\right), \mathcal{K}_i, v\right) = P\left(t, T_i\right) \Phi\left(d_{1,i}\right) - \mathcal{K}_i P\left(t, T_{i-1}\right) \Phi\left(d_{1,i} - v\right),$$

$$d_{1,i} = \frac{\ln \frac{P(t,T_i)}{\mathcal{K}_i P(t,T_{i-1})} + \frac{1}{2} v^2}{v}, \quad v = \sigma \sqrt{\frac{1 - e^{-2\kappa(T_{i-1} - t)}}{2\kappa}} B\left(T_{i-1}, T_i\right), \quad B(t, T) = \frac{1}{\kappa}\left(1 - e^{-\kappa(T-t)}\right). \tag{13.134}$$

Caps on interest rates are baskets of calls, that is, portfolios of puts on fixed coupon bonds, due to the inverse relation between prices and interest rates.

13.8.9 Swaptions

Let us elaborate on the S&L example of the previous sections. The benefits for the S&L to be long a cap is to be protected against upward movements in the short-term rates while ensuring the downside is freed up. These benefits arise period per period, so to speak: a cap is a basket of options with different maturities. A swaption works differently, in that the optionality kicks in "all together."

The S&L is now concerned about *future* inversions of the yield curve; therefore, it anticipates its need to go long a swap payer at some future date. At the same time, the S&L fears that in the future, swap rates will be lower relative to some reference strike. Swaptions allow to free up such a downside risk, because they offer the option to enter a swap contract on a future date. Let T_0 be the maturity date of this option. Come time T_0, the payoff for a *payer* swaption is the maximum between zero and the value of a *payer* interest rate swap at T_0. That is, and based on eq. (13.127),

$$\mathrm{IRS}\left(T_0, T_0, \cdots, T_n; K_{\mathrm{irs}}\right)^+ = \left(\sum_{i=1}^{n} \delta_{i-1}\left(F\left(T_0, T_{i-1}, T_i\right) - K_{\mathrm{irs}}\right) P\left(T_0, T_i\right)\right)^+. \quad (13.135)$$

By the FTAP, the value of the payer swaption at time t is

$$\begin{aligned} \mathrm{SW}_p(t) &= \mathbb{E}_t\left[e^{-\int_t^{T_0} r_\tau d\tau}\left(\sum_{i=1}^{n} \delta_{i-1}\left(F(T_0, T_{i-1}, T_i) - K_{\mathrm{irs}}\right) P(T_0, T_i)\right)^+\right] \\ &= \mathbb{E}_t\left[e^{-\int_t^{T_0} r_\tau d\tau}\left(1 - P(T_0, T_n) - K_{\mathrm{irs}} \sum_{i=1}^{n} \delta_{i-1} P(T_0, T_i)\right)^+\right], \end{aligned} \quad (13.136)$$

where we used the relation $\delta_{i-1}F(T_0, T_{i-1}, T_i) = \frac{P(T_0, T_{i-1})}{P(T_0, T_i)} - 1$.

Eq. (13.136) is the expression for the price of a *put* option *on a fixed coupon bond* struck at one. Therefore, we can price this contract in closed-form, through the models in section 13.8.4, in a way similar to how we did in the previous section while pricing caps. We have:

$$\mathrm{SW}_p(t) = \overline{\mathrm{Put}}\left(t, T_0; P_{\mathrm{fcb}}\left(t, T_n\right), 1, v\right),$$

where $\overline{\mathrm{Put}}(\cdot)$ satisfies the put-call parity in eq. (13.112). By the pricing formulae in section 13.8.6,

$$\begin{aligned} \overline{\mathrm{Call}}\left(t, T_0; P_{\mathrm{fcb}}\left(t, T_n\right), 1, v\right) = & K_{\mathrm{irs}} \sum_{i=1}^{n} \delta_{i-1} \mathrm{Call}\left(t, T_0; P\left(t, T_i\right), P_i^*, v\right) \\ & + \mathrm{Call}\left(t, T_0; P\left(t, T_n\right), P_n^*, v\right), \end{aligned}$$

where $\mathrm{Call}\left(t, T_0; P\left(t, T_i\right), P_i^*, v\right)$ is as in eq. (13.134), with $P_i^* = P\left(r^*, T_0, T_i\right)$, and r^* solution to eq. (13.122) for $K = 1$.

13.9 Market Models

13.9.1 Models and Market Practice

The previous section illustrates that models of the short-term rate (and their perfectly fitting extensions) lead to closed-form expressions for the price of important interest rate sensitive products. Yet practitioners evaluate caps, floors, or swaptions through Black's (1976) formula (see section 11.4.3 in chapter 11), as explained in detail below. The assumption underlying market practice is that the simply compounded forward rate is log-normally distributed. As it turns out, the analytically tractable (Gaussian) short-term rate models are *not* consistent with this assumption. Clearly, the (Gaussian) Vasicek model does not predict that the simply compounded forward rates are geometric Brownian motions.[55]

How to address these issues while relying on a non-Markovian HJM? Some qualifications are in order. A practical difficulty with HJM is that *instantaneous* forward rates are not observed, which at a first sight seems to be an hindrance to realistic pricing of caps, floors and swaptions. Brace, Gatarek, and Musiela (1997), Jamshidian (1997), and Miltersen, Sandmann, and Sondermann (1997) address this issue, and note that the HJM framework can be somehow "forced" to produce models ready to be used consistent with market practice. The result is known as "market model."

The key feature of market models is the emphasis on the dynamics of the *simply compounded* forward rates. One additional assumption is that these simply compounded forward rates are log-normal under the risk neutral probability Q. That is, we assume that given a nondecreasing sequence of reset times $\{T_i\}_{i=0,1,\cdots}$, each simply compounded rate, F_i, is the solution to[56]

$$\frac{dF_{i,\tau}}{F_{i,\tau}} = m_i(\tau)d\tau + \gamma_i(\tau)d\tilde{W}_\tau, \quad \tau \in [t, T_i], \quad i = 0, \cdots, n-1, \tag{13.137}$$

where $F_{i\tau} \equiv F(\tau, T_i, T_{i+1})$, and m_i and γ_i are some deterministic functions of time (γ_i is vector valued).[57]

We show that this simple framework can be used to apply the simple Black's (1976) formula to price caps and floors. Naturally, the short-term rate models of the previous sections are still valid alternatives to the framework in this section. The real advance of the market model is that it provides a rigorous foundation to the standard market practice to price caps, floors and swaptions by means of Black's (1976) formula.

13.9.2 No-Arbitrage Restrictions

By the definition of the simply compounded forward rates in eq. (13.6),

$$\ln\left(\frac{P(\tau, T_i)}{P(\tau, T_{i+1})}\right) = \ln\left(1 + \delta_i F_{i,\tau}\right). \tag{13.138}$$

The logic we follow, now, is the same as that underlying the HJM representation of section 13.7. We wish to express the volatility of bond prices in terms of the volatility of forward rates. To achieve this task, we first assume that bond prices are driven by Brownian motions and expand the LHS of eq. (13.138) (step 1). Then, we expand the RHS of eq. (13.138) (step 2). Finally, we identify the two diffusion terms derived from the previous two steps (step 3).

---

55. Indeed, $1 + \delta_i F_i(\tau) = \frac{P(\tau,T_i)}{P(\tau,T_{i+1})} = \exp\left[\Delta A_i(\tau) - \Delta B_i(\tau) r_\tau\right]$, where $\Delta A_i(\tau) = A(\tau, T_i) - A(\tau, T_{i+1})$, and $\Delta B_i(\tau) = B(\tau, T_i) - B(\tau, T_{i+1})$. Hence, $F_i(\tau)$ is not a Geometric Brownian motion, despite the fact that the short-term rate r is Gaussian and, hence, the bond price is log-normal. Black (1976) cannot be applied in this context.

56. Brace, Gatarek, and Musiela (1997) formulate a model in terms of the spot simply compounded LIBOR interest rates. Because $F_i(T_i) = L(T_i)$, the two derivations are essentially the same.

57. It is well known that log-normal *instantaneous* forward rates are problematic as they imply the money market account is ill-behaved. Sandmann and Sondermann (1997) provide a succinct overview on how this problem is handled with *simply-compounded* forward rates.

Step 1: Let $P_i \equiv P(\tau, T_i)$, and assume that under the risk neutral probability Q, P_i is the solution to:

$$\frac{dP_i}{P_i} = r d\tau + \sigma_{bi} d\tilde{W}.$$

In terms of the HJM framework in section 13.7,

$$\sigma_{bi}(\tau) = -\sigma^I(\tau, T_i) = -\int_\tau^{T_i} \sigma(\tau, \ell) d\ell, \tag{13.139}$$

where $\sigma(\tau, \ell)$ is the instantaneous volatility of the instantaneous ℓ-forward rate as of time τ. By Itô's lemma,

$$d \ln\left(\frac{P(\tau, T_i)}{P(\tau, T_{i+1})}\right) = -\frac{1}{2}\left(\|\sigma_{bi}\|^2 - \|\sigma_{b,i+1}\|^2\right) d\tau + \left(\sigma_{bi} - \sigma_{b,i+1}\right) d\tilde{W}. \tag{13.140}$$

Step 2: Applying Itô's lemma to $\ln(1 + \delta_i F_{i,\tau})$, and using eq. (13.137), yields:

$$\begin{aligned} d\ln(1+\delta_i F_i) &= \frac{\delta_i}{1+\delta_i F_i} dF_i - \frac{1}{2}\frac{\delta_i^2}{(1+\delta_i F_i)^2}(dF_i)^2 \\ &= \left(\frac{\delta_i m_i F_i}{1+\delta_i F_i} - \frac{1}{2}\frac{\delta_i^2 F_i^2 \|\gamma_i\|^2}{(1+\delta_i F_i)^2}\right) d\tau + \frac{\delta_i F_i}{1+\delta_i F_i}\gamma_i d\tilde{W}. \end{aligned} \tag{13.141}$$

Step 3: By eq. (13.138), the diffusion terms in eqs. (13.140) and (13.141) have to be the same. Therefore,

$$\sigma_{bi}(\tau) - \sigma_{b,i+1}(\tau) = \frac{\delta_i F_{i,\tau}}{1+\delta_i F_{i,\tau}}\gamma_i(\tau), \quad \tau \in [t, T_i].$$

By summing over i, we get the following no-arbitrage restriction applying to the volatility of the bond prices:

$$\sigma_{bi}(\tau) - \sigma_{b,0}(\tau) = -\sum_{j=0}^{i-1} \frac{\delta_j F_{j,\tau}}{1+\delta_j F_{j,\tau}}\gamma_j(\tau). \tag{13.142}$$

Eq. (13.142) is, thus, a restriction to the general HJM framework. In other words, assume the instantaneous forward rates are as in eq. (13.91) of section 13.7. As shown in section 13.7, the bond price volatility is, then, given by eq. (13.139). But if we also assume that simply compounded forward rates are solution to eq. (13.137), then, the bond price volatility needs to equal that in eq. (13.142). Comparing eq. (13.139) with eq. (13.142) produces,

$$\int_{T_0}^{T_i} \sigma(\tau, \ell) d\ell = \sum_{j=0}^{i-1} \frac{\delta_j F_{j,\tau}}{1+\delta_j F_{j,\tau}}\gamma_j(\tau).$$

The practical interest to restrict the forward-rate volatility dynamics in this way lies in the possibility to obtain closed-form solutions for some of the interest rates derivatives surveyed in section 13.8

13.9.3 Applications to Derivatives Evaluation

13.9.3.1 Forward rates as martingales

Forward rates are martingales under the forward probability. Regarding the continuously compounded notion, we have, by the definition of the instantaneous forward rate, the usual change of probability and standard regularity conditions,

$$\begin{aligned} f(t,T) &= -\frac{\partial \ln P(t,T)}{\partial T} \\ &= -\frac{\partial P(t,T)}{\partial T} \Big/ P(t,T) \\ &= \mathbb{E}_t\left(\frac{e^{-\int_t^T r_\tau d\tau}}{P(t,T)} \cdot r_T\right) \\ &= \mathbb{E}_t\left(\eta_T(T) \cdot r_T\right) \\ &= \mathbb{E}_{Q_F^T}\left(r_T\right) \\ &= \mathbb{E}_{Q_F^T}\left(f(T,T)\right), \end{aligned}$$

where the last equality holds as $r_t = f(t,t)$ as usual, and $\eta_T(T)$ is as in eq (13.108).

Similarly, and regarding simply compounded forward rates, we have that for a given sequence of dates $\{T_i\}_{i=0,1,\cdots}$,

$$F(\tau, T_i, T_{i+1}) = \mathbb{E}_{Q_F^{T_{i+1}}}\left(L(T_i, T_{i+1})\right) = \mathbb{E}_{Q_F^{T_{i+1}}}\left(F(T_i, T_i, T_{i+1})\right), \quad \tau \in [t, T_i], \tag{13.143}$$

where the second equality follows by eq. (13.7), that is, $L(T_i, T_{i+1}) = F(T_i, T_i, T_{i+1})$. To show eq. (13.143), note that by definition, the simply compounded forward rate $F(t,T,S)$ satisfies,

$$F(t,T,S) : 0 = \mathbb{E}_t\left(e^{-\int_t^S r_\tau d\tau} \cdot (L(T,S) - F(t,T,S))\right),$$

as explained in section 13.8.7.2. That is, by rearranging terms,

$$F(t,T,S) = \mathbb{E}_t\left(\frac{e^{-\int_t^S r_\tau d\tau}}{P(t,S)} L(T,S)\right) = \mathbb{E}_{Q_F^S}\left(L(T,S)\right). \tag{13.144}$$

We use this martingale property when pricing caps and floors.

13.9.3.2 Caps and floors

We provide analytical results for the price of caps only. We have:

$$\begin{aligned} p_{\text{cap}}(t) &= \sum_{i=1}^{n} \mathbb{E}_t\left(e^{-\int_t^{T_i} r_\tau d\tau} \delta_{i-1}\left(L(T_{i-1}, T_i) - K\right)^+\right) \\ &= \sum_{i=1}^{n} \mathbb{E}_t\left(e^{-\int_t^{T_i} r_\tau d\tau} \delta_{i-1}\left(F(T_{i-1}, T_{i-1}, T_i) - K\right)^+\right) \\ &= \sum_{i=1}^{n} \delta_{i-1} P(t, T_i) \cdot \mathbb{E}_{Q_F^{T_i}}\left(F(T_{i-1}, T_{i-1}, T_i) - K\right)^+, \end{aligned} \tag{13.145}$$

where $\mathbb{E}_{Q_F^{T_i}}(\cdot)$ denotes, as usual, the expectation taken under the T_i-forward martingale probability $Q_F^{T_i}$; the first equality is eq. (13.131); and the second equality follows by a change of probability, from the risk neutral to the forward.

A key point explained above is that $F_{i-1,\tau} \equiv F_{i-1}(\tau, T_{i-1}, T_i)$ is a martingale under $Q_F^{T_i}$ for $\tau \in [t, T_{i-1}]$ (see eqs. (13.143)–(13.144)), such that, by eq. (13.137), $F_{i-1,\tau}$ satisfies

$$\frac{dF_{i-1,\tau}}{F_{i-1,\tau}} = \gamma_{i-1}(\tau) dW_\tau^{Q_F^{T_i}}, \quad \tau \in [t, T_{i-1}], \quad i = 1, \cdots, n, \tag{13.146}$$

where $W_\tau^{Q_F^{T_i}}$ denotes a Brownian motion under $Q_F^{T_i}$. Therefore, the cap price in eq. (13.145) may be evaluated based on Black's (1976) formula discussed in chapter 11,[58] once we assume γ is deterministic

$$\mathbb{E}_{Q_F^{T_i}}\left(F\left(T_{i-1}, T_{i-1}, T_i\right) - K\right)^+ = F_{i-1,t}\Phi\left(d_{1,i-1}\right) - K\Phi\left(d_{1,i-1} - s_i\right), \tag{13.147}$$

where

$$d_{1,i-1} = \frac{\ln \frac{F_{i-1,t}}{K} + \frac{1}{2}s_i^2}{s_i}, \quad s_i^2 = \int_t^{T_{i-1}} \gamma_{i-1}^2(\tau) d\tau.$$

We can now price floors based on a put-call parity relation, an exercise left to the reader.

13.9.3.3 *Swaptions*

The main idea now is to elaborate on the payoff in eq. (13.130), rather than in eq. (13.127). Accordingly, the payoff of a *payer* swaption expiring at time T_0 is

$$\text{IRS}\left(T_0, T_0, \cdots, T_n; K_{\text{irs}}\right)^+ = \text{PVBP}_{T_0}\left(T_1, \cdots, T_n\right)\left(F_{\text{sw}}\left(T_0\right) - K_{\text{irs}}\right)^+,$$

where $F_{\text{sw}}(T_0) \equiv F_{\text{sw}}(T_0, T_0, \cdots, T_n)$. Therefore, by change of probability,

$$\begin{aligned} \text{SW}_p(t) &= \mathbb{E}_t\left(e^{-\int_t^{T_0} r_\tau d\tau} \text{PVBP}_{T_0}\left(T_1, \cdots, T_n\right)\left(F_{\text{sw}}(T_0) - K_{\text{irs}}\right)^+\right) \\ &= \text{PVBP}_t\left(T_1, \cdots, T_n\right) \mathbb{E}_{Q_{\text{sw}}}\left(F_{\text{sw}}(T_0) - K_{\text{irs}}\right)^+, \end{aligned} \tag{13.148}$$

where $\mathbb{E}_{Q_{\text{sw}}}$ denotes the expectation taken under the so-called *annuity*, or *forward swap probability*, defined by

$$\left.\frac{dQ_{\text{sw}}}{dQ}\right|_{\mathbb{F}_{T_0}} = e^{-\int_t^{T_0} r_\tau d\tau} \frac{\text{PVBP}_{T_0}\left(T_1, \cdots, T_n\right)}{\text{PVBP}_t\left(T_1, \cdots, T_n\right)}. \tag{13.149}$$

It is easy to see that $\mathbb{E}\left(\frac{dQ_{\text{sw}}}{dQ} | \mathbb{F}_{T_0}\right) = 1$, by using the definition of $\text{PVBP}_{T_0}\left(T_1, \cdots, T_n\right)$, the pricing equation, $P(t, T_i) = \mathbb{E}_t\left(e^{-\int_t^{T_0} r_\tau d\tau} P(T_0, T_i)\right)$, as anticipated in chapter 4 (see

58. See section 11.4 and appendix 11.B in chapter 11.

section 4.5). As also mentioned in chapter 4, Q_{sw} is sometimes referred to as *annuity probability*.

A key point underlying this change of probability is that the forward swap rate $F_{\text{sw}}(\tau, T_0, \cdots, T_n)$ is a martingale under Q_{sw} (see eq. (13.A19) in appendix 13.H) and is strictly positive. Therefore, it must satisfy

$$\frac{dF_{\text{sw}}(\tau,\cdot)}{F_{\text{sw}}(\tau,\cdot)} = \gamma_{\text{sw}}(\tau)\, dW_\tau^{\text{sw}}, \quad \tau \in [t, T_0], \tag{13.150}$$

where W_τ^{sw} is a Q_{sw}-Brownian motion, $\gamma_{\text{sw}}(\tau)$ is adapted and, for simplicity, we are using the short-hand notation $F_{\text{sw}}(\tau,\cdot) \equiv F_{\text{sw}}(t, T_0, \cdots, T_n)$.

If $\gamma_{\text{sw}}(\tau)$ in eq. (13.150) is deterministic, we can use Black's (1976) formula and price the payer swaption in eq. (13.148) in closed-form. We have

$$\text{SW}_p(t) = \text{PVBP}_t(T_1, \cdots, T_n)\, \mathbb{B}(F_{\text{sw}}(t,\cdot); T_0, K_{\text{irs}}, \sqrt{\bar{V}}), \tag{13.151}$$

where $\mathbb{B}(\cdot)$ is given by Black's (1976) formula

$$\mathbb{B}(F_{\text{sw}}(t,\cdot); T_0, K_{\text{irs}}, \sqrt{\bar{V}}) = F_{\text{sw}}(t,\cdot)\, \Phi(d_t) - K_{\text{irs}} \Phi(d_t - \sqrt{\bar{V}}),$$

$$d_t = \frac{\ln \frac{F_{\text{sw}}(t,\cdot)}{K_{\text{irs}}} + \frac{1}{2}\bar{V}}{\sqrt{\bar{V}}}, \quad \bar{V} = \int_t^{T_0} \gamma_{\text{sw}}^2(\tau)\, d\tau.$$

13.9.3.4 *A put-call parity in the swap space*

We derive a put-call parity relation for swaptions. The reasoning is standard. Consider the following identity

$$(F_{\text{sw}}(t, T_0, \cdots, T_n) - K_{\text{irs}})^+ = (K_{\text{irs}} - F_{\text{sw}}(t, T_0, \cdots, T_n))^+ + F_{\text{sw}}(t, T_0, \cdots, T_n) - K_{\text{irs}}.$$

Taking the expectations under Q_{sw} of both sides of the previous relation leaves

$$\text{SW}_p(t) = \text{SW}_r(t) + \text{PVBP}_t(T_1, \cdots, T_n) \cdot (F_{\text{sw}}(t, T_0, \cdots, T_n) - K_{\text{irs}})$$

where $\text{SW}_r(t)$ denotes a swaption receiver, struck at the same strike K_{irs}, and where we have used the property that the forward swap rate is a martingale under the annuity probability, $\mathbb{E}_{Q_{\text{sw}}}(F_{\text{sw}}(T_0, T_0, \cdots, T_n)) = F_{\text{sw}}(t, T_0, \cdots, T_n)$.

13.9.3.5 *Addressing inconsistencies*

If we assume that the forward rate is the solution to eq. (13.137), then, we cannot assume that γ_{sw} is deterministic. Conversely, if forward swap rates are log-normal, then, eq. (13.137) cannot hold. The implication of these simple statements is that we may only use Black's formula either to price caps or swaptions, but not both. Therefore, to implement the market model consistently, we need to rely on approximations or numerical solutions for the swaption values.

One well-known approach is based on a suggestion made by Rebonato (1998) (see also Rebonato, 1999), as discussed at length by Brigo and Mercurio (2006, section 6.15). The main idea of this approach consists in replacing the true pricing problem with an approximating one, where γ_{sw} is deterministic. In particular, consider the expression for the forward swap rate, $F_{sw}(t)$, in eq. (13.129). If we approximate the random weights $\omega(t, T_i)$ with weights frozen at the evaluation time 0, $\omega(0, T_i)$, the forward swap rate can be approximated as

$$F_{sw}(t) \approx \sum_{i=1}^{n} \omega(0, T_i)\, F(t, T_{i-1}, T_i).$$

By simple calculations, the instantaneous variance of $\frac{dF_{sw}(t)}{F_{sw}(t)}$ is, from the perspective of time 0,

$$\sum_{i,j=1}^{n} \frac{\omega(0, T_i)\, \omega(0, T_j)\, F(t, T_{i-1}, T_i)\, F(t, T_{j-1}, T_j)}{F_{sw}^2(t)} \rho_{i,j} \gamma_{i-1}(t)\, \gamma_{j-1}(t)\, dt,$$

where $\gamma_{i-1}(t)$ is the instantaneous volatility of the forward rate log-change (now a scalar), $\frac{dF(t,T_{i-1},T_i)}{F(t,T_{i-1},T_i)}$ (see eq. (13.137)), and $\rho_{i,j}$ is the instantaneous correlation between the log-changes of $F(t, T_{i-1}, T_i)$ and $F(t, T_{j-1}, T_j)$, which for simplicity we take to be a constant. Now, while further freezing forward rates and forward swap rates at the current levels, integrating, and rescaling by the swaption maturity, leaves the following expression

$$\hat{V} \equiv \frac{1}{T_0} \sum_{i,j=1}^{n} \frac{\omega(0, T_i)\, \omega(0, T_j)\, F(0, T_{i-1}, T_i)\, F(0, T_{j-1}, T_j)\, \rho_{i,j}}{F_{sw}^2(0)} \int_0^{T_0} \gamma_{i-1}(t)\, \gamma_{j-1}(t)\, dt.$$

We may now use the expression for $\hat{V}$ in (13.151) in lieu of $\bar{V}$ and obtain an approximating value for swaption prices.

A second approach is to rely on numerical approximations. Namely, assume that forward swap rates are log-normal. We may then price caps with Black's formula and price swaptions relying on the general HJM framework and its restrictions in eq. (13.142). While forward swap rates are not log-normal, we may calculate derivative values through numerical methods. Precisely, note that by a change of probability, the swaption value is

$$\begin{aligned} SW_p(t) &= \mathbb{E}_t\left[e^{-\int_t^{T_0} r_\tau d\tau} \left(\sum_{i=1}^{n} \delta_{i-1} \left(F(T_0, T_{i-1}, T_i) - K\right) P(T_0, T_i) \right)^+ \right] \\ &= P(t, T_0)\mathbb{E}_{Q_F^{T_0}} \left(\sum_{i=1}^{n} \delta_{i-1} \left(F(T_0, T_{i-1}, T_i) - K\right) P(T_0, T_i) \right)^+, \end{aligned} \tag{13.152}$$

where $F(T_0, T_{i-1}, T_i)$, $i = 1, \cdots, n$, can be simulated under $Q_F^{T_0}$.

Now, we know that $F_{i-1,\tau} \equiv F(\tau, T_{i-1}, T_i)$ is the solution to (13.146) and that, by results in appendix 13.B,

$$\begin{aligned} dW_\tau^{Q_F^{T_i}} &= dW_\tau^{Q_F^{T_0}} - \left(\sigma_{bi}(\tau) - \sigma_{b0}(\tau)\right) d\tau \\ &= dW_\tau^{Q_F^{T_0}} + \sum_{j=0}^{i-1} \frac{\delta_j F_{j,\tau}}{1 + \delta_j F_{j,\tau}} \gamma_j(\tau) d\tau, \end{aligned}$$

where the second line follows from eq. (13.142). Replacing this into eq. (13.146) leaves

$$\frac{dF_{i-1,\tau}}{F_{i-1,\tau}} = \gamma_{i-1}(\tau)\sum_{j=0}^{i-1}\frac{\delta_j F_{j,\tau}}{1+\delta_j F_{j,\tau}}\gamma_j(\tau)d\tau + \gamma_{i-1}(\tau)dW_\tau^{Q_F^{T_0}}, \quad \tau \le T_{i-1}, \quad i=1,\cdots,n. \tag{13.153}$$

The previous equation can be easily simulated with standard methods, such as those described by Kloeden and Platen (1992), and we may use the simulated values of $F_{i-1,T_0} = F(T_0, T_{i-1}, T_i)$ to approximate the expectation under $Q_F^{T_0}$ that delivers the swaption price in (13.152).

13.9.4 Multiple Curves

In the previous sections, interest rate swaps and other derivatives are priced assuming that no arb relations exist among LIBOR interest rates and the value of interbank deposits. These relations rely on the assumption that liquidity conditions are the same across all segments of the "swaption cube" (i.e., strikes, maturity, and tenors) and that the interbank market is exempt from default risk. The validity of these assumptions would deteriorate with the 2007–2009 global financial crisis (GFC, henceforth), as explained in more detail in the next chapter. Meanwhile, the regulatory landscape has led to better collateralization rules in OTC markets, making forward rate agreements safer than those implied by time-deposits (see section 13.9.4.3). This section is an introduction to the resulting "divergence" (i.e., the existence of different interest rate curves in different market segments) and pricing details.

13.9.4.1 Bootstrapping

Consider a contract that promises to deliver a series of known coupons $C(T_i)$ for a sequence of dates T_i. To evaluate this contract, we would need a series of discounting factors $P(t,T_i)$, say, some hypothetical zero-coupon bonds. Which type of bonds to use obviously depends on the risk of default of the issuing counterpart. For now, suppose we are given this series. We know very well that prices and coupons link through $B(t,T_n) - P(t,T_n) = \delta C(T_n)\sum_{i=1}^n P(t,T_i)$ (see chapter 12, eq. (12.3)), where $B(t,T_n)$ is the contract value, and δ^{-1} denotes the usual annualization factor.

Alternatively, and assuming $B(t,T_n) \equiv 1$, the previous equality may be interpreted as a "swap equation," in that the present value of fixed payments (its RHS) equals the present value of future (random) short term interest rates (the LHS). In this reinterpretation, $C(T_n)$ is the swap rate of fixed against variable interest rates for a given type of default risk. For example, section 13.8.7 relies on these relations while evaluating LIBOR rate swaps, and assuming that there is no counterparty risk in the LIBOR market (see eq. (13.128)). However, the same relations may describe other swaps, such as the overnight index swaps (OIS) described in chapter 12 (see section 12.2.1). In this section, we refer P to as the price of a generic zero, and specify which contracts it relates to when needed. Note, for now, that if the series of swap rates $C(\cdot)$ is mostly determined by market forces, we may bootstrap the corresponding zeros, by just inverting the swap equation,

$$P(t,T_m) = \frac{1 - \delta C(T_m)\sum_{i=1}^{m-1} P(t,T_i)}{1+\delta C(T_m)}. \tag{13.154}$$

Appendix 12.A in chapter 12 describes this procedure as "bootstrapping." We now describe market practice based on eq. (13.154) before and after the GFC.

13.9.4.2 *Pricing before the GFC: Single curve*

How to determine the LIBOR-based interest swap rate in practice? Eq. (13.128) and eq. (13.129) are, of course, equivalent, provided at least LIBOR deposits are exempt from default risk. In this case, one may use LIBOR discounts and calculate the corresponding zeros, denoted as P^{ℓ} from now on, and LIBOR-based theoretical bond values to calculate forward rates $F\left(t, T_{i-1}, T_i\right)$. Short-term zeros (i.e., up to one year) are obtained by the definition of LIBOR rates, and longer maturities zeros may be bootstrapped through eq. (13.154),

$$P^{\ell}(t, T_i) = \begin{cases} \dfrac{1}{1+(T_i - t)\, L(t, T_i)}, & \text{for } T_i - t < 1 \\ \dfrac{1 - \delta R_{\text{sw}}(t, T_m) \sum_{i=1}^{m-1} P^{\ell}(t, T_i)}{1 + \delta R_{\text{sw}}(t, T_m)}, & \text{otherwise} \end{cases}$$

where $R_{\text{sw}}(t, T_m)$ denotes the spot swap rate, i.e., $R_{\text{sw}}(t, T_m) = F_{\text{sw}}(T_0, T_0, \cdots, T_m)$, and $t = T_0$. Veronesi (2016) shows that, up to the GFC, this curve was substantially the same as that obtained through the OIS curve, consistent with the discussion in chapter 12 (see, e.g., figure 12.1). During and after the GFC, the two curves have diverged. Let us explain.

13.9.4.3 *Divergence*

An important assumption in this chapter is that LIBOR-based deposits are default free. Counterparty risk was a key element of the GFC. What happens in the presence of counterparty risk? Consider the value at t of a "time-deposit," that is, a deposit a counterparty (notably, a bank) makes with another for a period of time equal to $T - t$. Assuming that the short-term interest rate process, r_τ, is independent of default events, the value of a time-deposit is

$$D(t, T) = \mathbb{E}_t\left(e^{-\int_t^T r_\tau d\tau}\left(1 - \mathbb{I}_{\tau < T} l\right)\right) = P^{\text{ois}}(t, T)\left(1 - Q(t, T)\, l\right),$$

where τ denotes the default time of a generic bank counterparty, $l \in [0, 1]$ is the loss given a default event, $Q(t, T)$ is the probability that the borrower defaults by time T and, finally, $P^{\text{ois}}(t, T)$ denotes the price of a risk-free zero such as a value bootstrapped from a OIS, say. One assumption underlying this derivation is that, upon default, the recovery value, $1 - l$, is only paid off at maturity.

Thus, in the presence of counterparty risk, the LIBOR interest rate for the time interval $\delta = T_2 - T_1$ is

$$L(T_1, T_2) = \frac{1}{\delta}\left(\frac{1}{D(T_1, T_2)} - 1\right) = \frac{1}{\delta}\left(\frac{1}{1 - Q(T_1, T_2)\, l}\,\frac{1}{P^{\text{ois}}(T_1, T_2)} - 1\right). \quad (13.155)$$

Eq. (13.155) clearly generalizes our previous formulations of LIBOR rates, obtained under the assumption that $l \equiv 0$. Next, let us determine a LIBOR-based forward rate, $F(t, T_1, T_2)$.

We have

$$F(t,T_1,T_2):0=\mathbb{E}_t\left(e^{-\int_t^{T_1} r_\tau d\tau}\frac{\delta(L(T_1,T_2)-F(t,T_1,T_2))}{1+\delta L(T_1,T_2)}\right).$$

Indeed, the payoff of a FRA paid at T_2 is $\delta(L(T_1,T_2)-F(t,T_1,T_2))$, which is discounted back at T_1 through the LIBOR factor, $1+\delta L(T_1,T_2)$ and, then, at time t through the continuous time discounting factor. At time t, the FRA value is obviously zero.

Now, using the expression for $L(T_1,T_2)$ in eq. (13.155) leaves

$$F(t,T_1,T_2)=\frac{1}{\delta}\left(\frac{1}{1-\mathbb{E}_t(Q(T_1,T_2))\,l}\frac{P^{\text{ois}}(t,T_1)}{P^{\text{ois}}(t,T_2)}-1\right)>\frac{1}{\delta}\left(\frac{P^{\text{ois}}(t,T_1)}{P^{\text{ois}}(t,T_2)}-1\right). \tag{13.156}$$

That is, forward rates quotes for LIBOR-type contracts tend to be higher than forward rates implied by default-free bonds. Mercurio (2009) provides one of the earliest explanations of such a divergence based on counterparty risk. These conclusions generalize to interest rate swap contracts of any maturity and tenors: each contract has its own credit (and liquidity) risk and, then, its own curve. According to current market conventions, discounting is typically done with OIS, whereas forward LIBOR rates are determined through the corresponding forward curve (typically distinct from the OIS curve). We now describe the main features of this methodology.

13.9.4.4 *Pricing after the GFC: OIS discounting*

A key point of the methodology emerging after the GFC is that it relies on *quoted forward rates*, which tend to be lower than those implied by the LIBOR curve (i.e., $F(t,T_1,T_2)$ in (13.156)). That is, these quotes, $F^{\$}(t,T_1,T_2)$ say, tend to be lower than the LIBOR-based theoretical values, $F(t,T_1,T_2)$. One reason for this property is the presence of better collateralization rules for OTC derivatives such as FRA and interest rate swaps. Thus, the counterpart to eq. (13.127) to evaluate an interest rate swap is

$$\text{IRS}(t,T_0,\cdots,T_n;K_{\text{irs}})=\sum_{i=1}^{n}\delta_{i-1}\left(F^{\$}(t,T_{i-1},T_i)-K_{\text{irs}}\right)P^{\text{ois}}(t,T_i), \tag{13.157}$$

where $P^{\text{ois}}(t,T_i)$ is bootstrapped as in (13.154). Furthermore, to determine the forward swap rate, we replace eq. (13.129) with

$$F_{\text{sw}}(t,T_0,\cdots,T_n)=\sum_{i=1}^{n}\omega^{\text{ois}}(t,T_i)F^{\$}\left(t,T_{i-1},T_i\right),\quad \omega^{\text{ois}}(t,T_i)\equiv\frac{\delta_{i-1}P^{\text{ois}}(t,T_i)}{\sum_{i=1}^{n}\delta_{i-1}P^{\text{ois}}(t,T_i)}. \tag{13.158}$$

Furthermore, we can bootstrap market expected values of forward rates based on (13.158), viz

$$\hat{F}^{\$}(t,T_{n-1},T_n)\equiv F_{\text{sw}}(t,T_0,\cdots,T_n)+\frac{\sum_{i=1}^{n-1}\delta_{i-1}P^{\text{ois}}(t,T_i)\left(F_{\text{sw}}(t,T_0,\cdots,T_n)-F^{\$}(t,T_{i-1},T_i)\right)}{\delta_{n-1}P^{\text{ois}}(t,T_n)}.$$

To evaluate swaptions, combine, first, (13.157) and (13.158),

$$\text{IRS}\,(t, T_0, \cdots, T_n; K_{\text{irs}}) = \text{PVBP}_t^{\text{ois}}\,(T_1, \cdots, T_n)\,(F_{\text{sw}}\,(t, T_0, \cdots, T_n) - K_{\text{irs}}),$$

where $\text{PVBP}_t^{\text{ois}}\,(T_1, \cdots, T_n) = \sum_{i=1}^{n} \delta_{i-1} P^{\text{ois}}\,(t, T_i)$. Therefore, the payoff of a payer swaption at time T is $(\text{IRS}\,(T, T_0, \cdots, T_n; K_{\text{irs}}))^+$ and eq. (13.148) is modified as follows

$$\text{SW}_p\,(t) = \text{PVBP}_t^{\text{ois}}\,(T_1, \cdots, T_n)\,\mathbb{E}_{Q_{\text{sw}}^{\text{ois}}}\,(F_{\text{sw}}(T_0) - K_{\text{irs}})^+, \tag{13.159}$$

where $F_{\text{sw}}\,(T_0) \equiv F_{\text{sw}}\,(T_0, T_0, \cdots, T_n)$ (see Eq. (13.158)) and, now, $\mathbb{E}_{Q_{\text{sw}}^{\text{ois}}}$ is the expectation taken under the probability $Q_{\text{sw}}^{\text{ois}}$ defined as in (13.149), but with PVBP^{ois} replacing PVBP. Under standard assumptions, one may evaluate the expectation in (13.159) through Black's formula (see eq. (13.151)), but with the current forward rate given by (13.158).

13.10 Volatility Surfaces

13.10.1 Implied Volatilities

13.10.1.1 Caps and floors

Market practice quoting conventions rely on volatility surfaces stemming from the market models of the previous section, not on the approach in section 13.8.7–13.8.9. In principle, the models in section 13.8.7–13.8.9 may be used to produce volatility surfaces, albeit indirectly, after calibration of the two parameters κ and σ, as eq. (13.133) indicates. However, it is easier to provide volatility surfaces in the first place, through the models of this section. Quite simply, practitioners use eq. (13.147) and quote volatilities such that the market price of a cap equals to the value predicted by eq. (13.147) using the desired implied volatility s_i. In eq. (13.147),

$$s_i = \sqrt{T_{i-1} - t} \cdot \gamma\,(i),$$

for some $\gamma\,(i)$, although, then, practitioners simply quote the value of $\hat{\gamma}_n$ that satisfies

$$\hat{\gamma}_n : p_{\text{cap}}^{\$}\,(t; n) = \sum_{i=1}^{n} \delta_{i-1} P(t, T_i) \cdot \mathbb{B}\left(F_{i-1,t}; K, \hat{s}_{i,n}\right),$$

where $p_{\text{cap}}^{\$}\,(t; n)$ is the market price of the cap, and

$$\mathbb{B}\left(F_{i-1,t}; K, \hat{s}_{i,n}\right) = F_{i-1,t}\Phi\left(d_{1,i-1}^n\right) - K\Phi\left(d_{1,i-1}^n - \hat{s}_{i,n}\right),$$

$$d_{1,i-1}^n = \frac{\ln \frac{F_{i-1,t}}{K} + \frac{1}{2}\hat{s}_{i,n}^2}{\hat{s}_{i,n}}, \quad \hat{s}_{i,n} = \sqrt{T_{i-1} - t} \cdot \hat{\gamma}_n$$

Given n, we can bootstrap $\hat{\gamma}\,(i)$, that is, we can recursively solve for $\hat{\gamma}\,(i)$, as follows

$$0 = \sum_{i=1}^{n} \delta_{i-1} P(t, T_i) \cdot \left[\mathbb{B}\left(F_{i-1,t}; K, \hat{s}_{i,n}\right) - \mathbb{B}\left(F_{i-1,t}; K, \hat{s}_i\right)\right], \quad n = 1, \cdots, N,$$

where N is the latest available maturity, and $\hat{s}_i = \sqrt{T_{i-1} - t} \cdot \hat{\gamma}\,(i)$. The values of $\hat{\gamma}\,(i)$ amount to what is typically referred to as the term structure of caps volatilities.

13.10.1.2 *Swaptions*

As for swaptions, the situation is much simpler. The market practice is to quote swaptions through standard implied vols, that is, those vols IV_t such that, once inserted into eq. (13.151), deliver the swaption market price:

$$SW_p^{\$}(t) = PVBP_t(T_1, \cdots, T_n) \cdot \mathbb{B}(F_{sw}(t, T_0, \cdots, T_n); T_0, K_{irs}, IV_t).$$

13.10.2 Local Volatilities and SABR Models

How to evaluate illiquid derivatives while making sure that the existing products are fitted without error? When the "existing products" are derivatives, we can apply the same methodology relying on *local volatilities*, and put forward in chapter 11 (see section 11.7). However, Hagan, Kumar, Lesniewski, and Woodward (2002) (HKLW, henceforth) note that local volatility models may display some counterfactual properties. Consider the modeling of swaptions and assume, for simplicity, that local vols, denoted with $\sigma_{loc}(R_{n,\tau})$, are independent of calendar time, where $R_{n,\tau}$ denotes the forward swap rate at time τ for a given tenor T_n, i.e., $R_{n,\tau} \equiv F_{sw}(\tau, T_0, \cdots, T_n)$. Hagan and Woodward (1999) show that the implied Black's skew can be represented as

$$\sigma_{iv}(K, R_n) = \sigma_{loc}\left(\tfrac{1}{2}(K + R_n)\right)\left(1 + \frac{1}{24}\frac{\sigma''_{loc}\left(\frac{1}{2}(K+R_n)\right)}{\sigma_{loc}\left(\frac{1}{2}(K+R_n)\right)}(R_n - K)^2 + \cdots\right., \tag{13.160}$$

and argue that the terms omitted from this expansion may be very small for all intents and purposes.

How does the skew behave? To simplify, we approximate $\sigma_{iv}(\cdot,\cdot)$ with the first term on the RHS of eq. (13.160), and denote the result with $\hat{\sigma}_{iv}(K, R_n)$. Suppose, then, that the forward swap rate increases from R_n to $R_n + \Delta R_n$,

$$\hat{\sigma}_{iv}(K, R_n + \Delta R_n) \equiv \sigma_{loc}\left(\tfrac{1}{2}(K + R_n + \Delta R_n)\right) = \hat{\sigma}_{iv}(K + \Delta R_n, R_n).$$

If σ_{loc} is decreasing, the previous equality implies that the skew moves to the left as R_n increases, which does not seem to be consistent with empirical properties. Thus, a local vol model may lead to counterfactual properties. To illustrate this point, Mele and Obayashi (2016) provide the following example, a local volatility function $\sigma_{loc}(x) = 0.04 \cdot x^{-1/2}$. Figure 13.16 (left panel) plots the implied volatility, $\hat{\sigma}_{iv}(K, R_n)$ for two levels of R_n, i.e., $R_n = 3\%$ (solid line) and $R_n = 4\%$ (dashed line).

HKLW introduce a model that seems to fix some of these issues, which they refer to as SABR, for "Stochastic-$\alpha\beta\rho$." In this model, $R_{n,t}$ satisfies

$$\begin{cases} dR_{n,\tau} &= v_\tau R_{n,\tau}^{\beta} dW_{1\tau} \\ dv_\tau &= \xi v_\tau \left(\rho dW_{1\tau} + \sqrt{1-\rho^2} dW_{2\tau}\right), \quad v_t \equiv \alpha_t \end{cases} \tag{13.161}$$

where $W_{i\tau}$ are two standard Brownian motions defined under the forward swap probability; β, ρ, and ξ are constants; α_t is the initial condition for the stochastic volatility factor v_τ; finally, ρ is the instantaneous correlation of the forward swap rate and its stochastic volatility component, v_τ. Now, HKLW show that this model predicts the following skew

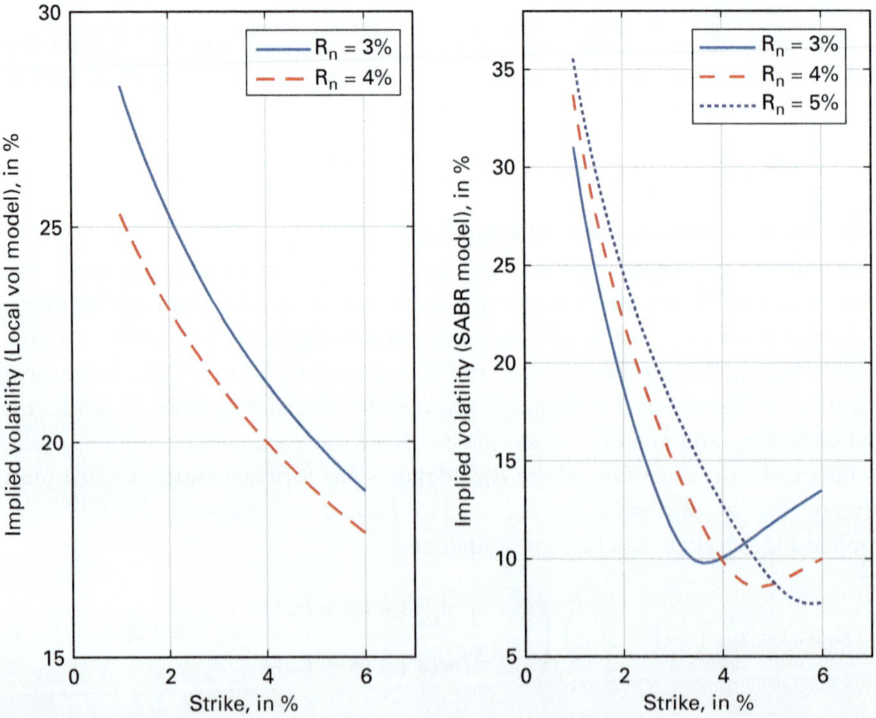

Figure 13.16
The left panel depicts the approximated skew $\hat{\sigma}_{\text{iv}}(K, R_n)$ when local volatility is $\sigma_{\text{loc}}(x) = 0.04 \cdot x^{-1/2}$; solid and dashed lines are the skews resulting from values of $R_{n,t}$ equal to 3% and 4%, resp. The right panel depicts the approximated skew $\sigma_{\text{iv}}(K, R_{n,t}; \alpha_t)$ in eq. (13.162) predicted by the SABR model in eqs. (13.161), with $\alpha_t = 0.02$, $\rho = -0.5$, $\beta = 0.5$, $\xi = 0.5$, and time to maturity $T = 1$; solid, dashed and dotted lines are skews resulting from values of $R_{n,t}$ equal to 3%, 4% and 5%, resp.

$$\sigma_{\text{iv}}(K, R_{n,t}; \alpha_t) = \frac{\alpha_t}{(R_{n,t}K)^{(1-\beta)/2}} \times \frac{1 + \left(\frac{(1-\beta)^2}{24} \frac{\alpha_t^2}{(R_{n,t}K)^{1-\beta}} + \frac{1}{4} \frac{\rho\beta\xi}{(R_{n,t}K)^{(1-\beta)/2}} \alpha_t + \frac{2-3\rho^2}{24} \xi^2 \right) T + \cdots}{\left(1 + \frac{(1-\beta)^2}{24} \ln^2 \frac{R_{n,t}}{K} + \frac{(1-\beta)^4}{1920} \ln^4 \frac{R_{n,t}}{K} + \cdots \right)} \frac{z_t}{u(z_t)}, \tag{13.162}$$

where

$$z_t \equiv \frac{\xi}{\alpha_t} (R_{n,t}K)^{(1-\beta)/2} \ln \frac{R_{n,t}}{K}, \quad u(z_t) \equiv \ln \frac{\sqrt{1 - 2\rho z_t + z_t^2} + z_t - \rho}{1 - \rho}.$$

Figure 13.16 (right panel) depicts the skew predicted by the model, and obtained through the first term of the RHS in (13.162). It is based on the same parameter values used by Mele and Obayashi (2016) and, hence, reproduces their Figure 20.6. The model seems to provide the right predictions: the skew shifts to the right as $R_{n,t}$ increases. The model also gives rise to a downward-sloping "backbone," defined as the curve traced by at-the-money volatilities as $R_{n,t}$ changes.

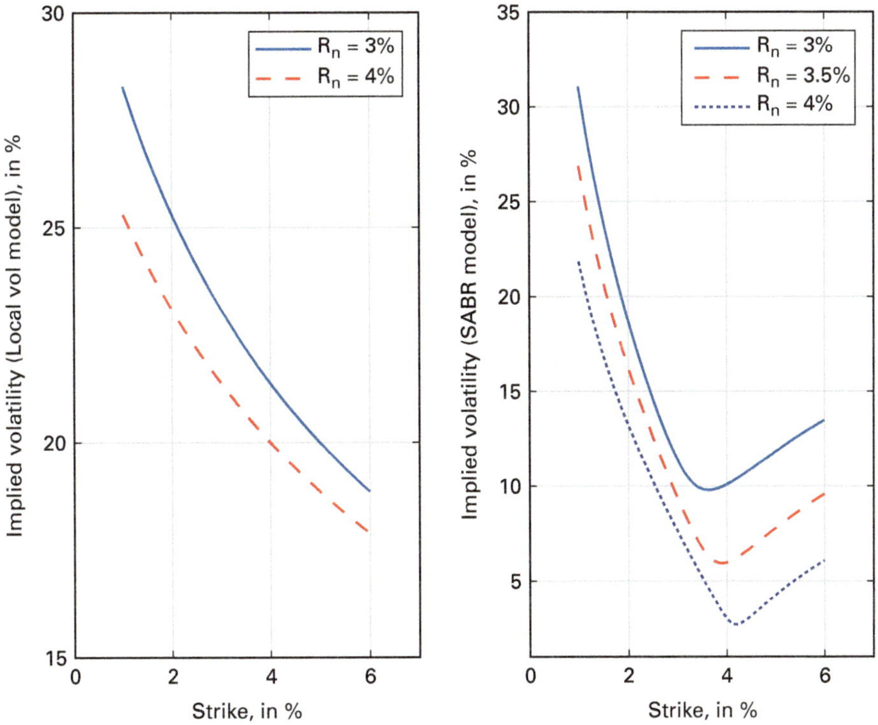

Figure 13.17
The left panel is the same as the left panel in figure 13.16. The right panel depicts the approximated skew $\sigma_{\text{iv}}\left(K, R_{n,t}; \alpha_t\right)$ in eq. (13.162) predicted by the SABR model in eqs. (13.161), obtained with the parameters values used in figure 13.16. Solid, dashed and dotted lines are skews resulting from values of $R_{n,t}$ equal to 3%, 3.5% and 4%, resp. The values of α_t in correspondence of the three values of $R_{n,t}$ are $\alpha_t = 0.02$, and then, two increments obtained consistent with the negative correlation in eqs. (13.161), $\Delta\alpha = \frac{\rho\xi}{R_n^\beta}\Delta R_n$.

The backbone is downward sloping because $\beta < 1$. HKLW also argue that their model predicts a skew (i.e., decreasing volatilities) due to two properties: (i) $\beta < 1$, and (ii) $\rho < 0$. Intuitively, by the first property, the instantaneous volatility in eqs. (13.161), $\upsilon R_n^{\beta-1}$, is decreasing in R_n; by the second property, the transition density of $\frac{dR_n}{R_n}$ is skewed to the left, as in standard explanations of Heston (1993) in the equity case (see section 11.5 in chapter 11). Furthermore, ξ is the volatility of volatility parameter, and explains the curvature of the skew. Finally, the skew shifts up as α_t increases, an intuitive property: in this model, option prices increase with α_t (see section 11.5.3.3 in chapter 11), a property inherited by the skew.

At the time of writing, market practice relies on SABR models in order to deal with the swaption skew. It goes without saying that the model does not enable one to perfectly match all liquid swaption prices—theoretically, local vols models do achieve this task. Finally, note that the comparative statics exercise in figure 13.16 regards a change in $R_{n,t}$. Because $R_{n,t}$ is correlated with volatility, an alternative comparative statics exercise is one in which both the forward swap rate and volatility change in accordance with their assumed correlation (see Bartlett, 2006). Figure 13.17 shows that in this case with negative correlation, an increase in the forward swap rate accompanied by a decrease in the volatility (consistent with the negative correlation) implies the skew shifts toward the left although the backbone is still downward sloping.

Appendix 13.A Bond Prices and Arbitrage Restrictions

We assume that available for trading are m pure discount bonds with prices $P_i \equiv P(\tau, T_i)$ satisfying:

$$\frac{dP_i}{P_i} = \mu_{bi} d\tau + \sigma_{bi} \cdot dW, \ i = 1, \cdots, m, \tag{13.A1}$$

where W is a Brownian motion in $\mathbb{R}^d$, and μ_{bi} and σ_{bi} (σ_{bi} is vector-valued) are such that there exists a strong solution to the previous system. The value of a self-financing portfolio in these m bonds and a money market account satisfies:

$$dV = \left(\pi^{\top}(\mu_b - \mathbf{1}_m r) + rV\right) d\tau + \pi^{\top} \sigma_b dW,$$

where π is some portfolio, $\mathbf{1}_m$ is a m-dimensional vector of ones, and

$$\mu_b = [\mu_{b1}, \cdots, \mu_{bm}]^{\top}, \quad \sigma_b = [\sigma_{b1}, \cdots, \sigma_{bm}]^{\top}.$$

Now suppose there exists a portfolio $\underline{\pi}$ such that $\underline{\pi}^{\top} \sigma_b = 0$. This is an arbitrage opportunity if there exist events for which at some time, $\mu_b - \mathbf{1}_m r \neq 0$. (Use as as usual (see chapter 4), $\underline{\pi}$ when $\mu_b - \mathbf{1}_m r > 0$, and $-\underline{\pi}$ when $\mu_m - \mathbf{1}_d r < 0$: the drift of V will then be appreciating at a deterministic rate that is strictly greater than r.) Therefore, arbitrage is ruled out if:

$$\pi^{\top}(\mu_b - \mathbf{1}_m r) = 0 \text{ whenever } \pi^{\top} \sigma_b = 0.$$

In other terms, there is no arbitrage as soon as every vector in the null space of σ_b is orthogonal to $\mu_b - \mathbf{1}_m r$, or when there exists a λ in $\mathbb{R}^d$ and satisfying a few integrability conditions, and such that $\mu_b - \mathbf{1}_m r = \sigma_b \lambda$, or

$$\mu_{bi} - r = \sigma_{bi} \lambda, \quad i = 1, \cdots, m. \tag{13.A2}$$

In this case,

$$\frac{dP_i}{P_i} = (r + \sigma_{bi} \lambda) \, d\tau + \sigma_{bi} \cdot dW, \ i = 1, \cdots, m.$$

Next, define $\tilde{W} = W + \int \lambda d\tau$, $\frac{dQ}{dP} = \exp(-\int_t^T \lambda^{\top} dW - \frac{1}{2} \int_t^T \|\lambda\|^2 \, d\tau)$. By Girsanov's theorem, the discounted bond price is a martingale under Q. Indeed, define, for a generic i, $P(\tau, T) \equiv P(\tau, T_i) \equiv P_i$, and

$$g_\tau \equiv e^{-\int_t^\tau r_u du} P(\tau, T), \quad \tau \in [t, T].$$

By Girsanov's theorem and Itô's lemma,

$$\frac{dg}{g} = \sigma_{bi} \cdot d\tilde{W}, \quad \text{under } Q.$$

Therefore, for all $\tau \in [t, T]$, $g_\tau = \mathbb{E}_\tau(g_T)$, implying that

$$g_\tau \equiv e^{-\int_t^\tau r_u du} P(\tau, T) = \mathbb{E}_\tau(g_T) = \mathbb{E}_\tau[e^{-\int_t^T r_u du} \underbrace{P(T,T)]}_{=1} = \mathbb{E}_t\left(e^{-\int_t^T r_u du}\right),$$

or

$$P(\tau, T) = e^{\int_t^\tau r_u du} \mathbb{E}_t\left(e^{-\int_t^T r_u du}\right) = \mathbb{E}_t\left(e^{-\int_\tau^T r_u du}\right), \quad \text{all } \tau \in [t, T],$$

which is eq. (13.2).

Note that no assumptions have been made regarding the number of zero coupon bonds, m. For example, suppose that $m < d$, and that there are no other assets traded in this market. Then, there exist an infinite number of risk neutral probabilities Q. If $m = d$, there exists one and only one risk neutral probability Q. If $m > d$, there exists one and only one risk neutral probability but then, the various bond prices have to satisfy some basic no-arbitrage restrictions. For example, take $m = 2$ and $d = 1$, such that eq. (13.A2) reduces to,

$$\frac{\mu_{b1} - r}{\sigma_{b1}} = \lambda = \frac{\mu_{b2} - r}{\sigma_{b2}}.$$

In other terms, the Sharpe ratio of any two bonds must be identical. Eq. (13.A2) is used several times in this chapter. In section 13.4, the market primitive is the short-term rate, solution of a multidimensional diffusion process, and μ_{bi} and σ_{bi} are derived via Itô's lemma. In section 13.7, μ_{bi} and σ_{bi} are restricted by a model for the forward rates.

Appendix 13.B Forward Probabilities

We provide results that complement those in chapter 4 on forward probability. Note that these results are being placed within one of the first appendixes of this chapter, due to the important role forward probabilities play in asset evaluation in fixed income markets.

13.B.1 Density Processes

Eq. (13.108) defines $\eta_T(T)$ as

$$\eta_T(T) = \frac{e^{-\int_t^T r_\tau d\tau} \cdot 1}{\mathbb{E}_t\left(e^{-\int_t^T r_\tau d\tau}\right)}$$

More generally, define a *density process* as

$$\eta_T(\tau) \equiv \frac{e^{-\int_t^\tau r_u du} \cdot P(\tau, T)}{\mathbb{E}_t\left(e^{-\int_t^T r_\tau d\tau}\right)}, \quad \tau \in [t, T]. \tag{13.A3}$$

By the FTAP, the numerator of $\eta_T(\tau)$ is a martingale under Q (see appendix 13.A in this chapter). Therefore, $\mathbb{E}(\frac{dQ_F^T}{dQ}\big| \mathcal{F}_\tau) = \mathbb{E}(\eta_T(T)| \mathcal{F}_\tau) = \eta_T(\tau)$ all $\tau \in [t, T]$, and in particular, $\eta_T(t) = 1$.

We demonstrate these claims under a slightly different angle. Let us consider the price dynamics of a zero coupon bond in eq. (13.A1), $P(\tau, T) \equiv P(\tau, T_i)$. Under the risk neutral probability Q,

$$\frac{dP}{P} = r \cdot d\tau + \sigma \cdot d\tilde{W},$$

where $\tilde{W}$ is a Q-Brownian motion and $\sigma \equiv \sigma_{bi}$. By Itô's lemma,

$$\frac{d\eta_T(\tau)}{\eta_T(\tau)} = -(-\sigma(\tau, T)) \cdot d\tilde{W}_\tau, \quad \eta_T(t) = 1.$$

The solution is:

$$\eta_T(\tau) = \exp\left(-\frac{1}{2}\int_t^\tau \|\sigma(u, T)\|^2 \, du - \int_t^\tau (-\sigma(u, T)) \cdot d\tilde{W}_u\right).$$

Under standard regularity conditions, we can use Girsanov's theorem and conclude that

$$W_\tau^{Q_F^T} \equiv \tilde{W}_\tau + \int_t^\tau \left(-\sigma(u, T)^\top\right) du \tag{13.A4}$$

is a Brownian motion under the T-forward probability Q_F^T.

Assuming for example that the driving state variable is the short-term rate, we have that the drift under Q_F^T of the same short-term rate is lower and that of the bond price is higher, due to negative bond price volatility, $\sigma < 0$.

Finally, note that for all i and nondecreasing sequences of dates $\{T_i\}_{i=0,1,\cdots,}$,

$$W_\tau^{Q_F^{T_i}} = \tilde{W}_\tau + \int_t^\tau \left(-\sigma(u, T_i)^\top\right) du, \quad i = 0, 1, \cdots.$$

Therefore,

$$W_\tau^{Q_F^{T_i}} = W_\tau^{Q_F^{T_{i-1}}} - \int_t^\tau \left(\sigma(u, T_i)^\top - \sigma(u, T_{i-1})^\top\right) du, \quad i = 1, 2, \cdots, \tag{13.A5}$$

is a Brownian motion under the T_i-forward martingale probability $Q_F^{T_i}$. Eqs. (13.A5) and (13.A4) are used in section 13.9 on interest rate derivatives.

13.B.2 Certainty Equivalents and Forward Prices

Multiply both sides of the pricing equation (13.2) by the amount S_T:

$$P(t, T) \cdot S_T = \mathbb{E}_t\left(e^{-\int_t^T r_\tau d\tau}\right) \cdot S_T.$$

Suppose momentarily that S_T is known at T. In this case, we have:

$$P(t, T) \cdot S_T = \mathbb{E}_t\left(e^{-\int_t^T r_\tau d\tau} \cdot S_T\right).$$

But in the context of this chapter, S_T is random. Define then its certainty equivalent by the number $\overline{S_T}$ that solves:

$$P(t, T) \cdot \overline{S_T} = \mathbb{E}_t\left(e^{-\int_t^T r_\tau d\tau} \cdot S_T\right),$$

or

$$\overline{S_T} = \mathbb{E}_t \left(\eta_T(T) \cdot S_T \right), \tag{13.A6}$$

where $\eta_T(T)$ has been defined in (13.108).

Comparing eq. (13.A6) with eq. (13.107) reveals that forward prices can be interpreted in terms of the previously defined certainty equivalent.

Appendix 13.C Factors and Components

This analysis provides some technical details regarding factor and principal component analysis that complement material in section 13.3.

13.C.1 Factor Analysis

Suppose that in eq. (13.22), $F \sim N(0, I)$, and that $\epsilon \sim N(0, \Psi)$, where Ψ is diagonal. Then, $R \sim N(\bar{R}, \Sigma)$, where $\Sigma = BB^\top + \Psi$. The assumptions that $F \sim N(0, I)$ and that Ψ is diagonal are necessary to identify the model, but not sufficient. Indeed, any orthogonal rotation of the factors yields a new set of factors that also satisfies eq. (13.22). Precisely, let T be an orthonormal matrix. Then, $(BT)(BT)^\top = BTT^\top B^\top = BB^\top$. Hence, the factor loadings B and BT have the same ability to generate the matrix Σ.

A unique solution obtains once we impose additional constraints on B. For example, Jöreskog (1967) develops a maximum likelihood approach to estimate a factor model, with a constraint that has some flavor of principal component analysis. Consider the log-likelihood function, $-\frac{1}{2}N\left[\ln|\Sigma| + \text{Tr}\left(S\Sigma^{-1}\right)\right]$, where S is the sample covariance matrix of R. The idea is to maximize this function under the constraint that $B^\top \Psi B$ is diagonal. The algorithm is: (i) for a given Ψ, maximize the log-likelihood with respect to B, under the constraint that $B^\top \Psi B$ is diagonal with elements arranged in descending order, thereby obtaining $\hat{B}$; (ii) given $\hat{B}$, maximize the log-likelihood with respect to Ψ, thereby obtaining $\hat{\Psi}$, which is fed back into step (i), etc. Knez, Litterman, and Scheinkman (1994) describe this approach and additional identification devices.

13.C.2 Principal Component Analysis

Principal component analysis transforms the original data into a set of uncorrelated variables, the principal components, with variances arranged in descending order. Consider the following program,

$$\max_{C_1} \left(var\left(Y_1\right) \right) \text{ s.t. } C_1^\top C_1 = 1,$$

where $var(Y_1) = C_1^\top \Sigma C_1$, and the constraint is an identification constraint. The first order conditions lead to,

$$(\Sigma - \lambda I)\, C_1 = 0,$$

where λ is a Lagrange multiplier. The previous condition tells us that λ must be one eigenvalue of the matrix Σ, and that C_1 must be the corresponding eigenvector. Moreover, we have $var(Y_1) = C_1^\top \Sigma C_1 = \lambda$ which is clearly maximized by the largest eigenvalue. Suppose that the eigenvalues of Σ are distinct, and let us arrange them in descending order, i.e.,

$\lambda_1 > \cdots > \lambda_p$. Then,

$$var(Y_1) = \lambda_1.$$

Therefore, the first principal component is $Y_1 = C_1^\top (R - \bar{R})$, where C_1 is the eigenvector corresponding to the largest eigenvalue, λ_1.

Next, consider the second principal component. The program, now, is

$$\max_{C_2} (var(Y_2)) \text{ s.t. } C_2^\top C_2 = 1 \text{ and } C_2^\top C_1 = 0,$$

where $var(Y_2) = C_2^\top \Sigma C_2$. The first constraint, $C_2^\top C_2 = 1$, is the usual identification constraint. The second constraint, $C_2^\top C_1 = 0$, ensures that Y_1 and Y_2 are orthogonal, that is, $E(Y_1 Y_2) = 0$. The first-order conditions for this problem are

$$0 = 2\Sigma C_2 - 2\lambda C_2 - \nu C_1$$

where λ is the Lagrange multiplier associated with the first constraint, and ν is the Lagrange multiplier associated with the second constraint. By premultiplying the first-order conditions by $C_1^\top$,

$$0 = 2C_1^\top \Sigma C_2 - \nu,$$

where we have used the two constraints $C_1^\top C_2 = 0$ and $C_1^\top C_1 = 1$. Now, because $C_1^\top \Sigma = \lambda_1 C_1^\top$ and $C_1^\top C_2 = 0$, the previous equality implies that $\nu = 0$. Therefore, the first-order conditions can be rewritten as

$$(\Sigma - \lambda I) C_2 = 0.$$

The solution is now λ_2, and C_2 is the eigenvector corresponding to λ_2. (Indeed, this time we cannot choose λ_1 as this choice would imply that $Y_2 = C_1^\top (R - \bar{R})$, implying that $E(Y_1 Y_2) \neq 0$.) It follows that $var(Y_2) = \lambda_2$.

In general, we have,

$$var(Y_i) = \lambda_i, \quad i = 1, \cdots, p.$$

Let Λ be the diagonal matrix with the eigenvalues λ_i on the diagonal. By the spectral decomposition of Σ, $\Sigma = C\Lambda C^\top$, and by the orthonormality of C, $C^\top C = I$, we have that $C^\top \Sigma C = \Lambda$ and, hence,

$$\sum_{i=1}^{p} var(R_i) = \mathrm{Tr}(\Sigma) = \mathrm{Tr}\left(\Sigma C C^\top\right) = \mathrm{Tr}\left(C^\top \Sigma C\right) = \mathrm{Tr}(\Lambda).$$

Hence, eq. (13.25) follows.

Appendix 13.D Jumps

13.D.1 Government Bond Volatility and Jumps

This section provides proofs related to the government bond volatility model of section 13.4.6.

Proof that $C(\tau) \geq 0$ in eq. (13.53). Differentiate eq. (13.52) with respect to v, and conclude that the bond price sensitivity to the jump intensity, $\Phi(r, v, t, T) = P_v(r, v, t, T)$, is the solution to

$$\left(r+k_v\right)\Phi=\frac{\partial\Phi}{\partial t}+k_r\left(r^*-r\right)\Phi_r+\frac{1}{2}\sigma^2\Phi_{rr}+k_v\left(v^*-v\right)\Phi_v+\frac{1}{2}\xi v\Phi_{vv}$$
$$+\left(P\left(r+q,v;t,T\right)-P\left(r,v;t,T\right)\right)+v\left(\Phi\left(r+q,v;t,T\right)-\Phi\left(r,v;t,T\right)\right), \tag{13.A7}$$

with the boundary condition $\Phi\left(r,v,T,T\right)=0$. We may extend the usual Feynman–Kac representation theorem (see section 4.2 in chapter 4) in order to deal with jumps, and conclude that

$$\Phi\left(r_t,v_t,t,T\right)=\mathbb{E}_t\left(\int_t^T e^{-\int_t^u\left(r_s+k_v\right)ds}\left(P\left(r_u+q,v_u;u,T\right)-P\left(r_u,v_u;u,T\right)\right)du\right).$$

A formal proof of the previous equation is left to the reader as an exercise. Note, now, that $P_r<0$ such that the integrand in the previous expression is negative. Thus, $\Phi<0$ and, hence, $C\left(\tau\right)\geq 0$, as claimed.

The yield curve increases with the interest rate jump size. We now prove a statement in the main text, namely, that the bond price in eq. (13.53) decreases with q, the jump size of the short-term rate. We rely on the same line of reasoning around "increasing risk" in appendix 8.D.2 of chapter 8 (see theorem 8.A1). Consider, then, two markets with different jump sizes: q_A and q_B, with $q_A>q_B$, and denote with P_j the resulting prices, with $j=A,B$. The price difference, $\Delta P\equiv P_B-P_A$, is the solution to

$$r\Delta P=\frac{\partial\Delta P}{\partial t}+k_r\left(r^*-r\right)\Delta P_r+\frac{1}{2}\sigma^2\Delta P_{rr}+k_v\left(v^*-v\right)\Delta P_v+\frac{1}{2}\xi^2 v\Delta P_{vv}$$
$$+v\left(\Delta P\left(r+q_B,v;t,T\right)-\Delta P\left(r,v;t,T\right)\right)+\varphi\left(r+q_B,v;t,T\right),$$

where

$$\varphi\left(r+q_B,v;t,T\right)=v\left(P_A\left(r+q_B,v;t,T\right)-P_A\left(r+q_A,v;t,T\right)\right)>0,$$

and the last inequality follows by the assumption that $q_A>q_B$. By arguments nearly identical to show that $\Phi<0$ in (13.A7), we conclude that $\Delta P>0$. That is, bond prices decrease with q.

Proof of eq. (13.56). Replace the expression for the log-price instantaneous variance in (13.55) into the definition of expected variance, and obtain

$$\begin{aligned}&(\mathcal{T}-t)\cdot\text{T-VIX}_t^2(\mathcal{T})\\&=\mathbb{E}_{Q_F^{\mathcal{T}}}\left(\int_t^{\mathcal{T}}V\left(v_u;u,\mathcal{T}\right)du\right)\\&=\mathbb{B}^2\left(t,T,\mathcal{T}\right)\sigma^2+\int_t^{\mathcal{T}}\mathbb{E}_{Q_F^{\mathcal{T}}}\left(C^2\left(T-u\right)\xi^2v_u\right)du+\int_t^{\mathcal{T}}\mathbb{E}_{Q_F^{\mathcal{T}}}\left(B^2\left(T-u\right)q^2dN_u\right)\\&=\mathbb{B}^2\left(t,T,\mathcal{T}\right)\sigma^2+\int_t^{\mathcal{T}}C^2\left(T-u\right)\xi^2\mathbb{E}_{Q_F^{\mathcal{T}}}\left(v_u\right)du+\int_t^{\mathcal{T}}B^2\left(T-u\right)q^2\mathbb{E}_{Q_F^{\mathcal{T}}}\left(v_{F\mathcal{T},u}\right)du,\end{aligned} \tag{13.A8}$$

where $\mathbb{B}^2(t,T,\mathcal{T}) \equiv \int_t^{\tau} B^2(\mathcal{T}-u)du$ and $v_{F\mathcal{T},t}$ denotes the intensity of N_t under the $\mathcal{T}$-forward probability. The last equality follows by results in appendix 4.F.3 in chapter 4 (see eq. (4.A34)): for any probability P_X,

$$\mathbb{E}_{P_X}(N_T) = \mathbb{E}_{P_X}\left(\int_t^T v_{P_X,u} du\right),$$

where $\mathbb{E}_{P_X}$ denotes the expectation under P_X and $v_{P_X,t}$ is the instantaneous intensity under under P_X. Next, we determine $v_{F\mathcal{T},t}$ and the dynamics of both v_t and $v_{F\mathcal{T},t}$ under $Q_F^{\mathcal{T}}$.

Consider the density process for the forward probability in appendix 13.B (see eq. (13.A3)), where the price $P(u,\mathcal{T})$ is, now, solution to Eq. (13.54). By Itô's lemma,

$$\begin{aligned}\frac{d\eta_{\mathcal{T}}(u)}{\eta_{\mathcal{T}}(u)} &= -\left(-\frac{1}{P_u}\frac{\partial P_u}{\partial r}\sigma\right)d\tilde{W}_{1u} - \left(-\frac{1}{P_u}\frac{\partial P_u}{\partial v}\xi\sqrt{v_u}\right)d\tilde{W}_{2u} + \frac{J_u}{P_u}(dN_u - v_u du)\\ &= -B(\mathcal{T}-u)\sigma d\tilde{W}_{1u} - C(\mathcal{T}-u)\xi\sqrt{v_u}d\tilde{W}_{2u} + \frac{J_u}{P_u}(dN_u - v_u du),\end{aligned}$$

with $\eta_{\mathcal{T}}(t)=1$, and where second lines follows by the expression for the bond price in eq. (13.53). Therefore, by Girsanov's theorem, $dW_{2t}^{Q_F^{\mathcal{T}}} = d\tilde{W}_{2t} + C(\mathcal{T}-t)\xi\sqrt{v_t}dt$ is a Brownian motion under $Q_F^{\mathcal{T}}$, such that, under $Q_F^{\mathcal{T}}$, v_t is the solution to

$$dv_u = (k_v v^* - G(\mathcal{T}-u)v_u)du + \xi\sqrt{v_u}dW_{2u}^{Q_F^{\mathcal{T}}}, \quad G(\tau) \equiv k_v + C(\tau)\xi^2. \tag{13.A9}$$

To determine $v_{F\mathcal{T},t}$, the intensity of N_t under $Q_F^{\mathcal{T}}$, note that, by results in appendix 4.F (see eq. (4.A27)), it must be that $\frac{J_u}{P_u} = \frac{v_{F\mathcal{T},u}}{v_u} - 1$, such that, using the definition of J_t, the expression for the bond price, and rearranging,

$$v_{F\mathcal{T},t} = e^{-B(\mathcal{T}-t)q}v_t. \tag{13.A10}$$

Based on eq. (13.A9)–(13.A10), we may now calculate the two conditional expectations appearing in the last line of eq. (13.A8). We have

$$\mathbb{E}_{Q_F^{\mathcal{T}}}(v_u) = k_v v^* \int_t^u e^{-\int_s^u G(\mathcal{T}-\tau)d\tau}ds + e^{-\int_t^u G(\mathcal{T}-\tau)d\tau}v_t,$$

$$\text{and} \quad \mathbb{E}_{Q_F^{\mathcal{T}}}(v_{F\mathcal{T},u}) = e^{-B(\mathcal{T}-u)q}\mathbb{E}_{Q_F^{\mathcal{T}}}(v_u).$$

Replacing these two expressions into eq. (13.A8), and rearranging terms, leaves eq. (13.56), with the two functions $\mathcal{A}(\mathcal{T}-t)$ and $\mathcal{B}(\mathcal{T}-t)$ given by

$$\begin{aligned}\mathcal{A}(\mathcal{T}-t) &= \frac{\mathbb{B}^2(t,T,\mathcal{T})}{\mathcal{T}-t}\sigma^2 + \frac{k_v v^*}{\mathcal{T}-t}\int_t^{\mathcal{T}}\left(\int_t^u e^{-\int_s^u G(\mathcal{T}-\tau)d\tau}ds\right)\Psi_u(\mathcal{T},T)du\\ \mathcal{B}(\mathcal{T}-t) &= \frac{1}{\mathcal{T}-t}\int_t^{\mathcal{T}} e^{-\int_t^u G(\mathcal{T}-\tau)d\tau}\Psi_u(\mathcal{T},T)du\end{aligned} \tag{13.A11}$$

where

$$\Psi_u(\mathcal{T},T) \equiv C^2(\mathcal{T}-u)\xi^2 + B^2(\mathcal{T}-u)q^2e^{-B(\mathcal{T}-u)q}.$$

Remark. Note that $v_{FT,\tau}$ is clearly lower than v_τ. This property is consistent with explanations in chapter 4 (see section 4.5.2): the forward probability assigns a higher weight to lower interest rate paths. Equally consistent with this explanation are the dynamics of v_t under Q_F^T. Indeed, the drift of v_t in eq. (13.A9) is uniformly lower than the drift of v_t under the risk neutral probability. Therefore, by a comparison theorem (e.g., Karatzas and Shreve (1991, 291–295)), the paths of v_t under Q_F^T are dominated by those under Q.

13.D.2 Comparison Results Regarding Defaultable Bonds

Next, we provide some proofs regarding the defaultable bond model in section 13.4.6. Consider two markets A and B where the default intensities are v^A and v^B, and assume that the coefficients of L are independent of v^i. The pre-default bond price in market i is $P^i(r,\tau,T)$, and by eq. (13.59), satisfies

$$0=(L-r)\,P^i+v^i(\bar{P}^i-P^i),\quad i=A,B,$$

with the usual boundary condition. Assuming that $\bar{P}^A=\bar{P}^B$, subtracting these two equations, and rearranging terms, leads to the result that the price difference $\Delta P(r,\tau,T)\equiv P^A(r,\tau,T)-P^B(r,\tau,T)$ satisfies

$$0=\left(L-(r+v^A)\right)\Delta P\,(r,\tau,T)+\left(v^A-v^B\right)\left[\bar{P}^B\,(\tau)-P^B\,(r,\tau,T)\right],$$

with the boundary condition $\Delta P\,(r,T,T)=0$ for all r. Because $\bar{P}^B<P^B$, one has that $\Delta P\,(r,\tau,T)<0$ whenever $v^A>v^B$, by an application of the maximum principle reviewed in appendix 8.D of chapter 8.

Appendix 13.E Exponential-Affine Models

13.E.1 Riccati's Equations

First, note that in these models, the vector Brownian motion under the risk neutral probability is defined as $d\tilde{W}_\tau=dW_\tau+\Lambda\,(y_\tau)\,d\tau$, where the risk premium vector Λ is as in eq. (13.70), such that, assuming that $\Pr\{V\,(y_t)_{(ii)}>0 \text{ all } t\}=1$, the factor dynamics under the risk neutral probability are

$$\begin{aligned} dy_\tau&=\left(\kappa\,(\mu-y_\tau)-\Sigma V^2\,(y_\tau)\,\lambda_1-\Sigma\lambda_2 y_\tau\right)d\tau+\Sigma V\,(y_\tau)\,d\tilde{W}_\tau\\ &=\kappa_Q\left(\mu_Q-y_\tau\right)d\tau+\Sigma V\,(y_\tau)\,d\tilde{W}_\tau, \end{aligned} \tag{13.A12}$$

for some matrix κ_Q and vector μ_Q. Then, by Itô's lemma, eq. (13.A12), and the assumption that the price function P is as in eq. (13.71), P satisfies

$$\begin{aligned} \mathbb{E}_\tau\left(\frac{dP}{P}\right)&=\frac{1}{P}\left(\frac{\partial P}{\partial \tau}+P_y\kappa_Q\left(\mu_Q-y\right)+\frac{1}{2}\mathrm{Tr}\left([\Sigma V\,(y)][\Sigma V\,(y)]^\top P_{yy}\right)\right)d\tau\\ &=\left(-\dot{\mathcal{A}}-\dot{\mathcal{B}}y+\mathcal{B}\kappa_Q\left(\mu_Q-y\right)+\frac{1}{2}\sum_{i=1}^n(\mathcal{B}\Sigma)_i^2\,\alpha_i+\frac{1}{2}\sum_{i=1}^n(\mathcal{B}\Sigma)_i^2\,\beta_i y\right)d\tau\\ &=(r^0+r^1 y)d\tau, \end{aligned}$$

where dots indicate differentiation with respect to time to maturity $x \equiv T - \tau$, and the last equality follows by the standard martingale property of the discounted bond price, and by eq. (13.67). Therefore, $\mathcal{A}(\cdot)$ and $\mathcal{B}(\cdot)$ are solutions to the following Riccati's equations

$$\begin{cases} \dot{\mathcal{A}}(x) = -r^0 + \mathcal{B}(x)\,\kappa_Q \mu_Q + \frac{1}{2}\sum_{i=1}^{n} (\mathcal{B}(x)\,\Sigma)_i^2\, \alpha_i \\ \dot{\mathcal{B}}(x) = -r^1 - \mathcal{B}(x)\,\kappa_Q + \frac{1}{2}\sum_{i=1}^{n} (\mathcal{B}(x)\,\Sigma)_i^2\, \beta_i^\top \end{cases} \tag{13.A13}$$

subject to the boundary conditions $\mathcal{A}(0) = 0$ and $\mathcal{B}(0) = 0$.

13.E.2 Application to Fong and Vasicek Model

The Fong and Vasicek (1991) model in section 13.5.1 (see eqs. 13.60) is an affine model. Indeed, set $r_\tau = y_{1\tau}$ and $v_\tau = y_{2\tau}$ (i.e., $r^0 = 0$ and $r^1 = [0\ \ 1]$), and note that under the assumptions in the main text, $y_{1\tau}$ and $y_{2\tau}$ are solutions to

$$\begin{cases} dy_{1\tau} = (\kappa_r(\bar{r} - y_{1\tau}) - \lambda_1 y_{2\tau})\, d\tau + \sqrt{y_{2\tau}}\, d\tilde{W}_{1\tau} \\ dy_{2\tau} = \kappa_{Q,v}\left(\bar{v}_Q - y_{2\tau}\right) d\tau + \xi_v \sqrt{y_{2\tau}}\left(\rho\, d\tilde{W}_{1\tau} + \sqrt{1-\rho^2}\, d\tilde{W}_{2\tau}\right) \end{cases}$$

where $\kappa_{Q,v} \equiv \kappa_v + \xi_v(\lambda_1 \rho + \sqrt{1-\rho^2}\lambda_2)$, $\bar{v}_Q \equiv \frac{\kappa_v}{\kappa_{Q,v}}\bar{v}$, $d\tilde{W}_{i\tau} = dW_{i\tau} + \lambda_i \sqrt{y_{2\tau}}\, d\tau$ are Brownian motions under Q, and λ_i are risk premium parameters defined in the main text. In terms of eq. (13.A12), we have $\alpha_i = 0$ and $\beta_i^\top = [0\ \ \xi_v^2]$ for $i = 1, 2$, and

$$\kappa_Q = \begin{bmatrix} \kappa_r & \lambda_1 \\ 0 & \kappa_{Q,v} \end{bmatrix}, \quad \mu_Q = \begin{bmatrix} \bar{r} - \bar{v}_Q \frac{\lambda_1}{\kappa_r} \\ \bar{v}_Q \end{bmatrix}, \quad \Sigma = \begin{bmatrix} \frac{1}{\xi_v} & 0 \\ \rho & \sqrt{1-\rho^2} \end{bmatrix},$$

$$V(y_\tau) = \begin{bmatrix} \sqrt{\xi_v^2 y_{2\tau}} & 0 \\ 0 & \sqrt{\xi_v^2 y_{2\tau}} \end{bmatrix}.$$

Therefore, the model predicts that the price is as in eq. (13.61), where the functions $A(\cdot)$, $B(\cdot)$ and $C(\cdot)$ satisfy eqs. (13.A13), i.e.,

$$\begin{cases} \dot{A}(x) = -\kappa_r \bar{r} B(x) + \kappa_{Q,v} \bar{v}_Q C(x) \\ \dot{B}(x) = 1 - \kappa_r B(x) \\ \dot{C}(x) = \lambda_1 B(x) - \kappa_{Q,v} C(x) + \frac{1}{2}\left(B^2(x) - 2\rho\xi_v B(x)\, C(x) + \xi_v^2 C^2(x)\right) \end{cases} \tag{13.A14}$$

subject to the boundary conditions, $A(0) = B(0) = C(0) = 0$.

13.E.3 Hull and White Model

As in the Ho–Lee model, the instantaneous forward rate $f(\tau, T)$ predicted by the Hull and White model is $f_\$(t, T) = -A_2(\tau, T) + B_2(\tau, T) r_t$, where functions A_2 and B_2 can be easily determined from eqs. (13.85) and (13.86) as:

$$A_2(\tau, T) = \sigma^2 \int_\tau^T B(s, T) B_2(s, T)\, ds - \int_\tau^T \theta_s B_2(s, T)\, ds, \quad B_2(\tau, T) = e^{-\kappa(T-\tau)}.$$

Therefore, the instantaneous forward rate $f(\tau, T)$ predicted by the Hull and White model is obtained by replacing the previous equations in eq. (13.80). The result is then equated to the observed forward rate $f_{\$}(t,\tau)$ so as to obtain:

$$f_{\$}(t,\tau) = -\frac{\sigma^2}{2\kappa^2}\left(1-e^{-\kappa(\tau-t)}\right)^2 + \int_t^\tau \theta_s e^{-\kappa(\tau-s)}ds + e^{-\kappa(\tau-t)}r_t.$$

By differentiating the previous equation with respect to τ, and rearranging terms,

$$\begin{aligned}\theta_\tau &= \frac{\partial}{\partial\tau}f_{\$}(t,\tau) + \frac{\sigma^2}{\kappa}\left(1-e^{-\kappa(\tau-t)}\right)e^{-\kappa(\tau-t)} + \kappa\left(\int_t^\tau \theta_s e^{-\kappa(\tau-s)}ds + e^{-\kappa(\tau-t)}r_t\right)\\ &= \frac{\partial}{\partial\tau}f_{\$}(t,\tau) + \frac{\sigma^2}{\kappa}\left(1-e^{-\kappa(\tau-t)}\right)e^{-\kappa(\tau-t)} + \kappa\left(f_{\$}(t,\tau) + \frac{\sigma^2}{2\kappa^2}\left(1-e^{-\kappa(\tau-t)}\right)^2\right),\end{aligned}$$

which reduces to eq. (13.87) after using simple algebra.

Appendix 13.F Expectation Theory and Embedding

We derive implications on expectation theory and embedding while relying on selected models.

13.F.1 Expectation Theory

Consider the HJM framework in section 13.7 and assume that

$$\sigma(\cdot,\cdot) = \sigma \text{ and } \lambda(\cdot) = \lambda, \tag{13.A15}$$

where σ and λ are constants. We derive the dynamics of r, compare them with f, and formulate some basic claims regarding the expectation theory. We have

$$r_\tau = f(t,\tau) + \int_t^\tau \alpha(s,\tau)ds + \sigma\left(W_\tau - W_t\right),$$

where

$$\alpha(\tau,T) = \sigma(\tau,T)\int_\tau^T \sigma(\tau,\ell)d\ell + \sigma(\tau,T)\lambda_\tau = \sigma^2(T-\tau) + \sigma\lambda,$$

such that

$$E_t(r_\tau) = f(t,\tau) + \frac{1}{2}\sigma^2(\tau-t)^2 + \sigma\lambda(\tau-t).$$

Even assuming that $\lambda < 0$, this model does not guarantee that $E_t(r_\tau) < f(t,\tau)$. The next example shows that, to establish this property, it is sufficient to remove the assumption of a non-stationary volatility function. Suppose, then, that instead of eq. (13.A15), we had

$$\sigma(t,T) = \sigma \cdot e^{-\gamma(T-t)} \text{ and } \lambda(\cdot) = \lambda,$$

where σ, γ and λ are constants. In this case, the instantaneous interest rate satisfies

$$r_\tau = f(t,\tau) + \int_t^\tau \alpha(s,\tau)ds + \sigma\int_t^\tau e^{-\gamma(\tau-s)}\cdot dW_s,$$

where

$$\alpha(s,\tau) = \sigma^2 e^{-\gamma(\tau-s)} \int_s^\tau e^{-\gamma(\ell-s)} d\ell + \sigma\lambda e^{-\gamma(\tau-s)}$$
$$= \frac{\sigma^2}{\gamma}\left(e^{-\gamma(\tau-s)} - e^{-2\gamma(\tau-s)}\right) + \sigma\lambda e^{-\gamma(\tau-s)},$$

such that,

$$E_t(r_\tau) = f(t,\tau) + \int_t^\tau \alpha(s,\tau)ds = f(t,\tau) + \frac{\sigma}{\gamma}\left(1 - e^{-\gamma(\tau-t)}\right)\left(\frac{\sigma}{2\gamma}\left(1 - e^{-\gamma(\tau-t)}\right) + \lambda\right).$$

Thus, $E_t(r_\tau) < f(t,\tau)$ for all τ, whenever the risk premium is sufficiently large in absolute value, i.e., $-\lambda > \frac{\sigma}{2\gamma}$: in other words, $\lambda < 0$, is a necessary condition, not sufficient.

13.F.2 Embedding

We now embed the Ho-Lee model in section 13.6.2 in the HJM format. In the Ho-Lee model,

$$dr_\tau = \theta_\tau d\tau + \sigma d\tilde{W}_\tau,$$

where $\tilde{W}$ is a Q-Brownian motion. By eq. (13.80) in section 13.6,

$$f(r,t,T) = -A_2(t,T) + B_2(t,T)r,$$

where $-A_2(t,T) = \int_t^T \theta_s ds - \frac{1}{2}\sigma^2(T-t)$ and $B_2(t,T) = 1$. Therefore, by Eqs. (13.99),

$$\sigma(t,T) = B_2(t,T)\cdot\sigma = \sigma,$$
$$\alpha(t,T) - \sigma(t,T)\lambda_t = -A_{12}(t,T) + B_{12}(t,T)r + B_2(t,T)\theta_t = \sigma^2(T-t).$$

Next, we embed the Vasicek model in section 13.4 into the HJM format. The Vasicek model is:

$$dr_\tau = (\theta - \kappa r_\tau)d\tau + \sigma d\tilde{W}_\tau,$$

where $\tilde{W}$ is a Q-Brownian motion. By results in section 13.4,

$$f(r,t,T) = -A_2(t,T) + B_2(t,T)r,$$

where $-A_2(t,T) = -\sigma^2\int_t^T B(s,T)B_2(s,T)ds + \theta\int_t^T B_2(s,T)ds$, $B_2(t,T) = e^{-\kappa(T-t)}$ and $B(t,T) = \frac{1}{\kappa}\left(1 - e^{-\kappa(T-t)}\right)$. By eqs. (13.99),

$$\sigma(t,T) = \sigma\cdot B_2(t,T) = \sigma e^{-\kappa(T-t)};$$
$$\alpha(t,T) - \sigma(t,T)\lambda_t = -A_{12}(t,T) + B_{12}(t,T)r + (\theta - \kappa r)B_2(t,T)$$
$$= \frac{\sigma^2}{\kappa}\left(1 - e^{-\kappa(T-t)}\right)e^{-\kappa(T-t)}.$$

Clearly this model cannot be embedded within HJM because it is not perfectly fitting. Condition (13.100) does not hold for the Vasicek model. However, the model may be embedded once θ is turned into an infinite dimensional parameter *à la* Hull and White (see section 13.6.3).

Appendix 13.G Strings

We prove eq. (13.102). We have, $\alpha^I(\tau,T)=\frac{1}{2}\int_\tau^T g(\tau,T,\ell_2)\,d\ell_2+cov(\frac{dP}{P},\frac{d\xi}{\xi})/d\tau$, where

$$g(\tau,T,\ell_2)\equiv\int_\tau^T\sigma(\tau,\ell_1)\,\sigma(\tau,\ell_2)\,\psi(\ell_1,\ell_2)\,d\ell_1.$$

Differentiation of the *cov* term is straightforward. Moreover,

$$\begin{aligned}\frac{\partial}{\partial T}\int_\tau^T g(\tau,T,\ell_2)\,d\ell_2&=g(\tau,T,T)+\int_\tau^T\frac{\partial g(\tau,T,\ell_2)}{\partial T}d\ell_2\\&=\sigma(\tau,T)\cdot\int_\tau^T\sigma(\tau,x)\,(\psi(x,T)+\psi(T,x))\,dx\\&=2\sigma(\tau,T)\cdot\int_\tau^T\sigma(\tau,x)\,\psi(x,T)\,dx.\end{aligned}$$

Appendix 13.H Changes of Numéraire

13.H.1 Jamshidian's (1989) Formula

Consider the following *change-of-numéraire* arithmetics. Let

$$\frac{dX_j}{X_j}=\mu_j d\tau+\sigma_j dW,\quad j\in\{A,B\}.$$

We have

$$\frac{d(X_A/X_B)}{X_A/X_B}=\left(\mu_A-\mu_B+\sigma_B^2-\sigma_A\sigma_B\right)d\tau+(\sigma_A-\sigma_B)\,dW. \tag{13.A16}$$

Next, we apply this result to the process $y(\tau,S)\equiv\frac{P(\tau,S)}{P(\tau,T)}$, under Q_F^S as well as under Q_F^T. We aim to derive the solution of $y(\tau,S)$ at T for Vasicek, namely

$$y(T,S)\equiv\frac{P(T,S)}{P(T,T)}=P(T,S)\text{ under }Q_F^S\text{ as well as under }Q_F^T.$$

This solution is needed to calculate the two probabilities in eq. (13.113).

By Itô's lemma, and the fact that $P_r=-BP$, we have that under the risk neutral probability Q,

$$\frac{dP(\tau,x)}{P(\tau,x)}=r d\tau-\sigma B(\tau,x)d\tilde{W}_\tau,\ x\geq T.$$

By applying eq. (13.A16) to $y(\tau,S)$,

$$\frac{dy(\tau,S)}{y(\tau,S)}=\sigma^2\left[B^2(\tau,T)-B(\tau,T)B(\tau,S)\right]d\tau-\sigma\left[B(\tau,S)-B(\tau,T)\right]d\tilde{W}_\tau. \tag{13.A17}$$

Next, we change probability with the tools of appendix 13.B. We have,

$$dW_\tau^{Q_F^x}=d\tilde{W}_\tau+\sigma B(\tau,x)\,d\tau$$

is a Brownian motion under the x-forward martingale probability. Replace then $W^{Q_F^x}$ into eq. (13.A17), then integrate, and obtain:

$$\frac{y(T,S)}{y(t,S)} = P(T,S)\frac{P(t,T)}{P(t,S)} = e^{-\frac{1}{2}\sigma^2\int_t^T[B(\tau,S)-B(\tau,T)]^2 d\tau - \sigma\int_t^T[B(\tau,S)-B(\tau,T)]dW_\tau^{Q_F^T}},$$

$$\frac{y(T,S)}{y(t,S)} = P(T,S)\frac{P(t,T)}{P(t,S)} = e^{\frac{1}{2}\sigma^2\int_t^T[B(\tau,S)-B(\tau,T)]^2 d\tau - \sigma\int_t^T[B(\tau,S)-B(\tau,T)]dW_\tau^{Q_F^S}}.$$

Rearranging terms gives eqs. (13.114) in the main text.

13.H.2 Proof of Eq. (13.132)

By the law of iterated expectations,

$$\begin{aligned}
&\mathbb{E}_t\left[\frac{e^{-\int_t^{T_i} r_\tau d\tau}}{P(T_{i-1},T_i)}[1-K_i P(T_{i-1},T_i)]^+\right] \\
&= \mathbb{E}_t\left[\mathbb{E}\left(\frac{e^{-\int_t^{T_i} r_\tau d\tau}}{P(T_{i-1},T_i)}(1-K_i P(T_{i-1},T_i))^+ \middle| \mathcal{F}_{T_{i-1}}\right)\right] \\
&= \mathbb{E}_t\left[e^{-\int_t^{T_{i-1}} r_\tau d\tau}(1-K_i P(T_{i-1},T_i))^+\right]. \qquad (13.A18)
\end{aligned}$$

13.H.3 Martingale Property of the Forward Swap Rate

By eq. (13.128), and a change of probability,

$$\begin{aligned}
\mathbb{E}_{Q_{swap}}[F_{sw}(\tau,T_0,T_1,\cdots,T_n)] &= \mathbb{E}_{Q_{sw}}\left[\frac{P(\tau,T_0)-P(\tau,T_n)}{PVBP_\tau(T_1,\cdots,T_n)}\right] \\
&= \mathbb{E}_t\left[\frac{e^{-\int_t^\tau r_\tau d\tau}(P(\tau,T_0)-P(\tau,T_n))}{PVBP_t(T_1,\cdots,T_n)}\right] \\
&= \frac{P(t,T_0)-P(t,T_n)}{PVBP_t(T_1,\cdots,T_n)} \\
&= F_{sw}(t,T_0,T_1,\cdots,T_n), \qquad (13.A19)
\end{aligned}$$

where $\mathbb{E}_{Q_{sw}}$ denotes expectations under the annuity probability.

Appendix 13.I Convexity Risks in Gaussian Markets

First, we show eq. (13.119). Note that, by eq. (13.113), the price of a call option predicted by the Jamshidian-Vasicek model is

$$C^b(r,K;t,T,S) = P(r,t,T)\underbrace{[Z(r,t,T,S)\Phi(d_1) - K\Phi(d_1-v)]}_{\equiv M(Z(r,t,T,S),K;v)}, \qquad (13.A20)$$

where

$$Z(r,t,T,S) = \frac{P(r,t,S)}{P(r,t,T)}, \quad d_1 = \frac{\ln \frac{Z(r,t,T,S)}{K} + \frac{1}{2}v^2}{v},$$

and v is as in eq. (13.116). Because the function $M(Z,K;v)$ is homogeneous of degree one in (z,k), we have, by standard arguments, that $M_Z(Z,K;v) = \Phi(d_1)$, such that

$$\begin{aligned} C_r^b(r,K;t,T,S) &= P_r(r,t,T)\, M(Z(r,t,T,S),K;v) \\ &\quad + P(r,t,T)\, M_Z(Z(r,t,T,S),K;v)\, Z_r(r,t,T,S) \\ &= P_r(r,t,T)\, M(Z(r,t,T,S),K;v) \\ &\quad + \Phi(d_1)\left(P_r(r,t,S) - P(r,t,S)\frac{P_r(r,t,T)}{P(r,t,T)}\right), \end{aligned}$$

where the second equality follows after substituting M_Z, and the partial derivative Z_r. Replacing M from eq. (13.A20) produces eq. (13.119). Given these expressions, it is easy to show that the expression for the stochastic duration in eq. (13.118) can be written as

$$D(r,t,T,S) = -\frac{1}{\kappa}\ln\left(1+\kappa\frac{P_r(r,t,S)\,\Phi(-d_1)+P_r(r,t,T)\,K\Phi(d_1-v)}{P(r,t,S)\,\Phi(-d_1)+P(r,t,T)K\Phi(d_1-v)}\right). \quad (13.A21)$$

References

Adrian, T., and H. S. Shin (2011). "Financial Intermediaries and Monetary Economics." In *Handbook of Monetary Economics* (Vol. 3A), edited by B. M. Friedman and M. Woodford, 601–650. Amsterdam: Elsevier.

Ahn, C.-M., and H. E. Thompson (1988). "Jump-Diffusion Processes and the Term Structure of Interest Rates." *Journal of Finance* 43, 155–174.

Ahn, D.-H., R. F. Dittmar, and A. R. Gallant (2002). "Quadratic Term Structure Models: Theory and Evidence." *Review of Financial Studies* 15, 243–288.

Aït-Sahalia, Y. (1996). "Testing Continuous Time Models of the Spot Interest Rate." *Review of Financial Studies* 9, 385–426.

Ang, A., and M. Piazzesi (2003). "A No-Arbitrage Vector Autoregression of Term Structure Dynamics with Macroeconomic and Latent Variables." *Journal of Monetary Economics* 50, 745–787.

Ang, A., G. Bekaert, and M. Wei (2008). "The Term Structure of Real Rates and Expected Inflation." *Journal of Finance* 63, 797–849.

Balduzzi, P., S. R. Das, S. Foresi, and R. K. Sundaram (1996). "A Simple Approach to Three-Factor Affine Term Structure Models." *Journal of Fixed Income* 6, no. 3, 43–53.

Barndorff-Nielsen, O. (1978). *Information and Exponential Families in Statistical Theory*. New York: John Wiley.

Bartlett, B. (2006). "Hedging Under SABR Model." *Wilmott Magazine*, July/August, 68–70.

Black, F. (1976). "The Pricing of Commodity Contracts." *Journal of Financial Economics* 3, 167–179.

Black, F., and M. Scholes (1973). "The Pricing of Options and Corporate Liabilities." *Journal of Political Economy* 81, 637–659.

Brace, A., D. Gatarek, and M. Musiela (1997). "The Market Model of Interest Rate Dynamics." *Mathematical Finance* 7, 127–155.

Brigo, D., and F. Mercurio (2006). *Interest Rate Models: Theory and Practice, with Smile, Inflation and Credit*. 2nd ed. Berlin: Springer Verlag Finance.

Brunnermeier, M. (2009). "Deciphering the Liquidity and Credit Crunch 2007-08." *Journal of Economic Perspectives* 23, 77–100.

Carverhill, A. (1994). "When Is the Short-Rate Markovian?" *Mathematical Finance* 4, 305–312.

Collin-Dufresne, P., and R. S. Goldstein (2002). "Do Bonds Span the Fixed-Income Markets? Theory and Evidence for Unspanned Stochastic Volatility." *Journal of Finance* 57, 1685–1729.

Conley, T. G., L. P. Hansen, E. G. J. Luttmer, and J. A. Scheinkman (1997). "Short-Term Interest Rates as Subordinated Diffusions." *Review of Financial Studies* 10, 525–577.

Cox, J. C., J. E. Ingersoll, and S. A. Ross (1979). "Duration and the Measurement of Basis Risk." *Journal of Business* 52, 51–61.

Cox, J. C., J. E. Ingersoll, and S. A. Ross (1985). "A Theory of the Term Structure of Interest Rates." *Econometrica* 53, 385–407.

Dai, Q., and K. J. Singleton (2000). "Specification Analysis of Affine Term Structure Models." *Journal of Finance* 55, 1943–1978.

Diebold, F. X., and C. Li (2006). "Forecasting the Term Structure of Government Bond Yields." *Journal of Econometrics* 130, 337–364.

Duffee, G. R. (2002): "Term Premia and Interest Rate Forecasts in Affine Models." *Journal of Finance* 57, 405–444.

Duffie, D., and R. Kan (1996). "A Yield-Factor Model of Interest Rates." *Mathematical Finance* 6, 379–406.

Duffie, D., J. Pan, and K. Singleton (2000). "Transform Analysis and Asset Pricing for Affine Jump-Diffusions." *Econometrica* 68, 1343–1376.

Duffie, D., and K. J. Singleton (1999). "Modeling Term Structures of Defaultable Bonds." *Review of Financial Studies* 12, 687–720.

Engle, R. F., D. F. Hendry, and J.-F. Richard (1983). "Exogeneity." *Econometrica* 51, 277–304.

Estrella, A., and G. Hardouvelis (1991). "The Term Structure as a Predictor of Real Economic Activity." *Journal of Finance* 46, 555–576.

Fama, E. F., and R. R. Bliss (1987). "The Information in Long-Maturity Forward Rates." *American Economic Review* 77, 680–692.

Filipović, D., M. Larsson, and A. B. Trolle (2017). "Linear-Rational Term Structure Models." *Journal of Finance* 72, 655–704.

Florens, J.-P., and M. Mouchart (1980). "Initial and Sequential Reduction of Bayesian Experiments." CORE Discussion Paper 8015. Universite Catholique de Louvain, Louvain-la-Neuve, Belgium.

Fong, H. G., and O. A. Vasicek (1991). "Fixed Income Volatility Management." *Journal of Portfolio Management* (Summer), 41–46.

Geman, H. (1989). "The Importance of the Forward Neutral Probability in a Stochastic Approach to Interest Rates." Unpublished working paper, ESSEC.

Geman H., N. El Karoui, and J. C. Rochet (1995). "Changes of Numéraire, Changes of Probability Measures and Pricing of Options." *Journal of Applied Probability* 32, 443–458.

Gerlach, S., and R. Stuart (2018). "The Slope of the Term Structure and Recessions: The Pre-Fed Evidence, 1857–1913." Centre for Economic Policy Research (CEPR) Discussion Paper 13013.

Goldstein, R. S. (2000). "The Term Structure of Interest Rates as a Random Field." *Review of Financial Studies* 13, 365–384.

Hagan, P. S., D. Kumar, A. S. Lesniewski, and D. E. Woodward (2002). "Managing Smile Risk." *Wilmott Magazine*, September, 84–108.

Hagan, P. S., and D. E. Woodward (1999). "Equivalent Black Volatilities." *Applied Mathematical Finance* 6, 147–157.

Harvey, C. R. (1991). "The Term Structure and World Economic Growth." *Journal of Fixed Income* 1, 4–17.

Harvey, C. R. (1993). "The Term Structure Forecasts Economic Growth." *Financial Analysts Journal* 49, no. 3, 6–8.

Heaney, W. J., and P. L. Cheng (1984). "Continuous Maturity Diversification of Default-Free Bond Portfolios and a Generalization of Efficient Diversification." *Journal of Finance* 39, 1101–1117.

Heath, D., R. Jarrow, and A. Morton (1992). "Bond Pricing and the Term-Structure of Interest Rates: a New Methodology for Contingent Claim Valuation." *Econometrica* 60, 77–105.

Heston, S. L. (1993). "A Closed-Form Solution for Options with Stochastic Volatility with Applications to Bond and Currency Options." *Review of Financial Studies* 6, 327–344.

Ho, T. S. Y., and S.-B. Lee (1986). "Term Structure Movements and the Pricing of Interest Rate Contingent Claims." *Journal of Finance* 41, 1011–1029.

Hördahl, P., O. Tristani, and D. Vestin (2006). "A Joint Econometric Model of Macroeconomic and Term Structure Dynamics." *Journal of Econometrics* 131, 405–444.

Hull, J. (2003). *Options, Futures, and Other Derivatives.* 5th ed. (International). Hoboken, NJ: Prentice Hall.

Hull, J., and A. White (1990). "Pricing Interest Rate Derivative Securities." *Review of Financial Studies* 3, 573–592.

Jamshidian, F. (1989). "An Exact Bond Option Pricing Formula." *Journal of Finance* 44, 205–209.

Jamshidian, F. (1997). "Libor and Swap Market Models and Measures." *Finance and Stochastics* 1, 293–330.

Jöreskog, K. G. (1967). "Some Contributions to Maximum Likelihood Factor Analysis." *Psychometrica* 32, 443–482.

Karatzas, I., and S. E. Shreve (1991). *Brownian Motion and Stochastic Calculus.* New York: Springer Verlag.

Karlin, S., and H. M. Taylor (1981). *A Second Course in Stochastic Processes.* San Diego, CA: Academic Press.

Kennedy, D. P. (1994). "The Term Structure of Interest Rates as a Gaussian Random Field." *Mathematical Finance* 4, 247–258.

Kennedy, D. P. (1997). "Characterizing Gaussian Models of the Term Structure of Interest Rates." *Mathematical Finance* 7, 107–118.

Kessel, R. A. (1965). "The Cyclical Behavior of the Term Structure of Interest Rates." National Bureau of Economic Research Occasional Paper No. 91.

Kloeden, P., and E. Platen (1992). *Numeric Solutions of Stochastic Differential Equations.* Berlin: Springer Verlag.

Knez, P. J., R. Litterman, and J. Scheinkman (1994). "Explorations into Factors Explaining Money Market Returns." *Journal of Finance* 49, 1861–1882.

Lamberton, D., and B. Lapeyre (1997). *Introduction au Calcul Stochastique Appliqué à la Finance.* Paris: Ellipses.

Langetieg, T. (1980). "A Multivariate Model of the Term Structure of Interest Rates." *Journal of Finance* 35, 71–97.

Laurent, R. D. (1988). "An Interest Rate-Based Indicator of Monetary Policy." *Federal Reserve Bank of Chicago Economic Perspectives* 12, 3–14.

Laurent, R. D. (1989). "Testing the Spread." *Federal Reserve Bank of Chicago Economic Perspectives* 13, 22–34.

Litterman, R., and J. Scheinkman (1991). "Common Factors Affecting Bond Returns." *Journal of Fixed Income* 1, 54–61.

Litterman, R., J. Scheinkman, and L. Weiss (1991). "Volatility and the Yield Curve." *Journal of Fixed Income* 1, 49–53.

Longstaff, F. A., and E. S. Schwartz (1992). "Interest Rate Volatility and the Term Structure: A Two-Factor General Equilibrium Model." *Journal of Finance* 47, 1259–1282.

Mele, A. (2003). "Fundamental Properties of Bond Prices in Models of the Short-Term Rate." *Review of Financial Studies* 16, 679–716.

Mele, A., and F. Fornari (2000). *Stochastic Volatility in Financial Markets: Crossing the Bridge to Continuous Time*. Boston: Kluwer Academic.

Mele, A., and Y. Obayashi (2015). *The Price of Fixed Income Market Volatility*. Springer Finance Series. New York: Springer Verlag.

Mele, A., and Y. Obayashi (2016). "Interest Rate Derivatives and Volatility," edited by Pietro Veronesi, 767–838. Handbook Series in Financial Engineering and Econometrics. Hoboken, NJ: John Wiley.

Mele, A., Y. Obayashi, and S. Yang (2020). "The Term Structure of Government Debt Uncertainty." SFI-USI Lugano. Discussion Paper no. 13874. Available from: https://antoniomele.org.

Mercurio, F. (2009). "Interest Rates and the Credit Crunch: New Formulas and Market Models."Bloomberg Portfolio Research Paper No. 2010-01-FRONTIERS. Available from: https://papers.ssrn.com/sol3/papers.cfm?abstract_id=1332205.

Merton, R. C. (1973). "Theory of Rational Option Pricing." *Bell Journal of Economics and Management Science* 4, 141–183.

Miltersen, K., K. Sandmann, and D. Sondermann (1997). "Closed Form Solutions for Term Structure Derivatives with Lognormal Interest Rate." *Journal of Finance* 52, 409–430.

Nelson, C. R., and A. F. Siegel (1987). "Parsimonious Modeling of Yield Curves." *Journal of Business* 60, 473–489.

Pagan, A., and A. Ullah (1999). *Nonparametric Econometrics*. Cambridge: Cambridge Univer-sity Press.

Piazzesi, M. (2010). "Affine Term Structure Models." In *Handbook of Financial Econometrics. Vol. 1, Tools and Techniques*, edited by Yacine Aït-Sahalia and Lars Peter Hansen, 691–766. North Holland: Elsevier.

Pritsker, M. (1998). "Nonparametric Density Estimation and Tests of Continuous Time Interest Rate Models." *Review of Financial Studies* 11, 449–487.

Rebonato, R. (1998). *Interest Rate Option Models*. Hoboken, NJ: Wiley.

Rebonato, R. (1999). *Volatility and Correlation*. Hoboken, NJ: Wiley.

Ritchken, P., and L. Sankarasubramanian (1995). "Volatility Structure of Forward Rates and the Dynamics of the Term Structure." *Mathematical Finance* 5, 55–72.

Sandmann, K., and D. Sondermann (1997). "A Note on the Stability of Lognormal Interest Rate Models and the Pricing of Eurodollar Futures." *Mathematical Finance* 7, 119–125.

Santa-Clara, P., and D. Sornette (2001). "The Dynamics of the Forward Interest Rate Curve with Stochastic String Shocks." *Review of Financial Studies* 14, 149–185.

Singleton, K. J. (2006). *Empirical Dynamic Asset Pricing*. Princeton, NJ: Princeton University Press.

Stanton, R. (1997). "A Nonparametric Model of Term Structure Dynamics and the Market Price of Interest Rate Risk." *Journal of Finance* 52, 1973–2002.

Stock, J. H., and M. W. Watson (1989). "New Indexes of Coincident and Leading Economic Indicators." In *NBER Macroeconomics Annual 1989*, edited by O. J. Blanchard and S. Fischer, 352–394. Cambridge, MA: MIT Press.

Stock, J. H., and M. W. Watson (2003). "Forecasting Output and Inflation: The Role of Asset Prices." *Journal of Economic Literature* 41, 788–829.

Vasicek, O. (1977). "An Equilibrium Characterization of the Term Structure." *Journal of Financial Economics* 5, 177–188.

Veronesi, P. (2010). *Fixed Income Securities: Valuation, Risk and Risk Management*. Hoboken, NJ: John Wiley.

Veronesi, P. (2016). "Discounting and Derivative Pricing Before and After the Financial Crisis: An Introduction." In *The Handbook of Fixed Income Securities*, edited by Pietro Veronesi, 414–434. Handbook Series in Financial Engineering and Econometrics. Hoboken, NJ: John Wiley.

14

Risky Debt and Credit Derivatives

14.1 Introduction

This chapter deals with the pricing of securities that carry credit risk. It examines the main conceptual approaches to deal with credit risk as well as how this risk can be transferred through dedicated *credit derivatives*. It is instructive to review the main historical developments leading up to the creation of these derivatives. The next subsection contains a very succinct account, a motivation for the whole chapter. Section 14.1.2 provides a roadmap to the chapter.

14.1.1 A Brief History of Credit Risk and Financial Innovation

The introductions to the previous two chapters have emphasized the size and the importance of fixed income markets. Markets around interest rate swaps began during the 1980s, but they grew very rapidly, and still constitute the dominant portion of the whole fixed income space. Growth came through the typical process of financial innovation. During the late 1980s, the appetite for interest rate sensitive products had proliferated and led to additional and fairly complex products. Innovation and competition were feeding on each other: financial innovation is relatively easy to imitate and may lead banks to increasing creativeness, the latter being required to keep the innovators' initial competitive advantage as long as possible.

The financial landscape during the early 1990s was extraordinarily propitious for innovation. On the one hand, interest rates were low amid concerns the US economy had still not recovered from the 1991 recession. On the other hand, financial market volatility was quite muted. Low interest rates and low capital market volatility are natural drivers for the introduction of new derivatives aimed at boosting investors' returns.[1] During this process, the 1994 financial turmoil brought the interest rate climate to suddenly change while some of these products were producing large losses. These losses would trigger a call for regulation by public opinion and some policy makers even while the International Swaps and

1. Examples of products introduced at the time are LIBOR squared, inverse floaters, or power options.

Derivatives Association (ISDA) would debate that more regulation would destroy market creativity.

Regulatory pressures would vanish by the mid-1990s, when the market started to innovate again amid a general consensus that derivative risks could be controlled through market discipline, not regulation. Interest rate swap markets recovered. They did so slowly though, as these derivatives were already in the end of the innovation cycle: the process of imitation had led interest rate swap related derivatives to become a "mass product," with profit margins eroded in the meantime. The market was ready for a new major innovation wave.

Credit risk was the next innovation stream. Global financial institutions (e.g., J.P. Morgan, Credit Suisse, Bankers Trust) soon realized that borrower defaulting was a source of substantial risk that could conveniently be reallocated through dedicated derivatives. While classic derivatives could transfer market risk, credit derivatives could transfer *credit* risk. Institutions such as J.P. Morgan had additional motivations to innovate in this space, given the vast pools of loans contained in their books: importantly, these loans required too many reserves and were therefore expensive.

One solution was to proceed with *securitization*. Securitization is a process by which some illiquid assets (say some loans) are gathered ("packaged") into a common pool that backs the issuance of new securities aimed at displaying an enhanced liquidity through packaging, credit, and liquidity enhancements. These new securities are, in fact, derivatives written on the initial illiquid assets. Two leading examples of this process include the securitization of mortgages and receivables. Financial institutions find the securitization process attractive, as they can carve out certain items in their balance sheet, thus boosting their return on investments; moreover, by securitizing assets, less capital is needed to meet capital requirements standards. For example, the accounts receivables of a corporation may be used to back the issue of commercial paper known as *asset-backed commercial paper*.

Securitization is a way to transfer and trade credit risk. However, chapter 5 explains that securitization needs to rely on a sound design model, one that would duly take moral hazard into account. To illustrate, in a model where loans are originated and distributed, securitization contracts would have to be incentive compatible. In particular, loans' originators should be incentivized to exert the efforts needed to ensure loans have good quality. Incentive compatibility may be implemented through "skin in the game," that is, the retention of a proportion of the securitized assets by the originators (see section 5.3.2 in chapter 5). Implicit in this model is a correct understanding of the risks affecting the securitized assets, a point furthered developed below.

During this process, global institutions would then repackage loans into derivatives, in a way that default risk and/or part of the securitized loans could be transferred to outside investors. Note that credit derivatives were also a regulatory mitigation device, partly useful as a response to regulation. The underlying ideas were (i) to turn loans into derivatives that could be sold and (ii) to create new insurance products such as *credit default swaps*. At the very beginning, derivatives were just designed to have single loans as the underlying. Afterward, the idea emerged to create structures organized in derivatives bundles, with cash flow indexed to baskets of loans—the ancestors to *collateralized debt obligations* (CDOs). For example, J.P. Morgan created "Bistro" (Broad Index Secured

Table 14.1
Stock and issuance of credit related derivative instruments during the credit derivatives boom and its debacle in the 2000s. In billions US dollars.

Year	US ABS (Outstanding)	Global CDO (Issuance)	US Agency MBS (Issuance)	US Agency CMO (Issuance)
2000	1084	68	474	586
2001	1230	78	1086	1455
2002	1381	83	1447	2019
2003	1507	87	2131	2762
2004	1814	157	1015	1379
2005	2111	251	983	1345
2006	2700	455	923	1240
2007	2945	430	1189	1471
2008	2599	62	1169	1339
2009	2326	4	1734	2022
2010	2034	7	1420	1885

Source: Securities Industry and Financial Markets Association (SIFMA).

Trust Offering), a structure relying on a variety of assets, ranging from corporate debt to public finance credits. During this innovation process, competition increased and profit margins fell again, leading to renewed motivation for additional innovation.

The response to increased competition was the creation of structured products referenced to riskier assets. Importantly, during the mid-1990s, derivatives teams began to interact with teams managing loans extended to borrowers with poor credit history—"subprime mortgages." Subprime loans would begin to be securitized and structured into CDOs with global financial institutions involved (e.g., Merrill Lynch or UBS), leading to a spectacular credit derivatives boom (see table 14.1 and figure 14.1). The mortgage banking model had shifted from one of "buy to hold" to one of "originate and distribute." The subprime crisis erupted in 2007, and sent the global financial system into nearly two years of turmoil, a condition in which the payments and settlement system was jeopardized.

The mechanics of the 2007–2009 crisis seem to be well understood. While low interest rates helped sustain the boom in the housing market, the originate-and-distribute model had operated in a way that lending standards were not in line with market expectations (see section 14.5.2). The subprime mortgage market would sink amid increasing interest rates and rapidly decelerating housing prices. All in all, defaults in this market began to spread in a way to contradict a perceived sense of "diversification." Securitizing debt originated in different spaces leads to diversification under the obvious assumption that the originating assets are not very correlated. The basic principle of diversification (discussed since chapter 1) breaks down when correlation is underestimated with, say, default rates in the mortgage space then appearing at the same time in different geographical areas. Note, also, that this market was characterized by derivative products with nonlinear payoffs. These payoffs give rise to tail risk. This chapter explains that tail risk becomes quite

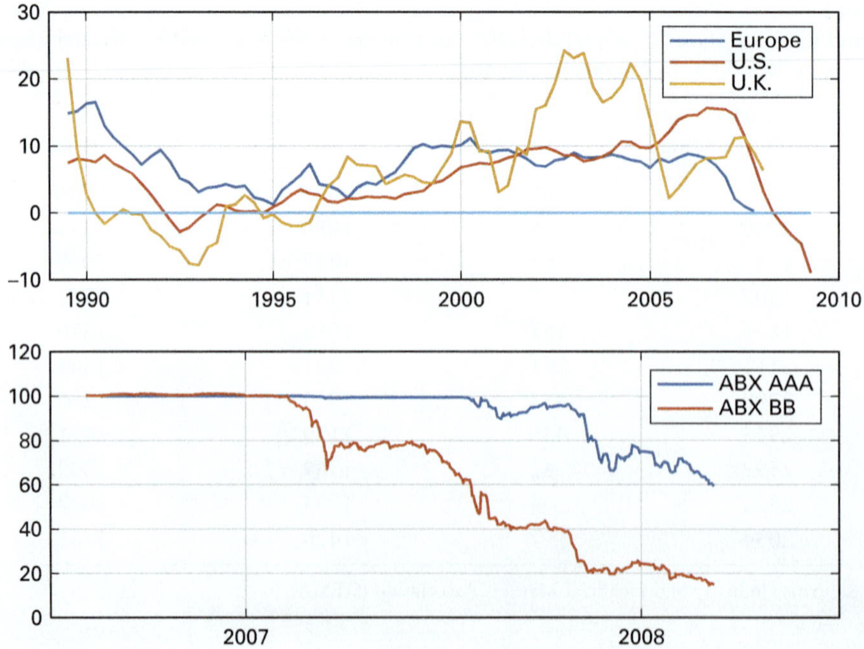

Figure 14.1
Top panel: U.S. and European House Price Change (year-to-year, in percentage). Bottom panel: Indices of CDS on US Mortgage-Related Securities Prices.
Source: IMF (2008).

relevant when correlation is underestimated. Financial institutions were affected by huge losses related to tail risk.

Added to these problems was the presence of a "shadow banking system." This shadow system helped sustain the originate-and-distribute model, and was an important piece of the crisis: the uncertainties related to the entities financing this system triggered a sharp liquidity dry-up and, then, a credit crunch, followed by a drop in the real economic activity, which magnified the credit crunch, over a spiral. Policy makers at the time had to intervene with extreme measures, both fiscal and monetary. In 2009, the primary fiscal deficit over GDP reached nearly 10%, i.e., the highest level since World War II. In 2014, the Fed had accumulated more than \$4 trillion in assets as a result of unconventional monetary policy known as *Quantitative Easing* (QE, henceforth). Calls for regulation culminated with the voluminous Dodd-Frank Wall Street Reform and Consumer Protection Act in 2010. The financial landscape changed. To illustrate, the notional value for credit default swaps fell from about \$60 trillion outstanding in 2007 to about \$7.5 trillion in 2019. This market is still very active though, and it may be susceptible to grow back to its previous levels. This chapter studies pricing details of both risky debt and its related derivatives.

14.1.2 Plan of the Chapter

This chapter reviews conceptual approaches to the pricing of defaultable securities as well as mechanics of additional derivatives that aim at transferring credit risk. Some of the exposition relies on models consistent with classical irrelevance results: capital structure does not affect firm value (Modigliani and Miller, 1958; see chapter 5). This fact should be taken as a consistent remainder in this chapter. For example, section 14.2 deals with "structural approaches" to debt evaluation, and relies on assumptions that are at times consistent and, at other times, inconsistent with Modigliani and Miller propositions. For example, this section discusses Merton's (1974) model (where capital structure doesn't matter) but also models in which default is costly and, yet, firms may find it convenient to default. In these models with strategic default, capital structure matters. Moreover, this section also deals with sovereign risk. Sovereign debt is obviously more subtle than corporate. Default events are quite different in these two cases, and evaluating sovereign debt requires the examination of incentives of economic agents that go well beyond those underlying the value of corporate debt. However, section 14.2 also deals with "reduced-form" models by which default risk is modeled as an exogenously given event. These models simply aim at providing pricing solutions that may be relatively easy to implement for the purpose of practical applications.

Section 14.3 reviews the main derivatives that aim to reallocate credit risk, such as credit default swaps and securitized obligations. We provide details regarding their usage and pricing based on reduced-form models (i.e., with exogenous default). This book has never really dealt with issues regarding risk management. Section 14.4 contains both broader introductory discussions, and detailed discussions regarding *credit* risk management. We deal with risk management conduct for financial institutions that may be consistent with the regulatory environment at the time of writing. We also provide discussions regarding macro-prudential monitoring instruments and measurement methods for systemic risk. Finally, section 14.5 provides a succinct account of the 2007–2009 financial crisis, which originally erupted while losses were mounting in credit markets right before their devastating effects would spread to the overall economy. We provide institutional details but also analytical tools to assess the risks involved into this crisis, tools that rely on some of the models in this chapter. Finally, this crisis notoriously represents an exemplary "case study" of endogenous risk, a notion discussed in several places in this book (see, e.g., chapters 9 and 11): some initial shock may be self-reinforcing to the extent that it results in a huge loss for the whole financial system. We discuss some simple models that illustrate these vicious circles. The chapter concludes while reviewing the rationale underlying the policy response to the crisis, as well as the implications of this policy on asset prices.

14.2 Conceptual Approaches to the Evaluation of Defaultable Securities

14.2.1 Firm Value, or Structural, Approach

A natural approach to the evaluation of defaultable securities relies on basic economic principles—in general, any approach based on first economic principles is known as *structural*. To illustrate, a structural approach allows us to identify default probabilities from a few assumptions underlying the firm that has issued the securities. By contrast, a reduced-form approach would take these probabilities as exogenous, as in section 14.2.5. This section deals with a model that illustrates how the structural approach would work in practice.

We review Merton's (1974) model. This model relies on the assumptions that lead to Modigliani-Miller propositions, by which the value of the firm is not affected by the leverage (see chapter 5). Note, then, the limitations of the model that we are about to describe: the model aims to evaluate debt in a market where leverage does not even affect the value of the firm that is issuing this debt. We will see extensions of this model later in this chapter (see, e.g., section 14.2.2).

Consider the following stylized balance sheet.

	Equity (E) (Shares)
Assets (A)	
	Debt (D) (Bonds)

Therefore, we have the accounting identity

$$A = E + D.$$

When debt expires, debt holders receive the minimum between the nominal value of debt and the value of the assets the firm can liquidate to honor its debt. Debt holders are senior claimants. Equity holders are juniors, i.e., they are residual claimants to the firm's assets. Shares and bonds can, then, be regarded as derivatives written on the firm asset value.

We use these basic insights and illustrate the first approach to the modeling of the risk-structure of interest rates—the Merton-KMV approach. In this approach, equity is the same as a European call option written on the firm's assets, with expiration equal to the debt expiration, and strike equal to the nominal value of debt. The current value of debt equals the value of the assets minus the value of equity, i.e. the value of a risk-free discount bond minus the value of a put option on the firm with strike price equal to the nominal value of debt, as shown by eq. (14.3) below.

Merton (1974) uses the Black–Scholes (1973) formula to derive the price of debt. The main assumption underlying this model is that the assets of the firm can be traded, and that their value A_t satisfies[2]

$$\frac{dA_t}{A_t} = r dt + \sigma d\tilde{W}_t, \tag{14.1}$$

where $\tilde{W}_t$ is a Brownian motion under the risk neutral probability, σ is the instantaneous standard deviation, and r is the short-term rate on riskless bonds.

Denote the nominal value of debt with N, the time to expiration of debt with $T - t$, and the time t value of debt with D_t, $t \leq T$. Bondholders are senior claimants, as explained. In other words, it is as if equity holders held a long position in a European call option

2. Eq. (14.1) could be generalized to one in which $dA_t = (rA_t - \delta_t)\, dt + \sigma A_t d\tilde{W}_t$, where δ_t is the instantaneous cash flow to the firm. This would make the firm value equal to $A_0 = \mathbb{E}\left(\int_0^\infty e^{-rt}\delta_t dt\right)$. For example, one could take δ_t to be a geometric Brownian motion with parameters g and σ, in which case $A_t = (r-g)^{-1}\, \delta_t$, forever, but we're just ignoring this complication.

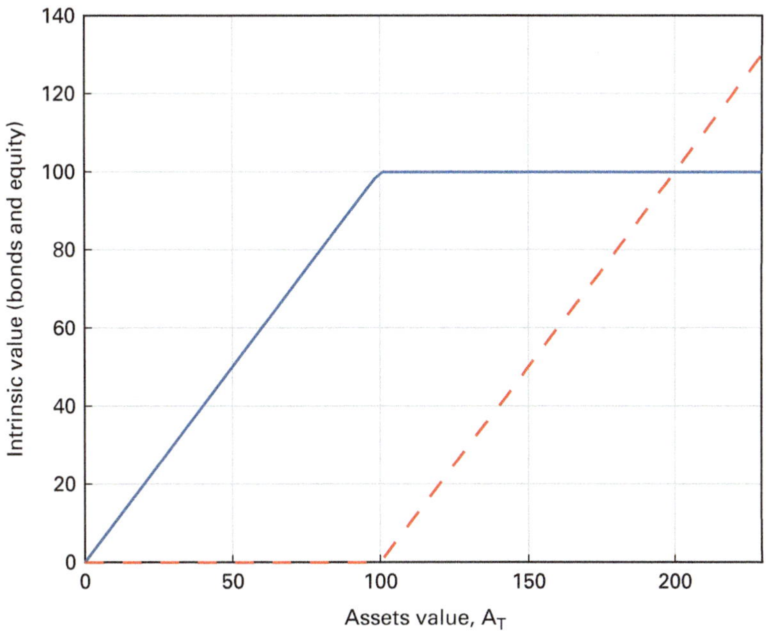

Figure 14.2
Dashed line: the value of equity at the debt maturity, T, max $\{A_T - N, 0\}$, plotted as a function of the firm asset value, A_T. Solid line: the value of debt at maturity, min $\{A_T, N\}$ as a function of A_T. Nominal value of debt is fixed to $N = 100$.

$$D_T = \begin{cases} A_T, & \text{if the firm defaults, } A_T < N \\ N, & \text{if the firm is solvent, } A_T \geq N \end{cases}$$

such that the firm assets value at time T can be decomposed into the sum of equity value plus debt value at T,

$$D_T = \min\{A_T, N\} = A_T - \underbrace{\max\{A_T - N, 0\}}_{\equiv \text{ Equity at } T}. \tag{14.2}$$

Furthermore, note that

$$D_T = \min\{A_T, N\} = N - \underbrace{\max\{N - A_T, 0\}}_{\equiv \text{ Put on the firm}}. \tag{14.3}$$

That is, credit risk raises the cost of capital. Let us explain. Debt can be understood as a risky asset, which provides the principal N, minus a nonnegative term. The nonnegative term reflects the optionality the debt holders are being short: it is as if the debt holders had sold a put option, which will be exercised when the firm is in default. This synthetic, short position, requires an increase in the cost of capital compared to a riskless loan.

Thus, equity holders face a convex payoff (see figure 14.2). This convexity may lead them to undertake a risk-taking behavior. Under conditions (see chapter 8), the expected payoff to equity holders is increasing in the asset volatility, σ. This property has been emphasized to explain adverse selection and credit rationing in chapter 9. Section 14.5.5 also relies on this basic property and explains how availability of credit and limited liability may lead to bubbles. Note, instead, that the terminal payoff to debt holders is concave,

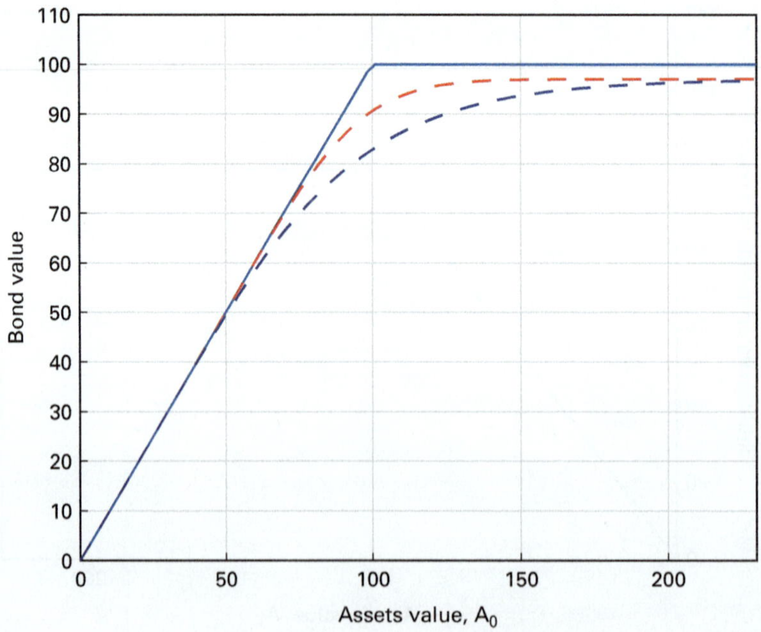

Figure 14.3
Solid line: the no-arbitrage bound, min $\{A_0, N\}$, depicted as a function of A_0, when the nominal value of debt is fixed to $N = 100$. The dashed lines depict the bond value predicted by Merton's model when $T = 1$, $r = 3\%$ and $\sigma = 20\%$ (middle curve) and $\sigma = 40\%$ (lowest curve).

such that debt value is, then, decreasing in the assets volatility, a property discussed further in the next section.

14.2.1.1 Merton

The *current* value of the bonds equals the current value of the assets, A_0, minus the current value of equity. The *current* value of equity can obtained through the Black–Scholes formula, as equity is a European call option on the firm, struck at N. By eq. (14.2), and standard risk neutral evaluation, the *current* value of debt, D_0, is,

$$D_0 = A_0 \Phi(-d_1) + Ne^{-rT}\Phi(d_1 - \sigma\sqrt{T}), \quad d_1 = \frac{\ln(A_0/N) + \left(r + \frac{1}{2}\sigma^2\right)T}{\sigma\sqrt{T}}, \tag{14.4}$$

where $\Phi(\cdot)$ denotes the distribution function of a standard normal variable.[3]

Bond prices are decreasing in the asset volatility as bad outcomes are exaggerated on the downside, due to the concavity properties illustrated by figure 14.2. It is useful to compare this property with others in the fixed income space. Chapter 13 (see section 13.5.1) explains

3. For the details, note that $D_0 = e^{-rT}\mathbb{E}[D_T | A_0]$ and, then, by eq. (14.2),

$$D_0 = e^{-rT}\mathbb{E}(A_T | A_0) - e^{-rT}\mathbb{E}[\max\{A_T - N, 0\} | A_0] = A_0 - \left[A_0\Phi(d_1) - Ne^{-r\tau}\Phi(d_1 - \sigma\sqrt{T})\right],$$

where the last equality follows by the Black–Scholes formula. Eq. (14.4) follows after rearranging terms in the previous equation.

that the yield curve relates to the volatility of the fundamentals (i.e., the short-term rate) in a complex way, due to two opposing effects at play: a "convexity" and a "risk premium" effect. In bad times, the risk premium effect should dominate, leading the yield curve to increase with volatility. In good times, a convexity effect would lead the yield curve to decrease with volatility. Instead, predictions in the defaultable case are very sharp: the term structure of interest rates increases with the volatility of the fundamentals. Naturally, this prediction relies on channels that are quite distinct from those discussed in chapter 13.

Next, consider the term structure of interest rates, defined as

$$R(T) \equiv -\frac{1}{T} \ln \left(\frac{D_0}{N} \right) = r + \mathcal{S}_0(T),$$

where

$$\mathcal{S}_0(T) = -\frac{1}{T} \ln \left(\frac{A_0}{N} e^{rT} \Phi(-d_1) + \Phi\left(d_1 - \sigma\sqrt{T}\right) \right). \tag{14.5}$$

We refer to $\mathcal{S}_0(T)$ as the "term-spread" for a given fixed maturity. The mapping maturity-spreads is known as the "risk-structure of interest rates."

Figure 14.4 depicts the spread predicted by this model. The left panel reveals that credit spreads shrink to zero as time-to-maturity becomes smaller and smaller. This property of the model stands in sharp contrast with the empirical behavior of credit spreads, which

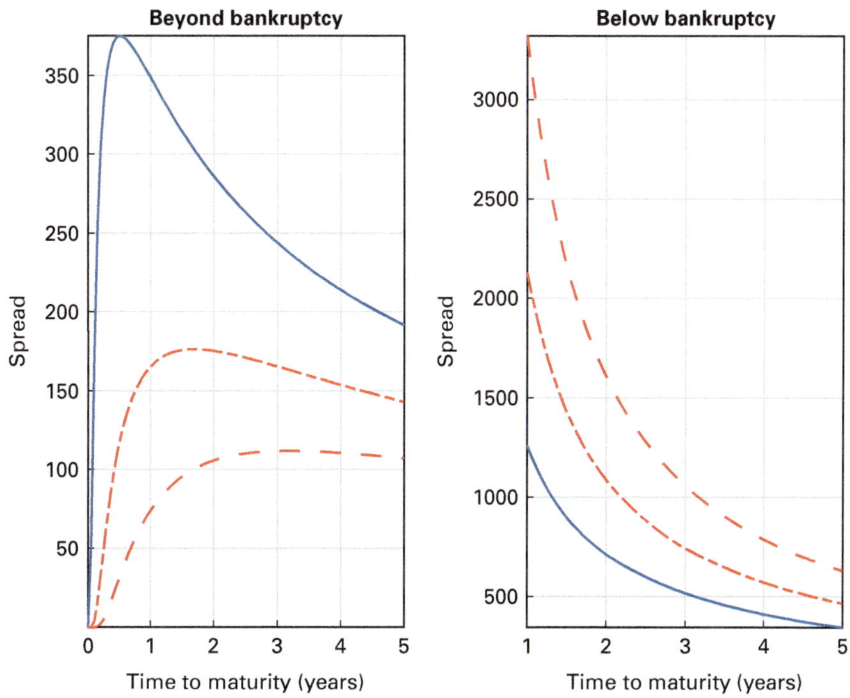

Figure 14.4
The term structure of spreads, $\mathcal{S}_0(T)$, in basis points, predicted by Merton's model. The left panel depicts eq. (14.5), when the initial asset values A_0 equal 110 (top line), 120, and 130 (bottom). The right panel depicts spreads for A_0 equal to 70 (top line), 80, and 90 (bottom). In both panels, $r = 3\%$, $\sigma = 0.20$, and $N = 100$.

are high even for short-maturity bonds. The property arises because the model is driven by Brownian motions, which have continuous sample paths, such that given a firm asset value $A > N$, the probability of bankruptcy, arising when A hits N from above, approaches zero very fast as time to maturity goes to zero. Because credit spreads reflect default probabilities, as explained in detail below (see eq. (14.9)), credit spreads shrink to zero quickly as time to maturity approaches zero.

Naturally, one might end up with credit spreads sufficiently high at short maturities, by assuming the firm asset value is sufficiently small. For example, in figure 14.4 (left panel) credit spreads are "high" for short maturities, when $A = 110$. However, even with $A = 110$, credit spreads are still close to zero at very short maturities. More fundamentally, requiring such a small value for A is problematic. Firms with such a low asset value would command a much higher spread than that in the left panel of figure 14.4. All in all, the Brownian motion model in this section lacks some source of risk driving the behavior of short-term spreads. In section 14.2.5, we will show that this issue can be addressed assuming that firm's default can be triggered by "jumps."

The shape of the term structure of credit spreads changes once the current firm asset value is below N. In this case, the probability the firm defaults is close to one when time to maturity is close to zero. The right panel of figure 14.4 illustrates that the spreads become larger and larger as we get closer and closer to maturity.[4]

What is the asymptotic behavior of the spread predicted by this model? If $r > \frac{1}{2}\sigma^2$, then, as $T \to \infty$, the probability of survival for the firm, which we shall show to be $\Phi(d_1 - \sigma\sqrt{T})$ below (see eq. (14.7)), approaches one, $\Phi(d_1 - \sigma\sqrt{T}) \to 1$. That is, the firm asset value is expected to grow so large that default will never occur, such that the bond becomes riskless and $\mathcal{S}_0(T) \to -\frac{1}{T}\ln\Phi(d_1 - \sigma\sqrt{T}) \to 0$. Intuitively, when $r > \frac{1}{2}\sigma^2$, the asset volatility is so small that the exponential trend for A_t will make it unlikely that the firm asset value will fall below the constant value N. In other words, Merton's model predicts that in the long run, things can only go well for the firm, a view quite opposite to that leading to positive spreads for long maturities.

To summarize, Merton's model predict that *short-term* spreads are zero and *long-term* spreads are likely also zero. Intensity models, such as those analyzed in section 14.2.5, help mitigate these counterfactual features. Intuitively, an intensity model is one where a firm can default at any time, thereby leading to positive short-term spreads. If the probability of default is time-varying and mean-reverting, long-term spreads may, then, be positive, especially when the current default probability is so low that it can be expected to increase significantly, due to mean-reversion.

14.2.1.2 *Credit quality I: Distance to default, survival probabilities*

We introduce a useful summary statistics to measure credit quality, called *distance-to-default* (under $\mathbb{Q}$). We can use the previous model to estimate the likelihood of default for a given firm. First, we develop eq. (14.2),

$$D_T = \min\{A_T, N\} = A_T \cdot \mathbb{I}_{\{A_T < N\}} + N \cdot \mathbb{I}_{\{A_T \geq N\}},$$

4. For visualization purposes, this figure only includes spreads for maturities beyond one year.

where $\mathbb{I}_{\{\mathcal{E}\}}$ is the indicator function, that is, $\mathbb{I}_{\{\mathcal{E}\}}=1$ if the event $\mathcal{E}$ is true and $\mathbb{I}_{\{\mathcal{E}\}}=0$ if the event $\mathcal{E}$ is false. Second, we have,

$$\begin{aligned} D_0 &= e^{-rT}\mathbb{E}\left(D_T\right) \\ &= e^{-rT}\left[\mathbb{E}\left(A_T\cdot\mathbb{I}_{\{A_T<N\}}\right)+N\cdot\mathbb{E}\left(\mathbb{I}_{\{A_T\geq N\}}\right)\right] \\ &= e^{-rT}\left[\mathbb{E}\left(A_T\right|\text{Default}\right)\mathbb{Q}\left(\text{Default}\right)+N\cdot\mathbb{Q}\left(\text{Survival}\right)\right], \end{aligned} \tag{14.6}$$

where $\mathbb{E}\left(A_T\right|\text{Default})$ is the expected firm asset value given the event of default, $\mathbb{Q}\left(\text{Default}\right)$ is the probability of default, and $\mathbb{Q}\left(\text{Survival}\right)=1-\mathbb{Q}\left(\text{Default}\right)$ is the probability the firm does not default.[5]

Comparing eq. (14.6) and eq. (14.4) reveals that for Merton's model,

$$\mathbb{Q}\left(\text{Survival}\right)=\Phi\left(d_2\right), \tag{14.7}$$

where for obvious reasons, the quantity,

$$d_2=\frac{\ln\left(A_0/N\right)+\left(r-\frac{1}{2}\sigma^2\right)T}{\sigma\sqrt{T}}, \tag{14.8}$$

is called *distance-to-default* (D-t-D). Distance-to-default is a useful summary statistics, providing an intuitive gauge of how far the firm is from defaulting: the higher d_2, the higher the (risk-adjusted) probability of surviving, $\Phi\left(d_2\right)$. The higher the current firm asset value A_0 is, the less likely it is the firm will default at T.

By eq. (14.1), we have that $\mathbb{E}\left(\ln A_T\middle| A_0\right)=\ln A_0+(r-\frac{1}{2}\sigma^2)T$, so eq. (14.8) tells us that distance-to-default is simply the difference $\mathbb{E}\left(\ln A_T\middle| A_0\right)-\ln N$, normalized by the standard deviation of the assets over the debt life. At times, then, we may use the slightly different formula,

$$\text{Distance-to-default}=\frac{\text{asset mkt value}-\text{default value}}{\text{asset mkt value}\times\text{asset volatility}}.$$

How do survival probabilities relate to debt maturity or assets volatility? Figure 14.5 reveals that the probability of survival decreases with assets volatility, but may be nonmonotone in debt maturity. To illustrate this nonmonotonicity, note that, for large T, the probability of survival approaches one, provided that $r>\frac{1}{2}\sigma^2$, as discussed earlier; this condition ensures that the assets value grows so large as to make default unlikely. In the top panel of figure 14.5, where we assume that $r>\frac{1}{2}\sigma^2$, the probability of survival does indeed begin revert to one as T grows large. At the same time, as T decreases, survival is more and more likely, provided $A_0>N$: a diffusion process has no jumps, a property further discussed in section 14.2.5.[6]

5. The last equality in eq. (14.6) follows because $\mathbb{E}\left(A_T\mathbb{I}_{\{A_T<N\}}\right)=\mathbb{E}\left(A_T\mathbb{I}_{\{A_T<N\}}\middle|\mathbb{I}_{\{A_T<N\}}=1\right)$ $\mathbb{Q}\left(\mathbb{I}_{\{A_T<N\}}=1\right)+\mathbb{E}\left(A_T\mathbb{I}_{\{A_T<N\}}\middle|\mathbb{I}_{\{A_T<N\}}=0\right)\mathbb{Q}\left(\mathbb{I}_{\{A_T<N\}}=0\right)=\mathbb{E}\left(A_T\middle| A_T<N\right)\mathbb{Q}\left(A_T<N\right)$.

6. Mathematically, assume that $A_0>N$ and $r>\frac{1}{2}\sigma^2$. Then the first term of d_2 in eq. (14.8) is decreasing in T, whereas the second is increasing. When T is small, the first term (and its sensitivity to T) dominates, such that distance-to-default decreases with maturity. But for large T, the second term of d_2 dominates and makes distance-to-default large.

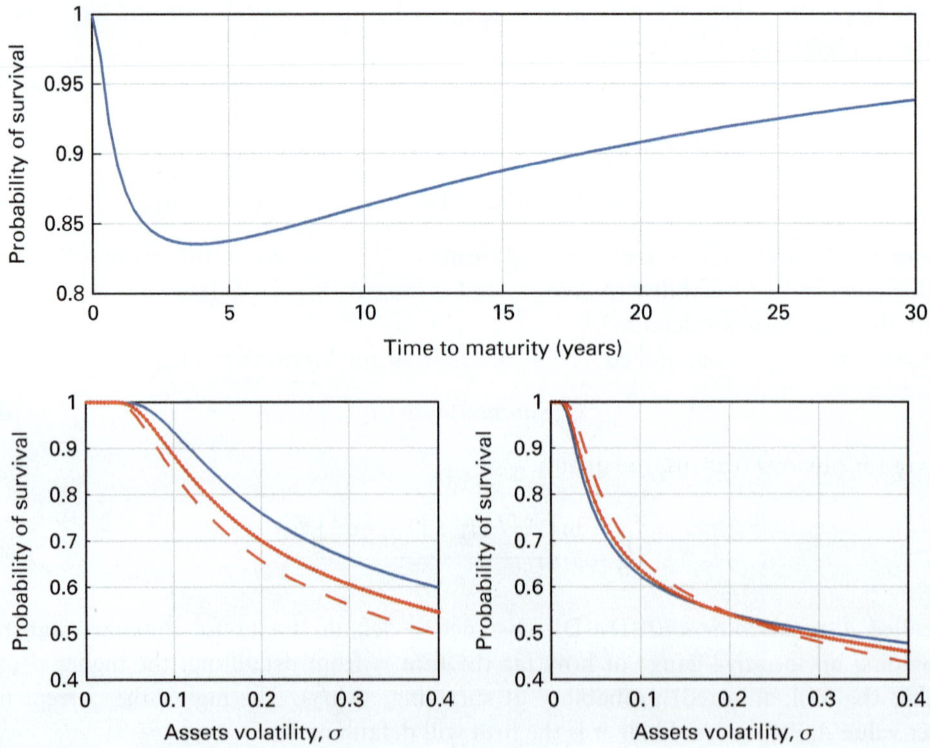

Figure 14.5
Probability of survival predicted by Merton's model, $\Phi(d_2)$, depicted as a function of time to maturity (top panel) and assets volatility (bottom panels). In both cases, face value of debt is $N=100$, and $r=3\%$. In the top panel, assets value $A_0=110$ and assets volatility is $\sigma=0.10$. The bottom left panel plots survival probabilities for maturities $T=0.5$ years (top line), $T=1$ and $T=2$ years (bottom), and assets value $A_0=110$. The bottom right panel plots the same probabilities for $A_0=101$. For sufficiently high σ, survival probabilities rank as in the left panel; for small σ, the ranking is reversed.

Note that when A_0 is small, some nonmonotonicities arise even for small maturities. In this case, survival probabilities can increase or decrease with maturities, depending on the values of σ (see the bottom panels in figure 14.5). Intuitively, when $A_0 \approx N$, the probability of survival is

$$\mathbb{Q}\left(\text{Survival}\right)=\Phi\left(d_2\right), \text{ with } d_2=\frac{\ln\left(\frac{A_0}{N}\right)+\left(r-\frac{1}{2}\sigma^2\right)T}{\sigma\sqrt{T}}\approx\frac{\left(r-\frac{1}{2}\sigma^2\right)}{\sigma}\sqrt{T},$$

which decreases in T for large σ although then it increases in T for small σ. Indeed, for large σ, the probability the assets value will end up below N from $A_0\approx N$ can only increase with time to maturity, T. That is, $\mathbb{E}\left(\ln A_T|\, A_0\right)=\ln A_0+\left(r-\frac{1}{2}\sigma^2\right)T\approx\ln N+\left(r-\frac{1}{2}\sigma^2\right)T$, such that the probability the assets value will be below N does indeed increase with σ.

14.2.1.3 *Credit quality II: Loss-given-default*

A useful concept is that of *loss-given-default*, which we denote with LGD. Comparing eq. (14.6) with eq. (14.4) reveals that, for Merton's model,

$$\mathbb{E}\left(A_T|\,\text{Default}\right)=\frac{A_0 e^{rT}\Phi\left(-d_1\right)}{\mathbb{Q}\left(\text{Default}\right)}=A_0 e^{rT}\frac{\Phi\left(-d_1\right)}{\Phi\left(-d_2\right)}=\mathbb{E}\left(A_T\right)\frac{\Phi\left(-d_1\right)}{\Phi\left(-d_2\right)}\leq\mathbb{E}\left(A_T\right).$$

Recovery rates are defined as the fraction of the bond value the bondholders expect to obtain at maturity and in the event of default, viz

$$\text{Rec}\equiv\frac{\mathbb{E}\left(A_T|\,\text{Default}\right)}{N}=\frac{A_0}{N}e^{rT}\frac{\Phi\left(-d_1\right)}{\Phi\left(-d_2\right)}.$$

We define *loss-given-default* as the fraction of the bond value that bondholders expect to lose at maturity in the event of default, i.e., LGD = 1 − Rec. Finally, by eq. (14.5),

$$\begin{aligned}\mathcal{S}_0\left(T\right)&=-\frac{1}{T}\ln\left(\frac{A_0}{N}e^{rT}\Phi\left(-d_1\right)+\Phi\left(d_2\right)\right)\\&=-\frac{1}{T}\ln\left(\text{Rec}\cdot\mathbb{Q}\left(\text{Default}\right)+\mathbb{Q}\left(\text{Survival}\right)\right)\\&\approx\frac{1}{T}\left[\text{LGD}\cdot\mathbb{Q}\left(\text{Default}\right)\right].\end{aligned}\qquad(14.9)$$

Eq. (14.9) follows by eq. (14.6) and is actually a general formula, one that goes beyond Merton's model. While it is intuitive, an important note is in order. The previous definitions of survival probabilities, distance-to-default, and LGD, are made under the risk-adjusted probability $\mathbb{Q}$. These quantities may defined under the true probability $\mathbb{P}$, by replacing r with the asset growth rate under the physical probability, μ, in all the relevant formulae (i.e., survival probabilities, $\Phi\left(d_2\right)$, distance-to-default, d_2, and LGD). However, it is well known that it is hard to estimate μ for many single names. Moody's KMV's Expected Default Frequencies (EDF^{TM}) methodology relies on dynamic structural models along the same lines as in this section, although the methodology details do not seem to be publicly known. Note that we can use historical data on *default frequencies* and estimate the probability that a given single name within a certain industry will default. These frequencies are based on samples of firms that have defaulted in the past, with similar characteristics to those of the firm under evaluation (in terms, for instance, of distance-to-default).

14.2.1.4 *Estimating assets value and volatility*

How does one estimate A_t and σ? One algorithm is to start with some σ equal to the volatility of equity returns, say $\sigma^{(0)}$, and use Merton's formula for equity, to extract $A_t^{(0)}$ for each date $t\in\{1,\cdots,\mathcal{T}\}$, where $\mathcal{T}$ is the sample size. Then, use $A_t^{(0)}$ to compute the standard deviation of $\ln(A_t^{(0)}/A_{t-1}^{(0)})$. This gives say $\sigma^{(1)}$, which can be used as the new input into Merton's formula to extract say $A_t^{(1)}$. We obtain a sequence of $(A_t^{(i)})_{t=1}^{\mathcal{T}}$ and $\sigma^{(i)}$, and we stop for i sufficiently large, according to some criterion.

14.2.1.5 One example

Assume a firm has asset value $A_0 = 110$, and that the asset value volatility is $\sigma = 30\%$, annualized. The safe interest rate is $r = 2\%$, annualized, and the expected growth rate of the asset value is $\mu = 5\%$, annualized. The firm has outstanding debt with nominal value $N = 100$, which expires in two years.

First, we compute the distance-to-default implied by Merton's model,

$$\text{D-t-D} = \frac{\ln\left(\frac{A_0}{N}\right) + \left(r - \frac{1}{2}\sigma^2\right)T}{\sigma\sqrt{T}} = \frac{\ln(1.1) + \left(0.02 - \frac{1}{2}0.3^2\right)2}{0.3\sqrt{2}} = 0.10680.$$

Accordingly, the probability of default is

$$1 - \Phi(0.10680) = 1 - 0.54253 = 0.45747.$$

We compute the same probability under the physical probability, by simply replacing $r = 2\%$ with $\mu = 5\%$, in the formula for Dist, obtaining

$$\text{Dist}^* = \frac{\ln\left(\frac{A_0}{N}\right) + \left(\mu - \frac{1}{2}\sigma^2\right)T}{\sigma\sqrt{T}} = \frac{\ln(1.1) + \left(0.05 - \frac{1}{2}0.3^2\right)2}{0.3\sqrt{2}} = 0.24822.$$

Therefore, the probability of default under the physical distribution is,

$$1 - \Phi(0.24822) = 1 - 0.59802 = 0.40198.$$

It is, of course, lower under the physical probability than under the risk neutral probability, due to the larger asset growth rate, $\mu > r$.

Finally, we can compute the spread on this bond,

$$\mathcal{S}_0(T) = -\frac{1}{T}\ln\left(\frac{A_0}{N}e^{rT}\Phi(-d_1) + \Phi(d_2)\right),$$

where $d_2 = \text{D-t-D}$, and $d_1 = d_2 + \sigma\sqrt{T}$. So we have,

$$\begin{aligned}\mathcal{S}_0(T) &= -\frac{1}{2}\ln\left(1.1e^{0.02\times 2}\Phi\left(-\left(0.10680 + 0.30\times\sqrt{2}\right)\right) + \Phi(0.10680)\right)\\ &= -\frac{1}{2}\ln\left(1.1e^{0.02\times 2}\times 0.29769 + 0.54253\right)\\ &= 6.20\%.\end{aligned}$$

14.2.1.6 Equity and debt volatility

Merton's model leads to precise predictions regarding equity and debt volatility. A simple example in chapter 9 (section 9.8) emphasizes that a positive probability of default may be responsible for a high volatility in equity returns. In this model, equity and bond return volatility are given by $\sigma_A A_t \frac{E'(A_t)}{E(A_t)}$ and $\sigma_A A_t \frac{D'(A_t)}{D(A_t)}$, resp., with obvious notation. Figure 14.6 plots these volatilities against asset values and default probabilities. Volatilities are decreasing in A_0, as expected: equity vol flattens out to σ_A; instead, bond vol flattens out to 0. Volatilities also correlate positively with default probabilities, for the simple reason that default probabilities are also decreasing in A_0; in the case of equity, volatility becomes very large for small values of A_0 (i.e., when default probability is high).

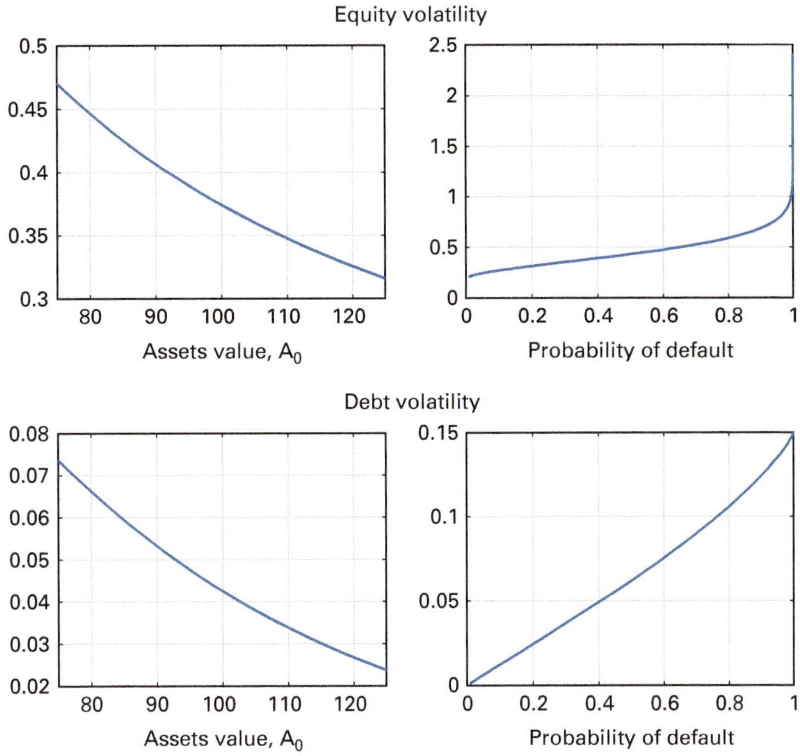

Figure 14.6
This picture depicts equity (top panel) and debt (bottom panel) volatility as a function of the assets value A_0 and default probabilities, $1-\Phi(d_2)$. In both cases, face value of debt is $N=100$, $T=10$ years, $r=3\%$, and assets volatility is $\sigma=0.15$.

14.2.1.7 *Stocks and bonds*

On August 5, 2011, the rating agency Standard and Poor's downgraded the US debt from AAA to AA+ for the first time in history. The US and global equity markets sank (the DJIA lost nearly 6%) on the first trading day (Monday, August 8) following the announcement. Somehow paradoxically, US Treasuries rallied on the very same day, a phenomenon many commentators described as a "flight-to-quality" response to a quite unique event. The reason this rally seems paradoxical is that the object of downgrade was US debt. Moreover, at the time, the US debt/GDP ratio was hovering at almost 100%, a fact that mitigates the case of US Treasuries as "safe-haven" assets.

But additional arguments made US Treasuries a safe haven. First, some of the signals leading to the downgrade regarded the political gaming about an increase in the debt ceiling, a gaming that could have led to delinquencies.[7] However, this gaming and its effects were arguably transitory. Moreover, AA+ debt is accepted as a collateral in many transactions, and considered to be high grade debt in most investment mandates. Furthermore, an issue at the time was to speculate whether other rating agencies (Moody's and Fitch) would proceed with similar downgrades of US debt that could have made the August 5

7. In the US, the Congress has to approve an increase in debt capacity.

decision more solidly grounded, so to speak. Finally, the Standard and Poor's decision was not totally unexpected, as rumors about it had started to circulate months earlier.

However, flight-to-quality does not seem to be an exhaustive explanation for the US Treasury rally during these events. First, during the period around the August 5, the US was flooded with bad news regarding the economic fundamentals, with many leading indicators reaching levels historically consistent with recessions. This news would make it likely (at the time) that the US economy would spiral toward a second recession in less than four years, i.e., right after that related to the subprime crisis (discussed in section 14.5). The unfolding of these events is entirely consistent with we learned in chapter 13: recession fears translate into an expectation future short rates will lower as a result of the Fed attempt to stimulate growth, whence the Treasury rally.

Therefore, the rally of US Treasuries at the time might merely reflect the expectation hypothesis that future rates would be lower. In this period of bad news (which also included adverse developments regarding the debt crisis in Europe), the Standard and Poor's downgrade might have come as yet another negative signal about the general health of the US system, which would further deteriorate the general investment climate. Therefore, a rally in US Treasuries could be explained by both flight-to-quality effects (i.e., an uncertainty premium about the occurrence of possible disorderly tail events) *and* the market expectations about the Fed response to particularly severe economic developments.

The model in this section suggests one additional potential channel conducive to the equity crash and the rally in US debt after Standard and Poor's downgrade decision. What happens to the price of a stock and a bond, after an adverse shock hits the fundamentals? According to Merton's model, they both fall after a decrease in A. But which of the two prices will drop more? After all, debt is less risky than stocks (due to subordination), and bad news about the fundamentals should affect stocks more than bonds.

Figure 14.7 depicts the value of bonds and stocks predicted by Merton's model. Naturally, Merton's model is a very raw approximation to the events we are discussing in this section. These events relate to sovereign debt, not firm's debt. At the same time, this model can shed some light into these events. It predicts that bond prices do not move too much when the probability of default is small (i.e., when A_0 is large enough), which might roughly correspond to the situation where an agency announces that a name is to be downgraded from AAA to AA+. Instead, stock prices fall, and substantially, due to convexity, following an increase in the probability of default (which occurs when A_0 falls in Merton's model).

While Merton's model does not obviously regard the joint behavior of stock and sovereign bond prices, it makes a sharp prediction regarding stock and bond prices for a firm. It is an open issue as to whether these predictions would also apply to market developments related to sovereigns. Naturally, the informal arguments of this section do not aim to rule out additional explanations around the events of August 2011, such as flight-to-quality effects and the expectation hypothesis. Rather, they suggest one additional hypothesis: even absent flight-to-quality effects or the expectation hypothesis, bond prices should not substantially fall, once the probability of default for a "name" still remains very small.

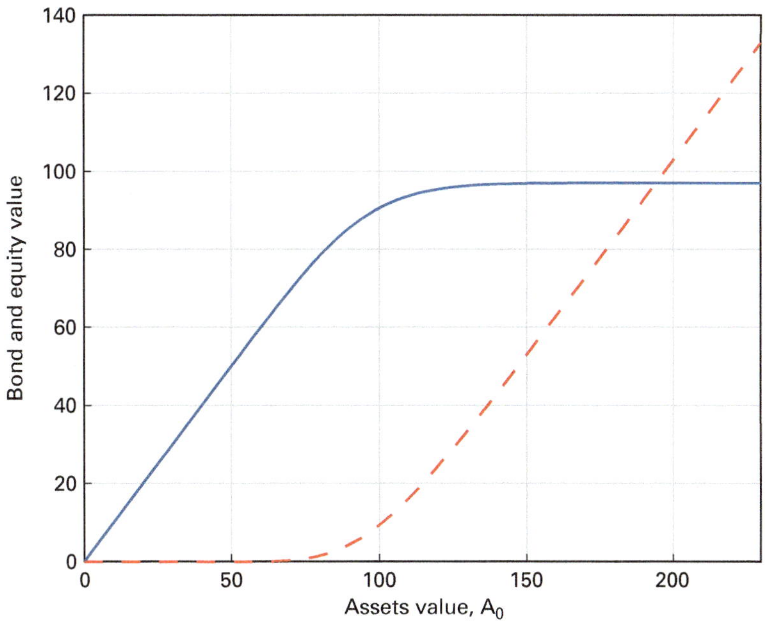

Figure 14.7
The solid and dashed lines depict the value of a bond and a stock predicted by Merton's model, when the nominal value of debt is $N = 100$, and $T = 1$, $r = 3\%$ and $\sigma = 20\%$, annualized.

14.2.1.8 First passage

The timing of default can be triggered by some exogenously specified events. For example, default occurs if the value of the assets hits some exogenous lower bound even before debt expiration. These models are known as "first passage" models, because they rely on mathematical techniques that solve for the probability the first time the asset value hits some exogenous "barrier," as in Black and Cox (1976). It is an interesting case of how asset evaluation theories can develop. The evaluation methods in this section mostly rely on the "option-pricing toolkit" available since Black–Scholes and Merton. However, the first passage approach of Black and Cox would then inspire further work on design and pricing derivatives with barriers (i.e., barrier options), such as down (or up-)and-out and down (or up-)and-in options.

14.2.2 The Structural Approach in Theory: Strategic Defaulting

The timing of default may be endogenous. We now describe a model, originally developed by Leland (1994), in which equity holders choose a defaulting barrier (i.e., the firm asset value that triggers bankruptcy) so as to maximize equity value. Thus, firms default strategically, contrary to the assumptions underlying the Modigliani-Miller theorem. Chapter 5 describes additional theoretical models that try to depart from the assumptions underlying the Modigliani and Miller propositions, with capital structure implications.

The model in this section resembles others in this chapter, in that it provides a natural extension to approaches with exogenous default. It predicts that the value of the firm will now depend on its capital structure. The mechanism of the model relies on well-known explanations that belong to the so-called trade-off theory. In its static version introduced by Kraus and Litzenberger (1973) and Scott (1976), this theory explains that firms solve a trade-off between (i) saving more taxes by issuing more debt and (ii) being more exposed to the risk of bankruptcy brought about by a higher leverage. This theory has received dynamic extensions. Hennessy and Whited (2005) provide an important contribution, which takes account of corporate income taxes, dividends, interest income, and distress costs. Leland (1994) provides one of the earliest dynamic extensions, setting up the standard for this type of analysis. The model works as follows. The firm issues debt and needs to ensure coupon payments could flow to the benefit of bondholders. If the value of the assets becomes low enough compared to the nominal value of debt, it would be beneficial for equity holders to default. In fact, the model carries additional implications. On the one hand, issuing debt adds value to the firm, because, in the model, debt acts as a tax-shielding device; therefore, the time to default is affected by this tax benefit: the higher the tax benefit, the higher the expected time to default. On the other hand, issuing debt exposes the firm to a risk of default and, thus, to higher expected default costs (e.g., legal expenses). The value of the firm, therefore, depends on its capital structure (how much debt compared to equity), and there may be optimal levels of leverage, that is, levels of leverage the maximize the firm value.

In more detail, the model assumes that equity holders finance debt coupons by continuously raising equity capital at each point in time the firm cash flows are not sufficient to honor the coupon payments. The firm cash flows include both asset performance and tax benefits associated with the issuance of debt. Then, a possibility of bankruptcy is opened to the firm, which occurs (endogenously) as soon as the equity holders consider that the value of the assets is too small to warrant them a lifetime positive expected return (in excess of debt services). Specifically, in bad times, when the assets perform poorly, the equity holders do not necessarily liquidate the firm, because there might be chances that the assets could perform better in the future. However, should the assets value become small enough, the equity holders will stop paying the coupons and will liquidate the firm. Naturally, equity holders choose the value of the asset that triggers bankruptcy to maximize the value of equity.[8]

Formally, the terms leading to strategic defaulting are as follows. First, to model the firm cash flows, we relax the assumption that the value of the assets, A_t, is the solution to eq. (14.1). Instead, we assume that the firm instantaneous cash flows are equal to a constant fraction δ of the assets A_t, such that, and generalizing eq. (14.1),[9]

$$\frac{dA_t}{A_t} = (r - \delta)\, dt + \sigma d\tilde{W}_t.$$

8. The model we analyze in this section is that in section VI.B of Leland (1994). This model was extended to one with finite maturity debt by Leland and Toft (1996). Anderson and Sundaresan (1996) consider cases of debt renegotiation. As explained, Leland's model considers firm liquidation as a strategic choice made by equity holders. In fact, the US bankruptcy code includes both a liquidation process ("Chapter 7") and a reorganization process ("Chapter 11"), but Leland's model only considers firm liquidation at bankruptcy. Broadie, Chernov, and Sundaresan (2007) generalize this setting to one where the firm may choose to default through a reorganization process, in which case no equity is issued to honour debt services as in the model of this section.

9. In particular, it is straightforward to check that the evaluation formula in Footnote 2 of this chapter collapses to $A_0 = \mathbb{E}\left(\int_0^\infty e^{-rt}\delta A_t dt\right)$, once the instantaneous cash flows $\delta_t = \delta A_t$.

Second, debt is infinitely lived, in that it pays off an instantaneous coupon equal to C, forever, conditional upon survival; in the absence of default risk, the value of debt would simply equal C/r. Third, tax benefits are assumed to be proportional to the coupon, θC. Fourth, there are bankruptcy costs: if the firm defaults at $A = A^B$, recovery is $(1-\alpha)\,A^B$. Equity holders choose A^B. Naturally, $A^B < A_0$.

The value of debt is a function of the firm asset value, A, say $D(A)$. Moreover, the firm finances the net cost of the coupon C by issuing additional equity, as explained above, and until the equity value is zero, i.e., until $A = A^B$, as seen below. That is, bankruptcy occurs when the firm cannot meet the instantaneous coupon payments. Under the risk neutral probability, the value of debt satisfies:

$$\underbrace{\frac{d}{dT}\mathbb{E}\left[D(A_T)|\,A_t\right]\bigg|_{T=t}}_{=\text{Expected capital gains}} + \underbrace{C}_{=\text{coupon}} = rD(A_t)\,. \tag{14.10}$$

Due to Itô's lemma, eq. (14.10) is an ordinary differential equation, subject to the following boundary conditions. First, at bankruptcy, $D\left(A^B\right) = (1-\alpha)\,A^B$. Second, for large A, debt is substantially riskless, i.e., $\lim_{A\to\infty} D(A) = \frac{C}{r}$. The solution to (14.10), which also satisfies these boundary conditions, is

$$D(A) = (1-\pi_B(A))\,\frac{C}{r} + \pi_B(A)\left[(1-\alpha)\,A^B\right], \tag{14.11}$$

where

$$\pi_B(A) \equiv \left(\frac{A^B}{A}\right)^{\gamma}, \tag{14.12}$$

and $\gamma > 1$ is a positive constant.[10] The function $\pi_B(A)$ is interpreted ad the present value in state A of \$1, contingent on future bankruptcy, as further explained in appendix 14.A. Accordingly, $(1-\pi_B(A))\,/r$ is the present value in state A of receiving a stream of payments equal to \$1 up to bankruptcy.

The total benefits arising from tax shielding and the present value of bankruptcy costs are, then, resp.,

$$TS(A) = (1-\pi_B(A))\,\theta\frac{C}{r}, \quad BC(A) = \pi_B(A)\,\alpha A^B.$$

Denoting equity with E, we have that

$$E + D = \text{Firm value} = A + TS(A) - BC(A)\,.$$

Summing up,

$$E(A) = A - (1-\pi_B(A))\,(1-\theta)\,\frac{C}{r} - \pi_B(A)\,A^B. \tag{14.13}$$

Equity equals (i) the firm assets value, A; minus (ii) the present value of debt contingent on no-bankruptcy, net of tax benefits, $(1-\pi_B(A))\,(1-\theta)\,\frac{C}{r}$; minus (iii) the present value

10. Notably, $\gamma = \sigma^{-2}(r-\delta-\frac{1}{2}\sigma^2+\sqrt{\left(r-\delta-\frac{1}{2}\sigma^2\right)^2+2\sigma^2 r})$.

of debt contingent on bankruptcy, and net of bankruptcy costs, $\pi_B(A)\,A^B$. The second term decreases with the default boundary, A^B or, equivalently, $\pi_B(A)$. The third term, instead, increases with A^B. So the time equity holders wait before declaring bankruptcy, which is inversely related to A^B, affects these two terms in opposite ways.

Equity holders choose A^B to maximize the value of equity. The solution is a default boundary, A^B, such that the value of equity does not change for small changes in the value of the assets A around A^B, or $A^B: E'(A)|_{A=A^B}=0$, a "smooth pasting condition" (see appendix 14.A). The result is

$$A^B=\frac{\gamma}{1+\gamma}\frac{(1-\theta)\,C}{r}. \tag{14.14}$$

It is easily seen that this value of A^B maximizes equity value, $E\left(A;A^B\right)\equiv E(A)$, in that $A^B:0=\partial E\left(A;A^B\right)/\partial A^B$. The expression for A^B is intuitive. Consider, for example, the case in which no tax benefits accrue to the firm while issuing debt, i.e., $\theta=0$. In this case, default occurs when the total assets value falls below a level "a bit lower" than the nominal value of debt, i.e., $A^B=\frac{\gamma}{1+\gamma}\frac{C}{r}$. As θ increases, the value of A^B in eq. (14.14) lowers and collapses to zero when the tax benefits exactly compensate for the "debt burden," $\theta=1$. In this case, $E(A)=A$.

We may derive the solution in (14.14) from a slightly different angle. Note that equity holders have access to an instantaneous dividend equal to $\delta A_t-C+\theta C$, and their optimization problem is

$$E(A_t)=\sup_{\tau}E_t\left(\int_t^{\tau}e^{-r(s-t)}\left(\delta A_s-(1-\theta)\,C\right)ds\right). \tag{14.15}$$

Appendix 14.A reviews the main lines of the argument and explains that the solution to this real option problem is that in eq. (14.14). That is, equity holders are willing to accept some temporary negative values of the dividends (and in this case, they would inject new equity capital to make sure debt is honored), although then they would declare bankruptcy as soon as the assets value reaches the threshold level A^B in (14.14), in which case the expected net present value of the dividends, and, hence, equity, E, is zero.

Figure 14.8 depicts debt and equity values as a function of the current assets value, A_0. Debt is increasing and concave and equity is increasing and convex in A_0, just as in Merton's model. The reason is that debt and equity are, resp., decreasing and increasing in $\pi_B(A)$, where $\pi_B(A)$ is decreasing and convex in A. Let us explain. When the current assets value A_0 is large, compared to A^B, bankruptcy is so unlikely that $\pi_B(A_0)\approx 0$, such that debt value approaches $\frac{C}{r}$; however, as the firm approaches bankruptcy, and $\pi_B(A_0)\approx 1$, debt value precipitates to its recovery value, $(1-\alpha)\,A^B$. The behavior of equity is interpreted similarly. When A_0 is high, bankruptcy is unlikely, such that equity grows linearly with A_0; as the firm value approaches the bankruptcy boundary, equity value approaches zero and becomes relatively insensitive to changes in the assets value: it will now take large changes in A before equity value may significantly move again.

Figure 14.8 shows that equity value increases with volatility. Moreover, debt value decreases with volatility when the firm is sufficiently far away from bankruptcy. However, in this example, debt may increase with volatility when the assets value is close

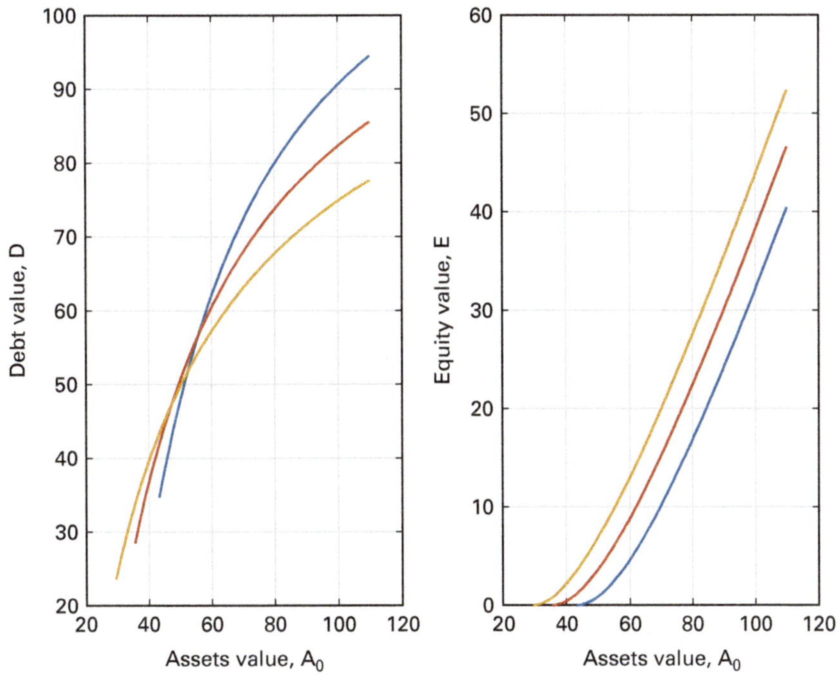

Figure 14.8
This picture depicts the bond (left panel) and equity values (right panel) predicted by Leland's model, against current assets value, A_0, when assets volatility is $\sigma = 0.20$, 0.25 and 0.30. Coupon value is $C = 4$ and remaining parameter values are $\alpha = 0.20$, $\theta = 0.35$, $r = 0.03$, $\delta = 0.02$. As volatility increases, equity value increases and, for sufficiently high levels of A_0, debt value decreases. For A_0 closer to the default boundaries, debt value increases in volatility.

to A^B. The reason is that the parameter γ and, then, A^B, is decreasing in σ^2. Thus, and consistent with intuition underlying real options theory (see section 4.8 in chapter 4), the value of the option to wait for action (i.e., bankruptcy) is increasing in uncertainty, σ^2.[11] So, A^B decreases with σ^2, such that debt value increases with σ^2 for values of A_0 close to A^B.

How does capital structure affect the firm value? Let us begin by assessing how bankruptcy affects debt value. The left panel of figure 14.9 illustrates the intuitive property that debt value, D, increases with its promised coupon, C, at least for small values of C; in fact, D decreases with C, provided C is sufficiently large. The reason for this nonmonotonicity is that bankruptcy becomes more likely, as C increases (see, e.g., eq. (14.14)): when C is large enough, this effect dominates the mechanical effect by which D increases with C. The right panel of figure 14.9 then reveals that the firm value inherits these nonmonotonicities: there exists a level of leverage that maximizes the firm value.

11. Note that $\gamma > 1$ is a solution to the same quadratic equation in section 4.8.6 of chapter 4 and, thus, is decreasing in σ^2. Intuitively, we have that $E(A_t) \approx \max\{0, (\delta A_s - (1-\theta)C) + e^{-r\Delta t} E_t(E(A_{t+\Delta t}))\}$. Waiting a little bit more time before defaulting is valuable as σ^2 increases, due to a higher value for the discounted expectation inside the max operator.

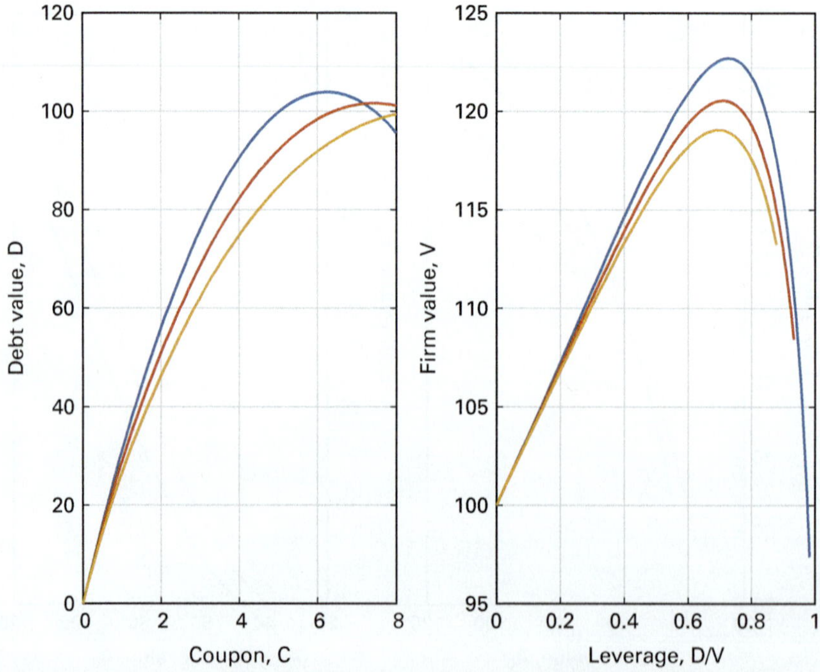

Figure 14.9
The left panel of this picture depicts the value of debt as a function of the coupon, C, when assets volatility is $\sigma = 0.20$, 0.25 and 0.30. Remaining parameter values are as in figure 14.8. Bond values decrease with assets volatility for low values of C. The right panel plots the firm value as a function of leverage, defined as $\frac{D}{V}$, with parameter values set to those in the left panel. Firm value decreases with assets volatility.

14.2.3 In Practice: The Pricing of Convertible Bonds

Convertible bonds offer bondholders the option to convert their bonds into shares of the firm.[12] Chapter 12 provides an introductory discussion of these assets (see section 12.7.3), along with a numerical example of how to price them through a binomial tree. This section analyzes convertible bonds in a continuous time model of the firm's capital structure. We assume the option to convert can be exercised at any time up to maturity. By definition, the face value of a convertible bond is

$$\$100 \equiv \mathrm{CR} \times \mathrm{CP}, \tag{14.16}$$

where CR is the *conversion ratio*, i.e., the number of shares this face value converts into, and CP is the *conversion price*, i.e. the stock price implicitly defined by eq. (14.16).

Typically, the bond is any like other fixed income instrument, with coupon payments, callable features, and credit risk. Callable features are almost invariably embedded into this type of contracts. The parity, or *conversion value*, is the value of the bond if the bondholders decide to convert. It is defined as

$$\mathrm{CV} = \mathrm{CR} \times S,$$

12. Strictly speaking, the "option" embedded into this kind of asset is a *warrant*, not an option. A warrant gives the holder a right to purchase new shares, i.e. shares issued by the firm.

where S is the price of the common share. Not only is the convertible bond price affected by interest rates, credit risk, or timing risk, it is also affected by the movements of the underlying stock price, due to a positive probability the bond might "become" a share in the future: convertible bonds are *hybrid* instruments. The embedded option offers bondholders the possibility to obtain equity returns (not just bond returns) in good times, while offering protection against the downside. As mentioned in chapter 12 (see section 12.7), convertible bonds are usually callable as well. In this case, bondholders are usually given the right to convert the bonds, once they are called. The rationale behind including an option to call is to induce bondholders to convert earlier.

Convertible bonds may be a means to trade volatility, through a type of strategy known as "convertible arbitrage." To illustrate this strategy, consider going long a convertible and short a Treasury. This trade is the same as holding a long position in an option on the firm. Therefore, convertible arbitrage is useful when there are no options on the firm available to trade, and/or when the options are very illiquid. Naturally, convertible arbitrage may also be a trading strategy aiming to profit from situations where options are available and sufficiently liquid, but their price is not aligned with the value of synthetic positions relying on a convertible bond and a Treasury.

The theoretical pricing of convertible bonds has been intensively studied. Ingersoll (1977) provides the first theoretical insights into the pricing of convertible and callable bonds. Let us define the *dilution factor*, denoted by γ, as the fraction of common equity that would be held by the convertible bondholders if the entire issue was converted. If there are n^{out} shares outstanding, and the convertible bond can be exchanged for n shares, then, in aggregate,

$$\gamma = \frac{n}{n+n^{\text{out}}}.$$

We assume that the market value of the firm is equal to the value of its assets, A, which is a geometric Brownian motion, as in eq. (14.1). Let $B^{\text{conv}}(A,\tau;N)$ be the aggregate value of the convertible bond with time to maturity τ and face value N. To simplify the presentation, we do not consider issues related to the option to call. However, we shall provide some intuition about this issue later. Let us assume that the stocks and the convertible bonds are the only two claims in the capital structure of the firm. Since, after conversion, only the stocks will remain, then, the post-conversion value of the convertible bonds is simply the conversion value of the convertible, i.e., γA. Moreover, we have that, for any $\tau \geq 0$,

$$\gamma A \leq B^{\text{conv}}(A,\tau;N) \leq A. \tag{14.17}$$

The first inequality in (14.17) holds for the following reasons: suppose that $B^{\text{conv}}(A,\tau;N) < \gamma A$; then, we can purchase the convertibles, convert them into shares and, finally, sell the shares for γA. The second inequality follows by the limited liability of the equity holders, and the Modigliani-Miller theorem.

At maturity,

$$B^{\text{conv}}(A,0;N) = \min\{A, \max\{N, \gamma A\}\}. \tag{14.18}$$

Indeed, $\bar{B} \equiv \max\{N,\gamma A\}$ is the value of the convertible, in case of no-default. Then, $\min\{A,\bar{B}\}$ is what the firm will pay to the bondholders: A in case of default, and $\bar{B}$ in case of no-default.

We can re-express the terminal payoff in eq. (14.18) in a manner that allows for a better understanding of the issues underlying the exercise of the convertibles. In particular, we have that

$$B^{\text{conv}}(A,0;N)=\min\{A,\max\{N,\gamma A\}\}=\max\{\gamma A,\min\{A,N\}\}. \tag{14.19}$$

Indeed, let $\hat{B}\equiv\min\{A,N\}$ the payment the firm is ready to supply if the bondholders do not convert. Then, $\max\{\gamma A,\hat{B}\}$ is obviously the payoff profile to the bondholders.

Inspection of the terminal payoff in eq. (14.19) reveals that convertible bonds embed an option to convert, on top of the plain vanilla nonconvertible bond. Intuitively, at maturity, a nonconvertible bond is worth $\min\{A,N\}$, and the option to convert is either worthless (in case of non conversion) or worth $\gamma A-N$ (in case of conversion), that is, it is $\max\{\gamma A-N,0\}$. This intuition is confirmed, mathematically, as we have that

$$\max\{\gamma A,\min\{A,N\}\}=\min\{A,N\}+\max\{\gamma A-N,0\}.$$

Therefore, the value of the terminal payoff is, by eq. (14.19),

$$B^{\text{conv}}(A,0;N)=\min\{A,N\}+\gamma\max\{A-N/\gamma,0\}. \tag{14.20}$$

One can show that it is not optimal to exercise the option to convert before maturity. Therefore, to price the convertible bond, we only need to deal with the terminal payoff in eq. (14.20).

Eq. (14.20) shows that the current value of the convertible bond is the sum of the value of a "straight" bond plus the value of γ options on the firm with strike price equal to N/γ. Accordingly, let $B(A,\tau;N)$ and $W(A,\tau;N/\gamma)$ be the prices of the straight bond and the option on the firm. We have,

$$B^{\text{conv}}(A,\tau;N)=B(A,\tau;N)+\gamma W(A,\tau;N/\gamma). \tag{14.21}$$

We may use Merton's (1974) model to find the price of the straight bond, $B(A,\tau;N)$. By results in section 14.2, it is

$$B(A,\tau;N)=A\Phi(-d_1)+Ne^{-r\tau}\Phi\left(d_1-\sigma\sqrt{\tau}\right),\quad d_1=\frac{\ln(A/N)+\left(r+\frac{1}{2}\sigma^2\right)\tau}{\sigma\sqrt{\tau}}, \tag{14.22}$$

where σ is the instantaneous volatility of the assets, r is the (constant) instantaneous short-term rate, and Φ is the cumulative distribution of a standard normal. Similarly, we may use the Black–Scholes formula to compute the function W:

$$W(A,\tau;N/\gamma)=A\Phi(d_{1\gamma})-\frac{N}{\gamma}e^{-r\tau}\Phi\left(d_{1\gamma}-\sigma\sqrt{\tau}\right),\quad d_{1\gamma}=\frac{\ln(A\gamma/N)+\left(r+\frac{1}{2}\sigma^2\right)\tau}{\sigma\sqrt{\tau}}. \tag{14.23}$$

Eq. (14.22) reveals the intuitive property that as A gets large, $B(A,\tau;N)\approx Ne^{-r\tau}$: the probability of default gets extremely tiny as the value of the assets gets large. Moreover, the Black–Scholes formula, eq. (14.23), suggests that $W(A,\tau;N/\gamma)\approx A-e^{-r\tau}N/\gamma$ as

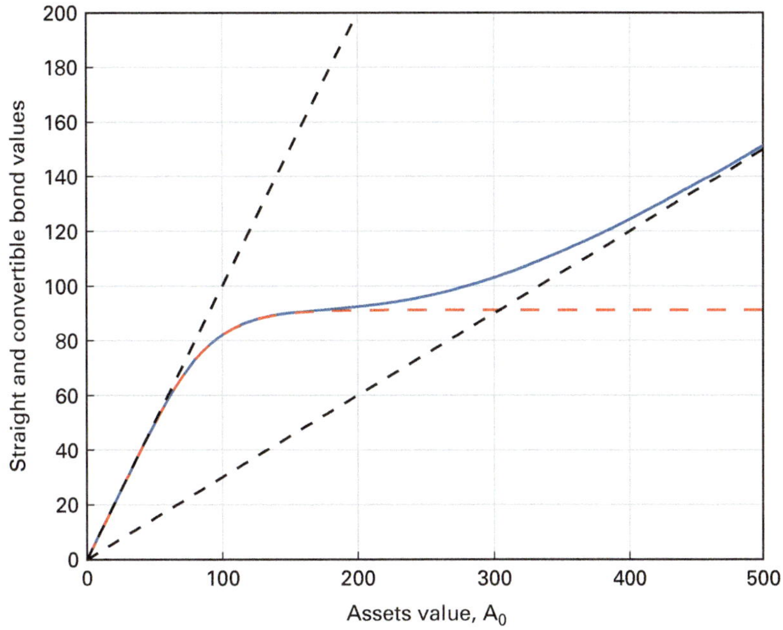

Figure 14.10
The value of convertible and straight bonds as a function of the current assets value, A_0, when the short-term rate $r = 3\%$, the asset volatility $\sigma = 0.20$, time to maturity $\tau = 3$ years, the dilution factor $\gamma = 30\%$, and nominal debt $N = 100$. The solid line depicts the value of the convertible bond. The dashed line starting from the origin, and flattening out to the constant $Ne^{-r\tau} = 91.3930$, is the value of the straight bond. The two dashed straight lines starting from the origin are the no-arbitrage bounds γA and A in eq. (14.17).

A gets large. Therefore, by eq. (14.21), we have that, for large A, $B^{\text{conv}}(A, \tau; N) \approx Ne^{-r\tau} + \gamma\left(A - e^{-r\tau}N/\gamma\right) = \gamma A$. Eq. (14.22) also shows that for small values of A, $B^{\text{conv}}(A, \tau; N) \approx 0$.

To sum up, the value of the convertible bond is less than the value of the firm, A, and larger than the conversion value, γA. Moreover, it approaches γA, as the value of the firm gets large. Figure 14.10 depicts the price of the convertible bond as a function of the assets value, A, as predicted by eq. (14.21), for a particular example. It is possible to show that the value of a callable convertible bond is between the value of the straight and that of the convertible.

14.2.4 Sovereign Risk

Financial history is constellated with default episodes by sovereign entities. Due to the binary nature of default risk, the cost of capital for potentially distressed nations may go through periods of violent fluctuations. This volatility, and the ensuing uncertainties, may affect a whole population for years. Allen and Gale (2007), and Reinhart and Rogoff (2009), among others, offer broad accounts of such financial crises as well as the interconnections between sovereign crises and banking crises.

How do we assess sovereign default risk? Studying sovereign crises and default premiums is actually very challenging. Consider the firm value approach in the previous sections. Our concern was to understand the conditions under which the balance sheet of a firm is conducive to default. Naturally, governments have budget constraints, too, and these constraints may lead to default. However, these constraints are different in nature than those in the firm case, for economic as well as mere accounting reasons. For example, government expenses may be the outcome of a decision process, whereby competing policy makers attempt to satisfy the electoral base, rather than maximize the welfare of a representative consumer, as explained in a seminal paper by Alesina and Tabellini (1990). In general, debt accumulation may well reflect political cycles and institutional details such as electoral laws or budget procedures.[13] While the political economy literature seems to provide useful indications regarding the determinants of national debt, the approach to pricing national debt seems to have evolved along a different line, one by which governments maximize the welfare of a representative consumer. Uribe and Schmitt-Grohé (2017, chap. 13) provide an overview of the literature. In this section, we succinctly survey the logic of a model in this pricing literature, which seems to emerge as a useful benchmark to think about the likelihood of default and the cost of capital for nations.

The roots of this model are in a very influential paper by Eaton and Gersovitz (1981). The authors consider an economy in which a benevolent government rebates to households the proceedings of its external debt, and defaults, strategically, whenever the costs of default are less than the costs of honoring debt services. The basic version of the model cannot account for the observed dynamics of default, debt levels, and the cost of capital. However, the model can conveniently be enriched to match the salient quantitative features in the data, as in Aguiar and Gopinath (2006) and Arellano (2008). We now review the basic assumptions and predictions of this model.

14.2.4.1 *Output and government objectives*

Output is the only source of randomness. Its level at time t is denoted with y_t, and assumed to be independent and identically distributed. Output is used for private consumption, c_t, for public consumption, g_t, and for net exports, $(X-M)_t$, that is,

$$y_t = c_t + g_t + (X-M)_t \,. \tag{14.24}$$

The government objective is to maximize the welfare of a representative consumer who has a CRRA utility function,

$$\max_{(c_t)_{t\geq 0}} E_0 \left(\sum_{t=0}^{\infty} \beta^t u\left(c_t\right) \right),$$

where β is the subjective discount factor and $u\left(c\right) = c^{1-\gamma} / \left(1-\gamma\right)$.

14.2.4.2 *Twin deficits*

The government issues short-term debt. At the end of time t, it issues b_{t+1} pieces of debt, which expire in one period, when they deliver \$1 conditional on no-default. The value at t of each of these pieces is denoted with q_t. Thus, q_t is the price of a zero coupon bond,

13. Alesina, Roubini, and Cohen (1997) provide an overview of the early political economy literature on public deficits and national debt.

such that the net debt issuance at time t is $b_{t+1}q_t - b_t$: the value of new debt minus the value of reimbursed debt. The government faces the following budget constraint

$$g_t + z_t - T_t = b_{t+1}q_t - b_t. \tag{14.25}$$

The RHS of eq. (14.25) is the net debt issuance, as explained. These proceeds are used for making government expenditures, g_t, and transfers to the representative consumer, z_t, net of taxes, T_t. Moreover, we assume that domestic output is not storable, or that domestic consumers cannot save and, hence, invest in national debt: debt is only issued abroad. Now, note that private consumption equals output plus government transfers, minus taxes, i.e., $c_t = y_t + z_t - T_t$. Replacing into eq. (14.25) leaves

$$g_t + c_t = y_t + \underbrace{b_{t+1}q_t - b_t}_{\text{trade balance}_t \equiv (M-X)_t} \tag{14.26}$$

where the equality below the terms indicated with *trade balance* follows by the accounting identity (14.24).

We have assumed that savings are equal to zero. Suppose, for a moment, that these savings, sav_t say, were positive, such that

$$c_t + \text{sav}_t = y_t + z_t - T_t. \tag{14.27}$$

Combining (14.27) with (14.24) leaves a famous accounting identity

$$g_t + z_t - T_t = \text{sav}_t + (M - X)_t. \tag{14.28}$$

That is, savings, sav_t, plus trade balance, $(M - X)_t$, equal the government primary deficit, $g_t + z_t - T_t$. Note that, in this case, $b_{t+1}q_t - b_t = \text{sav}_t + (M - X)_t$, such that the equality under the brackets of (14.26) does not hold anymore: now, the representative consumer also holds part of national debt.

We refer to "twin deficits" as the circumstance by which, due to these relations, government deficits should correlate with trade deficits. In the model we are studying, savings are zero, i.e., $y_t + z_t - T_t = c_t$, such that a government deficit is exactly equal to a trade deficit, where the latter mirrors the net debt issuance made abroad.[14]

The point of the previous calculations is to keep the presentation consistent with standard interpretations available in the international macroeconomics literature. The central identity that is needed in this model is (14.26). Moreover, for simplicity, we now set government expenditures equal to zero, i.e., $g_t = 0$.[15]

14.2.4.3 Default as a real option

At the beginning of each period, the government observes a realization of output, y_t, and decides whether to honor its debt burden or to default. In case of default, the government will enter into an absorbing state of financial autarky (an assumption relaxed below), and

14. In an economy with private investments, inv_t say, eq. (14.28) generalizes to $\text{inv}_t + \text{def}_t = \text{sav}_t + (M - X)_t$, where def_t denotes the government primary deficit.

15. All in all, replacing eq. (14.27) into eq. (14.25) leaves $c_t + g_t = y_t + b_{t+1}q_t - b_t - \text{sav}_t$. The model we are studying is one in which $\text{sav}_t = g_t = 0$.

its value at t, $v_d(y_t)$, say, would satisfy

$$v_d(y_t) = u(y_t) + \beta E_t(v_d(y_{t+1})).$$

Next, let $v(b_t, y_t)$ denote the government value function at t when debt is b_t, output is y_t, and assuming the government is not defaulting at t. We have

$$v(b_t, y_t) = \max_{b_{t+1}<\bar{b}} \left[u(y_t + b_{t+1}q_t - b_t) + \beta E_t(v_o(b_{t+1}, y_{t+1}))\right],$$

$$v_o(b_t, y_t) = \max\{v_d(y_t), v(b_t, y_t)\},$$

where $\bar{b}$ is an exogenous parameter. Thus, at time t, the government chooses next period debt. While the government is not defaulting at time t, it expects it may default at $t+1$; precisely, the government will default at $t+1$ if $v_d(y_{t+1}) > v(b_{t+1}, y_{t+1})$, i.e., for all values of output $y_{t+1} \in Y_d(b_{t+1}) \equiv \{y : v_d(y) > v(b_{t+1}, y)\}$. That is, government defaults when the welfare costs associated with default (i.e., financial autarky, and the lack of trade balance opportunities resulting thereof) is lower than the welfare costs associated with keeping on servicing debt. The government decision to default is, then, the solution to a real option problem, similarly as for the model of firm debt with strategic default of section 14.2.2.

14.2.4.4 *Model properties and extensions*

Unfortunately, the model cannot be solved in closed form. There are, however, some robust qualitative properties that one may infer while analyzing the default set, $Y_d(b_{t+1})$. First, defaults occur in bad times: if $y_2 \in Y_d(b_{t+1})$, then, $y_1 \in Y_d(b_{t+1})$, for all $y_1 \leq y_2$. Moreover, the default set, $Y_d(b_{t+1})$, widens with the level of b_{t+1}: the higher the debt, the higher the likelihood of default. Note, finally, that the zero coupon bond price is endogenous. We have

$$q_t \equiv q(b_{t+1}) = \frac{1 - \text{LGD} \cdot \Pr\{y_{t+1} \in Y_d(b_{t+1})\}}{1 + r^*},$$

where r^* is the interest rate for riskless loans, a given constant in the model.

The model, formulated in this way, cannot account for a number of quantitative properties of default experiences. There are, then, a number of extensions that are needed to make the model predictions consistent with data. First, financial exclusion has been historically limited in time, such that an empirically more accurate description of the value function in state of default is

$$v_d(y_t) = u(y_t - h(y_t)) + \beta E_t(\theta v(0, y_{t+1}) + (1-\theta) v_d(y_{t+1})),$$

where $h(y)$ is a function described in a moment, and θ is the probability of reentry, in which case the government is back to the markets with a debt level equal to zero, and a value function equal to $v(0, y_{t+1})$. Arellano (2008), for example, assumes an annualized average exclusion period, θ^{-1}, between about three and four years.

The function $h(y)$ is an output loss that the country experiences upon default, and needs to be given in advance. Last, but not least, a more realistic description of output is to assume it is a persistent process, for example, an autoregressive model. In this case, it is easy to see that the bond price schedule becomes a function of current output, $q(y_t, b_{t+1})$, because the default probability depends on the current output state, $\Pr\{y_{t+1} \in Y_d(b_{t+1}) | y_t\}$.

The literature on sovereign default that elaborates on these foundational building blocks is actually growing and shows promise in addressing practical issues regarding understanding and prediction of sovereign crises. Uribe and Schmitt-Grohé (2017, chap. 13) provide a very useful guide and additional motivation on this literature, in connection with the standard international macroeconomics literature and the extant empirical evidence, and further computational details.

14.2.5 Reduced Form Approaches: Rare Events or Intensity Models

Understanding credit risk through a fully-fledged economic model is an unavoidable objective. An economic model enables one to think about the complex interactions among the many constituents of a system, and allows for predictions based on sound reasoning. For example, in the case of credit risk, a structural approach allows us to understand complicated products and instruments easily, as in the case of the pricing of convertible bonds (see section 14.2.3). More generally, a structural approach leads to consistent relations among different securities issued by the same firm. A structural approach is also very useful in theoretical research. Finally, section 14.2.4 also explained how a structural approach may also help deal with sovereign risk.

While an economic model is a fundamental piece of knowledge, it may or it may not be of immediate practical use, and it may or may not lead to realistic quantitative predictions. Consider Merton's model in section 14.2.1. The firm assets value and volatility are not observed, and may only be estimated through dedicated calibration or estimation methods. Moreover, the bond prices generated by these models do not match market prices. We know from chapters 12 and 13 that, in the market practice, it is fundamental to have market evaluations be exactly matched by the models.

A particularly disturbing feature in these models is that they predict unrealistically low short-term spreads (see, e.g., figure 14.4). The intuition underlying this property is that diffusion processes are "smooth," in that the probability of default tends to zero as time to maturity approaches zero. In other words, diffusion processes are continuous (see chapter 4), such that default cannot just jump in an unexpected way: passage times are known, "locally," so to speak. These features are responsible for the low short-term spreads these models predict. However, empirical evidence suggests that short-term spreads may be substantial. This section contains a short description of how the "rare event" models introduced in chapter 4 (see section 4.9) may conveniently be employed to rationalize the empirical evidence on the short-term spreads. These models take into account a few, common and striking traits that accompany default of a private entity: default arrives unexpectedly, it is rare, and causes discontinuous price changes.

14.2.5.1 Poisson-driven defaults

As an alternative to Brownian motions, we may model defaults while assuming their arrival is a Poisson process, a process introduced in chapter 4. Suppose to "count" the number of times some event happens. Denote with N_t the corresponding "counting process" (see figure 14.11).

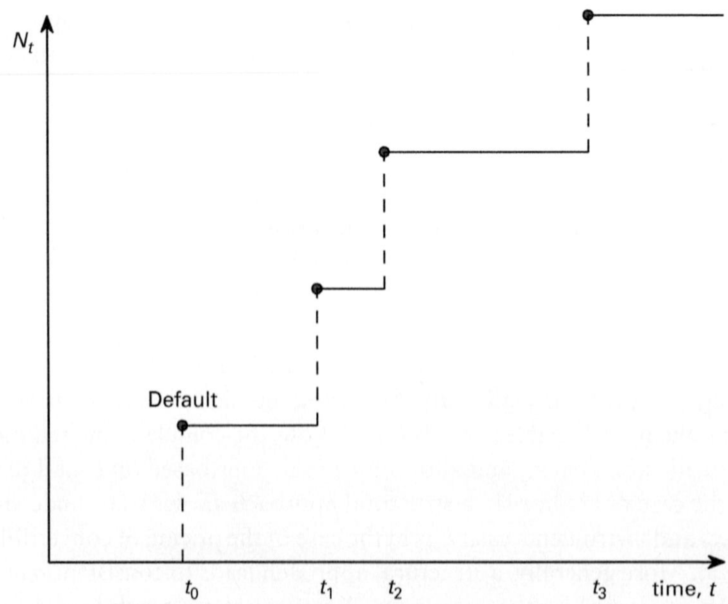

Figure 14.11
A hypothetical realization of a counting process.

The time of default is simply the first time N_t "jumps," for example, t_0 in figure 14.11. More in detail, assume we chop a given interval $[0, T]$ in n pieces, and consider each resulting interval $\Delta t = \frac{T}{n}$. Assume that the jump probability over each of these small intervals of time Δt is proportional to Δt, with proportionality factor equal to λ,

$$p \equiv \Pr\{\text{One jump over } \Delta t\} = \lambda \Delta t. \tag{14.29}$$

Assume the number of jumps over the n intervals follows a binomial distribution:

$$\Pr\{k \text{ jumps over } [0, T]\} = \binom{n}{k} p^k (1-p)^{n-k}, \quad \text{where } p = \lambda \frac{T}{n}.$$

For n large, or, equivalently, for small intervals Δt,

$$\Pr\{k \text{ jumps over } [0, T]\} \approx \frac{(\lambda T)^k}{k!}\left(1 - \frac{\lambda T}{n}\right)^{n-k} \approx \frac{(\lambda T)^k}{k!} e^{-\lambda T}.$$

We rely on these heuristic calculations and derive a few basic properties of default. We have,

$$\Pr\{\text{Survival by } T\} = \Pr\{0 \text{ jumps over } [0, T]\} = e^{-\lambda T}$$

$$\begin{aligned}\Pr\{\text{Default by } T\} &= \Pr\{\text{at least one jump over } [0, T]\} \\ &= 1 - \Pr\{\text{Survival by } T\} = 1 - e^{-\lambda T}\end{aligned}$$

$$\Pr\{\text{Default occurs at some } t\} = \lambda e^{-\lambda t} dt$$

Note that the expected time to default equals λ^{-1}.

We can use these probabilities to value debt subject to default risk. Consider a simple case, namely when default can occur over any $t \in (0, T]$, *but default implications do only occur at* T, in that, at T, the bond yields either the recovery value (in case of default) or the nominal value (in case of survival). In this case, we have, by eq. (14.6), that:

$$D_0 = e^{-rT} \underbrace{\left[\text{Rec}_N \mathbb{Q}\left(\text{Default}\right) + N\mathbb{Q}\left(\text{Survival}\right) \right]}_{\equiv B_0}, \tag{14.30}$$

where $\text{Rec}_N \equiv \text{Rec} \cdot N$ denotes the expected recovery face value of the asset. Using the probabilities predicted by the Poisson model, we obtain

$$B_0 = \text{Rec}_N \left(1 - e^{-\lambda T}\right) + Ne^{-\lambda T} = N \cdot \left(1 - \text{LGD}\left(1 - e^{-\lambda T}\right)\right), \tag{14.31}$$

where $\text{LGD} \equiv 1 - \text{Rec}$.

Appendix 14.B supplies an alternative derivation of eq. (14.31). The unattractive feature of the model is that there is no time variation in the term structure of credit spreads. But the model illustrates the main economic mechanisms underlying asset evaluation in the presence of default risk. Note how intuitive the expression for the bond price is. The second equality in (14.31) says that the price of defaultable bond is a "discount" that takes into account the expected loss, defined as LGD times the probability of default, $\left(1 - e^{-\lambda T}\right)$. Models with random intensity rates (λ) predict time variation in the term structure of credit spreads (see section 14.3.3), although the intuition underlying them follows that for the simple model in this section (see, e.g., eq. (14.55)).

14.2.5.2 *Predicted spreads*

The implications for the spreads corresponding to small maturities T can be easily seen after some approximations,

$$\text{Spread} = -\frac{1}{T} \ln\left(\frac{B_0}{N}\right) \approx -\frac{1}{T}\left(\frac{B_0}{N} - 1\right) = \frac{1}{T}\left(1 - e^{-\lambda T}\right) \cdot \text{LGD}.$$

Note that, in contrast to the structural models reviewed in section 14.2.1, the spread is not zero when T is small. Rather, it is given by the expected default loss per period, defined as the instantaneous probability of default times LGD,

$$\text{Short-term spread} = \lambda \cdot \text{LGD}.$$

Therefore, models with jumps have the potential to explain the empirical behavior of credit spreads at short maturities discussed in section 14.2.1. As explained, structural models, being typically driven by Brownian motions, cannot lead to positive spreads at very short maturities, as they imply that the probability of default decays quickly as time to maturity goes to zero. Instead, models with jumps predict a possibility the firm can experience a "sudden death": default can occur with positive probability at any time, even when the debt is about to expire.

A theoretical model by Duffie and Lando (2001) shows how a structural model of the firm can lead to positive short-term spreads, once we assume incomplete information and learning about the asset value. In their model, learning takes place with some delay, which

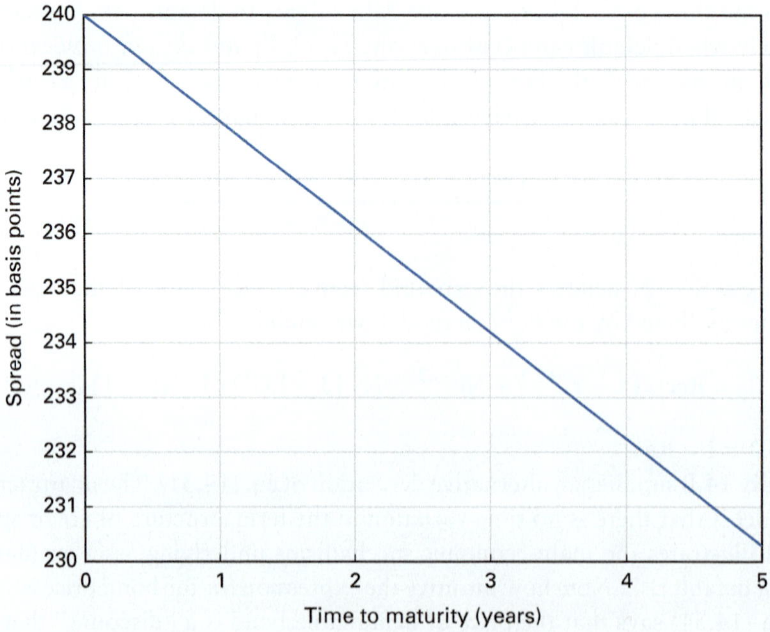

Figure 14.12
The term structure of bond spreads (in basis points) implied by an intensity model, with recovery rate equal to 40% and intensity equal to $\lambda = 0.04$, implying an expected time to default equal to $\lambda^{-1} = 25$ years.

leaves investors concerned about what they really know about the firm asset value. It is this concern to lead to positive credit spreads in their model, to an extent comparable to that generated by a jump process.

Figure 14.12 depicts the behavior of the spread predicted by the model at all maturities, given by

$$\text{Spread} = -\frac{1}{T}\ln\left(\frac{B_0}{\text{N}}\right) = -\frac{1}{T}\ln\left(\text{Rec}\cdot\left(1-e^{-\lambda T}\right)+e^{-\lambda T}\right).$$

In this example, spreads are decreasing in time to maturity. Eventually, as time to maturity gets large, the bond becomes somehow certain to default, with the unusual feature to deliver, for sure, some recovery rate at some point—the bond is certain to deliver the recovery rate. Indeed, in appendix 14.B, we show that, if the recovery value of the bond is not constant, but shrinks exponentially to zero as $\text{Rec}_T \equiv R \cdot e^{-\kappa T}$, for two constants R and κ, then, asymptotically, the spread is:

$$\lim_{T\to\infty} s(T) = \min\{\kappa, \lambda\}. \tag{14.32}$$

The interpretation of κ does not link to discounting. Rather, κ might be referred to as a "recovery dissipation rate" due to unfolding of time, in the following sense. As time unfolds, the likelihood of occurrence of bad events increases, which leads the expected recovery to worsen. Eq. (14.32) shows that if the dissipation rate is sufficiently large, term spreads can be increasing, as we discuss more comprehensively in a moment.

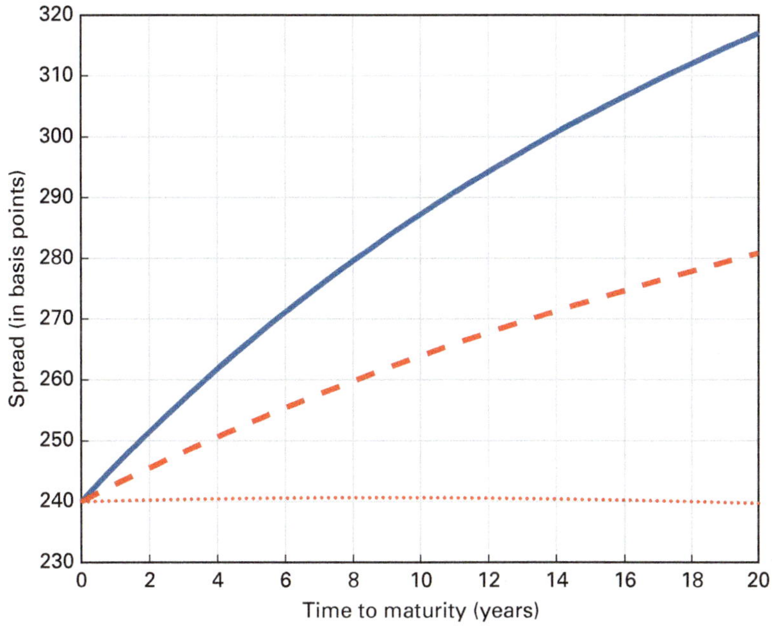

Figure 14.13
The term structure of bond spreads (in basis points) implied by an intensity model with recovery rate equal to $0.40e^{-\kappa\tau}$, where τ is time to maturity and κ is the recovery dissipation rate, taken to equal $\kappa = 0.05$ (solid line), $\kappa = 0.03$ (dashed line), and $\kappa = 0.013$ (dotted line). The instantaneous probability of default is taken to equal to $\lambda = 0.04$, implying an expected time to default equal to $\lambda^{-1} = 25$ years.

An instance leading to such an expected recovery rate is one where the recovery value of the bond equals R, if the firm defaults at any time T, and provided an hidden risk does not materialize, namely the risk that the firm will not distribute any recovery value at all, in case of bankruptcy. If this risk is independent of bankruptcy, and Poisson, with instantaneous risk neutral probability κ, the expected recovery is precisely $\text{Rec}_T = R \cdot e^{-\kappa T}$. This is indeed a quite simple way to model stochastic recovery rates.

Figure 14.13 plots the term structure of spreads predicted by this model, obtained with the same parameter values used to produce the spreads in figure 14.12, and utilizing three values for the dissipation rate: $\kappa = 0.05$, 0.03, and 0.013. Naturally, instantaneous spreads (i.e., those corresponding to time to maturity equal to zero) are $(1 - R) \cdot \lambda = 240$ (in basis points) in all cases. When $\kappa > \lambda$, long-term maturity spreads are always higher than short, by eq. (14.32). When $\kappa < \lambda$, instead, spreads for large maturities can be either higher or lower than short, according to whether κ is higher or lower than $(1 - R) \cdot \lambda$. In this particular example, long-term spreads equal 400 basis points, that is, the default intensity, λ. When $\kappa = 0.03$, which is lower than $\lambda = 0.04$, they are higher and when $\kappa = 0.013$, they are lower. In fact, when $\kappa = 0.013$, the term structure of the spreads may be hump-shaped, a feature not visible from the figure. This very simple model predicts features of both short-term and long-term spreads that Merton's model cannot account for.

We can interpret this behavior of term spreads as follows. Suppose we are in good times, when λ is small relative to κ. We are in good times precisely because we expect things would change adversely in the future, captured by a large value of κ. In this case, the term structure of spreads is increasing. Instead, in bad times, when λ is large compared to κ, we might expect future times to improve, which we might model by assuming κ is small.

Figure 14.13 shows that long maturity spreads are smaller in bad times. Naturally, we would expect that spreads should increase for any maturity in bad times, although this property is not captured by the numerical examples of figure 14.13, where we fix $\lambda = 0.04$. The point of this exercise is to show that the *slope* of the term structure of the spreads lowers as we enter bad times, when we only consider changes in the dissipation rate, κ. Allowing for a countercyclical λ would reinforce the conclusions of this exercise. While these conclusions rely on comparative statics, section 14.2.5 shows that they still hold in a dynamic context, where the intensity λ follows a mean-reverting continuous time process.

14.2.5.3 *One example*

Naturally, the intensity, λ, is the risk neutral instantaneous probability of default, not the physical, λ^* say. The ratio λ/λ^* is generally larger than one. Its inverse, λ^*/λ, is an indicator of the risk appetite in the credit market. Similarly, LGD is an expectation under the risk neutral probability, and should contain useful indications about market participants' risk appetite.

Assume that under the risk neutral probability, the instantaneous intensity of default for a given firm is $\lambda = 4\%$, annualized, and that under the physical, the instantaneous probability of default for the same firm is $\lambda^* = 2\%$, annualized. From here, we can compute the probability of survival of the firm within 5 years, under both probabilities. They are:

$$e^{-5\lambda} = e^{-5\times 0.04} = 0.81873, \quad e^{-5\lambda^*} = e^{-5\times 0.02} = 0.90484.$$

Naturally, the probability of survival is lower under the risk neutral probability.

Next, assume that the spread on a 5-year bond with face value $N = 1$, equals 3%. What is the implied expected recovery rate from this spread? We have

$$\begin{aligned} D_0 &= e^{-rT} \left[\text{Rec} \cdot \mathbb{Q}\,(\text{Default}) + N \cdot \mathbb{Q}\,(\text{Survival})\right] \\ &= e^{-rT} \left[\text{Rec} \times (1 - 0.81873) + 1 \times 0.81873\right]. \end{aligned}$$

The spread is,

$$3\% = -\frac{1}{5} \ln \left(\frac{\text{Rec} \times (1 - 0.81873) + 1 \times 0.81873}{1} \right).$$

Solving for Rec, gives, Rec = 23.16%.

14.2.6 Ratings

In practice, corporate debt is rated by rating agencies, such as Moodys or Standard and Poor's. Depending on the rating, corporate debt may be either investment grade or noninvestment grade ("junk"). Moodys ratings range from AAA to C. Standard and Poor's range from AAA to D. One can compute the probability of "migrations" based on past experience, leading to *transition probabilities*. Consider, for example, table 14.2:

We now base some discussion around this table. Note, for example, that its diagonal is "thicker" than its off-diagonal parts. This phenomenon is known as "credit rating inertia." The rating of your firm tends to be stable from year to year. However, transition probabilities should settle at some values under conditions, as we now explain.

14.2.6.1 Foundations

A natural approach to assess credit risk makes reference to probabilities of default built up on transition probabilities, like those in table 14.2. This approach is also known as "migration approach," and is somehow less drastic than that based on rare events, and hopefully more realistic. However, it is also technically more complex than the intensity approach of the previous section. We provide the most foundational issues of this approach, leaving some details to appendix 14.C.

At time t, there exist several rating classes, Z say, denoted as Rat_t,

$$\text{Rat}_t \in \{1, 2, \cdots, Z\}.$$

Transition probabilities of rating from time t to time T are,

$$P(T-t)_{ij} \equiv \Pr\left(\text{Rat}_T = j \middle| \text{Rat}_t = i\right), \quad i, j \leq Z.$$

We can build a Markov chain from here, by assuming that $P(T-t)_{ij}$ only depends on $T-t$. Finally, we must have that,

$$P(T-t)_{ij} \geq 0 \text{ and } \sum_{j=1}^{Z} P(T-t)_{ij} = 1.$$

For example, the probability of transition from rating $\text{Rat}_t = i$ to rating $\text{Rat}_{t+1} = j$ in one year is, $P(1)_{ij}$. Table 14.2 contains one possible example of $P(1)_{ij}$. The probability of transition from rating $\text{Rat}_t = i$ to rating $\text{Rat}_{t+2} = j$ in two years is $P(2)_{ij}$, and is

Table 14.2
One-year rating transition probabilities (%), Standard and Poor's 1981–1991.

From/to	AAA	AA	A	BBB	BB	B	CCC	D
AAA	89.10	9.63	0.78	0.19	0.30	0	0	0
AA	0.86	90.10	7.47	0.99	0.29	0.29	0	0
A	0.09	2.91	88.94	6.49	1.01	0.45	0	0.09
BBB	0.06	0.43	6.56	84.27	6.44	1.60	0.18	0.45
BB	0.04	0.22	0.79	7.19	77.64	10.43	1.27	2.41
B	0	0.19	0.31	0.66	5.17	82.46	4.35	6.85
CCC	0	0	1.16	1.16	2.03	7.54	64.93	23.19
D	0	0	0	0	0	0	0	100

obtained as follows,

$$P(2)_{ij} = \sum_{k=1}^{Z} \underbrace{P(1)_{ik}}_{\text{Pr(transition from } i \text{ to } k \text{ in one year)}} \times \underbrace{P(1)_{kj}}_{\text{Pr(transition from } k \text{ to } j \text{ in one further year)}}$$

More generally, we have, $P(T) = P(1)^T$, where $P(T)$ is the matrix with elements $\{P(T)_{ij}\}$.

For example, the probability transition matrix P in table 14.2 is

$$P = \begin{bmatrix} 89.1 & 9.63 & 0.78 & 0.19 & 0.3 & 0 & 0 & 0 \\ 0.86 & 90.1 & 7.47 & 0.99 & 0.29 & 0.29 & 0 & 0 \\ 0.09 & 2.91 & 88.94 & 6.49 & 1.01 & 0.45 & 0 & 0.09 \\ 0.06 & 0.43 & 6.56 & 84.27 & 6.44 & 1.6 & 0.18 & 0.45 \\ 0.04 & 0.22 & 0.79 & 7.19 & 77.64 & 10.43 & 1.27 & 2.41 \\ 0 & 0.19 & 0.31 & 0.66 & 5.17 & 82.46 & 4.35 & 6.85 \\ 0 & 0 & 1.16 & 1.16 & 2.03 & 7.54 & 64.93 & 23.19 \\ 0 & 0 & 0 & 0 & 0 & 0 & 0 & 100 \end{bmatrix}$$

The 15-year transition matrix is

$$P(15) \approx \begin{bmatrix} 20.01 & 35.82 & 23.91 & 9.92 & 4.05 & 3.06 & 0.43 & 2.66 \\ 3.38 & 30.28 & 32.71 & 15.91 & 6.38 & 5.11 & 0.77 & 5.34 \\ 1.17 & 13.12 & 34.21 & 21.93 & 9.69 & 8.01 & 1.29 & 10.33 \\ 0.64 & 6.76 & 22.21 & 22.40 & 12.42 & 11.93 & 2.09 & 21.39 \\ 0.33 & 3.22 & 10.71 & 13.616 & 11.36 & 14.68 & 2.78 & 43.16 \\ 0.14 & 1.65 & 5.01 & 6.75 & 7.48 & 13.17 & 2.64 & 63.04 \\ 0 & 1.08 & 3.54 & 3.90 & 3.51 & 5.60 & 1.22 & 81.02 \\ 0 & 0 & 0 & 0 & 0 & 0 & 0 & 100 \end{bmatrix}$$

14.2.6.2 *Evaluation*

The previous probabilities, $\{P(T)_{ij}\}$, are meant to be taken under the *physical*, not the *risk neutral*, world. They can be used for risk management purposes, but certainly not for pricing. Indeed, historical default rates are too low to explain the price of defaultable securities. A natural explanation relies on the presence of risk premiums. To use migration data for pricing, it is necessary to implement a number of steps.

The first step relates to cleaning up the data. For example, it might be that downgrades from class i to class $i+2$ are more frequent than downgrades from class i to class $i+1$, an occurrence which we wish to smooth. Moreover, we would need to remove zero entries: although some rating events did not happen in the past, they might well occur in the future. Finally, we need to add positive risk premiums to the previous smoothed data, to recover realistic asset prices.

As for the pricing details, the migration model relies on the assumption that there are Z classes of assets. Each single asset may migrate from one class to another. Because evaluation is a dynamic business, we cannot evaluate defaultable securities within a given class without simultaneously evaluate the defaultable securities in the remaining classes. For example, there could be a chance that a given asset will "mutate" into a different one over the next year (i.e., one belonging to another rating class). Therefore, the price of this asset, today, needs to reflect the price of the asset in the other classes where it can possibly migrate. As a result, we must simultaneously solve for all the asset prices in all the rating classes. This approach, developed by Jarrow, Lando, and Turnbull (1997), is quite complex and is given a succinct account in appendix 14.C.

Consider a simple case, arising when default can occur at any time before maturity T, but default implications arise only at maturity, in that the bond pays a recovery value only at T, should the firm default at any time prior to T. Let $\mathbb{Q}_i(T-t)$ denote the *risk neutral* probability the firm defaults, by time T, given it belongs to rating i at time T. By Eq. (14.6),

$$\frac{D_{0,i}}{N} = e^{-rT}\left[\mathrm{Rec}\,\mathbb{Q}_i(T-t) + (1-\mathbb{Q}_i(T-t))\right].$$

The risk neutral probabilities, $\mathbb{Q}_i(T-t)$, are found using migration frequencies such as those in table 14.2, "cleaned up" through appropriate risk premium corrections, as discussed.

14.2.6.3 *One example*

Consider the following transition matrix:

		To		
		A	B	Def
From	A	0.9	0.07	0.03
	B	0.15	0.75	0.10
	Def	0	0	1

where Def denotes the state of default. What is the probability that a name A will remain name A in two years? What is the probability that a name A will default in two years?

Consider the following two-year transition matrix:

$$\mathbb{Q}(2) = \underbrace{\begin{bmatrix} 0.90 & 0.07 & 0.03 \\ 0.15 & 0.75 & 0.10 \\ 0 & 0 & 1 \end{bmatrix}}_{\equiv \mathbb{Q}(1)} \cdot \underbrace{\begin{bmatrix} 0.90 & 0.07 & 0.03 \\ 0.15 & 0.75 & 0.10 \\ 0 & 0 & 1 \end{bmatrix}}_{\equiv \mathbb{Q}(1)},$$

such that

$$\begin{aligned}\Pr\{\text{A is A in 2 years}\} &= \underbrace{0.90\times 0.90}_{A\to A\to A} + \underbrace{(0.07)\times(0.15)}_{A\to B\to A} + \underbrace{0.03\times 0}_{A\to Def\to A} \\ &= 0.8205,\end{aligned}$$

and

$$\begin{aligned}\Pr\{\text{A defaults in 2 years}\} &= \underbrace{0.90\times 0.03}_{A\to A\to Def} + \underbrace{(0.07)\times(0.10)}_{A\to B\to Def} + \underbrace{0.03\times 1}_{A\to Def\to Def} \\ &= 0.064.\end{aligned}$$

In general, we have that:

$$\mathbb{Q}(2)_{ij} = \sum_{k=1}^{3} \mathbb{Q}(1)_{ik} \cdot \mathbb{Q}(1)_{kj},$$

and for any T,

$$\mathbb{Q}(T) = \mathbb{Q}(1)^T = \begin{bmatrix} 0.90 & 0.07 & 0.03 \\ 0.15 & 0.75 & 0.10 \\ 0 & 0 & 1 \end{bmatrix}^T .$$

Next, consider the following transition matrix, under the risk neutral probability:

		To		
		A	B	Def
From	A	0.80	0.20	0
	B	0.15	0.75	0.10
	Def	0	0	1

From here, we may easily compute, again, the (risk neutral) probability A will default in two years, and the probability B will default in two years. We have

$$\mathbb{Q}(2) = \underbrace{\begin{bmatrix} 0.80 & 0.20 & 0 \\ 0.15 & 0.75 & 0.10 \\ 0 & 0 & 1 \end{bmatrix}}_{\equiv \mathbb{Q}(1)} \cdot \underbrace{\begin{bmatrix} 0.80 & 0.20 & 0 \\ 0.15 & 0.75 & 0.10 \\ 0 & 0 & 1 \end{bmatrix}}_{\equiv \mathbb{Q}(1)},$$

such that:

$$\begin{aligned} \Pr\{\text{A defaults in 2 years}\} &= \mathbb{Q}(2)_{13} \\ &= \underbrace{0.80 \times 0}_{A \to A \to Def} + \underbrace{(0.20) \times (0.10)}_{A \to B \to Def} + \underbrace{0 \times 1}_{A \to Def \to Def} \\ &= 0.02. \end{aligned}$$

(multiply first row by the third column), and,

$$\begin{aligned} \Pr\{\text{B defaults in 2 years}\} &= \mathbb{Q}(2)_{23} \\ &= \underbrace{0.15 \times 0}_{B \to A \to Def} + \underbrace{(0.75) \times (0.10)}_{B \to B \to Def} + \underbrace{0.10 \times 1}_{B \to Def \to Def} \\ &= 0.175. \end{aligned}$$

(multiply second row by the third column).

Finally, suppose that the bonds issued by both A and B mature in two years. Furthermore, assume that if these two bonds default, they pay off the same recovery rate, equal to 30%, and only at the end of the second period. From here, we can compute the credit spreads for the two bonds. Denoting the bond price and spread for firm X with P_X and $s_{0,X}$,

$$e^{rT} \times P_A = (0.30) \times (0.02) + (1 - 0.02) = 0.986$$
$$\Rightarrow s_{0,A} = -\frac{1}{2} \ln(0.986) = 7.0495 \times 10^{-3}.$$

and,

$$e^{rT} \times P_B = (0.30) \times (0.175) + (1 - 0.175) = 0.8775$$
$$\Rightarrow s_{0,B} = -\frac{1}{2} \ln(0.8775) = 6.5339 \times 10^{-2}.$$

14.3 Credit Derivatives and Structured Products Based Thereon

14.3.1 Options and Spreads

14.3.1.1 Total return swaps

In a total return swap (TRS, henceforth), one party, who owns some asset, that underlying the TRS, receives from the counterparty payments based on a mutually agreed rate, either fixed or variable, and makes payments to the counterparty based on the *return* of the underlying asset, which includes both the income it generates and any capital gains. The underlying asset can be a loan, a bond, an equity index, or a basket of assets. The interest payments are typically based on LIBOR plus a spread. Consider the following example. Party A receives LIBOR + fixed spread equal to 3%. Party B receives the total return of the S&P 500 on a principal amount of \$1 million. If LIBOR is 7% and the S&P 500 is up by 12%, A pays B 12% and B pays A 7% + 3%. By netting, A pays B \$20,000, i.e. \$1 million × (12% − 10%).

While TRSs are usually considered credit derivatives, they combine both market risk and credit risk. The main benefit from going long a TRS is that the party with the asset on the balance sheet buys protection against loss in value. The main benefit from going short a TRS is that it allows the counterparty to receive the payoffs of the underlying without necessarily having to put this underlying in the balance sheet. Hedge funds find it quite convenient to short a TRS, as this allows them to have views with limited collateral upfront. The market for TRSs is over-the-counter and market participants include institutions only.

14.3.1.2 Spread options

Spread options (SO, henceforth) are options written on the difference between two indices. For example, let $S_1(T)$ and $S_2(T)$ be the prices of two assets at time T. The payoff promised by an SO entered at some time $t < T$, might be $\max\{S_1(T) - S_2(T) - K, 0\}$, where K is the strike of the SO. An SO can be written on the spread between two rates of returns too. Importantly, an SO can be written on the spread between the yield of a corporate bond and the yield of a Treasury bond. Examples include: (i) NOB spread (notes − bonds), which are spreads between maturities; (ii) Spreads between quality levels, such as the TED spread (treasury bills − Eurodollars); (iii) MOB spreads, i.e. the difference between municipal bonds and treasury bonds. More generally, the definition of an SO has now been extended to include payoffs written as a *linear combination* of indices, interest rates and yields.

14.3.1.3 *Credit spread options*

Credit spread options (CSO, henceforth) are options where the payoff is the difference between (i) the spread between two reference securities (say between Italian and German government bonds having the same maturity, or the spread between some stock return in excess of the LIBOR, or two credit instruments), and (ii) a given strike spread, for a certain maturity date. It may be an American or European option. So CSOs allow to hedge against, or take specific views about, changes in credit spreads. For example, an investor, while bullish on Italian bonds, might hedge against the uncertain outcome of a political election, which could trigger a widening of short-term spreads of Italian versus German bonds. The investor may, then, go long a CSO, with time to maturity around the days of the political election, where the underlying are the Italian-German spread for maturities equal to ten years, say. A possible payoff to the CSO holder is proportional to, $(\text{Spread} - K)^+$, where Spread is the ten-year Italian-German spread to prevail in three months, and K is the strike spread.

14.3.2 Credit Default Swaps

14.3.2.1 *Single name swaps*

TRSs provide protection against a general loss in asset value, which could be triggered by both market or credit risk, although it is obviously more often market risk than credit to kick in. Credit default swaps (CDS, henceforth) differ from TRSs insofar as they provide protection against a credit event.

The premium, assumed to be paid quarterly, on a CDS contract agreed at time t, is obtained by equating the expected discounted value of the protection (the *floating protection leg*), to the expected discounted value of all the premiums paid over the life of the contract (the *fixed premium leg*), i.e., at dates $t_i : t < t_1 < t_2 < \cdots < t_{4M}$, where $t_i = t + \frac{i}{4}$, and M is the number of years of the contract. The discounted expected floating protection leg is

$$\text{Protection}_t = \sum_{i=1}^{4M} e^{-r(t_i - t)} \text{LGD}(t_i) \Pr\{\text{Def.} \in (t_{i-1}, t_i)\}, \tag{14.33}$$

and the discounted expected fixed leg is

$$\text{Premium}_t = \sum_{i=1}^{4M} e^{-r(t_i - t)} \text{CDS}_t(M) \Pr\{\text{Surv. at } t_i\}, \tag{14.34}$$

where r is the (constant) risk free rate, $\text{CDS}_t(M)$ is the premium paid every quarter, prevailing at time t; $\text{LGD}(t_i)$ is the LGD at time t_i, which for simplicity is assumed to be known at time t; remaining notation is straighforward and regards probabilities of default and survival.

Equating Premium_t and Protection_t, and solving for $\text{CDS}_t(M)$, leaves

$$\text{CDS}_t(M) = \frac{\sum_{i=1}^{4M} e^{-r(t_i - t)} \text{LGD}(t_i) \Pr\{\text{Def.} \in (t_{i-1}, t_i)\}}{\sum_{i=1}^{4M} e^{-r(t_i - t)} \Pr\{\text{Surv. at } t_i\}}. \tag{14.35}$$

It is a forward premium, as long as $t < t_0$. We assume that the contract is terminated, should the obligor default prior to the starting date, t_0.

The denominator in the RHS of eq. (14.35),

$$v_{1t} \equiv \sum_{i=1}^{4M} e^{-r(t_i - t)} \Pr\{\text{Surv. at } t_i\}, \tag{14.36}$$

can be interpreted as the value of a basket of defaultable bonds with zero recovery value—a *defaultable*-PVBP (Present Value of a Basis Point), in perfect analogy with the expressions for the forward swap rate given in chapter 13. In other words, v_{1t} is the value of an annuity of \$1 paid at the dates $t_1, t_2, \cdots, t_{4M}$, until default or maturity of the default swap, whichever occurs first. For this reason, v_{1t} is also referred to as the value of a *defaultable annuity*. It plays a critical role for the evaluation of derivatives referenced on credit default swaps; we shall encounter this term very often in this chapter.

At first glance, the previous derivation looks like being "actuarial." It is not, because the probabilities in eq. (14.35) are *risk neutral* probabilities. These probabilities are, then, and obviously, the same as the probabilities we use to price the bonds underlying the CDS contract. Therefore, there are no-arb restrictions that link bond prices to CDS premiums, restrictions emphasized later (see section 14.3.3). This point illustrates in a remarkable way one key difference between a financial product and an insurance one. Even if we may end up pricing some insurance products through risk-adjusted probabilities, in the practice of financial asset evaluation, we typically end up having more traded risks than in insurance, risks that are tightly related through no-arb restrictions.

Eq. (14.35) is a general formula we can use, once we have a model determining the risk neutral probability of default. In this chapter, we implement eq. (14.35) through a reduced-form approach, which will allow us to find the quarterly premium (or spread) $\text{CDS}_t(M)$ quite easily. Consider the following derivations.

We have, denoting again with λ the instantaneous probability of default, that $\Pr\{\text{Surv. at } t_i\} = e^{-\lambda(t_i - t)}$, and that $\Pr\{\text{Def.} \in (t_{i-1}, t_i)\} = e^{-\lambda(t_{i-1} - t)} - e^{-\lambda(t_i - t)}$. Intuitively, if the name survives at t_i (event E_i), it must necessarily have survived at t_{i-1} (event E_{i-1}), but the converse is not true: $E_i \subset E_{i-1}$, and the complement of E_i to E_{i-1} is simply the event of default between t_{i-1} and t_i.[16] Substituting the previous probabilities into eq. (14.35) leaves

$$\text{CDS}_t(M) = \frac{\sum_{i=1}^{4M} e^{-r(t_i - t)} \text{LGD}(t_i) \left(e^{-\lambda(t_{i-1} - t)} - e^{-\lambda(t_i - t)} \right)}{\sum_{i=1}^{4M} e^{-(r+\lambda)(t_i - t)}}, \tag{14.37}$$

where the denominator, now, is the defaultable annuity v_{1t} for a constant hazard rate

$$v_{1t} = \sum_{i=1}^{4M} e^{-(r+\lambda)(t_i - t)}, \tag{14.38}$$

and will be discussed further in the next section.

16. We have that $\Pr\{\text{Def. at any } z \in (t_{i-1}, t_i)\} = \int_{t_{i-1}}^{t_i} \Pr\{\text{Def. at } z\} dz$, where $\Pr\{\text{Def. at } z\} = \lambda e^{-\lambda(z-t)}$. Note that we are assuming that a payment is made only at the end of a payment period. The evaluation formulae below (e.g., eq. (14.39)) slightly change when payment occurs at the very same time default occurs (see, e.g., Mele and Obayashi, 2015, chap. 5).

To illustrate eq. (14.37), assume that, for each t_i, LGD (t_i) is constant and equal to LGD, such that, for a generic $\Delta t = t_i - t_{i-1}$, eq. (14.37) simplifies to

$$\text{CDS}_t(M) = \text{LGD} \cdot \left(e^{\lambda \Delta t} - 1\right), \tag{14.39}$$

or, approximately, for small Δt,

$$\text{CDS}_t(M) \approx \lambda \cdot \text{LGD} \cdot \Delta t. \tag{14.40}$$

That is, $\text{CDS}_t(M)$ is approximately the same as the instantaneous spread on a defaultable bond (see section 14.2). This property is to be expected, because a purchase of a defaultable bond and protection on it amounts to a synthetic default-free bond. Therefore, there must be a no-arbitrage relation between CDS spreads and defaultable bond spreads.

The CDS premium thus proxies for the expected loss per unit of time, $\lambda \cdot \text{LGD}$, and over the small interval Δt. Naturally, λ is the *risk neutral* instantaneous probability of default for the security. Eq. (14.40) is also known as the "credit triangle," because it involves three variables: the spread, $\text{CDS}_t(M)$, the intensity, λ, and LGD, such that knowledge of two of these variables enables us to recover the third.

Note that, in this simple model, CDS premiums are constant, over time and across maturities. This property follows by the assumption that LGD, the intensity of default, λ, and the short-term rate, r, are constant. In practice, CDS premiums change over time. Moreover, we often observe CDS spreads increasing with maturity. Indeed, we may take interesting views. For example, buying CDS for two years and selling CDS for three is a view that default will not occur between the second and the third year from now. Section 14.3.3 deals with random intensity models that do allow to address these issues. We now continue with a description of additional products that are used to deal with credit risk.

14.3.2.2 CDS on indices

A CDS index is a basket of credit entities in which the protection buyer pays the same premium on all the names in the index, until a fixed expiration date. Credit events are typically bound to bankruptcy or delinquencies. After a credit event, the entity is removed from the index and the contract goes through with a reduced notional amount, until expiration, as explained in more detail below. To illustrate how a CDS index may facilitate risk-sharing, consider the macroeconomic risks that banks are exposed through the loans on their balance sheet. A bank may be a protection buyer on a CDS index that comprises names correlating with these macroeconomic risks. Hedge funds may provide insurance while being on the other side of the deal.

Credit products are typically over-the-counter. But while CDS on single names are typically illiquid, CDS indices are standardized and at the time of writing give rise to relatively more liquid markets, as historical data on bid-ask spreads show. In fact, it can be cheaper to hedge a portfolio of CDS or bonds with a CDS index than it would be to buy many CDS to achieve a similar effect. There exist two main indices: (i) CDX index, which contains North American and Emerging Market companies; and (ii) iTraxx index, which contains companies from the rest of the world.

14.3.2.3 Options on CDS indices

Credit default swaptions are options to enter a CDS—typically a CDS index. Consider, first, swaptions on single names. A payer swaption gives the right to buy protection at some future date at some CDS fixed strike, and a receiver swaption gives the right to sell protection. If default of the name occurs prior to the swaption maturity, the contract is terminated.

Credit default *index* swaptions work differently and will be dealt with in detail in section 14.3.4. As noted, at inception, a credit default index swap (CDIS) is referenced to a number of fixed names chosen by a market maker, each carrying a given weight. Buyers of CDIS are typically those who provide protection to market makers: they stand ready to pay a predetermined LGD for any default that occurs before maturity, which is constant and identical for all reference entities in the index. In exchange, the market makers pay the CDIS buyer a periodic fixed premium—the credit default index spread. After a default takes place, the nominal value of the CDIS is reduced by one, and no replacement of the defaulted firm would take place.

Note that credit default swaptions cannot be evaluated in the pricing context of this section, where CDS premiums are constant. Section 14.3.3 relies on a model of stochastic intensity rates, which supplies an evaluation framework for these products. Such a framework is described in section 14.3.4.

14.3.2.4 Fixed coupons and upfront payments

Single-name CDS were initially modeled as their interest rate swap counterparts (see chapter 13), being, thus, constructed to have zero value at entry. That is, they typically traded on a "par spread" or "running spread" basis, whereby the protection buyer pays a periodic premium determined such that the value of the contract is equal to zero at inception, just as in the previous section. Accordingly, the first payments would occur on the first coupon date. CDS contracts resembled, then, a type of "leveraged bet." High-yield names were an exception to this quoting convention: they traded, and still trade, with a fixed coupon and an upfront payment. This section provides an introduction to quoting conventions based on fixed coupons and upfront, and also explains some rationale behind these conventions.

First, let us determine the value of a CDS in case the contract is not necessarily zero at inception. We may still express this value as a function of the par spread, i.e., $\text{CDS}_t(M)$ in eq. (14.35). Consider the "present value" of the protection in (14.33), net of a premium calculated in correspondence of a periodic "coupon" payment C,

$$\text{Protection}_t - \text{Premium}_t = v_{1t}\left(\text{CDS}_t(M) - C\right), \tag{14.41}$$

where v_{1t} is as in (14.36). Eq. (14.41) follows by replacing the expression for $\text{CDS}_t(M)$ in (14.35) into the calculation of the protection leg, and by replacing $\text{CDS}_t(M)$ with C into the calculation of the premium in (14.34). Eq. (14.41) can now be used to explain the rationale behind a quote on an upfront basis.

In a quote on an upfront basis, the buyer of protection pays an immediate upfront fee and, then, a periodic payment of a fixed coupon C (typically, 100 or 500 basis points per annum according to whether entities are investment grade or high-yield, resp.). For example, consider the so-called quoted price, defined as[17]

$$quoted\ price = 100 - v_1\ (S) \times (S - C)/100, \tag{14.42}$$

where $v_1\ (S)$ will be defined in a moment, and S is the "spread" at the quoting time τ, that is, the par spread $CDS_\tau\ (M)$ in eq. (14.35) and for any τ.

Eq. (14.42) is the quoted price counterpart to eq. (14.41). The term $v_1\ (S)$ is known as the "flat defaultable annuity for the spread S." It is the defaultable annuity v_{1t} in (14.38) that is consistent with a spread level equal to S.[18] Note that the price in (14.42) is simply a quoting convention. The real payment made by the protection buyer is $100 - quoted\ price = v_1\ (S) \times (S - C)/100$, also known as the *PUF* (for Points Up-Front). In other words, the "payoff at origination" for the protection buyer is

$$-PUF = v_1(S) \times (C - S)/100. \tag{14.43}$$

The protection buyer, then, pays the coupons C over the life of the contract, with the protection seller proceeding to payments in case of default, such that the (credit-adjusted) *present value* of the overall position for both parties is zero at inception.

In the middle of the 2007–2009 financial crisis, more and more names started to quote upfront in face of increased financial distress. Highly distressed entities would indeed command high spreads, S, exposing protection buyers to pay huge premiums in the future in a "par spread quoting model." Alternatively, protection buyers might have preferred (and, indeed, began to pay) upfront, *PUF* in (14.43), and, then, proceed with the payment of much lower coupons during the life of the contracts. Changes to quotes on an upfront basis were typically triggered when the spread crossed a certain threshold.

Note that a strictly positive coupon in (14.43) also allows one to mitigate problems related to counterparty risk between protection buyer and protection seller: when S is very high, a positive C reduces the protection buyer disbursement at origination, which lessens the circumstance of a positive probability that the protection seller may default. Somehow, this scheme embeds an implicit debt contract (pertaining to C) that a seller of insurance extends to the buyer. Finally, quoting on an upfront basis allows one to lower the "risk of coupon payments" (i.e., the risk arising from default of the entity), as a big portion of these payments would be made upfront. This timing risk obviously increases with the riskiness of the very same entity.[19]

---

17. Note that S and C are expressed in basis points.

18. Note that the defaultable annuity v_{1t} is model-dependent: while r can be approximated by market data, λ needs to be calibrated. Market practice is to search for values of λ, such that $CDS_\tau\ (M)$ in eq. (14.37) matches the quoted spread, S. The result is a spread-dependent intensity, $\lambda\ (S)$. Replacing this $\lambda\ (S)$ into the expression for the defaultable annuity v_{1t} in (14.38), yields v_{1t} as a function of $\lambda\ (S)$, which we are denoting with $v_1\ (S)$.

19. To illustrate, consider the following example. Three months ago, you entered into a CDS contract as a protection buyer on a single name, ABC, with a par-spread equal to 200bps. Suppose that, now, the spread has increased to 450bps. To monetize, you should sell protection at 450bps, netting a positive 250bps per annum up to the maturity of the two contracts. However, the risk is that ABC will default in the meantime. Going for upfront allows you to lock in the present value of these positive net profits.

In 2009, ISDA released the so-called Big-Bang protocol, aimed at revamping the credit market through an effort at standardization. The protocol requires all CDS contracts to be traded upfront with fixed coupons. This feature makes payments standardized, thereby making it easier to offset contracts.

Conventions for CDS indices are very similar: for example, CDX indices have all fixed coupons set at the index launch (typically, again, 100bps for investment grade and 500bps for high-yields), such that entering into the index requires an upfront payment that is the index counterpart to (14.43).[20] In section 13.3.4.3, we explain that options to enter into CDS on single names and indices inherit the character of this upfront convention.

14.3.2.5 Disentangling default probability from risk appetite

A natural gauge of risk appetite in credit markets is the wedge between the probability of default adjusted for risk and the actual default frequency. Consider the following basic definitions. Let λ^p denote the instantaneous probability of default for a given security, under the *physical probability* P. Assume that LGD is constant. Then, the counterpart to eq. (14.40) under P is $\mathrm{EL}^p \equiv \lambda^p \cdot \mathrm{LGD} \cdot \Delta t$, and can be interpreted as the expected loss under P or "actuarial loss." If investors require compensation for default events, actuarial losses should be less than the CDS spread, i.e. $\mathrm{EL}^p < \mathrm{CDS}$, or, $\lambda > \lambda^p$. A simple measure of a *credit risk premium* is defined as the ratio of the CDS spread over EL^p, i.e.,[21]

$$\Lambda \equiv \frac{\lambda}{\lambda^p}. \tag{14.44}$$

Naturally, there exist sophisticated methods to implement the estimation of the risk premium suggested by (14.44). However, the basic idea underlying these methods remains the same: to compare the expected probability of default under Q and under P.[22] Early work focussing on ratios constructed in the same spirit as (14.44) include Amato (2005), Driessen (2005), and Berndt et al. (2005). These studies rely on information regarding Moody's KMV's EDFs, used in order to obtain proxies for λ^p. Amato and Berndt et al., then, make inference on λ using CDS data, whereas Driessen makes inference on λ relying on bond data. They all focus on aggregate credit market conditions, and suggest average estimates of Λ of about 2 or more.

Amato shows that both λ and λ^p dramatically decreased from end-2003 to end-2005, and that the credit premium was decreasing from 2003 too, at least up to events in 2005 related to the car industry. This risk appetite might have provided issuers of CDO (see section 14.3.5) with incentives to look for illiquid and relatively more complex assets to put as collateral in the process of issuance of instruments such as CDO referenced to ABS such as MBS. Fender and Hördahl (2007) is one of the earliest studies to document a repricing of risk in the period leading up to the subprime crisis that erupted in 2007. They show that, despite a downward trend in the average EDFs (a trend that would start to invert in 2007), the price of credit risk was rising even before the beginning of the crisis.

20. See Mele and Obayashi (2015), chap. 5.

21. Note that the definition of a credit premium in eq. (14.44) is distinct from, albeit related to, the definition of a credit premium as a spread of a defaultable security yield over a safe asset return.

22. Appendix 4.F in chapter 4 provides some technical details regarding the change in probability for intensity processes.

14.3.3 Evaluation with Random Intensity Rates

We may relax the assumption the instantaneous intensity of default, λ, is constant. This intensity is defined under the risk neutral probability and can change either because the intensity of default under the physical probability changes or because risk appetite changes, or both. We examine the asset pricing implications of time-varying intensities, by exploring how probabilities of survival change in a simple setting, where we do not single out the reasons leading to variations in λ.

14.3.3.1 *Survival probabilities: A heuristic derivation*

First, we assume the instantaneous probability of default can only change discretely, giving rise to random intensities λ_t, meaning that λ_t is the intensity of default in the time interval $[t-1, t]$. Let $\mathcal{F}_t$ be the information set as of time t. We assume that λ_t is $\mathcal{F}_t$-measurable. What is the probability of survival of any given name in this case? We have

$$\Pr\{\text{Surv at } t | \text{ Surv at } t-1\} = \frac{\Pr\{\text{Surv at } t\}}{\Pr\{\text{Surv at } t-1\}}. \tag{14.45}$$

By a repeated use of eq. (14.45),

$$\begin{aligned}\Pr\{\text{Surv at } t\} &= \Pr\{\text{Surv at } t | \text{ Surv at } t-1\} \Pr\{\text{Surv at } t-1\} \\ &= \cdots \\ &= \prod_{n=1}^{t} \Pr\{\text{Surv at } n | \text{ Surv at } n-1\}.\end{aligned} \tag{14.46}$$

So we are left with finding $\Pr\{\text{Surv at } n | \text{ Surv at } n-1\}$. Consider the following arguments. If λ_n was not random and fixed at some $\bar{\lambda}_n$, then, $\Pr\{\text{Surv at } n | \text{ Surv at } n-1\} = e^{-\bar{\lambda}_n}$. When λ_n is random, $e^{-\lambda_n}$ is the probability of survival, conditioned upon some particular value the intensity could possibly take. Heuristically, then, $\Pr\{\text{Surv at } n | \text{ Surv at } n-1\} = \sum_{s\in\mathcal{S}} e^{-\lambda_n(s)} \Pr\{s\}$, where $\lambda_n(s)$ is, so to speak, the value λ_n would take in state s, $\Pr\{s\}$ is the likelihood that state s occurs, and, finally, $\mathcal{S}$ is the set of all possible states, as illustrated by figure 14.14.

Therefore, $\Pr\{\text{Surv at } n | \text{ Surv at } n-1\} = \mathbb{E}\left(e^{-\lambda_n} \middle| \mathcal{F}_{n-1}\right)$, where $\mathbb{E}$ denotes the expectation taken under the risk neutral probability. Inserting this result into eq. (14.46), and using the law of iterated expectations, leaves:

$$\Pr\{\text{Surv at } t\} = \mathbb{E}\left(e^{-\sum_{n=1}^{t} \lambda_n}\right). \tag{14.47}$$

These results easily extend to a continuous time setting, under regularity conditions. We need to specify a random process for the intensity, λ, and, then, derive survival probabilities. We now describe a simple model, one in which intensities are generated by affine models. We, then, revisit the pricing of CDS and also deal with the pricing of related derivatives.

14.3.3.2 *Continuous time: Affine models of survival probabilities*

Eq. (14.47) shows that survival probabilities can be treated as pure discount bond prices, with intensities playing the same role as instantaneous interest rates. A natural

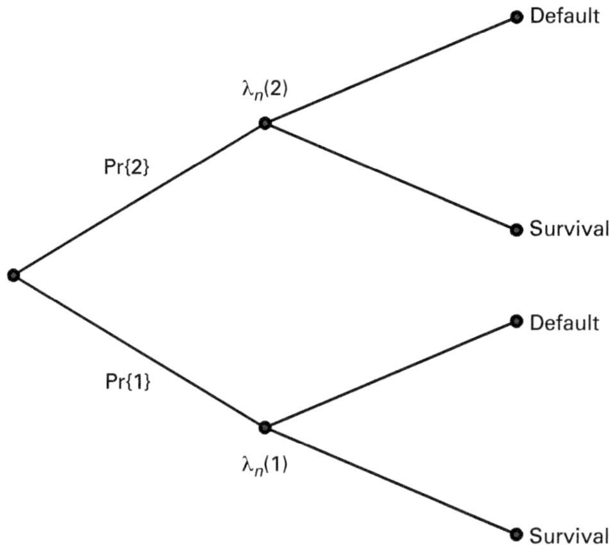

Figure 14.14
This picture depicts a tree for the survival probability with random default intensities in a one period and two states tree. At the beginning of period n, nature draws the event leading to the realization of a default intensity: $\lambda_n(1)$ with probability $\Pr\{1\}$ or $\lambda_n(2)$ with complementary probability. Then, the two paths leading to survival have probability of occurrence equal to $\Pr\{1\}e^{-\lambda_n(1)}$ and $\Pr\{2\}e^{-\lambda_n(2)}$, such that the total probability of survival is $\Pr\{1\}e^{-\lambda_n(1)} + \Pr\{2\}e^{-\lambda_n(2)}$.

continuous time model that matches the heuristic construction in the previous section is, then, one in which the risk neutral default intensity, λ_t, is the solution to

$$d\lambda_t = \phi\left(\bar{\lambda} - \lambda_t\right)dt + \sigma\sqrt{\lambda_t}d\tilde{W}_t, \quad \lambda_0 = \lambda, \tag{14.48}$$

where $\tilde{W}_t$ is a standard Brownian motion under the risk neutral probability, and ϕ, $\bar{\lambda}$ and σ are three positive constants. Note that this model is the same as the Cox, Ingersoll, and Ross (1985) (CIR) model for the short-term rate (see chapter 13). Therefore, under the parameter restrictions in chapter 13, λ_t is always positive, and the continuous time equivalent to (14.47) is

$$P_{\text{surv}}(\lambda, t) \equiv \Pr\{\text{Surv at } t\} = \mathbb{E}\left(e^{-\int_0^t \lambda_s ds}\right). \tag{14.49}$$

Eq. (14.49) is, formally, the same as the Feynman–Kac representation of a solution to a partial differential equation, and the solution is just the CIR pure discount bond price (see section 13.4.4.3). In other words, the survival probability in eqs. (14.48)–(14.49) is mathematically the same as the price of a zero coupon bond in the CIR model, viz

$$P_{\text{surv}}(\lambda, M) = \Phi(M)\, e^{-B(M)\lambda},$$

$$\Phi(M) = \left(\frac{2\gamma e^{\frac{1}{2}(\phi+\gamma)M}}{(\phi+\gamma)\left(e^{\gamma M}-1\right)+2\gamma}\right)^{\frac{2\phi\bar{\lambda}}{\sigma^2}}, \quad B(M) = \frac{2\left(e^{\gamma M}-1\right)}{(\phi+\gamma)\left(e^{\gamma M}-1\right)+2\gamma}, \tag{14.50}$$

$$\gamma = \sqrt{\phi^2 + 2\sigma^2}.$$

More generally, we can build up a whole family of models with a closed-form solution, the affine class reviewed in chapter 13, by assuming that:

$$\lambda_t = a_0 + a_1 \cdot y_t, \tag{14.51}$$

where a_0 is a constant, a_1 is a vector of constants, and y is a multivariate jump-diffusion process, with drift and diffusion terms as in chapter 13 (see section 13.5.3). This model is interesting, as we can judiciously choose the components of y_t which we suppose may affect the default intensity. For example, some of them could be unobservable, and others could be observable, and relate, say, to the business cycle or even the structure of the firm.

Given any solution for the survival probability predicted by any of these affine models when $y_0 = y$, $P_{\text{surv}}(y,t)$ say, we can easily derive the probability of default through the affine model

$$\Pr\{\text{Default} \in (t_{i-1}, t_i)\} = P_{\text{surv}}(y, t_{i-1}) - P_{\text{surv}}(y, t_i). \tag{14.52}$$

We can look at the bond spreads and the CDS spreads implied by this modeling choice. In appendix 14.D, we show the price of a defaultable pure discount bond expiring in M years is:

$$P(y, M) = e^{-rM} P_{\text{surv}}(y, M) + \int_0^M e^{-rt} \Pr\{\text{Default} \in dt\} \text{Rec}(t)\, dt, \tag{14.53}$$

where $\text{Rec}(t)$ denotes the recovery value in case of default, supposed to be known. Naturally, these derivations are perfectly consistent with similar derivations in chapter 13 (see section 13.4.6), although we are now emphasizing the aspects regarding survival probabilities.

As for the forward CDS spreads, we have, by eq. (14.35),

$$\text{CDS}_t(M) = \frac{\sum_{i=1}^{4M} e^{-r(t_i - t)} \text{LGD}(t_i) \left[P_{\text{surv}}(y, t_{i-1}) - P_{\text{surv}}(y, t_i) \right]}{\sum_{i=1}^{4M} e^{-r(t_i - t)} P_{\text{surv}}(y, t_i)}, \tag{14.54}$$

where M is, again, the number of years the CDS refers to, and $t_i = t + \frac{i}{4}$. Eq. (14.54) generalizes eq. (14.39) to random intensities.

Next, assume the short-term rate, r, is zero, and that LGD is constant. Then, as shown in appendix 14.D, the price of a defaultable pure discount bond, $P(\lambda, M)$, and the CDS premium, obtained from the forward once we set $t = 0$, $\text{CDS}_0(M)$, are given by:

$$P(\lambda, M) = 1 - \text{LGD}(1 - P_{\text{surv}}(\lambda, M)), \quad \text{CDS}_0(M) = \text{LGD} \frac{1 - P_{\text{surv}}(\lambda, M)}{\sum_{i=1}^{4M} P_{\text{surv}}(\lambda, t_i)}. \tag{14.55}$$

The expression for the price is a natural extension of the basic evaluation model in section 14.3.2 (see eq. (14.31)). The model, now, predicts time variation in credit spreads for both bonds and CDS premiums.

Figure 14.15 depicts the bonds spread, $\frac{-1}{M} \ln P(\lambda, M)$, and the annualized credit default spreads, $4 \times \text{CDS}_0(M)$, with parameters in eq. (14.48) fixed at $\phi = 0.30$, $\bar{\lambda} = 0.04$ and $\sigma^2 = \frac{1}{2}\bar{\lambda}$, and $\text{LGD} = 0.60$, and two values of the current intensity: $\lambda = \bar{\lambda} = 0.04$, and $\lambda = 0.02$.

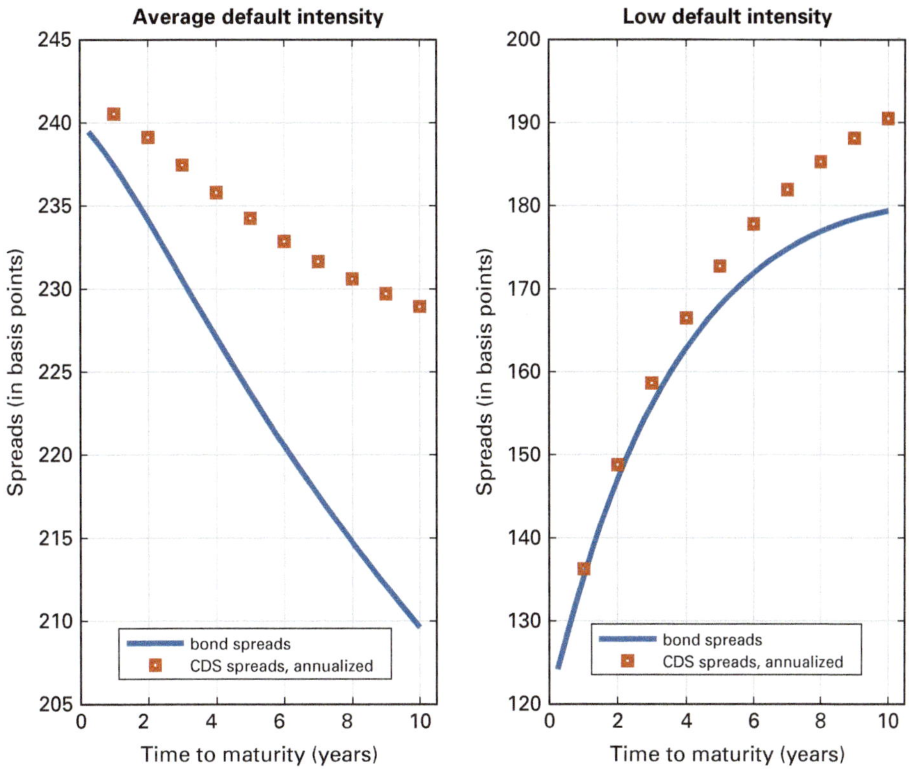

Figure 14.15
Spreads on bonds and CDS predicted by the affine model in eq. (14.48). The left panel depicts the spreads when the current default intensity equals the long-run mean, $\lambda = \bar{\lambda} = 0.04$. The right panel depicts the spreads in good times, i.e., when the current intensity of default takes a low value, $\lambda = 0.02$. In each case the recovery rate equals 40%.

The mechanism is that given the mean-reverting behavior of λ, good times are likely followed by bad, such that when $\lambda = 0.02$, we expect default rates to rise in the future. Spreads increase with maturity as a result. Moreover, bond spreads are approximately equal to CDS spreads at short maturities. At longer maturities, the two spreads diverge, with CDS spreads, $4 \times \text{CDS}_0(M)$, dominating bonds spreads, $\frac{-1}{M} \ln P(\lambda, M)$. Moreover, the two curves are decreasing in time to maturity even when the current value of the intensity equals the long-run one, $\bar{\lambda}$. This property is due to the assumption that recovery rates are constant, as explained in the constant intensity case dealt with in section 14.2.5. In appendix 14.E, we provide additional details and explanations regarding these properties.

14.3.3.3 Marking to market

You are long a CDS, that is, you are committing to a swap agreement at time t, a commitment to pay $\text{CDS}_t(M)$ at time t_i, if the name survives by time t_i, and to receive $\text{LGD}(t_i)$, if default occurs in the time interval $[t_{i-1}, t_i]$, for $4M$ time intervals. The payoff resulting from each of these swaps is

$$\text{cds}_t(t_i) \equiv \text{LGD}(t_i)\, \mathbb{I}_{\{\text{Def.} \in (t_{i-1}, t_i)\}} - \text{CDS}_t(M)\, \mathbb{I}_{\{\text{Surv. at } t_i\}}, \tag{14.56}$$

where

$$\text{CDS}_t(M): 0 = \sum_{i=1}^{4M} e^{-r(t_i - t)} \mathbb{E}_t\left(\text{cds}_t(t_i)\right),$$

and $\mathbb{E}_t$ denotes the expectation conditional upon the information set at time t, taken under the risk neutral probability. The solution to this equation is just that in eq. (14.35).

What happens to the value of this contract at any subsequent time $\tau \in (t, t_0)$? The marking to market value of the CDS is the present value of the risk neutral expectation of the single swaps payments $\text{cds}_t(t_i)$ in eq. (14.56). So the marking to market value of the CDS at τ is

$$\begin{aligned}
\text{MtM}_\tau(M) &\equiv \sum_{i=1}^{4M} e^{-r(t_i-\tau)} \mathbb{E}_\tau\left(\text{cds}(t_i)\right) \\
&= \sum_{i=1}^{4M} \Big[e^{-r(t_i-\tau)} \text{LGD}(t_i) \left(P_{\text{surv}}(\lambda_\tau, t_{i-1}) - P_{\text{surv}}(\lambda_\tau, t_i)\right) \\
&\qquad - \text{CDS}_t(M)\, e^{-r(t_i-\tau)} P_{\text{surv}}(\lambda_\tau, t_i) \Big] \\
&= v_{1\tau} \sum_{i=1}^{4M} [\text{CDS}_\tau(M) - \text{CDS}_t(M)], \quad v_{1\tau} \equiv \sum_{i=1}^{4M} e^{-r(t_i-\tau)} P_{\text{surv}}(\lambda_\tau, t_i),
\end{aligned}$$

where $v_{1\tau}$ is the defaultable annuity at time τ (see eq. (14.36)) predicted by the model, and the last line follows by the expression for $\text{CDS}_\tau(M)$, i.e., by setting $t \equiv \tau$ in eq. (14.54). These results perfectly match those in chapter 13 regarding forward swap rates and, indeed, relate to the present value of a CDS contract in eq. (14.41). However, note that, in this model, marking to market would collapse to zero if λ and LGD were constant.

14.3.3.4 A trading strategy

Bond prices and CDS spreads are driven by the same state variable, the default intensity, and so they are restricted to lie on some space, to be consistent with no-arbitrage. To illustrate, consider, first, the simple case where the default intensity is constant, such that CDS spreads are given by eq. (14.37). Given this model, we can look at the market data for CDS spreads, and infer the risk neutral intensity, as in figure 14.16.

CDS are indeed a function of the risk neutral intensity. Once we see a CDS quote, we may infer the market expectation of default, adjusted by risk. For example, if we had to observe a CDS premium equal to 200 basis points, as in figure 14.16, we would infer a risk neutral intensity approximately equal to $\hat{\lambda} = 0.033$. The key point is that this same $\hat{\lambda}$ should also be pricing the zero, such that for $M = 5$, $P(M) = 1 - \text{LGD}(1 - e^{-\hat{\lambda} M}) = 0.90874$, and so we go long both the bond and the CDS if the bond market price is less than 0.90874. The rationale behind this strategy is that the intensity implied by the current CDS premium is too low to justify the bond price, so bond prices and/or intensity (and, hence, CDS premiums) should increase. The exactly opposite reasoning applies when the bond price is higher than 0.90874.

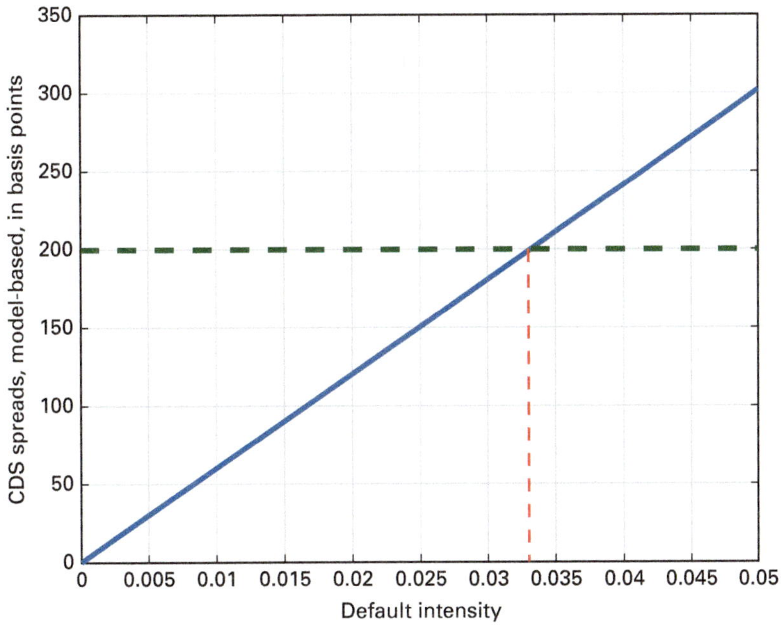

Figure 14.16
This picture depicts the CDS spreads predicted by eq. (14.37) as a function of the risk neutral intensity, λ, assuming $M = 5$ years, LGD $= 0.60$, and the short-term rate r is zero.

The previous example relies on a constant default intensity. However, the reasoning may be extended to cases in which default intensities are stochastic. Figure 14.17 depicts the no-arbitrage restrictions between bond spreads and CDS spreads, obtained through the random intensity model of this section. It also provides some rough indications on how one would proceed in order to exploit deviations from theoretical parity. For example, if market data happened to be in the northwest part of the diagram, one would like to buy bonds (which are cheap) and and buy protection (which is also relatively cheap). Theoretically, then, either bond prices increase or protection costs increase, or both, which will lead to profits. The opposite trade might be attempted if market data were on the southeast part of the diagram.

14.3.3.5 Hazard rates

In a pricing context, the relevant probabilities of survival are obviously conditioned upon the time of evaluation, time 0, say. For example, the probability of default in eq. (14.52) is only conditioned on the information we have at time 0. More generally, the probability of defaulting in the time interval (t_{i-1}, t_i), conditional upon survival at time $t < t_{i-1}$, is

$$\Pr\{\text{Def.} \in (t_{i-1}, t_i) \,|\, \text{Surv. at } t\} = \frac{P_{\text{surv}}(y, t_{i-1}) - P_{\text{surv}}(y, t_i)}{P_{\text{surv}}(y, t)}. \tag{14.57}$$

For example, for $t = t_{i-1}$, and (t_{i-1}, t_i) small, and λ deterministic, consider the following approximation to this conditional probability

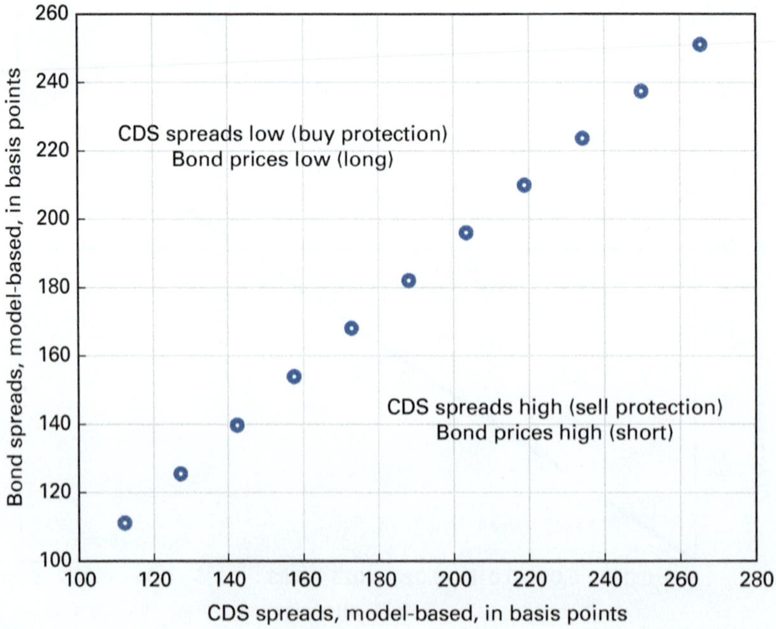

Figure 14.17
No-arb restrictions between bond spreads and CDS spreads for $M = 5$. This picture depicts the relation between CDS spreads and bond prices in the random intensity model where the intensity of default satisfies eq. (14.48). Parameter values are as in figure 14.15, and intensities λ_t are in the range from 0.0050 to 0.05.

$$\begin{aligned}\Pr\{\text{Def.} \in (t_{i-1}, t_i) | \text{Surv. at } t\} &\approx \frac{-\frac{\partial}{\partial t} P_{\text{surv}}(y,t)}{P_{\text{surv}}(y,t)}(t_i - t_{i-1}) \\ &\equiv \frac{p_{\text{def}}(y,t)}{1 - P_{\text{def}}(y,t)}(t_i - t_{i-1}) \\ &= \lambda_t (t_i - t_{i-1}),\end{aligned}$$

with straightforward notation. The previous expressions are known as *hazard rates*. They coincide with $\lambda_t dt$, when λ_t is deterministic. If λ_t is not deterministic, simple derivations in appendix 14.F reveal that, conditionally on information at time zero,

$$\Pr\{\text{Def.} \in (t, t+dt) | \text{Surv. at } t\} = \mathbb{E}_{Q_\lambda}(\lambda_t)\, dt, \tag{14.58}$$

where Q_λ is a new probability, with Radon-Nikodym derivative given by:

$$\left.\frac{dQ_\lambda}{dQ}\right|_{\mathcal{F}_t} = \frac{e^{-\int_0^t \lambda_s ds}}{P_{\text{surv}}(\lambda,t)}. \tag{14.59}$$

Accordingly, under Q_λ, the state variables in eq. (14.51) follow a diffusion process, with a tilted drift due to this change of probability. For example, in the simple setting of eq. (14.48), we have that, for a fixed t,

$$\begin{aligned}d\lambda_s &= \left(\mathcal{B}_0 - \mathcal{B}_1^t(s)\lambda_s\right) ds + \sigma\sqrt{\lambda_s} dW_{\lambda,s}, \quad s \in (0,t], \quad \lambda_0 = \lambda, \\ \mathcal{B}_0 &= \phi\bar{\lambda}, \quad \mathcal{B}_1^t(s) = \phi + B(t-s)\sigma^2, \quad B(\cdot) \text{ as in Eq. (14.50)},\end{aligned} \tag{14.60}$$

where W_λ is a Brownian motion under Q_λ. Therefore, by eq. (14.58),

$$\Pr\{\text{Def.} \in (t, t+dt) \mid \text{Surv. at } t\} = \left(\frac{\lambda}{G(t)} + \mathcal{B}_0 \int_0^t \frac{G(s)}{G(t)} ds \right) dt, \quad G(x) \equiv e^{\int_0^x \mathcal{B}_1^t (u)\, du}.$$

14.3.3.6 Extracting probabilities of default from market data

Markets obviously convey information about default probabilities, which could be extracted under a number of assumptions. To illustrate, assume zero recovery and that both the short-term rate and the default intensity are continuous time Markov and independent of each other. Then, the price of a defaultable zero is $P_{\text{def}}(\lambda, M) = P(M) \cdot P_{\text{surv}}(\lambda, M)$, where $P_{\text{def}}(\lambda, M)$ and $P(M)$ are the prices of a defaultable and a nondefaultable zero. Therefore, we can read the *risk neutral* probability of survival from the defaultable/nondefaultable price ratio:

$$P_{\text{surv}}(\lambda, M) = \frac{P_{\text{def}}(\lambda, M)}{P(M)}. \tag{14.61}$$

Naturally, surviving until some M_2 implies having survived until any $M_1 : M_1 < M_2$ and, from M_1 to M_2. Therefore, we have (approximately) that $P_{\text{surv}}(\lambda, M_2) = P_{\text{surv}}(\lambda, M_1) \cdot P_{\text{surv}}(\lambda, M_1, M_2)$, where $P_{\text{surv}}(\lambda, M_1, M_2)$ is the risk neutral probability of survival between M_1 and M_2. Using eq. (14.61), then, we can extract this probability, as follows:

$$P_{\text{surv}}(\lambda, M_1, M_2) = \frac{P_{\text{def}}(\lambda, M_2)}{P_{\text{def}}(\lambda, M_1)} \frac{P(M_1)}{P(M_2)}.$$

The previous example relies on the simplifying assumption of a zero recovery rate, but it can be generalized to the case where the recovery rate is nonzero. However, in this case, an identification issue arises, as prices would convey information about both default probabilities and recovery rates.

14.3.4 The Pricing of Credit Products

14.3.4.1 Credit default swaptions: On single names

With stochastic intensity rates, we can think about the pricing of the credit default swaptions that we briefly mentioned in section 14.3.2.3. We, now, actually assume that both default intensities and the short-term rate are stochastic: we assume that the short-term rate is a diffusion process, and that default arrives as a Cox process with intensity λ adapted to r.

Consider the following definition of a *default swap* in section 14.3.2.1—a contract whereby a party stands ready to pay its counterparty a loss determined by a credit event for a given flows of premiums, referred to as CDS premiums. At this level, we are not assuming that this swap is worthless at origination. We assume that LGD is constant. Denote the CDS premium, or "coupon," agreed at time t with C_t, $t \leq t_0$. Note that like in section 14.3.2, the contract we are dealing with is a *forward* default swap. We assume that the contract is terminated should the underlying obligor default prior to the start date, t_0.

In this contract, the protection buyer commits to a swap agreement whereby it pays the coupon C_t at time t_i, if the name survives by time t_i, and receives LGD if default occurs at some point in time $\tau^* \in [t_0, t_{4M}]$. Therefore, the value of the default swap originated at time t is

$$\mathrm{DS}_t = \sum_{i=1}^{4M} \mathbb{E}_t \left(e^{-\int_t^{t_i} r_\tau d\tau} \mathrm{cds}_t\left(t_i\right) \right) = \mathrm{LGD} \cdot v_{0t} - C_t \cdot v_{1t}, \tag{14.62}$$

where $\mathbb{E}_t$ denotes the risk neutral expectation, taken conditional upon the information set at time t, and, denoting the time to default with τ^*,

$$v_{0t} \equiv \mathbb{E}_t \left(e^{-\int_t^{\tau^*} r_\tau d\tau} \mathbb{I}_{\{\tau^* \in [t_0, t_{4M}]\}} \right), \quad v_{1t} \equiv \sum_{i=1}^{4M} \mathbb{E}_t \left(e^{-\int_t^{t_i} r_\tau d\tau} \mathbb{I}_{\{\text{Surv. at } t_i\}} \right). \tag{14.63}$$

The interpretation of v_{0t} is that of the value of \$1 paid off the first time after default, provided default occurs prior to the maturity of the default swap, $4M$.[23] Instead, v_{1t} is the value of a defaultable annuity, an expression that generalizes that in eq. (14.36) to the case of random intensity (and interest) rates.

The forward default spread is the value of C_τ such that $\mathrm{DS}_\tau = 0$. It is:

$$\mathrm{CDS}_\tau\left(M\right) = \mathrm{LGD} \frac{v_{0\tau}}{v_{1\tau}}, \tag{14.64}$$

such that the value of the default swap at time τ, agreed at time $t \leq \tau$, and denoted as $\mathrm{DS}_\tau\left(t, T\right)$, can be expressed as:

$$\mathrm{DS}_\tau\left(t, T\right) = \mathrm{LGD} \cdot v_{0\tau} - C_t \cdot v_{1\tau} = v_{1\tau} \cdot \left(\mathrm{CDS}_\tau\left(M\right) - C_t\right). \tag{14.65}$$

Note that the derivation leading to eq. (14.65) generalizes that underlying the marks-to-market updates in section 14.3.3.3.

Next, note that for any $\mathbb{F}_T$-measurable random variable X_T adapted to $(r_\tau)_{\tau \in [t,T]}$ and satisfying enough regularity conditions, we have that for fixed T, and by the law of iterated expectations,

$$\begin{aligned}
&\mathbb{E}_t \left(e^{-\int_t^T r_\tau d\tau} \cdot X_T \cdot \mathbb{I}_{\{\text{Surv. at } T\}} \right) \\
&= \mathbb{E}_t \left[\mathbb{E} \left(e^{-\int_t^T r_\tau d\tau} \cdot X_T \cdot \mathbb{I}_{\{\text{Surv. at } T\}} \middle| \mathbb{F}_T^r \right) \right] \\
&= \mathbb{E}_t \left[e^{-\int_t^T r_\tau d\tau} \cdot X_T \cdot \mathbb{E} \left(\mathbb{I}_{\{\text{Surv. at } T\}} \middle| \mathbb{F}_T^r \right) \right] \\
&= \mathbb{E}_t \left(e^{-\int_t^T \left(r_\tau + \lambda_\tau\right) d\tau} \cdot X_T \right),
\end{aligned} \tag{14.66}$$

where $\mathbb{F}_T^r$ is the information set at time T, which includes the path of the short-term rate only.

---

23. This evaluation framework does not generalize that in section 14.3.2, where it was assumed that premiums and protections are both paid at the end of the period. Instead, in the present section, we are assuming that protection is paid as soon as default occurs, as revealed by the expression for v_{0t} in eq. (14.63).

Define the probability Q_{sc} through the Radon-Nikodym derivative

$$\left.\frac{dQ_{sc}}{dQ}\right|_{\mathbb{F}_T} = e^{-\int_t^T (r_\tau + \lambda_\tau)\, d\tau} \frac{v_{1T}}{v_{1t}}, \tag{14.67}$$

where Q is the risk neutral probability. We shall argue in a moment that Q_{sc} does integrate to one.[24] Following Schönbucher (2003, 180), we refer to Q_{sc} as the *survival contingent probability*. Chapter 4 provides foundations on changes of probability, with this change of probability being a special case of a general framework.

We claim that for any $\tau \le t_0$,

$$v_{it} = \mathbb{E}_t \left(e^{-\int_t^\tau (r_s + \lambda_s)\, ds} v_{i\tau} \right), \quad i = 0, 1, \tag{14.68}$$

implying that Q_{sc} integrates to one. Indeed, note that v_{it} is the value of a basket of securities paying off contingent upon the event that the firm has not defaulted prior to time τ, $\tau \le t_0$, in which case the value drops to zero. Following derivations in chapter 13, we have that $Lv_i - rv_i + \lambda (0 - v_i) = 0$, where L is the infinitesimal generator for diffusions, whence eq. (14.68). Alternatively, eq. (14.68) follows by eq. (14.66).

Therefore, given the definition of Q_{sc} in eq. (14.67) and the martingale property of v_{0t} in eq. (14.68), we have that the forward default spread in eq. (14.64) is a martingale under the survival contingent probability:

$$\begin{aligned} &\mathbb{E}_t^{sc} (\text{CDS}_\tau (M)) \\ &= \mathbb{E}_t \left(e^{-\int_t^\tau (r_s + \lambda_s)\, ds} \frac{v_{1\tau}}{v_{1t}} \text{CDS}_\tau (M) \right) = \mathbb{E}_t \left(e^{-\int_t^\tau (r_s + \lambda_s)\, ds} \frac{v_{0\tau}}{v_{1t}} \text{LGD} \right) = \text{CDS}_t (M), \end{aligned}$$

where $\mathbb{E}_t^{sc}$ denotes the time t conditional expectation taken under the survival contingent probability, and where we have used the pricing equation (14.68) and the definition of $\text{CDS}_t (M)$ in eq. (14.64).

We evaluate default swaptions by relying on the survival contingent probability. By eq. (14.65), the payoff of a swaption payer is

$$\text{PDS}_T (t, T) = \mathbb{I}_{\{\text{Surv. at } T\}} v_{1T} (\text{CDS}_T (M) - K)^+, \quad T = t_0,$$

for a strike K. Relying on the property in eq. (14.66) leaves:

$$\begin{aligned} &\mathbb{E}_t \left(e^{-\int_t^T r_\tau d\tau} \text{PDS}_T (t, T) \right) \\ &= \mathbb{E}_t \left(e^{-\int_t^T (r_\tau + \lambda_\tau)\, d\tau} v_{1T} (\text{CDS}_T (M) - K)^+ \right) = v_{1t} \mathbb{E}_t^{sc} (\text{CDS}_T (M) - K)^+ . \end{aligned} \tag{14.69}$$

We know that $\text{CDS}_t (M)$ is a martingale under the survival contingent probability. Let W_τ^{sc} be a Brownian motion under Q^{sc}. Assume that

$$\frac{d\text{CDS}_\tau (M)}{\text{CDS}_\tau (M)} = \sigma dW_\tau^{sc}, \quad \tau \in [t, T],$$

24. See eq. (14.68); see also Schönbucher (2003, chap. 7) and Lando (2004, chap. 5).

where σ is the volatility parameter, a constant. We can apply Black (1976) to obtain evaluation formulae in this environment. However, this approach is actually not appropriate when dealing with contract designs with upfront and fixed coupon payments, such as that in section 14.3.2.4. These issues are dealt in some detail in section 14.3.4.3.

14.3.4.2 *Credit default swaptions: On CDS indices*

Consider, first, a *CDS index*, as succinctly described in section 14.3.2.3. Let n be the number of names in the index decided at time t. Each name has notional value equal to $\frac{1}{n}$, the same LGD and the same default intensity λ.

When any name j defaults at time τ_j, the index experiences a loss at τ_j equal to $\mathrm{LGD}\frac{1}{n}$, so in general $\mathrm{LGD}\frac{1}{n}\mathbb{I}_{\{t\leq\tau_j\leq T_{4M}\}}$ is the index loss generated by name j from t to the index expiry, which the protection seller stands ready to pay. The protection buyer pays a periodic premium, at t_i say, equal to a constant coupon C_t times N_{t_i}, the outstanding notional at t_i,

$$N_{t_i}\equiv 1-\frac{1}{n}\sum_{h=0}^{i}\mathcal{D}\left(t_{h-1},t_h\right)=\frac{1}{n}\sum_{j=1}^{n}\mathbb{I}_{\{\text{Surv}_j\text{ at }t_i\}},\quad N_t\equiv 1, \tag{14.70}$$

where $\mathcal{D}\left(t_{i-1},t_i\right)$ denotes the number of names having defaulted in the time interval $\left(t_{i-1},t_i\right)$,

$$\mathcal{D}\left(t_{i-1},t_i\right)\equiv\sum_{j=1}^{n}\mathbb{I}_{\{\text{Def}_j\in\left(t_{i-1},t_i\right)\}},$$

and $\mathcal{D}\left(t_{-1},t_0\right)$ is the number of defaults occurred in (t,t_0).

Given the assumptions that obligors are all the same ex ante, the value at t of the protection leg minus that of the premium leg over the life of the index is the same as in the single name case (see eq. (14.62)):

$$\begin{aligned}\mathrm{DSX}_t&=\mathbb{E}_t\left(\sum_{j=1}^{n}e^{-\int_t^{\tau_j}r_\tau d\tau}\mathrm{LGD}\frac{1}{n}\mathbb{I}_{\{t\leq\tau_j\leq T_{4M}\}}\right)-\mathbb{E}_t\left(\sum_{i=1}^{4M}e^{-\int_t^{t_i}r_\tau d\tau}C_tN_{t_i}\right)\\&=\mathrm{LGD}\cdot v_{0t}-C_t\cdot v_{1t},\quad\text{for } t\equiv t_0,\end{aligned}\tag{14.71}$$

where v_{0t} and v_{1t} are as in eqs. (14.63), and can interpreted as the values of securities indexed on default events of an hypothetical representative name.

The CDS index *spread* at the time of origination $t\equiv t_0$ is, then, simply, the value of C_{t_0} in eq. (14.71), which makes $\mathrm{DSX}_{t_0}=0$, viz

$$C_{t_0}(M)=\mathrm{LGD}\frac{v_{0,t_0}}{v_{1,t_0}}.$$

Next, consider a *forward starting credit default index*, which is an index starting at time t_0 and decided at some point $t\leq t_0$. Clearly, the value of the protection leg minus that of the premium leg is the same as that in eq. (14.71), for a generic $t\leq t_0$. Moreover, the value of the forward starting credit default index decided at t is, for any time $\tau \in (t, t_0)$,

$$\text{DSX}_\tau(t, t_0) = \text{N}_\tau (\text{LGD} \cdot v_{0\tau} - C_t v_{1\tau}), \tag{14.72}$$

where N_τ denotes the outstanding notion in eq. (14.70) (see appendix 14.G).

Finally, an *index default swaption payer* with strike K, gives the holder the option to enter a CDS index as a protection buyer with an index strike spread equal to K. Upon exercise, the protection buyer would also receive a *front-end protection*, defined as the losses occurring from the option origination to the exercise date. Let t be the option origination and $T = t_0$ the maturity of the swaption. The front-end protection is, $F_T = \text{LGD}\frac{1}{n}\mathcal{D}(t, T)$. In Appendix 14.G, we show that the value of the front-end protection is

$$v_\tau^{\text{F}} = \mathbb{E}_\tau \left(e^{-\int_\tau^T r_u du} F_T \right) = \text{LGD} \left(\frac{1}{n}\mathcal{D}(t, \tau) P(\tau, T) + \text{N}_\tau \left(P(\tau, T) - P_{\text{def}}(\tau, T) \right) \right), \tag{14.73}$$

where $P(t, T)$ and $P_{\text{def}}(t, T)$ denote the price of a nondefaultable and a defaultable zero expiring at time T, with zero recovery value and default intensity equal to that of the representative firm, λ. The underlying of a default swaption payer equals $\text{DSX}_T(t, T) + F_T$. Accordingly, we can define the *loss-adjusted forward default swap index*, as $\text{DSX}_\tau^L(t, T) \equiv \text{DSX}_\tau(t, T) + v_\tau^{\text{F}}$, and find the value of C_t such that newly issued forwards are worthless, $\text{DSX}_\tau^L(\tau, T) = 0$, denoted as $\text{CDX}_\tau(M)$, which is

$$\text{CDX}_\tau(M) = \text{LGD}\frac{v_{0\tau}}{v_{1\tau}} + \frac{v_\tau^{\text{F}}}{\text{N}_\tau v_{1\tau}}, \tag{14.74}$$

such that

$$\text{DSX}_\tau^L(t, T) = \text{N}_\tau v_{1\tau} (\text{CDX}_\tau(M) - C_t). \tag{14.75}$$

We wish to use $\text{N}_\tau v_{1\tau}$ as a numéraire such that $\text{CDX}_t(M)$ is a martingale under a suitable probability,[25] similarly as for the probability Q_{sc} in eq. (14.67). Define the probability $\hat{Q}_{\text{sc}}$ through the Radon-Nikodym derivative:

$$\left. \frac{d\hat{Q}_{\text{sc}}}{dQ} \right|_{\mathbb{F}_T} = e^{-\int_\tau^T r_u du} \frac{\text{N}_T v_{1T}}{\text{N}_\tau v_{1\tau}}. \tag{14.76}$$

The probability $\hat{Q}_{\text{sc}}$ is the index counterpart to Q_{sc} in eq. (14.67). For simplicity, we shall keep on referring to $\hat{Q}_{\text{sc}}$ as the "survival contingent probability." Appendix 14.G contains a proof that $\hat{Q}_{\text{sc}}$ does indeed integrate to one. It also shows that $\text{CDX}_t(M)$ in eq. (14.74) is a martingale under $\hat{Q}_{\text{sc}}$.

25. A technical issue with the definition of $\text{CDX}_t(M)$ in eq. (14.74) relates to a "denominator problem," i.e., the "armageddon" possibility of a total collapse of the index, $N_\tau = 0$. The occurrence of such an event has been taken into account by Rutkowski and Armstrong (2009) and Morini and Brigo (2011).

In the hypothetical, "idealized" case in which the holder of a swaption payer was allowed to enter into an index with a spread equal to K, the price of this contract would be, for any $\tau \in [t, T]$,

$$\mathrm{SW}_\tau^p(K,T) \equiv \mathbb{E}_\tau\left(e^{-\int_\tau^T r_u du} N_T v_{1T}(\mathrm{CDX}_T(M) - K)^+\right) = N_\tau v_{1\tau} \hat{\mathbb{E}}_\tau^{sc}(\mathrm{CDX}_T(M) - K)^+ ,$$

where $\hat{\mathbb{E}}_\tau^{sc}(\cdot)$ denotes the time τ conditional expectation under the survival contingent probability $\hat{Q}_{sc}$ in eq. (14.76).

We know $\mathrm{CDX}_\tau(M)$ is a martingale under $\hat{Q}_{sc}$. Therefore, we could use Black (1976) to evaluate the previous expression, once we assume that under $\hat{Q}_{sc}$, $\mathrm{CDX}_\tau(M)$ is a geometric Brownian motion with constant volatility. Unfortunately, this approach is not appropriate when indices cannot be issued with a spread equal to K.

14.3.4.3 *Evaluation of exotic payoffs: Pedersen's model*

The evaluation framework in the previous sections relies on the assumption that the holder of a payer (say) has the option to enter into a "par spread" contract with strike K. However, such contracts do not exist, and the "idealized" pricing in the previous sections is only a useful starting point. Section 14.3.2.4 explains indeed that entering a CDS contract or an index requires an initial upfront payment and a subsequent recurrent payment of a standardized coupon, C. The security design pertaining to credit default swaptions is built around the construct of section 14.3.2.4.

Suppose that a perspective buyer of protection wishes to hedge against the event that, in two months, the spread on a given single name may increase beyond some level, K. They may, then, go long a payer swaption on this single name with expiration equal to two months. The contract is structured as follows. If, at expiration, the payer's holder exercises, They will be (i) long the CDS contract at the prevailing spread, and (ii) compensated for the difference between the upfront required to enter the contract, $v_{1T}(\mathrm{CDS}_T(M) - C_t)$ say, *and* the upfront they would have paid if an hypothetical contract was available with a spread equal to K. The second upfront is equal to

$$H(C_t, K) \equiv (K - C_t)\, v_1(K),$$

where $v_1(K)$ denotes the flat defaultable annuity for a spread equal to K, i.e., the flat defaultable annuity under hypothetical market conditions with a spread equal to K (see eq. (14.42) and related explanations). Therefore, the payoff of the swaption at expiry T is

$$\Pi_T = (v_{1T}(\mathrm{CDS}_T(M) - C_t) - H(C_t, K))^+ .$$

Pedersen (2003) develops a pricing model for index options that is a standard in the market practice. We describe the salient features of this model in the simple single name case dealt with in this section. Assume interest rates are constant, and define a random variable $X_T : (X_T - C_t)v_1(X_T) = v_{1T}(\mathrm{CDS}_T(T,M) - C_t)$, and define the conditional *forward price*, $\mathcal{F}_\tau(T) \equiv \mathbb{E}_\tau(\mathrm{DS}_T(t,T))$, i.e., the price at τ, for "delivery" of a forward starting contract (at T) (contingent, of course, upon survival), which equals

$$\mathcal{F}_\tau(T) = e^{r(T-\tau)} v_{1\tau} \mathbb{E}_\tau^{sc}(\mathrm{CDS}_T(M) - C_t) = e^{r(T-\tau)} v_{1\tau}(\mathrm{CDS}_\tau(M) - C_t),$$

where the first line follows by the definition of $\mathcal{F}_\tau(T)$ and arguments similar to those used to achieve eq. (14.69), and the second equality follows by the martingale property of $CDS_\tau(M)$ under Q_{sc}.

The assumption underlying Pedersen's model is that, under the risk neutral probability,

$$X_T^{x^o} \equiv X_T = X_t \exp\left(-\frac{1}{2}s^2(T-t) + s\sqrt{T-t}\omega\right), \quad X_t \equiv x^o,$$

where ω is a standard Gaussian variable, x^o is some initial condition, and s is a constant volatility parameter. This log-normal assumption on X_T resembles that underlying the Black–Scholes model. The notable difference is that while the initial stock price is obviously known in the Black–Scholes market, the initial condition x^o is not in this credit context. However, for any given value of s, x^o can be calibrated to the forward price as the solution to the following nonlinear equation

$$\hat{x}^o : \mathcal{F}_\tau(T) = \mathbb{E}_\tau\left[\left(X_T^{\hat{x}^o} - C_t\right) v_1(X_T^{\hat{x}^o})\right].$$

Naturally, the calibrated value $\hat{x}^o$ depends on the spread volatility s. Given s and $\hat{x}^o$, we can now price a swaption (a payer, say) as

$$SW_\tau^p(C_t, K, T, M; \hat{x}^o, s) \equiv e^{-r(T-\tau)}\mathbb{E}_\tau\left[\left(\left(X_T^{\hat{x}^o} - C_t\right) v_1(X_T^{\hat{x}^o}) - H(C_t, K)\right)^+\right].$$

The expectation can be computed through simulations or numerical integration. One can, then, define an implied Pedersen's volatility as the value of s such that the swaption price predicted by the model matches the market price.

14.3.4.4 Extensions to index options

Index options feature, contractually, the same strike corrections we have just described for single names, and are priced exactly as in the previous section, once account is made of front-end protections and the shrinking notional, as originally illustrated by Pedersen (2003). At the time of writing, swaptions on indices have a further complication: while investment-grade indices are quoted in spreads, high yields and emerging market indices are quoted in prices (the index counterparts to *PUF* in eq. (14.43)). For a quotation in price, the payoff of a payer at T, say, is, then, $\left(DSX_T^L(t,T) - K_p\right)^+$, where $DSX_T^L(t,T)$ is as in (14.75), and K_p denotes the strike. Despite this quoting convention, Pedersen's model can obviously be applied to price the option through the procedure illustrated in the previous section, after having had regard of front-end protections and the shrinking notionals embedded into $DSX_T^L(t,T)$. O'Kane (2011) contains extensive examples regarding the implementation of the Pedersen's model.

14.3.5 Collateralized Debt Obligations

14.3.5.1 A crash description of structured finance

The US government perhaps provided a historically relevant example of securitization throughout a series of financial innovation initiatives. Until the 1970s, the financial system used to be in a "buy to hold" regime, whereby financial intermediaries, such as commercial banks, would extend loans to businesses or individuals, which they would typically hold in their balance sheets. The 1970s witnessed a new solid trend, whereby government-sponsored enterprises (widely known as GSE) such as the Government National Mortgage Association (GNMA or Ginnie Mae, created in 1968) would buy the mortgages from banks to incentivize them to extend more loans, with the purpose of making houses accessible to families. In a second step, GNMA would sell securities based on the cash flows generated by these mortgages. The Federal National Mortgage Association (Fannie Mae) and the Federal Home Loan Mortgage Corporation (Freddie Mac)[26] would subsequently take securitization to a higher level while securitizing the assets through "tranching." While this tranching model was being adopted, investment banks would begin to apply it to other types of securities, such as corporate bonds, student loans, small business loans, automobile loans, etc.

How does tranching work? The conceptual framework underlying this model is to create securitized shares from pools of assets. A collateralized debt obligation (CDO) is an example of such an instrument. The assets underlying a CDO, the "collateral," may include loans or debt instruments. A CDO may be a collateralized loan obligation (CLO) or a collateralized bond obligation (CBO), according to whether it relies only on loans or bonds, resp. CDO investors bear the credit risk of the collateral. Multiple tranches of securities are issued by the CDO, offering investors various maturity and credit risk characteristics. Tranches are categorized according to their degree of credit risk, and can be senior, mezzanine, or junior; junior tranches are also sometimes referred to as "subordinated" or "equity." When defaults occur, or otherwise the CDO's collateral underperforms, scheduled payments to senior tranches take precedence over those of mezzanine tranches, and scheduled payments to mezzanine tranches take precedence over those to junior tranches. Typically, senior tranches are rated, with ratings of A to AAA. Mezzanine are also rated, typically with ratings of B to BBB. In principle, these ratings should reflect both the credit quality of the collateral and the protection a given tranche is given by the tranches subordinating to it.

CDOs may be part of a complex securitization process, one that may also involve the inclusion of assets of different nature. The stylized example in figure 14.18 illustrates this process. In a first step, subprime mortgages are securitized. In a second step, a CDO is created out of the securitized subprime mortgages and additional asset backed securities (ABS); in a third step, the structuring process involves creating seniority rules. Investors in CDO *senior tranches* include banks and pension funds, which may benefit from both the expertise of the asset managers and risk-return profiles difficult to find in the marketplace. Investors in *junior tranches* are hedge funds in search for highly risky investment opportunities that bear a very high reward that is typically unavailable in the market. Additional investors in junior tranches may be dedicated off-balance-sheets entities such as "SIV," "conduits," and "SIV-lites" (see section 14.5).

---

26. We have already encountered Fannie Mae in chapter 13 (see section 13.8.5) while discussing negative convexity risks. Fannie Mae was created in 1938, as mentioned, in response to the Great Depression and to help the troubled housing market through long-term mortgages and affordable fixed rates and the support of the US federal government. Due to fiscal pressures determined by the Vietnam War, Fannie Mae was privatized under the Lyndon B. Johnson administration and acted as a GSE. To mitigate competition issues arising from the very few GSE in this space, Freddie Mac was created in 1970.

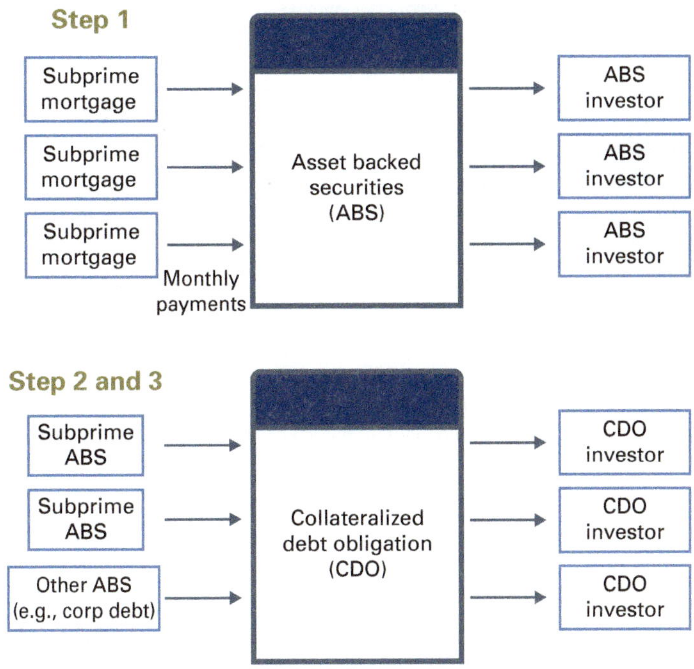

Figure 14.18
A stylized model of securitization through origination, formation of collateral and distribution through tranching.

Investment banks are typical CDO underwriters and enjoy generous fees, due perhaps to the complexity of the CDOs.[27] They work in close connection with the asset manager to create the "right" debt/equity ratio and they perform collateral quality tests. They liase with law firms and create the special purpose vehicle (SPV) (sometimes, in tax-haven systems) that is in charge of purchasing the assets from an arranger, issuing the tranches, pricing them and, obviously, finding the investors for these tranches, as illustrated in the example of figure 14.19. This example is inspired by the Committee on the Global Financial System (2005), but is stylized, because it ignores the role played by the ecosystem around the SPV. Involved into the structuring process are also the servicers (i.e., those who are in charge of collecting and distributing payments), compliance managers, accountants, and collateral administrators (i.e., those who distribute noteholder reports, check compliance, and execute priority of payments, perform due diligence on the CDOs collateral pool, verifying for example credit ratings for each asset) and last, but not least, rating agencies, which we shall discuss in the next subsection.

The economics behind structured finance is interesting. An originator may have private information about the quality of certain assets and/or a comparative advantage in evaluating these assets relative to other market participants. If the originator intends to sell some of its assets, an adverse selection problem arises: because investors do not know the true quality of the assets, they will demand a premium to purchase them or, even worse, a market might fail to arise (see section 5.3 in chapter 5 for a simplified model of this

27. According to Thomson Financial, top underwriters in 2006 were: Bear Sterns, Merrill Lynch, Wachovia, Citigroup, Deutsche Bank, and Bank of America Securities.

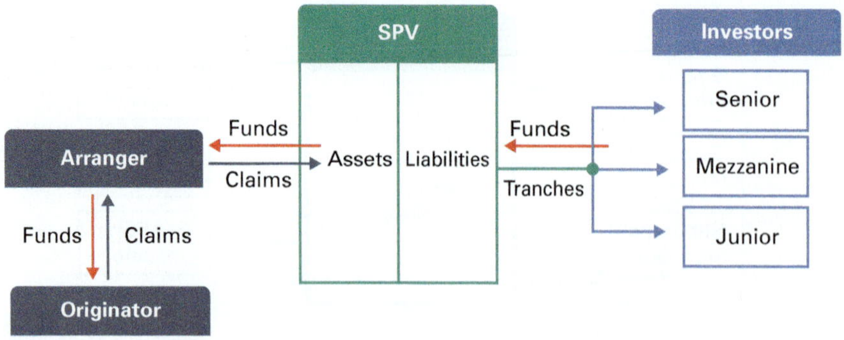

Figure 14.19
A stylized model of securitization through a SPV. Investors invest into securities issued by the SPV, the SPV liabilities. Returns originate from performance of collateral made available to the SPV collateral through origination and subsequent arrangement.

moral hazard problem). Structured finance helps originators mitigate this problem. First, by pooling the assets, diversification benefits can be achieved. Second, tranching allows relatively poorly informed investors to access senior tranches, and be relatively protected from default. In the process, the originator or arranger may retain subordinated exposure to alleviate investors' concerns about incentive compatibility. Section 14.5 revisits this model in light of the global financial crisis of the late 2000s.

14.3.5.2 The role of rating agencies

Structured finance has always been a "rated" market. Issuers of structured instruments had a natural appetite for a rating to occur at a scale comparable with that applying to debt: the main reason is that rating should facilitate the sale of these products to investors bound by ratings-based constraints defined by their investment mandates.

However, the involvement of rating agencies in the delivery of their opinion about credit risk differs from that related to traditional bonds. As regards traditional instruments, rating agencies simply aim to assess the risk of default, which they take as given. As regards structured finance transactions, rating agencies play a much more ex ante, reverse engineering role. A tranche rating reflects a view about both the credit risk of the asset pool and the extent of credit support to be provided. These two elements are organized to reverse engineer the tranche rating targeted by the deal's arrangers. Deal origination might involve rating agencies into the structuring process.

14.3.5.3 Types of CDOs

In practice, CDOs are considerably more complex than the previous stylized examples. There are a number of cases. We say that a CDO is *static*, if it holds the same set of assets. Instead, a CDO is *managed*, if the asset manager is allowed to change the composition of assets. If the claims to the CDO arise from the cash flows originated by the assets, we have a *cash-flow CDO*. If the claims to the CDO arise from the cash flows originated by the assets and/or active asset management, we have a *market-value CDO*. CDOs can also be created to carve out balance sheets, giving rise to *balance-sheet CDOs*. Moreover, and interestingly, CDOs can be created (i) to achieve investment-grade bonds through a pool of non-investment grade bonds, and (ii) to create riskier securities than those in the asset pool.

These cases lead to *arbitrage CDOs*. The term "arbitrage" CDOs is meant to emphasize the circumstance that these instruments achieve the goal of merely "reshuffling" risk and expected returns of the assets in the pool; that is, the total value of the CDO remains equal to the value of the assets in the pool, as illustrated by the examples in the next section. Moreover, arbitrage CDOs differ from balance-sheet CDOs, because issuers of arbitrage CDOs do not necessarily hold the underlying collateral in advance, which is obviously the case for issuers of balance-sheet CDOs. Therefore, the assets to enter into an arbitrage CDO pool have to be reasonably liquid. Furthermore, *synthetic CDOs* provide exposure to a pool of assets that are not strictly owned or in the asset pool, typically through CDS underwriting. Like a cash-flow CDO, the vehicle receives payments (the premiums), which are then transferred to the tranche holders; naturally, there may be default events that are also passed through the investors, in accordance with prespecified seniority rules.

A synthetic CDO is *funded*, if the relevant tranche holders bear the obligation to pay for credit events related to the collateral underlying the CDO. Typically, some funding is made available at the time of investment. At maturity, the investor receives a payoff equal to the funding minus the realized losses. Junior tranches are typically funded, and senior tranches are typically not. Naturally, senior tranche investors might have to make payments in the event losses had to erode their tranches. *Hybrid CDOs* are partly cash-flow CDOs and partly synthetic CDOs. In a *single-tranche CDO*, the entire CDO is structured to accommodate the specific needs of a small group of investors, with some remaining tranche held by the dealer. Finally, in a CDO^2, a large portion of the assets in the pool are tranches from other CDOs.

14.3.5.4 Stylized pricing models

CDOs repackage cash flows from a set of assets. We provide a few simple examples to show how to price the cash flows that result from this repackaging process. In these examples, we begin describing the cash flows promised by defaultable bonds. These defaultable bonds can be thought of as being the initial illiquid assets; the resulting CDO then aims to a liquidity enhancement. However, this chapter is being silent regarding the process through which the CDO becomes more liquid compared to the initial assets pools.

We begin with a simple example, in which we are given three one-year bonds with face value equal to 100. For each of these bonds, the *risk neutral* probabilities of default is 10% and the recovery rates are 40; finally, the safe interest rate for one year is 6%. Therefore, each bond price is[28]

$$b = e^{-0.06} \cdot (\underbrace{0.10}_{\equiv \text{Def. Prob}} \cdot 40 + \underbrace{0.90}_{\equiv \text{Surv. Prob}} \cdot 100) = 88.526,$$

such that the yield is $-\ln \frac{b}{100} = 12.19\%$.

A CDO restructures the bonds payoffs in such a way to transform the riskiness (and expected returns) of the initial assets base. Consider the following example:

28. The numerical values of default probabilities and recovery rates in this section are taken from McDonald (2006, 583). We use these values as benchmarks to elaborate the additional models in this section.

Asset pool	CDO claims
Face value = 300	Senior tranche = 140 Mezzanine tranche = 90 Junior tranche = 70

In this example, each tranche receives the minimum between (i) the nominal value claimed by the tranche and (ii) what is left available to the tranche after having satisfied the other tranches by order of seniority.

Let N_i be the nominal values claimed by the tranches, so that $N_1 = 140$, $N_2 = 90$ and $N_3 = 70$. Let $\tilde{\pi}$ be the realized payoff of the asset pool, defined as

$$\tilde{\pi} = \mathcal{N}^D \times 40 + \underbrace{\left(3 - \mathcal{N}^D\right)}_{\equiv \text{ No. of surviving bonds}} \times 100,$$

where $\mathcal{N}^D$ denotes the number of defaulted bonds. Naturally, $\tilde{\pi}$ is random because the number of defaulted bonds is random. At the expiration:

(i) The senior tranche receives the minimum between N_1 and $\tilde{\pi}$. For example, if only one bond defaults, $\tilde{\pi} = 240$, and the senior tranche receives 140. If, however, three bonds default, $\tilde{\pi} = 120$, which is less than the senior tranche nominal value; the senior tranche then receives 120. So a quite severe loss is needed to erode the senior tranche claims.

(ii) The mezzanine tranche receives the minimum between N_2 and the "left-over" from the senior tranche.

(iii) Eventually, the junior tranche receives the minimum between N_3 and the "left-over" from the senior and mezzanine tranches.

More formally, the payoff to ith tranche is

$$\pi_i = \min\left\{\text{left-over}_{i-1}, N_i\right\},$$

where left-over$_{i-1}$ denotes the left-over from previous tranches, and up to the $(i-1)$th tranche, namely

$$\text{left-over}_{i-1} \equiv \max\left\{\tilde{\pi} - \textstyle\sum_{k=1}^{i-1} \pi_k, 0\right\}.$$

That is,

$$\pi_i = \min\left\{\max\left\{\tilde{\pi} - \textstyle\sum_{k=1}^{i-1} \pi_k, 0\right\}, N_i\right\}.$$

All we need now is a model for the risk neutral probability of default for each firm. We assume the number of defaulted bonds follows a binomial distribution

$$\Pr\left(\mathcal{N}^D = k\right) = \binom{3}{k} p^k (1-p)^{3-k}, \quad p = 10\%, \quad k \in \{0, 1, 2, 3\},$$

and, initially, we assume that the default events are independent across firms. The following table summarizes the payoffs of each tranche in each state of nature:

Payoffs to CDO tranches and prices (w/ independent defaults)

		Pool payoff		Senior	Mezzanine	Junior
defaults	Pr(defaults)	$\tilde{\pi}$		π_1	π_2	π_3
0	0.729	300		140	90	70
1	0.243	240		140	90	10
2	0.027	180		140	40	0
3	0.001	120		120	0	0
			Price	131.82	83.40	50.34
			Yield	0.0601	0.0761	0.329

Notes: Pool payoff is $\tilde{\pi} = \mathcal{N}^D \times 40 + \left(3 - \mathcal{N}^D\right) \times 100$, and face values of tranches are $N_1 = 140$ (Senior), $N_2 = 90$ (Mezzanine), and $N_3 = 70$ (Junior).

The price of each tranche is computed as the tranche payoff, averaged across states, discounted at the safe interest rate. For example, the price of the mezzanine tranche is

$$P_M = e^{-0.06}\left(0.729 \times 90 + 0.243 \times 90 + 0.027 \times 40 + 0.001 \times 0\right) = 83.403,$$

and its yield is, $Y_M = -\ln \frac{83.403}{90} = 7.61\%$. Naturally, the sum of the three bond prices, $88.526 \times 3 = 265.58$, is equal to the total value of the three tranches, $131.828 + 83.403 + 50.347 = 265.58$. That is, a CDO doesn't add or destroy value: it is a mere repackaging device, redistributing risks (and returns).

The assumption defaults among names are uncorrelated is unrealistic, as argued in section 14.4.4. We now remove this assumption. We first analyze the special case where default events are *perfectly correlated.* In this case, either the three firms all default (with probability 10%) or none defaults (with probability 90%), such that the payoff matrix can be summarized as follows:

Payoffs to CDO tranches and prices (w/ perfectly correlated defaults)

		Pool payoff		Senior	Mezzanine	Junior
defaults	Pr(defaults)	$\tilde{\pi}$		π_1	π_2	π_3
0	0.9	300		140	90	70
1	0	na		na	na	na
2	0	na		na	na	na
3	0.1	120		120	0	0
			Price	129.96	76.28	59.33
			Yield	0.074	0.165	0.165

Notes: Pool payoff is $\tilde{\pi} = \mathcal{N}^D \times 40 + \left(3 - \mathcal{N}^D\right) \times 100$, and face values of tranches are $N_1 = 140$ (Senior), $N_2 = 90$ (Mezzanine), and $N_3 = 70$ (Junior).

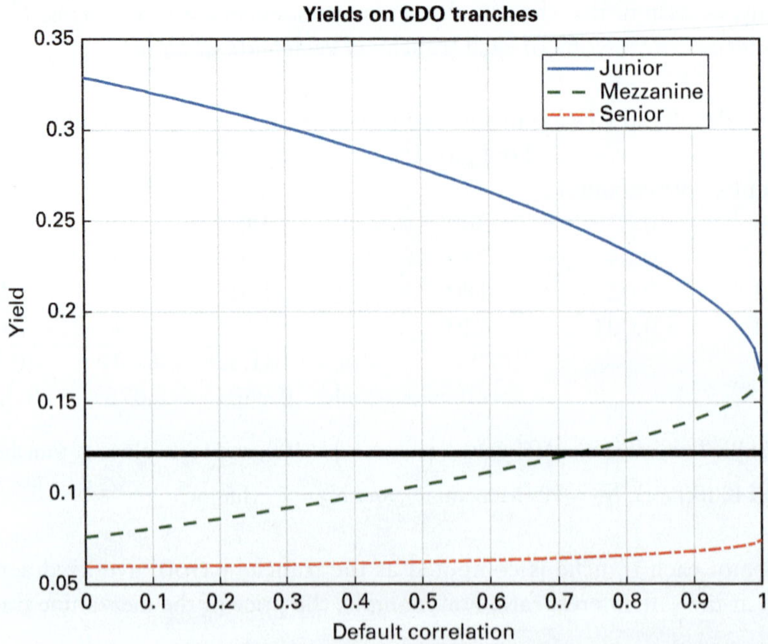

Figure 14.20
The yields on the three CDO tranches, depicted against the default correlation in the assets base, when the probability of default for each name is $p = 10\%$. The thick, horizontal, line is the yield on each securitized asset.

Note that the mezzanine and junior tranches now yield the same, because they each pay off either their nominal value or zero in exactly the same states of nature. In other words, default clustering implies that good times are really good, in that the probability of not having any default is now 90%, which is much higher than the 72.9% probability in the case of zero correlation.

The previous cases (with independent or perfectly correlated defaults) are extreme. When defaults are only imperfectly correlated, pricing becomes analytically more complex, requiring a model of default correlations. We rely on a model known as Gaussian copula (reviewed in appendix 14.H) and simulations (see appendix 14.I). Figure 14.20 depicts the yield on each tranche as a function of the default correlation in the CDO assets base.

"Arbitrage" CDOs Figure 14.20 illustrates how arbitrage CDOs work. The CDO has three assets yielding the same, 12.19% (the horizontal line in the picture). However, by restructuring the assets base through a CDO, we can create claims (senior and mezzanine) that yield less than 12.19%, as they are considerably less risky than the assets base, at least when the default correlation is low enough. In exchange, higher returns are "made available" to the holders of the junior tranche.

Note that this redistribution of risk works when the default correlation is relatively low. As the default correlation in the assets base increases, the situation may change dramatically, with the mezzanine tranche becoming more risky and, then, yielding a higher expected return than the base 12.19%. Finally, figure 14.21 depicts the output of a comparative statics exercise where we increase p from 10% to 20%. The yields are obviously

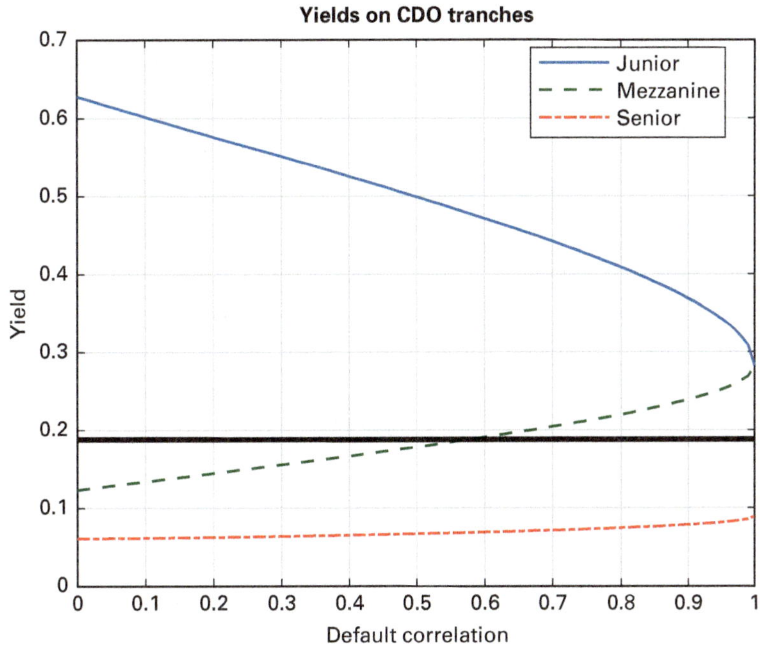

Figure 14.21
The yields on the three CDO tranches, depicted against the default correlation in the assets base, when the probability of default for each name is $p = 20\%$. The thick, horizontal, line is the yield on each securitized asset.

higher for each tranche, and the three assets now yield 18.78%, reflecting a higher marginal probability of default for each of the securities in the pool, p.

Correlation assumptions Figures 14.20 and 14.21 show that the yield on the junior tranche decreases with default correlation. This property follows from the assumption that the probability of default is fixed at $p = 10\%$ for each default correlation ρ (say). As ρ increases, the probability of clustering events increases, which makes the senior and mezzanine tranches relatively less valuable and, hence, the junior tranches more valuable. We shall go back to this property in section 14.4.4. An alternative assumption is that p increases with ρ; this assumption captures the idea that in bad times, both default correlation and default probabilities increase, driven as they should by common factors (e.g., the business cycle).

Accordingly, we replace the assumption that p and ρ are independent while positing that they are tied up through the following relation: $\rho = 3.8116 \times \ln(p+1)$; we vary p from 0.10 to 0.30, such that ρ varies from 0.3633 to 1. Figure 14.22 shows that pricing outcomes may change dramatically: not surprisingly, assumptions on default correlation may be of paramount importance for asset pricing. First, the yields on mezzanine and senior are still increasing in ρ, as ρ is also increasing in the probability of default. Second, the junior tranche has a yield that increases over a wide spectrum of values of ρ. Note that the junior tranche bends back as ρ gets closer to one, reflecting the fact that default clustering makes this tranche very valuable in good times, as explained earlier.

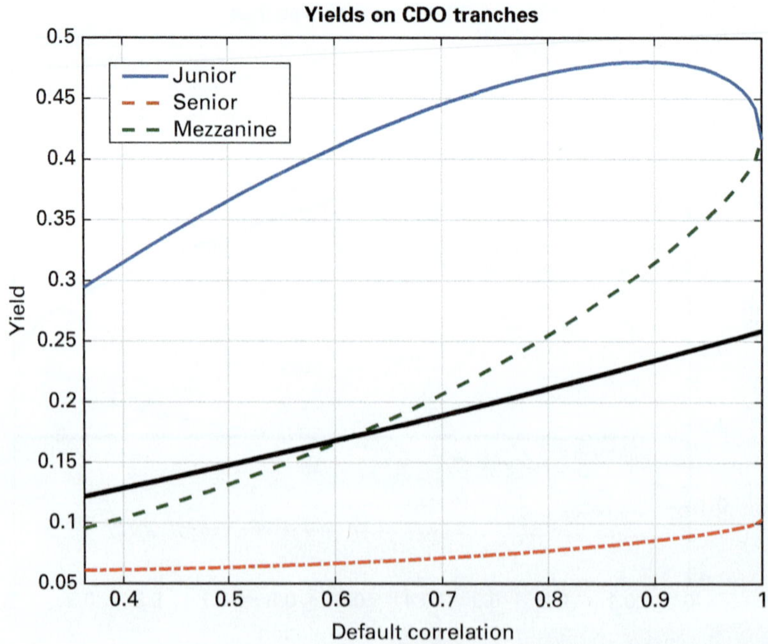

Figure 14.22
The yields on the three CDO tranches, depicted against the default correlation in the assets base, assuming that the default correlation, ρ, is increasing in the default probability, p, through the relation $\rho = 3.8116 \times \ln(p+1)$, $p \in [0.10, 0.30]$. The thick curve depicts the yield on each securitized asset.

14.3.5.5 Nth to default

In this contract, the owner of the first to default bears the risk of the first default that occurs in the asset pool, such that their payoff is:

$$\Pi_1 = \Pr(\mathcal{N}^D \geq 1) \times 40 + \Pr(\mathcal{N}^D < 1) \times 100,$$

where, as usual, $\mathcal{N}^D$ denotes the number of defaulted bonds. Likewise, the owner of the second to default bears the risk of the second default in the asset pool, and their payoff is:

$$\Pi_2 = \Pr(\mathcal{N}^D \geq 2) \times 40 + \Pr(\mathcal{N}^D < 2) \times 100.$$

Finally, the owner of the third to default bears the risk of the third default in the asset pool and their payoff is:

$$\Pi_3 = \Pr(\mathcal{N}^D = 3) \times 40 + \Pr(\mathcal{N}^D < 3) \times 100.$$

Let us assume that default correlation is zero for simplicity. We have already calculated the previous probabilities; they are $\Pr(\mathcal{N}^D \geq 1) = 0.243 + 0.027 + 0.001 = 0.271$, $\Pr(\mathcal{N}^D \geq 2) = 0.027 + 0.001 = 0.028$, and $\Pr(\mathcal{N}^D = 3) = 0.001$, such that the prices of the contracts are

$$P_{1^{st}\text{-to-def}} = e^{-0.06}\,[0.271 \times 40 + (1 - 0.271) \times 100] = 78.863$$

$$P_{2^{nd}\text{-to-def}} = e^{-0.06}\,[0.028 \times 40 + (1 - 0.028) \times 100] = 92.594$$

$$P_{3^{rd}\text{-to-def}} = e^{-0.06}\,[0.001 \times 40 + (1 - 0.001) \times 100] = 94.120$$

and the corresponding yields are $Y_{1^{st}\text{-to-def}} = -\ln(0.78863) = 23.74\%$, $Y_{2^{nd}\text{-to-def}} = -\ln(0.92594) = 7.69\%$, and $Y_{3^{rd}\text{-to-def}} = -\ln(0.94120) = 6.06\%$.

14.3.5.6 Numerical examples regarding stylized structured products

A. Defaultable bonds Suppose we observe the following risk structure of spreads ($s_{0,A}$ and $s_{0,B}$, say) related to two bonds maturing in two years

$$s_{0,A}(2\text{ years}) = 1.5\%, \quad s_{0,B}(2\text{ years}) = 2.5\%,$$

where A and B denote the rating classes the bond issuers belong to. Assume that the one-year transition rating matrix, defined under the risk neutral probability, is:

		To		
		A	B	Def
From	A	0.7	0.3	0
	B	0.3	0.5	0.2
	Def	0	0	1

where "Def" denotes default. We assume that in the event of default, the recovery value of the bond is paid off at the end of the second period. We want to determine the expected recovery rates for the two bonds, and which expected recovery rate is the largest. We have

$$e^{rT}\frac{D_{0,i}}{N} = \left[\text{Rec}_i \mathbb{Q}_i(2) + (1 - \mathbb{Q}_i(2))\right], \quad i \in \{A, B\}.$$

Therefore,

$$s_{0,A}(2\text{ years}) = 1.5\% = -\frac{1}{2}\ln\left[\text{Rec}_A \mathbb{Q}_A(2) + (1 - \mathbb{Q}_A(2))\right] \tag{14.77}$$

$$s_{0,B}(2\text{ years}) = 2.5\% = -\frac{1}{2}\ln\left[\text{Rec}_B \mathbb{Q}_B(2) + (1 - \mathbb{Q}_B(2))\right] \tag{14.78}$$

We have to find $\mathbb{Q}_A(2)$ and $\mathbb{Q}_B(2)$. The transition matrix for two years is

$$\mathbb{Q}(2) = \begin{bmatrix} 0.7 & 0.3 & 0 \\ 0.3 & 0.5 & 0.2 \\ 0 & 0 & 1 \end{bmatrix}\begin{bmatrix} 0.7 & 0.3 & 0 \\ 0.3 & 0.5 & 0.2 \\ 0 & 0 & 1 \end{bmatrix},$$

such that

$$\begin{aligned}\Pr\{\text{A defaults in 2 years}\} &= \mathbb{Q}_A(2) \\ &= \underbrace{0.70 \times 0}_{A\to A\to Def} + \underbrace{0.30 \times 0.20}_{A\to B\to Def} + \underbrace{0 \times 1}_{A\to Def\to Def} \\ &= 0.06\end{aligned}$$

and

$$\begin{aligned}\Pr\{\text{B defaults in 2 years}\} &= \mathbb{Q}_B(2) \\ &= \underbrace{0.20 \times 1}_{B\to Def\to Def} + \underbrace{0.50 \times 0.20}_{B\to B\to Def} + \underbrace{0.30 \times 0}_{B\to A\to Def} \\ &= 0.20 + 0.10 = 0.30.\end{aligned}$$

Hence, using eqs. (14.77)–(14.78), we have

$$\text{Spread}_A\,(2\text{ years}) = 1.5\% = -\frac{1}{2}\ln\left[\text{Rec}_A 0.06 + (1 - 0.06)\right]$$

$$\text{Spread}_B\,(2\text{ years}) = 2.5\% = -\frac{1}{2}\ln\left[\text{Rec}_B 0.30 + (1 - 0.30)\right]$$

Solving, yields

$$\text{Rec}_A = 50.7\%, \quad \text{Rec}_B = 83.7\%.$$

The expected recovery rate for the second bond is the largest. This is because the probability firm B defaults is much larger than the probability firm A defaults and yet the two spreads are relatively close to each other. So to rationalize the two spreads, we need a large recovery rate for the second bond.

What would happen to the two credit spreads, if we assumed that the recovery rates were the same, and equal to 50%? This question sheds additional light to the previous findings. If the recovery rates are the same and both equal 50%,

$$s_{0,A}\,(2\text{ years}) = -\frac{1}{2}\ln\left[0.50\mathbb{Q}_A(2) + (1 - \mathbb{Q}_A(2))\right]$$

$$s_{0,B}\,(2\text{ years}) = -\frac{1}{2}\ln\left[0.50\mathbb{Q}_B(2) + (1 - \mathbb{Q}_B(2))\right]$$

Then, using the previously computed transition probabilities for two years, we obtain:

$$s_{0,A}\,(2\text{ years}) = 1.52\%, \quad s_{0,B}\,(2\text{ years}) = 8.12\%.$$

When the recovery rates are the same, the spread on the second bond diverges substantially from that on the first bond.

B. Collateralized Debt Obligations Let us keep on using the same framework as before, but use different figures, so as to figure out the implications for CDOs pricing. Consider the following one-year transition matrix, under the risk neutral probability:

		To		
		A	B	Def
From	A	0.7	0.3	0
	B	0.1	0.6	0.3
	Def	0	0	1

where the column labeled "Def" identifies the state of default. Consider (i) 1 one-year bond issued by a company rated A, and (ii) 3 one-year bonds issued by a company rated B. Both bonds have face value equal to 100. We assume that the recovery values in case of default of all these bonds are the same, and equal to 50. Finally, we assume the safe interest rate is taken to be equal to zero.

Consider a CDO created out of the previous four bonds. The CDO has nominal value of 400, pays in one year, and has: (i) a senior tranche, with nominal value $N_0 = 150$; (ii) a mezzanine tranche, with nominal value equal to N_1; and (iii) a junior tranche, with nominal value equal to N_2. We assume that the CDO is such that $N_1 > 100$.

First, we determine the price and yields on all the four bonds. Since the safe interest rate is zero, and the company rated A is safe, up to the next year, the price of the A bond is 100, and its yield is zero. As for the three bonds rated B, we have:

$$P_B = 50 \times 0.3 + 100 \times 0.7 = 85.0, \quad Y_B = -\ln 0.85 = 16.25\%.$$

Second, we determine the yield on the junior tranche, and derive the yield on the mezzanine, as a function of its nominal value N_1. To determine the yield on the tranches, consider the following table

$\mathcal{N}^D$	Pr	$\tilde{\pi}$	π_0	π_1	π_2
0	0.7	400	150	N_1	N_2
1	0	na	na	na	na
2	0	na	na	na	na
3	0.3	250	150	100	0
4	4	na	na	na	na

where, as usual, $\mathcal{N}^D$ denotes the number of defaults, $\Pr \equiv \Pr(\mathcal{N}^D)$, $\tilde{\pi}$ is the pool payoff, defined as $\tilde{\pi} = \mathcal{N}^D \times 50 + (4 - \mathcal{N}^D) \times 100$, and, finally, π_0 is the payoff to the senior tranche, π_1 is the payoff to the mezzanine tranche, and, π_2 is the payoff to the junior tranche. Therefore, the tranches are priced as

$$P_{\text{mezz}} = 0.70 \times N_1 + 0.30 \times 100, \quad P_{\text{jun}} = 0.70 \times N_2,$$

such that

$$Y_{\text{mezz}} = -\ln\left(\frac{0.70 \times N_1 + 0.30 \times 100}{N_1}\right) = -\ln\left(0.70 + 0.30 \times \frac{100}{N_1}\right)$$

$$Y_{\text{jun}} = -\ln\left(\frac{0.70 \times N_2}{N_2}\right) = 35.67\%.$$

It is easy to verify that $Y_{\text{mezz}} < Y_{\text{jun}}$.[29]

We now consider the following reverse engineering exercise: to determine the nominal value of the mezzanine tranche N_1 such that the yield on the mezzanine tranche is equal to or greater than the yields on the bonds issued by the firm with credit rating B. The answer is $N_1 = 200$, for in this case, the mezzanine tranche would have the same payoff structure as the bond rated B: it would deliver (i) the face value, in the event the company rated B does not default; and (ii) half of its nominal value, 100, in the event the company rated B does default. A related reverse engineering exercise asks: which nominal value of the mezzanine tranche N_1 is needed to ensure that the yield on the mezzanine is equal to 18%? And, what is the corresponding nominal value of the junior tranche, N_2? To address these problems, note that we want to make sure that the yield on the mezzanine tranche is

$$Y_{\text{mezz}} \equiv -\ln\left(\frac{0.70 \times N_1 + 0.30 \times 100}{N_1}\right) = 18\%.$$

29. This inequality holds because $Y_{\text{jun}} = -\ln(0.70) > -\ln\left(0.70 + 0.30 \times \frac{100}{N_1}\right) = Y_{\text{mezz}}$.

Solving for N_1 yields, $N_1 = 221.78$. Therefore, $N_2 = 400 - N_0 - N_1 = 400 - 150 - 221.78 = 28.22$.

C. CDO: A second example Consider the following one-year transition rating matrix, defined under the risk neutral probability:

		To		
		A	B	Def
From	A	0.9	0.10	0
	B	0.3	0.50	0.2
	Def	0	0	1

We assume that available for trading are one bond rated A and two bonds rated B. The two bonds rated B are issued by the same firm. Each of these three bonds expires in one year, and has a face value of 100. We assume that the recovery rate for each bond is the same, and equal to 50%. Finally, we take the safe, short-term rate equal to zero.

We consider the following stylized CDO, one that pools the bond rated A and the two bonds rated B, and has, then, nominal value equal to 300. The CDO pays off in one year, and has three tranches: (a) a senior tranche, with nominal value N_1 equal to 150; (b) a mezzanine tranche, with nominal value N_2; and (c) a junior tranche with nominal value N_3. Given these assumptions, the prices of the bonds are $P_A = 100$ and $P_B = 50\mathcal{Q} + 100(1 - \mathcal{Q}) = 90$, where we have used the fact that the risk neutral probability of default for the second bond in one year is $\mathcal{Q} = 0.2$.

Suppose we want to set the nominal value of the mezzanine tranche, N_2, such that $N_2 \geq 50$. We wish to determine the price of each tranche, as a function of N_1, N_2 and N_3. Note that the realized pool payoff, Π, say, is $\tilde{\pi} = \mathcal{N}^D \times 50 + (3 - \mathcal{N}^D) \times 100$, with obvious notation. We know the bond rated A will not default. So we may only have that the two bonds rated B may default, if any. Moreover, the two bonds rated B are issued by the same firm such that, if one of these two bonds defaults, the other defaults as well. More generally, we know that with probability 0.2, there will be two defaults, and with probability 0.80, there will be no defaults at all. To summarize, we have the default probabilities in the following table:

$\mathcal{N}^D$	Pr	$\tilde{\pi}$	π_1	π_2	π_3
0	0.8	300	150	N_2	N_3
1	0	na	na	na	na
2	0.2	200	150	50	0
3	0	na	na	na	na

where π_1 is the payoff to the senior tranche, π_2 is the payoff to the mezzanine tranche, and π_3 is the payoff to the junior tranche.

Therefore, the price of the three tranches are: $P_{\text{sen}} = N_1 = 150$, $P_{\text{mezz}} = 0.8N_2 + 0.2 \cdot 50 = 0.8N_2 + 10$, and $P_{\text{jun}} = 0.8N_3$. Let us determine the yields on the junior and mezzanine tranche. The yield on the junior tranche is determined as $Y_{\text{jun}} = -\ln(P_{\text{jun}}/N_3) = -\ln(0.8) = 0.22314$. The yield on the mezzanine tranche cannot be determined before we choose its nominal value N_2:

$$Y_{\text{mezz}} = -\ln\left(\frac{P_{\text{mezz}}}{N_2}\right) = -\ln\left(\frac{0.8N_2 + 10}{N_2}\right).$$

The mezzanine yield is increasing in its face value. Intuitively, the higher N_2, the higher the LGD for this tranche. We can solve for N_2 while taking as given a desired yield on the mezzanine tranche. For example, if $Y_{\text{mezz}} = 12\%$, the nominal value of the junior tranche N_3 is $N_2 = 115.05$, which implies the face value of the junior tranche to be $N_3 = 150 - 115.05 = 34.95$.

14.4 Managing Loan Losses

How do financial institutions hedge against losses that may originate from holding illiquid assets such as a portfolio of loans? Obviously, banks can securitize loans; but the economics of structured finance suggests that hedging through securitization may fail due to moral hazard or adverse selection problems (see chapter 5), as during the 2007 subprime crisis (see section 14.5). Alternatively, how much capital should a bank set apart to cover such expected losses? Understanding and modeling "value at risk" is standard in the equity space. Value at risk became equally standard in the credit space, though the details are more elaborated in this case.

This section provides an introduction to the modeling of loan losses and foundations of risk management. Section 14.4.1 provides discussion regarding the extant regulatory framework; this overview also helps framing procyclicality issues dealt with later in this chapter (see section 14.5). Section 14.4.2 is an introduction to standard risk management tools, tools that are mostly suitable to deal with equity products. Section 14.4.3 surveys the literature regarding systemic risk. Section 14.4.4 deals with the relatively more challenging case of credit risk.

14.4.1 Regulatory Framework

Banks are required to set up capital buffers to guarantee the debt they issue against their risky activities of lending and investing. The Basel Committee on Banking Supervision (BCBS)[30] drafts accords aiming to create an international standard for the capital necessary to cope with these risks, together with rigorous tools for risk measurement and management. Simply, the greater the risk a bank is exposed to, the greater the amount of capital the bank needs to hold to safeguard its solvency, in the interest of overall economic stability. The main issue, then, is to correctly measure this risk.

The first accord of 1988, known as Basel I, focused on minimal capital requirements to cope with *credit risk*, and was enforced by law by the Group of Ten in 1992 and then by more than 100 countries. It relied on the so-called Cooke ratio (after Peter Cooke of the

30. The BCBS is a committee of banking supervisory authorities established by the central bank governors of the Group of Ten countries in 1975. It consists of senior representatives of bank supervisory authorities and central banks from Belgium, Canada, France, Germany, Italy, Japan, Luxembourg, the Netherlands, Spain, Sweden, Switzerland, the United Kingdom, and the United States. It usually meets at its permanent secretariat, located at the Bank for International Settlements in Basel.

Bank of England), a minimum capital adequacy standard of 8% of the total risk-weighted assets. The accord was quite coarse, in that it considered five broad classes of credit risk with which to weigh the assets, which did not discriminate about the credit quality across classes. For example, corporate loans had 100% weighting and loans to OECD countries had zero weighting, independently of the ratings of the borrowing entities.

The first amendment to Basel I occurred in 1996, and aimed to include tools to cope with *market risk*. In 1999, a first consultative paper was drafted on a new accord, known as Basel II. One of the main issues under reform was the "one-size-fits-all" approach of Basel I—the fact that default risk could be substantially lower for some of the assets within the same class of risk in the banks accounts. For example, banks could have securitized the loans with default risk lower than that implied by the flat rate within the same class, and hold those loans with higher default risk. This might have led to an increase in the overall riskiness of financial institutions. In 1998, the Federal Reserve chairman Alan Greenspan pointed to the existence of incentives left to banks to implement regulatory arbitrage:

> Banks arbitrage away inappropriately high capital requirements on their safest assets by removing these assets from the balance sheet via securitization. The issue is not solely whether capital requirements on the bank's residual risk in the securitized assets are appropriate. We should also be concerned with the sufficiency of regulatory capital requirements on the assets remaining on the book. In the extreme, such "cherry picking" would leave on the balance sheet only those assets for which economic capital allocations are greater than the 8 percent regulatory standard. [Greenspan, 1998, 166]

There is a consensus that Basel II did indeed considerably mitigate these issues, by paying more attention to risk sensitivity by means of a more precise set of indications about classes of risk and, also, by distinguishing among credit risk, market risk, and even operational risks.[31] Moreover, the Basel II accords aimed to a flexible supervisory system whereby banks could choose to measure and manage risks by following a "standardized" or an "internal" rating approach. The standardized approach would rely on the ratings supplied by rating agencies approved by national supervisors. Capital incentives would also be available to move toward more advanced, internal approaches, where banks calculate weightings through proprietary models. However, moving from mechanical rules to prop-generated ones requires a particular care as to the quality of the models, which have to be approved by national supervisors.[32] Therefore, Basel II encourages banks to improve their risk measurement and management systems.

Basel II relies on three "pillars," which impose increasingly stringent rules on capital adequacy:

---

31. Operational risk is defined as the risk of losses resulting from inadequate or failed internal processes, people, and systems, or external events. Examples of operational risk include two famous cases of "rogue trading": Nick Leeson, who in 1995 led Barings Bank to bankruptcy, through a loss of £1.3bn, and Jérôme Kerviel, who in 2008 led Société Générale to a loss of €5bn.

32. Note that within the internal rating approach, banks are not allowed to use internal models of credit risk. Banks that have received supervisory approval to use the internal approach may rely on their own internal estimates of risk components in determining the capital requirement for a given exposure. The risk components include: (i) measures of the probability of default, (ii) loss-given-default, (iii) exposure at default, (iv) effective maturity.

Pillar I: Minimal capital requirements. It defines a set of basic rules for measuring credit risk, market risk and operational risks (both "standardized" and "internal").

Pillar II: Supervisory review of capital adequacy. It increases the role of banking supervisors, by setting rules of conduct national supervisors should maintain to ensure that banks have capital adequacy over and above the minimal capital requirements of Pillar I.

Pillar III: Market disclosure. It increases the role of market discipline and disclosure, by relying on the publication of information by banks, relating to issues such as risk measurements, risk-rating processes, or risk management systems.

Pillar I defines a clear separation of three types of risk: (a) credit risk, (b) operational risk, and (c) market risk. The calculation rules rely on the concept of total risk-weighted assets (Total RWA), defined as

$$\text{Total RWA} = \text{Cr} + \text{M\&O},$$

where

$$\begin{aligned}
\text{Cr} &= \text{Risk-weighted assets for } \textit{credit} \text{ risk} \\
\text{M\&O} &= \text{Assets weighted for } \textit{market} \text{ and } \textit{operational} \text{ risk} \\
&= (\text{Capital requirements for } \textit{market} \text{ and } \textit{operational} \text{ risk}) \times \underbrace{12.5}_{=1/0.08}
\end{aligned}$$

For example, the capital requirements for market risk can be determined through VaR models (surveyed in sections 14.4.2 and 14.4.4) and, possibly, additional sophisticated methodologies. It goes beyond the scope of this book to review additional regulatory developments at the time of writing. The (total) minimum capital requirements are taken to be 8% of the total risk-weighted assets,

$$\frac{\text{Regulatory capital}}{\text{Total RWA}} \geq 8\%.$$

One immediate issue arising with Basel II is its heavy reliance on credit rating agencies for what counts as the standardized approach to credit risk. This approach might be misguided due to conflicts of interest between credit rating agencies and the firms whose debt these agencies rate. At the time of writing, rating agencies are mostly unregulated, with the credit risk estimates quality being obviously observable only with lags and, importantly, too late should serious mispricing take place.

A second issue is "procyclicality": in bad times, banks reduce lending, exacerbating the current economic developments, which makes banks reduce lending even further, in a vicious circle. Section 14.5 deals deal with procyclicality issues. The dangers of procyclicality in a regulatory context is that in bad times, when risks intensify, the banking system is given additional burden due to regulatory capital, which might lead to a further lending shrinkage. Basel III introduces a regulatory device that allow to mitigate procyclicality by requiring banks to build up capital buffers in good times with which to cope in adverse times.

Table 14.3
Capital requirements under Basel II and Basel III regimes.

	Capital requirements as a % of the Total RWA	
	Basel II	Basel III
Common equity	2%	4.5%
Tier 1	4%	6%
Total capital	8%	8%
Common equity (conservation)	–	2.5%

After a number of additional consultative papers, national regulators indicated to the Financial Stability Institute (FSI)[33] that they would implement Basel II by 2015. During the process when the European Union was implementing Basel II through its EU Capital Adequacy Directive (CAD III), the global financial crisis following the 2007 subprime events determined a rethinking of Basel II, leading to a new set of rules, known as Basel III. The main innovations of Basel III are summarized by the following points: (i) new capital requirements, such as those summarized in table 14.3, as well as a new mandatory capital conservation buffer of 2.5% of the Total RWA, to face economic stress; (ii) new rules that allow national supervisors to require banks to set up capital up to 2.5% of the Total RWA in times of high credit growth—countercyclical capital buffers; and (iii) a target for the leverage ratio, defined as the ratio of Tier 1 capital (i.e., equity plus reserves minus intangible assets) over total assets net of intangible assets, to be at least 3% ($\frac{\text{Tier 1}}{\text{Assets}} > 3\% \Leftrightarrow \text{Lev} \equiv \frac{\text{Non Tier 1}}{\text{Tier 1}} < \frac{1}{0.03} - 1$), as well as additional liquidity ratios. Table 14.3 summarizes the main differences in capital requirements that Basel III introduces against Basel II.

The next sections provide analytical tools to deal with capital requirements regarding the occurrence of loan losses. We begin with fundamental tools that are relevant in the equity space.

14.4.2 Foundations of Risk Management

This section develops foundational issues arising in the theory and practice of risk management, which relates to assessing and measuring *market risk*, and mostly in the equity space.

14.4.2.1 *Value at risk (VaR)*

Losses related to market risk obviously occur very frequently. However, sometimes these losses may be quite large. Financial history contains many instances of such "financial disasters," some of which related to adverse interest rate movements or an inappropriate use of derivative products. Such episodes occurred well before the subprime crisis; examples

33. The FSI, headquartered by the Bank for International Settlements in Basel, was established in 1999 in response to the Asian crisis of 1997.

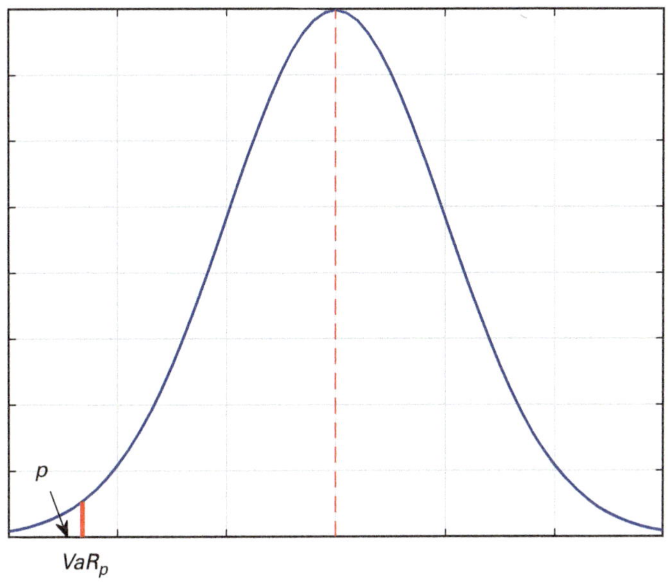

Figure 14.23
This picture depicts the dollar value of value at risk (VaR) for a confidence level equal to $1-p$.

include the Savings and Loans debacle of the 1980s, related to interest rate movements (see chapter 13), Barings Bank collapse, related to equity derivatives (see chapter 11), and other episodes of the early 1990s reviewed by Jorion (2001), including Orange County (interest rates movements) and Metallgesellschaft (oil derivatives), among others. Perhaps due to these episodes, the industry rapidly adopted new tools to monitor and manage market risk, such as the widespread *value at risk* (VaR). VaR measures the "worst" expected loss in a portfolio over a given horizon, under normal market conditions, and at a given confidence level. It also forms the basis for calculations of capital requirements for market risk reviewed in the previous section.

VaR addresses the following concerns. Let ΔV denote the change in value of a given portfolio. We would like to identify the threshold value of ΔV such that we are $(1-p)\%$ certain that the portfolio return shall not be below this threshold over the next 10 weeks, say. Thus, this threshold, denoted as VaR_p, satisfies: $\Pr(\Delta V < \text{VaR}_p) = p$. It is the pth percentile of the distribution of the portfolio change, that is, (minus) the most the portfolio can lose in a given time horizon with confidence level equal to $1-p$. The dollar value of this loss is simply $-\text{VaR}_p$, and is depicted in Figure 14.23.

Equivalently, we normalize this loss by the initial portfolio value, V_0, and define $\text{VaR}_p^r : \Pr(\frac{\Delta V}{V_0} < \text{VaR}_p^r) = p$. Thus, $-\text{VaR}_p^r$ is the highest relative loss that the portfolio may experience over a given time period at a confidence level equal to $1-p$. Naturally, we have: $\text{VaR}_p = \text{VaR}_p^r \cdot V_0$. Suppose, for example, that the portfolio return over the next two weeks is normally distributed with mean zero and unit variance. We know that $0.01 = \Pr(\frac{\Delta V}{V_0} < -2.32)$. Hence, $\text{VaR}_p = -2.32 \cdot V_0$. That is, we are 99% certain that our portfolio will not suffer of a *loss* larger than 2.32 times its current value over the next two weeks. More generally, suppose that the portfolio return over the next two weeks is normally distributed with mean μ and variance σ^2, i.e., $\frac{\Delta V}{V_0} \sim N(\mu, 1)$. Now, assuming $p = 0.01$, and by simple calculations, $\text{VaR}_p^r = \mu - 2.32\sigma$. For example, suppose that $\sigma^2 = \frac{2}{52}\sigma_y^2$, where $\sigma_y^2 = 0.15^2$ is the annualized variance, such that $\sigma \approx 0.03$, $\text{VaR}_p = (\mu - 0.0696)\, V_0$. Assuming that $\mu = 0$, which might be a reasonable assumption over a two-week horizon, $\text{VaR}_p^r \approx -7\%$: we are 99% certain that our portfolio will not suffer of a *loss* larger than 7% times its current value over the next two weeks.

14.4.2.2 *Refinements*

We discuss a few general issues related to VaR (estimation and backtesting), and also review some alternative measures of risk related to it (expected shortfall).

Distributional assumptions We know very well that asset returns are not normally distributed. In previous chapters of this part (e.g., chapter 11), and in part II (e.g., chapter 8), we explain that asset returns exhibit random volatility and are likely to be generated by unobserved factors. Furthermore, data are subject to changes in regimes or other nonlinearities. Particularly important to understand are the typical fat tails that characterize the density of asset returns. These tails define risks that matter when it comes to derivative pricing and risk management, as in the examples of section 14.4.4. Furthermore, security prices may be driven by a variety of market forces that need to be modeled, as in the case of baskets of derivatives. Finally, asset returns may be correlated, and their correlation may change randomly, often being high in bad times. This correlation may be a source of risk that needs to be adequately modeled.

In general, it seems difficult to come up with a set of solid statistical assumptions on asset returns. One possibility is to give up modeling asset returns through parametric models. Nonparametric methods are indeed promising avenues, even if they are also subject to important caveats. Nonparametric methods rely on an old and simple idea, to estimate the data distribution through histograms. Such histograms may readily be used to compute VaR. The reason for referring to these methods as "nonparametric" is that they do not rely on any model: they merely aim at replacing "rough" histograms with "smoothed" ones.[34] To illustrate, suppose we observe a time series of data x_n that is drawn from a given probability law with density $f(x)$. Consider the following estimate of $f(x)$,

$$\hat{f}_N(x) = \frac{1}{N}\sum_{n=1}^{N}\frac{1}{\lambda}K\left(\frac{x - x_n}{\lambda}\right),$$

where N is the sample size, and K is some symmetric function integrating to one. We may think of $\hat{f}_N(x)$ as a smoothed histogram, with window bin equal to λ.

It can be shown that, as N goes to infinity and λ goes to zero at a certain rate, $\hat{f}_N(x)$ converges in probability to $f(x)$, for all x. In principle, then, we may rely on Monte Carlo methods, simulate data out of $\hat{f}_N(x)$, and compute VaR. The caveat is that there are no simple rules to choose the "bandwidth," λ, and the "kernel," K. The choice of λ is notoriously difficult. Furthermore, and unfortunately, the "bias," $\hat{f}_N(x) - f(x)$, tends to be large exactly on the tails of $f(x)$, i.e., the region that we are mostly interested in.

34. Pagan and Ullah (1999) provide an extensive survey of the main properties of these methods.

Nonlinearities Furthermore, *portfolio* returns may exhibit nonlinearities, a likely circumstance in the case of portfolios of derivatives. Consider the value of a portfolio with m assets, $V \equiv \sum_{j=1}^{M} \alpha_i S_i$, where α_i and S_i denote the number and the price of the ith asset in the portfolio. Holding α_i constant, the change in the portfolio return within a given time interval is, simply, a weighted average of all the asset returns,

$$\frac{\Delta V}{V} = \sum_{j=1}^{M} \left(\frac{\alpha_i S_i}{V} \right) \frac{\Delta S_i}{S_i}.$$

The complication arises when the asset prices, S_i, are functions of some underlying state variables or interlinked through no-arb restrictions as, say, in the case of rate-sensitive derivatives. In this case, one would have to rely on factors in order to assess the overall riskiness of a portfolio of fixed income securities. Moreover, it is unlikely that the weights, α_i, are constant when the horizon of the VaR is large, as these weights may change over time, reflecting delta-hedging adjustments. The portfolio riskiness is, then, gauged while having regard to its risk-constituents, which may need to be carefully modeled. Numerical methods (e.g., Monte Carlo simulations) are typically employed for the purpose of implementing backtesting, stress testing and remaining standard statistical analysis.

One alternative to VaR: Expected shortfall VaR is subject to some practical and conceptual difficulties. For example, VaR tells us that for 1% of the time, losses will exceed the VaR figure, but it does not inform us about the magnitude of the loss. One useful complement to VaR is the *expected shortfall* (ES, henceforth), defined as the expected portfolio loss, conditional upon the event this loss has reached a given threshold. ES is attractive for a number of reasons. Note, indeed, that we expect a given measure of risk to satisfy a number of sensible properties. Artzner, Delbaen, Eber, and Heath (1999) note a number of them, and show that VaR does not satisfy the so-called *subadditivity* property, which states that the sum of the risk measures for any two portfolios should be larger than the risk measure for the sum of the two portfolios. Unfortunately, VaR does not satisfy the subadditivity property, which seems to be a contradiction with the principles of diversification. ES does satisfy subadditivity.

In more detail, ES is the expected value of all losses that exceed VaR_p^r, that is, the expected loss in the worst p% cases. If the loss distribution is continuous, the ES is the same as *conditional VaR*, defined as the expected VaR for all confidence levels above $1-p$. That is, and assuming that the portfolio returns distribution, F say, is continuous and differentiable with density f, we have that, for any return r_t, the ES at confidence level $1-p$ is

$$\text{ES}_p = E\left(r_t | \, r_t < \text{VaR}_p^r\right) = \frac{1}{p} \int_{-1}^{F^{-1}(p)} x f(x)\, dx = \frac{1}{p} \int_0^p \text{VaR}_u^r du, \tag{14.79}$$

where the second equality follows by the definition, $\text{VaR}_u^r = F^{-1}(u)$, for all $u \in [0, 1]$, and the second by the same definition and the change of variables $u = F(x)$. Eq. (14.79) may be generalized. Consider the following measure of risk, the ES corresponding to a drop of C%,

$$\text{ES}(\text{C}) \equiv E(r_t | \, r_t < \text{C}). \tag{14.80}$$

Section 14.4.3 builds upon this measure of risk while reviewing measures of *systemic* risk.

14.4.2.3 *Backtesting*

How do we ascertain whether VaR estimates have performed well in the past? How often did past losses exceed the reference period VaR calculated at, say, 99% confidence? Very simply, if the exceptions occur more than 1% of the time, there is evidence that the models leading to VaR estimates are "misspecified."[35] Backtesting, then, works as follows. Suppose the models leading to VaR are well-specified. By construction, the probability the VaR number is exceeded in any reference period is p, where p is the coverage rate for the VaR. Next, we go to our sample, which we assume comprises N days, and calculate the number of days the VaR is exceeded, M say. We wish to test whether the number of exceptions we observe is consistent, in statistical terms, with the expected number of exceptions based on VaR. For example, we could have observed a number of exceptions larger than expected, i.e., $M > pN$. We would like to test whether this circumstance was due to sample variability, rather than model misspecification.

A simple one-tail test relies on the theoretical probability that, in N days, the VaR is exceeded on more than M days. Assuming exceptions are binomially distributed, this probability is

$$\Pi_p(M,N) = \sum_{k=M}^{N} \frac{N!}{k!\,(N-k)!} p^k (1-p)^{N-k}.$$

Therefore, we can say the following. If, given M and N, we have that $\Pi_p(M,N) \leq 5\%$ (say), we reject the hypothesis that the probability of exceptions is p at the 95% level: the models we are using are misspecified. If, instead, $\Pi_p(M,N) > 5\%$, we cannot reject the hypothesis that the probability of exceptions is p at the 95% level: we can't say the models we are using are misspecified. This and additional tests are reviewed in more detail by Christoffersen (2003, chap. 8) and Hull (2007, chap. 8).

14.4.2.4 *Stress testing*

Stress testing allows one to generate artificial data from a range of possible *scenarios*. These scenarios help identify a range of factors that have the potential to create extraordinary losses or gains in trading portfolios, or to make the control of risk in those portfolios very difficult. These factors include low-probability events in all major types of risks, including the various components of credit, market, and operational risks. Stress scenarios need to shed light on the impact of such events on positions that display both linear and nonlinear price characteristics (i.e., options and instruments that have options-like characteristics).

Scenarios may be created by simulating (i) shocks that, although rare or even absent from the historical database at hand, are likely to happen anyway; and (ii) shocks leading to structural breaks and/or smooth transition in the data generating mechanism. One possible example is to set the percentage changes in all market variables in the portfolio equal to

35. Chapter 6 provides the standard definitions of model misspecification (see section 6.2).

the worst percentage changes that occurred ten days in a row during the subprime crisis of the late 2000s. Consider the following example, known as *historical simulation*. Let v_t the value of some market variable i in day t in our sample, where $t=0,\cdots,T$ (say). We may generate T scenarios for the next day, $T+1$, as follows.

- 1st scenario: each variable grows by the same amount it grew at time 1, $v_{T+1}=v_T\cdot\frac{v_1}{v_0}$.
- ⋯ tth scenario: each variable grows by the same amount it grew at time t, $v_{T+1}=v_T\cdot\frac{v_t}{v_{t-1}}$.
- Tth scenario: each variable grows by the same amount it grew at time T, $v_{T+1}=v_T\cdot\frac{v_T}{v_{T-1}}$.

The T scenarios are generated for all the market variables, which gives rise to an artificial multivariate sample of T observations. We can use this sample for many purposes, including VaR. Christoffersen (2003) and Hull (2007) provide additional details and extensions regarding stress testing and historical simulation.

14.4.3 Measures of Systemic Risk

A critical aspect of the global financial crisis of the late 2000s regarded the amplification mechanisms resulting from the impairment of large financial institutions (see section 14.5). In response to the crisis, the BCBS revised its capital adequacy measure recommendations along several dimensions, including *systemic risk*: the impact that a bank failure may exert on the global financial system and the wider economy, not only the risk that a single failure may occur.

The failure of certain banks may, indeed, entail too many externalities on the overall economy, due to factors such as the banks' size, interconnectedness, cross-jurisdictional activity, the complexity of the products dealt with (e.g., fixed income or other over-the-counter products) or, simply, lack of substitutability. To mitigate the likelihood of such failures, the BCBS recommends dedicated capital requirements that are based on the previous factors. Table 14.4 displays the list of Global Systemically Important Banks (G-SIBs) as of November 2019, as identified by the Financial Stability Board (FSB)[36] in consultation with the BCBS and national authorities. This list comprises 5 "buckets," where each represents the degree of systemic importance, with the 5th bucket identifying the highest degree. To each bucket corresponds a capital requirement rule (in parenthesis).

The list in table 14.4 is updated once a year. The academic literature complements this list throughout a series of indicators that are based on real-time market data. Consider, first, some preliminary estimate of the impact of a widespread shock (i.e., on the market) onto a single asset return. The *marginal expected shortfall* (MES) is a gauge of this impact based on (14.80) and is defined as:

$$\mathrm{MES}_{it}(C)\equiv E_{t-1}\left(r_{it}|\,r_{mt}<C\right).$$

36. The FSB provides policy recommendations about the global financial system while coordinating national financial authorities and international standard-setting bodies. It superseded the Financial Stability Forum (FSF) in April 2009, and comprises all G20 major economies, FSF members, and the European Commission. It is located at the Bank for International Settlements in Basel.

Table 14.4
List prepared by the FSB in 2019. The numbers in parentheses indicate requirements regarding additional common equity loss absorbency to be borne by each G-SIB in its bucket, expressed as a percentage of its risk-weighted assets.

Global Systemically Important Banks (G-SIBs)		
Bucket 5 (3.5%)	**Bucket 2 (1.5%)**	**Bucket 1 (1.0%)**
(Empty)	Bank of America	Agr. Bank of China
	Bank of China	Bank of New York Mellon
	Barclays	China Construction Bank
	BNP Paribas	Credit Suisse
	Deutsche Bank	Groupe BPCE
	Goldman Sachs	Groupe Crédit Agricole
	Ind. & Comm. Bank of China	ING Bank
	Mitsubishi UFJ FG	Mizuho FG
	Wells Fargo	Morgan Stanley
		Royal Bank of Canada
Bucket 4 (2.5%)		Santander
J.P. Morgan Chase		Société Générale
		Standard Chartered
Bucket 3 (2.0%)		State Street
Citigroup		Sumitomo Mitsui FG
HSBC		Toronto Dominion
		UBS
		UniCredit

It is the expected loss for some generic asset-i given that the market has dropped by $-C\%$.

Given MES, a *systemic risk measure* (SRISK) is the capital shortfall (if any) that occurs when, in a time of crisis, the market drops by more than $-C\%$, i.e.,

$$\text{SRISK}_{it}(C) \equiv \max\{0, \text{CS}_{it}(C)\},$$

where, and assuming that debt market value is unchanged over a reference period, and cannot be renegotiated in case of market distress, $\text{CS}_{it}(C)$ denotes the capital shortfall for a financial institution i, expected for a day $t+1$, and given the information available at time t, namely

$$\begin{aligned}\text{CS}_{i,t-1}(C) &\equiv E_{t-1}\left(-\text{Capital-buffer}_{it} \middle| r_{mt} < C\right)\\ &\equiv -E_{t-1}\left(W_{it} - \kappa\left(D_{it} + W_{it}\right) \middle| r_{mt} < C\right)\\ &= \kappa E_{t-1}\left(D_{it} \middle| r_{mt} < C\right) - (1-\kappa) E_{t-1}\left(W_{it} \middle| r_{mt} < C\right)\\ &= \kappa D_{it} - (1-\kappa)\left(1 + \text{MES}_{it}(C)\right) W_{i,t-1},\end{aligned}$$

and D_{it} is debt, W_{it} is equity and, finally, κ is a regulatory capital buffer ratio (e.g., $\kappa = 8\%$). One may now aggregate SRISK across B financial institutions and obtain the following aggregate gauge of risk measure:

$$\text{SRISK}_t(C) = \sum_{i=1}^{B} \text{SRISK}_{it}(C).$$

This gauge has been proposed by Brownlees and Engle (2017) and used by Acharya, Engle, and Richardson (2012). It is increasing in the aggregate leverage. Note that both MES and SRISK link to the comovements of the banks returns with the market.

Adrian and Brunnermeier (2016) consider alternative definitions of systemic risk, by linking them to a number of notions of tail dependence in the statistical literature. One particularly useful notion is CoVaR for a financial institution-i, defined as its VaR conditional upon some event $\mathbb{C}(r_{jt})$ regarding the asset return of some other institution-j, that is,

$$\text{CoVaR}_p^{i|\mathbb{C}(r_{jt})} : \Pr\left(r_{it} \leq \text{CoVaR}_p^{i|\mathbb{C}(r_{jt})} \middle| \mathbb{C}(r_{jt}) \right) = p.$$

For example, $\mathbb{C}(r_{jt})$ may be the event that the return-j hits its VaR, leading to the following definition

$$\text{CoVaR}_p^{i|j} : \Pr\left(r_{it} \leq \text{CoVaR}_p^{i|j} \middle| r_{jt} \leq \text{VaR}_p^j \right) = p,$$

where VaR_p^j denotes VaR for institution-j at level of confidence equal to $1-p$.

We may, then, define *delta-CoVaR*, as the portion of systemic risk of institution-i that can be attributed to institution-j as

$$\Delta\text{CoVaR}_p^{i,j} \equiv \text{CoVaR}_p^{i|j} - \text{CoVaR}_p^{i|r_{jt}=\text{VaR}_{0.50}^j}. \tag{14.81}$$

Note that $\text{VaR}_{0.50}^j$ is the median return of institution-j. Thus, delta-CoVaR may be interpreted as the incremental distress of institution-i when institution-j losses are higher than justified by normal market circumstances. Interestingly, eq. (14.81) may be employed to define financial distress for a set of institutions. To illustrate, we may define delta-CoVaR for the market, $\Delta\text{CoVaR}_p^{m,j}$, that is, the aggregate market drop that is attributable to institution-j being in financial distress.

14.4.4 Credit Risk, Correlation, and Loss Probabilities

14.4.4.1 Value at Risk

We may rely on VaR and assess and manage credit risk. However, VaR is conceptually challenging in the credit space, as it requires a thorough understanding of default risk, which is more difficult to model than market risk. In the credit space, we need to be able to generate and simulate rare events. Importantly, we need to model credit risk for a portfolio of loans, where default events may well be correlated. The input to the model reviewed in this section is the probability of default for a given name, which can be estimated through the models in section 14.2. Note, however, that this estimate is under the risk neutral probability and may, thus, be too conservative of the capital at risk involved into a portfolio of loans.

Default correlation is a key issue. In practice, defaults among names and loans are likely to be correlated due to many reasons. First, names or loans may be linked through direct relationships or, more generally, network effects. Second, the firms' economic performance may be driven by common factors. The model in this section is a one-factor model, originally developed by Vasicek (1987), and is at the heart of Basel II capital requirements. The model deals with correlations relying on the so-called copulae functions, a convenient statistical framework succinctly described in appendix 14.H. The model works as follows. Define the variable

$$z_i = \sqrt{\rho} F + \sqrt{1-\rho}\epsilon_i, \tag{14.82}$$

where F is a common factor among names in the portfolio of loans, ϵ_i is an idiosyncratic term, and $F \sim N(0,1)$, $\epsilon_i \sim N(0,1)$. As further explained in appendix 14.I, $\rho \geq 0$ is a coefficient that captures default correlation among the names.

Next, assume that the *physical* probability each firm defaults by T is the same for each firm and is given by $\Phi(\zeta_{\mathrm{PD}}) \equiv \mathrm{PD}$, where PD is the probability of default, and Φ is the cumulative distribution of a standard normal variable. That is, by time T, each firm defaults any time that

$$z_i < \zeta_{\mathrm{PD}} \equiv \Phi^{-1}(\mathrm{PD}),$$

where Φ^{-1} denotes the inverse of Φ. A simple economic interpretation of eq. (14.82) is that z_i is a shock hitting the value of a firm, and that this firm defaults whenever the shock value hits some exogenously given barrier ζ_{PD}.

Conditional upon the realization of the macroeconomic factor F, the probability of default for each firm is

$$p(F) \equiv \Pr(\mathrm{Default}|\, F) = \Phi\left(\frac{\Phi^{-1}(\mathrm{PD}) - \sqrt{\rho} F}{\sqrt{1-\rho}}\right). \tag{14.83}$$

By the law of large numbers, $p(F)$ is a good approximation to the default rate for a portfolio comprising a large number of assets falling within the same class of risk.

This conditional probability is decreasing in F: the higher the realization of the "common macroeconomic factor," the smaller the probability each firm defaults. Hence, we can always find values of F such that $p(F)$ is equal to any arbitrary value. Moreover, the probability F is larger than $-\Phi^{-1}(x)$ is just x:

$$\Pr\left(F > -\Phi^{-1}(x)\right) = \Pr\left(-F < \Phi^{-1}(x)\right) = \Phi\left(\Phi^{-1}(x)\right) = x.$$

Then, with probability x, the default rate will not exceed

$$\mathrm{VaR}_{\mathrm{Cr-Risk}}(x) = \Phi\left(\frac{\Phi^{-1}(\mathrm{PD}) + \sqrt{\rho}\Phi^{-1}(x)}{\sqrt{1-\rho}}\right). \tag{14.84}$$

Basel II sets $x = 0.999$ and, accordingly, imposes a capital requirement proportional to

$$\mathrm{LGD} \times \left(\mathrm{VaR}_{\mathrm{Cr-Risk}}(0.999) - \mathrm{PD}\right) \times \mathcal{M},$$

where $\mathcal{M}$ denotes some maturity adjustment. Note that this requirement is based on the difference $\mathrm{VaR}_{\mathrm{Cr-Risk}}(0.999) - \mathrm{PD}$, rather than just $\mathrm{VaR}_{\mathrm{Cr-Risk}}$, for the following reason. First, note that $\mathrm{VaR}_{\mathrm{Cr-Risk}}(x) = \mathrm{PD}$ for $\rho = 0$ and that $\mathrm{VaR}_{\mathrm{Cr-Risk}}(x)$ increases with ρ.

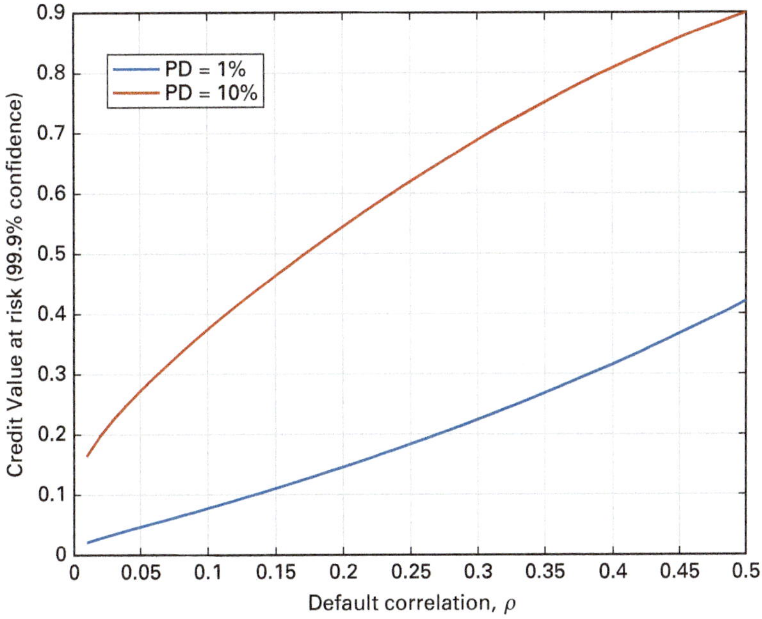

Figure 14.24
This picture depicts values of the "Credit value at risk" in eq. (14.84) as a function of default correlation ρ and two values for PD equal to 1% and 10%.

Figure 14.24 illustrates that this property may be quantitatively important, leading to considerable capital requirements for sufficiently high levels of default correlation. Basel II, then, targets capital *in excess* of the 99.9% worst-case loss over the expected idiosyncratic loss, PD, as well functioning capital markets should already discount the idiosyncratic losses.

An important issue concerns the estimate of ρ. Basel II requires banks rely on a formula for which ρ is inversely related to PD, a formula based on some empirical research (see Lopez, 2004): for a firm which becomes less creditworthy, the PD increases and its probability of default becomes less affected by market conditions. Finally, Basel II requires banks to compute a maturity adjustment factor that takes into account the fact that the longer the maturity the more likely it is a given name might eventually migrate toward a more risky asset class.

14.4.4.2 Fraction of defaulting loans

We ask: What is the probability that a fraction of loans will default? Note that, conditional on the realization of the macroeconomic factor F, defaults are obviously independent, being then driven by the idiosyncratic terms ϵ_i in eq. (14.82). Given N loans, and the realization of the macroeconomic factor F, these defaults are binomially distributed as:

$$\Pr\left(\text{No of defaults} = n \middle| F\right) = \binom{N}{n} p\,(F)^n\,(1 - p\,(F))^{N-n},$$

where $p(F)$ is as in eq. (14.83). Therefore, the unconditional probability of n defaults is:

$$\Pr\left(\text{No of defaults} = n\right) = \int_{-\infty}^{\infty} \Pr\left(\text{No of defaults} = n \middle| F\right) \phi(F)\, dF,$$

where ϕ denotes the standard normal density. This formula provides a valuable tool of analysis in risk management.

Next, we want to determine the probability density of the fraction of defaulting loans for large portfolios. Let ω denote the *fraction* of defaulting loans. For a large portfolio of loans, $\omega = p(F)$, such that:

$$\Pr(\omega \leq x) = \int_{-\infty}^{\infty} \Pr(\omega \leq x | F)\, \phi(F)\, dF = \int_{-\infty}^{\infty} \mathbb{I}_{p(F) \leq x} \phi(F)\, dF = \Phi\left(F^*\right), \tag{14.85}$$

where, due to eq. (14.83), F^* satisfies $-F^* : x = p(-F^*) = \Phi\left(\frac{\Phi^{-1}(\text{PD}) + \sqrt{\rho} F^*}{\sqrt{1-\rho}}\right)$. Solving for F^* leaves

$$F^* = \frac{\sqrt{1-\rho}\,\Phi^{-1}(x) - \Phi^{-1}(\text{PD})}{\sqrt{\rho}}.$$

It is the threshold value taken by the macroeconomic factor that guarantees a frequency of defaults ω less than x. Replacing F^* into eq. (14.85) delivers the cumulative distribution function for ω. The density function $f(x)$ for the frequency of defaults is then

$$f(x) = \sqrt{\frac{1-\rho}{\rho}}\, e^{\frac{1}{2}\left(\Phi^{-1}(x)\right)^2 - \frac{1}{2\rho}\left(\sqrt{1-\rho}\,\Phi^{-1}(x) - \Phi^{-1}(\text{PD})\right)^2}. \tag{14.86}$$

Figure 14.25 plots densities of default frequencies under different assumptions on default correlation. Note that, as ρ increases, density masses shift toward the extremes. This property is due to the "clustering" phenomenon already encountered in section 14.3.5: when the loans in a portfolio become more and more correlated, the portfolio performance is subject to some polarization, and becomes either quite good or quite poor. Naturally, all densities are such that the average default frequency, $E(\omega) = \text{PD}$. However, the tail behavior of these densities differs according to the level of default correlation. Securities that have a nonlinear payoff may be highly sensitive to the assumption on correlation. Pricing these securities while relying on only the first moment of the loss distribution may lead to a perceived, but wrong, sense of security. We shall return to this model and further examples in section 14.5.

Finally, note that we can generalize this model to one where the asset value of the firm, Z_i, is given by a multifactor model

$$Z_i = \sum_{j=1}^{K} \beta_{i,j} Y_j + \epsilon_i,$$

and, accordingly, interpret the event of default as that occurring as soon as $Z_i < \zeta_{\text{PD},i}$, where $\zeta_{\cdot,i}$ can now change across firms. Schönbucher (2003, chap. 10) provides an early survey on many additional details regarding these models.

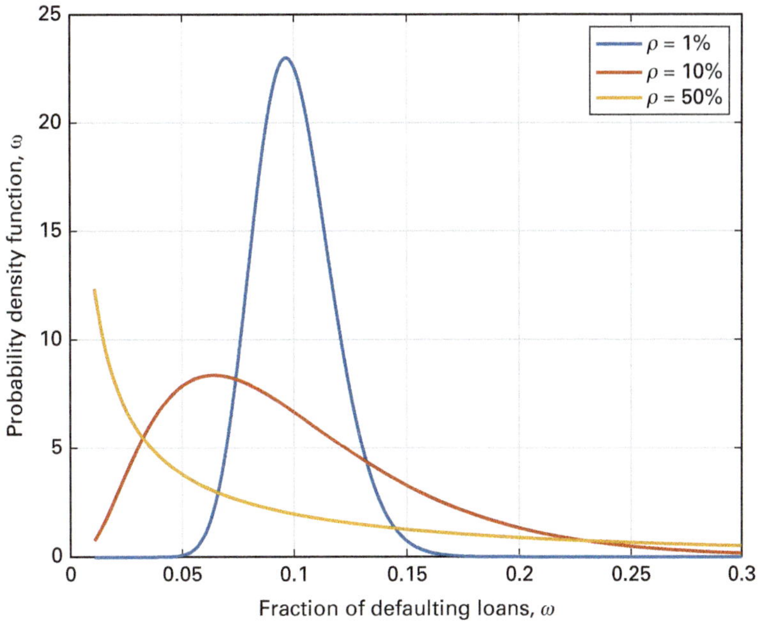

Figure 14.25
This picture depicts the probability density of the fraction of defaulting loans, $f(x)$ in eq. (14.86) under different assumptions on default correlation, i.e., for ρ equal to 1%, 10% and 50%.

14.5 The Global Financial Crisis of the Late 2000s

14.5.1 Credit Bubbles, Procyclicality, and "Quantitative Easing"

Credit risk is a very subtle space and its binary nature may lead to violent repricing and sudden losses. During summer 2007, the US financial system began to experience losses in credit-related products. While these losses seemed to be relatively small, they were perceived to be conducive to readjustments in the main architecture of this market. How is it that some relatively small losses had the power to lead to such important developments as the 2007–2009 crisis? After all, the initial losses did not amount to substantially more than one trillion US dollars. Note that these episodes were equally devastating regarding their effects on the real sphere of the economy, which experienced one of the deepest recessions since World War II, the "Great Recession." Finally, this crisis and its effects on real economic activity spread around the world. We refer to these episodes of the late 2000s as the global financial crisis.

The global financial crisis and its recovery rely on tightly concatenated events. First, the subprime crisis erupted in 2007. Second, and due to amplification mechanisms, the crisis turned into a systemic event: while the amount of losses was initially small, the very same losses were likely to be borne by a "shadow banking system." The uncertainty was that you did not properly understand the nature of your counterparty risk. The whole payment and settlement system was endangered. A global asset sell-off followed, feeding itself through an amplification mechanism, and leading, de facto, to a shutdown of financial markets, a credit crunch, with very quick spillovers into an already compromised economic activity.

Monetary authorities had to implement unconventional policies in order to deal with the intricate problems of the time.

We now provide some additional details of these mechanisms, before dealing with them in more detail in sections 14.5.2 through 14.5.5.

14.5.1.1 *The beginning of the crisis*

The crisis erupted during summer 2007, when investors reported losses in subprime-related products. Section 14.5.2 explains the mechanics of this crisis. Understanding its origins requires reviewing the investment climate leading up to the crisis. Since the 2001 recession, the Federal Reserve had conducted a policy of very low interest rates, as reviewed in the previous chapter. The Great Moderation, i.e., the historical period since 1982 characterized by low volatility in the real economic aggregates (see chapter 8) seemed to have left the investment community with the idea that financial markets were also going through a persistent regime with low volatility. Low interest rates and low volatility are strong incentives to financial innovation. As explained in the introduction, the innovation of the 2000s was in the credit space, and was particularly focused on mortgage-based securities.

Now, mortgage-based securities may not raise any particular issue if only they could be originated and, then, distributed through an informationally efficient market. But the products were mispriced, due to moral hazard problems, as well as additional institutional and technical details illustrated in section 14.5.2. The task of section 14.5.2 is to describe the main institutional details at the heart of the subprime crisis.

14.5.1.2 *Amplification*

The 2007 subprime crisis was sustained and, then, amplified by adverse selection mechanisms and by "procyclicality." Adverse selection was at play because investors were unable to know which institutions were involved in losses: lending money to potentially distressed institutions is prohibitive, especially in the absence of risk appetite. Risk appetite was indeed low at the time, due to many institutional constraints. For example, VaR constraints led institutions to "err on the conservative side"—notably, to sell into a depressed and volatile environment. Note that these constraints may be endogenous: the more volatile the environment, the more aggressive the sell-off may be, leading to additional volatility. In extreme cases, no buyers for any distressed products were available. These circumstances contributed to hinder price discovery and, hence, an ordered repricing of initially mispriced products.

Section 14.5.3 explains the general drop in the markets (not simply the collapse of the subprime market) through procyclicality: a trend in asset prices feeds an automatic mechanism, which, in turn, reinforces the asset price trend, thereby creating a feedback loop between the asset price trend and the mechanism. Under these circumstances, the equilibria are very different from the equilibria arising without such automatic mechanisms—and no equilibrium may even exist in the first place.

The mechanisms are automatic in that, once in place, they are not under control of any decision makers. Examples of procyclicality have been given throughout the whole book. For example, chapter 11 explains that procyclical hedging strategies may well have been at the origins of the Black Monday crash of October 19, 1987, and reviews many other similar episodes (see section 11.10). Chapter 9 deals with perhaps one of the oldest examples of procyclicality, which is more closely related to the topics studied in this section: the *financial accelerator*, that is, the amplification of business cycles due to capital market frictions (see section 9.11). The financial accelerator mechanism is fed through agency problems, which tend to worsen financial markets conditions and, then, the market support to the economy, which further deteriorates economic conditions, in a vicious circle.

Section 14.5.3 develops some simple models by which procyclicality results due to balance sheet effects originated by financial intermediaries. These models are similar in spirit to the balance sheet capacity models in chapter 9 (see section 9.11). For example, intermediaries may have concerns regarding their capital structure. Thus, following a negative shock hitting the assets in the balance sheet, banks need to restore their Tier 1 and Tier 2 capital (in short, their "top-tier capital") and leverage ratios. In the short run, banks cannot raise fresh capital and, thus, need to cash in by selling some of their assets. These sales create a vicious feedback loop whereby banks sell assets, contributing to a further drop in the assets' value, triggering further sales into a depressed market.[37] In some cases, this loop leads to a complete market dry-up: a liquidity shock may be amplified in a way to turn into a "liquidity black hole," in which no prices may clear the markets.

14.5.1.3 Credit crunch and QE

These markets may contribute to amplify some initial loss in the banking system, and ultimately lead to a dramatic lending shrinkage, a credit crunch. Section 14.5.4 discusses the monetary policy implemented in an attempt to mitigate the credit crunch during this crisis. A standard policy action to mitigate adverse developments (i.e., a recession) is to target low interest rates in the interbank markets for mandatory reserves. However, the cost of capital that matters to a recovery in economic activity is that faced by firms when demanding new funds to banks (through loans) and/or the market (through issuance of corporate bonds). In these episodes, this cost can be substantially higher than the interest rates targeted by the monetary authority. Firms had meager prospects, faced substantial uncertainty, and had severely hit collateral. We know from chapter 9 (see section 9.11) that a reduced collateral may be conducive to higher loan rates and also contribute to a credit crunch. It is a *borrower*-induced channel, in the language of macroeconomics with financial frictions; but chapter 9 also reviews explanations based on additional *lender*-induced channels, whereby a credit crunch goes hand in hand with an increase in the cost of capital faced by firms: banks with reduced capital require higher compensation for their risky activity.

Quantitative easing is an unconventional policy action, whereby monetary authorities engage in the purchase of some of the assets held by banks (including the most illiquid ones), so as to give banks incentives to start lending again. The dark side of QE is that it may lead to "distorted" prices. When credit becomes abundant, asset prices may be

37. Brunnermeier and Pedersen (2009) consider a model by which liquidity spirals may occur through margins: when price fall, margins increase, which reduces asset demands, inducing procyclicality. In their model, asset prices may be discontinuous in the exogenous shocks, a property the authors refer to as "fragility."

overpriced. Section 14.5.5 concludes this section and provides a discussion regarding the extent to which this unconventional policy may lead to bubbles.

14.5.2 The 2007 Subprime Crisis

Underlying the 2007 subprime crisis is an explosive mixture of a number of factors. One of these factors relates to institutional details: MBS securities were traded through a "shadow banking system" that escaped the official financial community, including supervisors. The market architecture underlying the trading of these securities relied on institutions with a high asset-liability duration mismatch and, accordingly, high liquidity risks. These risks carried a high potential for market failures. Moreover, the exposure of financial institutions to these risks was not properly understood in the marketplace.

A second factor is model misspecification. There is substantial evidence of moral hazard regarding mortgage origination[38] and final investors might have inadvertently acquired more exposure than desired in this space. There are many hints at concrete instances of model misspecification at the time. Investors used to rely on evaluation frameworks that incorporated unrealistic assumptions, such as stability of delinquencies, reliance on expected (linear) actuarial losses (not tail risk losses), or generous risk-aversion and liquidity adjustments.

Tail risk may be particularly relevant to the pricing of nonlinear products when default correlation is high. Consider the following stylized example, a large pool of loans with face value equal to 100, distributed through two tranches: a senior tranche with face value N_1 and a junior tranche with face value $100 - N_1$. We assume the market is risk neutral and that the safe interest rate is equal to zero. The pool payoff is $\tilde{\pi} \equiv 100 - \text{LGD} \cdot \omega$, where ω denotes the fraction of defaulted loans. The senior tranche payoff is given by

$$\pi_1 \equiv \min\{N_1, \tilde{\pi}\} = N_1 - \text{LGD} \cdot (\omega - \omega^*)^+, \quad \omega^* \equiv \frac{100 - N_1}{\text{LGD}}.$$

Accordingly, the price of the senior tranche is

$$E(\pi_1) = N_1 - \text{LGD} \cdot \int_{\omega^*}^{1} (\omega - \omega^*) f(\omega)\, d\omega, \tag{14.87}$$

where $f(\cdot)$ denotes the probability density of the fraction of defaulting loans.

Eq. (14.87) shows that tail risk matters. If $f(\cdot)$ has thick tails, loan losses may erode the senior tranche payoff. Accordingly, the price of the senior tranche should reflect this tail risk. Figure 14.26 plots the yield on the senior tranche, $-100 \ln \frac{E(\pi_1)}{N_1}$, based on the one-factor model of section 14.4.4, i.e., the density function $f(\cdot)$ in (14.86). The yield on the senior tranche increases with default correlation, reflecting the thick tail of $f(\cdot)$ in case of high default correlation (see figure 14.25).

Model misspecification may, then, be crucial. If you assume correlation is low, when it is not, you pay more for a senior, "safe" tranche than you should, and your losses may be more severe than you would have initially expected. The example in figure 14.26 leads to relatively low yields, as in the examples in section 14.3.5 (see figures 14.20 and

38. See Keys, Mukherjee, Seru, and Vig (2010).

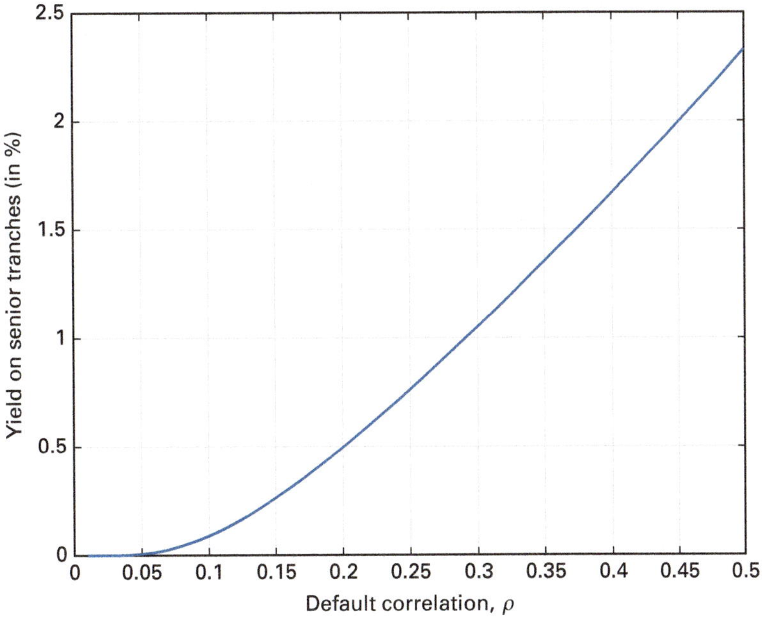

Figure 14.26
This picture depicts the yield on the senior tranche, $-100\ln\frac{E(\pi_1)}{N_1}$ in eq. (14.87), as a function of the default correlation in the asset base, based on the loss density given by eq. (14.86) and the following assumptions: $N_1=80$, PD = 10% and LGD = 80.

14.21), but the point may become even more relevant for other types of tranching that include mezzanine. This point helps us understand the importance of model misspecification, where investors relied on an inappropriate rating "mapping" system: during the structuring process described in section 14.3.5, rating agencies tended to rate structured products based on MBS, by using rating systems previously designed to assess corporate risks. Corporate risk has a much simpler nature than CDO risk, where tail risk plays a critical role. Finally, note that the model we are relying on in this section may not be particularly suitable for achieving the simultaneous scope of risk management and pricing, unless we consider risk neutrality to be a safe assumption. Reduced risk appetite should command a premium and shift probability masses toward the right and make tail risk more heavily discounted.

Default correlation is not easy to estimate. However, figure 14.27 shows delinquencies were actually traveling fast over the relatively newly created subprime mortgages. In retrospect, this informal piece of evidence might have helped predict an imminent crisis in the mortgage market. One additional reason default correlation might have been underestimated at the time of deal origination concerns the process of deterioration in economic conditions. This deterioration might have been due to poor macroeconomic performance, but also to poor performance of the ultimate mortgage borrowers. To illustrate, past data suggested a weak correlation between regional mortgages, which made investors perceive a sense of "diversification." However, the housing market grinding to a halt turned up to be a nationwide phenomenon. And the wide increase in interest rates at the time (discussed for example in chapter 13; see section 13.3) was leading to more clustered defaults.

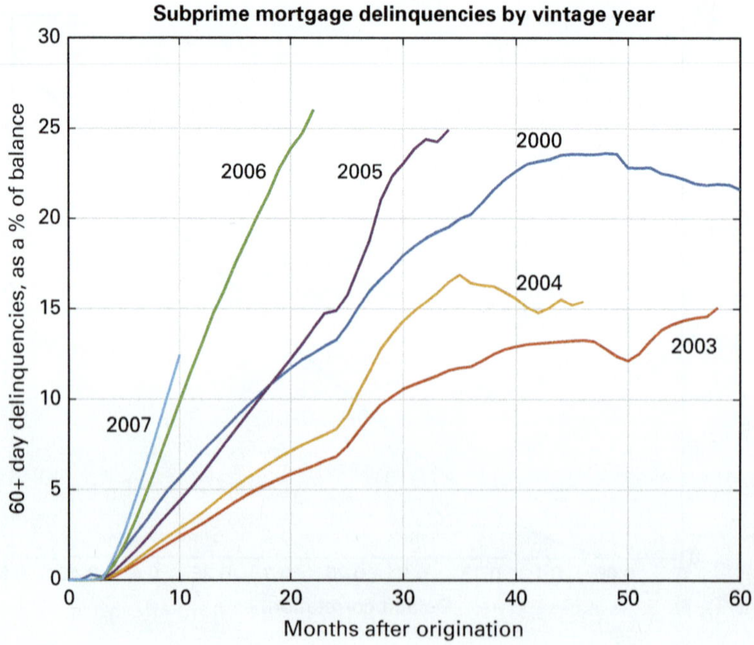

Figure 14.27
Subprime mortgage delinquency rates as a proportion of the outstanding balance.
Source: IMF (2008).

This section attempts a very succinct explanation of the subprime crisis that takes into account some of the previous discussion. The crisis erupted while MBS derivatives were producing losses in a market where the identity of the players was unclear: these products had been channelled through the off-balance-sheet vehicles in the shadow banking system. Therefore, we begin with a short description of the entities involved into the origination of these products. We, then, discuss the role of credit ratings. We conclude with a description of the meltdown.

14.5.2.1 The sell side of the shadow banking system

Asset-backed securities may be traded through off-balance-sheet entities that it is useful to describe. A preliminary distinction is order. A special purpose vehicle (SPV) is an entity that organizes the initial securitization of an asset pool. A structured investment vehicle (SIV) is a *fund* that manages asset-backed securities. SIV are virtual banks somehow, in that they borrow through low-interest securities and invest in longer-term securities, thereby promising large rewards (in exchange for high risk), as further discussed below.

Cousins to SIVs are conduits. SIVs and conduits both usually have an open-ended lifespan. On the funding side, SIVs issue long-maturity notes; on the asset side, they invest in assets that are relatively more complex than those conduits are invested in. Moreover, SIVs tended to be more leveraged than conduits. At the extreme lie "SIV-lites," which are less conservatively managed than SIV and are structured with greater leverage. Moreover, their portfolios are not very diversified, and are much smaller in size than SIVs. SIV-lites had a finite lifespan, with a one-off issuance vehicle. They were greatly exposed to the US subprime market, more so than SIVs.

These off-balance-sheet entities borrow in the shorter term, typically through commercial paper or auction rate securities with average maturity of 90 days, as well as medium-term notes with average maturity of a year. They purchase long-maturity debt, such as financial corporate bonds or asset-backed securities, which is high-yielding. Naturally, the profits made by these entities are paid to the capital note holders and the investment managers. The capital note holders are, of course, the first-loss investors. The obvious risk incurred by these entities is *solvency*, a risk that materializes when the value of long-term assets falls below the value of short-term liabilities. This risk has great chances of materializing when the assets in the balance sheet are mispriced, as explained earlier and further stressed below. A second risk is *funding liquidity*, the risk related to duration mismatch: refinancing occurs on a short-term frequency, but if short-term market conditions are bad, the entities need to sell the assets into a depressed market. To cope with this risk, the sponsoring banks granted credit lines.[39]

14.5.2.2 Conflicts of interest and credit ratings, liquidity, and model misspecification

The role of credit ratings was crucial in determining the riskiness of MBS-related derivatives. As explained in section 14.3.5, credit ratings were endogenous in the securitization and tranching process. That is, they would not be applied to an exogenously given tranching scheme; rather, they would be used to determine the riskiness of the tranching scheme.[40]

A second important point is that many of the MBS-based securitized assets were illiquid. Illiquidity does not facilitate pricing. The standard solution in this case is to look for somehow similar products that are priced in relatively more liquid markets. Thus, the pricing of structured products relied on the pricing of products that were similarly rated and for which quotes were available. For example, the price of AAA ABX subindices were used to estimate the value of AAA-rated tranches of MBS. Likewise, the price of BBB subindices were used to value BBB-rated MBS tranches. This is the "mapping role" credit ratings used to play in the pricing of customized or illiquid structured credit products.

However, the risk profile of structured products differs from that of corporate bonds. Even if a tranche has the same expected loss as an otherwise similar corporate bond, *unexpected loss or tail risk can* be much larger than that for corporate bonds given the complexity of the product, as in the simple example discussed earlier and underlying figure 14.26. Reality was indeed much more complex than in that example. Consider, for example, the "Matryoshka doll" scheme in figure 14.28. The structuring process was extremely granular and structured products ratings could hardly be extrapolated from those on corporate bonds. Typically, corporate bond ratings capture only the first moments of the distribution. Regarding structured products, tail risk may be responsible for destroying "credit rating inertia," a property observed for corporate bonds (see section 14.2.6).

39. Well-known sponsors at the time were Citibank ($100bn), J. P. Morgan Chase ($77bn), Bank of America ($60bn). In the European Union: HBOS ($42bn), ABN Amro ($40bn), HSBC ($32bn).

40. After the crisis, some rating agencies adopted internal reforms to mitigate conflicts of interest arising during their process of interaction with originators. Notable among them are those that aim to separate rating activities from sales, or to interdiction of agencies' analysts from participating in the originators' business development activities.

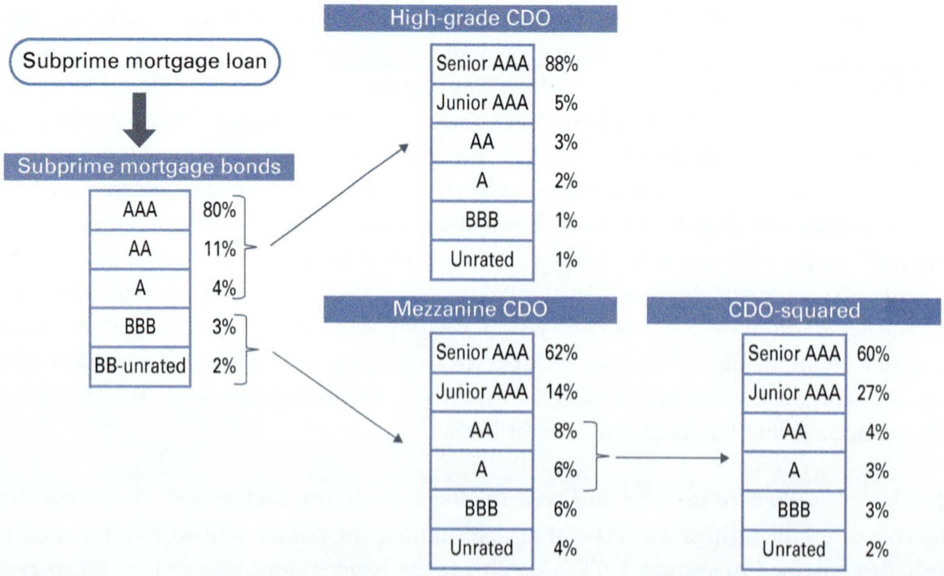

Figure 14.28
Multilayered structured credit products ("Matryoshka doll").
Source: IMF estimates (IMF, 2008).

Indeed, rating deterioration for structured products can travel very fast, as documented by the IMF in 2008 (see IMF, 2008).

Last, but not least, surrounding all these technical complications was an erosion in lending standards. Statistical models were calibrated to historically low mortgage default and delinquency rates that were typical of environments with tight credit standards. All in all, the products were "over-rated," that is, they appeared less risky than they were in reality. In this sense, these products were probably "toxic," in that they would not fit into some investors' optimal composition of their risk-return trade-offs; alternatively, these investors, if made aware of potential risks, would require only much lower doses of these products to be in their portfolios. Naturally, it is an open question as to whether these investors were, instead, fully aware of the risks they were going into, and, then, "riding a bubble."

14.5.2.3 The meltdown

A crucial feature of the crisis was the market fear of contagion from the rising level of defaults in subprime underlying instruments, many of which were incorporated in complex products. Fears of contagion began to regard safer tranches too. They came from the investors' understanding the pricing models were misspecified, and their lack of trust vis-à-vis the rating agencies: the price of safer tranches decreases with default correlation, as discussed earlier (see, e.g., figure 14.26).

Banks were affected for a number of reasons: (i) they had invested in subprime securities directly; (ii) they had provided credit lines to SIVs (indebted through commercial paper) and conduits that held these securities, thereby creating a shadow banking system, which escaped accounting and supervision rules; and (iii) this very same shadow system generated banks' loss of confidence in the ability of their counterparties to meet their contractual obligations. So the asset-backed commercial paper market dried up, triggering credit lines. The result was a sell-off of anything related to structured finance, from junk to AAA, which led to a complete "liquidity black-hole," and a severe reappraisal of structured finance.

The reappraisal of structured finance determined severe writedowns, and it was fueled by the liquidity black-hole, due to difficult repricing. Indeed, in the absence of a liquid market, writedowns largely rely on marking-to-model. But investors began not to trust the models and the rating process leading to them. Meanwhile, credit agencies proceeded to severe downgrades, confirming the investors' beliefs that previous ratings were based on misspecified assumptions, a self-reinforcing mechanism. These events escalated to a complete dry-up of capital markets and the bankruptcy of Lehman Brothers in September 2008, and subsequent painful bank bail-outs and recapitalizations. We refrain from reviewing details regarding the unfolding of this crisis, which can be found in many available publications, including, for example, Brunnermeier (2009).

14.5.3 Procyclicality

Treating volatility or credit risk as exogenous could be a good approximation when living in good times. The quality of this approximation deteriorates in times of crisis. The implicit assumption made in many instances of this and previous chapters is that one's own actions, based on a volatility forecast, do not affect future volatility, just as forecasting weather does not influence future weather. Arguably, the actions of many heterogeneous market participants should tend to cancel with each other, during periods of "calm." However, market participants tend to cluster their decision rules in periods of crisis. The literature on this "endogenous risk" is fascinating; Shin (2010) contains a survey of this literature that focuses on amplification mechanisms that are susceptible to lead to financial crises.

This book has dealt with procyclicality in many instances mentioned in section 14.5.1. This section develops a simple model of endogenous risk, where markets can be destabilized by one instance of procyclicality, arising because financial institutions need to comply with a given "top-tier capital" ratio (that is, in the terminology of section 14.5.1, the capital comprising Tier 1 and Tier 2). After a negative shock in the value of the assets on the balance sheet, a financial institution needs to restore its top-tier capital ratio. In the short-run, the institution can restore this ratio only through asset sales. Because every institution is doing the same, these asset sales have a market impact, collectively, determining a further fall in the value of the assets, and so on. The final outcome is an increased price volatility and a disproportionate asset sell-off, if compared to the initial shocks. The model is useful for thinking about the subprime events in 2007, as well as the ensuing credit crunch and the new solutions that monetary authorities have experimented with to help mitigate these adverse developments; these new solutions will be briefly discussed in the last subsections.

14.5.3.1 Model

We consider a model with many identical financial institutions that, for some (not modeled) reason, need to maintain a prespecified top-tier capital ratio against risky assets. Each institution has the following balance sheet:

Balance sheet, Time 1

A	E
C_b	D

The notation is a bit more elaborated than that used in section 14.2: while we still define E as equity (including past retained earnings) and D as debt, we now define A as the value of risky assets, no matter how liquid these can be. Moreover, we define C_b to equal cash and reserves. We suppose the 8% Cooke ratio is in place, or $E \geq 0.08A$ and, to simplify, we set $E = 0.08A$. Note that a top-tier capital rule does not determine a leverage rule: there are, obviously, many leverage ratios, $\frac{D}{E}$, consistent with a given top-tier capital ratio $\frac{E}{A}$. In fact, Basel III now explicitly considers leverage ratios, thereby innovating upon Basel II, as discussed in section 14.4.1. We shall deal with procyclicality induced by this new rule later in this section.

Next, assume that some exogenous shock takes place. Suppose that, following this shock, the risky assets value decreases by some amount, ΔA, such that each institution would have the following balance sheet:

Balance sheet, Time 2

$A - \Delta A$	$E - \Delta A$
C_b	D

But, each institution has to comply with its top-tier ratio target. Therefore, at time 2, the new top-tier capital, $E - \Delta A$, must be at least 8% of the risky assets, $A - \Delta A$, or,

$$E - \Delta A = 0.08\,(A - \Delta A)\,. \tag{14.88}$$

At time 1, financial institutions had set $E = 0.08A$. Therefore, eq. (14.88) cannot hold, and the intuition is simple. As the risky assets value falls, equity value falls relatively more, due to leverage: the value of risky assets falls by $-\frac{\Delta A}{A}$, whereas the value of equity falls by a larger percentage, $-\frac{\Delta A}{E}$, due to $E < A$.

Two solutions are available to financial institutions: (i) to inject fresh capital; (ii) to sell some of the risky assets. The first solution may not be viable in the short run. Let us analyze the second. We are looking for some quantity of the risky asset to sell, such that the reduction in assets value, say X^s, enables institutions to meet their top-tier capital ratio targets. The balance sheet would, then, be as follows:

Balance sheet, Time 3

$A - \Delta A - X^s$	$E - \Delta A$
$C_b + X^s$	D

How many assets should financial institutions get rid off? To maintain the new top-tier ratio, X^s must satisfy

$$E - \Delta A = 0.08\left(A - \Delta A - X^s\right).$$

Using $E = 0.08A$, and solving for X^s yields,

$$X^s = \frac{1 - 8\%}{8\%}\Delta A = 11.5 \cdot \Delta A.$$

That is, roughly, the number of risky assets to sell is proportional to the percentage loss in their value. In other words, the asset demand is *upward*-sloping.

In general,

$$\frac{X^s}{A} = \frac{1-\kappa}{\kappa}\frac{\Delta A}{A}, \quad \kappa \equiv \frac{E}{A}, \tag{14.89}$$

where κ denotes the top-tier capital ratio against risky assets. This result is intuitive: following a negative shock on the risky assets value, the amount of asset sales is decreasing in the prespecified top-tier capital ratio, κ: the closer κ is to 100%, the easier the adjustment is to maintain the same κ. Eq. (14.89) would end the description of this market, if the financial institution had no price impact.

We assume that financial institutions, collectively taken, have a market impact; that is, one single institution cannot affect the price of the risky asset; many institutions doing the same thing at the same time could, thereby creating price pressures, with the price of assets falling and triggering new sales in a depressed market, over a vicious feedback loop. Is there an equilibrium in this spiral? The answer relies on the way we think of the selling pressure. We model selling pressure by assuming that there is a continuum of financial institutions, and that the asset value changes according to:

$$\frac{\Delta A}{A} = \tilde{\epsilon} + \lambda\frac{X^s}{A}, \tag{14.90}$$

where, and adopting language from market microstructure (see chapter 10), λ is the "price impact." In words, the percentage change in the asset value is the product of two components: (i) the initial shock, $\tilde{\epsilon}$, and (ii) a selling pressure component, which will pump up endogenous volatility, as we shall show. Naturally, if the market was perfectly liquid, $\lambda = 0$. Moreover, in a world where financial institutions had no concerns about top-tier capital rules, we would have $X^s \equiv 0$ in the first place, and so

$$\frac{\Delta A}{A} = \tilde{\epsilon}. \tag{14.91}$$

Note that this is also the solution in the case the market is perfectly liquid, $\lambda = 0$. However, we assume price pressure, determined by the action of financial institutions that aim at maintaining a top-tier capital rule, leading them to a sale $\frac{X^S}{A}$ in eq. (14.89).

The loop we have created is, then, the following. After an initial shock affecting the risky asset value, $\tilde{\epsilon}$, financial institutions sell risky assets, to an extent proportional to the percentage change in the asset value, according to eq. (14.89). In turn, the sell-off entails a further percentage drop in the asset value, as determined by eq. (14.90). An equilibrium, provided it exists, is a fixed point in this feedback-loop, i.e. a situation where the loop stops because the drops in the risky asset value do not happen anymore, and the assets sell-offs are interrupted as a result, thereby providing no reasons for the asset value to fall any further.

To find this fixed point, we replace eq. (14.89) into eq. (14.90) and solve for $\frac{\Delta A}{A}$, and find that

$$\frac{\Delta A}{A} = c_A \cdot \tilde{\epsilon}, \quad c_A \equiv \frac{\kappa}{\kappa - \lambda(1-\kappa)}. \tag{14.92}$$

Note that an equilibrium exists if λ, the slope of the line $\frac{X^s}{A} \mapsto \frac{\Delta A}{A}$ in eq. (14.90), is less than $\frac{\kappa}{1-\kappa}$, the slope of the line $\frac{X^s}{A} \mapsto \frac{\Delta A}{A}$ in eq. (14.89). Intuitively, if the price impact λ were too large, the feedback from asset sales to the asset value drops would be strong enough to make the market collapse.

Eq. (14.92) shows, crucially, that the shock multiplier, $c_A > 1$. When financial institutions have a concern over top-tier capital ratios, the ultimate change in the asset value resulting from an initial shock is larger than we would have observed otherwise, say in eq. (14.91). For example, when $\kappa = 0.08$, a price impact $\lambda = 0.05$ implies a multiplier $c_A = 2.35$. Of course, these effects become less important as the market becomes more liquid, and do not matter any more in the limiting case of a perfectly liquid market, $\lambda = 0$.

What is the amount of asset sales resulting from this loop? Replacing eq. (14.92) into eq. (14.89) yields:

$$\frac{X^s}{A} = c_X \cdot \tilde{\epsilon}, \quad c_X \equiv \frac{1-\kappa}{\kappa - \lambda(1-\kappa)}. \tag{14.93}$$

Note that the feedback loop might exert substantial effects into the amount of asset sales. Assuming $\kappa = 0.08$, the multiplier c_X would equal 11.5 in the absence of feedback, $\lambda = 0$, as previously noted. The same multiplier more than doubles in the presence of feedbacks and a price impact of just $\lambda = 0.05$, attaining a value $c_X = 27.06$.

Thus, the model formalizes the idea that even a small shock affecting the risky assets held by financial institutions may lead to large-scale adjustments and price corrections, similarly as during the experience of the subprime events described in the previous sections. In the model, the concern of financial institutions about their top-tier capital ratios leads them to substantial asset sales in response to a shock, which are even more amplified in the presence of feedback effects induced by imperfectly liquid capital markets.

14.5.3.2 Multiple equilibria and market break-ups

In this model, an equilibrium exists under parameter restrictions that are independent of the realization of the initial shock, $\tilde{\epsilon}$. As noted, these restrictions are that the denominators of the multipliers c_A and c_X in eqs. (14.92) and (14.93) are strictly positive. We now introduce a simple variant of the model, in which an equilibrium may fail to exist, provided the initial shock $\tilde{\epsilon}$ is sufficiently large. Notably, in contrast to the assumption underlying eq. (14.90), we assume that the price pressure is nonlinear

$$\frac{\Delta A}{A} = \tilde{\epsilon} + \lambda \left(\frac{X^s}{A}\right)^2. \tag{14.94}$$

The quadratic term in eq. (14.94) formalizes the idea that the price impact of asset sales does not matter too much when the asset sales are limited, but becomes disproportionately high when the asset sales are at a large scale. This convexity makes the resulting feedback loop a bit more complicated. Indeed, replacing eq. (14.94) into eq. (14.89), we find that, in any equilibrium, the amount of asset sales is a solution to the following quadratic equation

$$0 = \varphi\left(\frac{X^S}{A}\right) \equiv \frac{X^S}{A} - \frac{1-\kappa}{\kappa}\lambda\left(\frac{X^S}{A}\right)^2 - \frac{1-\kappa}{\kappa}\tilde{\epsilon}. \tag{14.95}$$

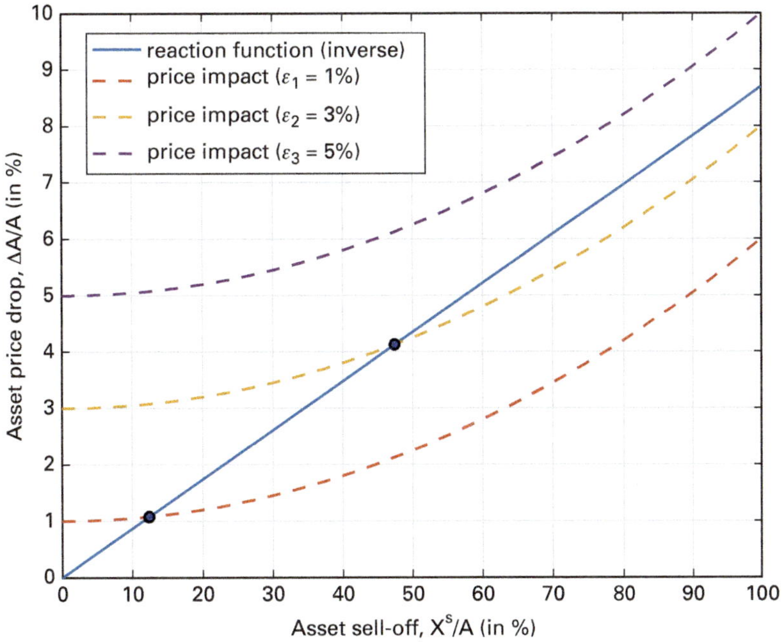

Figure 14.29

The solid line depicts the inverse reaction function in eq. (14.89), $\frac{\Delta A}{A}=R\left(\frac{X^s}{A}\right)\equiv\frac{\kappa}{1-\kappa}\frac{X^s}{A}$. The three dashed lines depict the price impact function in eq. (14.94), when the initial shock is $\tilde{\epsilon}=1\%$ (bottom curve), $\tilde{\epsilon}=3\%$ (intermediate), and $\tilde{\epsilon}=5\%$ (top), obtained assuming a top-tier capital ratio against risky assets $\kappa=8\%$, and a price impact $\lambda=0.05$. The equilibrium sales, if any, are those where the solid curve intersect the dashed ones.

Suppose that the market is hit by a series of shocks. Initially, we take $\tilde{\epsilon}=0$, such that two equilibria are possible: one, where the sell-off is just zero, $\frac{X^S}{A}=0$; and another, where the sell-off is $\frac{\kappa}{\lambda(1-\kappa)}$. We assume the sell-off is zero. Then, we assume that a first positive shock hits the market, with $\tilde{\epsilon}=1\%$. The solid line in figure 14.29 depicts the graph of the inverse of the reaction function in (14.89), i.e., $\frac{\Delta A}{A}=R\left(\frac{X^s}{A}\right)\equiv\frac{\kappa}{1-\kappa}\frac{X^s}{A}$. The dashed lines are the price impact in (14.94) when $\tilde{\epsilon}=1\%$, 3%, and 5%. There are two equilibria, corresponding to $x:\varphi(x)=0$ in (14.95). We assume that the market coordinates toward the leftmost one.

Next, the market is hit by one additional shock, say with $\tilde{\epsilon}=3\%$, such that the graph of $R(\cdot)$ shifts up, and the asset sales increase as a result, still being the leftmost zero of $\varphi(\cdot)$. Eventually, the market collapses when the shock is $\tilde{\epsilon}=5\%$: there are no points at which the inverse reaction function and the price impact function intersect, and no equilibria are possible as a result.

14.5.3.3 De-leveraging

So far, we have assumed that, following a shock affecting the assets in the balance sheet, financial institutions sell off their assets in order to restore their top-tier capital ratios. This section investigates additional adjustments that aim to restore leverage ratio targets. Denote the leverage ratio as $L\equiv\frac{D}{E}$. The timing of the shock and the banks' reaction is as in section 14.5.3.1, with the exception that, now, there is one additional constraint: at time 3, financial institutions also call portions of their debt, X^l say, so as to comply with leverage ratio targets. After a shock, then, the banks have the following balance sheet:

Balance sheet, Time 3
(De-leveraging with deep liquidity buffers)

$A - \Delta A - X^s$	$E - \Delta A$
$C_b + X^s - X^l$	$D - X^l$

The term X^s is the usual sell-off needed to maintain top-tier capital targets. Now, financial institutions also target to de-leverage for an amount equal to $X^l : \frac{D - X^l}{E - \Delta A} = L$, or

$$\frac{X^l}{A} = L \cdot \frac{\Delta A}{A}, \qquad (14.96)$$

and we initially assume that while doing so, they do not exhaust their liquidity buffers,

$$C_b + X^s - X^l \geq 0. \qquad (14.97)$$

Note that, if (14.97) holds true, de-leveraging does not produce a price impact because banks would simply be using cash to repay portions of their debt. In this case, X^s is the same as that in eq. (14.93). However, if $C_b + X^s$ is not large enough, financial institutions would have to sell additional assets, ΔX^s say, so as to have sufficient cash and meet leverage ratio targets. Precisely, if (14.97) does not hold, the asset sales ΔX^s need to leave the bank with positive liquidity buffers B,

$$\Delta X^s : B \equiv C_b + X^s - X^l + \Delta X^s \geq 0, \qquad (14.98)$$

such that the balance sheet financial institutions face at time 3 would be

Balance sheet, Time 3
(De-leveraging with exhausting liquidity buffers)

$A - \Delta A - X^s - \Delta X^s$	$E - \Delta A$
$C_b + X^s - X^l + \Delta X^s$	$D - X^l$

To determine the feedback effects of the asset sales, X^s and ΔX^s, assume that the banks keep on using the top-tier capital ratio rule in (14.89).[41] Replacing eq. (14.89) and the leverage condition, eq. (14.96), into eq. (14.98), and setting for simplicity $B = 0$, leaves

$$\frac{\Delta X^s}{A} = \frac{(1+L)\,\kappa - 1}{\kappa} \frac{\Delta A}{A} - \frac{C_b}{A}. \qquad (14.99)$$

This expression is positive because, by assumption, while de-leveraging, banks exhaust their liquidity buffers to the extent that (14.97) does not hold. This case arises precisely when leverage L is high enough. For example, assuming $\kappa = 0.08$, the loading for $\frac{\Delta A}{A}$ in eq. (14.99) is positive only when $L > 11.5$. We would need to observe values of L larger than 11.5 (and state-dependent, i.e., depending on the realization of $\frac{\Delta A}{A}$), for the condition in (14.97) to break down.

41. In this case, the top-tier condition will a fortiori hold with $\Delta X^s > 0$.

We determine an equilibrium for the feedback loop in this market. Replace eq. (14.99) into eq. (14.90), evaluated when the asset sales amount to ΔX^s, i.e. $\frac{\Delta A}{A}=\tilde{\epsilon}+\lambda\frac{\Delta X^s}{A}$, and solve for both the asset value drop and the asset sales,

$$\frac{\Delta A}{A}=c_{L,a}\cdot\tilde{\epsilon}-\lambda c_{L,a}\cdot\frac{C_b}{A},\quad \frac{\Delta X^s}{A}=c_{L,b}\cdot\tilde{\epsilon}-\frac{((1+L)\kappa-1)\lambda c_{L,a}+\kappa}{\kappa}\cdot\frac{C_b}{A}, \tag{14.100}$$

where the constants $c_{L,a}\equiv\frac{\kappa}{\kappa-\lambda((1+L)\kappa-1)}$ and $c_{L,b}\equiv\frac{(1+L)\kappa-1}{\kappa-\lambda((1+L)\kappa-1)}$. To ensure that an equilibrium exists, we need that λ, the slope of the line $\frac{X^s}{A}\mapsto\frac{\Delta A}{A}$ in eq. (14.90), be less than $\frac{\kappa}{(1+L)\kappa-1}$, the slope of the line $\frac{X^s}{A}\mapsto\frac{\Delta A}{A}$ in eq. (14.99), or that the denominators of $c_{L,a}$ and $c_{L,b}$ be strictly positive.

Finally, note that there is a third possibility available to banks: to sell additional assets even when the condition in eq. (14.97) holds. This possibility is relevant when financial institutions worry about maintaining liquidity buffers (some may be mandatory). For example, if the liquidity target $B=C_b$, we replace the inequality in (14.97) with $X^s-X^l\geq 0$, and we evaluate (14.98) at equality as $X^s-X^l+\Delta X^s=0$. The solutions for the asset value drop and sales are as in eqs. (14.100), but with the terms involving C_b dropped, i.e., $\frac{\Delta A}{A}=c_{L,a}\cdot\tilde{\epsilon}$, and $\frac{\Delta X^s}{A}=c_{L,b}\cdot\tilde{\epsilon}$. Figure 14.30 depicts the two multipliers of $\tilde{\epsilon}$ for $\frac{\Delta A}{A}$ and $\frac{\Delta X^s}{A}$ arising in this case, assuming the top-tier capital ratio target is $\kappa=0.08$, and the price impact of asset sales is $\lambda=0.05$.

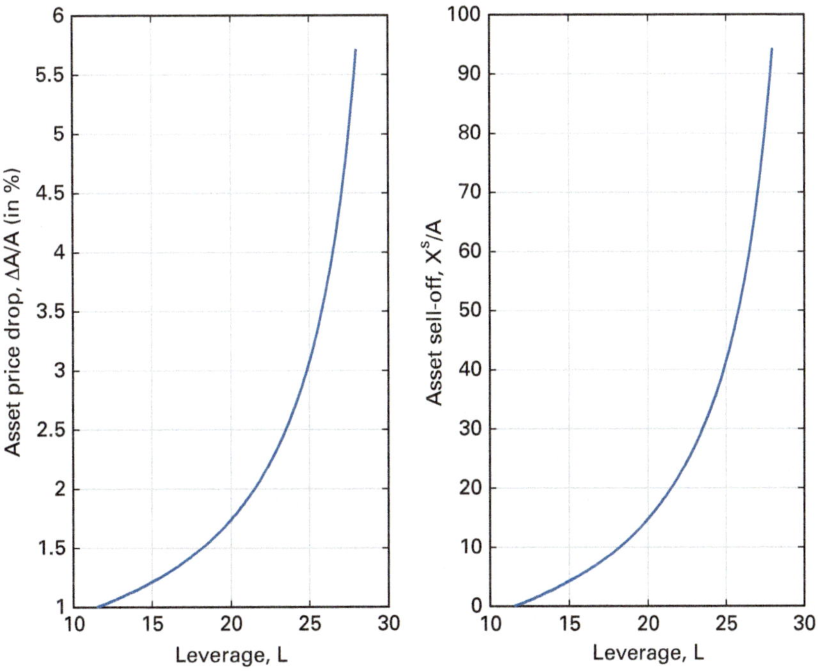

Figure 14.30
This picture depicts the graph the two multipliers, $c_{L,a}$ and $c_{L,b}$ in eqs. (14.100), as a function of the banks' leverage, L, when the top-tier capital ratio is $\kappa=0.08$, and the price impact of a sell-off is $\lambda=0.05$. When banks target to maintain cash and reserves equal to C_b (the level before the shock), the asset value drop and sales equal $\frac{\Delta A}{A}=c_{L,a}\cdot\tilde{\epsilon}$ and $\frac{\Delta X^s}{A}=c_{L,b}\cdot\tilde{\epsilon}$. The left panel depicts the graph of $c_{L,a}$ and the right panel depicts that of $c_{L,b}$.

Note that, given the assumption that $\kappa = 0.08$, the relevant range of variation for leverage is that for $L \geq 11.5$, as we are studying situations where de-leveraging leads to partial exhaustion of liquidity buffers. The effects of an initial shock on the asset price drop and asset sales may indeed be very substantial.

14.5.4 Credit Crunches and Quantitative Easing

14.5.4.1 The money multiplier

Loans make deposits. The well-known mechanics underlying the creation of money relies on the money multiplier, whereby new deposits made available to the banking system are partially used to extend new loans, which generate further deposits, and so on. By definition, money supply (M1 aggregates, say) includes cash held by the public plus deposits, $M = C_p + D$, with straightforward notation. Instead, the monetary base, or "high potential" money, is made of cash held by the public plus banks cash and reserves, $H = C_p + C_b$, where C_b denotes cash and reserves held by banks, as in the previous sections. Note the leakage banks create over the circuit of money creation: because banks face short-term liquidity needs (vis-à-vis their clients and/or other banks), and possibly need to maintain mandatory reserves with the central banks of the countries where they operate, they hoard C_b, which escapes the loans-make-deposits loop.

We assume that the ratios $\frac{C_p}{D}$ and $\frac{C_b}{D}$ are constant and equal to c_p and θ, resp., such that money supply equals a money multiplier times monetary base, namely

$$M = \frac{1 + c_p}{c_p + \theta} \cdot H. \tag{14.101}$$

The value of θ depends on a variety of factors, such as: (i) the discount rate at which a central bank lends money to banks; (ii) the interbank rates such as the LIBOR; (iii) the level of mandatory reserves banks have to keep with their central banks; (iv) the interbank rate for resources to allocate to mandatory reserves—the Federal Funds rate in the US; (v) the risk/return trade-off prevailing in other markets. Clearly, the value of θ increases with the values of the items from (i) to (iv), and decreases when the trade-off in (v) compares more favorably to banks.

14.5.4.2 Policy actions

Conventional policy strategies consist of actions aiming to affect the value of θ and H. For example, central banks can expand H through open market operations, by purchasing short-term government bonds. Note that this action likely affects θ as well, as the opportunity costs of holding excess reserves increase as markets are flooded with more and more liquidity.

There are obvious limits to open market operations, especially as short-term interest rates become small. Consider the events subsequent to the 2007 subprime crisis. We know that following a shock affecting the banks' books, the overall adjustments can be very substantial. For example, in the model in the previous section, banks have concerns over the top-tier capital ratio; after a shock takes place, banks aim to a shrinkage in the assets value equal to X^s. Moreover, the shrinkage can be even more substantial, $X^s + \Delta X^s$, should banks be high levered and willing to de-leverage, as we explained. Note that the model is silent regarding which particular assets (liquid or not) or loans are involved in the shrinkage plans, say X^s or $X^s + \Delta X^s$. We define a "credit crunch" as the situation where banks decide to cut on corporate loans and bonds—they hold more reserves, instead of lending money to the real sector.

A mechanical response to a credit crunch is to increase H through, say, open market operations. Simply, a credit crunch entails a higher value of θ, among other things. Monetary aggregates, M, are destroyed as a result, but can be restored through an injection of high potential money. Precisely, by eq. (14.101), the expansion of the monetary base needed to maintain the same supply of money, M, is $\Delta H = \frac{M}{1+c_p}\Delta\theta$, where $\Delta\theta$ is the increase in θ determined by the credit crunch. This policy action is quite fundamental as it helps keep interest rates low, yet it may not be enough when the credit crunch is so particularly severe as to lead to very substantial shrinkages in the economic activity, as we now explain.

The effects of a credit crunch on the real sector of the economy are quite obvious, with an increase in the cost of capital and a subsequent shrinkage in the economic activity. For example, the recession following the subprime events was spectacular, with industrial production falling by approximately 13% on a yearly basis in March 2009, the highest drop since World War II (excluding that resulting from the events related to Covid-19). The policy action was equally impressive: in less than two years after the subprime events, the Fed was capable of pushing short-term rates close to zero although during those periods it was already clear that this policy would not be likely to prevent an even deeper recession. All in all, even if the Federal Funds rate and short-term rates on safe assets were close to zero, the cost of capital firms had to bear were quite substantial as a result of the credit crunch.[42] Note that at that time, the credit crunch was also exacerbated by a freeze in the interbank lending market, a freezing arising from concerns financial institutions had about counterparty risk.[43]

The events following the 2007 turmoil can be described as those leading to a "liquidity trap," whereby banks hold abundant liquidity and short-term rates are close to zero. Arguably, the nature of this phenomenon might link to the standard Keynesian liquidity trap reviewed in chapter 1 (see appendix 1.D): a Keynesian liquidity trap arises when money demand is flat as a result of the expectations investors have that future interest rates may only increase. In this case, agents simply absorb any liquidity injections made by the monetary authority, and interest rates remain "trapped" at some minimum rate, coinciding with the lowest, shadow interest rate beyond which no investor is ready to

42. A high cost of capital to firms might occur during a credit crunch, as a result of one additional effect: a credit crunch leads to a contraction in aggregate demand, which makes defaults more likely.
43. A shrinkage in the economy activity suggests a natural extension of the models in the previous section, with one additional element of procyclicality: as the real economy plummets as a result of the credit crunch, the value of the assets decreases even more, thereby deepening the credit crunch, over a vicious feedback loop. Note that this feedback mechanism would be, quite naturally, part of the financial accelerator hypothesis, although distinct from the mechanism surveyed in chapter 9 (see section 9.11). In the version we suggest, the credit crunch is determined by concerns financial intermediaries have about their top-tier capital ratios and leverage exposures, rather than agency problems occurring over their relationships with clients. We do not examine this additional source of procyclicality to keep the analysis as simple as we can.

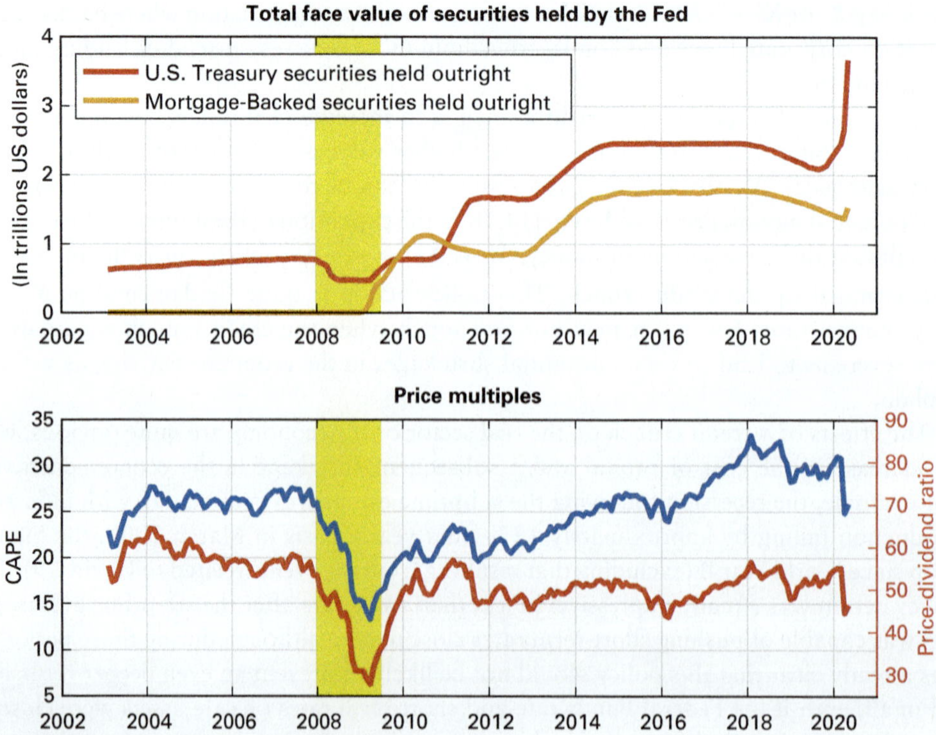

Figure 14.31
Top panel: US Treasury and mortgage-based securities held by the Federal Reserve. Bottom panel: Cyclically adjusted price-to-earning ratio (CAPE) and price-to-dividend ratio, both calculated by Robert Shiller. The yellow shaded area covers the 2007–2009 recession episode identified by the National Bureau of Economic Research.

bet against a decrease. At the time of the crisis, money supply was so abundant as to have made short-term rates close to zero, and the market expectation was that this circumstance would last for a long time. For many years, the whole yield curve up to ten years was locked in at nearly zero. That is, the market expected that investing in bonds (even long-maturity bonds) might only have led to losses. Consistent with this expectation, the Treasury bonds holdings of the Fed did increase in an unprecedented way, as further discussed below (see, e.g., figure 14.31). In any case, the economy was trapped in that a further increase in the monetary base would have no effects on short-term interest rates.

What was the initial policy reaction to this unusual circumstance? Note that a further difficulty at the time was that the liquidity trap was accompanied by a surge in corporate spreads resulting from the credit crunch. Quantitative Easing (QE, henceforth) is a policy action that aims at restoring the shrinkage in credit supply. This action would have possibly helped reduce corporate spreads and mitigate the adverse effects of the credit crunch on the real economic activity. Consider the following stylized balance sheets. The balance sheet on the left-hand side is that arising after financial institutions have reacted to a shock in their asset value, as formalized in previous sections. The portion of X^s that includes corporate loans and bonds is what we are terming the "credit crunch."

Balance sheets, Time 3 and beyond

$A-\Delta A-X^s$	$E-\Delta A$	$\rightarrow$	$A-\Delta A-X^s+Q^s$	$E-\Delta A$
C_b+X^s	D	$\leftarrow$	$C_b+X^s-Q^s$	D

The effects of QE can be seen through the balance sheet on the right-hand side. Banks can purchase new corporate bonds or extend new loans (securitized loans), which the central bank immediately purchases, leading to the "left arrow" of the previous diagram. The ideal, spontaneous, resolution of a credit crunch is when financial institutions are willing to extend corporate loans or purchase corporate bonds, to restore their credit shrinkage, at least partially, by some amount Q^s. We know this spontaneous resolution cannot occur until the value of the assets remains depressed. However, the central bank could step in and purchase the assets the banking system dislikes, to an extent at least equal to Q^s; this intervention would leave banks with their excess reserves compliant with their top-tier capital ratio targets. This policy action is the essence of QE, with assets typically involved being ABS and even long-term bonds. Its effects comprise both (i) an increase in H, equal to the amount of liquidity injected, and (ii) higher incentives given to banks to refinance the real sector, incentives resulting from the liquidity buffers supplied by the central bank.

14.5.5 Where Did Quantitative Easing Go?

This book has dealt with various frameworks that help rationalize the existence of bubbles (see, e.g., chapters 3, 4 and 9), but none of these frameworks explains that bubbles may actually link to the mere availability of credit to investors with limited liability. Yet, we know from chapter 9 (see section 9.11) that, when allowed to default on debt obligations, investors are incentivized to take more risks than they would without the possibility of bankruptcy opened to them. But wouldn't credit availability, then, lead investors to price assets above their fundamentals?

Figure 14.31 (top panel) plots the total value of US Treasury and MBS held by the Fed over nearly 20 years. The effects of the Fed's unconventional policy are clearly visible: the amount of US Treasury securities held by the Fed more than tripled in less than a decade after the 2007–2009 crisis; likewise, the value of MBSs went from nil to nearly \$2 trillion during the same time span. Note, incidentally, that the Fed implemented much more aggressive behavior in response to the Covid-19 pandemic crisis (which occurred at the time of writing), an episode we decided we shall not comment on in this book. The bottom panel of figure 14.31 depicts the behavior of price multiples related to the aggregate US stock market. Asset evaluations became roughly the same as (if not higher than) those in the pre-crisis period. In perspective, it might be argued that these evaluations might have been "excessive." Were they?

Figure 14.32 documents the well-known fact that the global financial crisis may be read as a *permanent* shock on real economic aggregates: GDP recovered after the crisis, but along a trend below that prior to the crisis. However, we know from chapter 8 that, in stylized models in which output is nonstationary, price multiples may be stationary,

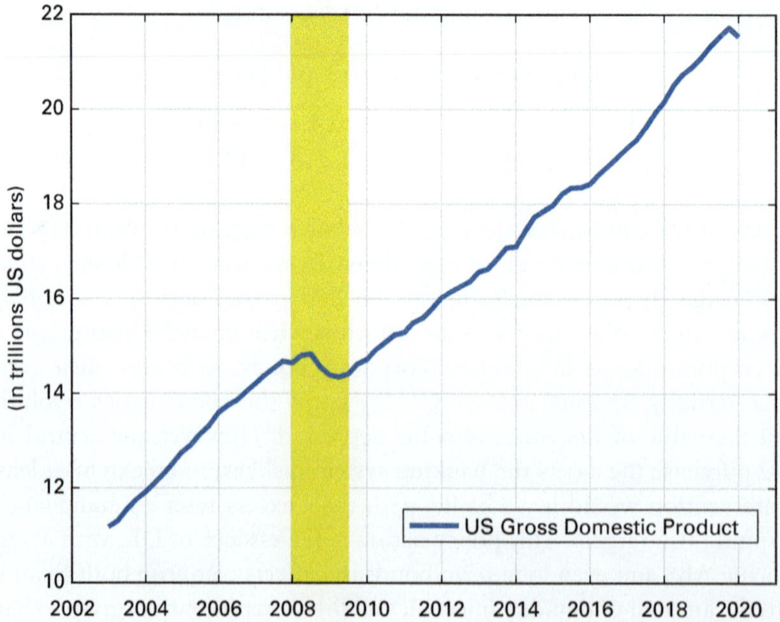

Figure 14.32
Quarterly sampled US *Nominal* GDP. The yellow shaded area covers the 2007–2009 recession episode identified by the National Bureau of Economic Research.

merely driven by output growth (see section 8.6.3). That is, a negative shock on output growth may be persistent (as in figure 14.32) and, yet, determine only a temporary decline in price multiples: price multiples may recover to levels prior to the shock in output growth even if output goes through a lower trend (see, e.g., figure 8.13 in chapter 8). Still, figure 14.33 shows that price multiples were well above their statistical averages; in fact, the cyclically adjusted price-to-earnings ratio (CAPE) was even higher than before the global financial crisis. We now describe some models by which persistently high evaluations may be explained by credit availability and investors with limited liability.

14.5.5.1 Bubbles and crises

Allen and Gale (2007) survey a number of models that formalize the idea that credit availability may lead to bubbles. The economic rationale behind these models links to famous episodes such as the Japanese stock and real estate bubbles of the 1980s to 1990s or the Southeast Asia bubbles of the 1990s. Typically, a period of credit expansion (fueled, for example, by financial liberalization) leads investors to take on risks that they would be unlikely to take were they fully liable for their investment decisions. The mechanism is known as *risk-shifting* (or "convexity"): limited liability leads investors to be interested in the upper part of the payoffs distribution because the risks regarding the lower part are shifted to the lenders. Risk-shifting (from investors to banks) may be responsible for bubbles, with investors indebted at relatively cheap conditions and, thus, incentivized to take positions in assets in finite supply that end up being overvalued. Eventually, a crisis erupts in bad times, i.e., when the investments performance is poor, and indebted investors default on the debt they had used to buy overvalued assets. These defaults may lead to banking

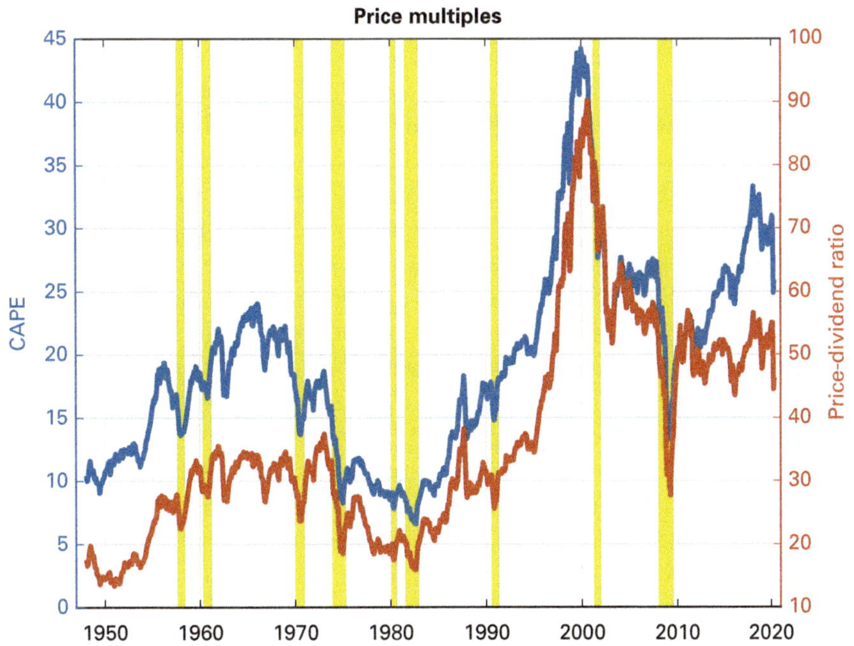

Figure 14.33
Cyclically adjusted price-to-earning ratio (CAPE) and price-to-dividend ratio, both calculated by Robert Shiller. The yellow shaded area covers the 2007–2009 recession episode identified by the National Bureau of Economic Research.

crises, with possible spillovers into the real economy. These mechanisms can also be part of explanations regarding credit market developments in the late 2000s (see, e.g., Reinhart and Rogoff, 2009). Relatively more controversial seems to be the question of whether these ideas help explain market developments subsequent to QE.

The deliberate scope of QE is to increase lending. But abundant credit availability also creates incentives to invest in risky activities more than it would have been the case without the possibility opened to investors to default on their debt. In the next section, we shall argue that these incentives actually increase as investments become riskier. At least theoretically, QE may produce the unintended consequence of detracting resources from the original targets set by central banks, and lead to bubbles. We now present a model along the lines of the work of Allen and Gale to illustrate how bubbles arise as a result of risk-shifting mechanisms.

14.5.5.2 Models of credit and bubbles

We consider a market for a risky security in fixed supply. First, there is a safe, fixed income security, in that investing F into it delivers $F(1+r)$ after one period, with $r \geq 0$. The risky security (say, real estate or stock) pays off $\tilde{x} = x_u$ in the good state with probability p and $\tilde{x} = x_l$ with complementary probability, with $\frac{1}{S}x_l < 1 + r < \frac{1}{S}x_u$, where S is the price of this security (to be determined in equilibrium). Investors are risk neutral, and can borrow \$1 to purchase $\frac{1}{S}$ units of the risky security. Their total expected returns are $\frac{1}{S}E(\tilde{x}) - (1+r)$, where E is the expectation under p. Due to risk neutrality, it must be that this total expected return is zero, such that the price of the risky security is $S_F = \frac{E(\tilde{x})}{1+r}$. We refer to S_F as the *fundamental value* of the risky asset.

Next, consider a friction: borrowers may default on their obligations. Moreover, we assume that potential borrowers may only search for resources through a banking system. For banks, borrowing and lending rates may differ, with borrowing rates, r_0 say, less than interest rate promised by the fixed income security, r. In other words, banks, now, may borrow \$1 at an interest rate $r_0 \leq r$, and we set $r - r_0 \equiv \sigma$. Thus, banks, by borrowing at r_0 and investing in fixed income securities at r, achieve an "intermediation margin" equal to σ. We may think of this margin as arising due to resources made available to banks through dedicated, nonstandard, monetary policy programs in times of particular distress, such as those that determined QE policies. We may think of σ approaching zero as the result of a "rate curve compression," resulting from leveraged purchases of securities fueled by nonstandard monetary programs.

We assume that banks do not have the ability to invest directly into risky projects; only borrowers can do so. This market "specialization" typically occurs in the case of real estate investments, and may actually result from bans on proprietary trading by commercial banks, as with the "Volcker rule" (i.e., section 619 of the Dodd-Frank Wall Street Reform and Consumer Protection Act, 2010). Finally, we assume that a collateral C is required to back any loan, and that this collateral is small, in that $C: \frac{1}{S}x_l + C < 1 + r_0 - \frac{p}{1-p}\sigma$. This collateral condition can be understood as follows. Suppose, first, that $\sigma = 0$; then, this condition simply means that, for a given price S, a borrower long in the risky security does default on their obligations in the bad state of nature. This condition becomes more stringent when $\sigma > 0$. The reason is that, in the model, we shall see, banks and investors (the borrowers) are required to make the same profits and, as it turns out, the higher σ, the lower C must be in order to ensure the existence of bubbles.

How do these new assumptions affect asset evaluation? To illustrate a simple case, assume that $\sigma = 0$; in this case, the total expected return from borrowing \$1 and investing it into the risky asset satisfies

$$\Pi(S) \equiv E\left(\max\left\{\frac{1}{S}\tilde{x} - (1+r), -C\right\}\right) = 0, \tag{14.102}$$

where the last equality is due to risk neutrality. An equilibrium price S^* satisfies $\Pi(S^*) = 0$. But by Jensen's inequality, $\Pi(S_F) \geq 0$, such that $S^* \geq S_F$. The difference, $S^* - S_F$, is a *bubble*. Moreover, it is easily seen that, due to convexity, S^* increases after a mean-preserving spread in $\tilde{x}$: the riskier the asset, the larger the bubble. We may further characterize this bubble.

For simplicity, we set $x_l = 0$, but consider the general case in which $\sigma \geq 0$. We define an equilibrium as the situation in which the borrowers' profits are the same as the banks' carry trade resulting from borrowing at r_0 and lending at r. Now, the carry trade profits from investing \$1 in the fixed income asset are $\pi \equiv \frac{1}{F} - (1 + r_0) = \sigma$. Therefore, the wedge between the levered expected returns from investing in the risky security and the carry trade are

$$\Pi_\sigma(S) \equiv \Pi(S) - \pi = p\left(\frac{1}{S}x_u - (1+r)\right) + (1-p)(-C) - \sigma.$$

The equilibrium price satisfies $S^*: \Pi_\sigma(S^*) = 0$. Any price $S < S^*$ is not an equilibrium, because investors would, then, only invest in the risky market, bidding up the price to S^* as the asset is in finite supply. A bubble arises whenever $S^* > S_F$. Solving for the equilibrium price leaves

$$S^* = \frac{p x_u}{p(1+r) + (1-p)C + \sigma}, \tag{14.103}$$

such that

$$S^* - S_F = \mathcal{B} = \frac{((1-p)(1+r_0 - C) - p\sigma)\, p x_u}{(1+r_0+\sigma)(p(1+r_0+\sigma) + (1-p)C + \sigma)}.$$

The term $\mathcal{B}$ is positive, due to the previous assumptions on collateral requirements. Therefore, $\mathcal{B}$ is a bubble.

Note that an "ultra-low interest rate environment" is not the economic channel for bubbles in this model. In this example, bubbles arise because banks provide investors with credit facilities, and investors may default. However, it is easy to show that, provided the intermediation margin σ and the required collateral C are sufficiently small, the bubble increases as r_0 lowers. Credit availability and default in this model lead to a true price "distortion": the possibility of defaulting on a credit expansion is such that the asset price fails factoring in all risks (notably, default). In fact, bubbles can be mitigated while increasing collateral requirements, C. When C is sufficiently large, bubbles disappear.

Appendix 14.A Strategic Defaulting

Present values contingent on future bankruptcy. The value of debt in Leland's (1994) model can be written as:

$$D(A) = \mathbb{E}\left(\int_0^{T_B} e^{-rs} C ds\right) + \mathbb{E}\left(e^{-rT_B}(1-\alpha)A^B\right), \tag{14.A1}$$

where T_B is the time at which the firm is liquidated. Eq. (14.A1) simply says that the value of debt equals the expected coupon payments plus the expected liquidation value of the bond. We have:

$$\mathbb{E}\left(e^{-rT_B}\right) = \int_0^\infty e^{-rt} f\left(t; A, A^B\right) dt \equiv \pi_B(A), \tag{14.A2}$$

where $f\left(t; A, A^B\right)$ denotes the density of the first passage time from A to A^B. It can be shown that $\pi_B(A)$ is exactly as in eq. (14.12) of the main text. Similarly,

$$\begin{aligned}
\mathbb{E}\left(\int_0^{T_B} e^{-rs} C ds\right) &= C \cdot \mathbb{E}\left(\int_0^{T_B} e^{-rs} ds\right) \\
&= C \cdot \int_0^\infty \left(\int_0^t e^{-rs} ds\right) f\left(t; A, A^B\right) dt \\
&= C \cdot \int_0^\infty \frac{1-e^{-rt}}{r} f\left(t; A, A^B\right) dt \\
&= \frac{C}{r} \cdot (1 - \pi_B(A)).
\end{aligned} \tag{14.A3}$$

Replacing eqs. (14.A2)–(14.A3) into eq. (14.A1) yields eq. (14.11).

Equity value as a real option. Note that the equity value $E(A)$ in eq. (14.15) is the solution to

$$LE(A) + \delta A - (1-\theta)\,C - rE = 0, \tag{14.A4}$$

where $LE = \frac{1}{2}\sigma^2 A^2 E'' + (r-\delta)\,AE'$ denotes the infinitesimal generator, and

$$E\left(A^B\right) = 0, \quad E'\left(A^B\right) = 0. \tag{14.A5}$$

The first equality in eqs. (14.A5) is a value matching condition (equity value is zero when the firm has defaulted, $A < A^B$, and at the very same moment it defaults). The second equality is a smooth pasting condition. The general solution to eq. (14.A4) is

$$E(A) = -(1-\theta)\frac{C}{r} + A + k_1 A^{x_1} + k_2 A^{x_2}, \tag{14.A6}$$

where x_1 and x_2 are the two roots of $0 = \frac{1}{2}\sigma^2 x^2 + \left(r - \delta - \frac{1}{2}\sigma^2\right)x - r$, i.e.,

$$x_{1/2} = \frac{-\left(r-\delta-\frac{1}{2}\sigma^2\right) \mp \sqrt{\left(r-\delta-\frac{1}{2}\sigma^2\right)^2 + 2r\sigma^2}}{\sigma^2}.$$

We have $x_2 > 0$ and, accordingly, we set $k_2 = 0$ in (14.A6), meaning that the effects of the option to default weaken as the assets value grows large. It is the equity analog assumption to the boundary condition for the bond formulated in the main text, by which the bond value is $\frac{C}{r}$ when the assets value is so large to make the likelihood of bankruptcy negligible. To determine k_1 and A^B, we use the value matching condition and the smooth pasting condition in (14.A5), which leaves the solution in (14.13), with A^B as in (14.14) and $\gamma = -x_1$.

Appendix 14.B Proof of Selected Results

Alternative derivation of eq. (14.31). Under the risk neutral probability, the expected change of any bond price must equal zero when the safe short-term rate is zero,

$$\frac{\partial B(t)}{\partial t} + \lambda\,(\text{Rec} - B(t)) = rB = 0, \quad \text{with } B(T) = N = 1,$$

where the first term, $\frac{\partial B(t)}{\partial t}$, reflects the change in the bond price arising from the mere passage of time, and $\lambda\,(\text{Rec} - B(t))$ is the expected change in the bond price, arising from the event of default, i.e. the probability of a sudden default arrival, λ, times the consequent jump in the bond price, $\text{Rec} - B(t)$.

The solution to the previous equation is,

$$B(0) = \int_0^T \text{Rec} \cdot \underbrace{\lambda e^{-\lambda t}}_{=\Pr\{\text{Default at } t\}} dt + Ne^{-\lambda T},$$

which is eq. (14.31).

Proof of eq. (14.32). The spread is given by:

$$s(T) = -\frac{1}{T}\ln\left(\frac{\text{Rec}_T\left(1-e^{-\lambda T}\right)+Ne^{-\lambda T}}{N}\right).$$

With $N=1$, and $\text{Rec}_T = R\cdot e^{-\kappa T}$, we have,

$$s(T) = -\frac{1}{T}\ln\left(Re^{-\kappa T}\left(1-e^{-\lambda T}\right)+e^{-\lambda T}\right) = \lambda - \frac{1}{T}\ln\left(Re^{-(\kappa-\lambda)T}\left(1-e^{-\lambda T}\right)+1\right),$$

or equivalently,

$$s(T) = -\frac{1}{T}\ln\left(Re^{-\kappa T}\left(1-e^{-\lambda T}\right)+e^{-\lambda T}\right) = \kappa - \frac{1}{T}\ln\left(R\left(1-e^{-\lambda T}\right)+e^{-(\lambda-\kappa)T}\right),$$

Therefore, if $\kappa \geq \lambda$, then, $\lim_{T\to\infty} s(T) = \lambda$, and if $\kappa \leq \lambda$, $\lim_{T\to\infty} s(T) = \kappa$.

Appendix 14.C Transition Probability Matrices and Pricing

Consider the matrix $P(T-t)$ for $T-t \equiv \Delta t$, $P(\Delta t)$, and write,

$$P(\Delta t)_{ij} \equiv \begin{cases} 1+\lambda_{ij}\Delta t, & i=j \\ \lambda_{ij}\Delta t, & i\neq j \end{cases} \tag{14.A7}$$

We are defining the constants λ_{ij} as they were the counterparts of the intensity of the Poisson process in eq. (14.29). Accordingly, these constants are simply interpreted as the instantaneous probabilities of migration from rating i to rating j over the time interval Δt. Naturally, for each i, we have that $\sum_{j=1}^{Z} P(\Delta t)_{ij} = 1$, and using this into eq. (14.A7), we obtain,

$$\lambda_{ii} = -\sum_{j=1, j\neq i}^{Z} \lambda_{ij}. \tag{14.A8}$$

The matrix Λ containing the elements λ_{ij} defined in eqs. (14.A7) and (14.A8) is called the *generating matrix*.

Next, let us rewrite eq. (14.A7) in matrix form,

$$P(\Delta t) = I + \Lambda\Delta t.$$

Suppose we have a time interval $[0, T]$, which we chop into n pieces, so as to have $\Delta t = \frac{T}{n}$. We have,

$$P(T) = P(\Delta t)^n = \left(I+\Lambda\frac{T}{n}\right)^n.$$

For large n,

$$P(T) = \exp(\Lambda T), \tag{14.A9}$$

the matrix exponential, defined as, $\exp(\Lambda T) \equiv \sum_{n=0}^{\infty} \frac{(T\Lambda)^n}{n!}$.

To evaluate derivatives "written on states," we proceed as follows. Suppose F_i is the price of derivative in state $i \in \{1, \cdots, Z\}$. Suppose the Markov chain is the only source of uncertainty relevant for the evaluation of this derivative. Then,

$$dF_i = \frac{\partial F_i}{\partial t} dt + [F_{\tilde{R}} - F_i],$$

where $\tilde{R} \in \{1, \cdots, Z\}$, with the usual conditional probabilities. In other words, the instantaneous change in the derivative value, dF_i, is the sum of two components: one, $\frac{\partial F_i}{\partial t} dt$, related to the mere passage of time, and the other, $[F_{\tilde{R}} - F_i]$, related to the discrete change arising from a change in the rating.

Suppose that $r = 0$. Then,

$$rF_i = 0 = \frac{E(dF_i)}{dt} = \frac{\partial F_i}{\partial t} + \sum_{j=1}^{Z} \lambda_{ij} (F_j - F_i) = \frac{\partial F_i}{\partial t} + \sum_{j \neq i} \lambda_{ij} (F_j - F_i),$$

with the appropriate boundary conditions.

As an example, consider defaultable bonds. In this case, we may be looking for pricing functions having the following form,

$$F_i(T-t) = xQ_i(T-t) + 1 - Q_i(T-t),$$

for some x, and then solve for $Q_i(T-t)$, for all $i \in \{1, \cdots, Z\}$. Naturally, we have

$$\begin{aligned} 0 &= xQ_i' - Q_i' + \sum_{j \neq i} \lambda_{ij} \left[x(Q_j - Q_i) - (Q_j - Q_i) \right] \\ &= x \left(Q_i' + \sum\nolimits_{j \neq i} \lambda_{ij} (Q_j - Q_i) \right) - \left(Q_i' + \sum\nolimits_{j \neq i} \lambda_{ij} (Q_j - Q_i) \right), \end{aligned}$$

which holds if and only if,

$$Q_i' = -\sum_{j \neq i} \lambda_{ij} (Q_j - Q_i) = -\sum_{j \neq i} \lambda_{ij} Q_j + \sum_{j \neq i} \lambda_{ij} Q_i = -\left(\sum\nolimits_{j \neq i} \lambda_{ij} Q_j + \lambda_{ii} Q_i \right).$$

That is, $Q' = -\Lambda Q$, which, solved through the appropriate boundary conditions, yields precisely eq. (14.A9).

Appendix 14.D Stochastic Default Intensity and Bond Spreads

We derive eq. (14.53), by relying on the pricing formulae of chapter 13. If the short-term rate is constant, the price of a defaultable bond derived in section 13.4.6 of chapter 13 is (using the notation of the present chapter)

$$P(y, N) = e^{-rN} \mathbb{E}_0 \left(e^{-\int_0^N \lambda_t dt} \right) + \int_0^N e^{-rt} \underbrace{\mathbb{E}_0 \left(\lambda_t e^{-\int_0^t \lambda_u du} \right)}_{= \Pr\{\text{Default} \in (t, t+dt)\}} \text{Rec}(t)\, dt. \qquad (14.A10)$$

The term indicated inside the integral of the second term is indeed the density of default time at t, because,

$$P_{\text{default by time } t}(\lambda) = 1 - \mathbb{E}\left(e^{-\int_0^t \lambda_s ds}\right),$$

such that differentiating with respect to t yields, under the appropriate regularity conditions, that Pr{Default$\in (t, t+dt)$} is just the term indicated in eq. (14.A10). So eq. (14.53) follows. Naturally,

$$\Pr\{\text{Default} \in (t, t+dt)\} = -\frac{\partial}{\partial t} P_{\text{surv}}(\lambda, t).$$

Replacing this into eq. (14.A10),

$$\begin{aligned} P(y, N) &= e^{-rN}\mathbb{E}_0\left(e^{-\int_0^N \lambda_t dt}\right) + \text{Rec}\int_0^N e^{-rt}\left(-\frac{\partial}{\partial t}P_{\text{surv}}(\lambda, t)\right)dt \\ &= 1 - \text{LGD}\left(1 - e^{-rN}P_{\text{surv}}(\lambda, N)\right) - (1 - \text{LGD})\int_0^N re^{-rt}P_{\text{surv}}(\lambda, t)\,dt, \end{aligned}$$

where the second equality follows by integration by parts and the assumption of constant recovery rates. Setting $r = 0$, produces eq. (14.55).

Appendix 14.E Bond and Credit Default Swap Spreads

We provide some analytical details regarding the behavior of bonds and CDS spreads depicted in figure 14.15. First, we show that it holds, approximately, that bond spreads are dominated by CDS spreads. We have:

$$\begin{aligned} \frac{-1}{N}\ln P(\lambda, N) &= \frac{-1}{N}\ln\left[1 - \text{LGD}\left(1 - P_{\text{surv}}(\lambda, N)\right)\right] \\ &\approx \text{LGD}\frac{1 - P_{\text{surv}}(\lambda, N)}{N} \\ &\leq \text{LGD}\frac{1 - P_{\text{surv}}(\lambda, N)}{\frac{1}{4}\sum_{i=1}^{4N} P_{\text{surv}}(\lambda, t_i)} \\ &= 4 \times \text{CDS}_0(N). \end{aligned}$$

Second, we show that, approximately, bonds and CDS spreads are bounded away by a function decreasing in time to maturity once the current λ is close to its long-term average under the risk neutral probability, $\bar{\lambda}$. For bond spreads, since $\mathbb{E}_0(\lambda_s) = \bar{\lambda} + e^{-\phi s}(\lambda - \bar{\lambda})$, we have, approximately, that:

$$\begin{aligned} \frac{-1}{N}\ln P(\lambda, N) &= \frac{-1}{N}\ln\left[1 - \text{LGD}\left(1 - P_{\text{surv}}(\lambda, N)\right)\right] \\ &= \frac{-1}{N}\ln\left[1 - \text{LGD}\left(1 - \mathbb{E}_0\left(e^{-\int_0^N \lambda_s ds}\right)\right)\right] \\ &\leq \frac{-1}{N}\ln\left[1 - \text{LGD}\left(1 - e^{-\int_0^N \mathbb{E}_0(\lambda_s)\,ds}\right)\right] \end{aligned}$$

$$\approx \text{LGD}\frac{1-e^{-\int_0^N \mathbb{E}_0(\lambda_s)\,ds}}{N}$$

$$=\text{LGD}\frac{1-e^{-\bar{\lambda}N-(\lambda-\bar{\lambda})\frac{1-e^{-\phi N}}{\phi}}}{N}.$$

Therefore, even if $\lambda=\bar{\lambda}$, bond spreads are bounded away by a function decreasing in N. Naturally, this property does not mechanically imply that bond spreads are decreasing in N too, although the existence of such a bounding function helps this happening.

Appendix 14.F Conditional probabilities of survival

We prove eqs. (14.58)–(14.60). First, for (t_{i-1}, t_i) small, the numerator in eq. (14.57) can be replaced by

$$-\frac{\partial}{\partial t}P_{\text{surv}}(\lambda, t) \equiv \mathbb{E}_0\left(\lambda_t e^{-\int_0^t \lambda_s ds}\right),$$

and rescaled by dt. Regularity conditions under which we can perform this differentiation can be found in a related context developed in Mele (2003). Eqs. (14.58)–(14.59) follow.

As for eq. (14.60), the proof follows the same lines of reasoning as that in appendix 13.B of chapter 13. That is, we can define a density process,

$$\eta_T(\tau)=\frac{e^{-\int_0^\tau \lambda_s ds}P_{\text{surv}}(\lambda_\tau,\tau,T)}{\mathbb{E}\left(e^{-\int_0^T \lambda_s ds}\right)}, \quad P_{\text{surv}}(\lambda_\tau,\tau,T)\equiv \mathbb{E}\left(e^{-\int_\tau^T \lambda_s ds}\middle| \mathcal{F}_\tau\right).$$

It is easy to show that the drift of P_{surv} is $\lambda_\tau d\tau$, such that by Itô's lemma,

$$\frac{d\eta_T(\tau)}{\eta_T(\tau)}=-\left(-\text{Vol}\left(P_{\text{surv}}(\lambda_\tau,\tau,T)\right)\right)dW_\tau,$$

where,

$$-\text{Vol}\left(P_{\text{surv}}(\lambda_\tau,\tau,T)\right)\equiv -\frac{\frac{\partial}{\partial\lambda}P_{\text{surv}}(\lambda_\tau,\tau,T)}{P_{\text{surv}}(\lambda_\tau,\tau,T)}\sigma\sqrt{\lambda_\tau}=B(T-\tau)\sigma\sqrt{\lambda_\tau},$$

where the second line follows by the closed-form expression of P_{surv} in eq. (14.50). Therefore, $W_{\lambda,\tau}$ is a Brownian motion under Q_λ, where

$$dW_{\lambda,\tau}=dW_\tau+B(T-\tau)\sigma\sqrt{\lambda_\tau}d\tau,$$

and eq. (14.60) follows.

Appendix 14.G CDS Index Swaps and Swaptions

In some of the derivations below, we shall use the following equality: for any fixed τ_A, τ_B, and $\tau\in[\tau_A,\tau_B]$,

$$\mathbb{I}_{\{x\in[\tau_A,\tau_B]\}}=\mathbb{I}_{\{x\in[\tau_A,\tau]\}}+\mathbb{I}_{\{x\geq\tau\}}\mathbb{I}_{\{x\in[\tau,\tau_B]\}}. \tag{14.A11}$$

This identity is helpful for calculating expectations conditional on information available at time τ. Consider, for example, the expectation $\mathbb{E}_\tau\left(\mathbb{I}_{\{x\in[\tau,\tau_B]\}}\right)$, where x can be interpreted as the default time of an entity. This expectation is $\Pr\{\text{Def}\in(\tau,\tau_B)\}$ if the entity has not defaulted by time τ, and zero otherwise, that is, $\mathbb{I}_{\{x\geq\tau\}}\Pr\{\text{Def}\in(\tau,\tau_B)\}$. Using the equality in (14.A11), we can easily determine conditional expectations of this type, as follows

$$\begin{aligned}\mathbb{E}_\tau\left(\mathbb{I}_{\{x\in[\tau_A,\tau_B]\}}\right)&=\mathbb{I}_{\{x\in[\tau_A,\tau]\}}+\mathbb{I}_{\{x\geq\tau\}}\mathbb{E}_\tau\left(\mathbb{I}_{\{x\in[\tau,\tau_B]\}}\right)\\&=\mathbb{I}_{\{x\in[\tau_A,\tau]\}}+\mathbb{I}_{\{x\geq\tau\}}\Pr\{\text{Def}\in(\tau,\tau_B)\}.\end{aligned}$$

We now rely on these equalities while determining mark-to-market updates of credit default swap products.

Proof of eq. (14.72). We have

$$\text{DSX}_\tau(t,t_0)=\mathbb{E}_\tau\left(\sum_{j=1}^{n}e^{-\int_\tau^{\tau_j}r_u du}\text{LGD}\frac{1}{n}\mathbb{I}_{\{t_0\leq\tau_j\leq t_{4M}\}}\right)-\mathbb{E}_\tau\left(\sum_{i=1}^{4M}e^{-\int_\tau^{t_i}r_u du}C_t\text{N}_{t_i}\right).\tag{14.A12}$$

The expectation of the first term in eq. (14.A12) is proportional to

$$\begin{aligned}&\frac{1}{n}\sum_{j=1}^{n}\mathbb{E}_\tau\left(e^{-\int_\tau^{\tau_j}r_u du}\left(\mathbb{I}_{\{\text{Def}_j\in(t,\tau)\}}+\mathbb{I}_{\{\text{Surv}_j\text{ at }\tau\}}\right)\mathbb{I}_{\{\text{Def}_j\in(t_0,t_{4M})\}}\right)\\&=\frac{1}{n}\sum_{j=1}^{n}\mathbb{I}_{\{\text{Surv}_j\text{ at }\tau\}}\mathbb{E}_\tau\left(e^{-\int_\tau^{\tau_j}r_u du}\mathbb{I}_{\{\text{Def}_j\in(t_0,t_{4M})\}}\right)=\text{N}_\tau\mathbb{E}_\tau\left(e^{-\int_\tau^{\tau_*}r_\tau d\tau}\mathbb{I}_{\{\tau_*\in(t_0,t_{4M})\}}\right),\end{aligned}\tag{14.A13}$$

where the last equality follows by the definition of the outstanding notional value in eq. (14.70), and the fact that the expectation in the first equality is the same for each name j, due to the assumption that the index names have the same credit quality.

The expectation of the second term in eq. (14.A12) follows by noticing that

$$\begin{aligned}&\mathbb{E}_\tau\left(e^{-\int_\tau^{t_i}r_\tau d\tau}\mathbb{I}_{\{\text{Surv}_j\text{ at }t_i\}}\right)\\&=\mathbb{E}_\tau\left(e^{-\int_\tau^{t_i}r_\tau d\tau}\mathbb{I}_{\{\text{Surv}_j\text{ at }\tau\}}\mathbb{I}_{\{\text{Surv}_j\text{ at }t_i|\text{Surv}_j\text{ at }\tau\}}\right)\\&=\mathbb{I}_{\{\text{Surv}_j\text{ at }\tau\}}\mathbb{E}_\tau\left(e^{-\int_\tau^{t_i}r_\tau d\tau}\mathbb{I}_{\{\text{Surv}_j\text{ at }t_i|\text{Surv}_j\text{ at }\tau\}}\right),\end{aligned}$$

and summing over the reset dates and all names, and using the fact that all names have the same default intensities.

Proof of eq. (14.73). The derivation of eq. (14.A13) relies on default events occurring after the swap origination, i.e. over the reset dates, after $T=t_0$. In evaluating the *front-end protection*, we need to price securities that pay off over defaults possibly occurring over the life of the swaption, i.e. before time $T = t_0$. We have,

$$
\begin{aligned}
v_\tau^{\mathrm{F}} &= \mathbb{E}_\tau\left(e^{-\int_\tau^T r_u du} F_T\right) \\
&= \mathrm{LGD}\frac{1}{n}\mathbb{E}_\tau\left(e^{-\int_\tau^T r_u du}\sum_{j=1}^{n}\left(\mathbb{I}_{\{\mathrm{Def}_j\in(t,\tau)\}} + \mathbb{I}_{\{\mathrm{Surv}_j \text{ at } \tau\}}\mathbb{I}_{\{\mathrm{Def}_j\in(\tau,T)\}}\right)\right) \\
&= \mathrm{LGD}\frac{1}{n}\mathcal{D}(t,\tau)\,P(\tau,T) + \mathrm{LGD}\frac{1}{n}\sum_{j=1}^{n}\mathbb{I}_{\{\mathrm{Surv}_j \text{ at } \tau\}} \\
&\quad\times \mathbb{E}_\tau\left(e^{-\int_\tau^T r_u du}\left(1 - \mathbb{I}_{\{\mathrm{Surv}_j \text{ at } T|\mathrm{Surv}_j \text{ at } \tau\}}\right)\right) \\
&= \mathrm{LGD}\left(\frac{1}{n}\mathcal{D}(t,\tau)\,P(\tau,T) + N_\tau\left(P(\tau,T) - P_{\mathrm{def}}(\tau,T)\right)\right),
\end{aligned}
$$

where the third equality holds by the assumption that the names have the same credit quality, and $P(\tau,T) = \mathbb{E}_\tau(e^{-\int_\tau^T r_u du})$ and $P_{\mathrm{def}}(\tau,T) = \mathbb{E}_\tau(e^{-\int_\tau^T (r_u+\lambda_u)du})$. Note that the first term in the brackets of the second equality is, obviously, always zero, when the timing of possible defaults does not overlap with the evaluation horizon, as for eq. (14.A13).

Proofs regarding the survival contingent probability. We show that $\hat{Q}_{\mathrm{sc}}$ in eq. (14.76) does integrate to one, and that $\mathrm{CDX}_\tau(M)$ in eq. (14.74), is a martingale under $\hat{Q}_{\mathrm{sc}}$. We rely on results that generalize the following equality:

$$
\begin{aligned}
\mathbb{E}_\tau(N_T) &= \mathbb{E}_\tau\left(\frac{1}{n}\sum_{j=1}^{n}\mathbb{I}_{\{\mathrm{Surv}_j \text{ at } T\}}\right) \\
&= \frac{1}{n}\sum_{j=1}^{n}\mathbb{I}_{\{\mathrm{Surv}_j \text{ at } \tau\}}\mathbb{E}_\tau\left[\mathbb{E}\left(\mathbb{I}_{\{\mathrm{Surv}_j \text{ at } T|\mathrm{Surv}_j \text{ at } \tau\}}\middle|\mathbb{F}_T^r\right)\right] \\
&= N_\tau\mathbb{E}_\tau\left(e^{-\int_\tau^T \lambda_u du}\right).
\end{aligned}
$$

For example, regarding the survival contingent probability $\hat{Q}_{\mathrm{sc}}$, we have that, under regularity conditions,

$$
\begin{aligned}
\mathbb{E}_\tau\left(e^{-\int_\tau^T r_u du} N_T v_{1T}\right) &= \mathbb{E}_\tau\left[\mathbb{E}\left(e^{-\int_\tau^T r_u du} N_T v_{1T}\middle|\mathbb{F}_T^r\right)\right] \\
&= N_\tau\mathbb{E}_\tau\left(e^{-\int_\tau^T (r_u+\lambda_u)\,du} v_{1T}\right) \\
&= N_\tau v_{1\tau},
\end{aligned}
$$

where the second equality follows by eq. (14.66) and the third by the definition of Q_{sc} in eq. (14.67).

As for the martingale property of $\mathrm{CDX}_t(M)$ under $\hat{Q}_{\mathrm{sc}}$, let $\hat{\mathbb{E}}_\tau^{\mathrm{sc}}(\cdot)$ be the time τ conditional expectation operator under the survival contingent probability $\hat{Q}_{\mathrm{sc}}$. We have, using the definition of $\hat{Q}_{sc}$ in eq. (14.76),

$$\begin{aligned}
\hat{\mathbb{E}}_\tau^{sc}\left(\mathrm{CDX}_T(M)\right) &= \mathrm{LGD}\cdot\hat{\mathbb{E}}_\tau^{sc}\left(\frac{v_{0T}}{v_{1T}}\right)+\hat{\mathbb{E}}_\tau^{sc}\left(\frac{v_T^{\mathrm{F}}}{N_T v_{1T}}\right)\\
&= \mathrm{LGD}\cdot\mathbb{E}_\tau\left(e^{-\int_\tau^T r_u du}\frac{N_T v_{1T}}{N_\tau v_{1\tau}}\frac{v_{0T}}{v_{1T}}\right)+\mathbb{E}_\tau\left(e^{-\int_\tau^T r_u du}\frac{N_T v_{1T}}{N_\tau v_{1\tau}}\frac{v_T^{\mathrm{F}}}{N_T v_{1T}}\right)\\
&= \mathrm{LGD}\frac{1}{v_{1\tau}}\cdot\mathbb{E}_\tau\left(e^{-\int_\tau^T r_u du}\frac{N_T}{N_\tau}v_{0T}\right)+\frac{1}{N_\tau v_{1\tau}}\mathbb{E}_\tau\left(e^{-\int_\tau^T r_u du}v_T^{\mathrm{F}}\right)\\
&= \mathrm{LGD}\frac{v_{0\tau}}{v_{1\tau}}+\frac{v_\tau^{\mathrm{F}}}{N_\tau v_{1\tau}},
\end{aligned}$$

where the last equality follows by the law of iterated expectations and eq. (14.68),

$$\begin{aligned}
\mathbb{E}_\tau\left(e^{-\int_\tau^T r_u du}\frac{N_T}{N_\tau}v_{0T}\right) &= \mathbb{E}_\tau\left[\mathbb{E}\left(e^{-\int_\tau^T r_u du}\frac{N_T}{N_\tau}v_{0T}\middle|\mathbb{F}_T^r\right)\right]\\
&= \mathbb{E}_\tau\left(e^{-\int_\tau^T (r_u+\lambda_u)\,du}v_{0T}\right)\\
&= v_{0\tau}.
\end{aligned}$$

Appendix 14.H Copulae

14.H.1 Statistical Independence and Correlation

If two random variables are independently distributed, they are always uncorrelated. Yet there are situations in which two random variables are not correlated and still exhibit statistical dependence. This appendix is a succinct introduction to copulae, which are an important tool to cope with these issues.

Consider two random variables Y_1 and Y_2. We relate Y_1 to another random variable Z_1 and we relate Y_2 to a second random variable Z_2, on a percentile-to-percentile basis, namely

$$F_i(y_i)=G_i(z_i),\quad i=1,2, \tag{14.A14}$$

where F_i are the cumulative marginal distributions of Y_i, and G_i are the cumulative marginal distributions of Z_i. That is, for each y_i, we look for the value of z_i such that the percentiles arising through the mapping in eq. (14.A14) are the same. We assume that Z_1 and Z_2 have a joint distribution and model the correlation between Y_1 and Y_2 through a function that links the marginals of Z_1 and Z_2. This indirect way to model the correlation between Y_1 and Y_2 is particularly helpful. It can be used to model the correlation of default times, as in the main text of this chapter. We now explain.

14.H.2 Copulae Functions

We begin with the simple case of two random variables. This case shall be generalized to the multivariate one with a mere change in notation. Given two uniform random variables U_1

and U_2, consider the function $C(u_1,u_2)=\Pr(U_1 \le u_1, U_2 \le u_2)$, which is the joint cumulative distribution of the two uniforms. A copula function is any such function C with the additional property of aggregating the marginals F_i into a summary of them, as follows

$$C(F_1(y_1), F_2(y_2)) = F(y_1,y_2), \tag{14.A15}$$

where $F(y_1,y_2)$ is the joint distribution of (y_1,y_2). Thus, a copula function is simply a cumulative bivariate distribution function, as $F(Y_1)$ and $F(Y_2)$ are obviously uniformly distributed. To justify eq. (14.A15), note that

$$\begin{aligned} C(F_1(y_1), F_2(y_2)) &= \Pr(U_1 \le F_1(y_1), U_2 \le F_2(y_2)) \\ &= \Pr\left(F_1^{-1}(U_1) \le y_1, F_2^{-1}(U_2) \le y_2\right) \\ &= \Pr(Y_1 \le y_1, Y_2 \le y_2) \\ &= F(y_1,y_2). \end{aligned} \tag{14.A16}$$

All in all, a copula function evaluated at the marginals $F_1(y_1)$ and $F_2(y_2)$ returns the joint density $F(y_1,y_2)$. Conversely, Sklar (1959) proves, in fact, that any multivariate distribution function F can be represented through some copula function.

The best known copula function is the so-called *Gaussian copula*, which has the following form

$$C(u_1,u_2) = \Phi\left(\Phi_1^{-1}(u_1), \Phi_2^{-1}(u_2)\right), \tag{14.A17}$$

where Φ denotes the joint cumulative normal distribution, and Φ_i denotes marginal cumulative normal distributions. So we have,

$$F(y_1,y_2) = C(F_1(y_1), F_2(y_2)) = \Phi\left(\Phi_1^{-1}(F_1(y_1)), \Phi_2^{-1}(F_2(y_2))\right), \tag{14.A18}$$

where the first equality follows by eq. (14.A16) and the second equality follows by eq. (14.A17).

For example, we can interpret Y_1 and Y_2 as being related to default events for two names, as in the examples of appendix 14.I. A simple assumption is that

$$F_i(y_i) = \Phi_i(z_i), \quad i = 1,2, \tag{14.A19}$$

for two random variables Z_i that are "stretched" just as explained in the previous section of this appendix. By replacing eq. (14.A19) into eq. (14.A18),

$$F(y_1,y_2) = \Phi(z_1,z_2).$$

This procedure can be generalized to the N-dimensional case, where

$$F(y_1,\cdots,y_N) = C(F_1(y_1),\cdots,F_N(y_N)) = \Phi(z_1,\cdots,z_N),$$

and

$$z_i : F_i(y_i) = \Phi_i(z_i).$$

We use this approach to model default correlation among names, as explained in the main text, and in appendix 14.I.

Appendix 14.I Pricing CDOs with Imperfect Correlation

We use a Gaussian copula to price the stylized CDOs in the main text. For each name, create the following random variable

$$z_i = \sqrt{\rho}F + \sqrt{1-\rho}\epsilon_i, \quad i = 1, 2, 3, \tag{14.A20}$$

where F is a common factor among the three names, ϵ_i is an idiosyncratic term, and $F \sim N(0, 1)$, $\epsilon_i \sim N(0, 1)$. Finally, $\rho \geq 0$ is meant to capture the default correlation among the names, as we now explain. Assume that the *risk neutral* probability each firm defaults by T is

$$\mathbb{Q}_i(T) = \Phi(\zeta_{0.10}) \equiv 10\%,$$

where Φ is the cumulative distribution of a standard normal variable. That is, by time T, each firm defaults whenever z_i hits its trigger

$$z_i < \zeta_{0.10} \equiv \Phi^{-1}(10\%).$$

Therefore, ρ is the default correlation among the assets in the CDO.

We can now simulate eq. (14.A20), build up payoffs for each simulation, and price the tranches by just averaging over the simulations. Precisely, simulate eq. (14.A20) and obtain values $\tilde{z}_{i,s}$, $s = 1, \cdots, S$, where S is the number of simulations and $i = 1, 2, 3$. At the sth simulation, we have

$$\tilde{z}_{1,s}, \tilde{z}_{2,s}, \tilde{z}_{3,s}, \quad s \in \{1, \cdots, S\}.$$

We use the previously simulated values as follows:

- For each simulation s, count the number of defaults across the three names, defined as the number of times that $\tilde{z}_{i,s} < \zeta_{0.10}$, for $i = 1, 2, 3$. Denote the number of defaults as of simulation s with Def_s.
- For each simulation s, compute the total realized payoff of the asset pool, defined as,

$$\tilde{\pi}_s = \text{Def}_s \cdot 40 + (3 - \text{Def}_s) \cdot 100.$$

- For each simulation s, compute recursively the payoffs to each tranche, $\pi_{i,s}$,

$$\pi_{i,s} = \min\left\{\max\left\{\tilde{\pi}_s - \textstyle\sum_{k=1}^{i-1} \pi_{k,s}, 0\right\}, N_i\right\},$$

  where N_i is the nominal value of each tranche ($N_1 = 140$, $N_2 = 90$, $N_3 = 70$).
- Estimate the price of each tranche by averaging across simulations

$$\text{Price senior} = e^{-r}\frac{1}{S}\sum_{s=1}^{S}\pi_{1,s}, \quad \text{Price mezzanine} = e^{-r}\frac{1}{S}\sum_{s=1}^{S}\pi_{2,s},$$

$$\text{Price junior} = e^{-r}\frac{1}{S}\sum_{s=1}^{S}\pi_{3,s}.$$

Finally, this model can be generalized to a multifactor model, where

$$z_i = \sqrt{\rho_{i1}} F_1 + \cdots + \sqrt{\rho_{id}} F_d + \sqrt{1 - \rho_{i1} - \cdots - \rho_{id}} \epsilon_i ,$$

with obvious notation. Moreover, this procedure may be applied to price tranches on CDOs with an arbitrary number of assets.

References

Acharya, V., R. Engle, and M. Richardson (2012). "Capital Shortfall: A New Approach to Ranking and Regulating Systemic Risks." *American Economic Review Papers & Proceedings* 102: 59–64.

Adrian, T., and M. K. Brunnermeier (2016). "CoVaR." *American Economic Review* 106, 1705–1741.

Aguiar, M., and G. Gopinath (2006). "Defaultable Debt, Interest Rates and the Current Account." *Journal of International Economics* 69, 64–83.

Alesina, A., and N. Roubini, and G. Cohen (1997). *Political Cycles and the Macroeconomy.* Cambridge, MA: MIT Press.

Alesina, A., and G. Tabellini (1990). "A Positive Theory of Fiscal Deficits and Government Debt." *Review of Economic Studies* 57, 403–414.

Allen, F., and D. Gale. (2007). *Understanding Financial Crises.* Clarendon Lectures in Finance. Oxford: Oxford University Press.

Amato, J. D. (2005). "Risk Aversion and Risk Premia in the CDS Market." *BIS Quarterly Review*, September, 55–68.

Anderson, R. W., and S. Sundaresan (1996). "Design and Valuation of Debt Contracts." *Review of Financial Studies* 9, 37–68.

Arellano, C. (2008). "Default Risk and Income Fluctuations in Emerging Economies." *American Economic Review* 98, 690–712.

Artzner, P., F. Delbaen, J.-M. Eber, and D. Heath (1999). "Coherent Measures of Risk." *Mathematical Finance* 9, 203–228.

Berndt, A., R. Douglas, D. Duffie, M. Ferguson, and D. Schranz (2005). "Measuring Default Risk-Premia from Default Swap Rates and EDFs." BIS Working Papers no. 173.

Black, F. (1976). "The Pricing of Commodity Contracts." *Journal of Financial Economics* 3, 167–179.

Black, F., and J. Cox (1976). "Valuing Corporate Securities: Some Effect of Bond Indenture Provisions." *Journal of Finance* 31, 351–367.

Black, F., and M. Scholes (1973). "The Pricing of Options and Corporate Liabilities." *Journal of Political Economy* 81, 637–659.

Broadie, M., M. Chernov, and S. Sundaresan (2007). "Optimal Debt and Equity Values in the Presence of Chapter 7 and Chapter 11." *Journal of Finance* 62, 1341–1377.

Brownlees, C., and R. F. Engle (2017). "SRISK: A Conditional Capital Shortfall Measure of Systemic Risk." *Review of Financial Studies* 30, 48–79.

Brunnermeier, M. K. (2009). "Deciphering the Liquidity and Credit Crunch 2007–2008." *Journal of Economic Perspectives* 23, 77–100.

Brunnermeier, M. K., and L. H. Pedersen (2009). "Market Liquidity and Funding Liquidity." *Review of Financial Studies* 22, 2201–2238.

Christoffersen, P. F. (2003). *Elements of Financial Risk Management.* Waltham, MA: Academic Press.

Committee on the Global Financial System (2005). The Role of Ratings in Structured Finance: Issues and Implications. Working paper. Basel: Bank for International Settlements.

Cox, J. C., J. E. Ingersoll, and S. A. Ross (1985). "A Theory of the Term Structure of Interest Rates." *Econometrica* 53, 385–407.

Driessen, J. (2005). "Is Default Event Risk Priced in Corporate Bonds?" *Review of Financial Studies* 18, 165–195.

Duffie, D., and D. Lando (2001). "Term Structure of Credit Spreads with Incomplete Accounting Information." *Econometrica* 69, 633–664.

Eaton, J., and M. Gersovitz (1981). "Debt with Potential Repudiation: Theoretical and Empirical Analysis." *Review of Economic Studies* 48, 289–309.

Fender, I., and P. Hördahl (2007). "Overview: Credit Retrenchement Triggers Liquidity Squeeze." *BIS Quarterly Review* (September), 1–16.

Greenspan, A. (1998). "The Role of Capital in Optimal Banking Supervision and Regulation." FRBNY Economic Policy Review, October, 163–168.

Hennessy, C. A., and T. Whited. (2005). "Debt Dynamics." *Journal of Finance* 60, 1129–1165.

Hull, J. C. (2007). *Risk Management and Financial Institutions*. Boston: Pearson Education International.

Ingersoll, J. E. (1977). "A Contingent-Claims Valuation of Convertible Securities." *Journal of Financial Economics* 5, 289–321.

International Monetary Fund (2008). *Global Financial Stability Report*. April.

Jamshidian, F. (1989). "An Exact Bond Option Pricing Formula." *Journal of Finance* 44, 205–209.

Jarrow, R. A., D. Lando, and S. M. Turnbull (1997). "A Markov Model for the Term-Structure of Credit Risk Spreads." *Review of Financial Studies* 10, 481–523.

Jorion, P. (2001). *Value at Risk*. 2nd ed. New York: McGraw-Hill.

Keys, B., T. Mukherjee, A. Seru, and V. Vig (2010). "Did Securitization Lead to Lax Screening? Evidence from Subprime Loans." *Quarterly Journal of Economics* 125, 307–362.

Kraus, A., and R. Litzenberger (1973). "A State-Preference Model of Optimal Financial Leverage." *Journal of Finance* 28, 911–922.

Lando, D. (2004). *Credit Risk Modeling: Theory and Applications*. Princeton, NJ: Princeton University Press.

Leland, H. E. (1994). "Corporate Debt Value, Bond Covenants and Optimal Capital Structure." *Journal of Finance* 49, 1213–1252.

Leland, H. E., and K. B. Toft (1994). "Optimal Capital Structure, Endogenous Bankruptcy, and the Term Structure of Credit Spreads." *Journal of Finance* 51, 987–1019.

Lopez, J. (2004). "The Empirical Relationship Between Average Asset Correlation, Firm Probability of Default and Asset Size." *Journal of Financial Intermediation* 13, 265–283.

McDonald, R. L. (2006). *Derivatives Markets*. Boston: Pearson International Edition.

Mele, A. (2003). "Fundamental Properties of Bond Prices in Models of the Short-Term Rate." *Review of Financial Studies* 16, 679–716.

Mele, A., and Y. Obayashi (2015). *The Price of Fixed Income Market Volatility*. Springer Finance Series. New York: Springer Verlag.

Merton, R. C. (1974). "On the Pricing of Corporate Debt: The Risk-Structure of Interest Rates." *Journal of Finance* 29, 449–470.

Modigliani, F., and M. Miller (1958). "The Cost of Capital, Corporation Finance and the Theory of Investment." *American Economic Review* 48, 261–297.

Morini, M., and D. Brigo (2011). "No-Armageddon Arbitrage-Free Equivalent Measure for Index Options in a Credit Crisis." *Mathematical Finance* 21, 573–593.

O'Kane, D. (2011). *Modelling Single-Name and Multi-Name Credit Derivatives*. Hoboken, NJ: John Wiley.

Pagan, A., and A. Ullah (1999). *Nonparametric Econometrics*. Cambridge: Cambridge University Press.

Pedersen, C. M. (2003). "Valuation of Portfolio Credit Default Swaptions." Lehman Brothers Quantitative Credit Research, November.

Reinhart, C. M., and K. S. Rogoff (2009). *This Time Is Different: Eight Centuries of Financial Folly*. Princeton, NJ: Princeton University Press.

Rutkowski, M., and A. Armstrong (2009). "Valuation of Credit Default Swaptions and Credit Default Index Swaptions." *International Journal of Theoretical and Applied Finance* 12, 1027–1053.

Schönbucher, Ph. J., 2003. *Credit Risk Pricing Models: Models, Pricing and Implementation*. Chichester, UK: Wiley Finance.

Scott, J. (1976). "A Theory of Optimal Capital Structure." *Bell Journal of Economics* 7, 33–54.

Shin, H. S. (2010). *Risk and Liquidity*. Clarendon Lectures in Finance. Oxford University Press.

Sklar, A. (1959). "Fonction de Répartition à *N* dimensions et Leurs Marges." *Publications de l'Institut Statistique de l'Université de Paris* 8, 229–231.

Uribe, M., and S. Schmitt-Grohé (2017). *Open Economy Macroeconomics*. Princeton, NJ: Princeton University Press.

Vasicek, O. (1987). "Probability of Loss on Loan Portfolio."KMV Working Paper. In *Risk* (December 2002), published under the title "Loan Portfolio Value."

Index

Publisher contact:
The MIT Press
Massachusetts Institute of Technology
77 Massachusetts Avenue, Cambridge, MA 02139
mitpress.mit.edu

EU Authorised Representative:
Easy Access System Europe, Mustamäe tee 50,
10621 Tallinn, Estonia
gpsr.requests@easproject.com

Printed by Integrated Books International,
United States of America